M000210691

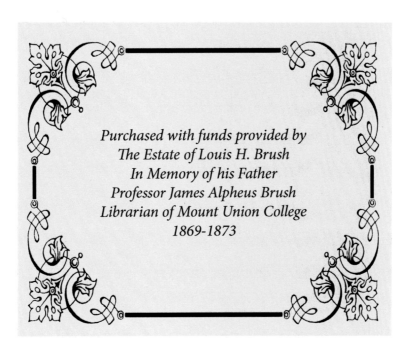

Purchased with funds provided by
The Estate of Louis H. Brush
In Memory of his Father
Professor James Alpheus Brush
Librarian of Mount Union College
1869-1873

Dictionary
of
Midwestern
Literature:
Volume
Two

The Midwest in 1872. *Colton's Common School Geography,* 1872.

Courtesy of David D. Anderson

Dictionary of Midwestern Literature

Volume Two: Dimensions of the Midwestern Literary Imagination

Philip A. Greasley, GENERAL EDITOR

Indiana University Press

BLOOMINGTON AND INDIANAPOLIS

REF
810.997703
D554g

This book is a publication of

Indiana University Press
Office of Scholarly Publishing
Herman B Wells Library 350
1320 East 10th Street
Bloomington, Indiana 47405 USA

iupress.indiana.edu

© 2016 by Indiana University Press

All rights reserved

No part of this book may be reproduced or utilized in
any form or by any means, electronic or mechanical,
including photocopying and recording, or by any
information storage and retrieval system, without
permission in writing from the publisher. The
Association of American University Presses'
Resolution on Permissions constitutes the only
exception to this prohibition.

The paper used in this publication meets the
minimum requirements of the American National
Standard for Information Sciences—Permanence
of Paper for Printed Library Materials, ANSI
Z39.48-1992.

Manufactured in the United States of America
Cataloging information is available from the Library
of Congress.
ISBN 978-0-253-02104-5 (cloth)
ISBN 978-0-253-02116-8 (ebook)

1 2 3 4 5 21 20 19 18 17 16

The Society for the Study of Midwestern Literature celebrates the lives and mourns the loss of David D(aniel) Anderson (1924–2011) and Patricia Ann Rittenhour Anderson (1930–2006), editorial board members for this volume as well as for volume 1 of the *Dictionary of Midwestern Literature*. David Anderson was a pioneer of Midwestern literary study, the founder of the Society for the Study of Midwestern Literature, a University Distinguished Professor at Michigan State University, and a prolific literary critic, theoretician, and creative writer. He was the inspiration for the *Dictionary of Midwestern Literature* series. Patricia Anderson, his wife of fifty-three years, was a Lansing, Michigan school librarian, a devotee of children's literature, and an active partner in David's literary study. Together, Patricia and David set the tone and created the friendly, encouraging, and generous atmosphere that have marked the Society for the Study of Midwestern Literature since its inception. This volume is dedicated to the memory of David and Patricia Anderson.

Contents

The Editorial Board

The Editorial Board of the *Dictionary of Midwestern Literature,* volume 2, consists of the following individuals:

GENERAL EDITOR:

PHILIP A. GREASLEY, Retired Associate Professor of English and Associate Vice President / Associate Provost, University Engagement, University of Kentucky

SENIOR EDITORS:

DAVID D. ANDERSON, University Distinguished Professor Emeritus, late of the Department of American Thought and Language, Michigan State University

PATRICIA A. ANDERSON, School Librarian, late of the Lansing Public Schools

MARILYN JUDITH ATLAS, Associate Professor of English, Ohio University

WILLIAM BARILLAS, Assistant Professor of English, University of Wisconsin–La Crosse

ROBERT BEASECKER, Director of Special Collections and University Archives, Grand Valley State University

ROBERT DUNNE, Professor of English, Central Connecticut State University

SARA KOSIBA, Associate Professor of English, Troy University

MARCIA NOE, Professor of English, The University of Tennessee at Chattanooga

MARY DEJONG OBUCHOWSKI, Professor of English Emerita, Central Michigan University

JOSEPH J. WYDEVEN, Professor Emeritus of English and Humanities and former Dean of the College of Arts and Sciences at Bellevue University, late of Bellevue University

ART EDITOR:

KAREN M. GREASLEY

ASSISTANT EDITORS:

ASHLEY HOPKINS

LAUREN BROWN SHEPHERD

Acknowledgments

Many people and entities contributed significant time, effort, expertise, encouragement, and financial support to making this volume a reality.

David D. Anderson and the Society for the Study of Midwestern Literature (SSML) provided the impetus for this volume and the *Dictionary of Midwestern Literature* series. Roger Bresnahan and the SSML Corporate Board set the priorities and provided financial resources. Marcia Noe, Robert Beasecker, and Loren Logsdon supplemented SSML funds with personal contributions, as did the estate of David D. Anderson. Partial funding for indexing this volume was provided by the Ohio University College of Arts and Sciences Humanities Research Fund.

The Editorial Board, originally David D. Anderson, Patricia Anderson, Marilyn Judith Atlas, William Barillas, Robert Beasecker, Robert Dunne, Philip Greasley, Sara Kosiba, Marcia Noe, David Newquist, Mary DeJong Obuchowski, Guy Szuberla, and Joseph Wydeven, provided strong guidance and important service as writers and editors. We regret that David and Patricia Anderson and Joseph Wydeven did not live to celebrate completion of this volume. Pressing commitments forced longtime board members Guy Szuberla and David Newquist to relinquish their positions, but their contributions remain significant and much appreciated.

Nearly one hundred literary scholars, librarians, teachers, and community members from across the United States and abroad contributed entries. The pages of this volume reflect their enthusiasm, varied perspectives, and wide-ranging expertise.

William Barillas and Robert Beasecker gave hundreds of additional hours to working with me in locating and securing permission to reprint the many images gracing this volume.

Karen Greasley, a graphic designer, began helping me, her father, by creating the maps and improving the images appearing throughout this volume. The Editorial Board recognized the quality and importance of her contributions by formally designating her as Art Editor.

Ashley Hopkins and Lauren Brown Shepherd advanced the volume through their work as Assistant Editors.

The University of Kentucky encouraged creation of the *Dictionary of Midwestern Literature* series and this volume and allowed my UK staff to support my work over many years. Grand Valley State University Libraries, Special Collections, and Robert Beasecker, Director of Special Collections and University Archives, provided invaluable assistance in suggesting and providing images of significant Midwestern works to accompany this volume. University of Kentucky Libraries Dean Terry Birdwhistell and Special Collections Director Gordon Hogg also made their collections available in support of this effort.

Sarah Jacobi and Nazareth Pantaloni III at Indiana University Press provided wise counsel and answered innumerable questions as we brought this volume to completion.

Finally, the families and friends of the team creating this volume supported and encouraged our work for more than a decade. This comprehensive study of the literature and culture of the Midwest remains deeply indebted to them and to all who fostered our efforts.

Philip A. Greasley
General Editor

ACKNOWLEDGMENTS FOR PUBLIC DOMAIN IMAGES

Anderson, Sherwood. *Winesburg, Ohio.* New York: B. W. Huebsch, 1919.

Aunt Sally; or, The Cross the Way of Freedom. Cincinnati: American Reform Tract and Book Society, 1859.

Baum, L. Frank. *The Wonderful Wizard of Oz.* Chicago: G. M. Hill Co., 1900.

Black Hawk. *Autobiography of Ma-ka-tai-me-she-kia-kiak, or Black Hawk.* St. Louis: Press of Continental Printing Co., 1882.

Boyhood Home of . . . Mark Twain (photo), 1902. Library of Congress Prints and Photographs Division.

Cather, Willa. *My Ántonia.* Boston: Houghton Mifflin Co., 1918.

———. *O Pioneers!* Boston: Houghton Mifflin Co., 1913.

The Centinel of the North-Western Territory 1.1 (November 9, 1793).

The Chap-Book 1.1 (May 15, 1894).

Charlevoix, Pierre-François-Xavier de. *Histoire et description generale de la Nouvelle France.* Paris, 1744.

Clemens, Samuel L. [Mark Twain]. *Adventures of Huckleberry Finn.* New York: Charles L. Webster and Co., 1885.

———. *The Adventures of Tom Sawyer.* Hartford, CT: American Publishing Co., 1876.

———. *A Connecticut Yankee in King Arthur's Court,* with illustrations after Daniel Beard. New York: Charles L. Webster and Co., 1891.

Colton's Common School Geography. New York: Sheldon and Company, 1872.

Delano, Jack. *Newsboy Selling the "Chicago Defender"* (photo), 1942. Library of Congress Prints and Photographs Division.

Drude Janson (photo), ca. 1920. Norwegian-American Historical Association, St. Olaf College, Northfield, MN.

Dubuque, Iowa (lithograph), 1857. Library of Congress Prints and Photographs Division.

Dunbar, Paul Laurence. *Lyrics of Lowly Life.* New York: Dodd, Mead, and Company, 1896.

Eggleston, Edward. *The Hoosier School-Boy.* New York: C. Scribner's Sons, 1883.

———. *The Hoosier School-Master.* New York: Orange Judd and Co., 1871.

Ellsbury, George H. *La Crosse, Wisconsin, 1873* (lithograph), ca. 1873. Library of Congress Prints and Photographs Division.

Eugene V. Debs . . . Set Free from Prison on Christmas Day, December 25, 1921. Library of Congress Prints and Photographs Division.

Filley, William. *The Indian Captive; or, The Long Lost Jackson Boy.* Chicago: Filley and Ballard, 1867.

Ford, Ed. *Malcolm X* (photo), 1964. Library of Congress Prints and Photographs Division.

Frank Leslie's Illustrated Newspaper (Haymarket Riot illustration), no. 1599 (May 15, 1886). Library of Congress Prints and Photographs Division.

Frederick, John T. *The Midland* 1.1 (January 1915).

Fuller, Henry Blake. *The Cliff-Dwellers.* New York: Harper and Brothers Publishers, 1893.

Garland, Hamlin. *Main-Travelled Roads.* Cambridge, MA: Stone and Kimball, 1893.

The Gerhard Sisters. *Jane Addams* (photo), 1914. Library of Congress Prints and Photographs Division.

Gift for the Grangers (detail). Cincinnati: J. Hale Powers and Co., 1873.

Great Lakes. Map adapted from S. S. Cornell, *Cornell's Primary Geography.* New York: American Book Co., 1888.

Hageboeck, August. *View of Minneapolis, Minn.* (engraving). A. Hageboeck, 1886. Library of Congress Prints and Photographs Division.

Haines, Richard. *Kansas Farming* (painting). U.S. Courthouse, Wichita, Kansas, 1936; photographed by Carol A. Highsmith for the General Services Administration, 2009. Library of Congress Prints and Photographs Division.

Highsmith, Carol M. *Robie House* (photo), ca. 1995. Library of Congress Prints and Photographs Division.

Howe, E. W. *The Story of a Country Town.* Atchison, KS: Howe and Co., 1883.

Howells, William Dean. *The Rise of Silas Lapham.* Cambridge, MA: Houghton Mifflin and Co., 1885.

Illinois: A Descriptive and Historical Guide (poster). Chicago: A. C. McClurg and Co., 1939.

In the Streets of St. Louis, Mo. (photo), 1890. Library of Congress Prints and Photographs Division.

John Muir (photo), 1875. Wisconsin Historical Society.

Johnston, Frances Benjamin. *Palace of the Mechanic Arts, World's Columbian Exhibition,* 1892. Library of Congress Prints and Photographs Division.

Jones, Alice Ilgenfritz, and Ella Marchant. *Unveiling a Parallel: A Romance.* Boston: Arena Publishing Co., 1893.

King, Frank. *Gasoline Alley. Chicago Tribune,* October 13, 1922.

Kirkland, Caroline M. *A New Home—Who'll Follow? or, Glimpses of Western Life,* with illustrations by F. O. C. Darley. 4th ed. New York: C. S. Francis, 1850.

Lewis, Sinclair. *Main Street.* New York: Grosset and Dunlap, 1921.

The Little Review 1.1 (March 1914).

Longfellow, Henry Wadsworth. *The Song of Hiawatha,* with illustrations from designs by Frederic Remington. Boston: Houghton Mifflin and Co., 1891.

Lorine Portrait (photo), ca. 1920. Hoard Historical Museum, Fort Atkinson, Wisconsin.

Macy, William. *Chicago Skyline* (painting). Kaufman and Fabry Co., 1927. Library of Congress Prints and Photographs Division.

Main Street . . . Kansas City. Detroit Publishing Co., ca. 1900. Library of Congress Prints and Photographs Division.

Masters, Edgar Lee. *Spoon River Anthology.* New York: Macmillan, 1915.

McCutcheon, John T. *The Restless Age.* Indianapolis: Bobbs-Merrill Company, 1921.

National Progressive Convention, Chicago, August 6, 1912. Kaufmann, Weimer and Fabry Co., 1912. Library of Congress Prints and Photographs Division.

Nowlin, William. *The Bark-Covered House.* Detroit, 1876.

Poetry: A Magazine of Verse 1.1 (October 1912).

Public Square . . . Cleveland (photo), 1906. Library of Congress Prints and Photographs Division.

Redwing, Morris. *The Young Bear Hunters.* New York: Beadle and Adams, 1885.

Reedy's Mirror 25.2 (January 14, 1916).

Sam Carley Blowsnake (photo), ca. 1900. Wisconsin Historical Society.

Sandburg, Carl. "Chicago." *Poetry: A Magazine of Verse* 3.6 (March 1914).

Sinclair, Upton. *The Jungle.* New York: Doubleday, Page and Co., 1906.

The Skyline, Cincinnati (photo), ca. 1910–1920. Detroit: Detroit Publishing Co. Library of Congress Prints and Photographs Division.

Sojourner Truth (photo). Detroit, 1864. Library of Congress Prints and Photographs Division.

Stephan G. Stephansson (photo), ca. 1917. Stephan V. Benediktson.

Stratton-Porter, Gene. *Freckles.* New York: Grosset and Dunlap, 1904.

Trifles (photo). Billy Rose Theatre Collection photograph, ca. 1916. The New York Public Library for the Performing Arts / Billy Rose Theatre Division.

Turner, Frederick Jackson. "The Significance of the Frontier in American History." *Proceedings of the State Historical Society of Wisconsin* 41 (1894).

Waldemar Ager (photo), ca. 1900. The Ager Association of Eau Claire, Wisconsin.

Wattles, William Austin. *Sunflowers: A Book of Kansas Poems.* Chicago: A. C. McClurg and Co., 1916.

Willa Cather (photo as a freshman at the University of Nebraska, 1891–1892). Nebraska State Historical Society.

Women Working in the Welding Department, Lincoln Motor Co., Detroit, Mich., 1914–1918. Library of Congress Prints and Photographs Division.

Dictionary
of
Midwestern
Literature:
Volume
Two

Introduction

Overview

The *Dictionary of Midwestern Literature, Volume Two: Dimensions of the Midwestern Literary Imagination* is the second in a projected three-volume series being created by the Society for the Study of Midwestern Literature. It complements the depiction in *Volume One: The Authors* of the lives, literary significance, leading works, and most important secondary sources on nearly four hundred Midwestern authors, poets, dramatists, and journalists from the advent of widespread European settlement in the region to the present. Both volumes are designed to meet the needs of many users, from literary scholars, college students, and university and community librarians to casual readers, high school students, and their parents. These volumes serve diverse purposes: each essay covers its topic fully, but some readers may choose instead to consult specific sections for historical background, analytical insights, leading primary works reflecting that topic, or secondary sources offering additional information.

The lead chapter for this series, "The Origins and Development of the Literature of the Midwest" by DAVID D. ANDERSON (1924–2011),

contextualizes the region's authors, literature, sites, centers, movements, and literary history. While the first volume consists of author biographies, analyses of their writings' Midwestern significance, and identification of the major critical sources on them, volume 2 makes clear the dimensions of the Midwestern literary imagination through coverage of the following topics:

• Thirty-five pivotal Midwestern literary texts: fiction, nonfiction, drama, and poetry written in English or experiencing rapid or simultaneous translation into English. These pivotal books represent an array of genres from picaresque novels and environmental literature to fantasy and humor. All assist in defining the literature, values, and culture of the Midwest and have become crucial texts in the evolving Midwestern and American literary canon. See also THE CHANGING MIDWESTERN LITERARY CANON.

• Entries representing the region's location and geography, including essays on states carved from the original Northwest Territory, ILLINOIS, INDIANA, MICHIGAN, OHIO, and WISCONSIN, and those trans-Mississippi states created from the Louisiana Purchase and the advancing western frontier, IOWA, KANSAS, MINNESOTA, MISSOURI, NEBRASKA,

NORTH DAKOTA, and SOUTH DAKOTA. Entries also examine the literatures of leading Midwestern cities: CHICAGO, CINCINNATI, CLEVELAND, DETROIT, KANSAS CITY, MINNEAPOLIS/ST. PAUL, and ST. LOUIS. Other essays highlight GREAT LAKES LITERATURE, RIVER LITERATURE, and the CHICAGO RENAISSANCE, the region's most influential literary site and movement. Coverage of Midwestern products of the FEDERAL WRITERS' PROJECT and the IOWA WRITERS' WORKSHOP, the nation's premier writing program, round out these geographically based depictions.

• Literatures of major Midwestern population groups, including those often overlooked because of erroneous assumptions of cultural homogeneity: AFRICAN AMERICAN LITERATURE, ARAB AMERICAN LITERATURE, ASIAN AMERICAN LITERATURE, JEWISH LITERATURE, LATINO/LATINA LITERATURE, NATIVE AMERICAN LITERATURE, and SCANDINAVIAN LITERATURE. Discussion of Midwestern DIALECTS confirms the movement of population groups to and through the Midwest, as well as the competition, conflict, and cultural enrichment marking interchanges between heterogeneous peoples. Explorations of Midwestern literary FEMINISM and of the region's LESBIAN, GAY, BISEXUAL, TRANSGENDER, AND QUEER LITERATURE further broaden the range of cultural heterogeneity and highlight contributions to Midwestern literature and culture by these many diverse but fully Midwestern groups.

• Historical and cultural developments, such as those producing IMMIGRANT AND MIGRANT LITERATURE and regional writing reflecting geographic contexts. The volume makes clear the literary, cultural, and political impacts of immigration and migration to and through the Midwest by Americans, as well as by those from other nations. A commentary on Midwestern and American writers who became EXPATRIATES chronicles their activities during the first half of the twentieth century. Together these treatments of Midwestern population groups and their political, social, and economic movements over the past two hundred years emphasize the diversity and continuing evolution shaping the region's literature and culture. These entries demonstrate Midwestern connections to the literature and life of the other regions of the United States and, indeed, of every region on the globe. They manifest the historical, geographic, and political evolution of the United States as embodied in the Midwest, shaped by Enlightenment ideas and created as the first regional product of the nascent federal government. In this context, they indicate the literary and cultural products of European exploration in the region that would become the Midwest. This historical perspective also appears in entries on Midwestern CAPTIVITY NARRATIVES, FRONTIER AND PIONEER ACCOUNTS, and NATIVE AMERICANS AS DEPICTED IN LITERATURE from the earliest years to the present, with significant perceptual shifts becoming evident over time. Essays on FARM LITERATURE and URBAN LITERATURE and on the SMALL TOWN and the SUBURB further depict Midwestern experience and perceptions. The final essay in this group considers the theory posited by CARL VAN DOREN (1885–1950): a Midwestern REVOLT FROM THE VILLAGE.

• Social movements and cultural change, capturing the ferment experienced in the region and across the nation. Analysis of SLAVE NARRATIVES brings to light the experience of slavery and its aftermath, as does the state entry for Kansas, the place where abolitionists and pro-slavery adherents clashed most vehemently before the Civil War. Similar divisions over issues like immigration, wage inequality, and class warfare have marked Midwestern experience and that of the nation in the past and continue to do so today. Also present are essays that detail responses to social conditions: PROGRESSIVISM, PROTEST LITERATURE, literary RADICALISM, and HULL-HOUSE, the first American embodiment of the international settlement-house movement. Pivotal Midwestern literary works regularly embody economic and social issues, protest, and even calls for revolution. Midwestern portrayal in literature of BUSINESS and of TECHNOLOGY AND INDUSTRY embodies Midwestern experience and response over two centuries. Alternative Midwestern attempts to achieve better lives also have literary embodiments, as in UTOPIAN LITERATURE, as well as in consideration of RELIGION and PHILOSOPHY.

• Literary genres such as AUTOBIOGRAPHY, CREATIVE NONFICTION, DRAMA, ENVIRONMENTAL LITERATURE, HUMOR, LITERARY MAPS, NEWSPAPER JOURNALISM, REALISM AND NATURALISM, REGIONAL THEATRE, and PRINTING AND PUBLISHING, as well as more popular forms of literature, among them CHILDREN'S AND YOUNG ADULT LITERATURE, COMIC STRIPS AND BOOKS, DIME NOVELS, FILM, GRAPHIC NOVELS, MYSTERY AND DETECTIVE FICTION, and SCIENCE FICTION AND FANTASY.

• Literary periodicals, including St. Louis's *REEDY'S MIRROR;* Chicago's literarily conservative *THE DIAL,* avant-garde *POETRY: A MAGAZINE OF VERSE,* and *THE LITTLE REVIEW;* and Iowa's *The MIDLAND,* the groundbreaking publication in Midwestern literary regionalism. A collective entry outlines the nature and contributions of other Midwestern LITERARY PERIODICALS.

• Regional studies featuring perspectives on Midwestern literary ANTHOLOGIES, ARCHETYPES, CULTURAL STUDIES, and a BIBLIOGRAPHY. These are supplemented by treatments of Midwestern ETHNOGRAPHY, FOLKLORE, and HISTORIOGRAPHY, as well as of the sister arts, ART and ARCHITECTURE. A brief history of the SOCIETY FOR THE STUDY OF MIDWESTERN LITERATURE, the central scholarly organization devoted to the creation and study of Midwestern literature and culture, rounds out this focus.

Methodologies

The volumes of the *Dictionary of Midwestern Literature* employ interdisciplinary methodologies. Literary analysis and the many schools of literary criticism dominate, but other disciplinary approaches, including those of anthropology, cultural and economic geography, educational and political theory, ecological thought, ethnic and racial studies, ethnography, folklore, gender and sexuality studies, history, linguistics, philosophy, and sociology, also contribute to the discussion. The volumes focus on the Midwest, its literature, and its culture, but they remain conscious of national and world literary, historical, political, and social movements as they impinge on and interact with the region.

Misconceptions

The volumes of the *Dictionary of Midwestern Literature* delineate the literature and culture of the region, but at the beginning of this second volume a brief statement and rebuttal of the three dominant misleading stereotypes of Midwestern life and literature is worthwhile. Consideration of these views recurs throughout the series, particularly in the essay on Midwestern archetypes, but they deserve brief discussion here. First is the notion that the region and its people are homogeneous, composed of uniformly white, middle-class people and communities. The second misconception perceives the Midwest as a cultural backwater devoid of literary and cultural merit, hopelessly behind the times, and only flyover country for those traveling between the more cultivated East and West Coasts. The third conceives of the Midwest as static, a region caught in the past like a prehistoric insect in amber, with no possibility for significant advancement over time and no awareness of or participation in regional, national, or global trends or movements.

The first stereotype, that of bland homogeneity, is false on its face. Diverse immigrant groups settled the Midwest and continue to do so. From the earliest days of white settlement in the region to the present, these groups have tended to form enclaves marked by a common language, nationality, ethnicity, or religion. These enclaves sometimes encompass large geographic areas, as, for example, the Scandinavian settlement of the upper Midwest, as referenced by writers and works like *GIANTS IN THE EARTH* (1927) by OLE EDVART RØLVAAG (1876–1931), and the Latino/Latina migration into and transformation of the Midwest, as reflected in *...Y NO SE LO TRAGÓ LA TIERRA / ...AND THE EARTH DID NOT DEVOUR HIM* (1971) by Tomás Rivera (1935–1984). More typically, these protective enclaves have been small rural communities or urban neighborhoods bordered by others different in some distinctive respects. Midwestern literary works describing Nebraska by WILLA CATHER (1873–1947) call attention to the region's adjacent but distinct ethnic and religious entities. The same is true of *STUDS LONIGAN: A TRILOGY* (1935) by JAMES T(HOMAS) FARRELL (1904–1979), documenting the encroachment of other groups on its Chicago Irish enclave. Many Midwestern works explore these distinctions, from uneasy coexistence to life-and-death struggles between competing groups in close proximity; representative of these are THE JUNGLE (1906) by UPTON (BEALL) SINCLAIR (JR.) (1878–1968), A STREET IN BRONZEVILLE (1945) by GWENDOLYN BROOKS (1917–2000), THE HOUSE ON MANGO STREET (1984) by SANDRA CISNEROS (b. 1954), and SONG OF SOLOMON (1977) by TONI MORRISON (b. CHLOE ARDELIA WOFFORD, 1931).

Another misperception associated with this presumed homogeneity is the belief that the Midwest consists solely of farms and small rural communities. Although farm experience and small-town life have significant places in Midwestern life and literature of the past and present, as of 2010 the twelve Midwestern states included ten of the nation's fifty largest cities. During the late nineteenth and early twentieth centuries Midwestern manufacturing cities were magnets for rural people seeking better lives; during the early and mid-twentieth century African Americans participated in two great migrations from the South to the Midwest, settling primarily in Chicago and Detroit industrial districts but also changing the demographics of the entire region. The Great Depression and the world wars saw the Midwest's cities energized by immigrant groups from across the region, the South, Appalachia, and the world. These diverse populations contributed to the workforce that made the Midwest and America what President Franklin D. Roosevelt called the "arsenal of democracy," in his 1940 radio address. In peacetime, for over a century the Midwest's urban-based businesses and industries have fed national and global appetites for automobiles, consumer goods, and a wide range of manufactures. Clearly, large cities and other urban areas are as quintessentially Midwestern as the region's universally recognized farms, small towns, and rows of corn stretching to the horizon. See also ARCHETYPES for fuller discussion of this topic.

The facts again are equally strong in considering the second erroneous stereotype, that of the Midwest as culturally defi-

cient. The Nobel Prize for Literature constitutes one standard of international acclaim, and four of the eight Nobel Prizes conferred on writers from the United States have gone to Midwesterners: (HARRY) SINCLAIR LEWIS (1885–1951), ERNEST (MILLER) HEMINGWAY (1899–1961), SAUL BELLOW (1915–2005), and Toni Morrison. Five Midwesterners are among the nineteen people awarded the title of Consultant in Poetry to the Library of Congress or the newer designation as Poet Laureate of the United States since 1985. Among these are Gwendolyn Brooks of Illinois, MONA VAN DUYN (1921–2004) of Iowa, RITA DOVE (b. 1952) of Ohio, Ted Kooser (b. 1939) of Nebraska, and Philip Levine (1928–2015) of Michigan.

In the late nineteenth and early twentieth centuries Midwestern writers led the nation in the development of American literary realism. Midwestern editors like WILLIAM DEAN HOWELLS (1837–1920), WILLIAM MARION REEDY (1862–1920) of Reedy's Mirror in St. Louis, HARRIET MONROE (1860–1936) of Poetry: A Magazine of Verse in Chicago, and MARGARET C. ANDERSON (1886–1973) of The Little Review, also in Chicago, and the literary movement of the Chicago Renaissance led the United States away from nineteenth-century poetic and prose fiction norms and toward modernist and other more contemporary poetic approaches.

The Midwest also claims an abundance of Pulitzer Prize recipients, some of whom have already been mentioned as Nobel laureates or U.S. poets laureate; others include, in drama, ZOË AKINS (1886–1958), ZONA GALE (1874–1938), SUSAN (KEATING) GLASPELL (1876–1948), WILLIAM (MOTTER) INGE (1913–1973), Tracy Letts (b. 1965), DAVID (ALAN) MAMET (b. 1947), Bruce Norris (b. 1960), SAM(UEL) SHEPARD (ROGERS III) (b. 1943), August Wilson (1945–2005), and Lanford Wilson (1937–2011); in poetry, Lisel Mueller (b. 1924), MARY OLIVER (b. 1935), THEODORE ROETHKE (1908–1963), CARL (AUGUST) SANDBURG (1878–1967), SARA TEASDALE (1884–1933), Mona Van Duyn, and James Wright (1927–1980); and in fiction, Robert Olen Butler (b. 1945), Willa Cather, (KAREN) LOUISE ERDRICH (b. 1954), Jeffrey Eugenides (b. 1960), EDNA FERBER (1885–1968), Jonathan Franzen (b. 1959), JOYCE CAROL OATES (b. 1938), Marilynne Robinson

(b. 1943), Sinclair Lewis, and BOOTH TARKING-TON (1869–1946). Syndicated Chicago commentator (MICHAEL) MIKE ROYKO (1932–1997) and journalist-autobiographer WILLIAM ALLEN WHITE (1868–1944) are also Pulitzer recipients. Collectively, these many recognitions document the Midwest's literary strength, quality, and strong cultural underpinnings.

Belief in a static Midwest with unchanging literature is the third misguided stereotype. Although perceptions of the region as a fixed point in a world of change and uncertainty lead to nostalgically endearing perceptions of the Midwest, the reality is different. Midwestern family farms are driven by national and global markets and have largely given way to the agribusiness described in *Shoeless Joe* (1982) by W(ILLIAM) P(ATRICK) KINSELLA (b. 1935), which was made into the movie *Field of Dreams* (1989). The region's small towns continue to lose population. Midwestern cities have been largely transmuted from smoke-belching, steel-producing industrial centers to postindustrial communities as national tax structures, global labor costs, and international trade agreements continue to alter the economic landscape. Midwestern populations are moving in step with those of the nation and the world. Political, social, and economic refugees from other nations have poured in, changing the makeup of Midwestern communities with the advent of African American, Asian, Arab, and Latino/Latina populations. One need only look at the rising Lebanese and Iraqi community centered on metropolitan Detroit, the Hmong enclave in and around St. Paul, Minnesota, or the Chicano/Chicana migration and Latin American immigration that have modified the complexion of the Midwest's cities and small towns. The ARCHETYPES entry in this volume makes clear the nature of and reasons for this ironically continuing misconception.

Volumes 1 and 2 of the *Dictionary of Midwestern Literature* and the projected volume 3, *The Literary History of the Midwest*, move beyond stereotypes. They portray the region and its people, culture, and literature as they have been in the past and as they are now.

How to Use This Volume and the Dictionary of Midwestern Literature *Series*

The organization of the *Dictionary of Midwestern Literature* series makes information easy to locate and use. The two existing volumes and the projected third volume complement one another, alerting readers to the availability of additional relevant information elsewhere in the series.

SMALL CAPS are the most obvious assistive tool, as seen in the preceding paragraphs on the contents and organization of this volume and the series. The presence of small caps indicates the existence of an entry in the *Dictionary of Midwestern Literature* series that adds to information at the reader's current location.

"See" and "See also" indicators appear where connections between coverage in the two locations are less direct but still valuable. "See" references also point out writers, groups, or entries identified by multiple names. For example, SAMUEL LANGHORNE CLEMENS (1835–1910) wrote under the pen name Mark Twain. Clemens's author entry appears alphabetically under Clemens, but the words "MARK TWAIN. See Samuel Langhorne Clemens" are placed alphabetically where Twain would appear in the first volume. Similarly, the "Latino/Latina Literature" entry in volume 2 appears alphabetized appropriately at Latino, but at the locations where "Mexican American Literature," "Chicano/Chicana Literature," and "Hispanic Literature" would occur, the guiding reference "See Latino/Latina Literature" directs the reader. Comprehensive indexes at the end of each volume further assist readers in locating information presented across the volumes.

Within each entry, the organization of sections structures information predictably. Each author essay in volume 1 has four parts. BIOGRAPHY supplies the writer's life history; SIGNIFICANCE outlines the Midwestern literary significance of the writer's works; SELECTED WORKS showcases the leading works by that writer; and FURTHER READING captures leading critical commentary on the writer's works, identifies biographical and bibliographic sources, and indicates repositories holding important manuscripts and related materials.

Organization is nearly identical for most entries in volume 2, but variants in first-level headings exist between major entry types appearing in this volume. Most entries begin with an OVERVIEW outlining the main thrust of the discussion. HISTORY AND SIGNIFICANCE explains the period of prevalence, relevance to Midwestern literature, and nature of each topic, whether it be SLAVE NARRATIVES or the CHICAGO RENAISSANCE. SELECTED WORKS indicates literary works most fully embodying and reflecting that topic. FURTHER READING points out valuable criticism and other secondary sources.

Volume 2's coverage of the twelve state literatures adds additional subheadings to better guide readers. Each begins by briefly stating the historical, geographic, political, and population information for that state. An OVERVIEW follows, outlining the state's cultural and literary experience at somewhat greater length and previewing the focus and ordering of topics in the discussion. HISTORY AND SIGNIFICANCE conveys the state's literary heritage, with material typically organized chronologically and by genre. The SELECTED WORKS section lists the state's most notable literature. FURTHER READING identifies leading secondary sources of information on the state and its literature. This structure initially seems the same as that of other subject essays, but the great length, the larger number of topics to be covered, the variability of the literatures of the states, and the extended chronological periods reported on for each state require additional organizational divisions. Thus, a state's HISTORY AND SIGNIFICANCE section typically also includes "Exploration and Travel," "Fiction," "Poetry," "Drama," and a number of subgenres under "Popular Literature." SELECTED WORKS subdivisions indicate the most central literary works, sometimes using many of these same subheadings. FURTHER READING divisions often include biography, bibliography, and literary archives. It must be noted that although the general organization of information within the state entries is fairly consistent, there are variations and departures among them. This variability reflects the individuality of each Midwestern state

and the predilection of the author in how the state's literature is presented and emphasized.

Discussions of pivotal Midwestern literary works also demand slightly modified treatment. They begin with HISTORY, which specifies the facts of composition and publication and includes the initial critical reaction. SIGNIFICANCE follows, setting forth the importance of the literary product over time. Because first editions are often difficult to access and because reprints, with or without changes, are frequent, IMPORTANT EDITIONS indicates the changes to the publication over time through authorial or editorial decisions, such as those associated with the evolving text of MAIN-TRAVELLED ROADS (1891) by (HANNIBAL) HAMLIN GARLAND (1860–1940) as the author moved beyond the first edition's six stories detailing the earliest stages of settlement and progressively added stories associated with later phases. This section also identifies the most accessible high-quality version of the book. Finally, FURTHER READING indicates the most important criticism.

To further clarify structure throughout this volume and the series, major headings appear in bold SMALL CAPS at the left-hand margin. Second-level headings are also in bold, use upper- and lower-case type, and appear at the left-hand margin but do not use small caps. Third-level headings, such as those often delineating the many genres of popular literature, are in bold italics and appear at the left-hand margin. The typical three levels of markers—for example, **HISTORY AND SIGNIFICANCE**, **Popular Literature**, *Juvenile and Young Adult Literature*—are readily identifiable and will help scholars, librarians, casual readers, and students perceive the structuring of entries and quickly locate elements of specific interest to them. Chronology and historical context are helpful in understanding individual entries, as well as the entire *Dictionary of Midwestern Literature* series. For that reason, where possible, the birth, death, or birth and death dates of authors are presented immediately after the first mention. Where exact dates cannot be definitively provided, as with the birth year of PAMILLA W. BALL (ca. 1790–1838), "ca." indicates "circa" or close to the year indicated. The indicator "fl.," meaning "flourished" or known to have been alive and active during the period listed, appears where very little definitive information exists about an author. Similarly, when the title of a literary work is first mentioned, the year of initial publication follows immediately.

The *Dictionary of Midwestern Literature* series organizes information to make it accessible and easily understandable regardless of whether the user reads the full presentation or consults only a specific section for its differentiated content. Therefore, readers may focus on SELECTED WORKS to learn the most significant literary works associated with a subject or FURTHER READING for the leading critical and secondary sources on an author or subject.

Finally, it is appropriate here to look at more than just functional use and to consider the larger literary and cultural significance of this volume and the full *Dictionary of Midwestern Literature* series. Collectively, the two extant volumes, setting forth the region's authors, its many literatures and diverse populations, literary landmarks, genres, movements, sites, centers, experiences, and sources, and the projected third volume, addressing the region's literary history, constitute the most wide-ranging, significant study of Midwestern literature and culture to date. These volumes recognize the American Midwest's continuing cultural vitality and its literary strength, distinctiveness, and value. Looking backward, we see that Midwestern literature written in or rapidly translated into English captures more than two centuries of widespread European settlement and cultural expression in the region. In encompassing Midwestern and American experience over those centuries, this volume demonstrates that the Midwest belies its stereotype as essentially rural, white, and middle class. Looking forward, we predict that Midwestern literature will continue to be rich, resilient, and regionally, nationally, and globally relevant. This literature is complex and ever evolving, reflecting diverse populations and wide-ranging experiences. The many scholars from across the United States and other nations who have been and will be involved in Midwestern studies testify to the importance of Midwestern regional literature and culture. The Society for the Study of Midwestern Literature, now over forty years old, continues to grow, attract new members, and support the creation and study of this important literature.

On behalf of the scholars and editorial board of the *Dictionary of Midwestern Literature* series and the Society for the Study of Midwestern Literature, I invite you to experience and enjoy this volume and the series.

Philip A. Greasley, General Editor
University of Kentucky

A

ADVENTURES OF AUGIE MARCH, THE

HISTORY: *The Adventures of Augie March*, the third novel by SAUL (C.) BELLOW (1915–2005) and the one that marked his maturity as a major American writer, was published in the fall of 1953. Set in Depression-era CHICAGO, the novel follows the adventures of Augie March, a street-smart, ambitious, and intellectual son of immigrant Russian Jewish parents. Reviews prominently featured in such journals as the *New York Times Book Review* and the *Saturday Review of Literature* revealed a critical ambiguity that continues to prevail.

The nature of these reviews reflects not only critics' attitudes but also Bellow's attitude toward the novel after its publication and in following years. Although he defended the novel against what he considered undue criticism, he is quoted in "The Art of Fiction XXXVII," *Paris Review* 36 (Winter 1966): 48–73, as thinking the novel too excessive and its style and structure in need of restraint (54). Nevertheless, in the same interview he said that he had written *Augie March* with "a great sense of freedom" (57). Later, in a May 1997 *Playboy* interview (59+), he asserted that *Augie March* had

liberated the American novel from "the English mandarin influence," as well as from Hemingway's (68). Hemingway, Bellow explained, "was a very marvelous and beautiful writer who was constricting. He produced novels with a highly polished surface. You didn't want to mar the surface of his beautifully constructed and polished stories or novels. But then it was too narrowing, because there were all kinds of experience which would never fit into that" (68). Significantly, the novel received the 1954 National Book Award for Fiction.

The critical ambiguity with which the novel has been regarded by reviewers, scholars, and Bellow himself may well be the result of what Bellow planned to do in the novel, as well as of the complex history of the novel's composition. *Augie March* appeared more than six years after the publication of *The Victim* in 1947. In that six-year period Bellow signed a contract for and abandoned a novel tentatively called *The Crab and the Butterfly*. He also applied for and, after two unsuccessful earlier applications, received a Guggenheim Award for $2,500, which he planned to spend on a year in Paris. Above all, he wrote, first on the novel that was later aborted and on other writing projects and then, increasingly furiously, on what was to become *The Adventures of Augie March.* The first tangible manifestation of the novel-to-be appeared in the November 1949 *Partisan Review* and was titled "From the Life of Augie March." In 1953 it would become chapter 1 of *The Adventures of Augie March.*

Subsequent appearances of works obviously related to the developing novel were frequent. "The Coblins," later to be chapter 2 of *Augie March,* appeared in the Autumn 1951 *Sewanee Review.* "The Einhorns," later to be chapter 5, appeared in the November–December 1951 *Partisan Review* and was reprinted in the Winter 1953 *Perspectives USA.* "Interval in a Lifeboat," later to be chapter 25, appeared in the December 27, 1952, *New Yorker.* "The Eagle," later to be chapters 15 and 16, was published in the February 1953 *Harper's Bazaar,* and "Mintouchian," later to be chapter 24, appeared in the Summer 1953 *Hudson Review.*

The Adventures of Augie March was largely the product of Bellow's Guggenheim, which gave him the freedom to write, as well as a unique perspective on his past. Both are evident throughout the novel. Freed from the relative formalism of his first two novels, as well as the perspective that governed both, he wrote furiously in a series of Parisian apartments, on café tabletops, and during excursions outside Paris. He was possessed by an exuberance he later decried, but also by the innocent adventurousness he discovered in his Midwestern antecedents from S AMUEL L ANGHORNE C LEMENS (1835–1910), writing as Mark Twain, to S HERWOOD A NDERSON (1876–1941), an influence he also later decried. He produced stories: "Dora" (*Harper's Bazaar,* November 1949, "Address by Gooley MacDowell to the Hasbeens Club of Chicago" (*Hudson Review,* Summer 1951), "A Sermon by Dr. Pep" (*Partisan Review,* May 1949), and others, but above all he worked on *Augie March.* When Bellow returned to the United States after his Guggenheim was not renewed, employment and a place to live became major problems. But after his slow tour of Europe, capped by six weeks of writing in Rome, he had the manuscript, more than 100,000 words long, well in hand.

Later, in an essay in the January 31, 1954, *New York Times Book Review* titled "How I Wrote Augie March's Story," he recounted his writing odyssey through southern Europe, concluding with the months back in the States during which he finished the novel: at the apartment of a friend, in a cold-water flat, in a Seattle hotel, in an Oregon motel, at the Yaddo artists' community, and even in Pennsylvania Station, a Broadway hotel, and the Princeton Library (3, 17). Oddly, however, he commented that not a single word of the novel was written in Chicago. With a one-year appointment as a creative-writing fellow at Princeton and with the novel finally at Viking, scheduled for spring 1953 publication, his first marriage ended but another on the horizon, Bellow felt confident about the future.

The novel was published at an auspicious time. Prominent critics had proclaimed the death of the traditional American novel even though the form endured; in the June 15, 1952, *New York Times Book Review* column "Speaking of Books," Diana Trilling (2) and, one week later in the June 22 issue,

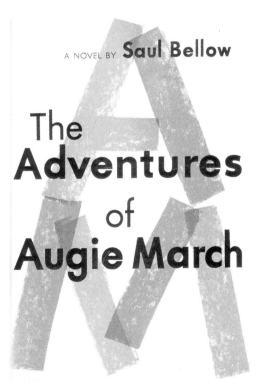

Saul Bellow's *The Adventures of Augie March.* **Dust-jacket design by Robert Hallock.**
© 1953 by Viking Press

John W. Aldridge had lamented the novel's demise (2). Others hoped that their pessimism would be refuted and believed that new young Jewish writers, Bellow among them, would introduce a new dimension into the American literary canon. *The Adventures of Augie March* was awaited with strong anticipation. Meanwhile, in a review of *Invisible Man* by Ralph Ellison (1914–1994) in the June 1952 issue of *Commentary*, Bellow insisted that the novel was hearty and strong, using Ellison's novel to support his almost passionate claims (608–10).

Before publication, the novel's success was clear. It was a selection by Readers' Subscription and an alternate selection by Book-of-the-Month Club, and it received enthusiastic blurbs by Robert Penn Warren and Lionel Trilling, as well as strong praise by Clifton Fadiman. By and large, these prepublication comments anticipated the postpublication reactions of prominent critics, both in the United States and abroad, often because they were so different. Pronouncements in the prepublication blurbs were invariably positive; the postpublication reviews were almost invariably tentative, if not ambiguous. Most reviewers were not sure what Bellow was trying to do, and most disliked his style. Nevertheless, most were sure that it was an important work.

In many ways typical of the critical responses to *The Adventures of Augie March* is that in the *Saturday Review of Literature* for September 19, 1953 (13). The cover of the issue is devoted to a drawing of Bellow against an urban neon background, thus suggesting the importance and the subject matter of the novel reviewed inside in Harvey Curtis Webster's lead review, titled "Quest through the Modern World." Webster begins the review by suggesting that reading *Augie March* in 1953 is comparable to reading *Ulysses* in 1923; he praises the story and the characterization but finds meaning "elusive." He concludes that Bellow "is perhaps a great novelist," and the book is "perhaps a great novel" (13). Robert Gorham Davis in the September 20, 1953, *New York Times* asserts that Bellow was a bit lavish in "adventures" and that Augie was not well drawn, but the novel was a major accomplishment (1, 36).

Other reviewers echo Webster's conclusions: *Time*'s anonymous September 21, 1953,

review praises the novel's "power and authenticity" but little else (114, 117). Granville Hicks in the *New Leader* for December 14, 1953, ranks it ninth among the ten best novels since 1945 and indicates that although he would recommend it to others, he would reread it himself only had he "but world enough and time" (12–14). However, Harvey Swados in the November 18, 1956, *New York Post* is unequivocal: *Augie March* is perhaps "the most significant and remarkable novel" in the past decade (11). Perhaps the most devastating review, by Anthony West in the September 26, 1953, *New Yorker,* describes parts of the novel as "frivolous," as an attempt by Bellow to seek literary fame or notoriety. West charges that the novel indulges in an "orgy of . . . loose political-sociological allegory" (128) and considers it a lesser version of Henry James's Christopher Newman in *The American* (128). Bellow took such offense at the review that he protested to the editors, who ultimately admitted that West was wrong, but Bellow never forgave or forgot either West or the review.

SIGNIFICANCE: The novel almost literally made Bellow's reputation as a major American writer, and although Bellow decried its exuberance and innocence on several occasions, it remains the cornerstone of his literary reputation and ranks high among twentieth-century works of fiction. Yet it is taught less frequently in American literature classes than it should be, primarily because of its length. A number of critics have suggested that the novel would benefit from extensive, judicious pruning.

The novel makes clear Bellow's penchant for using as models for characters people he had known in the past or even those who continued to be part of his life. Bellow admitted that his characterization of Augie drew on his Chicago neighbors, that Augie's brother, Simon, was based on Bellow's brother, Maurice, and that character names were freely borrowed from the world around him. He was equally free with the experiences of others; for example, he borrowed the eagle-training episode from the published experiences of Daniel and Jule Mannix. See D. W. Gunn, *American and British Writers in Mexico,* 1974.

Another important result of the novel was recognition that the Jewish American novel had come of age and that Bellow was a major practitioner of the art, a conclusion Bellow was quick to deny. "This whole Jewish writer business is sheer invention by the media, by critics, and by 'scholars,'" he said in one interview reprinted in the 1994 volume *Conversations with Saul Bellow* (103). He is, however, quoted in James Atlas's *Bellow* (2000) as frequently asserting that he was "an American, a Jew, a writer by trade" (128).

Publication of *The Adventures of Augie March* made Bellow a major writer and a famous man. It is often referred to as his most important work, and it has never been out of print. But Bellow grew and matured in his work, a fact he often suggested too many critics failed to acknowledge. Critics, scholars, and the reading public are now quick to acknowledge that the novel remains a major work by a major American writer.

IMPORTANT EDITIONS: The standard edition of *The Adventures of Augie March* is the fiftieth-anniversary edition, published by Viking in 2003. The text is essentially that of the 1953 edition, and the design of both the volume and the dust jacket faithfully reproduces the original, with the inclusion, however, of recognition in both that this is the fiftieth-anniversary edition; it also includes an introduction by Christopher Hitchens. Dust-jacket statements have also been updated.

Many other editions are in print in numerous languages. Most are in paperback, although hardcover editions are also widespread. The standard American paperback edition is published by Penguin Group (USA); its most recent publication date is February 2006.

FURTHER READING: No book devoted exclusively to *The Adventures of Augie March* has appeared, but many articles and essays discuss it. Bellow published "How I Wrote Augie March's Story" in the January 31, 1954, issue of the *New York Times Book Review*, and he commented on it many times in conversation and in interviews. The 1978 and 1985 bibliographies of Bellow and his critics are somewhat dated, but more general works on Bellow comment at length on Bellow's writing of *Augie March*. James Atlas's *Bellow* (2000) is definitive and extremely valuable in studying Bellow's writing of the work. Also valuable is Ruth Miller's *Saul Bellow: A Biography of the Imagination* (1991). Important critical works are Irving Malin's *Saul Bellow's Fiction* (1969) and Tony Tanner's *Saul Bellow* (1965). Other valuable works are *Conversations with Saul Bellow*, edited by Gloria Cronin and Ben Siegel (1994), and a collection of Bellow's occasional pieces, *It All Adds Up* (1994). David Mikics's "Bellow's Augie at Sixty," *Yale Review* 102 (2014): 30–42, looks back on the novel and compares it to Ellison's *Invisible Man*.

DAVID D. ANDERSON   MICHIGAN STATE UNIVERSITY

ADVENTURES OF HUCKLEBERRY FINN

HISTORY: By the time SAMUEL LANGHORNE CLEMENS (1835–1910), originally of MISSOURI, returned to his late frontier, early Midwestern youth in his best and most enduring, if most controversial, work, *Adventures of Huckleberry Finn* (London 1884; New York 1885), his nom de plume had all but supplanted his birth name in the popular mind and in the popular press. The author's name appeared as Mark Twain on the frontispiece of *Adventures of Huckleberry Finn* in 1884 in England, published by Chatto and Windus, and in Canada, published by Dawson, as well as on the title page of its first American edition, published in 1885 by Charles L. Webster and Company. Although the book was originally scheduled for simultaneous publication in the three countries in editions similar in all respects, including illustrations by Edward Windsor Kemble, American publication was delayed by copyright and pirating problems.

In a burst of pessimism, Clemens predicted a critical and financial failure that Webster was confident would not occur. Webster's optimism was more than justified when the first American edition of 30,000 copies was released to agents who had acquired thousands of advance orders. The official date of U.S. publication was February 18, 1885. The book was sold by agents in three formats for three prices: green or blue cloth at $2.75, leather at $3.25, and half morocco at $4.25. The cheapest binding had plain edges, the medium-priced library edition had sprinkled edges, and the most expensive had marbled edges (*The Annotated Huckleberry Finn* xcviii).

The Adventures of Huckleberry Finn
Chapter I.

YOU don't know about me, without you have read a book by the name of "The Adventures of Tom Sawyer," but that ain't no matter. That book was made by Mr. Mark Twain, and he told the truth, mainly. There was things which he stretched, but mainly he told the truth. That is nothing. I never seen anybody but lied, one time or another, without it was Aunt Polly, or the widow, or maybe Mary. Aunt Polly—Tom's Aunt Polly, she is—and Mary, and the Widow Douglas, is all told about in that book—which is mostly a true book; with some stretchers, as I said before.

THE WIDOW'S.

Now the way that the book winds up, is this: Tom and me found the money that the robbers hid in the cave, and it made us rich. We got six thousand dollars apiece—all gold. It was an awful sight of money when it was piled up. Well, Judge Thatcher, he took it and put it out at interest, and it fetched us a dollar a day apiece, all the year round—more than a body could tell what to do with. The Widow Douglas, she took me for her son, and allowed she would sivilize me; but it was rough living in the house all the time, considering how dismal regular and decent the widow was in all her ways; and so when I couldn't stand it no longer, I lit out. I got into my old rags, and my sugar-hogshead again, and was free and satisfied. But

2

Samuel L. Clemens's *Adventures of Huckleberry Finn,* opening page.
Charles L. Webster and Co., 1885

Before American publication in February 1885, three excerpts from the novel appeared in *Century* magazine for December 1884 and January and February 1885. The first excerpt, "An Adventure of Huckleberry Finn: With an Account of the Famous Grangerford-Shepherdson Feud," was drawn primarily from chapters 16 and 18; the second, "Jim's Investments and King Sollerman," was largely from chapters 8 and 14; the third, slightly bowdlerized to remove potentially offensive language, was "Royalty on the Mississippi: As Chronicled by Huckleberry Finn," from chapters 19, 20, 21, and 23. Periodical publication was a normal means of whetting the literary appetite for a new work. *Century* was a new, stylish magazine that had already serialized *The Rise of Silas Lapham* (November 1884–August 1885) by WILLIAM DEAN HOWELLS (1837–1920) and *The Bostonians* (1886) by Henry James (1843–1916) with good results. Clemens and Webster had hopes, ultimately justified, for the serialization of Huck's adventures.

As apparently complex as the prepublication history of *Adventures of Huckleberry Finn* was, the writing history of the book that led to its publication was even more complicated. Its evolution spanned nearly seven years. Bursts of sustained creative energy were punctuated by fallow weeks and months during which Clemens wrote or completed other works, including *A Tramp Abroad* (1880), *The Prince and the Pauper* (1882), and *Life on the Mississippi* (1883).

Clemens's initial intent in writing *Adventures of Huckleberry Finn* paralleled that of *The Adventures of Tom Sawyer* (1876). He had no clear reading audience in mind other than himself, and he wrote, as he told William Dean Howells, not for children but for adults. "It is *not* a boy's book at all. It will only be read by adults. It is only written for adults" (quoted in *Oxford Companion to Mark Twain* 13). Although Howells was enthusiastic about the book and proposed its serialization in the *Atlantic Monthly* under his editorship, he insisted that the book would be read by children and should be made suitable for them. Clemens agreed. The result was a book Clemens had not intended to write, one that remains an adult and children's classic well into its second century.

While *The Adventures of Tom Sawyer* was still in press, Clemens began *Huckleberry Finn*. Initially, he saw it as a continuation of *Tom Sawyer* and a book for adults about boyhood and its aftermath. He regretted not having written *Tom Sawyer* in the first person and planned to use the first person for *Huckleberry Finn*. He also planned to add a postscript or sequel to the new novel in which the boys of *Tom Sawyer* reunite as men to reminisce.

He wrote furiously in a burst of energy, completing nearly four hundred pages during the summer of 1876, and then stopped, writing Howells that he liked the book "only tolerably well" (quoted in *Oxford Companion to Mark Twain* 13) and planned to burn or pigeonhole the manuscript. He ultimately put it aside for nearly three years.

Clemens put the manuscript away near the end of chapter 16, when Huck and Jim, on the raft, drift past Cairo, Illinois, in the fog and miss their opportunity to sell the raft in Cairo and take passage on a steamboat up the Ohio River into free territory. At that point, however, after passing Cairo, a steamer runs down the raft, and the novel,

Clemens realized, had become something other than the quest for freedom of two runaways, a boy and a slave. Both had become creatures whose fate would be determined by chance and the river. Perhaps the shift resulted from his wish to write a book about boys for adults.

Nevertheless, Clemens ignored the book until the fall of 1879. Then, with no clear plan, he wrote chapters 17 through 22 between October 1879 and June 1883 and finished *Life on the Mississippi* that summer. The novel had become not an adventure but a portrayal of the underside of life on the banks of the river, sometimes comic but almost always with an undercurrent of horror and violence. Only on the raft in the middle of the river did sanity and virtue prevail.

At that point Clemens knew that the novel must end in ambiguity and that he had written a novel for adults, not for children. But he also knew that it would be seen as a boy's book, and he ended it not in the certainty of tragedy but in ambiguity as he reintroduced Tom Sawyer in a comic but inappropriate mistaken-identity subplot that borders on farce, with an unnecessary and absurd escape plot. The novel concludes on a final note of ambiguity when Huck asserts that he "reckons" that he's "got to light out for the territories" to make his ultimate escape. But the questions remain: Can he escape? Will he? And if he does, what follows escape? Or will he return to Aunt Polly, civilization, corruption, and ultimate adulthood? Huck is free of his father, and Jim is free of his chains, but Clemens suggests that the freedom regained is temporary, that civilization denies the possibility of escape, that rivers and journeys end not in freedom but in continued unsuccessful search. But Clemens's ending also suggests a happy ending, an ending that remains possible for boys but forever elusive for adults.

In the fall and winter of 1883 Clemens revised the entire manuscript, paying particular attention to the dialect and eliminating or changing any words or phrases suggesting an educated speaker, particularly in the language of both Huck and Jim. He also toned down scenes and rhetoric, particularly in the case of Colonel Sherburn.

He insisted that the book not be published until a substantial number of copies had been sold by subscription, but the final number of subscriptions fell 10,000 short of Clemens's goal, 40,000 copies, when the book appeared on February 18, 1885. Nevertheless, it was assured financial success. Few review copies were sent out, and critical reception was slow and mixed.

SIGNIFICANCE: Clemens's prefatory warning that "persons attempting to find a motive in this narrative will be prosecuted; persons attempting to find a moral in it will be banished; persons attempting to find a plot in it will be shot" is as deliberately disingenuous as his comments on the DIALECTS he insisted the characters speak. There is clearly a moral in the novel, evident not only in the treatment of characters as widely ranging as Pap Finn, Miss Watson, the Grangerfords and the Shepherdsons, and others but also in the clear moral growth of Huck as he senses Jim's humanity and recognizes the hypocrisy of social values and pronouncements, a moral growth paralleled by that of the shadowy Miss Watson.

Clemens apparently designed these prefatory remarks to deflect criticism directed at the novel's moral basis or its realism by leading its readers and critics to regard it as a book about boys for boys and a humorous work for all ages. Predictably, the keepers of the genteel tradition saw it as both real and humorous and condemned it on both counts. The *Springfield* (Massachusetts) *Republican,* as quoted in *Critic* 6 (March 28, 1885), reported that the Concord, Massachusetts, Library Committee considered it "rough, coarse, inelegant, more suited to the slums than to intelligent, respectable people"; it was, indeed, "veritable trash" (155).

Other critics, although seeing it as less than high literary art, nevertheless welcomed its publication. In England, the anonymous critic for *Athenaeum,* probably William Ernest Henley, wrote that "the book is Mark Twain at his best. . . . Jim and Huckleberry are real creations, and the worthy peers of Tom Sawyer" (December 27, 1884, 855). In a much longer review in the London *Saturday Review* of January 31, 1885, the anonymous critic, perhaps Brander Matthews, wrote that it is "autobiographic; it is a tale of boyish adventure along the Mississippi told as it appeared to Huck Finn. . . . Old maids of either sex will wholly fail to understand

him or to like him, or to see his significance and his value" (59).

Contemporary American critics saw the novel much as did their English colleagues, although among the Americans there was a much greater tendency to see it as realistic. T. S. Perry wrote in *Century* 30 (May 1885) that Huck and Jim "acquire full knowledge of the hideous fringe of civilization that then adorned [the Mississippi Valley]; and the book is a most valuable record of an important part of our motley American civilization." Nevertheless, "As to the humor of Mark Twain, it is scarcely necessary to speak. It lends vividness to every page" (171–72).

To Robert Bridges, humor was not only an important dimension of the novel; it was the novel. "Mark Twain is a humorist or nothing," he wrote in *Life* 5 (February 26, 1885): 19, and he itemized and described humorous incidents in detail in a tone that betrays a satirical intent: Huck's killing of the pig to fake his own death "can be repeated by any smart boy for the amusement of his fond parents"; the famous feud results in "an elopement and from six to eight choice corpses"; and the stage presentation by the King and the Duke would make good "Lenten parlor entertainments and church festivals."

Samuel Clemens's influence, particularly through his major work, *Adventures of Huckleberry Finn,* can hardly be overstated. The book has been declared an American—indeed, a world—masterpiece by such critics as H(enry) L(ewis) Mencken (1880–1956), T(homas) S(tearns) Eliot (1888–1965), Van Wyck Brooks (1886–1963), Lionel Trilling (1905–1975), and many others who insist on its significance in the American canon. However, the novel continues to receive adverse criticism, perhaps for matters that in Clemens's day would have remained unnoticed. A specific example is Huck's use of what we call today the unspeakable "n-word." In the mid-nineteenth-century Mississippi Valley it was the only word that Huck—and Jim—could have known. Clemens's use of this word is so frequent that in the novel's centennial year, 1985, a symposium of African American scholars concluded that the novel made them uncomfortable at best. Some condemned it outright, in at least one case without having read it.

Yet Clemens, the most American writer of his time, is claimed by Midwestern, western, and southern writers as their most important influence. Clemens's characters have become the grotesques of modernism in the works of Sherwood Anderson (1876–1941), William Faulkner (1897–1962), and others; his movement on the river has become the search in the works of Anderson, F(rancis) Scott (Key) Fitzgerald (1896–1940), Ernest (Miller) Hemingway (1899–1961), and others; and his dialects have become, in virtually all serious American writing of the twentieth century and beyond, the American vernacular.

Perhaps no assessment can be more meaningful and significant than the works of the writers who felt the power of Clemens's influence. William Dean Howells, his contemporary, wrote to him in 1899 that "you have pervaded your century almost more than any other man of letters, if not more" (quoted in Albert Bigelow Paine, *Mark Twain: A Biography,* volume 3, 1912, 1079). Sherwood Anderson wrote that Clemens is "among the two or three really great American artists" (Anderson, *Letters,* 1953: 3). Ernest Hemingway wrote in *Green Hills of Africa* (1935) that "all modern American literature comes from one book by Mark Twain called *Huckleberry Finn*" (22). William Faulkner, responding to a question about Sherwood Anderson's place and role in modern American literature in an interview later published as "The Art of Fiction" in the *Paris Review* 12 (Spring 1956), replied, "He [Anderson] was the father of my generation of American writers. . . . Dreiser is his older brother and Mark Twain the father of them both" (40). Contemporary writers including Thomas (Louis) Berger (1924–2014), Jim (James Thomas) Harrison (1937–2016), and Jane (Graves) Smiley (b. 1949) similarly reflect the influence of *Huckleberry Finn.*

The novel's many adaptations testify to its centrality in American popular and literary culture. John (Douglas) Seelye (b. 1931) wrote a revision, *The True Adventures of Huckleberry Finn* (1970), intended to heighten the novel's realism and address complaints about its final chapters. *My Jim* (2005) by Nancy Rawles (b. 1958) is told from the point of view of Jim's wife, and *Finn* (2007) by Jon Clinch (b. 1954) is narrated by Huck's father,

Pap. The musical *Big River: The Adventures of Huckleberry Finn* (1985) by William Hauptman and Roger Miller has enjoyed several revivals. At least eleven Film adaptations have been made: the best known may be the 1939 version directed by Richard Thorpe and starring Mickey Rooney; the most faithful, the four-hour version of 1985 directed by Peter H. Hunt and televised on PBS. These adaptations of *Adventures of Huckleberry Finn* reflect changes in how Americans imagine their nation's past and how they perceive the novel's perennial themes. Samuel Clemens and his greatest creation have endured in controversy and influence for more than a century, providing sheer reading pleasure that continues into the twenty-first century.

important editions: Since its original publication in 1884–1885, *Adventures of Huckleberry Finn* has appeared in hundreds of editions in dozens of languages, and it is in print in many today. Some are the product of impeccable scholarship; others, usually editions for children, exhibit bowdlerization that often can be considered crude or inept at best. Versions, whether scholarly or commercial, continue to differ on whether the correct title is *Adventures of Huckleberry Finn,* as it appears on the title page of the first American edition, or *The Adventures of Huckleberry Finn,* as it appears on the running heads of the first American edition, thus paralleling the title of *The Adventures of Tom Sawyer,* to which it has been considered a sequel. Scholarly consensus accepts the title as it appeared on the title page of the first American edition. However, the first illustration by E. W. Kemble on page 1, chapter 1, includes *The* as part of the title.

In addition to the first three printings of the novel in England, Canada, and the United States, the novel has been reprinted in dozens of fine editions for book collectors, and since 1990 many important Clemens scholars have edited scholarly editions. Among the most important and useful are those edited by Victor Fischer and Lin Salamo (2001, 2003) as part of the University of California Press edition of *The Collected Works of Mark Twain.* Also valuable are the New Riverside Edition, edited by Susan K. Harris and Lyrae Van Clief-Stefanon (2001), and that by Oxford University Press (1996) with a foreword by Shelley Fisher Fishkin, an introduction by Toni Morrison (b. Chloe

ARDELIA WOFFORD, 1931), and an afterword by Victor A. Doyno. The third edition of the Norton Critical Edition published in 1998 and edited by Thomas Cooley is both useful and readily available. The Random House edition (1996), with an introduction by Justin Kaplan, a forward and addendum by Victor Doyno, and Kemble's original illustrations, is attractive and handsome. The Centennial Facsimile Edition by Harper and Row (1987), with an introduction and bibliography by Hamlin Hill, is particularly interesting. *The Annotated Huckleberry Finn* (2001), edited by Michael Patrick Hearn, features exhaustively detailed commentary and illustrations.

FURTHER READING: Samuel Clemens and *Adventures of Huckleberry Finn* have been widely discussed in popular and scholarly literature since the book's publication, and writing about both shows no signs of diminishing. The biography *Mark Twain: A Life* (2005) by Ron Powers is well written and comprehensive, with insights into Clemens, his times, and his works. Other important works are Albert Bigelow Paine's *Mark Twain: A Biography* (1912), Justin Kaplan's *Mr. Clemens and Mark Twain* (1966), and Hamlin Hill's *Mark Twain, God's Fool* (1973).

Important works on *Adventures of Huckleberry Finn* include *Huck Finn's America: Mark Twain and the Era That Shaped His Masterpiece* (2015) by Andrew Levy; *Coming to Grips with "Huckleberry Finn": Essays on a Book, a Boy, and a Man* (1995) by Tom Quirk; *Writing "Huckleberry Finn": Mark Twain's Creative Process* by Victor A. Doyno (1991); *Born to Trouble: One Hundred Years of "Huckleberry Finn"* by Justin Kaplan (1985); and a particularly valuable collection of essays, *One Hundred Years of "Huckleberry Finn": The Boy, the Book, and American Culture; Centennial Essays,* edited by Robert Sattelmeyer and J. Donald Crowley (1985). In *"Huckleberry Finn" on Film: Film and Television Adaptations of Mark Twain's Novel, 1920–1993* (1994), Clyde V. Haupt reviews all major screen versions of the novel.

Numerous controversial essays and books have appeared over the years, among them Leslie A. Fiedler's "Come Back to the Raft Ag'in, Huck Honey!," in *An End to Innocence* (1955): 142–51. Also debatable are Shelley Fisher Fishkin's *Was Huck Black? Mark Twain and African-American Voices* (1993)

and Jane Smiley's "Say It Ain't So, Huck: Second Thoughts on Mark Twain's 'Masterpiece'" in *Harper's* (January 1996): 61–67.

Most of Clemens's manuscripts are in the Bancroft Library of the University of California at Berkeley. The typescripts of *Adventures of Huckleberry Finn,* on which Clemens made extensive revisions, were apparently lost, but the manuscript was finally reunited in 1990 after the first half had been mislaid for 103 years and considered lost.

DAVID D. ANDERSON   MICHIGAN STATE UNIVERSITY

AFRICAN AMERICAN LITERATURE

OVERVIEW: Discussions of Midwestern African American history often begin with the Great Migration, the mass movement of blacks out of the South between 1910 and 1930. Although many of these migrants moved to the West, New England, or the Mid-Atlantic states, large numbers headed for Midwestern cities, including CHICAGO and DETROIT, which offered industrial employment and the chance to create communities far from the increasingly oppressive Jim Crow South. Beginning with the Great Migration, the central narrative of African American history is dominantly urban. African American literature of the Midwest reflects that reality, and most well-known writers have portrayed black urban experience.

But the region's African American experience predates the twentieth century and encompasses rural as well as urban experience. African Americans have lived in the Midwest since the late eighteenth century, and their numbers grew in the nineteenth century, particularly after the Civil War and Emancipation. These earlier Midwesterners also produced literature, which this entry will review before discussing writers of the twentieth century and after. Although they are not present in all texts, certain themes recur in this writing, which has engaged in an ongoing conversation about the place of African Americans in a nation that first enslaved them and then withheld civil rights for over a century. Racial pride, resistance, and religion are perennial concerns, as are migration, community, and history. Stylistically, black writers have long found inspiration in rhetoric and rhythms drawn from black colloquial speech and the musical tradition that produced gospel, blues, jazz, soul, and hip-hop.

HISTORY AND SIGNIFICANCE: With the exception of small communities in northern states, the majority of people of African descent were in bondage in southern states until 1865. The North, including Midwestern states like OHIO, MICHIGAN, and INDIANA, represented the promised land, a place where African Americans could escape the yoke of slavery and enjoy the blessings of liberty, including paid labor and the chance to form communities with the mutual aid of churches, schools, and other organizations. This is not to say that the Midwest was a land of equality and good will. Despite anti-slavery provisions in the Northwest Ordinance and state laws, slavery existed in Midwestern states, and not only in the slave state of MISSOURI. Through both legal and extralegal means, northern whites also denied opportunities to free blacks and prevented their full participation in public life.

Yet African Americans were beginning to advance even before the Civil War, and in churches, black colleges like Wilberforce in Ohio, and abolitionist meetings, literary expression stirred. A famous example is the speech "Ain't I a Woman?" (1851), delivered at the Ohio Women's Rights Convention in Akron, Ohio, by SOJOURNER TRUTH (1797–1883). Born Isabella Baumfree, a slave in Swartekill, New York, she renamed herself in 1843 when she moved to Massachusetts and started to work for abolition and write her memoirs, published as *Narrative of Sojourner Truth: A Northern Slave* in 1850. In 1857 Truth bought a house in Harmonia, Michigan, where she lived for ten years before moving to nearby Battle Creek. Many of her speeches to abolitionist groups in Michigan and elsewhere were transcribed, as were addresses to the Michigan legislature after the Civil War. She also wrote a song, "The Valiant Soldiers," for the First Michigan Colored Regiment. *Sojourner Truth as Orator: Wit, Story, and Song* (1997), edited by Suzanne Pullon Fitch and Roseann M. Mandziuk, collects many of Truth's works.

Another black abolitionist was James Madison Bell (1826–1902). Born in Gallipolis, Ohio, Bell lived most of his life in CINCINNATI and Toledo. While living in Canada, he raised funds and recruited for John Brown,

I Sell the Shadow to Support the Substance.
SOJOURNER TRUTH.

Sojourner Truth, 1864.
Image courtesy of the Library of Congress

who conducted meetings at Bell's house. After Brown's raid on Harper's Ferry in 1859, Bell sought safe haven in San Francisco, where he started to write long poems to deliver as public orations. Bell's most celebrated poem, "The Day and War" (1864), deals with Brown, the Civil War, the heroism of African American troops, and the Emancipation Proclamation. He published *The Poetical Works of James Madison Bell* in 1901.

The Colored Aristocracy of St. Louis (1858) by Cyprian Clamorgan (1830–ca. 1906) is a rarity, a book by a free black living in a slave state. Clamorgan, who acquired wealth through barbering, real estate, and other ventures, provides portraits of educated and successful free blacks that were intended, as Julie Winch writes in her introduction to the annotated edition of 1999, "to convince white Americans that race was not an absolute, that the African American community was not a monolith, that class, education, and especially wealth, should count for something" (2).

SLAVE NARRATIVES, both published memoirs and transcriptions of interviews, are much appreciated for their literary value. African American writers have long drawn inspiration from slave narratives, many of which were written by former slaves in the Midwest or were dictated to interviewers from the FEDERAL WRITERS' PROJECT of the Works Progress Administration (WPA).

After the Civil War, African Americans were drawn to destinations in the Midwest by the promise of a better life and by other factors that spoke to their unique experience as former slaves. Many sought to escape overt discrimination and often violent treatment by individuals who wanted to reverse the political and economic gains made by blacks during Reconstruction. The proximity of former slave states like Kentucky and Tennessee to Midwestern destinations like Ohio made these migrations more attractive than a long trek to an eastern destination like New York. Work opportunities were plentiful in Ohio, Indiana, and ILLINOIS shortly after the Civil War because of farm labor shortages. Also, the Exoduster movement of 1879 involved an unplanned, mass migration from southern states to KANSAS, which was attractive to migrants because of its reputation as a place where African Americans could enjoy freedom, prosperity, and education.

Writers who emerged between the Civil War and World War I include CHARLES WADDELL CHESNUTT (1858–1932), born to free parents of mixed race in North Carolina. In 1883 he moved his family to CLEVELAND, Ohio, where he took a law degree and started to publish. Chesnutt's fiction reflects his experiences with the African American middle class in Cleveland and reveals the intraracial prejudice that ran rampant among the upper echelons of black society. His collections of stories, such as *The Wife of His Youth, and Other Stories of the Color Line* (1899), and novels, such as *The Marrow of Tradition* (1901), are pioneering works of African American fiction. In 2002 the Library of America published *Stories, Novels, and Essays.*

An acquaintance of Chesnutt's, Carrie Williams Clifford (1862–1934) was born in Chillicothe, Ohio, and grew up in Columbus. In 1886 she married William H. Clifford, a lawyer and one of the first black men to serve in the Ohio state legislature. They moved to Cleveland, where she founded literary societies and the Ohio Federation of Colored Women's Clubs, which worked for women's suffrage and racial justice. She also began publishing poetry, essays, and short stories and editing literary journals. In 1908 her family moved to Washington, D.C., where she held literary salons featuring such notables as Chesnutt and W(illiam E(dward) B(urghardt) Du Bois (1868–1963). An important early figure in the NAACP, Clifford published two books of poetry, *Race Rhymes* (1911) and *The Widening Light* (1922).

Late nineteenth-century poets working in black dialect constituted an important movement. Although these poets only occasionally confronted racism in their work, they testified to the dignity and worth of their African American subjects. Most also wrote poems in Standard English and courted white as well as black readers. Midwestern dialect poets included James Edwin Campbell (1867–1896). Born in Pomeroy, Ohio, Campbell worked as a teacher in Ohio and a school principal in West Virginia before moving to Chicago, where he worked in journalism and helped publish a literary journal called the *Four O'Clock Magazine.* He collected his poems in *Driftings and Gleanings* (1887) and *Echoes from the Cabin and Elsewhere* (1895). Although some of Campbell's poems are marked by stereotypes, he did capture aspects of black folk culture.

Campbell's poetry anticipated that of PAUL LAURENCE DUNBAR (1872–1906), who focused on aspects of the African American experience rather than on the Midwest's impact on that experience. The son of slaves who had migrated to Dayton, Ohio, Dunbar became well known for poetry in Standard English, as well as in dialect. Because he drew from the plantation tradition, some of his poems feature positive portrayals of pre–Civil War life in the South, with black characters content in their roles as servants. But Dunbar did express anger at racial oppression, and poems like "We Wear the Mask" (1895) have entered the literary canon. See THE CHANGING MIDWESTERN LITERARY CANON. Dunbar also published fiction, collected in *The Complete Stories of Paul Laurence Dunbar*

Lyrics of Lowly Life.

WE WEAR THE MASK.

WE wear the mask that grins and lies,
    It hides our cheeks and shades our
        eyes, —
This debt we pay to human guile ;
With torn and bleeding hearts we smile,
And mouth with myriad subtleties.

Why should the world be over-wise,
In counting all our tears and sighs?
Nay, let them only see us, while
        We wear the mask.

We smile, but, O great Christ, our cries
To thee from tortured souls arise.
We sing, but oh the clay is vile
Beneath our feet, and long the mile ;
But let the world dream otherwise,
        We wear the mask !

167

"We Wear the Mask" by Paul Laurence
Dunbar, from his *Lyrics of Lowly Life.*
Dodd, Mead and Company, 1896

(2007) and *The Collected Novels of Paul Laurence Dunbar* (2009).

Fenton Johnson (1888–1958) was born in
Chicago and attended Northwestern University and the University of Chicago. Taking
themes from African American history,
Johnson initially wrote lyrics influenced by
Dunbar, then dialect poetry, and, late in his
career, free verse influenced by CARL (AU-
GUST) SANDBURG (1878–1967). His three books
of poetry, *A Little Dreaming* (1913), *Visions of
the Dusk* (1915), and *Songs of the Soil* (1916), anticipated the Harlem Renaissance of the
1920s. Marked by a generally pessimistic
tone, Johnson's poetry equates a weariness
of laboring for whites for little compensation
with a general weariness of participating in
a society that fails to recognize the contributions of African Americans. He also published a collection of stories, *Tales of Darkest
America* (1920), and another of essays, *For the
Highest Good* (1920).

OSCAR MICHEAUX (1884–1951), novelist and
filmmaker, was born in Metropolis, Illinois,
and was raised in Great Bend, Kansas, the
child of former slaves. He worked as a railroad porter in Chicago and then farmed
in SOUTH DAKOTA, where he began writing
stories. In 1919 he made *The Homesteader,*
the first film by an African American and
the first of his forty-four features. He also
wrote several novels drawing on his experiences, including *The Conquest: The Story of a
Negro Pioneer* (1913).

Northern cities, including Chicago, Detroit, and Cleveland, became the primary
destination for African American migrants
during the Great Migration (1910–1930). Chicago emerged as a popular destination because it was a railroad hub, offered industrial
jobs, and received the advocacy of the *Chicago
Defender,* the nation's largest African American newspaper at the time. The paper
published letters from black migrants expressing frustration with the Jim Crow South
and their desperation to escape to better conditions in Chicago. These letters prompted
many to leave southern locales. The *Chicago
Defender* took great pains to describe the horrors of southern life, including lynching and
other acts of terror that African Americans
continued to experience. These stories were
intentionally run next to advertisements
for employment opportunities in order to
contrast life in Chicago with that in the
South. The *Defender* also published writers
like WILLARD F. MOTLEY (1909–1965), GWENDO-
LYN (ELIZABETH) BROOKS (1917–2000), and
LANGSTON (JAMES MERCER) HUGHES (1902–1967),
who wrote a column for the newspaper.

Specifically literary publications in the
mid-twentieth-century Midwest included
the bimonthly *Negro Story,* published in Chicago between 1944 and 1946 and edited by
Alice Browning and Fern Gayden. *Midwest
Journal: A Magazine of Research and Creative
Writing,* located at Lincoln University in Jefferson City, Missouri, from 1948 to 1956, published both Langston Hughes and DUDLEY
FELKER RANDALL (1914–2000).

Born in Joplin, Missouri, Langston
Hughes conveyed African American Midwestern experience through frequent use of
rhythms and images inspired by jazz and
blues, which were powerful presences in
KANSAS CITY, ST. LOUIS, and Chicago. His po-

etry used these musical styles throughout his career, from his early collection *THE WEARY BLUES* (1926) to *Ask Your Mama: 12 Moods for Jazz* (1961). Hughes also wrote a novel, *Not without Laughter* (1930), inspired by his childhood in Lawrence, Kansas, and two autobiographies, *The Big Sea* (1940) and *I Wonder as I Wander* (1956). His journalism is collected in *Langston Hughes and the "Chicago Defender": Essays on Race, Politics, and Culture, 1942–62* (1995), edited by Christopher C. De Santis.

Although RICHARD WRIGHT (1908–1960) was born in Mississippi, he revealed the great impact Chicago had on his literary imagination. In *NATIVE SON* (1940) he characterizes the South Side of Chicago as a hostile environment that determines the tragic fate of Bigger Thomas. Wright captures the coldness of Chicago, for his protagonist views it not as a thriving metropolis with a heart, but as an unfeeling monster that instigates Bigger's descent into violence. The geography in the novel echoes the migration experience of blacks who found urban life debilitating because it retained racist structures and failed to foster communal bonds. Chicago also figures in Wright's philosophical novel *The Outsider* (1953), which opens with the derailment of an el train in Chicago, after which the action moves to New York. Two posthumously published works draw significantly on Wright's experiences in Chicago. *Lawd, Today!* (1963), the first novel Wright wrote, follows a day in the life of an African American postal worker in 1930s Chicago. The autobiography *American Hunger* (1977) covers Wright's years in Chicago and his conflicts there with the Communist Party, of which Wright was a member from 1933 to 1942.

A number of black writers besides Wright also wrote about the Great Migration and African American experience in Chicago. Waters Turpin (1910–1968) was from Maryland, but his second novel, *O Canaan!* (1939), tells of southern blacks migrating to Chicago during the Great Depression. *Behold a Cry* (1947) by Alden Bland (1911–1992) dramatizes the travails of a migrant family in Chicago at the time of World War I. The novels of William Attaway (1911–1986) include *Blood on the Forge* (1941), in which three brothers find working in a Chicago steel mill as oppressive as sharecropping down south.

Although ROBERT HAYDEN (b. Asa Bundy Sheffey, 1913–1980), Consultant in Poetry to the Library of Congress (Poet Laureate), 1976–1978, insisted on being considered a poet rather than a black poet, his poetry drew on the experiences of African Americans. His first book, *Heart-Shape in the Dust* (1940), includes several poems about his early years in Paradise Valley, the African American inner-city Detroit neighborhood where he was raised by foster parents. These include "Those Winter Sundays," which famously portrays his troubled relationship with his father. Hayden returned to Detroit in a number of later poems, most notably in "Elegies for Paradise Valley" in his final volume, *American Journal* (1982). *Selected Poems* (1966) features a range of Hayden's poetry on a variety of themes, as well as his most popular poems.

Dudley Felker Randall, a friend of Hayden's, also grew up in Detroit, where he lived most of his life. Along with his career as a librarian and his work as a publisher, Randall wrote poetry in both fixed forms and free verse that showed a deep interest in Africa and in the fortunes of black America in the mid-twentieth century. Of special regional interest are poems touching on African American life in Detroit, such as "Laughter in the Slums" (1937) and "Detroit Renaissance" (1980). Melba Joyce Boyd has edited *Roses and Revolutions: The Selected Writings of Dudley Randall* (2009).

Poet Gwendolyn Brooks, Consultant in Poetry for the Library of Congress, later designated as Poet Laureate, 1985–1986, characterized Chicago's African American residents with dignity, humor, pathos, and resiliency. Brooks introduced Bronzeville, a black community in Chicago, in her first two books, *A STREET IN BRONZEVILLE* (1945) and *The Bean Eaters* (1960). "Of De Witt Williams on His Way to Lincoln Cemetery" takes the newly departed through his old city haunts. "Kitchenette Building" evokes residential and domestic life in Chicago tenements, while "A Song in the Front Yard" alludes to class stratification. Brooks's most anthologized poem, "We Real Cool," evokes the lack of opportunity that drives young people to reckless lifestyles and a sense of urgency they derive from their situation. With her exposure to the black nationalist poets of the 1960s, Brooks's poetry became more directly aimed at speaking to black audiences and less modernist, as in *In the Mecca* (1968) and *Primer for Blacks* (1980).

Other African American writers detailed harrowing experiences in the Midwest. Lorraine (Vivian) Hansberry (1930–1965) used the experience of the Younger family, a black family attempting to leave segregated and poverty-stricken inner-city Chicago for the white suburbs, to illustrate the tensions between integrationist and black nationalist ideologies in *A Raisin in the Sun* (1959). The title came from "Harlem" (1951), a well-known poem about African American struggle by Langston Hughes, who later retitled it "Dream Deferred" to universalize its message.

Malcolm X (b. Malcolm Little, 1925–1965) details his family's ordeal in Michigan as they faced anti-black forces in *The Autobiography of Malcolm X* (1965). In his autobiographies *The Quality of Hurt* (1972) and *My Life of Absurdity* (1976), Chester (Bomar) Himes (1909–1984) used his experiences growing up in Missouri to expound on the negative impact of racism on him as a young black man. In addition to his autobiographies, Himes produced novels of social protest, including *If He Hollers Let Him Go* (1945) and *Lonely Crusade* (1947). Frank London Brown (1927–1962) based his novel *Trumbull Park* (1959) on actual accounts of the integration of a Chicago public housing project, when African American families faced threats and attacks by white mobs.

The Black Arts Movement, the cultural arm of the Black Power movement of the 1960s and 1970s, emerged in New York City but developed a strong Midwestern contingent, especially in Chicago and Detroit. Social engagement was the central value of Black Arts, and the critical test for writers was the degree to which their work confronted racism and expressed pride in the beauty of black culture and black people. Malcolm X was an important influence, both as a political figure and for the rhetorical power of his speeches and autobiography. Writers associated with the Black Arts Movement in the Midwest include Dudley Randall, Margaret (Esse) Danner (1915–1986), Margaret Taylor Burroughs (1917–2010), James A(ndrew) Emanuel (1921–2013),

Mari Evans (b. 1923), Conrad Kent Rivers (1933–1968), Eugene B. Redmond (b. 1937), and Haki R. Madhubuti (b. Don L. Lee, 1942).

Literary journals and independent presses played a central role in the Black Arts Movement. In 1961 Johnson Publications of Chicago, publishers of *Ebony* and *Jet*, revived *Negro Digest*, which had run from 1942 to 1951, under the editorship of Hoyt Fuller. Fuller published poetry, fiction, drama, and criticism, often by Chicago writers, and provided a forum on the politics and aesthetics of Black Power. Sold at newsstands across the country, *Negro Digest* was renamed *Black World* in 1970 and ran until 1976. Broadside Press, run by Dudley Randall from 1965 to 1985 at his Detroit home, published established figures like Gwendolyn Brooks and emerging writers like Madhubuti and Etheridge Knight (1931–1991). It continues to operate as a nonprofit organization. Also emerging from the Black Arts Movement was Chicago's Third World Press, founded in 1967 by Madhubuti with Johari Amini (b. 1935), Roschell Rich, and Carolyn M. Rodgers (1945–2010); and Detroit's Lotus Books, formed in 1972 by Naomi (Cornelia) Long Madgett (b. 1923). Lotus has published dozens of volumes, including works by Detroit poets Toi Derricotte (b. 1941) and Paulette Childress (b. 1948). It continues today as a special imprint of Michigan State University Press.

Madgett is Poet Laureate of Detroit and professor of English at Eastern Michigan University. The first of her many books, *Songs to a Phantom Nightingale*, appeared in 1941; others include *One and the Many* (1956), *Star by Star* (1965), and *Pink Ladies in the Afternoon* (1972). Madgett's poetry is highly personal, even when it deals with social topics, drawing on her family history and personal experience. *Connected Islands: New and Selected Poems* appeared in 2004, and Madgett's autobiography, *Pilgrim Journey*, in 2006.

The fiction of Toni Morrison (b. Chloe Ardelia Wofford, 1931) focuses on the dynamics of blackness in Ohio locations. *The Bluest Eye* (1970) uses Lorain, Ohio, as a setting against which to explore tensions regarding black female beauty and white mainstream norms. *Sula* (1974) explores the need for tolerance by the African American community in Medallion, Ohio, necessitated by its segregated experience. *SONG OF SOLOMON* (1977) examines the impact of middle-class status on the cultural memory of African Americans. Ohio plays the largest role in *Beloved* (1987), in which former slaves grapple with the pain of their pasts in bondage. Morrison's other novels also develop her complex vision of race, social class, and the legacy of black history.

Born and educated in Chicago, RONALD L. FAIR (b. 1932) taught college English and wrote for *Encyclopaedia Britannica*. His second novel, *Hog Butcher* (1966), deals with the killing of a young African American man by Chicago police and was the basis for the 1975 film *Cornbread, Earl and Me*. *World of Nothing* (1970) consists of two novellas, both set in Chicago, as is the semi-autobiographical *We Can't Breathe* (1972). Fair, who has lived in Europe since 1971, has written several unpublished novels, including *The Migrants,* an epic of the Great Migration.

Born in Noblesville, Indiana, CYRUS COLTER (1910–2002) pursued a career in law and public service before starting to write in his fifties. KURT VONNEGUT (JR.) (1922–2007) chose Colter's *The Beach Umbrella* (1970), a collection of short stories about black Chicago, for the first University of Iowa Award for Short Fiction. Colter's first novel, *The Rivers of Eros* (1972), deals with a woman caring for her grandchildren in a Chicago ghetto. *The Hippodrome* (1973) involves a Chicago man who flees from the law after murdering his wife and her white lover. *The Amoralist, and Other Tales* (1988) collects Colter's short stories.

Leon Forrest (1937–1997) was highly regarded by critics. Born into a middle-class Chicago family, Forrest wrote four novels set in fictional Forrest County, Illinois: *There Is a Tree More Ancient than Eden* (1973), *The Bloodworth Orphans* (1977), *Two Wings to Veil My Face* (1983), and *Divine Days* (1992). He also published a book of essays, *Relocations of the Spirit* (1994). Other contemporary novels set in Chicago include *Faith and the Good Thing* (1974) by Charles Johnson (b. 1948), who uses the city as a backdrop for the protagonist's philosophical speculations, and *Where I Must Go* (2009) by Angela Jackson (b. 1951), based on her experience of racism and class snobbery at Northwestern University in the late 1960s.

A number of African American poets from the Midwest have published important work in recent decades. The career of Murray Jackson (1926–2002) is sampled in *Bobweaving Detroit: The Selected Poems of Murray Jackson* (2004), edited by Ted Pearson and Kathryne V. Lindberg. HERBERT WOODWARD MARTIN (b. 1933), formerly Professor of English and Poet-in-Residence at the University of Dayton, has published six books of poetry and several studies of Paul Laurence Dunbar. Born in Mississippi in 1940, poet Sterling Plumpp came to Chicago in 1962 and was now Professor of English and African American studies at the University of Illinois at Chicago. His many books include *Black Rituals* (1987) and *Blues Narratives* (1999). In *Thomas and Beulah* (1986) RITA DOVE (b. 1952) envisions a lifetime in Akron, Ohio, through the eyes of a married couple loosely based on her grandparents. Dove served as U.S. Poet Laureate from 1993 to 1995 and as co-laureate from 1999 to 2000. Patricia Smith (b. 1955), a leading figure in the POETRY SLAMS movement, is the author of *Life According to Motown* (1991), *Shoulda Been Jimi Savannah* (2012), and other collections. Born in Chicago, Smith often writes about her early life and family in that city. Detroit poet Kim Derrick Hunter (b. 1955) draws on a number of literary influences in his first book, *Borne on Slow Knives* (2001). Quraysh Ali Lansana (b. Ron Myles, 1964) was born in Oklahoma but has lived in Chicago for many years, teaching at Chicago State University and publishing such books as *Southside Rain* (2000).

Richard Wright's *Black Boy* (1945) and *The Autobiography of Malcolm X* may be the most celebrated and influential African American memoirs, but a number of other notable first-person narratives have emerged from the Midwest. In *Livin' the Blues: Memoirs of a Black Journalist and Poet* (1993) Frank Marshall Davis (1905–1987) tells of his youth in Kansas and later life in Chicago. *American Daughter* (1946) by Era Bell Thompson (1906–1986) recounts the author's upbringing in IOWA and NORTH DAKOTA. Thompson's was one of the very few African American families farming on the upper Great Plains. Her account ends in Chicago, where she later served as international editor for Johnson Publications. Nelson Peery (1923–2015)

Patricia Smith, 2009.
© Rachel Eliza Griffiths

recalls his youth in rural Wabasha, MINNE-
SOTA, and his radicalization during service in
World War II in *Black Fire: The Making of an
American Revolutionary* (1995). *Race and Re-
membrance* (2008) is the life story of Arthur L.
Johnson (1925–2011) of Detroit, an important
figure in the civil rights movement.

Janet Cheatham Bell (b. 1937) remembers
Indianapolis before the civil rights era in *The
Time and Place That Gave Me Life* (2007). Noted
writer and critic Mel Watkins (b. 1940) wrote
Dancing with Strangers (1998) about growing
up in Youngstown, Ohio, where his southern father came to work in the steel mills.
Incognegro: A Memoir of Exile and Apartheid
(2008) by Frank B. Wilderson III (b. 1956)
tells of Wilderson's role in the struggle
against apartheid as one of two African
Americans in the African National Congress. Wilderson's narrative alternates between South Africa and his youth in MINNE-
APOLIS as the child of academic parents. In
*Street Shadows: A Memoir of Race, Rebellion, and
Redemption* (2010) Jerald Walker (b. 1964)
contrasts his early years of poverty and

crime in South Side Chicago with his experience at the IOWA WRITERS' WORKSHOP and as
a college professor on the East Coast.

Also of Midwestern significance is
*Dreams from My Father: A Story of Race and In-
heritance* (1995) by Barack (Hussein) Obama
(b. 1961), forty-fourth President of the United
States and the first African American to hold
the office. The son of a Kenyan father and a
white mother with roots in Kansas, Obama
grew up in Hawaii and Indonesia but started
his political career as a community organizer on Chicago's South Side. After Obama
delivered the keynote address at the Democratic National Convention in July 2004, the
book became a best seller. *Dreams from My
Father* contributed to the positive impressions that led first to Obama's election as
a U.S. senator from Illinois in 2004 and then
as president in 2008.

Contemporary black writers in the Midwest represent a wide variety of styles and
aims, but they consistently demonstrate
awareness of the tradition that they are
modifying and extending. Although poets
like Hughes and Brooks and novelists like
Wright and Morrison continue to influence
writers of all ethnicities and to engage readers internationally, they are held in special
esteem by African American writers, who
find in their predecessors a standard of
excellence that continues to inspire. Midwestern African American literature has an
illustrious past, a lively present, and a promising future.

SELECTED WORKS: Volumes of Midwest-
ern African American poetry include Paul
Laurence Dunbar's *Lyrics of Sunshine and
Shadow* (1905), Carrie Williams Clifford's
Race Rhymes (1911), Fenton Johnson's *Visions of
the Dusk* (1915), Langston Hughes's *The Weary
Blues* (1926), Robert Hayden's *Heart-Shape in
the Dust* (1940), Gwendolyn Brooks's *A Street in
Bronzeville* (1945), Naomi Long Madgett's *Star
by Star* (1965), Mari Evans's *I Am a Black
Woman* (1970), Rita Dove's *Thomas and Beulah*
(1986), Patricia Smith's *Life According to Motown*
(1991), and Quraysh Ali Lansana's *Southside
Rain* (2000). Works of fiction include
Charles Chesnutt's *The Wife of His Youth,
and Other Stories of the Color Line* (1899), Oscar
Micheaux's *The Conquest: The Story of a Negro
Pioneer* (1913), Richard Wright's *Native Son*
(1940), Ronald L. Fair's *Hog Butcher* (1966),

Cyrus Colter's *The Beach Umbrella* (1970), Toni Morrison's *Song of Solomon* (1977), Leon Forrest's *Divine Days* (1992), and Angela Jackson's *Where I Must Go* (2009). Lorraine Hansberry's play *A Raisin in the Sun* (1959) enjoys periodic revivals on stage and screen and remains a classroom standard. Memoirs include *American Daughter* (1946) by Era Bell Thompson, *The Autobiography of Malcolm X* (1965), and *Dreams from My Father: A Story of Race and Inheritance* (1995) by Barack Obama.

Anthologies of Midwestern African American literature include *The Butterfly Tree: An Anthology of Black Writing from the Upper Midwest* (1985), edited by Conrad Balfour; *Isn't but a Place: An Anthology of African American Writings about St. Louis* (1998), edited by Gerald Early, which presents two centuries of writing; *Black Writing from Chicago: In the World, Not of It?* (2006), edited by Richard R. Guzman, which collects work from 1861 to the present; and *A Different Image: The Legacy of Broadside Press* (2004), edited by Gloria House and others.

A current literary journal is *Reverie: Midwest African American Literature,* published in Detroit. The scholarly journal *African American Review,* formerly *Negro American Literature Forum* and *Black American Literature Forum,* operates at Saint Louis University in St. Louis.

FURTHER READING: In *Emancipation's Diaspora: Race and Reconstruction in the Upper Midwest* (2009), Leslie Ann Schwalm documents African American life after the Civil War. The fundamental study of the Exoduster movement is Nell Painter's *Exodusters: Black Migration to Kansas after Reconstruction* (1977). Jack S. Blocker deals with postbellum migration in *A Little More Freedom: African Americans Enter the Urban Midwest, 1860–1930* (2008). James R. Grossman's *Land of Hope: Chicago, Black Southerners, and the Great Migration* (1989) is a detailed history. Stephen A. Reich's "The Great Migration and Literary Imagination" appeared in *Journal of the Historical Society* 9.1 (March 2009): 87–128. The period immediately after the Great Migration is the subject of Bill Mullen's *Popular Fronts: Chicago and African American Cultural Politics, 1935–46* (1999) and Maren Stange's *Bronzeville: Black Chicago in Pictures, 1941–1943* (2003), a collection of photos of Chicago's South Side by WPA photographers.

Ron Primeau published "Bibliography No. 3: Black Literature of the Midwest" in *Great Lakes Review* 2.1 (1975): 51–59. Literary scholarship focused on the Midwest includes Mary W. Burger's "I, Too, Sing America: The Black Autobiographer's Response to Life in the Midwest and Mid-Plains," *Kansas Quarterly* 7.3 (1975): 43–57; chapters on St. Louis and Indiana in Eric Gardner's *Unexpected Places: Relocating Nineteenth-Century African American Literature* (2009); Richard M. Breaux's "New Negro Arts and Letters Movement among Black University Students in the Midwest, 1914–1940," in *African Americans on the Great Plains: An Anthology* (2009), edited by Bruce A. Glasrud and Charles A. Braithwaite, 204–32; Maria K. Mootry's "Post–World War II African-American Literature in Illinois," *Illinois Libraries* 78.1 (Winter 1996): 36–42; and *The Black Press in the Middle West, 1865–1985* (1996), edited by Henry Lewis Suggs. "Black Theater and Writing" is chapter 7 of Paul Sporn's *Against Itself: The Federal Theater and Writers' Projects in the Midwest* (1995), 122–41. See also David Radavich's "African American Drama from the Midwest," *MidAmerica* 32 (2005): 95–119.

Studies focusing on Chicago include *The Chicago Black Renaissance and Women's Activism* (2006) by Anne Meis Knupfer; *Writers of the Black Chicago Renaissance* (2011), edited by Steven C. Tracy; *The Black Chicago Renaissance* (2012), edited by Darlene Clark Hine and John McCluskey Jr.; and *The Muse in Bronzeville: African American Creative Expression in Chicago, 1932–1950* (2011) by Robert Bone and Richard A. Courage. In "Overshadowed by Richard Wright: Three Black Chicago Novelists," *Negro American Literature Forum* 7.3 (Fall 1973): 75–79, Robert E. Fleming deals with Waters Turpin, Frank London Brown, and Alden Bland. Bill Mullen discusses Richard Wright, Gwendolyn Brooks, and the journal *Negro Story* in relation to black radicalism in *Popular Fronts: Chicago and African-American Cultural Politics, 1935–46* (1999). In "Desegregating the 1950s: The Case of Frank London Brown," *The Japanese Journal of American Studies* 10 (1999): 15–32, Mary Helen Washington discusses Brown in relation to black activism and other Chicago writers like Hughes, Hansberry, and Brooks. On writing from Detroit, see Dorothy H. Lee's "Black Voices in Detroit," *Michigan Quarterly Review* 25.2 (Spring 1986): 313–28, and "African-American Women Writers of Detroit," Ella Jean Davis's 1991 dissertation from the University of Michigan.

The Black Arts Movement is covered in James Edward Smethurst's *The Black Arts Movement: Literary Nationalism in the 1960s and 1970s* (2005) and David Lionel's "Chicago Poets, OBAC, and the Black Arts Movement," in *The Black Columbiad: Defining Moments in African American Literature and Culture* (1994), edited by Werner Sollors and Maria Diedrich, 253–64. See also *Dudley Randall, Broadside Press, and the Black Arts Movement in Detroit, 1960–1995* (2005) by Julius Eric Thompson.

Housed at the Carter G. Woodson Regional Library in Chicago, the Vivian G. Harsh Research Collection of Afro-American History and Literature is the largest African American history and literature collection in the Midwest. The Project on the History of Black Writing, originally known as the Afro-American Novel Project, began in 1983 at the University of Mississippi. In 1998 the project moved to the University of Kansas, where it maintains the most comprehensive online database of largely out-of-print and neglected novels published by African Americans, as well as programs for teaching and research.

CRYSTAL S. ANDERSON   ELON UNIVERSITY

AMERICAN BUFFALO

HISTORY: *American Buffalo* was written by DAVID (ALAN) MAMET (b. 1947) and was originally directed by Gregory Mosher for CHICAGO's Goodman Theatre in 1975 with William H. Macy as Bobby, J. J. Johnston as Donny, and several actors as Teach. When the play moved to the Saint Nicholas Theatre, Mike Nussbaum played Teach. Mosher mounted a new production in New York in 1976, winning an Obie for best new play. Mike Kellin won an Obie as Teach, and critics were very positive.

A new production of *American Buffalo* was mounted by Ulu Grosbard (1929–2012) for Broadway, with Robert Duvall as a terrifying Teach, in 1977. Reviewers divided on the play, but it won Best American Play from the New York Drama Critics' Circle. The play's often scatological language was among the elements that put off some critics. For example, Mamet's attack on simple Midwestern family values is unleashed when Teach enters, saying "Good Morning," and then, suddenly switching to invective, repeats "Fuckin' Ruthie" five times (9). The lines were terrifying and intimidating as an affront to middle-class propriety, particularly in the Broadway production with Duvall. There had never been such an aggressive burst of language on the American stage.

Emphasizing comic irony, Al Pacino revived the play periodically from 1980 to 1983 in New York, London, and Washington, D.C. The 1983 production, with J. J. Johnston as Donny, experienced an unexpected hiatus when James Hayden, playing Bobby, died of a drug overdose during the run. An unsuccessful film version was made in 1996 with Dustin Hoffman in the role of Teach. By the time Macy revived the play for his and Mamet's Atlantic Theatre in 2000, Teach's once-aggressive opening lines got tremendous laughs. They were no longer shocking, especially to the young audience; instead, they reflected language that had become clichéd, as signaled by Teach's cheesy moustache and checked suit. A Broadway revival with John Leguizamo as Teach failed in 2008. To bring the play full circle, Chicago's Steppenwolf Company mounted a production with Tracy Letts in 2009, which moved to the McCarter Theatre at Princeton in 2010.

SIGNIFICANCE: *American Buffalo* seems at first glance to take Chicago's Midwestern values and set them on their head. Instead of Midwestern ideals, which Cheryl Temple Herr, in *Critical Regionalism and Cultural Studies: From Ireland to the American Midwest* (1996), considers "traditionalism deployed in the 'family'; a largely unreflective patriotism; an ethic of hard work and democratic-socialist egalitarianism" (106), what is shown onstage seems the opposite. At first, the opening lines offer good homey advice: "Breakfast . . . is the most important meal of the day." "And it wouldn't kill you to take a vitamin" (8). But the lines parody the usual dramatic setting of the American family home and the lines usually spoken by the mother. Here, in the workplace, with a pseudofa-

Pictured (left to right) in the Goodman Theatre's 1975–1976 premiere production of David Mamet's *American Buffalo* are J. J. Johnston, Mike Nussbaum, and William H. Macy.
Courtesy of the Goodman Theatre

ther and son, the lines establish that the play is undercutting commonly accepted points of view.

Instead of conveying the value of "hard work," the setting is a junk shop full of the detritus of the 1933–1934 Century of Progress Chicago International Exposition. The "progress" depicted there was material rather than spiritual, and the play places the audience amid the scrap heap of worthless material values. Instead of the idyllic values of staunch Midwestern yeoman farmers, all working at one socioeconomic level, close to the land, and maintaining their integrity rather than selling out to money or position, we see junk, foul mouths, and degraded people. Instead of workers, the play features petty thieves who prey on those they think are upper class, thus discarding any sense of egalitarianism.

But interestingly, beneath these ironies, the old-fashioned Midwestern values continue to exist as traces appearing in *American Buffalo.* William H. Macy, who played the boy, Bobby, in the first production in 1975 and Teach in 2000, makes this clear to Les-

lie Kane, as quoted in her *Weasels and Wisemen: Ethics and Ethnicity in the World of David Mamet* (1999). Macy asserts: "It's about a man and his word. If a man's word is useless, then the man is useless. A man's character is defined by his action. . . . Everyone is trying to answer for himself: How can I live in a world . . . where nobody does what they say they are going to do? . . . All of . . . [Mamet's] characters want to be 'stand-up' people in the Chicago meaning of the term . . . people who you can rely on" (26). Thus although the play's plot seems to focus on betrayal and not being a "stand-up" guy, that very fact makes clear that following the old values would have been the right thing to do.

The plot of the play is simple, almost nonexistent for some early reviewers who misread the play's action as purely realistic. Using familial nicknames, Donny advises his gofer, Bobby, on living. Bobby has been watching the apartment of a man they plan to rob. That man had come into the shop and bought what Donny thought was a worthless buffalo nickel for ninety dollars. After the fact, Donny has decided that it must have been worth much more and wants to steal it back, along with the man's entire coin collection. Donny's friend Teach enters, having lost at poker the night before. In order to recoup his losses, Teach wants to displace Bobby from the robbery and do it himself. He talks Donny into the betrayal. Bobby, in the meantime, as an act of love, has gone out and bought a replacement nickel for Donny. But Teach thinks that Bobby has betrayed them, smashes him with a pig-iron ingot, and then discovers that Bobby had not really betrayed them after all. He had just lied when he said that the man would be away for the weekend. Teach leaves to get a car to take Bobby to the hospital.

By age twenty-seven Mamet had developed his theory of language, drama, and their confluence in the Midwest. In "A Playwright with the Chicago Sound" in the *Chicago Sun-Times,* January 7, 1976, Ron Powers quotes Mamet as saying: "Words cause specific behavior. The same phrase in Chicago will not produce the same behavior as it will in New York. Words involve a dynamic interchange; a moral interchange. It is impossible to perform a nonmoral action. And the type of language determines the type of action" (100). The use of language in *American Buffalo* is tricky and uniquely Chicago and Midwestern. When characters sound profound, they are the most vacuous; when they sound vacuous, their pronouncements have the most meaning. Reviewer Frank Rich seconds this view when he notes in his October 21, 1980, *New York Times* article "'American Buffalo' Is Revived with Pacino," "When a character says nothing—or, for that matter, mutters 'nothing'—it can mean everything" (C8).

The real delight of a Mamet production, therefore, is the game played with the audience as characters make pronouncements that sound realistic. But if one thinks about them, as Donny does not, they are actually vacuous: "Action talks and bullshit walks" (4); "That's what business *is.* . . . People taking *care* of themselves. . . . Cause there's business and there's friendship" (7), immediately followed by "Things are not always what they seem to be" (8).

Teach is similarly full of empty insights: "The only way to teach these people is to kill

them" (11). And he echoes Donny: "We're talking about money, for chrissake, huh? We're talking about cards. Friendship is friendship, and a wonderful thing. . . . But let's just keep it *separate,* huh" (15). When he gets on a roll, however, his eloquence is magnificent: "The Past is the Past, and this is Now, and so Fuck You" (16). If ever there was an embodiment of windy nothingness, it would be in these lines.

The aggressive talk is really empty and boastful. When characters understate in a typical Midwestern way, however, they avoid direct confrontation. Donny makes a call: "Lookit, sir, if I could get ahold of some of that stuff you were interested in, would you be interested in some of it?" (27). Twisted syntax makes the response even funnier: "The guy's an asshole or he's not, what do you care? It's business" (28). And Teach puts their views together as he tries to edge Bobby out of Donny's planned break-in: "All I mean, a guy can be too loyal, Don. Don't be dense on this. What are we saying here? Business" (34). The whole statement has to be decoded: do not be loyal to Bobby; this is not friendship, it is "business" as previously defined: "People taking care of themselves." The play, on one level, concentrates on this kind of betrayal of Bobby by Donny, with the former realizing only at the end that he has been treated unfairly.

The central metaphor of the American buffalo is indeterminate, like the play itself—full of implication, but nothing so concrete as to allow certainty. It implies symbolism of the disappearing Midwestern Great Plains frontier and its values, but no explicit allusions are ever made.

Similarly, the play opens with misdirection: Bobby reported that the coin collector left his apartment, but at the very end Bobby admits that he never saw the guy leave. So from the outset, what Donny, Teach, and the audience think is true is not. This is the case for much other misdirection as well. Donny depicts his friend Fletch as a superman: "You put him down in some strange town with just a nickel in his pocket, and by nightfall he'll have that town by the balls" (4). But at the end of the play Fletch does not show up for the break-in—superman has been beaten up by muggers. Teach's opening cursing of Ruthie is excessive. Only later do we realize that he lost badly at poker the night before—to Ruthie and Fletch, who won $600 between them. He is so penniless that he comes to scrounge breakfast and wants to commit the burglary to replace his lost cash.

So these are only pseudobusinessmen, and despite Teach's attempts to coat everything in the principles of BUSINESS, his view is warped—a wildly excessive view of capitalism: "You know what is free enterprise? . . . The freedom . . . Of the *Individual* . . . To Embark on Any Fucking Course that he sees fit. . . . In order to secure his honest chance to make a profit. Am I so out of line on this? . . . Does this make me a Commie? . . . The country's *founded* on this, Don. You know this" (72–73).

Teach's view of unbridled American individualism out solely for its own gain is key to Mamet's satire, not an endorsement. The first scholars to write books on Mamet, C. W. E. Bigsby and Dennis Carroll, both thought Mamet a playwright of community, implying the need for values through their negation. Here Teach's ideal of individual freedom is essentially a concept of total selfishness, and it ultimately leads Donny to betray Bobby and Teach to beat him. Yet in the last two lines of the play, Bobby apologizes and Donny consoles him, saying, "That's all right" (106). In a sense, this final stage picture reestablishes the pseudofamily harmony of the opening, reasserting those values that previous actions have violated.

Mamet's Midwestern egalitarian values originate with THORSTEN (BUNDE) VEBLEN (1857–1929), the Wisconsin-born University of Chicago economist and sociologist whose *Theory of the Leisure Class* (1899) was a major influence as it attacked the inequality of wealth and work. But instead of attacking the leisure class for uselessness, Mamet depicts their world from the upside-down perspective of the dregs of society. Arthur Holmberg quotes Mamet in *David Mamet and American Macho* (2012): "Veblen, also associated with Chicago, said behavior at the bottom of the food chain and the behavior at the top of the food chain are exactly the same" (21). Teach's view of capitalism parodies those of the upper classes when unrestrained greed typified the "Me Decade" of the 1980s. Mamet's play presciently recognizes this by depicting such capitalism in thieves who see themselves as simple businessmen following the American ideal. Thus Midwestern values are glimpsed, but almost through negation.

Mamet, however, would reject any attempt to classify the play in terms of theme; to him it is a tragedy, as it was to the first reviewer, Richard Christiansen, dean of Chicago critics. In his December 22, 1975, *Chicago Daily News* article "Bravos for a Play and a Theater," Christiansen asserted that "Mamet has reworked the play's ending, so that a kind of horrible awareness dawns in the brain of the poor, tortured Bobby, thus hammering a final nail of irony in the coffin of their wasted lives" (17). Amy Morton, who directed the Steppenwolf revival of the play in 2009, revealed all three characters coming to tragic recognitions at the end of the play.

IMPORTANT EDITIONS: The Grove first edition (1977) of *American Buffalo* remains the standard edition. All page citations from the play refer to that edition. Samuel French published the acting text in 1977. It is still in print. Methuen published the British edition in 1977; it was reprinted in *David Mamet: Plays,* volume 1 (1994).

FURTHER READING: Andrew Harris's *Broadway Theatre* (1994) explains the play's changes through early productions. Harris raises a key issue: a shift with Duvall from a play about Donny to one about Teach. Dennis Carroll's perceptive *David Mamet* (1987) notes a further change when Al Pacino played Teach with more irony. Ira Nadel's biography *David Mamet: A Life in the Theatre* (2008) also traces the play's early development, noting that director Mosher did not want the play to be done realistically "because it limited the metaphysical dimension of the play" (85). Steven Price gives the best overall survey of critics of Mamet in *The Plays, Screenplays and Films of David Mamet* (2008).

Language is a central concern in critical analysis of *American Buffalo.* Some critics see the debased language, mainly of Teach, creating debased thoughts and actions; these include Anne Dean in *David Mamet: Language as Dramatic Action* (1990), Stanton Garner in *Bodied Spaces: Phenomenology and Performance in Contemporary Drama* (1994), and

Thomas L. King in "Talk and Dramatic Action in *American Buffalo*," *Modern Drama* 34 (1991): 538–48. Other critics see Teach as more manipulative and in control of words; these critics include June Schleuter and Elizabeth Forsyth in "America as Junkshop: The Business Ethic in David Mamet's *American Buffalo*," *Modern Drama* 26 (1983): 492–500, and Robert Vorlicky in *Act like a Man: Challenging Masculinities* (1995). Christopher Hudgins, however, sees Teach in performance as comical in "Comedy and Humor in the Plays of David Mamet," in *David Mamet: A Casebook* (1991), edited by Leslie Kane (191–228).

Similarly, critics split over Mamet's view of business. If it is Teach's play, then it satirizes American business, as Jack Barbera argues in "Ethical Perversity in America: Some Observations on David Mamet's *American Buffalo*," *Modern Drama* 24 (1981): 270–75, and as Hersh Zeifman asserts in "Phallus in Wonderland: Machismo and Business in David Mamet's *American Buffalo* and *Glengarry Glen Ross*," in *David Mamet: A Casebook* (1991): 123–35. But if the play is focused on Donny, it is a tragedy of betrayal, as Kane argues in her study of Mamet's Jewish background, *Weasels and Wisemen: Ethics and Ethnicity in the World of David Mamet* (1999), and as Jeanette Malkin asserts in *Verbal Violence in Contemporary Drama* (1992).

The ending of the play is similarly a matter of debate. Some, like Kane and Vorlicky, find it comforting and healing; Brenda Murphy, in *Understanding David Mamet* (2011), sees the play ending with Donny's forgiveness of Teach and Bobby. Others, like Bigsby, Dean, and Malkin, find it despairing. Critics divide over Mamet as a misogynist. Carla McDonough makes that charge in *Staging Masculinity: Male Identity in Contemporary American Drama* (1997), while Janet Haedicke defends Mamet in "Plowing the Buffalo, Fucking the Fruits: (M)Others in *American Buffalo* and *Speed-the-Plow*," in *Gender and Genre: Essays on David Mamet*, edited by Hudgins and Kane (2001): 27–40.

Early reviews of note are Richard Christiansen's December 22, 1975, *Chicago Daily News* article "Bravos for a Play and a Theater," 17; Ron Powers's January 7, 1976, *Chicago Sun-Times* review "A Playwright with the Chicago Sound," 100; and Frank Rich's October 21, 1980, *New York Times* review "'American Buffalo' Is Revived with Pacino," C8. Cheryl Temple Herr's *Critical Regionalism and Cultural Studies: From Ireland to the American Midwest* (1996) addresses Midwestern values.

DAVID K. SAUER   SPRING HILL COLLEGE

AMERICAN INDIAN LITERATURE.
See Native American Literature

AMERICAN INDIANS AS DEPICTED IN MIDWESTERN LITERATURE.
See Native Americans as Depicted in Literature

. . . *AND THE EARTH DID NOT DEVOUR HIM*.
See . . . *y no se lo tragó la tierra*

ANTHOLOGIES
OVERVIEW: Midwestern literary anthologies have appeared throughout the region's history, gathering together representations of and perspectives on the Midwest as shown in poetry, prose, CREATIVE NONFICTION, and DRAMA. In addition to representing the entire Midwest, literary anthologies also represent subregions, including the Great Lakes, the upper Midwest, and others, as well as individual states. Whether authors have engaged in creative writing in a fictional realm or creative reflection based on memories and experiences, collections of literature have emerged about the Midwest, exploring its history, discussing its people, and contemplating its possibilities. These collections, which reflect the critical and popular trends of their times, constitute a record of THE CHANGING MIDWESTERN LITERARY CANON of Midwestern literature. If one considers the long history of this phenomenon, it is clear that exploring and collecting Midwestern literature will continue as long as the region itself.

HISTORY AND SIGNIFICANCE: The first Midwestern literary anthologies appeared in the early nineteenth century. The earliest was *The Western Souvenir, a Christmas and New Year's Gift for 1829*, edited by JAMES HALL (1793–1868) and published in CINCINNATI in 1828. A sophisticated volume of more than three hundred pages and with four engravings, it contained essays, poetry, and travel and natural history narratives as well as historical vignettes. In his prefatory remarks Hall states that the compilation is patterned after those published in the eastern states and that to give it originality, "it is written and published in the Western country, by Western men, and is chiefly confined to subjects connected with the history and character of the country which gives it birth" (iii).

A much more modest endeavor, *The Souvenir of the Lakes* (1831) is the second known literary anthology published in the Midwest. It was printed in DETROIT and is only one-tenth the size of *The Western Souvenir*. Its anonymous editor also selected examples of poetry, geographic descriptions, and natural history narratives. A number of contributions have been identified as the work of HENRY ROWE SCHOOLCRAFT (1793–1864), and it is possible that he was responsible for collecting, editing, and publishing this book.

Selections from the Poetical Literature of the West (1841), edited by William D. Gallagher (1808–1894), is generally recognized as the first attempt to gather verse by a variety of authors who were creating their works in what was then referred to as the northwestern, or simply the western, region of the United States. Published in Cincinnati, the poetry of Gallagher's anthology focuses on the Ohio Valley region and the country west of the Allegheny Mountains. Gallagher states in his preface that his goal is to assert a Western presence in the literary world and to show that the thirty-eight poets from that region were as talented as other writers of the time.

William T. Coggeshall (1824–1867), compiling his anthology *The Poets and Poetry of the West* (1860) almost two decades later, continued Gallagher's work. Coggeshall's anthology has a wider scope, including writers from MICHIGAN, WISCONSIN, IOWA, MINNESOTA, and other states. Both Gallagher and Coggeshall published works from a cross section of life, incorporating poetry by men and women from a variety of backgrounds and with various connections to the Midwest. Many of the poets and poems appear in both anthologies, and although they were recognized then, most are no longer well known. Coggeshall's anthology contains a more

extensive collection of poets and poetry; the most notable of these poets for contemporary readers may be ALICE CARY (1820–1871), PHOEBE CARY (1824–1871), and WILLIAM DEAN HOWELLS (1837–1920).

No other significant attempts to anthologize Midwestern literature appeared until the turn of the twentieth century. Beginning in 1900, more anthologies emerged that attempted to collect and express Midwestern ideas and creativity, focusing most on literature emerging from individual Midwestern states. The introductions to these anthologies argue that Midwestern literature is as worthy of recognition as other published work. These are also among the first anthologies to address the difficulty in understanding and defining Midwestern regional identity. Publications like the two-volume *Kansas in Literature* (1900), compiled by William Herbert Carruth, devote pages to identifying what characteristics are unique to their particular state or region and what qualifies authors to write authentically about that area. Other anthologies, like *Poets and Poetry of Indiana* (1900), edited by Benjamin S. Parker and Enos B. Heiney, seek to record and establish the history of a state or region. Parker and Heiney in particular set out to record the history of poetry in INDIANA from 1800 to 1900, establishing a state identity through the creative literature that emerged during its development.

As anthologies continued to be published, their arrangement and emphasis increasingly moved away from consideration of individual states to focus on the literature of the region as a whole. The collection *Stories from the Midland* (1924) by JOHN T(OWNER) FREDERICK (1893–1975), for example, compiles stories from *THE MIDLAND* magazine, which was created to encourage and publish creative writers, particularly those from the Midwest, such as Iowa's RUTH SUCKOW (1892–1960), who has two stories in the anthology. Similarly, short stories and novel segments are recorded in *Golden Tales of the Prairie States* (1932), an anthology by May Lamberton Becker; the volume includes work by (NEWTON) BOOTH TARKINGTON (1869–1946), SHERWOOD ANDERSON (1876–1941), UPTON (BEALL) SINCLAIR (JR.) (1878–1968), and others. In the introduction Becker expresses a desire to capture and record elements of the Midwest before they are lost amid the historical and social changes occurring in the region, a sentiment also found in introductions to other anthologies of the time. Despite this shift to consideration of the Midwest as a whole, state anthologies still outnumbered the broader regional anthologies. The New York publishing house of Henry Harrison published a variety of state poetry collections during the 1930s, including poetry from Iowa, ILLINOIS, KANSAS, OHIO, Michigan, and SOUTH DAKOTA and a combined volume on Minnesota and NEBRASKA poets. In addition, collections like *Poetry out of Wisconsin* (1937), edited by AUGUST (WILLIAM) DERLETH (1909–1971) and Raymond E. F. Larsson (1901–1991), and *North Dakota Singing* (1936), edited by Grace Brown Putnam (1870–1933) and Anna Ackermann (1894–1976), also compile voices from Midwestern states.

In the 1940s the focus of many Midwestern anthologies was shaped by the regionalist movement that governed critical literary scholarship of that time. These anthologies also began to incorporate figures from the Midwestern literary renaissance of the early twentieth century more consistently rather than always focusing on unknown or newly discovered talent. John T. Frederick's *Out of the Midwest: A Collection of Present-Day Writing* (1944) addresses the significance of regional characteristics and settings, particularly in writers producing work after 1910. Frederick's introduction discusses regionalism and what it means to be a regional writer, concerns that editors of previous volumes did not express. The argument for regional significance is continued in *Mid Country: Writings from the Heart of America* (1945), edited by Lowry C. Wimberly; it contains an introduction by the noted folklorist B. A. Botkin. Botkin defines what he sees as important characteristics of the Midwest, such as the region being the crossroads of the country and, because of that central location, containing qualities that are universally American. John T. Flanagan also establishes the Midwest as the "heartland" or center of the country in his anthology *America Is West: An Anthology of Middlewestern Life and Literature* (1945). By asserting that the Midwest is the heartland of the United States, Flanagan is arguing both for recognition of Midwestern identity in its own right and for the Mid-

west's fundamental role in American identity. The Midwest, therefore, becomes both specific and universal, its value increased by the view that the region inhabits a larger space within a common American identity. Anthologies such as these initiated the emphasis on regionalism and the heartland values of the Midwest that continued to be expressed long afterward.

Anthologizing Midwestern literature became even more popular during the mid-twentieth century, and editors were still concerned with establishing regional history and identity while at the same time countering negative regional stereotypes. The historical evolution of the Midwest and its states is developed in anthologies like *Land of the Long Horizons* (1960) edited by WALTER (EDWIN) HAVIGHURST (1901–1994), which includes writing from the early explorers of the Midwest to twentieth-century writers. This anthology is also the first to note in its introduction the stereotype of Midwestern

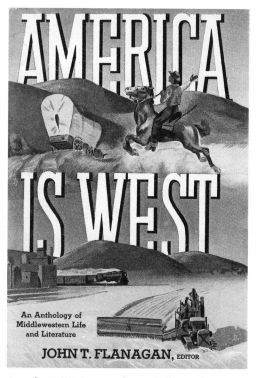

America Is West, an early anthology of Midwestern writing.
© The University of Minnesota Press, 1945

geographic and cultural sameness or flatness that is claimed to exist within American society. Havighurst and others try to counter those ideas in the introductions to their anthologies, arguing instead for Midwestern distinctiveness that is represented by the texts they compile. Havighurst also edited *The Great Lakes Reader* (1966), an anthology of GREAT LAKES LITERATURE.

LUCIEN (HENRY) STRYK (1924–2013), in his two volumes *Heartland: Poets of the Midwest* (1967) and *Heartland II* (1975), also argues against Midwestern stereotypes as he makes a case for the Midwest as being important in its role as America's heartland. These collections began what became a continuing argument by later editors of Midwestern anthologies, who reacted against the stereotypes of a homogenized Midwest with the

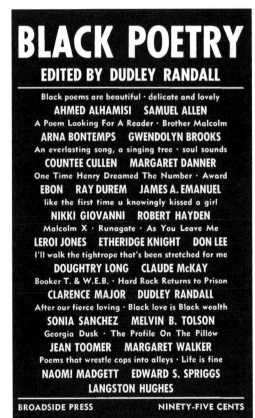

Black Poetry, a seminal anthology published in the Midwest.

© The Broadside Press, 1969. Reprinted by permission of the Dudley Randall Literary Estate

books they constructed to represent and record Midwestern vitality and creativity.

Although there were earlier anthologies that began to recognize racial diversity in the Midwest, such as *Black Poetry: A Supplement to Anthologies Which Exclude Black Poets* (1969), edited by Dudley Randall, which featured prominent voices such as GWENDOLYN BROOKS (1917–2000), ROBERT HAYDEN (1913–1980), LANGSTON HUGHES (1902–1967), and others, by the 1980s there was a concerted effort in anthology projects to focus on women writers and writers of various racial or ethnic backgrounds. *In the Middle: Ten Midwestern Women Poets* (1985), edited by Sylvia Griffith Wheeler, *Woman Poet: The Midwest* (1985), edited by Elaine Dallman and Martha Friedberg, and *The First Anthology of Missouri Women Writers* (1987), edited by Sharon Kinney-Hanson, show greater concern with the voices of Midwestern women than most previous anthologies. African American voices in the Midwest also gain their own arena of expression in the volumes *The Butterfly Tree: An Anthology of Black Writing from the Upper Midwest* (1985), edited by Conrad Balfour, and *On Being Black: Stories and Poems by Minnesota Authors* (1981), edited by Hazel Clayton, with a second volume published in 1991. GERALD VIZENOR (b. 1934) collects some Native American perspectives from the Midwest in his anthology *Touchwood: A Collection of Ojibway Prose* (1987). Although gender, racial, and ethnic perspectives do appear in other anthologies, collections published during this time place more emphasis on the individual voices speaking for themselves rather than on comparison with a variety of other points of view. At the same time, other anthologies continue to posit and assert elements of Midwestern identity. *A Place of Sense: Essays in Search of the Midwest* (1988) by MICHAEL A. MARTONE (b. 1955) continues the effort to delineate Midwestern values and experience suggested by earlier anthologies through its collection of essays by contemporary writers, including (KAREN) LOUISE ERDRICH (b. 1954).

The emphasis on recording a greater variety of voices from the Midwest continued into the next decade. *Reclaiming the Heartland: Lesbian and Gay Voices from the Midwest* (1996), edited by Karen Lee Osborne (b.

1954) and William J. Spurlin, appears to be the first anthology from the Midwest to address lesbian and gay perspectives within the region. See LESBIAN, GAY, BISEXUAL, TRANSGENDER, AND QUEER LITERATURE. Randy M. Brooks and Lee Gurga's *Midwest Haiku Anthology* (1992) is notable for collecting impressions of the Midwest through the Japanese form of haiku poetry. Contemporary perspectives on the Midwest again receive prominent attention in two anthologies edited by Mark Vinz (b. 1942) and Thom Tammaro (b. 1954): *Inheriting the Land: Contemporary Voices from the Midwest* (1993) and *Imagining Home: Writing from the Midwest* (1995). These two collections seek to understand how contemporary perspectives on the Midwest have developed and have been changed by the evolution of regional history and traditions. Vinz and Tammaro's collections help record yet another generation's responses to Midwestern literature and culture.

In the twenty-first century the desire to collect and explore Midwestern literature and perspectives through anthologies continues. Although individual Midwestern states continue to record voices from within their borders, many anthologies explore the Midwest as a whole. Edited by Richard O. Davies, Joseph A. Amato (b. 1938), and David R. Pichaske (b. 1943), *A Place Called Home: Writings on the Midwestern Small Town* (2003) collects written portrayals of small-town life in the Midwest from 1790 to the present, contrasting early perspectives by writers like (HANNIBAL) HAMLIN GARLAND (1860–1940) with those of contemporary Midwestern writers like GARY EDWARD KEILLOR (b. 1942), writing as Garrison Keillor. *In the Middle of the Middle West: Literary Nonfiction from the Heartland* (2003), an anthology edited by Becky Bradway, collects the point of view of contemporary writers relating to and interacting with the Midwest. Experimental literature from the Midwest has been highlighted in two collections from MINNEAPOLIS–based Sprout Press: *Blink* (2002), edited by John Colburn and Margaret Miles, and *Blink Again* (2011), edited by Colburn, Miles, and Michelle Filkins. Both volumes focus on flash fiction, stories of 1,000 to 1,200 words, by writers from Minnesota or the upper Midwest. The motivation behind these collections and other contemporary anthologies is not very different from what it was in the mid-nineteenth century when the first anthologies were published. Contemporary anthologies still strive to define the region and to recognize writing that stems from it.

Midwestern anthologies have specialized at times to address particular cultural elements of the region's population. Two anthologies collect and attempt to define Midwestern HUMOR. *Midland Humor: A Harvest of Fun and Folklore* (1947) by (JOHN WESLEY) "JACK" CONROY (1898–1990) records humor as it has evolved in the region from its beginnings among the trappers and explorers to its appearance in the literature of the early twentieth century. *So Ole Says to Lena: Folk Humor of the Upper Midwest* (2001), edited by James P. Leary, emphasizes a more ethnic approach to regional humor, building on Irish, German, Scandinavian, and other ethnic heritages in the stories it records. The anthology also addresses the humor found among loggers, miners, farmers, and other groups characteristic of the region. Beyond humor, *Third Party Footprints: An Anthology from Writings and Speeches of Midwest Radicals* (1966), edited by James M. Youngdale, collects writings of the radical political subculture that characterized the upper Midwest in the early twentieth century. Several writers have explored and attempted to define Midwestern food, as seen in anthologies such as *Fried Walleye and Cherry Pie: Midwestern Writers on Food* (2013), edited by Peggy Wolf. Such anthologies demonstrate a desire to collect not only the creative literature of the Midwest but also literature representing aspects of regional culture.

All these anthologies struggle with what it means to be Midwestern: whether one has to be born in the region to qualify, whether one can immigrate there and become part of the culture, or whether one can understand the Midwest simply by passing through. None of the anthologies follows a standard method of inclusion; they choose instead to define their authors and collected works by varying characteristics, often noting the possible problems associated with their choices or particular arguments that may be raised about them. Some include only works about the Midwest regardless of the author's place of birth or claim to the region. Others focus only on authors who have a Midwestern birthright, whether or not they chose to stay there their entire lives. The standards vary depending on the collection. Throughout the process of anthologizing Midwestern perspectives, ultimately both insiders and outsiders represent their views in many of these collections, providing an interesting cross section of perspectives on Midwestern life.

The creation of Midwestern literary anthologies appears to be motivated most by the desire to record written voices and establish validity for those voices, allowing them to express their ideas on the region they live in or on a region that has greatly influenced their lives. Whether the writers or anthologies aspire to literary greatness or simply desire to express themselves and their surroundings, all agree that literature from the Midwest has value. Midwestern anthologies have done a great deal to support the idea that a Midwestern literature is possible and that work from the region is worth reading, studying, and understanding.

SELECTED WORKS: Some recent anthologies manage to represent both the literary past and present in the Midwest and provide a good overview of writing from the region. For a general overview of contemporary writers in the Midwest, see Mark Vinz and Thom Tammaro's *Inheriting the Land: Contemporary Voices from the Midwest* (1993) and *Imagining Home: Writing from the Midwest* (1995), broad compilations of writers and styles. *In the Middle of the Middle West: Literary Nonfiction from the Heartland* (2003), edited by Becky Bradway, also contains a good cross section of contemporary authors, arranged by their experiences interacting with the Midwest and their ideas of place. *A Place Called Home: Writings on the Midwestern Small Town* (2003), edited by Richard O. Davies, Joseph A. Amato, and David R. Pichaske, contains a significant selection of authors who represent a historical overview of the Midwestern small town.

FURTHER READING: Nineteenth-century Midwestern anthologies are often cited in books or articles on the development of the region and its literature; however, no critical studies exist that look at the phenomenon of anthologizing literature in the Midwest as a whole. For scholars looking for a place to start researching and understanding Midwestern anthologies, *A Bibliographical Guide to Midwestern Literature* (1981), edited by Gerald Nemanic, provides a fairly comprehensive list of both general and state anthologies from their inception until the 1980s.

SARA KOSIBA   TROY UNIVERSITY

ARAB AMERICAN LITERATURE

OVERVIEW: The rapid rate at which Arab American novels, poetry, memoirs, plays, and short stories are being published marks an important period in the development of this literature, the beginnings of which can be traced back to the first half of the twentieth century. The Midwest constitutes an important regional base for many Arab American writers, even though their literary ancestors, like Gibran Khalil Gibran (1883–1931) and Ameen Rihani (1876–1940), gravitated toward the East Coast from 1885 to 1945 in what is regarded as the first wave of Arab immigration to the United States. During the second (1945–1967) and third waves (1967 to the present), the Midwest attracted more and more Arab immigrants; the DETROIT, MICHIGAN, area, for example, is currently home to the largest concentration of Arabs and Arab Americans living outside the Middle East. This community, in Michigan as well as other Midwestern states, encompasses a multiplicity of national, religious, and ethnic identities, including Muslim Shiites, Sunnis, and Alawites; Christian Catholics, Greek Orthodox, and Protestants; and regional sects like the Copts, Chaldeans, and Maronites, as well as Druze. The number of Arab Americans currently living in the United States is estimated at around 3.6 million; a large part of this population hails from the Levant area, encompassing Lebanon, Syria, Jordan, and Palestine. These diverse affiliations shape some of the major thematic concerns pervading Arab American literature: displacement, exile, identity politics, food, immigration, and transnationalism. Even though to date an exclusive focus on the Midwestern Arab American experience remains absent from most critical works in the field and from the available Arab American anthologies, Arab American literature of the Midwest features strong regional identifications that ground its writers in a distinct Midwestern locale.

HISTORY AND SIGNIFICANCE: The beginnings of Arab American literature can be traced to a group of early writers called the *mahjar*, or immigrant writers. The *mahjar* writers traveled from the Arab world to the United States in the late nineteenth and early twentieth centuries and wrote in both English and Arabic. In 1920 they established in New York what came to be known as Al-Rabita al-Qalamiyya, or the Pen League. The league consisted of Syrian and Lebanese writers like Gibran, Mikhael Naimy (1889–1988), and Elia Abu Madi (1890–1957). Although these early writers were mainly based on the East Coast, others from this period traveled and lectured in the Midwest, such as Abraham Mitrie Rihbany (1869–1944), who was eventually offered the position of resident minister in a Presbyterian church in Morenci, OHIO. Rihbany, who emigrated from Mount Lebanon, formerly part of Syria, to the United States when he was twenty-two, wrote about his background and his travels in his first book, *A Far Journey* (1914), which was followed in 1916 by *The Syrian Christ.* The period from the 1940s to the 1970s produced very few literary works characterized as Arab American, let alone Midwestern Arab American. Nevertheless, autobiographical works such as *Syrian Yankee* (1943) by Salom Rizk (1909–1973) and *Confessions of a Spent Youth* (1960) by VANCE (NYE) BOURJAILY (1922–2010) enjoyed great success when they were first published. Rizk, also known as Sam Risk, was born in a poor village in Syria and emigrated to the American Midwest when he was fourteen, while the second-generation Arab American Bourjaily was born in CLEVELAND, Ohio, to a Lebanese father and an American mother. Both writers' works underscore the strong urge felt by many Arab Americans during that period to assimilate into their U.S. surroundings and detach themselves from their Arab origins.

Contemporary Arab American writers differ from such early immigrant models and break from their literary forebears in notable ways, the most important being that their attachment to their Arab homelands is strong and typically devoid of nostalgia and sentimentalism. Starting in the 1970s and intensifying in the past couple of decades, Arab American literature has garnered increasing attention, and the events of September 11, 2001, have highlighted the need to bring the diversity of this community to the forefront of the nation's consciousness.

The regional concentration of Arab American writers in the Midwest is most apparent in the Detroit area. Influential writers from this region include poet and critic Lawrence Joseph (b. 1948), who was born in Detroit and attended the University of Michigan for his BA and JD degrees. A professor of law at St. John's University School of Law, Joseph is the author of several books of poetry, including *Into It* (2005). His first three books of poetry, *Shouting at No One* (1983), *Curriculum Vitae* (1988), and *Before Our Eyes* (1993), are collected in *Codes, Precepts, Biases, and Taboos: Poems, 1973–1993* (2005). He is also the author of *Lawyerland* (1997), a book of prose, and *The Game Changed: Essays and Other Prose* (2011). His Lebanese and Syrian Catholic grandparents were among the first Arab immigrants in Detroit, and Joseph writes poems that bear witness to the weight of history carried by immigrants across oceans. *Curriculum Vitae*, published to wide acclaim, features the poem "Sand Nigger," in which Joseph describes a childhood home in Detroit imbued with traces of Lebanon, not only in the sumptuous dishes and the revered saints that permeated the house, but also in the news of the Lebanese civil war that was circulated around the dining-room table and spilled into the children's ears.

This legacy of war, immigration, and loss is shared by another Detroit-born poet, Hayan Charara (b. 1972), author of *The Alchemist's Diary* (2001) and *The Sadness of Others* (2006). Detroit permeates Charara's work, in which images of assembly lines, racial tensions, and a sinking economy intermingle with haunting personal struggles, the most poignant of which is the death of his mother, a traumatic loss to which the poet returns often in his poems. Whether writing about the urge to leave Detroit in "Thinking American," teaching poetry to freshman students at a community college in Warren, Michigan, in "English 101," or describing how Warren Avenue became "Little Lebanon" in the poem "Home," Charara expresses through his poetry a strong rootedness in his Midwestern birthplace, "where / you were pulled from the womb / into the streets" (*The Alchemist's*

Hayan Charara, 2014.
Courtesy of Hayan Charara

Diary 13). Charara is also the editor of *Inclined to Speak: An Anthology of Contemporary Arab American Poetry* (2008). He edits the annual literary anthology *Graffiti Rag.*

Both Joseph and Charara have moved from their hometown to live and work elsewhere in the United States, Joseph to New York City and Charara to Texas, but many other Arab American writers still live and work in the Detroit area. This representative group of first- and second-generation writers forms a literary and creative pillar of the Arab American community in Michigan, and their works mirror and address this community's political, religious, and diasporic concerns. Deborah Al-Najjar (b. 1965), for example, writes about Chaldeans, or Eastern-rite Iraqi Catholics, in Dearborn. Her short story "A Cup of Tea," published in *Fork-Roads* (Fall 1995): 55–57, features the struggle between Selma, a second-generation Americanized Chaldean, and her mother, who is shocked at her daughter's rejection of a traditional marriage arrangement. Other short stories by Al-Najjar dealing with similar issues include "Selma's Weddings," *Michigan Quarterly Review* 31.4 (Fall 1992): 607–16; "Bebe Khomee," *Indiana Review* 12.1

(Winter 1988): 14–20; "Mariam Athra," *Artenews* (May 2006); and "No News," *Banipal: Magazine of Modern Arab Literature* 38 (2010): 83–85.

The novels of Iraqi American Weam Namou (b. 1970) also feature the Chaldean community. Her novels *The Feminine Art* (2004), *The Mismatched Braid* (2006), and *The Flavor of Cultures* (2008) explore the connections between America and Iraq in a post–Gulf War setting. Born into a Chaldean family in Iraq, Namou moved at the age of ten with her family to the United States, where she studied at Wayne State University and developed her skills in fiction and screenwriting. She works in both documentary and feature filmmaking and is cofounder and president of the Iraqi Artists Association. Members of the association who reside in Michigan include Marshall Garmo (b. 1953), whose self-published play *An Immigrant's Dream* (2002) is written in both English and Arabic.

Other writers from the Detroit/Dearborn community who focus on the political struggles plaguing their Arab homelands and the effect of this strife on their Arab American communities include Hasan Newash (b. 1942) and Dunya Mikhail (b. 1965), both first-generation Arab Americans who write about the injustice of war and despotic regimes in the Arab world. Poet and activist Newash was born in Jerusalem and is cofounder of the Palestine Office of Michigan. His poem "The Scream 98," included in Khaled Mattawa and Munir Akash's anthology *Post Gibran* (1999), enumerates the devastating effects of the U.S. sanctions against Iraq on the country's children; the poet states, "Sanctions allow no drugs for chemotherapy" (278). Mikhail, a Chaldean who left Iraq for the United States in 1996 and studied at Wayne State University, was awarded the United Nations Human Rights Award for Freedom of Writing in 2001. Her first book of poetry, *The War Works Hard* (2005), translated from the Arabic by Elizabeth Winslow, includes poems about the 1980–1988 Iraq-Iran War, post-Saddam Iraq, and life in the United States. Her poem "I Was in a Hurry" captures the exile's sense of loss: "Yesterday I lost a country. / I was in a hurry, / and didn't notice when it fell from me" (31). Her second book of poetry, *Diary of a Wave outside the Sea* (2009), is a bilingual English-Arabic poetic memoir that poignantly captures the personal effects of war and exile. Her third poetry collection, *The Iraqi Nights,* was published in 2014.

Also based in the Detroit/Dearborn area are poets Kevin Rashid (b. 1960), Alise Alousi (b. 1965), Glenn Shaheen (b. 1980), and Hedy Hebra (b. 1945). Rashid is curriculum and research coordinator in the Honors College at Wayne State University. His poems have appeared in several books and journals, including *The Academy of American Poets New Voices, 1989–1998* (1999), edited by Heather McHugh; *Arab Detroit: From Margins to Mainstream* (2000), edited by Nabeel Abraham and Andrew Shryock; *Abandon Automobile: Detroit City Poetry 2001* (2001), edited by M. L. Liebler and Melba Joyce Boyd; and journals such as the *Maxis Review* and *Graffiti Rag.* Rashid's poems "Thug Nun," "A Loved One Will Do," and "Keeping the Knife," published in the anthology *Inclined to Speak: An Anthology of Contemporary Arab American Poetry,* display concise and distinct images of childhood memories and disrupted adult relationships. With only a knife left from a failed relationship, the speaker states in "Keeping the Knife": "What's this knife / do for me now? / What safety? / What threat? / What now to cut at?" (273). Alise Alousi, born in Cleveland, Ohio, is also a Detroit resident and poet. She has worked as a writer-in-residence in the Detroit Public Schools and has published her work in several journals and poetry collections, including *I Feel a Little Jumpy around You* (1998), edited by Naomi Shihab Nye and Paul B. Janeczko, *Abandon Automobile: Detroit City Poetry 2001,* edited by M. L. Liebler and Melba Joyce Boyd, and *Poets against War* (2003), edited by Sam Hamill and Sally Anderson. Her chapbook, *Wearing Doors Away,* was published by Ridgeway Press in 1988, and her poems have appeared in the anthologies *Inclined to Speak: An Anthology of Contemporary Arab American Poetry* and *Al-Mutanabbi Street Starts Here* (2012), edited by Beau Beausoleil and Deema Shehabi. Glenn Shaheen, born in Halifax, Nova Scotia, currently resides in Michigan. His first book of poetry, *Predatory,* was published in 2011, and *Unchecked Savagery,* a chapbook of flash fiction, appeared in 2013. Hedy Habra, who was

born in Egypt to Lebanese parents, teaches Spanish at Western Michigan University. Her poetry and fiction, written in French, Spanish, and English, have appeared in various journals and anthologies. Her collection of short stories, *Flying Carpets* (winner of the 2013 Arab American Book Award's Honorable Mention in Fiction and finalist in the 2014 Eric Hoffer Book Award), and her book of poetry, *Tea in Heliopolis* (finalist in the 2014 International Poetry Book Award), were both published in 2013.

Other writers who hail from Michigan include Dahlia Petrus (b. 1977), whose short stories include "Is That All There Is?," *Mizna* 3.1 (2001), and "The Red Maverick," which appeared in *Ripe Guava: Voices of Women of Color at Brooklyn College* (2000); Heather Raffo (b. 1970), best known for her one-woman play *9 Parts of Desire* (2003); and Lara Hamza (b. 1974), whose poems and nonfiction have been published in *Inclined to Speak: An Anthology of Contemporary Arab American Poetry* and *Arab Detroit: From Margin to Mainstream,* respectively. The Arab American community in Dearborn has also been the focus of work by writers from the Arab world like Ahmad Baydoun (b. 1943), Lebanese history professor and author of *Bint Jibayl, Michigan* (1989), a travelogue that chronicles a trip to visit his family in Dearborn.

Emphasizing Michigan's pivotal position for Arab Americans, the Arab American National Museum, the first of its kind, was inaugurated in May 2005 in Dearborn, Michigan, and provides an important venue for the articulation and commemoration of Arab American history and culture. The museum hosts conferences, workshops, screenings, and performances that focus on Arab American arts and cultures and attract a wide range of Arab American writers, artists, critics, and performers. The Center for Arab American Studies at the University of Michigan–Dearborn is another venue that attracts Arab American writers and speakers from across the nation, as well as from the Arab world. The center's Arab and Arab American Writers' Series has featured many Arab American writers, including poet and scholar Khaled Mattawa (b. 1964), who currently teaches creative writing at the University of Michigan–Ann Arbor. He has published several books of poetry, including

Ismailia Eclipse (1995), *Zodiac of Echoes* (2003), *Amorisco* (2008), and *Tocqueville* (2010). His critical work *Mahmoud Darwish: The Poet's Art and His Nation* was published in 2014. The Arab American Studies program at the University of Michigan offers a variety of courses on Arab American culture, taught by faculty from various disciplinary backgrounds, including faculty members Rima Hassouneh, Khaled Mattawa, Andrew Shryock, Mathew Stiffler, and Evelyn Alsultany, whose book *Arabs and Muslims in the Media: Race, Popular Culture, and Cultural Politics* was published in 2012.

Other Midwestern states besides Michigan have long acted as a base for Arab American communities and writers. CHICAGO, for example, has become the final destination of many Arab immigrants seeking a home in the United States since the mid-nineteenth century. Ray Hanania (b. 1953), a Chicago-based journalist and comedian, chronicles the history and contribution of Arabs in the Windy City in his book *Arabs of Chicagoland* (2005). The book features a collection of interviews with Arab American personalities in the area, as well as profiles and photographs of them. Hanania, a well-known Arab American community spokesperson, has also published several books that emphasize his belief that humor is the best antidote to prejudice and discrimination. These include a book of essays titled *I'm Glad I Look like a Terrorist: Growing up Arab in America* (1996); *Tabouli Tales* (2003), featuring a variety of Palestinian recipes and family stories; and *Slice of Life* (2004), a collection of his humor columns. Hanania is the publisher of the *National Arab-American Times Newspaper,* published in English with select stories translated into Arabic.

Another notable Arab American literary voice in Chicago is that of Jamil Khoury (b. 1966), co-founder and artistic director of Silk Road Rising, a company that presents works by playwrights from Arab, Middle Eastern, and Mediterranean backgrounds. Born in Chicago to an American mother and a Syrian father, Khoury was constantly aware of the Middle East conflicts as he was growing up. He has spent time in the Arab world, working with the United Nations as a refugee affairs officer in the West Bank and traveling in various Middle Eastern

countries. Khoury's works include two plays, *Fitna: Chaos as Woman in the Arab World,* presented at the University of Chicago's University Theatre in 1995, and *Precious Stones* (2003), performed in ten U.S. cities. *Precious Stones,* which won *Gay Chicago Magazine*'s 2003 After Dark Award for Outstanding New Work, focuses on the Palestinian-Israeli conflict from the diasporic perspectives of two women, one Palestinian, the other Jewish, who break class, religious, political, and sexual boundaries when they fall in love. In 2010 Khoury organized and participated in Silk Road Rising's production of *The DNA Trail: A Genealogy of Short Plays about Ancestry, Identity, and Utter Confusion.* His short play *WASP: White Arab Slovak Pole* was included in *The DNA Trail* and became the basis of the documentary *Not Quite White: Arabs, Slavs, and the Contours of Contested Whiteness* (2012). His short video play *both/and* (2011) examines the construction of binaries governing Arab, American, and gay identities. Other works by Khoury include the short play *63rd and Kedzie,* which was adapted into the video play *The Balancing Arab* (2012), and the play *Mosque Alert,* which is part of an online interactive civic engagement project. See LESBIAN, GAY, BISEXUAL, TRANSGENDER, AND QUEER LITERATURE.

The Israeli-Palestinian conflict also resonates in the fiction of Chicago-based Arab American writer Sahar Mustafah (b. 1973). She won first place in the 2007 seventh annual Radius of Arab-American Writers' Competition in Creative Prose for her short story "An Unruly Life," published on the website of the Radius of Arab-American Writers (RAWI). Another short story by Mustafah, "Virgins in Paradise," also won RAWI's first prize in the 2005 creative-prose competition. It describes the desperation of I'ssa, a young man living in the Palestinian town of Khaleel, who is driven to become a suicide bomber by poverty and the need to find lodging for his family. "Shakespeare in the Gaza Strip" (2004) appeared in Pauline Kaldas and Khaled Mattawa's 2004 volume *Dinarzad's Children: An Anthology of Contemporary Fiction* (197–206). In this short story, Mustafah captures the innocent zeal of an American teacher trying to teach the tenets of English literature to her young female students in the Gaza Strip, not realizing what little meaning such texts as *A Midsummer's Night Dream* have for her students, whose lives are racked by senseless violence and the sudden disappearance and death of family members. Other stories by Mustafah include "Lovely Daughters," *Mizna* 5.2 (2003): 1–5, in which a snapshot of a Palestinian midwife's day is beautifully captured. Her short story "Shisha Love" won the 2012 Guild Literary Complex Fiction Award and was nominated for a 2013 Pushcart Prize. She is the co-founder and prose editor of the online literary journal *Bird's Thumb*. Another writer with strong roots in the Midwest is Randa Jarrar, who was born in Chicago in 1978 and studied creative writing at the University of Michigan. A novelist, short-story writer, essayist, and translator, Jarrar is the author of *A Map of Home* (2008), which won the 2009 Arab American Book Award, as well as the Hopwood and Geoffrey James Gosling Awards at the University of Michigan. In 2010 Jarrar was named one of the most gifted writers of Arab origin under the age of forty. Her writing has been featured in the *New York Times Magazine, Utne Reader,* Salon.com, *Guernica, Ploughshares, Five Chapters,* and other periodicals. She teaches creative writing at California State University, Fresno.

In addition to being home to many Arab American writers, Chicago is a strong thematic feature in several Arab and Arab American works, including *Chicago* (2007) by the Egyptian writer Alaa Al Aswany (b. 1957), author of the best-selling *The Yacoubian Building* (2002). The novel, written in Arabic and translated into English by Farouk Abdel Wahab, incorporates the author's experience of living in Chicago while studying dentistry at the University of Illinois in Chicago and focuses on the lives of an Arab American family. The city of Chicago also forms an important background for "Alone and All Together," a story by Joseph Geha (b. 1944) included in *Big City Cool: Short Stories about Urban Youth* (2002), an anthology edited by M. Jerry Weiss and Helen S. Weiss (51–63). Opening on 9/11, the story is told from the perspective of young Labibeh Tammouz, who eventually finds strength in claiming and defending her Arab American identity against the vengeful threats and physical assaults targeting Arab Americans

Joseph Geha, 2009. Photo by Ngaire West Johnson.
Courtesy of Joseph Geha

right after 9/11. By the end of the story, even the threat of an attack on Chicago leaves Labibeh unperturbed. Looking at the Sears Tower, she thinks: "Lit against the dark sky, its high beacons point right to Chicago, to us. Yes, it could happen here next time. And yet people are up there again, working. . . . Being afraid is catching, but so is being brave" (62).

Born in Zahle, Lebanon, Geha moved with his family in 1946 to Toledo, Ohio, where they lived in a largely Christian Lebanese American community. Several of the stories included in his collection *Through and Through: Toledo Stories* (1990; second edition 2009) reflect his experience of growing up in Toledo in an apartment above a grocery store owned by his father. Both "News from Phoenix" and "And What Else" feature young boys, Isaac and Habeeb, respectively, growing up around their fathers' stores in Toledo and witnessing the ways in which Arab culture and tradition are transplanted into Midwestern America. A professor emeritus of English at Iowa State University, Geha is a recipient of a National Endowment for the Arts fellowship and a Pushcart Prize, and his work is part of the permanent collection of the Smithsonian Institution's Arab-American Archive. His novel *Lebanese Blonde* was published in 2012. His other works include *Holy Toledo* (1987) and a one-act play, *The Pigeon* (1990). Another notable essayist and poet is Lebanese American Sam Hamod (b. 1936), who was born in Gary, IN-DIANA, and received a PhD from the University of IOWA WRITERS' WORKSHOP. Nominated for a Pulitzer Prize for Poetry in 1980, Hamod has published numerous books of poems and has taught at the Iowa Writers' Workshop, Princeton, Michigan, and Howard. A collection of his poetry appeared in 1980, titled *Dying with the Wrong Name: New and Selected Poems, 1968–1979*, which was followed by *The Arab Poems, The Muslim Poems* in 2000, *Just Love Poems for You* in 2006, and *Spring Will Come Soon* in 2013. Philip Metres (b. 1970) is another poet with roots in the Midwest. He grew up in the suburbs of Chicago, graduated with an MFA and a PhD from Indiana University, and currently teaches at John Carroll University in Ohio. His books of poetry include *To See the Earth* (2008) and *Abu Ghraib Arias* (2011), *and A Concordance of Leaves* (2013). His book *Behind the Lines: War Resistance Poetry on the American Homefront Since 1941* (2007) is a scholarly study.

The deep-seated effects of growing up in the Midwest surface in the works of various Arab American writers, including Mohja Kahf (b. 1968). Kahf, who as a child emigrated with her family from Syria and was raised in Indiana, tackles in her writing the sense of alienation resulting from growing up Arab and Muslim in a largely homogeneous Midwest. Poems in her book *E-mails from Scheherazad* (2003), such as "The Passing There" and "The Roc," emphasize the cultural disorientation experienced not only by Arab American immigrants but also by their children, who grapple with the complexity of hybrid identities in an unfamiliar and unsympathetic territory. In "The Passing There" a young Kahf and her brother are chased off an Indiana soybean field, which represents a terrain and a way of life that they have a hard time claiming as theirs despite all their efforts "to feel like Hoo-

siers" (18). Associate Professor of Comparative Literature and Middle East and Islamic Studies at the University of Arkansas, Kahf returns to her childhood memories of growing up in 1970s Indiana in her first novel, *The Girl in the Tangerine Scarf* (2006), although she insists that the book is not wholly autobiographical. As did Kahf, the novel's protagonist, Khadra Shamy, grows up in a devout Muslim community in Indiana, where members of this community are faced with hostility and even outright violence. The book's portrayal of a group of committed Muslims in that specific Midwestern setting typifies the particular tensions that arose during that period of national history between a mainly white Christian mainstream and a religious and ethnic Muslim minority. Although such depictions are not characteristic of all Muslim American experience across the United States, they portray a localized knowledge of the 1970s Midwest in which Kahf grew up.

Midwestern influences on multicultural perspectives can also be traced in the work of Lisa Suhair Majaj (b. 1960), who was born in Hawarden, IOWA, to a Palestinian father and an American mother. In her essay "Beyond Silence," published in *Homemaking: Women Writers and the Politics and Poetics of Home* (1996), edited by Catherine Wiley and Fiona R. Barnes, Majaj writes about the period in 1970 after she and her family fled Jordan and moved back to Iowa, where she was engulfed by a silence that inhibited her in Amman from talking about her experience of bullets, bombs, air-raid sirens, or hiding with her mother under the sink for protection. Even though she cannot imagine how accounts of such atrocities could be articulated and understood in a small town like Hawarden, Majaj states that such a Midwestern town, like many of its equivalents, has its own silenced stories of rape, teenage pregnancies, and incest.

Majaj further investigates her hybrid identity, one that straddles the Midwest and the Middle East, in her essay "Boundaries: Arab/American," which appears in Joe (formerly Joanna) Kadi's collection *Food for Our Grandmothers* (1994). The Midwest featured in this essay is represented not only by Iowa, which is always associated in Majaj's mind with her mother, but also by

Michigan, where she attended graduate school at the University of Michigan. Images of Iowa, with its farms and cornfields, emerge in Majaj's poetry, including "Recognized Futures," in which a heritage that she regards as half hers is represented by "cornfields golden / in ripening haze, green music / of crickets, summer light sloping / to dusk on the Iowa farm" (*Food for Our Grandmothers* 5). Her book of poetry, *Geographies of Light* (2009), features an intricate tapestry of poems; memory, identity, and cultural roots constitute some of the main thematic threads of this resonant collection.

Early memories of a Midwestern childhood also surface in several works by acclaimed poet Naomi Shihab Nye (b. 1952), who was born to an American mother and a Palestinian father in ST. LOUIS, MISSOURI. In "Being from St. Louis" from her book of poetry *Fuel* (1998), St. Louis images are recalled and pieced together from childhood memory, including "fallen gray leaves," "the gloomy wisdom of red brick," and "winter's fist that held and held" (24). Such images capture the essence of winter in this Midwestern city, lingering in Nye's memory and shaping her recollections of the city of her birth long after she moved to San Anto-

Naomi Shihab Nye, 1997.
By permission of Michael Nye, 2014

nio's warmer climate. Such mental revisitations are also enacted in the poem "The Brick" from Nye's collection *Words under the Words* (1980), in which the speaker finds herself, in those bleary moments before fully waking up, back in St. Louis's Pershing Avenue, looking for the building brick that she had touched with her mitten as a child in 1956. She pays tribute to such remembrances and locations, which she refers to as "the center of memory" ("The Brick" 119). Other references to the Midwest and St. Louis appear in Nye's young-adult novel *Habibi* (1997), the short essays "Newcomers in a Troubled Land," "The Cookies," "Tulips," and "Mint Snowball," included in *Never in a Hurry: Essays on People and Places* (1996), and the poems "Kansas," "First Things Last," and "Sure" in *Words under the Words*.

In *Thinking Class: Sketches from a Cultural Worker* (1996), essayist and poet Joe (formerly Joanna) Kadi (b. 1958), who is of Lebanese racial and cultural heritage, refers in the essay titled "Stupidity 'Deconstructed'" to the wide gulf that separates the working class from middle- and upper-middle-class academics who appropriate working-class experience. Beginning with a description of workers on a building site at the University of Minnesota, the essay outlines the process by which Kadi achieved an awareness of class and privilege within the university's elitist framework. Describing herself as "a working-class Arab halfbreed queer girl" (6), Kadi delineates in *Thinking Class,* often with brutal honesty, the contradictions of her background, which includes Canadian and Midwestern influences. Kadi is the editor of *Food for Our Grandmothers: Writings by Arab-American and Arab-Canadian Feminists* (1994) and has taught at the Center of Arts Criticism in Minneapolis (see MINNEAPOLIS/ST. PAUL) and the GLBTA Programs Office at the University of Minnesota. See GAY, LESBIAN, BISEXUAL, TRANSGENDER, AND QUEER LITERATURE.

Other writers of Arab background with connections to the Midwest include Mona Simpson (b. 1957), born in Green Bay, WISCONSIN, to a Syrian father and an American mother. Known for best-selling books including *Anywhere but Here* (1987), *The Lost Father* (1991), and *Off Keck Road* (2000), Simpson does not directly address Arab American or Midwestern issues as such. Nevertheless, some events in her novels reflect her family's history, including her parents' divorce when she was ten years old. In *The Lost Father* the female protagonist, a medical school student in New York, sets off in search of her Egyptian immigrant father, who had abandoned the family, while *Off Keck Road* is set in Green Bay, Wisconsin, Simpson's hometown, where the three main female characters have lived for most of their lives.

The Midwest's role in the development of Arab American literature is reflected in the 1999 launch of *Mizna*, the first journal of Arab American literature. Based in Minneapolis, *Mizna* features creative work focusing on Arab American themes encompassing poetry, fiction, essays, FILM, music, and visual art. Its annual Twin Cities Arab Film Festival and events such as the Mideast in the Midwest attract talent from across the country. *Mizna* also offers Arabic classes and organizes outreach programs in the community. Lebanese American Kathryn Haddad, co-founder of the journal, has co-written the play *With Love from Ramallah* (2004), which is set in St. Paul, MINNESOTA (see MINNEAPOLIS/ST. PAUL), and Ramallah and was performed at the Theatre in Minneapolis. Her play *Zafira the Olive Oil Warrior* (2011) was performed at Minneapolis's Pangea World Theater on the tenth anniversary of 9/11. Set in the near future, it focuses on the story of an Arab American woman who is subjected to internment after multiple suicide bombings turn all Arabs and Muslims in the United States into suspects.

Ismail Khalidi (b. 1984), who was born in Beirut to Palestinian parents and was raised in Chicago, acted in *With Love from Ramallah*, and in 2005 he co-wrote and acted in the one-person play *Truth Serum Blues*, which was performed in Minneapolis, New York City, Chicago, and Detroit. The play was selected as the Best Solo Performance of 2005 in Minneapolis's *Lavender* magazine. In 2010 his play *Tennis in Nablus* premiered at Atlanta's Alliance Theater. Khalidi is a winner of the Emerging Writers Grant from the Jerome Foundation, as well as the Many Voices Residency at the Playwrights Center in Minneapolis. His poems "Detour" (set in Dearborn), "Cold Hard Facts: Letter to the Editor, Part 1," and "Routine Procedure(s)" appeared in *Mizna* 6.2 (2004). *Mizna* has featured other writers affiliated with the Midwest, including journalist, fiction writer, and screenwriter Alia Yunis (b. 1969). Born in Chicago, Yunis grew up in the Twin Cities and Beirut and currently lives in Abu Dhabi, where she teaches film and television at Zayed University. Her autobiographical essay "Al-Manara" and the short story "The Lebanon-Detroit Express" both portray her Midwestern attachments. They appeared in *Mizna* 6.2 (2004) and 8.2 (2006), respectively. Yunis is a 2005 PEN Emerging Voices fellow and a 2006 Hedgebrook fellow. She is also the recipient of two comedy-writing awards, one from Warner Brothers and the other from Women in Film. Her first novel, *The Night Counter* (2009), explores the far-flung lives of members of the Arab American Abdullah clan, whose family roots straddle both Michigan and Lebanon. *Mizna* has also featured the works of various other Midwestern Arab American writers, including the Michigan-based scholar and creative writer Rosina Hassoun, whose poem "Accidental Hijacking" appears in *Mizna* 7.1 (2005).

SELECTED WORKS: Major works of early Midwestern Arab American fiction include Abraham Mitrie Rihbany's *A Far Journey* (1914), Salom Rizk's *Syrian Yankee* (1943), and Vance Bourjaily's *Confessions of a Spent Youth* (1960). Among later works are Mona Simpson's *Anywhere but Here* (1987), Joseph Geha's *Through and Through: Toledo Stories* (1990, second edition 2009), and Mohja Kahf's *The Girl in the Tangerine Scarf* (2006). Major books of poetry include Lawrence Joseph's *Shouting at No One* (1983) and *Curriculum Vitae* (1988), Hayan Charara's *The Alchemist's Diary* (2001) and *The Sadness of Others* (2006), Naomi Shihab Nye's *Words under the Words* (1980) and *Fuel* (1998), and Kahf's *E-mails from Scheherazad* (2003).

Several anthologies of Arab American literature have been published, and with the increasing interest in this ethnic literature, many more are scheduled to be published soon. One of the first anthologies that have marked a place for Arab American literature on the U.S. literary map is *Grape Leaves: A Century of Arab American Poetry*, edited by Gregory Orfalea and Sharif Elmusa. Published in 1988, this anthology focuses on first- and second-generation Arab American poets, including writers with roots in the Midwest, such as Sam Hamod. Another groundbreaking collection is *Food for Our Grandmothers: Writings by Arab American and Arab Canadian Feminists* (1994), edited by Joe Kadi. Featuring the poetry and essays of writers based in the Midwest, such as Leila Diab (b. 1946), Carol Haddad (b. 1965), Zana Macki (b. 1956), and Marilynn Rashid (b. 1955), this collection gives shape to a burgeoning Arab American FEMINISM. Such feminist investment has been further developed and emphasized by the essays featured in the collections *Scheherazade's Legacy: Arab and Arab American Women on Writing* (2004), edited by Susan Muaddi Darraj; *Shattering the Stereotypes: Muslim Women Speak Out* (2005), edited by Fawzia Afzal-Khan; and *Arab and Arab American Feminisms: Gender, Violence, and Belonging* (2010), edited by Rabab Abdulhadi, Evelyn Alsultany, and Nadine Naber.

Post-Gibran: Anthology of New Arab-American Writing (1999), edited by Khaled Mattawa and Munir Akash, is another landmark publication that emphasizes the emerging prominence and multiplicity of Arab American literature at the end of the 1990s. Writers with Midwestern connections in this anthology include Nuar Alsadir, who was born in Chicago; Evelyn Accad (b. 1943), Professor Emerita at the University of Illinois, Champaign-Urbana; and Saladin Ahmed (b. 1975) and Mechelle Zarou (b. 1974), both of whom were born in Michigan. Published by Detroit's Ridgeway Press and edited by D. H. Melhem and Leila Diab, *A Different Path* (2000) presents the works of some members of the RAWI organization, including Detroit's Ron David (b. 1939) and the Toledo-based Nada Najjar (b. 1951).

The period since 9/11 has witnessed an increase in the amount of literature by and about Arab Americans. This increased attention to Arab American studies can be ascribed to a need to educate the U.S. public about this community, as well as to assert the diversity of Arab American identities. Although not wholly dedicated to Midwestern Arab American literature, several anthologies present the works of authors with direct connections to the Midwest by birth, time spent in the area, or the content and themes of their work. Such collections include Nathalie Handal's *The Poetry of Arab Women* (2001); *Dinarzad's Children: An Anthology of Contemporary Arab-American Fiction* (2004; second edition 2009), the first anthology of Arab American short stories, edited by Khaled Mattawa and Pauline Kaldas; and Hayan Charara's *Inclined to Speak: An Anthology of Contemporary Arab American Poetry* (2008).

FURTHER READING: Scholarship on Arab American literature is notably on the rise, thus countering the scarcity of secondary materials that had until recently typified this field. Scholarly articles on Abraham Rihbany's *A Far Journey* and *The Syrian Christ* include the late Evelyn Shakir's "Mother's Milk: Women in Arab-American Autobiography," *MELUS* 15.4 (1988): 39–50, which also encompasses an analysis of Salom Rizk's *Syrian Yankee* (1943); and Sirène Harb's "Orientalism and the Construction of American Identity in Abraham Mitrie Rihbany's 'A Far Journey,'" *MELUS* 33.3 (2008): 131–45. Shakir also wrote on Vance Bourjaily's *Confessions of a Spent Youth* in "Arab Mothers, American Sons: Women in Arab-American Autobiographies," *MELUS* 17.3 (1991/1992): 5–15. William Parrill's "The Art of the Novel: An Interview with Vance Bourjaily" appears in *Louisiana Literature* 5.2 (Fall 1988): 3–20.

For an analysis of the religious aspects of Lawrence Joseph's poetry, refer to Andrew Krivak's "The Language of Redemption: The Catholic Poets Adam Zagajewski, Marie Ponsot and Lawrence Joseph," *Commonwealth* 130.9 (May 2003): 12–16. A review of Joseph's *Before Our Eyes* by David Yessi appears in *Parnassus: Poetry in Review* 19.2 (1994): 83–90. In "Delivering a Memory of Dearborn and Detroit: Debut of a New Arab-American Poet," in the Arab-American magazine *Al Jadid* 9.42/43 (Winter/Spring 2003): 46, New York–based Palestinian American poet Nathalie Handal reviews Hayan Charara's *The Sadness of Others*, while Dunya Mikhail's *The War Works Hard* is reviewed in *Publishers Weekly* (April 18, 2005): 58.

An analysis of Ahmad Baydoun's memoir *Bint Jibayl, Michigan* can be found in Rochelle Davis's "Language and Loss; or, How to Bark like a Dog and Other Lessons from al-Jahiz," *Critique: Critical Middle Eastern Studies* 13.1 (Spring 2004): 97–112. Praise for Jamil Khoury's work is featured in Lucia Mauro's review *Precious Stones: Silk Road Explores*

Conflict in Middle East, Chicago Tribune, January 24, 2003, 12; and Steve Street reviews Alaa Al Aswany's *The Yacoubian Building* in *Missouri Review* 3.1 (Spring/Summer 2007): 143–44.

For a comparison of Joseph Geha's work with that of other Arab American fiction writers, refer to Steven Salaita's "Sand Niggers, Small Shops, and Uncle Sam: Cultural Negotiation in the Fiction of Joseph Geha and Diana Abu-Jaber," *Criticism* 43.4 (Fall 2001): 423–44. Geha's literary style is also analyzed in Kenneth A. Robb's "The Fading Narrator in Joseph Geha's 'Through and Through,'" *Notes on Contemporary Literature* 22.3 (May 1992): 9–11; and Doris Safie's "Joseph Geha's Toledo Stories," *Paintbrush: A Journal of Contemporary Multicultural Literature* 18.35 (Spring 1991): 80–83. Donna Seaman's review of Mohja Kahf's *E-mails from Scheherazad* can be found in *Booklist* 1 (March 2003): 1141, and more praise for Kahf's work is featured in Lisa Suhair Majaj's online article "Supplies of Grace: The Poetry of Mohja Kahf," published on the web-based newsletter *ArteNews* in September 2006. Multiple critical pieces on Naomi Shihab Nye's poetry are available; a short list includes Louis McKee's "Ranting and Raving about Naomi Shihab Nye," *Swamp Root* (Spring 1989): 83–93; Gregory Orfalea's "Doomed by Our Blood to Care: The Poetry of Naomi Shihab Nye," *Paintbrush: A Journal of Contemporary Multicultural Literature* 18.35 (Spring 1991): 56–66; and Dima Hilal's "Bordering on the Borderless: The Poetry of Naomi Shihab Nye," *Al Jadid* 8.39 (2002): 7, 17. Bryce Milligan speaks to Nye in "Writing to Save Our Lives: An Interview with Naomi Shihab Nye," *Paintbrush* 18.35 (Spring 1991): 31–52. An overview of Arab American literature, including Midwestern writers like Nye, Simpson, Geha, and Hanania, is available in Elmaz Abinader's "Children of Al-Mahjar: Arab-American Literature Spans a Century" in *U.S. Society and Values* 5.1 (February 2000): 11–17. Other important articles that discuss the works of the major Midwestern Arab American writers include Lisa Suhair Majaj's "Two Worlds Emerging: Arab-American Writing at the Crossroads," *Forkroads: A Journal of Ethnic-American Literature* 1.3 (Spring 1996): 64–80, and "Arab-American Literature: Origins and Developments," in the unpaginated online *American Studies Journal* 52 (2008). Majaj has also published extensively on Arab American literature and discusses the works of writers such as Abraham Mitrie Rihbany, Salom Rizk, Vance (Nye) Bourjaily, Joseph Geha, and Naomi Shihab Nye in "Arab-American Literature and the Politics of Memory," in *Memory and Cultural Politics: New Approaches to American Ethnic Literatures* (1996), edited by Amritjit Singh, Joseph T. Skerret Jr., and Robert E. Hogan, 266–90.

A review of Joe Kadi's anthology *Food for Our Grandmothers,* Christina Civantos's "The Middle East in North America: Questions of Identity in *Food for Our Grandmothers,*" appears in the *Stanford Electronic Humanities Review* 5.1 (Spring 1996). Jonathan Coe reviews Simpson's *The Lost Father* in "Beautiful People," *London Review of Books,* July 23, 1992, 22–23; and Jonathan Bing writes about Simpson's background and writing in "Mona Simpson: Return of the Prodigal Father," *Publishers Weekly* (November 4, 1996): 50–51.

The years since 9/11 have witnessed the publication of various edited collections, books, and special journal issues on the topic of Arab American literature, including, for example, a special issue of *MELUS* 31.4 (December 2006) edited by Salah D. Hassan and Marcy Jane Knopf-Newman; *Arab Voices in Diaspora: Critical Perspectives on Anglophone Arab Literature* (2009), edited by Layla Al Maleh; *Contemporary Arab American Women Writers: Hyphenated Identities and Border Crossings* (2007) by Amal Talaat Abdelrazek; *Immigrant Narratives: Orientalism and Cultural Translation in Arab-American and Arab-British Literature* (2011) by Waïl Hassan; *Arab American Literary Fictions, Cultures, and Politics* (2007) and *Modern Arab American Fiction: A Reader's Guide* (2011) by Steven Salaita; *New Body Politics: Narrating Arab and Black Identity in the Contemporary United States* (2014) by Therí Pickens; and *Contemporary Arab-American Literature: Transnational Reconfigurations of Citizenship and Belonging* (2014) by Carol Fadda-Conrey.

Further depictions and analyses of Midwestern Arab Americans appear in books such as *Arabs in America: Building a New Future* (2000), edited by Michael Suleiman, particularly the essays by May Seikaly ("Attachment and Identity: The Palestinian

Community of Detroit"), Richard T. Antoun ("Jordanian Migrants in Texas and Ohio: The Quest for Education and Work in a Global Society"), and Louise Cainkar ("The Deteriorating Ethnic Safety Net among Arab Immigrants in Chicago"). Drawing on interviews, archives, and personal accounts of first- and second-generation Arab American women, Evelyn Shakir's book *Bint Arab: Arab American Women in the United States* (1997) presents an in-depth and firsthand portrayal of the lives of these women, some of whom were located in the Midwest.

The Arab American community in Michigan is the focus of various artistic, literary, and political studies, including Anan Ameri and Yvonne Lockwood's *Arab-Americans in Metro Detroit: A Pictorial History* (2001); Sally Howell and Andrew Shryock's "Cracking Down on Diaspora: Arab Detroit and America's 'War on Terror,'" *Anthropological Quarterly* 76.3 (Summer 2003): 443–62; Roland Hwang's *Civil Rights Issues Facing Arab-Americans in Michigan* (2003); and Rosina J. Hassoun's *Arab-Americans in Michigan* (2005). *Arab Detroit: From Margin to Mainstream* (2000), edited by Nabeel Abraham and Andrew Shryock, features essays, fiction, and poems that explore literary, immigrant, historical, cultural, political, religious, and demographic aspects of the Detroit area's Arab American community. The essays in other Detroit-focused collections handle the prejudice and discrimination faced by Arab and Muslim communities in Michigan; titles include *Arab Detroit 9/11: Life in the Terror Decade* (2011), edited by Nabeel Abraham, Sally Howell, and Andrew Shryock, and *Citizenship and Crisis: Arab Detroit after 9/11* (2009) by Wayne Baker and others. Other books focus on the targeting of Arab and Muslim communities in the United States, including Midwestern ones, such as *Race and Arab Americans before and after 9/11: From Invisible Citizens to Visible Subjects* (2008), edited by Amaney Jamal and Nadine Naber, and *Homeland Insecurity: The Arab American and Muslim American Experience after 9/11* (2009) by Louise Cainkar. Other works on Arab Americans include *Arab America: Gender, Cultural Politics, and Activism* (2012) by Nadine Naber; *Arabs and Muslims in the Media: Race and Representation after 9/11* (2012) by Evelyn Alsultany; and *Between the Middle East and the Americas: The Cultural Politics of Diaspora,* edited by Evelyn Alsultany and Ella Shohat (2013).

In addition to its literary components, the creative output of Midwestern Arab America encompasses film documentaries that include Joan Mandell's *Tales from Arab Detroit* (1995), depicting the relationships and connections among several generations of Arab Americans in Detroit. *Benaat Chicago: Growing Up Arab and Female in Chicago* (1996), directed by Jennifer Bin-Canar and Mary Zerkel, focuses on young Arab American women in Chicago struggling to reconcile their traditional backgrounds with their U.S. environment, while Neal AbuNab's *The Arabian Dream* (2005) depicts the Arab American community in the Detroit area. Also set in Detroit, Lebanese American Rola Nashef's film *Detroit Unleaded* (2012) portrays the daily life of Sami, a young Arab man who runs a gas station with his cousin Mike. *Amreeka* (2010), a feature film portraying the experiences of a mother and her son moving from Palestine to the Midwest, was written and directed by Cherien Dabis (b. 1976), a Palestinian American director, producer, and screenwriter who was born in NEBRASKA and grew up in Ohio and Jordan. Other screen depictions of Arabs and Muslims in the United States include *Fordson* (2011), which depicts the Arab American members of a high school football team in a Detroit suburb during the month of Ramadan, as well as *All-American Muslim,* a reality TV program that aired beginning in November 2011 for one season and followed the lives of five Lebanese American Muslim families who live in Dearborn, Michigan.

CAROL FADDA-CONREY   SYRACUSE UNIVERSITY

ARCHETYPES

OVERVIEW: The search for a definitive Midwest has occupied almost everyone who has studied the region. RUTH SUCKOW (1892–1960) writes in "Middle Western Literature," *English Journal* 21.3 (March 1932): 175–82, that "if any region has a right to its existence in art *as a region* . . . it must rest upon the one particular quality that is its own and differentiates it from all others" (178). For Suckow, that quintessential Midwestern quality is authenticity. Kent Ryden, in "Writing the Midwest: History, Literature, and Regional Identity," *Geographical Review* 89.4 (1999): 511–32, sees that quality as absence or lack. James Shortridge, in *The Middle West: Its Meaning in American Culture* (1989), finds pastoral idealism to be the quality most frequently associated with the Midwest. Jon Gjerde, in *The Minds of the West: Ethnocultural Evolution in the Rural Middle West, 1830–1917*, sees conflict between nativist and immigrant cultural traditions as the Midwest's defining characteristic. Frederick J. Hoffman, in *The Twenties: American Writing in the Postwar Decade* (1955), argues that the Midwest is a metaphor for all the most life-denying aspects of middle-class morality, while Margaret Stuhr in her article "The Safe Middle West: Escape to and Escape from Home," *MidAmerica* 14 (1987): 18–27, is struck by the double-sidedness of the Safe Middle West, experienced as a comforting haven from urban problems that is at the same time what Andrew R. L. Cayton in *The American Midwest: Essays on Regional History* (2001), edited by Cayton and Susan E. Gray, calls "the land of normalcy and niceness," dull, boring, and always ten years behind the times (141).

HISTORY AND SIGNIFICANCE: Despite these differing views of the Midwest, enduring archetypes—patterns of Midwestern experience—shape the way we see the region today and tell us who Midwesterners are, where they came from, and what they aspire to. More important, these archetypes perform important cultural functions that account for their endurance over the better part of two hundred years.

Many scholars have noted, with Stuhr, that the Midwest and Midwestern literature are characterized by dualisms, polarities, and contradictions, perhaps stemming from the region's central paradox: its geographic centrality but cultural marginality. The opening lines of "The Prairies" (1833) by William Cullen Bryant (1794–1878), "These are the gardens of the desert," exemplify this paradox as they introduce the archetype of the Midwest as both abundant garden, symbolizing the promise of a new life in the West, and what WILLA CATHER (1873–1947), in "The Sculptor's Funeral" (1905), in *The Troll Garden* (1905) termed "a desert of newness and ugliness and sordidness" (442), home to the virtuous yeoman farmer whose hard work, competence, and self-reliance have

made him into one of Thomas Jefferson's natural aristocrats, independent and self-supporting on his own farm.

One of Cather's best short stories, "Neighbour Rosicky" (1930), portrays the archetypal yeoman farmer in Anton Rosicky, a Czechoslovakian immigrant who has worked hard for a good life in rural NEBRASKA. Rosicky is connected to nature, beloved by his family, a kindhearted man who spent his youth in soul-destroying cities but has come into his own as an independent freehold farmer in the "happy land of farms and simple industries" (336) that (HERMAN) THEODORE DREISER (1871–1945) describes in *A Hoosier Holiday* (1916). Norwegian immigrant Per Hansa, the protagonist of *GIANTS IN THE EARTH* (1927) by OLE EDVART RØLVAAG (1876–1931), proudly surveying his acreage in the former Dakota Territory and dreaming of the imposing house and roomy barn he will one day build, is another yeoman farmer, as are the pioneer farmers of *SPOON RIVER ANTHOLOGY* (1915) by EDGAR LEE MASTERS (1868–1950): Rebecca Wasson, Lucinda Matlock, Aaron Hatfield, Conrad Siever, and Fiddler Jones.

Gift for the Grangers detail, 1873.
Image courtesy of the Library of Congress

But the self-made Midwestern farmer and the village dweller can also be materialistic philistines who neither value nor understand cultural amenities such as ART, music, or literature. In *Midwest at Noon* (1946) Englishman Graham Hutton (1904–1988) observes that "Midwesterners for a long time have put a lower value on the original and creative life of the mind than they have on material things, practical affairs, common sense, and what they term 'realism'" (192). Zury Prouder of *Zury* (1887) by JOSEPH KIRKLAND (1830–1894), John Wright of *TRIFLES* (1916) by SUSAN KEATING GLASPELL (1876–1948), Jesse Bentley of *WINESBURG, OHIO* (1919) by SHERWOOD ANDERSON (1876–1941), and Grant McLane of *MAIN-TRAVELLED ROADS* (1891) by (HANNIBAL) HAMLIN GARLAND (1860–1940) are just four examples of this very prevalent Midwestern materialistic philistine archetype. Cather might rhapsodize in *O PIONEERS!* (1913) and *My Ántonia* (1918) about the fertile farmland of Nebraska and the noble characters like Alexandra Bergson and Ántonia Shimerda Cuzak that life on the land engenders, but she is harshly critical of the Marshalls in "Neighbour Rosicky" and the Wheelers in *One of Ours* (1922), who acquire all the latest farm equipment at the expense of their families' comfort and convenience. Similarly, the townspeople in "A Sculptor's Funeral" are blinded by the prosaic realities of village life and cannot comprehend the artistic genius of their native son, sculptor Harvey Merrick. Viewed from another perspective, Aunt Georgiana of "A Wagner Matinee" (1905) and Mr. Shimerda find that their love of music has no place in their hardscrabble existence on the farm.

The notion of the Midwest as a cultural desert populated by philistines lives on in contemporary times. It exists in the reported characterization of his native Oak Park by ERNEST (MILLER) HEMINGWAY (1899–1961) as a place of broad lawns and narrow minds. It is also evident in the February 21, 1925, declaration by *New Yorker* editor Harold Ross that he was not editing his magazine for "the old lady in Dubuque" (2). It is equally present in films such as *Breaking Away* (1979) and in the perennial question "How will it play in Peoria?"

Other archetypes of the Midwest closely related to that of the philistine are the success-driven tycoon and the businessman-booster whose intellectual horizons do not extend beyond opportunities for making money. Erasmus Brainerd of *The Cliff-Dwellers* (1893) by HENRY BLAKE FULLER (1857–1929), Van Harrington of *The Web of Life* (1914) by ROBERT (WELCH) HERRICK (1868–1938), Curtis Jadwin of *The Pit* (1903) by (BENJAMIN) FRANK(LIN) NORRIS (1870–1902), and Frank Cowperwood of Dreiser's Cowperwood trilogy are Chicago titans of business and industry. They exemplify the assertion of Kenny Jackson Williams in "The Past Is Prologue: Chicago's Early Writing," *MidAmerica* 4 (1977): 56–73, that the early Chicago novel often portrays the businessman as the city's cultural hero, focused completely on BUSINESS and unmindful of the ethical standards of the East, "forging a city in an inhospitable wilderness" (57). The archetypal businessman-booster is George Babbitt, the protagonist of *Babbitt* (1922) by (HARRY) SINCLAIR LEWIS (1885–1951). Babbitt's bête noire is socialism, his favorite art form is the comic strip, and his raison d'être is the high-commission real estate deal. Babbitt's boosterism—as well as that of Colonel Beriah Sellers in *The Gilded Age* (1873) by SAMUEL LANGHORNE CLEMENS (1835–1910), writing as Mark Twain, George McDowell in *The Cliff-Dwellers*, and "Honest Jim" Blausser in Lewis's *MAIN STREET* (1920)—is reflected in the cartoon characters that many early twentieth-century Midwestern city newspapers created as public personae to inspire enthusiasm and support for their respective municipalities. Among these are the *Chicago Tribune*'s Miss Chicago and the *Columbus Dispatch*'s Kris Columbus. Such boosterism can be traced back to inflated claims about Midwestern lands and towns designed to lure investors and settlers to the region, as seen in *A Paper City* (1879) by DAVID ROSS LOCKE (1833–1888) and *Martin Chuzzlewit* (1843) by Charles Dickens (1812–1870). The boosters of burgeoning towns and small cities—including Lewis's Gopher Prairie and Zenith, and Midland City, which provides the setting for the novels constituting the growth trilogy of (NEWTON) BOOTH TARKINGTON (1869–1946)—are the fictional counterparts of the many members of commercial clubs, chambers of commerce, and service clubs that mushroomed in the late nineteenth and early twentieth centuries to promote growth, industrialization, and progress in Midwestern municipalities.

"The imagination of Midwesterners is almost universally confined to building or doing material things," Hutton observes in *Midwest at Noon*, providing a rationale for the prevalence of the tinkerer archetype in Midwestern literature (323). This archetype also reflects the region's nurturing a number of tinkerers like Orville and Wilbur Wright, John Deere, Cyrus McCormick, and Henry Ford, whose inventions revolutionized American society. This Midwestern penchant for inventiveness, Hutton argues, derives in part from the region's harsh climate: "It is no wonder that so many of the domestic mechanical contrivances and defenses against this climate were invented or manufactured in the Midwest" (7).

Although several fictional tinkerers appear in books by Midwestern authors, such as Lake Wobegon's handyman Carl Krebsbach and Spoon River's inventors Robert Fulton Tanner and Franklin Jones, the quintessential tinkerer in Midwestern literature is Anderson's Hugh McVey, the protagonist of *Poor White* (1920). He invents corn-cutting and coal-loading machines that transform his life and that of his hometown. Tarkington employs the tinkerer as a barometer of social change in *The Magnificent Ambersons* (1918). Inventor Eugene Morgan grows rich from his automobile factory, while the Ambersons languish and decline as they cling to their horse and buggy. The tinkerer archetype abounds in Lewis's novels, attesting to his faith that the American Dream would be achieved through technological progress. Among the Midwest's archetypal tinkerers presented in Lewis's fiction are engineer-mechanic Milt Daggett of *The Trail of the Hawk* (1915), aviator-inventor Carl Ericson of *Free Air* (1919), *Main Street's* handyman-engineer Miles Bjornstam, automaker Sam Dodsworth of *Dodsworth* (1929), and George Babbitt's son, Ted. One of the best-known characters in this vein is businessman-inventor Silas Lapham, whose values are tested in the unscrupulous business world of the East in *The Rise of Silas Lapham* (1885) by Ohioan WILLIAM DEAN HOWELLS (1837–1920). Reflecting the author's Midwestern ethic of accountability and honesty, Lapham ultimately rejects business success in order to recover his integrity, which he had previously subordinated to the pursuit of financial gain and social standing.

The yeoman farmer, the philistine, the tycoon, the tinkerer, and the businessman-booster could make life difficult for the nonconformist, the misfit, and the outsider. As DAVID D(ANIEL) ANDERSON (1924–2011) observes in "The Dimensions of the Midwest," *MidAmerica* 1 (1974): 7–15, the region has ironically signified both a space for freedom and growth and a place of oppression that limits opportunities. Despite the Midwest's reputation for egalitarianism, its literature is replete with the archetype of the "other." *Main Street* portrays the failure of three such misfits to be accepted in Gopher Prairie: schoolteacher Fern Mullins, socialist Miles Bjornstam, and tailor's assistant Erik Valborg. Each is ostracized and finally banished for failing to conform to the moral, political, and social norms, respectively, of the town. Anderson focuses extensively on this archetype in *Winesburg, Ohio*, peopling his book with "grotesques" who are too different to coexist comfortably in the town. They are people like Wing Biddlebaum, whose failure to control his hands has led to his being misunderstood and ostracized; Wash Williams, consumed with hatred for his adulterous wife; Enoch Robinson and his make-believe friends; the love-starved Seth Richmond; and the socially inept Joe Welling, whose verbosity ironically renders him unable to communicate. Closely related to Anderson's grotesques are the many misfits in the Spoon River cemetery, such as the Chinese Yee Bow, the African American blacksmith Shack Dye, the love-deprived Mabel Osborne, the misunderstood poetess Minerva Jones, and her father Indignation.

The immigrant pioneer settler became an increasingly dominant outsider archetype in Midwestern literature as Irish, Scandinavians, Czechs, Poles, and Germans continued to settle in the region in large numbers, bringing religious traditions, political affiliations, and mores greatly in contrast to those of the settlers from New England and the South. Rølvaag emphasizes the hardships these early pioneers experienced on the frontier; its harsh natural conditions and isolation ultimately take the life of

Per Hansa and the sanity of his wife, Beret. But other factors prove almost as challenging as nature; the Hansa family's Norwegian religious and cultural traditions clash with those of more materialistic and success-minded American-born settlers. Gjerde argues in *The Minds of The West: Ethnocultural Evolution in the Rural Middle West, 1830–1917* that these predominantly Catholic or Lutheran immigrants were shaped by cultural traditions that emphasized authority and hierarchy, while American-born migrants valued individualism, democracy, and independence. These cultural differences, in addition to social class distinctions that placed Yankee business owners on a higher stratum than Scandinavian farmers and working-men, produced the kind of cultural conflict seen in *Main Street* when members of the Jolly Seventeen complain about their "Scandahoofian" hired girls and boycott "Red Swede" Miles Bjornstam's wedding, as well as the funeral of his wife and child. A humorous portrayal of this conflict is seen in the early chapters of *Lake Wobegon Days* (1985) by GARY EDWARD KEILLOR (b. 1942), writing as Garrison Keillor, when the town's name alternates between New Albion and Lake Wobegon, depending on whether the immigrants or the Yankees have the current majority on the town council. Conflict between immigrant cultures in the upper Midwest— usually German Catholic versus Scandinavian Lutheran—is also seen in Keillor's novel, as well as in *Grand Opening* (1987) by JON (FRANCIS) HASSLER (1933–2008), in which religious affiliation determines which grocery store to patronize and who gets elected to the school board. Likewise, in Lake Wobegon there are competing German Catholic and Scandinavian Lutheran churches, car dealerships, Boy Scout troops, cemetery sections, and Memorial Day marching bands.

Movement has always been a major Midwestern dynamic, be it Twain's Huck and Jim floating down the Mississippi on their raft, Dreiser motoring through INDIANA in a Pathfinder touring car, or the Nevels family leaving Appalachia to search for a brighter economic future in DETROIT in *THE DOLL-MAKER* (1954) by HARRIETTE SIMPSON ARNOW (1908–1986). Although we most frequently think of Midwestern movement as a westward journey made by pioneer settlers to homestead in the region, the back-trailer who leaves the Midwest to pursue improved cultural or career opportunities elsewhere is an archetype that surfaces in post–Civil War Midwestern literature. Garland, who coined the term in his autobiographical narrative *Back-Trailers from the Middle Border* (1928), spent his formative years on farms in WISCONSIN and IOWA before moving to Boston and then to New York City, where he began to publish his fiction. One of the best-known stories in his *Main-Travelled Roads,* "Up the Coulé" focuses on successful New York City actor Howard McLane's return to the Wisconsin farm on which his brother has been struggling to make a living ever since Howard left the farm for the greater opportunities of the East. Many ambitious Midwesterners, actual and fictional, followed in Garland's and Howard McLane's footsteps, some after a stop in CHICAGO, to pursue careers in literature, theatre, or visual art. Cather moved to New York City to write her novels after having lived in Nebraska since the age of nine because, as she reportedly said, that was where books were bought and sold. Jim Burden, the narrator of *My Ántonia,* takes a path very similar to Cather's; after growing up in a small Nebraska town and graduating from college in Lincoln, he becomes a successful New York City railroad attorney.

Two back-trailers who continued to write about the Midwest although they no longer lived there were Glaspell and her husband, GEORGE CRAM COOK (1873–1924), descendants of Iowa pioneer settlers, who founded the Provincetown Players in Massachusetts in 1915 and subsequently wrote, directed, and acted in their own plays in Provincetown and New York until 1922. In their early one-act play *Suppressed Desires* (1915) Midwesterner Henrietta Brewster, now a sophisticated Greenwich Village intellectual, is visited by her naïve sister from Chicago. Cook and Glaspell were joined in their theatre venture by fellow Davenporter FLOYD DELL (1887–1969), who wrote fiction as well as DRAMA, and whose second novel, *The Briary-Bush* (1921), takes Felix Fay, the protagonist of his best-selling *Moon-Calf* (1920), from Davenport to Chicago. Two of Glaspell's novels also feature back-trailer characters: Ruth Holland in *Fidelity* (1915) and Irma Schraeder in *Fugitive's Return* (1929). Perhaps the best-known back-trailer in American literature is Nick Carraway, narrator of THE GREAT GATSBY (1925) by F(RANCIS) SCOTT (KEY) FITZGERALD (1896–1940), whose inability to reconcile the callous behavior of his East Coast friends with the moral norms of his MINNESOTA upbringing constitutes a major conflict in the novel.

Just as the post–Civil War period was marked by Midwestern back-trailing to the East Coast, the post–World War I period provided a similar backdrop for Midwestern EXPATRIATES in Europe. France, especially Paris—termed a "moveable feast" by Hemingway—was a cultural magnet for that writer, as well as for Fitzgerald, Anderson, JAMES T(HOMAS) FARRELL (1904–1979), ROBERT (MENZIES) MCALMON (1895–1956), GLENWAY WESCOTT (1901–1987), LOUIS BROMFIELD (1896–1956), (JOSEPH) BRAND WHITLOCK (1869–1934), and other Midwestern writers and artists. Their work from that period often reflects their determination to escape the repressive and conventional Midwest, break with the past, and "make it new" in the Old World. Thus, as SCOTT RUSSELL SANDERS (b. 1945) observes in *Writing from the Center* (1995), Midwestern literature is a literature of exile. "The most celebrated literature of the Midwest has been written by those who left," he asserts (25, 161). Hemingway's *The Sun Also Rises* (1926) and Fitzgerald's *Tender Is the Night* (1934), novels set and written in Europe by Midwestern-born authors, are perhaps the best evidence for Sanders's assertion. These novels enact the struggle with the post–World War I sense of loss and disillusionment of Jake Barnes and Dick Diver, respectively, played out against the frenzied moral confusion of expatriate activity in France and Spain. THE ADVENTURES OF AUGIE MARCH (1953) by SAUL (C.) BELLOW (1915–2005) also reflects the expatriate's quest for meaning and identity in a chaotic world.

Archetypes of place, as well as of character, depict the Midwest, often imagined as a land of contrasting horizontals and verticals: man-made grain elevators, silos, and skyscrapers silhouetted against the blue bowl of a Midwestern sky and the vast expanses of nature embodied in prairie, cornfield, and river. The last of these, the river, is one of the most identifiably Mid-western archetypes of place. It is first seen in the region's early travel narratives by voyageurs, pioneer settlers, and missionary priests, and it has continued as a dominant presence in the literature of the Midwest. Tellingly described by Leslie Fiedler in *Love and Death in the American Novel* (1960) as "a just-passed frontier, a defining limit between the realms of civilization and nature, a boundary which America touches and crosses on its way west . . . a passageway into the deep South" (386), the Mississippi is a liminal space that is all those things for Huckleberry Finn, whose boyhood experiences on the river, as related in *The Adventures of Tom Sawyer* (1876) and ADVENTURES OF HUCKLEBERRY FINN (London 1884; New York 1885), are echoed in boys' books—*Swatty* (1920), *Jibby Jones* (1923), and *Jibby Jones and the Alligator* (1924), all set in Riverbank (Muscatine), Iowa—by ELLIS PARKER BUTLER (1869–1937). *Adventures of Huckleberry Finn* also features a character type introduced by JAMES HALL (1793–1868) in *Letters from the West* (1828) and *The Western Souvenir* (1828), the boastful, tall-tale-telling raftsman whose prototype was Hall's keelboatman Mike Fink. This same character type is seen later in *A-Rafting on the Mississippi* (1928) by Charles Edward Russell (1860–1941). As he does in his masterpiece, Twain depicts the Mississippi as a crucible of initiation in his account of his early years as a steamboat pilot in *Life on the Mississippi* (1883). This theme is also employed by Iowan RICHARD PIKE BISSELL (1913–1977) in his autobiographical novel *A Stretch on the River* (1950). Like Twain and Bissell, artist George Catlin (1796–1872), historian George Bancroft (1800–1891), and novelists Charles Dickens, Anthony Trollope (1815–1882), and Herman Melville (1819–1891), among others, wrote of their experiences on the Mississippi, where Melville set one of his last works of fiction, *The Confidence Man* (1857). In that novel the central character is a slippery shape-shifter who comes aboard a steamboat docked in ST. LOUIS on April Fool's Day and challenges one of his marks to a game of cards for money. *Showboat* (1926) by EDNA FERBER (1885–1968) features a similarly mysterious rogue and riverboat gambler, Gaylord Ravenal, in her narrative of love and loss among three generations of a show-business family who make their living on the river.

The prairie, an equally multivalent Midwestern archetype of place, was often likened by travelers to a vast ocean, with its long grasses undulating like waves: a place of freedom, beauty, and opportunity, as well as of desolation and danger. An early visitor to the Illinois prairie was Englishman Morris Birkbeck (1764–1825). His *Notes on a Journey . . . to the Territory of Illinois* and *Letters from Illinois,* both published in 1818, emphasize the richness and vastness of the land. Similarly, Eliza (Woodson Burhans) Farnham (1815–1864) in *Life in Prairie Land* (1846) describes her first view of the Illinois prairie as "a sublime spectacle" (27), and (Sarah) Margaret Fuller (Ossoli) (1810–1850) records in *Summer on the Lakes, in 1843* (1844) that she responded with a "fairyland exultation" to the beauty of its jewel-like wildflowers (21). For Garland, the prairie represents the region's potential for abundant agricultural products, as seen in his memoir, *A Son of the Middle Border* (1917). Cather conveys the same notion in *My Ántonia* by employing the symbol of the silhouetted plow magnified against the setting sun. As Annette Kolodny has demonstrated in *The Land before Her: Fantasy and Experience of the American Frontiers, 1630–1860* (1984), many pioneer women in their diaries, journals, and letters conceptualized the prairie wilderness as a garden, representing home and community, in contrast to the masculine vision of a virgin land to be conquered and dominated.

The prairie was represented less benignly in many works written by female authors. For Caroline Kirkland (1801–1864) in *A New Home—Who'll Follow?* (1839), the prairie is a "Michigan mudhole," and its vast emptiness is suggestive of the frontier's lack of community institutions, emphasized in her account of her pioneering experiences near Ann Arbor, Michigan (5). The prairie also represents emptiness and loneliness, as well as a threat to sanity, for farmwives Minnie Foster Wright of *Trifles,* Mrs. Stockman of *A Window to the South* (1919) by Mary Katharine Reely (1881–1937), Lizzie Dalton of *The Prairie* (1925) by Walter J. Muilenburg (1893–1958), Beret Hansa of *Giants in the Earth,* and Lilice Black of *The Thresher* (1946) by Herbert Krause (1905–1976). Even in more recent times, some literary representations of the prairie emphasize absence or lack. For ex-

ample, Kathleen Norris (b. 1947), in her memoir, *Dakota: A Spiritual Geography* (1993), emphasizes the silence and separateness of the prairie, but she views these qualities as positive and beneficial in that the prairie, removed from urban-industrial noise and congestion, provides the means for individuals to find and center themselves. For her, then, the prairie is restorative rather than debilitating. Similarly, Mark Buechsel argues in *The Sacred Land* (2014) that Anderson, Cather, Fitzgerald, Suckow, and Smiley share a sacramental understanding of Midwestern nature that "is the necessary starting point for building a functional personal life and a functional culture" (14).

The archetype of the Midwestern Small Town survives as the embodiment of goodness, harmony, and community. This archetype has been perpetuated by every form of media, from McGuffey's readers to television commercials and situation comedies. "Spawned by an agricultural frontier where idealism, optimism, materialism, and an abiding faith in progress were strangely intermingled," as Lewis Atherton notes in *Main Street on the Middle Border* (1954), the archetypal Midwestern small town, unsurprisingly, dominates the literature of the Midwest (xvi).

Zona Gale (1874–1938) contributes to the construction of the Midwestern small town as a homey haven of neighborliness and Christian charity in her Friendship Village stories, a nostalgic view similar to that conveyed by Meredith Nicholson (1866–1947) in *The Valley of Democracy* (1918) and Howells in *The Kentons* (1902), among others. Although works of Midwestern Realism and Naturalism by Anderson, Lewis, Masters, and others have somewhat undermined this archetype, it has proved unusually resilient, even as, or perhaps especially as, American society has urbanized and industrialized. The Midwestern village that Lewis, with tongue in cheek, calls "the one sure abode of friendship, honesty, and marriageable girls" in *Main Street* lives on in the American cultural imagination, however out of sync with Midwestern reality it may be (264). The affectionate satire that Keillor directs at Lake Wobegon contributes to the endurance of this archetype, as do the fond memories of Muncie that Emily Kimbrough (1899–1989) relates in *How Dear to My Heart* (1944), the positive picture of Emporia that WILLIAM ALLEN WHITE (1868–1944) paints in his *Autobiography* (1946), and the nostalgic depiction of the small Midwestern town in *Farmington* (1904) by CLARENCE (SEWARD) DARROW (1857–1938). Musicals such as *The Music Man* (1957), set in River City, Iowa, and *Bye Bye, Birdie* (1959), set in Sweet Apple, Ohio, also perpetuate this idealized concept of the Midwestern small town.

Richard Slotkin in *Regeneration through Violence: The Mythology of the American Frontier, 1600–1860* (1973) argues that the frontier archetype and its concomitant myth of the hunter have legitimized American aggressive actions from the days of Manifest Destiny forward. In 1893 FREDERICK JACKSON TURNER (1861–1932), in his seminal essay "The Significance of the Frontier in American History," proclaimed the frontier to be the matrix of the American democratic character because the experience of settling the wilderness developed traits such as self-reliance, practicality, egalitarianism, and individualism in its pioneers. Slotkin concurs that this frontier archetype perpetuates "the concept of America as a wide-open land of unlimited opportunity for the strong, ambitious, self-reliant individual to thrust his way to the top," opening a space for those individuals to remake their lives (5). He asserts further that frontier narratives that recount the adventures of the hunter, such as those centering on Daniel Boone, and endorse the wilderness values that Turner identifies ultimately supported the nation's drive for western exploration and expansion and, later, overseas imperialism (323).

This concept of the frontier as opportunity, particularly for a new start, was developed in early American works of literature, including *Letters from an American Farmer* (1782) by J. Hector St. John de Crèvecoeur (1735–1813) and *The Prairie* (1827) by James Fenimore Cooper (1789–1851), and it functions similarly in the early literature of the Midwest. The Illinois frontier offers a second chance to the T——n family of *The Emigrants* (1793) by Gilbert Imlay (1754–1828), to Mabel Vaughan's brother Harry in *Mabel Vaughan* (1857) by Maria Susanna Cummins (1827–1866), and to Mark and Rosalie Sutherland

in *India: The Pearl of Pearl River* (1856) by Mrs. E. D. E. N. Southworth (1819–1899). The MISSOURI frontier functions in a similar way for the Hawkins family in *The Gilded Age,* as does the Kentucky frontier for Cuthbert Dangerfield in *Westward Ho!* (1832) by James Kirke Paulding (1778–1860).

Although the term "heartland" also designates a country music group, a style of rock and roll, and a movie set in Montana, it has proved to be the most dominant and enduring Midwestern archetype of all. Over time it has become a synonym for the Midwest itself. Ironically, although the Midwest has become increasingly urban, with a lengthy industrial history centered in cities such as Detroit, Chicago, St. Louis, Milwaukee, Indianapolis, Omaha, and KANSAS CITY, heartland images nevertheless dominate the region's national identity. Shortridge argues that the Middle West has been continually identified as rural despite the shift from an agrarian to an industrial economy. He sees the Midwest constructed in the popular imagination as an idyllic middle kingdom between the city and the wilderness, embodying the pastoral ideal and everything this term connotes (6). The assumption that Shoeless Joe Jackson makes in *Shoeless Joe* (1989) by W(ILLIAM) P(ATRICK) KINSELLA (b. 1935) epitomizes this attitude: "This must be heaven." "No. It's Iowa," he is told (6). The virtues that are said to develop from continuing contact with nature and work on the soil—industriousness, independence, self-reliance, honesty, frugality, egalitarianism—have come to be known as heartland values, with "heartland" connoting both the heart's centrality to the body and the positive emotions we associate with it.

Shortridge's argument is particularly compelling with respect to the region's poetry, which, as Lisel Mueller (b. 1924) observes in "Midwestern Poetry: Goodbye to All That," in *Voyages to the Inland Sea: Essays and Poems* 1 (1971), "owes its life to the heart of the heartland" (4). Unsurprisingly, the two collections of Midwestern poetry edited by LUCIEN STRYK (1924–2013) are titled *Heartland* (1967) and *Heartland II* (1975); the poems in these books offer ample support for Mueller's assertion. In the first volume, the outdoorsman in "Hunting Pheasants in a Cornfield" by ROBERT (ELWOOD) BLY (b. 1926), the old trainmen loafing in the tavern in "Old Davenport Days" by R. R. Cuscaden (1931–2005), the night watchman of "Autumn Begins in Martins Ferry, Ohio" by JAMES (ARLINGTON) WRIGHT (1927–1980), the fisherman in "Invitation to a Young River Queen" by DAVE ETTER (1928–2015), and the steelworkers in "Late Shift in the Mill" by JOHN (IGNATIUS) KNOEPFLE (b. 1923) evoke the everyday life of the heartland, inhabiting poems that trace their roots to CHICAGO POEMS (1916) and Cornhuskers (1918) by CARL (AUGUST) SANDBURG (1878–1967), as well as to Masters's Spoon River Anthology.

However, more recent literary constructions of the heartland have not been as adulatory. In the Heart of the Heart of the Country (1968) by WILLIAM H(OWARD) GASS (b. 1924) portrays a less benign Indiana small town than those described by Tarkington, Nicholson, and Kimbrough. Gass stresses instead its sterility and emptiness. Likewise, A Thousand Acres (1991) by JANE (GRAVES) SMILEY (b. 1949) focuses on an Iowa farm family whose head, Larry Cook, behaves irresponsibly and destructively toward both his family and his land. A Map of the World (1994) by JANE HAMILTON (b. 1957) portrays the death of the agrarian dream in the heartland in the failure of dairy farmers Alice and Howard Goodwin. Driftless (2008) by David Rhodes (b. 1946) details the challenges of contemporary Wisconsin farm life. Playwright WILLIAM (MOTTER) INGE (1913–1973) reveals the fear, misery, brutality, and despair that lurk under a façade of heartland normalcy in plays such as Come Back, Little Sheba (1950) and Picnic (1953). Intertextuality plays a big role in the persistence of this archetype as earlier small-town heartland texts are rewritten by later authors: Etter's Alliance, Illinois (1983) reflects and comments on Spoon River Anthology, as Grass Fires (1987) by DAN GERBER (b. 1940) does on Winesburg, Ohio.

"Movement made the Midwest, and the Midwest made movement," asserts Hutton (39), and if there is one enduring Midwestern story, it is the story of the journey: to the Midwest, within the Midwest, from the Midwest, and sometimes back again, a motif of departure and return that often centers on a quest. This archetypal Midwestern quest may not take the character far in actual miles but can nevertheless be life-changing, as seen in the Younger family's quest for a better home on Chicago's South Side in A RAISIN IN THE SUN (1959) by LORRAINE (VIVIAN) HANSBERRY (1930–1965) and Esperanza's search for a home in that city in THE HOUSE ON MANGO STREET (1984) by SANDRA CISNEROS (b. 1954). Sometimes the quest is for the essence of the Midwest itself, as is the case with John Wickliff Shawnessy and his search for the mystical raintree in RAINTREE COUNTY (1948) by ROSS (FRANKLIN) LOCKRIDGE JR. (1914–1948).

More often, this quest centers on personal goals. While Howard McLane, Nick Carraway, and Lewis's Carol Kennicott depart in search of opportunities on the East Coast, Rose Dutcher of Garland's Rose of Dutcher's Coolly (1895), Carrie Meeber of Dreiser's SISTER CARRIE (1900), and Anderson's George Willard of Winesburg, Ohio journey from their Midwestern hometowns to Chicago to construct new selves. Cather's Thea Kronberg of The Song of the Lark (1916), Kate Barrington of The Precipice (1914) by ELIA W(ILKINSON) PEATTIE (1862–1935), and Dell's semi-autobiographical Felix Fay from his novel The Briary-Bush (1921) travel to that city in search of fulfilling careers. Escape from the strictures of an oppressive society motivates Nick Adams in Hemingway's "Big Two-Hearted River" (1925) to travel to Michigan's Upper Peninsula and Huck Finn to abscond from St. Petersburg on his Mississippi River raft.

Some Midwesterners explore their home region by car, as Dreiser recounts in A Hoosier Holiday; others venture farther afield, as Lewis relates in Free Air (1919), his fictionalized account of his 1916 auto trip from Duluth to Seattle, and WILLIAM LEAST HEAT-MOON (b. William Lewis Trogdon, 1939) recounts in Blue Highways (1982), the story of his journey across the United States. But occasionally the Midwesterner departs for a more exotic locale, only to return to echo Dorothy Gale in the 1939 MGM film The Wizard of Oz: "There's no place like home."

Beyond reflecting aspects of Midwestern past or present reality, several archetypes discussed here have transcended Midwestern literature and culture to find a place in the national imagination. Among these are the frontier, the pioneer, the heartland, and Main Street, symbolizing the Midwestern small town derived from Lewis's novel and most recently employed to oppose Wall Street, a shorthand for the urban domain of big business and banking. These archetypes, largely positive in connotation, are now dead metaphors, particularly those relating to the frontier and the pioneer, which now usually describe places and individuals in the forefront of progress.

Beyond the elements of reality that they reflect, Midwestern archetypes have endured in part because the Midwest itself has come to function as a symbol for the nation as a whole. Andrew Cayton and Peter Onuf assert in *The Midwest and the Nation* (1990) that by the nineteenth century the region's inhabitants "believed that the Midwest embodied American culture; it *was* the United States" (84–85). R. Douglas Hurt writes in "Midwestern Distinctiveness," in *The American Midwest: Essays on Regional History* (2001), that by World War I the Midwest was considered "the most typical or American part of America" and that Midwesterners had come to be considered "the quintessential Americans" (163, 178). Shortridge concurs that "the Middle West came to symbolize the nation and to be seen as the most American part of America" (33).

One reason that the Midwest and, by extension, its archetypes have come to be equated with the nation as a whole is that Americans need to see them that way. David Radavich, in "Dramatizing the Midwest," *MidAmerica* 34 (2007), suggests that Americans have a psychological need for a national moral center or norm that the heartland archetype supplies: "The rootedness of the Midwest feeds on American nostalgia for a simpler life located somewhere in the mythic past . . . so deep is the longing in the American psyche for this imaginary heartland" (77). Although the region has become increasingly industrialized and urbanized, its pastoral image endures, and with it the belief in an innocent Midwest that functions as the foundation of our national myth: a democratic region where free, equal, and independent citizens can fulfill the promise of the Jeffersonian dream and live the good life as successful farmers, businessmen, workers, and professionals.

Other analyses move beyond the psychological and the personal. In *The Midwestern Pastoral*: *Place and Landscape in Literature of the American Heartland* (2006), William Barillas distinguishes between romantic and utilitarian pastoralism. He argues that the latter undergirds an individualistic ethos that promotes capitalism and views the Midwest as the locus of boundless natural resources that function as commodities to be put in the service of development, growth, and progress. This utilitarian pastoralism leads to the prevalence of the tinkerer archetype, a solitary genius who employs mechanical and technological acumen to harness these resources, make a fortune, and revolutionize society (33–35). Viewed from materialist and postcolonial perspectives, these images of the Midwest persist because they support the goals of the centers of national power. Although the Midwest has never been the colony of a foreign country, it has functioned as a cultural colony dominated by East and West Coast power structures, epitomized in the dismissive term "flyover country" that people from both coasts use to designate the region. The regularly used Main Street–Wall Street dichotomy of the early twenty-first-century investment-banking crisis underscores this political and cultural divide between the Midwest and the New York–Washington, D.C., axis. The titans of business, finance, and industry who inhabit our national centers of power, culture, wealth, and influence perpetuate images of the Midwest that serve their interests. These images include those of the Midwestern prairie as an abundant garden whose Edenic promise can be fulfilled by anyone willing to work hard enough to secure a competence; the frontier as the crucible of democracy where anyone can construct a new, more successful self; the pioneer as the risk-taking achiever; and the tycoon and the tinkerer as individuals who succeed because of their unique genius for business or technology.

The heartland archetype, in particular, is prevalent because it meets a double-sided national need. A Midwestern heartland characterized by agrarian values—goodness, honesty, integrity, and fortitude—exists in the American cultural psyche so that Americans can feel good about themselves. A nation increasingly dominated by greed, selfishness, and materialism needs the moral compass of the Midwest, just as Joel and Ethan Coen need Marge Gunderson, the righteous Minnesota sheriff in *Fargo* (1996), to balance the violence, stupidity, and greed of the other main characters. Edward Watts notes in *An American Colony: Regionalism and the Roots of Midwestern Culture* (2002) that the Midwestern heartland archetype serves a dual purpose. "So long as the Midwest preserved the innocence of agrarianism, industrial materialism was balanced in the national self-definition; so long as the Midwesterner was a 'hick,' the Easterner, by contrast, was more like the European model of polished accomplishment" (165). Thus the heartland is a powerful archetype in part because it gives Americans a place on which to project their best and displace their worst selves. Americans need the heartland to be America's great, good place so they can identify with it and like themselves. They also need it to be the epitome of dull mediocrity and conformity so they can distinguish themselves from the Babbitts and Zurys of the heartland and feel interesting, brilliant, and sophisticated. Diane Johnson (b. 1934), an Illinois native who now lives in Paris and San Francisco, rarely sets her fiction in the Midwest, although she sometimes writes of Midwesterners in cultural conflict when they are visiting or living in other locales. However, she, too, recognizes the significance of the archetypal Midwest to the nation, as she explains in "The Heart of the Heart of the Country," an article she published in the November 19, 1981, issue of the *New York Review of Books*. There, she asserts, "America has a calm center . . . defending its eccentricities against the frontier mentality of the West, the sissy affectations of the East, a rich storehouse of cultural certitudes trying to ignore the shifting values and faddish self-doubts of coastal America" (12).

SELECTED WORKS: Willa Cather's novels, particularly *O Pioneers!* (1913) and *My Ántonia* (1918), as well as her short story "Neighbour Rosicky" (1930), offer excellent examples of the yeoman farmer archetype. Cather's short story "The Sculptor's Funeral" (1905) and her Pulitzer Prize–winning novel *One of Ours* (1922) provide good illustrations of Midwestern philistinism. Theodore Dreiser wrote three novels about fictional Chicago tycoon Frank Cowperwood, loosely based on the life of streetcar magnate Charles T. Yerkes: *The Financier* (1912), *The Titan* (1914), and *The Stoic* (1947). Henry Blake Fuller's *The Cliff-Dwellers* (1893) and *With the Procession* (1895) portray a spectrum of Chicagoans engaged in business, industry, and commerce. Sinclair Lewis's *Babbitt* (1922) is the quintessential businessman-booster novel, just as Anderson's *Poor White* (1920) is the quintessential Midwestern tinkerer novel. Of the many Midwestern misfits or "others" who populate the region's literature, Anderson's grotesques in *Winesburg, Ohio* (1919) are perhaps the best examples. A representative Midwestern immigrant novel is Ole Rølvaag's *Giants in the Earth* (1927). Backtrailers can be seen in two of Hamlin Garland's stories in *Main-Travelled Roads* (1891)—"Up the Coulé " and "God's Ravens"—as well as in F. Scott Fitzgerald's *The Great Gatsby* (1925). The best-known Midwestern expatriate novel is Ernest Hemingway's *The Sun Also Rises* (1926); his memoir, *A Moveable Feast* (1964), is an excellent companion piece. The quintessential Midwestern river novel, of course, is Mark Twain's *Adventures of Huckleberry Finn* (1884, 1885), best read along with his memoir, *Life on the Mississippi* (1883). Insightful accounts of life on the Midwestern prairie can be found in Caroline Kirkland's *A New Home—Who'll Follow?* (1839) and in Hamlin Garland's *A Son of the Middle Border* (1917). The small-town Midwest can be accessed through many works of fiction, poetry, drama, and nonfiction. Representative works from each genre are Lewis's *Main Street* (1920), Edgar Lee Masters's *Spoon River Anthology* (1915*)*, William Inge's *Picnic* (1953), and William Allen White's *Autobiography* (1946), respectively. New starts on the Midwestern frontier can be seen in Twain's *The Gilded Age,* as well as in Maria Susanna Cummins's *Mabel Vaughan* (1857) and Mrs. E. D. E. N. Southworth's *India: The Pearl of Pearl River* (1856). The poems in Lucien Stryk's two collections, *Heartland,* and *Heartland II,* as well as those in Carl Sandburg's *Cornhuskers* (1918), offer excellent examples of the heartland archetype. More recent constructions of the heartland can be seen in William H. Gass's *In the Heart of the Heart of the Country* (1968), Jane Smiley's *A Thousand Acres* (1991), Jane Hamilton's *A Map of the World* (1994), and David Rhodes's *Driftless* (2008). The quest archetype is enacted in many Midwestern works, most centrally in Twain's *Adventures of Huckleberry Finn* and Ross Lockridge's *Raintree County* (1948).

FURTHER READING: A number of nonliterary studies offer perspectives that illuminate Midwestern experience and identity. Over a half century ago, Englishman Graham Hutton came to live in the region and recorded his impressions in *Midwest at Noon* (1946). Lewis Atherton contributes a social history of the Midwestern small town in *Main Street on the Middle Border* (1954). The prairie archetype is examined from a number of disciplinary perspectives in the collection *Recovering the Prairie* (1999), edited by Robert F. Sayre.

Historians have been especially prolific writers on Midwestern identity, beginning with Frederick Jackson Turner, who argued in his landmark 1893 essay "The Significance of the Frontier in American History" that the work of developing a civilization out of the Midwestern wilderness gave Americans their most salient character traits. Henry Nash Smith in *Virgin Land: The American West as Symbol and Myth* (1950) explains how the Midwest, once the Wild West, came to be seen as the Garden of the World and to symbolize the promise of the Jeffersonian dream. Book 3 of that work, which includes a discussion of Kirkland, Garland, and other Midwestern writers, is particularly pertinent. Richard Slotkin's *Regeneration through Violence: The Mythology of the American Frontier, 1600–1860* (1973) centers on the function of the hunter myth as an archetype that has structured our view of the settling of the frontier and influenced American attitudes toward expansion and intervention. Andrew Cayton and Peter Onuf began the postcolonial discussion of the region with *The Midwest and the Nation* (1990). Cayton, with co-editor Susan E. Gray, followed up with the collection *The American Midwest: Essays on Regional History* (2001), while Jon Gjerde examines the conflict between nativist and immigrant cultures of the region in *The Minds of the West: Ethnocultural Evolution in the Rural Middle West, 1830–1917* (1997). Over twenty-five years ago cultural geographer James Shortridge published his seminal study *The Middle West: Its Meaning in American Culture* (1989), examining how the re-gion came to be identified with the pastoral ideal and how its image became increasingly tarnished after 1920. It is an excellent starting point for beginning scholars of Midwestern literature and culture.

Scholars of Midwestern literature have dealt with regional archetypes in their books on the region's literature. Ronald Weber discusses several Midwestern archetypes briefly in the early pages of *The Midwestern Ascendancy in American Writing* (1992). William Barillas's *The Midwestern Pastoral: Place and Landscape in Literature of the American Heartland* (2006) discusses the yeoman farmer, booster, and tinkerer archetypes in his first chapter and goes on to examine pastoralism in the work of Cather, Wright and others. Mark Buechsel also focuses on pastoralism in *The Sacred Land: Sherwood Anderson, Midwestern Modernism, and the Sacramental Vision of Nature* (2014). Timothy Spears focuses on Midwestern movement from the small town to the big city in *Chicago Dreaming: Midwesterners in the City, 1871–1919* (2005), zeroing in on Dell, Sandburg, Dreiser, Anderson, Cather, Peattie, and others. Edward Watts, in *An American Colony: Regionalism and the Roots of Midwestern Culture* (2002), continues the postcolonial discussion, arguing that the region's marginality is the result of "an active program of metropolitan silencing and exclusion" (156).

Essays in journals and collections offer a rich trove of analyses of Midwestern identity. Early efforts include Booth Tarkington's "The Middle West," *Harper's Monthly Magazine* 106 (December 1902): 75–83; Mary Austin's "Regionalism in American Fiction," *English Journal* 21.2 (February 1932): 97–107; Ruth Suckow's "Middle Western Literature," *English Journal* 21.3 (March 1932): 175–82; and Lisel Mueller's "Midwestern Poetry: Goodbye to All That," in *Voyages to the Inland Sea* 1 (1971): 1–10. David D. Anderson's "The Dimensions of the Midwest," *MidAmerica* 1 (1974): 7–15, as well as his "Notes toward a Definition of the Mind of the Midwest," *MidAmerica* 3 (1976): 7–16, are seminal essays that laid the groundwork for much Midwestern literary scholarship from the mid-1970s to the present.

The effort to define Midwestern identity and a Midwestern literary tradition derived from it has occupied scholars from the 1970s to the present. David Radavich's "Dramatizing the Midwest," *MidAmerica* 34 (2007): 59–78, identifies several characteristics of regional identity, as do Jeffrey Gundy's "Humility and Literature: Is There a Plains Style?," *MidAmerica* 15 (1988): 19–26, and Margaret Stuhr's "The Safe Middle West: Escape to and Escape from Home," *MidAmerica* 14 (1987): 18–27. Scott Russell Sanders's "Imagining the Midwest," in *Writing from the Center* (1995), 22–51, surveys a number of canonical Midwestern works, exploring the paradoxes they enact and arguing for a conservationist and community-focused approach to living in the region. Kent C. Ryden's "Writing the Midwest: History, Literature, and Regional Identity," *Geographical Review* 89.4 (1999): 511–32, is a particularly thorough discussion of the evolution of Midwestern identity. Three of the essays in *The American Midwest: Essays in Regional History*, edited by Andrew R. L. Cayton and Susan E. Gray, examine Midwestern identity within a national context: Andrew R. L. Cayton's "The Anti-region: Place and Identity in the History of the American Midwest," R. Douglas Hurt's "Midwestern Distinctiveness," and Jon Gjerde's "Middleness and the Middle West." David Pichaske's "Where Now 'Midwestern Literature'?," *Midwest Quarterly* 48.1 (2006): 100–119, identifies some characteristics of Midwestern literature and argues for a distinct Midwestern literary tradition.

Essays are also good sources for studies of Midwestern archetypes, images, and symbols. Kenny J. Williams discusses the Chicago businessman-tycoon in "'The Past Is Prologue': Chicago's Early Writing," *MidAmerica* 4 (1977): 56–73, and Elizabeth Raymond focuses on the prairie archetype in "Learning the Land: The Development of a Sense of Place in the Prairie Midwest," *MidAmerica* 14 (1987): 28–40. Bruce Baker's "Nebraska's Cultural Desert: Willa Cather's Early Short Stories," *MidAmerica* 14 (1987): 12–17, David D. Anderson's "The Midwestern Town in Midwestern Fiction," *MidAmerica* 6 (1979): 27–43, and Guy Szuberla's "The Midwesterner as Out-of-Towner," *MidAmerica* 34 (2007): 44–58, are analyses that focus on Midwestern archetypes.

Several scholars have included chapters on Midwestern symbols and archetypes within broader studies of American literature. The third chapter of Frederick J. Hoffman's *The Twenties: American Writing in the Postwar Decade* (1955) focuses on the Midwest as metaphor (327–35). Leslie Fiedler discusses the Mississippi River as symbol in the last chapter of *Love and Death in the American Novel* (1960), and chapter 4 of Larzer Ziff's *The American 1890s: Life and Times of a Lost Generation* (1966) offers an extensive discussion of the Midwestern imagination (73–92). Annette Kolodny examines the distaff side of the westering experience with an emphasis on the writings of Kirkland, Farnham, Fuller, Southworth, and Cummins in *The Land before Her: Fantasy and Experience of the American Frontiers, 1630–1860* (1984).

MARCIA NOE
THE UNIVERSITY OF TENNESSEE AT CHATTANOOGA

ARCHITECTURE

OVERVIEW: Midwestern settlement transformed the region's landscape into living places, from the early log houses in OHIO and MICHIGAN to the sod houses of the Great Plains, the Greek revival structures of the 1893 Columbian Exposition, and the advent of the skyscraper in CHICAGO. The Midwest also produced two major American architectural movements—the Chicago school and the Prairie school. Exemplars of these two schools provide context for consideration of architecture as depicted in Midwestern literature.

Architecture houses people; it also serves as a sign and symbol of meaningful human activity. Architectural developments project cultural and technological concerns, as well as social values and aspirations. They contribute to our understanding of the Midwest as a distinctive region and to perceptions of the nature and significance of the region and its people. The following essay proceeds in roughly chronological sequence, focusing on historical developments in Midwestern architecture as they relate to the image of the Midwest as depicted in Midwestern literature.

HISTORY AND SIGNIFICANCE: The importance of place in Midwestern literature can hardly be overestimated. The maps found in Midwestern works as diverse as *WINESBURG, OHIO* (1919) by SHERWOOD ANDERSON (1876–1941), *RAINTREE COUNTY* (1948) by

ROSS (FRANKLIN) LOCKRIDGE JR. (1914–1948), *Ohio Town* (1962) by HELEN HOOVEN SANT-MYER (1895–1986), *The Situation in Flushing* (1965) by EDMUND G(EORGE) LOVE (1912–1990), and *Knockemstiff* (2008) by Donald Ray Pollock (b. 1954) underscore the importance of place in Midwestern literature. See LITERARY MAPS. These maps demand attention, for sketched in them are the architectural habitations through which themes are illustrated and settings humanized. Closely observed and richly detailed settings for Midwestern life extend throughout Midwestern literature, from *The Adventures of Tom Sawyer* (1876) and *ADVENTURES OF HUCK-LEBERRY FINN* (London 1884; New York 1885) by SAMUEL LANGHORNE CLEMENS (1835–1910), writing as Mark Twain, to the MINNESOTA musings of *Lake Wobegon Days* (1985) by GARY EDWARD KEILLOR (b. 1942), writing as Garrison Keillor.

The history of architecture in the Midwest goes back long before the arrival of the Europeans. Ancient American Indian mounds in the Ohio and Mississippi River valleys, for example, evince complex civilizations with sophisticated architecture, followed by more nomadic Indian architecture in the woodlands and plains. Timbered earth lodges and thatched houses were common in the Midwest. Elaborate structures such as Midewiwin and Drum Dance lodges served ceremonial purposes, while portable tepees served domestic purposes. Such structures are described in *LIFE OF MA-KA-TAI-ME-SHE-KIA-KIAK, OR BLACK HAWK* (1833) by BLACK HAWK (1767–1838), the works of CHARLES ALEXANDER EASTMAN (OHIYESA) (1858–1939), and *My People the Sioux* (1928) by LUTHER STANDING BEAR (1868–1939). They contribute to perceptions of Native Americans in the Midwest.

An interesting and thorough overview of Midwestern development is found in the Ohio trilogy by CONRAD (MICHAEL) RICHTER (1890–1968), consisting of the novels *The Trees* (1940), *The Fields* (1946), and *The Town* (1950). These three books offer an idealized history, richly imagining stages of Midwestern civilization before the Civil War, including the development of architectural structures in the appropriately named town of Americus.

Midwestern pioneer structures included log cabins, dugouts, and sod houses, the last most frequently on the treeless plains. The log cabin, the enduring staple of American frontier myth, was a ready symbol for generations and has become closely tied to the Midwest's quintessential myth, that of ABRAHAM LINCOLN (1809–1865) and his frontier origins, suggesting Midwestern egalitarianism, virtue, and the ability of common people to rise to high place through ability and hard work. Many immigrants reported log cabins glimpsed through the trees in passages down the Ohio River. Both CAROLINE KIRKLAND (1801–1864) in *A NEW HOME-WHO'LL FOLLOW?* (1839) and ELIZA FARNHAM (1815–1864) in *Life in Prairie Land* (1846) provide detailed glimpses of Midwestern frontier life and dismaying log-cabin conditions, as well as of developing town architecture that accommodated evolving cultural institutions. WILLIAM DEAN HOWELLS (1837–1920) in *My Year in a Log Cabin* (1893) detailed living in a cabin on the Little Miami River in Ohio in 1850. The same year Howells published his account, architect Daniel Burnham (1846–1912) had a log cabin built on the Wooded Island at the site of the Columbian Exposition in Chicago, close to his work as grand designer of the White City.

By the mid-nineteenth century Midwestern settlement had advanced beyond the Mississippi River and onto the Great Plains, a movement popularized in the *Little House* books of LAURA INGALLS WILDER (1867–1957), especially *Little House on the Prairie* (1935), which details the family's settlement in KANSAS. Wilder's work appealed especially to young adults. The televised series based on *Little House on the Prairie,* which ran for nearly a decade in the 1970s and 1980s, spoke to continued American nostalgia for "the good old days." The Midwest of (HANNIBAL) HAMLIN GARLAND (1860–1940), in such works as *MAIN-TRAVELLED ROADS* (1891) and *Son of the Middle Border* (1917), is considerably grimmer. Both Wilder and Garland were from families seeking better conditions while moving from WISCONSIN through various Midwestern landscapes—Minnesota, IOWA, MISSOURI, and SOUTH DAKOTA. In each of these places, living structures needed to be built, many of which are described in detail. Garland's *Main-Travelled Roads,* an early product of his Midwestern mobility, asserts the cultural deprivation and straitened circumstances in which Midwestern farmers and their families moving west were forced to live. Their homes, lacking beauty except for the surrounding natural landscape, were small, desolate, and often under threat of foreclosure.

Before the Homestead Act of 1862, settlement in the Midwest's western tier encouraged aggressive speculation. In a realistic picture of the chaos of speculation in Nebraska Territory, the diary of Erastus F. Beadle (1821–1894), *To Nebraska in '57* (1923; reprinted as *Ham, Eggs, and Corn Cake*, 2001), details proposed plans for a town that never came into existence. Although Beadle returned east, new settlers arrived, many of whom were forced to build dugouts hollowed from the earth and covered with sod. Descriptions of these primitive structures appear regularly in Midwestern immigrant and homestead literature, including GIANTS IN THE EARTH (1927) by OLE EDVART RØLVAAG (1876–1931) and *Old Jules* (1935) by MARI(E SUSETTE) SANDOZ (1896–1966). Solomon Butcher (1856–1927) in his *Pioneer History of Custer County, Nebraska* (1901) recorded typical primitive Midwestern structures in now-classic photographs and biographical sketches of their inhabitants. WILLA CATHER (1873–1947) observes in *O PIONEERS!* (1913) that "the houses on the Divide were small . . . tucked away in low places; you did not see them until you came directly upon them. Most of them were built of the sod itself, and were only the unescapable ground in another form" (*Willa Cather: Early Novels and Stories*, Library of America 1987 edition 147). In contrast is the Divide as it develops over time: the land becomes "a vast checkerboard, marked off in squares of wheat and corn," where Alexandra sees "gayly painted farmhouses," and "the gilded weathervanes on the big red barns wink at each other across the green and brown and yellow fields" (174).

In Chicago a truly Midwestern architectural style emerged—a response to the Great Chicago Fire of 1871 and rampant redevelopment afterward, especially in the 1880s and 1890s, as Chicago came into its own as a modern city. Architectural possibilities were virtually unlimited as innovative architects sought to impose order on the chaotic rebuilding of Chicago's core. The Chicago school emerged; its central group consisted of three major firms: Adler and Sullivan, Burnham and Root, and Holabird and Roche. These firms designed and engineered major innovations in architecture and urban planning to accommodate the city's soils and cultural needs. Rapid growth increased the city's size and made the skyscraper—and the elevator—inevitable. LOUIS (HENRI) SULLIVAN (1856–1924) was the poet-architect of the Chicago skyscraper. He insists, in "The Tall Office Building Artistically Considered," *Lippincott's Magazine* (March 1896), that the skyscraper must be "every inch a proud and soaring thing, rising in sheer exultation" (reprinted in *Kindergarten Chats and Other Writings*, 1979, 206). CHICAGO POEMS (1916) by CARL (AUGUST) SANDBURG (1878–1967) expresses the awed admiration of Chicago's laboring classes who worked in the city and built these soaring structures.

The Home Insurance Building (1884–1885), built in Chicago by William Le Baron Jenney (1832–1907), is usually considered the world's first metal-frame skyscraper. The steel-frame construction meant that architects no longer had to rely on heavy masonry to carry the weight of the building on exterior load-bearing walls; instead, steel columns and beams provided a frame on which the building's outer walls were "hung," reducing weight and introducing—with the enhancement of broad "Chicago windows"—more light into the interior.

Innovative buildings sprang from Chicago soil. William Holabird (1854–1923) and Martin Roche (1855–1927) built the Tacoma Building (1886–1889) and the Marquette Building (1894). Daniel Burnham and John Wellborn Root (1850–1891) designed the Reliance Building (1890–1894) and the Monadnock Building (1891–1893). For several years Burnham and Root's twenty-one-story Masonic Temple was the tallest building in the world, so high that EDGAR LEE MASTERS (1868–1950) reports in *Across Spoon River: An Autobiography* (1936) that he was told by "an old Polonius" that from its top he would be able to see Council Bluffs, the Iowa city four hundred miles distant (145). Root married the sister of poet HARRIET MONROE (1860–1936);

Monroe's tributes to Root are found in her autobiography, *A Poet's Life* (1938), and in her *John Wellborn Root: A Study of His Life and Work* (1896).

The firm of Dankmar Adler (1844–1900) and Louis Sullivan was responsible for the Auditorium Building (1887–1889), now part of Roosevelt University, a centerpiece of Chicago's late nineteenth-century cultural life. The impressive Auditorium Building incorporated a hotel, an office tower, and a world-class auditorium seating 4,200 patrons, employing acoustics Adler had learned in Germany. At the top of the tower, Adler and Sullivan had their offices, as did their employee FRANK LLOYD WRIGHT (1867–1959). Many literary characters—including Rose in *Rose of Dutcher's Coolly* (1895) by Hamlin Garland, Laura Dearborn in *The Pit* (1903) by (BENJAMIN) FRANK(LIN) NORRIS (1870–1902), and Thea Kronenberg in *Song of the Lark* (1915) by Willa Cather—attend performances in the Auditorium Theatre. Chicago's "the Little Room" group of artists and writers first gathered there after Friday matinee concerts, later in the Fine Arts Building (1885) next door.

Chicago cherished showing itself off through the Columbian Exposition in 1893, the architecture of which came to be called the White City. The man in charge, Daniel Burnham, was responsible for persuading America's chief architects to build monumental, if short-lived, architecture along classical lines, even if this decision meant ignoring the Chicago school's engineering and architectural advances. The classical Greek revival buildings, colonnades, and lagoons, which extremely displeased Louis Sullivan in his autobiography, bespoke reverence for the values and cultural institutions of the past rather than for the technologies that were moving Chicago to the forefront of American life. In 1893 Chicago, the "Hog Butcher for the World," as Carl Sandburg would later term it in his poem "Chicago," was recognized as a gritty, no-holds-barred industrial town more famous for its stockyards than for its cultural development. Thus, in choosing classical architecture for the fair, Burnham and the city leaders appeared to be attempting to put a "respectable" face on the city, emulating the eastern cultural establishment and European precedents. Even permission for nations to construct buildings in the White City reflected cultural and racial values; only U.S. states and prestigious European nations could house their exhibits there.

Carson Pirie Scott and Company Building, Chicago, 1899. Louis Sullivan, architect. Image courtesy of William Barillas, 2014.

Less developed and non-Caucasian nations, as well as less uplifting exhibits, like Little Egypt and Buffalo Bill's Wild West Show, were relegated to the less prestigious Midway Plaisance. Chicago's citizens were treated in the *Chicago Morning News* to sketches by John T. McCutcheon (1870–1949) of the exposition as it was being built, as well as to the column "Of the Streets and of the Town" by GEORGE ADE (1866–1944), in which Ade humorously commented on various Chicago blights.

The exposition generated several popular novels, most of which held the fair in reverent awe. These include *Samantha at the World's Fair* (1893) by Marietta Holley (1836–1926), in which characters see a "New Jerusalem" and a "City of Magic"; *Two Little Pilgrims' Progress* (1895) by Frances Hodgson Burnett (1849–1924), picturing a utopia for children; *The Adventures of Uncle Jeremiah and Family at the Great Fair* (1893) by Charles McClellan Stevens (1861–1942); and *Sweet Clover* (1896) by Clara Louise Burnham (1854–1927), in which the heroine finds her future husband; the novel is a romantic survey of the White City, and its Peristyle is understood as a symbol of divine love. *The Memoirs of an American Citizen* (1905) and *The Web of Life* (1900) by ROBERT HERRICK (1868–1938) both use the accidental burning of the White City in 1894 as a sign of confusion of identity. The flurry of architectural activity in downtown Chicago also generated works by Midwestern novelists, especially Robert Herrick and HENRY BLAKE FULLER (1857–1929). Herrick's novel *The Common Lot* (1904) concerns ethical dilemmas confronted by his architect protagonist Francis Jackson Hart, whose decision to trim building costs ends disastrously in a fire that kills at least ten people. The class implications of Fuller's *The Cliff-Dwellers* (1893) are worked out using the daytime inhabitants of an eighteen-story skyscraper Fuller calls the Clifton, probably based on Burnham and Root's Monadnock Building.

It is important to remember, however, that despite the splendor of these fabulous buildings, most Chicago inhabitants were mere onlookers to this phenomenon and were often forced to seek a living and a meaningful existence within dirty and squalid environments. These mean environ-

ments are spelled out in great detail in several works. In *SISTER CARRIE* (1900) by (HERMAN) THEODORE DREISER (1871–1945), Carrie Meeber makes her way despite ruthless circumstances and opportunistic men. In *THE JUNGLE* (1906) by UPTON (BEALL) SINCLAIR (JR.) (1878–1968), the narrator describes dismal lives in the environs of the Chicago stockyards—a sure breeding ground for socialism. Later, the *STUDS LONIGAN* trilogy (1935) by JAMES T(HOMAS) FARRELL (1904–1979) places Studs in a hostile Chicago environment in which he succumbs to defeat. Later in the century SANDRA CISNEROS (b. 1954), in the novel *THE HOUSE ON MANGO STREET* (1984), defies the effects of poverty and suggests the density of Latino/Latina life in the teeming streets and houses of Chicago's Pilsen neighborhood while intimately exploring the thoughts and feelings of her coming-of-age Latina protagonist, Esperanza. See LATINO/LATINA LITERATURE.

Chicago and its architecture became a subject for poets, sociologists, and reformers. The early Chicago settlement house HULL-HOUSE, created by JANE ADDAMS (1860–1935) and dedicated to amelioration and education for the city's poor and recent immigrants, is recorded in her *Twenty Years at Hull-House* (1910). For Carl Sandburg, Chicago is ragged and robust, and the building in "Skyscraper" that "looms in the smoke" "has a soul" because of the people who built it and give it life in its workday hours (*Chicago Poems* 67).

Decades later, African Americans living in racially segregated Chicago South Side housing found the city dense and dehumanizing, as exemplified in the poetry of GWENDOLYN BROOKS (1917–2000), beginning with *A STREET IN BRONZEVILLE* (1945). In tallying the number of children who have successively taken baths in "Kitchenette Building" and the ironic account of ostensibly charitable but actually self-aggrandizing white women who visit ghetto tenements in "The Lovers of the Poor," Brooks pinpoints the claustrophobic qualities inherent in leftover architecture. The contrast between downtown Chicago architecture and the housing for poor minorities is striking and grim, especially in Brooks's long poem about the search for a lost child, *In the Mecca* (1968), which is set in the once-opulent Mecca Building. This area of the city was also examined in *NATIVE SON* (1940), in which RICH-ARD WRIGHT (1908–1960), in telling the story of Bigger Thomas, contrasts the tenements with the houses of the rich.

Chicago was also home to another architectural development employing steel and glass. It is most closely associated with Ludwig Mies van der Rohe (1886–1969), who headed the architecture program at the Armour Institute of Technology, now the Illinois Institute of Technology, and designed buildings in the international or modernist style, anticipating the later work of Philip Johnson. Perhaps his most notable Chicago building is Crown Hall (1950–1956), a rectangular, glass-clad building suspended from four steel girders and supported by eight exterior columns. Another fine example of Mies's modernism is the Federal Center (1959–1974), composed of two office towers and the one-story Loop Post Office.

Although Chicago's skyscrapers are justly proclaimed, the architectural style most associated with the Midwest is that of the Prairie school, closely associated with Louis Sullivan and Frank Lloyd Wright, whose interest in organic residential architecture was its main impetus. Elements of Prairie-school style include horizontality, the buildings hugging the landscape as if in organic growth from it; flat or low-hipped roofs; broad overhangs; banding of art-glass windows in rows; and open interiors. Wright's Robie House (1908–1910) on the University of Chicago campus is an excellent example, emphasizing its spaciousness by a row of twelve French doors opening to a balcony, thus enhancing flow between inside and outside. Even today, in addition to the "pure" examples of Prairie-school architecture, signs of Prairie-school influence exist in houses and other structures throughout the Midwest. Oak Park, ILLINOIS, and Mason City, Iowa, are just two cities rich in Prairie-school buildings.

Literary depictions of architecture in Midwestern literature are many and varied. Because human experience takes place in specific locales—as a disaffected realtor says in "Icicles," from *In the Heart of the Heart of the Country* (1968) by WILLIAM H(OWARD) GASS (b. 1924), "Nothing happens—anywhere—that doesn't happen on a piece of property" (1981 Godine edition, 125–26)—architecture plays organic roles, often quite specific ones, in Midwestern literature. These works range from those that more or less incidentally employ architects and architecture to those that use architecture in substantive thematic ways.

Incidental use of architecture appears in *So Big* (1924) by EDNA FERBER (1885–1968), in which Selina DeJong's son Dirk becomes a Chicago architect. His downfall occurs when he leaves the profession for a more lucrative career as a bond salesman. Incidental architecture is also found in *Prairie Avenue* (1949) by Arthur Meeker (1902–1971). The novel explores the Prairie Avenue setting for many of Chicago's wealthy families—among them Armour, Field, Kimball, and Pullman—including the mansions that asserted their owners' social dominance. Another work employing an actual architectural site is *Anatomy of a Murder* (1958) by JOHN DONALD-SON VOELKER (1903–1991), writing as Robert Traver, set partially in the courthouse in Marquette, Michigan; the movie version also uses this setting. And in *Image of Josephine* (1945) by (NEWTON) BOOTH TARKINGTON (1869–1946), much of the action centers on a museum built to house and preserve art.

Substantive use of architecture in Midwestern literature is more compelling. Sherwood Anderson is extremely conscious of the buildings and environments in which his characters live in *Winesburg, Ohio* and other fictional works, as well as in his *Home Town* (1968), a paean to the SMALL TOWN accompanied by Depression-era Farm Security Administration photographs. Anderson is superb in presenting the small town and its streets and structures in *Winesburg*—the restaurants, grocery and hardware stores, the New Willard House, the office of the *Winesburg Eagle* where George Willard works, and the ubiquitous small-town railroad station. These were prefigured already in Anderson's first novel, *Windy McPherson's Son* (1916), set mostly in the small town of Caxton, Ohio. WRIGHT MORRIS (1910–1998), an admirer of Anderson, notes in his introduction to *Windy McPherson's Son* that Anderson's characters are often solitary walkers. In *Windy McPherson's Son* "The proper unit of measure . . . is the *walk*. A walk comprehends both space and time"; he adds, "To get back to Winesburg we need more than a map: we need to get out and walk" (University of Chicago Press 1965 edition vii, ix).

In his own work, novelist and photographer Wright Morris often combined photographs and words in what he called photo-texts. His second photo-text, *The Home Place* (1948), employs Morris's photographs of his Uncle Harry and Aunt Clara's run-down NEBRASKA farm, accompanied by a fictional text using his aunt and uncle as key characters. His emotional attachment to these people and their farm is obvious. Morris's best architectural metaphor appears in *The Field of Vision* (1956) as a model of the Midwestern mind. Morris describes his typical Midwestern character, McKee, as having

a simple frame-house sort of life with an upstairs and a downstairs, and a kitchen where he lived, a parlor where he didn't, a stove where the children could dress on winter mornings, a porch where time could be passed summer evenings, an attic for the preservation of the past, a basement for tinkering with the future, and a bedroom for making such connections as the nature of the house would stand. In the closets principles, salted down with mothballs. In the storm-cave, sprouting like potatoes, prejudices. (56)

Another Nebraska writer, already noted, is Willa Cather, whose work is essential to any discussion of architecture in Midwestern literature. Cather, as Marilyn Chandler points out in *Dwelling in the Text: Houses in American Fiction* (1991), is one of those novelists, like Henry James, who thought of writing itself as an architectural activity. Her first novel, *Alexander's Bridge* (1912), is about an engineer designing a great span, and her essay "The Novel Démeublé" (1922) is famous for its cautions against the use of "over-furnishing" in fiction. Perhaps her most important work involving architecture is *The Professor's House* (1925), set on Lake Michigan, in which Professor St. Peter resists moving into his new house because he is attached to the comforts and meanings in his old house, where he has clearly demarcated his own territory—specifically his garden and his study, both virtually free of domestic family dramas. The novel also dramatically contrasts modern houses with Tom Outland's Southwest adobe

houses and the fabulous Cliff City built of stone on Blue Mesa by an ancient Indian civilization.

(HARRY) SINCLAIR LEWIS (1885–1951) was another Midwestern author with a literary interest in architecture, and one who carefully studied what he considered the stultifying culture of Midwestern cities. Discontent with modern Midwestern houses is experienced by Lewis's Carol Kennicot in *MAIN STREET* (1920), where small-town architecture represents provincialism. In Minnesota towns she finds "the same two-story brick groceries with lodge-signs above the awnings; the same one-story wooden millinery shop; the same fire-brick garages; the same prairie at the open end of the wide street; the same people wondering whether the levity of eating a hot-dog sandwich would break their taboos" (Harcourt Brace 1948 edition 305). Her dream is to have her town razed and then rebuilt by "a great architect" who would "plan a town that would be suitable to the prairie" (140). In *Babbitt* (1922) George F. Babbitt, the epitome of the unreflective conformist, is a real estate agent who dearly loves his Dutch colonial house in Floral Heights, the section of Zenith in which he lives—in contrast to his neighbor's "comfortable house with no architectural manners whatever" (16). He is also pleased to see from his house's window "the top of the Second National Tower, an Indiana limestone building of thirty-five stories," a building that reassures him because of its qualities as "a temple-spire of the religion of business, a faith passionate, exalted, surpassing common men" (12–13).

LARRY WOIWODE (b. 1941) is considerably more sympathetic to the small town in his prelude titled "The Street" in *Beyond the Bedroom Wall* (1975). His adult narrator emotionally remembers a one-block street and its various buildings from his childhood in Hyatt, NORTH DAKOTA. The forces of fond memory also haunt the Michigan greenhouses of THEODORE ROETHKE (1908–1963) in such poems as "Big Wind" and "Otto," and the tenuous relationship between architecture and the fecund earth is palpable in such poems as "Forcing House" and "Root Cellar." A crucial landmark in the literature of Midwestern and American conservation is recorded in *A SAND COUNTY ALMANAC* (1949) by ALDO LEOPOLD

(1887–1948), which focuses on the restoration of a broken-down parcel of land in Wisconsin. In his foreword Leopold says that he and his family called this "refuge from too much modernity" "the Shack."

Although its primary settings are in New York, THE GREAT GATSBY (1925) by F(RANCIS) SCOTT (KEY) FITZGERALD (1896–1940) thematically contrasts the Midwestern childhood settings of Jay Gatsby and Nick Carraway with Long Island, where the drama's conflicting values are played out, largely inside symbolically representative houses. First, there is Gatsby's gigantic mansion, brilliantly lit to lure Daisy back to him; then Carraway's modest rental house, in which Gatsby makes his proposal to Daisy to leave her husband; and finally Tom and Daisy Buchanan's Georgian colonial mansion, a house designed to showcase their wealth. For Nick Carraway, these eastern houses are in explicit contrast with his family home back in the Midwest in "a city where dwellings are still called through decades by a family's name" (212). This sense of familial and cultural continuity is a factor that plays a role in making "Tom and Gatsby, Daisy and Jordan and I," all from the Midwest, "subtly unadaptable to Eastern life" (140).

One of the most interesting architectural structures in Midwestern literature is the troubled house at 124 Bluestone Road in CIN-CINNATI in *Beloved* (1987) by TONI MORRISON (b. CHLOE ARDELIA WOFFORD, 1931). The house is haunted by the memory of escaped slaves and finally by Beloved herself, the baby murdered on the property by her mother to keep her from being forced into slavery. In its history the house had been a way station of the Underground Railroad, thus linking the South and the Midwest while suggesting that the Midwest offers the best hope for freedom. Now the house is haunted by Beloved, who forces the issue between a life of slavery and the horrors of maternal murder.

Finally, no Midwestern architect has received more literary attention than Frank Lloyd Wright. Literary works that focus on his life and career include *The Architect* (1981), an admiring novel in which Meyer Levin (1905–1981) calls his hero Andrew Lane; *The Women* (2009) by T. C. Boyle (b. 1948), on Wright's difficult love relationships; and *Loving Frank* (2007) by Nancy Horan (b.

Robie House, Hyde Park, Chicago, 1909. Frank Lloyd Wright, architect.
The Carol M. Highsmith Archive, Library of Congress, Prints and Photographs Division. Image courtesy of the Library of Congress

1948), based on the tragic relationship between Wright and Mamah Cheney. Howard Roark in *The Fountainhead* (1943) by Ayn Rand (1905–1982) is sometimes said to have been based on Wright. In 1992 an opera focusing on the tragedy at Taliesen, *Shining Brow*, with a libretto by Paul Muldoon (b. 1951), was premiered in Madison, Wisconsin. *The Wright 3* (2006), a children's novel written by Blue Balliett, the pseudonym used by Elizabeth Balliett (b. 1955), concerns rescuing the Robie House from decay.

SELECTED WORKS: Examples of arresting architecture in the Midwest are abundant, especially in Chicago. Perhaps the greatest Chicago building is the Auditorium (1886–1890), built in Chicago's downtown by Adler and Sullivan, a major firm in the Chicago school. On Chicago's South Side is Frank Lloyd Wright's Robie House (1908–1910), a celebrated example of the Prairie-school style. Good examples of the modernist "second Chicago school" are embodied in Crown Hall (1950–1956) on the Illinois Institute of Technology campus and the three buildings in the Federal Center (1959–1974) in downtown Chicago, all designed by Ludwig Mies van der Rohe.

Significant literary works dealing substantively with architecture in the Midwest are *The Cliff-Dwellers* (1893) by Henry Blake Fuller and *The Common Lot* (1904) by Robert Herrick, both responding to the rapid rebuilding of Chicago at the turn of the twentieth century, while Gwendolyn Brooks's *A Street in Bronzeville* (1945) and *In the Mecca* (1968) deal with difficult and crowded conditions in Chicago's African American ghetto. Sinclair Lewis's *Main Street* (1920) and *Babbitt* (1922) address architecture in light of the Midwestern REVOLT FROM THE VILLAGE, while events in the houses of F. Scott Fitzgerald's *The Great Gatsby* (1925) mark differences in elite, middle-class, and laboring-class eastern and Midwestern sensibilities. Other great works employing Midwestern literary architecture are Willa Cather's *O Pioneers!* (1913) and *The Professor's House* (1925) and Wright Morris's photo-text *The Home Place* (1948). Toni Morrison's *Beloved* (1987) deals with a Midwestern house haunted by the impact of slavery.

FURTHER READING: Two excellent books on relations between literature and architecture are Ellen Eve Frank's *Literary Architecture* (1979), which deals only with Henry James and European figures but presents foundational theory, and Marilyn R. Chandler's *Dwelling in the Text: Houses in American Fiction* (1991). Chandler includes houses in works by Midwesterners Cather, Fitzgerald, and Toni Morrison.

Several historical studies focus on the small town as an environment supporting architectural structures. Two of these are Lewis Atherton's classic *Main Street on the Middle Border* (1954) and John Jakle's *The American Small Town: Twentieth-Century Place Images* (1982). On the homestead frontier, Everett Dick surveys the social history of the Midwest's four westernmost states in *The Sod-House Frontier, 1854–1890* (1954), including chapters on town building and the construction of dugouts and sod houses. Fred W. Peterson's *Homes in the Heartland: Balloon Frame Farmhouses of the Upper Midwest, 1850–1920* (1992) tackles a later stage of construction, discussing the nature of balloon-frame architecture and its impact on farm families and rural communities in the upper Midwest.

Studies of architectural activities in Chicago are abundant. Carl W. Condit's *The Chicago School of Architecture: A History of Commercial and Public Building in the Chicago Area, 1875–1925* (1964) is excellent on the development of technology. Carl Smith's *Chicago and the American Literary Imagination, 1890–1920* (1984) includes a chapter, "Chicago Building," on the significance of architecture in the works of Chicago writers. Smith's fine *The Plan of Chicago: Daniel Burnham and the Remaking of the American City* (2006) studies the history and significance of Burnham's 1909 *Plan of Chicago.* William Cronon's *Nature's Metropolis: Chicago and the Great West* (1991) and Timothy B. Spears's *Chicago Dreaming: Midwesterners and the City, 1871–1919* (2005) are essential on the relationship between Chicago and the Midwestern hinterlands. Both deal occasionally with literature. On the Columbian Exposition, Daniel Burg's *Chicago's White City of 1893* (1976) and Dennis B. Downey's *A Season of Renewal: The Columbian Exposition and Victorian America* (2002) assess the fair in its cultural context. Both discuss novels created in response to the event. Alan Trachtenberg's *The Incorporation of America: Culture and Society in the Gilded Age* (1982) includes a significant critique of the architecture and design of the exposition. Erik Larson's *The Devil in the White City* (2003) is a popular history with alternate chapters devoted to Daniel Burnham and the White City and chapters centered on mass murderer Henry H. Holmes, who built the "World's Fair Hotel," where he tortured and killed young women he lured from the White City.

The essential work on the Prairie school is H. Allen Brooks's *The Prairie School: Frank Lloyd Wright and His Midwest Contemporaries* (1972). David Gebhard's *Purcell and Elmslie: Prairie Progressive Architects* (2006) is a nicely illustrated introduction to this Prairie-school firm, as is Jennnifer Komar Olivarez's *Progressive Design: The Purcell-Cutts House and the Prairie School Collection at the Minneapolis Institute of Arts* (2000). Three autobiographies are excellent for the thinking behind the buildings. Louis H. Sullivan's *The Autobiography of an Idea* (1924) expands on "the Master's" architecture and theories of organic decoration and design. Frank Lloyd Wright's *An Autobiography* (1932) is a spirited account of Wright's philosophy and career. Wright's *Collected Writings* fills five volumes. Volume 1, *1894–1930* (1992), edited by Bruce Brooks Pfeiffer, includes essays about the Prairie style, written while Wright was designing in that manner. Two studies that explore romantic philosophy's influence on these architects are Naomi Tanabe Uechi's *Evolving Transcendentalism in Literature and Architecture: Frank Furness, Louis Sullivan, and Frank Lloyd Wright* (2013) and Lauren S. Weingarden's *Louis H. Sullivan and a 19th-Century Poetics of Naturalized Architecture* (2009). *The Autobiography of Irving K. Pond: The Sons of Mary and Elihu* (2009), by Irving K. Pond (1857–1939), edited by David Swann and Terry Tatum, covers sixty years of Chicago and other Midwestern architecture, including the buildings at Jane Addams's Hull-House and a variety of Midwestern university buildings, and is copiously illustrated. An intriguing book is *Inspiration: Nature and the Poet; The Collected Poems of Louis H. Sullivan* (1999), edited by Christian K. Narkiewicz-Laine. Another autobiography, that of Chicago architect and building commissioner Henry Ericsson (1861–1947), *Sixty Years a Builder: The Autobiography of Henry Ericsson* (1942), is an excellent insider's view of Chicago's architectural growing pains.

For Midwestern domestic architecture more generally, Robert Winter's *At Home in the Heartland* (2007) and George H. Berkhofer's *No Place like Home: A History of Domestic Architecture in Springfield and Clark County, Ohio* (2007) are quite useful. For images and discussion of an emerging modernist painter's avid interest in domestic architecture in Ohio—including his indebtedness to Sherwood Anderson and Hamlin Garland—see *Charles Burchfield, 1920: The Architecture of Painting* (2009), especially the essay "Charles Burchfield: Modern American" by Nannette V. Maciejunes and Karli R. Wurzelbacher (20–31). John Drury's *Historic Midwest Houses* (1947) emphasizes history over architecture, but it remains a useful survey, including many Midwestern writers' domiciles.

Several other works explore a variety of topics associated with Midwestern architecture. *The Midwest in American Architecture* (1991), edited by John S. Garner, includes essays on various aspects of Midwestern architecture from 1880 to 1920, among them Sullivan and Adler, Burnham and Root, S. S. Beman, and George Grant Elmslie. Robert Alan Benson's *Essays on Architecture in the Midwest* (1992) is useful on more recent architecture. For an interesting case of a Midwestern city with an abiding interest in

modern architecture, see *A Look at Architecture: Columbus, Indiana,* seventh edition, compiled by the Columbus Area Visitors Center (1998). For industrial architecture in the Midwest, Federico Bucci's *Albert Kahn: Architect of Ford* (2002) is a good beginning. Finally, *Midwestern Landscape Architecture* (2000), edited by William Tishler, deals with an often neglected topic.

JOSEPH J. WYDEVEN   BELLEVUE UNIVERSITY

ART

OVERVIEW: The history of visual art in the Midwest is complex and diverse. Written from the perspective of Midwestern literature, this essay highlights general movements and select Midwestern art landmarks, emphasizing those most typically considered Midwestern, and suggests further reading. Coverage, roughly chronological and based on the historical origins of the specific types of visual art found in the Midwest, begins with frontier artists and continues through Midwestern regionalism in the mid-twentieth century. Also included is a brief discussion of Midwestern photography.

HISTORY AND SIGNIFICANCE: For much of its early history, Midwestern art borrowed often from European and established eastern antecedents and sought to portray nature and culture as glimpsed and developed in newly settled areas of America. In sheer quantity and range of subject matter, Midwestern art was robust and exuberant. It is likely that frontier independence of spirit, however, prompted a wide range of approaches to Midwestern art, "whose development," William H. Gerdts writes in *Art across America: Two Centuries of Regional Painting, 1710–1920,* volume 2, *The South, and the Midwest* (1990), "was much more random and sporadic" than art in the East (175). Like their pioneer compatriots, Midwestern artists felt a wide range of strong emotions as they experienced firsthand the length and breadth of the Ohio, Mississippi, and Missouri Rivers; the unexpected diversity of Native American life; and the responses of their fellow settlers to frontier exigencies, town building, and adjustment of civic and cultural institutions to new circumstances. As Michael Hall and Nannette Maciejunes observe in "Field of Dreams: Heartland Regionalist Painting, 1925–1950," in *Illusions of*

Eden: Versions of the American Heartland (2000), edited by Robert Stearns, it was not until the advent of regionalism in the twentieth century that Midwestern artists identified "the Midwest as a discreet [*sic*] entity within the political, geographical, and mythological landscape of the United States" (84). This sense of being distinctively "in between" eastern industrialism and western wide-openness created a new set of imaginative parameters.

Midwestern art passed through a number of periods as it gained sophistication. Some of the early scenes of army life in the forts and in cultural conflict with Native Americans seem as primitive as much folk art, and the many portraits of important settlers in the new region offered little that distinguished it from portraiture produced in the East. Not until Karl Bodmer (1809–1893) were Native Americans carefully observed for significant detail and skillfully drawn and painted as human beings in their own right. With America's Native people often as background, Midwestern artists came to focus on the bounty and expansiveness of nature. Often this interest took the form of "views," pictured vistas of thriving Midwestern cities within their natural surroundings. Typically, these are proud attempts to place Midwestern cultural effort into a larger, nearly ethereal sphere. Many of the landscapes from the Civil War years and beyond are similar in tone to those of the Hudson River school. The panorama industries that later developed around Mississippi River views were distinctly Midwestern in their sense of awe at nature's bounty.

There was little early effort to distinguish character types or apply satire to the frontier or to landscape scenes, but by the time of the Civil War the Midwestern penchant for criticism was in full sway, particularly regarding politics and the sheer fun of observing American democracy in action, especially on Election Day. At this time, too, genre scenes of everyday life suggested the range of Midwestern humor, much of it self-effacing, as artists focused on broad character types, much as did writers like Eliza Farnham (1815–1864) and Samuel Langhorne Clemens (1835–1910), writing as Mark Twain.

By the 1880s a new realism emerged, along with a largely home-grown impressionism, and by this time the artistic arsenal included a range of styles and genres. By the second decade of the twentieth century, regionalism, the most important Midwestern movement, came into existence, spearheaded by Thomas Hart Benton (1889–1975), Grant Wood (1891–1942), and John Steuart Curry (1897–1946). The movement had a complicated history, subject to widely divergent interpretations during the brief years of its existence. Hall and Maciejunes assert that regionalism helps define Midwestern values "identified with corn" and associated with "the theme of home" (80, 94). They emphasize this domestic quality in the works of artists as diverse as Grant Wood, Charles Burchfield (1893–1967), Lois Ireland (b. 1928), and Clyde Singer (1908–1999). After regionalism, Midwestern art lost some of its unique regional distinctiveness, although its range of options continued to be wide, including the various styles of modernism and postmodernism.

The historical development of visual art in the Midwest affirms that where commerce thrives, culture follows. The importance of the Ohio River can hardly be overestimated in the early history of Midwestern art, for it was the Ohio, as Judith A. Barter noted in her 1977 book *Currents of Expansion* (11–15), that carried cultural influences into the interior and created Cincinnati, the first important center of Midwestern art. St. Louis was the next major city, a product of the Mississippi River and the city's proximity to the mouth of the Missouri. But the city that quickly surpassed the importance of Cincinnati and St. Louis was Chicago—a city of tremendous growth, largely because of its role as the Midwestern railroad center and its proximity to the Great Lakes.

From the beginning of Midwestern exploration, the American interior and its Native peoples were subjects of immense interest, and a number of artists emerged to satisfy this curiosity. George Winter (1809–1876) pictured Indian life in Indiana in the grip of severe change; Seth Eastman (1808–1875), commander at Fort Snelling in the 1840s, did sensitive sketches and watercolors of Minnesota and the Mississippi River, often incorporating aspects of Indian life. His *Ballplay of the Sioux on the St. Peter's River in Winter* (1848) is a memorable image of Native

Americans at vigorous recreation, with a te-pee village just beyond the frozen river shore. Henry Farny (1847–1916) of Cincinnati specialized in western themes; his *Song of the Talking Wire* (1904) depicts a Native American in a stark landscape holding his ear to a telegraph pole, probably contemplating a grim future.

The most famous of the Midwestern frontier artists, George Catlin (1796–1872), Karl Bodmer, and Charles (Carl) Wimar (1828–1862), were often associated with the Missouri River. These artist-explorers made their way up the Missouri from St. Louis to Fort Union and beyond; they are remembered mostly for their portraits of Native Americans and representations of customs and ceremonies. Catlin ascended the Missouri River in 1830, followed two years later by Bodmer, who accompanied Prince Maximilian von Wied. Wimar went up the Missouri in 1858 and 1859, employing an ambrotype camera that produced photographic images on glass. Of the three, Bodmer's work is the most accurate, for he was obligated to supply Maximilian with scientific detail and was therefore forced to see beyond prevailing European preconceptions and prevalent artistic norms.

Following eastern tradition, early Midwestern urban artists produced portraits and miniatures for prominent citizens. Aaron Corwine (1802–1830) was an important early Cincinnati portraitist, counting Andrew Jackson among those he painted. Jacob Maentel (1763–1863) was associated with Robert Owen's New Harmony colony; Sheldon Peck (1797–1868) did important portrait work in Chicago; and Jarvis Hanks (1799–1853) was an itinerant portrait painter in CLEVELAND. Sarah Miriam Peale (1800–1885), perhaps the preeminent woman artist of her generation, was born in Philadelphia but lived for more than a quarter of a century in St. Louis, where she specialized in portraits and still lifes.

By the time of the Civil War, many artists were scattered throughout the Midwest, and landscape and other pictorial traditions were becoming established. The experience of Cincinnati-born (Thomas) Worthington Whittredge (1820–1910) seems to have been typical. After experimenting with daguerreotypy and serving briefly as a housepainter,

Whittredge painted portraits before moving on to landscapes. Whittredge was typical also in having received artistic training in Germany. The Hudson River school had set the pictorial standard for landscape paintings in the United States, and like many others, Whittredge and the first successful African American painter, Robert Duncanson (1821–1872), fell under its spell. Duncanson's well-known *Blue Hole, Flood Waters, Little Miami River* (1851) pictures a quiet pond with three fishermen in the foreground; the picture generates a sense of peace that Duncanson might have desired for himself. His elaborate murals (ca. 1850–1852) for Nicholas Longworth's Cincinnati home, now the Taft Museum, are much admired.

George Caleb Bingham (1811–1879), the most famous MISSOURI artist in the nineteenth century, produced portraits and genre paintings but is best known now for his river scenes, such as *Fur Traders Descending the Missouri* (ca. 1845) and *The Jolly Flatboatmen* (1846), a well-composed genre scene of men relaxing from their labors as they make their way down the river. One man dances while two others play musical instruments; four other figures watch the action; and another man looks directly into the viewers' eyes. Bingham returned to this subject a number of times in his career.

Especially before and during the Civil War, genre paintings were a staple of American politics; many focused on democracy in action. Bingham's *The Verdict of the People* (1854–1855) is an excellent example. In it, democracy shows its many faces in a crowded canvas. The election verdict has been announced to a milling crowd under a large American flag. The general attitude of the picture is one of exuberance, but looming large in the foreground is a man kneeling on the ground, clearly inebriated; no one pays attention to him except an African American laborer rolling a wheelbarrow.

The most significant Midwestern genre painter of domestic incidents in women's lives was Lilly Martin Spencer (1822–1902), who lived near Marietta, OHIO, from 1833 to 1844. Her whimsical *Kiss Me, and You'll Kiss the 'Lasses* (1856) pictures a coquettish young woman dipping a spoon into the molasses dish on a fruit-covered table while she eyes the viewer. Spencer was also known for her portraits of children. Another genre painter, John Quidor (1801–1881), who had a studio in Quincy, ILLINOIS, from about 1837 to 1849, is best known for his genre scenes based on the work of his friend Washington Irving (1783–1859), such as *The Return of Rip Van Winkle* (ca. 1849). His Van Winkle appears deranged, while the crowd around him expresses emotional responses that range from incredulity to mockery and anger.

Immensely popular at midcentury were panorama paintings, many of which depicted the Mississippi River. Panoramas were huge works showing long stretches of scenery, usually on scrolls that were unrolled for audiences, with dramatic lighting and sound added. The most famous example is that of John Banvard (1815–1891), a panorama of the Mississippi River valley advertised as being three miles long. Another example is the 350-foot-long *Panorama of the Monumental Grandeur of the Mississippi Valley* (1850) that an early excavator of Midwestern Indian mounds, Montroville Wilson Dickeson (1810–1886), commissioned John J. Egan (1810–1882) to paint. Many Midwestern artists, including Leon Pomarede (1807–1892), who painted early St. Louis scenes, including *View of St. Louis from Illinois Town* (1835), and Henry Lewis (1819–1904), were involved in panorama painting. A thriving panorama industry, largely worked by German immigrants, operated in Milwaukee as late as the 1880s. Frederick Oakes Sylvester (1869–1915) made a career of work focused on the Mississippi. *The River's Golden Dream* (1911–1912) is a view of the river painted from a bluff rising above it; his book *The Great River: Poems and Pictures* (1911) remains memorable.

In the last two decades of the nineteenth century, an energetic interest in realism developed in Midwestern art. Two important Midwestern-born painters well known both for their own work and their roles as teachers are Frank Duveneck (1848–1919) and Robert Henri (1865–1929). Duveneck, of Cincinnati, learned his free brushwork style in Munich. His devoted followers, often called "the Duveneck Boys," play a minor role in the novel *Indian Summer* (1886) by WILLIAM DEAN HOWELLS (1837–1920), where he calls them "the Inglehart Boys." Robert Henri, best known as the leader of the rebellious group the Eight, as well as a member of the

Ashcan school, was the author of *The Art Spirit* (1923), observations and notes from his role as a teacher. Henri spent much of his childhood in a town his father founded, Cozad, NEBRASKA. SOUTH DAKOTA–born Frances Cranmer Greenman (1890–1981) testified to Henri's liberating effect as a teacher in her spirited autobiography, *Higher than the Sky* (1954). Another of Henri's Midwestern students was George Bellows (1882–1925), who spent his early years in Columbus, Ohio. MARI(E SUSETTE) SANDOZ (1896–1966) wrote of Henri's early life in her novel *Son of the Gamblin' Man* (1960).

The importance of the 1893 World's Columbian Exposition for Midwestern art can hardly be overestimated. Amid its White City architecture, the exposition boasted the cultural arrival of Chicago as a world-class city. In addition to an impressive display of eastern and European artists, Midwestern painters' works were exhibited at the Columbian Exposition. The collection, gathered by Halsey Cooley Ives (1847–1911), the founder of the St. Louis School and Museum of Fine Arts, included works by Kenyon Cox (1856–1919), Frank Duveneck, Elizabeth Nourse (1859–1938), T(heodore) C(lement) Steele (1847–1926), John Henry Twachtman (1853–1902), and Worthington Whittredge. Carl von Marr (1858–1936) exhibited his gigantic *The Flagellants* (1889) to great acclaim; and Robert Koehler (1850–1917) presented *The Strike* (1886), depicting a tense moment when striking workers assemble before a factory owner's house.

The Columbian Exposition gave evidence of major European influences on Midwestern art: the picturesque *plein air* work of the Barbizon school and the impressionism of Monet. The first important group of Midwestern painters associated with impressionism was the Hoosier Group, so named after (HANNIBAL) HAMLIN GARLAND (1860–1940) invited several Indiana painters to show their work in Chicago, resulting in an acceptance of bucolic Midwestern themes. The Hoosier Group included T. C. Steele, William J. Forsyth (1854–1935), Richard B. Gruelle (1851–1914), Otto Stark (1859–1926), and John Ottis Adams (1851–1927).

Realism and impressionism also lent themselves to cityscapes, as in *The Canal, Early Morning (Indianapolis)* (1894) by Richard Gruelle, an atmospheric view of a foregrounded canal and bridge, with the state capitol dome in the background; and *Rainy Evening on Hennepin Avenue* (ca. 1910) by Robert Koehler, a chilly view of a MINNE-APOLIS street with pedestrians and a trolley car diffusing golden light from its windows. Well-known Midwestern artists associated with impressionism were Twachtman and William Merritt Chase (1849–1916). Some attention has been paid to pioneer women impressionists from Minnesota, including Alice Hügy (1876–1971), Clara Mairs (1878–1963), and Ada Wolfe (1878–1945). In South Dakota, Harvey Dunn (1884–1952) often focused on the meaningful hardships of farm life, as in *Fixing Fence* (1944), depicting a young woman vigorously aiding an older man, presumably her father, in reattaching barbed wire to a fence post, and *The Prairie Is My Garden* (1950), showing a pioneer woman and two children cutting flowers from the tough prairie soil. Mari Sandoz wrote a fine homage to Dunn in "Dakota Country" (*American Heritage,* June 1961). *The Memories of an American Impressionist* (1980) is the autobiography of Abel Warshawsky (1883–1962), originally from Cleveland.

Regionalism is the movement most widely viewed as Midwestern, particularly in relation to Thomas Hart Benton, Grant Wood, and John Steuart Curry. Regionalism was typically concerned with rural themes and often incorporated elements from modernism and folk art. Iowan Grant Wood's *American Gothic* (1930), depicting a dour farm couple, the man with hay fork in hand, against a farmhouse in carpenter Gothic style, is the Midwest's most iconic image and the subject of numerous interpretations and parodies. It provides a hint of Wood's subtle humor in his depiction of people by whom he was both attracted and repelled. Although Wood employed as models his sister Nan and his dentist, B. H. McKeeby, thirty-two years apart in age, viewers typically interpret the two as a married couple. Their stolid stance, with the woman tucked slightly behind her mate, suggests rigid determination, a quality that might be admirable were it not so often understood as self-righteousness. The couple's intransigence is magnified by the man's stare into the viewer's eyes, coupled with the woman's absolute refusal to make eye contact. Because of the hay fork thrust between themselves and the viewers, they appear blatantly protective of isolationist values against intruding outsiders. Thus this Midwestern couple is presented as a subject of mixed admiration and scorn; the portrait, in Wanda Corn's words in "Grant Wood: Uneasy Modern" in *Grant Wood's Studio* (2005), edited by Jane C. Milosch, is "Wood's first narrative of confrontation" (122).

Outspoken Missourian Thomas Hart Benton produced many paintings and murals expressive of Midwestern scenes and values. His work was characterized by earthy social commentary and defined by swirling contours combined with diagonals expressing energy and drama. His murals range across a broad swath of American life: his works for the New School for Social Research in New York (1930–1931) deal with contemporary themes and the flux and flow of life, while *Independence and the Opening of the West* (1959–1962) in the Truman Library pictures frontier and settlement themes. Justly celebrated is *The Hailstorm* (1940), which pictures two farmers, one seeking shelter, the other continuing to plow, besieged by hail, wind, and shafts of lightning. More notorious is Benton's *Persephone* (1938–1939), which depicts an aging farmer as voyeur as he, abandoning his mules and wagon, spies from cover on a sleeping female nude.

The third essential regionalist, Kansan John Steuart Curry, is best known for his mural of John Brown in the state capitol in Topeka, *The Tragic Prelude* (1937–1942), depicting a fierce, Moses-like John Brown standing on the bodies of Civil War soldiers while a tornado whirls and potential homesteaders trek westward behind him. When many Kansans objected, Curry's commission was terminated, and he refused to sign the works he had already finished. Curry's paintings, such as *Baptism in Kansas* (1928), *The Line Storm* (1934), and *Wisconsin Landscape* (1938–1939), have generated much discussion. His *Tornado over Kansas* (1929), depicting a farm family making haste to their storm shelter as a terrifying tornado approaches, may have been the inspiration for the tornado scene in the 1939 film *The Wizard of Oz.* Many other Midwestern artists were associated with regionalism, among them William Sommer (1867–1949), Marvin Cone (1891–1965), William Dickerson (1904–1972), Dale Nichols (1904–1995), Doris Lee (1905–1983), Aaron Bohrod (1907–1992), Joe Jones (1909–1963), Bernece Berkman (1911–1979), and John Rogers Cox (1915–1990). The regionalist movement was over by the beginning of World War II, when, according to Benton, "Wood, Curry, and I found the bottom knocked out from under us" (quoted in Debra Bricker Balken's 2009 *After Many Springs: Regionalism, Modernism, and the Midwest*, 193).

Other significant Midwestern painters are African American artists Archibald Motley Jr. (1891–1981), the uncle of WILLARD F. MOTLEY (1909–1965), known for urban genre scenes, and Kansas-born Aaron Douglas (1898–1979). Georgia O'Keeffe (1887–1986), from WISCONSIN, is recognized primarily for her southwestern work. Ohio-born Charles Burchfield is noted for his watercolor scenes in which nature appears imbued with vitalistic energies. His *Night of the Equinox* (1917–1955) is a rich example, showing a town landscape soggy with rainfall and employing some of Burchfield's characteristic animated shapes; the water is so intensely evoked that in portions of the painting the lines are blurred between nature and culture. John Blake Bergers (1931–2011) painted many scenes from the works and Red Cloud environs of WILLA CATHER (1873–1947), while Swedish immigrant Birger Sandzén (1871–1954) was a distinctive painter and, from his faculty position at Bethany College in Lindsborg, an influential leader in the arts in KANSAS.

The Midwest also has a strong mural tradition, especially in public buildings. Many murals appeared in Midwestern post offices through the auspices of New Deal art programs. The most notorious mural is undoubtedly John Steuart Curry's work for the Kansas capitol, *The Tragic Prelude*. The best-known Midwestern muralist, however, is Thomas Hart Benton, who produced many murals, including, in addition to those noted previously, those at the Missouri state capitol in Jefferson City and controversial murals on Indiana history, first shown at the 1933 Century of Progress Exposition in Chicago and held now at Indiana University. Also significant are the murals of Di-ego Rivera (1886–1957) titled *Detroit Industry* (1932–1933) at the Detroit Institute of Arts.

In three-dimensional art, sculpture proved widely popular, especially as public art. Perhaps the most famous Midwestern sculptor is Hiram Powers (1805–1873), whose *The Greek Slave* (1846) fired the imaginations of Americans when it toured and tested American reactions to nudity in marble. Lorado Taft (1860–1936), one of the most important Chicago sculptors, created the sculpture of BLACK HAWK (1767–1838) called *The Eternal Indian* (1908–1911) and *Fountain of the Great Lakes* (1907–1913). Taft's *History of American Sculpture* (1903) was the first book to cover its subject.

Perhaps the best known of the modernist sculptors was Paul Manship (1885–1966) of St. Paul. His stylized figures of humans and animals grace the halls of many Midwestern museums. Two monumental works of Midwestern sculpture are located in South Dakota. The first, by Gutzon Borglum (1867–1941), depicts Presidents Washington, Jefferson, Lincoln, and Theodore Roosevelt at Mount Rushmore (1927–1941).The second is a work in progress, the *Crazy Horse Memorial*, begun in 1948, by Korczak Ziolkowski (1908–1982), perhaps the largest sculpture ever planned and executed. Works of sculpture have often served as signature icons for cities: well-known Midwestern examples include the *Chicago Picasso* (1967) by Pablo Picasso (1881–1973), Minneapolis's *Spoonbridge and Cherry* (1988) by Claes Oldenburg (b. 1929), and *La Grande Vitesse* (1969) by Alexander Calder (1898–1976) in Grand Rapids, MICHIGAN.

Folk art is composed of a vast array of work in different media, from quilts, ceramics, and jewelry to primitive sculptures and paintings, and has always been healthy in the Midwest. Memorable artists include Sheldon Peck (1797–1869), who painted in Chicago in the 1840s; Henry Church (1836–1908) of Chagrin Falls, Ohio, sculptor of the rock carving *The Rape of the Indian Tribes by the White Man* (1885); and Paul A. Seifert (1840–1921), a painter of detailed watercolors of Wisconsin farms. Some folk artists are associated with utopian religious communities, such as Olof Krans (1838–1916), a painter of portraits and landscapes at the Swedish Bishop Hill Colony in Illinois. Krans is per-

Kansas Farming mural, U.S. Courthouse, Wichita, Kansas, created for the U.S. General Services Administration. Painting by Richard Haines, ca. 1936. Photo by Carol M. Highsmith, 2009.
Image courtesy of the Library of Congress

haps best known for his nearly surreal *Corn Planting* (1896), featuring twenty-four bonneted and aproned women in a straight line with hoes at the ready in front of them. See also UTOPIAN LITERATURE.

Related to folk art is the phenomenon variously called "grassroots," "outsider," or "visionary" art; see, for example, the essays in *Backyard Visionaries,* edited by Barbara Brackman and Cathy Dwigans (1999): works produced by individuals with little training but considerable conviction. Examples include the extravagant *Grotto of the Redemption* in West Bend, IOWA begun in 1912 by the Catholic priest Paul Mathias Dobberstein (1872–1954) and continued by his successors; and the *Grotto of the Holy Ghost* in Dickeyville, Wisconsin (1925–1931), by Fr. Mathias Wernerus (1873–1931). Works of more secular interest include *The Garden of Eden* (1907–1928) in Lucas, Kansas, an array of Populist-inspired sculptures created by Samuel Perry Dinsmoor (1843–1932), and the Heidelberg Project (1986–present), in which African American Tyree Guyton (b. 1955) converts abandoned Detroit houses into "art environments."

As might be expected, the use of photography to record Midwestern realities has been ubiquitous. The second daguerreotype studio in the United States was established in Cincinnati in 1840. The first known

photograph of ABRAHAM LINCOLN (1809–1865) is a daguerreotype made in 1846 in Illinois by Nicholas H. Shepherd (1822–1902). Many Midwestern artists, including Worthington Whittredge and Anton Gág (1859–1908), father of WANDA (HAZEL) GÁG (1893–1946), used daguerreotype images for modeling painted portraits. Midwestern photographers who achieved national and international reputations include Gertrude Käsebier (1852–1934), Edward Curtis (1868–1952), Lewis Hine (1874–1940), Edward Weston (1886–1958), Berenice Abbott (1898–1991), Minor White (1908–1976), and John Szarkowski (1925–2007), along with Roy Stryker (1893–1975) and most of the photographers who worked for him in the Farm Security Administration.

Other important Midwestern photographers include Aaron Siskind (1903–1991), Harry Callahan (1912–1999), and Art Sinsabaugh (1924–1983), all associated with Chicago. Siskind manipulated his photographs of architecture and nature into examples of abstract impressionism. Callahan is best known for his pictures of his wife, Eleanor, taken in a variety of Midwestern settings. Sinsabaugh is well known for his wide-format Midwestern landscapes; in *6 Mid-American Chant / 11 Midwest Photographs* (1964) he paired his photographs with poems by SHERWOOD ANDERSON (1876–1941). In addition, numerous local photographers left behind archives of photographs of Midwestern towns; two memorable craftsmen were Otto Ping (1883–1975) of Brown County, Indiana, and Walter C. Schneider (1884–1964), of Kankakee, Illinois. David Plowden (b. 1932) has spent a lifetime recording rural images, many of them Midwestern, as found in his *Vanishing Point: Fifty Years of Photography* (2007). Terry Evans (b. 1944), best known for her aerial photographs of Illinois and Kansas, has contributed *Disarming the Prairie* (1998) and *The Inhabited Prairie* (1998).

Some of the most celebrated works combining Midwestern photography with words include *Pioneer History of Custer County, Nebraska* (1901) by Solomon Butcher (1856–1927), which joins Butcher's photographs of frontier families, some whimsically altered, to his historical commentary. His 1886 photograph of the John Curry sod house near West Union, Nebraska, pictures a farm couple, the man with pitchfork in hand, before their house and household furnishings. The photo suggests the later content of Grant Wood's *American Gothic;* according to Steven Biel, the Nebraska State Historical Society has come to call this photograph "Nebraska Gothic" (*American Gothic* 24). This is one of Butcher's altered images; Butcher has etched the form of an odd bird into his negative. Also from Nebraska is *The Home Place* (1948) by WRIGHT MORRIS (1910–1998), a photo-text novel featuring Morris's poignant photographs of his uncle and aunt's dilapidated farm. His photograph *Uncle Harry Entering Barn* (1947) has become something of a classic, picturing the old man entering the barn's dark interior, while the text alludes to Shakespearian "ripeness" raised in *King Lear.*

Another significant work joining pictures and words is the controversial *Wisconsin Death Trip* (1973) by Michael Lesy (b. 1945), a meditation on economic and emotional depression in Black River Falls, Wisconsin, from 1890 to 1910. Lesy juxtaposed newspaper stories and selections from GLENWAY WESCOTT (1901–1987), Hamlin Garland, and EDGAR LEE MASTERS (1868–1950) to images made by Charles Van Schaick (1897–1942), a professional photographer in Black River Falls. The best-known Midwestern African American photographer is Kansas-born GORDON (ALEXANDER BUCHANAN) PARKS

(1912–2006), famous for his Farm Security Administration photographs and photo essays in *Life* magazine and *Vogue*. Parks had a remarkably varied career as photographer, writer, film director, and composer.

SELECTED WORKS: The best-known artistic works from the Midwest are those of the regionalists. Perhaps the most iconic of all American paintings is Grant Wood's *American Gothic* (1930), which is still interpreted from a range of social perspectives. Thomas Hart Benton's murals in a variety of sites have drawn much attention. A good example is *Independence and the Opening of the West* (1959–1962); his painting *Persephone* (1938–1939) still retains its power to shock. John Steuart Curry's mural portrait of John Brown, *The Tragic Prelude* (1937–1942), remains powerful, and his *Tornado over Kansas* (1929) still reminds viewers of *The Wizard of Oz* (1939).

Many earlier visual works are redolent of the Midwest and its developing culture. George Caleb Bingham's *The Jolly Flatboatmen* (1846) is a famous scene à la Mark Twain, while his *The Verdict of the People* (1854–1855) is one of the best genre scenes of 1840s democratic politics.

African American Robert Duncanson is perhaps best known for his picturesque *Blue Hole, Flood Waters, Little Miami River* (1851), in the early tradition of the Hudson River school. Genre paintings reflecting women's culture are perhaps best found in the work of Lilly Martin Spencer, whose *Kiss Me, and You'll Kiss the 'Lasses* (1856) is a good example. Frederick Oakes Sylvester's passion for the Mississippi River is found in *The River's Golden Dream* (1911–1912), while selected poems and paintings are found in his book *The Great River: Poems and Pictures* (1911).

Two Midwestern photographers have achieved the status of classics. The first is Solomon Butcher, whose photographs of Nebraska homesteaders are found often in American history and social studies texts, as well as in his *Pioneer History of Custer County, Nebraska* (1901). His photograph of John Curry's sod house is a good example of both his portraits and his altered photographic work. The second photographer is Wright Morris, whose photo-text novel *The Home Place* (1948) combines photographs with words; the final photograph in the text is *Uncle Harry Entering Barn*. Two outstanding volumes of observations on art by Midwestern painters are Robert Henri's *The Art Spirit* (1923) and *Charles Burchfield's Journals: The Poetry of Place* (1993), edited by J. Benjamin Townsend.

FURTHER READING: The literature on Midwestern visual art is voluminous, although little of it deals specifically with the Midwest as a region. The best overview by individual states is William H. Gerdts's (b. 1929) three-volume *Art across America: Two Centuries of Regional Painting, 1710–1920* (1990), with excellent notes and bibliographies. Exhibition catalogs are often important sources for the study of Midwestern art as Midwestern. Perhaps the best single catalog is *Currents of Expansion: Painting in the Midwest, 1820–1940* (1977) by Judith A. Barter and Lynn E. Springer. For a fine overview of various visual arts in a crucial decade, see Jason T. Busch's *Currents of Change: Art and Life along the Mississippi River, 1850–1861* (2004). *Revisiting the White City: American Art at the 1893 World's Fair* (1993) is a substantial exhibition catalogue and superb study of art at the Columbian Exposition, including a catalog of American paintings and sculptures exhibited there.

The following works are among those that discuss various aspects of Midwestern art. *The Autobiography of Worthington Whittredge, 1820–1910* was published in the first issue of the *Brooklyn Museum Journal* (1942). On frontier conditions and Indian life, George Catlin's *Letters and Notes on the Manners, Customs and Condition of the North American Indians* (1841) is still relevant; *Indians and a Changing Frontier: The Art of George Winter* (1993), edited by Sarah E. Cooke and Rachel B. Ramadhyani, contains Winter's paintings and written observations; and *Karl Bodmer's North American Prints* (2004), edited by Brandon K. Ruud, is thorough and beautifully reproduces Bodmer's works.

Joseph D. Ketner's *The Emergence of the African-American Artist: Robert S. Duncanson, 1821–1872* (1993) offers a view of the volatile intersections of art and race in the mid-nineteenth century. On the role of women in Midwestern art, Judith Vale Newton and Carol Ann Weiss's *Skirting the Issue: Stories of Indiana's Historical Women Artists* (2004) introduces the essential issues and highlights the work of about one hundred artists. Rob-

ert Henri's example for American women artists is examined in *American Women Modernists: The Legacy of Robert Henri, 1910–1945* (2005), edited by Marian Wardle. *Growing Pains: Diaries and Drawings for the Years 1908–1917* (1940) by Wanda (Hazel) Gág is both delightful and instructive. On ethnic painting, a good source is *Painting by Minnesotans of Norwegian Background, 1870–1970* (2000) by Marion John Nelson.

Especially good studies of the visual art and culture of the plains and prairies are Joni L. Kinsey's *Plain Pictures: Images of the American Prairie* (1996), with a wide range of historical and contemporary images, and *Recovering the Prairie* (1999), edited by Robert F. Sayre; both include insightful essays. *Illusions of Eden: Versions of the American Heartland* (2000), edited by Robert Stearns, includes several compelling essays, especially "Field of Dreams: Heartland Regionalist Painting, 1925–1950" by Michael Hall and Nannette Maciejunes, and a superb selection of Midwestern images. For grassroots art, good sources include *Sacred Spaces and Other Places: A Guide to Grottos and Sculptural Environments in the Upper Midwest* (1993) by Lisa Stone and Jim Zanzi and *Backyard Visionaries: Grassroots Art in the Midwest* (1999), edited by Barbara Brackman and Cathy Dwigans. *An Open Land: Photographs of the Midwest, 1852–1982* (1983), edited by Victoria Post Ranney, offers a selection of photographs by major photographers, brief essays and poems, and a short bibliography.

A number of works published as guides, exhibition catalogs, or museum collection catalogs depict specific Midwestern states' artists or scenes. Among them are *Ohio Subjects and Ohio Artists: 18th and 19th Century Paintings* (1953); *Michigan on Canvas: The J. L. Hudson Company Collection* (1948); *The Michigan Experience: A Traveling Exhibition of Paintings of Michigan Themes by Michigan Artists in Celebration of the State's Sesquicentennial* (1986); the Indiana Art League's exhibit *The Edge of Town: Painting the Indiana Scene, 1932–1948* (1989); the Indiana Plein Air Painters Association–sponsored *Painting Indiana: Portraits of Indiana's 92 Counties* (2000); *Wisconsin as Seen by Wisconsin Artists: The Gimbel Wisconsin Centennial Art Collection* (1948); *100 Years of Wisconsin Art: 1888/1988; A Centennial Celebration* (1988); *The American National Bank*

Collection of Minnesota Art (1976); Dan Woodward's useful though not illustrated *Missouri Artist Guide: Of Artists Who Have Painted Missouri* (1993); Norman A. Geske's *Art and Artists in Nebraska* (1983); and *The Kansas Landscape* (1985), an exhibition catalog compiled by Don Lambert and Andrea Glenn.

Many good works exist on American regionalism. Matthew Baigell's *The American Scene: American Painting of the 1930's* (1974) provides excellent context, and his *Thomas Hart Benton* (1974) is a valuable overview of Benton's career. M. Sue Kendall's *Rethinking Regionalism: John Steuart Curry and the Kansas Mural Controversy* (1986) is superb, as are the reassessments in *John Steuart Curry: Inventing the Middle West* (1998), edited by Patricia Junker. Of the many works on Grant Wood, three are especially useful: Wanda M. Corn's *Grant Wood: The Regionalist Vision* (1983); *Grant Wood's Studio: Birthplace of "American Gothic"* (2005), edited by Jane C. Milosch; and Steven Biel's *"American Gothic": A Life of America's Most Famous Painting* (2005), a lively interdisciplinary account of the painting and its reception over time. Especially useful for students of literature is *Grant Wood's Main Street: Art, Literature and the American Midwest* (2004), by Lea Rosson DeLong and others, which focuses on Wood's illustrations for a special edition of MAIN STREET (1920) by (HARRY) SINCLAIR LEWIS (1885–1951). In *Renegade Regionalists: The Modern Independence of Grant Wood, Thomas Hart Benton, and John Steuart Curry* (1998) James M. Dennis probes the "regional" label customarily affixed to these three artists. Debra Bricker Balken studies the conflict between Alfred Stieglitz's version of modernism and regionalism and the latter's sometimes fierce defenders in *After Many Springs: Regionalism, Modernism, and the Midwest* (2009). Modernism is also the subject of *Against the Grain: Modernism in the Midwest* (2010), the catalog of an exhibition curated by Christine Fowler Shearer at the Massillon Museum in Ohio.

For New Deal murals, three useful works are Karal Ann Marling's *Wall-to-Wall America: A Cultural History of Post-Office Murals in the Great Depression* (1982), Marlene Park and Gerald E. Markowitz's *Democratic Vistas: Post Offices and Public Art in the New Deal* (1984), and John C. Carlisle's *A Simple and Vital De-* sign: *The Story of the Indiana Post Office Murals* (1995). Two primary works of value for comprehending regionalist motivations and irritations are Grant Wood's *Revolt against the City* (1935) and Thomas Hart Benton's autobiography, *An Artist in America* (fourth revised edition, 1983). Among several studies of Charles Burchfield's Ohio years is *Charles Burchfield, 1920: The Architecture of Painting* (2009), from an exhibition organized by the D. C. Moore Gallery in New York. *The Paintings of Charles Burchfield: North by Midwest* (1997) by Nannette Maciejunes and Michael Hall is also of much interest.

Midwestern novelists occasionally find subject matter in the lives of artists. Four diverse examples are the Christian novel *Barriers Burned Away* (1872) by E. P. Roe (1838–1888), about two artists—one Christian, the other a skeptic—at the time of the Great Chicago Fire; *The "Genius"* (1915) by (HERMAN) THEODORE DREISER (1871–1945), who also wrote much on art and artists as a journalist; *Orchard* (2003), a novel of an artist's affair with his model, set in Door County, Wisconsin, by Larry Watson (1947–2010); and *Shadow Tag* (2010) by (KAREN) LOUISE ERDRICH (b. 1954), about conflict between a married couple, the wife a doctoral student pursuing a dissertation on artist George Catlin, her husband an artist whose nude portraits of her are intensely emotional.

Irving Stone (1903–1989), who also wrote biographical novels about Van Gogh and Michelangelo, wrote *The Passionate Journey* (1949), a novel about Kansas-born artist John Noble. (NEWTON) BOOTH TARKINGTON (1869–1946) had a personal art collection of some value and also used visual art and art museums in his writings, as in the novel *Image of Josephine* (1945). Finally, in *Paintings in Taxicabs: Characteristics of Certain Art Consumers* (1965) painter and poet Richard Lyons (1920–2000) studied the consumption of American art historically and linked it to Midwestern practices, most specifically in NORTH DAKOTA. See also ARCHITECTURE.

JOSEPH J. WYDEVEN   BELLEVUE UNIVERSITY

ASIAN AMERICAN LITERATURE

OVERVIEW: Midwestern Asian American literary studies reflect the concept of Asian American identity that emerged from the student movement of the late 1960s and early

1970s. At that time students of Asian heritage at West Coast universities forged a tentative political coalition, as documented by Yen Le Espiritu in *Asian American Panethnicity: Bridging Institutions and Identities* (1992) and further elaborated with reference to recent Cambodian immigration by Aihwa Ong in *Buddha Is Hiding: Refugees, Citizenship, the New America* (2003). The field has already passed through several reformulations of its foundational premises, enumerated by Eric Hayot in "The Asian Turns," *PMLA* 124.3 (May 2009): 906–17.

Asian American literature is not a single tradition but multiple literatures emanating from the disparate histories of immigrant communities. This entry will inventory Midwestern Asian American writing with respect to those distinct communities. The separate history of each community will be reviewed, the work of major authors will be described, and briefer mention will be made of other authors, particularly younger authors of great promise. The majority of Midwestern Asian American writers are contemporary authors who are still producing. Many younger writers are graduates of creative-writing programs at Midwestern colleges and universities; their best work may be yet to come. It should be evident that this is a developing literature that presents considerable opportunities for research.

HISTORY AND SIGNIFICANCE: The first Asian American settlers in the Midwest were descended from Chinese immigrants who began to arrive in numbers during the California gold rush. An economic downturn in the 1870s prompted discriminatory legislation that culminated in the Chinese Exclusion Act of 1882, which prohibited further immigration from China except by individuals who could produce paperwork proving American citizenship by birth or paternity, hence the ruse of "paper sons," the most common means for Chinese to enter the United States until the repeal of the Chinese Exclusion Act in 1943.

Li-Young Lee (b. 1957) is the most distinguished contemporary Chinese American writer. Born to parents exiled from China to Indonesia, he came to the United States with his family in 1964. Lee lives in CHICAGO, where some of his poems are set. He has published five volumes of poetry, and his

memoir, *The Winged Seed: A Remembrance* (1995), won the American Book Award. Other Midwestern Chinese American writers are Eleanor Wong Telemaque (b. 1934), Andrea Louie (b. 1966), Sherry Quan Lee (b. 1948), and William Franklin Wu (b. 1951).

Chinese American texts reflecting the Midwest include Telemaque's novel *It's Crazy to Stay Chinese in Minnesota* (1978), which deals with the teenaged protagonist's alienation in a small town near the MINNESOTA border with IOWA; Andrea Louie's *Moon Cakes* (1995), about a Chinese American girl from OHIO who takes a six-week tour of China to explore her cultural roots; Li-Young Lee's second collection of poetry, *The City in Which I Love You* (1990), a Lamont Poetry Selection; and Sherry Quan Lee's poetry collection *Chinese Blackbird* (2002).

Japanese immigrants also faced an exclusionary movement borne of nativism and xenophobia. The 1907 Gentlemen's Agreement curtailed most Japanese immigration until it was nullified by the Immigration Act of 1924, which banned all Asian immigration except by Filipinos. Because Japanese had generally immigrated as families rather than as solitary laborers, these restrictions resulted in distinct generational categories in Japanese American communities: the issei, comprising the immigrant generation arriving before 1924 and especially before 1907; the nisei, the second generation, born in the United States and, therefore, American citizens; and their children, the sansei. The most prominent Japanese American writer in the Midwest is David Mura (b. 1952), a sansei who was born in Chicago, was educated at Grinnell College, and has lived much of his life in Minnesota. Mura has published two memoirs, four books of poetry, two novels, and a volume of literary criticism. *Famous Suicides of the Japanese Empire* (2008), his novel about the lingering effects of Japanese American internment during World War II, received mixed reviews.

Also of note is Kyoko Mori (b. 1957), author of nonfiction and poetry as well as novels and adolescent fiction. Born in Kobe, Japan, Mori came to the United States in 1977 and lived for many years in WISCONSIN, a state that figures in much of her writing. Her book of essays, *Polite Lies: On Being a*

David Mura, ca. 1996. Photo by Doug
Beasley.
© David Mura

Woman Caught between Cultures (1998), explores nuanced experiences of language,
gender, and culture. She is on the creative
writing faculty at George Mason University.
Other Japanese American Midwestern writers are poets Dwight Holden Okita (b. 1958)
and Yuko Taniguchi (b. 1975). Poetry by
Japanese Americans in the Midwest includes Mura's *Angels for the Burning* (2004)
and Taniguchi's *Foreign Wife Elegy* (2004).
Mori's novel *Yarn: Remembering the Way Home*
(2009) narrates a woman's collapsing marriage while subtly contrasting Japanese and
Midwestern knitting styles.

Koreans first migrated to Hawaii for
plantation work but were not numerous
enough to establish stable mainland communities because of the Japanese annexa-
tion of Korea in 1910, which brought Koreans under the Gentlemen's Agreement.
Large-scale Korean immigration did not
occur until after the immigration reforms
of the Immigration and Nationality Act of
1965. Much Midwestern Korean American
writing consists of the adolescent fiction
and memoirs of Korean adoptees. An exception is poet Myung Mi Kim (b. 1957),
who came to the United States with her
family from South Korea and lived in
Oklahoma and SOUTH DAKOTA before settling
in Ohio. Kim earned her MFA at the IOWA
WRITERS' WORKSHOP at the University of

Iowa. She has published six volumes of po-
etry, including *Penury* (2009). Other Mid-
western Korean American writers include
Marie G. Lee (b. 1964), who also goes by
the name Marie Myung-ok Lee; Sung Jung
Rno (b. 1967); Jane Jeong Trenka (b. 1972);
Sun Yung Shin (b. 1974); and Ed-Bok Lee (b.
1974), whose first book, *Real Karaoke People:
Poems and Prose* (2005), won a PEN/Beyond
Margins Award.

Most immigration from South Asia has
taken place since the immigration reforms of
1965, resulting in a highly educated workforce consisting of teachers, doctors, and
engineers. BHARATI MUKHERJEE (b. 1940),
who spent five years studying in Iowa (1961–
1966), has been a sometime chronicler of
these immigrants and their heartbreaks. Her
novel *Jasmine* (1989) follows its female protagonist from India to Iowa, vividly evoking
both locations. Chicago is strongly present
in the poetry of A(ttipat) K(rishnaswami)
Ramanujan (1929–1993). A distinguished
linguistics scholar at the University of Chicago, Ramanujan brought nostalgia for India and sometimes humor to his poetry. His
Collected Poems (1995) includes the three volumes published during his lifetime, as well
as the volume he was working on at the time
of his death. Although Shauna Singh Baldwin (b. 1962) writes mainly about India and
Canada, the title story of her collection *We
Are Not in Pakistan* (2007) is set in Wisconsin;
other stories in this collection allude to
Wisconsin locales. Zilka Joseph (b. 1963) is a
poet from India who now lives in MICHIGAN
and has begun to gain recognition. She has
so far published three books of poetry, *Lands
I Live In* (2007), *What Dread* (2011), and *Sharp
Blue Search of Flame* (2016).

From 1900, when the Treaty of Paris concluded the American victory in the Spanish-
American War, to the establishment of the
Philippine Commonwealth in 1935, Filipino
laborers entered the U.S. mainland as American nationals rather than aliens. By 1930
there were more than 45,000, including
sizable numbers in ILLINOIS and Michigan.
Much of the short fiction, including the novellas, of BIENVENIDO N. SANTOS (1911–1996)
recapitulates the Filipino "Old Timers" as
well as his own experiences as student, exile,
and sojourner. The 1965 immigration reforms brought educated professionals, par-

ticularly doctors, nurses, and engineers, from the Philippines. Paul Stephen Lim (b. 1944) arrived in the United States from the Philippines in 1968 and earned his BA and MA at the University of Kansas, where he became a Professor of English focusing on drama. *Conpersonas* (1977), his first published play, won the award for best original script from the American College Theatre Festival. His short stories were published as *Some Arrivals but Mostly Departures* (1982).

Immigration from mainland Southeast Asia was stimulated by the fall of Saigon in April 1975. From a total of 604 Vietnamese in the United States in 1964, the population rose to 643,200 by 1985. The Orderly Departure Program, which ran from 1980 to 1999, enabled an additional 500,000 family members from Vietnam to join their relatives in the United States. Because American allies in Laos were also in peril, some 70,000 Lao, 60,000 Hmong, and 10,000 Mien immigrated to the United States as refugees. After 1980, Cambodians who had suffered under Pol Pot's regime and then the Vietnamese invasion began arriving as refugees and settled around the United States, particularly in the upper Midwest. The Vietnamese American, Lao American, Hmong American, and Cambodian American writers who have begun to tell of their collective experience are the children of the refugee generation.

The most notable of these younger writers are Lao American poet and playwright Bryan Thao Worra (b. 1973), Vietnamese American novelist Bich Minh Nguyen (b. 1974), and Hmong American playwright Ka Vang (b. 1975). Adopted in Laos by an American pilot, Worra grew up in locations around the United States, including St. Paul. See MINNEAPOLIS/ST. PAUL. He has published *On the Other Side of the Eye* (2007), a book of poems touching on his Lao identity and life in the Midwest. Nguyen, whose family fled Vietnam in 1975, grew up in Grand Rapids, Michigan, and earned an MFA at the University of Michigan, where she received the Hopwood Award for Poetry. She teaches creative writing at the University of San Francisco and formerly taught at Purdue. In her first novel, *Short Girls* (2009), which won the American Book Award, grown daughters submerge their lifelong hostility for one an-

other as they return home to Michigan for their father's citizenship celebration. Ka Vang grew up in a refugee camp in Thailand and settled in St. Paul. Her plays *Disconnect, Dead Calling,* and *From Shadows to Light* were staged in the Twin Cities early in the twenty-first century. She is a columnist for the weekly *Minnesota Women's Press* and a frequent contributor to the Hmong literary periodical *Paj Ntaub Voice.*

Much Midwestern Asian American writing consists of memoirs and personal narratives. David Mura has published two personal narratives, *Turning Japanese: Memoirs of a Sansei* (1991), which recounts his Fulbright year in Japan and his immersion in contemporary Japanese culture, and *Where the Body Meets Memory: An Odyssey of Race, Sexuality, and Memory* (1996). In 1997 Mura dramatized Li-Young Lee's lyrical memoir *The Winged Seed* (1995). *American Paper Son: A Chinese Immigrant in the Midwest* (2000) chronicles three decades in the early life of Wayne Hung Wong (b. 1922), who became a prominent Wichita businessman and philanthropist. Yi-Fu Tuan (b. 1930), a retired geographer from the Universities of Minnesota and Wisconsin, published his

Bich Minh Nguyen, 2013.
© Bich Ming Nguyen. Image courtesy of the author

memoir as *Coming Home to China* (2007). In *Dream of Water: A Memoir* (1995) Kyoto Mori (b. 1967) describes her alienation in Japan after years of living in Wisconsin. *One Asian Eye: Growing Up Eurasian in America* (2004) by Jean Giovanetti (b. 1967) is a memoir of the author's youth in CLEVELAND as the daughter of an Italian American father and a Korean immigrant mother. In *The Language of Blood: A Memoir* (2003) Jane Jeong Trenka (b. 1972) recalls her experience growing up as a Korean adoptee in Minnesota. Other notable memoirs are *Bento Box in the Heartland: My Japanese Girlhood in Whitebread America* (2006) by Linda Furiya (b. 1966), *Stealing Buddha's Dinner: A Memoir* (2007) by Bich Minh Nguyen, *The Latehomecomer: A Hmong Family Memoir* (2008) by Kao Kalia Yang (b. 1980), and *The Good Hmong Girl Eats Raw Laab* (2012) by Ka Vang.

SELECTED WORKS: Contemporary Midwestern Asian American poetry forms a growing and accessible body of work. Especially recommended are Li-Young Lee's *The City in Which I Love You* (1990) and Sherry Quan Lee's *Chinese Blackbird* (2002). Also worthwhile are David Mura's *Angels for the Burning* (2004) and Myung Mi Kim's *Penury* (2009).

Bienvenido N. Santos best captured the poignancy and pathos of the Filipino "Old Timers" in his short stories collected in the volume *Scent of Apples* (1979). *Yarn: Remembering the Way Home* (2009) by Kyoto Mori and *Jasmine* (1989) by Bharati Mukherjee are two novels that portray immigrant women coping with life and memory in a strange land.

No anthology of Midwestern writing spans the spectrum of Asian American ethnicities. However, an anthology of women's experiences in the Midwest is *Voices of the Heart: Asian American Women on Immigration, Work, and Family* (2007), edited by Huping Ling. *Bamboo among the Oaks: Contemporary Writing by Hmong Americans* (2002), edited by Mai Neng Moua, a founder of *Paj Ntaub Voice,* encompasses a broad selection of emerging writers, mostly from the upper Midwest.

FURTHER READING: In "East of California: Points of Origin in Asian American Studies," *Journal of Asian American Studies* 1.1 (February 1998): 83–100, Stephen H. Sumida deals with Asian American texts and

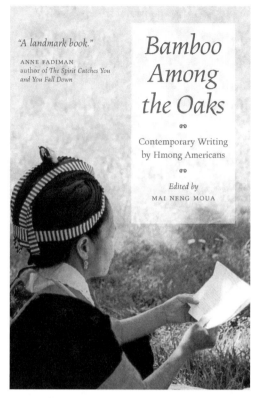

Bamboo among the Oaks, Hmong American anthology, 2002.
© Minnesota Historical Society, 2002. Photo courtesy of Minnesota Historical Society Press

experience in the Midwest going back to the early 1800s.

Among writers discussed in this entry, Li-Young Lee has attracted the most scholarly attention; the MLA database lists more than thirty articles and interviews. Earl G. Ingersoll has edited *Breaking the Alabaster Jar: Conversations with Li-Young Lee* (2006). Scholars have also started examining the work of David Mura. Xiaojing Zhou, for example, has published "David Mura's Poetics of Identity," *MELUS* 23.3 (Fall 1998): 145–66. For secondary sources on emerging writers, internet search engines and author websites remain the best option.

ROGER BRESNAHAN   MICHIGAN STATE UNIVERSITY

AUTOBIOGRAPHY

OVERVIEW: Reading autobiography is useful in understanding and interpreting the Midwest, for autobiography writers with

Midwestern roots or affiliations often reveal qualities of Midwesternness in their experiences of the region. Autobiography illustrates the intersection of personal lives with history in specific places, but the motives for writing autobiography are diverse. These motives may include a desire to relive the past, to correct public perception or biographical data, to justify oneself, or simply to create works of artistic beauty. In the last quarter century the study of autobiography has intensified, and the stories told, often with exaggerations, evasions, and omissions, have come under ever-closer scrutiny.

Although autobiography takes many forms, this entry will focus primarily on narrative works by Midwestern writers that offer a reasonably full account of their personal lives. Also included are memoirs of people and places, as well as journals and diaries, when these yield substantial information. The entry addresses not only works of literary artists but also selected nonfiction works that reveal Midwestern experience. Autobiography embedded in fiction is rarely included simply because claims that specific novelists or poets are autobiographical are too ubiquitous to be useful.

The entry considers a sampling of autobiographies from the Midwestern frontier, followed by longer sections on full formal autobiographies by literary figures, works focused only on Midwestern childhoods, works on specific Midwestern topics, and finally, ethnic autobiographies. Because so many Midwestern authors have written autobiographies and memoirs, this entry is necessarily selective, and subtitles are given only when they provide essential information.

HISTORY AND SIGNIFICANCE: Midwesterners have been interested in telling their personal stories for many reasons. The autobiographies most relevant to this entry are those that reveal aspects of social life and culture in given periods. As a group, they provide clues to the record of Midwestern history as lived by diverse individuals.

The first personal approaches to Midwestern experience appeared in journalistic accounts of hard journeys into the interior, although these are often only marginally autobiographical. Among early travel accounts that pay some attention to the authors' personal affairs are *A Journey to Ohio in 1810* (1912) by Margaret Van Horn Dwight (1790–1834), containing her sprightly observations as she made her arduous way into a sparsely inhabited territory; a series of letters by Timothy Flint (1780–1840) published as *Recollections of the Last Ten Years, Passed in Occasional Residences and Journeyings in the Valley of the Mississippi* (1826); and *Letters from the West* (1828) by James Hall (1793–1868), capturing life along the Ohio River in 1820.

The first formal autobiographies from the Midwest were written by Christian ministers and often combined personal experience with observations on social and religious manners. A fascinating account is the *Autobiography of Rev. James B. Finley; or, Pioneer Life in the West* (1853) by James B. Finley (1781–1856), which pictures an OHIO "redolent as Eden" and provides rich details on relations between whites and Indians and the settlement of Chillicothe (107). Another work is the *Autobiography of Peter Cartwright* (1856), which recounts sojourns in southern and Midwestern frontiers of preacher Peter Cartwright (1785–1872). A third, an important source for the novels of EDWARD EGGLESTON (1837–1902), is *Autobiography of a Pioneer* (1859) by Jacob Young (1776–1859); it tells of his life as a boy and later as an itinerant preacher. These works often combine detailed information concerning missionary activity with descriptions of difficult travel and exuberance for the newly discovered sections of the country.

An excellent autobiography about frontier life is *Recollections of Life in Ohio, from 1813 to 1840* (1895) by William Cooper Howells (1807–1894), written at the encouragement of his famous literary son, WILLIAM DEAN HOWELLS (1837–1920). Howells intimately describes his world, including observations on immigrants rafting down the Ohio, enthusiastic religious practices, the easy availability of alcohol, the problem of slavery, and the beginnings of journalism in frontier settings.

Women's autobiographical accounts of frontier conditions are particularly interesting for their depictions of the consequences of change on homemakers and mothers and their understanding of frontier democracy as a complex social leveler. *A NEW HOME— WHO'LL FOLLOW?* (1839) by CAROLINE KIRKLAND

(1801–1864), now considered an autobiographical novel, is perhaps the best-known Midwestern wilderness account by a woman. *Life in Prairie Land* (1846) by ELIZA FARNHAM (1815–1864) depicts frontier life in ILLINOIS; Farnham's humor is acerbic, and her powers of observation are acute as she surveys social and natural aspects of her new environment. The collection *Mother Theodore Guerin: Journals and Letters* (1937) presents the perspective of a Catholic nun on the frontier. Sister Theodore Guerin (1798–1856) traveled from France in 1840 to found the Sisters of Providence at St. Mary-of-the-Woods, INDIANA.

Autobiographies from frontiers west of the Missouri River are of interest for the light they cast on transitions between Midwestern and western frontiers and settlements. An important example is *The Life of Hon. William F. Cody, Known as Buffalo Bill, the Famous Hunter, Scout and Guide: An Autobiography* (1879), presumably by Buffalo Bill Cody (1846–1917), although authorship and veracity remain debatable. Cody's story presents a dynamic plains frontier in which Indians, whites, and slaves intermingle. Another example is *Buckskin and Blanket Days: Memoirs of a Friend of the Indians Written in 1905* (1957) by Thomas Henry Tibbles (1840–1928), which is especially valuable for its focus on the condition of the NEBRASKA tribes and on backgrounds of the 1879 trial of Standing Bear (1834–1908), a Ponca Indian chief, which established Native Americans as legal persons.

Several memorable works describe homestead conditions in the western Midwest. *Old Jules* (1935) by MARI(E SUSETTE) SANDOZ (1896–1966) is a powerful memoir of her father that depicts the harsh conditions in which early western development took place; *Sandhill Sundays and Other Recollections* (1970) is an excellent supplement. The autobiographical *Little House* books of LAURA INGALLS WILDER (1867–1957) portray homestead and town life; also revealing is Wilder's *On the Way Home: The Diary of a Trip from South Dakota to Mansfield, Missouri, in 1894* (1962).

The most important classification in this entry is Midwestern literary autobiography strictly understood, works by established writers who are important in the development of Midwestern literature. These works,

usually written toward the end of writing careers, often focus on the influences affecting the authors' perspectives. A good starting point is an examination of five celebrated writers at the core of the Midwestern canon; these writers were the most avid autobiographers, and in some, determining authenticity or establishing a critical text has proved difficult.

The case of SAMUEL LANGHORNE CLEMENS (1835–1910), writing as Mark Twain, is particularly intriguing because a definitive text has proved elusive. Two early semi-autobiographical works, *Innocents Abroad* (1869) and *Roughing It* (1872), used Twain's experiences as the basis for journalistic commentary. A decade later Twain included memories of boyhood and youth in *Life on the Mississippi* (1883). But when he attempted a full formal autobiography, Twain was indecisive. He seemed happiest when he was freed of chronological obligations and was able to range at will over memories of his lifetime. The result was a sprawling manuscript that incorporated letters, fictional works, and newspaper clippings. In 1906–1907 Twain published some portions, which later appeared in book form as *Mark Twain's Own Autobiography* (1990), edited by Michael J. Kiskis. *Mark Twain's Autobiography* (1924) was presented in two volumes by Albert Bigelow Paine; it adhered to Twain's theory that inspiration trumped chronology and some chapters were omitted at the request of Twain's daughter. In 1940 Bernard DeVoto incorporated fresh materials in *Mark Twain in Eruption*. Charles Neider edited *The Autobiography of Mark Twain: Including Chapters Now Published for the First Time* (1959); this volume has been criticized precisely because it rearranged Twain's material chronologically.

Finally, the three-volume *Autobiography of Mark Twain*, edited by Harriet Elinor Smith and Benjamin Griffin, was issued from 2010 to 2015. Smith writes in her introduction that "no [prior] text of the *Autobiography* so far published is even remotely complete, much less completely authorial. It is therefore the goal of the present edition to publish the complete text as nearly as possible in the way Mark Twain intended it to be published after his death" (volume 1, 4). This complete and unexpurgated edition restores the personal opinions that had been withheld from print for a century. A *New York Times* best seller, this latest *Autobiography* has been very well received by the reading public.

William Dean Howells, frequently a party to Mark Twain's indecisions, was more orderly in his approach to autobiography. Howells revisited his Ohio past several times in the 1890s, offering congenial portraits of post-pioneer life in *A Boy's Town* (1890), *My Year in a Log Cabin* (1893), and *My Literary Passions* (1895). The last and best, *Years of My Youth* (1916), focuses on Howells's days in Ohio, from his birth to his departure for his Venice consulship. Filled with references to his earlier memoirs, this late work seems intent on filling in gaps and reliving his youth.

A special note is necessary on Howells's *A Boy's Town*, one of the first in a genre Marcia Jacobson, in *Being a Boy Again: Autobiography and the American Boy Book* (1994), says provides "an entertaining and sometimes sentimentalized picture of a bygone age" (6). Howells never gives his protagonist a name other than "my boy" and claims that "every boy is two or three boys, or twenty or thirty different kinds of boys in one"—a happily construed mythical creature (171). As will be seen later, several other Midwestern writers appreciated this genre, which allowed them to wax eloquently nostalgic about their childhoods in exciting regions of the frontier.

(HANNIBAL) HAMLIN GARLAND (1860–1940) was another important Midwestern writer gripped by autobiography. The early *Boy Life on the Prairie* (1899) is a boy book, and many of the stories told there are retold in *A Son of the Middle Border* (1917), Garland's account of growing up on the agricultural frontiers of WISCONSIN, IOWA, and SOUTH DAKOTA. Garland dramatically details his father's drive for land, his mother's reluctance, and his own youthful dreams. The story continues in *A Daughter of the Middle Border* (1921), featuring Garland's marriage and the development of his writing career. Also of autobiographical interest are *Trail-Makers of the Middle Border* (1926), *Back-Trailers from the Middle Border* (1928), *Roadside Meetings* (1930), *Companions on the Trail* (1931), *My Friendly Contemporaries* (1932), and *Afternoon Neighbors* (1934).

(HERMAN) THEODORE DREISER (1871–1945) was also intensely attracted to telling his life story. His enthusiasm is found first in *A Traveler at Forty* (1913), describing a five-month trip to Europe, and *A Hoosier Holiday* (1916), narrating Dreiser's trip from New York to Indiana and presenting an intimate view of the conditions of automobile travel in 1915, as well as Dreiser's nostalgia and regret in revisiting his Indiana childhood houses. The history of Dreiser's subsequent full-blown autobiography is tangled, partially because of the sexual explicitness that unnerved his publishers. Dreiser completed the first volume by 1916 but decided against publication because of its too-revealing content until it was ultimately published as *Dawn* in 1931. A second volume, *A Book about Myself*, was published in 1922 and then was reissued with Dreiser's preferred title, *Newspaper Days*, in 1931. The University of Pennsylvania Press offered a restored *Newspaper Days* in 1991. *American Diaries, 1902–1926* (1982) added yet more information on Dreiser.

SHERWOOD ANDERSON (1876–1941) is a special case as an autobiographer because of his insistence that as a storyteller he should not be expected to tell the truth. Instead of literal truth, Anderson provided the felt sense of his experiences. He told his story three times over two decades. The first attempt, *A Story Teller's Story* (1924), has proved largely unreliable as a source of biographical information. The second, *Tar: A Midwest Childhood* (1926), is another example of a boy book. Anderson first called it "A Mid-American Childhood" and "Tar: The Story of a Mid-American Childhood"; the book is admirably complex because Anderson attempted to reproduce his protagonist's tentative thinking processes. In 1969 Ray Lewis White provided a possibly definitive critical edition, *Tar: A Midwest Childhood; A Critical Text*, edited from the original manuscripts. Anderson's final attempt at memoir was *Sherwood Anderson's Memoirs* (1942), the most detailed and thorough account. This book also had a history: initially encouraged by his fourth wife, Eleanor Copenhaver Anderson, he wrote these memoirs between 1933 and 1941 but left the manuscript unfinished at his death. Paul Rosenfeld edited the ultimate volume but modified the original documents to make them more accessible.

These examples suggest the difficulties of determining authenticity and truth in autobiography. No doubt the fame of the authors has much to do with the intensive scholarly attention their personal stories have generated. That kind of attention has rarely been given to the autobiographies in the next section. Presented in roughly chronological order, the following autobiographical works by Midwestern writers share a general intention to provide a comprehensive, if necessarily selective, overview of the subjects' entire lives.

One of the first is by LEW(IS) WALLACE (1827–1905), *Lew Wallace: An Autobiography* (1906), the first volume of which provides the Indiana backgrounds of this robust figure who became a Civil War general and wrote *Ben-Hur* (1880). Also from Indiana is GEORGE CARY EGGLESTON (1839–1911), whose *Recollections of a Varied Life* (1910) describe an assortment of careers: Confederate soldier, lawyer, journalist, editor, and novelist. As a frustrated teacher, he supplied literary materials for *The Hoosier School-Master* (1871) by his brother, Edward Eggleston. Iowan (JOHN) HERBERT QUICK (1861–1925) describes his first thirty years in *One Man's Life* (1925) and details his gradual education in literature and politics and his fascination with *Progress and Poverty* (1879) by Henry George (1839–1897). In his jaunty *Son of the Forests, an Autobiography* (1930) JAMES OLIVER CURWOOD (1878–1927) tells how he came to write adventure novels and reveals aspects of university life, newspaper life in DETROIT, and the life of a writer as professional journeyman.

Autobiographies by writers known primarily as journalists include two revealing works from KANSAS. The first is *Plain People* (1929) by E(DGAR) W(ATSON) HOWE (1853–1937), who edited the *Atchison Globe* for thirty years, published *E. W. Howe's Monthly* for another twenty, and wrote an important Midwestern novel of disillusionment, *Story of a Country Town* (1883). The second is *The Autobiography of William Allen White* (1946) by WILLIAM ALLEN WHITE (1868–1944), perhaps the most important book about the newspaper business and its links to Midwestern politics and history. White published and edited the *Emporia Gazette* for fifty years; his famous editorial "What's the Matter with Kansas?" first appeared there on August 15, 1896.

Other journalistic autobiographies include *I Remember* (1930) by OPIE PERCIVAL (POPE) READ (1852–1939), who recalls CHICAGO at the time of the Columbian Exposition and the journalists who congregated at the Press Club. Two important literary editors at the *Chicago Tribune* contributed personal works that highlight the city's culture: (ARTHUR) BURTON RASCOE (1892–1957), best known for his contentious reviews and support of Midwestern writers, wrote *Before I Forget* (1937) and *We Were Interrupted* (1947). Fanny Butcher (1888–1987), another Chicago fixture, was the author of *Many Loves—One Love* (1972), covering her long career at the *Tribune* and providing portraits of her literary friends. (ARNOLD) ERIC SEVAREID (1912–1992), best known as a CBS radio and television commentator, discusses his Midwestern development in *Not So Wild a Dream* (1946) and *This Is Eric Sevareid* (1964).

The Story of My Life (1932) by CLARENCE (SEWARD) DARROW (1857–1938) is devoted almost entirely to Darrow's career as a lawyer, including important names such as Eugene V. Debs, Nathan Leopold and Richard Loeb, and Darrow's antagonist in the Scopes trial, WILLIAM JENNINGS BRYAN (1860–1925); earlier, Darrow wrote a boy book, *Farmington* (1904). MARY (HUNTER) AUSTIN (1868–1934) employed interesting experimental devices to convey nuances in her psychological development in *Earth Horizon* (1932), the first half of which is set largely in Carlinville, Illinois; Austin richly details Midwestern social history and manners.

The candid *Homecoming: An Autobiography* (1933) by FLOYD DELL (1887–1969) is an important work. Dell, author of *Moon-Calf* (1920), knew many Midwestern literary figures of his time, as well as political writers like Jack Reed (1887–1920) and Randolph Bourne (1886–1918); edited the *Friday Literary Review* and *The Masses;* was a proponent of psychoanalysis; and played major roles in the CHICAGO RENAISSANCE and literary socialism. One of the most puzzling Midwestern autobiographies is *Across Spoon River* (1936) by EDGAR LEE MASTERS (1868–1950), which details the Midwestern literary resurgence and offers acute portraits of contemporaries while exhibiting the querulous disposition of a lawyer and poet who often saw himself as a victim of circumstances.

CARL (CLINTON) VAN DOREN (1895–1950), born in Hope, Illinois, wrote *Three Worlds* (1936), reporting his thoroughly Midwestern life in village and on farm before attending the University of Illinois and Columbia University and then working for the *Nation.* Van Doren recognized that American writers after World War I—including Midwesterners Masters, WILLA CATHER (1873–1947), Dreiser, (HARRY) SINCLAIR LEWIS (1885–1951), F(RANCIS) SCOTT (KEY) FITZGERALD (1896–1940), and ERNEST (MILLER) HEMINGWAY (1899–1961)—represented a new phenomenon; equally important is his diagnosis in "The Revolt from the Village: 1920," published in the *Nation* 113 (October 12, 1921): 407–12. See THE REVOLT FROM THE VILLAGE. His younger brother, the equable poet and teacher MARK VAN DOREN (1894–1972), contributed *The Autobiography of Mark Van Doren* (1958), chapters of which complement Carl's account of serene childhood. ORRICK JOHNS (1887–1946), believing that autobiography should include "a criticism of its times," contributed *Time of Our Lives* (1937), a rich historical document about his father's career at the *St. Louis Post-Dispatch* and his own involvement in journalism, the arts, and radical politics.

Several autobiographies from Chicago suggest the importance of the metropolis to the spirit and energy of Midwestern culture. An essential work is *Twenty Years at Hull-House* (1910) by JANE ADDAMS (1860–1935), which describes Addams's education and her social activism, in which the arts were intended to serve as amelioration. HARRIET MONROE (1860–1936), founder of *POETRY, A MAGAZINE OF VERSE*, contributed *A Poet's Life* (1938), which provides a broad view of the city and the Chicago Renaissance. An associate editor at *Poetry*, EUNICE (HAMMOND) TIETJENS (1884–1944) wrote *The World at My Shoulder* (1938). MARGARET C. ANDERSON (1886–1973), founder of *THE LITTLE REVIEW*, which competed with and complemented Monroe's *Poetry*, describes her bohemian life in *My Thirty Years' War* (1930); other autobiographical works by Margaret Anderson include *The Fiery Fountain* (1951), *The Unknowable Gurdjieff* (1962), and *The Strange*

Necessity (1969). *All Our Years* (1948) explains the role of ROBERT MORSS LOVETT (1870–1956) as a literary force, professor at the University of Chicago, supporter of the Chicago Renaissance, and resident at HULL-HOUSE.

In *A Peculiar Treasure* (1939) EDNA FERBER (1885–1968) provides a lively account of her upbringing in various Midwestern cities, her entry into journalism with the *Appleton Crescent,* and her creation of the character Emma McChesney; a second volume, *A Kind of Magic,* followed in 1963. RAY STANNARD BAKER (1870–1946) discusses his Wisconsin childhood in *Native American* (1941), and in *American Chronicle* (1945) he describes being a muckraking journalist in Chicago before moving on to *McClure's* and a close relationship with Woodrow Wilson. *Anatomy of Me* (1958) by FANNIE HURST (1885–1968) is rich in drama; childhood memories in Hamilton, Ohio, and ST. LOUIS are sprinkled throughout.

VERA CASPARY (1904–1987), most famous for the mystery novel *Laura* (1943), wrote *The Secrets of Grown-Ups* (1979); in early chapters she recalls growing up in Chicago. Novelist and photographer WRIGHT MORRIS (1910–1998) speaks with nostalgic exuberance about his childhood and adolescence in *Will's Boy* (1981) and *Solo: An American Dreamer in Europe, 1933–1934* (1983); "Photography in My Life," from *Photographs and Words* (1982), also found its way into *A Cloak of Light* (1985). Black Sparrow Press published all three works in one volume, *Writing My Life: An Autobiography* (1993). JIM (JAMES THOMAS) HARRISON (1937–2016) focuses on themes in his life rather than chronological sequence in *Off to the Side* (2002); autobiographical essays are also found in Harrison's *Just before Dark* (1991).

Many Midwestern autobiographies deal specifically with the authors' childhoods, suggesting that they saw childhood as the best and most formatively eventful period of life. In *Buckeye Boyhood* (1911), another boy book, WILLIAM HENRY VENABLE (1836–1920) remembers, through a protagonist named Tip, his life from 1836 to 1858. Describing his kind of memoir in the preface to *MY LIFE AND HARD TIMES* (1933) as a "manifestation of a twitchiness at once cosmic and mundane" (1986 Bantam edition, 10), JAMES

(GROVER) THURBER (1894–1961) tells boisterous comic tales of his childhood in Columbus, Ohio. In *The Age of Indiscretion* (1950) CLYDE BRION DAVIS (1894–1962) tells of his youth in Chillicothe, MISSOURI, attempting to refute the pronouncements on the decline of culture by T(HOMAS) S(TEARNS) ELIOT (1888–1965). *Time to Remember* (1951) nostalgically recalls the Ohio and Indiana boyhood of LLOYD C(ASSEL) DOUGLAS (1877–1951). *Always the Young Strangers* (1953) by CARL (AUGUST) SANDBURG (1878–1867) is a richly remembered account of the poet and Lincoln biographer's first twenty years, including a variety of jobs and the travel that widened his perceptions of American life.

The House on Jefferson Street (1971) by Horace Gregory (1898–1982) is an evocation of the impact of Milwaukee on the burgeoning poet and critic. JOHN G(NEISENAU) NEIHARDT (1881–1973) recalls his youth in *All Is but a Beginning: Youth Remembered, 1881–1901* (1972), a work continued in *Patterns and Coincidences* (1978). SUSAN ALLEN TOTH (b. 1940) writes memorably of growing up in Ames, Iowa in *Blooming: A Small-Town Girlhood* (1981), and later of college life in *Ivy Days: Making My Way out East* (1984). PAUL (HAMILTON) ENGLE (1908–1991) describes life in Cedar Rapids in *A Lucky American Childhood* (1996). WILLIAM (CHARLES) KLOEFKORN (1932–2011) wrote four memoirs, based on the four elements of earth, air, fire, and water: *This Death by Drowning* (1997), *Restoring the Burnt Child* (2003), *At Home on This Moveable Earth* (2006), and *Breathing in the Fullness of Time* (2009).

Midwestern autobiographies of farm and small-town life are numerous, and many are devoted to the impact of memories on adults who make nostalgic returns. LOUIS BROMFIELD (1896–1956) created several works that combine autobiography with philosophical reflections on nature and his Malabar Farm, especially *Pleasant Valley* (1945) and *From My Experience* (1955). CURTIS (ARTHUR) HARNACK (1927–2013) affectionately remembers his Iowa family's homestead life in *We Have All Gone Away* (1973) and *The Attic* (1993). Elements of autobiography in small-town MINNESOTA appear in *Lake Wobegon Days* (1985) by GARY EDWARD KEILLOR (b. 1942), writing as Garrison Keillor; of special interest is his *Homegrown Democrat* (2004). *Fugitive Spring* (1991) is an account by poet Deborah Digges

(1950–2009) of her Missouri girlhood in the 1950s and 1960s. Digges's *The Stardust Lounge: Stories from a Boy's Adolescence* (2001) is a memoir of her troubled son. Haven Kimmel (b. 1965) humorously explores her small-town childhood in *A Girl Named Zippy* (2001) and *She Got Up off the Couch: And Other Heroic Acts from Mooreland, Indiana* (2006). Two powerful memoirs of return attempt to come to terms with the meanings embedded in Midwestern roots: *Prairie Reunion* (1995) takes Barbara Scot (b. 1942) back to Scotch Grove, Iowa, where she reexamines her family history and her childhood within it; *Portable Prairie: Confessions of an Unsettled Midwesterner* (2005) carries M. J. Andersen (b. 1955) back to South Dakota.

Remembering Mark Twain, George Byron Merrick (1841–1931) contributed *Old Times on the Upper Mississippi: The Recollections of a Steamboat Pilot from 1854 to 1863* (1909). *If School Keeps* (1940) describes the experiences of PHIL(IP) (DUFFIELD) STONG (1899–1957) as student, high school teacher, and professor. The eight autobiographical essays in *The Crack-Up* (1945) by F(RANCIS) SCOTT (KEY) FITZGERALD (1896–1940) are powerful pieces about despair and burnout; also important is *Afternoon of an Author* (1957). *Down in My Heart* (1947) by WILLIAM STAFFORD (1914–1993) is an account of service as a conscientious objector during World War II. *A Memoir* (1952) concerns the childhood of RUTH SUCKOW (1892–1960) as a Congregationalist minister's daughter in Iowa and her attempt to overturn some stereotypes the image suggests. FINLEY PETER DUNNE (1867–1936) provides myriad reasons for not writing autobiography in "On Biography and Related Subjects" from *Mr. Dooley Remembers* (1963). Ernest Hemingway, author of much autobiographical fiction, remembers life in 1920s Paris in *A Moveable Feast* (1965). EDMUND G(EORGE) LOVE (1912–1990) wrote the charming *The Situation in Flushing* (1965), recalling his boyhood infatuation with the railroads running though his hometown; *Hanging On; or, How to Get through a Depression and Enjoy Life* (1972) discusses Love's college years in Ann Arbor and the effects of the Depression on Flint, Michigan.

All the Strange Hours (1975) by anthropologist-essayist-poet Loren (Corey) Eiseley (1907–1977) features sensitive autobiographical essays that connect dramatic events in his life to the long view of nature. In writing *Talking to Myself: A Memoir of My Times* (1977), (LOUIS) STUDS TERKEL (1912–2008) turned his famous interview approach on himself. *The Wind Blows Free: A Reminiscence* (1979) and *Prime Fathers* (1988) provide clues to the career of Minnesota novelist FREDERICK MANFRED (b. Feike Feikema, 1912–1994), including memories of influential role models.

In *A Hole in the World* (1990) Richard Rhodes (b. 1937) focuses on the absence of a mother in his Missouri childhood and the abuse he and his brother suffered before their rescue. In *Reports of My Death* (1990) KARL SHAPIRO (1913–2000) discusses his stint at the Library of Congress, his editorship of *Poetry,* and his decade at the University of Nebraska as editor of *Prairie Schooner.* JOSEPHINE (FREY) HERBST (1892–1969) contributed *The Starched Blue Sky of Spain, and Other Memoirs* (1991) on her life in radical literary politics. RUTH SEID (1913–1995), writing as Jo Sinclair, describes her relationship with mentor Helen Buchman in *The Seasons: Death and Transfiguration* (1993). Edmund White (b. 1940), noted gay novelist who grew up in CINCINNATI and Chicago and was a student in MICHIGAN, has published three memoirs: *Our Paris: Sketches from Memory* (1995), *My Lives* (2005), and *City Boy* (2009).

An account of life on the automobile assembly line at General Motors in Flint, Michigan, is found in *Rivethead: Tales from the Assembly Line* (1991) by Ben Hamper (b. 1956). Cheri Register (b. 1945) discusses her Minnesota working-class childhood in *Packinghouse Daughter* (2000). *What I Think I Did: A Season of Survival in Two Acts* (2000), the first of three projected volumes by LARRY (ALFRED) WOIWODE (b. 1941), focuses equally on the NORTH DAKOTA winter of 1996 and on Woiwode's coming of age as actor and writer, including relationships with actor Robert DeNiro and *New Yorker* editor William Maxwell; Woiwode's *A Step from Death: A Memoir* followed in 2008. Ted Kooser (b. 1939), U.S. Poet Laureate in 2004–2006, contributed *Local Wonders: Seasons in the Bohemian Alps* (2002) and *Lights on a Ground of Darkness* (2009) concerning country life in Nebraska and Iowa. Kooser's general approach is to focus gently on his experiences and the people he

Local Wonders by **Ted Kooser**
© University of Nebraska Press, 2002. Reproduced by permission

knew and with whom he currently lives in his community.

Critics have lauded the best-selling volume 1 of *Chronicles* (2004), by Bob Dylan (b. 1941) for its literary qualities. Intended as the first part of a projected three-volume memoir, the book jumps back and forth in time, paying considerable attention to the singer's early years in Minnesota, his development into the most celebrated lyricist of the 1960s, and his contact with cultural figures like poet ARCHIBALD MACLEISH (1892–1982).

Two works by Newbery Medal winners who wrote and illustrated children's books, some depicting Midwestern scenes and characters, are *Butter at the Old Price* (1971) by MARGUERITE (LOFFT) DE ANGELI (1889–1987) and *Journey into Childhood* (1972) by LOIS (LENORE) LENSKI (1893–1974). Two works that intimately connect the Midwestern identities of women with European kin are *In Search* of *Susanna* (1996) by Suzanne L. Bunkers (b. 1950) and *A Romantic Education* (1981) by PATRICIA HAMPL (b. 1946). Hampl has written several other memoirs, including *Virgin Time* (1992), concerning her quest for faith, and *The Florist's Daughter* (2007).

Architects LOUIS (HENRI) SULLIVAN (1856–1924) and FRANK LLOYD WRIGHT (1867–1959) left important personal records. Sullivan's *The Autobiography of an Idea* (1924) highlights his observations on the extravagant development of Chicago and the dynamic growth of the city's architecture after the fire of 1871. *An Autobiography: Frank Lloyd Wright* (1932) is a key document about the Prairie school and Taliesin, Wright's famous home in Spring Green, Wisconsin, as well as a revealing account of Wright's often difficult personal life. The autobiography of another architect, Irving K. Pond (1857–1939), important for his work at Hull-House and on Midwestern college campuses, remained unpublished until 2009: *The Autobiography of Irving K. Pond: The Sons of Mary and Elihu*.

Patricia Hampl, 2005. Photo by Barry Goldstein.
© Patricia Hampl, 2005

The diaries in *Growing Pains: Diaries and Drawings for the Years 1908–1917* (1940) by WANDA (HAZEL) GÁG (1893–1946) provide a rich sense of growing up in an artistic family in Minnesota. *An Artist in America* (1937; fourth revised edition, 1983) by the scrappy Thomas Hart Benton (1889–1975) evokes sometimes contradictory aspects of the twentieth-century American social world in which the arts sought a hearing.

Native American autobiographies are found frequently in the Midwestern canon; many were written to overcome stereotypes and educate whites about the reality of Native American life. Perhaps the earliest, first published as *LIFE OF MA-KA-TAI-ME-SHE-KIA-KIAK, OR BLACK HAWK* (1833), by Sauk warrior BLACK HAWK (1767–1838), is an important account of the ambiguities accompanying Caucasian Native American relations on a dynamic frontier and of narrowing horizons for central Midwestern tribes, culminating in the Black Hawk War of 1832. This autobiography, translated by a mixed-blood interpreter and edited by a Caucasian, highlights many of the problems inherent in determining authorial authenticity. Perhaps better known is the autobiographical *BLACK ELK SPEAKS* (1932), dictated by BLACK ELK (1863–1950) to the white poet John G(neisenau) Neihardt; the extent of Neihardt's intervention in the text is still debated. Two ethnographic autobiographies offer significant detail about tribal mores. *The Autobiography of a Winnebago Indian* (1920), edited and translated by Paul Radin, is an account by Sam Blowsnake (Hágaga; Ho-Chunk, 1875–1965) that is of interest for its views of religious ceremonies and conflicts between Christianity and the peyote cult. *Crashing Thunder: The Autobiography of an American Indian* (1926) is Radin's reworking of Blowsnake's memoir, with Blowsnake's name replaced with that of his brother, Crashing Thunder. *Mountain Wolf Woman, Sister of Crashing Thunder: The Autobiography of a Winnebago Indian* (1961) details the domestic life and travels of Blowsnake's sister, Mountain Wolf Woman (1884–1960), in Wisconsin and Nebraska. See NATIVE AMERICAN LITERATURE.

A lively insider account of life in a Christian mission school is *The Middle Five: Indian Schoolboys of the Omaha Tribe* (1900) by Francis La Flesche (1857–1932). Autobiographical essays from the female point of view are presented by Yankton Sioux ZITKALA-ŠA (RED BIRD) (1876–1938) in *American Indian Stories* (1921), originally printed in the *Atlantic Monthly* and *Harper's* in 1900–1901. CHARLES ALEXANDER EASTMAN (1858–1939), a physician at the Pine Ridge agency and witness to the Ghost Dance movement, tells of his early life in *Indian Boyhood* (1902) and of the transition from the "free wilderness life" to assimilation in *From the Deep Woods to Civilization: Chapters in the Autobiography of an Indian* (1916) (xvii). In *My People the Sioux* (1928) LUTHER STANDING BEAR (1868–1939) confronts white stereotypes and discusses the impact of white intrusion into Sioux territories. He wrote *My Indian Boyhood* (1931) primarily for white children. More recent works are *Choteau Creek* (1992) by Joseph Iron Eye Dudley (b. 1940), a memoir of life with his grandparents on the Yankton Reservation; and *Black Eagle Child: The Facepaint Narratives* (1992) by Mesquakie RAY (ANTHONY) YOUNG BEAR (b. 1950), a poetic narrative told through several personae and providing insights into Young Bear's personal life as well as the history of his people. Novelist and poet (KAREN) LOUISE ERDRICH (b. 1954) describes her life as a new mother in *The Blue Jay's Dance* (1995).

Richard Erdoes (1912–2008) collaborated with Native Americans on several autobiographical works that have received considerable attention: *Lame Deer, Seeker of Visions* (1972) with John Fire/Lame Deer (ca. 1903–1976), *Lakota Woman* (1990) with Mary Crow Dog (1954–2013), and *Crow Dog: Four Generations of Sioux Medicine Men* (1995) with Leonard Crow Dog (b. 1942). Mary and Leonard Crow Dog were political activists in the American Indian Movement and the 1973 siege of Wounded Knee.

Midwestern African American autobiographies abound and often confront American racism. In *The Big Sea* (1940) LANGSTON HUGHES (1902–1967) recounts his early life in Kansas, Illinois, and CLEVELAND, Ohio, before his move to New York as a key player in the Harlem Renaissance; a second volume, *I Wonder as I Wander* (1956), concerns Hughes's travels abroad. *Livin' the Blues* (1992) by FRANK MARSHALL DAVIS (1905–1987) highlights his youth in Kansas and his career as a journalist and poet in Chicago. *American Hunger*

(1977) by RICHARD WRIGHT (1908–1960) continues Wright's earlier *Black Boy* (1945), the two works narrating his flight to Chicago, his involvement with Depression-era arts projects, and his affiliation and disaffection with the Communist Party. The Library of America's *Richard Wright: Later Works* (1991) combines the two parts of the work as Wright originally intended it, with the title *Black Boy (American Hunger)*.

The first chapters in *The Quality of Hurt* (1971) by CHESTER HIMES (1909–1984) discuss his difficult life in Cleveland, leading to incarceration in the Ohio State Penitentiary, before his departure for New York and Europe; *My Life of Absurdity* (1976) highlights Himes's writing life in Europe. The autobiography of photographer, composer, filmmaker, and writer GORDON (ALEXANDER BUCHANAN) PARKS (1912–2006) consists of four volumes: *A Choice of Weapons* (1966), *To Smile in Autumn* (1979), *Voices in the Mirror* (1990), and *A Hungry Heart* (2005). *Half Past Autumn* (1997) is a collection of Parks's photography with autobiographical reflections. Kansas-born GWENDOLYN BROOKS (1917–2000) lived much of her life in Chicago and was made Poet Laureate of Illinois in 1968; her *Report from Part One* (1972) and *Report from Part Two* (1996) are miscellanies of information about her life as a poet and social activist. An American classic, THE AUTOBIOGRAPHY OF MALCOLM X (1965), written with Alex Haley (1921–1992), narrates the rise of MALCOLM X (1925–1965) from poverty in Omaha and Lansing to renown as an international leader.

Several Midwestern autobiographies focus on Jewish life. Ludwig Lewisohn (1882–1955) contributed *Up Stream: An American Chronicle* (1922), recounting the author's gradual migration from Berlin to The Ohio State University and his role as drama critic for *The Nation*. The emotional *Because I Was Flesh* (1963) by EDWARD DAHLBERG (1900–1977) focuses on Dahlberg's life with his mother in KANSAS CITY, highlighting urban despair, the inability of his mother to get ahead, and Dahlberg's failures as a son. In *My Last Two Thousand Years* (1972) HERBERT GOLD (b. 1924) portrays a search for his Jewish identity; two other works, *Fathers* (1967) and *Family* (1981), employ the ambiguous subtitle *A Novel in the Form of a Memoir*. *Messages from My Father*

(1996) by Calvin Trillin (b. 1935) is a warm memoir dealing with the author's Russian-born Jewish father and family relations in St. Joseph and Kansas City, Missouri.

Other notable ethnic autobiographies of Midwestern life include *With a Dutch Accent* (1944) by DAVID CORNEL DEJONG (1901–1967), which recounts his life in the Netherlands, the indignities of Ellis Island, and his difficult cultural acclimation in Grand Rapids, Michigan. HARRY MARK PETRAKIS (b. Haralampos Mark Petrakis, 1923), son of a Greek Orthodox priest, tells with good humor about his family and his development as a writer in *Stelmark* (1970), *Reflections* (1983), and *Tales of the Heart* (1999). *Memory's Fictions* (1993) by BIENVENIDO N(UQUI) SANTOS (1911–1996) is an account of life in the Philippines and the United States, with detailed commentary on Santos's writing career in Iowa City and Wichita.

Another important classification of Midwestern autobiography involves the many personal ways writers have approached the subject of nature. Midwestern writers appear to have developed especially down-to-earth approaches, often compounded of traditional nature writing, conservation, spiritual meanings, and even meditations on farming. See also ENVIRONMENTAL LITERATURE. Two important foundational figures are JOHN MUIR (1838–1914) and ALDO LEOPOLD (1887–1948). In *The Story of My Boyhood and Youth* (1913) Muir highlights his coming of age in Wisconsin after his family's emigration from Scotland, hard work enforced by his father's tyranny, observations of nature, and pleas for conservation. Aldo Leopold is famous for *A SAND COUNTY ALMANAC* (1949), which incorporates personal experience into his observations on recovering the vitality of his farm in Wisconsin. Most closely associated with the Minnesota wilderness, SIGURD F(ERDINAND) OLSON (1899–1982) in *Open Horizons* (1969) describes his wilderness travels and readings in history and exploration. Observing nature while living in a military munitions arsenal as a child provided SCOTT RUSSELL SANDERS (b. 1945) with the basis for *The Paradise of Bombs* (1987). *Writing from the Center* (1995) discusses Sanders's motives for writing. South Dakotan LINDA HASSELSTROM (b. 1943) exhibits her personal knowledge of environmental

issues in *Windbreak* (1987) and *Feels like Far* (2001). The nature reflections of Minnesota native PAUL GRUCHOW (1947–2004) are found in *The Necessity of Empty Places* (1988) and *Grass Roots* (1995). NORBERT BLEI (1935–2013) reveals aspects of himself in Door County, Wisconsin, in *Door Way* (1981) and *Meditations on a Small Lake* (1987). Because of illness, Iowa poet and playwright Mary Swander (b. 1950) found a schoolhouse in Amish country that fit her needs, as she recorded in her memoir *Out of This World: A Journey of Healing* (1993); she followed this with *The Desert Pilgrim: En Route to Mysticism and Miracles* (2003), in which she explains her recovery in New Mexico. In *Dakota: A Spiritual Geography* (1993) KATHLEEN NORRIS (b. 1947) combines nature with a meditative examination of the spirit of place. In *Field of Vision* (1996), *Flight Dreams* (1998), and *The Nature of Home* (2002), Lisa Knopp (b. 1956) mixes autobiography with observations on her social and natural worlds in Iowa and Nebraska. Robert Vivian (b. 1967) blends personal experience with social and natural observations in the essays of *Cold Snap as Yearning* (2001). Not to be neglected is John A. Jakle (b. 1939), geographer of the Midwest in many volumes, who brought fresh insights to his illustrated *My Kind of Midwest: Omaha to Ohio* (2008), which incorporates many of his photographs and much of his experience.

Finally, a very selective listing of autobiographies by important Midwestern political figures is included here. ABRAHAM LINCOLN (1809–1865), the sixteenth President of the United States, wrote no formal autobiography, but his life may be glimpsed in part from some of his letters and speeches; well-known sources of autobiographical information are the letter he wrote to Jesse W. Fell on December 20, 1859 and a third-person account by Lincoln, "Short Autobiography Written for the Campaign" in June 1860; both are found in the Library of America edition of *Abraham Lincoln: Speeches and Writings, 1859–1865* (1989): 106–08, 160–67. Another volume from the Library of America is *Ulysses S. Grant: Memoirs and Selected Letters*; *Personal Memoirs of U. S. Grant, Selected Letters, 1839–1865* (1990) by Ulysses S. Grant (1822–1885), whose *Personal Memoirs* were first published by Samuel L. Clemens, writing as

Mark Twain, in 1885. Theodore "Teddy" Roosevelt (1858–1919), the twenty-sixth President, lived off and on as a rancher and hunter in North Dakota. He bought two ranches there in 1883 and published two personal accounts, *Hunting Trips of a Ranchman* (1885) and *Ranch Life and the Hunting Trail* (1888). *Theodore Roosevelt: An Autobiography* appeared in 1913. Herbert C. Hoover (1874–1964), the thirty-first President, who had previously served as U.S. Secretary of Commerce and was a trained mining engineer and author, dealt among much else with his childhood in Iowa in *The Memoirs of Herbert Hoover: Years of Adventure, 1874–1920* (1951).

Gerald R. Ford (1913–2006), who was born in Omaha, Nebraska and reared in Grand Rapids, Michigan, became the thirty-eighth President of the United States when Richard M. Nixon (1913–1994) resigned that office in 1974 because of the Watergate scandal. In *A Time to Heal: The Autobiography of Gerald R. Ford* (1979) Ford discusses this turbulent time and detailed aspects of his political life. Ronald W. Reagan (1911–2004), the fortieth President, born in Tampico, Illinois, spent much of his early life in Dixon, Illinois; he published two autobiographical works: *Where's the Rest of Me?* (1965), with Richard G. Hubler, and *An American Life: The Autobiography* (1990).

Barack (Hussein) Obama (b. 1961), born in Hawaii, went on to Democratic politics in Illinois and finally became the forty-fourth President of the United States, the first African American to achieve that office. *Dreams from My Father: A Story of Race and Inheritance* (1995) was written partially to contribute to a larger understanding of race in American life.

Important political reform figures in Midwestern political life include the populist WILLIAM JENNINGS BRYAN (1860–1925), a voluminous author whose works include *The Memoirs of William Jennings Bryan, by Himself and His Wife, Mary Baird Bryan* (1925). The author of the Cross of Gold speech, Bryan was called "the boy orator of the Plains" and "the Great Commoner." Robert M. La Follette (1855–1925) of Wisconsin, a major progressive in Wisconsin and national politics who advanced many progressive policies, composed *La Follette's Autobiography: A Personal Narrative of Political Experi-*

ences (1913). George W. Norris (1861–1944), a fiery Nebraskan, wrote *Fighting Liberal: The Autobiography of George W. Norris* (1945; second edition, 2009). Norris was instrumental in the creation of the Tennessee Valley Authority and the Rural Electrification Act and attempted to overcome bipartisanship by supporting the Nebraska unicameral legislature.

SELECTED WORKS: For readers interested in pursuing a study of Midwestern autobiography, the following works are suggested as a varied representation of essential works, often illustrating the preoccupations of the periods in which they were written and sometimes focusing nostalgically on labor-intensive childhoods in exciting new locales, away from the restrictions of settled civilization. *Life of Ma-Ka-Tai-Me-She-Kia-Kiak, or Black Hawk* (1833) is the best single memoir dealing with frontier relations between American Indians and whites, especially as edited by Donald Jackson for the University of Illinois Press under the title *Black Hawk: An Autobiography* (1955). Another classic work is *Black Elk Speaks* (1932), as dictated to John Neihardt. Eliza Farnham's *Life in Prairie Land* (1846) is superb on frontier conditions described by an acute and often funny female observer, while William Cooper Howells's *Recollections of Life in Ohio, from 1813 to 1840* (1895), William Dean Howells's *Years of My Youth* (1916), and Mary Austin's *Earth Horizon* (1932) are good on the details of Midwestern social history. For his focus on harsh conditions on frontier and farm, Hamlin Garland's *A Son of the Middle Border* (1917) is a classic. Theodore Dreiser's *Dawn* (1931) is recommended for its sheer vitality and its powerful, detailed account of Midwestern poverty. The Chicago Renaissance is fully surveyed in Harriet Monroe's *A Poet's Life* (1938), while Floyd Dell's *Homecoming* (1933) provides an ample account of various aspects of American literary life and politics of the time. Perhaps the key central figure in all of Midwestern literature is Sherwood Anderson, and although *A Story Teller's Story* (1924) is often factually inaccurate, it is a pleasure. A scholarly edition of his *Tar: A Midwest Childhood*, edited by Ray Lewis White, was published in 1969; a fuller and more reliable work is *Sherwood Anderson's Memoirs* (1942), left unfinished at his death but edited and assembled by Paul Rosenfeld. For NEWSPAPER JOURNALISM on the Midwestern frontier, *The Autobiography of William Allen White* (1946) is superb; a shorter alternative is *Plain People* (1929) by E(dgar) W(atson) Howe. *Black Boy (American Hunger)* (1991) by Richard Wright is an archetypal work on African American northward migration and white reception in Chicago. *The Autobiography of Malcolm X* (1965), written with Alex Haley, provides insights into the author's life, African American dissent, and twentieth-century American race relations.

Useful collections of Midwestern autobiographical essays include *Growing Up in the Midwest* (1981), edited by Clarence A. Andrews; *A Place of Sense: Essays in Search of the Midwest* (1988), edited by Michael Martone; and *Imagining Home: Writing from the Midwest* (1995), edited by Mark Vinz and Thom Tammaro. Also noteworthy is *Diaries of Girls and Women: A Midwestern American Sampler* (2001), edited by Suzanne L. Bunkers.

FURTHER READING: Little scholarship deals specifically with Midwestern autobiography. Helpful guides are Albert E. Stone's *Autobiographical Occasions and Original Acts* (1982); *Telling Lies in Modern American Autobiography* (1990) by Timothy Dow Adams; and *Interpreting the Self: Two Hundred Years of American Autobiography* (1999) by Diane Bjorklund. A useful overview, including "Sixty Genres of Life Narrative," is found in the second edition of *Reading Autobiography* (2010) by Sidonie Smith and Julia Watson. Also recommended is Marcia Jacobson's *Being a Boy Again: Autobiography and the American Boy Book* (1994).

New and rediscovered Midwestern autobiographies are published perennially and are often found in the catalogs of the Midwest's university presses. Especially good are the Wisconsin Studies in Autobiography, the Iowa Singular Lives Series in North American Autobiography, and American Indian Lives from Nebraska. For those who want to dig deeper, the archives of the Midwest's state historical societies are repositories of many potentially publishable autobiographies. Midwestern autobiography is also the subject of numerous internet websites.

JOSEPH J. WYDEVEN   BELLEVUE UNIVERSITY

THE AUTOBIOGRAPHY OF MALCOLM X

HISTORY: *The Autobiography of Malcolm X* (1965), a classic of AFRICAN AMERICAN LITERATURE, was composed by Alex Haley (1921–1992) and was based on a series of interviews Haley conducted with MALCOLM X (1925–1965), leader of Temple Number Seven of the Nation of Islam (NOI) in Harlem, New York City, and an important public figure of the 1960s who inspired the Black Power movement. Malcolm first came to national prominence in 1959 as one of several NOI leaders portrayed in Mike Wallace's five-part documentary for CBS television, "The Hate That Hate Produced." From that time until his assassination on February 21, 1965, he was an unrelenting foe of white privilege and black integrationism. Signal moments included his description of the 1963 March on Washington as "the farce on Washington," his references to mainstream civil rights leaders as Uncle Toms, his characterization of the 1963 assassination of U.S. President John F. Kennedy (1917–1963) as "chickens coming home to roost," his break from the Nation of Islam, and his 1964 hajj to Mecca, which overturned his NOI-induced belief in racial separatism and the myth of Dr. Yacub, who supposedly created a bleached-out race of inferior humans who were actually white devils. Fundamental to Malcolm's perspective throughout his life was his early exposure through his parents to Marcus Garvey's black nationalist philosophy.

The idea for the book originated with Haley, who with Alfred Balk had co-authored "Black Merchants of Hate," which appeared in the January 26, 1963, issue of the *Saturday Evening Post*. That article juxtaposed Malcolm to NOI leader Elijah Muhammad, reciting well-known incidents from Malcolm's life and incorporating information fed to Balk by the FBI to sow discord within the NOI, according to Manning Marable in his 2011 biography *Malcolm X: A Life of Reinvention* (231). Haley's first series of interviews with Malcolm was published in *Playboy* in May 1963. Subsequently, the two met regularly at Haley's Greenwich Village apartment, where Malcolm narrated the events of his life, read over and marked up Haley's typescripts, and scribbled additional sentences on scraps of paper. Haley, a liberal Republican and proponent of racial integration, despised Malcolm's black nationalism but was moved by his personal story as an example of the destructive effect of racial segregation.

Haley and Malcolm agreed that Malcolm would have the final word on what appeared in the final typescript. As originally shopped to Doubleday, the book was to be co-authored. As the interviews continued, however, Haley began to understand how opposed he was to Malcolm's views. He informed his agent, Paul Reynolds, that it was to be an as-told-to book. Doubleday canceled its contract without explanation two weeks after Malcolm's death. The book was published by Grove Press in November 1965 with an introduction by *New York Times* journalist M. S. Handler, a longtime friend of Malcolm, and an epilogue by Haley.

The Autobiography of Malcolm X led to what Marable in his biography refers to as "Malcolm's popularity among millions of white Americans" and "the initial remaking of Malcolm's posthumous image" (265). The *Autobiography* was widely and positively reviewed. Notable reviews include "Making His Mark" by Bayard Rustin in the *New York Herald Tribune Book Week* (November 14, 1965): 1+ and "A Black Man's Quarrel with the Christian God" by Robert Bone in the *New York Times Book Review* (September 11, 1966): 407. After publication of the paperback edition in 1966, the book reached the *New York Times* best-seller list, where it remained for twenty-four weeks, as Jennifer Schuessler notes in "Inside the List" in the April 15, 2011 edition of the *New York Times Sunday Book Review* (22). In Marable's view (466), the most insightful reviewer was Rustin, who called the chapters on Malcolm's Midwestern years "essential reading for anyone who wants to understand the plight of American Negroes" (1).

SIGNIFICANCE: The *Autobiography* narrates Malcolm's early years and family history in Omaha, NEBRASKA, and Lansing, MICHIGAN, although its principal focus is his formative years in Boston and New York, his conversion to the NOI during a period of incarceration, his public persona as the minister of Temple Number Seven and subsequently as national minister, the 1964 pilgrimage to Mecca that led Malcolm to understand Is-

Malcolm X, 1964. Photo by Ed Ford.
Image courtesy of the Library of Congress

lam as a worldwide movement without reference to race, and the period after his public break with the NOI, when Malcolm converted to Sunni Islam and established Muslim Mosque, Inc., and the Organization of Afro-American Unity.

Events in the Midwest are related in the book because of their formative influence, for the most part destructive, on Malcolm's developing personality. Malcolm Little was born on May 19, 1925, in Omaha to Earl Little, a Georgia native, and Louise Langdon (Norton) Little, who was born and brought up in Grenada and immigrated to Canada at the age of nineteen. A carpenter by trade, Earl Little was also an itinerant Christian preacher. They met at a Montreal meeting of Garvey's United Negro Improvement Association (UNIA), married in 1919, and settled in Omaha to promote the Garveyite philosophy.

Forced to leave Omaha after a Ku Klux Klan attack on their home, the Littles settled briefly in Milwaukee and then in Lansing in 1929. Burned out of one Lansing house before the end of the year and stoned by white neighbors at another, they eventually settled south of Lansing proper. Earl continued his work with the UNIA, but according to *Seventh Child* (1998), a family history written by Malcolm's nephew Rodnell Collins, "The Littles found that blacks in Lansing were just as fearful of Garveyism as those in Omaha" (15). In the *Autobiography* Malcolm is bitter toward Lansing's middle-class blacks for adding to his family's woes.

Earl Little died after being run over by a streetcar in Lansing in 1931. The authorities ruled that he had fallen on the tracks in a drunken stupor, but Malcolm asserts in the *Autobiography* that he had been beaten by white supremacists and left on the tracks. After her husband's death, Louise was unable to provide for the family and was eventually committed to an asylum. Malcolm blames Michigan welfare authorities for his mother's mental illness and the destruction of their family. Fifteen-year-old Malcolm was placed in a juvenile detention home in Mason, south of Lansing. Malcolm acknowledges that the Swerlin family, the white couple who ran the home, treated him kindly and fostered his development. In hindsight, though, he came to believe that the Swerlins viewed him as a pet, ascribing to them what he considered popular notions among whites. Although Malcolm excelled in school, he later recalled racial jokes and slurs. One incident recounted in the *Autobiography* signaled for him the moment when he became apathetic about further education or professional aspirations. A teacher he refers to as Mr. Ostrowski advised Malcolm that his ambition to be a lawyer was unrealistic for a person of his race and that he ought to choose a menial trade.

After these formative experiences, Malcolm's involvement with the Midwest was largely incidental and occasional, but his Midwestern roots were evident during his hustler days in New York and Boston, when he was known as "Detroit Red" because of his striking red hair and because he told friends he was from DETROIT, knowing that they would not recognize Lansing; he also wanted to distinguish himself from his friend "Chicago Red," later known as the comedian Redd Foxx. Paroled from jail into his brother Wilfred's care in 1952, Malcolm

worked at a number of jobs and first proselytized for the NOI in Detroit, where W. D. Fard had founded the organization in 1931. He maintained Michigan family ties throughout his life. Wilfred became the NOI minister in Detroit, and another brother, Philbert, in Lansing; Malcolm's half brother Robert had a distinguished career at the Michigan Department of Social Services. Frequent trips to the NOI's CHICAGO headquarters to meet with Elijah Muhammad also speak to Malcolm's continuous association with the Midwest. Malcolm's life after prison was closely tied to Chicago and the dictates emanating from NOI offices there, as was his death. That Midwestern context is important for the *Autobiography,* even the scenes occurring in Harlem.

Although the *Autobiography* reads like a set of incontrovertible facts, it is a fictive work of literature, Malcolm's positioning of his life story as filtered by Haley's more conventional perspective. As a result, some readers have questioned its veracity. In his biography Manning Marable asserts that Malcolm continually remade himself to fit the image he sought, and that these reinventions appealed to black Americans largely because Malcolm "presented himself as the embodiment of the two central figures of African American folk culture, simultaneously the hustler/trickster and the preacher/minister" (11). As an example, Marable demonstrates that Malcolm Little's criminal record, from the time he went to live with his half sister Ella in Boston in 1941 to his 1946 incarceration in a Massachusetts state prison, was much milder than Malcolm portrayed. He embellished his criminality to illustrate the deleterious effects of racism and magnify the greatness of Elijah Muhammad in turning Malcolm from a life of self-destruction to one of self-respect.

Although Marable believed that Malcolm's self-reinventions applied only to his life after he moved to Boston, similar tropes occur in the narration of his early life in Michigan. Presenting no evidence that the Swerlins treated him with anything but dignity, he nevertheless finds fault with them to rule out the possibility that whites could positively contribute to black liberation. Likewise, his description of his father's frequent beatings of Louise and all the children except Malcolm is included to show that an uneducated man feels insignificant before an educated woman and that, for all his Garveyite black pride, Earl Little was so color conscious that he preferred the lighter-complected Malcolm. In the *Autobiography* and his preaching, Malcolm was a savvy storyteller, and all the stories carry meaning. The tropes he relied on in these reinventions are not those of *The Life and Times of Frederick Douglass* (1881) by Frederick Douglass (1818–1895), *Up from Slavery* (1901) by Booker T. Washington (1856–1915), or even the more contemporary *Black Boy* (1945) by RICHARD WRIGHT (1908–1960). They derive from earlier autobiographical and didactic works, including *The Autobiography of Benjamin Franklin* (1791) by Benjamin Franklin (1706–1790), as Carol Ohmann has described.

The *Autobiography* has enjoyed broad appeal and has exerted lasting influence on the Black Power movement and on the pride and determination of black youth. As Michael Eric Dyson writes in "Probing a Divided Metaphor: Malcolm X and His Readers," in *Teaching Malcolm X* (1996), edited by Theresa Perry, the *Autobiography* "is the urtext of contemporary black nationalism. Activists and intellectuals carry it in their back pockets and briefcases for ready reference in debates about black America, while rappers imitate its radical tones and students often quote it as scripture" (233). Given Malcolm's support for African nations seeking independence from European colonial powers, it is not surprising that his writings are valued by postcolonial, pan-African writers such as the Jamaican poet Mutabaruka (b. Allan Hope, 1952), who in "Dis Poem" (1992) lists Malcolm as a figure of worldwide significance along with Marcus Garvey and Haile Selassie. The annual celebration of Kwanzaa, promoted since 1966 by Maulana Karenga (b. 1941), was inspired by the *Autobiography*.

The book's influence on Midwestern writing and life has been significant. In the wake of the assassination and the publication of the *Autobiography*, the League of Revolutionary Black Workers was formed by worker-writer James Lee Boggs (1919–1993) and others at Detroit-area automobile plants to provide an alternative voice for African Americans in white-dominated

unions. The Black Arts Movement of the 1960s and 1970s was partly inspired by Malcolm's vision. The movement gained impetus from the shock of his assassination and spread from New York to other parts of the country, notably Chicago, where it had a major effect on the writing of GWENDOLYN BROOKS (1917–2000), LORRAINE (VIVIAN) HANSBERRY (1930–1965), and Haki R. Madhubuti (b. Don L. Lee, 1942).

Brooks and DUDLEY (FELKER) RANDALL (1914–2000) collaborated on a memorial anthology, *For Malcolm: Poems on the Life and Death of Malcolm X* (1969), published by Randall's Detroit-based Broadside Press and co-edited by Randall and Margaret G. Burroughs (1917–2010). Brooks's poem in the anthology, "Malcolm X," originally appeared in her collection *In the Mecca* (1967) and has been reprinted many times. The anthology includes poems by numerous writers within the Chicago Black Arts Movement and the greater Midwest, such as Clarence Major (b. 1936), ROBERT HAYDEN (b. Asa Bundy Sheffey, 1913–1980), and Etheridge Knight (1931–1991). Hayden included his poem about Malcolm, "El-Hajj Malik El-Shabazz," in *Words in the Mourning Time* (1970), a book confronting violence and war in the Vietnam-era United States.

Sheldon Jackson "Spike" Lee (b. 1957) directed the feature film *Malcolm X* (1992) with a script adapted from one by James Baldwin (1924–1987). Baldwin's unused screenplay appeared in print as *One Day, When I Was Lost: A Scenario Based on Alex Haley's "The Autobiography of Malcolm X"* (1972). Drawing largely on family sources and hewing close to the text of the *Autobiography*, Malcolm's third daughter, Ilyasah Shabazz (b. 1962), authored a brightly illustrated children's book aimed at grades one to five and titled *Malcolm Little: The Boy Who Grew Up to Be Malcolm X* (2013). In this treatment the rural settings of Omaha and Lansing are fundamental to the values inculcated in Malcolm and his siblings.

IMPORTANT EDITIONS: Simultaneously with the illustrated clothbound Grove Press edition (1965), a version was published by Castle of Secaucus, New Jersey. Grove brought out a paperback edition without illustrations in 1966, which was reissued in 1973 by Ballantine Books. This edition, with a foreword by Malcolm's eldest daughter, Attallah Shabazz, and an afterword by Ossie Davis, remains in print. Translations have appeared in several languages, including French (1966), Italian (1967), and Swedish (2003).

FURTHER READING: Manning Marable's *Malcolm X: A Life of Reinvention* (2011) was long awaited as an authoritative biography based on two decades of archival and documentary research. Even before it was awarded the 2012 Pulitzer Prize for History, the book elicited strong objections, including *A Lie of Reinvention: Correcting Manning Marable's "Malcolm X"* (2012), edited by Jared Ball and Todd Steven Burroughs. Marable's sudden death just days before his book was published means that these issues will not easily be resolved. Russell J. Rickford's *Betty Shabazz: A Remarkable Story of Survival before and after Malcolm X* (2003) touches on Malcolm's wife's role in producing the *Autobiography*. More information concerning the Shabazz family is found in *Growing Up X* (2002) by Ilyasah Shabazz, with Kim McLarin, and *Seventh Child: A Family Memoir of Malcolm X* (1998) by Malcolm's nephew Rodnell P. Collins, with A. Peter Bailey.

Alex Haley's initial interview with Malcolm X, published in the May 1963 issue of *Playboy*, is also available in *Alex Haley: The Playboy Interviews* (1993). M. S. Handler's *New York Times* articles appeared on March 9, March 13, and October 4, 1964. S. E. Gontarski discusses the editing of *The Autobiography* in Gilberto Sorrento's "The Novelist as Editor: An Interview with S. E. Gontarski" in *The Grove Press Reader, 1951–2001* (2001), which he edited (97–102).

Michael Eric Dyson examines books about Malcolm in "Probing a Divided Metaphor: Malcolm X and His Readers," in *Teaching Malcolm X* (1996), edited by Theresa Perry (231–41). Dyson also wrote *Making Malcolm: The Myth and Meaning of Malcolm X* (1995). In "Malcolm X: In Print, on Screen," *Biography* 23.1 (2000): 29–48, Thomas Doherty takes on controversies about the *Autobiography*'s veracity and Malcolm's legacy. In an untitled review published in the online journal *education review* (February 1999), Najee E. Muhammad describes the *Autobiography* as an "educational narrative of human possibility." Muhammad discusses Malcolm's Michigan years and school experiences and provides an extensive bibliography.

Literary treatments include Barrett J. Mandel's "The Didactic Achievement of Malcolm X's *Autobiography*," *Afro-American Studies: An Interdisciplinary Journal* 2 (1972): 269–74; Carol Ohmann's "The Autobiography of Malcolm: A Revolutionary Use of the Franklin Tradition," *American Quarterly* 22.2 (Summer 1970): 131–49; and Bashir M. El-Beshti's "The Semiotics of Salvation: Malcolm X and the Autobiographical Self," *Journal of Negro History* 82.4 (Fall 1997): 359–67. Particularly relevant for the information it provides on the Black Arts Movement in Chicago is *Malcolm X and the Poetics of Haki Madhubuti* (2006) by Regina Jennings. *The Malcolm X Encyclopedia* (2002), edited by Robert L. Jenkins, includes many entries pertaining to Midwestern locales and people.

The most comprehensive documentary film on Malcolm is *Malcolm X: Make It Plain* (1994), directed by Orlando Bagwell for the PBS series *The American Experience*. The film chronicles Malcolm X's entire life, including his Midwestern youth, through interviews and archival footage. The film's web page at the PBS website includes a complete transcript and other useful features.

Unknown quantities of Malcolm's papers were destroyed by Betty Shabazz in her raging grief after her husband's death. At her death in 1997, Betty Shabazz's papers and artifacts and the remaining papers of Malcolm X became the subject of disputes among the six daughters, one of whom allegedly placed her father's letters, speeches, and journals in storage but neglected to pay the bill. When the trove of Malcolm's papers turned up for sale at a San Francisco auction house in 2002, the estate paid more than $300,000 for their return. Subsequently, the Schomburg Center for Research in Black Culture, a Harlem branch of the New York Public Library, paid $400,000 to the estate for a seventy-five-year lease on the papers. These papers, including correspondence between Malcolm X and Alex Haley, may be viewed at the Schomburg Center. Other papers being contested by the daughters may include the autobiography that Betty Shabazz was apparently working on at the time of her death, according to John Eligon in

"Malcolm X Trove Hidden during Feud," *New York Times,* February 8, 2011, A22.

After Alex Haley's death in 1992, his estate auctioned off most of his papers. The typescript of the *Autobiography*, with annotations by both Malcolm and Haley and including the "lost" chapters, was purchased by a private collector, Detroit lawyer Gregory J. Reed. On what would have been Malcolm's eighty-fifth birthday, May 19, 2010, Reed staged a reading of the introduction and chapters missing from the original publication at the Malcolm X and Betty Shabazz Memorial and Educational Center, located in the former Audubon Ballroom, the site of Malcolm's assassination. Reed also announced plans to publish the whole work, with the lost chapters and a new preface by Malcolm's third daughter, Ilyasah Shabazz, but that project awaits resolution of probate issues. Reed presented parts of these chapters at a June 2010 symposium hosted by the Michigan State University Museum. The Alex Haley Archive at Texas A&M University's Cushing Memorial Library retains portions of typed pages from the *Autobiography* and a manuscript written by Haley titled "The Malcolm X I Knew."

ROGER BRESNAHAN   MICHIGAN STATE UNIVERSITY

B-C

BISEXUAL LITERATURE.

See Lesbian, Gay, Bisexual, Transgender, and Queer Literature

BLACK ELK SPEAKS

HISTORY: One of the most significant works of NATIVE AMERICAN LITERATURE, *Black Elk Speaks* (1932) has inspired an abundance of materials that document and examine the collaboration between BLACK ELK (1863–1950) and Midwestern writer JOHN G(NEISENAU) NEIHARDT (1881–1973). Scholars have compared the book with other accounts and have debated many questions regarding the reliability of the authorial process and the authenticity of the Native American voice that survived the dictation, translation, and writing process.

In 1930 Neihardt went to the Pine Ridge Reservation in SOUTH DAKOTA in search of elders who might explain to him the significance of the Ghost Dance among the Plains Indians as part of his research for *Song of the Messiah* (1935), the fifth part of his epic poem *A Cycle of the West* (1949). An Indian agent referred him to Black Elk, a second cousin of Crazy Horse and a participant of some prominence in spiritual matters of the Oglala Sioux and their neighbors and allies. Black Elk had received a sacred vision that empowered him to become a healer and spiritual adviser. He found the Ghost Dance congruent to his personal vision and became a participant.

In Neihardt, Black Elk found a compatible spirit with whom he was interested in sharing his spiritual knowledge. The two corresponded during the winter of 1930, and a series of meetings was arranged in the spring of 1931, during which the material out of which *Black Elk Speaks* was composed and transmitted to Neihardt. Black Elk, often in the company of his contemporary Oglalas, who contributed accounts and verifications, spoke in Lakota. His son, Ben, translated his statements into English, and Neihardt's daughter Enid took down the words in shorthand. The process required the English to be read back to Ben, who retranslated the sentences into Lakota for Black Elk to review. When the interviews on the Pine Ridge Reservation were completed, the Neihardt family returned to their home in Branson, MISSOURI, where Enid transcribed the notes. Neihardt stopped work on another project and immediately began writing *Black Elk Speaks*.

The first publication in 1932 was a popular and financial failure, but the book gath-

Black Elk and John G. Neihardt in 1944, their last time together.

Photo reprinted courtesy of the John G. Neihardt Trust, Coralee Hughes, Trustee

ered a modest and steady following. It gained a wider readership after World War II as interest in spiritual issues, minority cultures, and the natural environment intensified. With the Bison Book edition published by the University of Nebraska Press in 1961, *Black Elk Speaks* became a literary standard that has been reprinted and reissued in many editions.

SIGNIFICANCE: *Black Elk Speaks* is the most widely read book by a Native American author portraying traditional lifeways of an American Indian nation and the intellectual concepts that form them. As with all Native American materials told to English writers, disputes have arisen concerning how much of the book represents an authentic Native American account and how much of it is intrusion and imposition by an English-language author. Accounts of the collaboration between John Neihardt and Black Elk consistently state that Black Elk thought that Neihardt had been sent to him so that he could tell Neihardt what he knew, and Neihardt took this as a charge to tell the Lakota story as faithfully and effectively as he could. As Raymond J. DeMallie, editor of *The Sixth Grandfather: Black Elk's Teachings Given to John G. Neihardt* (1985), explains, "Neihardt perceived Black Elk's religion in terms of art; Black Elk perceived Neihardt's

art in terms of religion" (37). DeMallie further notes that Neihardt conceived the book as Black Elk's life story, while Black Elk conceived it as an account of old Lakota religion. However, Neihardt recognized the power of the story of Black Elk's life and rendered it through the literary repertoire he had at his command.

Neihardt's search for material for a multivolume epic poem about the frontier and the settling of the West led him to Black Elk. A Unitarian and a romantic, Neihardt incorporated conventions from classical literature, folklore, history, and mysticism into his work. As a poet, however, he understood the ultimate power of words as the projection of images on the mind of the reader or listener.

The central event in *Black Elk Speaks* is the power vision Black Elk received at the age of nine. The force of the book lies in the detailed images of that vision. Black Elk prefaces his relating of the vision with the statement that what happened "is not a story" but a revelation (1932 edition 20). He then presents a sequence of images that express the powers of the universe as they are identified with directions, seasons, and creative forces operating on the earth.

The significance of his account of the vision lies in the coherent and interconnected imagery much more than in the expository language. Native American literary accounts maintain that contemplative and abstract acts of thought are accomplished through mental images retained in personal and tribal memories in visual and aural form. In relating his vision, Black Elk transmits the imagery of interacting forces through a coherent symbolism drawn from his culture. Dreaming or having visions is a mode of thinking and perceiving, and the images from those visions are the form in which these complex matters are remembered, intellectualized, and transmitted. As a poet, Neihardt recognized the power and coherence of Black Elk's vision and retained Black Elk's thought structure and imagery. He used English literary conventions to translate the material into a story understandable to Western minds. As a collaborator, he undertook to do what Black Elk found daunting.

Black Elk was convinced that he had been given a charge in his vision to interpret and translate the vision for the benefit of his people. He says, "As I lay there thinking of my vision, I could see it all again and feel the meaning with a part of me like a strange power glowing in my body; but when the part of me that talks would try to make words for the meaning, it would be like fog and get away from me. . . . It was the pictures I remembered and the words that went with them" (49).

The words Black Elk refers to are the things that had been said to him by the powers in the vision and the songs he heard in it. In his youth he was afraid that people would ridicule his vision because he was so young when he had it and also because he might get something wrong in trying to relate it. His youth was lived with a pervasive sense of fear that he was not discharging the spiritual obligation conferred with the vision.

In late adolescence, with the assistance of elder holy men, Black Elk reconstructed his vision in the form of a horse dance. He taught the songs he had heard in his vision to the elder medicine men so that they could sing and lead others in the songs at appropriate times in the dance. The horse dance was a major production with thirteen horses and their riders, seven old men, and four young maidens, all costumed and painted to re-create what Black Elk saw in his vision, and a number of sets, including a painted tepee, and props of symbolic significance. The performance of the horse dance transmitted to the Lakota people what was revealed to Black Elk in his vision. The dance concluded with the observers participating in its finale.

The horse dance released Black Elk from his obsessive fear of failing to meet the charge given to him in his vision. He took up the duties of a medicine man to advise and heal, and he sought another vision to reinforce and clarify his powers. In his second vision Black Elk saw white people and their culture as an enemy that threatened his people. He was not designated to lead them to war or deliverance, but to make his people happier and stronger through the sustaining force of their beliefs and traditions.

An aspect of Black Elk's life not covered in *Black Elk Speaks* is that he became a Roman Catholic catechist and did missionary work on the reservation. Black Elk became familiar with Christianity while traveling with Buffalo Bill's Wild West Show, which Black Elk said he joined so that he might learn of some secret in white society that could help the Lakota. Rather, he found a selfish, uncaring culture that "could not be better than the old ways of my people" (221). Black Elk's account details how white culture subverts and destroys Native American life, but it does so in the context of explaining the vital and sustaining belief system of Lakota life.

The major arguments against Black Elk's account assert that it was compromised by doctrines Black Elk learned from the Roman Catholic Church or that John Neihardt contrived to shape it into a version that fit his literary orientation. Native American and literary scholars, however, have found that *Black Elk Speaks* is consistent with other accounts of Lakota cosmology and that Neihardt's work as a literary interpreter was faithful and diligent. Critics who assess the book as reliable and of great literary merit stress that Black Elk did not see a dichotomy between Catholicism and Lakota traditional religion; he found ecumenical commonalities that did not require the choice of one over the other, and he practiced his duties as both a catechist and a Lakota healer and teacher simultaneously. He saw concordant spiritual values that spanned the two cultures in which he operated.

However, *Black Elk Speaks* as Black Elk conceived it is not a story of his life. It is a story of a "people's dream" (276), he explains in the closing sentences of the book, as he was given to understand it. The dream, along with the book, ends with the Wounded Knee Massacre of December 29, 1890, when troops of the U.S. Seventh Cavalry Regiment killed at least 150 Lakota men, women, and children on the Pine Ridge Indian Reservation in South Dakota. Black Elk's subsequent life is not relevant to the spiritual vision he sought to make manifest. The rest of his life, not told in *Black Elk Speaks*, was spent trying to revive the dream and find spiritual values to replace what ended at Wounded Knee. The book is the story of a spiritual vision told through John Neihardt as Black Elk intended it to be.

The republication of *Black Elk Speaks* in 1961 not only reflected growing popular and scholarly interest in Native American history and culture but also provided impetus to the burgeoning Indian rights movement. In her memoir, *Lakota Woman* (1990), Mary (Brave Bird) Crow Dog (1954-2013) quotes Black Elk's lament that the Lakota "nation's hoop is broken . . . and the sacred tree is dead" (276). Crow Dog's participation in a Ghost Dance, performed during the 1973 occupation of Wounded Knee by activists in the American Indian Movement, moves her to assert that she and the other activists had "mended the nation's hoop. The sacred tree *is not dead!*" (155). Other Indian writers influenced by Black Elk include William Lewis Trogdon (b. 1939), writing as WILLIAM LEAST HEAT-MOON, formerly a student of Neihardt's at the University of Missouri. Trogdon follows Black Elk's example in linking narrative form to a sacred sense of place. In *Blue Highways: A Journey into America* (1982), an account of a trip around the United States in a van he named "Ghost Dancer," Trogdon reports that he took two books on his journey: *Leaves of Grass* (1855–1892) by Walt Whitman (1819–1892) and *Black Elk Speaks* (8).

Although no film version of *Black Elk Speaks* has been undertaken, Christopher Sergel (1918–1993) scripted a theatrical adaptation with the blessings of Black Elk's descendants. Sergel's play debuted in 1993 in Denver and was published in 1996.

IMPORTANT EDITIONS: The first edition of *Black Elk Speaks* was published in 1932 by William Morrow and Company, with illustrations by Stephen Standing Bear, a Minneconjou Lakota friend of Black Elk. Neihardt wrote new prefaces for the 1961 and 1972 editions from the University of Nebraska Press; the 1979 edition featured an introduction by Vine Deloria Jr. Nebraska's 2004 edition collected all previous introductory materials. SUNY Press has published *Black Elk Speaks: Being the Life Story of a Holy Man of the Oglala Sioux, the Premier Edition* (2008), edited and annotated by Raymond J. DeMallie and featuring illustrations, maps, extended commentary, and a new index. DeMallie has also edited the transcripts of Neihardt's interviews with Black Elk in *The Sixth Grandfather: Black Elk's Teachings Given to John G. Neihardt* (1985), along with a long essay. Reading *The Sixth Grandfather* alongside *Black Elk Speaks* allows a reader to distinguish more clearly Neihardt's literary shaping of the text.

FURTHER READING: The scholarly debate over *Black Elk Speaks* has been contentious and sometimes rancorous. Although the body of works provides useful perspectives, some authors claim exclusive franchises on Native American culture and expend much discussion in prosecuting those claims. The commentaries also are divided between those that treat the book as a literary text and those that treat it using the disciplinary approaches of sociology, anthropology, ethnology, and theology. In "Black Elk and Book Culture," *Journal of the American Academy of Religion* 67.1 (1999): 85–111, Philip P. Arnold discusses the textual controversy and the book's influence on later Native American writers and activists. He also contrasts Black Elk's worldview with what he terms the utopianism and consumerism of writer L(YMAN) FRANK BAUM (1856–1919), who, nine days before the Wounded Knee Massacre, wrote an editorial in a South Dakota newspaper that he edited in which he called for extermination of the Lakotas.

Drawing on interviews with Black Elk's friends and family, Michael F. Steltenkamp wrote *Black Elk: Holy Man of the Oglala* (1993), which details the last fifty years of Black Elk's life. Steltenkamp has also written the first complete biography, *Nicholas Black Elk: Medicine Man, Missionary, Mystic* (2009). Neihardt's daughter Hilda Neihardt Petri wrote a memoir of the collaboration, *Black Elk and Flaming Rainbow: Personal Memories of the Lakota Holy Man and John Neihardt* (1995). Also providing familial perspective is *Black Elk Lives: Conversations with the Black Elk Family* (2000) by Ester Black Elk DeSersa and others.

A book-length study focusing on the literary achievement of *Black Elk Speaks* is Brian Holloway's *Interpreting the Legacy: John Neihardt and "Black Elk Speaks"* (2003). A thorough look at Neihardt's poetics in the book is included in Michael Castro's *Interpreting the Indian: Twentieth-Century Poets and the Native American* (1991). Vine DeLoria Jr. edited a collection of essays that examine

Neihardt's role in *A Sender of Words: Essays in Memory of John G. Neihardt* (1984). Other literary studies include Anne M. Downey's "'A Broken and Bloody Hoop': The Intertextuality of *Black Elk Speaks* and Alice Walker's *Meridian*," *MELUS* 19.3 (Fall 1994): 37–45; and Carl Silvio's "*Black Elk Speaks* and Literary Disciplinarity: A Case Study in Canonization," *College Literature* 26.2 (Spring 1999): 137–50. Literary, historical, and philosophical themes are addressed by contributors to *The Black Elk Reader* (2000), edited by Clyde Holler.

In "The Soul of the Indian," *Wičazo Ša Review* 19.2 (Fall 2004): 79–104, David Martínez discusses the philosophies behind Native American vision quests and suggests how Native people may reclaim *Black Elk Speaks* after years of nonindigenous appropriation. Books dealing with religious issues include *Black Elk's Story: Distinguishing Its Lakota Purpose* (1991) by Julian Rice, *Black Elk's Religion: The Sun Dance and Lakota Catholicism* (1995) by Clyde Holler, and *Black Elk: Colonialism and Lakota Catholicism* (2005) by Damian Costello. Several studies are evaluated by Raymond J. DeMallie in "Black Elk in the Twenty-First Century," *Ethnohistory* 53.3 (Summer 2006): 595–601. Jerome McGann examines *Black Elk Speaks* as a prophetic Native American version of Euro-American history in "American Memory in *Black Elk Speaks*," *New Literary History* 44.3 (Summer 2013): 402–24.

DAVID L. NEWQUIST   NORTHERN STATE UNIVERSITY

BLACK HAWK.

See *Life of Ma-ka-tai-me-she-kiak; or Black Hawk*

BRANCH WILL NOT BREAK, THE

HISTORY: In the introduction to his important anthology *Contemporary American Poetry* (1962) DONALD HALL (b. 1928) heralds the arrival in the late 1950s and early 1960s of "a kind of imagination new to American poetry" (24). He very well could be describing *The Branch Will Not Break* (1963) by JAMES WRIGHT (1927–1980), as well as a cluster of books published between 1962 and 1964: *Silence in the Snowy Fields* (1962) by ROBERT (ELWOOD) BLY (b. 1926); *Traveling through the Dark* (1962) by WILLIAM STAFFORD (1914–1993); *The Moving Target* (1963) by W(illiam)

S(tanley) Merwin (b. 1927); and *Flower Herding on Mount Monadnock* (1964) by Galway Kinnell (1927–2014). Wright, like all these poets, had moved away from the academic formalism that had dominated American poetry of the 1950s, embracing instead free verse, vivid imagery, international influences, and a reflective inwardness. Five decades after its publication, *The Branch Will Not Break* is recognized as one of the most important books of poetry published since 1945.

Readers and critics familiar with Wright's work agreed that the poems in his third collection differ markedly in style, form, and tone from those in his two previous collections, *The Green Wall* (1957) and *Saint Judas* (1959). Circumstances in Wright's life contributed to this poetic evolution. Between 1957 and 1963 Wright experienced great personal and professional turmoil: separation and eventual divorce from his first wife in 1962, excessive drinking, and failure to receive tenure at the University of Minnesota in 1962. Yet it was also during this difficult time that he met Robert and CAROL BLY (1930–2007), of whom Wright said in an interview with Peter Stitt in *Paris Review* 62 (Summer 1975): 34–61, "They loved me and they saved my life. I don't mean the life of my poetry either" (49). Wright's friendships with the Blys and other writers who frequented the Blys' farm in Madison, MINNESOTA, such as JOHN (IGNATIUS) KNOEPFLE (b. 1923) and Louis Aston Marantz Simpson (1923–2012), gave him a sense of community and purpose. Reading foreign literature and collaborating on translations of European and Latin American poets enabled Wright to experiment with his own work as well. It was from this period that *The Branch Will Not Break* emerged, including some of Wright's most enduring poems: "Autumn Begins in Martins Ferry, Ohio," "Lying in a Hammock at William Duffy's Farm in Pine Island, Minnesota," and "A Blessing."

As both Nicholas Gattuccio and Kevin Stein have shown, the change in Wright's poetry had many causes. The first was Wright's discovery of the poetry of George Trakl (1887–1914) in Vienna in 1952, followed by his "rediscovery" of Trakl in 1958 when he read a translation of a Trakl poem in the first issue of Robert Bly's journal *The Fifties.* The long and complicated manuscript history of *The Branch Will Not Break* includes "Amenities of Stone," a partially abandoned manuscript falling chronologically between *Saint Judas* and *The Branch Will Not Break,* which links the two stylistically different collections. Twenty-eight poems from "Amenities of Stone" eventually found their way into *The Branch Will Not Break.* At one time or another, 113 poems were considered for inclusion. Over two years, with detailed revisions of five different full-length manuscript drafts, Wright carefully pared away poems from "Amenities in Stone" as he struggled to abandon the formalist voice of his earlier work to give shape to the mostly open forms of *The Branch Will Not Break.*

Although the Academy of American Poets lists *The Branch Will Not Break* as a "groundbreaking book," early reviews of the collection were mixed. In "Revelations of What Is Present," *The Nation* (July 13, 1963), Louis D. Rubin called Wright's new poems "arbitrary" and "unorganized" and claimed that "the images [didn't] combine to make poems" (39). Similarly, Thom Gunn, in "Modes of Control," *Yale Review* 53.3 (Spring 1964): 447–58, called the collection "a lightweight compared with [Wright's] two others" and hoped that Wright "will attempt to reconcile his new virtues with his old ones" (456–57). Others, however, found Wright's departure from his previous style and his "new imagination" refreshing and bold. Gene Baro, in "Curiosity and Illumination," in the September 1, 1963, *New York Times Book Review,* praised the collection for treating "symbolically, the world of contemporary experience" (5), and Harry Strickhausen, in "In the Open," *Poetry* 102 (September 1963), liked the book's "clarity and directness, the language bound intimately with idea and image; and the harshness, the precision, the sense of fitness and place for every syllable" (392).

SIGNIFICANCE: Wright's experiments with language and form, his use of Midwestern locales and landscapes, his attraction to the redemptive world of nature, and his visionary approach converged to create a collection that, in its time, transformed American poetry and continues to influence each new generation of poets. The metrical disci-

poems by JAMES WRIGHT

James Wright's *The Branch Will Not Break,* 1963. Cover design by William Van Saun. Published by Wesleyan University Press, Middletown, Connecticut. Used by permission

pline characteristic of poems in Wright's first two collections relaxed in *The Branch Will Not Break,* allowing Wright to capture the rhythms and cadences of his native "Ohioan" language. The book's radical departure from New Critical aesthetics shocked critics and readers alike. Wright's free-verse form, his easing away from tight iambic rhythms, and his experiments with short imagistic poems stand in direct contrast to the chiseled quatrains and sonnets found in *The Green Wall* and *Saint Judas.*

Of great importance to the poems in *The Branch Will Not Break* is their setting: in the Midwest, especially western Minnesota, the Dakotas, and, of course, Wright's OHIO, specifically, the gritty environs of Martins Ferry, Wright's hometown, a place that would haunt his poetry until his death. Place names abound in the titles and in the poems themselves—Mansfield, Bridgeport, and Marion, Ohio, as well as Minneapolis, Rochester, and Pine Island, Minnesota— as if Wright is determined to locate his universe in a real and knowable landscape. Although these are actual places, Wright is also creating a geography of the imagination and a dramatic arc based on the Midwest of his life experience. The book begins with poems set in Ohio, dominated by themes of loneliness and grief, and then shifts to Minnesota, whose roads and prairies promise renewal and redemption.

Perhaps no poems better illustrate this motion than the frequently anthologized "Autumn Begins in Martins Ferry, Ohio" and "A Blessing." Placed fifth in the collection, "Autumn Begins in Martins Ferry, Ohio" introduces the blighted landscape of Wright's early years, where the speaker "think[s] of Polacks nursing long beers in Tiltonsville, / And gray faces of Negroes in the blast furnace at Benwood, / And the ruptured night watchman of Wheeling Steel, / Dreaming of heroes" (15). Given its placement early in the collection, this poem stands as a kind of threshold guardian at the entrance to Wright's industrial wasteland.

The third-to-last poem in the collection, "A Blessing," may be Wright's most famous. "A Blessing" offers a kind of spiritual map for seeking the redemptive path by opening the self to the natural world and turning inward to the soul. "Just off the highway to Rochester, Minnesota," the speaker is welcomed by Indian ponies that he wishes to embrace. As the poem moves gracefully towards its famous end, toward its epiphanic moment— "Suddenly I realize / That if I stepped out of my body I would break / Into blossom" (57)—transcendence seems truly possible to the seeker.

Wright's friendships with the Blys, Knoepfle, and Simpson and their work editing *The Fifties* and *The Sixties* and translating foreign poets account, to some degree, for this visionary quality. Wright said in *Paris Review* that Robert Bly "made it clear to me that the tradition of poetry which I had tried to master, and in which I'd come to a dead end, was not the only one. He reminded me that poetry is a possibility, that although all poetry is formal, there are many forms, just as there are many forms of feeling" (49). The poems in *The Branch Will Not Break* share with Bly's *Silence in the Snowy Fields*, published a year before Wright's book, their inward turning, associative imagery, loose form, Midwestern settings, and colloquial language, all reaching toward transcendent moments. Eventually, these tendencies would come to be characterized by such terms as "leaping poetry" and "deep image poetry." Although Wright did not entirely abandon traditional prosody, he certainly moved toward more open forms as a way of exploring a new consciousness and developing a new voice.

The sustaining influence of *The Branch Will Not Break* can be measured to some degree by its staying power in the marketplace. Currently in its twentieth printing, *The Branch Will Not Break* has sold more than 25,000 copies in paperback. With an estimated 3,000 to 5,000 cloth copies printed early on, total sales figures approach 30,000. Its influence has been profound, especially on the poetry of the 1960s and 1970s and on writers such as Marvin Bell (b. 1937), JIM (JAMES RAYMOND) DANIELS (b. 1956), RITA DOVE (b. 1952), DAN GERBER (b. 1940), JIM (JAMES THOMAS) HARRISON (1937–2016), and JUDITH MINTY (b. 1937).

IMPORTANT EDITIONS: *The Branch Will Not Break* was published in 1963 by Wesleyan University Press. The collection contained forty-three poems, many of which had previously been published in such periodicals as *Harper's, Kenyon Review, The Nation*, the *New Yorker, Paris Review*, and *Poetry*. See *POETRY: A MAGAZINE OF VERSE*. Both *Collected Poems* (1972) and *Above the River: The Complete Poems* (1990) collect all the poems in the same order in which they first appeared in *The Branch Will Not Break*. In 2007 Wesleyan University Press published a special miniature (2.5" × 3.25") hardcover edition of *The Branch Will Not Break* to celebrate fifty years of publishing.

FURTHER READING: Wright comments on *The Branch Will Not Break* in his *Collected Prose* (1983), edited by Anne Wright, and in *A Wild Perfection: The Selected Letters of James Wright* (2005), edited by Anne Wright and Saundra Rose Maley with Jonathan Blunk. Given Robert Bly's relationship with Wright and especially his influence on Wright while he was writing *The Branch Will Not Break*, Bly's essays, interviews, and books, such as *Remembering James Wright* (1991), are invaluable. At this time, there is no biography of Wright nor any book that focuses solely on *The Branch Will Not Break.* However, several excellent chapters, essays, dissertations, interviews with Wright, and biographical sketches relevant to *The Branch Will Not Break* are available. All book-length critical studies of Wright's poetry contain bibliographies relevant to *The Branch Will Not Break.*

Each of the three substantial bibliographies of James Wright's poetry contains a section devoted to secondary sources related to *The Branch Will Not Break.* They include James R. Keegan's dissertation from the University of Delaware, "James Wright: An Annotated Secondary Bibliography" (1994); William H. Roberson's *James Wright: An Annotated Bibliography* (1995); and William Todd Copeland's dissertation from Texas A&M University, "A James Wright Research Guide: Bibliography of Primary Works, Bibliography of Secondary Works, and Other Reference Materials in English" (2000).

Chapters on *The Branch Will Not Break* are found in David C. Dougherty's *James Wright* (1987); Kevin Stein's *James Wright: The Poetry of a Grown Man* (1989); Andrew Elkins's *The Poetry of James Wright* (1991); and Dave Smith's *The Pure Clear Word: Essays on the Poetry of James Wright* (1982). William Barillas's *The Midwestern Pastoral: Place and Landscape in Literature of the American Heartland* (2006) has a chapter on Wright that asserts the regional dimensions of *The Branch Will Not Break* and Wright's other books. Peter Stitt and Frank Graziano have edited *James Wright: A Profile* (1988), with letters and an essay by Wright, photographs, tributes by other poets, and a bibliography; and *James Wright: The Heart of the Light* (1990), with essays, reviews, a biographical sketch, and a critical history.

Nicholas Gattuccio's "Now My Amenities of Stone Are Done: Some Notes on the Style of James Wright," *Concerning Poetry* 15 (Spring 1982): 61–76, and Kevin Stein's "A Redefinition of the Poetic Self: James Wright's *Amenities of Stone, Ohio Review* 33 (1984): 9–28, treat the evolution of Wright's manuscript, demonstrating that the change in Wright's poetry was not as sudden as it seemed when *The Branch Will Not Break* first appeared.

The largest repository of Wright's papers is held in the Literary Manuscripts Collection at the University of Minnesota Librar-ies, Minneapolis. This collection includes the corrected proof of *The Branch Will Not Break,* dated October 3, 1962, as well as a typed carbon draft of the manuscript from March 1962 with the title changed by hand from *The Blessing* to *The Branch Will Not Break.* Wesleyan University Press in Middletown, Connecticut, maintains correspondence and other materials related to the four volumes of Wright's poetry that it published, including four manuscript versions and the final form of *The Branch Will Not Break.* Additional Wright materials can be found in the special collections libraries of Kenyon College, the Martins Ferry Public Library, Ohio University, Princeton University, the University of Texas, and the University of Washington.

One enduring development related to Wright's life and poetry was the annual James Wright Poetry Festival, usually held in April, in Wright's hometown of Martins Ferry, Ohio. Beginning in 1981, the festival ran for twenty-seven consecutive years, featuring major figures in contemporary American poetry, such as Robert Bly, Carolyn Forché (b. 1950), Galway Kinnell, Yusef Komunyakaa (b. 1947), and Sharon Olds (b. 1942). The festival was sponsored by community organizations, among them the Martins Ferry Public Library, the Ohio Arts Council, the Eastern Ohio Arts Council, and Ohio University.

THOM TAMMARO

MINNESOTA STATE UNIVERSITY–MOORHEAD

BUSINESS

OVERVIEW: From the early 1800s to the present, business has increasingly pervaded Midwestern life. Tensions between farmers and banks and businessmen, between frontier romanticism and the often cynical realism of the business establishment, and between what Henry Nash Smith called "Virgin Land" and what Leo Marx called "the Machine in the Garden" appear regularly in Midwestern and American literature. Whether the focus is land speculation, banking, the stock or commodities markets, industry, or business, Midwestern writers have typically viewed business and those in business, their values, and their organizations negatively. The wealthy, especially those without direct connections to the land, are rejected. Even those who have parlayed farm backgrounds into significant financial success are suspect. Midwestern egalitarianism regularly opposes business's penchant for valuing corporate gain and personal wealth above human needs. Business and the businessman were especially prominent in writing from the late nineteenth and the early twentieth centuries, when the Midwest was at the center of American capitalism and the businessman was an iconic figure in popular culture. Although women figured in business life despite the strictures of sexism, business is generally imagined as a male domain in the literature of that period, and most fictional characters engaged in business are male.

HISTORY AND SIGNIFICANCE: Nineteenth-century America expanded into the frontier and saw isolated farmsteads grow into incipient frontier towns and established communities. The writings of CAROLINE KIRK-LAND (1801–1864) reflect early Midwestern views on banks and frontier people. She began writing to supplement her family income after DETROIT banks refused to honor their notes in 1837 and MICHIGAN wildcat banks collapsed in 1839. Her purpose, as stated in the preface of her first book, *A NEW HOME—WHO'LL FOLLOW?* (1839), is to provide "a veritable history; an unimpeachable transcript of reality; a rough picture, in detached parts, but photographed from life; a sort of 'Emigrants' Guide.'" The loosely disguised people in her book display the hard work and good character that are cherished as being the means to the American Dream, but they deal with nearly insurmountable frontier problems. Thirty-eight years later her son, JOSEPH KIRKLAND (1830–1894), in *Zury: The Meanest Man in Spring County* (1887), depicted an early Midwestern businessman. Zury, whose name plays on the word "usury," and who is financially shrewd and personally stingy. These qualities have made him a major local landholder in his rural ILLINOIS community. He uses his wealth to achieve his ends, including the woman he loves.

Realistic writers attempted to portray accurately the people and landscape of their region throughout the full cycle of community development. SAMUEL LANGHORNE CLEMENS (1835–1910), writing as Mark Twain, satirized various aspects of business, most

notably in the form of slaveholding as the basis of the southern economy, particularly in the characters of the Grangerfords and the Shepherdsons in *ADVENTURES OF HUCKLEBERRY FINN* (London 1884; New York 1885). In 1891 (HANNIBAL) HAMLIN GARLAND (1860–1940), who, as a child, was moved ever westward by a restless father, wrote of the nature of Midwestern frontier life in *MAIN-TRAVELLED ROADS* (1891). He presents the road of that life as "long and wearyful . . . [with] a dull little town at one end, and a home of toil at the other" (preface). Garland's story "Under the Lion's Paw" in that collection provides a metaphor for farmers' lives under a corrupt system that sanctions exploitative business practices. The wealthy and established business interests use the legal system to exploit those with less money or fewer local connections. Garland's volume makes clear the Darwinian nature of American capitalism.

At the next step in the settlement cycle, SHERWOOD ANDERSON (1876–1941) portrayed the movement from frontier landholdings to established small northwest OHIO towns in *WINESBURG, OHIO* (1919). In "Godliness" in that collection Anderson presents the four-part saga of Jesse Bentley, a ministerial student called home to take over his family's struggling frontier farmstead after the Civil War deaths of his four brothers and the incapacitation of his father. Jesse's felt need to find positive divine purpose in his family's terrible loss becomes twisted over time into a misguided quest for a sign of God's love for him. Jesse attempts to gain God's favor through the value of his land, the productivity of his farm, and the number of people doing his bidding. He becomes avaricious, exploiting the land, agricultural technology, family members, and all around him. Similarly, in her 1913 novel *O PIONEERS!* WILLA CATHER (1873–1947) portrays the negative transformation from struggling but community-oriented NEBRASKA frontier life to self-centered, materialistic lives in its established towns and cities.

Ohio-born WILLIAM DEAN HOWELLS (1837–1920), a leading late nineteenth-century American writer and critic, provided the classic literary study of business and morality. He set the novel *The Rise of Silas Lapham* (1885) in the elite section of Boston, where

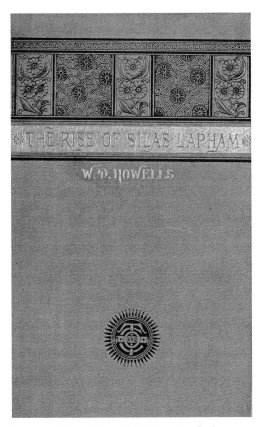

William Dean Howells's *The Rise of Silas Lapham*. Ticknor & Co., 1885.
Image courtesy of the University of Kentucky Special Collections Research Center

his protagonist, a wealthy paint company owner, is building his new home. Lapham is the product of rural upbringing and morality, but he conducts his business on the basis of power and advantage. Ultimately, when his life comes to a crisis, Lapham finds that immorality is the price of business success and a place among the Boston elite. Ultimately, he chooses a clear conscience over business success and returns to a simpler life in the rural place of his origins.

(HERMAN) THEODORE DREISER (1871–1945), born in Terre Haute, INDIANA, wrote SISTER CARRIE (1900), portraying the dreams of his naïve small-town WISCONSIN protagonist, Carrie Meeber, as she arrives in CHICAGO and experiences the economic, social, and sexual exploitation that mark the early twentieth-century laissez-faire industrial city. Unable to cope with work demands in the unregu-

lated industrial city, she is economically exploited by her sister and her husband and then sexually exploited by a salesman and a lounge manager. Over time Carrie learns to be as exploitative as those around her. In the process, she rises economically but will never achieve emotional fulfillment. Her major male counterpart in the novel, Hurstwood, is more specifically the businessman character. His fall is Dreiser's counterpoint to Carrie's rise. Ironically, the fullest justification Dreiser can provide for their otherwise immoral actions is naturalistic determinism, that they cannot control their needs, urges, or actions.

Dreiser also used non-Midwestern settings in some of his novels. Three of these, *The Financier* (1912), *The Titan* (1914), and *An American Tragedy* (1925), provide scathing indictments of the American businessman. The first two are based on the life and career of Charles Tyson Yerkes, a Philadelphia banker who eventually served a seven-month term in the penitentiary for embezzlement and later became an unscrupulous political figure. The third shows the ruination of Clyde Griffiths, a handsome, materialistic young man driven by aspirations for status and money; he eventually is found guilty of murdering a young woman with whom he has had an affair to avoid jeopardizing his chances for advancement.

In THE JUNGLE (1906) UPTON (BEALL) SINCLAIR (JR.) (1878–1968) depicts the interlocking directorate of business, government, and the courts controlling the Chicago meatpacking industry and, by extension, the city. The system ruthlessly exploits workers, including newly arrived Lithuanian immigrant Jurgis Rudkus and his family, for business efficiency, corporate profitability, and increased wealth for the elite. Jurgis's naïve Horatio Alger American Dream response to all setbacks, "I will work harder," becomes ever more ironic. Sinclair's novel makes plain his belief that Americans' dreams of upward mobility are empty dreams that are unscrupulously manipulated to benefit corrupt business interests. He advocates socialism instead, where worker solidarity will ensure that laborers benefit from their labor.

At another level of Midwestern urban and economic development, (BENJAMIN)

FRANK(LIN) NORRIS (1870–1902) depicts unscrupulous Midwestern commodity speculation in his unfinished *Trilogy of the Wheat*. The middle novel, *The Pit* (1903), portrays the trading floor of Chicago's futures exchange, where the fates of farmers are decided by traders who speculate wildly. The slightest price change can mean profit or ruin for farmers thousands of miles away, while those doing the trading are depicted as reckless and greedy, caring nothing about the impact of their actions. Similarly, in *The Octopus* (1901) the spread of the railroad and the behaviors of the unscrupulous businessmen who control it dictate the fortunes of farmers who rely on railroads to ship their crops. *The Octopus* strongly illustrates the clash between commercial and agrarian America in Midwestern literature.

In a number of novels (NEWTON) BOOTH TARKINGTON (1869–1946) takes on various aspects of business. *The Magnificent Ambersons* (1918), for example, chronicles the decline of the family fortune in the early days of automobiles.

CHICAGO POEMS (1916) by CARL (AUGUST) SANDBURG (1878–1967) positively portrays pre-industrial and industrial-age working-class men and women in poems that simultaneously attack the exploitative, self-seeking business interests of the city. From the title poem, "Chicago," forward, Sandburg's workers reflect dignity, while business and the elite are castigated. In poems like "They Will Say," "Mill-Doors," "Anna Imroth," "The Right to Grief," and "Muckers," Sandburg exhibits the inhuman pressure placed on those at the bottom in order to benefit business interests and the social elite. Sandburg's early solution, presented in poems like "I Am the People, the Mob," "Dynamiter," and "The Fence," is socialist revolution.

In 1925 Calvin Coolidge remarked to the Society of American Newspaper Editors, "The business of America is business," and generations of Americans have grown up believing the myths associated with the books written by Horatio Alger Jr. (1832–1899). Alger's books promise success to any boy willing to work hard and maintain high moral standards. In doing so, they reinforce the American myth that business is good and big business is better. In that same year, 1925, in *THE GREAT GATSBY*, F(RANCIS) SCOTT (KEY) FITZGERALD (1896–1940) responded with the story of a boy, James Gatz, the son of struggling NORTH DAKOTA parents. Gatz naïvely attempts to remake his life in accordance with the tenets of the American Dream; he changes his name, fictionalizes his history, and uses criminal business practices in a misguided and ultimately self-defeating effort to rise from poverty in the upper Midwest to the privileged class in the East. Fitzgerald made it clear that he rejected the American Dream, with its basis in business and its desire for social mobility.

To Have and Have Not (1937), a Depression-era novel by ERNEST (MILLER) HEMINGWAY (1899–1961), presents down-on-his-luck Florida Keys boat owner Harry Morgan, who is losing his battle to support his family. In desperation he resorts to illegal activities and is eventually killed. In the novel's coda Harry's boat is towed into the Key West harbor; aboard the large yachts in the harbor are characters who serve as foils for Harry Morgan. They are seen as the wealthy waste products of corrupt business lives; their angst is all they have in their meaningless world.

In *Babbitt* (1922) (HARRY) SINCLAIR LEWIS (1885–1951) conveys the self-delusion and everyday foibles motivating American businessmen in an era of local boosterism, industrial development, and suburban sprawl. In Lewis's ironically named city, Zenith, George Babbitt, the businessman, is not so much victimizer as misguided victim, mindlessly accepting the empty boosterish catchphrases of the day while struggling for financial gain or at least economic stability in a world he does not fully understand. Lewis's novel presages literary works attacking 1950s corporate culture, suburban life, and ever-present marketing. The novel's impact was such that "Babbitt" entered the English lexicon as a word signifying a conformist businessman or, by extension, any bourgeois materialist.

Midwestern writing of the late nineteenth and early twentieth centuries provides such a predominantly damning portrait of the businessman, from the feckless small-town entrepreneur to the exploitative big-city financier, that one might wonder how succeeding writers could have anything left to say. The themes persist, although they do not dominate later writing to the same degree as before, nor, with exceptions, in such purely black-and-white terms. MEREDITH (ROBERT) WILLSON (1902–1984) deals with the confidence man Harry Hill as a figure of HUMOR who brings hope and joy to a small Iowa town in *The Music Man* (musical, 1957 novel, 1962). In *Grand Opening* (1987) JON HASSLER (1933=2008) treats the difficulties of running a family grocery store in small-town MINNESOTA. *AMERICAN BUFFALO* (1976) by DAVID (ALAN) MAMET (b. 1947) explores the sleazy underside of marginal business operations, rivalry, and revenge; his *Glengarry Glen Ross* (1984) suggests the illegal lengths to which real estate salesmen might go to retain their jobs. In many of her novels (KAREN) LOUISE ERDRICH (b. 1954) shows the ways in which corruption touches Native American businesses; *LOVE MEDICINE* (1984, 1993) is only one of them. *The Businessman: A Tale of Terror* (1984) by Thomas M. Disch (1940–2008) is a gothic tale about a MINNEAPOLIS businessman haunted by the ghosts of his wife, whom he murdered, and others, including the late poet JOHN BERRYMAN (1914–1972). *A Voice from the River* (1990) by DAN GERBER (b. 1940) focuses on a man who reassesses his life, including his service in World War II, after retiring as chairman of a Michigan lumber company.

Writing about business and the businessman is not limited to the Midwest, and Midwestern authors have not confined their business-related writings to Midwestern characters or settings. The role of the businessman never quite disappears from literature, but it was particularly strong in the early part of the twentieth century. With few exceptions, Midwestern writers have typically rejected financial elitism and the valuing of personal and corporate gain above human needs and dignity.

SELECTED WORKS: Many Midwestern works portray business, businessmen, and the people they victimize. Among the best known and most important of these negative portrayals are Hamlin Garland's *Main-Travelled Roads* (1891), Theodore Dreiser's *The Financier* (1912) and *The Titan* (1914), and Frank Norris's *The Pit* (1903). Many Midwestern novels depict the negative impact of unbridled capitalism on its victims; most notable here are Dreiser's *Sister Carrie* (1900) and Upton Sinclair's *The Jungle* (1906). F. Scott Fitzgerald's *The Great Gatsby* (1925) and, more humorously, Sinclair Lewis's *Babbitt* (1922) portray the corrosive effect of the American dream of business success. More recent works include David Mamet's play *American Buffalo* and Dan Gerber's novel *A Voice from the River* (1990).

FURTHER READING: No book-length work presents views of business or the businessman in Midwestern literature. Secondary sources in American literature include Michael J. McTague's *The Businessman in Literature: Dante to Melville* (1979), Emily Stipes Watts's *The Businessman in American Literature* (1982), Lorne Fienberg's *A Cuckoo in the Nest of Culture: Changing Perspectives on the Businessman in the American Novel, 1865–1914* (1988), and Carl S. Horner's *The Boy inside the American Businessman: Corporate Darwinism in Twentieth-Century American Literature* (1992). Excerpts from scholarship on writers discussed in this entry appear, along with a bibliography, in "The Businessman in American Literature," edited by Dennis Poupard, *Twentieth-Century Literary Criticism* 26 (1988): 1–48.

STEPHEN C. HOLDER   CENTRAL MICHIGAN UNIVERSITY

CANON, THE CHANGING MIDWESTERN LITERARY

OVERVIEW: The definition of "literary canon" varies, but it generally involves judgment by scholars, critics, teachers, readers, or a combination of them as to which texts are particularly fine or important in a given time period or culture. Determining which artistic works do or do not merit consideration and inclusion in the canon reflects the range of political, ideological, and aesthetic values operating in a particular historical and cultural context. These acts of literary judgment are premised on a range of value structures that give a basis for making these decisions and disseminating and celebrating the works selected. Canon discussions always involve heated debate, and certain works excluded by one generation may be recovered and revalued by another. Such debate is not only inevitable but healthy. As M(eyer) H(oward) Abrams contends in *A Glossary of Literary Terms* (1999), "The boundaries of a literary canon remain indefinite, while inside those boundaries some authors are central and others more marginal" (29). This means that no single, authoritative canon exists for Midwestern literature, and that by its very nature the canon of Midwestern literature must be forever changing and finding strength in its fluidity, in the arguments made by scholars, critics, and general readers on behalf of authors they deem vital to the study of the Midwest.

HISTORY AND SIGNIFICANCE: In discussing issues of canon as they relate to the study of Midwestern literature, two distinct categories emerge: Midwestern authors whose work is acknowledged in the broader canon of American literary study, and authors whose work is included in the more focused regional canon of Midwestern literature, a canon established during the twentieth century, argued for by Midwestern literary scholars, and demonstrated by the efforts of such organizations as the SOCIETY FOR THE STUDY OF MIDWESTERN LITERATURE.

In the broader canon of American literature, the rise of literary figures who, by birth or life experience, come to be identified as Midwestern coincides with the celebration of regionalism in American culture. SAMUEL LANGHORNE CLEMENS (1835–1910), better known by his pen name, Mark Twain, was one of the earliest figures of Midwestern literature to cross the boundary from a writer of local-color stories highlighting several regions in America, including landscapes as disparate as MISSOURI and California, to a writer of international fame and influence whose place in the canon of American literature is seldom questioned. Like Twain, the earliest Midwestern authors to gain acceptance in the canon of American letters did so in the context of a literary establishment that valued the universal over the local, the national or international over the regional. For these authors to find success, their work had to possess some identifiable quality that a critic or scholar might argue had merit beyond the local or regional. For instance, although a story by Twain might be set in Hannibal, Missouri, or on the Mississippi River, the scholarly affirmation of that story would not focus its attention on the geographic location or the culture and customs of the Midwest, but rather would draw on the mythic or symbolic significance of these landscapes, demonstrat-

ing how events and locations transcended the literal place and time in which they were set.

One must keep in mind that acceptance by the academy of the merit of American literature and its validity for study came only in the late nineteenth and early twentieth centuries and was marked by movement away from the primary texts of classical Greek and Latin literature to the writing of America's own authors. This embrace of a national literature, which affected school curricula and areas of study in graduate and undergraduate programs in universities and colleges, did not come without accompanying baggage. As this shift occurred, the canon was shaped in part by editors as they composed ANTHOLOGIES that celebrated American life; in part by scholars who proposed arguments that would justify inclusion of particular writers in such anthologies; and in part by teachers and professors who taught the works of these authors in the newly instituted courses in American literary studies.

The most crucial debates tied to the growing discipline of American letters occurred during the heyday of modernism and the New Criticism. At this time authors and critics, among them T(HOMAS) S(TEARNS) ELIOT (1888–1965) and SHERWOOD ANDERSON (1876–1941), successfully argued that the most important literary works transcended their particular local context. The manner in which a particular writer represented a region like the Midwest played little or no role in determining the worth of that writer or his or her place in the canon. Although writers like ERNEST (MILLER) HEMINGWAY (1899–1961) and F(RANCIS) SCOTT (KEY) FITZGERALD (1896–1940) highlighted particular aspects of the Midwest in selected works, either by setting or by origin of the narrator, their rise to literary prominence was based on a modernist aesthetic that contends that the value of these writers does not lie in the particularity of the details but in the ways those details transcend their place in the real world and open outward toward some universal element in humanity.

Perhaps the most crucial step in the formation of a Midwestern literary canon occurred with the advent of contemporary critical theory. Schools of theory as diverse as

New Historicism, poststructuralism, reader-response criticism, and feminism, among others, established, over time, a space in which the idea of a single, universal literary canon was called into question. In certain postmodern schools of thought, the very idea of universal truth was attacked, and an embrace of local or regional truths was championed. In *The Postmodern Condition: A Report on Knowledge* (1984), Jean-François Lyotard argues that the only "truth" we have access to is through the local, through the *petites histoires* that are bound by their embedded cultural and temporal context. In other words, the very rules of canonicity were changing with the intellectual inroads associated with postmodernism and other rising critical theories. Where once the universal was considered the highest good—the principal prerequisite for inclusion in the canon—now the local took precedence. Instead of a single U.S. canon for literature, scholars began arguing for a multiplicity of canons.

In practice, during the first half of the twentieth century several scholars and writers in American literature began arguing for the value of regional diversity and distinctiveness. This happened across the United States, but the most coherent regional literary movements developed in the South and the Midwest. In 1915 JOHN T(OWNER) FREDERICK (1893–1975) founded the Midwestern literary journal *THE MIDLAND,* in which he published many writers from the region and gave the region a voice in the larger literary establishment. By the 1940s noted scholars such as John T. Flanagan (1906–1996) began writing critical articles and publishing anthologies, such as *America Is West: An Anthology of Middlewestern Life and Literature* (1945), that began to shape a common body of Midwestern authors and works. The argument in favor of a Midwestern literary canon continued to develop.

Within this context, in 1971 at Michigan State University, DAVID D(ANIEL) ANDERSON (1924–2011) founded the Society for the Study of Midwestern Literature. Perhaps no single group has done more to establish and shape the canon of Midwestern literature. Over the past four decades the members of this organization have founded and maintained two journals, *MidAmerica* and *Mid-western Miscellany;* a conference, the Cultural Heritage of the Midwest; a literary festival, the Midwest Poetry Festival; two annual awards, one given for contributions to the scholarly study of Midwestern literature, the MidAmerica Award, and one for the artistic creation of that literature, the Mark Twain Award; and up to four prizes for presentations at the annual conference. Many of the society's members have written scholarly essays and monographs arguing for the importance of a variety of Midwestern authors, produced anthologies that highlight the Midwest and its diversity, and created literary works that have found their way into the canon of Midwestern literature.

Arguably, the most important contribution to the formation of the modern Midwestern literary canon may be *Dictionary of Midwestern Literature,* volume 1, *The Authors* (2001), edited by Philip A. Greasley and composed of entries written by members of the Society for the Study of Midwestern Literature. As suggested previously, the creation of a canon involves a variety of forces and processes, but signal moments may be identified. At such moments a definable shift transpires, giving shape to certain aspects of the canon. For example, in each subsequent edition of *The Norton Anthology of American Literature* or *The Heath Anthology of American Literature*—to name two anthologies used in countless classrooms and influencing students and future scholars—certain writers find their place or role within the American canon either solidified or made more tenuous by their inclusion in or exclusion from these sources. Thus, at this point in American literary history, Midwestern authors like KURT VONNEGUT (1922–2007), TONI MORRISON (b. CHLOE ARDELIA WOFFORD, 1931), and JOYCE CAROL OATES (b. 1938) appear to have a strong foothold in the broader American canon. The *Dictionary of Midwestern Literature* serves as the most recent and likely the most forceful means of codifying the authors who will find their names written in the canon of Midwestern literature.

With entries on nearly four hundred Midwestern authors, the volume's range is formidable. It recognizes temporal boundaries, including some of the earliest writers in the region, such as CAROLINE KIRKLAND (1801–1864) and EDWARD EGGLESTON (1837–1902), as well as some of the most recent, such as JANE (GRAVES) SMILEY (b. 1949) and (KAREN) LOUISE ERDRICH (b. 1954). It attempts to capture the ethnic diversity of the region with such authors as OLE EDVART RØLVAAG (1876–1931), BHARATI MUKHERJEE (b. 1940), and RITA DOVE (b. 1952). At the same time it offers representation to writers who focus on the urban experience of the Midwest, such as (HERMAN) THEODORE DREISER (1871–1945) and JOHN BERRYMAN (1914–1972), as well as to authors whose work tends to concentrate on the rural aspects of the region, such as ALDO LEOPOLD (1887–1948) and MARY SWANDER (b. 1950). Additionally, the volume includes writers whose work has reached a broader popular audience, like GARY EDWARD KEILLOR (b. 1942), writing as Garrison Keillor, and ROBERT JAMES WALLER (b. 1939), and those writers whose work is firmly established in the canon of American literature—Hemingway, Fitzgerald, T. S. Eliot, and Toni Morrison, for instance—are included alongside less well-known authors like LUCIEN STRYK (1924–2013), JIM (JAMES THOMAS) HARRISON (1937–2016), and LINDA HASSELSTROM (b. 1943), whose contributions to the canon of Midwestern literature, despite less public awareness, remain extremely valuable.

Volumes such as the *Dictionary of Midwestern Literature*, however, can never be "complete" and important writers who undoubtedly deserve a place in the canon are inevitably overlooked. For example, in the first volume of *Dictionary of Midwestern Literature*, there is no entry for Ted Kooser (b. 1939), a Nebraskan who was named Poet Laureate of the United States in 2004 and who received the Pulitzer Prize for Poetry in 2005. Kooser, a prolific writer born in Ames, Iowa, has always identified himself as a Midwestern author; his friendships with the likes of Jim Harrison and his former role as editor and publisher of Windflower Press further solidify his regional significance. Such examples demonstrate that the work of canon formation is always in flux and depends on a range of forces.

The production of literary anthologies both reflects and guides the choices made by critics and readers. Although the breadth and depth of such anthologies are beyond the scope of this entry, a brief overview of the kinds of anthologies that help give shape to the canon may be useful. Some anthologies attempt to approach the Midwest as a whole, demonstrating the variety and range of the region through a select group of writers. For example, *Growing Up in the Midwest* (1981), edited by Clarence A. Andrews, is a collection of brief memoirs by such noted authors as MERIDEL LE SUEUR (1900–1996), LANGSTON HUGHES (1902–1967), GWENDOLYN BROOKS (1917–2000), Garrison Keillor, and PATRICIA HAMPL (b. 1946). Andrews explains in his introduction that he "ranged over the Middle West for these writings," attempting to represent "big cities, towns, villages, and rural areas," (viii) as well as an offering of the cross section of ethnic and occupational identities found in middle America.

Inheriting the Land: Contemporary Voices from the Midwest (1993), edited by Mark Vinz and Thom Tammaro, focuses more exclusively on the rural Midwest and its heritage and includes work by such noted Midwestern writers as CAROL BLY (1930–2007), ROBERT (ELWOOD) BLY (b. 1926), ALICE (RUTH) FRIMAN (b. 1933), THOMAS (MATTHEW) MCGRATH (1916–1990),WILLIAM STAFFORD (1914–1993), and LARRY WOIWODE (b. 1941). This collection of prose and poetry is organized thematically in sections titled "Climates," "The Presence of the Past," "Town and Country," and "Gains and Losses."

From the Heartlands: Photos and Essays from the Midwest (1988), edited by Larry Smith, strives to capture the sense of place endemic in much writing about the Midwest. As Smith suggests, landscape artists have always had the sense of personal and universal location engendered by a particular time and place. Smith collects work by such writers as Mark Vinz (b. 1942), SCOTT RUSSELL SANDERS (b. 1945), Michael Delp (b. 1948), and Jeff Gundy (b. 1952).

Two landmark anthologies of Midwestern poetry, *Heartland: Poets of the Midwest* (1967) and *Heartland II: Poets of the Midwest* (1975), edited by Lucien Stryk, influenced the course of the canon by marking already established careers in the first volume and launching other careers by highlighting work that up to that time had been recognized only in small-press periodicals. In *Heartland,* Stryk recognizes the achievement of such well-known poets as MARY OLIVER (b. 1935), Robert Bly, Gwendolyn Brooks, Thomas McGrath, and William Stafford. In *Heartland II,* Stryk introduces the work of such poets as DAN GERBER (b. 1940), Jim Harrison, Ted Kooser, JUDITH MINTY (b. 1937), and Michael Van Walleghen (b. 1938), who at this time in their careers had received little national exposure.

In addition to more general Midwestern anthologies, many other anthologies offer a more focused perspective, presenting an interesting counterpoint and distinguishing the unique landscapes that make up the region we call the Midwest. In this category are such books as *New Territory: Contemporary Indiana Fiction* (1990), edited by Michael Wilkerson and Deborah Galyan, which includes work by WILLIAM H(OWARD) GASS (b. 1924), Ron Hansen (b. 1947), and Scott Russell Sanders; *Benchmark: Anthology of Contemporary Illinois Poetry* (1988), edited by James McGowan and Lynn DeVore, which collects the work of such writers as Robin Behn (b. 1958), Dan Guillory (b. 1944), and Martha M. Vertreace-Doody (b. 1945); and *New Poems from the Third Coast: Contemporary Michigan Poetry* (2000), edited by Michael Delp, Conrad Hilberry, and Josie Kearns, which includes such writers as STUART DYBEK (b. 1942), Linda Nemec Foster (b. 1950), Thomas Lynch (b. 1948), Greg Rappleye (b. 1953), and Jack Ridl (b. 1944).

SELECTED WORKS: John T. Frederick's articles in *The Midland* and John Flanagan's *America Is West* (1945) are among the seminal documents establishing modern Midwestern literature and the Midwestern literary canon. Beyond these, the articles in the journals of the Society for the Study of Midwestern Literature, primarily *MidAmerica,* have developed and supported the evolving Midwestern literary canon.

FURTHER READING: Several articles and extended studies have been published that look at Midwestern authors or argue for a distinct Midwestern literature and canon. John T. Flanagan's "A Half-Century of Middlewestern Fiction," *Critique* 2 (Winter 1959): 16–34, and "The Reality of Midwestern Literature," in *The Midwest: Myth or Reality* (1961), edited by Thomas T. McAvoy, are strong examples of early arguments for a body of Midwestern writers 75–91. Ronald Weber's *The Midwestern Ascendancy in American Writing* (1992) is also a strong example of how regional literary history has significance in a national context and canon.

Although little has been written about the Midwestern canon, two available sources are Robert Dunne's "Not for White Men Only: The Methodology behind the *Dictionary of Midwestern Literature,*" *MidAmerica* 20 (1993): 40–47, and Philip A. Greasley's introduction to *Dictionary of Midwestern Literature,* volume 1, *The Authors* (2001): 1–8. Several key texts help construct the various arguments that have shaped the broader American canon. Richard Ruland and Malcolm Bradbury's *From Puritanism to Postmodernism: A History of American Literature* (1991) creates an intriguing narrative out of the cultural and historical forces that shape not only the writers and their texts but also the reception of those texts. *Columbia Literary History of the United States* (1988), edited by Emory Elliott, is a prodigious volume covering the breadth of American literary history. The section "Regionalism: A Diminished Thing" will prove especially interesting to the student of Midwestern literary studies. *Rewriting the Dream: Reflections on the Changing American Literary Canon* (1992), edited by W. M. Verhoeven, includes such chapters as "The Canonizers and the Canonized" by J. J. A. Mooij and "Rethinking Canonicity: Toni Morrison and the (Non) Canonic 'Other'" by Kofi Owusu. Judith Fetterley and Marjorie Pryse challenge the literary canon in *Writing Out of Place: Regionalism, Women, and American Literary Culture* (2003), arguing for the inclusion of women writers like Midwesterner ALICE CARY (1820–1871). Reassessing the work of F. Scott Fitzgerald, Joe Kraus addresses the critical tendency to devalue ethnic literature in "De-Centering the Canon: Understanding *The Great Gatsby* as an Ethnic Novel" in *Multiethnic Literature and Canon Debates* (2006), edited by Mary Jo Bona and Irma Maini, 127-44. In *American Literary Regionalism in a Global Age* (2007) Philip Joseph demonstrates how texts by (HANNIBAL) HAMLIN GARLAND

(1860–1940), WILLA CATHER (1873–1947), and others speak beyond their time and locale.

TODD F. DAVIS   PENN STATE ALTOONA

CAPTIVITY NARRATIVES

OVERVIEW: The "Indian" captivity narrative is one of the few literary genres, and among the first, to claim America as its birthplace. Typically, these narratives are accounts of white women captured and held captive by Native Americans, then referred to as Indians; however, captives also included white males, African Americans, and children. These narratives had their genesis in the early seventeenth century and include fictional and nonfictional accounts in the form of autobiographies, biographies, novels, DIME NOVELS, oral histories, plays, poems, and short stories. The reports, often penned by amateur writers, vary in literary merit and in length, from brief pamphlets to complete volumes. They evolved during a period spanning more than four centuries, geographically beginning in New England, moving across the Midwest, and ending in California. Midwestern captivity narratives are a unique subset within the captivity-narrative genre because of the time and place in which they were written. Although some narratives were straightforward and truthful, many were aggressively fictional, and many more fell somewhere in between. Often authenticity was subordinated to propaganda, whether political, religious, or historical. Whether these narratives were fictional, factual, or a combination, most were widely read. By the beginning of the twentieth century, the reality of captivity by Native Americans faded into history, but interest in captivity narratives remained strong and continues to the present with the publication of new ones, the writing of fictionalized renditions of true captivities, and the production of critical studies, films, and documentaries. See also NATIVE AMERICANS AS DEPICTED IN MIDWESTERN LITERATURE.

HISTORY AND SIGNIFICANCE: Captivity narratives underwent four major phases from the seventeenth to the nineteenth century. Within these four major phases the narratives also evolved. Overlapping progressions and characteristics exist and make it difficult to categorize individual captivity narratives, particularly those of the Midwest. The line between fiction and fact is blurred, and the agendas of editors and authors often conflict, complicating the task of distinguishing reality from fanciful embellishment. Despite these phases and transformations, all Indian captivity narratives have one element in common: they were written with specific historical and cultural purposes shaped by the demands of the times and the intended white readership. All had political, religious, or historical agendas.

The first phase of captivity narratives, largely confined to the eastern United States and based on events occurring in the late sixteenth and early seventeenth centuries, resulted primarily from New World colonization by European countries. These imperialistic narratives provided European readers with their initial views of indigenous peoples, perpetuating stereotypes that furthered the political objectives of the countries where they were published. An example of this type of captivity narrative is the account of Pocahontas and John Smith (1580–1630) found in Smith's *The Generall Historie of Virginia, New England, and the Summer Isles* (1624).

Written at the end of the seventeenth century, captivity narratives of the second phase were largely religious narratives in which captivity was translated into a religious or spiritual allegory meant to teach a lesson. One of the first narratives of this stage, and perhaps the most popular, is *The Sovereignty and Goodness of God, Together with the Faithfulness of His Promises Displayed* (1682) by Mary (White) Rowlandson (ca. 1636–1711). This captivity narrative, a best seller that saw thirty editions, was the first published as a full-length book by an Anglo American woman. Rowlandson incorporated elements of Puritan spiritual writing and interpreted her experience through her belief in God's providence, wisdom, mercy, and wrath. Puritans saw Indians as instruments of the devil; therefore, narratives of this second phase portrayed a captive's struggle against them as a struggle against the forces of Satan, and they could rationalize any action or retaliation against them as divinely ordained.

One of the Midwestern Indian captivity narratives to include religious elements is that of Father Louis Hennepin (1626–ca. 1705), a Franciscan friar captured by the Dakota in MINNESOTA in 1680. His account was included in his *Description de la Louisiane* (1683). Hennepin's narrative is not as overtly religious as many of the Puritan and Quaker captivity narratives, but he does discuss his desire to convert the Dakota and relates his baptism of a young Dakota child.

Another Midwestern captivity narrative incorporating religious elements is *A Short Biography of John Leeth, Giving a Brief Account of His Travels and Sufferings among the Indians for Eighteen Years Together with His Religious Exercises from His Own Relation* (1831) by Ewel Jeffries (1755–1832). At age seventeen, while living in New Lancaster, OHIO, John Leeth (1755–1832) was taken prisoner by the Delaware. The first half of Leeth's narrative details his life with the Delaware; the second half is devoted to his conversion and subsequent religious life. In a manner consistent with that of other late seventeenth-century writers, Leeth interprets captivity as God's way of disciplining and teaching his people. He sees his suffering as a redemptive aspect of captivity for which to praise God and as a lesson for both himself and the reader.

Captivity narratives of the third period, evolving during the eighteenth century and continuing in the nineteenth, were largely used to perpetuate stereotypes and spread propaganda against indigenous peoples, who were viewed as obstacles to European settlement. Most Midwestern captivity narratives were published during this phase, sometimes as dime novels. These narratives depicted Indians as murderous savages, justified their annihilation, and encouraged "civilization" of tribes and cultivation of the land by white men. These narratives accompanied the movement westward as Midwestern and western states were being settled. Rather than depicting captivity as a test of religious faith, many narratives interpreted captivity as a test of patriotic loyalty. Not only were new narratives written in the Midwest during the nineteenth century, but also narratives from the seventeenth and eighteenth centuries were reprinted to encourage removal or annihilation of Native peoples in the Midwest and West.

One typical Midwestern anti-Indian captivity narrative is the forty-eight-page *History of the Spirit Lake Massacre: 8th March, 1857: And of Miss Abigail Gardiner's [sic] Three Month's Captivity among the Indians, According to Her Own Account as Given to L. P. Lee* (1857) by Lorenzo Porter Lee (1800–1889). This narrative recounts the experiences of Abigail Gardner-Sharp (1843–1921) in IOWA. After her family was killed in the 1857 Spirit Lake Massacre, a precursor to the Minnesota Sioux Uprising of 1862, she was held captive by a group of Santee Sioux for three months. Lee's narrative depicts in gruesome detail the massacre of her family and two other captives, the hardships she endured, and her eventual rescue by "Christian Indians." Lee claims that he wrote and published the book so Gardner-Sharp could profit from its sales, but he also wrote it to meet the popular demand for sensational captivity narratives, feed readers' need for thrills and adventure, and evoke audience sympathy through descriptions of atrocities. Lee also compares Gardner-Sharp's captivity with others, implores readers to be thankful that they live in "civilized" areas of the country, and alludes to a future time in which the Midwest will be civilized and no longer ruled by "savages."

Twenty-eight years later Gardner-Sharp wrote her own version of the events, titled *History of the Spirit Lake Massacre and Captivity of Miss Abbie Gardner* (1885), which went through at least eleven editions. Surprisingly, Gardner-Sharp includes criticism of white expansion. While Lee's 1857 narrative praises Gardner-Sharp's father for obeying what he believed to be God's decree to move west and settle the land, Gardner-Sharp criticizes the idea that the white man must continually push westward. She blames her father for the massacre and her subsequent captivity. Rather than penning a rousing tale to entertain eastern readers, she believes that it is her responsibility to put down a historical record of the events that led to her captivity. She claims that writing her version of the events has been a trying task, but she reports that she hopes her narrative will pay tribute to the victims. Nonetheless, despite her purportedly noble purpose, Gardner-Sharp still exaggerates Indian violence, catering to public demand for sensationalistic captivity tales.

Oliver Spencer (1781–1838), in his narrative *Indian Captivity: A True Narrative of the Capture of Rev. O. M. Spencer* (1835), asserts that God decrees the westward march of white civilization and the removal of Native peoples as dispensable obstacles. He feels that whites must claim and cultivate undeveloped land that is thus wasted by the Indian inhabitants. In Spencer's narrative, even the Indians realize and accept the fact that the "pale faces . . . would not be satisfied until they had crowded the Indians to the extreme north, to perish on the great ice lake; or to the far west until, pushing those who should escape from their rifles, into the great waters, all would at length be exterminated" (117). Spencer, who was captured in 1792 in Ohio by the Shawnee, did not publish his narrative until over forty years after his captivity. It first appeared in serial form in 1834 in the *Western Christian Advocate,* and when it proved successful, Spencer published it in book form, achieving more than twelve editions. Scattered throughout the narrative are spiritual reflections and commentaries reminiscent of seventeenth-century religious captivity narratives. Thus Spencer is appealing to a dual audience: readers of the religious publication in which his narrative first appeared and patriotic settlers who believed in the civilization and cultivation of the Midwestern and western states.

As the narratives of this phase proved effective in conjuring hatred and encouraging white expansion and the simultaneous destruction of the indigenous peoples, kidnapping tales gradually became more fictitious, more exaggerated, and more focused on atrocities inflicted on white captives. These pulp thrillers, rather than being straightforward accounts of captivity and Native American life, became more stylized and literary, emphasizing horror to evoke pity for captives and promote retaliation by whites.

One example of a fictionalized captivity tale is *The Remarkable Adventures of Jackson Johonnet, a Soldier under General Harmar and General St. Clair, Containing an Account of His Captivity, Sufferings, and Escape from the Kickapoo Indians* (1793). Encouraging patriotism and westward expansion, this questionable anti-Indian narrative tells the tale of Jackson Johonnet, a young man taken captive in Ohio in 1791 by a party of Kickapoo. The book details his four-week suffering at the hands of his captors, the torture and eventual deaths of his comrades, and his incredible escape. After his escape he rejoins the army in time to attack the village where he was held captive. Although this was a popular narrative, no evidence exists for Jackson Johonnet's existence and many details contradict documented historical facts.

It was also not uncommon during this phase for entire anthologies of anti-Indian narratives to be published. Although these collections were not exclusively Midwestern, many of them did include Midwestern captivity narratives, and they were published for the sole purpose of promoting annihilation of Native Americans. *A Selection of Some of the Most Interesting Narratives of Outrages Committed by the Indians, in Their Wars, with the White People* (1808), edited by Archibald Loudon (1754–1840) and the anonymous *Indian Anecdotes and Barbarities: Being a Description of Their Customs and Deeds of Cruelty, with an Account of the Captivity, Sufferings and Heroic Conduct of the Many Who Have Fallen into Their Hands, or Who Have Defended Themselves from Savage Vengeance; All Illustrating the General Traits of Indian Character* (1837) were products of this phase.

While these sensational narratives continued to be written and were popular in the Midwest and West, where captivity was still a reality, in the East a new phase was beginning that would continue into the twentieth century. Narratives of this fourth phase saw Native Americans as a remnant of history, no longer the detested subjects of Anglo Americans. These narratives romanticized Native peoples, sometimes patronized them, and employed them as symbols of America's history and heritage. The third version of Abigail Gardner-Sharp's narrative, published in 1918, includes an additional chapter that is both sympathetic and condescending. In this final chapter Gardner-Sharp says that she now holds Indians in the highest regard and believes them capable of education and civilization with white

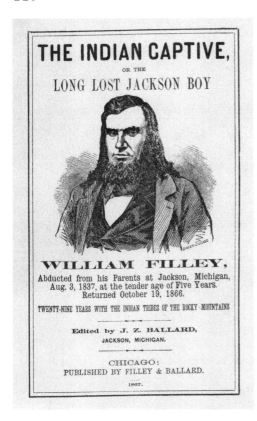

William Filley's *The Indian Captive*. Filley & Ballard, 1867.

intervention. Gardner-Sharp claims that after visiting reservations in Minnesota and SOUTH DAKOTA in 1892, she "wanted to see all of the Indians brought into harmony with the whites, and was very glad they were learning how to read, write, and do useful things" (336). She attributes her change of heart toward them to her religious conversion in 1889. Thus the final chapter is reminiscent of earlier religious captivity narratives. Although the bulk of Gardner-Sharp's later narrative would appeal to readers who still viewed Native people as opponents to be conquered and removed, she added the final chapter to appeal to readers who now were far enough removed to view indigenous peoples as a symbol of America's heritage.

William Filley (1832-ca. 1915) was abducted from his Jackson, MICHIGAN, farm when he was five years old, and over the following three decades he was taken further west by subsequent captors, eventually living with seventeen different tribes. His narrative, *Life and Adventures of William Filley ... and His Safe Return from Captivity ...* (1867), also published as *The Indian Captive, or the Long Lost Jackson Boy ...*, recounts his memories and observations among the Osage, Sioux, Comanche, and others in a straightforward and unsensational manner.

Although many narratives produced during the nineteenth and early twentieth centuries embraced traditional elements of earlier captivity narratives, they also adopted new elements in order to show captivity in ways uncommon at the time they were written. *A Narrative of the Life of Mrs. Mary Jemison, Who Was Taken by Indians in the Year 1755* (1824) by James E. Seaver (1787–1827) exhibits this new attitude toward Native Americans. Mary Jemison (1743–1833), who lived with her family in western Pennsylvania, was captured by a Shawnee and French raiding party in 1755, taken to Ohio, and given to two Seneca women as a replacement for their dead brother. Jemison was around twelve years old when she was captured, and although her early years of captivity were not easy, she did assimilate to her captors' culture and refused to return to white civilization. Jemison married twice, bore eight children, and lived with the Seneca for over seventy years. Although Jemison was critical of Seneca warfare and cruelties perpetrated on their enemies, she also believed that white attempts to "civilize" and educate Indians only made them act worse and would eventually lead to their extermination. Jemison not only justified and defended indigenous ways but also demonstrated little regard for, or trust in, white society. Despite the unique qualities of this narrative and its departure from typical narratives, it was a best seller that sold over 100,000 copies the first year and went through twenty-nine editions.

Another pioneering Midwestern captivity narrative is *Six Weeks in the Sioux Tepees: A Narrative of Indian Captivity* (1864) by Sarah Wakefield (1829–1899). Wakefield was captured with her two children during the 1862 Sioux Uprising and penned one of the most unusual narratives to emerge from the conflict. Her preface states her reasons for writing, none of which were typical of captivity narratives. She claims to have written the narrative as a legacy for her children, who were too young to remember what had happened. She also claims to have written the truth rather than embellishing and reports being protected from further harm by a "Christian Indian." Finally, Wakefield asserts no desire to make money from her narrative but wants to be vindicated from accusations concerning her attitude toward and defense of Native Americans. Before her captivity Wakefield and her family had moved to the Sioux reservation's Upper Agency, where her husband was a physician. At first, Wakefield feared her Dakota neighbors, but she later says that she grew to love the land and the Dakota. She credits her survival to her Christian faith and the kindness she had shown them before her captivity. Unlike most captives, Wakefield and her children had a protector, a Dakota man named Chaska. Throughout her captivity Wakefield shared his tepee. She vehemently claimed that Chaska never touched her and protected her from others who sought to rape her. Wakefield was criticized by her fellow captives during her captivity for having taken Chaska as her lover and by the public after her release. Fear of sexual "contamination" was common in female captivity narratives and was particularly problematic for Wakefield.

Wakefield's narrative is heavily religious, although its spiritual tone is significantly different from that of its Puritan predecessors. At the end of her narrative she calls on God to make things right and defend her from the blame directed at her by those who did not understand or condone her actions as a captive. Wakefield repeatedly claims that she did the Christian thing by helping her captors, cooperating with them in an effort to save herself and her children, and defending them after her release. She asserts her belief that God will vindicate her. Upon her release, Wakefield defended her protector, Chaska, and when he was unjustly hanged, she expressed guilt for not having been able to protect him as he had protected her. Wakefield not only defended Chaska but also criticized white males for disregarding her testimony at Chaska's trial and for showing disrespect to her. After her release

Wakefield was taken to a soldiers' camp and claimed that she had been "treated more respectfully by those savages, than I was by those [soldiers] in that camp" (quoted in *Women's Indian Captivity Narratives* 299). She also blames the 1862 uprising on white males who deliberately withheld food from the starving people. She is also angry that it took so long for soldiers to rescue the captives. Before, during, and after her captivity, Wakefield discovered that not all whites are honorable and trustworthy and not all Indians are loathsome heathens.

In "Narrative of Mary Schwandt," first published in Charles S. Bryant and Able B. Murch's *A History of the Great Massacre by the Sioux Indians, in Minnesota* (1864), Mary Schwandt (1848–1939) claims that she would have nothing to do with Wakefield because of her conduct. Schwandt admits having been raped several times during her captivity. She, too, had an Indian protector, a woman, and portrays herself as anything but cooperative when it came to men.

These four major phases of captivity narratives show that the narratives of the Midwest were complex, dynamic, and sometimes contradictory vehicles for expressing and decoding race relations, Manifest Destiny, and gender politics. They pushed the limits of reader comfort and acceptance and were often used to redefine political, geographic, and social boundaries.

SELECTED WORKS: Collections of captivity narratives include *American Captivity Narratives* (2000), edited by Gordon M. Sayre; *Women's Indian Captivity Narratives* (1993), edited by Kathryn Zabelle Derounian-Stodola; and *Captured by the Indians: 15 Firsthand Accounts, 1750–1870* (1961), edited by Frederick Drimmer. Sayre's text includes Rowlandson's narrative, accounts of African American captives, and the "inverse captivity narrative" of Geronimo (1829–1909). Zabelle Derounian-Stodola's book covers early Puritan captivity narratives, Sarah Wakefield's narrative, captivity poems, and the "Panther Captivity," a best-selling, completely fictionalized captivity narrative. Drimmer's compilation includes several Midwestern narratives. The definitive collection of captivity narratives is the 112-volume Garland Library of Narratives of North American Indian Captivities (1975–1983), which reprints

311 titles dating between 1682 and 1962; however, it is available in its entirety in only a few libraries. Many captivity narratives, including some discussed here, are available online as full original texts.

FURTHER READING: The first attempt at a scholarly examination of captivity narratives as a literary form was the anthology *Indian Captivities, Being a Collection of the Most Remarkable Narratives of Persons Taken Captive by the North American Indian* (1839), compiled by Samuel Gardner Drake. Drake reprinted original captivity accounts and appended historical notes and biographies. However, true objective study began with the work of C. Alice Baker in her *True Stories of New England Captives Carried to Canada during the Old French and Indian Wars* (1897), followed by *New England Captives Carried to Canada between 1677 and 1760* (1925) by Emma Lewis Coleman. Rebecca Blevins Faery's *Cartographies of Desire: Captivity, Race, and Sex in the Shaping of an American Nation* (1999) and *Captured by Texts: Puritan to Postmodern Images of Indian Captivity* (1995) by Gary L. Ebersole are both important studies. Midwestern captivity narratives are relatively uncharted territory and provide opportunities for research. However, the following texts provide insight into them: *White Captives: Gender and Ethnicity on the American Frontier* (1993) by June Namias; *Bound and Determined: Captivity, Culture-Crossing, and White Womanhood from Mary Rowlandson to Patty Hearst* (1996) by Christopher Castiglia; and *The Indian Captivity Narrative, 1550–1900* (1993) by Kathryn Zabelle Derounian-Stodola and James Arthur Levernier. Readers interested in a bibliographic approach will find the following texts useful: *Narratives of North American Indian Captivity: A Selective Bibliography* (1983) by Alden T. Vaughan and *Early Midwestern Travel Narratives: An Annotated Bibliography, 1634–1850* (1961) by Robert Rogers Hubach.

CRYSTAL STALLMAN   HAWKEYE COMMUNITY COLLEGE

CHICAGO

Chicago (from the Algonquin word *shikaakwa* for "wild leek" or 'skunk' and applied to onion fields, the lake, and then the city) was founded as a settlement in 1772 by Jean-Baptiste Point du Sable (ca. 1745–1818). Indian tribes ceded the land to the U.S.

© Karen Greasley, 2014

military in the Treaty of Greenville in 1795. Chicago was incorporated as a town (population 350) in 1833 and as a city in 1837.
Area: 234 square miles
Population (2010 census): 2,695,598

OVERVIEW: In *Writing Chicago: Modernism, Ethnography, and the Novel* (1993) Carla Cappetti asserts that Chicago stands as "the birthplace of American urban literature" (7). In the late nineteenth and early twentieth centuries Chicago novelists like (HERMAN) THEODORE DREISER (1871–1945) and HENRY BLAKE FULLER (1857–1929) wrote pioneering works of realism and naturalism; from the 1880s to the present Chicago has offered journalists and columnists a congenial home for the production of newspaper humor and fiction. Before 1920 the city's poets and dramatists laid the foundations for modern American poetry and theatre. These Chicago writers—novelists, poets, playwrights, and journalists working between roughly 1880 and 1920—are conventionally considered participants in the CHICAGO RENAISSANCE. In the 1920s the city produced a small body of African American writing that paralleled the more famous Harlem Renaissance. A decade later, as Cappetti maintains, Chicago novelists, like RICHARD WRIGHT (1908–1960), JAMES T(HOMAS) FARRELL (1904–1979), and NELSON ALGREN (1909–1981), wrote about the hard facts of urban experience, the city's racial divisions and ethnic neighborhoods, and its slums, gangs, and bare-knuckle politics. Although SAUL (C.) BELLOW (1915–2005), STUART DYBEK (b. 1942), GWENDOLYN BROOKS (1917–2000), and other Chicago writers who came to prominence after World War II did not exercise the same "sociological imagination" as their 1930s counterparts, they built on their predecessors' understanding of urban experience and on the literary traditions that they had begun (1). See also ILLINOIS and CHICAGO RENAISSANCE.

HISTORY AND SIGNIFICANCE: Chicago's reputation usually rests on its muscular industry, its rough-and-tumble politics, its violent criminal past, and its place at the vital center of commerce for the Midwest and the continent. But the city also deserves to be better known for its long, rich, and complex literary history, a history created in the less than two hundred years since its incorporation in 1837. After the Civil War, in a period of remarkable population growth, Chicago drew aspiring writers and the simply ambitious from the rural heartland and Midwestern small towns. Immigrants from Ireland, Germany, and eastern and southern Europe followed in greater numbers during the 1880s and 1890s; the Great Migration of African Americans from the South started about 1915 and continued for several decades. This mixing, massing, and melding of people—sometimes violently, sometimes with admirable civic and social

consciousness—charged the imagination of Chicago writers and contributed to the making of an important urban literature.

Chicago has been the setting for literary invention in fiction, poetry, drama, and nonfiction. The largest city in the Midwest has been the birthplace and home of hundreds of authors and a magnet for many who sought inspiration from the city's diverse people and neighborhoods. One of the earliest narratives is: The "Early Day" in the North-West (1856), about Chicago's Fort Dearborn and life on the frontier, by Juliette Kinzie (1806–1870). Two Native Americans are important in early Chicago literature. Translations of speeches by early nineteenth-century Potowatomi chief Metea (d. 1827) are available in Travels in the Central Portions of the Mississippi Valley (1825) by HENRY ROWE SCHOOLCRAFT (1793–1864). The speeches of BLACK HAWK (1767–1838) are available in Illinois Literature: The Nineteenth Century (1986), edited by John E. Hallwas, and in The Black Hawk War (1903) by Frank E(verett) Stevens (1856–1939)). Major John Richardson (1796–1852) is credited with the first Chicago novel, Hardscrabble; or, The Fall of Chicago (1850).

The Great Fire of 1871, the founding of HULL-HOUSE in 1889, and the World's Columbian Exposition in 1893 were signal events for Chicago writers and for the city's cultural identity. Two novels tell the story of the fire: The Fall of Chicago (1871) by Sophia B. Olsen (1846–1936) and Barriers Burned Away (1872) by E(dward) P(ayson) Roe (1838–1888). Hull-House, a settlement house founded by JANE ADDAMS (1860–1935) and Ellen Gates Starr (1859–1940) on the near West Side, caught the popular imagination and, in turn, generated

Chicago Skyline, 1927. Painting by William Macy. Kaufmann & Fabry Co., 1927.
Image courtesy of the Library of Congress

dozens of settlement-house novels, including *"Just Folks"* (1910) by CLARA E(LIZABETH) LAUGHLIN (1873–1941) and *The Precipice* (1914) by ELIA W(ILKINSON) PEATTIE (1862–1935).

The Columbian Exposition fascinated writers of the time like Clara Louise Burnham (1854–1927), who wrote *Sweet Clover: A Romance of the White City* (1894), and Daniel Oscar Loy (1851–1913), in his *Poems of the White City* (1893). Erik Larson (b. 1954) has written of the fair and, through careful research, has reconstructed the life of a serial murderer in *The Devil in the White City* (2003). In "Sharps and Flats," his column for the Chicago *Daily News*, EUGENE FIELD (SR.) (1850–1895) celebrated the fair even as he satirized Chicago's literary and cultural ambitions. Columnists GEORGE ADE (1866–1944) and FINLEY PETER DUNNE (1867–1936), working for competing Chicago papers and in different idioms, combined local color, political satire, and dialect humor. On their publication in 1890s, Ade's columns were titled "Stories of the Streets and Towns"; Dunne's representative works were collected in *Mr. Dooley in Peace and War* (1898) and *Mr. Dooley's Philosophy* (1900).

The Chicago Renaissance was a period of intense cultural energy, a confluence of genteel sensitivities, social upheaval, free experimentation, and the resulting literary production. By 1900 Chicago had become a major publishing center and by 1920, had produced a remarkable number of nationally acclaimed novelists, poets, and playwrights. All this led H(enry) L(ewis) Mencken (1880–1956) to proclaim in the April 17, 1920, issue of *The Nation* (London) that in the first two decades of the new century Chicago was "the literary capital of the United States" (92). No doubt CARL (AUGUST) SANDBURG (1878–1967) is the poet most often identified with the city, as in his books *CHICAGO POEMS* (1916), *Smoke and Steel* (1920), and *The People, Yes* (1936).

At the turn of the twentieth century several institutions and many less formal groupings fostered literary creativity in the city. Foremost were the clubs and "little-room" meetings of artists, writers, architects, and others gathering in places like the Cliff Dwellers' Club of (HANNIBAL) HAMLIN GARLAND (1860–1940) and Clara E. Laughlin's Chicago's Cordon Club and in the various studios of the Fine Arts Building on Michigan Avenue. The little-theatre movement and *POETRY: A MAGAZINE OF VERSE*, founded in 1912 by HARRIET MONROE (1860–1936), also played critical and defining roles. See also CLUBS, SALONS, AND SOCIETIES.

Chicago writers created a succession of works that pioneered literary REALISM AND NATURALISM. In Garland's *Rose of Dutcher's Coolly* (1895) a young writer comes to the city to find work; *With the Procession* (1895) by HENRY BLAKE FULLER (1857–1929) provides a portrait of the "new woman" in Susan Bates; Fuller's *The Cliff-Dwellers* (1893) satirizes Chicago's business classes and the belief that the city was undergoing a renaissance. Dreiser's *SISTER CARRIE* (1900) is often considered the strongest Chicago novel of this period. Several other works by Dreiser that reckon with the Midwest and Chicago's titanic power deserve attention: *Jennie Gerhardt* (1911), *The Financier* (1912), *The Titan* (1914), and *A Book about Myself* (1922). *The Pit: A Story of Chicago* (1903) by (BENJAMIN) FRANK(LIN) NORRIS (1870–1902) explores the life of Curtis Jadwin, "a great financial captain," both a victim and a symbol of the city's "sordid, material modern life" (21–22). *The Memoirs of an American Citizen* (1905) by ROBERT HERRICK (1868–1938) celebrates the city's financial patrons. *THE JUNGLE* (1906) by UPTON (BEALL) SINCLAIR (JR.) (1878–1968) exposes the abuses in the stockyards and the unbearably hard life of new immigrants and ends with a plea for socialism. FLOYD DELL (1887–1969) edited the *Friday Literary Review* and wrote a significant trilogy: *Moon Calf* (1920), *Briary Bush* (1921), and *Souvenir* (1930). The humor and satire are more scathing in *Erik Dorn* (1921), *The Front Page* (1928), and *A Jew in Love* (1931) by BEN HECHT (1894–1964).

Some writers of this time, like EDNA FERBER (1885–1968), SHERWOOD ANDERSON (1876–1941), and WILLA CATHER (1873–1947), lived elsewhere and wrote about Chicago or lived in Chicago and wrote famous books set elsewhere. Important works include *SPOON RIVER ANTHOLOGY* (1915) by EDGAR LEE MASTERS (1868–1950) and the many works of ERNEST (MILLER) HEMINGWAY (1899–1961).

Works of fiction associated with Chicago brought new prominence to the changing roles of women in American urban life. Among these were *The Glory of the Conquered*

(1909) and *The Visioning* (1911) by SUSAN (KEATING) GLASPELL (1876–1948), *A Woman of Genius* (1912) by MARY (HUNTER) AUSTIN (1868–1934), *The Penny Philanthropist* (1912) by Clara E. Laughlin, *The Main Road* (1913) by Maude Radford Warren (1875–1934), *The Precipice* (1914) by Elia W. Peattie, and *The Wine of Astonishment* (1919) by Mary Hastings Bradley (1882–1976).

Between 1932 and 1940 two landmark Chicago works were written: the Studs Lonigan trilogy by James T(homas) Farrell: *Young Lonigan: A Boyhood in Chicago Streets* (1932), *The Young Manhood of Studs Lonigan* (1934), and *Judgment Day* (1935); and *Native Son* (1940) by Richard Wright. Wright's and Farrell's novels were set on the South Side and, in different ways, traced the city's emerging racial conflicts. Wright began his novel while working for the FEDERAL WRITERS' PROJECT, sponsored by the Works Progress Administration.

Other Chicago writers employed on this program included Nelson Algren, Saul Bellow, WILLARD F. MOTLEY (1909–1965), and (LOUIS) STUDS TERKEL (1912–2008). Motley conducted some of the fieldwork and sociological study in Chicago that led to his novel *Knock on Any Door* (1947), a realistic narrative of a cop killer and the city's skid row. Algren went on to write *Never Came Morning* (1942), *The Man with the Golden Arm* (1949), and *Chicago, City on the Make* (1951), gritty explorations of the city and the North Side. Their works, characterized by an animating sociological imagination, are synonymous with what Sidney Bremer has called, in the chapter "Chicago's Residential Novels and Their Social Roots" in *Urban Intersections* (1992), the "Chicago tradition" in American fiction.

Together with poets Arna Bontemps (1902–1973) and Margaret Walker (1915–1998), Wright founded the South Side Writers' Group in 1936. Although the Chicago Black Renaissance may be given an earlier beginning date, the founding of the South Side Writers' Group was a crucial event in its history. Years before the high time of the Harlem Renaissance in the 1920s, the Chicago Black Renaissance had found a footing. The poem "Tired" by Fenton Johnson (1888–1958) was published in 1915; by 1918 OSCAR MICHEAUX (1884–1951) had founded the Micheaux Film and Book Company and had published three of his novels. His film *The Birth of a Race*—answering D. W. Griffith's *The Birth of a Nation*—debuted at Chicago's Blackstone Theatre. Micheaux's *Within Our Gates* (1920) responded powerfully to Chicago's race riots of 1919. Throughout this early period the *Chicago Defender*, the nation's leading black newspaper, published poetry and essays encouraging, wherever possible, the fine arts and the cultural aspirations of African Americans. Willard Motley published his Bud Billiken essays there in the 1920s, Gwendolyn Brooks placed her earliest poems on the *Defender*'s pages in the 1930s, and LANGSTON HUGHES (1902–1967) produced the first Jesse B. Semple tales for the *Defender* in 1943.

Gwendolyn Brooks, through her poetry and her abiding influence on younger black poets, was a groundbreaking figure in Chicago literature. Her initial success came with her portrayal of African American values and dignity amid the horrors of her South Side neighborhood in the poems collected in *A STREET IN BRONZEVILLE* (1945); this was followed by the Pulitzer Prize–winning collection *Annie Allen* (1949). At about the same time, Brooks spearheaded the second wave of the Chicago Black Renaissance through her neighborhood activities and work with younger writers like Carolyn (Marie) Rodgers (1940–2010), Angela Jackson (b. 1951), and Haki R. Madhubuti (b. Don L. Lee, 1942). With Brooks's help and encouragement, Madhubuti founded Third World Press, where she published her second autobiographical work, *Report from Part Two* (1996), continuing her *Report from Part One* (1972), published by DETROIT'S DUDLEY FELKER RANDALL (1914–2000) at his Broadside Press.

Chicago theatre flourished during most of the twentieth century, and its history and variety can only be suggested here. At the time of the Chicago Renaissance, the Players' Workshop in Hyde Park and the Little Theatre productions in the Fine Arts Building indicated the experimental direction the city's theatre was to take. George Ade, following the popular taste for light comedy, displayed his Midwestern wit and local color in *The Sultan of Sulu* (1903), *The Country Chairman* (1924), and *Just out of College* (1924). Chicago's newspaper heroics and political farce animated the comedy *The Front Page* (1928) by Ben Hecht and CHARLES (GORDON) MACARTHUR (1895–1956). Chicago's most famous play, A RAISIN IN THE SUN (1959) by LORRAINE (VIVIAN) HANSBERRY (1930–1965), attacked housing segregation and racism.

Chicago is famous for the Goodman Theatre and Steppenwolf, for many small theatres, and for improv at Second City, a company that in 1959 grew out of the Piven Theatre Workshop in Evanston and the Compass Players on 55th Street on the South Side. Arvid Sponberg's Chicago Theatre History Project has documented the remarkable expansion of professional companies and venues between 1950 and 2007. During those years Chicago developed a uniquely Midwestern talent base and highly responsive audiences. Examples include Hull-House Theater (revived 1963), Organic Theater, Pegasus Theatre at Harry Truman College, and the Chicago Shakespeare Festival at Navy Pier.

The city's most accomplished playwrights include DAVID (ALAN) MAMET (b. 1947), SAM(UEL) SHEPARD (ROGERS III) (b. 1943), and Sarah Ruhl (b. 1974). Mamet is most recognized for his *Sexual Perversity in Chicago* (1974), AMERICAN BUFFALO (1976), *The Blue Hour: City Sketches* (1979), and *Glengarry Glen Ross* (1984), which won a Pulitzer Prize. Shepard won a Pulitzer Prize for *Buried Child* (1978). Ruhl combines tragicomedy and theatre of the absurd in *Melancholy Play* (2002), *Eurydice* (2003), *The Clean House* (2005), and *Passion Play* (2006).

Shaped by the continuing influence of *Poetry* magazine, the city's rich ethnic traditions, and the powerful voices of the POETRY SLAMS, Chicago's poetry has grown to incorporate new urban tempos and idioms. The city can boast several Pulitzer Prize–winning poets: George Dillon (1906–1968), author of *The Flowering Stone* (1932); KARL SHAPIRO (1913–2000) for *V-Letter, and Other Poems* (1944); and Gwendolyn Brooks, for *Annie Allen* (1949). An important African American poet in Chicago just before and during the Harlem Renaissance was Fenton Johnson, who wrote *A Little Dreaming* (1913) and *Visions of the Dusk* (1915). John Frederick Nims (1913–1999) published distinguished poetry over a long period, writing *Knowledge of Evening: Poems, 1950–1960* (1960),

Of Flesh and Bone (1967), and *Selected Poems* (1994). A(ttipat) K(rishnaswami) Ramanujan (1929–1994) combined elements of his birthplace in India and Chicago in *The Striders* (1966), *Second Sight* (1986), and *The Black Hen: Complete Poems* (1995). MICHAEL ANANIA (b. 1939) has been Director of the Writing Program at the University of Illinois at Chicago and published *The Color of Dust* (1970), *Riversongs* (1978), *The Red Menace* (1984), and *Selected Poems* (1994). *Clinton* (1976) by Sterling Plumpp (b. 1940) won the Illinois Arts Council Literary Award. Barry Silesky (b. 1949) has edited *Another Chicago Magazine* since 1990 and wrote *The New Tenants* (1991) and *One Thing That Can Save Us* (1994). Carlos Cumpián (b. 1953), writer of *Coyote Sun* (1990), *Latino Rainbow* (1994), and *Armadillo Charm* (1996), founded the La Palabra readings at the Randolph Street Gallery. Li-Young Lee (b. 1957), one of the featured poets in Bill Moyers's *Power of the Word* TV series, has published *Rose* (1986) and *The City in Which I Love You* (1990). Native American poet Mark Turcotte (b. 1958) has written *Songs of Our Ancestors* (1995), *The Feathered Heart* (1995), and *Exploding Chippewas* (2002). Campbell McGrath (b. 1962) has published three books of poetry: *Capitalism* (1990), *American Noise* (1993), and *Spring Comes to Chicago* (1996), winner of the prestigious Kingsley Tufts Poetry Award. Lisel Mueller (b. 1924) won the Carl Sandburg Award for *Waving from Shore* (1989) and a Pulitzer Prize for *Alive Together: New and Selected Poems* (1996). Marc Kelly Smith (b. 1949), author of *Crowdpleaser* (1996), is the inventor and organizer of the1986 Chicago's Green Mill Lounge in July 1986, as well as the driving force behind many organizations supporting poetry in the city: Pong Unit One, Neutral Turf's Chicago Poetry Festival, and the Poetic Theatre Project.

Of the many novelists who took Chicago as a subject and theme after World War II, none holds a more powerful claim to understanding the city's humanity, cruelty, and sometimes violent, degraded beauty than Saul Bellow. His works range from the picaresque to social critiques, from jeremiads to low comedy. The playfulness and depth of THE ADVENTURES OF AUGIE MARCH (1953)—and the riffs on Chicago's polyglot language and street dialects—prompted comparison to *ADVENTURES OF HUCKLEBERRY FINN* (London 1884: New York 1885). *Herzog* (1964), winner of a National Book Award, presents a middle-aged intellectual ruminating about the world in crisis and Chicago's political corruption. *Humboldt's Gift* (1975) won a Pulitzer Prize in 1976. In the same year Bellow was awarded the Nobel Prize for Literature.

But Chicago has many more novelists who came to prominence after World War II. The writings of "HARRY" MARK PETRAKIS (b. 1923), including *Lion at My Heart (1959), Pericles on 31st Street* (1965), *The Waves of Night, and Other Stories* (1969), and *Ghost of the Sun* (1990), portray life in Chicago's Greektown. Longtime University of Chicago professor Richard Stern (1928–2013) has contributed many works described as fiction of ideas, most notably the novels *In Any Case* (1962), *Stitch* (1965), *Other Men's Daughters* (1973), and *A Father's Words* (1986). Leon Forrest (1937–1997) used experimental formats in several novels to chronicle the African American experience: *There Is a Tree More Ancient than Eden* (1973), *Two Wings to Veil My Face* (1983), and *Divine Days* (1992). In *Chin Music* (1985) James McManus (b. 1951) juxtaposes everyday pressures in the city to the bonding experienced by Chicago Bulls fans. *The Mixquiahuala Letters* (1986), the first novel by Ana Castillo (b. 1953), won the American Book Award, and her collection of stories, *Loverboys* (1996), shows the influence of magic realism. *THE HOUSE ON MANGO STREET* (1984) by SANDRA CISNEROS (b. 1954) is a collection of stories about a Mexican American girl growing up on Chicago's West Side. Tragicomic fiction by PETER DE VRIES (1910–1993) includes *Blood of the Lamb* (1961), *The Vale of Laughter* (1967), and *The Glory of the Hummingbird* (1974). Elizabeth Berg (b. 1948) wrote most of her works while living elsewhere, but she now lives in Chicago; her *Dream When You're Feeling Blue* (2007) is set in Chicago during World War II. *The Widows' Adventures* (1989) by Charles Dickinson (b. 1951) is a funny and sadly tragic tale of two Chicago ladies who take a road trip to California and return to a city decaying from within. His *Rumor Has It* (1991) explores ethical issues in newspaper work.

BETTE HOWLAND (b. 1937) addresses family, aging in the city, and the evolution of neighborhoods in *W-3* (1974), *Blue in Chicago* (1978), and *Things to Come and Go* (1983).

Other Chicago novelists who continue the street-wise traditions of Algren and Farrell include William Brashler (b. 1947) with *City Dogs* (1976), Isaac Rosenfeld (1918–1956) with *Passage from Home* (1946), and Sam Ross (1912–1998) with *Someday, Boy* (1948) and *Sidewalks Are Free* (1950). The novels of Morris (Harris) Philipson (1926–2011), author of *Bourgeois Anonymous* (1964), *The Wallpaper Fox* (1976), and *A Man in Charge* (1979), are satiric and witty. Tony Ardizzone (b. 1949) writes stories about baseball and growing up on the North Side, collected in *Heart of the Order* (1986) and *Taking It Home* (1996). *The Logic of a Rose: Chicago Stories* (2005) by Billy Lombardo (b. 1962) tells about growing up Italian in Bridgeport, Mayor Richard J. Daley's old Irish American neighborhood. CYRUS COLTER (1910–2002), in *The Beach Umbrella* (1970) and *The Rivers of Eros* (1972), captures the African American experience on Chicago's South Side in a variety of socioeconomic settings. Stuart Dybek has written poems and stories that recall and redact his experiences growing up in the Pilsen neighborhood of Chicago's lower West Side. *Brass Knuckles* (1979), *Childhood and Other Neighborhoods* (1980), and *The Coast of Chicago* (1990) combine meticulous realism and an expansive, sometimes fantastic imagination. In 2007 Dybek received both the distinguished Rhea Award for achievements in the short story and a MacArthur Genius Award.

Chicago has had a rich tradition of nonfiction, AUTOBIOGRAPHY, and imaginative reflection that started with the newspaper columnists and memoir writers of the late nineteenth and early twentieth centuries. Jane Addams's *Twenty Years at Hull-House with Autobiographical Notes* (1910) and *The Story of My Life* (1932) by CLARENCE (SEWARD) DARROW (1857–1938) are two early and illustrious examples. Studs Terkel, drawing on interview methods learned on the Federal Writers' Project, captures the sense of place and the people of Chicago in his many books of oral history, including, most prominently, *Division Street America* (1967), *Hard Times: An*

Oral History of the Great Depression (1970), and his Pulitzer Prize–winning *The Good War: An Oral History of World War II* (1984). (MICHAEL) MIKE ROYKO (1932–1997) is best known for his classic newspaper columns and for his probing *Boss: Richard J. Daley of Chicago* (1997). His columns have been collected in several works, from *Up against It* (1967) to *Dr. Kookie, You're Right* (1989).

Alex Kotlowitz (b. 1955) reports on social issues in Chicago in *There Are No Children Here: The Story of Two Boys Growing Up in the Other America* (1991) and *Never a City So Real: A Walk in Chicago* (2004). Carolyn Eastwood (1925–2014) has collected stories in her oral history *Near West Side Stories: Struggles for Community in Chicago's Maxwell Street Neighborhood* (2002). Ronne Hartfield (b. 1936), in *Another Way Home: The Tangled Roots of Race in One Chicago Family* (2004), shares the story of a mother's leadership in a multiracial South Side family. In *Pictures of Home* (2004) Douglas Bukowski (b. 1952) provides a photo-album-style account of growing up in Bridgeport at midcentury. In *Blue as the Lake: A Personal Geography* (1998) Robert B. Stepto (b. 1945), scholar of African American literature, relates his growing up in several neighborhoods on Chicago's South Side. SARA PARETSKY (b. 1947), author of the V. I. Warshawski detective stories, tells of her life in Chicago from 1966 to the present in *Writing in an Age of Silence* (2007). Along the way, the book sets down a scathing protest against the loss of personal freedoms under the Patriot Act.

Although Chicago literature is too voluminous to fit in any anthology, some collections stake out their territory carefully. Examples are *This Is Chicago: An Anthology* (1952), edited by Albert Halper; *Smokestacks and Skyscrapers: An Anthology of Chicago Writing* (1999), edited by David Starkey and Richard Guzman; and *The City Visible: Chicago Poetry for a New Century* (2007), edited by William Allegrezza and Raymond L. Bianchi. Ryan G. Van Cleave's *City of the Big Shoulders: An Anthology of Chicago Poems* (2012) is another resource. See also Bessie Louise Pierce, *As Others See Chicago*: *Impressions of Visitors, 1673–1933* (1933).

SELECTED WORKS: Chicago literature offers a wealth of great works, but as a starting point, readers should look at the following works of fiction: *Sister Carrie* (1900) by Theodore Dreiser, *The Jungle* (1906) by Upton Sinclair, *The Adventures of Augie March* (1953) by Saul Bellow, and *The Coast of Chicago* (1990) by Stuart Dybek. For poetry, start with *Spoon River Anthology* (1915) by Edgar Lee Masters, *Chicago Poems* (1916) by Carl Sandburg, and *A Street in Bronzeville* (1945) by Gwendolyn Brooks. For drama, consider *A Raisin in the Sun* (1959) by Lorraine Hansberry, *The Clean House* (2005) by Sarah Ruhl, and *Clybourne Park* (2010) by Bruce Norris. Among the many memoirs, sample *Another Way Home* (2004) by Ronne Hartfield and *Writing in an Age of Silence* (2007) by Sara Paretsky.

FURTHER READING: For the links between physical layout and the development of the arts in Chicago, see Robert A. Holland's *Chicago in Maps: 1612 to 2002* (2005). Lawrence Cortesi's *Jean du Sable*: *Father of Chicago* (1972) provides a good account of the city's founder. Excellent overviews are presented in Donald L. Miller's *City of the Century: The Epic of Chicago and the Making of America* (1996), Robert C. Bray's *Rediscoveries: Literature and Place in Illinois* (1982), and James Hurt's *Writing Illinois*: *The Prairie, Lincoln, and Chicago* (1992).

The best account of the dynamics of urban life before and after 1900 is Carl S. Smith's *Chicago and the American Literary Imagination, 1880–1920* (1984). For commentary on several of Chicago's neglected novels, see *Voices and Visions: Selected Essays* (2001) by Bernard F. Rodgers Jr. James A. Kaser's *The Chicago of Fiction: A Resource Guide* (2011) provides an annotated bibliography of novels and stories set in Chicago.

Good overviews of the Chicago Renaissance appear in Jan Pinkerton and Randolph H. Hudson's *Encyclopedia of the Chicago Literary Renaissance*: *The Essential Guide to the Lives and Works of the Chicago Renaissance Writers* (2004), Bernard Duffey's *The Chicago Renaissance in American Letters* (1954), and Dale Kramer's *Chicago Renaissance* (1966). H. L. Mencken's "The Literary Capital of the World," *The Nation* (London) 28 (April 17, 1920): 90–92, remains readable as a first report on the Renaissance. James DeMuth's

Small Town Chicago (1980) finds in humor writing an important nexus between the rural Midwest and Chicago. Sources on twentieth-century African American literature include *The Chicago Black Renaissance and Women's Activism* (2006) by Anne Meis Knupfer; *Writers of the Black Chicago Renaissance* (2011), edited by Steven C. Tracy; *The Black Chicago Renaissance* (2012), edited by Darlene Clark Hine and John McCluskey Jr.; and *The Muse in Bronzeville: African American Creative Expression in Chicago, 1932–1950* (2011) by Robert Bone and Richard A. Courage.

A useful discussion of "the standard Chicago novel" appears in Sidney Bremer's chapter "Chicago's Residential Novels and Their Social Roots" in *Urban Intersections* (1992). *Writing Chicago: Modernism, Ethnography, and the Novel* (1993) by Carla Cappetti persuasively defines Chicago literature, with special attention to Algren, Farrell, and Richard Wright.

An indispensable account of the development of plays, theatre companies, and venues in Chicago is Richard Christiansen's *A Theater of Our Own: A History and a Memoir of 1,001 Nights in Chicago* (2004). Arcadia Publishing's series Images of America provides dozens of informative and illustrated guides to events, literary developments, and neighborhoods in the city. One example is Paul M. Green and Melvin G. Holli's *World War II Chicago* (2003).

Additional studies of Chicago's historical context and literary image include Kenny J. Williams's *In the City of Men: Another Study of Chicago* (1974) and *Prairie Voices: A Literary History of Chicago from the Frontier to 1893* (1980); Clarence A. Andrews's *Chicago in Story: A Literary History* (1982); Hugh Duncan's *The Rise of Chicago as a Literary Center from 1885–1920: A Sociological Essay in American Culture* (1964); James Hurt's "Images of Chicago," in *Illinois: Its History and Legacy*, edited by Roger Bridges and Rodney Davis (1984); and a seminal article by DAVID D(ANIEL) ANDERSON (1924–2011), "Chicago as Metaphor," *Great Lakes Review* 1 (1974): 3–15.

Studies of expansion, mobility, and diversity include James R. Grossman's *Land of Hope: Chicago, Black Southerners, and the Great Migration* (1989), Melvin G. Holli and Peter d'A. Jones's *Ethnic Chicago: A Multicul-*

tural Portrait (1984), Harold Mayer and Richard C. Wade's *Chicago: Growth of a Metropolis* (1969), and Dominic Pacyga and Ellen Skerrett's *Chicago: City of Neighborhoods* (1986).

In *October Cities: The Redevelopment of Urban Literature* (1998), Carlo Rotella distinguishes between the "city of fact" and the "city of feeling" in reassessing writers' reimagining of Chicago after World War II. Rotella's emphasis on the key place of "the old neighborhood" provides insight into much of what has been called the "new" Chicago literature since the late twentieth century. Rotella returns to his exploration of neighborhood in "Return to South Shore," in *Playing in Time: Essays, Profiles, and Other True Stories* (2012). Thomas Dyja, in *The Third Coast* (2013), explores the impact of postwar Chicago literature on American culture. Robert A. Slayton's *Back of the Yards: The Making of a Local Democracy* (1986) shows how neighborhoods shape politics and literature. Two studies of what is always in the process of being lost as the city evolves are Alan Ehrenhalt's *The Lost City: The Forgotten Virtues of Community in America* (1995) and Ray Suarez's *The Old Neighborhood: What We Lost in the Great Suburban Migration, 1966–1999* (1999). Greg Holden's *Literary Chicago: A Book Lover's Tour of the Windy City* (2001) identifies homes, birthplaces, and museums of Chicago authors.

Chicago's popular literature, SCIENCE FICTION, crime and detective stories, little magazines, children's literature, and writing about sports and entertainment are too vast to attempt additional listing here. For references in these areas, see ILLINOIS.

The three most important collections that inform the literary history of Chicago are the papers assembled at the Chicago Historical Society, the Chicago Public Library, and the Newberry Library. Valuable materials are also housed at the Library of the University of Illinois at Chicago, the University of Chicago Library and the Art Institute of Chicago.

RONALD PRIMEAU   CENTRAL MICHIGAN UNIVERSITY

CHICAGO POEMS

HISTORY: *Chicago Poems* (1916) is a pivotal Midwestern work and a milestone of the CHICAGO RENAISSANCE and American literary

REALISM AND NATURALISM. It was created by CARL (AUGUST) SANDBURG (1878–1967), son of Swedish immigrants in Galesburg, ILLINOIS, and its impact rests on the confluence of local, national, and international social and literary movements. Sandburg's early Galesburg experiences with poetry and oratory at Lombard College, his time as a hobo and as a soldier in the Spanish-American War, his work as a platform speaker and organizer for the Wisconsin Social-Democratic Party and as secretary to Milwaukee's socialist mayor Emil Seidel, and his years as a CHICAGO journalist merged with advancing literary realism to produce the volume's striking subject matter and language. The success of *Chicago Poems* encouraged American poets to adopt aggressively realistic subjects and language and to confront the literary and political establishments.

In the late 1800s American urbanization and rapid, unregulated industrialization led to harsh working conditions, low pay, and destabilizing economic cycles. Prose writers like (HERMAN) THEODORE DREISER (1871–) in *SISTER CARRIE* (1900) and UPTON (BEALL) SINCLAIR (JR.) (1878–1968) in *THE JUNGLE* (1906) anticipated Sandburg in realistically depicting urban-industrial life.

American prose realism was well advanced by the early twentieth century. Fiction had significantly expanded the range of subjects and language, probed individual perception and motivation, and theorized on determinism, naturalism, and human nature. A realistic worldview and technique dominated Midwestern rural and urban fiction. Notable among these pioneering prose works were *The Story of a Country Town* (1883) by EDGAR WATSON HOWE (1853–1937); *Zury: The Meanest Man in Spring County* (1887) by JOSEPH KIRKLAND (1830–1894); *MAIN-TRAVELLED ROADS* (1891) by (HANNIBAL) HAMLIN GARLAND (1860–1940); *The Cliff Dwellers* (1893) by HENRY BLAKE FULLER (1857–1929); *Sister Carrie* (1900), *Jenny Gerhardt* (1911), *The Financier* (1912), *The Titan* (1914), and *An American Tragedy* (1925) by Dreiser; *The Pit* (1903) by (BENJAMIN) FRANK(LIN) NORRIS (JR.) (1870–1902); and *The Jungle* (1906) by Sinclair.

American poetry, however, remained tied to nineteenth-century romantic diction, technique, structure, and worldview. These retained romantic forms and values reflected increasingly desperate efforts to maintain America's sense of special providence. In reaffirming older literary, religious, and cultural values and rejecting change in language, style, and form, poetry became formulaic.

Yet poetic change began to manifest itself. *Leaves of Grass* (1855–1892) by Walt Whitman (1819–1892) massively expanded the range of poetic subjects and adopted vernacular speech and unrhymed verse. In 1891 WILLIAM MARION REEDY (1862–1920) began publishing what became *REEDY'S MIRROR*, calling for poetic change and proposing forward-looking models. Reedy's weekly literary pages gave direction to aspiring poets. In 1912 Chicago's HARRIET MONROE (1860–1936) created *POETRY: A MAGAZINE OF VERSE*, which aggressively fostered new poetic models and published and supported emerging poets. *Poetry* connected William Butler Yeats (1865–1939), Ezra Pound (1885–1972), and other leading poets to Chicago's poetic ferment. Amid this welter of change, Sandburg began writing poetry.

Penelope Niven's *Carl Sandburg: A Biography* (1991) recounts how Sandburg's financial difficulties and the plight of working-class Americans reinforced his personal sense of class injustice. Whitman's democratic, long-lined, oral-based poetics complemented Sandburg's developing social philosophy and provided democratic ideals and revolutionary poetic techniques that Sandburg first applied fully in *Chicago Poems*.

Sandburg's oratorical and journalistic work and his working-class experiences grounded his poetic orientation and his views on social issues, human nature, democracy, and America. But mastery came slowly. Several apprentice volumes and years as an orator and journalist preceded his poetic transformation. Work as a political organizer galvanized Sandburg's oratory and commitment to social justice (Niven 185; except where noted, all subsequent references are to this biography). His 1912 move to Chicago as a big-city journalist connected him to city realities, working people, and gifted writers and editors.

Reedy's complimentary letter on Sandburg's foreword to *The Dreamer* (1906) by Sandburg's first mentor, Philip Green Wright (1861–1934), encouraged him to continue writing poetry. In November 1906 Reedy rejected Sandburg's poetic submissions but gave him direction, calling his conventional romantic poems "too vague" but praising his "rough vigor" (113). For Sandburg, like Dreiser, EDGAR LEE MASTERS (1868–1950), and others, Reedy's mentorship and advocacy were critical. Sandburg continued writing and unsuccessfully submitting poems, including "Chicago," for publication. The best would ultimately appear in *Chicago Poems.*

SIGNIFICANCE: Sandburg's January 1914 submission to *Poetry* changed American poetry. It included "Chicago" and other poems that would form the core of *Chicago Poems.* *Poetry*'s publication of those radical experiments as the lead poems in the March 1914 issue advanced the poetic revolution.

Conservative literary journals, led by the *DIAL,* castigated the poems, but *Poetry*'s

VOL. III
No. VI

MARCH, 1914

CHICAGO POEMS

CHICAGO

OG Butcher for the World,
Tool Maker, Stacker of Wheat,
Player with Railroads and the Nation's
Freight Handler;
Stormy, husky, brawling,
City of the Big Shoulders:

They tell me you are wicked and I believe them, for I
have seen your painted women under the gas lamps
luring the farm boys.
And they tell me you are crooked and I answer: Yes, it
is true I have seen the gunman kill and go free to kill
again.
And they tell me you are brutal and my reply is: On the
faces of women and children I have seen the marks of
wanton hunger.

[191]

"Chicago" by Carl Sandburg, first publication in *Poetry: A Magazine of Verse,* March 1914. Image provided by the Modernist Journals Project (Brown University and the University of Tulsa), http://www.modjourn.org

May 1914 rejoinder in "The Enemies We Have Made" (4:61) signaled the end of the dominance previously enjoyed by genteel nineteenth-century poetics. *Poetry* asserted that it and its new poets had "taken chances, made room for the young and the new, tried to break the chains which enslave Chicago to New York, America to Europe, and the present to the past" (4:61).

Poetry's publication of Sandburg's poems and its spirited defense of his radical poetics brought him to the forefront. Later, his submissions were awarded *Poetry*'s 1914 Levinson Prize. Another seventeen Sandburg poems appeared in *Poetry* in October 1915. Two months earlier Dreiser had suggested that Sandburg collect his Chicago poems for book publication, and Sandburg began assembling, revising, and positioning poems for the collection (268). *Poetry*'s Alice Corbin Henderson connected Sandburg with Alfred Harcourt of Henry Holt and Company. He secured a contract for Sandburg by early February 1916 and worked with him to trim and focus the collection (270–71).

The resulting collection was notable. From the aggressively anti-poetic connotation of "Hog Butcher," the first two words of "Chicago," the volume's lead poem, Sandburg made it clear that *Chicago Poems* would make no accommodations to prevailing poetic norms or elite sensibilities (1916 edition, 3). Instead, it offered clear, realistic, Whitmanesque portraits of the city and its working people in aggressively simple, direct language counterposed with nuanced imagist and socialist anti-war poems.

Most of these poems starkly portray gross class injustice in a deterministic environment, but Sandburg's worker portraits regularly offer liberating expressions of joy, strength, spirit, hope, and aspiration. In poems like "Dynamiter," strong, committed working-class heroes fight on, sacrificing themselves to advance social justice. With few exceptions, *Chicago Poems* portrays working-class protagonists unbowed by circumstance: strong, noble figures in a hostile universe. They transcend injustice and identify with the city they are building.

The volume consists primarily of Whitmanesque oral poetry using parallelism and repetition for structure. These poems are linguistically sparer than Whitman's but reflect his social perspectives and vernacular speech. Brief, compressed, emotive imagist poems like "Fog" and "Nocturne in a Deserted Brickyard" counter the aggressively direct, harsh language and social commentary of Sandburg's Whitmanesque poems. These imagist poems offer visions of momentary beauty and release amid lives of travail. Most of the worker portraits and attacks on social injustice in *Chicago Poems* achieve emotional force through brutally direct, simple language and lengthening repetitive patterns, but the evocative imagist poems attune readers to every nuance. These complementary types make the abuses more biting, the beauty and heroism more poignant and uplifting. *Chicago Poems* also includes Sandburg's 1914–1915 socialist anti-war poems, broadening the portrayal of class injustice. These ironic war poems and their repeated references to "red" make Sandburg's working-class sympathies clear.

Chicago Poems had impact. Early response was predictably polarized, reflecting the massive shift in poetic subject, language, and form between those in vogue in the late nineteenth century and those characterizing twentieth-century poetry and subject matter. Avant-garde writers lauded the volume's strong, meaningful verse that addressed contemporary issues with force and impact. Conservative voices like the *Dial* attacked *Chicago Poems* for its brutality, referred to the "hog butcher" school of poetry, and called *Poetry* "a futile little periodical" (56: 231–32). *The Dial* asserted that *Chicago Poems* provided "no trace of beauty in the ragged lines . . . [and] admits no aesthetic claim of any description, and acknowledges subordination to no kind of law" (243).

By the late 1920s critical response to Sandburg's poetic experiments underlying *Chicago Poems* was almost universally positive. By the mid-1930s general affirmation of Sandburg's work meant that his major poetic innovations had now been widely adopted. The shock effect of his aggressively ungenteel diction dissipated as poets and prose writers adopted that standard. Sandburg's repetitive oral line no longer elicited shock. Free Verse had supplanted rhymed syllabic verse.

Over time, most social reforms Sandburg advocated were adopted. Child labor was abolished, the vote was extended to women, minimum-wage laws were enacted, unions became prevalent and protected, and employers became responsible for working conditions. Mandatory universal education and progressive taxation became the norm. Sandburg's social message was revolutionary no longer.

Sandburg continued experimenting with poetic diction, line length, and structure, but his major contributions had already appeared in *Chicago Poems.* Later work was less adversarial, lauding American democracy and common humanity. Much of the creative tension underlying his previous poetry had collapsed. Rather than chiseled portraits of individual heroic working-class Chicagoans, Sandburg increasingly substituted homage to mankind en masse. Picturesque idiom and experiments in the poetic line replaced compelling class-struggle portraits. Gone were his "muckers" digging wet yellow clay ditches for Chicago's subway; his "hunky" in "The Right to Grief" sweeping blood off the stockyards floor and paying a week's wages for his three-year-old daughter's coffin; and his "fish crier" joyfully dangling fish from a street-corner stand. Gone too were poems like "Mill-Doors," which captured industrial class injustice, and "Anna Imroth," which bitterly and ironically portrayed the arrogance and criminal negligence underlying the deaths of 146 garment workers in New York's criminally tragic 1911 Triangle Shirtwaist Factory fire.

Sandburg now placed greater emphasis on extended oral syntax, picturesque language, directness, clarity, and affirmation of America, in opposition to Modernist trends. Yet poets and prose giants, including LANGSTON (JAMES MERCER) HUGHES (1902–1967), ARCHIBALD MACLEISH (1892–1982), and ERNEST (MILLER) HEMINGWAY (1899–1961), paid homage to Sandburg. *A STREET IN BRONZEVILLE* (1945) by GWENDOLYN (ELIZABETH) BROOKS (1917–2000) is among the many volumes that adopt and extend Sandburg's realistic technique and social justice message. Poets and prose writers striving to capture the lives, speech, and dignity of common people owe him a great debt. Today *Chicago Poems* remains fresh and striking, asserting the dignity and heroism of "common" people.

IMPORTANT EDITIONS: Many poems in *Chicago Poems* first appeared elsewhere. Penelope Niven's *Carl Sandburg: A Biography* (1991) details these earlier publications. *Chicago Poems* was first published in 1916 by New York's Henry Holt and Company. Many editions have followed in nations and languages spanning the globe. As with most early twentieth-century literary works, access to first editions is typically limited to special collections. The 1992 University of Illinois Press edition of *Chicago Poems* features an introduction by John E. Hallwas. Dover's 1994 Thrift Edition of *Chicago Poems* is the cheapest edition available. It contains the unabridged 1916 first-edition text and adds a brief introductory note and list of titles. Most commonly available in libraries is the 1970 Harcourt Brace Jovanovich revised and expanded edition of *The Complete Poems of Carl Sandburg.*

FURTHER READING: No book-length works exist on *Chicago Poems,* but information on the volume and Sandburg can be found in several sources. Penelope Niven's *Carl Sandburg: A Biography* (1991) is the best source on Sandburg's life, writings, and criticism. The *Dictionary of Midwestern Literature,* volume 1 (2000), carries an entry on Sandburg by Philip A. Greasley.

Many books and book chapters address the Chicago Renaissance. Most important are Bernard I. Duffey's *The Chicago Renaissance in American Letters: A Critical History* (1954), Dale Kramer's *Chicago Renaissance: The Literary Life in the Midwest, 1900–1930* (1966), and Carl S. Smith's 1984 *Chicago and the American Literary Imagination, 1880–1920. The Vision of This Land: Studies of Vachel Lindsay, Edgar Lee Masters, and Carl Sandburg* (1976), edited by Hallwas and Dennis J. Reader, is a valuable addition. Greasley's "Big Shoulders, Cat Feet: The Midwestern Dimensions of Carl Sandburg's *Chicago Poems,*" in *Midwestern Literature* (2013), edited by Ronald Primeau (139–54) provides additional information on *Chicago Poems* and its author, as does Greasley's unpublished 1975 Michigan State University dissertation, "American Vernacular Poetry: Studies in Whitman, Sandburg, Anderson, Masters, and Lindsay."

MidAmerica, the journal of the SOCIETY FOR THE STUDY OF MIDWESTERN LITERATURE, has published multiple Sandburg articles. These include Paul J. Ferlazzo's "The Urban-Rural Vision of Carl Sandburg," in *MidAmerica* 1 (1979): 52–57, and his "The Popular Writer, Professors, and the Making of a Reputation: The Case of Carl Sandburg," in *MidAmerica* 6 (1979): 72–78; John T. Flanagan's "Carl Sandburg, Lyric Poet," in *MidAmerica* 4 (1977): 89–100; and Greasley's "Beyond Brutality: Forging Midwestern Urban-Industrial Mythology," in *MidAmerica* 11 (1984): 9–19.

William Alexander's "The Limited American, the Great Loneliness, and the Singing Fire: Carl Sandburg's *Chicago Poems"* appears in *American Literature* 45.1 (March 1973): 67–83. Robert L. Reid's "The *Day Book* Poems of Carl Sandburg," *Old Northwest: A Journal of Regional Life and Letters* 9.3 (Fall 1983): 205–18, considers Sandburg's poems in that newspaper around the time *Chicago Poems* was emerging. Mark Van Wienen's "Taming the Socialist: Carl Sandburg's *Chicago Poems* and Its Critics," *American Literature* 63.1 (March 1991): 89–103, provides information on politics and labor in early twentieth-century Chicago. John Marsh's "A Lost Art of Work: The Arts and Crafts Movement in Carl Sandburg's *Chicago Poems,*" *American Literature* 79.3 (September 2007): 527–51, evidences current American interest in *Chicago Poems* and Sandburg. *Endeavors at Self-Expression: Carl Sandburg, Poet and Man of Many Worlds* (2000) by Swedish scholar Ingegerd Friberg reflects international attention.

The University of Illinois at Urbana-Champaign Rare Book and Special Collections Library holds the manuscripts of Carl Sandburg's poetry as individual poems.

PHILIP A. GREASLEY   UNIVERSITY OF KENTUCKY

CHICAGO RENAISSANCE

OVERVIEW: Until recently the term "Chicago Renaissance" referred to literary activity in CHICAGO in the years before and immediately after World War I. Contemporary scholars, however, agree that the Chicago Renaissance spanned a longer period that can be divided into phases, each of which helped shape the development of American and world literature, and that these phases are fluid and overlapping, making it false and counterproductive to call one phase of it the Chicago Renaissance and the other phases or waves something else. According to Carlo Rotella, author of the "Chicago Literary Renaissance" entry in *The Encyclopedia of Chicago* (2004), edited by James R. Grossman, Ann Durkin Keating, and Janice L. Reiff, at least three surges of Chicago writing affected the development of American and world literature between the Great Chicago Fire of 1871 and the middle of the twentieth century (143–44).

The first wave, which crested at the turn of the century, featured "Midland realism." Some representative authors of this style were EDWARD EGGLESTON (1837–1902), HENRY BLAKE FULLER (1857–1929), (HANNIBAL) HAMLIN GARLAND (1860–1940), ROBERT (WELCH) HERRICK (1868–1938), WILLIAM VAUGHN MOODY (1869–1910), and (HERMAN) THEODORE DREISER (1871–1945), as well as popular humorists EUGENE FIELD (SR.) (1850–1895), GEORGE ADE (1866–1944), and FINLEY PETER DUNNE (1867–1936). See MIDLAND and REALISM AND NATURALISM.

The second wave of the Chicago Renaissance produced a fascinating gathering of writers, an amazing flowering of institutions, and an outpouring of writing between 1910 and the mid-1920s. Chicago writers during this period rejected the Genteel Tradition of nineteenth-century manners and style and embraced new forms and new perspectives, leading H(enry) L(ouis) Mencken (1880–1956) to pronounce that Chicago was now the "literary capital of the United States" in his famous 1920 essay with that title. Writers representative of this rich second and central wave of the Chicago Renaissance include HARRIET MONROE (1860–1936), EDGAR LEE MASTERS (1868–1950), SHERWOOD ANDERSON (1876–1941), CARL (AUGUST) SANDBURG (1878–1967), (NICHOLAS) VACHEL LINDSAY (1879–1931), Maurice Browne (1881–1955), EUNICE (HAMMOND) TIETJENS (1884–1944), ALICE (ERYA) GERSTENBERG (1885–1972), RING(GOLD WILMER) LARDNER (1885–1933), MARGARET C. ANDERSON (1886–1973), FLOYD DELL (1887–1969), Fenton Johnson (1888–1958), and BEN HECHT (1894–1964). Theodore Dreiser's career, which began in the Midland realist period, extended into this one.

The third wave crested in the 1940s and lasted through the 1950s, producing the novels of JAMES T(HOMAS) FARRELL (1904–1979), NELSON ALGREN (1909–1981), and SAUL (C.) BELLOW (1915–2005) and major works of AFRICAN AMERICAN LITERATURE by RICHARD WRIGHT (1908–1960), GWENDOLYN BROOKS (1917–2000), and others. Literary historians, such as Robert Bone in his seminal article "Richard Wright and the Chicago Renaissance," *Callaloo* 28 (Summer 1986): 446–68, demonstrate that a Black Chicago Renaissance, which existed between 1932 and 1959, should be included when the phrase "Chicago Renaissance" is used. This Black Chicago Renaissance emerged from the Great Migration that brought many African Americans to Chicago after Reconstruction failed them. During the Great Depression several black writers formed a community within the ILLINOIS branch of the FEDERAL WRITERS' PROJECT. Among them were Fenton Johnson, Marita Bonner (1899–1971), and Richard Wright.

In *Writing Chicago: Modernism, Ethnography, and the Novel* (1993) Carla Cappetti sees a strong connection between the Chicago school of sociology, the early urban literary tradition, and the important Chicago novels of the 1930s and 1940s by such writers as James Farrell, Richard Wright, and Nelson Algren. Science, Cappetti suggests, taught Wright the meaning of the environment that oppressed him. Wright explicitly acknowledged Chicago social scientists Robert (Ezra) Park (1864–1944), Robert Redfield (1897–1958), and Horace R(oscoe) Cayton Jr. (1903–1970) for helping him tell his story as an African American born in the South and living for a time in Chicago. In this third wave, as in the earlier two waves, many Chicago writers tied their interest in social justice to issues of style. In doing so, they brought their unique perspective of modernity in Chicago to America and the world.

Rotella suggests that we integrate the three waves, forming a single Chicago Renaissance "in which Chicago's writers, engaging with landscape and humanity in compelling motion around them, did much to give form and meaning to our imaginative encounter with modern urbanism" (144). This is the time frame the present entry uses: "The Chicago Literary Renaissance: 1880 to 1959." See URBAN LITERATURE.

HISTORY AND SIGNIFICANCE: The earliest wave of the Chicago Renaissance, which began after the Great Chicago Fire of 1871 destroyed one-third of the city, was a product of the intelligent, aesthetically innovative rebuilding of this Midwestern city. New thinking about urban space fostered not only architectural renewal projects but also literary realism and later modernist innovations. In the 1880s the City Beautiful movement, often associated with the 1893 World's Columbian Exposition and architect Daniel Hudson Burnham (1846–1912), was under way in Chicago, and architects were theorizing that buildings were ART forms, essential ingredients of a functional, thriving, and modern city. The 1890s witnessed the emergence of the first Chicago school of architecture, famous for Chicago's skyscrapers. This group included Daniel H. Burnham, John Wellborn Root (1850–1891), Dankmar Adler (1844–1900), and LOUIS (HENRI) SULLIVAN (1856–1924), who created functional but beautiful designs using materials such as glass and steel. In the 1890s Sullivan also established the Prairie School, in which architects such as FRANK LLOYD WRIGHT (1867–1959) led the way with new, modernist designs for homes, schools, and businesses. Prairie-style ARCHITECTURE became famous throughout the Midwest and the world. Sullivan and others effectively argued that modern buildings and homes were essential ingredients of a functional and world-class city.

Daniel H. Burnham was not only a major city planner associated with the 1893 Chicago World's Columbian Exposition but also one of the individuals credited with keeping the lakefront open to the people through a plan developed between 1906 and 1909. Other early city planners such as Frederick Law Olmsted (1822–1903) also helped balance the skyline and tone of Chicago by encouraging the creation of public space. Because Chicago's city planners were visionaries, the Lake Michigan coast remains accessible to citizens, and parks and green space interwoven into neighborhoods make the city more healthful and inhabitable for its citizens.

Literature, urban development, and PROGRESSIVISM reinforced one another in Chicago. Reformers in Chicago saw literature and the arts as necessary for progressive development of the city. During the first wave of the Chicago Renaissance, JANE ADDAMS (1860–1935) established a theatre at HULL-HOUSE, the famous Chicago settlement that she and Ellen Gates Starr (1859–1940) opened in 1889. Modern DRAMA had a significant place in this wave of the Chicago Renaissance. In 1900 Laura Dainty Pelham (1849–1924), a dramatist already established in Chicago, became director of the Hull-House Dramatic Association; she first staged melodramas but quickly changed course and staged more naturalistic works pushing Chicago toward modernism and toward connecting aesthetics to ethics and form to social action. In *Too Late to Lament* (1955) Maurice Browne, a co-founder with his wife, Ellen Van Volkenburg, of the Little Theatre in Chicago, credits Pelham with being the "true founder" of the American little-theatre movement (128).

In 1895, ten forward-looking women published *Hull-House Maps and Papers: A Presentation of Nationalities and Wages in a Congested District of Chicago,* honoring women's roles in reforming the city. Rema Lunin Schultz's introduction to the 2007 edition (1–42) establishes this collection as a worthy example of muckraking journalism, placing it alongside *An Economic Interpretation of the Constitution of the United States* (1913) by Charles A. Beard (1874–1948), *A Documentary History of American Industrial Society* (1910), edited by John R. Commons (1862–1945) and others, *History of the Standard Oil Company* (1904) by Ida Tarbell (1857–1944), *The Shame of the Cities* (1904) by Lincoln Steffens (1866–1936), *The Philadelphia Negro* (1899) by W. E. B. Du Bois (1868–1963), and *How the Other Half Lives* (1890) by Jacob Riis (1849–1914).

Hull-House Maps and Papers features a chapter written by Ellen Gates Starr titled "Art and Labor," in which Starr explains Hull-House's commitment to the arts as a bridge between races, classes, and ethnicities. Thus the first wave of the Chicago Renaissance anticipated the other waves, which in their own ways also connected art, social observation, and reform. Rima

Lunin Schultz discusses how Addams hoped that theatre would bring together Chicago clubwomen, business leaders, and residents of Hull-House so that those individuals working on a play would better understand and appreciate one another through their collaborative efforts. Seeing theatre as a cultural mediator, Addams helped foster little theatre and modernity in Chicago (Schultz 32). She first encouraged theatre associated with melodrama and revivals of classical Greek dramas, then naturalist and experimental European drama, and later, during the second wave of the Chicago Renaissance, original verse dramas and experimental Chicago plays such as *Grotesques* (1915) by Cloyd Head (1895–1969).

This first phase of the Chicago Renaissance was also encouraged by the Chicago World's Columbian Exposition of 1893, leaving the Midwest, the United States, and the world with the impression that there was a new center of creativity in Chicago that deserved national and even international at-tention. Dreams of prosperity and freedom led small-town and rural Midwesterners, both men and women, to Chicago during the next several decades.

Events such as the Haymarket riot in 1886, the founding of Hull-House in 1889, and the Pullman strike in 1894 fostered new ideas about citizenship, democracy, the role of nature in the city, and education. Hull-House developed summer camps for children and educational programming for adults and tried to be a place where adults could argue, share, play, and participate in experiential learning. Women and minorities were respected at Hull-House, and this nurturing institution colored how the world saw Chicago and how Chicago saw itself. By 1899, when THORSTEIN (BUNDE) VEBLEN (1857–1929) published *The Theory of the Leisure Class,* Jane Addams and her associates were demonstrating to Chicago and to the world that there were other, more fulfilling and ethical ways to view humanity than through the lens of social Darwinism. There were

Palace of Mechanic Arts and Lagoon, World's Columbian Exhibition, Chicago, 1893.
Image courtesy of the Library of Congress

many economic, political, and social tensions in the city, and a desire to write realistically, and sometimes humorously, about them developed during this first phase of the Chicago Renaissance. Journalists such as FRANCIS HACKETT (1883–1962) and Floyd Dell not only created world-class newspapers but also helped establish the arts in the city. INDIANA natives George Ade and John T. McCutcheon (1870–1949) described the Midwestern hinterlands with charm and wit in their columns and cartoons, amusing first a city caught between its rural past and its urban present and then a nation interested in their "Stories of the Streets and of the Town." Chicago's many newspapers, including the *Chicago Record,* the *Chicago Daily News,* the *Chicago Herald,* the *Chicago Tribune,* and the *Chicago Defender,* served as incubators for many literary careers. See NEWSPAPER JOURNALISM.

In the 1890s Chicago's middle-class and wealthy citizens were looking for ways to improve Chicago's cultural standing; they understood that one cannot have a world-class city without architecture, cultural institutions, and a flowering of the arts. Hosting the Columbian Exposition of 1893 brought money and status, along with several million guests, to Chicago. They admired the exposition's architecture and its state, national, and international exhibits, including displays of TECHNOLOGY AND INDUSTRY and demonstrations of women's creativity and contributions at the Women's Building. During this period Chicagoans also established a symphony, supported opera and dance, founded a major art museum and a world-class university, and built the city in such a way that it would affect the world and not simply be affected by it. Chicago became known for its interest and originality in the arts, particularly during this period when its architecture, journalism and fiction were internationally praised.

One major writer during this first phase of the Chicago Renaissance was poet and dramatist William Vaughn Moody. An anti-imperialist, Moody taught at the University of Chicago and examined the issues of the day in poetry and drama. His play *The Great Divide* (1906) is often described as a melodrama, but it may also be seen as an attempt to portray realistically the values of the day. Moody explores the harsh reality

that women were up against during the era of the Genteel Tradition, the era second-wave Chicago Renaissance writers would condemn both stylistically and thematically. In this drama, after a woman is kidnapped and raped, she condemns herself and is condemned by her peers. Moody implicitly encourages the reader to reject that condemnation in favor of values more accepting of physical bodies, fair play, and female empowerment.

Naturalist (BENJAMIN) FRANK(LIN) NORRIS (1870–1902) was another major Chicago writer during this first wave of the Chicago Renaissance. He set his novel *The Pit* (1903) in Chicago, exploring an indifferent world driven by unstoppable forces like the grain markets of Chicago's Board of Trade. Some find Norris's work too dark and more mythic than realistic, but one may also see him as a Midwestern realist concerned with an economic world that pays little attention to individuals.

Another important writer of this era was L(YMAN) FRANK BAUM (1856–1919), creator of THE WONDERFUL WIZARD OF OZ (1900). This classic of CHILDREN'S AND YOUNG-ADULT LITERATURE can be read as an allegory of the Midwest of the era, with the fabulous city of Oz representing the dubious promise of the White City, as the layout of Beaux-Arts buildings at the Chicago Columbian Exposition became known. If the White City was smoke and mirrors, Midwesterners still had real home bases, such as KANSAS or Chicago, to return to, cherish, examine, and improve. Baum's amazing story posits that escape will not fix the world.

Other significant writers from the first wave of the Chicago Renaissance included Hobart (Chatfield) Chatfield-Taylor (1865–1945), who supported the Chicago art movement financially as well as creatively. Between 1888 and 1891 Chatfield-Taylor published *America,* promoting the writings of such Midwesterners as Kate Chopin (1850–1904), Hamlin Garland, JOSEPH KIRKLAND (1830–1894), and Harriet Monroe. (JOSEPH) BRAND WHITLOCK (1869–1934) combined elements of romance, realism, and PROTEST in his early novels *The Thirteenth District* (1902), *The Happy Average* (1904), and *The Turn of the Balance* (1907). Finley Peter Dunne wrote humorous essays in dialect exploring Chicago through his Irish protagonist, Mr. Dooley. Columnist Eugene Field commented humorously on Chicago political and cultural affairs in both prose and poetry. UPTON (BEALL) SINCLAIR (JR.) (1878–1968) wrote *THE JUNGLE* (1906), an exposé that brought the meatpacking industry to its knees. Writers associated with the new University of Chicago, such as Robert Herrick and Henry Blake Fuller, and those from the hinterlands, such as Hamlin Garland, who wrote about the difficult transition as Americans moved from a rural to an urban economy, also helped shape the Chicago realist tradition.

Then, of course, there was Theodore Dreiser, whose novel *SISTER CARRIE* (1900) helped as much as any Chicago literary work to bring Midwestern realism to international prominence. In *Sister Carrie* Dreiser went further than the other realists. As an innovator willing to explore new ethics and character types, Dreiser created a female character who was not punished for her sexual exploits and who was not broken by her errors or appetites; he clearly made the novel modernist in its subject matter. Dreiser's language and form matched his content, and although critics did not immediately embrace the novel as a masterpiece, *Sister Carrie* has come to be seen as pushing the school of Chicago realist fiction into a new phase both culturally and stylistically.

Many types of literary CLUBS, SALONS, AND SOCIETIES were created during all three phases of the Chicago Renaissance to foster community and support creativity in the city. Some of the most famous salons founded during the first wave were the exclusive Fortnightly Club, the Cordon Club for women only, the Dill Pickle Club, the White Chapel Club, the Little Room, the reporters' round table at Schlogl's Restaurant, the 57th Street Colony, the Cliff Dwellers, and the Indiana Society of Chicago. During the second wave of the Chicago Renaissance, the Little Theatre and *POETRY: A MAGAZINE OF VERSE* created their own salons, and during the third wave, the South Side Community Art Center and the South Side Writers' Group were created to help foster black art. The dreamers and writers who came to Chicago from the villages and towns surrounding Chicago, from abroad, and from the South during the three waves of the Chicago Renaissance maintained their own communities while forging new connections as modernity blossomed in Chicago, the Midwest, America, and the world.

The many representative works from the first wave of the Chicago Renaissance begin with Edward Eggleston's *The Hoosier School-Master* (1871). In 1880 the first issue of *THE DIAL* appeared. Eugene Field began his "Sharps and Flats" column for the *Chicago Daily News* in 1883. In 1884 Lucy (E.) Parsons (1853–1942) published "To Tramps" in *Alarm*. Joseph Kirkland published *Zury: The Meanest Man in Spring County* (1887), an important novel in the realist tradition. In 1891 Hamlin Garland published *MAIN-TRAVELLED ROADS*, a major work that helped Chicago and the Midwest gain recognition as an area nurturing strong fiction writers concerned with farm, village, and city issues.

Speeches and public readings played an important role in the development of literature and social thought in Chicago. At a meeting of the American Historical Association held at the Columbian Exposition in 1893, FREDERICK JACKSON TURNER (1861–1932) delivered his famous address "The Significance of the Frontier in American History," which declared the American frontier officially closed and the national westward movement technically over. Frederick Douglass (1818–1895) also gave a speech at the exposition, "The Race Problem in America." After Douglass's talk PAUL LAURENCE DUNBAR (1872–1906) recited his poetry.

After the exposition Chicago continued to be an important American cultural center. In 1893 George Ade published his first "Stories of the Streets and Town" column, and William T. McCutcheon illustrated it for the *Chicago Record*. Henry Blake Fuller published *The Cliff-Dwellers* that same year. The Chicago publishing house Stone and Kimball was founded in 1894, the same year in which Finley Peter Dunne wrote his first "Mr. Dooley" column for the *Chicago Evening Post*. Stone and Kimball published the first issue of the *Chap-Book* in 1894. Henry Blake Fuller's *The Procession*, which explores the role of the Columbian Exposition, was published in 1895, as was *Hull-House Maps and Papers by the Residents of Hull-House*. George Ade published *Artie: A Story of the Street and the Town* in 1896. *The Spirit of an Illinois Town* by MARY HARTWELL CATHERWOOD (1847–1902) appeared in 1897, and *The Gospel of Freedom* by Robert Herrick in 1898. Finley Peter Dunne's *Mr. Dooley in the Hearts of His Countrymen* was published in 1899, and L. Frank Baum's *The Wonderful Wizard of Oz* in 1900. Henry Blake Fuller's *Under the Skylights* and George Barr McCutcheon's *Graustark* were published in 1901, and Jane Addams's *Democracy and Social Ethics* in 1902.

In 1903 WILLIAM DEAN HOWELLS (1837–1920) gave a name to the writing being done in Chicago, "the Chicago school of fiction." Frank Norris published *The Pit* that same year. In 1905 the first issue of the *Chicago Defender* appeared. *The Jungle* (1906) by Upton Sinclair soon followed.

The second wave of the Chicago Renaissance stabilized Chicago's position as a growing, young, and vital city, a metropolis, a great commercial center, a city on the cutting edge of avant-garde poetry, drama, and fiction, and a city actively engaged with experimental forms and, perhaps as significantly, new writing. Journals such as Harriet Monroe's *Poetry*, founded in 1912, and Margaret Anderson's THE LITTLE REVIEW, founded in 1914, attracted avant-garde writing from around the world. The ancient art of poetry became new during this era, renewed in form and content. The role of the narrator in fiction became increasingly complex and sophisticated: stream of consciousness and indirect discourse marked the prose of the modernist movement in Chicago, as elsewhere. International figures such as Emma Goldman (1869–1940), Gertrude Stein (1874–1946), James Joyce (1882–1941), and Hilda Doolittle (1886–1961) all had their place as writers or subjects in Chicago's little magazines.

While still tied to the Genteel Tradition, Chicagoans were brave enough to invite radical artists and theorists to their city and to engage with texts such as Gertrude Stein's *Tender Buttons* (1914). In 1913 at the New York Armory show, Chicagoans attempted, like modernists all over America and Europe, to understand and appreciate Marcel Duchamp's *Nude Descending a Staircase, No. 2*, a painting that had neither a nude nor a staircase, at least ones that were readily discern-ible by those who expected more realism in their art. Some saw obscenity and disrespect in the new arts: the police censored the image of a recognizably nude woman, and some Chicagoans tried to ban the Armory show from Chicago, but Chicago's avant-garde artists fought back. They learned to trust their own definitions of what made art. Earlier in the decade, when the young Margaret Anderson was hired by the *Friday Literary Review* to review books, she was told by Floyd Dell, then the editor, not to write about the books, but to write about herself. From March 1919 to December 1920, though no longer in Chicago, Anderson serialized James Joyce's *Ulysses* (1922) in *The Little Review* and went on to fight the courts over censorship. Whether in California, New York, or France, Anderson's association with Chicago remained part of her identity and that of the city.

Spirits were high in Chicago, and artists came from everywhere, particularly from the surrounding Midwestern villages and towns, to find community and discuss and create new art in a place where new forms and ideas commingled. World War I silenced some poets, but poetry remained a force in the city during the second wave of the Chicago Renaissance. Women, the ethnically identified, and minority writers found a safe-enough place in Chicago. Lake Michigan, industry, technology, a multiethnic population, good transportation, and artistic community: Chicago had it all, or so the boosters declared. Even if Chicago never became the center of American art, its advocates attempted to build a sophisticated city that could foster and contain artistic expression.

As the United States shifted from an agricultural to an industrial economy, Chicago's geographic position in America's heartland made it a natural destination. In *Chicago Dreaming: Midwesterners and the City, 1871–1919* (2005) Timothy B. Spears points out that railroad maps of the period demonstrated that the city was destined to become a great metropolis, a cosmopolitan center of the Midwest and the nation (xv). He also posits that the new citizens of Chicago never lost their rural identity, even while they acquired an urban sensibility (xvii), and that "city" and "rural" typically developed not as separate, exclusive entities but rather as mutually dependent cultures (205).

The large influx of immigrants led to complex social dynamics, as well as new art forms. People coming to Chicago from Europe, New England, and the South brought their music, art, dance, and languages. Chicago was seen as a growing metropolis that offered individuals opportunities beyond and within the stockyards, railroads, and merchandise marts, a city where one could earn money and be relatively free.

During the second wave of the Chicago Renaissance, Chicago writers continued to reject the Genteel Tradition. William Dean Howells's realism was perceived as tame and distorted by the Chicago modernists, who preferred to experiment with more taboo subjects, often sexual or violent, and edgier forms. Radical ideas from European art and PHILOSOPHY and access to the art and ideas of Africa, India, Japan, and China were influencing the way Chicago artists saw culture, creativity, and their own possibilities. The world shrank as transportation and communication became quicker and easier, and art, experienced from multiple sometimes simultaneous perspectives, became destabilized. Dance, painting, sculpture, literature, and architecture were sharing techniques, and artists were finding new ways to think about dialect and language. Harriet Monroe's *Poetry* and Margaret Anderson's *The Little Review* helped give space to these new ideas in literature and politics. Local publisher Herbert S(tuart) Stone (Sr.) (ca. 1871–1915) also cared about literary Chicago and supported Chicago art and artists.

In 1914, during this second phase of the Chicago Renaissance, Ellen Van Volkenburg and Maurice Browne opened the Little Theatre, where they staged not only the controversial plays of August Strindberg (1849–1912), George Bernard Shaw (1856–1950), and Henrik Ibsen (1828–1906) but also works of local experimental drama such as *Grotesques: A Decoration in Black and White* by Cloyd Head (1895–1968). Alice Gerstenberg acted and wrote for the Chicago Little

Theatre as well. She spent her career in Chicago, moving between theatre and radio and writing for children as well as avant-garde readers. Harriet Monroe, herself a writer of verse drama, honored the theatre. She gave Head's drama *Poetry*'s highest prize and published the play in her journal. Her associate editor, Eunice Tietjens, also demonstrated her commitment to Chicago and multiculturalism. She published a book of poems, *Profiles from China* (1917), about one Chicagoan's intimate encounter with a very different geography and culture.

The Dial, The Chap-Book, and Herbert Stone Publishers, along with the *Friday Literary Review,* the Little Theatre, Hull-House Theater, the Players' Workshop, *Poetry,* and *The Little Review,* orchestrated encounters between American and European artists and philosophers. Emma Goldman, Ezra Pound (1885–1972), William Butler Yeats (1865–1939), James Joyce, Rabindranath Tagore (1861–1941), D(avid) H(erbert Richards) Lawrence (1885–1930), and countless other writers from around the globe were part of the Chicago literary scene during this era, either in person or through their works.

Other writers during the second wave of the Chicago Renaissance, like EDNA FERBER (1885–1968), negotiated issues such as assimilation and religious identity and wrote with a less avant-garde audience in mind. Ferber wrote at least two versions of her life, first in her novel *Fanny Herself* (1917) and later in her AUTOBIOGRAPHY, *A Peculiar Treasure* (1939), exploring Midwestern geography and opportunities, female creativity, Judaism in the Midwest, and religious persecution. Ferber's extraordinary career included Hollywood FILM and best-selling fiction. See JEWISH LITERATURE.

Because Midwesterners of varied ethnicities were trying to find a new city from which to launch an international art movement to compete and converse with Vienna, London, and Paris, for a moment, New York had some competition. Artists came to Chicago to find community, to escape provincialism, and to discuss and create new art that reflected their experiences in the new, modern world.

World War I negatively affected the production of poetry, but *Poetry* continued its run, featuring multiple schools of experimental verse, some from abroad, some local, always honoring Walt Whitman and democracy. *Poetry* refused to define itself by identifying with one school of poetry, either regional or international. Yeats won an early major prize from *Poetry,* as did Vachel Lindsay and Carl Sandburg. Ezra Pound, international editor of *Poetry* for a while, was forced to accept Monroe's loyalty to Midwestern poets, not just the avant-garde ones he preferred. Edgar Lee Masters published SPOON RIVER ANTHOLOGY (1915) and Carl Sandburg published CHICAGO POEMS (1916), books of poetry that were read throughout the English-speaking world along with the work of Yeats and T(HOMAS) S(TERNS) ELIOT (1888–1965). Famous works of fiction written during the second wave of the Chicago Renaissance included *Song of the Lark* (1915) by WILLA CATHER (1873–1947) and *WINESBURG, OHIO* (1919) by Sherwood Anderson.

Chicago, a modern city, maintained its mythical status during this era, which made it attractive to writers as a setting for their work. For instance, although Cather was not a Chicagoan, Thea, the main character in *Song of the Lark,* comes to Chicago to be educated as an opera singer. Cather based her character on a real opera singer, but that singer had never studied in Chicago. Cather honored the power of the Midwest generally and Chicago in particular by situating her main character in this city, possibly because Chicago was where many ambitious Midwestern women went to study before they headed for New York or Paris. Cather may not have lived in Chicago during the second wave of the Chicago Renaissance, but she was aware of its art and its influence.

Free verse, then a radical school of poetry, transformed literature during this era; experimental, socially exploratory drama successfully competed with the pageantry and burlesque often performed in Chicago and throughout America; new fiction, ready for new narrative construction and subjects, found acceptance in Chicago; and new journals and editors brought the world to Chicago and sent Chicago out into the world.

Some writers became famous during the era. Edith Wyatt (1873–1958), whom some called the Jane Austen (1775–1817) of Chi-cago, published *True Love: A Comedy of the Affections* (1903) during the first wave of the Chicago Renaissance and during the second wave became a founding member of *Poetry.* ELIA W. PEATTIE (1862–1935) wrote *The Precipice* (1914), a well-received novel exploring the difficulty women continued to have if they wanted more than a domestic life. Although these writers were reprinted in the University of Illinois Press's Prairie State Book series of the 1980s and 1990s, they are little remembered today. Others like Carl Sandburg examined life in Chicago and in the surrounding countryside, attempting to give voice and honor to those who could not or did not articulate truths about their own lives. Sandburg's poem "Chicago" gives the Chicago of this period mythic dimensions, resonating as much today as it did during the second wave of the Chicago Renaissance.

Chicago was also enriched by writers' identification with various locales and ethnicities that gave multiple perspectives to their art. Writers like Sherwood Anderson and Willa Cather may not have used the word "hybrid," but the content and style of their works were informed by more than one consciousness. They intimately understood the modernist concepts of multiple perspective, subliminal text, and unavoidable or even preferable subjectivity. They understood and re-created the fight between the ideal and the pragmatic, the overt and the hidden, within character and text, and they were comfortable with the new, organic forms, the forms their unique vision of the world required. They found new, enduring ways to articulate their insights.

Some new Chicago writers chose to laugh at themselves and their generation's unrelenting focus on new forms and ideas. In 1916 Witter Bynner (1881–1968), ARTHUR DAVISON FICKE (1883–1945), and Marjorie Allen Seiffert (1885–1970) tired of the hoopla surrounding free verse and the numerous new schools of poetry, such as imagism, futurism, and expressionism, and decided to create a pseudoschool of poetry, purposefully incomprehensible in its theory and mocking in its example. Using pseudonyms, these writers decided to observe whether the avant-garde art world would review and publish work associated with their fake new school of poetry, "Spectra," whose theory and art they considered nothing more than dribble. In 1916 they sent their humorous and often garbled "modernist" poems out for review. The introduction to their collection indicated that they were new poets who had founded the Spectra school and that their poetry exemplified their theory. The hoax worked. Over a two-year period Ficke and others published spoofs in *Poetry* and *The Little Review,* as William Jay Smith (1918-2015) documents in *The Spectra Hoax* (1961).

Editors and reviewers were not too proud to laugh at their own gullibility once the hoax was revealed. They acknowledged that modernism's romance with experimental form sometimes went too far; new schools of art were not always to be embraced and supported. It was silly always to give high praise to the new.

The second wave of the Chicago Renaissance fostered cultures conscious of place and disrespectful of hegemony. Often writers who were transplants did not want to lose connection to the places from which they came, even if they felt compelled to examine their new urban geographies. They were interested not only in new art forms but also in examining the role of the city in their work.

The University of Chicago's Literature and Social Science Departments nurtured both the fictional and the scientific exploration of urban life. Although many of the early writers left Chicago during its second phase, they continued writing about this unique Midwestern city. Among the most famous who left but continued writing about Chicago were Sherwood Anderson, Floyd Dell, Theodore Dreiser, Edna Ferber, Ben Hecht, Ring Lardner, Vachel Lindsay, and Edgar Lee Masters. During this second wave of the Chicago Renaissance, women were in the forefront of the Chicago literary scene. Some of the women writing and editing in Chicago were Jane Addams, Mary Reynolds Aldis (1872–1949), Margaret Anderson, Mary Austin (1868–1934), Margery Currey (1877–1959), Alice Gerstenberg, SUSAN KEATING GLASPELL (1876–1948), Alice Corbin Henderson (1881–1949), CLARA E(LIZABETH) LAUGHLIN (1873-1941), Tennessee Claflin Mitchell (1874–1929) and Harriet Monroe, Elia W. Peattie. Eunice Tietjens, and Edith Wyatt. Amy

Lowell (1874–1925) and SARA TEASDALE (1884–1933) visited Chicago often and frequently published in the Chicago little magazines. They extended the conventional limits of women's participation in artistic, civic, and domestic life and left a feminist legacy as well as an artistic one.

The Great Migration that began in 1910 brought tens of thousands of southern blacks to Chicago, changing the city and leading to new developments in AFRICAN AMERICAN LITERATURE. Even earlier, in 1906, during the first wave of the Chicago Renaissance, Robert T. Motts (1861–1911), an African American, formed the Pekin Stock Company in Chicago. That same year, according to Anthony D. Hill and Douglas Q. Barnett (b. 1931), authors *of The Historical Dictionary of African American Theater* (2009), Henrietta Venton Davis produced the play *Dessalines* (1906) by William Edgar Easton Sr. (1861–1935) about the Haitian revolution. Fenton Johnson, a black poet, published during the second wave of the Chicago Renaissance and served, as Lisa Woolley points out in *American Voices of the Chicago Renaissance* (2000), as a bridge between black and white Chicago. Wealthy from birth, Johnson attended Northwestern University and Columbia University. In *A Little Dreaming* (1913), *Visions of the Dark* (1915), and his autobiography, *Tales of Darkest America* (1920), Fenton wrote of his anger at and frustration with a world where he was both insider and outsider. By doing so, he reminded readers how much the world of white Chicago artists and benefactors, such as Mary Reynolds Aldis and Arthur T. Aldis (1861–1933), was not affecting the lives of ordinary black Chicagoans.

During the second wave of the Chicago Renaissance, Mary Aldis, founder in 1911 of the Playhouse in Lake Forest, and her husband, Arthur T. Aldis, lawyer, real estate investor, and art patron, helped bring the Armory show to Chicago in 1913. Earlier, in 1911, Mary Aldis brought Lady Augusta Gregory (1852–1932) and the Irish Players of the Abbey Theatre to Chicago. Also in 1911 Mary Aldis presented plays by Lady Gregory, William Butler Yeats, and John Millington Synge (1871–1909).

Chicago's wealthy industrialists, builders, and robber barons supported the arts, though perhaps not well enough because the Little Theatre folded in 1917 and Margaret Anderson took *The Little Review* and left Chicago by 1916. But the journal's multi-year run helped establish Chicago as a place where young artists could experiment, be irreverent, and thrive. Anderson and Harriet Monroe, the city's transformational editors, believed that their journals were at the forefront of a global movement. Their importance is still being realized today as scholars around the world study the content of these journals and how they nurtured various forms of modernism. The University of Tulsa and Brown University recently began the Modernist Journals Project with the motto "Modernism began in the magazines." If this is accurate, then Chicago, as the home of two central and leading little magazines, can be seen as one of the most significant cities that helped create and foster modernism.

Women often led the way. Increasingly, scholars are acknowledging that Midwestern/Chicago modernism was significantly female and feminist. Ellen Van Volkenburg's and Maurice Browne's Little Theatre was created in 1912, the same year as *Poetry,* and local playwrights such as Alice Gerstenberg wrote innovative plays for it and other Chicago little theatres. The Chicago Little Theatre lasted only five years, but it was important to the development of little theatres throughout America. Other theatres in Chicago played a vital role in Chicago's burgeoning little theatre movement, but none were more receptive to European plays, innovative stage settings, classical theatre, and experimentation in Chicago than Van Volkenburg's and Browne's Little Theatre.

Because by 1919 many of the institutions such as the Chicago Little Theatre and the *Little Review* and individuals such as Floyd Dell, Susan Glaspell, Sherwood Anderson, and Theodore Dreiser were no longer in Chicago, many literary historians considered the Chicago Renaissance over by 1920. But many contemporary literary historians disagree, and rightfully so. The writers who left Chicago were still writing Chicago stories and coming to terms with their memories of the Midwestern prairies, villages, and towns they had left and the Chicago they perhaps loved but that had disappointed many of

them. New immigrant groups such as Jews and other post–World War II displaced people, African Americans exiting the hostile South, and farmworkers searching for employment, safety, or community were finding their voices in Chicago in this post-1920 era, and during the third wave of the Chicago Renaissance they would move front and center.

Floyd Dell, associated with the first wave of the Chicago Renaissance, arrived in Chicago from Davenport, Iowa, in 1908. The radical and exploratory *Friday Literary Review,* associated with Dell's major contribution to the city's art movement, began its run in March 1909. While Frances Hackett was the first major editor of that early and famous literary supplement, the twenty-one year old Dell worked on it almost from its inception, and by July 16, 1909, one of Dell's book reviews was on its front page. By 1911 he was the editor. Susan Glaspell published *The Glory of the Conquered* in 1909. *Poetry* was founded in 1912. In 1913 the poet Fenton Johnson published *A Little Dreaming,* and Mary Austin published her novel *A Woman of Genius.* Vachel Lindsay's "General William Booth Enters Heaven" was the lead poem in a 1913 issue of *Poetry,* and in 1914 Carl Sandburg's "Chicago" appeared in that journal as well. In 1914 Elia W. Peattie also published *The Precipice,* and Ring Lardner's "You Know Me Al" appeared in the *Saturday Evening Post.*

The year 1915 was a great year for Chicago literature, with Edgar Lee Masters's *Spoon River Anthology,* Willa Cather's *The Song of the Lark,* and Theodore Dreiser's *The Genius* seeing publication. Carl Sandburg's *Chicago Poems* and Edna Ferber's *Emma McChesney* followed in 1916. In 1919 Sherwood Anderson's *Winesburg, Ohio* and Henry Blake Fuller's *Bertram Cope's Year* were published. Both books deal with male homosexuality, and the issues they explore became part of modernity's conversations. See LESBIAN, GAY, BISEXUAL, TRANSGENDER, AND QUEER LITERATURE.

Miss Lulu Bett by ZONA GALE (1874–1938) and *Moon Calf* by Floyd Dell were published in 1920. In 1921 Ben Hecht published *Eric Dorn* and began his column "One Thousand and One Afternoons in Chicago" for the *Chicago Daily News.* (Nathan Eugene) Jean Toomer (1894–1967) published his brilliant *Cane* in 1922. In 1925 Theodore Dreiser published *An American Tragedy,* and Gʟᴇɴᴡᴀʏ Wᴇsᴄᴏᴛᴛ (1901–1987) published *The Grandmothers.* In 1927 Carl Sandburg published folk songs he had gathered in a book titled *The American Sandbag.* Fᴏʟᴋʟᴏʀᴇ expanded the definition of art. Saving what was popular became as essential as producing what was perceived as highbrow. In 1927 Ben Hecht and Charles MacArthur had their play *The Front Page,* a drama concerning Chicago journalists, produced in New York. Lᴀɴɢsᴛᴏɴ (Jᴀᴍᴇs Mᴇʀᴄᴇʀ) Hᴜɢʜᴇs (1902–1967) published *Not without Laughter,* and Jane Addams published *The Second Twenty Years at Hull-House* in 1930.

Literary memoirs show how significant writers from the second wave of the Chicago Renaissance reinvented themselves. Mary Reynolds Aldis's autobiography *Plays for Small Stages* (1915) is important for those interested in Chicago as a literary center and in its global connections during the first and second phases of the Chicago Renaissance. In *My Chicago* (1918) Anna Morgan (1851–1936) takes a look at her relationships with other artists and philanthropists of that era, as well as the role of little theatres in Chicago. It is also an important work if one wishes to understand Chicago's movement toward cultural awareness, an ethical stance, and modernist aesthetics. Expectedly, Fenton Johnson's *Tales of Darkest America* (1920) gives a very different perspective of Chicago. *Midwest Portraits: A Book of Memoirs and Friendships* (1923) by Henry Hansen (1884–1977) is another valuable memoir from this era. Susan Glaspell's memoir *The Road to the Temple* was published in 1927. Margaret Anderson wrote several memoirs. Her first, *My Thirty Years' War* (1930), covers the years she lived in Chicago. Floyd Dell published his autobiography, *Homecoming,* in 1933; Edgar Lee Masters's memoir *The Tale of Chicago* also appeared that year. In 1938, after Harriet Monroe's accidental death, her memoir *A Poet's Life: Seventy Years in a Changing World* (1938) was published, a must-read for any scholar of the Chicago Renaissance, as is Eunice Tietjens's *The World at My Shoulder* (1938). Ben Hecht's *A Child of the Century* (1954) also offers an important overview of the period, as does Maurice Browne's *Too Late to Lament* (1956).

The second wave of the Chicago Renaissance represents a complex mixture of artists looking for a new beginning in a modern world, often exploring community and place in ways that reflected where they came from. These men and women changed the world's understanding of literature, democracy, and the Midwest. Some authors of the second wave of the Chicago Renaissance, such as Sherwood Anderson, Edgar Lee Masters, and Carl Sandburg, are frequently discussed in studies of the Chicago Renaissance; others, such as Fenton Johnson, are only beginning to get the attention they deserve. Some, like Harriet Monroe, made the city famous; others, like Elia W. Peattie, are only now coming back into the light as literary scholars reevaluate this cultural movement.

The third wave of the Chicago Renaissance had multiple starts. Like its predecessors, it was a complex and fascinating flowering of the arts in this contradictory and fascinating city filled with disappointments and dreams, dirty, beautiful, powerful, broken, and at moments transcendent. This period was particularly rich in African American, ethnic, and working-class literature. Between 1910 and 1930, two million African Americans left the South for the Northeast, Midwest, and West, of whom tens of thousands moved to Chicago. The *Chicago Defender,* an African American newspaper, promoted and publicized the work of black artists and authors. Langston Hughes wrote a weekly column for the paper and published his first short stories featuring the character Jesse B. Semple there. Other immigrants were coming to America, so many that there was a backlash. The Immigrant Acts of 1921 and 1924 restricted immigration from southern and eastern Europe. The third phase of the Chicago Renaissance was filled with the voices of these new Midwesterners, extending the Chicago Renaissance into midcentury.

This third wave gathered momentum after the 1929 stock-market crash. Many of its writers were associated with the Federal Writers' Project of the 1930s, which operated in every state in the Union, providing much-needed jobs for ten thousand writers. Langston Hughes, Marita Bonner, Jack Conroy (1898–1990), Fenton Johnson, Meyer Levin (1905–1981), Margaret Walker (1915–1998),

Richard Wright, Nelson Algren, (LOUIS) STUDS TERKEL (1912–2008), Gwendolyn Brooks, Arna Bontemps (1902–1973), and Saul Bellow were among the many writers who benefited from Writers' Project employment. In *Soul of a People: The WPA Writers' Project Uncovers Depression America* (2009) David A. Taylor articulates how talented this group of writers was: "The Chicago office was an exceptional version of what Henry Alsberg could scarcely have hoped for when he said the WPA [Works Progress Administration] writers 'will get an education in the American scene': a community of talents that would absorb the local culture in each place with fresh eyes and imaginations" (44).

The WPA sponsored many projects in Chicago. One was the South Side Writers' Group, which was created in 1936 and lasted through the 1950s. Begun by Richard Wright, the group nurtured members such as Arna Bontemps and Margaret Walker. The WPA also helped support the South Side Community Art Center, which organized workshops for black citizens and gave black and white artists another chance to interact. One of its teachers, Inez Cunningham Stark, a wealthy white patron of the arts who sat on the board of *Poetry*, helped Gwendolyn Brooks find her poetic voice and her place in the avant-garde arts of Chicago. Brooks's first book, *A STREET IN BRONZEVILLE* (1945), gives voice to the residents of a poor black neighborhood on Chicago's South Side. Brooks won a Pulitzer Prize for *Annie Allen* (1949).

The WPA Federal Theatre Project was also active in Chicago. In *Against Itself* (1995) Paul Sporn notes that plays like *The Swing Mikado* (1938), a production of the black wing of the Chicago Theatre Project, transformed Gilbert and Sullivan's work. Featuring an original score based on the musical and lyrical idioms of jazz, *The Swing Mikado* is an example of nonelite art sensitive to race and ethnicity being fostered by the government and the city.

In his classic 1951 prose poem *Chicago, City on the Make*, Nelson Algren writes about the first and second phases of the Chicago Renaissance as the periods when Chicago literature became world literature, but he emphasizes that Richard Wright extended the Chicago Renaissance of Theodore Dreiser, John Peter Altgeld (1847–1902), and Eugene V. Debs (1855–1926) into the 1950s. Algren also reminds readers that in *NATIVE SON* (1940) Wright brilliantly created Bigger Thomas to grapple with "large feelings," offering readers another example of the people who inhabited "the city of the big shoulders" (66, 85). Algren loved Wright's novel but found 1940s Chicago disappointing. He believed that the Chicago Renaissance was over because Chicago had failed its artists. Other Chicago artists fled, and only Wright came: "Since the middle twenties the only party of over-average height to stop off here awhile was a Mississippi Negro named Wright. And he soon abandoned his potentialities. . . . Rumor has it, he preoccupies himself with the heady task of becoming a Café Flore intellectual" (53). Of course, Algren was wrong at least about the number of significant writers in the third wave of the Chicago Renaissance.

If one is looking to read additional work written during the third wave of the Chicago Renaissance, one can begin with Langston Hughes's first poetry collection, *THE WEARY BLUES* (1926), which he published with the help of CARL VAN VECHTEN (1880–1964), and the only novel he ever published, *Not without Laughter* (1930). In 1940 Hughes published his first autobiography, *The Big Sea*, in which he acknowledges being influenced by Sandburg and Lindsay. A year later, in 1941, he founded the Skyloft Players, which performed his musical *The Sun Do More*.

In 1987 Beacon Press published *Frye Street and Environs: The Collected Works of Marita Bonner*. This collection contains essays from the 1920s, Bonner's three plays, and short stories written between 1925 and 1941. Bonner is only beginning to get the attention she deserves, but already her place in the Chicago Renaissance, like Fenton Johnson's, is central and solid.

Jack Conroy's best-known novel, *The Disinherited*, was published in 1933. His *Anvil* stories were collected in *Writers in Revolt: The "Anvil" Anthology, 1933–1940*.

Meyer Levin published *The Old Bunch* in 1937, a novel about a group of American

Jewish friends in a Chicago neighborhood. Another of his novels, *Citizens* (1940), was highly praised by ERNEST (MILLER) HEMINGWAY (1899–1961), who said that it was one of the best novels he had ever read. In 1956 Levin published *Compulsion,* a fictionalization of the Leopold and Loeb murder case and one of the first documentary novels.

In 1935 Margaret Walker received her bachelor of arts degree from Northwestern University. In 1936 she began her work with the Federal Writers' Project. Her book of poems *For My People* (1942) won the Yale Series of Younger Poets competition in 1942; Walker's 1966 novel *Jubilee* was also well received.

Arna Bontemps graduated from the University of Chicago in 1943 with a master's degree in library science. He is honored for spending his career organizing and protecting primary documents from this era, but his association with the Harlem Renaissance, the Black Chicago Renaissance, and the third wave of the Chicago Renaissance is also one of artist and participant. He worked closely with both Langston Hughes and Jack Conroy and published works with both of them. In 1945 Bontemps and Conroy published *They Seek a City,* a study of the Great Migration.

Nelson Algren is best known for his collection of short stories *The Neon Wilderness* (1947) and his New Orleans novel *The Man with the Golden Arm* (1949). As an American from a complex ethnic background, he enriches our understanding of how important ethnicity was to the third wave of the Chicago Renaissance.

Saul Bellow published *Dangling Man* in 1944, THE ADVENTURES OF AUGIE MARCH in 1953, and *Henderson the Rain King* in 1959. One can connect Bellow's style not only to that of SAMUEL LANGHORNE CLEMENS (1835–1910), writing as Mark Twain, but also to the fiction of Theodore Dreiser and Sherwood Anderson. A Jew, an immigrant, and a Nobel Prize laureate, Bellow wrote brilliant work colored by Yiddishisms and wit. See JEWISH LITERATURE.

LORRAINE (VIVIAN) HANSBERRY (1930–1965) published *A RAISIN IN THE SUN* (1959) near the end of the third wave of the Chicago Renaissance, and Studs Terkel published his oral history *Division Street: America* in 1967. Although writers associated with the Black Arts Movement flourished in Chicago during the 1960s, and a number of Chicagoans have since produced distinguished literature about life in the city, critics address Chicago writing after 1959 separately from the three waves of the Chicago Renaissance. Chicago writing of the past half century bears the influence of earlier literary movements but has changed along with the city that inspired it.

SELECTED WORKS: Key texts from the first wave of the Chicago Renaissance include Edward Eggleston's *The Hoosier Schoolmaster* (1871), Hamlin Garland's *Main-Travelled Roads* (1891), Henry Blake Fuller's *The Cliff-Dwellers* (1893), Ida B. Wells's, Frederick Douglass's, Irvine Garland Penn's, and Ferdinand L. Barnett's *The Reason Why The Colored American Is Not in the World's Columbian Exposition* (1893; reprinted 1999), Theodore Dreiser's *Sister Carrie* (1900), Jane Addams's *Democracy and Social Ethics* (1902), Frank Norris's *The Pit* (1903), and William Vaughn Moody's *The Great Divide* (1906). Second-wave texts include Fenton Johnson's *A Little Dreaming* (1913), Cloyd Head's *Grotesques* (1915), Willa Cather's *Song of the Lark* (1915), Edgar Lee Masters's *Spoon River Anthology* (1915), Carl Sandburg's *Chicago Poems* (1916), and Sherwood Anderson's *Winesburg, Ohio* (1919). Significant memoirs include *The World at My Shoulder* (1938) by Eunice Tietjens and *I Came a Stranger: The Story of a Hull-House Girl* (1989) by Hilda Satt Polacheck (1882–1967). One might also look at the early volumes of *The Little Review* and *Poetry.* Important works from the third wave of the Chicago Renaissance include Richard Wright's *Native Son* (1940), Gwendolyn Brooks's *A Street in Bronzeville* (1945), Nelson Algren's *Chicago, City on the Make* (1951), and Saul Bellow's *The Adventures of Augie March* (1953). Also worthwhile are Lorraine Hansberry's poignant play *A Raisin in the Sun* (1959) and *Frye Street and Environs*: *The Collected Works of Marita Bonner* (1987). Anthologies include *Smokestacks and Skyscrapers: An Anthology of Chicago Writing* (1999), edited by David Starkey and Richard Guzman; *Illinois Voices: An Anthology of Twentieth-Century Poetry* (2001), edited by Kevin Stein and G. E. Murray; and *Black Writing from Chicago: In the World, Not of It?* (2006), edited by Richard R. Guzman.

FURTHER READING: Carl S. Smith's *Chicago and the American Literary Imagination, 1880–1920* (1984) is a well-written study of Chicago writing in a national context. Ronald Weber's *The Midwestern Ascendancy in American Writing* (1992) places the Chicago Renaissance in a broader context of regional history and culture. In *Writing Chicago: Modernism, Ethnography, and the Novel* (1993), Carla Cappetti convincingly extends the time frame for studying the Chicago Renaissance to include the 1930s, 1940s, and 1950s. Lisa Woolley explains in *American Voices of the Chicago Renaissance* (2000) why an extended timeline is needed for Chicago literary history, including the Black Chicago Renaissance. Likewise, in *Chicago Dreaming: Midwesterners and the City, 1871–1919* (2005), Timothy B. Spears convincingly argues that studying beyond 1919 is essential to an understanding of the diversity within the Chicago Renaissance. *The Genesis of the Chicago Renaissance: Theodore Dreiser, Langston Hughes, Richard Wright, and James T. Farrell* (2009) by Mary Hricko is also useful to those interested in a comparison between the 1890–1920 and 1930–1950 periods of the Chicago Renaissance. Hricko explores and compares patterns such as the rise of the city novel, the development of urban realism, and the shift to modernism. *The Muse in Bronzeville: African American Creative Expression in Chicago, 1932–1950* (2011) by Robert Bone and Richard A. Courage also examines the Black Chicago Renaissance. Two collections of essays on African American literature are *Writers of the Black Chicago Renaissance* (2011), edited by Steven C. Tracy, and *The Black Chicago Renaissance* (2012), edited by Darlene Clark Hine and John McCluskey Jr. Tracy's volume emphasizes overviews of major writers, whereas the essays assembled by Hine and McCluskey address diverse subjects. In *The Chicago Black Renaissance and Women's Activism* (2006), Anne Meis Knupfer places literature in a social context involving theatre, art, education, women's clubs, and protest movements. Part of the University of Illinois Press's New Black Studies series, Elizabeth Schroeder Schlabach's *Along the Streets of Bronzeville: Black Chicago's Literary Landscape* (2013) examines the Bronzeville community between the two world wars, exploring how "place" effected the lives of artists and wended its way into Black Chicago Renaissance texts. In this critical volume Schlabach also analyzes in detail how the South Side Community Art Center and the South Side Writers' Group engendered Black Chicago Renaissance political consciousness and aesthetics. Ayesha K. Hardison's book, *Writing through Jane Crow: Race and Gender Politics in African American Literature* (2013), explores women writers and female characters between World War I and II. This volume astutely examines the lives of and texts created by Black Chicago Renaissance writers Era Bell Thompson (1905-1986), memoirist and editor of *Ebony*, Richard Wright, and Gwendolyn Brooks.

In November 2007 Robert Bone, author of the seminal article "Richard Wright and the Chicago Renaissance" (1986), died and left behind the unfinished manuscript of a work that was to develop the core assertions of that article. Focusing on Richard Wright, Arna Bontemps, Gwendolyn Brooks, Margaret Walker, and Horace Cayton Jr., Bone argued that Chicago's South Side experienced a creative burst in the 1930s and 1940s comparable to the Harlem Renaissance. Richard A. Courage worked with him for several years near the end of his life, and this collaboration was published by Rutgers University Press in 2011 as *The Muse in Bronzeville: African American Creative Expression in Chicago, 1932–1950.* Amritjit Singh concludes his foreword to this critical study:

> Overall, Bone and Courage make a powerful case for moving Chicago's Bronzeville, long overshadowed by New York's Harlem, from a peripheral to a central position within African American and American Studies. In closing, I cannot help but note how Robert Bone, who had begun to be perceived as part of our past in his final years, would eventually leave us with a book that may mark the beginning of a new scholarly revival in U.S. literary and cultural studies. (xiv)

James R. Grossman, Ann Durkin Keating, and Janice L. Reiff edited *The Encyclope-*

dia of Chicago (2004). Over one thousand pages long, it attempts to do justice to many aspects of Chicago, including literary and artistic movements. Rema Lunin Schultz and Adele Hast edited *Women Building Chicago, 1790–1990: A Biographical Dictionary* (2001), which includes meticulously researched articles on women of the Chicago Renaissance. Jan Pinkerton and Randolph H. Judson edited *Encyclopedia of the Chicago Literary Renaissance: The Essential Guide to the Lives and Works of the Chicago Renaissance Writers* (2004), covering the beginnings through 1930.

Marianne DeKoven's essay " 'Excellent Not a Hull House': Gertrude Stein, Jane Addams, and Feminist-Modernist Political Culture," in *Rereading Modernism: New Directions in Feminist Criticism* (1994), edited by Lisa Rado, is an essential text on the role of the avant-garde in modernist discourse (chapter 15: 321–50). *The Old Guard and the Avant-Garde: Modernism in Chicago, 1910–1940* (1990), edited by Sue Ann Prince, shows how the various art movements cross-fertilized one another and describes the politics of presenting new ideas in a conservative and frightened city. Kenny J. Williams's *A Storyteller and a City: Sherwood Anderson's Chicago* (1988) not only informs the reader about Anderson's sense of place but also explains the complexities within the Chicago that Anderson knew.

Daniel J. Cahill's *Harriet Monroe* (1973) and Ellen Williams's *Harriet Monroe and the Poetry Renaissance: The First Ten Years of "Poetry," 1912–1922* (1977) document Monroe's talent as an editor. Williams's book will never be dated. In *Women Editing Modernism: "Little" Magazines and Literary History* (1995) Jayne E. Marek (b. 1954) examines Margaret Anderson's and Harriet Monroe's roles in shaping the Chicago Renaissance. Anna Massa's "Form Follows Function: The Construction of Harriet Monroe and *Poetry, A Magazine of Verse*," in *A Living of Word: American Women in Print Culture* (1995): 115-131, edited by Susan Albertine, is useful on Monroe, *Poetry*, women's roles, and print culture. William Drake's *The First Wave: Women Poets in America, 1915–1945* (1987) is an enlightening book if one wants to understand the role Monroe played in the lives of other women poets of that period.

Dorothy Chansky's *Composing Ourselves: The Little Theatre Movement and the American Audience* (2004) glances at Chicago's role in the turn-of-the-century little-theatre movement. *The Historical Dictionary of African American Theater* by Anthony D. Hill with Douglas Q. Barnett (2009) contains many entries pertaining to Chicago theatre, plays, and playwrights.

Those interested in the relationship between the Chicago Renaissance and other important writers in the 1920s may consult Frederick John Hoffman's *The Twenties: American Writing in the Postwar Decade* (1949) and Bernard Duffey's *The Chicago Renaissance in American Letters: A Critical History* (1954). Hugh Duncan's *The Rise of Chicago as a Literary Center from 1885–1920: A Sociological Essay in American Culture* (1964) contextualizes the social unrest that weaves through many Chicago Renaissance texts. Another classic study of the second wave of the Chicago Renaissance is Dale Kramer's *Chicago Renaissance: The Literary Life in the Midwest, 1900–1930* (1966). Also valuable are Clarence A. Andrews's *Chicago in Story: A Literary History* (1982), Robert C. Bray's *Rediscoveries: Literature and Place in Illinois* (1982), and James Hurt's essay "Images of Chicago," chapter 4 in *Illinois: Its History and Legacy* (1984): 169-179, edited by Roger Bridges and Rodney Davis.

Many texts examine ethnic Chicago. The University of Illinois Press publishes a series called the American Literature Initiative that includes *The Irish in Chicago* (1987) by Lawrence J. McCaffrey and others; *Swedish-American Life in Chicago: Cultural and Urban Aspects of an Immigrant People, 1850–1930* (1992), edited by Philip J. Anderson and Dag Blanck; and *The Jews of Chicago: From Shtetl to Suburb* (1996) by Irving Cutler. This last volume has a substantial section concerning the artistic dreams and production of Chicago Jews in Yiddish, English, and Polish. How these ethnic communities' literary productions connect to various elements of Chicago's literary renaissance, like the role of "magazine modernism" in the creation of global modernism, is still to be explored.

Bound copies of the *Friday Literary Review* of the *Chicago Evening Post* are available in the Newberry Library, which also holds the Tennessee Claflin Mitchell autobiography fragment, Sherwood Anderson letters, and boxes filled with material on Alice Gerstenberg, including her unpublished autobiography. The Harry Ransom Humanities Research Center at the University of Texas–Austin has the papers of many American modernists who spent time in Chicago. Other manuscript collections pertaining to the Chicago Renaissance can be found in the Houghton Library archives; the Illinois State Museum; and the Jane Addams Memorial Collection, Special Collections, the University Library, University of Illinois at Chicago.

There are many studies of the Federal Theatre and Writers' Projects in the Midwest. In *The Dream and the Deal: The Federal Writers' Project, 1935–1943* (1972), Jerre Mangione explores the roles of both Illinois and Chicago in the project. George Kazacoff's *Dangerous Theatre: The Federal Theatre Project as a Forum for New Plays* (1989) contains a chapter on the Midwest and an appended selection of new plays produced by the Federal Theatre Project. The Chicago Repertory Group, also known as the Chicago Workers' Theatre, and Studs Terkel's association with that group are examined in *Voices from the Federal Theatre* (2003) by Bonnie Nelson Schwartz. The Library of Congress holds "The Federal Theatre Project" (1986), a 350-page catalog-calendar of productions listing almost one hundred plays produced in Chicago between 1935 and 1939. There are also significant papers related to the Federal Theatre Project in the Loyola University, University of Chicago, and Marquette University archives.

The New York Public Library has an outstanding collection of American modernists. Emma Goldman's papers are at the International Institute of Social History in Amsterdam and the New York University Labor Special Collections.

Other libraries with pertinent archival collections include the Regional Studies Archives Library at Western Illinois University; the Schlesinger Library at Radcliffe College, the Sophia Smith Collection; Special Collections at the University of Illinois at Urbana-Champaign, which houses the Carl Sandburg archives; the Swarthmore College Peace Collection; the University Archives at the Iowa State University Library; the University of Chicago Special Collections, which has the *Poetry* archives; the University of Michigan Special Collections Library, which houses papers from many modernist writers; the University of Wisconsin Library archives.

Students of the Black Chicago Renaissance should visit the Chicago Public Library's Harsh Collection and the Schomburg Center for Research in Black Culture at the New York Public Library. The Illinois Writers' Project Papers are part of the Negro in Illinois Papers, box 35, folder 17, in the Vivian G. Harsh Collection. An extensive collection of Federal Writers' Project Papers are located at the Abraham Lincoln Library in Springfield, Illinois. The Richard Wright Papers are part of the Yale Collection of American Literature at the Beinecke Rare Book and Manuscript Library. In *The Historical Dictionary of African American Theater* Hill and Barnett list the Chicago Theater Company as an archival resource.

Study of Jewish writers in the Chicago Renaissance may be undertaken at the American Jewish Archives in CINCINNATI and at the Hebrew Union College–Jewish Institute of Religion campus in Cincinnati. The Art Institute of Chicago archives and the Chicago Historical Society archives are also useful.

MARILYN JUDITH ATLAS   OHIO UNIVERSITY

CHICANO/CHICANA LITERATURE.
See Latino/Latina Literature

CHILDREN'S AND YOUNG ADULT LITERATURE
OVERVIEW: Midwestern literature written for children and young adults has evolved considerably since the 1800s. In mid-nineteenth-century America relatively few books were written for the young, and those typically focused on adolescents and young adults rather than on younger children. Mid-nineteenth-century works regularly sought to inculcate morality and socially accepted traits. Many young-adult stories were coming-of-age tales portraying adolescents who, through their experiences, moved toward moral, socially sanctioned adulthood.

THE

ADVENTURES OF TOM SAWYER.

CHAPTER I.

' TOM !'
No answer.
' Tom !
' What's gone with that boy, I wonder ?   You Tom !
The old lady pulled her spectacles down and looked
over them about the room ; then she put them up and
looked out under them. She seldom or never looked
through them for so small a thing as a boy, for they were
her state pair, the pride of her heart, and were built for
' style ' not service ; she could have seen through a pair
of stove lids as well. She looked perplexed a moment
and said, not fiercely, but still loud enough for the
furniture to hear, ' Well, I lay if I get hold of you,
I'll——'

Opening page of Mark Twain's *The Adventures of Tom Sawyer*. Belford Bros., 1876.
Image courtesy of the University of Kentucky Special Collections Research Center

Writers like SAMUEL LANGHORNE CLEMENS (1835–1910), writing as Mark Twain, in works like *The Adventures of Tom Sawyer* (1876) and *ADVENTURES OF HUCKLEBERRY FINN* (London 1884; New York 1885), reflected the movement gaining force in the late nineteenth century to reject romantic idealization in favor of increasingly realistic portrayal of characters at or near the reader's level, from frontier locales, having experiences more like theirs, and speaking in dialect rather than standard English.

The twentieth-century impulse to recapture the early Midwestern frontier experience is evidenced in the continuing popularity of stories of frontier life and tall tales that amuse while giving a glimpse at the nature of life and values on the frontier. Twentieth-century advances in printing, along with rising affluence after World War II, also made books plentiful and resulted in increasing publication of books for younger children. Another major offshoot of enhanced printing capabilities has been a significantly increased emphasis on illustration, which has raised many children's books to works recognized as much for their illustrations as for their stories. This movement has paralleled the development of comic books, the increasing development of works prized primarily for their artistry, and the subsequent evolution of GRAPHIC NOVELS. See COMIC STRIPS AND BOOKS.

Television and the internet now allow nearly universal access to the media, and the greater frankness of contemporary society has made children more aware of issues previously deemed appropriate only for adults. Children's books have followed suit, introducing issues like poverty, illness, divorce, disease, and racism into literature written for younger children. These books have also made children more aware of multiculturalism and internationalism. But contemporary children's books do not all address problems or seek to indoctrinate young people on their place in the world. Many children's authors write strictly for their readers' enjoyment.

HISTORY AND SIGNIFICANCE: Much has been written about Midwestern literature and the people who produce it, but most has focused on works written for adults. Much less has been written about literature for children or young adults, particularly with respect to literature of the nineteenth and early twentieth centuries written by Midwesterners or having Midwestern settings or themes. The exceptions have been such early classics as *The Adventures of Tom Sawyer* and *Adventures of Huckleberry Finn*, THE WONDERFUL WIZARD OF OZ (1900) by L(YMAN) FRANK BAUM (1856–1919), and *Little House on the Prairie* (1935) by LAURA INGALLS WILDER (1867–1957).

In their book *The Literary Heritage of Childhood: An Appraisal of Children's Classics in the Western Tradition* (1987), Charles Frey and John Griffith included chapters on twenty-eight books, three of which are *The Wonderful Wizard of Oz, Little House on the Prairie,* and *The Adventures of Tom Sawyer*. Other lists sometimes omit Baum's or Wilder's books, but Twain's *The Adventures of Tom Sawyer* is always included.

An accurate evaluation of the nature and evolution of Midwestern literature for children and young adults must begin earlier than these universally recognized classics. When pioneer families began to settle the land that would become the Midwest, they typically carried few books on their journeys, perhaps the Bible or religious tracts for their children. Family reading was popular, and many early pioneers carried with them books from England, such as *Pilgrim's Progress* (1678), *Robinson Crusoe* (1719), or *Gulliver's Travels* (1826), to share with their children.

Before long, early settlers founded schools and began publishing newspapers and magazines. Ray Allen Billington in his *America's Frontier Heritage* (1966) wrote of travelers finding "extensive libraries . . . in remote log cabins," and that by 1796 Cincinnati had two bookstores selling, among a variety of books, some "for the instruction and entertainment of children" (81–82). Farther west, the same development occurred, and schools and libraries were established in areas having only a few families. Books were important to early settlers, as the story of their use by ABRAHAM LINCOLN (1809–1865) demonstrates.

Little has been written about the Midwestern writers who started producing literature for children and young adults. One early writer was WILLIAM (HOLMES) MCGUFFEY (1800–1873), a prominent OHIO educator who was asked by a CINCINNATI publisher to produce eclectic readers of interest to children while presenting important moral teachings about honesty, truthfulness, religious beliefs, and the importance of hard work. Six such readers appeared, beginning in 1836 with *The First Eclectic Reader*. Susan Bourrie, writing in *Dictionary of Midwestern Literature*, volume 1 (2001), points out that the stories, poems, and essays in the McGuffey readers reflected "a moral philosophy that encourages strong discipline—the tools required of a culture of pioneers" (360). The readers were very popular, and millions were purchased for and read by children. To this day, McGuffey readers remain in use, particularly by home schoolers.

ALICE CARY (1820–1871) and PHOEBE CARY (1824–1871) were sisters born near Cincinnati, Ohio. They wrote poetry for adults and children. Like the writing in McGuffey's eclectic readers, their poems were frequently moralistic. Some appeared in a new periodical, the *Riverside Magazine,* published from 1867 to 1870, and many of their poems were featured in readers and anthologies. *Stepping Stones to Literature: A Third Reader* (1897), edited by Sarah Louis Arnold and Charles B. Gilbert, includes "The Wise Fairy" by Alice and "The Good Little Sister" by Phoebe along with an essay about the sisters, with recommendations for further reading. The editors suggest that students read Alice's poem "An Order for a Picture," in which she describes her mother, and Phoebe's "Our Homestead," in which she portrays their Ohio home. Their poetry typically tells stories, like Alice's "The Leak in the Dike," a rhymed retelling of the story of the Dutch boy who saved the land from flooding. His courage and fortitude were recognized as desirable and even necessary traits for frontier people.

Twain's characters, like Tom Sawyer and Huck Finn, mark a new stage in the evolution of Midwestern and American literature for young adults and children. Writing in the emergent American literary realistic movement, Twain rejected dominant nineteenth-century romantic literary norms and portrayed dialect-speaking, lower- and middle-class adolescents from America's heartland in their first independent experiences of American civilization as they took early stands on some of its cardinal principles. Ironically, those works were considered unacceptable by nineteenth-century literary, cultural, and moral standards. *The Adventures of Tom Sawyer,* with its small-town MISSOURI setting, and *Adventures of Huckleberry Finn,* with its journey down the Mississippi River, were not intended by Twain as children's books, but through the years they have been read by all ages. Over time, both have appeared in abridged editions, comic books, and dramatic versions. They remain the works most people associate with Twain and the ones many young people have read.

Today we consider Twain's character Huck highly moral, and if there is debate about the morality of *Huckleberry Finn*, it centers on the use of the pejorative term to describe Jim's race and the crude humor, some of it at Jim's expense, rather than on Huck's moral stance against American

HUCKLEBERRY FINN.

Illustration of Huck from Mark Twain's *Adventures of Huckleberry Finn*. Charles L. Webster and Co., 1885. Image courtesy of the University of Kentucky Special Collections Research Center

greed, violence, dishonesty, and slavery. Thus, even with Twain's broadening of the range of setting, social class, and dialect in literature, he continued the tradition of providing models of moral action in coming-of-age stories.

The Wonderful Wizard of Oz by L. Frank Baum continued the evolution of works for children and young adults with a story centering on the first independent experience of his young female protagonist, Dorothy. The setting quickly shifts from stark Midwestern KANSAS to a fairy-tale or fantasy world. The Kansas farm is a hardscrabble, harsh environment, but after the cyclone carries Dorothy and her dog, Toto, to Oz, Dorothy comes to understand that she has courage and common sense and that home, family, and friends are critically important. Like Twain's *Tom Sawyer* and *Huckleberry Finn*, Baum's Oz books have often been abridged, and most children know the story from the 1939 film starring Judy Garland. Although

Baum wrote other Oz stories, his first book has been the most loved by American children. New editions are published regularly, in which illustrators depict their ideas about Oz and its characters.

In the late nineteenth century three Midwestern poets were writing poetry enjoyed by adults and children. In CHICAGO, EUGENE FIELD (1850–1895) entertained with his *Daily News* column "Sharps and Flats," which mixed wit, parody, sentimentality, and satire. His children's poems have remained his most popular works. "Wynken, Blynken, and Nod," "The Duel," "Jist 'Fore Christmas," "Sugar Plum Tree," and "Little Boy Blue" are his best-known children's poems. They have often been anthologized; some have appeared as illustrated books for young children.

JAMES WHITCOMB RILEY (1849–1916) was another newspaper reporter whose verse, often written in dialect, was very popular during his lifetime and continues to be read to some extent today. Riley, born in Greenfield, INDIANA, was writing for the *Indianapolis Journal* when his first book of verse, *The Old Swimmin' Hole, and 'leven More Poems* (1883), a collection from his newspaper work, was published. Riley's most popular poems for children are "Little Orphant Annie," "The Old Swimmin' Hole," "When the Frost Is on the Punkin'," and "The Raggedy Man." Like Eugene Field's most popular verse, some of these poems have been illustrated and published as individual books for children. One example is an adaptation of "Little Orphant Annie," *The Gobble-uns 'll Git You Ef You Don't Watch Out* (1975), illustrated by Joel Schick (b. 1945).

African American poet PAUL LAURENCE DUNBAR (1872–1906) was born in Dayton, Ohio, to parents who were former slaves. Dunbar wrote in many genres, but his dialect poetry is most remembered. Verses from his *Lyrics of the Hearthside* (1899) appear in children's anthologies. The short poem "Lullaby" appeared in *Story and Verse for Children*, selected and edited by Miriam Blanton Huber in 1940, but beginning in the 1960s many anthologies for older children have included his poems in volumes of African American poetry. A collection of Dunbar's poems for children, *Little Brown Baby*, was published in 1938.

Although she did not use Midwestern themes in her books for children, Lucy Fitch Perkins (1865–1937) deserves recognition in any history of Midwestern literature because of her Twins series, which introduced the world to the children of America. Living in Chicago, Perkins published *The Dutch Twins* in 1911, which was followed by more than twenty others, including *The Irish Twins* (1913), *The Italian Twins* (1920), and *The Norwegian Twins* (1933). Because so many immigrants were coming to the United States—and Perkins saw many of them in Chicago—she felt that American children should learn about children in other countries. In doing so, she was an early exemplar of a trend toward internationalism and depiction of diversity in all its forms that has become ever more evident since that time. She also wrote about American children from earlier periods, including *The American Twins of 1812* (1925), *The Pioneer Twins* (1927), and *The Farm Twins* (1928).

In 1899 *Boy-Life on the Prairie* by (HANNIBAL) HAMLIN GARLAND (1860–1940) appeared. Garland was born in WISCONSIN and later moved with his family to the IOWA prairies, which he vividly describes in the memoir of his youth in the years after the Civil War. In the essay "Books of My Childhood," which appeared in the *Saturday Review of Literature* 7 (November 15, 1930): 347, Garland writes of one of his boyhood favorite works of literature, *The Hoosier School-Master* (1871) by another Midwesterner, EDWARD EGGLESTON (1837–1902). Eggleston, born in Indiana, wrote other books for children and adults, but this one and one that followed, *The Hoosier School-Boy* (1893), were the most popular. Both give good historic pictures of Indiana life in the post–Civil War years. In the later book Eggleston writes of a favorite pastime of the boys:

All the boys in the river town thirty years ago—and therefore the boys in Greenbank, also—took a great interest in the steam-boats which plied up and down the Ohio. Each had his favorite boat, and boasted of her speed and excellence. Every one of them envied those happy fellows whose lot it was to "run on the river" as cabin-boys. Boats were a common topic of conversation—their build, their engines, their speed, their officers, their mishaps, and all the incidents of their history (210).

This love of Midwestern rivers, those often muddy routes to other places, frequently appears as a motif in much nineteenth-century Midwestern fiction for children and adults.

Love of nature dominated the young-adult and adult works of GENE STRATTON-PORTER (1863–1924). Books such as *Freckles* (1904) and *A Girl of the Limberlost* (1909) for a while rivaled the popularity of those by Charles Dickens.

Ruth Hill Viguers (1903–1971) was one of the four authors whose essays make up *A Critical History of Children's Literature* (revised edition 1969). Her lengthy section is titled "Golden Years and Time of Tumult." Viguers discusses the years from 1920 to 1967, a period she characterizes as marked by "a growing conscientiousness of the importance of books for children" (395). During

"Freckles' chickens were awaiting him at the edge of the clearing"

Illustration by E. Stetson Crawford for Gene Stratton-Porter's *Freckles*. Grosset & Dunlap, 1904. Image courtesy of Mary DeJong Obuchowski

this period major advances occurred in printing, and with greater availability of books and significantly increased family incomes, more books were written for children. Increasingly, illustrations were used in books, an important development in the evolution of Midwestern works for children and young adults.

WANDA (HAZEL) GÁG (1893–1946) was representative of artists producing illustrated works. Born in MINNESOTA and reading in German the fairy tales of the Brothers Grimm to keep up with her childhood language, Gág illustrated *Tales from Grimm* (1936). But before that, she had written and illustrated her own folktale, *Millions of Cats* (1928), a work that has remained a favorite since publication and is still in print. Gág also wrote and illustrated *The Funny Thing* (1929), *Snippy and Snappy* (1931), *The ABC Bunny* (1933), *Gone Is Gone: The Story of a Man Who Wanted to Do Housework* (1935), and *Nothing at All* (1941). She illustrated *Snow White and the Seven Dwarfs* in 1938. Gág, like many Midwesterners before her and since, went east to find success, but her books indicate that her sense of place and love of the Midwestern countryside remained with her.

This same period produced a rising "recognition of the need for books for 'young adults'" (401), according to Viguers. Because children now had to attend school for more years, there was an increased demand for books for adolescents, and authors and publishers worked together to produce them. This trend continued to develop in the mid- and late twentieth century, and the dominant market for literature for children and adolescents focused on younger children with each passing year.

As the frontier receded into myth, a rising tide of children's stories emerged, portraying the Midwestern frontier experience. In *Children's Literature: An Illustrated History* (1995) a picture shows eight grim-faced pioneers sitting in front of two covered wagons. The faces of these men, women, and children show fatigue but also determination. The caption indicates that although these settlers would not have had many books, their travels westward would be the subject of books for many years (122).

Reflection on the Midwestern pioneer experience has produced many books for children. Best known are the books of Laura Ingalls Wilder, born in Wisconsin in 1867. Wilder was over sixty years old when her first book was published. After many years of moving around the Midwest, from the Dakota Territory to Minnesota to Iowa, from farm to town to farm, Laura and her husband, Almanzo, had finally settled in Mansfield, Missouri. Their only daughter, ROSE WILDER LANE (1886–1968), was grown and working as a journalist when Wilder began to write down her childhood memories. Rose helped Laura, and her first book, *Little House in the Big Woods,* was published in 1932. Six more juvenile novels, or perhaps fictionalized autobiographies, followed, illustrating an era of migration spurred on by the Homestead Act of 1862. These included *Little House on the Prairie* (1935), *On the Banks of Plum Creek* (1937), *By the Shores of Silver Lake* (1939), *The Long Winter* (1940), *Little Town on the Prairie* (1941), and *These Happy Golden Years* (1943). During those years Wilder also wrote *Farmer Boy* (1933), the story of her husband's early years in New York State. In 1971 *The First Four Years* was published, featuring the story of Laura's and Almanzo's first years of marriage.

In the *Little House* books the Wilder family moves from Wisconsin to Minnesota to SOUTH DAKOTA. The books are full of details of pioneer life. In *Little House in the Big Woods,* for example, the reader learns how maple sugar was made, how a girl's hair was curled by using rags, how cheese was made, and how a gun was cleaned.

In 1985 another book about the frontier experience was published that went on to win the Newbery Medal. This was *Sarah, Plain and Tall,* written by Patricia MacLachlan and based on her family history. MacLachlan was born in Wyoming in 1938 and was educated in the East. Her book, however, takes place on the prairies, a flat, drab place not given a name in the book. The period is not indicated, but it appears to be the beginning of the twentieth century. MacLachlan's place of birth exemplifies settlers moving on, moving westward.

Sarah, Plain and Tall is told by Anna, whose mother has died after giving birth to Caleb. After some years her father, Jacob, places an advertisement in newspapers seeking a wife and mother for his children. He receives a letter from Sarah, who lives by the sea in Maine. Letters go back and forth, and one day Sarah arrives with her cat. Jacob has met her in town with his wagon, and they have agreed that she will visit for a month before deciding whether she will stay. Although Sarah misses the greenness of Maine and the sea, at the book's end she has decided that she would miss Jacob and the children more than what she left behind.

MacLachlan continues the story of this family in *Skylark* (1994). Here, Sarah is troubled by a severe drought that has caused fires and led her closest friends to give up and move away. After the family barn is destroyed by fire, Sarah takes the children to Maine. Jacob stays to take care of the farm. At the book's end, however, he travels to Maine, and Sarah and the children return to their prairie home with him, with Sarah expecting a child. Many similar works addressing the frontier experience were written by Midwestern authors and set in the Midwest. CAROL RYRIE BRINK (1895–1981) based *Caddie Woodlawn* (1935) on her grandmother's childhood in Wisconsin. In *Prairie Star* (1966) Nina Hermanna Morgan (1883–1970) presents her family's settling in NORTH DAKOTA. Some of these frontier stories introduce the issue of immigration. Among them is *Song of the Pines* (1949) by Marion Boyd Havighurst (1894–1974) and WALTER (EDWIN) HAVIGHURST (1901–1994), a story of Norwegian immigrants in Wisconsin.

Children have also vicariously experienced frontier life through return to the late nineteenth-century tall-tale genre. These stories portray Midwestern frontier roots and provide exemplars of pioneer strength, courage, and innovation. They have retained and increased their popularity with contemporary children. They carry an element of truth in their plots and characterizations, although many exaggerate for the sake of readers' enjoyment. These stories of Midwestern folk heroes provide appealing, larger-than-life models for young people. They include tales of Paul Bunyan, a North Woods logger; Johnny Appleseed, a horticulturalist and bringer of plant species to frontier lands; and ABRAHAM LINCOLN (1809–1865), a young person on the frontier, Midwestern statesmen, and American president. Among the writers in this genre are prominent Midwesterners like CARL (AUGUST) SANDBURG (1878–1967), with *Abe Lincoln Grows Up* (1928), and STERLING NORTH (1906–1974), with *Abe Lincoln, Log Cabin to White House* (1956).

The transition from oral tall tale to the printed story of Paul Bunyan was made by MICHIGAN journalist James MacGillivray, who first wrote an article about lumberjacks in the *Oscoda* (Michigan) *Press* on August 10, 1906, and published the first story about Paul Bunyan, "The Round River Drive," in the *Detroit News* on July 24, 1910. Presented as strong, brave, hardworking, honest, and larger than life, Paul Bunyan, with his giant blue ox, Babe, accomplished feats impossible for common men. Many writers since that time have taken great liberties in extending the Paul Bunyan story, according to noted Michigan State University and Indiana University folklorist Richard Dorson, who calls these extensions "fakelore" in his 1976 treatise *Folklore and Fakelore: Essays toward a Discipline of Folk Studies.*

Many children's books have also been written about John Chapman, or Johnny Appleseed, as he is better known. Born in Leominster, Massachusetts, in 1774, he lived in Licking County, Ohio, but traveled throughout Ohio, Indiana, and ILLINOIS, planting apple trees and passing out seeds. His peculiar appearance—barefoot, wearing poor clothing and a pot for a hat—and his simple, righteous lifestyle made him a popular folk hero, as well as an exemplar of morality and environmentalism. Mabel Leigh Hunt (1892–1971) of Coatsville, Indiana, was among the Midwestern writers on Chapman; her *Better Known as Appleseed* (1951) was a Newbery Honor Book.

Abraham Lincoln is the Midwest's and America's enduring democratic hero. He grew up poor on the frontier, educated himself, worked hard, and was known for honesty and a sense of humor. His rise from birth in a log cabin to youthful labor as a tall, awkward frontier rail-splitter and to storekeeper, lawyer, and president of the United States, holding together the Union and abolishing slavery, reflected Midwestern values and aspirations for upward social mobility. On this basis, Lincoln folk and hero stories link the tradition of moral tales with stories recounting American frontier values and aspiration for success. Many adult and children's books were published after Lincoln's death. Some were well documented; others took liberties in expanding Lincoln's mythic stature. *Abraham Lincoln, Friend of the People* (1950) by Clara Ingram Judson (1879–1960) was a runner-up for the Newbery Medal in 1951. More recent is *Our Abe Lincoln* (2009) by Illinois writer Jim Aylesworth (b. 1946).

Sterling North, in addition to his biography of Lincoln, wrote a biography of Twain for children and young adults, *Mark Twain and the River* (1961). He achieved distinction as the founder and editor of North Star Books, a series of American historical works for young people.

But North is best known for his work in another genre of books for children, works describing or implying difficult childhoods, realistically portraying problems, and describing the transformations of these children into moral adults through their experiences, particularly those associated with nature. He wrote *Rascal: A Memoir of a Better Era* (1963), a 1964 Newbery Honor Medal winner, and *The Wolfling: A Documentary Novel of the Eighteen-Seventies* (1969). Before moving to Chicago for college and jobs at the *Chicago Daily News,* North grew up on a farm near Edgerton, Wisconsin, where his parents instilled in him a love of animals and nature. In *Wolfling* a boy confronts the difficulties of raising a wild wolf pup. *Rascal* is a semi-autobiographical treatment of North's childhood adventures with his pet raccoon and his ultimate decision to return the animal to the wild, giving the raccoon its freedom and heralding his own metamorphosis into adulthood. *So Dear to My Heart* (1947), another story of a Midwestern farm boy and his pet, also became a best seller. Both *Rascal* and *So Dear to My Heart* were later made into movies.

Lois Lenski (1893–1971), a prolific children's writer and illustrator, was born in Springfield, Ohio. She attended Ohio State University, studied art in New York and London, England, and then lived most of her adult life in Harwinton, Connecticut. Although Lenski at first illustrated children's books for others, she soon began writing and illustrating her own books. Her first two books, *Skipping Village* (1927) and *A Little Girl of 1900* (1928), were based on her childhood

years in Ohio. Later she wrote books about areas beyond Ohio. Lenski was awarded the Ohioana Book Award for her first regional book, *Bayou Suzette* (1943). In 1946 another of her regional books, *Strawberry Girl,* was a Newbery winner. She also created many picture books, including the Mr. Small series, the Davy books, the Debbie books, several books of poetry, and children's historical novels. *Phoebe Fairchild: Her Book* (1936) and *Indian Captive: The Story of Mary Jemison* (1941), both historical novels, were Newbery Honor Books.

GARY PAULSEN (b. 1939), a MINNEAPOLIS native, is a popular novelist for young people with a similar perspective. He has three Newbery Honor Books to his credit, *Dogsong* (1985), *Hatchet* (1988), and *The Winter Room* (1990), the last of which also received the Northeastern Minnesota Book Award in 1989. Paulsen's childhood experiences growing up in a dysfunctional family, running away, and needing to support himself at seventeen gave him insight into troubled youths. His real-life skills in hunting, fishing, trapping, and dogsledding are applied in stories in which his teenage protagonists often escape their troubled lives and retreat to a family farm or the wilderness to achieve their transformation into maturity. Paulsen is a skilled writer who provides compelling descriptions of nature and treats coming-of-age themes. He received the Margaret A. Edwards Award for lifetime contributions to young-adult literature from the Young Adults Library Services Association in 1997. The American Library Association has also recognized a dozen or more of his books on its Best Books for Children and Best Books for Young Adults annual lists.

Richard Peck (b. 1934) is an Illinoisan who, as a former teacher, is aware of the modern teenage world and its many adult problems. Peck regularly writes about mature subjects for young adults. He has written prolifically in many genres, including novels, horror stories, and mysteries, as well as nonfiction. He won the 1999 National Book Award for *A Long Way from Chicago: A Novel in Stories* (1998) and the 2001 Newbery Medal for *A Year down Yonder* (2000). His *Are You in the House Alone?* (1976) won the Edgar Allan Poe Award for best juvenile writing.

With the advances of the twentieth and twenty-first centuries and nearly universal access by children to books, television, and movies, ever more adult material is being presented to younger children. Literature for children and young adults reflects that shift. Coming-of-age stories now increasingly focus on middle-school-age children rather than high school students. The greater openness of children's literature and the growing focus on younger children have increased children's awareness of contemporary social issues , including poverty, homelessness, disease, death, divorce, blended families, adolescent pregnancy, racism, and discrimination based on class, gender, or sexual orientation.

Two books by Christopher Paul Curtis (b. 1953) from Flint, Michigan, portray this trend. The first, *The Watsons Go to Birmingham—1963* (1995), was a Newbery Honor Book and appeared on many lists of best books, including that of the *New York Times Book Review.* Set in urban Flint, it is the story of an African American family of five and their automobile trip to Birmingham, Alabama, in the summer of 1963. The older son, Byron, thirteen, has been causing his parents to worry about his behavior, and they have decided that spending the summer with his grandmother in the South might improve it. In Birmingham the terrible church bombing occurs, killing four young girls. The family does not leave Byron in Alabama but rather returns to Flint. The short concluding chapter has them back home, trying to make sense of what has happened. Curtis's second novel, *Bud, Not Buddy* (1999), which won the Newbery Medal, is also set partly in Flint. Taking place during the Great Depression, the story involves ten-year-old Bud, an orphan who runs away from a foster family, hoping to find the father he has never known.

Stitches: A Memoir (2009) by David Small (b. 1945) from DETROIT, Michigan, carries this contemporary trend of presenting problem stories even further. It tells the story of a Detroit boy with cancer. His mother is a lesbian. In earlier decades this work, a 2009 National Book Award finalist in Young People's Literature, would have been considered an adult book if it had been allowed publication at all.

The second half of the twentieth century also fostered the continuing evolution in children's literature by presenting more works written purely for enjoyment. Shel Silverstein (1932–1999) exemplified this trend. In the mid-1960s Silverstein, a Chicago songwriter, screenwriter, and playwright, produced several best-selling books for children. He had written and drawn for *Stars and Stripes* while he was in the military and for *Playboy* later. He wrote hit songs for Johnny Cash, June Carter Cash, and the Irish Rovers. But it was his children's book *Uncle Shelby's Story of Lafcadio, the Lion Who Shot Back* (1963) that started his career of writing books for children. Following close behind was *The Giving Tree* (1964), a short but touching prose poem on love, compassion, the environment, and the cycle of life.

Silverstein's volumes revitalized interest in poetry for children. Poetry, as nursery rhyme, jump-rope chant, or simple poem, has always maintained some popularity with children, but Silverstein's books *Where the Sidewalk Ends* (1974), *The Light in the Attic* (1981), and *Falling Up* (1996) became best sellers and remain perennial favorites. They contain delightful, funny poems that children love to read and memorize and that adults enjoy as well. Readers and nonreaders enjoy the silliness of Silverstein's poetry books and his simple black-and-white drawings. The great success of these books inspired many other writers to create whimsical poetry for young people. One, Ohioan J. Patrick Lewis (b. 1942), has won many awards for his over fifty books and was children's Poet Laureate from 2011 to 2013.

Modern children have also been drawn in large numbers to a new genre of entertainment books for children: the horror story. R(obert) L(awrence) Stein, born in Columbus, Ohio, in 1943, is a renowned horror writer for preteens and teens. He has written over a hundred books in his Goosebumps series and Fear Street series. Stein's first teen horror book was *Blind Date* (1986).

Another trend in modern publishing arises out of advances in printing and publishing that have made high-quality books more affordable and that allow books to contain more and higher-quality illustrations. These advances have allowed children's literature to evolve toward picture books, which now constitute a significant proportion of publications for children. Picture books, unlike chapter books that may or may not have pictures, have illustrations that greatly enhance stories using paintings, drawings, unusual printing techniques, and photographs. Artist-authors use picture books to demonstrate their craft and draw interest to their works; other picture books are collaborations between authors and illustrators. Picture books can be for middle schoolers as well as younger children. The text determines their age appropriateness. Picture books for children represent a confluence with comic books and graphic novels for teenagers and adults, both treated elsewhere in this volume.

Many picture books depict Midwest locales and lifestyles. Hailing from just outside Lansing, Michigan, PATRICIA POLACCO (b. 1944) exemplifies Midwestern writers and illustrators who charm young audiences with simple stories about common people. Her illustrations, like her stories, are touching; the faces of her characters are reminiscent of those by Norman Rockwell, lifelike and often humorous. Her drawings give meaning to her text and add quality to her children's books. Most of Polacco's tales center on the stories and traditions of her rural Michigan family and those of her grandmother, who emigrated from Russia to Union City, Michigan. Among Polacco's many award-winning books are *The Keeping Quilt* (1988), which won the Sydney Taylor Book Award; *Rechenka's Eggs* (1988), which won the International Reading Association Award; and *Chicken Sunday* (1992), which received the Golden Kite Award. Polacco has continued her prodigious publication record.

Stories of Native Americans are another popular category of contemporary children's literature. These works connect children with their Midwestern forebears while simultaneously advancing awareness of cultural diversity. Paul Goble (b. 1933), born in Great Britain but a longtime resident of South Dakota's Black Hills, exemplifies this tradition. Goble has caught the spirit of Native American legends and stories and has presented them in colorful books for children. He is a prolific writer and illustrator for young people of the Yakinim and Oglad

tribes. Goble's Iktomi stories, told to him by Chief Edgar Red Cloud, the great-grandson of Chief Red Cloud, are very popular. Goble portrays Iktomi as a trickster and often a fool. His cultural tales are humorous but also continue the tradition of providing value lessons appreciated by adults and children.

Goble's *The Girl Who Loved Wild Horses* (1978), a Native American legend about a girl's love of horses and how she came to live with them, won the Caldecott Medal in 1979 and was selected as a Children's Book of the Year by the Library of Congress. The words are simple but captivating, and the Native American–influenced graphic designs and colors make the book enchanting. *Star Boy* (1983) won the Library of Congress Children's Book of the Year Award. *Mystic Horse* (2003) won the Children's Book Council Children's Choice Award. Goble continues to publish prodigiously, with over thirty books and many awards for his writing and illustration. 2015 saw publication of *Red Cloud's War: Brave Eagle's Account of the Fetterman Fight, December 21, 1866.*

SELECTED WORKS: Readers interested in classic works of Midwestern literature for children and young adults should begin with Mark Twain's *The Adventures of Tom Sawyer* (1876) or *Adventures of Huckleberry Finn* (1884, 1885) and L. Frank Baum's *The Wonderful Wizard of Oz* (1900). The McGuffey readers, beginning with *The First Eclectic Reader* (1836), reflect nineteenth-century didacticism in children's literature. Laura Ingalls Wilder's *Little House on the Prairie* (1935) is representative of works providing realistic yet nostalgic portrayals of growing up on the Midwestern frontier. *Rascal: A Memoir of a Better Era* (1963) by Sterling North is an excellent coming-of-age story. Gary Paulsen's *The Winter Room* (1990), David Small's *Stitches: A Memoir* (2009), and Richard Peck's *A Long Way from Chicago* (1999) reflect treatment of more adult subjects in works for children and young adults. Patricia Polacco's *Rechenka's Eggs* (1988) is representative of the many excellent picture books now being created for children. Paul Goble's *The Girl Who Loved Wild Horses* (1978) exemplifies the work of writers who are introducing children to Native peoples and those of other cultures. Shel

Silverstein's rollicking *The Light in the Attic* (1981) exemplifies contemporary books of humorous poetry for children and, more broadly, children's literature written solely for enjoyment.

FURTHER READING: Anyone studying Midwestern writing for children or young adults should first consult books addressing children's literature. Outstanding for its information on early children's books and periodicals is *A Critical History of Children's Literature*, revised edition (1969). Under the general editorship of Cornetta Meigs, the book has four sections written by Meigs, Anne Thaxter Eaton, Elizabeth Nesbitt, and Ruth Hill Viguers. The book begins with the earliest writings for children and continues through 1958. Viguers, writing about the most recent period, devotes several pages to regional literature.

Another basic book is *Children and Books*, fifth edition (1977), written by Zena (Bailey) Sutherland and May Hill Arbuthnot. In addition to giving critical summaries of many outstanding children's books, this volume contains lists of children's books and bibliographies, including research in the field. There is also a short section on popular literature, written by Larry N. Landrum and Michael T. Marsden.

Children's Literature: An Illustrated History (1995), edited by Peter Hunt, is outstanding for its discussion of literature written in English. The chapters on children's literature in America include many books that are Midwestern in subject matter.

The Kerlan Collection at the University of Minnesota is the best collection of children's books, authors' manuscripts, and memorabilia in the Midwest. Most state libraries contain collections of books written by authors born or living in their particular states. Libraries in the larger cities of the Midwest also have exceptional holdings of children's literature of this region.

PATRICIA A. ANDERSON   DIMONDALE, MICHIGAN
MARSHA O. GREASLEY   LEXINGTON, KENTUCKY

CINCINNATI

Cincinnati grew from three late 1700s settlements: Losantiville, Columbia, and North Bend. In 1790 Arthur St. Clair, then governor of the Northwest Territory, visited Los-antiville, the largest of the settlements based on the presence of Fort Washington. He changed the name to Cincinnati because of his position as a member of the Society of the Cincinnati and made the city the seat of Hamilton County. In time it grew to include the other two original settlements.

Area: 79.6 square miles

Population (2010 census): 296,943

OVERVIEW: Cincinnati was important in the early economic, military, and cultural development of the Midwest. By 1803, when OHIO was accepted into the Union, Cincinnati was already a chartered village, and it achieved incorporation as a city in 1819. Access to the Ohio River was economically vital, and the city served as a major manufacturing and meatpacking center. In the 1830s Cincinnati saw an influx of Germans and people of German descent. During this time citizens began calling it the "Queen City"; Henry Wadsworth Longfellow (1807–1882) reinforced this designation by referring to it as "the Queen of the West" in his poem "Catawba Wine." Cincinnati became the leading pork processor in the United States and was often referred to as "Porkopolis." The completion of the Erie and Miami Canal in 1845 helped swell Cincinnati's population to 100,000.

By the mid-1800s Cincinnati surpassed Lexington, Kentucky, as a cultural destination for traveling intellectuals and a residence for poets and other writers. Well over one hundred newspapers and magazines were being published in the city, and its pub-

© Karen Greasley, 2014

lishing houses were well known. Politically, Cincinnati was strongly Unionist and served as a major recruiting center for the Union Civil War effort. By 1890 Cincinnati's population was nearly 300,000; it was the largest city in Ohio at the time, and in the twentieth century it continued to grow. Surrounding communities added over 1.7 million people to the greater metropolitan area, and the city continued to thrive. Although its Midwestern cultural dominance had given way to CHICAGO in the late nineteenth century, influential intellectuals remained at work there in the twentieth and twenty-first centuries.

HISTORY AND SIGNIFICANCE: Although it was by no means the first literary work to be printed in Cincinnati, *The Western Souvenir, a Christmas and New Year's Gift for 1829* (1828), edited by JAMES HALL (1973–1868), is noteworthy for being the first literary annual published in the Midwest. Harriet Beecher Stowe (1811–1896) lived in Cincinnati from 1832 to 1850 and drew on her observations and experiences and the stories she had heard there in the writing of her anti-slavery masterpiece *Uncle Tom's Cabin* (1852). For further discussion of the important literary history of early Cincinnati, see LITERARY PERIODICALS and PRINTING AND PUBLISHING.

The city has been a setting for fiction for almost two centuries. Among the earlier works are *Tales and Sketches from the Queen City* (1838) by Benjamin Drake (1794–1841), who published the volume there; *The League of the Miami* (1850) by Emerson Bennett (1822–1905); and *Christie Bell of Goldenrod Valley: A Tale of Southern Indiana and of Cincinnati in the Olden Time* (1918) by Cincinnati-born Henry Thew Stephenson (1870–1957).

Twentieth-century works include *Process* (2001), originally written in 1925, an autobiographical novel by Kay Boyle (1902–1992). *The Frontiersmen* (1967) by Allan W. Eckert (1931–2011) is a work of historical fiction depicting the settling of Ohio and Kentucky; it sets much of the novel at Fort Washington. *Follow the River* (1969) by Albert I. Mayer (1906–1994) is a novel that concerns a Pennsylvanian settling in Cincinnati in the 1790s. Cincinnati serves as a partial setting for *Beloved* (1987) by TONI MORRISON (b. CHLOE

ARDELIA WOFFORD, 1931); she places the main character in a Cincinnati home. Cincinnati-born Joe David Bellamy (1941–2014) uses the city as the twentieth-century setting of his novel *Suzi Sinzinnati* (1989). Lynn S. Hightower (b. 1956) has created a series of mystery novels featuring a Cincinnati policewoman; the first of these is *Flashpoint* (1995). Among the many twenty-first-century works set in the Queen City is *Grand Avenue* (2001) by Joy (Tepperman) Fielding (b. 1945), in which she traces twenty years in the lives of four suburban Cincinnati women.

Major writers who lived in Cincinnati for a significant period include HARRIETTE SIMPSON ARNOW (1908–1986), CAROLINE LEE HENTZ (1800–1856), HENRY HOWE (1816–1893), and Nikki Giovanni (b. 1943). Unfortunately, their works consider the city only briefly or as a background; more positively, several important Midwestern writers lived in and wrote about the city and its surroundings. WILLIAM HENRY VENABLE (1836–1920) spent much of his life as a poet, novelist, and educator in the city. In the juvenile novel *Tom Tad* (1902) Venable uses local settings and deals with class struggle, education, and natural disasters in a small town near Cincinnati while also paying close attention to geographic details. FANNIE HURST (1885–1968) wrote a historical novel titled *Back Street* (1931), which is set in the 1890s and deals with the German American community of the downtown Over-the-Rhine district. Robert Lowry (1919–1994), a Cincinnati novelist and resident for most of his life, crafted many novels, including the autobiographical *The Big Cage* (1949), with its scathing portrait of Withrow High School and the University of Cincinnati. Thomas (Louis) Berger (1924–2014), best known for *Little Big Man* (1964), was born and educated in Cincinnati and based some of his writing on the city, particularly *Reinhart in Love* (1962), the second of Berger's four anti-hero Carlo Reinhart novels; it features post–World War II Cincinnati as a setting. Austin M. Wright (1922–2003)wrote many of his seven novels while he was Professor of English at the University of Cincinnati, including *First Persons* (1973), which deals with the mental torment of a University of Cincinnati professor who thinks that he is a notorious rapist and murderer in the

1960s, and *After Gregory* (1994), in which the protagonist, a Cincinnati teacher named Peter Gregory, experiences spiritual and mental rebirth after hurling himself into the Ohio River in a suicide attempt. The eleven-book series of Harry Stoner detective novels by JONATHAN LOUIS VALIN (b. 1948), beginning with *The Lime Pit* (1980), records the hero's various cases while he is traveling through the city. Cincinnati locales are described with great accuracy, both geographically and with respect to the social habits of the city's citizens. The last of the series, *Missing,* was published in 1995.

Cincinnati has also been the birthplace of and a subject for poets. Thomas Peirce (1786–1850) began writing poetry for local Cincinnati newspapers and in 1816 published his earliest known volume of verse, *A Present from the Carrier of the Western Spy to Its Patrons.* He later issued a collection of his newspaper satirical verse, *The Odes of Horace in Cincinnati* (1822). The most notable Cincinnati poets were the sisters ALICE CARY (1820–1871) and PHOEBE CARY (1824–1871). They grew up on Clovernook Farm north of the city, and although they relocated to New York in the early 1850s, much of their po-

etry dealt with natural and rural Ohio. Alice also wrote religiously didactic novels and sketches that dealt with the area. Of particular interest for studies of Cincinnati literature are *Poems of Alice and Phoebe Cary* (1850), *Clovernook; or, Recollections of Our Neighborhood in the West* (2 volumes, 1852–1853), *Clovernook Children* (1854), *Poems* [by Alice Cary] (1855), and *Pictures of Country Life* (1859). Although their verse was highly regarded at the time, excessive sentimentality limits its interest to modern readers.

Charles Milton Elam (1882–1944) operated a small Cincinnati printing press, Open Sesame Press, and published his own poetry and that of others. In 1928 he issued a small anthology, *Cincinnati Poetry of the Nineteenth Century.* Bertye Young Williams (1876–1951), the founder of the Cincinnati poetry quarterly *Talaria,* published several collections, including *House of Happiness* (1928) and *Garland for a City* (1946), the latter containing poems about Cincinnati.

Another major Cincinnati-born poet who focused at least some of his work on the city and its surroundings is JOHN (IGNATIUS) KNOEPFLE (b. 1923), who also wrote about other Midwestern cities, including Spring-

Cincinnati, Ohio, skyline, 1910–1920. Detroit Publishing, ca. 1915.
Image courtesy of the Library of Congress

field, ILLINOIS, Chicago, and ST. LOUIS. Richard Hague (b. 1947) has lived in Cincinnati since the 1960s and has allowed the regional influence of the city and surrounding areas to shape much of his poetry. Of his numerous books of poetry, *Crossings* (1978), *Garden* (2002), *The Time It Takes Light* (2004), and *Public Hearings* (2009) were published by Cincinnati presses, and he continues to teach in and write about the area.

Although Helen Steiner Rice (1900–1981) was born in Lorain, Ohio, she moved to Cincinnati in 1931, where she was employed by the Gibson Art Company. There she made a name for herself by writing sentimental, religious, and inspirational couplets for its greeting-card line. Numerous editions of her collected verse are in print, but there is little or no reference to Cincinnati in any of her poetry. Other poets of note who were born or lived for a long period in Cincinnati, although they may not have used it as a setting for the majority of their work, include Alvin (David) Greenberg (b. 1932), Pat(ricia) Mora (b. 1942), Andrew (Leon) Hudgins (Jr.) (b. 1951), Leah (David) Maines (b. 1962), and Deborah Pope (b. 1960).

Among the anthologies of Cincinnati poetry is *Up and down the Hills* (1953), published by the Anderson Hills Poetry Club of Cincinnati. In 1960 the Writers League of Greater Cincinnati produced *Thirty Years of Poetry: An Anniversary Anthology.* Judy Hennessy edited *Bridges: An Anthology of Poetry* by the Greater Cincinnati Writers League in 1988. Local Cincinnati poets' works were featured in two special issues of the University of Cincinnati's literary magazine, *Profile:* "A Handful of Pleasant Delights" (Spring 1971) and "This Cincinnati of the Heart" (Winter 1972).

Much juvenile fiction focuses on Cincinnati. Mary Prudence Wells Smith (1840–1930), a twenty-five-year resident of Cincinnati, wrote *The Browns* (1884) and *A Jolly Good Summer* (1895). Francis James Finn (1859–1928) wrote *Lucky Bob* (1917) about an orphan at a Jesuit boarding school in Cincinnati. Marjorie Hill Allee (1890–1945) wrote *Susanna and Tristram* (1929), the story of teenagers active in Cincinnati's Underground Railroad in the 1850s. In 1997 Susan Martins Miller (b. 1948) published *Danger on the Railroad* about a Cincinnati brother and sister helping a slave escape via the Underground Railroad. Sharon Mills Draper (b. 1952) published *Double Dutch* (2002), a story of three African American girls in Cincinnati.

Chicago's reputation in the late 1800s as the cultural capital of the Midwest came at the expense of Cincinnati. In past generations some critics have bemoaned the city's loss of preeminence. In 1981, for example, in *The Literary Guide to the United States* (1981), Jon Spayde put the matter most negatively, asserting that "to use the phrase [Cincinnati literature] at all may overstate the case for it" (96). This harsh judgment is certainly premature because the city, like many others in the Midwest, has been reinventing itself culturally and economically in the postindustrial landscape.

SELECTED WORKS: A glimpse of Cincinnati in the first decade of the 1800s is to be found in the melodramatic novel *The League of the Miami* (1850) by Emerson Bennett; the eighteenth-century settlements that would later become Cincinnati are mentioned in Allan W. Eckert's fictionalized historical narrative *The Frontiersmen* (1967). In *Beloved* (1987) Toni Morrison looks at the lives and predicaments of former slaves living near Cincinnati in the 1870s, while Fannie Hurst explores the city's sizable German community during the 1890s in *Back Street* (1931).

Other fiction that makes good use of Cincinnati as a background includes Robert Lowry's *The Big Cage* (1949); one of the four Carlo Reinhart novels, *Reinhart in Love* (1962), by Thomas Berger; Austin M. Wright's *After Gregory* (1994); and *Grand Avenue* (2001) by Joy Fielding. The mystery series by Jonathan Valin featuring his edgy detective Harry Stoner is worthy of mention for its detailed descriptions of Cincinnati, as in *The Lime Pit* (1980) and *Fire Lake* (1987).

Zan McQuade edited *The Cincinnati Anthology* (2014), a collection of essays about the city's physical geography and contemporary society. The poetry of Cincinnati is best explored in anthologies of verse. *Thirty Years of Poetry* (1960) showcases the work of members of the Writers League of Greater Cincinnati and was followed by a sequel, *Bridges* (1988), edited by Judy Hennessy. Cincinnati-born John Knoepfle has drawn on his early years in that city in a number of his poems, such as "Church of Rose of Lima, Cincinnati" in his *Rivers into Islands* (1965); and Richard Hague, a longtime resident of the city, has published a number of volumes of verse, such as *Garden* (2002) and *Public Hearings* (2009).

FURTHER READING: Cincinnati's history as an early center of publishing is recounted by Walter Sutton in two books: *Cincinnati as a General Publishing Center: The Middle Years, 1830–1860* (1958) and *The Western Book Trade: Cincinnati as a Nineteenth-Century Publishing and Book-Trade Center* (1961). These aspects are dealt with at length in many other books, including *The Literary Guide to the United States* (1981), edited by Stewart Benedict; Alvin Harlow's *The Serene Cincinnatians* (1950); and William Henry Venable's *Beginnings of Literary Culture in the Ohio Valley* (1891). DAVID D(ANIEL) ANDERSON (1924–2011) also has a brief but excellent chapter on Cincinnati publishing and the McGuffey readers in *Ohio: In Fact and Fiction; Further Essays on the Ohio Experience* (2006), 27–30.

In addition, Anderson includes an important chapter on Cincinnati's early literary development, "The Queen City and a New Literature," in his *Ohio: In Myth, Memory, and Imagination; Essays on the Ohio Experience* (2004). There he covers other important literary figures from Cincinnati, including the publishing pioneer William Maxwell (1755–1809) and the poets William Davis Gallagher (1808–1894), Otway Curry (1804–1855), and Charles A. Jones (1815–1851), all three of whom lived in and wrote about the Cincinnati area, although, as Anderson points out, they have been largely forgotten (50).

A discussion of the early literary ambitions of Cincinnati can be found in part 3, "The Empire of the Western Mind: Cincinnati and Colonial Culture," of Edward Watts's *An American Colony: Regionalism and the Roots of Midwestern Culture* (2002). A useful study of one of Cincinnati's numerous literary societies is Louis Tucker's "The Semi-colon Club of Cincinnati," *Ohio History* 73 (1964): 13–26. Dale Patrick Brown's *Literary Cincinnati: The Missing Chapter* (2011) presents information on Cincinnati writers in the late nineteenth and early twentieth centuries.

An extensive list of authors who were born or resided in Cincinnati can be found in *Ohio Authors and Their Books, 1796–1950* (1962), edited by William Coyle, but no extensive study of Cincinnati literature, fiction, or poetry has yet been published. The sole bibliography dealing with any of Cincinnati's literary output is Franziska C. Ott's *Cincinnati German Imprints: A Checklist* (1993), which lists all books printed in Cincinnati in the German language, including creative works.

The Cincinnati Public Library's Cincinnati Room has many historical documents and local history volumes that can aid students of Cincinnati literature. The library has a large collection of Cincinnati-based literature and poetry, including many works by lesser-known local writers. In addition, the Cincinnati Historical Society Library in the Cincinnati Museum Center at Union Terminal has an extensive collection of newspaper reviews of Cincinnati authors and Cincinnati-based works dating back to the turn of the twentieth century. The German-Americana Collection at the University of Cincinnati's Archives and Rare Books Library is a repository of German American writing that chronicles German heritage in the United States, particularly in the Ohio Valley.

EDWARD DAUTERICH   KENT STATE UNIVERSITY

CLEVELAND

Cleveland was named for General Moses Cleaveland, agent and chief surveyor of the Connecticut Land Company, who in 1796 founded the city near the mouth of the Cuyahoga River in northeastern OHIO on the southern shore of Lake Erie, about sixty miles west of the Pennsylvania border. It became a manufacturing center owing to its lakeshore location and its connections to numerous canals and railroad lines.

Area: 82.4 square miles

Population: (2010 census): 396,815

OVERVIEW: Cleveland is a quintessentially ethnic city built on heavy industry, especially steel and shipping, by immigrants from Europe and the South. It has seen slaves smuggled north on the Underground Railroad and rumrunners on Lake Erie. It is a city of smokestacks and church steeples, rib joints and sausage shops, the Indians and the Browns, Great Lakes freighters and the Rock and Roll Hall of Fame. All of these are

© Karen Greasley, 2014

elements of Cleveland as a Midwestern city and literary place.

Cleveland's history extends from the wilderness of Connecticut's Western Reserve through industrialization and manufacturing to the current era of globalization, outsourcing, and deindustrialization. The story of Cleveland is that of unionized urban America and the industrial Midwest, and the city's ups and downs reflect the changing American experience.

HISTORY AND SIGNIFICANCE: Literary figures commenting on the city have included Charles Dickens (1812–1870), who, in his *American Notes* (1842), described Cleveland as a "pretty town" (174), and SAMUEL LANGHORNE CLEMENS (1835–1910), writing as Mark Twain, who called Cleveland a "stirring, enterprising young city" and "a great manufacturing town." He called its Euclid Avenue "one of the finest streets in America" and, commenting on wealth and class in the United States, observed that to live on it, in what was known as Millionaires Row, "you have to be redolent of that odor of sanctity that comes with cash" (*Daily Alta California,* November 15, 1868, 1).

The writings of novelists, poets, essayists, short-story writers, journalists, and cartoonists in Cleveland's history have reflected the city. Many writers were born, were raised in, or later moved to Cleveland. Most wrote of the city; all were shaped by it and, to varying degrees, reflected its imprint. In *The Big Sea: An Autobiography* (1940) LANGSTON HUGHES (1902–1967) recounts that he com-

mitted himself to a writing career while growing up in Cleveland (28–29). He published his first stories and poems while he was a student at Cleveland's Central High School, where he became class poet and editor in chief of the yearbook. "Artemus Ward," a persona created by CHARLES FARRAR BROWNE (1834–1867) in his newspaper columns written for the *Plain Dealer,* achieved international fame as a stage character and in a series of collections beginning with *Artemus Ward, His Book* (1862). Civil War historian (CHARLES) BRUCE CATTON (1899–1978) was also a reporter in Cleveland, as were poet (HAROLD) HART CRANE (1899–1932), author of *White Buildings* (1926) and *The Bridge* (1930), and novelist DON ROBERTSON (1929–1999), whose eighteen works include three novels based on his experiences growing up in Cleveland: *The Greatest Thing since Sliced Bread* (1965), *The Sum and Total of Now* (1966), and *The Greatest Thing That Almost Happened* (1970). CHARLES WADDELL CHESNUTT (1858–1932), who has been credited with paving the way for the Harlem Renaissance and is recognized by many as the first great African American novelist, grew up in Cleveland and spent nearly all his life there. Treatments of the color line, "Negro" color consciousness, and the struggles of black migrants from the South are among his important contributions. His Groveland stories, published in the late nineteenth century and set in Cleveland, are stories of color, caste, and, in one instance, literary society. The most famous of these is "The Wife of His Youth" (1899). Educated at a Cleveland high school, CHESTER HIMES (1909–1984), an Ohio State University student, an Ohio state penitentiary inmate, and again a Cleveland resident through the late 1930s, wrote much highly regarded African American detective fiction, but his stories are set outside the Midwest. Himes moved to Paris in 1953 and never returned. His two autobiographies, *The Quality of Hurt* (1971) and *My Life of Absurdity* (1976), recount his life and shaping influences.

Nowhere in literature are the city of Cleveland and its history, politics, and culture more richly depicted than in the pages of *Crooked River Burning* (2001) by Mark Winegardner (b. 1961). As its epic story unfolds around the lives of its two main characters,

Cleveland public square, 1906.
Image courtesy of the Library of Congress

twentieth-century Cleveland materializes in a brilliant work of urban Midwestern fiction that follows the protagonists, as well as the city, from 1948 to 1969.

Novelist RUTH SEID (1913–1995), who wrote as Jo Sinclair, was born and lived most of her life in Cleveland; she is widely acknowledged as both a significant Jewish and lesbian writer and is best known for *Wasteland* (1946). Much of Sinclair's work unfolds in a fictionalized Cleveland. HERBERT GOLD (b. 1924), born in the Cleveland suburb of Lakewood, set five of his novels, including *Fathers: A Novel in the Form of a Memoir* (1967) and *The Prospect before Us* (1954), in the city. Lois Wedel (1906–1985) wrote short stories about Cleveland's early days in *Pioneer Tales of a Great City* (1944). Joyce Rebeta-Burditt (b.1938) wrote a fictional account of a Cleveland woman committed to a psychiatric hospital in *The Cracker Factory* (1977). Raymond De Capite (1924–2009) wrote novels such as *The Coming of Fabrizze* (1960) and *A Lost King* (1961) that portray the Italian community on the city's south side. Cleveland novelist Sarah Willis (b. 1954) wrote *A Good Distance* (2004) and *The Sound of Us* (2005).

Alice Mary Norton (1912–2005), writing as Andre Norton, and Roger (Joseph) Zelazny (1937–1995) are notable Cleveland

science-fiction writers. Popular westerns by Clevelander Jack (Warner) Schaefer (1907–1991) were the basis of two major Hollywood movies, *Shane* (1953) and *Monte Walsh* (1970). One of the important contemporary Cleveland writers of popular fiction is LES ROBERTS (b. Lester Roubert in 1937), whose numerous Milan Jacovich private detective novels feature the city, its ethnic neighborhoods, and its cuisine as if Cleveland were one of his characters. Among the novels in this series are *Pepper Pike* (1988), *Full Cleveland* (1989), *The Cleveland Connection* (1993), *The Lake Effect* (1994), *The Cleveland Local* (1997), *A Shoot in Cleveland* (1998), *King of the Holly Hop* (2008), *Cleveland Creep* (2011), *Whiskey Island* (2012), and *Win, Place or Die* (2013). Jerome "Jerry" Siegel (1914–1996) and Joseph Shuster (1914–1992) created the most famous fictional character invented in Cleveland, Superman, who first appeared in comics in 1938.

Cleveland has been the home of several children's writers, such as Florence M. (Casey) Everson (1887–1983) and Effie (Louise) Power (1873–1969). Their *Early Days in Ohio* (1928) provides a fictional presentation of two pioneer families who move to the Cleveland area in 1800. Marie Halun Bloch (1910–1998) wrote *Marya* (1957), the story of a girl in a Cleveland Ukrainian neighborhood. Best known for her juvenile books *Tears of a Tiger* (1994), *Forged by Fire* (1997), *Romiette and Julio* (1999), and *Darkness before Dawn* (2001), Cleveland-born Sharon M. Draper (b. 1952) has also published a series of picture books.

E(dmund) Burke Fisher (ca. 1799–ca. 1859) wrote what is perhaps the first poetry published about Cleveland in his verse satire *Wars of the Barnburners of Cuyahoga County* (1844). Cleveland has a vibrant poetry scene whose heritage includes Langston Hughes and Hart Crane, as well as local favorites like counterculture poet and underground-press publisher Darryl Allan Levy (1942–1968), writing as d. a. levy, and poet-activist Daniel R. Thompson (1935–2004). Traditional poetry, POETRY SLAMS, and underground verse are alive and thriving in Cleveland.

Lake Erie and shipping are central to the city and its culture; the genre of GREAT LAKES LITERATURE and the many nonfiction works of Dwight Boyer (1912–1978) reflect this heritage. So does the work of lifelong Clevelander Harvey Pekar (1939–2010). His *American Splendor,* an autobiography in comic-book form, debuted in 1976 and ran for many issues, drawn by a number of artists. A selection, *American Splendor: The Life and Times of Harvey Pekar,* appeared in 1986 and became a feature-film adaptation in 2003. See COMIC STRIPS AND BOOKS.

SELECTED WORKS: Readers wanting to get acquainted with Cleveland literature should begin with Don Robertson's Cleveland trilogy: *The Greatest Thing since Sliced Bread* (1965), *The Sum and Total of Now* (1966), and *The Greatest Thing That Almost Happened* (1970). Les Roberts also captures the texture, taste, and temperament of contemporary Cleveland in his many Milan Jacovich private eye stories, starting with *Pepper Pike* (1988) and continuing to the present. Mark Winegardner's *Crooked River Burning* (2001) is also a must-read of Cleveland literature, as is Harvey Pekar's *American Splendor,* a serial memoir in comics, of which *American Splendor: The Life and Times of Harvey Pekar* (1986) is one collection. Among Cleveland poetry anthologies are *Cleveland Anthology* (1975), edited by Geoffrey Singer and C. A. Smith, and *Voices of Cleveland: A Bicentennial Anthology of Poems by Contemporary Cleveland Poets* (1996). *Cleveland in Prose and Poetry* (2005), published by the Poets and Writers League of Greater Cleveland and edited by Bonnie Jacobson, is a sampler of Cleveland literature and an excellent introduction to contemporary poets. *Rust Belt Chic: The Cleveland Anthology* (2012), edited by Anne Trubek and Richey Piiparinen, collects essays about the city's industrial decline and attempts at cultural revival.

FURTHER READING: For historical background, the journalism and essays of George E(dward) Condon (1916–2011) will be of interest, along with *Cleveland: A Concise History, 1796–1996* (1997) by Carol Poh Miller and Robert A. Wheeler. An extensive list of authors who were born or lived in Cleveland can be found in *Ohio Authors and Their Books, 1796–1950* (1962), edited by William Coyle. The year 1991 saw the publication of *Catalog of Poetry Books Published by the Cleveland State University Poetry Center, 1971–1991. Remembering: Cleveland's Jewish Voices* (2011), selected by Judah Rubenstein and edited by Sally Wertheim and Alan D. Bennett, is an anthology of essays, short stories, and poems depicting Jewish life in Cleveland and northeastern Ohio.

The website of the Ohio Center for the Book at the Cleveland Public Library includes an interactive map of the state allowing for author searches by region. The Cleveland Memory project, based at Cleveland State University, is an internet venue at which one can search all things Cleveland, including manuscripts. The library at Cleveland State is also home to the Hazel Collister Hutchinson Poetry Room, maintained by the CSU Poetry Center.

DAVID PERUSEK   KENT STATE UNIVERSITY–ASHTABULA

CLUBS, SALONS, AND SOCIETIES

OVERVIEW: Many Midwestern literary clubs, salons, and societies existed as educational and creative outlets for men and women during the nineteenth and early twentieth centuries. Literary societies often distinguished themselves from other literary organizations by their more formal organizational structures and their maintenance of records of activities; salons tended to be more informal. A variety of rural and urban literary entities existed in the Midwest. These served the purpose of self-improvement for many and also were vehicles for self-expression; they also provided a basis for literary communities in some urban areas. Most originally attracted primarily white middle- and upper-class Protestants because of their association with religiously affiliated teacher training camps, but there were many exceptions. Fictionalized examples of these literary clubs, salons, and societies appear in several novels and short stories. Literary societies waned in the first decades of the twentieth century. In recent years many Midwestern cities have experienced revitalized interest in book clubs and literary salons.

HISTORY AND SIGNIFICANCE: Literary societies originated in Europe and date back to the sixteenth century. Several organizations of elite white males in England, such as the Kit Kat Club and the Scriblerus Club, enjoyed long tenures. The concept of the salon—social gatherings at private homes to discuss literary, artistic, and scientific topics—was popularized in France. Literary and philosophical salons provided a base for French writers such as Denis Diderot (1713–1784) in the eighteenth century and Charles Baudelaire (1821–1864) in the nineteenth century.

These literary entities were transplanted to the American colonies and drew members from the ranks of educated and affluent white males. One of the earliest examples was the Junto Club, formed in Philadelphia in 1727 and counting among its members Benjamin Franklin (1706–1790). According to his autobiography, it was created as a "club of mutual improvement" (1848 edition 103). Beginning with a dozen members, the group met every Friday and discussed morals, politics, or natural philosophy. Each member was required to prepare and read an essay on the subject of his choosing every three months. The organization continued for forty years and became the core of the American Philosophical Society.

In the nineteenth century, literary clubs and societies proliferated in the Midwest. These had characteristics distinguishing them from the earlier New England and East Coast literary entities. Although separate gender organizations were among the first to form, new coeducational models also emerged. Self-improvement was often an aim, and some members viewed participation as an alternative to advanced education.

Higher education eluded the majority of nineteenth-century Americans. In 1869–1870 only about two percent of the population graduated from high school. During the same period about one percent of college-aged Americans pursued education beyond high school, and twenty-one percent of these were women. The number of high school graduates remained below ten percent even as late as 1900. As a result, only a very limited number of men and women encountered collegiate literary societies, although academically affiliated literary societies proliferated in the Midwest and flourished between 1830 and 1920. These collegiate organizations formed as single-sex or coeducational clubs, depending on the institution, and focused on writing and reading essays. The clubs existed at both public and private institutions; some of the earliest formed at OHIO colleges, including groups at Ohio University in 1812 and Oberlin in 1833. Other well-known organizations included the Erodelphian and Union Literary Societies at Miami University of Ohio in the 1820s and the Athenian and Philomathean Societies in the 1830s at Indiana University.

Most Americans belonging to literary associations were middle aged or older and had occupational and familial responsibilities. Ladies' literary associations were among the earliest formed and were very popular in small and rural communities during the post–Civil War period. Some formed later in the century probably drew inspiration from Sorosis, a professional women's club founded in New York City in 1868, or the New England Women's Club, founded in Boston the same year.

There was also an ongoing tradition of Midwestern women forming library associations in the years before and right after the Civil War. As the momentum of the public library movement grew, many of these organizations emphasized literary pursuits and self-improvement. The Ladies' Library Association of Kalamazoo (Michigan) fit this model and was among the first library organizations, forming in 1852 and evolving into a literary society by the 1870s. Lucinda Hinsdale Stone (1814–1900), one of the founding members of the Kalamazoo organization, identified the programs of ladies' library and literary associations as the "'post-graduate' courses of study" for married women, according to Belle McArthur Perry (1856–ca. 1925) in her 1902 biography *Lucinda Hinsdale Stone, Her Life Story and Reminiscences* (165). The Kalamazoo Ladies' Library Association was particularly successful and claims the distinction of being the first women's organization in the United States to construct a women's club building, doing so in 1878–1879. Many of these organizations thrived at the end of the nineteenth century and found additional support and power by affiliating with the General Federation of Women's Clubs, organized in 1890.

Similar organizations for men often had occupational linkages. Farmers' organizations flourished in rural areas, and mechanics' organizations drew from more urban populations. Often these organizations had libraries and sponsored literary activities. The Western Literary Union in Tippecanoe County, INDIANA, was part of an umbrella organization called the Farmers' Institute. The literary and debating activities associated with the Western Literary Union became the center of intellectual activities in this rural county. Composed of Quakers, the Western Literary Union allowed both men and women to participate. This was somewhat unusual in the 1850s, when most Midwestern literary societies tended to be single sex. Reading lists and topics included religious and secular matters. The Western Literary Union began in 1851 and continued through the 1880s.

Self-improvement, especially for those lacking a formal education, was promoted by commercial programs available to literary clubs, such as those sponsored by the Chautauqua Literary and Scientific Circle. The Chautauqua movement began in upstate New York in 1874 as a Methodist Sunday school teachers' training camp. It grew into the Chautauqua Literary and Scientific Circle in 1878, with a four-year course of study culminating in a diploma. Offering a home-study course with a required four-book annual reading list supplemented by the organization's publication, the *Chautauquan*, the Literary and Scientific Circle provided the structure for many Midwestern literary societies. The membership of the Chau-

tauqua Literary and Scientific Circle was primarily female and heavily Midwestern. By 1900 some 10,000 circles had formed.

Although the Chautauqua Literary and Scientific Circle was probably the best-known program, others with comparable Protestant viewpoints emerged during this period. The Bay View (Michigan) Association had similar origins, initially organizing a camp meeting in 1875 and eventually selecting land on the shores of Little Traverse Bay in northwest MICHIGAN. The Bay View Reading Circle began in 1893 and continued through 1921, with membership numbering about 25,000 at one point.

Urban literary societies took on different characteristics. Some of the larger urban literary clubs mimicked established eastern organizations. Larger urban centers with more diverse populations saw more organizational variations, as well as societies consisting of Catholics, Jews, and African Americans.

The Chicago Literary Club began in 1874 as an organization of leading professional men of the city. Members prepared and read original works of nonfiction, fiction, biography, and critical essays. A female literary society, the Fortnightly of Chicago, founded in 1873, was among the most exclusive in CHICAGO. Both organizations have survived into the twenty-first century; however, the Chicago Literary Club counts both men and women among its members today.

The Young Irishmen's Society formed in Chicago in 1867. The organization lost most of its belongings during the 1871 Chicago fire but rebounded and reorganized as the Irish Literary Association of Chicago in the 1870s. Ellen Skerrett reports in *At the Crossroads: Old Saint Patrick's and the Chicago Irish* (1977) that programming celebrated the Irish literary heritage, and some events, such as the annual St. Patrick's Day banquet and ball, also involved women and children; the organization continued into the 1920s (9, 12).

In ST. LOUIS, MISSOURI, Jewish women formed the Pioneers Ladies' Literary Society in 1877. Modeled on similar Christian women's clubs, the organization covered a variety of literary subjects beyond Jewish literature. Rosa Sonnenschein (1847–1932), an active participant in the German cultural life of St. Louis, was one of the founding members and went on to publish *The American Jewess,* the first English periodical for Jewish women, in 1895.

African Americans also began forming literary societies in eastern cities in the years after the Civil War. By the 1880s similar organizations began to form in the Midwest. The Prudence Crandall Club in Chicago, named for the white abolitionist, formed in the mid-1880s and included Chicago's most prominent African American men and women. Fannie Barrier Williams (1855–1944), a reformer involved in the Frederick Douglass settlement house in Chicago, was among the organization's leaders. Williams also fought a long and eventually successful battle for membership in the influential Chicago Women's Club.

Toward the end of the nineteenth century, literary societies and salons began attracting leading writers, intellectuals, and artists in several Midwestern cities. In Chicago the Little Room brought together reformers, artists, and writers beginning in the early 1890s, drawing its name from a short story by Madeline Yale Wynne (1847–1918), published in 1895 in *Harper's New Monthly Magazine,* that described a room where visitors could find companionship and happiness. Little Room gatherings included JANE ADDAMS (1860–1935), Lorado (Zadoc) Taft (1860–1936), Ralph (Elmer) Clarkson (1861–1942), GEORGE ADE (1866–1944), HENRY BLAKE FULLER (1857–1929), (HANNIBAL) HAMLIN GARLAND (1860–1940), HARRIET MONROE (1860–1936), and Edith (Franklin) Wyatt (1873–1958). The organization met in one of the studios of Chicago's Fine Arts Building and continued into the 1930s.

In St. Louis in the early 1890s, Katherine O'Flaherty (1850–1904), writing as Kate Chopin, hosted a literary salon in her home named Thursdays for the day of the week on which it met. Chopin, a native of Missouri, is best known for her writing about Louisiana and her avant-garde novel *The Awakening* (1899). Chopin's salon included a diverse population of writers and thinkers, such as Sue V. Moore, editor of *St. Louis Life;* Dr. Frederick Kolbenheyer, an Austrian-born anarchist, freethinker, and family doctor; Charles Deyo, a *Post-Dispatch* journalist; George (Sibley) Johns (1857–1941), a *Post-Dispatch* reviewer; and WILLIAM

MARION REEDY (1862–1920), the editor of the *St. Louis Mirror.* See *REEDY'S MIRROR.*

Several Midwestern authors, including (HARRY) SINCLAIR LEWIS (1885–1951), ZONA GALE (1874–1938), and HELEN HOOVEN SANTMYER (1895–1986), have incorporated literary clubs into short stories, essays, and novels. Works by Isabella MacDonald Alden (1841–1930) and Bruce Bliven (1889–1977) illustrate the pervasiveness of the Chautauqua Literary and Scientific Circle in popular culture and the importance of the Chautauqua movement in the Midwest.

Lewis's *MAIN STREET* (1920) is based on the fictional town of Gopher Prairie, MINNESOTA, and brought him critical and commercial success. Lewis often drew from his experiences in his hometown, Sauk Centre, Minnesota, for inspiration in his writing and took a dim view of the conventions and provincialism of small Midwestern towns. In *Main Street* one of Lewis's objects of contempt is the local women's literary society, the Thanatopsis Club. Lewis describes the activities of the club, including rote memorization of facts and biographical studies of authors, and finds them less than intellectual. He lumps the women's literary society along with other aspects of small-town culture, including the annual appearance of the traveling Chautauqua, and treats it with much of the same disdain.

Another Midwestern author, Zona Gale, also drew from her hometown, Portage, WISCONSIN, for her writings. Gale's collection *Portage, Wisconsin, and Other Essays* (1928) includes an essay recounting the activities of a Chautauqua Literary and Scientific Circle, "Katytown in the Eighties." Her essay describes middle-aged men and women studying American history and classical works of literature. Although the Katytown group was coeducational, Gale describes a primarily female audience studying for the sake of study or possibly to earn a Chautauqua-issued diploma because opportunities for higher education have eluded most of the participants.

Helen Hooven Santmyer's "... *And Ladies of the Club"* (1982) focuses on a literary society in the fictional community of Waynesboro, Ohio. Santmyer also drew on her early experiences in Xenia, Ohio, for much of her adult writing. "... *And Ladies of the*

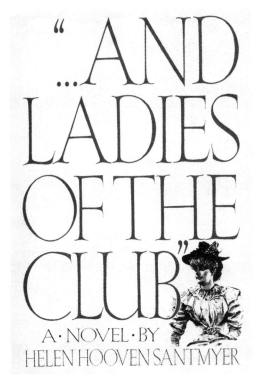

Helen Hooven Santmyer's . . . *And Ladies of the Club*, 1982.

Reproduced by permission from the Ohio State University Press

Club" follows the female members of a literary club in the years after the Civil War, chronicling changing political and social culture from 1868 to 1932. Santmyer's view of small Midwestern towns and literary societies is much more sympathetic than Lewis's or Gale's treatment of the subject. Santmyer thought that Lewis's view of small towns was too narrow. Santmyer's popular novel was eventually reissued as a Book-of-the-Month offering.

Isabella MacDonald Alden, more popularly known under the pseudonym Pansy, wrote numerous nineteenth-century works aimed at juvenile and young-adult audiences. Her 1882 work *The Hall in the Grove* focuses on what happens in a small town when a group of people form a Chautauqua Literary and Scientific Circle to study Rome, theology, and the Bible. Alden also wrote other books related to the movement, including a series called the Chautauqua

Girls, which focused on the camp experiences but did not share characters or plotlines with *The Hall in the Grove.*

Bruce Bliven also wrote about Chautauqua and its importance to the Midwest in a short essay, "Mother, Home, and Heaven," in the *New Republic* in 1924. Although his essay focuses on the circuit programs, it notes the importance of the movement for the intellectual development of Midwesterners. Sinclair Lewis's influence is obvious because Bliven references *Main Street.* Bliven, a product of Emmetsburg, IOWA, vacillates in his essay, criticizing the Puritan values promoted by Chautauqua and its limited scope but also finding value in one of the few avenues of intellectual stimulation open to small-town Midwesterners.

The literary societies of the nineteenth and early twentieth centuries faded in the first three decades of the twentieth century. Although some founded in the nineteenth century survive, their activities and focus have changed. A renewed interest in book clubs began in the 1990s, in which Oprah (Gail) Winfrey (b. 1954) and her Chicago-based television program played a major role when she initiated her book club in 1996. Winfrey featured both contemporary novels and classic works. The television-based book club ended with the conclusion of her talk show in May 2011. Oprah's Book Club 2.0 began in 2012 and is accessed via the internet. Literary salons geared toward authors have also reemerged. The Sunday Salon Chicago provides space for new and established literary voices. It is hosted by Natalia Nebel, Alexandra Sheckler, and Christine Sneed and was formerly co-hosted by Melanie Pappadis Faranello and Mike Zapata, the co-founder and publisher of *Make: A Chicago Literary Magazine.*

SELECTED WORKS: The Chautauqua Literary and Scientific Circle linked religious impulses with cultural uplift and educational self-improvement and was undoubtedly the most influential of the traditional literary organizations, providing the model for many Midwestern literary societies. Chicago's Little Room, functioning throughout the CHICAGO RENAISSANCE era, offered the most elite literary and intellectual gathering. The most significant fictional characterizations of these clubs, salons, and societies include Sinclair Lewis's negative portrayal in *Main Street* (1920), Zona Gale's collection *Portage, Wisconsin, and Other Essays* (1928), and Helen Hooven Santmyer's more positive depiction, *" . . . And Ladies of the Club"* (1982).

FURTHER READING: Some referenced authors have been considered in numerous studies, but Midwestern literary societies deserve additional research. To date, most coverage has been limited to specific issues or organizations. Karen Blair's *The Clubwoman as Feminist: True Womanhood Redefined, 1868–1914* (1980) looks at the activities of East Coast clubwomen and cites the existence of a limited number of literary clubs before the Civil War. Theodora Penny Martin's *The Sound of Our Own Voices: Women's Study Clubs, 1860–1920* (1987) brings the focus to the Midwest with a study of the Decatur, ILLINOIS, Art Class. Becky Bradway-Hesse's article "Bright Access: Midwestern Literary Societies, with a Particular Look at a University for the 'Farmer and the Poor,'" *Rhetoric Review* 17.1 (Fall 1998): 50–73, provides an excellent overview of Midwestern academic literary societies. The Chautauqua movement as it applies to Midwestern literary interests is explored by Julie R. Nelson in "A Subtle Revolution: The Chautauqua Literary and Scientific Circle in Rural Midwestern Towns, 1878–1900," *Agricultural History* 70.4 (Fall 1996): 653–71. Overviews of individual organizations often appear in county histories. Studies have been published about the Kalamazoo Ladies' Library Association in *Women with a Vision* (1997) by Grace J. Potts and Cheryl Lyon-Jenness and the Western Literary Union in David Hovde and John Fritch's "In Union There Is Strength: The Farmers' Institute and the Western Literary Union Library," *Libraries and Culture* 40.3 (Summer 2005): 285–306. Ellen Skerrett's *At the Crossroads: Old Saint Patrick's and the Chicago Irish* (1977) discusses Chicago's Young Irishmen's Society. Christopher Robert Reed's *Black Chicago's First Century: 1833–1900* (2005) discusses Chicago's Prudence Crandall Club. Kristin Mapel Bloomberg and Johanna Ganz's "The Violet Study Club of Minneapolis," *Hennepin History* 70.1 (2011): 4–17, focuses on this organization in Minnesota, which existed from 1906 to 1973. This club

served as the inspiration for the Violent Study Club in *Betsy's Wedding* (1955) in the Betsy-Tacy series by Maud Hart Lovelace (1892–1980).

Unpublished records of many of these organizations exist in large and small libraries throughout the Midwest. Some of the larger collections include minutes, correspondence, photographs, reports, and yearbooks. The records of the Chautauqua Literary and Scientific Circle are among the organizational records held by archives of the parent Chautauqua Institution in Chautauqua, New York. Records of local chapters may reside in public libraries and historical societies. The Bay View Reading Circle's records are included in the Bay View Archives in Michigan. Records of several Chicago organizations, including the Little Room, the Chicago Literary Club, and limited records of the Fortnightly Club, are held at the Newberry Library. The records of the Kalamazoo Ladies' Library Association are held at the Western Michigan University Archives and Regional History Collections. Similar records of other women's literary societies exist in public and university libraries throughout the Midwest.

SHARON CARLSON   WESTERN MICHIGAN UNIVERSITY

COMIC STRIPS AND BOOKS

OVERVIEW: Newspaper comic strips and comic books have reflected and affected American culture since their inception. The comic strip, a logical sequence of line drawings, usually compartmentalized into panels and telling a brief story, has existed since the late nineteenth century. The single-panel political cartoon has evolved internationally with the newspaper, but it was not until the 1890s that comic strips became a regular feature of newspapers in the United States. Originally, comic strips were designed as vehicles for HUMOR, with each appearance featuring a self-contained mini-narrative, or "gag." It was not until the early twentieth century that this new medium was employed to tell extended comedic or dramatic stories.

The first comic books, published as early as the 1890s, were collections of newspaper comic strips. In a stricter sense, the periodical format recognized today as the comic book first appeared in the 1930s. At that time comic books were saddle-stapled magazines with color covers and interiors and bore a price tag of ten cents. Although many still reprinted newspaper comic strips, they now also provided original stories scripted and drawn by people exclusively for comic-book publishers, not newspapers.

Despite their reputation as children's fare, these media have always attracted diverse readers with wide-ranging demographic backgrounds. Especially since the 1960s, many comics have been created specifically for adult readers. A number of cartoonists have begun their careers publishing in Midwestern newspapers, in many cases with strips portraying Midwestern scenes and characters. The Midwest has also been the setting of comic books by artists and writers with Midwestern origins or connections. Both comic strips and books have influenced GRAPHIC NOVELS, a form that has recently gained a wide readership and scholarly attention of its own. This entry traces the history of Midwestern comic strips and then that of comic books, emphasizing comics with Midwestern settings or other regional significance.

HISTORY AND SIGNIFICANCE: The first comic strips appeared in San Francisco and New York City newspapers, but some important early comics were created by transplanted Midwesterners. Richard F. Outcault (1863–1928) of Lancaster and CINCINNATI, OHIO, created the first popular comic. Outcault's *Hogan's Alley,* about children in a New York City slum, first appeared in Joseph Pulitzer's *New York Journal* in 1895. It became such a sensation that in 1896 rival publisher William Randolph Hearst hired Outcault away to produce his comic at the *New York World,* where it ran as *The Yellow Kid.* Outcault's central character is Mickey Dugan, a bald boy in a yellow nightshirt on which appear his comments in New York street slang. The term "yellow journalism," referring to the kind of sensationalism typical of newspapers of the time, originated with *The Yellow Kid.* Outcault's creation initiated the trend of newspapers using comics to increase circulation, as well as of secondary merchandising of cartoon characters in retail and advertising.

Winsor McCay (1869–1934), who grew up in MICHIGAN and started his career as a car-toonist in Cincinnati, created *Little Nemo in Slumberland,* one of the earliest strips with narrative continuity between episodes. *Little Nemo,* which first appeared in New York newspapers and ran from 1905 to 1914, features outstanding art nouveau graphics and surreal narratives occurring in the dreams of a small boy. Like *The Yellow Kid* and other early comics, *Little Nemo* appeared on Sundays. The first daily strip was *Mutt and Jeff,* created by Harry Conway "Bud" Fisher (1885–1954) of CHICAGO. It first appeared as *A. Mutt* in the *San Francisco Chronicle* in 1907 and achieved a large audience through syndication. Drawn first by Fisher and then by a succession of artists, *Mutt and Jeff* endured until 1982.

Although the single-panel editorial cartoon is outside the scope of this entry, it is important to acknowledge the influence of John T(inney) McCutcheon (1870–1949) not only on editorial cartoons but also on comics in general. Born in INDIANA and educated at Purdue University, he drew cartoons for the *Chicago Morning News* before moving to the *Chicago Tribune* in 1903, where he worked until his retirement in 1946. McCutcheon's cartoons on local, national, and international political issues earned him a Pulitzer Prize and the title "Dean of American Cartoonists." He was the leading figure in what is known as the Midwestern school of editorial cartooning, a group including Jay Norwood "Ding" Darling (1876–1962), Carey Orr (1890–1967), Vaughn Shoemaker (1902–1991), and Herb Block (1909–2001). McCutcheon also illustrated articles, as well as books like *New Fables in Slang* (1900) by GEORGE ADE (1866–1944). Along with publisher Joseph Medill Patterson, he mentored younger colleagues at the *Tribune,* including Gaar Williams (1880–1935), who drew sentimental cartoons based on his small-town Indiana childhood, and comic-strip artists (Robert) Sidney Smith (1877–1935) of *The Gumps,* Frank King (1883–1969) of *Gasoline Alley,* Frank Willard (1893–1958) of *Moon Mullins,* Carl Ed (1890–1959) of *Harold Teen,* Harold Gray (1894–1964) of *Little Orphan Annie,* and Chester Gould (1900–1985) of *Dick Tracy.* These strips, syndicated nationally by the Chicago Tribune Media Syndicate, made the *Tribune* an important center of comic strip art.

In addition to editorial cartoons and illustrations, McCutcheon drew humorous and sentimental cartoons for the *Tribune*. The most famous of these was "Injun Summer," which appeared on September 30, 1907, and was so well received that it was reproduced as a best-selling print and reprinted in the *Tribune* in 1910 and then every fall from 1912 to 1992. "Injun Summer" features two horizontally stacked panels. The first shows an old man sitting by a tree, smoking a pipe as he and a small boy stare at shocks of corn in a field in the approaching twilight. In the second panel dusk has arrived, and the scene is transformed, with the corn shocks transformed into tepees and campfire smoke evoking the spirits of Indians performing a ritual dance. In the accompanying text, written in Midwestern rural dialect, the old man explains Indian summer to the boy and encourages him to imagine the scene as portrayed by McCutcheon in the second panel. The cartoon evokes the myth of Indians as a vanishing race, also expressed in the famous sculpture *End of the Trail* (1894) by James Earle Frazier of MINNESOTA and SOUTH DAKOTA, and many works of literature. See NATIVE AMERICANS AS DEPICTED IN MIDWESTERN LITERATURE.

In 1917 Sidney Smith produced *The Gumps,* a strip that parodied the domestic lives of middle-class American families. This focus on ordinary life reflected the influence of literary REALISM AND NATURALISM. *The Gumps* proved crucial in the popularization of comics with ongoing, suspenseful narratives. Andy Gump and later his son Chester became enduring staples of the *Chicago Tribune* and newspaper comic pages everywhere. Smith lived in Bloomington, ILLINOIS, and Lake Geneva, WISCONSIN, where monuments to *The Gumps* still stand.

In 1918 Frank King from Tomah, Wisconsin, provided the Chicago Tribune Media Syndicate with another saga of middle-class America, although King's strip did not appear in the established comic-strip form until 1921. This was *Gasoline Alley,* featuring Walt Wallet and his foundling son, Skeezix, set in a small town surrounded by rolling countryside resembling that of Wisconsin. The first strip in which characters aged and eventually died, *Gasoline Alley* featured complex, extended stories that captured emotional nuances and the rhythms of daily life. King's large-format, full-color Sunday strips dispensed with narrative continuity and instead offered innovative graphics and ruminations on nature and companionship. *Gasoline Alley* has remained in syndication, drawn by a succession of cartoonists since King's death.

The most famous adventure-strip heroine appeared for the first time on August 25, 1924, in the *New York Daily News,* a paper owned by the Chicago Tribune Media Syndicate. She was Little Orphan Annie, created by Harold Gray, who grew up in rural Illinois and Indiana. The little waif with the red mop of hair is a Horatio Alger–like figure spouting moral philosophy as she struggles through life. Although her stepfather, the wealthy Daddy Warbucks, personifies free enterprise, Annie finds herself most often on the other side of the tracks. Gray lived in Kankakee, Illinois, some fifty miles south of

Frank King's *Gasoline Alley,* 1922.
From the collection of Rob Stolzer

Chicago. Annie's adventures occur in urban settings resembling Chicago, with occasional outings to flat, open landscapes recalling the Illinois countryside. *Little Orphan Annie* became the most popular comic strip of the 1930s and would be adapted for radio, FILM, and the musical theatre; *Annie*, by Charles Strouse (b. 1928), Martin Charnin (b. 1934), and Thomas Meehan (b. 1934), opened on Broadway in 1977. After Gray died in 1968, a succession of artists drew the strip until 2010, when it was discontinued.

The 1930s proved to be the golden age of the newspaper comic strip, when newspapers provided daily pages, as well as full-color Sunday supplements with individual strips occupying an entire page. This era produced the most famous detective comic strip, Chester Gould's *Dick Tracy*, which debuted in the *Detroit Mirror* on October 4, 1931. A descendant of Oklahoma Territory pioneers, Gould moved to Chicago in 1921 to pursue a career in comics. He made every effort to depict police procedure realistically by studying ballistics and related sciences, riding with Chicago-area police officers in squad cars, and reading newspaper accounts of gangsters. *Dick Tracy*, which has been drawn by a series of Gould's successors, remains in circulation and has been adapted for radio, television, and cinema.

Ohio's Milton Caniff (1907–1988) introduced *Terry and the Pirates* to newspapers via the Chicago Tribune Syndicate in 1934. The protagonist, Terry Lee, is an American boy coming of age in China. After the United States enters World War II, he serves as a fighter pilot with the Army Air Forces. Seeking both ownership of his work and more creative freedom, Caniff concluded the strip in 1946. He introduced *Steve Canyon*, another strip about a fighter pilot, in the *Chicago Sun-Times* and other newspapers in 1947 and continued these adventures until his death in 1988.

A later addition to the Chicago Tribune Media Syndicate's roster of talent was Dalia Messick (1906–2005). Born in South Bend, Indiana, Messick studied commercial art in Chicago, where she worked for a greeting-card company before moving to New York. She struggled initially to sell comic strip concepts because of sexism among male newspaper editors. To obscure her gender, she adopted the pen name Dale Messick. *Brenda Starr*, about a glamorous woman reporter, first appeared in 1940 and reached the peak of its popularity during the 1950s. The title character works at a Chicago newspaper, and story lines follow both Brenda's adventures as a journalist and her romantic life. As an independent professional woman, Brenda Starr resembles characters played by iconic film actresses of the 1940s; her appearance is modeled on Rita Hayworth. Messick drew *Brenda Starr* until she retired in 1980; thereafter, other female writers and artists produced the strip until 2011, when it was discontinued.

For most of the twentieth century, major newspapers did not employ African American cartoonists, and at least until World War II, comic strips rarely featured black characters that were not demeaning caricatures. It was left to black newspapers to offer comics about black people by black artists for black readers. The *Chicago Defender*, the most influential and widely distributed African American newspaper was also the first black newspaper to publish a full page of comics. Its longest-running strip was *Bungleton Green* (1920–1963). As drawn by its creator, Leslie Malcolm Rogers (1896–1935), from Gary, Indiana, *Bungleton Green* was a gag strip making light of black southerners recently arrived in Chicago. In these early strips the protagonist, Bungleton, is a buffoonish, luckless street hustler. Rogers drew the strip from 1920 to 1929, followed by a number of cartoonists. Three drew it for extended periods and made such significant changes as to create entirely new strips. Henry Brown (d. 1956), who had migrated to Chicago from Mississippi, took over in 1929 and continued until 1934. Under Brown, *Bungleton Green* became an adventure strip. Jay Jackson (1905–1954), originally from Oberlin, Ohio, drew the strip from 1934 to 1954, for a time portraying Bungleton as a stylish hepcat of the jazz era. From 1943 to 1947 Jackson produced *Bungleton Green and the Mystic Commandos*, an adventure strip drawn in a realistic, comic book style. Bungleton became a superhero, perhaps the first black character to fit that description, in science-fiction allegories touching on Nazism overseas and racism at home. In 1947

Jackson returned Bungleton to his comic origins. He also drew *Speed Jaxon,* about a black soldier of fortune, the gag panel *So What?* and the etiquette panel *Ravings of Prof. Doodle,* as well as editorial cartoons. Chester Commodore (1914–2004), originally from Racine, Wisconsin, drew *Bungleton Green* from 1948 to 1963 while also serving as the main editorial cartoonist at the *Defender.* He also drew *The Sparks* (1948–1962), about a black family, and continued Jackson's *So What?* and *Prof. Doodle.*

Minnesota's Charles M(onroe) Schulz (1922–2000) published the first of his famous *Peanuts* strips on October 2, 1950. *Peanuts* centers on a group of children and a humanized dog, the much-loved beagle Snoopy. The central character is Charlie Brown, a semi-autobiographical creation famed for his poor self-image. The world of *Peanuts* resembles Schulz's St. Paul, including its cold, snowy winters; early strips occasionally mention Minnesota place names like Hennepin County. See MINNEAPOLIS/ST. PAUL. One of Schulz's innovations was his creation and perpetuation of a comic strip designed for smaller spaces, as newspapers now demanded. Another was the strip's emotional complexity, with characters often facing loneliness, yearning, and spiritual doubt. Schulz developed long-running storylines, and some recurring narratives became iconic: Lucy pulling away the football just before Charlie Brown can kick it, for example, and Snoopy imagining his doghouse as an airplane and himself as a World War I fighter pilot. The heyday for *Peanuts* was the 1960s. Charlie Brown and his pals made their television debut in *A Charlie Brown Christmas,* an animated feature for CBS, in 1965. That program was followed by other television specials, a feature film, and the Broadway musical *You're a Good Man, Charlie Brown* (1967) by Clark Gesner (1938–2002). Such projects, along with endorsements and product marketing, made Schulz the most successful cartoonist in history, as well as one of the most influential. Featured at its peak in 2,600 newspapers in seventy-five countries, *Peanuts* ran daily for almost fifty years. The final strip appeared on February 13, 2000, the day after Schulz died. His strips are currently syndicated as *Classic Peanuts.*

A number of Midwesterners followed Schulz in making careers as syndicated cartoonists. Jim Davis (b. 1945), who introduced the highly successful *Garfield* in 1978, lives in Indiana, where he grew up on a farm. The title character of his strip is a gluttonous, lazy, anthropomorphic cat whose indulgent owner shares Davis's birthday and farm background. The strip is said to be set in Muncie, Indiana, although the city is never mentioned. Davis's other strips include *U.S. Acres* (1986–1989), about a group of barnyard animals.

Strips centering on female characters also appeared as the women's movement of the 1970s opened opportunities for artists like Cathy Guisewite (b. 1950), creator of the widely syndicated strip *Cathy.* Born in Dayton, Ohio, raised in Midland, Michigan, and educated at the University of Michigan, Guisewite drew *Cathy* from 1976, while she was living in DETROIT and working in advertising, until 2010. *Cathy* lampoons its main character's obsessiveness over her weight, her clothes, her dating life, and her relationship with her mother. A strip that more specifically espouses the ideals of FEMINISM is *Sylvia,* created by Nicole Hollander (b. 1939) of Chicago and syndicated from 1981 to 2012. An alter ego of her creator, Sylvia is often found sitting at her typewriter or across a table from a female friend wittily discussing gender politics and other issues. Hollander teaches at the School of the Art Institute of Chicago.

Bill (William Boyd) Watterson (b. 1958), creator of *Calvin and Hobbes* (1985–1995), grew up in Chagrin Falls, Ohio, studied at Kenyon College, and started his career drawing editorial cartoons at the *Cincinnati Post. Calvin and Hobbes* follows the adventures of Calvin, an imaginative, naughty only child of suburban parents, and Hobbes, a stuffed toy tiger that comes to life only when the two are alone together. The strip reflects the influence of *Peanuts* in depicting the Midwest's four seasons and a child's changing activities. Calvin's flights of imagination, such as his Spaceman Spiff alter ego, are related to Snoopy's fantasy life in *Peanuts* and the surreal adventures of McCay's Little Nemo. Watterson rejected lucrative offers to merchandise his characters and ended the strip at the peak of its popularity. He lives in CLEVELAND.

Aaron McGruder (b. 1974), who was born in Chicago, created *The Boondocks,* a strip about two young African American brothers from that city living in a Maryland suburb, where McGruder's family moved when he was six years old. First appearing in 1996, nationally syndicated in 1999, and running until 2006, *The Boondocks* commented on politics and black culture. It created controversy with its satires of race and social class and its criticism of public figures, both black and white. Three seasons of a television adaptation of *The Boondocks* were produced between 2006 and 2010 by Cartoon Network.

One of the most popular comic strips currently in syndication is *Zits,* written by Jerry Scott (b. 1955) and drawn by Jim (James Mark) Borgman (b. 1954). The protagonist, Jeremy Duncan, is a suburban Ohio high school student, and the strip follows his family life, friendships, studies, and relationship with his girlfriend. Much of the humor emerges from generational differences between Jeremy and his parents; social controversies are generally absent. Originally from South Bend, Indiana, Scott also co-created *Baby Blues* (1990–present) with Rick Kirkman (b. 1953). Borgman lives in Cincinnati, Ohio, where he is a Pulitzer Prize–winning editorial cartoonist for the *Cincinnati Enquirer.*

Other long-running comic strips created by Midwesterners include *Happy Hooligan* (1900–1932) by Frederick Burr Opper (1857–1937) of Ohio; *Bringing Up Father* (1913–2000) by George McManus (1884–1954) of MISSOURI; *Freckles and His Friends* (1915–1971) by Merrill Blosser (1892–1983) of Indiana; *The Bungle Family* (1918–1945) by Harry J. Tuthill (1886–1957) of Illinois and Missouri; *Thimble Theatre / Popeye* (1919–present) by E(lzie) C(risler) Segar (1894–1938) of Illinois; *Barney Google / Snuffy Smith* (1919–present) by Billy (William Morgan) DeBeck (1890–1942) of Missouri; *Etta Kett* (1925–1974) by Paul Dowling Robinson (1898–1974) of Ohio; *Blondie* (1930–present) by Chic (Murat Bernard) Young (1901–1973) of Missouri; *Alley Oop* (1932–present) by V(incent) T(rout) Hamlin (1900–1993) of IOWA; *Smokey Stover* (1935–1973) by Bill Holman (1903–1987) of Indiana; *Aggie Mack* (1946–1972) by Hal Rasmusson (1900–1962) of Minnesota; *Beetle Bailey* (1950–present) and *Hi and Lois* (1954–present) by (Addison) Mort(on) Walker (b. 1923) of Missouri; and *Mother Goose and Grimm* (1984–present) by Mike (Michael Bartley) Peters (b. 1943) of Missouri and Ohio.

Like comic strips, comic books have precedents in earlier forms. A collection of Outcault's Yellow Kid cartoons, titled *The Yellow Kid in McFadden's Flats* (1897), has been called the first significant predecessor of the modern comic book. The term "comic book" appeared for the first time on the back cover of that volume. Other collections of newspaper strips followed. *Dick Tracy* was one of the newspaper comic strips collected in and adapted for comic-book form in the 1930s. One of its early adaptations was as a Big Little Book from Whitman Publishing of Racine, Wisconsin. Big Little Books were important transitional media between newspaper comic strips and true modern comic books, which first emerged in 1933.

The first comic-book superhero has distinctly Midwestern origins and significance. Created by writer Jerome "Jerry" Siegel (1914–1996) and artist Joseph Shuster (1914–1992), Superman first appeared in *Action Comics,* a series produced by the firm that would become DC Comics, in 1938. Siegel was born and raised in Cleveland, Ohio; Shuster moved to Cleveland with his family from Canada when he was ten years old. They met at Cleveland's Glenville High School and formed a friendship sparked by a common interest in science fiction and comics. Superman, whose powers include flight, X-ray vision, and incredible strength, is from the fictional planet Krypton. His adoptive family and upbringing in agrarian and small-town KANSAS are central to his character; his morality and civic virtue are linked to those origins. Pastoral imagery in *Superman* comics and the double portrayal of the lead character associate the rural Midwest with innocence, nurture, and idealism, as opposed to the self-seeking life in large urban areas. Superman adopts the guise of Clark Kent, a seemingly shy, unsophisticated, socially inept character from the hinterland who is a figure of fun for the jaded, ambitious people he encounters in Metropolis. *Superman* comics have been in continual production since 1938, and their iconic presence in American popular culture has been reinforced by periodic adaptations for film and television.

Superman remains the one major mainstream comic-book series with strong Midwestern elements. Mainstream comics since the 1930s have been dominated by two New York firms, DC and Marvel. Although a number of artists at these companies have come from the Midwest, they have rarely touched on Midwestern themes. One must look outside the mainstream to find regionalism in comic books.

In the 1940s and 1950s comic books marketed by William Gaines at EC Comics featured themes of SCIENCE FICTION, crime, and horror. One popular writer of the day had a number of his stories adapted for publication by EC. This writer, who grew up in Waukegan, Illinois, was RAY (DOUGLAS) BRADBURY (1920–2012). Fresh off the success of his novels *The Martian Chronicles* (1950) and *The Illustrated Man* (1951), Bradbury saw the first illustrated versions of his work appear in *Tales from the Crypt, Weird Fantasy,* and other EC series. Some of these adaptations were reprinted in two paperbacks published under Bradbury's name, *The Autumn People* (1964) and *Tomorrow Midnight* (1966), although the illustrations were printed in black and white. Most of the EC line, including comic books featuring adaptations of Bradbury's works, is now available in full-color facsimiles. Bradbury later collaborated with artists on illustrated versions of additional stories, collected in several volumes of *The Ray Bradbury Chronicles,* and graphic-novel adaptations of such works as *Fahrenheit 451* (1953), which appeared in 2009.

The comic-book industry formed the Comics Code Authority in 1954 in response to public criticism, including U.S. congressional hearings, of violence and anti-authoritarian attitudes in comics, such as those produced by EC. The industry essentially banned graphic violence, sexual innuendo, and drug references, as well as comics about vampires and other staples of horror. Until the code was loosened in 1971, the strongest challenge to this censorship was the art known as underground comix, which emerged from the counterculture of the 1960s. Targeting college students and hippies, underground comix skirted the Comics Code because they were sold at record stores and head shops rather than newsstands, pharmacies, and grocery stores. Outrageous and anti-establishment, underground comix emphasized sex, drugs, politics, and violence—everything then forbidden by the mainstream comics industry.

Although San Francisco, California, became the mecca for underground cartoonists, including Midwesterners like S(teven) Clay Wilson (b. 1941) of NEBRASKA, significant underground comix also came out of Chicago and other Midwestern cities. In 1967 Jay "Jayzey" Lynch (b. 1945) and Mervyn "Skip" Williamson (b. 1944) started the *Chicago Mirror* in Chicago. A year later they renamed their publication *Bijou Funnies,* which became one of the most prominent underground comic books in the nation. Lynch's *Nard n' Pat,* which first appeared in the *Chicago Seed* in 1967, became a mainstay in *Bijou Funnies;* the strip follows the adventures of a human and his anthropomorphic cat friend. Williamson's highly political contributions included the countercultural adventures of Snappy Sammy Smoot. He also illustrated *Steal This Book* (1971) by anti-war activist Abbie Hoffman (1936–1989) and contributed with Lynch and others to *Conspiracy Capers* (1969), a one-off comic book about Hoffman and the conspiracy trial that resulted from protests at the 1968 Chicago Democratic Convention. Lynch subsequently collaborated with Gary Whitney (b. 1952) on the comic strip *Phoebe and the Pigeon People,* written by Lynch and drawn by Whitney. It was featured in the alternative newspaper the *Chicago Reader* from 1978 to 1990.

In 1972 *Bijou Funnies* was taken on by Kitchen Sink Press, which continued the comic up to its eighth and final issue. The publishing arm of Krupp Comic Works, Kitchen Sink also published such titles as *Mom's Homemade Comics, Dope Comix,* and *Bizarre Sex.* Founded in 1969 by Denis Kitchen (b. 1946) of Milwaukee, Wisconsin, Kitchen Sink operated until 1999. Kitchen cofounded the *Bugle-American,* an underground newspaper in Madison, Wisconsin, which appeared from 1970 to 1978, and founded the Krupp Syndicate, which provided weekly strips originating in the *Bugle-American* to alternative and college newspapers. These ventures offered publishing venues for Kitchen's own comics and those of other Wisconsinites, such as Jim Mitchell (b. 1949), Bruce (Walthers) von Alten (b. 1944), Don Glassford (b. 1946), and Wendel Pugh (b. 1943). Kitchen Sink also published *Super Soul Comix* by Richard Eugene "Grass" Green (1939–2002) of Fort Wayne, Indiana, the most prominent African American underground comix artist, as well as work by leading underground artists from elsewhere in the country, like R(obert) Crumb (b. 1943) and Art Spiegelman (b. 1948).

A later publication from Kitchen Sink Press, the erotic comic book *"Omaha" the Cat Dancer* was the creation of artist Reed Waller (b. 1949) and writer Kate Worley (1958–2004), who met in Minneapolis in the late 1970s. See MINNEAPOLIS/ST. PAUL. Their title character is a cat woman working as an exotic dancer in Mipple City, a cartoon version of Minneapolis populated by felines like Omaha. After appearing in underground comix in the late 1970s and early 1980s, *"Omaha"* was published as its own comic book series, first from Kitchen Sink (1984–1993) and then from Fantagraphics Books (1994–1995), with a conclusion appearing in *Sizzle* magazine in 2006. The entire run is available in the seven volumes of *The Complete "Omaha" the Cat Dancer* (2005–2008) from NBM Publishing.

An important figure in the development of autobiographical comic books was Harvey Pekar (1939–2010), author of *American Splendor.* Born to immigrant Polish Jewish parents in Cleveland, Pekar spent most of his life in the city and worked as a file clerk at the Veterans Administration Hospital. Drawn by many artists, *American Splendor* depicts Pekar's work, family, and daily life. The first issue, published in 1976, was drawn by R. Crumb, the central figure in underground comix. Pekar self-published most issues up to 1993; thereafter, *American Splendor* was published by Dark Horse Comics and then DC. Pekar became a celebrity through appearances on David Letterman's NBC-TV talk show, which he wrote into his comic books. The 2003 film adaptation, directed by Shari Springer Berman and Robert Pulcini, starred Paul Giamatti. Collections include *American Splendor: The Life and Times of Harvey Pekar* (1986).

By the 1980s many artists and publishers associated with underground comix had tired of the genre's bohemian themes, and a younger generation sought new approaches to comic art. The underground movement had demonstrated a market for unusual comics and that artists could reach that market while retaining rights to their work. Two trends emerged in response to that opportunity: independent comics and alternative comics. According to Charles Hatfield, author of *Alternative Comics: An Emerging Literature* (2005), the two are not always distinct, but independent comics lean toward "formula fiction inspired by the so-called mainstream . . . while 'alternative' more often denotes satirical, political, and autobiographical elements" (26). Midwestern artists and small presses have participated in both movements, which have benefited from the direct-market approach to selling comics, in which dedicated comic stores buy nonrefundable product from distributors. The comics industry adopted the direct market in the 1970s as drugstores and other retailers stopped selling comics.

Midwestern publishers of independent comics have included Caliber Comics of Detroit (1989–2000), Avatar Press of Rantoul, Illinois (1996–present), and First Comics, based in Evanston, Illinois, from 1983 to 1985 and then in Chicago until 1991. Like other independent comics companies, First Comics offered superhero and science-fiction serials tailored for adult readers. Two of their comics featured Midwestern scenarios. *American Flagg!* (1983–1989) by Howard Chaykin (b. 1950) is a science-fiction series set in Chicago in the 2030s. Chaykin satirizes TECHNOLOGY AND INDUSTRY as well as militarism, imagining a dystopian future in which a corporation runs the country and the U.S. government is based on Mars. From 1985 to 1991 First Comics published *Badger,* created by Mike Baron (b. 1949) and first published by Capital Comics of Madison, Wisconsin, where the series is set. Baron's protagonist is a Vietnam War veteran with multiple personalities; one of these, Badger, is a costumed superhero who fights evildoers in the Wisconsin capital. Baron was born in Madison but was raised in South Dakota; he completed high school in Madison and then worked there in journalism. In addition to creating other comic-book series, like *Feud* and *Spyke,* he has produced new series of *Badger* comics, as well as one-off issues from different publishers.

While independent comics adapt the conventions of mainstream comic books, alternative comics take a more personal approach and embrace a wider range of genres. Alternative comics also draw more from the fine arts and classic comic strips. Ambitious graphic design, high-quality printing, and a literary approach to storytelling frequently characterize alternative comics, which are mostly published in small press runs, sometimes by the artists themselves. They often appear in unusual formats quite different from standard comic books; many are one-time publications or part of an irregularly published serial. Many alternative artists have done strips as well as comic books; some have published graphic novels, working in a genre whose recent development has occurred in tandem with alternative comics.

The alternative-comics scene in Chicago has produced major artists like Dan Clowes (b. 1961), Archer Prewitt (b. 1963), Ivan Brunetti (b. 1967), Chris Ware (b. 1967), Anders Nilsen (b. 1973), Jeffrey Brown (b. 1975), Joshua W. Cotter (b. 1977), Paul Hornschemeier (b. 1977), Jeff Zwirek (b. 1977), Grant Reynolds (b. 1979), Jeremy Tinder (b. 1979), and Lilli Carré (b. 1983). The annual anthology *Blab!* was important to this scene. Edited by Monte Beauchamp and published from 1988 to 2007, *Blab!* featured the work of Clowes, Ware, and many others. Early issues appeared in a standard comic book format. With issue 8, the publication introduced a wider focus on graphic and fine arts. Fantagraphics published issues 9 to 18 in a large, square format influenced by LP record sleeves. *Blab!* concluded with issue 18 and has been superseded by *Blab World,* published in hardcover by Last Gasp. Beauchamp has curated gallery exhibits in Chicago and elsewhere by artists featured in *Blab!*

One common format of alternative comics is the minicomic, a short text that offers artists an inexpensive way to distribute their work. Since 1992 Archer Prewitt of Chicago has drawn *Sof' Boy,* a minicomic about a preternaturally cheerful boy made of bread dough who lives in a dirty, dangerous urban area. Initially self-published, *Sof' Boy* has become a cult favorite, distributed by presses like Kitchen Sink Press and Drawn and Quarterly and also appearing in alternative newspapers. An example of a longer text originating in a minicomic is *Skyscrapers of the Midwest* by Joshua W. Cotter. Cotter, who grew up on a farm near Barnard, Missouri, and later moved to Chicago, won the Isotope Award for this minicomic about anthropomorphic cat children in rural Missouri. He then expanded the narrative into four issues of a full-length comic book (2004–2007) that he gathered as a graphic novel in 2008.

One central figure in alternative comics is Chris Ware, who grew up in Omaha, Nebraska, but has lived in Chicago since 1993. He is best known for *Jimmy Corrigan, the Smartest Kid on Earth,* a graphic novel (2000) first published in installments in *Acme Novelty Library,* a comic book Ware started in 1993. *Jimmy Corrigan* follows a solitary, inarticulate man who meets for the first time the father who abandoned him; it also tells of Jimmy's great-grandfather, a child in Chicago at the time of the 1893 World's Columbian Exposition. Other features in *Acme Novelty Library,* such as *Quimby the Mouse, Rusty Brown,* and *Building Stories,* also develop themes of loneliness and alienation in modern urban society. Ware's elaborate graphic style complements the narrative with long asides, detailed footnotes, and extras such as flip-books. A scholar of comics history, Ware has written of his admiration for comics like *Gasoline Alley* and *Peanuts,* which influenced his graphic and narrative sensibilities.

Ivan Brunetti's family emigrated from Italy and settled in Chicago when he was a child. He draws in a simplified style influenced by classic cartoonists like Charles M. Schulz and Ernie Bushmiller (1905–1982). Brunetti's humor, however, inclines to twisted fantasies of violence, sex, and insanity. While he was enrolled at the University of Chicago, he drew the strip *Misery Loves Company* for the student newspaper; he later worked as a copy editor for the University of Chicago Press. The first volume of *Schizo* appeared in 1994; volumes 1 through 3 are collected in *Misery Loves Company* (2007; no relation to the comic strip). *Ho! The Morally Questionable Cartoons of Ivan Brunetti* (2009) is another collection. He also edited *An Anthology of Graphic Fiction, Cartoons, and True Stories* in two volumes (2006, 2008). Brunetti still lives in Chicago, where he teaches college courses on drawing comics and graphic novels. *Cartooning: Philosophy and Practice,* Brunetti's guide for aspiring artists, appeared in 2011.

ST. LOUIS, Missouri, also hosts a thriving alternative-comics scene, with artists like Ted May (b. 1969), Sacha Mardou (b. 1975), Dan Zettwoch (b. 1977), and Kevin Huizenga (b. 1977). Huizenga, who grew up in Harvey, Illinois, attended college in Grand Rapids, Michigan, before moving to St. Louis in 2000. His comics often center on Glenn Ganges, a suburban everyman whose experiences provoke philosophical speculation. Ganges figures in Huizenga's minicomic *Supermonster* (1993–2001), the comic book *Or Else* (2004–2009), the collection *Curses* (2006), and the *Ganges* series published by Fantagraphics since 2006. *Amazing Facts and Beyond! with Leon Beyond*, a weekly comic strip on which Huizenga collaborates with Zettwoch, made its debut in the *St. Louis Riverfront Times* in 2008.

Other respected alternative cartoonists live and work elsewhere in the Midwest. Carol Tyler (b. 1951) was born in Chicago and was raised there in a working-class Catholic family but now lives in Cincinnati. She teaches courses on comics at the University of Cincinnati. Highly praised by R. Crumb and (LOUIS) STUDS TERKEL (1912–2008), Tyler's generally autobiographical comics have appeared in many anthologies and periodicals, including the feminist comic books *Wimmen's Comix* and *Twisted Sisters*. Her first book, *The Job Thing* (1993), features graphic stories about bad work experiences. *Late Bloomer* (2005) is another collection. *You'll Never Know: A Graphic Memoir* is a trilogy about Tyler's relationship with her father, a World War II combat veteran, consisting of *Book One: A Good and Decent Man* (2009), *Book Two: Collateral Damage* (2010), and *Book Three: Soldier's Heart* (2012).

Jeff Smith (b. 1960) of Columbus, Ohio, created *Bone* (1991–2004), a fantasy epic inspired by *The Lord of the Rings* (1954–1955) by J. R. R. Tolkien (1892–1973) and the comic strip *Pogo* (1948–1975) by Walt Kelly (1913–1973). *Bone* involves bald, marshmallow-like characters exiled from their town who journey through strange lands menaced by frightful creatures. Originally drawn in black and white and serialized in fifty-five mostly self-published issues, the entire series was collected in *Bone: The Complete Cartoon Epic in One Volume* (2004), a massive 1,332-page book. Color editions of individual issues have also appeared, as well as sequels and prequels. *Bone* won awards and critical accolades and has become standard fare in school libraries, although it is not specifically tailored for young readers.

Comic strips and comic books are not merely entertainment; they are art forms capable of thematic complexity and depth. Teachers and school librarians no longer treat comics as contraband or associate them with delinquency but use them to encourage reading and creativity. Comics also yield aesthetic and intellectual rewards for adult readers. As graphic narrative or sequential art, Midwestern comic strips and books can be read alongside the region's poetry and prose and can be viewed in light of parallel developments in the fine arts in ways that enrich appreciation of both written and visual media.

SELECTED WORKS: *The Smithsonian Collection of Newspaper Comics* (1977) by Bill Blackbeard and Martin Williams and *The Comic Strip Century* (1995) by Blackbeard and Dale Crain are definitive collections of comic-strip art. Brian Walker's two-volume set *The Comics before 1945* (2004) and *The Comics since 1945* (2002) is also noteworthy. Herb Galewitz's *Great Comics Syndicated by the "Daily News"—"Chicago Tribune"* (1972) features many comic strips by Midwesterners. *The Smithsonian Book of Comic-Book Comics* (1982), edited by Martin T. Williams and J. Michael Barrier, offers a selection of classic comic-book texts.

R. F. Outcault's Yellow Kid: A Centennial Celebration of the Kid Who Started the Comics (1995), edited by Bill Blackbeard, collects the entire run of that seminal strip. Fantagraphics has published *The Complete "Little Nemo in Slumberland"* in multiple volumes; Taschen has produced the two-volume *Winsor McCay: The Complete Little Nemo* (2014). *The Best of "Little Nemo in Slumberland"* (1998), edited by Richard Marshall, features appreciations by artists like Charles M. Schulz and Bill Watterson. Peter Maresca has edited two volumes of full newspaper-size color reproductions: *Little Nemo in Slumberland: So Many Splendid*

Sundays! (2005) and *Little Nemo in Slumberland: Many More Splendid Sundays!* (2008).

Scribner's published the collection *Sidney Smith's "The Gumps"* (1974), edited by Herb Galewitz. Spec Productions has been publishing volumes titled *Frank King's "Gasoline Alley" Nostalgia Journal,* volume 1 (2003) begins with strips published in 1918. Drawn and Quarterly is publishing *Walt and Skeezix,* a multivolume collection of *Gasoline Alley* strips beginning in 1921, edited by Chris Ware, with introductions by Jeet Heer. In 2007, Sunday Press released *Sundays with Walt and Skeezix,* an oversize book of King's magnificent full-page, color Sunday *Gasoline Alley* comics. IDW Publishing is publishing *The Complete "Little Orphan Annie,"* *The Complete Chester Gould's "Dick Tracy,"* and *The Complete "Terry and the Pirates."* Hermes Press published volume 1 of *"Brenda Starr, Reporter": The Collected Daily and Sunday Newspaper Strips* in 2012.

During his lifetime Charles M. Schulz published many collections of *Peanuts* strips. Fantagraphics has published *The Complete "Peanuts"* (2004–2016) in twenty-five hardcover volumes. Each includes an introduction by a notable writer, artist, or public figure. Volume 1 (2004), covering 1950 to 1952, is introduced by GARY EDWARD KEILLOR (b. 1942), writing as Garrison Keillor, who, like Schulz, is a native-born Minnesotan. Publication of paperback editions of *The Complete "Peanuts"* volumes began in 2014. *My Life with Charlie Brown* (2010), edited by M. Thomas Inge, collects Schulz's writings from periodicals, book introductions, and other sources.

Many collections of Jim Davis's *Garfield* and Cathy Guisewite's *Cathy* are available. Nicole Hollander's books include *The "Sylvia" Chronicles: 30 Years of Graphic Misbehavior from Reagan to Obama* (2010). Bill Watterson's work is sampled in *The Essential "Calvin and Hobbes"* (1988); *The Complete "Calvin and Hobbes"* (2005) is a comprehensive two-volume set. Aaron McGruder's collections include *All the Rage: The Boondocks Past and Present* (2007); *My Bad: A "Zits" Treasury* (2009) is one from Jerry Scott and Jim Borgman.

The DC Archives reprint series includes volumes of the early *Superman* comics, such as *"Superman": The Action Comics Archives,* volume 1 (1998). A newer series, *The Superman Chronicles,* follows the original order of publication beginning in 1938; volume 1 appeared in 2006. The EC Comics of the 1940s and 1950s have also been reprinted in a variety of editions.

Midwestern underground comix are collected in *The Best of "Bijou Funnies"* (1974), edited by Jay Lynch; *The Oddly Compelling Art of Denis Kitchen* (2010); *The Complete " 'Omaha' the Cat Dancer"* by Reed Waller and Kate Worley; and Harvey Pekar's *American Splendor,* sampled in *American Splendor: The Life and Times of Harvey Pekar* (1986). Alternative comics include Archer Prewitt's *Sof' Boy,* Chris Ware's *Acme Novelty Library,* and Kevin Huizenga's *Ganges* and the books *The Job Thing* (1993) by Carol Tyler, *Bone* (2004) by Jeff Smith, *Misery Loves Company* (2007) by Ivan Brunetti, and *Skyscrapers of the Midwest* (2008) by Joshua W. Cotter.

FURTHER READING: Reference volumes include Ron Goulart's *The Encyclopedia of American Comics* (1991) and Allan Holtz's *American Newspaper Comics: An Encyclopedic Reference Guide* (2011). James Steranko's two-volume *History of Comics* (1970 and 1972), a landmark study of American comic books, features significant material on the Midwest. Scholarship also includes *The Art of the Funnies: An Aesthetic History* (1995) by Robert C. Harvey, *Comics, Comix and Graphic Novels: A History of Comic Art* (1996) by Roger Sabin, and *The Power of Comics: History, Form, and Culture* (2009) by Randy Duncan and Matthew J. Smith.

Timothy B. Spears discusses John T. McCutcheon and his collaborations with George Ade in *Chicago Dreaming: Midwesterners and the City, 1871–1919* (2005). See also Guy Szuberla's "Drawing from Memory: John T. McCutcheon on Chicago and the Midwest," *Midamerica* 30 (2003): 32–53.

The bibliography on artists from the Chicago Tribune Syndicate is substantial. In his essay "Dream Big and Work Hard," in volume 1 of *The Complete "Little Orphan Annie"* (2008), Jeet Heer discusses the strip's Midwestern dimensions. Stella Ress provides historical context in "Bridging the Generation Gap: Little Orphan Annie in the Great Depression," *Journal of Popular Culture* 43.4 (August 2010): 782–800. Garyn G. Roberts wrote *"Dick Tracy" and American Culture: Morality and Mythology, Text and Context* (1993). *Caniff: A Visual Biography* (2011), edited by Dean Mullaney, samples the full range of Milton Caniff's work while telling his life story in text and photography. On Dalia Messick and *Brenda Starr*, consult *Women and the Comics* (1985) by Trina Robbins and Catherine Yronwode.

Tim Jackson's *Pioneering Cartoonists of Color* (2016) is a landmark in comics studies and an essential resource on black artists. John D. Stevens published two articles touching on comics in the *Chicago Defender:* "'Bungleton Green': Black Comic Strip Ran 43 Years," *Journalism Quarterly* 51.1 (Spring 1974): 122–24, and "Reflections in a Dark Mirror: Comic Strips in Black Newspapers," *Journal of Popular Culture* 10.1 (Summer 1976): 239–44. See also Angela M. Nelson's "*Swing Papa* and *Barry Jordan:* Comic Strips and Black Newspapers in Postwar Toledo," *Ohio Academy of History Proceedings* (2004): 61–74.

David Michaelis wrote *Schulz and "Peanuts": A Biography* (2007). M. Thomas Inge links Schulz with F(RANCIS) SCOTT (KEY) FITZGERALD (1896–1940) in "Two Boys from the Twin Cities," in *A Comics Studies Reader* (2008), edited by Jeet Heer and Kent Worcester (94-100).

Lawrence F. Lowery's *The Collector's Guide to Big Little Books and Similar Books* (1981) is the definitive book on Big Little Books, the transitional medium that facilitated the collection of newspaper comic strips in comic-book form.

Umberto Eco's 1962 essay on Superman, translated from the Italian by Natalie Chilton in 1972 as "The Myth of Superman," appears in Eco's *The Role of the Reader: Explorations in the Semiotics of Texts* (1984): 107–24. Jeffrey K. Johnson discusses Superman in relation to pastoral ideology in "The Countryside Triumphant: Jefferson's Ideal of Rural Superiority in Modern Superhero Mythology," *Journal of Popular Culture* 43.4 (August 2010): 720–37. Books include *"Superman": The High-Flying History of America's Most Enduring Hero* (2012) by Larry Tye and *The Ages of "Superman": Essays on the Man of Steel in Changing Times*, edited by Joseph Darowski (2012).

A History of Underground Comics (1974) by Mark James Estren, *Rebel Visions: The Underground Comix Revolution, 1963–1975* (2002) by Patrick Rosenkranz, and *Kitchen Sink Press: The First 25 Years* (1994) by Dave Schreiner are illustrated histories. Denis Kitchen and James Danky include both essays and comics in *Underground Classics: The Transformation of Comics into Comix* (2009), the companion volume to an exhibition at the Chazen Museum in Madison, Wisconsin. Harvey Pekar is treated as a representative figure in *Comic Books as History: The Narrative Art of Jack Jackson, Art Spiegelman, and Harvey Pekar* (1989) by Joseph Witek.

On alternative and independent comics, consult Charles Hatfield's *Alternative Comics: An Emerging Literature* (2005) and the documentary film *The Cartoonist: Jeff Smith, "Bone" and the Changing Face of Comics* (2009), directed by Ken Mills. Two books have been published about Chris Ware's work: *Chris Ware* (2004) by Daniel K. Raeburn and *The Comics of Chris Ware: Drawing Is a Way of Thinking* (2010), edited by David M. Ball and Martha B. Kuhlman.

Jeet Heer's essay "Notes on the Midwestern School of Comics," dated December 29, 2009, appears in the online journal *Comics Comics*. In *Comics Wisconsin* (2009) Paul Buhle reviews the history of comics in his native state since *The Gumps* and *Gasoline Alley.* Britt Aamodt profiles twenty-three artists in *Superheroes, Strip Artists, and Talking Animals: Minnesota's Contemporary Cartoonists* (2011).

Extensive comics collections are held at the libraries of Michigan State University, Bowling Green State University, and Ohio State University, which together form the Consortium of Popular Culture Collections in the Midwest. Affiliated with Ohio State University, the Billy Ireland Cartoon Library and Museum in Columbus, Ohio, is the largest research facility in the field. Other institutions with significant holdings include the University of Missouri, the University of Iowa, Iowa State University, and Indiana University.

GARYN G. ROBERTS

NORTHWESTERN MICHIGAN COLLEGE

WILLIAM BARILLAS

UNIVERSITY OF WISCONSIN–LA CROSSE

CREATIVE NONFICTION

OVERVIEW: The term "creative nonfiction" refers to the practice of writing nonfiction as a literary genre and to the literary works that result from such writing. The origins and boundaries of creative nonfiction are difficult to determine. The tendency to see literature as a field composed of three genres and to use "nonfiction" as a blanket term for the broadest range of fact-based—and often "nonliterary"—writing has obscured the long history of nonfiction as a literary genre. The interchangeable terms "creative nonfiction" and "literary nonfiction" were promulgated in the 1980s to emphasize the literary qualities embodied in such forms as the personal or familiar essay, the memoir, the nature narrative, the travel narrative, personal cultural criticism, and literary journalism. Although its boundaries overlap with such fields as AUTOBIOGRAPHY, history, natural history, cultural criticism, and journalism, to name a few, the genre's inherent literary potential has made it a potent presence in literary journals, trade and university-press publications, writers' conferences and workshops, and college English programs usually affiliated with creative writing or composition and rhetoric. The leading program in the Midwest is the MFA in nonfiction program at the University of Iowa. Midwestern writers, capitalizing on nonfiction's capacity to foreground the author's role in interpretation, analysis, and research, have generated a wide range of works grounded in personal experience and focused on place. This is, as SCOTT RUSSELL SANDERS (b. 1945) puts it in his essay "Imagining the Midwest" from his 1995 *Writing from the Center*, "a literature of inhabitation" (50). In the same essay he also observes, "Becoming aware of the richness in long-settled, cultivated, often battered and abandoned country is the special calling of Midwestern writers" (36).

HISTORY AND SIGNIFICANCE: Creative nonfiction can be traced back to such works as the essays of Michel de Montaigne (1533–1592), the periodical writing of Joseph Addison (1672–1719) and Richard Steele (1672–1729), the Elia essays of Charles Lamb (1775–1834), and the Selburne epistles of Gilbert White (1720–1793). By the middle of the nineteenth century American literary antecedents of contemporary creative nonfiction were flourishing in periodical essays and articles, in travel memoirs such as *Lotus-Eating* (1852) by George William Curtis (1824–1892) and *Summer on the Lakes* (1844) by Margaret Fuller (1810–1850), and in re-

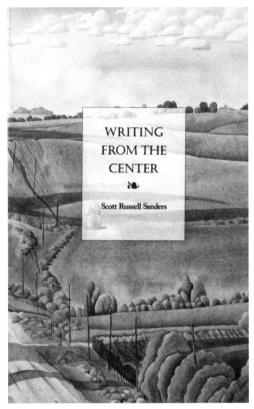

Dust jacket for *Writing from the Center* by Scott Russell Sanders.
© Indiana University Press, 1995

gional meditations and narratives, such as *Walden* (1854) by Henry David Thoreau (1817–1862) and *Rural Hours* (1850) by Susan Fenimore Cooper (1813–1894).

Midwestern writers were part of this movement. Notable early examples of the personal reportage typical of memoirs include *Life in Prairie Land* (1846) by ELIZA FARNHAM (1815–1864), set in pioneer ILLINOIS; *Wau-Bun: The "Early Day" in the North-West* (1856) by Juliette Kinzie (1806–1870), set in WISCONSIN and CHICAGO; and the three books *A NEW HOME—WHO'LL FOLLOW?* (1839), *Forest Life* (1844), and *Western Clearings* (1845) by CAROLINE KIRKLAND (1801–1864), that describe pioneer MICHIGAN. Michigan writer and painter Charles F. Lanman (1819–1895) published outdoor adventure narratives, such as *A Summer in the Wilderness* (1847), and collections of camping and fishing essays, such as *Essays for Summer Hours* (1841). Two prominent later practitioners of the travel narrative and the nature essay were the Missourian SAMUEL LANGHORNE CLEMENS (1835–1910), writing as Mark Twain, especially in *Life on the Mississippi* (1883), and the Wisconsin immigrant JOHN MUIR (1838–1914), notably in *A Thousand Mile Walk to the Gulf* (1916), as well as in his autobiographical memoir, *The Story of My Boyhood and Youth* (1913).

During the 1960s and 1970s the infusion of fictional elements of characterization, dialogue, plot, and setting into reportage generated work variously labeled as "the New Journalism," "literary journalism," "the nonfiction novel," and "narrative nonfiction." But such terms were limited as descriptions of the full range of literary work in nonfiction, and eventually the competing and complementary terms "literary nonfiction" and "creative nonfiction" replaced them, with varying degrees of enthusiasm and resistance, as umbrella terms for the entire genre. The two leading Midwestern nonfiction journals exemplify the competing perspectives on this genre. *Fourth Genre: Explorations in Nonfiction,* begun in 1999 and published at Michigan State University, emphasizes literary impulses with respect to the genre, particularly essays and memoirs; *River Teeth: A Journal of Nonfiction Narrative,* also begun in 1999 and published by Ashland University, emphasizes the connections of the form to roots in literary journalism. That some writers have been able to publish their work in both journals without adjusting their prose to satisfy editorial preferences suggests the extent to which an intuitive appreciation of the form's flexibility underlies editorial practices.

Contemporary creative nonfiction draws on similar impulses and forms as its historical antecedents, but it also takes full advantage of its license to be literary and draw on the narrative, lyric, dramatic, and contemplative resources of other forms. What Annie Dillard (b. 1945) observed of the essay in her introduction to *The Best American Essays, 1988* (1988) applies to the full range of creative nonfiction: "The essay can do everything a poem can do, and everything a short story can do—everything but fake it. The elements in any nonfiction should be true not only artistically—the connections must hold at base and must be veracious, for that is the convention and the covenant between the nonfiction writer and his reader" (xvii). For Midwestern writers, this perspective has licensed writing about the local, the familiar, and the personal with attention to literary language presentation uncommon in other, more academic or reportorial forms similarly derived from observation, research, and investigation. Scott Russell Sanders may be speaking not only for himself but for Midwestern writers in general when he declares in the title essay from his collection *Writing from the Center,* "I write from within a family, a community, and a landscape, concentric rings of duty and possibility. I refuse to separate my search for a way of writing from my search for a way of living" (164).

The range of forms in which Midwestern creative nonfiction writers work is suggested through the representative sampling that follows, but a caution is necessary: many writers' works overlap different subcategories and often challenge classification. For example, *Spillville* (1987) by PATRICIA HAMPL (b. 1946), a collaboration with the artist Steven Sorman, is both a parallel narrative of composer Antonin Dvořák's and Hampl's visits to the same IOWA community and a prose meditation on place. Scott Russell Sanders's essays often focus on place or nature but are also thoroughly imbued with a sense of the past and draw on elements of memoir. Throughout these examples, categories should be seen as fluid and flexible.

Memoir: Perhaps no other subgenre of creative nonfiction has been as prominent or popular in the last decades of the twentieth century and the first decades of the twenty-first century as the memoir. A good many works in all subgenres overlay elements of the memoir on other foundations, such as the travel narrative, the cultural investigation, or reportorial observation. Patricia Hampl has been a foremost practitioner as well as theorist of the memoir. *A Romantic Education* (1981), tracking her roots from MINNESOTA to Czechoslovakia, has been particularly influential. *Virgin Time: In Search of the Contemplative Life* (1992) is also a travel narrative of several pilgrimages. *I Could Tell You Stories: Sojourns in the Land of Memory* (1999) is an investigation of the memoir through a series of personal, critical, and theoretical essays; and *The Florist's Daughter* (2007) is an exploration of the relationship between the author and her parents. Other significant memoirs include *Off to the Side* (2002) by JIM (JAMES THOMAS) HARRISON (1937–2016), set partially in Michigan; *Blooming* (1981) by SUSAN ALLEN TOTH (b. 1940), set in Minnesota; *Prairie Reunion* (1995) by BARBARA J(UNE NORRIS) SCOT (b. 1942), *Out of This World: A Woman's Life among the Amish* (1995) by MARY SWANDER (b. 1950), *Flight Dreams: A Life in the Midwestern Landscape* (1998) by Lisa Knopp (b. 1956), and *Man Killed by Pheasant, and Other Kinships* (2008) by John T. Price (b. 1966), all set in Iowa; *The Prairie in Her Eyes* (2001) by Ann Daum (b. 1970) and *Windbreak: A Woman Rancher on the Northern Plains* (1987) by LINDA HASSELSTROM (b. 1943), both set in SOUTH DAKOTA; *Flood Stage and Rising* (2005) by Jane Varley (b. 1965), set in NORTH DAKOTA; *One Degree West: Reflections of a Plainsdaughter* (2000) by Julene Bair (b. 1949), set in KANSAS; *Rose City: A Memoir of Work* by Jean Harper (b. 1959), set in INDIANA; and *The Last Street before Cleveland* (2006) by Joe Mackall (b. 1958), set in OHIO.

Nature Writing: Midwestern literature has been remarkable for the quantity and quality of writing on nature, in narratives of wilderness travels and explorations, and in memoirs of farm living. Preeminent among American nature writers, especially in the Midwest, have been ALDO LEOPOLD (1887–1948), whose posthumously published book set on a "sand farm" in Wisconsin, *A SAND COUNTY ALMANAC* (1949), is one of the most influential classics of the subgenre; and SIGURD F(ERDINAND) OLSON (1899–1982), a Minnesota teacher and naturalist whose books about the Quetico-Superior region began with *The Singing Wilderness* (1956). Laurie Allman (Gorka) (b. 1958) toured the ecoregions of Minnesota, Wisconsin, and Michigan and blended science and personal observation in *Far from Tame: Reflections from the Heart of a Continent* (1996). Other Midwestern nature writers include Minnesotan PAUL GRUCHOW (1947–2004), author of *The Necessity of Open Spaces* (1987) and *Boundary Waters* (1997); Nebraskan Lisa Knopp, author of *Field of Vision* (1996) and *The Nature of Home* (2002); Illinoisan (Thomas) Tom Montgomery Fate (b. 1960), author of *Cabin Fever: A Suburban Father's Search for the Wild* (2011); and Iowan John Madson

(1923–1995), author of *Where the Sky Began* (1982) and *Up on the River: An Upper Mississippi Chronicle* (1985). This grouping also includes such records of country living as *A Country Year: Living the Questions* (1986) by Sue Hubbell (b. 1935), set in MISSOURI; *Eighty Acres: An Elegy for a Country Farm* (1990) by Ronald Jager (b. 1933), set in Michigan; *My Vegetable Love: A Journal of a Growing Season* (1996) and *Weathering Winter: A Gardener's Daybook* (1997) by Carl H. Klaus (b. 1932), set in Iowa; *Coop: A Family, a Farm, and the Pursuit of One Good Egg* (2009) and *Visiting Tom: A Man, a Highway, and the Road to Roughneck Grace* (2012) by Michael Perry (b. 1964), set in Wisconsin; and *A Community of Memory: My Days with George and Clara* (1995) by Jeff(rey Gene) Gundy (b. 1952), set in Illinois. The essays in *Prospect: Journeys and Landscapes* (2003) and *In the Mind's Eye: Essays across the Animate World* (2008) by Elizabeth (Caroline) Dodd (b. 1962), though chiefly centered on natural places, particularly in Kansas, also include considerable cultural observations and personal experiences and could easily be classified in several other subcategories, as could *Magpie Rising* (1988) by Merrill Gilfillan (b. 1945), a series of sketches and observations set in the High Plains. See ENVIRONMENTAL LITERATURE.

Personal / Familiar Essay: Preeminent among contemporary essayists is Joseph Epstein (b. 1937), a Chicagoan and former editor of *The American Scholar,* the Phi Beta Kappa quarterly. He divides his essays into two overlapping kinds, the familiar essays collected in such works as *The Middle of My Tether* (1983), *A Line Out for a Walk* (1991), and *Narcissus Leaves the Pool* (1999) and the cultural/critical essays collected in *Plausible Prejudices* (1985) and *Life Sentences* (1997), and *A Literary Education, and Other Essays* (2014). Thomas P. Lynch (b. 1948), a poet and mortician in Milford, Michigan, has also written essays that combine personal reminiscence and cultural commentary and are collected in *The Undertaking: Notes from the Dismal Trade* (1997) and *Bodies in Motion and at Rest* (2000). Scott Russell Sanders, who grew up in Ohio and taught for many years at Indiana University, has been particularly forceful as an advocate for essays about regional living, the theme of such collections as *Staying Put: Making a Home in a Restless World* (1993) and *Writing from the Center* (1995). He has also increasingly become an investigator of ethical and moral issues centered on daily living, the focus of *Hunting for Hope: A Father's Journeys* (1998), *The Force of Spirit* (2000), and *A Private History of Awe* (2006). Authors of significant collections of Midwestern regional essays include Minnesotan (WILLIAM JON) BILL HOLM (1943–2009), author of *The Music of Failure* (1985); Missourians Arthur M(ichael) Saltzman (b. 1953), author of the collection *Objects and Empathy* (2001), and William V. Holtz (b. 1932), author of *Gathering the Family* (1997); Nebraskans Ted Kooser (b. 1939), author of *Local Wonders: Seasons in the Bohemian Alps* (2002), and Robert Vivian (b. 1967), author of *Cold Snap as Yearning* (2001); Michiganians Kathleen Stocking (b. 1945), author of *Letters from the Leelanau* (1990) and *Lake Country* (1994), and Daniel Minock (b. 1944), author of *Thistle Journal, and Other Essays* (1998); Indianan MICHAEL A. MARTONE (b. 1955), author of *The Flatness and Other Landscapes: Essays* (2000); and Wisconsinian Michael Perry (b. 1964), author of *Population 485: Meeting Your Neighbors One Siren at a Time* (2002) and *Truck: A Love Story* (2006).

Personal Cultural Criticism / Expressive Academic Writing: CAROL BLY (1930–2007), in her collection *Letters from the Country* (1981) about the cultural life of small-town Minnesota, and KATHLEEN NORRIS (b. 1947), particularly in her studies of spirituality and place, *Dakota: A Spiritual Geography* (1993) and *The Cloister Walk* (1996), both set in South Dakota, draw on their personal experiences to anchor contemplations of regional living. LOREN (COREY) EISELEY (1907–1977), a native Nebraskan, similarly uses personal experience as a foundation for his speculations on the nature of human beings and the relationship between man and nature in such works as *The Immense Journey* (1957) and *The Night Country* (1971), both works of science and philosophy as well as literary works. *The Lonely Other: A Woman Watching America* (1996) by Diana Hume George (b. 1948) contains elements of memoir, personal essay, and cultural criticism. In *Not Just Any Land: A Personal and Literary Journey into the American Grasslands* (2004) John Price ranges across the Midwestern prairie states to interview authors of prairie books: Linda Hasselstrom, Mary Swander, Dan O'Brien (b. 1946), and WILLIAM LEAST HEAT-MOON (b. William Lewis Trogdon, 1939), and discuss the history of the grasslands and efforts to restore them. Stephanie Mills (b. 1948) has chronicled efforts at land restoration in the Midwest, including the site of Aldo Leopold's shack, in *In Service to the Wild: Restoring and Reinhabiting Damaged Land* (1995) and has argued for an appreciation of land as part of a fuller understanding of life's joys in *Epicurean Simplicity* (2002).

Literary Journalism: Much touted for his creative nonfiction work has been William Least Heat-Moon, a Missouri writer whose *Blue Highways: A Journey into America* (1982) was a best-selling travel narrative. His next book, *PrairyErth (a deep map)* (1991), rather than ranging widely, examines one county in Kansas in extreme detail. Similarly, Ian Frazier (b. 1951) has written an anecdotal travel narrative with considerable historical background, *Great Plains* (1989), and a more focused regional study, *On the Rez* (2000). He is also the author of *Family* (1994), which treats the history of his family in the twentieth century, principally in Ohio and Indiana, as an investigative journalism project. It is worthy of note that one of the most influential works of literary journalism was the "nonfiction novel" *In Cold Blood: A True Account of Multiple Murder and Its Consequences* (1965), by Truman Capote (1924-1984) and principally set in Kansas.

SELECTED WORKS: In *Writing from the Center* (1995) Scott Russell Sanders observes, "Much of our literature is the work of earnest pilgrims, idle drifters, travelers who write from a distance about places they have abandoned, or nomads who write about no place at all"; he claims to be "more attracted" by those writers who "have settled down and rooted their art in a chosen place" (158). F(RANCIS) SCOTT (KEY) FITZGERALD (1896–1940) is frequently alluded to by many writers as the prime example of the first kind of writer; Midwestern creative nonfiction writers may often feel the urge to "light out for the Territory," but in the end they tend to be the second kind of writer (375). In *The Florist's Daughter* (2007) Patricia Hampl, one of the most highly regarded American memoirists, writes of her parents, "These apparently ordinary people in an ordinary town, living faultlessly ordinary lives, and believing themselves to be ordinary, why do I persist in thinking—knowing—they weren't ordinary at all?" (14). Hampl has championed the idea of examining "relentlessly modest lives," and this memoir is an ideal place to discover the Midwestern conflict between a determination to send oneself into exile and a realization of the meaningfulness of a life of inhabitation; throughout her work Hampl tries to determine how she came to spend her life in St. Paul instead of following Fitzgerald's example. See MINNEAPOLIS/ST. PAUL. Scott Russell Sanders, one of the foremost American essayists, examines similar issues in *Writing from the Center,* a series of essays examining what it means to write from where you live and to be a writer in the Midwest. *Hunting for Hope: A Father's Journeys* (1998) is a more challenging and meditative collection of essays anchored in the need to uncover aspects of contemporary living that will give his children hope about their future. The most influential Midwestern nature writer has been Aldo Leopold. In *A Sand County Almanac* (1949) he rooted his art in a chosen place, a worn-out farm in central Wisconsin. His observations about nature throughout the year are perceptive and engaging, and his argument for a land ethic is persuasive and inspiring. Carol Bly's *Letters from the Country* (1981), a collection of essays written between 1973 and 1979, exemplifies the kind of powerful cultural criticism that arises from closely observed life in a small community that is akin to one of Fitzgerald's "lost Swede towns" far from the usual centers of art and culture and wrestling with the social heritage of its European roots and its local lifestyles. William Least Heat-Moon's *PrairyErth (a deep map)* (1991) is an ambitious work of immersion journalism, an attempt to "map" Chase County, Kansas, township by township, across space and time and, in the process, to reveal the complexities of place in what might be regarded as a typical and largely undistinguished prairie county. In *Walden West* (1941) AUGUST (WILLIAM) DERLETH (1909–

1971) profiles people in Sac Prairie, Wisconsin, where he spent his life, as well as providing nature interludes as a counterpoint to community life.

Many anthologies of Midwestern creative nonfiction exist. They include *A Place of Sense: Essays in Search of the Midwest* (1988) and *Townships* (1992), both edited by Michael Martone; *North Writers II: Our Place in the Woods* (1997), edited by John Erickson; *The Place to Which We Belong: Wisconsin Writers on Wisconsin Landscapes* (1998), edited by Dennis Boyer and Justin Isherwood; *In the Middle of the Middle West: Literary Nonfiction from the Heartland* (2003), edited by Becky Bradway; *Peninsula: Essays and Memoirs from Michigan* (2000), edited by Michael Steinberg; and *The Big Empty: Contemporary Nebraska Nonfiction Writers* (2007), edited by Ladette Randolph and Nina Shevchuk-Murray.

FURTHER READING: Useful starting points for exploring literary nonfiction are Annie Dillard's introduction to *The Best American Essays, 1988* (1988); Robert L. Root Jr. and Michael Steinberg's "Introduction: Creative Nonfiction, the Fourth Genre" in *The Fourth Genre: Contemporary Writers of/on Creative Nonfiction* (1999; 6th edition 2012), edited by Robert L. Root Jr. and Michael Steinberg; and Chris Anderson's "Introduction: Literary Nonfiction and Composition" in *Literary Nonfiction: Theory, Criticism, Pedagogy* (1989), edited by Chris Anderson. Travel writing about the Midwest is the focus of M. H. Dunlop's *Sixty Miles from Contentment: Traveling the Nineteenth-Century American Interior* (1995).

ROBERT ROOT   ASHLAND UNIVERSITY

CULTURAL STUDIES

OVERVIEW: As long as people of European ancestry have lived in the geographic area that over time has been referred to as the wilderness, the West, the Old Northwest, and, eventually, the Midwest or Middle West, studies have attempted to define and describe the culture of the region. As the Midwest has evolved through settlement and growth, historians, geographers, cultural critics, and other scholars have examined class dynamics, immigration, politics, history, ART, and popular thought in efforts to understand the region and to compare and contrast it with the nation as a whole. These studies

have ranged from consideration of the stories of the region's inhabitants to detailed
analysis of the archives of local and state
historical societies throughout the Midwest.
Central to all these studies has been the issue
of definition: how should the region be defined, and, on the basis of that definition,
what differentiates it from other parts of
the country?

HISTORY AND SIGNIFICANCE: The Midwest was an area of historical and cultural
interest well before the twentieth century.
One of the most comprehensive early studies is the two-volume collection *The Old
Northwest: With a View of the Thirteen Colonies
as Constituted by the Royal Charters* (1888) by
University of Michigan professor B(urke)
A(aron) Hinsdale. Hinsdale's study highlights the history of the Old Northwest
while placing it within the context of American history as a whole. He states in his
preface, "Save New England alone, there is
no section of the United States embracing
several States that is so distinct a historical
unit, and that so readily yields to historical
treatment, as the Old Northwest" (iii). Beginning with the exploration of the region
by the French in the 1600s, Hinsdale highlights the influence of the American Revolution on the region, notes the impact of the
Ordinance of 1787, and discusses the role of
slavery in the region. Hinsdale's work is
quite detailed, focusing primarily on historical facts and political dynamics, but it
provides a valuable early analysis of the
Midwest's role in American culture.

After the turn of the twentieth century,
the number of cultural analyses of the Midwest increased significantly. In 1934 two
comprehensive studies of the Midwest
began to record its evolving regional history.
In *The Civilization of the Old Northwest: A Study
of Political, Social, and Economic Development,
1788–1812* (1934), Beverley W. Bond Jr. provided a strong historical background for
the early Midwest. Bond's detailed research
into early newspapers and manuscripts from
the region's historical societies allowed
him to construct a view of the society and
the evolving civilization of the Midwest.
See NEWSPAPER JOURNALISM. Bond limited his
parameters for the Midwest to a focus predominantly on the settlement and development of the geographic area that would
eventually comprise OHIO, INDIANA, ILLINOIS,
and MICHIGAN.

The second study published in 1934 is
*Sources of Culture in the Middle West: Back-
grounds versus Frontier,* edited by Dixon Ryan
Fox. This study consists of three essays dealing with the evolution of civilization in the
Midwest, a response to those essays, and a
response to ideas proposed by the historian
Frederick Jackson Turner (1861–1932). Primarily a historical-political analysis, the
three essays discuss the evolution of a political government in the Midwest during the
rise of towns and increasing population;
the development of professions throughout
the region and the ways in which those
professions contributed to the changing
frontier landscape; and finally, the cultural
developments in the region that allowed it
to stand on its own in terms of definition
and identity.

Continuing the conversation about evolving regional identity, *The Culture of the Middle
West* (1944) is based on a series of lectures
given at Lawrence College in Appleton,
WISCONSIN, in the winter of 1942–1943. Howard Troyer, chairman of the lecture committee, remarks in his introduction that the
focus of the lectures is the exploration of regional distinctiveness:

If we speak like Middle Westerners, if more
recently we vote on political and social issues
like Middle Westerners, what are Middle
Westerners really like? Do we have a culture
sufficiently distinct from other regions to merit
the distinction of Middle Western? What are
its values and virtues? What are its shortcomings and failures? Will an honest appraisal
help us to understand ourselves, as well as our
own role in the national destiny? (vi)

The five lectures collected in the volume explore the region's geography, immigrant
history, political background, voice through
the work of SAMUEL LANGHORNE CLEMENS (1835–
1910), writing as Mark Twain, and art and
culture as represented by the city of CHICAGO.
Although these lectures are far from a comprehensive cultural study, they serve as a
starting point in examining the region's
emerging cultural awareness and criticism.

In the 1940s cultural studies of the Midwest took a more personal turn, incorporating individual responses and assessments.

America Is West: An Anthology of Middlewestern Life and Literature (1945), edited by John T. Flanagan (1906-1996), traces the region's development from the early pioneering days to the conflicted view of the Midwest found in many twentieth-century discussions, using a variety of perspectives from authors and historical figures including ABRAHAM LINCOLN (1809-1865), Louis Hennepin (1626–ca. 1705), (HARRY) SINCLAIR LEWIS (1885-1951), Grant Wood (1891–1942), and others. Flanagan comments in his introduction to the volume that even from its earliest days, the "great valley was developing a cultural life of its own" (vi).

Graham Hutton's 1946 cultural study *Midwest at Noon* is based largely on personal observations and experiences. Hutton brings an outsider's perspective to the region with his English nationality, frequently contrasting Midwestern culture with that of the rest of the United States, England, and Europe. His discussion covers many aspects of the Midwest, from the rural to the urban and from the agricultural to the industrial, and focuses on climate, culture, and personal characteristics of Midwesterners. Hutton states in his forward that he does not intend his book to be a comprehensive or strongly scientific examination of the region, but merely an early study or point of inspiration for other scholars and writers who, he hopes, will examine the region more closely.

By the mid-twentieth century, even as regionalism was diminishing as a major national concern for many scholars, the Midwest was still caught up in cultural debates about the definition and overall significance of the region. *Main Street on the Middle Border* (1954) by Lewis E. Atherton (1905–1989) presents "a cultural and economic history of Midwestern country towns from 1865 to 1950" (xvi). Combining historical and cultural details with a discussion of local biographies in and literary representations of small towns by authors such as (HANNIBAL) HAMLIN GARLAND (1860-1940), THORSTEIN (BUNDE) VEBLEN (1857-1929), Sinclair Lewis, WILLIAM DEAN HOWELLS (1837–1920), and others, Atherton constructs a well-rounded portrait of life in country towns spanning the Midwest. Although the book focuses primarily on literature, it also contains several appendixes that incorporate statistical information regarding population growth, surveys of rural shopping habits, and other details of Midwestern life.

John Murray's 1958 volume *The Heritage of the Middle West* is a collection of essays that again attempt to define and understand the region. He reports "The purpose of this book is not to catalogue all of the distinguishing characteristics of the Middle West, but to examine some of the factors which have produced them" (vii). In pursuit of that goal, the collection includes essays looking at cultural influences, agrarian aspects, politics, PHILOSOPHY, art, and other defining elements. Murray's study of Midwestern culture also includes a piece by Midwestern literary scholar John T. Flanagan titled "A Soil for the Seeds of Literature."

The Midwest: Myth or Reality? (1961) is a collection of essays based on an April 1960 University of Notre Dame symposium on the region. Edited by Thomas McAvoy and others, this series of essays looks at a wide range of regional issues, including RADICALISM, industrial issues, and the nature of Midwestern literature. Noted Midwestern scholars Russel B. Nye (1913–1993), John T. Flanagan, and JOHN T(OWNER) FREDERICK (1893–1975) contributed to this volume.

Douglas Waitley's 1963 *Portrait of the Midwest: From the Ice Age to the Industrial Era* is an attempt to lay out a geographic history of the Midwest. Focusing his definition of the Midwest on eight states—Illinois, Indiana, IOWA, Michigan, MINNESOTA, Ohio, Wisconsin, and northern MISSOURI—Waitley traces the development of the region from the glaciers that shaped the landscape to the people and history that made the region what it became. Waitley's discussion of the Midwest draws to a close in the 1920s with a discussion of how Henry Ford's automobile empire propelled the region into an industrial era very different from its pioneer past. Moving from cultural history to travelogue, Waitley also includes a "Vagabond" section in the back of his book for travelers to the Midwest, listing major cities and highlighting cultural and historical locations of interest for each state.

In *The Middle West: Its Meaning in American Culture* (1989), cultural geographer James R. Shortridge explores the regional characteristics and terminology of the Midwest more comprehensively than many others. The definition of the Midwest as it has evolved over time is Shortridge's primary interest, and he states that his "goal is not only to understand the Middle West as a cultural idea but also to reveal the important interplay that has occurred between this regional culture and that of the United States as a whole" (6). Beginning in the nineteenth century and continuing to the time of the book's publication, Shortridge examines the evolution of the words "Middle West" to describe an initially shifting perspective and then a more definitive recognition of the region as a section of the United States, the continuing focus on rural or pastoral imagery in connection with the region, and the way individual states define themselves as Midwestern.

Treating the historical evolution of the Midwest, historians Andrew R. L. Cayton and Peter S. Onuf examine the nineteenth-century Old Northwest in their 1990 book *The Midwest and the Nation: Rethinking the History of an American Region*. Cayton and Onuf study the social, cultural, and political forces

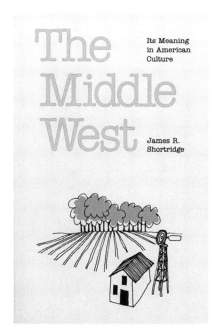

Dust Cover, James R. Shortridge's *The Middle West: Its Meaning in American Culture*. University Press of Kansas, 1989. Used by permission of the publisher

that have shaped the region in contrast to those shaping the rest of the country. Expanding transportation resources, economic conditions, and the rise of the middle class all inform their contrast between the Midwest's identity and that of the nation.

Cayton has continued his work on Midwestern history, editing *The American Midwest: Essays on Regional History* (2001) with Susan E. Gray. This collection of essays is based on an October 1998 Miami University history conference. Often examining a "dual regional consciousness," the essays incorporate a variety of perspectives that examine identity and regionality in multiple Midwestern locations and contexts (2).

In the late twentieth and early twenty-first centuries scholars incorporated broader aspects of literary, historical, and cultural theory into their analyses of the Midwest. In *The Minds of the West: Ethnocultural Evolution in the Rural Middle West, 1830–1917* (1997), Jon Gjerde (1953–2008) looks at the upper Midwest (NORTH DAKOTA, SOUTH DAKOTA, Minnesota, NEBRASKA, Iowa, Wisconsin, and Illinois) and the effects of settlement and immigration in the region. Although Gjerde's commentary is broadly based, he focuses primarily on Norwegian, German, and Swedish ethnic groups and examines the evolving sense of religious identity, family dynamics, and the construction of rural Midwestern communities among American and European settlers in the region during the nineteenth century.

An American Colony: Regionalism and the Roots of Midwestern Culture (2002) by Edward Watts incorporates aspects of postcolonial theory to address the development of the Old Northwest in the late eighteenth and early nineteenth centuries. Watts contends that the eastern United States and the forces of American nationalism influenced the development of the Midwest as it underwent settlement and growth, often provoking conflicts and responses similar to those of more formally colonized nations. Watts uses historical elements, cultural dynamics, and literary representations of the region to support his overall argument.

William Barillas's 2006 volume *The Midwestern Pastoral: Place and Landscape in Literature of the American Heartland* applies an interdisciplinary approach to his study of

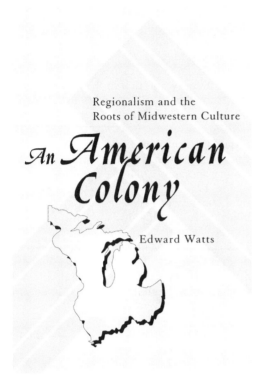

Dust jacket for *An American Colony: Regionalism and the Roots of Midwestern Culture* by Edward Watts. Cover design by Kari Rosenberg.
© Ohio University Press, 2002. Used by permission of Ohio University Press

Dust jacket for *The Midwestern Pastoral: Place and Landscape in Literature of the American Heartland* by William Barillas. *Madison Oaks,* drawing by Dan Beresford.
© Ohio University Press, 2006. Used by permission of Ohio University Press

Midwestern writers within the context of a pastoral aesthetic. He examines the connections between literature and nature in an attempt to better understand how landscape shapes and informs individual and artistic identity. Contrasting the work of authors WILLA CATHER (1873–1947), ALDO LEOPOLD (1887–1948), THEODORE ROETHKE (1908–1963), JAMES WRIGHT (1927–1980), and JIM (JAMES THOMAS) HARRISON (1937–2016), among others, Barillas places them within the larger discussions surrounding Midwestern literature and culture and the larger tradition of pastoral writing. Mark Bueschel's *Sacred Land: Sherwood Anderson, Midwestern Modernism, and the Sacramental Vision of Nature* (2014) expands Barillas's discussion of the pastoral and examines how spirituality also influences that connection to the land.

Study of Midwestern culture continues to draw interest. *The American Midwest: An*

Interpretive Encyclopedia (2007), edited by Richard Sisson, Christian Zacher, and Andrew Cayton, examines a broad swath of Midwestern culture. Cayton, in the "General Overview," states that the volume "introduces readers to the cultural diversity of the Midwest, including a vast array of foods, languages, styles, religions, and customs" (xxiv). The encyclopedia contains broad essays and short definitive pieces from a variety of contributors focused on Midwestern landscapes and people, society and culture, community and social life, economy and technology, and public life. Historian Jon Lauck traces the evolution of Midwestern HISTORIOGRAPHY and argues for continued Midwestern regional importance in *The Lost Region: Toward a Revival of Midwestern History* (2013).

SELECTED WORKS: *The American Midwest: An Interpretive Encyclopedia* (2007), edited by Richard Sisson, Christian Zacher, and Andrew Cayton, is an excellent starting point for scholars and students looking for a very broad overview of cultural dynamics in the Midwest. The introductory essay, "The Story of the Midwest," in Cayton and Gray's *The American Midwest: Essays on Regional History* provides context for that volume's collected essays but also presents a strong overview of the development of the region and the issues faced in establishing a distinctive Midwestern identity.

FURTHER READING: Significant room remains for more focused cultural studies of the Midwest. Jon Gjerde's *The Minds of the West: Ethnocultural Evolution in the Rural Middle West, 1830–1917* (1997), Edward Watts's *An American Colony: Regionalism and the Roots of Midwestern Culture* (2002), and William Barillas's *The Midwestern Pastoral: Place and Landscape in Literature of the American Heartland* (2006) are among the central works of Midwestern cultural studies. As their volumes attest, using larger theoretical frameworks and lenses provided by historical, literary, and cultural theory can result in greater understanding of the evolution of Midwestern culture and identity.

These books focus on broader analyses of Midwestern culture, but a large number of books and articles deal with more specific cultural movements or individual locations in the Midwest, particularly in the major cities. Dale Kramer's 1966 volume *Chicago Renaissance: The Literary Life in the Midwest, 1900–1930* defines the CHICAGO RENAISSANCE and the city's thriving literary scene. Hugh Dalziel Duncan's *Culture and Democracy: The Struggle for Form in Society and Architecture in Chicago and the Middle West during the Life and Times of Louis H. Sullivan* (1965) examines the influence of art and architecture on Chicago's cultural development. Timothy B. Spears's *Chicago Dreaming: Midwesterners and the City, 1871–1919* (2005) examines the changing literary and cultural landscape of the city during the late nineteenth and early twentieth centuries. Midwestern women have often been overlooked by cultural studies, but works such as *On Behalf of the Family Farm: Iowa Farm Women's Activism since 1945* (2013) by Jenny Barker Devine are working to fill in those gaps. These and other works make it clear that specific Midwestern localities have also had their own cultural movements. Further information on specific cultural movements or events in Midwestern history and literature can be found by browsing entries such as the CHICAGO RENAISSANCE, the FEDERAL WRITERS' PROJECT, RADICALISM, and others.

SARA KOSIBA   TROY UNIVERSITY

D–E

DETECTIVE FICTION.
See Mystery and Detective Fiction

DETROIT

Detroit (from the French *détroit*, "strait") was founded in 1701 by Antoine Laumet de la Mothe Cadillac (1658–1730). It was part of New France, 1701–1760; a British possession, 1760–1796; the capital of Michigan Territory, 1805–1836; and the Michigan state capital, 1837–1847.

Area: 139 square miles

Population (2010 census): 713,777

OVERVIEW: During its three-hundred-year existence, Detroit has played a substantial role on the local, regional, national, and international stages during two distinct periods. The first, in which it was a frontier settlement and bulwark against Native American depredations and European colonial rivals, dates from Detroit's founding by the French in 1701 to approximately 1815, when Anglo American armed conflict came to an end in the strategically important Great Lakes region. The second epoch, at the start of the twentieth century, saw a second-tier city become a manufacturing powerhouse within a relatively short time, especially in the burgeoning automobile industry. That once-dominant aspect of Detroit, as reflected in its "Motor City" appellation, has been on the decline for some time, and it remains to be seen what postindustrial identity it will ultimately assume. See also MICHIGAN.

HISTORY AND SIGNIFICANCE: The novel has been the most important vehicle in relating the Detroit scene and experience in literary form. A remarkable trio of historical romances, carefully based on documentary sources, was written over a three-year period by Mary Catherine Crowley (1869–1920). *A Daughter of New France* (1901), *The Heroine of the Strait* (1902), and *Love Thrives in War* (1903) cover three successive important events in Detroit history: the founding of the settlement by Antoine de la Mothe Cadillac in 1701; the siege of the fort in 1763 by Pontiac (ca. 1720–1769), leader of the Ottawas and allied tribes; and the British military operations in the area during the War of 1812. Although Crowley's novels were neither explicitly marketed to celebrate Detroit's bicentennial nor published as a trilogy, they clearly can be regarded from both these points of view.

Also telling the story of Cadillac and his struggle to establish a viable settlement are

© Karen Greasley, 2014

Hawk of Detroit (1939) by Arthur Pound (1884–1966), which covers the French settlement at Detroit and follows its progress through the subsequent ten years, and Robert Pico's (b. 1938) *Cadillac, l'homme qui fonda Détroit* (1995), which presents the fictionalized memoirs of Cadillac.

Pontiac coordinated Indian attacks on British forts throughout the Great Lakes area in 1763. His attempt to capture Detroit provides the setting for a number of novels, among which are Osgood Bradbury's (1798–1888) *Pontiac; or, The Last Battle of the Ottawa Chief* (1848), Randall Parrish's (1858–1923) *A Sword of the Old Frontier* (1905), and *Hatchet in the Sky* (1954) by Margaret Gay (1900–1957). In addition, there are no fewer than fifteen juvenile novels dealing with the legendary Ottawa chieftain and his exploits.

At the beginning of the War of 1812 General William Hull surrendered Fort Detroit to the British without a fight. This ignominious act has been fictionalized by a few writers, including John Richardson (1796–1852), whose *The Canadian Brothers* (1840) provides a British perspective on the event. On the American side, Ralph Beebe's *Who Fought and Bled* (1941) and *Trumpet in the Wilderness* (1940) by Robert Harper (1899–1962) are two examples.

Between the end of that war and Detroit's emergence as an industrial city at the beginning of the twentieth century, there is remarkably little distinctly Detroit literature that is worthy of notice. One exception is *Shoepac Recollections: A Way-Side Glimpse of American Life* (1856) by Orlando Bolivar

Willcox (1823–1907), which appeared under the pseudonym Walter March. It consists of fictionalized reminiscences of the author's boyhood in 1820s Detroit. Willcox went on to a distinguished career as a general in the Civil War, during which he was awarded the Medal of Honor.

The invention of the self-propelled gasoline-powered vehicle and the rise of the automobile industry in Michigan transformed not only the state of Michigan but the entire nation as well. The life of a fictitious Detroit inventor, based on that of Henry Ford (1863–1947), is traced in *The Onyx* (1982) by Jacqueline Briskin (1927-2014), and the exploitative beginnings of the Ford Motor Company are exposed in the novel *The Flivver King* (1937) by UPTON (BEALL) SINCLAIR (JR.) (1878–1968). The dangerous and dehumanizing work on the auto-factory assembly lines is explored in *The Disinherited* (1933) by (JOHN WESLEY) "JACK" CONROY (1898–1990), *Temper* (1924) by Lawrence H(enry) Conrad (1898–1982), and *F.O.B. Detroit* (1938) by Wessel Hyatt Smitter (1894–1951). Agitation for better working conditions led to the establishment of labor unions, but not without resistance by auto manufacturers that resulted in violence on both sides. Some of these issues are the subject of *Conveyor* by Robert Cruden (1909–1988), writing as James Steele; *The Underground Stream* (1940) by Albert Maltz (1908–1985); and *The Hard Rain* (1980) by Dinitia Smith (b. 1945). Other aspects of the automobile industry that many authors find interesting are the promotion and marketing of new car models. Examples of these works are *American Chrome* (1965) by Edwin Gilbert (1907–1976), *The Detroiters* (1958) by Harold Livingston (b. 1924), *Fireball* (1963) by Henry B. Hager (1926–2012), and *Motor City* (1992) by Bill Morris (b. 1952).

The image of industrial Detroit as a destination of opportunity for those seeking a better life is best described in *THE DOLLMAKER* (1954) by HARRIETTE SIMPSON ARNOW (1908–1986). There a Kentucky family encounters not an economic paradise but personal tragedy. The theme of European immigrants seeking the American Dream in Detroit is taken up in a few novels of the urban experience. *Papa's Golden Land* (1960) by Frita Roth Drapkin (1912–2006) is a fictionalized memoir about a Czechoslo-vakian family's new life in Detroit in the 1920s. In *Avenue of Dreams* (1990) Lucy Taylor (b. 1950) follows an Italian couple who arrive in Detroit in the 1920s with hopes of finding success and wealth. Although the literary émigré Russian is usually to be found in Paris, in *The Heart Returneth* (1943) by Vera Lebedeff (1910–1998) a group of refugees from the Russian Revolution form a supportive community in Detroit. In that same city Linda Crawford (b. 1938) shows an immigrant Scots family becoming gradually assimilated into American life in *Something to Make Us Happy* (1978).

The first novel with a Michigan setting written by an African American appears to have been *Appointed* (1894) by Walter H. Stowers (1859–1932) and William H. Anderson (b. ca. 1857), who used the joint pseudonym Sanda. Stowers and Anderson, co-founders of a black weekly newspaper in Detroit, later earned law degrees and were active in local politics. Their novel, partially set in Detroit, describes the frustration of black professionals at finding work within white society; it also delineates the far worse conditions in the Jim Crow South at the time, particularly the growing frequency of lynchings. Rosalyn McMillan (b. 1953) has written a number of novels that show the resolute and self-reliant aspects of African American women: *Knowing* (1996), *One Better* (1997), *Blue Collar Blues* (1998), and *The Flip Side of Sin* (2000). All have Detroit backgrounds. A young female Detroiter in *Fish Tales* (1983) by NETTIE (PEARL) JONES (b. 1941) gradually discovers the futility of finding happiness in casual sex and drugs. Jones's later novel *Mischief Makers* (1989) explores the concept of "passing," a common theme in African American literature; in this novel a professional Detroit couple sends their lighter-skinned daughter to northern Michigan to begin a new life as a white woman in the 1930s.

The history of Detroit race relations is highlighted by two notorious riots, one in 1943 that began on Belle Isle and the better-known civil disturbance in 1967, whose proximate cause was a police raid on an after-hours drinking establishment. It is surprising that these two watershed events in the history of Detroit do not figure in many fictional works. The 1943 event serves as a background to *The Hate Merchant* (1953) by Niven Busch (1903–1991), *Jitterbug* (1998) by LOREN D. ESTLEMAN (b. 1952), and *The Art Student's War* (2009) by Brad Leithauser (b. 1953). The 1967 riot is employed in both *Them* (1969) by JOYCE CAROL OATES (b. 1938) as the dramatic ending and *When the Fire Reaches Us* (1970) by Barbara Wilson Tinker (1909–1995), which shows the riot's effect on the inhabitants of the ghetto.

In titles such as *Whiskey River* (1990), *King of the Corner* (1992), *Jitterbug,* mentioned previously, and *Thunder City* (1999), episodes in the social history of Detroit are fictionally presented in the unofficially named Detroit series of novels by Loren Estleman. From the early beginnings of the auto industry, Prohibition, bootlegging, and midcentury motor-vehicle advertising to the often violent rust-belt cityscape of the 1990s, Estleman has deftly captured the mise en scène of Detroit during those periods.

A significant body of popular literature uses Detroit as the setting, notably in the crime and detective novel genre. For discussion and examples, see that section under MICHIGAN.

Dudley Randall, ca. 1972.
Reprinted by permission of the Dudley Randall Literary Estate

Philip Levine, 2002.
Photograph © Matt Valentine

Before the twentieth century Detroit poets and their poetry did not attain much regional or national acclaim, nor is their output of much critical interest today. Not until after World War II did the city inspire important poetic works by such writers as ROBERT HAYDEN (1913–1980), DUDLEY FELKER RANDALL (1914–2000), Philip Levine (1928–2015), and JIM (JAMES RAYMOND) DANIELS (b. 1956). Robert Hayden's first book of poetry, *Heart-Shape in the Dust* (1940), contains some verse based on his observations of ghetto life in Detroit. In most of his books, such as *They Feed They Lion* (1972) and *News of the World* (2009), 2011–2012 U.S. Poet Laureate Philip Levine creates verse vignettes of remembered Detroit from the 1930s to the 1950s, focusing especially on industrial work and his Russian Jewish immigrant family. *M-80* (1993), a collection of poems by Jim Daniels, juxtaposes working-class Detroit neighborhoods to urban crime and violence. For further information, see the section on poetry under MICHIGAN.

SELECTED WORKS: Historical fiction includes Mary Catherine Crowley's trilogy *A Daughter of New France* (1901), *The Heroine of the Strait* (1902), and *Love Thrives in War*

(1903). Although this trilogy is highly romantic in style, it still conveys a reasonably accurate picture of the first century of Detroit as a frontier settlement and important fort. *Who Fought and Bled* (1941) by Ralph Beebe depicts the surrender of the Detroit garrison to the British in the early days of the War of 1812. Detroit as a territorial capital in the 1820s serves as the setting for *Shoepac Recollections* (1856) by Orlando Willcox.

The trajectory of the automobile industry can readily be followed in *Temper* (1924) by Lawrence Conrad, *F.O.B. Detroit* (1938) by Wessel Smitter, *American Chrome* (1965) by Edwin Gilbert, and *Motor City* (1992) by Bill Morris. An interesting perspective on the relationship of the United Auto Workers union with the Ford Motor Company during the volatile 1930s is presented by Upton Sinclair in *The Flivver King* (1937).

The different aspects of life in twentieth-century Detroit are shown in Loren D. Estleman's six-book Detroit series, as well as in his Amos Walker detective novels. The industrial might of Detroit during World War II provides the background for *The Dollmaker* (1954) by Harriette Simpson Arnow and Brad Leithauser's *The Art Student's War* (2009). The grim realities of race relations in the city in 1967 are well described in separate viewpoints afforded by Barbara Tinker's *When the Fire Reaches Us* (1970) and *Them* (1969) by Joyce Carol Oates.

Anthologies devoted solely to Detroit literature are a fairly recent phenomenon. None appeared before 1983, although the collection assembled by the Detroit Women Writers Association, *Century of Voices* (1999), is a retrospective collection of its members' writing from 1900 to 1999 A substantial and important collection of verse, *Abandon Automobile* (2001), edited by Melba Joyce Boyd (b. 1950) and M. L. Liebler (b. 1953), contains the work of a number of poets writing about Detroit from 1930 to the present. Kurt Nimmo (b. 1952) and Christine Lahey-Dolega (b. 1949) edited *Planet Detroit: Anthology of Urban Poetry* (1983), which celebrates the culture of the modern city. Detroit's multiethnic diversity is exemplified by *Detroit Latin Sounds in Poetry: A Poetry Anthology,* which appeared in two volumes in 1985 and 1987, and in the two collections issued by the Detroit Black

Writer's Guild, *Inner Visions: A Poetry Anthology* (1994) and *Day's Dawn: A Short Story Anthology* (1996). *Detroit Noir* (2007), a collection of original short stories edited by E. J. Olsen and John C. Hocking (b. 1960), explores the darker aspects of the city's varied neighborhoods and those who inhabit them. *A Detroit Anthology* (2014), edited by Anna Clark, is a collection of stories, poems, essays, photographs, and art about Detroit aimed at an audience of Detroiters.

FURTHER READING:

Bibliography, Biography, and Criticism: Although Detroit has entered its fourth century of existence, no critical monograph or comprehensive survey of its literary production has yet been published. The literary history of Detroit has been largely subsumed in studies that cover the entire state of Michigan; for a representative list of these, see MICHIGAN.

A brief but good introduction to modern Detroit poetry and fiction can be found in "The Image of Detroit in Twentieth Century Literature" by Laurence Goldstein (b. 1943), *Michigan Quarterly Review* 25 (Spring 1986): 269–91. A chapter titled "Detroit in Letters" in *Detroit: Dynamic City* (1940) by Arthur Pound assesses a few Detroit authors and their works, although many of them are now obscure or forgotten. Silas Farmer's monumental *History of Detroit and Wayne County and Early Michigan* (3rd edition 1890) contains several chapters of modest literary interest, including information on city newspapers, publishers, literary societies, and local authors, including writers of nonfiction as well as poetry, fiction, and belles lettres; however, the author listings are more enumerative than evaluative.

Libraries and Repositories: The most important collection of all aspects of Detroit literature, both book and manuscript resources, resides in the Detroit Public Library as part of the Burton Historical Collection. The Michigan Collection at the Library of Michigan in Lansing also contains substantial Detroit-related fiction and poetry.

ROBERT BEASECKER   GRAND VALLEY STATE UNIVERSITY

DIAL, THE

OVERVIEW: Named after Margaret Fuller and Ralph Waldo Emerson's New England transcendentalist journal, between 1880 and 1918 *The Dial* was among Chicago's most influential magazines of literary criticism. Founded and edited by Francis Fisher Browne (1843–1913), *The Dial* generally consisted of reviews of important books, notices and lists of new books, literary news notes, publishers' announcements, and occasional pieces on the fine arts. *The Dial* 1.1 (May 1880) touted itself as a magazine for and by the "book-lover book-buyer" (17) and promised to distinguish between "literary criticism and literary cynicism" (18). *The Dial*'s contributors were predominantly Midwesterners from a variety of backgrounds and occupations. Despite this diversity, however, *The Dial* generally promoted Browne's conservative literary values and genteel literary tastes. In *Chicago: Creating New Traditions* (1976), Perry Duis indicates that *The Dial* favorably reviewed local CHICAGO writers like HENRY BLAKE FULLER (1857–1929) and nurtured the beginnings of the CHICAGO RENAISSANCE (122). It also served as the conservative literary foil to the more avant-garde *POETRY: A MAGAZINE OF VERSE* and *THE LITTLE REVIEW*, both Chicago-based supporters of progressive, modernist, and regionalist literature.

HISTORY AND SIGNIFICANCE: *The Dial* was not Browne's first journalistic attempt. As a teenager, Browne learned much about journalism and editing by helping his father, an editor of the Massachusetts-based *Chicopee Journal*. See NEWSPAPER JOURNALISM. Later, as an adult, Browne studied law at the University of Michigan but quickly found that his true passion was literature and left the university after less than a year.

In the late 1860s Browne moved to Chicago. After managing a print shop for a short time, he seized an opportunity to buy a portion of *Western Monthly*, a magazine recently established by H. V. Reed and E. C. Tuttle. Inspired by his commitment to bring a reading market to the Midwest and to establish a market for western literature in the East, Browne immediately worked to improve *Western Monthly*'s physical and literary qualities. In 1871 he changed the title of *Western Monthly* to *Lakeside Monthly* and worked to expand the magazine's influence to a national audience. Over time, New Englanders and even Europeans began reading *Lakeside Monthly*. Unfortunately, two major fires at the magazine's headquarters and the financial panic of 1873 eventually caused *Lakeside Monthly* to fold.

After *Lakeside Monthly* closed, Browne became very ill and was unable to work for several years. By 1877, however, he had recovered and was working as a literary editor for the *Chicago Alliance,* a religious journal. Shortly after that, Browne became an editor for Jansen, McClurg and Company, one of the largest book publishers in the Chicago area. While working for it, Browne envisioned a journal similar to the English monthly reviews that he cherished, such as the *Athenaeum* and the *Academy.* General A. C. McClurg shared Browne's vision and recognized his editorial talent. Therefore, in 1880, with the help of McClurg's publishing company, Browne started *The Dial: A Monthly Review and Index of Current Literature.*

From the beginning, Browne maintained high standards for *The Dial* and was meticulous about every aspect of its production. The magazine was consistently twenty to twenty-four pages long and contained no illustrations, even though readers in this period increasingly expected photos and line drawings. Advertisements were allowed only on the extra pages in the front and back of the magazine and never interfered with the magazine's main body of text. Books given good reviews could not be advertised in the magazine because Browne did not want his audience to think that a publisher could buy a good review. In order to further validate *The Dial*'s independence and integrity, in 1892 Browne bought the magazine from Jansen, McClurg and Company and began to publish the magazine himself under the auspices of The Dial Company. The same year, Browne changed the magazine's title to *The Dial: A Semimonthly Journal of Literary Criticism, Discussion, and Information.* He also hired two new associates, William Morton Payne and Edward Gilpin. Through all these changes, Browne upheld his high publishing standards and refused to pursue mainstream popularity. Perry Duis indicates in *Chicago: Creating New Traditions* (1976) that *The Dial* seldom achieved more than a thousand subscribers (122).

Browne was particular about the views presented in his journal. A New Englander by birth, he tended to prefer more conservative literature. To that end, he gathered a group of unpaid reviewers who reflected his conservative tastes. Some of the more famous contributors to *The Dial* were Woodrow Wilson (1856–1924), FREDERICK JACKSON TURNER (1861–1932), Henry Seidel Canby (1878–1961), JOSEPH KIRKLAND (1830–1894), EUGENE FIELD (SR.) (1850–1895), Chief Justice Melville W. Fuller (1833–1910), and Fred Lewis Pattee (1863–1950). Browne, through *The Dial,* supported the genteel tenor of the early Chicago Renaissance. Historian Perry Duis makes it clear that Browne "published articles about Chicago" that dispelled "the image of an unsophisticated, outgrown village" (122). If Browne was indirectly devoted to the development and advancement of Midwestern literature, he did not let this devotion preempt his values or critical judgment. In fact, in a letter responding to criticism by (HANNIBAL) HAMLIN GARLAND (1860–1940) that *The Dial* was too conservative and did not fully support Midwestern literature, Browne stated, "We must show that we are willing to have our literature tried by the standards of world literature, rather than the standards of the back settlement" (Francis Fisher Browne papers, Newberry Library, Chicago). Browne's refusal to rely on regionalism enabled *The Dial* both to bring world literature to the West and to introduce the world to genteel Midwestern literature.

FURTHER READING: Further information about *The Dial* can be found in *The Little Magazine: A History and a Bibliography* (1946) by Frederick J. Hoffman, Charles Allen, and Carolyn F. Ulrich; pages 196–206 discuss *The Dial.* Clarence A. Andrews's *Chicago in Story: A Literary History* (1982); *American Literary Magazines: The Twentieth Century* (1992), edited by Edward Chielens; Bernard Duffey's *The Chicago Renaissance in American Letters: A Critical History* (1954) and Frank Luther Mott's *A History of American Magazines: 1865–1885* (1930) are also valuable. Perry Duis, in *Chicago: Creating New Traditions* (1976), comments on the magazine's place in Chicago literature and the city's genteel "Upward Movement." "Literary Interests of Chicago III and IV," an article about *The Dial* by Herbert E. Fleming in the *Journal of Sociology* 11.4 (1906), was written while *The*

Dial was still being published. Biographical information about Francis Fisher Browne can be found on the *Contemporary Authors Online* database (2002) and in *American Magazine Journalists, 1850–1900* (1989) edited by Sam G. Riley. The University of Wisconsin–Madison owns one of the most extensive Little Magazine collections in the United States. This special collection contains the complete run of *The Dial,* including issues from the time when the magazine was based in Chicago and, later, New York.

RACHEL BRENEMAN

THE UNIVERSITY OF TENNESSEE AT CHATTANOOGA

DIALECTS

OVERVIEW: A popular misconception of the language of the Midwest is that of uniformity. For much of the twentieth century, the idea persisted that Midwesterners spoke an inflectionless "General American" dialect. But the diverse settlement history of the region suggests otherwise. The land was first occupied by Native Americans and then by the earliest European colonists, especially around the Great Lakes and the Mississippi Valley. They were French, but their numbers were never great, and the only noticeable remnant of French-language influence by the twentieth century appears in place names, such as DETROIT and Des Moines. In addition, there exist many examples of American Indian words appropriated by explorers and settlers as place names, for example, CHICAGO, Kankakee, Mississippi, and Topeka.

The chief reason that language of the Midwest is not uniform, then, is the dialects of its English-speaking settlers. In fact, dialectologists recognize five major regional dialects in the United States, and all but one contributed to the dialects of the Midwest. Dialects are identified by the use of "regionalisms," including vocabulary, pronunciation, or grammatical forms associated with the use of language in a particular area. This entry discusses the regionalisms that differentiate the Northern and Midlands dialect areas in the Midwest and the demographic origins of those regionalisms.

HISTORY AND SIGNIFICANCE: The first dialect is Inland Northern, so called to distinguish it from the more familiar dialect of New York City, Boston, and the rest of eastern New England. Many Boston speakers, for example, do not articulate the consonantal sound /r/ after vowels, hence the stereotypical "Pahk the cah in the yahd." Inland Northern, by contrast, flourished in western Vermont and upstate New York and was carried westward into the Great Lakes area by settlers from these regions. After about 1930 the Inland Northern dialect became the model for published pronunciation guides and manuals, which provide a readily available illustration of its pronunciation. The pronunciation features of this dialect became fairly standard among FILM and television actors during the 1950s. Northern settlers tended to found colonies and towns; therefore, Inland Northern frequently became the language of commerce. Because Inland Northern culture fostered an emphasis on education and literacy, and because many teachers in the early Midwest originated in New York and New England, Inland Northern often became associated with formal education and for some people became an unofficial norm.

Besides the Inland Northern dialect, the Midwest also became home to two varieties of the Midland dialect. This dialect originated largely in Pennsylvania with the arrival of thousands of Ulster Scots during the eighteenth century; it was this influence from Ulster that set the Midland dialect apart. Midland pronunciation is notable for the sound of /z/ instead of /s/ in *greasy* and *grease* and for a vowel system that makes *dawn* and *Don* sound alike; Midland speakers also insert an /r/ sound into words like *wash* and, also before /sh/, often raise the short *a* of *ash* or *national* into something more like a long *a.* Careful listeners from other regions might notice a Midland pronunciation of /r/ in words like *Laura* or *boring* that sounds stronger because the back of the tongue is somewhat retracted. Midland grammar differs from Inland Northern primarily in elliptical constructions like "The grass needs mowed," "The baby wants picked up," "The cat wants out," or "I want off." Midland speakers are also more likely to say "quarter till eleven" than the Northern "quarter to" or "quarter of eleven." Finally, the word *anymore* is used positively in sentences, as in "I tire easily anymore." Educational differences led to further divisions between Midland and Northern speakers.

The Ulster Scots who migrated south-ward from Pennsylvania encountered and absorbed much of the Southern dialect as they followed the mountain valleys into Virginia and the Carolinas and ultimately into Kentucky and Tennessee. These en-counters between Midland and Southern produced the South Midland or Upland Southern dialect. Before the settlers from New England arrived in the Midwest, these earlier arrivals came from Kentucky and Tennessee and from the uplands of Virginia and the Carolinas. In the Midwest they concentrated in the southern parts of ILLI-NOIS, OHIO, and INDIANA; some of them went farther west into MISSOURI, KANSAS, Okla-homa, and Texas. They usually spoke the southern version of the Midland dialect. Scholars disagree on whether South Midland and North Midland should be considered subdialects of Midland or, respectively, sub-dialects of the South and the North. Al-though South Midland retained some of the grammatical features that distinguish Mid-land from Northern, it also acquired many pronunciations and vocabulary features common with Southern. South Midlanders frequently pronounce *out* and *around* with a diphthong that begins with the short *a* of *cat* rather than the lower vowel of *pot*. An older feature of South Midland was the diphthong in words rhyming with *due* and *you;* some writers have tried to depict this pronuncia-tion by using the spelling *dew* or *yew.* South Midlanders may also pronounce *pin* and *pen* alike. A recent change in the Southern dialect has also affected some South Mid-landers: to a Northerner, the pronuncia-tion of *lake* might sound like *like.*

A second branch of the Midland dialect is variously called North Midland or West Midland. Its pronunciation has more in common with the North than with the South, except for the *dawn/Don* contrast, *greazy, warsh,* and the strong /r/ in *thirty.* The grammatical differences listed previously may be more frequent than they are in South Midland. North or West Midland di-alects moved west through central Ohio into Indiana and Illinois and across the Missis-sippi into parts of IOWA, NEBRASKA, NORTH DA-KOTA, and SOUTH DAKOTA.

In the past, Northern, North Midland, and South Midland dialects were also dis-tinguished by vocabulary. One vocabulary difference survives in place names appear-ing on maps. A small stream is generally called a *creek* or *brook* in New England, a *run* in the North Midland, or a *branch* in the South Midland or South; these names ap-pear on detailed maps of the Midwest as well.

Still other vocabulary differences involve food. What is termed *lunch* in the North may be *dinner* in the Midland or South; to some northerners *dinner* is an evening meal, which in the South and South Midland may be *supper.* In the South and South Midland a small amount of food between meals was a *snack* (which eventually became more general), but it was a *piece* in the West Mid-land. Before *cottage cheese* became a mass-market item, it was *Dutch cheese* in the North, *smearcase* in the North Midland, and *clabber cheese* in the South Midland. Finally, the South and South Midland have a *pulley bone—* elsewhere called a *wishbone—*in a chicken or turkey.

Wildlife offered another source of re-gional vocabulary. A *dragonfly,* probably orig-inally Northern, was a *devil's darning needle* or just *darning needle* in New England and parts of the Midwest. In the South it was a *mosquito hawk,* but in the West Midland it was a *snake feeder,* which competed with *snake doctor* in eastern Pennsylvania and the South.

The parts of a house often reflect regional vocabulary. The devices that catch rain run-ning off a roof are *eaves* or *eave troughs* in the North, but *spouting* in the North Midland. In the South and South Midland these are *gutters.* Most regions have no specific word for a bed made up on the floor, but in the South and South Midland this is a *pallet.*

Settlement history led to a Midwest that exhibits a very diverse dialect map. The ar-eas around the Great Lakes were largely In-land Northern, while the Ohio River valley was a mixture of North and South Mid-land, with a strong influence from western Pennsylvania extending west into Ohio, In-diana, and Illinois. Both North and South Midland dialects reached into Missouri and Kansas, while less distinctive Midland dia-lects also reached into Nebraska and the Dakotas. MINNESOTA received some Inland Northern settlements and dialect. But other factors led to an even greater complexity than has been described so far. For example, Canadian settlement affected the speech of the northern parts of MICHIGAN and WISCONSIN, especially the pronunciation of words such as *out* and *project*. A greater source of difference was possibly attitudes toward and the effects of formal education. Although the Northwest Ordinance made provision for public schools throughout the Northwest Territory, the response was not the same throughout the region. In the more southern parts of the Midwest, formal education appears to have had less impact than it did farther north. In Illinois by 1860, for example, fewer public high schools existed in the southern part of the state than in the northern part. And in those areas where settlers came from Europe and learned English in the New England–dominated school system, nonstandard English was less likely to prevail. This was true for those parts of Missouri heavily settled by Germans, as well as in northern states like Minnesota and Wisconsin where Germans and Scandinavians were concentrated.

Differences in the influence of formal education are most apparent in the distribution of nonstandard verb forms like *seen* for *saw, was* for *were, come* for *came, done* for *did*, and *wear* for *worn*. According to Virginia McDavid's 1956 University of Minnesota dissertation "Verb Forms of the North Central States and Upper Midwest," these nonstandard forms were much more common in the lower Midwest—again, the southern parts of Ohio, Indiana, and Illinois, along with Missouri—than farther north. In other words, one would be much more likely to hear "we was there" or "he come over yesterday" in central Illinois than in Minnesota. Although these nonstandard forms have no regional identification in the eastern United States, they have become parts of differing dialects in the Midwest.

Education played a greater role in the more recently settled parts of the northern Midwest, especially Minnesota and the Dakotas. In these areas schools were quickly established, and the large numbers of European immigrants were more likely to learn "school English." But the presence of large numbers of Scandinavians—and their language—also made a difference. Minne-

sota pronunciation is clearly close to Inland Northern, but one may also observe features like a briefer, more rounded version of the vowel in *house* and *out*. Many grammatical features can be identified with word-for-word translations from Swedish, Norwegian, German, or Finnish. Among these are *Do you want to go with?* ("Do you want to go with me?"), *Do you want go Hibbing* ("Do you want to go to Hibbing?") or *I didn't go prom* ("I didn't go to the prom").

This discussion has largely focused on the regionalism that divides the Midwest geographically. Urban areas of the Midwest are more complex. African Americans, who began to settle in Great Lakes cities in the early twentieth century, often use a dialect marked by grammatical differences. Omission of forms of *to be*, as in "he going," are well known, as is the use of uninflected *be* to indicate habitual action, as in "he always be over at my house." Pronunciation of African American English originally had much in common with the Southern dialect, but many Southern features have disappeared as speakers have taken up permanent residence in northern cities.

Besides African American dialects, other forms of English have begun to distinguish Midwestern cites from the surrounding countryside. Vowel pronunciation in Great Lakes cities has shifted for some speakers; for example, the pronunciation of *socks* in Chicago may sound more like *sacks* to someone from Minnesota. Chicago is also noted for the substitution of the sounds /d/ and /t/ for /th/, as in *da* for *the* and *tink* for *think* ("I tink da Bears will win").

SELECTED WORKS: Two linguistic atlas projects surveyed the dialects of the Midwest during the early and mid-twentieth century. "The Linguistic Atlas of the North Central States," covering Ohio, Indiana, Michigan, Indiana, Illinois, and Kentucky, was never published, but much of the research on Midwest dialects has used the project's records. Besides Virginia McDavid's dissertation, a good early overview is Raven I. McDavid and Virginia McDavid's "Grammatical Differences in the North Central States," *American Speech* 35.1 (February 1960): 5–19. Harold Allen edited the three-volume *Linguistic Atlas of the Upper Midwest* (1973–1976), which covered Minnesota, IOWA, the Dakotas, and Nebraska. A good collection of articles on the Midwest in general, as well as on Minnesota, Michigan, Wisconsin, Kansas, Missouri, and northern Illinois, appeared in a special issue of *Kansas Quarterly* 22.4 (Fall 1990). *"Heartland" English* (1993), edited by Timothy C. Frazer, is a book-length collection of essays on the Midwestern dialects.

FURTHER READING: A major six-volume treatment of dialects in the United States is the *Dictionary of American Regional English* (1985–2013), edited by Frederic G. Cassidy Joan Hall, and Luanne Von Schneidemesser. A landmark study of pronunciation in the United States and Canada is William Labov's *Atlas of North American English* (2006). An outstanding treatment of regional vocabulary, with regional maps for all parts of the United States, is Craig M. Carver's *American Regional Dialects* (1987).

TIMOTHY C. FRAZER   WESTERN ILLINOIS UNIVERSITY

DIME NOVELS

OVERVIEW: The dime novel has become a collective, and frequently pejorative, term for any nineteenth-century American fiction of dubious literary value, printed on cheap paper, bound in paper covers, selling for five or ten cents, and available at newsstands or by subscription. Like many other media designed for popular mass consumption, the dime novel was dismissed and vilified in many circles of the time as a corrupter of youth and for encouraging immorality in its readers. Nonetheless, its influence on literature and language has been significant in a number of ways, including providing reading matter to a wide population, establishing formulaic writing, and standardizing a spectrum of stereotypical characters.

HISTORY AND SIGNIFICANCE: Although its era of greatest popularity was from about 1860 to the end of that century, the dime novel had its beginnings as early as the 1840s. There was a parallel development in Great Britain, the products of which were known as "yellow-backs" and "penny dreadfuls." The two major factors contributing to the enormous success of the dime novel were the increasing number of literate people and the development of efficient high-speed printing presses capable of turning out vast numbers of these booklets to meet the public demand. The dime novel can be considered the antecedent of pulp fiction, as exemplified in the monthly detective and science-fiction magazines, as well as the comic book and the later mass-market paperback. See also COMIC STRIPS AND BOOKS, MYSTERY AND DETECTIVE FICTION, and SCIENCE FICTION AND FANTASY.

Most writers of dime novels, many of whom had newspaper backgrounds, were merely creating formulaic fiction designed to fit a prescribed number of pages. A few did go on to greater literary endeavors and renown, such as Louisa May Alcott (1832–1888), who anonymously and pseudonymously contributed more than thirty thrillers to the genre, and UPTON (BEALL) SINCLAIR (JR.) (1878–1968), who began his long writing career with similar efforts. The subjects of many of these novels were lurid and exciting narratives of frontier life, Indian fighters and scouts, naval and pirate adventures, and tales of the Revolutionary War, the War of 1812, and the Civil War, but some authors drew many of them from personal experience.

The best-known publisher of the dime novel was the New York firm Beadle and Adams (1860–1897), but there were many other proponents of the genre, including George P. Munro, Frank Starr and Company, and Street and Smith, also of New York, as well as the Boston publishers Elliott, Thomes and Talbot and Richmond and Company. Dime-novel publishers issued their books in a number of distinct series; for example, Beadle and Adams had a myriad of them under such titles as Beadles's Dime Novels, Beadle's Pocket Novels, Beadle's Boy's Library, Beadle's Popular Library, and others.

A number of authors with Midwestern backgrounds were active in the dime-novel industry. Some of the more prolific include Joseph E. Badger Jr. (1848–1909), who was born in ILLINOIS and lived in MISSOURI and KANSAS; Oliver "Oll" Coomes (1845–1921), who resided in IOWA; Thomas C. Harbaugh (1849–1924), who lived in OHIO; Charles Bertrand Lewis (1842–1924), who wrote under the pen name M. Quad and was a DETROIT newspaperman; James M. Merrill (1847–1936), who was born and lived in MICHIGAN; Metta V. Fuller Victor (1831–1885), who spent her early years in Ohio and Michigan;

John H. Whitson (1854–1936), who was born in INDIANA and later lived in Kansas; and Edward Willett (1830–1889), who was a staff writer for CHICAGO and ST. LOUIS newspapers.

SELECTED WORKS: Midwestern locales particularly favored by writers are Ohio, Missouri, and Chicago, but all twelve Midwestern states are represented in the dime-novel literature; two examples from each follow.

Illinois: James L. Bowen's (1842–1919) *The Frontier Scout; or, The Young Ranger's Life Mystery* (1865) deals with the Black Hawk War. *The On-the-Wing Detectives; or, Bolly Blair's Grand Exposition: A Romance of Chicago and the Depworth Millions* (1891) by Leon Lewis (1833–1920) is set in that city.

Indiana: Part of Joseph E. Badger's *The Mad Ranger; or, The Hunters of the Wabash: A Tale of Tecumseh's Time* (1871) features the Battle of Tippecanoe. *Tiger-Heart the Tracker; or, The Trapper of the Twin Cascades* (1874) by Thomas C. Harbaugh (1849–1924), writing as Charles Howard, has among its cast of characters William Henry Harrison and Tecumseh.

Iowa: *Rollo, the Boy Ranger; or, The Heiress of the Golden Horn* (1871) by Oliver "Oll" Coomes is set among pioneers on the Little Sioux River. Arthur F. Holt's *Little Lightfoot, the Pilot of the Woods; or, The Crooked Trail: A Story of the Northwest Woods* (1885) concerns wagon trains in the western part of the state.

Kansas: Outlaws and frontier justice are the subjects of Joseph E. Badger's *Black John, the Road-Agent; or, The Prairie Sink: A Tale of Early Kansas Life* (1873). The legendary Wild Bill Hickok is the hero of *Wild Bill, the Pistol Dead Shot; or, Dagger Don's Double* (1882) by Prentiss Ingraham (1843–1904).

Michigan: Life on the 1840s frontier is the background of Metta V. Victor's *Alice Wilde, the Raftsman's Daughter* (1860). *The Young Bear Hunters* (1882) by James M. Merrill, writing under the pseudonym Morris Redwing, takes place in the northwestern part of the state.

Minnesota: The 1862 Sioux uprising is the subject of *Indian Jim: A Tale of the Minnesota Massacre* (1864) by Edward S. Ellis (1840–1916). *The Squaw Guide; or, The Red River Rifles: A Tale of the North Frontier* (1872) by

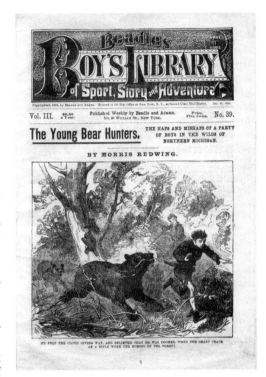

The Young Bear Hunters. Beadle and Adams, 1885.
Image courtesy of Special Collections, Grand Valley State University Libraries

Paul Bibbs concerns trapper life among the Indians.

Missouri: *Red Claw, the One-Eyed Trapper; or, The Maid of the Cliff* (1869) by a Captain Comstock is set in the Ozarks. In Joseph E. Badger's *The Outlaw Ranger; or, The Old Hunter's Last Trail: A Romance of the Missouri Settlements* (1872) a gang of outlaws terrorizes the northwestern part of the state.

Nebraska: Settlers battle Nebraska Territory land speculators in *The Land Claim: A Tale of the Upper Missouri* (1862) by Frances F. Barritt (1826–1902). *Wild Vulcan, the Lone Range-Rider; or, The Rustlers of the Bad Lands: A Romance of Northwest Nebraska* (1890) by William G. Patten (1866–1945) concerns cattlemen along the Niobrara River.

North Dakota: Henry M. Avery (b. 1840), writing as Major Max Martine, set his *Sharp-Eye, the White Chief of the Sioux: A Romance of the Far West* (1873) along the Missouri River. *Buckhorn Bill; or, The Red Rifle Team: A Tale of the Dakota Moonshiners* (1878)

by Edward L. Wheeler (ca. 1854–1885) deals with illicit liquor and a secret code.

Ohio: *The Riflemen of the Miami: A Tale of Southern Ohio* (1862) by Edward S. Ellis shows the interaction between rangers and the Shawnees in the 1790s, as does Edward Willett's *The Scioto Scouts; or, The Shawnees' Decoy* (1870).

South Dakota: Bigamy in a frontier town drives the plot of Thomas C(halmers) Harbaugh (1849–1924), writing as Captain Howard Holmes, in *Broadcloth Burt, the Denver Dandy; or, The Thirty Pards of Deadwood* (1884). *Border Bullet, the Prairie Sharpshooter; or, Yank Yellowbird's Black Hills Colony* (1888) by William H(enry) Manning (1852–1929) concerns army deserters among the Sioux.

Wisconsin: The Sioux uprising of 1862 spills into WISCONSIN in Lieut.-Col. Hazeltine's *The Silver Bugle; or, The Indian Maiden of St. Croix* (1864). *Nightingale Nat; or, The Forest Captains* (1878) by Thomas C. Harbaugh is set along the Lake Superior shore.

FURTHER READING: The first critical survey and history of the dime-novel phenomenon is Edmund Pearson's *Dime Novels; or, Following an Old Trail in Popular Literature* (1929). It provides a useful introduction to the genre, while *Pioneers, Passionate Ladies, and Private Eyes: Dime Novels, Series Books, and Paperbacks* (1996), edited by Larry Sullivan and Lydia Cushman Schurman, covers a wider field. The most important study of a particular dime-novel publisher is Albert Johannsen's *The House of Beadle and Adams and Its Dime and Nickel Novels: The Story of a Vanished Literature* (2 volumes, 1950; Supplement, 1962), which contains not only a detailed history of the firm but also a comprehensive bibliography of its books and biographies of its contributing authors. An encyclopedic approach to the genre is taken in *The Dime Novel Companion: A Source Book* (2000) by J. Randolph Cox. It features more than a thousand entries on dime-novel authors, titles, publishers, characters, and subjects.

ROBERT BEASECKER   GRAND VALLEY STATE UNIVERSITY

DOLLMAKER, THE

HISTORY: In her Kentucky trilogy *The Mountain Path* (1936), *Hunter's Horn* (1949), and *The Dollmaker* (1954), HARRIETTE SIMPSON ARNOW (1908–1986) captured the southeastern Kentucky Appalachian hill community whose existence was threatened by encroaching early twentieth-century social and economic changes. *The Dollmaker* chronicles the trials and tribulations endured by the Nevels family after migrating from the Kentucky hills to industrialized DETROIT during World War II, where it becomes a dislocated family struggling to adjust to the harsh realities of an alien culture in the North.

Arnow began to apply herself earnestly to her writing at age twenty-six after her 1934 move to CINCINNATI, OHIO. There she finished her first novel, which she had begun in Petoskey, MICHIGAN, and wrote some of her best short stories, those dealing with strong, self-reliant hill women as well as urban people downtrodden by the Great Depression. Arnow later revived and developed many of these characters and themes in her novels; for instance, a prototype of Gertie appears in the short story "Ketchup-Making Saturday," which was written in the 1930s but published posthumously in *The Collected Short Stories of Harriette Simpson Arnow* (2005).

In 1945, when Arnow's husband, Harold, found a job with the *Detroit Times*, the family moved to a Detroit wartime housing project similar to the one described in *The Dollmaker*. The migrants she met in the alley had a great impact on her imagination. Arnow admitted in several interviews that she kept wondering how a dislocated hill woman like Gertie would adjust to an industrialized environment. In Detroit she finished *Hunter's Horn* and began writing *The Dollmaker*. In 1950 the Arnows bought forty acres with a partially finished house near Ann Arbor. There she completed the book that would make her famous.

When she sent the manuscript to her editor at Macmillan Publishing Company in New York, "Much to my amazement a contract came in short order," she said in her last interview with John Flynn, "A Journey with Harriette Simpson Arnow," *Michigan Quarterly Review* 29.2 (Spring 1990): 258. In 1985 Flynn drove Arnow from Ann Arbor to her lecture at Morehead State University in eastern Kentucky. Along the way he experienced Arnow at her most natural and unguarded, smoking Lucky Strikes and confiding her need for her favorite liquor, Old Grand-Dad. Arnow recounted the extraordinary confrontation she had with a Macmillan editor who, as Arnow described it, wanted to increase "reader appeal" (258) and spent three days rewriting

almost everything Gertie had said or thought. She would say, "The sky looks like we'll soon have rain." . . . The rewriting had her say, "The sky appears cloudy; so perhaps it will rain." Perhaps was a word seldom heard in the back hills; they might say "perchance," or "I think," or "maybe," but not "perhaps." . . . I at last went to bed but could only think to myself, "To thine own self be true." The next morning I subtracted that young editor's advice and added, "And to your characters be true." (258–59)

Arnow threatened to sue to remove the revisions; her publisher acquiesced.

Convinced that ordinary advertising flyers would not properly convey the novel's extraordinary power, Macmillan took the unusual step of promoting the book before publication. Macmillan sent to critics and booksellers a thirty-two-page booklet containing the first chapter of *The Dollmaker* and excerpts of Arnow's notes on her writing process.

After publication on April 20, 1954, *The Dollmaker* became a critically acclaimed best seller and remained on the best-seller list for thirty-one weeks. In her review, "The Transplanted Folk," in the *New York Times Book Review* for April 25, 1954, Harnett T. Kane praised the book for its "rare gift of realism" (4). The novel also garnered numerous literary awards: it tied for best novel of the year in the *Saturday Review* national critics' poll; it was runner-up to *A Fable* (1954) by William (Cuthbert) Faulkner (b. Falkner) (1897–1962) for the National Book Award in 1955; and it also won Arnow the title "Kentucky Woman of the Year" for 1954 and the Friends of American Writers Award in 1955.

SIGNIFICANCE: *The Dollmaker* is Arnow's most artistically and thematically mature work, as well as a work of great cultural and historical import. It explores the tension between agrarian values and urban realities

during World War II. It also features Arnow's first female character asserting a creative spirit despite stifling and restrictive environments. Arnow's interview with Flynn makes clear what she sought to achieve in her writing: "To your characters be true" and "a style not exactly bleak, but not wordy, a narrative with no adverbs and few adjectives, a style of self" (259, 257). Arnow was at one time an aspiring poet, and her prose often sings like well-modulated musical phrases. Recognized by JOYCE CAROL OATES (b. 1938) in her afterword to the 1972 Avon edition of *The Dollmaker* as "our most unpretentious American masterpiece" (601), the novel established Arnow as a major American author.

The Dollmaker portrays the life of Appalachian woman Gertie Nevels from late autumn 1944 to late autumn 1945. She is a kindred soul to the mountain women portrayed by Sidney Saylor Farr in "Appalachian Women in Literature" in *Appalachian Heritage* 9.3 (Summer 1981): they love the land but love their husbands and children more, and their hardships under "geographic and social restrictions" have enabled them to retain "the self-reliant strength" of early pioneer women (11). Arnow repeatedly said that Gertie was not her favorite character because she was secretive, inarticulate, and difficult to work with. Once she grasped Arnow's imagination, however, Gertie would not leave the author alone, waking her up and demanding to be heard.

The novel opens by introducing big-boned but unassuming Gertie and her four interrelated passions: her family, a piece of land of her own, the Bible, and whittling, especially a block of cherry wood. By the end of the first chapter, with readers in awe at Gertie's heroic efforts to save her child by performing a roadside tracheotomy with her whittling knife, Arnow reminds readers of Gertie's fragile psyche. Despite her Amazonian appearance, Gertie turns timid and vulnerable when she reaches the doctor's office. This episode presages her difficulty in fending off later challenges. This self-contained first chapter is so well crafted that Robert Penn Warren (1905–1989) included it with a new title, "A Problem in Logistics," in the anthology *A New Southern Harvest* (1957).

Gertie grapples with what William Faulkner in his 1950 Nobel Prize acceptance speech had identified as "the problems of the human heart in conflict with itself." She faces debilitating conflicts whenever her instincts and inner reality clash with external forces. In Kentucky, Gertie is a self-reliant Appalachian woman completely in tune with nature, prompting Wilton Eckley in *Harriette Arnow* (1974) to call her "a kind of unconscious Transcendentalist" (94). In *The Dollmaker* Arnow describes her as physically strong and taller than her six-foot-four father, willing "to be th man in the settlement" (89). But when her hypochondriac mother moans that Gertie is about to sin by neglecting her wifely duty, she acquiesces meekly. After all, Gertie is a hill woman who is supposed to love the land but love her family more. Yet her self-reproach for not standing up to her mother for her own piece of heaven on earth is unforgiving. Arnow depicts Gertie's regrets: "She was a coward, worse than any of the others" (130). This is the first clear sign of her "heart in conflict with itself."

In Detroit, Gertie's heart is severely tested by mounting conflicts. Her hill values and personal passions seem delusional when they are set against urban realities: the crowded wartime housing project, economic hardships, and social and political persecution by bigots in the alley. Amid this chaos Arnow dramatizes the devastating impact of the mass migration of the 1950s, especially on the women who followed their husbands. As a result of World War II, the southern exodus to Midwestern industrial cities peaked while Arnow was writing *The Dollmaker*. Critics noted that grim, industrial Detroit seems like hell compared with Kentucky's pastoral hills. With her beloved piece of land forever out of reach, Gertie is no longer self-reliant; in her homesickness she often reminisces about a life of Thoreau-like simplicity in Kentucky "in her woolgathering ways" (290). Farr discusses Gertie as a dislocated Appalachian person for whom even a periodic homecoming is a necessary survival ritual (17).

Gertie fails to hold her family together. She is disheartened after losing Clytie and Enoch to the alley. She counsels Reuben and Cassie Marie to adjust to Detroit despite her misgivings, and she fails them both. In sorrow, Gertie seeks answers in the Bible; in grief, she turns to the block of cherry wood.

In Kentucky whittling was a luxury set against the demands of household chores; in Detroit, especially when tragedy hits, it becomes a necessity. Upon returning home from Cassie's funeral, she asks, "Th wood—where is th block a wood?" (378). The block provides nonverbal Gertie with a visual means of expressing herself, as well as of discovering her spiritual reality. The slowly emerging figure is "Judas after all" (536), Gertie admits, who "betrayed innocent blood" (328) as she has done with her children. She decides to chop up the unfinished but evocatively beautiful head to make figurines for a church bazaar.

Most critics see the ending positively: Gertie is heroic in coping with her overwhelming adversaries. She makes a painful but courageous journey, gaining insight into common humanity from her interaction with women in the alley; her sacrificing the cherished block of wood at the end signals her admirable attempt to adjust. The ABC-TV movie that first aired on May 13, 1984, provided an overtly promising end with Gertie returning to Kentucky.

Critical responses to Gertie have evolved over the years, reflecting women's improving social status. The emphasis on feminist research has shifted as well from women's "subjection" to their "subjectivity," as noted by Gisela Bock in her essay "Challenging Dichotomies in Women's History," originally published in 1991 and reprinted in *Major Problems in American Women's History* (2003), edited by Mary Beth Norton and Ruth M. Alexander (8). Initially, critics focused on Gertie's subjection, viewing her as a victim of her environments and attributing her travails to societal gender expectations. Criticism in the 1970s highlighted the harsh, oppressive realities Gertie faced in Kentucky and Detroit and treated the novel as a work of naturalistic determinism and proletarian social realism. At most, Arnow was a social realist, a self-proclaimed realist with a keen social conscience, but she did not find proletarian literature appealing. In "Starting Out in the Thirties, Harriette Arnow's

A page from the typescript of Harriette Simpson Arnow's
The Dollmaker.

© Thomas Arnow. University of Kentucky Special Collections Research Center

Literary Genesis," in *Literature at the Barricades: The American Writer in the 1930s* (1982), edited by Ralph F. Bogardus and Fred Hobson, Glenda Hobbs quotes Arnow: "Most [proletarian literature] seemed unable to create realistic characters" (149).

In the 1980s, when critics shifted their attention to Gertie's subjectivity and focused on her role in shaping her life, some feminists adored Gertie as a heroic woman; others were critical of Gertie's passivity and self-betrayal. Feminist readings have attempted to reconcile these seemingly contradictory critical strands. Elsa Dixler declared *The Dollmaker* required reading for feminists in her essay "Wanna Be a Feminist Intellectual?," *Ms.* (October 1983): 82–83. Arnow herself suggested that Gertie was trying to meet her family's basic needs, feeding them "a beef heart and some pork liver" (529). Arnow conceded, however, in her letter to Barbara H. Rigney, one of Gertie's harshest critics, in *Frontiers: A Journal of Women Studies* 1.2 (Spring 1976), that "it is the

reader who makes the novel . . . The doll has been and continues to be a different story for each reader" (147).

As an artist, Gertie decisively illustrates her subjectivity. Arnow said, "Gertie was no artist" (*Frontiers* 147); however, Gertie is the type of unconscious artist that Alice (Malsenior) Walker (b. 1944) writes about in *In Search of Our Mothers' Gardens: Womanist Prose* (1967) (232). An unconscious artist is unaware of her rich talent but must feed her creative spirit. Whether making a quilt or gardening, an unconscious artist, as Walker suggests, "is involved in work her soul must have, ordering the universe in the image of her personal conception of Beauty" (241). Gertie places little value on her carving, calling it "whittlen foolishness" (16). After Cassie's death, however, the block of wood becomes Gertie's primary means of maintaining sanity and survival. Clearly, Gertie could not have survived Cassie's loss without leaning on "the man in the wood" (476). Throughout the story Gertie never loses her creative spirit. In Kentucky, using wood as her material, she made hoe handles, door-knobs, and small dolls for her daughter Cassie. She continues in Detroit, spending extra time to carve additional details into a crucifix, compelled by her "personal percep-tion of Beauty," as Walker defines it. Gertie's anguished heart is in conflict with itself when she is about to bring the ax down on "the man," but being an unconscious art-ist makes it a bit easier to see him as "cherry wood" (548). Gertie will endure because her creative spirit will not remain stifled by cul-tural, religious, or sociopolitical restrictions. When she splits the block, she loses neither her creative spirit nor her soul.

In the introduction to the 1963 edition of *The Mountain Path*, Arnow explained why she changed the novel's title from *Dissolution* to *The Dollmaker*: "A combination of war and technology had destroyed a system of life, but people were not all destroyed to the point of 'dissolution.'" Her explanation is reprinted in Haeja K. Chung's 1995 volume *Harriette Simpson Arnow: Critical Essays on Her Work* (248). Arnow's statement harkens back to Faulkner's words: "The problems of the human heart in conflict with itself . . . alone can make good writing because only that is worth writing about." *The Dollmaker* is such a book; Arnow wrote about an Appalachian woman whose "heart is in conflict," but who does "endure and prevail" as Faulkner had asserted, because she has "a soul."

IMPORTANT EDITIONS: Macmillan Pub-lishing Company originally published the novel's hardcover edition in 1954 and re-printed the novel at least eleven times be-tween 1954 and 1976. The Collier Books edition (1961) and the HarperPerennial edi-tion (2003) were published by special ar-rangement with Macmillan. Avon issued the first paperback edition in 1972 with an afterword by Joyce Carol Oates. This edition was reprinted at least twenty-nine times and has been the most widely used edition. Even-tually, other paperback editions followed: Since June 2009 Scribner has printed the most recent trade paperback with renewed copyright permission from Marcella and Thomas Arnow, but this edition no longer carries Oates's afterword. The University Press of Kentucky printed a hardbound edi-tion in 1985 without Oates's article. Several

digital texts are available, including Scrib-ner's eBook, Google eBook, and Kindle eBook.

FURTHER READING: No book-length study of *The Dollmaker* exists, but many critical sources are accessible online. Twenty-five significant critical essays are available in full text from the Literary Resource Center by Gale Cengage in Detroit, a proprietary source. Most of these essays are also avail-able in *Contemporary Literary Criticism* 7 (1977) and 18 (1981) and in *Twentieth-Century Literary Criticism* 196 (2008).

The following sources and criticism are particularly relevant to study of *The Doll-maker*. Arnow's interviews offer invaluable insights into the novel. In addition to John Flynn's interview, "A Journey with Harri-ette Simpson Arnow," *Michigan Quarterly Review* 29.2 (Spring 1990): 258, two other no-table interviews are Dan Miller's "A *MELUS* Interview: Harriette Arnow," *MELUS* 9.2 (Summer 1982): 83–97, and Alex Kotlowitz's "The View from the End of the Road," *Detroit News*, December 4, 1983, 14–29. Haeja K. Chung's "Fictional Characters Come to Life: An Interview," in her *Harriette Simpson Arnow: Critical Essays on Her Work* (1995): 263–80, focuses primarily on *The Dollmaker*.

Renowned Appalachian culture scholar Cratis D. Williams pays great tribute to Ar-now for her exceptionally accurate analysis and description of the mountain woman. He acknowledges that Arnow is philosophically "a naturalistic determinist" in his pioneer-ing study "The Southern Mountaineer in Fact and Fiction," *Appalachian Journal* 3.4 (Summer 1976): 385–91.

Feminism is partially responsible for the resurgence of Arnow scholarship, and criti-cal views of Gertie continue to evolve. Bar-bara H. Rigney discusses Gertie as a tragic victim of Arnow's "grim and naturalistic world view" in "Feminine Heroism in Har-riette Arnow's *The Dollmaker*," *Frontiers* 1.1 (Fall 1975): 81–85. Upon receiving a copy of Rigney's essay, Arnow responded in the let-ter referenced previously. In "Free Will and Determinism in Harriette Arnow's *The Doll-maker*," *South Atlantic Review* 49.4 (November 1984): 91–106, Kathleen Walsh is critical of Gertie's habits of acquiescence that victimize her. In "Silence and Captivity in Babylon: Harriette Arnow's *The Dollmaker*," *Southern*

Studies 20.1 (Spring 1981): 84–90, Frances M. Malpezzi considers motherhood a hindrance to women's fulfillment, in that Gertie reluctantly sacrifices her art to meet her family's needs. Kristina K Groover discusses how Gertie's art is shaped by her commitment to her family and community in " 'Beholden to No Man': Artistry and Community in Harriette Arnow's *The Dollmaker*," *Kentucky Review* 13.3 (Winter 1997): 49–57. In " 'Carving Out a Life': *The Dollmaker* Revisited," *Appalachian Journal* 14.1 (Fall 1986): 46–50, William J. Schafer concurs, seeing that Gertie's victory is achieving "a sense of solidarity with her neighbors . . . through her art."

Michigan State University Press posthumously published additional work by Arnow that would further studies on *The Dollmaker*. Among these is *Between the Flowers* (1999), Arnow's second novel, whose publication was ultimately abandoned. It introduces Arnow's first female character who struggles with vague stirrings for freedom. *The Collected Short Stories of Harriette Simpson Arnow*, edited by Sandra L. Ballard and Haeja K. Chung (2005), provides insights into Arnow's writing process in developing the characters and thematic concerns that made possible the gripping narrative of *The Dollmaker*.

Special collections on Arnow exist at various university libraries. The most extensive archival materials and critical sources are available at the University of Kentucky Libraries in Lexington, Kentucky. On November 17, 2011, the university celebrated the opening of the Harriette Simpson Arnow papers, consisting of 145 boxes of correspondence with family, publishers, and editors; notebooks and manuscripts for her novels and social histories; photographs; and biographical materials. A digital finding aid is also available.

HAEJA K. CHUNG   MICHIGAN STATE UNIVERSITY

DRAMA

OVERVIEW: Midwestern drama arose in the nineteenth century and matured in the twentieth, establishing itself at center stage in terms of national theatre awards. The region has produced many Pulitzer Prize–winning plays, among them *Our Town* in 1938 by THORNTON WILDER (1897–1975), *Picnic* in 1953 by WILLIAM (MOTTER) INGE (1913–1973), *No Place to Be Somebody* in 1970 by Charles (Edward) Gordone (1925–1995), *Buried Child* in 1979 by SAM(UEL) SHEPARD (ROGERS III) (b. 1943), *Talley's Folly* in 1980 by LANFORD (EUGENE) WILSON (1937–2011), *Glengarry Glen Ross* in 1984 by DAVID MAMET (b. 1947), *Fences* in 1987 and *The Piano Lesson* (1990) by August Wilson (1945–2005), *August, Osage County* in 2008 by Tracy Letts (b. 1965), and *Clybourne Park* in 2011 by Bruce Norris (b. 1960). The Midwest has been particularly nurturing for female and African American playwrights. LORRAINE (VIVIAN) HANSBERRY (1930–1965) wrote the first African American play to be staged on Broadway. ZONA GALE (1874–1938) was the first woman to win a Pulitzer Prize for drama, and Gordone was the first African American to win this award.

Plays written by Midwesterners or set in the Midwest regularly share several features, and the most successful plays are the most likely to adopt these elements. They include (1) a focus on everyday rhythms—rising, eating, cleaning, sleeping—often universalized into a symbolic pattern; (2) grounding in the soil, with rootedness even in the town or city landscape that nurtures; (3) lack of pretension: honesty, straightforwardness, and understatement; (4) suppression of desire, often under communal pressure; intolerance for eccentricity; and (5) concentration on the home, usually as refuge and strength, neither transitory, as in the West, nor tormented by ancestral ghosts, as in the Northeast or South. An examination of major Midwestern plays reveals the ongoing vitality and prevalence of these elements.

HISTORY AND SIGNIFICANCE: *The Faith Healer* (1909) by WILLIAM VAUGHN MOODY (1869–1910) may be regarded as the first Midwestern dramatic masterpiece, although WILLIAM DEAN HOWELLS (1837–1920) and SAMUEL LANGHORNE CLEMENS (1835–1910), writing as Mark Twain, created noteworthy drama from the region decades earlier. Born in INDIANA and educated at Harvard, Moody wrote two great plays before his untimely death, both using geography to represent aspects of American character. *The Great Divide* (1906) is set in both an Arizona mining area and a Massachusetts sitting room, enacting a dialogue between East and West.

The Faith Healer is set in a "farm-house, near a small town in the Middle West" (Macmillan edition 3) and never leaves its rooted place. The entrance door "opens upon the side yard, showing bushes, trees, and farm buildings" (3). Although the weather improves from persistent fog to resplendent sunshine on Easter morning at the end, it seems to enwrap the play and its inhabitants, offering security, solace, and renewal.

The language and emotional longing are kept in check until the arrival of the Faith Healer, an otherworldly drifter from the West, who brings along an Indian boy, now called Lazarus, whom he had revived after three days. Biblical allusions permeate the play. Martha concerns herself with chores and running the household. Her sister Mary, incapacitated since the drowning of her brother five years before, and the emotionally wounded Rhoda respond immediately to the ministrations of the Faith Healer. Mary experiences compelling visions that annoy her down-to-earth husband, a devotee of Darwin and Spencer.

On one level, *The Faith Healer* enacts a contest between religion and science, belief and material evidence; on another, a clash between true religion and false. The Reverend Culpepper rejects the Faith Healer's brand of ministry as fakery and the multitude who surround the farmhouse as misguided idolaters. Mr. Beeler, on the other hand, rejects the Faith Healer as a modern-day Pan who seduces women and believers with "this hoodoo business" (58).

The Faith Healer experiences a crisis of faith while staying at the farmhouse and temporarily loses his healing powers. After decades of wandering in the West, he falls in love with Rhoda and sees "the vision of another life" in her (30). Initially, he shrinks from what he fears will be a contest between his divine calling and more earthly love. Eventually, he recognizes that Rhoda's pure, if wounded, heart is part of the "new-risen hope" (157), his confidence and healing powers return, and he enables Mary to walk after five years in her chair.

Mary, Rhoda, and the Faith Healer are renewed in this place, and religion has been restored to balance with science and pragmatism. *The Faith Healer* is a rich play moving from sickness, allied with guilt and loss, to renewal and health. The process takes place in a settled Midwestern home under biblical auspices undergirded by romance and realization of dreams. Common sense and pragmatism, embodied in domestic realism, do battle with idealistic or mystical longings, manifested in ritual, music, and religious experience.

Moody's neglected masterpieces feature strong female voices, and it seems no accident that the Midwest produced a surprising number of female playwrights throughout the twentieth century. Three early Pulitzer Prizes for Drama were awarded to plays by Midwestern female playwrights: *Miss Lulu Bett* in 1921 by Zona Gale, *Alison's House* in 1931 by SUSAN KEATING GLASPELL (1876–1948), and *The Old Maid* in 1935 by ZOË AKINS (1886–1958). ILLINOIS gave us Catherine (Gougher) Waugh McCulloch (1862–1945), Rachel Crothers (1878–1958), Mary Reynolds Aldis (1872–1949), and ALICE (ERYA) GERSTENBERG (1885–1972), while Gale, EDNA FERBER (1885–1968), Mary Katharine Reely (1881–1959), Calista Clark, and Marion Lucy Felton hailed from WISCONSIN, Glaspell from IOWA, and Akins from MISSOURI. Of these, Ferber and Glaspell were by far the most prominent, the former for her popular novels and Broadway hits with George S. Kaufman and the latter for her work with the Provincetown Players.

Glaspell was born in Davenport, Iowa, where her full-length plays *Inheritors* (1921) and *Alison's House* are set. Despite living for a brief time in Greece and extended periods in Provincetown, she never lost her ties to the Midwest. *TRIFLES* (1916), a one-act play, was based on an Iowa murder trial she covered as a Des Moines reporter. This jewel of a play is subtle and multilayered but direct and accessible; it is not surprising that *Trifles* appears in over sixty anthologies. The context is Midwestern, emphasizing family farming, canning, quilting, and membership in Ladies' Aid. At the same time, the atmosphere hovers at the edge of the West, embodied in the arrival of the sheriff and the county attorney investigating the recent death of John Wright, found mysteriously strangled in his own bed with no clear evidence of the murderer's identity.

Conflict unfolds on two levels. When the men enter, the dialogue remains investigative and male centered; the men dismiss the interests and concerns of the sheriff's wife and a neighboring farmwife, who seem deeply attuned to the social and emotional atmosphere of the home. Once the men leave, the women conduct their own investigation almost by accident as they examine Mrs. Wright's sewing, canning, and unbaked bread. They also speculate about the empty birdcage, only to discover the bird's corpse, carefully wrapped with its wrung neck, in her sewing box.

In the final conversation the women do not betray what they have discovered, and the men would not listen if they did. The play enacts a subtle and gendered meditation on law and justice. The men represent sanctioned legal authority, but the women consider two other "crimes" beyond the murder: (1) Mrs. Wright's pitiable decline from a bright, gay, artistically oriented young girl to a woman stunted and numb; and (2) the social indifference of neighbors to the downfall of what once had seemed a promising marriage. *Trifles* showcases female insights and delineates the shortcomings of patriarchal thinking. At the same time, the women do not challenge authority or assert their views, keeping instead that knowing silence so common in Midwestern discourse.

Another Midwestern Pulitzer Prize winner, Thornton Wilder, was born and raised in Madison, Wisconsin, and later taught in CHICAGO, but he lived in Shanghai and, during World War II, in North Africa and Italy and thus was among the most cosmopolitan of American writers. His plays and novels are set in a variety of locations and embody a sympathetic humanism that seems universal. Among the plays, only *Pullman Car Hiawatha* (1931) focuses in any detail on the Midwest, following the train from New York to Chicago and commenting especially on the people and landscape of OHIO.

Our Town (1938) ranks as one of the most frequently performed American plays. The setting is the fictitious Grover's Corners, New Hampshire, and Wilder dutifully comments on nearby mountains and topographic features. But the sensibility remains insistently Midwestern in all other respects. Wilder adopts the revolutionary theatrical techniques of Bertolt Brecht (1898–1956) to his

humanistic purposes, detaching the setting from any real place and creating instead a mythic "our town" purporting to represent typical American life of an earlier period. *Our Town* opens with metatheatrical character introductions by the narrating Stage Manager, along with background information about the town. Mild satire is made of the small town's xenophobia, social injustice to those in real need, and relative indifference to the arts. Action takes place in two imaginary homes, following the everyday preoccupations of the Gibbses and the Webbs, but is defamiliarized through the absence of scenery or props in a Brechtian foregrounding of *gestus*, the actors' physical expressions and attitudes. The language is emblematically quotidian.

The daily rhythms of act 1 lead into the ritual courtship and marriage of George and Emily in act 2 and a funeral procession in act 3. The most striking scene of the play occurs at the end as the dead Emily comes back to life in February 1899 and experiences the everyday rhythms both as she once did and as an otherworldly observer. This stroke of genius is not only metatheatrical and powerfully moving but also reinforces Wilder's humanism in surveying the species from within an individual character and at a generalized distance.

Our Town skillfully alludes to the most iconic Midwestern texts. MAIN STREET (1920) by (HARRY) SINCLAIR LEWIS (1885–1951) hovers like a specter, as does *WINESBURG, OHIO* (1919) by SHERWOOD ANDERSON (1876–1941). Simon Stimson, the choirmaster who never fits in, who drinks excessively, and of whom Dr. Gibbs says, "Some people ain't made for small-town life," seems straight out of Anderson's book (32). But the most overt allusion is to SPOON RIVER ANTHOLOGY (1915) by EDGAR LEE MASTERS (1868–1950). In act 2 the Stage Manager misquotes Masters: "It's like one of those Middle West poets said: You've got to love life to have life, and you've got to have life to love life. . . . It's what they call a vicious circle" (Coward-McCann edition 39). The actual line from "Lucinda Matlock" in the *Spoon River Anthology* is "It takes life to love life" (University of Illinois Press edition 295). However, Wilder has captured the spirit of the quotation, and the atmosphere of Masters's 1915 book pervades the third act of *Our Town*, in which the dead speak from their graves, discoursing on life in a way that incorporates many of the best features of Masters's poetic world.

Tennessee Williams (b. Thomas Lanier Williams, 1911–1983), a more restless traveler than Wilder, nonetheless spent twenty years in the Midwest, mainly in ST. LOUIS, where he acted with the Mummers there and won his first theatre awards with this company. He studied playwriting at the University of Missouri and later at the University of Iowa, graduating in 1938. Against the walls of apprentice years spent in St. Louis, the pearl of Tennessee Williams's art was formed and polished. By 1940 Williams was pursuing a theatrical career in New York; however, many of his plays written before 1938 are set either in St. Louis or in "a large mid-western American city" (*The Long Goodbye*, New Directions edition 203). One of his last plays, *A Lovely Sunday for Creve Coeur* (1978), is also set there. Williams returned frequently to the Gateway City and is buried there beside his mother.

Of Williams's dozen or so plays set in the Midwest, the most important is *The Glass Menagerie* (1945). The play encodes a struggle between romantic desires and memories associated with the southern past and the pragmatic imperatives of the Midwest. Even the physical details of the play—a no-nonsense Midwestern setting embellished with glass figurines and rose-colored lighting—reinforce this thematic conflict, while the central concerns of the plot involve finding a gentleman caller for Laura and, beyond that, sustaining the Wingfield family in a difficult economic environment. Amanda seems almost a caricature of the southern belle, but she is determined to survive and is not without "dignity and tragic beauty" (New Directions edition 96). She recreates her southern past in colorful language and wears a fantastic courting outfit from bygone days, whose glamour is vitiated by the more sordid details of her narrative. Her daughter, Laura, has been wounded by pleurisy and the challenges of life, but "Gentleman Caller" Jim O'Connor represents the Midwest at its pragmatic, self-confident best: he has goals and seems likely to succeed, at base "a nice, ordinary, young man" (xviii).

Narrator Tom Wingfield functions as a mediator between the outmoded, faded graciousness of the southern past and the insistent realism of the Midwestern present. But while his mother endeavors to work her way into St. Louis society, Tom longs to escape. He feels pushed to challenge his creativity, to pursue opportunity in a wider world. At the end of the play, he admits, "I left Saint Louis. . . . I was pursued by something" (96–97). Driven by Midwestern imperatives, Tom becomes Tennessee Williams in a moment when personal and public drama have merged into great art.

In what might be considered divine coincidence, the first interview Williams gave for *The Glass Menagerie*, during rehearsals, was with William Inge in St. Louis. This meeting functioned in retrospect as a passing of the torch to the dean of Midwestern playwrights, whose four hits—*Come Back, Little Sheba* (1950), *Picnic* (1953), *Bus Stop* (1955), and *The Dark at the Top of the Stairs* (1957)—dominated Broadway in the 1950s. Born and raised in southeastern KANSAS, Inge delineated Midwestern life at a time when the heartland had achieved a prominent place in the national consciousness. *Come Back, Little Sheba* radiates outward from domestic realism that symbolizes more fundamental psychic forces. The making of breakfast or cleaning house—for whom and with what prompting and intention—becomes a ritual enactment of deeper values and forces. *Sheba* also foregrounds neighbors and social pressures, situating the marriage of Doc and Lola in the crucible of "one of those semi-respectable neighborhoods in a Midwestern city" (Grove edition 5).

On one level, the central conflict in *Sheba* involves suppression and desire. At the outset the house is conspicuously dirty; Lola wears "a lumpy kimono" and looks disheveled (7). She has dreamed yet again of her missing Sheba, a cute white fluffy puppy. But Sheba has been gone for some time—vanished as so much else has in the life of this middle-aged couple—and Lola cannot cope with the loss. When Marie, the attractive boarder, brings home the athletic Turk, first to pose nearly naked for her drawing and later to make love upstairs, the held-together structures of the marriage begin to break apart.

Both Lola and Doc spend much of the play watching and witnessing the young couple. Sometimes the spectating is prompted by mere fascination, but often it borders on jealousy and Freudian displacement. The couple unleashes in Lola deep longings she has not faced in years, but that she nonetheless largely enjoys. Doc, on the other hand, recoils from this intrusive reminder of his transgressive past, when he was forced to marry Lola, the baby died, his dream of becoming a doctor collapsed, and he had to settle for being a chiropractor of limited means.

Doc's alcoholism, in fragile check at the outset, erupts in an astonishingly violent climax that shatters the quotidian rhythms that seemed so predictable earlier. Doc's repressed longings for Marie, combined with a visceral hatred of Turk, reignite his alcoholic destructiveness, and he attacks Lola with vicious words and finally with a hatchet. Two friends from Alcoholics Anonymous rescue the terrified Lola and take Doc off to the hospital.

As Marie departs blithely with her newly arrived fiancé, Lola struggles to hold the marriage together. Doc returns home, chastened, wanting to reconstruct his life with a new bird dog, while Lola finally admits that Sheba will never return. The disruptive spectacle of young lovemaking in their midst has purged the ghosts of their failures through a reenactment of the past before their eyes. The alchemy of this confrontation serves to transmute their life together into a new realm. The language and patterns of everyday Midwestern life confront and are transfigured by inscrutable forces.

Lorraine Hansberry's *A RAISIN IN THE SUN* (1959) brought an altogether new dimension to American theatre. Tragically, Hansberry died six years after the play debuted, but she launched a new wave of African American playwriting, much of it Midwestern, which continued in the work of Charles (Edward) Gordone, Adrienne (Lita Hawkins) Kennedy (b. 1931), Mari Evans (b. 1923), August Wilson, and many others. *Raisin* showcases Chicago in a high-profile way not seen since *The Front Page* (1928) by BEN HECHT (1894–1964) and CHARLES (GORDON) MACARTHUR (1895–1956). Grounded in realism, Hansberry's masterpiece transcends its material setting through considerations of race and the winds of change blowing from distant, exotic Africa.

The play opens on the South Side of Chicago, where "weariness has, in fact, won" (Signet Classic edition 11). Act 1 details the hard realities of everyday living, from cooking and ironing to sharing a bathroom with neighboring tenants. The adults all work at menial jobs in the service of others. The only hope for escape from stalled dreams is a life insurance check expected after the death of Big Walter. The anticipated windfall sets the various priorities of the family squarely against one another. Behind this domestic drama, however, lies a world where bombs explode and racial attacks on blacks make regular newspaper headlines. The Younger family is precariously positioned in a world of racial tensions and struggle for power, dignity, and equality of opportunity.

Raisin spins into more nonrealistic territory in act 2 as Beneatha, an aspiring medical student, dons the Nigerian outfit her Yoruba friend, Asagai, offers her. As Beneatha affects an imagined Africanism and performs a tribal welcoming dance, the lighting shifts, and Walter Lee Younger enters drunk and begins dancing on the table as a "warrior" addressing his "black brothers" (65–66). This imaginative scene grinds to a halt, however, with the arrival of George Murchison, Beneatha's assimilationist friend, who belongs to that category Walter derides as "these New Negroes" (93). The discussions of colonialism in Africa thus serve as both exotic counterpoint and grounding context for African American experience in urban postwar America.

The battles of Walter coming into his manhood, gender tensions in dating and marriage, and socioeconomic realities of raising children and maintaining a household unfold in a rich, multigenerational tapestry portraying the joys and defeats of a representative African American family. Obstacles include not only bigoted whites in the suburbs but also defeatist blacks like Mrs. Johnson, who rarely misses an opportunity to shoot down aspirations. At the end, the Younger family makes an adventurous leap into the unknown, moving to their new house in the suburbs. Mama takes along her "raggedy-looking old"

(101) house plant to a new life of hope and struggle, concluding this classic midcentury examination of racial politics and the American family.

The early plays of DAVID (ALAN) MAMET (b. 1947) are likewise set in Chicago but focus primarily on white male experience. AMERICAN BUFFALO (1975) established Mamet as a major new voice in American theatre with its incantatory, monosyllabic language and nebulous Pinteresque menace intimately connected to work and business. Don's Resale Shop, the setting of AMERICAN BUFFALO, serves as a home for three male characters who seem to have no other domicile. The shop frames and centers the lives of the men, who function as a biologically unrelated but emotionally dependent family. Teach claims, "I like you like a brother, Don" (Grove edition 45), and later emphatically says, "I am not your wife" (100). All the action takes place in the secondhand locus of their economic and emotional interdependency.

At the outset, Bobby apologizes for an unexplained trespass against Don, who endeavors to teach him about business and human nature. The dialogue is clipped, elliptical, and repetitive, achieving lyric power by means of syntactic distortions and omissions. Theirs is a male-centered, misogynistic underworld of shady deals, petty crime, and gangster-like compacts, with cops cruising ominously just outside. Interactions focus on economic transactions and a planned midnight raid on the nearby home of a customer who is apparently married to a beautiful woman, settled and comfortably well off.

Underneath the bravado and tough, often vulgar talk, however, friendships are maintained, power differentials are established, and psychic territories are defined. The dialogue in early scenes is extremely funny as Mamet exhibits his gift for mimicry and comic timing. But when Teach enters, the equilibrium between Don and Bobby is broken, and the stakes become more serious. Teach immediately begins attacking Bobby's qualifications and eventually assaults him so severely that they plan to take him to the hospital. He also taunts Don: "No wonder that you fuck this kid around." "You're a joke on this street, you

and him" (100–101). Don then attacks Teach, who in turn tears up the resale shop with a pig sticker. Both Bobby and Teach descend into self-loathing. At the end, Don and Bobby apologize to each other in a final exchange of intimacy.

A play that begins with bravado and abuse directed outward thus ends in wounding, recrimination, and, finally, forgiveness. The buffalo nickel Don sold before the play's onset weaves in and out, acquiring significance and ending up, mysteriously, in the hands of Bobby, seemingly the least experienced. Such mysteries are never resolved, and the language hovers between streetwise bluster and inchoate lyricism. The hyperrealism of *American Buffalo* becomes hypnotic and otherworldly, charting the sometimes violent terrain of men seeking dominance, companionship, and a kind of fundamental survival.

Three years after *American Buffalo* premiered in Chicago, Sam Shepard's *Buried Child* debuted in San Francisco. Born at Fort Sheridan, Illinois, Shepard spent his formative years in California and wrote many plays there before returning to the Midwest. In his Pulitzer Prize–winning play Shepard evokes his native region through the central contrast of the fecundity of the characters' land with their perverted relationships and guilty secrets. This contrast functions to comment ironically on the failure of the American Dream in the heartland.

Lanford Wilson's *5th of July*, which debuted, like *Buried Child*, in 1978, could not be more different in mood and style from Mamet's breakthrough play. Whereas *American Buffalo* is taut and menacing, with clipped, elliptical dialogue, *5th of July* is aleatory and laid back, with language that is ebullient and overflowing. The play forms the central part of Wilson's Talley trilogy, which also includes *Talley's Folly* (1979) and *Talley and Son* (1985). All are set in rural Missouri and showcase a slower, simpler lifestyle strongly connected to the land. *5th of July* is cheerfully Chekhovian, even down to a striking theatrical gloss on saving the house in *The Cherry Orchard* (1904). In this play the house is saved, while tragedy and comedy are finely intertwined in witty, off-the-wall dialogue and characters firmly rooted in the rural Midwest.

While *American Buffalo* and *Buried Child* focus on male experience with little attention to sex, *5th of July* revels in it. The central characters, Ken and Jed, are gay partners, current owners of the family estate. They kiss unselfconsciously early on and later embrace as Jed carries Ken, handicapped from wounds received during the Vietnam War, upstairs. John and Gwen, a hyperactive couple visiting from California, enjoy overheated sex upstairs. Comments about sex abound in this play, embodying the flower-child ethos of the post–Vietnam War era. Later, the audience learns that four of the characters lived together in a commune some years earlier in California, with consequences that are only now becoming manifest.

This play does not feature a traditional plot so much as clashes of ideas and values. The central conflict arises from the arrival of John and Gwen with their alien California mores. Whereas Ken and Jed take pleasure in daily rhythms and the slow unfolding of the garden, Gwen and John are stressed out and prescription dependent. Gwen, aged thirty-three, hyperventilates about her "crucifixion" year, seeking escape and regeneration. Weston, another Californian, comments dryly, "I've never seen so much air in my life" (Noonday edition 44). Many of the characters seek peace in growing, gardening, and the outdoors. Aunt Sally wants to bury the ashes of Uncle Matt, who died the year before, in the rose garden.

In *5th of July* the family is a constructed one, anchored by the central gay couple and including Ken's unmarried sister and child, as well as ex-lovers from the former commune. Most of the characters are wounded in some way. At the climax John pushes the defenseless Ken, who falls without his crutches and lies flat and motionless. We hear the moral on tape from Ken's brilliant, troubled student: "They knew it was up to them to become all the things they had imagined they would find" (127). In the enfolding serenity of the family property, the fertile Midwestern soil serves to ground and restore the human search for self-definition and fulfillment.

With *Ma Rainey's Black Bottom* (1984), set in Chicago, August Wilson began a ten-play cycle chronicling African American experience in the twentieth century. Following *Fences* (1985) and *Joe Turner's Come and Gone* (1986), *The Piano Lesson* (1990) presents a dynamic tension between past and present, its geographic pole radiating from rural South to industrial North. The setting is solidly Midwestern, a "sparsely furnished" (Dutton edition n.p.) living room and kitchen, but at the center sits an unforgettable piano with an intricately carved family history in Mississippi. The dialogue between the two regions is not only geographic but stylistic: Midwestern realism is haunted by the ghosts of racial oppression in the South.

Many elements in *The Piano Lesson* are lovingly detailed in realistic terms, from the cooking of breakfast to dressing for work and, perhaps most strikingly, Berniece's hot-curling of her daughter's hair in the final scene. In contrast to the rigged legal system and racial injustice in Mississippi, Pittsburgh offers freedom and opportunity: "They treat you better up here" (39). Berniece assures her brother's friend Lymon that he "shouldn't have too much trouble finding a job" (77). This situation stands in contrast to dismaying conditions in the South, where all the men in the play have served time in the penitentiary, largely on trumped-up charges.

The regional dichotomy is reflected in aesthetic dualities as well. Dreams play an important role; Berniece's suitor, Avery, offers an extended narrative of his vision calling him to the ministry, including sheep-headed people and his head on fire. But the really haunting visions involve Sutter's ghost when the light changes radically and chilling noises are heard. Near the end, Berniece's brother, Boy Willie, newly arrived and thoroughly dismissive of ghosts, must wrestle with the specter of the southern past.

The ghost is none other than Robert Sutter, who recently fell to his death in the backyard well. He is one of many whites who died in the same fashion, reputedly caused by the Ghosts of the Yellow Dog. After four blacks were deliberately burned in a boxcar, the fabled ghosts began their shadowy work. Their presence is embodied in the elaborately carved piano, created by Boy Charles, grandfather of the two siblings. Now the piano has become the focus of family conflict because Berniece wants to keep the piano to honor the family heritage, while Boy Willie wants to sell it so he can buy his own piece of land and escape being a servant to others.

The real battle emerges over the wisest way to live, preserving the past or pursuing one's own course. Berniece has become emotionally rigid since the death of her husband three years earlier in a racial shootout in Mississippi. She cannot yet accept Avery's offer of marriage and partnership. Boy Willie, at the other extreme, would sell the family legacy to enable a new start on his native land. Lymon and the siblings' Uncle Doaker are left to mediate between these extremes and find a constructive path into the future. *The Piano Lesson* enacts a rich exploration of African American heritage and choices, with colorful dialogue and haunting visitations of memory and history.

The success of these and other Midwestern plays derives from the region's characteristically direct, colloquial language. The heartland often seems appealing because of a straightforwardness that is neither exclusive nor condescending. With less focus on ancestry and tradition, Midwestern works can be more accessible than those from other regions. Their emphasis on everyday speech and rhythms speaks to the American mainstream with immediacy.

On a deeper level, the rootedness of the Midwest feeds on American nostalgia for a simpler life located somewhere in the mythic past. The myth includes comfortable daily ritual, reliable and meaningful hard work, and connectedness to the environment, whether rural or urban. In this construct, neighborliness is crucial to survival, and both people and life seem to matter. This is a sentimental notion, but so deep is the longing in the American psyche for this imaginary heartland that Midwestern drama resonates well.

Stylistically, the commonsense turn of Midwestern thinking and expression is embodied in domestic realism, mixed or in tension with fantasy, surrealism, or abstraction. This combination transfers easily to television and film, bridging the gap between American pragmatic materialism and a longing for spiritual or otherworldly experience. Midwestern plays seem tailor made

for the cinema in a way that those of Eugene O'Neill (1888–1953), for instance, do not. Inge's four major plays moved seamlessly from Broadway to Hollywood and became great hits in the 1950s, pulling the two coasts closer together. In the subsequent era of civil rights, feminism, and gay liberation, Midwestern plays gave voice to those concerns in a down-to-earth way that effectively integrated those ideals into a realistic context that permitted wider acceptance and dissemination.

The element of communal pressure restraining the individual in the Midwest may not resonate as well nationally in an era of rampant individualism. But for its other signature qualities, Midwestern drama remains central in American theatre, embodying many of the iconic preoccupations and conflicts in our national life. The very invisibility of Midwestern drama—the way playwrights like Howells, Twain, Glaspell, Wilder, and Mamet moved to New York, California, or beyond without notice or trespass—has been a hidden strength, permeating the culture and reflecting it to itself in a way that is neither surprising nor disconcerting. Midwestern drama is recognizable and comfortable, so deeply resonant with the national consciousness as to be accepted as simply American.

The plethora of musical plays and films that center on or take place in the Midwest reflects this tendency to conflate the region and the nation. Although it is set in Manhattan, *Wonderful Town* (1953) features Eileen and Ruth Sherwood, who sing a duet in which they wonder why they left Ohio. *Bye Bye, Birdie* (1960), set in the mythical Sweet Apple, Ohio, also plays off the contrast between the small-town Midwest and the Big Apple. The movie musicals *Meet Me in St. Louis* (1944) and *St. Louis Woman* (1946) evoke the urban Midwest, as does *Chicago*, which was staged on Broadway in 1975 and appeared in a film version in 2002. The classic *The Wizard of Oz* (1900) by L(YMAN) FRANK BAUM (1856–1919), which begins and ends in Kansas, inspired a 1903 Broadway musical, a 1939 movie musical, and a 1975 African American musical play, *The Wiz*, from which the 1978 film was adapted. Mark Twain's ADVENTURES OF HUCKLEBERRY FINN (London 1884: New York 1885) was brought to the

Broadway stage over one hundred years later as *Big River* (1988). Two Iowans, PHIL(IP) (DUFFIELD) STONG (1899–1957) and RICHARD PIKE BISSELL (1913–1977), wrote the books for *State Fair* (1945) and *The Pajama Game* (1954) respectively; Iowa is also the setting for *The Music Man* (1957; film, 1962), whose Mississippi River–town locale and Iowa-stubborn denizens invoke the boyhood of MEREDITH (ROBERT) WILLSON (1902–1984) in Mason City.

In 2008 Tracy Letts won the Pulitzer Prize for Drama with *August: Osage County*. Letts, originally from Tulsa, moved to Chicago at age twenty, where he worked with the Steppenwolf, Famous Door, and Bang Bang Spontaneous theatres. His *Man from Nebraska* was nominated for the Pulitzer Prize in 2004.

Bruce Norris won the Pulitzer Prize for Drama in 2011 with *Clybourne Park*. His drama extends the context and action of *A Raisin in the Sun* by Lorraine Hansberry, based on the Hansberry family's fight to purchase a home in a then-all-white Chicago South Side neighborhood. *Clybourne Park* uses that same house fifty years later in portraying continuing racial problems brought to the surface by the influx of whites associated with neighborhood gentrification. The work of Letts, Norris, and their contemporaries, David Auburn (b. 1970), Marcia Cebulska (b. 1944), Jeff Daniels (b. 1955), Steven Dietz (b. 1958), Diane Glancy (b. 1941), Tim Kaldahl (b. 1968), Kevin Kling (b. 1957), Shirley Lauro (b. 1933), Doug Marr (b. 1953), David Rush (b. 1940), Rick Shiomi (b. 1947), James Still (b. 1969), and David Wiltse (b. 1940), provides a good introduction to contemporary Midwestern drama.

SELECTED WORKS: *The Great Divide* and *The Faith Healer* can be found in volume 2 of *The Poems and Plays of William Vaughn Moody* (1969). *Trifles* is anthologized in *Plays by American Women, 1900–1930*, edited by Judith E. Barlow (1981), which also includes *Miss Lulu Bett*. Reely's *A Window to the South* (1919), Felton's *Goose Money* (1927), and Clark's *Dreams* (1929) are collected in *Wisconsin Rural Plays*, edited by Ethel Theodora Rockwell (1931). In 1911 the Illinois Equal Suffrage Association published McCulloch's *Bridget's Sisters; or, The Legal Status of Illinois Women in 1968*. Aldis's dramas can be found in her *Plays for Small Stages* (1922), while Ferber's collaborations with Kaufman—

Kristen Adele, Roya Shanks, and Daniel Morgan Shelley in the Geva Theatre Center's production of *Clybourne Park* by Bruce Norris, 2014.

© Huth Photography. Reprint courtesy of Ken A. Huth Photography

The Royal Family (1927), *Dinner at Eight* (1932), and *Stage Door* (1936)—have been published in the Library of America's *Kaufman and Co.* (2004). Gerstenberg's *Overtones* (1915) can be found in *American Plays of the New Woman,* edited by Keith Newlin (2000), which also includes Crothers's *A Man's World* (1909) and the winner of the first Pulitzer Prize for Drama, *Why Marry?* (1917) by Jesse Lynch Williams (1871–1929). *Pullman Car Hiawatha* was published in volume 1 of *The Collected Short Plays of Thornton Wilder* (1997); the Perennial paperback edition of *Our Town* (2003) includes an afterward by Wilder's nephew, Tappan Wilder, as well as Wilder's previously unpublished notes on the play and other documents. Grove Press published *William Inge: Four Plays* in 1958, which includes *Come Back, Little Sheba,* and a paperback edition of *American Buffalo* in 1977. In 1966 New Directions published a paperback edition of *The Glass Menagerie. Contemporary Black Drama from "A Raisin in the Sun" to "No Place to Be Somebody"* (1971), edited by Clinton F. Oliver and Stephanie Sills, includes Hansberry's and Gordone's masterpieces. In 1979 Hill and Wang published Lanford Wilson's *5th of July.* The Bantam paperback *Sam Shepard: Seven Plays* (1981) contains *Buried Child.* In 1990 Plume published a paperback edition of *The Piano Lesson.*

FURTHER READING: No book-length analysis of Midwestern drama has yet been published. *Midwestern Miscellany* 30 (Spring 2002) offers an overview of Midwestern drama, as well as essays on Gerstenberg, Gale, Reely, Clark, Felton, Inge, and Dietz. *American Playwrights, 1880–1945: A Research and Production Source Book,* edited by William W. DeMastes (1995), includes chapters on Akins, Crothers, Gale, Glaspell, Howells, Moody, and Wilder. *American Playwrights since 1945: A Guide to Scholarship, Criticism, and Performance,* edited by Philip C. Kolin (1988), offers chapters on Gordone, Hansberry, Inge, Mamet, Shepard, and Williams, as well as Lanford and August Wilson. C. W. E. Bigsby's three-volume work *Twentieth-Century American Drama* (1982, 1984, 1985) briefly discusses Glaspell and contains chapters on Wilder, Williams, Shepard, and Mamet, while his *Modern American Drama, 1945–1990* (1992) offers chapters on Williams, Mamet, and Shepard and a chapter on Broadway that discusses Inge, as well as the American musical theatre. His *Contemporary American Playwrights* (1999) contains a chapter on Lanford (Eugene) Wilson, as does William Herman's *Understanding Contemporary American Drama* (1987), which also offers chapters on Shepard and Mamet. An excellent source on individual playwrights is the Cambridge Companion series, which includes volumes on Mamet, Shepard, Williams, and August Wilson. *The Cambridge Companion to American Women Playwrights* (1991) contains essays on Crothers and Glaspell.

DAVID RADAVICH   EASTERN ILLINOIS UNIVERSITY

ENVIRONMENTAL LITERATURE

OVERVIEW: Environmental literature can be defined broadly as literature in which, according to ecocritic Lawrence Buell in his 1995 work *The Environmental Imagination,* human history is directly connected to natural history, human interests are not understood as the only legitimate interests, and human accountability to the environment is foregrounded in the text (13). The writings discussed in this entry either anticipate or enact these contemporary notions as they exemplify ways in which Midwestern landscapes have shaped the character, livelihoods, and attitudes of the region's people in both historical and contemporary times.

At the same time, the literature demonstrates the ways in which inhabitants of this area have shaped the landscape. A survey of Midwestern environmental literature provides testament to both the changes and the consistencies in thinking about the environment from frontier times to the present day. NATIVE AMERICAN LITERATURE texts, FRONTIER AND PIONEER ACCOUNTS, early arguments for wilderness preservation, pastoral fiction and poetry, and nonfiction—referred to as "nature writing"—indicate the diversity and changing complexion of Midwestern thoughts on the environment and their expression in literature.

Contemplation of nature has been and remains a significant trope for Midwestern writers, and the pastoral and frontier traditions popularized in the nineteenth and early twentieth centuries continue as significant Midwestern literary traits today. Although contemporary writers embrace these aspects of Midwestern heritage, they also draw on modern, more sophisticated historical and ecological understandings only intuited by their predecessors.

HISTORY AND SIGNIFICANCE: Frontier narratives and stories of life on the Midwestern frontier are the first literary endeavors that can be formally considered works concerned with the environment and its impact on Midwesterners. First appearing in the mid-nineteenth century as pioneers pushed into and settled in the untamed territories, these works of literature detail life in the Midwestern wilderness and the pioneers' struggles to survive and thrive in a foreign and unsettled land. Although the wilderness is often depicted as savage and unforgiving, there is also appreciation of its beauty and uniquely American qualities. The conversion of these wildlands into tamed environs capable of agriculture is a popular refrain in frontier fiction and nonfiction.

Although preservation of wilderness is not paramount in these texts, they establish groundwork for the nature-writing genre. As CAROLINE KIRKLAND (1801–1864), who wrote three novels about life on the MICHIGAN frontier, states in A NEW HOME—WHO'LL FOLLOW? (1839), the frontier landscape, though rough and difficult to thrive in, is nonetheless inspirational, and "the wild flowers of Michigan deserve a poet of their own" (20). Other accounts include those of ELIZA FARNHAM (1815–1864) and New England transcendentalist Margaret Fuller (1810–1850), who wrote Summer on the Lakes, in 1843 (1844), a reflection on her travels in the Great Lakes region. See GREAT LAKES LITERATURE.

Perhaps the most significant and famous Midwestern contributions to literature of the frontier come somewhat later from WILLA CATHER (1873–1947), who migrated to the NEBRASKA prairie as a child, and Carlinville, ILLINOIS, native MARY (HUNTER) AUSTIN (1868–1934). Cather is best known for her evocations of the wild prairie and its conversion into settled farmland. She perfected the narrative style established by her predecessors and fully realized the formative and sometimes debilitating influence of the landscape on settlers. As Cather observes in O PIONEERS! (1913), "this land was an enigma. It was like a horse that no one knows how to break to harness, that runs and kicks things to pieces" (18). The other key voice of the frontier and one of Cather's literary friends and correspondents was Mary Austin. Cather and Austin shared many values and understood the natural world in similar terms. Although much of Austin's fame rests on her depictions of the southwestern desert lands to which she migrated at the age of twenty, she reflects fondly on the Illinois landscape in her autobiography, Earth Horizon (1932).

While Americans were rapidly settling the Midwest, homesteading farther west, and confronting the challenges and beauty of the natural environment in both life and literature, Indian tribes living in the area were often displaced. When their earth-based ways of living and communal sensibilities were threatened, many took up the pen or narrated their stories to transcribers in order to defend their cultures, explain their ways of life, and record their histories for the public. Out of these narratives comes a keen insight into visions of the indigenous peoples about the environment and their connections to place. Their writings, which stress an interconnectedness and unity among people, spirit, and nature, anticipate ideals taken up in environmental movements a century later.

This early insight was made clear by one of the most prodigious and popular Native Americans writing about the frontier era, a Yankton Dakota Sioux from SOUTH DAKOTA, ZITKALA-ŠA (RED BIRD) (1876–1938). Her writings laid the groundwork for Native American intellectualism and activism and reveal nostalgia for a natural world uncorrupted by white settlement. Zitkala-Ša's American Indian Stories (1921) provides insight into the frontier from a Native American perspective and outlines early Sioux beliefs about nature in an easily accessible format.

Native American ideals are further supported in BLACK ELK SPEAKS (1932) by JOHN G(NEISENAU) NEIHARDT (1881–1973), in which the Oglala Sioux holy man BLACK ELK (1863–1950) explains his mystical calling. Other significant accounts of Midwestern Native American life and connections to nature can be found in the published works of Sauk warrior BLACK HAWK (Ma-ka-tai-me-she-kia-kiak, 1767–1838); Ottawa (Odawa)

ANDREW J. BLACKBIRD (Mack-a-te-be-nessy, 1814–1908); Ojibwa (also called Chippewa) WILLIAM W(HIPPLE) WARREN (1825–1853); and Teton Lakota (Sioux) LUTHER STANDING BEAR (1868–1939).

With the advent of the industrial age and the closing of the frontier, many Americans became nostalgic for the frontier period. In his famous article "The Significance of the Frontier in American History" (1893), Midwestern historian FREDERICK JACKSON TURNER (1861–1932) argues that the frontier was the primary force in shaping American character. Many Midwestern writers of the late nineteenth and early twentieth centuries echoed Turner's concerns. (HANNIBAL) HAMLIN GARLAND (1860–1940), JAMES OLIVER CURWOOD (1878–1927), and EDGAR LEE MASTERS (1868–1950) all emphasized conflict between "civilization" and "nature" and expressed primitivist longings for the rural lifestyle that was being rapidly altered toward the close of the nineteenth century. *SPOON RIVER ANTHOLOGY* (1915), Masters's classic collection of poetry, was a key text in what would later be termed the Midwestern literary REVOLT FROM THE VILLAGE.

Perhaps the most influential Midwestern voice in this genre was SHERWOOD ANDERSON (1876–1941), a native Ohioan who immortalized the rural small-town lifestyle of his youth in *WINESBURG, OHIO* (1919). Anderson's pursuit and love of the pastoral, defined by Leo Marx in *The Machine in the Garden: Technology and the Pastoral Ideal in America* (1964) as "an undefiled, green republic, a quiet land of forests, villages, and farms dedicated to the pursuit of happiness" (6), is reflected throughout his work. He sought spiritual truths in the Midwestern soil and expressed profound understanding of the natural processes that shape the Midwest. Seeing the rustic "middle state" between "civilization" and "wilderness" threatened by the invasion of the machine, Anderson records the historical interruption of the pastoral idyll and demonstrates how the extractive, materialistic forces of industry changed Midwestern people and landscape for the worse.

Anderson mentored ERNEST (MILLER) HEMINGWAY (1899–1961) early in his career and helped nurture Hemingway's well-documented love of and reliance on pastoral nature as a muse in his fiction. In stories such as "Big Two-Hearted River," set in northern Michigan, where the author learned as a boy to hunt and fish, Hemingway closely aligns wilderness recreation with masculinity and spiritual redemption, echoing the ideals of the "cult of the 'strenuous life'" popularized by figures such as Theodore Roosevelt. "Big Two-Hearted River" appeared in Hemingway's collection of stories *IN OUR TIME* (1925).

While Hemingway's pastoral narratives can be considered indirect arguments for preservation of wilderness, other twentieth-century Midwestern writers openly and directly took up the defense of the natural world. In fact, the Midwest can boast two of America's most prominent and influential preservationists and wilderness advocates, JOHN MUIR (1838–1914) and ALDO LEOPOLD (1887–1948). Muir, famous for starting the popular environmentalist organization the Sierra Club and for defending the forests and mountains of California in such environmental classics as *My First Summer in the Sierras* (1911), was influenced by transcendentalism and by his upbringing in frontier-era WISCONSIN. Muir, who believed that one could correspond directly with God through nature, attributed much of his sensibility to what he learned while growing up on his family's Wisconsin farm. Muir describes his early experiences in *The Story of My Boyhood and Youth* (1913).

John Muir went on to make his fame in areas farther west, but IOWA-born writer and naturalist Aldo Leopold remained closer to home, gaining posthumous fame and acclaim for his evocation of the Wisconsin landscape in the foundational text on ecology, *A SAND COUNTY ALMANAC* (1949). This work of literature, filled with personal narratives and ecological insights, is the first book that develops a defined "land ethic" that considers the earth and its creatures from a moral perspective, a fact that has earned Leopold the position of father of modern environmental ethics. As Buell observes in *The Environmental Imagination,* Leopold aimed to "create a symbiosis of art and polemic, such that environmental representation and lyricism exist for their own sakes, yet also, ex post facto, as a means to make the reader more receptive to environmental advocacy" (120).

John Muir, 1875.
Courtesy of the Wisconsin Historical Society

Since Leopold's time the nonfiction nature-writing genre has greatly expanded and has been enriched by myriad voices who have worked to preserve Midwestern flora and fauna and to maintain a semblance of our pastoral and frontier heritages. Midwestern nature writers have affected and continue to affect and reflect public perceptions of the environment. Their artistic efforts foster environmental consciousness and encourage the political and personal defense of endangered natural environments. As this entry has indicated, the pastoral impulse has driven both the loss, through development, of wild nature and its preservation. A survey of major nature writers demonstrates the trend toward more ecologically enlightened pastoralism.

FRANK LLOYD WRIGHT (1867–1959), celebrated American architect and Wisconsin native, was also a prolific writer. Midwestern landscapes not only influenced his architectural theories but also inspired him to express his love and understanding of nature in essays and books, such as *An Autobiography* (1943). LOUIS BROMFIELD (1896–1956), OHIO novelist and nonfiction writer, promoted Jeffersonian agrarian values and described his experiments in sustainable agriculture in books such as *Malabar Farm* (1948). Environmental activist SIGURD F(ERDINAND) OLSON (1899–1982), a primary defender, literary and political, of MINNESOTA's northern wilderness, published *The Singing Wilderness* (1956) and other books. Edwin Way Teale (1899–1980), one of the most popular nature writers of his generation, lived in the East but was born and raised in Joliet, Illinois, and spent summers at his grandparents' farm in INDIANA. He evokes the area in his memoir *Dune Boy: The Early Years of a Naturalist* (1943). Novelist and essayist JOHN DONALDSON VOELKER (1903–1991) celebrated Michigan's Upper Peninsula, with special affection for rivers and the trout within them; *Trout Madness* (1960) is one of his best-known works. Nebraska-born anthropologist LOREN COREY EISELEY (1907–1977) speculated on the natural world in essays, poems, and books such as *The Immense Journey* (1957). Josephine Johnson (1910–1990), who won a Pulitzer Prize for her novel *Now in November* (1934), about a Midwestern farm family, also wrote *Inland Island* (1968), a nonfiction account of the seasons on her land near CINCINNATI, Ohio, set against the Vietnam War and the increasing destruction of American landscapes. AUGUST (WILLIAM) DERLETH (1909–1971) eloquently traced the natural and human histories of the Wisconsin Sac Prairie region in books like *Walden West* (1961). FREDERICK (b. Feike Feikema, 1912–1994) earned a great literary reputation for his representations of specific places in the Dakotas, Iowa, Nebraska, and Minnesota.

More recent essayists include Wes Jackson (b. 1936), who leads scientific research at the Land Institute at Salina, KANSAS. Jackson writes about prairie ecology, alternative economics, and sustainable agriculture in *Becoming Native to This Place* (1994) and other books. WILLIAM LEAST HEAT-MOON (b. 1939) writes best-selling travel narratives, such as *PrairyErth (a deep map)* (1991), commenting on Midwestern landscapes and culture. The essays of SCOTT RUSSELL SANDERS (b. 1945) are deeply rooted in a sense of place and the defense of the bioregion against exploitation. His writings range from historical considerations of Indiana and the Ohio

GRASS ROOTS

THE UNIVERSE OF HOME

PAUL GRUCHOW

Paul Gruchow's *Grass Roots*. Minneapolis: Milkweed Editions, 1995.
Copyright by Paul Gruchow. Reprinted by permission from Milkweed Editions, www.milkweed.org

Lisa Knopp, 2014. Photo by Viveca Dilley.
© Lisa Knopp

River valley and attacks on nuclear programs to reflections on life and death and the possibility of renewal. *Staying Put: Making a Home in a Restless World* (1993) is a representative collection of his essays. KATHLEEN NORRIS (b. 1947) expresses a mystical sense of the rugged Great Plains landscape in books like *Dakota: A Spiritual Geography* (1993). In *Grass Roots: The Universe of Home* (1995) and other books, PAUL GRUCHOW (1947–2004) focuses on rural life in Minnesota, with special attention to prairie ecology and small farms. Stephanie Mills (b. 1948), author of *In Service of the Wild: Restoring and Reinhabiting Damaged Land* (1995), advocates bioregionalism, restoration ecology, and voluntary simplicity, drawing on her life in northern Michigan. MARY SWANDER (b. 1950) reflects on the simple life on the Iowa plains in books such as *Out of This World: A Woman's Life among the Amish* (1995). Susan Neville (b. 1951), author of *Sailing the Island

Sea: On Writing, Literature, and Land (2007), writes essays and fiction in which the geography, history, and literature of Indiana figure as central concerns. Lisa Knopp (b. 1956) grew up, like Aldo Leopold, in Burlington, Iowa. She lives in Lincoln, Nebraska, and has published four books on the area's ecology, including *The Nature of Home: A Lexicon and Essays* (2004). More recently, Kevin Koch (b. 1959) has contributed *The Driftless Land: Spirit of Place in the Upper Mississippi Valley* (2010).

Notable writers of Midwestern fiction have also written works that are especially readable from an ecocritical perspective. Originally from Michigan, JIM (JAMES THOMAS) HARRISON (1937–2016) wrote fiction that made him one of the Midwest's premier pastoralists, including novels like *Farmer* (1976) and *Dalva* (1988) that are set in rural and wild landscapes in Michigan, Nebraska, and elsewhere. Harrison also wrote poetry and essays about nature. *A Thousand Acres* (1991) by JANE (GRAVES) SMILEY (b. 1949) is a pessimistic reassessment of the agrarian myth seen in Cather. (KAREN) LOUISE ERDRICH (b. 1954), who figures among the most important Native American novelists and poets, investigates Native American life in modern times and provides historical discussions of the lives of Midwestern tribes. In works like LOVE MEDICINE (1984) Erdrich reminds her readers of the spiritual necessity of wild nature and shows how destruction of the land and violence against indigenous peoples coincide in Midwestern history. In 2003 she published her first work of nonfiction, *Books and Islands in Ojibwe Country,* an account of travel in the wild lake country of Minnesota and Ontario.

Midwestern poets have also speculated on the human-nature relationship. Important works that invite ecocritical analysis include *My Friend Tree* (1961) by LORINE NIEDECKER (1903–1970), THE LOST SON (1948) by THEODORE ROETHKE (1908–1963), *Silence in the Snowy Fields* (1962) by ROBERT (ELWOOD) BLY (b. 1926), THE BRANCH WILL NOT BREAK (1963) by JAMES WRIGHT (1927–1980), *American Primitive* (1983) by MARY OLIVER (b. 1935), *Lake Songs and Other Fears* (1974) by JUDITH MINTY (b. 1937), *The Theory and Practice of Rivers* (1985) by Jim Harrison, and *Weather Central* (1994) by Ted Kooser (b. 1939).

SELECTED WORKS: Important early texts of Midwestern environmental literature include Caroline Kirkland's *A New Home— Who'll Follow?* (1839), Margaret Fuller's *Summer on the Lakes, in 1843* (1844), John Muir's *The Story of My Boyhood and Youth* (1913), and Zitkala-Ša's *American Indian Stories* (1921).

Aldo Leopold's *A Sand County Almanac* (1949) is essential for anyone interested in ecology and conservation. Other important Midwestern works of nonfiction nature writing include Louis Bromfield's *Malabar Farm* (1948), Sigurd Olson's *The Singing Wilderness* (1956), August Derleth's *Walden West* (1961), Scott Russell Sanders's *Staying Put: Making a Home in a Restless World* (1993), Paul Gruchow's *Grass Roots: The Universe of Home* (1995), Louise Erdrich's *Books and Islands in Ojibwe Country* (2003), and Susan Neville's *Sailing the Island Sea: On Writing, Literature, and Land* (2007).

Essential pastoral fictions include Willa Cather's *O Pioneers!* (1913), Sherwood Anderson's *Winesburg, Ohio* (1919), Ernest Hemingway's short stories about Nick Adams, such as "Big Two-Hearted River" (1925), Jim Harrison's novels *Farmer* (1976) and *Dalva* (1988), Louise Erdrich's *Love Medicine* (1984), and Jane Smiley's *A Thousand Acres* (1991).

Midwestern poetic texts especially concerned with nature include Edgar Lee Masters's *Spoon River Anthology* (1915), Theodore Roethke's *The Lost Son* (1948), Robert Bly's *Silence in the Snowy Fields* (1962), James Wright's *The Branch Will Not Break* (1963), Judith Minty's *Lake Songs and Other Fears* (1974), Mary Oliver's *American Primitive* (1983), and Jim Harrison's *The Theory and Practice of Rivers* (1985).

Although an anthology of Midwestern nature writing has not yet appeared, several volumes treat the region's landscapes. Michael Martone's *A Place of Sense: Essays in Search of the Midwest* (1988) and *Townships* (1992) collect essays about rural and small-town life by many authors, as does *Inheriting the Land: Contemporary Voices from the Midwest* (1993), edited by Mark Vinz and Thom Tammaro. Joel R. Greenberg, who wrote *A Natural History of the Chicago Region* (2002), has edited *Of Prairie, Woods, and Water: Two Centuries of Chicago Nature Writing* (2008).

FURTHER READING: Formative texts about the American environment include Henry Nash Smith's *Virgin Land: The American West as Symbol and Myth* (1950), which includes commentary on literature of the Midwestern prairie frontier, and Leo Marx's *The Machine in the Garden: Technology and the Pastoral Ideal in America* (1964), which traces the pastoral and industrial impulses that have helped shape the American landscape. Roderick Frazer Nash's *Wilderness and the American Mind* (1967) discusses at length the impact of Midwesterners like Muir and Leopold on American thinking about nature. Annette Kolodny's *The Land before Her: Fantasy and Experience of the American Frontiers, 1630–1860* (1984) looks at nineteenth-century figures like Kirkland, Fuller, and Farnham from a feminist perspective. Lawrence Buell's *The Environmental Imagination* (1995) provides analyses of Midwesterners like Muir, Austin, and Leopold. M. H. Dunlop's *Sixty Miles from Contentment: Traveling The Nineteenth-Century American Interior* (1995) examines frontier-era travel writers in the

Midwest, including their impressions of the region's landscapes. Diane Dufva Quantic's *The Nature of the Place: A Study of Great Plains Fiction* (1995) deals with Midwestern as well as western texts. Susan J. Rosowski edited "Willa Cather's Ecological Imagination," a special issue of *Cather Studies* 5 (2003). Glen A. Love includes chapters on WILLIAM DEAN HOWELLS (1837–1920) and Ernest Hemingway in *Practical Ecocriticism: Literature, Biology, and the Environment* (2004). William Barillas's *The Midwestern Pastoral: Place and Landscape in Literature of the American Heartland* (2006), the first book on Midwestern environmental literature, devotes chapters to Cather, Leopold, Roethke, Wright, and Harrison. David Pichaske's *Rooted: Seven Midwest Writers of Place* (2006) focuses on Harrison, NORBERT BLEI (1935–2013), DAVE (PEARSON) ETTER (1928–2015), JIM HEYNEN (b. 1940), WILLIAM JON (BILL) HOLM (b. 1943), LINDA HASSELSTROM (b. 1943), and WILLIAM KLOEFKORN (1932–2011). In *Imagining the Forest: Narratives of Michigan and the Upper Midwest* (2011), John R. Knott addresses the human relationship to forests in Michigan, Wisconsin, and Minnesota from the early European explorers to the present, taking on environmental history as well as writers like John Muir and Jim Harrison. The publication of these monographs testifies to the contemporary growth of and interest in Midwestern environmental literature.

MIKE RYAN   PLEASANTVILLE, OHIO

ETHNOGRAPHY

OVERVIEW: Alongside the body of Midwestern literature as it is ordinarily perceived resides a vast but ill-defined, undifferentiated, and largely unremarked-on parallel literature of the Midwest. It, too, represents the region and the lives, habits, contradictions, and aspirations of its people. In doing so, this parallel body of Midwestern literature captures much of the Midwestern experience while making itself an important repository of Midwestern and American life. It is the ethnographic literature of the Midwest, an eclectic, nonfictional, social-scientific body of work and imagination unwittingly created as a latent consequence of research aimed not at the Midwest as "Midwest" but at society, culture, and life in the United States.

For students of Midwestern life, culture, and letters, ethnography may be an untapped reservoir of information extending from the Great Plains to the Great Lakes, the farms to the cities, the reservations to the slums and the suburbs, and the nineteenth century to the present. It is likely to expand throughout the twenty-first century.

HISTORY AND SIGNIFICANCE: Ethnography is both a type of research—the firsthand study of a community from the inside out—and a product of research, the monograph or book that brings it to light. The relationship of ethnography to American life has been peculiar owing to the academic division of labor that generally ceded the study of the United States to a relatively empiricist sociology driven by quantitative analysis while turning the anthropological lens and its developing ethnographic method of, in Clifford Geertz's phrase "thick description"—as presented in *The Interpretation of Culture: Selected Essays* (1973)—on the lives and communities of distant others. Growing up in association with the temporally distant and culturally alien, ethnography, when undertaken in the United States, historically gravitated toward Native American communities and toward discernible subcultural groups based on ethnic, occupational, or behavioral distinctiveness. Later, as sociologists embraced ethnography and anthropologists increasingly studied life and mainstream culture in the United States, their work was simply viewed as "Americanist" as against "Africanist," "Asianist," or "Latin Americanist" ethnography. Further distinctions of place were largely not made.

Attempts to outline further the body of Midwestern ethnographic literature are complicated by the intent, ethics, and scope of the literature itself. The intent of most ethnographic research conducted in the Midwest has been to describe the United States or some aspect of it, not the Midwest as such. Although that suggests a great deal about the Midwest as quintessential or even iconic "America," it does little to delineate this specific literature.

Ethically, as writers of nonfiction depicting living people and contemporary places, ethnographers often fictionalize the names not only of people but also of communities, sometimes with impenetrable success. Even

local landmarks that could betray specificity are sometimes distorted. The net effect,
of course, is to further obscure the outline
of the ethnographic Midwest.

Finally, there is the problem inherent in
the breadth of this literature unmarked as
Midwestern: finding it. Ethnographies exist
of virtually every Native American population for whom the Midwest has been home
from the historic period forward. Much of
what is known of these Native peoples and
of the Midwest outside those communities
resides here. So do life stories of the Hmong
in WISCONSIN, the Amish in INDIANA, Norwegians in Wisconsin, Poles in CHICAGO, African Americans in CINCINNATI, and Irish
Americans in CLEVELAND. Here reside accounts of Ghost Dancers on the Great Plains,
meatpackers in KANSAS, drug dealers in ST.
LOUIS, and autoworkers in MICHIGAN. Here
family farms and agribusiness collide, and
urban communities stare into the cold
winds of deindustrialization. Here gay farmers relate their adolescent struggles of isolation, identity, and place, and women sell
cars in Chicago and elsewhere. Here rural
family reunions are representations of the
American kinship system, high schools are
sites of initiation rituals, and hair salons facilitate constructions of self and other. Here
one finds descriptions of culture shock on
Chicago's Dan Ryan Expressway and the
confusion of newcomers confronted with
potluck dinners and vexing conventions of
speech like "How are you?" Here, in myriad
manifestations, resides the body of Midwestern ethnographic literature buried within
layered categories of ethnic, occupational,
generational, institutional, rural, urban, and
suburban American experience and awaiting its own archaeologists.

SELECTED WORKS: No canon of Midwestern ethnographic literature exists, but for
more than seventy-five years a single landmark work, still in print, has been synonymous with Midwest and American culture
and ethnographic attempts to describe them.
It is *Middletown: A Case Study in Contemporary
American Culture* (1929) by Robert S. Lynd
and Helen Merrell Lynd. By now, Middletown is synonymous with Muncie, Indiana, the actual Midwestern city chosen by
the Lynds to represent life and culture in the
United States. Conducted in 1924–1925, the

original study, organized in then-standard
ethnographic categories, examines the
experience and meaning of work, home
life, education, religion, leisure, and community life for the "Middletowners" among
whom the Lynds lived and whom they
studied.

A decade later Robert Lynd returned to
Muncie in the midst of the Great Depression
and from that experience wrote, again with
Helen, *Middletown in Transition: A Study in
Cultural Conflicts* (1937). Together, the Lynds'
Middletown studies tell a story of industrialization and emerging consumer culture, of
class stratification and racial segregation,
and of national values shifting toward individualism and away from community.

In addition to inspiring similar studies
throughout the country, the Lynds' original
works have generated a vast body of both
primary and secondary Middletown literature, including four notable further studies
of Muncie: Theodore Caplow's *Middletown
Families: Fifty Years of Continuity and Change*
(1982) and *All Faithful People: Change and Continuity in Middletown's Religion* (1983); *Back to
Middletown: Three Generations of Sociological
Reflections* (2000) by Rita Caccamo; and *The
Other Side of Middletown: Exploring Muncie's
African-American Community* (2004) by Luke
Eric Lassiter and others. Caplow's works are
more survey based than the original studies,
Caccamo examines Muncie and *Middletown*
from the perspective of a national outsider,
and the work of Lassiter and colleagues is a
collaboration of college students, ethnographers, and community members to tell the
story—omitted by the Lynds, who had chosen Muncie in part for the homogeneity they
saw there—of Muncie-Middletown's African American community.

In a body of literature with little self-
awareness and no clear outline, anthologies may be an excellent place to dig. In
this instance, two of them may be especially useful. At the University of Michigan, Horace Miner wrote a brief but brilliant ethnographic account of the "magic
ridden" Nacirema, "Body Ritual among the
Nacirema," *American Anthropologist* 58 (1956):
503–7. A classic, tongue-in-cheek turn of
the ethnographic lens on American society,
it is still widely anthologized today. "Nacirema" is "American" spelled backward, and

Miner's essay inspired a still-thriving genre of anthropological essays on American culture. James Spradley and Michael Rynkiewich compiled forty-one such essays in *Nacirema: Readings on American Culture* (1975); several of these describe life in specifically Midwestern settings. Also included is Ralph Linton's seminal essay on cultural diffusion, "One Hundred Percent American," originally published in *American Mercury* 40 (1937): 427–29, a must-read for students of culture, be it Midwestern, American, or any other.

Distant Mirrors: America as a Foreign Culture (third edition, 2002), edited by Philip R. DeVita and James D. Armstrong, is a collection of ethnographic essays by anthropologists and other scholars from outside the United States. Their takes on American life are fascinating, fresh, and insightful. A number of them are set in the Midwest. Historians and journalists sometimes bring elements of ethnographic style to their work; the extended interviews conducted by (LOUIS) STUDS TERKEL (1912–2008) with informants in such works as *Division Street America* (1967), *Hard Times* (1970), *Working* (1974), *The Good War* (1984), and *Coming of Age* (1995) are cases in point.

FURTHER READING AND OTHER SOURCES: The Center for Middletown Studies at Ball State University is a repository of Middletown literature ranging from the Lynds's papers to books, articles, dissertations, and essays, as well as a six-volume video series, *Middletown,* produced by Peter Davis and broadcast on PBS from 1979 to 1982. It also includes, as part of PBS's documentary, "The First Measured Century" (2000), a depiction of yet another Caplow restudy of Muncie conducted in 1998–1999 and now known as Middletown IV. Lassiter and colleagues' *The Other Side of Middletown* (2004) was published with a companion DVD, *Middletown Redux,* recounting the ethnographic fieldwork that went into the book. It is available through AltaMira Press.

The Center for the Ethnography of Everyday Life at the University of Michigan publishes research on work and family life in the Midwest and may become a valuable resource of both academic and popular works of Midwestern ethnographic literature.

DAVID PERUSEK   KENT STATE UNIVERSITY–ASHTABULA

EXPATRIATES

OVERVIEW: Extended periods of residence in England and continental Europe, although different from the early twentieth-century American "expatriation" that led to the expatriate movement of the 1920s in Paris, were nothing new to nineteenth-century American writers and artists, including Midwesterners. Examples of American literary sojourners to Europe in the nineteenth century included such distinguished writers as Washington Irving (1783–1859), James Fenimore Cooper (1789–1851), and Henry James (1843–1916). Midwestern expatriate writers of note in the late nineteenth century included WILLIAM DEAN HOWELLS (1837–1920), who held a consular appointment in Venice from 1861 to 1865, and SAMUEL LANGHORNE CLEMENS (1835–1910), writing as Mark Twain, who, although he mocked American tourists in *Innocents Abroad* (1869), lived most of the time from 1891 to 1900 in England and continental Europe.

Also in the later nineteenth century, with the advent of specialization and professionalism, many aspiring writers and art students, including Midwesterners attending East Coast schools, went abroad to live and study in internationally respected cultural centers such as London, Paris, and Munich. According to Warren Irving Susman's 1958 dissertation "Pilgrimage to Paris: The Background of American Expatriation, 1920–1934," many of these students would have been aware that the United States was still in some respects a postcolonial society that looked eastward to the "old countries" for the best graduate education possible (15).

The term "expatriate" used as a noun became current in the United States only between 1900 and 1910, and it was not until the flow of American writers and other artists to France after World War I that the terms "expatriate" and "expatriate movement" acquired their contemporary meaning. Therefore, it is likely that nineteenth-century American travelers, with the possible exception of Henry James, would not have regarded themselves as expatriates. Susman believed that the term "expatriate" became applicable to aspiring American writers, painters, or musicians who were alienated from their native land and who spent at least a year or two abroad to travel, enjoy European freedoms, and gain fresh perspectives (23). R. P. Blackmur in "The American Literary Expatriate," in *Foreign Influences in American Life* (1944), edited by David F. Bowers, provides a neater and shorter but perhaps too narrow definition of an expatriate as "the man or woman who chooses to live in a country not his own because he cannot do his serious work as well in his own country as he can in another" (126). Regrettably, neither of these definitions sheds much light on why expatriation had such broad appeal from 1920 to 1929.

Typically, 1920s expatriates settled in Paris, seeking cheap lodging in the vicinity of others like themselves in the Latin Quarter and frequenting popular sidewalk cafés along Montparnasse Boulevard on the left bank of the Seine. Some writers, notably ERNEST (MILLER) HEMINGWAY (1899–1961), were sufficiently disciplined to live the life of a working writer and to improve their writing in Paris while profiting from the cultural opportunities afforded by that great city. Sometimes, however, the line between the tourist in pursuit of pleasure and the cultural expatriate was fine indeed. Although most expatriates stayed in France at least a year or two, and some returned for more or less extended visits, a few stayed as long as ten or fifteen years, or until the onset of World War II. Although a trickle of expatriates to Paris continued into the 1930s, the great flood was over by the beginning of the Great Depression in 1929.

HISTORY AND SIGNIFICANCE: Several important manifestations of internationalism in late nineteenth- and early twentieth-century American society prepared the way for the expatriate movement of the 1920s. These included the celebrated World's Columbian Exposition of 1893 in CHICAGO; the "functional" architecture of LOUIS (HENRI) SULLIVAN (1856–1924) and FRANK LLOYD WRIGHT (1867–1959); and the CHICAGO RENAISSANCE, with such literary offspring as *POETRY: A MAGAZINE OF VERSE* and *THE LITTLE REVIEW*, both open to foreign as well as American contributors. In addition, Henry James, Gertrude Stein (1874–1946), and Ezra Pound (1885–1972) sought an international rather than a regional or national approach to ART.

In this same period influential American authors supported internationalism in art. Henry James focused attention in his novels on expatriation and the international theme in the life of the artist, inviting emulation by such authors as Edith Wharton (1862–1937) and encouraging others, like HOMER CROY (1883–1965), the MISSOURI author of *They Had to See Paris* (1926), to make a literary pilgrimage to Paris.

Gertrude Stein exerted a powerful influence on the writing careers of major authors, including SHERWOOD ANDERSON (1876–1941), Ernest Hemingway, and F(RANCIS) SCOTT (KEY) FITZGERALD (1896–1940), along with many lesser writers. It was Anderson, after a visit with Stein in Paris, who persuaded Hemingway and his new bride to go there rather than to Italy in pursuit of literary fame. Reflecting Stein's views on Paris as the cultural center of the Western world, Anderson told Hemingway that Italy was all right for tourists, but if one wanted to develop as an artist, Paris was the place to be.

As noted by George Wickes in *Americans in Paris, 1903–1939* (1969), Stein maintained that for an artist, Paris was the "right place to be," at least from 1900 to 1939 (3). Portraying England as refusing to leave the nineteenth century and America as "overwhelmed by the technology of the twentieth century," she viewed France as both modern and traditional, accepting change but not changing radically (3). Therefore, she concluded, Paris was the logical place for the pursuit of art. There, if anywhere, artists could capitalize on the strengths and avoid the pitfalls of English, American, and French culture. Wickes quoted with approval Stein's bold pronouncement on the importance of Paris to the creation of modern art: "So Paris was the place that suited those of us that were to create the twentieth century art and literature, naturally enough" (3). Summing up her self-image as the model of an internationally oriented American writer in Paris, Stein wrote in "An American and France" (a 1936 lecture collected in her 1940 book *What Are Masterpieces*), "America is my country but Paris is my home town" (61).

Another important contributor to internationalism in art was Ezra Pound, who successively settled in London, Paris, and Rapallo, Italy, where he spent much of the

American expatriates F. Scott and Zelda
Fitzgerald in Europe, 1929.
By permission of Harold Ober Associates Incorporated
on behalf of the Fitzgerald Trust

rest of his life. Struck by the need for better communication among writers from the United States, England, France, and other countries, Pound concluded that literature needed individuals like himself to tutor literary neophytes from different national and cultural backgrounds. In London he tutored T(HOMAS) S(TEARNS) ELIOT (1888–1965); in Paris he advised and assisted James Joyce (1882–1941) and Hemingway, who paid him this tribute, quoted by Howard Greenfeld in *They Came to Paris* (1975): "He helped poets, painters, sculptors and prose writers that he believed in, and he would help anyone whether he believed in them or not if they were in trouble" (116).

Pound's contributions to internationalism in art can be conveniently divided into the London, Paris, and Rapallo periods. In the London period Pound served as foreign correspondent for *Poetry: A Magazine of Verse*

from 1912 to 1919 and foreign correspondent of *The Little Review* from 1917 to 1919. Welcoming his contributions on such topics as imagism and vorticism, the editors of both magazines saw Pound as a supporter of communication between Europe and America. He served them as a brilliant and erudite, if often cranky, cultural ambassador determined to shape, if not control, the editorial policies of both magazines. In 1915, for example, although Harriet Monroe resisted Pound's pressure to publish Eliot's "Prufrock" in *Poetry,* he finally prevailed, and she published it. According to Bernard Duffey in *The Chicago Renaissance in American Letters: A Critical History* (1954), Monroe declared that her proudest achievement remained her discovery and publication of Midwesterners, but it is not clear that she regarded Eliot as one of them (187). Pound may have been more successful in influencing the editorial policy of *The Little Review,* which published not only Eliot but W. B. Yeats (1865–1939) and excerpts from Joyce's *Ulysses* (1922).

In addition to the rise of literary internationalism documented previously, R. P. Blackmur identified another reason for the expatriate movement: the Industrial Revolution and robber-baron capitalism as forces that reduced the country's political and cultural leaders, including its artists, to subservience. Blackmur felt that this process gave rise to alienation and rebellion that eventually impelled some artists and intellectuals to leave the country. They hoped that Paris would offer more artistic stimulation, respect, and influence than they could possibly obtain by staying home (133–34).

Other factors encouraging expatriation were the failure of the Progressive movement by the end of World War I and the advent of Prohibition, which greatly restricted Americans' personal freedom. Many of these Americans, ironically, had enjoyed more personal freedom in the military, especially in France, than they were permitted when they got back home. High unemployment and harsh anti-labor legislation followed by strikes and brutal police actions, all exacerbated by the corrupt Harding administration, were also factors.

Susman's perusal of the *Chicago Tribune*'s European edition and an article in the expatriate magazine *transition* (No. 14, 1928), titled "Why Do Americans Live in Europe?" turned up almost one hundred personal reasons for expatriation. According to Susman, disapproval of American conditions headed the list, but "the variety of reasons given is almost bewildering: to see the scene of previous wartime service, to escape from scandal in America, to forget unfortunate romances, to study, to get a better perspective on life and art, to find liberty and independence, to find an apartment . . . , to marry or celebrate a honeymoon, to get a divorce," and so on (212–13). Also in the early 1920s— though not necessarily later in the decade— the American dollar went much further in France than it did in the United States (148–60), making a small amount of American money sufficient for a surprisingly long stay.

African Americans maintained an equivocal relationship to the expatriate movement in the 1920s. After the early twentieth-century discovery by European artists and intellectuals of the beauty of African and Oceanian art, intense interest arose, especially in France and Germany, in the "primitive" and "exotic" aspects of African American culture. French writers and composers soon extended their appreciation of African visual art to jazz. European appreciation of African Americans contrasted sharply with the social status of blacks in the United States. Blacks in the North were segregated by custom, but in the South they were segregated by law. Given the warm welcome African Americans received in France in the 1920s, it is hardly surprising that they flocked there, especially in their much-appreciated roles as entertainers. The enormous success of such shows as the Revue Nègre opened the field for other entertainers as well. To the most successful of these entertainers, such as the legendary dancer Josephine Baker, Paris provided social as well as financial rewards. Susman asserts that even marriage to titled noblemen was not out of the question for the most attractive black female entertainers (221–22).

African American writers soon followed the entertainers to Paris, among them LANGSTON HUGHES (1902–1967), Claude McKay (1890–1948), Countee Cullen (1903–1946), and Jean Toomer (1894–1967). As Susman notes, "Almost every significant Negro figure in the fields of art and ideas could be discovered in Paris. Almost all the major editors and contributors to the outstanding American Negro publication *The Crisis,* for example, spent some time in Paris during the decade" (219).

In spite of the relatively large numbers of African Americans in Paris of the 1920s and the alienation from American society blacks might have felt, it is hard to find any who regarded themselves as expatriates. African Americans were not on the mastheads of expatriate magazines, and they did not have much to do with the expatriate community in Paris. Perhaps this detachment of blacks from the white expatriate community reflected the continuation abroad of long-established patterns of segregation at home. Susman concludes that the African Americans in Paris of the 1920s, unlike those who went to Paris after World War II, were not part of the main expatriate tradition. Many African Americans regarded Paris as only one stop among many in Europe, as well as Russia, Africa, and Asia, where they sought some "personal answer to the enormous problem of race prejudice in the United States" (225, 227). In 1937 Claude McKay, an American immigrant from Jamaica who had gone to Paris in 1923, summed up, in *A Long Way from Home* (1937), the situation of an African American traveler to Europe: "I never considered myself identical with the white expatriates. I was a kind of sympathetic fellow-traveler in the expatriate caravan. The majority of them were sympathetic toward me. But their problems were not exactly my problems. They were all white with problems which were very different from problems in black" (243).

Susman divides American expatriates to Paris into three chronological groups extending from 1920 to 1934. Whatever the very different historical and personal motivations of these groups, the first wave of expatriates, from 1920 to 1924, has been well described by Malcolm Cowley in *Exiles Return* (1934). They contrasted sharply with the two groups that followed (305). Most of the group from 1920 to 1924 came from prosperous, well-educated East Coast families. Many knew French culture and society from study of French literature in college or wartime service in American ambulance units or in the American Expeditionary Force in France. They strove idealistically to absorb the best of French culture and bring the best of American culture to France. They often struggled to make a living while preserving their individuality.

Susman asserts that the next wave, from 1924 to 1927, was much larger, including many from the Midwest: "In numbers there were more Americans in France from the area between the Great Lakes and the Rockies than from any other area in the United States" (320). On the basis of analysis of 462 of the 985 American expatriates on whom he had information, Susman concludes:

Slightly less than half had had a college education and slightly more than half had fought in the war. Generally they came from middle-class backgrounds, but usually lower-middle class and frequently rural backgrounds. A large percentage—over 60 percent—had known extensive travel, either within the United States or around the world, before they settled in France. More than half of the group worked as reporters at some time in their lives. Glenway Wescott, in his important "Good-Bye, Wisconsin," speaks of the Middle Westerners roaming the world as "a sort of vagrant chosen race like the Jews." This characterization seems, in terms of the research indicated here, especially apt. (321)

For many Midwesterners, the remove to Paris was part of the American literary revolt of the 1920s against the Midwest, with its odd mix of materialism, fundamentalism, and vestigial Puritanism arousing hostility to the arts. Although opposed to one another in many fundamental beliefs, these powerful forces found common ground in their conviction that the arts, including literature, were potentially dangerous and should be censored, especially where frank treatment of sex was concerned. The growing public support of censorship—as well as the hypocrisy that inevitably accompanied it—was anathema to Midwestern writers. They typically responded by leaving their hometowns to seek the anonymity, cultural opportunities, and comparative freedom of big cities such as Chicago and ST. LOUIS. From there, as local governments became more restrictive in the early 1920s, many moved eastward to sample the bohemian life of New York's Greenwich Village. By the

mid-1920s droves of aspiring Midwestern writers, now being described as "expatriates," made their way to London and Paris.

Midwestern literary expatriates, with a few exceptions like Ernest Hemingway, were not greatly interested in French literature or culture. Instead, they were eager in Paris or elsewhere to get a fresh perspective on the United States in order more aptly to portray the American life they had left behind. Susman reports that the contribution these expatriate Midwesterners made to the publishing history of the period was remarkable, as Ford Madox Ford (1872–1939), English editor of the short-lived Paris *transatlantic review* (1924–1925), repeatedly emphasized in his writings. Impressed by the quality and quantity of Midwestern authorship, he estimated that at least 80 percent of the material submitted to his magazine was from Midwesterners (320).

Although they called their works stories or novels, most Midwestern expatriates were, in fact, writing autobiographical narratives of their lives and observations of life back home. Examples include the grim portraits of Midwestern life in *Village: As It Happened through a Fifteen Year Period* (1924) by ROBERT (MENZIES) MCALMON (1895–1956); the three interrelated novels of American life, *Possession* (1925), *Early Autumn* (1926), and *A Good Woman* (1927), by LOUIS BROMFIELD (1896–1956); *What Happens* (1926) by JOHN (THEODORE) HERRMANN (1900–1959); and *Goodbye, Wisconsin* (1928) by Glenway Wescott. Despite their sense of alienation from American society and their often pessimistic criticism of it, these Midwestern expatriates had no desire to repudiate their country. On the contrary, Susman concludes that most of them continued to think of themselves not only as Americans but as Americans "with special responsibilities because of their European experience" (332).

Susman argues that the last relatively large group of American expatriates, the internationalists, came to Paris from 1927 to 1934 (333). Many were East Coast immigrants from Europe or children of immigrants returning to Europe from the United States. They are probably best represented in the first years by Eugene Jolas (1894–1952), editor of *transition* magazine. Karen L. Rood in *The Dictionary of Literary Biography*, volume 4,

American Writers in Paris, 1920–1939 (1980), asserts, however, that after 1934, the Paris publication date of *Tropic of Cancer* by Henry Miller (1891–1980), Miller and his friends Alfred Perlès (1897–1990) and Anaïs Nin (1903–1977) provided a formidable challenge to Jolas's leadership of the internationalists (300).

At least until 1928 Midwestern and other American expatriates and tourists were still pouring into France. By then, as F. Scott Fitzgerald reported in *The Crack-Up* (1945), "With each new shipment of Americans spewed up by the boom the quality fell off, until toward the end there was something sinister about the crazy boatloads"—a phenomenon cut short by the stock-market crash of late 1929 and the onset of the Great Depression (20). By 1931 even the reverse flow of expatriates returning to the States had dwindled.

Leadership roles among American expatriates from 1927 to 1934 were taken over by internationalists, few of whom came from the Midwest. In his widely acknowledged role as leader of the first group of internationalists, Jolas edited *transition* in Paris and elsewhere in France from 1927 to 1938, publishing in it translations of Russian, Spanish, French, and German authors, as well as American authors like Gertrude Stein, Kay Boyle, and (HAROLD) HART CRANE (1899–1932). Susman reports that Jolas, self-consciously in revolt against the "Middle-Westishness" that Ford Madox Ford had so much admired, offered instead of Midwestern naturalism and pessimism "the fabulous, the romantic, the magical in terms of the twentieth-century" (337–38). In pursuance of this policy, he published parts of Joyce's *Finnegans Wake* in *transition* as "Work in Progress." He also published psychoanalytic works influenced by Sigmund Freud and Carl Jung and surrealistic works somewhat resembling magic realism today. The contrast was sharp between the autobiographical, realistic or naturalistic, and generally pessimistic works composed by Midwestern expatriates and the multicultural, avant-garde, and romantic works published by Jolas.

One important Midwestern expatriate, JAMES T(HOMAS) FARRELL (1904–1979), came to Paris in 1931. Already at work on the character that would eventually become the protagonist of *STUDS LONIGAN: A TRILOGY* (1935), Farrell also wrote stories reflecting his and his bride, Dorothy's, poverty-stricken life in Paris. He later published thirteen of these realistic Parisian tales. Focusing on the creation of realistic sociological fiction, Farrell revealed how little he had in common with the internationalist, romantic, surrealistic concerns of the Jolas group. Farrell's sociological realism also set him off sharply from the art of Henry Miller and his friends, who were combining sociological awareness with revelations of their personal lives and fantasies. But even though Miller added to his realistic portrayal of slum life in Paris elements of fantasy and sexuality foreign to Farrell, these two writers were significantly similar. Far from trying to distance themselves emotionally from the poverty that constantly threatened to overwhelm them, both Farrell and Miller immersed themselves in Parisian slum life and capitalized on it in their writing. Farrell was positive about his sojourn in France: "When I had come to Paris, I thought that I knew what I was doing, and after about a year, I was returning, with more, not less, confidence. . . . A good and productive year had ended. A sad year had ended. And I could no longer consider myself a youth" (quoted in Rood 128, 131).

Frederick J. Hoffman, Charles Allen, and Carolyn F. Ulrich in *The Little Magazine: A History and a Bibliography* (1946) make it clear that two expatriate presses, Contact Publishing Company and Three Mountains Press, and two of the expatriate little magazines, the *transatlantic review* (January 1924–January 1925) and *This Quarter* (Spring 1925–June 1932), made particularly important contributions to the careers and reputations of Ernest Hemingway and other Midwestern authors (275, 279). Robert McAlmon, founder and owner of Contact Publishing Company, published not only his own naturalistic, uncompromising tales of Midwestern life, *A Hasty Bunch* (1922) and *Village* (1924), but also a small Hemingway booklet, *Three Stories and Ten Poems* (1923). This breakthrough for Hemingway was soon followed by a slim publication of *in our time* (1924) under the imprint of William Bird's Three Mountains Press. The generally favorable reception of this work was doubtless one of several factors leading to the 1925 Boni and Liveright publication of the book as *IN OUR TIME: Stories* in an enlarged and revised edition. This was Hemingway's first book to be published stateside, as well as his first important commercial success.

Hemingway's literary reputation had also been enhanced in 1924 by the publication of three stories in Ford Madox Ford's *transatlantic review*: "Indian Camp," "The Doctor and the Doctor's Wife," and "Cross-Country Snow" (Rood 198; Hoffman 275). As Frank MacShane makes clear in *The Life and Work of Ford Madox Ford* (1965), the publication of these stories put Hemingway in good company with other *transatlantic* contributors like Gertrude Stein, E(dward) E(stlin) Cummings (1894–1962), Ezra Pound, John Dos Passos (1896–1970), Djuna Barnes (1892–1982), James Joyce, and fellow Midwesterners Robert McAlmon and Glenway Wescott (156–59). Hemingway also wrote criticism for the review, read and helped select manuscripts for Ford, and edited one issue of the *transatlantic* during Ford's absence. In *Hemingway, the Writer as Artist* (1952) Carlos Baker comments on the review's contribution to Hemingway's development: "His year with the *transatlantic* . . . probably helped as much as any of his other serious literary activities to get Hemingway's name and fame into general circulation around Paris. . . . It offered him a focus, a kind of responsibility, and a sounding board such as he had not had up to that time" (264).

Ernest Walsh and Ethel Moorhead, editors of three brilliant issues of *This Quarter* in 1925–1926, also published fiction by McAlmon and Hemingway alongside work by Kay Boyle (1902-1992), Morley Callaghan (1903–1990), and James Joyce ("Work in Progress") and poets Yvor Winters (1900–1968) and Ezra Pound. In this review's resurrection from 1929 to 1932, its new editor, Edward Titus, published Midwestern fiction by Hemingway, Sherwood Anderson, James T. Farrell, and the now all-but-forgotten short-story writer Karlton Keim (1908–1987), together with such American poets as Robert Penn Warren (1905–1985), William Carlos Williams (1883–1963), and E. E. Cummings (Hoffman 279). Overall, the publication of Hemingway, McAlmon, and other Midwestern writers by Contact Publishing Company and Three Mountains Press provided invaluable name recognition. Similar benefits accrued to some Midwestern authors published by the *transatlantic review* and *This Quarter*.

By 1939 and the onset of World War II, all but a few stalwart expatriates like Gertrude Stein had returned to the United States. Even Henry Miller returned. In the years after the war, American expatriation to Paris became much less popular, and the number of expatriates living there diminished. Minorities, including homosexuals like Gore (Eugene Luther) Vidal (b. 1925) and African Americans like James Baldwin (1924–1987), however, were drawn to Paris and elsewhere in France and Europe as a refuge from American cultural oppression. Yet Jean Meral, in *Paris in American Literature* (1989), makes it clear that the more traditional mainstream theme of alienation from and disillusionment with American society in general still resonates in the expatriation of such writers as JAMES JONES (1921–1977), who lived in Paris from 1958 to 1974, and Irwin Shaw (1913–1984), who arrived in 1951 and stayed until 1975 (212). Perhaps the best-known Midwestern long-term expatriate writer from this period was RICHARD WRIGHT (1908–1960). After his acceptance of an invitation from the French Provisional Government in 1945, he settled in Paris in 1946–1947 and lived there until his death in 1960 (212). There Wright served as a mentor to other African American refugees from racism, including James Baldwin and Chester Himes (1909–1984), who went to Paris in 1953 and lived abroad the rest of his life (548).

Jean Meral asserts that the image of Paris since 1945 presented by American authors "is that of a slowly disintegrating city whose gradual decline seems irreversible" (238–44). All signs point to the end of its role as a creative catalyst for successive generations of writers. It does not seem to offer a challenge any more or elicit new and fresh responses from authors and shape the destinies of their heroes.

SELECTED WORKS: Four works published by Midwestern expatriates invite special attention. The first of these works is McAlmon's *A Hasty Bunch* (1922). The next two, both by Hemingway, are *In Our Time* (1925) and

The Sun Also Rises (1926); the last one is *Good-bye, Wisconsin* (1928) by Glenway Wescott.

McAlmon has been described by his biographer, Robert E. Knoll, in *Robert McAlmon: Expatriate Publisher and Writer* (1957) as "one of the least familiar and most important figures of 'the lost generation'" (ix). His first collection of stories, *A Hasty Bunch*, is an excellent early example of the realistic, generally pessimistic narratives written by many Midwestern expatriates. Autobiographical in that these stories deal mainly with the narrator's unvarnished personal or observed experience in the American plains states, they depend on the expatriate's Paris experience to provide a new perspective from which to examine life back home. In *A Hasty Bunch* the typical protagonist is a charming youth in rebellious pursuit of experience forbidden to members of his narrowly conformist small-town family.

A minor Midwestern classic, *A Hasty Bunch* nevertheless suffers by comparison with Hemingway's *In Our Time*, his first collection of stories, and even more by comparison with Hemingway's first novel, *The Sun Also Rises*. While most of the stories in *A Hasty Bunch* are individually absorbing, McAlmon's collection lacks the unifying structure and universality that Hemingway was reaching for in *In Our Time* and that he achieved in *The Sun Also Rises*. In *In Our Time* Hemingway uses his alter ego, Nick Adams, to unify some stories in his collection. Not content like McAlmon to restrict the significance of his individual stories to one place and time, Hemingway inserts beneath his stories' chapter headings epigraphs relating mostly to war and bullfighting. In so doing, he subtly extends the reach and implications of his art from childhood to adulthood, from the MICHIGAN stories to those with European settings, and from peace to war. Hemingway's emphasis on complexity, compression, and unity, due in large part to his study of Gustave Flaubert (1821–1880), Anton Chekhov (1860–1904), and Leo (Lev Nikolayevich) Tolstoy (1828–1910), his association with well-educated expatriates, and his acquaintance with contemporary writers like Gertrude Stein, Ezra Pound, and James Joyce, was crucial to his development.

These lessons were even more successfully applied to *The Sun Also Rises*. There Jake's narration of decadent expatriate intrigues in Paris and Pamplona is skillfully contrasted with the admirable American code of sportsmanship found in trout fishing in Burguete, and with the more demanding Spanish code of correct sporting behavior exhibited by the most dedicated bullfighters and aficionados of bullfighting in Pamplona.

Unlike most of Hemingway's stories, the title story of Wescott's *Good-bye, Wisconsin* (1928) is almost plotless. It describes the last part of his return journey from France to his rural WISCONSIN home on Christmas Eve and his train ride back to Milwaukee en route to Chicago and beyond. Compensating for this story's lack of plot, however, is the narrator's voice, vividly presenting not only the present moment but also memories and fantasies drawn from his early life in Wisconsin. Like the stories of many other Midwestern expatriates, this story is not only autobiographical but shrewdly topical. Passing by his hometown movie theatre, for example, the narrator dryly notes that Greta Garbo, with her "abnormally large and liquid eyes," is carrying out a formidable assault on Wisconsin's conservative religious values. Characteristically moving from specifics to generalizations about the secularizing impact of Hollywood on American society, he calls this theatre "the imagination's chapel . . . the small temple dedicated to licentiousness, aspiration, ideals" (24). Half seriously, half in fun, he broadens his indictment of Wisconsin weather and society to include even the "non-existent" Midwest: "There is no Middle West. It is a certain climate, a certain landscape; and beyond that, a state of mind of people born where they do not like to live" (39). As he returns to "civilization" after Christmas, he realizes that he must say good-bye forever to his childhood home, even as he recognizes that Wisconsin is more a part of him than he had imagined.

FURTHER READING: The history of little magazines, including those published in Paris, has been admirably encapsulated in Frederick J. Hoffman, Charles Allen, and Carolyn F. Ulrich's *The Little Magazine: A*

History and a Bibliography (1946). Warren Irving Susman's "Pilgrimage to Paris: The Background of American Expatriation, 1920–1964," a 1958 doctoral dissertation at the University of Wisconsin, is an extremely valuable resource on Midwestern expatriates in the context of nineteenth- and twentieth-century American expatriation to Europe. George Wickes's pleasantly gossipy *Americans in Paris, 1903–1939* (1969) is devoted to a few major expatriates, including Stein, Hemingway, and Henry Miller. A helpful reference work on many individual expatriates is *The Dictionary of Literary Biography*, volume 4, *American Writers in Paris, 1920–1939* (1980), edited by Karen Lane Rood. Jean Meral's *Paris in American Literature* (1989), translated by Laurette Long, provides a French scholar's perspective on American literature about Paris, with fascinating aperçus on numerous American expatriates from Henry James onward. In *American Expatriate Writing and the Paris Moment: Modernism and Place* (1996) Donald Pizer examines how such writers as Hemingway, Fitzgerald, and Dos Passos transformed their experience of Paris in the 1920s using modernist techniques.

Other resources include Arlen J. Hansen's *Expatriate Paris: A Cultural and Literary Guide to Paris of the 1920s* (2012), Paul Brody's *The Real Midnight in Paris: A History of the Expatriate Writers in Paris That Made Up the Lost Generation* (2012), and *Paris in American Literatures: On Distance as a Literary Resource* (2013), edited by Jeffrey Herlihy-Mera and Vamsi K. Koneru (2013), which features essays on Anderson, McAlmon, SAUL (C.) BELLOW (1915–2005), and (WILLIAM) TIM(OTHY) O'BRIEN (b. 1946). A significant primary source is *The Letters of Ernest Hemingway*, volume 2, *1923–1925*, edited by Sandra Spanier and others (2011), with correspondence touching on Hemingway's literary apprenticeship in Paris and his association there with Stein, Pound, Fitzgerald, Ford, Dos Passos, and others.

PAUL W. MILLER   WITTENBERG UNIVERSITY

EXPLORATION ACCOUNTS

OVERVIEW: Exploration in the region now comprising the American Midwest by Europeans or people of European ancestry extended from the early 1600s through and beyond American independence from Britain and included efforts by France, Britain, Spain, and the United States to create, extend, or maintain their spheres of influence on the North American continent. Midwestern explorations included, among others, such landmark journeys as the 1615 exploration of the Lake Huron region by Samuel de Champlain (ca. 1574–1635), the 1673–1674 exploration by Louis Joliet (1645–1700) and Jacques Marquette (1637–1675) from northern MICHIGAN to the Mississippi and Ohio Rivers, and the 1804–1806 Corps of Discovery exploration in and beyond the newly acquired Louisiana Purchase by Meriwether Lewis (1774–1809) and William Clark (1770–1838) in search of the fabled Northwest Passage.

The accounts of these explorations are seminal documents in Midwestern culture and literature and reflect the ideology of the explorers, the goals of their nations, and the earliest experiences by those of European ancestry in the region. Their importance to American and Midwestern history and culture is reflected in the fact that these accounts, some approaching four hundred years in age, remain available in published, often reprinted form, as well as via internet websites. This entry reviews the history of exploration accounts and lists the most readily available editions of original accounts.

HISTORY AND SIGNIFICANCE: Exploration accounts came about because explorers needed to describe where they had been and what they had seen for ideological, territorial, economic, and scientific purposes. Thus, for example, French exploration of the Midwest began in the seventeenth century to advance France's fur-trading and missionary interests and to hinder English expansion.

Champlain was among the earliest to leave an account of his travels. He began exploring the Saint Lawrence River and its tributaries, seeking a route to the interior of the North American continent. As part of this venture, he reached the Lake Huron region in 1615. The initial French account of Champlain's exploration of the Midwest appears in *Voyages et descouvertures faites en la Nouvelle France, depuis l'année 1615 jusques à la fin de l'année 1618* (1619). The first French edition presenting all of Champlain's voyages appeared in 1632. The English translation is provided in *Voyages of Samuel de Champlain. Translated from the French by Charles Pomeroy Otis. With Historical Illustrations, and a Memoir by the Rev. Edmund F. Slafter* (1878). Also valuable is *The Works of Samuel de Champlain* (1922–1936) in six volumes, edited by Henry P. Biggar.

Champlain realized that French exploration was heavily dependent on native cooperation and equipment. The most successful subsequent French explorations took these elements into account. Directed by Champlain, Étienne Brûlé (1592–1633) traveled to Sault Ste. Marie at the junction of Lakes Superior and Huron in 1621. He is believed to have been the first European to set foot in the future state of Michigan. Consul Willshire Butterfield provides the accounts of this exploration in *History of Brule's Discoveries and Explorations, 1610–1626: Being a Narrative of the Discovery by Stephen Brule of Lakes Huron, Ontario and Superior* (1898).

It was long believed that the Frenchman Jean Nicolet (also spelled Nicollet, 1598–1642), one of Champlain's interpreters, followed the shores of Lake Huron through the Straits of Mackinac to the bottom of Green Bay by 1634. He is now is thought to have traveled from Lake Huron to Lake Superior. An account of Nicolet's journey, written by Father Barthélemy Vimont (1594–1667), is found in *The Jesuit Relations and Allied Documents: Travels and Explorations of the Jesuit Missionaries in New France, 1610–1791* (1896–1901), edited by Reuben Gold Thwaites, volume 23, 275–79. Father Isaac Jogues (1607–1646) traveled with Jesuit missionary Charles Raymbaut (1602–1642) from Canada to Sault Ste. Marie; they were probably the first white men to see Lake Superior. Jérôme Lalemant (1593–1673), who traveled with them, wrote "Journey of Raymbault and Jogues to the Sault," found in Louise Phelps Kellogg's *Early Narratives of the Northwest, 1634–1699* (1917). Lalemant is believed to be the author of many of the narratives in the *Jesuit Relations*, which describe Jesuit explorations of the GREAT LAKES region in the seventeenth century and can be found in a number of editions, the most notable of which, previously cited, was edited by Thwaites. Written mainly between 1632 and 1673, they were originally intended to describe Jesuit conversion work but then became more focused on garnering wider public financial support for missions and settlement.

The first European accounts of the upper Mississippi come from Pierre Esprit Radisson (1636–1710), who traveled with his brother-in-law, Médard Chouart, Sieur des Groseilliers (1618–1696), around 1659. The problem with verifying Radisson's information is that he rarely gives the day of the month or the exact year; also, Radisson's narratives of his western explorations were written in 1665 after poor treatment by the French had driven him to seek patronage in England. These are recounted in Kellogg's *Early Narratives of the Northwest, 1634–1699* (34–65); *The Explorations of Pierre Esprit Radisson* (1961), edited by Arthur T. Adams, also documents this exploration.

A Jesuit priest, Jean Claude Allouez (1620–1689), stationed at Lake Superior between 1665 and 1667, provided some of the earliest accounts of the interior of the continent and the Indian peoples who occupied the eastern and northern plains. Allouez's *Journey to Lake Superior* (1665–1667) can be found on pages 95 through 137 in Kellogg's volume. In 1669 Allouez traveled from northern Lake Michigan through Green Bay and then up the Fox River into present-day WISCONSIN. After a French-Iroquois peace in 1666, the lower Great Lakes were thoroughly explored by François Dollier de Casson (1636–1701) and René de Bréhant de Galinée (1645–1678), Sulpician missionaries looking to establish bases. They followed the edge of Lake Ontario, traveled through Lake Erie and the straits of Detroit and St. Clair, and crossed Lake Huron to arrive at Sault Ste. Marie. Because Dollier de Casson destroyed his manuscript, the surviving account comes from Galinée in *Ontario Historical Society, Papers and Records* 4 (1903), edited by J. H. Coyne.

Dollier de Casson also accompanied René-Robert Cavelier, Sieur de La Salle (1643–1687), who set off from Canada on July 6, 1669, to North America but was specifically seeking the Ohio River. This he found and followed it to the junction with the Mississippi; years later the French claimed the

Ohio Valley because of this trip. He returned to Montreal but set off again in the spring of 1672 and that winter reached the Mississippi, which he called the Colbert in honor of the man whose patronage he needed. La Salle made no personal record of this voyage, but an account is found in the writings of Abbé Eusèbe Renaudot (1646–1720), to whom La Salle gave a description. This account is included in Francis Parkman's *La Salle and the Discovery of the Great West* (1869).

Also accompanying La Salle on his travels in the late 1670s was Recollect father Louis Hennepin (1626–ca. 1705), who was ordered by his superior to accompany La Salle on a voyage to explore the westernmost point of New France. He brought attention to what became Saint Anthony Falls in MINNESOTA, the only waterfall on the Mississippi River. He wrote accounts of his travels, but his veracity has been questioned. *Father Louis Hennepin, a New Discovery of a Vast Country in America* (1925, 1954) by Reuben Gold Thwaites details this exploration. This work was originally published in 1698; volumes 1 and 2 were combined in 1903.

Fur trader Louis Joliet (also spelled Jolliet) and Father Jacques Marquette, a Jesuit, reached the Mississippi and got within seven hundred miles of the Gulf of Mexico. Joliet's record is lost, but Marquette's notes of this expedition are among the best of the accounts by early explorers of the Mississippi. Some controversy exists about Marquette's actual writing of the narrative ascribed to him, but weighty evidence supporting his doing so appears in Raphael N. Hamilton's *Marquette's Explorations: The Narratives Reexamined* (1970). Marquette and Joliet were the first Europeans to view the land on which the city of CHICAGO was to stand. Another key settlement of the Midwest, DETROIT, was established not long after, in 1701, by the colorfully unscrupulous Antoine Laumet de Lamothe Cadillac (1658–1730). This exploration is described in *The Western Country in the Seventeenth Century: The Memoirs of Antoine Lamothe Cadillac and Pierre Liette; Life among the Indians of the Mississippi Valley from the Ohio River to North of Lake Superior* (1962).

French exploration and settlement in what is now the United States continued for well over two centuries, from the early 1500s

Title page of account of French exploration in North America by Pierre de Charlevoix. Pierre-François Giffart, Paris, 1744.
Image courtesy of Special Collections, Grand Valley State University Libraries

through the French loss of the French and Indian War to Britain in 1763. French Jesuit Pierre François Xavier de Charlevoix (1682–1761), an explorer, writer, and historian, wrote an influential history of French North America from its outset through the 1730s, including his own experiences in the early 1700s in Quebec and his travels through the Great Lakes region and down Lake Michigan to the Mississippi River, New Orleans, and the Gulf of Mexico. His work was published in 1744 as *Histoire et description generale de la Nouvelle France, avec le journal historique d'un voyage fait par ordre du roi dans l'Amérique septentrionnale*.

Mainly because of the barrier to east-west travel posed by the Appalachian chain, the English lagged behind other European explorers in traversing the interior, but by 1704 Anglo-Americans had made considerable strides in mapping this region. The first Anglo American to survey the Ohio River lands in southern OHIO was Christopher Gist (1706–1759). *Christopher Gist's Journals with Historical, Geographical and Ethnological Notes and Biographies of His Contemporaries* (2006), edited by William M. Darlington, contains Gist's account of his survey for the Ohio Company. Even before the French lost control of the area, British colonists began to expand into Ohio Country in the 1750s.

The most famous of the British explorers in the eighteenth century was probably Irish-born George Croghan (1720–1782). In the 1750s he was made a deputy to Sir William Johnson, superintendent of the Northern Department of Indian Affairs. He established diplomatic and trading contacts with a number of the Indian tribes in the Ohio area. "Croghan's Journal, 1765" appears in Reuben Gold Thwaites's *Early Western Travels, 1748–1846* (1904–1907), volume 1, 127–66. One of the earliest British accounts, as well as maps of the area between the Ohio River and the Great Lakes, was provided by Ensign Thomas Hutchins (1730–1789), a British army engineer sent by Croghan to map this area, recently acquired by Britain after the French and Indian War. *The Courses of the Ohio River Taken by Lt. Thomas Hutchins: Anno 1766 and Two Accompanying Maps* (1942), edited by Beverley W. Bond, describes this expedition.

Self-taught mapmaker and surveyor Jonathan Carver (1710–1780) was the first English-speaking explorer to travel west of the upper Mississippi River. Carver was hired in 1766 by Major Robert Rogers, who was interested in finding the Northwest Passage, in exploring the area west of Michilimacinac, and in documenting geography, the number and location of Indians, and the trading posts they encountered on their travels. Hoping to find out more about the Mississippi, Carver explored along the northern coast of Lake Michigan, eventually reaching what is now Green Bay, Wisconsin. He traversed the Fox and Wisconsin Rivers and from there followed the Mississippi to the trade encampment at Prairie du Chien near the confluence of the Wisconsin River and the Mississippi River. Rather than turn south, Carver's expedition turned north into what became Minnesota. He spent the winter in an Indian village in what became eastern IOWA. The next spring he continued exploring and mapping areas that form Minnesota and Wisconsin. Carver's accounts of his exploration contain wonderful details of the Indian tribes he encountered and renewed interest in routes to the Pacific, later pursued by Alexander Mackenzie (1764–1820) and by Lewis and Clark. The account of these explorations is presented in *Jonathan Carver's Travels through North-America, in the Years 1766, 1767, and 1768* (1778).

Spaniard Francisco Vásquez de Coronado (1510–1554) was the first European to explore the region now including NEBRASKA and KANSAS, looking for the fabled seven cities of gold. Instead, he found grass huts in a settlement of Wichita Indians on the Kansas River. *The Journey of Coronado, by Pedro Castaneda* (1904), edited by George Parker Winship, describes Coronado's explorations.

Concerned about French influence in the Great Plains, Pedro de Villasur (ca. 1686–1720) led a Spanish expedition north from Santa Fe and Taos in 1720. It reached central Nebraska, but the expedition ended in disaster when it was attacked by Indians and Villasur was killed. Alfred B. Thomas translated and edited the account of the expedition in *After Coronado: Spanish Exploration Northeast of New Mexico, 1696–1727* (1935).

The first recorded European exploration of what would become Nebraska was the expedition of Frenchman Étienne de Veniard, Sieur de Bourgmont (1679–1734). In 1713 he began writing *Exact Description of Louisiana, of Its Harbors, Lands and Rivers, and Names of the Indian Tribes That Occupy It, and the Commerce and Advantages to Be Derived There from the Establishment of a Colony*. In March 1714 he traveled to the mouth of the Platte River, which he named the Nebraskier River from the Otoe name for "flat water." He wrote "The Route to Be Taken to Ascend the Missouri River." This account reached the cartographer Guillaume Delisle, who noted that it was the first documented report of travels that far north on the Missouri River. The account is presented in Frank Norall's *Bourgmont, Explorer of the Missouri, 1698–1725* (1988).

John Evans (1770–1799), James MacKay (1761–1822), and David Thompson (1770–1857) all explored areas of Nebraska, SOUTH DAKOTA, NORTH DAKOTA, and northern Minnesota, providing information and maps that would later be of great help to Lewis and Clark. Their accounts are included in A. P. Nasatir's *Before Lewis and Clark: Documents Illustrating the History of the Missouri, 1785–1804* (2002).

Among the earliest explorers of the northern plains were the French Canadian La Vérendryes. Pierre Gaultier de Varennes, Sieur de la Vérendrye (1685–1749), and his sons were the first to explore what we now know as western North and South Dakota, and theirs are the first written records of the area and its native inhabitants. They have been compiled by G. Hubert Smith in *The Explorations of the La Vérendryes in the Northern Plains, 1738–43* (1980), edited by W. Raymond Wood. See also *Journals and Letters of Pierre Gaultier de La Vérendrye and His Sons* (1927), edited by Lawrence J. Burpee.

Meriwether Lewis and William Clark led the Corps of Discovery through North Dakota, where they spent the winter of 1804–1805 near Washburn at Fort Mandan. The narratives of the Lewis and Clark expedition appear in *The Definitive Journals of Lewis and Clark* (1983–2001) in thirteen volumes, edited by Gary E. Moulton. Useful one-volume condensations are Moulton's *The Lewis and Clark Journals* (2003) and Bernard De Voto's *The Journals of Lewis and Clark* (1953). A history of the various editions of the journals appears in Paul R. Cutright's *A History of the Lewis and Clark Journals* (2000).

As the nineteenth century progressed and settlers made their way into Louisiana Territory, literature of exploration gave way to FRONTIER AND PIONEER ACCOUNTS. However, the U.S. government and individual states continued to conduct explorations in remote areas of what would become known as the Midwest. In addition to his ethnological studies, HENRY ROWE SCHOOLCRAFT (1793–1864) published accounts of his explorations in the continental interior, beginning with *A View of the Lead Mines of Missouri* (1819) and *Journal of a Tour into the Interior of Missouri and Arkansaw* (1821). Schoolcraft's work in the Ozarks led to his participation in the 1820 expedition led by Michigan territorial governor Lewis Cass from Detroit to the Lake Superior and upper Mississippi regions. Schoolcraft wrote up the journey in *Narrative Journal of Travels through the Northwestern Regions of the United States* (1821). The Cass expedition mistakenly identified Cass Lake as the source of the Mississippi River, but Schoolcraft corrected the error during his expedition of 1831–1832 when he located the source in Lake Itasca, which he named. The story is told in Schoolcraft's *Narrative of an Expedition through the Upper Mississippi River to Itasca Lake* (1834).

Douglass Houghton, who acted as physician and naturalist on Schoolcraft's Itasca expedition, led surveys of the Great Lakes shores of both peninsulas of Michigan, conducted for the state of Michigan between 1838 and 1840. Houghton, who drowned on an 1845 federal survey of the Lake Superior country, did not live long enough to write accounts of his explorations. However, his assistant, Bela Hubbard (1814–1896), published *Memorials of a Half Century in Michigan and the Lake Regions* (1887), which may be considered one of the last true accounts of Midwestern exploration.

SELECTED WORKS: Champlain's explorations are recounted in *Voyages of Samuel de Champlain. Translated from the French by Charles Pomeroy Otis. With Historical Illustrations, and a Memoir by the Rev. Edmund F. Slafter* (1878). *The Jesuit Relations and Allied Documents* (1898, 1959), edited by Reuben Gold Thwaites, contains accounts of the journeys of Joliet and Marquette, along with those of other French explorers in the region. Gary E. Moulton edited the journals of the Lewis and Clark expedition in *The Definitive Journals of Lewis and Clark* (1983–2001).

Anthologies relating to exploration in the region that has now become the Midwest include *The First West: Writing from the American Frontier, 1776–1860* (2002), edited by Edward Watts and David Rachels; *North American Exploration* (1997), edited by John Logan Allen; *Voyages in Print: English Travel to America, 1576–1624* (1995) edited by Mary C. Fuller; *Up Country: Voices from the Midwestern Wilderness* (1985), compiled and edited by William Joseph Seno; and *The Exploration of North America, 1630–1776* (1974), edited by W. P. Cumming and others.

FURTHER READING: Louise Phelps Kellogg's *Early Narratives of the Northwest, 1634–1699* (1917), with fourteen translated narratives of journeys or episodes in the region of the Upper Great Lakes and Upper Mississippi, Robert R. Hubach's *Early Midwestern Travel Narratives: An Annotated Bibliography,*

1634–1850 (1961), and the internet site *American Journeys* provide excellent introductions to Midwestern exploration accounts. *American Journeys* reports having "more than 18,000 pages of eyewitness accounts of North American explorations from the sagas of the Vikings in Canada in A.D. 1000 to the diaries of mountain men in the Rockies 800 years later." Information on specific explorations in the Midwest can be found using the source documents identified previously.

Sources and documents on French occupation of the Northwest are found in *The French Foundations, 1689–1693* (1934), edited by Theodore C. Pease and Raymond C. Werner, and in *Old Cahokia: A Narrative and Documents Illustrating the First Century and Its History* (1949) by John McDermott. Many of the published accounts reported here also include commentaries on the explorations, as well as the original accounts. Other significant works covering exploration in the Midwest include *Champlain's Dream* (2008) by David Hackett Fischer. An excellent documentary film depicting the sites and relating the Lewis and Clark expedition is *Lewis and Clark: The Journey of the Corps of Discovery* (1997), directed by Ken Burns.

Bibliographies include Gerold L. Cole's *Travels in America: From the Voyages of Discovery to the Present; An Annotated Bibliography of Travel Articles in Periodicals, 1955–1980* (1984) and Robert R. Hubach's *Early Midwestern Travel Narratives: An Annotated Bibliography, 1634–1850* (1961).

CATHERINE TOBIN   CENTRAL MICHIGAN UNIVERSITY

F

FANTASY.
See Science Fiction and Fantasy

FARM LITERATURE

OVERVIEW: The poetry and fiction that constitute Midwestern farm literature, also referred to as "rural literature," regularly document writers' experiences with farm life and labor. Some renderings are idyllic and nostalgic, reflecting the positive value and reward of hard work on bountiful family farmsteads; others are grim accounts of unremitting labor that comes to naught through the vicissitudes of weather, health, or commodity prices.

Midwestern farm literature reflects a broad spectrum of time, experience, and thought, from frontier depictions of pioneers clearing forests and putting the first plows to prairie sod to portrayals of class injustice visited by local moneyed interests on those actually laboring on the farms but receiving little benefit from them, to negative characterizations of modern agribusiness, and even to contemporary eco-oriented primitivist expressions of faith that returning to the land can provide an antidote to sterile, dehumanizing city and suburban living. The narrative points of view adopted in works of farm literature further reflect and underscore this range of perspectives, whether the works are presented through the eyes of the farmer, the farm family, the hired hand, or an observer from outside the agricultural milieu.

HISTORY AND SIGNIFICANCE: Farm literature, especially the novel, was abundant in the Midwest, arising as it did from the rich agrarian experience of its first non–Native American settlers who were arriving directly from Europe or emigrating from eastern states throughout the nineteenth century. Most critics see the beginnings of the farm-novel genre as coinciding with the rise of naturalism, and its first proponent as (HANNIBAL) HAMLIN GARLAND (1860–1940) in his *MAIN-TRAVELLED ROADS* (1891), which, as Roy Meyer points out in *The Middle Western Farm Novel in the Twentieth Century* (1965), was not a novel but a collection of six stories (33). For a time, Garland dominated the genre of farm fiction with the publication of *Jason Edwards, an Average Man* (1892), *Rose of Dutcher's Coolly* (1895), and later books.

The farm novel, however, did not spring fully evolved onto the literary scene with Garland; an earlier tradition in rural fiction was the precursor to it. *A NEW HOME—WHO'LL*

Follow? (1839) and its sequel, *Forest Life* (1842), by Caroline Kirkland (1801–1864) are two of the earliest interpretations of Midwestern frontier life; both contain unflattering sketches of the Michigan farmer as rough, uncouth, and unlettered. Alice Cary (1820–1871) uses her somewhat romanticized experiences on a Cincinnati-area family farm as the basis for the stories in her two-volume collection *Clovernook; or, Recollections of Our Neighborhood in the West* (1852–1853).

Further along the road to the realism espoused by Garland is Edgar Watson Howe (1853–1937), whose *The Story of a Country Town* (1883) only tangentially mentions farming but emphasizes the drab and narrow-minded existence of both villager and farmer in a Kansas settlement. The first Midwestern farm novel that effectively set the stage for the hundreds that would follow was written by the son of Caroline Kirkland, Joseph Kirkland (1830–1894). His *Zury: The Meanest Man in Spring County* (1887), the story of a self-made Illinois farmer who rises from poverty to wealth and political influence out of shrewdness and force of will, is partly based on Kirkland's extensive agricultural background. John T. Flanagan in his 1942 article, "The Middle Western Farm Novel," believes that it is one of the most important literary pictures of an American farmer (115).

Midwestern farm fiction, like many other literary genres, exhibits recurring themes, situations, and stock characters. Among these are the resolute pioneer struggling to eke out an existence from an indifferent or openly hostile environment, as exemplified by Per Hansa in *Giants in the Earth* (1927) by Ole Edvart Rølvaag (1876–1931); the moral superiority of those who live and work on the land over those associated with the city, like Peter Oliver in *The Harvest Is Late* (1944) by John Hyatt Downing (1888–1973); the farm as a place of intellectual or spiritual stagnation or stultification, as shown by Paul (Frederick) Corey (1903–1992) in his Mantz Family trilogy; and the disillusionment with agricultural labor and the desire to escape it, naturalistically described in *Backfurrow* (1925) by G(eoffrey) D. Eaton (1894–1930).

Nineteenth-century Midwestern rural and farm fiction typically portrayed pioneer settlers or those more recently arrived from

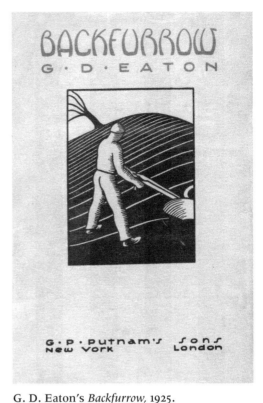

G. D. Eaton's *Backfurrow,* 1925.
© G. P. Putnam's Sons, 1925. Image courtesy of Special Collections, Grand Valley State University Libraries

New York or New England. In contrast, a significant portion of the output in the early twentieth century, when the form gained its full maturity, focused instead on European immigrants to the Midwest, including, for example, the Swedes and Bohemians of Willa Cather (1873–1947) in Nebraska, Rølvaag's Norwegians on the Dakota prairies, the West Frisians in Iowa depicted by Frederick Manfred (b. Feike Feikema, 1912–1994), and the Minnesota Swedes of Cornelia Cannon (1876–1969).

Willa Cather's two early novels of the Nebraska prairie, *O Pioneers!* (1913) and *My Ántonia* (1918), are concerned with the transformation of the Midwestern wilderness into arable land by immigrant Swedes and Bohemians, respectively. Using strong female central characters, Cather draws on the years she spent in Nebraska as a child and young woman to show both the rewards and the hardships of farm life.

Often singled out as the preeminent Midwestern farm novel, *Giants in the Earth* by O. E. Rølvaag follows the Norwegian immigrant family of Per and Beret Hansa in their move from Minnesota to the prairie of SOUTH DAKOTA in the 1870s. The rigors of farm work, religious faith, and cultural isolation are factors that lead to the tragic denouement. Near the beginning of the novel, the description of the emptiness of the featureless prairie that compounds the agoraphobia of Beret provides more than a foreshadowing: "At the moment when the sun closed his eye, the vastness of the plain seemed to rise up on every hand—and suddenly the landscape had grown desolate; something bleak and cold had come into the silence, filling it with terror" (10). That same looming darkness is echoed in the final lines as the snowstorm that will kill Per Hansa rages: "The swirling dusk grew deeper. . . . Darkness gathered fast. . . . More snow began to fall. . . . Whirls of it came off the tops of the drifts, circled about, and struck him full in the face" (464). Rølvaag continued his story of the Hansa family in two sequels, *Peder Victorious* (1929) and *Their Father's God* (1931), which are generally considered inferior to *Giants in the Earth.*

Notable for their diametrically opposed views of farming are two novels set in rural Michigan and coincidentally appearing in the same year. *Backfurrow* (1925) by G. D. Eaton is an unremittingly bleak picture of a young man desperately eager to leave the farm for what he hopes will be fame and fortune in the city; his failure forces him to return to the work he hates. On the other hand, in *Green Bush* (1925) JOHN T(OWNER) FREDERICK (1893–1975) shows the restorative powers of farmwork and rural living after a young man suffers a serious injury while pulling stumps.

Although RUTH SUCKOW (1892–1960) is better known for her novels of Iowa small-town life, she used the farm as the setting for her first novel, *Country People* (1924). It shows in understated prose the lives of a German family whose ultimate economic success is tempered by social and personal setbacks. Another Iowa-based first novel is *State Fair* (1932) by PHIL(IP) (DUFFIELD) STONG (1899–1957), which, in contrast to Suckow's protagonists, depicts a reasonably happy farm family of parents and children attending the annual agricultural fair in Des Moines.

The Pulitzer Prize–winning *Now in November* (1934), the lyrical first novel of Josephine Johnson (1910–1990), concerns a MISSOURI farm family harassed by the economic and weather-related troubles of the Depression, as well as by the emotional and mental instability of the three daughters. The image of sere farm fields evoked by the book's title is reflected in the grim telling of the story. A similar struggle against social and economic pressures, as well as the vagaries of nature, appears in *Wind without Rain* (1939) by HERBERT (ARTHUR) KRAUSE (1905–1976), who depicts the people and country he knew growing up on a farm in western Minnesota. The fictional portrayal of the northern OHIO ancestral farm of LOUIS BROMFIELD (1896–1956) and his forebears in *The Farm* (1933) is a reflection of the author's vehement disdain for modern industrial society and a paean to the agrarian ideal it has supplanted. One hundred years after its establishment, the farm has become an obstacle to "progress" in 1917: "For a long time the mills and factories had been spreading, to the north and the east, over the fields and along the altered channels of Toby's Run. . . . The Town would come nearer and nearer until presently the great barn and perhaps the rambling house itself would be pulled down" (343–44).

In addition to Rølvaag's trilogy of the prairie, other sequence novels of varying competence and quality also deal with Midwestern farm life. Dora Aydelotte (1878–1968) wrote *Long Furrows* (1935) and its sequel, *Full Harvest* (1939), both set in Illinois. *The Years of Peace* (1932) and *The Crowded Hill* (1934) by LeRoy MacLeod (1893–1983) are realistic portrayals of an INDIANA farm family. The trilogy by Paul Corey, consisting of *Three Miles Square* (1939), *The Road Returns* (1940), and *County Seat* (1941), follows the Mantz family in Iowa. Sophus K. Winther (1893–1983) wrote a trilogy about the Grimsens, a Nebraska Danish family: *Take All to Nebraska* (1936), *Mortgage Your Heart* (1937), and *This Passion Never Dies* (1938).

The number of farm novels set in the Midwest rapidly declined after the 1930s, but several are worthy of mention. The development of an early Ohio farming community is chronicled in *The Fields* (1946) by CONRAD (MICHAEL) RICHTER (1890–1968). In *The Shadow of My Hand* (1956) by Holger Cahill (1887–1960) a World War II veteran finds solace on a NORTH DAKOTA farm. The fictional narrator of *The Moonflower Vine* (1962) by Jetta Carleton (1913–1999) reminisces about her life on a Missouri farm. Frederick Manfred fictionalized his early years on an Iowa farm in *Green Earth* (1977). Canadian writer W(ILLIAM) P(ATRICK) KINSELLA (b. 1935) captures anti-agribusiness sentiment, as well as mystical feelings about the rural landscape, in *Shoeless Joe* (1982), his baseball novel set on an Iowa farm. *During the Reign of the Queen of Persia* (1983) by JOAN CHASE (b. 1936) seethes with the dissatisfactions of modern Ohio farm women.

Reflecting social issues such as changing gender roles and environmentalism, much fiction about Midwestern farm experience since the late twentieth century reassesses rural land-use patterns and social norms. A key text in this regard is the Pulitzer Prize–winning novel *A Thousand Acres* (1991) by JANE (GRAVES) SMILEY (b. 1949), who recasts Shakespearean tragedy on a twentieth-century Iowa farm. Attentive to fundamental flaws in the pioneer legacy, Smiley characterizes modern American agriculture as dominated by a ruthlessly patriarchal, utilitarian, and ultimately corporate ideology. Her *Some Luck* (2014), *Early Warning* (2015), and *Golden Age* (2015) comprise the Last Hundred Years trilogy that follows five generations of an Iowa farm family. Historical reassessment of Midwestern farming also characterizes *The Quickening* (2010), the debut novel by Michelle Hoover (b. 1972), about two women, neighbors and friends, who struggle both economically and with isolation and family tragedies during the Great Depression in Iowa. An entire oeuvre devoted to Midwestern farm life has been produced by Jerry Apps (b. 1934), a prolific scholar of agricultural practice and a writer of fiction and nonfiction. Apps's novels include *Cranberry Red* (2010), the fourth title in his Ames County, WISCONSIN, series tracing themes of community, family, economics, and land use from the post–Civil War era to the present. Apps portrays a present-day county agricultural agent whose principles are challenged when he takes a job promoting a genetically modified product that may have adverse health effects.

Fictional accounts of migrant farmworkers, although prevalent for western states, are nearly nonexistent for the Midwest. The one outstanding text, *...Y NO SE LO TRAGÓ LA TIERRA/...AND THE EARTH DID NOT DEVOUR HIM* (1971) by Tomás Rivera (1935–1984), challenges the pastoral myth of egalitarian Midwestern farm communities. Set in the early 1950s, Rivera's novel-in-stories narrates the experiences of a Mexican American boy and fellow laborers who spend the winter in Texas and the rest of the year working on farms in the upper Midwest. Rivera stresses the harshness of the migrants' working conditions and their exploitation and exclusion by white landowners and townspeople. Another novel that uses a Mexican American migrant child as a substantial character is *Clorinda of Cherry Lane Farm* (1945) by Caroline R. Stone (1884–1972), set mostly in the Saginaw, Michigan, area and written for young adults. Some *corridos* (Mexican American ballads) have been written by migrants about their experiences in the Midwest. See LATINO/LATINA LITERATURE. *Cloud of Arrows* (1950) by MARY FRANCES DONER (1893–1985) describes from a sympathetic outsider's perspective migrant workers in the sugar-beet fields of eastern Michigan.

CHILDREN'S AND YOUNG-ADULT LITERATURE abounds with farm stories set in the Midwest, and nearly all are idealized and romanticized visions of farm life, steeped in nostalgia and reflecting positive rural values. The first stories with a farm background for children were probably written in the nineteenth century as religious tracts emphasizing Christian values and using a panoply of rural hardships as examples of Christian forbearance. Like its adult counterpart, later children's rural fiction relies on memories of living on family farms. These recollections tend to be pleasant or to occur after some setback or problem is happily resolved. Two examples are *Little Rhody* (1953) by Neta Lohnes Frazier (1890–1990) and *Ken of Centennial Farm* (1959) by Bess Hagaman Tefft (1913–1977). Juvenile literature of this type sometimes employs a visit to a relative's farm by children who live in a city; in *Heedless Susan Who Sometimes Forgot to*

Remember (1939) by Emma L. Brock (1886–1974), the story line becomes a vehicle for explaining what farm life was like.

LAURA INGALLS WILDER (1867–1957) wrote her famous eight-book Little House series between 1932 and 1943, embodying memories of her family's homesteading adventures in Wisconsin, Minnesota, Kansas, and South Dakota in the late 1800s. The immensity of the open lands of the frontier impresses little Laura in *Little House on the Prairie* (1935): "That prairie looked as if no human eye had ever seen it before. Only the tall wild grass covered the endless empty land and a great empty sky arched over it" (26). Ohio-born LOIS (LENORE) LENSKI (1893–1974) locates her *Corn-Farm Boy* (1954) in Iowa; Mennonite farmers in Kansas are described in *Plow the Dew Under* (1952) by Helen C. Fernald (1888–1972); Mary Margaret McBride (1899–1976) fictionalizes her Missouri farm experiences in *The Growing Up of Mary Elizabeth* (1966); and a particular hazard of Michigan farm life is recounted by Verne T. Davis (1889–1973) in *The Time of the Wolves* (1962).

Several Midwestern autobiographies and memoirs focus on farm life. Among these are *Eighty Acres: Elegy for a Family Farm* (1990) by Ronald Jager (b. 1933), the seminal *A SAND COUNTY ALMANAC* (1949) by ALDO LEOPOLD (1887–1948), and *Going over East: Reflections of a Woman Rancher* by LINDA HASSELSTROM (b. 1943).

Poetry of the Midwestern farm and countryside generally corresponds to its fictional counterpart. Nineteenth-century farm poetry tended toward romanticized portrayal of farmers and rural life in general, with some leavening melodrama and humor, and most is based on personal experience and nostalgia for the family farm. Typifying the era are two authors, WILL(IAM MCKENDREE) CARLETON (1845–1912) of Michigan and JAMES WHITCOMB RILEY (1849–1916) of Indiana. Although they do not exclusively contain farm poems, Carleton's *Farm Ballads* (1873), *Farm Legends* (1875), and *Farm Festivals* (1881) were extremely popular and were reprinted continuously for more than thirty years. Sentimental and sometimes written in vernacular to imitate rural speech, some of the poems, such as "Gone with a Handsomer Man," do have an edge of naturalism that conveys the message that life on the farm could hold unpleasant surprises. Perhaps, however, Carleton's true feelings about the farm environment can be seen in his dedication in *Farm Legends:* "To the memory of a nobleman, my farmer father."

James Whitcomb Riley's substantial body of verse dealing with rural themes was first selected and published in the collection *Riley Farm-Rhymes* (1901). This verse is generally more lighthearted and humorous than that of his contemporary, Carleton, and also relies on rustic dialect to emphasize the "plain folks" uprightness of his subjects, as in "Thoughts fer the Discuraged Farmer," or the joys of a good harvest in "The Frost Is on the Punkin." Last reprinted in 1921, *Riley Farm-Rhymes* was a popular favorite, as were all of Riley's publications.

Poets have since moved away from nostalgic and romantic depictions of farm life in favor of more objective descriptions or vignettes of moments in time. Rooted in the regional arts movement that produced painter Grant Wood (1891–1942), JAMES HEARST (1900–1983) of Iowa produced thirteen books of carefully crafted poetry reflecting his work as a farmer and his close knowledge of nature. John Judson (b. 1930) uses rural and farm images in *Finding Words in Winter* (1973), a long meditation on landscape and people. Ted Kooser (b. 1939) of Nebraska, the first U.S. Poet Laureate from the Great Plains, has written many poems about rural places and people. "Abandoned Farmhouse," from Kooser's first book, *Official Entry Blank* (1969), features the close observation and skill with figurative language that have won him a wide readership, as well as critical acclaim. In his collection of poems *Old Man Brunner Country* (1987), LEO DANGEL (b. 1941) depicts farm life in South Dakota as seen through the eyes of the eponymous farmer, who is both tender and acerbic. Mark Vinz (b. 1942) recreates an abandoned farmhouse in the eleven stanzas of "North Dakota Gothic" from *Climbing Stairs* (1983). Norbert Krapf (b. 1943) has written about his German American farming background and landscapes of his native state in books such as *Somewhere in Southern Indiana: Poems of Midwestern Origins* (1993).

The future of Midwestern farm literature is uncertain. With the yearly decline in the number of farms and independent farmers in the United States, fewer and fewer writers have firsthand knowledge and experience of farmwork and life. It remains to be seen whether writers will produce fiction and poetry about industrialized agribusiness and factory farms in the Midwest, or about the countermovement of organic and sustainable agriculture. Such writing, along with nonfiction nature writing focused on farming, may emerge to extend and modify this distinctive genre of Midwestern literature. See ENVIRONMENTAL LITERATURE.

SELECTED WORKS: Further discussion and examples of farm fiction and poetry are found in entries on individual states, but some of the more important works are briefly mentioned here.

Main-Travelled Roads (1891) by Hamlin Garland is the enduring text of late nineteenth-century Midwestern farm fiction by the writer who dominated the genre in his era. The outstanding farm novels of the modernist era are Willa Cather's *O Pioneers!* (1913) and *My Ántonia* (1918) and O. E. Rølvaag's *Giants in the Earth* (1927). Novels written during and in some cases about the Great Depression include *The Farm* (1933) by Louis Bromfield, *Now in November* (1934) by Josephine Johnson, and *Long Furrows* (1935) by Dora Aydelotte. Later farm novels include *The Fields* (1946) by Conrad Richter, *The Moonflower Vine* (1962) by Jetta Carleton, *. . . y no se lo tragó la tierra/ . . . And the Earth Did Not Devour Him* (1971) by Tomás Rivera, *Green Earth* (1977) by Frederick Manfred, *A Thousand Acres* (1991) by Jane Smiley, and *Cranberry Red* (2010) by Jerry Apps.

Important works of farm literature for children and adolescents include *Little House on the Prairie* (1935) by Laura Ingalls Wilder, *Corn-Farm Boy* (1954) by Lois Lenski, and *The Growing up of Mary Elizabeth* (1966) by Mary Margaret McBride.

Poems expressing the mores and sentiments of nineteenth-century Midwestern farmers are collected in *Farm Ballads* (1873) by Will Carleton and *Riley Farm-Rhymes* (1901) by James Whitcomb Riley. Later poems about Midwestern farm life can be found in books by James Hearst, John Judson, Ted Kooser, Leo Dangel, Mark Vinz, and Norbert Krapf.

Anthologies or collections of farm literature are neither numerous nor specifically dedicated to the Midwest. Four that do contain some Midwestern writings and authors are *Late Harvest: Rural American Writing* (1991), edited by David R. Pichaske; *Handspan of Red Earth: An Anthology of American Farm Poems* (1991), edited by Catherine Marconi; and two compiled by LUCIEN STRYK (1924–2013), *Heartland: Poets of the Midwest* (1967) and *Heartland II: Poets of the Midwest* (1975).

FURTHER READING: At present no full-length survey or general critical work exists on Midwestern farm literature in all its forms. However, a useful introduction to the origins of farm literature in the nineteenth century and its evolution can be found in the chapter "The Agricultural West in Literature," in *Virgin Land: The American West as Symbol and Myth* (1950) by Henry Nash Smith.

One of the first descriptions and surveys of the then-emerging farm-novel genre was "Farm Life Fiction" by Caroline B. Sherman in *South Atlantic Quarterly* 27 (July 1928): 310–24. Sherman updated her discussion ten years later in "The Development of Rural Fiction," *Agricultural History* 12.1 (January 1938): 67–76. John T. Flanagan's critical survey with bibliography, "The Middle Western Farm Novel," was published in *Minnesota History* 23 (June 1942): 113–25, 156–58. It was not until 1965, however, that Roy W. Meyer's groundbreaking monograph *The Middle Western Farm Novel in the Twentieth Century* appeared. Besides detailed examination and categorization of the genre, it also contains a fully annotated bibliography of 140 Midwestern farm novels published from 1891 to 1962. Meyer's bibliography was updated by Herman Nibbelink in "Novels of American Rural Life, 1963–1984," *North Dakota Quarterly* 53 (Fall 1985): 167–72, but Nibbelink did not limit his compilation to works set in the Midwest.

The use of farm fiction as an important source of material for historians and social scientists is championed by Lewis Atherton in "The Farm Novel and Agricultural History," *Agricultural History* 40 (April 1966): 131–40. Much the same attitude toward the farm novelist as historian can be found in "Novels of the Middle Border: A Critical Bibliography for Historians" by Charles T. Dougherty in *Historical Bulletin* 25 (May 1947): 77–78, 85–88.

Farm literature is also touched on in William Barillas's *The Midwestern Pastoral: Place and Landscape in Literature of the American Heartland* (2006), which closely examines five Midwestern authors. In *Working the Garden: American Writers and the Industrialization of Agriculture* (2001) William Conlogue examines the literary response to the trend of family farms being subsumed by large agricultural conglomerates, citing and comparing a number of Midwestern texts. Janet Galligani Casey's *A New Heartland: Women, Modernity, and the Agrarian Ideal in America* (2009), a study of women's rural attitudes in the early twentieth century, includes a chapter on farm novels, many of them Midwestern.

ROBERT BEASECKER   GRAND VALLEY STATE UNIVERSITY

FEDERAL WRITERS' PROJECT

OVERVIEW: President Franklin D. Roosevelt created the Works Progress Administration (WPA) by issuing Executive Order No. 7034 on May 6, 1935. As administrator of the WPA, Harry Hopkins appointed federal directors of the arts programs. He selected Henry G. Alsberg to oversee the writers' projects. A small segment of the WPA, the Federal Writers' Project (FWP) employed about seven thousand people during its eight-year existence from July 1, 1935, to June 30, 1943. Although it was the least publicized of the arts programs, which also included music, arts, and theatre, the Federal Writers' Project is considered today to have been the most influential and valuable because of its publication of American Guide Series books, the Folklore Project, Social-Ethnic Studies, and SLAVE NARRATIVES.

HISTORY AND SIGNIFICANCE: In a series of 1934 meetings that included Jacob Baker, Harry Hopkins's Civil Works Administration assistant; Henry Alsberg, Baker's assistant; and Katherine Kellock, a professional writer, a project for all the arts emerged. It was labeled Federal One and was divided administratively by specialty area. The Writers' Project was approved for federal monies in June 1935, and Henry Alsberg was named director. Criticized for its attempt to democratize American culture, the FWP operated in the face of public skepticism; many Americans questioned whether writing projects deserved public support when so many Americans were suffering through the Depression.

Publicity poster for the Federal Writers' Project's *Illinois: A Descriptive and Historical Guide*.
© A. C. McClurg & Co., 1940

The Federal Writers' Project gave jobs to thousands of unemployed writers who produced publications on American topics. A number of these well-known writers with Midwestern connections received support. RICHARD WRIGHT (1908–1960) wrote *NATIVE SON* in his spare time while working for the FWP. SAUL (C.) BELLOW (1915–2005) contributed to the Illinois Writers' Project, in which he wrote on JOHN DOS PASSOS (1896–1970), SHERWOOD ANDERSON (1876–1941), and JAMES T(HOMAS) FARRELL (1904–1979). MAXWELL BODENHEIM (1892–1954) worked briefly for the FWP but was fired for his alleged Communist Party membership. (JOHN WESLEY) "JACK" CONROY (1898–1990) joined the Missouri Writers' Project in 1936 and the Illinois Writers' Project in 1938, where he contributed to early folklore studies. NELSON ALGREN (b. Nelson Ahlgren Abraham,

1909–1981) worked as a writer and editor for the Illinois Writers' Project. Poet LORINE NIEDECKER (1903–1970) contributed to the Wisconsin WPA guide, for which naturalist ALDO LEOPOLD (1887–1948) served as a consultant.

Perhaps no other American writer supported New Deal politics more strongly than ARCHIBALD MACLEISH (1892–1982), who served in several posts during the Roosevelt administration. MacLeish's involvement, however, drew fire from literary people who resented his support of New Deal policies for the arts.

Because the FWP was unpopular with conservative and right-wing Americans, its legacy is overshadowed by controversy. Most notable among its critics was Martin Dies, chair of the House Un-American Activities Committee, which found the American Guide Series fraught with Communist-inspired sympathies. Dies's allegations focused on the American guides for their efforts to incorporate racial and cultural minorities into accepted mainstream American identity. Individual guides also came under attack for their celebration of diversity at a time when many Americans sought a sense of unanimity, not difference.

As America prepared for World War II, however, the FWP became expendable and was eventually discontinued in 1943. Nonetheless, recent critical assessment of the FWP finds its efforts to rediscover American culture during the Depression a significant chapter in American literary history.

SELECTED WORKS: The Midwest is well represented in the American Guide Series and other FWP publications. All twelve Midwestern states produced guides. Examples from each state follow. *Illinois: A Descriptive and Historical Guide* (1939) is the best Illinois-related FWP publication. *Better Illinois Communities through WPA Projects* (1936) addresses the impact of the Depression on families and communities, as well as the positive impact of WPA programs in ILLINOIS. The 525-page *Indiana: A Guide to the Hoosier State* (1941) portrays INDIANA across time, from its archaeology, American Indians, and history to its then-contemporary agriculture, industry and labor, folklore, arts, music, theatre, architecture, cities, and state tours, and provides a bibliography.

Iowa: A Guide to the Hawkeye State (1938) commemorates the centenary of the organization of IOWA Territory. *Kansas: A Guide to the Sunflower State* (1939), a 538-page work, was overseen by the State Department of Education and included the normal topics, as well as sections devoted to the natural setting and sports and recreation. *Michigan: A Guide to the Wolverine State* (1941), at 696 pages the biggest of the state guides, maintains the standard format of the state guides and was overseen by the Michigan State Administrative Board. *Minnesota: A State Guide* (1938) has coverage much like that of the other states, as well as sections on immigration and racial elements and several canoe trips. *Missouri: A Guide to the "Show Me" State* (1941), at 652 pages, was a publication of the Missouri State Highway Department and maintained the standard divisions of the state guides. *Nebraska: A Guide to the Cornhusker State* (1939) was a project of the Nebraska State Historical Society; its coverage and format were like those of other states, but it included a section on ethnic elements. *North Dakota: A Guide to the Northern Prairie State* (1938) is a 360-page document sponsored by the State Historical Society of North Dakota. The volume is typical in its coverage but also includes a section titled "Playgrounds," which describes two state parks. *The Ohio Guide* (1940) covers all aspects of OHIO, including its first people, natural settings, history, farms and farmers, industry, labor, cities, government, press and radio, and tours. *WPA Guide to South Dakota* (1938), like that of several other Midwestern states, covers the state's natural setting, American Indians and their way of life, history, agriculture, education, religion, transportation, architecture, folklore and folkways, recreation, cities, the Black Hills, tours, and a bibliography. *Wisconsin: A Guide to the Badger State* (1941) is a 561-page guide following the standard general format but also includes WISCONSIN political history, the Cooperative movement, recreation, literature, painting and sculpture, theatre, religion, ARCHITECTURE, and cities.

All the American Guides have been reprinted by the Federal Writers' Project Staff of Irvine, California, and are found under the title *Collected Works of Federal Writers' Proj-*

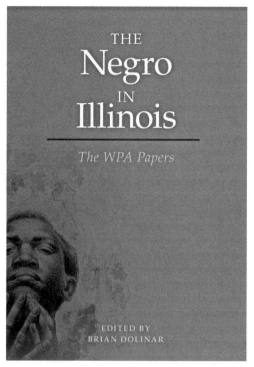

THE

Negro

IN

Illinois

The WPA Papers

EDITED BY
BRIAN DOLINAR

The Negro in Illinois: The WPA Papers, a WPA study of African Americans in Illinois, compiled and edited by Brian Dolinar, 2013.
Copyright 2013 by the Board of Trustees of the University of Illinois. Used by permission of the University of Illinois Press

ect include Monty Noam Penkower's *The Federal Writers' Project: A Study in Government Patronage of the Arts* (1977), focusing on the involvement of the New Deal in the FWP; Jerre Mangione's *The Dream and the Deal: The Federal Writers' Project, 1935–1943* (1972); and Jerrold Hirsch's *Portrait of America: A Cultural History of the Federal Writers' Project* (2003), relating the social and aesthetic features of the FWP projects. Paul Sporn's *Against Itself: The Federal Theater and Writers' Projects in the Midwest* (1995) considers Midwestern state politics, elite and popular arts, and class issues. It includes chapters on the Federal Writers' Project's effect on Polish, Finnish, and Jewish American culture, as well as a strong bibliography. George T. Blakey's *Creating a Hoosier Self-Portrait: The Federal Writers' Project in Indiana, 1935–1942* (2005) covers the Hoosier situation, the Indiana guide, oral history, finished and unfinished projects, research inventories, and a bibliography.

One book chapter and one article deal with the Federal Writers' Project and the Midwest: "Chicago and the Midwest," in David A. Taylor's 2009 volume *Soul of a People: The WPA Writers' Project Uncovers Depression America,* 39–74, which discusses Midwestern elements of the Federal Writers' Project; and Brian Dolinar's "The Illinois Writers' Project Essays: Introduction," *Southern Quarterly* 46.2 (Winter 2009): 84–90. Robert L. Carter's "Federal Writers' Project," in the Society for the Study of Midwestern Literature's *Newsletter* 9.1 (Spring 1979): 1–4, lists the Federal Writers' Project repositories and provides information on the degree to which they have been inventoried.

Valuable articles on Richard Wright and the FWP include Robert Bone's "Richard Wright and the Chicago Renaissance," *Callaloo* 28 (Summer 1986): 446–48, which discusses Wright's involvement in Chicago's Illinois Writers' Projects; Rosemary Hathaway's "Forgotten Manuscripts: Native Geography; Richard Wright's Work for the Federal Writers' Project in Chicago," *African American Review* 42.1 (Spring 2008): 91–108; and Thadious Davis's "Becoming: Richard Wright and the WPA," *Black Scholar* 39.1–2 (Summer 2009): 11–16.

Finally, Mindy J. Morgan's "Constructions and Contestations of the Authoritative

ect (1991). An important addition to the body of material in print is *The Negro in Illinois: The WPA Papers* (2013), edited by Brian Dolinar, who gathered writings, most previously unpublished, that were produced by a division of the Illinois Writers' Project. This division, directed by Arna Bontemps (1902–1973) and Jack Conroy and employing such writers as Richard Wright, Margaret Walker (1915–1998), and Fenton Johnson (1888–1958), focused on African American history, life, and culture, including literature. See also AFRICAN AMERICAN LITERATURE. *The Federal Writers' Project: A Bibliography* (1994), edited by Jeutonne P. Brewer, is a comprehensive compilation of books and articles attributed to the FWP. Several of the state guides can be read online.

FURTHER READING: Book-length scholarly treatments of the Federal Writers' Proj-

Voice: Native American Communities and the Federal Writers' Project, 1935–1941" appeared in *American Indian Quarterly* 29.1–2 (Winter/Spring 2005): 56–83.

JAMES M. BOEHNLEIN   UNIVERSITY OF DAYTON

FEMINISM

OVERVIEW: Since as early as 1405, with the publication of *The Book of the City of Women* by Christine de Pizan (1363–ca. 1430), the dialogue regarding women's rights and status has been debated in public discourse around the globe. By the early nineteenth century this discussion could be classified as a movement because many women and men were standing up more formally for women's rights. The women's movement began to take hold in the United States with speeches and publications devoted to the cause of women's rights and freedom. The most notable was the "Declaration of Sentiments" generated by the Women's Rights Convention in Seneca Falls, New York, in 1848, condemning social and legal discrimination against women. By the late nineteenth century this movement was often characterized as "feminism," and it led to a twentieth-century expansion of the fight for women's rights and equality on all levels. The movement reached a critical moment in the 1960s when a generation of students and younger faculty, steeped in feminist political inclinations emphasizing polemics, activism, and social concerns, became engaged in reinterpretive research and revisions of their course syllabi, casting aside the formalist assumptions and apolitical biases of New Criticism and affirming their newly found political passions. As *Historical Dictionary of Feminism* (2004), edited by Janet K. Boles and Diane Long Hoeveler, notes in its introduction, "The current consensus is that there is no one feminism but, in fact, many traditions within a larger movement dedicated to securing equity for women," a statement that characterizes the varied ways in which feminism and gender politics as a whole are currently debated (1). By exposing literary misogyny, recovering neglected women writers, and rethinking the conceptual grounds of literary study, literary feminism has transformed the study of literature by changing its center and standpoint.

In the Midwest the women's movement achieved the same strong presence it had elsewhere in the country. Many works of Midwestern literature detail ideas or attitudes related to the movement, and many Midwestern women and authors have lent their voices to the struggle. Therefore, women of the Midwest, like those of the United States as a whole, have benefited from a long history of individuals speaking out against gender injustice and for greater equality in society and under the law.

HISTORY AND SIGNIFICANCE: As the women's movement gained ground and developed throughout the United States, progress was felt in the Midwest. Early advocates of women's rights, such as Abigail Adams (1744–1818), SOJOURNER TRUTH (ca. 1797–1883), and Susan B. Anthony (1820–1906), were read and heard in the Midwest. Progressive measures were taken by Midwestern institutions of higher education; Oberlin College officially admitted women to the bachelor's degree program in 1837, and Kalamazoo College did the same in the 1840s. These schools were among the earliest in the nation to officially admit women. Novels such as *A NEW HOME—WHO'LL FOLLOW?* (1839) by CAROLINE KIRKLAND (1801–1864) reflect the pioneering efforts of women in the region during the nineteenth century, in Kirkland's case by presenting one woman's experience of Midwestern settlement and development. Although Kirkland's novel is not directly feminist in its message, it is one of the first to depict a strong female voice in the Midwest.

A very early feminist utopian novel came out of the Midwest. *Unveiling a Parallel: A Romance* (1893), by Alice Ilgenfritz Jones (1846–1905) and Ella Merchant (1857–1916) of Cedar Rapids, IOWA, focuses on a man who travels to Mars and finds a society there that allows far more equality for women than the society he left behind in America. The narrator is continually amazed by the power and equality that women have in the Martian world. Jones and Merchant even dare to suggest that women may explore their sexuality in the Martian community as easily as may some men on Earth.

ST. LOUIS–born writer Kate Chopin (1850–1904) explored women's rights in her writing. Neglected for decades as violating good

UNVEILING A

PARALLEL.

Decorative title page of the early Midwestern feminist novel *Unveiling a Parallel: A Romance*. Arena Pub. Co., 1893.
Courtesy of Hathitrust

taste and proper morals (and rediscovered in the 1960s), Chopin's novel *The Awakening* (1899) showcases her heroine, Edna Pontellier, who leaps off the page as an authentic malcontent and rebel against the gender prisons of Victorian womanhood, a heroine who is a metaphor and symbol for the new, politically driven critical age. Although Chopin was not part of feminist movements of her day, and although her work did not include representations of political feminists, her canon of fiction nevertheless echoed rebellious portraits of strong women characters searching for selfhood and sexual autonomy.

Some of Chopin's Midwestern contemporaries, including JANE ADDAMS (1860–1935), Ida B. Wells-Barnett (1862–1931), and ZITKALA-ŠA (RED BIRD, 1876–1938), also wrote texts that redefine women in contrast to late

nineteenth-century Victorian sexism and politics. Living and working in CHICAGO, Addams and Wells discussed race, class, and gender problems in that city and the nation. Addams's philosophical and political prose is informed by her life's work as a pioneer social worker at HULL-HOUSE (established in 1889), peace activist, and feminist. The combination of her social efforts, particularly in organizations such as the Women's International League for Peace and Freedom, led to Addams becoming the first American woman awarded a Nobel Prize in 1931. Born in Mississippi but based in Chicago for a good part of her life, African American journalist and activist Ida B. Wells-Barnett imbued her articles for the Chicago publication *The Conservator* with a passion for social justice for African Americans and supported anti-lynching crusades. She admonished white suffragists who forced black women to walk at the rear of a suffragist march in the South and urged them to build a multiracial women's movement against lynching. The fiction and essays of Zitkala-Ša, a Yankton Sioux from SOUTH DAKOTA, have been recovered and anthologized. In *American Indian Stories* (1921) Zitkala-Ša deals with painful memories of her childhood at a boarding school where forces of white Christian assimilation denied any value to her culture and ethnicity. As the first Native American woman to write independently and publish in *Harper's Monthly* and *Atlantic Monthly* about the double consciousness of her role as a woman within Indian and American societies, she left a legacy of elegant prose that affirms Indian identity, while her activism as a nationally recognized advocate for Native Americans contributed to the reformation of American laws regarding American Indians.

Other Midwestern women writers were advocates for women's rights and equality in their novels, stories, and plays. WILLA CATHER (1873–1947), who focuses on the NEBRASKA of her childhood and adolescence in many of her novels and stories, is recognized for her sympathetic rendering of women's lives. Alexandra Bergson in *O PIONEERS!* (1913), set in Nebraska, is a strong protagonist faced with balancing her own happiness with the expectations of society and the survival of her family farm. Cather's later novel *My Ántonia*

(1918) evokes the beauty of the Midwestern prairie and addresses the struggles of an immigrant woman farmer trying to make a home and build a strong family in a new country. SUSAN KEATING GLASPELL (1876–1948) deals with women's issues in many of her novels and plays, for example, *Fidelity* (1915) and *TRIFLES* (1916). Her female characters struggle to balance their sense of self with the conventions and constraints imposed by the small communities around them. EDNA FERBER (1885–1968) drew on her Midwestern upbringing and her knowledge of women's experiences in the region throughout much of her career for the novels *Fanny Herself* (1917) and *So Big* (1924). ZONA GALE (1874–1938) supported women's causes throughout her life, and her work often depicts strong female characters, most notably in *Miss Lulu Bett* (1920), which won a Pulitzer Prize in 1921 for a dramatic version of the novel. Gale's novel was so popular it shared the distinction of being the best-selling novel of 1920 with *MAIN STREET* by (HARRY) SINCLAIR LEWIS (1885–1951). Lulu is constrained by the expectations of her controlling family and the small town where she lives, perspectives biased by her status as an unmarried older woman; by the end of the novel she manages to escape the limiting viewpoints as she and her new husband are last seen heading in the direction of the railway station. *Miss Lulu Bett* represents a woman successfully liberating herself from the oppression of her family and those of larger social conditions.

In the first half of the twentieth century, literary modernism and radical socialist feminism emerged as two movements that attracted prominent Midwestern women writers. MARGARET C. ANDERSON (1886–1973), who lived for long periods in Chicago, was a leading exponent and practitioner of modernism. Anderson and Ezra Pound (1885–1972) were major architects of *THE LITTLE REVIEW* and profoundly influenced modernist style and taste. Anderson's lesbian relationships, rendered in her autobiographies *My Thirty Years War* (1930) and *The Fiery Fountains* (1951) and her lesbian novel *Forbidden Fires*, written in 1958 but not printed until 1996, are unusual for that time. These books resist heterosexist gender constructions and serve as examples of

lesbian discourse in feminist writing and thought.

Three Midwestern feminist socialist writers, TILLIE (LERNER) OLSEN (1912–2007), MERIDEL LE SUEUR (1900–1996), and Agnes Smedley (1892–1950), wrote about the intersections of class and gender, contributing to a tradition of radical women writers and activists. Born in Nebraska, Tillie Olsen was rediscovered by feminists more than three decades after her first literary flowering in the 1930s. Concerned with silences imposed on marginalized women writers, Olsen dramatizes motherly conflict and guilt in her soliloquizing story "I Stand Here Ironing," which gives voice to a beleaguered, guilt-ridden working mother-narrator. Born in Iowa, Meridel Le Sueur was also concerned with the plight of working-class Midwestern women and recorded the social realities of their lives in fiction, journalistic and historical essays, poetry, and autobiography. Her novel *The Girl*, written in 1936 but not published until 1978, takes the stories of women she met in the 1930s and synthesizes their experiences into the tale of a girl struggling to make a life away from her family and amid the challenges and temptations of the city. Agnes Smedley was born in Campground, MISSOURI, and lived in New York and as an expatriate in Germany, Russia, and China. Her dedication to detailing the hegemony of class on an American working-class feminist woman is illustrated in her novel *Daughter of Earth* (1929). Her portraits of Chinese peasant women are based on her travels with the Chinese Red Army in the 1930s. Although other women did not always declare themselves socialists during this time, they still wrote about and engaged in political issues prevalent during the period. JOSEPHINE (FREY) HERBST (1892–1969) published several novels set in the Midwest and depicting strong, independent female characters, including *Nothing Is Sacred* (1928) and *Pity Is Not Enough* (1933), and wrote journalistic pieces covering the farm struggles in the region during the 1930s.

From the late 1960s to the present, Midwestern women writers of diverse backgrounds and feminist sympathies have produced distinguished work that has been acclaimed nationally and internationally. The novel *THE DOLLMAKER* (1954) by HARRI-

ETTE SIMPSON ARNOW (1908–1986) was celebrated by feminists in the 1970s for its vivid, sympathetic depiction of a resourceful Appalachian woman whose dreams of owning a modest farm in Kentucky are crushed when she follows her husband to industrialized DETROIT during the 1930s. She survives her dismal life of disappointments, tragic compromises, and the death of one of her children through her artistry and indomitable loving spirit. The work of MARGE PIERCY (b. 1936) continues to attract interest. *Going Down Fast* (1969) and *Dance the Eagle to Sleep* (1970) have Midwestern settings, and *He She and It* (1992) uses a Nebraska setting for part of its dystopia. ALIX KATES SHULMAN (b. 1932) was born in CLEVELAND, and many of her characters are born in the Midwest and then leave the region for other places. Her novel *Memoirs of an Ex-Prom Queen* (1972) was well received in feminist circles of the 1970s. JOYCE CAROL OATES (b. 1938), one of the best-known American writers and perhaps the most prolific living writer in several genres, claims to be a feminist, an assertion borne out in *(Woman) Writer: Occasions and Opportunities* (1988) and in her fiction, which deals with the violent effects of patriarchy. The novels of JANE (GRAVES) SMILEY (b. 1949), especially *A Thousand Acres* (1991) and *Moo* (1995), are associated with the Midwest both through their settings and their vivid Midwestern women characters.

Exemplifying the diversity in recent Midwestern women writers, TONI MORRISON (b. CHLOE ARDELIA WOFFORD, 1931), the first African American woman to win the Nobel Prize for Literature, employs the contemporary feminist theme of selfhood as it is affected by the sexist and racist values of white culture in her first novel, *The Bluest Eye* (1970). She depicts the haunting effects of slavery, particularly through the perspective of a mother, in *Beloved* (1987). GWENDOLYN BROOKS (1917–2000), the Poet Laureate of ILLINOIS (1985–1986) and Consultant in Poetry to the Library of Congress, depicts African American characters and themes in much of her poetry; in poems such as "the mother" and "A Bronzeville Mother Loiters in Mississippi. Meanwhile, a Mississippi Mother Burns Bacon," she addresses the concerns of women and their experiences. Continuing a multicultural Midwestern

focus, the fiction of BHARATI MUKHERJEE (b. 1940), especially her acclaimed novel *Jasmine* (1989), details the clash between Indian immigrant women and dominant American culture set against an Iowa backdrop. SANDRA CISNEROS (b. 1954) gives voice to Chicago Chicanas in her novels, including *THE HOUSE ON MANGO STREET* (1984). The novels of MINNESOTA-born (KAREN) LOUISE ERDRICH (b. 1954), beginning with *LOVE MEDICINE* (1984), deal with both stories of Native American families and male-female relationships.

Feminist criticism and theory began and continues in leading women's studies journals. Contemporary criticism continues to reassess and recover women writers and their work and discuss issues of representation, definition, and politics related to women and, more broadly, gender studies as a whole. *Signs: A Journal of Women in Culture and Society* was founded in Chicago in 1975 and is one of the oldest academic journals to focus exclusively on women's studies. Other journals, including *Legacy: A Journal of American Women Writers, Feminist Studies*, and *NWSA Journal*, also publish articles addressing women's issues or focus on work by women writers.

Although women's rights have been firmly defended and established in the many centuries since Christine de Pizan and other early advocates for women's rights, it is clear that much remains to be understood and discussed regarding contemporary interpretations of gender and the role women play in the Midwest and around the globe.

SELECTED WORKS: Willa Cather's *O Pioneers!* (1913) and *My Ántonia* (1918) demonstrate classic themes surrounding women in Midwestern literature and culture. Meridel Le Sueur's *The Girl* (1978) represents a strong example of feminist issues and concerns in the Midwest. For students and scholars interested in more contemporary portrayals of Midwestern women or women's issues, Jane Smiley's *A Thousand Acres* (1991) or Louise Erdrich's *Love Medicine* (1984) would provide good introductions.

A few anthologies have focused on collecting or defining women's writing in the Midwest. *Jane's Stories: An Anthology of Work by Midwestern Women* (1994) and *Jane's Stories II: An Anthology by Midwestern Women* (2000) stem from the Jane's Stories Press Foundation writing collective, founded in the Midwest but encouraging women's writing around the world. There are also literary collections such as *In the Middle: Ten Midwestern Women Poets*, published by the KANSAS CITY, Missouri–based BKMK/University of Missouri-KANSAS CITY Press in (1985), edited by Sylvia Griffith Wheeler, and *Prairie Hearts: Women View the Midwest* (1996), edited by Whitney Scott.

Among anthologies that include Midwestern women writers are *American Women Writers: Diverse Voices in Prose since 1845* (1992), edited by Eileen Barrett and Mary Cullinan; *The Norton Anthology of Literature by Women* (1985), edited by Sandra M. Gilbert and Susan Gubar; *American Women Regionalists, 1850–1910* (1992), edited by Judith Fetterley and Marjorie Pryse; and *Women in the Trees: U.S. Women's Short Stories about Battering and Resistance, 1839–1994* (1996), edited by Susan Koppelman.

FURTHER READING: No critical texts are devoted to Midwestern literary feminism. Although it does not focus on the literature of the region, *On Behalf of the Family Farm: Iowa Farm Women's Activism since 1945* (2013) by Jenny Barker Devine is a valuable contribution to the study of feminist activism in farm communities in Iowa and the Midwest. Several other texts more generally address the struggles between regionalism and women's writing. Judith Fetterley and Marjorie Pryse have done significant work to recover women writers and discuss their regional significance. Their text *Writing out of Place: Regionalism, Women, and American Literary Culture* (2003) includes discussion of ALICE CARY (1820–1871), Willa Cather, and Zitkala-Ša. *Breaking Boundaries: New Perspectives on Women's Regional Writing* (1997), edited by Sherrie A. Inness and Diana Royer, explores women's writing and regionalism more broadly but includes Midwestern women Zitkala-Ša, Meridel Le Sueur, GENE STRATTON-PORTER (1863–1924), and LINDA HASSELSTROM (b. 1943). Although it focuses on western writers, Krista Comer's "Taking Feminism and Regionalism toward the Third Wave," in *A Companion to the Regional Literatures of America* (2003), edited by Charles L. Crow, 111–28, also contains useful insights about regionalism and women's writing.

Some works explore feminist boundary issues. Among these is the work of a relative newcomer, Achy Obejas, who was born in Cuba in 1956 and emigrated to Indiana and then to Chicago, where she lives and writes. An established poet, fiction writer, and journalist, Obejas won the 2002 Lambda Award for her novel *Days of Awe* (2001), which, like her other work, deals with the constructed boundaries of lesbian, bisexual, Cuban, and Sephardic-Jewish identities. See also LATINO/ LATINA LITERATURE. Karen Lee Osborne and William Spurlin, editors of *Reclaiming the Heartland*: *Lesbian and Gay Voices from the Midwest* (1996), present a wide range of Midwestern lesbian and gay writers who work in several literary genres. The collection presents another type of feminism, challenges the notion that the Midwest is repressive and backward, and explores the complexity of queer identity. The editors' underscored assertion is that the Midwest is a "perspective, a way of positioning oneself in the world" (xxi). See also LESBIAN, GAY, BISEXUAL, TRANSGENDER, AND QUEER LITERATURE.

Elaine Showalter's history of women's literature, *A Jury of Her Peers: Celebrating American Women Writers from Anne Bradstreet to Annie Proulx* (2009), provides a strong overview of American women writers and many of their key texts, including Midwesterners Caroline Kirkland, Kate Chopin, Susan Glaspell, Willa Cather, Meridel Le Sueur, Josephine Herbst (1892–1969), Gwendolyn Brooks, LORRAINE HANSBERRY (1930–1965), Joyce Carol Oates, Toni Morrison, SARA PARETSKY (b. 1947), Sandra Cisneros, Louise Erdrich, Jane Smiley, and others.

JOYCE LADENSON   MICHIGAN STATE UNIVERSITY
SARA KOSIBA   TROY UNIVERSITY

FILM

OVERVIEW: In *The Wizard of Oz* (1939), the movie version of *THE WONDERFUL WIZARD OF OZ* (1900) by L(YMAN) FRANK BAUM (1856–1919), Dorothy utters two lines that would solidify the popular perception of the Midwest throughout the twentieth century. Upon her arrival in Oz, she confides to her dog, "Toto, I've got a feeling we're not in Kansas anymore." Near the conclusion of the film, she comments, "There's no place like home." Ranked as the fourth and twenty-third most famous movie quotations in history by the American Film Institute in 2005, these lines symbolize how Hollywood has characterized the Midwest as the repository of homespun American values while subtly cautioning that life outside the Midwest is potentially threatening to such values. Both elements are clearly seen in dozens of dramas, comedies, and musicals.

A distinct exception to these depictions of the Midwest as the home of simple, honest values has been the CHICAGO film, which has frequently depicted this Midwestern capital as a vibrant but immoral metropolis visiting frontier justice on its ill-tempered, lawless populace. There have also been noteworthy revaluations of Midwestern popular myths in films that have critically deconstructed the props, plotlines, and ARCHETYPES of an innocent Midwestern psyche and have exposed a frigid or gritty lifestyle beneath the wholesome, upright veneer. Even though such locales as the South or cities like New York or Los Angeles have readily lent themselves to treatment in films, the Midwest has garnered significant attention of its own.

HISTORY AND SIGNIFICANCE: In the midst first of the Depression and then of World War II, Hollywood helped mythologize the Midwest as the refuge of longstanding American values and a bulwark against the social and political turbulence of the East and West Coasts and abroad. Regarded as America's heartland, the Midwest has been commonly portrayed in films as a repository for family, honesty, sincerity, and steadiness—even if such characteristics might be perceived as naïve or dull by outsiders. As Edward Recchia argues in "There's No Place like Home: The Midwest in American Film Musicals," *Midwest Quarterly* 39.2 (Winter 1998), "In our popular mythology, it is precisely the *lack* of excitement and sophistication that has become a virtue itself for the Midwest: Midwestern dullness has represented for the nation a kind of reassuring steadiness of human virtue and human values" (202). Frequently, Depression-era and World War II films depicted Midwesterners as withstanding the inroads of cutthroat capitalism, political chicanery, and fast-paced, burgeoning urbanization that more and more seemed to characterize the

nation. Not only did such films portray Midwesterners as withstanding "outside" threats, they often showed that Midwestern virtue could deal with external threats by using honest behavior to make outsiders reconsider the Midwest's largely pre-industrial philosophy and way of life. Although this portrayal was nostalgic at its core, it no doubt served as a psychic tonic to a nation otherwise preoccupied with turbulent social changes.

The musical genre best illustrates this depiction of the Midwest as bastion of homespun values. In such films the world outside the small-town Midwest poses a threat to the preservation of a simpler, more innocent, way of life. In *Meet Me in St. Louis* (1944), for instance, Alonzo Smith (Leon Ames) is ready to pack up his family for a job transfer to New York, but through the machinations of his three daughters (the eldest played by Judy Garland), involving the sentimental scenes surrounding major holidays, he is influenced to stay in ST. LOUIS. Similarly, *State Fair* (1945; other versions were made in 1933 and 1962), set during the annual IOWA State Fair, depicts two slick-talking easterners (Dana Andrews and Vivian Blaine) who nearly sweep a corn-fed sister and brother (Jeanne Crain and Dick Haymes) into marriage and eventual relocation. Ultimately, both siblings end up preferring to remain in their hometown, and the sister makes a convert of her big-city journalist lover. *The Music Man* (1962) gives us another such Midwestern conversion. There, con man Harold Hill (Robert Preston) is ready to abscond with funds collected to purchase band instruments and uniforms in a small Iowa town. The local music teacher (Shirley Jones) wins him over to the small-town honest life, and he stays for her, fulfilling his promise to start a boys' band. The story is similar in *Bye Bye Birdie* (1963). In that film the songwriter-agent (Dick Van Dyke) hopes to capitalize on his Elvis-like client by exploiting the gullibility of an OHIO small town for his own publicity; this too ends with the outsider rejecting the crass commercialism of New York to settle in the Midwest. Even in *The Wizard of Oz*, set mostly in Technicolor Oz, Dorothy (Judy Garland) yearns throughout to return to Auntie Em and her black-and-white Dust Bowl home in KANSAS.

Judy Garland as Dorothy Gale in the
Warner Brothers film *The Wizard of Oz*.
© Warner Brothers, 1939

A number of dramas have also perpetuated the mythology of a homespun Midwest. Set in NEBRASKA, *Boys Town* (1938) portrays how Father Flanagan (Spencer Tracy) achieves his dream of providing a second chance to troubled boys through the sincere generosity of everyday folks. Similarly, two films about ABRAHAM LINCOLN (1809–1865)— *Young Mr. Lincoln* (1939) and *Abe Lincoln in Illinois* (1940)—situate the future president's virtues in small-town ILLINOIS. *The Farmer's Daughter* (1947) shows how a simple Swedish farm girl from MINNESOTA (Loretta Young) could, while starting as a domestic for a congressman in Washington (Joseph Cotten), rise up to challenge right-wing politics by eventually running for Congress herself. Playing against the rustic Midwestern milieu, Alfred Hitchcock's *North by Northwest* (1959) follows the cross-country pursuit of adman Roger Thornhill (Cary Grant); in two of its most famous scenes, Thornhill is pursued by a crop-dusting pilot in rural Illinois and eludes his foreign-spy antagonists atop SOUTH DAKOTA's Mount Rushmore. In *The Out of Towners* (1970), a fish-out-of-water story of an innocent Ohioan couple

(Jack Lemmon and Sandy Dennis), the Midwesterners encounter every conceivable problem in New York, where Lemmon's character is lured by a promising job offer but rejects it to return to the Midwest. Finally, in *The Straight Story* (1999) David Lynch, breaking from his usual avant-garde style, directs Richard Farnsworth as an elderly widower who drives a riding mower from Iowa to WISCONSIN to visit his dying brother; it is a story that embodies an innocent, humble Midwest.

Many films in the sports genre sanctify traditional Midwestern values. *Breaking Away* (1979) portrays not only a town-and-gown conflict, with bicycling aficionado Dave Stohler (Dennis Christopher) living his life in Indiana University's Bloomington as a son of a limestone "cutter," but also his wistful desire to live as one of the great Italian bicycle racers. His trials and tribulations lead him to embrace Bloomington life. *Hoosiers* (1986) presents a story, loosely based on true events, of a discredited basketball coach (Gene Hackman) taking a small INDIANA high school basketball team to the state championships. *Rudy* (1993) replicates this theme, this time adapting the true story of the son of an Indiana steel-mill worker (Sean Astin) working hard to achieve his childhood dream to play football for Notre Dame. *Field of Dreams* (1989) solidifies the myth of Midwestern virtue through magic realism, by chronicling the construction of a baseball diamond in an Iowa cornfield by Ray Kinsella (Kevin Costner). The field provides second chances for those denied their dreams, including the ghost of "Black Sox" baseball player Shoeless Joe Jackson.

A glaring exception to the sepia-tinted film depictions of the Midwest as the mainstay of honest American values has been the Chicago film, which, from the 1930s on, has presented a continuous mythic depiction of the Midwest capital as a frontier metropolis fraught with graft and needing to apply frontier justice to keep the peace. In spite of—or perhaps because of—its social iniquities, Chicago is usually depicted as a dynamo of energy and vitality, consistently in stark contrast to the folksy, simpler ways depicted in small-town Midwest films. Even in the highly fictionalized *In Old Chicago* (1937), a sentimental film about Mrs. O'Leary (Alice

Kevin Costner as Eliot Ness in the Paramount Pictures film
The Untouchables.
© Paramount Pictures, 1987

Brady) and the rivalry of her two sons before her cow starts the Great Chicago Fire of 1871, the city is still depicted as a bastion of activity and power that will not be deterred in its progress, even by a devastating fire.

Prohibition-era gangster Al Capone became a frequently tapped resource for Chicago films set in the 1930s. *Little Caesar* (1930), *Public Enemy* (1931), and *Scarface* (1932) are all inspired by Chicago's gangster life during this time; and *Al Capone* (1959), *The St. Valentine's Day Massacre* (1967), and *The Untouchables* (1987) directly showcase Capone. *The Untouchables,* with a screenplay by DAVID (ALAN) MAMET (b. 1947), goes so far as to revise the frontier myth by presenting the city as the untamed wilderness, Capone (Robert DeNiro) as the dangerous prey, and Treasury agent Eliot Ness (Kevin Costner) as the untested novice hunter under the tutelage of beat cop Malone (Sean Connery), who teaches him how to get Capone.

Chicago gangster life is reflected in many other ways in film. The gangster environs of the 1920s inspire catchy tunes in *Robin and the 7 Hoods* (1964), featuring the Rat Pack and Frank Sinatra's crooning of "My Kind of Town." The lawless city is played for laughs in *The Sting* (1973), also set in Prohibition-era Chicago. The film invites the audience to root for two amiable con men (Paul Newman and Robert Redford) as they dupe ruthless gangster Doyle Lonnegan (Robert Shaw). More seriously, questionable police behavior involving a murder propels a crusading newspaperman (James Stewart) in *Call Northside 777* (1948). But even by the 1990s, when it was no longer an untamed wilderness, the city and its police force were still depicted as ruthless in *The Fugitive* (1993). *Candyman* (1992) ratchets up the dangers of the city even further by following the frightening actions of an African American supernatural killer who inhabits the city's Cabrini Green housing project.

An earlier film, *The Front Page* (1931, reworked as *His Girl Friday* in 1939 and remade in 1974), transforms the center of anarchic turbulence from law enforcement to the press. There, Chicago newspapermen vie with one another to get a scoop on a scheduled execution that goes awry, in part because of the corruption and ineptitude of the police force. Similarly, the musical *Chicago* (2002; earlier nonmusical versions in 1927 and 1942) satirizes the excesses of the press when working-class Roxie Hart (Renée Zellweger) murders her lover and hires flashy lawyer Billy Flynn (Richard Gere) to defend her. John Sayles's *Eight Men Out* (1988) also turns the tables on the venial press and the usual portrayals of Chicago gangsters by depicting the owners of the Chicago White Sox and other businesses as the true villains behind the White Sox's 1919 World Series scandal. *Medium Cool* (1969) presents a very different view of the media while continuing to reflect Chicago's non-typical Midwestern nature. This film follows a TV cameraman (Robert Forster) as he encounters racism, Vietnam War protests, government intrusion, and the riots surrounding the 1968 Democratic Convention.

Ferris Bueller's Day Off (1986), one of John Hughes's several films shot in Illinois, taps into the positive excitement and riches of the city as the title character (Matthew Broderick) skips school to attend a Cubs game and visit Chicago's Art Institute. In addition to Hughes's films, popular comedies set in Illinois include several starring famous alumni of Chicago's Second City comedy theatre, such as *The Blues Brothers* (1980), *Caddyshack* (1980), and *Wayne's World* (1992), which frequently draw humorous contrasts between Midwestern middle- and upper-class "normality" and the antics of nonconformist protagonists. At the other end of the socioeconomic spectrum, *A RAISIN IN THE SUN* (1961), based on the 1959 play by LORRAINE HANSBERRY (1930–1965), portrays African Americans struggling to survive in Chicago. The city's constant racial and ethnic struggles are also presented in *The Great White Hope* (1970), a fictionalized portrayal of prizefighter and club owner Jack Johnson. The film captures the racism the fighter endured for his successful boxing career and marrying a white woman. In *A Family Thing* (1996) a working-class white southerner (Robert Duvall) discovers that his biological mother was a black maid; he then travels to Chicago to find his black half-brother (James Earl Jones) and make sense of his mixed racial heritage.

In the midst of these sharply contrasting depictions of the Midwest are a number of films that do not follow neat black-and-white formulas. These films have variously presented critical revaluations of the mythic Midwest and have ranged from exposure of the unseemly side of the small-town heartland, including its provincialism and narrow-mindedness, to critiques of the small-town mind-set and its exploitation by more sophisticated outsiders. Another atypical thrust has been toward portrayals that deny the region its homespun symbolism and instead present it as a microcosm of pessimistic trends operating in the rest of the country. All these depictions challenge common perspectives of the Midwest as virtuous and genuinely American. *Kings Row* (1942), adapted from the 1940 novel by (Heinrich Hauer) HENRY BELLAMANN (1882–1945), portrays scandalous actions in a Midwestern small town that gradually erupts with incest, miscegenation, medical malpractice, and a host of other social sins. Similarly, *The Magnificent Ambersons* (1942), adapted from the novel by (NEWTON) BOOTH TARKINGTON (1869–1946), indicts the provincial snobbery of an Indianapolis family while also depicting how the nation's progress, symbolized by the advent of the automobile, is too great for an insulated Midwestern city to bear.

Set in a fictionalized CINCINNATI, *The Best Years of Our Lives* (1946) follows the difficulties of three World War II veterans reacclimating themselves to civilian life. Based on the novel *Glory for Me* (1945) by MACKINLAY (BENJAMIN) KANTOR (1904–1977), the film portrays a detached city unsympathetic to its returning veterans. Similar in theme, *Some Came Running* (1958) situates a discharged GI (played by Frank Sinatra) in his emotionally stifling Indiana hometown.

Also set in a fictionalized Cincinnati (or KANSAS CITY, as some have suggested), *The Asphalt Jungle* (1950) depicts the corrosive underbelly of the Midwestern city as it follows the planning and execution of an elaborate crime and its unsuccessful consequences. Politicians, police, and so-called upstanding citizens seem indistinguishable from the criminals in one of the first American "caper" films. Similarly, *Picnic* (1955), adapted from the popular play by WILLIAM (MOTTER) INGE (1913–1973), presents an outsider (William Holden) who tries to ingratiate himself in a small Kansas town but eventually leaves with the local girl (played by Kim Novak) after the judgmental town shows itself to be frigid and inflexible. Another Midwestern crime story, considered scandalous when it was released in 1959, *Anatomy of a Murder* dwells on graphic sexual details as attorney Paul Biegler (James Stewart) defends a murder suspect (Ben Gazzara) in MICHIGAN's Upper Peninsula. The film is an adaptation of the best-selling 1957 novel by JOHN DONALDSON VOELKER (1903–1991).

Much more starkly, *In Cold Blood* (1967), based on the best seller by Truman Capote (1924–1984), reconstructs the brutal murder of a Kansas family while simultaneously portraying the town as a virtual wasteland and the judicial system as brutal as the killers in its quest to execute them. Variations on this subject appear in *Capote* (2005) and *Infamous* (2006), which depict Capote researching and writing the book. Joel and Ethan Cohen's *Fargo* (1996) takes us mostly to Minnesota locales that become the setting of a kidnapping and multiple murders. In a clever updating of a Midwestern mythic character, the film portrays a pregnant police chief (Frances McDormand) as naïve and folksy but fully capable of solving the crime spree. The Cohen brothers return to their native Minnesota in *A Serious Man* (2009), which puts on display the downward spiral of a Job-like college professor in his stifling Jewish enclave. Set in the 1930s, Robert Altman's *Kansas City* (1996) showcases organized crime and political corruption, which provide a thriving environment for the rise of jazz. The critically acclaimed *Winter's Bone* (2010), set in the MISSOURI Ozarks, portrays a teenager's harrowing search for her missing father, exposing an impoverished, drug-addled rural community.

Among the few westerns set in the Midwest, *The Great Northfield Minnesota Raid* (1972) and *The Assassination of Jesse James by the Coward Robert Ford* (2007) are related not only by the appearance of the character Jesse James but also by their rather gritty depictions of the terrain. In the films' depictions of a violent and lawless society, Minnesota and Missouri seem little different from the Wild West. Ang Lee's *Ride with the Devil* (1999) showcases North-South rivalries and racial issues during the Civil War. Set in Missouri, the film points out the many conflicts in the only slave state that was pro-Union.

Midwestern innocence and naïveté are shown not to be virtues but detriments in a number of films. Adapted from the 1927 novel by (HARRY) SINCLAIR LEWIS (1885–1951), *Elmer Gantry* (1960) follows a Billy Sunday–like religious huckster (Burt Lancaster) as he travels throughout the Midwest and Southwest preying on the gullibility of small-town folks. *Paper Moon* (1973) follows the exploits of a Bible salesman and his pre-teen sidekick (Ryan and Tatum O'Neal) as they prey on the guilelessness of small-town folks in Missouri and Kansas. More gruesomely, *Badlands* (1973), inspired by the real-life Starkweather-Fugate criminal duo, follows the killing spree of a couple (Martin Sheen and Sissy Spacek) in 1950s Nebraska. The film portrays the killers as an amoral pair, bored with the banal life of the small town, who commence their killings on a whim and eventually enjoy the status of outlaws. Even the people they kidnap and rob (some of whom they later murder) seem thrilled by the experience, thus underscoring the bleak conditions of their lives.

Less typical approaches to undercutting Midwestern myths of idyllic pastoral life are many. *Waiting for Guffman* (1996), set in Blaine, Missouri, features bathetic local talents staging a musical about their town in hopes of attracting Broadway producers. It is a wry satire on the townsfolk's self-delusion. In the comedy *Grosse Pointe Blank* (1997) a professional killer (John Cusack) returns to his Michigan hometown with a contract to fulfill and a high school reunion to attend. World weary from the demands of his job, he is bemused that so little has changed in his town. After surviving several shootouts, he gains the admiration of his humdrum former classmates and leaves town with his former high school sweetheart. *Mr. and Mrs. Bridge* (1990) portrays the marital and family breakdown of an elderly couple (played by Paul Newman and Joanne Woodward) when their stifling, isolated Kansas City lifestyle is challenged by the return of their children from worldly experiences in the 1930s and 1940s. In Alexander Payne's *About Schmidt* (2002) Jack Nicholson plays a retired Omaha insurance actuary who comes to grips with the knowledge that he has lived a meaningless, banal life.

Payne revisits his home state in *Nebraska* (2013), which uses stark black-and-white photography to emphasize small-minded small-town ways when a cantankerous elderly alcoholic (Bruce Dern) returns to his home with the deluded intent to collect a prize in nearby Lincoln.

Other negative visions attack stereotypes of Midwestern life and people. *The Watermelon Man* (1970) showcases Godfrey Cambridge's portrayal of a bigoted white man in an Indiana town who one day wakes up transformed into a black man and has to suffer the prejudice of his town. More starkly, *Ordinary People* (1980), set in an upscale Chicago suburb, plays off the archetype that Midwesterners are "ordinary people" by focusing on an appearance-conscious family's attempts to cope with an accidental death, an attempted suicide, and the breakup of a marriage. Several films within the past thirty years have worked against the older formula of presenting the Midwest as a repository of nostalgic American values withstanding the inroads of national progress. In fact, these films have depicted stories and experiences that show the Midwest to be a microcosm of national issues and trends. *Stranger than Paradise* (1984) follows a New Yorker's cousin from Hungary as she moves from the Big Apple to CLEVELAND, meets up again with her cousin and his friend, and then travels to Florida. Using a minimalist approach and bleak black-and-white photography, writer-director Jim Jarmusch paints such a homogeneous picture of the American landscape that the three distinct locations seem almost interchangeable.

Among films about farm crises that emerged in the 1980s, two are set in the Midwest: In *Country* (1984) a long-standing Iowa farming family confronts natural disasters and—a far worse crisis—a government that turns its back on them. In *Miles from Home* (1988) two brothers inherit their father's award-winning farm, only to see it go bankrupt; this prompts them to torch the farm and become renegades. Both films, like other farm movies that came out of the decade, reflected a growing national issue as locally owned farms across the country failed or were bought out by huge agribusiness conglomerates.

Presenting a dystopian vision of the near future where crime is rampant and police forces are privatized by dubious corporations, *Robocop* (1987) blends black comedy and science fiction in a DETROIT setting emblematic of any American urban center. Set in Omaha, *Election* (1999) follows a cutthroat campaign for high school student government that holds up a mirror to myriad other campaigns for federal and state office. Serving as a microcosm for nationwide homophobia, *Boys Don't Cry* (1999) depicts the experiences of Brandon Teena (Hilary Swank), a transgender man who was born Teena Brandon. In the film Brandon relocates to a small Nebraska town, gets involved with a rough crowd, and is brutally raped and murdered by two men after they discover that he is anatomically and genetically female. Set in the burned-out inner city of Detroit, *8 Mile* (2002) traces a traditional saga of a young man who wants to break away from his bleak surroundings by pursuing his musical talents; the film radically updates the formula by portraying a white musician (Eminem) trying to surmount his origins through rap music, a genre then most associated with African Americans and East or West Coast urban locations. In *A History of Violence* (2005), an outsider who runs an Indiana diner (Viggo Mortensen) is hailed by his town as a hero for killing two criminals on the run but then endures an escalating string of violent episodes as his previous life in Philadelphia catches up with him. The cyclical nature of violence is shown to be just as much at home in the small-town Midwest as anywhere else in America.

Films about African Americans in the Midwest broaden viewers' sense of the region's past and present. Early films, many from black production companies, featuring black casts and marketed to black audiences, were known as "race films." OSCAR MICHEAUX (1884–1951), novelist and the first major black filmmaker, adapted his novel *The Conquest: The Story of a Negro Homesteader* (1913) as *The Homesteader* (1919). The film, now lost, drew on Micheaux's experience farming in South Dakota. His second film, *Within Our Gates* (1920), is the oldest known surviving film by a black director. A portrayal of a southern black woman going north to obtain funding for a black school, *Within Our Gates* deals with racist violence and the Great Migration of blacks out of the south. Micheaux's later films include *Underworld* (1936), a black take on the Chicago gangster film genre. Other race films included *Spirit of Youth* (1937), set in Detroit, with boxing champion Joe Louis starring as a version of himself, and *Chicago after Dark* (1946), by director Josh Binney.

Most films about black Midwesterners are set in Chicago. Two adaptations of *NA-TIVE SON* (1940) by RICHARD WRIGHT (1908–1960) have been produced, in 1951 and 1986. The first version starred the author himself as the main character, Bigger Thomas. *Cooley High* (1975), now a classic of black cinema, was directed by Michael Schultz, originally from Wisconsin. The film deals with the struggles of black high school students in 1960s Chicago. The romantic dramas *Love Jones* and *Soul Food*, both released in 1997, received strong reviews. The satirical drama *Chi-Raq* (2015), by director Spike Lee, confronts the issue of gang violence by adapting *Lysistrata* (411 BCE), by ancient Greek playwright Aristophanes (ca. 446–ca. 386 BCE), to contemporary Chicago. Notable black-centered films set elsewhere in the Midwest include *The Learning Tree* (1968), directed by GORDON (ALEXANDER BUCHANAN) PARKS (1922–2006) and based on his autobiographical 1963 novel about a boy in small-town Kansas; *Purple Rain* (1984), set in Minneapolis (see MINNEAPOLIS/ST. PAUL) and starring popular musician Prince; *Zebrahead* (1992), an interracial romance set in Detroit; *Beloved* (1998), an adaptation of the 1987 novel by TONI MORRISON (b. Chloe Ardelia Wofford, 1931), set near Cincinnati after the Civil War; and *Dreamgirls* (2006), a musical set in Detroit and loosely based on the story of Motown Records and the singing group, The Supremes.

Among the few notable documentaries set in the Midwest, two stand out as contributing to the cinematic trend of using the Midwest as a microcosm of the nation. In *Roger and Me* (1989) Michael Moore tracks down the General Motors chairman in order to challenge him about thousands of GM layoffs in Flint, Michigan. *Hoop Dreams* (1994) follows two inner-city Chicago teens as they struggle to make it to the NBA. These and

other films from the last thirty years may suggest that Midwestern regional distinctiveness in film is becoming blurred and perhaps blending into a more homogeneously negative picture of the nation as a whole.

SELECTED WORKS: Out of the films discussed here, moviegoers may best start out by viewing a few representative films. Films replicating the myth of the Midwest as the repository of old-fashioned values include *The Wizard of Oz* (1939), *State Fair* (1945), *The Farmer's Daughter* (1947), *The Music Man* (1962), and *Field of Dreams* (1989). Significant Chicago films include *The Front Page* (1931), *Scarface* (1932), *Medium Cool* (1969), and *The Untouchables* (1987). Important films that challenge traditional or formulaic depictions of the SMALL TOWN or the city include *The Magnificent Ambersons* (1942), *Badlands* (1973), *Fargo* (1996), and *Winter's Bone* (2010). Films portraying black experience in the Midwest include *Within Our Gates* (1920), *A Raisin in the Sun* (1959), *Cooley High* (1975), *Beloved* (1998), and *Chi-Raq* (2015).

FURTHER READING: Very little scholarly work has been done that focuses exclusively on film depictions of the Midwest. A fairly thorough overview is Rodney Hill's "Film and Theater," in the encyclopedic *The Midwest,* edited by Joseph W. Slade and Judith Yaross Lee (2004). Hill provides a solid groundwork for pre-1910 films and lists organizations, collections, and film festivals located in or dedicated to the Midwest. Edward Recchia, in "There's No Place like Home: The Midwest in American Film Musicals," *Midwest Quarterly* 39.2 (Winter 1998): 202–14, provides close studies of musicals set in the Midwest. John C. Tibbetts has an informative, compact entry on the Midwest in *The Columbia Companion to American History on Film,* edited by Peter C. Rollins (2006), 421–29. To better appreciate Midwestern musicals within the larger Hollywood musical genre, see Rick Altman's *The American Film Musical* (1987) and Stanley Green's *Hollywood Musicals Year by Year* (1990). To understand the full context of the many gangster films set in Chicago and other Midwestern locales, see Carlos Clarens and Foster Hirsch's *Crime Movies* (1997) and John McCarty's *Hollywood Gangland* (1993).

Cheryl Herr discusses a number of Midwestern rural films in an insightful study of the Midwest, especially Iowa, and comparable locales in Ireland in *Critical Regionalism and Cultural Studies: From Ireland to the American Midwest* (1996). Andrew Bergman closely analyzes films depicting the Depression era, many of which are set in the Midwest, in *We're in the Money: Depression America and Its Films* (1971). Arnie Bernstein deals with the history of filmmaking in Chicago, as well as the films set in the city, in *Hollywood on Lake Michigan: 100 Years of Chicago and the Movies* (1998). Sources on black film include *Blacks in Black and White: A Source Book on Black Films* (1977; second edition, 1995) by Henry T. Sampson and *Black City Cinema: African American Urban Experiences in Film* (2003) by Paula Massood. Several websites provide a plethora of details about individual films discussed in this entry, particularly the All Movie Guide and the Internet Movie Database.

ROBERT DUNNE

CENTRAL CONNECTICUT STATE UNIVERSITY

FOLKLORE

OVERVIEW: Folk language and literature are components of the total expressive culture with which folklore deals. Folklore also includes music, dance, games, mythology, ritual, customs, handicrafts, ARCHITECTURE, and other arts. In the Midwest, folk literature endures as a defining presence at a time when folklore scholars are divided into contending camps, arrayed on the spectrum of literary and anthropological approaches to the subject. Folklore conferences feature speeches and journals publish articles on the crisis and demise of folklore as a discipline of study. The Midwest does not escape the academic imbroglio, but accomplishments in the field of study centered on the Midwest must be reckoned within its defining history. The Midwest is the site of important collections and significant contributions to the theory, critical analysis, and interpretation of folk literature that stand as salient referents in the modish currents of scholarly unrest.

When the primary mode of transmission of folklore was word of mouth, it could be identified with regions and localities; but when, as media scholar Robert Thompson asserts, that personal mode has been displaced by "word-of-modem," the boundaries and dimensions that once defined folklore communities are no longer relevant and seldom operative. Identifying the role that regional communities play in the formation of the literary and general cultures is extremely complex and difficult but essential to understanding the diverse, global culture that subsumes those original, distinctive inventions of spirit that sustain cultural identities.

Midwestern collections begin with the incidental but comprehensive seventeenth-century accounts of *The Jesuit Relations and Allied Documents: Travels and Explorations of the Jesuit Missionaries in New France, 1610–1791; The Original French, Latin, and Italian Texts, with English Translations and Notes* (1896–1901), edited by Reuben Gold Thwaites in seventy-three volumes. Subsequent journals of EXPLORATION, travel, history, and observation are laden with folklore accounts, some incidental, but many deliberate in their intention and thorough in their accounts of lifeways and stories. As folklore became an organized discipline in the late nineteenth century with the formation of a professional society and more academic activity in the field, Midwestern collectors and scholars contributed significantly to and furthered its development. In the twentieth century, especially after World War II, the Midwest became an important collecting ground and the site of leading academic programs.

Seminal scholars Stith Thompson (1885–1976) and RICHARD M(ERCER) DORSON (1916–1981) did work that led to the formation of the Folklore Institute at Indiana University and the publication of journals on the subject. Other universities also developed programs and departments. Many of the programs grew out of literary study. Midwestern work in folklore retained a close relationship to language and literature. As the twentieth century ended, many programs shifted their focus to general cultural studies and closer identification with anthropology. Programs and publications with literary study as the main focus are being absorbed into programs of larger cultural purview, a trend that is provoking much self-examination and discussion of change in the field of folklore.

HISTORY AND SIGNIFICANCE: The Midwest has played an influential role in redefining folklore from its European origins as a diversion for the privileged to its current acknowledgment as the cultural matrix in which the arts are rooted. In its beginnings the study of folklore was concerned with expressions of the "backward classes or the less cultured classes of more advanced people," according to W. Edson Richmond in 1983 in his introduction to the *Handbook of American Folklore,* edited by Richard M. Dorson, and its major purpose was to preserve the cultural expressions of the folk before they were lost in the wash of history (xii). Folklore in the United States gained serious scholarly attention in the mid-nineteenth century, and its development as a formal branch of study coincided with the development of the Midwestern states and the dynamic interactions that formed their cultures. As it developed into a field of study in its own right, folklore dropped the old notion of being the study of the quaint antiquities of lesser cultures and shifted to treatment of its forms as pervasive forces that continue into the present. The Midwest is a prominent force in both the production of folklore materials and the institutions that lead in its study.

Initially, the study of folklore was a literary pursuit. Its earliest collectors and investigators were literary scholars and people with literary interests who extended their interest in texts to include oral and customary traditions. They established literary approaches in the study of folklore, which now embraces the arts and artifacts of the total folk culture. Folk literature, however, establishes more than the precedents for handling folk materials. It provides the cohering aspects in the transmission and study of folklore through its narrative and expository accounts. Departments of language and literature made the first academic offerings for the study of folklore and are the most common sites for these courses. The literary content and associations of folklore make it an essential aspect of our national and regional literature.

In *The Study of American Folklore* (1968) Jan Harold Brunvand reports that the American Folklore Society was founded in 1888 by a gathering of scholars and interested people at Harvard; its major purpose was "the collection of the fast-vanishing relics of folk-lore in America" (19). As the field gathered interest in America, the definition of folklore expanded to include all classes of people, all time embraced by the continuum of human culture, and all forms of cultural expression. Its study moved from being a subsidiary interest of people in related disciplines to a field of study in its own right that nevertheless retained the literary perspective in its interdisciplinary approaches. Part of its process of redefinition involved the need to accommodate the kinds of materials that collectors and scholars encountered as they moved their focus to the interior regions of America. Formal academic programs for the collection and study of folklore were not created until the 1950s. They grew out of work done in the Midwest, which, because of the wealth of materials and receptive attitudes, established some of the most extensive programs.

Although some scholars advocate the abandonment of folklore as a label and as a discipline, the question of what distinguishes folklore from other cultural expressions persists, at least in its historical context. Matters of distinctions make up a tremendous part of the discussion. However, a useful paradigm for placing folklore in its relative context is one that arrays cultural expressions under the categories of elite, normative, and folk. In the field of literature, elite works are serious novels and other works of literature of the kind studied in colleges and circulated as artifacts of high culture. Normative works are popular romances, films, and television shows of the kind often designed and promoted for commercial purposes without any pretense toward art. Folk literature is the tall tale or joke that represents the traditional and conservative concepts maintained by cultural communities. The categories define no discrete cultural entities, nor do they, as some insist, define levels of cultural stratification that presume a system of class. They do define levels of artistic intention and effort and the cultural motives of those who patronize and participate in the cultural forms. The lives of most individuals embrace all levels, but the folk level emerges as the one that most informs personal identity in family and regional contexts. It is the element that projects what is Midwestern in place, character, and personality and is thus useful as a defining concept.

The earliest systematic recordings of folk materials from the Midwest are contained in *The Jesuit Relations*. Although their purpose was to report the activities of Jesuit missionaries in New France to their ecclesiastical superiors, those first reports were so lively in narrative and rich in exotic detail that a Jesuit superior in France had them printed so they could be circulated. The reports in *The Jesuit Relations* fit into the early American genre of accounts of exploration, encounters, and founding. They record the geography and the folkways and include much written about "lower Canada," as the Midwest was designated in their parlance. Encounters with the Hurons, the Illini, and other Midwestern tribes of Native Americans provide important historical sources and early accounts of folk-centered literature written about and originating in the Midwest.

The development of texts from oral literature followed the interest generated by these early contacts with Native Americans in the Midwest. As scholarly work increased and formal organizations were established, the recording and saving of Native American materials was the predominant purpose.

The mission statement of the American Folklore Society indicated the driving force as scholars first organized its study: "The collection of the fast-vanishing relics of folklore in America" (19). Although the statement listed European, African American, and Native American sources, the latter received by far the preponderance of attention and scholarly effort during the last half of the nineteenth and the first half of the twentieth century. Conventional wisdom, as reflected in *The Vanishing American* (1925) by (Pearl) Zane Grey (1872–1939), was that Native Americans and their culture were disappearing from the face of the earth. The flurry of collection of materials on their folkways was spurred by complex motives, ranging from popular sympathy to the curiosity of a conquering race about just what it was conquering. Literature by and about Native Americans retained the kind of popularity and curiosity shown by the reports in *The Jesuit Relations*. Because the Midwest was

the frontier of the time, the tribes within its boundaries received significant and precedent-setting attention. Native American accounts of life and culture became staples of the publishing industry.

At the close of the Black Hawk War in 1832, BLACK HAWK (1767–1838) was taken on a tour of the eastern United States to show him the power of the nation and its government in order to discourage any thoughts he might entertain about future uprisings. Along the tour route people gathered by the thousands to catch sight of him and hear what he might say. He had attained the status of a celebrity. The tour set the stage for the writing and publication of his autobiography in 1833. Dictated by Blawk Hawk to interpreter Antoine LeClaire, it was edited into the acceptable Victorian prose of the time by newspaper editor J. B. Patterson as *LIFE OF MA-KA-TAI-ME-SHE-KIA-KIAK, OR BLACK HAWK* and was among the earliest Native American accounts in the as-told-to tradition. It focused on the Midwest and was a combination of national history, personal accounts, and ethnographic detail.

In 1839 HENRY ROWE SCHOOLCRAFT (1793–1864) and his wife, Jane Johnston Schoolcraft (1800–1842), published *Algic Researches, Comprising Inquiries Respecting the Mental Characteristics of the North American Indian: First Series; Indian Tales and Legends* (1839), which includes accounts of Midwestern Native American folklife. Another significant work was published in 1885, *The History of the Ojibways, Based upon Traditions and Oral Statements* by WILLIAM W(HIPPLE) WARREN (1825–1853); it includes folklore of this nation from WISCONSIN and MINNESOTA.

Government bureaus and scholarly societies were at the same time dispatching ethnologists throughout the country to gather and publish a steady outpouring of folklore-related materials. Truman Michelson (1879–1938) published numerous observations and collections in bulletins and annual reports of the Bureau of American Ethnology. He and a young Sauk anthropologist, William Jones (1871–1909), published the collection *Ojibwa Texts* in 1907 for the American Ethnological Society. The place of music in the verbal folk art of people received landmark scholarly presentations in *Chippewa Music* in 1910 and 1913 and *Chip-*

pewa Customs in 1929, both by Frances Dens-more (1867–1957).

The literary accounts of tribal folklife were consistently regarded as the most accessible and coherent. ZITKALA-ŠA (RED BIRD, 1876–1938) published important stories of Lakota life that were rich in folklore during the first three decades of the twentieth century, and the collaborative work BLACK ELK SPEAKS by BLACK ELK (1863–1950) with JOHN G(NEISENAU) NEIHARDT (1881–1973) was published in 1932. Both authors provided comprehensive accounts of physical and spiritual life and Lakota history in the western Dakotas, and their works are treated both as major literary achievements and as documents of folklife. See NATIVE AMERICAN LITERATURE.

Midwestern folklore activity intensified and expanded with the work of Richard M. Dorson. After obtaining a doctorate from Harvard and publishing a book on New England folktales, Dorson accepted a position at Michigan State University and made the Midwest the center of his research and writing. He gathered material on Michigan's Upper Peninsula, examined regional folklore of the Midwest, collected African American folktales in MICHIGAN, and published a book of folktales about the steel-making industry gathered in Calumet City, INDIANA. In his work on Midwestern folklore, Dorson looked for distinctive regional characteristics and found them in the way cultures of the Midwest mix and hybridize. He focused on folk literature and noted that it consisted of self-conscious stories through which people were articulating their identities. The landscape formed the setting and atmosphere of the stories and was further informed by its history. Folk brought their ethnic heritage and absorbed and used resources from other ethnic sources they encountered. In this paradigm of exchange, a locality formed a locus of cultural energies, and those energies could be traced to their origins. Folklore of a region, as Dorson asserted in *American Folklore* (1959), has its particular genius informed by local geography and the history played out on it (75), but it also maintains lines of descent that lead to other places, times, and cultures. He found that Native American stories provided the essential terms of geographic identity, and

so they have a seminal relationship to the general folklore of the Midwest.

The evolution in Dorson's approach to folklore set the pattern for the development of folklore study internationally. Kent C. Ryden (b. 1959), in *Mapping the Invisible Landscape: Folklore, Writing, and the Sense of Place* (1993), contends that Dorson approached his early work as an outsider for whom the Upper Peninsula of Michigan merely set a convenient boundary that established geographic limits to his collecting activities (60). In his later work, as represented in *Land of the Millrats* (1981), about the steel-making region of Indiana, Dorson approached his investigations from an insider's perspective. Dorson saw that the stories and other folklore "can be studied most profitably within an understanding of what the region—the physical entity itself—means to the people who inhabit it" (60). In pursuing the direction and method Dorson worked out for the study of folklore, Ryden stresses locality as the essential, defining feature that distinguishes a region's lore, and he formulizes the process through which physical features of the landscape and mental-cultural aspects interact as follows: "Local lore, especially material folklore, reveals the depth and intricacy of local knowledge of the nature and physical properties and limitations of the geographical milieu" (62–63); "Regional folklore encapsulates and transmits the intimate and otherwise unrecorded history of a place; it reveals the meaning of a place to be in large part a deeply known and felt awareness of the things that happened there" (63). Ryden asserts that "local lore provides a strong sense of personal and group identity" (64). "Most difficult to describe, regional folklore indicates the emotions which local residents attach to their place . . . feelings which arise from a knowledge of place-based history and identity which inevitably tinge their contemplation of their physical surroundings" (66). In these categories, Ryden identifies characteristics that folklore shares with more refined literary art. Just as early folklorists drew heavily on Native American oral accounts as works to collect and study for their shape and significance, Ryden also begins with the accounts of indigenous people to apprehend the depth and the reach of regional landscapes.

According to this theory for defining the characteristics that distinguish a regional folklore, any definition must acknowledge the processes of exchange, incorporation, and adaptation as it takes on its regional characteristics. The definition must also recognize the way folklore merges into the more formal arts. What distinguishes Midwestern folklore is the way it captures the landscape and history and reflects the creative ways in which people of diverse cultural heritages accommodate themselves to that landscape. This tie with a regional landscape in large measure defines the Midwestern character and personality of the region's folklore.

The Midwest received a massive infusion of African American sources during the Great Migration of blacks from the South, which brought jazz from New Orleans and the blues from the Mississippi Delta to CHICAGO. Chicago became a gathering place for blues performers, and Chicago-style blues took form. DETROIT became a creative center for rhythm and blues artists. Although the blues are still defined by the poetry of their lyrics, the importance of the music as cultural expression became more apparent and more interesting as the form gained popularity and commercial significance. The folk literature of the blues is in the song lyrics; literature about jazz and the blues remains largely oral or provided in fragments on record album covers and inserts.

The migration of other ethnic groups into the Midwest has contributed to a complex cultural intermixing for which collection and study are in their beginning stages. Latino and Asian American elements are prominent in the literary landscape of the Midwest, and literary courses and researches are leading the way to more comprehensive investigations of these cultures. At this time the transmission and study of the folk literature appears to be under the auspices of the various ethnic and cultural groups that have established academic programs under their own names. See LATINO/LATINA LITERATURE and ASIAN AMERICAN LITERATURE.

Indiana University has led the nation in the study of folklore. The evolution of its programs and publications reflects the evolution of folklore as it has moved from a literary orientation with class connotations to an inclusive democratic orientation, from a European orientation to a focus on how folk materials interact in a regional setting, and from a regional focus to a comparative, international focus.

In the introduction to the *Handbook of American Folklore*, W. Edson Richmond asserts that Stith Thompson came to Indiana University in 1921 and instituted the program in folklore that became "the foundation on which all folklore departments in the United States and Canada were based" (xvi). Thompson's published work, including *Motif-Index of Folk-Literature: A Classification of Narrative Elements in Folk-Tales, Ballads, Myths, Fables, Mediaeval Romances, Exempla, Fabliaux, Jest-Books, and Local Legends* (1932–1936) and *Tales of the North American Indians* (1929, 1966), is regarded as bringing to the study of folklore a methodical, analytical scholarship. He organized summer folklore institutes in the 1940s, and under his direction in 1953 the Indiana University English Department awarded its first doctorate in folklore. In 1956 Richard Dorson came to take charge of folklore studies. In 1965 he established the Folklore Institute as an academic department that granted baccalaureate through doctoral degrees.

The history of the department's journal demonstrates how the tracing of regional elements of folklore eventually led to an international focus. It also evidences how the drive toward globalization and diversity has moved scholars to eschew a focus on regions, such as the Midwest, in favor of placing their subject matter and their work on an international stage. In 1942 Indiana University began to publish the *Hoosier Folklore Bulletin*. In 1946 the journal became *Hoosier Folklore* and in 1951 expanded its scope to become *Midwest Folklore*. As the Folklore Institute was formalized by Dorson, the journal took on a global scope with the title *Journal of the Folklore Institute* in 1964 and was then renamed *Journal of Folklore Research* in 1982. This journal now contains almost no articles that concentrate on Midwestern materials. However, to maintain the regional focus, a new journal, *Indiana Folklore*, started in 1968 and continued through 1980. It reappeared as *Indiana Folklore and Oral History* from 1985 to 1987, publishing work with the focus that *Hoosier Folklore* once had. Similarly, in 1975 the Hoosier Folklore Society, headquartered at Indiana State University, began publication of the *Journal of Language and Midwestern Folklore*, renamed *Midwestern Folklore* in 1987. In 2000 the Folklore Institute at Indiana University joined a sister department, the Ethnomusicology Institute, to form the Department of Folklore and Ethnomusicology at Indiana. This institute reflects growing recognition of the fusing of verbal arts with other art and craft forms.

The controversies about what should be included in the study of folklore and what disciplinary approaches are relevant present barriers to a comprehensive perspective. Part of the confusion emanates from scholars of literature themselves. A reaction against structuralism was one of the major currents that concerned what is generally referred to as postmodernism. The New Criticism of the mid-twentieth century sought to focus on the internal coherence of literary works sufficient unto themselves. Structuralism sought to examine literary works in terms of their relationships to the general culture in which they occurred. Structuralism, as defined in Robert E. Scholes's *Structuralism in Literature* (1974), assumed a scientific posture and approached "literature as a system within the larger system of human culture" (10). It attempted to deal with disciplines of knowledge so fragmented and isolated by specialization that no coherent unity could ever be established. Although structuralism sought to restore some sense of coherence by placing literature in its larger context, many literary scholars perceived that their discipline was being subsumed by anthropological and political theory. Structuralist theory was attractive and convenient for literary folklorists because it attempted to establish the place of language and literature in the larger cultural context. However, the subordination of literature to culture took a patronizing tone, and it was countered by an abstruse, superior attitude in poststructuralist discourse. The poststructural reaction was to focus on the language of texts and whether language bore any correspondence to the world in which it exists. Whereas fragmentation of knowledge seemed to be the paramount problem that structuralists attempted to solve, pulverization of knowledge seemed to be the result of poststructuralist theory.

The theoretical bickering was repellent to many scholars within and outside the field of literature. Departments of English were barely tolerated on many college and university campuses, and during a time of declining resources, many English departments survive as service departments to offer instruction in writing and a few basic literature courses that qualify as the humanities component of general degrees. Folklore and literature have been casualties of this trend. Midwestern folklore receives scant attention because few places examine it as a respectable field of study or offer publications on the subject.

In the Midwest, folklore has often become part of ethnic and gender studies. Some ethnic, gender, and folklore programs indicate a direction that the study of folk literature seems to be taking in establishing a new purview. Jan Harold Brunvand's standard text *The Study of American Folklore* (1968) does not mention written diaries, letters, personal biographies, and family documents as materials for folklore study. He hews very closely to the "oral and traditional" premise for defining folklore. Outside courses in early American literature, such texts are not regarded as literature, but they receive attention in gender and ethnic programs, where they serve more as testimonies of plights than as cultural expressions. To literary scholars, however, these documents reflect a literary impulse and a cultural tradition that merit literary examination.

Studies of such texts appear in folklore journals. An essay by Marilyn Ferris Motz in the April/June 1987 issue of the *Journal of American Folklore* is "Folk Expression of Time and Place: 19th-Century Midwestern Rural Diaries." A book edited by Philip Gerber (1923–2005), *Bachelor Bess: The Homesteading Letters of Elizabeth Corey, 1909–1919* (1990), provides an incisive view into the life of a single woman who took out a homestead in SOUTH DAKOTA but had to teach school to support herself. An excellent recapitulation of SLAVE NARRATIVES collected by the Works Progress Administration is Ronald L. Baker's *Homeless, Friendless, and Penniless: The WPA Interviews with Former Slaves Living in Indiana* (2000).

Exemplary Midwestern collections that take an analytical approach but are careful to record stories and note their context include Harry Middleton Hyatt's *Folk-lore from Adams County, Illinois* (1935); Earl J. Stout's *Folklore from Iowa* (1936); Samuel J. Sackett's *Kansas Folklore* (1961); Roger L. Welsch's *A Treasury of Nebraska Pioneer Folklore* (1967); Linda Dégh's *Indiana Folklore: A Reader* (1980); and Richard Dorson's *Bloodstoppers and Bear Walkers* (1952), *Negro Folktales in Michigan* (1956), and *Land of the Millrats* (1981). These works evidence the literary imagination as it operates in a folk setting. Although Jan Harold Brunvand's *The Vanishing Hitchhiker: American Urban Legends and Their Meanings* (1981) does not focus primarily on the Midwest, it provides an essential discussion of urban legends, their regional occurrence and versions, and their relation to time and place. Two important collections of Native American oral cycles are Paul Radin's *The Trickster: A Study in American Indian Mythology* (1956) and William Jones's *Fox Texts* (1907). Radin presents the Ho-Chunk (Winnebago) stories from Wisconsin with care and thoroughness and avoids casting them to support anthropological theories. Jones, a Sauk ethnologist, is much more concerned about getting the language accurate in *Fox Texts*. The Meskwaki (Fox) syllabic versions and the English translations are displayed side by side. To literary scholars, the texts provide a chance to see the importance of the sounds and rhythms of the Meskwaki language in reading the texts. A translation of a trickster cycle geared to popular English stylistics appears in Thomas B. Leekley's *The World of Manabozho: Tales of the Chippewa Indians* (1965).

SELECTED WORKS: Jan Harold Brunvand's *The Study of American Folklore* (1968) is probably the most widely used text and provides a detailed discussion of the various genres of folklore and approaches to collecting and studying them. Richard Dorson's *Land of the Millrats* (1981) is widely cited. For both broad and specific approaches, Stith Thompson's *Tales of the North American Indians* (1929, 1964) and *Motif-Index of Folk-Literature* (1932–1936) are valuable.

FURTHER READING: Anyone investigating folklore and its state in the Midwest will find the paucity of current materials from a region so rich in folk literature puzzling. A helpful overview of what is taking place in the scholarship is Barbara Kirshenblatt-Gimblett's article, "Folklore's Crisis," *Journal of American Folklore* 111:441 (Summer 1998): 281–327. An illuminating companion piece to this essay is Barre Toeken's "The End of Folklore" in the Spring and Summer 1998 issue of *Western Folklore* (81–101). The overriding academic concern is bridging the disciplinary specialties and deciding which texts belong to folklife and which belong to popular, normative forms and deliberately artistic genres. Folk literature and cultural myths underlie the work of many writers, inspiring turf battles between literary and folklife specialists. A work that surmounts the academic squabbles, melds traditional folk accounts with oral and written personal and family accounts, and presents a comprehensive demonstration of how the strands of cultural materials are woven into rich, compelling narratives is *PrairyErth (a deep map)* (1991) by WILLIAM LEAST HEAT-MOON (b. 1939). He prospects a single county in KANSAS for a literary account of how and why culture converges into stories.

In addition to the journals mentioned previously, others that focus on folklore in the Midwest include *Heritage of the Great Plains*, which has been published at Emporia State University, Kansas; *Great Plains Quarterly*, published at the University of Nebraska; and *Missouri Folk Society Journal*, published at the University of Missouri. From 1975 to 1986 Indiana State University published the *Midwestern Journal of Language and Folklore*, which contained some essays focused on the Midwest but included folklore from throughout the world. Indiana State University also publishes a journal for the American Folklore Society, *The Folklore Historian: Journal of Folklore and History*, containing articles pertinent to the study of regional folklore.

DAVID L. NEWQUIST   NORTHERN STATE UNIVERSITY

FRONTIER AND PIONEER ACCOUNTS

OVERVIEW: Midwestern pioneer accounts can be found scattered across newspapers, short-lived periodicals of past generations, present-day periodicals, memoirs, travel accounts, proceedings of historical society journals, and pioneer life accounts. There is also noteworthy fiction written describing early settlement and community development. This literature runs the gamut from barely comprehensible anecdotes strung together to wonderfully crafted works. Some authors are of the caliber of WILLA CATHER (1873–1947), but most are unknown.

The hardy, undaunted pioneer battling nature's elements figures prominently in many of these works. Another salient theme in early travel documents is the opportunities and resources offered by the frontier areas. The rainbow of human emotions they convey saves many of these accounts from being mere catalogs of personal accomplishments or virtues of place; these stories capture the humor, sadness, bitterness, stubbornness, regret, and nostalgia that color life. Sometimes these emotions result from pioneers judging their new homes against the standards of their past experience. Often these travelers and immigrants did not go west to seek the wilderness; rather, they were determined to find and build something that re-created the life they had known elsewhere, and they were critical when their surroundings failed to meet their eastern notions of civilization. See also IMMIGRANT AND MIGRANT LITERATURE. If some were dismayed by their primitive surroundings, many more were fascinated by the newness, rawness, opportunities, and challenges of their frontier environment.

The era of widespread white settlement of the Midwest began in the early nineteenth century. Early nineteenth-century pioneer accounts differ from those late in that same century. For example, in the former, travel narratives by foreign travelers and Americans are common. Late in the nineteenth century, however, more literature was produced by people already resident on the frontier.

HISTORY AND SIGNIFICANCE: The GREAT LAKES region was the first area of the Old Northwest to be visited by Euro Americans. The earliest frontier accounts had exploration, fur-trading, and missionary purposes. Reuben Gold Thwaites (1853–1913) collected *The Jesuit Relations and Allied Documents* (1896–1901) into seventy-three volumes containing a multitude of materials describing early travel, Native American practices, and, of course, religious proselytizing. François Victor Malhiot, in "A Wisconsin Fur Trader's Journal, 1804–1805," *Collections of the State Historical Society of Wisconsin* 19 (1910): 163–233, for example, provides details about exchanging trade goods such as rum, ammunition, and tobacco for furs and wild rice. He bemoans the constant trouble caused by intoxicated Indians, but he supplies them with alcohol.

Early widespread movement into this area was encouraged by accounts such as that of Morris Birkbeck (1764–1825) in *Notes on a Journey in America from the Coasts of Virginia to the Territory of Illinois* (1818), in which he gives a glowing account of the environment and economic opportunities. Although such a report might have encouraged travel, others may have prompted a prospective migrant to think twice before traveling. Of this ilk was "An English Officer's Description of Wisconsin in 1837" by Frederick Marryat (1792–1848), *Collections of the State Historical Society of Wisconsin* 14 (1898): 137–154. He acknowledges that the soil was rich and the minerals plentiful in WISCONSIN, but snakes were also abundant and varied. Marryatt did not present Native inhabitants in glowing terms either, writing that the Winnebago Indians at Prairie du Chien were almost always intoxicated and dirty. HENRY ROWE SCHOOLCRAFT (1793–1864) in *A View of the Lead Mines of Missouri* (1819) described resources for the enterprising in this region; a compilation of works by him can be found in *Schoolcraft's Narrative Journal of Travels* (1953). The panic of 1837 and the resulting depression put a dent in the enthusiastic expansion that followed publication of many of these frontier accounts. However, published travel accounts by visitors, both foreign and American, increased as travel conditions improved and helped placate concerns about the hostile frontier land.

For many, the decision to move to the frontier was economic. Many settlers were young and often newly married; others just wanted a fresh start. They traveled down the Ohio River, moved overland by horse and wagon, or walked. Migrant letters and travel diaries testify to the difficulty of travel. For instance in an entry entitled "Lankford Burdick, One More of the Old Settlers

THE BARK COVERED HOUSE—1834

William Nowlin's *The Bark Covered House*, Detroit, 1876.
Image courtesy of Special Collections, Grand Valley State University Libraries

Gone," Lankford (Robert) Burdick's journey to MICHIGAN with his three sons and their young families is recounted. It took them a week to cross Lake Erie on a steamer. They purchased a wagon and a yoke in DETROIT; then the trip progressed at an even slower pace. It took two days to go ten miles, and Burdick's young granddaughter wrote back to her eastern friends that there "was a great deal of water and no bridges, a great many farms with no fences and one hundred and two mud holes" (*Michigan Pioneer and Historical Collections* 10 (1886): 189–90.

Pioneer experiences with Native American populations often depended on who the author was, the time of writing, and the place. Charles Joseph Latrobe (1801–1875), for instance, in *The Rambler in North America, 1832–33* (1835), has little admiration for members of the Osages, whereas Washington Irving (1783–1859), writing "A Tour of the Prairies" in *The Crayon Papers* (1835) around the same time, describes them favorably. Outside the War of 1812, attitudes toward Native Americans were surprisingly benign. See NATIVE AMERICAN LITERATURE and

NATIVE AMERICANS AS DEPICTED IN MIDWESTERN LITERATURE. William Nowlin (1821–1884) in his memoir on pioneering in Michigan, *The Bark Covered House* (1876), says that his and his siblings' fear of them proved to be groundless; Joseph Pritts (d. 1848), in *Incidents of Border Life, etc.* (1841), describing frontier life in the Ohio River valley area, remarks openly on Native American sexual customs, gender relations, and styles of personal ornamentation. Emily Foster (b. 1945), editor of *The Ohio Frontier: An Anthology of Early Writings* (2000), provides excerpts from firsthand accounts of early encounters of Europeans with Native Americans from the 1750s to the 1840s. These accounts reveal the dispossession and displacement of Indians in the settlement of OHIO.

The Native Americans may have been fascinating and the land rich, but life was crude and hard. In *A NEW HOME–WHO'LL FOLLOW?* (1839), CAROLINE KIRKLAND (1801–1864), who came to Pinckney, Michigan, in the 1830s, observed that travelers were in for a rude shock if they were expecting the same kind of conditions they were accustomed to back east. When her book on frontier life was published, Kirkland's neighbors were displeased at her descriptions of their foibles.

Self-sufficiency was clearly imperative on the frontier. In *Seventy Years on the Frontier* (1893) Alexander Majors (1814–1900), whose firm operated the Pony Express across the plains, claimed that in frontier MISSOURI "from ninety-five to ninety-seven per cent of the entire population manufactured at home almost everything necessary for good living" (27). Among the goods people took along to Missouri were "a pair of chickens, ducks, geese, and, if possible, a pair of pigs, their cattle and horses. The wife took her spinning wheel, a bunch of cotton or flax, and was ready to go to spinning as soon as she landed on the premises" (28).

For women, the frontier experience was especially startling. *Birchbark Belles: Women on the Michigan Frontier* (1993), edited by Larry Massie, is a collection of excerpts from thirty-one narratives by women on the Michigan frontier. Included in this collection are such luminaries as Harriet Martineau (1802–1876), Caroline Kirkland, Margaret Fuller (1810–1865), and Frederika Bremer (1801–1865). Lesser-known figures in this collection were like Nancy Howard, who came to settle with her family in Michigan in 1812. Her family farm was attacked by Indians during the War of 1812, but although the Indians plundered her home, her family members were allowed to escape unmolested. Another early account is that of Mary Ann Brevoort Bristol (1812–1894), who, in her "Reminiscences of the North-West," *Collections of the State Historical Society of Wisconsin* 8 (1879): 293–308, reported her mother's tales of housekeeping in Detroit in the early 1800s, where washing was done at the river using some kind of washboard. She also tells of the fear that riveted her parents during the War of 1812.

A woman's lot on the plains seems to have been even more difficult than it had been on the Great Lakes frontier, probably because by the late nineteenth century the notions of the cult of domesticity held more sway over women's expectations. Glenda Riley, in "Women's History from Women's Sources: Three Examples from Northern Dakota," *North Dakota History* 52.2 (Spring 1985): 2–9, examines the various stereotypes of pioneer women in scholarly and popular writing.

Apart from physical hardship and material deprivation, what seemed to bother women most was isolation. Remarks on such imposed loneliness in Michigan can be found in *"Time by Moments Steals Away": The 1848 Journal of Ruth Douglass* (1998), edited by Robert L. Root. Some, though, made the best of their situation by relying on humor, as recalled in the reminiscences of Mary C. Moulton (b. 1851) in *True Stories of Pioneer Life* (1924). *Wau-Bun: The "Early Day" in the North-West* (1856) by Juliette Kinzie (1806–1870) is inspiring as it recounts how she managed to make the best of her situation despite such conditions as camping in the snow and having the tent cave in. But Kinzie, as the wife of an Indian agent and businessman, would not have had to deal with the wearying drudgery of physical labor.

Civilization came slowly but irrevocably. Schools were hard to come by, and few accounts reported good school teachers. *Autobiographical Notes* (1905) by Ebenezer Lakin Brown (1809–1899) tells of a teacher who almost choked a young boy for failing to learn a lesson. Only when the whole school was in an uproar did she desist. Elaine Goodale Eastman (1863–1953), with Kay Graber (b. 1938), gives a personal recollection of her years as a schoolteacher in *Sister to the Sioux: The Memoirs of Elaine Goodale Eastman, 1885–1891* (1978).

The church was an especially important "civilizing" institution on the early frontier, and the quest to establish organized religion is the subject of many accounts. By the 1820s Methodist missionaries organized in Michigan with the goal of converting the Indian population. One expressed his ire at the mining communities to which he ministered. Alfred Brunson, DD (1793–1882), in "A Methodist Circuit Rider's Horseback Tour from Pennsylvania to Wisconsin, 1835," *Collections of the State Historical Society of Wisconsin* 15 (1900): 264–291, tells of miners more interested in carousing than in religion. He wrote of Dubuque that "the lead mines in its neighborhood are of the wealthiest character, and have given independent fortunes to the most degraded men of our species" (288). INDIANA-born frontier writer EDWARD

EGGLESTON (1837–1902), in *The Circuit Rider: A Tale of the Heroic Age* (1874), fictionalizes the preacher's life on the frontier. Although Eggleston experienced the tail end of the heroic age of frontier Methodism, in his writing he drew heavily from the work of Jacob Young (1776–1859), *Autobiography of a Pioneer: or, The Nativity, Experience, Travels and Ministerial Labors of Rev. Jacob Young with Incidents, Observations, and Reflections* (1857). A Catholic missionary to the Great Lakes region, Bishop Frederic Baraga (1797–1868), recounts the trials of establishing missions between 1852 and 1863 in *The Diary of Bishop Frederic Baraga: First Bishop of Marquette, Michigan* (1990). One of his major challenges was to try to wean fur traders away from bartering alcohol with local Native people.

Settlement of the western Midwest depended on overcoming people's preconceptions, undermining Native American resistance, improving transportation, and casting lures by local entrepreneurs. For example, the biggest settlement problem in ILLINOIS was populating the prairies because settlers had a prejudice against treeless land. Only by 1850 were these feelings overcome. Improved plows to work tough sod probably helped the process. In IOWA settlement increased gradually as a series of Indian treaties in the 1830s and 1840s made land available to whites. Farming spread slowly from Iowa and WISCONSIN into the forested lake country of MINNESOTA; settlers included homesteaders lured into the cutover timber areas of Minnesota by lumbermen needing food for their logging camps. Missouri benefited from being a major launching pad for overland migration. The beginning of settlement in KANSAS and NEBRASKA was spurred primarily by transportation improvements. One account of early travel to Nebraska territory appears in "A Journey through the Nebraska Region in 1833 and 1834: From the Diaries of Prince Maximilian von Wied," edited by William J. Orr and Joseph C. Porter, *Nebraska History* 64.3 (Fall 1983): 325–453.

The Santa Fe Trail crossed Kansas, the Mormon Trail crossed Nebraska, and the Oregon and California Trails crossed them both. In the Dakotas early settlements were linked with Native Indians, explorers, and forts. Pre–Civil War migrants only glanced at the eastern part of Kansas and Nebraska. Settlers moving into the western part of these areas after that war found themselves facing a new variety of problems associated with frontier life, namely, shortage of wood, lack of moisture, and unfriendly Native Americans.

The harsh life on rural frontier farms is evocatively portrayed by (HANNIBAL) HAMLIN GARLAND (1860–1940), especially in his *MAIN-TRAVELLED ROADS* (1891). In the story "Up the Coulé," when the son returns to the old homestead after being absent for a number of years, he finds his mother marked by a "sort of dumb despair in her attitude" (80) because of life on the relentlessly challenging plains. In "Under the Lion's Paw" a family's crop is so devastated by grasshoppers that they would even eat "fork-handles" (203). However, Garland at times looks beyond the harshness and sees the good, acknowledging the spirit of community help that prevailed on the frontier. In *The Sod House* (1930) Cass G. Barns (1848–1942) observes that even the widespread loss of cattle in 1894 due to lack of forage "was not all bad" because the farmers ultimately had to get rid of "all manner of scrub stock of horses, cattle and hogs" (93). BESS STREETER ALDRICH (1881–1954) presents evidence of a determined frontier spirit in such novels as *A Lantern in Her Hand* (1928) and its sequel, *A White Bird Flying* (1931), drawing on the experiences of her homesteading family in Nebraska.

After 1830 increasing numbers of immigrants settled in Ohio, Illinois, Wisconsin, Michigan, and Iowa; they are the subjects of a voluminous literature. Among their stories are "Anders Wiberg's Account of a Trip to the United States in 1852–1853," translated and edited by John Norton in *Swedish Pioneer Historical Quarterly* 29.2 (1978): 89–116 and 29.3 (1978): 162–69. Similar accounts by northern European immigrants, including Danes, Norwegians, and German Russians, describe the hardships of their early years and their struggle to become established farmers. *Sod and Stubble* (1936) by John Ise (1885–1969) tells of his family's homesteading experience in the wind-swept plains of Kansas. The author's mother, who was of German immigrant parents, married a young German farmer at age seventeen and moved to Kansas. There she reared eleven of her twelve children and sent nine of them through various colleges, including Harvard, Yale, Columbia, Stanford, the University of Chicago, and the University of Zurich, Switzerland.

The immigrant experience in the plains is the subject of some of the most notable novelists of the late nineteenth and early twentieth centuries. Both Willa Cather and OLE EDVART RØLVAAG (1876–1931) were familiar with the land they portrayed. Like their subjects, Cather and Rølvaag were not native to the region. Rølvaag was born in Norway and did not come to SOUTH DAKOTA until he was twenty. In GIANTS IN THE EARTH (1927), *Peder Victorious* (1929), and *Their Father's God* (1931), he dealt with the cost of frontier settlement on the plains. Willa Cather, born in Virginia, came with her family to Nebraska when she was a young girl. In *O PIONEERS!* (1913) she provides details of pioneering life, of planting, harvesting, and church bazaars. In *My Ántonia* (1918) Cather writes about the life of Bohemian and Scandinavian immigrants and about human relations in frontier society.

Robert (Ball) Anderson (1843–1930) recounts his life on the plains of Nebraska in *From Slavery to Affluence: Memoirs of Robert Anderson, Ex-Slave* (1927). Mattie Bradshaw and Sam Dicks reprinted a story written by Mattie Leatha Bradshaw about her grandmother's experiences as an exoduster to Kansas in the late 1870s in "Eliza Bradshaw: An Exoduster Grandmother," *Kansas History* 26.2 (2003): 106–11.

Accounts of life on frontier military posts constitute another form of pioneer literature. Widely scattered military posts were built for reservations, defense against Native Americans, safeguards for the building of the railroad, and protection of mail routes. Martha Gray Wales wrote of her childhood in military forts on the Dakota frontier in "When I Was a Little Girl: Things I Remember from Living at Frontier Military Posts," edited by Martha Gray Wales and Willard B. Pope, *North Dakota History* 50.2 (1983): 12–22. She remembers the loneliness and drudgery, the constant Indian threat, and the challenges of the frontier environment.

Establishing communities required the development of social infrastructure, including professional services, churches, and schools. Such efforts are the subject of many accounts. For example, Daniel Drake (1785–1852), in his *Physician to the West: Selected Writings of Daniel Drake on Science and Society* (1970) and other works, discusses health issues. A folksy personal memoir of a successful pioneer life in the Dakotas from 1871 to 1898 can be found in Mark Wentworth Sheafe's "Mark Wentworth Sheafe: Pioneer, Businessman and Politician," *South Dakota History* 8.3 (Summer 1978): 250–67; this narrative describes starting and operating a business, transportation, fighting grasshoppers, floods, dealing with early local politics, and establishing relations with Native Americans.

SELECTED WORKS: The many journals, articles, and other firsthand nonfiction accounts of frontier settlement and life are valuable for historians and readers alike, and for both, fiction is the best place to start. Major writers who depicted this time and place include Daniel Drake in his nonfiction *Physician to the West: Selected Writings of Daniel Drake on Science and Society* (1970). Among the novels are Edward Eggleston's *The Circuit Rider: A Tale of the Heroic Age* (1874); Hamlin Garland's *Main-Travelled Roads* (1891); Willa Cather's *O Pioneers!* (1913) and *My Ántonia* (1918); Ole Rølvaag's *Giants in the Earth* (1927), *Peder Victorious* (1929), and *Their Father's God* (1931); and Bess Streeter Aldrich's *A Lantern in Her Hand* (1928) and *A White Bird Flying* (1931). *Romance of Western History; or, Sketches of History, Life and Manners in the West* (1857) by James Hall (1793–1868) provides early pioneer accounts.

On early days of contact between Europeans and Indians in the Great Lakes area, see *A Collection of Documents Relating to Jacques Cartier and Sieur de Robertval* (1930), edited by H. P. Biggar (1872–1938); and Reuben Gold Thwaites's *The Jesuit Relations and Allied Documents*, 73 vols. (1896–1901). Fur-trade journals include *A Winter in the St. Croix Valley: George Nelson's Reminiscences, 1802–03* (1948) by George Nelson.

State historical societies collected and published an abundance of interviews with first-generation migrants, reminiscences by them or their descendants, diaries, and travel accounts in the late nineteenth and twentieth centuries. Among the most comprehensive collections are those of the *Indiana Historical Collections* (1916–1994); *Reports and Collections of the Michigan Pioneer and Historical Society* (1877–1929); *Collections of the State Historical Society of Wisconsin* (1896–1901), edited by Lyman C. Draper and Reuben G. Thwaites; and *Collections of the Illinois State Historical Society* (1903–1975). These may be most easily found at historical libraries. The Clarke Library at Central Michigan University has compiled published accounts of Detroit between 1700 and 1837 and has made them available on its website.. The *Ohio State Archaeological and Historical Society Publications* (1887–1939) contains a number of pioneer accounts as well as few essays of literary interest.

FURTHER READING: A useful background resource on settlement of the Midwest is *Westward Expansion: A History of the American Frontier* (1982) by Ray Allen Billington (1903–1981) and Martin Ridge (b. 1949); one on women is *Prairie Voices: Iowa's Pioneering Women* (1996), edited by Glenda Riley. The *Farmers' Frontier, 1865–1900* (1966) by Gilbert C. Fite deals with the agricultural frontier in the Midwest. *The Middle West in American History* (1966) by Dan Elbert Clark, a revision of his earlier 1937 work, is a general survey but contains information on the frontier experience.

An excellent annotated bibliography of travel narratives is *Early Midwestern Travel Narratives: An Annotated Bibliography, 1634–1850* (1961) by Robert R(ogers) Hubach. Mark Wyman's *The Wisconsin Frontier* (1998) has a good annotated bibliography of resources on early Wisconsin. The classic and still-valuable bibliography of early pioneer accounts is *The Voice of the Frontier* (1949) by R(obert) W(illiam) G(lenroie) Vail (1890–1966). Another important source is Ralph Rusk's *The Literature of the Middle Western Frontier* (1925). Specific to the prairie states and women's experience is *Farm Women on the Prairie Frontier: A Sourcebook for Canada and the United States* (1983) by Carol Fairbanks and Sara Brooks Sundberg.

CATHERINE TOBIN   CENTRAL MICHIGAN UNIVERSITY

G–H

GAY LITERATURE.
See Lesbian, Gay, Bisexual, Transgender, and Queer Literature

GIANTS IN THE EARTH

HISTORY: *Giants in the Earth*, a novel first published in English in 1927, became the most popular and memorable work by OLE EDVART RØLVAAG (1876–1931). Rølvaag's novel tells the story of Norwegian immigrant families and their community founded in the Dakota Territory of 1873. The saga of Per Hansa, his wife, Beret, their children, and three other immigrant families reenvisions the Midwestern frontier prairie as a harsh and unforgiving force. After several years of prosperity and hardships, the winter of 1880–1881 brings a tragic climax. Per Hansa dies in the middle of a blizzard while searching, at the behest of his disturbed wife, for the minister to perform the last rites for his dying friend.

Rølvaag chose the setting for *Giants in the Earth* from his own experience living in SOUTH DAKOTA. At the age of twenty he moved from Norway and worked on a farm during his first two years in America. His firsthand accounts of images and life on the prairie become crucial to the realism inte-grated into *Giants in the Earth*. Specifically, he modeled the time and setting of this novel after the life of his father-in-law, who arrived in South Dakota the same year Per Hansa did. Rølvaag's father-in-law provided him with a wealth of information about frontier life and the trials of starting a community.

In the decade after World War I, the United States, including its farmers, became disenchanted with the romantic, idealized portrayal of life in literature. Rølvaag, like many other writers in the 1920s, shifted toward gritty realism in his literary work. The accidental drowning of his son, Paul Gunnar, may have pushed Rølvaag even more into discussing the perilous aspects of nature. *Giants in the Earth* was the result of an outside catalyst. In 1923 Rølvaag discovered that the well-known Norwegian novelist Johan Bojer (1872–1959) was visiting the United States with plans to write a novel about Norwegian immigration and settling there. Rølvaag, who believed that his experience as a farmhand in South Dakota and his knowledge of stories from the Norwegian settlers entitled him to write a novel such as this, determined to write a story that would take into account the psychological

Manuscript page from Ole Rølvaag's *Giants in the Earth*.
Courtesy of the Norwegian-American Historical Association, Northfield, Minnesota

and emotional aspects of pioneering on the prairie. He applied for a year's sabbatical from St. Olaf College (1923–1924) and, in an effort to cull realistic life from nature, spent part of his time writing in a summer cabin he had built the previous year along Big Island Lake, Itasca County, MINNESOTA.

Giants in the Earth appeared first in Norway in two volumes: *I De Dage—Fortælling om Norske Nykommere i Amerika* (*In Those Days: A Story about Norwegian Immigrants in America*) in 1924 and *De Dage—: Riket Grundlægges* (*Founding the Kingdom*) in 1925, both published by H. Aschehoug and Company. Rølvaag then set his sights on getting an English version published, but his novel was rejected by Knopf. With the help of Lincoln Colcord, Rølvaag not only translated his two volumes into what became books 1 and 2 of *Giants in the Earth* but also found a connection to Harper's, which published it in 1927.

Giants in the Earth was an instant success and was marketed as a modern classic. Rølvaag's realistic portrayal of successes and defeats on the prairie portrayed Manifest Destiny in a new light. The volume was chosen for the Book-of-the-Month Club, which guaranteed an initial 30,000 copies, and before 1928 it had sold approximately 80,000 copies. *Giants in the Earth* was also a critical success, receiving positive reviews in numerous publications, such as the *New York*

Times, the *Atlantic,* the *Nation,* the *Boston Transcript,* the *Independent,* and the *Saturday Review of Literature.* Furthermore, it fared well with academics, most notably with Vernon Parrington (1871–1929), a Pulitzer Prize winner and historian of American literature. Parrington not only wrote an introduction to a subsequent edition of *Giants in the Earth* but also included a discussion of this work in his unfinished third volume of *Main Currents in American Thought* (1930). Parrington believed that Rølvaag in *Giants in the Earth* had more thoroughly approached and addressed the perils of the frontier than others such as WILLA CATHER (1873–1947) and (HANNIBAL) HAMLIN GARLAND (1860–1940).

SIGNIFICANCE: *Giants in the Earth* is noteworthy for its treatment of Norwegian and American experience. Originally written in Norwegian and later translated into English, this novel reveals an American historical period of settling the Midwest through a Norwegian immigrant's eyes. Throughout, Rølvaag depicts the plight of the European immigrant settler in ways other novels do not, and he also displays a master touch in conveying their hardships through day-to-day reporting; nevertheless, these seemingly simple accounts of experiences involving the Midwest frontier translate into a moving epic.

The epic content of *Giants in the Earth* revolves around three important themes. First, it questions the frontier myth. Popular novels had presented America and the American West as a land of opportunity and untold riches, but this novel, mainly through Beret's perspective, presents the Midwestern frontier as anything but warm and hospitable. She constantly struggles to find a felicitous space in a land so open and vast, a place where, she regularly remarks, a person has no place to hide. Per Hansa—joyous at the opportunity to construct the biggest house of the settlement and to sow seeds in such fertile land—considers himself nothing less than a king in his own fairy tale. Beret sees in the open frontier a dangerous myth and a diabolical force.

A major issue connected to this questioning of the frontier myth is the conflict between man and nature, specifically the Midwestern land itself. Instead of a blessed, benevolent promised land of the Old Testament Israelites, Rølvaag personifies the frontier as a living force that challenges humans to succeed in settling in the vast stretch of land. This challenge becomes quite vindictive in various forms, such as harsh weather, recurring plagues of locusts, and, for Beret, the eeriness of the night. Her depression progresses into a form of insanity: to fight the malevolent outside spaces, she covers the windows with clothes and hides in their immigrants' trunk. Per Hansa, on the other hand, heartily accepts nature's challenge, fights back through vigorous farming, and believes that someday he and other settlers will conquer the land. Tragically, however, Per Hansa ultimately loses his fight with the land and dies in the terrible blizzard of 1880–1881.

Finally, the novel expresses the ambiguously detrimental effects of immigration on identity. Just as Per Hansa's death serves as a metaphor for the struggle to tame the Midwest, so does Rølvaag reveal the progressive clash between the traditional Norwegian identity and the budding American one in the Spring Creek community. Rølvaag shows that although settling the Midwestern frontier may provide immigrating families a chance for a new life, this new life—specifically through Beret's eyes—threatens to assimilate them completely into American culture while erasing their Norwegian heritage. From the very beginning of *Giants in the Earth,* Rølvaag depicts a feeling of isolation through language gaps. Although Per Hansa proves that body language with the Native Americans can surpass any linguistic boundaries, he cannot claim his land at the town office or communicate outside his community without the help of his English-speaking neighbor, a language barrier that initially instills a cantankerous relationship between the Norwegians and the Irish. Even though the members of this new Norwegian community struggle to conform to American standards, they also, in their attempts to educate their children, infuse their makeshift school curriculum with tales and songs from Norway. Nevertheless, Per Hansa and the rest start to assimilate into their new lives by Americanizing their names. This issue of heritage versus American conformity plays a part in the rest of the trilogy (*Peder Victorious,* 1929; *Their Fathers' God,* 1931).

Rølvaag and his literary antecedents were concerned with issues surrounding humanity and its psychological connections with nature. Rølvaag was interested in creating a story of epic proportions while still focusing on the common farmer. Because he was an immigrant himself, his literary forebears were connected to Norway. They and their works included *Markens Gröde* (1917; translated as *The Growth of the Soil,* 1921) by Nobel Prize winner Knut Hamsun (1859–1952); Nobel Prize winner Sigrid Undset (1882–1949); *Den Siste Viking* (1921; translated as *Last of the Vikings,* 1923) by Johan Bojer, a fellow Lofoten fisherman; and *De Norske Settlementers Historie* (1908; translated as *History of the Norwegian Settlements,* 1978) by Hjalmar Rued Holand (1872–1963), who devoted significant passages to the prairie in his book. Rølvaag's influence can be seen in Vilhelm Moberg's (1898–1973) *Utvandrarna* (1949; translated as *The Emigrants,* 1951). Moberg writes about a Swedish settlement in 1850s Minnesota, and his story revolves around a couple like Per Hansa and Beret. The same migration theme can be seen in novels by RUTH SUCKOW (1892–1960) and HERBERT (ARTHUR) KRAUSE (1905–1976).

IMPORTANT EDITIONS: *Giants in the Earth* was both a popular and a critical success. By 1929 it had become one of Harper's Modern Classics; the inexpensive edition included an introduction by noted critic Vernon Parrington. By 1965 it was published in the Perennial Classics paperback series, and it continues in print in the 1999 Harper Perennial Modern Classics series edition. *Giants in the Earth* has maintained its popularity and has been translated into such languages as Portuguese, Finnish, Swedish, German, French, Hungarian, and Italian.

FURTHER READING: Theodore Jorgenson and Nora Solum's *Ole Edvart Rølvaag: A Biography* (1939) is the benchmark biography and contains translations of his personal writings. Paul Reigstad's *Rølvaag: His Life and Art* (1972) and Einar Haugen's *Ole Edvart Rølvaag* (1983) also provide insight into Rølvaag's works written in Norwegian and English. In addition to giving an excellent introduction to the works of Rølvaag in her book *Ole Edvart Rølvaag* (1987), Anne Moseley examines the effects of the Midwest in "The Land as Metaphor in Two Scandina-

vian Immigrant Novels," *MELUS* 5.2 (Summer 1978): 33–38. Erica Haugtvedt has contributed "Abandoned in America: Identity Dissonance and Ethnic Preservationism in *Giants in the Earth,*" *MELUS* 33.3 (Fall 2008): 147–68. Other significant critical works include an anthology of essays, *Ole Rølvaag, Artist and Cultural Leader* (1975), edited by Gerald Thorson, and *Prairies Within: The Tragic Trilogy of Ole Rølvaag* (1987) by Harold P. Simonson. In *Twofold Identities: Norwegian-American Contributions to Midwestern Literature* (2004) Øyvind T. Gulliksen, professor emeritus of American studies at Telemark University College in Norway, focuses not only on the popularity of *Giants in the Earth* but also on the issues surrounding dual identities for immigrants. The main collection of Rølvaag's writings is in the Rølvaag Collection in the Norwegian-American Historical Association Archives at St. Olaf College in Northfield, Minnesota. See also SCANDINAVIAN LITERATURE.

LANCE WELDY   FRANCIS MARION UNIVERSITY

GRAPHIC NOVELS

OVERVIEW: For decades, newspaper comics and comic books were seen as a genre with little literary merit, filled with superheroes and funny animal characters and written mainly for children and adolescents. See COMIC STRIPS AND BOOKS. As this medium matured and began to use more adult themes and subjects and added sophisticated character development, a new descriptive term was needed to define this new entity and separate it from the comic book: the graphic novel. Graphic novels generally extend the comics form. Often dealing with adolescence or coming-of-age moments, many graphic novels have explored Midwestern landscapes, histories, and cultures, producing their meanings through the combination of drawings and text.

HISTORY AND SIGNIFICANCE: Graphic novels are a relatively recent classification or genre. Paul Gravett traces the origin of the term "graphic novel" to Richard Kyle, a comics critic and publisher who first used it in 1964. In *Graphic Novels: Everything You Need to Know* (2005) Gravett comments that the term is far from a finite definition because "many are shorter, or consist of collections of short stories, and they can come in all shapes, square, oblong, from minuscule to gigantic. Even more important, a great many are definitely not fictional at all but belong in the categories of non-fiction—history, biography, reportage, documentary, or educational" (8). Douglas Wolk's definition of the graphic novel in *Reading Comics: How Graphic Novels Work and What They Mean* (2007) is just as general. He notes that the term became more mainstream with the publication of *A Contract with God, and Other Tenement Stories* (1978), written and illustrated by Will Eisner (1917–2005), and highlights the debate surrounding its usage, most typically to assert higher quality and artistic status than the more commercially appealing comic book. Gravett's and Wolk's broad definitions encapsulate the breadth of subjects and ideas encompassed by Midwestern graphic novels.

At the apex of the universe of graphic-novel creators is, arguably, the multitalented Chris Ware (b. 1967). Born in NEBRASKA and living in CHICAGO, he creates, writes, and illustrates a variety of works that include comic books, series strips, paper assemblages, and three-dimensional items. His recurring characters exhibit some psychological or physical flaw, such as his version of Superman, a sociopathic man who still clings to childish proclivities, or a young woman who has lost part of her leg. Ware is best known for the graphic novel *Jimmy Corrigan, the Smartest Kid on Earth: An Improvisatory Romance, Pictographically Configured* (2000), set in Chicago and southwestern MICHIGAN. In it the emotionally impaired title character visits his father, whom he has never previously met, and learns disturbing things about his family. One of Ware's projects, *Building Stories* (2012), plays with the very definition of a graphic novel because the various components of the text (books, pamphlets, newspaper-style publications) are randomly ordered in a box. There is a central narrative theme in the focus on various families located in a Chicago apartment building; however, because of the fragmented nature of the box's contents, the various familial threads can merge past and present in a multitude of nonlinear readings and perspectives. Ware's highly literate narrative skills and distinctive artwork are reminiscent of the renowned newspaper comic strip *Krazy Kat* (1913–1944) by George Herriman (1880–1944).

Graphic novels with Midwestern settings and characters regularly focus on childhood or adolescence. Although some might imagine that an adolescent audience would be most attracted to these novels, the perspective they contain often reflects a maturity that comes only with years of postadolescent self-awareness. One example is the autobiographically based novel *My War with Brian* (1998) by Ted Rall (b. 1963), which focuses on his adolescence in Kettering, OHIO. Rall, a writer and illustrator of several graphic novels and comics, provides an honest and brutally emotional depiction of the bullying he received throughout junior high school and includes reflections on the overall effect those experiences had on his life. Like other coming-of-age graphic novels with Midwestern settings, Rall's novel portrays the Ohio town where he lived as a backward, culturally limited place that he claims to be happy to have "escaped" (59).

Blankets (2003), written and illustrated by Michigan-born author Craig Thompson (b. 1975), is based on his youth growing up in a small WISCONSIN town. Thompson's novel explores the often heartbreaking realities he faced as an adolescent, from the strain of being in abusive situations to the humiliation of being taunted by fellow students and the personal difficulty of trying to understand and reconcile himself with the strict religious influences around him. One of the great strengths of Thompson's novel is his artistic depiction of the world into which his character, Craig, escapes to avoid the reality that surrounds him. The images range from frames of the character Craig's artistry on paper to Thompson's illustrations of beautiful Midwestern landscapes, often filled with snow; together, the images balance and lighten the difficulties the characters face. Craig ultimately befriends a girl named Rayna and through their friendship and ultimate relationship finds hope and skills to cope with the world around him. Thompson's novel captures the frustrations and confinement that can characterize rural Midwestern life, yet it shows the beauty that exists there as well.

An example of the graphic novel-as-memoir is *Stitches* (2009) by the children's book illustrator David Small (b. 1945). In it, Small explores his childhood and adolescence in Detroit, where, to deal with chronic sinus difficulties, his unscrupulous physician father overexposed him to X-rays that in turn caused cancer of the throat and other health problems. The horrific subject is reflected in the somber pen-and-ink washes in black and gray, and the cityscapes and hospital interiors are likewise sterile and depressing.

Reinforcing the definitions of graphic novels as covering a broad spectrum of artistic and literary possibilities, Chicago-born writer Sarah Grace McCandless (b. 1974) presents a graphic novel at one end of the spectrum in *Grosse Pointe Girl: Tales from a Suburban Adolescence* (2004). Rather than being a story told solely or even primarily through narrative illustrated panels, McCandless's 178-page written text follows a more conventional novel format but includes twenty-three graphic illustrations by Christine Norrie (b. 1974) along the way. Depicting the adolescence of a girl named Anna in the upscale Grosse Pointe area north of Detroit, Michigan, during the 1980s, McCandless includes details characteristic of the period. She mentions Trapper Keepers, a brand of loose-leaf binder, and bands like Wham! and Poison and refers to locally specific details, such as the prevalence of auto companies in the area, trips across the bridge to Canada, where drinking is legal at a younger age, and fellow high school students going on to study at the University of Michigan. It is a tale of struggling to find where one fits in with friends, peer pressure, and growing up, culminating in a high school ten-year reunion at the end of the novel that reflects on the implications of the earlier experiences.

Skyscrapers of the Midwest (2008) is an eclectic collection of images and short graphic sequences by self-declared "Midwestern cartoonist" Joshua W. Cotter (b. 1977); this work was first published as a four-part serial from 2004 to 2007. The novel's back cover states that it is the "winding tale of a young cat, his little brother, and the creeping shadow of imminent adolescence in the American heartland," and it lives up to this description. Reminiscent of the adolescent transition described in Thompson's

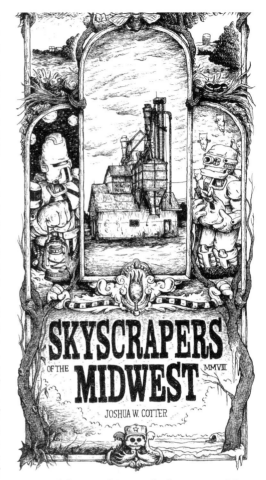

Cover of the graphic novel *Skyscrapers of the Midwest*.
© Joshua W. Cotter, 2008

Blankets, Cotter's two young cats cope with a rocky home life, peer pressure and bullying, and the struggle of trying to fit into their family's religious expectations in Missouri. Interspersed within the short graphic segments that make up the overall story are humorous fictional advertisements and other commentary that deepen the novel's Midwestern elements.

Midwestern history is explored in graphic novels like *Road to Perdition* (1998) by Iowa-born writer Max Allan Collins (b. 1948), which was made into a movie starring Tom Hanks in 2002. *Road to Perdition* builds on the real history of gangsters and Mafia activity in the Midwest during the early twentieth century through the fictional story of Michael O'Sullivan and his work as a hit man for the infamous Looney family in the tri-cities area of Rock Island, ILLINOIS, and Moline and Davenport, IOWA. Collins interweaves aspects of the real-life Looney history with appearances by figures like Eliot Ness, Al Capone, and Frank Nitti to create a story of a man who loses his family while serving as a mob soldier. The illustrations by British artist Richard Piers Rayner (b. ca. 1953) add to the story and portray a harsh, dark landscape befitting the start of the Great Depression, when the story is set. Collins expanded on this story line in several graphic-novel sequels.

Abel (1998) by writer William Harms (b. 1969) and illustrator Mark Bloodworth (b. 1963), both of whom have Midwestern connections by way of Nebraska and Detroit, respectively, is the story of two brothers living in ironically named Friend, Nebraska, during World War II. The novel is starkly illustrated with sepia-toned images, and the contrast between the compassion and uncertainty of John and the cruelty of his violent older brother Philip is at the center of this story. Told primarily from John's perspective, this graphic novel navigates the hard life growing up on a farm, John's struggle to try to understand his brother's behavior, and his confusion over the conservatism and racism he witnesses in the town around him. The novel's violent and angry ending reflects sadly on the small town and leaves open the question of what impact that environment will ultimately have on John.

Other graphic novels simply offer commentary on the landscape or the culture as a whole through Midwestern settings and characters. *A History of Violence* (1997) by Pennsylvanian-turned-British writer John Wagner (b. 1949) plays on widely accepted ideas of safety and security in the Midwest to build suspense for the violent tale. A conventional Midwestern family, located in Ravens Bend, Michigan, finds their lives upended when two criminals hold up the family diner. The father's violent response to the attempted robbery and his hidden history taint the innocence and security of the town and the family as they become exposed to New York gangsters and criminals. Vince Locke (b. 1966), a Michigan illustrator, deftly mixes tranquil scenes of rural softball games

with the darkness of the novel's violent episodes and gloomy New York streets.

Harvey Pekar (1939–2010), well known for his *American Splendor* comics, and his wife, Joyce Brabner (b. 1952), venture a longer graphic novel in *Our Cancer Year* (1994). The novel highlights the struggle Pekar and Brabner went through in the year he was diagnosed with cancer and the ways they dealt with the emotional trauma. The illustrations by Frank Stack (b. 1937) continue the images fans would recognize from Pekar's other comics dramatizing the CLEVELAND landscape and local characters.

Midwestern cities have long served as settings for literary novels, and many of those novels are now evolving into graphic form. *Welcome to the Jungle* (2008), a graphic novel by Missouri native Jim Butcher (b. 1971), represents the first graphic depiction of his ongoing fantasy series, the Dresden Files. In an alternate, magical Chicago, professional wizard Harry Dresden investigates mysterious circumstances at the Lincoln Park Zoo. Full-color illustrations by Indonesian artist Ardian Syaf depict the characters and setting, complete with notable elements of the Chicago skyline and references to UPTON (BEALL) SINCLAIR (JR.) (1878–1968), and provide a sense of place within the story.

Laurell K. Hamilton (b. 1963) is another writer who is transforming her novels into graphic form. Known for her popular novel series Anita Blake: Vampire Hunter, which began in 1993 with *Guilty Pleasures,* the stories featuring her eponymous protagonist have taken on visual form. Set in ST. LOUIS, the full-color panels rendered by Brett Booth and Ron Lim (b. 1965) tell of Blake's adventures in volumes adapted from the novels, such as *Guilty Pleasures,* published in twelve parts (2006–2008), and in stories written especially for the graphic form, such as the two-part *The First Death* (2007), illustrated by Wellinton Alves, who lives in Brazil.

James O'Barr (b. 1960) wrote and illustrated his four-part fantasy *The Crow* (1989), set in Detroit. It concerns a young man and his fiancée who are murdered by a gang and how the dead man returns to exact violent retribution on the perpetrators. Drawn in black and white, the story and art deftly capture the noir aspect of the subject and locale. *The Crow* was collected into one volume in 1993 and was made into a feature film in 1994 starring Brandon Lee; it has become a cult classic.

The Midwestern landscape also provides a focus for fantasy storytelling in the special-edition graphic-novel spin-off by Bill Willingham (b. 1956) of his popular *Fables* comic-book series, *Fables: Werewolves of the Heartland* (2013), illustrated by Jim Fern (b. 1964). Willingham's comic-book series draws on common folklore tales and characters, and in this special edition, a recurring character from the series, Bigby Wolf, has his own epic adventure and ends up in Story City, Iowa, a town occupied by werewolves. Wisconsin-born writer Tim Seeley (b. 1977) and illustrators Mike Norton (b. 1973) and Mark Englert (b. 1979) have collected four volumes so far of their *Revival* series (2012–2015), a graphic narrative of mystery and intrigue in Wausau, Wisconsin, described as "rural noir" on the cover, where the dead have come back to life.

SELECTED WORKS: As a starting point for reading or research, Max Allan Collins's *Road to Perdition* (1998), Chris Ware's *Jimmy Corrigan, the Smartest Kid on Earth* (2000), and Craig Thompson's *Blankets* (2003) are strong graphic novels for anyone interested in understanding how the Midwest is portrayed in the genre. *Abel* (1998) by William Harms and Mark Bloodworth and *A History of Violence* (1997) by John Wagner also portray Midwestern characters and settings.

FURTHER READING: No major studies of Midwestern graphic novels have yet appeared, nor have any bibliographies of the regional genre been composed; however, Daniel K. Raeburn (b. 1968) has written *Chris Ware* (2004), a substantial critical appraisal of the author-artist with a generous full-color sampling of Ware's work. Some general sources regarding graphic novels do note Midwestern contributions. Paul Gravett's *Graphic Novels: Stories to Change Your Life* (British edition, 2005), republished in the United States as *Graphic Novels: Everything You Need to Know* (2005), provides a strong written and illustrated discussion of graphic novels, highlighting thirty "essential" works in the genre that form a place to start understanding them. Gravett examines the ways the novels can address coming of age, war, superheroes, fantasy realms, HUMOR, and other themes. Although Gravett's analysis of genre and subject is broad, he does note the work of Midwesterners Harvey Pekar and Craig Thompson. Douglas Wolk's *Reading Comics: How Graphic Novels Work and What They Mean* (2007) provides a critical overview of the genre and reviews several prominent comics and graphic-novel writers, including Thompson.

A number of additional general sources exist on the evolution and artistry of comics, comic books, and graphic novels. *Understanding Comics: The Invisible Art* (1993) by Scott McCloud (b. 1960) provides a comprehensive overview of the techniques and characteristics of comics writing and ultimately the basic elements of graphic novels as well. It is based on McCloud's experiences working in the comics genre and is thoroughly illustrated in comics form. In *Comics, Comix and Graphic Novels: A History of Comic Art* (1996), Roger Sabin gives a glimpse of the genre from a worldwide perspective. Jan Baetens has edited a collection of critical essays, *The Graphic Novel* (2001). Two general works that outline the history and development of the form are *Faster than a Speeding Bullet: The Rise of the Graphic Novel* (2003) by Stephen Weiner and *The Rough Guide to Graphic Novels* (2008) by Danny Fingeroth. A special issue of *English Language Notes* 46.2 (Fall/Winter 2008), edited by William Kuskin, is titled "Graphia: Literary Criticism and the Graphic Novel." A comprehensive guide to what Gene Kannenberg considers the most important works of the genre is his *500 Essential Graphic Novels: The Ultimate Guide* (2008); it includes listings of the novels by subject, as well as information on the authors and artists.

SARA KOSIBA   TROY UNIVERSITY

GATSBY.
See *Great Gatsby, The*

GAY LITERATURE.
See Lesbian, Gay, Bisexual, Transgender, and Queer Literature.

GREAT GATSBY, THE
OVERVIEW: In the five years between the publication of his first novel, *This Side of Paradise* (1920), and *The Great Gatsby* (1925), F(RANCIS) SCOTT (KEY) FITZGERALD (1896–

1940) established himself as the literary voice of his generation, the spokesman for what he called the Jazz Age. *The Great Gatsby* is a short novel, the tragic story of an obscure young Dakotan named James Gatz who re-creates himself on the basis of "his Platonic conception of himself" (1995 edition 104) as the romantic and fabulously wealthy Jay Gatsby of West Egg, Long Island. It is also the story of another Midwesterner, Nick Carraway, the novel's narrator, recently arrived in the East and fascinated by his mysterious neighbor, Gatsby.

There was more than a little of both Gatsby and Carraway in their creator. Fitzgerald virtually willed himself into prominence with a soaring ambition that attracted the kind of romantic fascination that surrounded his title character. He was also like Gatsby in his pursuit of love. Just as Gatsby was driven by his unsuccessful attempt to win Daisy Fay Buchanan, Fitzgerald was obsessed with the rejection by his first love, Ginevra King (1898–1980), and his successful wooing of his second, Zelda Sayre Fitzgerald (1900–1948). Like Nick Carraway, Fitzgerald was a product of an affluent urban Midwestern family and brought an intelligent outsider's critical eye to the vortex of dreams and heartbreak that was New York of the 1920s. And perhaps there was more of the Buchanans, Tom and Daisy, and their friend Jordan in Fitzgerald than he would have liked to admit. Nick calls them "careless people," and in some ways the wreckage they left in their wake was not totally unlike that which Scott and Zelda and others of their circle would leave in the coming years (187).

Fitzgerald, like his friend ERNEST (MILLER) HEMINGWAY (1899–1961), was fortunate to have Maxwell Perkins as his editor; Perkins ably shepherded the novel through its publication by Scribner's in April 1925. Reviews were positive; most were enthusiastic, although no reviewer treated the novel as a major addition to the American canon. Despite the favorable notices, however, sales were disappointing, and *The Great Gatsby* at best hovered for a short time near the middle of the best-seller lists, never approaching the commercial success of Fitzgerald's earlier books. The two printings, totaling slightly less than 24,000 copies, had not sold out by the time of his death in 1940. The Pulitzer Prize for Fiction for 1925 was awarded to fellow Midwesterner (HARRY) SINCLAIR LEWIS (1885–1951) for *Arrowsmith*. Lewis declined the honor that Fitzgerald, we must think, would have embraced proudly.

HISTORY AND SIGNIFICANCE: Members of the generation that came of age in the wake of the Great War experienced a dramatically different world and life than had their parents, who had reached maturity at the end of the nineteenth century. In his earliest works Fitzgerald had helped define the way this new generation understood itself in the postwar world. In those works, the novels *This Side of Paradise* and *The Beautiful and the Damned* (1922) and the story collections *Flappers and Philosophers* (1921) and *Tales of the Jazz Age* (1922), Fitzgerald had thrilled his readers with the shimmering, if somewhat ephemeral, world of a new youth in a new age. In *The Great Gatsby* he not only created more nuanced characters and situations but also expanded the scope of his portrayal of modern American society. This new novel was self-consciously and successfully topical, but Fitzgerald also found a way to evoke a historical America, a tragic America in which the comings and goings of a clique of wealthy and spoiled would-be sophisticates were inexorably connected to the great persons and events of American history and myth.

When, in the opening pages of the novel, Nick says that "Gatsby . . . represented everything for which I have an unaffected scorn" and then immediately says that "there was something gorgeous about him, some heightened sensitivity to the promises of life" (6), he suggests the tension that drives the novel. If *The Great Gatsby* is a celebration of the American Dream of unlimited possibility, it is also a novel of the failure of that dream—its corruption and the devastation that results from it. When Nick describes his commute into Manhattan, he exults: "The city seen from the Queensboro Bridge is always the city seen as if for the first time, in its first wild promise of all the mystery and beauty in the world" (73), but on this particular day he is to meet Gatsby's friend Meyer Wolfsheim, the man who could "play with the faith of fifty million people" (78) by fixing the 1919 World Series.

If the unlimited opportunity of the American Dream could lead to the extraordinary opulence of the Buchanan mansion and the spectacular acquisitiveness of Jay Gatsby, its by-product is the valley of ashes, "a fantastic farm where ashes grow like wheat into ridges and hills and grotesque gardens" (27). Fitzgerald's valley of ashes certainly owes a debt to *The Waste Land,* the 1922 T(HOMAS) S(TEARNS) ELIOT (1888–1965) poem in which Eliot dissected the malaise of the modern world by portraying it as a physically, emotionally, and spiritually barren place, a despoiled Garden of Eden. But if Eliot's poem presented images of symbolic dust, Fitzgerald darkened the imagery by suggesting that America actually grows the life-choking detritus of modern life in a "fantastic farm" that is an ironic inversion of both the Edenic myth that has always been a central part of American dreaming and the Jeffersonian vision of America as an agrarian paradise. In *The Great Gatsby* Jefferson's yeoman farmer has become one of those "ash-grey men" who "move dimly and already crumbling through the powdery air" (27).

But if Jefferson's agrarian vision is corrupted, so is the ideal of America imagined by its preeminent urbanite and practical moralist, Benjamin Franklin (1706–1790). His prescription for moral living and his plan for practicing it as recorded in *The Autobiography* are transmuted into a "Schedule" and list of "General Resolves" that Gatsby had written out as a youth and that has been preserved as a holy relic by his father. Franklin's original plan has been criticized by D(avid) H(erbert Richards) Lawrence (1885–1930) and others for its reduction of morality to a series of easily enumerated exercises in right living, but the young Gatsby's plan is particularly quotidian and simplistic. It is as if he had filtered Franklin through Horatio Alger, with such resolves as "Bath every other day" and "Read one improving book or magazine per week" (182).

Moreover, in *The Great Gatsby* Fitzgerald alludes to other historical figures from America's past, particularly from the process of the western pioneering experience. There are references, for example, to real pathfinders such as Daniel Boone (1734–1820), fictional ones like Hopalong Cassidy, and dubious, self-mythologizing ones like (William) Buffalo Bill Cody (1846–1917). It is in the final words of the novel that Fitzgerald most powerfully and poetically evokes the American past. With Gatsby dead, murdered by one of those "already crumbling . . . ash-grey men," Nick decides to move back to the Midwest. Before leaving, he takes one last look at Gatsby's house, becomes aware of "the old island here that flowered once for Dutch sailors' eyes—a fresh green breast of the new world," and imagines that "for a transitory enchanted moment man must have held his breath in the presence of this continent . . . face to face for the last time in human history with something commensurate to his capacity for wonder" (189).

Earlier in the novel Nick had imagined Gatsby in a state of apprehension much like that of those Dutch sailors as he stood silently, arms outstretched, reaching toward the green light at the end of Daisy Buchanan's dock. It is at this moment of heartbreaking longing, of unfulfilled dreams and passions, that Gatsby is most attractive to Nick, who recognizes in Gatsby "an extraordinary gift for hope, a romantic readiness" (6). Richard D. Lehan, in *F. Scott Fitzgerald and the Craft of Fiction* (1966), argues that just such romantic readiness is also the key to understanding Fitzgerald and his writing. He suggests that as a result of the failure of his youthful courtship of Ginevra King, Fitzgerald "came to believe that such yearning was an end in itself; he believed in the need to preserve a romantic state of mind where the imagination and the will are arrested . . . by an idealized concept of beauty and love. The loss creates an eternal striving and keeps the world beautifully alive" (95). Yet the novel suggests that such a romantic state of mind—the very thing that makes Gatsby so attractive to Nick—would seem to be a tragic flaw in the decidedly unromantic modern world. This possibly autobiographical link between the author and his doomed character lends heartbreaking poignancy to the novel.

Gatsby and Fitzgerald are outside the norms of their time in their romanticism, but the novel exploits the motif of the outsider in other ways as well. In its obvious examination of social class and wealth and its more subtle consideration of race and ethnicity, the novel explores what it means to be perceived as inside or outside the American Dream. Ultimately, Fitzgerald, through Nick, considers this motif in geographic terms. Near the end of the novel Nick realizes that "this has been a story of the West, after all—Tom and Gatsby, Daisy and Jordan and I, were all Westerners, and perhaps we possessed some deficiency in common which made us subtly unadaptable to Eastern life" (184).

Nick never explains what that supposed deficiency is or means. On that point, as on so many others, Fitzgerald asks us to live without specific explanation. What we do know, however, is that Nick writes his fictional memoir of his adventures in the East after returning to the Midwest. And even though Nick had found incredible Gatsby's belief that he could simply repeat the past, he finds in the Midwest the comforting past of his own memories. He tells us, "That's my Middle West . . . the thrilling returning trams of my youth and the street lamps and sleigh bells in the frosty dark and the shadows of holly wreaths thrown by lighted windows on the snow." And after his recent experiences he has come to realize that "I am part of that, a little solemn with the feel of those long winters, a little complacent from growing up in the Carraway house in a city where dwellings are still called through decades by a family's name" (184). In the opening pages of the novel Nick tells us that when he returned from the East, he had wished the world "to be in uniform and at a sort of moral attention forever" (6), but presumably through the writing of *The Great Gatsby* he has come to realize the fatal impossibility of that. Instead, he seems to find in his native Midwest the stability, the diminished expectations, and the human pace of life that allow him to frame a moral tale but still follow his father's injunction to reserve judgment, to accept the necessary ambiguities of life.

In the decade after Fitzgerald's death, critics and scholars began to reconsider the writer and his achievement. Today *The Great Gatsby* is widely believed to be among the

Warner Baxter (second from left) as Gatsby in the 1926 film adaptation of *The Great Gatsby,* directed by Herbert Brenon.

© Paramount Studios, 1926

very finest, most serious, and most influential American novels. In the years since the novel's publication, there have been an extraordinary number of critical studies of the novel, as well as a proliferation of adaptations, including two major ballets; four major-studio film adaptations, starring Warner Baxter (1926), Alan Ladd (1949), Robert Redford (1974), and Leonardo DiCaprio (2013); a graphic novel by Nicki Greenberg (2007); a major opera by John Harbison (b. 1938), which debuted at New York's Metropolitan Opera in 1999; and the celebrated off-Broadway play *Gatz* (2010), produced by the Electric Repair Service ensemble, in which actors read the text of the novel in its entirety over the course of seven hours. All of this attests to the continuing allure of *The Great Gatsby.*

IMPORTANT EDITIONS: The first American edition of April 1925 by Charles Scribner's Sons was followed by the English edition of February 1926. From April through August 1926 the novel was serialized in five parts in *Famous Story Magazine.* Since then there have been many dozens of editions in English, and the novel has been translated into nearly forty languages, including Hindi, Estonian, Arabic, and Basque. In 1991 Cambridge University Press began an ambitious plan to publish Fitzgerald's complete works in twelve volumes with extensive introductions, critical apparatuses, and notes. *The Great Gatsby* was the first volume, edited by Matthew J. Bruccoli. Although the Cambridge volume may be considered the definitive text, a popular version, *The Great Gatsby: The Authorized Text,* based on the Cambridge edition and published in paperback by Scribner and Simon and Schuster in 1995, may be the most accessible and most used text.

FURTHER READING: All major Fitzgerald biographies treat *The Great Gatsby* and its composition and reception in some detail. Arthur Mizener's *The Far Side of Paradise* (1951) was the first important biography and a key work in establishing Fitzgerald's posthumous reputation. Andrew Turnbull's *Scott Fitzgerald* (1962) further fleshed out his life. Matthew J. Bruccoli's *Some Sort of Epic Grandeur: The Life of F. Scott Fitzgerald* (1981) and Jeffrey Meyers's *Scott Fitzgerald: A Biogra-*

phy (1994) have made use of new materials for a more complete view of the man and writer.

Fitzgerald was a prolific letter writer and often discussed his writing, including his aims for and attitudes about *The Great Gatsby.* Several general collections exist, each of which offers some letters not contained in the others. Andrew Turnbull edited the first important gathering of the correspondence in *The Letters of F. Scott Fitzgerald* (1963). Matthew J. Bruccoli has edited two volumes: *Correspondence of F. Scott Fitzgerald* (1980), with Margaret Duggan; and, with Judith S. Baughman, *F. Scott Fitzgerald: A Life in Letters* (1994). Of particular interest for students of *The Great Gatsby* is Fitzgerald's correspondence with his legendary editor gathered in *Dear Scott / Dear Max: The Fitzgerald-Perkins Correspondence* (1971), edited by John Kuehl and Jackson R. Bryer.

A number of monographs focus on *The Great Gatsby,* including Kathleen Parkinson's *"The Great Gatsby"* (1987); two volumes by Ronald Berman, *"The Great Gatsby" and Modern Times* (1994) and *"The Great Gatsby" and Fitzgerald's World of Ideas* (1997); and Sarah Churchwell's *Careless People: Murder, Mayhem and the Invention of "The Great Gatsby"* (2013). Several important collections of essays suggest the changes in Fitzgerald criticism and the emerging critical opinion of the novel, as can be inferred from their dates of publication; among these are Frederick J. Hoffman's *"The Great Gatsby": A Study* (1962), Ernest Lockridge's *Twentieth Century Interpretations of "The Great Gatsby"* (1968), Henry Dan Piper's *Fitzgerald's "The Great Gatsby": The Novel, the Critics, the Background* (1970), Scott Donaldson's *Critical Essays on F. Scott Fitzgerald's "The Great Gatsby"* (1984), and Matthew J. Bruccoli's *New Essays on "The Great Gatsby"* (1985).

Andrew T. Crosland's *A Concordance to F. Scott Fitzgerald's "The Great Gatsby"* (1974) and Bruccoli's *F. Scott Fitzgerald's "The Great Gatsby": A Literary Reference* (2002) are valuable tools for anyone doing scholarly work on the novel. The manuscript and galley proofs are housed at Princeton University Library. Bruccoli prepared an impeccable facsimile, *"The Great Gatsby": A Facsimile of the Manuscript* (1973).

JOHN ROHRKEMPER   ELIZABETHTOWN COLLEGE

GREAT LAKES LITERATURE

Lake Erie: 9,910 square miles
Lake Huron: 23,000 square miles
Lake Michigan: 22,300 square miles
Lake Ontario: 7,340 square miles
Lake Superior: 31,700 square miles

OVERVIEW: The Great Lakes are among the most significant features of the Midwestern landscape, and their beauty, violent weather, and varied cultures have inspired storytellers for millennia. Native peoples' literatures about the lakes include sacred origin stories and descriptions of an underwater monster who causes the furious storms encountered while fishing and trading. See also NATIVE AMERICAN LITERATURE. European explorers, often accompanied by priests, came to the lakes seeking furs in the seventeenth century. Their accounts began a five-century tradition of writers documenting their experiences traveling the lakes. See also EXPLORATION ACCOUNTS. By the nineteenth century many descriptions of the lakes were written by women who found a ready market for portrayals of a place then considered as exotic as Russia or China. The Industrial Revolution, which led to massive lakeside cities, also created a freshwater merchant marine that would inspire a maritime literature that is unique in the world. What happened elsewhere in the Midwest—trade, war, immigration, industrialization, resource extraction, environmental degradation—also happened on the Great Lakes and is reflected in lakes literature. The lakes are a highway into one of the continent's richest regions.

HISTORY AND SIGNIFICANCE: The Great Lakes came into literature ten thousand years ago, when the first Paleo-Indian big-game hunters pushed north onto the tundra that was springing up as the glaciers retreated and discovered vast lakes. These hunters and the archaic cultures that followed them also fished, encountering whales in Lake Huron and giant sturgeon in the other Great Lakes, and told stories about their experiences. From their worlds of water, wind, and stars, Native peoples learned earth-diver origin stories of Aataentsic, or

Great Lakes map adapted from *Cornell's Primary Geography*. D. Appleton & Co., 1888.
Courtesy of Special Collections, Murphy Library, University of Wisconsin–La Crosse

Sky Woman, who falls pregnant from the sky toward the endless waters. She is saved by the animals who cluster beneath her to break her fall and keep her from drowning. Great Turtle offers her shelter on his back for the birth of her child, and the least of the animals—Muskrat or Toad—dives to find soil to spread on Turtle's back to create the land world. The best version of this story is by Skanawati (John Buck) in "Iroquoian Cosmology, First Part" by J. N. B. Hewitt, in *Twenty-First Annual Report of the Bureau of American Ethnology to the Secretary of the Smithsonian Institution, 1899–1900* (1903): 127–339.

Native peoples also have stories about underwater monsters, one of whom, during the Woodland and protohistoric cultures before European contact, came to be known as Micipijiu (Missipeshu), a mythic demon lover portrayed as a great lynx or panther who raises storms, kidnaps women and children, and grants great powers for good or evil. Arrogance or failure to appease the underwater spirits frequently resulted in harm, as is reflected in "Peeta Kway" [*biitekwe*, "Foam Woman"] ("The Tempest"), collected from an unidentified Odawa storyteller by HENRY ROWE SCHOOLCRAFT (1793–1864) and his wife, Jane Johnston Schoolcraft (1800–1842), in *Algic Researches, Comprising Inquiries Respecting the Mental Characteristics of the North American Indians: First Series; Indian Tales and Legends* (1839). The story describes a beautiful young woman kept on a raft offshore on Lake Michigan. Her mother refuses an offer of marriage for her, hoping for a more distinguished match. To punish the mother's arrogance, the underwater beings raise a storm that carries the raft to the islands in the strait near present-day DETROIT, where the young woman is married to the old ruler of an island. Native peoples did not romanticize the lakes, as would successor cultures; from long experience they treated them with respect even as they built their camps on the most beautiful promontories, such as Mackinac (Great Turtle) Island, and traveled across them in birch and dugout canoes that were liable to capsize even in moderate waves.

European contact with Native Americans was first recorded in the seventeenth century by explorers such as Samuel de Champlain (ca. 1574–1635) in *The Voyages of 1604–1618* (1906, 1907). These explorers were looking for a northwest passage to China but found furs instead, and the ensuing trade was an economic engine that drove the North American continent for over two centuries. The lakes travels it required were described in accounts such as *Le Grand Voyage du Pays des Hurons* by Father Gabriel Sagard (1614–1636), published in *The Jesuit Relations*, 73 volumes (1896–1901), edited by Reuben Gold Thwaites (1853–1913); *A New Discovery of a Vast Country in America* (1698) by Father Louis Hennepin (1626–ca. 1705); *History and General Description of New France and Journal of a Voyage to North America* (1761) by Pierre François Xavier de Charlevoix (1682–1761); *Voyages* (1885) of Pierre-Esprit Radisson (1636–1710); and later autobiographies such as the *Narrative of the Travels and Adventures of a Merchant Voyageur in the Savage Territories of Northern America Leaving Montreal the 28th of May 1783 (to 1820)* (1978) by Jean-Baptiste Perrault (1761–1844).

Although the fur trade was finished by about 1840, its afterlife as a fictional subject was just beginning in romanticized DIME NOVELS, juvenile adventure stories, and middlebrow adult historical fictions that persist to the present. For example, *The Loon Feather* (1940) by IOLA FULLER (GOODSPEED MCCOY) (1906–1993) filters the cultural conflicts brought by trappers, traders, and military encroachments through the eyes of a young Native woman on Mackinac Island in the nineteenth century. The reality was quite different, as lamented in one voyageur chanson collected by Marius Barbeau and published as "Le Voyage, C'est Un Mariage" in the Canadian journal *The Beaver* (now renamed *Canada's History*) 273 (June 1942): 19. These lines from "Le Voyage" are translated here by Carl Masthay:

Je plains qui s'y engage
Sans y être invite.
Léve tôt, couché tard,
Il faut subir son sort,
S'exposer á la mort.

I pity whoever does it
Without being a guest.
Early to rise, late to sleep,
Submit to your lot,
While risking your death.

The Great Lakes were a battleground not only commercially but also in at least nineteen Native, European, and American wars, beginning with the French-English Beaver Wars in the 1640s. A multitude of documents exist from these wars, including the speeches of Pontiac (ca. 1720–1769) during the siege of Detroit and the *History of the Ojibway People* (1885) by WILLIAM W(HIPPLE) WARREN (1825–1853), which describes the attack on Fort Michilimackinac. The *Journals* (1765) of Major Robert Rogers (1731–1795) also come from this period; his description of his late fall trip from New York to Detroit to relieve the French of their Great Lakes forts is particularly interesting. The War of 1812, much of which was fought on or near the Great Lakes, inspired not only *Ned Myers: A Life before the Mast* (1843) but also a firsthand account, *Battle of Lake Erie* (1854), by Dr. Usher Parson (1788–1868), surgeon on Commodore Oliver Hazard Perry's ship. *The Travels and Adventures of David C. Bunnell during Twenty Three Years of Seafaring Life* (1831) by David C. Bunnell (b. 1793) is a narrative of the battle, as well as this sailor's capture by the British afterward.

Although Native Americans had always used the lakes for commerce—Lake Superior copper has been discovered in the southeastern United States, and furs and agricultural products were regularly traded between northern and southern lakes nations—the European introduction of ships capable of carrying substantial cargoes refigured the traditional Great Lakes theme of storm and disaster. The subsequent industrialization of the Great Lakes basin in the nineteenth century eclipsed all previous economic development in the region. The lakes became a busy, crowded highway for moving the products of resource extraction and agriculture to the East and ferrying immigrants westward in an ever-expanding cycle. See also IMMIGRANT AND MIGRANT LITERATURE. With few harbors of refuge, explosive storms, little sea room, and scant regulation of vessels, the results were calamitous. Not surprisingly, death and danger became twin themes that drove Great Lakes seafaring literature from its beginning. Wreck statistics support the literary tropes—the Great Lakes are still ranked by Lloyd's of London as the fifth most dangerous waters in the world—and the theme of a ship in a storm is the most romantic, most popular, and seemingly most enduring plot of Great Lakes maritime literature.

"The Wreck of the *Edmund Fitzgerald*" (1976), a ballad by the Canadian singer Gordon Lightfoot (b. 1938), is one recent example of a musical and literary genre of storm and disaster that began with Hennepin's *A New Discovery*, which describes the prophetic career of the first European ship on the upper lakes, La Salle's *Griffon*, piloted by a captain familiar only with the Atlantic. The *Griffon* promptly went to the bottom in a storm after Natives had warned him not to leave safe anchorage (90). Like most saltwater sailors who first see the lakes, her captain scoffed before he met his reckoning, a theme that endures in the stories written about the lakes. Fiction entered the literature of the Great Lakes in 1836 with the anonymous *Scenes on Lake Huron* and reached its artistic apogee with the 1943 novel *November Storm* by Jay McCormick (1919–1997). James Fenimore Cooper (1789–1851), who had sailed the lakes in the War of 1812, highlighted the excellent ship-handling skills required of Great Lakes sailors in *The Pathfinder; or, The Inland Sea* (1840). Cooper also edited one of the most interesting personal accounts to come from the War of 1812, *Ned Myers; or, A Life before the Mast* (1843); it describes in horrific detail the foundering of the *Hamilton* and the *Scourge* in a night squall on Lake Erie, resulting in the greatest single loss of life in the entire war on the lakes. Herman Melville (1819–1891) incorporated the figure of a tough, freedom-loving Great Lakes sailor as Steelkilt in chapter 51 of *Moby-Dick* (1851) while noting, as would many others, that Great Lakes sailing required extraordinary skill, another rebuke to saltwater sailors who described the lakes as puddles unworthy of notice.

The first fiction about shipwreck on the lakes, however, was written by a woman, Constance Fenimore Woolson (1840–1894), who had often traveled as a child with her father on steamers around the still-wild lakes in the 1850s. After her ship sinks in Lake Michigan, the heroine of Woolson's story "Margaret Morris," published in *Appletons' Journal* on April 13, 1872, is saved by her pluck, anger, and refusal to give up, a common theme in Woolson's writings. She wrote about the lakes and their wild weather in several other stories, most of which were collected in *Castle Nowhere* (1875), and lake storms appeared in her fiction until nearly the end of her life.

Woolson made her living as a writer and early learned that travel narratives about the lakes would sell to eastern magazines. Indeed, by the time she wrote "Round by Propeller," published in *Harper's New Monthly Magazine* in September 1872, the form had become so common that she could mock the travelers, the ship, and the form itself. Travel narratives about the lakes had begun almost as soon as Europeans could arrange passage and guides. Vicomte de Chateaubriand (1768–1848) published *Travels in America and Italy* in 1828, followed shortly by Charles Dickens (1812–1870), who described with great tenderness immigrants moving west but worried irascibly about steamboat explosions in *American Notes* (1842). Charles Lanman (1819–1895), a genteel painter who normally worked with government subjects in Washington, D.C., wrote *Summer in the Wilderness: Embracing a Canoe Voyage up the Mississippi and around Lake Superior* (1847). In 1850 Dr. John Bigsby (1792–1881), the physician to the U.S.-Canadian boundary survey party, wrote *The Shoe and Canoe* (1880), recounting his travels with the party and on his own. William Cullen Bryant (1794–1878) wrote of his trip to the lakes in *Letters of a Traveller; or, Notes of Things in Europe and America* (1850). Captain Frederick Marryat (1792–1848), who had previously derided Great Lakes sailing, related his comeuppance in *A Diary in America* (1839). In the same vein, Rudyard Kipling (1865–1936) penned what is arguably the epitome of stunned European reaction to the lakes in *Letters of Travel, 1892–1913* (1920): "Lake Superior is all the same stuff towns pay taxes for (fresh water), but it engulfs and wrecks and drives ashore like a fully accredited ocean—a hideous thing to find in the heart of a continent" (159).

While male travelers were preoccupied with danger and overcoming death, women travel writers found a vehicle that freed them from the constraints of nineteenth-century decorum and allowed them to act independently on an international stage.

One of the first was political economist Harriet Martineau (1802–1876), who used her trip to the lakes to contrast the free North of the Great Lakes and its noble-appearing Natives with the degraded, slave-holding South in *Society in America* (1837). She was followed by Anna Jameson (1794–1860), who, to escape her ill-fated marriage to a drunken Canadian administrator, set off across present-day Ontario. The result was *Winter Studies and Summer Rambles in Canada* (1838). Jameson was the first woman of European origins to venture into the lakes with only her male guides; she was also the first to run the rapids of Sault Ste. Marie in a canoe, a feat that earned her the sobriquet Wahsàh-gewahnòquà, the Woman of the Bright Foam, from her Native paddlers. She knew that descriptions of Native American cultures and the inclusion of Native stories culled from Schoolcraft's work would be highly marketable and thus ensure sales to sophisticated Europeans and urban Americans who were beginning to mythologize a frontier that was now no longer as dangerous. Even very young writers, such as Victoria Stuart-Wortley (1837–1912), who was twelve when she wrote *A Young Traveller's Journal of a Tour in North and South America during the Year 1850* (1852), knew that there would be a market for their work. Jameson, Martineau, and the women writers who followed them, such as Isabella Lucy Bird (1831–1904) of *The Englishwoman in America* (1856), wrote not only to make money but also to engage with national and international issues in a female autobiographical form that challenged the traditions of masculine exploration and travel narratives. Another example is *Summer on the Lakes, in 1843* (1844) by Boston transcendentalist (Sarah) Margaret Fuller (Ossoli) (1810–1850).

Fuller was perhaps the first to recognize that the Great Lakes travel genre was becoming bankrupt, since by the 1840s, and increasingly throughout the rest of the century, all travel writers were compelled by fashion and readers' expectations to describe the grandeur of Niagara Falls, the quaintness of Detroit, the fairy-like beauty of Mackinac Island, the noble/fearsome/degraded Natives, the industriousness of Milwaukee, and the confusion of CHICAGO. After the Civil War, literary treatments of travel on the Great Lakes coincided with the popularity of local-color realism, which featured descriptions of remote places and strange characters that attracted curious readers. Magazines such as *Harper's, The Atlantic Monthly,* and *Appletons' Journal* regularly presented accounts of the Great Lakes alongside descriptions of Europe or the Far East, destinations that were harder for women to reach.

Schoolcraft met nearly all of the travelers as they tramped through his home and agency at Mackinac or Sault Ste. Marie and was little impressed, as he related in the August 16, 1837, entry in his *Personal Memoirs of a Residence of Thirty Years with the Indian Tribes on the American Frontiers* (1851): "It seems to me that Englishmen and Englishwomen, for I have had a good many of both sexes to visit me recently, look on America very much as one does when he peeps through a magnifying glass on pictures of foreign scenes, and the picturesque ruins of old cities. . . . It is difficult to realize that such things are. It is all an optical deception" (566). His *Personal Memoirs* is interesting for what it reveals about someone who collected Native American stories for profit, as well as scholarship, and changed them as he and his wife saw fit. His *Memoirs* also provides detailed observations of waves and weather and the frequent difficulties of traveling on the lakes on business before the advent of large steamships.

The industrialization of the Great Lakes basin and the coming of steamships, which were accompanied by the professionalization of the craft of sailing, led to a romanticizing of earlier sailing ships in fiction and autobiography that continues in the present. Morgan Robertson (1861–1915), the son of a lakes captain, best captured the change in "The Survival of the Fittest," from *The Three Laws and the Golden Rule* (1898), in which an itinerant seaman, scalded in a boiler explosion, rigs a dismasted, abandoned sailing ship to ride out a storm. Older captains responded to the change by penning memoirs about early lakes sailing. *Reminiscences of Early Sailing Vessels and Steam Boats on Lake Ontario* (1879) by James Van Cleve (1808–1888) was followed by later publications of journals and logbooks of captains, such as *Diary of Soren Kristiansen: Lake Michigan Schooner Captain, 1891–1893* (1981) and *The Schooner*

"La Petite": Journal of Captain Oscar B. Smith (1970). The folksongs from this era collected by Ivan H. Walton (1893–1968) have been edited and compiled by Joe Grimm in *Windjammers: Songs of the Great Lakes Sailors* (2002).

The new economic reality below decks on a Great Lakes steamboat is described in the 1916 novel *Trial by Fire: A Tale of the Great Lakes* by Richard Matthews Hallet (1887–1967), whose protagonist is a stoker in the firehold. Writers who had not worked on the lakes capitalized on the popularity of the genre by adapting the work of others. Eugene O'Neill (1888–1953), for example, derived most of the material for his play *The Hairy Ape* (1922) from *Trial by Fire* without crediting it.

As the first-generation steamboats and their captains were being superseded by ever-larger, more technologically sophisticated vessels, the autobiographical impulse began anew. *An Ancient Mariner Recollects* (1966) by Merwin Stone Thompson (1875–1967), *Winds over Lake Huron* (1977) by Captain Robert A. Sinclair (1898–1982), and *Life on the Great Lakes: A Wheelsman's Story* (1981) by Fred Dutton (ca. 1900–1980) all follow a traditional trope of maritime autobiography: mistakes may be made when the writer is young, but after one becomes a captain or a higher-ranking officer, all errors and problems disappear. *Life on the Mississippi* (1883) by SAMUEL LANGHORNE CLEMENS (1835–1910), writing as Mark Twain, adheres to this pattern. Twenty-first-century entries in this genre are *Lake Effect: A Deckhand's Journey on Great Lakes Freighters* (2008) by Richard Noel Hill (b. 1952) and Nelson Haydamacker's *Deckhand: Life on Freighters of the Great Lakes* (2009).

Until the mid-twentieth century the Great Lakes maritime world remained a romantic subject, a regional literature that thrived on disaster or the possibility of it, perhaps because the men who sailed the ships did not control their own destinies, despite the common shipboard belief in captains as minor gods. The industrialists in the cities ringing the lakes controlled who sailed and where. This romanticism inspired many historical novels, including *The Courage of Captain Plum* (1908) by JAMES OLIVER CURWOOD (1878–1927), concerning the settlement of Mormons on Beaver Island and the death of their leader, "King" Strang. The Mormons were a popular subject for lakes fiction, including dime novels such as Beadle and Adams's *The Flying Glim; or, The Island Lure* (1887) by Leon (Julius Warren) Lewis (1833–1920), about shipwrecking in the Beaver Islands, based on the historic practices of the Mormons. *The Merry Anne* (1904) by SAMUEL MERWIN (1874–1936) and *The Adventures of Captain McCargo* (1956) by William Ratigan (1910–1984) feature other adventures involving smuggling and romance. MARY FRANCES DONER (1893–1985), the daughter of a Great Lakes captain and a popular writer from the 1930s through the 1950s, set several books on the Great Lakes. *Chalice* (1940) concerns the life of a captain; *Not by Bread Alone* (1941) details the conflicts between work and family of a female cook on a Great Lakes ore carrier. Writers have continued to incorporate the past into Great Lakes fiction. *The Long-Shining Waters* (2011) by Danielle Sosin (b. 1959) tells three separate stories of Lake Superior, about a precontact Native, an early fisherman, and a contemporary woman.

The growth of railroads and car ferries that hauled railcars across Lake Michigan inspired *The Indian Drum* (1917) by WILLIAM (BRIGGS) MACHARG (1872–1951) and EDWIN BALMER (1883–1959), a best-selling novel that grafted a romantic pastiche of Native American culture onto the shipwreck plot. This plot continued unabated after the sinking of the *Edmund Fitzgerald* in 1975 with novels such as *The Survivor of the "Edmund Fitzgerald"* (1985) by Joan Skelton (b. 1929), which combines the sinking with the Native character of Micipijiu, and plays such as *Ten November* (1988) by Steven Dietz (b. 1958) and Eric Peltoniemi (b. 1949).

What the romantic shipwreck genre seldom acknowledges, however, is that by the 1980s a sharply reduced number of vessels carrying ever-diminishing cargoes in safer conditions made shipwreck a rare event. This prompted DAVID MAMET (b. 1947) in *Lakeboat* (1981) to parody the genre with a realistic farce in which the crew sails forever in an endless circle between Lake Superior and Chicago carrying the same cargo in a dead summer calm. In Mamet's work Great Lakes maritime literature changed from Kipling's "fully accredited ocean—a hideous thing to find in the heart of a continent" to boring wage labor leavened only by unsubstantiated gossip and ironic jokes about who would bring the skipper a sandwich—a highly accurate portrayal of life on a contemporary Great Lakes bulk carrier.

By the beginning of the twenty-first century the *Edmund Fitzgerald* sinking had become an industry, and it was becoming difficult to find a lakes maritime subject that had not already become predictable. Romance novelists had used the Great Lakes maritime world as a setting for decades, including a groundbreaking genre of advertising novels designed to promote trips on the Detroit and Cleveland Steamship Company ships to Mackinac Island. Artists had been showcased in exhibitions such as *Great Lakes Marine Painting of the Nineteenth Century* (1983) by J. Gray Sweeny and in photography collections like *End of an Era: The Last of the Great Lakes Steamboats* (1992) by David Plowden. Folksong groups proliferated, writing new sailing-era songs while performing authentic ones; fishermen memorialized their dying industry in books like *A Great Lakes Fisherman: The Classic Story of a Boy, a Grandfather, and the Fishing Heritage That Binds Them Together* (1983) by Ed (Edward R.) Landin (b. 1933).

When there did not appear to be any frontiers left to exploit, writers created new ones, describing their voyages on the lakes in small motorboats (Ann Davison, *In the Wake of the Gemini* [1962]), sailboats (Marlin Bree, *In the Teeth of the Northeaster: A Solo Voyage on Lake Superior* [1988]), replica sailing ships (*The Living Great Lakes: Searching for the Heart of the Inland Seas* [2004] by Jerry Dennis [b. 1954]), and even, in *Deep Water Passage* (1995) by Ann Linnea (b. 1945), a kayak named *Grace*. Linnea, suffering through a frigid summer circumnavigating Lake Superior and finding herself in the process, is the latest in a lineage of women who came to the lakes for health, marriage, travel, or a dare and discovered that they could use their experiences to free themselves from the confines of domesticity and make a living in the process.

As one would expect because of the dramatic nature of Great Lakes fictional themes, many children's books employ Great Lakes settings. *Paddle-to-the-Sea* (1941), written and illustrated by Holling Clancy Holling (1900–

1973), is well known, but it misunderstands a Native tradition of setting figures or insects afloat in tiny canoes as sacrifices to the underwater spirits during storms. See also NATIVE AMERICANS AS DEPICTED IN MIDWESTERN LITERATURE. The earliest novels for adolescents are two volumes by William Taylor Adams (1822–1897), writing as Oliver Optic: *Out West; or, Roughing It on the Great Lakes* (1877) and its sequel, *Lake Breezes; or, The Cruise of the "Sylvania"* (1878). Both are adventure stories that contain the staples of later boys' Great Lakes novels: encounters with dangerous criminals, ship chases, smuggling of illicit cargoes, mysterious passengers, and violent storms. In addition, many series for boys include at least one book with a Great Lakes setting. Edward Stratemeyer (1862–1930), writing as Arthur M. Winfield, set *The Rover Boys on the Great Lakes* (1901); the pseudonymous Allen Chapman issued *The Darewell Chums on a Cruise* (1909) as the fourth entry in that series; John Henry Goldfrap (1879–1917), writing as Dexter J. Forrester, published *The Bungalow Boys on the Great Lakes* (1912); and *Larry Dexter and the Stolen Boy; or, A Young Reporter on the Lakes* (1912) was written by the prolific Howard Roger Garis (1873–1962). Frank G. Patchin (1861–1925), writing as James R. Mears, offered *The Iron Boys on the Ore Boats* (1913), and the probably pseudonymous Ross Kay wrote *The Go Ahead Boys on Smugglers' Island* (1916). A later coming-of-age story about the son of a cargo-ship captain working for the first time on his father's vessel is told in *Cabin Boy* (1956) by Vincent Dempsey (1924–1989). The best juvenile/young-adult works are *The Gill Netters* (1979) by Alice Nancy Behrend (1913–1993), writing as Jolie Paylin; *Great Lakes Sailor* (1952) by (Eva) Jane (Klatt) Rietveld (b. 1913), about commercial fishing with pound boats using sails; and *The Cruise of the "Gull-Flight"* (1937) by Sidney Corbett (1891–1961).

Fewer stories for girls use the Great Lakes as settings or backgrounds. Two high school girls become involved in stolen mail while taking a steamer to a Lake Michigan island in *The Island Mail* (1926) by Clarice N. Detzer (1895–1982). Josephine Lawrence (1899–1978) wrote *Honey Bunch: Her First Trip on the Great Lakes* (1930) using the pseudonym Helen Louise Thorndyke. Three girls spend a summer living aboard a derelict ship off Isle Royale in *The Phantom Violin* (1934) by Roy (Judson) Snell (1878–1959); and in *Daughter of the Coast Guard* (1938) by Betty Baxter (Anderson) (1908–1966), fur smugglers on the waters of Lake Michigan occupy the interest of two adolescent girls. The Mackinac Island trilogy by Gloria Whelan (b. 1923) beginning with *Once on This Island* (1995) opens in 1812 and traces the developing relationship of young Mary O'Shea and her friend White Hawk. Even Nancy Drew came to the lakes in *Danger on the Great Lakes* (2003) by an author using the name Carolyn Keene, the collective authorial pseudonym for the Nancy Drew stories.

Poetry set on the Great Lakes, like regional poetry elsewhere, can range from doggerel to sublime verse. The Federalist poet Philip Freneau (1752–1832) wrote several poems about the lake battles in the War of 1812. Henry Wadsworth Longfellow (1807–1882) used the name of a Haudenosaunee leader as the hero of sacred Ojibwe trickster stories gleaned from Schoolcraft's *Algic Researches* for *The Song of Hiawatha* (1855). This well-known literary text is not faithful to indigenous traditions; it should be understood as reflecting romantic stereotypes of Natives as noble savages and nineteenth-century Anglo American anxieties about national identity and race. More accurate transcriptions of trickster stories are available, particularly versions by Sam Blowsnake (Hágaga, 1875–1965) in *The Trickster* (1956), by Paul Radin; Charles Dutchman (Naehcīwehtok, b. 1856) in *Menomini Texts* by Leonard Bloomfield, *Publications of the American Ethnological Society* 12 (1928); and Wāsāgunäckank in *Ojibwa Texts,* edited by William Jones and Truman Michelson, 2 volumes, *Publications of the American Ethnological Society* 7 (1917, 1919). See also NATIVE AMERICANS AS DEPICTED IN MIDWESTERN LITERATURE.

Much early Great Lakes poetry is no longer easily readable or relevant. *The Heroes of the Lake* (1814), attributed to Samuel Woodworth (1784–1842), consists of 103 pages of heroic couplets celebrating the victory of the American naval squadron under Oliver Hazard Perry in the Battle of Lake Erie in 1813. Detroit minister George Duffield (Jr.) (1818–1888), author of many religious writings, privately printed his eight-page narrative poem *Angelique: A Story of Lake Superior, A.D. 1845*, based on the true story of a woman who survived alone on Isle Royale during a winter with no supplies. Will(iam) J(eremiah) Massingham (1848–1933) wrote *Lake Superior, and Other Poems* (1904); the poems are supplemented by photographs. Later collections inspired by one or more of the inland seas include *Songs of the Lakes, and Other Poems* (1899) by Louise McCloy Horn (1868–1956) and *Blue Water Ballads: The Inland Seas* (1928) by Clarence P. Milligan (b. 1889).

HARRIET MONROE (1860–1936) describes the lakes in several poems such as "By Lake Michigan" in *Valeria and Other Poems* (1892). CARL SANDBURG (1878–1967) describes a "picnic boat," common during his era in Chicago, in *CHICAGO POEMS* (1916). EDGAR LEE MASTERS (1869–1950) wrote "In Michigan," published in *Songs and Satires* (1916), and "The Lake Boats," which appeared in *Toward the Gulf* (1918). Noted objectivist poet LORINE NIEDECKER (1903–1970) of WISCONSIN placed her long poem "Lake Superior" in the collection *North Central* (1968) and wrote other poems about the lakes as well. JUDITH MINTY (b. 1937) examines her relationship with the lakes in *Lake Songs and Other Fears* (1974) and *In the Presence of Mothers* (1981). *Hangdog Reef: Poems Sailing the Great Lakes* (1989) by Stephen Tudor (1933–1994) is more recent, as are *Inland Sailing: A Collection of Poetic Sketches Concerning Work on the Great Lakes during the 1970s* (2001) by Alan MacDougall (1935–1999) and *Blue Lash* (2006) by James Armstrong (b. 1957).

If the industrial era in the Great Lakes basin ends in the twenty-first century, it will not bring an end to writing about the lakes. Readers and critics have only begun to think about the relationships between literature and place in North America, and about the challenges of defining regionalism as a subject of study. In this evolving debate the Great Lakes can offer an instructive example. Because many Native peoples of the Great Lakes region were not removed, their literatures, both oral and written, provide a link to a prehistoric past many regions cannot access. The lakes were also home to a métis culture, people of mixed English, French, and Native heritage who played key roles in the fur trade, early territorial gov-

ernments, and the merchant marine; we are just now beginning to appreciate the complications of métis culture, including its literature. The texts of the Underground Railroad and its relationship to Great Lakes shipping remain to be collected and analyzed; there were many African American ship owners and workers, but their stories are frequently hidden in archives. The evolution of technology in a maritime world— from birch-bark canoes to thousand-foot bulk carriers—and humans' reactions to it permeates Great Lakes literature, an instructive subject for study as technology becomes more prevalent in the twenty-first century. The evolution of travel literature from the early 1800s to the present in the lakes region is another subject that has not been explored. The future of Great Lakes literature can be a bright one if scholars can look beyond the usual idea of what constitutes "Midwestern" and recognize the freshwater oceans before them.

SELECTED WORKS: The most interesting early exploration narrative is Pierre de Charlevoix's *History and General Description of New France and Journal of a Voyage to North America* (1761). Collections of later works of exploration and travel buckle library shelves, but readers may also wish to consider Anna Jameson's *Winter Studies and Summer Rambles in Canada* (1838), Charles Lanman's *Summer in the Wilderness: Embracing a Canoe Voyage up the Mississippi and around Lake Superior* (1847), Dr. John Bigsby's *The Shoe and Canoe* (1850), Henry Rowe Schoolcraft's *Personal Memoirs* (1851), Isabella Lucy Bird's *The Englishwoman in America* (1856), and Constance Fenimore Woolson's "Round by Propeller," which appeared in *Harper's New Monthly Magazine* in September 1872. Later works include *Deep Water Passage* (1995) by Ann Linnea and *The Living Great Lakes: Searching for the Heart of the Inland Seas* (2004) by Jerry Dennis.

Fiction that still appeals to contemporary readers begins with James Fenimore Cooper's *The Pathfinder; or, The Inland Sea* (1840) and continues with any of the short stories by Morgan Robertson or Constance Fenimore Woolson, Richard Mathews Hallet's *Trial by Fire: A Tale of the Great Lakes* (1916), William MacHarg and Edwin Balmer's *The Indian Drum* (1917), and Jay McCormick's

November Storm (1943). Some Beadle and Adams dime novels remain interesting, particularly *The Flying Glim* (1887) by Leon Lewis.

Significant depictions of the Great Lakes in poetry by American writers include *Lake Songs and Other Fears* (1973) by Judith Minty, *Hangdog Reef: Poems Sailing the Great Lakes* (1989) by Stephen Tudor, and *Blue Lash* (2006) by James Armstrong. David Mamet's *Lakeboat* (1981) is an effective contemporary drama about life on the Great Lakes.

Notable books for adolescents include *The Island Mail* (1926) by Clarice N. Detzer; *The Gill Netters* (1979) by Alice Nancy Behrend, writing as Jolie Paylin; *Great Lakes Sailor* (1952) by (Eva) Jane (Klatt) Rietveld; and *The Cruise of the "Gull-Flight"* (1937) by Sidney Corbett.

A number of anthologies provide overviews of Great Lakes literature. *The Great Lakes Reader* (1966), edited by WALTER (EDWIN) HAVIGHURST (1901–1994), offers an introduction to the literature of the lakes region, although it has few narratives by women and none by Native Americans. *The Women's Great Lakes Reader* (2000), edited by Victoria Brehm, is a comprehensive collection of women's narratives about living, working, and traveling on the Great Lakes from the eighteenth century to the twenty-first. *Star Songs and Water Spirits: A Great Lakes Native Reader* (2010), also edited by Brehm, collects in one volume samples of literature from all major Great Lakes Native American nations, including a section on Micipijiu. A collection of contemporary creative nonfiction, *Fresh Water: Women Writing on the Great Lakes* (2006), was edited by Alison Swan.

FURTHER READING: Little secondary writing about Great Lakes literature exists; most scholarly writing has been concerned with history or shipwreck research. A brief, useful survey of novels and short stories is "Great Lakes Maritime Fiction" by Victoria Brehm in *MidAmerica* 16 (1989): 19–28. DAVID D(ANIEL) ANDERSON (1924–2011) identifies and explicates nautical themes and stereotypes in five novels in "The Fiction of the Great Lakes," *Northwest Ohio Quarterly* 34.1 (Winter 1961–1962): 18–28. The frequently encountered argument that the freshwater lakes can be equated with the oceans is made by Jill B. Gidmark in "Fresh Salt Water: The Great Lakes as Literature of the Sea,"

MidAmerica 26 (1999): 147–55. Gidmark also edited the *Encyclopedia of American Literature of the Sea and Great Lakes* (2001), which features a number of Great Lakes–related entries.

Bibliographies include *Literature of the Great Lakes Region: An Annotated Bibliography* (1991) by Donald W. Maxwell and *The Great Lakes Region in Children's Books: A Selected Annotated Bibliography* (1980) by Donna Taylor. *Michigan in Literature* (1992) by Clarence A. Andrews includes a chapter reviewing the Great Lakes in books about MICHIGAN.

Myriad manuscript accounts of life on the Great Lakes are held in the collections of the Institute for Great Lakes Research at Bowling Green State University, Bowling Green, Ohio; the special collections departments of the Milwaukee, Detroit, and Chicago public libraries; the Bentley Historical Collections of the University of Michigan; the Chicago Historical Society; the Buffalo Historical Society in Buffalo, New York; the Western Reserve Historical Society in CLEVELAND, OHIO; and the Minnesota and Wisconsin Historical Societies. Because the lakes share a border and a maritime culture with Canada, interested readers may also wish to consult the archives at the Toronto Public Library, the Ontario Archives, and the Centre Canadien d'Études at Université Laval in Québec.

VICTORIA BREHM   TUSTIN, MICHIGAN

HISPANIC LITERATURE.
See Latino/Latina Literature

HISTORIOGRAPHY
OVERVIEW: The historiography of the American Midwest has encompassed at least three major subgenres: regional history as boosterism, which originated in the nineteenth century and has persisted until the present day; regional history as a microcosm of the history of the United States as a whole, which developed in the late nineteenth century and thrived until the middle of the twentieth century; and regional history as Midwestern exceptionalism, an early twenty-first century phenomenon.

HISTORY AND SIGNIFICANCE: As soon as settlers arrived in the geographic areas later to be known as the Midwest, they began constructing narratives that legitimized their conquest while emphasizing the inevitability of Native American defeat and the bright promise of their community or state. Migrants from New England and New York especially sought to counter perceptions of the West as an uncivilized wilderness. Ohioan Benjamin Drake (1794–1841) and Hoosier John B(rown) Dillon (ca. 1808–1879) were among those who explained how enterprising pioneers had endured physical hardships and overcome powerful but doomed Native Americans in order to fashion in a matter of decades a great society of farms and towns, merchants and lawyers, and Protestant churches and public schools.

By the late nineteenth century local historians and organizations were producing scores of weighty tomes devoted to the origins and progress of states, counties, and cities. These books exuded a sense of satisfaction with the accomplishments of local pioneers and their descendants and argued implicitly that the development of the Midwest was right and good. Authors mixed oral traditions with facts and focused almost exclusively on people whose families had persisted rather than those that had disappeared. To the extent that they mentioned conflict, they examined sectional tensions among settlers that pitted stereotypes of reform-minded Yankees against democratic southerners.

Boosterism continues to dominate local history. But in the late nineteenth century, with the rise of professional scholarship, there was a growing emphasis on the degree to which the history of the Midwest epitomized the history of the United States as a whole. By far the most famous of this school of historians was FREDERICK JACKSON TURNER (1861–1932), a native of WISCONSIN who was trained at Johns Hopkins University. In 1893 Turner, then a young professor at the University of Wisconsin, delivered a paper titled "The Significance of the Frontier in American History" at the annual meeting of the American Historical Association conducted at the World's Columbian Exhibition in CHICAGO. The published version became the most influential essay ever written by an American historian. It and other essays by Turner appear in his 1920 collection *The Frontier in American History.*

Turner argued that the settlement of the frontier, of which the Midwest was his prime example, had decisively shaped the United States by encouraging political democracy, social equality, and individualism. Echoing these themes, a host of academic historians, no longer eager to prove that they were civilized by eastern or European standards, wrote monographs and state histories that put the Midwest at the center of American culture. In many ways their collective work was a more intellectually sophisticated and expertly researched version of the by-now-common assertion of the character building inherent in the Midwestern triumph over nature and adversity.

State historical societies were the primary sponsors of the new professional history. Under the direction of Lyman C(opeland) Draper (1815–1891) and Reuben Gold Thwaites (1853–1913), the State Historical Society of Wisconsin, founded in 1846, became a model institution in preserving records, promoting professional standards of evidence and objectivity, and encouraging democratic access to information. Professional scholars, including Dorothy (Hubbard) Schwieder (1933–2014) in IOWA, Gayle Thornbrough (1914–1999) and Emma Lou Thornbrough (1913–1994) in INDIANA, and Theodore C(alvin) Pease (1887–1948) in ILLINOIS spent their lives editing and interpreting vast collections of manuscripts and public records. Their findings usually appeared in journals or books published by state historical societies. The societies also supported or encouraged multivolume state histories.

A handful of scholars, including John D(onald) Barnhart (1895–1967), Beverley W. Bond Jr. (1881–1961), and R(oscoe) Carlyle Buley (1893–1968), bucked the state-centered nature of Midwestern historiography by writing regional histories. But they, too, ultimately told familiar progressive tales that stressed the ability of democratic, pragmatic Midwesterners to adjust to the challenges of industrialization, immigration, and modernization. These authors tended to be native-born individuals who asserted the values of pioneer origins and small-town life and the view of non-English-speaking, nonwhite, and non-Protestant Midwesterners as threats

THE SIGNIFICANCE OF THE FRONTIER IN AMERICAN HISTORY.[1]

BY FREDERICK JACKSON TURNER, PH. D.

[Address delivered at the Forty-First Annual Meeting of the State Historical Society of Wisconsin, December 14, 1893.]

In a recent bulletin of the superintendent of the census for 1890 appear these significant words: " Up to and including 1880 the country had a frontier of settlement, but at present the unsettled area has been so broken into by isolated bodies of settlement that there can hardly be said to be a frontier line. In the discussion of its extent, its westward movement, etc., it cannot, therefore, any longer have a place in the census reports."[2] This brief official statement marks the closing of a great historic movement. Up to our own day American history has been in a large degree the history of the colonization of the Great West. The existence of an area of free land, its continuous recession, and the advance of American settlement westward, explain American development. Behind institutions, behind constitutional forms and modifications, lie the vital

---

[1] The foundation of this paper is my article entitled, " Problems in American History," which appeared in The Ægis, a publication of the students of the University of Wisconsin, November 8, 1892. This address was first delivered at a meeting of the American Historical Association, in Chicago, July 12, 1893. It is gratifying to find that Professor Woodrow Wilson — whose volume on " Division and Reunion," in the Epochs of American History series, has an appreciative estimate of the importance of the West as a factor in American history—accepts some of the views set forth in the papers above mentioned, and enhances their value by his lucid and suggestive treatment of them in his article in The Forum, December, 1893, reviewing Goldwin Smith's History of the United States.

[2] Extra Census Bulletin, No. 2, April 20, 1892.

"The Significance of the Frontier in American History" by Frederick Jackson Turner, first published in *Proceedings of the State Historical Society of Wisconsin*, volume 41, 1894.

Courtesy of the Wisconsin Historical Society

to a social order successfully established in the pioneer period.

In the second half of the twentieth century academic historians' attention to social history and traditionally marginalized groups led to an explosion of studies focused on Native Americans, early French settlements, the twentieth-century Great Migration of African Americans and white Appalachians, working-class communities and immigrant cultures, and the lives and contributions of rural women. Focusing on cities or rural areas defined by social networks rather than political boundaries, historians highlighted the lives of people who resisted or dissented from the supposedly mainstream values of Protestantism, capitalism, and white middle-class society. Although their overall story was no longer consensual or triumphal, these writers continued to see the Midwest primarily as an exemplar of generic American problems. Unlike students of the South and the West, they had little interest in considering whether the region was distinctive.

Geographers have long been more interested in thinking about the Midwest as a region. Only since the late twentieth century have historians done the same. Perhaps the most successful is William Cronon (b. 1954), whose 1991 book *Nature's Metropolis: Chicago and the Great West* details the complex commercial networks that united Chicago and a vast rural hinterland. Rather than assuming that the significance of the Midwest lies in its role as the United States in microcosm, many historians now think about the extent to which the region has diverged from the rest of the nation or how its history amounts to a variation on global themes. To be sure, Midwestern regional history—built around the idea of the region as an exceptional place—does not approach southern and western regional history in either scale or tradition, but it is showing signs of life.

SELECTED WORKS: Readers interested in Midwestern history should start with any of the authors mentioned previously. In addition to those, excellent examples of Midwestern history include Lizabeth Cohen's *Making a New Deal: Industrial Workers in Chicago, 1919–1939* (1990); Kathleen Neils Conzen's *Immigrant Milwaukee, 1836–1860:*

Jon Lauck's *The Lost Region: Toward a Revival of Midwestern History*, 2013.

Cover image of *The Lost Region* © 2013 by the University of Iowa Press. Cover art, *Island in the Corn,* © Genie Hudson Patrick. Used by permission of publisher and artist. All rights reserved

Accommodation and Community in a Frontier City (1976); John Mack Faragher's *Sugar Creek: Life on the Illinois Prairie* (1986); Jon Gjerde's *The Minds of the West: Ethnocultural Evolution in the Rural Midwest, 1830–1917* (1997); Susan E. Gray's *The Yankee West: Community Life on the Michigan Frontier* (1996); and Thomas J. Sugrue's *The Origins of the Urban Crisis: Race and Inequality in Postwar Detroit* (1996).

FURTHER READING: Recent overviews of Midwestern historiography include David Scott Brown's *Beyond the Frontier: The Midwestern Voice in American Historical Writing* (2009); Andrew R. L. Cayton and Peter S. Onuf's *The Midwest and the Nation: Rethinking the History of an American Region* (1990); *The American Midwest: Essays on Regional History* (2001), edited by Andrew R. L. Cayton and Susan E. Gray; Jon K. Lauck's "The Prairie

Historians and the Foundations of Midwestern History," *Annals of Iowa* 71 (Spring 2012): 137–73; Jon K. Lauck's *The Lost Region: Toward a Revival of Midwestern History* (2013); James H. Madison's *Heartland: Comparative Histories of the Midwestern States* (1988); and Edward Watts's *An American Colony: Regionalism and the Roots of Midwestern Culture* (2002). Two important biographies of Frederick Jackson Turner are Ray Allen Billington's *Frederick Jackson Turner: Historian, Scholar, Teacher* (1973) and Allan Bogue's *Frederick Jackson Turner: Strange Roads Going Down* (1998). *Middle West Review*, an interdisciplinary journal devoted to Midwestern history, was launched in 2014.

ANDREW R. L. CAYTON   LATE OF MIAMI UNIVERSITY

HOUSE ON MANGO STREET, THE

HISTORY: The 1984 publication of *The House on Mango Street* by SANDRA CISNEROS (b. 1954) marked the entry of Chicano/Chicana (Mexican American) and, more broadly, LATINO/ LATINA LITERATURE into the national mass market for fiction in the United States. Narrated by a Mexican American girl named Esperanza Cordero, the novel chronicles life in an urban barrio through a series of forty-four vignettes about Esperanza, her family, and their neighbors. The barrio is presumably located in CHICAGO, ILLINOIS, the author's birthplace and hometown, although the narrator never names the city in which the action occurs. Throughout the narrative the house on Mango Street symbolizes Esperanza's poverty and her unfulfilled desire for material comfort, safety, and independence.

Cisneros has stated in interviews that the idea for the book arose while she was a graduate student at the elite IOWA WRITERS' WORKSHOP at the University of Iowa from 1976 to 1978. She was troubled by her unfamiliarity with the privileged life typical among her classmates and accepted as the American cultural norm. A classroom discussion of *The Poetics of Space* (1958) by French philosopher Gaston Bachelard (1884–1962) proved particularly frustrating. The class sought to apply Bachelard's theories to writing about houses they had lived in, with attics, basements, and other spaces representing aspects of psychology. But the residences, mostly tenements, of Cisneros's childhood bore little resemblance to Bachelard's model or to the houses in which Cisneros's mostly white, middle-class classmates had grown up. The conversation led Cisneros to recognize her unique ability to represent experiences virtually unknown within the United States Anglo American mainstream. She started writing stories set in a large Midwestern city, with a Mexican American family's run-down house as a central image. These stories formed the nucleus of *The House on Mango Street*.

After graduating from the University of Iowa in 1978, Cisneros worked as a counselor at a Chicago high school for at-risk Latino/Latina students, whose experiences suggested narratives and details for her stories. She developed a sense of herself as a social advocate whose writing voiced realities of the disenfranchised. A grant from the National Endowment for the Arts allowed Cisneros to concentrate on the manuscript in 1981, while she was living in Provincetown, Massachusetts, and 1982, when she traveled to Europe.

In 1982 Cisneros signed a contract with Arte Público Press of Houston, Texas, a publishing house specializing in Latino/Latina literature. She finished the book while she was living on an island in Greece, submitting chapters by mail. Editors wanted additional revisions, which took two years, during which Cisneros worked in France and in San Antonio, Texas. Arte Público published *The House on Mango Street* on January 1, 1984.

Although Esperanza's age is never specified, her diction and certain references suggest that she is about twelve years old. Esperanza speaks of her parents, her two brothers, her younger sister, their neighbors, and strangers she encounters. The neighborhood consists mostly of working-class Latinos and Latinas, like Esperanza's family, who hope for a better life beyond their oppressive circumstances. There are immigrants, both Mexican and Puerto Rican, struggling with homesickness and lack of English fluency, and women who face cultural and economic oppression, as well as the tyranny of patriarchal power vested in fathers and husbands. In the small world of this impoverished Chicago barrio, Esperanza plays with her friends and discovers a desire to write about herself and the world as she sees it.

Reviews of the first edition were positive, often focusing on the poetic quality of Cisneros's prose and her ability to capture a child's voice. *The House on Mango Street* won the 1985 American Book Award from the Before Columbus Foundation. The book's success launched Cisneros's career and led to residencies at a series of universities and a 1995 MacArthur Fellowship, which supported the writing of her first long-form novel, *Caramelo* (2002).

SIGNIFICANCE: Cisneros's text is known for its expression of a class, gender, and race consciousness in the deceptively simple language of a child. Esperanza's narrative is characterized by her yearning for a house she can be proud to live in, one she is not ashamed to identify as her own. Thematically, however, this longing is overridden by the novel's commentary on the place of women within a social structure that the young narrator struggles to understand. Although Esperanza's observations about her life and the lives of those around her are communicated in a voice that is inexperienced and naïve, her descriptions reveal much about the circumstances of girls and women living under the oppressive regimes of patriarchy and poverty in an urban environment.

These observations are at times focused on women older than Esperanza, for example, Marin, who dreams of her boyfriend in Puerto Rico as she stays imprisoned in the house of her aunt and uncle, relegated to watching children and forbidden from venturing beyond the streetlight. Although she is unmarried and has no children of her own, Marin is unable to explore her surroundings or her opportunities because her relatives deem her untrustworthy. Marin's confident sexuality makes her a target not only of male attention but also of the policing mechanisms of the family. In "Minerva Writes Poems" Esperanza tells of Minerva, a young woman not much older than herself with two children and a physically abusive husband, who is "sad like a house on fire" (1991 edition, 84), writes poems after feeding her kids their dinner, and slips her writing to Esperanza, her only audience. The confinement of these women is associated with

Sandra Cisneros's *The House on Mango Street,* 1991.

Image reprinted by permission from *The House on Mango Street,* © Arte Público Press–University of Houston

their gender and status as property within the patriarchal domestic sphere.

The narrative further suggests that these women's situations are exacerbated by poverty. Minerva has only flour, water, and sugar to feed her children, and Marin's escape is forever deferred by a limited income derived from babysitting and selling Avon products. In "A Smart Cookie" Esperanza speaks of her mother's advice to stay in school and make something of herself. By revealing to her daughter her own longing for what life might have been, Esperanza's mother hints at the degree to which she, too, has experienced the negative effects of self-denial and male oppression.

Other themes include that of emergent sexuality as Esperanza reveals her attempts to come to terms with her changing body and identity. As she negotiates this difficult terrain, Esperanza becomes cognizant of the ways in which women's status as sexual objects can sever their connections to one another. This theme is developed in narratives about Sally, who is confined, first by her abusive father and then by her husband. Esperanza feels betrayed by Sally, who is absent when a boy sexually assaults Esperanza in "Red Clowns." The impressionistic manner in which Cisneros handles Esperanza's rape and then does not mention it again suggests the extent to which the social system is set against working-class women of color. Esperanza, whose name means both "hope" and "waiting," does not seek support or understanding from civil authorities or family in this traumatic circumstance; instead, she turns to her inner resources of imagination and creativity.

The book closes with Esperanza's anticipated departure from Mango Street as she envisions a house of her own and productive work as a writer. Cisneros, however, does not present Esperanza's coming of age in terms of Anglo American individualism. She imagines her future home as a symbolic refuge for the dispossessed, accepting the mandate of her old aunts in "The Three Sisters," who say, "You will always be Mango Street. . . . You must remember to come back. For the ones who cannot leave as easily as you" (105). In this way Cisneros binds the writer's task to the well-being of community and the solidarity of Latinas.

Throughout the book Cisneros diverges from literary conventions representing predominantly Anglo Midwesternness. The urban environment in which the action takes place is not characterized as explicitly Midwestern, perhaps because these are tales of marginalized subaltern people who have not been incorporated into the grand narratives of urban centers in the United States. *The House on Mango Street* provides a window into experiences that differ from the dominant white, middle-class, rural images of Midwesterners. As a labor force, Latinos and Latinas, like earlier immigrant populations, play significant, if largely unrecognized, roles contributing to the functioning of Midwestern cities such as Chicago. Cisneros's novel is marked as Midwestern through this focus on Latinos and Latinas, a population that has long maintained a presence in the Midwest, but has been recognized as a vital force in the region only in recent decades.

Historical contexts for *The House on Mango Street* include Latina FEMINISM of the 1970s and 1980s, including work by Gloria Anzaldúa (1942–2004), Cherríe Moraga (b. 1952), and Ana Castillo (b. 1953), writers who both inspired Cisneros and took heart from her example. The success of *The House on Mango Street* played a significant role in the Latino/Latina literary boom of the 1980s and early 1990s. Until then, Latino and Latina writers were generally published by small presses. The high sales of Arte Público's initial editions anticipated not only Cisneros's contract with Random House for trade publication but also other best-selling Latino/Latina novels like *The Mambo Kings Play Songs of Love* (1989) by Oscar Hijuelos (1951–2013) and *How the García Girls Lost Their Accents* (1991) by Julia Alvarez (b. 1950).

Over two million copies of *The House on Mango Street* have been sold. Initially marketed by Arte Público as a Young Readers selection, it is now a common text in high school curricula. *The House on Mango Street* was also one of the first Chicano/Chicana literary works to be incorporated into the canons of U.S. literature and women's literature at the college level. It has been translated into Spanish, Korean, and other languages. A theatrical adaptation by Amy Ludwig played at Chicago's Edgewater Theatre Center in 1992, and one by Tanya Saracho at Chicago's Steppenwolf Theatre in 2009.

IMPORTANT EDITIONS: *The House on Mango Street* was first published in 1984 by Arte Público Press of Houston, Texas. Arte Público reprinted the novel in 1985 and 1986 and issued a slightly revised edition in 1988. Random House republished the revised edition under the Vintage Contemporaries imprint in 1991; in 1992 they released a recording of Cisneros reading the novel. 1992 also saw the publication of *Una casa en Mango Street*, Enrique De Hériz's translation into Peninsular Spanish, by Ediciones B of Barcelona, Spain. In 1994, Random House published *La casa en Mango Street*, a translation into Mexican Spanish by the celebrated Mexican writer Elena Poniatowska (b. 1932); also in 1994, Knopf issued the first hardcover edition. Vintage's twenty-fifth anniversary edition, published in 2009, features a new introduction by Cisneros.

FURTHER READING: Cisneros extends the architectural metaphor announced by the title of her first novel in *A House of My Own: Stories from My Life* (2015), a collection of essays, lectures, and other texts that constitute a discursive memoir. She includes in the book many anecdotes about the writing and reception of *The House on Mango Street*. Cisneros also discusses *The House on Mango Street* in her essay "Do You Know Me? I Wrote *The House on Mango Street*," *Americas Review* 15.1 (Spring 1987): 77–9, and in a number of interviews, such as "On the Solitary Fate of Being Mexican, Female, Wicked and Thirty-Three: An Interview with Sandra Cisneros" by Pilar E. Rodríguez, *Americas Review* 19.1 (Spring 1990): 64–80, and "Sandra Cisneros: Two Interviews," in *Conversations with Contemporary Chicana and Chicano Writers* (2007) by Hector A. Torres, 191–243.

Collections of essays about the book include *Sandra Cisneros's "The House on Mango Street"* (2010), edited by Harold Bloom, and *"The House on Mango Street," by Sandra Cisneros* (2011), edited by María Herrera-Sobek, which features "Midwest Raíces: Sandra Cisneros's *The House on Mango Street*" by Amelia María de la Luz Montes (21–35). For a biographical overview, see *Border Crossings and Beyond: The Life and Works of Sandra Cisneros* (2009) by Carmen Haydée Rivera.

Book-length studies of Chicano/Chicana literature have devoted significant attention to Cisneros's novel. See Ramón Saldívar's *Chicano Narrative: The Dialectics of Difference* (1990), Alvina Quintana's *Home Girls: Chicana Literary Voices* (1996), Sonia Saldívar-Hull's *Feminism on the Border: Chicana Gender Politics and Literature* (2000), and José David Saldívar's *Trans-Americanity: Subaltern Modernities, Global Coloniality, and the Cultures of Greater Mexico* (2012).

The scholarly bibliography on the novel is large and growing. Essays addressing the issue of space in the novel include Julián Olivares's "Sandra Cisneros's *The House on Mango Street* and the Poetics of Space," *Americas Review* 15.3–4 (Fall–Winter 1987): 160–70; Karen W. Martin's "*The House (of Memory) on Mango Street*: Sandra Cisneros's Counter-Poetics of Space," *South Atlantic Review* 73.1 (Winter 2008): 50–67; and Elisabetta Careri's "Home, Streets, Nature: Esperanza's Itineraries in Sandra Cisneros' *The House on Mango Street*," in *Landscapes of Writing in Chicano Literature* (2013), edited by Imelda Martín-Junquera, 13–22. Feminist readings are provided by Jacqueline Doyle in "More Room of Her Own: Sandra Cisneros's *The House on Mango Street*," *MELUS* 19.4 (Winter 1994): 5–35; Leslie Petty in "The 'Dual'-ing Images of la Malinche and la Virgen de Guadalupe in Cisneros's *The House on Mango Street*," *MELUS* 25.2 (Summer 2000): 119–32; and Robin E. Field in "Revising Chicana Womanhood: Gender Violence in Sandra Cisneros's *The House on Mango Street*," in *Feminism, Literature and Rape Narratives: Violence and Violation* (2010), edited by Sorcha Gunne and Zoë Brigley Thompson, 54–67. Lee Kihan takes on stylistic issues in "Towards the Poetics of Sandra Cisneros' *The House on Mango Street*," *Studies in Modern Fiction* 12.2 (Winter 2005): 151–76. Anna Nogar compares the novel's two Spanish translations in "Hamandeggs: Dual Translation in Elena Poniatowska's *La casa en Mango Street*," *Confluencia* 28.1 (Fall 2012): 52–66.

A number of essays compare the novel with the work of other authors. One such article is "Growing Up Chicano: Tomás Rivera and Sandra Cisneros" by Erlinda González-Berry (b. 1942) and Tey Diana Rebolledo (b. 1937), in *International Studies in Honor of Tomás Rivera* (1986), edited by Julián Olivares, 109–20. Delia Poey discusses the novel's use in classrooms in "Coming of Age in the Curriculum: *The House on Mango Street* and *Bless Me, Ultima* as Representative Texts," *Americas Review* 24.3–4 (1996): 201–17, as does Alayne M. Sullivan in "Mango Street and Malnourished Readers: Politics and Realities in an 'At-Risk' Middle School," *Journal of Latinos and Education* 6.2 (2007): 151–75.

Two books intended for high school students are *A Reader's Guide to Sandra Cisneros's "The House on Mango Street"* (2010) by Ann Angel and *Sandra Cisneros: Latina Writer and Activist* (1998) by Caryn Mirriam-Goldberg (b. 1959). Curricular materials have also been published for secondary teachers.

Studies of reviews and scholarship include María Elena de Valdés's "The Critical Reception of Sandra Cisneros's *The House on Mango Street*," in *Gender, Self, and Society* (1993), edited by Renate von Bardeleben, 287–300;

and Felicia J. Cruz's "On the 'Simplicity' of Sandra Cisneros's *House on Mango Street*," *Modern Fiction Studies* 47.4 (2001): 910–46.

SHEILA MARIE CONTRERAS
                    MICHIGAN STATE UNIVERSITY
WILLIAM BARILLAS
                UNIVERSITY OF WISCONSIN–LA CROSSE

HUCKLEBERRY FINN.
See *Adventures of Huckleberry Finn*

HULL-HOUSE
OVERVIEW: Hull-House was founded on September 18, 1889, and operated through 1963 as Chicago's first social settlement house and, according to Louise W. Knight's *Citizen: Jane Addams and the Struggle for Democracy* (2005), the most important in the United States (192, 463). It was intended to be a meeting point where diverse nationalities and social classes, Americans and immigrants alike, could form a new community emblematizing what settlement-house workers often termed "social unification." JANE ADDAMS (1860–1935) and Ellen Gates Starr (1859–1940), the founders, took inspiration and some of their ideas for residence among the poor from London's Toynbee Hall and People's Palace. Their aim, as Addams recalled in *Twenty Years at Hull-House with Autobiographical Notes* (1910), was "to provide a center for a higher civic and social life . . . , and to investigate and improve the conditions in the industrial districts of Chicago" (89). For this social experiment, they chose a neighborhood on Chicago's near West Side, a stretch of South Halsted Street crowded with factories, sweatshops, and saloons. What they began at Hull-House proved to be, especially in the first decades of the twentieth century, a model for other settlement houses and for the programs and reforms of the Progressive movement. See PROGRESSIVISM. This entry will review literature written by people associated with or inspired by Hull-House.
HISTORY AND SIGNIFICANCE: Addams and Starr began by renting the second floor of a run-down house at 335 South Halsted, a once-elegant mansion built in 1856 for Charles J(erald) Hull (1820–1889). Their neighbors in the Nineteenth Ward were "new immigrants" and their children, mostly German, Greek, Irish, Italian, Rus-

sian Jewish, and Polish, almost all poor and uneducated. Although it was first called a Chicago Toynbee Hall or a "Toynbee Hall" experiment, their social settlement soon became known as Hull-House. When Helen Culver (1832–1925), Hull's niece, donated the building and surrounding land, the name Hull-House was formally affixed in Charles Hull's honor. Within twenty years of its founding, the Hull-House complex grew to occupy thirteen buildings and a full city block. Two reform-minded architects, the brothers Allen Pond and I. K. Pond, designed the buildings and oversaw the restoration and enlargement of the Hull mansion. The group of buildings in the complex included the Butler Art Gallery, a coffeehouse supplying low-cost meals, a gymnasium, a theatre, the Mary Crane Nursery, the Jane Club for working women, public baths, workshops, a textile or labor museum, rooms and apartments for the residents, and multipurpose spaces. From the start, Hull-House supported an ever-changing array of classes, clubs, and social causes, including a Penny Bank for children, day care, a kindergarten, citizenship classes, the Hull-House Juvenile Protective Association, a theatre group, a music school, an industrial arts department, and some of the nation's first college extension courses. Hilda Satt Polacheck (1882–1967), a Polish Jewish girl from the neighborhood, writes in her autobiography, *I Came a Stranger: The Story of a Hull-House Girl* (1989), about taking an extension course at the University of Chicago and documents her firsthand experience as someone who wrote and acted in Hull-House plays, taught classes in English as a second language, and benefited from Jane Addams's largesse.

Between 1900 and 1914 Hull-House reached what Mary Lynn McCree Bryan and Allen F. Davis in *100 Years at Hull-House* (1990) describe as "the peak of its reputation and influence" (63). In the early 1890s newspapers had ridiculed Hull-House as a "salon in the slums" and had attacked it for giving anarchists and socialists a place to speak and debate. But the reform programs of the settlement and the social work of its residents soon won national and international renown. Addams, with her genius for writing and speech making, enlisted the support of the city's women's clubs and the socially prominent, people like Edward Butler, Louise deKoven Bowen, and Anita McCormick Blaine. She drew on Chicago's civic pride and the philanthropic spirit of many wealthy citizens. Writing in "The Upward Movement in Chicago" in the October 1897 *Atlantic Monthly* (80:538), the CHICAGO novelist HENRY BLAKE FULLER (1857–1929) characterized the work of Hull-House as an important part of the cultural forces, civic energy, and social reforms that came to be known as the first CHICAGO RENAISSANCE. The political action and social causes Hull-House promoted, particularly the formation of labor unions, city sanitation and health reforms, child-labor laws, and good government, both defined and helped create the American Progressive movement.

In many ways these reforms reflected Midwestern values. Addams, in her autobiographical *Twenty Years at Hull-House,* attributed such democratic ideals to what she called the "influence of Lincoln" (the title of chapter 2 in *Twenty Years at Hull-House*) and the community values of Cedarville, ILLINOIS, the small Midwestern town where she

Jane Addams, ca. 1914. Photo by the Gerhard Sisters, ca. 1914.

Image courtesy of the Library of Congress

grew up. After her death in 1935, Hull-House passed through a series of crises in funding and leadership. Most of the buildings known as Hull-House were razed in 1963 to make way for the University of Illinois at Chicago campus, although Hull-House and a restored coffeehouse still survive. These two Hull-House buildings continue today as a library and a museum, both important resources for the study of settlement-house history, urban history, and the Progressive movement. When Hull-House faced demolition in the 1960s, Senator Paul H(oward) Douglas (1892–1976) contended that "Hull-House and Lincoln's home are the two great inspiration centers in Illinois" (quoted in *100 Years at Hull-House* 265–66).

SELECTED WORKS: No better starting point for understanding Hull-House and its history exists than Jane Addams's *Twenty Years at Hull-House with Autobiographical Notes* (1910). *Hull-House Maps and Papers: A Presentation of Nationalities and Wages in a Congested District of Chicago* (1895), written by the "Residents of Hull-House," illustrates the settlement's program of "residence, research, and reform" with a "map of nationalities," a "wage map," and essays on such topics as the Chicago ghetto by Charles Zueblin (1866–1924) and art and labor by Ellen Gates Starr. The book *100 Years at Hull-House* (1990), edited by Mary Lynn McCree Bryan and Allen F. Davis, gathers original writings and photographs detailing the history of Hull-House.

FURTHER READING: Biographies of Jane Addams provide a useful view of Hull-House. Louise W. Knight's *Citizen: Jane Addams and the Struggle for Democracy* (2005) ends in 1898–1899, and so her story of Addams and the settlement is necessarily incomplete, although it is richly documented and artfully told. Also important is *Jane Addams: A Writer's Life* (2004) by Katherine Joslin, who emphasizes the development of Addams's prose style and her relation to her literary contemporaries. In *The Education of Jane Addams* (2003) Victoria Bissell Brown analyzes the ideas, life, and work of Addams and explores what led to the creation of this successful settlement community; Brown's introduction to the Bedford/St. Martin's edition of *Twenty Years at Hull-House* (1999) is also excellent. Allen F. Davis's *American*

Heroine: The Life and Legend of Jane Addams (1973), like his earlier *Spearheads for Reform* (1967), stresses the lines connecting Hull-House and the settlement-house movement to Progressive politics and reforms. Rivka Shpak Lissak's *Pluralism and Progressives: Hull-House and the New Immigrants, 1899–1919* (1989) questions the extent of the settlement's oft-stated commitment to "cosmopolitan" and "democratic" ideals. *Division Street: America* (1967) by (LOUIS) STUDS TERKEL (1912–2008), in telling the story of Florence Scala's efforts to preserve Hull-House, outlines the meaning that the settlement held for those in its surrounding neighborhood. More recent is Louise W. Knight's *Jane Addams: Spirit in Action* (2010).

About a dozen novels were written about Hull-House and Chicago settlements in the 1890s and early 1900s. Some, like *Two Women and a Fool* (1895) by HOBART (CHATFIELD) CHATFIELD-TAYLOR (1865–1945), satirized the high-minded motives of the settlement-house workers; others, like *"Just Folks"* (1910) by CLARA E(LIZABETH) LAUGHLIN (1873–1941) and *The Precipice* (1914) by ELIA W. PEATTIE (1862–1935), expressed faith in the promises of their social work and programs of reform. *Hull-House Magazine* and the settlement's sponsorship of other literary efforts helped launch the careers of Chicago writers like WILLARD F. MOTLEY (1909–1965). For its near-comprehensive view of Hull-House history with many links to photos and illustrations, the University of Illinois at Chicago website "Urban Experience in Chicago: Hull-House and Its Neighborhoods, 1889–1963," has no rival.

GUY SZUBERLA   UNIVERSITY OF TOLEDO

HUMOR

OVERVIEW: For almost as long as an idea of the Midwest has existed, the region has had its jokesmiths, comic writers, tavern wits, rustic sages, and all manner of camp followers tramping after the muse of laughter. From SAMUEL LANGHORNE CLEMENS (1835–1910), writing as Mark Twain, to JAMES (GROVER) THURBER (1894–1961), from GEORGE ADE (1866–1944) to RING (GOLD WILMER) LARDNER (1885–1933) and PETER DE VRIES (1910–1993), from JEAN SHEPHERD (1929–1999) to Max Shulman (1919–1988), Erma Bombeck (1927–1996), and GARY EDWARD KEILLOR (b. 1942),

writing as Garrison Keillor, the heartland has nurtured important humorists. At their best and most characteristic, Midwestern humorists have held to a rough-hewn, democratic line. Their type characters, colloquial inflections, and stock situations have, with due exaggeration, exploited the region's reputation for rustic innocence and an absence of sophistication. Neither as crude and scatological as typical southern humorists and seldom as well mannered, cerebral, or self-consciously literary as New England and northeastern writers, they have played up or played on the virtues of naïve wisdom. Midwestern humor writers have held at arm's length the urbanity that marked the Knickerbocker wits and the *New Yorker* writers, and they have been wary of the racial caricatures and class consciousness haunting the humorists of the modern South and the "Old Southwest." They have generally tried to present themselves as defenders of pragmatic thinking and populist values. The region's humorists, even when they delight in the grotesque and the foolish, strive to stand foursquare for simple and unaffected common sense.

The Midwest and Midwesterners have inspired a raft of jokes and comic stories. They have been made, fairly and unfairly, into caricatures and comic grotesques. They have embodied the perception of the region as the home of the all-too-normal and middling middle class and the bland and boring flyover country between the glamour of the two coasts. These traits have become the objects of commonplace beliefs, the stage properties of stand-up comics and countless American humorists. The region's writers have woven these old jokes and outworn caricatures into their story lines. They have also written humor running counter to the belief in the heartland's deadening normality. Perhaps in response to superior bicoastal airs, Midwestern humor tends to be deflating, piercing cultural pretensions and high-flying social ambitions. George Ade's parodies of Horatio Alger heroics, like Garrison Keillor and his much-quoted line about the "above average" children of Lake Wobegon, typify this leveling spirit and the shticks that so often give it flesh and body. The Midwesterner as the innocent "out-of-towner," a figure of fun ready to be fleeced or belittled, pops up in the play with that title (1969) by (Marvin) Neil Simon (b. 1927), in *The Corrections* (2001) by Jonathan Franzen (b. 1959), and in the humor literature of nearly every region. Lardner's stories of the Gullibles in *Gullible's Travels, Etc.* (1917) and the tales by Ruth McKenney (1911–1972) of her first New York days in *My Sister Eileen* (1938) are among the most notable treatments of this character type by Midwestern writers.

To this short list of old jokes, formulaic story lines, and type figures must be added one more commonplace character: the sage of the rural Midwest or cracker-barrel oracle. George Ade, FINLEY PETER DUNNE (1867–1936), JAMES WHITCOMB RILEY (1849–1916), and LANGSTON HUGHES (1902–1967) variously translated him. Herb Shriner, Jean Shepherd, Ronald Reagan, Johnny Carson, Garrison Keillor, and David Letterman, among many others, brought this same wisely innocent figure to life in the second half of the twentieth century.

Midwestern humor came late to American literature. The region's representative writers, type characters, and important literary traditions did not emerge in fully localized colors until after the Civil War. In his book *The Midwestern Ascendancy in American Writing* (1992), Ronald Weber places the "ascendancy" in the period from the 1880s through the 1920s, a time that coincided with the rise and recognition of the region's humor writers. In *The Middle West: Its Meaning in American Culture* (1989) James R. Shortridge asserts that not until near the end of the nineteenth century did the Midwest or "Middle West" find its name and an identity as a farmland or, in the popular imagination, as an idealized pastoral landscape (92). Humorists like John T. McCutcheon (1870–1949) and (FRANK MCKINNEY) "KIN" HUBBARD (1868–1930), starting in the 1890s, helped formulate this rural identity in the region's big-city newspapers. They stressed the Midwest' small-town roots and the farm-bred character of its people, and they developed certain enduring character types to reflect a golden past.

Far into the twentieth century, long after CHICAGO, CLEVELAND, DETROIT, MINNEAPOLIS/ST. PAUL, and other large and industrialized cities filled the heartland, the region's humorists still posed as rustic sages and country bumpkins. In keeping with their small-town personae, they masked their urbanity and left the wearing of cultural pretenses and literary airs to *New Yorker* writers and others. Despite such self-conscious innocence and exaggerated rusticity, or because of a general belief in such fixed ideas and character types, Midwestern humorists were able to turn their native democratic values into an original comic art.

HISTORY AND SIGNIFICANCE: The history of Midwestern humor falls into four fairly conventional literary-historical periods: 1830–1865, 1865–1915, 1916–1945, and 1945 to the present. Although the region was originally referred to as "the West" and its precise cultural boundaries remained indeterminate, humorists were already using regional differences in their tall tales and dialect stories, playing up character types like ILLINOIS "suckers" and INDIANA "Hoosiers." Such literary creations anticipated the period just before and during the Civil War, when local newsmen like CHARLES FARRAR BROWNE (1834–1867), writing as Artemus Ward, and DAVID ROSS LOCKE (1833–1888), working behind a character mask, came to national prominence.

In the period from 1865 to 1915 Mark Twain shaped humor writing, particularly in his use of dialect speech as a literary language; he opened the way for later American humorists, including those marked by the imaginative experience of the Midwest. The rise of Chicago as a literary center in the 1880s and 1890s followed on the work of its newspaper columnists, the most important being EUGENE FIELD (SR.) (1850–1895), George Ade, and Finley Peter Dunne. As the region grew more industrialized and urban, many of its humorists paradoxically adopted the character and dialect speech of the rustic sage. Ethnic humor and ethnic characters, often grossly exaggerated and flatly stereotyped, appeared in newspaper columns and comic strips (see COMIC STRIPS AND BOOKS) and on the vaudeville and burlesque stage.

Between 1916 and 1945 James Thurber, DON(ALD ROBERT PERRY) MARQUIS (1878–1937), and Ring Lardner, starting out in the Midwest, reworked and recast certain Midwestern type characters: the wise boob, the little man, and the rustic sage. In *American Humor*

(1978) Walter Blair and Hamlin Hill asserted that although these humorists sometimes used nineteenth-century local-color conventions, they tended to parody its colloquial style and ridicule the commonsensical philosophizing of the "rustic sage" (369). Such humor, though strongly influenced by Ade and Twain, turned toward twentieth-century complexities and complexes: nervousness, the war between the sexes, and the chaos of modern, urban life. The writings of EDNA FERBER (1885–1968), BEN HECHT (1894–1964), Langston Hughes, and others illustrated the nexus of urban and ethnic humor.

From 1945 on, James R. Shortridge asserts in *The Middle West: Its Meaning in American Culture*, the region became "romanticized" in farm novels, the popular press, and political discourse as a home of "traditional . . . values" and as an idealized pastoral landscape (71), as the careers and small-town public personae of Herb Shriner (1918–1970), Max Shulman, Garrison Keillor, and others might suggest. Humorists like Erma Bombeck, Peter De Vries, (MICHAEL) MIKE ROYKO (1932–1997), and Jean Shepherd reflected the shift to urban and suburban angst already evident in the comic foibles of Lardner and Thurber's characters.

1830–1865:

Frontier Humor: In the years from 1830 to 1865 Midwestern humorists were a restless and transient lot, often writing for a dozen newspapers in the stretch of a few years and moving on when the local money played out or when another opportunity farther west beckoned. Midwestern writers, if they sought national recognition and larger incomes, looked to New York and Philadelphia to publish their work. Not until the late 1840s and early 1850s did newspapers and literary magazines in cities like CINCINNATI, ST. LOUIS, and Chicago begin to open a significant marketplace and a local audience for the region's comic writing.

During the 1830s, when the first Midwestern journalists began to publish comic sketches, stories, and newspaper columns, two large, loosely formed schools dominated American humor: the writers of the Old Southwest, composed of the states and territories of the South, and the Knickerbockers and Yankees of the urban Northeast

and New England. New York's Washington Irving (1783–1859), Yankees like Thomas Chandler Haliburton (1796–1865), and southwesterners like Georgia's Augustus B. Longstreet (1790–1870) and Johnson J. Hooper (1815–1863) exerted powerful and inescapable influences. But then and later, some Midwestern humorists followed their own comic bent and the raw spirit of their locale. They generally steered away from the high-minded and book-learned didacticism of their Yankee cousins. At the same time, they were almost never as violently physical, as ready with references to filth, feces, or the obscene, or as downright raunchy as the southwestern school, and they were seldom given to the same comic delight in the grotesque that animated Longstreet and later southern writers.

By the 1830s two type characters, the frontiersman and the Yankee, had moved front and center in American humor. During this high time of Jacksonian democracy, the squatter, the keelboatman, the roarer, and a gang of assorted roughs and backwoods characters exercised a fascination for the southwestern school and, in turn, for the first Midwestern comic writers. The frontiersmen's hollers and whoops, heroic deeds, practical jokes, bloody fights, and tall tales represented the young nation's energetic spirit. For some writers, including St. Louis's enterprising Joseph M. Field (1810–1856) and John S. Robb (ca. 1813–1856), the western frontier and frontiersman yielded brand-new subjects, at once native, popular, and salable in the Midwest and the East.

Among the earliest creators of Midwestern humor, Field and Robb, co-editors of the *St. Louis Reveille*, rank as the most important. From 1844 to 1850 their writing and editing made the short-lived *Reveille* what Hennig Cohen and William B. Dillingham have called "one of the country's leading journals of humor" (*Humor of the Old Southwest* 142). With their co-editor, Solomon Smith (1801–1869), they filled its daily columns with tall tales and humorous stories of squatters, settlers, and "a worthless and criminal character" that Robb, in *Streaks of Squatter Life* (1847), called "the *border harpy*" (ix). Robb and Field also burlesqued Illinois "Suckers" and downstate Indiana "Hoosiers" and touted the exploits of hard-drinking riverboat "roarers" like Mike Fink.

Field collected about two dozen Mike Fink tales in *The Drama of Pokerville: The Bench and Bar of Jurytown, and Other Stories* (1847) and published them through Carey and Hart of Philadelphia. His "Dedication" obliquely outlined his intentions: to "[open] out a native literary path, which albeit not the most elevated, nevertheless hath its pleasant ways . . . and amusement to the public" (3). This formal, ironic bow to elevated taste gave few hints that Field would write about such low and violent subjects as the death of Mike Fink. His account, nominally written to strip away the legends and myth surrounding Fink, dramatized the comic in the frontiersmen's violence, giving life to their drunken frolics, tall talk, and wild feats. In stories like "The Bench and Bar of Jurytown" Field turned to freewheeling farce and sharp satire. Here the noisome behavior of a courtroom crowd—their "hawking" and "spitting," cursing and "blowing of noses"—upset the fragile dignity of Judge Frill, a "refined man [who] was 'ever so long at college'" (94). Field's broadstroke caricatures of "republican character" and western "etiquette" (93) pointed the way to Twain's comic courtroom scenes, as well as to the half-comic satire of the Tecumseh, Indiana, divorce proceedings at the close of the novel *A Modern Instance* (1882) by WILLIAM DEAN HOWELLS (1837–1920).

John S. Robb's designs can be gleaned from his book's serpentine title, *Streaks of Squatter Life, and Far-West Stories: A Series of Humorous Sketches Descriptive of Incidents and Characters of the Wild West* (1847). His use of "West" belonged to the period, since before the turn of the nineteenth century the term took in both the expanding western frontier and what is now commonly called the Midwest. In his preface Robb addresses an audience back east, readers who were expected to find humor in the "oddity and originality" of this far-off place. He informs them that "the west abounds with incident and humor, and the observer must lack an eye for the comic who can look upon the panorama of western life without being tempted to laugh." He adds, alluding to the violence and killing along the frontier, that there are "dark streaks in western life" (viii–ix).

Robb's "Nettle Bottom Ball" (59–64) illustrates nicely both the dark streaks and the comic. It is a story of squatter life in the Illinois bottomlands, set near a fictive Equality, Illinois, somewhere along the Mississippi. Robb expresses his debt to the southwestern school in his preface, where he speaks of his admiration for both T. B. Thorpe (1815–1878) and Johnson J. Hooper (viii). Unlike most southwestern humorists, though, he was not haunted by the specter of slavery or the questions of race. Robb's stories, for the most part, took their local color and political flavor from the odd characters found in backwoods MISSOURI, Illinois, and river towns along the Ohio. The fictive towns of Equality, Illinois, and Liberty, Missouri, where these characters fight and frolic, are presented as places largely free from antebellum conflicts and the political crises bound up in the iniquities of slavery.

Somewhat like CAROLINE KIRKLAND (1801–1864), Juliette Kinzie (1806–1870) embedded comic stories into her larger narrative. When she drew her tales from oral sources, she carefully marked off her authorial voice from the characters' dialect speech. For example, in recasting a conventional western story, the squatter or westerner "doing a dandy," she had the local country "bumpkins" trick some well-dressed city gentlemen in an expected comic reversal. But instead of giving the locals' dialect speech, as Twain and others later did, she muted the words and laughter in sober and grammatically correct summary. Kinzie, like many other regional writers in the period, felt obliged to defer to literary conventions and attitudes established outside the region. She smoothed down the rough edges of Midwestern character types and translated their speech and manners according to decorous eastern codes of behavior.

Literary Comedians: At the height of their powers and popularity in the 1860s, Charles Farrar Browne and David Ross Locke addressed their newspaper columns to audiences that, so far as the divided times allowed, were national. They both wrote for OHIO newspapers: Browne, for the *Cleveland Plain Dealer;* Locke, first for the *Findlay Hancock-Jeffersonian* and later for the *Toledo Blade.* Like other literary comedians, they seldom relied on local material. They invented character types and personae that belonged to places either indefinitely located or set somewhere outside the Midwest. In *American Humor* (1978) Walter Blair and Hamlin Hill, commenting on Locke and other literary comedians, observe that such "professional comic writers handed over to local colorists . . . the fun of evoking provincial ways of feeling, living, and talking" (291). Browne, born in Waterford, Maine, wandered for many years as a journeyman printer and newspaper writer before finding steady employment at the *Plain Dealer.* In January 1858 he wrote his first column in the voice and persona of Artemus Ward, a blustering illiterate and self-described "genial showman." Ward scattered puns, malapropisms, and fortuitous misspellings in every wandering and disjointed sentence of his comic letters. He packed his paragraphs with ingeniously constructed flips and flops into anti-climax (*American Humor* 278). As Ward says in *Wit and Humor of the Age* (1883), "My Fort is the grate moral show bizniss & ritin choice famerly libertaoor for the noospapers. That's what's the matter with *me*" (112–13). On the lecture platform Browne, as Ward, imitated the earnest and deadly serious style of temperance lecturers and parodied the high-flying oratory of the day's political speakers, most famously in a performance titled "Shall the Star-Spangled Banner Be Cut Up into Dish-cloths?" (*The Complete Works of Artemus Ward* 59).

Locke learned much from Ward. He created his own illiterate alter ego in Petroleum Vesuvius Nasby, a character who lives, according to the title page of *Ekkoes from Kentucky* (1868), at "Confederit X Roads (wich is in the Stait uv Kentucky)." Using Nasby as a medium, Locke mimicked and attacked racial prejudice, Confederate sympathies, disloyal Democratic Copperheads, and the South's pathological hatred of Lincoln. Nasby's speech and orthography were as barbaric as Ward's; his political illogic, because it so faithfully reproduced certain popular prejudices, seemed more extreme and at times peculiarly vicious. Locke's writing, like much humor writing in this period, was adversarial, a precisely tuned expression of political and cultural sentiments in the North and the Midwest.

1865–1915: The next generation of humorists found a liberating example in the wandering monologues of Ward and Nasby. Browne and Locke had freed these humor characters from conventional framing devices, especially the controlling presence of the literate narrator and gentleman-author. Despite their general indifference to local color, their writings and lecture-platform performances proved valuable for succeeding Midwestern humorists, who would increasingly dramatize the peculiarities of regional speech, manners, and mores.

Mark Twain did this with fidelity and high comic art through the voices, dialect humor, and characters of Huckleberry Finn, Tom Sawyer, Jim, Aunt Polly, and scores of others. His memories of Hannibal, Missouri, and his sense of place fired his imagination all his creative life. In the fictive Midwestern small towns he created—St. Petersburg, Dawson's Landing, and Hadleyburg—he brought back this past and made it "as real as it ever was, and as blessed" (*The Autobiography of Mark Twain* [1959], edited by Charles Neider, 12). Twain also re-created the practical jokes, boyhood pranks, and cruel humor of that time and place. Early in his adolescent years he had taken the measure of the southwestern school, drawing out of newspaper exchanges the old jokes, squibs, and formulaic stories that his comic art required. Working in his brother Orion's print shops, in Hannibal, Missouri, and in Muscatine and Keokuk, IOWA, he copied, reworked, and refined the crudities of newspaper jokesters, the work of literary comedians, and the tall tales that he heard in his travels.

Twain left Hannibal, Missouri, in 1853 and for much of the rest of his life wandered far from the Midwest. He spent six months in Cincinnati in 1856–1857 and remembered the time and the town as wearisome. According to local tradition, as quoted in William Baker's "Mark Twain in Cincinnati: A Mystery Most Compelling," *American Literary Realism* 12 (Autumn 1979), Twain said, "When the end of the world comes, I want to be in Cincinnati—it is always ten years behind the times" (299). That the Midwest he had known somehow lagged behind the culturally superior East was a common-enough belief in the late nineteenth and early twentieth centuries. Boston, Philadelphia, New York, and other eastern seaboard cities housed the nation's publishers, its major cultural institutions, and its important newspapers and literary journals. Twain, ever ambitious to succeed as a writer, moved east, making his home for many years in Hartford, Connecticut and upstate New York. A southerner in the North, a Midwesterner in the East, he forged a career as a humorist, platform performer, and serious writer that gave every section and school of American humor reason to claim him. Yet from his apprentice efforts, crude and derivative sketches written in the 1850s, to the poetic descriptions and brutal jokes of *Huckleberry Finn* and on through the black humor of his final years, Twain drew on the experience, the memories, and the language of Hannibal and his youth. For Midwestern humorists and writers as different as Don Marquis, James Thurber, and KURT VONNEGUT (1922–2007), and for American literature in general, Twain's influence and importance run beyond summary reckoning.

Those writers closely identified with Chicago humor near the turn of the twentieth century were not bound tightly by a single style or dominant influence. Eugene Field, Finley Peter Dunne, and George Ade—and lesser lights like Charles Harris (1841–1892), Henry Ten Eyck White (1853–1942), and Keith Preston (1884–1927)—were among the many humorists who wrote columns for Chicago newspapers in this period. Field, a poet, children's author, and short-story writer, opened the way for others in his column "Sharps and Flats." Writing for the *Chicago Daily News* between 1885 and 1895, he produced playful verse, political commentary, musings on Chicago's weather, satires of the city's wealthy and its cultural aspirations, tributes to old books and theatregoing, and thoughts on almost any topic that fed his fancy. Remembered now for the sentimental children's poem "Little Boy Blue," he was also known in his time to display a "Rabelaisian nature" when he spoke before men's groups. In his columns Field exercised a freedom and whimsical range that his rivals and successors found liberating.

Finley Peter Dunne was a competitor of Field, writing for the rival *Chicago Evening Post*. For the *Post* in October 1893, he first created the fictional tavern owner Martin Dooley, an Irish immigrant living in Bridgeport on Chicago's near West Side. Since his tavern was said to be on Archer Avenue, he was soon dubbed the "Archey Road Philosopher." As he topped off schooners of beer, he dispensed political wisdom and neighborhood gossip, mixing in stories and legends of old Ireland. He emphasized common sense with a rolling brogue and casually dropped epigrammatic sayings and durable insights, as in the 1938 collection *Mr. Dooley at His Best:* "No matther whether th' Constitution follows th' flag or not, th' Supreme Coort follows th' iliction returns" (77).

At such moments Dunne reprised and transformed the literary tradition so long associated with the rustic sage and cracker-barrel oracle of the small town. The character of Dooley just as importantly gave life and significance to the language of the new immigrant and the experience of urban America. At the time Dunne wrote, in the so-called nativist nineties, African Americans and the new immigrant groups were routinely paraded as comic stereotypes in humor magazines like the old *Life*. They were also grotesquely caricatured in Sunday comic strips, as well as in the humor sections of high-toned literary magazines. Not until the late 1890s did the *Chicago Tribune* drop its Paddy jokes from its back pages. Well into the 1920s, comic strips in the *Tribune* and other Midwestern papers represented blacks in cruel racist forms. The national syndication of Dunne's columns, however small a step, marked a shift away from such stereotypes.

George Ade's fables and short fiction kept alive a rural Midwest that was fast vanishing into memory and the mythic past. Like Field and Dunne, Ade perfected his humor while reporting and writing a column for a Chicago paper. In mid-September 1897 he created the first of his hundreds of "fables in slang" for the *Chicago Record*. More often than not, the humor in these brief stories turns on clever inversions of copybook wisdom and rewrites of Horatio Alger success stories. "The Patient Toiler Who Got It in the Usual Place" and "The Fable of Sister Mae Who Did as Well as Could Be Expected," in *Fables in Slang* (1899), typify his ironic tributes to the American Dream and the work ethic behind it.

Ade wrote in a "slang" of his own invention and spelled out his stories through the shorthand of character types. He strung out his characters between the simple ways of Midwestern small towns and the hard-and-fast demands of urban life. In his measured nostalgia for rustic old-fashioned ways, he showed his kinship with two fellow Hoosiers, the poet James Whitcomb Riley and the cartoonist and writer John T. McCutcheon. With sharper humor and a more insistent skepticism, Ade played up the confusions and comic quandaries of country people new to Chicago. He lampooned the citizens of Nubbinville and those "undersized towns" who tried to keep up with big-city fashions. His short novels *Artie* (1896), *Pink Marsh* (1897), and *Doc' Horne* (1899) sympathetically fit urban experience into middle-class values and Victorian mores even as Ade gently makes fun of his lead characters' retrograde ideas of courtship, love, and gallantry.

Summing up his understanding of Chicago humorists in the February 1917 *Harper's Monthly,* William Dean Howells said that in Ade and other Chicago writers, "the refining grace of the New England Spirit" met the rude "democracy" of the West (445). He found these values fully illustrated in Ade's short story "Effie Whittlesy," published in *In Babel: Stories of Chicago* (1903), a tale comically pitting the manners and snobbishness of Chicago society against "the democracy of a small community" (51).

1916–1945: Although Ade wrote and produced popular work into the 1920s and was to influence later writers as different as H(enry) L(ouis) Mencken (1880–1956), S(idney) J(oseph) Perelman (1904–1979), and Jean Shepherd, critics and readers now generally agree that his most interesting and significant writing dated from the 1890s, when he first created his "fables in slang." Don Marquis and Ring Lardner, who started their writing careers a little more than ten years after Ade's first newspaper publica-

tions, turned out to be somewhat better guides to early twentieth-century Midwestern humor. They laughed at the nation's popular manias, confronted some of its darker moods, and comically paraded the grotesque character of those who had succumbed to either. Their humor may have sometimes used the same small Midwestern town settings and cast of characters that Ade had carried into his fables, but Marquis and Lardner, far more than Ade, helped create what Walter Blair and Hamlin Hill, in *America's Humor,* call "the shift from predominantly 'rustic' to predominantly 'urbane' humor" (368–69).

Marquis and Lardner straddled a transitional moment. Both established themselves as columnists in the years just before World War I and did their best work from the war years through the 1920s. Masters of the mock oral narrative, both relied on and burlesqued colloquial speech, small-town manners, and the tale-telling style of nineteenth-century Midwestern humorists. Although they came from small Midwestern towns, they wrote their first important fiction as columnists for big-city dailies. Marquis was born in Walnut, Illinois, wrote for his hometown paper, and, after several years of apprenticeship under Joel Chandler Harris (1845–1908), established himself as a columnist for the *New York Evening Post* in 1912. Lardner's career followed an almost parallel track. Born in Niles, Michigan, he began writing for a South Bend paper in 1905 and found his way to Chicago, where he wrote for the *Chicago Tribune* between 1908 and 1918. It was Marquis who reinvented the rustic sage for big-city readers in his "Sun Dial" columns. Archy, the *vers libre*–writing cockroach, Mehitabel the cat, and Clem Hawley, the "Old Soak," commented on the era's new sexual freedoms, criticized the day's intellectual and artistic fads, and joked about controversies over evolution, the wars between labor and capital, and the strife splitting anarchists from socialists.

Through "certain maxims of archy" Marquis had Archy mimic the moral certitude and pithy expressions of the cracker-barrel philosophers (*The Lives and Times of Archy and Mehitabel,* 1927, 50–55). As moralist, good citizen, rebel, and *poète maudit,* Archy worries about humanity's hubris and the ways of city folk like Mehitabel the cat. She dresses and struts like a flapper, sings of her sexual freedom, and swoons over spiritualism and metempsychosis. In language both oratorical and homely, Clem Hawley, the "Old Soak," takes on the iniquities of Prohibition, parodies temperance literature, and remembers fondly the good old days of the saloon. Through such comic characters and parodic devices, Marquis addressed serious contemporary issues.

Lardner, on the other hand, seldom dealt directly with philosophy or troubling social issues in his characters' wandering monologues. In writing his *Tribune* column "In the Wake of the News," he drew on the example of Ade's and Dunne's colloquial personae. Dunne, in particular, pointed the way to masking controversial views behind the words of a "wise boob." Dunne's Mr. Dooley, talking with the workingmen and fellow Irish immigrants who visit his tavern, mingles political satire with gossip about the old neighborhood. Lardner's typical characters are much too self-absorbed to consider political questions or philosophical ideas. More often than not, he pictured the "average man" and his wife as nothing more than conspicuous consumers, clawing and climbing their way up the social ladder. He found humor in their petty quarrels, cliché-ridden speech, and social pretensions. Critic Norris Yates concludes in *The American Humorist* (1964) that Lardner wrote "largely about the limited interests of mass-man" (166). His illiterate baseball players, blustering Broadway producers, spoiled middle-class children, and small-town Midwesterners live lives of noisy desperation. What they do from day to day and what they say in explaining their narrow lives seems by turns comic, pathetic, and vicious. The babbling nurse-trainee in "Zone of Quiet," a story first collected in *The Love Nest, and Other Stories* (1926), tells us on the opening page that "the doctors treat us like they thought we were Mormons or something." "Haircut," Lardner's much-anthologized tale of small-town Michigan, also first collected in *The Love Nest, and Other Stories,* exposes the cruelty of practical jokes and the social pressures that can debase a whole community. Gone is the idealized Midwestern small

town that glows so warmly in Ade's "Effie Whittlesy." Gone, too, are the manners and spirit Ade attributes in *In Babel: Stories of Chicago* to "the democracy of a small community" (51). Travel, suburban affluence, and urban experience do not diminish the innocence, stupidity, or obnoxiousness of Lardner's typical characters. *Gullible's Travels, Etc.* (1917), the adventures of a young Chicago couple, charts the Gullibles' innocence and crudity even as it burlesques their pretensions to sophistication. As Gullible says, "We was both hit by the society bacillus" (45).

In the 1920s and 1930s the Midwest's most important and representative humorists created characters who were formed by urban experience. Edna Ferber had already cataloged, with humor and pathos, the city life of shop girls, hotel maids, and white-collar workers in short-story collections like *Buttered Side Down* (1912) and *Cheerful, by Request* (1918). In the 1920s more and more newspaper columnists and humorists dropped the conventional mask of rustic innocence and assumed an urbane and sophisticated stance toward the common man. Expressing themselves in witty and knowing glances at "the so-called human race," Ben Hecht, Bert Leston Taylor (1866–1921), FRANKLIN (PIERCE) ADAMS (1881–1960), and other Chicago columnists adopted what Kenney J. Williams and Bernard Duffey in their *"Chicago's Public Wits": A Chapter in the American Comic Spirit* (1983) called the "superior eye" (210).

The shift to urban humor did not, however, spell an immediate and final end to the Midwestern school of "hoss sense" or the traditional values that sustained it. Even as Hecht was turning out the columns collected in *1001 Afternoons in Chicago* (1922) and co-writing the comedy *The Front Page* (1927), Kin Hubbard's "Abe Martin" cartoons and columns were appearing in national syndication. Through countless reprints, this raggedy, rustic character and his sayings remained popular long after Hubbard's death in 1930.

In a 1924 series of cartoons and narratives, John T. McCutcheon published his "Corn Fed Philosophy" for *Cosmopolitan Magazine*. Like Hubbard, McCutcheon was putting on the mask of the village philosopher, telling jokes and stories that had gotten laughs in the 1890s. Such humor was part of a rearguard action waged against a younger generation of novelists, poets, and humorists, who, it was said, were in REVOLT FROM THE VILLAGE. Hubbard's and McCutcheon's humor recalled pleasant days in the country and the intimacies of Midwestern village life, but it also sought to answer the criticisms of small-town values in WINESBURG, OHIO (1919) by SHERWOOD ANDERSON (1876–1941) MAIN STREET (1920) by (HARRY) SINCLAIR LEWIS (1885–1951), and the world-weary humor of the "lost generation."

Among the humorists who emerged in the 1920s and 1930s, James Thurber seems the most important and interesting. Critic Adam Gopnik says in "A Critic at Large," in the New Yorker (June 27, 1994), that Thurber gave American writing "a plain, modern voice that perfectly suited the American comedy" (169). Thurber, he demonstrates, did this through great talent and discipline, but also by discovering that he could tune his voice to a cosmopolitan and urbane pitch while posing as the innocent Ohio boy that he always was. Thurber was born in Columbus, Ohio, wrote a column for the Columbus Dispatch in the early 1920s, and began steadily contributing pieces to the New Yorker in 1927. His views of the Midwest and Columbus were conflicted, if not flatly contradictory. Stephen L. Tanner, in his Fall 1992 American Studies article "James Thurber and the Midwest," asserts that Thurber felt that Anderson's and Lewis's novels had "hysterically maligned" the Midwest, but he also enjoyed H. L. Mencken's attacks on "Babbitry" and the satirical renderings of Columbus and Ohio State University written by Ludwig Lewisohn (1882–1955) (65).

Thurber knitted up the loose ends of his love and hate for his hometown in MY LIFE AND HARD TIMES (1933), a book that tells of his strangely eccentric and oddly funny family. Throughout the loosely joined series of episodes that composed his narrative, Thurber displays a precise feeling for colloquial speech and the crossfire of dialogue, reminders of his debt to Twain and a result of his powers of observation. Thurber also shows himself to be literate and literary, a devotee of Henry James and a student of word games and wordplay. Although he never puts on the mask of the cornpone philosopher, he persistently assumes the role of the innocent with a nervous ease, fitful grace, and a talent for the tall tale. His much-anthologized stories "The Secret Life of Walter Mitty" (1939) and "The Catbird Seat" (1942) present this innocent in all his timid glory. In such human comedies he wrote out his versions of the "little man," a sensitive character who, in his imagination and in his actions, comically triumphs over stronger and more powerful antagonists. Thurber sometimes feigned indifference to politics and world affairs, but he wrote and drew The Last Flower in 1939 as an anti-war "parable." He created it, he says in the dedication, in the "wistful hope" that his daughter's "world will be better than mine." In the same year, he collaborated with Elliott Nugent (1896–1980) on the play The Male Animal (1940), an eloquently comic put-down of the political intolerance of the times. He set the action at a fictionalized but easily recognizable Ohio State University.

The Great Depression and the years of protest it brought made many Midwestern writers and artists into political radicals and, on occasion, turned some of the radicals into writers of humor. By the end of the 1930s Ruth McKenney had joined the Communist Party and had written Industrial Valley (1939), a prize-winning novel about a violent Akron strike. At about the same time, she wrote the novel My Sister Eileen (1938). This series of loosely connected episodes sketch her childhood and adolescence in East Cleveland with light humor and some deft satiric flourishes. Eileen and her sister, as rendered in these fictions, strives to be sophisticated beyond their years but inevitably betrays an innate and comic innocence. Once in New York, they are typical and gullible Midwesterners, prey to big-city boyfriends and a conniving landlord. Some of the final scenes, those showing the sisters fleeing Brazilian naval officers, match the speed and zaniness of 1930s screwball comedy films. McKenney's stories, particularly the New York chapters, served as the basis for a play, two successful films, and the musical titled Wonderful Town.

The radical politics of Langston Hughes informed his creation of the character and tales of Jesse B. Semple. Semple, also known as Simple, is presented as a barroom philosopher, a working-class African

American who, through his down-home diction and mother wit, exposes the iniquities of American racial beliefs, attacks Jim Crow law, and ridicules the peculiar institutions behind the segregated armed forces. Some readers detected the influence of Finley Peter Dunne in the neighborhood tavern setting, the humorous dialect speech, and the political themes. Hughes wrote the first of his Jesse B. Semple columns on January 19, 1943, for the African American newspaper the *Chicago Defender* and ended the column in 1966. He developed the stories into five books, beginning with *Simple Speaks His Mind* (1950). *Simply Heavenly,* a play in 1957 and a television presentation in 1959, brought the Simple stories to a larger, national audience.

1946 to the Present: The representative Midwestern humorists who arrived in the years just after World War II did not faithfully continue the literary traditions drawn from nostalgia for the farm or country village, nor did they often find a reason to ridicule or mimic those humorists who still sounded like the old-time rustic sages and cracker-barrel philosophers. Their monologues edged closer to the language and urbanized spirit of stand-up comics. Writers like Peter De Vries and Max Shulman mimicked the speech of immigrant parents, took up the comedy of manners found in the melting pot of the city, and usually drew, for their loose and wandering plots, on the simple patterns of love stories and the war between the sexes. Blair and Hill, in *American Humor,* assert that readers in postwar America had developed a taste for a "combination of slapstick and subtle humor in fiction" (470).

Shulman's humor catered to the taste for slapstick, generously mixing juvenile jokes, superficial book learning, and a fistful of outrageous puns. From his first novel, *Barefoot Boy with Cheek* (1943), to *Potatoes Are Cheaper* (1971), Shulman told and retold stories of his early years in St. Paul (see MINNEAPOLIS/ST. PAUL) and his college days at the University of Minnesota. His characters, as their exotic and implausible names suggest, are character types or caricatures. The innately innocent Midwesterner Asa Hearthrug, his cousin "Yanqui Imperialismo," and a boy called "Kyrie Eleison" ap-

peared in his first novel. Dobie Gillis and young innocents like him followed in later books and plays. For the most part, Shulman steered away from serious satire or social commentary. *Potatoes Are Cheaper* sketches the hard lives of St. Paul's Jewish community during the Depression, although taken in bulk, the novel is as farcical in handling adolescent love and sex as were many of Shulman's syndicated columns for college newspapers.

Peter De Vries's humor, unlike that of Ade and other turn-of-the-century Midwestern humorists, insistently showed off book learning and traded on urban and suburban experience. He invented city-bred comic heroes who, however street wise, remain innocent and unsophisticated. Despite their usually befuddled condition and clownish behavior, the main characters in his many novels have a flair for educated talk, a literary consciousness, and an unfulfilled desire for the finer things. Like Thurber, whom he much admired, De Vries delighted in complicated wordplay, took pleasure in parodying contemporary writers, and quoted, usually with mock sentimentality, the words of old-fashioned standard authors. His churning mix of literary modes and language often makes for characters who speak in an odd yet literary patois. Louie in *The Blood of the Lamb* (1961) recites Shelley and Swinburne but yokes their poetic diction to speech filled with the "deses," "dems," and "doses" of Chicago's South Side. *Slouching towards Kalamazoo* (1983) alludes to Yeats in the title, parodies, transplants, and updates the plot of *The Scarlet Letter,* and, riding on the same comic wave, reworks some vaudeville-style jokes about Kalamazoo, Kenosha, Fond du Lac, and Muncie. In De Vries's other novels his lead characters mimic the broken English of their immigrant parents and sprinkle the pages with their own malapropisms. In *Into Your Tent I'll Creep* (1971) the conniving Al Banghart, to sell his wares door-to-door, slips into "a kind of all-purpose Eastern-European speech you can't pin down" (147). Whether living in the exurbia of Connecticut or passing through Chicago's better neighborhoods, De Vries's comic heroes remain outsiders, prone to social blunders and given to ridiculous faux pas.

What some have called "the Great Midwestern Joke" sits near the center of Jean Shepherd's humor and close to the heart of Garrison Keillor. The joke, as critic Peter Scholl summarizes it in *Garrison Keillor* (1993), springs from Midwesterners' feeling that they are "doomed to insignificance, to lives of provincial obscurity and sameness" (153). Trying to escape the Midwest and dreaming of lives of bicoastal glamour, they inevitably find themselves drawn home by a "backward tug," a contradictory "longing for what they left behind in the great void of the Heartland" (153). In *The America of George Ade* (1960) Shepherd suggests that "almost all of [Midwestern] humor is of the school of Futility" (12). Although Shepherd and Keillor occasionally borrowed tricks and dodges from earlier local-color writers, and the spirit of George Ade hovers over both of them, their humorous writings bring to life the small Midwestern town with a cast of characters and a set of stories that appeal to modern and urban readers. Shepherd set many of his tales in Hohman, a stylized version of his hometown, Hammond, Indiana. Hohman, like Hammond, is a steel-mill town, hard by Whiting's refineries and a Mazola plant, part of that industrial stretch of northwest Indiana called "da region." Shepherd used this setting for *In God We Trust, All Others Pay Cash* (1966), a

collection of stories cast as remembrances of childhood. "Duel in the Snow, or, Red Ryder Nails the Cleveland Street Kid," since its conversion into film as *A Christmas Story* (1983), may be the best known of these. Like his many other tales of childhood angst and desire in the 1930s, its humor intermittently folds in pathos and irony. If a "backward tug" of nostalgia exerts a force over the telling, it is an ambivalent one, countered by the narrator's ironic perspective and some astringent asides.

Keillor's *Lake Wobegon Days* (1985) has often been seen as a pastoral. Its humor, however, owes more to Midwestern humorists like Twain, Ade, and Thurber than it does to Theocritus and the conventions of the pastoral. Without slipping into sharp satire or hard social criticism, Keillor plays up the eccentricities of small-town Midwesterners and the peculiar stasis of their lives. Telling the stories of Lake Wobegon, a town in rural MINNESOTA, he lends an ear to the people's repetition of well-worn jokes and listens to idiosyncratic rhythms in the clichés and conversational taglines that have been carried from generation to generation. As Ade did before him, Keillor trades on recognizable character types and regularly takes up the town's folk beliefs and familiar sayings in a spirit of anti-proverbialism. Yet if he comically exaggerates the eccentricities of

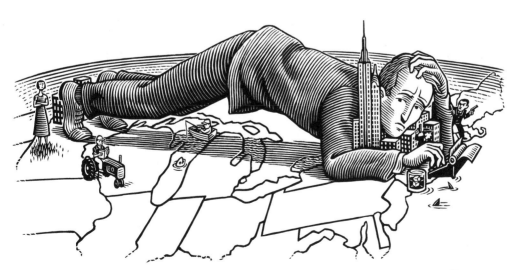

Love Me, illustration by Gregory Nemec humorously depicting New York City's pull on Midwesterner Garrison Keillor, 2003.
© Gregory Nemec, 2003

the Wobegonians, he still treats them with affectionate and nostalgic indulgence; the crude country manners of "Norwegian bachelor farmers," the oddities of the narrator's family beliefs, and the stubborn religious ideas of the town's Protestants and Catholics may sometimes seem outlandish but never appear odious. In the introduction to *We Are Still Married* (1989), Keillor states his version of the "Great Midwestern Joke" as the "Law of the Provinces": *"Don't think you're somebody. If you were, you wouldn't be here, you'd be on the Coast"* (xviii). That overstatement and the fixed assumptions about the small and narrow life of the Midwest beneath it pull and tug at the wandering protagonist of Keillor's novel *Love Me* (2003). Larry, a failing novelist, bounces crazily between the glamour of New York celebrity and his old life in blue-collar St. Paul, a place that, for a time, seems to him a soul-killing backwater.

Some patterns in Midwestern humor writing have held over the past thirty or forty years, even as its intended readers have been distracted and diverted to the comic wares of the newer media. As in the past, newspaper columnists have masked themselves behind humorous personae and built jokes and stories on carefully measured exaggerations. Mike Royko, using the character of Slats Grobnik and the warm and familiar surroundings of a Chicago tavern, skewered the city's political graft and greed and thus continued a literary tradition that had started with Finley Peter Dunne in the 1890s. Erma Bombeck, who found important inspiration in the work of Shulman and Thurber, sketched and burlesqued the trials of family life in the small towns and tract suburbs of Dayton. Although she first wrote only for local papers, from the start she made little direct reference to the Midwest and almost never drew on local color. *At Wit's End* (1967), her first book collection of columns from the *Dayton Journal-Herald* and *Newsday* syndication, seemed aimed straight at a national audience.

Although Michael Feldman (b. 1949) has had himself introduced on radio as "the sage of WISCONSIN," he is not ready to revive nineteenth-century cracker-barrel humor so much as he is intent on parodying and deploying its faux-naïf character. Like Garri-

son Keillor, he subtly mixes wisecracks and folk wisdom in humor driven by the well-paced delivery of a stand-up comic. Feldman has written *Wisconsin Curiosities: Quirky Characters, Roadside Oddities, and Other Offbeat Stuff* (2004). He also compiled and comically deconstructed many of the myths and several pieces of faulty folk wisdom about the Midwest in the essay "The Midwest: Where Is It?" (1983), reprinted in *Mirth of a Nation: The Best Contemporary Humor* (2000), edited by Michael J. Rosen. There, Feldman puts on a deadpan face, mimicking the voice of the serious sociologist or cultural geographer: "Recent survey results suggest that most people don't know where the Midwest is, including many who live there (or would, if they only knew where they were)" (*Mirth of a Nation* 154).

"Humor," says Constance Rourke in her celebrated study *American Humor* (1931), "is a matter of fantasy" (20). The Midwest, for many readers and literary critics, stands for a literature of hard facts, the grinding machinery of naturalism, and the baking heat and killing cold associated with prairie realism. This is a place, it seems, that was made for the brooding muses of (HANNIBAL) HAMLIN GARLAND (1860–1940), (HERMAN) THEODORE DREISER (1871–1945), and OLE EDVART RØLVAAG (1876–1931). Its flat landscapes, decaying cities, and rusting steel mills do not appear to make a comfortable place for fantasy, for comic turns and joy-filled diversions, or for those habits of imagination and exaggeration that, when expressed in art and laughter, can mask, deny, and erase reality. Yet, paradoxically, fantasy is what the Midwest's humorists have generously supplied, even when they have delivered it wrapped up as common sense and disguised as the hard facts of daily life.

SELECTED WORKS: By common consent, the most significant works of American humor and the most important works of Midwestern humor belong to Mark Twain. Although *The Adventures of Tom Sawyer* (1876), *ADVENTURES OF HUCKLEBERRY FINN* (1884, 1885), *The Tragedy of Pudd'nhead Wilson* (1894), and his humorous sketches and stories can be read in any of a number of editions, the Library of America's volumes are accessible, intelligently annotated, and authoritative. George Ade's "fables in slang" appear in multiple collections and editions. Jean Shepherd's *The America of George Ade* (1960), however, offers in one book an insightful introduction to Ade, some taut observations on Indiana and Midwestern humorists, and a generous helping of Ade's best fables, short stories, and essays. Oddly enough, Shepherd does not include Ade's short story "Effie Whittlesy," the story Howells once cited as the finest example of Midwestern humor. Ade published his story in *In Babel* (1903).

Ring Lardner's 1925 short story "Haircut," collected in *Haircut, and Other Stories* (1926), and his short novel *Gullible's Travels, Etc.* (1917) can stand as an introduction to the Midwest and to twentieth-century humor. *The Thurber Carnival* (1945) opens up the full range of Thurber's genius, collecting his stories, essays, and cartoons published through 1944. It includes the full text of *My Life and Hard Times* (1933) with a "Preface to a Life" that may help define what humor and humorists do. Langston Hughes's *The Best of Simple* (1961) presents an accessible grouping of the Jesse B. Semple tales. *The Blood of the Lamb* (1961) has often been judged Peter De Vries's finest novel. Although it turns from his expected farce and comedy toward a series of tragic scenes, the book may still be read as a representative example of De Vriesian humor. First-time readers of De Vries may find a quicker and more direct route to grasping his comic art in early short stories like "Tulip," collected in *No, but I Saw Movie* (1952). Jean Shepherd's *In God We Trust, All Others Pay Cash* (1966) and Garrison Keillor's *Lake Wobegon Days* (1985), with the passage of time, come ever closer to being seen as canonical works of humor and Midwestern literature. Michael Feldman's essay "The Midwest: Where Is It?" in *Mirth of a Nation: The Best Contemporary Humor*, edited by Michael J. Rosen (2000), 154–57, reminds us that even the idea of the Midwest remains elusive. *The Best of Bombeck* (1987), which includes *At Wit's End* (1967), *"Just Wait Till You Have Children of Your Own!"* (1971), and *I Lost Everything in the Post-natal Depression* (1973), gives ample evidence for the dust-jacket claim that Erma Bombeck is "America's favorite humorist."

Jack Conroy's anthology *Midland Humor: A Harvest of Fun and Folklore* (1947) provides a useful, if now dated, introduction to Midwestern humor. Conroy introduces and samples humor from an expansively defined Midwest, ranging from almanac writers of the early nineteenth century to a larger grouping called "modern voices." The collection includes writers like CAROLINE KIRKLAND (1801–1864), Finley Peter Dunne, and James Thurber, as well as some interesting and forgotten minor humor writers, such as Opie Read (1852–1939), Henry Ten Eyck White, and Keith Preston. For additional examples of nineteenth-century humorists like Charles Farrar Browne and ROBERT JONES BURDETTE (1844–1914), see the anthology edited by Melville D. Landon, *Wit and Humor of the Age* (1883). *Chicago's Public Wits: A Chapter in the American Comic Spirit* (1983), edited by Kenny J. Williams and Bernard Duffey, complements Conroy's collection in other ways, gathering up more recent writers and defining both Chicago's and the Midwest's importance in American humor writing. *Chicago's Public Wits* begins with political satire and humor of the 1840s and finishes with some modern counterparts of the 1980s. Some of Mike Royko's Slats Grobnik stories and the Bill Granger essay "Talkin' Chicawgo," accordingly, round out the collection. Not so long ago, popular anthologies of humor like Bennett Cerf's *An Encyclopedia of American Humor* (1954) routinely set aside a section for writers from the Midwest. In these spaces editors usually collected some short pieces by Thurber, Lardner, and Max Shulman and a miscellany of personal favorites. For the most part, such gatherings of Midwestern humor have ceased.

FURTHER READING: Scholarly studies coupling "Midwestern" with "humor" have appeared infrequently in the past few years. Compilations of humorous stories and systematic studies of oral traditions like Richard Dorson's *Land of the Millrats* (1981), Ronald L. Baker's *Jokelore: Humorous Folktales from Indiana* (1986), and James P. Leary's *So Ole Says to Lena: Folk Humor of the Upper Midwest* (2001) sketch rough starting points for understanding a larger Midwestern region and its humor writing. But such collections, despite the strong regional flavor of their jokes and stories, lean toward anthropology or folklore. The kind of paradigmatic listing of literary subjects, folk sources, and character types that Hennig Cohen and William B. Dillingham provide in *Humor of the Old Southwest* (1964) has yet to be fully attempted.

Nancy Walker's *A Very Serious Thing: Women's Humor and American Culture* (1988) yields insights into individual Midwestern writers like Erma Bombeck and Caroline Kirkland. But Walker's book, like other gender-based studies of American humor, can give only incidental attention to Midwestern humor and its dominating character types. Her deftly formed catalogs of perfection-seeking housewives, "lovelorn women," and "dumb blondes" are seldom set into a definition of place or region (11). Kenny J. Williams and Bernard Duffey's short section "The Rise of Ethnic Humor and Disturbing Laughter" in *Chicago's Public Wits* (1993) suggests that a study binding together regionalism, ethnicity, and humor can be profitable. They discuss Charles Harris (1841–1892), the creator of *Carl Pretzel's Magazine Pook*, sample nineteenth-century ethnic jokes, and reproduce a small portfolio of cartoons (97–114).

Neither Constance M. Rourke (1885–1941) in her groundbreaking study *American Humor: A Study of the National Character* (1931) nor Walter Blair's equally important *Native American Humor* (1960) take up Midwestern humor or group the region's humorists in any direct, sustained way. Nevertheless, these pioneer scholarly works on American humor can, if only by implication and suggestion, prove useful in defining the place and importance of Midwestern humor writing. Both contain rich commentary on individual Midwestern humorists, even if their regional affinities are largely left undefined. If scholars have given generous tribute to the achievements of individual Midwestern humorists like Twain, Ade, Thurber, and Lardner, they have been less willing to recognize or study in an integrated or comprehensive way a Midwestern school or tradition. Norris Yates's book *The American Humorist* (1964) outlines the significance of the "little man" character type in Thurber and analyzes the treatment of the "mass man" in Lardner. Given the high quality of Yates's commentary and the additional discussions of Ade, Dunne, Hubbard, and Marquis, his book qualifies as required reading. Walter Blair and Hamlin Hill's generally comprehensive *America's Humor* (1978) is detailed, readable, and authoritative, although it finds no particular place to group Midwestern humor writers. William Dean Howells's "Editor's Easy Chair" essay in *Harper's Monthly Magazine* (February 1917): 442–45 touches on Midwestern humor for only a few pages, but after all these years, his remarks on the democratic spirit of the region's humorists and the significance of the Chicago writers remain relevant and true.

From most perspectives, then, we have had individual Midwestern humorists but no such thing as Midwestern humor. If a comprehensive perspective on Midwestern humor is to be reached, it must almost necessarily be drawn from the various studies of individual authors. Four seem particularly valuable. James DeMuth in *Small Town Chicago: The Comic Perspective of Finley Peter Dunne, George Ade, and Ring Lardner* (1980) presses a suggestive thesis about the link between Chicago writers and the outlying small towns of the Midwest—and the kind of urban humor such a cultural connection defines. Stephen L. Tanner's article "James Thurber and the Midwest," *American Studies* 33 (Fall 1992): 61–72, has implications for understanding other Midwestern humorists and their ambivalence about the Midwest. Thurber's humor, like that of others, turned on being a "partially unreconstructed Midwesterner." In *Not So Simple: The "Simple" Stories by Langston Hughes* (1996), Donna Akiba Sullivan Harper demonstrates how Hughes developed his comic character first in newspaper columns and then in books. She emphasizes Hughes's racial concerns and portrayals of women rather than his leftist politics. Peter A. Scholl, in his Twayne series study *Garrison Keillor* (1993), sets down a concise definition of "the great Midwestern joke." He points out that in certain turns of humor, Midwesterners are caricatured as people who believe that they are "doomed to insignificance, to lives of provincial obscurity and sameness" (153–55, 171). Like Howells's brief comments on Ade and Dunne and like DeMuth's and Tanner's critical readings of individual authors, what Scholl has to say about Keillor tells even more about Midwestern humor writers in general.

Guy Szuberla   University of Toledo

I–J

ILLINOIS

In 1763 England gained title to the French territory east of the Mississippi that would become the Northwest Territory; Illinois was part of the Northwest Territory from 1787 until 1800, when it became part of Indiana Territory. Congress established the Illinois Territory in 1809, which originally included what became Illinois, Wisconsin, eastern Minnesota, and the western part of Michigan's Upper Peninsula. Illinois was admitted to the Union on December 3, 1818, as the twenty-first state.

Area: 57,914 square miles

Land: 55,519 square miles

Water: 2,395 square miles

Population (2010 census): 12,830,632

OVERVIEW: Illinois is distinguished not only by the amount of literature it has produced but also by the number of authors who have achieved national and international reputations as fiction writers, poets, playwrights, and journalists. CHICAGO is the hub of much of this literary activity and innovation, but distinguished writers come from all areas of the state.

Positive portrayals of Illinois appear in much of the state's early literature and find expression in the folksong "El-a-noy," which was popular around 1850. Depictions of Illinois as a garden state or an Eden reflect the abundance of its wildlife, the beauty of its prairies, the fertility of its land, and the promise of the American Dream. "El-a-noy" divides Illinois into two parts: Chicago and the rest of the state. Chicago is "a great commercial city" (162), and the rest of the state is agricultural. This division reflects a political reality that continues today: Chicago and "downstate," the latter including everywhere else in Illinois.

HISTORY AND SIGNIFICANCE:

Exploration and Travel Accounts: The first Europeans in Illinois were French. Determined to find a route to the western sea through the great western river, which Native American accounts referred to as the "Great Water" or "Missipi," New France administrator Jean Talon chose Louis Joliet (1645–1700) to head the expedition. Beginning on May 17, 1673, Joliet and his companion, the Jesuit priest Jacques Marquette (1637–1675), explored the Mississippi; on their return they traveled up the Illinois River. It is speculated that the first description of Illinois was recorded in Joliet's journal, but that journal was lost when his canoe capsized. Joliet was, however, the first

© Karen Greasley, 2014

to visualize the great potential of the Illinois country. He provided passionate verbal descriptions of the land and proposed a canal to transport boats from Lake Erie to the Mississippi and on to the Gulf of Mexico.

Marquette's journal did survive; *Voyage et Découverte du P. Marquette et Sr. Jolliet dans l'Amérique Septentrionale* (1681) contains written descriptions of the rich Illinois country, the Illinois River, and Native American customs. In fact, the Works Progress Administration (WPA) guidebook *Illinois: A Descriptive and Historical Guide* (1939), edited by HARRY HANSEN (1884–1977), credits Marquette with the commencement of Illinois's literary record (22).

In 1680, thirty-three friars and artisans, including René-Robert Cavelier, Sieur de La Salle (1643–1687), Henri de Tonti (ca. 1650–1704), and Father Louis Hennepin (1626–ca. 1705) traveled down the Illinois River to Lake Peoria; Hennepin was convinced that a water passage could be found through Illinois to the West. Illinois town names such as Joliet, La Salle, and Hennepin reflect this French heritage and those explorers who were the dominant forces in Illinois until the French and Indian War.

Accounts of Illinois by military men appeared in the eighteenth century. The journals of George Rogers Clark (1752–1818) describing his expedition through Vincennes and Kaskaskia in 1778 were published in 1920 as *The Conquest of the Illinois*. Other explorers and travelers who recorded impressions of the state included William Newnham Blane (1800–1825), who wrote *An Excur-*

sion through the United States and Canada during the Years 1822–1823 (1824), and John Woods (1771–1829), who published his account in *Two Years' Residence in the Settlement on the English Prairie, in the Illinois Country, United States* (1822). Edmund Flagg (1815–1890) provided another description of Illinois in *The Far West; or, A Tour beyond the Mountains* (1838), recounting his travels in the Mississippi Valley.

The Emigrant's Guide to the Western States of America (1852) by John Regan (1818–1893) recounts the struggles of an Illinois settler. Two nineteenth-century female travelers contributed to the cultural construction of Illinois as a New Eden where the American Dream might be fulfilled. Margaret Fuller (1810–1850) described her visit to Oregon, Illinois, in *Summer on the Lakes, in 1843* (1844). ELIZA (WOODSON) FARNHAM (1815–1864) settled near her brother and sister in Groveland and related her experiences on the Illinois frontier in *Life in Prairie Land* (1846). Like Fuller, she advocated women's rights, prison reform, and abolition of slavery.

The most noteworthy of the first travelers to write about Illinois, Englishman Morris Birkbeck (1764–1825), wrote *Notes on a Journey in America, from the Coast of Virginia to the Territory of Illinois* (1818) and *Letters from Illinois* (1818), the first significant nonfiction works about Illinois. In *Illinois Literature: The Nineteenth Century* (1986) John Hallwas observes that Birkbeck was the state's first and only writer of significance until the 1830s, when Illinois literature began in earnest, largely because of his grasp of the importance of Illinois to the American Dream (11).

Among Illinois's early Native American authors were Metea (ca. 1760–1827), a Potawatomi chief who addressed the Chicago Council four times in 1821, and BLACK HAWK (1767–1838), a Sauk war chief. Black Hawk's life story, *LIFE OF MA-KA-TAI-ME-SHE-KIA-KIAK, OR BLACK HAWK*, dictated in 1833 with several later revised versions, was the first Native American autobiography published in America.

Speeches, Sermons, and Oratory: Illinois's response to slavery was complex. The French were the first colonists, but most left after England gained title to the Northwest Territory. The first wave of settlers came through southern Illinois from southern states. Although these settlers did not favor making Illinois a slave state, they did sympathize with those southern states where slavery already existed, and many of these southerners opposed the abolitionists.

One of the most influential abolitionists was Elijah P. Lovejoy (1802–1837), editor of an anti-slavery newspaper, who was murdered in Alton on November 7, 1837, while defending his press from an angry mob. Lovejoy's Market House speech is one of the most famous Illinois speeches. His eloquence survives also in his letters, which were collected in 1838. Another influential enemy of slavery was Lovejoy's friend Edward Beecher (1803–1895), who served as the first president of Illinois College from 1830 to 1844; his most important work is *Narrative of Riots at Alton: In Connection with the Death of Rev. Elijah P. Lovejoy* (1838), which includes Lovejoy's speech and accounts of the riot. Owen Lovejoy (1811–1864), younger brother of Elijah P. Lovejoy, was a dedicated abolitionist, an eloquent speaker, and a conductor of the Underground Railroad in Illinois. Owen Lovejoy has been recognized as having had tremendous influence on ABRAHAM LINCOLN (1809–1865), who acknowledged him as a generous friend. His speeches were never collected, but part of his most famous speech, "Human Beings, Not Property," is included in *Illinois Literature* (122–26).

Peter Cartwright (1785–1872), a frontier preacher, published his *Autobiography of Peter Cartwright, the Backwoods Preacher* in 1857. Cartwright's sermons could have been a rich source of information and insight, but they were lost because Cartwright did not preach from a printed text. Another frontier preacher who wrote and spoke in opposition to slavery was John Mason Peck (1789–1858), whose career also included writing newspaper articles and histories. Peck's *Gazetteer of Illinois, in Three Parts* (1837) is his most famous publication. Hallwas asserts that "Peck presented Illinois as the foremost embodiment of America's renowned identity, the land of opportunity" (*Illinois Literature* 40).

ROBERT (GREEN) INGERSOLL (1833–1899) was one of America's most famous nineteenth-century orators. In 1867 he was appointed attorney general of Illinois; his speech nom-

inating James Blaine for president in 1876 is a classic in political oratory. Examples of his wide-ranging interests are seen in "An Address to Colored People" (1867), "About Farming in Illinois" (1877), "My Chicago Bible Class" (1879), "A Tribute to Walt Whitman" (1882), and "Civil Rights" (1883). WILLIAM JENNINGS BRYAN (1860–1925), "the Great Commoner," was a native of New Salem and a graduate of Illinois College. His 1896 Cross of Gold speech and his *Memoirs* (1925) are his most enduring works.

Of all the nineteenth-century Illinois orators, Abraham Lincoln is the most renowned. His 1858 debates throughout Illinois with Stephen Douglas, his opponent for a US Senate seat, brought him national recognition and the 1860 Republican presidential nomination. Lincoln's leadership in abolishing slavery in the United States and his determination to keep the Union together are reflected in his Gettysburg Address (1863), his letters, and his addresses to Congress.

Social Criticism and Humor: The 1890s were noteworthy for Illinois social criticism and HUMOR writing. OPIE PERCIVAL (POPE) READ (1852–1939) brought his *Arkansas Traveller* to Chicago in 1887 and lived there for fifty years, publishing humorous sketches in that weekly periodical. Several humorists worked as Chicago newspaper

Abraham Lincoln's home in Springfield, Illinois, restored to its 1860 appearance.
© Philip Greasley, 2014

columnists before collecting their columns in books. *Byrd Flam in Town* (1894) by Le Roy Armstrong (1854–1927) and *Artie: A Story of the Streets and Town* (1896) and *Doc' Horne* (1899) by GEORGE ADE (1866–1944) were among the early popular works of humor. In the last years of the decade FINLEY PETER DUNNE (1867–1936) gave Illinois one of its most famous characters in Mr. Dooley, a homespun philosopher who was the subject of several books: *Mr. Dooley in Peace and War* (1898), *Mr. Dooley's Opinions* (1901), and *Observations by Mr. Dooley* (1902). Contemporary Illinois humorists include JEAN SHEPHERD (1929–1999), who wrote *In God We Trust, All Others Pay Cash* (1966), *A Fistful of Fig Newtons* (1981), and *A Christmas Story* (1983), and *Chicago Daily News* columnist and 1972 winner of the Pulitzer Prize for Commentary (MICHAEL) MIKE ROYKO (1932–1997), who published his Slats Grobnik columns in *Slats Grobnik and Some Other Friends* (1973). Novelist Robert (Lowell) Coover (b. 1932) wrote *Whatever Happened to Gloomy Gus of the Chicago Bears?* (1987), a work of political satire.

The most famous nineteenth-century work of social criticism and cultural analysis was *The Theory of the Leisure Class: An Economic Study of Institutions* (1899) by THORSTEIN (BUNDE) VEBLEN (1857–1929). Many of Veblen's conclusions about the leisure class were based on his observations of Chicago life. (LAURA) JANE ADDAMS (1860–1935), the first American woman to win the Nobel Peace Prize (1931), initiated the American settlement-house movement in Chicago and, with Ellen Gates Starr, founded HULL-HOUSE in 1889. Her writings include *Democracy and Social Ethics* (1902), *The Newer Ideals of Peace* (1907), *Twenty Years at Hull-House* (1910), and *The Second Twenty Years at Hull-House* (1930).

Peoria native Betty Friedan (1921–2006) wrote *The Feminist Mystique* (1963) and other gendered critiques of American culture, sparking and sustaining the second wave of the American women's movement. Two contemporary Illinois fiction writers have turned to social criticism. Sociologist ANDREW M. GREELEY (1928–2013) is the author of *A Stupid, Unjust, and Criminal War: Iraq, 2001–2007* (2007) and *Chicago Catholics and the Struggles within Their Church* (2011). Curtis

White (b. 1951) is the author of *The Middle Mind: Why Americans Don't Think for Themselves* (2003), *The Barbaric Heart: Faith, Money, and the Crisis of Nature* (2009), and other works of cultural critique.

Fiction: The first published novel set in what would become Illinois was written by Gilbert Imlay (1754–1828), a man of many trades, including that of Revolutionary War captain. His travels through the region inspired his novel *The Emigrants* (1793), which employs pastoral conventions in its story of a British family who rebuild their lives on the Edenic Illinois frontier. In 1828 *Western Monthly Review* editor Timothy Flint (1780–1840) published the first Illinois novel by an American, *Life and Adventures of Arthur Clenning*, the story of South Seas castaways who settle in the state.

Fiction set in the years before statehood may be grouped in the following categories: the French explorers, George Rogers Clark, Native Americans, Kaskaskia and southern Illinois, and Fort Dearborn. *This Land Is Ours* (1940) by Louis Zara (1910–2001) presents the story of the exploration and settlement of the Old Northwest, partially set in the Illinois territory.

MARY HARTWELL CATHERWOOD (1847–1902) wrote a series of novels about the French in Illinois, including *The Story of Tonty* (1890) and *Old Kaskaskia* (1893). Later novels include *Antoinette of Illinois: A Story of Early America* (1950) by Edward Davis (1874–1964), *Touched with Fire* (1952) by John Tebbel (1912–2004), *The Wilderness Way* (1954) by Merritt Parmelee Allen (1892–1954), and *The Gilded Torch* (1957) by IOLA FULLER (GOODSPEED McCOY) (1906–1993).

George Rogers Clark is the focus of two early twentieth-century novels: *Conquest: The True Story of Lewis and Clark* (1902) by Eva Emery Dye (1855–1947) and *Long Knives* (1907) by GEORGE CARY EGGLESTON (1839–1911). Among several later novels about Clark are *Waters of the Wilderness* (1941) by Shirley Seifert (1889–1971) and *George Rogers Clark, Soldier and Hero* (1954) by JEANNETTE COVERT NOLAN (1896–1974).

In 1836 John Russell (1793–1863) published "The Piasa: An Indian Tradition of Illinois," a legend first related by Jacques Marquette in 1673. Other fiction about Native Americans includes *Hearts Undaunted: A*

Romance of Four Frontiers (1917), a fictional biography by Eleanor Atkinson (1863–1942) of fur trader and early Chicago settler John Kinzie (1763–1828) and Eleanor Kinzie, who was an Indian captive as a child. Twentieth-century works about Black Hawk include *Thunder on the River* (1949) by Charlton Laird (1901–1984); *Black Hawk* (1957), a sympathetic fictional autobiography by Arthur J. Beckhard (1899–1961); *Sparrow Hawk* (1950) by MERIDEL LE SUEUR (1900–1996); and *The Good Journey* (2001) by Micaela Gilchrist (b. 1962). Fictional works about Kaskaskia and southern Illinois include *Tales and Sketches* (1829) by William Leggett (1801–1839), *Jackknife Summer* (1958) by Ota Lee Russell (1905–1996), and *Wide River, Wide Land* (1976) by William Faherty (1914–2011).

Fort Dearborn, situated on the south bank of the Chicago River, is famous for an 1812 Indian attack on its soldiers and civilians, who had evacuated the fort and were en route to Fort Wayne. Two early fictional treatments of events at Fort Dearborn are *Narrative of the Massacre at Chicago, [Saturday,] August 15, 1812, and of Some Preceding Events* (1844) by Juliette Kinzie (1806–1870) and her later work, *Wau-Bun: The "Early Day" in the North-West* (1856), which influenced future accounts of the Fort Dearborn legend through its favorable treatment of her father-in-law, John Kinzie. Major John Richardson (1796–1852) also produced two fictional accounts of that event: *Wau-Nan-Gee; or, The Massacre at Chicago* (1852), which presented the opposing, pro-military version of the massacre, and *Hardscrabble; or, The Fall of Chicago: A Tale of Indian Warfare* (1856).

Among several twentieth-century fictional treatments of Fort Dearborn are *Shadow of Victory: A Romance of Fort Dearborn* (1903) by Myrtle Reed (1874–1911) and *Old Chicago* (1933) by Mary Hastings Bradley (1882–1976), the latter comprising four novellas about Chicago from the time of Fort Dearborn to 1893. Part of the novel *Wolves against the Moon* (1940) by Julia Altrocchi (1893–1972) covers the Fort Dearborn massacre, as does *Gateway to Empire* (1983) by Allan W. Eckert (1931–2011).

JAMES HALL (1793–1868), an early Illinois editor and author, wrote *Legends of the West* (1832) and *Tales of the Border* (1835). Hall's short story "The Dark Maid of Illinois," collected in the latter volume, is a humorous sketch of a Frenchman's encounter with an Indian princess. "The Indian Hater," included in *Legends of the West,* presents the sinister upshot of the encounter of Indians and whites and was Herman Melville's source for his Indian-hater character in *The Confidence Man* (1857). *The Harpe's Head, a Legend of Kentucky* (1833) is a fictional account of the bloodthirsty frontier outlaws Micajah and Wiley Harpe; it introduces Hank Short, a prototype of Huckleberry Finn.

Mrs. E. D. E. N. Southworth (1819–1899) was a prolific novelist who penned many nineteenth-century narratives of the Illinois frontier; she takes Mark and Rosalie Sutherland of *India: The Pearl of Pearl River* (1856) to Rock River country to homestead in bucolic bliss. Maria Susanna Cummins (1827–1866) depicts the Vaughan family finding the state's pastoral environment redemptive when they move to eastern Illinois in *Mabel Vaughan* (1857). *The Captain of Company K* (1891) by JOSEPH KIRKLAND (1830–1894) is a fictionalized account of Kirkland's Civil War experiences. Other fiction writers in this period cover a variety of topics. John McConnel (1826–1862) wrote three novels: *Talbot and Vernon* (1850), *Grahame; or, Youth and Manhood, a Romance* (1850), and *Glenns, a Family History* (1851). *Banditti of the Prairies* (1850) by Edward Bonney (1807–1864) is set in Rock Island and Nauvoo and provides insight into Mormon history. *Prairie Fire! A Tale of Early Illinois* (1854) by William Bushnell (1823–ca. 1909) takes place in central Illinois. *Barriers Burned Away* (1872) by Edward Roe (1838–1888) describes the 1871 Great Chicago Fire in a novel.

In *A Reader's Guide to Illinois Literature* (1985) James Hurt identifies four main emphases in Illinois fiction since 1915, highlighting the richness and diversity of the state's literature: the coming of modernism, the Chicago tradition, the Chicago anti-tradition, and the contemporary novel (49–57). Hurt discusses "Milk Bottles," published in *Horses and Men* (1923) by SHERWOOD ANDERSON (1876–1941), as an example of Illinois literary modernism. The action of this Chicago short story is slight, taking place in a single evening, and several possible stories exist within the narrative. Hurt connects Anderson's modernist fictional techniques to those in *Dubliners* (1914) by James Joyce (1882–1941) (50). ERNEST (MILLER) HEMINGWAY (1899–1961), the winner of the Pulitzer Prize for Fiction in 1953 and the Nobel Prize in Literature in 1954, is the most famous Illinois modernist, but his home state is only tangentially present in his fiction. The Oak Park native's early Nick Adams stories are set in MICHIGAN before World War I, as are his stories of Nick's return after the war. Another modernist writer, Chicago native JOHN DOS PASSOS (1896–1970), used modernist experimental techniques in *Manhattan Transfer* (1925) and his trilogy *U.S.A.: The 42nd Parallel* (1930), *1919* (1932), and *The Big Money* (1936).

The second emphasis in Illinois fiction after 1915, the Chicago tradition, is a continuation of the naturalism of (HERMAN) THEODORE DREISER (1871–1945) and (BENJAMIN) FRANK(LIN) NORRIS (JR.) (1870–1902). Hurt sees it as characterized by naturalistic elements best exemplified in the works of JAMES T(HOMAS) FARRELL (1904–1979), especially *STUDS LONIGAN: A TRILOGY* (1935): excessive detail, portrayal of life as a war or a jungle, and emphasis on male initiation ending in death or defeat (51–52). Another major Illinois writer in this tradition is NELSON ALGREN (1909–1981), whose *The Man with the Golden Arm* (1949) won the first National Book Award in 1950. His novels include *Somebody in Boots* (1935), *Never Come Morning* (1942), and *The Neon Wilderness* (1947). His *Chicago, City on the Make* (1951) exposes the city's dark, corrupt side. Albert Halper (1904–1984) is a third Chicago-tradition writer; he wrote several novels about industrial Chicago, including *The Chute* (1937) and *The Foundry* (1934). *The Old Bunch* (1937) by Meyer Levin (1905–1981) is set in Chicago during the Depression and recounts the coming of age of several Jewish youths. Meyer also drew on Chicago material for his 1956 novel *Compulsion,* based on the Chicago Leopold and Loeb murder trial.

NATIVE SON (1940) by RICHARD WRIGHT (1908–1960) and *Knock on Any Door* (1947) by WILLARD F. MOTLEY (1909–1965) are significant works in the Chicago tradition by African American writers. Wright's naturalistic novel features Bigger Thomas, tried for and convicted of the murder of his white employer's daughter, although the death was

accidental. Motley's crime novel, also set in Chicago, features protagonist Nick Romano and was made into a major motion picture with the same title in 1949. RONALD L. FAIR (b. 1932) is a third twentieth-century African American writer who focuses on black life in Chicago; his *Hog Butcher* (1966) was adapted for the screen as *Cornbread, Earl and Me* in 1975.

Hurt's third emphasis, the Chicago anti-tradition, rejects Chicago-tradition naturalism. This emphasis is seen in the novels *O Canaan!* (1939) by Waters Turpin (1910–1968), *Maud Martha* (1953) by GWENDOLYN (ELIZABETH) BROOKS (1917–2000), and *THE ADVENTURES OF AUGIE MARCH* (1953) by SAUL (C.) BELLOW (1915–2005), winner of the 1976 Pulitzer Prize for Fiction and the Nobel Prize, as well as in the novels of Chicago Greek life by "HARRY" MARK PETRAKIS (b. 1923). Hurt observes that Bellow's *The Adventures of Augie March* "might well be read as an ironic inversion of the naturalistic novel, a sort of reply to *Studs Lonigan*" (53). He regards Brooks's *Maud Martha* "as the sharpest contrast imaginable to *Studs Lonigan*" (53) and points out the lyric quality, the internal focus, and the lack of a well-defined plot. He asserts that Petrakis, who has been writing about Greek American life in Chicago for five decades, is also a major figure in the Chicago anti-tradition (53). Petrakis's collections of short stories *Pericles on 31st Street* (1965) and *The Waves of Night, and Other Stories* (1969) and his novels *In the Land of Morning* (1973) and *Nick the Greek* (1979) reveal his literary kinship to Brooks and Bellow. *The Twilight of the Ice* (2003) is set in early 1950s Chicago, while the protagonist of *The Orchards of Ithaca* (2004) is a Halstead Street restaurant owner. RAY (DOUGLAS) BRADBURY (1920–2012) is another important writer in the Chicago anti-tradition. Although he is generally regarded as a science-fiction writer, he considers himself a fantasist. Bradbury, like Hemingway and Bellow, was born in Illinois but also has international status; the success of *The Martian Chronicles* (1950) opened the doors of major publishing houses for science-fiction writers.

The fourth emphasis in Illinois literature, operating from 1960 onward, is characterized by complexity reflecting the changing political, social, and cultural scene in Illinois and the nation. The 1960s ushered in the civil rights movement, led by Dr. Martin Luther King Jr. (1929–1968), as well as the sexual revolution and the feminist movement. Hurt argues that contemporary Illinois fiction writers make an almost complete break with the traditions of the past but retain from those traditions a modernist "ironic self-consciousness and the freedom from forms" (55). WILLIAM MAXWELL (JR.) (1908–2000) is Hurt's example of a contemporary Illinois writer. Hurt calls Maxwell's novel *So Long, See You Tomorrow* (1980), reflecting his boyhood in Lincoln, "one of the finest written about Illinois life" (55) for its "rich and sophisticated modernist conception of fiction" (57). He connects the novel with the *Studs Lonigan* trilogy and *Maude Martha* as examples of "a modern Illinois fiction that rises above the academic conception of 'regional' fiction to a genuine and permanent distinction" (57).

The unique blend of comedy, satire, and tragedy by Chicago novelist PETER DE VRIES (1910–1993) illustrates Hurt's idea that post-1960 Illinois literature finds new forms. In fact, Diane Bishop argues in her 1975 master's thesis "Tragic Elements in the Work of Peter De Vries" that a new literary term, "comi-tragedy," best describes De Vries's vision. Set in Chicago, *The Blood of the Lamb* (1961) is at times hilarious and at other times sad to the point of despair. De Vries's special blend of humor and tragedy can be found in novels such as *The Vale of Laughter* (1967), *Into Your Tent I'll Creep* (1971), and *The Glory of the Hummingbird* (1974).

The works of Robert (Lowell) Coover are considered examples of metafiction and fabulation. His widely anthologized short story "The Babysitter" (1969) is a narrative using multiple points of view in which reality and fantasy are so convincingly mixed that at the end the reader is not sure what is real. Coover's novel *The Universal Baseball Association, Inc., J. Henry Waugh, Prop.* (1968) explores the mythic qualities of baseball in the complex mixture of the fantasy life and the real life of the protagonist.

Richard Powers (b. 1957), LUIS J. RODRÍGUEZ (b. 1954), Ward Just (b. 1935), Robert Olen Butler (b. 1945), STUART DYBEK (b. 1942), and NORBERT BLEI (1935–2013) are among the state's important contemporary fiction writers. Powers, of the University of Illinois, has published several novels, including the much-honored *The Gold Bug Variations* (1991), *The Echo Maker* (2006), and *Generosity: An Enhancement* (2009). *Gain* (1998) is set in rural Illinois. Ward Just, a Waukegan native, has written eighteen novels, most recently *Rodin's Debutante* (2011), set in a boy's school in Chicago's suburbs. Robert Butler, winner of the 1993 Pulitzer Prize for Fiction for his story collection *A Good Scent from a Strange Mountain* (1992), is the author of twenty-one fiction works, including *Wabash* (1987), a Depression-era labor novel in a downstate steel town resembling his native Granite City, a location that also furnishes a partial setting for *They Whisper* (1994). Dybek and Blei are Chicago natives who use that city and its environs in their fiction. Dybek writes about his Chicago childhood neighborhood in his story collections *Childhood and Other Neighborhoods* (1980) and *The Coast of Chicago* (1990). Blei makes similar use of Chicago-area settings in *Adventures in American Literature* (1982) and *The Ghost of Sandburg's Phizzog, and Other Stories* (1986).

Village and Small-Town Novels: Several small-town novels use central Illinois as their locale. *A Paper City* (1879) by DAVID ROSS LOCKE (1833–1888) takes place in "New Canton" and satirizes the era's real estate bubble. EDWARD EGGLESTON (1837–1902), usually associated with INDIANA, wrote *The Graysons: A Story of Illinois* (1888), a central Illinois romance in which Abraham Lincoln defends Tom Grayson, who is wrongfully accused of murder. Mary Hartwell Catherwood blended romanticism with realism in *The Story of an Illinois Town* (1897). *The Valley of the Shadows: Recollections of the Lincoln Country, 1858–1863* (1909) by Francis Grierson (1848–1927) is a memoir employing fictional techniques in its portrayal of the central Illinois frontier as an Edenic garden, linking back to nineteenth-century novels and travel narratives with the same theme. DON(ALD ROBERT PERRY) MARQUIS (1878–1937) evoked his Walnut upbringing in his first novel, *Danny's Own Story* (1912), and Ray Bradbury set one of his best-loved novels, *Dandelion Wine* (1957), in "Greentown," Illinois, modeled on Waukegan. Like *ADVENTURES OF HUCKLEBERRY FINN* (London 1884;

New York 1885), it is a book about children for both children and adults. Although the focus is on the adventures and initiation of adolescent Douglas Spaulding, the spiritual wisdom he gains in the summer of his twelfth year is applicable to all.

Farm Novels: Joseph Kirkland's *Zury: The Meanest Man in Spring County* (1887) is perhaps the best-known nineteenth-century Illinois FARM novel. The novel is noted for its dialect, its descriptions of the Illinois landscape as Edenic, and its fully developed, convincing protagonist, Zury Prouder, all of which give the novel authenticity. Kirkland's sequel to *Zury*, *The McVeys: An Episode* (1888), the story of Zury's marriage to New England schoolteacher Anne Sparrow, takes place in "Springville" in central Illinois. In *The Middle Western Farm Novel in the Twentieth Century* (1965) Roy Meyer says that in *Zury* Kirkland asserts a theme prominent in twentieth-century farm novels: the rewards in store for those who persevere through the hardships of settling the frontier (28). Four such novels are listed in the annotated bibliography of Middle-Western farm fiction appended to Meyer's study: *Long Furrows* (1935) by Dora Aydelotte (1878–1968), *The Memoirs of Dunstan Barr* (1959) by Jonathan Fields, *East of Eden* (1925) by Lynn Montross (1895–1961), and *American Years* (1938) by Harold Sinclair (1907–1966).

Historical Fiction: Several Illinois writers at the turn of the twentieth century focused on the past, writing Illinois adventure novels that can be called historical romances. They provide valuable insight into life in the early times after statehood, the years leading up to the Civil War, and the Reconstruction period. Examples include *The Prairie Schooner: A Story of the Black Hawk War* (1900) by William Barton (1861–1930), *Diane: A Romance of the Icarian Settlement on the Mississippi River* (1904) by Katharine Holland Brown (1876–1931), and *The Boss of Little Arcady* (1905) by Harry Wilson (1867–1939).

Urban Novels: The high tide of early Illinois literature occurred in Chicago at the turn of the twentieth century. "Chicago as Metaphor" by DAVID D(ANIEL) ANDERSON (1924–2011), *Great Lakes Review* 1.1 (1974): 3–15, captures the spirit of the CHICAGO RENAISSANCE and reflects Chicago's status as the literary center of America from 1890 to 1915.

Chicago was a prime example of unprecedented urban growth in the years after the Civil War and the problems that followed from that growth, including the 1886 Haymarket riot and the 1894 Pullman strike. It provided a case study in the social Darwinism prevalent in the business world. See also CHICAGO

Many novelists attempted a realistic portrayal of life in Chicago between 1890 and 1915, practicing the sociological realism developed by WILLIAM DEAN HOWELLS (1837–1920). *The Cliff-Dwellers* (1893) by HENRY BLAKE FULLER (1857–1929) is one of the first critical treatments of big-city life; its title ironically contrasts the businessmen who work in Chicago's sterile concrete canyons with a more authentic Native American culture. Fuller's *With the Procession* (1895), a study of a businessman's decline amid his upwardly mobile counterparts, contains the famous characterization of Chicago as "the only great city in the world to which all its citizens have come for the one common, avowed object of making money" (248). *The Pit: A Story of Chicago* (1903) by Frank Norris takes the reader inside the city's commodities market. However, the most famous Chicago novel of this era is THE JUNGLE (1906) by UPTON (BEALL) SINCLAIR (JR.) (1878–1968), which depicted the meatpacking industry so graphically that instead of galvanizing socialist revolution, it led readers to focus on unscrupulous, unsanitary meatpacking and to demand the 1906 Pure Food and Drug Act.

ROBERT (WELCH) HERRICK (1868–1938), who was lured to the University of Chicago by William Raney Harper in his raid on eastern intellectuals, was one of the most prolific Chicago novelists of this period. Herrick's 1926 novel *Chimes* is a fictionalized account of his years as a professor there. His protagonists included lawyers, physicians, businessmen, architects, and professors, and his novels addressed almost every social issue of the era. *The Memoirs of an American Citizen* (1905) can be read as a companion piece to *The Jungle*. Unlike Sinclair's working-class protagonist, Jurgis Rudkus, Herrick's Van Harrington rises to success and becomes one of the top movers in the meatpacking industry. Other Herrick novels are *The Gospel of Freedom* (1898) and *The Web of Life*

(1900), a grittily realistic portrait of late nineteenth-century Chicago.

A fourth major Chicago novelist, EDNA FERBER (1885–1968), moved from Michigan to Illinois at age twelve. A prolific fiction and drama writer, Ferber introduced her most memorable character, traveling saleslady Emma McChesney, in 1911. Two of her three collections of Emma McChesney short stories, *Roast Beef Medium* (1913) and *Emma McChesney and Company* (1915), are set partly in Chicago; her 1925 Pulitzer Prize–winning novel *So Big* (1924) takes place in the Near South suburbs.

Other realistic Chicago novels during this period include *The Man of the Hour* (1905) by ALICE FRENCH (1850–1934), writing as Octave Thanet; *By Bread Alone* (1901) by Isaac Friedman (1870–1931); *He Knew Lincoln* (1907) by Ida Tarbell (1857–1944); and four novels by Opie Read: *The Colossus* (1893), *Judge Elbridge* (1899), *The Mystery of Margaret* (1907), and *The New Mr. Howerson* (1914). Much of Sherwood Anderson's first two novels, *Windy McPherson's Son* (1916) and *Marching Men* (1917), takes place in Chicago, where Anderson served his literary apprenticeship.

As Timothy Spears observes in *Chicago Dreaming: Midwesterners and the City, 1871–1919* (2005), a significant subset of Chicago novels of this era consists of books featuring a young protagonist from a SMALL TOWN coming to make a career and a new self in Chicago. Journalist ELIA W(ILKINSON) PEATTIE (1862–1935), whose writings on Jane Addams and the settlement-house movement were responsible for conveying information about settlement-house work to the general public, also published *The Precipice* (1914), which takes its protagonist, Kate Barrington, to Chicago, where she becomes involved in social welfare work. *The Song of the Lark* (1915) by WILLA CATHER (1873–1947) relates the story of Thea Kronborg from Moonstone, Colorado, who revises her goal of teaching music to become an opera star under the city's cultural influence. Rose Dutcher, in *Rose of Dutcher's Coolly* (1895) by (HANNIBAL) HAMLIN GARLAND (1860–1940), moves to Chicago to become a poet but meets and marries her sweetheart there and settles for a less glamorous life. Dreiser's *SISTER CARRIE* (1900) and *Jennie Gerhardt* (1911) focus on the plight of working-class women in Chicago and were notorious in their day for Dreiser's explicit account of the way sex facilitates Carrie and Jennie's upward mobility. *The Briary-Bush* (1921), the sequel to *Moon-Calf* (1920) by FLOYD DELL (1887–1969), takes protagonist Felix Fay from his hometown, Port Royal, modeled on Davenport, IOWA, to Chicago, where he becomes involved in settlement-house work and literary journalism.

Lesbian and Gay Literature: Most lesbian and gay literature from Illinois has come from Chicago, whose lesbian and gay community has deep historical roots. HENRY BLAKE FULLER (1857–1929), an important figure in REALISM AND NATURALISM and the early Chicago Renaissance, wrote *Bertram Cope's Year* (1919), the first gay-themed novel by a major American writer. In 1924 in Chicago, Henry Gerber (1892–1972) started the Society for Human Rights, the first gay rights organization in American history; the society's short-lived journal, *Friendship and Freedom*, was the nation's first gay periodical. Lesbian and gay writers associated with Chicago have included MARGARET C. ANDERSON (1886–1973), founder of the *LITTLE REVIEW*, Nella Larsen (1891–1964), Mark Turbyfill (1896–1991), Willard F. Motley, JAMES (OTIS) PURDY (1914–2009), LORRAINE (VIVIAN) HANSBERRY (1930–1965), Jon-Henri Damski (1936–1997), Linnea Johnson (b. 1946), Carol Anshaw (b. 1946), Jim Elledge (b. 1950), Robert Alexander (b. 1952), Ana Castillo (b. 1953), Rane Arroyo (1954–2010), Robert Rodi (b. 1956), and Achy Obejas (b. 1956). See LESBIAN, GAY, BISEXUAL, TRANSGENDER, AND QUEER LITERATURE.

Writers from elsewhere in Illinois have included two well-known authors of lesbian pulp novels of the 1950s and 1960s. Ann Weldy (b. 1932), originally of Joliet, published several novels as Ann Bannon. The first of these, *Odd Girl Out* (1957), is based on her life in a sorority at the University of Illinois. *Whisper Their Love* (1957) and other novels by Valerie Taylor (1913–1997), born Velma Nacella Young in Aurora, are generally set in Chicago. Edmund White (b. 1940), a key figure in the development of fiction by and about gay men, spent part of his teenage years in Evanston and fictionalized that period in his novel *A Boy's Own Story* (1982). In addition to stories and mystery fiction, Martha Miller (b. 1947) of Springfield has published *Tales from the Levee* (2005), a novel-in-stories about a district in Springfield where lesbian and gay culture thrived during the late 1960s and early 1970s.

Gay-themed young-adult novels from Illinois include *Love Drugged* (2010) by James Klise (b. 1967), about a high school boy in Chicago going to extremes to hide his homosexuality, and the best-selling *Will Grayson, Will Grayson* (2010), by John Green (b. 1977) and David Levithan (b. 1972), about two teenage suburban Chicago boys with the same name, one gay but closeted and the other straight, with a talented, self-confident gay friend. An older work also discussed in this context is *The Folded Leaf* (1945) by William Maxwell, about a young man, a student at the University of Illinois, who hero-worships his friend, a handsome, athletic classmate.

Poetry: From 1831 to 1846 the *Sangamo Journal* published poems by a poet who signed them as "H." John Hallwas edited and collected many of these poems in *The Poems of H.: The Lost Poet of Lincoln's Springfield* (1982). Although William Cullen Bryant (1794–1878) was not an Illinois citizen, he must be mentioned here because his poem "The Prairies" was inspired by his visit to Jacksonville in 1832. The description of Illinois as an Eden in Bryant's other Illinois poem, "The Hunter of the Prairies," may have influenced the folksong "El-a-noy." Eliza R. Snow (1804–1887), who wrote about the Mormon experience in MISSOURI and Illinois, lived briefly in Nauvoo and then left for Utah. Lucy Larcom (1824–1893), another poet of that era who sojourned in Illinois, used this experience in *Similitudes, from the Ocean and the Prairie* (1853). Later nineteenth-century Illinois poets included the brother of William Cullen Bryant, John Howard Bryant (1807–1902), who wrote several poems about Lincoln and a famous poem titled "Temperance" (1840); JOHN HAY (1838–1905), famous, in addition to his diplomatic career, for his collection of poems, *Pike County Ballads, and Other Pieces* (1871); and EUGENE FIELD (SR.) (1850–1895), the most popular Illinois poet in the 1880s, who published much of his verse in his *Chicago Daily News* column "Sharps and Flats." His fame rests primarily on children's poems,

including "Little Boy Blue" (1888) and "Wynken, Blynken, and Nod" (1889). The poems of University of Chicago professor WILLIAM VAUGHN MOODY (1869–1910), such as "An Ode in Time of Hesitation" (1912) and "On a Soldier Fallen in the Philippines" (1919), frequently appeared in American literature anthologies.

Poetry in Illinois at the turn of the century was not particularly noteworthy. HARRIET MONROE (1860–1936) wrote the unremarkable "The Columbian Ode" (1893), the commemorative poem for Chicago's World's Columbian Exposition, but she made much greater contributions to the genre in 1912 when she founded *POETRY: A MAGAZINE OF VERSE*. Her magazine was especially important in providing an outlet and editorial support for Illinois poets like 1919 and 1951 Pulitzer Prize for Poetry winner CARL (AUGUST) SANDBURG (1878–1967), (NICHOLAS) VACHEL LINDSAY (1879–1931), and EDGAR LEE MASTERS (1868–1950), as well as for other American poets like Robert (Lee) Frost (1874–1963), T(HOMAS) S(TEARNS). ELIOT (1888–1965), and Ezra Pound (1885–1972) and leading European poets, including William Butler Yeats (1865–1939).

Lindsay, Sandburg, and Masters were all honored by *Poetry* magazine with the Helen Haire Levenson Prize during its early years. Lindsay was famous for his travels, performances, and lectures. His experiences in his native Springfield are reflected in *The Village Magazine* (1910) and *The Golden Book of Springfield* (1920); he also drew on Illinois material for his tribute to Illinois governor John Peter Altgeld, "The Eagle That Is Forgotten" (1913), as well as "Abraham Lincoln Walks at Midnight" (1914).

Sandburg, sometimes compared to Walt Whitman (1819–1892) for his democratic orientation and oral poetic structuring, wrote widely of Illinois and Midwestern experience. Urban scenes inspired *CHICAGO POEMS* (1916), Sandburg's first volume of mature poetry, but "Prairie Waters at Night," from *Cornhuskers* (1918), and other poems set in rural Illinois are also significant.

Masters's *SPOON RIVER ANTHOLOGY* (1915), a who's who of alienated citizens depicting the narrowness of small-town life in many of the collection's poems, is one of the most important books in Illinois literary history, reflecting Masters's youth in Petersburg and Lewistown and chronicling the decline of the Jeffersonian dream in the Midwest. DAVE (PEARSON) ETTER (1928–2015) presents a more balanced view of downstate small-town life in *Alliance, Illinois* (1983), a collection of contemporary dramatic monologues recalling Masters's landmark work.

Contemporary downstate Illinois poetry reflects activity from five major regions. The southern region has Carbondale at its center. Among those associated with that region are Rodney Jones (b. 1950), whose volumes include *Transparent Gestures* (1989) and *Kingdom of the Instant* (2002), and Eugene B. Redmond (b. 1937), a noted scholar and Poet Laureate of East St. Louis.

The central region is dominated by Champaign-Urbana, Springfield, Bloomington-Normal, and Charleston. Hope native MARK VAN DOREN (1894–1972) won a Pulitzer Prize in 1940 for his *Collected Poems*. The University of Illinois, located in Urbana-Champaign, published two volumes of verse, *Illini Poetry: 1918–1923* (1923) and *Illini Poetry: 1924–1929* (1929), edited by Bruce Weirick, who acquired a large amount of Sandburg memorabilia for the school's library. Other poets who achieved distinction at the university are Michael Van Walleghen (b. 1938) and Laurence Lieberman (b. 1935). Another prominent group from the Champaign-Urbana area was the Red Herring Poets, organized in 1974 by Robert Bensen (b. 1947), with Kathryn Kerr (b. 1946) and Ron Deverman (b. 1950) as major participants. Eastern Illinois University in Charleston has been home to Bruce Guernsey (b. 1944), John Guzlowski (b. 1948), and David Radavich (b. 1949), a poet and playwright now living in North Carolina.

Decatur is home to a group called Pomoja, which reads and performs the work of African American poets, and the Blue Pike Poets, which includes Michael Johnson (b. 1954) and Carol Massat (b. 1954). Still another group was associated with Millikin University, most prominently Dan Guillory (b. 1944), author of *The Lincoln Poems* (2008). The Springfield area has contributed significantly to Illinois poetry. The best-known contemporary poet from this area is JOHN (IGNATIUS) KNOEPFLE (b. 1923), who has published over twenty books, including *Rivers*

into Islands (1965), *poems from the sangamon* (1985), and *A Prayer against Famine, and Other Irish Poems* (2004). Two other leading poets from the area are Osmond Guy (1933–1974) and David Curry (b. 1942).

In the Bloomington-Normal area, William Wantling (1933–1974) published several books of poetry, among them *The Awakening* (1967) and *San Quentin's Stranger* (1973). James McGowan (b. 1932) brought distinction to Illinois Wesleyan University with *Each Other—Where We Are* (1980). Joanne M. Riley (b. 1959) published *Earth Tones* (1979) and *Pacing the Moon* (1985). Lucia Getsi (b. 1944), at Illinois State University, has published such books as *Teeth Mother Letters* (1984) and *Intensive Care* (1992). Poems by Forrest Robinson (b. 1931) can be found in *The Champaign Letters* (1979) and *After the Fire* (1989). *Family Scraps: Ten Poems in the Voice of Parley Porter* by Duane Taylor (b. 1950) was published in 1986. Bradley University's Kevin Stein (b. 1954), an Illinois poet laureate, has published several books, including *American Ghost Roses* (2005) and *Sufficiency of the Actual* (2008). David Pichaske (b. 1943), formerly of Bradley University, is an editor, scholar, publisher, and poet now based in MINNESOTA; his work includes *Jubilee Diary*, a collection of poems published in 1982, and *The Father Poems* (2005).

The northern region's main centers of activity are the Quad Cities, De Kalb, and Rockford. Quad Cities poets include Kathleen L. Cox (b. 1938), Michael Sheridan (b. 1943), and Anthony Kallas (b. 1947). At Northern Illinois University LUCIEN STRYK (1924–2013) published *Selected Poems* (1976) and *Collected Poems: 1953–1983* (1984) and edited two anthologies, *Heartland: Poets of the Midwest* (1967) and *Heartland II* (1975); the former includes the work of Illinois poets Dave Etter, 1997 Pulitzer Prize for Poetry winner Lisel Mueller (b. 1924), John Frederick Nims (1913–1999), and John Knoepfle, as well as that of canonical Midwestern poets from other states: JAMES (ARLINGTON) WRIGHT (1927–1980), THOMAS McGRATH (1916–1990), and JAMES HEARST (1900–1983). *Heartland II* includes poems by MICHAEL ANANIA (b. 1939), Ralph Mills Jr. (1931–2007), David Curry, and Michael Sheridan. Also residing in the De Kalb area is Dave Etter. Noted for his strong sense of place and his command of the spoken idiom, Etter has published thirty works of poetry, including *How High the Moon* (1996), *Looking for Sheena Easton* (2004), and *Dandelions* (2010). Rockford-area poets include Christine Swanberg (b. 1949), who wrote *Tonight on This Late Road* (1984), and Todd Moore (b. 1937), noted for *The Devil's Backbone* (2001).

Since 1915 Chicago has been the home of many accomplished Illinois poets, several of whom were closely associated with *Poetry* magazine. A major poetry movement in the 1920s and 1930s was the Chicago school of poets; prominent in this group was George Dillon (1906–1968), editor of *Poetry* from 1937 to 1942, whose *The Flowering Stone* (1931) won a Pulitzer Prize in 1932. Another member of the group, KARL (JAY) SHAPIRO (1913–2000), the editor of *Poetry* from 1950 to 1956, won a Pulitzer Prize in 1945 for *V-Letter, and Other Poems*. Elder Olson (1909–1992) of the University of Chicago published his *Collected Poems* in 1963 and *Last Poems* in 1984. John Frederick Nims left Chicago to join the University of Illinois faculty; his *Selected Poems* was published in 1982.

Gwendolyn Brooks's Chicago South Side is reflected in her first poetry collection, *A STREET IN BRONZEVILLE* (1945), which contains many of her landmark poems. She was a popular speaker and a generous philanthropist during her lengthy term as Illinois's third Poet Laureate and as Consultant in Poetry to the Library of Congress. Chicano poet and activist Carlos Cumpián (b. 1953) has published books such as *Armadillo Charm* (1996) and has served as an editor for March/Abrazo Press, which specializes in Latino/Latina and Native American poetry. Li-Young Lee (b. 1957), now living in Chicago, has received many awards for his volumes of poetry, among them *The Winged Seed: A Remembrance* (1995) and *Behind My Eyes* (2008). Lisel Mueller, whose family emigrated from Germany when she was an adolescent, has published many books since her first, *Dependencies*, appeared in 1965. Mueller's *Alive Together: New and Selected Poems* (1996) won the 1997 Pulitzer Prize for Poetry. MAXINE CHERNOFF (b. 1952) was born and educated in Chicago but moved to California. She is a short-story writer, novelist, and poet whose publications include *A Plain Grief* (1991) and *American Heaven* (1996). Simone Muench (b.

1969) of Lewis University won the 2000 Marianne Moore Prize for Poetry with *The Air Lost in Breathing* (2000), and her *Lampblack and Ash* (2003) won the Kathryn A. Morton Prize for 2004.

Two Chicana poets from Chicago have won national honors. SANDRA CISNEROS (b. 1954), author and winner of the American Book Award for *THE HOUSE ON MANGO STREET* (1984), has published three books of poems: *Bad Boys* (1980), *My Wicked, Wicked Ways* (1987), and *Loose Woman* (1994). Ana Castillo, also a winner of the American Book Award and author of *The Mixquiahuala Letters* (1986), has published several books of poems, including *Otro Canto* (1977), *Women Are Not Roses* (1984), and *I Ask the Impossible* (2001).

Illinois has been served by four poets laureate: Howard Austin (1886–1962), Carl Sandburg, Gwendolyn Brooks, and Kevin Stein, the current Poet Laureate of Illinois. In 1985 Gwendolyn Brooks was named consultant in poetry to the Library of Congress, the predecessor title to Poet Laureate of the United States. Earlier Carl Sandburg was offered the same position but declined.

Drama: In 1847 the first Chicago theatre was built to host traveling stock companies. The years from 1870 to 1895 saw theatres in that city mushroom as Chicago formed the nucleus for early twentieth-century theatre in Illinois, anchored by Maurice Browne and Ellen Van Volkenberg's Chicago Little Theatre and Laura Dainty Pelham's Hull-House Players. Founded in 1912, the Chicago Little Theatre performed classics such as *The Trojan Women*, as well as plays by Strindberg and local playwrights, including ALICE (ERYA) GERSTENBERG (1885–1972), who wrote over three dozen plays and founded the Junior League Children's Theatre in 1921 and the Playwrights Theatre in 1922. Her *Overtones* (1913) was an early staging of the unconscious and a forerunner of *Strange Interlude* (1928) by Eugene (Gladstone) O'Neill (1888–1953). The Lake Forest Players, founded by Mary (Reynolds) Aldis (1872–1949), also provided a stage for Chicago playwrights; Aldis wrote, produced, and acted in her own plays, the best known of which is *Mrs. Pat and the Law* (1915). The best-known dramatist of this period was William Vaughn Moody, whose plays include *The Masque of*

Judgment (1900), *The Fire-Bringer* (1904), and *The Great Divide* (1909). His *The Faith Healer* (1909) is considered the first major play set in the Midwest. Robert Herrick, Don Marquis, and George Ade were also active turn-of-the-century playwrights.

A prolific playwright for New York's Liberal Club and the Provincetown Players, Barry native Floyd Dell adapted his novel *An Unmarried Father* (1927) for the Broadway stage. Set in Chicago, *Little Accident* (1928) became a hit, running for 289 performances. Another big stage hit in 1928 was *The Front Page* by BEN HECHT (1894–1964) and CHARLES (GORDON) MACARTHUR (1895–1956), based on their experiences as Chicago reporters. For the first three decades of the twentieth century, Bloomington's Rachel Crothers (1878–1958) was a prolific and successful Broadway playwright, director, and producer whose plays, such as *He and She* (1920) and *Mary the Third* (1923), explored gender and generational conflicts among the upper middle class. During the Depression the Federal Theatre Project's Midwest Play Bureau was headquartered in Chicago and was directed from 1936 to 1938 by Pulitzer Prize–winning playwright SUSAN KEATING GLASPELL (1876–1948); the Negro unit of the bureau debuted *Big White Fog* by Chicagoan Theodore Ward (1902–1983) in 1938. Although Robert Emmett Sherwood (1896–1955) was not an Illinois writer, he deserves mention here for his play *Abe Lincoln in Illinois* (1938).

Illinois African American playwrights include LANGSTON (JAMES MERCER) HUGHES (1902–1967), who founded the Skyloft Players in Chicago in 1941, where he mounted his musical, *The Sun Do Move* (1942). *A RAISIN IN THE SUN* (1959) by Lorraine Hansberry, set in South Side Chicago and one of the most important and successful plays of the twentieth century, takes place on the eve of a decade of great social change in American life. In the play Walter Lee, Lena, and Beneatha Younger achieve a decisive family victory against racism, but they must pursue their individual dreams in an atmosphere of changes coming soon. MELVIN VAN PEEBLES (b. 1932), a playwright and filmmaker of international status, is significant in Illinois literature because his FILM *Sweet Sweetback's Baadasssss Song* (1971) was written in response to the deaths of Black Pan-

ther Party leaders Mark Clark and Fred Hampton, who were killed in a 1969 Chicago police raid.

DAVID (ALAN) MAMET (b. 1947) and SAM(UEL) SHEPARD (ROGERS III) (b. 1943) are two internationally known contemporary playwrights from the Chicago area. Mamet served a lengthy theatre apprenticeship in Chicago and used settings in that city for *AMERICAN BUFFALO* (1977), *Sexual Perversity in Chicago* (1978), and *Glengarry Glen Ross* (1984), for which he won a 1984 Pulitzer Prize. Shepard has won eleven Obies over the course of his theatre career; his play most closely connected to Illinois, *Buried Child,* won a Pulitzer Prize in 1979. The Pulitzer Prize–winning *Proof* (2001) by David Auburn (b. 1970) is set in Chicago, as is the 2011 Pulitzer Prize winner *Clybourne Park* (2010) by Bruce Norris (b. 1960), evoking *A Raisin in the Sun* in its exploration of fifty years of race relations in the neighborhood where the Younger family came to live.

Illinois's vibrant contemporary theatre scene nurtures both emerging and established playwrights. Bloomington's Heartland Theatre, founded in 1986, offers a statewide playwriting competition through its Emerging Illinois Playwrights Project. Timberlake Playhouse in Mt. Carroll has been hosting summer playwriting labs since 2001, and Fox Valley Repertoire in St. Charles gives new playwrights the opportunity to develop new work through its summer festivals.

Chicago's many theatres, companies, and collectives have been a major source of support for Illinois playwrights and other Midwestern dramatists. One of the best known is Steppenwolf Theatre Company, which has been producing Midwestern classics such as *The Fifth of July* (1978) and *The Glass Menagerie* (1944) since 1974. Chicago's Goodman Theatre, through its New Works Development Department, commissions plays, sponsors concert readings of original work through its New Stages Series, and mounts the world premiere of a new play each year. Chicago Dramatists, led by resident playwright Keith Huff (b. 1959), has been developing new playwrights and plays since 1979 through workshops, readings, classes, and special programs. In 2009 Huff's Chicago police drama *A Steady Rain* (2007) was mounted on Broadway, starring Hugh Jackman and Daniel Craig. A recent play is *The Detective's Wife* (2011).

David Rush (b. 1940), professor emeritus of the playwriting program at Southern Illinois University at Carbondale and a resident playwright at Chicago Dramatists, has written over twenty-five plays and musicals, drawing on Illinois history for *Leander Stillwell* (1995), about an Illinois boy who joins the Union army, and *The Prophet of Bishop Hill* (1999), which enacts the conflict between Swedish immigrant Erik Janson and the utopian community he founded in that western Illinois town. Plays by Rush set in Chicago include *Dapples and Greys* (1997), *Police Deaf Near Far* (2000), and *Cuttings* (2003). Bloomington native Kellie Powell (b. 1983) is an actor, director, and playwright with nineteen plays and seventeen productions to her credit. *Bargaining* (2007) begins and ends with scenes set in Chicago.

Juvenile Literature: IRENE HUNT (1902–2001), a native of Pontiac, set two Newbery Award–winning books in Illinois: *Across Five Aprils* (1964) and *Up a Road Slowly* (1966). *Class Ring* (1951), *Boy Trouble* (1953), and *One of the Crowd* (1961) are works for teens by Rosamond du Jardin (1902–1963). Jerome Brooks (1931–2004) published six young-adult novels, including *Naked in Winter* (1990) and *Knee Holes* (1992). Raymond Bial (b. 1948) has written twenty-five books for children, including *County Fair* (1992) and *Amish Home* (1993). Richard Peck (b. 1934) has written many books for children and young adults, among them *A Long Way from Chicago* (1999), a Newbery Honor winner in which two siblings journey to rural Illinois each summer to visit their eccentric grandmother. Peck won the Newbery Medal in 2001 for *A Year down Yonder;* a recent book is *Secrets at Sea* (2011). Jim Aylesworth (b. 1943) has written more than thirty children's books, including *Tale of Tricky Fox* (2001) and *Naughty Little Monkeys* (2003). Blue Balliett, the pseudonym of Elizabeth Balliett (b. 1955), won the 2004 Edgar Award, Juvenile division, for *Chasing Vermeer* (2004) and followed that juvenile mystery with *Wright 3* (2006), *The Calder Game* (2008), and *The Danger Box* (2010).

Illinois children's books include Newbery Honor winner *On My Honor* (1986) by Marion Dane Bauer (b. 1938), *Color Me Dark* (2000) by Patricia McKissack (b. 1944), *Project Mulberry* (2005) by Linda Sue Park (b. 1960), and *Deliver Us from Normal* (2005) and its sequel, *Far from Normal* (2006), by Kate Klise (b. 1963). Dorothy Haas (1924–2007), a prolific juvenile-fiction writer, published an extensive bibliography of this genre in *A Reader's Guide to Illinois Literature.*

Popular Literature:
Mystery and Detective Fiction: Early Illinois writers of MYSTERY AND DETECTIVE FICTION include Robert Casey (1890–1962), who wrote *The Secret of 37 Hardy Street* (1929), *The Secret of the Bungalow* (1930), *The Third Owl* (1934), and *Hot Ice* (1933); Milton Ozaki (1913–1989), who wrote *Dressed to Kill* (1954) and *A Time for Murder* (1956); and Marvin Albert (1924–1996), whose *Party Girl* was published in 1958. Prolific novelist, playwright, and screenwriter VERA CASPARY (1904–1987) is best known for *Laura* (1943), which was made into a motion picture the following year. See FILM for other movies made in the state, especially Chicago. Another prolific writer was Ralph McInerny (1929–2010) with twenty-one novels, including *The Grass Widow* (1983) and, under the pseudonym Monica Quill, *Let Us Prey* (1982). McInerny gave this genre two famous characters in Father Dowling and Sister Mary Teresa, who later rose to television fame. Andrew M. Greeley is another popular crime writer. His Blackie Ryan series, which includes *The Bishop and the Missing L Train* (2000), *The Bishop Goes to the University* (2003), and *The Bishop at the Lake* (2007), features a priest-detective who solves mysteries in Chicago and abroad. Other crime-genre writers are Ross Spencer (1921–1998), whose fourteen novels include *Monastery Nightmare* (1986) and *The Devereaux File* (1990); and Eugene Izzi (1953–1996), whose ten novels written under the pseudonym Nick Gaitano include *Bad Guys* (1988) and *Special Victims* (1994). Attorney Scott Turow (b. 1949) sets his crime novels in Chicago; his *Presumed Innocent* (1987) was made into a film. Other crime novels by Turow include *The Burden of Proof* (1990), *Pleading Guilty* (1993), *The Laws of Our Fathers* (1996), and *Innocent* (2010), the sequel to *Presumed Innocent*. See also MYSTERY AND DETECTIVE FICTION.

Several Illinois crime writers have created memorable female protagonists. Eleanor M. Taylor Bland (1944–2010), an African American mystery writer from Waukegan, wrote twelve novels, including *Windy City Dying* (2002) and *A Cold and Silent Dying* (2004), several of which feature African American female police detective Marti McCallister. SARA PARETSKY (b. 1947) often has V. I. Warshawski do her detecting in the Chicago business world; her novels include *Indemnity Only* (1982), *Tunnel Vision* (1994), *Hardball* (2009), and *Body Work* (2010). Cassidy McCabe solves her mysteries in Oak Park, where her creator, Alex Matthews (b. 1940) resides, while Skye Dennison is the detective protagonist of the Scumble River series by Morris native Denise Swanson (b. 1956).

Dime Novels: A number of DIME NOVELS have been written by Illinois natives or have been set in the state. *The Frontier Scout; or, The Young Ranger's Life Mystery* (1865) by James L. Bowen (1842–1919) and its sequel, *Scouting Dave; or, The Winnebago Renegade* (1865), both concern the Black Hawk War. *The On-the-Wing Detectives; or, Bolly Blair's Grand Exposition: A Romance of Chicago and the Depworth Millions* (1891) by Leon Lewis (1833–1920) takes place in that city. *Tim, the Scout; or, Caught in His Own Toils: A Tale of Tecumseh's Time* (1867) by Charles Dunning Clark (1843–1892) is partially set in northeastern Illinois. *Chicago Charlie, the Columbian Detective; or, The Hawks of the Lakeside League: A Story of the World's Fair* (1893) and *Chicago Charlie's Diamond Dash; or, Trapping the Tunnel Thieves: A Story of the White City* (1893) are both by John H. Whitson (1854–1936), writing under the pseudonym A. K. Sims. George C. Kelly (1849–1895) wrote *Tracked to Chicago; or, Thad Burr's Great Trunk Mystery* (1894) under the pseudonym Harold Payne.

Romance Novels: Chicago's Patricia Rosemoor (b. 1947) has written over eighty books, including fifty in the Harlequin Intrigue series; two of her titles are *Silent Sea* (1994) and *Velvet Ropes* (2004). Susan Carroll (b. 1952) writes historical romances, including *The Dark Queen* (2005) and *Twilight of a Queen* (2009). Springfield's award-winning novelist Dee Henderson (b. 1966) wrote the O'Malley series of romantic suspense novels, including *The Guardian* (2001) and *The*

Rescuer (2003), as well as the Uncommon Heroes series of military romance novels, including *True Devotion* (2005) and *True Valor* (2005). In 2002 *The Guardian* won the Christy Award, Romance category. Native Chicagoan Angie Daniels (b. 1968), who won the 2003 Romance in Color Reviewer's Choice Award, wrote, among others, *Love Uncovered* (2005) and *The Playboy's Proposition* (2008). Sylvia Shults (b. 1968), a Bloomington native who now lives in Pekin, writes fiction and romance novels, including *Timeless Embrace* (2007) and *Ghosts of the Illinois River* (2010).

Science Fiction and Fantasy: Although most SCIENCE FICTION by Illinois writers occurs in the future and outside Illinois, the state has produced some impressive writers in that genre. Perhaps the earliest is Edgar Rice Burroughs (1875–1950), who wrote eleven books in his Martian series, beginning with *A Princess of Mars* (1912). *The Sinful Ones* (1953), by Fritz Leiber (1910–1992), takes place in Chicago in the 1940s. *The Martian Chronicles* (1950) and *Fahrenheit 451* (1953) are two classic Ray Bradbury science-fiction works.

Peoria's PHILIP JOSÉ FARMER (1918–2009) wrote several unique science-fiction works and is known for his Riverworld series. In *Venus on the Half-Shell* (1975) he used the pen name Kilgore Trout, taken from a character in the fiction of KURT VONNEGUT (JR.) (1922–2007). (John) Michael Crichton (1942–2008) wrote several science-fiction novels, among them *The Andromeda Strain* (1969), *The Terminal Man* (1972), and *Jurassic Park* (1990). Although relatively new to science fiction, Steven Burgauer (b. 1952) has published thirteen novels to date, among them *Fornax* (1994), *In the Shadow of Omen* (1997), and *The Grandfather Paradox* (1998). A recent novel is *The Railguns of Luna* (2013).

Religious Literature: *Jericho Road: A Story of Western Life* (1877) by John Habberton (1842–1921) focuses on Illinois religion in the 1840s. A best seller of this era that is still in print and deserves special consideration is *In His Steps* (1897), subtitled *What Would Jesus Do?* by Charles Sheldon (1857–1946), a KANSAS minister, who began the novel in an Illinois town and concluded it in Chicago.

Archbishop Fulton J. Sheen (1895–1979), born in El Paso, Illinois, was one of the most prolific American Catholic writers. His first book was *God and Intelligence in Modern Philosophy* (1925); his last was the autobiography *Treasure in Clay* (1982). He wrote over seventy books and was famous in the 1950s for his weekly television program. Chicago's Andrew M. Greeley wrote about one hundred books, among them works on the Catholic faith and Catholic education, such as *The Catholic Revolution: New Wine, Old Wineskins, and the Second Vatican Council* (2004) and *The Making of the Pope, 2005* (2005). Jacksonville native J. F. POWERS (1917–1999) is another significant Catholic author; his two novels, *Morte d'Urban* (1962) and *Wheat That Springeth Green* (1988), employ Illinois settings and feature priest protagonists struggling to balance the sacred and the secular in their ministries. *Do Black Patent Leather Shoes Really Reflect Up?* (1975) and *The Last Catholic in America* (1973) are two John R. Powers (b. 1945) novels that satirize growing up Catholic; both were made into popular stage plays.

Graphic Novels: The most famous Illinois graphic novel was written by an Iowan. *The Road to Perdition* (1998) by Max Allan Collins (b. 1948) is based on the exploits of Rock Island gangster John Looney; it was later made into a motion picture starring Tom Hanks. Chris Ware (b. 1967), born in NEBRASKA and now living in Chicago, is another noteworthy graphic novelist. His *Jimmy Corrigan: The Smartest Kid on Earth* (2000) is set partly in Chicago. Other Illinois graphic novelists include Aaron Reynolds (b. 1970) of Fox River Grove with the Tiger Moth series; Jeff Weigel (b. 1958) of Belleville with *Atomic Ace* (2004) and *Atomic Ace and the Robot Rampage* (2006); and Joshua Elder (b. 1980), formerly of Carmi and now of Chicago, with his Mail Order Ninja series.

War Novels: Robinson native JAMES JONES (1921–1977) wrote three important war novels: *From Here to Eternity* (1951), *The Pistol* (1958), and *The Thin Red Line* (1962); his *Some Came Running* (1958) is the story of a World War II veteran who returns to his downstate hometown to write a war novel. La Salle native Jeffrey Miller (b. ca. 1958) published *War Remains,* a Korean War novel, in 2011. Three works about the Vietnam War by Larry Heinemann (b. 1944) are *Close Quarters* (1977); *Paco's Story* (1986), winner of the 1987 National Book Award; and *Black*

Virgin Mountain (2005). Ward Just's *Stringer* (1974) and Robert Olen Butler's *A Good Scent from a Strange Mountain* (1992) also address Vietnam.

Printing, Small Presses, and Journalism: The first newspaper in Illinois, *the Illinois Herald,* began publishing in May 1814. Founded by Matthew Duncan in Kaskaskia, it was sold in 1816 and continued under the title *Western Intelligencer.* The *Illinois Emigrant,* established in Shawneetown in 1818, was the state's second newspaper, followed by the *Edwardsville Spectator* in 1819. James Hall edited Shawneetown's *Illinois Gazette* in the early 1820s and the *Illinois Intelligencer* in 1827 after moving to Vandalia. In the years after 1824, the population of the Illinois River valley, like that of the state's central region, began mounting rapidly, and with it grew the newspaper industry. Within the next fifteen years Illinois became home to forty-three newspapers. Jersey County's John Russell, editor of the *Backwoodsman,* which began publishing in 1837, wrote "The Venomous Worm" (1838), a temperance jeremiad published in McGuffey's readers. Robert Jones Burdette began writing for the *Peoria Transcript* in 1869 before moving on to Iowa.

Chicago's first weekly newspaper, the *Democrat,* began in 1833. The year 1839 saw the advent of the *American,* the city's first daily. In 1848 John L. Scripps purchased a one-third interest in the new *Chicago Tribune* and, as senior editor, gained journalistic esteem for the newspaper. Scripps developed a unique editorial style, introduced market reviews, and broadened the *Tribune*'s news service. The poet Bert Leston Taylor (1866–1921) also contributed to the *Tribune*'s legacy; the wit with which he wrote "A Line o' Type or Two" made him one of the most beloved columnists of his time, while (ARTHUR) BURTON RASCOE (1892–1957) made his mark as the paper's drama and book critic.

By 1861 Illinois boasted almost three hundred newspapers, and in the decade between 1870 and 1880 that number doubled. In 1871 every newspaper establishment in Chicago was damaged during the Great Fire; nevertheless, all the major dailies resurfaced within two days, and the Chicago press expanded during that decade. In 1880 the census reported 1,017 state newspapers and noted that each of Illinois's 102 counties housed at least one. Illinois also boasted French, Polish, and German foreign-language publications. In 1876 Melville Stone and others founded the *Chicago Daily News;* the newspaper continued to publish for over one hundred years and soon became famous for its columnists. Eugene Field, George Ade, and Ben Hecht were some of the earliest; later *Daily News* luminaries included literary editor Harry Hansen and John Gunther (1901–1970), a fledgling member of the Schlogl's Restaurant coterie. Gunther later wrote a series of "inside" books, including *Inside Europe* (1936), *Inside Asia* (1939), *Inside USA* (1947), and *Inside Africa* (1955), based on his work for the foreign bureaus of the *Daily News.* Mike Royko, columnist and author, won a Pulitzer Prize for Commentary in the *Daily News* in 1972; *Boss* (1971) is his incisive unauthorized biography of Chicago mayor Richard J. Daley. The *Chicago Daily News* ceased publication in 1978.

Chicago produced newspapers representing diverse ethnic and social groups and political views. Chicago's *Broad-Ax,* founded in 1890, and the *Chicago Defender,* founded in 1905 and still publishing today, were two of the nation's few turn-of-the-century Democratic African American periodicals. Langston Hughes wrote a column for the latter paper in the 1940s. When the *Chicago Tribune*'s perspective narrowed in the 1930s, the Field family founded the *Chicago Sun* in order to offer a more international point of view. The *Sun* and the *Times* merged in 1948 to form the *Sun-Times,* where Urbana native Roger (Joseph) Ebert (1942–2013) began writing film reviews in 1967; in 1975 he won the Pulitzer Prize for Criticism for his columns. In the 1880s more than 1,000 newspapers served the state's 3 million residents; today just over 450 remain for Illinois's 12 million people.

Several twentieth-century Illinois journalists, primarily those from Chicago, achieved national prominence and later became respected authors. Elia Peattie reported on art and society for the *Chicago Tribune,* served as that paper's literary critic, and published two novels and a short-story collection. RING (GOLD WILMER) LARDNER (SR.) (1885–1933), later known for his short stories, became a *Chicago Tribune* sports reporter in 1908; by 1913 he was writing a daily *Tribune* column, "In the Wake of the News." Chicago radio and television personality (LOUIS) STUDS TERKEL (1912–2008) is known for his oral histories, including *Working* (1974), *Division Street: America* (1967), and *Hard Times* (1970). He won a Pulitzer Prize in 1985 for *"The Good War"* (1984). BOB GREENE (b. 1947), Illinois journalist of the year in 1995, is a former *Chicago Tribune* columnist who has published his columns in a number of books, including *He Was a Midwestern Boy on His Own* (1991) and *Chevrolet Summers, Dairy Queen Nights* (1997). Downstate Illinois journalists of note include Jerry Klein (b. 1926), columnist and author of *Played in Peoria* (1980), and Bill Knight (b. 1949), a Western Illinois University journalism faculty member whose books include *R.F.D. Notebook* (1994), *Fair Comment: Essays on The Air* (2003), and *Video Almanac* (2003).

Illinois small presses have made major contributions to the state's literature. The western region substantially supported poetry through the Decker Press in Prairie City, which published poetry and fiction from 1938 to 1949. James Decker's first publication was *The Ship of Gold* (1937) by Warren Van Dine (1902–1983). He also published two collections by Edgar Lee Masters: *Illinois Poems* (1941) and *Along the Illinois* (1942). This press, in a tiny Illinois town, achieved national recognition by publishing authors such as AUGUST (WILLIAM) DERLETH (1909–1971), Kenneth Patchen (1911–1972), and Kenneth Rexroth (1905–1982). From 1939 through 1949 the Decker Press published twelve issues of *Compass,* a poetry journal that became the *Beloit Poetry Journal* after the press folded. At Illinois State University, James R. Scrimgeour (b. 1934) and Robert Sutherland (b. 1937) founded the Pikestaff Press; Fred Brian's Pilot Rock Press was another important press in the area. David Pichaske founded Spoon River Poetry Press in Peoria in 1978 and Ellis Press, dedicated to prose publications, there in 1983. Morris Philipson (1926–2011) served for more than thirty years as the director of the University of Chicago Press, the most important press in Illinois.

The Federal Writers' Project in Illinois: JOHN T(OWNER) FREDERICK (1893–1975) became director of the FEDERAL WRITERS'

PROJECT for Illinois in 1937. Besides the Illinois volume in the American Guide Series, Frederick supervised the Life Histories from Illinois project (1936–1940), which included first-person narratives by Chicagoans from various occupations, for example, bartenders, taxi drivers, meatpackers, and steelworkers. He also spearheaded the Illinois Historical Records Survey (1935), which located and described archives throughout the state. The Federal Writers' Project provided a valuable training ground for Illinois authors such as Nelson Algren, JACK CONROY (1898–1990), and Margaret Walker (1915–1998). Willard Motley, Richard Wright, Saul Bellow, Arna Bontemps (1902–1973), and Studs Terkel also worked for the Illinois Writers' Project. African American writers were involved in the Illinois Federal Writers' Project to a larger extent than in most other states. Wright, Walker, and Bontemps gathered material for "The Negro in Illinois, 1779–1942," a book left unfinished when the project ended in 1943; this experience led to the formation of the South Side Writers' Group, founded by Wright in 1936, which included Bontemps, Walker, and Langston Hughes. Many decades later Brian Dolinar located, reconstructed, and edited the scattered papers, publishing *The Negro in Illinois: The WPA Papers* in 2013.

Literary and Scholarly Periodicals: The first literary magazine in Illinois was James Hall's Vandalia-based *Illinois Monthly Magazine* (1830). Another early Illinois literary magazine was established in Tilton in 1864: *The Prairie Chicken* was edited by Joseph Kirkland and his siblings in honor of their mother, Michigan frontier chronicler CAROLINE KIRKLAND (1801–1864). Chicago saw the founding of a plethora of literary journals, beginning with Kiler Kent Jones's *The Gem of the Prairie* in 1844, followed by Francis Fisher Browne's *Lakeside Monthly* in 1869. After the fire of 1871 Browne regrouped with the DIAL in 1880. The most important and enduring literary magazine is Harriet Monroe's *Poetry: A Magazine of Verse,* begun in 1912, although that era also saw the birth of several other Chicago literary periodicals, most notably the LITTLE REVIEW, edited by Margaret Anderson.

John T. Frederick took his MIDLAND from Iowa City to Chicago in 1930; it suspended publication three years later after playing a major role in the careers of James T. Farrell, Mark Van Doren, and other Illinois writers. Another Illinois literary magazine that thrived for a time but now is gone is *Direction: A Quarterly of New Literature,* founded in 1934 by J. Kerker Quinn (1911–1969). The magazine was renamed *Accent* when Quinn joined the University of Illinois faculty in 1940. Also at the University of Illinois, poet and fiction writer DANIEL CURLEY (1918–1988) established *Ascent* in 1975. David Pichaske founded *Spoon River Quarterly* in 1976; this journal later moved to Illinois State University, where it became *Spoon River Poetry Review,* edited by Lucia Getsi from 1987 until 2006. Other literary magazines of note were *Apple,* founded and edited by David Curry, and the *Mississippi Valley Review,* founded and edited by Steve Tietz, Michael Clippinger, and Forrest Robinson at Western Illinois University; Tietz also served as poetry editor for the *Eureka Literary Magazine.* Duane Taylor was the founding editor of *Illinois Writers Review* and *IWI Monthly.*

Illinois currently has a wealth of LITERARY PERIODICALS. Among those published in the northern area of the state are *Another Chicago Magazine, Baffler, Chicago Poetry, Chicago Review, Rambunctious Review, Journal of Ordinary Thought,* and *Whetstone,* published by the Barrington Area Arts Council. *Off the Rocks* fosters gay literature and is published by the Newtown Writers.

Literary magazines based at universities and colleges include the *Awakenings Review* at the University of Chicago, *Tri-Quarterly Online,* originally *Tri-Quarterly,* at Northwestern University, *Crab Orchard Review* at Southern Illinois University, and *Oyez Review* at Roosevelt University. Other significant literary magazines include *Cosmoetica,* located in the Bloomington-Normal area; *Downstate Story,* founded and edited by Elaine Hopkins; and *A Summer's Reading,* founded and edited by Ted Morrissey in the Lincoln area.

State Literary Awards: The Society of Midland Authors, which celebrated its centennial in 2015, gives several annual awards, grants, and fellowships to authors residing in one of the twelve Midwestern states. For over forty years Illinois literature has been supported and encouraged by the Illinois Arts Council, headquartered in Chicago; it

continues to grant awards for prose and poetry and also provides annual fellowships
in poetry and prose. The Illinois Association of Teachers of English supports Illinois
literature with its Illinois Author of the
Year award. The Illinois Center for the
Book, the State Library, and the Secretary
of State sponsor the annual Illinois Emerging Writers Competition. Also supporting
in-state talents are the Gwendolyn Brooks
Poetry Awards and the James Jones Creative Writing Awards. The Illinois Reading
Council names a Prairie State Author of the
Year in the field of children's or young-
adult literature. The Illinois State Poetry
Society sponsors several writing contests,
and the *Spoon River Poetry Review* gives an
annual $1,000 Editors' Prize to the first-
prize poem in its annual contest.

**Literary Societies and Writers'
Organizations:** During the last quarter of
the nineteenth century, Chicago's literary
societies were instrumental in establishing that city as an important cultural center. The Fortnightly Club, founded in 1872,
boasted 176 female members; two years later
its all-male counterpart, the Chicago Literary Club, was founded. Both clubs, the latter
now open to both men and women, continue
to meet in the twenty-first century. The Little
Room was organized in the early 1890s, as
was the Contributors Club; the Twentieth
Century Club began to meet in 1899; the
Cliff Dwellers Club was founded by Hamlin
Garland in 1907; and the Society of Midland
Authors, organized in 1915, still exists today.

Literary societies also became part of the
cultural infrastructure of downstate cities
and towns. Lisle had a literary society as
early as 1869, and Mary Augusta Safford
founded the Hawthorne Literary Society in
Hamilton in 1871. A literary society was
functioning in Franklin County as early as
1874 and in Towanda as early as 1915. Pontiac's Athenia Literary Club celebrated its centennial in 2011, and three other literary
societies still function in that city: the Clio-
nian Society, founded in 1877, the Twentieth
Century Club, and the Dialectic Literary
Society.

The forerunners of today's Greek-letter
fraternities, literary societies were the heart
of social and intellectual life at nineteenth-
century Illinois colleges and universities and
provided crucial training in oral and written
communication for future professionals,
such as William Jennings Bryan, a member
of Sigma Pi at Illinois College. These organizations sponsored debates, discussions of
current events, and oratorical and essay contests and hosted speakers, such as Abraham
Lincoln, who lectured at Illinois College's
Phi Alpha Men's Literary Society in the
1850s.

Many contemporary Illinois literary
societies and writers' organizations have
promoted writing, literacy, and book culture. In 1987 the Illinois Center for the Book,
in cooperation with the Read Illinois program, the Illinois State Library, the Illinois
Association of Teachers of English, and the
Chicago *Tribune,* produced a poster map of Illinois writers. This organization also maintains an online directory that offers basic
biographical and bibliographic information
on hundreds of Illinois authors. The Illinois
State Poetry Society was founded in 1991 to
promote poetry writing and appreciation in
the state and sponsors several poetry contests. The Northern Illinois Literary Society
publishes an annual anthology that it distributes to area libraries, hospitals, and nursing homes, while the James Jones Literary
Society in Robinson sponsors a short-story
award and the James Jones Chair in World
War II Studies at Eastern Illinois University.
Two current groups that support writers in
the Springfield area are the Vachel Lindsay
Association and the Springfield Poets and
Writers, formerly known as the Poets and
Writers Literary Forum. A Mary Austin
literary society exists in her hometown,
Carlinville.

SELECTED WORKS: *Illinois Poets: A Selection*
(1968) is a valuable anthology compiled
by E. Earle Stibitz. The best source for surveying nineteenth-century Illinois literature
is *Illinois Literature: The Nineteenth Century*
(1986), edited by John Hallwas; it includes
chronologically arranged stories, speeches,
essays, poems, letters, and newspaper articles and excerpts from autobiographies
and novels. Kevin Stein and G. E. Murray
edited *Illinois Voices: An Anthology of Twentieth
Century Poetry* (2001). *This Is Chicago* (1952),
edited by Albert Halper, has been called
"the best collection of Chicago writing" by
Hurt (62).

The earliest published descriptions of Illinois appear in Jacques Marquette's *Voyage et Découverte du P. Marquette et Sr. Jolliet dans l'Amérique Septentrionale* (1681). George Rogers Clark's eighteenth-century journals were published in 1920 as *The Conquest of the Illinois*. Morris Birkbeck published *Notes on a Journey in America from the Coast of Virginia to the Territory of Illinois* (1818) and *Letters from Illinois* (1818). Other notable travelers' narratives are *Summer on the Lakes, in 1843* (1844) by Margaret Fuller and *Life in Prairie Land* (1846) by Eliza Farnham. Joseph Kirkland's *Zury* (1887) is a prime example of prairie realism. Francis Grierson's *The Valley of the Shadows* (1909) also looks at pioneer life in central Illinois, while Edgar Lee Masters's *Spoon River Anthology* (1915) offers 244 dramatic monologues that record the end of agrarian culture in that region. Clark E. Carr's *Illini: A Story of the Prairies* (1904) is especially good in presenting the slavery issue in central Illinois in the 1850s, with Abraham Lincoln, Stephen Douglas, and Owen Lovejoy as characters.

Early twentieth-century portraits of Chicago life are Theodore Dreiser's *Sister Carrie* (1900), Upton Sinclair's *The Jungle* (1906), and Carl Sandburg's *Chicago Poems* (1916). MARGARET AYER BARNES in her 1931 Pulitzer Prize–winning *Years of Grace* (1930) chronicles Chicago's growth from the 1893 World's Columbian Exposition through the 1920s from an upper-middle-class perspective, while James T. Farrell's *Studs Lonigan: A Trilogy* (1935) and Richard Wright's *Native Son* (1940) explore the intersections of race, class, and ethnicity in Depression-era Chicago. Gwendolyn Brooks in *A Street in Bronzeville* (1945) and *The Bean Eaters* (1960) and Lorraine Hansberry in *A Raisin in the Sun* (1959) depict African American life in Chicago during the middle decades of the twentieth century. During the second half of the twentieth century, Saul Bellow's Chicago novels, notably *The Adventures of Augie March* (1953) and *Humboldt's Gift* (1975), dominated the city's literary scene, as did David Mamet's Chicago plays, *American Buffalo* (1977) and *Glengarry Glen Ross* (1984). Ray Bradbury's *Dandelion Wine* (1957), Dave Etter's *Alliance, Illinois* (1983), and John Knoepfle's *poems from the sangamon* (1985) evoke the ambiance of mid- to late twentieth-century downstate life.

Scott Turow's crime novels, notably *Presumed Innocent* (1987) and *Innocent* (2010), evoke the political, social, and moral complexities of life in contemporary Chicago.

FURTHER READING:

Literary Guides and Bibliographies: *A Reader's Guide to Illinois Literature* (1985, second edition 1987), edited by Robert C. Bray, with John Hallwas, James Hurt, Babette Inglehart, and John Knoepfle contributing specific sections, provides a useful guide to Illinois literature with overviews of major genres. Two important sources for fiction with an Illinois setting are *Illinois! Illinois! An Annotated Bibliography of Fiction* (1979), edited by Thomas Kilpatrick and Patsy-Rose Hoshiko, and *Illinois! Illinois! An Annotated Bibliography of Fiction: Twenty-Year Supplement, 1976–1996* (1998) edited by Kilpatrick. A detailed bibliography of the works of African American writers is available in *A Reader's Guide to Illinois Literature* by Steven Cameron Newsome. Babette Inglehart's bibliography in that volume includes the literature of Illinois's many ethnic groups and women writers, and Nicolás Kanellos has compiled a bibliography of Illinois Hispanic writers that also appears in it. Scholarly books to consult about Illinois literature include Robert C. Bray's *Rediscoveries: Literature and Place in Illinois* (1982), James Hurt's *Writing Illinois: The Prairie, Lincoln, and Chicago* (1992), and David Pichaske's *Rooted: Seven Midwest Writers of Place* (2006), which includes chapters on Dave Etter and Norbert Blei. Gerald Nemanic's *A Bibliographical Guide to Midwestern Literature* (1981) is another useful source.

For the history of Illinois newspapers and magazines, the essential source, although dated, is Franklin William Scott's *Newspapers and Periodicals of Illinois, 1814–1879* (1910). A current database of Illinois newspapers and where they can be located is maintained by the Illinois Newspaper Project under the aegis of the University of Illinois. A comprehensive listing of early printing and publishing in the state is *A Bibliography of Illinois Imprints, 1814–58* (1966) by Cecil K. Byrd. In 1938 the American Imprints Inventory of the WPA in Illinois published *Check List of Chicago Ante-Fire Imprints, 1851–1871*, a listing of nearly 1,900 publications printed in Chicago before the disastrous fire in 1871. This list was extended in 1944 by Douglas C. McMurtrie in *A Bibliography of Chicago Imprints, 1835–1850*.

H(enry) L(ewis) Mencken (1880–1956) described Chicago as "the literary capital of America" in his article with that title in *Nation* 17 (April 1920): 90–92. David D. Anderson's essay "Chicago as Metaphor," *Great Lakes Review* 1.1 (1974): 3–15, presents a useful study of the Chicago Renaissance, as do *The Chicago Renaissance in American Letters* (1954) by Bernard Duffey; *The Rise of Chicago as a Literary Center from 1885 to 1920* (1964) by Hugh Dalziel Duncan; *Chicago Renaissance* (1966) by Dale Kramer; *Prairie Voices: A Literary History of Chicago from the Frontier to 1893* (1980) by Kenny J. Williams (1927–2003); *Chicago in Story: A Literary History* (1982) by Clarence A. Andrews (ca. 1913–2002); *Chicago and the American Literary Imagination, 1888–1920* (1984) by Carl S. Smith; James Hurt's "Images of Chicago," in *Illinois: Its History and Legacy* (1984), edited by Roger D. Bridges and Rodney O. Davis; *Writing Chicago: Modernism, Ethnography and the Novel* (1993) by Carla Cappetti; and *Chicago Dreaming: Midwesterners and the City, 1871–1919* (2005) by Timothy B. Spears.

Libraries and Archives: Western Illinois University's Archives and Special Collections Library houses the Illinois Regional Archives Depository, a rich collection of materials, including local government records and documents from sixteen counties in west central Illinois. Chicago's Newberry Library holds the papers of many Illinois writers, including George Ade, Sherwood Anderson, Floyd Dell, Henry Blake Fuller, and Joseph Kirkland. The University of Chicago Library's Special Collections Research Center holds the William E. Barton Collection of Lincolniana, the editorial files of *Poetry* magazine, and the papers of Saul Bellow, John Gunther, and other Illinois authors. The Chicago Public Library's Woodson Regional Library houses the Vivian G. Harsh Research Collection of Afro-American History and Literature, the largest such collection in the Midwest. The University of Illinois at Chicago's Richard J. Daley Library holds books from Jane Addams's personal library and the Chicago Pre-Fire Imprints Collection of nearly five hundred items published in Chicago before the Great Fire of 1871. The University of Illinois at Urbana-Champaign's Rare Books and Manuscript Library holds the papers of James Jones, William Maxwell, Willard Motley, and Carl Sandburg.

LOREN LOGSDON   EUREKA COLLEGE

IMMIGRANT AND MIGRANT LITERATURE

OVERVIEW: Although the point should be obvious, it bears repeating: with the exception of Native Americans, the United States is a nation of immigrants, and the Midwest follows the national pattern. Historians recognize that the Midwest experienced several waves of migration from other regions in the United States, as well as from other nations. This entry will survey literature by and about immigrants and migrants who have played a part in the development of the Midwest. This literature typically portrays one or more of the following aspects of the migratory experience: economic and social conditions that cause people to leave their native country or region; the actual journey from that homeland to the Midwest; initial struggles to survive and prosper in the new physical and social environment; the importance of family and ethnic community; language and DIALECT; the experience of prejudice and discrimination; assimilation and loss of tradition; conflicts between immigrants and their children, second-generation Americans; and a search for identity.

HISTORY AND SIGNIFICANCE: In the late eighteenth century creation of the Northwest Territory via the Ordinances of 1784, 1785, and 1787 laid the groundwork for what is now known as the Midwest. With the Ordinance of 1787, Congress set the template for the ultimate creation of the twelve Midwestern states. Noteworthy in this ordinance was the prohibition of slavery in the region. That prohibition motivated migration from the South to the Midwest. Unfortunately, the prohibition of slavery did not prevent these states from prohibiting migrating African Americans in the first decades of the nineteenth century or requiring them to show legal documentation or provide a cash bond to live in the area. The Midwest was not without its share of controversy surrounding slavery. In order for

Maine to be admitted as a free state, the Missouri Compromise of 1820 dictated that MISSOURI be a slave state. Nevertheless, African Americans began to move to the Midwest around the 1840s.

The migration of American-born people to the Midwest, especially beginning in the 1830s, 1840s, and 1850s, originated from three major U.S. regions: the Northeast, the Middle Atlantic, and the upper South. The previously mentioned ordinances, especially the 1785 ordinance, provided an incentive for American migrants to the Midwest by selling land north and west of the Ohio River to mitigate overpopulation in the East. Pragmatically, the migration from all three American regions, as well as that from abroad, was dependent on the available means of transportation at the time, including waterways like the Erie Canal, which began in the mid-1820s, and railroads, which rose to prominence in the second half of the nineteenth century. The general model of migration to the Midwest followed multiple east-west routes. Those from or traveling through the Northeast, including New England and New York, tended to migrate to the upper Midwest, particularly MICHIGAN, WISCONSIN, and Dakota Territory. Sometimes referred to as "Yankees," these migrants left a distinct mark on the cultural landscape of the upper Midwest, including town plans, educational institutions, dialects, and literature. FRONTIER AND PIONEER ACCOUNTS by these people often begin with narratives of migration. Representative texts of upper Midwestern Anglo American migration include *A NEW HOME—WHO'LL FOLLOW?* (1839) by CAROLINE KIRKLAND (1801–1864), about New Yorkers transplanted to frontier Michigan, and *MAIN-TRAVELLED ROADS* (1891) by (HANNIBAL) HAMLIN GARLAND (1860–1940), which depicts pioneers facing hardships in the upper Midwest.

Those from the Middle Atlantic region, with the help of the National Road, tended to settle the lower Midwest, including OHIO, INDIANA, and ILLINOIS. WILLA CATHER (1873–1947), herself a representative migrant from Virginia to NEBRASKA, wrote extensively about the immigrant experience in novels like *My Ántonia* (1918), about a Czech family's difficult transition to the Nebraska plains in the late nineteenth century.

The Shimerda family at the train station. Illustration by W. T. Benda for Willa Cather's *My Ántonia*. Houghton Mifflin Co., 1918.
Image courtesy of the University of Kentucky Special Collections Research Center

Those coming from or through the South saw an opportunity for better soil for farming and land that was more legally certain in places such as southern Illinois and Indiana, Missouri, and KANSAS. African Americans seeking a better life in the post–Civil War South found that they were not always welcome. By the mid-nineteenth century a considerable number had moved to Indiana and Ohio from Virginia and North Carolina, looking for greater freedom than the South afforded them and thus beginning a longstanding tradition of Midwestern African American writers, including SOJOURNER TRUTH (ca. 1797–1883), GWENDOLYN BROOKS (1917–2000), and VIRGINIA (ESTHER) HAMILTON (1936–2002). Portrayals of these early migrants are found in the short stories and novels of CHARLES WADDELL CHESNUTT (1858–1932), who wrote about African Americans in Ohio cities during the late nineteenth century, and *Beloved* (1987) by TONI MORRISON (b. CHLOE ARDELIA WOFFORD, 1931), which illustrates the experience of one African American family that migrates from slavery in Kentucky to Ohio before and during the era of Reconstruction. See AFRICAN AMERICAN LITERATURE.

Westward expansion created a need for labor that encouraged a laissez-faire stance in federal immigration policy. Beginning in the 1840s, the Midwest experienced a phenomenal rise in immigration, primarily from western European nations like Ireland and Germany and from regions of Scandinavia. Nationwide, the Irish constituted the largest immigrant influx in the 1840s, and although the numbers of Irish in the Midwest never rose to those in the Northeast, their influence in the Midwest was significant. Reasons for leaving Ireland ranged from political dissatisfaction and religious conflict resulting from English rule to the potato famine of the mid-to late 1840s. Millions of Irish people sought a better life in America, often by way of "chain migration," a form of immigration involving already established family members sending money or a ticket back home for another family member to join them. The greatest contribution of the Irish to the Midwestern cultural fabric during the mid- to late nineteenth century was religious. With the support of resident German Catholics, the Irish managed to establish Catholicism as a major American religion. Among the Irish American writers were FINLEY PETER DUNNE (1867–1936) and JAMES T(HOMAS) FARRELL (1904–1979), whose STUDS LONIGAN (1935) showcases a coming-of-age story in Irish CHICAGO and explores the difficulties of the Depression era. Mary Deasy (1914–1978) wrote a series of novels about Irish Americans in the Midwest. *The Hour of Spring* (1948) follows three generations of a family from County Kerry, beginning with their immigration to Ohio in the 1870s.

Although German immigration to the United States began before the 1850s, it was not until then that Germans emerged as one of the most influential Midwestern immigrant groups. Several reasons underlay the large-scale German migration of that era. The Napoleonic Wars undercut economic stability, while the revolutions of 1848 made remaining in Germany dangerous. German influence grew to be so widespread in the Midwest by the 1890s that the area between CINCINNATI, ST. LOUIS, and Milwaukee came to be known as the "German Triangle." Many writers published in German in these cities, and some work was translated in later years. For example, Emil Klauprecht (1815–1896), a German American newspaper editor, wrote *Cincinnati; oder, Geheimnisse des Westens* (1854–1855), a novel about Germans in Cincinnati, translated by Steven Rowan as *Cincinnati; or, The Mysteries of the West* (1996). Henry Boernstein (1805–1892) wrote *Die Geheimniss von St. Louis* (1851), which shares the anti-clerical perspective of Klauprecht's novel. Although (HERMAN) THEODORE DREISER (1871–1945) is not often discussed in relation to the immigrant experience, he was the son of German immigrants in Indiana and portrayed German immigrants in such works as the story "Old Rogaum and His Theresa" (1901) and the novel *Jennie Gerhardt* (1911). A twenty-first-century novel about German immigrant experience in the Midwest is *The Master Butchers Singing Club* (2003) by (KAREN) LOUISE ERDRICH (b. 1954). Best known for fiction about Native Americans in MINNESOTA and NORTH DAKOTA, Erdrich turned fully toward her German heritage for the first time in this novel.

People from the Netherlands came to the Midwest because of economic hardships from the 1840s to the early twentieth century. Western Michigan, especially the Holland and Grand Rapids area, reflects Dutch tradition and influence to this day. Writers from this Dutch American community include two brothers, DAVID CORNEL DEJONG (1905–1967) and MEINDERT DEJONG (1906–1991); the former conveys the struggles of being newly arrived foreigners in his 1934 novel *Belly Fulla Straw*. Dutch immigrants also settled further west in IOWA; a fictionalized account of the founding of Palla in 1847 is given in *Roofs over Strawtown* (1945) by Sara Elizabeth Gosselink (1893–1982).

Scandinavians represented another significant immigrant community, especially in the second half of the nineteenth century. Norway and Sweden contributed the largest numbers of Scandinavian immigrants to the Midwest in the decades after the Civil War. Norwegian immigration to the Midwest was spurred by dramatic population increase at home and the scarcity of arable land. Swedes experienced scant harvests and began massively emigrating in the 1870s and 1880s. Both of these countries' immigrants settled in the Midwest as its frontier reached toward the Great Plains. Scandinavians flourished in U.S. regions at the same latitudes as their former home countries, so the Dakotas, Iowa, and northern Illinois were natural targets for their immigration. Although it was perhaps not as well known as the German Triangle, the so-called Swedish Triangle existed in Minnesota between the St. Croix and Mississippi Rivers. Notable novels about Swedish immigrants include *Charli Johnson, syenk-amerikan* (1909) by Gustav Nathaniel Malm (1869–1928) and *O PIONEERS!* (1913) by Willa Cather, both set in Nebraska. Swedish author Vilhelm Moberg (1898–1973) wrote *The Emigrants,* a series of novels about a Swedish family coming to Minnesota in the late nineteenth century. The second book in the series, *Invandrarna* (1952), translated by Gustaf Lannestock as *Unto a Good Land* (1954), deals with the family's journey from New York to Minnesota and their initial efforts to start a farm. The novel *Falconberg* (1878) by Hjalmar Hjorth Boyesen (1848–1895) deals with Norwegians settling in Wisconsin. *GIANTS IN THE EARTH* (1927), the most popular work by OLE EDVART RØLVAAG (1876–1931), recounts the lives of Norwegians as they migrated to Dakota Territory during the 1870s and 1880s. Literature was also produced by immigrants to the Midwest from Denmark, Finland, and Iceland. See SCANDINAVIAN LITERATURE.

From the end of the Civil War through the early twentieth century, the Midwestern urban population grew through migration and immigration. During this time the social and racial restrictions placed on African Americans in the South by Jim Crow laws and the rising opportunities for employment in industrial jobs in the North precipitated what has come to be known as the Great Migration. Factories in the North, which relied heavily on European immigrant labor, suffered a shortage of workers during World War I. As a result, African Americans saw an opportunity to leave the South for economic gain and a better life. Millions moved to Midwestern urban areas like DETROIT, Chicago, CLEVELAND, St. Louis, and KANSAS CITY. A great deal of literature has depicted these experiences. RICHARD WRIGHT (1908–1960) represents the African American Great Migration to the North in his works, which include the classic novel *NATIVE SON* (1940) and his autobiography, *Black Boy* (1945). CARL (AUGUST) SANDBURG (1878–1967) cap-

tures an incident involving white reaction to the Great Migration in *The Chicago Race Riots, July, 1919* (1919).

White southerners from Appalachian Tennessee, Kentucky, and West Virginia were also drawn to the Midwest for economic reasons in the twentieth century, especially during the Great Depression and the decades thereafter. Seeking a life free of poverty, these migrants moved to nearby urban-industrial areas such as Cleveland, Cincinnati, or Chicago. HARRIETTE SIMPSON ARNOW (1908–1986) reflects the Appalachian migration to the Midwest in her Kentucky trilogy, which culminates in her best-known work, *THE DOLLMAKER* (1954), set in Detroit.

During the early twentieth century Midwestern immigration began to include peoples from outside western Europe. Cities like Chicago, with their industrial employment and growing ethnic neighborhoods, drew large numbers of people from eastern and southern Europe; their experiences have since provided material for many writers. A notable early example is *THE JUNGLE* (1906) by UPTON (BEALL) SINCLAIR (JR.) (1878–1968), an important work of PROTEST LITERATURE that provides a vivid portrayal of the Lithuanian community in Chicago shortly after the turn of the twentieth century.

Chicago also produced fiction about Jewish immigrants from eastern Europe. Louis Zara (1910–2001) wrote *Blessed Is the Man* (1935), about the rise of a Russian Jewish immigrant in Chicago. *The Old Bunch* (1937) by Meyer Levin (1905–1981) deals with second-generation eastern European Jews coming of age in Chicago. Nobel laureate SAUL (C.) BELLOW (1915–2005) created deep and complex characterizations of Jewish immigrants and their children in Chicago, as in *THE ADVENTURES OF AUGIE MARCH* (1953). See JEWISH LITERATURE.

Literature of the Italian American experience includes *Rosa: The Life of an Italian Immigrant* (1970) by Marie Hall Ets (1895–1984). Ets interviewed Rosa Cassettari (1866–1943), whom she renamed Rosa Cavalleri, at the Chicago Commons settlement house shortly after World War I. Cavalleri told of her early life in Italy, her emigration in 1884, and her difficult but often rewarding life in Chicago and elsewhere, including a period in a Missouri mining town. Another notable book is

Paper Fish (1980) by Tina De Rosa (1944–2007), a lyrical novel about a third-generation Italian American girl in Chicago whose immigrant grandmother helps her connect with her heritage as she comes of age.

Greeks also came to the Midwest in the first half of the twentieth century, seeking both opportunity and refuge from Greek political instability. HARRY MARK PETRAKIS (b. 1923) writes about Greek American life in Chicago in his novels and autobiographies, including *Pericles on 31st Street* (1965). Also distinctly Midwestern in setting and plot is the Pulitzer Prize–winning novel *Middlesex* (2002) by Jeffrey Eugenides (b. 1960), in which the intersex narrator traces generations of his family from Greece through the rise and fall of industrial Detroit.

Also at the beginning of the twentieth century Mexicans migrated to the Midwest, seeking work in agriculture and industry. See LATINO/LATINA LITERATURE. Although the Great Depression slowed Mexican immigration, a little later in that century Mexican migrant workers came from regions in the South like Texas and worked their way north into the Midwest, gravitating to seasonal work in agriculture and increasingly to the big cities. Tomás Rivera (1935–1984) depicts the Mexican American migrant experience in his best-known work, . . . *Y NO SE LO TRAGÓ LA TIERRA* / . . . *AND THE EARTH DID NOT DEVOUR HIM* (1971), the protagonist of which is a boy whose family migrates annually to and from Texas and the upper Midwest. *THE HOUSE ON MANGO STREET* (1984) by SANDRA CISNEROS (b. 1954) portrays Mexican and Puerto Rican immigrants in Chicago from the point of view of a Mexican American girl. Cisneros's semi-autobiographical *Caramelo* (2002) follows a girl whose family travels annually between Chicago and her grandmother's home in Mexico City.

Nativist prejudice against immigrants rose in the early twentieth century because of economic pressures, as well as racism and ethnic animosity. A series of federal laws began to restrict immigration in regard to numbers and nations of origin. The Emergency Quota Act of 1921 limited the number of immigrants from any country, excluding Latin America, to 3 percent of their nationality already living in the United States as of 1910. During and after World War II, however, immigration policy changed. The Chinese Exclusion Act of 1882 was suspended in 1943, and the 1965 Immigration and Nationality Act allowed greater numbers of people to immigrate and ended quotas based on nations of origin.

India is one of the countries that have benefited from the 1965 Immigration Act. Millions of Indians have immigrated to the United States in general, and to the Midwest in particular, for many reasons, including a need for more technologically skilled workers. Upon their arrival, immigrants from India headed toward Midwestern university cities, particularly Indianapolis, St. Louis, Chicago, and Detroit. BHARATI MUKHERJEE (b. 1940), who immigrated to the Midwest from India in 1961, portrays the merging and crossing of cultural boundaries in such works as *Jasmine* (1989), whose titular character moves from India through Iowa as she crosses the United States. Other groups of Asian Americans in the Midwest who are beginning to produce literature include Hmong Americans, exiles from Laos and their descendants who form communities in Minnesota and Wisconsin. See ASIAN AMERICAN LITERATURE.

Surpassing African Americans as the largest American minority nationwide, Hispanic or Latino people have constituted the most significant Midwestern immigrant population in the second half of the twentieth century and the twenty-first century. Latinos hailing from Mexico, Puerto Rico, Cuba, and other Latin American countries began migrating to the Midwest in the early 1900s, seeking political freedom and economic gain. The Mexican Revolution near the beginning of the twentieth century, the Cuban crisis from the 1960s onward, and civil wars in Central America in the 1980s all brought documented and undocumented immigrants to the Midwest. Significant numbers of these immigrants are found in the bigger Midwestern cities, but many have located in rural areas. Latino Midwesterners writing of the immigrant experience include Rane Arroyo (1954–2010), a Puerto Rican poet from Chicago and long resident in Ohio, and Omar S(igfrido) Castañeda (1954–1997), who portrayed Guatemalan immigrants in Indiana in his books.

Immigration to the United States has not ceased, nor will it cease any time soon. The past half century has seen a rise in immigration stimulated by world events, including the Cuban Revolution and the Vietnam War. Since the 9/11 terrorist attacks in 2001, Americans have been even more keenly aware of Arab immigrants and undocumented workers and have engaged in political debates that have at times been vitriolic. See ARAB AMERICAN LITERATURE. Immigration, however, remains a main source of both economic development and cultural production in the United States. Literature about the immigrant and migrant experience continues to inform our understanding of the Midwest and the nation as a whole.

SELECTED WORKS: Hamlin Garland's *Main-Travelled Roads* (1891), Richard Wright's *Black Boy* (1945), Harriette Simpson Arnow's *The Dollmaker* (1954), Tomás Rivera's *. . . y no se lo tragó la tierra / . . . And the Earth Did Not Devour Him* (1971), and Toni Morrison's *Beloved* (1987) showcase the experience of migrants in the Midwest. Reflections of immigration include Willa Cather's *My Ántonia* (1918), O. E. Rølvaag's *Giants in the Earth* (1927), Meindert DeJong's *Belly Fulla Straw* (1934), *Rosa: The Life of an Italian Immigrant* (1970) by Marie Hall Ets, and *Middlesex* (2002) by Jeffrey Eugenides.

Two useful anthologies that include Midwestern texts are *Visions and Divisions: American Immigration Literature, 1870–1930* (2008), edited by Tim Prchal and Tony Trigilio, and *Crossing into America: The New Literature of Immigration* (2005), edited by Louis Mendoza and Subramanian Shankar.

FURTHER READING: For an excellent visual presentation of migration in America, see Stephan A. Flanders's *Atlas of American Migration* (1998). Although the book's scope extends beyond the American Midwest, the centrality of the Midwest's geography cannot help but factor into the majority of the book's discussions. Chad Berry's *Southern Migrants, Northern Exiles* (2000) explores Appalachian migration to Midwestern cities during the Depression era. *The Great Migration in Historical Perspective: New Dimensions of Race, Class, and Gender* (1991), a collection edited by Joe William Trotter Jr., focuses on several aspects of this movement and includes a chapter devoted to the urban Midwest. Roger Daniels provides a broad historical overview in *Coming to America: A History of Immigration and Ethnicity in American Life* (revised edition, 2002). Jon Gjerde focuses on the confluence and clashing of a multitude of immigrant groups in the upper Midwest in the second chapter of *The Minds of the West: Ethnocultural Evolution in the Rural Middle West, 1830–1917* (1997). A more exhaustive approach to immigration on a larger scale can be found in John Powell's *Encyclopedia of North American Immigration* (2005). For literary studies, consult the "Further Reading" sections of entries in this volume on particular ethnic or national groups.

LANCE WELDY   FRANCIS MARION UNIVERSITY

IN OUR TIME

HISTORY: When *In Our Time* was published in 1925, mainstream critics immediately recognized ERNEST (MILLER) HEMINGWAY (1899–1961) as a major American postwar voice. His first American short-story collection, *In Our Time* showed Hemingway's emerging talent and the literary and artistic influences of European modernism. His presence in Paris during the 1920s placed him in a key American expatriate collective that would significantly shape American literature of the twentieth century. The collection of stories and short untitled vignettes built on many of Hemingway's life experiences, including details from his adolescence and young adulthood in ILLINOIS and MICHIGAN, the education he received as a journalist in KANSAS CITY, his observations in Italy during World War I, and his knowledge of European and expatriate life. The fictional character of Nick Adams, prominent in many of the *In Our Time* stories, was loosely based on Hemingway himself.

Boni and Liveright published the first American edition of this collection, consisting of fifteen stories interspersed with vignettes, later called chapter headings, in 1925. The collection included three stories, "Up in Michigan," "Out of Season," and "My Old Man," from *Three Stories and Ten Poems*, Hemingway's first book, which had been published in Paris in 1923, but Boni and Liveright balked at the sexual content of "Up in Michigan." Hemingway wrote a

Frontispiece and title page of Ernest
Hemingway's *in our time.*
© Three Mountains Press, Paris, 1924

new Nick Adams story, "The Battler," to replace the objectionable story. The vignettes were short experimental pieces, mainly secondhand descriptions of war and bullfighting, which had been published as *in our time* (1924), the last of the Inquest into the State of Contemporary English Prose series edited by Ezra Pound (1885–1972) and published by Three Mountains Press. In the 1925 Liveright edition of *In Our Time,* two vignettes, "A Very Short Story" and "The Revolutionist," became titled stories. The book's structure contrapuntally shifts among early Nick Adams stories, the interspersed vignettes of a world that has lost its innocence, and the final Nick Adams stories in which Nick's contrasting innocence becomes a metonymy for America and the Midwest. The collection was published to positive reviews, many of which noted the stylistic influence of Gertrude Stein (1874–1946) and SHERWOOD ANDERSON (1876–1941) on Hemingway's writing.

SIGNIFICANCE: *In Our Time* constituted an experiment in form in which its components were inseparable from the work's Midwestern significance. *WINESBURG, OHIO* (1919) by Anderson—an earlier radical experiment with related short stories as a novel and a book with which Hemingway was familiar through his friendship with Anderson—provided a literary mode for inquiring into Midwestern and American identity. Eight of the fifteen stories in the

1925 Boni and Liveright edition feature Nick Adams, Hemingway's fictional alter ego. The first five stories in that edition sequentially trace Nick Adams from young boyhood in "Indian Camp," witnessing an Indian woman giving birth and discovering her husband's suicide, to the young man adventurously riding the rails in "The Battler." The Midwestern setting of these stories is emphasized in many references, including the Indian characters speaking Ojibwa, the language of a Native American tribe local to the upper Great Lakes, in "The Doctor and the Doctor's Wife." References to the lumbering town of Hortons Bay, Michigan, in "The End of Something" and "The Three-Day Blow" also reflect the Michigan setting.

Early shadowy themes of death and suffering now emerge more strongly in the tone, voices, and events of later stories. In "A Very Short Story," the first non–Nick Adams story, for example, the emotionless voice of the unnamed speaker tersely marks the aftermath of war and romance, saying that he "contracted gonorrhea from a loop department store sales girl while riding in a taxicab through Lincoln Park" (66). "A Very Short Story" also deepens the Midwestern connections in Hemingway's stories; the Lincoln Park neighborhood reference firmly places the story in CHICAGO. Paul Smith, in *A Reader's Guide to the Short Stories of Ernest Hemingway* (1989), also notes that in the original 1924 publication of *in our time* the "loop department store" was specified as The Fair, a famous early Chicago department store. That reference was changed in later publications due to fear of libel charges (26).

Hemingway returns to Chicago material in chapter 15, located between sections of "Big Two-Hearted River" at the end of collection. Chapter 15 refers to the hanging of murderer Sam Cardinella (ca. 1868–1921), which occurred in Chicago on April 15, 1921. In a letter to his father published in *Ernest Hemingway: Selected Letters, 1917–1961* (1981), edited by Carlos Baker, Hemingway refers to passing the county jail on the day of the execution, again showing that he drew on his Midwestern experiences in composing his fiction (46).

"Soldier's Home" is the second of four stories featuring Americans returning to the

Midwest from the war. Krebs's difficult homecoming closely parallels Hemingway's own. The Nick Adams tales are transparently autobiographical, lifting events directly from Hemingway's life. Nick's mother is a preachy moralist; his father is a physician and hunter. In "The End of Something" Nick colludes with his friend Bill, modeled on Hemingway's friend William B. Smith Jr., to break up with Marjorie just as Hemingway had broken up with Marjorie Bump, a seventeen-year-old Petoskey waitress, at his friend's urging.

Early critics treated *In Our Time* mainly as a "promising" short-story collection, but preliminary and implicitly inferior to novels to come. Only gradually did criticism begin to see that *In Our Time* was more than a thematically related short-story collection. Each story can stand alone, but the stories clearly modify one another, adding complexity and tone. The critical discussion of *In Our Time* as a thematically related collection of short stories or an integrated work, even a novel, hinges on the relationship of the Nick Adams narrative to the non–Nick Adams stories.

Some critics argued for a "nearly novel" status by focusing on the Nick Adams narrative and ignoring the other stories. Later critics found unity by emphasizing thematic relationships. In 1990 Debra A. Moddelmog suggested a new perspective. Focusing on nine pages Hemingway had initially intended to conclude "Big Two-Hearted River"—which he had deleted at Gertrude Stein's suggestion and which were subsequently published as "On Writing" in *The Nick Adams Stories* (1972)—Moddelmog argues that Nick is the author of the non–Nick Adams stories. This emphasis alerts readers to the metafictional nature of *In Our Time*. Each story is part of an evolving literary manifesto. The inarticulateness of Krebs, for example, in "Soldier's Home" resembles Hemingway's challenges in talking about the war to an audience dulled by romantic exaggeration. In "Cat in the Rain" the narrator calls attention to artists who come out to paint only in good weather, implicitly distinguishing their aesthetic preference from the narrator's creed that insists on looking at experience in bad weather. Even

"The Three Day Blow" provides early signs of Nick's aesthetic interests.

The meaning of *In Our Time* lies in the relationship between the portrayal of Nick Adams's coming of age as a man and artist from the Midwest and the portrayal of American and European voices and experiences in the vignettes and non–Nick Adams stories. The arrangement of stories, settings, and times, especially in relation to war, contradicts the essential contrast between American innocence and European experience. "On the Quai at Smyrna," for example, establishes associations that reverberate across stories. The story's opening description of the screaming war refugees—"The strange thing was, he said, how they screamed every night at midnight" (11)—resonates with the screaming Indian woman in the ensuing "Indian Camp." The opening story's narrator tells how they turned the "searchlight on them to quiet them" (11), linking jaded British postwar experience with young Nick, who, as he listens to the screaming Indian woman, cries out to his father, "Oh, Daddy, can't you give her something to make her stop screaming?" (16). The screaming recurs across time, culture, and experience. The women refusing to give up their dead babies in "On the Quai at Smyrna," the Indian woman screaming in pain during childbirth in "Indian Camp," the suffocating maternalism in "Soldier's Home," the joyless couple trying to make babies in "Mr. and Mrs. Elliot," the implied pregnancy in "Out of Season," and the pregnancies of Nick's wife and the Swiss girl in "Cross Country Snow" similarly create a community of female experience uniting pre- and postwar experience and connecting American, Indian, Armenian, and Greek refugees, silly American academic poets, British upper classes, and Swiss serving girls. This was Hemingway's special triumph in *In Our Time*. The novel's formal properties—Midwestern coming-of-age narrative interspersed with other American and European experiences—express Hemingway's, the Midwest's, and America's relationship to the world at large, especially to Europe. *In Our Time* reveals that the dark tragedy of the quai at Smyrna also lay at the heart of Hemingway's beloved Michigan woods.

In Our Time celebrates the American Midwest and the uninflected mid-American voice. Nick Adams's voice and experience contrast with the experiences of the novel's other American characters, notably the empty, narcissistic American tourists in "Cat in the Rain" and the impotent American easterners with their idiotic aspirations in "Mr. and Mrs. Eliot." Nick Adams's voice and experience also contrast with European alternatives found in the introductory "On the Quai at Smyrna" and later in "Out of Season." In "Cross Country Snow" we see Nick's growing aesthetic qualities and desires that make him superior to his Anglophile pal George. Nick sees things George misses, like the barmaid's pregnancy. In response to George's displeasure at what he considers the girl's grumpiness, Nick reveals a rich, empathic novelist's imagination based on his complex knowledge. The most important differences between the two Americans, however, are their attitudes toward Europe and home. George reflects thoughtless American celebration of things European and does not want his youthful joy to end. He says to Nick, "Don't you just wish we could bum together?" (110) and "I wish we were Swiss" (112). But Nick does not. Although Nick has enjoyed his youthful European adventure, he knows that it must end, that it is time to go home.

The book comes home in its concluding story, "Big Two-Hearted River," which returns to Nick Adams in his Midwestern setting, on a fishing trip to the burned-out landscape outside the town of Seney, in Michigan's Upper Peninsula. Nick is no longer the callow youth of "The Battler." In these final stories Nick tries to come to grips with the transformative experiences of his past. Although the war is not specifically mentioned in the final edited version, it is implied in the burned-out remnants of the Michigan woods through which he travels and in his desire to leave his past behind. "He felt he had left everything behind," Hemingway writes, "the need for thinking, the need to write, other needs. It was all back of him" (134).

Nick is an artist, seeing in ways that imply Hemingway's own aesthetic styles and values. Nick sees beneath the surface water's swirl to the trout holding steady through minute, alert adjustments to the powerful current. The trout represent the deft control and balanced intimacy with natural forces that Hemingway sought in his art. Nick's alert notation also describes how the artist must see. He looks past the surface, "down into the clear, brown water" (133). Nick knows the difference between appearance and actuality, knows that the water is not really brown but takes its color "from the pebbly bottom" (133). He is patient, attentive, and focused. Through knowledge and careful, patient watching, the artist sees beyond the surface to greater depths, suggesting the dark borders of meaning and consciousness.

In an earlier story, "Cat in the Rain," a maid asks a wandering American tourist whether she has lost something: "Ha perduto qualque cosa, Signora?" (92). Her question reverberates through all of Hemingway's fiction, effectively interrogating not just the American characters of *In Our Time* but all the questing American tourist-EXPATRIATES of Hemingway's later fiction. His Americans search the world for something they think they have lost. In *In Our Time* Hemingway suggests that the answer lies in an intimate relationship with home, not a home characterized by any conventional, bucolic, or romantic narratives of the Midwest, but a Midwestern woods as sinister as the Congo in *Heart of Darkness* (1902) by Joseph Conrad (b. Józef Teodor Konrad Korzeniowski, 1857–1924) and as mythically suggestive as the forests in "Young Goodman Brown" (1935) by Nathaniel Hawthorne (b. Nathaniel Hathorne, 1804–1864). Hemingway presents a young Midwestern man in control, or moving toward control, of his moral perspective, experience, and voice. We contrast Nick Adams's mature and maturing certainties, his careful, unflinching examination of his experience, not only with his earlier selves but also with competing European selves, like the British speaker in "On the Quai at Smyrna."

These final stories offer us a Nick Adams significantly different from the Nick of the first five stories, one who exhibits compelling contrasts with his British or continental

European counterparts in stories like "Out of Season." The character in that story is led by a besotted Italian peasant on a fishing trip that never occurs because no one really wants to fish. They want only the pleasures that come without fishing. Most important, Nick Adams, Midwestern American hero, in these morally conclusive stories stands entirely on his own. Nick, like the Hemingway narrator toward whom he is growing, speaks authoritatively and with increasing moral and aesthetic confidence from his Midwestern center.

In Our Time launched Hemingway's career and announced his aesthetic, themes, and philosophical stance to a wide readership. The collection has been translated into several languages, including Chinese, German, and Dutch. Along with his success as a novelist, Hemingway continued writing important short stories. He folded *In Our Time* and subsequent story collections into *The Fifth Column and the First Forty-Nine Stories* (1938). That volume, followed by its later versions—currently *The Complete Short Stories of Ernest Hemingway: The Finca Vigia Edition* (1987)—became the most widely distributed edition of Hemingway's short fiction, which has profoundly influenced generations of writers worldwide, including Midwesterners like JIM (JAMES THOMAS) HARRISON (1937–2016) and THOMAS (FRANCIS) MCGUANE (III) (b. 1939), who have set fiction in Nick Adams's northern Michigan woods, and (WILLIAM) TIM(OTHY) O'BRIEN (b. 1946).

Several stories from *In Our Time* have been adapted for cinema and television. Jean Negulesco directed *Under My Skin* (1950), a version of "My Old Man"; John Erman directed *My Old Man* (1979). Paul Newman played the punch-drunk boxer in "The Battler" (1955), directed by Arthur Penn for the NBC Television program *Playwrights 56*. Two scripts by Hemingway friend and memoirist A(aron) E(dward) Hotchner (b. 1920) weave stories from *In Our Time* into coherent, if somewhat contrived, longer-form narratives: "The World of Nick Adams" (1957), produced for the CBS program *Seven Lively Arts,* and Martin Ritt's *Hemingway's Adventures of a Young Man* (1962). Robert Young directed *Soldier's Home* (1977) for PBS.

IMPORTANT EDITIONS: Boni and Liveright published the first edition of *In Our Time* in 1925. When Scribner published its 1930 edition, editor Maxwell Perkins requested an introduction. Hemingway suggested that critic Edmund Wilson contribute an introduction, which he did, and that Scribner add the opening story, "On the Quai at Smyrna," which was simply called "Introduction by the Author" in the 1930 edition. (It took its current title in the 1938 Scribner short-story collection and retained that title in subsequent editions.) Quotations from *In Our Time* in this entry are drawn from the 1996 Simon and Schuster reprint of the 1930 Scribner edition. There is currently no critical edition available.

FURTHER READING: Prominent Hemingway biographies include Carlos Baker's *Ernest Hemingway: A Life Story* (1969, 1980) and James R. Mellow's *Hemingway: A Life without Consequences* (1993). Peter Griffin's *Along with Youth: Hemingway, the Early Years* (1987) provides a comprehensive overview of Hemingway's Midwestern upbringing. Michael Reynolds's five-volume biography is now the exhaustive standard. Reynolds's first two volumes, *The Young Hemingway* (1987, 1998) and *The Paris Years* (1989), are invaluable for Hemingway's formative Midwestern years, with specific background of the stories of *In Our Time* and its complicated publishing history.

Understanding of Hemingway's stories can be greatly enriched by reading his correspondence. Carlos Baker's *Ernest Hemingway: Selected Letters, 1917–1961* (1981) has been the scholarly standard, but Cambridge University Press's *The Letters of Ernest Hemingway* incorporates all existing correspondence written by Hemingway from his earliest letters until his death. Volume 1 of *The Letters* (2011), covering the years 1907–1922, Volume 2 (2013), covering the years 1923–1925, Volume 3 (2015), covering the years 1926–29, and forthcoming volumes provide valuable insights into Hemingway's experiences and craft.

The Nick Adams stories are often separately collected and discussed, incorporating stories from *In Our Time*, some of Hemingway's later story collections, and manuscript fragments. *The Nick Adams Stories* (1972) was chosen by the Michigan Humanities Council in 2007–2008 as part of its literacy program the Great Michigan Read, in which over five hundred programs and events related to the book took place throughout the state. One of the best scholarly examinations of those stories is Joseph Flora's *Hemingway's Nick Adams* (1982).

In *Hemingway's "In Our Time": Lyrical Dimensions* (1992), Wendolyn E. Tetlow considers the influence of Ezra Pound and T(HOMAS) S(TERNS) ELIOT (1888–1965) on the book's structure and language. Matthew Stewart provides a companion to the book in *Modernism and Tradition in Ernest Hemingway's "In Our Time": A Guide for Students and Readers* (2001). An excellent study of the earliest version of the collection is Milton A. Cohen's *Hemingway's Laboratory: The Paris "in our time"* (2005). The best criticism of *In Our Time* occurs in examinations of its individual stories. A few collections have incorporated these essays, including *Critical Essays on Hemingway's "In Our Time"* (1983), edited by Michael Reynolds. Other articles appear primarily in the *Hemingway Review*. Three articles examining *In Our Time* as an aesthetically integrated work deserve mention: Debra Moddelmog's "The Unifying Consciousness of a Divided Conscience: Nick Adams as Author of *In Our Time*," in *New Critical Approaches to the Short Stories of Ernest Hemingway* (1990), edited by Jackson J. Benson, 17–32; Harbour Winn's "Hemingway's *In Our Time*: 'Pretty Good Unity,'" *Hemingway Review* 9.2 (Spring 1990): 124–41; and Stephen Clifford's "Hemingway's Fragmentary Novel: Readers Writing the Hero in *In Our Time*," *Hemingway Review* 13.2 (Spring 1994): 12–23.

CLARENCE B. LINDSAY   UNIVERSITY OF TOLEDO

INDIAN CAPTIVITY NARRATIVES.
See Captivity Narratives

INDIANA
Indiana was admitted to the Union on December 11, 1816, as the nineteenth state. Before that, it was part of the Old Northwest territory (1783–1803) and Indiana Territory (1803–1816). Its present boundaries were not established until statehood.
Area: 36,418 square miles

Land: 35,867 square miles
Water: 551 square miles
Population (2010 census): 6,483,802
OVERVIEW: Nicknamed the "Crossroads of America" because of the many highways running like arteries through the state, Indiana occupied for many years a central position within the nation, geographically, demographically, and culturally. From 1861 to 1951, of the 136 most widely read books, 15 percent were by Hoosier authors. During Indiana's golden age, the fifty-year period between 1871 and 1921, Indiana rivaled the East by producing a disproportionate number of best sellers, its writers ranking a close second to New York in number published. Even up to 1965 Indiana writers still garnered second place.

Several factors contributed to this early flowering just fifty years after statehood in 1816. First, the state was settled by people from the South, OHIO, Pennsylvania, New Jersey, New York, and New England and also from Europe. For a while, geography encouraged Indiana to become a true melting pot without islands of nationality or an intellectual center. From 1890 to 1950 Indiana was the statistical center of the U.S. population. Contributing to local pride in being the real America, Indianans tended to vote with the majority of Americans in national elections, making the state a reliable political bellwether. As a result, the entire population became vocal.

Second, educational opportunities—or lack thereof—played a large role. Several denominational colleges created a favorable

© Karen Greasley, 2014

atmosphere for writers, but Indiana was poor in primary and secondary education relative to other states. In 1840 Indiana ranked sixteenth of twenty-six states in adult literacy. Many inhabitants turned to FOLKLORE, oral tales that stirred the imagination, and a rich language of colloquialisms, DIALECTS, and bad grammar. A close relationship exists between rich language and literary output, as witnessed in Elizabethan England. The lack of educational opportunities in Indiana increased library usage and encouraged formation of literary societies. This form of self-education fostered a people interested in reading and producing quality literature.

Third, at the beginning of the twentieth century Indiana possessed a community of writers who supported and encouraged one another. The proximity of publishing opportunities in CINCINNATI, Ohio, and Lexington, Kentucky, to the south, as well as the Bobbs-Merrill Company in Indianapolis, encouraged literary output. As a result, many Indiana authors chose to remain in the state rather than move to eastern publishing and artistic centers.

Although its literature tended toward the popular rather than the stellar, Indiana writers affected the course of American literary movements. They played a major role in shaping a truly American literature by redirecting it toward realism and contributing to the idea of America as the New World, the new frontier, and the new Eden, with the American frontiersman as the new Adam in a land that was both paradise and sinister wilderness. Indiana literature shares many themes with other Midwestern states, but its combination of geography and history, its writers' ambivalence toward the Hoosier landscape, and its preoccupation with the agrarian dream and garden myth make it unique.

HISTORY AND SIGNIFICANCE: Given the astounding number of works published by Indiana authors before World War II, Hoosier humorist GEORGE ADE (1866–1944) joked that every Hoosier considered himself a writer. Abe Martin, a fictional Brown County character created by (FRANK MCKINNEY) "KIN" HUBBARD (1868–1930), declares, "I'm told by transcontinental tourists who cross Indianny west on the ole historic Na-tional road that they no sooner hit Richmond on the Eastern border till plots fer novels an' rhymes fer verses come o'er 'em so fast an' thick that they kin hardly see the road, an' often go in the ditch" (quoted in Richard Banta, *Hoosier Caravan* [1975]: xi–xii). Although the record cannot support this inflated view of the inhabitants, Indiana's literary output has been substantial.

Early Exploration, Travel, and Captivity Narratives: The first Europeans in Indiana were probably French fur traders and Roman Catholic missionaries. Trader Louis Joliet (1645–1700) and Father Jacques Marquette (1637–1675) may have spent time in northern Indiana as they voyaged across Lake Michigan some time shortly after 1673. Joliet's original narrative has been lost, but Marquette's travels are recorded in *Voyage et Découverte du P. Marquette et Sr. Jolliet dans l'Amérique Septentrionale* (1681). In December 1679 René-Robert Cavelier, Sieur de La Salle (1643–1687), and his party portaged at South Bend on their way from the GREAT LAKES to the Mississippi. Some historians believe that they may have discovered the southern boundary of Indiana a decade earlier when they traveled from Lake Erie to the Ohio River. La Salle's explorations were recorded in his own writings and in four narratives by an Italian companion, Henri de Tonty (1650–1704).

The earliest English narrative primarily addressing the Indiana territory is the unpublished "Diary of a Journey into the Indian Country, 1765–1766," probably written by Charles Andre Barthe (fl. 1765), who traveled into the Miami, Wabash, and White River regions before going on to DETROIT. The journal of Colonel Henry Hamilton (ca. 1734–1796), published in the *Journal of Henry Hamilton and George Rogers Clark in the American Revolution, with the Unpublished Journal of Henry Hamilton* (1951), edited by R. E. Banta, recounts his trek to Fort Vincennes, which he recaptured for the British from George Rogers Clark in late 1778. Clark retook the fort in February. The diary of Virginian major Joseph Bowman (ca. 1752–1779), the only known journal by any of Clark's men, tells of Clark's recapture of the post. Two notable War of 1812–era diaries are the *Journal of the Life, Travels, and Gospel Labours of William Williams* (1828) by William Williams (Jr.)

(1763–1824), covering events and descriptions of Quaker meetings in the Indiana territory during 1814–1816, and the 1809 diary of Quaker Edward Bond (1740–1821).

Published travel narratives about Indiana after 1816, when it became a state, fall roughly into two types: those written by migrants from the eastern United States or other countries who assess the possibilities of the new state; and those written by Indiana residents traveling within the state.

Of the migrant literature, four works are noteworthy. *Memorable Days in America* (1823) by the Englishman William W. Faux is like much British literature for emigrants—satirical and abusive. Although Faux liked much of the Midwest, he found Indiana wild and nearly savage, with unprincipled residents. Another Englishman, William (Newnham) Blane (1800–1825), recounts his visit to the social experiment at New Harmony in *An Excursion through the United States and Canada during the Years 1822–23* (1824). His is considered the most unbiased and, therefore, the best English book about the Midwest. Other recorders of the New Harmony experiment were Paul Brown (fl. 1827) with *Twelve Months in New-Harmony* (1827) and Robert Dale Owen (1801–1877), son of founder Robert Owen, with *Threading My Way: Twenty-Seven Years of Autobiography* (1874). Both reveal disharmony within the utopian community.

Two Indiana immigrants who produced guides were John Scott (1793–1838) and Henry William Ellsworth (1814–1864). Scott left Pennsylvania for Brookville, Indiana, and later for Centerville, where he published in 1826, with William M. Doughty, the *Indiana Gazetteer, or Topographical Dictionary, Containing a Description of the Several Counties, Towns, Villages, Settlements, Roads, Lakes, Rivers, Creeks, Springs, &c. in the State of Indiana*. Unlike previous immigrant literature, the *Gazetteer* is optimistic, possessing a quaint charm and style. After a later move to Logansport, Scott started northern Indiana's first newspaper, the *Potawattimie and Miami Times*, in 1829. Ellsworth's *Valley of the Upper Wabash, Indiana, with Hints on Its Agricultural Advantages: Plan of a Dwelling, Estimates of Cultivation, and Notices of Labor-Saving Machines*, published in New York in 1838, gives an almost utopian vision of the area's fertility, climate, inhabitants, markets, and opportunities.

Of the travel literature written by Indiana residents, two works stand out: *The Christian Traveller. In Five Parts. Including Nine Years and Eighteen Thousand Miles* (1828) by Isaac Reed (1787–1858) and *The Journals and Indian Paintings of George Winter, 1837–1839* (published posthumously in 1948) by George Winter (1809–1876). Reed, a Presbyterian minister and circuit rider covering Indiana, Kentucky, and ILLINOIS, frankly describes small-town moral and cultural conditions. Winter came west in 1837 to paint Indians and settled in the frontier town of Logansport. First published piecemeal as a series of articles in the Logansport newspaper, Winter's journal realistically portrays Indians and their customs with understanding unusual for his time.

The last travel narrative to be considered is a most unusual one. Kate Rabb (1866–1937) disguised her work of historical fiction, *A Tour through Indiana in 1840*, as the edited diary of a relative, John Parsons, who travels from Petersburg, Virginia, through parts of Indiana, including Richmond, Indianapolis, Terre Haute, and Vincennes. Many travel narratives border on the fictional in their exaggerated descriptions of new lands and inhabitants, but Rabb's main character existed only in her imagination despite the frontispiece photograph of him. The date in the title belies the fact that it does not truly belong in the early literature category since it was published in 1920.

The captivity narrative that most grasped the nation's imagination was that of the 1778 capture of five-year-old Frances Slocum by the Lenape tribe. She was taken from her home in Wyoming Valley, Pennsylvania, to the Indiana territory, where she spent the rest of her life. Her brothers finally found her fifty-nine years later on an Indian reservation near Peru, Indiana, but she refused to leave her family, having married twice and given birth to four children. Her tale was told many times: by William Leete Stone (1835–1908) in *The Poetry and History of Wyoming* (1841), by John Todd (1800–1873) in *The Lost Sister of Wyoming* (1842), by James Slocum in *Frances Slocum, the Indian Captive* (1878), by Charles Elihu Slocum (1841–1915)

Edward Eggleston's *The Hoosier School-Boy*. C. Scribner's Sons, 1883.
Image courtesy of Special Collections, Grand Valley State University Libraries

in *History of Frances Slocum, the Captive* (1908), and by Ethel Leah Rosenberg (1915–2003), writing as Eth Clifford, in the children's book *Search for the Crescent Moon* (1973). The most complete retelling is by John F. Meginness (1827–1899) in *Biography of Frances Slocum, the Lost Sister of Wyoming* (1891).

Fiction: Before publication of *The Hoosier School-Master* in 1871 by EDWARD EGGLESTON (1837–1902), Indiana, and perhaps even the entire Midwest, did not appear to have a viable literary tradition of its own. As Eggleston complained in his novel's preface, Midwesterners found it difficult to see their own experience in the literature of the day because, no matter where it was written or by whom, "the manners, customs, thoughts, and feelings of New England country people filled so large a place in books, while our life, not less interesting, not less romantic, and certainly not less filled with humorous and grotesque material, had no place in literature" (1–2).

Not until 1843 was a novel set in Indiana: *The New Purchase; or, Seven and a Half Years in the Far West* by Baynard Rush Hall (1798–1863). Hall became one of the first professors in Indiana, teaching in the seminary that later became Indiana University. He published this thinly disguised autobiography under the pseudonym Robert Carlton. *The New Purchase* is important for its portrait of pioneer life, and Hall's disappointment in the area is evident in his descriptions of the rude state of Bloomington culture. Eunice (Bullard White) Beecher (1812–1897), wife of the famous Reverend Henry Ward Beecher (1813–1887), wrote *From Dawn to Daylight; or, The Simple Story of a Western Home* (1859) under the pseudonym A Minister's Wife. It, too, was an unflattering account of the ten years she spent with her husband as he led the Second Presbyterian Church in Indianapolis. Both Hall and Beecher wisely published these books after they returned east, but ironically, because they were so notorious, they became the most widely read fiction within the state until the 1870s—the latter despite or perhaps because of being banned from local library shelves.

Most early Hoosier fiction was sensational, didactic, or romantic, with romance ruling the day. The setting was little more than a backdrop to the exciting lives of the characters, so it made little difference where the action occurred. Even the most widely received work of this era was not set primarily in the state. The short-story collection *Life Sketches from Common Paths: A Series of American Tales* (1856) by JULIA LOUISA CORY DUMONT (1794–1857) was the second Midwestern book to gain favorable acceptance in the East. Although some of the stories can be considered realistic pictures of life along the Ohio River, many are sentimental and romantic and not about Indiana or its people. Interestingly, Dumont taught both novelists Edward and GEORGE CARY EGGLESTON (1839–1911) as children, and Edward Eggleston acknowledged his great debt to her in a March 1879 *Scribner's Monthly* article.

With the publication of Eggleston's *The Hoosier School-Master*, Indiana literature claimed its own identity, and the so-called golden age (1871–1921) began. Over a dozen Indiana fiction writers emerged as significant in American literature during this period. Many are still read, including LEW(IS) WALLACE (1827–1905), Edward Eggleston, George Cary Eggleston, AMBROSE (GWINETT) BIERCE (1842–ca. 1914), (JAMES) MAURICE THOMPSON (1844–1901), MARY HARTWELL CATHERWOOD (1847–1902), CHARLES MAJOR (1856–1913), GENE STRATTON-PORTER (1863–1924), George Ade (1866–1944), MEREDITH NICHOLSON (1866–1947), (NEWTON) BOOTH TARKINGTON (1869–1946), GEORGE BARR McCUTCHEON (1866–1928), and (HERMAN) THEODORE DREISER (1871–1945). Several prominent Hoosier writers have emerged since the golden age, but Hoosier fiction's major subjects and themes had developed by the onset of World War I.

The landscape was one of the first subjects. Mountains, deserts, and seas often become symbols for withstanding time or human intervention, but the Indiana landscape lacks such features. Frontier Indiana lay shrouded by nearly impenetrable hardwood forests. Early travelers found the forests either dangerous to physical and psychic survival or an escape from the evils of civilization. Images of the trees, of solitude, darkness, and stillness, or of being swallowed, buried, or lost abound. Being attracted to the wilderness yet desiring to tame or even break it for human habitation became a motif in works such as George C. Eggleston's *Jack Shelby: A Story of the Indiana Backwoods* (1906), George Barr McCutcheon's *Kindling and Ashes* (1926), and *Leafy Rivers* (1967) and *The Massacre at Fall Creek* (1975) by (MARY) JESSAMYN WEST (1902–1984). Charles Major's *The Bears of Blue River* (1901), purportedly for juveniles, thrilled his adult audiences with its primal lust to conquer nature. Another novel touching on this motif is *The Cubical City* (1926) by Janet Flanner (1892–1978), in which a young woman is unaware of the influence of her Indiana roots on the way she tries to introduce rural influences into her New York apartment.

Other authors explored the garden myth, sometimes using the Indiana landscape as a kind of Eden—lost but with the possibility of being regained. Among these are the autobiographical *Laddie* (1913) by Gene Stratton-Porter, as well as her nonfiction *Music of the Wild* (1910); *RAINTREE COUNTY* (1948) by ROSS (FRANKLIN) LOCKRIDGE JR. (1914–1948); *Miss MacIntosh, My Darling* (1965) by Marguerite

(Vivian) Young (1908–1995); *God Bless You, Mr. Rosewater* (1965) by KURT VONNEGUT (JR.) (1922–2007); and *A Serpent's Tooth* (1946) by Marthedith Furnas (1904–1991).

The works of MICHAEL A. MARTONE (b. 1955), including *Alive and Dead in Indiana* (1984), *Fort Wayne Is Seventh on Hitler's List* (1990), and *Double-Wide* (2007), play with the border between fact and fiction to encourage readers to search for their own mythic Midwest. Martone shapes the lives of several historical figures with Indiana ties as he explores what is omitted when famous people are reduced to dates and actions: Alfred Kinsey, James Dean, John Dillinger, and Ezra Pound (1885–1972) are but a few. *Indiana Winter* (1994) and *In the House of Blue Lights* (1998) by Susan Neville (b. 1951) also combine fact and fiction to reveal Indiana's outer and inner landscapes.

State historical events prompted literary works, and the historical novel was a favorite of Hoosier romance writers, especially from 1900 to 1910. The founding of the first Jesuit mission at the mouth of the White River became the subject of the romance *Dionis of the White Veil* (1911) by CAROLINE VIRGINIA KROUT (1852–1931), writing as Caroline Brown and inspired by her reading of an Indiana Historical Society account. Fort Vincennes, called Fort Sackville in the novel, also captured her attention in another romance, *On the We-a Trail* (1903), involving the recapture of the fort by George Rogers Clark. Maurice Thompson's *Alice of Old Vincennes* (1900) also features the Clark's recapture of Fort Vincennes. George Rogers Clark's life is the basis for *Long Knife* (1979) and *From Sea to Shining Sea* (1984) by James Alexander Thom (b. 1933). Thom's *Panther in the Sky* (1995) is based on the life of Tecumseh.

Tecumseh and the Battle of Tippecanoe feature in *Me-Won-I-Toc: A Tale of Frontier Life and Indian Character* (1867) by Solon Robinson (1803–1880). This short novel is a weak imitation of James Fenimore Cooper's writing but does contain a good description of the prairie during the frontier era. Jessamyn West's *The Massacre at Fall Creek* explores a true event that occurred on the Indiana frontier in 1824 when whites were executed for murdering Indians. The novel raises issues about the cultural clash between whites and Native Americans (see NATIVE AMERICANS AS DEPICTED IN MIDWESTERN LITERATURE), especially concerning land-ownership, capital punishment, and justice.

The New Harmony experiment was treated fictionally in *Seth Way: A Romance of the New Harmony Community* (1917) by Caroline Dale Snedeker (1871–1956). The story is based on the life of the natural scientist Thomas Say (1787–1834). Robert Dale Owen's *Beyond the Breakers: A Story of the Present Day* (1870) addresses his social reform ideas by idealizing New Harmony in the fictitious Chicksanga and himself in the hero, Franklin Sydenham. Other individuals from New Harmony make it into the novel under fictitious names. *Angel in the Forest: A Fairy Tale of Two Utopias* (1945) by Marguerite Young (1908–1995) tells of the Owenite and Rappite social experiments.

The Civil War era in Indiana found its way into several novels. *The Test of Loyalty* (1864) by James M. Hiatt, set mostly near Indianapolis, reveals the growing discontent within the federal army and the sympathizers who sheltered deserting soldiers who returned home. The semi-autobiographical *Thad Perkins: A Story of Indiana* (1899) by Frank A. Myers (1848–ca. 1928) reveals pioneer life in southern Indiana, including such dangerous groups as the White Caps and the anti-Union Knights of the Golden Circle. Southern sympathizers are the subject of *A Knight of the Golden Circle* (1911) by Ulysses Samuel Lesh (1868–1965). *Bates House* (1951), a novel by Clarence Benadum (1889–1978) inspired by a bronze plaque on the Claypool Hotel in Indianapolis, reveals the hatred Indianapolis residents felt for the Knights of the Golden Circle. Indiana Copperheads figure in Caroline Krout's *Knights in Fustian: A War Time Story of Indiana* (1900) and in *The Glory of His Country* (1910) by Frederick Landis (1872–1924), later dramatized as *The Copperhead* (1922). John Hunt Morgan's raid into Indiana is the subject of two novels: the romance *The Legionaires: A Story of the Great Raid* (1899) by Millard Cox (1856–1914), writing under the pseudonym Henry Scott Clark, and *The Raiders* (1955) by William E. Wilson (1906–1988). Ambrose Bierce's *Tales of Soldiers and Civilians* (1891) is based on his experiences in the Civil War, but Indiana does not figure in these tales.

Two novels that look at the home front during the world wars are *First Fiddle* (1932) by Margaret Weymouth Jackson (1895–1974) and *Under the Apple Tree* (1998) by DAN WAKEFIELD (b. 1932). Centered in Indianapolis, *First Fiddle* is the account of a World War I veteran, John Moore, who finds that the good jobs have been taken by those who remained home. Because his wife has advanced further in her career than he in his, he plays second fiddle in the family. Set in Illinois, Hoosier Wakefield's *Under the Apple Tree* examines the home front during World War II through the eyes of a ten-year-old.

Life in Indiana villages and small towns is another important subject in the state's literature. In the more realistic fiction, small-town inhabitants appear as insular, primitive, narrow-minded, suspicious of education, and hostile to those who do not make a living through physical labor. Examples can be found early and continue throughout Indiana literary history, including the two fictionalized autobiographies, Hall's *The New Purchase* and Beecher's *From Dawn to Daylight;* Mary Catherwood's short stories in *The Queen of the Swamp, and Other Plain Americans* (1899) and in various issues of *Lippincott's Magazine;* and the short-story collection *An Idyl of the Wabash* (1898) by Anna Nicholas (1849–1929). In *The Walking Stick* (1930) C(harles) E(lbert) Scoggins (1888–1955) criticizes both small-town conformity and the rebel who leaves, in this case a young musician who returns home after gaining fame in New York. In *Second Best* (1933) JEANNETTE COVERT NOLAN (1897–1974) chronicles the spiritual decline of a young woman who cannot follow her dream of a stage career in New York and must settle for small-town life.

Later writers, many of them exiles from their native state, find small-town life bleak. The short-fiction collection by WILLIAM H(OWARD) GASS (b. 1924), *In the Heart of the Heart of the Country* (1968), shows the careless neglect by the town's inhabitants of their landscape. Susan Neville's short-story collection *The Invention of Flight* (1984) decries the unimaginative clinging to place, while the characters in the 1957 collection *The Passionate Shepherd* (1988) by Samuel Yellen (1906–1983) attempt to reconnect to the place of their childhood. *Binding Spell* by

Elizabeth (Ann) Arthur (Bauer) (b. 1953) spoofs small-town isolationism. Even the state capital is criticized for its provincialism: Dan Wakefield's *Going All the Way* (1970) describes Indianapolis as limited and limiting to the two returning war vets.

On the other hand, Booth Tarkington, in *The Gentleman from Indiana* (1899), paints small-town life as being able to help eastern-born protagonists find themselves. Jessamyn West lovingly draws her small-town and rural characters in her collection of Quaker stories, *The Friendly Persuasion* (1945). Kurt Vonnegut—who includes characters hailing from Indiana in most of his novels—uses Indiana as a way to convey these characters' innocence, wholesomeness, rusticity, or lack of sophistication. SCOTT RUSSELL SANDERS (b. 1945) focuses on rural life in his essays and fiction, making his works prophetic calls for individuals to connect to local communities and take responsibility for the land. *Fetching the Dead* (1984), a collection of short fiction, and the essay collections *Staying Put: Making a Home in a Restless World* (1993) and *Writing from the Center* (1995) are good introductions to Sanders's themes. The trilogy by Haven Kimmel (b. 1965), including *The Solace of Leaving Early* (2003), *Something Rising (Light and Swift)* (2004), and *The Used World* (2007), captures both the tedium and the grace of small-town life.

Surprisingly, given the state's agricultural heritage, Indiana has produced only two significant writers of farm novels, LeRoy (Oliver) MacLeod (1893–1983) and DON(ALD LESTER) KURTZ (b. 1951). In the trilogy *Three Steeples* (1931), *The Years of Peace* (1932), and *The Crowded Hill* (1934), MacLeod follows Tyler Peck and his southern Indiana community just after the Civil War. Kurtz's *South of the Big Four* (1995) chronicles a failing farm operation.

Maurice Thompson's *Hoosier Mosaics* (1875) and Edward Eggleston's *The Hoosier School-Master* and *The Circuit Rider* (1874) reveal vivid details of farming communities in the early nineteenth century, an age Eggleston recognized as past when he wrote about it. A novel by Louis (Leon) Ludlow (1873–1950), *In the Heart of Hoosier-Land: A Story of the Pioneers, Based on Many Actual Experiences* (1925), celebrates with humor and pathos the spirit, simplicity, and purity of the rather crude rural society of southeastern Indiana. George McCutcheon's *The Sherrods* (1903), a tale about bigamy, shows what evils happen when a young man leaves the farm for the city. Gene Stratton-Porter's novels frequently portray the farm—with its hard work and drudgery and its joy and rustic beauty—as an adjunct to the pristine woods and nature that give her characters sanctuary. *What This River Keeps* (2009) by Gregory L. Schwipps (b. 1972) explores the price of deeply loving the land. In this case, a dam project threatens to swallow an elderly couple's southern Indiana farm.

Running through much Hoosier agrarian and small-town fiction is the sense of flatness, of a country long settled, long battered and used, often neglected, but with a beauty of its own. As a whole, the literature tells the story of clearing dark, dangerous woods to establish farm and family and later abandoning the rural and agricultural for the urban and industrial. These conflicts among the pristine, the agricultural, and the industrial states of the land capture the imagination of Hoosier writers.

One writer who focused on the urban and industrial was Booth Tarkington. After a stint writing romance novels, Tarkington turned to realism, although, like most early realists, he was not as concerned with exploring large social issues as with capturing the flavor of his time. His *Growth* trilogy—*The Turmoil* (1915), *The Magnificent Ambersons* (1918), and *The Midlander* (1924)—narrates the decline of the older aristocratic families as industrialization changes the social and economic character of the community, giving power to the brawny businessmen capable of hustling after success. *Alice Adams* (1921), originally planned to be part of the trilogy, is probably his best novel. It deals with a family that fails to rise in the socioeconomic world despite their efforts.

John Calvin Mellett (1888–1976), sometimes writing as Jonathan Brooks, extolled the virtues of high-mindedness and civic responsibility in his novels about cities feeling the pangs of industrial growth. *High Ground* (1928) follows a newspaper editor, and *Chains of Lightning* (1929), a public utilities magnate.

These more optimistic viewpoints were not shared by Theodore Dreiser, a naturalist whose novels portray a morally indifferent world where vice and virtue might be accidents, if not mere irrelevancies in life. Exterior forces control his characters, whose weak wills appear to be the result of circumstance, not failing, but they are destroyed in the crucible of social Darwinism. Although none of his novels is set in Indiana, at least four are considered to have elements of the lives of Dreiser's family members: SISTER CARRIE (1900), *Jennie Gerhardt* (1911), *The "Genius"* (1915), and *An American Tragedy* (1925).

A fourth novelist dealing with urban themes, DAVID GRAHAM PHILLIPS (1867–1911), wrote several muckraking novels dealing with the exploitation of workers by big business monopolies and political corruption. *The Reign of Gilt* (1905) is his most important. His later books, including *Susan Lenox, Her Fall and Rise* (posthumously published in 1917) reveal women's uncertain status in an era when commercial success took a tremendous toll on the individual. Although Phillips shared some of Dreiser's social Darwinist views, he wrote to effect social change rather than to record current conditions. (Lela) Lee (Ann) Zacharias (b. 1944) described the pollution and urban sprawl of Hammond in her short-story collection *Helping Muriel Make It through the Night* (1975). Bloomington fares better in *Lessons* (1981), her novel set in that locale.

As for industry, Indiana had little manufacturing until the mid-nineteenth century when small factories appeared. By 1900 Indiana was ranked eighth in the nation in the value of its manufactured goods.

The automobile figures in Tarkington's *The Magnificent Ambersons* and *The Winner* (1915) by William (West) Winter (1881–1940). The latter is the success story of a young engineer who designs a radically new automobile engine that is tested in an important automobile race. The Indianapolis 500-Mile Race is remembered specifically in *High Cotton* (1992) by Darryl Pinckney (b. 1953); this novel is told from the perspective of a young black man who eventually escapes Indianapolis for New York. The protagonist's grandfather calls race day "White Trash Day" because of the garbage left by the predominantly white race fans.

Three novels by David Anderson (1878–1947), all set in the Wabash River area, explore minor and little-known Indiana occupations. Pearl hunting is the occupation in *The Blue Moon: A Tale of the Flatwoods* (1919) and *Thunderhawk: A Tale of the Wabash Flatwoods* (1926), while *The Red Lock: A Tale of the Flatwoods* (1922) describes the adventures of a boy bound to a moneylender in 1849 to satisfy his family's debts.

Indiana's educational system has proved fertile ground for Hoosier writers, perhaps a reflection of the fact that Indiana, in its 1816 constitution, was the first state to provide for free public education, which it did not fund with taxes, however, until 1849. Eggleston's *The Hoosier School-Master* gives a glimpse into the rural schoolteacher's life, based in part on his boyhood and the experiences of his brother George as a rural teacher. Hall's *The New Purchase* recounts his negative opinions of the Indiana State Seminary, which was created by the state legislature and later opened at Bloomington, becoming the Indiana State College in 1828. He changes the names of all characters and places in the book. Wabash College, fictionalized as Madison College, in its early years is the background for Meredith Nicholson's *A Hoosier Chronicle* (1912), which was well received and did much to increase the interest of non-Hoosiers in the state. Rose Polytechnic Institute, now Rose Hulman Institute of Technology, in Terre Haute, is perhaps the setting of *A Fearsome Riddle* (1901) by MAX(IMILIAN) EHRMANN (1872–1945), a mystery about the strange death of a professor. Elmer (Holmes) Davis (1890–1958) wrote several humorously satirical novels about respectable people placed in doubtful circumstances. Those involving educators include *Times Have Changed* (1923), about a principal whose innocent attention to an alumna results in misunderstanding; *I'll Show You the Town* (1924), about a similar predicament involving a professor and three women; and *Strange Woman* (1927), about a college president and a seductive opera singer.

Given its status as crossroads and melting pot, Indiana has not produced a noteworthy body of immigrant, ethnic, or racial fiction. Darryl Pinckney in *High Cotton* (1992) considers whether enduring legacy or ever-changing social definition determines blackness. He explores this question in a world of upper-middle-class blacks; his unnamed character moves physically from conservative Indianapolis to Harlem to Paris and psychically through various definitions of blackness. Mohja Kahf (b. 1967), in *The Girl in the Tangerine Scarf* (2006), creates a heroine who, like her, is a Syrian immigrant to Indiana struggling to live her Muslim faith in a culture frequently hostile to it.

It is also not surprising that Indiana has not produced many Native American writers. See NATIVE AMERICAN LITERATURE.. When French explorers ventured into the territory, they found it practically deserted because the native inhabitants had fled from the northern Iroquois, encouraged by the rivalry between the French and British. When the Indians did return, they had to contend with French traders and later white settlers who drove them west. But three Native American fiction writers should be counted within Indiana's literary history borders. ZITKALA-ŠA (RED BIRD) (1876–1938), born Gertrude Simmons in SOUTH DAKOTA, was educated in Indiana at Quaker-funded schools, first as a child at White's Manual Labor Institute in Wabash and then at Earlham College in Richmond. Her most important work is *American Indian Stories* (1921). In this collection of short stories and autobiographical essays, she chronicles her traditional Sioux upbringing, criticizes the harshness of American Indian boarding schools and the corruption of government institutions, and outlines her struggle to find her identity without succumbing to the restrictions of reservation life or complete assimilation into white culture. Although she is better known for her poetry, Kimberly M. Blaeser (b. 1955), an Ojibwa raised in MINNESOTA and educated at the University of Notre Dame in South Bend, has also written prose. She edited and contributed to *Stories Migrating Home: A Collection of Anishinaabe Prose* (1999). Dark Rain Thom (b. 1942), a Shawnee, co-wrote *Warrior Woman: The Exceptional Life Story of Nonhelema, Shawnee Indian Woman Chief* (2004), a novelized biography, with her husband, James Alexander Thom.

Poetry: During Indiana's frontier era, poetry was the only purely literary form deemed acceptable for writing and reading by settlers. Some have speculated that this was because of the mind-set that came with building something new in a new world.

The settlers were concerned with the practical, focused on the future, and too busy for formal education. But the poetry of this period provided them, in the words of Daniel Drake's 1834 address to Miami University, with a new language "superior in force, variety, and freshness," so it took root in the newly plowed soil and flowered early in the state (*Oxford* [Ohio] *Addresses,* 1835, 214). *Poets and Poetry of the West* (1860) by William Turner Coggeshall (1824–1867) lists 23 Hoosier poets among the 152 poets included from a ten-state area. In the years from statehood until the end of the Civil War, the subject matter and skill level varied, but for the most part, Coggeshall asserts that these poets wrote "respectable" poetry, such as the "melodious sermons" of SARAH T(ITTLE BARRETT) BOLTON (1814–1893).

The first Indiana poet was Mrs. Lard, perhaps Rebecca H. Lard, who emigrated from Vermont to Indiana in 1820, several years after her husband, only to divorce him and return to her native state. Her twelve-page poem *The Banks of the Ohio* (1823) takes the history of the Ohio Valley as its subject and praises the state.

John Cain (1805–1867) claims two firsts: first published book by a Hoosier poet and first poetry book published within the state. However, no copies of his *Miscellaneous Poems* (1832) now exist. The first book of poetry still extant by a Hoosier poet is *Harp of the West: A Volume of Poems* (1839) by Dr. Joseph S. Welsh (d. ca. 1846), and the first published in Indiana still extant is *Elskwatawa; or, The Moving Fires, and Other Poems* (1840) by George Washington Cutter (1801–1865). Welsh's "The Indiana Warrior's Reflections, on the Banks of Coal Creek, and His Description of the Combat at Tippecanoe" is unusual for its time in that it presents the Indian point of view. Cutter's poems were widely known, especially "Buena Vista," about the Mexican War battle, and the patriotic "E Pluribus Unum"; both were from *Buena Vista, and Other Poems* (1848). Cutter was considered the state's leading literary figure at the time.

Other early poets were Horace P. Biddle (1811–1900), whose first book, *A Few Poems* (1852), was praised by Washington Irving (1783–1859). Biddle wrote seven more volumes. The best volumes of Dr. Orpheus

Everts (1826–1903), *O-Na-We-Quah, and Other Poems* (1856) and *The Spectral Bride, and Other Poems* (1857), were published in La Porte and were not widely known. Mary Louisa Chitwood (1832–1856), after showing much promise, died at twenty-three. Her poems were collected and published posthumously as *Poems* (1857). *Recollections of the Early Settlement of the Wabash Valley* (1860) by Sandford C. Cox (1811–1877) is significant for the glimpses it provides of early state history and life, including the organization of two colleges: Wabash and Indiana Asbury, now DePauw University.

Ohio-born sisters ALICE CARY (1820–1871) and PHOEBE CARY (1824–1871) spent a few years in Indiana, which inspired their poems of rural life and nature. Alice's "The West Country" and "Pictures of Memory" and Phoebe's "Field Preaching," "The Lamp on the Prairie," "The Maize," "The Prairie Fire," and "Nearer Home" all reflect their stay at Oxford in Benton County. They were published in *The Poems of Alice and Phoebe Cary* (1849).

Sarah T. Bolton was the most beloved poet of this period. She published four volumes: *Poems by Sarah T. Bolton* (1865), which was reissued with additional poems as *The Life and Poems of Sarah T. Bolton* (1880); *Songs of a Life-Time* (1892); and *Paddle Your Own Canoe, and Other Poems* (1897) published posthumously. Although she explored various themes and techniques, she wrote predominantly sentimental verse about real and imagined death and loss, religious subjects, and the lost past.

John Finley (1797–1866) wrote a poem that brought fame to the word "Hoosier," although he was not the first to use that term. "The Hoosier's Nest," published in *Palladium* in 1830, was tremendously popular and made it all the way to England. Critics cited it as an example of backwoods poetry and the best Indiana poem of its day. Whether or not this judgment was valid, "The Hoosier's Nest," celebrating the virtues of the state and of hard work, was the earliest western poem to attract such attention.

After the Civil War, Indiana literature entered a golden age. Although the novel dominated the next fifty years of the state's literary production, Hoosier poets also experienced critical success, most notably SISTER MARY MADELEVA (1887–1964), Evaleen Stein (1863–1923), Max Ehrmann, JAMES WHITCOMB RILEY (1849–1916), known as "Mr. Indiana," and WILLIAM VAUGHN MOODY (1869–1910). Golden-age poetry tends to be romantic, even sentimental, with realism a minor refrain.

Although Sister Mary Madeleva's work spanned several decades, she is included in the golden age. Born Mary Evaline Wolff, she published twelve volumes of verse, much of it religious, but she also explored secular and spiritual love and her European travels in free verse and sonnets. *The Four Last Things: Collected Poems* (1959) is a good introduction to her work.

Evaleen Stein has the honor of being the state's first true nature poet in *One Way to the Woods* (1897) and *Among the Trees Again* (1902). Previous poets had merely used nature as a backdrop for plot or moral lessons. She also wrote children's books and romantic tales.

Max Ehrmann wrote fiction and drama but did his best work in poetry. *A Prayer and Other Selections* (1906) and *Desiderata* (1927) were very popular. In all his many volumes of verse, he extols the worth of toil, the need for reflection, love of humanity, and care for the unfortunate.

The writer most associated with Indiana is James Whitcomb Riley, loved by many for his glimpses into remembered childhood, his sentimental praise of a life that never existed, his use of folksy dialect, and his humor emphasizing peculiarity of character in figures such as Little Orphant Annie, the Raggedy Man, and old Aunt Mary. He is sharply criticized by others for those very qualities. Without ignoring the darker sides of poverty and crime, he looked at the world through the eyes of a child, in the process extolling the virtues of common sense, cheerfulness, and wholesomeness. He came to be called the Hoosier Poet. Some of the most popular of his numerous volumes were *The Old Swimmin' Hole, and 'Leven More Poems* (1883), *Afterwhiles* (1888), *Rhymes of Childhood* (1890), *Poems Here at Home* (1893), and *The Book of Joyous Children* (1902).

William Vaughn Moody was a meticulous craftsman who destroyed what displeased him and therefore published little. The verse drama *The Fire-Bringer* (1904), the first part of a projected trilogy he died before completing, secured his reputation. The trilogy uses the myth of Prometheus to assert human dependence on God and explore sin and evil. His place in American letters suffered when the imagists gained dominance. Thus ended the golden age of Indiana's poetry. Nineteen Hoosier poets achieved popularity during this period. Only Riley and Moody remain well known.

In the remaining decades of the twentieth century, several poets should be noted. Marguerite Young (1908–1995) published *Prismatic Ground* (1937) and *Moderate Fable* (1944) that reveal her as an intellectual, if sometimes obscure, poet. The twelve books by E. Merrill Root (1895–1973) cover nature, philosophy, humor, love, and history. *Before the Swallow Dares* (1947) is considered his best. Margaret E. Bruner (1886–1971) wrote nine books, had poems appear in 160 publications, and won forty cash prizes during her career, earning her the title of Poet Laureate from both the Indiana Federation of Poetry Clubs and the Indiana Poetry Society. *The Deeper Need* (1957) presents poems about Indiana.

During her years in Indianapolis, ALICE (RUTH) FRIMAN (b. 1933) felt alienated from the state's conservatism and open landscape but produced poems that explore the link between nature and human identity. *Reporting from Corinth* (1984) and *Inverted Fire* (1997) are two of her works. Michael Martone has published two volumes of poetry, *At a Loss* (1977) and *Return to Powers* (1985). Thomas R. Thornburg (b. 1937), an expatriate, writes of central Indiana in *Saturday Town and Other Poems* (1976) and *Munseetown* (2001). *Jagged with Love* (2005) by Susanna Childress (b. 1978) features poems reflecting her childhood in Madison and events in the state. Indianapolis residents Etheridge Knight (1931–1991) and Mari E. Evans (b. 1923) write poetry reflective of their African American identity, as does University of Notre Dame professor Cornelius Eady (b. 1954).

Other Hoosiers using the state's landscape in their poetry include John Woods (1926–1995) with *The Deaths of Paragon, Indiana* (1955); Philip D. Appleman (b. 1926) with *Kites on a Windy Day* (1967) and *Open Doorways* (1976); Richard Pflum (b. 1932) with *Moving into Light* (1975); Darlene Mathis

Eddy (b. 1937) with *Leaf Threads, Wind Rhymes* (1986); Charles Isley (1910–2000) with *Dune Trail* (1949) and *Dune Song* (1982); Samuel Yellen (1906–1983), author of *The Convex Mirror: Collected Poems* (1971); and Arthur Mapes (1913–1986) with *Indiana Memories* (1980), including the state's official poem, "Indiana." The works of Jared Carter (b. 1939) and F(RANKLIN) RICHARD THOMAS (b. 1940) are grounded in the Midwest. Carter's mythic Mississinewa County, somewhere north of the Ohio River, is the setting of many poems in *Work, for the Night Is Coming* (1981), *After the Rain* (1993), and *Cross This Bridge at a Walk* (2006). Thomas describes himself as a domestic poet; his poems reflect southern Indiana and MICHIGAN. He has published six volumes, including two in the same year: *Frog Praises Night* (1980) and *Alive with You This Day* (1980). Shari Wagner (b. 1958), Indiana Poet Laureate for 2016 and 2017, grew up in the Mennonite culture. Her books include *The Harmonist at Nightfall: Poems of Indiana* (2013). Her poetry exhibits close knowledge of Indiana's landscape and history.

Drama: *Pocahontas* (1837) by Robert Dale Owen is considered the first play written by a Hoosier. During the golden age of Indiana literature, many writers known principally for their work in other genres, including Lew Wallace, Booth Tarkington, Max Ehrmann, William Dudley Foulke (1848–1935), Meredith Nicholson, and Theodore Dreiser, also wrote plays. George Ade wrote thirteen comic dramas and musicals; two that portray the Hoosier scene and character are *The County Chairman* (1924) and *The College Widow* (1924). In addition to his verse dramas, William Vaughn Moody wrote prose plays *The Great Divide* (1906) and *The Faith Healer* (1909). *The Faith Healer* is the first drama of importance set in the Midwest and embodying its themes.

Only two individuals functioned primarily as playwrights during this era: Joseph Arthur (b. Arthur Hill Smith, ca. 1848–1906) and William O. Bates (1852–1924). Arthur's melodramas were popular and successful in the late nineteenth century, and many of them employed machinery—such as a saw, fire engine, or elevator—in the climactic scenes. *Blue Jeans* (1890) is set in Rising Sun. Bates wrote mostly one-act plays, such as *Polly of Pogue's Run* (1917) about a Copperhead uprising in Indiana. His influence was most important in the Little Theatre Society of Indiana, founded in 1915, which produced plays by Hoosier writers.

Morning's at Seven (1939) by Paul Osborn (1901–1988) won a Tony Award. Joseph Arnold Hayes (1918–2006), sometimes using the pseudonym Joseph Arnold, wrote comedies during his long career, beginning with *And Came the Spring* (1942). Charles (Edward) Gordone (1925–1995), author of *No Place to Be Somebody* (1967), was the first African American to earn the Pulitzer Prize for Drama (1970). Mari Evans, another African American writer from Indiana, wrote several plays during the 1970s, including *Eyes* (1979), based on Zora Neal Hurston's *Their Eyes Were Watching God*.

Film: Indiana writers have also contributed to the FILM industry. Gene Stratton-Porter formed her own film company, Gene Stratton-Porter Productions, to film her novels. Jessamyn West helped with the filming of her book *The Friendly Persuasion*. Emily Kimbrough (1899–1989), Alan LeMay (1899–1964), and cousins Lois Christine Eby (1908–1998) and John Fleming (1906–1964) were screenwriters. Bill Peet (b. William Bartlett Peed, 1915–2002) worked for Disney Studios. Serbian American Steve Tesich (1942–1996) wrote an Academy Award–winning coming-of-age screenplay for the film *Breaking Away* (1979), set in Bloomington, as well as the novel *Summer Crossing* (1982), set in East Chicago, Indiana. Angelo Pizzo (b. 1948) wrote and co-produced two films about Hoosier sports legends: *Hoosiers* (1986), based on the Milan basketball team's state championship, and *Rudy* (1993), about a walk-on to Notre Dame's football team. *Hoosiers* has been named the best sports film of all time by ESPN and *USA Today* and has earned placement in the Library of Congress National Film Registry. Don Boner (b. 1944), an Indianapolis-based independent filmmaker, released *Somewhere in Indiana* (2004). The film chronicles the characters' journey of self-discovery as they physically journey to the Indiana birthplace of fictional actor Eddie Ray. *Home of the Giants* (2007, Heartland Film Festival) by Rusty Gorman is another movie about Hoosier high school basketball.

To date, over seventy films and television episodes have been filmed in Indiana, including *Hoosiers, Rudy, Rain Man* (1988), *Pearl Harbor* (2001), and *Eight Men Out* (1988). One such film, *Madison* (2005), starring Jim Caviezel, explored the importance of hydroplane racing to the town of the same name. Although the television series *Close to Home* (2005–2007) was filmed in Southern California, it centered on the prosecutor's office in Indianapolis. *The Middle* (beginning in 2009) is set in fictional Orson, Indiana, and *Parks and Recreation* (also beginning in 2009), in fictional Pawnee, Indiana. Popular radio (1930s) and television (1950s) personality Richard (Bernard) "Red" Skelton (1913–1997) wrote many of the sketches for his performances.

Popular Literature:

Children's Literature: Indiana authors have written several juvenile series novels that had an important influence on children: the Elsie Dinsmore books (1867–1905) by Martha Finley (1828–1909); the twelve Little Colonel books (1895–1930) by Annie Fellow Johnston (1863–1931), which led to the Shirley Temple movie; the Brownie books (1905–1927) by Nathaniel Moore Banta (1867–1932); the Twins series (1911–1938) by Lucy Fitch Perkins (1865–1937); and Raggedy Ann (1918–1943) by Johnny Gruelle (1880–1938), which was exceeded in sales only by *Alice in Wonderland*. Clifford, the Big Red Dog, the 1963 creation of Norman (Ray) Bridwell (b. 1928), and Garfield the Cat by Jim Davis (b. 1945), first syndicated in 1978, have become widely known.

Prolific children's authors who have made use of the state include George Cary Eggleston, who wrote many idealized tales for boys; Mabel Leigh Hunt (1892–1971), who published nearly thirty books, many with Indiana settings; and Miriam Mason (1900–1973), some of whose fifty-seven books are based on Indiana heritage, as is the case with the eighteen books by Elisabeth H. Friermood (1903–1992). Eth Clifford set eleven of her forty-five books in Indiana, and Crystal Thrasher (b. Faye Knight; 1921–2007) wrote five books that follow the Robinson family during Indiana's Depression years. Author-illustrator Bill Peet has produced more than thirty-five books. Two of the sixteen novels by Dorothy Hamilton (1906–1983) focus on Indiana: *Rosalie at Eleven* (1980) and *Anita's Choice* (1971), the latter about migrant workers near New Castle. Phyllis Reynolds Naylor (b. 1933) has written nearly fifty books; *The Witch's Sister* (1975) and its two sequels and several Bessledorf books have plots that occur in Indiana.

Many children's authors make use of the state's history or merely use Indiana as a plot backdrop. However, one book that explores frontier life is *Log Cabin in the Woods* (1988) by Joanne Landers Henry (b. 1927). Representative examples of descriptions of small-town life are Friermood's *The Luck of Daphne Tolliver* (1961), about Mason, Indiana, around 1918; Hunt's *Ladycake Farm* (1952), about racist attitudes in rural communities; and Pamela Service's (b. 1945) *When the Night Wind Howls* (1987), perhaps about Bloomington, where the author lives. The protagonist of Hamilton's *Anita's Choice* grows to feel a part of the community because of the school and the friends she makes.

Schools furnish the backdrop for *Pageant* (1986), by Kathryn Lasky (b. 1944), a semi-autobiographical account of a Jewish girl in a Christian private school, and Hunt's *Cupola House* (1961), another semi-autobiographical account of a family's move to a college town for better education.

Peet has written two books about industries, *Smokey* (1962), a switch engine, and *The Caboose Who Got Loose* (1971), as well as *Pamela Camel* (1984) about circus life, stemming from his hometown experience in Peru, Indiana, the winter quarters of the Barnum and Bailey circus.

Adult novelists who also wrote for children include Charles Major, with *The Bears of Blue River*; Tarkington, with books about Penrod, "the worst boy in town" (*Penrod* 125), including *Penrod* (1914), *Penrod and Sam* (1916), and *Penrod Jashber* (1929); and Stratton-Porter, with *Freckles* (1904), *A Girl of the Limberlost* (1909), and *Laddie* (1913). Riley's *Joyful Poems for Children* (1892) includes many favorites.

In 1988 the National Endowment for the Humanities published a reading list for high school seniors; it contained 115 books, from the Bible through Homer and Shakespeare to a cutoff date of 1960. A handful of Hoosier authors' works made the list: Wallace's *Ben Hur: A Tale of the Christ* (1880), *The Robe* (1942) by LLOYD C(ASSEL) DOUGLAS (1877–1951), *The Big Sky* (1947) by A(lfred) B(ertram) Guthrie (Jr.) (1901–1990), and Dreiser's *Sister Carrie* (1900) and *An American Tragedy* (1925).

Mysteries and Crime Fiction: Most crime novels by Indiana writers are not set in the state, perhaps because Indiana has few large cities, the preferred locale for plots by the early writers of the genre. During the 1930s and 1940s, however, several writers emerged. Years in government service led Herbert (Osborne) Yardley (1859–1958) to write three novels about international espionage: *The Blonde Countess* (1934), about World War I; *Red Sun of Nippon* (1934), about Japan; and *Crows Are Black Everywhere* (1945), set in Chungking, China. Rex (Todhunter) Stout (1886–1975) created several characters in his fifty-plus novels: the widely known detective team of Nero Wolfe and Archie Goodwin, Tecumseh Fox, Alphabet Hicks, and the female detectives Theodolinda "Dol" Bonner and Sylvia Raffray. During this same period (H.) Bill Miller (1920–1961) co-wrote several novels with Californian Robert (Allison) Wade (1920–2012), using the pseudonyms Wade Miller, Dale Wilmer, or Whit Masterson. Their San Diego hotel detective Max Thursday first appeared in *Guilty Bystander* (1947). Mildred Gordon (1912–1979) and Gordon Gordon (1912–2002), writing under the name the Gordons, published twenty novels, including the Undercover Cat series in the 1960s, which became the film *That Darn Cat!* (1965). Thomas B. Dewey (1915–1981), using the pseudonyms Tom Brandt and Cord Wainer, wrote forty novels and numerous short stories. His characters include Singer Batts, introduced in *Hue and Cry* (1944), the CHICAGO detective Mac, introduced in *Prey for Me* (1954), and Pete Schofield. Known primarily as a playwright, Joseph Hayes was the author of nine suspense novels, including *The Desperate Hours* (1954), which was later turned into a Tony Award–winning play.

During the later decades of the twentieth century JOHN (WILLIAM) JAKES (b. 1932), who also wrote historical and science fiction, began the Johnny Havoc series in 1960. Spy novelist Richard O'Connor (1915–1975), writing as Frank Archer and Patrick Wayland, developed the characters of Lloyd Nicholson, whom he introduced in *Counterstroke* (1964), and Joe Delaney, who appeared first in *The Naked Crusader* (1964). Joe L. Hensley (1926–2007), an African American judge, wrote *The Color of Hate* (1960), addressing racism in the legal system. He also created, in *Deliver Us to Evil* (1971), the character of Donald Robak, criminal lawyer. University of Notre Dame professor Ralph McInerny (1929–2010) wrote the popular Father Roger Dowling mystery series, beginning with *Her Death of Cold* (1977). He also created Sister Mary Teresa in *Not a Blessed Thing* (1981).

Novels set in Indianapolis include two series by Michael Z. Lewin (b. 1942), one featuring private eye Albert Samson and the other police lieutenant Leroy Powder, and the series by Ronald Tierney (b. 1944) about Indianapolis detective Deets Shanahan: *The Stone Veil* (1990), *The Steel Web* (1991), and *The Iron Glove* (1992). The Lace White series by Jeannette Covert Nolan uses several Indiana locales, although with fictional names: Brown County and Indianapolis in *Where Secrecy Begins* (1939) and New Harmony in *Final Appearance* (1943).

Dime Novels: An early writer of DIME NOVELS, Symmes M. Jelley (b. 1855), writing under the pseudonym Le Jemlys, published a work of crime fiction, *Shadowed to Europe: A Chicago Detective on Two Continents* in 1885. James Buchanan Elmore (1857–1942), who wrote of rural life, marketed his works so cheaply and effectively that at his death he owned five hundred acres of land, much of it purchased with the earnings from his dime books. Most of them were of poetry, including the famous poem "The Monon Wreck," but he also wrote prose. His books are sought by collectors: *Love among the Mistletoe, and Poems* (1899); *Poems* (1901); *A Lover in Cuba, and Poems* (1901); *Twenty-Five Years in Jackville, a Romance in the Days of "The Golden Circle"* and *Selected Poems* (1904); and *Autumn Roses* (1907). John Whitson (1854–1936) wrote nineteen books, most of dime-novel quality. George Ade wrote a burlesque of the genre in *Bang! Bang!* (1928).

Romance Novels: It is not a coincidence that Indiana's golden age coincided with the flourishing of romance and sentimental fiction in America. Romance novels fall into two forms: those set in exotic locales and involving courtly romance, and those using more familiar, local settings complete with the requisite adventure, danger, and romance. Americans at the end of the nineteenth century, although still enamored with the exotic, became more intrigued with the familiar setting made unfamiliar. Hoosier writers, with their focus on Midwestern settings and characters and their experimentation with the realistic and the romantic, found a ready market. Many were published by the Indianapolis-based Bowen-Merrill Company.

Three Hoosier works became national standards of the romance genre, all within the exotic category: Charles Major's *When Knighthood Was in Flower* (1898); Booth Tarkington's *Monsieur Beaucaire* (1900), set in Bath, England; and George Barr McCutcheon's *Graustark* series, introduced in 1901, about a mythical Balkan kingdom. Among those works that used local color and achieved large sales were Tarkington's *The Gentleman from Indiana,* Maurice Thompson's *Alice of Old Vincennes,* Major's *The Bears of Blue River,* Meredith Nicholson's *The House of a Thousand Candles* (1905), and Gene Stratton-Porter's *Freckles.* Each of these writers also produced more realistic novels.

Science Fiction: Although Indiana writers known primarily for their work in other genres experimented with science fiction, the state has produced three writers important to the field: Kurt Vonnegut, PHILIP JOSÉ FARMER (1918–2009), and John Jakes. Although Vonnegut's novels use Hoosier characters, only one has an Indiana setting: *God Bless You, Mr. Rosewater* (1965). Farmer published *The Green Odyssey* (1957) and six Riverworld books, the first being *To Your Scattered Bodies Go* (1971). Jakes, also the author of historical and crime novels, wrote the Brak the Barbarian series and fourteen more science-fiction works.

Another work deserves mention because of its Indiana locale. *Alternities* (1988), by Michael P. Kube-Mcdowell (b. 1954), has the protagonist travel to a parallel universe by using a gate in the Scottish Rite Cathedral in Indianapolis. The tale also features a scene in a southern Indiana forest where the trees are seen as a sanctuary from the highly technological world—a motif portrayed in much of the state's literature.

Religious Fiction: Two important and highly successful works of religious fiction emerging from Indiana are Lew Wallace's *Ben Hur: A Tale of the Christ* and Lloyd C. Douglas's *The Robe*. Both became feature films. A prolific novelist of biblical subjects is Walter Wangerin (b. 1944) with titles such as *Paul* (2001) and *Jesus* (2005).

As for early fiction, *Mrs. Ben Darby; or, The Weal and Woe of Social Life* (1853) by Angelina Maria Lorraine Collins (1805–1885); *The Scroll and Locket; or, The Maniac of the Mound* (1858) by James Hervey (1819–1905); *Nora Wilmot: A Tale of Temperance and Woman's Rights* (1858) by Henrietta Rose; and the short-story collection *Hot Corn* (1854), set mainly in New York City, by Solon Robinson (1803–1880) are representative.

A bitter and wild anti-Catholic novel, *Light, More Light* (1855) by Isaac Kelso, is set at the convent of St. Mary-of-the-Woods, near Terre Haute. It was popular enough to go through ten editions. A much more positive view of Catholics is portrayed in books and short stories by Maurice Egan (1852–1924), including *That Girl of Mine* (1877), *The Life around Us* (1885), and *A Marriage of Reason* (1893). A poorly written but highly autobiographical novel of Quaker life in early Indiana is *In the Days of My Youth: An Intimate Personal Record of Life and Manners in the Middle Ages of the Middle West* (1923) by James Baldwin (1841–1925). Indiana Amish farmers are the subject of *Straw in the Wind* (1937), the first novel by Ruth (Lininger) Dobson (1911–1985). Her second novel is about a minister's wife in a small Indiana town: *Today Is Enough* (1939).

Humor: HUMOR appears frequently in Indiana literature regardless of genre. Hoosier humor is characterized by dry wit, drollery, and the story told with a straight face, often ironically, regularly at the expense of the narrator, but always at the expense of other inflated egos. George Ade is one of the state's most famous and prolific authors; he wrote short stories, fables, plays, and musicals. SAMUEL LANGHORNE CLEMENS (1835–1910), writing as Mark Twain, and WILLIAM DEAN HOWELLS (1837–1920) were fans of his early collections of stories that used continuing characters: *Artie* (1896), *Pink Marsh* (1897),

and *Doc' Horne* (1899). His *Fables in Slang* (1899) secured his fame and wealth, and he went on to write stage plays.

Kin Hubbard was another popular American humorist. He began as an artist, specializing in caricatures, many of which were political. Hubbard's rural character Abe Martin captured the nation's interest. Collections of these drawings with Martin's quips were issued annually, beginning in 1907 with *Abe Martin of Brown County, Indiana* and continuing until 1929 with *Abe Martin's Town Pump*. Through his informality, keen observation, ability to coin catchy sayings and aphorisms, use of dialect, and satire that allowed readers to laugh at themselves while laughing at the characters, Hubbard was widely accepted.

The boyhood home of humorist JEAN SHEPHERD (1929–1999) in Hammond, Indiana, provides the setting and imaginative fodder for much of his short fiction, especially *In God We Trust, All Others Pay Cash* (1966), *Wanda Hickey's Night of Golden Memories and Other Disasters* (1971), and *A Fistful of Fig Newtons* (1981). Several of his stories have been adapted for television, and his 1982 screenplay reflected in the 1983 film *A Christmas Story* is a popular seasonal classic. Like Woody Allen, Shepherd is fascinated with the popular culture embraced by working-class America between the world wars.

Philip Gulley (b. 1961) and Tom (James) Mullen (1934–2009) continue the Hoosier humor tradition, turning it toward religious subjects. Gulley's popular works are *Front Porch Tales* (2001) and the series of novels set in the fictional small town of Harmony. Mullen wrote nonfiction.

Printing, Private Presses, and Journalism: Printers followed the movement of white settlers in the slow settlement of the state. Before 1820 only one printer opened shop: Elihu Stout (1786–1860) began the *Indiana Gazette* in Vincennes on or around July 31, 1804. No copies are now known to exist. In 1820 Brookville, Charlestown, Corydon, Jeffersonville, Lexington, Madison, Salem, and Vevay also had newspapers. By 1830, fifteen towns in the southern two-thirds of the state boasted printing presses.

The Evansville *Southwestern Sentinel* claimed in 1840 to be the first in the world to print on a continuous sheet. Josiah Warren (1798–1874), one of the New Harmony utopians, invented the press; it printed so fast that the printing crew at Evansville repeatedly sabotaged it.

The slow mail system bringing news to the frontier forced printers to fill papers with literary matter. This provided an opportunity for writers, especially poets, to publish.

One of the earliest magazines in the state was the *Western Ladies' Casket,* beginning in 1823 in Connersville; its contents ranged from chemistry treatises to reprinted articles from the *Edinburgh Encyclopedia* and the *London Magazine.* The first literary magazine was the *Madison Museum* (1832), dedicated to "chaste and elevated" literature. An anti-slavery press in Newport published tracts and became the center of Indiana's abolition movement in the first half of the 1800s. All told, at least thirty-nine magazines existed in the state before 1850.

Today Indiana is home to several literary magazines, including the *Indiana Review; Indiana English,* begun as the *Indiana English Journal; Snowy Egret,* devoted to nature writing; *Southern Indiana Review; Sycamore Review,* which sponsors the Wabash Prize in Fiction; and many college-run journals. The *Saturday Evening Post* also hails from Indiana.

Two journalists of note are Eugene (Victor) Debs (1855–1926) and (ERNEST) "ERNIE" (TAYLOR) PYLE (1900–1945). Debs, a prominent labor and Socialist Party leader, edited several journals: the Terre Haute *Fireman's Magazine* (1878) and the national socialist weeklies *Appeal to Reason* (1904) and *American Appeal* (1925). Pyle provided World War II coverage, writing about how America's boys lived and fought with such sensitivity and humor that he became a much-loved reporter. His columns were collected into eight books, including *Here Is Your War* (1943) and *Brave Men* (1944). His posthumous collection *Home Country* (1947) reveals pre–World War II Indiana.

Newspaper presses were responsible for any book printing done during the frontier age. Eight books were printed in 1830, and the total was 574 for the period up to 1850, mostly on politics, education, and religion. Lexington and Louisville, Kentucky, and

Cincinnati, Ohio, provided greater opportunities for authors to get their writings into print. The New Harmony community was a notable exception. The original German Rappite founders began printing their own books in 1824, and the Owenites continued this trend, publishing books of their scientific research. When the community collapsed in 1827, the area remained an intellectual center for twenty-five more years. The Working Men's Library, which the community organized, has the best collection of New Harmony imprints.

In 1883 Merrill, Meigs and Company began production with a second reprint of Riley's *The Old Swimmin'-Hole.* In 1885 it became known as the Bowen-Merrill Publishing Company, which later became Bobbs-Merrill. Besides Riley, Meredith Nicholson, Gene Stratton-Porter, Charles Major, and many other Hoosier authors published their works through that house.

Today the *Literary Market Place* lists forty publishers in the state. Indiana University Press in Bloomington publishes trade and scholarly nonfiction, literature, folklore, and more. The University of Notre Dame and Purdue University maintain scholarly presses. Barnwood Press in Selma publishes poetry; Delirium Press in North Webster publishes horror; Patria Press in Carmel publishes children's historical fiction. The religious market is the focus of such Catholic presses as Abbey, Ave Maria, Cross Cultural, Our Sunday Visitor, and St. Augustine. Other religious presses include the Quaker Friends United, the Brethren in Christ Evangel Press, and the Wesleyan and Winters presses.

The Indiana Federal Writers' Project: Ross (Franklin) Lockridge Jr. headed the Indiana branch of the FEDERAL WRITERS' PROJECT (FWP) from its beginnings in 1935 until he was forced to resign in 1937 for not adhering to federal guidelines. Those guidelines put the priority on the state guide rather than on gathering the folklore, slave interviews, and local histories he was coordinating. Another complaint was that Lockridge was often out of the Indianapolis office, staging his traveling historical pageants throughout the state, as he continued to do into the 1940s. His successor was New Yorker Gordon Briggs, who oversaw all Indiana Writers' Project (IWP) publications.

Unlike projects in other states, the IWP did not provide financial support for famous writers or, with the exception of Lockridge, a venue for writers who later became famous. Indiana was already doing well as a literary center and held a literacy rate higher than the national norm. Tarkington and Ade had retired; Dreiser and Pyle lived elsewhere; and Nicholson wrote only as a sideline to his diplomatic career. Those who needed help were educated, middle-class professionals, including journalists, teachers, librarians, ministers who had been displaced by the Depression-era economy and the declining print trade with the advent of radio. The IWP offered jobs to several hundred Hoosiers, not more than 150 at any one time, who were employed primarily as field-workers doing research. Indiana's project hired more women and fewer members of racial minorities than other states. Notable Indiana fieldworkers included Lauana Creel, Iris Cook, Elizabeth Kargacos, Merton Knowles, Albert Strope, Emery C. Turner, and William W. Tuttle. James Clarence Godfroy, a descendant of Frances Slocum and the Miami Indian chief Francis Godfroy, specialized in collecting folklore and Native American customs. Charles Bruce Millholland (1903–1991) later wrote about his experience traveling the rails. His work became the Broadway show *Twentieth Century* (1932) and later a Hollywood film (1934). He also wrote the play *Faun* (1935).

The major accomplishment of the project was the publication of the state guide, *Indiana: A Guide to the Hoosier State,* in September 1941, the forty-seventh of the forty-eight state guides produced. Rebecca Pitts wrote most of the essays, and Lockridge, Briggs, and Mildred Schmitt contributed others. Clay Stearley edited the guided-tours section. Kurt Vonnegut and Stith Thompson (1885–1976) were among the many consultants who volunteered to read the drafts for accuracy. The guide received favorable reviews and was considered one of the better products of the FWP series for its readability, interest, and attention to Hoosier authors. The guide was updated and expanded in 1989 by the Indiana Historical Society and published as *Indiana: A New Historical Guide.*

The IWP completed four other publications: *Hoosier Tall Stories* (1937), a pamphlet edited by Lockridge; *Calumet Region Historical Guide* (1939), edited by Naomi Harris Phillips; *Indiana: Facts, Events, Places, Tours* (1941), a pamphlet edited by Briggs; and *A Text for Americanization and Naturalization Classes* (1942), a pamphlet by Ray Thurman. Briggs's staff also wrote "It Happened in Indiana," a column carried for two years by seventy newspapers. When the IWP ended in 1942, it left many unfinished works, including three oral history projects: interviews of surviving witnesses of Morgan's raid, Native American materials, and slave narratives.

Indiana also had a branch of the Federal Theatre Project, another WPA initiative. Indiana University professor Lee Norvelle headed the project from 1935 to 1937, staging numerous plays in Keith's Theater, Indianapolis.

Literary Awards and Prizes: Indiana hosts two major film festivals: the Indianapolis International Film Festival and the Heartland Film Festival. The latter's mission is to recognize filmmakers who focus on the human condition and convey integrity. Heartland annually presents cash awards in several categories and has a video-distribution initiative.

For playwrights, the Basile Festival of Emerging American Theatre at Phoenix Theatre, Indianapolis, presents awards and staging, as does the Waldo M. and Grace C. Bonderman Playwriting for Youth Symposium at the Indiana Repertory Theatre, Indianapolis.

Indiana has a history of unofficially recognizing a poet laureate that dates back to 1929 with Emory A(aron) "Big Rich" Richardson (1886–1965). From 1945 through 2005 the Indiana State Federation of Poetry Clubs had the responsibility of appointing an individual to this unofficial post. In 2005 the Indiana General Assembly passed legislation honoring Joyce Brinkman (b. 1944) as the first official state Poet Laureate through 2008. Norbert Kraff (b. 1943) served from 2008 to 2010; Karen Kovacik (b. 1959) from 2012 to 2013; and George Kalamaras (b. 1956) from 2014 to 2015.

Other literary awards include the Ernest Sandeen and Richard Sullivan Prizes in Fiction and Poetry awarded by the University of Notre Dame Press for authors who have published one volume of short fiction or poetry. Both Kappa Delta Pi and the Indiana Center for the Book present book-of-the-year awards in several categories. The American Legion Fourth Estate Award is presented annually for excellence in journalism.

Literary Societies: Although Indiana had several private schools and institutions of higher learning, a public education system did not arrive until after the Civil War. But citizens were interested in the life of the mind from Indiana's earliest days. Literary societies and reading circles for men, women, and children encouraged reading and provided an audience for many Hoosier writers. See LITERARY CLUBS, SALONS, AND SOCIETIES. The frontier town of Vevay boasted a literary club three years after the town's founding in 1814. Because of the paucity of available published materials, members of these early clubs often produced their own original material.

The state's earliest recorded women's club may be the oldest in the United States. Founded as the Minerva Club in 1858 by Constance Fauntleroy Runcie (1836–1911), it followed her to Madison in 1861. After various name changes and gender changes in membership, it survives as the Alcuin Club. The oldest recorded mixed club began meeting as the College Corner Club of Indianapolis in 1872. Probably the most famous Hoosier literary society is the Western Association of Writers in Indianapolis. It lasted twenty years after its organization in 1886. Its membership roster included James Whitcomb Riley, Lew Wallace, Charles Major, Mary Hartwell Catherwood, Maurice Thompson, Meredith Nicholson, and Booth Tarkington. Every year the club met at Eagle (now Winona) Lake in northern Indiana for a weeklong literary festival.

The period after the Civil War saw the formation of many literary clubs. The financial panic of 1873–1874 surprisingly instigated more clubs. By 1893 Indiana had an estimated 179 clubs and college societies. The Indiana State Teachers' Association formed teachers' reading circles in 1883, children's reading circles in 1887, and farmers' reading circles in 1891. The Indiana Union of Literary Clubs formed around 1890.

These clubs and the spirit underlying them were long lived. Thirty-seven of those founded in the 1830s were still surviving 150 years later, and many continue today. A modern Chautauqua-like festival, Spirit and Place, has been staged annually since 1996 in Indianapolis. This seventeen-day, community-wide festival began as a model for engaging the arts, humanities, and religion to promote careful reflection, mutual respect, public imagination, and civic change.

SELECTED WORKS: Readers seeking an overview of Indiana literature should begin with anthologies. *The Indiana Experience* (1977) by Arnold Lazarus is a good starting point, covering sixty-nine authors. For early works, consult the state's first anthology, *Poets and Poetry of Indiana* (1900), compiled by Benjamin Parker and Enos B. Heiney. Other anthologies include *Hoosier Caravan: A Treasury of Indiana Life and Lore* (1975), edited by Richard Banta; *Loaves and Fishes: A Book of Indiana Women Poets* (1983), edited by Alice Friman; and *New Territory: Contemporary Indiana Fiction* (1990), edited by Michael Wilkerson and Deborah Galyan.

Consideration of Indiana fiction should include Eggleston's *The Hoosier School-Master* (1871), Dreiser's *Sister Carrie* (1900), Thompson's *Alice of Old Vincennes* (1900), Major's *The Bears of Blue River* (1901), Nicholson's *The House of a Thousand Candles* (1905), Stratton-Porter's *A Girl of the Limberlost* (1909), Tarkington's *Alice Adams* (1921), West's *The Friendly Persuasion* (1945), Lockridge's *Raintree County* (1948), Vonnegut's *God Bless You, Mr. Rosewater* (1965), and Martone's *Alive and Dead in Indiana* (1984).

For poetry, read Riley's *The Best of James Whitcomb Riley* (1982), edited by Donald Manlove; Thomas's *Frog Praises Night* (1980); Jared Carter's *After the Rain* (1993); and Friman's *Inverted Fire* (1997). The following works in other genres are also significant: George Ade's *The Best of George Ade* (1985), Moody's *The Faith Healer* (1909), Neville's *Indiana Winter* (1994), and Sanders's *Staying Put: Making a Home in a Restless World* (1993). Sanders's *Writing from the Center* (1995) is an excellent place to start for Indiana and Midwestern CREATIVE NONFICTION writing.

FURTHER READING: The earliest listing of Hoosier writers can be found in William

Coggeshall's *Poets and Poetry of the West* (1860), which includes twenty-three Hoosier poets. *Poets and Poetry of Indiana* by Benjamin Parker and Enos Heiney is a collection of poets writing from 1800 to 1900. Henry Harrison's *Indiana Poets* (1935) includes the works of forty-eight writers living at that time.

Early bibliographic works covering the state include Orah Cole Briscoe's published Indiana University master's thesis, *Indiana Fiction before 1870* (1934), and Thomas J. Barry's unpublished thesis, "A Bibliographical and Biographical Dictionary of Indiana Authors" (University of Notre Dame, 1943). Richard E. Banta's *Indiana Authors and Their Books, 1816–1916* (1949), containing 955 Hoosier authors, was supplemented by two later volumes, edited by Banta and Donald Eugene Thompson, for the years 1917–1966 (1974) and 1967–1980 (1981), adding an additional 2,751 and 3,113 names, respectively. *Bibliographical Studies of Seven Authors of Crawfordsville, Indiana* (1942), by Dorothy Ritter Russo and Thelma Lois Sullivan, updated in 1952 by Russo, Sullivan, and Bruce Rogers, provides a biographical and bibliographic listing for Lew and Susan Wallace, Maurice and Will Thompson, Mary Hannah and Caroline Krout, and Meredith Nicholson.

However, the best work to date on Indiana's literary history is *A History of Indiana Literature* (1962) by Arthur W. Shumaker (1913–2000). The earlier criticism focused on individual writers, especially those of greatest importance, but Shumaker evaluates authors from all genres and traces their role within the development of the state's literature. Concentrating on authors writing before World War II, he divides the literature into three periods: early (from about 1821 until 1879 after the end of the Civil War), the golden age (1871–1921), and since the golden age (1922–1939). This entry attempts to continue his work beyond World War II.

Another important work for the study of Hoosier fiction is Jeanette Vanausdall's *Pride and Protest: The Novel in Indiana* (1999). Vanausdall examines Indiana's place within the larger American literary heritage, particularly its development of themes by Hoosier writers, and focuses on authors whose works capture, as she explains, the "profound and fundamental ways of Indiana" (xi).

Some works dealing with Midwestern literature are also useful for the study of Indiana's literary heritage. Ronald Weber's *The Midwestern Ascendancy in American Writing* (1992) and Scott Russell Sanders's essay "Imagining the Midwest" from his essay collection *Writing from the Center* (1995) are two good sources, the first for a historical perspective and the second for prevalent themes. *A Place of Sense: Essays in Search of the Midwest* (1988), edited by Michael Martone, is also thematically based.

For CHILDREN'S AND YOUNG-ADULT LITERATURE, the *Directory of Indiana Children's Authors and Illustrators* (third edition, 1997), by Sara Laughlin provides an extensive catalog of authors but merely lists their works. For bibliographic annotations, see *Reading for Young People: The Midwest* (1979) by Dorothy Hinman and Ruth Zimmerman. Hinman and Zimmerman survey the authors of Illinois, IOWA, MISSOURI, and Ohio, as well as Indiana. Ruth Gillis's *Indiana Books by Indiana Authors: A Guide to Children's Literature* (1990) also provides bibliographic entries and essays that give an overview of each genre surveyed.

For Indiana's printers and publishers, *The Beginnings of Printing in the State of Indiana* (1934, with an update in 1937) by Mary Alden Walker and others provides a brief overview of the state's literary publication up to 1850, with lists of book titles published, newspapers and magazines in operation, printers' names, and towns where printing was done. Walker's effort was later considerably expanded by Cecil K. Byrd and Howard H. Peckham in *A Bibliography of Indiana Imprints, 1804–1953* (1955). George Blakey's *Creating a Hoosier Self-Portrait: The Federal Writers' Project in Indiana, 1935–1942* (2005) provides a history of the project and its place in the context of the time.

Indiana's State Library in Indianapolis has one of the largest and broadest collections of Hoosier interest. It includes the largest collection of Indiana newspapers and houses nearly three million items in its Manuscript Section, including eighteenth-century fur traders' papers. Indiana University's Lilly Library also has a substantial collection, including materials on Vonnegut, Riley, and Dreiser. The Indianapolis–Marion County Public

Library houses collections for Indiana authors, as well as Indianapolis authors.

Materials from the Indiana Federal Writers' Project are housed in the Library of Congress, in the National Archives, and at Indiana State University, Terre Haute. Under its previous name, Indiana State Teachers College, the university sponsored the IWP when the federal government restructured the Works Progress Administration in 1939.

SUSAN YANOS   EARLHAM SCHOOL OF RELIGION

INDUSTRY.

See Technology and Industry

IOWA

Iowa was admitted to the Union on December 28, 1846, as the twenty-ninth state. Before statehood it was part of the District of Louisiana (1804–1805), the Territory of Louisiana (1805–1812), the Territory of Missouri (1812–1821), unorganized territory (1821–1834), Michigan Territory (1834–1836), Wisconsin Territory (1836–1838), and Iowa Territory (1838–1846).

Area: 56,273 square miles

Land: 55,857 square miles

Water: 416 square miles

Population (2010 census): 3,046,355

OVERVIEW: Situated between two rivers, the land later known as Iowa was inviting to the American military and to westward-bound immigrants because of its proximity to water and its location as a gateway to the greater frontier. On the east lies the Mississippi River, prized for its path to the Gulf of Mexico, its potential for trade, and its easy access to settlement. To the west is the Missouri River, once a launching point for journeys into uncharted territories in hopes for land and wealth. Iowa's pioneer communities began primarily at its eastern border and

DES MOINES

© Karen Greasley, 2014

then spread westward; the newly formed state developed an agricultural identity from the promise of its soil.

Fictional tracts describing prosperous Iowa farms were commonly sold as immigration recruitment tools in America's eastern states; farming's drudgery, financial risks, and the state's weather extremes played little role in the stories. Early settlers' reliance on agriculture for survival, the development of frontier communities, and the ensuing rise of towns and cities formed common threads in the first significant Iowa novels. The farm novel dominated from 1880 to 1930.

HISTORY AND SIGNIFICANCE: This entry examines Iowa's earliest literature in EXPLORATION ACCOUNTS and travel narratives, as well as its diverse fiction, divided according to themes or subject matter. Chronological discussions of significant poetry, drama, and playwrights are included; subgenres of popular literature are noted. PRINTING AND PUBLICATION and journalism history, the FEDERAL WRITERS' PROJECT, state literary awards and prizes, literary societies, and notable repositories of Iowa's literature conclude the offerings.

Early Exploration and Travel: Journals written by European explorers are the first literary works to describe Iowa's landscape, native peoples, and natural resources. The surviving journal of Father Jacques Marquette (1637–1675) was published in *The Jesuit Relations* for 1675, an annual report of missionary work Marquette undertook with the fur trader Louis Joliet (1645–1700), whose journal was lost in a canoe mishap near present-day Montreal. The pair are commonly credited with being the first white men to step onto Iowa land, doing so near the mouth of the Des Moines River on June 25, 1673. Marquette's accounts of the Illinois tribe and the subsequent landing are included in his journal, the earliest published work to reflect firsthand exploration of the state.

Historical evidence for Iowa's first permanent white settler, Julien Dubuque (1762–1810), derives mainly from legal land claims submitted in an effort to press the Spanish government for full rights to profitable lead mines in present-day Dubuque. A native of Quebec and a shrewd businessman, Dubuque held an exclusive agreement with the Mesquakie tribe, also known as the Fox, to work the lead mines, the only white settler ever offered a claim.

The journals of the Lewis and Clark expedition (1804–1806) were first published under the title *History of the Expedition under the Command of Captains Lewis and Clark, to the Sources of the Missouri, Thence across the Rocky Mountains and down the River Columbia to the Pacific Ocean* (1814). They note the death of Kentucky native Sergeant Charles Floyd on August 20, 1804, and his burial in present-day Sioux City.

Assigned to discover the origins of the Mississippi River and to seek sites for military fortification, Zebulon Montgomery Pike (1779–1813) arrived at the mouth of the Des Moines River on August 20, 1805. Pike's Iowa travels, duly noted in his journal, published as *An Account of Expeditions to the Sources of the Mississippi* (1810), included his visits with a Sac Indian tribe, his campsites at Fort Madison and Burlington, and his brief visit with Julien Dubuque on September 1, 1805.

Future general Stephen Watts Kearny (1794–1848), commonly called the "Father of the U.S. Cavalry," led an expedition in 1820 to chart an overland route between the mouths of the Minnesota and Missouri Rivers. As a captain of the Second Infantry, Kearny considered the route through northern Iowa and southeastern MINNESOTA impractical because of its rugged hills and lack of timber and water. The story, recounted in *The 1820 Journal of Stephen Watts Kearny, Comprising a Narrative Account of the Council Bluff–St. Peter's Military Exploration and a Voyage down the Mississippi River to St. Louis* (1908), documents one of the U.S. Army's first efforts to establish a post west of the Mississippi River.

Albert Miller Lea (1808–1891), a lieutenant in the United States Dragoons, participated as cartographer and journalist in an 1835 mapping expedition between the Des Moines and Mississippi Rivers. Lea's notes on this portion of Wisconsin Territory are credited with giving the state of Iowa its name; *Notes on Wisconsin Territory* (1836) is also responsible for providing the first in-depth description in maps and narrative of Iowa's prairies. In 1844 a second dragoon company led by Captain James Allen (1806–1846) traversed northwestern Iowa and

southwestern Minnesota seeking the source of the Des Moines River. The eighteen-page *Letter from the Secretary of War, Transmitting the Report, Journal, and Map of Captain J. Allen, of the First Regiment of Dragoons, of His Expedition to the Heads of the Rivers Des Moines, Blue Earth, &c., in the Northwest, in Compliance with a Resolution of the House of Representatives of the 29th of January, 1845* (1846) briefly describes his journey to the Big Sioux River and was later used to attract settlers to Iowa.

The CAPTIVITY NARRATIVE, usually featuring a European American woman abducted by Native Americans, fared well as popular pioneer literature. SEE NATIVE AMERICANS AS DEPICTED IN MIDWESTERN LITERATURE. Among Iowa titles in this genre are *Left by the Indians: The Story of My Life* (1892) by Emeline Fuller (1847–ca. 1923) and *History of the Spirit Lake Massacre and Captivity of Miss Abbie Gardner* (1885) by Abigail Gardner Sharp (1843–1921), a firsthand account of Iowa's only Native American attack against white settlers in 1857.

Fiction: The first Iowa novels include *A Home in the West; or, Emigration and Its Consequences* (1858) by M. Emilia Rockwell (ca. 1835–ca. 1915), an emigration recruitment tract. It was the first novel physically published in Iowa and was marketed as a domestic novel to encourage Midwestern settlement. *The Pet of the Settlement: A Story of Prairie-Land* (1860) by Caroline A(ugusta) Soule (1824–1903) features Iowa as its setting. A fictionalized account of Soule's years in a central Iowa log cabin, the story depicts pioneers battling weather, the land, and personal limitations to establish a homestead. Successful newspaper columnist Rebecca Harrington Smith (1831–1917), writing as Kate Harrington, wrote the first novel by an Iowa inhabitant, *Emma Bartlett: Prejudice and Fanaticism by an American Lady* (1856); the book was published in Kentucky while Smith lived in Farmington, Iowa. Neither the book's content nor its setting is directly connected to Iowa. A majority of Iowa's early fiction chronicles the transformation of the prairie into small villages and towns. Novels about the state's pioneer history came long after actual settlement; significant titles based on the colonial, Native American, or frontier experience did not appear until the 1920s.

Conquering Horse (1959) by FREDERICK MANFRED (1912–1994) presents Iowa's first white settlers venturing into the author's "Siouxland," a quadrant including land in SOUTH DAKOTA, NEBRASKA, Minnesota, and Iowa. *The Shining Trail* (1943) by IOLA FULLER (GOODSPEED McCOY) (1906–1993) is an adolescent novel presenting the shared Fox and Sauk tribal village, Saukenuk. Set roughly a dozen years before the Black Hawk War of 1832, Fuller's novel shows Native Americans struggling to accommodate and to establish a peaceful coexistence with white settlers. A rather factual account of the war follows this failed attempt. *Thunder on the River* (1949) by Charlton G(rant) Laird (1901–1984) traces major events in the later years of BLACK HAWK (1767–1838), a chief of the Sac and Fox tribes, all culminating in the 1832 battle known as the Bad Axe Massacre.

State Librarian of Iowa Johnson Brigham (1846–1936) chronicled the years 1843–1846 at old Fort Des Moines in *The Sinclairs of Old Fort Des Moines* (1927). PHIL(IP) (DUFFIELD) STONG (1899–1957) introduced the fictional village of Pittsville in *Buckskin Breeches* (1937); the area is portrayed as an 1837 southern Iowa settlement founded by OHIO pioneers. *Spirit Lake* (1961) by Pulitzer Prize–winning novelist MACKINLAY KANTOR (1904–1977) relates the 1857 Santee Sioux uprising against white settlers at the settlements founded at Spirit and Okoboji Lakes. *Spirit Lake* features some fifty characters recounting their roles in the events leading up to the massacre.

Iowa's transition from prairie outposts to small villages and towns is the subject of a significant body of fictional writing. ALICE FRENCH (1850–1934), who often published under the name Octave Thanet, was a longtime resident of Davenport, where her *Stories of a Western Town* (1893) is set. Considered Iowa's first major literary figure, French gathered her local-color stories into several volumes, including *Otto the Knight, and Other Trans-Mississippi Stories* (1891), *A Book of True Lovers* (1897), and *The Heart of Toil* (1898). (JOHN) HERBERT QUICK (1861–1925) began his Iowa trilogy with *Vandemark's Folly* (1922), which focuses on eastern families who came to the Midwest in search of land and financial success. As modern amenities came

Dubuque, Iowa, 1857. Illustration by Henry Lewis.
Image courtesy of the Library of Congress

with growth, novels addressed the cycles of social and industrial change, as shown in *A Lantern in Her Hand* (1928) by BESS STREETER ALDRICH (1881–1954) and in two novels by Margaret Wilson (Steel Deans) (1882–1973): *The Able McLaughlins* (1923), which won the Pulitzer Prize for Fiction in 1924, and *The Law and the McLaughlins* (1936).

Country People (1924) by RUTH SUCKOW (1892–1960) chronicles three generations of German immigrants on their eastern Iowa farm. Suckow portrays the dynamics of small-town life through middle-class families in *Iowa Interiors: Sixteen Stories* (1926), *The Folks* (1934), and *New Hope* (1942). An alternative but nonetheless positive vision comes through the eyes of prominent local citizens. A minister serves as the vehicle in *Dominie Dean* (1917) by ELLIS PARKER BUTLER (1869–1937) and in *The Bonney Family* (1928) by Ruth Suckow. *Sioux City: A Novel* (1940) and *Anthony Trant* (1941), both by J(ohn) Hyatt Downing (1888–1973), follow a banker as he chases and loses great wealth. Despite personal struggle, the inability of common people to change levels in a town's social hierarchy remains clear in *The Cutters* (1926) by Bess Streeter Aldrich, *Cora* (1929) by Ruth Suckow, and the quasi-historical novel *Young and Fair Is Iowa* (1946) by Matthias (Martin) Hoffman (1889–1961).

Small-town habits and the development of urban society cause chaos in Phil Stong's *The Rebellion of Lennie Barlow* (1937) as the young hero battles prejudice in fictional

Pittsville. RICHARD PIKE BISSELL (1913–1977) describes the clash between preservers of historic areas and promoters of economic growth for a Mississippi riverfront community in his novel *Goodbye, Ava* (1960).

To escape the mundane aspects of contemporary life, modern novels offer their protagonists drastic measures, such as the call of a mysterious voice to build a baseball diamond and to take the reclusive J(erome) D(avid) Salinger (1919–2010) to a baseball game in *Shoeless Joe* (1982) by W(ILLIAM P(ATRICK) KINSELLA (b. 1935). *The Bridges of Madison County* (1992) by ROBERT JAMES WALLER (b. 1939) features the four-day romance of a nature photographer and a farm wife while her husband and children attend the state fair. A small town's reaction to the end of life receives modern treatment in several contemporary novels. Studies of abandonment or death reflecting a healing journey are notably seen in MacKinlay Kantor's *Happy Land* (1943), *At Paradise Gate* (1981) by JANE (GRAVES) SMILEY (b. 1949), *An Ocean in Iowa* (1997) by Peter Hedges (b. 1962), and *Gilead* (2004) and *Lila* (2014) by Marilynne Robinson (b. 1947).

Popular Literature:

The Farm Novel: Synonymous with Iowa's identity is the farm as a symbol of its settlement, self-reliance, productivity, and wealth. A significant body of Iowa literature details the struggle to secure land and harness its power. Realism in portraying the farm's demands and drudgery marks the short-story collections MAIN-TRAVELLED ROADS (1891) and *Prairie Folks* (1893) that placed sometime Iowa resident (HANNIBAL) HAMLIN GARLAND (1860–1940) on the American literary stage. Two classic examples exploring prairie life on the Midwestern plains are his reminiscences of his youth, *Boy Life on the Prairie* (1899) and *A Son of the Middle Border* (1917). As communities developed around farms, cultural mores and economic changes brought new concerns to rural America.

Farming families faced hardships from weather, economics, and the lure of adventure in cities, losing children to the promise of better fortune elsewhere. Often strife between a father and son forms the major conflict of a story, involving passage of the land between generations despite protests from the young for a different life. Herbert Quick's

The Hawkeye (1923), the second volume of his Iowa trilogy, traces a man's break with his family farm to begin a life in law and politics. When women are forced to choose a life off the farm, education and marriage rise as the prime alternatives. Quick's *The Invisible Woman* (1924), the third volume of his Iowa trilogy, follows an 1890s farm woman who embraces urban living and marries her employer. Divorce, transferred possession of the family farm, and unrequited love for a local farmer envelop Phil Stong's protagonist in *Stranger's Return* (1933).

The Iowa farm also projects an image of wealth and symbolizes the rise of modern agribusiness. Often loss of humanity and social values accompanies supposed economic progress. The Mantz family trilogy, *Three Miles Square* (1939), *The Road Returns* (1940), and *County Seat* (1941), by PAUL (FREDERICK) COREY (1903–1992) chronicles the gradual demise of the family farm as large-scale operations, worker unions, and world markets affect a small Iowa town, leading to corruption and fear. *Acres of Antaeus* (1946), Corey's fictional treatise on corporate influence in farming, never offers a solution to its dilemma and uses the 1932–1933 American farm protests and world grain-market crashes as backdrops. *Wapsipinicon Tales* (1927) by Jay G. Sigmund (1885–1937) presents dark views of modern country life, revealing undercurrents of death, racism, and emotional isolation. Largely labeled a comic novel in spite of its controversial content, Phil Stong's *State Fair* (1932) finds the Frake family at the Iowa state fair, hoping to gain what is unattainable at the farm—recognition, financial success, and, for the youth, sexual experience. *State Fair*, which was adapted as a feature film in 1945 and again in 1962, became a major theatre event during 1996, marking its New York debut. The belief that land is the only item of worth sets Jane Smiley's Pulitzer Prize–winning *A Thousand Acres* (1991) apart as a consummate example of the modern farm novel. Doubts about a family corporation spawn a chain of events leading to madness, isolation, and death. By severing his working ties to the land, Larry Cook, the protagonist, destroys himself and his children.

School and College Novels: Iowa's educational beginnings in the one-room schoolhouse are captured in two short-story collections by Jim Heynen (b. 1940), *The One-Room Schoolhouse: Stories about the Boys* (1993) and *The Boy's House: Stories* (2001). The simplicity of early school settings does not appear in the majority of academic literature set in Iowa. Instead, most tales are set on college or university campuses, such as *Miss Bishop* (1933) by Bess Streeter Aldrich, set in "Oak River, Iowa" and at "Midwestern College" from 1876 to 1932. Robert James Waller's second novel about forbidden Iowa love, *Slow Waltz in Cedar Bend* (1993), pairs a tenured economics professor and a colleague's wife for the central romance. Jane Smiley's comedy *Moo* (1995) is set at a land-grant institution similar to Iowa State University in Ames, particularly with respect to its agriculture and humanities programs.

Significant IOWA WRITERS' WORKSHOP alumni often portray their experiences as graduate students, using local landmarks and academic culture in their fiction. Capturing the University of Iowa's campus spirit in the 1950s is *Letting Go* (1962) by Philip (Milton) Roth (b. 1933). Academia of the 1960s provides the basis of *The Water-Method Man* (1972) by John Wallace Blunt Jr., writing as John (Winslow) Irving (b. 1942). *Moving On* (1970) by Larry (Jeff) McMurtry (b. 1936) follows a 1960s Texas student as he journeys northward and enrolls at the Writers' Workshop. Anti-war protests seen from campus and off-campus perspectives are common elements of 1970s settings. *Live from Earth* (1991) by Lance Olsen (b. 1956) follows an Iowa native and Vietnam veteran as he transitions to the life of a Writers' Workshop graduate student. Against a backdrop of student war protests and opera rehearsals, *Now Playing at Canterbury* (1976) by VANCE (NYE) BOURJAILY (1922–2010) is set at a cultural center modeled on the University of Iowa's Hancher Auditorium.

Immigrant and ethnic novels were also important in Iowa's settlement and development. Immigration into the state was actively solicited. Part of the Black Hawk Purchase (1833), Iowa's highly prized farmland appealed to American families from congested eastern states and from central states—INDIANA, Ohio, Kentucky, and Virginia. Published by the state's Board of Immigration, *Iowa: The Home for Immigrants, Being a Treatise on the Resources of Iowa and Giving Useful Information with Regard to the State, for the Benefit of Immigrants and Others* (1870), had an initial printing of 65,000 copies and was distributed to every American newspaper and advertised in major magazines.

The adventures of a German American farmer in 1890s Iowa are brought to life by Johannes Gillhoff (1861–1930) in his best-selling novel *Jürnjakob Swehn der Amerikafahrer* (1917). Similarly, the Norwegian immigrant experience in northeastern Iowa is revealed in *How Halvor Became a Minister* (1936) by Peer O(lsen) Strømme (1856–1921), the first English translation of a story serialized in the WISCONSIN Norwegian-language newspaper *Superior Posten* from 1892 to 1893. It was later reissued as *Halvor: A Story of Pioneer Youth* (1960) by Luther College Press in Decorah.

Later treatments of the Iowa immigrant experience include *Iowa Outpost* (1948) by Katherine Buxbaum (1885–1975), set in the fictional Moravian village of Lapham. *Sign of a Promise, and Other Stories* (1979) by James C. Schaap (b. 1948) offers tales of Dutch immigrants and their struggles to plant a community in Iowa. The search for identity permeates the novel *Jasmine* (1989) by BHARATI MUKHERJEE (b. 1940), about a young Punjabi widow's experiences in India, New York City, and Iowa, where she is married to a paraplegic banker. RAY (ANTHONY) YOUNG BEAR (b. 1950), a native Iowan and resident of the Meskawki Tribal Settlement (Tama), blends folklore, visions, and history to create tales based on his life experience in the 1950s and 1960s. Young Bear began publishing poems in the 1960s, gaining recognition with *Waiting to Be Fed* (1975) and *Winter of the Salamander* (1980). *Black Eagle Child: The Facepaint Narratives* (1992) and *Remnants of the First Earth* (1996) highlight Young Bear's journeys. Tomás Rivera (1935–1984), author of *. . . Y NO SE LO TRAGÓ LA TIERRA / . . . AND THE EARTH DID NOT DEVOUR HIM* (1971), set some of his stories and poems about Mexican American migrant workers in Iowa; among these is "Zoo Island" from *Harvest* (1989).

Children's and Young Adult Literature: CHILDREN'S AND YOUNG ADULT LITERATURE with an Iowa setting has its early roots in a Horatio Alger (1832–1899) morality tale titled *Bob Burton; or, The Young Ranchman of the Missouri* (1888). The boy, in typical Alger fashion, achieves success through hard work and diligence, outwitting his nemesis, a scheming real estate agent. *Swatty, a Story of Real Boys* (1920) by Ellis Parker Butler is set in the 1870s lumber boomtown of Muscatine. This book was followed by *Jibby Jones: A Story of Mississippi River Adventure for Boys* (1923), an honest and endearing portrait of an 1800s Iowa town told through Jones's Tom Sawyer–like escapades. Phil Stong's *Farm Boy: A Hunt for Indian Treasure* (1934) is set in the early 1900s. *Maudie in the Middle* (1988) by Phyllis Reynolds Naylor (b. 1933) focuses on a mischievous girl in a large farming family. A twelve-year-old girl's story is brought to life in catalog reprints and advertisements in Richard Pike Bissell's *Julia Harrington, Winnebago, Iowa, 1913* (1969). Zebulon Pike's Iowa expedition forms the backdrop for *As the Crow Flies* (1927) by Cornelia Meigs (1884–1973). *Prairie Anchorage* (1933) by Marjorie Medary (1890–1980) charts the desperate journey of an English family to establish a home in Iowa. *Farm on the Hill* (1936) by Madeline Darrough Horn (1888–1978) focuses on the daily demands of an Iowa pioneer farm. Family friend Grant Wood (1891–1942) created the book's popular illustrations. See also ART. LOIS (LENORE) LENSKI (1893–1974) published the Midwestern installment of her regional fiction for children, *Corn-Farm Boy,* in 1954. The book blends experiences of responsibility and pleasure to create an accurate view of a 1950s Iowa farm family. *McBroom's Wonderful One-Acre Farm* (1972), an early book by Sid Fleischman (1920–2010), weaves tall tales about a magical small Iowa farm.

Literature exploring coming-of-age issues dominates modern Iowa fiction offerings for young adults. Henry Gregor Felsen (1916–1995), a prolific children's author from Des Moines, is most recognized for a single title from a long-running series, *Hot Rod* (1950). Felsen's best-selling books explore social problems and their consequences in moral tales pairing Iowa teenage boys and their cars. Hadley Irwin, the pseudonym of two authors, Ann(abelle) Irwin (1915–1998) and Lee Hadley (1935–1995), worked in a sub-

genre called "problem novels," based on teens exploring complex issues, including racism, aging, and suicide. The authors' *Moon and Me* (1981) features a rural Iowa farming community and the friendship between two girls, each battling her own insecurities. An Iowa boy who recently lost his father in the Korean War befriends a former Negro League player in *Stumptown Kid* (2005) by Carol Gorman (b. 1952). Jealousy of a popular girl triggers humorous revenge in *Dagmar Schultz and the Powers of Darkness* (1989) by Lynn Hall (b. 1937). In *Switcharound* (1985) by Lois Lowry (b. 1937) two New York City kids spend an Iowa summer with their divorced father, vowing to be difficult to their new stepmother.

Mystery and Detective Fiction: The earliest mystery set in Iowa appears to be *Shyster Lawyer* (1929) by Leo F(rancis) Schmitt (1891–1963), a collection of twenty-six short stories about the cases of a lawyer named Jim Asbestos. Mary Meigs Atwater (1876–1956) shows that even an Iowa farm community is not immune from drugs and abortion in *Crime in Corn-Weather* (1935). Crime novels by the prolific pulp-fiction author Frank Gruber (1904–1969) that use Iowa settings include *The Laughing Fox* (1940), *The Mighty Blockhead* (1942), and *The Fourth Letter* (1947). Elizabeth Hardwick (1916–2007) provides a gripping account of a murder trial in a small Iowa town in *The Simple Truth* (1955). *Nine Seven Juliet* (1969) by Laurence D. Lafore (1917–1985) features a sleuth who is a retired literature professor and amateur pilot. In *Fatal Obsession* (1983) by Stephen Greenleaf (b. 1942) John Marshall Tanner, the protagonist of a detective series usually set in San Francisco, returns to his Chaldea hometown for the disposition of the family farm. While he is there, a distant nephew is murdered, and Tanner searches for the boy's killer. In *Sweet Eyes* (1991) JONIS AGEE (b. 1943) pairs a town's shock over an interracial affair with its silent complicity in an unresolved death. Depression-era murders fascinate an Iowa medical examiner in *Just Bones* (1996) by Jeffrey Denhart (b. 1950).

Modern mysteries may allude to the classic detective model even as they radically differ in character design and crime solving. Max Allan Collins (b. 1948) wrote the

Mallory series, centered on an Iowa mystery writer, including *The Baby Blue Rip-Off* (1983), *No Cure for Death* (1983), and *Nice Weekend for a Murder* (1986). The investigator's exploits occur in fictional Port City, a community based on Collins's hometown of Muscatine. Iowa detective Robert Payne, a criminal psychologist, makes his first appearance in the novel *Blood Moon* (1994) by Edward Gorman (b. 1941), in which he tracks the vicious killer of an eight-year-old girl. Payne's later cases are captured in *Hawk Moon* (1996), *Harlot's Moon* (1997), and *Voodoo Moon* (2000). Another Gorman detective, Sam McCain, is a young lawyer and part-time private eye who reluctantly investigates crime in Black River Falls. *The Day the Music Died* (1999) launched the series; later installments include *Fools Rush In* (2007), *Ticket to Ride* (2009), and *Bad Moon Rising* (2011). Donald Harstad (b. 1945), a retired northeastern Iowa deputy sheriff, uses his work experiences to develop the character of Carl Houseman, a sheriff solving brutal crimes in quiet Iowa towns. *Eleven Days: A Novel of the Heartland* (1998), *Known Dead* (1999), *The Big Thaw* (2000), *Code 61* (2002), and *A Long December* (2003) portray Houseman as a traditionally minded criminologist, employing intuition and observation in battles against thieves, murderers, and drug kingpins.

Pitting a lesbian protagonist against murderers, Midwestern sports fanatics, and corporate America uniquely sets the Mara Gilgannon novels by Mary Vermillion (b. 1964) apart in their Iowa treatments. See LESBIAN, GAY, BISEXUAL, TRANSGENDER, AND QUEER LITERATURE. The hamlet of Aldoburg is the setting for *Death by Discount* (2004); a controversial rape case and its aftermath at the University of Iowa inspired Gilgannon's second tale, *Murder by Mascot* (2006). Parenting crises and death in a sperm bank frame the third Gilgannon novel, *Seminal Murder* (2012). A collaborative writing effort involving seventeen Iowa fiction authors and edited by Barbara Lounsberry (b. 1946) began with the novel *Time and Chance: An Iowa Murder Mystery* (1998), a whodunit set in a sleepy river town. The next novel, *16,000 Suspects* (1999), which features a murder during the annual across-the-state bike ride, was followed by

Politics Is Murder (2000) and *Orchestrated Murder* (2001).

Dime Novels: One of the most inexpensive and successful American publishing efforts to reach a mass population, DIME NOVELS typically offered formulaic tales of adventure, humor, and mystery, sometimes using historical events and personages and employing stereotypical racial and ethnic characters. Among these classic examples of escapist literature are tales with Iowa settings, most penned by Oliver "Oll" Coomes (1845–1921), a farmer from Wiota. An Ohio native who came to Iowa at age eleven, Coomes briefly attended college and spent much of his life farming in Cass County. In a fifty-year period Coomes wrote roughly one hundred dime novels using the pen name Oll Coomes. *Thornpath, the Traitor; or, The Perils of the Prairie* (1870), set in 1820 near Des Moines on the mouth of the Raccoon River, follows its hero as he chases, captures, and kills renegade Sioux who have burned a local outpost. A white man, driven by vengeance, haunts an island in the middle of Storm Lake in northwestern Iowa in the novel *Bald Head, the Hunter; or, Red Star, the Spirit of the Lake* (1871). Border outlaws, a secret cavern in the bluffs overlooking the Missouri River, and hostile Native Americans vie for the archery ability of the protagonist in *Silent Shot, the Slayer; or, The Secret Chamber of the Hunter* (1871).

Oll Coomes created *Antelope Abe, the Boy Guide; or, The Forest Bride: A Tale of the North-West* (1872) and cast a fearless hunter of Sioux, who lives east of Des Moines, as his main character. *The Boy Spy; or, The Young Avenger* (1876) centers on Frank Bell, a young man driven to recover a stolen map and to avenge his parents' murder by Natives. In the serial *Ole Hurricane; or, The Dumb Spy of Des Moines* (1873) native Kentuckians come to 1842 Iowa, staking claims along the Des Moines River; and the serial *Hawkeye Harry, the Young Trapper Ranger* (1872) follows Harry Houston on the banks of the Boyer and Raccoon Rivers in northwestern Iowa. In *The Boy Chief; or, The Doomed Twenty* (1872), the sequel to Coomes's *The Boy Spy*, Frank Bell is falsely accused of murder and seeks to clear his name.

Two further examples of dime novels with Iowa settings are the pseudonymous

Henry J. Thomas's *Old Kyle, the Trailer; or, The Renegade of the Delawares* (1869), which features a scout who saves lost hunters, and in which most of the action is set on the banks of the fictional Rattlesnake River in Iowa; and *Mori, the Man-Hunter; or, The Counterfeiters of the Border* (1873) by Maro Orlando Rolfe (1852–1925), which follows a searcher for a notorious counterfeiting ring based in an 1835 Iowa tavern near the Mississippi River.

Romance Novels: The contrast between Midwestern predictability and the spontaneity of romance is an obvious catalyst for novelists and is found in several tales set in rural Iowa towns or on farms. Clear Lake's Dorothy Garlock (b. 1942) has written over thirty-five romance novels. *Homeplace* (1991) unfolds love and family secrets on an 1880s Dubuque-area farm. Most of her tales focus on small communities where relationships struggle against social conventions, twists of circumstance, and past indiscretions. Garlock's *More than Memory* (2001) centers on a 1950s businesswoman whose life is immediately changed when her high school boyfriend returns. The first American author to write for the Harlequin series, Independence's Janet Dailey (1944–2013), published almost one hundred novels. Her Americana series comprises fifty novels, each set in a different state; *The Homeplace* (1976) is the Iowa book in the series.

Lee Ann Lemberger (b. 1954), writing as Leigh Michaels, is the author of some seventy-five novels, several with Iowa settings. *Kiss Yesterday Goodbye* (1984), *Once and for Always* (1989), and *Family Secrets* (1994) feature rural communities and modern characters, including single parents. The dramatic romance *Leap of Faith* (2001) by Danielle Steel (b. 1947) centers its action on an orphaned French girl who spends her early life in Iowa and then returns to the family chateau, where she encounters old secrets and a handsome suitor.

Science Fiction: Robert A. Heinlein (1907–1988), considered a master of the SCIENCE-FICTION genre, composed two tales with Iowa settings. The first, *The Puppet Masters* (1951), finds American secret agents battling mind-controlling alien invaders who have landed near Grinnell. *The Cat Who Walks through Walls* (1985) follows a former military leader and his new bride as they leave Earth to thwart an assassination attempt. Numerous scenes in Iowa fill this story, considered one of Heinlein's best works. Philip K. Dick (1928–1982), another legendary science-fiction writer, alters reality when a Des Moines businessman, presumed dead in an explosion, communicates with his employees in *Ubik* (1969).

Horror, Fantasy, and Techno-thrillers: The popular fiction categories of horror, fantasy, and techno-thrillers have representatives with Iowa settings. *Morning Ran Red* (1986) by Stephen Bowman (b. 1948) offers an account of the infamous 1912 axe murders in Villisca. *Dark Iowa, Bright Iowa* (1994) by Robert P. James (b. 1960) collects eleven "dark fantasy" stories and three poems with Iowa settings. Uncle and nephew George F. Jewsbury (b. 1941) and Neal Town Stephenson (b. 1959), the former writing as J. Frederick George, co-authored *The Cobweb* (1996), a story detailing a murder investigation that leads to Iraqi students performing hidden bioterrorism research at an Iowa university.

Religious Fiction: Contemporary Christian fiction featuring inspirational Iowa settings is exemplified in the Ann of the Prairie series by Nick Harrison (b. 1947) and Kenneth W. Sollitt (1907–2001). *These Years of Promise* (1987) and *While Yet We Live* (1991) focus on an 1800s Osceola County farming community, detailing its inhabitants' settlement troubles and ever-enduring faith. Quaker history and beliefs appear in novels by Susan McCracken (b. 1950); *For the Love of a Friend* (1994) traces a family moving to the Iowa prairie. After marriage the protagonist faces life on the frontier in *For the Gift of a Friend* (1995); the teen daughter's coming of age highlights McCracken's third installment, *For the Call of a Friend* (1997).

Poetry: The state's first published verse collection, *The Heart-Lace, and Other Poems* (1856) by Hiram Alvin Reid (1834–1906), a self-described promoter, is noteworthy mainly for its early evocations of Davenport. A visit to Iowa's Chickasaw County inspired William Savage Pitts (1830–1918), a Wisconsin teacher and music student, to pen the words and melody to "The Little Brown Church in the Vale" (1857). A historian and pioneer schoolteacher from Fort Des Moines, Tacitus Hussey (1833–1919), released *The*

River Bend, and Other Poems (1896). A two-line excerpt from a single poem set to music by Horace Towner (1855–1937) briefly became the state song—"Iowa, the Beautiful Land."

Samuel Hawkins Marshall Byers (1838–1933), a major in B Company, Fifth Iowa Infantry, was captured by Confederate forces at the Battle of Missionary Ridge in Tennessee and spent sixteen months as a prisoner, ultimately housed in South Carolina. There, in 1864, Byers heard of General Sherman's march across Georgia and composed the poem "Sherman's March to the Sea." Smuggled out of the prison, the poem was widely circulated and became a national sensation. Byers's verse was later set to music and reprinted nationally (1896) with the title "March to the Sea." *Poets and Poetry of Iowa* (1894), presumed to be the first published anthology of living Iowa poets, was edited by Thomas William Herringshaw (1858–1927) and offered biographical sketches of its selected writers.

Iowa academic writing programs were influential in advocating for the literature of the state. Lewis Worthington Smith (1866–1947) was both a literary critic and a prominent voice in launching the farm-fiction era associated with Iowa's literary history. Smith, an English professor, poet, and dean at Drake University in Des Moines, published widely in various Iowa author anthologies. Raymond Kresensky (1897–1955), a high school English teacher, published a single-poem volume, *Luke 24, 13–35* (1931); tirelessly promoted literary magazines; aided the production of *Lyrical Iowa*, an annual compilation by the Iowa Poetry Association; and researched the solid anthology *A List of Iowa Poets* (1953). Edwin Ford Piper (1871–1939), whose writing first appeared in a 1917 issue of THE MIDLAND, remains indelibly associated with Midwestern pioneer life and the prairies because of his noteworthy *Barbed Wire and Wayfarers* (1924).

Iowa's celebrated association with regionalism is reflected in the poetry of Jay G. Sigmund. The Cedar Rapids writer, naturalist, and insurance company executive incorporated images and themes from the Wapsipinicon River valley in the poems and tales in *Pinions* (1923), *Land o' Maize Folk* (1924), *Drowsy Ones* (1925), and *The Ridge Road:*

Short Stories and Poems (1930). JAMES (SCHELL) HEARST (1900–1983), considered Iowa's greatest farm poet by many critics, held an academic appointment at the University of Northern Iowa in Cedar Falls. *Country Men* (1937) placed Hearst at the forefront of farm writing; *The Sun at Noon* (1943), *Man and His Field* (1951), *Limited View* (1962), and *A Single Focus* (1967) solidified his reputation.

Davenport's literary circle included two poets, FLOYD DELL (1887–1969) and ARTHUR DAVISON FICKE (1883–1945). Dell, an ILLINOIS native and versatile writer, embraced Iowa culture and traditional mores even as he promoted emerging feminist and Marxist ideologies. His *Homecoming: An Autobiography* (1933) incorporates several of his own poems, as well as examples by Ficke, a successful lawyer who abandoned his practice to pursue poetry. A man who heartily detested Davenport's small-town milieu, Ficke wrote poetry that had little relation to Midwestern life. *From the Isles* (1907) and *The Happy Princess* (1907) were inspired by an around-the-world trip. The first issue of POETRY: A MAGAZINE OF VERSE (1912) offered a sonnet by Ficke titled "Poetry." *Sonnets of a Portrait Painter* (1914) showcases his expertise in that verse form.

Among Iowa's most recognized poets is PAUL (HAMILTON) ENGLE (1908–1991), a Cedar Rapids native who, as a high school student, was mentored by Jay G. Sigmund. His University of Iowa master's project, among the first creative theses accepted in fulfillment of a degree, was titled "One Slim Feather" (1932). Published that year as *Worn Earth* in the Yale Series of Younger Poets, the volume includes sonnets and longer works. In 1933 *Poetry* magazine selected "America Remembers" from the volume *American Song* (1934) for its Century of Progress prize, and in 1941 Engle began directing the Iowa Writers' Workshop, guiding the program for over twenty years. Engle also edited the O. Henry Prize annual volume of short stories; published an Iowa literary anthology of workshop writers, *Midland: Twenty-Five Years of Fiction and Poetry Selected from the Writing Workshops of the State University of Iowa* (1961); and authored several poetry collections.

Iowa's poetic voices emerging in the 1950s broke conventional barriers in theme, structure, and use of language even as they incorporated classic Midwestern rural topics: agriculture, determinism, self-reliance, and the natural landscape. *The Green Town* (1956) by JOSEPH (THOMAS) LANGLAND (1917–2007) was nominated for the National Book Award; Langland's second book, *The Wheel of Summer* (1963), garnered a second nomination. Donald (Rodney) Justice (1925–2004), former faculty member of the Iowa Writers' Workshop, won the 1959 Lamont Poetry Selection Prize for his first book, *The Summer Anniversaries,* and the 1980 Pulitzer Prize for *Selected Poems* (1979). Recognized as a master teacher and writer, Justice won the Bollingen Prize for Poetry in 1991. After founding the Pittsburgh Poetry Series and chairing its university press, poet Paul J. Zimmer (b. 1934) directed the University of Iowa Press from 1994 to 1998. Zimmer's writing life includes three Pushcart Prizes and eleven books of poetry, including *The Great Bird of Love* (1989) and *Crossing to Sunlight: Selected Poems, 1965–1995* (1996).

Waterloo native MONA VAN DUYN (1921–2004) launched her national poetry career with the book *Valentine to the Wide World* (1959). Her collection *To See, To Take* (1970) won the National Book Award; *Near Changes* (1990) was awarded the Pulitzer Prize. Van Duyn, also a recipient of the Bollingen Prize, served as the first female poet laureate of the United States from 1992 to 1993.

Marvin Bell (b. 1937) and Robert Dana (1929–2010) launched their respective careers with modest volumes from small presses. Bell, a New York native, holds master's degrees from the University of Chicago and the Iowa Writers' Workshop, where he joined the poetry faculty in 1965. That same year he published *Two Poems* with Hundred Pound Press. *Poems for Nathan and Saul* and *Things We Dreamt We Died For* followed in 1966. The Academy of American Poets awarded Bell the 1969 Lamont Poetry Prize for *A Probable Volume of Dreams*. Bell was selected as the first Iowa Poet Laureate, serving from 2000 to 2004; a later publication is *Mars Being Red* (2007).

Born in Massachusetts, Robert Dana attended Drake University and then earned a master's degree from the Iowa Writers' Workshop in 1954. Dana immediately joined the faculty of Cornell College in Mount Vernon, honored as the youngest tenured faculty member. During his forty years as the college's poet-in-residence, Dana published thirteen books of poetry, starting his career with *My Glass Brother* (1957). While holding his professorship, Dana revived the *North American Review* and moved the publication from Boston to the University of Northern Iowa, edited it from 1964 to 1968. A Pulitzer Prize nomination for *Starting Out for the Difficult World* (1988) led to Dana's selection for the 1989 Delmore Schwartz Memorial Poetry Award. His significant collections include *In a Fugitive Season: A Sequence of Poems* (1980), *What I Think I Know: New and Selected Poems* (1991), and *The Morning of the Red Admirals* (2004). In 1985 and 1993 Dana was awarded poetry fellowships by the National Endowment for the Arts; he served two terms as Iowa Poet Laureate from 2004 to 2008.

Iowa State University's creative writing faculty has featured two poets, Neal Bowers (b. 1948) and MARY SWANDER (b. 1950). Bowers is the author of *The Golf Ball Diver* (1983), *Lost in the Heartland* (1990), and *Night Vision: Poetry* (1992). The Society of Midland Authors awarded Bowers its 2002 poetry prize for his book *Out of the South: Poems,* inspired by his 1950s Tennessee childhood and racial struggles. Bowers now devotes his talents to novels and nonfiction, including *Words for the Taking: The Hunt for a Plagiarist* (2007). Swander is an Iowa native and a graduate of the Iowa Writers' Workshop. Her first collection, *Succession* (1979), marked the genesis of a focus on Iowa's landscape and people as inspiration. *Driving the Body Back* (1986) explores Midwestern oddities and the mundane, seeking truth in both situations. The poetry volume *Heaven-and-Earth House* (1994) was followed by the memoirs *Out of This World* (1995) and *The Desert Pilgrim: En Route to Mysticism and Miracles* (2003). Swander received the Chicago Public Library's Carl Sandburg Literary Award in 1981, the Iowa Library Association's Johnson Brigham Plaque in 1996, and the Des Moines Public Library Foundation's Iowa Author's Award in 2006. In 2009 she was named Iowa Poet Laureate; in that year she also published *Girls on the Roof,* an account of the 2008 Iowa flood, and adapted it as a performance piece.

Amy Clampitt (1920–1994), an Iowa native and Grinnell College graduate, spent most of her life in New York City and began composing poems in her forties. In 1983 Clampitt had her first major release with *The Kingfisher,* followed by *What the Light Was Like* (1985), *Archaic Figure* (1987), and *Westward* (1990). Clampitt received a 1984 Academy of American Poets fellowship and was a 1992 MacArthur Foundation fellow. She published her last collection of poems, *A Silence Opens,* in 1994. James McKean (b. 1946), an English professor retired from Mount Mercy College in Cedar Rapids and a graduate of the Iowa Writers' Workshop, is noted for his poetry and nonfiction, particularly sports writing. McKean had further critical success with an Iowa Poetry Award for *Tree of Heaven* (1994).

Other Iowa poets include Ann Struthers (b. 1930), writer-in-residence at Coe College in Cedar Rapids and author of two poetry collections, *Stoneboat* (1988) and *The Alcott Family Arrives* (1993). Debra Marquart (b. 1956), Iowa State University creative writing professor, won the Minnesota Voices Award for her 1995 book *Everything's a Verb.* Another poetry collection is *From Sweetness* (2002). Marquart's memoir, *The Horizontal World: Growing Up in the Middle of Nowhere* (2006), explores her early years on a NORTH DAKOTA farm. Michael Carey (b. 1954), farmer, poet, and Iowa Writers' Workshop graduate, is the author of *The Noise the Earth Makes* (1990), *Honest Effort: Poems* (1995), *Nishnabotna: Poems, Prose, and Dramatic Scenes from the Natural and Oral History of Southwest Iowa* (1995), and *Carpenter of Song* (1998). A promoter of Iowa writers and the poetry genre, Carey is the founding editor of Loess Hills Books and published the anthology *Voices on the Landscape: Contemporary Iowa Poets* in 1996.

Drama: Among the earliest works for the stage by Iowans are three plays written by Helen Sherman Griffith (1873–1961) in 1899: *The Minister's Wife, The Burglar Alarm,* and *A Borrowed Luncheon.* The politically charged dramas of John Wesley DeKay (1874–1938), including *Longings* (1908), *Love, and Other Songs* (1916), and *Women and the New Social State* (1918), focused on expanding roles for women in modern society. The first American play produced with Works Progress Administration (WPA) funds was *The Unconquered* (1934), staged at the Federal Portable Theatre in New York City. The work's author, Marshalltown native and actor Carl Glick (1890–1971), soon returned to Iowa to establish one of the state's first community theatres in Waterloo. Iowa's 1947 centennial statehood gala offered a University of Iowa theatre performance of *The Chancellor's Party* (1949) by Don C. Liljenquist (1921–2013), the winning entry in a statewide drama contest.

In charting Iowa's literary history from 1890 to 1935, two playwrights remain prominent, not only for their individual talents but also for their contributions to the American theatre. GEORGE CRAM COOK (1873–1924) and his wife, SUSAN KEATING GLASPELL (1876–1948), founded the Provincetown Players in 1915 and the following year presented Glaspell's one-act play TRIFLES (1916), based on a murder trial Glaspell covered in Indianola. Glaspell and Cook were the team that staged the early plays of Eugene (Gladstone) O'Neill (1888–1953), Floyd Dell, Edna St. Vincent Millay (1892–1950), Djuna Barnes (1892–1982), and others who became prominent in the arts. Cook co-authored two plays with his wife and penned three solo efforts but focused primarily on production, direction, and management of the playhouse and acting company. Glaspell wrote eleven plays for the group, including five with Iowa settings: *Trifles, Close the Book* (1917), *Inheritors* (1921), *Chains of Dew* (1922), and *Alison's House* (1930), winner of the 1931 Pulitzer Prize.

MEREDITH (ROBERT) WILLSON (1902–1984), beloved son of Mason City, both charmed and shocked the musical theatre establishment with the release of *The Music Man* in 1957. A Juilliard graduate, alumnus of John Philip Sousa's band, and former orchestra leader for two television networks, Willson put his Midwestern childhood stories into comedic form. As author, lyricist, and composer of the musical, Willson saw *The Music Man* run at the Majestic Theater in New York City from 1957 to 1961, breaking box-office records. The classic tale of Harold Hill, a con man who persuades the River City townspeople to begin a boys' band, won five 1958 Tony Awards, including best musical. Roughly a dozen years later, in the midst of national tension, Dubuque native and Vietnam veteran David (William) Rabe (b. 1940) launched his war trilogy with *Sticks and Bones* (1969), winning the 1972 Tony for best play. *The Basic Training of Pavlo Hummel* (1971) followed, earning Tony accolades for its 1977 Broadway revival. The trilogy's closing installment, *Streamers* (1976), was directed by Mike Nichols (1931–2014) and was nominated for the 1977 Tony for best play. Rabe's later writing includes the play *Hurlyburly* (1984) and screenplays for the feature films *Casualties of War* (1989) and *The Firm* (1993).

Shirley Lauro (b. 1933), born in Des Moines, has authored ten full-length and six one-act plays, including *I Don't Know Where You're Coming From at All* (1982). The award-winning playwright's most recognized work is *Open Admissions* (1984), a Tony-nominated drama about an urban female teacher and her illiterate student who seeks a university education.

Iowa has also produced its share of screenwriters. Born in MISSOURI and raised in Keokuk, Rupert Hughes (1872–1956) enjoyed sixty years in Hollywood, where he distinguished himself as a master screenwriter and a prolific novelist. Writer and director of some fifty silent and sound motion pictures, Hughes also wrote plays, novels, and short stories that served as the inspiration for over fifty feature films. While little of his fiction is set in Iowa, *In a Little Town* (1917) features stories about people in small towns resembling Keokuk.

In the mid-1950s Richard Pike Bissell adapted his comic novel *7 and ½ Cents* (1953) for the stage and later for the screen as *The Pajama Game* (1957). Set in a fictional Junction City during a strike at the Sleep-Tite pajama factory, the work is a humorous interpretation of an actual labor crisis at Bissell's family garment business in Dubuque. The original Broadway production (1954–1956) won the Tony Award for best musical. The 1957 movie version starred Doris Day and John Raitt. The 2006 Broadway production won Tony Awards for best revival of a musical and best choreography.

Born and raised in Des Moines, Peter Hedges (b. 1962) wrote the screenplays for adaptations of his novels *What's Eating Gilbert Grape* (1991) and *An Ocean in Iowa* (1997), both set in the state. He followed those efforts with the screenplay for *A Map of the World* (1999), based on the novel by JANE HAMILTON (b. 1957). Hedges also wrote the 2002 screen adaptation of *About a Boy* (1998) by Nick Hornby (b. 1957) and earned accolades for *Pieces of April* (2003), which he wrote and directed. He also wrote and directed the 2007 feature film *Dan in Real Life*.

The state's most successful screenwriter and mystery novelist is Max Allan Collins, a native and current resident of Muscatine. Writer for the Dick Tracy comic strip (1977–1993), independent filmmaker, and musician, Collins is considered one of the publishing industry's leading authors of movie and television tie-in novels. *See* COMIC STRIPS AND BOOKS. Among his screenplay credits are *The Expert* (1995), *Mommy* (1995), *Mommy's Day* (1997), Mike Hammer's *Mickey Spillane* documentary (1999), and *Real Time: Siege at Lucas Street Market* (2000). He is recognized for a prolific career in short fiction and the GRAPHIC-NOVEL format; his most acclaimed project in the latter category, *Road to Perdition* (1998), was adapted as a feature film with the same title in 2002, starring Tom Hanks and Paul Newman.

Printing, Private Presses, and Journalism: Iowa's first newspaper, the *Du Buque Visitor,* founded in May 1836 by John King (1803–1871), a local mining businessman and law official, hoped to foster community relations even as it suffered constant financial stress. By 1860 over one hundred of Iowa's earliest newspapers had ceased publication. Despite the local prestige held by an editor, most presses struggled under the weights of unpaid subscriptions and nearby competing newspapers. Pioneer journalism continued until the establishment of the *Rock Rapids Review,* a weekly, in January 1873, marking the end of Iowa's uncharted western frontier.

In 1860 brothers James S. Clarkson (1842–1918) and Richard P. Clarkson (1840–1905), along with their father, Coker F. Clarkson (1810–1890), bought a Des Moines newspaper, the *Iowa State Register,* and renamed it the *Des Moines Register.* In 1903 Gardner Cowles Sr. (1831–1946) bought the heavily in-debt publication; once the executive paired his talents with Harvey Ingham (1858–1949), supervisor of the editorial and news departments, the team quickly acquired competing local newspapers, and subscriber numbers soared. The rapid rise in the *Register*'s popularity can be attributed to the impact of political cartoonist Jay Norwood "Ding" Darling (1876–1962), two-time winner of a Pulitzer Prize and nationally known conservationist. In his forty-five years with the newspaper, Darling drew roughly 15,000 cartoons and held a front-page designation. The *Des Moines Register* celebrated its sesquicentennial year of operation in 1999, marked from the establishment of a precursor newspaper, the *Des Moines Leader* in 1849, as one of the nation's few remaining statewide newspapers. The state's second-largest city, Cedar Rapids, offers a daily newspaper that is still locally owned, the *Cedar Rapids Gazette.* The press is part of the greater Gazette Communications Group and celebrated its 125th year of operation in 2007.

The pairing of newspapers with agriculture was an early state publishing venture. *Iowa Farmer and Horticulturist,* founded in 1853 in Burlington by James W. Grimes, soon moved to Des Moines and dissolved in 1860. *Northwestern Farmer and Horticultural Journal,* later named *Iowa Homestead,* was begun by Mark Miller in Dubuque in 1855, survived the Civil War, and eventually reached over 150,000 customers by 1920. The publication was eventually absorbed by the most prominent Iowa agricultural newspaper, *Wallace's Farmer,* which has been publishing continuously since 1874. That publication was founded by "Uncle" Henry Wallace (1836–1916), a former minister and farming reporter who suffered creative differences with Miller and chose to launch his own newspaper. Wallace's son, Henry C(antwell) Wallace (1866–1924), an Iowa State University dairy science professor, joined efforts with an academic colleague, C. F. Curtiss, and his brother, John C. Wallace, to create *Wallace's Farmer and Dairyman* (1894), a publication for both academics and the larger industry. The paper bought its rival, the *Iowa Homestead,* for $2 million in October 1929 and immediately sank into bankruptcy during the stock-market crash. After *Wallace's Farmer* was bought by a creditor in a sheriff's sale, Henry A. Wallace (1888–1965), grandson of "Uncle Henry" and son of Henry C. Wallace, edited the publication, which endorsed

New Deal programs and won back its circulation, reaching almost 300,000 subscribers in 1955. Despite accolades, the paper was sold to a Chicago farming press, *Prairie Farmer,* as part of a 1957 media-deal package.

Iowa's most widely circulated agricultural periodical, *Successful Farming,* first published in Des Moines in 1902, was envisioned as a regional service title offering family-appropriate content. Paid advertising was included when the periodical reached 100,000 subscribers in 1906; by 1914 the monthly circulated in over 500,000 homes. *Successful Farming* remains America's largest paid-circulation magazine targeting farmers and ranchers.

Today the Meredith Corporation is recognized as one of the nation's leading media and marketing companies. Among its well-known titles are *Family Circle, Ladies' Home Journal, Midwest Living, Parents,* and *Better Homes and Gardens,* the first home magazine to circulate widely without featuring fiction. Begun in 1922 as *Fruit, Garden, and Home,* the flagship publication was renamed in 1924 and became America's highest mass-circulation magazine, reaching over 6 million paid subscribers by 1963, the largest audience ever recorded for an Iowa-based periodical. Meredith's book-publishing arm offers the highly visible *Better Homes and Gardens Cookbook,* launched in 1930 with its familiar red plaid cover. Other special-interest Meredith Books titles include volumes on gardening, home repair and renovation, decorating, and handicrafts.

The State Historical Society of Iowa began its first magazine project in 1863, founding the *Annals of Iowa,* one of the first historical quarterlies published in the United States. The *Iowa Journal of History and Politics* (1903–1960) primarily featured scholarship by leading state historians; the *Palimpsest* (1920–1995), known as *Iowa Heritage Illustrated* since 1996, offers state history with a general public appeal. Now celebrating its sixth decade of production, the *Iowan* magazine promotes the state's people, communities, culture, and traditions.

Both education and religious magazines proliferated in Iowa, the former appealing to teachers and administrators, the latter based on the wide variety of denominations and churches. The *District School Journal of Education of the State of Iowa*, issued in Dubuque from 1853 to 1854, was the state's earliest teaching journal. The state's first religious journal, *The Christian Evangelist* (1850–1864), originating in Fort Madison, reflected its readership's dedication to missionary work in the American West. Quaker, Adventist, Episcopal, Latter-Day Saints, Methodist, Unitarian, Baptist, and Catholic publishing ventures fill the state's magazine history. The *Witness*, the newspaper of the Archdiocese of Dubuque, continues to publish parish news for a thirty-county area and has been active since 1921.

With the 1894 premiere of a literary magazine, the *Midland Monthly*, Johnson Brigham broke new publishing ground, promoting the works of Hamlin Garland, Alice French, Ellis Parker Butler, and other notable Iowa authors. The magazine quickly rose to prominence for its quality, and many Iowa poets were launched within its pages. In 1898 the magazine moved to ST. LOUIS, Missouri, and ceased publication in 1899. The journal focused on "literature of the middle border" and inspired the *Midland*, edited by JOHN T(OWNER) FREDERICK (1893–1975) and published at the University of Iowa from 1915 to 1930 and then in CHICAGO until 1933. Frederick emphasized texts and poetry with Midwestern settings, choosing to discover and promote new Iowa poets and fiction writers.

Students and faculty writing from Iowa's colleges and universities made appearances as early as 1870 in the *Iowa Classic* (1870–1875) at Iowa Wesleyan College and the *College Quarterly* (1878–1880) at Iowa State College, now Iowa State University. Over fifty campus literary magazines have been associated with the state. Significant titles in this group include Grinnell College's *Tanager* (1925–1948), Cornell College's *Husk* (1922–1937), and *American Prefaces* (1935–1943), produced by the School of Journalism at the University of Iowa. That university is also the headquarters of *Philological Quarterly*, which has been publishing scholarship pertaining to classical and modern languages and literatures continuously since 1922, as well as the *Iowa Review*, which has been publishing creative work continuously since 1970.

Iowa's publishing industry features university presses and private printers devoted to scholarly and educational offerings. The Iowa State University Press, affiliated with Blackwell Publishing since 2000, was founded as the Collegiate Press in 1924 and specializes in scholarly research. The University of Iowa Press, established in 1938, was formally organized with a board of faculty advisers in 1969. The press averages thirty to thirty-five new titles each year and offers books in literature, poetry, history, architecture, music, natural science, regional studies, and Iowa history. In the area of commercial publishing, Perfection Learning Corporation, based in Logan, has progressed radically from its first offerings of school forms in the 1920s. The company is now recognized as a leading producer of teacher and student materials for children from preschool through grade twelve. The company creates and markets literature, vocabulary, writing, and reading-readiness tools for the classroom. Kendall-Hunt Publishing Company, a Dubuque-based entity for over fifty years, focuses on K–12 teacher materials, college textbooks, and business-related manuals and publications.

Iowa's national reputation for excellence in handmade book production began its legacy through the efforts of a core group of printers. Carroll Coleman (1904–1989), operator of the Prairie Press in Muscatine from 1935 to 1965 and director of the Typography Laboratory at the University of Iowa, envisioned a regional press with a Midwestern focus. Considered one of America's most gifted book designers, Coleman organized and created Iowa's first private press, building Prairie Press's reputation on finely crafted volumes of original poetry and prose. Harry Duncan (1916–1997) founded the Cummington Press in 1939 in Massachusetts before coming to Iowa as Coleman's successor. Duncan maintained his direct campus ties while influencing contemporary American publishing. Cummington Press promoted relatively unknown poets with fine workmanship; it operated from 1956 to 1972 and ultimately moved to West Branch. Duncan published work by Rainer Maria Rilke (1875–1926), William Carlos Williams (1883–1963), Allen Tate (1899–1979), Wallace Stevens (1879–1955),

Robert Lowell (1917–1977), and Mona Van Duyn. After his retirement in 1985, he moved to Omaha and resumed publishing under the Cummington imprint.

Arguably Harry Duncan's most gifted student, Karl Kimber "Kim" Merker (1928–2013) enrolled at the University of Iowa and took a typography class with the master in 1957. Immediately thereafter, Merker began Stone Wall Press, another Iowa imprint recognized for publishing first books by major poets, including U.S. Poet Laureate Philip Levine (1928–2015), Mark Strand (1934–2014), and Marvin Bell. Stone Wall's press runs were typically small and offered superb quality in printing and design. By 1966 Merker's efforts also persuaded the University of Iowa to launch a press specifically for the teaching of hand-printed book production. The resulting company, Windhover Press, operated from 1967 to 1995; Merker produced immaculately crafted books at one of the first fine presses sponsored by a public university. Stone Wall Press ceased production in 1976. Merker's legacy includes helping found the University of Iowa's Center for the Book. In 1964, book designer Neil Shaver (b. 1924) made contact with Merker, who instructed him in the use of a Washington press. Shaver later enrolled in a printing class taught by Harry Duncan and in 1979 founded the Yellow Barn Press in Council Bluffs. Unique to Shaver's efforts was his focus on works about printing and the history of books; the direction of his press was determined by strong sales of "The Old Printing Office," an essay by Pulitzer Prize–winning historian Frank Luther Mott. Yellow Barn Press averaged two titles per year, relying on the talents of master engraver John DePol (1913–2004), before it closed in 2005 after having produced thirty books.

Other notable private presses in Iowa have included Torch Press, based in Cedar Rapids from 1907 to 1959 and founded by Luther Albertus Brewer (1858–1933). Torch was well known for its Christmas books, an annual tradition from 1912 to 1959 for special friends of the press. Clio Press, launched in 1930s Iowa City by Frank Luther Mott, specialized in Midwestern fiction, nonfiction, and poetry; the press released Grant Wood's regionalist treatise *Revolt against the City* in 1935. Toothpaste Press (1970–1984), located

in West Branch, is now known as Coffee House Press and is based in MINNEAPOLIS. The press's founders, Allan and Cinda Kornblum, bought Harry Duncan's former home and followed local sentiment that embraced actualism, the belief in using common objects as subject matter for poetry.

Iowa's active private publishing ventures include Ice Cube Press, located in North Liberty since 1993, which publishes books that focus on how people interact with the natural world and foster community. Proprietor Steve Semken developed the Harvest Book series in 2000, featuring titles exploring the relationship between Iowa's natural environment and the human spirit. Prominent poet and farmer Michael Carey founded Loess Hills Books in 1996, dedicated to the promotion of Midwestern literature from its headquarters in Farragut. Final Thursday Press in Cedar Falls, led by proprietor Jim O'Loughlin since 2001, specializes in chapbooks by Iowa authors and signed and numbered editions of poetry and fiction. The press maintains an Iowa poetry series and actively seeks manuscripts from regional writers. In 2002 an internationally acclaimed study of camouflage launched Bobolink Press in Cedar Falls. The press's founder, sole author, and designer, Roy Behrens, produces titles that present little-known aspects of Iowa history in relation to the arts. In 2004 Russell (Scott) Valentino, a University of Iowa professor, began Autumn Hill Books in Iowa City with an emphasis on publishing English translations of international literature.

Iowa Federal Writers' Project: Iowa's history with the FEDERAL WRITERS' PROJECT began with the appointment of Jay DuVon as state director in 1935. DuVon's responsibility was to locate and hire talented writers for the state guide project. His tenure was brief since he was soon promoted to a regional director position. The state director associated with the Iowa state guide is the poet Raymond Kresensky, who, from his central office in Des Moines, supervised the production and printing of *Iowa: A Guide to the Hawkeye State* (1938), published by Viking Press. Research and assembly of the state volume occurred mainly from 1936 to 1938 and involved several writers of note: Mae L. Christensen, Henry G. Felsen, Vivian Fisher, Jane T. Irish, Fred Langenberg, James S. Martin, William E. Myers, and Raymond Rooney. The writer Opal Shannon was lauded for her significant work on the book; Henry M. McCullough served as a project editor. The book includes essays and photographs of farms and rural life, descriptions of major crops, profiles of seventeen cities, and roughly twenty-three driving tours.

In addition to the state guide, the writing team produced histories for the following Iowa counties: Cherokee, Monroe, and Van Buren (1940); Crawford, Franklin, and Johnson (1941); and Buena Vista, Dubuque, Jackson, Lee, Osceola, Page, Ringgold, Scott, and Woodbury (1942). Specialized regional guides include the *Guide to Cedar Rapids and Northeast Iowa* (1937) and *A Guide to Estherville, Iowa, Emmet County, and Iowa Great Lakes Region* (1939). The cities of Dubuque (1937), Burlington (1938), McGregor (1938), and Bentonsport (1940) received their own treatments. A geological and history guide for southwestern Iowa was published in 1936; the state's general recreational guide was released in 1941. The Iowa Federal Writers' Project was terminated in 1942, a result of the dissolution of the Works Progress Administration, laws mandating releases of all WPA-associated staff, and the absence of viable funding.

State Literary Awards and Prizes: Created by the Des Moines Public Library Foundation in 2000, the annual Iowa Author Awards Dinner raises funds to support library programs and services and to promote Iowa's rich literary offerings. Among the recipients of the award are Robert James Waller (2002), Jane Smiley (2003), CURTIS (ARTHUR) HARNACK (1927–2013) (2004), Marilynne Robinson (2005), Mary Swander (2006), Debra Marquart (2009), and Elvin McDonald (2011). The Iowa Library Association's Johnson Brigham plaque is named in honor of the founder of the *Midland Monthly* and is presented every three years to an Iowa author who has published a critically respected work in the previous award period. Winners include Ruth Suckow (1935), Paul Engle (1940), Bess Streeter Aldrich (1949), Frederick Manfred (1980), Leigh Michaels (2003), Michael Carey (2007), and Dorothy Garlock (2009).

The University of Iowa Press has offered the annual Iowa Short Fiction Award since 1969. Competitors submit a volume of short stories as part of a national search; entries are juried by the fiction faculty of the Iowa Writers' Workshop. In 1988 the John Simmons Short Fiction Award was created to honor the press's first director. This award complements the traditional short-fiction prize, thereby recognizing two prose works published by the press in a calendar year.

Originally known as the Edwin Ford Piper Poetry Award and renamed in 1993, the Iowa Poetry Prize is also sponsored by the University of Iowa Press. Until 2001 only those poets who had previously published at least one collection were eligible for the competition. After that year the contest was redesigned to honor new poets' debuts as well, always bestowing the prize on two book-length collections in English. Writers are selected only once for the honor.

The Iowa Association of School Librarians, a division of the state's library association, sponsors an annual statewide campaign to encourage student reading that allows children to nominate their favorite works and select the award recipients. The Iowa Children's Choice Award, begun in 1979, targets titles appropriate for students in third through sixth grades; honorees may be fiction or nonfiction but must have been written by an American author within the last five years. In 2010 Iowa elementary students selected *Stolen Children* by Peg Kehret (b. 1936). The Iowa Teen Award, inaugurated in 1985, allows students in grades six through nine to vote for their favorite title. The association also sponsors a relatively new prize, the Iowa High School Book Award, first presented in 2004 to Nicholas Sparks (b. 1965) for his novel *A Walk to Remember* (1999). Selected as the 2011 winner was *The Hunger Games* (2008) by Suzanne Collins (b. 1962).

State Literary Societies: Affiliated with the National Federation of State Poetry Societies and founded in 1945, the Iowa Poetry Association publishes *Lyrical Iowa,* an annual collection of verse by Iowa residents. The organization offers semi-annual critique workshops and is a sponsor of the Des Moines International Poetry Festival. Recognized for its signature publication that began in 1946 and for its past leadership role in the statewide Iowa Poetry Day celebration (1943–1984), the association celebrates original unpublished poetry by Iowa writers.

Founded in 1997, the Iowa Scriptwriters Alliance includes both professional and novice playwrights and screenwriters. The group offers monthly workshops for evaluative readings and professional education. The Des Moines–based organization supports script development and the performance of works in film and on stages within the state. The Society of Children's Book Writers and Illustrators of Iowa is affiliated with its national organization, the Society of Children's Book Writers and Illustrators. Membership is designed for writers with interest or previous experience in publishing, writing, or illustrating for children in magazines, multimedia, television, and books. The Iowa Storytellers Roundtable, a division of the Iowa Library Association, is dedicated to the art of storytelling in libraries and other public venues. Membership consists primarily of Iowa school media specialists, elementary and high school children's and young-adult librarians, and those involved in special adult outreach programs.

Iowa's university libraries house many specialized collections pertaining to the literature of the state. Iowa State University's archives contain thousands of titles, including fiction and nonfiction, by faculty, staff, and alumni. The University of Northern Iowa has long acquired small-press publications reflecting creative efforts in Iowa and the greater Midwest. The campus library also offers the American Fiction Collection, some 5,300 first editions of novels published between 1960 and 1980. The principal collection of state literature is housed in the Department of Special Collections at the University of Iowa Main Library. The department's Iowa Authors Collection, established in 1945, includes writers in three categories: natives of the state; those associated with the state who have published a book; and those writers who have resided in Iowa for at least twenty years. Over 20,000 volumes and 2,000 authors are represented; the collection offers generous holdings in history and prose, emphasizing fiction.

SELECTED WORKS: Iowa's seminal literature primarily reflects its rich history in fic-

tion and poetry. The state's pioneer era is vividly shown in MacKinlay Kantor's *Spirit Lake* (1961), a retelling of events associated with the Spirit Lake Massacre. Frederick Manfred's focus on "Siouxland," a corner of northwestern Iowa, sets the backdrop for *Conquering Horse* (1959), set during the time of Iowa's earliest white settlement. The state's transition from undeveloped prairie to homesteading is charted in numerous farm novels. Among the most prominent and well crafted is Paul Corey's *Three Miles Square* (1939), the first installment of his Mantz trilogy, mapping southwestern Iowa's agricultural history from 1910 to 1916. *Vandemark's Folly* (1922) by Herbert Quick profiles pioneers moving into 1850s Iowa and struggling to begin new lives. Modern farm novels are represented by two Pulitzer Prize winners, Jane Smiley's *A Thousand Acres* (1991) and Marilynne Robinson's *Gilead* (2004). Smiley's book explores the destruction of a family and its enduring reliance on the land; Robinson's text weaves memory and past experience to develop connections between an elderly minister and his newborn son.

The evolution from organized farmsteads to small prairie towns marks the next body of significant Iowa fiction. Two talented female authors, Ruth Suckow and Bess Streeter Aldrich, crafted classics of this genre. *The Folks* (1934), Suckow's exemplary tale of life in an early Iowa community, is critically praised as her strongest work. Aldrich's *A Song of Years* (1934), one of her later novels, captures eastern Iowa's transition from the agrarian pre–Civil War era to loosely developed townships, focusing on the period from 1854 to 1865. Hamlin Garland, the author who first portrayed the brutal realism of late nineteenth-century Midwestern farm life in fiction, chronicles his childhood in Wisconsin and his later Iowa life in *A Son of the Middle Border* (1917).

The psychological and economic complexities of urbanization were also addressed by Iowa writers exploring the tangible changes that began in the early twentieth century. Alice French, commonly remembered for her adept use of local color in the short-story genre, gathered high critical accolades for the novel *Man of the Hour* (1905). A searing view of labor and industrial struggles in Davenport, the tale is ultimately an indictment of political power and wealth gained at the cost of individuals' well-being. Ellis Parker Butler, venturing from his typical humorist publications, created a powerful vision of a developing Iowa town along the Mississippi River in the novel *Dominie Dean* (1917). Susan Glaspell studied class differences and conventions in tightly structured communities, as well as the consequences of personal choice, in novels such as *The Visioning* (1911) and *Fidelity* (1915). JO-SEPHINE (FREY) HERBST (1892–1969), born in Sioux City, composed the Trexler-Wendel farm trilogy, considered the best of her fiction, including *Pity Is Not Enough* (1933), *The Executioner Waits* (1934), and *Rope of Gold* (1939). The novels profile farmers and industrial laborers struggling against the devastation of the Dust Bowl, failing government relief programs, and personal debts, both monetary and spiritual. Satirical views of Iowa's farm culture and its homogeneous population spur the irony in Phil Stong's humorous masterwork *State Fair* (1932). Stong's immediate device is to pair the central family's parents' quest for fair honors in cooking and swine showing with the sexual explorations of their children at the fairgrounds.

Two of Iowa's most prominent modern poets, Jay G. Sigmund and Paul Engle, shared a lasting friendship and talent with language. *The Ridge Road: Short Stories and Poems* (1930), a collection representing the best of Sigmund's efforts, searches humanity's dark nature, drawing inspiration from the Wapsipinicon River valley of eastern Iowa. "One Slim Feather," Engle's graduate thesis, was published as *Worn Earth*, the 1932 volume from the Yale Series of Younger Poets. An illustrious career followed, including numerous literary prizes and a lengthy tenure as director of the Iowa Writers' Workshop. Iowa native and critically praised farm poet James Hearst earned honors for his strong collection *Country Men* (1937). Current Iowa poets blend rural imagery, modern themes, and language conventions to produce memorable verse. Among those of the highest rank is Marvin Bell, a National Book Award nominee for his volume *Stars Which See, Stars Which Do Not See* (1977). Mary Swander delves into both ordinary and bi-zarre aspects of Midwestern life in the memorable collection *Driving the Body Back* (1986).

Iowa's poetic and prose history is shown in three lauded anthologies. *Prairie Gold by Iowa Authors and Artists* (1917) is the first significant collection from the state. A publication of the Iowa Authors Club, the volume includes leading fiction authors and poets, as well as a thorough discussion of Iowa's literary beginnings by historian Johnson Brigham. *Out of This World: Poems from the Hawkeye State* (1975), edited by Gary and Judith Gildner, is a compilation reflecting national and regional poets of strong reputation. Efforts in poetry revival and appreciation by Michael Carey, award-winning writer and founder of the Loess Hills Press, led to the book *Voices on the Landscape: Contemporary Iowa Poets* (1996). Poets in the anthology represent major voices in Iowa; most have won regional and national awards.

FURTHER READING: Early efforts toward a comprehensive bibliography on Iowa history produced three notable projects, all guided to print by the State Historical Society of Iowa. The works, titled *One Hundred Topics in Iowa History* (1914), *Two Hundred Topics in Iowa History* (1932), and *A Reference Guide to Iowa History* (1942), were research projects of the historian William J. Petersen (1901–1989). In 1952 the culmination of Petersen's energies, a volume that would appeal to the general public, was released as *The Iowa History Reference Guide*. Students, educators, and county historical societies were target audiences, and the book thereby encouraged a growing interest in Iowa history. Petersen's work draws a majority of its references from State Historical Society of Iowa publications; however, as a general-application bibliography, the contents remain strong and reflect a core of significant, historical research for the state.

The state's next notable history bibliography appeared in 1989, once again under the auspices of the State Historical Society of Iowa. Patricia Dawson, a librarian at Drake University, and David Hudson, a reference librarian at the University of Iowa, compiled their findings to produce *Iowa History and Culture: A Bibliography of Materials Published between 1952 and 1986*. Comprehensive but not exhaustive, the work appeals to students, librarians, historians, and members of the general public seeking knowledge about the state's history. The authors offer regional, state, and local histories; coverage of immigration and religion; a section on science; and women's history. The book is considered essential for Iowa history and literature collections.

Dawson and Hudson continued their professional collaboration and updated the 1989 publication in a series of articles in the *Annals of Iowa* during 1993. In lieu of a formal volume, Dawson compiled the team's findings and released "Iowa History and Culture: A Bibliography of Materials Published from 1987 to 1991" in three issues of the journal. The listings follow the main bibliography's arrangement scheme and add some citations not included in the 1989 book. Motivated to compile a bibliography of books set in Iowa, Kristy Raine and Marilyn Murphy, both affiliated with Mount Mercy University's Busse Library, refined their research efforts to produce the internet's largest comprehensive list of fiction set in Iowa for both children and adults. The staff has added numerous appendixes since the project's original launch in March 2002. Recent expansions of the website, Iowa: A Literary Landscape, highlight media formats, such as feature films, electronic works, audio works, and non-English translations of featured novels.

State librarian and historian Johnson Brigham edited *A Book of Iowa Authors by Iowa Authors* (1930), which offers an essay on Iowa literary history and critical studies of seventeen major authors. *Who's Who among Prairie Poets: Centennial Edition, 1938*, edited by Lou Mallory Luke, is a celebration of the state's 1838 founding and a publication affiliated with the Iowa Authors' Club, a group involving Iowa's most recognized authors. The compilation is a biographical dictionary offering a valuable list of club membership and a geographic index. Poet profiles include birth and parent data, educational and employment details, a list of primary publications, personal interests, and residence information.

Released through the Friends of the University of Iowa Libraries, Frank Paluka's *Iowa Authors: A Bio-Bibliography of Sixty Native Writers* (1967) was inspired by the Iowa Authors Collection. This bibliography includes authors who were born in the state or who lived there for twenty or more years. Sixty writers are profiled, all Iowa natives with five or more original books.

The first statewide effort to assemble a list of books by Iowa authors was prepared and published under the guidance of the Iowa Library Commission. Anna Belknap Howe's resulting compilation, *List of Books by Iowa Authors: Collected by the Auxiliary Committee of the Iowa Commission, Louisiana Purchase Exposition, for the Exhibit of Books by Iowa Authors in the Iowa State Building, St. Louis, 1904* (1904), presents authors born in Iowa or who were identified with the state and were producing literary work at the time of the list's publication. The majority of works are nonfiction, although some works of poetry and fiction are included.

Independent of any library-sponsored effort was the Iowa State Historical Society's attempt to chronicle Iowa authors and their works dating from 1880 to 1918. Preliminary findings by Assistant Curator Alice Marple were released in 1918 as *Iowa Authors and Their Works: A Contribution toward a Bibliography*. Criteria for inclusion required that an author be born in Iowa or be employed in the state. Once again, nonfiction items represent the bulk of entries, but this work offers a literature section, reflecting poetry, fiction, and drama.

Betty Jo Buckingham, editor and chairperson of a statewide committee to create an Iowa history bibliography for school libraries, led efforts to produce a document in 1969, 1974, and 1982. These versions were published independently through the Iowa Association of School Librarians; later editions fall under the jurisdiction of the Iowa Department of Education. *Iowa and Some Iowans: A Bibliography for Schools and Libraries* (1996), currently in its fifth edition, is designed primarily for school media specialists, with an emphasis on elementary and secondary levels. The bibliography is unique in its target audience and in its annotations for appropriateness and reading levels within a given age group.

Johnson Brigham's essay "Iowa as a Literary Field," featured in the 1917 anthology *Prairie Gold by Iowa Authors and Artists*, focuses on the state's publishing history during the nineteenth and early twentieth centuries. Frank Luther Mott emphasizes the direct relationship between fictional guidebooks that romanticized the Midwest and the rapid arrival of eastern pioneers in his lecture *Literature of Pioneer Life in Iowa: An Address Delivered before the Academy of Science and Letters at Sioux City in March, 1923,* which offers a historical and literary framework to trace the rise of Iowa's earliest fiction. An annotated bibliography is included, notable for its exhaustive approach to the state's first significant publishing efforts.

Jessie Welborn Smith, editor of Iowa entries in the *North American Book of Verse* (1939) and an advocate for poets, produced a small volume of literary commentary published by the New York City poetry house Henry Harrison. A combination of biography, textual criticism, and general commentary, *What of the Iowa Poets?* (1941) gives readers a retrospective view of the state's poetry offerings beginning in the pioneer era. Literary folklore is integrated; of particular worth are the discussions of emerging writers and of the role of the Iowa Federation of Women's Clubs in disseminating literature and encouraging poetry appreciation.

Clarence A. Andrews's *A Literary History of Iowa* (1972) remains the standard study of the state's authors and is essential for Iowa history and literature collections. Andrews uses criteria associated with the Iowa Authors Collection; novels, short stories, and poetry are main emphases. In 1992 Andrews's update, "Iowa Literary History, 1971–1991," appeared in *Books at Iowa.*

For information on early Iowa printing and publishers, see *A Check List of Iowa Imprints, 1838–1860,* published by the American Imprints Inventory of the WPA in 1940; although it is dated, it is still useful. This work enlarged and supplemented an earlier bibliography compiled by Alexander Moffitt and published in the *Iowa Journal of History and Politics* (January 1938). Joseph A. Michaud's *Iowa City, City of the Book: Writing, Publishing, and Book Arts in the Heartland* (2011) focuses on writing and publishing in that city.

KRISTY NELSON RAINE   MOUNT MERCY UNIVERSITY

IOWA WRITERS' WORKSHOP, THE

OVERVIEW: The University of Iowa's Graduate Program in Creative Writing, more commonly known as the Iowa Writers' Workshop, is a two-year residency program culminating in the submission of a creative thesis and the awarding of a master of fine arts degree. The Iowa Writers' Workshop is the most prestigious and notably the oldest graduate creative writing program in the country, and with about one hundred students attending each year—fifty in fiction and fifty in poetry—it is also the largest of the top-ranked programs. Since the program's inception the Writers' Workshop has become a seminal force in American literature and has helped turn its hometown, Iowa City, IOWA, into a major hub of both American and international literary culture. Writers affiliated with the workshop have won twenty-eight Pulitzer Prizes, seventeen by graduates of the program, and at least four Writers' Workshop graduates have been appointed U.S, poets laureate. Notable alumni of the workshop include many luminaries of American literature, such as Raymond Carver (1938–1988), Flannery O'Connor (1925–1964), Jorie Graham (b. 1950), John Irving (b. John Wallace Blunt Jr., 1942), Denis Johnson (b. 1949), Galway Kinnell (1927–2014), and W. D. Snodgrass (1926–2009), as well as many others. Notable former faculty members include JOHN BERRYMAN (1914–1972), John Cheever (1912–1982), Philip Roth (b. 1933), KURT VONNEGUT (1922–2007), and Pulitzer Prize winners James Alan McPherson (b. 1943) and Marilynne Robinson (b. 1943), who are current faculty members. In 2003 the workshop received a National Humanities Medal from the National Endowment for the Humanities, the first such medal awarded to a university and only the second given to an institution rather than an individual. The Writers' Workshop has been greatly influential in originating and popularizing the concept of creative writing classes in American academia, as well as in molding the ways in which creative-writing workshops are traditionally taught. This entry focuses on the history and development of the program, the increasing impact it exerted on American literature throughout the twentieth century, and the current life of the Iowa Writers' Workshop, which continues to hold great literary prominence and influence.

HISTORY AND SIGNIFICANCE: Classes in creative writing had been a curricular eccentricity particular to the University of Iowa since 1897, when poet and teacher GEORGE CRAM COOK (1873–1924) first offered a course in "Verse-Making." During the three decades that followed, various teachers offered courses in the writing of poetry and short stories. In the early twentieth century JOHN T(OWNER) FREDERICK (1893–1975), Frank Luther Mott (1886–1964), and Edwin Ford Piper (1871–1939)—whose courses were the first to be informally called workshops—taught classes in creative writing at the University of Iowa, forming a bedrock of tradition on which the Iowa Writers' Workshop would later be built. Piper is often regarded as a godfather figure to the workshop. It was Piper who first developed the now-familiar writing workshop structure of round-robin peer critique of student work and who in 1922 helped persuade the university to award graduate credit for creative work; because of Iowa's status as a public state university, it was in a unique position to experiment freely with such an extraordinary rarity at the time in higher education—a risk that prestigious private universities such as Harvard and Yale were not yet willing to take.

In 1930 Norman Foerster (1887–1972), the Director of the university's School of Letters, began to push for the innovative idea of a semi-autonomous program in creative writing within the English Department. Foerster strongly believed that the creative writer must necessarily also be a literary critic. In the same year in which Foerster began his push for the creation of the writing program, the tradition of writing at Iowa was already alive enough for the poet and short-story writer Edward J(oseph Harrington) O'Brien (1890–1941), the founder of *Best American Short Stories,* to declare, "Two generations ago Boston was the geographical centre of American literary life, one generation ago New York could claim pride of place, and I trust that the idea will not seem too unfamiliar if I suggest that the geographical centre to-day is Iowa City" (quoted in Frank Luther Mott, *A History of American Magazines,* vol. 5, *1905–1930,* 188). The following year, 1931, the English Department awarded its first Master of Arts degree for a creative the-

sis. Although courses in creative writing were already unofficially called workshops, in 1939 the title of the course was first listed officially as "Writers' Workshop, credit arranged." Norman Foerster and Wilber (Lang) Schramm (1907–1987), the first official director of the writing program, somewhat disparagingly considered the writers who taught at Iowa regionalists interested primarily in writing that reflected the culture of the Midwest. Foerster and Schramm actively sought to expand this narrow focus to the creation of imaginative literature in a wider sense. Wilber Schramm continued as director of the workshop until he left the program in 1941 to help with the war effort abroad before returning a year later to take over the administration of the Journalism School. The poet and teacher PAUL (HAMILTON) ENGLE (1908–1991) then replaced him as director of the program. Under the leadership of Engle—an energetic personality of great charm, talent, and entrepreneurial zeal—the Iowa Writers' Workshop rose to fame and international prestige.

Over the course of his twenty-three-year tenure as director, Engle greatly expanded enrollment and brought to Iowa City writers such as NELSON ALGREN (1909–1981), Robert Penn Warren (1905–1989), Robert Lowell (1917–1977), John Berryman, Kurt Vonnegut, and Philip Roth. Under Engle, the administrative structure of the workshop took form. Engle split the program into fiction and poetry as enrollment swelled. During the 1940s, 1950s, and 1960s Engle helped turn Iowa City into a famous training ground for young writers, overseeing many students who would later achieve literary renown and influence, including Flannery O'Connor, Philip Levine (1928–2015), Donald Justice (1925–2004), ROBERT (ELWOOD) BLY (b. 1926), and Wallace Stegner (1909–1993). By 1961 the Writers' Workshop offered both graduate and undergraduate courses in fiction and poetry, and ranking faculty members included Engle, VANCE (NYE) BOURJAILY (1922–2010), Donald Justice, and Ray B(enedict) West, Jr. (1908–1990). During his tenure Engle raised millions of dollars in support of the writing programs. The workshop, as it grew under Engle, became the essential model on which hundreds of other creative writing programs at American colleges and universities were molded.

Engle retired from the directorship in 1965 amid a period of tumult in the program, resulting in part from the program's growing pains and in part from political friction between Engle and the university's English Department. In 1967, with his future wife, Hualing Nieh (b. Nieh Hualing in 1925), Engle co-founded the University of Iowa's International Writing Program, which to this day provides for authors from all over the world to converge in Iowa for three months each year. In 1976 Paul and Hauling Nieh Engle were nominated for a Nobel Peace Prize for their work with the International Writing Program.

Meanwhile, John C. Gerber, then the head of the English Department, took over unofficially in 1965 as director of the creative writing program. Poet and workshop faculty member George Starbuck ran the program as the interim director from 1966 through 1969, and John "Jack" (Ward) Leggett (1917–2015) was appointed acting director in 1970 and became the fourth director of the workshop in 1971. Leggett directed the workshop for seventeen years. By this time the workshop was a solidly famous institution with a rotating faculty composed each year of writers of worldwide distinction and with alumni going on to win every major literary prize. In the 1970s John Cheever, John Irving, Raymond Carver, Gail Godwin (b. 1937), and many others taught such writers of future acclaim as T(homas) C(oraghessan) Boyle (b. 1948), Ron Hansen (b. 1947), James Alan McPherson, Thom Jones (b. 1945), Denis Johnson, STUART DYBEK (b. 1942), JANE (GRAVES) SMILEY (b. 1949), Allan Gurganus (b. 1947), SANDRA CISNEROS (b. 1954), Michael Cunningham (b. 1952), and Jayne Anne Phillips (b. 1952). Several poets who graduated from the workshop during this time went on to win Pulitzer Prizes, including RITA DOVE (b. 1952), Jorie Graham, Philip Schultz (b. 1945), and James Tate (1943–2015).

When John Leggett retired in 1987, Frank Conroy (1936–2005) replaced him as the fifth director of the workshop. Conroy came to Iowa after having directed the literary program at the National Endowment for the Arts. Conroy, a former teacher and jazz pianist, was best known for his 1967 memoir *Stop-Time.* Like Paul Engle, Conroy was a forceful and charismatic personality who presided over the workshop's continued growth and rising prominence for the next eighteen years. Under Conroy's directorship a new generation of fiction writers and poets continued to carve out acclaimed careers in literature: Kathryn Harrison (b. 1961), Elizabeth McCracken (b. 1966), A(my) M. Homes (b. 1961), Chris(topher John) Offutt (b. 1958), Charles D'Ambrosio (b. 1960), current director Lan Samantha Chang (b. 1965), and (Zuwena) "ZZ" Packer (b. 1973), among many others. James Salter (James Arnold Horowitz, 1925–2015) wrote in his *New York Times* obituary of Conroy in May 2005,

As director . . . Conroy read every submission and made final decisions himself. It was the way the great cities of Europe were built, not by committee but by royal decree. The faculty was assembled the same way. There were permanent members, Frank being one of them, but others were there by invitation for a year or two. The workshop ran like a clock, due also to a chief administrator, Connie Brothers, who looked after all the details Frank could treat somewhat offhandedly and who acted as a kind of foster mother for the students. Between them was the power.

After a battle with colon cancer, Frank Conroy died in 2005. In 2006 his former student Lan Samantha Chang (b. 1965) replaced him as both the first woman and the first Asian American to direct the program. Current permanent faculty members include Chang, Ethan (Andrew) Canin (b. 1960), Charles D'Ambrosio (b. 1958), James Galvin (b. 1951), Mark Levine (b. 1965), Margot Livesey (b. 1953), Ayana Mathis (b. 1973), James Alan McPherson (b. 1943), Marilynne Robinson (b. 1943) and Elizabeth Willis (b. 1961). The Iowa Writers' Workshop continues to thrive under Chang's directorship, each year admitting about fifty new students divided between fiction and poetry, and it continues to make Iowa City not only a central hive of Midwestern literature but also an internationally recognized gathering place for writers.

FURTHER READING: Probably the most expansive and helpful introduction to the Iowa Writers' Workshop is *The Workshop: Seven Decades of the Iowa Writers' Workshop;*

Forty-Three Stories, Recollections, and Essays on Iowa's Place in Twentieth-Century American Literature (1999), edited by Tom Grimes. This book provides a concise history of the workshop, an excellent critical analysis and defense of teaching creative writing by Grimes, copious anecdotes and recollections of times spent in the workshop, and forty-three short stories written by workshop alumni, spread out across the history of the program. It is arguable that the one weakness of this otherwise excellent book is that it ignores poetry almost entirely while focusing on the teachers and students of fiction who have passed through the program over the years. This book was published in the same year as *The Eleventh Draft: Craft and the Writing Life from the Iowa Writers' Workshop* (1999), edited by Frank Conroy, a collection of personal essays by workshop alumni and teachers about the writing life at Iowa. Those interested in a very careful, lively, and thorough history of the early days of the workshop through the 1960s should certainly consult *The Iowa Writers' Workshop: Origins, Emergence, and Growth* (1980) by Stephen Wilbers. *A Community of Writers: Paul Engle and the Iowa Writers' Workshop* (1999), edited by Robert Dana (1929–2010), is an excellent book of personal and critical essays and reflections on the history, philosophy, and literary significance of the Iowa Writers' Workshop. *Seems like Old Times* (1986), edited by Edward Henry Dinger, is a collection of reminiscences distilled from the manuscripts submitted by alumni and friends of the Iowa Writers' Workshop in anticipation of its golden jubilee in 1986, celebrating the fiftieth anniversary of the program. Eric Olsen and Glenn Schaeffer edited *We Wanted to Be Writers: Life, Love, and Literature at the Iowa Writers' Workshop* (2011), with reminiscences of several major writers. Ann Patchett's acclaimed memoir *Truth and Beauty: A Friendship* (2004) touches on the experiences of Patchett and the late Lucy Grealy (1963–2002) when the two friends attended the workshop in the 1980s; workshop alumnus Tom Grimes's *Mentor: A Memoir* (2010) tells the story of his coming of age as a writer and his friendship with workshop director Frank Conroy. Mark McGurl outlines the rise of creative writing programs and their influence in *The Program Era: Postwar Fiction and the Rise of Creative Writing* (2011), discussing at length Paul Engle and the Iowa Writers' Workshop. In *Workshops of Empire: Stegner, Engle, and American Creative Writing during the Cold War* (2015), Eric Bennett demonstrates how Cold War politics shaped the theory and pedagogy of creative writing programs.

BENJAMIN HALE   THE UNIVERSITY OF IOWA

JEWISH LITERATURE

OVERVIEW: The Spanish Inquisition unleashed its terror in 1483. Queen Isabella of Spain expelled the Jews in 1492; many fled to the more tolerant Netherlands, a center for international trade and commerce. Descendants of these original immigrants later relocated to Dutch colonies in Brazil, but when the Portuguese captured Recife in 1654, the Jews, fearing persecution from the Portuguese Inquisition, escaped yet again, some back to the Netherlands, some to the Dutch colonies of the Caribbean and Guyana, and twenty-three to New Amsterdam in 1654.

Despite the inhospitable greeting of director general Peter Stuyvesant, the twenty-three were allowed to remain in the colony that would become New York a decade later when the British captured it from the Dutch. The new immigrants found their way in the New World, settling in port cities along the East Coast where they could use their talents as merchants most effectively. These Sephardic Jews were later joined by Ashkenazi brethren from Germany and Poland who had been driven from their homes by the Thirty Years' War (1618–1648).

By 1820, the beginning of the great migration of Jews from central and eastern Europe, the Jewish population of America numbered approximately 3,000. By 1880 the number was closer to 300,000. Many new arrivals, seeking the freedom granted by the First Amendment to the U.S. Constitution, gradually spread westward, opening general merchandise stores or providing such essential services as tailoring or shoemaking and thereby establishing an important Jewish presence.

Jews were relatively invisible in Midwestern small towns and cities. Non-Jewish writers DAWN POWELL (1896–1965) in *Dance Night* (1925) and SHERWOOD ANDERSON (1876–

1941) in WINESBURG, OHIO (1919) noted their presence and painfully marginal status. EDNA FERBER (1885–1968), an assimilated Midwestern Jewish writer, described her difficulty growing up as a Jew in Midwestern small towns. Ferber's stories of uncomfortable Midwestern Jewish childhoods are told in *Fanny Herself* (1917) and *A Peculiar Treasure* (1939). She continued examining her life in a later autobiography, *A Kind of Magic* (1963).

By 1925, after the European migration, approximately 4.5 million Jews lived in the United States. After New York, the largest Jewish community was in CHICAGO, and there were sizable additional populations in CINCINNATI, CLEVELAND, and DETROIT and smaller numbers in Midwestern rural areas. Quickly, the work of these immigrant Jews began to define their new land. They became important figures in politics, the labor movement, the popular arts, and, by the early twentieth century, English-language literature. In time, their contributions to Midwestern literature became significant.

HISTORY AND SIGNIFICANCE: The first generation of important Midwestern Jewish writers includes some, like journalist and novelist Elias Tobenkin (1882–1963), who were born in Europe and immigrated to the Midwest. Tobenkin graduated from the University of Wisconsin in 1905 and then pursued a career in journalism before publishing his first novel, the autobiographical *Witte Arrives* (1916), which deals with the Jewish immigrant experience in America. His 1925 novel *God of Might* is set in a small ILLINOIS town and explores interfaith marriage.

But the vast majority of Jewish Midwestern writers were born in America and wrote of America, and not always—or even often— of Jewish America. FANNIE HURST (1885–1968), for one, was born in Hamilton, OHIO, was raised in ST. LOUIS, MISSOURI, and attended Washington University. Her eighteen novels and eight collections of stories made her one of the most popular writers of her time. Several of Hurst's novels were adapted for FILM, including *Back Street* (1931), which tells of Ray Schmidt's lifelong and ill-fated love for her married Jewish lover, Walter Saxel. The controversial *Imitation of Life* (1933), the story of white Bea Pullman

and black Delilah Johnston, single mothers who together raise their daughters and build a restaurant empire, was produced twice for the screen. *Humoresque* (1919) is an early collection of stories; *Anitra's Dance* (1934) and *Lonely Parade* (1942) demonstrate her talent and her importance to the Midwestern literary canon.

Other authors of this early generation are equally significant. Proletarian novelist and journalist JOSEPHINE HERBST (1892–1969) was born in Sioux City, IOWA. Today she is most remembered for her Trexler family trilogy, *Pity Is Not Enough* (1933), *The Executioner Waits* (1934), and *Rope of Gold* (1939). Poet and novelist MAXWELL BODENHEIM (1892–1954) was born in Mississippi, moved to Chicago, and was more notorious for his bohemian life and violent death—he and his wife were murdered in New York—than famous for his ten books of poetry and thirteen novels. His poetry, such as *Minna and Myself* (1918), *The King of Spain* (1928), and *Lights in the Valley* (1942), and his Chicago novels, *Blackguard* (1923) and *A Virtuous Girl* (1930), demonstrate his literary range. BEN HECHT (1893–1964) was a close friend of Bodenheim; he was born in New York, lived in Racine, WISCONSIN, and was most famous for his screenplays of the ur-gangster movie *Scarface* (1932), as well as for *Barbary Coast* (1935), *Wuthering Heights* (1939), *A Farewell to Arms* (1957), and many others. His *Erik Dorn* (1921) and *A Jew in Love* (1931) deserve rediscovery. Hecht's autobiography, *A Child of the Century* (1954), sheds light on the role of Jews and the Midwest in twentieth-century literature. *Laura* (1943), the suspense novel by Chicago novelist and playwright VERA CASPARY (1899–1987), became a highly successful film. EDWARD DAHLBERG (1900–1977), who was born in Boston and then lived in KANSAS CITY and Cleveland, wrote the autobiographical novel *Bottom Dogs* (1929). The popular novel *Compulsion* (1956) by Chicago's MEYER LEVIN (1905–1981) was based on the horrific Leopold and Loeb murder case.

Of this generation, the works of Kalamazoo, Michigan, native Edna Ferber have most endured in literary memory. Ferber's groundbreaking creation, the traveling saleswoman Emma McChesney, first brought her work to national attention, and although she was awarded the Pulitzer Prize for *So Big* (1925), she is perhaps better known for the novels *Show Boat* (1926) and *Giant* (1952). *Show Boat* was adapted into a popular musical play and three films. *Giant*, Ferber's novel of Texas, became a blockbuster film starring Elizabeth Taylor, Rock Hudson, and James Dean.

But it is in Ferber's early novel *Fanny Herself*, her only fictional work to deal overtly with Jewish concerns, that Emma McChesney makes an appearance. The novel is the coming-of-age story of Fanny Brandeis of Winnebago, WISCONSIN, as well as the story of her witty and indefatigable mother, Molly, who runs the general store left to her by her husband. The book explores small-town Midwestern Jewish life, as well as the challenges to a career faced by a young Jewish working woman in the late nineteenth and early twentieth centuries.

The next generation produced many significant writers. NELSON ALGREN (1909–1981) was born Nelson Ahlgren Abraham in Detroit, lived in Chicago, and wrote the 1950

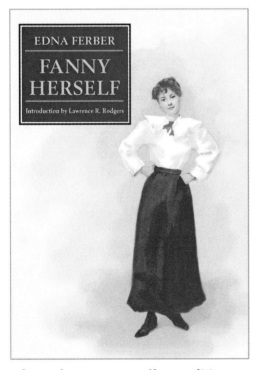

Edna Ferber's *Fanny Herself*, 2001 edition.
© University of Illinois Press, 2001. Used by permission of the University of Illinois Press

National Book Award winner *The Man with the Golden Arm* (1949) and *A Walk on the Wild Side* (1956). Pulitzer Prize–winning journalist and oral historian (LOUIS) STUDS TERKEL (1912–2008) authored several notable Midwestern texts, including *Working: People Talk about What They Do All Day and How They Feel about What They Do* (1974) and *The Good War: An Oral History of World War II* (1985). Nebraska short-story writer and novelist TILLIE OLSEN (1912–2007) is noted for her collection of stories *Tell Me a Riddle* (1961) and her novel *Yonnondio: From the Thirties* (written in the 1930s but first published in 1974); it is set in the period preceding the Great Depression and dramatizes its effects on the lives of a poor, working family. The much-neglected novel *The Changelings* (1955) by novelist RUTH SEID (1913–1995), writing as Jo Sinclair, is best known for *Wasteland* (1946), a novel that deals with second-generation Jewish immigrants coming to terms with their family history. Chicago-born author of horror and crime fiction Robert Bloch (1917–1994) was the creator of the novel *Psycho* (1959), on which Alfred Hitchcock's acclaimed 1960 film was based. Popular novelist Irving Wallace (1916–1990) was born in Chicago, was raised in Kenosha, Wisconsin, and based his best seller *The Chapman Report* (1960) on the Kinsey reports. Novelist Sidney Sheldon (1917–2007), also of Chicago, created *The Other Side of Midnight* (1973) and *The Doomsday Conspiracy* (1991). Isaac Rosenfeld (1918–1956) was a much-neglected major critic and writer of the post–World War II era; a Chicagoan and a friend of SAUL (C.) BELLOW (1915–2005), he is finally receiving the attention he deserves. Steven J. Zipperstein published his biography, *Rosenfeld's Lives* (2009). Rosenfeld's book *Passage from Home* (1946) explores 1940s Chicago. His work has been collected posthumously in *An Age of Enormity: Life and Writing in the Forties and Fifties* (1962), edited and introduced by Theodore Solotaroff with a foreword by Saul Bellow; and in *Alpha and Omega* (1966) and *Preserving the Hunger: An Isaac Rosenfeld Reader*, edited and introduced by Mark Shechner (1988). Each work sheds light on the Midwest in Jewish American literature and on a generation of Jewish writers and critics who emerged from what was still a Yiddish-speaking immigrant world.

Nobel laureate Saul Bellow is the star of this generation. Some, including Bellow himself, prefer the pure delight of *Henderson, the Rain King* (1959). In this novel a millionaire Protestant, Eugene Henderson, feels very much that he is the primordial wandering Jew filled with dissatisfaction and desire; in this case, however, he wears the identity of the upper-class Christian traveling in Africa. Others, including Martin Amis and Christopher Hitchens, consider THE ADVENTURES OF AUGIE MARCH (1953) a contender for the great American novel.

Augie, "an American, Chicago born," is a compendium of all things American (2003 Viking edition, 1). He is Huck Finn and Walt Whitman, possessed of optimism and wonder and, like F(RANCIS) SCOTT (KEY) FITZGERALD's (1896–1940) Jay Gatsby and Augie's— and Bellow's—Chicago, corrupt around the edges and charming. His quest is that of the American in the new America in the largest city in the middle of America, and the quest of the Jew in a land that is not quite his. Augie is on a pilgrimage, a picaresque journey to find his fate, to define himself. On his way, he encounters swindlers, wheeler-dealers, and sundry disreputable but always brilliantly articulate characters who clothe him and remake him over and over again as he searches for that elusive fate.

In this Chicago, Midwestern American, and European novel, Augie March discovers that finding one's place means making one's place. Augie, like Chicago itself, is always rising. The stomach, another character insists, cannot freeze while one is singing, and Augie sings from Chicago throughout the world, forever the optimist that Chicago, that great Midwestern city, taught him to be. Other Bellow novels, such as *Dangling Man* (1944), *Herzog* (1964), *Mosby's Memoirs* (1968), and *Ravelstein* (his examination of Isaac Rosenfeld's life and career, 2000), are essential works for those trying to understand the depth and breadth of Saul Bellow's canon.

Many Jewish authors born in America before World War II are associated with the generation that followed Bellow's. Detroit, Michigan, working-class poet Philip Levine (1928–2015) was the recipient of the Pulitzer Prize for Poetry in 1995 and became the Poet Laureate of the United States in 2011; he used Detroit as the subject and setting of many of his poems. Harold Brodkey (1930–1996), who was born Aaron Roy Weintraub in Staunton, Illinois, and was raised in University City, Missouri, produced short stories, novels, and nonfiction works, including *This Wild Darkness: The Story of My Death* (1996), which deals with his battle with AIDS. William Goldman (b. 1931) was born in Chicago and is a novelist and screenwriter of such films as the Oscar-winning *Butch Cassidy and the Sundance Kid* (1969) and *All the President's Men* (1976); he is the brother of librettist and screenwriter James Goldman (1927–1998), who created the scripts for *The Lion in Winter* (1968) and *White Nights* (1985). Kansas City, Missouri–born Calvin (Marshall) Trillin (b. 1935) is a journalist, novelist, and humorist best known for his food writings. The collection of stories *Blue in Chicago* (1978) by BETTE HOWLAND (b. 1937) gives a powerful and vivid sense of that city's people and neighborhoods.

This was also the generation that produced influential feminist writers. They include Betty Friedan (1921–2006), who was born in Peoria, Illinois, and was the co-founder of the National Organization for Women and the author of the highly influential *The Feminine Mystique* (1963). E. M. Broner (1930–2011) was a Detroit novelist and "Seder Sister," a member of a group of women, including Bella Abzug, Gloria Steinem, and feminist psychologist Phyllis Chesler, who met for over thirty years at a Passover seder they created using new, inclusive rituals highlighting the roles of women in Jewish history; Broner was also the author of two important feminist experimental novels, *Her Mothers* (1975) and *A Weave of Women* (1978). ALIX KATES SHULMAN (b. 1932) was born in Cleveland and wrote, most notably, *Memoirs of an Ex-Prom Queen* (1972), a significant novel of the women's liberation movement in the form of a coming-of-age story of a Midwestern woman whose experiences reflect the anti-feminist mores of her times. MARGE PIERCY (b. 1936) is a Detroit novelist, science-fiction writer, poet, memoirist, and essayist who continues her role as a Jewish public intellectual committed to the concept of *tikkun olam*, the Jewish requirement to help repair the world. Piercy's *Braided Lives* (1982), *Gone to Soldiers*

(1987), and *He, She and It* (1991) are all Midwestern based. *Small Changes* (1973) established her as a feminist novelist. *The Art of Blessing the Day* (1999), a collection of Jewish-themed poems, is important for those interested in one Midwestern Jewish woman's attempt to modernize Judaism and make it accessible to Jewish feminists. Piercy continues to explore both geography and human nature in her creative work.

Now an established part of the Jewish Midwestern community, this generation of writers has not forgotten where it came from. HERBERT GOLD (b. 1924) of Lakewood, Ohio, focuses in his fictionalized autobiography *Fathers* (1967) on his father's past to explain his own place in the present. At thirteen, hidden in a cart to avoid the czar's police, Sam Gold left his Ukrainian village to journey to America. The story follows Sam from New York to Canton, Ohio, to Indianapolis, to Cleveland, to marriage and sons, to his sometime dalliance with the "dee-vor-see" Myrna, a clerk in his grocery store, to the Great Depression and anti-Semitism, and to Sunday mornings at the Turkish baths.

The fictional Herbert Gold, the eldest of Sam's sons, who will become the youngest of the titular "fathers," tells Sam's story, his own story, and, in the "Epilogue and Beginning" of his novel, the story of an even earlier generation. In 1938, when Herbert is fourteen years old and the European madness is in progress, Sam Gold receives a letter from his own grandfather in Russia. In the 1830s, as a boy, he had been blinded in one eye by "the Crippler," who maimed the sons of Jews so they would not be taken away from their families to enter the czar's army, never to be heard from again. Now he is 107 years old and dying. The eventual death of Herbert's great-grandfather marks the severing of the final connection to the European past. It was his mutilation as a young boy that ultimately enabled Sam to escape to America and his son Herbert to write the book that would tell their story.

The current generation of Jewish Midwestern writers was born after World War II. Their earliest literary productions date from the 1970s and 1980s. *Indemnity Only* (1982), for example, is the first work of popular detective novelist SARA PARETSKY (b. 1947), who was born in Ames, Iowa, and raised in Kansas; this work introduced her female protagonist, V. I. Warshawski, P. I. Paretsky's novel *Bleeding Kansas* (2008) examines the role of religion in the American prairie during the Civil War era. AMERICAN BUFFALO (1977), one of the earliest works of Chicago playwright and screenwriter DAVID (ALAN) MAMET (b. 1947), considers American and Midwestern values.

Other current Midwestern Jewish writers include novelist and short-story writer Max Apple (b. 1941) of Grand Rapids, Michigan, whose works include the collection *The Jew of Home Depot, and Other Stories* (2007). St. Louis, Missouri, poet, fiction writer, and Jewish folklorist and reteller of tales Howard Schwartz (b. 1945) is the author of *Elijah's Violin, and Other Jewish Fairy Tales* (1983), *Lilith's Cave: Jewish Tales of the Supernatural* (1987), and other works. Poet and naturalist Diane Ackerman (b. 1948) of Waukegan, Illinois, examines the hiding of Jews in a Warsaw zoo in *The Zookeeper's Wife: A War Story* (2007). Chicago-born Scott Turow (b. 1949) is the author of eleven bestselling novels of legal intrigue, as well as of nonfiction works. Chicago novelist and poet Maxine Chernoff (b. 1952) has described residents of that city in the stories in *Signs of Devotion* (1993). Playwright, actress, and comedian Lisa Kron (b. 1961) of Ann Arbor, Michigan, wrote the prize-winning autobiographical play *Well,* which was produced on Broadway in 2006. Her first musical, *Fun Home* (with music by Jeanine Tesori), opened to rave reviews at the Public Theater in New York in 2013. Lev Raphael (b. 1954) has lived and taught for many years in MICHIGAN; he is the creator of a series of academic mysteries that take place in and around the "State University of Michigan." Raphael, the son of Holocaust survivors, is another inheritor of the past. In his Midwestern fictional universe, to be Jewish and to be homosexual are fraught with danger, sometimes from within, often—still—from without. In Raphael's collection of stories *Dancing on Tisha B'Av* (1990), the new Nazis take many forms. They are the titular "Cossacks" defacing the Hillel Foundation house of a university in Ohio or, in the aptly titled "Abominations," burning a dorm room in Michigan. Sometimes the enemy is our own fear of who we are: John Bedford in "Sanctuary," Jewish despite his name, surrounds himself with sterility, hiding in academe in a life of his own invention. Elsewhere, a woman, a survivor of the concentration camps, is desperate for the "fresh air" of the title of her story after she runs a red light intending to kill a man crossing the street because she is certain that he is the Nazi guard who killed her brother. The enemy, born in the past, is everywhere in Raphael's stories, pursuing the present. *The German Money* (2003) explores Paul Menkus's relationship to his inheritance: German reparation money and a troublesome maternal relationship for himself and his siblings.

STUART DYBEK (b. 1942), author of *Childhood and Other Neighborhoods* (1980), *The Coast of Chicago* (1990), and *I Sailed with Magellan* (2003), is receiving extraordinarily positive attention as a Midwestern and Jewish writer. Jaimy Gordon (b. 1944) published the novel *Lord of Misrule* in 2010; it won the National Book Award. *Lord of Misrule* explores a Jewish outlaw, Two-Tie, and the underworld of horse racing. Maggie Koderer, a rebellious but nice Jewish girl, breaks the rules but also breaks down Jewish stereotypes. She, like the original Jewish characters, finds an original way to heal the world.

Lorrie Moore (b. 1957), formerly Delmore Schwartz Professor in the Humanities at the University of Wisconsin–Madison and currently on the faculty at Vanderbilt University, was a finalist for the 2010 PEN Faulkner Award for Fiction and the Orange Prize. Her novel *A Gate at the Stairs* (2009) examines a Jewish mother and a half-Jewish protagonist, Tassie, in a novel that explores motherhood, adoption, the meaning of family, and what ethnicity and racism foster. The novel is set in Wisconsin and demonstrates how difficult it is to be a Jew in the heartland. Another of Moore's works, the short story "The Jewish Hunter," published in the *New Yorker* 65 (November 13, 1989): 48–58, examines how Jews fail to fit into the Midwest: the harder they try, the more their culture collides with the dominant one. A wonderful stylist, Moore is able to be funny and emotionally serious simultaneously. In her hands and through her insight, readers see the implications of the ordinary with new eyes.

Peter Orner (b. 1968) has also been praised as a talented Chicago fiction writer using a novel-in-stories approach. *Esther Stories* (2001) moves from examining unrelated strangers to looking at two Jewish families, one from the East Coast and the other from the Midwest. His novel *Love and Shame and Love* (2011) wittily and unpredictably explores Chicago literature and history.

SELECTED WORKS: Most Midwestern Jewish authors have produced substantial bodies of writing, and the current generation is still a collective work in progress. The following are suggested works through which to gain familiarity with Midwestern Jewish writing. Elias Tobenkin's *God of Might* (1925), set in small-town Illinois, deals with problems arising from interfaith marriage. Of Fannie Hurst's many works, *Humoresque* (1919), her early collection of stories, and her novels *Anitra's Dance* (1934) and *Lonely Parade* (1942) are good stylistic and thematic examples. Maxwell Bodenheim's works include the collections of poetry *Minna and Myself* (1918), *The King of Spain* (1928), and *Lights in the Valley* (1942) and the Chicago novels *Blackguard* (1923) and *A Virtuous Girl* (1930). Of Ben Hecht's canon, the novels *Erik Dorn* (1921) and *A Jew in Love* (1931) and his autobiography, *A Child of the Century* (1954), are helpful in understanding twentieth-century Midwestern Jewish writing. Edna Ferber's autobiography *A Peculiar Treasure* (1939) written, not coincidentally, during Hitler's rise to power, details her experiences growing up as a Jew in the Midwest and her subsequent fame. Ferber followed with a second autobiography, *A Kind of Magic*, in 1963. Studs Terkel's *Working: People Talk about What They Do All Day and How They Feel about What They Do* (1974) and *The Good War: An Oral History of World War II* (1985) are quintessential books. Jo Sinclair's *Wasteland* (1946) deals with second-generation Jewish immigrants coming to terms with their family history.

Of Saul Bellow's works, *Dangling Man* (1944), *The Adventures of Augie March* (1953), *Henderson, the Rain King* (1959), *Herzog* (1964), and *Ravelstein* (2000) reflect the depth and breadth of his career. E. M. Broner's *A Weave of Women* (1978) has as its center the importance of ritual for a group of women living in a house in Jerusalem. Marge Piercy's *The Art of Blessing the Day* (1999) is a collection of poems on Jewish themes, and her novels *Small Changes* (1973) and *Braided Lives* (1982) show that she is a popular writer of sensitivity and intelligence. Of newer writing, Maxine Chernoff's collection of stories *Signs of Devotion* was a *New York Times* Notable Book for 1993. Lev Raphael's *The German Money* (2003) tells the story of Paul Menkus, who inherits the German reparation money paid to his mother, a Holocaust survivor whose coldness has had severe emotional consequences for Paul, his brother, and his sister. His later works *Rosedale in Love* and *The Vampyre of Gotham* (both 2014) continue his focus on Jewish characters and themes. Diane Ackerman's *The Zookeeper's Wife: A War Story* (2007) is the tale of the Zabinski family, keepers of the Warsaw Zoo, who hid Jews in the zoo during World War II under the eyes of the Nazis. Sara Paretsky's novel *Bleeding Kansas* (2008), whose title refers to the state's battle over slavery in the 1850s, takes on extreme right-wing religious belief as the latest cause of the bleeding of the American prairie.

Stuart Dybek's *The Coast of Chicago* (1990) is a classic collection of short Midwestern fiction and should be read by those interested in contemporary fiction. Jaimy Gordon's *Lord of Misrule* (2010) will delight those interested in breaking stereotypes. Lorrie Moore's *A Gate at the Stairs* (2009) examines the pain, cost, and humor of outsider status with artistic integrity. Peter Orner's *Esther Stories* (2001) and *Love and Shame and Love* (2011) should be read by those interested in Midwestern history and in contemporary, innovative Jewish Midwestern fiction.

FURTHER READING: Many book-length and shorter studies exist on individual Midwestern Jewish authors referenced here. The following list provides a starting point for further research. For general sources, begin with the *Handbook of American-Jewish Literature: An Analytical Guide to Topics, Themes, and Sources* (1988) by Lewis Fried, Gene Brown, Lewis Chametzky, and Louis Harap; another good general resource is *Contemporary Jewish-American Novelists: A Bio-Critical Sourcebook* (1997), edited by Joel Shalzky and Michael Taub. *Jewish Life in*

Small-Town America: A History (2005) by Lee Shai Weissbach will help readers understand the difficulty of ethnic difference in small towns. Ava F. Kahn's *Jewish Life in the American West: Perspectives on Migration, Settlement, and Community* (2002) provides perspectives on Western migration. Eleanor Kaugman's article "Fargo Jewish Archive Malady," *Oxford Literary Review* 25 (2003): 261–80, is a valuable look at one Midwestern culture. Kenneth Libo and Irving Howe's *We Lived There Too: In Their Own Words and Pictures—Pioneer Jews and the Westward Movement of America, 1630–1930* (1984) is also valuable. Linda Mack Schlof's *"And Prairie Dogs Weren't Kosher": Jewish Women in the Upper Midwest since 1855* (1998) provides a focused look at Midwestern Jewish women's lives. Also of interest to those who study Jewish popular culture are several books on Jewish writers from the Midwest and the superheroes they created, including *From Krakow to Krypton: Jews and Comic Books* (2008) by Arie Kaplan and *Jews and American Comics: An Illustrated History of an American Art Form* (2008) by Paul Beuhle.

ELLEN SERLEN UFFEN   NEW YORK, NEW YORK

JOURNALISM.
See Newspaper Journalism

JOURNALS.
See Periodicals, Literary

JUNGLE, THE
HISTORY: With the publication of *The Jungle* in 1906, UPTON (BEALL) SINCLAIR (Jr.) (1878–1968) started a firestorm of public outrage. The novel chronicles the difficulties of Jurgis Rudkus, a Lithuanian immigrant who brings his wife and their extended family to CHICAGO's "Packingtown" in search of a better life and finds nothing but heartbreak. After losing his wife, his son, and his home, Jurgis becomes a wanderer and eventually stumbles into a meeting where he finds salvation in the form of socialism. This powerful novel, with its gruesome depictions of horrific conditions in Chicago's packinghouses, affected American consumers for decades to come.

Upton Sinclair grew up poor, the only son of an alcoholic liquor salesman. He was often sent to spend time with wealthy relatives, and he became aware at an early age of the stark contrast between rich and poor, which was to plague Sinclair and emerge in his writings throughout his life. While he was at college in New York, he started writing pulp fiction for boys' weeklies and thus achieved some financial independence. At the turn of the twentieth century Sinclair began writing novels, but these early works received little recognition. His first major novel, *Manassas,* was published in 1904; critics have since viewed it as the necessary stepping-stone toward the writing of *The Jungle.*

Sinclair joined the Socialist Party in the early 1900s and began writing for *Appeal to Reason,* a popular socialist paper published in KANSAS by Julius A. Wayland (1854–1912). His first effort was a series of articles chronicling a failed strike in Packingtown and exposing corruption in the beef trust. Fred D. Warren, the editor of *Appeal to Reason,* challenged Sinclair to write another novel like *Manassas,* this one dealing with wage slaves rather than chattel slaves, and offered him a $500 advance. Macmillan, the publisher of *Manassas,* also expressed interest and offered Sinclair another $500. Sinclair accepted the challenge and headed for Chicago to do research for his novel.

The seven weeks Sinclair spent in Packingtown haunted him for the rest of his life. He interviewed workers and toured the packinghouses, witnessing firsthand the horrors he later depicted so graphically. He wrote the first part of the novel at a hectic pace and then experienced difficulties when the time came to introduce socialism. Giving in to pressure from publishers and the socialist elite, Sinclair wrote the final four chapters of the novel in the fall of 1905.

During 1905 *The Jungle* was first published serially in *Appeal to Reason* and *One-Hoss Philosophy,* another socialist magazine edited by Wayland. Despite its original expression of interest in the novel, Macmillan declined to publish it, citing concerns about libel, but perhaps also concerned by the book's unrelieved negative tone and expectations of small sales. Four other publishers also turned down *The Jungle.* Sinclair was preparing to publish the novel himself when, in February 1906, Doubleday, Page and Company agreed to print the volume.

The novel instantly became a best seller and catapulted Sinclair to international fame. Its initial reception was highly favorable, although even then critics expressed concerns about the ending, with its shift away from a proletarian perspective and loss of narrative continuity.

SIGNIFICANCE: The practical impact of *The Jungle* was significant; it has been credited with speeding the passage of the Pure Food and Drug Act (1906), which had been mired in Congress, as well as with helping improve working conditions in the packinghouses. In addition to its practical impact, *The Jungle* changed American literature. It is widely recognized as the most powerful of the muckraking novels and as the earliest true proletarian novel. It was also one of the first novels to focus on the lives of eastern European immigrants to the Midwest.

It was no coincidence that Sinclair chose a Lithuanian hero for his novel of wage slavery. Rapid industrialization of the Midwest after the Civil War brought an influx of immigrants, many of them from eastern Europe. Sinclair's visit to Packingtown brought him into contact with many Lithuanian

Upton Sinclair's *The Jungle.* Doubleday, Page & Co., 1906.

Image courtesy of Special Collections, Grand Valley State University Libraries immigrants, and the Rudkus family is a composite of the numerous families whose homes he visited. Sinclair became somewhat familiar with Lithuanian customs and culture during his visits, and this familiarity informed his writing. In fact, the Lithuanian wedding feast, or *veselija,* in the first chapter is often cited as the best-realized scene in the novel. However, most critics agree that it was not Sinclair's intention to provide an entirely accurate portrayal of Lithuanian culture. Rather, his goal was to create a character who could represent all victims of wage slavery. Although the Lithuanian background of the Rudkus family is addressed, Jurgis emerges as a distinctly American, and Midwestern, character.

Jurgis's faith in his ability to create a better life for his family, inspiring at the beginning of the novel, becomes almost pathetic in later chapters. When the Rudkus family moves to Chicago, Jurgis is confident that his remarkable strength will bring them prosperity. Even when that strength fails to improve his family's fortunes, Jurgis refuses to lose hope. Throughout the first part of the novel, in the face of repeated setbacks and against insurmountable odds, Jurgis clings to his motto, "I will work harder." His story and the novel directly repudiate the Horatio Alger "rags-to-riches" American Dream myth.

At the beginning of the novel Jurgis also displays a fascination with progress. As he tours the packing plant, he is almost entranced by its efficiency. In fact, Sinclair himself seems similarly entranced, expending a great deal of time and ink detailing the processes involved in producing America's meat products. The packinghouses, the first truly modern assembly-line production facilities, served as an ideal setting for a novel in which human beings become mere cogs in the industrial wheel.

A society that views human beings as expendable resources is Sinclair's target in *The Jungle.* Sinclair, along with his hero, exhibits a certain wariness regarding the rich. Not all the wealthy characters in *The Jungle* are nefarious, however; Freddie is merely frivolous, and Schliemann is paternalistic. In spite of an occasional positive experience with a wealthy figure, Jurgis regards the

rich with a healthy suspicion. He is right to do so. He and his family are exploited by the elite from the very beginning, when they are tricked into paying an exorbitant price for a dilapidated house that has been painted to look new.

It is this relentless and merciless exploitation that finally drives Jurgis into a meeting hall where he encounters socialism. This part of the novel has drawn the most critical attention since the novel's publication. From the beginning, Sinclair made no secret of his intention to promote socialism through *The Jungle.* However, his original intention was to do so subtly, without preaching. Despite Sinclair's best intentions, the last four chapters of the novel read more like a socialist tract than a work of fiction. After Jurgis's conversion to socialism, a scene that evokes comparison with religious salvation, he disappears almost completely from the narrative, leaving in his wake a string of socialist proselytizers.

Several possible explanations for this incongruous ending have been suggested, including Sinclair's straitened finances, pressure from publishers, and persistent writer's block. Around the time he was writing the end of the novel, Sinclair had a great deal of contact with the socialist elite, including Jack London, who may have influenced him to introduce socialism into the novel more forcefully than he had originally intended. In his 1977 biography of Sinclair, William Bloodworth presents the last four chapters as a breakdown of Sinclair's attempt to write from a proletarian perspective, noting that unlike the majority of *The Jungle,* the final chapters seem to "take on qualities of paternalism and condescension" (63). Whatever the cause, Sinclair himself was unhappy with the ending of *The Jungle,* and it has continually been cited by critics as the novel's greatest weakness.

This weak ending may finally be viewed as the result of Sinclair's struggles with form. His goal was to write a naturalistic novel in the pattern of Émile Zola's *Germinal,* and for the first twenty-one chapters he succeeded in doing just that. However, Sinclair also hoped to create a work like Harriet Beecher Stowe's *Uncle Tom's Cabin* (1852) but focusing on wage slaves, and to accomplish this goal, he needed to end the novel on a note of hope. It does not seem to have occurred to Sinclair in the beginning that these two impulses might be contradictory. However, when the time came to move from naturalism to socialism, Sinclair found himself unable to make a smooth transition. Perhaps for some of the reasons listed here, he simply tacked on the socialist ending and hoped that readers would accept it.

Although they duly noted its flaws, readers did accept *The Jungle*, as did other writers. Sinclair's novel became the flagship of the muckraking movement, and it lent some credibility to the socialist movement as well. Although Sinclair appreciated the book's impact on food safety regulations, his main concern was with social justice. In his article "What Life Means to Me," published in *Cosmopolitan* 41.6 (October 1906), Sinclair wrote, "As I have phrased it elsewhere, I aimed at the public's heart and by accident I hit it in the stomach" (594).

The novel also paved the way for the advent of proletarian literature in America. Its influence on foreign writers, such as Bertolt Brecht (1898–1956) and George Orwell (1903–1950), has also been documented.

IMPORTANT EDITIONS: Despite having fallen somewhat out of favor in the years immediately following World War II, *The Jungle* has been continuously in print for more than a century. Sinclair's difficulty in finding a publisher had led him to advertise and prepare to publish the novel himself. He had the printing plates ready when Doubleday agreed to publish a trade edition on Sinclair's terms. Both editions were published simultaneously; Sinclair's was issued under the rubric "The Jungle Publishing Co."

The Doubleday, Page and Company edition, originally published in 1906 after the novel's serialization, is considered the authoritative text. However, the discovery of some correspondence in 1980 between Sinclair and his publishers led to a search for the original text of the novel as it appeared in *Appeal to Reason* and resulted in the publication of *Upton Sinclair's "The Jungle": The Lost First Edition* in 1988, edited by Gene De-Gruson. This text differs significantly from the Doubleday, Page version in length and

content: the latter is five chapters shorter, possesses an alternate ending, and has lost some of its ethnic Lithuanian coloration. These changes, however, are more indicative of authorial rewriting than of suppression by potential publishers, as DeGruson has claimed. A Norton Critical Edition, *"The Jungle": An Authoritative Text, Contexts and Backgrounds, Criticism,* edited by Clare Virginia Eby, was published in 2003. It contains the full Doubleday text and significant passages from the *Appeal to Reason* version; its focus is on the historical context of the novel, but it does provide a critical overview, although several important sources are omitted. *The Jungle* has been translated into more than twenty foreign languages.

FURTHER READING: *The Jungle* had an immense professional and personal impact on Sinclair, and he frequently discussed the novel in his letters and memoirs. In *The Autobiography of Upton Sinclair* (1962) he discusses at length the circumstances surrounding the writing of the novel. This work also contains an interesting discussion of Sinclair's reaction to the initial popularity of the novel and his dismay at seeing it become famous as an exposé of unsanitary packinghouses rather than as a socialist novel. Sinclair's statement about aiming "at the public's heart" appears in "What Life Means to Me," *Cosmopolitan* 41.6 (October 1906): 594.

There are several excellent biographies of Sinclair. Leon Harris's *Upton Sinclair: American Rebel* (1975) and William Bloodworth's *Upton Sinclair* (1977) both contain valuable discussions of the writing of *The Jungle* and of the novel's significance. Later accounts of Sinclair's life include *Radical Innocent: Upton Sinclair* (2006) by Anthony Arthur and *Upton Sinclair and the Other American Century* (2006) by Kevin Mattson. Lauren Coodley's *Upton Sinclair: California Socialist, Celebrity Intellectual* (2013) contains material on the film productions of *The Jungle*. For additional information about this period in Sinclair's life, see Christine Scriabine's article "Upton Sinclair and the Writing of *The Jungle*," *Chicago History* 10.1 (Spring 1981): 26–37.

Critical studies of *The Jungle* are numerous. For studies that focus on the accuracy of the novel, including its portrayals of Chicago and of the conditions in the packinghouses, see *Upton Sinclair's "The Jungle"* (2002), a collection of critical essays edited by Harold Bloom; Louise Carroll Wade's "The Problem with Classroom Use of Upton Sinclair's *The Jungle*," *American Studies* 32.2 (Fall 1991): 79–101; and James Harvey Young's essay "The Pig That Fell into the Privy: Upton Sinclair's *The Jungle* and the Meat Inspection Amendments of 1906," *Bulletin of the History of Medicine* 59.4 (Fall 1985): 467–80. For studies that focus on the accuracy of Sinclair's portrayal of Lithuanian culture and characters in *The Jungle,* see Antanas Musteikis's "The Lithuanian Heroes of *The Jungle*," *Lituanus* 17.2 (Summer 1971): 27–38; Alfonsas Šešplaukis's "Lithuanians in Upton Sinclair's *The Jungle*," *Lituanus* 23.2 (Summer 1977): 28–29; and Suk Bong Suh's "Lithuanian Wedding Traditions in Upton Sinclair's *The Jungle*," *Lituanus* 33.1 (Spring 1987): 5–17. A detailed examination of the use of the ethnic protagonist and background in *The Jungle* can be found in *Upton Sinclair, the Lithuanian Jungle: Upon the Centenary of "The Jungle" (1905 and 1906) by Upton Sinclair* (2006) by Geidrius Subačius.

For a general overview of the critical reception of the novel, see *Critics on Upton Sinclair: Readings in Literary Criticism* (1975), edited by Abraham Blinderman, which contains short excerpts from several discussions of *The Jungle* and *"The Jungle": An Authoritative Text, Contexts and Backgrounds, Criticism* (2003), edited by Clare Virginia Eby. For perspectives on teaching the novel, see Christopher Phelps's "How Should We Teach *The Jungle*?," *Chronicle of Higher Education*, March 3, 2006, and Russ Castronovo's "Teaching the Good," *Journal of Narrative Theory* 41.2 (Summer 2011): 167–74. Although the manuscript of *The Jungle* was destroyed by fire in 1907, some fragments and related materials are among the Upton Sinclair manuscripts held by Indiana University's Lilly Library.

SHEENA DENNEY BORAN   UNIVERSITY OF MISSISSIPPI

K-L

KANSAS

Kansas was admitted to the Union on January 29, 1861, as the thirty-fourth state. Before statehood it was part of Kansas Territory (1854–1861).

Area: 82,279 square miles
Land: 81,759 square miles
Water: 520 square miles
Population (2010 census): 2,853,118

OVERVIEW: Geography, politics, and the historical framework of Kansas's entry into the Union define the Sunflower State. During his two-year search for the fabled Seven Cities of Gold in what was to become the American Southwest, Francisco Vásquez de Coronado (1510–1554) trekked as far north as central Kansas in 1541, where he had been told that a rich civilization called Cibola was to be found.

Kansas was part of the Louisiana Purchase of 1803, and its northeast corner, defined by the Missouri River, was traversed by the 1804 Lewis and Clark expedition. Other early explorers also crossed the state, Zebulon Montgomery Pike in 1806, Stephen Harriman Long in 1819, and John Charles Frémont in 1842 among them. Long's map labeled much of western Kansas as part of the Great American Desert, and the image of "desert," in contrast with early promotions of Kansas as "garden," persists as a dichotomy in Kansas literature to this day.

Later, via Westport in KANSAS CITY, MISSOURI, Kansas became the first leg of the Santa Fe Trail, patrolled and protected by soldiers from Fort Leavenworth, Fort Larned, and others. These forts, along with Fort Riley and Fort Hays, were instrumental in prosecuting the Indian Wars. In 1830 Kansas was the destination of Native American tribes forcibly relocated through the federal policy of Indian removal. Reservations for such tribes as the Potawatomis, Ottawas, Kickapoos, Shawnees, and Delawares were located in territories formerly belonging to such indigenous tribes as the Kansas, Osages, and Pawnees.

By 1854, when Kansas was opened as a territory, the United States was on the verge of civil war over slavery. The 1854 Kansas-Nebraska Act gave those settling in Kansas "popular" or "squatter sovereignty," the right to decide for themselves whether Kansas would enter the Union as a free or a slave state. Abolitionists flocked to Kansas under the auspices of the New England Emigrant Aid Company. John Brown (1800–1859) followed his sons to a farm near Osawatomie.

© Karen Greasley, 2014

Free-state towns—Topeka, Lawrence, Manhattan—sprang up, as did the pro-slavery towns of Tecumseh, Lecompton, and Atchison. Kansas entered the Union as a free state in 1861 and gave more troops per capita to the Union cause than any other state.

After the Civil War, Kansas was settled predominantly by Union army veterans, and hence Republicans, and has been dominated by that political party ever since. But nineteenth-century Republicanism supported all kinds of reforms, and writers analyzing the state remarked on Kansas as a bellwether. In his 1910 essay "Kansas," historian Carl Lotus Becker, as quoted in *PrairyErth (a deep map)* (1991) by WILLIAM LEAST HEAT-MOON (b. 1939), noted that "the Kansas spirit is the American spirit double distilled" (7). WILLIAM ALLEN WHITE (1868–1944) in his *Emporia Gazette* of 1922 wrote, "When anything is going to happen in this country, it happens first in Kansas." Among these, he mentions abolition, Prohibition, Populism, and other reform movements, including women's suffrage.

Unfortunately, much of what happened in Kansas might be said to reinforce the state motto, *Ad astra per aspera* (To the Stars through Difficulties). Eastern Kansas was settled primarily before the Civil War, amid political difficulties. The central third of Kansas was settled from the late 1860s through the 1870s. Plagued by economic depression, drought, and grasshopper invasion, those Kansans must have often felt like a character in the 1936 biography *Sod and Stubble: The Story of a Kansas Homestead* by John Ise (1885–1969): "When we have rain and crops, we don't want to go, and when there ain't no crops we're too poor to go; so I reckon we'll just stay here till we starve to death" (quoted in Kansas Literature over-view, online). Western Kansas, on the High Plains, saw the most difficulties. The 160-acre claims of the Homestead Act of 1862 were insufficient to sustain life in such a dry climate. Settlers struggled mightily because rainfall rarely exceeded fifteen inches per year. As a result of these geographic differences, the farm literature of eastern and central Kansas tends to focus on success, while works set in the western third of the state often end in failure. That western Kansas story, coupled with the devastating effects of the Dust Bowl, makes for bleak reading.

Out of the western Kansas struggles came the most viable third-party movement in U.S. history, Populism. Together with the Democrats, the Populists nominated WILLIAM JENNINGS BRYAN (1860–1925) to run against Republican William McKinley Jr. in the 1896 presidential election. A body of political poetry rose from this movement.

Kansas settlement and development were tied closely to the railroads, particularly the Union Pacific and the Santa Fe. As a result, by 1868, when the Union Pacific reached Abilene, the cattle industry was given a boost in supplying beef to post–Civil War America. Out of the cattle industry came new developments in literature, from cowboy songs and poetry to outlaw-rustler adventures, agricultural works, and accounts of lawmen charged with maintaining order in towns given to gambling, prostitution, and saloons. No wonder the state's version of Prohibition passed the Kansas legislature in 1881, just before the last cattle drives to Dodge City in 1882.

Twentieth-century Kansas literature was dominated by rebellion against the SMALL TOWN, the hardships endured during the Dust Bowl, the rise of corporate farming after World War II, and, from the 1970s forward, the rediscovery of the state's subtle landscape, coupled with environmental awareness.

HISTORY AND SIGNIFICANCE: The literary history of Kansas is extensive and involves many genres. Among these are EXPLORATION ACCOUNTS, travel, fiction, AUTOBIOGRAPHY and memoirs, poetry, DRAMA, and several divisions of popular literature. Other major topics included are PRINTING

AND PUBLISHING, the Kansas FEDERAL WRITERS' PROJECT, and literary awards in Kansas. A "Selected Works" section suggests essential literary works to read to begin a study of the literature. The last section, "Further Reading," includes bibliographic and critical sources and manuscript collections and repositories.

Exploration and Travel: Coronado's expedition from Mexico into what is now central Kansas was chronicled by Pedro de Castañeda de Nájera in *The Journey of Coronado, 1540–1542: From the City of Mexico to the Grand Canyon of the Colorado and the Buffalo Plains of Texas, Kansas, and Nebraska, as Told by Himself and His Followers* (1904), translated and edited by George Parker Winship. Although he found similarities between Spain and the plains his company traversed, his impressions were ultimately negative, given the expectation of finding Cibola, the Seven Cities of Gold. Of greater importance was the Santa Fe Trail. Lewis Hector Garrard (1829–1887) traveled throughout the West and wrote *Wah-to-yah, and the Taos Trail; or, Prairie Travel and Scalp Dances* (1850), full of descriptions of Kansas landscapes and Native American tribes. Francis Parkman (1823–1893) wrote "The Oregon Trail," published serially in *Knickerbocker's Magazine* (1847–1849) and then as *The California and Oregon Trail: Being Sketches of Prairie and Rocky Mountain Life* (1849).

The military presence in Kansas gave rise to such accounts as *Tenting on the Plains; or, General Custer in Kansas and Texas* (1887) by Elizabeth B. Custer (1842–1933). *Before Kansas Bled* (2007), edited by Douglass Wallace, gives a complete history and description of the geology, geography, Native American culture, and pre-white settlement history of Shawnee County.

Fiction: The first novel to use Kansas as its setting, according to Benjamin Fuson's *Centennial Bibliography of Kansas Literature, 1854–1961* (1961), was *The Border Rover* (1857) by Emerson Bennett (1822–1905). It treats settler conflicts with Native Americans along the Santa Fe Trail. See NATIVE AMERICANS AS DEPICTED IN MIDWESTERN LITERATURE. The first novel written by a Kansas inhabitant was *Ravenia; or, The Outcast Redeemed* (1872) by Annie Hamilton Nelles Dumond

(1837–1903), although much of the book is set outside Kansas.

Early fiction set in Kansas often treats the territorial fighting of "Bleeding Kansas." Among these are DIME NOVELS: *Guerrillas of the Osage; or, The Price of Loyalty on the Border* (1864) by Stephen Holmes Jr.; *The Spy of Osawatomie; or, The Mysterious Companions of Old John Brown* (1881) by Mary E. Jackson (b. 1849); and *The Squatter Sovereign* (1883) by Mary Anne Vance Humphrey (1838–1916).

Early Kansas homesteading novels include *Westward: A Tale of American Emigrant Life* (1870) by Julia McNair Wright (1840–1903), *Sons of the Border: Sketches of the Life and People of the Far Frontier* (1873) by James William Steele (1840–1905), and *Two Young Homesteaders* (1880) by Theodora Robinson Jenness (1847–1935). Military settings include Fort Hays in *The Colonel's Daughter; or, Winning His Spurs* (1883) by Charles King (1844–1933) and in another work by James William Steele, *Frontier Army Sketches* (1883).

Paul Iselin Wellman (1898–1966), a prolific writer and one of the best-selling authors from Kansas, started his saga with *Bowl of Brass* (1944), set in southwestern Kansas. From there, he moved east to Wichita and Kansas City in *The Walls of Jericho* (1947), *The Chain* (1949), and *Jericho's Daughters* (1956).

Later novels, particularly the work of Don Coldsmith (1926–2009), often treat Native American life on the Great Plains. His *Tallgrass* (1997) is a saga of the tallgrass land of Kansas, spanning the arrival of the Spanish conquistadors through the nineteenth-century pioneer boom. This story encompasses the lives of the Native peoples, a freed slave with the Corps of Discovery, and those who came to settle from other lands.

John Brown strides through the territorial literature of Kansas as main and minor character, catalyst, villain, hero, or mythic figure. He is such an important figure that he continues as a subject for fiction by Kansans and others attracted to that period in American history. *Sons of Strength: A Romance of the Kansas Border Wars* (1899) by William R. Lighton (1866–1923) details Lawrence, John Brown, and the Wakarusa War. *Free Soil* (1920) by Margaret Lynn (1869–1958) is set in

Lawrence and is dedicated "to the ever-loving memory of those men and women who ventured greatly and endured nobly that the new state they were establishing might also be a free state." *A Wind like a Bugle* (1954) by Leonard Nathan (1915–ca. 1981) maintains more distance from Brown, questioning the methods of the prophetic advocate of bloodshed in the fight against slavery.

Pillar of Cloud (1957) by Jackson Burgess (1927–1981) is set in the fictional town of Whitaker in 1858. Marguerite Allis (1887–1958) wrote an account of settlement in which a southern belle becomes a Kansas woman in *Free Soil* (1958). Janice Young Brooks (b. 1943) adds to these territorial accounts the novel *Seventrees* (1981), set at Grinter's Ferry, a crossing on the Kaw (Kansas) River, at the Shawnee Methodist Mission, and at Chouteau's Four Houses, a trading settlement in Kansas City, Kansas.

Contemporary novelists have continued this interest in John Brown's Kansas. Russell Banks (b. 1940) tells the story of John Brown from the perspective of his son in *Cloudsplitter* (1998). JANE (GRAVES) SMILEY (b. 1949) became interested in the problem of political violence and "Bleeding Kansas" after the Oklahoma City bombing. Her finely researched novel *The All-True Travels and Adventures of Lidie Newton* (1998) is set in Lawrence in 1856.

William Clark Quantrill, Confederate guerrilla who raided Lawrence on August 21, 1863, has spawned such novels as *The Dark Command: A Kansas Iliad* (1938) by William R. Burnett (1899–1982) and *Woe to Live On* (1987) by Daniel Woodrell (b. 1953), which was filmed as *Ride with the Devil* in 1999.

As might be expected, much fiction has been written about Kansas farm life. *Sod and Stubble* (1936), a biography by John Ise, written like a novel and often taught in literature courses, appears to be a call for courage. It is the story of Ise's mother's life from 1873 to 1909 near Downs, Kansas. Henry and Rose Ise and their eleven children saw their share of hardship from blizzards, prairie fires, drought, grasshoppers, and even Native Americans. A counterpoint to *Sod and Stubble* is *Dust* (1921) by E(MANUEL) HALDEMAN-JULIUS (1889–1951) and Marcet Haldeman-Julius (1887–1941), she the vice president of a

bank, an Episcopalian, and the niece of (LAURA) JANE ADDAMS (1860–1935) of HULL-HOUSE, and he a socialist newspaper editor and founder of the Little Blue Books. Set in the same period, this novel tells the story of Martin Wade, whose father dies shortly after the family establishes a homestead in southeastern Kansas. Traumatized by his youth and the hardship of settlement, Wade finds solace only in work, in driving himself and those around him toward a prosperity that is meaningless to him.

Chaff in the Wind (1964) by Edna Walker Chandler (1908–1982) shows pioneering from the point of view of a younger generation of women who, aided by the example of their strong mothers, learn both to appreciate and to transcend the work of farming. In *Come Spring* (1986) Charlotte Hinger (b. 1940) writes about the settlement of western Kansas, including the homesteaders' problems with entrepreneurs, developers, and the growing influence of the railroads in the late nineteenth century.

Plow the Dew Under (1952) by Helen Clark Fernald (1888–1972) treats Crimean immigrants, especially the second generation, who live in the world of their parents' past, as well as in the America of their own future. In her autobiographical novel *The Story of Evaliz: Shukar Balan, the White Lamb* (1976) Mela Meisner Lindsay (1903–1989) divides her setting between the steppes of Russia and the plains of Kansas, where this Volga-German family emigrates in 1905 in quest of American citizenship and landownership. Dell H. Munger (b. 1862) begins her novel *The Wind before the Dawn* (1912) with the grasshopper invasion of 1874. A somewhat romantic tale, it captures the hardships and triumphs typical of the Kansas farm novel.

ROBERT (MENZIES) McALMON (1895–1956) was born in Clifton, Kansas. One of the "lost generation," he lived and worked in Paris for many years. His collection of short stories *A Hasty Bunch* (1922) includes several stories set in rural Kansas. See also EXPATRIATES. MERIDEL LE SUEUR (1900–1996), who spent some time growing up in Fort Scott, wrote about farm life in her classics *Harvest* (1977) and *The Girl* (1978). One of the most evocative and darkest of Kansas books is *The Narrow Covering* (1956) by Julia Ferguson Siebel (1915–

1991), who grew up in Colby in far western Kansas, the daughter of a banker. She understood her town and its surroundings in both human and economic terms.

Village and small-town novels are numerous in Kansas literature. EDGAR WATSON HOWE (1853–1937), editor of the *Atchison Globe,* published *The Story of a Country Town* to much critical acclaim in 1883. Although he did not initiate the literature that skewers the American small town, he was certainly important in its development. Like his friend H(enry) L(ouis) Mencken (1880–1956), Howe did not have a high opinion of humanity, and his later novels, including *The Mystery of the Locks* (1885), *A Man Story* (1889), and *An Ante-Mortem Statement* (1891), are pessimistic and misogynistic. Howe's daughter, Mateel Howe Farnham (1883–1957), followed in her father's footsteps. Her first novel, *Rebellion* (1927), is about the difficulties of a daughter living with a depressed and authoritative father. The book was critically acclaimed, but although E. W. Howe himself admired it, he cut Mateel out of his will.

Joseph Stanley Pennell (1903–1963), whose family settled in Junction City, wrote *The History of Rome Hanks and Kindred Matters* (1944). He followed this book with *The History of Nora Beckham: A Museum of Home Life* (1948). *Salt of the Earth* (1941) by Kenneth Haun Kitch (1907–1987), writing as Victor Holmes, treats small-town Grand City from the perspective of a country editor writing about its denizens—preacher, lawyer, doctor, bum—in the early twentieth century.

Kenneth Sydney Davis (1912–1999), in *The Years of the Pilgrimage* (1948) and *Morning in Kansas* (1952), delves beneath the surface of Kansas small towns. In the former work he portrays what he sees as a watered-down early twentieth-century Kansas, not the one of the past that "could bleed for an idea. . . . The blood of Kansas is thin. . . . The wild-eyed idealists are dead. . . . Their inheritance . . . [is] dissipated among the earnest advocates of petty prohibitions" (3–5). Davis and others often acknowledge the vivid past of Kansas and even use it to criticize the present.

Harveyville, Kansas, during the Depression and the Dust Bowl forms the backdrop of *The Persian Pickle Club* (1996) by Sandra Dallas (b. 1939). In it a murder has been committed, and it takes the persistence and community of a club of women to solve the case. *Ditch Valley* (1972) by Daryl Henderson (b. 1941) is a series of interconnected stories set from the 1930s to the 1970s and centered on a single mother trying to leave a small-minded town.

Edwin Moses (b. 1943) captures 1950s Kansas in *One Smart Kid* (1982). When a stranger comes to Fox Creek, Kansas, suspicions abound, even about Marvin Hollowell, the novel's thirteen-year-old narrator. The book dramatizes the troubles that ensue when McCarthyism strikes at the heart of America. PBS news anchor (James Charles) Jim Lehrer (b. 1934), however, finds charm in the Kansas small town. His *Kick the Can* (1988) is about One-Eyed Mack, who, blinded in a childhood game, is unable to pursue his dream of becoming a state trooper. Instead, he opts for more picaresque adventures amid the sensibilities and politics of the 1950s Midwest.

Max Yoho (b. 1934), both humorous and insightful, was voted a favorite Kansas author by the Kansas Center for the Book. *The Revival* (2001) examines small-town RELIGION, and *Moon Butter Route* (2006) reflects Kansas's love-hate relationship with its many years of Prohibition. *The Slow Air of Ewan MacPherson* (2003) by Thomas Fox Averill (b. 1949) brings Scotland to a small town in Kansas during the 1970s and 1980s. Part coming-of-age account, part love story, part tale of immigration, the novel shows the best and worst of the Kansas small town. Laura Moriarty (b. 1970), in *The Center of Everything* (2003), captures the experience of the Kansas small town of the 1980s for a single mother, including the promise of education to provide opportunities outside the narrow choices allowed in small towns. In Moriarty's *The Chaperone* (2012) a Wichita woman who came to Kansas on an orphan train accompanies the fifteen-year-old, soon-to-be-famous Louise Brooks (Cherryvale/Wichita) to New York and seeks her own identity. The character, Cora, embodies so many of the social issues and conventions of her time that she might be considered the chaperone of the twentieth century itself.

Although Kansas is hardly an urban state, it does have its share of city novels.

EARL THOMPSON (1931–1978) wrote the most urban of Kansas novels, the gritty *A Garden of Sand* (1970), about the Wichita poor. In the novel Wilma MacDeramid and her son Jacky struggle for work, money, and housing. Jacky's obsessive sexuality, including his interest in his mother, keeps this book from being widely read despite its raw power and its examination of Wichita during the Depression.

EVAN S(HELBY) CONNELL JR. (1924–2013) contributed two important novels of urban experience in *Mrs. Bridge* (1959) and *Mr. Bridge* (1969). In these novels, being upper class comes with isolation and loneliness, which can be ruinous psychologically. Although in these books Connell writes mostly of suburban Kansas City, Missouri, he describes well the Kansas territory of the suburbs. The two novels were combined in a film version, *Mr. and Mrs. Bridge* (1990), starring Paul (Leonard) Newman (1925–2008) and Joanne (Gignilliat Trimmier) Woodward (b. 1930). Another novel of suburban Kansas City is Whitney Terrell's (b. 1967) *The King of King's County* (2005), which deals with issues of class and race, as well as outrageous real estate development.

Originally from Russia, Paullina Simons (b. 1963) set her debut novel, *Tully* (1994), in Topeka from the late 1970s to 1990. It tells the story of Tully, the daughter of an abusive mother and a girl who suffers further abuse from the men in her life, who, through abandonment, abortion, promiscuity, and marriage, finds some sense of self. Tully's mother works in the Topeka refuse plant, a detail that defines how this novel treats the city.

Antonya Nelson (b. 1961) grew up in Wichita and centers her fiction in that city. Her rich and sympathetic *Living to Tell* (2000), a layered novel that uses Wichita well, concerns a dysfunctional family living together while trying to focus their rambling lives. The divorced daughter, a single mother, has cancer, the second daughter has addiction issues, and the son is just out of prison, where he served time for manslaughter. In Nelson's 2011 novel *Bound*, also set in Wichita, the main character is twice surprised: she has been named the guardian of the teenage daughter of a now-dead friend, and the serial killer who haunted Wichita during her youth has resurfaced.

Kansas also cannot be characterized as an industrial state, although agriculture—farming and ranching—and oil and gas extraction are certainly moving toward industrial practices. Some agricultural novels have already been discussed as farm novels. Kansas has yet to see a literature develop from the feedlots and the immigrants who work there. William Allen White wrote the best novel about agribusiness, *A Certain Rich Man* (1909), about the rise and fall of a local boy from Sycamore Ridge, a fictionalization of White's Emporia, who corners the markets in grain, controls the elevators, holds a patent for a railcar part crucial to shipping grain, and conspires with the railroads to control shipping costs. He also deals in land mortgages, so he controls the flow of grain from land to mill. His ultimate fall from economic and social grace is White's way of showing the power of the Progressive, trust-busting Republican reforms of the early twentieth century.

A second novel by White, *In the Heart of a Fool* (1918), treats the coal-mining industry of southeastern Kansas, showing the brutal working conditions, the strikes and strike busters, and the exploitation of workers—all seen as ameliorated by Progressive reform. A later novel of the coal mines is *The Overlord* (1978) by Les V. Roper (1931–1998). Roper was also a romance writer, probably the first ever to serve in the Kansas legislature.

Kansas fiction about school and college life includes *A Master's Degree* (1913) by Margaret Hill McCarter (1860–1938), a work about Sunrise College, perhaps modeled on Southwestern College in Winfield. An educator herself, McCarter wrote over a dozen novels and novelettes and has the distinction of being one of Kansas's best-selling authors; she frequently combined her subjects—education, town building, and trail sagas—with romance. DOROTHY (DOROTHEA FRANCES CANFIELD) FISHER (1879–1958) was born in Lawrence and lived there for twelve years. Her novel *The Bent Twig* (1915) shows Lawrence and university life through the eyes of a professor's child.

Evan S. Connell Jr. attended the University of Kansas, and his short story "The Anatomy Lesson," in *The Anatomy Lesson, and Other Stories* (1957), is set in a Kansas University art classroom. A professor awaits the one student who will be a true artist, seeing beyond and into, rather than simply looking at, the nude model presented to the squeamish students. The story is an interesting distillation of the role of the university as it stands against the conventions of Kansas. Irving Stone (1903–1989) wrote *The Passionate Journey* (1949), a novel about the education of Kansas artist John Noble. In *Astonishment of Heart* (1984) Edwin Moses wrote about a university professor on sabbatical who returns to the farmstead of his mother to discover truths about her life, as well as his own.

Like other Midwestern states, Kansas has a considerable amount of immigrant and ethnic literature, some of which has already been discussed, particularly under the category of farm novels. John Ise's *Sod and Stubble* is decidedly German, as were many Kansas settlers in the 1870s. The Mennonite presence in Kansas is also important, making the state the highest in the nation per capita in conscientious objectors.

In *Kansas Irish* (1943), the first book of a trilogy, Charles Driscoll (1885–1951) captured the Kansas experience of the Irish, a group usually associated with the city rather than the prairie. Mary Molek (1909–1982) wrote *Immigrant Woman* (1976) in an attempt to capture life as experienced by women like her mother, who came to Pittsburg, Kansas, with the mining industry and lived in "camps" provided by the mining companies. Al Ortolani (b. 1952) wrote about what was left of the camps in *The Last Hippie of Camp 50* (1989) and again in *Finding the Edge* (2011). When he was at Wichita State University, BIENVENIDO N(UQUI) SANTOS (1911–1996) wrote *Scent of Apples* (1979) about the Filipino immigrant experience in the United States.

Several fictional works by African Americans are set in Kansas. *Not without Laughter* (1930) by LANGSTON HUGHES (1902–1967) is a novel set in Stanton, a fictionalized Lawrence, Kansas, around the time of World War I. African American Sandy Rodgers comes of age in an atmosphere of racial prejudice. Many influences and philosophies clamor for attention in his life, and finally he sets out to live up to his grandmother's dream that he will someday become a great man and help the whole black race. GORDON (ROGER ALEXANDER BUCHANAN) PARKS (1912–2006) wrote *The Learning Tree*

(1963), his "novel from life," at a time of racial unrest. This coming-of-age story takes place in Cherokee Flats, a fictionalized Fort Scott, between 1924 and 1928. Parks has said that he was lucky to survive Kansas, and the violence and racial prejudice in the novel show why he made that assertion. On the other hand, Kansas is where Newt Winger learns the important lessons of courage, bravery, and truth telling. There he finds the tools to propel him to a better life after the death of his mother.

Rattlebone (1994) by Maxine Clair (b. 1939) is a group of connected stories of the coming of age of Irene Wilson in her all-black neighborhood in Kansas City, Kansas, in the 1950s. Irene must weather racial prejudice, adulterous parents, death, her budding sexuality, and challenges to her friendships as she learns to realize her promise and stand up for herself.

Widow Man (1953), a short novel by Edgar Wolfe (1906–1989), is set in the early 1950s, the era of *Brown v. Board of Education,* in the Argentine district of Kansas City, Kansas. Tom Way, a white man newly widowed by the death of his black wife, must decide whether to move from his predominantly black neighborhood or to stay. A courtship with Tunsie, a black neighbor, helps him make up his mind. Carol Ascher (b. 1941) was also influenced by *Brown v. Board of Education* in her novel *The Flood* (1987). Against the backdrop of desegregation and the flood of 1951, Eva Hoffman is the precocious ten-year-old daughter of a Jewish psychiatrist who recently immigrated to Topeka to work at the Menninger Clinic. Eva and her family struggle to understand a new country, with its awkward race relations. They are all tested when Eva's mother takes in a "redneck" family from across the river.

Kansas has a unique relationship to the western myths of law enforcement, the cowboy, and cattle drives. Although we admire the independent cowboy and seem prone to celebrate the American addiction to violence, most cowboy and western novels are about settling down. Andy Adams (1859–1935) wrote an early novel, *The Log of a Cowboy* (1903), about a trail drive to Dodge City, a town famous as the last destination before the railroad was built far enough to make the long cattle drive a thing of the past.

Mack Cretcher (1868–1946) wrote *The Kansan* (1923) about a Kansas town caught between bankers and rustlers and the agricultural people who want peace. *The Last Cattle Drive* (1977) by Robert Day (b. 1941) is set in 1970s Kansas and is narrated by the tenderfoot schoolteacher Leo, who takes a summer job with a local rancher and ends up on a cattle drive from Gorham/Hays, Kansas, all the way to the Kansas City stockyards. In addition to its rollicking humor and accurate geography, the novel is an excellent introduction to the big differences between eastern and western Kansas.

In a more contemporary novel Greg Matthews (b. 1949) reconfigures the western with his *Heart of the Country* (1985), about a half-Indian man who becomes a buffalo hunter, a bone gatherer, and a settler. Philip Kimball (b. 1941) spins a tall tale in *Liar's Moon* (1999), presenting a romping collage of the western myth, the Kansas answer to the classic *Little Big Man* (1964) by Thomas (Louis) Berger (1924–2014). In *Prince of the Plains* (2002) Troy Boucher (b. 1940) explores the life of a character named Henry Newton Brown, who typically played both sides of the law, riding with Billy the Kid and then becoming marshal of Caldwell, Kansas.

Kansas appears to have a love-hate relationship with western outlaws and criminals. Kansans never tire of talking about Quantrill and his 1863 raid on Lawrence or of pointing out that the James and Younger brothers rode with the Confederate guerrilla. Kansas literature is replete with stories of crime and criminals. The Dalton gang, the focus of two Kansas museums, is also the subject of *The Dalton Gang* (1963) by Harold Preece (1906–1992) and *The Sixth Rider* (1991) by southeastern Kansas writer Max McCoy (b. 1958).

Between 1871 and 1873 the Bender family of Labette County ran a wayside inn where they robbed and murdered as many as eleven people. Besides a small museum in Cherryvale, their legacy is sensationalized in *The Bloody Benders* (1970) by Robert Adleman (1919–1995) and chronicled in a well-researched history, *The Benders: Keepers of the Devil's Inn* (1992) by Fern Morrow Wood (1922–2012). Sarah Smarsh (b. 1980) includes the Benders and many other famous Kansas desperadoes in her *Outlaw Tales of Kansas*

(2010). Her historical *It Happened in Kansas: Remarkable Events That Shaped History* (2010) is another lively look at the state's traditions.

The best-known Kansas crime book is *In Cold Blood* (1965). When Herb Clutter and his family in Holcomb, Kansas, were murdered in 1959, Truman Capote (1924–1984) set out for Kansas, determined to write what he would call the "nonfiction novel." The result is a classic work that captures our fascination with Middle America both as a safe and innocent place and as a place where violence can erupt quickly and as devastatingly as a cyclone. Kansas native Ralph Voss (b. 1943), now at the University of Alabama, has examined the relationships among the murders, Kansas, and Capote in *Truman Capote and the Legacy of "In Cold Blood"* (2011).

Lori Roy (b. 1965), who grew up in Manhattan and graduated from Kansas State University, has had great success with her first novel, set in western Kansas in the 1960s. Half literary novel, half thriller, *Bent Road* (2011) won the 2011 Edgar Award for Best First Novel by an American Author and was named a 2011 *New York Times* Notable Crime Book.

William Gibson (1914–2008) came to Topeka with his psychiatrist wife and got his start as a playwright working with the new Topeka Civic Theatre. His novel *The Cobweb* (1954) is set in a Midwestern mental hospital modeled after Topeka State Hospital.

The short story is typically underrepresented in discussions of Kansas literature. William Allen White was prolific in the genre. Robert Day is one of its best practitioners, as in *Speaking French in Kansas* (1989). So is Evan S. Connell Jr. in *The Anatomy Lesson*. But one of the most unusual writers of short stories was Edythe Squier Draper (1882–1964). *As Grass*, a collection of six of her short stories, was published in 1994. These are works set in southeastern Kansas between the world wars and concern themselves with abused women and neglected children, poor blacks, and other people at the fringes of the small towns and communities in which they live. Contemporary Kansas in all its regions is the setting of *Ordinary Genius* (2004) by Thomas Fox Averill. The work offers stories of common people in common places who, as WILLIAM STAFFORD (1914–1993) would have directed, find a way to see into and transcend their lives, even if momentarily. Native Kansan Andrew Malan Milward (b. 1979), a graduate of the IOWA WRITERS' WORKSHOP, has written a group of short stories set in Kansas; they are collected in *The Agricultural Hall of Fame* (2012).

Autobiography and Memoir: Fiction is of crucial importance to Kansas literature, but also of interest are the many memoirs, autobiographies, and other personal histories Kansans have felt compelled to write. Harry Kemp (1883–1960) made his mark as an American tramp, but part of his travel found him at the University of Kansas, where he became involved with the state's poets. *Tramping on Life: An Autobiographical Narrative* (1922) provides an overview of his life. Charles Leroy Edson (1881–1975) wrote biting poems in free verse in the 1920s, taking on the romantic vision of pioneering and criticizing Kansas icons like John Brown. His autobiography, *"The Great American Ass"* (1926), gives an excellent glimpse of Kansas at that time.

Howard Ruede (1854–1925) came to Osborne County and wrote letters home to Pennsylvania for a year, providing a detailed account of daily pioneer life in central Kansas. These letters were collected by John Ise in *Sod House Days: Letters from a Kansas Homesteader, 1877–78* (1937). Arthur Hertzler (1870–1946) describes the trials and advances of medicine in the early twentieth century in *The Horse and Buggy Doctor* (1938), a fascinating account of the doctor who later founded a clinic in Halstead and taught at the University of Kansas Medical Center.

Martin Johnson (1884–1937) married Osa Helen Johnson (1894–1953) when she was just sixteen and ten years his junior. She proved to be his match, learning to fly a plane, traveling as an equal partner all over the world, and filming people in the South Sea islands, Borneo, and Africa. Explorers, lecturers, photographers, filmmakers, and writers, the two were famous all across the nation. Three years after Martin's death, she wrote *I Married Adventure: The Lives and Adventures of Martin and Osa Johnson* (1940). Ralph Moody (1898–1982), in *Horse of a Different Color: Reminiscenses* [*sic*] *of a Kansas Drover* (1968), chronicled the ranching in-

dustry but also wrote children's books in his nine-volume Little Britches series (1950–1968). James F. Hoy (b. 1939) discovered and edited a cowboy biography *Cowboy's Lament: A Life on the Open Range* (2010) by Frank H. Maynard (1853–1920).

African American FRANK MARSHALL DAVIS (1905–1987) chronicled his growing up in Arkansas City in *Livin' the Blues* (1992). Davis's work has seen a renaissance thanks to Kansas native John Edgar Tidwell (b. 1945), who is also the editor of Davis's *Black Moods: Collected Poems* (2002).

Lawrence Svobida (1908–1984) wrote *Farming the Dust Bowl* (1986) about his experiences in southern Kansas during drought years. He quit farming in 1939, just before the rains returned and wheat began to grow again. In *Garden City: Dreams in a Kansas Town* (1988) Holly Hope (b. 1956), daughter of U.S. senator Clifford Ragsdale Hope Jr. (1923–2010) and granddaughter of U.S. representative Clifford Ragsdale Hope Sr. (1893–1970), wrote a social history of her town and a personal coming-of-age story.

No history of the state would be complete without a chronicle of the 1960s "hippie" movement, which was very strong at the University of Kansas. Roger Martin, David Ohle, and Susan Brosseau have edited a volume to satisfy curiosity about that era in *Cows Are Freaky When They Look at You: An Oral History of the Kaw Valley Hemp Pickers* (1991). Keith Waldrop (b. 1932) grew up in Emporia and wrote a moving and poignant memoir about his development as an artist in *Light While There Is Light* (1993).

Carol Brunner Rutledge (1938–2004) found herself traveling regularly from her home in Topeka to her childhood home in Hope to visit her dying mother. The journey resulted in *Dying and Living on the Kansas Prairie* (1994), a meditation on hope, the human spirit, and deep understanding of place. James Dickenson (b. 1931) recalls his growing up in McDonald, population 200, and expands on the history and culture of the Great Plains in *Home on the Range: A Century on the High Plains* (1995). Arnold J. Bauer (b. 1930) recalls his youth on a 160-acre Clay County farm, attending a one-room school, and surviving the Great Depression in his memoir, *Time's Shadow: Remembering a Family Farm in Kansas* (2012).

Journalist Bruce Bair (b. 1944) uses an ironic title in *Good Land: My Life as a Farm Boy* (1997). Bair grew up on a western Kansas wheat farm near Goodland and writes a chip-on-the-shoulder account of life with a difficult father in a difficult landscape during a time of transition to bigger and bigger farms. Bruce Bair's sister, Julene Bair (b. 1949), wrote *One Degree West: Reflections of a Plainsdaughter* (2000), in which she meditates on the challenges of family dynamics and farming in western Kansas and the complexity of gender roles that enter into both. This book provides a female perspective on the family story recounted in her brother's *Good Land*. A later memoir, *Ogallala Road* (2014), examines water use.

Poetry: Kansas can claim several famous poets who were born in the state but did not write about it. EDGAR LEE MASTERS (1868–1950) was born in Garnett but moved very early to ILLINOIS; there he found the inspiration for his *SPOON RIVER ANTHOLOGY* (1915). GWENDOLYN BROOKS (1917–2000) was born in Topeka while her mother was visiting from CHICAGO. As is the case for Masters, Langston Hughes, Gordon Parks, and others who moved while young, Kansas lays small claim to being part of her career.

The first Kansas poems were written by those who used Kansas as a word to conjure freedom during the territorial struggles against slavery. Lucy Larcom (1824–1893) wrote "A Call to Kansas" (1855), which has the crowing refrain "We'll sing upon the Kansas Plains / A song of liberty!" (*Kansas in Literature*, part 1, *Poetry*, 31). John Greenleaf Whittier (1807–1892) wrote "The Song of the Kansas Emigrant," which begins, "We cross the prairies as of old / The pilgrims crossed the sea, / to make the West, as they the East, / the homestead of the free." Indigenous poetry soon surfaced, like "Juanita: An Idyl of the Plains" by Henry Brace Norton (1836–1885), who wove Anglo, Hispanic, and Native American threads into a tragic western romance.

Dr. Brewster Higley (1823–1911) was not a great poet, but in the tradition of amateur poems published in local newspapers, his "My Western Home" has an illustrative history. Once set to music by Daniel E. Kelley (1845–1905), the song immediately went into the folk tradition, carried mostly by cowboys up and down the Great Plains. They called it "Home on the Range" and changed and added verses. When "Home" was named Franklin D. Roosevelt's favorite song, copyright issues sent lawyers sleuthing until they found the original in an 1873 issue of the *Smith County Pioneer*. "Home on the Range" became the Kansas state song in 1947.

Thomas Brower Peacock (1852–1919) contributed poems about Kansas in *Poems of the Plains and Songs of the Solitudes together with "The Rhyme of the Border War"* (1888), the "Rhyme" being something of a Miltonic epic. Another poetic chronicler, Richard Realf (1834–1878), also began by writing about the territorial struggles in such poems as "The Defense of Lawrence." His *Poems by Richard Realf: Poet . . . Soldier . . . Workman* (1898) was published twenty years after his death by suicide. Another versifier was Fort Scott lawyer Eugene Fitch Ware (1841–1911), who wrote under the pen name Ironquill. His work was published and republished as his body of poetry grew. *Some of the Rhymes of Ironquill* (1902) is full of Kansas subjects,

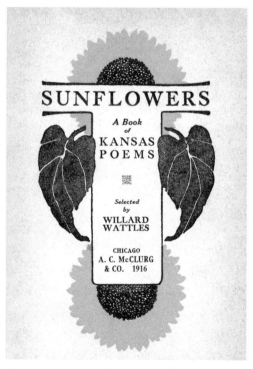

Kansas poetry anthology, *Sunflowers*. A. C. McClurg & Co., 1916.

mostly celebrating the struggles and triumphs of pioneering.

Kansas poetry began to come into literary stature in the early twentieth century, when poets like Willard Wattles (1888–1950) and Harry Kemp began to see Kansas as a cultural center, a place that could express itself free of eastern decadence and industrialization. Wattles compiled *Sunflowers: A Book of Kansas Poems* in 1916. Helen Rhoda Hoopes (1878–1973) edited *Contemporary Kansas Poetry* (1927) and published the work of many of the women poets writing at the time, including Nora B. Cunningham (1887–1975) and May Williams Ward (1882–1975), who together briefly edited a literary magazine, the *Harp*. A collection of Cunningham's poems, *NBC Decades* (1977), was brought out after her death. A collection of poems by May Williams Ward, *In That Day,* appeared in 1969. Lana Wirt Myers (b. 1952) has written a biography, complete with poetry and photographs: *Prairie Rhythms: The Life and Poetry of May Williams Ward* (2010).

Kenneth Wiggins Porter (1905–1981) is a seminal Kansas poet from this period, the author of *The High Plains* (1938) and *No Rain from These Clouds* (1946). His colloquial style, deep understanding of place, and celebration of the people while also challenging Kansans to make better use of the environment are important qualities in these collections written during the Dust Bowl years. Although Porter was trained as an economic historian, his work, with its Christian socialist leanings, gave a new voice to Kansas poetry and encouraged others to create from the idea of place rather than from the traditions of academic verse or English poetry. Certainly William Stafford adopted that position, as do later poets of importance to the Kansas tradition.

The next generation of poets included many associated with academic institutions. At Kansas State University was W. R. Moses (1911–2001), who wrote powerful lyrical poetry of very particular observation in *Identities* (1965) and *Passage* (1976). *The Kansas Poems* (1987) by Dallas Wiebe (1930–2008), a Mennonite associated with the University of Wisconsin and the University of Cincinnati, shows his minimalist form and wry humor about the state. Another Mennonite, Elmer F. Suderman (1920–2003) of Gustavus

Adolphus College, wrote *What Can We Do Here?* (1974), containing many poems about the settlement of the state by this religious group. BRUCE CUTLER (1930–2001) published extensively during and after his stint as director of the Master of Fine Arts in Writing program at Wichita State University. Among his many books are *A West Wind Rises: The Marais des Cygnes Massacre* (1962), *Sun City* (1964), and *The Massacre at Sand Creek: Narrative Voices* (1995). *A West Wind Rises* was written to honor and explore Kansas at its centennial of statehood. Cutler did comprehensive research to create multiple voices and perspectives exploring the "Bleeding Kansas" heritage.

William Stafford is the best-known and most highly revered twentieth-century Kansas poet. He is considered not only the most accomplished, having won the National Book Award for his second book, *Traveling through the Dark* (1962), and the most prolific but also the poet who most defined Kansas and Great Plains poetry. Amy Fleury said of his work, "The simple language of complicated life, the respect for the landscape of Kansas and the Great Plains and the welcoming inclusiveness in these poems are the region's quintessence" (quoted in *Kansas Poetry, an Overview,* online). Beyond style, Stafford's work contains a powerful commitment to the region, as well as to certain life principles—peace, racial equality, and modesty. Stafford's posthumous collection *The Way It Is: New and Selected Poems* (1998) consists of new and collected poems, including one written on the day of his death. His *Down in My Heart* (1947) is an account of his time spent as a conscientious objector during World War II.

Kansas has a group of poets who took their places in the experimental, beat, surreal, and imagistic schools. Among them are Michael McClure (b. 1932), author of *Dark Brown* (1961) and *Rare Angel* (1974). Ronald Johnson (1935–1998), a prolific member of the Black Mountain school of poetry, contributed *A Line of Poetry, a Row of Trees* (1964), *The Book of the Green Man* (1967), *Radi Os* (1977), *Ark* (1996), and *The Shrubberies* (2001). James (Vincent) Tate (1943–2015), from Kansas City and Pittsburg, won the Yale Younger Poets prize for *The Lost Pilot* (1967) and has had a prolific career. Lawrence was identified

William Stafford near El Dorado, Kansas, November 1986.

© Vince Wixon. Reprinted courtesy of Lewis and Clark College Aubrey Watzek Library Archives & Special Collections

with the beat poets, hosting readings by poets like Allen Ginsberg (1926–1997), who wrote "Wichita Vortex Sutra," and WILLIAM S(EWARD) BURROUGHS (II) (1914–1997), who chose to live there at the end of his life, finding a nurturing community of writers.

Jonathan Holden (b. 1941) served as the first Poet Laureate of Kansas from 2005 to 2007. He has won awards for all his poetry collections, from the Associated Writing Programs Award Series selection of *Leverage* in 1983 through the Vassar Miller Prize in Poetry for *The Sublime* (1996). None of his seven books of poems is specifically about Kansas, but many individual poems treat Kansas as landscape and idea. Holden wrote the first critical book about William Stafford, *The Mark to Turn: A Reading of William Stafford's Poetry* (1976).

James F. Hoy grew up on a Flint Hills ranch and has written history, FOLKLORE, and memoir about that experience. His *Prairie Poetry: Cowboy Verse of Kansas* (1995) shows all facets of this still-vital genre. B. H. Fairchild (b. 1942) wrote *The Art of the Lathe* (1998) and *Early Occult Memory Systems of the Lower Midwest* (2003); both combine strong narrative with lyrical poetry that reveals the nature of Kansas people. Max Douglas (1949–1970) was a brilliant young poet at the University of Kansas who wrote in spare lines, stark and exacting, about compressed insights and concise moments. His *Collected Poems* (1978) was published after his death from a heroin overdose.

The number of poets in the academy has increased significantly with the teaching of creative writing and with graduate programs dedicated to writing. Michael Paul Novak (1935–2006) taught at the University of Saint Mary at Leavenworth. His first book, *The Leavenworth Poems* (1972), includes "English 101—The State Prison," based on his experiences teaching in Lansing, Kansas. His final book was *A Story to Tell* (1990). Novak was a lyric poet and a fine observer of life with a darkly humorous intelligence. Stephen Meats (b. 1944), the poetry editor of *Midwest Quarterly,* has written *Looking for the Pale Eagle* (1993). Steven Hind (b. 1943) is particularly adept at capturing the Flint Hills. Influenced by William Stafford, he has published four collections of poetry: *familiar ground* (1980), *That Trick of Silence* (1990), *In a Place with No Map* (1997), and *The Loose Change of Wonder* (2006). Albert Goldbarth (b. 1948), a National Book Critics Circle Award winner for *Heaven and Earth: A Cosmology* (1991), is prolific, intellectual, and accessible, although Kansas is rarely his subject.

Elizabeth Dodd (b. 1962) of Kansas State University treats some Kansas subjects in her *Archetypal Light* (2001), and she has carved out a CREATIVE NONFICTION niche with *Prospect: Journeys and Landscapes* (2003). *Retrieving Old Bones* (2002) by William Sheldon (b. 1962) is a meditation on life and landscape in central Kansas, and Sheldon, who teaches English at Hutchinson Community College, has also published a chapbook, *Into Distant Grass* (2009), and a full-length collection, *Rain Comes Riding* (2012). *Beauti-*

ful Trouble (2004) by Amy Fleury (b. 1970) won the Crab Orchard Award; her poetry has been described by 2004–2006 U.S. Poet Laureate Ted Kooser (b. 1939) as "ordinary words placed with perfect precision" in the service of consciousness of the relationship between people and place (*Beautiful Touble*, 52). Later collections are *Reliquaries of the Lesser Saints* (2010), a chapbook, and *Sympathetic Magic* (2013). Visual artist and poet Harley Elliott (b. 1940) brings his painter's eye and sense of humor to his poetry about Kansas. For example, in his collection *Darkness at Each Elbow* (1981), "The Mountain Men of America" is set in a laundromat. Patricia Traxler (b. 1944) came to Kansas from California and has been a vital part of the Salina arts community. Two of her poetry collections are *The Glass Woman* (1983) and *Forbidden Words* (1994). Her novel is *Blood* (2001). With roots in more than one place, Kathleen Johnson (b. 1959) divides her time between New Mexico and Kansas. Her poetry collections are *Burn* (2008) and *Subterranean Red* (2012). She is the editor of the *New Mexico Poetry Review*. Mark Hennessy (b. 1969), who grew up in Kansas City, Kansas, and took his master of fine arts at the University of Kansas, is the author of *I Lost It All the Night the Day the Circus Came to Town* (2010).

A generation of young poets has come out of Topeka. Kevin Young (b. 1970), one of the nation's most prolific poets, has published *Most Way Home* (1995), *To Repel Ghosts* (2001), *Jelly Roll: A Blues* (2003), *Black Maria* (2005), *For the Confederate Dead* (2007), *Dear Darkness* (2008), *Ardency* (2010), and *The Grey Album: On the Blackness of Blackness* (2012), works that evoke Langston Hughes and Gwendolyn Brooks, with a playful sense of language and an avid interest in the multigenre arts experience of music, FILM, television, and visual art. He has edited numerous anthologies as well. Ed Skoog (b. 1971) is well known among young poets; his chapbook is *Field Recordings* (2003), and his books are *Mister Skylight* (2009) and *Rough Day* (2013) Eric McHenry (b. 1972) has Topeka roots through several generations. His *Potscrubber Lullabies* (2006) tends toward formal lines and shapes and is full of rich humor and gentle insights; McHenry also reviews contemporary poetry for the *New York Times Book Review*. A later book is a collection of

light verse, *Mommy, Daddy, Evan Sage* (2011). *The Lichtenberg Figures* (2004), the first book by Ben Lerner (b. 1979), contains loosely structured sonnets and masterful lyrical poems. His *Angle of Yaw* (2006), a finalist for the National Book Award, is a critique of contemporary American culture using that culture's own images and obsessions. His third collection is *Free Mean Path* (2010), which was followed by a novel, *Leaving the Atocha Station*, which garnered attention and awards in 2011. Cyrus Console (b. 1977) has written a collection of prose poems, *Brief under Water* (2008). His second collection is *The Odicy* (2011). Another Topekan, Matthew Porubsky (b. 1979), is the author of three volumes of poems: *voyeur poems* (2006), *Fire Mobile (The Pregnancy Sonnets)* (2011), and *Ruled by Pluto* (2013). Nick Twemlow (b. 1973) is the author of a chapbook, *Your Mouth Is Everywhere* (2010). His first full-length collection is *Palm Trees* (2012). Israel Wasserstein (b. 1981) published his first collection of poetry, *This Ecstasy They Call Damnation*, in 2012.

Drama: WILLIAM (MOTTER) INGE (1913–1973) is the preeminent playwright in the state and the only Kansan to win a Pulitzer Prize for Drama, for *Picnic* (1953). His *Four Plays* (1958) includes his blockbusters of the 1950s: *Come Back, Little Sheba* (1950), *Picnic*, *Bus Stop* (1955), and *The Dark at the Top of the Stairs* (1957). Along with Tennessee Williams (1911–1983) and Arthur Miller (1915–2005), Inge defined Broadway theatre until the negative reviews and quick closing of *A Loss of Roses* (1959). After that, Inge left New York for California, where he won an Oscar for best original screenplay for *Splendor in the Grass* (1961). Inge wrote two novels, *Good Luck, Miss Wyckoff* (1970) and *My Son Is a Splendid Driver* (1971). He committed suicide in 1973 at age sixty. Although his work has fallen out of favor, he captured the American Midwest of the 1920s with accuracy, sympathy, and a true sense of voice. Ralph Voss wrote the definitive biography, *A Life of William Inge: The Strains of Triumph* (1989). Inge is honored in Kansas with the William Inge Theatre Festival, held annually in Independence.

For the twenty-fifth anniversary of the Inge Theatre Festival, Marcia Cebulska (b. 1944) wrote *Touched* (2006), a play about the life of William Inge commissioned by the Inge Center. Cebulska was also commissioned to write for the celebration of the fiftieth anniversary of *Brown v. Board of Education.* Her *Now Let Me Fly* (2004) was the centerpiece of events that included the opening of the National Park Service *Brown v. Board of Education* site in Topeka. Before Inge, Kirke Field Mechem (1889–1985) wrote plays, among them *John Brown* (1939). His son, Kirke Mechem (b. 1925), is a composer whose opera *John Brown* (2008) also treats the famous abolitionist.

Allen Crafton (1890–1966), of the University of Kansas, wrote poetry, plays, and novels, as well as a technical guide, *The Complete Acted Play from Script to Final Curtain* (1946). Topeka playwright Phil Grecian (b. 1948) wrote a dramatic version of Charles Sheldon's *In His Steps* (1994) to commemorate that book's hundredth anniversary.

Other recent playwrights include Ric Averill (b. 1950), also a screenwriter, who has written numerous children's theatre works, especially for his own Lawrence company, the Seem-to-Be Players. Two of his works are *Alex and the Shrink World* (1998) and, with William Averill, a film, *Riding the Pine* (2009). Junction City native Kevin Willmott (b. 1958) is both a playwright and a filmmaker. His work includes *Ninth Street* (1999), about the demise of the African American business district that served Junction City and Fort Riley for years; and *C.S.A.: The Confederate States of America* (2004), a "mock-umentary" that imagines historical conditions if the South had won the Civil War. Later films are *Bunker Hill* (2008), *The Only Good Indian* (2008), *Destination Planet Negro* (2013), *and Jayhawkers* (2014), all set in Kansas.

Although African American novelist and pioneer filmmaker OSCAR MICHEAUX (1884–1951) did not write about Kansas, he grew up and is buried in Great Bend. Paul Stephen Lim (b. 1944) ran the English Alternative Theatre at the University of Kansas. His *Conpersonas* (1976) was performed at the Kennedy Center, and his *Flesh, Flash and Frank Harris* (1981) is set partly in Lawrence. Originally from Pomona, James Still (b. 1969) has written numerous plays. His *Amber Waves* (1991) covers a year in the life of a Kansas farm family. *False Creeds* (2007) by Topeka native Darren Canady (b. 1982) won the third annual Kendeda Graduate Playwriting

Competition at the Alliance Theatre in Atlanta. Later awards include the Lorraine Hansberry Playwriting Award, the Theodore Ward Prize for African American Playwrights, and the M. Elizabeth Osborn New Play Award 2012, which recognized *Brothers of the Dust* (2011).

Popular Literature:

Mystery and Detective Fiction: Rex (Todhunter) Stout (1886–1975) grew up in Topeka and attended the University of Kansas. He created Nero Wolfe and assistant Archie Goodwin in *Fer-de-Lance* (1934). After 1938 he published annually up to his death. James P. Girard published a literary novel, *Changing All Those Changes* (1976), and the literary detective novels *The Late Man* (1993) and *Some Survive* (2002), both set in Wichita.

Nancy Pickard (b. 1945) wrote a series of detective novels set in Massachusetts before private investigator Jenny Cain came to the Kansas Flint Hills in *Bum Steer* (1990). Pickard's *The Virgin of Small Plains* (2006) and *The Scent of Rain and Lightning* (2010) are also set in Kansas. Gaylord Dold created P.I. Mitch Roberts in his six Wichita novels, beginning with the 1987 publication of two novels: *Hot Summer, Cold Murder* and *Snake Eyes. Bone Pile* (1988), *Muscle and Blood* (1989), *Disheveled City* (1990), and *Semedi's Knapsack* (2001) followed. Dold has also published literary novels and travel books.

SARA PARETSKY (b. 1947) was raised in Lawrence, but most of her mystery novels have been set in Chicago, where both she and her detective, V. I. Warshawski, live. Her *Bleeding Kansas* (2007), not a mystery novel, is about two families who have been in Kansas for 150 years and how their lives are affected by war and by changing sexual and religious values.

Children's and Young Adult Literature: Kansas young-adult literature is dominated by two iconic books set in the state. LAURA INGALLS WILDER (1867–1957) lived on Cherokee land about fourteen miles from Independence, Kansas, in 1869–1870. The government forced the Ingallses to move, but the experience, remembered and researched years later, became *Little House on the Prairie* (1935). L(YMAN) FRANK BAUM (1856–1919), who set foot in Kansas only once, as an actor with a traveling theatre company, set *THE WONDERFUL WIZARD OF OZ* (1900) in the state, probably to avoid offending relatives who still lived in Aberdeen, SOUTH DAKOTA. The opening description of Kansas in his book is probably the bleakest of any writer on the state, but the last line of his book reflects joy in Midwestern place: "And oh, Aunt Em! I'm so glad to be home again!" The movie version also gives Kansas the distinction of being the home of Dorothy's lines "There's no place like home" and the less flattering "Toto, I don't think we're in Kansas anymore." Baum included the Kansas setting in three other Oz books. Thomas Fox Averill has written on Baum's use of Kansas in "Oz and Kansas Culture," *Kansas History* 12.1 (1989): 2–12. Baum's work has inspired several Kansas- and Oz-based books for adult readers: *Wicked: The Life and Times of the Wicked Witch of the West* (1995) by Gregory Maguire (b. 1954), *Was* (1992) by Geoff Ryman (b. 1951), and *My Life with Corpses* (2004) by Kansas-born Wylene Dunbar (b. 1949).

Other early children's literature focuses on equally iconic images of Kansas: the Oregon and Santa Fe Trails, sod houses, cowboys and cattle drives, the Pony Express, and romanticized western figures associated with the state—(Christopher Houston) Kit Carson (1809–1868), (William Frederick) Buffalo Bill Cody (1846–1917), Wyatt (Barry Stapp) Earp (1848–1929), and (James Butler) Wild Bill Hickok (1837–1876). Some specific titles include one of the earliest books for young people, *Stories for Kansas Boys and Girls* (1895) by Carolina Wade Baker (ca. 1850–1920). Henry Inman (1837–1899) wrote *The Ranche on the Oxhide: A Story of Boys' and Girls' Life on the Frontier* (1898). *Immortal Dream Dust: A Story of Pioneer Life on a Kansas Homestead* (1931) by May Griffee Robinson (ca. 1890–1960) is set near Sterling. Bernice Goudy Anderson (1894–1997) wrote *Topsy Turvy's Pigtails* (1930) and *Topsy Turvy and the Tin Clown* (1932). *Treasure Aboard* (1931) by Charles Driscoll is about boys who, while camping on the Arkansas River near Wichita, discover treasure in a buried ship.

The 1950s saw such titles as *The Phantom Steer* (1953) by Floyd Benjamin Streeter (1888–1956) and Helen D. Francis (1915–1992) and *Sod House Adventure* (1956) by Bonnie Bess Worline (1914–2006). Don Wilcox (1905–2000) wrote *Joe Sunpool* (1956), about an Indian boy attending Haskell Institute in Lawrence. Another book about Native Americans, *Blue Jacket: War Chief of the Shawnees* (1969), is by Allan W. Eckert (1931–2011).

The Motoring Millers (1969) by Alberta Wilson Constant (1908–1981) is set in the fictional town of Gloriosa. Peter Zachary Cohen (b. 1931) wrote *Foal Creek* (1972). Patricia Beatty (1922–1991) set her young-adult novel *Jayhawker* (1991) in territorial Kansas. In *Climbing Kansas Mountains* (1993) by George Shannon (b. 1946), a boy's father takes him to climb the town's grain elevator, the "mountain" in the town, and he sees a wide vista of checkerboard fields that bring food to dining tables. Lois Ruby (b. 1942) has written several young-adult books set in Kansas, among them *Pig Out Inn* (1987) and *Steal Away Home* (1994), the latter about a house in Lawrence in which the current inhabitants discover a skeleton. The parallel historical story is about the runaway slave whose body they have discovered. The Newbery Award–winning novel *Moon over Manifest* (2010) by Clare Vanderpool (b. 1965) has a similar plot structure. Set in southeastern Kansas in the coal mines near Pittsburg, it uses the 1918 flu epidemic and the Great Depression in its exploration of a tandem father/daughter story.

Best-selling writer of the psychological self-help "dance" books, Harriet Lerner (b. 1944) has co-authored two children's books with her sister, Susan Goldhor: *What's So Terrible about Swallowing an Apple Seed?* (1996) and *Franny B. Kranny, There's a Bird in Your Hair!* (2000). Richard Jennings (b. 1945) has written *The Great Whale of Kansas* (2001), about a young man digging a pond in his backyard who discovers a fossil that his teacher and a Native American man believe to be a whale. Interestingly, this fictional use of the abundance of fossil evidence from when Kansas was covered by the great inland sea appeared around the time at which the Kansas Board of Education was restricting the testing of evolution as part of state science standards. Lisa Harkrader (b. 1962) has created a winning combination of small-town basketball, uncertain parentage, and a trip to see the KU Jayhawks in the famous Allen Fieldhouse in *Airball, My Life in Briefs* (2005). Brian Meehl (b. 1952) sets his humorous young-adult novel *Out of Patience* (2006) in the fictional Patience, Kansas. Stephen T. Johnson (b. 1964), trained as a fine artist, not only writes books but also constructs them so children can experience them physically. His hands-on offerings are *My Little Red Toolbox* (2000), *My Little Blue Robot* (2002), and *My Little Yellow Taxi* (2006). Illustrator-turned-author Brad Sneed (b. 1966) creates tall tales with illustrations in the style of Thomas Hart Benton (1889–1975), colorful, elongated, exaggerated, and perfectly evocative of his subjects. His *Deputy Harvey and the Ant Cow Caper* (2005) was named a Kansas Notable Book. Some new young-adult literature is being produced by Maynard Knepp (b. 1956) and Carol Duerksen (b. 1954), as in their *Runaway Buggy* (1995). Another contribution to Kansas books for children, *Noco* (2010) by Topeka artist Justin Marable (b. 1982), contains rich drawings of the central Kansas landscape.

Romance: Wichita resident Janice Graham (b. 1947) set her first novel, *Firebird* (1998), in the Kansas Flint Hills. Since then she has continued to publish, although she does not always set her novels in the state. Rebecca Brandewyne (b. 1955) makes her home in Wichita and has published over thirty romance novels. Monica Jackson (1959–2012) was an African American romance writer. Her *Never Too Late for Love* (2000) carries the Arabesque (Black Entertainment Network) imprint.

Science Fiction: In *The Gods Hate Kansas* (1964) by Joseph Millard (1908–1989), nine meteors hit the Sunflower State and then turn into automatons that must be stopped. James Gunn (b. 1923), a winner of the Hugo Award, founded the Center for the Study of Science Fiction at the University of Kansas. His futuristic novel *Kampus* (1977) is perhaps a response to the protests and violence at the university during the mid-1970s. Karen Lee Killough (b. 1942), writing as Lee Killough, mixes genres, seemingly equally comfortable with horror, detective, and science fiction. Her first novel, *A Voice out of Ramah* (1978), is fantasy. *The Doppelganger Gambit* (1979) combines the detective novel, a futuristic Topeka, and starships. Her Bloodwalk series combines detectives and vampires, as in *Blood Hunt* (1987). Robert Chilson (b. 1945) uses the fact that Kansas was once at the bottom of the great inland sea to create

a pulp time-travel novel in *The Shores of Kansas* (1976). Warren Fine (1943–1987) published *The Artificial Traveler* (1968) when he was twenty-four years old. The book is not quite science fiction but moves from realism into dream, myth, and fantasy. David Ohle is the author of *Motorman* (1972), *The Age of Sinatra* (2004), and *The Pisstown Chaos* (2007). See SCIENCE FICTION AND FANTASY.

Lesbian and Gay Fiction: Mysterious Skin (1995) by Scott Heim (b. 1966) is the only novel of growing up homosexual in Kansas, providing a view of what it means to be unique in sexual preference, taste, and experience in a state typically seen as quintessentially, even relentlessly, "normal." His later novels are *In Awe* (1997) and *We Disappear* (2008).

Religious Literature: Charles Sheldon (1857–1946) wrote serial fiction to deliver as his weekly sermons at what is now Central Congregational Church in Topeka. One series, titled *In His Steps* (1896), became a best-selling novel and posed the still-popular question "What would Jesus do?" HAROLD BELL WRIGHT (1872–1944), also a minister, wrote *That Printer of Udell's* (1903) in Pittsburg, also first delivered as a series of sermons. Wright later became famous for *The Shepherd of the Hills* (1907), which is still performed as a play in Branson, Missouri.

For his *Elmer Gantry* (1927), (HARRY) SINCLAIR LEWIS (1885–1951) came to Kansas City to research the narrowness of evangelical religion. The first part of that novel is set in Kansas, where Elmer Gantry attends Terwilliger College, perhaps based on Ottawa University in Ottawa, Kansas.

Graphic Novels: Ande Parks (b. 1964) drew on several sources for his graphic novel *Capote in Kansas* (2005), a Kansas Notable Book in 2006. His *Union Station* (2004) is about the 1933 massacre involving a shootout between criminals and the FBI in Kansas City, Missouri.

Folklore: VANCE RANDOLPH (1892–1980) was born in Pittsburg and went on to become a leading folklorist, particularly of the Ozarks. *Hedwig* (1935) is his novel about a young woman coming of age. David Dary (b. 1934) writes folklore in such books as *The Buffalo Book* (1974), *True Tales of Old-Time Kansas* (1984), and *Cowboy Culture: A Saga of Five Centuries* (1989). After years of research,

William Trogdon (b. 1939), writing as WIL-LIAM LEAST HEAT-MOON, created an in-depth historical, biographical and geographic examination of Chase County, in the heart of the Flint Hills, in his *PrairyErth (a deep map)*.

Health-Related Literature: Because Kansas is home to the Menninger Clinic, founded by Karl Menninger and his brothers in 1925, the state has also developed a literature that portrays mental illness and institutions. Karl Menninger's father was an early Topeka physician, and his mother, Flo Menninger (1863–1945), wrote *Days of My Life* (1939), recounting life in the state in the late nineteenth century. Karl Menninger was a brilliant psychiatrist whose *The Human Mind* (1930) was followed by four more books about human psychology that spoke to a popular audience. *Dear Dr. Menninger: Women's Voices from the Thirties* (1997), edited by Howard Faulkner (b. 1945) and Virginia Pruitt (b. 1943), consists of correspondence from his column, "Mental Hygiene in the Home," in the *Ladies' Home Journal*. Faulkner and Pruitt also edited two volumes of *The Selected Correspondence of Karl A. Menninger* (1989).

Harriet Lerner came to Topeka to work at the Menninger Clinic and wrote best-selling books that explained Bowen Family Systems therapy to a wide audience. *The Dance of Anger: A Woman's Guide to Changing the Patterns of Intimate Relationships* (1985) was followed by five more "dance" books, as well as a collection of her advice columns, *Life Preservers: Staying Afloat in Love and Life* (1996). A later book is *Marriage Rules: A Manual for the Married and the Coupled Up* (2012).

Topeka's Washburn University was the birthplace of art therapy; there, early pioneer Mary Huntoon studied the effect of doing art in a psychiatric environment. Art literally saved Elizabeth "Grandma" Layton (1910–1993), who began self-portrait contour drawing at age sixty-seven after struggling for years with chronic depression. Her life and art are chronicled in *Through the Looking Glass: Drawings by Elizabeth Layton* (1984) and *The Life and Art of Elizabeth "Grandma" Layton* (1995) by Don Lambert (b. 1950).

Printing and Journalism: The first newspaper in Kansas was the *Siwinowe Kesibwi* (*Shawnee Sun*), introduced by mis-sionary Jotham Meeker (1804–1855) in 1835 and printed for nearly a decade for the Indians at Shawnee Baptist Mission. Meeker carried a printing press with him when he entered Kansas in 1833 and printed the first book in Kansas, *Delaware Prime and First Book* (1834). The first English-language newspaper in Kansas was the Democratic, pro-slavery *Kansas Weekly Herald* in Leavenworth, first published on September 15, 1854. Others soon followed, such as the *Herald of Freedom*, a free-state newspaper in Lawrence, first published on October 21, 1854.

As in any newly established territory in the Midwest, newspapers were abundant. A good source for Kansas territorial newspapers is the website of the Kansas State Historical Society, a major organization founded by the Kansas Editors' and Publishers' Association in 1875 to save historical records, particularly newspapers. As a result, that institution has a collection of newspapers touted as one of the most comprehensive in the nation.

Some of the earliest names in Kansas journalism include Marshall Murdock (1837–1908), founder of the *Wichita Eagle* in 1872, and his son Victor Murdock (1871–1945), its longtime editor. Henry Allen (1868–1950), of the *Wichita Beacon* and the *Topeka State Journal*, was also governor of Kansas. Edgar Watson Howe of the *Atchison Globe* was a Kansas H. L. Mencken. W(illiam) Y(ost) Morgan (1866–1932) made the *Hutchinson News* an important paper. Noble Prentiss (1839–1900) worked on a number of Kansas newspapers and wrote *A Kansan Abroad* (1878). His *History of Kansas* (1899) was used for years in Kansas schools. See NEWSPAPER JOURNALISM.

Many early journalists were also writers of literature, from verse to sketches to novels. William Allen White, for example, wrote fiction but also won a Pulitzer Prize twice for columns appearing in his *Emporia Gazette*. The most famous of those was about the death of his daughter, Mary White (ca. 1904–1917). His many collections of short fiction read as much like journalism as they do like short stories, being sketches of small-town life. Typical of those is *In Our Town* (1906). Thomas A. McNeal (1853–1942) was a journalist and publisher who wrote *When*

Kansas Was Young (1922). Walt Mason (1862–1939) was a longtime employee of the *Emporia Gazette.* His musings were popular and resulted in books that he called "prose poems," one of which was simply titled *Uncle Walt* (1910). Arthur Capper (1865–1951) was the founder of Capper Publications and served as Kansas governor and U.S. senator.

William Lindsay White (1900–1973), son of William Allen White and a journalist in his own right, wrote a significant novel, *What People Said* (1938), directly based on the Finney bond scandal that rocked Kansas. Ronald Finney and White were boyhood friends. Nelson Antrim Crawford (1888–1963) was the editor of *Household Magazine,* a Capper publication, and also wrote two novels, *A Man of Learning* (1928) and *Unhappy Wind* (1930). Clyde M. Reed (1871–1949) was the publisher of the *Parsons Sun* and also served as Kansas governor and U.S. senator. Rolla Clymer (1888–1977), "the Sage of the Flint Hills," editor of the *El Dorado Times* for over half a century, wrote affectionately about small-town life; his poem "The Majesty of the Hills" won him the popular designation "Poet Laureate of the Flint Hills." Zula Bennington Greene (1895–1988) found herself in Kansas by the 1920s. During the Great Depression she secured a berth at the *Topeka Daily Capital* and then the merged *Topeka Capital-Journal* as "Peggy of the Flint Hills." *Skimming the Cream* (1983) collects fifty years of her popular columns. Her autobiography, edited by poet Eric McHenry, is *Peggy of the Flint Hills: A Memoir* (2012). A later columnist, Cheryl Unruh (b. 1959), associated with the *Emporia Gazette,* has collected her columns into a book, *Flyover People: Life on the Ground in a Rectangular State* (2010).

Vivien Sadowski (1930–2004) worked her way up to publisher and editor of the *Abilene Reflector-Chronicle.* In 1994 she became the first woman president of the Kansas Press Association. Bruce H. Thorstad (b. 1946), a western novelist, wrote about early Kansas journalism in *The Wichita Times* (1992).

The Kansas Professional Communicators began as Kansas Press Women in 1941 and was open to "factual writers." Now open to men as well as women and to all kinds of communicators, it is an affiliate of the National Federation of Press Women and holds an annual conference each spring.

Crane and Company of Topeka was one of the earliest publishers of books by Kansans, books about Kansas, and bibliographies of Kansas writing. However, this legacy has not been well studied, and the books are difficult to find outside special collections. The University Press of Kansas, though not as regionally active as Oklahoma and Nebraska university presses and for the most part eschewing fiction and poetry, nevertheless publishes a range of books centered on the Kansas environment, Kansas figures, and Kansas culture.

Emanuel Haldeman-Julius, with his wife, Marcet, began publishing the Little Blue Books in 1919, striving for inexpensive paperback books that would constitute "a University in Print," including classics of Western literature from the Greeks to Shakespeare and Voltaire. But the Haldeman-Juliuses also published regional work concerning Kansas history and biography, social issues like the Scopes monkey trial, and Margaret Sanger on birth control. They persuaded Will(iam James) Durant (1885–1981) to write popular PHILOSOPHY; the result was the widely popular *The Story of Philosophy* by Will and Ariel Durant.

Woodley Press was founded in 1980 by writer and Washburn University professor Robert Lawson (1928–2013) to print the literary work of writers close to Bob Woodley (d. 1976), who taught creative writing at Washburn University. After publishing books by Topeka-area writers—Eleanor Bell's *Flights through Inner Space* (1980), Larry McGurn's *The Printer, and Other Stories* (1981), and *4* (1982) by Thomas C. Kennedy (b. 1943)—the press expanded its mission to publication of contemporary literature for a statewide audience by writers who might benefit from a first book to help launch their careers. Some of those writers, such as Thomas Fox Averill, Denise Low (b. 1949), and James P. Girard (b. 1944), have gone on to publish books in wider venues. The Woodley Press has thirty-five books available through its website.

Watermark Books of Wichita was founded by Bruce Jacobs in 1977 and became a literary publishing venture in 1988, with

Gaylord Dold (b. 1947) as editor. The press published dozens of books before stopping the venture, but at least a dozen titles remain available on its backlist. Sunflower University Press of Manhattan, later bought by KS Publishing, has published a significant number of nonfiction titles about the state.

The Washburn University Center for Kansas Studies has dedicated itself to reprinting classic and contemporary texts of value to the classroom. Important classics include *Dust* (1921) and *Short Works* (1992) by Marcet and Emanuel Haldeman-Julius; *As Grass* (1994) by Edythe Squier Draper; *The Kansas Poems* (1982) by Kenneth Porter; and Bruce Cutler's *A West Wind Rises* (1962). The more contemporary poems of Steven Hind are in three volumes, *That Trick of Silence* (1990), *In a Place with No Map* (1997), and *The Loose Change of Wonder* (2006). The novellas and short stories of Robert Day are printed in *Speaking French in Kansas* (1989). Some of these books are available electronically on the Center for Kansas Studies website.

Beginning in 1872, the literary journal *Kansas Magazine* was the voice of Kansas. Although its nineteenth-century manifestation lasted only a few years, a revival beginning in 1933 oversaw the creation of a Kansas literary voice. Langston Hughes, Karl (Augustus) Menninger (1893–1990), Kenneth Wiggins Porter, and William Allen White were among the contributors. Published annually and featuring ART along with poetry, fiction, and essays, *Kansas Magazine* is still important to any discussion of Kansas literary culture as it developed in the twentieth century. In 1965 *Kansas Magazine* morphed into *Kansas Quarterly,* which became the finest literary magazine in Kansas as edited by W. R. Moses, Harold Schneider, and Ben Nyberg. Once voted among the top ten nonpaying literary magazines in the United States, *Kansas Quarterly* ceased publication in 1993.

The *Harp,* published in Larned in the mid- to late 1920s, was edited by poet May Williams Ward with help from Nora B. Cunningham in 1927–1928. *Cottonwood* began in the early 1970s as the literary magazine of the Department of English at the University of Kansas. Often edited by students, among the first being Robert Day, and publishing regional work, it has also reached outside Kansas. Early work by Denise Low, Harley Elliott, Thomas Fox Averill, Robert Day, and Steven Hind appears in the magazine. At one time *Cottonwood* published book-length manuscripts.

Naked Man was a relatively short-lived magazine published by graduate student Michael Smetzer (b. 1950) when he was in the English Department at the University of Kansas. Another Lawrence magazine, *Tellus,* was edited by Stephen Bunch (b. 1949) between 1978 and 1988. Bunch's later collection of poetry is *Preparing to Leave* (2011).

Tansy started as a bookstore and then became both a magazine and a press run by John Moritz (1946–2007) of Lawrence. Moritz, a poet in his own right, published the work of experimental poets like Kenneth Irby (1936–2015), who practices projective verse, with "line" breaths and physical speech as form. Irby's *To Max Douglas* (1974) is important for understanding Lawrence in the 1960s. For a representative sampling of his work, see *The Intent On: Collected Poems, 1962–2006* (2009).

The *Little Balkans Review,* focusing primarily on the lore of southeastern Kansas, was edited by poet and librarian Gene DeGruson (1932–1997). DeGruson's collection of poetry, *Goat's House* (1986), had the same focus. The *Little Balkans Review* operated from 1980 to around 1989 and was revived by poet Al Ortolani and others in the fall of 2009.

Midwest Quarterly was first published in 1959 and is housed at Pittsburg State University. Although it is primarily a scholarly journal, it runs a creative issue each summer. The journal has featured work by Kansans on regional subjects and tributes to Kansas writers like William Stafford and Jonathan Holden and has published some of the finest new work by emerging Kansas writers. *Flint Hills Review,* a yearly literary magazine published by Emporia State University, began in 1996. *Ark River Review* was the literary magazine at Wichita State University during the 1970s and 1980s. *Coal City Review,* first published in 1989, is edited by poet Brian Daldorph (b. 1958). The review also serves as a press, publishing, for example, *Bird's Horn* (2007) by Kevin Rabas (b. 1974), a collection of jazz-inspired poetry. Rabas has also published *Lisa's Flying Electric Piano* (2009).

Kansas State Federal Writers' Project: *Kansas: A Guide to the Sunflower State* was written by the Federal Writers' Project of the Works Progress Administration for the state of Kansas and was published as part of the American Guide Series in 1939. The second book to come out of this federal project was *Lamps on the Prairie: A History of Nursing in Kansas,* sponsored by the Kansas State Nurses' Association and published by William Allen White's Emporia Gazette Press in 1942. The complete papers of the Federal Writers' Project of Kansas are housed at Wichita State University.

Kansas Literary Awards and Literary Societies: In 2005 Kansas instituted the position of poet laureate, whose recipients were selected by a panel of the Kansas Arts Commission; Jonathan Holden, Denise Low, and Caryn Mirriam-Goldberg (b. 1959) have each served. Now defunct, the Kansas Arts Commission also gave Literary Fellowships and Governor's Arts Awards to writers. The reconfigured Kansas Center for the Book makes yearly Kansas Notable Book designations, honoring fifteen to twenty books by or about Kansas each year. The Kansas Center for the Book once sponsored the Kansas Book Festival (now produced through the Governor's Office as a project of First Lady Mary Brownback), as well as a statewide reading program, Kansas Reads.

Each year since 1953 the schoolchildren of Kansas have chosen a book to receive the William Allen White Award. A selection committee of Kansas educators and librarians nominates books, and children read and vote. In the category of picture books, the Bill Martin, Jr., Award from the Kansas Reading Association honors that children's book author. Born in 1916, Martin died in 2004.

Kansas has had a number of literary societies. The oldest continuing literary society in Kansas, the Kansas Authors Club, began in Topeka in 1904. The most prominent early member was George P(ierson) Morehouse (1859–1941), who oversaw the founding and early growth of the organization. Early members included William Allen White, Emanuel and Marcet Haldeman-Julius, and Karl Menninger. Margaret Hill McCarter was the first woman president of the organization. The Authors Club website contains archives and historical notes.

The Kansas Association of Writing Programs was active in the 1980s and early 1990s as a loose-knit affiliation of creative-writing teachers from across the state. It held annual conferences each spring.

SELECTED WORKS: The most iconic Kansas books and staples of American popular culture are L. Frank Baum's *The Wonderful Wizard of Oz* and Laura Ingalls Wilder's *Little House on the Prairie,* two books that not only define home but explore the Kansas *love* of home while celebrating American virtues of determination, independence, and self-reliance.

William Stafford, undoubtedly the most important and most revered of Kansas poets, echoes the importance of home in the beginning of "One Home" in *The Way It Is: New and Selected Poems* (1998), saying, "Mine was a midwest home—you can keep your world." This posthumously published volume is an excellent introduction to his work. An earlier poet, Kenneth Wiggins Porter, is also crucial to the Kansas tradition, as seen in *The High Plains* (1938) and *No Rain from These Clouds* (1946) and in his encouragement to other poets to focus on the concrete idea of place.

Other poets important to the Kansas tradition are Jonathan Holden, author of *The Sublime* (1996), and the Kansas Poet Laureate for 2007–2009, Denise Low; her book *Words of a Prairie Alchemist: The Art of Prairie Literature* (2006) combines interviews, poetry, essays, and criticism. During her tenure as Poet Laureate she created broadsides about Kansas poets that were collected into a book, *To the Stars: Kansas Poets of the Ad Astra Poetry Project* (2009). Later books are *Ghost Stories of the New West* (2010) and *Natural Theologies: Essays about Literature of the New Middle West* (2011). The third Poet Laureate designated by the now-defunct Kansas Arts Commission (the functions of that agency are now part of what is called Creative Industries, which also houses the Kansas Film Commission) was Caryn Mirriam-Goldberg. During the

150th-anniversay celebration—the sesqui-centennial of Kansas—she created a poetry blog that was then published as *Begin Again: 150 Kansas Poems* (2011). Mirriam-Goldberg is also the author of *Landed* (2009). *The Divorce Girl* (2012), a novel, is not set in Kansas. Wyatt Townley (b. 1954) served as Kansas Poet Laureate for 2013–2014. Eric McHenry (b. 1972) was appointed for 2015–2017.

Kansas literature often deals with the important element of the environment. The classic pioneering saga, John Ise's *Sod and Stubble* (1936), was written by an economics professor who saw pioneering as an economic venture; any romance in the experience was offset by its punishing cost in human terms. No discussion of the state's literature can be complete without an understanding of this book. Another critical portrait of Kansas pioneering is *Dust* (1921) by Marcet and Emanuel Haldeman-Julius. It can be read as a critique of capitalism's habit of treating land, people, and animals solely as commodities.

Since Kansas is a state of many environments, occupations, attitudes, and even cultures, those who understand the differences and tensions among them are essential to Kansas literature. William Allen White's first collection of fiction, *The Real Issue* (1899), exhibits a deep understanding of the several Kansas environments and the challenges they represent. Paul I. Wellman's Kansas novels, including *Bowl of Brass* (1944), *The Walls of Jericho* (1947), *The Chain* (1949), and *Jericho's Daughters* (1956), may not be lasting literature, but they are essential to understanding the mid-twentieth-century Kansas mind-set.

Race is significant in Kansas, from the "Bleeding Kansas" fight against slavery to the Exoduster movement, the first black migration from the South after the failure of Reconstruction, and to *Brown v. Board of Education,* which resulted in the landmark U.S. Supreme Court decision to desegregate America's schools. Three Kansas African American writers show the reality of the black experience in Kansas: Langston Hughes in *Not without Laughter* (1930), Gordon Parks in *The Learning Tree* (1963), and Maxine Clair in *Rattlebone* (1994).

Kansas attitudes toward social class are found in Joseph Stanley Pennell's *The History of Rome Hanks and Kindred Matters* (1944) and Laura Moriarty's *The Center of Everything* (2003), which present views of the Kansas small town. Add to those Evan S. Connell Jr.'s important American novels of suburban life, *Mrs. Bridge* (1959) and *Mr. Bridge* (1969), and Whitney Terrell's *The King of King's County* (2005), essential to understanding class, race, and white flight from Missouri into Kansas.

Finally, playwright William Inge wrote in all his plays, including his screenplay for *Splendor in the Grass* (1961), of have-nots and the small-town prejudices against them. Kansas short stories also provide an acute picture of life in Kansas, among them William Allen White's *The Real Issue* (1899) and *In Our Town* (1906), Edythe Squier Draper's *As Grass* (1994), Robert Day's *Speaking French in Kansas* (1989), and Thomas Averill's *Ordinary Genius* (2004).

The state's literature is perhaps best presented in ANTHOLOGIES. Most helpful to an understanding of Kansas literary traditions are *Sunflowers: A Book of Kansas Poems* (1916), edited by Willard Wattles; *Contemporary Kansas Poetry* (1927), edited by Helen Rhoda Hoopes; and *Kansas Poets* (1935), edited by the House of Harrison Publishing Company.

The next push to understand the state's literature came with the centennial celebration of statehood. *Kansas Renaissance* (1961), the first multigenre anthology, was edited by Warren Kliewer and Stanley Solomon.

The Kansas Art Reader (1976), edited by Jonathan Wesley Bell, is very useful for understanding the cultural history of the state. One essay, "Kansas Poetry," by Lorrin Leland (b. 1950), became the basis for a fine review of Kansas poetry, Leland's *The Kansas Experience in Poetry* (1978), which collects poems that best help readers understand the history and culture of Kansas.

FURTHER READING: *What Kansas Means to Me: Twentieth-Century Writers on the Sunflower State* (1991), edited by Thomas Fox Averill, is a collection of analysis, essays, and poetry appreciative of the hold Kansas has had on so many of its citizens.

Bibliographies: Early bibliographies, such as William Carruth's *Kansas in Literature* (1900), were published by Crane and Company of Topeka. Benjamin Willis Fuson took on the mammoth project of creating *Centennial Bibliography of Kansas Literature, 1854–1961* (1961). Fuson also produced an updated supplement, *Kansas Literature of the Nineteen Sixties* (1970). Work on Kansas literature is being done extensively on the internet. Useful websites exist for various organizations, including the Map of Kansas Literature, the Center for Kansas Studies, Kansas Poets, Poetry of Kansas, and the Kansas Center for the Book, including an Author Database Index. Denise Low maintains a blog featuring poems and analysis of poets she admires.

For the study of early Kansas printing and publishing, *Check List of Kansas Imprints, 1854–1876,* published by the American Imprints Inventory of the Works Progress Administration in 1939, is the standard work. *Kansas Imprints, 1854–1876: A Supplement* (1958), compiled by Lorene Anderson Hawley and Alan W. Farley, adds over four hundred items to the earlier publication. *Jotham Meeker, Pioneer Printer of Kansas, with a Bibliography of the Known Issues of the Baptist Mission Press at Shawanoe, Stockbridge, and Ottawa, 1834–1854* (1930) by Douglas C. McMurtrie and Albert Allen is a detailed study of the first Kansas printer and his productions.

Libraries and Repositories: Significant collections of Kansas literature are found in many places throughout the state. The Axe Library at Pittsburg State University has a significant collection, especially of the Little Blue Books published by Emanuel Haldeman-Julius. The Spencer Research Library at the University of Kansas and the University Archives contain books, manuscripts, letters, and other personal papers important to the study of Kansas literature. Wichita State University has extensive collections and archives, and Kansas State University has some holdings pertinent to the literary history of the state, as do Emporia University and Fort Hays State University. Public libraries, especially those in Wichita, Larned, Salina, Pittsburg, and Topeka and Shawnee County all have valuable collections of local literature. Fort Scott Community College opened the Gordon Parks Center for Culture and Diversity in 2004 to honor Parks's life and continue his work. In 2010 the author of this entry do-

nated half of his Kansas Library to Mabee Library on the Washburn University campus to start the Thomas Fox Averill Kansas Studies Collection. Eventually, his entire collection, including manuscripts, letters, posters, and other literary ephemera, will be on display and available to researchers.

THOMAS FOX AVERILL   WASHBURN UNIVERSITY

KANSAS CITY

Kansas City, Missouri, was incorporated as the Town of Kansas in 1850, and officially became Kansas City with a state-approved charter in 1853. Across the state line and the Kansas River, Kansas City, KANSAS, is a separate, smaller municipality.

Area: 318 square miles
Population (2010 census): 459,787

OVERVIEW: Kansas City history can be segmented into four eras: western settlement and conflict; economic expansion and cultural crossroads; the "wide-open town" in the Prohibition years and later, when the city earned a reputation for political corruption, crime, booze, and jazz; and the postwar metropolis. The details and textures of each can be found in a wide variety of books, from nineteenth-century DIME NOVELS to solid regional histories and personal memoirs revealing the complex dynamics that led to the making of a prosperous, though racially divided, metropolitan area. Thematically, many of those books investigate the nature of a place whose identity has always been in flux, a city in the middle of the nation where East meets West and North meets South in a flurry of mixed signals and meanings.

Literary representations of Kansas City can be found in the writings of well-known

© Karen Greasley, 2014

travelers, who contribute outsiders' perspectives. Writers ranging from Walt Whitman (1819–1892) to Jack Kerouac (1922–1969) have left brief accounts of their passage through Kansas City. Whitman, writing of western travels in *Specimen Days* (1882), was unimpressed with the demeanor of the women he watched outside a store window. Kerouac astutely questioned why the city center had disconnected itself from the Missouri River, a geographic complaint that can still be made today.

HISTORY AND SIGNIFICANCE: Kansas City has long been a national crossroads. Its location at the confluence of the Missouri and Kansas Rivers signifies its two-state identity. The period of western settlement and conflict can be traced to the early eighteenth century, when frontier voyages by French explorers began European and Euro-American interest in the area's prairie lands and river bluffs that were already home to numerous Native American tribes, including the Osages, the Missouris, the Kansas, the Otoes, and the Iowas. The Lewis and Clark expedition of 1804–1806 and the subsequent arrival of French traders accelerated the momentum toward settlement.

Fort Osage, a nearby trading outpost on the Missouri River, contributed to the traffic, and in the early decades of the nineteenth century the waterfront became commercialized and settled. In 1850 the Town of Kansas was incorporated, and trading posts in nearby Westport and Independence outfitted fortune seekers and migrants launching their wagons on the Santa Fe, California, Mormon, and Oregon Trails. Along with its part in settlement of the West, the Kansas City area was the focal point of a border war that raged after passage of the Kansas-Nebraska Act in 1854 and culminated in the Civil War.

The late nineteenth century initiated the period of economic expansion and cultural crossroads. Through decades of boom and bust Kansas City grew into a centrally located agricultural market and hub for diverse industries. The arrival of the cattle market and railroads, using an important river crossing built in 1869, furthered the crossroads activity, and the city took on the reputation of a civic-minded community somewhat more tolerant than most of urban

grit and temptation. Community leaders with eastern educations and experience traveling to Europe fostered interest in art, music, and theatre. Lumber barons, bankers, and business leaders forged a can-do attitude in the twentieth century, symbolized by the heroic rebuilding of the city's Convention Hall, which had burned to the ground just three months before the scheduled Democratic National Convention of 1900.

Civic development progressed with significant contributions from powerful and corrupt influences, especially the political machine controlled in succession by brothers James and Tom Pendergast. The latter helped Kansas City become by the 1920s and 1930s a "wide-open town" where all sorts of sin and hedonistic pursuits could be found, often to a jazz soundtrack. By 1941, after Pendergast's arrest and imprisonment, city leaders began to reform the political culture and lay the groundwork for the postwar metropolis. A diverse economy helped the city prosper in the second half of the century. The coming of the federal highway system in the 1950s sparked a significant exodus from the city's core to the suburbs, magnifying racial divisions, creating a period of urban decline, and forging a substantial, well-heeled sprawl. As the twenty-first century began, both entities known as Kansas City entered a new period of economic development, and Kansas City, MISSOURI, especially experienced a prosperous and creative rekindling of its urban core.

The recorded history of Kansas City began in 1724 with the journals of a French voyageur, military commander of Missouri River territory, and ad hoc ambassador to the region's Indian tribes, Étienne de Véniard, Sieur de Bourgmont (1679–1734). His party ventured to the Kansa village, upriver from what is now Kansas City, and beyond on a mission to maintain tribal alliances and forestall Spanish advances. Bourgmont's journals can be found in *Bourgmont: Explorer of the Missouri, 1698–1725* (1988) by Frank Norall (1918–2001). Various editions of the published journals of the Corps of Discovery expedition led by Meriwether Lewis (1774–1809) and William Clark (1770–1838) also contain brief accounts of several days of exploration as they passed through the area on and along the Missouri River in 1804 and 1806. The novel *The Melancholy Fate of Capt. Lewis* (2007) by Michael Pritchett (b. 1961) investigates the troubled psyche of Lewis through the metafictional device of a Kansas City writer's work and life.

Kansas City's importance as the epicenter of the mid- to late nineteenth-century struggle over slavery and the westernmost front of the Civil War is captured in several major novels. Russell Banks (b. 1940) portrays abolitionist John Brown (1800–1859), who spent several turbulent years across the state line in Kansas, in *Cloudsplitter* (1998), a novel written from the perspective of Brown's son Owen. Brown, as seen through the eyes of a former slave child, is the subject of the comic and trenchant *The Good Lord Bird* (2013) by James McBride (b. 1957), winner of the National Book Award. The brutal war between Kansas Jayhawkers and Missouri Bushwhackers provides the background and emotional landscape of novels such as *Woe to Live On* (1987) by Daniel Woodrell (b. 1953), filmed by director Ang Lee as *Ride with the Devil* (1999), and *Enemy Women* (2003) by a Missouri native, Paulette Jiles (b. 1943). G. P. Schultz (b. 1948) imagines the post–Civil War years in the bustle of Kansas City's waterfront settlement in the novel *Gully Town: A Novel of Kansas City* (1990). Lenore Carroll (b. 1939) creates a fictional portrayal of a prominent Kansas City madam in *Annie Chambers* (1990).

Myths and legends about Jesse (Woodson) James (1847–1882) and other western outlaws were encouraged by journalists of the day and fueled by innumerable dime novels of the late nineteenth century and beyond. The James gang's long presence in Kansas City and nearby towns made them local folk heroes and admired villains. Typical of the regional interest in James is *Death of a Legend* (1954) by Will Henry, a pseudonym of Henry Wilson Allen (1912–1991), a prolific Kansas City–born writer of popular western fiction. Henry's novel, which skewers the heroic myth of Jesse James, also appeared in later years retitled *The Raiders* (1974). Ron Hansen (b. 1947) explores the dynamics of the Jameses and their circle and depicts post–Civil War Kansas City in his novel *The Assassination of Jesse James by the Coward Robert Ford* (1983). Susan Dodd (b. 1946) narrates the story from the perspective of the James boys' mother, Zerelda, in *Mamaw* (1988).

(William Frederick) Buffalo Bill Cody (1846–1917), (James Butler) Wild Bill Hickok (1837–1876), (Phoebe Ann Mozee) Annie Oakley (1860–1926), and other colorful figures of the late nineteenth century West, all of whom passed through the city, also populate countless pulp novels and works of history. Courtney Ryley Cooper (1886–1940), onetime Kansas City journalist and noted crime reporter, collaborated with Cody's widow, Louisa (Maud) Frederici Cody (1843–1921), on *Memories of Buffalo Bill* (1919) and produced a biography, *Annie Oakley, Woman at Arms* (1927), among other books.

Newspaper publisher William Rockhill Nelson introduced his *Kansas City Star* in 1880 and by the early twentieth century had built it into one of the most respected papers in the nation. Nelson's influence on journalism and the city was enormous, a story best captured in a biography written by the newspaper staff and published soon after his death, *William Rockhill Nelson: The Story of a Man, a Newspaper and a City* (1915). The *Star* contributed to the literary culture of the city by excerpting popular novels and employing a brand of ambitious, itinerant journalists who could quote Fyodor Dostoyevsky (1821–1881) in a crime story or stuff notes in their desks toward the proverbial great American novel.

ERNEST (MILLER) HEMINGWAY (1899–1961) got his professional writing start at the news-

Main Street, Kansas City, Missouri, 1900–1910. Detroit Publishing Co., ca. 1905. Image courtesy of the Library of Congress

paper. He joined the staff as an eighteen-year-old high school graduate in late 1917 and stayed for six and a half months until he left to serve in Italy with the Red Cross ambulance corps. Hemingway's legacy as a forefather of hard-boiled and noir fiction can be traced to the period he spent covering Kansas City crime and other subjects. Two Hemingway short stories, "A Pursuit Race" (1927) and "God Rest You Merry, Gentlemen" (1933), explicitly reflect his Kansas City experience, and although his novels and nonfiction books are set elsewhere, several include remembrances of Kansas City. In *Across the River and into the Trees* (1950), for example, Hemingway's protagonist, the Colonel, promises his Italian lover that when they visit Kansas City, they will stay in the Muehlebach Hotel, "which has the biggest beds in the world," and "pretend we are oil millionaires" (241). In *A Moveable Feast* (1964), his posthumously published memoir, Hemingway, while having wine and oysters with a Paris friend, records a lurid passing thought about Kansas City prostitutes, whom he encountered or heard about from emergency-room doctors and police.

Other *Star* alumni produced fictional accounts reflecting their time in Kansas City. In *Sam* (1939) John Selby (1897–1980) imagines the life of a newspaper publisher not unlike Nelson, whose legend he got to know on the newspaper's staff. Paul I. Wellman (1898–1966), a prolific novelist and Hollywood screenwriter, includes vivid Kansas City scenes in *The Walls of Jericho* (1947), which is largely set in a fictional Kansas town. Marcel Wallenstein (1893–1986) returned to Kansas City's tawdry noir precincts of the early 1920s in *Tuck's Girl* (1953).

One of the most significant and controversial works of fiction inspired by Kansas City came from (HARRY) SINCLAIR LEWIS (1885–1951). Lewis spent a few months in the city, attending church services and befriending pastors, to write *Elmer Gantry* (1927), a tale of religious hypocrisy. Lewis portrayed Gantry as a small-town Kansan who becomes an evangelical preacher with a penchant for sin. Although the settings are fictional, readers had no trouble associating the Bible Belt satire with Kansas City because of Lewis's gift for publicity. Lewis

was convinced that his research locale was "a kind of crossroads for American religious practices where he would find all the material he needed," as the scholar Mark Schorer noted in the afterword to the 1967 Signet Classic edition (420). The novel caused a social stir across the nation and civic hand-wringing in Kansas City.

Kansas City's literary record also exists in nonfiction, especially in notable works of history and memoir. A comprehensive, illustrated overview of the city's history from its origins to the present can be found in *Kansas City: An American Story* (1999) by Rick Montgomery (b. 1960) and Shirl Kasper (b. 1948). The story of the city's domination by the Pendergast political machine is best told in a midcentury history, *Tom's Town: Kansas City and the Pendergast Legend* (1947; reprinted 1986) by William M. Reddig (1900–1968), a onetime reporter and book critic. Reddig's book has since been joined by *Truman: The Rise to Power* (1986) by Richard Lawrence Miller (b. 1949), which connects future president Harry S. Truman's early political life to the Pendergast machine in unprecedented detail, and *Pendergast!* (1997) by Lawrence H. Larsen (b. 1931) and Nancy J. Hulston (b. 1944). Other significant accounts of this important period include the monumental biography *Truman* (1992) by David McCullough (b. 1933) and *Truman and Pendergast* (1999) by Robert H. Ferrell (b. 1921).

ST. LOUIS journalist Harper Barnes (b. 1937) crafted a fictional portrait of Pendergast's wide-open town of the 1930s. His novel, *Blue Monday* (1991), focuses on the jazz clubs and people who gave the city its musical reputation and wraps it in a tale of political corruption and racial division. Similarly, Lise McClendon (b. 1952) set a crime novel against the fabric of the jazz era with *One O'Clock Jump* (2001) and a second one, *Sweet and Lowdown* (2002), in World War II Kansas City. Bandleader (William) Count Basie (1904–1984) portrays the city's jazz scene from a musician's perspective in his autobiography, *Good Morning Blues* (1985), co-written with Albert Murray (1916–2013). Numerous musicians recall the Kansas City jazz heyday in two oral histories: *The World of Count Basie* (1980) by Stanley Dance (1910–1999) and *Goin' to Kansas City* (1987) by Nathan W. Pearson Jr. (b. 1951). Jazz historians

Frank Driggs (1930–2011) and Chuck Haddix (b. 1951) recount the era in *Kansas City Jazz: From Ragtime to Bebop—A History* (2005).

Director Robert Altman (1925–2006) was born and grew up in Kansas City, where he set and filmed his first movie, *The Delinquents* (1956). Altman's film *Kansas City* (1996) is set in 1934 amid the city's lively jazz scene and corrupt politics. The same era provides the backdrop for *Pete Kelly's Blues* (1955), directed by (John) Jack (Randolph) Webb (1920–1982) and featuring a musical performance by Ella Fitzgerald (1917–1996); *City Heat* (1984), directed by Richard Benjamin (b. 1938) and starring Clint(ton) Eastwood (Jr.) (b. 1930); and Eastwood's film portrait of Charlie Parker, *Bird* (1988).

A rare fictional view of African American life in pre–World War II Kansas City appears in a posthumously published novel by Vincent O. Carter (1924–1983), a black writer who, like James Baldwin (1924–1987), resettled in Switzerland in the early 1950s. His novel *Such Sweet Thunder* (2003) portrays an urban boyhood from the 1920s to the 1940s, based on Carter's experience. Another fictional portrait of African American life, this one set in the 1950s in Kansas City, Kansas, is *Rattlebone* (1994), a story collection by Maxine Clair (b. 1939). Clair followed that with a novel inspired by schoolteachers she knew in her hometown, *October Suite* (2001).

A matched pair of novels by EVAN S(HELBY) CONNELL (JR.) (1924–2013), *Mrs. Bridge* (1959) and *Mr. Bridge* (1969), portrays upper-crust residents of Kansas City in the 1920s and later, the world in which the author grew up. Connell's episodic, fictive mosaics suggest a certain degree of autobiography or memoir. The two novels served as the basis for director James Ivory's film *Mr. and Mrs. Bridge* (1990), starring Paul Newman (1925–2008) and Joanne Woodward (b. 1930). Kansas City's influence on Connell, who departed early for points west, can be found in his other work, including *At the Crossroads* (1965), a collection of stories.

Kansas City as a shaper of character and lives is addressed much more directly in autobiographies and memoirs by a wide variety of writers. Frenchman André Maurois, born Émile Salomon Wilhelm Herzog (1885–1967), spent six months in 1946 as a visiting lecturer at the University of Kansas City, now the University of Missouri–Kansas City, and devoted one hundred pages to that stay in *From My Journal: United States; 1946* (1947). He put the city on a kind of literary high bar when he pronounced it "one of the loveliest cities on earth" (22).

Among those who lived in Kansas City for longer periods, EDWARD DAHLBERG (1900–1977) depicted the "luckless" world of his single mother and his boyhood in the first decades of the twentieth century in *Because I Was Flesh: The Autobiography of Edward Dahlberg* (1964). He had covered similar territory in his first novel, *Bottom Dogs* (1929).

The journalist and historian Richard Rhodes (b. 1937) writes of his World War II–era boyhood as an orphan in *A Hole in the World* (1990). He also reports on other aspects of Kansas City in an earlier essay collection, *The Inland Ground: An Evocation of the American Middle West* (1970), and he set his novel of a crumbling marriage, *Holy Secrets* (1978), in Kansas City of the 1970s. Journalist and humorist Calvin (Marshall) Trillin (b. 1935) has written frequently of Kansas City in his travel and food reportage and in memoirs, including the book-length account of his father, *Messages from My Father* (1998). Hilary Masters (1928–2015), son of the poet EDGAR LEE MASTERS (1868–1950), recalls his Kansas City childhood in *Last Stands: Notes from Memory* (1982; reprinted 2004).

Bruce Lowery (1931–1988), an expatriate in Paris, wrote a coming-of-age story about a thirteen-year-old Kansas City boy tormented by a harelip scar. It first appeared in French as *La cicatrice* (1960) and won the Prix Rivarol in 1961. An English edition, *Scarred*, was published in 1961. Two novels by one-time Kansas Citian Jetta Carleton (1913–1999) have come to light, one long out of print and one never before published: *The Moonflower Vine* (1962; reprinted 2009) and *Clair de Lune* (2012). Both are set in rural Missouri, although Kansas City, especially in the latter, is a landmark and a destination for her characters. Race and race relations serve as themes of two contemporary novels about Kansas City's divisive history. Whitney Terrell (b. 1967) reveals secrets of the country-club set in *The Huntsman* (2001) and explores the consequences, racial and otherwise, of real estate development and sprawl in *The King of King's County* (2005). Thomas Fox Averill (b. 1949) invents and populates a southwestern-style restaurant in Kansas City, complete with recipes, in his novel *Secrets of the Tsil Café* (2001).

Among the contemporary writers whose stories or novels reflect their connection to Kansas City are James C(ourtwright) McKinley (Jr.) (1935–2015), Catherine Browder Morris (b. 1944), and Elaine Kagan (b. 1942); mystery writers Nancy Pickard (b. 1945), Joel Goldman (b. 1952), and Linda Rodriguez (b. 1947); and the best-selling author Gillian Flynn (b. 1971). No substantial anthology of Kansas City writing has been compiled, but local writers are represented in small-press roundups such as *Exposures: Essays by Missouri Women* (1997), edited by Sarah Morgan (b. 1953); *Missouri Short Fiction* (1985), edited by Conger Beasley Jr. (b. 1940); and *These and Other Lands* (1986). Fourteen writers with local connections, including Woodrell, Morris, and Pickard, are included in a short-story collection, *Kansas City Noir* (2012), edited by Steve Paul (b. 1953).

Notable poets with roots in Kansas City and work that reflects their memories of life there include Melvin B. Tolson (1898–1966), Edward Sanders (b. 1939), and James (Vincent) Tate (1943–2015). The city today has a small but lively poetry community, fostered over the years by university faculty and small literary presses. *New Letters,* which began as *University Review,* published at the University of Missouri–Kansas City since the 1930s, has earned a reputation for publishing high-quality poetry, fiction, and essays. Contemporary poets who published widely distributed books while based in Kansas City include David Ray (b. 1932), Michelle Boisseau (b. 1955), Mbembe Milton Smith (1946–1982), Wayne Miller (b. 1976), Kevin Prufer (b. 1969), H. L. Hix (b. 1960), and Gloria Vando Hickok (b. 1936). Hickok also launched a literary journal, *Helicon Nine,* and publishing house of the same name featuring poetry and fiction by women. Local poets have been collected in two volumes from a small press, both titled *Kansas City Out Loud* (1975, 1990). See PRINTING AND PUBLISHING.

SELECTED WORKS: Presettlement accounts of the river, terrain, and Indian tribes of Kansas City and vicinity can be found in the 1724 journal of Étienne de Véniard, Sieur de Bourgmont, published in *Bourgmont: Explorer of the Missouri, 1698–1725* (1988), by Frank Norall and posted online at the nebraskastudies.org website. An all-in-one historical survey of the city from settlement through the twentieth century appears in *Kansas City: An American Story* (1999) by journalists Rick Montgomery and Shirl Kasper. Notable fiction of the nineteenth-century border-war era and the post–Civil War exploits of Jesse James includes Daniel Woodrell's *Woe to Live On* (1987), Ron Hansen's *The Assassination of Jesse James by the Coward Robert Ford* (1983), and Susan Dodd's *Mamaw* (1988), a novel told from the point of view of Zerelda (Elizabeth Cole) James (Simms Samuel) (1825–1911), the outlaw's mother.

Among the best historical accounts of the Pendergast era and political machine are *Tom's Town: Kansas City and the Pendergast Legend* (1947) by William Reddig, *Truman: The Rise to Power* (1986) by Richard Lawrence Miller, and David McCullough's magisterial biography *Truman* (1992). Ernest Hemingway captured some of the city's seedier undercurrents encountered during his Kansas City newspaper apprenticeship in 1917–1918 in two short stories: "A Pursuit Race," about a drug-addled bicycle-race advance man, and "God Rest You Merry, Gentlemen," involving two doctors, a reporter, and a young man intent on self-mutilation. See NEWSPAPER JOURNALISM.

Such Sweet Thunder (2003), a posthumously published novel by Vincent O. Carter, takes readers inside the consciousness of an African American boy growing up in the 1920s and 1930s. Autobiographical books by Calvin Trillin, especially *Messages from My Father* (1998), and Richard Rhodes's *A Hole in the World* (1990), Evan S. Connell's episodic Kansas City novels *Mrs. Bridge* (1959) and *Mr. Bridge* (1969), and Whitney Terrell's *The King of King's County* (2005) portray aspects of the social scene at midcentury, from Rhodes's portrayal of troubled orphanhood to Connell's and Terrell's depictions of high society. Rhodes's essay collection *The Inland Ground* (1970) offers astute perceptions of culture and other topics in the 1960s. Because of its multiplicity of voices, *The World of Count Basie* (1980), an oral history gathered by Stanley Dance, remains one of the livelier accounts of the Kansas City jazz era. *Kansas City Jazz* (2005) by Chuck Haddix and Frank Driggs is extensively researched and detailed.

FURTHER READING: A statewide literary survey, published at midcentury, can be found in an article, "Missouri: The Mother of Authors," by Thomas Layne Sanders in the *Wilson Library Bulletin* 31.10 (June 1957): 791–95. Some commentary on Kansas City literature appears in *Encyclopedia of the Great Plains* (2004), edited by David J. Wishart, although its geographic scope is much wider, and *The American Midwest: An Interpretive Encyclopedia* (2007), edited by Richard Sisson, Christian K. Zacher, and Andrew R. L. Cayton, which includes Kansas City–referenced entries on Hemingway, LANGSTON HUGHES (1902–1967), and others. One of the most detailed accounts of Ernest Hemingway's journalistic training in Kansas City appears in *The Apprenticeship of Ernest Hemingway: The Early Years* (1954) by Charles A. Fenton (1919–1960). Most later biographies of Hemingway rely on the Kansas City pages of Carlos Baker's *Hemingway: A Life* (1969). Matthew J. Bruccoli (1931–2008) collected many of Hemingway's unsigned *Kansas City Star* articles in *Ernest Hemingway, Cub Reporter* (1970).

Essential collections of Kansas City literature and archival material are located in the Kansas City Public Library's Missouri Valley Room. Other major collections exist at the State Historical Society of Missouri Research Center–Kansas City and the Special Collections Department of the Miller Nichols Library at the University of Missouri–Kansas City, which includes the Marr Sound Archives, a vast collection of jazz and other recordings. The Missouri Center for the Book has compiled an online directory of authors and other resources.

STEVE PAUL   *KANSAS CITY STAR*

LATINO/LATINA LITERATURE

OVERVIEW: Latino/Latina literature in the United States has gained a large popular readership and extensive treatment by scholars and teachers. Although attention has focused mainly on writing from regions other than the Midwest, places with larger Latino/Latina populations, the Midwest has a large and long-standing population of Latinos and Latinas, the terms for men and women, respectively, with greater currency in the humanities than "Hispanic." "Latino/a" is used for gender inclusiveness. Midwestern Latino/as, whether native-born U.S. citizens or immigrants from Mexico, the Caribbean, Central America, or South America, have created a diverse body of writing. By turns local and international in subject and stylistic derivation, written mostly in English but also in Spanish and in combinations of the two languages, Latino/a literature is a significant and growing part of the Midwestern literary heritage.

Midwestern Latino/a literature before the 1970s remains a relatively unexplored field of inquiry. Thereafter, a distinct movement is evident, beginning with writing associated with the Mexican American civil rights movement. As Latino/as come to represent an ever-greater portion of the Midwestern population, the stature of their literature will continue to rise.

After briefly considering Spanish exploration, this entry treats the literature of three groups: Mexican Americans, or Chicano/as, as some contemporaries refer to themselves; Puerto Ricans; and other Latino/as, with origins in the Caribbean, Central America, and South America. One should be careful about generalizing about these distinct groups. Some themes, however, recur: migration, family and community, biculturalism, and resistance against prejudice and assimilation. Many Latino/as integrate Spanish into English-language poetry and prose. To a greater degree than most U.S. writers, they draw on international literatures, especially Latin American. To establish further these aspects of Midwestern Latino/a literature, this entry also considers writing by Latino/as from other U.S. regions who have lived temporarily in the Midwest, Latino/as in the Midwest who write in Spanish, and major Latin American writers who have written about the Midwest.

HISTORY AND SIGNIFICANCE: The Latino/a presence in the Midwest predates the United States by more than two centuries if we consider early Spanish explorers such as Francisco Vásquez de Coronado (1510–1554), who in 1541 led the first European expedition to present-day KANSAS. Accounts by Coronado and his men appear in *The Journey of Coronado, 1540–1542* (1904) by George Parker Winship (1871–1952), who also translated *The Narrative of the Expedition of Coronado by Castañeda* (1896) by Pedro de Castañeda de Nájera (b. ca. 1512). See also Juan de Oñate's account of his 1601 expedition to the same area, translated by George P. Hammond (1896–1993) and Agapito Rey (1892–1997) in *Don Juan de Oñate: Colonizer of New Mexico* (1953). These historically important texts feature early descriptions of the prairie, the vastness of which struck the explorers as strange and even frightening.

Scholars need to examine records of Spanish officials and traders in Louisiana Territory, claimed by Spain in 1763. Accounts may emerge of incursions into MICHIGAN (1781) and WISCONSIN (1797), when Spanish forces took British forts in support of the fledgling United States. Diaries and other texts by nineteenth-century Latino/a residents of MISSOURI, Kansas, and other states may also fill in the historical record.

Mexican Americans: The early modern history of Midwestern Latino/a literature awaits rediscovery in Spanish-language periodicals published in the early 1900s. During that period Mexicans and Mexican Americans from Texas and the Southwest first arrived in large numbers, attracted by work on railroads, on farms, and in factories. Prose, poetry, and song lyrics by those migrants await translation and publication.

Corridos, ballads recounting the heroism of ordinary folk, have long been sung in Midwestern migrant communities, as well as along the U.S.-Mexico border. Scholars have collected many of relevance to Midwestern literary studies. Versions of "Kiansis" (ca. 1870), the earliest known corrido, depict the fabled cattle drives from Texas to Kansas. Other corridos, as María Herrera-Sobek points out in *Northward Bound: The Mexican Immigrant Experience in Ballad and Song* (1993), "describe the migrant experience from Texas to other states," including "ILLINOIS, Michigan, MINNESOTA, and the Midwest in general" (90). These songs are a corrective to the egalitarian pastoral myth of the Midwest. Mexican laborers, who did not figure in that myth, sang songs like "Versos de los betabeleros," about the beet harvest in Michigan, to reinforce group solidarity. Although many Mexican Americans made lives of the seasonal peregrination to and from the Midwest, others found work in DETROIT, CHICAGO, and other cities, where they formed communities that persist to this day. Some Midwestern migrant lyrics and stories have been collected, but most have yet to be recovered.

From the Mexican American migrant experience emerged the classic novel *... Y NO SE LO TRAGÓ LA TIERRA/ ... AND THE EARTH DID NOT DEVOUR HIM* by Tomás Rivera (1935–1984), published simultaneously in Spanish and English in 1971. Born in Texas into a family of migrant workers, Rivera worked half the year in the upper Midwest from childhood until early adulthood. As an adult, Rivera devoted himself to Chicano/a advancement as a professor of Spanish and as the first Mexican American chancellor in the University of California system. A foundational text in Chicano/a letters, *... y no se lo tragó la tierra* consists of thirteen stories and thirteen vignettes, set both in Texas and the Midwest, documenting migrants in the early 1950s. The novel depicts a boy's coming of age during a year that Rivera does not render chronologically, but in a manner representative of the boy's family and community.

Other texts by Rivera also reflect Midwestern experience, such as his essay "The Great Plains as Refuge in Chicano Literature" (1982), which includes reminiscences of his early days in Midwestern states. Among four stories intended for inclusion in *... y no se lo tragó la tierra* but omitted by the book's editors were four set in the Midwest, "On the Road to Texas: Pete Fonseca," "The Harvest," "Eva and Daniel," and "Zoo Island." These were subsequently published in *The Harvest* (1989) and *The Complete Works* (1992). Another story, "The Salamanders," involves a migrant family in Minnesota. Many of Rivera's poems are ambiguous in setting, whether in the Midwest or in Texas. One poem's title implies that the ambiguity is intentional, that the author claimed both places, just as he considered both Spanish and English his native tongues: "The Rooster Crows en Iowa y en Texas."

Rivera's novel emerged during a period of cultural awakening. The Chicano/a civil rights movement of the 1960s and 1970s gave Mexican Americans not only a new name ("Chicano") but also a myth of common origins and destiny: Aztlán, a vision of a Mexican American homeland in the southwestern United States and an ethnic identity rooted in Native American heritage. Political organizing on the basis of Chicano/a nationalism brought Midwestern Chicano/as in contact with counterparts in other regions and encouraged literary production.

Chicano/a nationalism, however, has its critics in the Chicano/a community. In "Exiles, Migrants, Settlers, and Natives: Literary Representations of Chicano/as and Mexicans in the Midwest," *Midwestern Miscellany* 30 (Fall 2002): 27–45, Theresa Delgadillo argues that the movement "tended to exaggerate cultural homogeneity and to enshrine the Southwest as the sole site of Chicano/a unity" (27–28). Midwestern Chicano/as countered that bias by forming outlets for their work, which had been ignored almost as much by Latino/as in other regions as by colleges and major publishers. Just as Chicago periodicals like *POETRY: A MAGAZINE OF VERSE* nurtured Anglo writers in the early twentieth century, small presses and journals founded during the heyday of Chicano/a nationalism promoted Midwestern writers of all Latino/a backgrounds.

One journal evolved into the oldest and largest publisher of Latino/a literature. Nicolás Kanellos and Luis Dávila published the first issue of *Revista Chicano-Riqueña* at Indiana University Northwest in Gary in 1973. The journal, renamed the *Americas Review* in 1986, published creative and scholarly writing until 1999. Kanellos founded Arte Público Press in 1979 and in 1980 accepted a position at the University of Houston, where Arte Público still thrives. Its projects include the Recovering the U.S. Hispanic Heritage series, which reprints early texts and studies of such works. A selection from the *Americas Review* appears in *The Floating Borderlands: Twenty-Five Years of U.S. Hispanic Literature* (1998), edited by Lauro Flores.

Norma Alarcón (b. 1943), who worked on *Revista Chicano-Riqueña,* founded *Third Woman,* a journal for women of color. *Third Woman* ran from 1981 to 1989 and, except for the final volume, was published at Indiana University Northwest. It drew on feminist theory in linking Latina Midwesterners, Latinas elsewhere in the United States, and Latin American women. The journal's first issue, "Of Latinas in the Midwest" (1981), included writers from several states. Since moving to Berkeley, California, Alarcón has directed Third Woman Press, which publishes literature and studies of gender and ethnicity.

Carlos Cumpián (b. 1953) edits Chicago's MARCH/Abrazo Press as part of the Movimiento Artístico Chicano, founded in 1975 by artist José González. Tia Chucha Press was founded in 1991 by LUIS J. RODRÍGUEZ (b. 1954) as the imprint of the Guild Complex, created in 1989 to promote multicultural arts in Chicago.

Chicago produced SANDRA CISNEROS (b. 1954), whose *THE HOUSE ON MANGO STREET* (1984) is one of the most popular Latino/a texts. Consisting of short pieces narrated by a Mexican American girl in a poor Chicago neighborhood, *The House on Mango Street* subverts conventions of the bildungsroman to fit the experience of a working-class woman of color. The fictional street of the title embodies Chicano/as' claim to the Midwest as their rightful home, one to which they bring their own history and cultural flavor.

Most of the selections in Cisneros's *Woman Hollering Creek, and Other Stories* (1991) are set in Texas, where the author now lives. "Barbie-Q," however, is narrated by a Chicago girl, and "Eleven" and "Salvador Early or Late" suggest Cisneros's childhood in Chicago and experience teaching in the city. Cisneros also evokes Chicago in her poetry collections *My Wicked, Wicked Ways* (1987) and *Loose Woman* (1994). Her novel *Caramelo* (2002) follows a Mexican American family through three generations, from Mexico City to San Antonio and Chicago. She has also published *Have You Seen Marie?* (2012), a fable for adult readers illustrated by Ester Hernández, and *A House of My Own: Stories from My Life* (2015), a memoir in essays, occasional writings, poems, and photographs.

Chicago-born Ana Castillo (b. 1953) writes fiction that suggests ideas about gender, ethnicity, and spirituality addressed directly in her poems and essays. *The Mix-*

quiahuala Letters (1986) consists of letters between a Mexican American poet in Chicago and an Anglo artist in New York. The protagonist of *Sapagonia* (1990) migrates from a mythical Latin American country to France, Spain, and then Chicago. *Peel My Love like an Onion* (1999) follows a Chicana flamenco dancer in Chicago's gypsy subculture. The stories in *Loverboys* (1996) confound conventional notions of sexual orientation. Castillo's poems appear in such books as *My Father Was a Toltec, and Selected Poems* (1995). She has published a book for adolescents, *My Daughter, My Son, the Eagle, the Dove* (2000); a play, *Psst . . . I Have Something to Tell You, Mi Amor* (2005); and a study of Chicana feminism, *Massacre of the Dreamers: Essays on Xicanisma* (1994). The essay "Illinois" appeared in *These United States* (2003), edited by John Leonard (122–32). Castillo has edited or co-edited several anthologies, like the influential *This Bridge Called My Back: Writings by Radical Women of Color* (1988), with Cherríe Moraga.

Another vision of Chicago appears in *The Last Laugh, and Other Stories* (1988) and *Steeling Chicago: South Side Stories* (2014) by Hugo Martínez-Serros (b. 1930). Born in Chicago to parents from Zacatecas, Mexico, Martínez-Serros studied at the University of Chicago and Northwestern Univesrsity. He taught Spanish at Lawrence University in Appleton, Wisconsin, from 1966 to 1995. His stories take place in the Mexican section of Chicago during the Great Depression and World War II. Martínez-Serros's novel *Enamored Dust* (2013) is set in a fictional Mexican town at the time of the Mexican Revolution.

Notable Mexican American poets include Carlos Cortéz (1923–2005), born in Milwaukee but a Chicago resident after 1964. An accomplished artist in print media, Cortéz wrote in solidarity with working-class people. His poems, published in *Industrial Worker* and the books *Crystal-Gazing the Amber Fluid, and Other Wobbly Poems* (1990), *De Kansas a Califas & Back to Chicago* (1992), and *Where Are the Voices, and Other Wobbly Poems* (1997) call for resistance against exploitation, racism, and war.

One poet who benefited from mentorship by Cortéz is Carlos Cumpián, author of *Coyote Sun* (1990), *Armadillo Charm* (1996), and *14 Abriles: Poems* (2010). Cumpián spent his early years in Texas and California but

Carlos Cortéz and Carlos Cumpián, Chicago. Photo by William Barillas, 2004.

moved to Chicago with his family in 1967. His poetry is strongly urban, colloquial, and political, with a strong feeling for indigenous cultures. In his essay "Without Reservation or Passport, the Next Round Is Ours," *Rattle* 5.2 (Winter 1999): 123–32, Cumpián addresses challenges he has faced as the editor of MARCH/Abrazo Press. Other Midwestern Mexican American poets include Trinidad Sánchez Jr. (1943–2006), Rubén Medina (b. 1955), Raúl Niño (b. 1961), Brenda Cárdenas (b. 1961), and Paul Martínez Pompa (b. 1976).

Significant memoirs include those of Luis Leal (1907–2010), a celebrated scholar of Mexican and Chicano/a literatures who studied and taught at the Universities of Chicago and Illinois. Leal collaborated on two memoirs that speak of his Chicago years: *Don Luis Leal, una vida y dos culturas* (1998), with Victor Fuentes, and Mario T. Gracia's *Luis Leal: An Auto/Biography* (2000). Other memoirs include *Harvest of Hope: The Pilgrimage of a Mexican American Physician* (1989) by Jorge Prieto (1918–2001), president of the Chicago Board of Health, and *Gabriel's Fire* (2000) by Luis Gabriel Aguilera (b. 1973).

Puerto Ricans: Puerto Ricans first came in large numbers to cities like Chicago and Milwaukee in the late 1950s and early 1960s as a result of federal programs encouraging mainland migration. Midwestern Puerto Rican writers include novelist Sandra Benítez (b. 1941), who lives in Edina, Minnesota. Benítez was born Sandy Ables in 1941 to a Puerto Rican mother and an Anglo father who worked for the U.S. State Department in Mexico and then El Salvador, where Benítez spent most of her early life. She attended high school and college in northeastern Missouri while living on her grandparents' farm. At thirty-nine she started writing novels, beginning with *A Place Where the Sea Remembers* (1993), a family drama set in a Mexican fishing village. *Bitter Grounds* (1997) and *The Weight of All Things* (2001) deal with El Salvador's civil war. *Night of the Radishes* (2004) involves a Minnesota woman who travels to Mexico in search of her estranged brother.

The parents of Rane Arroyo (1954–2010) met in Chicago, each having emigrated from Puerto Rico. They lived in Lincoln Park and other North Side neighborhoods before moving to Chicago's western suburbs when Arroyo was a teenager. In his dissertation "Babel USA: A Writer of Color Rethinks the Chicago Renaissance" (1994), Arroyo examines how Chicago writers were admitted into the canon only after critics displaced their politics in favor of aesthetic issues. Arroyo published several chapbooks and books of poetry, including *The Buried Sea: New and Selected Poems* (2008), and a book of stories, *How to Name a Hurricane* (2005). Frequently alluding to popular culture as well as literature, Arroyo's writings reflect his identity as a gay man, a Puerto Rican, a Midwesterner, a teacher, and a writer. He was Director of Creative Writing at the University of Toledo.

Other Puerto Rican poets in the Midwest include Gloria Vando Hickok (b. 1936), author of *Shadows and Supposes* (2002); David Hernández (1946–2013), author of *Rooftop Piper* (1991); and Frank Varela (b. 1949), author of *Serpent Underfoot* (1993) and *Bitter Coffee* (2001).

A different side of Chicago is depicted in *My Bloody Life: The Making of a Latin King* (2000) and *Once a King, Always a King* (2003), the harrowing memoirs of the pseudonymous Reymundo Sánchez (b. 1963). Sánchez, whose mother brought him as a child to Chicago from Puerto Rico, escaped an abusive household by joining the Latin Kings, a notorious gang often as brutal toward its members as toward rivals.

Writers of Other Latin American Origins: Mexican American and Puerto Rican writers in the Midwest may turn to long-established communities for cultural solidarity and inspiration. Writers of other Latin American origins, who generally lack such ethnic networks, have maintained connections to their nations of origin and have stressed familial ties.

Beatriz Badikian (Gartler) was born in 1951 in Buenos Aires, Argentina, to an Armenian father and a Greek mother. In 1970 her parents left Argentina and settled in Chicago, where Badikian worked first as a translator and then as a teacher. Badikian's poetry, collected in *Mapmaker Revisited: New and Selected Poems* (1999), addresses exile and multinational identity from a feminist perspective. Her novel *Old Gloves: A 20th-Century Saga* (2005) is based on her family's migrations in Europe and the Americas. Her essays include "A Necessary Evil: My Love/

Omar S. Castañeda, Zacapa, Guatemala, 1991.
© Quetzil Castañeda

Hate Relationship with Translation," *Metropolitan Review* 2.1 (1999): 10–15.

Omar S(igfrido) Castañeda (1954–1997) wrote fiction for adults, adolescents, and children. Born in Guatemala and raised in Michigan and INDIANA, Castañeda completed an MFA in creative writing at Indiana University, studying under SCOTT RUSSELL SANDERS (b. 1945) and others. While teaching at Rollins College and then Western Washington University, Castañeda often traveled to Guatemala to conduct research.

Castañeda's finest work appears in two astonishing books of stories, *Remembering to Say "Mouth" or "Face"* (1993) and *Naranjo the Muse* (1997), which draw on the phantasmagoria of Edgar Allan Poe (1809–1849), Franz Kafka (1883–1924), and Jorge Luis Borges (1899–1986); South American magic realism; postmodernist metafiction; and Maya mythology. *Remembering* establishes semi-autobiographical characters and alternation between U.S. and Guatemalan settings as motifs and introduces Clowerston, Indiana, a fictional city featured in several stories.

Castañeda's Clowerston stories, such as "Shell and Bone," "Under an Ice Moon," and "Crossing the Border" in *Remembering* and "Dogs of Clowerston" in *Naranjo the Muse*, dramatize tensions between North and Central American perspectives.

Castañeda's novels, all set in Guatemala, involve Maya women caught between tradition and modernity. *Cunuman* (1987) was followed by *Among the Volcanoes* (1991) and *Imagining Isabel* (1994). Castañeda's book for children, *Abuela's Weave* (1993), illustrated by Enrique O. Sánchez, tells of a Maya girl selling traditional weavings. Although Castañeda's final novel, *Islas Coloradas*, has not appeared, an excerpt was published in *Latino Heretics* (1999), edited by Tony Diaz.

Daisy Cubias (b. 1944) left El Salvador in 1965 for New York before moving to Milwaukee in 1970. Her activism in support of Central American refugees intensified after the Salvadoran military murdered her brother, sister, and brother-in-law in the early 1980s. Her poems, collected in *Children of War / Los hijos de la guerra: Poems of Love, Pain, Hope and Determination* (1989), detail the violence of U.S.-supported governments and connect consumerism in the United States to Third World poverty. See also *Journey of the Sparrows* (1991), an adolescent novel Cubias co-wrote with Fran Leeper Buss, about a girl fleeing El Salvador for Chicago. A Spanish translation, *El viaje de los gorriones*, appeared in 1993.

The family of Achy Obejas (b. 1956) left Cuba after the 1959 revolution and settled in Michigan City, Indiana. Her journalism has appeared in Chicago gay and lesbian periodicals, the *Chicago Sun-Times*, and the *Chicago Tribune*, which carried "An Island of Harmony: Cuban-Americans in Chicago—From One Melting Pot to Another" in the *Chicago Tribune Magazine* for February 3, 2002, sec. 10: 17, 28. See also LESBIAN, GAY, BISEXUAL, TRANSGENDER, AND QUEER LITERATURE.

Obejas's books reflect her multilayered identity as a Cuban exile, a Chicagoan, and a lesbian. The stories in *We Came All the Way from Cuba So You Could Dress Like This?* (1994) feature characters rarely seen in Midwestern fiction, from gays and lesbians to HIV-positive individuals and drug users. Marked by an edgy prose style and sexual candor, the stories established geographic

Achy Obejas, 2007. Photo by Ovie Carter.
© Achy Obejas

specificity as a central element of Obejas's writing. The characters move through a Midwest given spatial dimension through descriptions of the Loop, Lake Michigan, ST. LOUIS, and other places.

Obejas's novels focus on Cuban Americans in Chicago. The narrator of *Memory Mambo* (1996) tries to understand her family's history while coping with a troubled love life and conflicts between Cubans and Puerto Ricans, homophobes and lesbians, and chauvinistic men and assertive women. Although it is less verbally audacious than Obejas's earlier books, *Days of Awe* (2001) is a significant advance in characterization and use of multiple time frames. The novel's protagonist leaves Cuba with her parents in 1959 at age two. As a young woman in Chicago, she contemplates her father's hidden Judaism, which she understands better after traveling to Cuba. *Ruins* (2008), set entirely in Cuba, concerns a married man's struggles in Havana in the 1990s.

Latino/a Visitors to the Midwest: Related study may be undertaken of Latino/a writers from other regions who have sojourned in the Midwest. These writers generally evince little awareness of Midwestern Latino/as and express feelings of isolation in the region. This is the case with the Dominican American writer Julia Alvarez (b. 1950), who considered writing a novel inspired by her husband's upbringing in rural NEBRASKA. Instead, she wrote the essay "In the Name of the Novel" in *Something to Declare* (1998), about a controversial Catholic shrine in Wisconsin. A Vermont resident who frequently returns to the Dominican Republic, Alvarez has mixed feelings about the Midwest, where she once lived. "I didn't take to it," she told interviewer Hilary McClellen in "In the Name of the Homeland," *Atlantic Online*, July 19, 2000. "It scared me, how landlocked it was, the lack of diversity, the distance from the centers of ethnicity and color." Alvarez also responded positively: "I do feel drawn to the Midwest, and I do want to go back, on paper, and explore the place that formed my husband and that has informed so much of North American culture." See also Alvarez's bilingual fable *A Cafecito Story / El Cuento del Cafecito* (2002), about a Nebraska man who decides to grow fair-trade coffee in the Dominican Republic.

Martín Espada (b. 1957), a Puerto Rican poet from Brooklyn who teaches at the University of Massachusetts, lived in Wisconsin from 1977 to 1982 while studying at the University of Wisconsin–Madison. He has written many poems set in Wisconsin, most based on his experience as a bouncer in a bar, a night clerk at a transient hotel, a caretaker at a primate laboratory, and an attendant at mental institutions. These poems appear in several books, including *Trumpets from the Island of Their Eviction* (1987), *Rebellion Is the Circle of a Lover's Hands* (1990), and *Imagine the Angels of Bread* (1996). Although not all of the Wisconsin poems mention the state by name, they comprise a significant segment of Espada's work, respected for its narrative thrust and advocacy on behalf of working-class immigrants.

Gustavo Pérez Firmat (b. 1949) left Florida in 1973 to pursue a doctorate at the University of Michigan. In his memoir *Next Year in Cuba: A Cubano's Coming-of-Age in America* (1995; revised 2000), Pérez Firmat speaks of "both entering and escaping exile" in the Midwest, since he yearned for Miami just as his father "had always longed for Cuba." Ann Arbor represented the beginning of an "irreversible voyage of discovery" in which the graduate library, rather "than a safe haven . . . turned out to be a perilous, unpredictable book world" (191–92).

Luis J. Rodríguez grew up in Los Angeles but established his reputation in Chicago. His memoir *Always Running: Gang Days in L.A., La Vida Loca* (1993) concludes in Chicago, where he relocated in 1985. *Poems across the Pavement* (1989) focuses on urban struggles for social justice. The one poem unquestionably set in his adopted city, "Walk Late Chicago," evokes a night at a homeless shelter. Although the poems in *Concrete River* (1991) are mostly set in Los Angeles, they consistently reveal the fact of their composition in the Midwest. Rodríguez begins "City of Angels," for example, by musing that "somewhere out there, lies the city." This places him in Chicago, looking west to Los Angeles, a city he describes as "awaiting [his] return" (110). Chicago served as neutral ground where Rodríguez could evaluate his past and develop as a writer and activist. His Chicago poems portray a transitional period, as in "Lips," a poem in *Concrete River* that finds him sitting "in Chicago traffic / waiting for a light to change" (78).

Chicago's cultural life is a central theme in *Trochemoche* (1998), Rodríguez's third book of poetry. Chicago figures in poems like "Notes of a Bald Cricket," which describes how bringing poetry to the streets saved Rodríguez from despair for a life of social commitment. See also Rodríguez's *América Is Her Name* (1998), a children's book illustrated by Carlos Vasquez, set in the Pilsen barrio of Chicago. Although Rodríguez moved back to Los Angeles in 2000, his time in Chicago significantly affected his writing.

Spanish-Language Writers: Latin American immigrants in the Midwest have written notable literature in Spanish. Chicago, in particular, is a center of Spanish-language publication. Although they are relatively neglected by English-only readers and, for the most part, by literati in their home countries, Spanish-language writers in the Midwest are steadily developing an audience for their work. The increasing bilingualism of the United States makes these writers bellwethers of major cultural and demographic changes already underway.

Mario Andino is the pen name of Mario Lopez (b. 1934), a journalist from San Felipe, Chile, who has lived in Chicago since 1961. His novels, all with Chilean settings, are *Oratorio para herejes* (1989), *El capo y las amazonas* (1991), *Prohibido para mayores* (1992), *La loba* (2000), *Actos de misterio* (2000), and *Angel del más allá* (2003). Andino's other books are *Fuera de juego* (2001), an adolescent

novel; *Cuentos para el siglo XXI* (1997), a collection of short stories; and *Versos para no versados* (1995), a collection of poetry.

Ricardo Armijo (b. 1959) emigrated to the United States from Nicaragua in 1980 and has lived in Chicago since 1991. His stories and essays have appeared in journals in the United States, Mexico, and Nicaragua. More than most Chicago-based Spanish-language writers, Armijo writes about Midwestern experience, particularly immigrants confronting materialism in urban environments. In 2005 he was awarded the first John Barry Award for New Fiction in Spanish from Chicago.

José Castro-Urioste (b. 1961) was born in Montevideo, Uruguay, but grew up in Tacna, Peru. He has taught Latin American literature at Purdue University–Calumet since 1998. Castro-Urioste's book of stories, *Desnudos a medianoche* (1996), was followed by the novellas *Aún viven las manos de Santiago Berríos / ¿Y tú qué has hecho?* (2001). His play *Ceviche en Pittsburgh* appears in the anthology *Dramaturgia Peruana* (1999), which Castro-Urioste edited with Roberto Ángeles. His essay "Más allá del último acto: Reflexiones sobre el teatro latino de Chicago" appeared in *Pie de página* 2 (2004): 10–14, and "Una historia poco (re)presentada: Tres grupos teatrales latinos de Chicago" in *Teoria y practica del teatro hispánico* 18.36 (November 2003): 167–76.

Alfonso Díaz (1943–1999) grew up in Riosucio, a town in northwestern Columbia, where his stories are set. The bilingual volume *Recordando a Alfonso: Cuentos, poemas y recuerdos de Alfonso Díaz* (2002), edited by Henry Russell, includes testimonials by fellow writers.

Born in Punta Arenas, Chile, in 1945, Alejandro Ferrer served in the government of President Salvador Allende. He was arrested after the 1973 coup and was confined at the Chilean military's notorious prison camp on Magallanes Island. Since moving to Evanston, Illinois, in 1976, he has taught in the Chicago Public Schools and at Saint Augustine University. His short stories, collected in *Cuentos de la Patagonia* (1996), are set in Chile.

Born in Mexico City in 1957, poet Olivia Maciel came to Chicago in 1989 and completed a doctorate in Romance Languages at the University of Chicago in 2004. She has published four bilingual volumes: *Más salado que dulce / Saltier than Sweet* (1995), *Limestone Moon / Luna de cal* (2000), *Filigrana encendida / Filigree of Light* (2002), and *Sombra en plata / Shadow in Silver* (2005). She writes in Spanish and collaborates with translators. Maciel's poetry has a metaphysical emphasis; its graceful syntax and imagery suggest kinship with the French symbolists and international strains of modernism, including Spanish poets like Juan Ramón Jiménez (1881–1958) and Latin Americans like Octavio Paz (1914–1998).

Bernardo Navia (b. 1967), originally of Chillán, Chile, took graduate degrees in Spanish at the University of Illinois–Chicago and now teaches at DePaul University. He has published a book of philosophical poetry, *Doce muertes para una resaca* (2000), and stories in Chilean, Puerto Rican, and U.S. journals.

Graciela Reyes (b. 1944), from Buenos Aires, Argentina, has been a linguist and professor of Spanish at the University of Illinois–Chicago since 1979. In addition to her scholarship, she has published four books of poetry, *Poemas para andar por casa* (1982), *Reflexiones de una mujer sola* (1982), *Que la quiero ver bailar* (1988), and *Poems* (1991), as well as four books of stories, *El caracol mensajero* (1994), *Dos historias de mujeres* (1999), *Cuentos de amor* (2000), and *Cuentos para niños chicos y grandes* (2001).

Armando Romero (b. 1944), from Cali, Columbia, has taught at the University of Cincinnati since 1983 and has published fiction, poetry, and scholarship. During the 1960s he was associated with the literary movement known as *el nadaismo*. He left Columbia in 1967 and traveled for five years throughout the Americas and Europe, living for a time in Chicago. Drawing on that experience, the novel *La rueda de Chicago* (2004) is at once a love story, a critique of U.S. society, and an appreciation of U.S. art and literature, especially Chicago blues and writers like NELSON ALGREN (b. Nelson Ahlgren Abraham, 1909–1981) and SAUL (C.) BELLOW (1915–2005). Many of the poems in Romero's *De noche el sol* (2004) evoke CINCINNATI and the Ohio River.

Leda Schiavo (b. 1935), from Buenos Aires, Argentina, was a professor of Spanish at the University of Illinois–Chicago from 1976 to 2004. In addition to scholarly studies, Schiavo has published *Con las debidas licencias* (2000), a bilingual edition of her poetry, as well as individual stories and *La diosa del volcán* (1997), co-written with Graciela Reyes.

Febronio Zatarain was born in 1958 in Concordia, a town in the Mexican state of Sinaloa. In 1989 he came to Chicago, where he has played an important role in Spanish-language literary journals. Zatarain teaches Spanish at Truman College in Chicago and also works in journalism. His two books of poetry are *Faltas a la moral* (1991) and *Desesperada intención* (1994).

Spanish-language journals in Chicago have included *Tres Américas: Revista cultural* (1989–1996); *Fe de Erratas* (1992–1995); *Cardinal* (1993); *Abrapalabra* (1995); *Zorros y erizos* (1997–1998); *Tropel* (1999–2000); *Arena Cultural,* the cultural magazine of the newspaper *La Raza* (1999–2002); and *Contratiempo* (since 2003). Publishers of books in Spanish include Ediciones Grupo Esperante, Tres Américas, and Black Swan / El Cisne Negro Ediciones.

Latin American Commentators: Additional perspectives may be sought in works by Latin American authors who have contemplated the Midwest. Although they do not constitute Latino/a literature in the sense here discussed, such writings offer valuable insights into Midwestern culture. Three examples follow, from works by José Martí (1853–1895), Pablo Neruda (1904–1973), and Gabriel García Márquez (1928–2014).

Martí, the Cuban journalist, poet, and patriot who spent fifteen years in exile, mainly in New York, wrote three essays on the 1886 Haymarket Square bombing and the subsequent trial of anarchists implicated in the deaths of Chicago policemen. Whereas the first two, written during the trial, convey the same xenophobia as other accounts of the time, the third, published more than a year after the trial, expresses solidarity with the anarchists and criticizes the conditions that fostered the violence. The essays appear in *Obras Completas* (1963): "Grandes motines de obreros" (1886) in volume 10 (443–64), "El proceso de los siete anarquistas de Chicago" (1886) in volume 11 (55–61), and "Un drama terrible: La guerra social en

Chicago" (1887) in volume 11 (333–56). Esther Allen translated the last as "Class War in Chicago: A Terrible Drama," in *José Martí: Selected Writings* (2002): 195–219.

Chilean Nobel laureate Neruda often employs Chicago as a synecdoche for the United States and ABRAHAM LINCOLN (1809–1865) as a national archetype. Neruda's pan-American epic *Canto general* (1950) includes two elegies to Lincoln. In "El viento sobre Lincoln" ("The Wind over Lincoln") the president's tomb in Springfield, Illinois, symbolizes the struggle for racial equality. The title of "Que despierta el leñador," a section of *Canto general,* has been translated as "Let the Woodcutter Awaken" and, to clarify the allusion to Lincoln, as "I Wish the Railsplitter Would Wake Up." Neruda addresses "The Woodcutter" to a personified United States, with the Midwest as its apotheosis. He praises landscapes of Wisconsin, Missouri, and Illinois, along with farmers, workers, and writers like ROSS (FRANKLIN) LOCKRIDGE JR. (1914–1948), as representative of what is best about the United States. These aspects contrast with U.S. foreign policy, which supported Latin American dictatorships and engineered the overthrow of democratically elected governments, as in Chile in 1973. Jack Schmitt, a Latin Americanist originally from Minnesota, published a complete English version of *Canto general* in 1991. ROBERT (ELWOOD) BLY (b. 1926), also from Minnesota, rendered the first part of "The Woodcutter" in a Midwestern idiom. See Bly's *Neruda and Vallejo: Selected Poems* (1971), which also features an essay on Neruda and a 1966 interview. Bly's volume reflects the impact Spanish-language poets had on him and other Midwesterners, such as JOHN (IGNATIUS) KNOEPFLE (b. 1923) and JAMES WRIGHT (1927–1980), whose translations are included. Bly's translation also appears in *The Poetry of Pablo Neruda* (2003), edited by Ilan Stavans.

Finally, the rural Midwest is glimpsed in Columbian Nobel laureate García Márquez's epic *Cien años de soledad* (1967), translated by Gregory Rabassa as *One Hundred Years of Solitude* (1970). At the end of the novel, a young Columbian becomes the first in his family to abandon the ancestral town. Consistent with the novel's magic realism, Álvaro buys "an eternal ticket on a train that never stopped traveling" (408). The train takes him through North America, evoked in poetic images of Louisiana, Kentucky, Arizona, and finally the Midwest. The region is symbolized by "the girl in the red sweater painting watercolors by a lake in Michigan who waved at him with her brushes, not to say farewell but out of hope, because she did not know that she was watching a train with no return passing by" (408). The episode serves as an homage to the United States that García Márquez knew through literature, the country of SAMUEL LANGHORNE CLEMENS (1835–1910), writing as Mark Twain, and ERNEST (MILLER) HEMINGWAY (1899–1961). It also indicates that for García Márquez, as for Martí, Neruda, and other Latin Americans, the Midwest represents something essential about the United States. Such passages suggest that literate Latin Americans understand the United States better than most *estadounidenses* understand their neighbors to the south. America is a hemisphere, not a single nation, and what we refer to as "American" or "Midwestern" is at once more provincial and more cosmopolitan than we tend to acknowledge.

The work of Latino/a writers, be they native-born Midwesterners, migrants, immigrants, visitors from other U.S. regions, or foreign exiles, similarly expands our understanding of this part of the Americas. As the Midwest and the entire nation become increasingly multicultural and multilingual, Latino/a literature is an important source for understanding what we have been and what we are becoming.

SELECTED WORKS: Major works of Midwestern Latino/a fiction include Tomás Rivera's *. . . y no se lo tragó la tierra / . . . And the Earth Did Not Devour Him* (1971), Sandra Cisneros's *The House on Mango Street* (1984), Ana Castillo's *The Mixquiahuala Letters* (1986), Hugo Martínez-Serros's *The Last Laugh, and Other Stories* (1988), Omar S. Castañeda's *Remembering to Say "Mouth" or "Face"* (1993), Achy Obejas's *We Came All the Way from Cuba So You Could Dress Like This?* (1994), and Armando Romero's *La rueda de Chicago* (2004). Key volumes of poetry include Carlos Cumpián's *Armadillo Charm* (1996), Luis J. Rodríguez's *Trochemoche* (1998), Beatriz Badikian's *Mapmaker Revisited: New and Selected Poems* (1999), Olivia Maciel's *Limestone Moon /*

Luna de cal (2000), and Rane Arroyo's *The Buried Sea: New and Selected Poems* (2008).

Although a comprehensive anthology of Midwestern Latino/a writing has yet to appear, several volumes set a precedent. Some compile the work of seasoned writers, while others are populist in their inclusiveness. The latter type is exemplified by Joy Hintz's *An Anthology of Ohio Mexican American Writers* (1974) and *Mexican American Anthology II: Poetry, Prose, Essays, Stories, Songs, Dichos, Corridos, Art* (1976). Both document migrant labor in OHIO during the heyday of Chicano/a nationalism. The first includes exhortations to ethnic pride, speeches by labor leader César (Estrada) Chávez (1927–1993), and children's writings. The second volume, more professionally printed and bound, features sections on culture, history and identity, migrant experience, and protest. Of particular literary interest are lyrics and corridos, found on pages 278–310 and 321–26, about migrant experience in Ohio.

Several anthologies deal with Midwestern states and cities. These include *A Confluence of Colors: The First Anthology of Wisconsin Minority Poets* (1984), edited by Angela Lobo-Cobb, and *I Didn't Know There Were Latinos in Wisconsin: Three Decades of Hispanic Writing* (2014), the third anthology of Wisconsin Latino/Latina writing edited by Oscar Mireles. The "Nosotros Anthology" edition of *Revista Chicano-Riqueña* 5.1 (1977), edited by David Hernández, collects work by Chicago-based writers. A strong selection of Chicago poets appears in *Shards of Light / Astillas de luz* (1998), edited by Olivia Maciel. The Latino Writers Collective of Kansas City, Missouri, published *Primera Página: Poetry from the Latino Heartland* (2008) and *Cuentos del Centro: Stories from the Latino Heartland* (2009).

Women's anthologies redress past editorial imbalances and highlight Latina experience in the Midwest. See *Winter Nest: A Poetry Anthology of Midwestern Women Poets of Color* (1987), edited by Lobo-Cobb, and *Between the Heart and the Land / Entre el corazón y la tierra: Latina Poets in the Midwest* (2001), edited by Brenda Cárdenas and Johanny Vázquez Paz.

The late John Barry, the first scholar to focus on Spanish-language literature of Chicago, edited two anthologies, *Voces en el viento: Nuevas ficciones desde Chicago* (1999) and

Into the Wind's Eye: Latino Fiction from the Heartland / En el ojo del viento: Ficción latina del Heartland (2004). The first collects stories in the original Spanish, whereas the second also features Barry's English translations.

Ray González has edited anthologies such as *Muy Macho: Latino Men Confront their Manhood* (1996), with essays by Arroyo, Castañeda, Espada, and Rodríguez, and *Under the Pomegranate Tree: The Best New Latino Erotica* (1996), with selections by Castañeda and Brenda Cárdenas.

FURTHER READING: One important center for Latino/a studies is the Julian Samora Research Institute at Michigan State University. The institute's reports appear on its website. Periodicals include *Latino Studies*, a peer-reviewed journal at the University of Illinois–Chicago since 2003, and the bilingual *Diálogo*, at DePaul University since 1996.

For early Spanish history in the present-day Midwest, consult *The Hispanic Presence in North America from 1492 to Today* (1987; updated edition 1999) by Carlos M. Fernández-Shaw. On Coronado's expedition, see Herbert T. Bolton's *Coronado: Knight of Pueblos and Plains* (1949) and Bernard DeVoto's *The Course of Empire* (1952).

Mexican Americans: Mexican American histories include *Al Norte: Agricultural Workers in the Great Lakes Region, 1917–1970* (1991) by Dionicio N. Valdes and *Mexicans in the Midwest, 1900–1932* (1996) by Juan R. García. Zaragosa Vargas deals with social class and ethnicity in *Proletarians of the North: A History of Mexican Industrial Workers in Detroit and the Midwest, 1917–1933* (1993).

Research into corridos should begin with María Herrera-Sobek's *Northward Bound: The Mexican Immigrant Experience in Ballad and Song* (1993), which includes the lyrics to "Kiansis" ("Kansas"), "Los reenganchados a Kansas" ("The Kansas Contractees"), and "Versos de los betabeleros" ("Verses of the Beetfield Workers").

In "Exiles, Migrants, Settlers, and Natives: Literary Representations of Chicano/as and Mexicans in the Midwest," *Midwestern Miscellany* 30 (Fall 2002): 27–45, Theresa Delgadillo discusses texts by southwestern Chicano/as who equate "the Midwest with exile, isolation, alienation, and assimilation" (28). She contrasts such texts with writings by Rivera, Castillo, Cisneros, and Martínez-Serros in which Chicano/as claim the Midwest as home, despite emotional and cultural ties to the Southwest and Mexico.

The scholarship on Tomás Rivera is extensive; the MLA database lists dozens of studies in several languages. The Tomás Rivera Library at the University of California–Riverside holds the author's papers. The Tomás Rivera Policy Institute, with offices in Los Angeles and New York, sponsors sociological studies of U.S. Latino/as.

On the journal *Third Woman,* see Catherine Ramírez's "Alternative Cartographies: *Third Woman* and the Respatialization of the Borderlands," *Midwestern Miscellany* 30 (Fall 2002): 47–62.

Entries on Sandra Cisneros in *Dictionary of Literary Biography* by Eduardo F. Elías in 122 (1992): 77–81 and by Cynthia Tompkins in 152 (1995): 35–41 include bibliographies of early criticism. Caryn Mirriam-Goldberg's *Sandra Cisneros: Latina Writer and Activist* (1998) is an illustrated biography. Reviews of *Caramelo* include Ilan Stavans's "Familia Faces," *The Nation* (February 10, 2003): 30. Juanita N. Heredia and Bridget Kevane interview Cisneros in *Latina Self-Portraits: Interviews with Contemporary Women Writers* (2000).

The extensive commentary on Ana Castillo is sampled in *Contemporary Literary Criticism* 151 (2002): 1–120. Sara Spurgeon's *Ana Castillo* (2004) is a biographical and critical study. Rolando Romero reviews *Last Laugh and Other Stories* by Hugo Martínez-Serros in *Hispania* 73 (September 1990): 671–72.

Marc Zimmerman's *U.S. Latino Literature: An Essay and Annotated Bibliography* (1992) includes many Midwestern writers. Zimmerman's articles include "Transplanting Roots and Taking Off: Latino Writers in Illinois," in *Writers in Illinois* (1989), edited by John Hallwas, 77–116; "Chicago and the Poets of Aztlán: The Most Forgotten of the Forgotten," *Critica: A Journal of Critical Essays* 2.2 (Fall 1990): 230–48; and "The Poetic Voice of Carlos Cortéz," in *Carlos Cortéz Koyokuikatl, Soapbox Artist and Poet: A Catalog,* edited by Victor Sorrell (2002), 86–99. Zimmerman also wrote three articles for *Dictionary of Literary Biography* 209 (1999): "Carlos Cortéz" (45–51), "Carlos Cumpián" (52–60), and "Raúl Niño" (167–69). On Trinidad Sánchez,

see Sandra Cisneros's review of *Poems by Father and Son* in *Tonantzin* 1.4 (June/July 1984): 17, and Gilbert Garcia's "The Poet's Poet" in *San Antonio Current,* August 2, 2006, 18.

Kathleen Leal Unmuth profiles Luis Leal in "Un Hombre de Letras," *Northwestern* 6.2 (Winter 2003): 22–25. Three essays on Leal appear in *Palabra: Revista de Literatura Chicana* 4–5.1–2 (Spring–Autumn 1982–1983). Bob Herguth's "Dr. Jorge Prieto" appears in the *Chicago Sun-Times,* December 4, 1989, 16. James Janega's informative obituary of Prieto appears in the *Chicago Tribune,* August 23, 2001, 2. On Luis Gabriel Aguilera's *Gabriel's Fire,* see Valerie Menard's "A Kinder, Gentler Urban Tale," *Hispanic,* October 2000, 94.

Puerto Ricans: For ethnography, consult Félix M. Padilla's *Puerto Rican Chicago* (1987) and Ana Y. Ramos-Zavas's *National Performances: The Politics of Class, Race, and Space in Puerto Rican Chicago* (2003). *The Rican: A Journal of Contemporary Puerto Rican Thought* was published at Northeastern Illinois University from 1971 to 1975. The Puerto Rican studies journal *Centro* published a special issue on Chicago, 13.2 (Fall 2001).

Barbara Belejack's "In the Midst of Terror," a review of Sandra Benítez's *Bitter Grounds,* appears in *Women's Review of Books,* June 1998, 24. Andrea O'Reilly Herrera deals with *A Place the Sea Remembers* in "Sandra Benítez and the Nomadic Text," in *Postmodern Approaches to the Short Story* (2003), edited by Farhat Iftekharrudin and others, 51–64.

Marvin A. Lewis establishes a critical history in "Neorican Poetry of Chicago: Some Sociolinguistic and Thematic Considerations," *Chiricú* 3.1 (1982): 90–100. See also Marc Zimmerman's "Defendiendo lo suyo en el frío: Puerto Rican Poets in Chicago," *Latino Studies Journal* 1.3 (September 1990): 39–58. Julie M. Schmid has published "A *MELUS* Interview: David Hernández, Chicago's Unofficial Poet Laureate," *MELUS* 25.2 (2000): 147–62.

Commentary on Rane Arroyo includes Glenn Sheldon's entry in David William Wallace's *Latin American Writers on Gay and Lesbian Themes: A Bio-Critical Sourcebook* (1994), 43–46. In "The Already Browned Skin of 'American' Modernism: Rane Arroyo's *Pale Ramón,*" *Midwestern Miscellany* 30 (Fall 2002): 15–26, María DeGuzmán argues that

Arroyo revises the New World consciousness of the modernist poets. Arroyo's papers are held at El Centro de Estudios Puertorriqueños at Hunter College.

Writers of other Latin American Origins: On Beatriz Badikian, consult the entry by Tara Betts and Catherine Cucinella in *Contemporary American Women Poets* (2002), edited by Cucinella, 23–27.

On Omar S. Castañeda, see Terri Lee Grell's "Straddling the Volcanoes: Interview with Omar Castañeda," *Left Bank* 1 (Winter 1991): 77–83; Shirley Strand Guess's "An Interview with Omar S. Castañeda," *Bloomsbury Review* 14.6 (November–December 1994): 5, 11; and Jonathan Harrington's "A Truly Immense Journey: Profile of Omar S. Castañeda," *Americas Review* 23.3–4 (Fall–Winter 1995): 204–16. Vincent Spina analyzes Castañeda's "On the Way Out" in "Three Central American Writers: Alone between Two Cultures," in *A Companion to US Latino Literatures* (2007), edited by Carlota Caulfield and Darién J. Davis, 120–39. In "Cultural Transgressions in Omar S. Castañeda's *Remembering to Say 'Mouth' or 'Face,'*" *Studies in 20th and 21st Century Literature* 37.2 (Summer 2013): 131–46, Alicia Ivonne Estrada addresses how parallels to Maya history and myth complicate characters' ethnic and national identities. On the circumstances of Castañeda's death, which ironically resembled situations in his fiction, read Peter Monaghan's "A Professor's Death from Heroin Overdose Stuns a Campus: Colleagues Say More Compassion Might Have Averted a Tragedy," *Chronicle of Higher Education*, June 27, 1997, A12–A13. Also of interest is the "Self-Profile" written by Castañeda's father, the distinguished philosopher Héctor-Neri Castañeda (1924–1991), in *Hector-Neri Castañeda* (1986), 3–76. The elder Castañeda recounts family history, his early years in Guatemala, and his academic career in Detroit and Bloomington, Indiana.

Achy Obejas speaks with Jorjet Harper in "Dancing to a Different Beat: An Interview with Achy Obejas," *Lambda Book Report* 5.3 (September 1996): 1, 6–7. Scholarship includes Linda J. Craft's "Truth or Consequences: Mambos, Memories, and Multiculturalism from Achy Obejas's Chicago," *Revista de Estudios Hispánicos* 35 (2001): 369–87; and Sara Cooper's "Queering Family: Achy Obejas's *We Came All the Way from Cuba So You Could Dress like This?*" *Chasqui: Revista de Literatura Latinoamericana* 32.2 (November 2003): 76–88.

Latino/a Visitors to the Midwest: In "Exiles, Migrants, Settlers, and Natives," cited previously, Theresa Delgadillo discusses Chicano/a writers who visited the Midwest. "In the Name of the Homeland," Hilary McClellen's interview with Julia Alvarez, appears in *Atlantic Online,* July 19, 2000. Robert Carballo's "Gustavo Pérez Firmat's *Next Year in Cuba:* The Exile Experience as Formative Influence upon the Literary Imagination" is in *Revista/Review Interamericana* 25.1–4 (January 1994–December 1995): 139–48. On Martín Espada, see Eric Goldscheider's "The People's Poet," *On Wisconsin* 111.1 (Spring 2010): 42–47. In "'Running' and Resistance: Nihilism and Cultural Memory in Chicano Urban Narratives," *MELUS* 25.2 (Summer 2000): 133–47, Vincent Perez compares Rodríguez's *Always Running* to RICHARD WRIGHT'S *NATIVE SON* (1940).

Spanish-Language Writers: John Barry's scholarship includes "La periferia en el centro: La marginación de los escritores latinos de Chicago," *Tres Américas* 7 (Fall 1996): 32–36; "Writing(s) in Spanish from Chicago," *Tropel* 6 (February 2000): 9; and "Persistencia de la memoria: Prosa en español desde Chicago," *Pie de página* 2 (2004): 54–57.

Ricardo Armijo's "Historia silvestre de las revistas literarias en español de Chicago" appears in *Pie de página* 1 (May–August 2002): 17–27. Notices of Armando Romero's writing include Jim Dexter's "Out of Isolation Comes a Highly Original Voice," *McMicken* 6.1 (Fall–Winter 1996): 13–15. José Cardona-López's "Violencia, amor y exilio en la narrativa de José Castro Urioste" appears in *Con-Textos* 31 (2004): 41–48. On Olivia Maciel's poetry, see Humberto Gamboa's "Poesía de colores y sabores," *Exito,* October 26, 1995, 11.

Latin American Commentators: On Martí's Haymarket essays, consult Sebastiaan Faber's "The Beautiful, the Good, and the Natural: Martí and the Ills of Modernity," *Journal of Latin American Cultural Studies* 11.2 (2002): 173–93. On Neruda, see James Nolan's *Poet-Chief: The Native American Poetics of Walt Whitman and Pablo Neruda* (1994) and *Pablo Neruda and the U.S. Culture Industry*

(2002), edited by Theresa Longo. *Gabriel García Márquez* (1999), edited by Harold Bloom, includes articles on the author's U.S. influences.

WILLIAM BARILLAS
UNIVERSITY OF WISCONSIN–LA CROSSE

LESBIAN, GAY, BISEXUAL, TRANSGENDER, AND QUEER LITERATURE

OVERVIEW: Same-sex love and nonnormative gender identity are as old as humanity, and their depiction in literature is as ancient as *Gilgamesh*. Yet when we speak of "gay literature" or "lesbian literature," we are using terms that embody modern ideas about sexuality. The term "homosexual," which first appeared in print in 1869, began to enter wide usage only in the late nineteenth and early twentieth centuries. That same period, between the Civil War and World War I, witnessed the economic and cultural rise of the Midwest. Since then, Midwestern writers have contributed significantly to a long-standing literary tradition reflecting the experience of people who today refer to themselves as lesbian, gay, bisexual, transgender, or queer, commonly abbreviated as LGBTQ.

Particularly in the developed world, a strong sense of common cause has developed among these groups. The acronym LGBTQ includes people of every social class, race, and ethnicity, with diverse sexual orientations and gender identities. Although lesbians and gay men may be more prominent, bisexuals are also a significant part of the population. Transgender individuals include biological males who identify as women and females who identify as men; transsexuals are people who feel that their biological sex does not match their inner self, and who wish to change their sex by means of surgery. Transgender and transsexual people may feel sexual attraction to men, women, or both. "Queer" is used by people who prefer it as a term for any orientation or identity that defies heterosexual norms. Although many older individuals are uncomfortable with the word, which has a long history as a vicious epithet, the rehabilitation of "queer" demonstrates the ability of the LGBTQ community to meet adversity with defiance. Among letters standing for other identities, "I" is sometimes used to identify intersex individuals, people born with ambiguous genitalia or atypical chromosomes.

Although LGBTQ writers deal with universal concerns, certain themes distinguish this literature, marking a historical change from secrecy and fear to openness and pride made possible by a long struggle for social acknowledgment and legal rights. These themes include a childhood sense of difference; recognition of same-sex attraction; sexual initiation; the experience of one's sexuality as a secret and attendant feelings of loneliness and fear; struggles to accept one's sexuality; encounters with homophobia; discovery of the LGBTQ community, typically in cities; expressions of subculture, such as camp and drag; and social activism on behalf of LGBTQ causes. More recent literature has also dealt with "coming out," HIV/AIDS, same-sex marriage, adoption rights, and the right to serve openly in the military.

This entry surveys the development of Midwestern LGBTQ literature in the following periods: the late nineteenth and early twentieth centuries; the period during and between the world wars; the post–World War II era of the 1950s and 1960s; and the contemporary period, kicked off by the 1969 Stonewall uprising in New York City, which signaled the rise of the gay rights movement. Although it emphasizes writing by lesbians, gay men, bisexuals, transgender individuals, and queer authors, this entry places the LGBTQ tradition in a broad historical and literary context that includes heterosexuals. This inclusion is consistent with the new field of queer studies and the practice of "queering" texts by apparently heterosexual writers or queer writers who have presented their experience in heterosexual guise.

HISTORY AND SIGNIFICANCE: The development of a queer literary tradition in the Midwest parallels and to some degree accounts for the social progress of LGBTQ people. Where writers once found it necessary to hide their sexuality or gender identity, their counterparts today speak of "gay pride" and act on it as citizens and as writers. The success of this ongoing struggle owes much to the personal sacrifice and literary expression of individuals who lived and worked under oppressive conditions.

A necessary background for the study of LGBTQ literature is the transition from the nineteenth century to the twentieth, from Victorian to modern ideas about sexuality. Victorian morality, which proscribed sexual expression other than procreative intercourse, imagined women as either "pure" or "fallen" and men as lustful creatures requiring control by the state and religion. Sexual acts between women were barely acknowledged, and relations between men were described in terms of effeminacy, sin, disease, and crime. Yet passionate friendships between men or between women were celebrated, and homosocial physical intimacy, including the sharing of beds, was common. Many such arrangements undoubtedly involved sex, but documentation is scarce.

ABRAHAM LINCOLN (1809–1865), for example, lived with Joshua Fry Speed in Springfield, ILLINOIS, for four years; the two young lawyers shared a bed and a notably close friendship. Lincoln also shared a bed with his White House bodyguard, Captain David Derickson. At one point Lincoln wrote a poem, perhaps humorously intended, about two men marrying. These and other aspects of Lincoln's life have led to claims that the sixteenth President was either gay or bisexual. CARL (AUGUST) SANDBURG (1878–1967) hints as much in the first edition of *Abraham Lincoln: The Prairie Years* (1926) when he writes that Lincoln and Speed shared "a streak of lavender, and spots soft as May violets" (264). Queer theorists, however, are less interested in "proving" that Lincoln was gay than they are in challenging the heterosexist assumption that all people in the past were straight unless "proved" otherwise, a bias arguably evident in the strenuousness with which some Lincoln scholars have denied the possibility of his being other than strictly heterosexual.

Cohabitation of unmarried women, referred to as "Boston marriage," was an accepted way of life, particularly among the upper classes. Social reformer (LAURA) JANE ADDAMS (1860–1935) had committed, intimate relationships, living first with Ellen Gates Starr (1859–1940), who co-founded HULL-HOUSE in CHICAGO with Addams, and

then with Mary Rozet Smith (1868–1934), who was essentially Addams's spouse from 1890 (the same year, incidentally, in which the term "lesbian" first appeared in print) until Smith's death. Addams's social philosophy drew on her conviction that women needed to counteract the aggressive, selfish tendencies of male-dominated society. Her ideals operated both at the level of community, as seen in writings like *Twenty Years at Hull-House* (1910), and in personal relations, documented in private poems and correspondence with Starr and Smith.

The homosexuality of Walt Whitman (1819–1892) is generally acknowledged. From the first edition of *Leaves of Grass* (1855) to the last (1892), Whitman prophesies an American republic based on companionate love, both sexual and nonsexual, between men. In "Whitman and the Gay American Ethos," in *A Historical Guide to Walt Whitman* (2000), edited by David S. Reynolds, 121–51, M. Jimmie Killingsworth asserts that Whitman "helped to invent gayness" as an identity (122). Although he was a product of the Middle Atlantic region, Whitman idealized the landscapes and people of the continental interior. This is evident in his many references to the GREAT LAKES, the Mississippi River, and especially the Midwestern prairies. In the poems "For You O Democracy," "The Prairie-Grass Dividing," "A Leaf for Hand in Hand," and "To a Western Boy," from the homoerotic "Calamus" sequence of 1860, the prairie constitutes "leaves of grass" writ large, a whole ecoregion embodying Whitman's master symbol of nature, mystical transcendence, and democratic reconciliation of self and society. In "The Prairie-Grass Dividing," for example, Whitman associates the prairie with "the most copious and close companionship of men . . . Those of earth-born passion, simple, never constrain'd, never obedient, / Those of inland America" (*Complete Poetry and Collected Prose*, 1982, 281). Images of vigorous, virtuous Midwesterners and the prairie also appear in "Night on the Prairies" (1860), "O Tan-Faced Prairie-Boy" (1865), "The Prairie States" (1880), and "A Prairie Sunset" (1888), as well as writings about Lincoln like the great elegy "When Lilacs Last in the Dooryard Bloom'd" (1865). Prose pieces in *Specimen Days* (1882) about Whitman's 1879 trip through OHIO, INDIANA, Illinois, MISSOURI, and KANSAS also praise landscapes of the Midwest and predict social and literary greatness for the region's people in a manner consistent with his views on companionate love.

Whitman was a prophet; the "Calumus" poems became almost sacred texts for gay and lesbian writers of succeeding generations. These writers were constrained, however, from writing about same-sex love with the same directness because new medical theories about sexuality made the guise of "companionship" untenable: living or sleeping together now implied sex. As the terms "heterosexual" and "homosexual" gained currency in the decade after Whitman's death, the new binary understanding of sexual orientation added a new rationale for persecution. Homosexuality, still seen as sinful and criminal, was now considered a mental illness as well. Even as the idea of homosexuality gave many people a sense of identity, it was used as a weapon against them. As a result, writers adapted another of Whitman's strategies: the use of hints, symbols, and references to a personal "secret." Some transmuted homosexual themes into safe, heterosexual narratives or simply remained silent about their sexuality.

The period between 1890 and 1920 saw the urbanization and industrialization of the United States. In addition to economic motivations shared by all Americans of that era, gays and lesbians moved to cities like Chicago, DETROIT, and CINCINNATI seeking safer companionship and community. They also participated in reform movements of the era, such as women's suffrage, Prohibition, and the labor movement. The development of Midwestern cities owes much to LGBTQ labor and cultural production, even if the sexual orientation of many important figures has gone unacknowledged or remains unknown.

In literature, HENRY BLAKE FULLER (1857–1929) made important contributions. Associated with the early stages of the CHICAGO RENAISSANCE, Fuller was seen in his time as the leading figure in Chicago letters. Two of Fuller's works have been reassessed by scholars of gay literature: his play At Saint Judas's (1896), a tragic story of men in love, and his novel Bertram Cope's Year (1919),

about the romantic relationships of an English instructor at Northwestern University. Because of its subject, Bertram Cope's Year was rejected by publishers, and Fuller had to publish it himself. It is the first gay-themed novel by a major American writer.

The Story of a Life (1901) by the pseudonymous Claude Hartland (b. 1871) is the first autobiography of a gay man published in the United States. Presenting his memoir as a case study, Hartland tells of his rural youth and later life in ST. LOUIS, Missouri, in a manner reflecting both nineteenth-century sensibilities and the new medical model of sexuality. After decades of obscurity, the book was reprinted in 1985 and has attracted the interest of queer studies scholars.

In the aftermath of World War I, the urban scene that embraced jazz, bootleg liquor, and modern art also produced a queer counterculture, expressed both in nascent activism and in literature. Of particular note is Henry Gerber (1892–1972) of Chicago. After internment as an alien during the war, the German-born Gerber served in the U.S. Army in occupied Germany, where he came into contact with the German homophile movement. In 1924 he founded the Society for Human Rights in Chicago, the first gay rights organization in American history. Although the society lasted less than a year before Gerber and its other officers were arrested, they published two issues of a journal, Friendship and Freedom, the first gay periodical in the United States. Gerber returned to military service and later lived in New York, continuing to write essays in defense of homosexual rights.

Literary modernism also challenged the status quo with a new frankness about sex and an examination of gender roles. The story "Hands," for example, in WINESBURG, OHIO (1919) by SHERWOOD ANDERSON (1876–1941) depicts a victim of small-town homophobia. In "Paul's Case" (1905) by WILLA CATHER (1873–1947), an adolescent faces the disapproval of his teachers. Cather codes Paul's behavior, dress, and fascination with theatre as gay, and his self-destruction as internalized homophobia.

In her essay "The Novel Démueblé" (1922) Cather argues that fiction should be free of excessive detail; what matters is "the

Willa Cather, freshman at the University of
Nebraska, 1891–1892.

Nebraska State Historical Society, RG 2639. Copy and
reuse restrictions apply

inexplicable presence of the thing not
named . . . the overtone divined by the ear
but not heard by it" (*Stories, Poems, and Other
Writings*, 1992, 837). According to Sharon
O'Brien, the phrase "the thing not named"
suggests the aspect of Cather's life on which
she maintained silence: her lesbianism. Biographers have documented Cather's early
male identification and the homosocial pattern of her life. As a youth in NEBRASKA, she
dressed in masculine clothes, cropped her
hair, and referred to herself as "William
Cather." Cather experienced great passion
for her friends Louise Pound and Isabelle
Hambourg; her longest relationship was
with Edith Lewis, who lived with Cather
from 1912 until the author's death, when she
became Cather's literary executor.

A strong case has been made that Cather
develops lesbian themes by heterosexualiz-
ing her narratives, partly by using male
characters in place of female ones. Joanna
Russ so argues in "To Write 'Like a Woman':
Transformations of Identity in the Work of
Willa Cather," in *Historical, Literary, and Erotic
Aspects of Lesbianism* (1986), edited by Monika Kehoe, 77–87. According to Russ, the
perspective of characters like Jim Burden in
My Ántonia (1918) is "inconsistent with the
male persona, but instead resembles lesbian experiences: the inaccessibility . . . of
women who are nonetheless accessible to
other men, the absolute heartbreak at the
untouchability of the women rather than
anger or guilt or the search for sexual release
elsewhere, and the women's intimacy with
the men involved . . . without any suggestion of sexual involvement or explicit sexual history" (77). This gender switching
should be seen in the light of Cather's coming of age in the 1890s, the decade of Whitman's death and the trial of Oscar Wilde
(1854–1900), when, as Russ reminds us, "the
social invention of the morbid, unhealthy,
criminal lesbian had intervened" (79). Lacking the cover of sublimated friendship
available to an earlier generation, Cather
nurtured a public image of chaste aestheti-
cism and employed gender masquerade as
a fictive technique.

Lesbians, gay men, and bisexuals played
important roles in the publication and promotion, as well as the writing, of Modernist
literature. MARGARET C. ANDERSON (1886–
1973) grew up in Indiana and Ohio and
moved to Chicago in 1908 to pursue a career
in publishing. In 1914 she founded THE LITTLE
REVIEW, which played a central role in the
Chicago Renaissance and modernism in
general. In 1915 she met Jane Heap (1883–
1964), who became Anderson's lover and
assistant editor (later editor) of *The Little Review*. Anderson wrote three autobiographies,
including *My Thirty Years War* (1930), and one
novel, *Forbidden Fires* (1996).

Another important publisher was ROBERT
(MENZIES) McALMON (1895–1956), who grew
up in Kansas and SOUTH DAKOTA and studied
at the University of Minnesota. While living in New York, he co-edited the journal
Contact with William Carlos Williams
(1883–1963). A brief marriage provided an
endowment that enabled McAlmon to live
in Paris, where he turned *Contact* into a literary press that published *Three Stories and*

Ten Poems (1923), the first book by ERNEST (MILLER) HEMINGWAY (1899–1961), and other modernist texts. McAlmon's fiction, which employs modernist fragmentation and non-linear narrative, tends to semi-autobiography. The stories in *A Hasty Bunch* (1922) and the novel *Village: As It Happened Through a Fifteen Year Period* (1924) both feature men in Midwestern towns furtively interested in other men. McAlmon conveys his bisexuality in *Distinguished Air: Grim Fairy Tales* (1925), an avant-garde collection that garnered praise from both James Joyce (1882–1941) and Ezra Pound (1885–1972). See also EXPATRIATES.

Mark Turbyfill (1896–1991) had success in dance and painting as well as poetry. Born in Oklahoma when it was still Indian Territory, Turbyfill moved with his family to Chicago in 1911 and began publishing as a teenager. His poems frequently appeared in *The Little Review* and POETRY: A MAGAZINE OF VERSE; the latter devoted its entire May 1926 issue to his long poem "A Marriage with Space." Turbyfill's imagism and precise phrasing mark him as a contemporary of T(HOMAS) S(TEARNS) ELIOT (1888–1965) and E(dward) E(stlin) Cummings (1894–1962), whose poetry appeared in many of the same journals and anthologies as Turbyfill's. *The Living Frieze* (1921) includes poems like "Chicago," an answer to Carl Sandburg's famous poem with the same title, and "The Adventurer," which hints at the poet's sexual orientation. Introducing his poems as "trinkets you may toy," Turbyfill tells the reader, "I cannot tell you of what they are made / Or where I found them" (13). Turbyfill also published *Evaporation: A Symposium* (1923; with Samuel Putnam) and *The Words beneath Us: Balletic Poems* (1951).

(HAROLD) HART CRANE (1899–1932) is best known for *The Bridge* (1930), a classic of modernist poetry. Crane, who was born in Garrettsville, Ohio, tends to encode his homosexuality, as in "C33" (1916), an early poem about Oscar Wilde (the title refers to Wilde's prison identification number), and "Modern Craft" (1918). Poems like "Porphyro in Akron" (1921) convey Crane's alienation in the Midwest, a state of mind partly attributable to the secret of his homosexuality. Crane wrote "Voyages" in *White Buildings* (1926) for his lover, Emil Opffer. Also worth considering for their gay implications are sections of

Mark Turbyfill. Frontispiece from *The Living Frieze*. M. Wheeler, 1921

The Bridge such as "The Harbor Dawn" and "Cape Hatteras," as well as poems uncollected during Crane's lifetime, such as "Episode of Hands," "The Visible the Untrue," and "Reply."

Ernest Hemingway has been reassessed by scholars who find his writing much more nuanced in regard to gender and sexuality than did earlier critics. Although he embraced the cult of rugged masculinity associated with Theodore Roosevelt (1858–1919) and Rudyard Kipling (1865–1936), Hemingway was also influenced by the sexual freedom of 1920s Paris, where he enjoyed friendships with lesbians like Gertrude Stein (1874–1946). Despite his macho persona, Hemingway frequently depicts sexually dominant women and heterosexual couples who reverse conventional gender roles in the bedroom. "If we can identify Hemingway as heterosexual but not quite straight," Richard Fantina asserts in *Ernest Hemingway: Machismo and Masochism* (2005), "we can do worse than refer to him as a queer heterosexual or as transgendered" (76). Hemingway, according to Fantina, "affirm[ed] the patriarchal social mandate while undermining it in sexual relationships" (77).

Hemingway's gender conflicts originated in childhood; his mother "twinned" him with an older sister until school age, cutting their hair and dressing them identically as either boys or girls. Twinning and identical haircuts, or references to them, frequently appear in Hemingway's stories and novels, most notably in *The Garden of Eden*, edited for publication in 1986. This novel involves a young couple on their honeymoon on the French Riviera in the early 1920s; Catherine and David Bourne have their hair identically cut and colored, engage in sexual play in which he becomes a "girl" and she a "boy," and share a female lover. Hemingway's long struggle to complete *The Garden of Eden* suggests that his hypermasculine public image interfered with a desire to explore his transgressive sexuality in writing.

An acquaintance of Hemingway's in Paris was GLENWAY WESCOTT (1901–1987), whom Hemingway portrayed disparagingly as Robert Prentiss in *The Sun Also Rises* (1926). Born on a WISCONSIN farm, Wescott studied at the University of Chicago and lived much of his life in Europe and on the East Coast. Although his stories, such as "Adolescence" from *Good-bye, Wisconsin* (1928), occasionally hint at homosexuality, Wescott withheld his gay-themed stories from publication. One, "A Visit to Priapus" (1938), can be found in *The New Penguin Book of Gay Short Stories* (2003), edited by David Leavitt and Mark Mitchell. His journals, published as *Continual Lessons: The Journals of Glenway Wescott, 1937–1955* (1990), are also candid about his sexuality.

Born in Missouri and raised in Kansas, Illinois, and Ohio, poet LANGSTON HUGHES (1902–1967) is best known as a central figure of the Harlem Renaissance. His iconic status has been predicated on critical omission of his sexuality, an oversight that Hughes encouraged. Biographers have established Hughes's homosexual affairs, as well as his close friendships with gay men such as Countee Cullen (1903–1946) and Claude McKay (1889–1948), fellow participants in the Harlem Renaissance who, like Hughes, admired Whitman not only as a populist poet but as one who encoded homosexual desire. "Focusing on such poems as 'Joy,' 'Desire,' 'Café: 3 A. M.,' 'Waterfront Streets,' 'Young Sailor,' 'Trumpet Player,' 'Tell Me,'

and many poems in *Montage of a Dream Deferred* (1951)," Alden Reimonenq writes in his entry on Hughes in *Gay and Lesbian Literary Heritage* (revised edition 2002), edited by Claude J. Summers, "we can identify homoeroticism and other gay markings" (350). Also significant is Hughes's story "Blessed Assurance," in *Something in Common and Other Stories* (1963), in which an effeminate man's gift for song briefly earns him the respect of his homophobic community.

Better Angel (1933) by Forman Brown (1901–1996) has been rediscovered as a pioneering work of gay fiction. Writing under the pseudonym Richard Meeker, Brown drew on his youth in Otsego, MICHIGAN, his college years in Ann Arbor, and his career as a composer for the musical theatre. Most fiction of the era portrays homosexuals as unhappy and self-destructive, but *Better Angel* features a self-confident protagonist and a happy ending. Brown's other books are *Walls* (poems; 1925), *The Pie-Eyed Piper, and Other Impertinent Plays for Puppets* (1933), *Punch's Progress* (1936), *Small Wonder: The Story of the Yale Puppeteers and the Turnabout Theatre* (1980), and *The Generous Jefferson Bartleby Jones* (1991), a children's book about gay parents.

In the quarter century after World War II, LGBTQ Americans faced renewed repression. Popular culture and mores pressured people to conform to stereotypical gender roles, and Cold War fears of communism were directed against homosexuals, as well as leftists in government and the media. This "Lavender Scare" resulted in myriad forms of harassment. Medical stigmatization was reinforced by the American Psychiatric Association's 1952 listing of homosexuality as a sociopathic personality disturbance, which was not rescinded until 1973.

At the same time, however, homophile organizations like the Mattachine Society, founded in 1950, and the Daughters of Bilitis, founded in 1955, made subtle steps toward equal rights. Sexologist Alfred (Charles) Kinsey (1894–1956) at Indiana University created a new discourse about sexual variation that blurred the binary absolutism of heteronormativity. In 1962 Illinois became the first state to repeal sodomy laws, although police harassment of LGBTQ citizens continued and even intensified in Chicago and elsewhere. The pattern in the LGBTQ community was to maintain anonymity.

This situation is documented in *The Evening Crowd at Kirmser's: A Gay Life in the 1940s* (2001), the memoir of journalist Ricardo J. Brown (1927–1999), who was born in Stillwater, MINNESOTA. Focusing his narrative on a bar in St. Paul, Minnesota (see MINNEAPOLIS/ST. PAUL), Brown depicts Midwestern working-class gay life in a time when gay men and lesbians lived in fear of violence, blackmail, and legal harassment. Bars like Kirmser's offered Brown and his friends a tenuous refuge in a difficult time.

Developments in postwar literature suggested that change was under way. Beat Movement writers like the famously gay Allen Ginsberg (1926–1997) challenged censorship and the dominant academicism of American letters. Meanwhile, scholars began to identify the parameters of gay literary history. A Midwesterner who contributed to this trend was Jeannette Howard Foster (1895–1981), author of *Sex Variant Women in Literature: A Historical and Quantitative Survey* (1956), the first major study of lesbians in literature. Born in Oak Park, Illinois, Foster earned her doctorate in library science at the University of Chicago and was the first librarian at Kinsey's Institute for Sex Research. She influenced generations of scholars and activists, including Valerie Taylor (1913–1997) and Marie J. Kuda (b. 1939), who were inspired by Foster to organize the world's first lesbian literary conference in Chicago in 1974. Foster also published short fiction, including the story "Lucky Star," which appeared in *Harper's* in October 1927, and stories printed in the lesbian journal *The Ladder* during the 1950s and 1960s. She also co-wrote with Valerie Taylor *Two Women: The Poetry of Jeannette Foster and Valerie Taylor* (1976).

Wasteland (1946) by RUTH SEID (1913–1995), writing as Jo Sinclair, has been called the first lesbian-themed Jewish novel and the first novel in the United States to offer a well-rounded and positive characterization of a lesbian. Set in CLEVELAND, Ohio, during World War II, Seid's first novel follows a young Jewish man's progress through psychotherapy. The protagonist overcomes his self-loathing by embracing the example of his sister, who came to accept her lesbianism with the help of the same psychologist. Published with a glowing tribute from RICHARD WRIGHT (1908–1960) on the dust jacket, *Wasteland* was well received by critics and treasured by lesbian readers. Seid had a distinguished career but did not publish another novel with a lesbian character.

Writers for stage and screen still found it necessary to disguise gay themes in the years after World War II. One example is WILLIAM (MOTTER) INGE (1913–1973), who set most of his work in his native state of Kansas. Several of Inge's plays became hits on Broadway and were adapted into popular films. Like writers associated with the early twentieth-century REVOLT FROM THE VILLAGE, Inge portrays the tragic consequences of thwarted desire, caused by the social conservatism of the small towns where his plays are set. The sexual orientation of some of Inge's characters is unclear; two openly gay characters are Pinky in *Where's Daddy?* (1966) and Archie in *The Disposal* (1968). Inge's most direct treatment of gay themes appears in two one-act plays that he wrote in the 1950s but did not publish until 1962: *The Boy in the Basement* and *The Tiny Closet*. As their titles suggest, these plays involve secretly gay men who suffer from isolation and fear of discovery. Inge's writing dramatizes his anxiety as a closeted gay man; years of psychotherapy did not prevent him from taking his life at the age of sixty.

An important medium for gay and lesbian writers of the 1950s and 1960s was pulp fiction—paperbacks typically published with lurid covers. Although much pulp fiction was no more durable than the cheap paper on which it was printed, it included works by talented writers like WILLARD F. MOTLEY (1909–1965), whose tough naturalism drew comparisons to JOHN DOS PASSOS (1896–1970) and (HERMAN) THEODORE DREISER (1871–1945). Motley was African American but never revealed that fact in his novels, which portray ethnic whites. Motley's *Knock on Any Door* (1947) follows a Chicago hustler. The 1949 film adaptation starred Humphrey Bogart and John Derek, who delivers the famous line "Live fast, die young, and leave a good-looking corpse."

Between 1957 and 1962 Ann Weldy (b. 1932), writing as Ann Bannon, published a sequence of pulp novels known as the Beebo Brinker Chronicles. The books follow young Midwestern women who come out as lesbians in Greenwich Village during the 1950s. Born in Joliet, Illinois, Bannon attended the University of Illinois; her experiences at a sorority there inspired *Odd Girl Out* (1957), the first novel in the series. *Odd Girl Out* broke with the conventions of lesbian-themed fiction of the time, which followed publishers' insistence that lesbian characters not end up happily. Bannon's novels became iconic among lesbian readers, who avidly sought such positive representations of lesbian experience. *Odd Girl Out* was followed by *I Am a Woman* (1959), *Women in the Shadows* (1959), *Journey to a Woman* (1960), and *Beebo Brinker* (1962). Cleis Press began reprinting the entire series in 2001, with new introductory essays by Bannon.

Novelist, poet, and activist Valerie Taylor was born Velma Nacella Young in Aurora, Illinois. Taylor acceded to social expectations by marrying at age twenty-two and having two children. She acknowledged her attraction to women in her thirties and thereafter alternated between identifying herself as lesbian and as bisexual. Divorced in 1953, she lived in Chicago between 1962 and 1975, participated in the Daughters of Bilitis, and co-founded Mattachine Midwest in 1965. Her lesbian-themed pulp novels, which typically feature Chicago settings, include *Whisper*

Cover of Ann Bannon's *Odd Girl Out*. Gold Medal Books, 1957.
© Fawcett Publications

Their Love (1957), *The Girls in 3-B* (1959), and *A World without Men* (1963). Her later books include *Prism* (1981) and *Ripening* (1988).

The work of JAMES (OTIS) PURDY (1914–2009) drew high praise from writers like Edith Sitwell (1887–1964) and Susan Sontag (1933–2004). Purdy's novels, which often depict men torn between homosexual desire and internalized homophobia, are by turns realistic, surrealistic, and gothic, featuring sex, racial and social class conflicts, and extreme violence. Born in Fremont, Ohio, Purdy studied at the University of Chicago and taught at Lawrence University in Appleton, Wisconsin, from 1949 to 1953. After another period in Chicago, he moved to New York, where he lived thereafter. Purdy set much of his fiction, such as *The Nephew* (1960) and *Jeremy's Version* (1970), in small Midwestern towns. Other novels are set in Chicago, such as *Malcolm* (1954), *63: Dream Palace* (1957), and the controversial *Eustace Chisholm and the Works* (1967), the first book in which Purdy focused on gay characters.

LGBTQ Americans participated in the social revolutions of the 1960s, including the civil rights and anti-war movements. The activism of those years fueled the gay liberation movement of the 1970s as LGBTQ individuals came to see themselves as belonging to an oppressed minority. The summer of 1969 saw the Stonewall uprising in New York City, which began when patrons of a gay bar fought back against a police raid. Stonewall quickly assumed national significance, representing a shift from the gradualist approach of groups like the Mattachine Society to strategies of protest, lobbying, and electoral politics. Gay politics now emphasized "gay pride" and "coming out."

Although Greenwich Village in New York and San Francisco's Castro District were the nationally recognized centers of gay culture, significant advances took place in Midwestern cities and college towns in the decade after Stonewall. In 1970 the *Detroit Gay Liberator* newspaper started its two-year run; the Amazon Bookstore Cooperative, the first feminist/lesbian bookstore, opened in Minneapolis; and University of Nebraska professor Louis Crompton taught one of the first gay studies courses. In 1973 Jerry DeGrieck and Nancy Wechsler, who served on the Ann Arbor, Michigan, City Council, became the first elected officials to declare their homosexuality. The following year Kathy Kozachenko won a seat on the same council, becoming the first openly lesbian or gay candidate to win an election. Steve Endean (1948–1993), who was born in IOWA and raised in Illinois and Minnesota, became a major figure in gay politics in this period. After fighting for gay rights in Minnesota, Endean moved to Washington, D.C., where he became the first gay rights lobbyist in 1978. In 1980 Endean founded the Human Rights Campaign Fund, which became the Human Rights Campaign, the largest LGBTQ political action committee. Vicki L. Eaklor edited Endean's memoir, *Bringing Lesbian and Gay Rights into the Mainstream: Twenty Years of Progress* (2006). The leadership exerted by Midwesterners in the 1970s anticipated subsequent political advances. In 1982 Wisconsin became the first state to outlaw discrimination based on sexual orientation. In 1998 Tammy Baldwin, Democrat of Wisconsin, became the first openly lesbian, nonincumbent candidate to win election to the U.S. House of Representatives; in 2012 she became the first lesbian elected to the U.S. Senate. In 2009 Iowa became the first Midwestern state, and only the third nationally, to legalize same-sex marriage.

The 1970s saw unabashed depictions of LGBTQ experience in print. The impulse was autobiographical; many writers depicted childhood in the repressive 1950s, adolescence in the turbulent 1960s, and young adulthood in the 1970s heyday of discos and bathhouses. At the same time, scholars like Jonathan Katz constructed a gay social and literary history. In the 1980s writers assumed a new soberness as the AIDS crisis decimated the gay male population and homophobic backlash affected people throughout the LGBTQ community.

No writer better exemplifies these trends than Edmund White (b. 1940). Born into an upper-middle-class family in Cincinnati, Ohio, White was raised there and in Evanston, Illinois. He studied at the Cranbrook Boys' School in Bloomfield Hills, Michigan, and at the University of Michigan. In 1980 and 1981 he participated in the Violet Quill, a group in New York whose members saw themselves as gay writers writing for a gay audience, not simply writers who happened to be gay. White's memoirs and semi-autobiographical novels reflect his Midwestern upbringing. *A Boy's Own Story* (1982), a gay coming-of-age novel set in the Midwest, has become a classic; its sequel, *The Beautiful Room Is Empty* (1988), follows the narrator from his Midwestern prep school to New York City. *The Farewell Symphony* (1997) deals with the AIDS epidemic. *States of Desire: Travels in Gay America* (1980) documents gay culture, including that in the Midwest, just before the AIDS crisis. White also co-wrote *The Joy of Gay Sex: An Intimate Guide for Gay Men to the Pleasures of a Gay Lifestyle* (1977) with Dr. Charles Silverstein.

Another post-Stonewall writer is novelist and playwright Daniel R. Brown (b. 1938), writing as Daniel Curzon. Born in Litchfield, Illinois, he grew up in Detroit, studied at Kent State and Wayne State Universities, and later became professor of English at City College of San Francisco. Curzon's *Something You Do in the Dark* (1971), an early gay protest novel, involves a gay man seeking vengeance on a Detroit police officer. Curzon's other books include *The World Can Break Your Heart* (1984), a novel about growing up gay and Catholic in working-class Detroit, and *Dropping Names: The Delicious Memoirs of Daniel Curzon* (2004), which touches on Curzon's years in Detroit and notable people he has known, including novelist JOYCE CAROL OATES (b. 1938).

Transsexual memoirs appearing after the landmark publication in 1967 of *Christine Jorgensen: A Personal Autobiography* include *Emergence: A Transsexual Autobiography* (1977) by Mario Martino (b. 1938). Born a girl in a conservative Italian Catholic family in a Midwestern city, Martino felt from an early age that he was a male trapped in a female body. His autobiography describes his family life, attempts to escape his inclinations at a convent school for girls, and, ultimately, sex reassignment surgeries. Martino went on to counsel and advocate for female-to-male transsexuals.

Another memoir was written by Deirdre N. McCloskey (b. 1942), a distinguished economist. Born Donald N. McCloskey and raised in Boston, she underwent sex reassignment surgery in 1995 while she was a professor at the University of Iowa. In *Crossing: A Memoir* (1999), McCloskey describes her early female identification and her transition into a woman, including her generally positive postoperative reception by colleagues and students in Iowa City and mixed reactions from family members.

Chicago's cultural diversity and internationalism are apparent in LGBTQ writing from that city. Post-Stonewall authors include Ifti Nasim (1946–2011), a Pakistani businessman and gay activist who studied at Wayne State University in Detroit before moving to Chicago in 1974. In addition to books in Urdu dealing with the marginalization of gays in Asia, he published the English-language *Myrmecophile: Selected Poems, 1980–2000* (2000). Poet Dwight Okita (b. 1958) speaks to his Japanese ancestry, as well as his experience as a gay man, in *Crossing with the Light* (1992). His first novel, *The Prospect of My Arrival* (2012), is a work of SCIENCE FICTION set in Chicago. LGBTQ Latino/Latina writers from Chicago include novelist Ana Castillo (b. 1953), author of such books as *Loverboys* (stories; 1996); poet Rane Arroyo (1954–2010), author of *Pale Ramón* (1998) and several other works; and novelist Achy Obejas (b. 1956), whose publications include *Memory Mambo* (1996). *See also* LATINO/LATINA LITERATURE.

MARY OLIVER (b. 1935) did not publicly acknowledge her lesbianism until she won the National Book Award for *New and Selected Poems* (1992). In her acceptance speech Oliver thanked her life partner, Mary Malone Cook, to whom she had dedicated most of her books. Readers immediately began to reassess Oliver's work in light of this new knowledge about her personal life. Generally seen as an heir to romantics like Whitman and Henry David Thoreau (1817–1862), Oliver first nurtured her intimate knowledge of nature as a child, exploring the country outside her hometown of Maple Heights, Ohio. Oliver shares Whitman's joy in direct, bodily experience of American landscapes. In "The Gardens," the final poem in the Pulitzer Prize–winning *American Primitive* (1983), Oliver envisions an unnamed lover as "a sea creature, except / for your two human legs / which tremble / and open / into the dark country / I keep dreaming of" (86). Although Oliver has

lived most of her adult life away from her home state, she continually returns to Midwestern subjects, including the rivers, fields, and woods where she first discovered her sensuous and mystical love of nature.

Another Midwestern lesbian poet is Linnea Johnson (b. 1946). Born and raised in Chicago, Johnson earned a doctorate in English from the University of Nebraska and currently lives in Topeka, Kansas. In *The Chicago Home* (1986) Johnson deals with Midwestern history and landscape. In "Because They Could Not Be Entirely Honest" she considers whether Willa Cather should be criticized "for her living in the bosom of a woman / yet for not daring the edge of things: / not writing those frontiers, those pioneers, / but the other ones instead" (28). Johnson's *Making Sense: Nine Love Poems* (1989) is marked by frank eroticism. Her second full-length book, *Augury,* appeared in 2010.

Contemporary gay male poets with strong ties to the Midwest include Robert Peters (1924–2014), Antler (b. 1946), and William Reichard (b. 1963). Peters established himself as a scholar of Victorian literature before publishing *Songs for a Son* (1967), the first of many books of poetry. *Songs for a Son* bears the influence of ROBERT (ELWOOD) BLY (b. 1926) and THEODORE ROETHKE (1908–1963), particularly Roethke's book *THE LOST SON* (1948). Born in Eagle River, Wisconsin, and raised on a nearby farm, Peters saw army service in Europe during World War II before earning degrees in English at the University of Wisconsin and embarking on an academic career. He focuses on his Wisconsin youth in *Familial Love and Other Misfortunes: Poems of My Early Years* (2002) and in a series of memoirs, the first of which, *Crunching Gravel: Growing up in the Thirties,* appeared in 1993. *Poems: Selected and New, 1967–1991* was published in 1992.

The best-known Midwestern disciple of the Beat Movement, Brad Burdick (b. 1946), writing as Antler, has been a lifelong resident of Milwaukee, Wisconsin. Influenced by Walt Whitman and Allen Ginsberg, Antler's poetic catalogs evoke an eroticized landscape and express yearnings for wild nature, sexual ecstasy, and social justice. *The Selected Poems* (2000) is Antler's most readily available volume. William Reichard grew up in the village of Smith's Mill, Minnesota, before moving to St. Paul. His poetry, which often focuses on family and history, has been read by GARY EDWARD KEILLOR (b. 1942), writing as Garrison Keillor, on National Public Radio. His collections are *An Alchemy in the Bones* (1999), *To Be Quietly Spoken* (2001), *How To* (2004), *This Brightness* (2007), and *Sin Eater* (2010).

The Pulitzer Prize–winning novel *Middlesex* (2002) by Jeffrey Eugenides (b. 1960) is both a family saga about Greek immigrants in Detroit and a first-person coming-of-age narrative about an intersexed man. Cal, the narrator and protagonist, has a chromosomal condition that produced indeterminate genitalia. While raised as a girl, Caliope, Cal comes to realize his fundamental masculinity, which he must struggle to claim and even preserve when Cal's parents accede to a doctor's plans for sex assignment surgery. Since Eugenides is heterosexual, this novel might be described as written by an LGBTQ ally.

Other LGBTQ authors with Midwestern connections include CARL VAN VECHTEN (1880–1964); Nella Larsen (1891–1964); THORNTON (NIVEN) WILDER (1897–1975); Edward Harris Heth (1909–1963); Samuel Morris Steward (1909–1993), writing as Phil Andros; WILLIAM S(EWARD) BURROUGHS (II) (1914–1997); Alma Routsong (1924–1996), writing as Isabel Miller; LORRAINE (VIVIAN) HANSBERRY (1930–1965); Jon-Henri Damski (1936–1997); LANFORD (EUGENE) WILSON (1937–2011); Jack Fritscher (b. 1939); George Klawitter (b. 1942); Carol Anshaw (b. 1946); Martha Miller (b. 1947); Ellen Hart (b. 1949); Jim Elledge (b. 1950); Robert Alexander (b. 1952); Lev Raphael (b. 1954); Karen Lee Osborne (b. 1954); Terri Lynn Jewell (1954–1995); Holly Hughes (b. 1955); Sheila Packa (b. 1956); Robert Rodi (b. 1956); Barrie Jean Borich (b. 1959); Gregg Shapiro (1959); Lori L. Lake (b. 1960); Brian Malloy (b. 1960); James Cihlar (b. 1961); Scott Heim (b. 1966); Dale Peck (b. 1967); Therese Szymanski (b. 1968); Carol Guess (b. 1968); Christopher Hennessy (b. 1973); Julie Gard (b. 1974); Mark A. Roeder (b. 1974); Laura Madeline Wiseman (b. 1978); Valerie Wetlaufer (b. 1982); and Stephen S(cott) Mills (b. 1982).

A number of LGBTQ-themed films have been set in the Midwest. *Agora* (1992), directed by Robert and Donald Kinney, involves a closeted gay man's encounter at a hotel with lesbian and gay couples. Tom Kalin's *Swoon* (1992), a postmodernist retelling of the Leopold-Loeb murder case in 1920s Chicago, focuses on the infamous pair's homosexuality. David Moreton's *Edge of Seventeen* (1998) is a gay coming-of-age story set in Ohio during the 1980s. Jane Anderson (b. 1954) directed *Normal* (2003), a televised adaptation of her play *Looking for Normal* (2002), about a middle-aged married man in Ohio who undergoes sex reassignment surgery. The film starred Jessica Lange and Tom Wilkinson and was filmed in Chicago. *Boys Don't Cry* (1999), directed by Kimberly Peirce, adapts the true story of Brandon Teena, a young transgender man from Nebraska who was raped and murdered in 1993. Hillary Swank won the Academy Award for Best Actress for her role as Brandon. The tragedy is also recounted in the documentary film *The Brandon Teena Story* (1998), directed by Susan Muska and Gréta Olafsdóttir.

Midwestern LGBTQ literature contradicts the mistaken assumption of Midwestern heteronormativity and the image of Midwesterners as essentially rural, conservative, bourgeois, and straight. (The 1930 painting *American Gothic* by Grant Wood of Iowa is popularly viewed as a representation of that stereotype; it is not widely known that Wood was a closeted gay man. See also ART.) It also challenges a "metropolitan" and "coastal" bias in queer studies, which, according to William J. Spurlin in "Remapping Same-Sex Desire: Queer Writing and Culture in the American Heartland" (2000), holds "that the seaboard cities are the only centres of queer culture and the primary locations from which queers can speak" (183). The Midwest, in this view, is a place to escape from, like Dorothy leaving Kansas in THE WONDERFUL WIZARD OF OZ (1900) by L(YMAN) FRANK BAUM (1856–1919) or in Victor Fleming's film adaptation, *The Wizard of Oz* (1939), which has become iconic in the LGBTQ community, particularly among gay men. Yet despite popular belief, the Midwest is and always has been a queer space. LGBTQ Midwesterners, both those who have lived their lives in the region and those who have left, have made and continue to make significant contributions both to literature and to the political and social advancement of the LGBTQ community.

SELECTED WORKS: Major texts of Midwestern LGBTQ literature include Claude Hartland's *The Story of a Life* (1901), Jane Addams's *Twenty Years at Hull-House* (1910), Willa Cather's *My Ántonia* (1918), Henry Blake Fuller's *Bertram Cope's Year* (1919), Mark Turbyfill's *The Living Frieze* (1921), Glenway Wescott's *Good-bye, Wisconsin* (1928) and *Continual Lessons* (1990), Margaret Anderson's *My Thirty Years War* (1930), Forman Brown's *Better Angel* (1933), Ruth Seid's *Wasteland* (1946), Willard Motley's *Knock on Any Door* (1947), Ann Bannon's *Odd Girl Out* (1957), James Purdy's *Eustace Chisholm and the Works* (1967), Robert Peters's *Songs for a Son* (1967), Daniel Curzon's *Something You Do in the Dark* (1971), Mario Martino's *Emergence: A Transsexual Autobiography* (1977), Edmund White's *A Boy's Own Story* (1982), Mary Oliver's *American Primitive* (1983), Ana Castillo's *Loverboys* (1996), Achy Obejas's *Memory Mambo* (1996), Rane Arroyo's *Pale Ramón* (1998), and Antler's *The Selected Poems* (2000).

The first anthology of Midwestern LGBTQ writing is *Reclaiming the Heartland: Lesbian and Gay Voices from the Midwest* (1996), edited by Karen Lee Osborne and William J. Spurlin. Handtype Press of Minneapolis published the anthologies *Among the Leaves: Queer Male Poets on the Midwestern Experience* (2012), edited by Raymond Luczak, and *When We Become Weavers: Queer Female Poets on the Midwestern Experience* (2012), edited by Kate Lynn Hibbard. *Windy City Queer: LGBTQ Dispatches from the Third Coast* (2011), edited by Kathie Bergquist, collects contemporary writing from Chicago. *Farm Boys: Lives of Gay Men from the Rural Midwest* (1996), edited by Will Fellows, consists mainly of oral histories. *The Columbia Anthology of Gay Literature: Readings from Western Antiquity to the Present Day* (1998), edited by Byrne R. S. Fone, features Whitman, McAlmon, Crane, and White. *Lesbian Pulp Fiction: The Sexually Intrepid World of Lesbian Paperback Novels, 1950–1965* (2005), edited by Katherine V. Forrest, includes selections by Bannon and Taylor.

FURTHER READING: Vicki L. Eaklor's *Queer America: A GLBT History of the 20th Century* (2008) may be supplemented by *Out and Proud in Chicago: An Overview of the City's Gay Community* (2008), edited by Tracy Baim; *Queer Twin Cities* (2010), edited by the Editorial Board of the Twin Cities GLBT Oral History Project; *Land of 10,000 Loves: A History of Queer Minnesota* (2012) by Stewart Van Cleve; and *Chicago Whispers: A History of LGBT Chicago before Stonewall* (2012) by St. Sukie de la Croix.

Reference texts on literature include *The Gay and Lesbian Literary Heritage: A Reader's Companion to the Writers and Their Works, from Antiquity to the Present* (revised edition 2002), edited by Claude J. Summers, and the two-volume *Encyclopedia of Contemporary LGBTQ Literature of the United States* (2009), edited by Emmanuel S. Nelson.

William J. Spurlin contributed "Remapping Same-Sex Desire: Queer Writing and Culture in the American Heartland" to *Decentering Sexualities: Politics and Representations beyond the Metropolis* (2000), edited by Richard Phillips, Diane Watt, and David Shuttleton (179–94). Spurlin contests the domination of queer studies by coastal perspectives and examines Midwestern texts that challenge assumptions both about LGBTQ people and the Midwest. In *Foundlings: Lesbian and Gay Historical Emotion before Stonewall* (2001) Christopher S. Nealon deals with Cather, Crane, and Bannon, identifying an archetypal coming-of-age story in their texts with an alienated figure, the foundling of the title.

Abraham Lincoln's poem about men marrying each other appears in *Herndon's Lincoln* (1889) by William Henry Herndon and Jesse W. Weik; it can be found on pages 47–48 of the 2006 edition edited by Douglas L. Wilson and Rodney O. Davis. C. A. Tripp's *The Intimate World of Abraham Lincoln* (2005), which argues unequivocally that Lincoln was gay, was savaged by reviewers. Lincoln is given careful consideration by Jonathan Katz in *Love Stories: Sex between Men before Homosexuality* (2001) and by Charles E. Morris III in "My Old Kentucky Homo: Abraham Lincoln, Larry Kramer, and the Politics of Queer Memory," in *Queering Public Address: Sexualities in American Historical Discourse* (2007), edited by Charles E. Morris: 93–120.

On Walt Whitman, see Katz's *Love Stories*, as well as Gary Schmidgall's *Walt Whitman: A Gay Life* (1997) and M. Jimmie Killingsworth's "Whitman and the Gay American Ethos," in *A Historical Guide to Walt Whitman* (2000), edited by David S. Reynolds (121–51). On Midwestern themes, consult Ed Folsom's "Walt Whitman's Prairie Paradise," in *Recovering the Prairie* (1999), edited by Robert F. Sayre (47–60).

Katherine Joslin's *Jane Addams: A Writer's Life* (2004) places the reformer in the context of Theodore Dreiser, HARRIET MONROE (1860–1936), JAMES T(HOMAS) FARRELL (1904–1979), and other Chicago writers. See also Lillian Faderman's *Odd Girls and Twilight Lovers: A History of Lesbian Life in Twentieth-Century America* (1991).

On Henry Blake Fuller, see Keith Gumery's "Repression, Inversion, and Modernity: A Freudian Reading of Henry Blake Fuller's *Bertram Cope's Year*," *Journal of Modern Literature* 25.3–4 (Summer 2002): 40–57; and Anthony Slide's *Lost Gay Novels: A Reference Guide to Fifty Works from the First Half of the Twentieth Century* (2003): 94–97.

Adam Sonstegard analyzes Claude Hartland's *The Story of a Life* in "Performing the 'Unnatural' Life: America's First Gay Autobiography," *Biography* 25.4 (Fall 2002): 545–68. Discussions of Hartland also appear in Katz's *Love Stories* and James Gifford's *Dayneford's Library: American Homosexual Writing, 1900–1913* (1995).

Passages from the writings of Henry Gerber appear in Jonathan Katz's *Gay American History: Lesbians and Gay Men in the U.S.A.: A Documentary* (1976). "Henry Gerber (1895–1972), Grandfather of the American Gay Movement" by Jim Kepner and Stephen O. Murray can be found in *Before Stonewall: Activists for Gay and Lesbian Rights in Historical Context* (2002), edited by Vern L. Bullough (24–34).

Sharon O'Brien's essay " 'The Thing Not Named': Willa Cather as a Lesbian Writer," *Signs* 9 (1984): 576–99, and her biography *Willa Cather: The Emerging Voice* (1987) are foundational. Joanna Russ's "To Write 'like a Woman': Transformations of Identity in the Work of Willa Cather," is in *Historical, Literary, and Erotic Aspects of Lesbianism* (1986), edited by Monika Kehoe (77–87). Marilee Lindemann reassesses Cather's oeuvre in *Willa Cather: Queering America* (1999). John P. Anders connects Cather with gay male sensibilities in *Willa Cather's Sexual Aesthetics and the Male Homosexual Literary Tradition* (1999), as does Eric L. Haralson in *Henry James and Queer Modernity* (2003).

Peter Revell's entry on Mark Turbyfill in *Dictionary of Literary Biography* 45, *American Poets, 1880–1945, First Series* (1986): 410–17, is the best source on the poet. Turbyfill's papers at the Newberry Library in Chicago include his unpublished autobiography, *Whistling in the Windy City: Memoirs of a Poet-Dancer-Painter,* which touches on his friendships with literary figures like Margaret Anderson, Henry Blake Fuller, and Harriet Monroe. Special Collections at Southern Illinois University holds a collection of Turbyfill's letters.

Scholarship on Hart Crane includes Thomas E. Yingling's *Hart Crane and the Homosexual Text: New Thresholds, New Anatomies* (1990) and Ernest Smith's "Spending out the Self: Homosexuality and the Poetry of Hart Crane," in *Literature and Homosexuality* (2000), edited by Michael J. Meyer (161–81). Also consult Robert K. Martin's *The Homosexual Tradition in American Poetry* (second edition 1998) and Paul L. Mariani's *The Broken Tower: The Life of Hart Crane* (1999).

Relevant books about Ernest Hemingway include Carl P. Eby's *Hemingway's Fetishism: Psychoanalysis and the Mirror of Manhood* (1998), Debra Moddelmog's *Reading Desire: In Pursuit of Ernest Hemingway* (1999), and Richard Fantina's *Ernest Hemingway: Machismo and Masochism* (2005). Also see *Papa: A Personal Memoir* (1976) by Gregory H. Hemingway, Ernest's youngest child, who struggled not only with depression and alcoholism, like his father, but also with gender dysphoria. A cross-dresser his entire life, Gregory underwent sex reassignment surgery in 1995 and thereafter alternated between calling himself Gregory and Gloria. He died in 2001 under tragic circumstances. John Patrick Hemingway, one of Gregory's sons, tells the story in *Strange Tribe: A Family Memoir* (2007).

Jerry Rosco's *Glenway Wescott Personally: A Biography* (2002) details Wescott's career and ultimately more public homosexuality. A briefer narrative appears in Marc Vargo's *Noble Lives: Biographical Portraits of Three Remarkable Gay Men—Glenway Wescott, Aaron Copland, and Dag Hammarskjöld* (2005). See also Kegan Doyle's "The Moral of Glenway Wescott: The Closet and the Second Act,"

Canadian Review of American Studies 28.1 (1998): 43–61; and Edmund White's "The Loves of the Falcon," *New York Review of Books* 56.2 (February 12, 2009): 34–38.

A. B. Christa Schwarz devotes a chapter of *Gay Voices of the Harlem Renaissance* (2003) to Langston Hughes. Also consult Charles I. Nero's "Re/Membering Langston: Homophobic Textuality and Arnold Rampersad's *Life of Langston Hughes*," in *Queer Representations: Reading Lives, Reading Cultures* (1997), edited by Martin Duberman (188–96); and Shane Vogel's "Closing Time: Langston Hughes and the Queer Poetics of Harlem Nightlife," *Criticism* 48.3 (Summer 2006): 397–425.

Forman Brown's *Better Angel* is featured in Anthony Slide's *Lost Gay Novels* (2003), 125–29, and discussed by John Rechy in "Sixty Years Later a Gay Classic Enters (Almost) the Mainstream," in *Beneath the Skin: The Collected Essays of John Rechy* (2004): 145–49. Joanne Ellen Passet's *Sex Variant Woman: A Life of Jeannette Howard Foster* appeared in 2008. Two unpublished novels by Foster are held in the Barbara Grier / Donna McBride Collection at the San Francisco Public Library.

For information on Ruth Seid's *Wasteland*, consult Monica Bachmann's "'Someone like Debby': (De)Constructing a Lesbian Community of Readers," *GLQ: A Journal of Lesbian and Gay Studies* 6.3 (2000): 377–88; and Warren Hoffman's *The Passing Game: Queering Jewish American Culture* (2009). On William Inge, see Albert Wertheim's "Dorothy's Friend in Kansas: The Gay Inflections of William Inge," in *Staging Desire: Queer Readings of American Theater History* (2002), edited by Kim Marra and Robert A. Schanke (194–217); and Jeff Johnson's *William Inge and the Subversion of Gender: Rewriting Stereotypes in the Plays, Novels, and Screenplays* (2005).

Robert E. Fleming's *Willard Motley* (1978) is an introduction to the novelist. Also consult M. E. Grenander's "Criminal Responsibility in Native Son and *Knock on Any Door*," *American Literature* 49.2 (May 1977): 221–33; and the entry on *Knock on Any Door* in Anthony Slide's *Lost Gay Novels*, 135–36.

For LGBTQ involvement in pulp novels, see Susan Stryker's *Queer Pulp: Perverted Passions from the Golden Age of the Paperback*

(2001). Scholarship on Ann Bannon includes Suzanna Danuta Walters's "As Her Hand Slowly Crept up Her Thigh: Ann Bannon and the Politics of Pulp," in *Sexual Politics and Popular Culture* (1990), edited by Diane Christine Raymond, 81–101. Yvonne Keller's "'Was It Right to Love My Brother's Wife So Passionately?' Lesbian Pulp Novels and U.S. Lesbian Identity, 1950–1965," *American Quarterly* 57.2 (June 2005): 385–410, discusses both Bannon and Valerie Taylor. An interview with Taylor appears in *Coming of Age: The Story of Our Century by Those Who've Lived It* (1995) by (Louis) Studs Terkel (1912–2008).

James Morrison's entry on James Purdy in *Contemporary Gay American Novelists: A Bio-Bibliographical Critical Sourcebook* (1993), edited by Emmanuel S. Nelson, 328–39, provides a good overview. Nelson's volume also includes a profile of Daniel Curzon, written by John Gettys (89–95). On Deirdre N. McCloskey, see *Identity's Strategy: Rhetorical Selves in Conversion* (2007) by Dana Anderson. Robin Wilson's "Leading Economist Stuns Field by Deciding to Become a Woman" appears in the February 16, 1996, issue of the *Chronicle of Higher Education*, A17–A18. Michael A. Gilbert reviews *Crossing: A Memoir* in *Archives of Sexual Behavior* 31.2 (April 2002): 222–25.

Stephen Barber's *Edmund White: The Burning World* (1999) is a biography. Scholarship includes Nicholas F. Radel's "(E)racing Edmund White: Queer Reading, Race, and Sexuality in *A Boy's Own Story*," *Modern Fiction Studies* 54.4 (Winter 2008): 766–90; and Tony Purvis's "America's 'White' Cultural and Sexual Dissensus: The Fictions of Edmund White," *Journal of American Studies* 42.2 (August 2008): 293–316. The Edmund White Papers are held at Yale University's Beinecke Library.

Sue Russell's "Mary Oliver: The Poet and the Persona" appears in *The Harvard Gay and Lesbian Review* 4.4 (Fall 1997): 21–22. In "Landscapes Strange and Manifold as Morning: The Poetry of Mary Oliver," *Ohioana Quarterly* 45.1 (Spring 2002): 6–13, Terry Hermsen considers Oliver's Ohio poems. Susan Swartwout's "Filling in Between: The Lesbian Love Poems of Linnea Johnson" can be found in *Illinois Writers' Review* 11.1 (1992): 22–29. Charles Hood's entry on Robert Peters appears in *Dictionary of Literary Biography* 105, *American Poets since World War II, Second Series* (1991): 192–99. Selected reviews appear in *Contemporary Literary Criticism* 7 (1977): 303–304, and interviews are presented in Peters's *The Great American Poetry Bake-off, Fourth Series* (1991). Peters's papers are held by the Kenneth Spencer Research Library at the University of Kansas and the Geisel Library at the University of California, San Diego. Howard Nelson contributed "The Work of Antler" to the *Twayne Companion to Contemporary Literature in English* (2003), edited by Richard. H. W. Dillard and Amanda Cockrell, 21–34. Thomas March's "Translation Skill: A Review of *How To* by William Reichard" appears in *Lambda Book Review* 12.8–9 (March/April 2004): 20.

On Jeffrey Eugenides's *Middlesex*, see Leland S. Person's *"Middlesex:* What Men Like in Men," *American Literary History* 17.4 (2005): 753–64; Susan Frelich Appleton's "Contesting Gender in Popular Culture and Family Law: *Middlesex* and Other Transgender Tales," *Indiana Law Journal* 80.2 (2005): 391–440; and Morgan Holmes's "Cal/liope in Love: The 'Prescientific' Desires of an Apolitical 'Hermaphrodite,'" *Journal of Lesbian Studies* 11.3–4 (August 2007): 223–32.

New Queer Cinema: A Critical Reader (2004), edited by Michele Aaron, features critical debate over queer-themed films of the 1990s. Derek Dalton considers *Swoon* in "The Deviant Gaze: Imagining the Homosexual as Criminal through Cinematic and Legal Discourses," in *Law and Sexuality: The Global Arena* (2001), edited by Carl Franklin Stychin and Didi Herman, 69–83. In "This Is Normal? A Theatre Coach Works in Film," in *Film, Broadcast and Electronic Media Coaching* (2003), edited by Rocco Dal Vera (33–43), dialect coach Eric Armstrong describes helping the cast of *Normal* with Midwestern speech patterns and Tom Wilkinson with shifting from a masculine to a feminine voice.

On Brandon Teena and *Boys Don't Cry*, see *In a Queer Time and Place: Transgender Bodies, Subcultural Lives* (2005) by Judith Halberstam; Melissa Rigney's "Brandon Goes to Hollywood: *Boys Don't Cry* and the Transgender Body in Film," in *Queer Youth Cultures* (2008), edited by Susan Driver (181–98) and Sherri Helvie's "Willa Cather and Brandon Teena: The Politics of Passing," *Women and Language* 20.1 (Spring 1997): 35–40.

Periodicals have played an important role in the development of LGBTQ literature in the Midwest. *RFD,* a magazine for rural gay men, was founded in 1974 in Grinnell, Iowa. After two years *RFD* relocated; it now operates in Massachusetts. *Common Lives / Lesbian Lives* was published in Iowa City, Iowa, from 1981 to 1996. Devoted to writing by gay men, *The James White Review* was published in Minneapolis from 1983 to 1998 and thereafter in Washington, D.C., until 2004. *Windy City Times,* a Chicago gay and lesbian newspaper founded in 1985, includes coverage of books and authors. The *Evergreen Chronicles,* founded in Minneapolis in 1985, publishes writing by diverse members of the LGBTQ community.

Founded in 1981, Gerber/Hart Library in Chicago is the most prominent gay and lesbian library and archive in the Midwest. The Jean-Nickolaus Tretter Collection in Gay, Lesbian, Bisexual, and Transgender Studies at the University of Minnesota also has significant holdings. The Labadie Collection, an archive at the University of Michigan devoted to modern radical movements, collects documents of gay and lesbian activism. The Kinsey Institute for Research in Sex, Gender, and Reproduction at Indiana University also has an enormous collection of LGBTQ materials.

WILLIAM BARILLAS

UNIVERSITY OF WISCONSIN–LA CROSSE

Life of Ma-Ka-Tai-Me-She-Kia-Kiak, or Black Hawk

HISTORY: The autobiography of BLACK HAWK (1767–1838), published as *Life of Ma-Ka-Tai-Me-She-Kia-Kiak, or Black Hawk* (1833), established two literary precedents. It was the first best-selling book produced on the Mississippi Valley frontier and the first account in American letters dictated by a Native American–language speaker to an English-language writer. See FRONTIER AND PIONEER ACCOUNTS and NATIVE AMERICAN LITERATURE. Although the circumstances surrounding its creation and transmission led to serious questioning of the volume's authenticity, it has earned a place as a Midwestern and American classic. Black

BLACK HAWK.

Frontispiece, *Autobiography of Ma-ka-tai-me-she-kia-kiak, or Black Hawk*. **Press of Continental Printing, 1882.**
Image courtesy of University of Kentucky Special Collections Research Center

Hawk dictated the account to Antoine LeClaire, a French-Potawatomi who spoke French, English, and twelve Native languages and served as the U.S. interpreter for the Sac and Fox Agency on Rock Island adjacent to Saukenuk, the major Sauk village. LeClaire certifies in the first edition of the book that Black Hawk approached him in August 1833, a year after the conclusion of the Black Hawk War, about writing and publishing an account of his thoughts and actions that resulted in that war. LeClaire translated Black Hawk's account and supplied it to newspaperman John B. Patterson, who wrote it in English and had it published in CINCINNATI.

The tripartite collaboration stirred skepticism from the outset. In the popular press, advocates of Manifest Destiny dismissed any account by Native Americans on the racist grounds that Indians were incapable of truth. Literary commentators were suspicious of the process of dictation, translation, and writing, which seemed to obscure the form and substance of Black Hawk's statements while leaving much to Patterson's discretion and possible contrivance. No manuscripts, correspondence, or personal papers pertaining to the book's publication have been found, so scholars have no evidence regarding the working relationships and procedures of Black Hawk, LeClaire, and Patterson beyond statements attributed to them in the first edition.

Conjecture about the writing process and the degree of accuracy with which it captures Black Hawk's thoughts and intentions remains rampant, but the book stands as a literary document providing a Native American perspective on events associated with the loss of lands the Sauk had occupied since the early eighteenth century. Although the controversy over the book's authenticity and the integrity of the rendering of Black Hawk's voice persists in criticism, the book accords with works of history, ETHNOGRAPHY, and literature. Patterson's stilted Victorian stylistics are intrusive at times, but the general critical consensus is that the book accurately portrays Sauk history and conveys the values and cultural perceptions of a Sauk warrior.

SIGNIFICANCE: After the Black Hawk War, Black Hawk was held prisoner at Jefferson Barracks in ST. LOUIS and was then taken by government officials and military leaders on a tour of the eastern United States to see the nation's power and to discourage him and other Native American dissidents from further uprisings. Editors and critics of recent editions conjecture that this tour resulted in the idea for the book.

Black Hawk's reception by white Americans on the tour and the reaction to his autobiography demonstrate the ambiguity with which he and Native Americans generally were regarded by the white American public. Those who coveted the land occupied by the Sauk saw Black Hawk as a degraded savage who stood in the way of civilized settlement. On the other hand, as he toured the United States, crowds came out to see him, the press covered his appearances, and the public often accorded him a heroic dignitary's reception. Although a few incidents reported by military officers who accompanied him were menacing, people saw in him courage, dignity, and resoluteness projected by an aesthetically striking bearing that reflected their own values.

This interest and fascination partly explain the success of his autobiography. In the last years of his life Black Hawk became a cult figure to settlers and visitors. Similarly, anti-Indian attitudes among whites in America did not deter settlers from appropriating large aspects of Native American culture. Black Hawk's autobiography provided a vehicle by which advancing settlers could sublimate Native dispossession by paying tribute to notable Native American figures. The volume also filled the demand for a heroic literature grounded in the American land and experience.

In their tendency to read the book as an account of a warrior hero in the western tradition, early readers missed many details of Sauk ethnography and the complex interplay of culture, personality, and character that establish the book as a unique story of the Midwest and an important work of Native American literature. The public persisted in calling Black Hawk "Chief" even though he never attained the stature required of a designated leader in the Sauk council.

In the volume Black Hawk explains how his leadership in the Black Hawk War resulted from a factional divide within the Sauk nation between those who refused to be removed and those who thought that removal was inevitable and resistance futile. He maintains that the treaty of 1804, which ceded the lands in western ILLINOIS, was invalid because it was negotiated with Sauk individuals not authorized to represent their nation and did not follow the procedures required by the Sauk for relinquishing land.

Two considerations were paramount among those who resisted the land transfer. As a place where generations of Sauk were buried, the land was the site of important cultural and sacred rites; it was also the place where extensive fields for crops had been established. The women, who had charge of the fields and would have to break ground for new ones, supported Black Hawk.

His open rebellion against the order to remove, however, was prompted by neighboring tribal leaders who assured him that his resistance would inspire many warriors from other nations to join him.

Much of the war was actually an attempt by the Black Hawk band to evade the army and the militia and seek refuge in IOWA. As the band attempted to cross the Mississippi River from WISCONSIN into Iowa at the mouth of Bad Axe Creek, it was met by a gunboat that opened fire, killing twenty-five of the band and cutting off its retreat. All members of the Black Hawk band were killed or captured.

The autobiography is not rendered in English in an effort to capture Black Hawk's voice through literary manipulation of tone, attitude, and verbal characteristics, as are some dictated accounts by Native Americans. However, a compelling literary characteristic that speaks to its authenticity is the central consciousness of the narrative, which is consistently and coherently Black Hawk's. The narrative draws on traditional forms of Native American oral literature, further evidence that the essential story originated in Black Hawk's Sauk mind. The book also conforms to a format used by Native Americans in treaty negotiations and councils with other governments. These councils were conducted according to stringent rules of order that required formalities to be observed in the presentation of subjects or grievances to be addressed. These formalities included a gracious acknowledgment of the other party in stating the purpose of the council, a statement that indicated the tribal identity and the interests inherent in that identity, a statement of achievements that qualified a speaker to address the council, and a review of problems or grievances that one party wished to be resolved. At such councils held by the British, the proceedings were recorded by two or three amanuenses. Black Hawk's appearances at such councils are recorded and provide materials to compare with the autobiography.

The autobiography contains six sections, or rhetorical movements, that conform to Native American traditions. After some ceremonial statements, the book opens with a mythic history of the Sauk nation. The second narrative movement deals with Black Hawk's recitation of accomplishments in the tradition of "counting coups" or relating military achievements. The third movement is a rhetorical summary of the movement of American settlers into the Mississippi Valley. It is followed by the fourth section, which is a pleasant recounting of the Sauk way of life and landscape that the settlers were disrupting. The fifth section presents the grievances that the Sauk had at what they regarded as the depredations of the settlers. The sixth section has two parts. The first of these covers the specific events and circumstances that led to the Black Hawk War; the second deals with Black Hawk's life after he was captured and made a prisoner of war.

The controlling point of Black Hawk's story is that the Sauk were wronged, and each movement of the book is a rhetorical demonstration of that point. In his edition of the autobiography, Donald Jackson asserts that it is the story of "a stubborn warrior brooding upon the certainty that his people must fight to survive," a man who "chose a bitter last stand against extinction" (31).

A contemporaneous text providing a counterpoint to Black Hawk's *Autobiography* is the well-known poem "The Prairies" (1832) by William Cullen Bryant (1794–1878). Bryant wrote the poem during a visit to Illinois coinciding with the Black Hawk War. Ignoring current events and distorting Native prehistory, Bryant conveys romantic cultural nationalism and sentimentality regarding the pioneers. Midwestern authors have since demonstrated an awareness of Black Hawk and his *Autobiography*. Elbert Herrick Smith, an early Milwaukee poet, published the best-selling *Ma-ka-tai-me-she-kia-kiak, or Black Hawk, an Epic Poem, and Scenes in the West* (1848). Smith's formulaic, derivative poem is sympathetic to Native Americans, although it stereotypes them as noble savages. In her novel *My Ántonia* (1918) WILLA CATHER (1873–1947) changed the name of her NEBRASKA hometown from Red Cloud, named after a Sioux war chief, to Black Hawk, an alteration that places the issue of violence against Native Americans at a geographic and historical remove. *The Shining Trail* (1943) by IOLA FULLER (GOOD-

SPEED MCCOY) (1906–1993) and *Sparrow Hawk* (1950) by MERIDEL LE SUEUR (1900–1996) are historical novels about the Black Hawk War written for young readers. LORINE NIEDECKER (1903–1970) lived most of her life in Wisconsin on Black Hawk Island, near Fort Atkinson, named for General Henry Atkinson, who led American forces in the Black Hawk War; she wrote a tightly rendered, untitled poem that contrasts the Sauk view of land with that of whites, represented by Atkinson and ABRAHAM LINCOLN (1809–1865), who also served in the Black Hawk War. The poem, which begins "Black Hawk held," appears in Niedecker's *My Friend Tree* (1961) (n.p.) and in her 2004 *Collected Works* (99). Michael Borich (b. 1949), originally from Iowa, published *The Black Hawk Songs* (1975), a book of poetry about the Sauk leader and his people's struggle. Black Hawk is one of thirty-five Illinois authors whose names are engraved on the frieze of the Illinois State Library, dedicated in 1990.

IMPORTANT EDITIONS: The first edition of *Life of Ma-Ka-Tai-Me-She-Kia-Kiak, or Black Hawk* was published in 1833 in Cincinnati, OHIO. The book has been continually reprinted ever since. The 1882 version, published in Oquawka, Illinois, added J. B. Patterson's history of the Black Hawk War. The Lakeside Press edition of 1916, edited by Milo Milton Quaife, is currently in print in a Dover edition titled *Life of Black Hawk* (1994). There are two scholarly editions of the book. *Black Hawk: An Autobiography*, edited by Donald Jackson, was published by the University of Illinois Press in 1955 and continues to be reprinted. *Black Hawk's Autobiography*, edited by Roger L. Nichols, was published in 1999 by Iowa State University Press.

FURTHER READING: Benjamin Drake's *The Life and Times of Black Hawk* (1838), published five years after the autobiography, uses interviews and contemporary sources. Perry Armstrong's *The Sauks and the Black Hawk War* (1887) is sympathetic to the Sauk, whereas Frank E. Stevens's *The Black Hawk War, Including a Review of Black Hawk's Life* (1903) favors the settlers' belief in Manifest Destiny. Cyrenus Cole's *I Am a Man: The Indian Black Hawk* (1938) tries for objectivity in recapping the warrior's life.

Ellen M. Whitney's four-volume collection of documents and papers, *The Black Hawk War, 1831–32* (1970–1978), is an essential resource for putting the autobiography in context. Anthony F. C. Wallace's *Prelude to Disaster: The Course of Indian-White Relations Which Led to the Black Hawk War of 1832* (1970) is a comprehensive account of Sauk governance and the failure of the United States to observe the rules of treaty negotiation required for the valid transfer of lands. Wallace's work supports Black Hawk's contentions in his autobiography; it was referred to by the Indian Claims Commission in accepting the Sauk contention that the treaty of 1804 was invalidly negotiated. Cecil Eby's *"That Disgraceful Affair," the Black Hawk War* (1973), is a generalized account of the events leading up to and during the war. Roger L. Nichols's *Black Hawk and the Warrior's Path* (1992) is a useful biography. Notable speeches of Black Hawk that reveal his thought and expression include one, edited by John E. Hallwas, in *Illinois Literature: The Nineteenth Century* (1986), and another from an 1817 meeting between Black Hawk and the British on Drummond Island, appended to a doctoral dissertation, David L. Newquist's "A Reading of Black Hawk's 'Autobiography' " (1980). One chapter of Cheryl Walker's *Indian Nation: Native American Literature and Nineteenth-Century Nationalisms* (1997) discusses Black Hawk's autobiography in relation to Native American views of U.S. nationality; Walker also comments on Elbert H. Smith's epic poem. Two histories, Kerry A. Trask's *Black Hawk: The Battle for the Heart of America* (2007) and Patrick J. Jung's *The Black Hawk War of 1832* (2007), provide narratives of the war and deal with the production of the autobiography.

The *Autobiography* has commanded the attention of literary scholars, as well as historians. Literary studies include Scott L. Pratt's "The Given Land: Black Hawk's Conception of Place," *Philosophy and Geography* 4.1 (2001): 109–26; Laura L. Mielke's " 'Native to the Question': William Apess, Black Hawk, and the Sentimental Context of Early Native American Autobiography," *American Indian Quarterly* 26.2 (2002): 246–70; David L. Newquist's "A Rereading of Black Hawk's *Autobiography*," *MidAmerica* 29 (2002): 78–90;

Eric Gary Anderson's "Indian Agency: Life of Black Hawk and the Countercolonial Provocations of Early Native American Writing," *ESQ: A Journal of the American Renaissance* 52.1–2 (2006): 75–104; and Kendall A. Johnson's "Peace, Friendship, and Financial Panic: Reading the Mark of Black Hawk in *Life of Ma-Ka-Tai-Me-She-Kia-Kiak*," *American Literary History* 19.4 (2007): 771–'99. Arnold Krupat contrasts Black Hawk's authorial perspective as the life story of an identity defined by the tribal community with the Euro-American convention of a personal, individual account in "Patterson's *Life:* Black Hawk's Story, Native American Elegy," *American Literary History* 22.3 (2010): 527–52. Mark Rifkin correlates excerpts of the text to illustrate the conflicting concepts of land occupation between the Sauk and the Americans in "Documenting Tradition: Territoriality and Textuality in Black Hawk's Narrative," *American Literature* 80.4 (2008): 677–705.

DAVID L. NEWQUIST   NORTHERN STATE UNIVERSITY

LITERARY MAPS.
See Maps, Literary

LITERARY PERIODICALS.
See Periodicals, Literary

LITTLE REVIEW, THE
OVERVIEW: Although circulation never rose much above a thousand subscribers and the magazine was published only sporadically because of its financial difficulties, *The Little Review* played a pivotal role in the development and promotion of Midwestern writers and modernist literature, publishing Midwesterners such as SHERWOOD ANDERSON (1876–1941), EDGAR LEE MASTERS (1868–1950), and ERNEST (MILLER) HEMINGWAY (1899–1961), as well as leading European poets, critics, and authors, including William Butler Yeats (1865–1939), Aldous Huxley (1894–1963), and James Joyce (1882–1941).

Founded in CHICAGO in March 1914 by MARGARET C. ANDERSON (1886–1973), *The Little Review* was groundbreaking in its content and its independent, staunchly feminist editor. It launched and supported CHICAGO RENAISSANCE writers, asserted emerging regional, national, and international norms for poetry

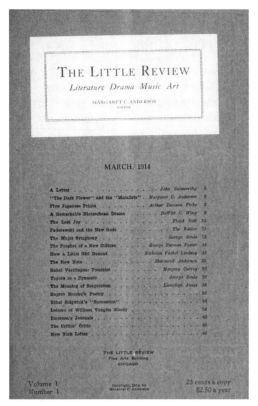

The Little Review

Literature Drama Music Art

MARGARET C. ANDERSON
EDITOR

MARCH, 1914

THE LITTLE REVIEW
Fine Arts Building
CHICAGO

Volume 1   25 cents a copy
Number 1   Copyright, 1914, by $2.50 a year
                Margaret C. Anderson

First issue of Margaret Anderson's *The Little Review*, March 1914.

Image files © The Modernist Journals Project. Image provided by the Modernist Journals Project (Brown University and the University of Tulsa), http://www.modjourn.org

and fiction, and enhanced Chicago's stature as a leading national and international literary center. *The Little Review* later moved to New York and finally to Paris, but CHICAGO was its impetus and home during its formative years.

HISTORY AND SIGNIFICANCE: *The Little Review*, like POETRY: A MAGAZINE OF VERSE, grew out of the Chicago cultural movement of the early 1900s. Anderson's previous magazine experience included writing book reviews for *The DIAL* and serving as literary editor for the *Interior*, a Chicago religious magazine. Within a few years *The Little Review* adopted the slogan "A Magazine of the Arts: Making No Compromise with the Public Taste." At its best, the publication—though often whimsical and sometimes erratic—was inspired by and fostered avant-

garde literature. Its goal as stated in the first issue was "to practice criticism of books, music, art, drama, and life that shall be fresh and constructive, and intelligent from the artist's point of view" (3). In the same issue Anderson widened the publication's range prospectively, declaring her intent to "print articles, poems, stories that seem to us definitely interesting, or . . . vital" (9).

The first issue was a potpourri of genres and topics, including poems, some by (NICHOLAS) VACHEL LINDSAY (1879–1931); an expressionistic "book review" by FLOYD DELL (1887–1969); a review of *Mr. Faust* as a Nietzschean drama by Arthur Davidson Ficke (1883–1945); the first part of Sherwood Anderson's "The New Note," calling for "a reinjection of truth and honesty into the craft" (23); and multiple opinion pieces on art and music, letters from and articles on European writers, and multiple pieces on feminism. Lindsay, Ficke, and Anderson went on to become frequent contributors. Sherwood Anderson ultimately published stories from *WINESBURG, OHIO* and "The Struggle" there. Lindsay contributed "How a Little Girl Danced" and "I Went Down to the Desert." Ficke published "Portrait of Theodore Dreiser" and "Rupert Brooke (A Memory)." *The Spring Recital*, a play by (HERMAN) THEODORE DREISER (1871–1945), also appeared in an early issue.

These early years also featured several other Midwestern works, including "Gone" and "Graves" by CARL (AUGUST) SANDBURG (1878–1967); "So We Grew Together" by Masters; and "The American Family," "Broken Necks," and "Autumn Song" by BEN HECHT (1894–1964). As time passed, however, the magazine's contents included more and more East Coast and European writers, poetry, and international matters. Anderson and Jane Heap (1883–1964), who joined *The Little Review* in 1916, as well as their devoted following of regional writers, wanted the magazine to capture the shifting nature of modernist poetry.

Trying to break new ground took its toll. After Anderson published "Letters from Prison" by Emma Goldman (1869–1940) in 1915, the magazine lost some financial support on the grounds that the letters were anarchist propaganda. Undeterred, Anderson and Heap continued to publish what they chose regardless of risk. Early controversial poems by MAXWELL BODENHEIM (1892–1954) found a place in *The Little Review,* as did "In Shadow" and "The Real Question" by (HAROLD) HART CRANE (1899–1932).

The year 1916 saw the infamous half-blank issue when Anderson felt she had few contributions worth publishing; during other months her publication overflowed with groundbreaking, controversial material. The two women launched a birth-control campaign and published a defense of Margaret Sanger (1879–1966), further exacerbating their fiscal woes when this decision upset some of their subscribers. Personal and professional friends contributed to keep *The Little Review* afloat, and the editors made personal sacrifices to keep the magazine going.

In 1917 Anderson and Heap moved the magazine to New York in search of a wider audience and a broader circulation, but the move did not stop the suppression and censorship; publication of "Cantleman's Spring-Mate" by Wyndham Lewis (1882–1957) caused the October issue to be confiscated by the post office. Financial backing proved hard to find, and some issues were omitted because the women could not meet production costs.

Even though *The Little Review* published many Midwestern authors, Anderson and Heap also showed an affinity for European writers because one of the magazine's ultimate purposes was to blend American and European literature into one new, innovative form. In 1917 Ezra Pound (1885–1972) became the magazine's foreign correspondent. William Butler Yeats's "The Wild Swans at Coole," "A Song," and "Presences," as well as some works by Lady Gregory (1852–1932), Aldous Huxley, and, most famously, James Joyce were all published in *The Little Review.* American EXPATRIATES, including several from the Midwest, found a voice in the *Review.* "Advice to a Young Poet" and "A Study in French Poets" by Ezra Pound, Ernest Hemingway's first six stories from *in our time,* and "The Hippopotamus" and "Eeldrop and Appleplex" by T(HOMAS) S(TEARNS) ELIOT (1888–1965) appeared in its pages. Perhaps *The Little Review* is best known as the first American literary magazine to publish parts of Joyce's *Ulysses* (1922), serialized between 1918 and 1920. For doing so, both Anderson and Heap were prosecuted for obscenity, fined $100, and fingerprinted.

Despite efforts to keep the magazine financially viable while publishing cutting-edge writing, finances continued to degenerate. According to Anderson in her autobiography, *My Thirty Years' War* (1930), "as *The Little Review* became more articulate, more interesting, its subscription list became less impressive. It is much easier to find a public for ideals than for ideas. The subscriptions dwindled during the whole of the L. R.'s best period" (146). The emotional strain of supporting a declining magazine with personal finances, continuing censorship, and the growing strain on Anderson and Heap's relationship closed the first chapter of *The Little Review*'s history. Shortly after the *Ulysses* controversy, Anderson, feeling that nearly ten years was enough of one's life to dedicate to one pursuit, left for Europe and relinquished most responsibilities to Heap, who took official control in 1923. The publication remained in New York until 1927, publishing quarterly when possible and annually the rest of the time. Then it moved to Paris, where it remained until 1929, when Heap finally agreed that the publication had run its course.

SELECTED WORKS: The University of Wisconsin–Milwaukee holds many editorial copies and correspondence related to *The Little Review.* The University of Delaware has some manuscripts in its Florence Reynolds Collection. The Library of Congress, the University of Michigan, Yale University, and the University of Texas at Austin all hold some Anderson and Heap manuscripts and papers. Anderson herself edited *The Little Review Anthology* (1953). Finally, the New York Public Library holds a compiled index of *The Little Review.*

FURTHER READING: Frank Luther Mott's fifth volume of *A History of American Magazines* (1938) and Margaret Anderson's autobiography, *My Thirty Years' War* (1930), are good sources on *The Little Review.* Both Jayne E. Marek's *Women Editing Modernism: "Little" Magazines and Literary History* (1995) and Lisa Woolley's *American Voices of the Chicago Renaissance* (2000) contain chapters on the publication. See also Marilyn J. Atlas's "Harriet Monroe, Margaret Anderson, and the Spirit of the Chicago Renaissance," *Midwestern Miscellany* 9 (1981): 43–53; and Philip A. Greasley's "Mid American Poetry in Midwestern Little Magazines," *MidAmerica* 5 (1977): 50–65.

Ashley Hopkins
                    The University of Tennessee at Chattanooga

Lost Son and Other Poems, The

history: The publication of *The Lost Son and Other Poems* in 1948 placed Theodore Roethke (1908–1963) in the first rank of American poets. His first book, *Open House* (1941), was a competent collection of formalist poetry, but *The Lost Son* revealed a truly original style and subject matter. The book's twenty-nine poems, mostly in free verse, introduced the poet's central imagery: the plant life nurtured in and around the greenhouses run by Roethke's father and uncle in Saginaw, Michigan. The symbolic power of that pastoral imagery and the beauty of Roethke's language make *The Lost Son* one of the most important books of twentieth-century poetry and a singular contribution to Midwestern literature.

Roethke wrote the book between 1942 and 1947 while teaching at Bennington College and Pennsylvania State University and while visiting Saginaw. Several poems first appeared in *Harper's, The New Republic,* and other periodicals. During this period Roethke benefited from friendships with poet William Carlos Williams (1883–1963) and scholar Kenneth Burke (1897–1993). Williams encouraged Roethke to write in more natural, specific language, and Burke's investigations into Freudian psychology suggested how poetry could delve into unconscious desires and fears. Roethke suffered from clinical depression, experiencing his second major manic episode requiring hospitalization during this period. He came to see writing as a quest for self-knowledge, mental health, and mystical union with the forces of life.

The Lost Son is arranged in four parts. Part 1 contains the verses known as "the greenhouse poems," which describe the plants, the greenhouses, and the work of Roethke's father and others to keep the operation running. Part 2 consists of seven poems, three in rhyme and meter, on topics varying from the poet's father playing with young Theodore in the often anthologized "My Papa's Waltz" to expressions of loneliness in factories, offices, cinemas, and homes. Part 3 returns to imagery of nature, beyond the greenhouses in five poems that relate natural forms and evolution to human consciousness. The book culminates in the four long poems of part 4. The first and most significant of these is "The Lost Son," a symbolic journey through the landscape of Roethke's early years, proceeding through a psychic terrain of grief, mania, regression, and, ultimately, consolation and hope. The last three poems in the book, concluding with "The Shape of the Fire," substantiate the experience of joy through means consistent with those of the title poem: imagery of nature, stream of consciousness, and wordplay reminiscent of Mother Goose.

Dissatisfied with Knopf, the publisher of *Open House,* Roethke submitted his manuscript to Doubleday and Company of Garden City, New York, in early 1947. *The Lost Son* was published on March 11, 1948, by which time Roethke was completing his first year as associate professor of English at the University of Washington. Early reviews were laudatory. In the *New York Herald-Tribune,* for example, Babette Deutsch credited Roethke with "aural virtues that reach out and lay hands upon the nerves of the listener. . . . What emerges at the end is a history of a man's soul" (quoted in Allan Seager's *The Glass House: The Life of Theodore Roethke* [1968], 158).

The autobiographical nature of Roethke's work and his depiction of extreme psychological states have led some critics to associate him with "confessional" poets like John Berryman (1914–1972), Robert Lowell (1917–1977), Anne Sexton (1928–1974), and Sylvia Plath (1932–1963). All these poets lived with depression and wrote about their suffering; Berryman, Sexton, and Plath committed suicide. Roethke differed from these others not only in style but also in his emphasis on place, his mysticism of nature, and his depiction of joy in equal measure with despair. In some ways his closest contemporary was Welsh poet Dylan Thomas (1914–1953), a friend and mutual admirer who, like Roethke, was fundamentally romantic in spirit. Both poets alternated free verse with traditional forms; both possessed lyrical expertise, using figurative language and sound devices to great effect. Roethke remains arguably the most popular and critically respected American poet of his generation. That high regard stems from the accomplishment that is *The Lost Son.*

SIGNIFICANCE: Whether they see the book as Roethke's best or as the foundation for even greater accomplishment in his later poetry, critics have consistently praised *The Lost Son.* His startling imagery, dense syntax, and symbolic complexity are cited as evidence of his originality and lyrical power. Scholars have stressed Roethke's relation to British romantics like William Blake (1757–1827) and the Americans Ralph Waldo Emerson (1803–1882), Henry David Thoreau (1817–1862), and Walt Whitman (1819–1892). Roethke also drew from and saw himself in competition with the modernists, who were still publishing important work in the 1940s. *The Lost Son* represents an effort to write something as notable as works by Williams, T(HOMAS) S(TERNS) ELIOT (1888–1965), and Ezra Pound (1885–1972).

Also central to an understanding of *The Lost Son* is its autobiographical, Midwestern dimension. As a child in Michigan, Roethke observed his father, German immigrant Otto Roethke, working with plants, maintaining the greenhouses, and running the business. At an early age Theodore was given jobs pulling weeds and arranging flowers. His father was, by all accounts, a perfectionist and a stern taskmaster. In 1923, when Theodore was not yet fifteen, Otto died of cancer. "His father's death," Allan Seager argues in *The Glass House,* "was the most important thing that ever happened to him. . . . The love and fear he felt for Otto Roethke were the deepest emotions he ever had and his complex feelings for nature were tied to his father" (104).

Those feelings underlie Roethke's second book, leading Walter B. Kalaidjian to assert in *Understanding Theodore Roethke* (1987) that the "loss of the father is the central subject of *The Lost Son*" (6). Awareness of mortality contends with the will to live in the book's first two poems, "Cuttings"

Young Theodore Roethke in his family's greenhouse, Saginaw, Michigan, ca. 1920.
Courtesy of the Roethke Family Collection, Local History and Genealogy Department,
Public Libraries of Saginaw, Michigan

and "Cuttings (*later*)," which describe how "starts," pieces of plants made to grow in a nitrogen-rich solution, begin to wither before taking root and moving toward the light. Here and elsewhere Roethke identifies human consciousness with the smallest, most primitive elements of nature. "I can hear, underground, that sucking and sobbing," he writes in the second poem. "In my veins, in my bones I can feel it" (*Collected Poems,* 1975 edition, 35).

Subsequent greenhouse poems like "Root Cellar" and "Orchids" similarly portray the instinctual life force of plants as simultaneously beautiful and frightening. Roethke describes his childhood tasks in "Weed Puller" and "Moss-Gathering." In the latter he recalls hiking in one of his father's private forests, charged with harvesting moss, "the kind for lining cemetery baskets." That his return trip follows a "logging road" subtly correlates the experience to Michigan's logging era, which by the time of Roethke's childhood had devastated the forests of upper Michigan. This ecological parable ends with the child feeling "mean . . . / As if I had committed, against the whole scheme of life, a desecration" (*Collected Poems* 38).

For the most part, however, Roethke depicts the greenhouse as a place of meaningful labor, where ingenuity and competence yield an aesthetic harvest. In "Big Wind," for example, workers spend a worrisome night making sure the greenhouses survive a violent storm. In "Old Florist," a catalog of ways in which Otto tended his plants, the poet marvels at his father's life-giving powers.

Those powers figure prominently in "The Lost Son," described by Jay Parini in *Theodore Roethke: An American Romantic* (1979) as "the central poem in Roethke's canon" (96). "The Lost Son" involves a spiritual journey into and beyond the self, beginning with Roethke's grief over his father's death, followed by a mythological dark night of the soul, and concluding with clearly remembered scenes of the greenhouses in winter. Using archetypal images like water, light, shadows, and the sun and moon, Roethke captures rhythms of the unconscious mind along with the perspectives of childhood and adolescence. "The Lost Son" conjoins subjective, inner experience with the actual Midwestern landscape of Roethke's Saginaw: the cemetery where his father was buried, the Tittabawassee River, and the greenhouses, described in one of Roethke's essays, collected in *On the Poet and His Craft: Selected Prose of Theodore Roethke* (1965), as "both heaven and hell, a kind of tropics created in the savage climate of Michigan, where austere German-Americans turned their love of order and their terrifying efficiency into something truly beautiful" (8–9).

Roethke's impact on American poets has been profound, particularly on those concerned with nature and place. He influenced younger poets even during his lifetime, as evidenced by echoes of *The Lost Son* in poetry by Plath and by her husband, England's Ted Hughes (1930–1998). Major Irish poets influenced by Roethke's work, especially the greenhouse poems, include Richard Murphy (b. 1927), John Montague (b. 1929), and Seamus Heaney (1939–2013); Murphy and Montague knew Roethke, and all three have written about him. Native American poets like Duane Niatum (b. 1938) and Sherman Alexie (b. 1966) refer admiringly to Roethke. In "A Conversation: Sherman Alexie and Diane Thiel" (2004), available on the Poetry Society of America website, Alexie said, "I've spent my whole career rewriting 'My Papa's Waltz' with an Indian twist." In *"The Edge Is What I Have": Theodore Roethke and After* (1977) Harry Williams identifies a "Roethkean mode" in the work of poets sharing Roethke's "repugnance for a high-speed, technocratic society" (155), including Midwesterners ROBERT (ELWOOD) BLY (b. 1926) and JAMES WRIGHT (1927–1980). Wright, a former student of Roethke's, made a similar transition from formalism to free verse with his third book, THE BRANCH WILL NOT BREAK (1963). Poets from Roethke's home state cannot help but be aware of the greenhouse poems, especially poets attuned to Michigan ecology like JIM (JAMES THOMAS) HARRISON (1937–2016), JUDITH MINTY (b. 1937), and DAN GERBER (b. 1940).

IMPORTANT EDITIONS: The first edition of *The Lost Son* was published by Doubleday in 1948; John Lehmann's British edition followed in 1949. The poems in part 4 appear in *Praise to the End!* (1951) in an extended "Lost Son" sequence featuring nine additional poems. The poem "O, Thou Opening,

O" concludes the sequence in *The Waking: Poems, 1933–1953* (1954), which also includes poems from *The Lost Son*. Selections also appear in *Words for the Wind: The Collected Verse of Theodore Roethke* (1958) and *Selected Poems* (2005). *The Collected Poems of Theodore Roethke* (1966) contains *The Lost Son* in its entirety. Pagination varies slightly between the 1966 text and Doubleday's 1975 paperback, still in print, which adds the poem "Frau Bauman, Frau Schmidt, and Frau Schwartze" at the end of part 1. Roethke incorporated that poem, which did not originally appear in *The Lost Son*, into subsequent appearances of the greenhouse sequence. In *Theodore Roethke: The Poet and His Critics* (1986) Randall Stiffler presents the textual controversy surrounding "Frau Bauman" (46–48), as well as alternative orderings of the "Lost Son" sequence (82–87). Most scholars use the 1975 paperback, the most readily available text and the one cited here.

FURTHER READING: Authorial comments on *The Lost Son* appear in *On the Poet and His Craft: Selected Prose of Theodore Roethke* (1965), expanded and republished as *On Poetry and Craft* (2001), and *The Selected Letters of Theodore Roethke* (1968), edited by Ralph J. Mills Jr. Journal entries from the period leading up to the publication of *The Lost Son* appear in *Straw for the Fire: From the Notebooks of Theodore Roethke, 1943–1963* (1972), edited by David Wagoner.

Allan Seager's *The Glass House: The Life of Theodore Roethke* (1968) is the only full-length biography. Seager includes a chapter on the genesis, publication, and reception of *The Lost Son*.

The first important scholarly study of Roethke's poetry, Kenneth Burke's "The Vegetal Radicalism of Theodore Roethke," analyzes psychological dimensions of *The Lost Son*. The essay appeared in *Sewanee Review* 58 (1950): 68–108 and in *Profile of Theodore Roethke* (1971), edited by William Heyen (19–46). Since Burke's essay, many articles and books on Roethke's work have appeared. Randall Stiffler reviews the earlier scholarship in *Theodore Roethke: The Poet and His Critics* (1986). Books treating *The Lost Son* at length include Harry Williams's *"The Edge Is What I Have": Theodore Roethke and After* (1977), Jay Parini's *Theodore Roethke:*

An American Romantic (1979), and Walter B. Kalaidjian's *Understanding Theodore Roethke* (1987). Don Bogen's *A Necessary Order: Theodore Roethke and the Writing Process* (1991) contains chapters on the writing of poems in the book and the extended "Lost Son" sequence. *Northwest Review* 11.3 (Summer 1971), a special issue on Roethke, includes Brandan Galvin's "Kenneth Burke and Theodore Roethke's 'Lost Son' Poems" (67–96), which was reprinted in Harold Bloom's 1988 collection *Theodore Roethke* (85–113).

In *"My Toughest Mentor": Theodore Roethke and William Carlos Williams (1940–1948)* (1999) Robert Kusch makes skillful use of the poets' correspondence in the years leading up to the publication of *The Lost Son*. On Roethke's impact on Irish poetry, see Elmer Kennedy-Andrew's *Writing Home: Poetry and Place in Northern Ireland, 1968–2008* (2008) and *Northern Irish Poetry: The American Connection* (2014). *The Midwestern Pastoral: Place and Landscape in Literature of the American Heartland* (2006) by William Barillas has a chapter on Roethke that stresses the poet's regional context and the centrality of *The Lost Son* to his poetic career.

The Friends of Theodore Roethke Foundation maintains Roethke's childhood home in Saginaw, Michigan and sponsors lectures, readings, and tours of Roethke House. The greenhouses no longer exist; houses occupy the land where they once stood. The poet's ashes are interred in a family plot in nearby Oakwood Cemetery, called "Woodlawn" in the title poem of *The Lost Son*.

Roethke's papers at Special Collections of the University of Washington Libraries include the manuscript of *The Lost Son*.

WILLIAM BARILLAS

UNIVERSITY OF WISCONSIN–LA CROSSE

LITERARY MAPS.
See Maps, Literary

LITERARY PERIODICALS.
See Periodicals, Literary

LOVE MEDICINE
HISTORY: In the years since 1984, when (KAREN) LOUISE ERDRICH (b. 1954) published *Love Medicine*, the novel has earned many awards, including the National Book Critics Circle Award for Best Work of Fiction

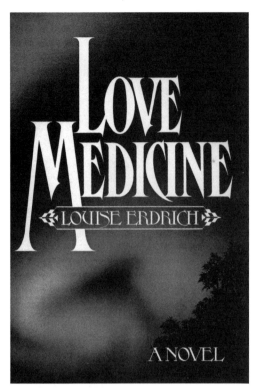

Louise Erdrich's *Love Medicine*, 1984. Cover design by Honi Werner.
© Honi Werner, 1984

(1984), the Sue Kaufman Prize for Best First Fiction from the American Academy and Institute of Arts and Letters (1984), and the *Los Angeles Times* Award for Fiction (1985), among others. Perhaps the best-known novel in Erdrich's series of four located on the same fictional reservation, *Love Medicine* is also the most critically acclaimed of Erdrich's works. Several chapters of *Love Medicine* were initially published as individual short stories in various reviews, magazines, and quarterlies, including "Saint Marie" in the *Atlantic Monthly*, March 1984, 78–84; "The Red Convertible" in the *Mississippi Valley Review*, Summer 1981, 10–17; and "Scales" in the *North American Review*, March 1982, 22–27; many individual chapters have since been reproduced in anthologies and textbooks. Furthermore, the novel as a whole is taught frequently in academic programs.

Well received by U.S. critics and the public alike, Erdrich's *New York Times* best-seller novel has been similarly embraced by an in-ternational audience and has assisted in ushering in, as Hertha D. Sweet Wong observes in *Louise Erdrich's "Love Medicine": A Casebook* (1999), a "second wave" of interest in Native North American writers—the first beginning with N. Scott Momaday's Pulitzer Prize–winning *House Made of Dawn* in 1969 (3).

Born to a German American father and a French and Ojibwa mother and raised in Wahpeton, NORTH DAKOTA, where her parents worked for the Wahpeton Indian Boarding School, as a child Erdrich spent time with her family on the Turtle Mountain Ojibwa Reservation in North Dakota. That experience provided her with the model for her fictional reservation. After receiving a BA from Dartmouth College in 1976 and an MA from Johns Hopkins University in 1979, she became the communications director and editor of the *Circle*, a Native American newspaper published by the University of Minnesota, that same year. In 1982 Erdrich received the Nelson Algren Fiction Award for "The World's Greatest Fisherman," a short work that would become the first chapter of *Love Medicine*. It was selected from over two thousand entries for the award by a panel of judges including Donald Barthelme (1931–1989), Kay Boyle (1902–1992), and (LOUIS) STUDS TERKEL (1912–2008), and was published in the October 1982 *Chicago* magazine.

SIGNIFICANCE: *Love Medicine* is an intricate collection of interrelated short stories narrated by one or more characters, woven into a novel through the movement toward a resolution and larger vision. The first to be published of a series of four novels that span over eighty years from 1912 through 1995, chronologically *Love Medicine* falls in the series after *Tracks* (1988), dating from 1912 through 1924, and *The Beet Queen* (1986), covering the time from 1932 through 1984, and before *The Bingo Palace* (1994), chronicling the period from 1981 through 1995. The chapters of *Love Medicine* begin in 1981, jump backward to 1934, and progress through 1984. The elaborate exchange between stories, with ties to both the postmodern concept of metafiction and the traditional method of Native American storytelling, works to place each individual character at the center of the story, forcing the reader, according to Kathleen M. Sands in her essay *"Love Medicine:* Voices and Margins," in *"Love Medicine": A Casebook*, to "shift position, turn, ponder, and finally integrate the story into a coherent whole" (34).

This structural tie between Native American oral tradition and the adapted postmodernist style of the novel is just one of the links between the cultures of the Ojibwas and the white community that impinges on the reservation life Erdrich creates in *Love Medicine*. Additionally, the multiple narrators and the repetition of stories, rather than further fragmenting the already frail identity of Native American people or the isolation associated with the modern Western world, serve instead to emphasize the search for individual and cultural identity that Erdrich's characters experience. Through the multiple voices and autobiographical elements, Erdrich is able to place the individual in a larger community identity. It is the search for identity that all of *Love Medicine*'s protagonists seem to share as they love, fight, and dream, are broken down, and attempt to build anew. Above all, *Love Medicine* becomes a network of stories about survival and family portrayed through the gaps in the multiperspective narration.

Leslie Marmon Silko, in "Here's an Odd Artifact for the Fairy-Tale Shelf: Review of the *Beet Queen," Studies in American Indian Literature* 10.4 (Fall 1986): 177–84, criticized Erdrich's *The Beet Queen* for lacking political commitment. Yet Erdrich's fiction uses the idea of place to make subtle observations on Native American reservation life. Drawn from Erdrich's experiences growing up in North Dakota as a mixed-blood member of the Turtle Mountain Band of the Ojibwas, Erdrich's concept of place ties in closely to conceptions of identity, assimilation, community, and healing. Considerable critical commentary has linked her writing to that of William Faulkner (1897–1962). Erdrich herself lists Faulkner as an influence on her work in several interviews, and the themes of her novels and stories—race, family, the past, community, and regionality—reflect those in Faulkner's fiction.

Love Medicine is a novel of all these themes and also a narrative in the tradition of an Ojibwa trickster tale as its protagonists change roles and—often humorously—subvert the rules. Through Gerry Nanapush's repeated escapes from prison, Lipsha Morrissey's love potion from supermarket-bought turkey hearts, and Marie Kashpaw's switching the placement of Nector's note from under the sugar canister to the salt, each character carves out a particular role in the reservation community.

And just as the fictional reservation is modeled on the Turtle Mountain Reservation, many of the settings are taken straight off maps of the Midwest. Williston, North Dakota, Fargo, Minnesota, and the Twin Cities provide scenes and physical backdrops for the chapters in *Love Medicine*. The policy of land allotment is mentioned several times. Beyond geographic names and places, the novel's sense of place, the community itself, and its links outside the reservation firmly anchor the work as characters marry outside the reservation, worship, and form relationships with the encroaching white community. Characters developed through the loosely connected stories of several reservation families, the Kashpaws, Lamartines, Morrisseys, and Pillagers, gradually become blended through intermarriage, thus blurring the distinction between full-blood and mixed-race members.

Assimilation of the white culture into Ojibwa traditions is also evident, especially in the economic improvement of the community and the practices of younger generations. Lulu Lamartine's house, which has long been located on the reservation, is targeted as the location for a new factory, and tribal members are divided, the more traditional members of the community arguing with the younger and more assimilationist members. The same is true with respect to education and healing. Lipsha, the son of June Kapshaw and Gerry Nanapush, fails in his schooling and returns to the reservation to cultivate traditional Ojibwa healing practices and "the secrets in [his] hands that nobody ever knew to ask" (1993 Harper Perennial edition 231), but his cousin Albertine enters a medical school that teaches Western medicine. Religion also reflects the divisions and linkages between Native American culture and that of the surrounding white Midwest. For example, in one scene Zelda Kashpaw exclaims about her daughter, Albertine: "My girl's an *Indian. . . .*

I raised her an Indian, and that's what she is" (24). But earlier in the chapter it is reported that Zelda was raised Catholic, and when Zelda asked Albertine whether she had met any marriageable boys in Fargo, her daughter "knew she meant Catholic" (14).

Erdrich's complicated relationship to the Midwest landscape of *Love Medicine* begins in the novel's first chapter, "The World's Greatest Fisherman." June Kapshaw, "walking down the clogged main street of oil boom-town Williston, North Dakota," is waiting for the noon bus that will take her "home" (1). After drinking the evening away with Andy, a mud engineer she met at a bar in Williston, she slips out of the pickup truck they just drove out of the city and "[crosses] the wide fields" back to the reservation (6). Although June never physically makes it back to the reservation, the "pure and naked part of her" finally does return home (7).

In a 1989 interview with Mickey Pearlman published in *Conversations with Louise Erdrich and Michael Dorris* (1994), Erdrich explains how the open spaces of the Midwest landscape are associated with her fiction and more generally with the Native American nations:

> It had a lot to do with where I grew up. I set myself back in that pure, empty landscape whenever I am working on something . . . [because] there's nothing like it. . . . June headed out into that open space, she was going across it, but she was heading home. She was heading into that wonderful and difficult mixture of family and place that mysteriously works on a person, that is home. (152–53)

However, the interaction between land and people is complicated by the struggle with identity that the characters experience as they navigate life on the reservation and in the outside world. As Lyman Lamartine struggles with his brother Henry Junior's death, it is not the "wind and the earth" that revitalize his identity, but an IRS account (301). Lyman explains, "I could die now and leave no ripple. Why not! I considered, but then I came up with the fact that my death would leave a gap in the BIA records, my IRS account would be labeled incomplete" (300). There is no clear and absolute identification between the protagonists and the land; it must be cultivated and maintained

through the community itself. The land is not as stable as it seems: because it is a reservation, it is a place to which the families were displaced generations ago as a home created through the loss of a home. Moreover, the land allotment is dwindling because of "how much of the reservation was sold to whites and lost forever" (12).

It is the cultivation of the reservation as home that links the novel's characters to a community. Characters constantly attempt to flee the physical and emotional borders of the reservation, but no escape is ever complete. Many find their way back home, just as June did. Albertine, Nector, several of the Lamartine boys, Lipsha, and King all make desperate attempts to define their lives by place and seek their identities by movement. The individuals' movements are echoed by the movement of the story, fragmented and jumping between place and time and from narrator to narrator.

Ultimately, the individual's identity is found in the identity of the whole. Several stories are told twice or, rather, are told by one speaker and then again through a different narrator and point of view. The first-person narration speaks directly to readers in a way James Ruppert explains in his essay "Celebrating Culture: *Love Medicine*," in *"Love Medicine: A Casebook"*, "as if they were chatting around a kitchen table. They speculate, remember, complain, come to conclusions, and describe their actions" (68). This shifting narration echoes and reinforces the struggle to form a cohesive and complete identity as the reader is forced to see that identity is not simple or united. We learn about characters before we hear their voices, and we often know their secrets before they do. This narrative method leads readers to identify or distance themselves from characters' identity, culture, and memories. Erdrich's narrative approaches lead readers to struggle with characters as we see the difficulties of forming an identity through the trials of assimilation and the combination of two often clashing cultures.

Infusing the complex relationships of Native American and European traditions with tales of everyday life, *Love Medicine* expands the scope and possibilities of Native American fiction, as well as the body of literature as a whole. Through the telling, retelling, and weaving together of individual stories in the novel, a stable and individual identity is formed that is linked inextricably to community and family. Erdrich's novel explores the complex relations between individual and community, human and land. It does not limit the definition of Ojibwa or Native American or become essentialist in its representations.

IMPORTANT EDITIONS: The first edition of *Love Medicine*, containing fourteen chapters, was published in 1984 by Henry Holt and Company. In 1993 Holt printed an expanded hardcover edition, containing four extra chapters and a new section in the chapter "The Beads"; by arrangement with Holt, Harper Perennial reprinted this version. In 2009 the book was reprinted with the inclusion of selected interviews and supplemental material, and in 2010 Odyssey Editions made *Love Medicine* available to Kindle users. Although the only edition currently in print is the 2009 expanded edition, much of the criticism focuses on the earlier work, and the 1993 edition is still widely available. Readers who wish to think and write critically on the work should consider all editions. This entry cites the 1993 Harper Perennial version.

FURTHER READING: Several of Erdrich's novels, including *Tracks, The Beet Queen, The Bingo Palace, Tales of Burning Love* (1996), *The Last Report on the Miracles at Little No Horse* (2001), and *Four Souls* (2004), overlap with *Love Medicine*'s time periods and character plots, referencing one another and forming a much larger entity.

Many interviews with Erdrich have been conducted, and Allan Chavkin and Nancy Feyl Chavkin's 1994 *Conversations with Louise Erdrich and Michael Dorris* collects many of these for the ideas behind, the thoughts on, and the reception of her works. Allan Chavkin edited a collection of essays under the title *The Chippewa Landscape of Louise Erdrich* (1999). Other critical works include another collection of essays edited by Hertha D. Sweet Wong, titled *Louise Erdrich's "Love Medicine": A Casebook* (1999), and Lorena Laura Stookey's *Louise Erdrich: A Critical Companion* (1999). Teachers may wish to examine *Approaches to Teaching the Works of Louise Erdrich* (2004), edited by Greg Sarris, Connie A. Jacobs, and James Richard Giles. Additionally, E. Shelly Reid's essay "The Stories We Tell: Louise Erdrich's Identity Narratives," *MELUS* 26.3–4 (Autumn 2000): 65–86, is a compelling argument focusing on how Erdrich modifies characters' biographies into a larger narration that represents Native Americans as individuals and as part of a larger community. See NATIVE AMERICAN LITERATURE.

EMILY CHURILLA   STONY BROOK UNIVERSITY

M

MAGAZINES.
See Periodicals, Literary

MAIN STREET

HISTORY: One of the best-selling novels of the 1920s, *Main Street* (1920) is a major work of that decade, presenting a caustic and knowing look at small-town Midwestern life. The fictional village of Gopher Prairie, MINNESOTA, created by (HARRY) SINCLAIR LEWIS (1885–1951) is a much more complex and less pleasant place than similar villages that had been presented positively in early twentieth-century American fiction by Midwestern writers such as ZONA GALE (1874–1938) and (NEWTON) BOOTH TARKINGTON (1869–1946). With his critique of the insularity of the SMALL TOWN, Lewis joined writers like EDGAR LEE MASTERS (1868–1950) and SHERWOOD ANDERSON (1876–1941) in the REVOLT FROM THE VILLAGE literary movement, as CARL VAN DOREN (1885–1950) called it, presenting the Midwestern small town much more realistically than before.

Main Street was the start of a controversial and highly productive decade for Lewis that was capped by his becoming the first American to win the Nobel Prize for Litera-ture in 1930. His novels of the 1920s explore aspects of American society, including BUSINESS in *Babbitt* (1922) and *Dodsworth* (1929); medicine in *Arrowsmith* (1925); and religion in *Elmer Gantry* (1927). His satirical presentation of middle-class Americans' hopes and expectations touched a nerve in both readers and critics.

Lewis created Gopher Prairie out of his ambivalence toward his hometown, Sauk Centre, Minnesota. It became for him a representation of all that was both good and bad about the Midwest and, by extension, America. Lewis, who had long wanted to write a novel satirizing small-town life, found inspiration during a trip home to Sauk Centre in 1916, by which time he had already published two novels and stories in major venues like the *Saturday Evening Post*. Along with his wife, Grace, Lewis stayed with his family in Sauk Centre for two months, where he attended dinner parties, gave lectures, studied the local newspaper, worked on his writing, and took voluminous notes about the town and its people. He began writing *Main Street* in 1919 and completed a draft in February 1920. After making extensive revisions that summer, Lewis deliv-

Cover of Sinclair Lewis's *Main Street,* 1922.
Grosset & Dunlap, 1921.
Courtesy of the Minnesota Historical Society

ered the manuscript to his publisher, Alfred Harcourt, in July. The novel was published on October 23, 1920.

Main Street was a phenomenal success, selling 180,000 copies within its first seven months and helping establish the new publishing firm of Harcourt, Brace and Howe. Because of its subject matter and frankness in challenging American ideals, critic Mark Schorer, in *Sinclair Lewis: An American Life* (1961), noted that its publication was "the most sensational event in twentieth-century American publishing history" (268). The novel received much critical acclaim and was recommended for the Pulitzer Prize. Because of its success, Lewis was able to give up his editorial job and become a full-time writer.

SIGNIFICANCE: With *Main Street* Lewis fulfilled his artistic potential and created a novel that still has much relevance today. He provides a sympathetic portrayal of an intelligent woman who feels stifled by her lack of opportunity in her small prairie town. Carol Milford, a librarian in St. Paul, marries Dr. Will Kennicott and moves to his hometown of Gopher Prairie. Carol is expected to exist primarily as the doctor's wife, supporting his endeavors and bearing his children. She hopes that she will have the influence to improve the town in ARCHITECTURE, landscaping, and the arts.

Carol is disappointed not only in the flat and uninspiring landscape of central Minnesota but in Gopher Prairie itself. Typical of small Midwestern prairie towns, it has few sidewalks, flimsy-looking buildings, and a sense of impermanence. Lewis carefully and brilliantly contrasts Carol's disappointment with the exultation of Bea Sorenson, a young farm girl who has arrived on the same train as Carol and sees the town through rural eyes, fascinated and overwhelmed by the stores and the hotel.

Carol matures during the course of the novel, learning that she cannot accomplish anything of substance without the cooperation of the rest of the town and that she often has to compromise. Her suggestions mirror early twentieth-century urban planning. She recommends architectural changes in the town, is derided because of the cost, and settles for redecorating her husband's office. Her attempt to start a little-theatre group is undermined by gossip and the group's wish to perform moralistic melodrama rather than Shaw. She is invited to join the Thanatopsis Club, a women's organization that provides both social opportunities and intellectual development, but she quickly despairs when they discuss all the British poets in one meeting. Her greatest success is in helping set up a waiting room for farmers' wives. This gives a safe and comfortable place for farm wives who come to town with their husbands and is modeled after one that Lewis's stepmother, Isabel, established in Sauk Centre.

Carol's despair leads to two flirtations, one with lawyer Guy Pollack, who identifies her ennui as "the village virus," a term Lewis considered for the title of his novel (157). The second and more serious relationship is with the tailor's assistant, Erik Valborg, who shares Carol's love of the arts and feels like an outsider, as she does.

Admonished for this flirtation, Carol breaks it off and tries to find solace in the traditional woman's occupation of childbearing and rearing but finds that it is not enough.

After a series of depressing incidents, including the death of her maid, Bea, and Bea's son, Olaf, the town's xenophobia during World War I, and the banishment of schoolteacher Fern Mullins, who has been unsuccessful in avoiding the sexual abuse of the town bully, Cy Bogart, Carol leaves her husband and his town and moves to Washington, D.C., to look for fulfilling work. However, the Main Street mentality of gossip and narrow-mindedness exists everywhere, even in the nation's capital. Eventually Will persuades her to return, and with the birth of her next child, a daughter, she hopes that the possibility of living a rewarding life will be easier for her daughter's generation. She contends that her struggle to improve life on the prairie has not been wasted even if much of what she attempted failed: "But I have won in this: I've never excused my failures by sneering at my aspirations, by pretending to have gone beyond them. I do not admit that Main Street is as beautiful as it should be! I do not admit that Gopher Prairie is greater or more generous than Europe! I do not admit that dish-washing is enough to satisfy all women! I may not have fought the good fight, but I have kept the faith" (451).

Thousands of women identified with Carol Kennicott and her village virus. James Hutchisson, in *The Rise of Sinclair Lewis, 1920–1930* (1996), notes that although critical reception in general was quite good, critics "tended to praise the book on social rather than literary grounds" (46). That many were made uncomfortable by the America that Lewis presented is evident from the number of parodies written after *Main Street*. In *The Revolt from the Village, 1915–1930* (1969), Anthony Channell Hilfer notes that "Lewis's talent lies precisely in the incisiveness and suggestiveness of his delineations of the social surface, his unmasking of the dominant middle class" (158).

Lewis's interest in detail, characterization, and social issues was heavily influenced by American realists (HANNIBAL) HAMLIN GARLAND (1860–1940) and WILLIAM DEAN HOWELLS (1837–1920). He has contin-

ued to influence writers, especially those who use dense realism and choose a broad canvas on which to critique American society, including (Thomas Kennerly) Tom Wolfe (Jr.) (b. 1931), John (Hoyer) Updike (1932–2009), and Philip (Milton) Roth (b. 1933). *Main Street* has remained in print since its first publication, usually available in several different editions. It was made into a silent film in 1923 and a sound film, *I Married a Doctor,* in 1936. There have been several dramatic adaptations, including one by Craig Wright for the Great American History Theatre in St. Paul in 2003.

IMPORTANT EDITIONS: *Main Street* was first published by Harcourt, Brace and Howe in 1920 and was a huge best seller. Because of the number of copies that exist and the widely available reprint by Grosset & Dunlap from the same page plates as the original, most scholarly articles refer to these page numbers. Grosset and Dunlap also published a photoplay edition with pictures from the silent-film adaptation. A Nobel Prize edition was published by P. F. Collier shortly after Lewis was awarded the Nobel Prize for Literature, and a Limited Editions Club edition was published in 1937 with illustrations by Grant Wood (1891–1942). The novel was well received abroad and has been translated into dozens of languages, including French, German, and Japanese. There is no critical edition, although current reprints include a Signet Classics edition, a Barnes and Noble Classics edition, and a Library of America volume of *Main Street* and *Babbitt,* edited by George Killough, Brooke Allen, and John Hersey, respectively, as well as several electronic and audio editions.

FURTHER READING: The only major collection of letters by Lewis is *From Main Street to Stockholm: Letters of Sinclair Lewis, 1919–1930* (1952), edited by Harrison Smith. These letters show Lewis's thoughts on his writing of the 1920s, including the genesis of *Main Street,* and focus primarily on correspondence between him and Alfred Harcourt. Lewis never wrote an autobiography, but some of his essays on a variety of topics, from his boyhood to his literary views to social questions, are reprinted in *The Man from Main Street: Selected Essays and Other Writings, 1904–1950* (1953), edited by

Harry E. Maule and Melville H. Cane. The introduction that Lewis wrote for the Limited Editions Club edition of *Main Street* is included there.

Two early short stories, "A Woman by Candlelight" (1917) and "A Rose for Little Eva" (1918), are set in Gopher Prairie, as is part of *Free Air* (1919), inspired by an automobile trip Lewis and his wife took across much of the Midwest, where they encountered rutted and muddy roads, bad food, and car breakdowns. Gopher Prairie continued to be a touchstone for Lewis, who set two later pieces there, "Main Street's Been Paved!" (1924) and "Main Street Goes to War" (1942). All four pieces that Lewis set in Gopher Prairie are included in *Sinclair Lewis: The Minnesota Stories* (2005), edited by Sally E. Parry. The first two stories also appear in volumes 2 and 3, respectively, of *The Short Stories of Sinclair Lewis* (2007), edited by Samuel J. Rogal.

The University Museums of Iowa State University exhibited the Grant Wood illustrations for the 1937 edition of *Main Street* in 2004 and published Lea Rosson DeLong's *Grant Wood's Main Street: Art, Literature and the American Midwest* (2004), an appreciation of both the novelist and the illustrator.

There are two major biographies of Lewis. *Sinclair Lewis: An American Life* (1961) by Mark Schorer is a detailed, if at times unflattering, account of Lewis's life. Schorer had access to most of Lewis's papers and interviewed many of Lewis's contemporaries. A more sympathetic biography is *Sinclair Lewis: Rebel from Main Street* (2002) by Richard Lingeman. Both biographies provide much valuable information on Lewis's writing of *Main Street*. *Sinclair Lewis Remembered* (2012), edited by Gary Scharnhorst and Matthew Hofer, is a comprehensive portrait of Lewis that covers his whole career through memoirs by his contemporaries.

There have been more essays written about *Main Street* than about any other novel by Lewis, as well as one book-length study, *"Main Street": The Revolt of Carol Kennicott* (1993) by Martin Bucco, which provides literary and historical context, as well as a critical reading of the novel. James M. Hutchisson's *The Rise of Sinclair Lewis, 1920–1930* (1996) is valuable for its presentation of Lewis's creative process, from his notes

through the typescript to the finished copy. The book focuses on Lewis's five major novels of the 1920s and shows the changes that Lewis made during the composition process, including a deleted chapter from *Main Street*. Also important is *The Art of Sinclair Lewis* (1967), in which D(avid) J(oseph) Dooley (b. 1921) discusses the aesthetics of all of Lewis's novels, focusing in one chapter on *Main Street* and *Babbitt*.

Critical Essays on Sinclair Lewis (1986), edited by Martin Bucco, includes reviews of most of Lewis's novels, including "Consolation," a review of *Main Street* by H(enry) L(ouis) Mencken (1880–1956), and more general appraisals of Lewis's writing that use *Main Street* as the focus. *Sinclair Lewis: New Essays in Criticism* (1997), edited by James M. Hutchisson, offers five essays with a variety of critical perspectives on *Main Street*. The centennial of Lewis's birth became the occasion for many essays on *Main Street*, including those in *Sinclair Lewis at 100: Papers Presented at a Centennial Conference* (1985), edited by Michael Connaughton, and a special issue of *Modern Fiction Studies* 31 (1985). Anthony Channell Hilfer presents Lewis's centrality to the attack on American provincialism in *The Revolt from the Village, 1915–1930* (1969). The three-volume *A Guide to the Characters in the Novels, Short Stories, and Plays of Sinclair Lewis* (2006), edited by Samuel J. Rogal, provides useful references to all the characters in Lewis's writing.

The Sinclair Lewis Society Newsletter, the publication of the Sinclair Lewis Society, publishes articles related to Lewis's life and writings and maintains a website. A partial manuscript of *Main Street* is held by the University of Texas at Austin.

SALLY E. PARRY   ILLINOIS STATE UNIVERSITY

MAIN-TRAVELLED ROADS

HISTORY: Although CAROLINE KIRKLAND (1801–1864), EDWARD EGGLESTON (1837–1902), and EDGAR WATSON HOWE (1853–1937) were well-regarded authors who made life in the Midwest their subject, (HANNIBAL) HAMLIN GARLAND (1860–1940) is generally credited with bringing the Midwest into literary prominence. In *Main-Travelled Roads* (1891), a book widely acknowledged as a central text of American literary naturalism, Garland presents the difficulties and beauties of rural Midwestern life. The short stories in *Main-Travelled Roads* do not focus on one group of characters; instead, they create a stunning overview of nineteenth-century farm life. Unlike predominantly sentimental literary portraits of the Midwest, Garland's stories depict farm life beset by economic exploitation, drudgery, and boredom, a view reflected in the Populist movement of the 1890s. See PROTEST LITERATURE. Garland balanced this depiction with a redeeming portrait of the Midwestern landscape, harmonizing human toil with natural splendor.

Garland began his literary career in 1885 in Boston, studying and lecturing on literature and writing book reviews, poetry, and sketches of farm life for newspapers and magazines like the *Boston Evening Transcript* and *Harper's Weekly*. Having grown up on WISCONSIN, IOWA, and SOUTH DAKOTA farms, Garland was largely self-educated. Although his early fiction and poetry were not always technically sound, editors were impressed with his depictions of farm life. His growing literary reputation in Boston allowed him to meet WILLIAM DEAN HOWELLS (1837–1920) and JOSEPH KIRKLAND (1830–1894). Acting on Howells's advice to write about the rural Midwest, in 1887 Garland returned to gather material in Iowa and what would become the state of South Dakota in 1889. From 1888 to 1890 Garland published rural stories in *Harper's Weekly* and the *Arena*. In the summer of 1891 the *Arena* published a selection of Garland's farm stories as *Main-Travelled Roads: Six Mississippi Valley Stories.*

Although Garland would later claim otherwise, *Main-Travelled Roads* received favorable reviews; critics praised his characterization of Midwestern people and landscapes and defended his dark depiction of farm life. Howells's "Editor's Study" in the September 1891 issue of *Harper's Monthly* is typical, noting Garland's gloomy characterizations while defending their artistry. "The type caught in Mr. Garland's book is not pretty, it is ugly and often ridiculous, but it is heart-breaking in its rude despair" (639). Despite positive reviews, *Main-Travelled Roads* initially sold poorly. Because Garland continued to publish new and expanded editions of *Main-Travelled Roads,* many versions exist.

THE ride from Milwaukee to the Mississippi is a fine ride at any time, superb in summer. To lean back in a reclining-chair and whirl away in a breezy July day, past lakes, groves of oak, past fields of barley being reaped, past hay-fields, where the heavy grass is toppling before the swift sickle, is a panorama of delight, a road full of delicious surprises, where down a sudden vista lakes open, or a distant wooded hill looms darkly blue, or swift streams, foaming deep down the solid rock, send whiffs of cool breezes in at the window.

It has majesty, breadth. The farming has nothing apparently petty about it. All seems vigorous, youthful, and prosperous. Mr. Howard McLane in his chair let his newspaper fall on his lap, and gazed out upon it with dreaming eyes. It had a certain mysterious glamour to him; the lakes were cooler and brighter to his eye, the greens fresher, and the grain more golden than to any one else,

71

Opening page of "Up the Coulé" from Hamlin Garland's *Main-Travelled Roads,* 1891. Stone and Kimball, 1893.
Image courtesy of Special Collections, Grand Valley State University Libraries

SIGNIFICANCE: The six stories in the 1891 *Arena* edition of *Main-Travelled Roads* are generally regarded as Garland's best work. Many critics, including Donald Pizer, have commented that Garland's later additions resulted in a less unified collection. While the six Mississippi Valley stories maintain a consistent theme of farm toil set against the redeeming natural landscape, the stories added in subsequent editions reflect increasing intrusions of more urbanized life.

In *Main-Travelled Roads* Garland found a place for "Up the Coulé" and "A Branch Road," two novelettes too long for publication in the *Arena*. In these stories Garland explores a character's escape from and return to his rural home. In "Up the Coulé," Garland juxtaposes Howard McLane, a successful actor and world traveler returning to his rural boyhood home, to his brother, Grant McLane, who has remained on the farm, disheartened and disaffected. The reader first looks on the farm landscape of the Midwest through Howard's eyes and sees refreshing natural beauty. To Grant, however, the rural landscape is one of mud, manure, and incessant work. Although Howard endeavors to buy the family farm for his brother, the land has beaten Grant; he sees himself as "a dead failure. . . . Life's a failure for ninety-nine per cent of us" (Perennial Classic edition 85).

"A Branch Road" follows Will, a farm boy with a seminary education, and Agnes, his sweetheart. When farmers taunt Will about his romance with Agnes, he becomes enraged, wanting to keep private what the farmers consider public. Will's jealousy drives him away from Agnes, and he wanders out west and makes his fortune as a gambler. Will returns seven years later to find that Agnes has married an abusive husband and has a child. At the story's end, Will has persuaded Agnes to leave her husband and come with him. Despite the romantic reunion and Will's acceptance of her child, readers are left unsure of their future; "[Agnes] smiled again, in spite of herself. Will shuddered with a thrill of fear, she was so weak and worn. But the sun shone on the dazzling, rustling wheat, the fathomless sky, blue as a sea, bent above them—and the world lay before them" (42).

"The Return of a Private" and "Under the Lion's Paw" demonstrate Garland's Populist leanings and the plight of Midwestern farmers. Originally published in the December 1890 *Arena*, "Return" is based on Garland's father's return from the Civil War. Here Private Smith, an old, ailing veteran, makes a weary march home. Too poor to afford a hotel room, Smith sleeps overnight at the train station before walking to his farm, where "he saw himself sick, worn out, taking up the work on his half-cleared farm, the inevitable mortgage standing ready with open jaw to swallow half his earnings" (110). Despite the difficulties awaiting him, his need for rest, and the fact that his youngest children do not recognize him, Smith toils on, for "his heroic soul did not quail" (126). The farmer's spirit counters his bleak prospects.

"Under the Lion's Paw," originally published in *Harper's Weekly* in September 1889, follows the Haskins family. At the outset, they are returning from Dakota, where grasshoppers have destroyed their crops. They are aided by Council, a farmer who has connections to set Haskins up on a rented farm, supplying him seed corn and supporting the family for a year. With hard work, the farm thrives. When Butler, the farm owner, finds it in such good condition, he doubles its original price because of Haskins's improvements. Despite the bounty the family has wrested from the land, Butler controls their fate.

The outlook is brighter in "Mrs. Ripley's Trip" and "Among the Corn-Rows," both originally published in *Harper's Weekly* in November 1888 and June 1890. "Mrs. Ripley's Trip" differs from the other five Mississippi Valley stories in its focus on Mrs. Ripley, an old woman entrenched in her farm labor. To the surprise of all, Mrs. Ripley is determined to visit her relatives back East. When Mr. Ripley questions the need, she reminds him of her relentless labor: "For twenty-three years, Ethan Ripley, I've stuck right to the stove an' churn without a day or a night off. . . . And now I'm a-goin' back to Yaark State" (168–69). Mrs. Ripley makes her trip and takes up her burden again, "never more thinking to lay it down" (179). She shines in her determination to take the trip and in her resolve in returning to her ceaseless toil.

"Among the Corn-Rows" follows Rob, a NORTH DAKOTA homesteader who decides to return to Wisconsin, where "girls are thick as huckleberries" (89). Rob is ridiculed by other bachelor farmers for planning to come back in ten days with a wife, but there he finds Julia behind a plow. Her father values Julia not much more highly than a farm animal, and Rob understands that his offer of a partnership of toil would be appealing to her. Like Mrs. Ripley, Rob and Julia toil on the land fairly and willingly, and therefore, they may be successful.

If the original six stories of *Main-Travelled Roads* focus on the life, love, and labor of Midwestern farmers, Garland's later added stories depict changing rural life. "The Creamery Man," originally published in *Outlook* in December 1897 as "The Creamery

Man of Molasses Gap," is the story of Claude, a young, good-looking creamery driver. As he visits the local farms, Claude flirts with the young women along his route, notably Lucindy Kennedy, heiress to a large, productive farm, and Nina Haldeman, an immigrant girl. Claude's eventual decision to marry Nina reflects the growing dominance of Midwestern immigrant populations.

The characters of Mr. and Mrs. Ripley return in "Uncle Ethan Ripley," originally published in the *Arena* in December 1891 as "Uncle Ripley's Speculation." Here Ethan Ripley is taken in by a patent-medicine salesman who offers ten bottles of medicine in exchange for permission to paint an advertisement on Ripley's barn. Ripley agrees, thinking that he will sell the extra medicine, but he soon finds that the salesman has made the same deal with several other local farmers. Although the outcome is humorous, Garland portrays the intrusion of commercialism as it disturbs the Ripleys' quiet life. Less humorous is "A 'Good' Fellow's Wife," originally published in the *Century* in April 1898. Here a young man and his family move to a small town to start a bank. When he and his partner speculate and lose the townspeople's money, he wants to leave town, but his wife is determined to stay and pay the debt. In the end she succeeds through hard work and good relations with the community, but Garland infers that her husband's actions are more typical.

In his later stories Garland also began characterizing the SMALL TOWN as a stepping-stone between urban and rural. "God's Ravens," originally published in *Harper's Monthly* in June 1894, shows a CHICAGO writer's return to his childhood small town. It is not as idyllic as he remembers it, however, and he fails to connect with the villagers and their way of life. Similarly, in "A Day's Pleasure," originally published in *Ladies' Home Journal* in July 1898 as "Sam Markham's Wife," a farm wife seeks relief from farm labor through a trip to town. There she finds herself hopelessly out of place and ends up wandering up and down the main street. Eventually, the outsiders in each story are comforted by small-town insiders: a townswoman invites the farm wife to tea, and the town rallies around the

Chicago writer in his illness. In both stories the idealized town fails initially to meet the outsider's expectations, and only through uncharacteristically charitable actions are the outsider's dreams actualized.

In some ways "The Fireplace" does not fit with the other stories in *Main-Travelled Roads.* Garland wrote it after the turn of the century and first published it as "Martha's Fireplace" in the *Delineator* in December 1905. It was not added to the collection until 1930. Nonetheless, "The Fireplace" serves as a fitting final story in *Main-Travelled Roads,* depicting the end of the pioneering farm era. Here a farmer retires to a cramped small-town house to please his wife. Town life comes to represent the death of his heroic pioneer lifestyle, for he is unable to adjust to town inactivity and longs for the rustic and impractical fireplace he loved in his pioneer homestead.

IMPORTANT EDITIONS: The original *Arena* edition of 1891 featured an opening epigraph and epigraphs for each story: "A Branch Road," "Up the Coulé," "Among the Corn-Rows," "The Return of a Private," "Under the Lion's Paw," and "Mrs. Ripley's Trip." The 1893 Stone and Kimball edition added an introduction by Howells, illustrations, and minor changes to Garland's stories. In this edition Garland seemed primarily concerned with making the stories less sentimental. The 1899 Macmillan and Company edition included illustrations and epigraphs for all stories and added "The Creamery Man," "A Day's Pleasure," and "Uncle Ethan Ripley." Harper and Brothers purchased the contract for Garland's work in 1909 and in 1911 published *Main-Travelled Roads* as part of the eight-volume Sunset Edition. The 1920 Harper edition also included "God's Ravens" and "A 'Good' Fellow's Wife" for a total of eleven stories. Harper's twelve-volume collection of Garland's works, the Border Edition (1922), included these eleven stories and a new forward by Garland, and although the introductory epigraph remained, the epigraphs for each story were removed. Garland added a final story, "The Fireplace," to the 1930 Harper edition, which included individual and opening epigraphs.

Most recent editions of *Main-Travelled Roads* contain either the original six sto-

ries from the 1891 *Arena* edition or the 1922
Harper edition's eleven stories. The
Charles E. Merrill standard edition (1970)
presents a facsimile copy of the 1891 six-story
edition with an introduction and background material by Donald Pizer. The
University of Nebraska Press's Bison Books
edition (1995) follows the eleven-story 1922
Harper and Row edition and includes introductory material by Joseph B. McCullough.
Readers interested in the twelve-story
edition should consult the 1956 Harper and
Row Perennial Classic edition. It is out of
print but is generally available in libraries
and used bookstores.

FURTHER READING: The University of
Southern California's Doheny Library is the
primary archive of Garland's work, containing an extensive collection of unpublished
manuscripts, diaries, letters, and journals.
Jean Holloway's *Hamlin Garland: A Biography* (1960) is an essential starting point for
study of Garland; its bibliography and
chronology of Garland's publications are
especially useful. Keith Newlin's *Hamlin
Garland: A Life* (2008) is the most comprehensive and current Garland biography. In *Hamlin Garland's Early Work and Career* (1960),
Donald Pizer mixed biographical information with insightful readings of Garland's
early work, and his *Hamlin Garland: Prairie
Radical* (2010) provides essential context
concerning Garland's early writing career.
The collection edited by Charles Silet and
others, *The Critical Reception of Hamlin Garland, 1891–1978* (1985), provides an overview
of changing perceptions of Garland's work
over time. Newlin's *Hamlin Garland: A Bibliography, with a Checklist of Unpublished Letters*
(1998) is a useful catalog of Garland scholarship. The Hamlin Garland Society website provides useful biographical and critical
resources and an illustrated listing of *Main-
Travelled Roads* editions.

JEFFREY SWENSON   HIRAM COLLEGE

MAPS, LITERARY

OVERVIEW: In general terms, a literary
map functions as a supplement to a work of
fiction, locating the action in an imaginary
place. Usually printed on the endpapers or
inserted as a frontispiece, such a map is intended to give the reader of that work the
impression that the setting of the story is au-

thentic and to enable the reader to follow the
movements of the characters more easily.
The maps appended to *Treasure Island* (1883)
by Robert Louis Stevenson (1850–1894) and
Absalom, Absalom! (1936) by William Faulkner
(1897–1962) are two examples of this device.

A second kind of literary map, usually
produced by libraries or teachers' organizations, depicts the leading exemplars of a
national, regional, state, or city literature,
often with portrait vignettes of important
authors and scenes from their works super-
imposed on a map of the area in question.
A variation of this type portrays how more
circumscribed geographic areas feature in
the literary works, usually enumerated, of a
particular author or authors. These maps are
printed in a colorful, oversized format suitable for display in schools and libraries to
honor a region's authors and literature, but
for the most part they are more decorative
than of literary significance.

HISTORY AND SIGNIFICANCE: The literary map as a deliberate adjunct to works of
fiction has been in use for centuries. Its direct antecedents are the maps illustrating
sixteenth-century travel and geography
books, such as the idealized picture of the
perfect state described by Sir Thomas More
(1478–1535) in his *Utopia* (1516). Such maps
became a necessity in the imaginary-voyage
genre that flourished in the 1700s. Since the
nineteenth century, however, a good proportion of literary maps have been used to
illustrate children's books, such as A. A.
Milne's (1882–1956) "Hundred Acre Wood"
in *Winnie-the-Pooh* (1926), the twelve-book
Swallows and Amazons series (1930–1947) by
Arthur Ransome (1884–1967), and *The Hob-
bit* (1936) by J. R. R. Tolkien (1892–1973).

Few Midwestern novels in their first appearances have included literary maps as
part of the text. The first edition of WINES-
BURG, OHIO (1919) by SHERWOOD ANDERSON
(1876–1941), however, has a bird's-eye-view
map of the town on its endpapers with eight
specifically identified places that have significance in the story. The map, drawn by
Harald Toksvig, is included in many of the
book's subsequent reprintings. In *Raintree
County* (1948) by ROSS (FRANKLIN) LOCKRIDGE
JR. (1914–1948), the prominence of the frontispiece map underscores the importance of
that fictional INDIANA county setting to the

novel. Among Midwestern historical novels employing literary maps are *This Land Is Ours* (1940) by Louis Zara (1910–2001), a chronicle of the Old Northwest between 1755 and 1855; a novel about the MICHIGAN frontier, *Once a Wilderness* (1934) by Arthur Pound (1884–1966); and *Bright Journey* (1940) by AUGUST (WILLIAM) DERLETH (1909–1971), the story of a fur trader in WISCONSIN.

Some Midwestern mystery novels written in the 1930s and 1940s have endpaper or frontispiece maps that elucidate the stories and provide the reader with clues to the solution of the puzzle. Frances Moyer Ross Stevens (1895–1947), writing as Christopher Hale, uses such maps in at least three of her Crime Club novels set in Michigan.

The more generalized literary map is of relatively recent origin. The earliest example in English appears to be one created by Walton Van Loan (1834–1921) in 1891 and devoted to James Fenimore Cooper and his Leatherstocking Tales. There, points of interest from these novels are marked on a map of the Otsego Lake region in upstate New York. England was the subject of the first national literary map in 1899. It was issued, coincidentally, by two publishers in two separate editions that appeared in London and Boston. *Booklovers Map of America* (1926) was the first literary map of the United States and was subsequently republished three times (1933, 1939, and 1949) in revised and updated editions. The first literary map devoted to a single state was that for New Jersey (1927). It lists eighty-two Garden State authors and their works. Since the 1950s there has been a concerted effort by most state associations affiliated with the National Council of Teachers of English to issue literary maps for individual states. The initiative for the publication of these state maps probably came from the national association. Since the 1980s with the establishment of the Center for the Book at the Library of Congress and similar centers at the state level, literary maps have been appearing from these groups as an educational vehicle to promote state authors and literary works.

The earliest Midwestern literary map was published in 1932 for NORTH DAKOTA, followed by one for IOWA in 1934. Although some regions of the United States, such as the South and New England, as well as a few cities, have their own literary maps, none has yet been published for the entire twelve-state Midwest area or for any Midwestern city.

SELECTED WORKS:

Midwestern Authors:

The Adventures of Mark Twain. Hollywood, CA: Warner Bros., 1944. 21½×31 in.

Annand, George. *A Map of Sinclair Lewis' United States as It Appears in His Novels.* New York: Doubleday, Doran, 1934. 13×21½ in.

Heide, Florence Parry, and Roxanne Heide. *Kenoska, Home of the Spotlight Club Mysteries* [Kenosha, Wisconsin]. Chicago: Albert Whitman, 1978. 10½×16½ in.

Hirsch, Tim. *Edna Ferber Walking Tour* [Appleton, Wisconsin]. Eau Claire: University of Wisconsin, Eau Claire, 1992. 7½×8½ in.

Maguire, Molly. *The Ernest Hemingway Adventure Map of the World.* Los Angeles: Aaron Blake, 1986. 19×22½ in.

The Old Jules Home Region [Mari Sandoz]. New York: J. F. Carr, 1965. 22½×17 in.

Oullahan, A. C. *The Bret Hart Trail, Map Showing the Land of Romance and Gold Immortalized by Bret Hart & Mark Twain* [in central California]. Stockton, CA: Stockton Chamber of Commerce, 1922. 35×58½ in.

Illinois:

Hook, J. N., Ellen Burkhart, and Louise Lane. *Illinois Authors and a Literary Map of Illinois.* Urbana: Illinois Association of Teachers of English, 1952. 34×22 in.

Anderson, Judie, Arn Arnam, and Tom Heinz. *Illinois Authors.* Chicago: Chicago Tribune Educational Services, 1987. 31×23½ in.

Indiana:

Indiana Council of Teachers of English. *A Literary Map of Indiana.* Terre Haute: Indiana Council of Teachers of English and Indiana College English Association, 1956. 27½×19 in.

Blackwell, Edward M. *A Literary Map of Indiana.* Terre Haute: Indiana Council of Teachers of English, 1974. 28×20 in.

Indiana Center for the Book. *1816–2016 Literary Map of Indiana; 200 Years—200 Writers.* Indianapolis: Indiana State Library, 2016. 24×18 in.

Iowa:

Shellenberger, Grace. *Historical and Literary Map of Iowa.* Davenport: Davenport Public Library, 1934. 17×28 in.

Larkin, Harriet. *Literary Map of Iowa.* Cedar Falls: Iowa State Teachers College, 1952. 17×23 in.

Kansas:

Fuson, Benjamin Willis. *Centennial Literary Map of Kansas, 1861–1961.* Topeka: Kansas Association of Teachers of English, 1961. 20×27½ in. Accompanied by the booklet

Centennial Bibliography of Kansas Literature, 1861–1961, compiled by Fuson.

Filkel, Janet. *Kansas Bicentennial Literary Map.* Dodge City: Kansas Heritage Center, 1976. 18×23 in.

Averill, Thomas Fox. *A Map of Kansas Literature.* Lawrence: Kansas Association of Teachers of English, 1994. 12½×19½ in.

Michigan:

Michigan Council of Teachers of English. *A Literary Map of Michigan.* Ann Arbor: Michigan Council of Teachers of English, 1965. 33×22 in.

Michigan Center for the Book. *Portraits of Literary Michigan.* Lansing: Library of Michigan, 1994. 22×17 in.

Michigan Center for the Book. *Michigan Award-Winning Authors & Illustrators.* Lansing: Library of Michigan, 2005. 24×19 in.

Minnesota:

Martz, Eugene V. *A Literary Map of Minnesota.* Minneapolis: Minneapolis English Teachers Club, 1954. 29×23 in.

Barron, Ronald. *Minnesota Writers.* Bloomington: Minnesota Council of Teachers of English, 1994. 34½×25 in.

Missouri:

Clemenson, Bill. *A Literary Map of Missouri.* Columbia: Missouri Association of Teachers of English, 1955. 30×22 in.

McReynolds, Ronald W. *A Literary Map of Missouri.* Warrensburg: Department of English, Central Missouri State University, 1988. 37×24 in.

Nebraska:

Brodie, Jack and Bernice Kauffman. *Nebraska Centennial Literary Map and Guide to Nebraska Authors.* Omaha: Nebraska Centennial Non-Profit Association, 1967. 16½×23 in.

Eckersley, Dika. *Nebraska Authors.* Omaha: University of Nebraska at Omaha and Nebraska Center for the Book, 1991. 18×24 in.

Cox, Gerry, and Carol Gulyas. *Nebraska Literary Map, with Native Wild Flowers.* Lincoln: Nebraska English Language Arts Council, 1996. 16×35 in.

North Dakota:

Rosvold, Charlotte S., and Catharine Phillips. *North Dakota Literary Trails.* Mayville, ND: Hazel Webster Byrnes, 1932. 17×22½ in.

Maxwell, Nancy. *North Dakota Writers.* Bismarck: North Dakota Center for the Book, 1994. 11×17 in.

Ohio:

Russell, Mark. *A Literary Map of Ohio.* Columbus: Martha Kinney Cooper Ohioana Library, 1957. 23×35 in.

Wentz, Donald. *A Literary Map of Ohio.* Columbus: Martha Kinney Cooper Ohioana Library Association, 1983. 23×35 in.

Mahan, Benton. *Ohioana Ohio Literary Map.* Columbus: Ohioana Library Association, 1995. 19×32½ in.

Hengst, Linda R., Merce Robinson, Kate Templeton Fox, and Linda T. Parsons, eds. *Ohio Literary Map.* Columbus: Ohioana Library Association, 2007. 18×20 in.

South Dakota:

South Dakota Council of Teachers of English. *Literary Map of South Dakota.* Rapid City: South Dakota Council of Teachers of English, 1994. 23×34 in.

Wisconsin:

Roen, Duane, and Maureen Roen. *Wisconsin Authors.* N.p.: Wisconsin Council of Teachers of English, 1978. 29×23 in. Accompanied by the booklet *Wisconsin Authors,* WCTE Service Bulletin no. 37, prepared by the Roens.

FURTHER READING: The subject of literary maps has been ignored or overlooked by scholars, with a few notable exceptions. Ben W. Fuson gives a brief history and detailed descriptions of state maps, including maps of eight Midwestern states, in "Halfway Point: State Literary Maps," *English Journal* 59.1 (January 1970): 87–98. Jules Zanger, in "'Harbors like Sonnets': Literary Maps and Cartographic Symbols," *Georgia Review* 36 (Winter 1982): 773–90, promotes the idea that authors employ maps as rhetorical devices in their works to affect the reader's interpretation of the text. The Library of Congress, in cooperation with its Geography and Map Division and Center for the Book, developed an exhibit of literary maps that traveled throughout the United States from 1993 to 1996. The research done for this exhibit resulted in a fully illustrated descriptive catalog of the holdings of literary maps in the Library of Congress, *Language of the Land: The Library of Congress Book of Literary Maps* (1999), compiled by Martha Hopkins and Michael Buscher. This work constitutes the definitive study of the genre to date. Aside from the sources just mentioned, secondary critical writing relating to this subject is lacking, and the term itself is not defined or mentioned in the standard dictionaries, handbooks, or other reference books on general or American literature.

ROBERT BEASECKER

GRAND VALLEY STATE UNIVERSITY

MEXICAN AMERICAN LITERATURE.
See Latino/Latina Literature

MICHIGAN

Michigan was admitted to the Union on January 26, 1837, as the twenty-sixth state. Before statehood it was, in succession, part of the Northwest Territory, 1787–1803; Indiana Territory, 1803–1805; and Michigan Territory, 1805–1837.

Area: 96,716 square miles

Land: 56,804 square miles

Water: 39,912 square miles

Population (2010 census): 9,883,640

OVERVIEW: The literary heritage of Michigan has its beginnings as early as the seventeenth century. The state, owing to its position in the midst of the Great Lakes, was a crossroads for European explorers and traders, as well as for a number of Native American nations, such as the Ojibwa, Huron, and Potawatomi. Its strategic location astride the routes of communication, commerce, and invasion made Michigan and the connecting Great Lakes a vital region during the struggle between England and France for mastery of North America. That same important location later gave the state an advantage in the development and use of its natural resources, industries, and agricultural produce.

The themes and subjects of Michigan literature reflect all aspects of its history, geography, natural resources, rural and city life, businesses and manufacturers, and social and intellectual life and all classes of its population: Native Americans, subsequent pioneers, settlers, and rustic and urban

© Karen Greasley, 2014

dwellers of many origins. This output by the state's writers follows that of the nation as a whole in that it closely corresponds to literary trends and fashions then current in other parts of the country. The single indigenous subject for literary exploration that could have arisen in no other state is that of Michigan's pioneering efforts in the automobile industry, revolutionizing travel and communication and at the same time giving rise to the assembly line and labor unions. The juxtaposition of heavy industry with vast tracts of forest and farmland also provides fertile field for literary exploitation.

HISTORY AND SIGNIFICANCE: Michigan's literary output comprehends a variety of genres. Included among these are exploration and travel, fiction, poetry, DRAMA, and a number of subgenres under popular literature. Other major topics examined are PRINTING AND PUBLISHING, the FEDERAL WRITERS' PROJECT, and Michigan literary awards. The last section, "Further Reading," includes biographical, bibliographic, and critical sources and literary and manuscript collections and repositories.

Exploration and Travel: The earliest literary accounts from Michigan were reports of French explorers and missionaries in New France describing the geography, natural history, mineralogy, and ethnology of the areas through which they traveled. Although the authors generally attempted to be objective, their reports often contained exaggerations and fanciful constructions that make them not only travel narratives but also works of literary imagination. The first mention of the lands that now encompass Michigan was recorded in *Des sauvages* (1604) by Samuel de Champlain (ca. 1574–1635) as a report of his initial trip to Canada the previous year. Because he did not travel farther into the interior than Montreal, his descriptions of lands farther west relied on secondhand descriptions he had heard from the Algonquins. The first published account of a firsthand observer of Michigan, Étienne Brûlé (ca. 1592–1632), who lived among the Hurons for a number of years, appeared in *Le grand voyage du pays Hurons* (1632) by Gabriel Sagard-Théodat (fl. 1614–1636). Other French narratives of Michigan exploration and description include *Relation de ce qui s'est passé de plus remarquable aux missions des* *pères de la Compagnie de Jésus, en la Nouvelle France les années 1670 & 1671* (1672) by Claude Dablon (1618–1697); *Recueil de voyages de Mr Thevenot* (1681) by Melchisédich Thévenot (1620–1692), which contained the first appearance of the word "Michigan" on a map; and *Description de la Louisiane, nouvellement découverte au sud'oüest de la Nouvelle France* (1683) by Louis Hennepin (1626–ca. 1705).

Another form of travel literature extremely popular in its day was the Indian captivity narrative. These were purportedly true accounts written by or about a white prisoner after he or she was freed or rescued and returned to civilization; however, many of these stories had propensities for exaggeration and hyperbole that border on fiction. The first published narrative in which a captive is taken to Michigan is *An Account of the Remarkable Occurrences in the Life and Travels of Col. James Smith . . . during His Captivity with the Indians, in the Years 1755, '56, '57, '58, & '59* (1799). Col. James Smith (1737–1812), a British soldier, was captured in Pennsylvania and taken to Fort Duquesne, northern Ohio, and DETROIT before finally making his escape. An eleven-year forced sojourn among the Indians in the late 1770s is described in *Memoirs of Charles Dennis Rusoe D'Eres, a Native of Canada* (1800), including his trip from Detroit to Michilimackinac, although part of the book seems a fabrication. Probably the latest captivity narrative with a Michigan connection is *Life and Adventures of William Filley, Who Was Stolen from His Home in Jackson, Michigan, by the Indians, August 3d, 1837, and His Safe Return from Captivity, October 19, 1866, after an Absence of 29 Years* (1867). Filley (b. 1832) was five when he was taken by Indians, and he spent most of his subsequent life among tribes in California before being freed. See also CAPTIVITY NARRATIVES.

Fiction: The first novel that uses Michigan as a setting, albeit only partially, is *The Champions of Freedom; or, The Mysterious Chief: A Romance of the Nineteenth Century, Founded on the War between the United States and Great Britain* (1816) by Samuel Woodworth (1784–1842). In this novel the young soldier protagonist receives aid from the spirit of a Miami chief during the War of 1812. Only a few pages of this three-volume

epic are set at Fort Detroit. Until about 1875 the Michigan novel concentrated on the military in frontier forts guarding settlers from Indian depredations, conditions on isolated homesteads, and the often ridiculed parochial mores of the village and its people.

The early French colonial experience in New France is represented in stories of explorers, missionaries, and voyageurs. Robert La Salle's seventeenth-century forays in the Great Lakes and Michigan areas are recounted in only three novels, interestingly all written within five years of one another: *The Wilderness Way* (1954) by Merritt Parmelee Allen (1892–1954), *The Gilded Torch* (1957) by IOLA FULLER (GOODSPEED MCCOY) (1906–1993), and *Touched with Fire* (1952) by John Tebbel (1912–2004). In addition, Virginia C. Watson (1872–1971) wrote the young-adult novel *With La Salle the Explorer* (1922). The journeys of Father Jacques Marquette (1637–1675) likewise have three exemplars, all fictionalized biographies: *The Marks of the Bear Claws* (1908) by Henry S. Spalding, SJ (1865–1934), written for Catholic children; *The Explorations of Père Marquette* (1951) by James Kjelgaard (1910–1959); and *Blackrobe* (1937) by Charles T. Corcoran (1893–1955), which was written to celebrate the tercentenary of the birth of Marquette. The travels of Daniel Greysolon, sieur Duluth (1636–1710) from Montreal to Lake Superior in the 1670s are the subject of *Daniel Du Luth; or, Adventuring on the Great Lakes* (1926) by Everett McNeil (1862–1929). French fur traders and voyageurs have been the subject of a number of novels; among the most notable are *Wolves against the Moon* (1940) by Julia Cooley Altrocchi (1893–1972), *Bright Journey* (1940) by AUGUST (WILLIAM) DERLETH (1909–1971), and Iola Fuller's *The Loon Feather* (1940). Besides appearing in the same year, all three are set at least partially on Mackinac Island.

Great Britain, as a result of its successes in the French and Indian War and the provisions of the subsequent Treaty of Paris, took control of New France, including Michigan, which it held for the next thirty-three years. The signal event during the British superintendency of Michigan was the attempt by the Ottawa chieftain Pontiac (ca. 1720–1769), with an unprecedented alliance of Native American tribes, to force the British back across the Allegheny

Mountains. His dramatic 1763 siege of Fort Detroit and the massacre at Fort Mackinac have provided the background for dozens of novels since 1832. For some examples, see DETROIT.

The War of 1812 witnessed military operations between the United States and Great Britain in a number of Michigan locales, as well as on the Great Lakes. Among novels that use these as the background are *The Champions of Freedom* (1816) by Samuel Woodworth, the first novel set in Michigan; *Oak Openings, or, The Bee-Hunter* (1848) by James Fenimore Cooper (1789–1851), which pits an intrepid American woodsman against a British spy and depicts a Potawatomi attack near Kalamazoo; and the section of *The Tory's Daughter* (1888) by Albert Gallatin Riddle (1816–1902) that takes place in the Raisin River area. This war on the Michigan frontier was also a popular background for a number of adventure novels for boys. For other examples, see also DETROIT.

The establishment of permanent settlements in Michigan occurred over a long period, beginning in the eighteenth century and finally ending in the early part of the twentieth century in remote areas of the Upper Peninsula. *A Table in the Wilderness* (1959) by Lulu J. Dickinson (1874–1962) tells of a pioneer family in Livingston County from 1818 to 1900. The three-volume sequence by Merritt W. Greene (1897–1972), *The Land Lies Pretty* (1959), *Curse of the White Panther* (1960), and *Forgotten Yesterdays* (1964), follows the adventures of a New York immigrant teacher in Hillsdale County from 1832 to 1839. *Born Strangers* (1949) by Helen Topping Miller (1884–1960) is based on the author's family, whose 1820 homestead was located in Genesee County. Henry Ormal Severance (1867–1942) also recounts fictionally his family's pioneer experience in 1830s Oakland County in *Michigan Trailmakers* (1930). Not surprisingly, the hardships and dangers of frontier Michigan are a very popular subject for juvenile novels. Some of the better ones are *Little Mossback Amelia* (1939) by Frances Margaret Fox (1870–1959), *The Secret of the Rosewood Box* (1937) by Helen Fuller Orton (1872–1955), *Moccasined Feet* (1929) by Irene Hollands Wolfschlager (1866–1948), and *Next Spring an Oriole* (1987) by Gloria Whelan (b. 1923). *Next Spring an Oriole* is the first book of a trilogy

concerning the settling of the Michigan frontier and the concomitant displacement of Native Americans; it was followed by *Night of the Full Moon* (1993) and *Shadow of the Wolf* (1997).

In Michigan fiction the frontier village and later small-town life are regularly pilloried for coarse manners and insular views. The earliest such castigation occurs in two books by CAROLINE KIRKLAND (1801–1864), *A NEW HOME—WHO'LL FOLLOW?* (1839) and *Forest Life* (1842). These fictionalized narratives describing her time in Pinckney are so savagely satiric that Kirkland wrote them under the pseudonym Mary Clavers. A similar but somewhat kinder look at village characters in Constantine is presented by Henry Hiram Riley (1813–1888) in *Puddleford and Its People* (1854). The civilizing force of Christianity on a rough backwoods town is shown in the religious tract *The Clevelands* (1860) by Electa M. Sheldon (1817–1902). Later depictions of the small-minded ugliness rampant in small-town Michigan include *Welcome to Thebes* (1962) by GLENDON (FRED) SWARTHOUT (1918–1992), *Hour upon the Stage* (1929) by Ann Kramer Pinchot (1905–1998), and *Tamarack* (1940) by Edith Roberts (1902–1966). The novels of Allan Seager (1906–1968), such as *Amos Berry* (1953), are nearly forgotten now but deserve to be rediscovered for their devastating portrayal of the small rural town with its prejudices and guarded secrets. DAN GERBER (b. 1940) has fictionalized his hometown of Fremont in some of his writing, such as *Grass Fires* (1987), a collection of stories. CHARLES (MORLEY) BAXTER (b. 1947) has looked at the variety of interactions within families and between couples, using Michigan towns as backdrops in such novels as *First Light* (1987) and *Saul and Patsy* (2003).

Since the emergence of the farm novel as an identifiable type in the 1890s, most have been set in the Midwest and many in Michigan. Possibly the most interesting of these, because of their diametrically opposite views of farm life, are *Green Bush* (1925) by JOHN T(OWNER) FREDERICK (1893–1975) and *Backfurrow* (1925) by Geoffrey Dell Eaton (1894–1930). Eaton shows that life on a farm was not only physically exhausting but also intellectually deadening; Frederick agrees that farm life is difficult, but at the same time he sees it as spiritually invigorating and rewarding. Other farm novels of note are *Clay in the Sand* (1953) by Katherine Neuhaus Haffner (1909–1982), *Lightning before Dawn* (1938) by David McLaughlin, and *Measure My Love* (1959) by Helga Sandburg (Crile) (1918–2014), the daughter of CHICAGO poet CARL SANDBURG (1878–1967). An early fictional depiction of migrant workers, in this case connected with the Michigan sugar-beet industry, can be found in *Cloud of Arrows* (1950) by MARY FRANCES DONER (1893–1985). Scores of juvenile novels employ Michigan farms as the background, almost always shown in a positive light. See FARM LITERATURE.

Logging was the first major industry to establish itself in Michigan, and between 1860 and 1910 the state was virtually clear-cut of both hardwoods and pines. It is said that Michigan white pine rebuilt the city of Chicago after the fire of 1871. Stewart Edward White (1873–1946) wrote novels about Michigan logging drives, *The Blazed Trail* (1902) and *The Riverman* (1908), that provide excellent descriptions of lumber-camp life and logging techniques along with melodramatic plots. *"Timber"* (1922), *Below Zero* (1932), and *The Man from Yonder* (1934) by Harold Titus (1888–1967) also use the lumber industry as the background. *Glory of the Pines* (1914) by Rev. William Chalmers Covert (1864–1942) tells of the problems faced by a minister trying to bring religion to impious lumbermen. *Nick of the Woods* (1916) by Alaska Blacklock, the pen name of George Edward Lewis (1867–1942), follows the adventures of two brothers in lumber camps in the northwestern part of the state. Many novels with logging subjects have been written for the juvenile market. They include *Connie Morgan with the Forest Rangers* (1925) by James B. Hendryx (1880–1963) and *The Eagle Pine* (1958) by Dirk Gringhuis (1918–1974).

Many writers have used the waters of the four Great Lakes adjoining Michigan as dramatic settings. Neither commercial fishing nor sport fishing, however, has seen much literary exploitation. *White Gold* (1936) by Myron David Orr (1896–1986) describes the bad feelings between rival fishing companies, and *Bay Mild* (1945) by Louis J. Kintziger (1906–1990) shows a young commercial fisherman questioning the social acceptability of his profession. The use of fly-fishing by ERNEST (MILLER) HEMINGWAY (1899–1961) in his Nick Adams stories set in Michigan, particularly "Big Two-Hearted River" (1925), is well known. On the other hand, commercial shipping in Michigan waters of the Great Lakes has been a popular subject for fiction. One of the earliest is the anonymous *Scenes on Lake Huron* (1836), which fictionalizes a trip by schooner from Green Bay to Detroit and is noteworthy for equating the dangers of the open ocean with those of the inland seas. Richard Matthews Hallet (1887–1967) places a privileged young man down on his luck in the filthy stokehold of a freighter in *Trial by Fire; a Tale of the Great Lakes* (1916). Mary Frances Doner draws on memories of her father's captaincy of a lakes freighter to give a detailed picture of the shipping industry in a number of her novels, particularly *Some Fell among Thorns* (1939), *Chalice* (1940), *Not by Bread Alone* (1941), and *Glass Mountain* (1942). The fury and terror of Great Lakes storms are prominent features in the work of SAMUEL MERWIN (1874–1936), particularly *His Little World* (1903), as well as in *November Storm* (1943) by Jay McCormick (1919–1997); the former tells of the sinking of a lumber schooner off Manistee, and in the latter a coal freighter succumbs to the elements on its planned final voyage of the season. As of this writing, probably the most famous shipwreck on the lakes, the 1975 sinking of the freighter *Edmund Fitzgerald* in Lake Superior, has not been the subject of a major novel. Adventuring on the Great Lakes was a staple of boys' series books, most dating from the early twentieth century. A few examples include *The Rover Boys on the Great Lakes* (1901) by Edward Stratemeyer (1862–1930), writing as Arthur M. Winfield; Allen Chapman's *The Darewell Chums on a Cruise* (1909); *Motor Boat Boys on the Great Lakes* (1912) by St. George H. Rathborne (1854–1938), writing as Louis Arundel; and Ross Kay's *The Go Ahead Boys on Smuggler's Island* (1916). See also GREAT LAKES LITERATURE.

The mineralogical surveys of the Upper Peninsula by Douglass Houghton and others in the 1840s established the existence of vast and valuable deposits of copper and iron ore. The resultant mining industry brought jobs, immigrants, and wealth to the state. One of the earliest novels about mineral exploration in Michigan is *Manita of the Pictured Rocks; or, The Copper Speculator* (1848) by Osgood Bradbury (1798–1886). Technical details about mining play a large role in *Where Copper Was King* (1905) by James North Wright (1838–1910). *Not without Honor* (1941) by Vivian Parsons (1907–1950) and *The Long Winter Ends* (1941) by Newton G. Thomas (b. 1878) look at the mining industry through the eyes of individual miners.

Since its rise in the early 1900s, the automobile industry has had a significant economic and social impact not only on Michigan's major manufacturing centers, such as Detroit and Flint, but also on the entire state. Many novels set in Michigan have exploited this subject, the first being *An Auto-Biography* (1915) by Edward Henry Peple (1869–1924), which features a sentient motor vehicle explaining how it was made. A fuller account of fiction dealing with the Michigan automobile industry will be found under DETROIT.

Unique to Michigan was the short-lived Mormon colony the Kingdom of St. James, established on Beaver Island by James Jesse Strang (1813–1856) in 1847 after he and his followers separated from Brigham Young's group in WISCONSIN. This colony and its leader, the self-proclaimed "King" Strang, have been the subject of a few novels. Focusing on the more lurid and sensational aspects of the polygamous Mormon colony is *Harem Island* (1961) by Eugene (Gene) Lee Caesar (1927–1986), writing under the pseudonym Anthony Sterling, a novel masquerading as a factual exposé. Karl W. Detzer (1891–1987) writes of Strang's notoriety among the mainland fishing community in *The Pirate of the Pine Lands* (1929). Somewhat more objective, if not sympathetic to Strang and his Mormon splinter group, are *The Gallant Spirit* (1982) by Willo Davis Roberts (1928–2004) and *Queen of the Island* (1993) by Jo Ann Mazoué (b. 1924).

Michigan's educational systems, as seen by teachers and pupils, have been explored in many works of fiction. Primary and secondary education is represented largely by stories of frontier and rural schools. *Theophilus Trent: Old Times in the Oak Openings* (1887) by Benjamin Franklin Taylor (1819–1887) concerns a young New York schoolteacher who travels to a frontier school on the Raisin River in the 1830s. *Country Schoolma'am* (1941), one of the novels by DELLA THOMPSON LUTES (1866–1942), makes use of her experiences as a sixteen-year-old teacher at a one-room school in Jackson County in the 1880s. A more contemporary setting appears in *Farmer* (1976) by JIM (JAMES THOMAS) HARRISON (1937–2016). The protagonist of *Farmer* not only teaches in the local high school but also tries to run a small northern Michigan farm. Harrison returns to a farm locale in *The English Major* (2008), from which the sexagenarian protagonist embarks on a road trip. The loneliness of a young female teacher assigned to an isolated school district near Harbor Springs is the subject of *The Shadow of the Crooked Tree* (1965) by Helen Fernald (1888–1972). Many juvenile novels look at school from the student's point of view, concentrating mostly on adolescent angst, peer groups, and the heartbreaks and embarrassments of first love. Ann Hunter Lowell's twelve-book Sorority Girls series (1986–1987) deals with a suburban Detroit high school social club, and *Daughters of Eve* (1979) by Lois Duncan (b. 1934) concerns a faculty adviser's malignant influence on a high school sorority. Gloria Whelan in *Indian School* (1996) portrays a mission school for Native American children in northern Michigan in the late 1830s.

Higher education is well represented in Michigan fiction, although most works use the state's first university, the University of Michigan, as their setting. One of the first and of special interest is *An American Girl and Her Four Years in a Boys' College* (1878) by Sola, an anagram of the initials of the author's name, Olive San Louie Anderson (1852–1886). One of the first female students admitted to the University of Michigan, where she earned a bachelor of arts in 1875, Anderson relates her coeducational experiences with a veneer of fiction in this novel. Katharine Holland Brown (1876–1931) also fictionalized two years of a female student at the university in *Philippa at Halcyon* (1910). *Ann Arbor Tales* (1902) by Karl E. Harriman (1875–1935) is a collection of short stories about undergraduate life at the University of Michigan. Ann Arbor clergyman and bestselling author LLOYD C(ASSEL) DOUGLAS (1877–1951) pits a young medical student against an arrogant doctor at the University of Michigan Medical School in *Disputed Passage* (1939). The "University of Winnemac" is a thinly disguised University of Michigan in *Arrowsmith* (1925) by (HARRY) SINCLAIR LEWIS (1885–1951). Jean Hamilton (1878–1958), a onetime dean of women at the University of Michigan, wrote *Wings of Wax* (1929) under the pseudonym Janet Hoyt. It is a roman à clef about the liberal student policies a college president institutes, which cause his ultimate downfall. A series of mysteries featuring a female computer consultant by Michigan alumna Susan Holtzer (b. 1940) is set in Ann Arbor and at the University of Michigan. A small college in southwestern Michigan is the setting for *Disguises of Love* (1952) by Robie Macauley (1919–1995) and is probably based on Olivet College, where the author spent some time. Calvin College in Grand Rapids is used by FREDERICK MANFRED (b. Feike Feikema, 1912–1994), in his highly autobiographical novel *The Primitive* (1949).

Juvenile novels about college life tend to concentrate on intercollegiate athletics. C. Paul Jackson (1902–1991) wrote four books about Michigan college football. In *Blaine of the Backfield* (1937) Donal Hamilton Haines (1886–1951) tells of a young man trying out for varsity football at the University of Michigan; and in *On the Campus Freshman* (1925) by James Schermerhorn Jr. (1897–1956), a first-year football player is accused of purposely throwing a game.

Michigan's immigrant experience is reflected in a broad fictional literature. The first immigrants to the lands that would become Michigan in the seventeenth and eighteenth centuries were the French and English colonists and settlers. Before statehood the majority of the incoming population came from New York and the New England states; even by 1860 only about one-fifth of Michigan inhabitants were foreign born. Nonetheless, significant numbers of Germans, Dutch, Scandinavians, and Canadians came to the state to escape political repression, enjoy religious freedom, or find better economic conditions and employment opportunities. Albert Grimm (1864–1922), writing as Alfred Ira in the German language, shows the hardships and joys of a German miner's family in the Upper Peninsula copper fields in *Das Stiefmütterchen* (1898). *Juell Demming* (1901) by Albert Law-

rence (1865–1924) tells of a Canadian migrant making a small town on the shore of Lake Michigan his home. Writing as Jolie Paylin, Alice Behrend (1913–1993) describes a family of Danish immigrants trying to make a living at Green Bay and Menominee as commercial fishermen in *The Gill Netters* (1979); and in *A Bashful Woman* (1944) by Kenneth Horan (1886–1983) a successful wagon-making business established by Welsh immigrants evolves into the nascent auto industry in a southern Michigan city. See also DETROIT for examples of the immigrant experience there.

A number of novels, mostly published in the 1940s, commemorate the centennial of the 1847 founding of Holland, Michigan, by Albertus Van Raalte (1811–1876) and his company of Dutch settlers and recount the hardships they faced and overcame. Among them are *Landverhuizers* (1947), a two-volume Dutch-language saga by Pieter Johannes Risseeuw (1901–1968); *Instead of the Thorn* (1941) by Bastian Kruithof (1902–1990); *A Land I Will Show Thee* (1949) by Marian Schoolland (1902–1984); and *De Man met de Berenhuid* (1898), written in Dutch by Johannes Keuning (b. ca. 1860) and translated into English in 1925 as *The Man in the Bearskin*. Juvenile fiction concerning Dutch pioneer life at the Holland settlement is represented by *Hope Haven,* written in 1947 by Dirk Gringhuis. See also IMMIGRANT AND MIGRANT LITERATURE.

No clear line of demarcation exists between immigrant and ethnic literatures. In many fictional representations of the immigrant experience, first-, second-, and third-generation descendants of arrivals from the "old country" relate not only stories of their forebears' first years in America but also descriptions of ethnic city neighborhoods or ethnic rural settlements. Common themes running through these books include acclimatizing to new surroundings, language difficulties, cultural differences, and the misunderstanding, suspicion, or outright hostility of neighbors or co-workers. Examples include *The Dominie of Harlem* (1913), *Bram of the Five Corners* (1915), and *The Outbound Road* (1919), pictures of disaffected youth in western Michigan Dutch communities by Arnold Mulder (1885–1959). The process of acclimatization of a Grand Rapids

Dutch family over twenty years is explored in *Belly Fulla Straw* (1934) by DAVID CORNEL DEJONG (1905–1967). In *Seedtime and Harvest* (1935) and *Wherever I Choose* (1938) by Eleanor Blake Pratt (1899–ca. 1953), the daughter and granddaughter of Norwegian immigrants, respectively, aspire to leave the restrictive world of the farm for better opportunities; the patriarch of a Swedish family in the Upper Peninsula instructs his young daughter in customs of the old country in *Latchstring Out* (1944) by Skulda V. Banér (1897–1964). In the juvenile novel *Inga of Porcupine Mine* (1942) by Caroline R. Stone (1884–1972), aspects of an Upper Peninsula girl's dual heritage from her Finnish mother and Cornish father are explored.

African Americans in Michigan have been depicted in a wide range of novels written by both black and white authors. The earliest appearance of an African American in a novel set in Michigan can be found in *Eine neue Welt* (1843), a German-language work by Robert Wilhelm Heller (1814–1871). The story concerns events in the Kalamazoo River valley in the early 1800s that involve an army officer, his black companion, and two Ojibwas. Two African American Detroit lawyers, Walter H. Stowers (1856–1932) and William H. Anderson (b. 1858), under the pen name Sanda, wrote *Appointed* (1894), part of which is set in Detroit.

It was not until seventy-one years later that the next noteworthy Michigan African American novel appeared. The critically acclaimed *Ladies of the Rachmaninoff Eyes* (1965) by Henry Van Dyke (1928–2011) concerns the complicated relationship, by turns pleasant and nasty, between an elderly Jewish widow and her African American widowed companion of similar age. Van Dyke draws on Allegan, his hometown, as the setting of the book. The third novel of Nobel Prize winner and OHIO native TONI MORRISON (CHLOE ARDELIA WOFFORD) (b. 1931), *SONG OF SOLOMON* (1977), is based on the folk myth that Africans could fly, and part of the story takes place in an unnamed Michigan city. Morrison's deft and lyrical use of African American culture and heritage in her writing has inspired a number of black authors to emulate her success. *Linden Hills* (1985) by Gloria Naylor (b. 1950) is set in suburban Detroit and shows a black middle-class community that has lost its racial and cultural identity in the pursuit of success. *Mama* (1987), the first and very successful novel by Terry McMillan (b. 1951), traces the struggle a black woman undergoes as she raises her five children single-handedly in Port Huron. Two novels by Pearl Cleage (b. 1948), *What Looks like Crazy on an Ordinary Day* (1997) and *I Wish I Had a Red Dress* (2001), use the once-prosperous black summer resort Idlewild, located in Lake County, as a setting where women gather for mutual support and a feeling of community. See also DETROIT.

Native Americans, particularly the indigenous Ojibwas, Hurons, and Potawatomis, have been portrayed in Michigan fiction from the earliest time. Their many dime-novel depictions nearly always mirror the nineteenth-century stereotypes of cunning and bloodthirsty forest dwellers or, in the case of the Ottawa chief Pontiac, the tragic "noble savage" for whom grudging admiration is allowed. Most of this literature is set during times of colonial and frontier conflict, usually in the 1763 attacks on Michilimackinac and Detroit, and during the War of 1812. For a representative list of such titles, see "Dime Novels" later in this entry.

Re-creating ancient and pre-Columbian days among Michigan's Native Americans has also occupied the imagination of some authors. The earliest work, a fantasy titled *The Heroines of Petoséga* (1889) by Frederic Alva Dean (1859–1936), postulates the existence and destruction of an advanced civilization located in the Little Traverse Bay and Straits of Mackinac areas three thousand years ago. More soundly based on the archaeological record are *Winged Moccasins* (1933) by Abbie J. Grosvenor (1865–1948), in which a young American Indian attempts to warn villages of his people of the approach of a hostile war party; and *People of the Lakes* (1994) by Kathleen Gear (b. 1954) and W. Michael Gear (b. 1955), which re-creates the role that spirits and shamanism play among Native American clans in Ohio and Michigan. Frederick Burton (1861–1909) shows the life of one Great Lakes Indian family through three generations just before the advent of European explorers in *Redcloud of the Lakes* (1909).

The recurring theme of enduring and escaping Indian captivity can be found in many boys' adventure stories and DIME NOVELS and some mainstream fiction. Those written in the 1800s are in most cases directly influenced by the allegedly nonfiction Indian captivity narratives that proliferated at that time. The earliest example with a Michigan scene is *Edward Wilton; or, Early Days in Michigan* (1851) by Frances Traver (ca. 1815–1855), writing as Fanny Woodville. The novel relates the story of a boy taken from his family by a Potawatomi war party and returned to white society years later. Clara F. Guernsey (1836–1893) provides a Christian message in her novel *The Shawnee Prisoner: A Borderer's Story* (1877); the story tells of the capture of a young Virginian in the late 1700s and his travels to Detroit before being reunited with his family. Examples of works with Michigan settings written for younger audiences include *Lost in the Fur Country* (1914) by Dietrich J. Lange (1863–1940), *The White Captive: A Tale of the Pontiac War* (1915) by Richard Clyde Ford (1870–1951), and *Red Wing's White Brother* (1956) by Elisabeth Webster (1881–1965).

In spite of the obvious sexual overtones that the captivity of white females by Native Americans connotes, this aspect has not been explored to any degree by Michigan novelists. Social and sexual relations between Native Americans and whites, however, have been occasional themes in Michigan fiction since the nineteenth century. The shame of a mixed-race heritage, especially in women, and the prejudice it engenders in polite society are exemplified in *The Fatal Secret* (1873) by Cynthia M. Roberts Gorton (1829–1894), writing under the pseudonym Ida Glenwood. In this story an attractive young woman from Mackinac Island has her reputation and social advance thwarted when her "secret," that one of her parents is Native American, becomes public knowledge. *The Water Dancers* (2003) by Terry Gamble (b. 1955) examines similar prejudices during World War II, involving a wealthy Harbor Springs family, their severely wounded son, and a local sixteen-year-old Indian girl. A more liberal view of the attraction between whites and Native Americans has been expressed in a number of historical romance novels. In *Savage Passions* (1996) by Cassie Edwards (b. 1936) an Ottawa chief is the object of desire by a preacher's daughter on the 1840s Michigan frontier; and Gail Oust (b. 1943), writing as Elizabeth Turner, follows a romance between a French-Indian métis forest ranger and an Englishwoman at Fort Mackinac during the War of 1812 in *Wild and Sweet* (2000).

Varieties of social problems have harried the Native American inhabitants of the state since the coming of the white man, and some appear as themes in Michigan fiction. *Indian Paul* (1945) by John Moore (1913–1989) shows the consequences when an enraged crowd in Mackinaw City takes the law into its own hands to deal with a young Native American accused of murdering his mother. Another view emerges, however, in *Joe Pete* (1929) by Florence McClinchey (1889–1946), in which a young Native American boy on Sugar Island makes a success of himself through dedication to his family and education. The contentious establishment and proliferation of gambling casinos on Native American land and run for the benefit of the tribes is a more recent phenomenon. What should be fertile ground for exploration of the moral, social, and criminal aspects of the industry has not yet been fully used in fiction. In *Michigan Roll* (1988) Thomas E. Kakonis (b. 1930) looks at the Leelanau casino milieu through the eyes of a professional gambler, and in *The Murmurings* (2002) David Walks-As-Bear (b. 1957) uses the background of a tribal casino to juxtapose modern ways to lost Native American traditions. See also the various subtypes of ethnic and racial literature, for example, NATIVE AMERICAN LITERATURE and AFRICAN AMERICAN LITERATURE.

Among the most distinguished twentieth-century fiction writers with strong Michigan ties are Ernest Hemingway and Jim Harrison. Several of the Nick Adams stories are based on Hemingway's experiences and imaginative transformations associated with his family's summer home on Walloon Lake near Petoskey in northern Michigan. Among Hemingway's Michigan literary products are "Indian Camp," "The Doctor and the Doctor's Wife," "The Three-Day Blow," "The End of Something," "The Last Good Country," and, most famously, "Big Two-Hearted River." All are collected in *The Nick Adams Stories* (1972). Jim Harrison has published many popular and critically respected novels and collections of novellas, as well as poetry, essays, and Hollywood screenplays. Although some of Harrison's best-known fiction is set elsewhere, novels like *Wolf* (1971), *Farmer* (1976), *Sundog* (1984), *Returning to Earth* (2007), and *The Big Seven* (2015) and the collected novellas concerning the title character of *Brown Dog* (2013) vividly portray rural and wild northern Michigan settings.

Poetry: The earliest original literary work published in the state that also uses Michigan as a background is most likely the anonymous poem *The Emigrant* (1819). It has been attributed to Henry Whiting (1788–1851), who wrote at least two similar verse narratives on Native American subjects and was also the author of a biography of the explorer Zebulon Pike. Whiting began his career as a soldier and served in the war with Mexico.

The most famous verse work using a Michigan locale is arguably *The Song of Hiawatha* (1855) by Henry Wadsworth Longfellow (1807–1882). Set on the south shore of Lake Superior, the narrative poem relates the life of a legendary Ojibwa warrior and chief. One of Longfellow's sources was *Algic Researches* (1839), an ethnographic study that HENRY ROWE SCHOOLCRAFT (1793–1864) compiled with assistance from his wife, Jane Johnston Schoolcraft (1800–1842) while he was an Indian agent at Sault Ste. Marie.

The sentimental poetry of WILL(IAM MCKENDREE) CARLETON (1845–1912) became nationally popular during the nineteenth century, expressing in homey vignettes everyday life in a succession of collections, beginning with *Farm Ballads* (1873). Many of his poems, such as "Betsey and I Are Out" and "Over the Hill to the Poor-House," became staples of school recitations. Carleton was named Poet Laureate of Michigan, and for many years his birthday, October 21, was celebrated as Will Carleton Day in the schools of the state.

The verse of JULIA A. (DAVIS) MOORE (1847–1920), who promoted herself as the "Sweet Singer of Michigan," was considered so bad even in its day that she was ridiculed in print and during her frequent pub-

lic readings. In *ADVENTURES OF HUCKLEBERRY FINN* (London 1884; New York 1885) by SAMUEL LANGHORNE CLEMENS (1835–1910), writing as Mark Twain, she appears as the deceased amateur poetess Emmeline Grangerford, whose "Ode to Stephen Dowling Bots, Dec'd" is a direct parody of Moore's style and subject matter. There is some evidence that suggests that Moore was aware of her compositional shortcomings but shrewdly capitalized on them by staging well-advertised personal performances.

The humorous poetry of Ben King (1857–1894), another self-styled "sweet singer," this time of St. Joseph, often relies on the rural dialect of his southwestern Michigan home and the juxtaposition of the archetypical country bumpkin to the sophisticated city dweller. A volume of his collected poems, *Ben King's Verse* (1894), was rushed into print soon after King's death, and his popularity assured its reprinting through 1912.

Born in Wayne County, Michigan, Ivan Swift (1873–1945) moved to Harbor Springs at an early age. He exemplifies the complete artist who is comfortable and competent in many media, in his case painting, photography, graphic design, and poetry. He illustrated his only book of poems, *Fagots of Cedar* (1907), with his photographs and drawings of the Michigan landscape. This book was reissued at least three times in the next twenty years, sometimes with additional material.

John Couchois Wright (1874–1939) was born in Harbor Springs and spent much of his life there. In 1896 he established and edited the Harbor Springs weekly newspaper the *Standard,* but he became better known for his lyrical verse using the picturesque Little Traverse Bay area, such as *Lays of the Lakes* (1911) and *Northern Breezes* (1917). He retells Indian legends of northwestern Michigan in *Stories of the Crooked Tree* (1915). A volume of his collected poems, provisionally titled "Signal Smoke," was in preparation at the time of his death in Alma but was never published.

EDGAR A(LBERT) GUEST (1881–1959), a journalist for the *Detroit Free Press,* published a poem each day in his column, which eventually was syndicated to three hundred newspapers and made him nationally known. Guest was another poet of the commonplace, the simple life, and nostalgia; his newspaper verse was gathered into dozens of collections, typical titles of which include *Heap o' Livin'* (1916) and *Rhymes of Childhood* (1924).

Lew Sarett (1888–1954), who, like Ben King, was from southwestern Michigan, enjoyed widespread appeal for verse dealing with nature, local Native Americans, and Benton Harbor locales. Poems appearing in volumes such as *Slow Smoke* (1925) and *Wings against the Moon* (1931), while exhibiting some technical merit, are now considered quite old fashioned by most critics.

Gwen Frostic (1906–2001) of Benzonia was an author of nearly two dozen volumes of inspirational poetry with Michigan themes and settings. They include such titles as *My Michigan* (1957), her first effort, and *Lilies of the Fields* (1999). Her work was literally a cottage industry: she illustrated all these volumes with her own block prints, published them at her own press, and sold them through her studio to tourists and enthusiasts.

THEODORE ROETHKE (1908–1963), a native of Saginaw and a graduate of the University of Michigan, spent much of his professional and writing career outside the state. The romantic agrarianism in his poetry was drawn significantly from memories of his early life in Saginaw, where his parents worked as florists, and he often evoked images of the Michigan landscape, as seen in *THE LOST SON* (1948) and *The Waking* (1953); the latter won Roethke the Pulitzer Prize.

Black poets ROBERT HAYDEN (b. Asa Bundy Sheffey, 1913–1980), DUDLEY FELKER RANDALL (1914–2000), Naomi Cornelia Long Madgett (b. 1923), and Murray Jackson (1926–2002) mine the African American experience in the streets and neighborhoods of Detroit for much of their subject matter, which also contains significant autobiographical material.

Pulitzer Prize winner and U.S. Poet Laureate Philip Levine (1928–2015) was born in Detroit, and although he lived most of his postgraduate life in California, his poetry effectively uses his memories of the city and experiences in its factories and particularly champions working-class people and their inherent nobility.

Dan Gerber and Jim Harrison, both born in small Michigan towns, also share a simi-

Theodore Roethke's childhood home, Saginaw, Michigan, 2006. Photo by William Barillas.

larity not only in poetic style but in their themes, most notably rural and small-town life. Gerber and Harrison met while attending Michigan State University, became good friends, and subsequently co-founded the literary magazine *Sumac* (1968–1971), to which they both contributed early poetry. Both have written of places in Michigan in a manner reflecting the influence of American transcendentalism and Zen Buddhism. Gerber's *Snow on the Backs of Animals* (1986) evokes western Michigan landscapes; *A Last Bridge Home: New and Selected Poems* (1992) collects the best of his early work. Harrison drew on international literary currents, including poetry from Latin America and Asia as well as Europe. Most of his poetry is included in *The Shape of the Journey: New and Collected Poems* (1998); later collections include *In Search of Small Gods* (2009) and *Songs of Unreason* (2011).

The poetry of Detroit native JIM (JAMES RAYMOND) DANIELS (b. 1956) reflects his blue-collar background as the son of an autoworker. Class and racial divides, urban violence, and industrial landscapes are among

Dan Gerber and Jim Harrison, Traverse City, Michigan, 1992. Photo by William Barillas.

the themes explored in his spare, prize-winning verse, as exemplified in *M-80* (1993).

Besides older poets who have not yet received proper recognition for their works, many new and emerging poets born in Michigan or writing on Michigan themes have already made names for themselves through their chapbooks or published collections and their contributions to little magazines and literary reviews. Among the poets and works in these two categories are Patricia Clark (b. 1951) with *North of Wondering* (1999); Linda Nemec Foster (b. 1950) with *Amber Necklace from Gdansk* (2001); Alice Fulton (b. 1952) with *Cascade Experiment* (2004); Linda Gregerson (b. 1950) with *Waterborne* (2002); Robert Haight (b. 1955) with *Water Music* (1993); Bob Hicok (b. 1960) with *Insomnia Diary* (2004); Conrad Hilberry (b. 1928) with *Player Piano* (1999); Patricia Hooper (b. 1941) with *At the Corner of the Eye* (1997); Jonathan Johnson (b. 1967) with *Mastodon, 80% Complete* (1997); Laura Kasischke (b. 1961) with *Gardening in the Dark* (2004); Josie Kearns (b. 1954) with *New Numbers* (2000); Faye Kicknosway (b. 1936) with *Mixed Plate* (2003); David Dodd Lee (b. 1959) with *Arrow Pointing North* (2002); Kathleen McGookey (b. 1967) with *Whatever Shines* (2001); JUDITH MINTY (b. 1937) with *Walking with the Bear*

(2000); Anne Ohman Youngs (b. 1939) with *Thirty Octaves above Middle-C* (1998); John Palen (b. 1942) with *Open Communion* (2005); Miriam Pederson (b. 1948) with *This Brief Light* (2003); Greg Rappleye (b. 1953) with *Figured Dark* (2007); John Rybicki (b. 1961) with *Yellow-Haired Girl with Spider* (2002); F. Richard Thomas (b. 1940) with *Extravagant Kiss* (2007); Robert Vander Molen (b. 1947) with *Breath* (2000); Diane Wakoski (b. 1937) with *The Butcher's Apron* (2000); and TERRY WOOTEN (b. 1948) with *Child of War* (2007).

The Poetry Society of Michigan was established in 1933 as an organization for the mutual benefit and support of state poets. Its periodical, *Peninsula Poets,* which began in 1946 as a quarterly but in 1988 changed to twice yearly, publishes the poetry of its members.

Drama: An early play with a Michigan background, and in fact the second dramatic work written and published by an American, is *Ponteach; or, The Savages of America: A Tragedy* (1766). Its author, Major Robert Rogers (1731–1795), was the commander of the famous military unit Rogers' Rangers during the French and Indian War and later governor of Michilimackinac. The play cynically views the duplicity and savagery of both whites and Native Americans and is loosely based on Pontiac's conspiracy, which Rogers witnessed firsthand.

Avery Hopwood (1882–1928), a graduate of the University of Michigan, was a nationally recognized playwright who wrote a number of popular and successful works for the stage, although none had elements that particularly identified him with Michigan. By far his most important influence on the literature of the state was the establishment, through the terms of his will, of cash prizes for outstanding creative writing by students at his alma mater. The Hopwood Awards have been given annually since 1931 and have marked the beginning of many acclaimed literary careers. See also "Michigan Literary Awards" later in this entry.

Native Michiganian Milan Stitt (1941–2009) wrote *The Runner Stumbles* (1976), a drama based on an incident in northern Michigan in the 1920s involving illicit relations between a Catholic priest and a nun and the latter's mysterious death. The play was named Best Broadway Play of 1976, and a revised motion-picture version appeared in 1979.

Brothers Paul Schrader (b. 1946) and Leonard Schrader (1943–2006) were both born and grew up in Grand Rapids and collaborated on many screenplays that received positive critical notice. Some of their films have been directed by Martin Scorsese and explore the violence and alienation in modern society; among these are *Taxi Driver* (1976), *American Gigolo* (1979), and *Raging Bull* (1980). Two of Paul Schrader's screenplays use Michigan themes and settings: *Blue Collar* (1978), co-written with Leonard Schrader, which concerns autoworkers confronting a corrupt labor union in Detroit, and *Hardcore* (1979), which follows a Grand Rapids man searching for his missing daughter, who has turned up as an actress in a pornographic film. Both screenplays were later rewritten as novels by Leonard Schrader.

Chelsea, Michigan, native Jeff Daniels (b. 1955), better known as a film and stage actor, established the not-for-profit Purple Rose Theatre in his hometown in 1991. He intended it primarily for Midwestern directors, playwrights, and actors. He has written a number of plays that have been performed in this venue, among them *Shoe Man* (1990), *The Vast Difference* (1993), and *Escanaba in da Moonlight* (1995); he subsequently produced the last as an independent film that enjoyed significant commercial success.

Popular Literature:

Dime Novels: No fewer than two dozen dime novels written between 1860 and 1903 use Michigan as a locale. The War of 1812 is the subject of *One-Armed Alf, the Giant Hunter of the Great Lakes* (1881) by Oliver "Oll" Coomes (1845–1921). Pontiac and his conspiracy of 1763 provide the background for *Red Lightning; or, The Black League* (1872) by Charles Dunning Clark (1843–1892), writing as W. J. Hamilton. *The Trader Spy; or, The Victim of the Fire Raft* (1869) was written by Edward Willett (1830–1889) under the pen name J. Stanley Henderson; and *Caribou Zip; or, The Forest Brothers* (1874) is by Joseph E. Badger (1848–1909). Life on the Michigan frontier is covered in *Trapper Joe; or, The Outlaw of Lake Huron* (1869) by Ar-

thur Meserve (1838–1896), *The Young Bear Hunters* (1882) by James M. Merrill (1847–1936), and *The Backwoods' Bride* (1860) by Metta V. Fuller Victor (1831–1885). Big-city crime and perpetrators being hunted down by intrepid detectives form the plot of *Deadwood Dick, Jr. in Detroit* (1889) by Edward L. Wheeler (ca. 1854–1885) and *Nick Carter's Battle against Odds; or, The Mystery of the Detroit Pawnbroker* (1903) by John R. Coryell (1851–1924).

One dime novel in particular needs to be mentioned for its interesting premise and probable debt to Jules Verne. The protagonists in *Under Five Lakes; or, The Cruise of the Destroyer* (1886) by Charles Bertrand Lewis, writing as M. Quad, build a submarine that they use to explore the Great Lakes and plunder the shipwrecks they locate therein.

Mystery and Detective Fiction: Michigan has been a much-used setting in the mystery, detective, and crime genre. The first non-dime-novel mystery that uses the state as a background is *The Spiritualists and the Detectives* (1877) by Allan Pinkerton (1819–1884), in which the action occurs in Kalamazoo and Detroit, but the actual flood of titles began in the 1930s, roughly corresponding to the national trend. Some of these authors are prolific.

Frances Moyer Ross Stevens (1895–1947), writing as Christopher Hale, produced a series of ten mysteries published from 1935 to 1948 featuring Lieutenant Bill French of the Michigan State Police investigating crimes committed throughout the state. *Stormy Night* (1937), *Dead of Winter* (1941), and *Midsummer Nightmare* (1945) are three examples of her classic "whodunit" puzzles.

JOHN DONALDSON VOELKER (1903–1991), writing as Robert Traver, won national acclaim for his criminal courtroom novel *Anatomy of a Murder* (1958), set in an Upper Peninsula city and based on a 1952 murder and subsequent trial in which Voelker was the defense attorney. The novel went on to become a best seller and an Oscar-winning film the following year. Voelker also wrote two other legal mysteries with Michigan settings, *Laughing Whitefish* (1965) and *People versus Kirk* (1981), along with fictionalized portrayals of his experiences as a prosecuting attorney, essays, and musings on law, life, society, and nature.

Two early novels by Mark Smith (b. 1935), *Toyland* (1965) and *The Middleman* (1967), are closely linked, although no contemporary reviewers took notice. They tell the same story, from different vantage points, of the hired kidnapping and attempted murder of two children arranged by their uncle in Charlevoix, who is the beneficiary of their insurance policies.

Probably the best-known and most popular—nationally and internationally—crime novelist writing about Michigan is ELMORE LEONARD JR. (1925–2013), a master of dialogue. Many of his novels are set in Detroit and its suburbs and use these locales to excellent effect, and the casts of fully limned thieves, murders, con artists, grifters, and mob bosses are ably counteracted by the police and ordinary citizens caught up in Leonard's intricate plots. His Michigan-based novels include *The Big Bounce* (1969), *Swag* (1976), *Killshot* (1989), and *Up in Honey's Room* (2007), among many others.

The indigenous violence and hopelessness of life in the Detroit ghetto are themes that African American novelist Donald Goines (1938–1974) returns to in many of his books, some written under the pseudonym Al C. Clark, such as *Dopefiend* (1971), *Street Players* (1973), and *Death List* (1974). His characters range from drug dealers, hit men, and prostitutes to a cynical and world-weary mixed-race police detective team.

The mean streets of Detroit as portrayed by LOREN D. ESTLEMAN (b. 1952) in his continuing Amos Walker mysteries are as well known and evocative as Raymond Chandler's Los Angeles and have become a continuing character in his books. Private investigator Walker, no matter how tempted he may be by femmes fatales or the promise of easy money, remains faithful to his personal code. Two of Estleman's twenty-five novels through 2015 that feature Amos Walker are *Motor City Blue* (1980) and *The Sundown Speech* (2015). WILLIAM X(AVIER) KIENZLE (1928–2001), also writing about murder and mayhem in Detroit, did so from the vantage point of a parish priest in his series of twenty-four Father Koesler mysteries. Although the novels are about man's depravity, they also are quite humane in the way in which the priest discovers the perpetrator and at the same time offer a look into the workings of the modern Catholic Church. *The Rosary Murders* (1979) and *The Gathering* (2002) are two examples.

Two series employ the brooding vastness and beauty of Michigan's Upper Peninsula as an effective setting. In the ongoing series Woods Cop Mysteries by Joseph Heywood (b. 1943), criminal activity in the western Upper Peninsula forests is usually stumbled on by a conservation officer in such titles as *Killing a Cold One* (2013). Ex-cop-turned-private investigator Alex McKnight operates his investigative business out of the eastern Upper Peninsula town of Paradise in volumes by Steve Hamilton (b. 1961), including *Misery Bay* (2011).

Children's and Young Adult Literature: Clarence Budington Kelland (1881–1964) was the author of the eight-book Mark Tidd series, whose eponymous protagonist, overweight and possessing a stutter, is the antithesis of the usual boy hero. He and his friends experience a variety of adventures, mostly in and around a small Michigan town, in such titles as *Mark Tidd: His Adventures and Strategies* (1913) and *Mark Tidd, Manufacturer* (1918).

Margaret Isabel Ross (1897–1986), the sister of mystery novelist Frances Moyer Ross Stevens, was a popular author of juvenile fiction, some of which, like *Morgan's Fourth Son* (1940), has Grand Traverse and other northern Michigan area settings.

Gloria Whelan began her writing career relatively late but has made up for lost time. Since her first book in 1978, she has written at least twenty novels set in or around Mancelona, Mackinac Island, and other Michigan areas. Her novel imagining Ernest Hemingway's sixteenth summer at Horton Bay, *The Pathless Woods* (1981), and *The Wanigan* (2002), about lumbering on the Au Sable River in 1875, are typical of her work.

Most of the young-adult books by Ann Arbor writer Alfred Slote (b. 1926) deal with youth sports teams and boys who must overcome some defect or obstacle in their personal life, such as parental divorce or disapproval, serious illness, or difficulties with peer acceptance. Two of his fifteen books set in "Arborville" are *Stranger on the Ball Club* (1970) and *Finding Buck McHenry* (1991).

John Bellairs (1938–1991) used his hometown, Marshall, and one of its houses as the setting for three of his horror novels that feature ten-year-old Lewis Barnavelt: *The House with a Clock in Its Walls* (1973), *The Figure in the Shadows* (1975), and *The Letter, the Witch, and the Ring* (1976). The popularity of these books is attested by the fact that the publisher has commissioned Brad Strickland (b. 1947) to continue the series, and six more titles have appeared, the latest being *The Sign of the Sinister Sorcerer* (2008).

Hilda Stahl (1938–1993) holds the distinction of being the most prolific Michigan novel writer. Of her more than 150 books written between 1972 and 1993, at least 59 are set in Michigan. They include a number of adult mysteries and historical novels; however, the vast majority of her output consists of six children's series. Examples of individual titles are *Teddy Jo and the Terrible Secret* (1982), *Mystery of the Missing Grandfather* (1988), and *Roxie's Mall Madness* (1993).

PATRICIA POLACCO (b. 1944) presents her memories of life on a farm near Union City and the importance of family in a number of delightful picture books, including *Meteor!* (1987), *My Rotten Redheaded Older Brother* (1994), and *When Lightning Comes in a Jar* (2002).

The strange twilight world of adolescence is deftly captured in the novels of Margaret Willey (b. 1950), whose young people are faced with adult problems and must make difficult choices, sometimes with tragic results. *The Bigger Book of Lydia* (1983) and *The Melinda Zone* (1993) are set in small western Michigan lakeshore towns, much like the one in which she grew up.

Romance: The love story, written by women and intended primarily for a female audience, has found Michigan to be a sympathetic setting since the 1930s. With the rise of specialty romance publishers in the 1980s, such as Harlequin and Silhouette, and the growing market for this popular literature, it has been difficult to keep track of the scores of such novels appearing each month.

Louise Marks Breitenbach Clancy (1876–1963), writing as Louise Jerrold, employed Detroit as the background for her three romance novels, one of which, *Love Isn't Important* (1932), involves a hatcheck girl seeking a rich husband.

Mary Frances Doner bracketed her successful mainstream novels of the 1940s and 1950s by writing a baker's dozen of romances with settings on both coasts of the state. In *Forever More* (1934) a woman is married to a farmer she thinks she does not love on Lake St. Clair, and her last book, *The Darker Star* (1974), follows the growing relationship between a waitress and a wealthy man in Ludington.

The majority of the romance novels by Pat Warren (b. 1936) are set in Detroit, although the Upper Peninsula is also a locale of interest. *Final Verdict* (1987) features an attractive lawyer interested in a Detroit prosecuting attorney, and a romance ensues when a widower engages a caregiver for his child in *Keeping Kate* (1996).

Maris Soule (b. 1939) has written many romance novels that feature a variety of state settings. The owner of a tavern in *Sounds like Love* (1986), set in Grand Rapids and Holland, develops an interest in a musician she hires; and a regional director of an Ann Arbor public relations firm tries not to jeopardize her career when she becomes attracted to her neighbor in *No Promises Made* (1994).

The novels of Jill Culby (b. 1948) also use many Michigan locales, ranging from the crowded Detroit metropolis to the Upper Peninsula. Written under the pseudonym Jeanne Grant, *Wintergreen* (1984) concerns a widow falsely accused of infidelity who falls in love with her brother-in-law. In a later effort, *The Woman Most Likely to . . .* (2002), written under the name Jennifer Greene, an older woman handles difficulties with a daughter while being reacquainted with a former love.

Many of the romance novels of Lisa Childs (b. 1969) have used the locales around Grand Rapids and western Michigan near the author's hometown. Among these are *Bridal Reconnaissance* (2004) and *His Baby Surprise* (2010).

Science Fiction: The inherent danger to earthlings from extraterrestrial visitors has been a major plotline of science fiction since H. G. Wells's (1866–1946) *The War of the Worlds* in 1898. In his novel *VOR* (1958) James Blish (1921–1975) has a UFO land in a remote northern Michigan forest. It eventually proves to be a great danger to the earth.

The idyllic-sounding *Down on the Farm* (1987) by John Stchur (b. 1947) is anything but benign as a long-buried alien craft and its centipede-like pilot begin to exert a malign influence over the local fauna in rural Lenawee County.

Another popular science-fiction theme is nuclear war and its aftermath. *Testament XXI* (1973) by Guy Snyder (b. 1951) posits the existence of a theocratic republic under the rubble of Detroit; it is in conflict with a democratic enclave among the ruins of Chicago some years after a devastating atomic war.

Some of the action of the German-language *Hans Hardts Mondfahrt* (1928) by Otto Willi Gail (1896–1956), translated into English in 1931 as *By Rocket to the Moon*, takes place in Detroit as an American newspaper reporter is asked to accompany a young German inventor on a trip to the moon in a rocket ship. In the classic science-fiction novel *When Worlds Collide* (1933) by EDWIN BALMER (1883–1959) and Philip Wylie (1902–1971), part of the human race is selected to escape the imminent destruction of the earth on a spaceship that is built and launched in the Upper Peninsula.

Time travel has been employed in a few juvenile works with Michigan settings, mostly as a means to explore historic aspects of the state's past. In *Potawatomi Indian Summer* (1974) by E. William Oldenburg (1936–1974), some Grand Haven children are magically transported to the 1600s and learn about Native American life in that age. In her Dream Quest Adventures series Janie Lynn Panagopoulos (b. 1955) didactically looks at a variety of early Michigan societies and industries, such as *Journey Back to Lumberjack Camp* (1993) and *Train to Midnight* (1999), set in the nineteenth century.

Gay and Lesbian Novels: An emerging genre is the novel with gay and lesbian themes and characters. See also LESBIAN, GAY, BISEXUAL, TRANSGENDER, AND QUEER LITERATURE. Although this literature has been around since at least the 1920s, it has until recently been considered obscene or pornographic through most of the twentieth century and was sold and distributed surreptitiously. The first gay novel with a Michigan background is *Better Angel* (1933) by Forman G. Brown (1901–1996), writing as Richard Meeker; it follows a gay man's youth in a small Michigan town and his subsequent career as a musician in New York City. This book was finally reissued under Brown's name in 1995 and has become a gay classic. The acclaimed gay novels by Edmund White (b. 1940), *A Boy's Own Story* (1982) and *The Beautiful Room Is Empty* (1988), are actually fictionalized renderings of his early life, some of which occurs in Michigan schools.

Legal and societal persecution of homosexuals is grimly outlined in *Something You Do in the Dark* (1971) by Daniel R. Brown (b. 1938), writing as Daniel Curzon. Brian Bouldrey (b. 1963) in *The Genius of Desire* (1993) charts the gradually developing self-awareness of a young Catholic boy in mid-Michigan and how his sexual orientation affects his family.

In *Legacy of Love* (1997) by Marianne K. Martin (b. 1945), a lesbian moves from New York City to rural Michigan in an attempt to make a new life for herself after being raped. *Licking Our Wounds* (1997) by Elise D'Haene (b. 1959) is partially set in Michigan, where a lesbian tries, after being jilted by her lover, to recover and deal with deteriorating relations with her family.

When Some Body Disappears (1999), one of a series of mystery novels by Therese Szymanski (b. 1968), features a pair of Detroit lesbians and touches on organized crime and drug rings as the protagonists move to what they hope is the safer town of Alma. Lev Raphael (b. 1954) wrote a well-received seven-book series about a gay English professor at Michigan State University who finds himself involved in various academic crimes, such as enmity among faculty that leads to murder in *The Edith Wharton Murders* (1997).

Printing and Journalism: Michigan can claim the second printing press established within the twelve Midwestern states: there is dated evidence of one operated by John M'Call in Detroit not later than 1796. The supposed existence of a French Jesuit press at the L'Arbre Croche mission, as well as a Bible allegedly printed there in the Ottawa language in the 1750s, has never been substantiated.

The state's best-known journalist and humorist, often compared with Mark Twain, is Charles Bertrand Lewis (1842–1924), who appropriated the printer's term "em quad" to create his professional sobriquet, M. Quad. He began his newspaper career as a printer's apprentice and later advanced to manager of publications in Flint and Lansing before working as legislative reporter for the *Detroit Free Press* in 1869. When the state legislature was not in session, he wrote articles that poked fun at current topics of interest. His work employed stock characters speaking in humorous dialect and soon attracted a great number of readers throughout the country and even abroad. Collected reprints of his newspaper columns, such as *Quad's Odds* (1875) and *Sawed-Off Sketches* (1884), also proved popular with the public. In addition, Lewis wrote dime novels and published a volume of his Civil War memoirs. See also PRINTING AND PUBLISHING.

Perhaps the most significant literary publication to come out of Michigan is the Broadside Press, which operates out of Detroit. It was established in the early 1960s by Dudley Felker Randall, who initially planned to use it to issue his own poetry, but it soon became one of the most important vehicles for the publication of black poetry in the country. Both emerging and established authors were featured, among them GWENDOLYN BROOKS (1917–2000), Robert Hayden, Naomi Long Madgett, Nikki Giovanni (b. 1943), and many more. Randall sold Broadside Press in 1985, but it continues its original mission to publish the works of black poets, although on a much reduced scale since 2000.

Michigan Federal Writers' Project: A part of the Works Progress Administration, the FEDERAL WRITERS' PROJECT (1935–1943) was intended as a means to provide relief for unemployed writers in America during the Great Depression. As in all other states, the primary project undertaken by writers in the Michigan Federal Writers' Project was the preparation of the state guidebook, *Michigan: A Guide to the Wolverine State* (1941). Other publications issued under its auspices include *Northwestern High School, 1914–1939: A History* (1939); *Cosmopolitan Edu-*

cation: A History of Hamtramck High School (1940); *Knowing the Thunder Bay Region* (1941); *Michigan Log Marks: Their Function and Use during the Great Michigan Pine Harvest* (1941); and, as part of the Michigan Historical Records Survey, *Preliminary Check List of Michigan Imprints, 1796–1850* (1942).

Sources of information on the Federal Writers' Project in Michigan are generally fragmentary or anecdotal, and no comprehensive bibliography exists. Paul Sporn's *Against Itself: The Federal Theater and Writers' Projects in the Midwest* (1995) is the best history to date, but it is concerned primarily with theater.

Michigan Literary Awards:

Michigan Author Award: The Michigan Author Award was established in 1992, largely through the effort of a Michigan librarian, Roger Mendel, who believed that there should be a statewide recognition for Michigan authors. The first few awards were made as part of the annual Thunder Bay Literary Conference with support from the Michigan Center for the Book. The award is currently sponsored by the Michigan Center for the Book and the Michigan Library Association. Recipients of the annual award, listed in chronological order from 1992 through 2015 are Dan Gerber, Charles Baxter, NANCY WILLARD (b. 1936), Janet Kauffman (b. 1945), Elmore Leonard, Loren D. Estleman, Gloria Whelan, Jerry Dennis (b. 1954), Janie Lynn Panagopoulos, Thomas Lynch (b. 1948), Nicholas Delbanco (b. 1942), Diane Wakoski, Patricia Polacco, Christopher Paul Curtis (b. 1953), Steve Hamilton, Sarah Stewart (b. 1939), Tom Stanton (b. 1960), Dave Dempsey (b. 1957), John Smolens (b. 1949), Gary Schmidt (b. 1957), Bonnie Jo Campbell (b. 1962), Laura Kasischke (b. 1961), Jim Harrison, and David Small (b. 1945).

Hopwood Awards: Although the Avery and Jule Hopwood Awards are restricted to currently enrolled students at the University of Michigan, they are significant because of their age, national reputation, and roster of illustrious winners. Established in 1931 and funded through the terms of the will of Avery Hopwood, the substantial cash awards are given in a number of categories of creative writing: novel, short fiction, poetry, drama, screenplay, and essay. Some of the more notable Hopwood laureates include Max Apple (b. 1941), John Ciardi (1916–1986), Robert Hayden, Lawrence Kasdan (b. 1949), Laura Kasischke, Jane Kenyon (1947–1995), Jay McCormick, Arthur Miller (1915–2005), Frank O'Hara (1926–1966), MARGE PIERCY (b. 1936), Alfred Slote, Milan Stitt, Harvey Swados (1933–1983), Glendon (Fred) Swarthout (1918–1992), Henry Van Dyke, Chad Walsh (1914–1991), Edmund White, Nancy Willard, and Maritta (Martin) Wolff (Stegman) (1918–2002).

SELECTED WORKS: An excellent starting point for sampling a cross section of the rich literature of Michigan is the collection chosen and edited by DAVID D. ANDERSON (1924–2011), *Michigan: A State Anthology; Writings about the Great Lake State, 1641–1981, Selected from Diaries, Journals, Histories, Fiction, and Verse* (1983). Historical novels dealing with aspects of the fur trade on Mackinac Island during the British control of the area are *Wolves against the Moon* (1940; reissued 1994) by Julia Altrocchi and *The Loon Feather* (1940; reissued 1998) by Iola Fuller. A pioneer narrative containing humorous and unflattering sketches of early Michigan settlers is *A New Home—Who'll Follow?* (1839; reissued 1990) by Caroline Kirkland. The War of 1812 in southwestern Michigan is the subject of the mediocre effort by James Fenimore Cooper in *Oak Openings; or, The Bee-Hunter* (1848; reprinted often).

Della Thompson Lutes fictionalizes her life in a small town and a nearby farm during the 1880s in *Country Schoolma'am* (1941), among other works. A landmark firsthand account of the beginnings of coeducation at the University of Michigan, in the form of a novel, is *An American Girl and Her Four Years in a Boys' College* (1878; reissued 2006) by Olive Anderson. Two widely different perceptions of Michigan farm work are best exemplified in novels published in the same year: *Green Bush* (1925) by John T. Frederick and *Backfurrow* (1925) by Geoffrey D. Eaton. Contemporary farm settings are used in some of Jim Harrison's novels, such as *Farmer* (1976) and *The English Major* (2008). Michigan industries are represented by Stewart Edward White's *The Blazed Trail* (1902; reissued 1968), which thoroughly and accurately describes logging. *The Long Winter Ends* (1941)

by Newton G. Thomas concerns copper mining in the Upper Peninsula; and shipping on the Great Lakes is the subject of Jay McCormick's *November Storm* (1943). The automobile industry is covered in DETROIT.

Varieties of ethnic and racial experience in Michigan are sympathetically related for the Native American in *Joe Pete* (1929) by Florence McClinchey; the Dutch communities of western Michigan in Arnold Mulder's *Bram of the Five Corners* (1915) and *Belly Fulla Straw* (1934) by David Cornel DeJong; African American family life in *Mama* (1987) by Terry McMillan; and the mixed Ojibwa and Finnish heritage of the Upper Peninsula protagonist in *Returning to Earth* (2007) by Jim Harrison.

Much Michigan verse can be circumscribed by the pastoral poets Will Carleton and Theodore Roethke. The former's *Farm Ballads* (1873) and its sequels are a mixture of sentimentality and naturalism that offer a glimpse of nineteenth-century Michigan characters and situations. *The Collected Poems of Theodore Roethke* (1966), on the other hand, shows the author's twentieth-century neoromanticism and use of nature, greatly influenced by his Michigan roots. *A Last Bridge Home: New and Selected Poems* (1992) is a good introduction to Dan Gerber's poetry. Much of Jim Harrison's verse is included in *The Shape of the Journey: New and Collected Poems* (1998).

No list of Michigan writing is complete without mention of Ernest Hemingway's early short stories about his alter ego, Nick Adams, many of which are based on the young Hemingway's experiences on the lakes and streams of northern Michigan, such as "Big Two-Hearted River" (1925) and "Now I Lay Me" (1927). A collected edition, *The Nick Adams Stories*, was published in 1972.

Despite its rich literary heritage, Michigan has not been well represented in anthologies of its literature. The earliest such volume known to contain works by Michigan authors is *The Souvenir of the Lakes*, printed in Detroit by George L. Whitney in 1831. Its limited but eclectic contents include a travel essay, poetry, and Native American legends and tales. One of the tales is attributed to Henry Rowe Schoolcraft. Not until a century later did the second important state anthology appear. Edited by Edith R.

Mosher and Nella D. Williams, *From Indian Legends to the Modern Book-Shelf: An Anthology of Prose and Verse by Michigan Authors Prepared for the Youth of the State* (1931) contains a wide sampling of stories, verse, essays, and excerpts from novels illustrating many of the state's literary and historical highpoints. The best one-volume cross section of Michigan's literary experience is the previously mentioned *Michigan: A State Anthology*, edited by David D. Anderson, which is more than just an anthology; each literary selection is accompanied by a critical essay and notes that chart the evolution of Michigan's literary history. James Tipton and Robert Wegner have edited an important collection of contemporary authors, *The Third Coast: Contemporary Michigan Fiction* (1982). An annual anthology, *Voices of Michigan*, began publication in 1999, and each issue published short fiction and poetry from Michigan authors who had been winners in a statewide refereed writing contest. It ceased publication after four volumes.

The sole anthology devoted to a single Michigan city is Laurence Goldstein's *Writing Ann Arbor: A Literary Anthology* (2005). Goldstein, the longtime editor of the University of Michigan's literary journal, *Michigan Quarterly Review*, has assembled a comprehensive sampling of fiction, poetry, drama, memoirs, and essays, all relating to Ann Arbor in its many facets from 1824 to the present.

Other than the collected poetry of individual Michigan authors and members of various state poetical societies and associations, there have been few extensive anthologies of Michigan poets. The first seems to be *Michigan Poets and Poetry* (1904), compiled by Floyd D. Raze (1873–1928) and Warren W. Lamport (1855–1948). Although it features a few well-known poets, the majority of the selections are from the less famous, including the two editors. Similarly, the volume edited by the poetry-publishing firm of Henry Harrison, *Michigan Poets: An Anthology of 36 Contemporaries* (1936), selected verse that is best described as mediocre. By far the best collection published to date is *The Third Coast: Contemporary Michigan Poetry* (1976), edited by Conrad Hilberry, Herbert Scott, and James Tipton, in which the work of thirty important Michigan poets

is presented. It has been followed by two further collections: *Contemporary Michigan Poetry: Poems from the Third Coast* (1988), edited by Michael Delp, Conrad Hilberry, and Herbert Scott, which offers selections from fifty-three writers; and *New Poems from the Third Coast: Contemporary Michigan Poetry* (2000), edited by Michael Delp, Conrad Hilberry, and Josie Kearns, in which sixty Michigan poets are featured. See also ANTHOLOGIES.

FURTHER READING:
Bibliography, Biography, and Criticism: An interesting collection of essays and bibliographies about Michigan's fiction, poetry, and screenwriting was published in 1988 as *Literary Michigan: A Sense of Place, a Sense of Time* by the Michigan Council for the Humanities. In *Michigan: A Guide to the Wolverine State* (1941), the product of the Michigan Writers' Program, the section on state literature is discussed in only seven pages (145–51), but the breadth of coverage of fiction, poetry, and nonfiction is remarkable.

Although Clarence A. Andrews made an impressive effort to provide a detailed literary history of the state in his *Michigan in Literature* (1992), the volume unfortunately suffers from a number of errors and omissions, so there is still a need for a comprehensive literary history of Michigan. Over the years a number of works have appeared that list Michigan authors; the best of these are Madge Knevel Goodrich's *A Bibliography of Michigan Authors* (1928) and the third edition of *Michigan Authors* (1993), edited by Carol Smallwood. The former contains information on writers' works, as well as biographical sources, and the latter, although highly selective, lists many emerging authors. A continuously updated internet version is also available through the auspices of the Library of Michigan, the Michigan Association of Media in Education, and the Michigan Center for the Book at http://libraryofmichigan.state.mi.us/Authors/

A comprehensive list of more than 2,700 works that employ Michigan as a setting can be found in *Michigan in the Novel, 1816–2006: An Annotated Bibliography* (2013), compiled by Robert Beasecker, a revised and augmented edition of his 1998 work. The electronic version is available at http://scholarworks.gvsu

.edu/library_books/6/. An important contribution to the literature of travel and exploration is Robert R. Hubach's *Early Midwestern Travel Narratives: An Annotated Bibliography, 1634–1850* (1961), which contains much information on Michigan examples.

Douglas C. McMurtrie provides a dated but still useful review of the history and development of early printing and publishing in Michigan in *Early Printing in Michigan: With a Bibliography of the Issues of the Michigan Press, 1796–1850* (1931). *A Selective Bibliography of Important Books, Pamphlets and Broadsides Relating to Michigan History* (1958) by Albert Harry Greenly is also recommended.

Besides being long out of date and incomplete, *Michigan Bibliography: A Partial Catalogue of Books, Maps, Manuscripts and Miscellaneous Materials Relating to the Resources, Development and History of Michigan from the Earliest Times to July 1, 1917* (1921) by Floyd Benjamin Streeter was based on the holdings of only a few large libraries. In spite of what should be fatal shortcomings, this bibliography is still an important list of all types of Michigania up to the first two decades of the twentieth century.

Libraries and Repositories: The largest and most important collection of published works of Michigan authors, as well as books dealing with Michigan subjects and locales, is held in the Michigan Collection of the Library of Michigan in Lansing.

In East Lansing, the Special Collections Division of Michigan State University Libraries houses its Michigan Writers Collection, whose mission is to acquire the manuscripts and publications of certain contemporary Michigan writers, some of them MSU alumni, and make them available to scholars and researchers for study. Included in this collection are holdings by Dan Gerber, Jim Daniels, Richard Ford (b. 1944), Jim Harrison, and Thomas McGuane (b. 1939), among many others.

At the University of Michigan in Ann Arbor, the Special Collections Library has among its holdings literary manuscripts of some recipients of the University's Hopwood Awards, including Marge Piercy and Nancy Willard. It is also the repository of the Hopwood Awards Committee records.

The best collection of novels that employ Michigan as a setting is to be found in the Special Collections of Grand Valley State University Libraries in Allendale, where Jim Harrison's papers are also housed. In Mount Pleasant, the Clarke Historical Library at Central Michigan University has a similar collection.

Many small public libraries throughout the state have small collections that highlight local authors and literary groups whose publications have had limited publicity and distribution but represent regional efforts otherwise unknown.

ROBERT BEASECKER   GRAND VALLEY STATE UNIVERSITY

MIDLAND, THE

OVERVIEW: *The Midland* (1915–1933) was the best-known and most influential of the little magazines espousing Midwestern literary regionalism in the early part of the twentieth century. It was founded and then carefully edited and published throughout its existence by JOHN T(OWNER) FREDERICK (1893–1975), mostly from Iowa City. Three years before it was absorbed by the University of Montana *Frontier* in November 1933, Frederick moved his magazine to CHICAGO to capitalize on its growing national reputation. *The Midland* published almost four hundred short stories and one thousand poems, largely by aspiring Midwestern writers. Frederick's editorials consistently advocated a Midwestern regionalism to counter the increasing standardization, urbanization, and commercialization of American literature. Although the journal's circulation was usually less than five hundred, an enthusiastic H(enry) L(ouis) Mencken (1880–1956) wrote in the July 1923 *Smart Set* that it was "probably the most influential literary publication ever set up in America" (141).

HISTORY AND SIGNIFICANCE: In January 1915 the somewhat reserved Frederick was an unlikely person to launch a major regional magazine. He had no family connections or wealth and at nearly twenty-two was still working his way through the University of Iowa. But he did have the editorial, financial, and emotional support of his mentor, C(lark) F(isher) Ansley (1869–1939), head of the Iowa English Department and Dean of the College of Fine Arts.

Until its last three years Frederick ran the magazine from Iowa City except for two

The Midland

VOLUME 1   JANUARY 1915   NUMBER 1

The First Person Plural

THE MIDLAND is not a commercial enterprise, and it is not endowed. Its publishers, editors and contributors receive no payment for their work. Obviously, miscellaneous advertising is not sought or accepted. Possibly subscriptions will meet the only expenses of the magazine,—the cost of printing and mailing. With that faint hope its commercialism ends.

The magazine is merely a modest attempt to encourage the making of literature in the Middle West. The region is already renowned for certain material products and for financial prosperity; but the market of its literary and other artists has commonly been beyond the mountains, and the producers have commonly gone to their market. Possibly the region between the mountains would gain in variety at least if it retained more of its makers of literature, music, pictures, and other expressions of civilization. And possibly civilization itself might be with us a somewhat swifter process if expression of its spirit were more frequent. Scotland is none the worse for Burns and Scott, none the worse that they did not move to London and interpret London themes for London publishers.

First issue of John Towner Frederick's *The Midland*, 1915.

Courtesy of Hathitrust

periods. From 1917 to 1921 he took it first to Moorhead, MINNESOTA, where he chaired the English department at the State Normal School, and then to the cutover country in Alcona County, MICHIGAN, where he homesteaded. He also spent the academic year 1922–1923 with the English Department at the University of Pittsburgh because he did not think that the University of Iowa was giving proper due to creative writing—as it later would by establishing the IOWA WRITERS' WORKSHOP. Throughout his various moves the carefully edited and handsomely printed magazine, usually a monthly, remained totally noncommercial and independent. Frederick never sought advertising, never paid writers, and accepted support from the University of Iowa only in the form of office space and a part-time student assistant. In most years the magazine ran a financial deficit, which Frederick paid for from lecture tours on Midwestern literature and from his meager teaching salary.

The Midland was clearly the lengthened shadow of its remarkable editor, who was also a novelist, critic, and greatly admired teacher almost until his death at eighty-one in 1975. But three other men lent crucial support to the journal at different times in its history. After its first year Edmund J. O'Brien (1890–1941), editor of the annual *Best American Short Stories* from 1914 to 1940, credited *The Midland* with paving the way for the wealth of Midwestern writing coming out of Chicago. In the 1920s H. L. Mencken championed *The Midland* in *The Smart Set* and *The American Mercury* because he admired Frederick's Midwestern challenge to the New York hegemony and his remarkably patient nurturing of Midwestern writers. And in 1925 Frank Luther Mott (1886–1964) became Frederick's co-editor for what were probably the five most productive years of the journal. Mott, who later authored the definitive, five-volume history of American magazines, wrote that "never was there a happier partnership" (from *Time Enough* [1962], quoted in *A History of American Magazines,* volume 5, *1905–30* [1968]: 172).

The more outgoing and urbane Mott shared Frederick's abiding interest in the realistic fiction of the rural and small-town Midwest, where both had grown up. He agreed with the regional point of view Frederick had expressed on the first page of the magazine's first, slim issue in 1915: "Scotland is none the worse for Burns and Scott, none the worse that they did not move to London and interpret London themes for London publishers." In their book reviews and editorials of the late 1920s, both men disparaged genteel and romantic best sellers, as well as the contrived, overplotted stories that filled the pages of *The Saturday Evening Post* and other commercial magazines. Instead, they looked for realistic slices of life that depicted the richness of traditional life in the Midwest, which they defined as the "great valley" between the Alleghenies and the Rockies. In many of the stories in *The Midland* there is a preoccupation with nature and the rhythms of agriculture; the importance of the traditional family takes precedence over any prodigal child; love emerges slowly between a husband and wife over time rather than from some fleeting, romantic, golden moment; the young are less engaging and interesting than the old; and human existence is satisfying rather than either ecstatic or grim.

On the whole, *The Midland*'s fiction today seems somewhat anachronistic. With urbanization and industrialization, the rural and small-town life the editors favored became less and less important. The magazine's strong regional perspective also undervalued the importance of the fragmented, post–World War I world that Midwestern expatriate writers like T(HOMAS) S(TEARNS) ELIOT (1888–1965), ERNEST (MILLER) HEMINGWAY (1899–1961), and F(RANCIS SCOTT (KEY) FITZGERALD (1896–1940) were depicting.

Frederick's greatest accomplishment was in painstakingly encouraging—at least once with an exchange of eighty letters before first publication—many writers who went on to become well-known authors, critics, journalists, and naturalists: Cleanth Brooks Jr. (1904–1994), Marquis (William) Childs (1903–1990), AUGUST (WILLIAM) DERLETH (1909–1971), LOREN COREY EISELEY (1907–1977), PAUL (HAMILTON) ENGLE (1908–1991), JAMES T(HOMAS) FARRELL (1904–1979), Howard Mumford Jones (1892–1980), MACKINLAY KANTOR (1904–1977), JOHN G(NEISENAU) NEIHARDT (1881–1973), RUTH SUCKOW (1892–1960), and MARK VAN DOREN (1894–1972). Its most frequently published writers are now less well known: Grace Stone Coates (1881–1976), William March (b. William Edward Campbell, 1893–1954), Walter J(ohn) Muilenburg (1893–1958), Jay G. Sigmund (1885–1937), Father Leo L(ewis) Ward (1898–1953), and Raymond L. Weeks (1863–1954).

The Midland was less well known for its poetry, about half of which is conventionally mediocre even for its time. But the accomplished verse of Eiseley, James Hearst (1900–1983), Edwin Ford Piper (1871–1939), and Jay G. Sigmund retains a surprising freshness and interest even today.

SELECTED WORKS: Complete copies of *The Midland* were rare until 1967, when the Kraus Reprint Company reprinted five hundred complete sets, making the magazine widely available. Milton M. Reigelman's *"The "Midland": A Venture in Literary Regionalism* (1975) contains an index of stories, poems, and book reviews.

FURTHER READING: The only book-length treatment of the magazine is Milton (M.) Reigelman's *The "Midland": A Venture in Literary Regionalism* (1975). The most authoritative essays on the magazine are two standard works: Frederick J. Hoffman, Charles Allen, and Carolyn F. Ulrich's *The Little Magazine: A History and a Bibliography* (1946) and Frank Luther Mott's *A History of American Magazines,* volume 5, 1905–30 (1968). Much *Midland* material, including correspondence, can be found in the Special Collections Department of the University of Iowa Library.

MILTON REIGELMAN   CENTRE COLLEGE

MIGRANT LITERATURE.

See Immigrant and Migrant Literature

MINNEAPOLIS/ST. PAUL

Minneapolis (from the Dakota *mine,* "of the waters," and the Greek *polis,* "city") was chartered in 1856; before the 1803 Louisiana Purchase the area was a Spanish and French possession.

St. Paul (from Fr. Lucien Galtier's 1841 log chapel of the same name) was the capital of Minnesota Territory, 1849–1858, and became the Minnesota state capital in 1858.

Area: Minneapolis: 58.4 square miles; St. Paul: 56.2 square miles

Population (2010 census): Minneapolis (382,578); St. Paul (285,068)

© Karen Greasley, 2014

OVERVIEW: The twin cities of Minneapolis and St. Paul are perceived as one entity. However, separated by the Mississippi River, they are historically different and socially and culturally distinct. St. Paul, the older city, founded by French and French Canadians, was an early trade and transportation center marking the northern terminus for riverboats traveling upriver on the Mississippi. Many European immigrants from northern and southern Europe settled there in the second half of the nineteenth century. St. Paul was the MINNESOTA territorial capital and continues as the state capital and government center. It was also the home of early railroad magnates whose majestic mansions along famed Summit Avenue feature in literature about the city. Since the mid-1970s large numbers of Hmong people, refugees from Southeast Asia, have made St. Paul their home.

Minneapolis, built on the west bank of the Mississippi River on land ceded by the Sioux, grew larger than St. Paul by 1890. Flowing water and St. Anthony Falls provided abundant power for nineteenth- and early twentieth-century saw, grist, and cotton mills. Business success in Minneapolis has made it the more prosperous of the Twin Cities. As the tide of immigration moved westward after the Civil War, Minneapolis became not only a waypoint for Scandinavians, the majority of whom were Norwegians, but also a destination, so that by the 1890s it had become the cultural capital of that group.

HISTORY AND SIGNIFICANCE: The first white settlement was associated with the 1819 establishment of Fort Snelling at the confluence of the Mississippi and Minnesota Rivers between St. Paul and Minneapolis. Maud Hart Lovelace (1892–1980) created a charming historical novel about that time, *Early Candlelight* (1929), in which she mixed historical figures and fictional characters and detailed life in the white settlements while dealing sympathetically with American Indians. Books appearing in the second half of the nineteenth century that describe life in early St. Paul include *Dakota Land; or, The Beauty of St. Paul* (1868) by Colonel Charles Ashton Hankins (b. ca. 1825) and *Allisto: A Romance* (1884), a typical late nineteenth-century melodrama by Josie G.

Oppenheim (1851–1915), writing under the pseudonym John Emersie. *The God-Seeker* (1949), a less well-known novel by (HARRY) SINCLAIR LEWIS (1885–1951), describes the life of a New England missionary who settles in St. Paul. Other early novels that use Minneapolis and St. Paul as settings include *A Tale of the Twin Cities: Lights and Shadows of the Street Car Strike in Minneapolis and St. Paul, Minnesota, Beginning April 11, 1889* (1889) by Eva Gay (1827–1903), the anonymous *Federal City: Being a Reminiscence of the Time before St. Paul and Minneapolis Were United* (1891), and *Pards: A Story of Two Homeless Boys* (1891) by Effie Woodward Merriman (1857–1937).

Most early white settlers in the area were from the northeastern United States, but European immigrants soon discovered the healthful climate. *En Saloonkeepers Datter: Fortaelling* (1889) by Drude Krog Janson (1846–1934) describes immigrants' struggles in dealing with American society and culture and, for some, their success at finding a place in the new land. This exemplar of immigrant literature was made more accessible when it was translated into English by Gerald Thorson as *A Saloonkeeper's Daughter* in 2002. It is one of only a few novels written by Scandinavian immigrants in their native language. Another excellent account of immigrant life, *The Boat of Longing* (1933) by OLE EDVART RØLVAAG (1876–1931), reflects the challenges faced by immigrants to the upper Midwest. See also MINNESOTA. *They Sought a County* (1950) by Norman E. Nygaard (1897–1971) also documents the lives of nineteenth-century Norwegian immigrants. Other early novels written in Norwegian about life in early Minneapolis are *Bag Gardinet* (1889) by Kristofer Janson (1841–1917) and *Stenholts Politihistorier: Billeder af Minneapolis Bystyre* (1903) by Lars Andreas Stenholt (1850–1911). In *I Love You like a Tomato* (2003) Marie K. Chapian (b. 1938), writing under her family name, Marie Giordano, narrates the experiences of an Italian immigrant family in the Twin Cities after World War II. The situations are different, but the experiences are similar to those of the Scandinavian immigrants.

St. Paul has been enjoying a renaissance of immigration in the late twentieth and early twenty-first centuries. Hmong

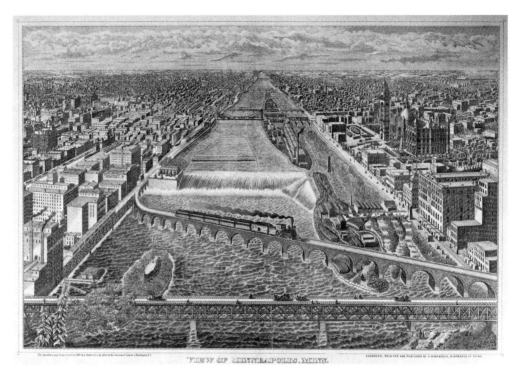

View of Minneapolis, Minnesota, ca. 1886, by August Hageboeck.
Image courtesy of the Library of Congress

immigrants are just beginning to describe their experiences. Of the many pieces included in *Bamboo among the Oaks: Contemporary Writing by Hmong Americans* (2002), edited by Mai Neng Moua, the short stories "Ms. Pac-Man Ruined My Gang Life" by Ka Vang (b. 1975) and "943" by M. S. Vang exemplify the troubles of young Hmong in St. Paul and the difficulties generally faced by the Hmong attempting to assimilate into a different culture. Kate Green (b. 1950) in *If the World Is Running Out* (1983) also points out the struggles of the Hmong immigrants in her prose poem "The Community": "Yeng, Yang, Vang, Kang, Kong, Blia, Dia and Nou sit straight at big desks writing words for things that we all know: Sun moon. My mother say what time it is? Snow fall like little rices" (57).

In *Upon Thy Doorposts* (1936) Jennie Rosenholtz (1882–1956) tells the story of a family of orthodox Jews in pioneer St. Paul. Norman Katkov (1918–2009) wrote about St. Paul Jewish families in *Eagle at My Eyes* (1948) and *A Little Sleep, a Little Slumber* (1949); their experiences mirror those of immi-

grants with regard to assimilation, feelings of difference, and reactions from the mainstream white community. Evelyn Fairbanks (1928–2001) published a charming memoir about St. Paul's black community, *Days of Rondo* (1990). It evokes the African American storytelling tradition as she narrates stories about her youth in the 1930s and 1940s. Lesbian and gay literature is also represented in the Twin Cities. Barrie Jean Borich (b. 1959) describes her south Minneapolis neighborhoods in *My Lesbian Husband* (1999). *Innuendo* (1999) by R(obert) D(ingwall) Zimmerman (b. 1952) provides insights into gay men in Minneapolis. See also LESBIAN, GAY, BISEXUAL, TRANSGENDER, AND QUEER LITERATURE.

American Indians, the original residents of the area, have interacted with both cities much like newly arrived immigrants, but literature about them in the Twin Cities is scarce. *Wordarrows: Indians and Whites in the New Fur Trade* (1978) by GERALD (ROBERT) VIZENOR (b. 1934) is a realistic, painful description of the lives of urban Indians. (KAREN) LOUISE ERDRICH (b. 1954) writes in *The Ante-*

lope Wife (1998) about an Ojibwa family in Minneapolis as they balance traditional Indian ways and customs and the mainstream white culture of which they are also a part.

The finest literature about early twentieth-century St. Paul centers on the lives of society and the wealthy residents of Summit Avenue. Novels by Grace Flandrau (1886–1971), such as *Being Respectable* (1923), cover the same social milieu as those of F(RANCIS) SCOTT (KEY) FITZGERALD (1896–1940), but her characters are unhappy insiders in the same society that Fitzgerald's characters often yearn to join. For more on Fitzgerald, see MINNESOTA.

Three contemporary writers provide a contrasting view of the Summit Avenue milieu, juxtaposing the lives of minority or immigrant women to those of the upper class. In *A Romantic Education* (1981) PATRICIA HAMPL (b. 1946) tells about her Czech grandmother, who worked as a maid and cook on Summit Avenue. Louise Erdrich's 2004 novel *Four Souls* shows the collision of two worlds as an Ojibwa woman goes to St. Paul to seek revenge on the wealthy lumber baron who stole her native land. In *Summit Avenue* (2000) Mary Sharratt (b. 1964) narrates a beautifully told story of love and life in the German American community on Summit Avenue. Here the tensions between poor and wealthy, immigrant and American-born members of the German American family are complicated by lesbian love. In both Erdrich's and Sharratt's novels the wealthy residents of Summit Avenue are no longer the lively, dazzling characters represented by Fitzgerald and Flandrau. They are worn and burdened by their possessions, reflecting the postmodern sensibilities of the writers. The 2010 novel *Freedom,* the fourth by Jonathan Franzen (b. 1959), considers the nature of freedom in following the values, choices, and lives of an upper-middle-class St. Paul family, the Berglands, from the 1970s to the near present.

Popular fiction written since the 1930s examines particular events, geography, and climate. Winter is a feature of many books about the Twin Cities; notable are two popular fiction works: *The Treasure Hunt* (1992) by Roger Barr (b. 1951) and *Sherlock Holmes and the Ice Palace Murders* (1998) by Larry Mil-

lett (b. 1947), both of which focus on activities during the St. Paul Winter Carnival.

The decade of the 1930s is a popular era for writers. Steve Thayer (b. 1953) in *Silent Snow* (1999) revisits the kidnapping of the Lindbergh baby. He also evokes the gangster era in St. Paul in *Saint Mudd: A Novel of Gangsters and Saints* (1988). *Sons of Adam* (1980) by FREDERICK MANFRED (b. Feike Feikema, 1912–1994) describes young men growing up in Minneapolis during the Depression. Feminist MERIDEL LE SUEUR (1900–1996) portrays the lives of working-class women in Depression-era St. Paul in *The Girl* (1978). Two mystery novels of the 1930s successfully employ Minneapolis as a setting: *Murder Goes to Press* (1937) by Noel M. Loomis (1905–1969) and *The Man with the Magic Eardrums* (1939) by Harry Stephen Keeler (1890–1967).

The Twin Cities are the setting of much genre fiction, especially mysteries. See MINNESOTA for a discussion. John Roswell Camp (b. 1944), writing as John Sandford, is the author of more than thirty books, but he is best known for his Prey series, centering on a Minneapolis police detective, Lucas Davenport, and his cases, most of which are set in Minneapolis and St. Paul and exhibit a strong sense of place, such as *Rules of Prey* (1989) and *Field of Prey* (2014). Sandford's other major fiction series are the Kidd and Virgil Flowers series. Two fantasy/science-fiction novels feature Minneapolis as their location. *Flying Saucers over Hennepin: A Novel about an Avenue* (1997) by Peter Gelman is a witty, alternative view of the city in the state of "Minne-snow-ta." *Archangel* (1995) by Michael Conner (b. 1951) is set in the alternate universe of Milltown in the late 1920s, where whites are dying from the plague. This science-fiction thriller is also a powerful commentary on racial issues.

Contemporary fiction set in Minneapolis often provides little sense of place. The characters do not interact with their urban environment; they just inhabit the city, a city that could be any Midwestern urban area, such as CHICAGO or Milwaukee, because of the homogeneity of late twentieth- and early twenty-first-century American culture. Two novels set in Minneapolis exemplify this trend: *Amnesia Nights* (2004) by Quinton Skinner (b. 1968) and *Where No Gods Came* (2003) by Sheila O'Connor (b.

1959). Each concerns troubled protagonists who recently moved to the city to escape past difficulties. Max Shulman (1919–1988), born in St. Paul, set two of his early humorous novels in Minneapolis: *The Feather Merchants* (1944) and *The Zebra Derby* (1946) deal with the World War II home front and returning veterans.

Minneapolis poets of renown include JOHN BERRYMAN (1914–1972), ROBERT (ELWOOD) BLY (b. 1926), JAMES WRIGHT (1927–1980), CHARLES BAXTER (b. 1947), and David Mura (b. 1952), all of whom have drawn on the city as a subject for their verse. Berryman's "Mpls, Mother," collected in the posthumous collection *Henry's Fate* (1977), is a critical look at the metropolis, which is described in unflattering terms. Wright similarly explores the darker side of the city and its denizens in "The Minneapolis Poem," published in *Shall We Gather at the River* (1968). Mura, a third-generation Japanese American, has published books of poetry like *Angels for the Burning* (2004), as well as memoirs and essays that often touch on the cultural diversity of Minneapolis. In *Twin Cities* (2011) Carol Muske-Dukes (b. 1945) describes the different natures of these two municipalities.

Arthur Wheelock Upson (1877–1908) of St. Paul was a talented young poet who taught at the University of Minnesota. In addition to his books of poetry, he wrote a stanza for "Hail! Minnesota," which would become the Minnesota state song. His *Collected Poems* (1909) was published in two volumes after his death by drowning in Lake Bemidji. St. Paul inaugurated the position of city Poet Laureate in 2006 and named lifelong St. Paul resident Carol Connolly (b. 1934) to the position. Her books include *All This and More: New and Selected Poems* (2009).

Books set in St. Paul do a much better job of situating the story and characters in the city; one example is *Twelve Branches: Stories from St. Paul* (2003), a collection of twelve short stories by four authors that were compiled and published under the aegis of the St. Paul Public Library. See also MINNESOTA. A delightful book of fiction by GARY EDWARD KEILLOR (b. 1942), writing as Garrison Keillor, *Love Me* (2003), describes the life of a novelist and advice columnist and is nicely situated in the city.

SELECTED WORKS: An early fulsome and sometimes fictional description of pioneer St. Paul as seen through contemporary eyes is *Dakota Land; or, The Beauty of St. Paul* (1868) by Colonel Charles Ashton Hankins. Later novels describing the first settlers in the area are *Early Candlelight* (1929) by Maud Hart Lovelace and Sinclair Lewis's *The God-Seeker* (1949). Various aspects of life in the twentieth-century Twin Cities are to be found in the novels of Grace Flandrau, such as *Being Respectable* (1923); Frederick Manfred's *Sons of Adam* (1980); and *Freedom* (2010) by Jonathan Franzen.

Scandinavian immigrants also provided fictionalized versions of their experiences coming to St. Paul and Minnesota. The most important of these is *En Saloonkeepers Datter: Fortaelling* (1889) by Drude Krog Janson, originally published in Norwegian and now made more accessible in an English translation. Also noteworthy are two English-language novels that describe Norwegian immigrants in the twin cities: O. E. Rølvaag's *The Boat of Longing* (1933) and *They Sought a Country* (1950) by Norman E. Nygaard.

Important fictional representation of other immigrant and minority groups in Minneapolis and St. Paul include Louise Erdrich's novels *The Antelope Wife* (1998) and *Four Souls* (2004), both about Ojibwas; and Evelyn Fairbanks's memoir of the black community in *Days of Rondo* (1990). An Italian immigrant family is recounted in *I Love You like a Tomato* (2003) by Marie Giordano; in *Upon Thy Doorposts* (1936) Jennie Rosenholtz tells of orthodox Jews in early St. Paul; and the experiences of the recently arrived Hmong are described in the anthology of fiction and poetry *Bamboo among the Oaks* (2002).

In later genre fiction the Twin Cities are used as more than just a backdrop, as shown in the police procedurals of John Sandford, beginning with his *Rules of Prey* (1989), and the science-fiction novel *Flying Saucers over Hennepin* (1997) by Peter Gelman. Gay and lesbian characters and culture appear in R. D. Zimmerman's *Innuendo* (1999) and *My Lesbian Husband* (1999) by Barrie Jean Borich.

Poetry that features the Twin Cities is best sampled in a number of anthologies. Among these collections are *Minneapolis*

Skyline (1940), edited by Nan Fitz-Patrick; *Minneapolis Muse* (1983), compiled by the Minneapolis Poetry Society; and *Women Poets of the Twin Cities* (1975). A number of Minneapolis and St. Paul poems appear in the larger anthology edited by Robert Hedin, *Where One Voice Ends Another Begins: 150 Years of Minnesota Poetry* (2007). An anthology of mystery and detective stories set in St. Paul and Minneapolis is *Twin Cities Noir* (2006), edited by Julie Schaper and Steven Horwitz.

FURTHER READING: Most published biographical and critical information about the literature of Minneapolis and St. Paul is included in works about Minnesota. Two useful books are *Minnesota Writers: A Collection of Autobiographical Stories* (1961), edited by Carmen Nelson Richards, and Ron Barron's *A Guide to Minnesota Writers* (1987; revised 1993). For more sources, see MINNESOTA. John T. Flanagan's excellent essay "Thirty Years of Minnesota Fiction," *Minnesota History* 31.3 (September 1950): 129–144, contains analysis of a few early writers. Focusing on St. Paul literature, Frances Sontag's article "Romance, Melodrama, Murder, Mayhem: The Novelist in Not-So-Fictional St. Paul," *Ramsey County History* 28.1 (Spring 1993): 10–18, 24, provides detailed description and analysis of significant works.

The fine public libraries in each city hold significant collections of literature related to their cities. The University of Minnesota Libraries contains much of the older fiction in its general and special collections, as well as literary manuscripts of selected Minnesota authors. The library of the Minnesota Historical Society contains a comprehensive collection of the literature of St. Paul and Minneapolis.

LESLIE CZECHOWSKI   UNIVERSITY OF PITTSBURGH
ROBERT BEASECKER   GRAND VALLEY STATE UNIVERSITY

MINNESOTA

Congress established Minnesota as a territory on March 3, 1849. Before this, it was not identified as one unified landmass but as two, separated by the Mississippi River. Its eastern portion has been part of the Northwest Territory (1787–1800), Indiana Territory (1800–1809), Illinois Territory (1809–1818), Michigan Territory (1818–1836), and Wisconsin Territory (1836–1848). West

© Karen Greasley, 2014

of the Mississippi, Minnesota was part of Louisiana Territory (1803–1812) and Missouri Territory (1812–1821). Minnesota was admitted as the thirty-second state in the Union on May 11, 1858.

Area: 86,939 square miles
Land: 79, 610 square miles
Water: 7,329 square miles
Population (2010 census): 5,303,925

OVERVIEW: Minnesota's literary heritage, economy, and culture spring from its geography and geology. The northernmost state of the contiguous United States, Minnesota is equidistant between the East and West Coasts. Celebrated as "our northern star" in the official state hymn, Minnesota routinely records the lowest winter temperatures in the contiguous forty-eight states. Its northernmost point, the Northwest Angle, created by the Treaty of Paris to end the Revolutionary War in 1783, is surrounded by the Lake of the Woods and appears as an odd appendage jutting thirty miles into western Ontario. Anonymous authors mythologized the distant and mysterious northern Minnesota woodlands with yarns about Paul Bunyan, a mythical giant lumberjack whose companion was Babe the Blue Ox.

The state is well inland, but freshwater is abundant. On the northeast, Minnesota abuts the north shore of Lake Superior for nearly two hundred miles. The major shipping port, Duluth, named for French explorer Daniel Greysolon, sieur Duluth (1636–1710), has been active since 1855, when construction of the Sault St. Marie locks opened up shipping. Split Rock Lighthouse, fifty miles northeast of Duluth, was built in 1905 and may be the most photographed site in the state.

Glaciers left the state's terrain rugged and created thousands of lakes glittering in its rocky inlets. The state's nickname, "Land of Ten Thousand Lakes," is, however, an understatement; the Minnesota Department of Natural Resources' official tally is 11,842. The Boundary Waters Canoe Area Wilderness in the northeast, stretching over one hundred miles along the Ontario border, contains 1,000 of these lakes and 1.3 million acres of unbroken forest. It is a haven for wild animals and an attractive venue for tourism, recreation, and literary contemplation.

The mighty Mississippi begins in Minnesota. Its source, Lake Itasca, was pinpointed by HENRY ROWE SCHOOLCRAFT (1793–1864) on July 13, 1832. The search for this source occupied several early expeditions and filled many explorers' diaries. From its headwaters tucked deep within Itasca State Park, the Mississippi undulates eastward down from north central Minnesota for nearly 680 miles before forming the border with WISCONSIN for nearly 140 miles. The Red River, flowing north, forms Minnesota's western border with NORTH DAKOTA.

Farming dominates the southern and central portions of the state. Wild rice grows in the north, and white-pine logging occurs in the east, but Minnesota's industry is most firmly rooted in iron-ore mining and meatpacking. Those participating in the 1865 gold rush were disappointed, but geologists uncovered the state's real treasure: iron-ore deposits in the north. Early immigrants flocked to the state to work in its four iron-ore ranges. The Vermilion Range, between Tower and Ely, rich in hematite, was in production from 1884 to 1967, shipping 104 million tons of ore. The Mesabi Range, the largest domestic iron range and one of the biggest ore bodies in the world, zigzags for 120 miles from Hoyt Lakes to Grand Rapids and has yielded over 3 billion tons of ore. Margaret Culkin Banning (1891–1982), a Duluth resident whose second husband was the president of the Oliver Iron Mining Company, wrote *Mesabi* (1969), a mining novel. Poet John Caddy (b. 1937) was likewise inspired by the area, publishing spiritual nature poems in *The Color of Mesabi*

Bones (1989) and *Morning Earth: Field Notes in Poetry* (2003). The Cuyuna Range to the south near Crosby yielded roughly 100 million tons of ore before it was exhausted. Gunflint Range in the extreme north extends into Canada.

The fortunes of George A. Hormel (1860–1946), king of Spam, spawned the town of Austin in south-southeastern Minnesota. His meatpacking business began operations in 1891 and expanded to twenty-fourth among food companies in the Fortune 500; sales in the mid-1990s exceeded $3 billion.

Minneapolis's Guthrie Theater, acclaimed since 1963, and GARY EDWARD KEILLOR (b. 1942), writing as Garrison Keillor, hosting weekly radio segments of *The Prairie Home Companion* since 1974, have secured Minnesota's place on the national cultural map. Singers LaVerne (Sophia), Maxene (Angelyn), and (Patricia Marie) Patty Andrews; Prince (Rogers Nelson) (1958–2016); the pianist (Yiannis Hrysomallis) Yanni; and singer-songwriter Bob Dylan (b. 1941), born Robert Allen Zimmerman in Hibbing, have put the state on the musical map of America, and the Minnesota Orchestra, the St. Paul Chamber Orchestra, and the Minnesota Opera have established Minnesota's classical music reputation.

HISTORY AND SIGNIFICANCE: For a state with a relatively short history, Minnesota has produced a diverse and rich literature. Two Minnesotans have been awarded the Nobel Prize for Literature: the Norwegian immigrant Knut (Pedersson) Hamsun (1859–1952) in 1920 and Sauk Centre's (HARRY) SINCLAIR LEWIS (1885–1951), the first American-born winner of the prize, in 1930.

Exploration and Travel: From 1620 to 1820 travelogues were the main literary output in Minnesota. (Antoine) Louis Hennepin (1626–ca. 1705), a Franciscan friar, produced the first printed account of Minnesota and its Native peoples, the Sioux, or Dakota, in his book *Description of Louisiana* (Paris, 1683), which details his journey to the upper Mississippi in 1680. Many other travel accounts exist in manuscript; one of the few to be published is *Découvertes et établissements des Français dans l'Ouest et dans le Sud de l'Amérique Septentrionale* by Pierre Margry (1818–1894) (Paris, 1879–1886). This work contains Minnesota travel accounts from 1650 to 1763. A modern perspective is found in *The Voyageurs' Highway* (1941) by Grace Lee Nute (1895–1990), who trained guides and foresters in north-country canoeing. Her book covers the area from Rainy Lake east to Lake Superior, chronicling famous explorers, the great fur traders, voyageurs, Indians, and loggers who passed that way three hundred years before she did. See also EXPLORATION ACCOUNTS.

New Englander Captain Jonathan Carver (1710–1780), in his popular *Travels through the Interior Parts of North-America, in the Years 1766, 1767, and 1768* (1778), was one of the earliest British colonials to describe Minnesota. Alexander Henry (1739–1824), another colonial, reported his travels via Grand Portage on Lake Superior in *Travels and Adventures in Canada and the Indian Territories between the Years 1760 and 1776* (1809). The boundary waters between Minnesota and Canada were well used for exploring, canoeing, and trading by French Canadian voyageurs, but the first American account of travel here was by Zebulon Montgomery Pike (1779–1813), who thought that he had found the source of the Mississippi River when he turned back from Leech Lake in 1806 and recorded his journey as *An Account of a Voyage up the Mississippi River from St. Louis to Its Source* (1807). Mississippi River travel narratives became enormously popular and were authored by Major Stephen H(arriman) Long (1784–1864), Giacomo (Costantino) Beltrami (1779–1855), General Lewis Cass (1782–1866), Henry Rowe Schoolcraft, Joseph (Nicolas) Nicollet (1786–1843), and others. Captain Frederick W. Marryat (1792–1848), who published *Diary in America, with Remarks on Its Institutions* (1839), stopped short of the Mississippi headwaters, as did many travelers.

The sketches of Indians and frontiersmen that William Joseph Snelling (1804–1848), a fur trader and guide from 1821 to 1827, published as *Tales of the Northwest* (1830) anticipate the American short story. During the 1830s missionaries began putting the Sioux and Ojibwa languages into print in the form of hymns, grammars, and parts of the Bible and even printed a Sioux newspaper, *Dakota Tawaxitku Kin; or, The Dakota Friend* (1850). Examples of books published by missionaries are *Mary and I* (1880) by Stephen R. Riggs

(1812–1883), *Two Volunteer Missionaries among the Dakotas* (1893) by Samuel W. Pond (1808–1891), and *Dahcotah; or, Life and Legends of the Sioux around Fort Snelling* (1849) by Mary Henderson Eastman (1818–1887), which is believed to have influenced Henry Wadsworth Longfellow (1807–1882) when he wrote *The Song of Hiawatha* (1855).

A fur trader and Minnesota's first governor, Henry Hastings Sibley (1811–1891), erected the first stone house in Minnesota. He was also one of the earliest sports writers, using the pen names Hal, a Dakota and Walker in the Pines. Ojibwa WILLIAM W(HIPPLE) WARREN (1825–1853) chronicled his tribe's history and culture in *History of the Ojibways* (1885). In the area around St. Cloud where he lived, two female newspaper editors reached some prominence: Jane Grey Swisshelm (1815–1884), who advocated for women's rights and against slavery, and Julia Sargent Wood (1825–1903), writing as Minnie Mary Lee, who published novels, poems, and short stories. Another newspaper writer, Christopher Columbus Andrews (1829–1922), produced sketches of early frontier life along the Red River Trail and was an acquaintance of EDWARD EGGLESTON (1837–1902), a leading early realist in Minnesota, OHIO, and INDIANA. Eggleston's novel *The Mystery of Metropolisville* (1873) focused on land speculation in Minnesota.

Fiction: Dillon O'Brien (1817–1882), a lawyer from St. Paul (see MINNEAPOLIS/ST. PAUL), penned what is presumably the first novel written by a Minnesotan and published in Minnesota, *The Dalys of Dalystown* (1866), which he followed with *Frank Blake* (1876). Charles Hoag (1808–1888), educator and superintendent of schools, was the writer of *Henry Clay* (1857), the first full-length popular book printed in Minnesota. He is also credited with having named the city "MINNEAPOLIS," a word coined from the Dakota *minne*, meaning "of the waters," and the Greek *polis*, "city." The 1850s brought IGNATIUS LOYOLA DONNELLY (1831–1901) from Philadelphia to Minnesota, where he was active as a politician, lecturer, newspaperman, and author of a dystopian novel, *Caesar's Column* (1890). Published under the pen name Edmund Boisgilbert, this best seller is reminiscent of the fiction of WILLIAM

DEAN HOWELLS (1837–1920) and SAMUEL LANG-
HORNE CLEMENS (1835–1910), writing as Mark
Twain.

Two of the best novels of Minnesota
frontier life are *Unto a Good Land* (1952), a
narrative of Swedish immigration by
Vilhelm Moberg (1898–1973), and *Scarlet
Plume* (1964), an Indian captivity novel by
Frederick Manfred (b. Feike Feikema, 1912–
1994). See also CAPTIVITY NARRATIVES. Also
noteworthy is *The Black Angels* (1926), a vivid
portrayal of Minnesota in the 1860s and 1870s
by Mankato's Maud Hart Lovelace (1892–
1980), as are two of her novels about pioneering along the Minnesota River: *Early
Candlelight* (1929) and *One Stayed at Welcome*
(1934).

Sinclair Lewis's childhood home, Sauk
Centre, Minnesota, 2000. Photo by William
Barillas.

Charles Flandrau (1871–1938), son of a
Minnesota pioneer, explored university life
and travel in his *Harvard Episodes* (1897), *The
Diary of a Freshman* (1901), and *Viva Mexico*
(1908). His sister-in-law, Grace Flandrau
(1886–1971), wrote *Being Respectable* (1923), a
drawing-room comedy protesting the rigid
social life she experienced in St. Paul, and
Indeed This Flesh (1934), about a settler's son
who seeks to escape his background. Mary
Ellen Chase (1887–1973) wrote about her
Minnesota education and teaching in *A
Goodly Fellowship* (1939). The best-known
novel by William James McNally (1891–1967)
is *House of Vanished Splendor* (1932), set in the
old Mississippi River town of Frontenac near
Lake Pepin; his plays were produced on the
New York stage. Novelist Clara Chapline
Thomas Aldrich (1884–1967), writing as Dar-
ragh Aldrich, was a radio commentator and
journalist as well as a novelist; she set *Peter
Good for Nothing* (1919) in northern Minne-
sota logging camps and *Red Headed School
Ma'am* (1935) along the Minnesota border.
Born in St. Paul, Kay Boyle (1903–1992) is a
two-time winner of the O. Henry Memo-
rial Prize (1936 and 1941); some of her nov-
els are *Wedding Day* (1931), *Plagued by the
Nightingale* (1931), *Year before Last* (1932), and
The White Horses of Vienna (1936).

Two giants of Minnesota fiction who
quickly earned national acclaim are Sinclair
Lewis and F(RANCIS) SCOTT (KEY) FITZGERALD
(1896–1940). In his sardonic, cynical portrayal of small-town central Minnesota
inhabitants and their intolerance for "the
other," Lewis anticipates examination of

the same population by contemporary
writer Garrison Keillor, although Keillor's
treatment is, by contrast, warm, gently reflective, and humorous. Until his sixth
novel, Lewis's literary output was not memorable, although he did publish over forty
short stories. It was MAIN STREET (1920), set
in fictional Gopher Prairie, a thinly disguised Sauk Centre, that won him fame,
along with his later novels *Babbitt* (1922),
Arrowsmith (1925), *Elmer Gantry* (1927), and
Dodsworth (1929). Although *Arrowsmith* garnered a Pulitzer Prize in 1926, Lewis refused
to accept it because *Main Street* had been
named but passed over for the prize in 1921.

Born and raised in St. Paul, to which he
returned in 1919 after writing advertising
copy in New York City, F. Scott Fitzgerald,
chronicler of the Jazz Age, had a flamboy-
ant career that included school at Princeton; an army commission; an extended
stay in France, where he became friends
with ERNEST (MILLER) HEMINGWAY (1899–
1961); a reckless and hedonistic lifestyle;
and a scriptwriting stint in Hollywood. THE
GREAT GATSBY (1925) and *Tender Is the Night*
(1934), both about failed lives, secure his
prominence as one of the most important
fiction writers of the twentieth century. A
number of his short stories take place in
St. Paul: "Winter Dreams" (1922), the last
story Fitzgerald wrote before he left St. Paul
in 1922; "The Ice Palace" (1920), one of
Fitzgerald's most famous stories, born of his
wondering whether Swedes were melancholy because of the cold; "The Camel's

Back" (1920), inspired by a party at a Summit Hill mansion; "A Short Trip Home" (1927), which includes a description of St. Paul's Seven Corners; "A Freeze-Out" (1931), the final reference to his hometown in his fiction; the autobiographical Basil Duke Lee stories about his adolescent friends, most of which were first published in 1928 and 1929 in the *Saturday Evening Post;* "Babes in the Woods" (1919), "Bernice Bobs Her Hair" (1920), and "At Your Age" (1929). Although Minnesota and the Midwest are more elusive in Fitzgerald's novels, they resonate as places of nurture, departure, moral centering, and renewal. In *The Great Gatsby* Nick Carraway differentiates between the East and the Midwest, saying:

That's my Middle West—not the wheat or the prairies or the lost Swede towns, but the thrilling returning trains of my youth, and the street lamps and sleigh bells in the frosty dark and the shadows of holly wreaths thrown by lighted windows on the snow. I am part of that, a little solemn with the feel of those long winters, a little complacent from growing up in the Carraway house in a city where dwellings are still called through decades by a family's name. I see now that this has been a story of the West, after all—Tom and Gatsby, Daisy and Jordan and I, were all Westerners, and perhaps we possessed some deficiency in common which made us subtly unadaptable to Eastern life. (1925 edition 212)

MERIDEL LE SUEUR (1900–1996), socialist and feminist, settled in St. Paul and became active in Midwestern reform and labor movements. Her poignant pictures of the working-class poor during the Depression, particularly women, include stirring reportage in her novel *The Girl* (1939) and her fictional essay "Women on Breadlines" (1932).

Frederick Manfred produced a number of novels that, despite his peripatetic earlier life, ground his reputation in southern and southwestern Minnesota near Luverne and Pipestone, an area, which also included parts of IOWA, SOUTH DAKOTA, and NEBRASKA, he affectionately dubbed Siouxland. His output was large, and most of his fiction was successful. Best known are his historical novels—*Lord Grizzly* (1954), *Riders of Judgment* (1957), *Conquering Horse* (1959), *Scarlet Plume* (1964), and *King of Spades*

(1966)—and the farm novels *The Golden Bowl* (1944), *This Is the Year* (1947), and *Green Earth* (1977). Other notable titles are *Boy Almighty* (1945), *The Chokecherry Tree* (1948), and *Morning Red* (1956). Walter O'Meara (1897–1989) published two historical novels: *The Trees Went Forth* (1947), concerning Finnish farmers and lumberjacks, and *Grand Portage* (1951), based on an early nineteenth-century fur trader's diary.

The characters in the fiction and drama of JON (FRANCIS) HASSLER (1933–2008) reflect the people he knew in the small Minnesota towns in which he spent most of his life. Such novels as *Simon's Night* (1979) and the Staggerford trilogy—*Staggerford* (1977), *The Green Journey* (1985), and *Dear James* (1993)—as well as *Grand Opening* (1987) and *The Love Hunter* (1981), treat with humanity and compassion the ways in which very ordinary people face extraordinary challenges, such as terminal illness, fear of dementia, betrayals large and small, and even murder, potential or real. Hassler creates or re-creates a wide variety of residents with comical faults, seriously flawed personalities, generosity, stoicism, and enduring friendship and love.

Minnesota fiction is often autobiographical. *Recovery* (1973) by JOHN BERRYMAN (1914–1972), poet and professor at the University of Minnesota from 1955 to 1972, addresses his alcohol addiction; a short story, "Wash Far Away," is partially set near Lake Superior. CAROL(YN) BLY (1930–2007) wrote about rural people, a sense of community, and self-reliance in *Backbone* (1985) and *My Lord Bag of Rice: New and Selected Stories* (2000). Worthington native (WILLIAM) TIM(OTHY) O'BRIEN (b. 1946), best known for his Vietnam novels *Going after Cacciato* (1978) and *The Things They Carried* (1990), wrote an open-ended mystery, *In the Lake of the Woods* (1995), about the disappearance of the protagonist's wife from a cabin in that city in Minnesota's North Woods, also the setting of his earlier novel *Northern Lights* (1974). His *July, July* (2002) takes place at a Minnesota high school reunion. Two significant contemporary Minnesota novelists are Elizabeth Berg (b. 1948) and Charles Baxter (b. 1947). Berg, a St. Paul native, has written over twenty-four works of fiction, several of which are set in Minnesota, including *Tapestry of Fortunes* (2013). Baxter, who hails from Minneapolis, is the author of more than twelve works of fiction, including *Gryphon: New and Selected Stories* (2011).

Immigrant and Ethnic Fiction: Minnesota's heavily Scandinavian population is reflected in its early immigrant literature. Drude Krog Janson (1846–1934) published *Ein Saloonkeepers Datter: Fortaelling* (1889), translated into English as *A Saloonkeeper's Daughter* in 2002; the novel chronicles the struggles of Norwegian immigrant Astrid Holm in frontier Minneapolis in the realist tradition of (HERMAN) THEODORE DREISER (1871–1945) and (BENJAMIN) FRANK(LIN) NORRIS (1870–1902). Knut Hamsun, a Norwegian who spent a few peripatetic years in Madelia, Minneapolis, and the Red River valley in the 1880s, wrote fiction marked by a deep aversion to civilization and the belief that man's only fulfillment lies with the soil. His works include *Hunger* (1890) and *Growth of the Soil* (1917). See also IMMIGRANT AND MIGRANT LITERATURE and SCANDINAVIAN LITERATURE.

More renowned for his portraits of Minnesota rural life is OLE EDVART RØLVAAG (1876–1931), who came to the state as a university student via SOUTH DAKOTA after emigrating from his native Norway. Although *GIANTS IN THE EARTH* (1927) is his most famous novel, *The Boat of Longing* (1933) more precisely follows the arc of Rølvaag's life, from fisherman in the islands off the northern coast of Norway to immigrant to Minneapolis and to frustrating attempts at assimilation. The search for cultural and artistic identity looms large in this novel.

The Red River valley proved fertile soil for fiction. Martha Ostenso (1900–1963) exposed the bleak realism of the lives of Red River valley Scandinavians in her novels *The Mad Carews* (1928), *The Young May Moon* (1929), and *O River, Remember* (1943). HERBERT (ARTHUR) KRAUSE (1905–1976) also used the Red River valley as the setting for his novels that recount the bleak farm life of German American pioneers and farmers: *Wind without Rain* (1939), *The Thresher* (1946), and *Oxcart Trail* (1954).

Contemporary Minnesota fiction has a significant multicultural voice. Native American novelist, short-story writer, and poet GERALD (ROBERT) VIZENOR (b. 1934) writes postmodern novels, such as *Darkness in Saint Louis: Bearheart* (1978). His *Walking the Rez Road* (1993) blends short fiction and poetry and centers on protagonist Luke Warmwater, a Vietnam veteran of Ojibwa heritage. Similarly gifted, (KAREN) LOUISE ERDRICH (b. 1954) transformed short fiction into her first novel, *LOVE MEDICINE* (1984, 1993), one of a cluster of books set mainly in North Dakota but also moving back and forth into Minnesota, particularly the Twin Cities. Ojibwa families living on and around the Turtle Mountain Band Reservation intertwine and interrelate over several generations. Multiple narrators in *Love Medicine, The Beet Queen* (1986), *Tracks* (1988), *The Bingo Palace* (1994), and succeeding books tell of events from their various perspectives, spotlighting ambiguities, conflicts among the various families and ethnic groups, injustices, and issues between and among tradition, assimilation, and Christian and American Indian religions. The cultural and psychological consequences are woven together into a rich and often surprising mix. Jim Northrup (b. 1943) writes short fiction consisting of humorous short sketches about life on northern Minnesota's Fond du Lac Reservation; his poetry addresses Vietnam and its aftermath. Not published until 1983, *Night Flying Woman: An Ojibway Narrative* by Ignatia Broker (1919–1987) recounts the lives and culture of several generations of Ojibwa people in Minnesota during the early nineteenth century.

Novelist Sandra Benítez (b. Sandy Ables, 1941) relies heavily on her experiences in Mexico and El Salvador in *A Place Where the Sea Remembers* (1993), winner of the Minnesota Book Award, and *Bitter Grounds* (1997), winner of an American Book Award. Alexs D. Pate (b. 1950) grapples with African American fatherhood in two novels, *Losing Absalom* (1994) and *Finding Makeba* (1996); he also co-wrote *Amistad: A Novel* (1997). *Twelve Branches: Stories from St. Paul* (2003), edited by Nora Murphy, Diego Vazquez Jr., Julia Klatt Singer, and Joanna Rawson, layers an underpinning of historical research into the fictional stories of contemporary multiethnic activist neighborhoods in St. Paul. Taiwan-born Catherine Liu (b. 1964) wrote the fictionalized coming-of-age autobiography *Oriental Girls Desire Romance* (1997).

Minnesota is the state with the second-largest Hmong population; St. Paul's large community supports the first Hmong ABC, the first Hmong bookstore in the United States. From *Paj Ntaub Voice,* the Hmong literary arts journal she edits in St. Paul, Mai Neng Moua selected twenty-two Hmong writers' stories to anthologize in *Bamboo among the Oaks* (2002).

Poetry: Although national life, disillusion, and social reform were in the minds of Minnesota poets after the 1920s, a number established international reputations and ventured into genres other than poetry. Arthur Upson (1877–1908) moved from New York to St. Paul, joining the University of Minnesota faculty two years before his death. Somewhat reminiscent of poetry by Percy Bysshe Shelley (1792–1822) and Francis Thompson (1859–1907), his volumes include *At the Sign of the Harp* (1900*), Octaves in an Oxford Garden* (1902), *Westwind Songs* (1902), *The City* (1904), and *The Tides of Spring* (1907). Joseph Warren Beach (1880–1957), who taught at the University of Minnesota for many years, published several books of literary criticism, as well as three volumes of poetry: *Sonnets of the Head and Heart* (1903), *Beginning with Plato* (1944), and *Involuntary Witness* (1950), as well as poems in POETRY magazine and the *Atlantic Monthly.*

Master of the long Whitmanesque line, poet THOMAS (MATTHEW) McGRATH (1916–1990) is best known for his *Letter to an Imaginary Friend,* published separately in 1962, 1970, and 1985 and collectively in 1997, a wide-ranging epic about twentieth-century American society that incorporates Christianity, Greek myth, and Hopi legend. Much of the poetry of ROBERT (ELWOOD) BLY (b. 1926), also a translator and editor, is visionary and nonacademic, whether it is based in the natural world, as in *Silence in the Snowy Fields* (1962), or is political and surrealist, as in *The Light around the Body* (1967), which won a National Book Award. Named the first Minnesota state Poet Laureate (2007–2011), Bly has published more than twenty books of poetry, including *What Have I Ever Lost by Dying?* (1992) and *Talking into the Ear of a Donkey* (2011). Joyce Sutpen followed Bly as Poet Laureate in 2011; one of her recent books is *Modern Love and Other Myths* (2015).

Robert Bly, 1972. Photo by William Stafford.
© William Stafford. Reprinted courtesy of Lewis and Clark College Aubrey Watzek Library Archives & Special Collections

Michael Dennis Browne (b. 1940) writes music based on children's stories and lyrical long poems, such as *Smoke from the Fires* (1984). PATRICIA HAMPL (b. 1946) received initial encouragement from Garrison Keillor; her poems are collected in *Woman before an Aquarium* (1978) and *Resort, and Other Poems* (1983). Cary Waterman (b. 1942), Marisha Chamberlain (b. 1952), and Kate Green (b. 1950) are among the state's other academic women who publish poetry.

Native American poet Gerald Vizenor writes allusive and cryptic poetry, such as that collected in *Raising the Moon Vines* (1964), out of a strong oral tradition, violence and desertion in his childhood, and years spent in Japan and China. Louise Erdrich has published three volumes of verse: *Jacklight* (1984), *Baptism of Desire* (1989), and *Original Fire: New and Selected Poems* (2003); the last two juxtapose Christian and Anishinaabe beliefs blended with occasional magic realism. Her sister, Heid E. Erdrich (b. 1963), has also published three volumes of poetry: *Fishing for Myth* (1997), *The Mother's Tongue* (2005), and *National Monuments* (2008); she is also the co-editor of *Sister Nations: Native American Women Writers on Community.* David Mura (b. 1952), a third-generation Japanese American, deals with racism, sexuality, ethnicity, and identity in his poetry collections *After We Lost Our Way* (1989), which won the National Poetry Series contest in 1989, *The Colors of Desire* (1995), and *Angels for the Burning* (2004). See also NATIVE AMERICAN LITERATURE.

The celebrated poets John Berryman and JAMES WRIGHT (1927–1980) taught at the University of Minnesota, Berryman from 1955 until his death by suicide in 1972 and Wright from 1957 to 1963. Both wrote poems reflecting their residence in Minnesota, including Berryman's "Minnesota Thanksgiving," included in *Collected Poems, 1937–1971* (1989). *Dream Songs* (1969) is the most highly regarded of Berryman's books. Although Wright is more closely associated with OHIO, he wrote many poems set either in Minneapolis or the western Minnesota prairie, most famously "The Blessing" from *THE BRANCH WILL NOT BREAK* (1963).

Other poets with significant Minnesota ties include Diane Glancy (b. 1941), Phebe Hanson (b. 1928), Margaret Hasse (b. 1950), (William Jon) Bill Holm (1943–2009), Louis Jenkins (b. 1942), Jim Moore (b. 1943), Mark Vinz (b. 1942), and David Wojahn (b. 1953). Joyce Sutphen (b. 1949), author of *Naming the Stars* (2004) and other books, was named Minnesota Poet Laureate in 2011. Also worthy of note is Bob Dylan, from Hibbing, who is often cited as the most influential lyricist of the past half century. Dylan's songs, which have influenced poets as well as musicians, often reflect Minnesota in their imagery, dialect, and populist ideals.

Drama and Screenplays: Oscar Firkins (1862–1932), a critic and poet as well as a playwright, wrote a volume of one-act plays in 1928, *Two Passengers from Chelsea*. Another early playwright, F. Scott Fitzgerald, gained his primary reputation on the basis of novels and short stories; however, he staged three early two-act musical comedies—*Fie! Fie! Fi-Fi!* (1914), *The Evil Eye* (1915), and *Safety First* (1916)—at Princeton University and published them in pamphlet form to distribute at performances. A collection of his early dramatic work, *St. Paul Plays, 1911–1914*, was published in 1978, but *The Vegetable; or, From President to Postman* (1923) is better remembered. In Hollywood, Fitzgerald produced a screenplay, *Three Comrades* (1938), and worked on film scripts for *A Yank at Oxford* (1937), *Infidelity* (1938), *Madame Curie* (1938), *The Women* (1939), *Winter Carnival* (1939), and *Cosmopolitan* (1940). By all accounts, the most successful screenplay on which he collaborated was *Gone with the Wind* (1939), although his contribution was limited to polishing dialogue. See also DRAMA and FILM.

Like Fitzgerald, humorist Max Shulman (1919–1988) was born in St. Paul and moved to Hollywood. Before he left the Midwest, he lampooned college life in *Barefoot Boy with Cheek* (1943), a novel adapted as a musical comedy and produced on Broadway. His novel *Rally Round the Flag, Boys* (1957) was produced as a film, and his play *The Tender Trap* (1955) was a hit on Broadway and in Hollywood. His musical comedy *How Now, Dow Jones* (1968) was produced on Broadway in 1967. While he was a columnist at the University of Minnesota's *Minnesota Daily*, Shulman carried on a playful journalistic feud with Minnesotan Thomas Orlo Heggen (1919–1949), whose work about life aboard a cargo freighter, *Mister Roberts*, won acclaim as a novel (1946), a Broadway play (1948), and a film (1955). Minnesota-born Frank Gruber (1904–1969), one of the "kings of pulp fiction," also wrote original screenplays and over two hundred teleplays, notably *Tales of Wells Fargo* (1957) and *77 Sunset Strip* (1958). Scriptwriter Pat(rick) Proft (b. 1947), one of the most prominent and prolific members of Hollywood's so-called Minnesota Mafia, has nearly thirty titles to his credit, including three versions of *The Naked Gun* (1988, 1991, and 1994). Minnesota filmmakers Joel (b. 1954) and Ethan Coen (b. 1957), born in St. Louis Park, have the reputation of being idiosyncratic, ironic, and wryly humorous. *Fargo* (1996), a violent crime comedy set in Minnesota, earned them a Best Original Screenplay Oscar; their nineteen films include *Blood Simple* (1984), *Raising Arizona* (1987), *Miller's Crossing* (1990), *Barton Fink* (1991), *O Brother, Where Art Thou?* (2000), *Burn after Reading* (2008), and *A Serious Man* (2009). Separately, Joel Coen has published *Crimewave* (1985), and Ethan Coen *The Naked Man* (1998).

August Wilson (1945–2005), transplanted from Pittsburgh to St. Paul in 1978, became the first Minnesota playwright to win a Pulitzer Prize, for *Fences* (1986), which also won four Tonys, including one for Best Play of the 1986–1987 Broadway season, and the Drama Critics' Circle Award for best play. *The Piano Lesson* (1990) earned Wilson a second Pulitzer. Both plays are part of Wilson's cycle of ten plays characterizing the black experience in twentieth-century America; one is set in each decade and focuses on a particular problem of that time. Other plays in the cycle include *Ma Rainey's Black Bottom* (1984), *Joe Turner's Come and Gone* (1986), *Two Trains Running* (1990), *Seven Guitars* (1995), and *Gem of the Ocean* (2003).

The important drama that has emerged from Minnesota is being written by younger, still-living dramatists and screenwriters. Diane Glancy, of Cherokee and German heritage, grounds her novels, poems, and drama in Native American culture; *War Cries,* a collection of her plays, was published by Duluth's Holy Cow! Press in 1995. Born in Minneapolis and now teaching at Rutgers, Lee Blessing (b. 1949) has written nearly thirty plays and screenplays. He was nominated for both a Tony Award and a Pulitzer Prize for *A Walk in the Woods* (1988), about superpower arms negotiations. His *Two Rooms* (1988) is about an American prisoner of war in the Middle East who is put to death; *Thief River* (2000), set in Thief River Falls, concerns gay men confronting their sexual identity; and *Going to St. Ives* (1996) turns on a clash of postcolonial perspectives between a British woman and an African woman. Blessing was in Minneapolis for the Playwright Lab's reading of *A Body of Water,* which premiered at the Guthrie Laboratory in 2005. *Heaven's My Destination,* adapted from the Thornton Wilder novel, premiered at Ohio's Cleveland Playhouse in 2008.

Steven Dietz (b. 1958), who was born in Denver and divides his time between Seattle and Austin, Texas, lived in Minneapolis during the eleven years in which he was becoming established as a playwright. He often grounds his plays in historical events and family history: *God's Country* (1990) focuses on the white supremacist movement, and *Ten November* (1987) chronicles the disappearance of an ore freighter on Lake Superior. *Lonely Planet* (1994) concentrates on two gay men mourning friends who have died of AIDS. *Fiction,* produced off-Broadway in 2004, is about married writers who tell the truth about themselves and each other only in their journals. Jeffrey Hatcher (b. 1958), born in Ohio, moved to Minneapolis from New York in the 1990s; besides his plays *Murder by Poe* (2003), based on short stories by Edgar Allan Poe (1809–

1849), and *The Turn of the Screw* (1996), adapted from the novella by Henry James (1843–1916), Hatcher has written plays based on works of George Bernard Shaw (1856–1950) and Jean Anouilh (1910–1987). Kevin Kling (b. 1957), born, raised, and educated in Minnesota, wrote *21A* (1986), which follows passengers on a south Minneapolis bus route and won the Heideman Award for Best Short Play. Other works by Kling that are set in Minnesota are *Fear and Loving in Minneapolis* (1991), *The Ice Fishing Play* (1993), *Mississippi Panorama* (2001), and *Tales from the Charred Underbelly of the Yule Log* (2003). His musical *Northern Lights / Southern Cross* debuted at the Guthrie Theater in 2009.

Newer playwrights include Jordan Harrison (b. 1977), who wrote *Kid-Simple: A Radio Play in the Flesh* (2003); Melanie Marnich (b. 1962), author of *Quake* (2001), *Blur* (2002), and *Tallgrass Gothic* (2003); and Kira Obolensky (b. 1962), a Minneapolis magazine editor and bookmaker born in New York and raised in Houston, who uses the power of the imagination as a theme in her plays *Lobster Alice* (2000), *Quicksilver* (2003), and *Hiding in the Open* (2004).

Three Minneapolis theatres contribute to the state's diverse performance scene. The Penumbra Theatre was founded in 1976 by artistic director Lou Bellamy, whose self-stated mandate is to present proactive and culturally based productions by well-known black playwrights, such as August Wilson, and newer writers, such as Carlyle Brown (b. 1946), whose plays include *The Fula from America* (2004), *Pure Confidence* (2005), and *Point of Revue* (2006). In January 2000 Danny Glover presented Penumbra with the Jujamcyn Award, a national award for the development of artistic talent that has been earned by top regional theatres such as the Yale Repertory Theatre and the Mark Taper Forum. Mixed Blood, "dedicated to the spirit of Dr. King's dream since 1976," is a professional multiracial theatre company that promotes cultural pluralism by producing plays with culture-conscious casting, taking artistic risks in the selecting and producing of plays, and catering to a nontraditional audience. In 1992 third-generation Japanese Canadian Rick Shiomi (b. 1947) relocated to Minneapolis and became founding artistic director of Theater

Mu. In 2004 Theater Mu merged with the Taiko drum group Mu Daiko to become Mu Performing Arts. Shiomi's *Mask Dance* (1995) was Theater Mu's inaugural production; his play *The Walleye Kid* (2003) addresses issues Korean adoptees face growing up in Minnesota. See also REGIONAL THEATRE.

Creative Nonfiction: A number of personal narratives present rich and diverse views about living in the state. *Old Rail Fence Corners: Frontier Tales Told by Minnesota Pioneers* (1914) by Lucy Leavenworth Wilder Morris (1865–1935) presents personal stories of hardship and happiness told by early Minnesota settlers, re-creating everyday frontier life from the 1840s to the 1860s. Chester G. Anderson edited *Growing Up in Minnesota: Ten Writers Remember Their Childhoods* (1976), organized generally from age to youth. It contains a lyrical portrait by Meridel Le Sueur, a journalistic essay by reporter Harrison Salisbury (1908–1993), sharp vignettes by Gerald Vizenor, an essay about confinement and liberation by Keith Gunderson (1935–2013), sensuous exuberance from Shirley Schoonover (b. 1936), and memorable imagery from Robert Bly. Notable in the volume are an African American perspective full of joy and agony by Toyse Kyle (1938–2010) and an Asian American family chorus written by Edna Hong (1913–2007), Howard Hong (1912–2010), and Mary Hong Loe (b. 1944). *The Minnesota Experience: An Anthology* (1979), edited by Jean Ervin (b. 1925), groups selections under the titles "The Land," "The Town and the City," "Childhood and the Family," and "Old Age." Peg Meier (b. 1946), a former columnist for the *Minneapolis Star Tribune,* brought together letters, diaries, government documents, and photographs from people who lived through Minnesota's early history, from territory to early statehood, in *Bring Warm Clothes: Letters and Photos from Minnesota's Past* (1981). Explorers, farmers, homemakers, socialites, children, laborers, lawyers, and lumberjacks are all represented. See also AFRICAN AMERICAN LITERATURE and ASIAN AMERICAN LITERATURE.

Single-author works offer unified perspectives. CHARLES ALEXANDER EASTMAN (1858–1939) published *Indian Boyhood* in 1902, his account of growing up with the Sioux. *The Singing Wilderness* (1956) by North Woods naturalist, activist, and adventurer SIGURD F(ERDINAND) OLSON (1899–1982) is superior nature writing and presents the story of one man's unfolding appreciation of the natural world. *Canoeing with the Cree* (1935) by (ARNOLD) ERIC SEVAREID (1912–1992) traces his adventures from Minneapolis to Hudson Bay while reliving early Midwestern history. His memoirs *Not So Wild a Dream* (1946) and *This Is Eric Sevareid* (1964) reflect on his Midwestern upbringing. Charles A. Lindbergh (1902–1974), who grew up on a farm near Little Falls, won a Pulitzer Prize for *The Spirit of St. Louis* (1953), about his solo transatlantic flight to Paris in 1927. He also wrote *Boyhood on the Upper Mississippi* (1972) and *Lindbergh Looks Back: A Boyhood Reminiscence* (2002), both published by the Minnesota Historical Society Press. Walter O'Meara (1897–1989) recounts his tenth year growing up in the sawmill town of Cloquet in *We Made It through the Winter: A Memoir of Northern Minnesota Boyhood* (1974); the lumber industry forms the backdrop for the family saga, reflecting his father's work experience in a logging camp, and the conflicts of family life are central to the book.

Contemporary female accounts of growing up in the Midwest are offered by SUSAN ALLEN TOTH (b. 1940), who earned a PhD in English at the University of Minnesota in 1969 and joined the English faculty at Macalester College that year. Her memoirs *Blooming: A Small-Town Girlhood* (1981) and *Ivy Days: Making My Way out East* (1984) are steeped in Midwestern small-town sensibilities and powerfully portray coming of age and undergraduate life. Patricia Hampl's *A Romantic Education* (1981) and *The Florist's Daughter* (2007) recount growing up in a Czech family in St. Paul. Male accounts of Minnesota life include *Letters from Side Lake: A Chronicle of Life in the North Woods* (1992) by Peter M. Leschak (b. 1951), a humorous description of building a log home and forging a life in a North Woods community. Another eloquent spokesperson for nature and the rural life, PAUL GRUCHOW (1947–2004), published *Journal of a Prairie Year* (1985) and *Grass Roots: The Universe of Home* (1995). In *The Language of Blood: A Memoir* (2003) Jane Jeong Trenka (b. 1972) writes from the perspective of a Korean adoptee, using art, imagination, and memory to tell her story.

Other works by Minnesotans that provide insight into the cultural environment of the state are *Letters from the Country* (1981) by Carol Bly, a collection of essays, both descriptive and polemic, about rural life; *How to Talk Minnesotan* (1987) by HOWARD MOHR (b. 1939), a humorous tour of the idiosyncrasies of Minnesota speech, mannerisms, attitudes, and habits; and *The St. Paul Stories of F. Scott Fitzgerald* (2004), edited by Patricia Hampl and Dave Page (b. 1954), which collects for the first time Fitzgerald's fiction set in Minnesota, most of which consists of fictionalized versions of his experiences there as an adolescent and young adult. But no list of representative Minnesota literature would be complete without referring to the nostalgic works of Garrison Keillor. His local-color radio monologues and books are unparalleled in voicing the themes, subjects, and emotions of middle-class central Minnesota; its sense of community and conformity; its traditions of morality, innocence, and repression; its adventures in escape and reconciliation; and its certainty of mortality. In addition to his Lake Wobegon and radio novels, Keillor has published *Homegrown Democrat: A Few Plain Thoughts from the Heart of America* (2004).

Popular Literature:

Children's and Young Adult Literature: Among the many contemporary Minnesota writers for children are Janet Shaw (b. 1937), with *Kirsten's Story Collection* (1990); Dori Hillestad Butler (b. 1965), with *M Is for Minnesota* (1998); and Betsy Bowen (b. 1949), author of *Antler, Bear, Canoe: A Northwoods Alphabet Year* (2002).

Other writers of juvenile literature are well known to literary scholars. PHIL(IP) (DUFFIELD) STONG (1899–1957), who taught high school near Duluth, published *Honk, the Moose* in 1935. Social activist Meridel Le Sueur's female-centered short stories and novels often eclipse her juvenile title, *Johnny Appleseed* (1945). Although CAROL RYRIE BRINK (1895–1981) became famous for her novel *Caddie Woodlawn* (1935), which won the Newbery Medal, she has other juvenile titles to her credit: *Anything Can Happen on the River* (1934), *Harps in the Wind* (1947), *Family Grandstand* (1952), and *Four Girls on a Homestead*

(1977). Emma Brock (1886–1974), who illustrated her own books, fictionalizes life on an island in Lake Superior near Split Rock Lighthouse in *Then Came Adventure* (1941). LAURA INGALLS WILDER (1867–1957), who, with her daughter ROSE WILDER LANE (1886–1968), wrote the Little House books (1932–1941), lived briefly in Minnesota; she based these tales on her experiences growing up on the Midwestern frontier. WANDA (HAZEL) GÁG (1893–1946) wrote and illustrated the highly successful *Millions of Cats* (1928), as well as *Gone Is Gone: The Story of a Man Who Wanted to Do Housework* (1935), based on her New Ulm childhood. Dietrich Lange (1863–1940) published nature stories and historical works for young readers, such as *On the Trail of the Sioux* (1911) and *Nature Trails* (1927). Maud Hart Lovelace set her beloved Betsy-Tacy books in Deep Valley, a fictionalized Mankato. Three-time Newbery Award winner GARY (JAMES) PAULSEN (b. 1939) sets his powerful fiction for young adults primarily in the wilderness, where survival skills and respect for nature are all-important; he also realistically depicts Minnesota small towns, the North Woods, and farm communities. *Winterkill* (1976), *Hatchet* (1987), and *Dancing Carl* (1983) are among Paulsen's works that have won literary awards. Paulsen has written over a hundred books, including two series for children, the Culpepper Adventures and World of Adventures. Louise Erdrich's novel for children, *The Game of Silence* (2005), is set on an island in Lake Superior in 1847. This novel, the first in a projected cycle centering on a young Ojibwa girl and her family, was nominated for a National Book Award in the Young People's Literature category.

Mystery and Detective Fiction: Minnesota provides the settings for many mystery stories and novels and is home to many mystery writers. In fact, two Minneapolis bookstores specialize in murder mysteries: Once upon a Crime and Uncle Edgar's Mystery Bookstore. Nonfiction murder narratives make up *Murder in Minnesota: A Collection of True Cases* (1962) by Walter N. (1917–2012); the other works discussed here, however, are fiction. See MYSTERY AND DETECTIVE FICTION.

Born in Herman, Mabel Seeley (1903–1991) was one of the best-known mystery writers of her time. Seven of her novels are detective stories, all using Midwestern characters or locales. *The Listening House* (1938) made the *New York Herald*'s list of the best detective-crime-mystery fiction in the two decades preceding 1938. Typical of her work are *The Crying Sisters* (1939), set at a Minnesota lake resort; *The Chuckling Fingers* (1941), which makes use of the Paul Bunyan myth and Indian legends and is set at a resort on Lake Superior; and *The Whispering Cup* (1940), perhaps her best mystery, set in a Minnesota farming community. Ruth Sawtell Wallis (1895–1978), an anthropologist as well as a mystery writer, drew on her knowledge of archaeology to color her mysteries *Too Many Bones* (1943), *No Bones about It* (1944), *Blood from a Stone* (1945), and *Cold Bed of Clay* (1947). William A. Swanberg (1904–1992), born and educated in Minnesota, won the Centennial Book Prize for *First Blood* (1958). Walter O'Meara's *Minnesota Gothic* (1956) is a novel of crime and punishment set in Minnesota, as is *Killing Time in St. Cloud* (1988) by JUDITH (ANN) GUEST (b. 1936) and Rebecca Hill (b. 1944).

Several contemporary mystery writers either grew up in Minnesota or worked and lived there. James Allen Simpson (b. 1934) writes under the pseudonym M. D. Lake; his novels feature Peggy O'Neill, a fictional law-enforcement officer drawn from a real-life University of Minnesota campus police officer. *Amends for Murder* (1989) was the first of his novels to feature this resourceful character; other titles include *Cold Comfort* (1990), *Murder by Mail* (1993), *Once upon a Crime* (1995), and *Death Calls the Tune* (1999). Thomas Gifford (1937–2000) moved to Minnesota after earning a bachelor of arts from Harvard; his novels *The Wind Chill Factor* (1975) and *The Cavanaugh Quest* (1976) use northern Minnesota and Minneapolis as settings. (Barbara Jean) Babs Lakey (b. 1942) moved to Minneapolis in her late teens and centers her writing in various Minnesota cities: Northfield, Sauk Centre, Menahga, and Minneapolis. Her psychological suspense novels include *Spirit of the Straightedge* (2001), *Spirit of the Silent Butler* (2002), and *Spirits of the Once Walking* (2002). Her heroine, Elsie Sanders, braves Minnesota blizzards and encounters ancient American

spiritualists and healers along the Mississippi River.

A prolific author, John Roswell Camp (b. 1944), writing under the name John Sandford, moved to the Twin Cities from Iowa via Florida in 1978. He published *The Fool's Run* (2001) under the name John Camp, initiating his Kidd series, whose hero is an adventurous jack-of-all-trades—artist, cat lover, and student of karate and tarot. *Rules of Prey* (1989), published under the name John Sandford, introduced Minneapolis police officer Lucas Davenport, a brilliant games inventor, and inaugurated his Prey series, comprising over twenty-four titles. R(obert) D(ingwall) Zimmerman (b. 1952), writing under the pseudonym Robert Alexander, has writtenover fifteen psychological thrillers, among them *Deadfall in Berlin* (1990), *Death Trance* (1992), and *Blood Trance* (1993). *The Red Encounter* (1986) involves stealing software programs from a Minneapolis computer firm. *Tribe* (1996) also unfolds in Minneapolis and depicts homosexuality and homophobia.

Ellen Hart (b. 1949) initiated the Jane Lawless series in 1989 with *Hallowed Murder,* set in Minneapolis; *This Little Piggy Went to Murder* (1994), set in Duluth, began her Sophie Greenway series. Gail Frazer (1943–2013), who lived north of Elk River, collaborated with Mary Monica Pulver Kuhfeld (b. 1943) to write the Sister Frevisse tales, a seventeen-book series, under the name Margaret Frazer. Writing as Monica Ferris, Kuhfeld has also published *Crewel World* (1999), a novel in her Needlepoint series, as well as a number of other mystery titles under various names. Tami Hoag (b. 1959) sets her not-at-all Minnesota-nice thrillers in her home state: *Ashes to Ashes* (1999) and *Dust to Dust* (2000) take place in Minneapolis, *Guilty as Sin* (1996) is set at Deer Lake, and *Still Waters* (1992) and *Night Sins* (1995) are set in the fictional town of Still Creek.

Dime Novels: The Sioux massacres of 1862 inspired several Minnesota DIME NOVELS. Neither Edward S. Ellis (1840–1916) nor Paul Bibbs was a Minnesota native or resident; however, Ellis's *Indian Jim: A Tale of the Minnesota Massacre* (1864), *The Lost Trail* (1864), and *The Hunter's Escape* (1864) are set in the state and draw on Minnesota historical materials, as does Bibbs's *The Squaw Guide; or, The Red River Rifles: A Tale of the North Frontier* (1872). Other Minnesota dime novels are *The Indian Avenger* (1868) by Charles Dunning Clark (1843–1892), writing as W. J. Hamilton; and *Dusky Dick; or, Old Toby Castor's Great Campaign: A Story of the Last Sioux Outbreak* (1872) by Joseph E. Badger (1848–1909).

Romance Novels: An early Minnesota romance writer was Frances Roberta Sterrett (1869–1947), whose *Up the Road with Sallie* (1915) traces the romantic adventures of a young woman and her great aunt traveling up the Mississippi River Road. Darragh Aldrich had such a big hit with her romance of mistaken identities, *Enchanted Hearts* (1917), that George M. Cohan adapted it for the stage as *A Prince There Was* in 1918, and Waldemar Young adapted it for the screen, using Cohan's title, in 1921. Contemporary romance authors include Edna Curry (b. 1928), who sets her novels in the Dalles area of the St. Croix River valley; her *Circle of Shadows* (1994) was a Golden Heart Finalist, as was the first novel of Kathleen Eagle (b. 1947), who uses the folklore of Minnesota Native Americans in novels such as *The Night Remembers* (1997), a *Chicago Tribune* notable book. A top-selling author worldwide, with over 15 million copies of her works in print and several film adaptations, Minnesota's most popular romance novelist is LaVyrle Spencer (b. 1943), a Stillwater resident. Among her Minnesota novels are *The Fulfillment* (1979), set during World War I in rural Minnesota; *The Endearment* (1982), set on the Minnesota frontier; *Bygones* (1992), set in the Twin Cities; *November of the Heart* (1993), set in the Victorian era at a White Bear Lake resort and also in St. Paul; *Family Blessings* (1994), set in Anoka; *Home Song* (1995), set in suburban St. Paul; and *Then Came Heaven* (1997), set in a 1950s Polish community in Browerville, Spencer's hometown. Tami Hoag, better known for her mysteries, began writing romance novels in 1988, publishing *Magic* (1990) and *Sarah's Sin* (1991).

Science Fiction and Fantasy: CLIFFORD D(ONALD) SIMAK (1904–1988), a reporter, news editor, and science writer at the *Minneapolis Star Tribune* from 1939 to 1976, won many awards for his science fiction, much of

which draws on his Midwestern boyhood. Among his many writing honors are three Hugo Awards: in 1959, for Best Novelette (*The Big Front Yard*, 1958); in 1964, for Best Novel (*Way Station*, 1963); and in 1981, for Best Short Story ("Grotto of the Dancing Deer," 1980). He was inducted into the Science Fiction Hall of Fame in 1973. Three notable contemporary Minnesota authors who write in these genres are Lois McMaster Bujold (b. 1949), who inaugurated her Vorkosigan series in 1996 with *Dreamweaver's Dilemma*; Steven Brust (b. 1955), whose Vlad Taltos novels include *Teckla* (1987), *Taltos* (1988), *Phoenix* (1990), *Athyra* (1993), *Dragon* (1998), *Issola* (2001), and *Iorich* (2010); and Joel Rosenberg (1954–2011), whose science-fiction titles are *Ties of Blood and Silver* (1984), *Emile and the Dutchman* (1986), *Not for Glory* (1988), and *Hero* (1990). His Guardians of the Flame series includes *The Sleeping Dragon* (1983); *Paladins* (2004) initiated his Mordred's Heirs series. See also SCIENCE FICTION AND FANTASY.

Religious Literature: Minnesota's large Lutheran immigrant population from Norway, Sweden, and Germany is reflected in the number of significant books that center on RELIGION and spirituality. Ole Rølvaag's realistic writing about the Norwegian American immigrant experience, particularly in the trilogy *Giants in the Earth: A Saga of the Prairie* (1927), *Peder Victorious: A Tale of the Pioneers Twenty Years Later* (1929), and *Their Father's God* (1931), centers on the myth of the Promised Land and frontier morality. Margaret Culkin Banning was a social activist and early feminist with over forty books and four hundred short stories to her credit. Raised Roman Catholic, she explored women and work, divorce, contraception, and religious conviction in fiction such as *This Marrying* (1920), *Money of Her Own* (1928), and *Women for Defense* (1942). *Fallen Away* (1951) focuses on marriages between people of differing religious faiths. In *Elmer Gantry* (1927) Sinclair Lewis exposes the dangers of evangelical religion; this story centers on a charismatic revival preacher whose sole interests are the money, sex, and power his position brings him.

J(AMES) F(ARL) POWERS (1917–1999), jailed as a conscientious objector for refusing to serve in World War II, taught at St. John's University and the College of Saint Benedict and wrote about the conflict between spirituality and the secular world. Considered by many to be the premier Catholic writer in the United States, Powers makes his central characters in *Morte d'Urban* (1962) and *Wheat That Springeth Green* (1988) Catholic priests. Father Joe Hackett, the protagonist of the latter novel, is a principled man drawn with humor. Powers presents Hackett's foibles and triumphs against a trenchant analysis of the pitfalls of modern society. In both works Powers deftly satirizes a church and a priesthood whose daily efforts to reconcile the secular with the sacred make for some humorous scenes, a theme also explored in his short-story collections: *Prince of Darkness, and Other Stories* (1947), *The Presence of Grace* (1956), and *Look How the Fish Live* (1975).

Thomas Gifford, better known for his mystery novels, wrote *The Assassini* (1990), based on a medieval legend about a group of hired killers used by the Catholic clergy to preserve their power. Updated to 1982, the novel centers on two rivals who want to succeed the dying pope. Peter Leschak, who grew up a miner's son in Chisholm and still lives in northern Minnesota, wrote *Bumming with the Furies* (1993), which deals with the Leschaks' experiences with a fundamentalist Christian organization.

Born in Minneapolis, Kent Michael Nerburn (b. 1946), who trained in theology and studied the wisdom literature of many cultures, lives in Bemidji, where he directs an oral history project on the Red Lake Ojibwa reservation. His *Native American Wisdom* (1991) quotes tribal leaders past and present; *The Soul of an Indian, and Other Writings from Ohiyesa* (1993) presents the thought of Santee leader Ohiyesa, also known as Charles Alexander Eastman. One of his most popular books, *A Haunting Reverence: Meditations on a Northern Land* (1996), is inspired by the North American plains.

Louise Erdrich's fiction springs from her German American and Turtle Mountain Ojibwa heritages. Of her many books of fiction, *The Last Report on the Miracles at Little No Horse* (2002) most directly focuses on religion. The novel centers on Father Damien Modeste, who entered holy orders as Sister Cecilia and was baptized and reborn to the priesthood in a body-and-soul-cleansing flood. Miracles abound in this epic tale, recorded in Father Damien's "reports" to the Holy See, which raise questions about the nature of faith and the role of the church in the unraveling of Native American cultures. Characters in her Ojibwa saga—*Love Medicine* (1984), *The Beet Queen* (1986), *Tracks* (1988), *The Bingo Palace* (1994), and *Four Souls* (2004)—reflect Erdrich's Christian and Anishinaabe beliefs.

Jon Hassler focuses on faith and inspiration in his gentle novels. Three of these, *The Green Journey* (1985), *North of Hope* (1990), and *Dear James* (1993), pit the strength in small-town living against the challenges and crises of faith that Roman Catholic priests can experience. The Catholic-Lutheran conflict often seen in small Minnesota towns is portrayed in *Grand Opening* (1987). Bill Holm examines how religion and the church affect the lives of Minnesotans of Icelandic heritage in essay collections such as *Boxelder Bug Variations: A Meditation on an Idea in Language and Music* (1985) and *The Dead Get By with Everything* (1991). *Peace like a River* (2001) by Leif Enger (b. 1961), set in 1960s rural Minnesota, is a novel crowded with miracles and biblical allusions. The haunting penultimate chapter, "Be Jubilant, My Feet," describes the meeting between a character and his father in the next world. *Jesus Sound Explosion* (2003) by Mark Curtis Anderson (b. 1961) is an affectionate and humorous chronicle of growing up evangelical; Anderson depicts the allure of salvation, on the one hand, and sex, drugs, and rock and roll, on the other.

Like Hassler, Garrison Keillor often renders German Catholic and Norwegian Lutheran conflicts with gentle humor as the two cultures coexist in Lake Wobegon, a fictionalized Anoka. Their respective rituals, eccentricities, and values are treated in a humorous evocation that is half parody and half nostalgia for bygone morality and mores. Life in Lake Wobegon seems at first glance more wholesome and simple than life in the small-town Midwest today, but beneath the surface lurk some irredeemably quirky and melancholic elements. Keillor's most popular books, *Happy to Be Here* (1982) and *Lake Wobegon Days* (1985), as well as *We Are Still Married* (1989), *The Book of Guys*

(1993), and *WLT: A Radio Romance* (1991), are largely drawn from monologues he composed for his radio broadcasts. Several of the later Lake Wobegon books, such as *Pontoon* (2007), *Liberty* (2008), and *Pilgrims* (2010), are notable for their sidesplitting humor.

Comic Strips, Comic Books, and Graphic Novels: A household name to comic-strip readers, Charles M(onroe) Schulz (1922–2000) was born in Minneapolis and raised in St. Paul, studied cartooning in a Minneapolis correspondence school, and quickly became nationally syndicated. With four full-length films, forty books, and thirty television specials to his credit, Schulz was selected Humorist of the Year by Yale University in 1958 and received the Emmy and Peabody Awards for the television specials "A Charlie Brown Christmas" (1965) and "A Charlie Brown Thanksgiving" (1974). His books include *Good Ol' Charlie Brown* (1957), *The World According to Lucy* (1960), *The Meditations of Linus* (1967), *Peanuts Treasury* (1968), and *It's a Mystery, Charlie Brown* (1975). In 2010 M. Thomas Inge edited *My Life with Charlie Brown by Charles M. Schulz.* In 2004 Fantagraphics Books began publishing *The Complete Peanuts* in twenty-five volumes.

After spending more than a decade painting houses while drawing comics on the side, self-taught artist Sam Hiti (b. 1975) began sketching illustrations for the *New York Times.* He published a demon-hunter saga called *End Times / Tiempos Finales* (2004) and produced a comic-book adaptation of *Lemony Snicket's "A Series of Unfortunate Events,"* a 2004 film starring Jim Carrey. (Michael Joseph) Mike Mignola (b. 1960), creator of the Hellboy series, has called *End Times* the best graphic novel of 2004, saying that it is a powerful representation of what an independent artist can do. See also COMIC STRIPS AND BOOKS and GRAPHIC NOVELS.

Printers, Small Presses, and Journalism: Shortly after settlement began, land speculation and politics spurred the development of Minnesota publishing. Firms in Ohio and Wisconsin vied to establish newspapers in the state. The first to arrive was James Madison Goodhue (1810–1852), publisher of the *Grant County Herald* in Lancaster, Wisconsin, bringing his press by boat shortly before the state became a terri-

tory. On April 28, 1849, in a building in St. Paul, using a primitive press, he published the first issue of the *Minnesota Pioneer.* The paper, and Goodhue in particular, became famous for caustic editorials and trenchant political commentary. A rival press in CINCINNATI, however, claimed to have established the first newspaper, publishing the *Minnesota Register* there, which it sent to St. Paul, bearing printing dates of April 7 and 27, 1849, although its presses in Minnesota did not actually print copies until July 14. Another Ohio press rushing to St. Paul issued its first *Minnesota Chronicle* on May 31, 1849. In August of the same year these Ohio presses combined forces to publish the *Minnesota Chronicle and Register.* Also in 1849 an Ojibwa mission in Cass Lake began printing religious material in both Ojibwa and English. Beginning in 1850, Christian Sioux could read the *Dakota Friend,* edited by Indian missionary Gideon Pond in St. Paul.

The present-day *Minneapolis Star Tribune* evolved from the *St. Anthony Express,* which appeared at St. Anthony Falls in 1851 and was co-published by Elmer Tyler, a tailor, and Isaac Atwater, a lawyer, both Whigs. The *North-Western Democrat,* founded in 1853, ceased publication in 1857. Competition was fierce. During that first decade of pioneer journalism, ninety papers were established, the following twelve of which have survived: the *St. Paul Pioneer Press* (1849), the *Minnehaha* (1855), the *Winona Republican Herald* (1855), the *Chatfield News* (1856), the *Hastings Gazette* (1856), the *Hoka Chief* (1856), the *Stillwater Post-Messenger* (1856), the *Mantorville Express* (1857), the *Monticello Times* (1857), the *Red Wing Republican* (1857), the *St. Cloud Daily Times and Daily Journal-Press* (1857), and the *Wabasha County Herald-Standard* (1857). Major Minnesota newspapers today target specific interests, such as *Business Journal, Minnesota Law and Politics, Minnesota Politics,* the *St. Paul Legal Ledger,* and the University of Minnesota newspaper *Minnesota Daily.* Of a more general nature are the *Minneapolis Star Tribune,* the *St. Paul Pioneer Press,* and the free news and arts weekly, *City Pages.* See also NEWSPAPER JOURNALISM.

Several editors from the 1850s and 1860s have developed lasting reputations: Earle S. Goodrich, who edited the Goodhue paper;

Arctic explorer Sam K. Whiting, who edited papers in Winona; Pennsylvanian Ignatius Loyola Donnelly, who founded the *Emigrant Aid Journal;* and Jane Grey Swisshelm, Minnesota's most famous newspaperwoman, who set up shop in St. Cloud. Joseph A. Wheelock (1831–1906), affiliated with the *Pioneer Press,* is acknowledged as the dean of Minnesota journalism. Foreign-language papers became established as immigrants settled; these were mainly in German, Swedish, and Norwegian, but for over forty years a French newspaper was also published.

Two twentieth-century Minnesota journalists have achieved national prominence. Eric Sevareid, a 1935 University of Minnesota alumnus, wrote for the *Minneapolis Star* and the *Minneapolis Journal* before moving on to a career in radio and television journalism with CBS News. He published collections of his columns in *In One Ear* (1952) and *Small Sounds in the Night* (1956). Mystery writer John Sandford, also known as John Roswell Camp, was a 1980 Pulitzer Prize finalist for a series of stories on Native American culture in the *Pioneer Press* and won a Pulitzer in 1986 for Non-deadline Feature Writing about how the Midwest farm crisis affected southwestern Minnesota farmers.

Although the small-press scene in contemporary Minnesota is a changing landscape, it is thriving. Graywolf Press, a nonprofit literary press, publishes novels, short stories, memoirs, essays, and poetry; among its authors are Charles Baxter and Robert Bly. Graywolf was founded in 1974 by Scott Walker; in 1985 he moved the press from Port Townsend, Washington, to St. Paul. Graywolf is currently located in Minneapolis and has been directed by Fiona McCrae since 1994. Graywolf Press poets have won two Pulitzer Prizes, one National Book Award, and a National Book Critics Circle Award.

Several of the best-known Minnesota small presses are collaborative efforts. Milkweed Chronicle / Milkweed Editions attends to high-quality literary and visual art, at times collaborating with Bieler Press, which hand-assembles books, and publishes such established authors as Carol Bly. New Rivers Press, founded by C(alvin) W(illiam) Bill Truesdale (1929–2001) in 1968 and based

at Minnesota State University–Moorhead, publishes regional writers and ethnic writers; the press has two series—a Minnesota Voices competition for area authors and Many Minnesotas, showcasing ethnic writers. Coffee House Press, established in 1970 in Iowa as Toothpaste Press, moved to Minneapolis in 1984 and publishes both limited editions and trade paperbacks. Sing Heavenly Muse! is the quaint name of a Minneapolis small press that publishes both a feminist journal and occasional books featuring women writers. Minneapolis's *Evergreen Chronicles,* a venue for gay and lesbian writers and artists, was established in 1985. Former Minnesota resident Jim Dochniak, publisher of Shadow Press and *SEZ* magazine, asserts that the mission of the latter is to provide a forum for voices that have been disenfranchised by both mainstream and small presses. See also LESBIAN, GAY, BISEXUAL, TRANSGENDER, AND QUEER LITERATURE.

Minnesota Federal Writers' Project: Under the aegis of the Works Progress Administration, the FEDERAL WRITERS' PROJECT (1935–1943) argued successfully for state support of the arts, producing, among other things, the American Guide Series; the WPA guide to Minnesota was published in 1938. *Minnesota: A State Guide* was directed by Mabel S. Ulrich (1876–1945), a physician and former bookstore owner. Because of pressure to produce the volume quickly, it cannot be considered a scholarly reference on Minnesota history and culture, but it does contain much valuable information. The book is divided into three parts, with appendixes that contain a chronology, maps, and a classified bibliography. Part 1, "Minnesota: Past and Present," features sections on geology and climate, early settlement, agriculture, immigration, transportation, industry, education, the press and radio, sports, recreation, and the arts. Part 2, "Minnesota: Cities and Towns," concentrates on Minneapolis, St. Paul, Duluth, St. Cloud, Winona, and Rochester. Part 3 details twenty scenic automobile tours and fifteen canoe trips within the Superior National Forest. See also LITERARY MAPS; PRINTING AND PUBLISHING; ART; and MINNEAPOLIS/ST. PAUL.

The Minnesota Writers' Project also produced the *St. Cloud Guide* (1936), *Minneapolis, Story of a City* (1940), *Minnesota* [Recreation

Series] (1941), *Bohemian Flats* (1941), *The Minnesota Arrowhead Country* [American Guide Series] (1941), *Kittson County: A School History* (1940), *Logging Town: The Story of Grand Rapids, Minnesota* (1941), *The Mayors of St. Paul, 1850–1940* (1940), and *Wabasha County* (1938). Books about the WPA in Minnesota are *Works Progress Administration Accomplishments: Minnesota, 1935–1939* (1939), Nancy A. Johnson's *Accomplishments: Minnesota Art Projects in the Depression Years* (1976), and *Wall-to-Wall America: A Cultural History of Post-Office Murals in the Great Depression* (1982) by Karal Ann Marling (b. 1943). The Minnesota Historical Society holds the papers of the Minnesota WPA. See also CULTURAL STUDIES.

Minnesota Literary Awards and Prizes: In 2006 the Friends of the St. Paul Library resumed sponsorship of the Minnesota Book Awards, which have been given to Minnesota's writers and publishers since 1988. In 2014 Ethan Rutherford (b. 1991) won in the Novel and Short Story category, Matt Rasmussen (b. 1975) won in the Poetry category, and Carrie Mesrobian (b.1975) won in the Young People's Literature category. The John Flanagan Prize, offered between 1997 and 2000, recognized outstanding achievement in the literature and culture of the Midwest; winners were Bill Holm in 1997, Paul Gruchow in 1998, Richard "Fred" Arey (b. 1954) and Gaylord Schanilec (b. 1956) in 1999, and Jon Hassler in 2000. The Minnesota Humanities Prize for Literature, established in 2001, annually recognizes contributions to literature and the advancement of the humanities; recent winners have been Carol Bly in 2001, Louise Erdrich in 2002, Senator Paul Wellstone (1944–2002) posthumously in 2003, Paul Gruchow in 2004, Joseph A. Amato (b. 1938) in 2005, and Robert Bly in 2006. The Honor Award recognizes works with strong Minnesota content that fall outside established categories. The Kay Sexton Award, named for a book buyer at Dayton's and B. Dalton Bookstores, is presented to the individual or organization that best fosters reading and literary activity.

Established in 1988 to recognize books that reveal the history, culture, heritage, or lifestyle of northeastern Minnesota, the Northeastern Minnesota Book Award has been given in six categories: General Nonfiction, Fiction, Art/Photography, Children's Literature, Poetry, and Memoir and Creative Nonfiction. The Maud Hart Lovelace Book Award, named for the author of the Betsy-Tacy books, has been awarded since 1980 for titles suitable for grade-school-level readers. The Kerlan Awards in Children's Literature, named for children's book collector Irvin Kerlan, have been conferred annually since 1975 on such recipients as Wanda Gág and Carol Ryrie Brink. See also CHILDREN'S AND YOUNG-ADULT LITERATURE and CREATIVE NONFICTION.

SELECTED WORKS: The experience of Minnesota, particularly in the early years but lingering into the present, is largely that of immigrants. Minnesota's most important writer on the Norwegian immigrant experience in frontier Minnesota and the Dakotas is Ole Rølvaag with his trilogy *Giants in the Earth* (translated into English in 1927), *Peder Victorious* (translated 1929), and *Their Father's God* (1931), all depicting the experience of immigrant Norwegians in frontier Minnesota and the Dakotas and their multigenerational attempts to assimilate. *Unto a Good Land* (1952) by Vilhelm Moberg (1898–1973) portrays the Swedish immigrant experience in frontier Minnesota. Another work detailing the Scandinavian immigrant experience is Drude Krog Janson's *En Saloonkeepers Datter: Fortaelling* (1889), translated into English in 2002 as *A Saloonkeeper's Daughter*. Jon Hassler's much later novel *Grand Opening* (1987) portrays small-town Minnesota divisions based on religion and national origins. Humorous treatment of the late twentieth- and early twenty-first-century immigrant experience in Minnesota and the ongoing issues of assimilation, sometimes dividing Minnesota German Catholics from Norwegian Lutherans, appears in Garrison Keillor's *Lake Wobegon Days* (1985) and his many subsequent volumes, most based on his on-air "reports from Lake Wobegon." See also IMMIGRANT AND MIGRANT LITERATURE.

Perhaps the best-known treatment of Minnesota in fiction is that of Sinclair Lewis in *Main Street* (1920). Lewis scathingly portrays Midwestern life and culture in his fictional Gopher Prairie. This bitingly negative portrayal led Carl (Clinton) Van Doren (1885–1950) to posit in 1921 a REVOLT FROM THE

VILLAGE that rejected Midwestern small-town culture and to cite Lewis among the writers in this "revolt." Lewis's 1922 novel *Babbitt* continues the assault, attacking Midwestern and American materialism, boosterism, and the rise of superficially attractive but culturally void suburban subdivisions. A more positive, albeit brief, presentation of St. Paul, Minnesota, and the Midwest they represent appears in *The Great Gatsby* (1925) by F. Scott Fitzgerald. His many early short stories set in St. Paul also provide a perspective on aspiring middle-class youth and young adulthood in the Jazz Age.

Historical novels present Minnesota's early experience, as evidenced by Frederick Manfred's *Scarlet Plume* (1964), a novel in the Indian captivity mold of a woman captured by the Sioux in the 1860s. The state's juvenile fiction also includes many historical novels, most notably *On the Banks of Plum Creek* (1937) by Laura Ingalls Wilder and Rose Wilder Lane, reflecting the family's farm life near Walnut Grove, Minnesota, in the late 1800s, and the Betsy-Tacy stories of Maud Hart Lovelace. These latter stories, published from 1940 to 1953, depict the experiences of two female friends growing up in small-town Minnesota during the first decade of the 1900s. See also CAPTIVITY NARRATIVES.

Meridel Le Sueur's *The Girl* (1939) and "Women on Breadlines" (1932) reflect working-class, feminist, and socialist views during the Depression era. The values and experiences of the Midwest's other less completely assimilated population groups, including Native Americans, Asians, and Latinos/Latinas, are reflected in the works of Gerald Vizenor, Louise Erdrich, Sandra Benítez, and many others. Vizenor's *Darkness in Saint Louis Bearheart* (1978) is his first novel. Erdrich's *Love Medicine* (1984) is perhaps her best-known work. Her *Four Souls* (2004) is partially set in Minnesota. See also LATINO/LATINA LITERATURE.

Minnesota poetry is well reflected in the works of Thomas McGrath, particularly his *Letter to an Imaginary Friend* (1962, 1970, 1985, and 1997); Robert Bly, with his National Book Award winner *The Light around the Body* (1967); and John Berryman, with his *Dream Songs* (1969) and *Collected Poems, 1937–1971*, edited by Charles Thornbury (1989).

Dramatist August Wilson has captured Midwestern life and problems in theatrical productions that include his Pulitzer Prize–winning *Fences* (1986) and *The Piano Lesson* (1990).

Sigurd F. Olson's *The Singing Wilderness* (1956) and Eric Sevareid's *Canoeing with the Cree* (1935) reflect excellent Minnesota nature writing and, more broadly, creative nonfiction.

Clifford D. Simak is Minnesota's premier science-fiction and fantasy writer; his award-winning works include his novelette *The Big Front Yard* (1958); his novel *Way Station* (1963); and his short story "Grotto of the Dancing Deer" (1980). Mystery and detective fiction can be experienced in *In the Lake of the Woods* (1995) by Tim O'Brien and *Rules of Prey* (1989) and *Field of Prey* (2014) by John Sandford.

Anthologies of Minnesota writing have appeared at intervals over the past century and a half. An early collection is *The Poets and Poetry of Minnesota* (1864), edited by Harriet N. K. Arnold. Twentieth-century volumes of poetry include *Minnesota Verse: An Anthology* (1934), edited by Maude Colgrove Schilplin; and *Minnesota Skyline: Anthology of Poems about Minnesota* (1944), edited by Carmen Nelson Richards. Two later anthologies are *To Sing along the Way: Minnesota Women Poets from Pre-territorial Days to the Present* (2006), edited by Joyce Sutphen and others; and *Where One Voice Ends Another Begins: 150 Years of Minnesota Poetry* (2007), edited by Robert Hedin.

Two collections of short memoirs are *Minnesota Writers: A Collection of Autobiographical Stories* (1961), edited by Carmen Nelson Richards; and *Growing Up in Minnesota: Ten Writers Remember Their Childhoods* (1976), edited by Chester G. Anderson, which features Bly, Le Sueur, and Vizenor. Other prose anthologies include *The Minnesota Experience* (1979) and *The North Country Reader: Classic Stories by Minnesota Writers* (2000), both edited by Jean Ervin.

FURTHER READING:

Biographies and Bibliographies: The best sources for biographies of Minnesota authors are in need of updating and expansion. The seminal work, *Minnesota Writers: A Collection of Autobiographical Stories by Minnesota Prose Writers*, edited by Carmen Nelson Richards (1891–1978), was published in 1961;

an earlier version, titled *Minnesota Writes*, appeared in 1945. Although this volume does not provide birth and death years for the authors, the biographies and commentaries are useful, and the appendix contains a detailed bibliography of authors by genre and interest area. Another monograph, *A Selected Bio-Bibliography: Minnesota Authors* (1958), produced by the Minnesota Statehood Centennial Commission, contains listings for some seven hundred authors, beginning with Snelling's *Tales of the Northwest*. Grace Lee Nute's *A History of Minnesota Books and Authors* (1958) is useful, as is *Twenty-Six Minnesota Writers* (1995) edited by Emilio DeGrazia (b. 1941) and Monica DeGrazia (b. 1956), which contains brief biographies; *25 Minnesota Poets* (1974), edited by Seymour Yesner (1925–2009), and *Minnesota Writes: Poetry* (1987), edited by Jim Moore and Cary Waterman, employ a similar format. *Minnesota's Literary Visitors* (1993) by John T(heodore) Flanagan (1906–1996) depicts Minnesota as literary sojourners found it between 1838 and 1890.

A Guide to Minnesota Writers (1987) by Ron Barron (b. 1940) offers portraits of forty representative writers; a later edition with the same title (1993) presents sixty additional entries, including bibliographies, "Representative Works," and "Biographical and Critical Sources" for each author. The Minnesota Author Biographies Project, a collaboration among the Minnesota Historical Society, Metronet, and the Minnesota Center for the Book, has a pilot online database that provides biographical sketches of thirty-six Minnesota authors; the bibliography of significant works that accompanies each entry lists both print and web-based sources of additional information.

Two essays are useful, though dated: John T. Flanagan's "Some Minnesota Fiction, 1920–1950," *Minnesota History* 31.3 (September 1950): 145–47, and "These Books on Our Shelves: Minnesota Prose Writers" by J. Ruth Stenerson (1924–2002), *Minnesota English Journal* 11.2 (Fall 1975): 20–29. The most comprehensive study of fiction written by early Minnesota settlers is a master's thesis, "Fact and Fiction: Historical Fiction Set in Pioneer Minnesota" (University of Minnesota, 2004), by Leslie J. Czechowski (b. 1948). This project is a scholarly compendium of novels depicting life on the frontier and interactions with Indians; the final chapter focuses extensively on Vilhelm Moberg's *Unto a Good Land* and Frederick Manfred's *Scarlet Plume*.

Libraries, Archives, and Other Repositories: Minnesota literary collections and manuscripts exist in two major repositories: the University of Minnesota Libraries system and the Minnesota Historical Society. At the University of Minnesota, most research materials are located in the Elmer L. Andersen Library, which houses the Hess Collection, an archive of popular literature of the nineteenth and twentieth centuries that includes the largest library collection of dime novels in the United States. The collection comprises more than 50,000 related items, such as story papers, Big Little Books, dime novels, series books, early paperbacks, and comic books; more than 7,000 of the dime novels have been microfilmed. The story papers in this collection include a fifteen-year run of *Golden Days* and a seven-year run of *Good News*. Titles in the Dave Fearless and Nat Ridley series are also part of the collection, as well as dime-novel adaptations by Edward Stratemeyer (1862–1930). In 1986 the university acquired a similar archive, the Denis R. Rogers / Edward S. Ellis Collection, with fifty-seven different periodicals and dime novels in over sixty different series. The Kerlan Collection, internationally recognized, contains over 100,000 children's books, manuscripts, and artworks.

The Andersen Horticultural Library at the Minnesota Landscape Arboretum includes books and periodicals on horticulture, botany, natural history, and landscape architecture, including one of the largest collections of seed and nursery catalogs in the country, dating from the early 1800s. The Charles Babbage Institute preserves and interprets the history of information technology and computing worldwide. The Immigration History Research Center locates, collects, and preserves the records of ethnic groups that settled in Minnesota but originated in Europe and the Near East. The James Ford Bell Library's collection of rare books, maps, and manuscripts from 1400 to 1800 documents the expansion of Europe relating to international trade. See also ARCHITECTURE.

The Manuscripts Division of the University of Minnesota comprises several collections. The Literary Manuscripts Collection contains personal papers of Minnesota authors and poets, as well as a poster collection from World War I and World War II. The Performing Arts Archives traces the history of professional and amateur performing arts groups, including the Minnesota Orchestra, the Guthrie Theater, and the Minnesota Dance Theatre The Northwest Architectural Archives preserves the records of architects, engineers, and contractors from the Minnesota region. The Social Welfare History Archives holds documents from voluntary-sector social service and social reform organizations, as well as the personal papers of leaders in the field; within this archive is the Upper Midwest Jewish Archives, the most important collection of the Jewish Historical Society of the Upper Midwest. The Special Collections and Rare Books division is the university's general repository for items needing special attention because of age, value, or fragility. Under this aegis is the Archie Givens Sr. Collection, one of the country's richest collections of African American literature, biography, social science, art, and manuscripts; the Sherlock Holmes Collections; and the Tell G. Dahllof Collection of Swedish Americana.

The Minnesota Historical Society's Library offers documentation about the state, its people, and its culture and a collection of 500,000 volumes, particularly strong in early Minnesota imprints, histories of Minnesota organizations and families, and atlases and plat books. This library contains the largest collection in the world of Minnesota fiction and works from local private presses. All told, the society owns nearly 8,000 separate manuscript collections, which occupy over 38,000 cubic feet of storage space.

JILL BARNUM UNIVERSITY OF MINNESOTA–TWIN CITIES

MIRROR.
See *Reedy's Mirror*

MISSOURI
Missouri was admitted to the Union on August 10, 1821, as the twenty-fourth state. Before statehood it was, in succession, part of Louisiana Territory (1803–1812) and of Missouri Territory (1812–1821).
Area: 69,707 square miles
Land: 68,742 square miles
Water: 965 square miles
Population (2010 census): 5,987,580
OVERVIEW: Missouri has a long precolonial, colonial, and territorial past that lends a particular flavor to its current population and culture. Before European settlement, Native Americans (see NATIVE AMERICAN LITERATURE and NATIVE AMERICANS AS DEPICTED IN MIDWESTERN LITERATURE) found a habitable location at the point where the Ohio and Missouri Rivers join the Mississippi. The area then was explored and settled by the French, ceded to the Spanish, returned briefly to French rule, and finally acquired by the United States. For most of the eighteenth century the area that encompasses Missouri today was known as the ILLINOIS Country. After 1770, when it came under Spanish control, it was called both Spanish Illinois and Upper Louisiana. After the Louisiana Purchase in 1803, the area was known as the Territory of Louisiana until 1812, when it was renamed Missouri Territory to distinguish it from the newly admitted state of Louisiana.

Missouri has been a borderland where Native Americans, white Europeans, African slaves, free blacks, and their descendants interacted. During its frontier period Missouri was a starting point for westward migration. Its admission to the Union was calculated to maintain a balance between free and slaveholding states; Missouri's status as a slaveholding state affected immigra-

JEFFERSON CITY

© Karen Greasley, 2014

tion to the state, as well as the distribution of population within the state.

Missouri has been popularly regarded in two ways. Its location near the center of the nation has led it to be called the most American of American states and the most Midwestern of Midwestern states; alternatively, it is seen as a state consisting of distinct regions, each of which contributes its own characteristics to Missouri culture.

In themes, subjects, and literary movements, Missouri literature generally follows the nation, but two intellectual interests differentiate the state. Journalism has been particularly central to Missouri cultural life; from the pioneer period through the twenty-first century, journalists have written, professionally and recreationally, in all literary genres, promoting political views and literary movements. Rivalries between newspapers, individual editors or publishers, and cities have marked the state. Ethnic immigrants have achieved national reputations, and female and minority editors or journalists have made their mark in print, as well as in broadcasting.

Interest in FOLKLORE and regional history also sets Missouri apart. Many residents of the Ozarks became experts in local stories and history, writing down and recording tales and songs. The existence of organizations such as the Missouri Folklore Society and Southwest Missouri State University's Center for Ozarks Studies attests to general and professional interest in folklore.

HISTORY AND SIGNIFICANCE:

Exploration and Travel: The first European to set foot in what is now Missouri was probably the Spaniard Hernando De Soto (ca. 1498–1542), who briefly passed through extreme southeastern Missouri in 1541 during his three-year expedition. The French explorers Father Jacques Marquette (1637–1675), a Jesuit, and Louis Joliet (1645–1700) descended the Mississippi River in 1673 as far as Arkansas; and in 1682 René-Robert Cavelier, Sieur de La Salle (1643–1687), explored the Mississippi to the Gulf of Mexico. Although both groups observed the Missouri littoral, neither ventured farther into the interior.

Missouri, part of the Louisiana Purchase of 1803, was more thoroughly explored by

successive American expeditions that produced detailed travel narratives. The Lewis and Clark expedition of 1804–1806, commissioned by President Thomas Jefferson, traveled the Missouri River at the beginning of the journey and again on its return. The official report by Meriwether Lewis (1774–1809) and William Clark (1770–1838), *History of the Expedition under the Command of Captains Lewis and Clark, to the Sources of the Missouri, Thence across the Rocky Mountains and down the River Columbia to the Pacific Ocean* (1814), followed at least four earlier, briefer accounts published from 1806 to 1809. Another member of the expedition, Patrick Gass (1771–1870), contributed his own narrative: *A Journal of the Voyages and Travels of a Corps of Discovery, under the Command of Capt. Lewis and Capt. Clarke* [*sic*] . . . (1807).

During 1806 Zebulon Montgomery Pike (1779–1813) traveled up the Missouri River from ST. LOUIS to the Osage River. The report of this trip is included in his *An Account of Expeditions to the Sources of the Mississippi . . . during the Years 1805, 1806, and 1807 . . .* (1810). In 1818 HENRY ROWE SCHOOLCRAFT (1793–1864) and a companion embarked on a geological and topographic survey of Missouri and Arkansas, resulting in the book *A View of the Lead Mines of Missouri . . .* (1819), which identified an important mineralogical resource of the state. Major Stephen Harriman Long (1784–1864), an army topographic engineer, commanded a two-year geographic and ethnographic expedition to the West that traversed the entire state using the Missouri River. Although Long did not write the formal report of this journey, one of his party, Edwin James (1797–1861), compiled an important narrative using Long's notes and diaries. The *Account of an Expedition from Pittsburgh to the Rocky Mountains, Performed in the Years 1819 and '20* was published in 1822–1823 with a separate portfolio of maps.

Timothy Flint (1780–1840) arrived in Missouri in 1816. His *Recollections of the Last Ten Years Passed in the Occasional Residences and Journeyings in the Valley of the Mississippi* (1826) reflects the environs and people of OHIO, Kentucky, and Missouri. Edmund Flagg (1815–1890), a teacher, lawyer, newspaper contributor and editor, diplomat, and government administrator, published a journal of his travels in Missouri and Illinois titled

The Far West: or, A Tour beyond the Mountains in two volumes in 1838. Flagg edited three St. Louis newspapers briefly at various times: the *St. Louis Evening Gazette,* the *St. Louis Times,* and the *St. Louis Daily Commercial Bulletin.*

British travelers were among Missouri's social-political observers. They included Thomas Ashe (1770–1835), who wrote *Travels in America, Performed in 1806, for the Purpose of Exploring the Rivers Alleghany, Monongahela, Ohio, and Mississippi, and Ascertaining the Produce and Condition of Their Banks and Vicinity* (1808); and William Faux with his 1823 volume *Memorable Days in America.*

Some gazetteers, guides, and manuals were not of literary importance but reflected the flow of immigration to the frontier. In 1797 Jedidiah Morse (1761–1826) mentioned what was then the West in his *The American Gazetteer.* Similar books multiplied thereafter. Samuel R. Brown (1775–1817) contributed *The Western Gazetteer* (1817). Robert Baird (1798–1863) contributed another early perspective in *View of the Valley of the Mississippi* (1834). Gottfried Duden (1789–1856), a German lawyer, came to the United States to find land for Germans to settle and reached St. Louis in 1824. His book, *Report of a Journey to the Western States of North America and a Residence of Several Years . . . Dealing with the Question of Emigration and Excess Population* (1829), written in the form of personal letters, influenced German immigration to Missouri in the 1830s. The *Gazetteer of the State of Missouri* (1837) by Alphonso Wetmore (1793–1849) included several entries by firsthand observers.

Captivity Narratives: Eliza Swan (fl. 1815) published her captivity experience, *An Affecting Account of the Tragical Death of Major Swan, and of the Captivity of Mrs. Swan and Infant Child, by the Savages in April Last . . .* (ca. 1815), which tells of the family's capture near St. Louis and their subsequent privations before their release. Another account, *Narrative of the Captivity and Sufferings of Mrs. Hannah Lewis, and Her Three Children, Who Were Taken Prisoners by the Indians, near St. Louis, on the 25th May, 1815 . . .* (1817), relates a heartbreaking denouement in which the mother and her eldest son escape but leave the other two children behind. Both these booklets consist of twenty-four pages and were issued by the same publisher, perhaps an indication of the formulaic nature of the genre, as well as of its popularity. A third captivity tale, *A Narrative of the Horrid Massacre by the Indians, of the Wife and Children of the Christian Hermit, a Resident of Missouri . . .* (1840), was published in St. Louis. It is, however, quite similar to an earlier publication, *Narrative of the Massacre, by the Savages, of the Wife and Children of Thomas Baldwin . . .* (1835), whose events purportedly took place in Kentucky, in which names and some details have been altered. It is unlikely that the writer lived in Missouri, and the account itself is probably fictitious. See also CAPTIVITY NARRATIVES.

Fiction: Many early works of Missouri fiction focused on recording frontier descriptions and dynamics. One of the earliest Missouri novelists was Timothy Flint. His novel *George Mason, the Young Backwoodsman; or, Don't Give Up the Ship* (1829) was set in Mississippi. Flint also wrote *The Shoshonee Valley: A Romance* (1830). Elijah L. Jacobs and Forrest E. Wolverton, in their book *Missouri Writers: A Literary History of Missouri, 1780–1955* (1955), contend that the content of Flint's novel draws on autobiographical details from his time in Missouri. Edmund Flagg's literary work was well known during his lifetime and includes such historical novels as *The Howard Queen, a Romance of History* (1848). Alphonso Wetmore's *Gazetteer of the State of Missouri* provided short stories conveying the spirit and dialect of the Missouri frontier. Nathaniel Beverley Tucker (1784–1851) was born in Virginia and came to Missouri in 1815 to work as a judge. One of his novels, *George Balcombe* (1836), is set in Missouri and Virginia and is a story of frontier life; it was declared to be "the best American novel" in a review by Edgar Allan Poe published in the January 1837 issue of *Southern Literary Messenger* (50). The novel begins on the Missouri prairie with an heir in pursuit of a misplaced or stolen will. Eventually, the situation faces final judgment in Virginia, and the money is returned to the rightful legatees.

Popular novelist and successful editor John Beauchamp Jones (1810–1866) wrote the best-selling *Wild Western Scenes: A Narrative of Adventures in the Western Wilderness, Forty Years Ago* (1841), a minor frontier classic because of its portrayal of local environments and humorous, colorful characters. *The Western Merchant: A Narrative* (1849), the only one of his novels written under the pseudonym Luke Shortfield, is based on Jones's life as a New Franklin and Arrow Rock storekeeper in the 1830s. Tucker and Jones wrote additional novels addressing regional conflicts that foreshadowed issues leading to the Civil War.

Collections of fictional and humorous tales also characterized early Missouri fiction. *The Drama in Pokerville* (1847) by Joseph M. Field (1810–1856) draws on small-town stories and tall tales for much of its content. John S. Robb (ca. 1813–1856), a St. Louis journalist who used the pseudonym Solitaire, wrote a collection of humorous frontier tales titled *Streaks of Squatter Life, and Far Western Scenes* (1847), many of which were set in Missouri.

Many early works of fiction about Missouri were published in cities in the eastern United States. Records show that the earliest fictional work published in Missouri was originally in German; Heinrich von Zschokke's *Die Rose von Disentis* (1846) took place in Europe. The first English-language novel published in Missouri appeared the following year. *Taos, a Romance of the Massacre, Founded upon the Terrible Events of January and February, 1847, in Taos Valley* (1847), was written by Joseph M. Field under the pseudonym Everpoint; it tells of the tragedy when Mexicans and Indians attempted to overthrow American leadership in New Mexico, resulting in the death of Charles Bent, a prominent former St. Louis resident. The first novel published in St. Louis by a St. Louis author was *The Unknown: A Prize Tale* (1849) by attorney Pierce C. Grace; it focused more on English life than on that in Missouri and was set in London and Charleston.

The Mysteries of St. Louis (1852) by Heinrich Börnstein (1805–1892), a German author and journalist, originally published serially in German as *Die Geheimnisse von St. Louis* in 1851, was set in the region but was considered scandalous for its harsh depiction of Catholicism. Women writers also began to publish in St. Louis in the 1850s, among them Anne T(uttle) J(ones) Bullard (1808–1896) and Sallie Rochester Ford (1828–1910);

Mark Twain's boyhood home, Hannibal, Missouri, 1902.
Image courtesy of the Library of Congress

their novels generally take place outside the region and attempt to convey moral and religious teachings.

Production of fiction diminished in Missouri during the Civil War but regained prominence with the work of SAMUEL LANGHORNE CLEMENS (1835–1910), writing as Mark Twain. One of the most famous Missouri writers, Twain was born in Florida, Missouri, and grew up in Hannibal. Although Twain's life took him to both sides of the United States, as well as abroad, he returned to the Missouri region in the late 1850s to train as a riverboat captain along the Mississippi River and later in his life as he collected material for *Life on the Mississippi* (1883). Although Twain produced a large body of work, Missouri appears most prominently in *The Adventures of Tom Sawyer* (1876), *ADVENTURES OF HUCKLEBERRY FINN* (1884, 1885), and *Pudd'nhead Wilson: A Tale* (1894), later expanded and republished as *The Tragedy of Pudd'nhead Wilson, and the Comedy of Those Extraordinary Twins* (1894). This series of novels focuses on life along the Mississippi and coincides with the expansion of literacy in Missouri.

Twain's Missouri novels were heavily based on his childhood. All three take place in pre–Civil War Missouri and develop ideas related to small-town life, the circumstances of slavery, and the culture and atmosphere along the Mississippi River. *Adventures of Huckleberry Finn*, in particular, solidified Twain's status in American literature and was admired by prominent twentieth-century writers, including SHER-WOOD ANDERSON (1876–1941), ERNEST (MILLER) HEMINGWAY (1899–1961), and William Faulkner (1897–1962).

For Missouri writers, as well as those from across the Midwest, the SMALL TOWN was increasingly a focal point of their novels. One example is *The Story of a Country Town* (1883) by EDGAR WATSON HOWE (1853–1937). Howe was born in INDIANA; when he was a young child, his family moved to Harrison County, Missouri. *The Story of a Country Town* critiques the small-town life of Fairview and Twin Mounds, Missouri, using characters and scenarios to convey a sense of unhappiness rather than a romanticized treatment of an idyllic Midwestern rural community.

Regional characteristics and dialect became increasingly prevalent in Missouri fiction, particularly in descriptions of life in the Ozark Mountains. The Reverend John B. Monteith (1833–1918) came to St. Louis in 1866 to organize a church and continued to live in the state until his death. During a period of ill health around 1870, he spent time on a farm in Iron Mountain, Missouri; it provided him with insight into the traditions and culture in the southern part of the state. He later wrote *Parson Brooks, a Plump Powerful Hardshell* (1884), an entertaining novel about a former Union soldier who relocates to southern Missouri and encounters Parson Brooks and his family, who are tenants on a portion of his farm. The volume reproduces the character and dialect of the Ozark region. Interest in the Ozark region continued in books such as *The Ozark Post Office* (1899) by John Henton Carter (1832–1910) and, less successfully, *The Little Fiddler of the Ozarks* (1913) by John Breckenridge Ellis (1870–1956), a Missouri writer known for writing over twenty books, mainly historical romances. He also wrote juvenile fiction.

Kentucky-born James Newton Bassett (1849–1925) moved to Missouri as a child, eventually working as an engineer and surveyor and undertaking some scientific study. He also wrote three novels with a strong foundation in Missouri life. *At You-All's House* (1898) depicts Missouri life and landscapes, *As the Light Led* (1900) addresses religious differences, and *Sweetbrier and Thistledown* (1902) contrasts city and rural life.

Kate Chopin (1850–1904), a native of St. Louis, moved to Louisiana after she married Oscar Chopin, a New Orleans cotton broker. Although Chopin set most of her fiction in Louisiana locales, she began publishing her work only after she moved back to St. Louis after the death of her husband. She drew on her experience as a Midwestern outsider trying to come to terms with the South in her benchmark novel of female emancipation, *The Awakening* (1899), in which the protagonist, Edna Pontellier, a native of Kentucky, comes to grief in part because she fails to understand Creole customs. Her first novel, *At Fault* (1890), is set partly in St. Louis and features several characters from that city who visit Louisiana; Chopin exploits the humor resulting from their fish-out-of-water status. St. Louis also features prominently in a number of her short stories, eleven of which were published in St. Louis periodicals.

The turn of the twentieth century continued to produce Missouri writers drawn to historical fiction. Winston Churchill (1871–1947), born and raised in St. Louis, became a popular novelist of historical fiction, although he did not write much about the region, and his career ultimately took him outside the state. His novel *Richard Carvel* (1899), which treats the American colonial period through the Revolution, was extremely popular at the time it was published. Churchill drew on St. Louis as a site in his novel *The Crisis* (1901), which depicted the period just before, during, and after the Civil War. St. Louis native Roswell Martin Field (1851–1919), brother of EUGENE FIELD (SR.) (1850–1895), also wrote several works of fiction, although many of them drew on his travels and experiences outside the region. His one story collection qualifying as Missouri regional fiction, *In Sunflower Land: Stories of God's Own Country* (1892), used elements of farm and village life in KANSAS and Missouri and incorporated humor.

Journalist Eugene P. Lyle Jr. (1873–1961) was born in Texas but spent much of his childhood in KANSAS CITY; he wrote a number of short stories and novels later in his career. His most notable historical novel concerning the region was *The Missourian* (1905). The main character in the novel, Din Driscoll, is a soldier in General Shelby's army on his way to Mexico as part of an effort to avoid surrendering after the Civil War.

Missouri writers continued their exploration of local life, and much of it interested the burgeoning Hollywood movie industry. HAROLD BELL WRIGHT (1872–1944) was not a native Missouri writer, but the time he spent living in the Ozark Mountains for his health and the interaction he had with locals while preaching there significantly influenced his writing. His best-known novel, *The Shepherd of the Hills* (1907), takes place just outside Branson, Missouri, and follows a character from the city as he seeks refuge among the people of the Ozark hill country. Although the novel contains a definite religious tone, it was highly popular and was adapted for FILM several times during the first half of the twentieth century, including a 1941 version starring John Wayne.

The Ozarks played a significant role in some of the novels of ROSE WILDER LANE (1886–1968) as well. The daughter of LAURA INGALLS WILDER (1867–1957), Lane moved to Mansfield, Missouri, with her parents while she was a child and integrated her experiences in the region into some of her fiction. Her novels *Hill-Billy* (1925) and *Cindy: A Romance of the Ozarks* (1928) are set in the Ozark hill country and use aspects of local dialect. In *The Old Home Town* (1935) Lane explored this same region through the perspective of a young girl much like herself in a series of short stories centered on a pre–World War I Ozark town.

The Missouri-based work of HOMER CROY (1883–1965) belongs to the same REVOLT FROM THE VILLAGE tradition that characterized the work of other Midwestern writers such as Sherwood Anderson and (HARRY) SINCLAIR LEWIS (1885–1951). Born and raised on a farm near Maryville, Missouri, Croy attended the University of Missouri before embarking on a career as a journalist. His career took him far away from his Missouri upbringing, but he returned to it in some of his fiction. In particular, his two novels, *West of the Water Tower* (1923) and *R.F.D. No. 3* (1924), take place in the fictional town of Junction City, Missouri. *West of the Water Tower* was originally published anonymously because its serious treatment of small-town life clashed with the reputation Croy had established as a humorist. A later novel, *They Had to See Paris* (1926), describes a Missouri family in Europe. Several of his works, including *West of the Water Tower* and *They Had to See Paris,* were made into motion pictures; the latter starred Will Rogers (1879–1935) in his first speaking film role.

Writer (Heinrich Hauer) HENRY BELLAMANN (1882–1945) brought aspects of his hometown of Fulton, Missouri, into his novels *Kings Row* (1940) and *Parris Mitchell of Kings Row* (1948). Bellamann employed the small fictional town of Kings Row to demonstrate the problems and issues that often underlie the pristine, idyllic image that many small towns project. The follow-up novel, *Parris Mitchell of Kings Row,* finished by Bellamann's wife after his death, carries the narrative through World War I. *Kings Row* was made into an Oscar-nominated motion picture in 1942, featuring a character played by future American president Ronald Reagan, and in the 1950s was further adapted for a television series that ran for seven episodes.

Screenwriter and short-story writer Sally Benson (1897–1972) was born in St. Louis; she published a number of stories, including many in the *New Yorker.* Several of these stories were collected in *Meet Me in St. Louis* (1942). They offer monthly glimpses of a St. Louis family before the 1904 World's Fair and led to a successful Hollywood film with the same title in 1944.

Examining the small town a bit more sympathetically and emphasizing the good were writers such Elizabeth Gasporotti (1897–1983) of Moberly, Missouri, writing under her maiden name, Elizabeth Seifert. She evokes the life of a small-farming-town doctor in *Young Doctor Galahad* (1938), winner of the Dodd, Mead–*Redbook* $10,000 novel contest. Prolific Missouri novelist Louise Platt Hauck (1883–1943) moved to the state as a child and wrote novels and stories while raising a family. Among her many works, *Missouri Yesterdays: Stories of the Romantic Days of Missouri* (1920) and *Wild Grape: A Novel of the Ozarks* (1931) exemplify her borrowing from the people of the region for her fiction.

FANNIE HURST (1885–1968) was among the successful writers who were born or lived in the state but did not use that biographical or regional material significantly in their writing. The St. Louis of her childhood and young adulthood does appear in some of her short stories and novels, such as *Hallelujah* (1944), a novel partially reflecting the life of prominent St. Louis publisher WILLIAM MARION REEDY (1862–1920). However, her novels and stories also drew from other places, including Ohio and New York City. Josephine Winslow Johnson (1910–1990) anchored some of her fiction in details from her Missouri childhood, but her career took her to other regions as well. Her first novel, *Now in November* (1934), the story of a family devastated by the Great Depression, was written while Johnson was still in Missouri and won a Pulitzer Prize in 1935.

(JOHN WESLEY) "JACK" CONROY (1898–1990) was born in Monkey Nest, a coal-mining camp near Moberly in northern Missouri. Growing up among the mining community had a profound effect on Conroy and shaped both his politics and his writing. He based his novels *The Disinherited* (1933) and *A World to Win* (1935) on his experiences and observations as a member of an itinerant working class trying to stay employed during the struggles of the Great Depression. As one involved in the Midwestern radical movement of writers, Conroy edited a socialist literary bimonthly magazine, the *Anvil* (1933–1935), which published proletarian short fiction. He also took part in the Missouri Writers' Project in the 1930s and worked to record the literary history of the state.

MACKINLAY KANTOR (1904–1977) was originally from IOWA and never lived in Missouri, but he did travel throughout the state. Kantor's influence on Missouri literature is most notable in his portrayal of a Missouri dog in *The Voice of Bugle Ann* (1935). This novel takes place in the Ozark Mountains, describes fox hunting, and demonstrates the love between a man and his dog. *The Daughter of Bugle Ann* (1953) continues where the first novel ended.

Both EDWARD DAHLBERG (1900–1977) and CLYDE BRION DAVIS (1894–1962) were born outside the state but were raised in KANSAS CITY and Chillecothe, respectively. Dahlberg brought the struggles he experienced as a child in Kansas City into his first novel, *Bottom Dogs* (1929). The last third of Davis's *The Great American Novel* (1938), about a newspaperman, takes place in Kansas City, and his later work *The Big Pink Kite* (1960) follows a small-town Missouri man whose life becomes overwhelmed by tragedy and circumstance.

Famed counterculture writer WILLIAM S(EWARD) BURROUGHS (1914–1977) was born in St. Louis, although his birthplace never significantly factored into his fiction. Among his books are *Junkie* (1953) and *Naked Lunch* (1959, 1962).

EVANS(HELBY) CONNELL JR. (1924–2013) was born in Kansas City, Missouri, and derived many of his characters and locales from the Midwest. His *Mrs. Bridge* (1959) and the companion novel *Mr. Bridge* (1969) develop the relationship of an upper-middle-class couple living in a Kansas City suburb. He captured both benefits and flaws within this context and explored how they affect the characters. Connell also used Midwestern settings in many of his short stories.

Ntozake Shange (b. 1948) lived in St. Louis for several years as a child, and those experiences shape her novel *Betsey Brown* (1985). In it, an African American seventh grader, her family, and her friends adapt to life in the often tumultuous world of St. Louis during the late 1950s and 1960s.

The fiction of Jonis Agee (b. 1943) spotlights various parts of the Midwest, including her home state of NEBRASKA, Iowa, MINNESOTA, and the boot heel of Missouri. Set in a tiny town on the Mississippi, *The River Wife* (2007) follows for over a century the lives of women touched by a fur-trader, innkeeper, and river pirate and his grandson. Agee explores themes of love, loyalty, betrayal, and tragedy among earthquakes and other upheavals along the river. Another writer born in Nebraska, Ron Hansen (b. 1947), has produced a variety of fiction and nonfiction. His historical novel *The Assassination of Jesse James by the Coward Robert Ford* (1983), focusing on Missouri native Jesse (Woodson) James (1847–1882), deals with love and obsession and was released as a film in 2007. *She Loves Me Not* (2012), a collection of Hansen's short stories, uses Missouri and other Midwestern settings.

Jonathan Franzen (b. 1959) grew up in Webster Groves, a suburb of St. Louis, and two of his novels take place in that area: *The Twenty-Seventh City* (1988) in St. Louis and *The Corrections* (2001) in a Midwestern city, "St. Jude," a suburb of St. Louis. Franzen's fiction probes family relationships, often in dysfunctional situations; *Freedom* (2010), however, focuses on a St. Paul, Minnesota, family. His memoir, *The Discomfort Zone: A Personal History* (2006), treats his childhood and adolescence in Webster Groves and observes the life of his family and his own development.

Most of the fiction of Daniel Woodrell (b. 1953) deals with crime in the Ozarks in a dark mode he calls "country noir," a term taken from his 1996 book *Give Us a Kiss: A Country Noir. Woe to Live On* (1987) became the film *Ride with the Devil* (1999); *Winter's Bone* (2006), a somewhat lighter novel, was produced as a film in 2010. *The Maid's Version* (2013) is based on a 1920s explosion in an Ozark dance hall.

The first novel of Whitney Terrell (b. 1967), *The Huntsman* (2001), explores racial issues, past and present, in his hometown, Kansas City. *The King of Kings County* (2005) traces the effects produced by a greedy developer on a Kansas City suburb and the consequent white flight from the city.

Popular Literature:

Dime Novels: Missouri was a frequent locale of DIME NOVELS published in the second half of the nineteenth century. Many were set in St. Louis or Independence, where fur traders, explorers, or wagon-train pioneers began their journeys farther west. *Mountain Max; or, Nick Whiffles on the Border: A Tale of the Bushwhackers in Missouri* (1859) by John Hovey Robinson (1820–1867) is an early Missouri dime novel that uses the Ozark Mountains as its background.

Joseph E. Badger Jr. (1848–1909) was one of the most prolific dime-novel authors; he placed no fewer than nine novels in Missouri. These include *The Outlaw Ranger; or, The Old Hunter's Last Trail: A Romance of the Missouri Settlements* (1872), *The Wood King; or, Daniel Boone's Last Trail: A Romance of the Osage Country* (1873), *Sweet William, the Trapper Detective; or, The Chief of the Crimson Clan* (1882), and *Big Bandy, the Brigadier of Brim-*stone Butte; or, The Secrets of the Hollow Hill* (1890).

The bitter and bloody conflict between Union and Confederate supporters in Civil War Missouri was the subject of three dime novels. Two companion stories by the pseudonymous Lieut.-Col. Hazeltine are *The Border Spy; or, The Beautiful Captive of the Rebel Camp: A Story of the War* (1863) and *The Prisoner of the Mill; or, Captain Hayward's "Body Guard"* (1864). Another unknown author, writing as Stephen Holmes Jr., wrote *The Guerrillas of the Osage; or, The Price of Loyalty on the Border* (1864).

Mystery and Detective Fiction: Missouri has long been a locale of MYSTERY AND DETECTIVE FICTION, which has used both its rural scenes and its larger cities, particularly St. Louis and Kansas City. Among Mark Twain's later writings were a few in this genre. In *Pudd'nhead Wilson* (1894) the title character, a young lawyer, comes to Dawson's Landing, a Missouri village on the Mississippi River. Here, aided by his hobby, collecting fingerprints, Wilson is able to exonerate his clients, who were being tried for a murder they did not commit. Twain's use of this now-common criminologist's tool was among the first in fiction, anticipating Sherlock Holmes by nine years. The 1896 novella *Tom Sawyer, Detective* takes place the year after the events recounted in *Adventures of Huckleberry Finn*. The story involves Tom and Huck traveling down the Mississippi River from Hannibal to Arkansas. There they save their uncle Silas from a murder charge and recover a pair of diamonds stolen in St. Louis. *Huckleberry Finn* also uses plot elements seen in mystery fiction. In chapter 7 Huck kills a pig and uses its blood and carcass to fake his own death. In chapter 9 Huck and Jim encounter the body of a man in a derelict house; he is later revealed to be Huck's Pap, but the murder plot is not developed, and the perpetrator is not identified.

Other nineteenth-century mystery novels include *Joshua Humble: A Tale of Old St. Louis* (1899) by Edgar Rice Beach (1841–1930), a convoluted story about the murder of a millionaire and the fraudulent business dealings in the city uncovered by the subsequent investigation. One number of a pulp-novel series featuring the outlaw James

Brothers and the Dalton Boys is *Frank James in St. Louis; or, The Mysteries of a Great City* (1898) by the pseudonymous W. B. Lawson; in it Frank James rescues a young woman from the clutches of a Pinkerton agent who has been hired to return her to her abusive father.

St. Louis has served as the locale of many other mysteries. Silas Bent (1882–1945) used his experiences as a *St. Louis Post-Dispatch* reporter in *Buchanan of "The Press"* (1932). *Death Makes a Merry Widow* (1938) by Robert George Dean (1904–1989) exemplifies hard-boiled detective fiction. There a pair of private investigators tries to prove the innocence of their client, who has been charged with murder. *Murder's Web* (1950) by St. Louis resident Dorothy Dunn (b. 1913) features a compelling murder mystery, as well as a midcentury portrait of that city. Richard Deming (1915–1983), writing under the pseudonym Max Franklin, demonstrated his fondness for St. Louis in the well-plotted *Justice Has No Sword* (1953), an intriguing story of police investigating gang killings and ultimately uncovering a criminal syndicate.

The Twenty-Seventh City (1988), the ambitious first novel by Jonathan Franzen, is among the later St. Louis–based crime novels; it deals with a female police chief from Mumbai, India. Robert J. Randisi (b. 1951) sets his Joe Keough private detective series in St. Louis, starting with *In the Shadow of the Arch* (1998); others in that series include *Blood on the Arch* (2000) and *Blood of Angels* (2004). Based at a St. Louis hospital, trauma nurse Molly Burke investigates mysterious deaths in *Bad Medicine* (1995) and *Head Games* (2004) by Eileen Dreyer (b. 1952), who has also written *If Looks Could Kill* (2012), in which a celebrated author becomes involved in a series of murders in a small Missouri town. Alo Nudger, the detective in the long-running series of John Lutz (b. 1939), is featured in eight novels and one collection of short stories set in St. Louis, including *Nightlines* (1985) and *Death by Jury* (1995).

Laurell K. Hamilton (b. 1963) has created an alternate universe in which a St. Louis federal marshal, Anita Blake, is empowered to hunt vampires, reanimate zombies, and investigate paranormal murders for the police. This series, beginning with *Guilty Pleasures* (1993), now encompasses twenty-five titles with the publication of *Kiss the Dead* (2012); *Affliction* (2013); *Dancing*, a novella (2013); Jason, a novella (2014); and *Dead Ice* (2015). In *Hanging Curve* (1999), a Mickey Rawlings mystery by Troy Soos (b. 1957), the baseball detective finds himself playing with the St. Louis Browns during the 1922 season when he becomes involved with murder and racial tensions. The investigation of the killing of two police officers leads to a methamphetamine ring in *The Betrayers* (2007) by James Patrick Hunt (b. 1964) in his series featuring St. Louis homicide detective George Hastings.

Despite their relatively similar populations, fewer mysteries have been set in Kansas City than in St. Louis.. *Federal Bullets* (1936) by George F. Eliot (1894–1971) is an early mystery that takes place partly in Kansas City. The story of a psychopath who murders two women in Paris and Kansas City is told in *The Accomplice* (1947) by Matthew Head, the pseudonym of John Edwin Canaday (1907–1985). Two private investigators employed by the Hargrave Detective Agency office in Kansas City, John Roscoe (1921–1983) and Michael Ruso, turned their experiences into five novels featuring their fictional detective, Johnny April, written under the joint pseudonym Mike Roscoe. Three of these are set in Kansas City: *Death Is a Round Black Ball* (1952), *Riddle Me This* (1952), and *One Tear for My Grave* (1955).

Another series describing Kansas City locales in detail includes *Hot Wire* (1989), *Blind Spot* (1991), and *Caught Looking* (1992) by Randy Russell; all concern a former car thief who has run afoul of the local Kansas City mob and law-enforcement officials. Lou Jane Temple (b. 1944) has created an edgy protagonist in Heaven Lee, a Kansas City chef and master caterer who finds herself caught up in a number of murders in *Death by Rhubarb* (1996), *A Stiff Risotto* (1997), and *Death Is Semisweet* (2002).

Rural and small-town Missouri are also venues of mystery and detective fiction. The southern Missouri Ozark region is a favorite because of its topographic beauty and inhabitants, who are presented both as resourceful fonts of folk wisdom and as sinister hillbillies. Co-written by Vance Randolph (1892–1980) and the pseudonymous

Nancy Clemens, *The Camp-Meeting Murders* (1936) occurs in an Ozark mountain village. A large country house in the Ozarks is the scene of *Remind Me to Forget* (1942) by Carolyn Byrd Dawson (1905–1987).

Ozark native Daniel Woodrell uses the area as an evocative setting in his *Give Us a Kiss* (1996) and *Tomato Red* (1998). Located in the Ozarks, Branson is the site of popular country music festivals used by at least three authors as scenes of mysteries, including Donald E. Westlake (1933–2008) in his *Baby, Would I Lie?* (1994), *Electric Country Roulette* (1996) by W. L. Ripley (b. 1952), and *Evil Harmony* (1996) by Kathryn Buckstaff (b. 1947).

Deeds Ill Done (1939) and *3 Blind Mice* (1942) by Missourian Adele Seifert (1891–1986) also have rural settings; the latter takes place on a Missouri homestead. Prolific mystery writer Frank Gruber (1904–1969) sets *The Hungry Dog* (1941) on a large Missouri estate that has passed to one of the protagonists on the death of his uncle. *Saint Louie Blues* (1992) by Jake Tanner, the joint pseudonym of Stephen Schermerhorn (1944–1993) and Laura Museo (b. 1949), shows the corrupting influence of illicit drug activity in a small town thirty miles from Kansas City; and W. L. Ripley in *Dreamsicle* (1993) tells of a hunter discovering a Missouri field full of marijuana that leads to the killing of the local sheriff.

Romance Novels: Many romance novels have featured Missouri locales. *Dreams to Keep* (1985) by LeAnn Lemberger (b. 1954), writing as Leigh Michaels, concerns a woman who hopes to rise to full partnership in a prestigious St. Louis architectural firm but has to be wary of relationships with men in the office. Phyllis Rossiter (1938–2007) explores the professional and personal life of a Missouri policewoman in *On the Scent of Danger* (1989). Rival radio personalities in a Kansas City station discover compelling affinities in *One Night* (1994) by Debbie Macomber (b. 1948). LaVyrle Spencer (b. 1943), in *Small Town Girl* (1997), shows how love comes to a famous country singer when she returns to Missouri to care for her mother.

Missouri resident Suzann Ledbetter (b. 1953) has written romantic mysteries featuring Hannah Garvey, the resident manager of an upscale Ozarks retirement community. They include *East of Peculiar* (2000), *South of Sanity* (2001), *North of Clever* (2001), *West of*

Bliss (2002), and *Halfway to Half Way* (2007). The four-book Missouri series by Dorothy Garlock (b. 1942) takes place in a fictional small town, Fertile, and follows a number of characters in the 1920s and 1930s; the works include *The Edge of Town* (2001), *High on a Hill* (2002), *A Place Called Rainwater* (2003), and *River Rising* (2006).

Some prolific Missouri romance writers use their state sparingly in their novels. Most of the more than one hundred romances by Janet Dailey (b. 1944) take place in the West; only *Show Me* (1976) and *Can't Say Goodbye* (2002) use Missouri locales. Like Dailey, Lori Copeland (b. 1941) prefers western settings for her nearly one hundred romance novels; *Avenging Angel* (1987), *Simple Gifts* (2007), and *The Christmas Lamp* (2009) are the Missouri exceptions.

Science Fiction: Science Fiction has not had a large presence in Missouri literature; however, the state did give birth to a significant twentieth-century science-fiction writer. Robert A. Heinlein (1907–1988), of Butler, Missouri, published dozens of novels and short-story collections, including *The Puppet Masters* (1951), *Starship Troopers* (1959), and *Stranger in a Strange Land* (1961). See SCIENCE FICTION AND FANTASY.

Children's and Young Adult Literature: Samuel L. Clemens created several books often considered works for children. Most notable are *The Adventures of Tom Sawyer, The Prince and the Pauper* (1881), and *Adventures of Huckleberry Finn*. In his preface to *The Adventures of Tom Sawyer*, Twain wrote:

Most of the adventures recorded in this book really occurred; one or two were experiences of my own, the rest of those of boys who were schoolmates of mine. Huck Finn is drawn from life: Tom Sawyer also but not from an individual—he is a combination of the characteristics of three boys whom I knew and therefore belongs to the composite order of architecture.

Adventures of Huckleberry Finn has drawn both praise and condemnation. Although *Huckleberry Finn* is a sequel to *Tom Sawyer*, Twain's writing there deals with much more than a boy's adventure. In *The Singular Mark Twain* (2003) Fred Kaplan details its early banning by a Connecticut library because of its coarse language and its treatment of slavery-related issues (210–11). *Adventures of Huckleberry Finn* rapidly came to be thought of as inappropriate for youth. In *Mr. Clemens and Mark Twain: A Biography* (1966) Justin Kaplan quotes Louisa May Alcott as saying, "If Mr. Clemens cannot think of something better to tell our pure-minded lads and lasses, . . . he had best stop writing for them" (268). Others, including Ernest Hemingway, praised it for its use of language, its writing style, and its honesty and declared it a great American novel. Although many books and films have provided sanitized editions of the *Huckleberry Finn* story, controversy continues to this day whether Clemens's book as originally written should be high school reading. In 2011 NewSouth Books released a version of *Adventures of Huckleberry Finn* that substitutes the word "slave" for Twain's usage to satisfy teachers who need those changes to make the book acceptable in their schools.

Also included in the list of Clemens's books for the young is the classic *Prince and the Pauper* (1881), a tale of two boys in the Tudor era. The story relates the boys' adventures and lessons when they trade places. Later Clemens wrote *Tom Sawyer, Detective* (1896) and *Tom Sawyer, Abroad* (1896). One year after the last of Twain's works discussed here appeared, John R. Musick (1849–1901) provided *Stories of Missouri* (1897), a collection of tales for children reflecting Missouri history.

Laura Ingalls Wilder was living on the Rocky Ridge Farm near Mansfield, Missouri, when she began writing the Little House series. Once a teacher and writer for an area newspaper, she was encouraged by her daughter, Rose Wilder Lane, an accomplished writer in her own right and a sounding board for her mother, to write about her life as a pioneer girl. Wilder's books include *Little House in the Big Woods* (1932), *Farmer Boy* (1933), *Little House on the Prairie* (1935), *On the Banks of Plum Creek* (1937), *By the Shores of Silver Lake* (1939), *The Long Winter* (1940), *Little Town on the Prairie* (1941), and *These Happy Golden Years* (1943).

Several contemporary Missouri writers for children and young adults have gained acclaim. David L(ee) Harrison (b. 1937) has written over seventy children's books, including fiction, nonfiction, poetry, and picture books: *The Book of Giant Stories* (1972), *When Cows Come Home* (1994), *Johnny Appleseed: My Story* (2001), *Dylan the Eagle-Hearted Chicken* (2002), *The Alligator in the Closet* (2003), *Pirates* (2008), *Paul Bunyan: My Story* (2008), and *Mammoth Bones and Broken Stones* (2010), a Christopher Award winner.

Vicki Grove (b. 1948) writes books for adolescents. They include *Rimwalkers* (1993), *The Starplace* (1993), *Reaching Dustin* (1998), *Destiny* (2000), and *Crystal Garden* (2001), a 2001 winner of the Midland Authors Award for Children's Fiction. Constance Levy (b. 1931) writes poetry for children, including *I'm Going to Pet a Worm Today, and Other Poems* (1991), *When Whales Exhale, and Other Poems* (1996), *A Crack in the Clouds, and Other Poems* (1998), and *Splash! Poems of Our Watery World* (2002), the winner of the 2003 Lee Bennett Hopkins Award at Pennsylvania State University. Riki (Lola Ricena) Lipe (b. 1934) writes books for middle school children. They include *The Secret of Ricena's Pond* (1991), *The Mystery at Ricena's Pond* (1998), and *Wonder What Would Happen If* (2001).

Judy Young (b. 1956) has written more than fifty well-illustrated children's poetry books. Among these are *S Is for Show Me: A Missouri Alphabet* (2001), *R Is for Rhyme: A Poetry Alphabet* (2006), *Lazy Days of Summer* (2007), *H Is for Hook: A Fishing Alphabet* (2008), *The Lucky Star* (2008), *Minnow and Rose* (2009), *The Missouri Reader* (2010), *The Hidden Bestiary of Marvelous, Mysterious, and (Maybe Even) Magical Creatures* (2010), *A Book for Black-Eyed Susan* (2011), *A Pet for Miss Wright* (2011), *Little Missouri* (2012, *Tuki and Moka: A Tale of Two Tamarins* (2013), *Digger and Daisy Go on a Picnic* (2014), and *Promise* (2015). *R Is for Rhyme: A Poetry Alphabet* received the 2006 Missouri Writers' Guild Best Juvenile Book Award, the 2006 National Parenting Publication Association Honor Award for Ages Nine and Up, and the 2008 Educators' Choice Award. *Lucky Star* won the 2010–2011 Missouri Show Me Readers' Award List. *Minnow Rose* was included on the Missouri Show Me Readers Award List and won the 2010 Storytelling World Award for Preadolescent Listeners.

Biographies and Memoirs: Among biographies and memoirs associated with Missouri is *Bohemian Life; or, The Autobiography of a Tramp* (1884) by Thomas Manning Page (1841–1900), who was born in St. Louis and contributed to the St. Louis humor newspaper the *Hornet* under the pseudonym Sidney Harrington. Poet, dramatist, and novelist ORRICK JOHNS (1887–1946), the son of a *St. Louis Post-Dispatch* editor, also wrote a memoir, *Time of Our Lives: The Story of My Father and Myself* (1937). Missouri-born radio personality and writer Mary Margaret McBride (1899–1976) contributed *A Long Way from Missouri* (1959). In 1937 the controversial regionalist painter Thomas Hart Benton (1889–1975), born in Neosho, Missouri, published the first edition of his *An Artist in America.*

Poetry: Missouri has produced many significant poets. Some left the state early in life, leaving it to readers to seek Missouri references in their verse; others, both native born and transplants to the state, have made Missouri people and places sources for their writings. Missouri poetry is diverse in form and content, ranging from sentimental verse to high modernism, with every variety in between.

As in every Midwestern state, poetry emerged in Missouri during the frontier era and early years of settlement. A poem from the period of Spanish rule is "Chanson de l'année du coup" (1780), about a British and Indian attack on St. Louis, written by French Canadian fur trader Jean Baptiste Trudeau (1748–1827).

In addition to books about his travels and geological work in Missouri, Henry Rowe Schoolcraft wrote *Transallegania; or, The Groans of Missouri* (1820), an allegorical poem that deals with a meeting of the personifications of Missouri's subterranean mineralogical riches, who decide to create the series of New Madrid earthquakes of 1811–1812 to discourage settlers from moving to the area. In St. Louis, Angus Umphraville (b. 1798) created *Missouri Lays and Other Western Ditties* (1821), consisting mostly of poems about Missouri scenes. Parley P. Pratt (1807–1857) defended his fellow Missouri Mormons in *The Millennium, and Other Poems* (1840). Anna Peyre Dinnies (1805–1886), who came to St. Louis from South Carolina, was a popular pre–Civil War poet. Her collection *The Floral Year* (1847) features the sentimentality then favored by many readers.

Missourians who were producing poetry in the late 1800s and early 1900s were typically otherwise engaged in law, journalism, or other professions. These included George Henry Walser (1834–1910), a lawyer and Civil War veteran from Indiana who founded the town of Liberal in 1880 as an atheist, freethinking community. Walser wrote several volumes of verse, including *Poems of Leisure* (1890) and *The Bouquet* (1897). Will Ward Mitchell (1871–1909), a Higginsville newspaper editor, brought together his poems in *Jael, and Other Rhymes* (1898), *Sonnets* (1905), and other books. Eugene Field, a St. Louis and Kansas City journalist, also created poetry, much of which appeared first in his newspaper columns. His children's verse, which entertains rather than moralizes, was published in such books as *Love Songs of Childhood* (1894) and still appears in anthologies for children. Field's books for adult readers, such as *A Little Book of Western Verse* (1889), alternate among parody, dialect, and sentimental expression.

Mary Elizabeth Mahnkey (1877–1948) was born in Arkansas but grew up in Taney County, Missouri, and became a longtime Springfield journalist. Referred to as the "poet laureate of the Ozarks," she wrote sentimentally but specifically about farmwork and Ozark mountain culture. *Ozark Lyrics* (1934) collects some of her verse.

SARA TEASDALE (1884–1933) was born in St. Louis. Her short, elegant poems in traditional forms found favor with the generation coming of age just before World War I. Her early work appeared in REEDY'S MIRROR and POETRY: A MAGAZINE OF VERSE. On trips to CHICAGO beginning in 1913, she was befriended by CHICAGO RENAISSANCE writers like HARRIET MONROE (1860–1936) and (NICHOLAS) VACHEL LINDSAY (1879–1931). Her book *Love Poems* (1917) was the first winner of the forerunner of the Pulitzer Prize for Poetry. After years of ill health, Teasdale committed suicide. Posthumously published books include *Strange Victory* (1933) and *Collected Poems* (1937).

T(HOMAS) S(TERNS) ELIOT (1888–1965) was born in St. Louis, where his family had lived for decades. Eliot became a British subject and espoused a cosmopolitan aesthetic that emphasized dimensions of time over particularities of place, but he carried strong memories of St. Louis and the Mississippi River. Without exaggerating the Midwestern elements in Eliot's poetry, one can read the fog that appears in "The Love Song of J. Alfred Prufrock" (1915) as St. Louis factory smoke, and the river that introduces "The Dry Salvages" (1941) from *Four Quartets* (1943) as the mighty Mississippi.

H(arold) H(arwell) Lewis (1901–1985), known as the "Plowboy Poet" of Missouri, achieved recognition in the 1930s as a left-wing advocate for migrant workers and a poet of farm labor. Befriended by literary lights of the time like Malcolm Cowley (1898–1989), William Carlos Williams (1883–1963), and Jack Conroy, Lewis published books like *Red Renaissance* (1930) and poems like "Farmhand's Refrain" (1938) while engaging in political activism and working the family farm near Cape Girardeau.

Poet and nonfiction writer LANGSTON (JAMES MERCER) HUGHES (1902–1967) was born in Joplin, Missouri, although he moved soon after birth and the state never played a large role in his writing. The years that Hughes spent in Kansas City and Chicago introduced him to jazz and the blues and nurtured his ear for gospel, the rhythms of which appear in his poetry in books such as THE WEARY BLUES (1926, 1939). Hughes's well-known "The Negro Speaks of Rivers" was written near St. Louis and evokes the Mississippi.

Charles Guenther (1920–2008) translated poetry from many languages and wrote free and formal verse, sometimes about nature and Missouri scenes. Born in St. Louis and educated at Webster College and St. Louis University, he wrote reviews for the *St. Louis Post-Dispatch* from 1953 to 2003. *Phrase/Paraphrase* (1970) was nominated for a Pulitzer Prize. *Moving the Seasons: The Selected Poetry of Charles Gunther* appeared in 1994.

A group of distinguished poets gathered in the late twentieth century at Washington University in St. Louis. U.S. Poet Laureate for 1992–1993 MONA VAN DUYN (1921–2004) co-founded the MFA program there in 1975. She drew on local subjects in poems like "Earth Tremors Felt in Missouri" from *A Time of Bees* (1964) and "In the Missouri Ozarks" from *Letters from a Father, and Other Poems* (1982). Howard Nemerov (1920–1991) won the trifecta of American poetry prizes—the National Book Award, the Pulitzer Prize, and the Bollingen Prize—for his *Collected Poems* (1977). Constance Urdang (1922–1996) came to St. Louis in 1960 and started teaching at Washington University in 1974. Her poems with a Missouri sense of place include "Reflections on History in Missouri" from *The Lone Woman and Others* (1980). Donald Finkel (1929–2008), Urdang's husband, taught at Washington University from 1960 to 1991. His books include *Not So the Chairs: Selected and New Poems* (2003). John N. Morris (1931–1997), who was born in England, taught at Washington University for almost thirty years. *John N. Morris: Selected Poems* (2002) features some of his best work.

The position of Missouri Poet Laureate was established in 2008 when Walter Bargen (b. 1948) was named to the post. He spent his childhood in Germany, where his father was stationed with the U.S. Army, and in Belton, Missouri, near Kansas City. He has written about war, nature, and other themes in more than a dozen books. *Days like This Are Necessary: New and Selected Poems* (2009) and *Trouble behind Glass Doors* (2013) offer samples from his work. *Harmonic Balance* (2001) and *Theban Traffic* (2008) feature narratives set in fictional Midwestern towns, an approach that aligns Bargen with EDGAR LEE MASTERS (1868–1950).

Born in Jefferson City, Deborah (Leah Sugarbaker) Digges (1950–2009) was a child of Dutch immigrants. *Late in the Millennium* (1989), one of her four books of poetry, reflects her Missouri childhood, as does *Fugitive Spring: Coming of Age in the '50s and '60s* (1992), one of her two memoirs.

David Clewell (b. 1955), who directs the creative-writing program at Webster University, was named Missouri Poet Laureate in 2010. Although he was born and raised in New Jersey, Clewell writes far-ranging, witty poetry grounded in Missouri experience. His books include *Room to Breathe* (1977) and *Taken Somehow by Surprise* (2011).

A lively poetry scene has long existed in Kansas City. David Ray (b. 1932) taught for many years at the University of Missouri–Kansas City. A socially conscious poet, Ray co-founded American Writers against the Vietnam War with ROBERT (ELWOOD) BLY (b. 1926). See PROTEST LITERATURE. Selections from Ray's many books appear in *Music of Time: Selected and New Poems* (2006). Dan Jaffe (b. 1933), a founding editor of BkMk Press at the University of Missouri–Kansas City, was befriended by Langston Hughes, who encouraged Jaffe's interest in jazz. Jaffe's books include *Playing the Word: Jazz Poems* (2001). Gloria Vando Hickok (b. 1936), a Puerto Rican poet from New York, has been part of the Kansas City scene since 1980. Her books include *Shadows and Supposes* (2002). The poetry of Mbembe Milton Smith (1946–1982) approaches hard realities of black urban experience from a spiritual perspective. His work is sampled in *Selected Poems* (1986). Linda Rodriguez (b. 1947), author of *Heart's Migration* (2009), has played a leadership role in organizations like Kansas City's Latino Writers' Collective. She is of Cherokee, Choctaw, and Irish descent. Stanley E. Banks (b. 1956), who teaches at Avila University, draws on the blues tradition in which Hughes also distinguished himself. *Blue Beat Syncopation: Selected Poems, 1977–2002* (2002) surveys Banks's earlier work.

Missouri-born poets with varying connections to the state include Marianne Moore (1887–1972), Langston Hughes, Maya Angelou (1928–2014), Quincy Troupe (b. 1939), Pattiann Rogers (b. 1940), Diane Glancy (b. 1941), James Tate (1943–2015), and Howard Schwartz (b. 1945). Poets who teach or have taught at Missouri colleges and universities include Jim Thomas (1930–2009), Jim Barnes (b. 1933), Nanora Sweet (b. 1942), 2012 Missouri Poet Laureate William Trowbridge (b. 1944), Michael Castro (b. 1945), Howard Schwartz, Mary Jo Bang (b. 1946), Robert Stewart (b. 1946), Sherod Santos (b. 1948), Cornelius Eady (b. 1954), Michelle Boisseau (b. 1955), Eamonn Wall (b. 1955), MARCUS CAFAGÑA (b. 1956), Aliki Barnstone (b. 1956), Carl Phillips (b. 1959), Devin Johnston (b. 1970), Hadara Bar-Nadav (b. 1973), and Wayne Miller (b. 1976).

The St. Louis Poetry Center, founded in 1946, and the Missouri State Poetry Society, organized in 1998, sponsor workshops, readings, and contests. The Missouri Cowboy Poetry Festival, held in Mountain View, Missouri, began in 1999.

Drama: According to Elijah L. Jacobs and Forrest E. Wolverton in their *Missouri Writers* (1955), "The history of Missouri drama is a relatively short story" (246), at least until 1955, because Missouri playwrights were not particularly interested in presenting drama about their home state in what was then the American West. What drama did appear in the early years, much of it not well documented, was presented in St. Louis. Nevertheless, interest in dramatic production has continued throughout Missouri's history.

The condition of frontier drama may be deduced in part from the shenanigans of the "actors," the rapscallion Duke and the King, in *Adventures of Huckleberry Finn* by Samuel Langhorne Clemens. Many plays were performed on the Mississippi on steamboats and showboats such as the Cotton Blossom Floating Palace Theatre depicted in *Show Boat* (1926) by EDNA FERBER (1885–1968). Farce, melodrama, and plays written with moral fervor were favorite genres, as were productions of Shakespeare. Theatre generally was quite popular, but Missourians had little interest in plays about the frontier.

William E. Foley in his *A History of Missouri,* volume 1 (1971), reports that a few St. Louis enthusiasts put together an amateur drama group in 1814 and offered the state's first performances in 1815. The Works Progress Administration guide, *Missouri: A Guide to the "Show Me" State* (1941), provides more detailed information. Apparently that first performance was put on by a group called the Roscians; it staged two plays, *The School for Authors* and *The Budget of Blunders,* on January 6, 1815, in the state's first theatre, a much-used building of many purposes. The short-lived Roscians and the Thespian Society, which came into existence shortly afterward, appear to have shared at least some of the same members. The Thespian Society survived for about twenty years. Missouri's first professional theatrical production was the February 1819 performance of *Isabella; or, The Fatal Marriage,* staged by the Thespians.

The first important drama written in Missouri was *The Pedlar: A Farce in Three Acts;*

Written for the St. Louis Thespians, by Whom It Was Performed with Great Applause (1821) by Alphonso Wetmore, also the author of *Gazetteer of the State of Missouri.* Mary Barile adapted Wetmore's play for the University of Missouri at Columbia stage in 2007.

Western authors regularly adapted plays. Among these was *East and South,* an adaptation of *A Yankee among the Nullifiers,* which was performed in St. Louis in 1837. *The Partisan, a Tale of the Revolution* played in St. Louis in 1837 and 1838.

Three men important to the St. Louis theatre scene were John H. Vos, Noah M. Ludlow, and Samuel Drake, who carried on the Thespians' work, emphasizing production of plays on European themes, performed in the New Theatre and, for a short time, the Old Salt-House Theatre, which operated from 1825 to 1827. The new St. Louis Theater opened in 1837, one stop on the CINCINNATI, Louisville, and Lexington theatre circuit begun in 1834. Stock circuits and the advent of the starring system in the East brought famous actors west. Ellen Tree, an internationally known actress, appeared in St. Louis during an 1838–1839 tour. Edwin Forrest appeared first in 1839.

In the fourth volume of *A History of Missouri* (1971), Lawrence O. Christensen and Gary R. Kremer report that

Thespian Hall, built in Boonville prior to the Civil War, enjoyed great success during the "golden years" of the 1870s. One of the frequent performers on its stage was George T. Ferrel, a local newspaper man widely referred to as "The Poet Laureate of Missouri." Ferrel's first statewide recognition as a poet and journalist came in May 1875 at the ninth annual convention of the Missouri Press Association, held at Thespian Hall. (72–73)

Other early Missouri theatres included St. Louis's Varieties Theater, which opened in 1852, managed by Heinrich Börnstein, and the German Apollo Garten Theater, which opened in 1862 under the direction of Alexander Pfeiffer. In the 1840s and 1850s theatre groups formed in smaller cities, including Jefferson City, St. Joseph, Palmyra, Boonville, and Columbia (*Missouri: A Guide to the "Show Me" State* 153–54).

Alfred Henry Nolle in *The German Drama on the St. Louis Stage* (1917) indicates that a distinctly German theatre in St. Louis existed as early as 1842. The St. Louis Opernhaus opened in 1859, but it was short lived, closing in 1861.

A number of playwrights wrote often on American, though seldom Missouri, themes. These included Hugh A. Garland (1835–1864), author of *Life of John Randolph of Roanoke* (1850) and a tragedy about Jamestown titled *Opachancanough* (1853); Denton J. Snider (1841–1925), author of a verse play titled *Clarence* (1872); William Busch (b. 1836), a prolific playwright whose titles include *The Commandant of La Tour* (1902), on the Louisiana Purchase; and Roswell Field (1851–1919) and Henrietta Dexter Field (b. 1863), whose plays for children were published as *The Muses up to Date* (1897).

Augustus Thomas (1857–1934) was Missouri's first great playwright; he was associated with a dramatic group called the McCullough Club. His most famous play was *In Mizzoura* (1893; revised in 1916), a play in four acts set in Pike County, Missouri. Also by Thomas are *The Witching Hour* (1908), which was also made into a novel, and *The Copperhead* (1917). His memoirs are found in *The Print of My Remembrance* (1922). A contemporary of Thomas's, metallurgical engineer Henry William Charles Block (b. 1854), wrote *John Carver* (1902), which concerns St. Louis municipal corruption.

Born in Humansville, Missouri, Zoë Akins (1886–1958) was often called a writer of society plays. She began her writing career in St. Louis with her play *Papa* (1914). Three of her plays can be easily accessed in the volume *Déclassée; Daddy's Gone A-Hunting; and Greatness—A Comedy* (1923). *The Greeks Had a Word For It* (1930) became three different films: *The Greeks Had a Word for Them* (1932), *Three Blind Mice* (1938), and *How to Marry a Millionaire* (1953), featuring Marilyn Monroe, then a rising star. Akins received a Pulitzer Prize for her stage adaptation of Edith Wharton's *The Old Maid* (1935).

(Thomas Lanier) Tennessee Williams (1911–1983) received early training in St. Louis. In his introduction to *27 Wagons Full of Cotton* (1946), Williams praised the St. Louis Mummers theatre group for its "dynamism" and theatrical "disorderliness" under the direction of Willard Holland (ix). From 1929 to 1931 Williams attended the University of Missouri at Columbia, majoring in journalism but finding his classes tedious; from Columbia he sent off many of his early creative- writing efforts. His *Memoirs* (1975) presents aspects of his life in St. Louis and Columbia.

Williams's *The Long Goodbye* (1940), *The Strangest Kind of Romance* (1942), and *Hello from Bertha* (1946) are one-act plays that take place in a tenement building in a Midwestern city, no doubt St. Louis. Proletarian themes prevail in all three plays; the most poignant is *The Long Goodbye,* in which the writer-protagonist, Joe, prepares to move out of his tenement home and sadly remembers his mother's suicide and his sister's decline into prostitution. The best known of Williams's full-length plays set in St. Louis is *The Glass Menagerie* (1945), an innovative, haunting memory play in which the handicapped Laura Wingfield collects glass animals and is disappointed in a potential suitor while her brother seeks to find his way in the world. The late, poignant one-act play *A Lovely Sunday for Creve Coeur* (1979) features four St. Louis women, three of them in difficult circumstances; Dorothea wants to escape her surroundings, with its "vistas that suggest the paintings of Ben Shahn: the dried-blood horror of lower middle-class American urban neighborhoods" (*The Theatre of Tennessee Williams* 8:119).

Arna Bontemps (1902–1973) and Countee Cullen (1903–1946) created the play *St. Louis Woman* (1944) from Bontemps's novel *God Sends Sunday* (1931). It was made into a popular musical (1946) with music by Harold Arlen (1905–1986) and lyrics by Johnny Mercer (1909–1976); Pearl Bailey starred in the Broadway performance (1946).

LANFORD WILSON (1937–2011) is the most famous Missouri playwright of the late twentieth and early twenty-first century.. Early experiences playing Tom Wingfield in a high school production of *The Glass Menagerie* and his interest in touring productions of other important plays led Wilson to study playwriting in Chicago. Wilson's early plays set in the Midwest include *This Is the Rill Speaking* (1965) and *The Rimers of Eldritch* (1966). Among his best-known works are three plays set in Lebanon, Missouri, his hometown: *5th of July* (1978); *Talley's Folly* (1979), which won a Pulitzer Prize; and *Talley and Son* (1985).

Stardust (1978) by James Nicholson (b. 1946) is a play about a St. Louis burlesque club that runs into zoning difficulties; it is included in *A Missouri Playwrights' Anthology: Six Plays by Missouri Playwrights* (1981), edited by Robert E. Knittel.

Dr. Patricia McIlrath, at the then newly designated University of Missouri–Kansas City, established the Repertory Theatre in 1964; it remains active. Among smaller theatre efforts is the Unicorn Theatre in Kansas City, which originated in 1974 as a theatre workshop; it changed its name to the Unicorn in 1981 and remains an active, innovative theatre.

Film: Missouri has been represented in FILM in often contrasting ways. *Meet Me in St. Louis* (1944), based on short stories by Sally Benson, probably best represents the theme of the Midwest as a haven of straight-thinking, unpretentious values serenely insulated from the influences of big cities in the Northeast; the conclusion of the film shows how three daughters, the eldest played by Judy Garland, ultimately convince their father not to take a job in New York and to remain in St. Louis. This theme is turned on its head in *Mr. and Mrs. Bridge* (1990), based on two novels by Evan S. Connell, in which an elderly couple played by Paul Newman and Joanne Woodward encounter marital and family conflicts brought on when their children return from worldly experiences in the 1930s and 1940s to the staid, insulated confines of their Kansas City home.

This inversion of more typical portrayals of the Midwest as a bastion of small-town simplicity, depicting it instead as a parochial home of bumpkins, has had longer traction in films set in the state. *Paper Moon* (1973), adapted from the novel *Addie Pray* (1971) by Joe David Brown (1915–1976), for instance, follows the travails of a Bible salesman and his pubescent sidekick, played by Ryan and Tatum O'Neal, as they exploit small-town gullibility in such locales as St. Joseph. *Waiting for Guffman* (1996), adapted from the play *Waiting for Godot* (1953) by Samuel Beckett (1906–1989), is set in Blaine and satirizes traditional Midwestern ARCHETYPES as local talents delude themselves into thinking that their staging of a musical in town will attract the attention of Broadway.

Like many Chicago films, those associated with Kansas City have often portrayed that locale as an arena of organized crime and shady public officials. *Pete Kelly's Blues* (1955), starring and directed by Jack Webb and featuring musical performances by Ella Fitzgerald and Peggy Lee, takes place there during the Prohibition era. Similarly, Kansas City native Robert Altman's *Kansas City* (1996) features the rise of jazz amid the milieu of gangsters and crooked politicians. His first film, *The Delinquents* (1957), depicts the exploits of teenage gangs in the city.

Until recent decades, few films used frontier or rural Missouri. *Belle of the Nineties,* also known as *That St. Louis Woman,* a 1934 "western" starring Mae West and based on a work by her, begins in St. Louis but quickly shifts to New Orleans. One of the earlier films, *Ride with the Devil* (1999) by Ang Lee (b. 1954) and based on *Woe to Live On* (1987) by Daniel Woodrell, centers on North-South rivalries and racial issues as pro-South Bushwhackers face off against Union troops during the Civil War; highlighting southwestern Missouri, the film calls attention to the inherent conflicts in the only pro-Union slave state. A revisionist western, *The Assassination of Jesse James by the Coward Robert Ford* (2007), based on a 1983 book by Ron Hansen, explores the last days and eventual murder of Jesse James in a gritty, violent Missouri town. *Winter's Bone* (2010), based on a 2006 novel by Daniel Woodrell, is a highly acclaimed independent film shot in the rural Ozarks. It follows a teenager searching for her missing father while revealing backwoods life as impoverished and laden with crime and drug abuse.

Gay and Lesbian Literature: Writing by gay and lesbian writers has a long history in Missouri, although most texts have appeared since the gay rights movement of the 1970s. An early landmark is *The Story of a Life* (1901) by the pseudonymous Claude Hartland (b. 1871), believed to be the first gay autobiography in the United States. Hartland details his life in St. Louis, addressing his book to medical specialists. *The Story of a Life* can be contrasted with *America's Boy:*

A Memoir (2006) by Wade Rouse (b. 1965), a book about growing up gay and overweight in the Missouri Ozarks.

A number of other gay- or lesbian-themed novels are set in Missouri. *Aquamarine* (1992) by Carol Anshaw (b. 1946) presents three alternative life experiences of an athlete after competition in the 1968 Olympics: she is either married, single, or divorced; straight or lesbian; and living in her Missouri hometown or in New York. Janet McClellan (b. 1951) has written a series of mysteries about Tru North, a lesbian police detective in Kansas City. The series includes *K.C. Bomber* (1997), *Penn Valley Phoenix* (1998), *River Quay* (1998), and *Chimney Rock Blues* (1999). *Bilal's Bread* (2005) by Sulayman X (b. 1963) tells of a Kurdish teenager in Kansas City struggling with his homosexuality and also with local prejudice, the murder of his father by the Iraqi secret police, and sexual abuse by his older brother. *Missouri* (2006) by German novelist Christine Wunnicke (b. 1966) is a violent but moving gay love story set during the nineteenth-century frontier era. David Miller's English translation appeared in 2010.

Novels about gay and lesbian experience in Missouri have been also been written for young-adult readers. Set in Kansas City in 1958, *What Happened to Mr. Forster?* (1981) by Gary W. Bargar (1947–1985) involves a sixth grader whose teacher becomes the target of homophobic suspicion. In *Deliver Us from Evie* (1994) by M. E. Kerr, a pseudonym of Marijane (Agnes) Meaker (b. 1927), a teenager and his family deal with prejudice in their Missouri town when his older sister comes out as a lesbian. *Almost Perfect* (2009) by Brian Katcher (b. 1975) is about a teenage boy in a small town who falls in love with a girl who turns out to be a transgender male. Katcher's novel won the 2011 Stonewall Children's and Young Adult Literature Award from the American Library Association. See LESBIAN, GAY, BISEXUAL, TRANSGENDER, AND QUEER LITERATURE.

Printing and Journalism: The earliest printer in what was then Louisiana Territory was Joseph Charless (1772–1834), who moved to St. Louis from Kentucky in 1808. He had obtained a contract from the territorial governor naming him the official government printer before he moved west. Shortly after his arrival in St. Louis, Charless established the weekly *Missouri Gazette,* the earliest newspaper in what was to become Missouri, as well as the first west of the Mississippi River. It began on July 12, 1808, and continued under his editorship until 1820, when he transferred it to James C. Cummins.

Because of the editor's connection with the territorial government, some local citizens accused Charless and his newspaper of partisanship, a charge he vehemently denied. Indeed, he later became so critical of some territorial officials that he lost his exclusive government contract. The *Missouri Gazette,* renamed, merged, and absorbed over the years, finally ceased publication in 1986 as the *St. Louis Globe-Democrat.*

Charless, by virtue of his position as official printer, published *The Laws of the Territory of Louisiana* (1808). Charless also published a speech by Frederick Bates, the secretary of Louisiana Territory, *An Oration Delivered before Saint Louis Lodge, No. 111* (1809); that publication is now deemed the first book printed in Missouri. His shop was also responsible for the territory's earliest almanac, *Charless' Missouri and Illinois Magazine Almanac for 1818* (1817).

The *Western Journal* was St. Louis and Missouri's second newspaper, beginning in March 1815; it was edited and printed by Joshua Norvell, formerly of Kaskaskia, Illinois. Norvell was hired in 1815 by St. Louis politicians and military officers to counter the criticisms of Joseph Charless in his *Missouri Gazette and Illinois Advertiser,* then the *Missouri Gazette.* However, Norvell sold his paper less than a year later. After a succession of owners and a name change to the *Emigrant and General Advertiser,* it finally found stability in August 1818 as the *St. Louis Enquirer* under the editorship of Thomas Hart Benton (1782–1858). Benton, formerly on the staff of General Andrew Jackson, had arrived in St. Louis a few years earlier to practice law and ultimately was elected to the U.S. Senate.

Verse and other literary efforts occasionally appeared in early Missouri newspapers, but it was not until January 1837 that St. Louis saw a monthly specifically devoted to poetry. James Ruggles published the *Western Mirror, and Ladies Literary Gazette,* edited by a Mrs. H. A. Ruggles, probably his spouse,

but it did not survive to the end of the year. A second important literary serial was *Weekly Reveille* by Charles Keemle (1800–1865), a prolific St. Louis printer. Ostensibly a newspaper, it also often included stories, sketches, and tall tales, the most notable of which was "Death of Mike Fink" (1844) by Joseph M. Fields (1810–1856), adding to the growing mythical status of that famous keelboatman.

Missouri journalists of note included Samuel L. Clemens, who worked as a typesetter for his older brother's newspaper, the *Hannibal Journal,* and contributed humorous sketches before leaving Hannibal for New York at age eighteen. In St. Louis, Carl Schurz (1829–1906), the influential editor of the city's daily German-language *Westliche Post,* hired Hungarian immigrant Joseph Pulitzer (1847–1911) as a reporter in 1867. By 1869 Pulitzer became city editor. In 1879 he purchased two St. Louis newspapers, the *Post* and the *Dispatch,* and combined them into the *St. Louis Post-Dispatch,* which, through hard-hitting editorials, exposed corruption and championed the common man. Having transformed his St. Louis newspaper into a respected regional and national medium, Pulitzer moved to New York City in 1883, having purchased the *New York World.* In the mid-1890s he began his long and bitter rivalry with William Randolph Hearst and his *New York Morning Journal.*

Missouri native and poet Eugene Field began as a *St. Louis Evening Journal* reporter before moving to stints as editor at a succession of newspapers, including the *St. Joseph* (Missouri) *Gazette,* the *St. Louis Times-Journal,* and the *Kansas City Times.* His popular contributions were reprinted in other regional newspapers.

William Marion Reedy was influential in promoting the region's authors, as well as a distinctive Midwestern literature. Born in St. Louis, Reedy first worked as a reporter for the *Missouri Republican* before contributing freelance articles to the *St. Louis Sunday Mirror.* After James Campbell, its owner, appointed Reedy editor in 1896, the magazine became a venue for new Midwestern authors and a nationally known arbiter of and advocate for regional, national, and international literature, as well as a vehicle for social and political commentary. It was known as *Reedy's Paper* until 1913, when its name was changed to REEDY'S MIRROR. A few months after Reedy's death in 1920, it ceased publication. Among the authors championed in this journal were Zoë Akins, Sara Teasdale, and Edgar Lee Masters.

Shortly after graduating from high school in Oak Park, Illinois, Ernest (Miller) Hemingway worked as an eighteen-year-old cub reporter for the *Kansas City Star* from October 1917 to April 1918. The stories attributed to him at the *Star* show the beginnings of his trademark spare, understated writing developed by studying the newspaper's style sheet and through the mentorship of its editor, C. G. Wellington. Hemingway's experiences as a young man in Kansas City were later recast as scenes in a few of his novels and short stories.

Contemporary Missouri literary magazines include *Big Muddy, Boulevard,* the *Cape Rock, Center, Chariton Review, Elder Mountain, Gingko Tree Review, Green Hills Literary Lantern, I-70 Review, Laurel Review, Margie: The American Journal of Poetry, Missouri Review, Mochilla Review, Moon City Review, Natural Bridge, New Letters, Paintbrush, Pleiades, River Valley,* and *River Styx.*

Missouri Federal Writers' Project: *Missouri: A Guide to the "Show Me" State,* published in 1941, was the sole publication of the Missouri Federal Writers' Project, one of the state programs of the Federal Writers' Project (1935–1943). Jack S. Balch, assisted for a time by Jack Conroy and later by Charles van Ravenswaay, supervised the Missouri office. Coverage by the guide, sponsored by the Missouri State Highway Department, is extensive, including chapters on the arts and culture of the state. Project writers also collected two brief interviews called "American Life Histories," one of which was with Rose Wilder Lane. These handwritten manuscripts are held by the Library of Congress. In addition, a number of former slaves were interviewed. The Library of Congress holds approximately eighty of these typescripts. They and slave narratives from other states made during this period were gathered into a nineteen-volume work titled *Slave Narratives: A Folk History of Slavery in the United States from Interviews with Former Slaves* (1941). It was reprinted in 1976. The Missouri content appears in volume 10.

Missouri Literary Awards: Missouri has a Humanities Council, an Arts Council, and a Missouri Center for the Book. These entities have generated literary awards, including the Governor's Humanities Award for works that increase understanding and appreciation of Missouri history and culture. The University of Missouri Press distributes literary and critical awards. Among the regional awards is one sponsored by the Missouri Western State University Prairie Lands Writing Project, the Missouri Writing Projects Network, and the Missouri Association of Teachers of English. The Prairie Lands Writing Project is divided by areas: Northwest, Central Eastern and St. Louis, Northeast, Southwest, and South Central. The Missouri Writing Region, an affiliate of the Alliance for Young Artists and Writers, is sponsored by the Missouri Western State University Prairie Lands Writing Project, the Missouri Writing Projects Network, and the Missouri Association of Teachers of English and offers literary prizes. The University of Missouri offers the Francis W. Kerr Writing Prize for excellence in undergraduate writing; the Missouri Writers' Guild and the St. Louis Writers Guild maintain their own awards. A Big River writing contest in Chesterfield celebrates Mark Twain and the Missouri River valley. The Missouri Literary Festival is an annual event that launches a Civil War Challenge Short Fiction Contest in Springfield, Missouri; the *Missouri Review* sponsors the Jeffrey E. Smith Editor's Prize.

Anthologies: *A Little Book of Missouri Verse* (1897), edited by James Samuel Snoddy, is an early anthology of Missouri poetry featuring works by seventy-three authors. Richard R. Jesse and Edward A. Allen edited *Missouri Literature* (1901), a comprehensive collection of poetry and fiction. John T. Frederick's *Out of the Midwest* (1944) includes a section, "Missouri and Eastern Kansas," that includes works by Thomas Hart Benton, Edgar Watson Howe, Langston Hughes, and MacKinlay Kantor set in or addressing the state. The *Missouri Reader* (1964), edited by Frank Luther Mott, divides its selections among different stages of Missouri history and culture.

Later poetry anthologies include *The Missouri Poets* (1971), edited by Robert Killoren and Joseph Clark; *Five Missouri Poets* (1979), edited by Jim Barnes; *Voices from the Interior: Poets of Missouri* (1982), edited by Robert Stewart; and *Missouri Poets: An Anthology* (1982), edited by Robert C. Jones and Maryfrances Wagner. Anthologies focusing on areas of the state or poetic genres include *Kansas City Outloud II: 32 Contemporary Area Poets* (1990), edited by Dan Jaffe; *Missouri Cowboy Poetry* (2001), from the Missouri Cowboy Poets Association; and *Balancing on a Bootheel: New Voices in Poetry from Southeast Missouri* (2006), edited by Jon Thrower and Susan Swartwout.

A Missouri Playwrights' Anthology (1981), compiled by Robert E. Knittel, brings together several works of drama from the region. *The First Anthology of Missouri Women Writers* (1987), edited by Sharon Kinney-Hanson, collects the stories and poems of eighty Missouri women.

SELECTED WORKS: The work of Samuel Longhorne Clemens, writing as Mark Twain, is a necessary starting place in Missouri fiction, particularly the novels *The Adventures of Tom Sawyer* (1876) and *Adventures of Huckleberry Finn* (1884, 1885). *The Story of a Country Town* (1883) by Edgar Watson Howe and John Wesley "Jack" Conroy's novel *The Disinherited* (1933) are additional strong examples. The fiction of Daniel Woodrell invokes modern-day conditions in poor Ozark communities.

Significant poetry volumes by Missourians include: *Love Poems* (1917) by Sara Teasdale; *Red Renaissance* (1930) by H. H. Lewis, *Ozark Lyrics* (1934) by Mary Elizabeth Mahnkey, *A Time of Bees* (1964) by Mona Van Duyn, *Phrase/Paraphrase* (1970) by Charles Guenther, *The Lone Woman and Others* (1980) by Constance Urdang, *Blue Beat Syncopation: Selected Poems, 1977–2002* (2002) by Stanley E. Banks, *Days like This Are Necessary: New and Selected Poems* (2009) by Walter Bargen, and *Taken Somehow by Surprise* (2011) by David Clewell.

Readers may sample several Missouri plays. Three good examples are Augustus Thomas's versatile frontier play *In Mizzoura* (1893; revised in 1916), Tennessee Williams's famous St. Louis tenement drama *The Glass Menagerie* (1945), and the Pulitzer Prize–winning *Talley's Folly* (1979) by Lanford Wilson.

FURTHER READING: Significant sources on Missouri include Ralph Leslie Rusk's *The Literature of the Middle Western Frontier,* volume 1 (1925; reprinted in 1975), and Elijah L. Jacobs and Forrest E. Wolverton's *Missouri Writers: A Literary History of Missouri, 1780–1955* (1955). Although they are dated, both remain authoritative sources for early Missouri literature. A statewide literary survey published in the mid-twentieth century can be found in "Missouri: The Mother of Authors" by Thomas Layne Sanders, *Wilson Library Bulletin* 31.10 (June 1957): 791–95. Some commentary on Kansas City literature appears in *Encyclopedia of the Great Plains* (2004), edited by David J. Wishart, although its geographic scope is much wider. *The American Midwest: An Interpretive Encyclopedia* (2007), edited by Richard Sisson, Christian K. Zacher, and Andrew R. L. Cayton, includes entries on Hemingway and Langston Hughes with references to Kansas City; and the website of the Missouri Center for the Book is a comprehensive source for literary history and contemporary literature. The online St. Louis Mercantile Library: Literary St. Louis; A Research Guide includes sources and research materials for all Missouri literature.

For extended biographies of early Missouri writers, readers may wish to consult Alexander N. DeMenil's "A Century of Missouri Literature," *Missouri Historical Review* 20 (October 1920): 74–125. The chapter "Literature" in *Missouri: A Guide to the "Show Me" State* (1941) is a short but wide-ranging discussion of the state's authors, newspapers, and literature. *Missouri's Literary Heritage: Traveling through the Centuries* (1996), a booklet issued by the Missouri Center for the Book, lists authors connected with the state by region from the earliest time to the 1990s.

For poetry, "The Good Poets of Missouri" by Robert Stewart appears in the *Antioch Review* 38.2 (Spring 1980): 237–45. Minnie M. Brashear published the three-part "Missouri Literature since the First World War" in *Missouri Historical Review:* part 1, "Verse," in 40.1 (October 1945): 1–20; part 2, "Drama, Juvenilia, and Non-fiction," in 40.3 (April 1946): 330–48; and Part 3, "The Novel," in 41.3 (April 1947): 241–65.

Alfred Henry Nolle's *The German Drama on the St. Louis Stage* (1917) is a significant source. Jacobs and Wolverton's *Missouri Writers: A Literary History of Missouri, 1780–1955* also provides important information on Missouri drama.

Little scholarly work has focused on film depictions of Missouri, except for specific films that happen to be set there. An informative overview of Midwestern films in general is Rodney Hill's "Film and Theater," in the encyclopedic *The Midwest,* edited by Joseph W. Slade and Judith Yaross Lee (2004). Edward Recchia, in "There's No Place like Home: The Midwest in American Film Musicals" (*Midwest Quarterly* 39:2 [Winter 1998]: 202–14) studies themes of several musicals set in the Midwest, including *Meet Me in St. Louis.* Several owebsites, including the Internet Movie Database, provide information on individual films discussed in this entry.

Newspapers, their editors, and journalism on the Missouri frontier are discussed at length in "A Century of Journalism in Missouri" by William V. Byars in *Missouri Historical Review* 20 (October 1920): 53–73. *The Pioneer Editor in Missouri, 1808–1860* (1965) by William H. Lyon is also valuable. Important sources on early printing and publishing in Missouri include *A Preliminary Check List of Missouri Imprints, 1808–1850* (1937), the first state volume by the Historical Records Survey of the Works Progress Administration; and Viola A. Perotti's *Important Firsts in Missouri Imprints, 1808–1858* (1967). The latter expands and corrects some of the information in the earlier work.

Significant collections of Missouri literature are found throughout the state. The online Missouri Literary Directory lists significant information. Washington University has an archive for National Book Award–winning Missouri novelist William Gaddis (1922–1998). The Langston Hughes papers are archived in the Yale Collection of American Literature. The State Historical Society of Missouri in Columbia, Missouri, has literary archives, as do the four campuses of the University of Missouri: Columbia, Kansas City, Rolla, and St. Louis. This system houses the papers of Mary Hartwell Catherwood, Samuel L. Clemens, Eugene Field, and Hamlin Garland, as well as the Missouri Writers' Guild Papers from 1916 to 1980 and the JOHN G(NEISENAU) NEIHARDT (1881–1973) letters, 1912–1925, and owns material important to scholars studying both

Neihardt's *A Cycle of the West* (1949) and *Black Elk Speaks,* as well as information on the literary editors of the *St. Louis Post-Dispatch* (1929–1938).

DICTIONARY OF MIDWESTERN LITERATURE EDITORIAL BOARD

My Life and Hard Times

HISTORY: *My Life and Hard Times* (1933) by JAMES (GROVER) THURBER (1894–1961) has been called a short novel, a comic memoir, and, with guarded seriousness, an autobiography. No single designation can hold it firmly in place. Whatever else it may be called, it is first and foremost a work of HUMOR, mingling fact, fiction, and generous helpings of invention. In it Thurber recalls his childhood and college days in Columbus, OHIO. His family, as re-created there, seems at once eccentric, mildly mad, Midwestern, and middle-class. So are most of the rather zany Columbus citizens he chooses to describe and caricature. Upon publication, Thurber's recollections troubled some in Columbus, including his father, mother, and two brothers. Whether Thurber's comic darts and exaggerations amount to an attack on Midwestern values or constitute a warm and nostalgic homage to his hometown cannot easily be said. Throughout his narrative he follows a line running elusively between tall tales and the verisimilitude of autobiography.

The volume unfolds as a series of episodes, loosely bound by repeating characters and its early twentieth-century Columbus, Ohio, setting. Although the book begins with the narrator as a boy and ends with his college days at Ohio State University, Thurber does not follow the traditional literary form of an "education" or a bildungsroman. The most important characters, Thurber's family members, are comically possessed by fixed, unchanging ideas and psychological tics. Given the comic logic of his narrative, the family that he invents seems wonderfully right and strangely plausible. His two brothers are folded into the character of Roy, a prankster who finds his father easy prey. His father's fears of machinery, especially the newfangled automobile, put in motion some of the funniest stories. Without much stretching of his mother's character, Thurber shows her to be a woman who believes that "electricity was dripping invisibly all over the house" and finds a "bright side" in the chaos that the family regularly creates (*Thurber Carnival* 186, 181). Grandpa Fisher, in life an upstanding Columbus businessman, traipses through the stories as a loony Civil War veteran unstuck in time. In one episode, "The Night the Ghost Got In," he mistakes the city police for Union army deserters. Thurber's preface recites with mock seriousness Benvenuto Cellini's rules for autobiographers; he then proceeds to parody and burlesque the conventional autobiography rather than write one.

Thurber wrote most of the book for 1933 publication in the *New Yorker*. Eight of the book's nine chapters were published there in installments between July 8 and September 30. For the completed book, published in the late fall of that year, Thurber added "Preface to a Life," "The Dog That Bit

People," and "A Note at the End." An important clue to the book's composition history and its substance comes in the first paragraph of "The Night the Bed Fell," a story of Thurber's family on one confused, alarm-filled night. Acknowledging that his story might work better as a "recitation" than as a written piece, he explains that when he performed it for his friends, he found it necessary to "throw furniture around, shake doors, and bark like a dog" (176). He had, in short, rehearsed his tales and their comic incidents, slapstick violence, and vaudeville dialogue many times. If his stories carry the flavor of an oral telling, it is because much of Thurber's writing began in dramatized performances. His biographers point out that Thurber used letters to try out rough drafts of some stories. Harrison Kinney, in his voluminous biography *James Thurber: His Life and Times* (1995), indicates that Thurber's

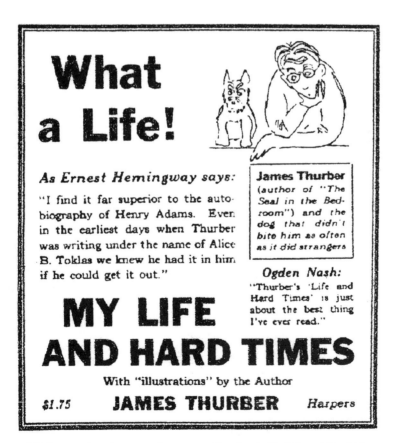

Publisher's advertisement for James Thurber's *My Life and Hard Times*. Harper & Bros., 1933.

friends remembered him performing the entire text of *My Life and Hard Times* at late-night parties (477–78). Thurber settled in New York in 1926, and being away from his hometown seems to have intensified his interest in family gossip and memories of pre–World War I Columbus.

Many readers have observed that although Thurber's title is *My Life and Hard Times* and its publication date is 1933, he makes no reference to the Great Depression. Apart from his half-joking assertion in the preface that he "knows vaguely that the nation is not much good any more," he ignores political upheavals and economic dislocations. He says in the preface that he will not be painting a picture of his time. Instead, he offers "his own personal time, circumscribed by the short boundaries of his pain and embarrassment" (*Thurber Carnival* 174–75). Thurber biographer Kinney reports speculation that Thurber raced to finish *My Life and Hard Times* before Clarence Day Jr. (1874–1935) could place his own comic recollections of his father and family in the *New Yorker* (526). The evidence for this claim seems slight, since Day had for some years been writing and publishing the stories that would be collected in *God and My Father* (1932) and *Life with Father* (1935). It is more likely that Thurber moved on his own schedule or on one imposed by his editor, Harold Ross.

My Life and Hard Times was Thurber's fourth book and established his importance as a writer and as America's leading humorist. With E(lwyn) B(rooks) White (1899–1985), he had written *Is Sex Necessary?* (1929). He followed with his own *The Owl in the Attic, and Other Perplexities* (1931) and *The Seal in the Bedroom, and Other Predicaments* (1932). None brought him the critical acclaim that *My Life and Hard Times* would. Reviewers heaped praise on the stories and what some called Thurber's "slapstick" humor. Robert M. Coates, writing in the *New Republic,* found it "the pleasantest possible mixture of fantasy and understanding" and "*the* funniest" book of recent times (December 13, 1933, 137). In an early notice in the *New York Times,* John Chamberlain said that he laughed so often that he wound up falling to the floor "pretty hard" (November 16, 1933, 21). A few reviewers struggled with the notion that a book so filled with obvious half-truths and tall-tale exaggerations could be autobiography. ERNEST (MILLER) HEMINGWAY (1899–1961) supplied a facetious dust-jacket statement calling Thurber's book "far superior to the autobiography of Henry Adams." With similar extravagant praise from Ogden Nash (1902–1971), Hemingway's words were prominently placed in advertisements, as in the *New York Times Book Review,* November 19, 1933, 18. According to Kinney in *The Thurber Letters* (2002), Thurber's cartoons and the book's popularity made him "a literary star by 1934" (165).

SIGNIFICANCE: Thurber's comic exaggeration of the fears, foibles, and psychological tics of his characters has been obvious to most readers. Yet this book, for all its comic distortions, was built on sharp observation and specific memories. Whether the view of his hometown and the Midwest should be taken as an expression of warm nostalgia or cool, distant, cosmopolitan ridicule raises still other questions. In any case, Thurber's stress on the oddities of his family's behavior and the quirks of Columbus citizens undercuts commonplace ideas defining the Midwest as the home of the bland and boring.

Critics and readers have differed over the cumulative meaning of the slapstick humor, improbable stories, and inflated caricatures and have tended to take one of two positions. Walter Blair contends that Thurber, Robert Benchley (1889–1945), S(idney) J(oseph) Perelman (1904–1979), and other twentieth-century humorists abandoned the pragmatic values of common sense and self-reliance implicit in frontier humor. Quoting at length from the preface of *My Life and Hard Times,* Blair outlines the ways in which Thurber as narrator assumes the persona of a nervous, neurotic character. Not surprisingly, Thurber creates characters who are hapless and helpless in an irrational world where common sense no longer matters. Blair finds a "fine illustration" of this in the chapter titled "The Day the Dam Broke." In *Native American Humor* (1937) he says that Thurber, telling of the crowd's panic before an imagined flood, mocks "human dignity" (174–79).

Norris Yates, on the other hand, in *The American Humorist: Conscience of the Twentieth*

Century (1964), reads the oddities and idio-syncrasies of the Thurber family as asser-tions of individuality and resistance to the machine-made and system-grinding deper-sonalization of the modern world. He asserts that Thurber's helpless "little man," unable to cope with machinery or fend off the com-plexities of modern times, represents the courage and "humor of despair" (275, 287).

In *Without a Stitch in Time* (1972) humor-ist and novelist Peter De Vries (1910–1993) included the essay "James Thurber: The Comic Prufrock." De Vries found evidence not of neuroticism but of "poetic sensitiv-ity" in Thurber's "filterings and transfor-mations" of everyday reality (309, 304). He also compares Thurber's comic genius to that of modern poets, specifically T(homas) S(tearns) Eliot (1888–1965). De Vries's com-ments suggest a way of understanding Thurb-er's imaginative power and explain his startling leaps from pedestrian facts of life to high-flying fantasy.

Many contend that Thurber continued to think of Columbus, his family, and their old-fashioned values as centers of emotional stability and comfort. Thurber pointed out in the chapter titled "A Note at the End" that in his futile efforts to pass himself off as a Conradian wanderer, his "Ohio accent" in-evitably betrayed him (240). As a descrip-tion of Columbus, Ohio, its people, and his family, *My Life and Hard Times* is neither as factual nor as sympathetically detailed as his later memoir, *The Thurber Album* (1952). Kin-ney asserts in his biography that Thurber's family never quite understood his comic in-tentions or recognized their antic shadows in *My Life and Hard Times* (52). Instead, they felt insulted by the representations, particu-larly the portrayal of the father as fumbling and ineffective. According to Burton Bern-stein in *Thurber* (1975), Charles Thurber once shouted his displeasure over his son's book loudly enough to "scare the squirrels over in the State House yard" (219–20). In "James Thurber and the Midwest," *American Studies* 33.2 (Fall 1992): 61–72, Stephen L. Tanner ar-gues that *My Life and Hard Times* revealed a "complicated and equivocal" attitude toward the Midwest. In it, he says, Thurber pre-sented himself as "the naïve Ohio boy just awakening to the perplexities" of a bewil-dering modern world (67). Columbus and

the eccentricities of his family represent, at different points in the narrative, a stubborn, admirable individualism and, alternatively, a confused and backward provincialism. The Columbus created here and in other writ-ings was part of his "idealized Midwest" (66–69). Charles S. Holmes in *The Clocks of Columbus: The Literary Career of James Thurber* (1972) judges *My Life and Hard Times* to be "the peak achievement of Thurber's early career," adding that "for many readers it is his one unquestioned masterpiece" (148). Over the years, individual stories excerpted from it, like "The Night the Bed Fell" and "The Dog That Bit People," have won ac-claim nearly equal to that given to Thurb-er's much-reprinted cartoons and "The Se-cret Life of Walter Mitty."

Thurber graced the pages of *My Life and Hard Times* with his own line drawings. His figures, almost without exception, stand fro-zen in moments of panic, alarm, or confu-sion. In these drawings, even the characters absorbed in thoughtful reflection seem just a bit daft. Thurber's handling of their facial expressions and stylized gestures no doubt owed a debt to comic strips, silent films, and vaudeville acts he had once watched. Thurb-er's irascible family dog Rex is drawn so that he possesses a dignity and a look of in-telligence equal to any of the human beings on the pages surrounding him. For *The Thurber Album* (1952), a largely serious and respectful memoir, Thurber used old family photographs and newspaper-file images. The book's "photograph gallery" lent everyone an austere dignity. In contrast, the cartoons in *My Life and Hard Times* framed the same cast of parents, grandparents, football he-roes, and Columbus citizens in comic poses and overwrought emotional states. In his biography, Kinney indicates that some crit-ics saw in Thurber's art a modern spirit and handling of line like that of Matisse's sinuous early drawings (458–59). If so, Thurber had paradoxically illustrated the old-fashioned early twentieth-century world in the idiom of radically contemporary art.

Anthologies and textbooks once magni-fied the influence and importance of se-lected *My Life and Hard Times* chapters. "The Night the Bed Fell," "More Alarms at Night," and "University Days" appeared in collections like Bennett Cerf's popular *An*

Encyclopedia of Modern American Humor (1954). In the 1940s and after, such Thurber stories were frequently placed under the heading "The Midwest." "University Days" was reprinted in high school textbooks often enough to attain canonical status.

IMPORTANT EDITIONS: *My Life and Hard Times* was published in November 1933 by Harper and Brothers in an edition of 3,000 copies, and by October 1964 it had been reprinted twenty-four times. A British edition was published in London in 1934, and it was subsequently translated into at least eight languages, including Bengali and Arabic. Paperback printings began with the Armed Forces Edition in 1944, followed by Bantam Books in 1947, which reprinted it numerous times into the 1970s. The text is available in the collection *The Thurber Carnival* (1945, 1999), which Thurber edited for Harper and Brothers. The book also constitutes part of the Library of America's *James Thurber: Writings and Drawings* (1996), the contents of which were chosen by GARY EDWARD KEILLOR (b. 1942), writing as Garrison Keillor.

FURTHER READING: Burton Bernstein in *Thurber* (1975) and Harrison Kinney in *James Thurber: His Life and Times* (1995) track the composition history, the circumstances of publication, and the initial reception of *My Life and Hard Times*. Kinney's account draws on interviews and materials Bernstein had no access to. Bernstein's book has the virtues of compactness and cogency that Kinney sometimes loses in his 1,238 pages. Thurber himself offers useful background material in chapter 8 of his memoir, *The Years with Ross* (1958). Harold Ross, his editor at the *New Yorker*, worked with Thurber during the year when he completed *My Life and Hard Times*. *The Thurber Letters* (2002), edited by Harrison Kinney and Rosemary A. Thurber, provides additional information on the book and its critical reputation. Critics and biographers, reckoning with skewed family biographies and fictional re-creations of Columbus, have often had recourse to *The Thurber Album* (1952). Thurber carefully researched that book and made it into a group biography of his family, his nineteenth-century forebears, and some noteworthy Columbus people. Stephen L. Tanner uses comparisons of the two books as a key to his study "James Thurber and the Midwest,"

American Studies 33.2 (Fall 1992): 61–72. Charles S. Holmes, in *The Clocks of Columbus* (1972), compares the Thurber family represented in the two books in sorting through what he calls the "confusion, chaos, and eccentricity" Thurber ascribed to his boyhood (153).

For understanding Thurber and *My Life and Hard Times* in the context of American humor traditions and history, Walter Blair's *Native American Humor* (1960) and *America's Humor: From Poor Richard to Doonesbury* (1978), the second of which he co-wrote with Hamlin Hill, remain necessary reading. Chapters 40 through 43 in *America's Humor* consider Thurber, define his prominent place in modern American humor, and outline his relation to his predecessors and contemporaries, including Robert Benchley, E. B. White, and others. Peter De Vries's essay "James Thurber: The Comic Prufrock" places him in the literary tradition of T. S. Eliot and modern poetry. It first appeared in *POETRY: A MAGAZINE OF VERSE* 63.3 (December 1943): 150–59 and was reprinted in *Without a Stitch in Time* (1972).

From 1913 to 1917 Thurber, his parents, his brothers, and occasional boarders lived at 77 Jefferson Avenue, near downtown Columbus. The Thurber House, restored beginning in 1984, appears much as it did when the Thurbers lived there. For *My Life and Hard Times*, Thurber changed the address to 77 Lexington. A walk through the house today makes clear that many of the stories, including "The Night the Ghost Got In," took inspiration and borrowed from the floor plan of this 1873 Victorian-style home. Appropriate passages from *My Life and Hard Times* are quoted on wall plaques that guide visitors through the rooms Thurber re-created in his book. The attic rooms of the house have served as a residence and studio for visiting writers. Next door, at 91 Jefferson Avenue, the Thurber Center houses archives, a gallery, and conference rooms. The James Thurber Family Collection there includes manuscripts, family photos, taped interviews, period sheet music, and memorabilia. The largest and most important collection of Thurber manuscripts is held in Ohio State University's Rare Books and Manuscripts Library.

GUY SZUBERLA   UNIVERSITY OF TOLEDO

MYSTERY AND DETECTIVE FICTION

OVERVIEW: With antecedents in the Bible and in the Greek and Roman classics, modern mystery and detective fiction has been one of the mostly widely read types of popular literature since its emergence as a separate genre in the nineteenth century. Like the DIME NOVEL, westerns, and romances, the mystery and detective novel can be formulaic, using stereotypical characters and familiar plot devices. The genre has often been denigrated for precisely these written-to-formula aspects, as well as the perceived lack of literary quality; however, many works in the genre rise to excellence as their authors find new ways to work within the formulas or manipulate and expand on them. Some writers have self-consciously separated their mysteries from their "literary" novels by using pseudonyms; Graham Greene (1904–1991) called his forays into the form "entertainments." Nevertheless, mystery and detective fiction continues to be consumed by a broad spectrum of readers and figures prominently on best-seller lists.

HISTORY AND SIGNIFICANCE: Most critics agree that with the appearance of the story "The Murders in the Rue Morgue" in the April 1841 issue of *Graham's Lady's and Gentleman's Magazine,* Edgar Allan Poe (1809–1849) established the modern mystery and detection genre. In this story and several others he initiated several standard conventions of the form, including a murder committed in a locked room and a brilliant, if eccentric, detective who successfully interprets clues that baffle the authorities. Mystery writer Dorothy L. Sayers (1893–1957) in the introduction to her anthology *Omnibus of Crime* (1929) refers to Poe's groundbreaking story as "almost a complete manual of detective theory and practice" (17).

Taxonomic subdivisions of the mystery and detective novel include, among others, police procedural novels (*romans policiers*), those with legal or courtroom backgrounds, whodunits, and works featuring private investigators, some of whom are referred to as "hard-boiled." In addition, a number of related types of fiction are often subsumed under the mystery and detective rubric: gothic, thriller, suspense, horror and supernatural, and spy novel number among them. The varieties and combinations of plot, char-

acter, setting, point of view, and sleuth personality would seem to prove that this genre, far from being hidebound and predictable, is similar to mainstream fiction in its breadth and depth.

In the nineteenth and early twentieth centuries the most important feature of the detective novel was solving the puzzle or mystery itself; the setting was often secondary and usually in a large city on either the East or the West Coast, if a locale was specified at all. CHICAGO's growing Prohibition-era notoriety for gang-controlled illicit liquor inspired novels that used this criminal activity for colorful background, with works like *Little Caesar* (1929) by W. R. Burnett (1899–1982); *Scarface* (1930) by Maurice Coons (1902–1930), writing as Armitage Trail; and *The Public Enemy* (1931) by Kubec Glasmon (1889–1938). All were made into memorable motion pictures.

Beginning in the 1980s, more and more mystery and detective novels were set in the Midwest, both in small towns and in the larger metropolitan areas; for example, according to Allen J. Hubin's bibliography of crime fiction, *Crime Fiction IV: A Comprehensive Bibliography, 1749–2000* (2003), 70 percent of those set in CLEVELAND were written between 1980 and 2000. It is not clear what is causing this developing interest in regional settings, but the trend continues.

SELECTED WORKS: Mystery novels with settings in some of the Midwestern states appeared fairly early; other Midwestern states were surprisingly ignored until much later. The presumed earliest mystery novels set in each Midwestern state, half of them in the nineteenth century, are listed here in chronological order: OHIO: *Oakshaw; or, The Victims of Avarice* (1855) by William Turner Coggeshall (1824–1867); MINNESOTA: *The Mystery of Metropolisville* (1873) by EDWARD EGGLESTON (1837–1902); MICHIGAN: *The Spiritualists and the Detectives* (1877) by Allan Pinkerton (1819–1884); ILLINOIS: *Dyke Darrel, the Railroad Detective; or, The Crime of the Midnight Express* (1886) by A. Frank Pinkerton, probably a pseudonym; MISSOURI: *Pudd'nhead Wilson* (1894) by SAMUEL LANGHORNE CLEMENS (1835–1910), writing as Mark Twain; NEBRASKA: *Like a Gallant Lady* (1897) by Kate M. Cleary (1863–1905); INDIANA: *The House of a Thousand Candles* (1905) by MEREDITH

W. R. Burnett's *Little Caesar*, the first gangster novel.
© Dial Press, 1929

NICHOLSON (1866–1947); KANSAS: *The Amateur Detectives* (1926) by Christopher B. Booth (b. 1887); WISCONSIN: Carolyn Wells's (1869–1942) *Deep-Lake Mystery* (1928) and *Into Thin Air* (1928) by Horatio G. Winslow (1882–1972) and Leslie Quirk (b. 1882); IOWA: *Crime in Corn-Weather* (1935) by Mary M. Atwater (1878–1956); SOUTH DAKOTA: *Murder at St. Dennis* (1952) by Margaret Ann Hubbard (1909–1992); and NORTH DAKOTA: *The Affair of Chief Strongheart* (1964) by Frank O'Rourke (1916–1989), writing as Patrick O'Malley, and *The Score* (1964) by Donald E. Westlake (1933–2008), writing as Richard Stark.

Several examples exist of the Midwestern lone private detective, based on the hard-boiled variety perfected by Raymond Chandler (1888–1959) and Dashiell Hammett (1894–1961). Among these is the creation of LOREN D. ESTLEMAN (b. 1952), Amos Walker, who walks the mean streets of Detroit. Arnold Magnuson, the aging founder of his detective agency, trails a murderous madman through many Chicago locales and its sub-

urbs in *The Death of the Detective* (1974) by Mark Smith (b. 1935), a remarkable novel that was a finalist for the American Book Award.

Modern police-department methods and investigations are subjects of the series featuring Lt. French of the Michigan State Police, beginning with *Smoke Screen* (1935), by Frances Moyer Ross Stevens (1895–1947), using the pseudonym Christopher Hale. John Roswell Camp (b. 1944), writing as John Sandford, follows the career of Lt. Lucas Davenport of the Minneapolis Police Department in his ongoing Prey series, which began in 1989 with *Rules of Prey*.

The Midwest is well represented in the field of ecclesiastical detectives. ANDREW M(ORAN) GREELEY (1928–2013) placed his Monsignor (later Bishop) Blackie Ryan in Chicago, where he began a long series with *Happy Are the Meek* (1985), solving many locked-room mysteries. The Detroit parish priest Father Robert Koesler was introduced in *The Rosary Murders* (1979) by WILLIAM X(AVIER) KIENZLE (1928–2001) and continued his church-related investigations in twenty-three subsequent novels. Charles Merrill Smith (1918–1985) created a Methodist minister, C. P. Randollph, who becomes involved in mysteries while at his Chicago church in a six-book series that began with *Reverend Randollph and the Wages of Sin* (1974). Ralph McInerny (1929–2010) was the creator of two Midwestern religious sleuths: Father Roger Dowling, a parish priest in the fictional Fox River, Illinois, in a thirty-two book series whose detecting began in *Her Death of Cold* (1974); and Sister Mary Teresa Dempsey, an elderly Chicago nun who in her nine books typically solves mysteries from her armchair, as in *Not a Blessed Thing!* (1981).

Crimes are not committed solely in cities, and the Midwest is no exception. Rural settings are common, as are those in isolated, self-contained locales. Esther Haven Fonseca (1900–1995) places a murderer on a Wisconsin island cut off by rising floodwaters in *Death below the Dam* (1936). Mignon G. Eberhart (1899–1996) writes of a murder at an isolated hunting lodge in the Nebraska Sandhills in *The Mystery of Hunting's End* (1930). A woman is menaced by her stepchildren in a lonely Illinois beach cottage in *I Am Afraid* (1949) by Elma K. Lobaugh (1907–

1997), and a murderer stalks a patient in an Illinois mental hospital in *Shock Treatment* (1961) by Winfred Van Atta (1910–1990).

Further discussion and listings of mystery and detective fiction and its authors can be found in the sections on this genre in the literature entries on most of the Midwestern states and in the entries on CINCINNATI, CLEVELAND, and MINNEAPOLIS/ST. PAUL

FURTHER READING: The secondary literature concerning detective and mystery fiction is vast, but among these works are the following regularly cited sources. Dorothy L. Sayers's seminal discussion, brief history, and classification of the mystery and detective fiction genre, printed as an introduction to her anthology *Omnibus of Crime* (1929), is still an important survey of the genre. *The Oxford Companion to Crime and Mystery Writing* (1999), edited by Rosemary Herbert, is an essential and authoritative reference containing entries of various lengths on the history and development of the genre, the many recognizable types of detectives, the variety of settings, biographies of noteworthy authors and fictional characters, and the surprising numbers of subgenres in mystery and detective fiction.

The unsurpassed cornerstone bibliography of the genre is Allen J. Hubin's five-volume *Crime Fiction IV: A Comprehensive Bibliography, 1749–2000* (2003), the fourth edition of his efforts that began in 1984 to list all English-language works. Its listings of over 100,000 titles are alphabetic by author and include novels, short stories, and plays; especially valuable are the detailed indexes of settings, which include all Midwestern states and a number of Midwestern cities. For mysteries with a Chicago locale, he lists no fewer than 850 titles. Hubin continues to revise and update this bibliography through his website.

Few sources deal specifically with Midwestern mystery and detective fiction. A significant part of *The American Regional Mystery* (2000) by Marvin Lachman concerns the Midwest as setting and lists a number of novels exemplifying this section of the United States. Each of the twelve Midwestern states is discussed separately, as are Chicago and Detroit. These chapters first appeared in issues of the *Mystery Reader's Newsletter* and *Armchair Detective* in the 1970s and were revised and updated for the book. A number of short articles on Chicago mysteries appeared as a special issue of *Mystery Readers Journal* 15.2 (Summer 1999). Andrew Cayton's brief three-page entry "Crime Fiction" in *The American Midwest: An Interpretive Encyclopedia* (2007), edited by Richard Sisson, Christian K. Zacher, and Andrew R. L. Cayton, focuses on only a few major authors from the late twentieth century.

ROBERT BEASECKER   GRAND VALLEY STATE UNIVERSITY

N

NARRATIVES.
See Captivity Narratives; Slave Narratives

NATIVE AMERICAN LITERATURE

OVERVIEW: Stories have long served many functions in Native American families, communities, and nations. Largely passed along through the oral tradition, stories describe everything from the creation of the world to cultural norms, history, religion, relations with other tribes, and internal governance. These stories, which were shaped both by the storytellers and by listeners, centered a people's place in the world and the cosmos. In modern times, stories have been recorded and written and have taken on a variety of forms and functions. In addition, there are clear influences, such as repetition, derived from oral tradition, that are present in many contemporary written works. Furthermore, contemporary literature serves many of the same functions as the oral tradition.

Native Americans have been publishing short stories, poetry, novels, autobiographies, and nonfiction since at least the early nineteenth century. Yet it was not until Kiowa author N(avarre) Scott Momaday (b. 1934) won the Pulitzer Prize for *House Made of Dawn* (1968) that contemporary publica-

tion of Native American literature grew to wide popularity. Momaday's novel is both nonlinear and nonchronological, two characteristics that link it with the tradition of oral storytelling. Midwestern Native American writers have used nonlinear and nonchronological forms. Other connections also exist between oral and written forms in Native American literature, especially in poetry. The repetition and form of poetry easily relate to the oral tradition. However, Native American writers in the Midwest have published in a wide variety of genres, both adapting elements of oral tradition and incorporating new forms that allow them to better express themselves. No single form or theme alone can characterize Native American literatures of the Midwest. In fact, diversity is one of the most useful descriptions of Native American literatures. The vast political, cultural, economic, and religious diversity of the more than five hundred nations that encompass the category "Native American / American Indian" is reflected in the literature.

Native Americans historically have maintained large populations in the Midwest and continue to do so in the present. Native American nations in the Midwest include the Anishinaabe (also called Ojibwe, Ojibwa, and Chippewa), Arikira, Brothertown Mohican (Stockbridge-Munsee), Hidatsa, Ho-Chunk (formerly called Winnebago), Mandan, Menominee, Meskwaki (Fox) and Sac (Sauk) Miami, Omaha, Oneida, Ottawa (or Odawa), Ponca, Potawatomi, Shawnee, and Sioux (Lakota, Dakota, and Nakota). Several popular and influential Native American writers live in the Midwest or have tribal connections to the area. Most literature published by Native Americans in the Midwest is in English, but current language-revitalization efforts include publication of works in Native languages. Wiigwassi Press in conjunction with Birchbark Books, for example, is publishing texts in the Anishinaabe language.

The field of Native American literature has grown in scope, and Midwestern authors continue to make significant contributions to the field. An increasing number of writers are using literature as a means to delineate Native concepts of sovereignty, nationalism, and transnationalism. Many themes are found in Native American literature of the Midwest; for example, both HUMOR and trickster themes are common in Native American literature of the Midwest. These themes have their roots in Native American cultures and serve to invert tragic images while encouraging fortitude and offering hope for the future. Place is also central to many Native Americans, and this sense of place is reflected in the literature. Nature writing and other themes relating to place are frequently found in Native American literatures of the region. Challenging the popular portrayals of historical figures and events is another prominent theme. Finally, identity is perhaps the most common theme in Native American literatures of the Midwest. Authors delineate their identity in relation to their tribal nation, their family, and the outside world.

This entry will discuss oral literature, including stories, songs, and oratory; nineteenth-century writers and memoirists; twentieth- and twenty-first-century memoirists; and twentieth- and twenty-first-century literary writers. In addition, the aforementioned categories will be divided by tribal nation. Historical and cultural contexts are essential for understanding Native American literatures of the Midwest. As with any literature, multiple, layered meanings will come to light when they are placed within their proper context. Many readers will find it useful to know biographical information about the authors because it will often give insight into the themes and topics of their writing.

HISTORY AND SIGNIFICANCE: Native Americans have been present in the Midwest since time immemorial. Many tribes believe that they originated in the region or came to be there through divine directives. The first encounter of many Native American nations with non-Indians was with the French, the leaders in the GREAT LAKES fur trade. The widespread introduction of European goods, including beads, metal goods, and weapons, changed life for Native Americans; however, the fur trade also brought about exchanges of information and worldviews. As European populations grew, Native American nations of the Midwest signed many treaties to establish boundaries, alliances, and peace, but by the nineteenth century the sale of land became a primary impetus for treaties. Native nations sold millions of acres of land to the United States, generally reserving hunting, fishing, and gathering rights on ceded territories, as well as possession of smaller portions of land, which would become reservations.

The U.S. government began to see Native American nations as an impediment to the nation's progress and, consequently, launched assimilation programs aimed at cultural and political genocide. Education was a primary tool in this endeavor, and many Native Americans learned the English language at government schools. As a result of these policies, significant language loss among Native Americans has occurred, and most literature published by them today is in English. During the twentieth century Native American populations also shifted from reservations to urban areas. The U.S. government's policy of relocation during the 1950s accelerated this shift, but Natives have also been attracted to urban areas because of education and employment opportunities.

Oral Literature: Native American oral literature includes stories about creation and origin; tribal tricksters and culture heroes; sacred songs and prayers, spoken and sung; and political, social, and ceremonial oratory. Since the time Native Americans first encountered Euro-Americans, these spoken forms have been recorded, transcribed, and published by both Indians and non-Indians. Because oral literature reflects the great diversity of Native American religious beliefs, social structures, cultural customs, and languages, it is useful to study oral literature within the social and historical contexts of individual tribes.

Motivated by the desire to record Native American stories and songs before they "disappeared," non-Indian ethnographers and anthropologists collected traditional stories and songs from several tribes. Ethnologist and Indian agent HENRY ROWE SCHOOLCRAFT (1793–1864), published several collections, such as *Algic Researches* (1839), which includes such stories as "The Summer-Maker" (Anishinaabe) and "The Celestial Sisters" (Shawnee). Because it is unknown how much editing Schoolcraft did, it is useful to compare these stories with other renditions. Philip Mason and Mentor Williams have edited Schoolcraft's work and published it as *Schoolcraft's Ojibwa Lodge Stories: Life on the Lake Superior Frontier* (1997) and *Schoolcraft's Indian Legends from "Algic Researches," the Myth of Hiawatha, Oneota, the Red Race in America, and Historical and Statistical Information Respecting . . . the Indian Tribes of the United States* (1991). Schoolcraft's *The American Indians: Their History, Condition and Prospects, from Original Notes and Manuscripts* (1851) was reprinted in 2008.

Many tribes in the Midwest divide their stories into a variety of categories. Often those that deal with spiritual aspects of tribal life can be told only at specific occasions, whereas those dealing with secular affairs can be told at any time. For example, Paul Radin (1883–1959) in *The Trickster: A Study in American Indian Mythology* (1956) notes that the Ho-Chunk classify their narratives as *waikan* (what is sacred) and *worak* (what is recounted). *Waikan* are told only during the winter and after dark; they frequently have a spirit as the central character. *Worak*, which can be told at any time, generally deal with recent events and feature human or earthly protagonists.

Many traditional Native American stories deal with a trickster or culture hero like Nanabozho, the trickster/culture-hero figure of the Anishinaabe, who is known by a variety of names, including Wenabozho and Nanapush. Nanabozho stories instruct the Anishinaabe how they should and should not behave, as well as on the origin of many things. These stories carry many broad and deep meanings and are understood in a wide variety of ways. Nanabozho is fallable, and the Anishinaabe learn from his misfortunes. Anthropologists were eager to record Nanabozho stories because of the cultural significance of the stories, as well as because of their fear that there would come a time when the stories would no longer be told.

The stories in Victor Barnouw's *Wisconsin Chippewa Myths and Tales* (1977) were recorded by anthropologists and were told primarily by five members of the Lac Court Oreilles and Lac du Flambeau bands of Ojibwa: Julia Badger, Tom Badger, Prosper Guibord, John Mink, and Delia Oshogay; they contain several tales about Nanabozho and his adventures. Other collections that include stories about Nanabozho are Katharine B. Judson's *Native American Legends of the Great Lakes and the Mississippi Valley* (1914), Dorothy M. Reid's *Tales of Nanabozho* (1963), and Alethea K. Helbig's *Nanabozhoo, Giver of Life* (1987). Native Americans not working with anthropologists have published their own collections of stories that include Nanabozho. For example, Anne M. Dunn (Anishinaabe, b. 1940) has published several collections of Anishinaabe stories that contain some of the adventures of Nanabozho, including *When Beaver Was Very Great* (1995), *Grandmother's Gift* (1997), and *Winter Thunder* (2000).

Native American songs carry cultural information and have a significant place in many Native American cultures. Songs play a critical role in religious and social ceremonies, as well as on an individual level. They are often highly regulated and classed into a variety of types, which determine who can sing them and when. According to Brian Swann in *Song of the Sky: Versions of Native American Song-Poems* (1993), the first Native American song to be transcribed was one from the Illinois, taken down by Father

Jacques Marquette (1637–1675) in 1674 (vii). Close study of songs awaited late nineteenth-century scholars like anthropologist Alice Cunningham Fletcher (1838–1923), who, with the collaboration of Francis La Flesche (1857–1932) and other Omaha peoples, wrote *A Study of Omaha Music* (1893). That book contains the musical scores for ninety-two songs, as well as the native-language words for the songs. Likewise, ethnomusicologist Frances Densmore (1867–1957) published *Chippewa Music* (1913) and *Poems from Sioux and Chippewa Songs* (1917), which were based on her fieldwork with the Anishinaabe and the Sioux. Densmore also wrote *Teton Sioux Music* (1918) and *The Indians and Their Music* (1926).

Oratory was a central part of Native American political life before the twentieth century. Since Native Americans used a variety of forms of governance,, oratory and a leader's ability to use oratory to persuade constituents were critical. After contact with non-Indians, Native American oratory was translated, transcribed, and, on some occasions, published. The best-known works of Native oratory are speeches given by Native leaders to officials of the U.S. government. Questions about accuracy abound; however, when the speeches are placed in historical and cultural context, they are excellent sources for understanding the views and desires of Native Americans, as well as seeing the ways in which Natives employed words as a political strategy. *Great Speeches by Native Americans* (2000), edited by Bob Blaisdell, includes speeches by several Midwestern leaders, such as "Englishman! You Know That the French King Is Our Father" by Minavavana (Ojibwa) and "The Master of Life" by Pontiac (Ottawa), as well as several speeches by Tecumseh (Shawnee), including "Let the White Race Perish" and "Father! Listen to Your Children!" Native leaders used oratory to raise awareness about a variety of issues and to incite change.

Nineteenth-Century Writers and Memoirists: AUTOBIOGRAPHY arose as a form during the Enlightenment and is generally thought to be the story of an individual's life written by the person himself or herself. For Native Americans, the line between autobiography and anthropological forms such as ethnographic life story has been blurred. Before the arrival of Europeans, Native people told their personal stories through a variety of means, including wampum belts and pictographs. It was not until the early 1800s that autobiographies in forms recognizable as such to Europeans were written. These early autobiographies were often written and translated by a second or third party. Many whites thought that Native Americans were going to disappear and were interested in learning about Natives before they did so. In addition, romantic stereotypes about Native Americans and their relationship with nature created interest as industrialization raised questions about American identity and culture. Native Americans were eager to have an opportunity to pass along the wisdom they acquired from experiences with both Natives and non-Indians.

In 1833 the famous Sauk leader BLACK HAWK (Ma-ka-tai-me-she-kia-kiak; 1767–1838) dictated his life story to Antoine LeClaire (1797–1861), U.S. interpreter for the Sauk and Fox tribes. LeClaire translated it into English, and then the text was edited by ILLINOIS newspaperman John B. Patterson. Although both men swore that the result was faithful to Black Hawk's words, translation is always challenging, and even with the best intentions some concepts are not likely to be adequately explained. The memoir, published as *LIFE OF MA-KA-TAI-ME-SHE-KIA-KIAK, OR BLACK HAWK* (1833), is still in print. Black Hawk begins by recalling his youth and early accomplishments; he then devotes much of the book to explaining his motives and relating his experiences in the Black Hawk War of 1832. Although the text is mediated by two non-Indians, it is considered a Native American classic.

Jane Johnston Schoolcraft, or Bame-wa-was-ge-zhik-a-quay (Anishinaabe, 1800–1842), who was raised in MICHIGAN and married Henry Rowe Schoolcraft, is the first known Native American literary writer. *The Sound Stars Make Rushing through the Sky: The Writings of Jane Johnston Schoolcraft* (2007), edited by Robert Dale Parker, features many previously unpublished texts along with cultural history, biography, and a critical introduction to Schoolcraft's work. Parker notes that Schoolcraft is the first known Native American woman writer, the first known Native American poet, the first known poet to write in a Native American language, and the first known Native American to write out traditional Indian stories herself—as opposed to transcribing and translating from someone else's oral delivery, which she also did.

George Copway (Kah-ge-ga-gah-bowh; Anishinaabe, 1818–1869) was born in Canada but spent a significant period of his life in the United States in the upper Great Lakes region. Copway wrote one of the first Native American autobiographies, *The Life, History and Travels of Kah-Ge-Ga-Gah-Bowh (George Copway), a Young Indian Chief of the Ojebwa Nation, a Convert to the Christian Faith, and a Missionary to His People for Twelve Years* (1847), in which he describes his childhood, conversion to Christianity, and work as a minister. Copway demonstrates the value of traditional Anishinaabe life and the humanity of Indian people, arguing that the Anishinaabe and, more broadly, Native Americans have the ability and intellectual capacity to adapt to European and European American society. Popular and well received by non-Indians, the book was expanded in 1850 to include speeches and letters. Copway also wrote *The Traditional History and Characteristic Sketches of the Ojibway Nation* (1851). A. Lavonne Brown Ruoff and Donald B. Smith published *Life, Letters and Speeches: George Copway (Kahgegagahbowh)* (1997).

ANDREW J. BLACKBIRD (Mack-e-te-be-nessy; Ottawa, ca. 1814–1908) was born in the area now known as Harbor Springs, Michigan, a son of the Ottawa chief Macka-de-pe-nessy. *Makade-binesi*, meaning "black hawk," was mistranslated as "black bird." Blackbird was well educated in Ottawa traditions and also received some formal schooling in Michigan and OHIO. In 1887 Blackbird published *History of the Ottawa and Chippewa Indians of Michigan; A Grammar of Their Language, and Personal Family History,* one of the first authoritative accounts of the Ottawa and Anishinaabe peoples. The book not only imparts historical information but also explains traditional beliefs held by the two tribes. In addition, it delineates particulars of how the Ottawa and Ojibwa hunted, fished, and trapped. The book includes a basic grammar of the Ottawa and Anishi-naabe languages. Blackbird also published *Complete Both Early and Late History of Ottawa and Chippewa Indians of Michigan: A Grammar of Their Language, Personal and Family History of the Author* (1897) and *The Indian Problem, from the Indian's Standpoint* (1900), in which he advocated that Native Americans be given U.S. citizenship.

SIMON POKAGON (Potawatomi, ca. 1830–1899) spent much of his life in Michigan and Illinois. He was a celebrated literary figure in his day, was an honored guest at the 1893 World's Columbian Exposition in CHICAGO, and gave a speech there. At the exposition he distributed *The Red Man's Rebuke*, which was printed on birch bark, discussed his criticisms of U.S. treatment of Native Americans, and predicted that by the mid-twentieth century there would be no more Indian reservations and that Natives would amalgamate into the dominant society. He subsequently published it as *The Red Man's Greeting* (1893). Pokagon was a popular lecturer and published a number of essays, including "An Indian on the Problems of His Race" (1895), "The Future of the Red Man" (1897), "An Indian's Plea for Prohibition" (1898), "Massacre at Fort Dearborn at Chicago" (1899), and "Algonquin Legends of Paw Paw" (1900). He was also an early advocate for treaty rights and played an important role in securing payment for the sale of Potawatomi land that became Chicago. His autobiographical novel *Queen of the Woods* (1899) gives a romantic account of the Potawatomi and warns both Indians and non-Indians of the dangers of alcohol; the volume was published posthumously. In *Indian Nation: Native American Literature and Nineteenth-Century Nationalisms* (1997) Cheryl Walker describes Pokagon's *Queen of the Woods* as "the first novel about Native Americans by a Native American" (209).

Francis La Flesche (Omaha) wrote *The Middle Five: Indian School Boys of the Omaha Tribe* (1900), a touching memoir focused on the author's years at the Presbyterian mission school in NEBRASKA. He dedicates the book to the "Universal Boy" and writes to "reveal the true nature and character of the Indian boy" (xv). La Flesche also wrote a number of short stories, few of which were published in his lifetime, which have been edited by Daniel F. Littlefield and published as *Ke-ma-ha: The Omaha Stories of Francis La Flesche* (1998). The text also includes a biographical sketch by James W. Parins. The stories were designed to show similarities between Native Americans and European Americans.

CHARLES ALEXANDER EASTMAN (Ohiyesa; Santee Dakota, 1858–1939) was born in MINNESOTA but spent several years in Canada. He returned to the United States at the age of fifteen and went on to become a physician. He penned several autobiographies, including *Indian Boyhood* (1902), *The Soul of the Indian: An Interpretation* (1911), and *From the Deep Woods to Civilization: Chapters in the Autobiography of an Indian* (1916). His works remain popular today and deal with ethical and cultural questions surrounding assimilation and religion.

Ella Cara Deloria (Yankton-Nakota, 1889–1971) was born in SOUTH DAKOTA and attended Columbia University, where she studied under the famed anthropologist Franz Boas (1858–1942). Deloria was an excellent translator and interpreter of Lakota narratives. She published *Dakota Texts* (1932), which focused on translations and analysis, and *Dakota Grammar* (1941), which has a linguistic focus. Her best-known work is *Waterlily*, which was completed in 1944 but not published until 1988. *Waterlily* is a fictional work set primarily in the precontact era. The protagonists, Blue Bird and her daughter, Waterlily, illustrate the complex networks of Dakota kinship and thus reveal the intricacies of communal identity.

BLACK ELK (Oglala Sioux, 1863–1950) witnessed the Battle of the Little Bighorn in 1876, joined Buffalo Bill's Wild West Show, and supported the Ghost Dance movement before converting to Catholicism late in life. Black Elk told his story to JOHN G (NEISENAU) NEIHARDT (1881–1973), but the process was complicated by the fact that Ben Black Elk translated and Neihardt's daughter transcribed the meetings. Neihardt is considered the author, not just the editor, of BLACK ELK SPEAKS (1932), and questions about the accuracy of the text have persisted. The book describes Black Elk's development as a spiritual leader and gives a narrative of Lakota history. In 1972 *Black Elk Speaks* was reissued in paperback and gained significant popularity. A new edition, annotated by Raymond J. DeMallie, was released in 2008. Black Elk describes seven primary Sioux spiritual practices in *The Sacred Pipe* (1953), drawn from interviews and edited by Joseph E. Brown.

LUTHER STANDING BEAR (Ota Kte/Mochunozhin; Lakota, 1868–1939) grew up on the Pine Ridge Reservation in South Dakota and attended Carlisle Indian School in Pennsylvania. He worked a variety of jobs and wrote *My People, the Sioux* (1928), the *Land of the Spotted Eagle* (1933), and *Stories of the Sioux* (1934). Like Standing Bear, ZITKALA-ŠA (RED BIRD / Gertrude Simmons Bonnin; Yankton Dakota Sioux, 1876–1938) was raised on the Pine Ridge Reservation in South Dakota. She attended and later taught at Carlisle Indian School in Pennsylvania. An activist for Indian rights, she published essays in the *Atlantic Monthly*, including "Impressions of an Indian Childhood" (January 1900), "School Days of an Indian Girl" (February 1900), "An Indian Teacher among Indians" (March 1900), and "Why I Am a Pagan" (1902). She also wrote two volumes of traditional stories, *Old Indian Legends* (1901) and *American Indian Stories* (1921).

Twentieth- and Twenty-First-Century Memoirists: Native American memoirists from the twentieth century forward describe diverse experiences, illustrating the wide range of knowledge, understanding, and feelings that exist among modern Native Americans. Anthropologists and other scholars continue to play a role in many autobiographies, working as collaborators with Natives. Like nineteenth-century autobiographers, Native autobiographers of the twentieth and twenty-first centuries write to counter continuing stereotypes and show that Native Americans have not vanished but, in fact, are thriving.

Anishinaabe memoirists include John Rogers (Chief Snow Cloud / Way Quah Gishig, b. 1890), who wrote *A Chippewa Speaks* (1957), republished as *Red World and White: Memories of a Chippewa Boyhood* (1996). Rogers's narrative begins when he returns home at age twelve to the White Earth Reservation from boarding school in Flandreau, South Dakota. He critiques his educational experience and Christianity. The narrative continues until 1909, when he is reunited with his father, a Midewiwin leader and lumberman, at Cass Lake, Minnesota. The University of Oklahoma Press edition of 1996 includes a forward by Melissa Meyer that provides useful historical context.

Maude Kegg (Naawakamigookwe; Anishinaabe, 1904–1996) was born in a birch bark wigwam near a wild rice harvesting camp in Crow Wing County, Minnesota. In 1969 she began working with linguist John D. Nichols, relating stories of her childhood. She published *Portage Lake: Memories of an Ojibwe Childhood* (1993), as told to John D. Nichols, and *Nookomis Gaa-Inaajimotawid: What My Grandmother Told Me* (1990), a special edition of *Oshkaabewis Native Journal*. Kegg describes her life in relation to seasonal activities like maple sugaring, muskrat and beaver trapping, gardening, berry picking, swimming, wild rice harvesting, camping, hunting, and fishing. Her stories focus on her childhood but also include references to significant historical events. The bilingual presentation of these texts provides an opportunity for language students to explore the intricacies of the Anishinaabe language. In 1990 Kegg received a National Heritage Fellowship from the National Endowment for the Arts in recognition of her achievements as a folk artist and cultural interpreter.

Keewaydinoquay Peschel (Anishinaabe, ca. 1919–1999) grew up in Michigan and went on to work in anthropology and ethnobotany. Published after her death, *Keewaydinoquay: Stories from My Youth* (2006) was edited by Lee Boisvert. Keewaydinoquay describes her early childhood and education, including her experiences at public school and her apprenticeship to the highly regarded Anishinaabe medicine woman Nodjimahkwe.

Ron(ald J.) Paquin (Anishinaabe, b. 1942) wrote *Not First in Nobody's Heart: The Life Story of a Contemporary Chippewa* (1992) with Robert Doherty. In this autobiography Paquin gives a candid account of his life in Michigan. He describes the abuse he suffered at the hands of his parents, his teenage alcoholism, his prison experiences, his attempted suicide, and, finally, his marriage, the birth of a son, his activism with regard to Native fishing rights, and his efforts to support his family. *While the Locus Slept* (2001), the powerful Minnesota Book Award–winning memoir by Peter Razor

(Anishinaabe, b. 1928), also tells a story of strength and resilience, detailing the abuse he suffered as a child at a Minnesota orphanage in the 1930s.

In *Women of White Earth* (1999) Vance Vannote compiles photographs and interviews with forty-three female citizens of the White Earth Anishinaabe nation. Illustrating a wide range of diverse experiences, the women discuss politics, education, religion and spirituality, identity, and their goals and dreams. *Memories of Lac du Flambeau Elders* (2004), edited by Elizabeth M. Tornes, similarly compiles photographs and interviews with fifteen Anishinaabe elders from Lac du Flambeau, WISCONSIN. The elders discuss their varied life experiences, including both the survival of tribal traditions and their adaption in the face of adversity.

Sioux memoirs include *Madonna Swan: A Lakota Woman's Story* (1991) by Madonna Swan (Lakota, 1928–1993) and Mark St. Pierre and *Standing in the Light: A Lakota Way of Seeing* (1996) by Severt Young Bear (Lakota, 1934–1996) and R. D. Theisz. Richard Erdoes has collaborated on several Native American memoirs, including *Lakota Woman* (1990) and *Ohitika Woman* (1993) by Mary Crow Dog (Brave Bird, 1954–2013), *Crow Dog: Four Generations of Sioux Medicine Men* (1995) by Leonard Crow Dog (b. 1942), *Ojibwa Warrior: Dennis Banks and the Rise of the American Indian Movement* (2005) by Dennis Banks (b. 1937), and *Lame Deer, Seeker of Visions* (1972) by John (Fire) Lame Deer (Tháhča Hušté; Lakota, ca. 1903–1976).

Autobiographies by Native Americans of other Midwestern tribes include two books by Sam Blowsnake (Hágaga; Ho-Chunk, 1875–1965), an important informant of ethnologist Paul Radin. Blowsnake's *The Autobiography of a Winnebago Indian* (1920) was translated into English by Radin and describes his extraordinary life, including cultural changes he experienced and observed, his initiation into the Medicine Dance, his marriage, traveling with a circus, his alcoholism, and his murder of a Potawatomi man. Radin later edited the work and published it as *Crashing Thunder: The Autobiography of an American Indian* (1926). (Crashing Thunder was Blowsnake's brother, whose name Radin substituted in the volume because he preferred the sound of that name.)

Sam Carley Blowsnake, ca. 1900. Photo by
Charles Van Schaick.
Courtesy of the Wisconsin Historical Society

Anthropologist Nancy O. Lurie interviewed Blowsnake's sister, Mountain Wolf
Woman (Ho-Chunk, 1884–1960), and wrote
down Mountain Wolf Woman's life story.
It was published as *Mountain Wolf Woman,
Sister of Crashing Thunder: The Autobiography
of a Winnebago Indian* in 1961. In the book
Mountain Wolf Woman discussed her marriages and religious practices, including her
use of peyote.

*Oneida Lives: Long-Lost Voices of the Wiscon-
sin Oneidas* (2005), edited by Gerald L. Hill, L.
Gordon McLester III (Oneida), and Herbert S. Lewis (Oneida), contains sixty-five
chronicles told by fifty-eight Oneidas; the
stories were drawn from a large collection
of handwritten accounts of the Works Progress Administration FEDERAL WRITERS' PROJ-
ECT undertaking called the Oneida Ethnological Study (1940–1942). These accounts are
grouped thematically and describe everything from work and economic struggles to
family dynamics and religious practices.

**Twentieth- and Twenty-First-Cen-
tury Writers:** Several themes characterize Native American writers in the modern era. Foremost is identity. Many Native
American authors write to counter stereotypes while delineating their own experiences and perspectives. During the twentieth century the population of Native
American shifted from a majority living on
reservations to a majority living in urban
areas, often to attend school and find employment. Native American writers in the
Midwest have depicted their experiences
living in urban areas, as well as their connections, or lack thereof, to their home reservations. Native American resilience and
ability to adapt to new living conditions
are extraordinary.

Many Native American writers use multiple characters to narrate a single text. This
usage illustrates multiple perspectives shifting the balance of authority and truth. Another theme is "survivance," a term coined
by GERALD (ROBERT) VIZENOR (Anishinaabe, b.
1934) that combines "survival" and "resistance." Vizenor asserts in *Manifest Manners*
(1994) that "the shadows and language of
tribal poets and novelists could be the new
ghost dance literature, the shadow literature
of liberation, that enlivens tribal survivance"
(106). Echoing many Native American

writers, Vizenor attests to the power of words and stories, arguing that literature can provide liberation and support cultural endurance.

Underlying many of the aforementioned themes is sovereignty. Native authors deal directly and indirectly with the many definitions and manifestations of sovereignty. As citizens of tribal nations, Native Americans have a distinct political status and often use literature as a means to support the political, cultural, and intellectual sovereignty of their specific nations. In a similar vein, Native authors consider nationhood and nationalism. In *American Indian Literary Nationalism* (2005), Jace G. Weaver (Cherokee, b. 1957), Robert A. Warrior (Osage, b. 1963), and Craig S. Womack (Muscogee Creek–Cherokee) argue that approaching Native American literature from a "nationalist" perspective, which is one approach to the interpretation of literatures centered on political implications, can provide meaningful insights, as well as support for sovereignty. Critics are now examining Native American literatures for the ways in which they might define and articulate native forms of nationalism.

Two of the best-known, most prolific, and most influential Native American writers are Anishinaabe. The works of Gerald Vizenor and (Karen) Louise Erdrich (b. 1954) have transformed the field of Native American literature. Both have employed trickster themes in their work and subvert major stereotypes, including the perception that Natives exist only in the past and on isolated reservations. Vizenor is well known both for creative and scholarly work, while Erdrich's books are extraordinarily popular.

Vizenor grew up in Minneapolis (see Minneapolis/St. Paul) and has taught at several universities, including the University of Minnesota, the University of California–Berkeley, and the University of New Mexico. He is currently retired in Naples, Florida. Vizenor has published more than forty books in a variety of genres, including fiction, poetry, autobiography, history, and critical studies. He had an interest in haiku and began publishing in that genre. He published his first collection, *Two Wings the Butterfly*, in 1962 and went on to publish *Raising the Moon Vines* (1964), *Seventeen Chirps* (1964), *Slight*

Abrasions with Jerome Downs (1966), *Empty Swings* (1967), *Matsushima: Pine Islands* (1984), *Cranes Arise* (1999), and *Favor of Crows* (2014). Many of Vizenor's haiku focus on nature and turn on an uncommon juxtaposition or ironic twist, thereby avoiding romantic images and gesturing beyond the poem toward experience.

A primary theme of his work is the fight against the victimization of Native Americans and the static identities often assigned to Natives. Vizenor's distinct style includes the introduction of new terms, such as "postindian," "imagic," and "survivance," of which the last has gained currency among scholars. Vizenor's novel *Darkness in Saint Louis: Bearheart* (1978; republished as *Bearheart: The Heirship Chronicles* in 1990) is told as a story within a story. Saint Louis Bearheart, an Indian working at the Bureau of Indian Affairs, has just completed a novel titled *Cedarfair Circus: Grave Reports from the Cultural Word Wars*, at the time of the takeover of the bureau. The manuscript describes the journey of Proude Four, an Anishinaabe shaman, his wife, and a number of pilgrims from Wisconsin to New Mexico. Their journey is spurred by oil shortages, and they encounter on their journey a number of fantastic figures out of the trickster tradition. Vizenor won the American Book Award for *Griever: An American Monkey King in China* (1990). His other novels include *The Heirs of Columbus* (1991), *Chancers: Novel* (2001), *Father Meme* (2008), and *Shrouds of White Earth* (2010). *Blue Ravens* (2014) explores the experiences of two brothers from White Earth in World War I and their lives after the war. Vizenor's recurrent themes of chance, survivance, and irony underlie the novel's narrative. Vizenor's theoretical works include *Manifest Manners: Narratives on Postindian Survivance* (1999) and *Fugitive Poses: Native American Indian Scenes of Absence and Presence* (2000). Vizenor's epic poem *Bear Island: The War at Sugar Point* (2006) tells of a little-known battle in 1898 between the U.S. Army and the Anishinaabe at Sugar Point on the Leech Lake Reservation in Minnesota, when the Anishinaabe defeated the U.S. Army despite being outnumbered three to one.

Louise Erdrich is one of the best-known and best-selling contemporary Native American authors. Erdrich grew up in Wahpeton, NORTH DAKOTA, where her parents taught at the Bureau of Indian Affairs School. She currently resides in Minneapolis, where she continues to write and operate an independent bookstore, Birchbark Books. Her debut novel, *LOVE MEDICINE* (1984), won the National Book Critics Circle Award. Her novels *Tracks* (1988), *The Beet Queen* (1986), *The Bingo Palace* (1994), *Four Souls* (2004), and *The Plague of Doves* (2008), which center on a fictional Anishinaabe community in North Dakota, are connected through the use of multiple overlapping narrators. The novels illustrate connections between generations, impacts of government policies, and the resilience of the Anishinaabe. In addition, they directly and indirectly address the powers of words and stories. For example, in *Tracks* Nanapush attests to the healing power of story: "I saved myself by starting a story. . . . I got well by talking. Death could not get a word in edgewise, grew discouraged, and traveled on" (46). *The Round House* (2012) is also set on a fictional reservation in North Dakota, but this time a single narrator, Joe, grapples with the complexities of justice, including jurisdictional issues that are very real in Native nations today, and the violence in his community as he comes of age.

Erdrich has also published several children's books, including *The Birchbark House* (1999), *The Game of Silence* (2005), and *The Porcupine Year* (2008), a series that chronicles the life of an Anishinaabe girl. These books follow Anishinaabe history and include interactions with Anglo Americans. Erdrich has also published the poetry volumes *Jacklight* (1984), *Baptism of Desire* (1989), and *Original Fire: Selected and New Poems* (2003). Her works of nonfiction include *The Blue Jay's Dance* (1996), a memoir of early motherhood that eloquently describes the bond between mother and baby, and *Books and Islands in Ojibwe Country: Traveling through the Land of My Ancestors* (2006), an account of her travels though southern Ontario, where she sees sacred rock paintings created centuries ago. Erdrich's sister Heid E. Erdrich (b. 1963) writes about spirituality, her family's Ojibwe and German heritage, and other subjects in several books of poetry including *Cell Traffic: New and Selected Poems* (2012). Her nonfiction book *Original Local: In-*

digenous Foods, Stories, and Recipes from the Upper Midwest appeared in 2013. She also makes short films, directs Wiigwaas Press, an Ojibwe language publisher, and collaborates with her sister Louise on writing workshops and programs supporting indigenous languages.

Kimberly M. Blaeser (Anishinaabe, b. 1955) grew up on the White Earth Reservation in Minnesota and currently resides near Milwaukee, where she teaches at the University of Wisconsin–Milwaukee. She has published three collections of poetry: *Trailing You* (1994), *Absentee Indians, and Other Poems* (2002), and *Apprenticed to Justice* (2007). Blaeser's poetry explores many themes, including identity, motherhood, place/nature, and justice. She has also written several critical works, including "New Frontier of Native American Literature: Dis-arming History with Tribal Humor," in *Native American Perspectives on Literature and History* (1994), edited by Alan R. Velie, 37–50, in which she explores the ways in which Native American

Wisconsin Poet Laureate (2015–2016) Kimberly Blaeser, 1999. Photo by Vance Vannate.

© Kimberly Blaeser

writers defy binary constructions of literature and history. Blaeser was selected to serve as Wisconsin state Poet Laureate for 2015–2016.

Gordon Henry Jr. (Anishinaabe, b. 1955) was born in Philadelphia and grew up on various military bases because his father served in the U.S. Navy. He teaches at Michigan State University. Henry's first novel, *The Light People* (1994), won the American Book Award in 1995. The novel is set on the fictional Fineday Reservation and begins with Oskinaway's quest to find his mother, who "vanished on the powwow trail" (3). As he seeks the advice of tribal elders, the story continues through a large cast of characters, each of whom narrates part of the story. The novel is humorous but deals with important themes of cultural identity and history. Henry's poetry has been featured in a number of ANTHOLOGIES, including *Songs from This Earth on Turtle's Back* (1983), *Returning the Gift* (1994), and *Traces in Blood, Bone, and Stone* (2006), and he has published a book of poetry, *The Failure of Certain Charms* (2008).

David Treuer (Anishinaabe, b. 1970) was raised on the Leech Lake Reservation in Minnesota. Before earning his doctorate in anthropology at the University of Michigan, he took degrees at Princeton University, where his thesis adviser in the creative-writing program was TONI MORRISON (CHLOE ARDELIA WOFFORD, b. 1931). He currently teaches at the University of Southern California. Treuer is the author of four novels featuring Anishinaabe characters, set in a variety of locations but predominantly in Minnesota: *Little* (1996), *The Hiawatha* (2000), *The Translation of Dr. Apelles* (2006), and *Prudence* (2015). In 2012 he published *Rez Life*, his first work of nonfiction. Treuer has also written a critical work, *Native American Fiction: A User's Manual* (2006), in which he examines a selection of novels by several prominent Native American authors. Treuer questions the very term "Native American fiction" and the validity of debates of authenticity that have surrounded Native American literature. This literature is generally defined as being written by a Native American; however, questions about who is "really" Native abound. In addition, some would like to create other criteria, for example, subject matter or writing style, and use those markers to define Native American literature.

A number of Sioux writers have distinguished themselves. Elizabeth Cook-Lynn (b. Elizabeth Bowed Head Irving; Dakota, 1930) was raised on the Crow Creek Reservation in South Dakota. Her family has been active in tribal politics, and she has continued this tradition of activism through literature. She has written in a variety of genres, including two novels, *From the River's Edge* (1991) and *That Guy Wolf Dancing* (2014); a series of short stories, *The Power of Horses, and Other Stories* (1990); a book of poetry, *I Remember the Fallen Trees: New and Selected Poems* (1998); and a book of novellas, *Aurelia: A Crow Creek Trilogy* (1999). Cook-Lynn's multigenre work *Then Badger Said This* (1983) combines essays, traditional narratives, and poems. In 2007 Cook-Lynn received the Lifetime Achievement Award from the Native Writers' Circle of the Americas.

Frances Washburn (Lakota/Anishinaabe, b.1949) grew up on the Pine Ridge Reservation in South Dakota. In her debut novel, *Elsie's Business* (2006), a modern retelling of the Lakota Deer Woman story, the narrator seeks to find out the truth about the 1969 rape and murder of Elise Roberts, the daughter of an African American father and a Native American mother. She has also published *The Sacred White Turkey* (2010) and *The Red Bird All-Indian Traveling Band* (2014).

Joseph M. Marshall III (Sicunga Lakota Sioux, b. 1945) grew up on the Rosebud Reservation in South Dakota, where he was raised by his grandparents. He has been active in education and helped found Sinte Gleska University (1971) on the Rosebud Reservation. Marshall is a prolific writer and has published in a variety of genres. In *Walking with Grandfather: The Wisdom of Lakota Elders* (2005) Marshall shares stories and lessons his grandfather taught him. Two of his works deal specifically with resilience: *Keeping Going: The Art of Perseverance* (2009) and *The Lakota Way of Strength and Courage: Lessons in Resilience from the Bow and Arrow* (2012). His novels *Hundred in the Hand: A Novel* (2007) and *The Long Knives Are Crying* (2008) are westerns that transcend the genre and depict Lakota experiences at the Fetterman Fight of 1866 and at the Battle of the Little Bighorn. He has also published a collection of stories, *The Dance House: Stories from Rosebud* (1998), and a children's book, *How Not to Catch Fish: And Other Adventures of Iktomi* (2005).

Susan Power (Dakota, b. 1961) grew up in Chicago, Illinois, where her mother was very active in the Native American community. She now lives in St. Paul. See MINNEAPOLIS/ST. PAUL. Power wrote *The Grass Dancer* (1994), which won the 1995 Ernest Hemingway Award for best first work of fiction. Set on a North Dakota reservation, *Grass Dancer* is a series of intricately interconnected stories that flow backward and forward in time between 1864 and 1982. Power has published a book of fiction and nonfiction, *Roofwalker* (2002), which won the Milkweed National Fiction Prize. In *Sacred Wilderness* (2014) four women from different backgrounds and eras help heal and restore a mixed-blood woman who has found that the American Dream is a life of emptiness.

Gwen Nell Westerman (Santee Dakota, b. 1957) has published *Follow the Blackbirds* (2013), a collection of poetry in English that often shifts to the Dakota language. Her poems evoke the Great Plains landscape and express deep concern for family, community, and cultural survival, based on the spiritual power of language. Professor of English at Minnesota State University, Mankato, Westerman is also co-author with Bruce White of *Mni Sota Makoce: The Land of the Dakota* (2012), a study of Dakota history in Minnesota based on tribal narratives and early historical documents.

Contemporary writers of other Native American origins include Nas'Naga / Roger Russell (Shawnee, b. 1941), whose novel *Indians' Summer* (1975) involves U.S. and Canadian Indians joining with India to overthrow the American and Canadian colonial governments. He also has written two volumes of poetry, *The Darker Side of Glory* (1979) and *Faces beneath the Grass* (1979). Diane Glancy (Cherokee, b. 1941) was born in ST. LOUIS, MISSOURI, but spent many years living in Minnesota as an English professor at Macalester College in St. Paul. She won the North American Indian Prose Award for *Claiming Breath* (1996), a mixed-genre, non-linear work in which she describes her life as a woman, mother, and Native American. Her novels include *Pushing the Bear* (1998), *The Only Piece of Furniture in the House* (2001), *The Mask Maker* (2002), *Designs of the Night Sky* (2002), *Stone Heart: A Novel of Sacajawea* (2004), *Flutie* (2007), and *The Reason for Crows* (2009). Her poetry collections include *The Relief of America* (2000), *The Stones for a Pillow* (2001), *The Shadow's Horse* (2003), and *Asylum in the Grasslands* (2007). She received the Juniper Poetry Prize from the University of Massachusetts Press for *Primer of the Obsolete* (2004). *In-Between Places* (2005) is a collection of eleven essays that takes the reader along on a journey with Glancy through New Mexico and to China while discussing the craft of writing.

Although Roberta J. Hill (formerly Roberta Hill Whiteman; Oneida, b. 1947) has spent the majority of her life in the Midwest, she grew up among the Oneida community in western Wisconsin, as well as in Green Bay. The movements of her family between those two locations and the removal of her Oneida ancestors from New York State have informed her poetry. She earned her undergraduate degree at the University of Wisconsin and her doctorate at the University of Minnesota. Hill has published two collections of poetry: *Star Quilt* (1984) and *Philadelphia Flowers* (1996). Her poems have also appeared in numerous anthologies, including *Songs from This Earth on Turtle's Back* (1983), *That's What She Said* (1984), and *Reinventing the Enemy's Language* (1998). Her poems cover a range of topics; many of them describe vivid nature scenes, while others are personal, detailing her roles as daughter, mother, and wife; still others engage with social and political issues. She has taught for many years at the University of Wisconsin.

RAY (ANTHONY) YOUNG BEAR (Mesquakie; b. 1950) wrote *Black Eagle Child* (1996) and *Remnants of the First Earth* (1998); both are narrated by Edgar Principal Bear. The mixed-genre texts chronicle Edgar's life at the Black Eagle Child Settlement in IOWA. Young Bear has received high acclaim for his ability to connect past, present, and future, as well as tribal histories and personal experiences. Young Bear is also known for his powerful poetry, which explores everything from TV dinners to the natural world. His volumes of poetry include *Winter of the Salamander* (1980), *The Invisible Musician* (1996), and *The Rock Island Hiking Club* (2001).

SELECTED WORKS: Major texts by nineteenth-century Native Americans in the Midwest include *Life of Ma-ka-tai-me-she-kia-kiak, or Black Hawk* (1833), George Copway's *The Life, History and Travels of Kah-Ge-Ga-Gah-Bowh (George Copway)* (1847), Andrew J. Blackbird's *History of the Ottawa and Chippewa Indians of Michigan* (1887), and Charles Alexander Eastman's *Indian Boyhood* (1902). Although it has been the subject of much scholarly debate, John G. Neihardt's *Black Elk Speaks* (1932) remains a classic.

Important twentieth-century autobiographies include Sam Blowsnake's *The Autobiography of a Winnebago Indian* (1920), Maude Kegg's *Portage Lake: Memories of an Ojibwe Childhood* (1993), and John Rogers's *A Chippewa Speaks* (1957). Major works of fiction include Gerald Vizenor's *Darkness in Saint Louis: Bearheart* (1978), Louise Erdrich's *Love Medicine* (1984), Elizabeth Cook-Lynn's *From the River's Edge* (1991), Gordon Henry Jr.'s *The Light People* (1994), and Diane Glancy's *Pushing the Bear* (1998). Books of poetry include *Winter of the Salamander* (1980) by Ray A. Young Bear, *Star Quilt* (1984) by Roberta Hill, *Trailing You* (1994) by Kimberly Blaeser, *Cell Traffic* (2012) by Heid E. Erdrich (b. 1963), and *Follow the Blackbirds* (2013) by Gwen Nell Westerman.

Several anthologies compile Midwestern texts from Native American oral traditions. Anton Treuer's *Living Our Language: Ojibwe Tales and Oral Histories* (2001) is a bilingual anthology of stories told by Ojibwa-language speakers and transcribed by Treuer. Biographical information for each speaker is given. The stories provide an opportunity for Ojibwa-language learners to engage with contemporary texts in the language. Songs by Midwestern tribes may be found in Brian Swann's *Song of the Sky: Versions of Native American Song-Poems* (1993) and Victoria Lindsay Levine's *Writing American Indian Music: Historic Transcriptions, Notations, and Arrangements* (2002). *Great Speeches by Native Americans* (2000), edited by Robert Blaisdell, includes oratory by Pontiac (Ottawa), Tecumsah (Shawnee), Black Hawk

(Sauk), and other Midwestern figures. See also *Native American Speakers of the Eastern Woodlands: Selected Speeches and Critical Analyses* (2001), edited by Barbara Alice Mann. Victoria Brehm's *Star Songs and Water Spirits: A Great Lakes Native Reader* (2011) is a substantial volume that contains a range of historic and contemporary narratives, including traditional/sacred stories, songs, poetry, speeches, and fiction.

Selections by Black Hawk, Black Elk, Charles A. Eastman, Sam Blowsnake, and Gerald Vizenor appear in *Native American Autobiography: An Anthology* (1994), edited by Arnold Krupat. Gerald Vizenor and Diane Glancy contributed to *I Tell You Now: Autobiographical Essays by Native American Writers* (2005), edited by Brian Swann and Arnold Krupat.

Literary anthologies featuring contemporary Midwestern Native American writers include Duane Niatum's *The Harper's Anthology of 20th Century Native American Poetry* (1988), Clifford Trafzer's *Earth Song, Sky Spirit: Short Stories of the Contemporary Native American Experience* (1997), and John L. Purdy and James Ruppert's *Nothing but the Truth: An Anthology of Native American Literature* (2000). Kimberly Blaeser has edited *Stories Migrating Home: A Collection of Anishinaabe Prose* (1999) and *Traces in Blood, Bone, and Stone: Contemporary Ojibwe Poetry* (2006). Kathleen Tigerman's *Wisconsin Indian Literature: Anthology of Native Voices* (2006) emphasizes oral traditions as shared by elders and educators from Wisconsin's twelve Native tribes and bands. Jane Katz's *Messengers of the Wind: Native American Women Tell Their Life Stories* (1995) includes the life stories of several Wisconsin writers. *Sister Nations: Native American Women Writers on Community* (2002), an anthology of fiction, prose, and poetry, was edited by Heid E. Erdrich (Anishinaabe) and Laura Tohe (Navajo/Dine), with a forward by Winona LaDuke (Anishinaabe). This anthology contains the writings of many contemporary Midwestern Native Americans, including Roberta J. Hill (Oneida), Elizabeth Cook-Lynn (Dakota), Marcie R. Rendon (Anishinaabe, b. 1952), and Kimberly M. Blaeser.

FURTHER READING: Many readers will find it useful to familiarize themselves with Native American history to provide political, social, and cultural context for literary works. *Enduring Nations: Native Americans in the Midwest* (2008), edited by R. David Edmunds, shows how the region's Native peoples have influenced Midwestern culture even while adapting to changing circumstances. Tribes in the region's western reaches are covered in Loretta Fowler's *The Columbia Guide to American Indians of the Great Plains* (2003). Helen Hornbeck Tanner's *Atlas of Great Lakes Indian History* (1987) provides invaluable information and includes many beautiful maps and illustrations. Patty Loew's (Anishinaabe) *Indian Nations of Wisconsin: Histories of Endurance and Renewal* (2001) devotes a single chapter to each Native nation now located in Wisconsin. Nancy Oestreich Lurie's *Wisconsin Indians* (revised edition, 2002) is an excellent and concise account of Wisconsin's Native peoples.

For background on the Anishinaabe, consult Bruce White's *We Are at Home: Pictures of the Ojibwe People* (2007), a collection of photographs of Anishinaabe people in Minnesota up to 1950, accompanied by White's conscientious introduction and contextual information. Thomas Vennum Jr.'s *Wild Rice and the Ojibway People* (1988) delineates the cultural and economic importance of wild rice to the Anishinaabe and includes historical and ethnological accounts combined with the author's fieldwork, in which he privileges the words of his informants. *Ojibwe Waasa Inaabidaa: We Look in All Directions* (2001) by Thomas Peacock (Anishinaabe) and Marlene Wisuri gives a wide range of historical and cultural information about the Anishinaabe. Canadian Anishinaabe author Basil Johnston's *Ojibway Ceremonies* (1990) and *Manitous: The Spiritual World of the Ojibway* (2001) are useful for understanding Anishinaabe spiritual practices. In *Those Who Belong: Identity, Family, Blood, and Citizenship among the White Earth Anishinaabeg* (2015), Jill Doerfler describes how the Anishinaabe have alternately resisted and acceded to the U.S. government's use of blood quantum to determine Native identity.

On the Sioux, consult *Mni Sota Makoce: The Land of the Dakota* (2013) by Gwen Westerman and Bruce White, which is an important contribution to the history of the Dakotas in Minnesota, including their fortitude in the face of forced removal. Guy Gibbon's *The Sioux: The Dakota and Lakota Nations* (2002) covers history and culture from prehistory to 2000 in a single volume. Jeffrey Ostler's *The Plains Sioux and U.S. Colonialism from Lewis and Clark to Wounded Knee* (2004) has received scholarly acclaim for its exemplary analysis of primary texts. Donovin Arleigh Sprague (Cheyenne River Sioux) drew on photographs, personal interviews, and family stories to write *Cheyenne River Sioux* (2003) and *Standing Rock Sioux* (2004).

For a broad introduction to Native American literatures, see Suzanne Lundquist's *Native American Literatures* (2004) and *The Columbia Guide to American Indian Literatures of the United States since 1945* (2006), edited by Eric Cheyfitz. Literary scholarship focused on the Midwest includes Blair Whitney's "American Indian Literature of the Great Lakes," *Great Lakes Review: A Journal of Midwest Culture* 2.2 (Winter 1976): 43–53; P. Jane Hafen's "Native American Writers of the Midwest," in *Updating the Literary West* (1997), edited by the Western Literature Association, 711–19; and "'Hey! Get Up! You Got No Relations Here!' Native American Humorous Narratives of Cultural Renewal in Michigan" by Mary Magoulick, *Midwestern Folklore* 27.1 (Spring 2001): 18–36.

For commentary on important speeches, consult *Oratory in Native North America* (2002) by William M. Clements. Frederick W. Turner's *The Portable North American Indian Reader* (1977) contains speeches by Tecumseh (Shawnee), Senachwine (Potawatomi), and Sitting Bull (Hunkpapa Lakota). In *The Native American Oral Tradition: Voices of the Spirit and Soul* (2000) Lois J. Einhorn gives a thorough account of Native American oral tradition and includes some Midwestern examples. A valuable source on the functions of Ojibwa songs is Michael D. McNally's *Ojibwe Singers: Hymns, Grief, and a Native Culture in Motion* (2000).

In "The Anishinaabe Point of View: The History of the Great Lakes Region to 1800 in Nineteenth-Century Mississauga, Odawa, and Ojibwa Historiography," *Canadian Historical Review* 73.2 (June 1992): 194–210, Peter MacLeod discusses the work of Andrew J. Blackbird, George Copway, and other Native American writers in relation to European

American sources. An excellent article on Black Hawk's *Life of Ma-Ka-Tai-Me-She-Kia-Kiak, or Black Hawk* (1833) is Mark Rifkin's "Documenting Tradition: Territoriality and Textuality in Black Hawk's Narrative," *American Literature* 80.4 (December 2008): 677–705. On Francis LaFlesche, see Sherry Smith's "Francis LaFlesche and the World of Letters," *American Indian Quarterly* 25.4 (Fall 2001): 579–604. On Jane Johnston Schoolcraft, see Robert Dale Parker's *The Sound the Stars Make Rushing through the Sky: The Writings of Jane Johnston Schoolcraft* (2007). Chapter 3, "Between the People and the Land: Luther Standing Bear, Mother Earth, and Assimilation," in *Listening to the Land: Native American Literary Responses to the Landscape* (2008) by Lee Schweninger, 57–74, examines the works of Luther Standing Bear for the ways in which the earth is described. In *Interpreting the Legacy: John Neihardt and "Black Elk Speaks"* (2003), Brian Holloway explores some of the issues relating to the collaborative nature of the text and argues that Neihardt attempted to maintain as much of Black Elk's views as possible.

Hertha Dawn Wong discusses Charles A. Eastman, Sam Blowsnake, Black Elk, and Mountain Wolf Woman in *Sending my Heart Back across the Years: Tradition and Innovation in Native American Autobiography* (1992). H. David Brumble III includes chapters on Eastman and Blowsnake in *American Indian Autobiography* (2008). Two other important studies with Midwestern coverage are Arnold Krupat's *For Those Who Come After: A Study of Native American Autobiography* (1985) and Stephanie A. Sellers's *Native American Autobiography Redefined* (2007).

On Eastman, see Drew Lopenzina's "'Good Indian': Charles Eastman and the Warrior as Civil Servant," *American Indian Quarterly* 27.3–4 (Summer/Fall 2003): 727–57; and *Dakota Philosopher* (2009) by David Martinez (Pima). For analysis of Zitkala-Ša, see P. Jane Hafen's "Zitkala-Ša: Sentimentality and Sovereignty," *Wíčazo Ša Review* 12.2 (Fall 1997): 31–41; Ruth Spack's "Re-visioning Sioux Women: Zitkala-Ša's Revolutionary *American Indian Stories*," *Legacy* 14.1 (1997): 25–42; and Gary Totten's "Zitkala-Ša and the Problem of Regionalism: Nations, Narra-

tives, and Critical Traditions," *American Indian Quarterly* 29.1–2 (Spring 2005): 84–123.

On Ella Deloria, see Susan Gardner's "Speaking of Ella Deloria," *American Indian Quarterly* 24.3 (Summer 2000): 456–82; and Maria Eugenia Cotera's "'All My Relatives Are Noble': Recovering the Feminine in Ella Cara Deloria's 'Waterlily,'" *American Indian Quarterly* 28.1/2 (Winter/Spring 2004): 52–72. On Keewaydinoquay Peschel, see Nan J. Giblin's "Keewaydinoquay, Woman-of-the-Northwest-Wind: The Life and Philosophy of a Native American Teacher," *Counseling and Values* 42.3 (April 1998): 226–33.

The Cambridge Companion to Native American Literature (2005), edited by Joy Porter and Kenneth M. Roemer, includes "Gerald Vizenor's Post-Indian Liberation" by Kimberly M. Blaeser (257–70) and "Louise Erdrich's Storied Universe" by Catherine Rainwater (271–82). For more on Vizenor, consult Deborah L. Madsen's *Understanding Gerald Vizenor* (2009), Kimberly Blaeser's *Gerald Vizenor: Writing in the Oral Tradition* (1996), A. Robert Lee's *Loosing the Seams: Interpretations of Gerald Vizenor* (2000), and Alan R. Velie's *Four American Indian Literary Masters: N. Scott Momaday, James Welch, Leslie Marmon Silko, and Gerald Vizenor* (1982). Arnold Krupat's edited collection *New Voices in Native American Literary Criticism* (1993) contains two essays on Gerald Vizenor's work. *Studies in American Indian Literature* devoted a special issue to Gerald Vizenor (Spring 1997), as did *American Indian Quarterly* (Winter 1985).

On Louise Erdrich, consult P. Jane Hafen's *Critical Insights: Louise Erdrich* (2013), Lorena L. Stookey's *Louise Erdrich: A Critical Companion* (1999), and Peter G. Beidler and Gay Barton's *A Reader's Guide to the Novels of Louise Erdrich* (2006). Collections include *The Chippewa Landscape of Louise Erdrich* (1999), edited by Allan Chavkin, and *Approaches to Teaching the Works of Louise Erdrich* (2004), edited by Greg Sarris, Connie A. Jacobs, and James R. Giles. On Kimberly Blaeser, see Molly McGlennen's "Seasonal Reverberations: Kimberly Blaeser's Poetry of Place," *Midwestern Miscellany* 32 (Spring–Fall 2004): 7–20. On David Treuer, see Padraig Kirwan's "Remapping Place and Narrative in Native

American Literature: David Treuer's *The Hi-awatha*," *American Indian Culture and Research Journal* 31.2 (2007): 1–24; and David Stirrup's "Life after Death in Poverty: David Treuer's 'Little,'" *American Indian Quarterly* 29.3/4 (Summer/Fall 2005): 651–72. On Elizabeth Cook-Lynn, see Thomas Matchie's "Spiritual Geography in Four Midwestern Novels," *Midwest Quarterly* 39.4 (Summer 1998): 373–89; and James Stripes's "'We Think in Terms of What Is Fair': Justice versus 'Just Compensation' in Elizabeth Cook-Lynn's *From the River's Edge*," *Wičazo Ša Review* 12.1 (Spring 1997): 165–87.

On Susan Power, see Lee Schweninger's "Myth Launchings and Moon Landings: Parallel Realities in Susan Power's *The Grass Dancer*," *Studies in American Indian Literatures* 16.3 (2004): 47–69. For scholarship on Diane Glancy, see Jennifer Andrews's "A Conversation with Diane Glancy," *American Indian Quarterly* 26.4 (Fall 2002): 645–58; and Amy J. Elias's "Fragments That Rune up the Shores: Pushing the Bear, Coyote Aesthetics, and Recovered History," *Modern Fiction Studies* 45.1 (Spring 1999): 185–211.

For scholarship on Ray A. Young Bear, see Robert F. Gish's "Memory and Dream in the Poetry of Ray A. Young Bear," *Minority Voices: An Interdisciplinary Journal of Literature and the Arts* 2.1 (1978): 21–29; Robert Dale Parker's "To Be There, No Authority to Anything: Ontological Desire and Cultural and Poetic Authority in the Poetry of Ray A. Young Bear," *Arizona Quarterly: A Journal of American Literature, Culture, and Theory* 50.4 (Winter 1994): 89–115; and Elias Ellefson's "An Interview with Ray A. Young Bear," in *Speaking of the Short Story: Interviews with Contemporary Writers* (1997), edited by Farhat Iftekharuddin, Mary Rohrberger, and Maurice Lee, 35–44.

Studies in American Indian Literatures, published by the Association for the Study of American Indian Literatures with the University of Nebraska Press, is the preeminent journal in the field. *Yellow Medicine Review*, founded in 2007 and based at Southwest Minnesota State University, publishes writing by indigenous peoples around the world. Although it is not exclusively devoted to Native American literatures, *American Indian Quarterly*, which is currently based at the University of New Mexico and is published with the University of Nebraska Press, publishes a significant number of articles relating to Native American literatures. Likewise, *Wičazo Ša Review*, which was founded by Elizabeth Cook-Lynn, is published at the University of Minnesota and contains articles on Native American literatures.

JILL DOERFLER (WHITE EARTH ANISHINAABE)
UNIVERSITY OF MINNESOTA–DULUTH

NATIVE AMERICANS AS DEPICTED IN MIDWESTERN LITERATURE

OVERVIEW: The portrayal of Native Americans in Midwestern literature reflects past trends in American literature. The first images of Native Americans came from Christopher Columbus in the fifteenth century. He provided both positive and negative images of natives with whom he came in contact, and although these images combined direct descriptions with the preconceptions and prejudices of fifteenth-century Italy, they were quickly replaced with more inaccurate, racist, and stereotyped images. Familiar descriptors of the natives as barbarians, heathens, and noble savages were also popularized. As Native Americans were pushed farther west, killed, or placed on reservations, their portrayal was reimagined by each generation of authors as a reflection of then-current white fears, suspicions, and government agendas. See also NATIVE AMERICAN LITERATURE.

Although it is impossible to place depictions of Native Americans in all genres of Midwestern literature in easily definable chronological categories, the general trend of literary representation from the mid-sixteenth century to the present has been an evolution of often sensationalistic and shocking depictions finally giving way to more historically accurate portrayals. Early Midwestern travel narratives in the sixteenth and seventeenth centuries often gave relatively accurate representations of Native Americans, who were not yet seen as threats requiring extermination. Many CAPTIVITY NARRATIVES of the seventeenth, eighteenth, and nineteenth centuries were embellished and sensationalistic, aimed at shocking readers and promoting anti-Indian sentiment. Later, novels, DIME NOVELS, and westerns of the nineteenth and twentieth centuries tended to justify the destruction of Indians or portray them as romantic American relics doomed to die out in the face of white expansion. Unfortunately, the images bore little to no resemblance to historical Native Americans. Because Native Americans continue to be a topic of interest to non-Native writers today, there is a need for more in-depth analysis of American Indians as depicted in Midwestern literature.

HISTORY AND SIGNIFICANCE: Travel narratives of the sixteenth and seventeenth centuries were the first American literary genre to depict Native Americans. Because travel narratives were often written by explorers and early settlers rather than by professional writers, they tended to portray life more realistically than other forms of literature, and the authors were generally more sympathetic toward indigenous people. Jesuit priests penned the first significant travel narratives describing the native peoples. Their early Midwestern accounts include meticulous descriptions of Native Americans and their ways. Although many Jesuit narratives labeled the natives savages or barbarians, they also showed respect and awe at their abilities to survive in the wilderness. Midwestern travel narratives were published as early as 1542. One of the most successful was *Description de la Louisiane . . .* (1683) by the Recollect friar Father Louis Hennepin (1626–ca. 1705). Although he was accused of exaggeration and plagiarism, Hennepin demonstrated admiration for Native people as he described their community customs and natural abilities—men as warriors and women as workers.

Because of the expansion of exploration and settlement of the West, the number of travel narratives coming out of the trans-Mississippi area increased during the eighteenth and nineteenth centuries. One of the most valuable and popular narratives written at this time was *Three Years among the Indians and Mexicans* (1846) by General Thomas James (1782–1847). This adventure tale presents an accurate representation of several Midwestern tribes and customs, as well as James's observations of and interaction with them. Although he does include some images of their brutality, he also emphasizes

their hospitality and the kindness they extended to him and his fellow travelers.

Travels through the Interior Parts of North-America, in the Years 1766, 1767, and 1768 (1778) by Jonathan Carver (1710–1780) was also widely popular. It went through at least twenty-three editions and was translated into German, French, and Dutch. Carver, thought to be the first English-speaking traveler to explore the trans-Mississippi area, visited many Native American tribes living in the Midwest. His narrative provides readers with a largely objective description of the manners, religions, customs, and languages of these Native Americans and contains the first published descriptions of some of the Sioux and Ojibwas.

One of the best-known travel narratives, albeit not entirely Midwestern, is *History of the Expedition under the Command of Captains Lewis and Clark, to the Sources of the Missouri, Thence across the Rocky Mountains and down the River Columbia to the Pacific Ocean: Performed during the Years 1804–5–6 by Order of the Government of the United States* (1814), compiled from the journals of Meriwether Lewis (1774–1809) and William Clark (1770–1838) and edited by Paul Allen. Lewis and Clark's expedition came into contact with nearly fifty tribes, many of which were Midwestern. The narrative contains meticulous descriptions of these various tribes, including the Osage of KANSAS and MISSOURI, the Otoe and Missouri who inhabited the land on the border of Missouri and NEBRASKA, the Teton and Yankton Sioux of SOUTH DAKOTA, and the Arikari of northern South Dakota.

Captivity narratives were the second major literary genre focusing significantly on Native Americans in the Midwest, and the bulk of these narratives were published during the seventeenth and eighteenth centuries. Most Midwestern captivity narratives encouraged anti-Indian sentiment with shocking tales of massacres, torture, and unfettered brutality or portrayed Native Americans sympathetically as remnants of history and symbols of America's heritage. *Narrative of the Capture and Providential Escape of Misses Frances and Almira Hall . . .* (1832) is a good example of an embellished captivity narrative meant to encourage hatred of Indians. On the other hand, *A Narrative of the Life of Mrs. Mary Jemison, Who Was Taken by the Indians in the Year 1755 . . .* (1824) by James E. Seaver (1787–1827) was one of the first captivity narratives to exhibit a new attitude of sympathy toward and acceptance of Native Americans. Jemison assimilated to her captors' culture, lived with them for over seventy years, and showed little regard for or trust in white men.

As captivity narratives became more fictionalized toward the end of the eighteenth century, they heavily influenced many other rising literary forms in the Midwest, especially novels, dime novels, and westerns. During this period Native Americans began finding their way into plays, poems, autobiographies, and even children's literature. See also CHILDREN'S AND YOUNG ADULT LITERATURE. Many Midwestern works of the early nineteenth century presented the Indian as a brutal savage bent on torturing and murdering white settlers. These literary works, in turn, were used for the extraliterary purpose of justifying any and all actions whites took against Native Americans. Many authors portrayed Indians as fated for destruction and even extermination and therefore encouraged their removal from Midwestern lands, either peaceably or by force, to make way for white settlement and civilization. The belief that Native Americans were fated to die out in the face of white progress helped ease guilty consciences over their removal and destruction. The play *Logan, the Last of the Race of Shikellemus, Chief of the Cayuga Nation* (1823) by Joseph Doddridge (1769–1826), set along the Ohio River, encourages the extermination of the Indian and promotes white settlement of the land many asserted the Indians had no claim to and did not deserve.

In similar fashion, Francis Parkman (1823–1893) believed that what he considered civilized progress controlled history and that the supposedly primitive, inferior, and static Indians deserved their doom. In 1846 Parkman lived with a Midwestern Sioux tribe for several weeks while on a hunting expedition, and although he lived with them at a time when he could witness their struggles with the effects of white encroachment, his visit only reinforced his views that civilization must conquer savagery and that displacement of the Indian was a natural effect of progress. Parkman's

beliefs are evident in *The California and Oregon Trail: Being Sketches of Prairie and Mountain Life* (1849), a best seller of the nineteenth century.

SAMUEL LANGHORNE CLEMENS (1835–1910), writing as Mark Twain, is another Midwestern author who portrayed Native Americans negatively. In 1870 he published "The Noble Red Man," a satirical essay mocking James Fenimore Cooper's overly romanticized Indian characters. Clemens ridicules and criticizes their appearance, manners, and lifestyle, but the essay's ambivalent tone makes it nearly impossible for readers to discern whether they should take him seriously or dismiss his rhetoric as simple contempt for unrealistic and highly romanticized narratives. His portrayal of Injun Joe, the villain in *The Adventures of Tom Sawyer* (1876), one of his most popular novels, has also been problematic for readers. Injun Joe is presented as a malevolent character motivated by the desire for revenge on those who have even only slightly offended or wronged him in any way. Injun Joe not only murders the town doctor but also fantasizes about torturing a woman. He is the embodiment of evil for Tom Sawyer and Huckleberry Finn and several times throughout the novel is said to be evil because of his Indian blood. "The Noble Red Man," *The Adventures of Tom Sawyer,* and *Roughing It* (1872), a narrative of Clemens's adventures in the West, all depict images of Native Americans that unequivocally defy the theme of the noble savage.

Dime novels, or penny dreadfuls, which originated in the 1840s and remained popular until the turn of the twentieth century, took negative images of Native Americans to the extreme. The more exciting the episodes, the more embellished the language, the bloodier the battles, the more gruesome the torture, and the more horrific the descriptions, the better. Although the dime-novel Indian is often seen torturing his victims, scalping them, or burning them at the stake, he is also predictable and, at best, a flat character whose sole purpose is to antagonize the main character and make a hero of him. One dime novel that takes place in the Midwest and presents these themes is *Adventures of Buffalo Bill from Boyhood to Manhood . . .* (1881) by Colonel Prentiss Ingraham (1843–1904), one of the most prolific dime-novel authors. In this narrative young Billy kills his first Indian, gains the nickname "Boy Indian Killer," and is made a hero for his actions.

The western novel, or the western, an offshoot of the dime novel that maintained the traditional white stereotypes of Native Americans, gained popularity during the nineteenth century. Many authors of westerns felt no need to attempt accurate portrayals of Native Americans and often gave them one of two roles to fill: the good Indian or the bad Indian. The good Indian was the white hero's faithful sidekick, the noble savage standing side by side with good whites to fight the white outlaws and bad Indians. The bad Indian was the stereotypical bloodthirsty savage bent on revenge, torture, and murder of innocent whites. However, the Indian usually served as the background rather than the focus of the novel. This technique allowed the author to simplify the Native American character and to use him as a prop or tool.

At the turn of the twentieth century, westerns were more popular than ever, but the twentieth-century emergence of pro-Indian westerns marked the continuing evolution of that genre. Native Iowan FREDERICK MANFRED (b. Feike Feikema, 1912–1994) is often considered an author of westerns. However, his novels are unique in that they do not follow the typical western formulas popular in the early part of the twentieth century. His novel *Manly-Hearted Woman* (1975) takes place before the arrival of the whites in the Midwest. Manfred avoids the good-Indian/bad-Indian dichotomy and the trivial romance of many early westerns; instead, he focuses on realistic themes and provides a more truthful picture of Native Americans. Beneath the simple story line of two young Indians who meet but are not destined to be together are many complex themes, such as native community life, religion, and homosexuality. Manfred's novel *Scarlet Plume* (1964), the third novel in his Buckskin Man Tales, also stands apart from other westerns. The setting is the Minnesota Uprising of 1862. Although he does employ the good-Indian/bad-Indian theme, and although the novel is in some ways reminiscent of nineteenth-century captivity narratives, it also contains highly sexualized descriptions of the Indians and their relationships with white women.

A later exemplar of the evolving western genre is *Dances with Wolves* (1988) by Michael (Lennox) Blake (b. 1945). This novel, set in 1863 on the far western edge of the Midwest, reverses the bad-Indians/good-whites theme and presents many whites as cruel, deceitful, and greedy. The Native Americans, with the exception of the Pawnees, are shown to be noble, helpful, and trustworthy. In 1990 *Dances with Wolves* hit the big screen and became one of the top-five-grossing western movies of all time, perhaps signifying contemporary audiences' desire for more realistic and respectful portrayals of Native Americans.

Prevalent stereotypes of Native Americans have evolved markedly over time. James Fenimore Cooper (1789–1851) maintained a romanticized view of Native Americans. The third novel written in his Leatherstocking Tales, although chronologically the last in the series, *The Prairie* (1827) is set in Nebraska; however, Cooper had no extensive experience with Native Americans, and he wrote this novel while he was living in Paris. Nevertheless, Cooper is able to tell the story of the American frontier through the adventures and interactions of his characters, both white and Indian, and through the theme of nature versus civilization. In each of his novels Cooper includes both the savage Indian and the noble Indian, and he clearly differentiates between the two. However, in the constant progress of civilization, both are seen as fated to die out.

A stereotype of Native Americans that developed in opposition to the brutal savage is the noble Indian brave. The noble Indian in American literature was a nineteenth-century invention; Indians could be viewed as noble only after the Indian threat was eliminated or far removed from white civilization. Authors of novels, plays, and poems usually portrayed the Indian as noble only before contact with the corrupting influence of the white man or in the very early stages of contact. One work that follows this tradition is the popular narrative poem *The Song of Hiawatha* (1855) by Henry Wadsworth Longfellow (1807–1882), set in the forests of upper MICHIGAN before the arrival of the white man. Longfellow, influenced by Indian

Frederic Remington's illustration of Longfellow's *The Song of Hiawatha,* 1891 edition.
© Houghton, Mifflin & Co, 1891. Image courtesy of
the Library of Congress

legends collected by HENRY ROWE SCHOOL-
CRAFT (1793–1864), sentimentalized the Indian by combining the ballad form with a
legend that would take readers back to a
time long ago when the Indian could be
viewed with sympathy and tenderness.
Longfellow presents a humanized, civilized, and Christianized Indian with whom
his readers could be comfortable. Although
Longfellow met with criticism for confus-
ing and intermixing Iroquois and Ojibwa
customs and legends, the poem sold 38,000
copies the first year, testifying to readers'
needs to simplify and sentimentalize American history, which was in reality fraught
with violence, bloodshed, and broken
treaties.

Although the savage-Indian and noble-
Indian stereotypes of Native Americans did
nothing to positively portray the reality of
Native life and tradition, perhaps what is not
said about Native Americans in white literature is just as damaging. Although WILLA

CATHER (1873–1947) did approach the subject
of Native Americans in some of her works,
such as *Death Comes for the Archbishop* (1927),
she essentially ignored their presence on the
Nebraska frontier in *O PIONEERS!* (1913) and
glossed over the brutality of the extinction of
the Pawnees, the Poncas, and other tribes
of the plains. She disregarded both centuries
of Native American habitation in the Midwest and the recent history of Native American extinction and removal. As William
Barillas points out in *The Midwestern Pastoral:
Place and Landscape in Literature of the American Heartland* (2006), the Plains War took
place from 1862 to 1890, and the narrative
timeline of *O Pioneers!* covers the period from
1883 to 1900. Cather, Barillas notes, makes
no mention of the war or its effect on Native
Americans (68–69).

The mid- to late nineteenth century and
the twentieth century saw attempts at realism in fiction, biographies, and other writings. Many Midwestern authors moved
away from the stereotyped Indian of the
earlier centuries and began portraying
Native Americans in new ways. One such
work that appeared before its time was *History of the Indian Tribes of North America, with
Biographical Sketches and Anecdotes of the Principal Chiefs* (1836–1844) by Thomas McKenney (1785–1859) and James Hall (1793–1868).
McKenney, who was superintendent of
Indian trade for six years and then the first
director of the Office of Indian Affairs, became closely acquainted with various tribes
of the Midwest and West and deeply concerned for their welfare and survival. McK-
enney partnered with lawyer and author
James Hall, and together over a span of six
years they created a portfolio of portraits
and biographical sketches to preserve Midwestern and western Native American
culture.

Explorer, travel writer, ethnographer,
and Indian agent Henry Rowe Schoolcraft
also did much to record and preserve an accurate portrayal of Native American life and
customs. Schoolcraft was married to the
granddaughter of an Ojibwa chief and was
thus able to observe Native American culture firsthand. Despite having come from a
family that had fought against Native Americans on the Revolutionary War frontier, and
despite the fact that his early works reflect

his family's bias against Native Americans, Schoolcraft developed sensitivity toward Native Americans, and his later works were mainly ethnographic. Schoolcraft wrote many volumes containing realistic portrayals of Native American life, culture, tradition, and religion. Two of them are *Algic Researches: Comprising Inquiries Respecting the Mental Characteristics of the North American Indian* (1839), which was Longfellow's inspiration for *Hiawatha,* and *Historical and Statistical Information Respecting the History, Condition, and Prospects of the Indian Tribes of the United States,* published in six volumes from 1851 to 1857.

JOHN G(NEISENAU) NEIHARDT (1881–1973), Nebraska author and employee of the Bureau of Indian Affairs, truthfully revealed the brutal treatment Native Americans received at the hands of white conquerors and emphasized the spiritual heroism of Native Americans. Many of Neihardt's works, including *A Cycle of the West* (1949), a collection of five poems, and *When the Tree Flowered* (1951), his last novel, demonstrate the results of white settlement from the Native American point of view. *BLACK ELK SPEAKS* (1932), Neihardt's collaborative biography of Oglala Sioux medicine man BLACK ELK (1863–1950), paints a positive, albeit difficult, picture of Native American life. Black Elk agreed to share his life's narrative and visions with Neihardt, expressing his desire to reveal the reality of Oglala life, customs, and religious ceremonies. Although it did not initially receive the attention it gained in the decades after it was published, its popularity now shows a growing interest in social, ethical, and religious analysis of Native Americans. However, contemporary debates surrounding the biography focus on the extent of Neihardt's literary license with Black Elk's dictation. Some critics and scholars have gone so far as to claim that the biography displays more of Neihardt's beliefs than of Black Elk's.

Along with this attempt at realism, the twentieth century witnessed a back-to-nature movement that involved a surge of interest in all things Native American. MARI(E SUSETTE) SANDOZ (1896–1966) is one Midwestern author who fed this interest with her biography of Oglala Sioux war chief Crazy Horse in *Crazy Horse, the Strange Man*

of the Oglalas (1942). The daughter of a frontiersman who was respectful toward his Indian visitors—as frequently depicted in her *Old Jules* (1935)—Sandoz grew up in close proximity to the lands where Crazy Horse lived, fought, and died, and she held a deep respect and sympathy for the war chief. This respect is evident in *Crazy Horse* through the language and point of view, which make readers feel as though they are one with the characters. Sandoz's profound consideration for Native Americans continued in *Cheyenne Autumn* (1953), as well as in many other biographical and fictional works.

An important novel that portrays Native Americans with realism and sympathy is *Dalva* (1988) by JIM (JAMES THOMAS) HARRISON (1937–2016). Set in Nebraska, *Dalva* is a complex novel interweaving several plotlines with complicated characters while at the same time raising ethical questions about Indian policy of the late nineteenth century. Although the novel is set in 1986, passages from the journals of a nineteenth-century ancestor of the novel's main character allow the reader to experience life on the Nebraska frontier during the Plains War, to sympathize with Native Americans, and to question the government's treatment of them.

From the simple and straightforward descriptions of Native Americans in the travel narratives of early explorers to the politically motivated racist representations of captivity narratives, dime novels, and westerns and to the multifaceted characters found in the novels of the twentieth century, Native Americans continue to be a subject of fascination for many writers. However, the long history of often inaccurate, insensitive, and brutal white literature dealing with Native Americans has provided an important motivation for Native Americans to portray themselves in their own words. It has paved the way for Midwestern Native American authors such as GERALD (ROBERT) VIZENOR (b. 1934), (KAREN) LOUISE ERDRICH (b. 1954), and many others to finally portray Native American culture and life honestly and candidly.

SELECTED WORKS: One of the earliest published accounts of white contact with the indigenous people of the Midwest is Father Louis Hennepin's *Description de la Louisiane . . .* (1683). In this account Hennepin admires Native Americans for their skills and way of life. For readers interested in captivity narratives, *A Narrative of the Life of Mrs. Mary Jemison, Who Was Taken by Indians in the Year 1775* (1824) by James Seaver portrays a woman who assimilated to the Indian way of life and chose to live with her captors rather than return to white civilization. *Narrative of the Capture and Providential Escape of Misses Frances and Almira Hall . . .* (1832), however, presents a skewed picture of captivity designed to promote hatred of Indians.

Marking the movement from captivity narratives to works of fiction, the dime-novel *Adventures of Buffalo Bill from Boyhood to Manhood* (1881) by Colonel Prentiss Ingraham concerns a protagonist who is made a hero for killing Indians. Similarly, Joseph Doddridge's play *Logan, the Last of the Race of Shikellemus* (1823) encourages hatred and extermination of Indians. On the other hand, the novel *Manly-Hearted Woman* (1975) by Frederick Manfred more accurately portrays Indian life before white settlement of the Midwest. The novel *Dances with Wolves* (1988) by Michael Blake also presents a positive view of Midwestern Indians. Mari Sandoz's biography *Crazy Horse* (1942) and Jim Harrison's novel *Dalva* (1988) show respect toward Native Americans and allow readers to question their treatment at the hands of whites.

Authors of biographies and other works of nonfiction have also attempted more genuine and credible pictures of Native Americans. Thomas McKenney and James Hall's *History of the Indian Tribes of North America, with Biographical Sketches and Anecdotes of the Principal Chiefs* (1836–1844) falls into this category. Two of the many works by Henry Rowe Schoolcraft carefully portray Native Americans: *Algic Researches: Comprising Inquiries Respecting the Mental Characteristics of the North American Indian* and *Historical and Statistical Information Respecting the History, Condition, and Prospects of the Indian Tribes of the United States* (1839). John Neihardt's *Black Elk Speaks* (1932) offers a candid picture of Native American life.

FURTHER READING: Analysis of Native Americans in Midwestern literature has been neglected and thus provides significant opportunity for research. *Savagism and Civilization: A Study of the Indian and the American Mind* (1967) by Roy Harvey Pearce contributes much to the study of white attitudes toward Native Americans and dedicates many pages to discussion of the noble-savage stereotype. Another text on the same theme is *The White Man's Indian: Images of the American Indian from Columbus to the Present* (1978) by Robert F. Berkhofer Jr. Valuable but limited information on Midwestern literary representations of Native Americans appears in *The Ignoble Savage: American Literary Racism, 1790–1890* (1975) by Louise K. Barnett; *The Indian in American Literature* (1933) by Albert Keiser; *White on Red: Images of the American Indian* (1976), edited by Nancy B. Black and Bette S. Weidman; and *Born for the Shade: Stereotypes of the Native American in United States Literature and the Visual Arts, 1776–1894* (1994) by Klaus Lubbers. A similar text is *The Demon of the Continent: Indians and the Shaping of American Literature* (2001) by Joshua David Bellin, an examination of how contact between Europeans and Native Americans shaped and influenced American literature.

A thorough analysis of the image of Native American females in American literature from 1799 to 1911 is provided in *Pocahontas and Co.: The Fictional American Indian Woman in Nineteenth-Century Literature; A Study of Method* (1984) by Asebrit Sundquist. Although it is limited in examining Midwestern Native American females, this is an area largely ignored by scholars and critics to date. Another valuable text is *The Return of the Vanishing American* (1968) by Leslie (Aaron) Fiedler which focuses primarily on the western genre in American literature. It also discusses four myths depicting the possibilities of encounters between red men and white men in the wilderness and how these myths are presented in literature, including Midwestern literature. *Facing West: The Metaphysics of Indian-Hating and Empire-Building* (1980) by Richard T. Drinnon explores the U.S. government's racial attitudes and actions against minorities, particularly Native Americans; the writings of Thomas McKenney are evaluated under this theme. *Going Native: Indians in the American Cultural Imagination* (2001) by Shari M. Huhndorf examines how, in films and texts, whites have exploited Native Americans for their own gain. A valuable text for readers interested in the image of the Native American on the silver screen is *Making the White Man's Indian: Native Americans and Hollywood Movies* (2005) by Angela Aleiss. It not only addresses some movies set in the Midwest but also draws parallels between images of Native Americans in literature and FILM. Readers interested in a bibliographic approach to the study of Native Americans in literature will find the following texts useful: *Early Midwestern Travel Narratives: An Annotated Bibliography, 1634–1850* (1961) by Robert R. Hubach; *Literature by and about the American Indian: An Annotated Bibliography* (1979) by Anna Lee Stensland; *A Bibliographical Guide to Midwestern Literature* (1981), edited by Gerald Nemanic; and *The Native American in American Literature: A Selectively Annotated Bibliography* (1985) by Roger O. Rock.

CRYSTAL STALLMAN   HAWKEYE COMMUNITY COLLEGE

NATIVE SON

HISTORY: With the March 1940 publication of *Native Son*, RICHARD WRIGHT (1908–1960) became one of America's most important chroniclers of the social experience of African Americans in the urban Midwest. *Native Son* stood apart from earlier articulations of African American identity because it identified an emerging racial type in the figure of Bigger Thomas, who openly rebelled against the social norms of the dominant culture and of the African American community. *Native Son* also presents the first realistic fictional portrayal of the conditions under which many blacks lived in the urban Midwest.

Wright's family experienced racism and difficult lives in the South, and the family was uprooted several times. In 1927 Wright and his aunt Maggie left Memphis for CHICAGO. This move marked the first phase of Wright's literary development, during which he read widely, notably the work of Midwestern writers, including (HERMAN) THEODORE DREISER (1871–1945) and (HARRY) SINCLAIR LEWIS (1885–1951), as well as European writers, including Joseph Conrad (1857–1924), Fyodor Dostoyevsky (1821–1881), and Émile Zola (1840–1902). In the mid-1930s Wright began publishing short stories and poetry. He also increased his involvement in the literary community, affiliating himself with the Chicago chapter

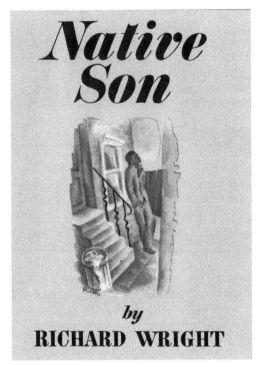

Richard Wright's *Native Son*.
© HarperCollins Publishers, 1940

of the John Reed Club, writing for the FEDERAL WRITERS' PROJECT, becoming active in the South Side Writers Group, and participating in the Middle West Writers' Congress.

In 1938 Wright published *Uncle Tom's Children* to much critical praise. In 1939 he won a Guggenheim Fellowship and used it to complete *Native Son*, which he had begun drafting in 1937. In late 1939 Wright was notified that the Book-of-the-Month Club was interested in *Native Son* on condition that substantial changes be made to the manuscript. Wright's changes focused on an early scene in which Bigger Thomas and his friend masturbate in a theater. Wright also toned down the novel's use of sexually explicit language and revised plot details elsewhere in the novel.

Even with these changes and the Book-of-the-Month Club's choice of the book as a dual selection, *Native Son* was met with critical controversy. However, the consensus was positive, with critics hailing the novel as a landmark for its treatment of American racial issues. *Native Son* sold over 200,000 copies in its first month of publication and became the number one best seller by April 1940. In 1941 the National Association for the Advancement of Colored People awarded Wright the Spingarn Medal for greatest achievement by an African American during the preceding year.

Native Son affected perceptions of race then and continues to do so now. The novel depicts the effects of racial discrimination and social oppression on a character living in the heart of Chicago. Wright's innovative approach, his attention to narration and voice, and his misogyny and general refusal to be politically correct ensured that the critical debate surrounding *Native Son* will always be lively, securing for Wright a position among the Midwest's most important writers.

SIGNIFICANCE: Discussions of *Native Son*'s literary merit cannot easily be separated from analysis of its social impact, especially since the novel's main character was conceived by Wright as a product of the social conditions prevalent in 1930s Midwestern America. In his March 12, 1940, Columbia University lecture "How 'Bigger' Was Born," published with later editions of the novel, Wright emphasized the importance of his Chicago setting, calling it "an indescribable city, huge, roaring, dirty, noisy, raw, stark, brutal; a city of extremes: torrid summers and sub-zero winters, white people and black people, the English language and strange tongues, foreign born and native born, scabby poverty and gaudy luxury, high idealism and hard cynicism!" (1993 edition, 453).

Native Son presents an unflinching portrait of Bigger Thomas, whose violent behavior and racial anomie set him apart from previous characterizations of blacks in American fiction. The significance of this portrait is its relation to previous portrayals of African American identity, including Wright's own. His aim with *Native Son* was to write something "so hard and deep" that readers "would have to face it without the consolation of tears" (454).

The success of Wright's effort can be measured by the early critical response to the novel, partially documented in the introduction to Robert J. Butler's *The Critical Response to Richard Wright* (1995). Writing for the Book-of-the-Month Club, Henry Seidel

Canby praised the book as one so true to African American experience that "only a Negro could have written it" (xxvii). Butler also records that Sterling Brown (1901–1989) felt that *Native Son* was the first novel about blacks that conducted a "psychological probing of the consciousness of the outcast, the disinherited, the generation lost in the slum jungles of American civilization" (xxvii). *Native Son* also provoked negative reactions, most notably what John M. Reilly in *Richard Wright: The Critical Reception* (1978) identifies as an ad hominem attack by Burton Rascoe that "recount[s] a literary luncheon at which Wright appeared to have been consumed by hatred for the whites present" (xvii). The widespread differences in initial reactions to *Native Son* are well summarized in the March 4, 1940, issue of *Time,* as quoted online, which carried a review titled "Bad Nigger." The writer of that review asserts that "only a Negro could have written it; but until now no Negro has possessed either the talent or the daring to write it." This review concludes: "Bigger's murders only pull the trigger of Author Wright's bigger story—the murderous potentialities of the whole U.S. Negro problem" (72).

As *Time*'s review signals and as Wright had signaled in "How 'Bigger' Was Born," *Native Son* suggests that in the industrial heart of the Midwest, social oppression, political disenfranchisement, and economic deprivation crystallize the murderous protest of African Americans (439–43). Personal experience directly informs *Native Son*'s depiction of Chicago's Black Belt. After the stock-market crash of 1929, Wright, his mother, and brother lived in slums much like those portrayed in the novel. In *Black Boy,* as quoted in *Later Works* (1991), Wright shares the difficulty of his life in Chicago during that period: "The depression deepened and I could not sell insurance to hungry Negroes. I sold my watch and scouted for cheaper rooms; I found a rotting building and rented an apartment in it. . . . When my mother saw it, she wept. I felt bleak" (285).

Before the 1929 crash, however, Wright perceived the Midwest as much more accommodating than the South he had left behind. The "Chronology" addendum of the Harper Perennial edition stresses this position in its "1928" section: "Wright finds

Chicago stimulating and less racially oppressive than the South, but is often dismayed by the pace and disarray of urban life" (466–67). Chicago's urban landscape in *Native Son* becomes the environment in which Wright, in "How 'Bigger' Was Born," asserts that African American men are "trying to react to and answer the call of the dominant civilization" (439) but are by social custom forbidden from answering that call. The disjunct between this "call of the dominant civilization" and the inability of African Americans like Bigger Thomas to answer produces the urban Midwest's disinherited and alienated native sons.

In the novel the call of dominant civilization comes to Bigger in the form of work as a chauffeur for the wealthy Dalton family. The family members do not see Bigger as human. They are blind to his individual existence. Mr. Dalton uses Bigger as an object on which to exercise his philanthropic impulse, attempting to assuage the guilt he feels for economically exploiting blacks living in slums he owns. Mrs. Dalton, who is literally blind, views Bigger as an unformed being in need of educational refinement. Mary Dalton and Jan Erlone treat Bigger and blacks in general as live subjects for the social experiment of communism, a philosophy that in the novel disregards Bigger's heartfelt desires to "blot out" the society that has shaped him. Boris A. Max, arguably the person who comes closest to understanding Bigger, is horrified at the novel's end when Bigger affirms his satisfaction at having killed out of racial hatred.

Bigger is alienated from the dominant white culture by which he is oppressed; he is also estranged from the black community. Bigger rejects his family and friends, all of whom he considers blind to the meaning of his murders. Critic Burton Rascoe, in his May 1940 *American Mercury* essay "Negro Novel and White Reviewers," argues that Bigger's distance from his fellow blacks is a fault of the novel (113). Wright foresees this type of criticism and responds to it in "How 'Bigger' Was Born" by pointing to the black men who were the models for Bigger Thomas. Such men, Wright explains, rejected everything the black community had to offer even as they rejected the white world that restricted them.

Native Son's bleak Chicago industrial landscape, coupled with the limited choices of Bigger Thomas to determine his own fate, has led many critics to identify the novel as urban naturalism. Wright himself testifies to the influence of naturalism in his autobiographical *Black Boy*. When he was a young reader still living in the South, realism and naturalism were conflated in his mind: "I read Dreiser's *Jennie Gerhardt* and *Sister Carrie* and they revived in me a vivid sense of my mother's suffering; I was overwhelmed. I grew silent, wondering about the life around me. It would have been impossible for me to have told anyone what I derived from these novels, for it was nothing less than a sense of life itself" (239). It is fitting, given Wright's identification with naturalism, that the inexorable conclusion of Bigger's life is traced in the arc of the novel's three main sections: "Fear," "Flight," and "Fate."

In addition to the actual 1938–1939 Robert Nixon murder trial, parts of which Wright fictionalized for inclusion in *Native Son*, critics have identified several significant literary sources for the novel. In *"Native Son": The Emergence of a New Black Hero* (1991) Robert Butler identifies characters in the work of Fyodor Dostoyevsky, Henrik Ibsen (1828–1906), and Émile Zola as literary ancestors of Bigger Thomas (112). Other critics see different literary influences on *Native Son*. Dale E. Peterson, in "Richard Wright's Long Journey from Gorky to Dostoevsky," *African American Review* 28.3 (Fall 1994): 375–87, credibly argues that *Native Son* was substantially influenced by Dostoyevsky's *Crime and Punishment* (1866). Noel Polk remarks on William Faulkner's *The Sound and the Fury* (1929) and its influence on Wright in "Richard Wright Award Address: Notes of Another Native Son," *Southern Quarterly: A Journal of the Arts in the South* 44.2 (Winter 2007): 126–37. Seymour Gross argues in "Native Son and 'The Murders in the Rue Morgue': An Addendum," *Poe Studies* 8 (1975): 23, that Poe's 1841 poem influenced the novel (23). In the *College Language Association Journal* 12.4 (1969): 358–59, Keneth Kinnamon suggests that Shakespeare's *Othello* left its mark on *Native Son*. In "Black Folklore and the Black American Literary Tradition," in *Long Black Song* (1972), Houston Baker identifies figures from black folk culture as kin to Bigger Thomas, including Brer Rabbit and heroes like Nat Turner (18–42).

In the years after the publication of *Black Boy,* Wright was unable to match the success achieved with *Native Son.* This perceived flagging of his literary talent led critics, for a time, to diminish their esteem for his earlier achievements, *Native Son* in particular. The nadir of negative reaction occurred in the early 1960s when James Baldwin (1924–1987) and Irving Howe (1920–1993) asserted that Wright had gone wrong when he abandoned naturalism for existentialism and critics such as Richard Gilman (1923–2006) proclaimed Wright an incompetent writer. The pendulum of critical favor began to swing the other way in the late 1960s. Readers in the wake of the civil rights movement and the start of the Black Arts movement were disposed to identify Wright as one of the most politically and socially relevant writers of his time. Lawrence P. Jackson, however, argues that Wright's fall from favor has been exaggerated. In *The Indignant Generation: A Narrative History of American Writers and Critics, 1934–1960* (2010) he asserts that Wright's art and vision, although controversial, were essential to Chicago and America even before the civil rights movement began in 1960. Positive responses to *Native Son* were many and deep between its publication and the beginning of the civil rights and Black Arts movements. The graphic violence portrayed in *Native Son* became an asset during the age of black militancy. In the field of women's studies, *Native Son* has been interpreted as a novel that displays hostility toward women, signaling that even negative critical assessments of Wright's masterwork judge the novel to be a serious work of literature.

Native Son has influenced later writers as they have articulated their versions of African American identity, most notably Ralph Ellison (1914–1994) in *Invisible Man* (1952) and TONI MORRISON (CHLOE ARDELIA WOFFORD) (b. 1931) in *The Bluest Eye.* As Robert Butler notes in *"Native Son": The Emergence of a New Black Hero* (1991), before *Native Son* no fiction by any writer, white or black, contained "detailed, realistic portraits of the impoverished masses of urban blacks" (9). In the twenty-

first century, when the CHICAGO RENAISSANCE and the Black Chicago Renaissance are discussed, Richard Wright and *Native Son* remain central to the conversation.

IMPORTANT EDITIONS: *Native Son* was first published in 1940 by Harper. That edition was a radical alteration of the original manuscript Wright submitted in June 1939. The changes Wright made to the text under the advice of Edward Aswell, Wright's editor at Harper, are considered by many critics acts of voluntary censorship. In 1942 Harper added Wright's essay "How 'Bigger' Was Born" to printings of *Native Son.* In 1991 Harper Perennial published *Richard Wright: Early Works,* which included *Native Son* as restored by the Library of America, the basis of the 1993 Harper Perennial restored edition, which is introduced by Arnold Rampersad. Since its initial publication *Native Son* has been translated into at least seventeen languages. In 1941 (George) Orson Welles (1915–1985) and John Houseman (Jacques Haussmann, 1902–1988) produced a theatrical version of *Native Son.* In 1951 and 1986 film adaptations of *Native Son* were directed by, respectively, Pierre Chenal (1904–1990) and Jerrold Freedman.

FURTHER READING: Among the book-length studies addressing Richard Wright's *Native Son,* Keneth Kinnamon's 1972 *The Emergence of Richard Wright* is among the best known and provides a close account of the ideology and biography undergirding *Native Son.* Joyce Ann Joyce's 1986 *Richard Wright's Art of Tragedy* deemphasizes the biographical and social influences on Wright's novel and focuses instead on Wright's literary craft. Robert Butler's 1991 *Richard Wright's "Native Son": The Emergence of a New Black Hero* also discusses the literary structure of *Native Son.*

The paucity of authoritative book-length treatments of *Native Son* is offset by the plenitude of book chapters and articles devoted to the novel. Perhaps the most notable defense of *Native Son*'s importance to American literature is Irving Howe's "Black Boys and Native Sons," in *A World More Attractive: A View of Modern Literature and Politics* (1963). The introduction to Robert J. Butler's 1995 *The Critical Response to Richard Wright* provides a boon to scholarship on *Native Son* by giving a comprehensive and detailed overview of the critical opinion surrounding the novel. *Richard Wright: An Annotated Bibliography of Criticism and Commentary, 1983–2003* (2006), compiled by Keneth Kinnamon, is also valuable as an overview of *Native Son* criticism. Ayesha K. Hardison's *Writing through Jane Crow: Race and Gender Politics in African American Literature* (2013), particularly in chapter 1, "At the Point of No Return: A Native Son and His Gorgon Muse," offers scholars a nuanced examination of Wright's misogynist depiction of female characters in *Native Son* and a fascinating discussion of how Wright attempted to correct that perception in "Black Hope," an unfinished novel manuscript archived in the Richard Wright Papers in the Yale Collection of American Literature at the Beinecke Rare Book and Manuscript Library.

Houston A. Baker Jr. (b. 1943), in "Richard Wright and the Dynamics of Place in Afro-American Literature," in Keneth Kinnamon's *New Essays on Native Son* (1990), 85–116, discusses the role of place in the novel, as does Charles Scruggs in "The City without Maps in Richard Wright's *Native Son*," in Kinnamon's *Critical Essays on Richard Wright's "Native Son"* (1997), 147–79, reprinted from *Sweet Home: Invisible Cities in the Afro-American Novel* by Charles Scruggs (1993). Two chapters from Elizabeth Schroeder Schlabach's *Along the Streets of Bronzeville: Black Chicago's Literary Landscape* (2013)—"From Black Belt to Bronzeville" and "The South Side Community Art Center and South Side Writers Group"—may be of particular interest to *Native Son* scholars. They examine daily life in Bronzeville locations and remind readers that places such as the Regal Theater where Bigger Thomas viewed the double feature *The Gay Woman* and *Trader Horn* were real and that Wright's relationship to the South Side Community Art Center and the South Side Writers Group immeasurably nurtured his creativity.

For a fellow Chicagoan's response to Richard Wright, read "Remembering Richard Wright" by NELSON ALGREN (b. Nelson Alghren Abraham, 1909–1981) in *The Nation* 192 (January 28, 1961): 85. For those interested in the Chicago Renaissance and the Black Chicago Renaissance, Robert Bone's essay "Richard Wright and the Chicago Re-naissance," *Callaloo* 28 (Summer 1986): 446–68, is the place to begin.

For a biographical treatment of Richard Wright, read Michel Fabre's *The Unfinished Quest of Richard Wright* (1973). Hazel Rowley's *Richard Wright: The Life and Times* (2001), particularly her chapter "The South Side of Chicago" (50–73), will aid Richard Wright scholars in their quest for an accurate understanding of his aesthetic, ideas, and history.

Wright's papers are held in the Beinecke Rare Book and Manuscript Library at Yale University; 136 boxes were sold in 1976 by Ellen Wright, his widow. This material was added to Yale's collection after Fabre completed his important biography and contains intimate 1930s and 1940s letters from Chicago friends Abe Aaron and Abe Chapman.

The James Weldon Johnson Collection of the Beinecke Library at Yale has the majority of the material related to the publication of *Native Son*, including the bound page proofs sent to the Book-of-the-Month Club. The Fales Collection of the New York University Library and the Firestone Library at Princeton University hold other significant material related to *Native Son*'s publication. Horace Cayton left recorded interviews with several of Wright's Chicago friends and colleagues; these are in the Vivian G. Harsh Research Collection of Afro-American History and Literature at the Carter Woodson branch of the Chicago Public Library. The State Department files at the National Archives in Washington also include forty-two pages on Richard Wright.

JOHNNIE WILCOX   OHIO UNIVERSITY
MARILYN JUDITH ATLAS   OHIO UNIVERSITY

NATURALISM.
See Realism and Naturalism

NATURE WRITING.
See Environmental Literature

NEBRASKA
Nebraska was admitted to the Union on March 1, 1867, as the thirty-seventh state. Before statehood it was part of Louisiana Territory (1805–1812) and then part of Missouri Territory (1812–1821). From 1821, when

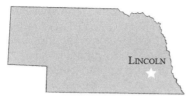

© Karen Greasley, 2014

Missouri became a state, to 1854, the land comprising the future state of Nebraska was without official government as part of a vast, unorganized "Indian Country." Finally, through the Kansas-Nebraska Act, it became part of Nebraska Territory (1854–1867).

Area: 77,348 square miles

Land: 76,824 square miles

Water: 524 square miles

Population (2010 census): 1,826,341

OVERVIEW: Nebraska's literary history began with sporadic passages by explorers and fur traders in the early nineteenth century based primarily on the state's location on the Missouri River. The state takes its name from an Omaha and Otoe word meaning "flat water," a reference to the shallowness of Nebraska's major river, the Platte. Because the Platte River, running west to east across the state, was developed early into the Great Platte River Road, Nebraska was a crucial place for travelers participating in the great migration to Utah, Oregon, and California. The land that became Nebraska was home to many American Indian tribes, including the Pawnee and Arikari; the Omaha, Ponca, and Otoe, who arrived in the eighteenth century; and others, including the Teton Sioux, Cheyenne, Arapaho, Santee Sioux, and Winnebago.

Nebraska literature began in earnest after the Kansas-Nebraska Act in 1854, when the state was brought in as a free territory in contrast to KANSAS. Nebraska's territorial status spurred development of the region, especially after the Homestead Act of 1862. With settlement, interest in literature developed rapidly, inspired by Chautauqua and literary societies intended to build and maintain culture.

Important early themes of Nebraska literature include exploration and cultural and political development, as well as the debate over slavery. A perennial theme is that of homesteading in a difficult and sometimes unforgiving terrain, often involving accounts of travel to or through the state. In this respect Nebraska literature is similar to that of Midwestern states to the east, but as in the other states in this western tier, geography is essential. Nebraska is crossed by the ninety-eighth meridian, roughly marking the start of the Great Plains, with its different terrain—shorter grass, less rainfall—an area earlier dubbed the "Great American Desert." To the west, farms give way to ranches, and population density decreases severely.

HISTORY AND SIGNIFICANCE: This section considers Nebraska literature by genre, subject, and theme. Included in genres are exploration and travel, fiction, poetry, DRAMA, and significant aspects of popular literature. Discussion follows of Nebraska journalism, the Nebraska Federal Writers' Project, state literary societies and awards, and Nebraska literary archives and collections.

Exploration and Travel: Nebraska's central position on the Great Plains, its two great rivers, the Missouri and the Platte, and the conflicting claims of Spain and France made the land area associated with the present-day state the focus of much westward exploration, at least until the Louisiana Purchase in 1803. As early as 1540 Francisco Vásquez de Coronado (1510–1554) is thought to have entered Nebraska. An interesting fictional account is *The Quest of Coronado: An Historical Romance of the Spanish Cavaliers in Nebraska* (1901) by Rev. Denis Gerald Fitzgerald (b. 1858). Any Spanish claim ended in 1720 with the deaths of Pedro de Villasur and many of his men in a battle with the Pawnee on the Platte River.

The most important expedition into Nebraska was that of Lewis and Clark in 1804 as the Corps of Discovery ascended the Missouri River. The party explored Nebraska locations from July to September. In early August its members held their first official council with American Indians, a party of Otoe and Missouria, north of present-day Omaha, the later site of Fort Atkinson. Nebraska's early reputation as an uninhabitable "Great American Desert" resulted from reports by Zebulon Montgomery Pike (1779–1813) in 1806 and Major Stephen Long

(1784–1864) in 1820, a reputation that still needed correction fifty years later.

A year after the artist George Catlin (1796–1872) ascended the Missouri River on the steamboat *Yellowstone,* Prince Maximilian von Wied (1782–1867), followed in 1833, accompanied by Karl Bodmer (1809–1893), perhaps the most important of the explorer-artists. Maximilian kept diaries in which he recorded Indian life and observations about flora and fauna that were published in German in 1839, and translated into English as *Travels in the Interior of North America* (1843). John Treat Irving (1812–1906), a nephew of Washington Irving (1783–1859), had an intense interest in aboriginal Indian life and traveled into Kansas and Nebraska, where he closely observed many tribes, including the Pawnee and the Otoe. He published his experiences in *Indian Sketches* (1835). See also ETHNOGRAPHY.

Among the many early missionaries to Nebraska Indians were Moses Merrill (1803–1840) and Pierre-Jean de Smet (1801–1873). Baptists Moses and Eliza Merrill moved to Bellevue in 1833, where they ministered to the Otoes. Moses's translation of parts of the Bible into Otoe is sometimes considered the first book published in Nebraska. The Jesuit priest Pierre-Jean de Smet was much admired by Indian tribes along the Platte River. His chief work is *Letters and Sketches: With a Narrative of a Year's Residence among the Indian Tribes of the Rocky Mountains* (1843). Two memoirs by Methodist ministers are *Solitary Places Made Glad: Being Observations and Experiences for Thirty-Two Years in Nebraska* (1890) by Henry Turner Davis (b. 1832) and *A Frontier Life: Being a Description of My Experience on the Frontier the First Forty-Two Years of My Life* (1902) by Rev. Charles Wesley Wells (1843–1927). Several guidebooks were available for immigrants, including *Nebraska in 1857* by James M(ills) Woolworth (1829–1906), *Kansas and Nebraska Handbook for 1857–8* (1857) by Nathan Parker, and *Nebraska: Its Advantages, Resources and Drawbacks* (1875) by Edwin A. Curley.

The diary of Erastus F. Beadle (1821–1894), first published as *To Nebraska in '57* (1923), provides a detailed account of land speculation for a proposed town, Saratoga, to be located near Omaha, but which perished in 1857. The diary also gives details of the rigors of travel and life in a new territory, along with glimpses into politics and social life. Beadle went on to be a major partner, along with Robert Adams, in the DIME-NOVEL industry. Another firsthand account is *Mollie: The Journal of Mollie Dorsey Sanford in Nebraska and Colorado Territories, 1857–1866* (1959) by Mollie Sanford (1838–1915). It includes an account of homesteading on the Little Nemaha River. Solomon Butcher (1856–1927), the photographer who first recorded the homes of homestead families with their possessions prominently displayed, compiled *S. D. Butcher's Pioneer History of Custer County: And Short Sketches of Early Days in Nebraska* (1901).

Works by renowned writers traveling in Nebraska include *The California and Oregon Trail: Being Sketches of Prairie and Mountain Life* (1849) by Francis Parkman (1823–1893); *The Adventures of Captain Bonneville* (1850) by Washington Irving, based on the famous fur trader's journals; and *Roughing It* (1872) by SAMUEL LANGHORNE CLEMENS (1835–1910), writing as Mark Twain. *Roughing It* describes the author's adventures in Nebraska Territory in 1861, including extended descriptions of the coyote, the "jackass rabbit," and the class structure of stagecoach riders. A visit to Nebraska by Stephen Crane (1871–1900) in February 1895 occasioned a brief meeting with WILLA CATHER (1873–1947) and precipitated "The Blue Hotel" (1899).

Fiction: Some of the earliest fiction written about Nebraska centers on conflicts between Indians and whites. The first Nebraska novel is *The Hunters of the Prairie; or, The Hawk Chief: A Tale of the Indian Country* (1837) by John Treat Irving. The volume is a romance about a young Pawnee chief and includes all the classic romance elements: Indian-white warfare, captivity and rescue, a love triangle, and epigraphs from Shakespeare and the English romantic poets.

Another early writer on Native American life in Nebraska was William Justin Harsha (1853–1931), who was sympathetic to Indians and studied the cultural dynamics by which they were suppressed during white encroachment. His *Ploughed Under: The Story of an Indian Chief, Told by Himself* (1881) appears to be the first novel about American Indians by a white person living in Nebraska. Harsha appears to have had help from Thomas Henry Tibbles (1840–1928) and Omaha Indian Inshta Theamba (Susette La Flesche) (1854–1903). Another novel by Harsha is *A Timid Brave: The Story of an Indian Uprising* (1886), which details the theft of the "Maha" Noah's cattle, his tribe's revolt against the Indian agent, and the Indians' inevitable defeat. Tibbles wrote the novel *Hidden Power: A Secret History of the Indian Ring, Its Operations, Intrigues, and Machinations: Revealing the Manner in Which It Controls Three Important Departments of the United States Government* (1881). It posits a "Black Code" by which Indians were manipulated by government officials. Tibbles also wrote *The Ponca Chiefs: An Account of the Trial of Standing Bear* (1880), which focused on the case in which Native Americans were first judged persons with legal status; and *Buckskin and Blanket Days: Memoirs of a Friend of the Indians* (1905).

The Middle Five: Indian Schoolboys of the Omaha Tribe (1900) by Francis La Flesche (1857–1932) is a series of lighthearted sketches based on La Flesche's life in a Presbyterian mission school. La Flesche also published ethnographic short stories, which were collected in 1995 in *Ke-ma-ha: The Omaha Stories of Francis La Flesche*. Susette La Flesche, sister of Francis and wife of Thomas Henry Tibbles, was active in art and writing, creating the illustrations for Fannie Reed Giffen's *Oomah-ha Ta-wa-tha (Omaha City)* (1898), said to be the first book illustrated by an American Indian.

The importance of JOHN G(NEISENAU) NEIHARDT (1881–1973) to the literature depicting American Indians cannot be overestimated. Neihardt's short stories about the Omaha were first published in the opening decade of the century, when Neihardt was a Nebraska resident, and were collected by his daughter, Hilda Neihardt Petri, in *The End of the Dream, and Other Stories* (1991). Neihardt's *When the Tree Flowered* (1951) is a fictional autobiography of a Sioux named Eagle Voice. Neihardt's most important book is *BLACK ELK SPEAKS* (1932), his influential collaborative interpretation of the life of the "holy man of the Oglala Sioux" as reported to him by BLACK ELK (1863–1950).

Signal Lights: A Story of Life on the Prairies (1906) by Louise M. Hopkins (b. 1860) is about the Indian Wars in 1858; in it eighteen-year-old Newton Bolt is captured by Sioux and escapes to rejoin his party, in the process learning to respect his captors, including young Red Cloud and Sitting Bull. *The Long Land* (1977) by Budington Swanson (ca. 1913–1991) is a novel of Fort Atkinson, active north of Omaha from 1818 to 1827, written from the perspective of a regimental surgeon. May Roberts Clark (1867–1937) wrote short stories about homesteading and Native American life, as well as a novel about a Pawnee Indian, *Taka, the Man Who Would Be White* (1938).

Another important contributor to the literature depicting Native Americans was MARI(E SUSETTE) SANDOZ (1896–1966), whose carefully researched historical studies of Native American figures were often rendered through controversial fictional devices. Two such works are *Crazy Horse: The Strange Man of the Oglalas* (1942) and *Cheyenne Autumn* (1953); the latter is Sandoz's account of the return of a band of Cheyenne from Oklahoma to their ancestral home in western Nebraska and their imprisonment and escape from Fort Robinson, concluding with many dead. A movie version directed by John Ford appeared in 1964.

Native American life and relations with whites are a staple of Nebraska literature, especially in popular genres, such as *Behold the Brown-Faced Man,* appearing in *Warwhoop: Two Short Novels of the Frontier* (1952) by MACKINLAY KANTOR (1904–1977), a tale of Indian fighting in 1864. In *The Road Home* (1998) JIM (JAMES THOMAS) HARRISON (1937–2016) continued his saga of his heroine Dalva and her family, begun in his novel *Dalva* (1988), tracking back to Nebraska and its tangled history of white and Indian relations through the fictional diaries of Dalva's great-grandfather John Northridge. There appear to be no novels published by Native Americans in Nebraska's history.

A number of Nebraska novels have focused primarily on westward travel. One of the earliest is *Shadow of a Great Rock* (1907) by William Rheem Lighton (1866–1923), which conveys the spirit energizing the westward movement. *A Prairie-Schooner Princess* (1920) by Mary Katherine Maule (b. 1861) portrays a family's move from OHIO to Nebraska Territory in 1856 and the rescue of an immigrant girl whose parents had been killed by Indians. *A Cry of the Soul: A Romance of 1862* (1917) by Anne Newbigging (1869–1921) concerns the Mormon trek; several chapters are set near Omaha. A lighter novel written from a Catholic perspective is *A Bridal Trip in a Prairie Schooner* (1921), apparently by Sister Mary Angela (fl. 1920s), writing as Gilbert Guest. Hayden Carruth (1862–1932) published a comic variation on the travel novel, *The Voyage of the Rattletrap* (1897), in which three men leave their homes in Dakota Territory to seek their fortunes farther west, making their way through the Sandhills before changing their minds and returning home. *Bob Hardwick: The Story of His Life and Experiences* (1911) by Henry Howard Harper (1871–1953) has picaresque elements and is apparently based on the author's childhood experiences with a restless father.

Sometimes slighted as a genre is the literary sketch, exemplified by works such as those of Anson Uriel Hancock (1856–1899), a humorous observer of frontier life. His *Old Abraham Jackson and His Family: Being an Episode in the Evolution of Nebraska Dug-Outs* (1891) is a fictionalized social history of the development of a community, from primitive dugout to the construction of frame houses, the development of farming, and the building of institutions. Hancock used Dickens-like characters named Flipperty and Fizzlepate. Hancock also contributed *Silhouettes from Life: On the Prairie, in the Backwoods* (1893), sketches about attorneys, editors, and various rascals. *Thrice a Pioneer: A Story of Forests, Plains, and Mountains* (1901) by P. M. Hannibal (1849–1935) is a fictionalized account, telling the story of Thomas Rugby in WISCONSIN, Nebraska, and the Rockies. Hannibal employed three thematic concerns in his work: slavery, warfare, and, most important, intoxicants, a topic carried into his *Uncle Sam's Cabin: A Story of a Mighty Mystery* (1910); the cabin in the title is a "dram house." William Rheem Lighton's *Uncle Mac's Nebrasky* (1904) is about settlement, relations between whites and Pawnee, Sioux, and Winnebago, and Uncle Mac's meeting with John Brown. Lighton's novel *The Ultimate Moment* (1903), set on an

Willa Cather's childhood home, Red Cloud, Nebraska, 1999. Photo by William Barillas.

Elkhorn Valley farm and in Omaha, details the idealistic departure and later return of a chastened native. Some of John Neihardt's frontier fiction appears in *Indian Tales and Others* (1926); *The Ancient Memory* (1991), edited by Hilda Neihardt Petri, collects other Neihardt stories published from 1905 to 1908.

Nebraska novels with political implications also appeared early. The first is *Golden-Rod: A Story of the West; By a Daughter of Nebraska* (1896), whose author was later identified as Anna M. Saunders; the book is apparently an argument for WILLIAM JENNINGS BRYAN (1860–1925), populism, and free silver. *Out of the West* (1902) by Elizabeth Higgins Sullivan (b. 1874) may be the first novel published by a woman born in Nebraska; it is a story of love, politics, and the efforts of Frank Field to get elected to Congress, overcome corruption, and sponsor a bill limiting railroad freight rates. *The Promoters: A Novel without a Woman* (1904) by William Hawley Smith (1845–1922) follows four business partners who choose Cherry County, Nebraska, as the site for a plan to realign the earth on its axis by firing 100,000 cannons in sequence; they hope, under the guise of a promise to bring rain, to have Nebraska inhabitants buy into the scheme.

As might be expected, many literary works were written about Nebraska homestead farm life. Perhaps the first of these is by ELIA W. PEATTIE (1862–1935), who lived in Nebraska for only a few years. Her collection of stories *A Mountain Woman* (1896) contains powerful examples: two stories are set on Nebraska farms. Peattie was one of twelve women who wrote an experimental novel, *Inasmuch: A Story of the West* (1898), for the Woman's Home Missionary Union of Nebraska. In *Impertinences: Selected Writings of Elia Peattie, a Journalist of the Gilded Age* (2005), Susanne George-Bloomfield collected articles, editorials, and sketches Peattie wrote from 1888 to 1896 while she worked at the *Omaha World-Herald*. The most important works on homestead Nebraska were written by Willa Cather. Cather arrived from Virginia with her family in 1883, moved to Lincoln in 1890, and attended the University of Nebraska before moving east in 1896. Her first novel, *Alexander's Bridge* (1912), is set mainly in Boston and London but nonetheless evinces some of Cather's later thematic interests. In some of her early shorter works, such as "Peter" (1892), "On the Divide" (1896), "A Sculptor's Funeral" (1903), and "A Wagner Matinée" (1904), Cather's view of the Nebraska landscape is dark and somewhat negative. As Cather matured, however, her sensitivities to landscape deepened. "The Bohemian Girl" (1912) foreshadows Cather's novel *O PIONEERS!* (1913), which is usually considered the first indispensable novel written about Nebraska. Set on a homestead farm, *O Pioneers!* focuses on Alexandra Bergson and details immigrant heroism, thwarted love, and fulfillment through mature love of the land. *O Pioneers!* was followed by *My Ántonia* (1918), a story about Bohemian Ántonia Shimerda, who homesteads with her family and endures years of difficulty on the intensely evoked Nebraska prairie. *One of Ours* (1922), which won a Pulitzer Prize, carries its protagonist, Claude Wheeler, to college in Lincoln and then to war in France. "Neighbor Rosicky" (1930), first published as a magazine story and later collected in *Obscure Destinies* (1932). is a tender story of a decent man who confronts his death with philosophical equilibrium while setting the tone for flight from twentieth-century cities, industrialism, and modern life. In *Lucy Gayheart* (1935) a woman leaves Nebraska to pursue music in CHICAGO and beyond.

Mildred Burcham Hart (b. ca. 1888) wrote two Nebraska farm novels. In *Dead Wom-*

an's Shoes (1932) a reluctant housekeeper works for a widower who continues to mourn his dead wife but nevertheless impregnates and marries Virgie. The novel details how she gradually wins his love. Hart's *Strange Harvest* (1936) concerns a family run by a strict German with a passion for land who forces his daughter to marry a man she despises. Another story of a controlling father is told by Howard Farrens (1901–1983) in *Hilda* (1940), but here the family is Swedish, and the father's motives are even more psychologically vicious.

Dorothy Thomas (1898–1999) published two collections of humorous and closely detailed stories about Nebraska farm and family life: *Ma Jeeter's Girls* (1933) and *The Home Place* (1936). Christine Pappas edited another collection by Thomas, *The Getaway* (2002). *Spring Storm* (1936) by Alvin Johnson (1874–1971) is a novel set in the Nebraska of Johnson's youth and tracks the protagonist from his first arrival in the West at fourteen to his departure for college. Johnson's *The Battle of the Wild Turkey* (1961) is a collection of short stories.

In Friends We Trust (1938) by Marjorie Bayley (1902–1979) is a Depression novel that tells how Johnny Hincks enlists the aid of freight-yard "bums" to help run his farm and overcome the machinations of the local banker. *Footprints across the Prairie* (1930) by Carolyn Renfrew (ca. 1858–1948), an earnest tale of flawed character, includes a scene in which a church wedding is disrupted. *Seeds of Time* (1938) by Ethel Doherty (1889–1974) and Louise Long (1886–1966) concerns three generations of a family on a farm near Beatrice from the 1880s to the 1930s. The novel debates the utility of machines and the conflicts between capitalism and communism. In *Nebraska Coast* (1939) CLYDE BRION DAVIS (1894–1962) presents an often humorous picture of the newly settled Nebraska Territory, when steam wagons were in competition with the development of the cross-country railroad.

WRIGHT MORRIS (1910–1998), the most important Nebraska novelist after Cather, developed a new genre in the photo-text novel *The Home Place* (1948). It examines traditional farm values as exemplified in a Nebraska farmstead. The novel incorporates a complex plea for the disappearing value of privacy in American life and contains about ninety of Morris's photographs of rural structures and objects. In his final novel, *Plains Song* (1980), which won the American Book Award, Morris traces the lives of three generations of women in relation to their sense of attraction-repulsion for the plains. In *Homefield: Sonata in Rural Voice* (2000) Robert Richter (b. 1948) tells the story of a Vietnam War resister's encounter with the Nebraska farm crisis in the 1970s. David Kubicek (b. 1952) edited *The Pelican in the Desert, and Other Stories of the Family Farm* (1988).

The ranch novel set in cattle country is a frequent Nebraska genre. *The Sand Hiller* (1944) by John Coleman (1871–1959) and Beatah H. Coleman (1876–1949) is an adventure set in the 1890s concerning a man who encounters rustlers and romance. *Too Tough to Die* (1987) by John B. Davis is a short, appreciative ranching novel set near Cody, a Sandhills town. JONIS AGEE (b. 1943) contributed *Strange Angels* (1993) and *The Weight of Dreams* (1999), books employing Sandhills settings and incorporating action based on family conflicts; *The Weight of Dreams* was the first novel to win the Nebraska Book Award. In *Slogum House* (1937) Mari Sandoz's fascist heroine brutally accumulates land. Ladette Randolph (b. 1957), who served as the executive editor at the University of Nebraska Press, wrote the lyrical novel *A Sandhills Ballad* (2009) and *Haven's Wake* (2013), the latter concerning a Nebraska Mennonite family.

In addition to homestead fiction, many works about village and small-town life have been written about Nebraska. Among the first were those of Kate M. Cleary (1863–1905), who migrated with her husband from Chicago to Hubbell, Nebraska, in 1884. Cleary's *Like a Gallant Lady* (1897) is a novel involving insurance fraud. In *A Lost Lady* (1923) Willa Cather tells the story of an enigmatic western woman in Sweet Water, a town based on Red Cloud; the novel is important for its portrayal of the loss of frontier values.

The immensely popular interpreter of Midwestern prairie experience, BESS STREETER ALDRICH (1881–1954), moved to Elmwood, Nebraska, from IOWA in 1909. Aldrich is best known for her stories of small-town domestic life, which are romantic works intended to be uplifting. She may have been the first writer to place a series of family stories in American magazines. Many of these are collected in her first book, *Mother Mason* (1924). Aldrich's other works include the novels *The Rim of the Prairie* (1925); the much-lauded *A Lantern in Her Hand* (1928) and *A White Bird Flying* (1931), featuring Abbie Deal's family; *Spring Came On Forever* (1935); and *The Lieutenant's Lady* (1942). The novel *Prairie Women* (1930) by Ivan Beede (1896–1946) is a series of sketches about disappointments, guilt, and telling moments of passion and anger. Weldon Kees (1914–1955) wrote short stories in a similar vein; they are collected in *Ceremony* (1984) and *Selected Short Stories* (2002).

Wright Morris wrote several works focused ironically on memories evoked by small-town life. Morris's central theme involves the problem of relying too heavily on the past for meaning. He first addressed this theme in *The World in the Attic* (1949), where he discusses the "home-town nausea" produced by excessive nostalgia (26). *The Field of Vision* (1956), which won the National Book Award, and *Ceremony in Lone Tree* (1960) are comic novels on this theme. In the former, set at a Mexico City bullfight as observed by Nebraskans, Morris examines implications of living in the past; *Ceremony in Lone Tree* is set against a murder spree based on the Starkweather-Fugate murder rampage across Nebraska in 1957. *The Works of Love* (1952) explores the pathos of the life of a man based on Wright Morris's father; the author also explored this life in his memoir, *Will's Boy* (1981).

Omaha-born Ron Hansen (b. 1947) has written several celebrated novels, including *Mariette in Ecstasy* (1991), *Atticus* (1996), and *The Assassination of Jesse James by the Coward Robert Ford* (1983); the last was made into a movie with the same title in 2007, starring Brad Pitt and Casey Affleck. Hansen employs Nebraska settings sparingly in *Nebraska: Stories* (1989), including "Nebraska" and "Wickedness," a memorable fictional account of the blizzard of 1888. His *Isn't It Romantic? An Entertainment* (2003) is something of a screwball comedy involving two French tourists who find themselves as guests in a town called Seldom, Nebraska (population 395). The celebrated and often anthologized TILLIE (LERNER) OLSEN (1912–2007), whose works have been praised for the beauty of her language, was brought up in a Russian Jewish neighborhood in Omaha. Olsen wrote the famous *Tell Me a Riddle* (1961), which includes "I Stand Here Ironing" and the title story, the winner of the First Prize O. Henry Award in 1961. "Tell Me a Riddle" was made into a movie starring Melvyn Douglas and Lila Kedrova in 1980.

Many novels portray the development of Nebraska towns. In *The Wine o' the Winds* (1920) Keene Abbott (1876–1941) narrates the adventures of Dr. Harry North and a place called Tecon City in the Elkhorn River valley. This novel presents a picture of the Pawnee Scouts in action. *Retreat of a Frontier* (1950) by Kathryn Fingado O'Neil (1874–1959) is based on personal experiences homesteading in what she calls "Willow Grove." *The Call of the Western Prairie* (1952) by Elizabeth Jane Leonard (1881–1955) does something similar for central Nebraska. Two novels about the development of actual Nebraska towns are *A City Grew on the Sod* (1952) by George O. Criswell (1875–1952), about Loup City from pioneer days to the 1950s, and Mari Sandoz's *Son of the Gamblin' Man* (1960), a fictionalized biography of the artist Robert Henri, whose father founded Cozad, Nebraska.

Mari Sandoz's *Miss Morissa* (1955) tells the story of a young female doctor on the frontier near Sidney, Nebraska, in the 1870s. *Hang Up the Fiddle* (1954) by Frederic Babcock (1896–1979) concerns small-town Nebraska life before World War I. *The Proud Walk* (1960) by Nancy Moore (b. 1929) deals with provincial attitudes toward a young woman transplanted from Virginia to 1930s Nebraska.

In recent years Nebraska fiction has become more complex, often troubled by the tension between traditional Midwestern values and the complexities of contemporary life. For example, in "Starkweather's Eyes," from *River Street: A Novella and Stories* (1994) by Phil Condon (b. 1947), a son narrates the story of his father's disappearance at the time of Charles Starkweather's murderous rampage. Condon's novel *Clay Center* (2004)

concerns two Nebraskans' attempts to find meaning in Vietnam-era politics. The sometimes redemptive qualities of small-town life are explored in works by contemporary writers like Tom McNeal (b. 1947), author of *Goodnight, Nebraska* (1998), and Dan Chaon (b. 1964). Chaon's books include *Fitting Ends* (1995), stories about family and small-town narrow-mindedness; *Among the Missing* (2001); and *You Remind Me of Me* (2004), his first novel. *Await Your Reply* (2009) is more complex and is only partly set in Nebraska. His latest collection of stories is *Stay Awake* (2012). *The Phantom Limbs of the Rollow Sisters* (2002) by Timothy Schaffert (b. 1968) is about two sisters forced to come to grips with their father's suicide and abandonment by their mother; *The Singing and Dancing Daughters of God* (2005) deals with a recently divorced man who seeks to pull his scattered family members back together; *Devils in the Sugar Shop* (2006) is a comedy focused on the art scene in Omaha; and *The Swan Gondola* (2014) is set during the 1898 Omaha World's Fair. In 2011 Robert Vivian (b. 1967) completed his somewhat apocalyptic Tall Grass Trilogy, *The Mover of Bones* (2006), *Lamb Bright Saviors* (2010), and *Another Burning Kingdom* (2011). The first two novels feature visionary preachers and preacher-like figures roaming the Nebraska plains offering forgiveness and redemption. The final novel principally concerns two brothers: the older brother, Lem, is driving from the West Coast to interrupt his younger brother Jackson's plan to bomb the Nebraska state capitol in Lincoln. His 2012 novel *Water and Abandon* probes the emotions of a Nebraska family after the death of their seventeen-year-old daughter. Karen Gettert Shoemaker (b. 1957) explores the rising hatred of all things German during World War I and how it affects a Nebraska farm family in *The Meaning of Names* (2014).

Wide-ranging contemporary short-story collections, often on small-town themes, include *The Summer before the Summer of Love* (1995) by Marly Swick (b. 1949), *Are We Not Men?* (1996) by Brent Spencer (b. 1952), *The Dirty Shame Hotel* (1998) by Ron Block (b. 1955), *Troublemakers* (2000) by John McNally (b. 1965), and *Night Sounds* (2002) by Karen Gettert Shoemaker. Nebraska folklorist and humorist Roger Welsch (b. 1936) has written about rural and small-town life in such books as *It's Not the End of the Earth, but You Can See It from Here: Tales of the Great Plains* (1990). Ladette Randolph's short stories have appeared in *This Is Not the Tropics* (2005).

Several urban novels have employed Omaha and Lincoln as settings. The first Omaha novel appears to be *Joe Jason of Omaha* (1897) by Anson Eby (1867–1941). It tells the story of a Kentuckian who settles in Omaha, courts a young woman, loses her through a moral lapse, and then, repenting, marries her. *The Main Chance* (1903) is the first novel by MEREDITH NICHOLSON (1866–1947) and the first to use Omaha, here called Clarkson, as the setting for a BUSINESS novel. It involves an attempt by two business leaders to gain financial control of the city's cable-car system.

Social problems have occasionally been the subject of Nebraska urban novels. *Captain Martha Mary* (1912) by (Mabel) Avery Abbott (1870–ca. 1960) provides a picture of the lives of the poor in turn-of-the-century Omaha. The expressionistic *Bill Myron* (1927) by Dean Fales (1897–1965) follows Myron as he tries to succeed in a dismal city called Prospect. Coincidences abound in this tale of class and the social forces and personal flaws that keep the protagonist down. Carr Hume (1916–1999), a former Cudahy Packing Company accountant turned minister, wrote *Hodgepodge* (1971) to consider inner-city problems in the troubled Vietnam era. Tillie Olsen's unfinished novel *Yonnondio: From the Thirties* (1974) takes place partly in the South Omaha packinghouse district. *Capital City* (1939) by Mari Sandoz is a bitter Depression-era proletarian protest novel set in a state capital, Kenawa, intended to represent Midwestern state capitals in general but nevertheless understood to be Lincoln, Nebraska.

The Red Menace (1984) by MICHAEL ANANIA (b. 1939) is an autobiographical "fiction" about growing up in 1950s Omaha and coming to terms with identity and sexuality in the wake of the atomic bomb. *Dirty Bird Blues* (1996) by Clarence Major (b. 1936) concerns an African American blues musician who moves to Omaha in the 1950s to get a new start in life. The novel presents powerful descriptions of African American life and racism.

The Water's Edge (1958) by Allen Dale (b. 1923) is about the Missouri River flood of 1952 and its impact, especially on two reporters sent to Omaha to write about it. Omaha-born Carl Jonas (1913–1976) wrote a series of satires set in Gateway City. They include *Jefferson Selleck* (1952), *Riley McCullough* (1954), *Lillian White Deer* (1964), *The Observatory* (1966), and *The Sputnik Rapist* (1973). In *Star Smash* (1984) Sumner Hayward (1916–2013) depicts the retreat to Omaha of a budding actress who has been disfigured and put under the care of a plastic surgeon. James Magorian (b. 1942) is a prolific poet and writer of children's stories, as well as a novelist; his *Hearts of Gold* (1996) is a comic novel in which a member of the Omaha Flying Saucer Spotters Club seeks to find the Lost Dutchman Gold Mine, pursued by a host of oddballs and inept government agents.

In addition to *The Middle Five* by Francis La Flesche, novels about Nebraska school life include *The Cracker Box School* (1917) by Elizabeth Miller Lutton (1869–1945), which portrays the development of a progressive school devoted to practical realities. Willa Cather's last story, "The Best Years," published in *The Old Beauty, and Others* (1948), celebrates the life of a Nebraska schoolteacher. *Winter Thunder* (1951) by Mari Sandoz is based on the blizzard of 1949 and concerns a teacher and her pupils as they cope with their overturned bus.

The first Nebraska novel about university life was *John Auburntop, Novelist: His Development in the Atmosphere of a Fresh Water College* (1891) by Anson Uriel Hancock (1856–1899). Set in the 1870s at the newly opened University of Nebraska, the novel presents a detailed picture of literary debates. Dean Fales's satirical *Bachelor of Arts* (1932) focuses on a football star at Cornucopia University. Barney is a failure as a student and ends up working at his father's creamery business. The novel was made into the musical comedy *College Humor* (1933), starring Bing Crosby, George Burns, and Gracie Allen. Around 1940 Weldon Kees wrote the satirical college novel *Fall Quarter,* first published in 1990.

Miss Bishop (1933) by Bess Streeter Aldrich takes place largely at Midwestern College in a generalized Iowa and Nebraska, where Ella Bishop teaches for half a century. The novel was made into the movie *Cheers for Miss Bishop* (1941), which gave Lincoln its first movie premiere. Elizabeth Atkins (1891–1963) wrote the comic *Holy Suburb* (1941), set at Epworth College and based on Nebraska Wesleyan University; it is a gentle satire directed at college politics and the Methodism supporting the institution. In his novel *Edsel* (1971) iconoclastic KARL SHAPIRO (1913–2000) takes on the excesses of the 1960s in a city called Milo (Lincoln)—particularly the roles of certain poets and administrators in politicizing the university.

As the Nebraska homestead era saw a great influx of Europeans, primarily from Scandinavia, Germany, and Bohemia, many immigrant novels appeared, including several written in the author's original language and not translated. A good introduction is found in the videotape *The Nebraska Frontier in Swedish and Danish Ethnic Literature* (1985) by Dorothy Skardal. Perhaps the best known of the immigrant writers was Sophus Keith Winther (1893–1983). Winther was born in Denmark and wrote the Grimsen Trilogy, employing some of his family's experiences near Weeping Water, Nebraska. The first novel, *Take All to Nebraska* (1936), carries Danish immigrants Peter and Meta Grimsen and their children to a rented farm, where they encounter unexpectedly harsh conditions. In the second, *Mortgage Your Heart* (1937), the family is evicted, and the children grow up and leave; protagonist Hans makes his way to the university, where his values are severely tested. In *This Passion Never Dies* (1938) the family's difficulties continue, and Hans returns to the farm. Kristian Ostergaard (1855–1931), writing in Danish, set at least four novels in Nebraska, only one of which, *A Merchant's House* (1909), has been translated into English. It is set in 1870s Omaha, the first book of a trilogy about the Krogh family, whose members attempt to define themselves in the new world but are eventually overwhelmed by the surrounding culture.

Two Swedish writers whose novels have not yet been translated are Gustav Malm (1869–1928) and Leonard Stromberg (1871–1941). Malm's *Charli Johnson: Svensk-Amerikan* (1909) concerns a student who visits America and works on a Nebraska farm, marries the Swedish farmer's daughter, and introduces the community to European classical music. Stromberg, a Methodist minister, wrote a trilogy of Nebraska novels published in Sweden between 1933 and 1940.

Poetry: The first poem appearing in print in Nebraska was apparently "A Lady Type Setter" by T. D. Curtis, published in the first issue of the *Nebraska Palladium* on July 15, 1854. The first book-length poem employing the name of the territory was *Nebraska: A Poem, Personal and Political,* published in Boston in 1854 and attributed to Samuel R. Phillips (1824–1880) and George W. Bungay (1818–1892). Written in blank verse, it is largely a political work concerned with the implications of the Kansas-Nebraska Act.

Nebraska's first important poet, Orsamus Charles Dake (1832–1875), was born in Portage, New York, and was ordained in the Episcopal Church before migrating to Omaha in 1862. In 1871 he became the first professor of belles lettres at the University of Nebraska. Dake published two books, *Nebraska Legends and Poems* (1871) and *Midland Poems* (1873), the latter including many poems found in the earlier volume. The two most important works are long poems developed from Native American legends. In "The Raw Hide," about white incursion into Pawnee territory, a white man deliberately murders a Pawnee woman and is subsequently flayed to death by the woman's husband. The second poem, "The Weeping Water," tells the story of an Otoe man who marries an Omaha woman and lives with her in the Omaha camp, precipitating a battle in which the men of the two tribes destroy one another. The tears of the women and children who find them form the stream henceforth called Weeping Water.

Another epic poem on the naming of a river is *Niobrara's Love Story: An Indian Romance of Prehistoric Nebraska; Of the Fabled Ancient Empire of Quivera* (1900) by E. E. Blackman (1865–1942). In the poem the warrior Keya Paha falls in love with a goddess-like being named Niobrara. When Keya Paha is killed in battle, Niobrara mourns him extravagantly, and her father gives his daughter's name to the beautiful Nebraska River.

Isabel Grimes Richey (b. 1863), perhaps the first woman in Nebraska to publish books of poetry, wrote *A Harp of the West* (1895), which included no specifically Nebraska material, and *When Love Is King* (1900). The latter book is of interest primarily because of its introduction by J. Sterling Morton, a champion of Nebraska causes. Other early efforts include the work of Herbert Bates (1868–1929) in *Songs of Exile* (1896). *A Gallery of Farmer Girls* (1900) by Schuyler Miller (1868–1914) is an attempt to write verse about "real" things through the use of phonetic spelling and colloquial language paralleling the dialect verse of FINLEY PETER DUNNE (1867–1936), JAMES WHITCOMB RILEY (1849–1916), and others. William Reed Dunroy (1869–1921) published *Corn Tassels: A Book of Corn Rhymes* (1899), *Tumbleweeds* (1901), and *Rubaiyat of the Roses* (1907). Mary French Morton's (1832–1902) *Leaves from Arbor Lodge* (1901) is a collection of nature poems. Willa Cather's first book, a volume of poetry titled *April Twilights* (1903), only occasionally hints at Nebraska themes.

The most significant early Nebraska poet was John G. Neihardt, the state's first poet laureate, who held the title from 1921 to 1973. His first books were *The Divine Enchantment* (1900) and *A Bundle of Myrrh* (1907). Neihardt's major poetic work is the epic *A Cycle of the West* (1949), concerning western history from the beginnings of the MISSOURI fur trade to the massacre at Wounded Knee in 1890. It is composed of five parts: *The Song of Hugh Glass* (1915), *The Song of Three Friends* (1919), *The Song of the Indian Wars* (1925), *The Song of the Messiah* (1935), and *The Song of Jed Smith* (1941).

Another influential Nebraskan was Hartley Burr Alexander (1873–1939). He wrote poetry, plays, philosophical studies, works on Indian life, and the inscriptions for architect Bertram Goodhue's Nebraska state capitol building in Lincoln. Among Alexander's volumes of poetry are *The Mid Earth Life* (1907), *The Mystery Of Life: A Poetization Of "The Hako"—A Pawnee Ceremony* (1913), and *Odes and Lyrics* (1922).

Poems and Sketches of Nebraska (1908) by Addison Sheldon (1861–1943) is of greater historical than literary interest. Sheldon was a dedicated Nebraskan, superintendent of

the Nebraska State Historical Society from 1917 to 1943, the founder of *Nebraska History,* and a prolific writer. His poems deal with historical figures, landscape, architecture, and weather—even the 1903 Kansas-Nebraska football game.

As was the custom at the time, newspaper columnists published verse, sometimes collected in book form. A. L. "Doc" Bixby (1856–1934) published *Driftwood* (1895) and *Memories, and Other Poems* (1900) from his "Daily Drift" column for the *Nebraska State Journal.* Will M. Maupin (1863–1948), who wrote for the *Omaha Bee,* the *Omaha World-Herald,* and William Jennings Bryan's *Commoner,* was less overtly political. He published *Whether Common or Not* (1903) and *Sunny Side Up* (1926). Grace Sorenson (1880–1952) published *Home Made Jingles* (1908), originally written for the *Omaha World-Herald.*

Several landmark Nebraska volumes have been written on historical subjects. Among these are *Barbed Wire and Wayfarers* (1924) by Edwin Ford Piper (1871–1939), on conflicts between ranchers and homesteaders; *The Copper Kettle, and Other Poems* (1925) by Cora Phebe Mullin (1866–1923), long poems devoted to Manuel Lisa, Omaha chief Logan Fontenelle, and the Mormons at Winter Quarters; and *The True Story of Parker the Outlaw* (1927) by William Earl Hill (1880–1943), including "Sagas of the Sand Hills" and poems about the murders of two homesteaders by Sandhills cattlemen. *The Trumpeting Crane* (1934) by Helene Magaret (1906–1998) is a book-length poem about love and duty on the prairie. *The*

Ted Kooser, Garland, Nebraska, 2006. Photo by María Ghiggia.

Great Horse (1937) concerns the Mormon trek west. Dan Jaffe's (b. 1933) *Dan Freeman* (1967) highlights the nation's first homesteader, who filed his claim, now the Homestead National Monument in southeastern Nebraska, just after midnight on January 1, 1863.

LOREN COREY EISELEY (1907–1977) was also a poet of considerable force. His *Notes of an Alchemist* (1972), *The Innocent Assassins* (1973), *Another Kind of Autumn* (1977), and *All the Night Wings* (1979) provide meditations on the wonders of nature and oblique references to Eiseley's plains childhood and days as a "bone-hunter." Three Nebraska poets of merit for their sophistication and influence were Virgil Geddes (1897–1989), Weldon Kees, and Karl Shapiro. Geddes wrote *Forty Poems* and *Poems 41 to 70* (1926). Kees's works, *The Last Man* (1943), *The Fall of the Magicians* (1947), and *Poems, 1947–1954* (1954), are easily accessible now only in *The Collected Poems of Weldon Kees* (1975). Shapiro was editor of *Prairie Schooner* from 1956 to 1966.

Three of Michael Anania's books contain poems pertinent to Nebraska: *The Color of Dust* (1970), *Riversongs* (1978), and *The Sky at Ashland* (1986). The poems in *Walking along the Missouri River* (1977) by John McKernan (b. 1942) deal with personal responses to life and the death of his father in Nebraska.

WILLIAM KLOEFKORN (1932–2011), Nebraska State Poet from 1982 until his death, focused largely on farm and village life in such volumes as *Alvin Turner as Farmer* (1974), based on Kloefkorn's grandfather; *Cottonwood County* (1979), written with Ted Kooser (b. 1939); *Platte Valley Homestead* (1981); *Welcome to Carlos* (2000), on a small-town boy discovering poetry through a friend; and *Loup River Psalter* (2001). The monumental collection *Swallowing the Soap: New and Selected Poems* (2010), edited by Ted Genoways, is admirable and contains a generous selection of poems from across Kloefkorn's career. *This Death by Drowning* (1997), *Restoring the Burnt Child: A Primer* (2003), *At Home on This Moveable Earth* (2006), and *Breathing in the Fullness of Time* (2009) are memoirs.

Ted Kooser, one of Nebraska's best-known poets, was named Poet Laureate of the United States in 2004. For most of his writing years, Kooser worked at the Lincoln Benefit Life Company, retiring as vice president. Among his books are *Shooting a Farmhouse / So This Is Nebraska* (1975); *Sure Signs* (1980), winner of the Society of Midland Authors Prize; *Weather Central* (1994); and *Delights and Shadows* (2004). *The Blizzard Voices* (1986) concerns the famous blizzard of 1888. Kooser's friendship with Jim Harrison is reflected in *Winter Morning Walks: One Hundred Postcards to Jim Harrison* (2000) and *Braided Creek: A Conversation in Poetry* (2003). His *Local Wonders: Seasons in the Bohemian Alps* (2002) contains prose observations and reminiscences.

Contemporary Nebraska poetry is strong and vital, with too many poets to note in detail. The following books are representative: *Gay . . . Some Assembly Required* (1995) by Brian E. Bengtson (1966–2015); *Dismal River* (1990) by Ron Block; *Cheyenne Line* (2001) by J(ames) V(ernon) Brummels (b. ca. 1951); *The Dark Is a Door* (1984) by Susan Strayer Deal (1948–2014); *Bullroarer: A Sequence* (2001) by Ted Genoways (b. 1972); *How to Live in the Heartland* (1992) by Twyla Hansen (b. 1949); *In a River of Wind* (2000) by Neil Harrison (b. ca. 1952); *A Quiet I Carry with Me* (1994) by Nancy Peters Hastings (b. 1953); *Disciples of an Uncertain* Season (2001) by Larry Holland (1937–1999); *Skies of Such Valuable Glass* (1990) by Art Homer (b. 1951); *Nobody Lives Here Who Saw This Sky* (1998) by Greg Kosmicki (b. 1949); *Nebraska: A Poem* (1977) and *Selected Poems* (1996) by Greg Kuzma (b. 1944); *Freezing* (2001) by Steve Langan (b. 1965); *From the Dead Before* (2000) by Clif Mason (b. 1950); *Old Froggo's Book of Practical Cows* (1998) by Matt Mason (b. ca. 1968); *Girl Talk* (2002) by Nancy McCleery (b. 1933); *Divine Honors* (1997) by Hilda Raz (b. 1938); *Lost in Seward County* (2001) by Marjorie Saiser (b. 1943); *Before We Lost Our Ways* (1996) by Mark Sanders (b. 1955); *Pointing Out the Sky* (1985) by Roy Scheele (b. 1942); *The Upside Down Heart* (2003) by Barbara Schmitz (b. 1945); *Prairie Air Show* (2000) by Steven P. Schneider (b. 1951); *Dead Horse Table* (1975) by Don Welch (b. 1932); and *Lights along the Missouri* (1979) by Fredrick Zydek (b. 1938). Kathleene West (1947–2013), who grew up near Genoa, Nebraska, has explored farm life and her family's Nebraska roots in such works as *Land Bound* (1978), *Water Witching* (1984), *Plainswoman: Her First Hundred Years* (1985), and *The Farmer's Daughter* (1988).

In *Frankenstein Was a Negro* (2002) African American Charles Fort (b. 1951) presents a series of near-surrealistic prose poems, some involving a recurrent character, Darvil. Fort also has written *As the Lilac Burned the Laurel Grew* (1999) and *Immortelles* (2000); these cast an African American light on the Nebraska frontier. Nebraska State Penitentiary death-row inmate Harold Lamont Otey (1952–1994) published the chapbooks *And Me I Am like the Leaf* (1981) and *Singing for Mooncrumbs* (1985). Native American poetry from Nebraska is found in *La-ta-we-sah (Woman of the Bird Clan): Her Poetry and Prose* (1989), the work of Eunice W. Stabler (1885–1963); and *Up River: Good Medicine Poems* (1973) by Frank V. Love.

The first anthology of Nebraska poetry was *Nebraska Poets: One Hundred Pages of Prairie Poems* (1893) with work by thirty-two poets, including Kate Cleary and Elia Peattie. Some others are *Minnesota and Nebraska Poets* (1937), edited by Robert Cary; and the two-volume collection *Poems by Nebraska Poets* (1940), edited by Frederick Blaine Humphrey. Later anthologies include *The Sandhills and Other Geographies* (1980), edited by Mark Sanders; *Wellsprings: A Collection of Poems from Six Nebraska Poets* (1995), edited by Susanne George Bloomfield, with fresh introductions to Hansen, Kloefkorn, Kooser, Saiser, Strayer, and Welch; and *The Plains Sense of Things* (1997), in two volumes, edited by Mark Sanders. Greg Kuzma has edited several anthologies, including *Nebraska Poets* (1975) and *Forty Nebraska Poets* (1981). *On Common Ground: William Kloefkorn, Ted Kooser, Greg Kuzma, and Don Welch* (1983), with interviews, was edited by Mark Sanders and J. V. Brummels. *Nebraska Presence: An Anthology of Poetry* (2007), edited by Greg Kosmicki and Mary K. Stillwell, is a collection of work by nearly eighty contemporary poets, with thoughtful introductions on the condition of poetry and the audience for poetry in Nebraska.

Two anthologies have focused on Nebraska women poets. Judith Sornberger edited *All My Grandmothers Could Sing: Poems by Nebraska Women* (1984), and Elizabeth Banset, William Kloefkorn, and Charles Stubblefield edited *Adjoining Rooms* (1985), with poems by five poets. Another collection is broader in scope; *Times of Sorrow / Times of Grace: Writing by Women of the Great Plains / High Plains* (2002), edited by Marjorie Saiser, Greg Kosmicki, and Lisa Sandlin, collects poetry, fiction, and memoir. Twyla M. Hansen was named State Poet in 2013.

Drama: The first professional dramatic group performed in Omaha in 1857, and several theatres were built in Omaha in the 1860s. Early theatre focused on known talent rather than on development of an indigenous Nebraska drama. The Omaha Drama League originated in 1915 and awarded prizes for new drama. (Mabel) Avery Abbott, an Omaha fixture, won the league's prize in 1923 for *Mr. Enright Entertains.* Allena Harris (b. ca. 1887) wrote mostly one-act plays, like *Old Walnut* (1926). The Omaha Community Playhouse opened in 1924. This very active theatre is currently the largest community theatre in the United States.

The pageant, a form of entertainment in Nebraska that combined words, music, and spectacle, was intended primarily to instill pride and patriotism. Well-known pageants are *The Pageant of Lincoln* (1917) and *Coronado in Quivera* (1922) by Hartley Burr Alexander. Grace Welsh Lutgen (1888–1969) wrote *Goldenrod Sprays: Pageants* (1943).

Nebraska was home to a number of playwrights who wrote little on Nebraska subjects, including Colin Campbell Clements (1894–1948) and Frederick Ballard (1884–1957). Ballard's *320 College Avenue* (1938), written with mystery novelist Mignon G. Eberhart (1899–1996), is a comic whodunit set in a sorority house in College City, U.S.A. Mabel Conklin Allyn (1894–1941) wrote a number of unpublished plays about farm life, as well as published works such as *Maggie Fixes It* (1929) and *Big Brother* (1934).

Notable Nebraska dramatic works include *Home Light of the Prairies* (1920) by Gilbert Guest and *Sod: A Drama of the Western Prairie in One Act* (1934) by Stuart M. Hunter (1883–1957). *Sod* is set in a sod house in 1900; a mother plans to have her daughter escape life on the prairie by sending her to school in INDIANA, but her hope is thwarted when the daughter elopes. Virginia Faulkner (1913–1980) wrote the libretto for *Songs from out of the Wind* (1977), a musical drama based on Cather's "Eric Hermannson's Soul." Grace Sorenson published plays for children, including *Juvenile Comedies* (1926) and *Holiday Plays for Young Actors* (1950). Virginia Bradley (1912–2003) produced plays for teenagers; they include *Is There an Actor in the House?* (1975) and *Stage Eight: One-Act Plays* (1977).

Two unreasonably neglected Nebraska playwrights are E. P. Conkle (1899–1994) and Virgil Geddes. Conkle's work includes over fifty plays, among them *Prologue to Glory,* a drama about ABRAHAM LINCOLN (1809–1865) that played on Broadway and was acclaimed one of the best plays of 1938. *Crick Bottom Plays: Five Mid-Western Sketches* (1928) contains five humorous one-act plays about common Nebraska folks; among them are *Minnie Field, Sparkin',* and *'Lection. In the Shadow of a Rock* (1937) is a more ambitious play set in Peru, Nebraska, in 1849; frontier life, slavery, and politics come together as the protagonist reluctantly accepts runaway slaves—two small children. This play served as part of Conkle's doctoral thesis at the University of Iowa in 1936.

Virgil Geddes, like Eugene O'Neill (1888–1953), was interested in the Greek mythology that inspired Freudian themes. In *The Earth Between* (1929) Nat Jennings removes all obstacles to his daughter's affections, including possibly committing murder, and the play also suggests that Floy will "replace" her mother. Such dark Oedipal themes are continued in *Native Ground: A Cycle of Plays* (1932), including *Native Ground, The Plowshare's Gleam,* and *As the Crow Flies.*

Memorable playwriting continues in Nebraska. David G. Wiltse (b. 1940) uses southeastern Nebraska settings to explore themes of marital conflict, infidelity, and general menace, as in *A Grand Romance* (1982), *A Dance Lesson* (1991), and *Temporary Help* (1999). Doug Marr (b. 1953) has written many plays, including *Back at the Blue Dolphin Saloon* (1988), about an Omaha packing plant in the 1970s; *The Big Band Boys Grow Old* (1992); *Voices* (1995), containing an extended monologue by Mari Sandoz; *East of Denver Christmas Eve* (2000), starring a disc jockey at an isolated Nebraska radio station; and the multimedia drama *Starkweather* (1989). Tim Kaldahl (b. 1968) has written several one-act plays, including *West Omaha Soul Sucker* (2001), and the full-length *Marlin Perkins under Glass* (2004), employing the Mutual of Omaha *Wild Kingdom* emcee as the narrator in a comic play that examines Midwestern restlessness.

Omaha premiered three plays featuring significant Nebraska stories: *Minstrel Show* (1998) by Max Sparber (b. 1968), the story of William Brown, a black man dragged by a mob from Omaha's Douglas County Jail and lynched in 1919, as told by two fictional minstrel players; *Something Is Wrong* (1999) by Robert Vivian; and *Ink and Elkskin* (2004) by Carson Grace Becker (b. 1964), chronicling the first official meeting of Lewis and Clark with American Indians, the Otoe and Missouria, in 1804 Nebraska.

Several plays use Nebraska as a generic setting to focus on contemporary cultural conditions. Among these are the anti-violence and anti-child-abuse play *Goona Goona* (1991) by Megan Terry (b. 1932), *The Swan* (1994) by Elizabeth Egloff (b. 1953), and *Nebraska* (1989) by Keith Reddin (b. 1956). The last of these is set on an air force base and links modern angst to the responsibilities of characters tending a missile silo. The comic *Man from Nebraska* (2005) by Tracy Letts (b. 1965) is about a man suddenly stricken with a conviction that God does not exist.

Film: Nebraska's first movie theatre, the Parlor, opened in Omaha in 1905. Many films are associated with Nebraska. Terrence Malick's *Badlands* (1973) is based on the Starkweather-Fugate killing spree and stars Martin Sheen and Sissy Spacek. *Terms of Endearment* (1983), set in Lincoln and starring Jack Nicholson, Shirley Maclaine, and Debra Winger, garnered many Academy Awards. Dan Mirvish (b. 1967) made *Omaha: The Movie* (1994), the first independent film made in Nebraska by a native Nebraskan. The most acclaimed Nebraska filmmaker is Alexander Payne (b. 1961). His credits include *Citizen Ruth* (1996), *Election* (1999), and *About Schmidt* (2002), all filmed in Nebraska. Payne's *Sideways* (2004), a comedy set in California wine country, won an Academy Award for Best Writing in an Adapted Screenplay. Hilary Swank won an Academy Award for her performance in *Boys Don't Cry* (1999), in which she played Brandon Teena, a troubled young transgender man who is ultimately murdered in Falls City. *The Indian Runner* (1991) by Sean Penn (b. 1960) was filmed in Plattsmouth, Nebraska.

Popular Literature:

Dime Novels: The most famous figure in the dime-novel tradition was (William Frederick) "Buffalo Bill" Cody (1846–1917), although not many Buffalo Bill titles were actually set in Nebraska. Cody was born in Iowa, was raised in Kansas, and lived much of his adult life in Nebraska. Prentiss Ingraham (1843–1904) wrote well over one hundred Buffalo Bill dime-novel adventures. These included *Adventures of Buffalo Bill from Boyhood to Manhood* (1881), the first of Beadle's Boy's Library of Sport, Story, and Adventure, and *Buffalo Bill's Life-Stake; or, The Pledged Three: A Story of the Marked Shadower of Rocky Ridge* (1895), which is set in Nebraska. Ingraham also wrote *Dashing Charlie's Pawnee Pard; or, Red Hair, the Renegade: A Romance of Real Heroes of Borderland* (1892). Another writer was Edward Zane Carroll Judson (1821–1886), using the pseudonym Ned Buntline, who often employed the character of Buffalo Bill.

Other recurrent dime-novel characters were Pawnee Bill and Nebraska Charlie. The latter is found in Ingraham's *The Adventurous Life of "Nebraska Charlie," the Boy "Medicine-Man" of the Pawnees* (1882). Three different writers employed the pseudonym Edward C. Taylor; titles include the Ted Strong novels in the Western Story Library, among them *Ted Strong in Nebraska; or, The Trail to Fremont* (1904) and *Ted Strong's Nebraska Ranch; or, Fun and Frolic in the West* (1905). Oliver "Oll" Coomes (1845–1921) wrote two dime novels set on the Platte River, *Wild Raven, the Scout; or, The Missing Guide* (1870) and *Old Strategy, the Trapper Ventriloquist* (1870). William G. Patten (1866–1945) wrote *Wild Vulcan, the Lone Range-Rider; or, The Rustlers of the Bad Lands: A Romance of Northwest Nebraska* (1890).

Western Novels: Nebraska generated many popular westerns. Noel B. Gerson (1914–1988), writing as Dana Fuller Ross, wrote *Nebraska!* (1979), the second volume of Gerson's Wagons West series, about a wagon train crossing the plains in 1837. *Blood on the Republican* (1992) by Jeff O'Donnell (b. 1953) opens in 1861 when Lute North's family is attacked by Cheyennes. Lute is a fictionalized version of the scout Luther North (1846–1935), leader of the Pawnee Scouts. (PEARL)

ZANE GREY (1872–1939) fictionalized Edward Creighton's feat in stringing the telegraph lines through Nebraska and the West in *Western Union* (1939). The more traditional popular western is found in the works of George G. Shedd (1877–1937), including *Cryder* (1922). Wayne C. Lee (1917–2010) wrote popular westerns, such as *Barbed-Wire War* (1983), set in the Sandhills. Another prolific writer was Wayne D. Overholser (1906–1996); as Joseph Wayne he wrote *The Long Wind* (1953), a story about conflict among promoters, settlers, and cattleman in western Nebraska.

Mystery and Detective Fiction: The best-known Nebraska mystery writer is Mignon G. Eberhart; she wrote nearly sixty novels and was the second-highest-paid mystery writer in America. She set her third novel, *The Mystery of Hunting's End* (1930), in the Sandhills. It was later made into the movie *Mystery House* (1938) with Ann Sheridan. Crime pulp writer Jim Thompson (1906–1977) wrote *Heed the Thunder* (1946), an untidy novel set in a Sandhills town roughly from 1890 to 1910. The novel involves unsavory characters in the Fargo clan.

Jo(sephine) Frisbie (1903–1996) and Gunnar Horn (1912–2001) wrote four mysteries set in Nebraska: *Murder in the Old Mill* (1979), *Murder in the Museum* (1980), *Murder in the Church Yard* (1982), and *Murder on Maple Street* (1984). David Wiltse has written crime novels featuring Billy Tree, a Secret Service agent who has lost his nerve and returns home to Falls City, Nebraska, in *Heartland* (2001) and *The Hangman's Knot* (2002), where he confronts bullies, drugs, and buried racial prejudice. Wiltse's *Home Again* (1986) is also set in Nebraska. *Teardrops Are Red* (2000) by psychiatrist John Schepman (b. 1937) involves murder, rape, and a doctor who claims to have a "violence cure." The novel's protagonist, Zed Taggert, is another detective drawn back to Nebraska to solve a crime. *Outside Valentine* (2004) by Liza Ward (b. ca. 1976) is a suspense novel employing the Starkweather-Fugate murders.

Several writers have set mystery novels in Omaha locations. William J. Reynolds (b. 1956) wrote a series of novels featuring an Omaha detective named Nebraska: *The Ne-*

braska Quotient (1984), *Moving Targets* (1986), *Money Trouble* (1988), *Things Invisible* (1989), *The Naked Eye* (1990), and *Drive-By* (1995). Richard Dooling (b. 1954) specializes in medical satire and suspense. *Critical Care* (1992) was made into a film directed by Sidney Lumet. *Bet Your Life* (2002) is a novel about an insurance-fraud investigation in Omaha. Dooling collaborated with Stephen King on the television miniseries *Kingdom Hospital* (2004). Sharon Kava (b. 1960), writing as Alex Kava, has written several thrillers starring Maggie O'Dell, a retired FBI profiler. *A Perfect Evil* (2000) deals with serial murder in Platte City, Nebraska. Kava's *One False Move* (2004) concerns a bank robbery in which six people are killed and the killers escape to Platte River State Park near Omaha. Sean Doolittle (b. 1971) has set two of his fast-moving suspense novels with down-and-out protagonists in Nebraska locations: *Rain Dogs* (2005) in the Sandhills and *The Cleanup* (2006) in Omaha.

Graphic Novels: The poet Ted Kooser wrote a work titled *Hatcher* (1978) that is sometimes called a GRAPHIC NOVEL, although it does not meet strict criteria for that genre. It is an amusing, if slight, work composed largely of borrowed prints—many of them apparently German prints from the nineteenth century—to which Kooser added cartoon dialogue boxes in which figures in the prints comment on the romantic pursuits and sexual prowess of the mysterious poet and lover Hatcher. William Harms (b. 1969) published a graphic novel titled *Abel* (2002), set in a small Nebraska community and concerning a boy growing up with a violent brother; when the brother kills a young woman, the town blames a Chinese servant in town, and the book ends with a lynching and the boy's emotional accommodation to the murder. The best-known graphic novelist originally from Nebraska, although he is now based in Chicago, is Franklin Christenson Ware (b. 1967), usually writing as Chris Ware. His work has won numerous awards and has been exhibited in important art museums. His best-known graphic novel is *Jimmy Corrigan: The Smartest Kid on Earth* (2000), and he has created at least twenty volumes so far in his Acme Novelty Library, beginning in 1994, among a variety of other works.

Children's and Young Adult Literature: Early Nebraska works for juveniles often focused on animal life, as in *Fairy Tales of the Western Range* (1902) by Eugene O. Mayfield (1860–1943). These were animal fables and adventure stories. As Uncle Ross, Frank A. Secord (1867–1954) wrote about animals in *Wonder Tales: Gabby Crow and Mud-and-Sticks Stories* (1933). Dan V. Stephens (1868–1939), a U.S. congressman from 1911 to 1919, tells homey tales in *Cottonwood Yarns*: *Being Mostly Stories Told to Children about Some More or Less Wild Animals That Live at "the Cottonwoods" on the Elkhorn River in Nebraska* (1935). In *Passing of the Buffalo at the Cottonwoods* (1938) he tells of having to slaughter buffalo.

The frontier has remained a staple of fiction for juveniles. Marion Marsh Brown (1908–2001) wrote copiously for children and teenagers, sometimes telling tales from her homesteader grandfather. Among her most popular books is *Stuart's Landing: A Story of Pioneer Nebraska* (1953; originally *Frontier Beacon*), the story of a young man who wants to be a writer in pioneer Nebraska. Jean Bothwell (1892–1977) wrote many books for juveniles, including *The Tree House at Seven Oaks: A Story of the Flat Water Country in 1853* (1957), a novel about Bellevue that incorporates historical figures Peter Sarpy and Joseph La Flesche. *Wires West* (1957) by Leo V. Jacks (1896–1972) concerns an Irishman who comes to Omaha to work for Edward Creighton stringing telegraph wires across the plains. *San Domingo: The Medicine Hat Stallion* (1972) by Marguerite Henry (1902–1997) deals with a boy's emergence as a Pony Express rider. *Prairie Songs* (1985) by Pam Conrad (1947–1996) won acclaim for its treatment of pioneer sod-house life. *A Pony for Jeremiah* (1997) by Robert H. Miller (b. 1945) is about an African American slave family that escapes to Nebraska.

The cultures of American Indian tribes are popular subjects for juvenile fiction. *Beaver: The Pawnee Indian* (1918) by Stephen. M. Barrett (1865–1948) is a fictional account of the Pawnees, tracing tribal history from their life in the Platte River valley to their removal to Indian Territory. *A Bow for Turtle* (1960) by Dorothy Heiderstadt (1907–2001) is a short novel about a Pawnee child's official acceptance into the life and culture of his people before the coming of the whites. Mari Sandoz wrote several works for young adults, including *The Horsecatcher* (1957), the story of a Cheyenne teenager, and *The Story Catcher* (1963), on Sioux society in the 1840s. See also CHILDREN'S AND YOUNG-ADULT LITERATURE.

Many juvenile books have orphans as heroes. Among these is *Young Sand Hills Cowboy* (1953) by Francis Lynde Kroll (1904–1973). *Massacre at Ash Hollow* (1960) by Robert T. Reilly (1923–2004) portrays the coming of age of the orphaned protagonist on the Nebraska frontier. *An Orphan for Nebraska* (1979) by Charlene Joy Talbot (1924–2013) focuses on an Irish boy sent by the Children's Aid Society to Nebraska, where he works for a newspaper. *The Great American Elephant Chase* (1993) by Gillian Cross (b. 1945) presents a fifteen-year-old who takes an elephant from Pennsylvania to Nebraska in 1881. The companion volumes *Gratefully Yours* (1997) and *Hank's Story* (2001) by Jane Buchanan (b. 1956) are set in 1923 when the protagonists are sent west by orphan train. *My Face to the Wind: The Diary of Sarah Jane Price, a Prairie Teacher* (2001) by Jim Murphy (b. 1947) reconstructs the life of a nineteenth-century orphan who became a teacher in Nebraska. In *Holding Up the Earth* (2000) by Dianne Gray (b. 1944) the heroine learns about the Nebraska past through letters and diaries she discovers in her stepmother's house.

Trella Lamson Dick (1889–1974) wrote several novels of contemporary life for juveniles, among them *Tornado Jones* (1953) and *Tornado's Big Year* (1956), set in the Sandhills. *A Bee in Her Bonnet* (1944) by Eva Margaret Kristoffersen (1901–1954) carries a MICHIGAN family to an inherited Nebraska farm during World War II. Virginia Bradley (1912–2003) wrote *Bend to the Willow* (1979), in which a transplanted schoolteacher comes to terms with the car accident that killed her parents. Bradley's *Who Could Forget the Mayor of Lodi?* (1985) portrays small-town life and mental health in the 1930s. Florence Laughlin's (1910–2001) *The Seventh Cousin* (1966) is a mystery novel set in an old Lincoln mansion where someone is threatening to harm the heir to the family fortune. Gail Rock (b. 1940) wrote a series of novels based on her Nebraska childhood in the 1940s. Among these is *The House without a Christmas Tree* (1974), also a TV movie (1972) starring Jason Robards and Lisa Lucas. *The Night of the Twisters* (1984) by Ivy Ruckman (b. 1931) centers on reaction to seven separate tornadoes that touched down on Grand Island in June 1980. Tom Frye's (b. 1956) *Scratchin' on the Eight Ball* (1982) depicts a fourteen-year-old boy in Lincoln who faces issues with drugs and crime. Two young-adult books on religious themes are *Davey in the Sand Hills* (1951) by Anne M. Halladay, which concerns the impact of home missionary activities on children; and *Calling Me Home* (1998) by Patricia Hermes (b. 1936), which treats a teenage girl's struggle to accept her life on the Nebraska prairie in the 1850s.

Romance Novels: The love story remains healthy in Nebraska, and several romance organizations and writers have fueled the genre. Barbara Bonham (b. 1926) is best known for her historical romances, including *Challenge of the Prairie* (1965), in which a homestead family copes with squatters; *Passion's Price* (1977), about a young widow who enters a relationship with a "family man"; and *Green Willow* (1982). *The Woman I Am* (1979) and *Dear Stranger* (1982) by Catherine Kidwell (1921–2002) are "feminist romances" set in Lincoln at the University of Nebraska and the Cornhusker Hotel during World War II. Barbara Leigh's *Web of Loving Lies* (1993) concerns a woman's relationship with an Indian scout. Pam Hart's *Lies and Shadows* (1993) is about a woman who hires an unusual nanny—a handsome young man—to help her raise her three troubled children. In *Land of Dreams* (1995) by Cheryl Ludwigs (b. 1951), writing as Cheryl St. John, two adults vie for the care of a young orphan girl, and the protagonist builds a mill based on the historic mill at Neligh. *A Husband by Any Other Name* (1996), set near the apple orchards of Nebraska City, concerns twin brothers, one with amnesia, the other carrying the first's identity. The Gypsy in *Lady Gypsy* (2001) by Pam Crooks (b. 1955) encounters conflict and love with a railroad man in the northern Nebraska of 1876. Kim

Louise Whiteside (b. 1962), writing as Kim Louise, an African American romance writer, wrote *Destiny's Song* (2000) and *A Touch Away* (2001), about an African American woman's belated return to college in Omaha. *Walks the Fire* (1995) and *Soaring Eagle* (1996) by Stephanie Grace Whitson (b. 1952) and *Unforgettable Faith* (2000) by Cynthia Rutledge (b. 1954) are inspirational Christian romances. Other authors associated with Nebraska, among them Victoria Alexander (b. 1965), Barbara Blackman, writing as Jeanne Allan, Victoria Morrow (b. 1957), Judith Nelson, and Kathleen Pieper (b. 1951), also write romances.

Science Fiction and Fantasy: In *The Fork River Space Project* (1977), set in Nebraska and Kansas, Wright Morris has his characters confront an expansion of consciousness by way of a mysterious space show. In *Deus ex Machina* (1989) the writer character constructed by J. V. Brummels (b. 1951) faces the end of the world and is forced to choose between staying on Earth or transporting himself into space.

Lesbian and Gay Fiction: Little Nebraska fiction deals explicitly with gay and lesbian themes. Some exceptions are *Walkin' Matilda* (1984) by Larry Paul Ebmeier (1950–2011), writing as Clayton R. Graham, a comedy about a gay exchange student from Australia with a wooden leg; *Nebraska* (1987) by George Whitmore (1945–1989), a sexual coming-of-age novel in which a boy gradually discovers that his uncle has been given electroshock treatment as a response to his homosexuality; and *Omaha's Bell* (1999) by Penny Hayes (b. 1940), involving a lesbian triangle and the purchase of a bell for a local school in nineteenth-century Omaha. See also LESBIAN, GAY, BISEXUAL, TRANSGENDER, AND QUEER LITERATURE.

Nonfiction Literary Genres: In addition to fiction, two kinds of personal writing are of special importance in Nebraska: memoirs and personal essays. Homesteader memoirs are abundant. Among the most useful collections are *Nebraska Pioneer Reminiscences* (1916), issued by the Nebraska society of the Daughters of the American Revolution; *Sod House Memories* in three volumes (1972), edited by Frances Jacobs Alberts; and *Paradise on the Prairie: Nebraska Settlers Stories* (1986) by Baldwin F. Kruse

(1902–1980), edited by his son, Lowen V. Kruse. The best-known homesteader account is Mari Sandoz's first book, *Old Jules* (1935), the famous biography of Sandoz's complex father and an insider's account of life on the frontier.

Other popular accounts are *Them Was the Days: An American Saga of the '70's* (1950) by Martha Ferguson McKeown (1903–1974), *The Buffalo Wallow* (1953) by Charles Tenney Jackson (1874–1955), and *Thunder and Mud: A Pioneer Childhood on the Prairie* (1996) by Julia Brown Tobias (1902–2001). Well-known Sandhills memoirs are *Western Story: The Recollections of Charley O'Kieffe, 1884–1898* (1960) by Charley O'Kieffe (1879–1967) and *No Time on My Hands* (1963) by Grace Snyder (1883–1983), assisted by Nellie Snyder Yost (1905–1992). *Trails of Yesterday* (1921) by John Bratt (1864–1918) is considered a classic on ranching.

Memoirs of famous Nebraska citizens include those of Luther North (1846–1935), the head of the Pawnee Scouts, *Man of the Plains: Recollections of Luther North, 1856–1882* (1961); and Buffalo Bill's *The Life of Hon. William F. Cody, Known as Buffalo Bill: The Famous Hunter, Scout, and Guide; An Autobiography* (1879). Political autobiographies include those of William Jennings Bryan, *Memoirs of William Jennings Bryan* (1925); Bryan adviser Alfred P. Mullen (1873–1938), *Western Democrat* (1940); and George W. Norris (1861–1944), *Fighting Liberal: The Autobiography of George W. Norris* (1945).

Two memoirs involving Omaha are of significant interest. *The Face of a Naked Lady: An Omaha Family Mystery* (2005) by Michael Rips (b. 1954) philosophically connects some intriguing family mysteries to Omaha history. In *Omaha Blues: A Memory Loop* (2005) Joseph Lelyveld (b. 1937), executive editor at the *New York Times* from 1994 to 2001, explores his feelings of abandonment within his troubled family in the years when they lived in Nebraska.

Because much of Nebraska is rural and sparsely populated, a literature of science and reflection on nature emerged early in poetry and the personal essay. That tradition may have started with *Forests and Orchards in Nebraska: A Handbook for Prairie Planting* (1884) by James Thomas Allan (1831–1885). The best-known naturalist writer is Loren

Eiseley, who wrote what he called "concealed essays," reflections on nature and science connected to autobiographical anecdotes. His most popular book, *The Immense Journey* (1957), contains poetic accounts of evolutionary highlights; similar essays make up his autobiographies, *The Night Country* (1971) and *All the Strange Hours: The Excavation of a Life* (1975). Paul A. Johnsgard (b. 1931) and John Janovy Jr. (b. 1937) are prolific scientific writers. Johnsgard's works include *The Platte: Channels in Time* (1984) and *The Nature of Nebraska: Ecology and Biodiversity* (2001). Janovy's work includes *Keith County Journal* (1978) and other books. Several lyrical books are *Hawk Flies Above: Journey to the Heart of the Sandhills* (1996) by Lisa Dale Norton (b. 1956), *The Last Prairie: A Sandhills Journal* (2000) by Stephen R. Jones (b. 1947), *Cold Snap as Yearning* (2001) by Robert Vivian, and *The Nature of Home: A Lexicon and Essays* (2002) by Lisa Knopp (b. 1956).

Printing and Journalism: Given the intensely heightened activity resulting from the 1854 Kansas-Nebraska Act and the frontier traffic flowing through Nebraska, it was not long before newspapers took root. The first newspaper, the *Nebraska Palladium*, began in mid-July 1854, but was actually printed in Iowa until October of that year when it moved to Bellevue. It was followed by the *Omaha Arrow* at the end of July 1854 and then by the *Omaha Nebraskian* in January 1855. The *Nebraska City News* began in November 1854; its first editor was J. Sterling Morton. In Brownsville Robert W. Furnas began the *Nebraska Advertiser* in 1856 and the *Nebraska Farmer* in 1859. An early newspaper, *Huntsman's Echo*, was established in Wood River Center, now known as Shelton, in 1859. Other early newspapers included the *Daily Nebraskan Republican* (1858) in Omaha; the *Nebraska State Journal* in Lincoln (1869), for which Willa Cather began to write in 1893; and the *Omaha Bee*, founded by Edward Rosewater in 1871. The *Omaha Daily World*, founded by Gilbert M. Hitchcock in 1885, combined with the *Omaha Daily Herald* in 1889 to form the *Omaha World-Herald*.

Early specialized newspapers included the *Progress*, begun in Omaha in 1889 as the first newspaper in the state for African Americans. Mary Fairbrother owned and edited the *Woman's Weekly* in Omaha from 1894 to 1901; it served as the official organ of the Omaha Women's Club. Thomas Tibbles edited the *Independent*, a weekly Populist paper in Lincoln in the 1890s. J. Sterling Morton started the weekly *Conservative* in Nebraska City in 1898. WILLIAM JENNINGS BRYAN (1860–1925) began the *Commoner*, a weekly, in Lincoln in 1901. There were also several immigrant newspapers, such as the German *Nebraska Deutsche Zeitung*, begun in Nebraska City in 1861, and the Czech *Pokrok Zapadu*, begun in Omaha in 1871.

Literary magazines and journals published in Nebraska include immigrant literary periodicals such as the Czech *Květy Americké*, begun in Omaha in 1884. The quarterly *Nebraska Literary Magazine*, first published in 1895, was the first devoted to student literary efforts at the University of Nebraska. It was followed by the monthly *Kiote* (1898–1899). Important journals of national distinction included *Mid-West Quarterly* (1913–1918), edited by Prosser Hall Frye, and the ongoing *Prairie Schooner*, a literary quarterly with an international reputation for quality, established in 1926 by Lowry C. Wimberly.

The University of Nebraska Press, established in 1941, is a major national press that publishes in a number of specialties, including Midwestern and Western regional books; its series called Flyover Fiction includes new work by regional writers. Many small presses are devoted primarily to Nebraska poetry, such as Backwaters Press (Greg Kosmicki), Logan House Press (J. V. Brummels and Jim Reese), Best Cellar Press (Greg Kuzma), and Sandhills Press (Mark Sanders). Harry Duncan (1916–1997) was well known for producing fine books through Cummington Press and Abattoir Edition Books. Bradypress (Denise Brady), associated with the Nebraska Book Arts Center, publishes letterpress editions of poetry.

Nebraska Federal Writers' Project: The Nebraska Federal Writers' Project developed out of the Emergency Relief Act of 1935 and was headquartered in Lincoln under Elizabeth Sheehan, then J. Harris "Jake" Gable, and finally Rudolph Umland until its termination in March 1942. According to Jerry Mangione in *The Dream and the Deal* (1972), the Nebraska unit was considered one of the most successful in the country. It produced thirteen books in addition to the state guide and over thirty pamphlets on Nebraska folklore. Some of the books were *Nebraska: A Guide to the Cornhusker State* (1939), *Old Bellevue* (1937), *Origin of Nebraska Place Names* (1938), *A Military History of Nebraska* (1939), *Negroes of Nebraska* (1940), and *Italians of Omaha* (1941). Its most popular title was *Lincoln City Guide* (1937), which sold 16,000 copies.

Nebraska Literary Societies and Awards: Writers in Nebraska early sought association with others. In 1898 the English Club at the University of Nebraska established the *The Kiote,* self described as "a literary monthly dedicated to the prairie yelper." The Quill, for women writers in Lincoln, began informally in 1921; the Omaha Women's Press Club was created in 1946. The still-active Nebraska Writers Guild began in 1925, at the start including such figures as Cather, Neihardt, Bess Streeter Aldrich, and Louise Pound (1872–1958). The Nebraska Poetry Association produced *Sandbars and Cattails: The Nebraska Poetry Association 1976 Anthology* (1976). The Omaha Writers Group was organized in 1946.

Important current groups supporting literature in Nebraska include the Nebraska Humanities Council, the Nebraska Arts Council, and the Nebraska Center for the Book, which has generated a number of literary awards. These include the Mildred Bennett Award for contributions to "the literary tradition in Nebraska"; the Jane Geske Award for organizations or schools for long-time commitment to writing in Nebraska; and the Nebraska Book Awards Competition for best annual books in several categories, including adult and juvenile fiction and poetry.

SELECTED WORKS: A good place to start an exploration of Nebraska writing is with four classic works: Willa Cather's *O Pioneers!* (1913) and *My Ántonia* (1918), farm novels that put Nebraska fully into American consciousness; Mari Sandoz's fictionalized biography of her father, *Old Jules* (1935); and John Neihardt's *Black Elk Speaks* (1932), which inti-

mately explores spiritual Native American life on the plains.

Useful approaches to early Nebraska poetry are found in *Nebraska Legends and Poems* (1871) by Orsamus Charles Dake, which incorporates mythic materials, and the first anthology, *Nebraska Poets: One Hundred Pages of Prairie Poems* (1893). Later works include Neihardt's saga *A Cycle of the West* (1949), Weldon Kees's *The Collected Poems of Weldon Kees* (1975), and Loren Eiseley's works, including *Another Kind of Autumn* (1977). Nebraska state poet William Kloefkorn's many works include *Welcome to Carlos* (2000) and *Loup River Psalter* (2001). U.S. Poet Laureate Ted Kooser's works include *Weather Central* (1994), *Winter Morning Walks: One Hundred Postcards to Jim Harrison* (2000), and *Delights and Shadows* (2004).

Nebraska drama is well represented by *Crick Bottom Plays: Five Mid-Western Sketches* (1928) and *In the Shadow of a Rock* (1937) by E. P. Conkle, as well as by the Oedipal dramas of Virgil Geddes in *Native Ground: A Cycle of Plays* (1932). David G. Wiltse, a contemporary playwright of interest, has contributed suspenseful plays such as *Temporary Help* (1999).

Nebraska fiction is rich in subjects and themes. Native American life is glimpsed in the novel *Ploughed Under: The Story of an Indian Chief, Told by Himself* (1881) by William Justin Harsha and in *The Middle Five: Indian Schoolboys of the Omaha Tribe* (1900) by Francis La Flesche. Danish immigrant life is explored by Sophus Keith Winther in the Grimsen Trilogy, beginning with *Take All to Nebraska* (1936). The Nebraska frontier is the subject of *A Lantern in Her Hand* (1928) by Bess Streeter Aldrich and of Willa Cather's classic works noted previously. Another Cather novel, *A Lost Lady* (1923), is important for portraying the decline of frontier values. Tillie Olsen's *Yonnondio: From the Thirties* (1974) is a work of urban life in the Depression. Wright Morris pictures Nebraska farm life in the photographs and text of *The Home Place* (1948) and explores post-frontier conditions ironically in *Ceremony in Lone Tree* (1960).

In addition to those already noted, several anthologies should be mentioned. Virginia Faulkner edited *Roundup: A*

Nebraska Reader (1957), collecting essays and excerpts putting the literature into historical perspective. *Nebraska Voices: Telling the Stories of Our State* (1993) consists of newspaper columns selected by the Nebraska Humanities Council and occasioned by the 125th anniversary of Nebraska statehood. *Rural Voices: Literature from Rural Nebraska* (2002), edited by Christopher Rand Gustafson, includes a broad variety of short poems and prose pieces by both established writers and newcomers. Ladette Randolph edited *A Different Plain: Contemporary Nebraska Fiction Writers* (2004) and, with Nina Shevchuk-Murray, a nonfiction collection, *The Big Empty: Contemporary Nebraska Nonfiction Writers* (2007). These volumes suggest the rich diversity of contemporary Nebraska writing. *Road Trip: Conversations with Writers* (2003) contains excellent interviews with twelve Nebraska writers conducted by Shelly Clark and Marjorie Saiser. Several important sources on folklore include *Nebraska Folklore* (1959) by Louise Pound and *A Treasury of Nebraska Pioneer Folklore* (1966) and *Omaha Tribal Myths and Trickster Tales* (1981) by Roger Welsch.

FURTHER READING:

Bibliography, Biography, and Criticism: Although no history of Nebraska literature has yet been written, several valuable bibliographies exist. The first is by Sophia J. Lammers, *A Provisional List of Nebraska Authors* (1918). Margaret Badollet Shotwell and Henry F. Kieser compiled *First Nebraska Authors' Week—Also Containing a Directory of Nebraska Authors* (1923). Alice G. Harvey's *Nebraska Writers* (1934), claiming some four hundred Nebraska writers, is quite useful; the second edition (1964) does not significantly expand the field. Jack Brodie and Bernice Kauffman's *Nebraska Centennial Literary Map and Guide to Nebraska Authors* (1967) is short but well annotated, while Emily Jane Uzendoski's doctoral thesis, "Handlist of Nebraska Authors" (1977), is extensive but not annotated. A later bibliography is *Guide to Nebraska Authors* (1998) by Gerry Cox and Carol MacDaniels. The online website Nebraska Center for Writers at Creighton University is indispensable.

Biographical and critical works on Willa Cather are extensive, and new studies appear every year. Two standard works are the biography *Willa Cather: A Literary Life* (1987) by James Woodress and *The Voyage Perilous: Willa Cather's Romanticism* (1986) by Susan Rosowski. Scholarly editions from the Willa Cather Archive are available for several novels, including *O Pioneers!* (1992) and *My Ántonia* (1994). An introduction to Wright Morris's work in fiction and photography is found in *Wright Morris Revisited* (1998) by Joseph J. Wydeven. Mari Sandoz is well served by Helen Winter Stauffer's biography *Mary Sandoz: Story Catcher of the Plains* (1982). Stauffer also edited *Letters of Mari Sandoz* (1992). Useful books for approaching John G. Neihardt include *A Sender of Words: Essays in Memory of John G. Neihardt* (1984), edited by Vine Deloria Jr., and *Black Elk and Flaming Rainbow* (1995), Hilda Neihardt Petri's memories of the relationship between her father and Black Elk. James Reidel wrote *Vanished Act: The Life and Art of Weldon Kees* (2003). Carol Miles Petersen's *Bess Streeter Aldrich: The Dreams Are All Real* (1995) is a useful biography. Good introductions to Kate Cleary are found in *The Nebraska of Kate McPhelim Cleary* (1958), a miscellany of stories, poems, recipes, and sketches, and *Kate M. Cleary: A Literary Biography with Selected Works* (1997) by Susanne George-Bloomfield.

No one can explore the Nebraska experience in any depth without the expansive resources of the Nebraska Historical Society and its quarterly journal, *Nebraska History,* first published in 1918. Several of the society's publications are of value, including *Published Sources on Territorial Nebraska: An Essay and Bibliography* (1956) by John Browning White, *The Great Platte River Road: The Covered Wagon Mainline via Fort Kearny to Fort Laramie* by Merrill J. Mattes (1969), and *Conquering the Great American Desert: Nebraska* (1975) by Everett Dick. John D. Unruh Jr.'s revisionist *The Plains Across: The Overland Emigrants and the Trans-Mississippi West, 1840–60* (1979) emphasizes cooperation rather than individualism. For the Midwestern states on the Great Plains, a vital resource is the *Encyclopedia of the Great Plains* (2004), edited by David J. Wishart.

Libraries, Archives, and Other Repositories: Significant collections of Nebraska literature are found throughout the state, but especially in Lincoln. The Jane Pope Geske Heritage Room of Nebraska Authors in the Bennett Martin Public Library in Lincoln has the largest general collection, along with a special Weldon Kees collection and the Dorothy Thomas Archive. The Nebraska State Historical Society Archives also has a broad collection. The University of Nebraska Love Library Archives has special collections on Cather, Kees, Morris, Neihardt, and Sandoz. Other important repositories are found at the Willa Cather Pioneer Memorial and Educational Foundation in Red Cloud, the Mari Sandoz High Plains Heritage Center at Chadron State College, and the John G. Neihardt Historical Site in Bancroft.

JOSEPH J. WYDEVEN   BELLEVUE UNIVERSITY

NEW HOME—WHO'LL FOLLOW? A, OR, GLIMPSES OF WESTERN LIFE

HISTORY: The 1839 publication of *A New Home—Who'll Follow? or, Glimpses of Western Life* by CAROLINE KIRKLAND (1801–1864) presented the American public for the first time with a realistic, conversational account of a woman settler's experience in the West. An autobiographical narrative employing pseudonyms for real people and places in MICHIGAN, *A New Home—Who'll Follow?* offers first-person impressions of settlement by a well-educated East Coast émigré, Mrs. Mary Clavers, Kirkland's *nom de plume*. Chronicling the establishment over a three-year period of Montacute, a stand-in for the actual town of Pinckney, Michigan, Kirkland portrays the complex forces and diverse peoples propelling the creation of "a new home" in the West.

Born Caroline Mathilda Stansbury, Kirkland grew up in a supportive middle-class family in New York City. Her father, Samuel Stansbury, was employed by an insurance company, and her mother, Eliza Alexander Stansbury, was an avid reader and writer. Kirkland received a strong formal education. In 1809, at the age of eight, she enrolled at a Quaker school where her aunt, Lydia P(hiladelphia) Mott, was headmistress. A gifted student, Kirkland became a schoolteacher in New Hartford, New York. In 1819 she met her future husband, William Kirk-

land (1800–1846), who was also an educator. After marrying in 1828, William and Caroline administered a girls' school in Geneva, New York, from 1828 to 1835. In 1835, with their four children, including the future writer JOSEPH KIRKLAND (1830–1894), the family moved to DETROIT, Michigan, where William Kirkland became a principal at the Detroit Family Seminary. Two years later, in 1837, the family moved to Pinckney, Michigan, a town that William Kirkland founded on an eight-hundred-acre land purchase. Caroline Kirkland's experiences in Pinckney inspired her first book, *A New Home—Who'll Follow?* and two subsequent works, *Forest Life* (1842) and *Western Clearings* (1845), all published under the pen name Mrs. Mary Clavers. The Kirklands returned to New York City in 1843 because of financial pressures caused by the panic of 1837. After William's untimely death in 1846, Caroline Kirkland supported her family through her editorship from 1847 to 1850 of *Union Magazine of Literature and Art*, which was renamed *Sartain's Union Magazine* in 1848. She was a prolific magazine contributor and wrote several books before her death in 1864.

In the preface to *A New Home—Who'll Follow?* Kirkland describes her central premise: "I claim for these straggling and cloudy crayon-sketches of life and manners in the remoter parts of Michigan, the merit of general truth of outline" (v). The first eleven chapters recount Mrs. Clavers's travel from Detroit to Montacute, offering humorous sketches of people and places. The seminal image of chapter 1 is the omnipresent Michigan bog hole. The remaining chapters cover such topics as housekeeping and house building in the West, the development of the local economy, the nuances of wildcat bank scandals, and the contrasting fortunes of two towns, Montacute and Tinkerville. Throughout, Kirkland depicts the people, particularly the women, who make up fledgling western communities.

In 1839 C. S. Francis and Company published the single-volume first edition of *A New Home—Who'll Follow?* in New York. In 1840, under the title *Montacute: Or, A New Home—Who'll Follow?*, E. Churton published the book in London in two volumes. The

"Now if our ponies would only have gone a little faster! But they would not: so we were wet to the skin—travelling jets d'eau."
p. 138

Illustration by Felix Octavius Carr Darley for the 4th edition of Caroline Kirkland's *A New Home—Who'll Follow?*, 1850.
Image courtesy of the University of Kentucky Special Collections Research Center

work was popular with the American public and was acclaimed by American and British reviewers alike. By 1842, three editions had been printed in the United States, and three editions had been published in England. C. S. Francis and Company had published five American editions by 1855. As a testimony to its durability and continued interest among readers, it was reissued in 1872 as *Our New Home in the West: or, Glimpses of Life Among the Early Settlers* by James Miller in New York and reprinted in 1874.

Initial reception was celebratory. Cornelius Conway Felton's sixteen-page review in the *North American Review* 50 (January 1840): 206–23 heralds the work's "striking merit," different from other works defined by "repetition and imitation" (206). The review describes Kirkland as a "person who sees for herself, and understands what she sees" and characterizes her as possessing "the happy art of representing what she

undertakes to describe, with a fidelity and reality, which at once fix the reader's attention, and make him feel, that no common intellectual power is at work" (206). The review extracts lengthy sections and praises their originality and artistry.

Favorable notices appeared in American magazines, including *Godey's Lady's Book,* the *Knickerbocker,* and the *New York Review.* The "Editors' Book Table" notice in *Godey's Lady's Book,* January 1840, 45 describes the work as "very clever" and "one that must have been written from actual experience." Noting the text's "graphic sketches of life in Michigan" and ability to convey "the interest which sober reality can assume," the editors also praised its comedic merit: "We commend the book to every dyspeptic gentleman, and nervous lady as a special antidote for low spirits." The review in the *Knickerbocker* 14 (November 1839): 452–56 begins with a strong endorsement: "Unhesitatingly, with the impressions derived from its perusal fresh upon us, do we pronounce this unpretending volume one of the most natural, pleasant, and entertaining books that we have read for a twelvemonth" (452). Lambert Lilly, in the *New York Review* 6 (January 1840): 250, called the work "one of the cleverest productions of the season; containing very interesting and lively pictures of western life, character, and manners."

The English press carried similarly favorable notices. The review in the *Athenaeum* 635 (December 28, 1839): 981–82 describes the work as "lively, freshly-coloured, and characteristic" and suitable for those with "any appetite for what is humorous and graphic." The *Literary Gazette,* no. 1190 (November 1839): 713, calls it "a more minute and faithful account of their [the settlers'] daily life than any book of travels that has been published."

In the 1840s and 1850s positive assessments of Kirkland's career appeared. In "American Literature: Its Position in the Present Time, and Prospects for the Future," in *Papers on Literature and Art,* part 2 (1846), 121–59, the review by Margaret Fuller (Ossoli) (1810–1850) highlights Kirkland's "spirited delineations" of settlers and "the features of Hoosier, Sucker, and Wolverine life . . . peculiar to the soil . . . [which] indicate its hidden treasures" (130). John S.

Hart in *Female Prose Writers of America* (fifth edition 1855) praises Kirkland's writing for its "racy wit, keen observation of life and manners, and a certain air of refinement which never forsakes her, even in the roughest scenes." Hart adds, "These sketches of western life were entirely without a parallel in American Literature" (116–17).

Edgar Allan Poe's series "The Literati of New York," *Godey's Lady's Book,* August 1846, 75–76, assesses Kirkland's career enthusiastically. It describes *A New Home—Who'll Follow?* as having "wrought an undoubted sensation" and explains that "the cause lay not so much in picturesque description, in racy humor, or in animated individual portraiture, as in *truth* and novelty" (75; Poe's emphasis). The review commends her realism: "With a fidelity and vigor that prove her pictures to be taken from the very life, she has represented 'scenes' that could have occurred only *as* and *where* she has described them" (75). Poe ranks Kirkland as a top-tier American author: "Unquestionably, she is one of our best writers, has a province of her own, and in that province has few equals" (76).

Rufus Griswold's first edition of *The Prose Writers of America* (1847), a study of seventy-one American writers, includes five women writers: Caroline Kirkland, Catharine M. Sedgwick (1789–1867), Eliza Leslie (1787–1858), Lydia M. Child (1802–1880), and Margaret Fuller. About Kirkland's three western texts, Griswold's book maintains, "No works of their class were ever more brilliantly successful than these original and admirable pictures of frontier scenery, woodcraft, and domestic experience" (463). Griswold heralds Kirkland's art as a paragon, "free from the tyranny of British examples" (463).

Although the general public welcomed the book, residents of Pinckney, Michigan, bristled at the portrayal of them. In the preface to *Forest Life* (1842) Kirkland expresses caution about literary depictions of people, commenting on her neighbors' disapproval: "I am credibly informed that ingenious malice has been busy in finding substance for the shadows which were called up to give variety to the pages of a 'A new Home,' [*sic*]—in short, that I have been accused of substituting personality for imper-sonation. This I utterly deny" (3–4). Although she admits some regret, she also claims artistic freedom: "In matters of opinion I claim the freedom which is my birthright as an American, and still further, the plainness of speech which is a striking characteristic of this Western country, the land of my adoption" (4).

SIGNIFICANCE: *A New Home—Who'll Follow? or, Glimpses of Western Life* is an important work in American literature and a significant contribution to Midwestern literature for four reasons. First, Kirkland's account of settlement in the Old Northwest Territory challenges masculine depictions of the West prevalent at this time. Discussing women's friendships, contributions, and hardships, Kirkland underscores the centrality of women's experience in the process of migration and settlement. Second, Kirkland's account is an early work of American realism. Published one year before a work considered a forerunner of American realism, *Two Years before the Mast* (1840) by Richard Henry Dana Jr. (1815–1882), Kirkland shares many of the commitments to verisimilitude noted in Dana's work. Third, Kirkland's artistry anticipates the mid- to late nineteenth-century interest in regionalism and local color that proliferated after the Civil War. Kirkland's narrative voice displays a range of response that includes alternating detachment and close identification with characters, a technique typical of local-color prose. Fourth, Kirkland's depiction of Michigan documents the "First West"—territories immediately west of the thirteen colonies—as a dynamic, heterogeneous site. Kirkland emphasizes demographic and topographic diversity in a manner that defies any easy classification of the Midwest as a particular type of place. She captures the complex, chaotic forces behind the establishment of new western communities.

Kirkland's influence is evident in the hybrid narrative style of Fuller's *A Summer on the Lakes, in 1843* (1844). Fuller's first sentence—"Since you are to share with me such footnotes as may be made on the pages of my life during this summer's wanderings"—echoes Kirkland's presentation of her work as "straggling and cloudy crayon-sketches of life and manners."

More generally, Kirkland's blending of realism and sentimentalism and her mixing of social commentary with humor place her among the major American female authors of the nineteenth century. Kirkland contributes to, and belongs within, a woman's tradition of nineteenth-century American literature that includes, among others, Lydia Maria Child, Catharine Maria Sedgwick, Fanny Fern (Sara Willis Parton) (1811–1872), Harriet Beecher Stowe (1811–1896), and E. D. E. N. Southworth (1819–1899).

IMPORTANT EDITIONS: *A New Home—Who'll Follow?* remained out of print for nearly eighty years until 1953, when John Nerber edited *A New Home; or, Life in the Clearings,* which included selected chapters from both *A New Home—Who'll Follow?* and *Forest Life,* for G. P. Putnam's Sons. In 1965 the College and University Press published an edition of *A New Home—Who'll Follow?,* edited by William S. Osborne. In 1990 Sandra A. Zagarell contributed an edition for Rutgers University Press's American Women Writers Series. Using the 1839 C. S. Francis and Company first edition, Zagarell includes an extensive introduction, explanatory notes, and a bibliography. Hers is the definitive critical edition.

FURTHER READING: Despite its initial success, Kirkland's *A New Home—Who'll Follow?* garnered little scholarly attention in the first half of the twentieth century. Langley C. Keyes's 1935 Harvard University dissertation "Caroline Matilda Kirkland: A Pioneer in American Realism" is the most substantial criticism before 1965. This limited response mirrors early twentieth-century scholarly resistance to nineteenth-century women writers.

William S. Osborne's 1965 edition of the novel and his 1972 biography *Caroline M. Kirkland* marked a shift in reception. Building on feminist criticism and the recovery of women's texts, Annette Kolodny's *The Land before Her: Fantasy and Experience of the American Frontiers, 1630–1860* (1984) made another important contribution, arguing that Kirkland revises masculine visions of the frontier. Since then, Kirkland's first book has generated a body of criticism. Studies focus on domesticity, female bonding, gender identity and gender community, consumerism, depictions of Native Americans, and representations of social class and classism.

Osborne's 1972 *Caroline M. Kirkland* remains the only major biography. The four Kirkland entries in *Dictionary of Literary Biography* 3, 73, 74, and 250 are exceptionally informative, as is Stacy L. Spencer's profile in *Legacy* 8.2 (Fall 1992): 133–40, which includes a bibliography of primary and secondary sources. Erika M. Kreger's 1999 bibliographic essay "A Bibliography of Works by and about Caroline Kirkland," *Tulsa Studies in Women's Literature* 18.2 (Fall 1999): 299–350, provides an annotated bibliography of Kirkland scholarship through the mid-1990s.

Five notable studies of the text since 2000 include a chapter on Kirkland and Sedgwick in Lori Merish's *Sentimental Materialism: Gender, Commodity Culture, and Nineteenth-Century Literature* (2000), 88–134; Elizabeth C. Barnes's 2003 essay "The Politics of Vision in Caroline Kirkland's Frontier Fiction," *Legacy* 20.1–2 (January 2003): 62–75; Mary DeJong Obuchowski's essay "'Murdered Banquos of the Forest': Caroline Kirkland's Environmentalism," *Midwestern Miscellany* 33.1 (Spring 2005): 73–79; Jeffrey Hotz's essay "Imagining a New West, a Midwest, in Caroline Kirkland's *A New Home, Who'll Follow?*," *Midwestern Miscellany* 38 (Spring/Fall 2010): 8–23; and Rachel Azima's essay "Promotion, Borrowing, and Caroline Kirkland's Literary Labors," *ESQ: A Journal of the American Renaissance* 57.4 (2011): 390–426. These interpretations focus, respectively, on consumerism, visual textual dynamics, environmental consciousness, regional representations, and Kirkland's textual borrowing as an economic commentary. Obuchowski has also contributed "Caroline Kirkland" to *Early American Nature Writers: A Biographical Encyclopedia,* edited by Daniel Patterson (2008), 235–41.

Kirkland's papers are held in a number of libraries, including the Clifton Waller Barrett Library at the University of Virginia, the Cornell University Library, the Massachusetts Historical Society, the New York Public Library, the Historical Society of Pennsylvania, the Michigan Historical Collections, the University of Michigan, and the Cincinnati Historical Society.

JEFFREY HOTZ   EAST STROUDSBURG UNIVERSITY

NEWSPAPER JOURNALISM

OVERVIEW: Journalism has become a profession noted for its rapid processing of facts and information for distribution through the mass media, and American reporters have earned a reputation for reliable, nonpartisan reporting of major events and issues. Newspapers had been the major news medium since colonial settlement in North America, but the nature of newspapers changed in the early nineteenth century at the same time as settlers moved into the Midwest. Before that time newspapers had been partisan promoters of political and mercantile interests, mostly written by elites for other elites.

Nineteenth-century newspaper editors faced new urban audiences with diverse language and literacy backgrounds. These new readers purchased news on the street about crime, sex, social issues, HUMOR, and other working-class people. Popular papers were sometimes sold on the street for as little as a penny rather than through annual subscriptions. While urban newspapers in the East built larger and faster printing presses to print newspapers for mass audiences, editors headed for the Midwest with the simple Washington hand press with hollow legs to make it lighter to transport via covered wagons. See also PRINTING AND PUBLISHING.

This entry emphasizes the late nineteenth and early twentieth centuries in the Midwest, when newspapers were the dominant mass medium. Editors in the Midwest usually promoted towns and, in competitive areas, often supported opposing political cliques in hopes of winning printing contracts when their patrons won elections. Daily and Sunday newspapers published not only journalism but also poetry, humor, fiction, and essays. Many literary figures began in Midwestern journalism, which provided a training ground, a rich source of material, and a place to be published.

HISTORY AND SIGNIFICANCE: The *New York Tribune* under Horace Greeley (1811–1872) advocated westward expansion as a "safety valve" to relieve poverty in New York City, and he borrowed and often repeated the advice "Go West, young man." This oft-quoted statement promoted opportunities in the Midwest, and Greeley published weekly and semiweekly *Tribune* editions that supplied agricultural news, advice, and moral support for people settling the frontier.

Individualistic, cantankerous, and opinionated Midwest editors often seemed more independent than they were. They depended on their communities for advertising and subscriptions, and they often needed political, economic, or religious sponsors. Boosterism sometimes replaced political patronage. Mary Wheelhouse Berthel, in *Horns of Thunder: The Life and Times of James M. Goodhue* (1948), quotes editor James M. Goodhue (1810–1852) of the *Minnesota Pioneer* as saying, "I dwell upon Minnesota and St. Paul; for they are ever in my thoughts and a part of my very existence. There is not a party tie or political association that I would not instantly sever, to promote their welfare" (75–77). Goodhue printed extra copies to celebrate MINNESOTA's virtues to the entire world and distributed his message through the networks by which editors exchanged copies with one another to share news with distant cities.

As an editor of the *Ohio State Journal* in Columbus, WILLIAM DEAN HOWELLS (1837–1920) edited a regular column of items lifted or summarized from exchanges. Thomas Wortham in *The Early Prose Writings of William Dean Howells* (1990) quotes Howells as saying in a December 22, 1858, column of items, "We think that the business of itemizing has a tendency to blunt the keen edge of the sense of honesty" (126). Some newspapers tended to reprint items without credit, Howells continued, and then other newspapers would reprint those items. An agitated reader once complained that the *Toledo Blade* had printed something he had written without credit. Then a Columbus newspaper reprinted that item, giving credit to the *Blade*. Howells said that it was often "a matter of some difficulty to indicate the original proprietorship of an item, and requires a prodigious effort to hunt up the pencil, and affix a credit" (126). Nonetheless, the Toledo man's item was "going the rounds of a predatory press—tossed upon a newspaper sea, a helmless boat, with no clearance papers abroad." Howells began his literary career at the *Hamilton* (Ohio) *Intelligencer,* which his father owned, and may have been influential in creating a perception of journalism as lowbrow culture and literature as high culture.

The war of words over whether KANSAS would become a free or a slave state began under an elm tree near the future site of Leavenworth when the *Kansas Weekly Herald* first appeared in 1854. A second pro-slavery paper began at Kickapoo, and free-state papers soon followed at Lawrence, reflecting the national debate begun by the Kansas-Nebraska Act passed that year. Free-state papers—the Kansas *Herald of Freedom,* the *Kansas Free State,* and the *Kansas Tribune*—began in Lawrence in the mid-1950s. More than one hundred newspapers were published in Kansas's territorial period between 1854 and 1861, and both sides invited settlers to come and vote on whether Kansas would be slave or free. Raiders from MISSOURI often targeted newspaper offices because they were influential in the abolitionist movement. After the Civil War, African American editors boosted Kansas by encouraging the migration of freed slaves into small towns founded on the prairie.

Trying to avoid the sectional strife and the Civil War, SAMUEL LANGHORNE CLEMENS (1835–1910), who would write as Mark Twain, headed west from his native Missouri. Before that, however, he worked as a writer or printer on newspapers in ST. LOUIS, CINCINNATI, and Keokuk, IOWA. Clemens had served as an apprentice to his older brother Orion on two Missouri newspapers before becoming a riverboat captain and later following him to Nevada, where ABRAHAM LINCOLN (1809–1865) had appointed the older Clemens territorial secretary. Clemens wrote serious news and satire—sometimes without a clear difference—for the *Territorial Enterprise* in Virginia City, Nevada. From Carson City he wrote a series of exaggerated articles, one of which he signed "Mark Twain," a nom de plume derived from a river term meaning two chalk marks, or twelve feet of water, and appropriated by his Nevada associates in drinking contests. Clemens's humor borrowed from CHARLES FARRAR BROWNE (Artemus Ward) (1834–1867) and William Wright (Dan De Quille) (1829–1898), whom he met in Nevada and California. He both copied and parodied the method of borrowing news from the exchanges.

Perhaps the most partisan and creative editor, although not in a literary sense, was Wilbur F. Storey (1819–1884), who, as quoted in Justin E. Walsh's *To Print the News and Raise Hell: A Biography of Wilbur F. Storey* (1968), said in 1861 that a newspaper's duty is "to print the news and raise hell" (4). As the nineteen-year-old editor of the *La Porte Herald* in INDIANA, as quoted by Walsh, he attacked an opposing editor as "a degraded being, an abandoned reprobate, entirely reckless of truth, deceitful and treacherous, a filthy and loathsome blackguard, an object of pity and contempt rather than of ridicule" (18). Later, in South Bend he supported a candidate who fell so hopelessly behind in a congressional race that Storey ran a front-page story saying that his Whig opponent had died, forcing residents to vote for Storey's Democrat. Readers were not intimidated, however, and the Whig candidate won despite Storey's dirty trick. After the election Storey said that he had relied on an unfounded rumor. During the Civil War, Storey was the publisher of the *Chicago Times* and sent correspondent Franc B. Wilkie (1832–1892) to cover the war with this oft-quoted and misquoted instruction: "Telegraph fully all the news, and when there is no news, send rumors." Wilkie, as quoted in *Personal Reminiscences of Thirty-Five Years of Journalism* (1891), said that the comment emphasized the telegraph, stressing that reporters should send news often and quickly (114–15). Nonetheless, General U. S. Grant banished one of Storey's annoying reporters from the war, but two others—Wilkie and Sylvanus Cadwallader—were respected Civil War journalists. Nonetheless, Union Major General Ambrose Burnside moved his army into the *Chicago Times* to shut down this Copperhead newspaper for three days in June 1863 before President Lincoln intervened.

In contrast to Storey, Abraham Lincoln, also in ILLINOIS, exploited newspapers to launch his political career. He sometimes wrote for newspapers, and his first known newspaper letter appeared in the *Sangamon Journal* (sometimes called the *Sangamo Journal*) of Springfield. After election to the Illinois legislature, Lincoln sent reports to the *Sangamon Journal* under pseudonyms that reflected his sense of humor: Johnny Blubberhead, Citizen of Sangamon, Conservative, Our Correspondent, Sampson's Ghost, Old Settler, and Rebecca. When Lincoln became the Whig floor leader, the *Sangamo Journal* began publishing his speeches.

Lincoln seemed awkward among crowds, but he knew how to spin his message for newspapers. Seeking to represent Illinois in the U.S. Senate in 1858, Lincoln began stalking the incumbent and taking the platform to rebut each of his speeches. Senator Stephen A. Douglas, the incumbent, became so frustrated that he finally allowed Lincoln to join him on the platform, creating the famous Lincoln-Douglas debates. Unlike today's sound-bite campaigns, these debates allowed uninterrupted statements ranging from half an hour to an hour and a half. In this era newspapers reprinted documents more than they wrote stories. The Lincoln-Douglas debates pushed newspapers a step toward political independence because correspondents knew that the opposition was covering the same event and tried to report as accurately as possible. After he was elected president, Lincoln ended a complex patronage system for national, state, and local newspapers by creating the Government Printing Office.

After the Civil War, CHICAGO emerged as both an agricultural and an urban center, and Chicago newspapers produced key literary figures, including playwright GEORGE ADE (1866–1944), muckraker RAY STANNARD BAKER (1870–1946), humorist FINLEY PETER DUNNE (1867–1936), novelist (HERMAN) THEODORE DREISER (1871–1945), columnist EUGENE FIELD (SR.) (1850–1895), and authors (HANNIBAL) HAMLIN GARLAND (1860–1940), RING(GOLD WILMER) LARDNER (SR.) (1885–1933), and CARL (AUGUST) SANDBURG (1878–1967). Dreiser, Lardner, and Garland derived much of their somber realism from reporting on Chicago. Chicago journalists BEN HECHT (1894–1964) and CHARLES (GORDON) MACARTHUR (1895–1956) re-created many of the people and events they knew in the Windy City in their classic comedy *The Front Page,* which opened on Broadway on August 14, 1928.

Independence preceded objectivity. In St. Louis, immigrant Joseph Pulitzer (1847–1911) purchased the bankrupt *Dispatch* for $2,500 and within days combined

it in 1879 with the *Post* to begin the *Post-Dispatch,* one of the nation's most influential newspapers, based on independence from political parties and support for the working poor. In Chicago, Melville Stone founded the *Daily News* in 1876 as an alternative to the solidly Republican *Tribune* with a pledge that the publisher would have no economic interests other than the newspaper. Stone even investigated his advertisers, and he provided sympathetic coverage of striking railroad workers in 1877 despite business pressure to ignore them. Stone became general manager of the Associated Press in 1900 after the wire service became a cooperative. Edward Willis Scripps (1854–1926) became even more independent, starting a newspaper that spurned advertisers, and counted Sandburg among his reporters.

The tumultuous urban growth and change in journalism from the Civil War through the 1920s stimulated a creative period even as journalism moved toward glorification of fact and objectivity over creativity. Several newspapers made distinctive impacts on the region's culture. The *Chicago Defender* stimulated a large migration to Chicago of African Americans from the South, where discrimination, mob violence, and lack of civil rights infected everyday life. LANGSTON (JAMES MERCER) HUGHES (1902–1967) later wrote a column for the *Defender,* which

Chicago newsboy selling the *Chicago Defender,* 1942. Photo by Jack Delano.
Image courtesy of the Library of Congress

also printed work by other major African American writers, like GWENDOLYN BROOKS (1917–2000) and WILLARD F. MOTLEY (1909–1965). By contrast, WILLIAM ALLEN WHITE (1868–1944) attracted national attention to the *Emporia Gazette* with his political commentaries and columns about life in small-town Kansas. Novelist EDNA FERBER (1885–1968) began her career writing for newspapers in Appleton and Milwaukee, WISCONSIN; she later applied journalistic research techniques to her fiction, as well as a certain reportorial style. A number of Ferber's contemporaries followed a similar career path. By the end of the twentieth century, however, as newspapers began to decline, fewer literary writers made their start in journalism. The consolidation of media and the cult of objectivity posed difficulties for literary voices in daily journalism, while academic creative-writing programs like THE IOWA WRITERS' WORKSHOP became the new launching pad for literary careers.

The situation for newspapers has worsened in the new millennium as readers have fled to the internet. Many papers have been forced to combine in joint operating agreements, move operations partly or completely online, or cease publication entirely. Many small-city newspapers have reduced page count and shifted their focus to local coverage. Positive signs, however, can be seen in continued efforts to maintain quality of writing and cultural coverage. These include the columns of (MICHAEL) MIKE ROYKO (1932–1997) in a succession of Chicago newspapers from 1959 through 1997; the careers of novelists like Chicago-based Cuban American Achy Obejas (b. 1956), beginning in newspaper work; and the recent syndication of "American Life in Poetry," a free weekly column distributed nationally, featuring a poem by a contemporary American writer with a brief introduction by Ted Kooser (b. 1939) of NEBRASKA, the 2004–2006 Poet Laureate of the United States. The future of newspapers is uncertain, but such efforts have demonstrated that there is still a place for literate journalism in the Midwest.

SELECTED WORKS: Newspaper databases, to which college libraries are the primary subscribers, have made nineteenth- and twentieth-century newspapers from both large cities and small towns across the country available in an easily searchable format that has revolutionized HISTORIOGRAPHY and journalistic studies. The online versions of some newspapers, such as the *Chicago Tribune,* offer archival access to their subscribers. The Library of Congress maintains Chronicling America, a free online database of digitized historical newspapers. Keyword searches on these databases will yield many articles written by authors of importance to literary history.

The Early Prose Writings of William Dean Howells (1990), edited by Thomas Wortham, includes columns Howells wrote for Ohio newspapers. An authoritative collection of Samuel Langhorne Clemens's journalism has not been published, but a number of volumes collect his newspaper writing; the two-volume set *Mark Twain: The Collected Tales, Sketches, Speeches, and Essays* (1992), edited by Louis J. Budd, provides a good start. Clemens provides a mix of fact and autobiographical fiction in *Roughing It* (1872), as does Theodore Dreiser in *Newspaper Days: An Autobiography* (1931), originally published in 1922 as *A Book about Myself.*

Stories of the Streets and of the Town: From the "Chicago Record," 1893–1900 (1941) collects articles by George Ade, many with illustrations by John T. McCutcheon. The book was reprinted in 2003 as *Stories of Chicago*. Collections of journalism by Ray Stannard Baker include *Our New Prosperity* (1900). Finley Peter Dunne published several volumes of his pieces written in the voice of an Irish bartender for the Chicago *Sunday Post,* including *Mr. Dooley's Philosophy* (1900). *Sharps and Flats* (1900), a two-volume set edited by Slason Thompson, collects Eugene Field's newspaper columns. *By-line, Ernest Hemingway: Selected Articles and Dispatches of Four Decades* (1967), edited by William White, presents some of ERNEST (MILLER) HEMINGWAY's (1899–1961) best journalism.

The Broadway comedy *The Front Page* (1928) by Chicago journalists Ben Hecht and Charles MacArthur satirizes Midwestern newspaper work. Christopher C. De Santis has edited *Langston Hughes and the "Chicago Defender": Essays on Race, Politics, and Culture, 1942–62* (1995). Mike Royko's columns were collected in many volumes, such as *Sez Who? Sez Me* (1982).

FURTHER READING: Although few studies consider the development of journalism or literary journalism of the Midwest alone, two succinct readable histories tell of the origins of journalism in Missouri and MINNESOTA. William E. Lyon, in *The Pioneer Editor in Missouri, 1808–1860* (1965), looks at editors and their place in frontier life at a time when street fights between editors could coincide with their court battles. George S. Hage in *Newspapers on the Minnesota Frontier* (1967) provides an in-depth and entertaining look at the earliest newspapers in Minnesota. These editors doggedly attacked political corruption, but such corruption, of course, usually ran rampant among the opposition and seldom, if ever, on the editor's own side.

Aurora Wallace's *Newspapers and the Making of Modern America: A History* (2005) explores the contributions to their communities of different types of newspapers, including the African American *Chicago Defender,* the *Des Moines Register* in Iowa, and William Allen White's *Emporia Gazette* in Kansas. Studies of individual newspapers and journalists abound, but Michael Robertson's *Stephen Crane, Journalism, and the Making of Modern American Literature* (1997) links the journalism and literature of Midwestern authors Howells, Dreiser, and Hemingway with the works of Crane, showing how their journalism informed their literature and how they used reporters as characters in their fiction. Lincoln's use of newspapers is outlined by Robert S. Harper in *Lincoln and the Press* (1951), by Lincoln scholar Harold Holzer in *Lincoln and the Power of the Press: The War for Public Opinion* (2014), and by Gregory A. Borchard and David W. Bulla in *Lincoln Mediated: The President and the Press through Nineteenth-Century Media* (2015).

Several comprehensive histories of the U.S. mass media have been written, but none focuses exclusively on the Midwest. Like the histories of journalism, discussions of literary journalism seldom look at the craft from a regional perspective, even though they always include *In Cold Blood* (1966) by Truman Capote (1924–1984), with its focus on Kansas murders.

Journalism history scholars have debated when the idea of an independent press and the myth of objectivity displaced overt partisanship. William E. Huntzicker's *The Popular Press, 1833–1865* (1999) looks at the transition as a slow, gradual change over much of the century. David T. Mindich in *Just the Facts: How Objectivity Came to Define American Journalism* (2000) traces objectivity to the news releases of Lincoln's Secretary of War, Edwin Stanton (1814–1869), who used factual reporting and numbers to manipulate the truth. Richard L. Kaplan's *Politics and the American Press: The Rise of Objectivity, 1865–1920* (2002) looks at DETROIT newspapers to challenge the idea of a contrast between partisan and commercial journalism, saying that publishers found that market segmentation appealed to commercial and political constituencies. Duane C. S. Stoltzfus, in *Freedom from Advertising: E. W. Scripps's Chicago Experiment* (2007), looks at a newspaper without advertising and Sandburg's role in it. Hazel Dicken-Garcia's *Journalistic Standards in Nineteenth-Century America* (1989) considers professionalism and ethics in the field.

Outsiders in 19th-Century Press History: Multicultural Perspectives (2002), edited by Frankie Hutton and Barbara Straus Reed, examines African American, Native American, Chinese American, and other minority newspapers. Patrick S. Washburn gives special attention to the *Chicago Defender* in *The African American Newspaper: Voice of Freedom* (2006) and *A Question of Sedition: The Federal Government's Investigation of the Black Press during World War II* (1986).

In *Chicago Journalism: A History* (2009) Chicago reporter-editor Wayne Klatt applies his journalistic concern for accuracy and flair for writing to a survey of the Windy City's journalism and occasionally weaves into his story the literary figures and others "for whom the news business was just a phase" (108). Richard Junger ties early Chicago journalism to city boosters in *Becoming the Second City: Chicago's Mass News Media, 1833–1898* (2010), and Jon Bekken adds additional social context in "Shaping Chicago's Sense of Self: Chicago Journalism in the Nineteenth Century," published online in *H-Net Reviews,* August 2011. The best critiques linking journalism to literature are James DeMuth's *Small Town Chicago* (1980), emphasizing Ade, Dunne, and Lardner; and

Shelly Fisher Fishkin's *From Fact to Fiction: Journalism and Imaginative Writing in America* (1985), with sections on Midwestern newspapermen Clemens, Dreiser, and Hemingway. Fishkin, who has edited an extensive Oxford edition of Clemens's writings, focuses on Twain's literature and journalism in *Lighting Out for the Territory: Reflections on Mark Twain and American Culture* (1998). James Edward Caron has contributed *Mark Twain: Unsanctified Newspaper Reporter* (2010), which places Clemens's early journalistic career in a historical context.

Much scholarship touches on Ernest Hemingway's apprenticeship and later work in journalism. Elizabeth Dewberry's "Hemingway's Journalism and the Realist Dilemma," in *The Cambridge Companion to Hemingway* (1996), edited by Scott Donaldson, 16–35. is a good start for inquiry into the topic.

WILLIAM E. HUNTZICKER   ST. CLOUD STATE UNIVERSITY

NONFICTION.
See Creative Nonfiction

NORTH DAKOTA

North Dakota was admitted to the Union on November 2, 1889, as the thirty-ninth state. Before statehood parts of North Dakota were claimed by France, Spain, and England. The Louisiana Purchase transferred the North Dakota area drained by the Missouri River to the United Sates in 1803. In 1818 North Dakota became part of Missouri Territory.

The area east of the Missouri River was, in succession, part of Michigan Territory (1834–1836), Wisconsin Territory (1836–1838), Iowa Territory (1838–1849), and Minnesota Territory (1849–1858); the area was without territorial oversight when Minnesota became a state in 1858. The North Dakota area west of the Missouri River was part of Nebraska Territory (1854–1861). The whole of North Dakota was part of Dakota Territory (1861–1889).

Area: 70,699 square miles

Land: 69,001 square miles

Water: 1,698 square miles

Population (2010 census): 672,591

OVERVIEW: North Dakota, the state at the geographic center of North America, has a small population, and its Midwestern his-

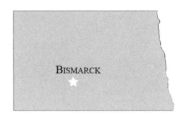

© Karen Greasley, 2014

tory and culture often blend into those of MINNESOTA, SOUTH DAKOTA, and Montana, as well as the Canadian prairie provinces to the north. The northern-flowing Red River of the North sets its eastern border, and the Missouri River, which served as an important early means of EXPLORATION, travel, and commerce, tends to break the state into sections. The map of tribal territory in 1850 published in Elwyn B. Robinson's *History of North Dakota* (1966) includes Mandan, Hidatsa, and Arikara in the center and west, Teton Dakota in the southwest, Assiniboin in the northwest, Ojibwa in the northeast, and Yanktonai Dakota in the largest land area, the southeast and center. Reservations include Fort Berthold, Standing Rock, Turtle Mountain, and Spirit Lake.

The first literature in North Dakota was that of American Indian tribes, which was passed down in oral accounts. The next body of literature was written by European adventurers, explorers, fur traders, and missionaries and in business reports, letters, journals, and religious writings. The first adventurers and explorers were typically sent from European centers of government and commerce, and their utilitarian motives were mixed with greed as natural resources were discovered.

In the later decades of the nineteenth century, immigrants from over forty countries, with high percentages from Germany and Norway, settled in the state, bringing their native cultures with them. Homesteader literature reflected optimism that the new land would be an improvement over their recent experiences in their home countries. These narratives emphasized their formative years in the state and often described harsh natural landscapes, brutal weather conditions, and the rigors of farming.

HISTORY AND SIGNIFICANCE: The following sections provide roughly chronological accounts of literary development in North Dakota, beginning with American Indian literature and proceeding to accounts of exploration and travel before statehood and to AUTOBIOGRAPHY, memoir, and biography, followed by fiction, poetry, DRAMA, printing and journalism, the FEDERAL WRITERS', PROJECT, and significant popular literature categories. These sections are followed by a brief account of North Dakota's literary awards..

American Indian Literature: Marie L(ouise Buisson) McLaughlin (1842–1933), who was one-quarter Sioux, wrote down the stories her grandmother had told her in *Myths and Legends of the Sioux* (1916), first published by the *Bismarck Tribune*. "A Legend of Devil's Lake" is included in *Indian Boyhood* (1902) by CHARLES ALEXANDER EASTMAN (Ohiyesa) (1858–1939). Gilbert (Livingstone) Wilson (1868–1930) recorded lives of the Mandan and Hidatsa Indians in *Goodbird the Indian: His Story* (1914) and *Wahenee: An Indian Girl's Story as Told by Herself to Gilbert L. Wilson* (1921). In *Essie's Story: The Life and Legacy of a Shoshone Teacher* (1998) Esther Burnett Horne (Shoshone) (1909–1999), who taught at the Wahpeton Indian School from 1930 to the 1950s, tells her story in collaboration with anthropologist Sally McBeth.

Other works about the state's American Indians have been written or edited by white authors. Orin G(rant) Libby (1864–1952), University of North Dakota professor of history and longtime director of the State Historical Society of North Dakota, interviewed men who were at the Little Bighorn and wrote *The Arikara Narrative of the Campaign against the Hostile Dakotas, June, 1876* (1920), which is volume 6 in the State Historical Society of North Dakota's North Dakota Historical Collections. Libby's grandchildren, Robert Barr and Martha Barr Liebert, published *Corn Silk* (2004), a summary of which had been printed by the State Historical Society. James McLaughlin (1842–1923), an Indian agent at Devils Lake and Standing Rock, wrote *My Friend the Indian* (1910) about his life and career. Frank (Bennett) Fiske (1883–1952), a photographer who spent much of his life at Fort Yates,

wrote about Indian life in *The Taming of the Sioux* (1917) and *Life and Death of Sitting Bull* (1933). *Earth Lodge Tales from the Upper Missouri: Traditional Stories of the Arikara, Hidatsa, and Mandan* (1978), edited by Douglas R(ichard) Parks (b. 1942), A. Wesley Jones, and Robert C. Hollow, incorporates both native and English texts. Mary Jane Schneider, author of *North Dakota Indians: An Introduction* (1986) and *North Dakota's Indian Heritage* (1990), wrote, with Carolyn (Ives) Gilman (b. 1954), *The Way to Independence: Memories of a Hidatsa Indian Family, 1840–1920* (1987). Native traditions are incorporated in *Teton Sioux Music* (1918) and *Mandan and Hidatsa Music* (1923) by Frances Densmore (1867–1957). *The First Sioux Nun: Sister Marie-Josephine Nebraska, 1859–1894* (1963) by Sister Mary Ione Hilger (1897–1971) is a biography for young readers.

The best-known North Dakota Native American fiction writer is (KAREN) LOUISE ERDRICH (b. 1954), who has been writing her saga for nearly three decades, employing stories she heard from her Ojibwa and German ancestors. Her novel LOVE MEDICINE (1984), awarded the 1984 National Book Critics Circle Award, introduces the Kashpaw and Lamartine families; its chapters are set between 1934 and 1984 and are told by various family members. Erdrich's novels also include *The Beet Queen* (1986), *Tracks* (1988), *The Bingo Palace* (1994), *Tales of Burning Love* (1996), *The Antelope Wife* (1998), *The Last Report on the Miracles at Little No Horse* (2001), *The Master Butchers Singing Club* (2003), *Four Souls* (2004), *The Painted Drum* (2005), *The Plague of Doves* (2008), *Shadow Tag* (2010), and *The Round House* (2012). *The Crown of Columbus* (1991), written with Michael Dorris (1945–1997), presents a Native response to the "discovery" of the New World by Columbus.

Louise Erdrich's poetry collections include *Jacklight* (1984), *Baptism of Desire* (1989), and *Original Fire: Selected and New Poems* (2003). Her sister, Heid E. Erdrich (b. 1963), has published several books of poetry, including *Fishing for Myth* (1997), *The Mother's Tongue* (2005), and *National Monuments* (2008).

Susan Power (b. 1961), an enrolled member of the Standing Rock Sioux tribe, has contributed two fictional works about American Indian life: *The Grass Dancer* (1994) and *Roofwalker* (2002). *The Grass Dancer,* winner of the PEN/Hemingway Award in 1995, is a wide-ranging series of tales covering four generations. In the short-story collection *Roofwalker* (2002) Power emphasizes the power of past traditions over contemporary people.

Gordon Henry (Jr.) (b. 1955), an enrolled member of the White Earth Ojibwa tribe of Minnesota, earned a PhD from the University of North Dakota, where he received the Thomas McGrath Award for poetry. Henry uses traditional Anishinaabe stories and storytelling techniques in his fiction. In the novel *The Light People* (1994; American Book Award winner for 1995) his character Oskinaway seeks his American Indian identity and finds it through a variety of stories and storytellers. Another examination of identity and consciousness is *The Failure of Certain Charms and Other Disparate Signs of Life* (2008).

Exploration and Travel: Like other Midwestern states, North Dakota has a history of exploration and missionary work before white settlement. The first Europeans came to explore the region or pursue the salvation of souls in the New World at a time when France, Spain, and England were vying for dominance. Fur companies—the Hudson's Bay Company, the North West Company, and the American Fur Company—kept business records, and some individuals kept journals. The coming of the railroad in the 1880s, coinciding with the great Dakota boom, facilitated both the travel of immigrants to the region and the transportation of farm crops to distant markets.

The journey of Pierre Gaultier de Varennes, Sieur de La Vérendrye (1685–1749), who came west from Montreal, claiming land for France and setting up trading posts before reaching the Mandan villages along the Missouri River in 1738, is recorded in *The Journals and Letters of Pierre Gaultier de Varennes de La Vérendrye and His Sons* (1927). Alexander Henry (ca. 1765–1814) wrote about his years with the North West Company, including his establishment of a trading post at Pembina in 1801; his account was published in *New Light on the Early History of the Greater Northwest: The Manuscript Journals of Alexander Henry . . . and of David Thompson . . . ,*

1799–1814 (1897). David Thompson (1770–1857) explored and mapped the Mouse and Missouri River basins in 1797–1798.

After the Louisiana Purchase in 1803, Meriwether Lewis (1774–1809) and William Clark (1770–1838) explored the region, collecting plant and animal specimens and making reports about everything they saw. When they reached the Mandan villages along the Missouri River in 1804, they remained until spring, their longest stop at any location. Among the many books based on the journals by Lewis and Clark is Clay (Straus) Jenkinson's (b. 1955) compilation *A Vast and Open Plain: The Writings of the Lewis and Clark Expedition in North Dakota, 1804–1806* (2003), incorporating the North Dakota portions of the journals of Lewis and Clark, John Ordway (ca. 1775–ca. 1817), Patrick Gass (1771–1870), and Joseph Whitehouse (1775–1817).

Other explorers whose journals have been published include those of Henry M(arie) Brackenridge (1786–1871), who traveled to the Knife River villages with Manuel (de) Lisa (ca. 1772–1820) and compiled his *Journal of a Voyage up the Missouri River, in 1811* (1814). The artist George Catlin (1796–1872) sketched scenes at Fort Union in 1832, recorded in *The Manners, Customs, and Condition of the North American Indians* (1841). Prince Maximilian von Wied (1782–1867), accompanied by the painter Karl Bodmer (1809–1893), spent a winter at the Knife River villages, as recorded in *Travels in the Interior of North America* (German, 1839–41; English translation, 1843). *The North American Journals of Prince Maximilian of Wied,* volume 1, from May 1832 to April 1833 (2008), and volume 2, from April through September 1833 (2010), include the full text of the journals and annotations. Ornithologist John James Audubon (1785–1851) traveled as far as the Mandan villages in 1843, as reflected in *Audubon and His Journals* (1897). Fur trader Henry A. Boller (1836–1902), who was at Fort Atkinson from 1858 through 1860, wrote *Among the Indians: Eight Years in the Far West, 1858–1866* (1868). His journals were published as *Twilight of the Upper Missouri River Fur Trade: The Journals of Henry A. Boller* (2008). Yet another account of North Dakota and other states is found in *Sketches of Frontier and Indian Life on the Upper Missouri and Great Plains* (1889) by Joseph H(enry) Taylor (1845–1908), who was a hunter and trapper near Bismarck beginning in 1869.

Among the missionaries who left written records, the Jesuit father Pierre-Jean de Smet (1801–1873), who visited northern Dakota several times between 1839 and 1868, wrote *Letters and Sketches: With a Narrative of a Year's Residence among the Indian Tribes of the Rocky Mountains* (1843) and miscellaneous writings published as *Life, Letters and Travels of Pierre-Jean de Smet* (1905). Father George A. Belcourt (1803–1874) built a mission near Pembina in 1848 and a second mission and the state's first flour mill several years later at St. Joseph, now Walhalla. Proficient in linguistics, Belcourt wrote an important Ojibwa-language grammar, *Principes de la langue des sauvages appelés Sauteux* (1839), and a dictionary, *Dictionnaire français-sauteux, ou, odjibway* (1877).

Missionary life is also the subject of *Experiences from My Missionary Life in the Dakotas* (1926) by Rev. Peter Bauer (1855–1942) and *100 Years at Fort Berthold: The History of Fort Berthold Indian Mission, 1876–1976* (1977), compiled by Harold and Eva Case, who served at Fort Berthold from 1922 to 1965. The lives of early missionaries are the subject of *Father de Smet in Dakota* (1962) and *James McLaughlin: The Man with an Indian Heart* (1978) by Louis Pfaller, OSB (1923–1979). See also *Memoirs of Father Anthony Kopp* (1999) by Father Anthony Kopp (1891–1964), which recounts his life serving five parishes in the Bismarck diocese.

Autobiographies, Memoirs, and Biographies: North Dakota has a strong autobiographical and biographical tradition. Like earlier writing about exploration and travel, these personal stories capture the spirit of a pioneering people. They are discussed here in roughly topical and chronological order.

Accounts of army life include works by George Armstrong Custer (1839–1876) and his wife, Elizabeth Bacon Custer (1842–1933), who came to Dakota Territory in 1873. George Custer's articles published from 1872 to 1874 in *The Galaxy* magazine were reprinted as *My Life on the Plains; or, Personal Experiences with Indians* (1874). Elizabeth Bacon Custer wrote three books about army life in the west: *"Boots and Saddles"; or, Life in*

Dakota with General Custer (1885), *Tenting on the Plains; or, General Custer in Kansas and Texas* (1887), and *Following the Guidon* (1890). Linda Warfel Slaughter (1843–1911), who moved to Fort Rice near Bismarck in 1871 and later to Camp Hancock with her physician husband, published a series of articles in 1893–1894, later republished by her granddaughter, Hazel Eastman, as *Fortress to Farm; or Twenty-Three Years on the Frontier* (1972).

Ranch life in the territory is also an important subject of North Dakota autobiography. Theodore Roosevelt (1858–1919), the state's best-known resident, came first to hunt but in 1883 decided to ranch. Roosevelt eventually owned five thousand cattle on his two ranches, the Maltese Cross and Elkhorn, before heavy snow and cold weather in the winter of 1886–1887 doomed the venture. Roosevelt wrote poetic descriptions of his life on the ranch, his hunting trips, and even winter storms. Most significant in depicting North Dakota are his *Ranch Life and the Hunting-Trail* (1888), reflecting his experiences as a cattle rancher in the Medora area of Western Dakota, and *The Wilderness Hunter* (1893). Roosevelt's appealing accounts of his experiences captured the imaginations of readers who would never travel to the West. Lincoln A(lexander) Lang (b. 1867), who called himself "a companion rancher," contributed the memoir *Ranching with Roosevelt* (1926).

Several other accounts focus on early ranch life. A colorful Frenchman is the subject of *The Marquis de Mores: Dakota Capitalist, French Nationalist* (1972) by D. Jerome Tweton (b. 1933) and *The Marquis de Mores: Emperor of the Bad Lands* (1970) by Donald W. Dresden (1910–1982). A(rthur) C(lark) Huidekoper (1845–1928) recorded his memoirs in *My Experience and Investment in the Bad Lands of Dakota and Some of the Men I Met There* (1947). Edson Carr Dayton (1860–1942), who came to Dakota to raise sheep in 1886, explored his career in *Dakota Days: May 1886–August 1898* (1937). William Timmons (1878–1965), who worked for Charles Goodnight in Texas and ranched near Dickinson from 1896 to 1910, wrote *Twilight on the Range: Recollections of a Latter Day Cowboy* (1962). Harry V. Johnston (b. ca. 1876), who lived in the Badlands area from 1900 to 1916, wrote *My Home on the Range: Frontier Life in the*

Badlands (1942), as well as a novel, *The Last Roundup* (1950). *Yet She Follows: The Story of Betty Freeman Dearborn* (1931) by Edna LaMoore Waldo (1893–1999), whose brother Louis L'Amour (1908–1988) also wrote about the West, portrays the "westering" roots of her family. Waldo also wrote *Dakota: An Informal Study of Territorial Days* (1936). The life of rancher Harriet T. Beckert is recorded by Irving Speed Wallace (1916–1990) in *Stardust to Prairie Dust* (1976).

Settlement in the territory gave rise to many accounts of life in what would become North Dakota. One volume's lengthy title summarizes many writers' experiences of pioneering, settlement, and ranching: *Tom's Experience in Dakota: Why He Went, What He Did There; What Crops He Raised, and How He Raised Them; What They Cost Him, and What He Received for Them; and All about His Ups and Downs, Successes and Failures; His Talks with Old Friends, and His Advice to Them about Going West, Who Ought to Go, and Who Ought Not; What Men and Women with Money and with None Can Do There; Why Some Succeed, and Others Do Not; with Practical Information for All Classes of People Who Want Homes in the West, Pointing Out Plainly the Way to Success* (1883) by A. P. Miller. Although he did not give his real name to avoid being "overrun with letters of inquiry," the narrator provided information about his expenses and warned the reader to listen cautiously to tales of big crops and winter weather.

North Dakota attracted immigrants from many European countries, and some kept diaries and journals suggesting their motivations for risky emigration, discussing the ordeals of the journey, and exploring what they found upon arrival. Rachel Bella Calof (1876–1952) left Russia alone to marry a man she met through correspondence. In 1936 she wrote about life from her birth in 1876, and about the lure of free land and the shock and despair of the early years on the homestead near Devils Lake. Years after her death, her daughter found the manuscript, which was translated from Yiddish into English and later published as *Rachel Calof's Story: Jewish Homesteader on the Northern Plains* (1995).

Dakota Diaspora: Memoirs of a Jewish Homesteader (1984) by Sophie Trupin (1903–1992) is a series of sketches about a group of Jewish immigrants who fled anti-Semitism in Russia and came to Burleigh County, where Trupin's father tried farming before setting up a butcher shop. Barrie Barstow Greenbie uncovered his family's buried history in the Jewish utopian Garske Colony near Devils Lake in *The Hole in the Heartland: An American Mystery* (1996). Philo T. Pritzkau (1902–2004) wrote of growing up in a sod house in *Growing Up in North Dakota* (1996), published by the Germans from Russia Heritage Collection at North Dakota State University.

Many autobiographical works concern growing up during the early years of North Dakota. Among these are *Along the Trails of Yesterday: A Story of McIntosh County* (1941) by Nina Farley Wishek (1869–1957); and *Grass of the Earth: Immigrant Life in the Dakota Country* (1950) and *Measure of My Days* (1953) by Aagot Raaen (1873–1957). Dorothy Berry de St. Clement (1879–1984) contributed *White Gumbo* (1951), which describes the experiences of her homesteading family, and later a book of poems, *Prairies and Palaces* (1963), dedicated to "my beloved husband, Count Giulio de Sauteiron de St. Clement, last scion of his noble family on the borderline of France and Italy." Mary Dodge Woodward (1826–1890) lived in Dakota Territory on a bonanza farm, a large farm operation employing many workers. The Dodge farm covered about 1,500 acres, and some operations were larger. Excerpts from Woodward's diary, written between 1884 and 1888, were published by her granddaughter Mary Boynton Cowdrey as *The Checkered Years* (1937).

I Remember (1978) and *The Day of the Pioneer* (1980) by Russell Duncan (b. 1910) provide short autobiographical sketches from pioneer days to the 1970s. Harvey Sletten (1912–2002) focused on personal episodes in the years 1918 to 1932 in Hannaford in *Growing Up on Bald Hill Creek* (1977). Ann Marie Low (1912–1998) used her diary from 1928 to 1937 in *Dust Bowl Diary* (1984). Kathy L. Plotkin (b. 1930) authored *The Pearson Girls: A Family Memoir of the Dakota Plains* (1998), addressing the loss of farm life for the children and grandchildren of immigrants. Dean Hulse (b. 1955) wrote *Westhope: Life as a Former Farm Boy* (2009) about his boyhood on the family farm and his failed efforts to hold on to it. Edward F. Keller (b. 1927), a dentist in Dickinson, wrote *My First World* (1995) and *Memory Stories* (1997), recalling incidents from his childhood around Strasburg. *Amateur Writer* (2000) concerns his adventures in self-publishing. See FARM LITERATURE.

Three noted journalists have written about their lives in North Dakota as touchstones for their later success. *Canoeing with the Cree* (1935), the first book by (ARNOLD) ERIC SEVAREID (1912–1992), tracks the 2,250-mile canoe trip he and a high school friend made from MINNEAPOLIS to York Factory on Hudson Bay, partially along the Red River of the North. Sevareid's "history in personal terms" is found in his *Not So Wild a Dream* (1946), beginning with his boyhood in Velva, which he praises for its equality among all people. Commentaries and interviews include *In One Ear* (1952), *Small Sounds in the Night* (1956), *This Is Eric Sevareid* (1964), and *Conversations with Eric Sevareid* (1976).

In the foreword to the 1967 reprint of her autobiography, *American Daughter* (1946), Era Bell Thompson (1905–1986) writes, "Usually an autobiography is written near the end of a long and distinguished career, but not taking any chances, I wrote mine first, then began to live." As a young girl living near Driscoll, North Dakota, Thompson and her family, one of the few black families in the area, found kindness among the immigrant families. In Bismarck and Grand Forks she found acceptance and encouragement. Later, as an editor for *Ebony*, Thompson wrote many articles and books, including *Africa, Land of My Fathers* (1954). St. Thomas native Edward K(rammer) Thompson (1907–1996) wrote about his years at *Life* and *Smithsonian* magazines in *A Love Affair with "Life" and "Smithsonian"* (1995).

Distinguished North Dakota journalist Richard (Patrick) Critchfield (1931–1994) reported on war and life in the Third World for decades. He also wrote important works on North Dakota, American experience, and values. These works carry the strength of Critchfield's Third World experience and have strong implications for North Dakota, the Midwest, and America. *Those Days: An American Album* (1986) describes Critchfield's family's life in the rural Midwest from the 1880s through 1940. *Trees: Why Do You Wait? America's Changing Rural Culture* (1991) describes the impacts of technology and agribusiness on Midwestern farms and rural communities.

North Dakotans involved with music and the music industry have also written autobiographical accounts. The best known of these is the "Champagne Music Maker," Lawrence Welk (1903–1992), who wrote with Bernice McGeehan about his life in the Strasburg area and his career in music. Welk was a son of immigrant parents, and his German American dialect is reflected in the titles of two books, *Wunnerful, Wunnerful!* (1971) and *Ah One, Ah Two! Life with My Musical Family* (1974). *My America, Your America* (1976) and *This I Believe* (1979) express Welk's appreciation for his life in America and the reasons for his success. *You're Never Too Young* (1981) includes his business plans for a resort and museum in Escondido, California.

Jamestown native Peggy Lee (1920–2002), born Norma Delores Egstrom, began her singing career in North Dakota. *Miss Peggy Lee: An Autobiography* (1989) describes her life and career, which included a Grammy for "Is That All There Is?" in 1969 and a Grammy Lifetime Achievement Award in 1995. Her songwriting credits include songs from Disney's *Lady and the Tramp* (1955) and a Broadway production, *Peg* (1983). As an actress, she was nominated for an Academy Award for her role as a singer in *Pete Kelly's Blues* (1955).

Composer (Johann) Peter Schickele (b. 1935), who studied music theory with Sigvald Thompson, conductor of the Fargo-Moorhead Symphony Orchestra, created *The Definitive Biography of P. D. Q. Bach, 1807–1742?* (1976). Photographs in the volume include several of the fictional University of Southern North Dakota at Hoople. Finally, rock music journalist Chuck Klosterman (b. 1972) discusses the influence of rural North Dakota in *Fargo Rock City: A Heavy Metal Odyssey in Rural North Dakota* (2001) and *Killing Yourself to Live: 85% of a True Story* (2005).

Other important North Dakota figures in the arts have written accounts of their experiences. The actress Dorothy Stickney (1896–1998) is best known on Broadway for her role as Mother in the long-running *Life with Father*. She also wrote and acted in *A*

Lovely Light, based on the poems and letters of Edna St. Vincent Millay (1892–1950). Her autobiography, *Openings and Closings* (1979), begins with her memories of Dickinson, where her father was a friend of Theodore Roosevelt. Levon West (1892–1969), who also used the pseudonym Ivan Dmitri, wrote books about his artistic methods, *Making an Etching* (1932) and *Kodachrome and How to Use It* (1940). James Rosenquist (b. 1933), the well-known pop artist and creator of the epic painting *F-111,* has contributed *Painting below Zero: Notes on a Life in Art* (2009), in which he devotes chapters to his early life with his amateur aviator parents and among Scandinavian farmers in North Dakota and Minnesota.

In the field of sports, Phil(ip Douglas) Jackson (b. 1945), an athlete at Williston and the University of North Dakota, wrote *Maverick: More than a Game* (1975) with Charles Rosen, which begins with his childhood and early years as a professional player with the New York Knicks before coaching the Chicago Bulls and the Los Angeles Lakers to several national championships. Jackson has also written *Sacred Hoops: Spiritual Lessons of a Hardwood Warrior* (1995).

Arctic explorer Vilhjalmur Stefansson (1879–1962) wrote *My Life with the Eskimo* (1913), beginning with his memories of Dakota Territory. Stefansson wrote more than twenty volumes about his explorations. *Discovery: The Autobiography of Vilhjalmur Stefansson* appeared in 1964. Dick Grace (1898–1965) wrote *Squadron of Death*: *The True Adventures of a Movie Planecrasher* (1929), *I Am Still Alive* (1931), and *Visibility Unlimited* (1950) about his experiences during World War I and his early days as a Hollywood pioneer stunt pilot.

In *Chances of a Lifetime* (2001) Warren Christopher (1925–2011), statesman and secretary of state in the first Clinton administration, recalled what he learned in North Dakota that helped him negotiate with national and world leaders.

Contemporary literary memoirs include *What I Think I Did: A Season of Survival in Two Acts* (2000) and *A Step from Death: A Memoir* (2008) by Larry (Alfred) Woiwode (b. 1941). Like his fiction, which explores relationships among family members and how families work to overcome difficulties,

Woiwode's memoirs are about his family's struggle on a family farm near Mott, where mental and physical survival is as difficult as it was for earlier generations. In addition to the elements of nature, Woiwode's family dealt with their son's near-fatal injuries on the farm; Woiwode was severely injured when an arm was pulled into a bailer. Along with the difficulties of life on the farm, Woiwode writes about his struggles as an actor and writer in New York City, where he was guided as a writer by the extraordinary *New Yorker* editor William (Keepers) Maxwell (Jr.) (1908–2000). Woiwode also wrote *Aristocrat of the West: The Story of Harold Schafer* (2000). *The Blue Jay's Dance: A Birth Year* (1995) by Louise Erdrich combines experiences of pregnancy and the births of her three daughters. In *Education of a Wandering Man* (1989) Jamestown native Louis L'Amour, born Louis Dearborn LaMoore, describes his self-education, including diary entries from the 1930s about books he had read.

Timothy Murphy (b. 1951) contributed *Set the Ploughshare Deep: A Prairie Memoir* (2000), which combines his poetry and prose with his father's reminiscences about the qualities of a North Dakota life. *The Horizontal World: Growing Up Wild in the Middle of Nowhere; A Memoir* (2006) by German Russian Debra Marquart (b. 1956) explores the conflict between her desire to flee North Dakota and her strong feelings of attachment to its history and environment. Marquart has also published *Everything's a Verb* (1995) and *From Sweetness* (2002), collections of poetry; and *The Hunger Bone: Rock and Roll Stories* (2001), about her years as a rock and heavy metal musician.

Fiction: In a young state where the drama of daily life has been so crucial to memoir and autobiography, the relatively comfortable circumstances for writing fiction developed slowly. The first work of fiction in the state was by Linda Warfel Slaughter, already a published writer when she arrived in North Dakota. "The Amazonian Corps: A Romance of Army Life," an autobiographical novella about an officer's wife, was published in the *Bismarck Tribune* in 1874–1875.

Given the state's ethnic history, much of North Dakota's fiction is based on immigrant and ethnic experience. Some works have not been translated. OLE EDVART RØLVAAG (1876–1931), who wrote *GIANTS IN THE EARTH* (1927) and other novels based on immigrant experiences, spent time in North Dakota, and Knut Hamsun (1859–1952) worked on threshing crews before writing *Growth of the Soil* (1920). Simon Johnson (1874–1970), who arrived in 1882 with his parents, wrote novels about immigrant experiences, most of which have not been translated. His works include *From Fjord to Prairie; or, In the New Kingdom* (1916), *Et Geni* (A Genius) (1907), *Lonea* (1909), *Fire Fortellinger* (Four stories) (1917), *Fallitten paa Braastad* (Bankruptcy at Braastad) (1922), and *Frihetens Hjem* (Freedom's home) (1925). Hans A. Foss (1851–1929) wrote romantic novels, including *The Cotter's Son* (1884; translation, 1963), *Kristine: En Fortaelling fra Valders* (Kristine: A tale from Valdres) (1886), and *Valborg* (1927). As a leader in the Dakota Temperance Society, Foss wrote *Tobias: A Story of the Northwest* (1899), *Hvide Slaver: en social-politisk skildring* (White slaves: A social-political portrayal) (1892), and *Livet i Vesterheimen* (Life in the western home) (1886). Johan Bojer (1872–1959) wrote primarily of his native Norway, but *The Emigrants* (Norwegian, 1924; translation, 1925) tells a story of Norwegian emigration to La Moure County in the 1880s.

Olga Overn (1897–1988) contributed *Challenge: A Saga of the Northwest* (1949), in which young Bjorn becomes a pioneer in the North Dakota Badlands and interacts with such historical figures as the Marquis de Mores and Theodore Roosevelt. In *The Coffee Train* (1953) Margarethe Erdahl Shank (1910–2004) re-creates her childhood in the 1920s in fiction in a town she calls Prairie; Shank also wrote the novel *Call Back the Years* (1966), reflecting on questions of Norwegian immigration to America. Anna O. Bertinuson (1888–1972) wrote *Echoes* (1962) about homestead life in North Dakota; an earlier book by Bertinuson, *Amalie of Solvang* (1955), is about daily life in Norway around 1900. In *The Rag Rug* (1955) Martha Reishus (1888–1980) weaves a family story of immigration and settlement involving the home country and WISCONSIN, Minnesota, and North Dakota. Nina Hermanna Morgan (b. ca. 1875) wrote *Prairie Star* (1955), which deals with a young Norwegian immigrant and his pioneering experiences in the mid-1850s; and E(dgar) Palmer Rockswold (b. 1916) wrote *Per: Immigrant and Pioneer* (1981).

Nora Fladeboe Mohberg (1903–1995) relied heavily on biographical materials but employed fictional techniques in *The Straddlebug* (1968) and *A Home for Agate* (1966); *Sarah, Your Sister Needs You* (1977) concerns Icelandic immigrants to North Dakota. Her *Duke of Dunbar* (1971) is about a horse told from the horse's point of view and is perhaps best categorized as young-adult fiction. Carrie Young (b. 1923), who had written her mother's biography in *Nothing to Do but Stay: My Pioneer Mother* (1991), followed with seven short stories in *The Wedding Dress: Stories from the Dakota Plains* (1992).

Rodney Allen Nelson (b. 1941) is primarily a poet but has written a number of novels, including *Home River* (1984) and the more introspective *Villy Sadness* (1987), two novellas of the mid-twentieth century pertinent to Scandinavian American social and political identity in the Red River valley near Fargo. Much of Nelson's work is now published only online. Wishek native Ron(ald J.) Vossler (b. 1948) often uses the experiences of the Black Sea Germans who came to Dakota from Russia. His many books include *Horse, I Am Your Mother: Stories* (1988); an edited collection of correspondence, *We'll Meet Again in Heaven: Germans in the Soviet Union Write Their Dakota Relatives, 1925–1937* (2001); and *Dakota Kraut: A Memoir; Collected Notes on How I Learned to Love My Accent and My Ancestry, 1983–2003* (2003).

Ranch and farm life is a staple of North Dakota literature, including fiction. Zdena Trinka (1888–1987) wrote the novel *Medora* (1940), which concerns the days of the Marquis de Mores in the Badlands of western North Dakota. Bea Agard (1888–1983) wrote a biographical novel of her parents' homesteading experience in *Lark against the Thunder* (1953), set in Larimore, Dakota Territory, beginning in 1886. Lois Phillips Hudson (1927–2010) wrote about the effects of the Depression on her family, particularly her mother and herself, in the celebrated classic novel *The Bones of Plenty* (1962), describing Midwestern farmers' responses to the drought and the Depression. Hudson's *Reapers of the Dust* (1964) is a collection of short stories concerning this same period. *Victoria* (1953) by Hannah (Ulness) Perhus (b. ca. 1895) takes place on a North Dakota farm during World War II; the plot asserts the importance of farming to the United States during the war years. Harvey Sletten wrote a novel set in the Sheyenne River valley, *Over These Steps* (1979), and a sequel, *Erich Collins Comes Home* (1992); *Walking Arrow* (1992) tells an American Indian story set in the 1860s.

School and college fiction from North Dakota writers is exemplified by the work of Devils Lake native Lynn C. Miller (b. 1951), who has written two academic novels, *The Fool's Journey* (2002) and the mystery *Death of a Department Chair* (2006). Walter Ellis (1943–2004) in *Reflections on the Academic Life in North Dakota* (2002) focuses on the relationship between a history professor at a North Dakota university and a graduate student, as well as their tour of the Holy Land.

Keith Wheeler (1911–1994) wrote autobiography and fiction based on his experiences as a war correspondent for the *Chicago Sun-Times* during World War II. *The Pacific Is My Beat* (1943) and *We Are the Wounded* (1945) present his experiences, and *The Reef* (1951) and *Small World* (1958) are fiction based on those experiences. Wheeler also wrote many books about the Old West and World War II for Time-Life. In a novel, *Peaceable Lane* (1960), which won the Brotherhood Award in 1961 from the National Council of Christians and Jews, Wheeler raises questions about prejudice, integration, and problems relating to race relations.

The important Midwestern philosophical critic and fiction writer WILLIAM H(OWARD) GASS (b. 1924) was born in Fargo, but his family moved to OHIO when he was still an infant. North Dakota's most famous writer is the novelist Larry Woiwode, who writes often about the experiences of three generations of a North Dakota family from homesteading through the Depression to the 1970s. Woiwode has written several books of fiction based on his experiences in North Dakota, most notably *Beyond the Bedroom Wall: A Family Album* (1975), which won the

Friends of American Writers Award and was nominated for the National Book Award and the National Book Critics Circle Award. "The Street," the "Prelude" to the novel, describes the main street and the narrator's memories of particular buildings and people. This main street is like the one-block main streets of many small towns in North Dakota and the Midwest during the 1940s and 1950s. Woiwode's first novel, *What I'm Going to Do, I Think* (1969), won the William Faulkner Foundation Award. Other works of fiction include *Poppa John* (1981), *Born Brothers* (1988), *The Neumiller Stories* (1989), *Indian Affairs* (1992), and *Silent Passengers* (1993).

Larry Watson (b. 1947) has written several novels, a collection of stories, and a chapbook of poetry, *Leaving Dakota* (1983). Watson won awards from the Wisconsin Library Association for *Montana 1948* (1993) and *Orchard* (2003), set in Door County, Wisconsin. Watson's first book, *In a Dark Time* (1980), is a suspense novel about the murder of several students in a Minneapolis high school. *Mavis* (1996), by Brenda K. Marshall (b. 1953), concerns six sisters who were reared on a North Dakota farm and the murder of the husband of one of the sisters. Marshall's *Dakota; or, What's a Heaven For* (2010), is set in Dakota Territory from 1874 to 1883. Much of the acclaimed first novel by Leif Enger (b. 1961), *Peace like a River* (2001), takes place in the Badlands of North Dakota.

Poetry: According to Richard Lyons (1920–2000) in his preface to *Poetry North: Five Poets of North Dakota* (1970), North Dakota poetry begins with poems written as early as 1865 by Captain Enoch Adams, who was stationed at Fort Rice near Bismarck. Adams published his poems in the *Frontier Scout*, a newspaper he edited.

North Dakota's poets often write about the natural beauty of the state and the pioneering spirit, the intense labor involved in working the land, the loneliness as well as the promise of the wide open spaces, and the opportunities available to those who are willing to work hard. These poems are generally optimistic. Some of the state's early poetry was written and published by individuals, and from the 1920s through the 1940s the North Dakota Poetry Society provided a community of writers.

Some of the state's poets were immigrants who wrote in their first language. Perhaps the most important was Stephan G. Stephansson (1853–1927), who emigrated from Iceland and lived in Dakota Territory from 1880 to 1889; he was a remarkable Icelandic farmer-poet, according to Jane W. McCracken, author of *Stephan G. Stephansson: The Poet of the Rocky Mountains* (1982). Stephansson wrote six volumes of *Andvokur* (Wakeful nights) between 1909 and 1938. *Stephan G. Stephansson: Selected Translations from "Andvokur"* (1982) also includes some letters and correspondence. Paul Bjarnason (b. 1882), an important translator of Stephansson, contributed original poetry and translations in *Odes and Echoes* (1954) and *More Echoes* (1963), published in English; *Fleygar* (1953), a work of fiction, was published in Icelandic. The many poetic dramas of the prolific Jon Norstog (1877–1942), often based on biblical themes, have apparently not been translated in their entirety from Norwegian; his works include *Moses: Drama i fem vendingar* [Moses: A Drama in Five Acts] (1914), *Josef: Dit episk dikt* [Joseph: An Epic Poem] (1918), and *Tone, Forteljing* [Tone: A Tale] (1920), among many others. Some selected translations from Norstog's work appear in Inga Bredesen's account in "Jon Norstog, the Book-Maker" in volume 30 of *Poet Lore* (1919).

Much of the state's early poetry is optimistic and was written primarily for family and friends. Among these poems are *Infinity; or, Nature's God* (1909) by F. J. Duggan (b. 1851) and *Poems of Home Life* (1912) by Mrs. John Heffernan (Elinor F. Heffernan; b. 1869), including poems about religious reverence and the poet's family. Some later volumes in this vein are *Whispering Wings* (ca. 1955) by Snorri Thorfinnson (1901–1986), *Prairie Poems: Poetic Dreams of Prairie Themes* (1974) by Arnold H. Marzolf (1916–1998), and *In My Own Way* (1975) by Marge L. Stroklund (1918–1993).

Aaron McGaffey Beede (1859–1934), a missionary and attorney who spent much of his life among the Sioux, credits Indian culture for some of his poems. In addition to two volumes of poetry, *Toward the Sun* (1916) and *Self Sloughed-Off Person Free: Heart and Pluck in This Epoch* (1934), Beede also wrote *Sitting Bull and Custer* (1913), *Large Indian Cornfields in North Dakota Long Ago: and an Indian Drama Petite for School Children* (1914), and *Heart-in-the-Lodge* (1915).

Modern Poems for Modern People (1919) by Florence Borner (1888–1962) includes political poetry dealing with two topics of the time, patriotic poems about World War I and the rise of North Dakota's Nonpartisan League (NPL) and NPL songs. The Nonpartisan League emerged in several states in the Midwest as citizens sought greater control of their economic conditions and successfully nominated and elected state officials. In North Dakota, the State Mill and Elevator and the State Bank were established to counter the power and influence of businesses outside the state.

Although he was never officially recognized by the North Dakota legislature, "Poet Laureate" James W. Foley (1874–1939), author of more than thirty volumes of verse, was well known to the people of the state, and James Foley Day was observed with programs of his poetry. Among Foley's best-known works are "North Dakota Hymn," designated the state's official song in 1947, and "Letter Home," a poem celebrating freedom and opportunity in North Dakota. His themes are found in the three volumes of *The Verses of James W. Foley* (1911), *Book of Boys and Girls, Book of Life and Laughter,* and *Book of Plains and Prairie.* Florence F. Renfrow (1926–1996) published three volumes of verse, *Poems from North Dakota* (1979), *Country Poems* (1984), and *Poems from Our Town* (1990), the "town" of the title being Turtle Lake, North Dakota.

From the late 1920s through the 1940s many of the state's poets were members of the North Dakota Poetry Society. The society published news and poetry in its newsletter, *Prairie Wings. North Dakota Singing* (1936), edited by Grace Brown Putnam (1870–1933) and Anna Ackerman (1894–1976), includes works of sixty-eight poets and reflects the poetry of the time; much is written in iambic pentameter with strict rhyme patterns and deals with traditional themes that include death, friendship, love, natural beauty, home life, and trust in God. The poets in the collection are "singers" of the state. The volume contains seven poems about travel experiences by Louis L'Amour, now better known for his fiction, and in his biographical note L'Amour created the image he used throughout his career: "He has been at times a miner, seaman, deep-sea diver, lumberjack, pugilist, reporter, tourist guide, and actor, adventurer and wanderer." L'Amour's first published volume was a book of poetry, *Smoke from This Altar* (1939).

Some local chapters, or "stanzas," of the North Dakota Poetry Society also published collections of poetry. *Beta Stanzas* (1940) was printed on a press in the Bismarck basement of two members, Clell G. Gannon (1900–1962) and Ruth Gannon. Clell G. Gannon, an artist as well as a poet, also wrote and illustrated *Songs of the Bunch-Grass Acres* (1924) and *How Christmas Came to North Dakota* (1929). After Gannon's death, his family published *Ever and Always I Shall Love the Land* (1965).

Other members of the North Dakota Poetry Society published collections of poetry. Eva K. Anglesburg (1893–1976) wrote *Of the Level Land* (1935) and *For Many Moods* (1938). Richard Beck (1897–1980), who wrote in Icelandic and English and also translated Icelandic poetry, published *Icelandic Lyrics: Originals and Translations* (1930) and *A Sheaf of Verses* (1945; enlarged 1966). Paul Southworth Bliss (1889–1940) created collections including *Spin Dance and Spring Comes to Shaw's Garden* (1934), *Cirrus from the West* (1935), and a hand-bound volume, *The Rye Is the Sea* (1936), all with illustrations by Harold J. Matthews. Mary Brennan Clapp (1884–1966) wrote *And Then Re-mold It* (1929), reprinted as part of *Collected Verse* (1951); Gottfried (Emanuel) Hult (1869–1950) published *Reveries, and Other Poems* (1909) and *Outbound* (1920). Huldah Lucile Winsted (1884–1959) wrote *In the Land of Dakota: A Little Book of North Dakota Verse* (1920), *America Makes Men, and Other Poems* (1924), and *North Dakota—Land of the Sky, and Other Poems* (1927). Finally, Nina Farley Wishek created *Rose Berries in Autumn* (1938).

The North Dakota Poetry Society encouraged North Dakota's best poet, THOMAS (MATTHEW) McGRATH (1916–1990); some of his early poetry was published in *Prairie Wings*. McGrath wrote more than twenty volumes, including poetry, books for children, two novels, and critical essays. As a poet, McGrath stresses the importance of

place. *Letter to an Imaginary Friend* (four parts, 1962–1985) emphasizes understanding one's home and the relationship of that home to other places. McGrath's collections of poetry include the four parts of *Letter to an Imaginary Friend, The Movie at the End of the World: Collected Poems* (1972), and *Passages toward the Dark* (1982). McGrath's political novel, *This Coffin Has No Handles* (written 1947, published 1988) pits New York longshoremen against owners. The editor of the definitive edition of *Letter to an Imaginary Friend,* Dale Jacobson (b. 1949), has also written collections of poetry, including the chapbook *Dakota Incantations* (1973), *Factories and Cities* (2003), and *A Walk by the River* (2004).

The North Dakota state legislature has officially recognized several poets laureate: Corbin A. Waldron (1899–1978), Henry R. Martinson (1883–1981), Lydia O. Jackson (1902–1984), and Larry Woiwode. Waldron, laureate from 1957 to 1978, wrote *Voice of the Valley* (1968), *Lines and Lyrics from Dakota* (1943; revised 1956), and *Footprints in America's Fields* (1975). Henry R. Martinson, laure-

Thomas McGrath, ca. 1964.
Courtesy of North Dakota State University Archives

ate from 1979 to 1981, was a farmer and organizer for the Socialist Party and later for the Nonpartisan League. Martinson's poetry includes *Old Trails . . . and New* (1958); his autobiographical sketches are found in *Village Commune Barefoot Boy* (1976). Lydia O. Jackson, Poet Laureate from 1979 to 1984, wrote *Rhymes for Every Season* (1943), *Selected Poems* (1962), *Pardon My Gaff* (1967), and *A Trilogy Trimmed in Lace* (1984). Larry Woiwode was named North Dakota's Poet Laureate in 1995. His poetry is found in *Even Tide* (1977).

In 1989 David R. Solheim (b. 1947) was named North Dakota's centennial poet. Solheim has published several collections of poetry, including *On the Ward* (1975), *Inheritance* (1987), *West River: 100 Poems* (1989), and *The Landscape Listens* (1999). A volume compiled in preparation for celebration of the state's centennial, *A Long Way to See: Images and Voices of North Dakota* (1987), includes a selection of poems by Fargo-born Michael Moos (b. 1949), photographs by Wayne Gudmundson, and an introduction by Lois Phillips Hudson.

Richard Lyons edited *Poetry North: Five Poets of North Dakota* (1970), which includes works by him, Thomas McGrath, John R. Milton (1924–1995), Anthony Oldknow (b. 1939), and Larry Woiwode. His poem "Prairie Wife" appears in the small collection *Six Poets of the Red River* (1971) along with poems by David Martinson (1946–2010), McGrath, Oldknow, Mary Ann Pryor, and Mark Vinz (b. 1942). Lyons and Prudence Gearey Sand (1908–1984) contributed the chapbook *Stackers of Wheat* (1951). Lyons also wrote *Men and Tin Kettles* (1956); *Gallery B: Portraits* (1963), indebted in technique to EDGAR LEE MASTERS (1868–1950); and *Enough to Be a Woman* (1994). *Scanning the Land: Poems in North Dakota* (1980) combines poetry and photographs.

Mark Vinz wrote several collections of poetry, including *Climbing the Stairs* (1983), *Mixed Blessings* (1989), and *Long Distance* (2005). He was also the co-editor of many ANTHOLOGIES, including *Inheriting the Land: Contemporary Voices from the Midwest* (1993) and *Imagining Home: Writing from the Midwest* (2000), both with Thom Tammaro. With Grayce Ray he edited *Dacotah Territory*, a journal published just across the Red River at Moorhead State University in Minnesota;

it attracted regional and national poets from 1971 through 1981. *Dacotah Territory: A 10 Year Anthology* (1982) includes a selection of poems from the seventeen issues. Vinz was editor of *Dakota Arts Quarterly,* a publication devoted to literature, visual art, and music and published from 1977 to 1984.

Roland Flint (1934–2001) published several volumes of poetry, including *Resuming Green: Selected Poems, 1965–1982* (1982) and *Hearing Voices* (1991), with William Stafford. *This House Is Filled with Cracks* (1994) is by Madelyn Camrud (b. ca. 1939). Her poem "The River Leaps," a meditation on the devastating Red River flood, is found in the book of photographs *Under the Whelming Tide: The 1997 Flood of the Red River of the North* (1998). Jamie Parsley (b. 1969), ordained an Episcopalian priest in 2004, is a prolific poet with at least ten books and chapbooks, including *The Loneliness of Blizzards* (1995) and *No Stars, No Moon: New and Selected Haiku* (2004). *Cloud: A Poem in Two Acts* (1997) considers the bombing of Hiroshima in 1945. Rodney Allen Nelson, noted previously under fiction, has published poetry books and chapbooks often centered on his Scandinavian heritage; *Red River Album* (1982), *Thor's Home* (1983), and *Mere Telling* (2009) are representative. Much of Nelson's work since the mid-1980s, such as *Swede Poems* (2007) and the novel *Harvestman* (2004), appears only online.

North Dakota has a number of cowboy poets. In 1987 Bill Lowman (b. 1947), author of *Riders of the Leafy Spurge* (1985), *The Blueberry Roan* (1986), and *Walk ah Mile in My Bones* (1988), organized a Dakota Cowboy Poetry Gathering in Medora. Rodney (Rod) Nelson (b. ca. 1949) has written *Good Clean Fun* (1989) and *Cowboy Laundry, and Other Poems of Wit and Humor* (1995); *Up Sims Creek: The First 100 Trips* (2001) is a collection of his humorous columns from *Farm and Ranch Guide. Wilbur's Christmas Gift* (2000) is a book-length poem for children illustrated by Scott Nelson. A public performer, Nelson once appeared on *The Johnny Carson Show.* Shadd Piehl (b. 1967) is the author of a chapbook, *Towards Horses: Poems* (1999).

Students in public schools and universities throughout the state produce chapbooks and collections of literature. One example of poetry by high school and grade school students is *Sparks in the Dark: Student Writing from the North Dakota Writers-in-Residence Program* (1983), edited by Joan Eades and Mark Vinz.

Drama: Even before statehood in 1889, many North Dakota communities built opera houses in which touring groups performed operas, plays, and patriotic historical pageants. Pulitzer Prize–winning playwright Maxwell Anderson (1888–1959) saw his first professional production in Grand Forks, and New York Broadway actress Dorothy Stickney saw her first professional performance in Dickinson.

The dramatic heritage of North Dakota centers on its schools, from the one-room schoolhouses once found by the thousands across the state to the state's colleges and universities. When Frederick Koch (1877–1944) came to the University of North Dakota in 1905, he brought with him the idea of "folk plays" and quickly organized a group of student actors. Koch believed that theatre should come from the people, so he introduced a class in playwriting and founded the Sock and Buskin Society in 1910, renamed the Dakota Playmakers in 1917. By 1914 Koch was instrumental in establishing Bankside Theatre. *The Pageant of the North-West*, performed there, was the first ambitious theatre project in North Dakota. It was published as *The Book of a Pageant of the North-West* (1914) by eighteen undergraduate members under the direction of Koch and Orin G. Libby.

Of all North Dakota playwrights, Maxwell Anderson, a charter member of the Sock and Buskin Society, has received the most critical attention. Following the folk-play tradition, Anderson's first play for Broadway, *White Desert* (1923), concerns newly married immigrants who settle in North Dakota in 1888. *Both Your Houses* (1933), a political satire, was awarded a Pulitzer Prize, and *Winterset* (1935) and *High Tor* (1937) won New York Drama Critics' Circle Awards. In 1936–1937 Anderson had the distinction of having three plays running simultaneously on Broadway—*The Wingless Victory, High Tor,* and *The Masque of Kings*. In his bibliography in *The Life of Maxwell Anderson* (1983), Alfred S. Shivers lists thirty-one individually published plays and twenty complete play manuscripts; numerous books of poetry, fiction, and criticism; and many individual essays, articles, and reviews.

Dakota Playmakers' Vera Kelsey (1892–1961) published *Free* in the *Quarterly Journal of the University of North Dakota* in 1917, and *Sigrid* by Margaret Radcliffe was published in *American Folk Plays* (1939). Mattie Crabtree (b. ca. 1896) produced two outdoor pageants, *Dickey County Historical Pageant* in 1917 and *A Patriotic Pageant of Dickey County* in 1918. Margaret Plank Ganssle (1893–1934) produced *The New Day: A Masque of the Future* in 1918. Lauga Geir (1888–1968) produced "Expressions of Icelandic Heritage in Pembina County."

Franz Rickaby (1889–1925) continued the Koch tradition, encouraging original plays, establishing the Junior Playmakers for high school students, writing plays, and editing *Dakota Playmaker Plays* (1923) on "colonial themes." With his wife, Lillian, Rickaby wrote *The Christmas Spirit: A Poetic Fantasy* (1921), presented by the Dakota Playmakers. Rickaby's *Ballads and Songs of the Shanty-Boy* (1926) is based on ballads he collected from lumber camps in MICHIGAN, Wisconsin, and Minnesota.

In 1914 Alfred G. Arvold (1882–1957) established a theatre program at North Dakota State University. Arvold's *The Little Country Theater* (1922) is about the importance of theatre to rural life and includes original plays produced by his students and others. Arvold also staged pageants, including *Covered Wagon Days* in 1920 and a pageant for the bicentennial of George Washington's birthday in 1932. Reminiscences and miscellanea are collected in *Alfred . . . in Every Man's Life* (1957). See REGIONAL THEATRE.

Frederick G. Walsh (1915–1999), who came to North Dakota State University and the Little Country Theater in 1952, was also committed to regional theatre. Walsh developed outdoor theatre programs in Medora in 1958 and Mandan in 1959. For the Theodore Roosevelt centennial in 1958, Walsh coordinated production and directed *Old Four Eyes*, a play about Teddy Roosevelt's ranching days, at the Burning Hills Ampitheatre at Medora. Walsh co-authored with W. T. Chichester and was consulting director for *Trail West: An Historical Drama Produced on the Exact Locale Where Custer's Last March Began* (1959). *Trail West* was presented over three seasons at Mandan and recounted the life of General George Armstrong Custer, the Seventh Cavalry, and the events leading to the Battle of the Little Bighorn.

For the fiftieth anniversary of the Little Country Theatre in 1964, Walsh wrote *The Trial of Louis Riel* (1965); Riel was a leader of the "Riel Rebellions" in Manitoba and Saskatchewan to secure rights for the Métis. Walsh also created the Prairie Stage touring company, which presented approximately five hundred performances in eighty communities from 1971 through 1976. Among Walsh's students, Doug Fosse of Grand Forks directed *Dakota Land* (1987), a community production in the tradition of the first folk plays.

William Borden (1938–2010) won many credits for his work in drama. *When the Meadowlark Sings* (1989) was selected by the North Dakota Centennial Commission as the state's official drama. Other plays include *Sakakawea: The Woman with Many Names* (1989), *Turtle Island Blues* (2000), and *Bluest Reason: The Winter of Their Discontent; The Untold Story of Lewis and Clark* (2001). Joan Eades (b. 1947) wrote several plays, including *Beacon over Our Western Land* (1983) for the centennial of the University of North Dakota.

Ev Miller (b. 1935) is a Bismarck playwright whose plays are based on North Dakota events and people. Miller's first play, *A Dusty Echo* (1990), based on his family's experiences on a farm near Bismarck, won the North Dakota Bicentennial Playwriting Contest in 1976 and was selected for a tour of thirty North Dakota communities. Among many other plays, Miller has written *Crying from the Earth* (1997) and *Here's to the Winner* (2003). In 1995 he received a Bush Foundation Grant for *Playwrights of North Dakota,* which Miller says in his introduction is "the only complete listing of North Dakota playwrights ever done."

Rodney Allen Nelson wrote *Detriment: A Radio Play* (1981) and *The Popcorn Man: A Norwegian Immigrant Verse-Play* (1982). His *Cowboy Village* (2005), set "in the western Dakotas," is available online from *Scene4 Magazine.*

Printing and Journalism: The first newspaper published in northern Dakota Territory appears to have been the *Frontier Scout,* which was first issued at Fort Union on July 7, 1864, and moved to Fort Rice in 1865, when for a few issues it became a weekly. Clement A. Lounsberry (1843–1926) founded the weekly the *Bismarck Tribune* in July 1873. On July 6, 1876, he published an "extra," "First Account of the Custer Massacre," within hours of the return of the steamer *Far West* from the Little Bighorn in Montana. Other early newspapers include the *Fargo Express,* the *Daily Plaindealer* (Grand Forks), and the *Jamestown Alert.* See also NEWSPAPER JOURNALISM and PRINTING AND PUBLISHING.

Lounsberry published a three-volume history, *North Dakota: History and People; Outlines of American History* (1916); the second and third volumes were composed of biographical sketches of pioneers and other citizens of importance. "The Press of North Dakota," chapter 30 of the first volume, is about newspapers established through 1890. In *History of the Red River Valley* (1909) George B. Winship, founder of the *Grand Forks Herald* in 1879, writes that the first publication in North Dakota's Red River valley was Father George A. Belcourt's "little missionary paper" in French in the 1850s "descriptive of his work among the Indians." Among newspapers published in languages other than English, Lounsberry includes *Der Pioneer,* established in 1883 at Jamestown. Winship lists two Scandinavian papers established in Grand Forks, *Tidende* in 1885 and *Normanden* in 1888, and the *Fargo Posten,* established in 1889. *Dakotans Are Reading People: The Continuing Story of the North Dakota Newspaper Association, 1886–2003* (2003) by Danny Butcher and Marah De Meule is a history of North Dakota journalism.

Three North Dakota newspapers have won Pulitzer Prizes. In 1938 the *Bismarck Tribune* won a Pulitzer for articles and editorials about the Dust Bowl. The *Fargo Forum* won a Pulitzer for its coverage of a June 10, 1957, tornado. The *Grand Forks Herald* won a Pulitzer Prize for Public Service for never missing a publication although the 1997 flood covered the city, and the newspaper offices and other downtown buildings burned while standing in floodwaters. Mike Jacobs, editor of the *Grand Forks Herald,* was previously editor of his independent newspaper, the *Onlooker,* and wrote *One Time Harvest: Reflections on Coal and Our Future* (1975).

The Red River Valley Historical Society published a collection by Roy P. Johnson (1899–1963), *Roy Johnson's Red River Valley: A Selection of Historical Articles, First Printed in the "Forum" from 1941 to 1962* (1982). Frances Wold (1889–1994) collected some of her writing from *Farm and Ranch Guide* in *Prairie Scrapbook* (1982) and *Guide Country—Then and Now* (1987). Thomas D. Isern (b. 1952) has written *Dakota Circle: Excursions on the True Plains* (2000).

A number of presses and publications have printed literary material over the years. The official publication of the North Dakota Poetry Society from May 1936 until February 1948 was the monthly *Prairie Wings.* The North Dakota Institute for Regional Studies, established in 1950 at North Dakota State University, continues to publish diverse volumes on regional literature, biography, history, agriculture, and other topics. *North Dakota Quarterly* is a literary journal established in 1910 at the University of North Dakota. *North Dakota History: Journal of the Northern Plains,* originally the *North Dakota Historical Quarterly,* began publication in 1926. Many little magazines also originated in North Dakota. Scopcraeft Press was begun by Anthony Oldknow as a literary journal at North Dakota State University in Fargo in 1966; it became a nonprofit press in 1975.

Since 1971 the Greater North Dakota Association has been publishing the quarterly *North Dakota Horizons.* For the North Dakota centennial, editor and photographer Sheldon Green, photographer Russ Hanson, and writer Nancy Edmonds Hanson produced a five-volume series about the state: *'Cross the Wide Missouri: Bismarck and the West River Country* (1984), *Bread Basket of the World: Fargo, Grand Forks and the Red River Valley* (1985), *Heart of the Prairies: Minot, Jamestown and Valley City* (1986), *Sagebrush, Buttes and Buffalo: Williston, Dickinson and the Badlands* (1985), and *Getting to Know Dakota: An Insiders Guide to North Dakota* (1985).

North Dakota journalists have written works centering on important issues to North Dakota and the nation. The economic crisis in the 1980s is the setting for journalist James Corcoran's *Bitter Harvest: Gordon Kahl and the Posse Comitatus; Murder in the Heartland* (1990). After the bombing in Oklahoma City in 1995, the book was republished as *Bitter Harvest: The Birth of Paramilitary Terrorism in the Heartland* (1995). In *Coyote Warrior: One Man, Three Tribes, and the Trial That Forged a Nation* (2004) Paul VanDevelder tells about one fight by American Indians for their native lands. Parshall native Martin Cross argued several cases and also successfully represented the Mandan, Arikara, and Hidatsa—the Three Affiliated Tribes—in lobbying for compensation for land taken by Congress for the construction of Garrison Dam on the Missouri River. As noted by the publisher, Cross's father, Martin Cross, was the tribal chairman who unsuccessfully protested the taking of land for construction of the dam and also the great-grandson of chiefs who had helped Lewis and Clark during the winter the expedition spent among the tribes.

North Dakota Federal Writers' Project: As one of many relief projects in the United States and Midwest, the North Dakota Federal Writers Project produced *North Dakota: A Guide to the Northern Prairie State* (1938) under the direction of young journalist Ethel Schlasinger. It was reprinted as *The WPA Guide to 1930s North Dakota* (1990). The volume lacks any discussion of North Dakota's literary history.

Popular Literature:

Western Novels: Louis L'Amour is perhaps the best-known writer of popular westerns and helped create the popular image of the American West in such books as *How the West Was Won* (1962). L'Amour wrote over ninety books and four hundred short stories. Many are still in print, and several have been made into movies. His first novel, *Hondo* (1953), was made into a movie (1953) starring John Wayne. The continuing popularity of the western provided a market for Robert Kammen (b. 1931), a former postmaster from Mott, who wrote more than twenty-five western stories between 1985 and 1995, including *Bloody Dakota Summer* (1992). Peter Brandvold (b. 1953) wrote short fiction before he began to write westerns; since writing *Once a Marshal* (1998), he has written more than twenty-five westerns, including *Dakota Kill* (2000).

Mystery and Detective Fiction: Vera Kelsey, who wrote several travel books about China and South America, also wrote mystery novels, among them *The Bride Died Alone* (1943) and *Whisper Murder* (1946), a novel based on events in Grand Forks. Lynn M. Boughey (b. 1956), a lawyer in Bismarck and formerly commander of the Fifth Fighter Interceptor Squadron at Minot Air Force Base, has written a Cold War spy thriller, *Mission to Chara* (2001), featuring the SR-71 Blackbird aircraft. *The Guys from Fargo* (2007) by Delray Dvoracek (b. ca. 1940), who also writes westerns under the pseudonym Kent Kamron, is a detective story founded on blackmail, centered on the streets of Fargo, and featuring the Powers Coffee House there. *The Murdered Family* (2010) by Vernon Keel (b. 1940) is a novel based on the actual 1920 murders of seven members of a farm family in McLean County, North Dakota.

Children's and Young Adult Literature: Ralph "Doc" Hubbard (1886–1980), who spent his lifetime gathering and preserving Indian heritage, wrote *Queer Person* (1930) and *The Wolf Song* (1935), the latter about Kiowa "wolf wisdom," concluding with a detailed story of two orphaned Indian children who find their way home over a great distance by following the "song" of the wolf. *Queer Person,* a Newbery Honor Book in 1931, concerns a young deaf-mute Indian boy who is adopted by an old woman and grows up with honor.

Bigelow Neal (1891–1962) published hundreds of stories about pioneer life and wild animals for children's publications such as *Blue Book* and *American Boy. The Last of the Thundering Herd* (1933) concerns the last days of the buffalo herds. Neal also wrote *The Valley of the Damned* (1949) about the construction of North Dakota's Garrison Dam, begun in 1947 by the U.S. Army Corps of Engineers to provide control of Missouri River and Mississippi River flooding.

Lucy Johnston Sypher (1907–1990) wrote four fictionalized autobiographical works based on her memories of Wales, North Dakota, in 1916–1917: *The Edge of Nowhere* (1972), *Cousins and Circuses* (1974), *The Spell of the Northern Lights* (1975), and *The Turnabout Year* (1976). After teaching English and modern history at a Massachusetts college, Sypher began writing about her childhood for her grandchildren. The four books take the young girl, Lucy, from her childhood in Wales to the cusp of adulthood as she be-

comes aware of the world around her. In the first book Sypher describes "the prairie village of Wales, on the northmost edge of North Dakota" (1). *Cousins and Circuses* centers on the excitement of a family vacation to Lake Minnetonka in Minnesota. *The Spell of the Northern Lights* concerns her increasing maturity, and in *The Turnabout Year* the young girl begins to plan her future.

Erling Nicolai Rolfsrud (1912–1994) wrote thirty books of reminiscence, history, fiction, and biography, including *Extraordinary North Dakotans* (1954). His first work of fiction was *Gopher Tails for Papa* (1951). Zdena Trinka published a novel for children based on life in the old country, *Jenik and Marenka: A Boy and Girl of Czechoslovakia* (1937). Borghild Margarethe Dahl (1890–1984) used her Norwegian heritage to write several books, including *Karen* (1947), the story of a Norwegian girl who immigrates to America, marries, settles on a stretch of land in North Dakota, and successfully faces frontier hardships. *Homecoming* (1953) is about a young Norwegian American girl who becomes a teacher in Minnesota. Skulda Vanadis Báner (1897–1964) wrote *First Parting* (1960), based on her teaching experiences in North Dakota. *Against the Wind* (1955) by Harriett H. Carr (1899–1977) is based on farming experiences in homestead days.

Rutherford G. Montgomery (1894–1985), using A. A. Avery and other pen names, wrote more than one hundred books, including animal stories for children. Among his works that won writing awards, *Kildee House* (1949) was a Newbery Award Honor Book in 1950, and *The Stubborn One* (1965) was given the Western Writers of America Golden Spur Award in 1965. Lyla Hoffine (1897–1984) wrote several books about her knowledge of Indian life, including *Wi Sapa: Black Moon* (1936), reprinted as *Sioux Trail Adventure* (1957); *White Buffalo: A Story of the Northwest Fur Trade* (1939); *Running Elk* (1957); *Jennie's Mandan Bowl* (1960); *The Eagle Feather Prize* (1962); and *Carol Blue Wing, What Is Your Pleasure?* (1967).

Emily Rhoads Johnson (b. 1936), who founded the Writers' Conference in Children's Literature at the University of North Dakota in 1980, has written *Spring and the Shadow Man* (1984), *A House Full of Strangers* (1992), and *Write Me If You Dare!* (2000). Many who have attended the conference have published books, including Esther Allen Peterson (b. 1934), with *Frederick's Alligator* (1979), and Priscilla Homola (b. 1947), who wrote *The Willow Whistle* (1983). Faythe Dyrud Thureen (b. 1941) has written *Jenna's Big Jump* (1993) and *Troll Meets Trickster on the Dakota Prairie* (2005). Jane Kurtz (b. 1952), who lived and taught in Grand Forks for twelve years, has written more than twenty books, including *River Friendly, River Wild* (2000) about the 1997 Red River flood.

Thomas McGrath's books for young children include *Clouds* (1959) and *The Beautiful Things* (1960). Louise Erdrich's books for children include *Grandmother's Pigeon* (1996), *The Birchbark House* (1999), *The Range Eternal* (2002), *The Game of Silence* (2005), and *The Porcupine Year* (2008).

Romance Novels: Lauraine Snelling (b. 1942) has written many works of Christian fiction for adults and children, including six novels focused on Norwegians in North Dakota in her Red River of the North series, starting with *An Untamed Land* (1996). Later series are Return to Red River and Dakotah Treasures. Judy Baer (b. 1951) has written over seventy Christian and traditional romances, including *Shadows along the Ice* (1985), *Dakota Dream* (1986), and *Be My Neat-Heart* (2006). Kathleen Eagle (b. 1947), who taught at Fort Yates for seventeen years, has written more than forty books, including *A Class Act* (1985). Janet Spaeth (b. 1950) has written several romances, including *Angels Roost* (2003) and *Rose Kelly* (2006), as well as the critical study *Laura Ingalls Wilder* (1987). Lois Greiman is the author of over twenty romance novels, including works in multiple series, such as the Highland Brides, the Highland Rogues, Sedonia, Chrissy McMullen, and the Witches of Mayfair. Roxanne Henke (b. 1953) writes Christian and inspirational novels dealing with medical and family problems. Among these are *After Anne* (2002), *Finding Ruth* (2003), and *Learning to Fly* (2008).

Science Fiction: Poet Thomas McGrath published a futuristic, dystopian satire in *The Gates of Ivory, the Gates of Horn* (1957), in which "the Investigator," overcome by guilt, indicts himself in a smog-filled world in which robotic squirrels collect plastic acorns amid tin trees and the Dakotas have become part of an "Unoccupied Country" between the two coasts. William Borden's *Superstoe* (1967) is a satiric novel about peace in an increasingly small world threatened with destruction and a plan to control government and improve society. Much of *Ancient Shores* (1996) by Jack McDevitt (b. 1935) is set in North Dakota and deals with the consequences after a farmer unearths a strange sailboat in his wheat field.

Literary Awards and Prizes: According to the Office of the Governor, the Theodore Roosevelt Roughrider Award, established during the Dakota Territory Centennial in 1961, recognizes "present or former North Dakotans who have been influenced by this state in achieving national recognition in their fields of endeavor, thereby reflecting credit and honor upon North Dakota and its citizens." Literary North Dakotans who have received the award include Eric Sevareid, Louis L'Amour, Era Bell Thompson, Larry Woiwode, and Louise Erdrich.

Since 1977 the North Dakota Council on the Arts has recognized those "individuals and organizations that have made outstanding contributions to the arts in the state." Frederick Walsh (1987) and Peter Schickele (1991) have been recognized.

Since 1992 the English Department at the University of North Dakota has presented awards to outstanding BA and MA or PhD graduates. Named for Maxwell Anderson, the Maxi Awards have been presented to one excellent writer annually.

SELECTED WORKS: North Dakota's literary heritage is rich and varied. Readers interested in familiarizing themselves with some of the most important works are directed especially to the following. For the early period, Marie L. McLaughlin's *Myths and Legends of the Sioux* (1916) and *Earth Lodge Tales from the Upper Missouri: Traditional Stories of the Arikara, Hidatsa, and Mandan* (1978), edited by Douglas R. Parks, A. Wesley Jones, and Robert C. Hollow, are important written sources of oral storytelling; the latter provides the stories in their original American Indian languages with parallel English translations. Gilbert L. Wilson's *Goodbird the Indian: His Story* (1914) contains Mandan and Hidatsa Indian stories. Clay Jenkinson's *A Vast and Open Plain: The Writings of the Lewis and Clark Expedition in North*

Dakota, 1804–1806 (2003) compiles journals produced by various members of the Lewis and Clark expedition. Two books about the transition between the Indian and military periods are Elizabeth Bacon Custer's *"Boots and Saddles": or, Life in Dakota with General Custer* (1885), presenting a woman's view of the Great Plains and detailed descriptions of military life; and James McLaughlin's *My Friend the Indian* (1910), which provides interesting views of the life of an Indian agent.

Ranch Life and the Hunting-Trail (1888) by Theodore Roosevelt describes the early years of open ranching in western Dakota. Mary Dodge Woodward's *The Checkered Years* (1937) presents the bonanza farm period from 1884 to 1888. Lucy Johnston Sypher's fictionalized autobiographical books for children, starting with *The Edge of Nowhere* (1972), are based on her memories of 1916–1917 in Wales, North Dakota. Erling Nicolai Rolfsrud's many books for children include *Gopher Tails for Papa* (1951).

The difficult years of the Great Depression are a source for powerful autobiography and fiction. Era Bell Thompson's *American Daughter* (1946) and Eric Sevareid's *Not So Wild a Dream* (1946) both emphasize a state where neighbors helped one another through difficult times. Lois Phillips Hudson's *The Bones of Plenty* (1962) and *Reapers of the Dust* (1964) concern the reactions of a young girl rejecting a sense of helplessness. Ann Marie Low's *Dust Bowl Diary* (1984) uses elements of her own diary entries from 1928 to 1937.

Good examples of ethnic writing in North Dakota are Norwegian Hans A. Foss's romantic novel *The Cotter's Son* (1884, translation 1963) and Ron Vossler's stories of German Russians in North Dakota in *Horse, I Am Your Mother* (1988). Memorable autobiographies include Lawrence Welk's *Wunnerful, Wunnerful!* (1971) and *Rachel Calof's Story: Jewish Homesteader on the Northern Plains* (1995).

Modern novels about North Dakota include Larry Woiwode's *Beyond the Bedroom Wall* (1975) and *Born Brothers* (1988), exploring his fictional Neumiller family, and Louise Erdrich's LOVE MEDICINE (1984), the best book with which to begin the saga of Erdrich's Ojibwa ancestors. Popular novels such as *How the West Was Won* (1962) were produced by the prolific Louis L'Amour; L'Amour's autobiography is *The Education of a Wandering Man* (1989).

Dramatist Maxwell Anderson's folk play *White Desert* (1923) concerns newly married North Dakota immigrants; his *Both Your Houses* (1933) is a satire about an ineffective Congress. Thomas McGrath's long and influential poem *Letter to an Imaginary Friend* (1962–1985) begins with his experiences as a child during the Great Depression and contains content pertinent to modern American life.

No comprehensive anthology of the whole range of North Dakota literature has yet been compiled. Of the anthologies available, poetry has been best served. Poetry collections include Grace Brown Putnam and Anna Ackerman's *North Dakota Singing* (1936), *Beta Stanzas: Poems by Members of the Beta Stanza of the North Dakota Poetry Society* (1940), and Lydia O. Jackson's *A Peace Garden of Verses* (1967), containing the work of nine North Dakota women poets. *Dacotah Territory: A 10 Year Anthology* (1982) includes a selection of poems from 1971 to 1981. Martha and Jay Meek's *Prairie Volcano: An Anthology of North Dakota Writing* (1995) is the most comprehensive anthology to date, including poetry and prose, but it is limited to fifty contemporary writers.

FURTHER READING:

Bibliographies, Biographies, and Criticism: A study of the state should begin with Elwyn B. Robinson's *History of North Dakota* (1966) and its extensive bibliography. Helen J. Sullivan's *Know Your North Dakota: A Handbook of Information for the Schools of North Dakota* (1929) includes a chapter with summaries of books about North Dakota and by North Dakota authors. Charlotte S. Rosvold and Catherine Philips compiled a literary map of authors published by State Librarian Hazel Webster Byrnes in 1932. See LITERARY MAPS. Edna LaMoore Waldo and Huldah Lucile Winsted compiled *Who's Who among North Dakota Writers* in 1935. The State Library Commission created *North Dakota Books Published within the Past Twenty Years* (1956), *North Dakota Books and Authors: Books Published 1930–1962 and Selected Earlier Books* (1962), and *North Dakota in Print* (1972). The State Library and the State Department of

Public Instruction have periodically compiled lists of books about North Dakota. The Plains Humanities Alliance's Digital Initiative and the North Dakota Center for the Book/North Dakota Humanities Council have also compiled useful listings.

William C. Sherman has written about settlement patterns and cultures. His *Prairie Mosaic: An Ethnic Atlas of Rural North Dakota* (1983) includes settlement maps and discussions of the various cultures. Sherman and Playford V. Thorson edited *Plains Folk: North Dakota's Ethnic History* (1988), with essays by Warren A. Henke, Timothy J. Kloberdanz, Theodore B. Pedeliski, and Robert P. Wilkins.

The Germans from Russia Heritage Collection at North Dakota State University, established in 1978, provides much information about this immigrant group. Some earlier research about the Germans from Russia includes George P. Aberle's *From the Steppes to the Prairies* (1963) and his two-volume *Pioneers and Their Sons* (1964–1969). Shirley Fischer Arends presents the lives and customs of North Dakota immigrants in *The Central Dakota Germans: Their History, Language, and Culture* (1989). David Dreyer and Josette S. Hatter wrote *From the Banat to North Dakota: A History of the German-Hungarian Pioneers in Western North Dakota* (2006).

The lives of North Dakota women are the subject of several studies. Mary Barnes Williams contributed *Fifty Pioneer Mothers of McLean County, North Dakota* (1932). Angela Boleyn's *Quarter Sections and Wide Horizons* (1978) is a two-volume collection of brief biographies of pioneer women published in the *Fargo Forum* from 1931 to 1934. H. Elaine Lindgren's *Land in Her Own Name: Women as Homesteaders in North Dakota* (1991) is a richly illustrated historical study. Barbara Handy-Marchello's *Women of the Northern Plains: Gender and Settlement on the Homestead Frontier, 1870–1930* (2005) considers the role of women in homesteading families. Ann Rathke's *Lady, If You Go into Politics: North Dakota's Women Legislators, 1923–1989* (1992) is about the seventy-two women elected between 1923 and 1989, from women's suffrage to consideration of an equal rights amendment.

A series of four books commissioned in anticipation of the state's centennial in 1989 includes Sherman and Thorson's *Plains Folk: North Dakota's Ethnic History* (1988); *The North Dakota Political Tradition* (1981) by Charles Nelson Glaab and Thomas William Howard; and *North Dakota's Indian Heritage* (1990) by Mary Jane Schneider. A fourth book in the series titled *Dakota: The Literary Heritage of the Northern Prairie State* (1990) by Kathie Ryckman Anderson provides the first comprehensive account of the state's literature; in the epilogue Anderson discusses prior compilations of writers and publications. In 1994 the North Dakota Center for the Book presented a program, *Language of the Land: Journeys into Literary North Dakota*, featuring Kathie Ryckman Anderson, Larry Woiwode, David Solheim, Larry Watson, Louise Erdrich, Lois Phillips Hudson, Kathleen Norris, and Richard Critchfield; some excerpts were published in *North Dakota History*. For that series of programs Anderson provided a literary map of the state that was published in the special literary issue of *North Dakota History* 62.3 (Summer 1995).

Libraries and Repositories: Collections in the state are located at the State Historical Society of North Dakota in Bismarck, at the North Dakota Institute for Regional Studies at North Dakota State University in Fargo, and in the Elwyn B. Robinson Department of Special Collections at the University of North Dakota in Grand Forks. Larry Woiwode has donated some of his papers to his parents' alma mater, Valley City State University. Maxwell Anderson donated some of his manuscripts to the University of North Dakota; other manuscripts are found at the Harry Ransom Center at the University of Texas at Austin, including that of Anderson's first play for Broadway, *White Desert* (1923), set in North Dakota. The Burdick Collection at the State Historical Society of North Dakota preserves some early American Indian narratives. Audrey Porsche's *Yuto'keca: Transitions: The Burdick Collection* (1987) includes photos of many items and an essay about Burdick and the collection.

KATHIE RYCKMAN ANDERSON   JESSIE, NORTH DAKOTA

O–Q

O PIONEERS!

HISTORY: Although she had already published a novel, *Alexander's Bridge,* in 1912, WILLA CATHER (1873–1947) considered *O Pioneers!* (1913) her first novel, meaning that the book was the first full-length work in which she had made use of her most natural source of materials: the westering generation she had come to know intimately and to admire during her girlhood in and around Red Cloud, NEBRASKA. Since the 1890s she had used these youthful experiences to produce a number of well-received shorter works of fiction, some of which had been collected in her volume *The Troll Garden* (1905). These early stories, generally dark in tone and at times even morose, served as forerunners to *O Pioneers!* In them Cather demonstrated her tendency, one she later disavowed, to follow the lead of naturalistic writers of the day, including (HANNIBAL) HAMLIN GARLAND (1860–1940), (HERMAN) THEODORE DREISER (1871–1945), and (BENJAMIN) FRANK(LIN) NORRIS (JR.) (1870–1902), whose vision of life was generally downbeat and sometimes even tragic. See also REALISM AND NATURALISM.

Early magazine stories such as "Lou, the Prophet" (1892), "On the Divide" (1896), and "Peter Sadelak, Father of Anton" (1900) tend to be naturalistic and heavily laced with the bitterness of characters who suffer physically and psychologically from the harshness and loneliness rampant on Nebraska's barren plains. But in *O Pioneers!* Cather managed to look away from many of the extreme hardships she had observed in frontier Nebraska to achieve a more balanced viewpoint by focusing instead on a successful and somewhat larger-than-life heroine, Alexandra Bergson. Cather's new determination was to avoid emphasizing the more unpleasant aspects of establishing a new society on the harsh plains of Nebraska. This change is strongly implied by her omission of sixteen years between parts 1 and 2 of Alexandra's story, the years of greatest trial, of slogging through the discouragements of drought and severe plagues of insects, and of strong temptation to retreat to eastern areas where the conditions of farming seemed less forbidding.

O Pioneers! had its beginnings in a story called "Alexandra," which Cather started in 1911 after completing revisions of *Alexander's Bridge.* By the middle of 1912 she had written another story, "The White Mulberry Tree," about the murder of adulterous lovers by the woman's jealous husband. Perceiving the close connections between these two stories, Cather linked them, creating what she, as quoted by Elizabeth Shepley Sergeant (1881–1965) in *Willa Cather: A Memoir* (1953), referred to as a "two-part pastoral," one an epic of the pioneer era and the other a tragic romance (86).

The novel appeared in June 1913. Reviewers, by and large, were quick to recognize Cather's unique contribution. Gardner W. Wood, writing in the July 1913 issue of *Mc-Clure's Magazine,* took note of the many authors who by that time had treated the West in fiction, but declared *O Pioneers!* "a totally new kind of story" out of the prairie (199). FLOYD DELL (1887–1969) noted in the July 25, 1913, issue of the *Chicago Evening Post's Friday Literary Review* that Cather's renewal of the theme of taming western lands was accomplished with a touch of genius. Other reviewers were generous with the use of such terms as "herculean" and "honestly wrought." Wood, in his *McClure's* article, praised Cather's vital portrait of Alexandra as an image of "triumphant womanhood—a sort of Nebraskan Valkyr" (199). Cather's writing was described as "solid," "profoundly true," and "well-balanced," and her book was praised as a work to "read and enjoy, and to read again." To more modern eyes it may seem surprising that only one reviewer, in the October 1913 *Sewanee Review,* called attention to Cather's "feminist theme" (509–10), an emphasis that contemporary readers recognize and appreciate.

SIGNIFICANCE: With helpful advice from her fellow writer Sarah Orne Jewett (1849–1909), Cather was able to make unique use of the materials she naturally possessed: stories that stemmed from the life in which she had been immersed as a child during the 1880s and 1890s. She frankly acknowledged that much of her writing was grounded in the experience of riding her horse about the countryside of Webster County in south central Nebraska. Here she encountered the new farms established by recent immigrants. She was drawn particularly to the Swedish, Bohemian, and German farm wives, observing them with care, hearing their tales drawn from fascinating family histories, and participating vicariously in their American histories on wild plains only

ALEXANDRA

Willa Cather's *O Pioneers!* frontispiece illustration of Alexandra by Clarence F. Underwood. Houghton Mifflin Co., 1913. Image courtesy of the University of Kentucky Special Collections Research Center

recently recognized officially as parts of a state of the Union.

In *O Pioneers!* Willa Cather took as her theme the human struggle to create on the untamed Midwestern plains a successful society grounded in agriculture. The difficulties of accomplishing this agrarian vision were daunting. The land was windswept both summer and winter, rainfall was barely adequate to produce a crop, and the countryside was subject to enormous temperature fluctuations that produced long, arctic winters and brief, tropical summers. This struggle is introduced on the opening page of *O Pioneers!* which depicts a January day on which "the little town of Hanover, anchored on a windy Nebraska tableland, was trying not to be blown away" (1992 edition 11).

Writing without a traditional plotline, Cather composed her novel in a fashion that would typify her later fiction: a chronological series of narrative vignettes, like panels in a broad mural, in each of which her Swedish heroine, Alexandra Bergson, would be important. The novel's consistency of place and its ever-forward-moving sequence in time help the story achieve unity, but in the end it is Alexandra who ties the novel together. It is her story, and other characters serve to display her hopes and strengths, often by way of contrast.

The Bergsons move into a partially settled Nebraska in which the only available and affordable lands are high on the underwatered divide between streams (capitalized in the novel as a place name, "the Divide). It is a polyglot neighborhood up there. The "Americans," the first wave of settlers, have already claimed the valuable river bottoms, leaving the Divide to be settled by a rich diversity of immigrant Swedes, Norwegians, French, Russians, Germans, and Bohemians. Alexandra soon develops a love for the untamed land and trusts in its ability to provide a settler with a good living and eventually to serve as a basis for a prosperous farm community. But the weather cannot always be counted on, and when lack of rain causes crop failures, many are discouraged, ready to sell out and retreat to the more dependable East. Among these are Alexandra's brothers, Lou and Oscar Bergson. "There's no use of us trying to stick it out, just to be stubborn," argues Lou. "There's something in knowing when to quit" (57). But Alexandra responds from the depth of her feeling: "Down there [on the bottoms] they have a little certainty, but up here with us there is a big chance. We must have faith in the high land" (63).

Her instinct is to stick it out, purchasing nearby farms as their discouraged owners surrender, many returning to wage-earner jobs in eastern factories. Time bears out the wisdom of Alexandra's choice. When the plentiful rains return after a period of drought, the Bergson properties are among the richest farms in the territory, and everyone knows "that the farmer [is] a woman, Alexandra Bergson" (80).

Each section of the novel advances the plot and the sequence of time as Alexandra's story is told. "Part I: The Wild Land" concerns her girlhood and then the years of hardship farming the Divide. "Part II: Neighboring Fields" takes place sixteen years later and concerns the growth of Alexandra's brother Emil and her developing feelings for neighbor Carl Linstrum. "Part III: Winter Memories" tells of the deteriorating marriage between a pair of young Bohemians, Frank and Marie Shabata, and depicts Alexandra's closeness to Emil and to Carl, both of whom travel far away from Nebraska but keep in touch with Alexandra by mail. "Part IV: The White Mulberry Tree" centers on the adulterous love of Emil Bergson and Marie Shabata, on Frank Shabata's discovery of this liaison, and on his precipitate murder of Emil and Marie. "Part V: "Alexandra" completes the novel with Alexandra's forgiveness of Frank Shabata, now in the penitentiary for his crime, and the return of Carl Linstrum, who, Cather strongly suggests, will soon marry Alexandra.

A powerful secondary theme in *O Pioneers!* is loss, especially the conviction that human beings face inevitable failure in their attempts to control circumstances. Cather sounds this theme in the novel's epigraph, her poem "Prairie Spring," which contains a portrait of Nebraska's countryside: "Rich and sombre and always silent / Sullen fires of sunset, fading, / The eternal unresponsive sky." Against this immutable fact is set the impatient force of "Youth with its insupportable sweetness, / Its fierce necessity, / Its sharp desire" (5). Challenging nature with its hopes and efforts, youth seems destined to lose because, as Alexandra acknowledges, "the land belongs to the future. . . . That's the way it seems to me. How many of the names on the county clerk's plat will be there in fifty years? . . . We come and go, but the land is always here." Because life is so fleeting, the best an individual can hope for is to own the land "for a little while" (272–73).

Scholars of Midwestern literature have noted the novel's importance as the first book in Cather's great pastoral trilogy, which includes *My Ántonia* (1918) and *A Lost Lady* (1923), depicting the beginning, apex, and decline of the westering movement. The ethic of *O Pioneers!* prefigures the "land ethic" of WISCONSIN environmentalist ALDO

LEOPOLD (1887–1948), exemplified by the hermit Ivar, who lives in harmony with the land and treats wild creatures with respect. Alexandra's protection of Ivar, together with her loving transformation of the hostile Nebraska wilderness into an orderly and productive farm, links her to this ethic and establishes her as an embodiment of Jeffersonian agrarianism. The novel also serves to document, through the story of the Swedish Bergsons' pioneering experiences, the significant Scandinavian influx into the Midwest in the nineteenth century.

Given the status of *O Pioneers!* as a classic, it is not surprising that later novels about women on the Midwestern prairies, such as *Dalva* (1988) by JIM (JAMES THOMAS) HARRISON (1937–2016) and *A Thousand Acres* (1991) by JANE (GRAVES) SMILEY (b. 1949), bear its influence. The novel's legacy also includes a 1992 film adaptation, directed for television by Glenn Jordan and starring Jessica Lange, and a 1990 musical, starring Mary McDonnell, with a script by Darrah Cloud and music by Kim D. Sherman. This version was filmed for PBS's *American Playhouse* series in 1991, directed by Kirk Browning and Kevin Kuhlke. The script was published in 1996.

IMPORTANT EDITIONS: *O Pioneers!* was published in June 1913 by Houghton Mifflin simultaneously with an English edition by William Heinemann. After its debut *O Pioneers!* retained a wide readership and was reprinted from the original plates dozens of times throughout the 1920s and 1930s, its author seemingly content with her novel as originally written and published. Even in the "Scholarly Edition" of 1937, Knopf editors made fewer than one hundred minor changes in punctuation and spelling, including the change in the flower name from "zenias" to "zinnias." The result has been that every printing of *O Pioneers!* has been very much the same book, differing only in binding, paper, and pagination. The readership of the novel has also endured, one mark of a classic. Whereas early reprintings were produced in the range of 1,000 to 2,000 copies, recent reprints have averaged above 12,000 copies. Susan J. Rosowski and Charles W. Mignon edited the scholarly edition of *O Pioneers!* published in 1992 by the University of Nebraska Press. Cather scholars will appreciate the exten-

sive back matter, which includes a historical essay, explanatory notes, and textual commentary. The novel has been translated into many languages, including Bengali, Chinese, German, Italian, Japanese, and Swedish.

FURTHER READING: Cather comments on *O Pioneers!* in her 1931 essay "My First Novels (There Were Two)," in the 1949 volume *On Writing: Critical Studies on Writing as an Art* (89–98). Elizabeth Shepley Sergeant, Cather's close friend, deals with the production of the novel in *Willa Cather: A Memoir* (1953), as does Cather's companion Edith Lewis in *Willa Cather Living: A Personal Record* (1953). Helpful biographical and critical studies include Sharon O'Brien's *Willa Cather: The Emerging Voice* (1987) and Philip Gerber's *Willa Cather* (revised edition 1995). Valuable critical studies of *O Pioneers!* include "The Brave Are Homeless," in Joseph R. Urgo's *Willa Cather and the Myth of American Migration* (1995); and Demaree C. Peck's "A Pioneer in Art: Staking Out the Claim to Consciousness in *O Pioneers!*" in *The Imaginative Claims of the Artist in Willa Cather's Fiction* (1996), which identifies the influence of Ralph Waldo Emerson's *Nature* (1836) and Henri Bergson's *Creative Evolution* (1907; English translation, 1911) on Cather's attempts to preserve her inner self from the annihilating threat of the barren Nebraska landscape during her most impressionable years. A chapter in Susan J. Rosowski's *The Voyage Perilous: Willa Cather's Romanticism* (1986) appraises *O Pioneers!* as a modern pastoral grounded in Virgil's *Eclogues* and Ovid's *Metamorphoses*. A chapter in Sally Peltier Harvey's *Redefining the American Dream: The Novels of Willa Cather* (1995) discusses *O Pioneers!* as an example of Willa Cather's belief that it is possible, though difficult, to achieve both material prosperity and genuine happiness in America. In *Cosmopolitan Vistas: American Regionalism and Literary Value* (2004) Tom Lutz discusses the multiple perspectives of *O Pioneers!* as an example of the kind of cosmopolitanism that he believes characterizes the best regional literature. William Barillas's chapter on Cather in *The Midwestern Pastoral: Place and Landscape in Literature of the American Heartland* (2006) includes a critique of *O Pioneers!* that emphasizes the novel's elision of the injustices done by the

pioneers both to the original Native American inhabitants and to the environment.
PHILIP GERBER

THE COLLEGE AT BROCKPORT,
STATE UNIVERSITY OF NEW YORK

OHIO

Ohio was admitted to the Union as the seventeenth state by act of Congress on February 19, 1803. Before statehood it was part of the Northwest Territory (1787–1803).
Area: 44,826 square miles
Land: 40,861 square miles
Water: 3,965 square miles
Population (2010 census): 11,536,504

OVERVIEW: Ohio, the first Midwestern state, is marked by a number of large, industrialized cities, such as its capital, Columbus, and CINCINNATI, CLEVELAND, and Toledo. Yet despite these large urban areas, much of Ohio still remains agricultural. For over two hundred years Ohio has experienced change and diversity, and the state's literature reflects that. As part of the Northwest Territory from 1787 to 1803, the Ohio Valley attracted foreign explorers who generated a significant amount of travel literature.

Ohio's rich contributions to Midwestern and U.S. literature lie in a number of areas tracing the settlement and development of the Midwest, particularly exploring the territory and setting up burgeoning farms in the fertile plains and valleys. Early tracts describe this exploration, partly by those who would exploit the new region's resources, partly by those who would convert the Native Americans and support new congre-

© Karen Greasley, 2014

gations in the tiny villages and growing communities, and partly by those with an eye to political advantage. The first novels record these efforts and trace village and town life both from an idealistic and nostalgic point of view and through the eyes of those who rebelled against restriction and parochialism. As the cities increased along with industry, education, modernity, and corruption, the state's literature became more sophisticated, and poetry and drama reflected those trends.

Cincinnati was the literary center of Ohio's early history, but today the state's literary output is more widely diffused, as is its variety of literary products. From journalism to children's books and from poetry to realistic fiction, literature has been produced by native Ohioans, as well as by those who passed through the state or remained for a time.

Ohio writers have excelled in a number of specialized genres. Because the state was home to authors of early full-length detective novels like *Oakshaw; or, The Victims of Avarice: A Tale of Intrigue* (1855) by William T. Coggeshall (1824–1867), it is not surprising that some of the nation's finest detective and mystery writers have hailed from Ohio. Children's literature is also an area of strength. Because many large cities possessed major newspapers, many prominent Ohio writers and humorists spent part of their lives as journalists. Since the mid-nineteenth century Ohio literature has also maintained a powerful African American voice, and a number of prominent poets have called Ohio home. As the first Midwestern state, Ohio has shaped a number of talented writers, and a distinctive, diverse body of literature has emerged.

HISTORY AND SIGNIFICANCE: The diverse and voluminous nature of the literary contributions about Ohio and by its authors begins with early discovery and EXPLORATION ACCOUNTS. There is a substantial body of fiction; its subgenres include FARM LITERATURE, AUTOBIOGRAPHY and memoirs, poetry, and DRAMA. More popular forms of fiction also include MYSTERY AND DETECTIVE FICTION, the DIME NOVEL, romance novels, SCIENCE FICTION AND FANTASY, religious literature, CHILDREN'S AND YOUNG-ADULT LITERATURE, GRAPHIC NOVELS and COMIC BOOKS, and lesbian and gay literature. As the first site of PRINTING AND PUBLISHING and NEWSPAPER JOURNALISM in the Midwest, Ohio's importance in these areas is significant. Ohio's participation in the Federal Writers Project and the state's literary accomplishments and awards to Ohio authors are mentioned.

Exploration Accounts: The area that came to be known as Ohio has provided substantial travel literature by explorers, representing the first writing in the region. Although the Ohio region was part of the French Pays des Illinois territory, it did not generate the published exploration accounts that the GREAT LAKES and the Mississippi River inspired, such as those associated with Pierre François Xavier de Charlevoix (1682–1761), Jacques Marquette (1637–1675), and Louis Joliet (1645–1700). The earliest known account by a European explorer of the Ohio country is that of Pierre Joseph Céloron de Blainville (1683–1759). In 1749 Blainville (also known as Bienville), a native of Montreal, Canada, was charged with leading an expedition into Ohio to claim lands for France and prevent the English Ohio Company from acquiring it by right of settlement. However, Blainville's narrative, *Journal de la Campagne, que moy Céloron . . . dans la Belle Rivière . . .* , was not published until it appeared in Pierre Margry's (1818–1894) six-volume collection *Découvertes et établissements des Français dans l'ouest et dans le sud de l'Amérique Septentrionale, 1614–1754* (1876–1886).

Christopher Gist (1706–1759) was the first to write a description of the Ohio country in English. As a surveyor for the Ohio Company of Virginia, he explored the area in 1750 and again with George Washington in 1753. His diary from the first trip, "A Journal of Christopher Gist's Journey . . . down the Ohio . . ." was published as an appendix to *A Topographical Description of Such Parts of North America as Are Contained in the (Annexed) Map of the Middle British Colonies and in North America* (1776) by Thomas Pownall (1722–1805). As geographer of the United States, Thomas Hutchins (1730–1789) began to survey the land subsumed in the Northwest Territory, but before doing so he published a description of the Ohio region as part of his *A Topographical Description of Virginia, Pennsylvania, Maryland, and North Carolina . . .* (1778), based on his personal reconnaissance as a British soldier in the late 1760s. John May (1748–1812) of Boston traveled through Ohio; his notes on the country and its early settlers were published much later as *Journal and Letters of Colonel John May . . . Relative to Two Journeys to the Ohio Country in 1788 and '89 . . .* (1873).

Rev. Thaddeus Mason Harris (1768–1842) compiled his 1803 experiences in the Ohio backwoods and published them, along with supplementary maps, as *The Journal of a Tour into the Territory Northwest of the Allegheny Mountains; Made in the Spring of the Year 1803: With a Geographical and Historical Account of the State of Ohio* (1805). Thomas Ashe (1770–1835), a British traveler, wrote a disdainful, vituperative account in *Travels in America, Performed in 1806, for the Purpose of Exploring the Rivers Alleghany, Monongahela, Ohio and Mississippi . . .* (1808). To counter Ashe's exaggerations and falsehoods, Christian Schultz (ca. 1770–1814) traveled in the same areas and wrote *Travels on an Inland Voyage through the States of New York, Pennsylvania, Virginia, Ohio, Kentucky and Tennessee . . .* (1810), including a substantial Ohio component. British literary ridicule of Americans was a recurring theme. It reappeared in Frances Milton Trollope's (1779–1863) well-known *Domestic Manners of the Americans* (1832), based on her experiences and observations while living in Cincinnati. A more accurate and objective account of Ohio residents and topography by a British tourist, *A Ramble of Six Thousand Miles through the United States of America* (1832), was written by Simon Ansley Ferrall (d. 1844).

Fiction: Ohio's earliest published fictional works appear to have been reprints of other popular works. First among these is *History of the Captivity and Sufferings of Mrs. Maria Martin, Who Was Six Years a Slave in Algiers . . . Written by Herself,* a very popular fictitious Barbary pirate CAPTIVITY NARRATIVE originally published in 1806. The Ohio edition was printed in St. Clairsville in 1815. Another Ohio reprint of a popular novel first published in London in 1791 was *Charlotte Temple: A Tale of Truth* by Susanna Haswell Rowson (1762–1824). The Ohio edition was published in 1827 and was reprinted numerous times.

The earliest short story with what is believed to be an Ohio setting is "Bass-Island Cottage" (1824), a work by Benjamin Drake (1795–1841), which appeared in the first issue of the *Cincinnati Literary Gazette* on January 1, 1824. More than a decade later, Drake's collection of short stories, *Tales and Sketches, from the Queen City* (1838), explored frontier life in the Cincinnati area.

The anonymously written *Morton: A Tale of the Revolution* (1828), first published in Cincinnati, was among the earliest novels published in Ohio. The first novel published in Ohio by an Ohio resident appears to have been *The Shoshone Valley* (1830), published in Cincinnati by the author, Timothy Flint (1780–1840). The novel's fictional setting, however, is in the far West, not in Ohio. Flint wrote several novels, including *Francis Berrian; or, The Mexican Patriot* (1826) and *George Mason, the Young Backwoodsman; or 'Don't Give Up the Ship.' A Story of the Mississippi* (1829). He also helped develop the legend of Daniel Boone by compiling the *Biographical Memoir of Daniel Boone, the First Settler of Kentucky* (1833).

The Young Emigrants: A Tale Designed for Young Persons (1830) by Susan Anne Livingston Ridley Sedgwick (1788–1867) relates the story of an immigrant family of five from England who establish a homestead near Cincinnati. A novel partially set in Ohio was penned by James Strange French (1807–1886). His *Elkswatawa; or, The Prophet of the West* (1836) features the Shawnee leader Tecumseh, his brother, Tenskwatawa the Prophet, and William Henry Harrison. PAMILLA W. BALL (1790–1838) published a number of fiction and nonfiction pieces on pioneer life in local newspapers, including "The Maid of the Muskingum" (1837), which favorably compares Ohio's western setting with that of Virginia. JULIA LOUISE CORY DUMONT (1794–1857) published most of her short stories in periodicals, including "Ashton Grey" (1832), which concerns an Ohio River boatman; it was included in her collection *Life Sketches from Common Paths: A Series of American Tales* (1856).

Philadelphian Emerson Bennett (1822–1905) lived in Cincinnati from 1844 to 1850 and while there wrote several sensational frontier adventures using Ohio settings and characters. Some of these are *The League of the Miami* (1845), concerning a band of horse thieves operating in the Miami valley; *Mike Fink: A Legend of the Ohio* (1848), which relates episodes in the life of a famous keelboatman; *Kate Clarendon; or, Necromancy in the Wilderness* (1848), which features the environs of the Little Miami River; and *The Forest Rose: A Tale of the Frontier* (1850), a story about early settlers near Lancaster and the Hocking River in the 1790s. Henry Barnes (fl. 1850), a physician, wrote *The Faithful Hostler; or, Retributive Justice* (1850), a tale set in Medina and Cincinnati in 1838.

Uncle Tom's Cabin (1852), the famed antislavery novel by Harriet Beecher Stowe (1811–1896), was one of the most influential novels to come out of Ohio. Stowe drew on stories she heard during her eighteen-year residence in Cincinnati to help craft this story. First published serially in *The National Era* starting in 1851, the volume was extremely successful and is marked by many memorable scenes depicting the impact of slavery, such as that of Eliza escaping across the ice of the Ohio River. A contemporary of Stowe's, fellow Cincinnati resident CAROLINE LEE (WHITING) HENTZ (1800–1856), published a rebuttal, the novel *The Planter's Northern Bride* (1854). Although she wrote a number of other works, it is this pro-slavery work for which Hentz is remembered. While in Cincinnati she wrote and published the novel *Lovell's Folly* (1833), which used recognizable Cincinnatians and was withdrawn to avoid charges of libel.

MARY HARTWELL CATHERWOOD (1847–1902) contributed *Craque-o'-Doom* (1881), an autobiographical novel based on her unhappy childhood in the fictional town of Barne, a thinly disguised Hebron, Ohio. Her collection of short stories *Queen of the Swamp, and Other Plain Americans* (1899) contains a number of works using Ohio as a setting, including "The Queen of the Swamp," "The Stirring-Off," "Sweetness," "Serena," and "Rose Day."

A native of Meigs County, Ohio, AMBROSE (GWINNETT) BIERCE (1842–ca.1914) is best known for his short stories of horror and the macabre and those based on his experiences during the Civil War. Of the former, two stories in the collection *Tales of Soldiers and Civilians* (1891), "The Suitable Surroundings" and "The Boarded Window," are set in rural forested areas near Cincinnati.

One of Ohio's favorite literary sons is Martins Ferry, Ohio, native WILLIAM DEAN HOWELLS (1837–1920). Although his journalistic résumé is impressive, Howells is most widely recognized for his realistic fiction. As the author of hundreds of works in a variety of genres, Howells strongly reflected the influence of his home state. The discovery of natural gas fields at Findlay and its subsequent industrialization provided the inspiration for the fictional town of Moffitt, INDIANA, in *A Hazard of New Fortunes* (1890). *The Kentons* (1902) follows an Ohio family's trip to Europe. Ohio's significant fiction authors also include CHARLES WADDELL CHESNUTT (1858–1932), an African American from Cleveland, Ohio. Chesnutt, better known for his dialect stories and novels set in the South, wrote a number of stories based on his experiences and observations in Cleveland. Among these "Groveland" (Cleveland) stories are "The Wife of His Youth," "Uncle Wellington's Wives," and "A Matter of Principle"; they are included in his collection *The Wife of His Youth, and Other Stories of the Color Line* (1899).

CLARENCE DARROW (1857–1938), the renowned lawyer from Farmdale, Ohio, earned his literary stripes with his fictional memoir *Farmington* (1904), focusing on a boy growing up in a small Ohio town. Zanesville's (PEARL) ZANE GREY (1872–1939) was a tremendously successful writer of westerns, blazing a trail for those who followed him. He was the author of more than ninety books; his three-volume Ohio River trilogy consists of *Betty Zane* (1903), *The Spirit of the Border* (1906), and *The Last Trail* (1909).

Ohio's largest cities figure prominently in a number of novels. DOROTHY (DOROTHEA FRANCES CANFIELD) FISHER (1879–1958) drew on her experiences in Columbus in writing *The Bent Twig* (1915) and *The Deepening Stream* (1930); her earlier novel *The Squirrel Cage* (1912) takes place in the fictional town of Endbury, Ohio. Fisher portrays Ohio and the Midwest generally as places from which to escape. Henry Thew Stephenson (1870–1957) looks backward to the Cincinnati of "olden time" in *Christie Bell of Goldenrod Valley: A Tale of Southern Indiana and Cincinnati in the Olden Time* (1918). See also CINCINNATI and CLEVELAND.

Noted realist (JOSEPH) BRAND WHITLOCK (1869–1934) used the town of Macochee as a fictional substitute for his actual hometown, Urbana, Ohio, in *The Happy Average* (1904) and *The Fall Guy* (1912). More than a decade later, Whitlock returned to Macochee with his novel *J. Hardin and Son* (1923), in which mass-produced, flashy, and cheap but shoddily made buggies displace the much superior and long-lasting but more expensive buggies of the town's master buggy craftsman, J. Hardin. Macochee appeared yet again in *Brand Whitlock's "The Buckeyes": A Story of Politics and Abolitionism in an Ohio Town, 1836–1845* (1977), an unfinished novel edited by Paul Miller. In addition, several short stories in Whitlock's collection *The Gold Brick* (1910) also feature Macochee as a locale.

SHERWOOD ANDERSON (1876–1941), one of Ohio's most remarkable and influential writers, wrote one of the state's signature novels, *WINESBURG, OHIO* (1919), a group of interrelated short stories that delve into life in an Ohio small town. Although he was born in Camden, Ohio, Anderson eventually settled in Clyde, which provided the basis for his fictional town, Winesburg. Anderson followed this acclaimed work with *Poor White* (1920), a novel tracing the transformation of Bidwell in southeastern Ohio from an agrarian community into an industrial center. Short stories by Anderson, including "Corn Planting" and "I'm a Fool," focus on Ohio farm life. Anderson again used Bidwell in a number of short stories, including "The Egg," collected in *The Triumph of the Egg* (1921), and "The Sad Horn-Blowers" and "An Ohio Pagan," collected in *Horses and Men* (1924). Other significant Anderson works not set in Ohio include *Windy McPherson's Son* (1916), *Marching Men* (1917), and *The Triumph of the Egg* (1921).

JIM TULLY (1888–1947), born near St. Marys, Ohio, was a novelist and journalist who spent part of his life as a hobo. He wrote several autobiographical novels, all of which drew on his Ohio experience. *Emmett Lawler* (1922) and *Shanty Irish* (1928), in particular, focus on his family life in St. Marys. *Beggars* of Life: A Hobo Autobiography (1924) details Tully's life on the road.

FANNIE HURST (1885–1968) of Hamilton used Ohio locales as the setting of her books A President Is Born (1927) and Back Street (1931). Ohio small towns are featured in her short fiction as well, including stories she wrote for Cosmopolitan Magazine: "Back Pay" (1919), "A House of Men" (1925), and "Song of Life" (1926). DAWN POWELL (1896–1965) of Mount Gilead, a village north of Columbus, published six novels set in Ohio: She Walks in Beauty (1928), The Bride's House (1929), Dance Night (1930), The Tenth Moon (1932), The Story of a Country Boy (1934), and My Home Is Far Away (1944). Powell was a satirist whose works expressed great dissatisfaction with the small-town life she herself lived.

Born in Columbus, JAMES (GROVER) THURBER (1894–1961) is widely recognized as one of America's great humorists. Among his twenty-seven books are The Owl in the Attic, and Other Perplexities (1931) and The Thurber Carnival (1945). Thurber also published two volumes of sketches steeped in social consciousness: Fables for Our Time and Famous Poems (1940) and Further Fables for Our Time (1956). His best-known story is "The Secret Life of Walter Mitty" (1942). In a statement prepared for his acceptance of the 1953 Ohioana Sesquicentennial medal, Thurber acknowledged his enduring connection to the Buckeye State: "I am never very far away from Ohio in my thoughts, and the clocks that strike in my dreams are often the clocks of Columbus."

Central Standard Time (1937) was penned by Ironton-born HARLAN HENTHORNE HATCHER (1898–1998). This proletarian novel about striking industrial workers in a small Ohio town is one of three novels using Ohio River valley settings. Tunnel Hill (1931) and Patterns of Wolfpen (1934) both examine the development of that valley. Living in Springfield, Ohio, for his first twenty-eight years before moving to CHICAGO, W(illiam) R(iley) Burnett (1899–1982) wrote Goodbye to the Past: Scenes from the Life of William Meadows (1934), describing the arrival of a young man with a small fortune in a middle-sized Ohio town and his gradual rise to prominence. His novel King Cole (1936) concerns the reelection campaign of an Ohio governor hoping to

use that victory as a stepping-stone to the White House.

WALTER (EDWIN) HAVIGHURST (1901–1994) wrote many Ohio novels. The Quiet Shore (1937) is considered his best work; it follows multiple generations of a family living along Lake Erie. Signature of Time (1949) fictionalizes Kelleys Island, which serves as a refuge for a returning war correspondent.

CONRAD (MICHAEL) RICHTER (1890–1968) published a trilogy set in the southeastern Ohio wilderness. The Trees (1940) was the first novel in the series, followed by The Fields (1946), which explores the emergence of a wilderness community. The final volume, The Town (1950), portrays the development of a pioneer town. These three novels were later collected into one volume and issued as The Awakening Land (1966). HERBERT GOLD (b. 1924) was born in Cleveland and grew up in nearby Lakewood, which served as the setting in his debut novel, Birth of a Hero (1951). He also wrote of his Ohio years in Fathers: A Novel in the Form of a Memoir (1967), and Family: A Novel in the Form of a Memoir (1981).

In the 1950s Marguerite Allis (1887–1958) published four historical novels that explored Ohio pioneer life through the experiences of the fictional Field family. Now We Are Free (1952) concerns their migration to the Western Reserve wilderness from Connecticut after the Revolutionary War. To Keep Us Free (1953) continues their story through the War of 1812 with visits to Marietta and Chillicothe. Brave Pursuit (1954) covers the years from 1815 to the 1820s, using as background the development of the Ohio and Erie Canal. The final book, Rising Storm (1955), finds the family in Cincinnati in the 1830s amid the growing anti-slavery movement and Underground Railroad activities. These books may have been written to commemorate Ohio's sesquicentennial.

A Cleveland native, DON ROBERTSON (1929–1999), used that city as a vital backdrop for his so-called Cleveland trilogy: The Greatest Thing since Sliced Bread (1965), The Sum and Total of Now (1966), and The Greatest Thing That Almost Happened (1970). These novels concern the youth and adolescence of a boy from 1944 to 1953. In Paradise Falls (1968) Robertson uses a small Ohio town to exemplify America's growth and changes during the final third of the nineteenth century.

During his career Jack M. Bickham (1930–1997) authored more than seventy-five novels under a variety of pseudonyms, many of them westerns and mysteries. His 1982 novel *I Still Dream about Columbus* shows the effect of the Depression on one family in Columbus during the 1930s as seen through the eyes of a twelve-year-old boy. In *Owen Glen* (1950) Ben Ames Williams (1889–1953) describes the gritty Appalachian mining region and the nascent United Mine Workers of America of the 1890s as a young coal miner steadily rises in the union hierarchy.

Goodbye, Columbus (1959), the novella and short-story collection by Philip Roth (b. 1933), won the National Book Award in 1960, but rather than telling of life in Columbus, Ohio, it focuses instead on Jewish American life and social climbing. JACK MATTHEWS (1925–2013), a product of the Columbus suburbs, has published more than a dozen books, some of them focusing on Ohio. His short-story collections *Tales of the Ohio Land* (1980) and *Storyhood As We Know It, and Other Tales* (1993) make significant use of the Ohio milieu, while *The Charisma Campaigns* (1972) features a used-car dealer in a small Ohio town who, while successful in his business, is a failure in other aspects of his life. Toledo native ROBERT (JAMES) FLANAGAN (b. 1941) published two volumes of short fiction, *Naked to the Naked Goes* (1986) and *Loving Power* (1990), that contain stories set in the Columbus and Toledo areas. Donald Ray Pollock (b. 1954) of Chillicothe has published *Knockemstiff* (2008), a collection of linked stories about violence, drug abuse, and petty crime among working-class people, set in the southern Ohio village named in the title. Pollack's first novel, *The Devil All the Time* (2011), is also set in Knockemstiff and deals with similar themes.

Allan W. Eckert (1931–2011) was one of the more popular Ohio writers during the second half of the twentieth century. His six-book series the Winning of America is a sweeping historical narrative with a thin veneer of fiction that portrays colonial America and the early Republic in what would become the Old Northwest from the 1700s to the 1830s. Four of these books, *The Frontiersmen* (1967), *Wilderness Empire* (1968), *The Conquerors* (1970), and *Gateway to Empire* (1982), include persons and events prominent in early Ohio history. All four were nominated for the Pulitzer Prize for History; the first won the 1968 Ohioana Book Award for History. TONI MORRISON (CHLOE ARDELIA WOFFORD) (b. 1931), winner of the 1993 Nobel Prize for Literature, stays close to her Lorain roots in a trio of novels. The earliest, *The Bluest Eye* (1970), is set in her hometown and tells the story of a poor black girl impregnated by her father. The fictional town of Medallion, Ohio, is the backdrop for *Sula* (1974), which follows the lives of two black girls. *Beloved* (1987) portrays the life of a former slave in post–Civil War Cincinnati who is haunted by the spirit of the two-year-old daughter she killed while escaping from a Kentucky plantation.

Later contributions to Ohio's literary legacy include the novel *Middle C* (2013) by WILLIAM H(OWARD) GASS (b. 1924); it presents a coming-of-age tale set in the fictional town of Woodbine, Ohio. The 2012 Ohioana Book Award–winning short-story collection *Memory Wall* (2011) by Cleveland native Anthony Doerr (b. 1973) features "Afterworld," which focuses on an elderly Ohio woman who has visions of her childhood in Nazi Germany.

Farm Novels: A number of Ohio's most prominent authors have drawn inspiration from farm life. In spite of the importance of agriculture to the state's history and economy, it has not resulted in as many farm novels as in other Midwestern states. The earliest is a series of interconnected sketches written by ALICE CARY (1820–1871) and issued in two sequentially published volumes under the same collective title, *Clovernook; or, Recollections of Our Neighborhood in the West* (1852–1853). In these volumes Cary fictionalizes and sentimentalizes her childhood experiences on a farm near Cincinnati. THOMAS BEER (1889–1940) used Bucyrus as the model for the fictional Ohio town Zerbetta in a number of short stories. Originally published in the *Saturday Evening Post* and other magazines, these stories about the Egg family and their neighbors are collected in *Mrs. Egg and Other Barbarians* (1933) and the posthumous *Mrs. Egg and Other Americans* (1947).

Thomas Alexander Boyd (1898–1935) drew inspiration from his birthplace, Defiance, Ohio, to publish *Samuel Drummond* (1925), in which a Civil War veteran and his wife descend into debt and struggle to save their farm. In *Rosscommon* (1940) CHARLES ALLEN SMART (1904–1967) tells the story of a farm near Chillicothe that became the property of a writer and subsequently failed. LOUIS BROMFIELD (1896–1956) was a prolific writer, publishing more than thirty books and other works. He used his hometown, Mansfield, Ohio, in *The Farm* (1933), which portrays the gradual decline of an Ohio family farm over a century in which rural ways are supplanted by growing industrialization. Bromfield's Malabar Farm, a 1,800-acre plot originally composed of three separate failed farms that he purchased and began reclaiming in 1939, served as his home until his death. It became a source for his later nonfiction works on rural life and his passion, sustainable agriculture.

Glass (1933) by Howard P. Stephenson (1893–1978) explores the vicissitudes of one Ohio farmer's life and the ramifications of building a glass-manufacturing plant in his small farming community. Herman Fetzer (1899–1935), using the pseudonym Jake Falstaff, wrote a series of stories and sketches that were collected and published after his death. His *Come Back to Wayne County* (1942) consists of observations of rural life by a New York boy who spends the summer on his cousin's northeastern Ohio farm. Armin Frank (1904–1988), in *The Flesh of Kings* (1958), focuses more on the violent and deadly feud between two southern Ohio families than on the everyday business of farming.

Ellen Bromfield Geld (b. 1932), Louis Bromfield's daughter, wrote *A Timeless Place* (1971), concerning the owners of a large farm trying to prevent a politician from commercializing a nearby tract of land. JOAN CHASE (b. 1936) details three generations of farm life in northern Ohio in *During the Reign of the Queen of Persia* (1983). George Dell (1901–1992) presents *The Earth Abideth* (1986), beginning in 1866, the story of three generations of a family with a Fairfield County, Ohio, farm.

Gene Logsdon (b. 1932) has contributed a pair of Ohio farm novels. The first, *The Man Who Created Paradise* (2001), focuses on a factory worker who transforms the site of an old southeastern Ohio strip mine into a successful farm. The second, *The Last of the Husbandmen: A Novel of Farming Life* (2008), relates the story of two friends in the 1940s who own competing farms in the fictional village of Gowler, Ohio.

Autobiographies and Memoirs: Some of the earliest Ohio memoirs, apart from those that deal with frontier exploration, detail the experiences of citizens in the Civil War. Sandusky-born John Beatty (1928–1914) wrote about his experiences in the Third Ohio Volunteer Infantry during the Civil War in *The Citizen Soldier; or, Memoirs of a Volunteer* (1879).

Ohio has also been the birthplace of several American presidents. In the first volume of *Personal Memoirs of U. S. Grant* (1885) Ulysses S. Grant (1822–1885) describes his childhood in Point Pleasant and Georgetown, Ohio. This set is also notable because it was published by SAMUEL LANGHORNE CLEMENS (1835–1910) shortly after Grant's death.

A number of prominent Ohio authors have shared their experiences of growing up in the Buckeye State. *A Boy's Town* (1890), *My Year in a Log Cabin* (1893), and *Years of My Youth* (1916) by William Dean Howells depict Howells's years in Hamilton, Ohio, from 1840 to 1848. Several works by Sherwood Anderson are autobiographical. *Tar: A Midwest Childhood* (1926) provides a sketch of Anderson's life while growing up in Camden. *A Story Teller's Story* (1924), *Sherwood Anderson's Notebook* (1926), and *Sherwood Anderson's Memoirs* (1942) depict elements of his life and musings. The autobiography of Clarence Darrow, *The Story of My Life* (1932), compares favorably with those of Howells and Anderson. In *MY LIFE AND HARD TIMES* (1933) James Thurber humorously presents what it was like growing up in Columbus. This autobiography is often regarded as his best work. The autobiography of RUTH SEID (1913–1995), writing as Jo Sinclair, *The Seasons: Death and Transfiguration* (1993), describes her experiences and education living and working in Cleveland.

Poetry: In 1811 Ohio's first original literary work was published in Cincinnati: *The Dagon of Calvinism,* an anonymous satirical poem attacking Calvinism. Gorham A.

Worth (1783–1856) followed, anonymously publishing *American Bards: A Modern Poem in Three Parts* (1819) in Cincinnati.

Otway Curry (1804–1855) was one of Ohio's earliest known poets. Born in Greenfield, he spent parts of his life as a journalist, legislator, and lawyer. His verse appeared in newspapers and periodicals and was collected in 1948 as a master's thesis. His most famous contribution to Ohio verse may be "The Buckeye Cabin Song" (1840), a campaign song for Whig candidate and later president William Henry Harrison.

Two of Ohio's prominent early poets came from the same family. Sisters Alice Cary and PHOEBE CARY (1824–1871) grew up on Clovernook Farm near Cincinnati and were among the first well-known Midwestern poets. Alice published her first major poem, "The Child of Sorrow," in 1838. Her poetry often draws on her Ohio farm experiences; she even titled one of her collections *Clovernook Children* (1854). Phoebe published two volumes of poems: *Poems and Parodies* (1854) and *Poems of Faith, Hope and Love* (1868). Together they published an anthology, the *Poems of Alice and Phoebe Cary* (1849).

A number of distinguished African American poets were Ohioans, the earliest being Dayton's PAUL LAURENCE DUNBAR (1872–1906). The son of former slaves, he became the first prominent African American poet, as well as a prolific writer of short stories and novels. Dunbar published his first book of poems, *Oak and Ivy* (1893), in Dayton at his own expense. It was followed by a number of dialect poetry collections, such as *Poems of Cabin and Field* (1899), *Candle-Lightin' Time* (1901), and *When Malindy Sings* (1903).

(HAROLD) HART CRANE (1899–1932) was a noted and influential poet before his suicide at the age of thirty-two. The Garrettsville, Ohio, native published just two volumes in his brief lifetime: *White Buildings* (1926) and *The Bridge* (1930). Crane's notable poem specifically about Ohio, "Porphyro in Akron," was a precursor of the elements he would use later. It appeared in the little magazine the *Double Dealer* (August–September 1921) and reflects Crane's disdain for the Midwest: "Akron, 'high place,'—/ A bunch of smoking hills / Among rolling Ohio hills" (53).

Niles native Kenneth Patchen (1911–1972) was a poet who also worked in the visual

Martins Ferry, Ohio, 2001. Photo by William Barillas.

arts. Famous for his "picture poems," Patchen wrote more than forty books of poetry, prose, and drama. Youngstown steel mills are referenced in the poems "May I Ask You a Question, Mr. Youngstown Sheet & Tube?" (1936) and "The Orange Bears" (1957).

Alberta Turner (1919–2003) of Oberlin co-founded the poetry journal *Field* and taught for many years at Cleveland State University, where she directed the CSU Poetry Center. In addition to several books of poetry, such as *Learning to Count* (1974), *Beginning with And: New and Selected Poems* (1994), and *Tomorrow Is a Tight Fist* (2001), Turner published studies of poetic form and technique.

JAMES WRIGHT (1927–1980), an important Ohio poet who often wrote about the landscapes and people of his native state, won the 1972 Pulitzer Prize for *Collected Poems* (1971). His hometown is featured prominently in poems such as "Autumn Begins in Martins Ferry, Ohio" from THE BRANCH WILL NOT BREAK (1963). Wright's other Ohio poems include "Beautiful Ohio," "In Ohio," "The Old WPA Swimming Pool in Martins

Ferry, Ohio," "The Sumac in Ohio," and many others found in *Above the River: The Complete Poems* (1990).

A number of Ohio poets have followed in Wright's footsteps. Richard Howard (b. 1929), born in Cleveland, is the former chancellor of the Academy of American Poets and a distinguished poet who now teaches at Columbia University, his alma mater. His collections of poems include *Quantities* (1962), *Two-Part Inventions* (1974), *Lining Up* (1984), *Like Most Revelations* (1994), *Talking Cures* (2002), *The Silent Treatment* (2005), and *Without Saying* (2008). He received the Pulitzer Prize for *Untitled Subjects* (1969).

HERBERT WOODWARD MARTIN (b. 1933) is a celebrated African American poet, scholar, and professor emeritus at the University of Dayton. Although he has written on many subjects, Martin has often focused on the city of Dayton, home also to Paul Laurence Dunbar, whom Martin has portrayed in performance, and on whom he has published scholarship. His collections include *Escape to the Promised Land* (2005) and *Inscribing My Name: Selected Poems; New, Used, and Repossessed* (2007).

MARY OLIVER (b. 1935), from Maple Heights, has written a number of poetry collections, as well as some prose. She began her career by publishing the collection *Voyage, and Other Poems* (1963) and has since published several books, including *The River Styx, Ohio* (1972). Poems that incorporate Ohio settings include "The Black Walnut Tree" and "Stark County Holidays" in *Twelve Moons* (1979) and "Tecumseh" in the Pulitzer Prize—winning *American Primitive* (1983).

STANLEY (ROSS) PLUMLY (b. 1939) is a noteworthy poet who has drawn on his Barnesville upbringing in his poetic works, specifically "Buckeye" from *Giraffe* (1973) and "Tree Ferns" from *Summer Celestial* (1983). DAVID CITINO (1947–2005) enjoyed an academic career that spanned three decades at Ohio State University. Poems specifically referencing the Buckeye State include "Homage to the Corn," "Basic Writing, Marion Correctional," and "Cleveland, Angels, Ogres, and Trolls," all in *The Discipline: New and Selected Poems, 1980–1992* (1992). William Greenway (b. 1947), a faculty member at Youngstown State University since 1986, has published seven poetry collections, including *Ascending Order* (2003) and *Everywhere at Once* (2008), which received the Ohioana Poetry Book Award in 2009.

Bruce Weigl (b. 1949) was born in Lorain and now teaches at Lorain Community College. In addition to highly acclaimed poetry about his Vietnam War service, Weigl has written about his working-class Ohio youth. His books include *Song of Napalm* (1988), *Sweet Lorain* (1996), *Archeology of the Circle: New and Selected Poems* (1999), and *Declension in the Village of Chung Luong* (2006).

RITA DOVE (b. 1952), an Akron native and another powerful African American voice, served as Poet Laureate of the United States from 1993 to 1995. She has received numerous literary awards, including the 1987 Pulitzer Prize for Poetry for her collection *Thomas and Beulah* (1986). "The Gorge" and "The Buckeye" from *Grace Notes* (1989) and "Wingfoot Lake" from *Thomas and Beulah* draw specifically on her Ohio heritage.

Amit Majmudar (b. 1979) was named Ohio's first Poet Laureate in 2015. His books of poetry include *Heaven and Earth* (2011).

Other Ohio poets with multiple book publications include Hollis Summers (1916–1987), Wayne Dodd (b. 1930), James C. Kilgore (1930–1988), Robert Wallace (1932–1999), John Clarke (1933–1992), Leonard Trawick (b. 1933), Hale Chatfield (1936–2000), David Young (b. 1936), Imogene Bolls (1938–2010), Myrna Stone (b. 1944), David Lee Garrison (b. 1945), Elton Glaser (b. 1945), Cathryn Essinger (b. 1947), William Greenway (b. 1947), Maggie Anderson (b. 1948), Don Bogen (b. 1949), George Bilgere (b. 1951), Jeff Gundy (b. 1952), David Baker (b. 1954), and Kathy Fagan (b. 1958).

Drama: The earliest play with an Ohio setting may be *Logan, the Last of the Race of Shikellemus, Chief of the Cayuga Nation* (1823) by Joseph Doddridge (1769–1826). It was first printed in Virginia and was reprinted in Cincinnati in 1868.

Famed poet Paul Laurence Dunbar wrote the lyrics for *In Dahomey* (1903), a musical comedy widely recognized as the first Broadway musical written and performed by African Americans. Poet and playwright Ridgely Torrence (1875–1950) was born in Xenia, Ohio, and drew on his memories of African American life there in the plays published in *Granny Maumee, The Rider of*

Dreams, Simon the Cyrenian: Plays for a Negro Theater (1917). The three-act play *Outside Looking In* (1925) by Maxwell Anderson (1888–1959) is a dramatization of Ohio novelist Jim Tully's life, based on his 1924 autobiography *Beggars of Life.* Anderson's play was first performed in 1925 but was not published until 1928.

George S. Kaufman (1889–1961) and Moss Hart (1904–1961) wrote the three-act comedy *The Man Who Came to Dinner* (1939). Set during the Christmas season in the small fictional town of Mesalia, Ohio, in the 1930s, this play focuses on New York City radio personality Sheridan Whiteside, who is invited to dinner at the home of an Ohio businessman. The play enjoyed a number of revivals and was made into a feature film in 1942 and a television movie in 2000.

(Rollie) Lynn Riggs (1899–1954), one of the most prominent Native American playwrights, wrote *Toward the Western Sky* (1951), a six-scene musical play set in Ohio from 1825 to 1951. Riggs is most famous for his play *Green Grow the Lilacs* (1931), which was adapted into the musical *Oklahoma!* (1943).

A collection of short stories about two Ohio sisters living in New York City, *My Sister Eileen* (1938) by Ruth McKenney (1911–1972), was developed into a two-act comedy for the stage in 1940 under the same title by Joseph A. Fields (1895–1966) and Jerome Chodorov (1911–2004). Film versions appeared in 1942 and 1955, and *Wonderful Town,* with music by Leonard Bernstein (1918–1990), in 1953. McKenney's novel *The Loud Red Patrick* (1947) was adapted for the stage by John Boruff (1910–1993), and his three-act play, using the same title, debuted in 1956. Set in Cleveland in 1912, this comedy focuses on Patrick Flannagan, an Irish widower committed to women's rights.

Tony Award–winning *Bye Bye Birdie* (1960) used the fictional town of Sweet Apple, Ohio, as its setting. A stage musical written by Michael Stewart (1929–1987), with lyrics by Lee Adams (b. 1924) and music by Charles Strouse (b. 1928), this famous satire is set in 1958 and was inspired by Elvis Presley's 1957 induction into the U.S. Army. This musical has enjoyed several major revivals, spawned a sequel, and was later adapted into a 1963 film and a 1995 television production.

Allan Eckert's Pulitzer Prize–nominated book *The Frontiersman* (1965) has been adapted into *Tecumseh!* This outdoor drama began in 1973 and continues to run at the Sugarloaf Mountain Amphitheater near Chillicothe.

Jerome Lawrence (1915–2004) and Robert E. Lee (1918–1994), two prominent modern playwrights, hail from Ohio. Their play *Jabberwock: Improbabilities Lived and Imagined by James Thurber in the Fictional City of Columbus, Ohio* (1974), commissioned by Ohio State University, dramatizes the early life of writer James Thurber and his family and was first performed in 1972. Although Lawrence and Lee's contributions to the field are numerous, this is their only work with an Ohio setting.

Robert (James) Flanagan wrote a two-act drama, *Jupus Redeye* (1988), set in Liberty Center, Ohio, in 1912, which focuses on a twelve-year-old girl torn between her parents' religious belief and nonbelief. Robin Rice Lichtig (b. 1941), author of more than forty plays, set one of her comedies in Yellow Springs, Ohio. *Evening Primrose in Ohio* (1991) is a one-act play in which all the action occurs in a laundromat in that town.

Popular Literature:

Mystery and Detective Fiction: Ohio has been the setting for many works of fiction in the mystery and detective genre. The earliest appears to have been a story by Cincinnati newspaperman William T. Coggeshall. His *Oakshaw; or, The Victims of Avarice: A Tale of Intrigue* (1855), first published as a newspaper serial in 1851, concerns an old man, his lovely daughter, and a villainous blackmailer in rural Ohio.

In *The Veil Withdrawn* (1900) Berton J. Maddux (1871–1952) writes of a detective who investigates an Ohio district attorney's murder. Among the poems and stories of May Stranathan (1865–1952) is a short mystery novel, *The Huff Case* (1912), set in eastern Ohio. The novel *Find the Woman* (1929) by Helen Joan Hultman (1891–1985) explores the mystery of a philandering husband's poisoning in Dayton, while, in a similar vein, Leonard Falkner (1900–1977) tells the tale of an Ohio man's murder, possibly by his wife's lover, in *M* (1931). Hultman, a resident of Dayton, set another of her mysteries, *Murder on Route 40* (1940), at a tearoom along the nearby National Road.

Ohio's biggest cities have been the stage for a number of detective novels. Fenn McGrew, the joint pseudonym of Caroline K. Fenn (1908–1982) and Julia McGrew (ca. 1882–ca. 1968), wrote three novels that feature a Columbus police lieutenant: *Murder by Mail* (1951), *Taste of Death* (1953), and *Made for Murder* (1954).

The metropolitan areas of Cleveland and Cincinnati have been popular settings for a number of mystery novels. For Cleveland, among the more important authors are Robert Martin (1908–1976), Les Roberts (b. 1937), and Max Allen Collins (b. 1948), while Cincinnati is represented by JONATHAN LOUIS VALIN (b. 1948). For more extensive lists and discussions of mystery and detection fiction and its writers in these two locales, see those sections of the city entries for Cleveland and Cincinnati.

Crime, however, is not restricted to the big cities. Ohio small towns and rural areas are also settings for mystery and detective fiction. A country estate is the scene of a double murder in *Death at the Manor* (1938) by Molly E. Corne (1907–1954). The protagonist in the story collection *Diagnosis: Murder* (1941) by Rufus King (1893–1966) is a young physician in the small town of Laurel Falls. Another Ohio physician-detective, Dr. Daniel Webster Coffee, is the creation of Lawrence G. Blochman (1900–1975); Dr. Coffee's exploits in a hospital at Northbank are recounted in the short-story collections *Diagnosis: Homicide* (1950) and *Clues for Dr. Coffee* (1964).

Florence V. Morse (1887–1962) wrote about foul play on a model farm and estate near Van Wert in *Black Eagles Are Flying* (1942). The fictional town of Preston is the setting for four early novels by Thomas B. Dewey (1915–1981); there, beginning with *Hue and Cry* (1944), a small-hotel owner and Shakespeare aficionado is a reluctant detective. The systematic murders of nuns in an Ohio convent is the story line of *The Eighth Sacrament* (1977) by Thomas P. Cullinan (1919–1995). Ben Safford, an Ohio congressman, is the lead character in a seven-book mystery series by Mary Jane Latsis (1927–1997) and Martha Hennisart (1929–1997), writing under the joint pseudonym R. B. Dominic; however, only one of these, *Attending Physician* (1980), is set in Ohio.

Best-selling author Richard North Patterson (b. 1947) used the fictional town of Lake City as the site of a murder trial in *Silent Witness* (1997). *Rainbow's End* (2002) by Bob Adamov (b. 1949) is the first book in a series of five set at Lake Erie's Put-in-Bay Island.

Wooster resident Paul L. Gaus (b. 1949) is the author of a well-received mystery series set among the Millersburg Amish community; the first of these is *Blood of the Prodigal* (1999), and the seventh and latest is *Harmless as Doves* (2011). Karen S. Harper (b. 1945) also uses the Ohio Amish background; her four Amish mysteries set in fictional Maple Creek include *Dark Road Home* (1996), *Down to the Bone* (2000), *Dark Harvest* (2004), and *Dark Angel* (2005). Harper began a new series about the Home Valley Amish with *Fall from Pride* (2011).

Ohio is the setting for quite a few mysteries set in college or university towns. Marion Margaret Havighurst (1894–1974), using her maiden name, Marion Boyd, wrote *Murder in the Stacks* (1934), which focuses on the death of a reclusive librarian at Kingsley University, a fictionalized Miami University in Oxford. Mary Elizabeth Campbell (1903–1984) tells the story of stolen exam questions and the murder of a dean at an unidentified institution, probably Ohio University in Athens, in her novel *Scandal Has Two Faces* (1943). The University of Cincinnati is the locale of *Cap and Gown for a Shroud* (1960) by Esker N. Gilla (1922–1983), in which a beautiful coed who blackmails students and faculty alike is found murdered.

William Dale Smith (1930–1986), writing under the pseudonym David Anthony, authored *The Midnight Lady and the Mourning Man* (1969). This novel features Morgan Butler, a security officer investigating a campus murder in the fictional small town of Jordan City, Ohio. *Monkey Puzzle* (1985) by Paula Gosling (b. 1939) concerns violent death in the English Department of the fictitious Grantham University in northern Ohio. Ralph McInerny (1929–2010) is much better known for his mysteries set in ILLINOIS and at Notre Dame, but *The Search Committee* (1991) is set at the imaginary University of Ohio Fort Elbow campus, where competition for the vacant chancellorship results in two fatal poisonings.

Dime Novels: Ohio has many connections with the popular nineteenth-century publishing phenomenon the DIME NOVEL. Sandusky native Orville J. Victor (1827–1910) became the chief editor for Beadle and Adams, the best-known publisher of dime novels, in 1861, where he worked until 1897. He and his wife, Metta V. Victor (1831–1885), a prolific writer of dime novels herself, may have collaborated on *The Hunter's Vow* (1864), issued under the pseudonym Louis LeGrand and set on the Ohio frontier during the aftermath of the twin defeats of Generals Harmer and St. Clair in 1790 and 1791.

Another Ohio native, Edward S. Ellis (1840–1916), was a prominent dime-novel writer who produced scores of stories under his own name and at least fourteen different pen names. A number of them are set in Ohio. *The Riflemen of the Miami: A Tale of Southern Ohio* (1862) relates the story of four hunters among the Shawnees in the 1790s. *The Hunter's Cabin: An Episode of the Early Settlements of Southern Ohio* (1862) depicts the trouble between the Shawnees and the Moravian settlers in the 1790s; its sequel, *Oonomoo, the Huron* (1862), was published a few months later. *The Settler's Son; or, Adventures in Wilderness and Clearing: A True Story of Early Border Life* (1882) details the progress of a young man who rises from working in an Ohio sawmill to become a congressman. Under the pseudonym Boynton Belknap, he wrote *Lewis Wetzel, the Scout; or, The Captives of the Wilderness* (1868), which focuses on the Shawnee attack on Chillicothe in 1779.

Other dime novels using the state as a setting include *The Marked Bullet; or, The Squaw's Reprieve* (1864) and *Gottlieb Gootsoock; or, The Bride of the Wilderness* (1865) by George Henry Prentice, which are set in backwoods frontier Ohio. In *Simple Phil; or, The Pineville Massacre: A Story of the Settlements* (1866), James L. Bowen (1842–1919) deals with Indian raids and captivity in early frontier Ohio. He also wrote *Smooth-Face, the Scout: A Tale of Early Ohio* (1876). *Red Jacket, the Huron; or, The Belle of the Border* (1870) by Paul Bibbs takes place in the Scioto River valley. *Abdiel, the Avenger; or, The Madman of the Miami* (1873) by Edward Willett (1830–1889)

focuses on George Rogers Clark and the Shawnees in 1780. Under the pseudonym J. Stanley Henderson, Willett also wrote *The Willing Captive; or, The Woodyard Mystery: A Tale of Ohio River Life* (1865).

Thomas C. Harbaugh (1849–1924), writing under the pseudonym Charles Howard, uses the Miami country in 1782 as the setting in *Phil Hunter, the Boy Scourge; or, The Shawnee Maid's Sacrifice* (1873). An Englishman, Percy Bolingbroke St. John (1821–1889), wrote *Queen of the Woods; or, The Shawnee Captives: A Romance of the Ohio* (1868), which had been published serially the previous year. *The Old River Sport; or, A Man of Honor* (1886), written by an unknown writer using the pseudonym Daniel Boone Dumont, explores illicit activities involving moonshiners and horse thieves in Cincinnati.

Edward L. Wheeler (ca.1854–1885) contributed *Deadwood Dick, Jr., in Cincinnati; or, The Clincher Campaign* (1889). *Jaunty Joe, the Jockey Detective; or, Big Stakes for the Winner!* (1889) by George C. Jenks (1850–1929) tells of corruption and horse racing in Cleveland. Albert W. Aiken's (1846–1894) *Joe Phenix's Double Deal; or, The Diamond Dagger: A Story of the Queen City of the Ohio* (1897), previously issued serially in 1893–1894, is set in Cincinnati.

Romance Novels: Romance novels were written early in Ohio, although they were set in the East and elsewhere. Examples are Caroline Lee Hentz's *Lovell's Folly* (1833) and Cincinnati writer Robert Burt's *The Scourge of the Ocean* (1837).

James Ball Naylor (1860–1945) authored many novels set in southern Ohio, including the historical romance *In the Days of St. Clair: A Romance of the Muskingum Valley* (1902). The Civil War also served as historical inspiration for love stories. *McLean: A Romance of the War* (1904) by John Beatty (1828–1914) is a fictional work based on Colonel Edward M. Driscoll's escape from the Confederacy during his time in the Third Ohio Volunteer Infantry. Although much of the novel focuses on the escape of two prisoners, Captain Northrup and Captain Lindsay, from Confederate hands and their travel northward, a parallel plot involves the capture and ransom of a Southerner, Alice Brevar. The two men find her while making their way north, and Northrup and Alice fall in love and eventually marry by the end of the novel, despite the travails of the war and their place on opposite sides. Judge John S. Cochran (1841–1926) also drew on the era before and during the war in his romance novel *Bonnie Belmont: A Historical Romance of the Days of Slavery and the Civil War* (1907).

Suzi Sinzinnati (1989) by Joe David Bellamy (1941–2014) is set in Cincinnati during the 1960s. The title character is a stripper who captures the attention of a young college student. Bellamy, a Cincinnati native, won the Editor's Book Award for this, his first novel. Joy Fielding (b. 1945) also employs the Cincinnati area as the setting in her novel *Grand Avenue* (2001). Jeannette Haien (1922–2008) uses the World War II era as a backdrop in her novel *Matters of Chance* (1997), which begins in a fictional Cleveland suburb before moving to other locations.

Best-selling author and Wapakoneta native Jennifer Crusie (b.1949) has published more than fifteen romance novels, two of which use her home state as a primary locale. *Welcome to Temptation* (2001) is set in the aptly named fictional small town of Temptation, Ohio, while the action in *Faking It* (2002) takes place in Columbus's German village. This locale also serves as the setting in the vampire romance novel *Rapture in Moonlight* (2002), the second entry in a five-book series by Rosemary Laurey (b. 1946).

Science Fiction and Fantasy: Ohio has served as the setting for a pair of stories focusing on a child capable of altering reality. Jerome Bixby (1923–1998) used the town of Peaksville, Ohio, in his short story "It's a Good Life," published in *Star Science Fiction Stories* (no. 2, 1953). This tale, which focuses on a three-year-old whose every wish comes true, was later adapted into one of the most memorable episodes of the classic television series *The Twilight Zone*. Stephen King (b. 1947), using the pseudonym Richard Bachman, creates the fictional town of Wentworth, Ohio, to serve as the setting for his novel *The Regulators* (1996), which also features a young boy able to transform reality.

Cincinnati native Kathleen Ann Goonan (b. 1952) imagines a futuristic dystopia in *Queen City Jazz* (1994). The book depicts an Ohio, including major cities such as Dayton and Cincinnati, transformed and corrupted by nanotechnology. Dayton also served as the setting in the short story "Chronicles of a Comer" (1972), published in the collection *And Walk Now Gently through the Fire* (1972) by Barry N. Malzberg (b. 1939), writing as K. M. O'Donnel; this short story portrays a mathematician using statistical correlations in looking for the second coming of Christ.

Two of the most prominent twentieth-century science-fiction authors incorporated Ohio as a setting. Harlan Ellison (b. 1934), born in Cleveland and author of more than one thousand works in various media formats, used this locale in his short story "The Voice in the Garden," published in *Lighthouse* (June 1967). The novel *Changing Planes* (2003) by award-winning science-fiction and fantasy author Ursula K. Le Guin (b. 1929) features a protagonist who hails from Cincinnati. Other award-winning science-fiction writers from Ohio include Andre Norton (1912–2005), Roger Zelazny (1937–1995), Stephen Donaldson (b. 1947) and Lois McMaster Bujold (b. 1949).

Religious Literature: Presbyterian minister Lyman Beecher (1775–1863), father of Harriet Beecher Stowe, became the first minister of Lane Theological Seminary in Cincinnati after a lengthy pastorship in Boston. While he was at Lane, Beecher published *A Plea for the West* (1835), a foundational jeremiad for the cause of nativism. Alarmed at the rising population of Catholic immigrants in the East, Beecher called for Protestants in the Midwest (the West of his title) to stand their ground against the supposed threats that he felt the mostly Irish immigrants and their Catholic priests represented. Beecher's *Plea* helped launch the first great wave of nativism in the country, which culminated in the nationwide Know-Nothing movement of the 1850s.

Jewish life and literature also developed in Ohio. By the mid-nineteenth century Judaism was being modernized. Theoreticians such as Abraham Geiger (1810–1874) established the movement in Germany and then South Carolina, and it quickly took root in Ohio. In the words of Carolyn S. Blackwell in "Jews," in *Peopling Indiana: The Ethnic Experience* (1996), edited by Robert M. Taylor

Jr., and Connie A. McBirney: "Along the river highways of the Ohio and the Wabash, individual Jewish settlers found their way to frontier settlements. Early Jewish immigrants were scattered and often the only Jews in the community. Religious practices were difficult to observe" (314). Reform Judaism was a simpler, easier, and less divisive way to be both Jewish and American. Cincinnati, the center of Reform Judaism in America, helped make assimilation acceptable by fostering the German Reform movement. For much of the nineteenth century the Cincinnati Jewish community was the largest and most important west of the Alleghenies; its reform spirit emanated throughout the Midwest and America.

Rabbi Isaac Mayer Wise (1819–1900), a German-speaking immigrant from Prague, came to the United States in 1846 and settled in Cincinnati. Wise's ideas spread. His desire for access to prayer by translation and modernization, accessibility, and "union" was disseminated in the columns he wrote in the Philadelphia-based the *Occident,* which contained many articles written by Ohioans and fostering Reform Judaism. Wise was the author of many books, including *The Essence of Judaism,* published in Cincinnati in 1861. In his early years he wrote novels, which appeared first as serials in the *Israelite,* among them *The Convert* (1854). He also wrote plays in German. The English-language the *Israelite,* established in 1854, was the first Jewish newspaper published in Cincinnati; it helped explain, spread, and codify Reform Judaism's tenets. Rabbi Wise was its founder and editor and also founded the German-language *Die Deborah* in 1855. The *Israelite,* now the *American Israelite,* still exists and is the longest-running Jewish newspaper in the United States.

In 1873, twenty-five years after Wise had first broached the idea of a unified group of reform congregations, the Union of American Hebrew Congregations was organized in Cincinnati (in 2003, the organization changed its name to the Union for Reform Judaism). It published many newsletters and magazines. Over the years the organization's newsletter changed its name from the *Union Bulletin* to the *Union Tidings. The Jewish Teacher,* a quarterly magazine, was first published in 1932 and by 1966 became *Di-*

mension. Started as a newsletter in 1911, by 1930, Gary P. Zola asserts in "Reform Judaism," in *Popular Religious Magazines of the United States* (1995), the *Union Tidings* contained noteworthy articles and editorials (435).

Ohio literary works reflecting religious thought also include *The Leatherwood God* (1916) by William Dean Howells, which explores religious fanaticism in telling the story of a preacher who comes to Ohio, claiming to be God. *The Circuit Rider: A Tale of the Heroic Age* (1874) stayed close to Edward Eggleston's roots, following a Methodist preacher's travels into areas that included parts of Ohio. Albert Benjamin Cunningham (1888–1962) wrote *The Chronicle of an Old Town* (1919), in which a pastor is voted out of his church in the East and is reassigned to the small Ohio town of Paxton. In *The Soul's Fire* (1936) Jeremiah Stokes (1877–1954) used Kirtland, Ohio, as a partial setting for his historical-fiction account of the Mormon Church and its founder, Joseph Smith (1805–1844), in the region.

The recurring search for meaning in life and the need for divine guidance are present in Ohio literature. For example, the story "Godliness" in *Winesburg, Ohio* by Sherwood Anderson describes religion-obsessed Jesse Bentley and the shift in values from the frontier Ohio of the mid-1800s to that of the small-town era of the early twentieth century. "The Strength of God," also in *Winesburg, Ohio,* follows the moral crisis of Reverend Curtis Hartman, who becomes a minister out of weakness, seeking a safe career and life, rather than through the strength of his religious feeling.

Children's and Young Adult Literature: William Holmes McGuffey (1800–1873), a Miami University faculty member and minister, working with Cincinnati publisher Truman and Smith, created the nation's first graded readers. The first, *The Eclectic First Reader,* was published beginning in 1836. The Eclectic School Series, as it was formally known, taught moral lessons, reading, and related studies at progressively higher levels using writings by well-known authors. The series was used widely in classrooms across the United States for over one hundred years. Although the series included six readers, the most popular were the first and second readers, which are still used by some religious schools and homeschoolers.

Hostetler; or, The Mennonite Boy Converted: A True Narrative (1848) was originally published anonymously by "a Methodist preacher." It is now generally considered to have been written by Adam Miller (1810–1901), who seemingly drew on his life's experiences to craft this tale. As a child, Miller lived in western Ohio and later became a preacher in Cincinnati. With *Our Cousins in Ohio* (1849) Mary Botham Howitt (1799–1888) contributed a fictionalized account for children of her younger sister Emma's experiences with her family on a prosperous farm on the Ohio River.

Ohio contains a wealth of books for children and young people and many authors who specialize in that literature. One early and significant contributor to this genre was LOIS (LENORE) LENSKI (1893–1974), who illustrated nearly one hundred of her own books. Her first fictional novels, *Skipping Village* (1927) and *A Little Girl of 1900* (1928), were autobiographical, drawing on her experiences growing up in Ohio. *A-Going to Westward* (1937) tells the story of a family's migration from Connecticut to Franklin County in 1811.

(JOHN) ROBERT MCCLOSKEY (1914–2003) of Hamilton, Ohio, was named a living legend by the Library of Congress in 2000. McCloskey used the streets, parks, and characters of his hometown, which he called Alto, in *Lentil* (1940); in Hamilton a statue of Lentil playing his harmonica, followed by his dog, commemorates the book. A Tom Sawyer–like protagonist, Homer Price, and small-town Midwestern eccentrics populate *Homer Price* (1943) and *Centerburg Tales* (1949). The humor, the exaggerations, and McCloskey's drawings progress through the three books until they reach the proportion of tall tales, with the accents, dialect, and regionalisms of southern Ohio. His picture book *Make Way for Ducklings,* set in Boston, was the 1942 Caldecott Medal winner.

VIRGINIA (ESTHER) HAMILTON (1936–2002) is another prominent, award-winning children's author. A product of Yellow Springs, she published a number of novels; the first was *Zeely* (1967), followed by *The House of Dies Drear* (1968), a mystery about a house in her hometown that had been a stop on the Underground Railroad. She won the American Book Award in 1974 and the Newbery Medal in 1975 for *M. C. Higgins, the Great* (1974), which focuses on a black man and his family's struggles living in the eastern Ohio mining region.

Ohio is featured in a number of other significant children's works. *The Secret of the Ruby Locket* (1943) by Harriet T. Evatt (1891–1983) takes place on an Ohio farm. Mildred D. Taylor (b. 1943), a prominent African American Newbery Award–winning author, drew on her experiences in Ohio's Franklin County to write *The Gold Cadillac* (1987), set in Toledo during the 1950s. She also employed an Ohio setting in *Time Pieces* (2002). In *Out of the Storm* (1995) Patricia Willis (b. 1933) relates the story of an unhappy girl's experiences on her aunt's northern Ohio sheep farm in 1946. Lynda Durrant (b. 1954) has won the Ohioana Book Award on two occasions for the novels *The Beaded Moccasins: The Story of Mary Campbell* (1998), which fictionalizes the captivity narrative story of twelve-year-old Mary Campbell, who was taken to Ohio in the 1760s by Delaware Indians, and *Betsy Zane, the Rose of Fort Henry* (2000), set in West Virginia on the Ohio River. *Fat Angie* (2013) by e. E. Charlton-Trujillo focuses on the struggles of a high school girl in the fictional town of Dryfalls, Ohio; it was the winner of the 2014 Stonewall Book Award, sponsored by the American Library Association's Gay, Lesbian, Bisexual, and Transgender Round Table.

Even when Ohio does not serve as the location, the contributions of native Ohioans have helped shape this genre. Mildred Wirt Benson, writing under the pen name Carolyn Keene (1905–2002), created the iconic teenage heroine Nancy Drew. Beginning with *The Secret of the Old Clock* (1930), Benson authored twenty-three of the first thirty Nancy Drew novels. Columbus native Robert Lawrence Stine (b. 1943) has earned his place as one of America's most successful adolescent authors, publishing hundreds of fantasy novels, including the famous Goosebumps and Fear Street series.

Graphic Novels and Comic Books: Ohio has brought the world a number of prominent graphic novelists, cartoonists, and comic-book authors. Perhaps none, however, has been as influential as Lancaster, Ohio, native Richard F. Outcault (1863–1928), who is widely acknowledged as the inventor of the modern newspaper comic strip with his two series, *The Yellow Kid* (1895) and *Buster Brown* (1902). Massachusetts-born Ted Rall (b. 1963) was raised in Kettering, Ohio, and has published a quartet of graphic novels and an equal number of cartoon collections. His graphic novel *My War with Brian* (1998) deals with bullying in an Ohio suburb during the 1970s.

Jeff Smith (b. 1960), a longtime Columbus resident, is famous for his award-winning graphic-novel series *Bone*, which ran for fifty-five issues from 1991 to 2004. In 2008 Smith was honored with a pair of museum exhibits in Columbus: *Jeff Smith: "Bone" and Beyond* at the Wexner Center for the Arts and *Jeff Smith: Before "Bone"* at the Cartoon Research Library at Ohio State University.

Cleveland has provided the comic-book genre with influential contributors. Harvey Pekar (1939–2010) is best known for his autobiographical *American Splendor* comic series, set in Cleveland, which ran for 39 issues from 1976 to 2008. Co-written with his wife, Joyce Brabner (b. 1952), *Our Cancer Year* (1994), also a Cleveland-based graphic novel, explores Pekar's treatment for lymphoma.

Lesbian and Gay Literature: A number of distinguished gay and lesbian writers have come from Ohio or have lived in the state. The family of Natalie Clifford Barney (1876–1972) lived in Dayton until the future poet, novelist, and playwright was ten years old. Barney was a fixture among EXPATRIATES in Paris, where she maintained a salon that hosted major writers like Rainer Maria Rilke (1875–1926), T(HOMAS) S(TERNS) ELIOT (1888–1965), and F(RANCIS) SCOTT (KEY) FITZGERALD (1896–1940). She published many lesbian-themed texts and inspired others. A state historical marker honoring Barney was dedicated in Dayton in 2009.

JAMES (OTIS) PURDY (1914–2009) of Hicksville, Ohio, was a prominent writer who published more than a dozen novels. His first collection, *Don't Call Me by My Right Name, and Other Stories* (1956), employs small-town settings evocative of Ohio. Two novels

embrace his Ohio heritage more strongly. The location in *The Nephew* (1960) is Rainbow Center, actually depicting Bowling Green, Ohio, the home of Purdy's alma mater. *Jeremy's Version* (1970) uses the towns of Findlay and Hicksville as the models for its locales, despite changing the names to Boutflour and Hittisleigh, respectively.

Contemporary gay and lesbian writers include Edmund White (b. 1940), author of *A Boy's Own Story* (1982), a landmark gay coming-of-age novel. Although the novel curiously lacks place names, it reflects White's upbringing in an upper-middle-class Cincinnati family that summered in MICHIGAN. Keith Banner (b. 1965) of Cincinnati has written *The Smallest People Alive* (2004), a collection of stories, some set in Ohio, about rural gay men who work marginal jobs and struggle with problems like alcoholism and obesity. Columnist and commentator Kathy Y. Wilson (b. 1965) collected many of her essays in *Your Negro Tour Guide: Truths in Black and White* (2004), examining the intersection of race, class, and sexuality in Cincinnati. Lesbian and gay poets from Ohio include Hart Crane, Mary Oliver, and Rane Arroyo (1954–2010). See also LESBIAN, GAY, BISEXUAL, TRANSGENDER, AND QUEER LITERATURE.

Journalism: Ohio is home to several major metropolitan cities, and many prominent writers spent some of their time as journalists. Ohio State University houses a Journalism Hall of Fame, which honors writers including Warren G. Harding (1865–1923), Whitelaw Reid (1837–1912), and William Dean Howells.

Ohio's journalistic tradition began in 1793 when William Maxwell (ca. 1755–1809) published the weekly newspaper *Centinel of the North-Western Territory* in Cincinnati. Maxwell was responsible not only for writing the content but also for setting the type and doing the printing. Concurrent with Maxwell's discontinuation of the *Centinel* in June 1796, the father-and-son team of Samuel and Edmund Freeman began their weekly, *Freeman's Journal*, in Cincinnati. In 1800, presumably to take advantage of the opportunity offered by the naming of Chillicothe as the capital of Ohio Territory, the paper was relocated to that town, but by the end of the year it had been sold, and its name had been changed to the *Scioto Gazette.* Other early Ohio weekly newspapers include the *Western Spy* (1799), printed in Cincinnati under a variety of subsequent names until the 1840s; the *Ohio Gazette* (1801) of Marietta; Steubenville's *Western Herald,* which began in 1806 and survived into the 1920s; the *Western Star* (1807), published in Lebanon; and the *Muskingum Messenger* (1809), which was printed in Zanesville until it ceased in 1820.

One of Ohio's most prominent journalistic figures was DAVID ROSS LOCKE (1833–1888), who became famous writing under the pseudonym Petroleum V. Nasby. As editor of the *Hancock Jeffersonian* in Findlay, Locke established a name for himself by publishing the satirical Nasby letters. These were written in a semi-literate fashion to help illustrate Nasby's ignorance and overtly racist and sexist attitudes, expressing Southern views but showing the Confederates in a negative light. The letters succeeded in rallying support for the Union cause. Locke became editor and part owner of the *Toledo Blade* in 1865. A number of volumes collecting Locke's Nasby letters were published; among these were *The Nasby Papers* (1864), *Swingin' 'Round the Cirkle* (1867), and *The Nasby Letters* (1893).

CHARLES FARRAR BROWNE (1834–1867) was another prominent Ohio journalist and the creator of an alter ego, Artemus Ward, under whose name he wrote humorous columns. Artemus Ward first saw publication in 1858 in the *Cleveland Plain Dealer.* Ward's writings reflected the ideas of a poorly educated man and contained regular puns, misspellings, and malapropisms, and as his writings gained national popularity, Browne began to appear on the lecture stage impersonating his creation. The success of Browne's Artemus Ward columns and personal appearances led to the publication of *Artemus Ward, His Book* (1862) and *Artemus Ward, His Travels* (1865) among others, all reprinted many times.

Mildred Wirt Benson (1905–2002) crafted many of the famous Nancy Drew novels and other girls' book series. She spent most of her professional career as a Toledo journalist, enjoying fifty-eight years with the *Toledo Times* and the *Toledo Blade,* and was inducted into the Ohio Women's Hall of Fame in 1993.

Ohio Federal Writers Project: The Federal Writers Project, developed by the Works Progress Administration to employ out of work writers and artists during the Great Depression, produced several interesting volumes documenting urban and rural history in the state. Books and pamphlets included *They Built a City: 150 Years of Industrial Cincinnati* (1938), *Chillicothe and Ross County, Ohio* (1938), and *Ohio's Capitols* (1941). Other books and pamphlets highlight the state's nature and beauty, including *The Beautiful River* (1940), which described the life and landscape along the Ohio River, and *Ohio Nature Trails* (1941). From 1936–1938, project workers recorded several dozen slave narratives from around the state and deposited those narratives in the Library of Congress. The project also generated an all-inclusive book about the state *The Ohio Guide* (1940), which contains a series of photographs of small town or rural life by artist Ben Shahn.

Ohio Literary Awards: The Dayton Literary Peace Prize has the distinction of being the only annual literary award in the United States recognizing the power of literature to promote peace. Established in 2006, this award honors one fiction and one nonfiction work each year.

Since 1942 the Ohioana Book Awards, sponsored by the Ohioana Library Association, have brought state and national attention to Ohio authors and their books. Up to six awards may be given annually in categories including fiction, nonfiction, juvenile literature, poetry, and books about Ohio or Ohioans. Among the annual fiction winners have been Toni Morrison, Don Robertson, HELEN HOOVEN SANTMYER (1895–1986), JOHN JAKES (b.1932), and Jo Sinclair. Juvenile winners have included Virginia Hamilton, Robert McCloskey, and Lois Lenski. Among the annual nonfiction winners have been Bruce Catton (1899–1978), Arthur Schlesinger (1888–1965), Walter Havighurst, and SCOTT RUSSELL SANDERS (b. 1945). Rita Dove, David Citino, Mary Oliver, James Wright, Kenneth Patchen, and John Crowe Ransom (1888–1974) have been winners in poetry. David Hassler (b. 1964) was the 2007 winner in the Books about Ohio or Ohioans category. DAVID D(ANIEL) ANDERSON (1924–2011) was a 2009 Ohioana Career Award winner.

Ohio Literary Organizations and Societies: Established in 1977, the Ohio Center for the Book at the Cleveland Public Library is an online presence promoting Ohio's literary heritage. The Poets' and Writers' League of Greater Cleveland promotes northern Ohio writers.

Ohio recognizes a number of its famous writers in locations throughout the state. The James Wright Poetry Festival was held annually in Wright's home town, Martins Ferry, Ohio, from 1981 through 2007. The Paul Laurence Dunbar House in Dayton honors its namesake with literary and personal exhibits. James Thurber is similarly honored with the Thurber House and Museum, a literary center for readers and writers located in Columbus, the historic former home of the famed author and cartoonist. The Harriet Beecher Stowe House in Cincinnati, famous in conjunction with Stowe's writing of *Uncle Tom's Cabin,* is another noted Ohio historical and cultural site. Malabar Farm, the home of Louis Bromfield, has been immortalized as Malabar Farm State Park and holds many of Bromfield's papers.

SELECTED WORKS: Perhaps the state's most famous literary product, and one that identifies Ohio in its title, is Sherwood Anderson's *Winesburg, Ohio* (1919). This collection of interrelated short stories, set in the fictionalized town of Winesburg, draws heavily on Anderson's Ohio roots, most specifically in Clyde, Ohio. *Winesburg, Ohio* is Anderson's most famous work, one of the most important pieces of Midwestern literature, and, arguably, Ohio's most iconic work.

An argument can be made, however, that because of its long-lasting historical and cultural impact, Harriet Beecher Stowe's *Uncle Tom's Cabin* (1852) should also be regarded as one of Ohio's most important books. Although Stowe was not a native Ohioan, the events of the novel take place on the Kentucky-Ohio border and draw on her experiences in Cincinnati.

No list of essential Ohio works of literature would be complete without works by William Dean Howells, whose novels *The Kentons* (1902) and *The Leatherwood God* (1916) capture Ohio life in a fictionalized but realistic manner. His autobiography *A Boy's Town* (1890) is also worthy of consideration.

Another noteworthy Ohio autobiography is James Thurber's *My Life and Hard Times* (1933), which humorously depicts life in Columbus and has been widely praised. Although Thurber's famed and widely anthologized short story "The Secret Life of Walter Mitty" does not employ Ohio as its setting, it may be the most famous and enduring work by this prominent Ohioan.

Louis Bromfield's novel *The Farm* (1933) captures Ohio farm life, as well as the decline of the family farm. Though not as highly regarded, his nonfiction work *Malabar Farm* (1948) reflects Bromfield's commitment to sustainable agriculture.

Ohio has a long history of prominent African American writers, including Paul Laurence Dunbar, Charles Chesnutt, and Rita Dove. The most prominent late twentieth-century and early twenty-first-century African American writer and Ohio writer in general is Toni Morrison. Three of her novels rank among Ohio's finest works; *The Bluest Eye* (1970), *Sula* (1974), and *Beloved* (1987) all employ locations in Ohio as their setting and help represent the voice of African American women.

Ohio's strong presence in poetry has resulted in a number of Pulitzer Prize–winning collections, including James Wright's *Collected Poems* (1971), Mary Oliver's *American Primitive* (1983), and Rita Dove's *Thomas and Beulah* (1986). Hart Crane's brief career produced a pair of collections, of which *White Buildings* (1926) was received much better than *The Bridge* (1930). Similarly, several of Paul Laurence Dunbar's poetry collections can be considered seminal Ohio books, but none more so than *Lyrics of Lowly Life* (1896), which caught the attention of prominent Ohioan William Dean Howells.

Several anthologies sample Ohio writing from various periods and genres. Both nineteenth- and twentieth-century literature are collected in *Anthology of Western Reserve Literature* (1992), edited by David Rollin Anderson and Gladys Haddad. *Home Material: Ohio's Nineteenth-Century Regional Women's Fiction* (1998) was compiled by Sandra Parker. Emily Foster edited *The Ohio Frontier: An Anthology of Early Writings* (1996).

Prose anthologies include *Ohio Short Fiction: A Collection of Twenty-Two Stories by Ohio Writers* (1995), edited by Jon Saari; and *Good Roots: Writers Reflect on Growing Up in Ohio* (2007), edited by Lisa Watts, a collection of reminiscences by a score of contemporary Ohio authors. One of the first poetry anthologies of state authors is *The Poets and Poetry of the West: With Biographical and Critical Notices* (1860), collected by William Turner Coggeshall and published in Columbus; of the 152 poets included, 60 are Ohioans. Another, edited by Emerson Venable, is the substantial and still-important *Poets of Ohio: Selections Representing the Poetical Work of Ohio Authors, from the Pioneer Period to the Present Day, with Biographical Sketches and Notes* (1909). Ohio poetry is found in *Ohio Poets: An Anthology of 90 Contemporaries* (1934), edited by Henry Harrison; and *Contemporary Ohio Poetry: An Anthology of Mid-century Ohio Poetry* (1959), edited by George Abbe and sponsored by the Ohio Poetry Society. David Citino edited both *73 Ohio Poets* (1978) and *Poetry Ohio, Art of the State: An Anthology of Ohio Poems* (1984), published as special issues of the *Cornfield Review*. Elton Glaser and William Greenway edited *I Have My Own Song for It: Modern Poems of Ohio* (2002). Audrey A. P. Lavin and Ruth V. Tams Fuquen co-edited *Made in Ohio: Poetry and Prose* (2000). *An Anthology of Ohio Mexican American Writers* (1974) was edited by Joy Hintz of Heidelberg College.

FURTHER READING: No comprehensive literary history of Ohio has been published, but a number of sources provide useful starting points. Among the earliest is Peter Gibson Thomson's *A Bibliography of the State of Ohio* (1880); the majority of its fourteen hundred entries deal with the history of the state, but a few relate to literature. W. H. Venable's *Beginnings of Literary Culture in the Ohio Valley* (1891) is a survey of cultural elements, including the press, periodicals, libraries, and literature, through the end of the Civil War. *A Study of the Local Literature of the Upper Ohio Valley* (1921) by Mary Meek Atkeson examines pioneer and Indian tales of the early 1800s. A brief but useful introduction to the state's literature can be found in *The Ohio Guide* (1940), a volume in the Works Progress Administration (WPA) American Guide Series.

Sources dealing with PRINTING AND PUBLISHING in Ohio include one volume of the American Imprints Inventory of the WPA Historical Records Survey, *A Check List of Ohio Imprints, 1796–1820* (1941), which lists 590 items. For the state's newspapers, the indispensible reference is *Guide to Ohio Newspapers, 1793–1973* (1974), edited by Stephen Gutgesell, which expands and updates Osman Castle Hooper's *History of Ohio Journalism, 1793–1933* (1933). Although they are limited specifically to Cincinnati, two publications are worthy of note in relation to the history of publishing in Ohio: *The Western Book Trade: Cincinnati as a Nineteenth-Century Publishing and Book-Trade Center* (1961) by Walter Sutton and *Cincinnati German Imprints: A Checklist* (1993), Franziska C. Ott's comprehensive bibliography of German-language works.

W. Ralph Janeway's mimeographed compilation *A Selected List of Ohio Authors, and Their Books* (1933) was superseded by William Coyle's comprehensive *Ohio Authors and Their Books, 1796–1950* (1962), which provides substantial biographical information and listings of books for 4,700 authors from 1796 to 1950; however, its lack of a comprehensive index makes accessing its wealth of information difficult.

The series of antiquarian book catalogs from Robert G. Hayman (1921–2002) of Carey, Ohio, provides a very important but little-known source for bibliographic information on Ohio authors, literature, and publishing. In 150 catalogs, mostly titled "Americana" or "Literature of the Middle West" and issued from 1961 to 1994, there are many listings of obscure novels and poetry from obscure Ohioans; for the researcher and literary historian of the state, these are a valuable untapped resource.

A number of works include Ohio in their discussions, but not as the sole focus. All are out of date but still contain much worthwhile historical material. The oldest is Ralph Leslie Rusk's two-volume set *Literature of the Middle Western Frontier* (1925). Gerald Nemanic's *A Bibliographical Guide to Midwestern Literature* (1981) provides a great deal of information on prominent authors and works, many with Ohio connections. Because of Ohio's strong presence in children's literature, Donna Taylor's *The Great Lakes Region in Children's Books*

(1980), which contains an entire section on Ohio, is important for that genre.

The Ohioana Library maintains a website, Ohio Reading Road Trip, which contains biographies of prominent Ohio authors and bibliographies of their major works; it is designed primarily for middle school students and their teachers and offers DVDs and curriculum guides as adjuncts to the website.

Libraries and Repositories: An adjunct to the State Library of Ohio in Columbus, the Ohioana Library was established in 1929 by Martha Kinney Cooper (1884–1964), the wife of then governor Myers Cooper, as a home for publications by Ohio authors. The present mission, according to the statement approved by its board in 2002, is to "recognize and encourage the creative accomplishments of Ohioans, preserve, and expand a permanent archive of books, sheet music, manuscripts, and other materials by Ohioans and about Ohio, and disseminate information about the work of Ohio writers, musicians, and other artists to researchers, schools, and the general public." With more than 45,000 books, 10,000 pieces of sheet music, and approximately 20,000 biographical files on Ohio writers, musicians, and artists of note, it is undoubtedly the largest collection of Ohio literature in the state. In addition to fiction, poetry, and juvenile literature, the noncirculating collection also contains scrapbooks, original illustrations, pamphlets, and county histories and atlases.

DANIEL P. COMPORA   UNIVERSITY OF TOLEDO

PERIODICALS, LITERARY

OVERVIEW: From the rough-and-tumble journalists of CINCINNATI frontier days to modernist female editors HARRIET MONROE (1860–1936) and MARGARET C. ANDERSON (1886–1973) and contemporary poet-editors JIM (JAMES THOMAS) HARRISON (1937–2016) and DAN GERBER (b. 1940), the men and women at the helm of little magazines have nurtured the Midwestern voice, providing a publication venue to women, people of color, feminists and other progressives, and the imagist poets and pioneers of what Bernard Duffey in *The Chicago Renaissance in American Letters* (1954) called the Liberation, the Chicago Renaissance's second genera-

tion of poets and fiction writers who rejected earlier "genteel" literary norms, as well as subsequent authors of creative works. Midwestern literary magazines like *THE LITTLE REVIEW* and *REEDY'S MIRROR* have taken on the characters of their editors and publishers as they shaped the region's literary identity. These pioneers made seminal contributions to Midwestern and American literature, publishing writers such as EDGAR LEE MASTERS (1868–1950), (HERMAN) THEODORE DREISER (1871–1945), CARL (AUGUST) SANDBURG (1878–1967), SHERWOOD ANDERSON (1876–1941), and (HANNIBAL) HAMLIN GARLAND (1860–1940); several, including *POETRY: A MAGAZINE OF VERSE* and *Prairie Schooner*, have established national and international profiles as well.

HISTORY AND SIGNIFICANCE: Literary periodicals have been part of Midwestern culture since the early nineteenth century. Although almost every state had a fledgling literary periodical, such as *Illinois Monthly Magazine*, begun in Vandalia in 1830 and edited and published by JAMES HALL (1793–1868), and the *Chip Basket*, begun in Davenport, IOWA, in 1856 and printed and published by Hiram Reid (1834–1906), Cincinnati's frontier culture provided a particularly fertile matrix for literary periodicals. The earliest, Timothy Flint's *Western Monthly Review*, was published there from 1827 to 1830. Another such periodical, the *Western Messenger*, was published in Cincinnati, the Queen City, from 1835 to 1836 and 1839 to 1841 by a group of New England Unitarians. The *Western Messenger* professed to explain the often misunderstood principles of Unitarianism and disseminate ideas on literature and education. Originally edited by Ephraim Peabody, the magazine moved to Louisville, Kentucky, in April 1836 when James Freeman Clarke took over the editorship. It returned to Cincinnati in May 1839. Throughout its run the *Western Messenger* published the work of Christopher Pearse Cranch (1813–1892), Ralph Waldo Emerson (1803–1882), and Margaret Fuller (1810–1850).

The *Ladies' Repository*, published monthly in Cincinnati from 1841 to 1876, was founded by Samuel Williams to offer Christian women a magazine suited to their religious sensibilities. Contributors included Frances E(lizabeth Caroline) Willard (1839–1898), the founder of the Women's Christian Temperance Union; ALICE CARY (1820–1871); and PHOEBE CARY (1824–1871). In 1877 the magazine was superseded by the *National Repository,* also published in Cincinnati, and continued under that title until 1880. The Queen City was also home to the short-lived *Western Literary Journal and Monthly Magazine,* published by Lucius A. Hine in 1844–1845, which ceased after only six issues. *Golden Hours,* a Cincinnati children's magazine that operated from 1869 to 1880, published the early works of MARY HARTWELL CATHERWOOD (1847–1902).

As the frontier moved west, periodicals were founded to mark the spread of civilization. In Des Moines, Johnson Brigham (1846–1936) began publishing the *Midland Monthly* in 1894, featuring the work of ALICE FRENCH (1850–1934), writing under the name Octave Thanet, and Hamlin Garland; it ended publication in 1899. Farther south, in ST. LOUIS a veritable literary institution was born in the weekly publication the *Mirror,* later *Reedy's Mirror,* the most interesting aspect of which was, arguably, the personality at its helm—WILLIAM MARION REEDY (1862–1920), who edited it from 1896 until 1920. According to Max Putzel's *The Man in the Mirror* (1963), Reedy, dubbed the "Literary Boss of the Midwest" by Edgar Lee Masters, worked to subvert some of the genteel traits of traditional literary works and develop a native voice in poetry. The verse of Amy Lowell (1874–1925), SARA TEASDALE (1884–1933), Carl Sandburg, Ezra Pound (1885–1972), and (NICHOLAS) VACHEL LINDSAY (1879–1931) was featured in the magazine, as was the short fiction of Theodore Dreiser and Alice French. Particularly noteworthy were Reedy's advocacy and mentoring leading to the serial publication of Edgar Lee Masters's Spoon River poems before they appeared in book form in 1915. Renamed *Reedy's Mirror* in 1913, the magazine also published essays, articles, and even some literary gossip.

CHICAGO became a fertile field for literary journalism in the 1880s and 1890s. The *Current,* a weekly magazine second in literary importance in Chicago only to THE DIAL, was edited by Edgar L. Wakeman from 1883 to 1888 and published the work of Joaquin Miller (1837–1913) and OPIE PERCIVAL (POPE)

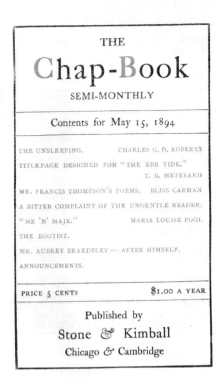

First issue of *The Chap-Book*. Stone & Kimball, 1894.
Image courtesy of Special Collections, Grand Valley State University Libraries

READ (1852–1939), among others. Another important publication was the semi-monthly *The Chap-Book,* an attempt to emulate the popular English *Yellow Book;* it published a wide variety of reviews, poems, and stories from May 1894 until July 1898, when it merged with *The Dial.* Selected stories from the *Chap-Book* were separately issued by the publisher, Herbert S. Stone, in *Chap-Book Stories* (1896). The *Chicago Ledger,* a weekly tabloid newspaper that featured serialized fiction, began publishing in 1872 and enjoyed the second-longest run of any Chicago literary magazine, publishing until 1924, when it merged with the *Saturday Blade* to form the *Blade and Ledger.*

The story of the literary magazines of the CHICAGO RENAISSANCE is tightly woven. Bernard Duffey argues in *The Chicago Renaissance in American Letters* that one of the three main shaping forces of the Renaissance was

Harriet Monroe's magazine *Poetry.* However, the seeds of the Renaissance began to take root earlier in the more literarily conservative *Dial,* founded by Francis Fisher Browne in 1880. *The Dial* was not Browne's first foray into editing; previously he had edited the *Lakeside Monthly,* published from 1869 to 1874, which Clarence Andrews considered the best Chicago-based literary magazine before the *Dial.* Issued by A. C. McClurg until Browne began publishing it in 1892, the *Dial* was Browne's attempt to disseminate works that reflected current Chicago literary trends, but it was not supportive of the poetic innovations that *Poetry: A Magazine of Verse* fostered. Browne believed that the citizens of Chicago were readers but not necessarily writers; therefore, the early issues mainly consisted of book reviews. Later the *Dial* published Chicago-based writers, including staff member Margaret Anderson. Although the *Dial* was literary, it was also known for publishing lengthy reviews of nonfiction, as well as editorials. The *Dial* moved to New York in 1918.

Browne's influence spilled over into another famous literary magazine of the Chicago Renaissance, *The Little Review.* The idea for the publication originated with free-spirited Margaret Anderson, a former book reviewer for the Chicago Presbyterian periodical *Interior* and a clerk in Browne's bookstore. Through her association with Browne, Anderson became acquainted with writers such as Theodore Dreiser and SUSAN KEATING GLASPELL (1876–1948). First published in March 1914, *The Little Review* was founded in the spirit of freedom that permeated the Liberation era and published essays, poems, fiction, and articles, using no guidelines other than Anderson's personal taste. However, that taste turned out to be discerning: *The Little Review* introduced the early works of Sherwood Anderson, BEN HECHT (1894–1964), ERNEST (MILLER) HEMINGWAY (1899–1961), and other Midwestern writers, as well as printing selections from *Ulysses* by James Joyce (1882–1941) as a work in progress. Anderson moved the magazine to New York in March 1917, where it was published until 1922. It then moved to Paris, where it was published sporadically until 1929. See PRINTING AND PUBLISHING.

A very prominent and influential magazine of the Chicago Renaissance was POETRY: A MAGAZINE OF VERSE, the brainchild of Harriet Monroe, a daring, talented writer and editor. Although Monroe was enamored of Chicago, she perceived that the city lacked a poetic voice. There was poetry in Chicago, but Monroe believed that none of it was alive, vital, or new; her goal was to promote more forward-looking verse. With that vision in mind, Monroe published the first issue of *Poetry* in October 1912. This issue included two poems by Ezra Pound along with his prediction of a complete poetic renaissance in America. *Poetry* published many of the early works of Carl Sandburg and Edgar Lee Masters, as well as early poems by Vachel Lindsay, GWENDOLYN BROOKS (1917–2000), and T(HOMAS) S(TEARNS) ELIOT (1888–1965).

An important *Poetry* tradition began when Monroe took strong editorial issue with *The Dial* over its extremely negative response to Sandburg's poems. When *The Dial* attacked Sandburg's work, Monroe responded by defending him editorially and awarding him the first Helen Haire Levinson Prize. The magazine has given the award to a worthy poet every year since 1914 except 1932. Other Levinson Prize winners include Edgar Lee Masters, Vachel Lindsay, Robert Frost (1874–1963), Amy Lowell, future *Poetry* editor KARL SHAPIRO (1913–2000), Edna St. Vincent Millay (1892–1950), and Dylan Thomas (1914–1953). Still published and financially secure today, *Poetry* continues to provide a venue for some of the nation's most celebrated poets.

Early in the twentieth century Midwestern colleges and universities began publishing little magazines that focused mainly on creative work and literary criticism. The *Kenyon Review,* issued by Kenyon College in Gambier, OHIO, began publishing in 1939; *Triquarterly,* initially a student literary publication of Northwestern University in Evanston, ILLINOIS, in 1958; *Midwest Quarterly,* a product of Pittsburg State University in Pittsburg, KANSAS, in 1959; *Michigan Quarterly Review,* at the University of Michigan, in 1962; and the *Beloit Poetry Journal,* a product of Beloit College in Beloit, WISCONSIN, in 1950. These are only a few of the major literary journals that have been affiliated with Midwestern institutions of higher learning.

One of the earliest and most influential of these was the MIDLAND, published at the University of Iowa from 1915 until 1930 by JOHN T(OWNER) FREDERICK (1893–1975) and carrying the subtitle *A Magazine of the Middle West*. The *Midland* introduced RUTH SUCKOW (1892–1960), PAUL (FREDERICK) COREY (1903–1992), and AUGUST (WILLIAM) DERLETH (1909–1971) to the reading public. In 1930 Frederick moved the *Midland* to Chicago, where it remained until it merged with the University of Montana's *Frontier* in 1933 to become *Frontier and Midland*. That title ceased in 1939.

Prairie Schooner, first published in January 1927, is a quarterly publication of the University of Nebraska–Lincoln's English Department. With Professor Lowry Wimberly (1890–1959) serving as the catalyst, *Prairie Schooner* was created by student members of the national literary society, Sigma Upsilon, who met at Wimberly's home. Their goal was to show the world that the Midwest had serious contributions to make to American literature. By the 1950s the magazine had an international list of subscribers and had been translated into several languages. Some of the magazine's prominent contributors include Truman Capote (1924–1984), (MARY) JESSAMYN WEST (1902–1984), Eudora Welty (1909–2001), BESS STREETER ALDRICH (1881–1954), and JOYCE CAROL OATES (b. 1938). This little magazine is among the oldest Midwestern literary magazines still publishing today.

New Letters began as the *University Review* in 1934. In 1944 its name changed to the *University of Kansas City Review*, but the magazine reverted to its original name in 1963 when its publisher became the University of Missouri–Kansas City. Since 1971 it has been known as *New Letters*. When publication began, its mission was to offer a selection of the finest writing by Midwestern writers. Since then, the magazine has adjusted its mission to include the finest writing from writers across the country. It has published work by Pearl S(ydenstricker) Buck (1892–1973), J(erome) D(avid) Salinger (1919–2010), E(dward) E(stlin) Cummings (1894–1962), Joyce Carol Oates, and RICHARD WRIGHT (1908–1960).

In 1946 the University of Chicago began the *Chicago Review*, a literary journal focused on maintaining a contemporary standard of good writing to counteract the overemphasis on the history and analysis of literature at the expense of creative writing. Despite its title, the *Chicago Review*, which is still being published, is not a regional journal; it publishes fiction, poetry, reviews, and essays by international as well as American writers. Some of the more noteworthy contributors to this magazine include William Carlos Williams (1883–1963), Marshall McLuhan (1911–1980), Philip (Milton) Roth (b. 1933), Susan Sontag (1933–2004), Adrienne (Cecile) Rich (1929–2012), Joyce Carol Oates, Kenneth Burke (1897–1993), and E(dward) E(stlin) Cummings.

During the years of the Beat Generation and beyond, the magazines of the Midwest have continued to publish works by up-and-coming authors. During its single-year run (1948–1949) the *Golden Goose* published the early works of poets Robert Creeley (1926–2005) and Charles Olson (1910–1970), both of whom counted Ezra Pound among their influences. That journal, which superseded *Cronos* and was located in Columbus, Ohio, also published works by William Carlos Williams, Kenneth Patchen (1911–1972), Kenneth Rexroth (1905–1982), and Lawrence Ferlinghetti (1919–2003). Another landmark little magazine was the quarterly edited by ROBERT (ELWOOD) BLY (b. 1926), the *Fifties* (subsequently renamed the *Sixties* and later the *Seventies*), founded in 1958 to publish the work of younger poets and foreign poetry in translation. Published in Pine Island, MINNESOTA, Bly's magazine encouraged the transition in American poetry from formalism and New Critical aesthetics to free verse influenced by world literature and surrealism.

In 1963 the English Department at the University of South Dakota established the *South Dakota Review*. Like the *Chicago Review*, the *South Dakota Review* does not confine itself to regional literature. Although there is a slight western regional emphasis, the journal is primarily a national literary publication, as well as a scholarly journal, publishing the works of both emerging and well-published writers. *Sumac*, short lived but nonetheless influential, was the creation of poets Jim Harrison and Dan Gerber. Published in Gerber's hometown of Fremont, MICHIGAN, beginning in 1968, *Sumac* was quickly lauded as a first-tier literary publication. Submissions were eclectic, including the works of four Pulitzer Prize winners and the early poems of James Tate (1943–2015), Denise Levertov (1923–1997), 2011–2012 U.S. Poet Laureate Philip Levine (1928–2015), Carl Rakosi (1903–2004), and (Dušan) Charles Simić (b. 1938). It also included translated works by poets originally writing in French, Chinese, Spanish, and Russian. Over its seven issues, *Sumac* published nine hundred poems before ceasing publication with the Fall 1971 issue.

In the late 1960s and early 1970s regional literature became the focus of serious literary study with the founding of the Western Literature Association (1965), the Society for the Study of Southern Literature (1968), and THE SOCIETY FOR THE STUDY OF MIDWESTERN LITERATURE (1971). The last organization has published *MidAmerica* annually since 1974. Along with its sister publication, *Midwestern Miscellany*, it features scholarly articles that continually grapple with questions of Midwestern place, voice, and boundaries.

Several publications dedicated to Midwestern culture began in the mid-twentieth century. Some of these have ceased publication, including the *Great Lakes Review*, based in Chicago and operating from 1974 to 1985; the *Old Northwest* from Miami University in Oxford, Ohio, which was published from 1975 to 1992; and *Western Illinois Regional Studies*, a Western Illinois University journal that was published from 1978 to 1991. Other Midwestern literary publications that began in the mid-twentieth century are continuing. Among these are *Inland Seas*, published continuously since 1945 by the Great Lakes Historical Society, and *Ohioana Quarterly*. The latter, published by the Martha Kinney Cooper Ohioana Library Association in Columbus, was founded in 1958 to collect, preserve, and promote the work of Ohio's artists, writers, and musicians and keep readers informed about the arts in Ohio. The *Ohioana Quarterly*, now published twice a year, provides reviews of recent books, articles, and essays about the literary and cultural arts in Ohio and an annotated list of new books received.

In 2000 Susan Swartwout and Frank Nickell began publishing a semi-annual periodical, *Big Muddy: A Journal of the Mississippi River Valley*. Published by Southeast Missouri State University Press, the magazine focuses on the ten states that border the Mississippi and features CREATIVE NONFICTION, essays, poetry, fiction, and research-oriented pieces. Three new literary periodicals, also inaugurated since the turn of the twenty-first century, are the *Lake Region Review*, published by the Lake Region Writers network in Battle Lake, Minnesota; *Ink Lit Mag*, published by the Iowa Writers Living-Learning Community in Iowa City, Iowa; and *Midwestern Gothic*, published quarterly in Ann Arbor, Michigan.

Many Midwestern publishers focus on women's literary and political writings. *Primavera*, an annual founded in Chicago by Janet Ruth Heller and others and dedicated to women's interests and literature, first appeared in 1975. It suspended publication in 2007. *Black Maria*, a quarterly published from 1972 to 1984, grew out of the Chicago Women's Liberation Union and focused on current issues in the women's movement and literature. In 1975 the University of Chicago Press began publishing *Signs: Journal of Women in Culture and Society*, a journal dedicated to issues of gender, culture, class, and sexuality that is still published today. Five years later, the University of Wisconsin began publishing a pedagogically focused journal that offers reviews focused on teaching and research in women's studies, *Feminist Collections: A Quarterly of Women's Studies Resources*; it is now part of a joint subscription with *Feminist Periodicals*. *Bridges: A Jewish Feminist Journal* began publication in 1990 in Ann Arbor, Michigan, moved to Indiana University Press, and ceased publication in 2011.

Midwestern protest and revolt are reflected in its little magazines. The inaugural issue of the socialist periodical *Tri-City Worker's Magazine* in November 1905 included a poem by FLOYD DELL (1887–1969), soon to become a leader in the Chicago and Greenwich Village liberation movements. In 1906 Dell became editor of this Rock Island, Illinois, publication and contributed several muckraking articles and published book reviews and poems before the magazine ceased publication later that year after eleven issues. Although the Davenport, Iowa, radical journal the *Left,* founded in 1931, published only two issues, those numbers included works by John Cheever (1912–1982), Norman Macleod (1906–1985), (JOHN WESLEY) "JACK" CONROY (1898–1990), Horace Gregory (1898–1982), and Louis Zukofsky (1904–1978). The *Anvil: The Proletarian Fiction Magazine,* a slightly longer-lived magazine edited by Jack Conroy, was published in Moberly, MISSOURI, from 1933 to 1935 and included many writings on race and class. Conroy, who was eager to encourage new writers who were sympathetic to the proletarian literary movement, published "Daughter" and "Blue Boy" by Erskine Caldwell (1903–1987) after mainstream publications refused them because they dealt with sensitive race issues. The *Anvil* was also home to works by authors such as JAMES T(HOMAS) FARRELL (1904–1979), LANGSTON (JAMES MERCER) HUGHES (1902–1967), and Norman Macleod. It combined with the *Partisan Review* in 1935.

Chicago became a major center for African American periodicals in the 1940s when John H. Johnson (1918–2005) founded his publishing empire. Johnson published *Ebony* (1945), *Jet* (1951), and *Negro Digest* (1942), which was renamed *Black World* in 1970 after it increasingly began to reflect the values, goals, and spirit of the Black Power movement. Edited by Hoyt W. Fuller, *Black World* published essays, articles, short stories, and poems. Its global outlook was reflected in its anti-colonial editorial position that blacks in the United States would not be completely free until all vestiges of colonialism were eliminated in Africa and blacks controlled its wealth and governments. It ended publication in 1976. The first scholarly black journal in the United States, *Midwest Journal,* was founded in Jefferson City, Missouri, at Lincoln University. This periodical, published from 1948 to 1956, focused on research in the social sciences and humanities and published articles and book reviews, as well as literary theory, literary criticism, history, some creative writing, and seminal essays on race and culture, such as W(illiam) E(dward) Burghardt Du Bois's (1868–1963) famous essay "The Freedom to Learn."

The momentum of the civil rights movement in the 1960s generated several black publications in the Midwest. The *Negro American Literature Forum,* first published in Terre Haute at Indiana State University in 1967, was a quarterly that published essays on black American literature, art, and culture, as well as bibliographies, interviews, poetry, and book reviews. In 1976 its name changed to *Black American Literature Forum;* since 1992 it has been known as *African American Review. AIM: America's Intercultural Magazine* was published in Chicago starting in 1974. *The Black Writer,* a Chicago quarterly published from 1983 to 1988, presented the poetry, articles, and fiction of African Americans. In 1982 the *Afro-Hispanic Review,* a bilingual journal of literature and culture aimed at the Spanish-speaking black diaspora, was founded at the University of Missouri. This journal publishes literary criticism, book reviews, translations, and creative writing and is now located at Vanderbilt University.

The first major Latino/Latina periodical published in the Midwest was *The Rican: Journal of Contemporary Puerto Rican Thought,* founded in 1971 at Northeastern Illinois University in Chicago to promote Puerto Rican culture; it was published under the aegis of the Midwest Institute of Puerto Rican Studies and Culture until it ceased in 1975. Edited by Samuel Betances, the journal published essays in the social sciences and original writing by Puerto Ricans living in the United States. A more broadly based periodical, *Revista Chicano-Riqueña,* was the first national magazine devoted to U.S. LATINO/LATINA LITERATURE. Founded by Nicolás Kanellos and Luis Dávila at Indiana University-Northwest in Gary in 1972 this journal moved to the University of Houston in 1982, changed its name to *Americas Review* in 1986, and ceased publication in 1999. In 1981 *Third Woman* began publishing semi-annually at Indiana University, featuring poetry, creative prose, visual art, book reviews, and scholarly essays by and about Chicanas, other Latinas, and Latin American women. *Third Woman* frequently dealt with issues of Chicana, Latina, and borderland feminism. This journal, which ceased publication in 1986, also helped emphasize the prominence of Latino/Latina culture in the Midwest. A more recent addition to Chicago's diverse literary publications is

Revista Chicano-Riqueña, volume 3, issue 1, 1975.
Reprinted by permission from Revista Chicano-Riqueña. © Arte Público Press–University of Houston

Mizna: Prose, Poetry, and Art Exploring Arab America, volume 14, issue 1, 2013. Cover art by Osama Esid.

the semi-annual *Diálogo,* published by the Center for Latino Research at DePaul University since 1996, although it has recently become irregular. The magazine's mission is to publish creative and scholarly works that forge links between the academic community and the increasing Latino/Latina population.

Another groundbreaking periodical is *Mizna,* the first and still the only journal of ARAB AMERICAN LITERATURE. Based in St. Paul, Minnesota (see MINNEAPOLIS/ST. PAUL), where it has been published since 1999, *Mizna* features poetry, prose, and artwork that expose "American audiences to the breadth and depth of the current, vital culture of the Middle East and of Arabs in America" while countering "stereotypes of Arabs that bombard Americans on a daily basis" (*Mizna* website). The Mizna organization also produces an Arab Film Festival and arts events at its center in St. Paul.

SELECTED WORKS: *Prairie Schooner, Poetry, MidAmerica, Ohioana Quarterly, Big Muddy, Diálogo, New Letters,* and *Mid-American Review* are among the literary periodicals of the Midwest that are still active. The entire run of *The Little Review* was reprinted in 1967. Readers interested in sampling the contents of some of these magazines can consult, for example, *Stories from the "Midland"* (1924), *The "Prairie Schooner" Caravan* (1943), *"The Little Review" Anthology* (1953), *The "Sumac" Reader* (1996), and *The "Poetry" Anthology, 1912–2002* (2002). Full or partial runs of some of these periodicals have also become available electronically, for example, *Ladies' Repository, The Dial, The Chap-Book,* and *Poetry.* The Black Maria Collective published *The Black Maria: Women Speak* (1984).

FURTHER READING: Those interested in learning more about William Marion Reedy will find Max Putzel's *The Man in the Mirror: William Marion Reedy and His Magazine* (1963) worthwhile; similarly, Margaret Anderson's autobiography, *My Thirty Years' War* (1930), will provide inside information on the trajectory of *The Little Review* and its iconoclastic editor. More information about *Third Woman* can be found in Catherine Ramírez's article "Alternative Cartographies: *Third Woman* and the Respatialization of the Borderlands," *Midwestern Miscellany* 30 (Fall 2002): 47–62. Books discussing the literary periodicals of the Chicago Renaissance include Bernard Duffey's *The Chicago Renaissance in American Letters* (1954), Ellen Williams's *Harriet Monroe and the Poetry Renaissance: The First Ten Years of "Poetry,"* 1912–22 (1977), Clarence A. Andrews's *Chicago in Story: A Literary History* (1982), Carl S. Smith's *Chicago and the American Literary Imagination, 1880–1920* (1984), Dale Kramer's *Chicago Renaissance: The Literary Life in the Midwest, 1900–1930* (1966), and *Writers of the Black Chicago Renaissance* by Steven C. Tracy (2011).

Frank Luther Mott's five-volume series *A History of American Magazines* (1938–1968) covers centuries of American publication history and includes valuable information on Midwestern periodicals. John T. Frederick wrote sections of the last volume, published after Mott's death. Also valuable is the two-volume *American Literary Magazines* (1986 and 1992), edited by Edward E. Chielens; the first volume covers the eighteenth and nineteenth centuries, and the second, the twentieth century. *The Little Magazine: A History and a Bibliography* (1946) by Frederick Hoffman, Charles Allen, and Carolyn Ulrich, while dated, is an important source on the early history and development of the form, and its comprehensive chronological listing of magazines includes both well-known and obscure Midwestern titles. Information on Midwestern periodicals can also be found in Ralph Rusk's two-volume *The Literature of the Middle Western Frontier* (1925); in *The Little Magazine in America: A Modern Documentary History* (1978), edited by Elliot Anderson and Mary Kinzie; and in Gerald Nemanic's *A Bibliographical Guide to Midwestern Literature* (1981). A later book on this subject is *Paper Dreams: Writers and Editors on the American Literary Magazine* (2013), edited by Travis Kurowski

The John T. Frederick Papers at the University of Norte Dame Library include materials relating to his editorship of the *Midland*. The University of Wisconsin Library at Madison holds one of the most extensive collections of twentieth-century magazines in the United States. Many of the periodicals discussed in this entry can be found in this collection.

RACHEL BRENEMAN, JENNIFER CATHEY, ASHLEY HOPKINS, AND MARCIA NOE

THE UNIVERSITY OF TENNESSEE AT CHATTANOOGA

PHILOSOPHY

OVERVIEW: In considering Midwestern philosophy, one must begin by distinguishing it from the philosophy of the Midwest. The possible existence of the latter depends on the highly suspect notion that there is or might be a way of viewing the world that could be authentically Midwestern despite the demonstrable diversity of viewpoints held by Midwesterners of the past and present. On the other hand, the possible existence of Midwestern philosophy depends on the more likely prospect that philosophers have given theoretical expression to ideas and themes that reflect the influence of Midwestern life and express aspects of Midwestern culture. It should also be emphasized that questions about the history and content of Midwestern philosophy cannot be answered simply by enumerating philosophers born and raised in the Midwest or by listing those whose professional careers have been spent in the Midwest. The works of a philosopher born and raised in the Midwest or who spent his or her professional career in the Midwest would be irrelevant to this inquiry unless those works could be shown to have been decisively influenced by the Midwestern locale and to express some aspect of Midwestern culture. If one applies this standard, only a few philosophers can be said to have written works that exemplify Midwestern philosophy.

The first philosophers in the Midwest were a group of Ohioans influenced by G(eorg) W(ilhelm) F(riedrich) Hegel (1770–1831), including Johann B. Stallo (1823–1900), August Willich (1810–1878), and Peter Kaufmann (1806–1869). Willich was a leftist Hegelian and a political revolutionary, while Stallo emphasized Hegel's significance for the philosophy of science, and Kaufman argued that Hegelianism could be reconciled with Christianity. Whatever their differences, it is not clear that the philosophy of any of the three could be characterized as Midwestern in inspiration. In contrast, another group of thinkers influenced by Hegel formed a school of philosophy, the St. Louis movement, whose inspiration clearly derived from its Midwestern locale. The school originated around 1860 in Sᴛ. Loᴜɪs and remained a major force in American philosophy throughout the second half of the nineteenth century.

In the twentieth century the University of Chicago provided a home to many prominent philosophers. In the first quarter of the century a Cʜɪᴄᴀɢᴏ school of psychology, sociology, and education developed under the philosophical leadership of John Dewey (1859–1952) and George Herbert Mead (1863–1931). After the reorganization of the University of Chicago under Robert Maynard Hutchins (1899–1977), who served as president and chancellor from 1930 to 1951, recognizable Chicago schools emerged in law, economics, sociology, and literary criticism. In most cases, however, any connection between the Midwest and the Chicago schools is speculative at best. On the other hand, the inspiration for philosophical work of Alvin Plantinga (b. 1932) may be traced to the Calvinist religious culture that has flourished in communities scattered throughout the Midwest.

HISTORY AND SIGNIFICANCE: The St. Louis movement in philosophy began with the meeting of William Torrey Harris (1835–1909) and Henry Conrad Brokmeyer (1818–1906) in 1858. Their shared interest in German idealism and especially the thought of Hegel led them to found the St. Louis Philosophical Society in 1866. Other important members of the group were Denton Jacques Snider (1841–1925), Thomas Davidson (1840–1900), and George (Holmes) Howison (1834–1916). The best-known and most influential member of the group was Harris, not only because of his editorship of the *Journal of Speculative Philosophy* and his writings but especially because of his work as an educational administrator, first as superintendent of schools in St. Louis and then as the U.S. commissioner of education for seventeen years (1889–1906).

Perhaps the movement's most important contribution to American philosophy was the founding of the *Journal of Speculative Philosophy*. Edited by Harris, it quickly became what William H. Goetzmann (1930–2010) in *The American Hegelians* (1973) calls "the most important philosophical journal in America from 1867 to 1893," its years of publication (8). As Goetzmann points out, the journal published articles by virtually all the important American philosophers of the era, including the founders of pragmatism, Charles Sanders Peirce (1839–1914), William James (1842–1910), and John Dewey, as well as essays by members of the St. Louis school. One of the key works of the movement, Brokmeyer's translation of Hegel's *Logic,* has remained unpublished. Circulating in manuscript among the members of the society, it provided the basis for the discussions of Hegel that dominated the society's sessions.

Despite their respect for Hegel, the members of the society saw their philosophy as an expression of the new society and culture forming in St. Louis and the Midwest. Denton Snider, the historian of the movement, described the spirit of the group, as quoted in Goetzmann's *The American Hegelians,* as "fresh, native to the soil, sprung of the place and the time" (29). While the New England transcendentalists, who also drew on German idealism, were concerned primarily with the individual rather than society, the St. Louis thinkers followed Hegel in arguing that the individual could find fulfillment only within society. They stressed the importance of education in creating the new kind of citizen required for the growth of the new democratic republic.

One of the most successful projects of the St. Louis movement was the Concord Summer School of Philosophy and Literature, operating from 1879 to 1888, where Harris, Snider, and other Midwesterners lectured and taught as equals alongside well-known eastern transcendentalists like Bronson Alcott (1799–1888) and even Ralph Waldo Emerson (1803–1882). According to a source quoted in Herbert Schneider's *History of American Philosophy* (1946), the school was "a Midwestern triumph of culture" (391).

The St. Louis movement appears to have been the only school of thought of any prominence that claimed to speak for a peculiarly Midwestern philosophical vision. The approaches of the various Chicago schools in the social sciences, literary criticism, and law that developed in the twentieth century owed much more to the intellectual orientation of specific academic departments at the University of Chicago than to any broader intellectual currents in the city of Chicago or the Midwest. The success of the University of Chicago as a new home for philosophical ideas originating outside the United States may derive, paradoxically, from the very absence of philosophy as a recognizable and significant part of Midwestern life. In *The Closing of the American Mind* (1987) by Allan (David) Bloom (1930–1992), who grew up in Indianapolis before becoming a professor in the University of Chicago's Committee on Social Thought, Bloom suggests that his capacity for philosophic wonder derived in large part from a philosophical innocence attributable to his Midwestern upbringing. This innocence made possible a "naïve profundity" (345) that allowed him to take philosophy and its ideals seriously. The same pervasively middle-class Midwestern culture that impelled both the fictional literary character James Gatz, alias Jay Gatsby, and his creator, F(RANCIS) SCOTT (KEY) FITZGERALD (1896–1940), to believe that the rich are different allowed a later Midwesterner, Bloom, to believe that it is not the rich but the philosophers who are truly different.

Whether or not philosophy has been a major factor in Midwestern culture at least since the demise of the St. Louis movement, it is demonstrably true that RELIGION has always played a prominent role. The outlook of Alvin Plantinga, one of the most prominent contemporary philosophers, derives from the form of Calvinism first articulated in Holland, especially the province of Friesland, and brought to the Middle West by immigrants such as his grandparents in the nineteenth century. Western Michigan, especially the Grand Rapids area, became one of the centers of Dutch Reformed life in the United States. Plantinga asserts that the intellectual turning point of his life was his decision after his freshman year at Harvard University to leave for Calvin College in Grand Rapids. Plantinga's father taught psychology at Calvin, but even more important for Plantinga, the leading figure in the Department of Philosophy, William Jellema, defended the intellectual validity of Christianity by seriously engaging the most impressive versions of the anti-religious arguments Plantinga had encountered at Harvard. After earning a PhD at Yale and teaching at Wayne State University in Detroit, Plantinga returned to Calvin in 1963 as a professor, replacing his mentor, Jellema. In 1982 he began teaching at Notre Dame University in INDIANA. In books such as *God and Other Minds* (1967), *The Nature of Necessity* (1974), *God, Freedom and Evil* (1974), *Does God Have a Nature?* (1980), and *Warranted Christian Belief* (2000), Plantinga has offered an intellectual justification for belief in God in a project that has come to be known as reformed epistemology.

Philosophical study continues in the Midwest. To date, the St. Louis movement of the second half of the nineteenth century and the thought arising from Calvinism, Alvin Plantinga, and the Dutch Reformed Church in western MICHIGAN constitute the fullest embodiment of organic Midwestern philosophy.

SELECTED WORKS: None of the works of the founders of the St. Louis movement are in print, but William Goetzmann's anthology *The American Hegelians* (1973) includes generous excerpts from the writings of William Torrey Harris, Henry Brokmeyer, and Denton Snider, as well as selections from the Ohio Hegelians Johann Stallo, August Willich, and Peter Kaufmann. Loyd D. Easton's *Hegel's First American Followers* (1966) includes excerpts from the works of Moncure Conway (1832–1907), Stallo, Willich, and Kaufmann. John Dewey's works are available in many editions; a scholarly edition of his complete works, *The Collected Works of John Dewey, 1882–1953* (1996), has been edited by Jo Ann Boydston and published by Southern Illinois University Press. A convenient source for the work of George Herbert Mead is *Selected Writings: George Herbert Mead* (1964), edited by Andrew J. Reck. Almost ignored in the controversy over *The Closing of the American Mind* (1987) by Allan Bloom is its interest as a Midwestern intellectual autobiography. Alvin Plantinga is the author of many books. An introduction to his thought is available in *The Analytic Theist: An Alvin Plantinga Reader* (1998), edited by James F. Sennett. Plantinga's "Spiritual Autobiography" can be found on the Calvin College website.

FURTHER READING: Volume 2 of Elizabeth Flower and Murray Murphey's *A History of Philosophy in America* (1977) begins with a chapter on the St. Louis Hegelians. Herbert Schneider's *A History of American Philosophy* (1946) is a standard work. Two books by Henry Pochmann discuss the St. Louis movement: *German Culture in America* (1957) and *New England Transcendentalism and St. Louis Hegelianism* (1948). For the debates arising over *The Closing of the American Mind,* see *Essays on "The Closing of the American Mind"* (1989), edited by Robert L. Stone; and *Beyond Cheering and Bashing: New Perspectives on "The Closing of the American Mind"* (1992), edited by William K. Buckley and James Seaton. Alvin Plantinga's thought is considered in D. Z. Phillip's *Faith after Foundationalism* (1988).

JAMES SEATON   MICHIGAN STATE UNIVERSITY

PIONEER ACCOUNTS.
See Frontier and Pioneer Accounts

PLAYS.
See Drama

POETRY: A MAGAZINE OF VERSE
OVERVIEW: *Poetry,* originally subtitled *A Magazine of Verse* and published in CHICAGO throughout its 104 year history, is one of the longest continuously running magazines in the United States. Launched by HARRIET MONROE (1860–1936), a poet, playwright, and journalist, its first issue appeared in October 1912. In its early years, because of Monroe's influence, as well as that of other leading advocates of new poetic norms, *Poetry* opened doors to new poets and regularly sounded a note of rebellion against late nineteenth-century poetics. Today *Poetry* enjoys a circulation of nearly 30,000, receives more than 90,000 submissions from around the world each year, and enjoys an assured financial future.

Poetry published many of the most influential poets of the twentieth century, among

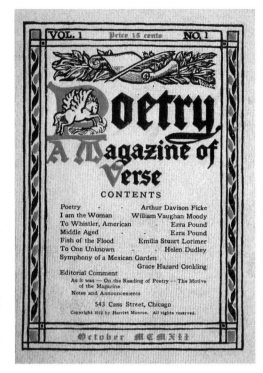

First issue of Harriet Monroe's *Poetry: A Magazine of Verse,* October 1912.
Image files © The Modernist Journals Project. Image courtesy of the Modernist Journals Project (Brown University and the University of Tulsa), http://www.modjourn.org

them T(HOMAS) S(TEARNS) ELIOT (1888–1965), Marianne (Craig) Moore (1887–1972), Wallace Stevens (1879–1955), William Carlos Williams (1883–1963), William Butler Yeats (1865–1939), CARL (AUGUST) SANDBURG (1878–1967), and GWENDOLYN BROOKS (1917–2000). *Poetry*'s advocacy of Midwestern poets like Sandburg, (NICHOLAS) VACHEL LINDSAY (1879–1931), EDGAR LEE MASTERS (1868–1950), and Gwendolyn Brooks was important to the emergence and recognition of twentieth-century Midwestern and American poetics, as well as of the CHICAGO RENAISSANCE.

HISTORY AND SIGNIFICANCE: At the beginning of the twentieth century American periodicals were oriented toward serious prose, not poetry, and the poetry they published and reviewed favorably reflected late nineteenth-century genteel American romanticism. In ST. LOUIS the *Sunday Mirror,* or *REEDY'S MIRROR,* as it was later titled was the leading exception, and the amount of space it could devote to literature and poetry was very limited. Much more representative was THE DIAL, a Chicago-based literary journal with very conservative literary tastes.

Poetry has always focused exclusively on poetry. The magazine owed its initial funding to notable Chicago business leaders, including the Sears Roebuck Company, the McCormick family of International Harvester fame, and the Chicago area's major utility magnates. They funded Poetry to support the local literary initiative, secure their personal reputations as not only corporate but also cultural leaders, and rebut Chicago's negative turn-of-the-century image as a culturally void, gritty industrial, railroad, commercial, and slaughterhouse center. Their motivation with Poetry was the same as that driving their support for the 1893 Chicago World's Columbian Exposition and the early purchase of impressionist art by the Chicago Art Institute.

From the beginning, Harriet Monroe advocated for new poetics and movement away from established genteel romantic form and content in poetry. The first issue, October 1912, carried Monroe's editorial statement, "The Motive of the Magazine," which was "to publish in Poetry some of the best work now being done in English verse. . . . The test . . . is to be quality alone; all forms . . . will be acceptable" (24). Despite her apparent welcome to all poetic forms and styles, little traditional verse found its way onto Poetry's pages.

During 1914 and 1915 Poetry flourished in what are often regarded as its most fecund years. The firm editorial guidance of Harriet Monroe and the remarkable support and contributions of many leading poets and literary theoreticians of the day, such as Ezra Pound (1885–1972), F(rank) S(tuart) Flint (1885–1960), Amy Lowell (1874–1925), and Ford Madox Ford (1873–1939), were critical to the emergence and recognition of new poetry. Poetry provided significant new opportunities for publication to aspiring new poets, the luxury of payment for accepted contributions, ongoing instruction by leading national and international poets and critics, advocacy for realist, imagist, impressionist, and modernist poetics and

for the poets who practiced them, and staunch editorial defense against attacks from more traditional literary journals.

Among the many important poetic contributions in the first few years were Carl Sandburg's March 1914 publication of "Chicago Poems" (3:191) and T. S. Eliot's June 1915 "The Love Song of J. Alfred Prufrock" (6:130). Significant early Poetry articles defining and supporting new poetics included Ezra Pound's March 1913 "A Few Don'ts by an Imagiste" (2: 202–06), F. S. Flint's "Imagisme" in the same issue (198–200), Harriet Monroe's November and December 1913 "Rhythms of English Verse, Parts I and II" (3:61–68, 100–111), Amy Lowell's March 1914 "Vers Libre and Metrical Prose" (3:213–20), her October 1914 "Nationalism in Art" (3:33–38), and Ford Madox Ford's August and September 1913 "Impressionism–Some Speculations" (2:182–85, 280–87).

Poetry was equally strong in defending new writers and poetics. For example, when The Dial attacked Edgar Lee Masters's SPOON RIVER ANTHOLOGY (1915) with a very negative review, citing its "deliberate unloveliness," "extraordinary study in mortuary statistics," and "cruel and unusual" events that occur, Alice Corbin Henderson (1881–1949) rose to the defense, saying in her August 1916 response, "Our Friend and Enemy," "Is Mr. Alden's criticism of a type to guide or instruct in any way the professional craft of poets? I do not think so. Its tendency is simply to discourage the public. . . . The Dial is one of the few journals in America devoted exclusively to the interests of literature. It is a sad commentary on the present state of criticism that it should be recorded of The Dial . . . that it recognizes merit only after the fact. For the initial recognition, genius must look to other tribunals" (6:259, 261). Poetry clearly intended to be chief among those tribunals.

In this heady environment Poetry thrived. In doing so, it also played a key role as a medium in the Chicago Renaissance, a literary movement that, in the words of Carla Cappetti (b. 1956) in Writing Chicago: Modernism, Ethnography, and the Novel (1993), "brought the world to Chicago and Chicago to the world" (7). The Renaissance brought many Midwestern poets, fiction writers, and journalists to national and international attention, among them Sandburg, Lindsay, and Masters.

In 1914, 1915, and 1916, respectively, these three won *Poetry's* Helen Haire Levinson Prize, a $500 prize endowed by Salmon O(liver) Levinson (1865–1941) and awarded annually to a single author from 1914 to the present. The choice of Sandburg, Lindsay, and Masters during the first three years of the prize further established Chicago as a significant cultural center, *Poetry* magazine as a rallying point for new poets, and Midwestern literature as a trendsetter on the national and international literary scene.

By 1916, however, problems multiplied. Although significant early funding had come from Chicago's leading citizens, it became evident that Monroe had downplayed *Poetry's* financial problems. She had also tried to ignore questions of her overt censorship in late 1915. After a spring 1916 meeting in New York, she attempted to repair the breach and reached out to poets who had come to associate themselves with a rival magazine, *Others,* including Skipwith Cannell (1888–1957) and William Carlos Williams, but was rebuffed. More positively, the November 1916 issue of *Poetry* saw the second publication by Robert Frost (1874–1963), "Snow" (9:57), as well as the now-famous poems "Marriage," "Naked," and "Summer Song" by Williams (9:81).

World War I contributed to *Poetry's* malaise. Both Williams and Sandburg continued to be productive poets, but only Sandburg contributed extensively to *Poetry* during the war. Over time, the Chicago Renaissance gave way to the Harlem Renaissance, and *Poetry's* pivotal era was behind it.

With Monroe's unexpected death in 1936, leadership passed to her assistant, Morton Dauwen Zabel (1902–1964), who oversaw *Poetry* for a year. A number of others followed in the decades to come. In 1937 George Dillon (1906–1968) assumed the editorship. During this time the Harriet Monroe Poetry Award was established, as stipulated in her will. The importance of this award grew as its recipients came to include Marianne Moore, E(dward) E(stlin) Cummings (1894–1962), Robert Penn Warren (1905–1989), Elizabeth Bishop (1911–1979), Allen Ginsberg (1926–1997), Wallace Stevens, and Robert Lowell (1917–1977). Dillon edited *Po-*

etry through 1942 and again from 1946 through 1949, while PETER DE VRIES (1910–1993) edited the magazine during the intervening years. Hayden Carruth (1921–2008) followed in 1949. His emphasis on prose works proved unpopular, and *Poetry* passed into the hands of Pulitzer Prize–winning poet KARL (JAY) SHAPIRO (1913–2000), who edited it for five years. Shapiro's leadership included an emphasis on poetry in translation, particularly from the post–World War II era in Spanish, Portuguese, and Greek. Shapiro left *Poetry* in 1956 turning the reins over to Henry Rago (1915–1969), a confident editor and gifted fund-raiser whose fourteen-year tenure provided continuity and hospitality to more diverse schools of poetry, including the poems of Sylvia Plath (1932–1963). During Daryl Hine's tenure *Poetry* shed its official politically neutral stance and published a full anti-war issue in September 1970. Joseph Parisi (b. 1944) began his twenty-one-year editorship in 1983.

In 1984 *Poetry* was dropped from the *Reader's Guide to Periodical Literature,* among other indexes, during a period of cutbacks in library budgets. However, it rebounded from these setbacks, regained its readership, and received an unprecedented $100 million Lilly Foundation grant in 2002. That grant has had a profound impact on the magazine. Receipt of the Lilly gift was followed by the arrival of Christian Wiman (b. 1966) as editor. The Poetry Foundation, which now oversees the magazine, currently includes such electronic resources as *harriet: the blog* and a podcast, *Off the Shelf,* which was picked up by National Public Radio in 2007.

SELECTED WORKS: Many of the manuscripts reviewed by Harriet Monroe and Ezra Pound are available through the "Harriet Monroe Modern Poetry Library Record, 1936–1970" at the Special Collections and Manuscripts division of the Special Collections Research Center at the University of Chicago. Joseph Parisi and Stephen Young edited *The "Poetry" Anthology: Ninety Years of America's Most Distinguished Verse Magazine* (2002). Don Share and Christian Wiman edited *The Open Door: 100 Poems, 100 Years of "Poetry" Magazine* (2012). Past issues of *Poetry,* beginning with October 1912, may be read on the searchable online archive found on the Poetry Foundation website.

FURTHER READING: The creation and development of *Poetry* are covered by Ellen Williams's *Harriet Monroe and the Poetry Renaissance: The First Ten Years of "Poetry," 1912–22* (1977). On the Chicago Renaissance and its role in the Midwest, see Dale Kramer's *Chicago Renaissance: The Literary Life in the Midwest, 1900–1930* (1966), an author-centered study that includes a chapter each on Lindsay, Masters, and Sandburg. Chapter 10 of Bernard I. Duffey's *The Chicago Renaissance in American Letters* (1954) discusses *Poetry* along with THE LITTLE REVIEW and the *Friday Literary Review* of the *Chicago Evening Post* as three major voices of the Liberation, the nongenteel second generation of the Chicago Renaissance. Philip A. Greasley discusses the significance of *Poetry* in "Mid American Poetry in Midwestern Little Magazines" in *Mid America* 5 (1977): 50–65. Additional sources include a chapter devoted to *Poetry* in *The Little Magazine: A History and a Bibliography* (1946) by Frederick J. Hoffman, Charles A. Allen, and Carolyn F. Ulrich and *Between the Lines: A History of "Poetry" in Letters* (2006) by Joseph Parisi and Stephen Young. For a broader view of Chicago and literary trends surrounding that city, see Carl S. Smith's *Chicago and the American Literary Imagination, 1880–1920* (1984). *The Encyclopedia of Chicago* (2004), a print and an online reference work edited by Janice L. Rieff,, summarizes the leading figures and trends of the Chicago Renaissance in its entry "Chicago Literary Renaissance." The editorial files of *Poetry* are held at the University of Chicago library's Special Collections Research Center.

HANNAH COFFEY
THE UNIVERSITY OF TENNESSEE AT CHATTANOOGA

POETRY SLAMS

OVERVIEW: Although the term "poetry slam" has become synonymous with performance poetry competitions, it was originally coined by Chicagoan Marc Kelly Smith (b. 1949) to describe the cabaret-style poetry show he began at Chicago's Green Mill Tavern in July 1986. Interactive by design, poetry slams encourage an audience to respond energetically and honestly to the poems presented on stage. Cheering, booing, hissing, finger snapping, and foot stomping are customs. Most slams have an open-microphone policy, a segment of guest performances ranging from solo poets to multimedia presentations, with a slam competition closing out the night.

The slam competitions that evolved out of Smith's original show have spread across the world. Slam is a format for performance, not a genre. Simply, it marries the art of performance with the art of poetry. At most competitions judges are selected randomly from the audience and are instructed to give numerical scores on a scale of zero to ten or one to ten based on the poet's content and performance. The competitive atmosphere compels the audience to listen and adds an extra element of entertainment to a literary event.

Since the first poetry slams in 1986, the show's popularity has increased exponentially. Today poetry slams are held throughout the Midwest, as well as in every state in the nation and many European and Asian countries. The slam has rejuvenated poetry and has created new opportunities for poets to share their work. It has also challenged traditional institutions to redefine poetry, has spawned new careers in the literary arts, has inspired poets outside academia to join MFA programs, and has become one of the most successful tools for teaching and engaging grade school and high school students in the reading and writing of poetry. In doing so, the poetry slam has established its place in the literary landscape.

HISTORY AND SIGNIFICANCE: In 1984 poetry had little audience outside academic institutions. In that year Marc Kelly Smith, a former construction worker, began experimenting with poetry and cabaret performance art at the Get Me High Lounge in CHICAGO. He encouraged the audience to express their disapproval with groans and appreciation with applause. In July 1986 Smith initiated a second show at Chicago's Green Mill Tavern to provide a weekly outlet for the antics of the Chicago Poetry Ensemble, a performance troupe he had formed in 1985. To inject pageantry and surprise into these performances, Smith and the ensemble donned costumes, wielded props, and interwove poetry with music and spectacle. The three-hour event was capped by a mock competition between rival poets. Smith called the show the Uptown Poetry Slam, an event he has hosted ever since, playing to

Marc Kelly Smith on stage at the Green Mill Tavern, Chicago.
Courtesy of Emily Thornton Calvo

standing-room-only audiences every Sunday night. The show has attracted tens of thousands of poets and fans and has evolved into a mecca for performance poets.

Not long after, slams modeled on the Uptown show appeared in Ann Arbor, MICHIGAN, and Milwaukee, WISCONSIN. In 1989 Gary Mex Glazner, a florist from California, visited the Green Mill and took the idea home to San Francisco, where he produced the first National Poetry Slam in October 1990, with Marc Kelly Smith as consultant. Smith, Dean Hacker, Cindy Salach, and Patricia Smith (b. 1955) formed the CHICAGO team, which won the team competition. Patricia Smith won the first national individual competition; she went on to become the only four-time national champion.

In 2009 Chicago slam advocates established Chicago Slam Works (CSW), a nonprofit organization, to push slam's horizon beyond coffeehouses and bars into theatres and concert halls to elevate the form and debunk the notion that slam poetry exists only with scoreboards and prizes. Through its Poets with Class program, CSW works to make poetry a vital part of language arts education by making performance poetry an integral part of every school's poetry curriculum. Reinforcing Chicago's reputation as the true mecca of slam poetry, CSW collaborates with international slam organizations to produce translations and interpretations wherein both languages are presented simultaneously in performances that bring to life both the meaning and the sound of the material presented.

The poetry slam's democratic nature welcomes newcomers from all sectors of society. It is not unusual to find senior citizens performing alongside teenagers, or scientists scoring plumbers and vice versa. Honest criticism and openness are at the root of most slams and have fostered their growth. Over the years poets who attended poetry slams in one city have returned home and established their own shows.

Over the past two decades, performance poetry has spread to hundreds of cities, universities, high schools, festivals, and cultural centers. Long-running Midwestern slams are held in DETROIT, Omaha, MINNEAPOLIS, and elsewhere. Although Poetry Slam Inc. maintains a directory of registered slam venues on its website, scores of other slams, large and small, are held every year without official sanction from the national organization. The slam has taken root internationally in Germany, the United Kingdom, France, Sweden, Australia, and many other countries.

One sign of slam poetry's recognition by mainstream culture was an event held at the White House, hosted by President Barack Obama and First Lady Michelle Obama on May 12, 2009. Billed as a "poetry jam" because no competition was involved, this event featured a performance by Chicago native Mayda del Valle, 2001 individual champion of the National Poetry Slam. That President and Mrs. Obama are also Chicagoans reinforced the Midwestern origins of the poetry slam.

The national stage has inspired a keen interest in keeping traditional poetry alive while at the same time challenging it. Audiences push poets to innovate and take risks with their performances and writing. Many forms of spoken word performance, such as cowboy poetry and hip-hop, have infiltrated the slam and have become part of the mix. These converging camps have forced discussions about how to define contemporary poetry. Just as rock and roll challenged traditionalists to redefine music, so the poetry slam has prompted academics to broaden their definition of poetry.

SELECTED WORKS: Two anthologies edited by Mark Eleveld, *The Spoken Word Revolution: Slam, Hip Hop and the Poetry of a New Generation* (2005) and *Spoken Word Revolution*

Redux (2007), present a wide view of the diverse voices and poetic styles the poetry slam has inspired. Each book includes an audio CD of poetry performances. Marc Kelly Smith's two how-to books, *Take the Mike* (2009) and *Stage a Slam* (2009), present to readers the early philosophy and history of the poetry slam, as well as practical advice for entering the slam arena. Wordsmith Press, of Whitmore Lake, Michigan, publishes books, CDs, and DVDs of slam poetry, including collections such as *(off the mic): Ann Arbor Poetry Slam Anthology* (2004), edited by Larry Francis, Ester Hurwitz, and Vince Cavasin, and *Slamma Lamma Ding Dong: An Anthology of Nebraska's Slam Poets* (2005), edited by J. M. Huscher, Matt Mason, and Don Leamen. Books by Midwestern slam poets include Marc Kelly Smith's *Crowdpleaser* (1996) and Patricia Smith's *Life according to Motown* (1991).

FURTHER READING: Susan B. A. Somers-Willett wrote *The Cultural Politics of Slam Poetry: Race, Identity, and the Performance of Popular Verse in America* (2009), the first scholarly book on the slam. See also Tyler Hoffman's "Treacherous Laughter: The Poetry Slam, Slam Poetry, and the Politics of Resistance," *Studies in American Humor* 3.8 (2001): 49–64; and Julie Schmid's "Spreading the Word: A History of the Poetry Slam," *Talisman: A Journal of Contemporary Poetry and Poetics* 23–26 (2001–2002): 636–45. Gary Mex Glazner's *Poetry Slam: The Competitive Art of Performance Poetry* (2000) collects a variety of articles and poems. Eric Murphy Selinger reviews several books about slam poetry and books by slam participants in "Trash, Art, and Performance Poetry," *Parnassus: Poetry in Review* 23.1–2 (1998): 356–82. The 2009 poetry jam at the White House is covered by John McCormick in "Poetry, Not Politics, at White House," *Chicago Tribune*, May 13, 2009, 12.

The originator of the slam is profiled in "Marc Smith: An Interview," *Another Chicago Magazine* (Spring–Summer 1997), 32ff. Smith's concerns about the future of the poetry slam are addressed in Larry Rohter's "Is Slam in Danger of Going Soft?" *New York Times*, June 3, 2009, C1. *Rattle* 27 (Summer 2007) has a section on slam poetry, featuring interviews with Marc Kelly Smith and Patricia Smith. The most influential film

documentaries about and inspired by slam are Paul Devlin's *Slam Nation: The Art of the Spoken Word* (1998) and Siskel/Jacobs Productions's *Louder than a Bomb* (2010). Additional material can be found on the websites of Poetry Slam Inc. and Chicago Slam Works.

EMILY THORNTON CALVO AND MARC KELLY SMITH
CHICAGO, ILLINOIS

PRINTING AND PUBLISHING

OVERVIEW: As the American frontier moved westward across the Alleghenies in the eighteenth century, civilization and culture in the form of the printed word followed the early settlers of the Old Northwest. Printers and publishers in those places that would ultimately become part of the Midwest not only saw into print newspapers, broadsides, legal forms, government reports, and ephemera related to social and religious activities but also, in time, gave native and indigenous authors of imaginative literature their outlet to the larger public. Although they never rivaled New York, Boston, or Philadelphia, a few Midwestern cities did become regional publishing centers, most notably CINCINNATI, CHICAGO, and Indianapolis.

Beginning in the 1890s and extending into the next century, the fine printing component of the Arts and Crafts movement and the establishment of private presses produced a significant presence in the Midwest. The formation of university presses to disseminate scholarship, culture, and literature also began at about this time in the Midwest these were both important and influential. For coverage of the vast periodical literature, little magazines, and other literary journals, see LITERARY PERIODICALS.

HISTORY AND SIGNIFICANCE: In most cases early printing in the Midwestern states served practical purposes: news reports; promulgation of territorial and state laws; proceedings of their legislatures; notices from local merchants, land agents, and railroads; and almanacs and other useful handbooks. In most frontier settlements and nascent towns where people were struggling to eke out a living in what was often a hostile environment, the need for the relative luxury of printed creative literature, other than the standard authors of the East and Europe, was limited at best.

A few of the most active early printers in the Midwestern states were those affiliated with religious organizations, such as the Baptists in a number of locales, the Mormons in Nauvoo, ILLINOIS, before they were expelled from that state, and the New Harmony community in INDIANA. Their products included minutes of meetings, promotion of beliefs, and defensive tracts in answer to attacks from detractors. Fraternal organizations, such as the Odd Fellows, also actively produced similar materials, and in early KANSAS the viciously contending political parties issued a huge number of broadsides and pamphlets offering their respective views.

The following section lists the Midwestern states in order of the date of the arrival of the first printing press and the earliest work published.

Ohio: Owing to its advantageous location on the Ohio River, Cincinnati became an important early gateway for settlers moving into the Northwest Territory and consequently saw rapid growth. Revolutionary War veteran William Maxwell (ca. 1755–1809) arrived in the OHIO settlement in 1793, where he established the Midwest's earliest print shop. In November of that year he began the first newspaper to appear in the region, *The Centinel of the North-Western Territory*, a weekly that ceased in mid-1796 when he went into politics. Perhaps more noteworthy is the earliest book printed in the Northwest Territory, *Laws of the Territory of the United States North West of the River Ohio*, which came from his Cincinnati press in 1796. Although he had nothing to do with the writing of the text, it soon became known as Maxwell's Code.

Ohio's earliest printed literary work was a two-volume edition of the contemporary English satirist John Wolcot (1738–1819), *The Poetical Works of Peter Pindar*, which appeared in Cincinnati in 1797. However, it was not until 1811 that the state's first original literary work was produced, also in Cincinnati: *The Dagon of Calvinism*, an anonymous satirical poem attacking that religious denomination.

Other Ohio towns that saw the arrival of presses in the early nineteenth century were Chillicothe (1800), Marietta (1801), and Co-lumbus (1814). Chillicothe and Columbus were designated the state capital in succession, so it was natural that they would need to print official documents issued by the state government.

Cincinnati, however, continued to be the most important Ohio settlement. Because of its location and growth, Cincinnati was the preeminent publishing capital of the Midwest before the Civil War. By the 1830s it had already obtained what was necessary for self-sufficiency: paper mills, type foundries, steam presses, and means of distribution via the Ohio River.

Although most of the early Cincinnati output served utilitarian purposes through such products as city directories, river guides, grammars, and, later, schoolbooks, a number of short-lived literary periodicals appeared there in the 1820s. The earliest literary annual published in the Midwest was *The Western Souvenir, a Christmas and New Year's Gift for 1829*; it was edited by JAMES HALL (1793–1868) and was printed in Cincinnati in November 1828. Cincinnati firms offered a wide range of options, including reprints of classical literature, textbooks, legal forms and blank books, music, religious tracts, cheap paperbacks, and books sold by subscription.

Three Cincinnati publishers flourishing between 1830 and 1880 deserve special mention. In 1834 the firm of Truman and Smith began operating in Cincinnati, but its fame rests on a single series introduced in 1836 and sold in the millions through the years, becoming a ubiquitous feature of most schools in the country and influencing generations of schoolchildren: the *McGuffey Eclectic Readers*. WILLIAM HOLMES MCGUFFEY (1800–1873) was an Ohioan, a professor of language at Miami University in Oxford, Ohio.

H. W. Derby Company was founded by Henry W. Derby (1820–1892), who had arrived in Cincinnati in 1844 from Columbus via New York. He created a typical array of books but also had a special interest in Midwestern authors and titles of regional interest, such as Jacob Burnet's (1770–1853) *Notes on the Early Settlement of the North-Western Territory* (1847) and *History of the State of Ohio. First Period, 1650–1787* (1854) by James W. Taylor (1819–1893). Derby retired from business in 1858.

First issue of *The Centinel of the North-Western Territory,* November 9, 1793.

Image courtesy of Special Collections, Grand Valley State University Libraries

The Western Methodist Book Concern, established in Cincinnati in 1820 as a distribution depot of its New York parent, did not begin issuing its own titles until 1837. As would be expected, most of its output was Methodist or generally religious in nature. In 1841 it began the monthly magazine *The Ladies' Repository and Gatherings of the West,* which offered articles on religion as well as ART and literature and continued until 1880. The Western Methodist Book Concern was one of the few early Cincinnati publishers to survive into the twentieth century. Cincinnati's dominance in this area continued until the 1860s, when Chicago began to overtake it. By the 1880s the decline of Cincinnati as a printing and publishing center was nearly complete.

Michigan: A tenuous record of the initial publication exists in one copy of a pamphlet, *An Act Passed at the First Session of the Fourth Congress of the United States of America,* produced at DETROIT in 1796 by John McCall. No other products from his press are extant, and it is probable that both his establishment and its output were consumed in the 1805 fire that also destroyed the entire town. Printing does not seem to have been resurrected in Detroit until a Catholic priest, Fr. Gabriel Richard (1767–1832), brought a press to that place in 1808. Under his direction the Richard Press issued an impressive variety of works in both French and English, including a spelling book and other schoolbooks for children, local laws and pronouncements, a newspaper, religious works, and literary reprints.

The earliest literary work printed in Michigan appears to have been a Detroit edition of a selection of French poetry originally published in Paris in 1749, *Les ornamens de la memoire; ou, Les traits brillans des poetes francois* (1811), but the first original work is the long pastoral poem by Henry Whiting (1788–1851) about life in Michigan, *The Emigrant* (1819), also issued at Detroit. Detroit remained the sole Michigan locale with a printing press until 1825, when Monroe obtained one, followed by Ann Arbor (1829), Pontiac (1830), and White Pigeon (1833).

Indiana: Elihu Stout (1786–1860) emigrated from Kentucky to Vincennes, Indiana, opened the first print shop in the newly organized Indiana Territory, and began the weekly newspaper the *Indiana Gazette* at the end of July 1804. Appointed the official printer of Indiana Territory, Stout began his tenure with *Laws for the Government of the District of Louisiana* (1804); this was typical of his output throughout the rest of his career, which lasted into the 1840s. Other early Indiana printers were located in Madison (1813), Corydon (1816), Indianapolis (1822), and Harmony (1824).

The Vision of Columbus (1824) was the first literary product from an Indiana press. It was a reprint of Joel Barlow's (1754–1812) Miltonian epic poem from 1787. In 1832 John Cain (1805–1867) allegedly issued his *Miscellaneous Poems*, the earliest original literary work of an indigenous author published in the state; however no copy is now extant. The second such work is *A Poem Read before the Whig Society of Hanover College* (1838) by Caroline Lee Hentz (1800–1856).

Bobbs-Merrill opened in 1850 as Hood and Merrill. After a number of subsequent name changes, the Indianapolis company adopted the Bobbs-Merrill name from 1903 until its dissolution in 1985. Bobbs-Merrill was arguably the most important and influential Midwestern company devoted to regional literature and authors. Starting in 1885 with the publication of the second edition of *The Old Swimmin' Hole* by James Whitcomb Riley (1849–1916), the company began its long association with Indiana and other Midwestern authors, including L(yman)

Frank Baum (1856–1919), James Oliver Curwood (1878–1927), Emerson Hough (1857–1923), Ring(gold Wilmer) Lardner (Sr.) (1885–1933), (John) Herbert Quick (1861–1925), James Whitcomb Riley, Sam(uel) Shepard (Rogers III) (b. 1943), and (Joseph) Brand Whitlock (1869–1934), among others. By the 1920s it was known as the Hoosier House, not only for its physical location but also for its strong ties to Indiana authors and their writings.

Missouri: Another Kentucky printer, Joseph Charless (1772–1834), made his way to the mostly French-speaking settlement of St. Louis in 1808. In July of that year he began a weekly newspaper, the *Missouri Gazette*. From dated advertisements in that newspaper it has been determined that Charless issued the earliest book printed in Missouri, *The Laws of the Territory of Louisiana*, in December 1808. As the population and importance of St. Louis grew as an emigrant waypoint to western settlement, many more establishments supplied the need for published material, although never on the scale that Cincinnati, and ultimately Chicago, provided. Following St. Louis, printing in Missouri next appeared in Franklin (1819), Jackson (1819), and St. Charles (1820). In 1832 a press was operating in Independence, but Kansas City did not have one until 1851.

Illinois: After the old French settlement of Kaskaskia was designated the capital of Illinois Territory in 1809, another Kentucky printer, Matthew Duncan (1790–1844), moved there and in the spring of 1814 began a weekly newspaper, *The Illinois Herald*, which he produced for the next two years. In 1815 he was responsible for the inaugural book in Illinois, *Laws of the Territory of Illinois*, also in Kaskaskia.

Early settlement of Illinois occurred predominantly in the southern portions, and printing came initially to those places: Shawneetown (1818), Edwardsville (1819), and, when the capital moved there, Vandalia (1820) and later Springfield (1827). It was not until 1833 that John Calhoun (1808–1859) arrived in Chicago from New York and began putting out the town's earliest newspaper, the *Chicago Democrat*. A rival Whig paper, the *Chicago American*, began there in 1835.

Chicago's rise to prominence as a regional and subsequently a national publishing center has its roots in the 1840s with the formation of the firm Ellis Fergus. Its initial effort was *The Quid Nunc* (1842), the first daily one-cent newspaper west of the Alleghenies. It was followed by *Gleanings of Thought* (1843), a ninety-five-page collection of poems by a Chicago resident, Horatio Cooke, likely the earliest publication of a literary work there. Later the company was better known for its city directories, histories, and textbooks; bankruptcy ended its operations in 1900.

S. C. Griggs Company was founded as a publishing house in Chicago in 1849. By the time of the Civil War the firm had expanded to include schoolbooks and was the largest distributor of American books in the Midwest and the leading importer of foreign titles in the nation. In 1875 the company expanded its line to include fiction; children's literature followed the next year. Its most famous and lucrative title, *Robert's Rules of Order,* appeared in 1874 and has never been out of print since. When Griggs retired in 1896, he sold the entire business and inventory to Scott, Foresman and Company, one of the largest textbook companies in the country, now operating out of Evanston, Illinois, as a division of Pearson Education.

Rand, McNally Company, founded in Chicago in 1858, has long been a noted supplier of atlases, maps, and guidebooks; however, its trade list expanded in the 1880s to include western Americana, potboiler fiction in paperback format, and later general fiction and textbooks. Some of the fiction titles included works by Chicago authors such as OPIE PERCIVAL (POPE) READ (1852–1939) and Stanley Waterloo (1846–1913).

Another Chicago company, R. R. Donnelley Sons, began in 1864 as Church, Goodman and Donnelley and eventually became one of the largest and most important publishing houses in the Midwest. Although it was among the casualties of the 1871 Chicago fire, the company soon reestablished itself and by 1873 was back in business. Besides its normal printing activities, it began a successful paperback series, the Lakeside Library, which reprinted previously issued fiction and nonfiction titles at greatly reduced prices. In 1903 R. R. Donnelley introduced its well-known continuing annual series, Lakeside Classics, putting out small-format, beautifully designed volumes of out-of-print classics that deal with pioneer accounts, personal narratives, and the literature of Chicago, Illinois, and the Midwest, among other subjects.

At the turn of the nineteenth century two companies were formed that took advantage of Chicago's maturing literary and cultural scene and interest in fine printing. Stone & Kimball, later Herbert S. Stone Company, began operation in 1893 and ceased in 1905. Although Way & Williams was in operation only from 1895 to 1898, it, like Stone & Kimball, not only was influential in the book arts for its design and typography but also was particularly noted for its publication of works by Chicago and other Midwestern authors. Among these were (HANNIBAL) HAMLIN GARLAND (1860–1940), WILLIAM ALLEN WHITE (1868–1944), EUGENE FIELD (SR.) (1850–1895), ROBERT HERRICK (1868–1938), GEORGE ADE (1866–1944), Stanley Waterloo, and ELIA W. PEATTIE (1862–1935). Upon the demise of Way & Williams, Herbert S. Stone Company took over its trade list.

Wisconsin: Green Bay was the site of the earliest printer in WISCONSIN, then still part of Michigan Territory. Albert G. Ellis (1800–1885) arrived from New York and began the irregularly published newspaper the *Green-Bay Intelligencer* in December 1833. That same month, or early in 1834, he produced Wisconsin's earliest book, an almanac in the Ojibwa language. Printing then spread to Pike River, Milwaukee, and Belmont (all 1836), followed by Burlington (1837) and Racine and Madison (both 1838).

Wisconsin's initial published literary endeavor is a three-column poetry broadside entitled *The Critic's Report.* Written by G. Ihrie Wallace, presumably a local resident, it was printed in Southport (now Kenosha) in 1842. Noah Cressy's (1776–1867) *The Burning of the "Phoenix,"* a long poem commemorating an 1847 marine disaster in Lake Michigan near the city of Sheboygan, was the initial book-length literary publication; it was produced in Milwaukee in 1848.

Kansas: Twenty years before Kansas achieved territorial status, Jotham Meeker

(1804–1855), a minister and printer from Cincinnati, came to the Shawnee Baptist Mission a few miles west of the Missouri state line. There he established a press and early in 1834 began printing religious booklets in the Shawnee language. Meeker also founded the earliest newspaper in Kansas, the *Siwinowe Kesibwi* (*Shawnee Sun*), which began in March 1835. *Siwinowe Kesibwi* is also important as the first periodical printed in a Native American language in the United States.

Subsequently, printing appeared near Highland at a Presbyterian mission (1843) and at Stockbridge (1846) and Ottawa (1849); the last two used Meeker's press, which had been relocated to these places. The earliest Kansas newspaper in English was the *Kansas Weekly Herald*, printed in Leavenworth beginning in September 1854, shortly after the region had been organized into Kansas Territory.

Considering the troubles associated with "Bleeding Kansas" among the pro-slavery and anti-slavery factions from the 1850s through the Civil War, it is no wonder that no creative writing was issued in the state until after that war. Although the long epic poem *Osseo, the Spectre Chieftain* (Leavenworth, 1867) by Evender C. Kennedy (1842–1893) has long been regarded as the first literary work put out in Kansas, the seventeen-page *The Unpublished Poetic Writings of Lieut. Lucius O'Brien, Deceased, 8th U.S. Infantry* was published in Leavenworth in 1866. The son of Lucius O'Brien (ca. 1817–1841) saw the verses into print.

Iowa: Dubuque was still part of Wisconsin Territory when John King, a local settler engaged William Carey Jones and Andrew Keesecker, from Ohio and Illinois respectively, to print the first issues of the weekly *Du Buque Visitor* in May 1836. Other IOWA towns quickly established shops: Burlington (1837), Davenport and Fort Madison (1838), Bloomington (1840), and Iowa City (1841). For nearly twenty years Iowa printers produced mainly newspapers, official government publications, and religious, Masonic, and temperance tracts and orations.

Iowa's earliest published creative work appears to have been a poem by Richard H. Sylvester (1830–1896) that accompanied Charles O. Waters's dedicatory address on the occasion of the laying of the cornerstone for the Iowa Female Collegiate Institute in Iowa City in 1853. Hiram Alvin Reid (1834–1906) self-published *The Heart-Lace, and Other Poems* (1856) in Davenport, and this book is generally considered the first literary work by an Iowan.

Nebraska: The first printed document from NEBRASKA was *General Epistle from the Council of the Twelve Apostles,* an eight-page product of the Mormon press in December 1847 under the signature of Brigham Young (1801–1877), giving the particulars of the sect's travels and travails since quitting Nauvoo, Illinois. It indicates that it was produced at "Winter Quarters, Omaha Nation," near the current location of Omaha, where the Mormons camped before moving on to Utah in the spring of 1848.

Among rival claimants for the true first permanent printing press in Nebraska Territory is the one established to print the *Omaha Arrow,* commencing at the end of July 1854. Technically the short-lived *Nebraska Palladium,* which began in mid-July 1854, was the first newspaper in the territory, but it was printed in Iowa until October 1854 when it moved to Bellevue. The press brought to Nebraska City from Iowa in November 1854 printed the *Nebraska News* and was edited by Dr. Henry Bradford (b. 1812). Printing next appeared in Brownville (1856) and Plattsmouth (1858).

Nebraska Territory's inaugural literary work is probably the anonymous broadside titled *The Carrier's Address.* It contained three columns of verse and was issued on January 1, 1861 by the *Platte Valley Herald* in Plattsmouth; it seems likely that this was intended as a New Year's greeting to the newspaper's subscribers. The collection *Midland Poems* by Orsamus Charles Dake (1832–1875) was the state's earliest substantial work of literature; it was published in Lincoln in 1873. Dake was chair of the Belles Lettres Department at the University of Nebraska at the time.

Minnesota: In April 1849 New Hampshire native James Madison Goodhue (1810–1852) began the newly organized Minnesota Territory's first newspaper, the weekly *Minnesota Pioneer* in St. Paul. As official printer to the territorial government, Goodhue issued the first booklets to appear in MINNESOTA that same year, containing messages of the governor. Later in 1849 missionaries at Cass Lake obtained a press and put out a bilingual hymn as a broadside in English and Ojibwa. Printing appeared next in St. Anthony (1851), Red Wing (1854), Minneapolis (1855), and Winona (1856).

The initial creative work printed in Minnesota was issued in 1857 for a Christmas Eve musical festival at Hastings. It was a reprint of the cantata *The Flower Queen*, previously published with music by George F. Root (1820–1895) and words by Fanny Crosby (1820–1915) in New York in 1852. Before 1866 no original imaginative literary work was printed in Minnesota; however, in the wake of the Sioux War in 1862, a number of CAPTIVITY NARRATIVES appeared.

South Dakota: The initial printing in what was to become SOUTH DAKOTA, an election notice, was by Samuel J. Albright (1829–1913) in Sioux Falls in 1858, three years before the official creation of Dakota Territory. It also antedates the inaugural issue of the irregular *Dakota Democrat* newspaper, also printed by him in July 1859. It is alleged that his press was the one used to print Minnesota's earliest newspaper. Printing then moved to Yankton and Vermillion (both 1861), Canton (1872), and Deadwood (1876).

South Dakota's earliest printed literary work appears to have been *Gothamites: A Society Drama in Five Acts* by C. A. Rounds and H. T. Root. It was published in Sioux Falls in 1884; the authors were employees of a local bank.

North Dakota: Fort Rice, one of the frontier forts guarding against depredations by the Sioux, was the site of the first newspaper in NORTH DAKOTA. The *Frontier Scout* debuted in July 1864, under the direction of Lt. Charles H. Champney, Company C, First U.S. Volunteer Infantry, with the assistance of other soldiers. Not until 1873 did another press begin work within the confines of the future state of North Dakota, this one at Bismarck; other cities followed: Fargo and Grand Forks (both 1874) and Jamestown (1878).

The earliest creative work printed in North Dakota also came from Fort Rice. This was *Ballad of Love's Independence*, an 1865 broadside containing fourteen stanzas of sentimental verse written by Sgt. Pinck-

ney A. Morgan (1843–1878) of Company E, First U.S. Volunteer Infantry. It was issued from the press used to print the fort's newspaper.

Fine Presses: The Arts and Crafts movement began in England in the 1880s as a reaction against machine-made, mass-produced objects and promoted a return to handmade and craftsman ideals. One product of this movement was the revival of well-designed books, pamphlets, and broadsides printed on small presses with hand-set type and in small editions, typically no more than a few hundred copies. By the 1920s hundreds of these small presses were operating, and some of the more important ones were located in the Midwest. Much of the output consisted of reprints and new editions of standard works, as well as works by some avant-garde authors, but many also produced works of local authors.

Dard Hunter (1883–1966) was perhaps the dean of the craftsman-printers. He not only operated his Chillicothe, Ohio, press but also made his own paper and designed, cast, and set his own type. In Cincinnati the long-lived Fleuron Press (1923–1984) and the Stratford Press (1922–1965) operated. Chicago was home to many craftsman-printers, including Ralph Fletcher Seymour (1876–1966) and his Alderbrink Press, which operated from 1897 to 1963; Blue Sky Press (1899–1906); Will Ransom's private operation (1921–1930); Black Cat Press (1932–1984); Trovillion Private Press (1908–1958); and the Art Institute of Chicago's Department of Printing Arts (1921–1932). Under the aegis of the city's bibliophilic organization the Caxton Club, fine limited editions of local and regional histories and literature were issued from time to time, many of which were printed by Chicago's R. R. Donnelley Sons.

The Cranbrook Press of newspaper publisher and philanthropist George G. Booth (1864–1949) operated in Detroit from 1900 to 1902; Booth was an influential proponent of the Arts and Crafts movement; he later established the Cranbrook Educational Community northwest of Detroit.

DUDLEY FELKER RANDALL (1914–2000) began his Broadside Press in the basement of his Detroit home in 1965 primarily to promote his own poetry, but he soon expanded to include other new and established African

American voices, among whom were Midwesterners GWENDOLYN BROOKS (1917–2000), ROBERT HAYDEN (b. Asa Bundy Sheffey, 1913–1980), LANGSTON HUGHES (1902–1967), and Haki Madhubuti (b. 1942). Randall sold the press in 1985.

Torch Press of Cedar Rapids, Iowa, was founded in 1907 by Luther Albertus Brewer (1858–1933) and existed as both a commercial and a specialty printer until its demise in 1959. During that time it issued not only its own books but also limited editions for other entities, including the Chicago Bookfellows, the Rowfant Club of Cleveland, and the Bibliophiles of Boston, and small runs of Christmas books for Iowa businessman and collector T. Henry Foster. Many Torch Press items were of Iowa and Midwestern interest.

University Presses: Although private presses were associated with American higher education as early as 1640, publications issued under the aegis of a university for the purpose of disseminating knowledge and scholarship did not have a true beginning until the second half of the 1800s with Cornell (1869) and Johns Hopkins (1878). In the Midwest, in 1891, only a year after its founding, the University of Chicago established a press, the third such American institution to do so. Other Midwestern university presses followed, including the University of Illinois Press (1918), Iowa State University Press (1924), the University of Minnesota Press (1925), the University of Michigan Press (1930), the University of Wisconsin Press (1937), the Press of Western Reserve University (1938), the University of Nebraska Press (1941), Wayne State University Press (1941), the University of Kansas Press (1946), Michigan State University Press (1947), Indiana University Press (1950), Southern Illinois University Press (1953), the University of Notre Dame Press (1954), Northwestern University Press (1957), Ohio State University Press (1957), the University of Missouri Press (1958), and Ohio University Press (1964).

The vast majority of books and journals issued by university presses dealt with the sciences, social sciences, and classic literary texts. It was not until the 1960s that Midwestern regional studies, including poetry and fiction, began to be published in this venue. Most university presses produce regional titles, and some acknowledge their commitment to them by establishing discrete series within their programs. Indiana University Press has a Library of Indiana Classics series; Wayne State University Press has been issuing books under the Great Lakes Books rubric since 1986. Other presses publish original fiction and poetry, the authors of which are not necessarily Midwestern.

SELECTED WORKS: Of all the pioneer Midwestern newspaper editors, four are particularly important for their first publications of early territorial laws: William Maxwell, with *Laws of the Territory of the United States North West of the River Ohio* (Cincinnati, 1796; Elihu Stout, with *Laws for the Government of the District of Louisiana* (Vincennes, 1804); Joseph Charless, with *The Laws of the Territory of Louisiana* (St. Louis, 1809); and Matthew Duncan, with *Laws of the Territory of Illinois* (Kaskaskia, 1815).

Commercial publishers of note that brought culture to the Midwest in the form of the printed word include H. W. Derby Company and the Western Methodist Book Concern, both of Cincinnati; and the Chicago firms Rand, McNally & Company and R. R. Donnelley & Sons. Especially influential in the printing and promulgation of Midwestern literature were the relatively short-lived Chicago publishers Stone & Kimball and Way & Williams; however, probably the most important of all in bringing Midwestern authors to national attention was Bobbs-Merrill, the Hoosier House, in Indianapolis.

Of Midwestern university presses only Indiana University Press and Wayne State University Press have series that are devoted to regional literature: the Library of Indiana Classics and Great Lakes Books, respectively. The private press of Detroit poet Dudley Felker Randall, the Broadside Press, provided an outlet for Midwestern African American poets.

FURTHER READING: No substantial history concentrating on Midwestern printers or publishers has yet been written; however, John Tebbel's four-volume survey *A History of Book Publishing in the United States* (1972–1981) contains detailed information on regional publishing and individual publishers by state. The dated but still-unsurpassed comprehensive bibliography of the literature of printing and publishing in the United States is the two-volume *Guide to the Study of United States Imprints* (1971) by G. Thomas Tanselle (b. 1934). Among its contents are especially useful listings of published sources dealing with regional and state imprints.

Study of the output of early presses in the individual states is dependent on bibliographies published by the American Imprints Inventory, a subunit of the Works Progress Administration's Historical Records Survey endeavor under the general editorship of Douglas C. McMurtrie (1888–1944), a prolific print historian. From 1937 until the WPA was terminated in 1943, twenty-four bibliographies were completed, including ones on eight Midwestern states and one city. These are *A Preliminary Check List of Missouri Imprints, 1808–1850* (1937); *Check List of Minnesota Imprints, 1849–1865* (1938); *Check List of Chicago Ante-Fire Imprints, 1851–1871* (1938); *Check List of Kansas Imprints, 1854–1876* (1939); *A Check List of Iowa Imprints, 1838–1860* (1940); *A Check List of Ohio Imprints, 1796–1820* (1941); *A Check List of Wisconsin Imprints, 1833–1863* (4 volumes, 1942); *A Check List of Nebraska Non-Documentary Imprints, 1847–1876* (1942); and *Preliminary Check List of Michigan Imprints, 1796–1850* (1942).

Those Midwestern states not included in the American Imprints Inventory project were later covered in separate publications. These include *Dakota Imprints, 1858–1889* (1947), edited by Albert H. Allen; *A Bibliography of Indiana Imprints, 1804–1853* (1955) by Cecil K. Byrd and Howard H. Peckham; and Cecil K. Byrd's *A Bibliography of Illinois Imprints, 1814–58* (1966). Iowa City is the subject of the 2011 volume *Iowa City, City of the Book: Writing, Publishing, and Book Arts in the Heartland* by Joseph A. Michaud.

McMurtrie had previously examined many early Midwestern imprints and publishers, and his writings, although dated, remain valuable for their information and insights. Still useful is his "The Westward Migration of the Printing Press in the United States, 1786–1836," *Gutenberg-Jahrbuch,* 1930, 269–88. McMurtrie's article provides a partial history of printing in Ohio, Indiana, Illinois, Michigan, Wisconsin, and Iowa.

Some of McMurtrie's other publications that concern the Midwest include *The First Printing in Peoria, Illinois* (1929); *Beginnings of Printing in the Middle West* (1930); *Early Printing in Michigan* (1931); *Preliminary Check List of North Dakota Imprints, 1874–1890* (1943).

Many of McMurtrie's publications listed here are brief summaries and overviews rather than longer in-depth works. A valuable and detailed history of the rise and decline of printing, publishing, and allied arts in Cincinnati is Walter Sutton's *The Western Book Trade: Cincinnati as a Nineteenth-Century Publishing and Book-Trade Center* (1961).

Unlike their eastern counterparts, only a handful of monographs or other studies exist on individual publishing houses in the Midwest. One of the most important firms in the region, Bobbs-Merrill of Indianapolis, is the subject of a detailed history by Richard J. Schrader, *The Hoosier House: Bobbs-Merrill and Its Predecessors, 1850–1985* (2004). Two short-lived Chicago publishers are memorialized in *A History of Stone & Kimball and Herbert S. Stone Co., with a Bibliography of Their Publications, 1893–1905* (1940) by Sidney Kramer and *A History of Way & Williams: With a Bibliography of Their Publications, 1895–1898* (1984) by Joe W. Krause (1917–2010). Some Midwestern publishers have issued brief self-congratulatory pamphlets on their firms; others have distributed promotional literature that contains outlines of company history.

ROBERT BEASECKER   GRAND VALLEY STATE UNIVERSITY

PROGRESSIVISM

OVERVIEW: The Midwest was the home of the Progressive Party at the turn of the twentieth century, as the region had been the home of the Republican Party in the middle of the nineteenth century. More a blend of concurrent movements than a homogeneous political entity, Progressivism brought together rural and urban people, native-born and immigrant Americans, and men and women from different but overlapping racial and ethnic cultures, all with the goal of ameliorating the strains of industrial capitalism on communal life in the United States, as typified by life in the Midwest.

Progressivism grew from grassroots struggles over such ethical and political issues as social justice, civil liberties, universal suffrage, workplace safety, a living wage, health insurance, and conservation, together with a suspicion of corporate power and military expansion. As conceived by such Midwestern leaders as WISCONSIN governor and U.S. senator Robert M. La Follette (1855–1925), Progressivism called for reform to end the patronage system and political machines, to redistribute wealth through equitable income and inheritance taxes, to protect union organizers and members, and to regulate utilities. Rethinking the parameters of democracy, Progressives sought purity in food, health in the workplace, and education of the young, including support of public universities. As stated in *La Follette's Autobiography: A Personal Narrative of Political Experiences* (1913), "In a high sense the university has been the repository of progressive ideals; it has always enjoyed both free thought and free speech" (28–29).

Midwestern Progressive literature includes the overtly political writings of Robert M. La Follette, Belle Case La Follette (1859–1931), WILLIAM JENNINGS BRYAN (1860–1925), and William Howard Taft (1859–1932), as well as the sociological writings of (LAURA) JANE ADDAMS (1860–1935) and Florence Kelley (1859–1932), the muckraking journalism of RAY STANNARD BAKER (1870–1946), Ida B. Wells Barnett (1862–1931), DAVID GRAHAM PHILLIPS (1867–1911), and WILLIAM ALLEN WHITE (1868–1944), the editing of Richard T. Ely (1854–1943) and Paul U. Kellogg (1879–1958), and the environmental writings of JOHN MUIR (1838–1914), together with the literary naturalism of such fiction writers as (HERMAN) THEODORE DREISER (1871–1945), ZONA GALE (1874–1938), (HANNIBAL) HAMLIN GARLAND (1860–1940), (BENJAMIN) FRANK(LIN) NORRIS (1870–1902), and UPTON (BEALL) SINCLAIR (JR.) (1878–1968). The Progressives provided plenty of material for Midwestern humorists, especially FINLEY PETER DUNNE (1867–1936).

HISTORY AND SIGNIFICANCE: The pressures of economic and social life in the nineteenth century opened sizable fissures between social classes in the United States. On the prairies of Midwestern rural America, grassroots political movements, including the Farmers' Alliance and the Grange, questioned the rise of capitalist monopolies, the power of the railroads, and what farmers saw as the waste of public lands. Rural farmers' groups continued to grow throughout the nineteenth century and merged into the People's Party in 1891, a group that joined forces with the Democratic Party in 1896, running Midwesterner William Jennings Bryan, who was defeated by Republican William McKinley. Failing in the national election, Midwestern farmers continued to work at the state and local levels to create a viable third political party, finding much in common with urban labor groups and women suffragists.

Between 1889, when Jane Addams and Ellen Gates Starr (1859–1940) opened the social settlement at HULL-HOUSE in CHICAGO, and 1912, the year the Bull Moose Convention of the National Progressive Party convened in that same Midwestern city and nominated Theodore Roosevelt (1858–1919), over 12 million immigrants entered the United States, most of them from countries in southern and eastern Europe, as well as from Mexico and Asia. Chicago had grown rapidly in the late nineteenth century, becoming America's second-largest city by 1900 with a population of over 1,500,000 and setting the stage for much of the Progressive Era legislation that would be proposed to ease newly arrived immigrants into American culture. As Addams looked out of her Hull-House window on the "Bloody Nineteenth" Ward, she cautioned her readers in *Newer Ideals of Peace* (1907), "Insanitary housing, poisonous sewage, contaminated water, infant mortality, the spread of contagion, adulterated food, impure milk, smoke-laden air, ill-ventilated factories, dangerous occupations, juvenile crime, unwholesome crowding, prostitution, and drunkenness are the enemies which the modern city must face and overcome would it survive" (182).

In the early 1890s Florence Kelley, Julia Lathrop (1858–1932), and Jane Addams conducted a study of the Halsted Street neighborhood and published *Hull-House Maps and Papers: A Presentation of Nationalities and Wages in a Congested District of Chicago together with Comments and Essays on Problems Growing out of the Social Condition* (1895) under the editorship of Richard T. Ely, a professor at the University of Wisconsin. Kelley, an ardent socialist, became the director of the National Consumer League and wrote books about

National Progressive Convention, Chicago,
August 6, 1912.
Image courtesy of the Library of Congress

political reform, *Ethical Gains through Legislation* (1905) and *Modern Industry* (1914). Lathrop became an inspector of charities and was appointed by President Taft to head the Children's Bureau in Washington, D.C., in 1912, the first woman to serve the U.S. government in such an appointment. The women of Hull-House focused attention on the disparity between the idling wealthy and the working poor, calling for fair wages and working hours, health care, and workplace safety. They sought the release of children from labor and argued for the protections of public education and juvenile courts.

Midwestern Progressive ideas gained national appeal, moving between the Republican and Democratic Parties, whose leaders nervously eyed the successes of the movement. President McKinley's assassination in 1901 put Theodore Roosevelt into the White House, and when he assumed power, he took up many Progressive causes in what he called the "Square Deal," including a progressive income tax and an inheritance tax. When the Senate was debating the pure-food bill in 1906, INDIANA senator Albert Beveridge (1862–1927) sent Roosevelt a copy of Upton Sinclair's *THE JUNGLE* (1906), a novel meant to expose the harsh working conditions that Lithuanian immigrants endured in Chicago's meatpacking plants but that instead alarmed the public with news that they were eating dangerously contaminated meat. Roosevelt invited Sinclair to the White

House and championed passage of the Pure Food and Drug Act.

John Muir, a Scottish immigrant raised in Wisconsin, campaigned for the protection of wilderness areas, especially Yosemite, and the organization of the Sierra Club. His environmental sensitivity, articulated in *The Story of My Boyhood and Youth* (1913), developed in the woods and meadows of frontier Wisconsin. He escorted Theodore Roosevelt through Yosemite in 1903 and schooled him in the interlocking nature of human and animal life. In 1907 Roosevelt proved himself a forceful conservationist by securing twenty-one national forests and expanding eleven existing ones in the western states of Colorado, Idaho, Montana, Oregon, Washington, and Wyoming.

Even as Roosevelt traveled and dined with Progressive writers, he worried about the power of "the Man with the Muckrake," a figure from John Bunyan's *Pilgrim's Progress.* In a speech to the Gridiron Club on March 17, 1906, Roosevelt warned about the excessive pessimism of the muckraker, a term that stuck with crusading journalists such as Midwesterners Ray Stannard Baker, David Graham Phillips, and William Allen White. Baker, a writer for *McClure's Magazine,* joined Lincoln Steffens (1866–1936) and Ida Tarbell (1857–1944) in 1905 to buy the *American Magazine,* a publication dedicated to the "New Journalism." Investigative journalists followed a pattern of research and reporting that Ida B. Wells-Barnett had used in writing *A Red Record* (1895), an exposé of lynching in the United States. Ida Tarbell wrote the famous exposé of John D. Rockefeller's Standard Oil Company, and Phillips wrote an equally scathing indictment of the U.S. Senate, titled "The Treason of the Senate," a series that ran in *Cosmopolitan* in 1906 and infuriated Roosevelt. White had drawn national attention for his criticism of William Jennings Bryan in an 1896 editorial "What's the Matter with Kansas?" and went on to become an ardent Progressive. In 1921 White wrote a series of editorials in the *Emporia Gazette* attacking the Ku Klux Klan.

The term "muckraker" came to define literary naturalists, including the Midwesterner novelists Sinclair, Theodore Dreiser, and Frank Norris. Dreiser encountered considerable opposition from social purity groups for trying to tell an accurate story about how his sisters fared as they left Terre Haute, Indiana, for Chicago and then New York. In SISTER CARRIE (1900) and *Jennie Gerhardt* (1911) he recorded the precise economic discomforts of poverty and, at times, took to task the complacency of those calling themselves Progressives. *Jennie Gerhardt* carried his message: "Out of this total income of fifteen dollars a week, all of these eight individuals had to be fed and clothed, the rent paid, coal purchased, and the regular monthly installment of three dollars paid on the outstanding furniture bill of fifty dollars. How it was done, those comfortable individuals, who frequently discuss the social aspects of poverty, might well trouble to inform themselves" (107).

When Theodore Roosevelt left office in 1909, the OHIO Republican William Howard Taft came to the White House, questioning the power of trusts and supporting such reforms as a federal income tax, the direct election of Senators, and the power of the Interstate Commerce Commission to set railroad rates. Progressives, however, grew wary of Taft and formed the National Progressive Party in 1911 as they sought a nominee for the 1912 election, an honor that La Follette, known as "Fighting Bob," expected to receive. Roosevelt, spurned by the Republicans in favor of Taft at the Republican Convention, returned to Chicago in August as the hero of the Bull Moose Convention and claimed the nomination of the National Progressive Party. The platform, written by a coalition of farmers, unionists, women, African Americans, and Socialist Party members, called for government ownership of railroads and utilities, support for farmers' credit, union organization, civil liberties, women's suffrage, and an end to child labor and to U.S. imperialism in Latin America. Even as Progressives denounced the activities of the Ku Klux Klan, Roosevelt compromised on the color line at the convention, seating African American delegates from the North but not those from the South. Jane Addams, the first major female speaker at a national convention, seconded the nomination and worked hard in a campaign that succeeded in splitting Republicans and, ironically, putting the Democrat Woodrow Wilson into office.

In 1913 La Follette published his autobiography in order to give his account of the Progressive movement, a coalition that began to fail with Roosevelt's defeat. In his introduction La Follette declared, "I have no literary intent whatsoever" (ix). The tone and style of his writing, however, belie his claim. Consider this apt caricature of the Rough Rider president: "This cannonading first in one direction and then in another filled the air with noise and smoke which confused and obscured the line of action, but when the battle cloud drifted by and quiet was restored, it was always a matter of surprise that so little had really been accomplished" (205). La Follette's portrait of Roosevelt has the look of those drawn by the humorist Finley Peter Dunne, whose droll persona Mr. Dooley, after reading *The Rough Riders,* observes, "'Tis 'Th' Account iv th' Desthruction iv Spanish Power in th' Ant Hills,' as it fell fr'm th' lips iv Tiddy Rosenfelt an' was took down be his own hands" *Harper's Weekly* 48 (25 November 1899): n.p.

During his presidency Woodrow Wilson took up Progressive reform, supporting the passage of workingmen's compensation, the banning of most child labor, the expansion of farmers' credit, and the creation of the Federal Reserve Board, the Federal Trade Commission, and the Tariff Commission. The force of Wilson's Progressivism had the intended effect of draining strength from the National Progressive Party.

The movement of the United States into World War I split the Progressives more deeply than battles over domestic issues ever did. Roosevelt and, eventually, Woodrow Wilson supported war, but other Progressive leaders, including Robert M. La Follette and Jane Addams, remained pacifists. Addams headed the International Congress of Women at The Hague in 1915, a group that sent delegations of women to meet with heads of state to urge warring nations to engage in mediation. The group became known as the Women's International League for Peace and Freedom, and its members were widely condemned as traitors, especially after the United States joined the fighting in 1917. Addams wrote *Women at The Hague* (1915) and *Peace and Bread in Time of War* (1922) to articulate her ideas and defend her opposition to World War I.

The Vigilantes, a group of writers who supported U.S. entry into the war, attacked pacifists such as La Follette, whom they characterized as a German sympathizer. The split among Progressives never healed, and although La Follette was reelected to the U.S. Senate from Wisconsin in 1922, his run for the presidency as a Progressive Party candidate failed decisively in 1924, and he died a year later.

Franklin Delano Roosevelt (1882–1945) took up Progressive causes after he was elected president in 1932, offering the country what he dubbed the "New Deal" in an echo of the "Square Deal." The pressures of the Great Depression again called attention to the fissures between social classes in America. The New Deal included such Progressive programs as Social Security, the Civil Works Administration, the Civilian Conservation Corps, the Public Works Association, and the Works Progress Administration. The FEDERAL WRITERS' PROJECT gave work to artists, including MICHIGAN poet ROBERT HAYDEN (1913–1980), whose research on the Underground Railroad led to his poem "Middle Passage." Eleanor Roosevelt (1884–1962) proved to be more of a Progressive than her husband in her advocacy of workers' rights and her opposition to racism. She supported the Iowan Henry A. Wallace (1888–1965), Franklin Roosevelt's vice president from 1941 to 1945, who ran for president in 1948 on the Progressive Party ticket.

Progressive issues have emerged in the administrations of New Englander John Kennedy; southerners Lyndon B. Johnson, Jimmy Carter, and Bill Clinton; and Hawaiian-born, Chicago-trained Midwesterner Barack Obama. The questions posed by Midwestern Progressives at the turn of the twentieth century remain at issue in the early years of the twenty-first century in the ongoing debates over privatizing Social Security, Medicare, and Medicaid, reversing Obamacare, cutting income and inheritance taxes for the wealthy, reducing wages in a global economy, undermining unions and collective bargaining, drilling for oil and fracking for gas on nature preserves, and expanding military operations in the Middle East. In resisting such policies, Midwestern activists and writers continue to draw on the region's Progressive tradition. Twenty-first-century texts include *Dude, Where's My Country?* (2003) by Michael Moore (b. 1954), *Homegrown Democrat: A Few Plain Thoughts from the Heart of America* (2004) by GARY EDWARD KEILLOR (b. 1942), writing as Garrison Keillor, and *Uprising: How Wisconsin Renewed the Politics of Protest, from Madison to Wall Street* (2012) by John Nichols (b. 1959).

SELECTED WORKS: At the beginning of the twentieth century Midwesterners edited Progressive magazines that featured political and imaginative writing worth reading today. From Wisconsin, Robert M. La Follette and his wife, Belle Case La Follette, founded *La Follette's Weekly Magazine,* a publication they later called the *Progressive*. *La Follette's Autobiography,* published in 1913, is available in a 1960 edition that includes a useful introduction by Allan Nevins. Paul U. Kellogg, from Kalamazoo, founded and edited *Survey* and *Survey Graphic*. Michigan-born and Wisconsin-raised Ray Stannard Baker, together with Lincoln Steffens and Ida Tarbell, edited the *American Magazine*. Baker later supported Wilson and wrote the Pulitzer Prize–winning eight-volume *Woodrow Wilson: Life and Letters* (1927–1939).

Midwestern politicians wrote speeches, editorials, and essays that are, for the most part, earnest in tone and didactic in style. In *William Jennings Bryan: Selections* (1967), Ray Ginger offers characteristic speeches, many of them presented in Midwestern Lyceum and Chautauqua circuits, by the populist and sometimes Progressive politician born and raised in ILLINOIS. The Midwest was also home to conservationist John Muir, who in *The Story of My Boyhood and Youth* (1913) explains how Wisconsin shaped his ideas about the environment. Ida B. Wells-Barnett, who moved to Chicago from the South, cataloged lynchings in the United States in her book *A Red Record* (1895).

Jane Addams was a very influential Midwestern Progressive writer who authored ten books and collaborated on three others. Her three early books *Democracy and Social Ethics* (1902), *Newer Ideals of Peace* (1907), and *The Spirit of Youth and the City Streets* (1909) articulated Progressive ideals that social settlement workers put into practice at Hull-House. Her autobiography, *Twenty Years at Hull-House* (1910), has become a classic in American literature. She also wrote *A New Conscience and an Ancient Evil* (1912), detailing the horrors of what was called "white slavery," the sexual traffic in young women, another Progressive cause early in the century.

Upton Sinclair wrote dozens of books exposing the ills of American society but is best known for his novel *The Jungle* (1906), which depicts working-class life in immigrant Chicago. In *Sister Carrie* (1900) and *Jennie Gerhardt* (1911) Theodore Dreiser tells similar stories about young rural women new to the city. See the 1992 Penguin edition of *Jennie Gerhardt,* edited by James L. W. West III, for a history of the censorship of the early manuscripts. Chicago-born novelist Frank Norris similarly set the imaginative stage for Midwestern Progressivism in the first two parts of his proposed trilogy about wheat, *The Octopus* (1901) and *The Pit* (1903). Other Midwestern writers associated with Progressivism include the Wisconsin playwright and novelist Zona Gale, whose novel *Heart's Kindred* (1915) features Jane Addams as a heroine at the International Women's Congress at The Hague. Hamlin Garland, also born in Wisconsin, expressed Midwestern Progressive views in *A Son of the Middle Border* (1917). The Midwestern humor of Finley Peter Dunne, born in Irish Chicago, served to counterbalance the sober tone of the Progressives in collections such as *Mr. Dooley's Philosophy* (1900) and *Mr. Dooley's Opinions* (1901).

FURTHER READING: The Jane Addams Papers Project makes available eighty-two reels of microfilm, including her papers, both personal and professional, as well as papers associated with Hull-House. The University of Illinois at Chicago Library houses the Jane Addams Papers, and the University of Illinois Press has issued new editions of her books. Katherine Joslin's *Jane Addams, a Writer's Life* (2004) tells the story of her as a Progressive writer, and Rivka Shpak Lissak's *Pluralism and Progressivism: Hull House and the New Immigrants* (1989) gives a wider history and analysis of the social settlement house. Donald Springen's *William Jennings Bryan: Orator of Small-Town America* (1991) places him in the Midwest. Nancy C. Unger's *Fighting Bob La Follette: The Righteous Reformer* (2000) offers a thorough account of his political ideas. Patricia O'Toole's *When Trumpets Call: Theodore Roosevelt after the White House* (2005) details his encounters with La Follette, Bryan, Addams, and other Midwesterners struggling to build a third major political party. William M. Gibson, in *Theodore Roosevelt among the Humorists* (1980), places Finley Peter Dunne, WILLIAM DEAN HOWELLS (1837–1920), and SAMUEL LANGHORNE CLEMENS (1835–1910), writing as Mark Twain, in the company of the Progressives.

KATHERINE JOSLIN   WESTERN MICHIGAN UNIVERSITY

PROTEST LITERATURE

OVERVIEW: Protest literature is writing intended to bring about social change. It documents injustice and promotes a new understanding of society. It may urge readers to take action, often through collective efforts such as demonstrations, strikes, boycotts, unions, and political parties. Protest writers express dissent, sometimes angrily, as they seek to create solidarity among activists, oppressed people, or individuals sympathetic to a cause. They reject the status quo and offer alternatives to the established social order.

The American protest tradition is rooted in eighteenth-century texts. The political essays of Thomas Jefferson (1743–1826) and the pamphlets of Thomas Paine (1737–1809) signal the origins of this perennial genre in Enlightenment ideals of representative government and human rights. Later expressions of this tradition were influenced by the transcendentalist writings of Ralph Waldo Emerson (1803–1882), Margaret Fuller (1810–1850), and Henry David Thoreau (1817–1862), who stressed nonconformity and the individual conscience. Protest literature has emerged from social movements seeking the abolition of slavery, temperance, women's rights, and collective bargaining for labor, Native American rights, civil rights, gay rights, and environmental protections. In addition, anti-war movements, which were particularly strong during World War I and the Vietnam War, have also produced much protest literature.

Midwestern writers have participated in all these movements, from the nineteenth century to the present day, supporting social causes with prose and poetry in many genres and styles. Later writers are conscious of their predecessors, in some cases citing or alluding to them as they take part in a controversy that may have parallels to past historical events. Although this entry touches on several movements in the Midwest, it will leave in-depth discussion of particular literary traditions to entries devoted to those traditions. On writing about labor issues and social class struggle, see RADICALISM. On writing from the late nineteenth and early twentieth centuries advocating political reform, see PROGRESSIVISM. For more on literary traditions with elements of protest, see AFRICAN AMERICAN LITERATURE, ENVIRONMENTAL LITERATURE, FEMINISM, LATINO/LATINA LITERATURE, and LESBIAN, GAY, BISEXUAL, TRANSGENDER, AND QUEER LITERATURE.

HISTORY AND SIGNIFICANCE: The nineteenth century witnessed the birth of several important protest movements in the United States. Abolitionists sought the immediate and uncompensated end of slavery. Suffragists sought to win women the right to vote; they were sometimes aligned with abolitionists and with the temperance movement, which sought to outlaw the production, distribution, and use of alcohol. SOJOURNER TRUTH (ca. 1797–1883) and Francis Ellen Watkins Harper (1825–1911), for example, were active in abolitionism, suffrage, and temperance.

The abolitionist movement had a strong base in various churches, and prominent ministers and other activists flooded the country with anti-slavery literature and helped produce two political parties, the Liberty Party and the Free-Soil Party, in the 1840s. A strong Christian message underlay much abolitionist literature, such as *Uncle Tom's Cabin* (1852) by Harriet Beecher Stowe (1811–1896) of CINCINNATI, the most influential anti-slavery novel ever written.

The greatest voice against slavery was that of Frederick Douglass (1818–1895), whose memoir *The Narrative of the Life of Frederick Douglass, an American Slave* (1845) introduced audiences to a firsthand account of the evils of slavery. His escape from slavery also helped forge the powerful and poignant features of the SLAVE NARRATIVES, which emerged as a genre of American literature. In the antebellum period slave narratives served to illustrate the injustice of slavery and to humanize slaves. Slave narratives from the Midwest include *An Address to All the Colored Citizens of the United States* (1846) by John Berry Meachum (1789–1854), a ST. LOUIS minister and teacher; *From Fugitive Slave to Free Man: The Autobiographies of William Wells Brown* (1847) by William Wells Brown (ca. 1814–1884); and *Aunt Sally; or, The Cross the Way of Freedom: A Narrative of the Slave-Life and Purchase of the Mother of Rev. Isaac Williams of Detroit, Michigan* (1859) by Isaac Williams (b. ca. 1821).

The women's suffrage movement also began during the antebellum era. Women had always been kept politically and legally subordinate to men; they could not own property, make wills, vote, attend college, or retain wages they had earned. At a meeting in 1848 in Seneca Falls, New York, women's right to vote was given national prominence. Elizabeth Cady Stanton (1815–1902), Lucy Stone (1919–1893), Julia Ward Howe (1819–1910), and Susan B. Anthony (1829–1906) championed this cause. Their Midwestern associates included Helen Jackson Gougar (1843–1907) of Lafayette, INDIANA, a lawyer and a leading figure in the Women's Christian Temperance Union and the National Women's Suffrage Association. A noted orator, Gougar also promoted temperance and suffrage in newspaper columns, first in the *Lafayette Daily Courier* (1878–1880) and thereafter in her own newspaper, *Our Herald.* Gougar's writings have attracted the interest of historians and specialists in women's studies.

Another prominent suffragist was May Wright Sewall (1844–1920), who was born Mary Eliza Wright in Milwaukee, WISCONSIN, but lived for many years in Indianapolis. An associate of Gougar's, Sewell served as president of the National Congress of Women and of the International Congress of Women. Sewell held a regular salon at her home, hosting literary and activist notables like JANE ADDAMS (1860–1935). A noted spiritualist and peace activist, as well as a feminist, Sewell published such books as *Women, World War and Permanent Peace* (1915).

Intending to awaken the country to the evils of drink, a campaign against the manufacture and consumption of alcohol took place under the banner of the temperance movement. Its leading crusader, Carry Nation (1846–1911) of KANSAS, sought total eradication of alcohol by smashing saloons from San Francisco to New York, including ones in Midwestern cities such as KANSAS CITY, MISSOURI, and towns such as Holly, MICHIGAN. Nation tells her story and argues for a ban on alcohol in her autobiography, *The Use and Need of the Life of Carry A. Nation* (1905). Nation's sensational demonstrations attracted a following in the Midwest, including DAVID ROSS LOCKE (1833–1888), an OHIO journalist and newspaper editor who delivered speeches and wrote essays supporting temperance, often under the pseudonym Petroleum V. Nasby. Locke published such temperance tracts as *Beer and the Body: Testimony of Physicians against This Great Evil* (1884).

The second half of the nineteenth century saw a proliferation of publications that discussed moral and ethical issues about which many Americans believed strongly. Jane Addams, SAMUEL LANGHORNE CLEMENS (1835–1910), writing as Mark Twain, and THORSTEIN (BUNDE) VEBLEN (1857–1929), to name a few, wrote compellingly and provocatively and are among many nineteenth-century Midwestern writers for whom aesthetics and rhetoric affected societal ills. An underlying belief was that power was aggressive and always seeking to erode liberty. In addition, the agrarian spirit of the Midwest became the impetus behind many humanitarian and revolutionary ideas of the nineteenth century.

As MINNESOTA lieutenant governor and U.S. congressman, IGNATIUS LOYOLA DONNELLY (1831–1901) championed freed slaves, land reform, and education while opposing social Darwinism, racism, and anti-Semitism. WILLIAM ALLEN WHITE (1868–1944) and (JOSEPH) BRAND WHITLOCK (1869–1934) opposed segregation and corruption, respectively. White's work as a journalist anticipated that of the muckrakers of the turn of the twentieth century. Whitlock's novels, such as *J. Hardin and Son* (1923), focus on the Midwestern underclass who became victims of national trusts and mass production.

Noted for provocative lectures and essays treating scientific humanism, freethinking, and rational criticism of Christianity, ROBERT GREEN INGERSOLL (1833–1899) developed the reputation of an infidel who supported Darwinism. WILLIAM JENNINGS BRYAN (1860–1925), his political and religious opposite, supported agrarian interests and prohibition while opposing tariffs, monopoly, and impe-

rialism. Together, Ingersoll and Bryan represented the broad spectrum of issues and concerns that typified the Midwest of their times.

The last years of the nineteenth century saw increased journalistic efforts to remedy social problems in the Midwest. Against this background, DAVID GRAHAM PHILLIPS (1867–1911), UPTON (BEALL) SINCLAIR (JR.) (1878–1968), and Thorstein Veblen contributed reportage that exposed corruption and indicted the powerful. Phillips's "The Treason of the Senate" (1906) attacked members of the Senate for serving wealthy lobbyists. Sinclair's *THE JUNGLE* (1906) shocked the nation with its depiction of the CHICAGO meatpacking industry. Veblen's *The Theory of the Leisure Class* (1899) argued that working people wasted time and money in a futile imitation of higher economic classes. These writers believed that the Industrial Revolution was causing more social disruption and inequality than positive change in the Midwest and in the United States as a whole.

Ethnic literatures have foregrounded protest during periods of heightened social struggle for rights and recognition. Native American concerns in the Midwest were taken up by BLACK ELK (1863–1950) and JOHN G (NEISENAU) NEIHARDT (1881–1973). Their collaborative work *BLACK ELK SPEAKS* (1932) reflects talks by Black Elk, with Black Elk's son as interpreter, and provides a vivid account of Lakota life during the nineteenth century. *Black Elk Speaks* expressed a powerful indictment of American conquest and the subjugation of indigenous people and inspired later Native American writers and activists, such as Mary Brave Bird (Mary Crow Dog, 1954–2013) and Winona LaDuke (b. 1959), who emerged from the Indian rights movement of the early 1970s.

Protest is one important strand of African American literary history, from antebellum slave narratives to the civil rights era and after. A number of famous poems by black Midwesterners may be described as literary protests. "We Wear the Mask" (1895) by PAUL LAURENCE DUNBAR (1872–1906), for example, and "I, Too, Am America" (1924) by LANGSTON (JAMES MERCER) HUGHES (1902–1967) assert black pride in the struggle against oppression, whether from without by institutional racism or from within by defeatism and self-rejection. *NATIVE SON* (1940) by RICH-ARD WRIGHT (1908–1960) created a template for the mid-twentieth-century novel of black protest, further developed by CHESTER (BOMAR) HIMES (1909–1984) in *If He Hollers Let Him Go* (1945) and GWENDOLYN BROOKS (1917–2000) in *Maud Martha* (1953). Dramatists, too, protested white supremacism, as in *A RAISIN IN THE SUN* (1959) by LORRAINE HANS-BERRY (1930–1965), who titled the play using a line from Hughes's 1951 poem "Harlem," also known as "Dream Deferred." The afore-mentioned texts, along with *THE AUTOBIOG-RAPHY OF MALCOLM X* (1965) by MALCOLM X (b. Malcolm Little, 1925–1965), influenced the aesthetics and politics of the Black Arts movement of the 1960s and 1970s, which prioritized social advocacy in literature. Gwendolyn Brooks, whose poetry already featured an element of protest, aligned her-self with the movement, as did other black Midwesterners, including DUDLEY FELKER RANDALL (1914–2000) and Margaret Danner (1915–1986).

The African American civil rights move-ment of the 1960s took great inspiration from music of the era, which provided a sense of solidarity among activists and sympathizers. Bob Dylan (b. 1941) began his storied career with protest songs in support of civil rights and against militarism. Some songs directly reflect Dylan's Midwestern origins, such as "The Death of Emmett Till" (1962), about the Chicago boy whose lynching in Mississippi in 1955 provoked indignation that helped fuel the civil rights movement. Others, such as the classic "Blowin' in the Wind" (1963), em-ploy imagery and language that, as David Pichaske shows in *Song of the North Country: A Midwest Framework to the Songs of Bob Dylan* (2010), reflect the dialect, the landscape, and even the weather of Dylan's native northern Minnesota. Sam Cooke (1931–1964), the fa-mous gospel and soul singer from Chicago, was directly inspired by "Blowin' in the Wind" to write "A Change Is Gonna Come" (1964), a civil rights song of such enduring power that Barack Obama alluded to it at the beginning of his victory speech in Chicago after his election as U.S. president on No-vember 5, 2008. Other gospel-influenced soul songs that gave courage and comfort to civil rights activists were written by Curtis

Mayfield (1942–1999) of Chicago, who sang with the Impressions. Mayfield's best-known civil rights songs include "Keep On Pushing" (1964), "People Get Ready" (1965), and "Choice of Colors" (1969).

Anti-war literature has played an impor-tant role in political debates in the United States, and Midwestern writers have made significant contributions. Samuel Lang-horne Clemens stridently opposed Ameri-can imperialism, writing numerous essays, such as "To the Person Sitting in Darkness" (1901), against the U.S. war in the Philip-pines and serving as vice president of the Anti-Imperial League from 1901 to 1910. Written in 1906 and first published in 1923, his story "The War Prayer" has become a protest classic. Clemens's anti-war writings are collected in *Weapons of Satire: Anti-imperialist Writings on the Philippine-American War* (1992), edited by Jim Zwick. Another relevant collection is *A Pen Warmed-Up in Hell: Mark Twain in Protest* (1972), edited by Frederick Anderson.

Speeches by early twentieth-century Midwestern political figures may also be read for their enduring rhetorical value and social relevance. On April 4, 1917, two days after President Woodrow Wilson urged U.S. entrance into World War I, Robert M. La Follette Sr. (1855–1925), U.S. senator from Wisconsin, delivered a speech before Con-gress sometimes referred to as "The People Do Not Want This War." Also opposed to the war was Eugene V. Debs (1855–1926), labor leader and perennial Socialist candidate for U.S. president from Terre Haute, Indiana. On June 16, 1918, Debs delivered a speech in Canton, Ohio, "The Subject Class Always Fights the Battles," that cost him a ten-year sentence under the Espionage Act of 1917. Debs's statement to the court upon convic-tion, delivered on September 18, 1918, is an eloquent defense of his right to protest. After serving more than two and a half years in prison, Debs was pardoned by President Warren G(amaliel) Harding. These and other speeches by Debs and La Follette often appear in anthologies of protest literature.

Debs, as well as Clemens, deeply influ-enced novelist KURT VONNEGUT (1922–2007), who accepted the Eugene V. Debs Award from the Debs Foundation in 1981. Vonnegut often quoted the famous Socialist leader and

Socialist candidate for president Eugene V. Debs being set free from prison on Christmas Day, 1921.

Image courtesy of the Library of Congress

fellow Indiana native and even named fictional characters after him. Vonnegut opposed the Vietnam War and other military actions by the United States; much of his writing, including late editorials denouncing the U.S. war in Iraq that began in 2003, speaks to the obscenity and absurdity of war. Vonnegut's novels *Cat's Cradle* (1963) and *Slaughterhouse-Five* (1969) contributed artistically and intellectually to the anti-war counterculture of the 1960s and have become classics of protest literature, as well as SCIENCE FICTION.

Another leading Midwestern writer who opposed the Vietnam War was ROBERT (ELWOOD) BLY (b. 1926) of Minnesota, who co-founded American Writers against the Vietnam War with fellow poet David Ray (b. 1932) in 1965. The group protested the war through public demonstrations and readings. Bly and Ray also edited an anthology, *A Poetry Reading against the Vietnam War* (1966), intended for use at anti-war events. Several poems in Bly's second book, *The Light around the Body* (1967), protest the Vietnam War by means of surrealistic imagery and bitter irony. When the book won the National Book Award in 1968, Bly used his acceptance speech as an opportunity to encourage draft resistance and to donate the prize money to anti-war efforts. Bly's third book, *Sleepers Holding Hands* (1973), includes "The Teeth Mother Naked at Last" (1970), a powerful long poem attacking the war as a perverse extension of

American Puritanism, frontier attitudes, and industrialism.

Anti-war activism during the Vietnam War involved a good deal of literary activity, including manifestos, broadsides, and underground periodicals. Much of this took place in college towns like Ann Arbor, Michigan, and Madison, Wisconsin, which were major sites of protest. One of the main anti-war groups, Students for a Democratic Society (SDS), was formed at the University of Michigan by DETROIT-born activist (Thomas Emmet) Tom Hayden (b. 1939) and others. The founding document of SDS, the Port Huron Statement, is a key text of the anti-war movement. In their autobiographies anti-war radicals who were active in the Midwest during this period explain their actions and seek to make their past struggles relevant to present-day activism. Texts include *Fugitive Days: A Memoir* (2003) by William Charles (Bill) Ayers (b. 1944), *Reunion: A Memoir* (1989) by Tom Hayden, *Ravens in the Storm: A Personal History of the 1960s Antiwar Movement* (2008) by Carl Oglesby (1935–2011), *Prairie Radical: A Journey through the Sixties* (2001) by Robert Pardun (b. 1941), and *Lost from the Ottawa: The Story of the Journey Back* (2004) by Lawrence "Pun" Plamondon (b. 1945). Documents of the Weather Underground, an extremist offshoot of SDS that was particularly active in Chicago, are collected in *Sing a Battle Song: The Revolutionary Poetry, Statements, and Communiqués of the Weather Underground, 1970–1974* (2006), edited by Bernardine Dohrn, Bill Ayers, and Jeff Jones. Also of interest are writings by John Sinclair (b. 1941) of Michigan, leader of the White Panther Party and manager of the radical Detroit rock band MC5, collected in *Guitar Army: Street Writings / Prison Writings* (1972) and *It's All Good: A John Sinclair Reader* (2009).

As in the civil rights movement, music played an important role in protests against the Vietnam War, and popular songs figured among the most influential anti-war texts. Although Bob Dylan had stopped writing protest lyrics by 1965, some of his earlier songs served as anti-war anthems, and he remained a hero to the counterculture. Dylan was a major influence as popular music lyrics became more poetic and political. Increasing demand for such lyrics, particularly among young people, led record companies to release socially relevant music. Even Motown Records of Detroit, which had avoided controversy as part of the company's successful effort to win a large white audience for black artists, had major hits with such anti-war songs as "War" (1970), written by Norman Whitfield (1940–2008) and Barrett Strong (b. 1941) and sung by Edwin Starr, and "What's Going On" (1971), written by Renaldo "Obie" Benson (1936–2005), Al Cleveland (1930–1996), and Marvin Gaye (1939–1984) and sung by Gaye. Gaye's album *What's Going On* (1971), which begins with the title song, took on issues such as environmentalism and inner-city despair, as well as the Vietnam War; it routinely turns up in lists of the ten best albums. In the rock genre, one of the most notable protest songs was "Ohio" (1970) by Neil Young (b. 1945), recorded by Crosby, Stills, Nash, and Young and released soon after four students were shot to death at Kent State University by soldiers from the Ohio National Guard. These songs remain radio staples that become sadly relevant again in times of war.

From the tragedy at Kent State University also emerged the quirky, ironic songs of Devo, an alternative rock band from Ohio that achieved fame in the late 1970s and early 1980s with songs and videos satirizing TECHNOLOGY AND INDUSTRY, consumerism, and conformity in modern America. Devo was formed at Kent State by art students who were present during the shootings; founding member Gerald Casale (b. 1948) was a member of SDS. Their overarching concept, "de-evolution," holds that humanity is not evolving but regressing. Behind the humor and surrealism of Devo's lyrics, music, and visual media reside the anger and intelligence that have always informed the best protest literature, and that attended the band's founding in the midst of dissent and tragedy. Songs representative of Devo's conceptual approach to social protest include "Jocko Homo" by Mark Mothersbaugh (b. 1950), from the album *Q: Are We Not Men? A: We Are Devo!* (1978), and the title song from Devo's third album, *Freedom of Choice* (1980), by Mothersbaugh and Casale.

The sardonic but idealistic work of Michael Moore (b. 1954), Michigan-born and based director of films like *Fahrenheit 9/11* (2004) and author of books like *Dude, Where's My Country?* (2004), constitutes a major contribution to the Midwestern protest tradition. Moore's jeremiads against militarism, gun culture, and corporate malfeasance descend directly from the efforts of Clemens, Debs, and 1960s activists.

The protest tradition that began with abolition, suffrage, and labor activism and continued with anti-war protesters and activists for civil rights and other causes is alive and well in the Midwest today. In addition to traditional literary genres, it is apparent in music and film and on activist websites and blogs. These contemporary voices echo those of past dissenters from the Midwestern American status quo.

SELECTED WORKS: Important texts of Midwestern protest include *An Address to All the Colored Citizens of the United States* (1846) by John Berry Meachum; *The Theory of the Leisure Class* (1899) by Thorstein Veblen; *The Use and Need of the Life of Carry A. Nation* (1905) by Carry A. Nation; "War Prayer" (1905) by Samuel Langhorne Clemens; *The Jungle* (1906) by Upton Sinclair; *Women, World War and Permanent Peace* (1915) by May Wright Sewall; *Black Elk Speaks* (1932) by John G. Neihardt; *Native Son* (1940) by Richard Wright; "Blowin' in the Wind" (1963) by Bob Dylan; "A Change Is Gonna Come" (1964) by Sam Cooke; "People Get Ready" (1965) by Curtis Mayfield; *The Light around the Body* (1967) by Robert Bly; *Slaughterhouse-Five* (1969) by Kurt Vonnegut; "Ohio" (1970), recorded by Crosby, Stills, Nash, and Young; "What's Going On" (1971), as sung by Marvin Gaye; *Guitar Army: Street Writings / Prison Writings* (1972) by John Sinclair; and Michael Moore's film *Fahrenheit 9/11* (2004).

The contents of several anthologies suggest the strength of Midwestern contributions to a canon of American protest literature. Drawing on work from around the world and across the centuries, Upton Sinclair helped define the genre by editing the early anthology *The Cry for Justice: An Anthology of the Literature of Social Protest* (1915). Ralph F. Young has edited *Dissent in America* (2005), an anthology of protest literature in two volumes. Zoe Trodd includes many Midwestern figures in *American Protest Literature* (2006), and Patrick McCarthy and John McMillian, the editors of *Protest Nation: Words That Inspired a Century of American Radicalism* (2010), include selections by Sinclair, Debs, and Malcolm X.

Poets against the War (2003), edited by Sam Hamill and published in opposition to the U.S. war in Iraq, includes Midwestern writers like Antler (b. 1946), Robert Bly, Patricia Clark (b. 1951), PATRICIA HAMPL (b. 1946), and JIM (JAMES THOMAS) HARRISON (1937–2016). An online version of Hamill's anthology, maintained by Poets against War, features more than 20,000 poems from around the world.

FURTHER READING: Scholarship about nineteenth-century protest movements abounds and provides a good starting point for research about Midwestern involvement. Broad treatments of the social, cultural, and historical underpinnings of the abolition movement include *Of One Blood: Abolitionism and the Origins of Racial Equality* (2000) by Paul Goodman and *Abolitionism* (2010) by Reyna Eisenstark. The women's suffrage movement is treated in Sylvia D. Hoffert's *When Hens Crow: The Women's Rights Movement in Antebellum America* (1995) and Rosalyn Terborg-Penn's *African-American Women in the Struggle for the Vote, 1850–1920* (1998). Treatments of the temperance movement are found in Joseph R. Gusfield's *Symbolic Crusade: Status Politics and the American Temperance Movement* (1963) and Carol Mattingly's *Well-Tempered Women: Nineteenth-Century Temperance Rhetoric* (2000).

Studies of the Native American campaigns for equity during the nineteenth century include Francis Paul Prucha's *The Great Father: The United States Government and the American Indians* (1984) and Colin G. Calloway's *First Peoples: A Documentary Survey of American Indian History* (1999).

Scholars of Midwestern literature have sometimes focused on social protest. John T. Flanagan did so in "Literary Protest in the Midwest," *Southwest Review* 34 (Spring 1949): 148–57, as did Felton O. Best in "Paul Laurence Dunbar's Protest Literature: The Final Years," *Western Journal of Black Studies* 17.1 (Spring 1993): 54–63. One critical debate over Richard Wright's *Native Son* has to do with whether, in serving its function as social protest, the novel sacrifices believability of characterization and plot. This was the argument of James Baldwin (1924–1987) in "Everybody's Protest Novel" (1949), an essay

that ended Baldwin's friendship with Wright and continues to provide a point of reference in scholarship about Wright and other mid-twentieth-century black writers. See, for example, "Everybody's Protest Novel: The Era of Richard Wright" by Jerry W. Ward Jr. in *The Cambridge Companion to the African American Novel* (2004), edited by Maryemma Graham, 173–88, and "Anybody's Protest Novel: Chester Himes and the Prison of Authenticity" by Stephanie Brown in *Invisible Suburbs: Recovering Protest Fiction in the 1950s United States* (2008), edited by Josh Lukin, 62–84.

James Donal Sullivan's *On the Walls and in the Streets: American Poetry Broadsides from the 1960s* (1997) includes a chapter on the Black Arts movement and the broadside as a medium for protest. On protest in soul music lyrics, consult *Just My Soul Responding: Rhythm and Blues, Black Consciousness, and Race Relations* (1998) by Brian Ward, *Dancing in the Street: Motown and the Cultural Politics of Detroit* (1999) by Suzanne E. Smith, and *Higher Ground: Stevie Wonder, Aretha Franklin, Curtis Mayfield, and the Rise and Fall of American Soul* (2004) by Craig Werner.

Patricia D. Netzley includes entries on *Fahrenheit 451* (1953) by RAY (DOUGLAS) BRADBURY (1920–2012) and *Player Piano* (1952) by Kurt Vonnegut in *Social Protest Literature: An Encyclopedia of Works, Characters, Authors, and Themes* (1999).

Books on Vietnam-era anti-war protest include *Dissent in the Heartland: The Sixties at Indiana University* (2002) by Mary Ann Wynkoop and *Prairie Power: Voices of 1960s Midwestern Student Protest* (2004), in which Robbie Lieberman compiles oral histories of campus activists. Entries on Bob Dylan, Tom Hayden, and John Sinclair appear in *Leaders from the 1960s: A Biographical Sourcebook of American Activism* (1994), edited by David De Leon. On anti-war poetry of the Vietnam era, see Michael Bibby's *Hearts and Minds: Bodies, Poetry, and Resistance in the Vietnam Era* (1996) and Subarno Chattarji's *Memories of a Lost War: American Poetic Responses to the Vietnam War* (2001).

Protest in popular music is examined in *33 Revolutions per Minute: A History of Protest Songs, from Billie Holiday to Green Day* (2011) by Dorian Lynskey. The vast bibliography on Bob Dylan includes "Bringing It All Back

Home; or, Another Side of Bob Dylan: Midwestern Isolationist," *Journal of American Studies* 26.3 (December 1992): 337–55, by Tor Egil Foorland; *Highway 61 Revisited: Bob Dylan's Road from Minnesota to the World* (2009), edited by Colleen Josephine Sheehy and Thomas Swiss; and *Song of the North Country: A Midwest Framework to the Songs of Bob Dylan* (2010) by David Pichaske. Matthew Bernstein has edited *Michael Moore: Filmmaker, Newsmaker, Cultural Icon* (2010), a collection of scholarly essays.

JAMES M. BOEHNLEIN   UNIVERSITY OF DAYTON

PUBLISHING.
See Printing and Publishing

QUEER LITERATURE.
See Lesbian, Gay, Bisexual, Transgender, and Queer Literature

R

RADICALISM

OVERVIEW: A marginal tradition rather than a movement or a genre, Midwestern literary radicalism derives its continuity from the historical succession of political, cultural, and social circumstances. Contingent on nature and practices, its distinctive features include creating an alternate literary discourse separate from the dominant discourse of capitalistic commodity culture and establishing a system of literary production that gives access to those who, as a class, typically do not write. The importance of Midwestern literary radicalism lies in the effort to sustain a democratic culture for which Walt Whitman's *Democratic Vistas* (1871) may serve as a definition. Whitman calls for "a programme of culture, drawn out, not for a single class alone, or for the parlors or lecture-rooms, but with an eye to practical life, the west, the working-men, the facts of farms and jack-planes and engineers, and of the broad range of the women also of the middle and working strata, . . . and of a grand and powerful motherhood" (40). Such a culture requires a literate society, access to channels of communication, and a consensus that views democracy, in John Dewey's phrase from *Democracy and Education* (1916), as a "conjoint communicated experience" (101).

From the early settlement of the Midwest to the present, a small but significant number of writers, editors, and publishers have sought to create a literature pertinent to Whitman's view of common existence. Central to this project are "the people" and their relation to the government that best represents their interests. ABRAHAM LINCOLN (1809–1865) in his November 19, 1863, Gettysburg Address defined the relationship broadly in calling for a government "of the people, by the people, for the people." The contested areas of workers' rights and economic justice elude broad definition, however, and require vigorous leadership, discussion, and, on occasion, activism.

Building on previous traditions and movements such as critical realism, PROTEST LITERATURE, socialist writings, progressive reform, and a resurgent left-wing movement after World War I, literary radicals in the Midwest constructed a rough-hewn tradition of political and cultural discourse. Working-class issues neglected in the national cultural discourse found alternate avenues of expression bypassing the hierarchical institutions that generally decide the

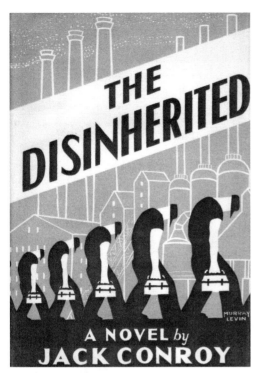

Jack Conroy's *The Disinherited*. Illustration by Murray Levin. Covici, Friede Publishers, 1933.
Image courtesy of Special Collections, Grand Valley State University Libraries

social status of literary works. In the 1930s a generation of young writers, little-magazine editors, and mainstream publishers created a literature drawing on everyday experience and the rituals, idioms, and customs that give expression to a class historically excluded from both popular and elite literature.

The attempt to join the interests of the writer with those of the reader in a common discourse separate from the dominant system of commodity production and mass marketing sets Midwestern literary radicalism apart as an alternate cultural tradition rooted in working-class experience. Distinguishing it from its Marxist counterparts are the decentralized and anarchistic tendencies characteristic of the Midwest that have often brought it into conflict with East Coast radical traditions, which draw on European antecedents. Rooted in American traditions of dissent and protest, Midwestern literary

radicalism achieves common purpose through its commitment to democratic ideals and social justice for common people, who, in Andrew Jackson's words, form "the great body of the people of the United States . . . men who love liberty and desire nothing but equal rights and equal laws" (Farewell Address, March 4, 1837).

Linked to events in labor history beginning with early industrialism in the mid-nineteenth century, Midwestern literary radicalism reflects the long struggle for workplace equity and worker expression. Its legacy offers instructive models for both individuals and marginal groups while seeking social and economic justice in the face of centralizing and hierarchical forces in society.

Evolving from early unpublished workers' narratives and autobiographies in the nineteenth century through union and socialist journals of the early twentieth century, Midwestern literary radicalism represents a significant, if neglected, tradition unique to the Midwest. Its influences and sources are eclectic, following no one school or movement or ideology but rather representing tendencies as unorthodox as the writers, editors, printers, and publishers who gave it life.

Like a network of subterranean streams, Midwestern literary radicalism burst through the landscaped surface of institutionalized culture when the pressure for change could no longer be contained. As a part of a broader heritage of Midwestern literature, the legacy of Midwestern literary radicalism deserves recovery and critical attention because it provides the language of resistance and embodies the spirit of dissent that Thomas Jefferson (1743–1826) and Henry David Thoreau (1817–1862), among others, have argued are essential to sustain a robust democracy.

HISTORY AND SIGNIFICANCE: Radical expression in America can be traced back to early polemicists like Thomas Paine (1737–1809), finds eloquent use in Jefferson's writings, and was invoked by Lincoln in describing the Civil War as a revolution against the inner spirit of slavery. According to Maxwell (David) Geismar (1909–1979) in *American Moderns* (1958), "It was the 'atheists,' the radicals, the immigrant dreamers of social justice in the late nineteenth century, who mainly inherited and preserved our true cultural heritage" (36–37). Less likely than their eastern counterparts to join radical organizations, Midwesterners from the earliest days have participated in protest movements when they pursued specific aims, such as the Farmers' Holiday Association in the 1930s. Typically, however, participation ended and organizations dissolved when those aims were achieved or proved impossible to attain. Dissent and protest are deeply rooted in Midwestern life and history. They are linked to anti-authoritarian and egalitarian tendencies, as well as to the rebellious iconoclasm of certain notable individuals, for example, John Brown (1800–1859) and Kate Richards O'Hare (1877–1948).

The problematic settings of rural, village, and industrial urban life have long provided Midwestern writers with subjects. The harsh conditions of rural life and the misery of industrial cities in the decades before World War I gained readers' attention through the works of celebrated Midwestern writers such as IGNATIUS LOYOLA DONNELLY (1831–1901), (HERMAN) THEODORE DREISER (1871–1945), (HANNIBAL) HAMLIN GARLAND (1860–1940), WILLIAM DEAN HOWELLS (1837–1920), (BENJAMIN) FRANK(LIN) NORRIS, (JR.) (1870–1902), and OLE EDVART RØLVAAG (1876–1931). Garland's MAIN-TRAVELLED ROADS (1891), for instance, portrays the straitened lives of small farmers in helpless dependence on weather and distant markets. The disillusion that follows the settlers' initial mood of expectation finds only fleeting release in sensuous appreciation of natural beauty on the prairies. Responsible for the farmers' plight, Garland suggested, were the power brokers of eastern capitalism, together with the monopolistic practices of railroads. Similar perceptions gave rise in the late nineteenth century to a spirit of rural insurgency bitterly opposed to the joint influence of money and monopolistic control. That insurgency coalesced into social-political movements such as the Grange and the Farmers' Alliance.

In the 1880s the People's Party was born, reflecting the long-held grievances of rural populations in Midwestern and southwestern states. Populism achieved few victories on the national level but succeeded in the formulation of principles of economic justice and popular rule that were mainly unheeded in the face of a declining rural economy, the unwillingness of industrial unions to make common cause, and the increasing bureaucratization of government.

Among the significant literary works of social protest fiction to emerge from the Populist movement was Ignatius Donnelly's futuristic romance *Caesar's Column* (1890). Donnelly portrays the proletarian masses of the world rising up in revolt against a brutal oligarchy, a prophecy echoed in his preamble to the Populist Party's first national platform (1892). There he cites the class division between rich and poor in American society and warns of a vast international conspiracy poised to take possession of the world.

Midwestern literary radicalism grew in part from seeds planted by early prairie realists and authors of protest fiction such as EDWARD EGGLESTON (1837–1902), JOSEPH KIRKLAND (1830–1894), and (JOSEPH) BRAND WHITLOCK (1869–1934). Eggleston's *The Hoosier School-Master* (1871) employs vernacular speech, as does Kirkland, whose *Zury: The Meanest Man in Spring County* (1887) brings to the surface the brutality of frontier life. In *The Turn of the Balance* (1907) and *J. Hardin and Son* (1923) Whitlock exposes the corrupting influence of financial speculation and new money on a small OHIO community.

Most early protest fiction called for reform, not fundamental change, in the socioeconomic system. Critical realism, best known through Howells's dual role as author and editor, was prompted in part by the materialism of industrial capitalism in the late nineteenth century. In *A Hazard of New Fortunes* (1889) Howells centers his narrative on ethical questions relating to social justice rather than on issues attending actual labor conflicts. A streetcar strike plays a relatively small role in the story. Promoting realism as the proper discourse of democratic life and values, Howells, in *The Rise of Silas Lapham* (1885), redeems, through Lapham's moral choices, the corruption inherent in industrialization.

The earliest radical novel calling for fundamental systemic change, according to Walter Rideout's *The Radical Novel in the United States, 1900–1924*, is *By Bread Alone* (1901) by Isaac Kahn Friedman (1870–1931).

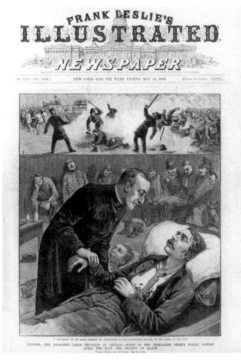

Frank Leslie's Illustrated Newspaper portraying the Haymarket riot, May 15, 1886.
Image courtesy of the Library of Congress

Born to a wealthy family in CHICAGO in 1870, Friedman was educated at the University of Michigan and later gained experience in settlement-house work, where he studied Chicago steelworkers and joined the Socialist Party. Situated in Homestead, Pennsylvania, during the violent events of the 1892 strike against the Carnegie Steel Company, Friedman's novel represented new stirrings in literary realism linked with the growing socialist movement in a time when romance literature continued to attract wide readership among all social classes.

Certain radical moments served to catalyze the demand for social transformation. Many of these moments took place in Chicago: the 1877 railroad strike, including the so-called Battle of the Halstead Viaduct, in which thirty protesters were killed; the Haymarket massacre (May 4, 1886) that led to a world labor holiday and created, in Eugene V(ictor) Debs's February 1898 words to the *New York Times,* "the first martyrs in the cause of industrial freedom" (E. V. Debs Internet Archive); and the 1894 Pullman

strike, from which Debs emerged as the leading figure of the Socialist Party. Other similar events sparked the imaginations of Midwestern writers. These included the invasion of the Philippines in 1898; the Ludlow, Colorado, mine strike in 1913–1914; the Centralia, Washington, IWW (Industrial Workers of the World) massacre in 1919; the 1922 great railroad strike; the 1927 Sacco and Vanzetti executions; and the crest of labor protest in the 1930s.

Literary responses to these events include poems on the Haymarket Square martyrs by (NICHOLAS) VACHEL LINDSAY (1879–1931) and EDGAR LEE MASTERS (1868–1950), as well as the searing indictment of American imperialism in the Philippine rebellion by SAMUEL LANGHORNE CLEMENS (1835–1910), writing as Mark Twain. Missouri-born Agnes Smedley (1892–1950) portrays her childhood memories of deadly tensions between mine owners and miners in her autobiographical novel *Daughter of Earth* (1929). Other responses include IWW, or Wobbly, poetry on the Centralia massacre, collections of angry poems occasioned by the Sacco-Vanzetti executions that helped catalyze the incipient literary radical movement of the 1930s, and the novel *Citizens* (1940) by Meyer Levin (1905–1981), dealing with the 1937 Memorial Day massacre of steel strikers in Chicago.

Hamlin Garland complained that William Dean Howells's brand of realism lacked the fiber to portray failure and impoverishment on the Middle Border. Closer in critical spirit to Garland's "Veritism," *The Story of a Country Town* (1883) by EDGAR WATSON HOWE (1853–1937) reveals the dark corners of human existence in small-town people's lives. Their longing, isolation, and frustrations anticipate *WINESBURG, OHIO* (1919) by SHERWOOD ANDERSON (1876–1941), whose argument for "crudity" in literature influenced Midwestern literary radicals in the 1930s. Focusing on an economic system that extracted wealth from the work of poor small farmers, Frank Norris's *The Pit* (1903) attacks the ruthless practices of laissez-faire capitalism. The Chicago native portrayed the means by which speculators on the Chicago Board of Trade wreaked devastation on the lives of farmers and small-town merchants.

No Midwestern novel of radical pedigree, however, had elicited the response accorded

THE JUNGLE when it was published in 1906. UP-TON (BEALL) SINCLAIR (JR.) (1878–1968) described Chicago packing-plant conditions in graphic terms, shocking readers and prompting government legislation. Likewise, the muckraking studies of Midwesterner RAY STANNARD BAKER (1870–1946), which revealed social injustice and monopolistic business practices, played an important role in Progressive Era reforms and helped set the stage for radical expression in the following decades. Theodore Dreiser counted the terrible costs incurred by working-class people who, thirsting for life, engage a society that cares little for individual lives. *SISTER CARRIE* (1900), like Stephen Crane's *Maggie, a Girl of the Streets* (1893) and Jack London's *People of the Abyss* (1903), allows readers a glimpse inside the world of prostitutes, taverns, unemployed factory workers, and the criminal milieu in the late nineteenth century. With the broad sweep of social history, (JOHN) HERBERT QUICK (1861–1925) continued the work of the prairie realists into the early decades of the twentieth century with his trilogy of rural life, *Vandemark's Folly* (1922), *The Hawkeye* (1923), and *The Invisible Woman* (1924).

Conditions of industrial life in the cities prompted socialist and Progressive writers to reject the dreary fatalism of literary naturalism in favor of programs for rational political action and socialist ethics. See REALISM AND NATURALISM. Six years after the Pullman strike in 1894, the Chicago publishing firm of Charles H. Kerr started the *International Socialist Review* (*ISR*), which later absorbed the Socialist literary magazine the *Comrade*, begun in 1901. The aim was to educate workers by introducing them to European socialist thought and the classics of socialist and realist literature, including Debs, Upton Sinclair, Karl Marx (1818–1883), and Maxim Gorky (1868–1936). CARL (AUGUST) SANDBURG (1878–1967) wrote articles for the *ISR* on workers' rights and strikes. Socialist fiction focused on the marginalized worker, the unemployed slum dweller, and the wage slave, weighing the grim facts of American economic life against the anticipation of economic justice.

One of many writers and intellectuals drawn to the informal salon of JANE AD-DAMS (1860–1935) at Chicago's HULL-HOUSE was Henry Demarest Lloyd (1847–1903), an editorial writer for the *Chicago Tribune*. Infused with the critical spirit of Garland, Donnelly, Norris, and Dreiser, Lloyd, a native of New York City, drew his material for *Wealth against Commonwealth* (1894) from the Haymarket riot and the ensuing Pullman strike. Yet neither the middle-class moral sentiments of socialist literature nor the socialist vision of a "cooperative commonwealth" were in tune with what most people experienced in their work lives or hoped to achieve. Working-class speech and attitudes were lacking in socialist fiction, which echoed the moral idealism of Victorian reform measures and employed the language of genteel literature. Despite their progressive convictions and the popular appeal of their verse, Carl Sandburg and Vachel Lindsay offered little sustenance to working-class readers in the struggle for workplace justice. Their poems spoke to what Raymond (Henry) Williams (1921–1988) in *Culture and Society, 1780–1950* (1958) calls the "embodied spirit" (34) of the people, not to the angry, insurrectionary miners in Ludlow, Colorado, and the steelworkers in Chicago.

The most successful publication to reach a working-class readership was the Socialist newspaper *Appeal to Reason* (1895–1922). Initially published in KANSAS CITY, *Appeal* relocated two years later to Girard, KANSAS, where Julius A. Wayland (1854–1912) and co-editor Fred Warren first serialized Sinclair's *The Jungle. Appeal* was a primary force in the Socialist Party's bid to elect Debs in the 1912 presidential race. Printing personal narratives and opinions by workers along with contributions by well-known figures such as Howells, London, O'Hare, Debs, William Morris (1834–1896), and John Ruskin (1819–1900), it pioneered methods of radical literary production, including a volunteer "Appeal Army" of 80,000 who sold subscriptions and distributed copies at union halls and train stations. Succeeding as publisher in 1919, E(MANUEL) HALDEMAN-JULIUS (1889–1951) began to issue pocket-sized books called the Appeal Pocket Series, later changed to Little Blue Books, in an effort to bring classic and socialist literature into low-income homes.

In 1922 Haldeman-Julius replaced *Appeal* with the *Haldeman-Julius Weekly*, which, like the *Oklahoma Leader,* edited by Oscar Ameringer (1870–1943), sought readers among farmers and workers. Although Haldeman-Julius lacked Ameringer's folksy humor and incisive wit, he proved to be a better businessman. Yet neither socialist convictions nor business instinct enabled these publications to continue into the succeeding decade, when new realities and political alignments imposed new credos. Nevertheless, socialist editors and publishers like Wayland, Ameringer, and Haldeman-Julius were successful in preparing the way for a new generation of Midwestern literary radicals who had acquired a taste for literature from reading William Shakespeare (1564–1616), (Joseph) Rudyard Kipling (1865–1936), Percy Bysshe Shelley (1792–1822), and Oscar Wilde (1854–1900) in five-cent Little Blue Book editions and who had found a willing publisher for their early stories in the Haldeman-Julius newspapers.

If protest literature, critical realism, and socialist literature planted the seeds, working-class life was the soil that nourished Midwestern literary radicalism. Pre-literary expression in the form of worker correspondence and personal narratives appeared in factory and union journals such as the *United Mine Workers Journal,* first published in Columbus, Ohio, in 1891 and subsequently in Indianapolis; magazines such as Hamilton Holt's *The Independent* (1902–1906), B. O. Flowers's *Arena* (1889–1909), Charles H. Kerr's *International Socialist Review* (1900–1918), *The Comrade* (1901–1905), *The Masses* (1911–1917), *The American Mercury* under H(enry) L(ewis) Mencken's (1880–1956) editorship (1924–1933), *The New Masses* in its early years (1926–1935), and the spirited little magazines of the 1930s like *The Anvil* (1933–1935), whose slogan was "We prefer crude vigor to polished urbanity." In addition, the IWW occasionally issued pamphlets.

Worker narratives functioned as subtexts for Twain's *Life on the Mississippi* (1883), Dreiser's *An Amateur Laborer* (written in 1904, first published in 1983), *The Disinherited* (1933) by Missourian (JOHN WESLEY) "JACK" CONROY (1898–1990), and *Waiting for Nothing* (1935) by Tom Kromer (1906–1969). Indeed, the novels of greatest influence in the American proletarian literary movement were novelized worker autobiographies: the trilogy by Maxim Gorky and *Jews without Money* (1930) by Michael Gold (1894–1967). Historically, worker narratives represent restless stirrings prompted by working-class literacy and the powerful desire to communicate. They serve to foster workers' self-awareness and confidence, as they did in the Chartist movement in England a century earlier.

Critics and literary historians of the 1930s tended to gather the work of writers on the left whose subject matter involved working-class people into a loosely defined category called "proletarian literature." The writers themselves frequently invoked the term without precisely knowing its meaning. "Proletarian" was a politically loaded term suggesting alignment with the Communist-led cultural program in the 1930s that viewed society from a class perspective and sought to enroll industrial workers in a worldwide revolutionary movement. To young Midwestern radical writers like NELSON ALGREN (1909–1981), Sanora Babb (1907–2005), Jack Conroy, PAUL (FREDERICK) COREY (1903–1992), Robert Cruden (1909–2004), EDWARD DAHLBERG (1900–1977), JOSEPHINE (FREY) HERBST (1892–1969), LANGSTON HUGHES (1902–1967), Joseph Kalar (1906–1972), MERIDEL LE SUEUR (1900–1996), H(arold) H. Lewis (1901–1985), and Joseph Vogel (1904–1995), the term "proletarian literature" sounded like a foreign import awkwardly translated to American working-class life. They referred to the term without fully appreciating its origin or implications. "Class," in contrast, and "racial bias" had unmediated meanings grounded in personal experience.

Possessing little Marx and less Engels, the Midwest literary radicals of the Depression decade drew on indigenous traditions of protest and progressive thought in responding to economic crises and the perceived failure of government to deal with the specter of mass unemployment, dispossession, and hunger. The generation of Midwestern radicals who came of age in the 1920s and produced most of their work during the Depression responded to the proletarian movement because it appeared to translate class interests into conscious goals for organized action. Most Midwesterners showed little interest in the ideological debates among leftist intellectuals in New York City. The latter's propensity for fruitless polemics and their ignorance of events and people in the hinterland were frequently satirized in Midwestern radical circles.

Fostered by magazine editors like H. L. Mencken, JOHN T(OWNER) FREDERICK (1893–1975), Jack Conroy, and others, Midwestern novelists such as JAMES T(HOMAS) FARRELL (1904–1979) and Nelson Algren, like Dreiser, Norris, and Anderson before them, stripped bare harsh social realities. Sherwood Anderson's reference to "crudity" meant a rejection of genteel writing and the facade of conventional morality. The cold-water bath of the early Depression years toughened a new radical temper that stressed the activist function of a literary work and the social responsibilities of the author. The Midwestern radicals refashioned the genres of everyday speech to represent the events and lives of ordinary people they had known on farms and in factories, mines, and lumber mills. Their aim was to write from within their own experiences, telling how they arrived at radical perceptions. Their written testimonies were conceived as a social act; in Marx's terms they represented an interaction in which participants' consciousness is transformed.

The Midwestern literary radicals came of age in an era of labor militancy and a revolutionary leftist movement fostered by the Communist Party of America. The party's successes in organizing demonstrations and strikes and for a time promoting workers' culture drew writers and publishers, both radical and mainstream, to participate. Intended to give voice to workers, the Left's proletarian movement produced only limited results since most workers, then and now, lack time to pursue writing. Those who attempted to write had to pursue their literary ambitions during available moments of their work life or while looking for work. Moreover, the hyphenated condition of worker-writer introduced contradictions and ambivalences that only a few Midwesterners, such as Le Sueur, Conroy, Babb, and TILLIE (LERNER) OLSEN (1912–2007), successfully explored.

Radically different from traditional ideas of authorship and literary production, worker writing typically is multivoiced and episodic, and the events often portray the difficult circumstances in which the writing came into existence. The writers' status is not always clearly defined, and their work, sensitive to the marginalized voices of their culture, is anti-canonical. Nonetheless, the work of the 1930s literary radicals was a considerable achievement, for in different ways they all succeeded in giving voice to the working class. The tragedy is that in doing so, these writers, the rightful heirs of the great protest and naturalist-realist writers of the Midwest, slipped into obscurity.

The shift away from worker writing in the Popular Front era, heralded by the First American Writers' Congress in 1935, coincided ironically with signal victories in labor's struggle for workplace justice. The little magazines were short lived; literary journalism would soon move to the universities. Mainstream publishers like Alfred A. Knopf and Viking Press that had for a time discovered publishable writing among the literary radicals followed the lead of readers attracted to subjects that stayed discreetly away from the question of revolutionary change. Literary modernism, the hardboiled novels of the 1950s, and writings that tapped mainstream interests and the usual best-seller topics—scandal, sex, violent exploits—were among these subjects.

Cold War anxiety, the House Un-American Activities Committee, and the anti-Communist crusade of Senator Joseph Raymond McCarthy chilled the market for critical realism while promoting revisionist examinations of radical writers and the political causes in which they engaged. Viewed as rubber-stamped copies of Stalinist orthodoxy and in some instances seditious, the work of the pre–World War II literary radicals remained in obscurity until the work of recovery and evaluation began in the late 1950s. This work continues today and has resulted in new editions of radical novels and poetry collections, as well as numerous scholarly studies that place in proper perspective the neglected heritage of literary radicalism in the Midwest.

If Midwestern literary radicalism tends to rise and fall with periods of labor activism, this cyclical pattern may account for its present relative silence. By contrast, FILM documentaries, video productions, and still photographs, representing the visual counterpart of literary radicalism, are making significant contributions that in another era would have appeared in book form. Notable examples include the popular and controversial documentaries by Academy Award–winning director Michael Moore (b. 1954), which frequently refer to his working-class upbringing in industrial Flint, MICHIGAN, and which feature present-day Flint as Moore challenges industrial policy, militarism, American gun culture, and capitalism. New technologies for networking and low-cost production methods, historically the instrumental elements of literary radicalism, are available to users through the internet and web publishing. A sweeping transformation in communication is taking place that few literary radicals could have foreseen. The question remains open whether these new electronic media will give meaningful expression to the timeless questions of social justice and workplace equity and, therefore, extend the proud tradition of Midwestern literary radicalism.

SELECTED WORKS: Readers unfamiliar with the tradition of Midwestern literary radicalism should start with the twelve most significant novels representing the diversity of this tradition: Edgar Watson Howe's *The Story of a Country Town* (1883); Ignatius Donnelly's *Caesar's Column* (1890); Hamlin Garland's *Main-Travelled Roads* (1891) (including the short story "Under the Lion's Paw"); Theodore Dreiser's *Sister Carrie* (1900); Upton Sinclair's *The Jungle* (1906); Jack Conroy's *The Disinherited* (1933); Nelson Algren's *Somebody in Boots* (1935); Langston Hughes's *Good Morning Revolution* (1973); Sanora Babb's *Whose Names Are Unknown* (written in the 1939, first published in 2004), Paul Corey's trilogy, beginning with *Three-Miles Square* (1939–1941); *Letter to an Imaginary Friend* (1962) by THOMAS (MATTHEW) McGRATH (1916–1990); and Meridel Le Sueur's *Ripening* (1982).

Readers interested in a historical study of Midwestern literary radicalism are advised to begin with the prairie realists, including Edward Eggleston's *The Hoosier School-Master* (1871); Joseph Kirkland's *Zury: The Meanest Man in Spring County* (1887); Ole E. Rølvaag's *GIANTS IN THE EARTH* (1927); and Herbert

Quick's *Vandemark's Folly* (1922). Carl Sandburg's *CHICAGO POEMS* (1916) and Vachel Lindsay's *Collected Poems* (1923) express important radical convictions. A good sample of Midwestern radical writings from the Depression years includes Jack Conroy's *The Disinherited* (1932) and *A World to Win* (1935); Nelson Algren's *Somebody in Boots;* Tillie Olsen's *Yonnondio: From the Thirties* (first published in 1974); Langston Hughes's poems collected in *Good Morning Revolution* (1973); Joseph Vogel's *Man's Courage* (1938); Josephine Herbst's *Pity Is Not Enough* (1933); and Edward Dahlberg's *Bottom Dogs* (1929). Significant works of literary radicalism published since World War II include *Knock on Any Door* (1947) by WILLARD F. MOTLEY (1909–1965); Joseph Kalar's *Papermill: Poems, 1927–35* (2006); Alexander Saxton's *The Great Midland* (1948); and Sanora Babb's *The Lost Traveler* (1958) and *Whose Names Are Unknown* (written in 1939, first published in 2004).

Three films by Michael Moore that have received critical acclaim and wide distribution are *Roger and Me* (1989), about the abandonment of Flint, Michigan by General Motors; *Fahrenheit 9/11* (2004), about President George W(alker) Bush (b. 1946) and his administration's reaction to the terrorist attacks of September 11, 2001; and *Capitalism: A Love Story* (2009), which centers on the economic crisis of 2008 and the federal bailout of large banks. David Sutherland's *The Farmer's Wife* (1998) explores the emotional costs incurred by a young farm couple facing the loss of their land and home in rural Nebraska. *Hard Earned,* produced by Al Jazeera America, is a six-part series that aired in 2015. The film examines urban realities in Chicago, Milwaukee, and elsewhere, focusing on the struggles of American families to maintain dignity while attempting to provide their basic needs.

A selection of useful anthologies includes *Rebel Voices: An I.W.W. Anthology* (1964), edited by Joyce L. Kornbluh; *Haymarket Scrapbook* (1986), edited by Dave Roediger and Franklin Rosemont; *Echoes of Revolt: "The Masses", 1911–1917* (1966), edited by William L. O'Neill; *Social Poetry of the 1930s* (1978), edited by Jack Salzman and Leo Zanderer; *Writing Red: An Anthology of American Women Writers, 1930–1940* (1987), edited by Charlotte Nekola and Paula Rabinowitz; and *Calling Home: Working-Class Women's Writing* (1990), edited by Janet Zandy.

FURTHER READING: An indispensable guide to a study of Midwestern literary radicalism is Walter Rideout's *The Radical Novel in the United States, 1900–1954* (1956). Daniel Aaron's *Writers on the Left* (1961) justly underscores the fact that the scope of American literary radicalism in the first half of the twentieth century extended across national borders, establishing links in some cases with its counterparts abroad. A shortcoming in Aaron's seminal work, however, is that relatively little attention is given to regional differences within the American literary radical tradition. Other important studies include H. Wayne Morgan's *American Writers in Rebellion: From Mark Twain to Dreiser* (1965) and Eric Homberger's *American Writers and Radical Politics, 1900–39* (1986). Critical work focusing on reevaluation and recovery include Alan Wald's *Exiles from a Future Time* (2002) and Cary Nelson's *Repression and Recovery* (1989).

Useful companions to the study of Midwestern literary radicalism are standard labor histories such as *A History of Labor in the United States* (4 volumes, 1921–1935) by John Commons and others and *Labor and the Left: A Study of Socialist and Radical Influences in the American Labor Movement, 1881–1924* (1970) by John H. M. Laslett. In *Labor's Text: The Worker in American Fiction* (2001) Laura Hapke studies the connection between labor history and literary narrative.

Specific topics related to Midwestern radical cultural and literary traditions include *Freethought on the American Frontier* (1992), edited by Fred Whitehead and Verle Muhrer; Roy W. Meyer's *The Middle Western Farm Novel in the Twentieth Century* (1965); Douglas Wixson's *Worker-Writer in America: Jack Conroy and the Tradition of Midwestern Literary Radicalism, 1898–1990* (1994); Lawrence Goodwyn's *The Populist Moment: A Short History of the Agrarian Revolt in America* (1978); *Yours for the Revolution: "The Appeal to Reason," 1895–1922* (1990), edited by John Graham; Elliot Shore's *Talkin' Socialism: J. A. Wayland and the Role of the Press in American Radicalism, 1890–1912* (1988); and Meridel Le Sueur's *Crusaders: The Radical Legacy of Marian and Arthur LeSueur* (1955). Useful for a study of Wobbly writings is *Rebel Voices: An I. W.W. Anthology* (1964), edited by Joyce L. Kornbluh. On the role of *New Masses* and proletarian literature in Midwestern literary radicalism, *"New Masses": An Anthology of the Rebel Thirties* (1969), edited by Joseph North, is an essential reference work. For a general study of the Communist movement in the United States, see Irving Howe and Lewis Coser's *The American Communist Party* (1957). To explore differences between Midwestern literary radicalism and its New York counterpart, one should consult James Burkhart Gilbert's *Writers and Partisans* (1968).

Reference works dealing with little magazines include Frederick J. Hoffman, Charles Allen, and Carolyn F. Ulrich's *The Little Magazine: A History and a Bibliography* (1946) and *American Literary Magazines: The Twentieth Century* (1992), edited by Edward E. Chielens. Subjects related to Midwestern literary radicalism today appear in *Mid-America, Midwestern Miscellany, North Dakota Quarterly, New Letters,* and publications of the university presses of ILLINOIS, MISSOURI, Oklahoma, North Carolina, New Mexico (including West End Press), and Kansas. Correspondence, unpublished memoirs, manuscripts, and other materials are located in various archives, but much remains to be preserved. The Jack Conroy collection, housed at the Newberry Library in Chicago, is an important resource on Midwestern literary radicalism from World War I to the present. The Moberly, Missouri, Area Community College houses Jack Conroy's private library of Midwestern literature, including many titles of radical literature, in a permanent collection. The Harry Ransom Humanities Research Center in Austin, Texas, maintains invaluable collections related to Midwestern literary radicalism, as does the Labadie Collection at the University of Michigan. Other archives include the Minnesota Historical Library in St. Paul (see MINNEAPOLIS/ST. PAUL) and the Pittsburg State University Library in Kansas. Web links and sites exist for individual writers and for the general topic of Midwestern literature. See also CHICAGO POEMS; FARM LITERATURE; GIANTS IN THE EARTH; THE JUNGLE; NEWSPAPER JOURNALISM; PROTEST LITERATURE; and SISTER CARRIE.

DOUGLAS WIXSON   UNIVERSITY OF MISSOURI–ROLLA

RAINTREE COUNTY

HISTORY: Set in a fictionalized Indiana county, *Raintree County* (1948), the only novel by ROSS (FRANKLIN) LOCKRIDGE JR. (1914–1948), narrates the life of John Wickliff Shawnessy through a series of flashbacks prompted by events within the passing of a single day, July 4, 1892. A small-town schoolteacher and aspiring writer, fifty-three-year-old Shawnessy relives his life, deeply embedded in the larger historical events and cultural forces of nineteenth-century America. Although most of the 1,060-page novel was written in the East, when Lockridge was supposedly writing a Harvard doctoral dissertation on Whitman, the principal setting is the Midwest. Many of the characters have counterparts in Lockridge's mother's forebears, and Raintree County is modeled on Henry County, INDIANA, where they were born and raised and lived most of their lives. The novel is structured around the celebratory homecoming to Waycross of notable Raintree County denizens who have made their fame beyond its borders: a U.S. senator, a railroad magnate, an army general, and a columnist for *THE DIAL*. Only Shawnessy, still obscure, is living in the county of his origin.

Lockridge hand-delivered the unsolicited twenty-pound manuscript in a battered suit-case to a junior editor at Houghton Mifflin in Boston on April 24, 1946, the day before his thirty-second birthday. Just as it was about to be rejected, two friends with Houghton Mifflin connections persuaded senior editors to take a look. Generating much in-house enthusiasm, the novel was accepted on May 27. Lockridge immediately resigned a $2,500 teaching position at Simmons College and moved with his wife and four children to a lakeshore cottage in Manistee, MICHIGAN, where he undertook an extensive revision. During this period he renewed ties with his cousin Mary Jane Ward (1905–1981), author of the best-selling novel *The Snake Pit* (1946), based on her incarceration for mental illness at Rockland State Hospital, New York. He also engaged in a bitter contract dispute with his publisher and visited Hollywood.

Not unlike Shawnessy himself but no longer obscure, Lockridge returned to his hometown, Bloomington, Indiana, with his family in time for the much-heralded publication of *Raintree County* on January 5, 1948, the same day fellow Bloomingtonian Alfred Kinsey published *Sexual Behavior in the Human Male*. The novel had already been excerpted as "The Great Footrace" in the September 8, 1947, issue of *Life* magazine (108–27). It was the main selection of

Ross Lockridge Jr. in the Lockridge family home, Bloomington, Indiana, 1939. Photo by Vernice Baker Lockridge.

© the Lockridge family, 1939

Book-of-the-Month Club, had secured a very lucrative movie contract with MGM, and had sold out a prepublication edition of 50,000 copies. On March 6, 1948, just as his novel reached the top of the *New York Times* best-seller list, Lockridge took his own life by carbon monoxide poisoning in the family garage. He was thirty-three years old.

The initial popularity of the novel owed much to the postwar letdown and a widely felt need throughout the United States for renewal of its cultural mission in a world that had witnessed the Holocaust and Hiroshima and was then settling into the Cold War. Many early reviews of *Raintree County* emphasized its idealism, vitality, anchorage in American history, and affirmation of American values. But the novel was also deemed controversial because of its eroticism and blasphemy. In the prepublication run Jerusalem Webster Stiles, a Mephistophelean character, remarks, "Nature puts no premium on chastity. My God, where would the human race be if it weren't for the bastards? Wasn't Jesus God's? Pass the perfectos, John" (1994 edition 152). In the remaining first-edition run, the Book-of-the-Month Club edition, and all subsequent printings until 1994, "Wasn't Jesus God's?" was deleted. Prominently condemned by a Jesuit professor at Fordham, the novel was seized in late March 1948 by the Philadelphia vice squad in bookstores throughout the city. Houghton Mifflin won an injunction against further seizures and eventually prevailed in United States District Court (Houghton Library, Ross Lockridge Jr. Correspondence and Documents).

SIGNIFICANCE: The title *Raintree County* is familiar to Americans more because of the movie version MGM released in 1957 than because of the novel itself. Frequently shown on television, the movie—directed by Edward Dmytryk, with a screenplay by Millard Kaufman, and starring Elizabeth Taylor, Montgomery Clift, and Eva Marie Saint—bears slight resemblance to the novel, whose length has limited any potential for college course adoption. Although it has occasioned a fair number of critical essays and one monograph, *Raintree County* to date has had few serious readers in academe and has been on the fringe of the American canon.

Lockridge's ambition was encyclopedic, and the resulting novel might best be termed "encyclopedic" in Northrop Frye's sense of a work that attempts to embody the life cycle and culture of a people. It explicitly incorporates a large number of well-known works, from the Bible, *Oedipus Rex,* and *The Republic* to *Uncle Tom's Cabin,* the Gettysburg Address, *Leaves of Grass,* and *The Golden Bough.* The plot is based on Hawthorne's short story "The Great Stone Face." Its single-day framework comes from James Joyce's *Ulysses,* although, unlike Joyce's novel, the flashbacks are fully narrated episodes. Lockridge felt that Joyce's novel, which he deeply admired in other respects, was inaccessible to the common reader. "The emotions are there, but not for the reader, who is too busy deciphering." (This comment, as well as all of Lockridge's comments on Midwestern writers, is taken from Lockridge's unpublished notes on his reading, ca. 1939–1943.) Lockridge attempted a polyphony of voices, prose styles, and subgenres, but early critics heard mostly Thomas Wolfe. Having read the southern novelist, Lockridge disliked this comparison because of what he took to be Wolfe's egotism and formlessness. He thought of his novel as epic, even cosmic, and was dismayed when Hamilton Basso in the *New Yorker* treated it as the raw produce of a Hoosier hick, mistakenly calling him "Lockwood" throughout.

Lockridge did pay his respects to Midwestern writers, taking notes on his reading of them as he geared up to write *American Lives,* an earlier 2,000-page manuscript he began in 1941. He abruptly turned it over one summer evening in 1943 and started writing *Raintree County* on the other side. *American Lives,* of which some 200 pages survive on versos of the fragmentary *Raintree County* manuscript, was set in twentieth-century instead of nineteenth-century Henry County. It was more single-mindedly agrarian and small town than *Raintree County,* which has portions set in New York City, Philadelphia, Washington, D.C., Indianapolis, New Orleans, and many Southern sites associated with the Civil War.

For *American Lives* he opportunistically read *The Story of a County Town* (1883) by EDGAR WATSON HOWE (1853–1937) and called that work "a punk book, without even the historical importance generally ascribed to it." He wrote ten pages of nonjudgmental notes on *A Son of the Middle Border* (1917) by (HANNIBAL) HAMLIN GARLAND (1860–1940) and plot summaries of the stories in *WINESBURG, OHIO* (1919) by SHERWOOD ANDERSON (1876–1941). On (HARRY) SINCLAIR LEWIS'S (1885–1951) *MAIN STREET* (1920) he commented, "An American version of *Madame Bovary,* but lacking the intensity and classic effect of Flaubert's masterpiece."

Responses to other Midwestern writers suggest that Lockridge rarely felt that they lived up to the ambitions he had set for himself. He thought *An American Tragedy* (1925) by (HERMAN) THEODORE DREISER (1871–1945) "very impressive, though the reader is nearly drugged to sleep in the first few hundred pages. Style and artistic presentation as bad as ever. . . . A very depressing book." On *The Bridge of San Luis Rey* (1927) by THORNTON (NIVEN) WILDER (1897–1975), he wrote, "Certainly a second-rate book and scarcely worth the popularity it has attained." On *Oil!* (1927) by UPTON (BEALL) SINCLAIR (1878–1968) he wrote, "The usual strong socialist doctrine. Artistically weak . . . but a noble book, and of course on the right side."

Lockridge had a higher estimate of *U.S.A.* (collected 1938) by JOHN (RODERIGO) DOS PASSOS (1896–1970) and wrote a lengthy, impassioned defense of the novel when he ran into trouble at Simmons College for assigning portions to female undergraduates. Among Midwestern works, *U.S.A.* had the single greatest influence on *Raintree County,* more for its journalistic and cinematic techniques than for its literary sensibility. Not much taken by William Faulkner (1897–1962), Lockridge read most of ERNEST (MILLER) HEMINGWAY (1899–1961) up through *For Whom the Bell Tolls* (1940), admiring the "tough, honest writing" and dialogue. He envied Hemingway for his war experience. Declared 4-F for the draft, Lockridge wrote to his publisher that "while the Republic was bleeding, I hid behind a thousand skirts and let J. W. S. bleed for me all over the thousands of MS. pages of *Raintree County.*" He fought World War II from his writing desk.

Apart from growing up in it, Lockridge's greatest debt to Midwestern culture came by way of his parents. Ross Sr. (1877–1952) was known throughout the state as "Mr. Indiana," a state historian who wrote middle school biographies of George Rogers Clark (1752–1818) and ABRAHAM LINCOLN (1809–1865) and the standard textbook of Indiana history. He was better known for his "historic site recitals," in which he told stories of the famous dead and orated their words on the very spot where great events had taken place. As a boy and high school student, Ross Jr. participated in these recitals and other historical pageants arranged by his father. But he began to chafe at the tasks his father set for him and, in time, developed a more critical view of American history.

He had small interest in the Lockridge side of the family and found his main character, Shawnessy, in his maternal grandfather, John Wesley Shockley (1839–1907), a Hoosier schoolmaster who wrote belletristic poetry and dreamed of a larger life. Lockridge dedicated his novel to his mother, Elsie Shockley (1880–1961), who told him many stories of her Henry County childhood and of her revered father, who had died seven years before Ross Jr. was born.

Lockridge's mysterious suicide, which prompted a spate of editorials, encouraged darker readings that emphasized the novel's pervasive sense of loss. Its critical stance toward racism and slavery, as America's "original sin," toward commercialism from the Gilded Age on, and toward a loss of mythic consciousness began to lead some critics to find in it the makings of cultural critique. Lockridge unabashedly attempted the great American novel. His novel has twice been termed at least the "Great American Studies Novel"—by Joel M. Jones in "The Presence of the Past in the Heartland: *Raintree County* Revisited," in *Myth, Memory, and the American Earth,* edited by David D. Anderson, 53; and by Charles Trueheart, "The Great American Studies Novel," *Atlantic Monthly* 274.3 (September 1994), 105–10.

The novel's dominant themes of homecoming, attachment to the land, eros, time and mortality, memorials, racism, FEMINISM, politics, war, RELIGION, and the power of myth are large and perennial at the same time at which they are anchored in nineteenth-century Midwestern culture. Asked by his publisher for promotional material, he wrote in July 1947 that, among other large aims, he wished to "embody in fiction a profound analysis of the social, anthropological, and sexual characteristics of Nineteenth Century American life" and to "provide a living document of the religious and political 'rites' of the American People" (Houghton Library, Ross Lockridge Jr. Correspondence and Documents). *Raintree County* is an album of Midwestern county fairs, grand patriotic programs, revival meetings, county atlases, courthouse and marketplace culture, footraces, saloons, picnics, buggy rides, rough country weddings, temperance dramas, and outdoor sex. Lockridge spent untold hours in the journalistic archives of the Boston Public Library reading old newspapers of Henry County and environs to get a better sense of the immediacy of events, both local and national. He revisited the old family sites in Henry and Miami Counties with a historian's passion for repossession of the past. He read the manuscripts of his grandfather Shockley's poetry and pondered the *Illustrated Historical Atlas of Henry County* (1875).

John Wickliff Shawnessy is the rememberer, but one so weighed by the past that he cannot get on with the epic he has in mind to write. Jerusalem Webster Stiles, the "Perfessor," tells Shawnessy that the past cannot be repossessed, sadly so since "all lovely things are old things." And all myths of homecoming are myths of death. The Perfessor enters into philosophical dialogue with Shawnessy in the "Day" sequences throughout the novel. He had left Raintree County for the East after the death of his mother and then had returned as a philologist and classicist, heading up Pedee Academy, where Shawnessy became his student. Learning the trade as a war correspondent, the Perfessor then becomes a successful eastern journalist. The novel's large element of classical allusion sustains Lockridge's evocation of nineteenth-century Midwestern classicism, whose gentility attempted to civilize rubes by means of extracts from Cicero and Virgil. Although he is a Hermes figure, a messenger of the gods

spreading such culture, the Perfessor is also a skeptic and debunker of the very myths he peddles. He is deeply anti-Christian. His dark humor owes something to the writings of SAMUEL LANGHORNE CLEMENS (1835–1910), writing as Mark Twain, which Lockridge was teaching at Simmons College. Clemens's *Gilded Age* (1873) influenced the novel's "City" section.

Shawnessy amicably counters with the values, convictions, and dreams of an American romantic visionary. Much of what he says and feels has its source in eros and worship of the land. *Raintree County* has been called an "ecological novel" by Fred Erisman in "*Raintree County* and the Power of Place," *Markham Review* 8 (Winter 1979): 36–40. The Great Swamp, the Shawmucky River, the Raintree, and even the Danwebster graveyard—overrun by myrtle, wild carrot, blackberries, and poison ivy—affirm the continuance of life amid tragic loss. Nell Gaither, Shawnessy's first doomed love, is seen by him rising naked from the Shawmucky, suddenly transformed from a fig-leafed Eve into a seductive Venus. The Shawmucky, whose original is Miami County's Eel River, the Kenapocomoco, is symbolic of the male life force, just as the Great Swamp is female. That the eponymous Raintree, symbol of fecundity, renewal, and beauty, actually exists in Raintree County is only a legend Shawnessy would like to believe. There is no doubt that raintrees exist in New Harmony, Indiana, the site of two early nineteenth-century utopian experiments. In his mid-twenties, for fifty dollars, as arranged by his father, Ross Jr. had written *A Pageant of New Harmony* (1937), some thirteen hundred lines of blank verse. He was ashamed of this work and did not attend the performance, but material produced under coercion fed later into his representation of the erotic life. It is under the raintree in the Great Swamp that Shawnessy loses his virginity to Susanna Drake, his second doomed love, a southern woman haunted by the probability that she is the daughter of a mulatto.

Throughout, the erotic life is hedged in by hoopskirts and disrupted by death, but erotic yearning persists. "Raintree County was itself the barrier of form imposed upon a stuff of longing, life-jet of the river" (116).

Having lived through tragic loss, the Civil War, and a thwarting of professional ambition, Shawnessy settles down with his second wife and three children in a Victorian gingerbread house. His wife, Esther, a former student and part Native American, always addresses him as "Mr. Shawnessy." Eros has been domesticated but lives on in the strong current of feeling that dominates even the "Day" episodes.

Beyond eros, Shawnessy argues another value against the Perfessor's clever, affable pessimism: the constructive power of myth. Shawnessy's own life has borne out the truth of the old stories. In beating frontier braggart Flash Perkins in the great Raintree County footrace, he lives out James Frazer's thesis that one hero will usurp another, often killing him. In having sex with Susanna under the raintree and paying quite a price, he lives out the truth of Genesis. In coming home from the war after being reported dead, he lives out the story of Lazarus. In being almost tarred and feathered by a righteous mob near the end of the "Day" section, he lives out the myth of Christ. The old stories still have power over us, but they need to be remembered and recited, and Lockridge, not unlike his father, recites them in his novel.

The Perfessor laments, "I wish I could believe in sacred places. . . . But beauty and the gods can't survive the era of Darwin and the Dynamo" (912). Shawnessy disagrees, drawing on a tradition of cultural humanism that Lockridge is implicitly tapping into: from Vico and Schiller to Carlyle and Emerson, and anticipating Northrop Frye's "myth of freedom." New mythmakers are much needed. We think up our institutions, and, as Schiller had argued, it is only through the strong imaginings of aesthetic culture that a new politics is possible. As America's representative "dreamer," Shawnessy sees at the day's conclusion the possibility of a new republic that will connect with America's original promise. Whether he will now be able to write the great epic of the American people is unresolved, but in a real sense Lockridge has attempted to write it for him.

Shawnessy's is, of course, a fragile idealism that since 1892, not to mention since 1948, history has not treated kindly. Where is the evidence that "courageous dreamers" are prevailing? But for the duration of his novel's composition, Lockridge tried to believe that Shawnessy was getting the better of the argument with the Perfessor.

Subsequent writers have rarely acknowledged a *Raintree County* influence. Pablo Neruda (1904–1973) mentions Lockridge in a 1948 poem, "Que despierte el leñador." *The Riddle of Genesis County* (1958) by Lynne Doyle (b. ca. 1940) is an explicit brief adaptation. *Paradise Falls* (1968) by DON ROBERTSON (1929–1999) parallels *Raintree County* in some respects and was initially publicized with references to the novel. John (Hoyer) Updike (1932–2009) on occasion referred to it, as in *In the Beauty of the Lilies* (1996). Thomas Mallon (b. 1951) makes Lockridge's suicide a leitmotif in *Dewey Defeats Truman* (1997), but his narrator is critical of *Raintree County* itself. *Tears of the Mountain* (2010) by John Addiego (b. 1951) is a direct homage, taking place in a single day, July 4, 1876, with flashbacks beginning in 1831, and set in Sonoma County, California; it also makes use of the technique of one chapter leading linguistically into the next. Some important novelists and poets have indicated to this writer a felt, if indirect, influence: for instance, Marguerite (Vivian) Young (1908–1995), Herman Wouk (b. 1915), Philip D. Appleman (b. 1926), Joseph (Prince) McElroy (b. 1930), and Thomas (Michael) Keneally (b. 1935). Edna Rydzik Buchanan (b. 1939), a Pulitzer Prize–winning novelist-journalist, has said that *Raintree County* is her all-time favorite novel, but her genre is crime fiction.

MGM/Turner has thus far blocked many initiatives by producers for a new film adaptation. Lockridge reserved only live stage rights in his confining 1947 contract with MGM; and all attempts at operatic, musical, and dramatic adaptations have failed as of this writing.

IMPORTANT EDITIONS: *Raintree County* was initially published by Houghton Mifflin in 1948. Concurrently, a Book-of-the-Month edition was issued. In 1949 a British hardcover was published by Macdonald. In connection with the MGM movie, a paperback was released in 1957 by Popular Library, and an abridged version by Dell. The novel was issued in a 1984 Arbor House paperback with a preface by Joseph Blotner. The Book-of-the-Month Club printed a facsimile hardcover edition in 1992. The 1994 Penguin Books paperback, edited by Larry Lockridge, corrected a few typos and restored the censored words "Wasn't Jesus God's?" A new edition of *Raintree County* was published by Chicago Review Press in 2007; it features a notable foreword by Herman Wouk. *Raintree County* has been translated, in abridged form, into Japanese, Spanish, Dutch, German, French, and three Scandinavian languages, Norwegian, Swedish, and Finnish.

FURTHER READING: The first book-length study of Lockridge's novel is Fred Waage's *"Raintree County": The Foremost American Environmental Novel; Uncovering the Deep Message of an Undervalued Text* (2011), published with a foreword by Barbara Stedman by the Edwin Mellen Press. Other extended discussions include Larry Lockridge's "The Author in the Epic," chapter 8 of *Shade of the Raintree: The Life and Death of Ross Lockridge, Jr.* (1994), 271–309. DAVID D(ANIEL) ANDERSON (1924–2011) edited two collections of critical essays: *Myth, Memory, and the American Earth: The Durability of "Raintree County"* (1998), with essays by Ray Lewis White, Gerald D. Nemanic, Joel M. Jones, Park Dixon Goist, Dean Rehberger, Douglas A. Noverr, David D. Anderson, and Larry Lockridge; and *Midwestern Miscellany* 26 (Spring 1998), with new essays by some of these critics, as well as essays by Patricia Ward Julius and Theodore R. Kennedy. See also *Twentieth-Century Literary Criticism* 109 (2001): 316–74. Raintreecounty.com, maintained by Ross Lockridge III, contains many manuscript materials, photographs, and links to other sites. The small portion of the original *Raintree County* manuscript that Lockridge did not burn is in the Lilly Library, Indiana University. In late 2011 the four Lockridge heirs—Ernest, Larry, Jeanne, and Ross III—donated forty-seven organized cartons of Ross Lockridge Jr.'s papers and related materials to the Lilly Library. Containing 75,000 items, the archive is inventoried in a two-volume, 457-page descriptive bibliography, compiled by Larry Lockridge, available in the reference room at the Lilly Library, which has also made it available online. An inventory can be found on the Lilly Library website: http://www.indiana.edu/~liblilly/lilly/mss/index.php?p=lockrdg3. This archive and other Ross Lockridge Jr. papers are available without restriction to scholars and critics. An exhibition, *Raintree County: A Celebration of the Life and Work of Ross Lockridge, Jr.,* containing about 300 items from the Ross Lockridge Jr. Collection, occupied the Main Gallery of the Lilly Library, January 21 through May 19, 2014, marking the centennial of the author's birth. In conjunction with this exhibition, Indiana University Press reissued Larry Lockridge's *Shade of the Raintree* with a new preface by the author. For a fuller bibliographic survey, consult the *Dictionary of Midwestern Literature,* volume l (2001), 328–29.

LARRY LOCKRIDGE   NEW YORK UNIVERSITY

RAISIN IN THE SUN, A

HISTORY: *A Raisin in the Sun* (1959) holds a central place in THE CHANGING MIDWESTERN LITERARY CANON and is one of the great classics of American theatre. The play changed American theatre and culture through its brilliant exploration of race in middle-class Midwestern America. It was also the first play by an African American woman to be performed on Broadway. Its author, playwright LORRAINE HANSBERRY (1930–1965), was born in CHICAGO on May 19, 1930, the fourth child of Carl A. and Nanny Perry Hansberry. Lorraine Hansberry's parents were born to middle-class African American families in the South. In Chicago, despite segregation, her father was a successful businessman and real estate investor. In 1938 the Hansberrys purchased a home in Chicago's racially segregated South Side neighborhood just south of Washington Park but encountered racial violence and legally enforced discrimination when an ILLINOIS court ordered the family to vacate the home they had purchased. The Hansberry case went to the U.S. Supreme Court, which in 1940 ruled in their favor, declaring racially restrictive covenants unconstitutional.

A Raisin in the Sun ends with the fictional Younger family, like Hansberry's, moving into a hostile white Chicago neighborhood. The play dramatizes the generational and cultural tensions, greatly exacerbated, if not caused, by poverty and racism, that tear the Younger family apart. Walter Lee Younger's final decision, supported by the rest of the family, to reject the money offered by a white homeowners' association to stay out of the neighborhood marks the dramatic climax of the play.

Lorraine Hansberry attended Chicago public schools, but a large part of her education took place in the family home, where the family received visitors like W(illiam) E(dward) B(urghardt) Du Bois (1868–1963), LANGSTON HUGHES (1902–1967), Paul Robeson (1898–1976), and Lorraine's uncle, William Leo Hansberry, who taught African history at Howard University. After graduating from Englewood High, she attended the University of Wisconsin. In 1950 she moved to Greenwich Village in New York, where she studied writing at the New School in New York City and African history under Du Bois at the Jefferson School for Social Research and wrote for Paul Robeson's *Freedom*.

Hansberry completed *A Raisin in the Sun* in 1957; it played to good reviews before opening on Broadway at the Ethel Barrymore Theatre on March 11, 1959. The play was immediately recognized as a masterpiece, running for 538 performances on Broadway and winning the year's New York Drama Critics' Circle Award for Best Play against *Sweet Bird of Youth* by Tennessee Williams (1911–1983) and *A Touch of the Poet* by Eugene O'Neill (1888–1953). It also won Tony Awards for best play, director, actor, and actress. Hansberry also wrote the screenplay for the successful 1961 film version, in which Sidney Poitier again starred as Walter Lee Younger Jr.

HISTORY AND SIGNIFICANCE: Although *A Raisin in the Sun* was a great popular and critical success from the beginning, its stature as a play of enduring significance has become clear only over time. At first, some critics thought that its popularity was dependent on the topical relevance of racial restrictive housing covenants, which would inevitably diminish. Leonard R. N. Ashley in his essay "Lorraine Hansberry and the Great Black Way," in *Modern American Drama: The Female Canon* (1990), edited by June Schlueter, argues that the play is too "safe" to be great and that it is "relevant without being radical and sweet without being saccharine," a commercially appealing play, if not "a great play" (158), so mixed opinions exist concerning its aesthetic and political contributions, but over the years

Ruby Dee and Sidney Poitier in the film adaptation of *A Raisin in the Sun*, 1961.
© Columbia Pictures, 1963

critics have overwhelmingly asserted the play's significance.

The play remains compelling fifty years after its opening because it is beautifully crafted and because it continues to address the still-contentious issues of racial integration. It is also true, however, that the issue of racial integration, in housing and elsewhere, no longer has the centrality it did when *A Raisin in the Sun* opened. This loss of topical relevance has not lessened interest in the play but instead has led to a new appreciation of its permanent value as a literary work and a study of African American life. In an essay in the twenty-fifth anniversary edition of *A Raisin in the Sun*, Amiri Baraka (1934–2014) admitted that those who, like himself, had once condemned the play as "'middle class' in that its focus seemed to be on 'moving into white folks' neighborhoods" had "missed the essence of the work" (19).

The passage of time has made it easier to appreciate the play's richness in that audiences and critics are no longer tempted to believe that the Younger family's one-family "integration" of Clybourne Park provides an uplifting but unearned happy ending and, by implication, an all-too-simple solution to racial problems. Hansberry commented that those who supposed that the conclusion offered a fairy-tale-like happy ending were invited to move themselves to a neighborhood like the fictional Clybourne Park and find out for themselves.

The plot turns on the Younger family's decision to buy a house in the white Clybourne Park neighborhood, modeled on Chicago's Washington Park area, whose residents seem unalterably and perhaps violently opposed to racial integration of their white Chicago South Side neighborhood. Mr. Lindner, the representative of the Clybourne Park Improvement Association, urges the Youngers to think twice about "moving into a neighborhood where you just aren't wanted," warning that "people can get awful worked up when they feel that their whole way of life and everything they've ever worked for is threatened" (1959 edition, act 2, scene 3, 105; all subsequent quotations from the play are from this edition). Similarly, although Walter saves his own and the family's honor by refusing the money Lindner offers to buy back the house from the Youngers, he has no way to return the family money entrusted to him by his mother. Beneatha also has no fairy-tale happy ending: she still does not know where she will get the money to go to medical school. Ruth, too, must worry about how to pay for the baby she is expecting, and Lena may have to return to domestic work despite her age. Walter himself will be lucky to hold on to a job as a chauffeur for a wealthy white family—the same job that Bigger Thomas in NATIVE SON (1940) by RICHARD WRIGHT (1908–1960) held briefly in the same Chicago South Side as that of the Youngers.

Just as the play provides no happy ending or easy solution to racial problems, so there is no resolution to the family conflicts that make for some of the play's most effective theatre. Throughout the play Walter, dreaming about somehow making big money, and his sister Beneatha, who hopes to become a doctor, argue about many things, including her African suitor. After Walter finally gathers his strength and refuses the money offered by the neighborhood association to buy back their house, he is not so transformed that he is ready to accept Asagai as a viable husband for Beneatha. Despite Asagai's political radicalism, however, he agrees with Walter that marriage should be the goal of any woman. Although Asagai is much more attractive to Beneatha than George Murchison, his sexism diminishes him. Beneatha wants to be a medical doctor and her own person. She effectively points out that Asagai knows little about women's hearts because his sense of womanhood has been formed by reading novels written by men. Hansberry's feminist play strongly suggests that love is not and ought not to be enough for a woman. Walter may advise Beneatha, "You better marry yourself a man with some loot" (act 3, 141), and Ruth may prefer Beneatha's college beau, George Murchison, as husband material because he represents middle-class, materialistic black Chicago, but Beneatha has her own dreams.

The Norton Anthology of African American Literature (2004) notes in its introduction to the play that in 1957 "Hansberry was 'coming out' as a lesbian and ending her marriage. In several letters to *The Ladder*, an early lesbian publication, she analyzed the political connections between homophobia and antifeminism, as well as the economic and psychological factors that pressure lesbians into marriage" (1770). These new perspectives only increase the play's significance as an artistic as well as a historical artifact. See also LESBIAN, GAY, BISEXUAL, TRANSGENDER, AND QUEER LITERATURE.

"Mama" Lena Younger is surely the matriarch of the family, but she is far from a stereotypical earth mother. It is she, after all, who has bought the house in Clybourne Park, although she disclaims any motive other than getting the best house for the least money. The one act of violence in the play occurs when she slaps Beneatha for denying belief in God. Strong as she is, however, after making the down payment on the house she turns over the remainder of the insurance money, and with it leadership of the family, to her son, Walter Younger Jr. Beneatha and Lena Younger are of two different generations and have very different ideas, but Hansberry does not demand that the audience choose one character's value system over another's. Just as moving into Clybourne Park is not offered as a solution, so no one character presents a philosophy or point of view that provides an "answer" to the many dilemmas posed by the play. Beneatha is certainly the most ambitious and intellectual character, but her naïveté about the Africa she envisions is a source of affectionate comedy. When she attempts to dress like "a well-dressed Nigerian woman," she looks instead "more like Butterfly than any Nigerian that ever was," according to Hansberry's stage direction. Beneatha, it is clear, misses the mark when her enthusiasm for Africa leads her to condemn a "good loud blues" playing on the radio as "assimilationist junk" (act 2, scene 1, 67).

Lorraine Hansberry was certain that the play's larger relevance depended on her ability to capture the particular aspect of African American experience represented by life in 1950s South Side Chicago. In an interview in *To Be Young, Gifted and Black* (1969), Hansberry declared, "Not only is this a Negro family, specifically and definitely culturally, but it's not even a New York family or a southern Negro family. It is specifically Southside Chicago" (114). Previously, in her article "What Could Happen Didn't" in the *New York Herald Tribune* (March 26, 1961): 8, she had described herself as "born to the romance of the Sandburg image of the great city's landscape" and hoped that the film version would allow her to emphasize even more strongly the significance of Chicago for the drama. In the introduction to the 1994 Signet edition of *A Raisin in the Sun: The Original Unfilmed Film Script,* Margaret Wilkerson states that "Hansberry's cinematic vision was indeed of Sandburgian sweep as she sought to make her characters quintessential Chicagoans" (xxx). When the wealthy George Murchison tries to show his sophistication by his knowledge of New York, Walter insists, "New York ain't got nothing Chicago ain't. Just a bunch of hustling people all squeezed up together—being 'Eastern.'" George questions whether Walter has been there, and Walter responds with a bold lie, "Plenty of times." His wife Ruth, stage directions indicate, is supposed to act shocked at the lie. When she says his full name out loud, Walter reacts without shame, vehemently underlining his feeling that a Chicagoan has nothing to learn from New York by repeating the word "plenty" and then changing the subject (act 2, scene 1, 73–74). Chicago is Walter's city.

In the play's second act, when Walter is trying to find out who he can be in the city, temporarily running from Ruth and her new pregnancy and chasing his dream to own his own bar, he experiences a broader Chicago. He is studying his city, and he is unraveling, drinking heavily without much sense of who he has become. Earlier he has revealed pride in a place that refuses to allow him dignity. He trusts his friend, Willy Harris, with his mother's $6,500, and his friend leaves town with it. Walter is ready to swallow his pride and take a bribe to keep him out of Clybourne Park, but at the last minute he decides to honor his father and refuses to be an accomplice in his own humiliation. He will not be "bought" out of moving into a middle-class white neighborhood. Walter's last and most significant speech points toward his redemption: "We called you over here to tell you that we are very proud and that this is—this is my son, who makes the sixth generation of our family in this country, and that we have all thought about your offer and we have decided to move into our house because my father—my father—he earned it" (act 3, 138). Significantly, Walter decides that place, space, and home in Chicago, in the Midwest, are worth the fight.

Raisin, a musical based on the play, won the 1974 Tony Award for Best Musical, and *A Raisin in the Sun* was successfully revived on Broadway in 2004 and 2014. The 2010 play *Clybourne Park* by Bruce Norris (b. 1960) extends and provides a controversial commentary on *A Raisin in the Sun.* Written in response to Hansberry's play and underlining its continuing significance, *Clybourne Park* won the Pulitzer Prize for Drama on April 18, 2011. Norris's Midwestern urban play continues the exploration, focusing on racial tensions in today's Midwest, as well as on problems associated with neighborhood gentrification, keeping Lorraine Hansberry's original play, *A Raisin in the Sun,* as relevant as when it first appeared.

IMPORTANT EDITIONS: *A Raisin in the Sun* (1959) is available in a paperback edited by Robert Nemiroff, the literary executor and former-husband of Lorraine Hansberry. A 1987 New American Library edition and a 1988 Signet edition are available in an expanded and reedited form. The 1987 edition also includes an additional play and three critical essays. Nemiroff explains that the version appearing in both the 1987 and 1988 editions, which he considers definitive, restores to the play two scenes unknown to the general public and a number of other key scenes and passages staged for the first time. It is the version Nemiroff believes Hansberry would have preferred had she had the final word when *Raisin in the Sun* was first published in 1959.

FURTHER READING: *To Be Young, Gifted and Black: Lorraine Hansberry in Her Own Words*, adapted by Robert Nemiroff (1969), is a collection of Lorraine Hansberry's writings and interviews, including much that directly or indirectly illuminates *A Raisin in the Sun*. Important essays by James Baldwin (1924–1987), Nikki Giovanni (b. 1943), Alex Haley (1921–1992), Adrienne Rich (1929–2012), and Margaret B. Wilkerson appear in "Lorraine Hansberry: Art of Thunder, Vision of Light," a special issue of *Freedomways* 4 (1979) edited by Jean Carey Bond. In 1996 John Maitino and David Peck edited a book of nineteen essays, *Teaching American Ethnic Literature*, that contains Meanne-Marie Miller's article " 'Measure Him Right': An Analysis of Lorraine Hansberry's *A Raisin in the Sun*" (133–45). Those interested in critical reception should consult Robin Bernstein's "Inventing a Fishbowl: White Supremacy and the Critical Reception of Lorraine Hansberry's *A Raisin in the Sun*," *Modern Drama* 42.1 (Spring 1999): 16–27. Feminists and those interested in comparative studies will benefit from reading Diana Adesola Mafe's "Black Women on Broadway: The Duality of Lorraine Hansberry's *A Raisin in the Sun*" and Ntozake Shange's "*For Colored Girls*," *American Drama* 15.2 (Summer 2006): 30–47. Michelle Gordon's " 'Somewhat like War': The Aesthetics of Segregation, Black Liberation and *A Raisin in the Sun*," *African American Review* 42.1 (Spring 2008): 121–33, and GerShun Avilez's "Housing the Black Body: Value, Domestic Space, and Segregation Narratives," in the same issue, 135–47, are two modern examples of the type of work being done as scholars continue to examine the play. Sandra Seaton's "*A Raisin in the Sun*: A Study in Afro-American Culture," *Midwestern Miscellany* 20 (1992): 40–49, and Yomna Saber's "Lorraine Hansberry: Defining the Line between Integration and Assimilation," *Women's Studies* 39.5 (July 2010): 451–69, will be of interest to literary and cultural historians. Another provocative article that examine the politics and aesthetics of the play is Zachary Ingle's " 'White Fear' and the Stu-

dio System: A Re-evaluation of Hansberry's Original Screenplay of *A Raisin in the Sun*," *Literature/Film Quarterly* 37.3 (2009): 184–93.
ANN LOUISH SEATON   BARD COLLEGE

REALISM AND NATURALISM

OVERVIEW: Literary realism and naturalism are not exclusively Midwestern phenomena, but writers from the Midwest contributed significantly to the literary movement that came to dominate American literature from the mid-nineteenth century to the first decade of the twentieth century and extended its influence to modernism and even to the present day.

Realism came to the United States after the Civil War, the product of many forces and changes occurring in the nation. In addition to the shock of the Civil War, with its 625,000 deaths and many times that number of injuries and families affected, Reconstruction ushered in the Gilded Age with the visibly corrupt administration of President Ulysses S. Grant and the public cynicism it engendered. The emergence and growth of the Industrial Revolution pulled the Midwest's population from family farms to anomie in amoral industrial cities lacking protection for employees or a social safety net for the unsuccessful. Rising immigration in the last decades of the nineteenth century made competition all the more cutthroat and lowered wages as employers cynically played desperately poor workers and their families against one another. See also TECHNOLOGY AND INDUSTRY.

Realism also found a congenial environment as a result of westward expansion and the interest of those in the East in experiencing, if only vicariously, the events, settings, people, and DIALECTS of the Midwestern frontier and the SMALL TOWN. Portrayals in literature of harsh, demanding, but also imaginatively compelling locales and the people there widened the range of literary coverage. Although easterners could feel smug about their purported cultural superiority over the people portrayed in this writing, they also wanted to experience something of the growing nation, as well as the lives and speech of the uncouth but strong people who were advancing the Republic. And although frontier and small-town people were often illiterate, their stories and their pride in transforming wilderness into farms and communities were regularly captured in frontier oral tales and stories. As literacy rose in the East and earlier-settled areas of the Midwest, working-class people also clamored to see people like themselves in literature: real people doing real jobs in real American settings distant from the nation's long-settled urban and cultural centers.

Together, these factors increasingly led Americans to favor literature more connected to the realities of everyday life among common people. This thrust toward greater realism was complimented by a revolt against nineteenth-century romanticism, with the unrealistic types of characters it typically portrayed, the settings it reflected, and the actions it presented. By the late nineteenth century New England could no longer purport to represent the country as a whole and could no longer sustain the great romantic tradition of Ralph Waldo Emerson (1803–1882). Nathaniel Hawthorne (1804–1864), and Herman Melville (1819–1891). Highly optimistic varieties of romanticism were especially called into question by social change and the negative experiences of Americans during the second half of the nineteenth century.

Realism initially came to be recognized abroad in the works of such French writers as Émile Zola (1840–1902) and Gustave Flaubert (1821–1880) and later by such Russians as Leo (Lev Nikolayevich) Tolstoy (1828–1910) and Fyodor Dostoyevsky (1821–1881). Opposed to the idealized characterizations and situations of romanticism, realists sought to deal with the actualities of a materialist rather than a spiritual understanding of human life. This evolution meant shifting, over time, from idealistic views and idealized characters to secular, often amoral, evolutionary models developed primarily by Charles Darwin (1809–1882) and Herbert Spencer (1820–1903). The earlier obligations of romantic writers to be didactic, to teach and inspire morality, to produce works of beauty, and to write solely about "acceptable" people in "polite" language gave way to wider themes and topics and a focus on common people. In matters of style, realist writing tended toward journalistic approaches that could produce a kind of poetry of the quotidian and immediate or devolve into a heaping up of details and facts.

Although the transition from romantic worldviews and techniques to those of realism was gradual rather than immediate, realism moved toward capturing American life and people as they were. According to the strictures of WILLIAM DEAN HOWELLS (1837–1920), novelist and literary critic from OHIO, realism's principal aim was to present a simple, honest treatment of contemporary life without the perceived excesses and distortions of romantic authors. Fiction, Howells believed, should avoid sentimentality or sensationalism, narrate plausible events, and emphasize character rather than plot. Realism, as embodied in Howells's fiction and that of many of the writers he published and promoted, deals with the aspirations and ethical dilemmas of middle-class characters; middle-class life represented for these writers the average and therefore representative human experience. By the end of the nineteenth century realism had institutionalized itself as the dominant mode of writing in American publishing and criticism. This was in no small part due to Howells. Particularly in his role as editor of the *Atlantic Monthly,* Howells became so influential that he was called the "dean of American letters."

One relatively late stage of realism is social-critical realism, in which protagonists and other characters tend to be low in socioeconomic status and unfairly exploited by the social, economic, and political elite who wield power in society and the workplace. Although the hero-victims have little control over their situations and are likely to be defeated or even destroyed, they continue their heroic fight for changes that will right social wrongs and create greater opportunity in the future. Narrators of these stories affirm the existence of right and wrong, applaud the courage and resolve of those being imperiled, and call for social change and collective action to bring about that change. *THE JUNGLE* (1906) by UPTON (BEALL) SINCLAIR (JR.) (1878–1968) and "worker portraits" by CARL (AUGUST) SANDBURG (1878–1967), like "Dynamiter" in *CHICAGO POEMS* (1916), reflect Midwestern social-critical realism.

Naturalism is a pessimistic form of realism that turned from Howells's emphasis on middle-class life and average experience toward portrayals of working-class life, both urban and rural, and more extreme situations involving struggle for survival. Naturalism also adds the concept of determinism and in so doing imposes a quasi-philosophical interpretation of life. In naturalistic fiction characters are "determined" by forces beyond their control. They are victims of biological, economic, and social influences, and readers are frequently given what amounts to a case history. The tone of this literature is pessimistic, as writers often leave their characters and readers in despair or retreating into a mitigating stoicism. In a naturalistic universe there is no transcendent moral order, only strength, cunning, and luck or lack thereof. Naturalistic characters sometimes resemble animals in a world of survival of the fittest. Even if they are successful in the short term, they will be defeated in time. Sometimes, to avoid the logical conclusion of their interpretation of life, naturalistic writers like (HERMAN) THEODORE DREISER (1871–1945) merge their work with social protest or message fiction or seek refuge in traditional humanistic values.

Midwestern writers played significant roles in the genesis and maturation of American literary realism, although placing writers and their works into specific literary movements always entails some oversimplification. Some of the authors discussed in this entry reflect early stages of American literary realism as it adopted attitudes and techniques of local color and regional writing. Local color can best be viewed as a mixture of sentimentalism and realism focused on a specific frontier or rural locale previously little depicted in literature. It frequently employs dialect; its province is the short story. Regionalism, on the other hand, attempts to universalize the locale treated. It is local color writ large, covering a broader geographic area. Regionalism is typically more honest or more fully developed in detail than local color, more artistic in its selection of details, more expansive thematically, and less journalistic in style. Howellsian realism sets this literary mode on a more serious, sustainable path but remains tied to teaching morality and maintaining some elements of Victorian decorum.

Other Midwestern writers illustrate movement toward social-critical realism or full-blown naturalism.

The Midwestern authors who best evince the style, technique, worldview, and content of realism and naturalism as presented and qualified in the foregoing include CAROLINE KIRKLAND (1801–1864) and JOSEPH KIRKLAND (1830–1894) of MICHIGAN; SAMUEL LANGHORNE CLEMENS (1835–1910), writing as Mark Twain, of MISSOURI; William Dean Howells, AMBROSE (GWINETT) BIERCE (1842–ca. 1914), CHARLES WADDELL CHESNUTT (1858–1932), PAUL LAURENCE DUNBAR (1872–1906), and SHERWOOD ANDERSON (1876–1941) of Ohio; EDWARD EGGLESTON (1837–1902), EDGAR WATSON HOWE (1853–1937), and Theodore Dreiser of INDIANA; (HANNIBAL) HAMLIN GARLAND (1860–1940) of WISCONSIN; EDGAR LEE MASTERS (1868–1950) of KANSAS and ILLINOIS; HENRY BLAKE FULLER (1857–1929), ROBERT HERRICK (1868–1938), (BENJAMIN) FRANK(LIN) NORRIS (JR.) (1870–1902), and Carl Sandburg of Illinois; and WILLA CATHER (1873–1947) of NEBRASKA.

HISTORY AND SIGNIFICANCE: Caroline Kirkland was a significant forerunner of the Midwestern realists. She began writing in hopes of improving her family's finances after the collapse of the Michigan wildcat banks in 1839, when Michigan was only beginning to be settled. Her writing portrays the harshness of the environment for the pioneers who first moved westward. She published *A NEW HOME—WHO'LL FOLLOW?* (1839) under the pseudonym Mary Clavers in order to avoid conflict with people in her Michigan community who provided models for her characters. Directed at an eastern audience, the novel counters distorted, idealized perceptions of frontier life as a kind of pastoral refuge. Kirkland followed *A New Home* with *Forest Life* (1842) and *Western Clearings* (1845). All three books celebrate the common people and belief in hard work and good character as the chief ingredients of success in America; at the same time, they offer an unflinching view of the hardscrabble existence of the impoverished settler. Kirkland's works are free of any notion that divine predetermination controls outcomes in life. See also FRONTIER AND PIONEER ACCOUNTS.

A key text in the development of American realism after the Civil War is *The Hoo-*

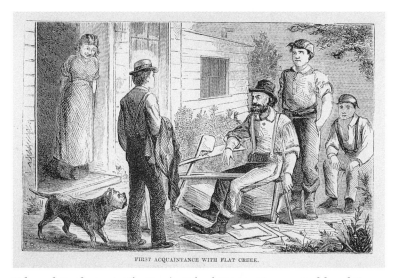

FIRST ACQUAINTANCE WITH FLAT CREEK.

Edward Eggleston's *The Hoosier School-Master*. Orange Judd and Co., 1871.

Image courtesy of the University of Kentucky Special Collections Research Center

sier School-Master (1871) by Edward Eggleston. Born and raised in Indiana, Eggleston had a varied career as a farmworker, Methodist clergyman, and journalist before writing novels and studies of American history. *The Hoosier School-Master* draws on his memories of frontier-era Indiana, as well as the experiences of his brother, GEORGE CARY EGGLESTON (1839–1911), as a rural schoolteacher. Although it features stock characters and conflicts typical of the era's popular fiction, Eggleston's first novel is notable for its portrayal of backwoods manners and its innovative use of dialect, both features of what is sometimes called prairie realism. When later writers like Joseph Kirkland and Hamlin Garland credited Eggleston with leading the transition from sentimentalism to realism in American fiction, they had in mind *The Hoosier School-Master*. Literary scholars have since reaffirmed that assessment of the novel's historical significance.

Another important early figure in Midwestern realism, Edgar Watson Howe, was born in Indiana, was reared in Missouri and Nebraska, and settled finally in Kansas. In 1883 Howe published *The Story of a Country Town*, a naturalistic novel about the deterministic forces controlling a boy's life as he comes of age. *The Story of a Country Town* is an uneven novel, with parts devoted to ex-

position, parts to description, and parts to intrusive authorial comments on such subjects as temperance and bigotry; it is held together by a melodramatic plot about the maturation of the narrator, Ned Westlock, and his friend, Jo Erring. Howe's characters are colorful, and their diction is that of rural Midwesterners of the era. Despite the novel's tendency toward sentimentalism and its frequently stilted descriptive language, Howe's plot is not marked by contrivances. Although he offers some optimism to temper his pessimistic determinism, Howe is unstinting in his realistic portrait of Midwestern small-town life.

Joseph Kirkland, Caroline Kirkland's son, did not turn to serious writing until later in life, after experiencing a variety of occupations. In his roles as businessman, government employee, publisher, and attorney, Kirkland traveled much and met many of the leading figures in the country at the time. His Illinois novels, *Zury: The Meanest Man in Spring County* (1887) and its sequel, *The McVeys: An Episode* (1888), depict Midwest country life in much the same ways as did Caroline Kirkland's books, and her influence is clear, but his novels come much closer to realizing the form than Caroline's. Joseph Kirkland's writings are marked by well-developed, dynamic characters,

E. W. Howe's *The Story of a Country Town*, Howe & Co., 1883.

Image courtesy of Special Collections, Grand Valley State University Libraries

suspenseful plots, and plausible conflicts, as well as regionally accurate diction. Although his plots occasionally yield to sentimentalism, the landscape itself, as Kirkland describes it, is indifferent and unyielding. There are droughts, floods, and windstorms; poverty, hunger, and farm failures are common. Kirkland also turns a critical eye on economic exploitation; the title *Zury* is the nickname of the novel's central character, Usury Prouder, the "meanest" man in Spring County because of his usurious acquisition of mortgages on others' land. See also FARM LITERATURE.

No other writer of the realist period in American literature exemplifies its defining characteristics as unmistakably and infuses them with as high a degree of aesthetic excellence as Samuel Langhorne Clemens, writing as Mark Twain. The trajectory of his writing career spans an involvement with the oral tradition, the tall tale, frontier hu-

mor, local color, regionalism, dialect, and strong social-critical realism. All these elements reach their refinement in a masterpiece that ERNEST (MILLER) HEMINGWAY (1899–1961) later proclaimed no less than the source of all modern American literature.

Like many other realists of his time, Clemens manifests a rejection of romanticism. Yet his portrayal of Huck and his feeling for the Mississippi River in *ADVENTURES OF HUCKLEBERRY FINN* (London 1884, New York 1885) recall romantic idealism even while he satirizes through Tom Sawyer and the poetry of Emmeline Grangerford the tendency of romanticism to sentimentalism and impracticality. The river functions as a moral force beyond the orthodox notion of morals and manners adhered to by many of Twain's fellow realists, while Huck Finn reaffirms the potential for goodness in the individual uncorrupted by social norms and practices. Twain's writing after *Huckleberry Finn* increasingly reflects the perspectives associated with naturalism. Such works as "The Man That Corrupted Hadleyburg" (1900), "The Mysterious Stranger" (1916), and "The War Prayer" (written in 1906 and first published in 1923) are decidedly pessimistic in outlook and deterministic in their view of human nature.

Without doubt, the most influential of the realists with Midwestern ties was Ohioan William Dean Howells, who promoted the careers of such writers as Sarah Orne Jewett (1849–1909) and Stephen Crane (1871–1900), as well as Midwestern realists like Clemens, Dunbar, and Garland. He articulated his ideas primarily in *Criticism and Fiction* (1891) and in his editorship of the *Atlantic Monthly* and *Harper's Magazine*.

Howells wrote three introspective autobiographical books about his youth: *A Boy's Town* (1890), *My Year in a Log Cabin* (1893), and *Years of My Youth* (1916). Taken together, Howells's three memoirs show the making of his mind, as well as his interest in multiple literary genres, including poetry, plays, criticism, and fiction; they recount his years from boyhood until President ABRAHAM LINCOLN (1809–1865) appointed him to the post of consul at Venice. Although religion held little interest for Howells, he did inherit from his parents a strong sense of ethics and the elements of good character, as well as the obligation for continuous self-improvement. A recurring theme in Howells's works is the search for an objective morality that does not depend on the doctrines of organized religion.

Howells's best-known novel, *The Rise of Silas Lapham* (1885), dramatizes the tension between the moral and the legal for the Lapham family of Boston. Although the novel is set in the East, the basic values extolled in it are those of Howells himself, a Midwesterner during his formative years. In the novel, Silas, a simple man with country values and a war hero, has been lucky enough to inherit a property on which he establishes a paint company. He becomes wealthy and, at the same time, develops social aspirations for his wife and daughters while remaining unpolished himself. Lapham decides to drive his partner out of the business on the eve of a huge windfall profit from the sale of a milling property. As Lapham rises financially, he declines morally; in following his wife, Persis's, guidance, Lapham ruins himself financially but regains his moral values. Symbolically, at the same time Lapham makes the right moral choice, the garish house he has built in Boston's Back Bay area is destroyed by fire, and the Laphams are forced to leave the city for the simpler life of their origins. After years of bickering about social status, material possessions, and finding the socially "right" husbands for their daughters, the Laphams have regained their happiness through their moral decision. The novel also indicates, by way of the privileged Corey family, the moral vacuity of the elite class.

New Leaf Mills (1913) is a fictional rendering of the rise and fall of a utopian community founded by Howells's father near CINCINNATI. For *The Leatherwood God* (1916), Howells took another real event and fashioned it into the tale of an unscrupulous preacher whose gullible followers consider him an actual deity until he meets an unfortunate demise. The characters and landscapes are drawn from rural Ohio.

Like other writers of realism, Howells grew up in a time when good taste demanded the eschewal of the sordid in life. Howells recognized that all life is the purview of the realist, although, like many other Midwestern writers of the time, he re-mained Victorian in regard to the portrayal of sexuality in literature. In *Criticism and Fiction* he rails against "the writers who now almost form a school among us, and who may be said to have established themselves in an easy popularity by the study of erotic shivers and terrors" (152). Howells and other Midwestern realists were bound to the standards of good taste by personal preference, as well as by the preferences of the reading public. Neither Kirkland nor Howells shied away from problem areas—Kirkland's *Zury* and Howells's novel *A Modern Instance* (1882) address the problem of adultery—but specific details are left to the reader's imagination.

Nine years after Howells's *A Modern Instance,* a leading figure in American naturalism, Hamlin Garland, published MAIN-TRAVELLED ROADS (1891), a collection of stories set in the rural upper Midwest. Garland's father had repeatedly uprooted the family, compulsively moving to new and unsettled places without consulting Garland's mother, who resigned herself to the role of dutiful wife. Garland never lost sight of the injustices to women in such situations, and his stories reflect this. "A Branch Road," the long story that Garland placed first in his book, presents a dark, realistic depiction of marriage. Agnes has married the plodding, mean-spirited Ed after believing that her real suitor, Will, has jilted her. When Will returns after some years to find Agnes living in squalor, he explains that a broken wagon wheel was responsible for his not taking her to the fair years earlier, and he urges her to leave her farmer husband and go with him. He says, "There's just one way to get out of this, Agnes. Come with me. He [Ed] don't care for you; his whole idea of women is that they are created for his pleasure and to keep house. Your whole life is agony. Come! Don't cry. There's a chance for life yet" (59–60). Will and Agnes, together with her baby, drive off through the wheat fields into a new life, leaving Ed to come home to an empty house.

The Midwestern landscape is treated realistically in Garland's work as well. He describes the "main-travelled" road as "long and wearyful," with "a dull little town at one end and a home of toil at the other. Like the main-travelled road of life it is traversed by many classes of people, but the poor and the weary predominate" (preface). Garland dedicates the collection "to [his] father and mother whose half-century pilgrimage on the main-travelled road of life has brought them only toil and deprivation." Starting with the book's front material, Garland rejects sentimentality about the frontier and rural life. His depictions of tenant farmers, Civil War veterans, and ruthless land speculators convey both a sense of social determinism and a populist idealism aimed at identifying injustices and encouraging their amelioration.

The rise of cities, with their dense populations and industrialism, also drew the attention of writers. Henry Blake Fuller and Robert Herrick, novelists associated with the first phase of the CHICAGO RENAISSANCE, wrote some of the first important American works of URBAN LITERATURE. Fuller earned the praise of Howells and other critics for *The Cliff-Dwellers* (1893), which follows the rise and fall of a CHICAGO banker. The "cliff-dwellers" of the title are the business and professional people working in the city's new skyscrapers, people whom Fuller characterizes as having sacrificed cultural values in favor of crass materialistic pursuits. The novel's publication in the year of the World's Columbian Exposition drew an uncomfortable contrast between the idealized image of Chicago presented in the exposition and the hard urban-industrial realities addressed in the book. Fuller's next novel, *With the Procession* (1895), deals with an established Chicago family whose fortunes and social status falter as newcomers to the city bring new development and creative energies. Fuller was also a pioneering gay writer; his play *At Saint Judas's* (1896) and novel *Bertram Cope's Year* (1919) are by many accounts the first direct treatments of male homosexuality in American literature in their respective genres. See also LESBIAN, GAY, BISEXUAL, TRANSGENDER, AND QUEER LITERATURE.

Massachusetts-bred and Harvard-educated Robert Herrick brought a newcomer's perspective to Chicago fiction. Like Fuller, he saw Chicago as a representative setting in the era of American industrialization and urbanization, but he was even more critical of the city's shortcomings. Herrick taught at the University of Chicago,

wrote a column for the *Chicago Tribune,* and published realist novels set in the city, the most notable being *The Web of Life* (1900) and *Memoirs of an American Citizen* (1905). *The Web of Life* is a love story about a Chicago surgeon, set against a tumultuous scene of unemployment, poverty, and the Pullman railway strike. *Memoirs of an American Citizen* deals with corruption at the highest levels of Chicago's meatpacking industry and the rush to judgment in the notorious Haymarket trial of 1887. These novels, with their frank descriptions of the urban landscape and unflattering depictions of Chicago's economic and political elite, did not endear Herrick to the city's boosters. In *Robert Herrick: The Development of a Novelist* (1962) Blake Nevius quotes Herrick, later defending his approach: "I had taken my literary creed of realism seriously and felt morally bound to represent by words what my mind saw when it looked forth upon Chicago,—its streets, its buildings, its dirt, its noise, its slovenly incompleteness, its rather crude social life" (87).

Among the most naturalistic writers of the period was Dreiser, who was born in Terre Haute, Indiana. His exceptionally poor and dysfunctional family was dominated by a father whose obsession with religion and sin kept him from remaining long in one job and a mother who loved her children dearly but had little control over them. The separations of Dreiser's parents became longer over time, and the children were largely on their own. Early in life Dreiser concluded that spiritual concerns were largely irrelevant, and material success was the only important goal; he was also obsessed with sex. He loosely based his characters on family members and others he knew. His sisters, for example, maintained common-law marriages and provided rough models for the title character of SISTER CARRIE (1900). Carrie, a bright and pretty but shallow young woman, has the chameleon-like ability to emulate people who possess those things in life she perceives as desirable, copying them so perfectly that people perceive her as the image she projects. Early in the novel she allies herself with Drouet, a traveling salesman who provides her with an apartment, necessities, and some luxuries. In the middle of the novel Carrie leaves Drouet for Hurstwood, a club manager who empties his employer's safe and abandons his wife to run off with Carrie. Carrie's relationships with both men are monogamous but unmarried. Never satisfied with what she has, by the end of the novel Carrie is a star on the New York stage, although her roles lack any intellectual qualities. After a long downward spiral Hurstwood commits suicide, and we last see Carrie in her rocking chair as she considers her prospects. Dreiser makes it clear that no level of success will bring her fulfillment. Carrie's rise, as much as Hurstwood's fall, is the result of chance and deterministic forces beyond her control.

Like Carrie, Clyde Griffiths, the protagonist of Dreiser's *An American Tragedy* (1925), is driven by his desires for material success and is presented as a victim of chance. The son of impoverished missionaries in KANSAS CITY, but a handsome and hardworking young man, Clyde begins his socioeconomic climb when he is taken in by a rich uncle and given a menial job in the uncle's collar factory in New York. Drawn to the "fast" crowd, Clyde finds acceptance among the members of the small town's elite society although he is still quite poor, a fact he successfully conceals. Unfortunately, Clyde also begins a sexual relationship with Roberta Alden, a factory girl. When she becomes pregnant, Clyde lures her to a remote lake for a romantic getaway after her attempts at securing an abortion fail; in actuality he intends to drown her in order to be free to pursue Sondra Finchley, the rich girl with whom he has become infatuated. After they are far out on the water, Clyde lacks the courage to murder Roberta, but a boating accident leads to her drowning. Clyde is convicted of murder and sentenced to death. After Clyde's execution, the novel continues for a few more pages in which Dreiser replicates the opening scene, in which a poor but alert young boy accompanies street missionaries on a hot summer evening, and the cycle begins again.

Like other regional realists, Paul Laurence Dunbar conveyed the diction of his characters in poems and fiction, capturing the authentic speech of slaves and ex-slaves. During Dunbar's formative years many of the gains made during early Reconstruction

were undone as southern states passed "black codes" that imposed de jure segregation. Between 1890 and 1896 the events leading to the Supreme Court's 1896 decision in *Plessy v. Ferguson* were unfolding, and the Ku Klux Klan and other racist groups were rampant in the South. Dunbar's use of plantation diction is still a topic of academic debate, as in the introductory material in *In His Own Voice: The Dramatic and Other Uncollected Works of Paul Laurence Dunbar* (2002), edited by HERBERT WOODWARD MARTIN (b. 1933) and Ronald Primeau.

Dunbar's transition from romanticism to naturalism was not unusual for a writer of his day. His early influences were the British and American romantic writers. During his high school years at Dayton Central High School in Dayton, Ohio, Dunbar gave readings of their works to any available audiences. By the time his novel *The Uncalled* was first published in 1898, Dunbar had completed the transition. Like the opening chapters of the naturalistic novel *Maggie: A Girl of the Streets* (1893) by Stephen Crane, the first scenes of Dunbar's novel depict a squalid and violent home, a place where no good can come to its inhabitants, and it becomes immediately obvious that grinding socioeconomic determinism is a major theme of the novel. *The Uncalled* is the story of Fred Brent, left orphaned after the disappearance of his divorced alcoholic father and the death of his alcoholic mother. Fortunately, Fred falls into "saving hands" when he is taken in by a prim lady of the community, brought up in the church, and pointed to a life in the ministry. That happenstance, however, does not provide Fred with a completely satisfactory life. Like George in Crane's *George's Mother* (1896), Fred is torn between the attractions of a dissolute cosmopolitan lifestyle and the safety offered by the church. But unlike George, Fred is saved from ruin by a chance meeting with his newly reformed father, who has become a temperance advocate.

Dunbar's best-known novel, *The Sport of the Gods* (1902), delivers one shock after another, driving the reader on to see what else bad can happen to the Hamilton family. Berry Hamilton, the father of the family, is ill served by the virtues typically associated with success in America, perhaps because the virtues he personifies are his downfall. He is trustworthy but too trusting. He is loyal but lacks the capacity for skepticism. He is simple and hardworking but naïve and lacking in self-direction. He is happy to have been emancipated but remains in the same situation as when he was a slave. He believes in the American system but fails to understand that, in the South at least, it is the white man's system. On first reading, it appears that Dunbar has sentimentalized Berry Hamilton, but subsequent readings reveal the ironic and cynical tone of Dunbar's narration. The economic and racial determinism of the Hamiltons' situation is inexorable; Hamilton goes to prison for a crime he did not commit, and the systematic destruction of his family begins after they flee in disgrace to New York. Fannie, Berry's wife, enters into a common-law marriage to a violent and abusive man. Joe, Berry's son, ends up in prison for the murder of a woman. And Kit, the daughter who is the apple of Berry's eye, has become a dancer in a sleazy stage troupe. What might have been a happy ending, after Berry Hamilton's vindication and the death of Fannie's vicious common-law husband, does not come to pass. Instead, Berry and his wife come to the realization that they are "powerless against some Will infinitely stronger than their own" (255).

At about the same time at which Dunbar was working on *The Uncalled,* another naturalist, Frank Norris, was writing *Vandover and the Brute* (1914). Born in Chicago, Norris moved with his parents to California when he was a teenager. Norris, too, was encouraged by Howells and, in turn, advanced the publication of Theodore Dreiser's naturalistic novel *Sister Carrie* by using his success and influence with his publisher in support of Dreiser's manuscript. A favorite technique of both Norris and Dreiser is systematically to strip away the acculturation of their characters to reveal animalistic, instinctual behaviors; their characters are driven by the fundamental urges of hunger, self-preservation, and sex. In both *Vandover and the Brute* and *McTeague* (1899), however, Norris illustrates the conflict between the outwardly civilized individual and the inner animal much more graphically than does Dunbar in any of his works.

Writers of a younger generation influenced by Garland, Howells, and other realists included Willa Cather, who was nine years old when she moved with her family from Virginia to a farm near Red Cloud, Nebraska. Her early stories about the Nebraska frontier, such as "On the Divide" (1896) and "A Matinée" (1904), emphasize the harshness of farm life in the pioneer era and show sensitive, cultured migrants and immigrants as particularly isolated and vulnerable. That naturalistic strain in Cather's work is softened in *O Pioneers!* (1913), her first novel set on the Midwestern frontier. Her protagonist, Alexandra Bergson, brings up her brothers on the farm, the success of which remains in question for many years. Ultimately, her labor and management, as well as her imagination and spiritual feeling for the Nebraska landscape, bring the family through difficult times. Jim Burden, the narrator of *My Ántonia* (1918), who arrives in Nebraska at about the same age as Cather did, watches other settlers face sometimes overwhelming challenges: an often hostile climate and landscape, failing agricultural practices, disease and death of heads of family, and unscrupulous money lenders. In her prairie novels and later stories like "Neighbour Rosicky," Cather expresses her realism through rich descriptions of the grueling labor of breaking land and growing crops, the constant battle with shortages, the brutal winters, and the bias against outsiders. Yet these conditions are balanced by a transcendental feeling for nature and the stalwart qualities of some of the principal characters. They see beauty and spiritual significance in the undulation of the wheat and grass, the scent of spring, and the caress of breezes on the skin, and they maintain a sound perspective on the virtues and shortcomings of their fellow workers on the land.

Major writers of the Chicago Renaissance's second phase, from about 1910 to 1925, should also be understood in relation to realism. Some of the best writing published in Chicago during this period was about life in small Midwestern towns. A key text in what would later be described as the Midwestern literary Revolt from the Village was Edgar Lee Masters's *Spoon River Anthology* (1915), a book of poetry that startled and even outraged the reading public of the time.

Using the device of epitaphs in a small-town graveyard, he has its residents reveal their secrets of greed, egotism, cruelty, ambition, and sexuality. Exposing the underside of supposed Edenic village life in compact free verse, Masters challenges romantic idealism. He never repeated the success of his first book, which portrays small-town Midwesterners realistically, even naturalistically, but not without compassion.

In many volumes of poetry, beginning with *Chicago Poems* (1916), Carl Sandburg carried on the free-verse tradition of Walt Whitman (1819–1892), supplemented by folk idioms and techniques drawn from the imagist movement. His purview includes the harsh realities that common people face, whether in country life, city life, or industry, such as crime, corruption, exploitation, and brutally hard labor. At the same time, he celebrates the life, courage, and diversity of his subjects with enthusiasm and often with romantic optimism.

Midwestern writers of the early twentieth century increasingly focused on the plight of the individual. Ohioan Sherwood Anderson, for example, depicted the personal isolation experienced by many people in small-town America. Like many other Midwestern writers of the time, Anderson was largely self-educated and a voracious reader. He was particularly interested in the psychology of individuals, especially as related to sexuality. Anderson's characters are victimized by the self, as well as by the forces of geographic and social circumstances. Eschewing plot-driven strategies in his best works, particularly in the short-story form, Anderson became tremendously influential in advancing psychological realism, or impressionism, portraying life as it is felt. Therefore, he is a precursor of this particular direction that realism increasingly followed in the modern period and beyond.

A collection of two dozen stories that some have argued constitute a loosely woven novel, WINESBURG, OHIO (1919) is the most sustained and successful example of Anderson's psychological realism. The book's prefatory tale, "The Book of the Grotesque," explains the overall theme of the stories: "It was the truths that made the people grotesques . . . . The moment one of the people took one of the truths to himself,

called it his truth, and tried to live his life by it, he became a grotesque and the truth he embraced became a falsehood" (1997 Oxford University Press edition, 9).

Anderson shows his characters to be people frustrated by their inhibitions or by past experiences in society. Often they suffer a kind of paralysis because of the limitations of language and communication. For example, in "Queer," Elmer Cowley has a paranoid loathing of the town because he feels that his unsuccessful family is always under scrutiny; he, like many other grotesques in the book, seeks out George Willard in an effort to find someone who will understand him, but he fails and instead leaves town. In "Adventure," Alice Hindman lives her life saving herself for the return of the man who took her virginity, even though she knows that he will never return. Eventually she becomes isolated and desperate for human companionship, but her attempt to break out of her self-imposed bondage fails, and the narrator concludes, in the last line of the story, that "many people must live and die alone, even in Winesburg" (92). It is only in "Sophistication," wherein George Willard and Helen White verge on grotesqueness via the "sadness of sophistication," that Anderson comes the closest to prescribing a cure for the grotesque by showing that George and Helen can achieve "the thing needed" only by nonverbal, intuitive means (200). Anderson's innovations in underscoring the inefficacy of language had a powerful impact on subsequent generations of writers.

Realism and naturalism began to wane as a literary movement around 1920 as many younger writers embraced new aesthetic principles at odds with those of realism. Leading modernists departed from realism in rejecting highly detailed and chronological narrative in favor of fragmentation and stream of consciousness and in privileging subjective perception over purported objectivity. These writers were still concerned with "reality," but their depiction of human experience drew from new ideas in psychology, philosophy, and the arts.

Yet in defining their art against realism and the "genteel tradition" of Victorian moralism, modernist writers worked in creative tension with the accomplishments of their realist predecessors, from whom they borrowed as well as diverged. Continuities between realism and modernism are seen, for example, in the work of Ernest Hemingway, who acknowledged not only Clemens and Anderson as formative influences but also naturalists like Crane and Dreiser. As had Crane and Dreiser, Hemingway began his career in NEWSPAPER JOURNALISM, which encouraged a reportorial, declarative style. Their narratives of extreme experiences in war or in settings both urban and rural also helped inspire the stories that make up IN OUR TIME (1925) and The Sun Also Rises (1926), Hemingway's first major novel.

(HARRY) SINCLAIR LEWIS (1885–1951), on the other hand, wrote novels like MAIN STREET (1920) that combine realist verisimilitude with the irony and hyperbole of social satire. His descriptive cataloging of early twentieth-century material culture— ARCHITECTURE, furniture, clothing, and so forth—has a precedent in Howells and Dreiser, and his critical perspective on small-town life in Masters and Anderson. Willa Cather, who was also influenced by the realists and naturalists, turned in midcareer to what she called the "novel démeublé," or "unfurnished" novel. In her 1922 essay "The Novel Démeublé," Cather speaks of discarding what she saw as the descriptive excess of realism in favor of a highly aestheticized economy of language. She employed this approach, a kind of modernist realism, in A Lost Lady (1923) and other late works.

The influence of realism and naturalism is also apparent in major works from the third and final phase of the Chicago Renaissance. Novels such as STUDS LONIGAN (1935) by JAMES T(HOMAS) FARRELL (1904–1979), NATIVE SON (1940) by RICHARD WRIGHT (1908–1960), and THE ADVENTURES OF AUGIE MARCH (1953) by SAUL (C.) BELLOW (1915–2005) detail physical and social environments of Chicago and portray characters whose fates are largely determined by those environments. The naturalistic impulse also emerges in Midwestern MYSTERY AND DETECTIVE FICTION, including works by LOREN D. ESTLEMAN (b. 1952), SARA PARETSKY (b. 1947), and Scott Turow (b. 1949), who narrate from the skeptical and tragic perspective associated with the detective genre. Works of what might be termed postmodernist realism include . . . Y

NO SE LO TRAGÓ LA TIERRA / . . . AND THE EARTH DID NOT DEVOUR HIM (1971) by Tomás Rivera (1935–1984), A Thousand Acres (1991) by JANE (GRAVES) SMILEY (b. 1949), In the Lake of the Woods (1995) by (WILLIAM) TIM(OTHY) O'BRIEN (b. 1946), The Corrections (2001) by Jonathan Franzen (b. 1959), and Middlesex (2002) by Jeffrey Eugenides (b. 1960). These Midwestern works play with time and narrative point of view in innovative ways while maintaining the realist concern for social commentary and historical perspective.

Finally, realism has given rise to magic realism, developed by mid-twentieth-century European and, especially, Latin American writers as a combination of realism and fantasy. Midwestern works of magic realism include the novels Shoeless Joe (1982) by W(ILLIAM) P(ATRICK) KINSELLA (b. 1935), which was adapted into the popular 1989 film Field of Dreams by director Phil Alden Robinson; SONG OF SOLOMON (1977) and Beloved (1987) by TONI MORRISON (CHLOE ANTHONY WOFFORD) (b. 1931); and Peace like a River (2001) by Leif Enger (b. 1961), as well as stories by Omar S(igfrido) Castañeda (1954–1997) such as "Shell and Bone" in Remembering to Say "Mouth" or "Face" (1993) and the title story in The River Swimmer (novellas; 2013) by Jim Harrison (1937–2016). In these works fantastic elements like ghosts or miracles are accepted by characters as part of the world they inhabit. Realist verisimilitude and social commentary remain but are extended by means consistent with mythology, folklore, and surrealism.

Midwestern realism and naturalism, then, can be defined in two ways. First, it was a literary movement with roots in the pre–Civil War frontier era that achieved its fullest expression between the Civil War and World War I. Second, it is a current running through works by later writers. Understanding and appreciation of modern and contemporary Midwestern literature are strengthened by study of the region's realist classics.

SELECTED WORKS: A New Home—Who'll Follow? (1839) by Caroline Kirkland is an early work of Midwestern realism. Major works of Midwestern prairie realism include The Hoosier School-Master (1871) by Edward Eggleston, The Story of a Country Town (1883) by Edgar Watson Howe, and Zury: The Mean-

est Man in Spring County (1887) by Joseph Kirkland. Henry Blake Fuller's *The Cliff-Dwellers* (1893) and Robert Herrick's *The Web of Life* (1900) are realist Chicago novels significant in the development of urban literature in the United States. Hamlin Garland moves into naturalism in *Main-Travelled Roads* (1891), as does Paul Laurence Dunbar in *The Uncalled* (1898), Frank Norris in *McTeague* (1899), and Theodore Dreiser in *Sister Carrie* (1900). Upton Sinclair's *The Jungle* (1906) and Carl Sandburg's *Chicago Poems* (1916) are strong works of social-critical realism. William Dean Howells portrays Ohio realistically in *The Leatherwood God* (1916). *Winesburg, Ohio* (1919) by Sherwood Anderson is a work of psychological realism, or impressionism. Works published in the century after the period of realism and naturalism that fulfill many of the movement's stylistic and philosophical directives include *Native Son* (1940) by Richard Wright, *The Adventures of Augie March* (1953) by Saul Bellow, *A Thousand Acres* (1991) by Jane Smiley, and *Middlesex* (2002) by Jeffrey Eugenides.

FURTHER READING: Important studies of American realism that deal with Midwestern writers include Warner Berthoff's *The Ferment of Realism: American Literature, 1884–1919* (1981) and Amy Kaplan's *The Social Construction of American Realism* (1992). *American Realism* (2000), edited by Christopher Smith, features essays by noted scholars on subjects relevant to Midwestern studies, including regionalism, the small town, and urban life. Phillip J. Barrish also takes a thematic approach in *The Cambridge Introduction to American Literary Realism* (2011), which features chapters on Howells, Clemens, and Dreiser. In *The Midwestern Ascendancy in American Writing* (1992) Ronald Weber surveys the development of realism in the Midwest and discusses the artistic merits and cultural contexts of books discussed in this entry.

Ronald M. Grosh acknowledges both the literary faults and the accomplishments of Eggleston and other writers in "Provincialism and Cosmopolitanism: A Re-assessment of Early Midwestern Realism," *Midwestern Miscellany* 21 (1993): 9–18. Grosh has also contributed "Early American Literary Realism I: The National Scene," *MidAmerica* 15 (1988): 132–44; "Early American Literary Realism

II: The Midwestern Matrix," *MidAmerica* 16 (1989): 122–30; and "Early American Literary Realism III: Patterns of Anomaly," *MidAmerica* 17 (1990): 118–24.

Donald Pizer has published many books and essays on the movement and on writers like Garland, Dreiser, and Norris. His *Realism and Naturalism in Nineteenth-Century American Literature* (1966; revised edition, 1984) is a standard text. Also useful are Pizer's *The Theory and Practice of American Literary Naturalism: Selected Essays and Reviews* (1993); *Twentieth-Century American Literary Naturalism: An Interpretation* (1982), which includes chapters on *Studs Lonigan* and *The Adventures of Augie March*; and *American Naturalism and the Jews: Garland, Norris, Dreiser, Wharton, and Cather* (2008), an examination of literary anti-Semitism.

A comprehensive treatment of the rise of prairie literature can be found in Dorothy Anne Dondore's *The Prairie and the Making of Middle America: Four Centuries of Description* (1926). In *The Great Prairie Fact and Literary Imagination* (1989) Robert Thacker links early Midwestern prairie realism to portrayals of life on the western Great Plains.

The central role of William Dean Howells in the development of realism and naturalism makes scholarship on his life and work helpful to a broader understanding of the movement. Edwin Cady's two-volume study, consisting of *The Road to Realism: The Early Years, 1837–1885, of William Dean Howells* (1956) and *The Realist at War: The Mature Years, 1885–1920, of William Dean Howells* (1958), is considered definitive. Susan Goodman and Carl Dawson's *William Dean Howells: A Writer's Life* (2005) delineates Howell's interactions with other writers of his time. Also insightful is Hamlin Garland's *Roadside Meetings* (1930), based on diary accounts of encounters with leading literary figures.

STEPHEN C. HOLDER   CENTRAL MICHIGAN UNIVERSITY

REEDY'S MIRROR

OVERVIEW: For almost thirty years *Reedy's Mirror* was a pivotal force in the development of Midwestern writers and recognition of and advocacy for avant-garde literary movements. Originally called the *Sunday Mirror* in 1891, shortened to the *Mirror* in 1895, it was renamed *Reedy's Paper* in 1896 when WILLIAM MARION REEDY (1862–1920) became the editor; it did not officially become *Reedy's Mirror* until 1913. Initially the periodical presented both regional and national authors, such as Kate Chopin (1850–1904), Robert Frost (1874–1963), AMBROSE (GWINETT) BIERCE (1842–ca. 1914), SARA TEASDALE (1884–1933), (NICHOLAS) VACHEL LINDSAY (1879–1931), (HERMAN) THEODORE DREISER (1871–1945), and EDGAR LEE MASTERS (1868–1950). Although the magazine struggled after Reedy died suddenly in 1920, *Reedy's Mirror* played a crucial role in the development and recognition of Midwestern literature, its traditions, and its themes.

HISTORY AND SIGNIFICANCE: Begun in February 1891 as the *Sunday Mirror* in ST. LOUIS, MISSOURI, the magazine that later became renowned as a prestigious literary journal originally printed gossip, sports, and other amusements under the subtitle: *A Journal Devoted to Literature, Art, Society, the Drama.* But within two years the *Sunday Mirror* was out of funds and was rescued from bankruptcy by James Campbell, shortly after Reedy, a co-founder, was named editor. However, it was not long before fiscal problems reemerged despite Campbell's infusion of funds; he walked away from the *Mirror,* exasperated, in early 1894, ceding control to Reedy.

Reedy was the driving force behind the *Sunday Mirror*'s progression from a gossip-column and sports newspaper to a leading journal of literature. Changing its subtitle to *A Journal of Comment on Anything of Human Interest,* Reedy subtly began to shift the content to political opinion, emerging and groundbreaking literary works, and other topics he thought would be of interest to Americans. By dropping the price from a dime to a nickel shortly after the paper went bankrupt, Reedy was able to gain new subscriptions quickly. With a circulation that peaked at nearly 33,000 in 1898, the *Mirror* rivaled other well-established literary journals of the time.

Convinced that Europe was offering better literature, Reedy recognized European literary leaders, including Oscar Wilde (1854–1900) and Ezra Pound (1885–1972), and struggled hard to give voice to American works that could compete. He sought to print works that, according to Max Putzel's *The Man in the Mirror: William Marion Reedy and His Magazine* (1963), rivaled "the very nature of poetry" and "called in question the essentials of the art" (162). Ezra Pound and Lindsay were among the writers Reedy felt capable of achieving this goal. Among Reedy's contributions were advancing American literary realism in prose and poetry and recognizing new literary trends and talented writers, including several from the Midwest.

Reedy sought to promote poets and writers who were overlooked or, in his opinion, underestimated. Early in his editorship, he published the poems of Emily Dickinson (1830–1886) and ALICE FRENCH (1850–1934). During these years Reedy was not just looking for poetry; he was looking for a native poetic tradition. As Reedy drew nearer to this goal, he again changed the subtitle of the paper, this time to *A Weekly Journal Reflecting the Interests of Thinking People.* Reedy worked hard to establish the *Mirror* as a periodical of regional importance and to build a reputation for advocacy of Midwestern writers.

One of the first Midwesterners Reedy fostered was Midwestern reporter and fiction writer Theodore Dreiser after Doubleday, Page and Company attempted to suppress publication of his *SISTER CARRIE* (1900) because of Doubleday's assertion of the volume's immorality. In *The Man in the Mirror: William Marion Reedy and His Magazine* Max Putzel reports that in December 1900 Reedy read a copy of the novel provided by Dreiser himself and wrote a series of positive reviews and comments, beginning on January 3, 1901, intent on presenting the novel as a work of advanced realism and building reader demand for it (124–27). The continuing professional and personal assistance Reedy provided over the next several years were important to Dreiser. This support may well have given Dreiser the confidence to buy back the printing plates for *Sister Carrie,* invest $1,000, and have the volume made available by B. W. Dodge and Company in 1907. Even after *Sister Carrie* had gained international fame, Reedy continued to give space to Dreiser's short stories. Dreiser, in return, dubbed Reedy "The Literary Boss of the Middle West."

Reedy's impact on other talented Midwestern writers was also positive. He hired

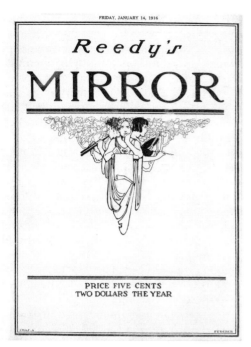

Reedy's Mirror, January 14, 1916.
Courtesy of the State Historical Society of Missouri

ZOË AKINS (1886–1958) in 1905 to review plays; she went on to become a New York playwright who won the Pulitzer Prize for Drama in 1935. Sara Teasdale's early poetry appeared in the *Mirror* around this time as well. FANNIE HURST (1885–1968), then a Washington University student, also began publishing in the *Mirror* in the late 1910s. ORRICK JOHNS (1887–1946), who succeeded Akins as play reviewer, saw many of his radical articles appear in the *Mirror* before moving to New York.

In 1914 and 1915 Reedy serially printed some of Edgar Lee Masters's Spoon River poems in the *Mirror* under the pseudonym Webster Ford. Ironically, Masters had sent the initial group of poems not as serious submissions but as a mocking rebuke of Reedy's repeated rejections of his many earlier traditional poetic submissions. Reedy, in correspondence, had accompanied his rejections with advocacy for the brevity, directness, and simplicity that marked the newly translated *Greek Anthology*. Upon seeing his poems in the *Mirror,* Masters was first appalled and then delighted to find that his Spoon River poems had made him

a literary sensation. His SPOON RIVER ANTHOLOGY (1915), which grew out of his submissions in *Reedy's Mirror,* became a national best seller and has never been out of print. Under the influence of Reedy's tutoring, Masters comments negatively on traditional poetics in his *Spoon River Anthology* poem "Petit, the Poet."

Reedy's advocacy for and his printing of Masters's poetry, which was then considered radical for its realistic language and depiction of previously taboo aspects of Midwestern village life, brought more renown to the *Mirror* and sparked a national debate over the appropriate subject matter and language for poetry. THE DIAL, a conservative CHICAGO literary journal, attacked *Spoon River Anthology;* POETRY: A MAGAZINE OF VERSE, another Chicago magazine advocating new approaches to poetry, staunchly defended the volume and further advanced the CHICAGO RENAISSANCE, its avant-garde literary tastes, and Midwestern writers like Masters and Lindsay. The Reedy-inspired *Spoon River Anthology* later became a leading exemplar, along with WINESBURG, OHIO (1919) by SHERWOOD ANDERSON (1876–1941) and MAIN STREET (1920) by (HARRY) SINCLAIR LEWIS (1885–1951), of Midwestern literary texts identified by CARL (CLINTON) VAN DOREN (1885–1950) in his article "The Revolt from the Village, 1920," *The Nation* 113 (October 12, 1921): 407–12, sparking decades of critical debate over the purported Midwestern REVOLT FROM THE VILLAGE.

Reedy's relationships with writers and his innovative eye for groundbreaking poetry firmly established the *Mirror* as a Midwestern institution with a national reach. Babette Deutsch (1895–1982) sought publication in the *Mirror* in the mid-1910s; Edna St. Vincent Millay (1892–1950), whose poems had appeared in the *Mirror* a few years earlier, presented her play *Aria da Capo* on the pages of the magazine in the late 1910s. Carl Sandburg thanked Reedy in the preface to his CHICAGO POEMS (1916) after Reedy printed some of them, and he reported that he never missed an issue of the *Mirror.*

In 1920 Reedy died suddenly of a heart attack, and the magazine printed a long eulogy on August 5, 1920. It was briefly taken over by editor J. J. Dickinson but lasted only two months under its new supervision. One of the original founders, Jack Sullivan, tried to revive *Reedy's Mirror* in 1929, but it appeared only sporadically and ceased publication completely in 1947.

Despite its untimely demise, *Reedy's Mirror* was pivotal both in helping develop a Midwestern voice and in transforming the shape of American prose and poetry. The magazine encouraged Midwestern writers and gave them a venue from which to become nationally known and respected.

FURTHER READING: The fourth volume of Frank Luther Mott's *A History of American Magazines* (1957) is a useful source on the magazine and its eccentric editor. Max Putzel's *The Man in the Mirror* (1963) also contains pertinent information about the literary magazine and the man whose name it ultimately bore. *Reflections of Reedy: A Biography of William Marion Reedy of "Reedy's Mirror"* by Ethel M. King was published in 2011.

Twenty-seven volumes of *Reedy's Mirror* are held at the St. Louis Public Library, as are incomplete indexes of the periodical. The Mercantile Library at the University of Missouri–St. Louis and the University of Pennsylvania also hold incomplete indexes of *Reedy's Mirror*. The Missouri History Museum has many early copies of the *Sunday Mirror;* the University of Wisconsin library holds issues of *Reedy's Mirror* between 1913 and 1920. In 2009 the Newberry Library in Chicago opened a collection of Reedy's papers from 1906 to 1919.

ASHLEY HOPKINS
THE UNIVERSITY OF TENNESSEE AT CHATTANOOGA

THEATRE, REGIONAL

OVERVIEW: The Midwest is historically rich in theatre. Although the focus is appropriately on the DRAMA being performed, attention must also be given to the important role of regional theatre companies performing these works and the performance spaces they create and maintain. Some theatrical productions originating in the Midwest do move to Broadway, but the mission of Midwestern regional theatres is and has been to enhance their communities, eschewing notions that they exist as tributaries to New York stages.

Nineteenth-century theatre in the Midwest included regional stock companies, showboats, and touring tent theatres. In the early twentieth century the Midwest had some of the most significant little theatres influencing the development of university drama programs and, in turn, community theatres. During the 1930s the Midwest Play Bureau was an important part of the Federal Theatre Project, and state-sponsored playwriting contests helped keep community theatres flourishing as Broadway theatres struggled. The 1950s through the 1960s, concurrent with the development of off- and off-off-Broadway theatres, saw the formation of regional not-for-profit professional theatres. These groups formed to keep theatre alive outside New York and were financially supported by federal and state grants, as well as season subscriptions and box-office sales. Some regional theatres remain in operation today and, in addition to professional groups founded since the 1970s, represent important American theatre companies. Writing contests, too, have continued. Currently, the Midwest features the Hopwood Writing Contest at the University of Michigan and the Algonquin Project in Indianapolis.

HISTORY AND SIGNIFICANCE: In the nineteenth century many large Midwestern cities had resident stock companies managed by someone local who leased the building and hired actors; that era also saw touring troupes that moved by boats to theatres situated by rivers. One example was that of the Chapman family. In 1831 English actor William Chapman (1764–1839) and his family converted a flatboat and gave performances while floating down the Ohio River to the Mississippi from Pittsburgh to New Orleans, junking the flatboat once they arrived. Five years later, according to Philip Graham in *Showboats: The History of an American Institution* (1951), the Chapman family traded in their floating theatre for a small steamboat that allowed them to return upriver (18). Steamboat theatres, or floating palaces, became a practical and popular method of touring in the Midwest between 1875 and 1900. Minstrel shows, circuses, and productions of Shakespeare were among the dramatic fare performed from showboats.

Overland touring to rural areas, spanning the period from the late 1800s through the early 1900s, was called repertoire theatre, and groups performed in tent theatres.

Most popular were performances of Toby shows, skits featuring Toby, a freckled farm boy from the Midwest, and his girlfriend, Susie, who outsmarted the villainous city slicker. An important collection from the tent repertoire was founded in 1973 by ex-troupers Neil and Caroline Schaffner; the Theatre Museum of Repertoire Americana in Mt. Pleasant, IOWA, housing those artifacts and a library, is open to the public.

In the early twentieth century, influenced by independent theatres in Europe such as André Antoine's (1858–1943) Théâtre Libre and the Irish folk plays of Dublin's Abbey Theatre, American noncommercial theatres were organized to produce new plays. Before World War I the term "little theatre" typically referred to art theatres run by amateurs for small audiences, often in converted spaces seating fewer than a hundred spectators and staging an eclectic mix of new American and European plays. The little theatres introduced American audiences to new European stagecraft in productions that experimented with techniques of symbolism and expressionism. After World War I and through the 1920s, the term referred to the activities of noncommercial private, community, and university theatres. A major goal of little theatre producers was to create an enlightened, discriminating audience for quality drama; they cited Walt Whitman (1819–1892) in his "Ventures, on an Old Theme" in *Complete Prose Works. Walt Whitman* (1892) saying: "To have great poets there must be great audiences, too." The movement succeeded in developing an audience for community theatre that continued to grow through the 1930s and laid the groundwork for the not-for-profit professional companies that organized in the 1950s and 1960s.

A pioneer in the little theatre movement was Maurice Browne (1881–1955), who founded the Chicago Little Theatre with his wife, Ellen Van Volkenburg (1882–1978); their company staged performances for five seasons from 1912 to 1917. Like many little theatre practitioners, Browne formed the Chicago Little Theatre to introduce audiences to a serious, provocative repertoire, and he was more interested in a play's literary merits than in its broad appeal. Browne staged plays by European writers such as W. B. Yeats (1865–1939), Henrik Ibsen (1828–1906), George Bernard Shaw (1856–1950), August Strindberg (1849–1912), and Arthur Schnitzler (1862–1931), as well as works by CHICAGO playwrights including ALICE (ERYA) GERSTENBERG (1885–1972), GEORGE ADE (1866–1944), and BEN HECHT (1894–1964), in what was originally a storage space on the fourth floor of the Fine Arts Building. The theatre appealed to what Sheldon Cheney describes in *The Art Theater* (1917) as an ever-small but "highly cultivated audience" (130). Influenced by English stage designer Edward Gordon Craig (1872–1966), Browne and his directors created the Little Theatre Puppets for young audiences.

Although his Chicago theatre was short lived, Browne was not alone in his desire to elevate the cultural taste of American theatre audiences. In 1910 the Drama League of America was founded in Evanston, ILLINOIS, to create an audience for high-quality theatre. Its first president, Marjorie A. Starr Best, wrote in a 1925 Drama League pamphlet that the league aimed at restoring "the drama to its honorable place as the most intimate, most comprehensive, and most democratic medium for the self-expression of the people" (4). The Drama League grew out of the interest of local women's club members in reading quality plays and attending league-sanctioned productions then on tour, and women's clubs supported the productions with tickets bought in bulk. As touring road productions originating in New York waned, the league concentrated on its education campaign. It worked with publishers such as Longmans, Green and Company to print affordable editions of plays and put together study guides and pamphlets on methods of theatre production. These were then distributed across the country and reached small towns and rural areas. The publishing campaign of the Drama League led remote communities to organize little-theatre groups to perform the plays in distribution. The league published *Drama: A Quarterly Review of Dramatic Literature* and *Drama League Monthly* from 1912 to 1919. The two periodicals merged in 1919, forming *Drama Magazine,* which featured a "Little Theatre Monthly" section that kept groups connected. The league also sponsored, with publisher Longmans, Green and Company, the Little Theatre Tournament, a national playwriting contest held annually in New York from 1923 to 1930. The Drama League ceased operation in 1931.

The Lake Forest Players, founded by poet and playwright Mary Reynolds Aldis (1872–1949), was contemporary with the Chicago Little Theatre and operated from 1911 to 1915. It was an amateur group that performed for invited audiences in the Aldis Playhouse, a small house converted into a theatre next door to Aldis's home in Lake Forest, Illinois. Aldis wrote plays for the group, and other members adapted short stories or translated European one-act plays. In the preface to her book *Plays for Small Stages* (1915) Aldis writes that the Players produced intellectual drama in which the "expressed word, the mental attitude and the interplay of character [were] of more importance than the physical action" (xv). The Lake Forest Players performed at Mrs. Lyman Gale's Toy Theatre in Boston and garnered positive reviews for simple, truthful acting. Aldis also belonged to the Chicago Players' Workshop, founded in 1916 to perform the work of Chicago playwrights; the group included Alice Gerstenberg, Ben Hecht, Oscar Wolff (1876–1934), and Kenneth Sawyer Goodman (1883–1918).

The Hull-House Players, formerly the Hull-House Dramatic Association, was another Midwestern little theatre; it was organized by Laura Dainty Pelham (1849–1924) in 1897 at Jane Addams's Chicago HULL-HOUSE. In Galesburg, Illinois, the Prairie Playhouse was founded by Allen Crafton (1890–1966), later head of the Department of Speech and Drama at the University of Kansas, along with playwrights Abby Marchant and Mark White Reed. The three created a theatre out of an abandoned saloon in Galesburg, where Crafton had attended Knox College. As was the case with many little theatres, the Prairie Playhouse, interrupted by World War I, ran for only two seasons. In 1916 Sam Hume, a student of Craig's, organized the Arts and Crafts Theatre in DETROIT; Hume, with the assistance of Sheldon Cheney and Edith J. R. Isaacs, started *Theatre Arts Magazine,* a journal celebrating new stagecraft.

In 1915 the Cleveland Play House was founded by drama and music critic Raymond O'Neill. Six years later Frederic McConnell (1890–1968), a student of Thomas Wood Stevens at the Carnegie Institute of Technology and an assistant director to Sam Hume at the Arts and Crafts Theatre, was hired as the theatre's first professional executive director. McConnell helped design the Play House's Euclid Avenue Theatre, built in 1949, which, with its thrust stage, was a departure from the conventional nineteenth-century proscenium stage. McConnell set the Play House apart from other noncommercial theatres by hiring a permanent company of paid actors, a decision that ensured quality productions and steady audience attendance. He led the Play House for thirty-seven years and was succeeded by associate K. Elmo Lowe. The Cleveland Play House continues today under the artistic direction of Michael Bloom.

Instrumental in the growth and maturity of little theatre activity was the work of college professors and students who helped foster community theatres. American drama programs, just beginning to form at colleges and universities, were particularly important to the spread of noncommercial theatre because drama program directors usually stayed for an extended period, which allowed the work to develop. A key figure was Thomas H. Dickinson (1877–1961), a University of Wisconsin English professor. Dickinson taught a class in modern European drama and wanted his students to stage the plays. When the administration forbade the use of university facilities, Dickinson founded the Wisconsin Dramatic Society with the help of students, faculty, and community members, including playwright ZONA GALE (1874–1938) of Portage, WISCONSIN. The society operated in Madison from 1911 to 1915.

In its first few years the society staged plays such as *The Intruder* (1890) by Maurice Maeterlinck (1862–1949) and *The Master Builder* (1892) by Ibsen; however, as Dickinson writes in *The Insurgent Theatre* (1917), the group became known as a playwrights' theatre, producing regional drama written by society members (71). Out of their work came two volumes, *Wisconsin Plays: Series One* (1914), which includes Gale's little-theatre classic *The Neighbours,* and *Wisconsin Plays: Second Series* (1918). In the introduction to the first volume, Dickinson wrote that the "majority of the plays in the series belong to the repertory of the Society and have been presented in regular performances in Madison and Milwaukee, and on tour in other places of the Middle West" (i). When Dickinson left Madison in 1915 to join the Department of Drama at Carnegie Tech, the society dissolved, but it had fostered an interest in community theatre that spread across the state. The Milwaukee branch, the Wisconsin Players, founded in 1909 by playwright Laura Sherry (1876–1947), continued into the 1930s. In 1928 the Wisconsin Dramatic Guild formed to lend organizational support to the numerous amateur groups.

In NORTH DAKOTA noncommercial theatre was organized through the work of two college professors, Frederick H. Koch (1877–1944) in Grand Forks and Alfred G. Arvold (1882–1957) in Fargo. Koch, who later organized the Carolina Playmakers at the University of North Carolina, began his career at the University of North Dakota in 1905. After receiving his MA at Harvard, where he studied with George Pierce Baker from 1908 to 1909, he returned to Grand Forks and formed a student theatre group, the Sock and Buskin Society. The society wrote and performed *The Book of a Pageant of the North-West* (1914), for which Koch created the Bankside Theatre, an outdoor amphitheater. Two years later the group, now renamed the Dakota Playmakers, focused on raising the "folk-consciousness" of its audience by staging student-authored plays of prairie life, some of which were anthologized in *The Dakota Playmakers* (1918). Playwright Maxwell Anderson (1888–1959), a member of the Sock and Buskin Society, compared its one-acts to the folk plays of the Irish Players, particularly those by J. M. Synge (1871–1909).

Alfred Arvold, head of the Department of Public Discussion and Social Service at the North Dakota Agricultural College, now North Dakota State University, founded his community theatre in 1914 to help the people of the region. According to Arvold's *The Little Country Theater* (1923), the people of the region lived in geographic isolation and cultural starvation. The theatre, originally a chapel on the second floor of the administration building at the college, resembled a country town hall on which communities

modeled their own little theatres. The facilities included a lending library of scripts and production manuals. Arvold's list of nonroyalty one-act plays circulated through the Little Country Theater Program Service for rural communities' neighborhood programs. His theatrical outreach began with student tours of classic plays and Broadway hits to rural areas; later, and most important, Arvold assisted rural people in creating pageants and showed them how to produce plays on their own in home talent tournaments so that they might, in his words, "become better satisfied with the community in which they live[d]" (56).

In 1925 the Kenneth Sawyer Goodman Memorial Theatre and School was founded at the Art Institute of Chicago and was led by Thomas Wood Stevens. The Goodman School offered professional training of actors, highlighted by experience in the Goodman's repertory company. In 1957 Austrian John Reich headed the Goodman School, whose alumni include noted actors such as Geraldine Page. In 1969 he transformed the Goodman Theatre into a fully professional resident company, hiring equity actors, and led the theatre until his retirement in 1972. Acting instruction was taken over by eminent teacher Charles McGaw, author of *Acting Is Believing* (1955). In 1978 the Goodman School was acquired by DePaul University and is known today as the Theatre School at DePaul University. An essential part of student training at DePaul is acting in children's theatre, a tradition inherited from the Goodman. Since its inception the Goodman Theatre for Children has led the nation in creating drama for children. Most renowned was children's theatre director and playwright Charlotte Chorpenning (1873–1955), who headed the theatre for twenty-four years. The Goodman Theatre, now under the artistic direction of Robert Falls, remains one of Chicago's most respected professional theatres.

Another Midwestern drama program was initiated by E(dward) C(harles) Mabie (1892–1956) at the University of Iowa. Mabie had been hired to head the Department of Public Speaking in 1920, but he was more interested in theatre and was appointed head of the Department of Speech and Dramatic Arts in 1925. That department became one of the leading programs in the country at both undergraduate and graduate levels. Mabie created an academically rigorous program of study that included playwriting. Mabie encouraged students to write regional drama that would be relevant to the community. During his university tenure, which lasted until his death, Mabie found funding for the University of Iowa Theatre, which was completed in 1936.

As Kenneth Macgowan (1888–1963) points out in his history of the little-theatre movement, *Footlights across America: Towards a National Theatre* (1929), increased costs for train travel and the popularity of the movies nearly brought to an end the touring Broadway road shows that had formerly visited large Midwestern cities (73). In the 1930s the Depression aggravated an already dire situation for many theatre professionals. In 1935 the Federal Theatre Project, one of five art projects sponsored by the Works Progress Administration, was created to provide jobs for unemployed theatre workers. Directing the project was Iowan Hallie Flanagan (1889–1969), who had taught drama at Grinnell College and had assisted George Pierce Baker at Harvard before heading the Vassar Experimental Theatre. The project attempted to provide, on a national scale, high-quality theatre at low prices to areas that had as yet no access to theatre. Like the producers in the little-theatre movement, Flanagan insisted on high standards for all productions and was more concerned with the artistic and social qualities of theatre than with commercialism. Flanagan wrote in *Arena: The History of the Federal Theatre* (1940) that "any theatre sponsored by the government of the United States should do no plays of a cheap or vulgar nature but only such plays as the government could stand behind in a planned theatre program national in scope, regional in emphasis, and democratic in allowing each local unit freedom under general principles" (45). Although the Federal Theatre Project was active for only three and a half years, it reached a wide audience, and interest in theatre spread and continued with amateurs involved in community theatres.

The Federal Theatre Project was divided into five regions. Organizational centers were located in major cities in the Midwest, such as CINCINNATI, CLEVELAND, Detroit, Gary, and Peoria. At the centers, theatre companies were formed, actors were retrained, and tours to rural areas were organized. Flanagan brought together prominent Midwestern theatre professionals as part of the first planning meeting for regional and state directors. Mabie, of the University of Iowa, was chosen to lead the Midwest region; Stevens, of the Goodman School, headed the Chicago unit; and McConnell, director of the Cleveland Play House, represented OHIO.

The Midwest Play Bureau, part of the National Play Bureau, contributed to the theatrical vitality of the region. Playwright SUSAN KEATING GLASPELL (1876–1948) headed it for two years. She was succeeded by Don Farran (1902–1986), also a playwright, who had worked on the Iowa guidebook for the FEDERAL WRITERS' PROJECT. The Play Bureau oversaw the work of regional playwrights such as Arnold Sundgaard (1910–2006), author of the Living Newspaper's play *Spirochete* (1938), and George Murray and David Peltz, who collaborated on a political satire about Social Security, *Pie in the Sky*. Other Midwest plays of note were the religious play *Within These Walls* (1936) by Marcus L. Bach and *Big White Fog* (1938) by THEODORE "TED" WARD (1902–1983). *Big White Fog* was produced by the Chicago unit on Chicago's South Side and ran for ten weeks. From its headquarters in the Merchandise Mart in downtown Chicago, the Play Bureau also sent out lists of approved plays intended to ensure high-quality drama for community theatre productions.

During the 1930s community theatres remained active in the Midwest. To meet the needs of groups wanting plays, playwriting contests and writing workshops were conducted. The search for new playwrights and facilitating their development had been the concern of university drama programs for years, in large part because of the demand from community theatres, which then competed in drama tournaments. Wisconsin community theatre activity in the 1920s through the 1930s was supervised by Ethel Theodora Rockwell (1884–1971), chief of the Bureau of Dramatic Activities at the University of Wisconsin's Extension Division. Rockwell had been a student of Thomas

Dickinson at the University of Wisconsin and an original member of the Wisconsin Dramatic Society. Rockwell continued Dickinson's investment in shaping both the social and the artistic awareness of audiences primarily by developing writers. To encourage amateur playwrights, Rockwell coordinated annual tournaments sponsored by the Wisconsin Dramatic Guild. In 1931 she edited *Wisconsin Rural Plays,* containing five prize-winning plays entered in contests she had juried, and, in 1935, a second volume, *Wisconsin Community Plays.*

Another important Midwest playwriting contest that began in 1931 is the Hopwood Program at the University of Michigan. Avery Hopwood (1882–1928), a playwright, alumnus, and member of the class of 1905, left money in his will for prizes for students enrolled in University of Michigan writing courses. The Hopwood Contest continues to offer prizes in five genres, one of which is drama/screenplay. One well-known recipient is director, producer, and screenwriter Lawrence Kasdan (b. 1949), who won the award four times. Kasdan has since started a scholarship in his name and donated a collection of screenplays to the Hopwood Room, a library and meeting room for contestants.

The Indiana Theatre Association in Indianapolis, formed in 1974 to develop theatre in the state, merged with the Algonquin Project in 2002, a group that fosters growth among theatre artists in the community, with a special emphasis on playwrights. The merged Indiana Theatre Association / Algonquin Project sponsors the Algonquin Project Play, readings of work by local, regional, and national playwrights. A Writers' Salon also facilitates a works-in-progress seminar for members.

In the 1950s and 1960s Midwestern professional companies began to form in order to meet the needs of communities desiring high-quality theatre, which amateur groups could not consistently supply. As early as 1921 Frederic McConnell, director of the Cleveland Play House, identified the ingredients necessary to maintain a regional not-for-profit theatre supported by its community: an excellent theatre facility, a professional staff, and a repertoire that attracts and holds excellent actors. In 1961 the

Ford Foundation formed the Theatre Communications Group (TCG) to assist regional theatres then forming, provide a central casting office, hold annual auditions for university students, and offer limited financial assistance, as Joseph Wesley Zeigler writes in 1973 in *Regional Theatre* (235). By 1967 only thirteen theatres, considered the most promising, had received Ford Foundation TCG support. In addition to the previously mentioned Goodman Theatre, which became a professional company in 1969, the other Midwestern theatre companies that received TCG funds were the Fred Miller Theatre (1954), later renamed the Milwaukee Repertory Theater; the Cincinnati Playhouse in the Park (1960); and Minneapolis's Tyrone Guthrie Theater (1963). In addition to these, however, other significant Midwestern theatres were founded in the 1960s: the Detroit Repertory Theatre (1957), the Firehouse Theatre of Minneapolis (1963–1969), the Boars-Head Theater in Lansing, MICHIGAN (1966), and the Magic Theatre Foundation of Omaha (1968).

The Fred Miller Theatre, founded by a group of Milwaukee people who wanted to produce current Broadway plays with well-known actors, was named after the head of the Miller Brewing Company. In 1963 the board changed the theatre's name to the Milwaukee Repertory, consonant with the theatre's refigured mission, staging classic plays and new works with a resident acting company. The Milwaukee Repertory currently resides in the Patty and Jay Baker Theatre Complex, which houses three theatres. A mainstay of the community for fifty years, the Milwaukee Repertory is one of the Midwest's most respected theatres.

The site of the original Cincinnati Playhouse in the Park, founded in 1960, was a pavilion in Eden Park converted into a theatre with a thrust stage. Its seasons were restricted to spring and summer. Now the Playhouse, committed to bringing classic plays and new works to the region, includes two theatres and runs from September to June. Since 1986 the Playhouse has toured productions to area schools.

Perhaps the most noteworthy theatre to be founded in the United States in the 1960s was the Guthrie Theater. As Guthrie

Guthrie Theater, Minneapolis. Photo by Sally Wagner.
Reprinted courtesy of the Guthrie Theater

explains in *A New Theatre* (1964), he sought to start an institution that would be "more permanent and more serious in aim than a commercial theatre can ever be" (9). Guthrie and his co-founders, Peter Zeisler and Oliver Rea, chose MINNEAPOLIS after seeking applications from interested cities. According to Julius Novick in *Beyond Broadway: The Quest for Permanent Theatres* (1968), Minneapolis citizens raised more than $2 million to build a theatre with a seating capacity equal to that of a large Broadway house (106). After four and a half years of planning, the theatre opened with a production of *Hamlet* directed by Guthrie, thus beginning the staging of a classical repertoire featuring some of America's finest actors, including Hume Cronyn, Jessica Tandy, and Zoe Caldwell. The Guthrie Theater was particularly significant because it set a standard of excellence and attained critical respect that brought legitimacy to the work of other resident professional theatres. Theatre professionals in other companies saw the potential for national recognition, and actors realized that acting at a resident theatre provided a place away from

the commercial pressure of Broadway where they could grow and be challenged, not a stepping-stone to Broadway. The Guthrie Theater remains active today under the artistic direction of Joe Dowling. In 2006 the Guthrie moved to a new building designed by French architect Jean Nouvel.

Two months after the Guthrie was founded, the Firehouse Theatre opened. With playwright Sydney Shubert Walter at the helm, the Firehouse staged both avant-garde classics and new plays. The productions featured experiments in nonnaturalistic acting and the use of film, projections, and strobe lighting. The Firehouse operated as a collective in which members shared all duties and received nominal pay. It introduced audiences from Minneapolis and the upper Midwest to environmental theatre techniques then being explored in the work of Joseph Chaiken (1935–2003) and the Open Theatre, where Walter had worked. In 1969 the Firehouse Theatre moved to San Francisco.

The BoarsHead Theater, founded by John Peakes and Richard Thomsen and committed to nurturing area writers and artists, was the center for theatre in central Michigan. As with other resident theatres, the vitality of the BoarsHead depended on the involvement of new audiences, which the theatre attempted to reach through a relevant repertoire and statewide touring. Declining ticket sales doomed the company, and the theatre closed in early 2010.

Another important Michigan theatre is the Detroit Repertory Theatre, founded by Bruce Millan, a Detroit native who still serves as its artistic director. Millan and his company are dedicated to seeking out an audience reflecting the diversity of southeastern Michigan. From 1957 to 1963 Millan toured shows for children, reaching communities in Michigan, INDIANA, Ohio, and western Pennsylvania.

The Magic Theatre Foundation of Omaha, founded by artistic director Jo Ann Schmidman, is run by a group of women artists. The theatre features new plays, many written collaboratively by resident playwright Megan Terry (b. 1932) and Schmidman, both of whom also perform with the ensemble in their production facility, once a department store. Their book *Right Brain Vacation Photos* (1992) is a compilation of the plays and photographs of their productions staged between 1972 and 1992.

Since 1970 over forty-five Midwestern resident professional theatres have formed, including the Steppenwolf Theatre Company of Chicago (1975), the Mixed Blood Theatre Company of Minneapolis (1976), and the Purple Rose Theatre Company of Chelsea, Michigan (1991). The Steppenwolf Theatre, now with an international reputation gained through actors John Malkovich, Joan Allen, and Gary Sinise, was started by Terry Kinney, Jeff Perry, Sinise, and others. Its first performance space was a Catholic school in Highland Park, Illinois; in 1991 the company, which had grown to thirty members, moved to its state-of-the art facility in Chicago and has since added a studio theatre for new work. Minneapolis's Mixed Blood Theatre Company, founded by Jack Reuler, the current artistic director, was created to showcase a multiracial staff of artists and to encourage attendance through low ticket prices. Mixed Blood tours productions and maintains a training program. The Purple

Rose Theatre Company, founded in 1991 by Jeff Daniels, Bartley Bauer, Doug Beaumont, and T. Newell Kring, has contributed greatly to southeastern Michigan culture in a relatively short time. Now under the artistic direction of Guy Sanville, the theatre seeks out original plays by regional writers and, like other Midwestern companies, is dedicated to bringing theatre to a large audience through affordable ticket prices and an exciting repertoire.

FURTHER READING: Jack Poggi's *Theater in America: The Impact of Economic Forces* (1968) offers an excellent overview of the development of American theatre with emphasis on regionalism. Jere C. Mickel's *Footlights on the Prairie: The Story of the Repertory Tent Players in the Midwest* (1975) includes memoirs of Midwest tent troupers of the nineteenth and early twentieth centuries. Clarence A. Perry's *The Work of the Little Theatres: The Groups They Include, the Plays They Produce, Their Tournaments, and the Handbooks They Use* (1933), a key text on the little-theatre movement, describes Midwest groups, their repertoire, and play contests. Robert Gard, who was a professor at the University of Wisconsin, discusses the relationship between community theatre and university drama programs in *Grassroots Theater: A Search for Regional Arts in America* (1955) and *Community Theatre: Idea and Achievement* (1959), co-authored with Gertrude S. Burley. Naima Prevots describes Frederick Koch's pageant work in North Dakota in *American Pageantry: A Movement for Art and Democracy* (1990). Books on the little-theatre movement include Dorothy Chansky's *Composing Ourselves: The Little Theatre Movement and the American Audience* (2004) and Shannon Jackson's study of Chicago's Hull-House Players, *Lines of Activity: Performance, Historiography, Hull-House Domesticity* (2001). On the growth of federally funded Midwest rural community theatres in the 1930s, see Marjorie Patten's *The Arts Workshop of Rural America: A Study of the Rural Arts Program of the Agricultural Extension Service* (1937). Albert McCleery and Carl Glick report on the growth of community theatre in the 1930s in *Curtains Going Up* (1939), a regionally arranged account. Norris Houghton's *Advance from Broadway: 19,000 Miles of American Theatre* (1941) covers the author's tour of noncommercial theatres in 1940. The Midwestern Play Bureau of the Federal Theatre Project is discussed in Jane Sherron De Hart and Jane De Hart Matthews's *The Federal Theatre, 1935–1939: Plays, Relief, and Politics* (1967). A later study is Paul Sporn's *Against Itself: The Federal Theater and Writers' Projects in the Midwest* (1995). The Federal Theatre Project website offers a tremendous amount of material; included is Don Farran's account of his experience as director of the Midwest Play Bureau. The work of not-for-profit professional regional resident theatres in the context of noncommercial theatres in the 1960s is covered in Robert Gard, Marston Balch, and Pauline B. Temkin's report for the National Theatre Conference, *Theater in America: Appraisal and Challenge* (1968). The most comprehensive reference guide listing not-for-profit professional theatres is the Theatre Communications Group's *Theatre Profiles,* a biennial series that started in 1973 and concluded with the twelfth edition in 1995. The TCG now offers current information about member theatres online.

ANNE BECK   EASTERN NEW MEXICO UNIVERSITY

RELIGION

OVERVIEW: Religion enters into Midwestern literature, like the literature of the United States as a whole, in a multiplicity of ways, ranging from the profoundly spiritual to the political and from the transcendent to the satiric and vitriolic. The fact that people of many faiths have moved through or settled in Midwestern states adds to the richness religion infuses into the customs, values, culture, and writing of the area. In the United States, which cherishes religious freedom, and particularly in the twentieth and twenty-first centuries, orthodox and nonorthodox believers profess a wide variety of faiths. Recognizing this important dimension of American life, Midwestern writers have portrayed religious beliefs and practices ranging from traditional religious thought to New Age explorations of psychic phenomena and esoteric forms of spiritualism.

These religious or spiritual stances are diverse and not exclusive to the Midwest, but religious beliefs and spiritual values tend to be affected by geography and cultural experience. Some Midwesterners believe that their characteristic confidence may derive from the sense that something or someone is looking out for them. Others take a stewardship perspective, maintaining that anything that improves the environment is moral or even divinely ordained. Midwestern religious beliefs seem to be influenced by the region's farms, the nature of life in rural towns in the nation's breadbasket, and the stoicism farms seem to engender, as well as by the very different experiences associated with life in Midwestern cities and work in their industrial settings and retail businesses.

Once religious groups are established in communities, they often divide over theology, politics, or customs. They re-form, merge with others, and may divide again. When different faiths and cultures meet, conflict often results. Prejudice, with its concomitant discrimination, harassment, and persecution, still occurs, and the resulting conflicts are reflected in the literature of the Midwest. Deeply held beliefs may be evident as the central values underlying thought and action and providing the thematic center of novels, poems, drama, and nonfiction. Cultural change can make religion, particularly in its conservative forms, a predictable target for writers. In any case, faith and its manifestations influence character, plot, and content, as well as style, imagery, and symbolism. Because it is impossible to include every work in which some form of religious belief inheres in Midwestern literature, a heavily restricted but representative sampling follows. Together these examples provide a sense of the spiritual tone of much Midwestern literature.

HISTORY AND SIGNIFICANCE: The first known residents of the Midwest were Native Americans. Writings transcribed from tribal oral tradition abound with myths recounting the interaction of gods and other supernatural beings with humans and their environment and explaining the origins of customs and values permeating everyday life. Many representations of Native American religious and cultural thought appear in Midwestern literature. See NATIVE AMERICANS AS DEPICTED IN MIDWESTERN LITERATURE. HENRY ROWE SCHOOLCRAFT (1793–1864), his wife, Jane Johnston Schoolcraft (1800–1842), and her Ojibwa family re-

corded large numbers of oral tales and histories dominated by myth and spiritual
matters and compiled them into the ethnographic *Algic Researches* (1839). This work
contains creation stories of the Algonquin,
the Iroquois, and other tribes, mainly of
the upper Midwest, along with legends that
address people and animals, good and evil,
and the changing of the seasons. The use of
place, including the shores of Lake Superior, and the animals and plants characteristic of the area is notable. In some tales the
figure of Manabozho, a descendant of the
god Manitou, has encounters with musk-
rats and sturgeons. Other featured animals
include the fisher, the red squirrel, and the
wolverine.

Another representative Midwestern literary expression of Native American Indian
religious thought is *BLACK ELK SPEAKS* (1932),
one of the most powerful American Indian
spiritual documents. It records a vision experienced by BLACK ELK (Hehake Sapa, 1863–
1950), a Teton Lakota holy man. Black Elk
dictated his statement through a translator
to JOHN G(NEISENAU) NEIHARDT (1881–1973),
who structured the English-language work
and passed it back through the translator to
Black Elk to ensure its accuracy.

Native American and other writers regularly turn to indigenous spirituality in expressing concern for the land and a sense of
oneness with it. (KAREN) LOUISE ERDRICH (b.
1954) exemplifies twentieth- and twenty-
first-century Native American writing in
exploring issues raised by the confronta-
tions and syntheses among tribal ritual,
mysticism, and Roman Catholicism in *LOVE
MEDICINE* (1984, 1993) and other works. LINDA
HASSELSTROM (b. 1943), a non–Native American rancher, poet, and essayist, reflects
some Native American thought as she communicates her identification with the land,
calling herself pagan and expressing herself poignantly through the concept of the
sacred hoop in *Land Circle* (1991). For more
on religious writing by Native Americans,
see NATIVE AMERICAN LITERATURE.

Accounts by Roman Catholic missionaries provide the earliest Christian reactions to
the frontier, beginning in the early seventeenth century. *The Jesuit Relations and Allied
Documents: Travels and Explorations of the Jesuit Missionaries in New France, 1610–1791; The*
*Original French, Latin, and Italian Texts, with
English Translations and Notes* (1896–1901), edited by Reuben Gold Thwaites (1853–1913) in
seventy-three volumes, provides abundant
material on the proselytizing work of missionaries and their minute observations of
Native Americans. A Protestant evangelist,
James B. Finley (1781–1856), similarly recorded missionary activity and the settling
of the frontier, mainly in Kentucky and
OHIO, in his *Autobiography of James B. Finley;
or, Pioneer Life in the West* (1853).

As easterners began to move west, they
built churches, often in communities centered on religion. Some religious colonies
that sprang up include those by Mormons
on their way west in Kirtland, Ohio, Beaver
Island, MICHIGAN, and Nauvoo, ILLINOIS; separatists from the Lutheran church in Bethel,
MISSOURI; pacifists in Zoar, Ohio, and
Amana, IOWA; Pietists in Bishop Hill, Illinois; and Amish communities throughout
much of the Midwest. Most no longer exist, other than the widely dispersed Mormons, Amish communities, and the Amana
colonies. With a few notable exceptions,
these groups produced no literature. Some
books, written mostly by outsiders, portray
them unfavorably. For example, the Mormons on their trek across the United States
from New York to Utah encountered problems along the way. JAMES OLIVER CURWOOD
(1878–1927), in *The Courage of Captain Plum*
(1908), sensationalizes the death of the
breakaway Mormon leader James Jesse
Strang (1813–1856), self-proclaimed "King,"
on Beaver Island. Long after the fact, Tom
Roulstone (b. 1939) recorded the conflicts at
Nauvoo and the departure of the Mormons
from there in *One against the Wilderness*
(1996). Orson Scott Card (b. 1951) gave a
more favorable depiction of the situation at
Nauvoo in *Saints* (1984). Transcendentalist
Unitarians from New England took up residence briefly in the Ohio and Mississippi
Valleys and founded the *Western Messenger,*
a periodical publishing religious articles
and literature, particularly poems. It originated in CINCINNATI and flourished from
1835 to 1841. See PRINTING AND PUBLISHING.

Groups from denominations experiencing oppression or discrimination in Europe
often immigrated to the United States
and particularly to the Midwest. In some

instances a church would send a few members to find a suitable place to settle, and part or all of a congregation would follow. Many of these enclaves persist, and churchgoing and strong family values still direct the culture into the twenty-first century. Thus, for instance, Dutch Reformed churches sprang up in Michigan, Ohio, Illinois, and Iowa. FREDERICK MANFRED (b. Feike Feikema, 1912–1994), portrays in *Green Earth* (1977) the rather harsh influence of Christian Reformed theology on a farming family in early twentieth-century Iowa. In *Wind without Rain* (1939) HERBERT KRAUSE (1905–1976) conveys an even harsher environment, a failing farm family run by an angry and brutal father in a small Midwestern community dominated by a fire-and-brimstone German Lutheran pastor. With gentle but pointed humor marking a different characterization, GARY EDWARD KEILLOR (b. 1942), writing as Garrison Keillor, delineates the apparent contrasts between the stern Norwegian Lutherans and the somewhat more lighthearted German Catholics who populate the MINNESOTA town he calls Lake Wobegon in *Lake Wobegon Days* (1985) and other books. Still more immigrants, traveling as families or alone to large cities, found like-minded people in the Catholic churches, whose priests served as liaisons with the English-speaking residents, businesses, the police, and other important elements of the community.

The nineteenth century saw the burgeoning of Midwestern belles lettres, and realism was the dominant mode in the latter part of the century. SAMUEL LANGHORNE CLEMENS (1835–1910), writing as Mark Twain, takes Christianity to task in that most Midwestern of his works, *ADVENTURES OF HUCKLEBERRY FINN* (London 1884, New York 1885). His humor is directed at such targets as the Grangerfords and Shepherdsons, who take their guns to church to hear a sermon on brotherly love, only to massacre each other over a disagreement they have long since forgotten. The satire on religion in Twain's novel sounds a more somber and dismissive note when he has his hero reject Christianity because of what Twain sees as its hypocrisy and spiritual bankruptcy in contrast to the spirituality that Twain discerns in nature. WILLIAM DEAN HOWELLS

(1837–1920) provides a similar exposé of religious charlatanism in *The Leatherwood God* (1916). The novel is set in rural Ohio, where an evangelist generates a small sect of gullible believers who revere him as a god. But positive approaches still existed, as in the treatment of Methodism in *The Circuit Rider: A Tale of a Heroic Age* (1874) by EDWARD EGGLESTON (1837–1902).

Two Minnesota writers present a sympathetic, though sometimes gently satirical, view of traditional Roman Catholicism. Born in Illinois, J(AMES) F(ARL) POWERS (1917–1999) portrays the conflicts of priests in small-town Minnesota, human in their failings but able to grow in their spiritual gifts, notably in *Morte d'Urban* (1962). Agatha McGee, in a trilogy by JON (FRANCIS) HASSLER (1933–2008), including *Staggerford* (1977), *The Green Journey* (1985), and *Dear James* (1993), struggles to maintain the conservative aspects of her Catholic faith and practice as she navigates teaching in a small town, the murder of a colleague, and her surprising friendship through correspondence with a like-minded priest in Ireland. A third, PATRICIA HAMPL (b. 1946), who grew up in St. Paul (see MINNEAPOLIS/ST. PAUL), reflects on her movement away from and return to Catholicism throughout her nonfiction and poetry, particularly in *Virgin Time* (1992). The Midwestern novels of WILLA CATHER (1873–1947) display less explicit admiration of the Catholic Church and its priests than the non-Midwestern novels do, but sympathy for the church can be seen, for instance, in *O PIONEERS!* (1913). Born in DETROIT to Lebanese Maronite Catholics, poet Lawrence Joseph (b. 1948) depicts the gritty streets, racial violence, exploitation, and factories of that city in *Shouting at No One* (1983) and *Curriculum Vitae* (1988) and moves to the horror of 9/11 in *Into It* (2005). Despite the significant challenges portrayed in each of Joseph's works, all are marked by a sense of the sacred that offers comfort and hope through faith and love.

On the other hand, the anonymous protagonist in Tomás Rivera's (1935–1984) novel *... Y NO SE LO TRAGÓ LA TIERRA/ ... AND THE EARTH DID NOT DEVOUR HIM* (1971), a Mexican migrant child working at times in Midwestern fields and brought up to be profoundly Catholic, encounters such wrenching experiences that he rejects his faith. JAMES T(HOMAS) FARRELL (1904–1979) implies that in the Irish Catholic neighborhoods of *STUDS LONIGAN* (1935) the Catholic churches—and the Detroit priest Father Charles Edward Coughlin (1891–1979)—not only abetted racism but also bore some responsibility for the spiritual and material poverty of the Irish to whom they ministered. These indictments occur in, but are not exclusive to, *Young Lonigan: A Boyhood in Chicago Streets* (1932), *The Young Manhood of Studs Lonigan* (1934), and *Judgment Day* (1935).

WILLIAM MAXWELL (1908–2000) tracks a history of the relationships among Protestant denominations as he traces his family history to his youth in small-town Illinois in his memoir, *Ancestors* (1971). It remains easier to criticize an institution than to praise it in fiction, and so such writers as (HARRY) SINCLAIR LEWIS (1885–1951), whose charlatan evangelist takes advantage of credulous citizens of small Midwestern towns in *Elmer Gantry* (1927), set about exposing the flaws in ill-directed fundamentalism.

Others, like writers in the rest of the country, mirror increasingly eclectic approaches to faith and yet return in their own particular ways to the churches of their childhood. Iowa poet MARY SWANDER (b. 1950) follows a circuitous route back to Roman Catholicism, via insights from other faiths, in her autobiographical *Out of This World* (1995) and *Desert Pilgrim: En Route to Mysticism and Miracles* (2003).

Struggles with the Christian faith dominate many contemporary novels. Of Christian Reformed background, PETER DE VRIES (1910–1993) records in the semi-autobiographical *The Blood of the Lamb* (1961) a rending struggle between faith and unbelief. Marilynne Robinson (b. 1943) in *Gilead* (2004), *Home* (2008), and *Lila* (2014) explores tensions in families, particularly in regard to manifestations of faith.

The diversity of denominations and the thirst for spiritual wholeness lead others to highly personal theologies. Thus poet and essayist KATHLEEN NORRIS (b. 1947) reports in *Dakota* (1993) that she may preach on a Sunday morning in a Presbyterian church and at the same time be an oblate of a Benedictine abbey isolated in the SOUTH DAKOTA landscape.

Highly fallible and idiosyncratic preachers are found in a number of Midwestern novels, including *Omensetter's Luck* (1966) by WILLIAM H(OWARD) GASS (b. 1924), set in nineteenth-century Ohio, and two novels by Robert Vivian (b. 1967). In *The Mover of Bones* (2006) and *Lamb Bright Saviors* (2010), the first two novels of what Vivian calls his Tall Grass Trilogy, odd, peripatetic, and visionary preachers make their way across NEBRASKA; the third, *Another Burning Kingdom* (2011), presents a more ambiguous situation, with a messianic terrorist, elements of the supernatural, and possible redemption in the end. *The Faith Healer* (1909), a play by WILLIAM VAUGHN MOODY (1869–1910), dramatizes the loss and restoration of the faith and powers of an itinerant minister.

Taking their readers into the realm of magic realism, such novelists as W(ILLIAM) P(ATRICK) KINSELLA (b. 1935) in *Shoeless Joe* (1982), TONI MORRISON (b. CHLOE ARDELIA WOFFORD, 1931) in *Beloved* (1987), and Leif Enger (b. 1961) in *Peace like a River* (2001) add miracles to the mix of doubt, faith, forgiveness, and transcendence.

Father ANDREW M. GREELEY (1928–2013), WILLIAM X(AVIER) KIENZLE (1928–2001), and Ralph McInerny (1929–2010), respectively a priest and sociologist, a former priest, and a philosopher-theologian, make Midwestern religious life, customs, and experiences in CHICAGO, Detroit, and South Bend the grist of mystery novels. Greeley is perhaps best known for his Blackie Ryan series with works like *Happy Are the Meek* (1985). Kienzle's murder novels centering on Father Robert Koesler begin with *The Rosary Murders* (1979). McInerny's collections include the well-known Father Dowling mysteries, starting with *Her Death of Cold* (1977), the Andrew Broom series, and the Notre Dame mysteries.

Midwestern Jewish writers provide a range of perspectives on the role of faith and culture throughout the Midwest. *Fanny Herself* (1917) by EDNA FERBER (1885–1968) illustrates the influence of the Jewish faith on a girl in a small WISCONSIN town, and how the death of her mother and the necessity of forging a living for herself suppress that belief. Its metamorphosis into a compassionate social consciousness possibly accompanied by a return to religion runs through the plot like a refrain. Sam Gold, the principal father in *Fathers: A Novel in the Form of a Memoir* (1967) by HERBERT GOLD (b. 1924), rejects the religion and the Russia of his father and grandfather and relies only on his will to bring about the material success that replaces his faith. He enjoys the pursuit but never achieves contentment. SAUL (C.) BELLOW (1915–2005), ranging further, has a character, in his search for meaning or transcendence, explore the esoteric spirituality of Rudolf Steiner's anthroposophy in *Humboldt's Gift* (1975).

Muslims emigrated from many countries in the twentieth century. At the same time, some African Americans joined the Nation of Islam. Among them was Malcolm Little, who became MALCOLM X (1925–1965). In *THE AUTOBIOGRAPHY OF MALCOLM X* (1965), with the assistance of Alex) Haley (1921–1992), he presents his conversion to, work in, and later repudiation of the movement, followed by his becoming a Muslim in a more orthodox sense. Recently discovered additional chapters may be appended to new editions of the book. *The Girl in the Tangerine Scarf* (2006) by Mohja Kahf (b. 1967) chronicles the experiences of a Syrian girl transplanted to Indianapolis and growing up with conflicts among Muslim custom, ritual, and spirituality, as well as internal and external pressures to assimilate. Fortified by what Westerners might call an epiphany, she accepts her Midwestern neighbors as having the same qualities and values as her family does: "Set in their ways, hardworking, steady, valuing God and family. . . . My folks are the perfect *Hoosiers!*" (438). She draws sympathetic parallels between her family and the Mormon family next door. Still, she continues to cherish her Muslim beliefs and practices. One of the opening poems in *Dying with the Wrong Name: New and Selected Poems, 1968–1979* (1980) by Sam Hamod (b. 1936), "After the Funeral of Assam Hamady," shows his Lebanese-born father and relatives stopping by the side of a South Dakota highway for six o'clock prayer. It expresses the conflicts of the son, who was born in INDIANA, between traditional beliefs and contemporary sensibility.

The protagonist of *Jasmine* (1989) by BHARATI MUKHERJEE (b. 1940) sees the Midwest through the lenses of her Hindu religion and upbringing. Her husband in the poverty of India falls victim to a religious fanatic; her lover, a banker in drought-stricken rural Iowa, is shot by a bankrupt client; but she sees each event as a tiny particle in the life of the world, surviving on the belief that "every second of your existence is a possible assignment from God" (61).

Bich Minh Nguyen (b. 1974), who came to Grand Rapids, Michigan, with her family as a refugee from Vietnam, explores what it means to be an Asian Buddhist among blonde Protestants and Mexican Americans in *Stealing Buddha's Dinner: A Memoir* (2007). As a child, she struggles with the shifting prejudices and traditions of cultures she cannot comprehend and uses Buddhism as her anchor, even though she does not understand that religious orientation well. The metaphor of craving American junk food as opposed to the concept of food as offering to Buddha crystallizes the tension between the desire for acceptance and the need for secure roots.

Beyond traditional religion, searchers find their way to belief by moving from one orthodoxy to another through New Age practices, the cosmologies of SCIENCE FICTION, and environmentalism, among many other approaches. Even a traditionalist like THORNTON WILDER (1897–1975) in *The Eighth Day* (1967) turns to Eastern religious beliefs to explore and fathom his characters' lives, positing karma as a far more illuminating and satisfying conception for explaining human life than the scientific thinking of the modern world affords.

Science-fiction and fantasy author RAY (DOUGLAS) BRADBURY (1920–2012) incorporates Christian and other religious values and elements in his work; *Fahrenheit 451* (1953), for instance, posits a world in which books are destroyed, but at the end, characters concentrate on memorizing the Bible in order to preserve it. PHILIP JOSÉ FARMER (1918–2009) creates alternate cosmologies in such works as the Riverworld trilogy (1971–1980). In *American Gods* (2001), Neil Gaiman (b. 1960) sets a conflict between religious and mythological avatars brought to the U.S. by immigrants against such contemporary powers as technology; parts of the preparations for this war take place in the Midwest. Hints of the multiple themes in this novel appear in other works by Gaiman.

Among environmentally oriented writers, GENE STRATTON-PORTER (1863–1924) asserts in *Music of the Wild* (1910) that the forest is a cathedral, inspiring awe. ALDO LEOPOLD (1887–1948) develops a "land ethic" that, as expressed in *A SAND COUNTY ALMANAC* (1949), sometimes takes on a spiritual dimension. Willa Cather shows the weather on the Midwestern plains as sometimes destructive, but her landscapes often inspire awe, reverence, and a sense of eternal life. THEODORE ROETHKE (1908–1963) feels a powerful unity with growing plants as expressed in such poems as "Cuttings (later)" and "Moss Gathering" in *The Collected Poems of Theodore Roethke* (1966).

Romantic nature mysticism is modified by Zen Buddhism in the work of DAN GERBER (b. 1940), JIM (JAMES THOMAS) HARRISON (1937–2016), and LUCIEN STRYK (1924–2013), three Midwesterners whose poetry and prose reflect Zen principles and practice. Books of Zen-inspired poetry include Gerber's *The Chinese Poems* (1978) and Harrison's *After Ikkyū* (1996). Harrison speaks at length about Zen in *Just before Dark: Collected Nonfiction* (1991) and *The Etiquette of Freedom: Gary Snyder, Jim Harrison, and the "Practice of the Wild"* (2010), edited by Paul Ebenkamp. Susan Porterfield provides a selection of Stryk's writings, along with commentaries on his work, in *Zen, Poetry, the Art of Lucien Stryk* (1993). A talented translator, Stryk also published many anthologies, such as *The Penguin Book of Zen Poetry* (1987), with Takashi Ikemoto, and books of commentary like *Encounter with Zen: Writings on Poetry and Zen* (1981).

Mingling of orthodoxies, struggles between doubt and faith, and finding spiritual fulfillment appear in a multitude of writings, fiction, nonfiction, poetry, and drama. In this respect, the Midwestern religious experience mirrors that of the rest of the country, with perhaps less self-consciousness and possibly greater steadfastness in the farms, cities, and landscapes of the region.

SELECTED WORKS: Readers who seek a sense of religion and its diverse expressions in Native American Midwestern literature might well begin with William Rowe Schoolcraft's *Algic Researches* (1839) and *Black Elk Speaks* (1932), transcribed by John G. Neihardt. For histories of the establishment of Christianity, one could consult, for example, *The Jesuit Relations and Allied Documents* (1896–1901), edited by Reuben Gold Thwaites; documents such as *Autobiography of James B. Finley* (1853); or William Maxwell's *Ancestors* (1971).

Prose works in which Christianity plays a central role include Willa Cather's *O Pioneers!* (1913), Jon Hassler's Staggerford trilogy (1977–1993), and Marilynne Robinson's *Gilead* (2004). Powerful satire of religion in general and fundamentalism in particular dominates Mark Twain's *Adventures of Huckleberry Finn* (1884, 1885) and *Elmer Gantry* (1927) by Sinclair Lewis.

Fanny Herself (1917) by Edna Ferber expresses Jewish faith, and *The Autobiography of Malcolm X* (1965) provides a Muslim perspective. Immigrants from India and Vietnam reflect Hinduism in *Jasmine* (1989) by Bharati Mukherjee and Buddhism in *Stealing Buddha's Dinner* (2007) by Bich Minh Nguyen.

FURTHER READING: No definitive work has yet appeared on religion in Midwestern literature, and even comprehensive reference works on American literature and American and British literature and religion are lacking. Although many books exist on spiritual matters and particular groups of authors, their coverage of Midwestern writers is spotty. Readers with an interest in religion in the writing of a particular author should consult works on that author. One periodical, *Religion and Literature,* successor to *NDEJ: A Journal of Religion in Literature,* occasionally prints articles on Midwestern authors.

MARY DEJONG OBUCHOWSKI

CENTRAL MICHIGAN UNIVERSITY

REVOLT FROM THE VILLAGE, THE

OVERVIEW: In 1921 CARL (CLINTON) VAN DOREN (1885–1950) fired the first shot in a literary war that, for the better part of the twentieth century, would engage writers, critics, scholars, and readers in continual skirmishes over the construction of the

Midwest and its meaning in American culture. Focusing on SPOON RIVER ANTHOLOGY (1915) by EDGAR LEE MASTERS (1868–1950), WINESBURG, OHIO (1919) by SHERWOOD ANDERSON (1876–1941), *The Anthology of Another Town* (1920) by E(DGAR) W(ATSON) HOWE (1853–1937), MAIN STREET (1920) by (HARRY) SINCLAIR LEWIS (1885–1951), *Miss Lulu Bett* (1920) by ZONA GALE (1974–1938), and *Moon-Calf* (1920) by FLOYD DELL (1887–1969), Van Doren argued that these books rejected what he called the cult of the village: the notion that life in American small towns was happy, harmonious, virtuous, and peaceful.

Although the writers Van Doren discussed at greatest length in his essay later denied that they had participated in any such movement, the term "revolt from the village" became widely accepted and was employed uncritically throughout the rest of the century and into the new millennium. During the second half of the twentieth century, however, "revolt from the village" became a contested term. Some scholars worked to refine the concept, others rejected it completely, and still others sought to situate the movement within a larger cultural perspective on the Midwest, generating a lively conversation about exactly what the revolt from the village was, whether such a revolt in fact existed, and, more significantly, how perceptions about this movement have participated in the cultural construction of the Midwest.

HISTORY AND SIGNIFICANCE: In "The Revolt from the Village: 1920," *Nation* 113 (October 12, 1921): 407–12, Van Doren began by noting that during the second decade of the twentieth century a number of American books were published that reflected a change in attitude toward the American small town. This essay, the tenth in a series in the *Nation* on contemporary American novelists, heralded what he termed "the newest style in American fiction" (407), a fresh breath of candor that blew away the facade of innocence from American small-town life and exposed the raw emotions that made up its inner core. He presented Masters's *Spoon River Anthology* as the urtext of the revolt from the village, lingered on the "scandal" and "affairs of sex" (407) that he felt the poems stressed, and stated that the book's

John T. McCutcheon's illustration from his *The Restless Age*, 1921. Bobbs-Merrill Co., 1921.

influence had been widely felt, as reflected by the number of "deliberate imitations" (408) published within the next few years. The first of these, Anderson's *Winesburg, Ohio,* Van Doren termed "the 'anthology' 'transprosed'" (408). He noted that, like Masters, Anderson dealt with scandal, but that while the former touched scandal with irony, Anderson touched it with beauty (408). Likewise, Van Doren's discussion of *The Anthology of Another Town* emphasized Howe's refusal to perpetuate "the sentimental traditions" of the village (408).

Van Doren gave more space to Lewis's *Main Street* than to any other book he discussed, possibly because, as he carefully noted, the novel was a runaway best seller that introduced more people to the "village virus" of dullness and conformity than any of the other revolt-from-the-village books. Again, Van Doren credited to Masters's influence *Main Street*'s indictment of dullness and noted that a former idealist of the village, Gale, had also published a scathingly critical village novel, *Miss Lulu Bett,* in 1920. Van Doren also discussed another novel published that year, Dell's *Moon-Calf,* emphasizing that its protagonist, Felix Fay, rebels against the Midwestern village without the hatred, reproach, or vengefulness that Van Doren believed characterized the other revolt-from-the-village books; the critic also praised Dell's narrative stance that neither sentimentalized nor vilified the Midwestern town. Van Doren continued with a long summary paragraph remarking on the unusually large number of novels published in 1920 that were critical of the village. He concluded with a discussion of *This Side of Paradise*, also published in 1920 by F(RANCIS) SCOTT (KEY) FITZGERALD (1896–1940), emphasizing the novel's energy and intelligence.

Although Van Doren devoted more ink to this alleged literary movement than did other critics and, therefore, was arguably most responsible for its perpetuation, the notion of a revolt from the village found a fertile field in the cultural conversation of the era. Several observers were already broaching an idea that Van Doren had implied: that the revolt-from-the-village authors' depiction of the stultifying Midwestern village was a synecdoche for American cultural limitations.

Thus George Jean Nathan (1882–1958) and H(enry) L(ewis) Mencken (1880–1956) wrote in *The American Credo: A Contribution toward the Interpretation of the National Mind* (1920) that Americans were unique in their compulsion to social mobility, which manifested itself in a conformity to middle-class conventions that they termed "the herd mentality." In this and many of the essays he published in his *Prejudices* series, Mencken attributed the herd mentality to farmers and townspeople.

Van Wyck Brooks (1886–1963) in "The Literary Life in America," in *America's Coming-of-Age* (1958), echoed these ideas in his critique of America as a materialistic and culturally bankrupt nation. Moreover, he blamed the pioneer experience "with its burden of isolation, nervous strain, excessive work, and the racial habits these have engendered" (197) for the literary deficiencies of the culture at large. In an earlier collection of essays, *Letters and Leadership* (1918), Brooks had praised *Spoon River Anthology* as an accurate account of the culturally and spiritually impoverished American village and, as Van Doren would do two years later, had overstated Masters's case by suggesting that everyone in Spoon River lived in spiritual isolation. In *The Ordeal of Mark Twain* (1920) Brooks focused on the struggle of SAMUEL LANGHORNE CLEMENS (1835–1910), writing as Mark Twain, with his village environment, blaming the deficiencies in Twain's fiction on his repressive and culturally deprived upbringing in Hannibal, MISSOURI; he noted as substantiation of his claim that a number of "books have been published of late years letting us behind the scenes of the glamorous myth of pioneering" (29). Among these, he cited Howe's *Story of a Country Town* (1883) and *A Son of the Middle Border* (1917) by (HANNIBAL) HAMLIN GARLAND (1860–1940).

Van Doren continued to beat the drum of literary and cultural revolt for the next twenty years. He republished his essay in *Contemporary American Novelists* (1922) as a chapter titled "The Revolt from the Village," which he updated in 1940 as two chapters, "The Revolt from the Village" and "Sinclair Lewis," in *The American Novel, 1789–1939*. In 1923 Van Doren included an essay titled "On Hating the Provinces" in the collection *The Roving Critic* (1923). There he asserted that "voice after voice is added to the regiments of criticism being raised against suburban Philistia and the vilatic bourgeoisie" (83), adding, "Those novelists and dramatists who now hate our provinces most are nearly all dissatisfied men lately escaped from stodginess and devoted to getting their revenges" (85). Van Doren reiterated this notion in 1925 in the textbook he published with his brother, Mark, *American and British Literature since 1890*, and again in a 1936 biographical sketch of Lewis. Here, as well as in his landmark 1921 essay, he used a sustained battle metaphor that would control the way the revolt from the village would be conceptualized and written about for decades:

> Thousands who had suffered from their villages rose to shouts of triumphant recognition and turned missionary. Tens of thousands who had not felt dull in their villages defended them and any like them. Rival prejudices, having found in the book a cause for war, read it chiefly to pick up ammunition. *Main Street* made a flag and a target, became a symbol, and was blamed for all the war's excesses. (*American and British Literature since 1930*: 23–24)

As the 1920s waned, the literary movement whose existence Van Doren asserted found new acolytes. Dorothy Dondore (1894–1946) discussed the revolt in *The Prairie and the Making of Middle America* (1926) as part of a movement away from romanticism, referring to Van Doren and his essay and emphasizing, as he did, that the rebellion was a cultural movement led by Lewis, Dell, and Anderson. By the 1930s the revolt had escalated into an all-out war, at least in the language of some scholars, who picked up on and elaborated the martial images dominating Van Doren's discourse. Among these was Ima Honaker Herron (1899–1987), who seemed to have been so heavily influenced by Van Doren's revolt theory that she devoted her entire career to writing about the literature of the small town, the focus of her 1926 MA thesis and her 1935 PhD dissertation, published in 1939 as *The Small Town in American Literature*. This book, which was republished in 1959 and again in 1971, echoed Van Doren's military metaphors as Herron conceptualized "the battle of the village," opposing the "village apologists," including WILLIAM ALLEN WHITE (1868–1944), JAMES WHITCOMB RILEY (1849–1916), MEREDITH NICHOLSON (1866–1947), (NEWTON) BOOTH TARKINGTON (1869–1946), and Gale, to the "prophets of the new age," among whom she included Masters, Anderson, Lewis, Dell, and WILLA CATHER (1873–1947). Herron expanded on Van Doren's theory by situating the literature of revolt within the larger mode of rebellion characteristic of early twentieth-century literature. Van Doren's influence pervaded Herron's scholarship, reappearing in her second book, *The Small Town in American Drama* (1969), which included a section titled "The Flight from Main Street."

Russell Blankenship, in *American Literature as an Expression of the National Mind* (1931), also constructed the revolt from the village similarly in a chapter titled "The Battle of the Village," exploiting Brooks's familiar shibboleths of the puritan and the pioneer as those elements of village life that had provoked the rebellion: "As the home of such elements the village drew the first fire of the critics. The defenders of the small town had not waited for the attack of the hostile party" (650). Such military images were further developed by the structure of the chapter, which first discussed "the defense," including White, Tarkington, and DOROTHY (DOROTHEA FRANCES CANFIELD) FISHER (1879–1958), and then "the attack," represented by Lewis and Anderson. Blankenship's innovation was to include a third subsection, "Beyond the Village," in which he praised Cather's work.

This construction of the revolt from the village as literary war was also seen when HARLAN (HENTHORNE) HATCHER (1898–1998), in *Creating the Modern American Novel* (1935), noted, "RUTH SUCKOW [1892–1960] has joined no side in the controversy between Main Street and Friendship Village" (106).

The 1940s and 1950s saw influential New York critics embracing and elaborating on the notion of a revolt from the village. In *On Native Grounds* (1942) Alfred Kazin (1915–1998) devoted a chapter to Anderson and Lewis, linking them as "two stories of revolt against small-town life in the Middle West" that "signalized even more the coming of a fresh new realism to fiction" (205). Like Van Doren, Kazin saw the revolt through a modernist lens, stressing the element of postwar liberation from the old conventions and the freedom to describe the common experiences of ordinary Midwesterners (206–7). In *The Twenties: American Writing in the Postwar Decade* (1955) Frederick J. Hoffman reflected Mencken and Nathan's emphasis on the herd mentality in his conceptualization of the literature of revolt as an attack on conformity. Further, he stated that the Middle West had become a metaphor for middle-class conventions and virtues, using the term Ford Madox Ford (1873–1939) had coined—"Middle Westishness," which Ford equated with "disillusionment . . . and an enormous awakening" (327)—to describe the mood of the literature of revolt. Hoffman emphasized that the motif of escape linked the novels of revolt and provided a detailed outline of their structure, noting that the young man or woman had to go east instead of west to find freedom, a style, culture, and sophistication or moral maturity (328).

By midcentury the revolt from the village had, in the words of Anthony Channell Hilfer (1936–2008) in *The Revolt from the Village, 1915–1930* (1969), "become an accepted rubric of historical criticism" (3). Henry Steele Commager (1902–1998) devoted a chapter of *The American Mind: An Interpretation of American Thought and Character* (1950) to "the literature of revolt" and joined in the chorus of critics who portrayed this literature as a protest against middle-class values (261). The revolt also made an appearance in Robert Spiller's *The Literary History of the*

United States (1948), where it transmogrified from a war to a deadly pestilence. Spiller asserted that

writers like Sherwood Anderson and Sinclair Lewis were now ready to report that the infection had spread to the village where, so their countrymen wanted to believe, the democratic virtues still lingered. Masters's Spoon River was the first village to have its shroud of decency violently removed. Anderson's Winesburg and Lewis's Gopher Prairie were not spared for long. (1181)

Arthur Hobson Quinn (1875–1960) concurred, stating in *The Literature of the American People* (1951) that "what Carl Van Doren was soon to label 'the revolt from the village' began in Spoon River" (870). In 1955 no less a scholar of Midwestern literature than John T(heodore) Flanagan (1906–1996) in "Literary Protest in the Midwest," *Southwest Review* 34.2 (Spring 1949): 148–57, recognized the massive attack on the Midwest and its culture, arguing that "by the early 1920s, what Carl Van Doren called the revolt from the village was in full swing, the Midwest small town had been recorded as an ugly, gossip-ridden, materialistic, hypocritical, prurient, stolid community, death at once to the imagination and to the artist" (152). Hatcher, in *Creating the Modern American Novel* (1935), situated the revolt within the contexts of realism and modernism and emphasized its role in undermining traditional Victorian morals and conventions: "Greenwich Village (and its equivalent in a dozen large cities) became the symbol of escape, the dream Mecca where life was joyous and love was free. Young college men and women fled their Western villages for the absolution of a hall bedroom and a stool in the Village Café" (77).

Thus, although its legitimacy would be challenged in the coming decades, the term "revolt from the village" was used continually by scholars and critics as if everyone agreed on what it was and what it meant. Robert B(ingham) Downs included a chapter on *Main Street* titled "The Revolt from the Village" in his *Famous American Books* (1971) that touted the Van Doren line, as did George F. Day, who, in *A Literary History of the American West* (1987), discussed the revolt as one of four major themes in Midwestern

literature. In *The Middle Western Farm Novel in the Twentieth Century* (1965), Roy W(illard) Meyer (1925–2007) invoked the term to emphasize the difference between the Middle Western farm novel and the Middle Western village novel. Ronald Weber also discussed the movement in *The Midwestern Ascendancy in American Writing* (1992), as did Jon Gjerde in his essay "Middleness and the Middle West," in *The American Midwest: Essays on Regional History* (2001), edited by Andrew R. L. Cayton and Susan E. Gray.

In the second half of the twentieth century, however, closer analysis of the revolt-from-the-village movement began, perhaps stimulated by the interest in regional literature signaled by the founding of the Western Literature Association in 1965, the Society for the Study of Southern Literature in 1968, and the SOCIETY FOR THE STUDY OF MIDWESTERN LITERATURE in 1971. This period also saw the first dissertations and books specifically focused on the revolt from the village. Hilfer in his 1965 dissertation, later revised as *The Revolt from the Village, 1915–1930* (1969), did not challenge the validity of the concept; rather, he conceptualized the revolt as an attack on the pastoral myth of the village constructed by Oliver Goldsmith (1730–1774), Philip Freneau (1752–1832), Timothy Dwight (1752–1817), Sarah Orne Jewett (1849–1909), and others and historicized it by showing that the two main themes of the revolt, the buried life and the herd mentality, had been discussed much in contemporary writings by critics such as Brooks and Mencken. Hilfer emphasized another theory of earlier observers: the revolt was not an attack on the village per se but rather on the village as a synecdoche for middle-class values and conventions. He also advanced the notion that there were two revolts from the village and characterized the prairie realism of EDWARD EGGLESTON (1837–1902), E. W. Howe, JOSEPH KIRKLAND (1830–1894), and others as constituting the first revolt before discussing the writers of the second revolt whom Van Doren had designated as village rebels (Anderson, Masters, Gale, and Lewis), a case that Philip H. Ford had advanced a few years earlier in "Evidence of a Revolt from the Village in the Eighteen Nineties," *Philological Papers* 10 (May 1956): 40–54.

In her 1971 dissertation and in an article, "The Revolt from the Village and Middle Western Fiction, 1870–1915," *Kansas Quarterly* 5.6 (1973): 5–16, Diane Dufva Quantic sought to clarify rather than challenge the notion of the revolt from the village. She framed her discussion of the works of White, Gale, and Cather within the context of the revolt-from-the-village movement, stressing links between selected texts by these authors and the later literature of revolt. Further, she questioned the notion itself, noting that it had become a vague designation for any book that was critical of small-town life and seeking to develop a precise definition of the term. Like Hilfer, Quantic also noted that many critics saw the revolt from the village as an attack not so much on the village itself as on a state of mind typical of middle-class residents of Middle Western towns. However, she argued that a critical stance against the middle class was still too broad a definition to characterize the movement accurately. She delineated the characteristics of a revolt-from-the-village book: (1) it is set in a contemporary Middle Western small town for the major part of the action; (2) it features a character who rebels against restrictive middle-class mores; and (3) it is set in a stagnant community composed of complacent residents who are hostile to change, thus provoking the conflict in the work between the character who must either reject this stifling environment or come to terms with it (5–9). And, like Hilfer and Ford, Quantic took issue with critics who posited 1915 as the beginning of the movement, noting that it was strongly rooted in the literature of nineteenth-century prairie realism, in which authors such as Eggleston, Kirkland, Howe, and Garland articulated the paradoxical archetype of the village as both flowering garden and cultural desert (22–23).

Other scholars joined Hilfer and Quantic in seeking clarification, refinement, and qualification. In 1964 Thomas Tanselle warned in "Sinclair Lewis and Floyd Dell: Two Views of the Midwest," *Twentieth-Century Literature* 9.4 (January 1964): 175–84, that "the phrase [revolt from the village] can be misleading if we take it to signify a complete rejection of the Midwest by the writers to whom it is applied" (175). Tanselle

cautioned against lumping together in the "revolt" category all writers who wrote unsentimentally about the Midwest and used the examples of Dell and Lewis, who both published novels in 1920 that Van Doren discussed in his famous essay. The differences between these novels, Tanselle maintained, "reveal the pointlessness of trying to classify either simply as a revolt-from-the-village writer, for their individual attitudes are too complicated to be adequately summed up in such a phrase" (175). Another scholar who attempted to define the phenomenon more precisely was Park Dixon Goist (b. 1936). In *From Main Street to State Street: Town, City, and Community in America* (1977) Goist acknowledged Hilfer's view of the revolt as an attack on village conformity but added that many so-called revolt-from-the-village authors, namely, Gale and Dell, were ambivalent about their small-town settings, finding in them community as well as conformity (21–22). And, like Quantic, Charles Wordell in "The Revolt from the Village and the Exquisites: Carl Van Vechten's *The Tattooed Countess*" *Chu-Shikoku Studies in American Literature* 20 (1984): 5–18, attempted to clarify the concept more specifically, arguing that there were four common characteristics of revolt novels: (1) an emphasis on the negative side of village life that lies beneath the surface of harmony and pleasantry, (2) the village's interference with personal development, (3) the necessity to leave the village for self-realization, and (4) the acceptance of the village as a social reality that has strengths as well as weaknesses (10–11).

While these scholars sought to refine the fuzzy edges of the term "revolt from the village," others opposed the notion itself. Perhaps the first skeptic was AUGUST (WILLIAM) DERLETH (1909–1971), himself a chronicler of WISCONSIN village life, who interviewed Masters, Lewis, and Anderson in the 1930s and 1940s and carefully questioned them, as reflected in his *Three Literary Men: A Memoir of Sinclair Lewis, Sherwood Anderson, Edgar Lee Masters* (1963), about their views on the "revolt." Masters, the man who supposedly started it all, took exception to the notion: "There never was anything to this revolt from the village business. We didn't do any such thing. Maybe Lewis backed away from something that hurt him, but he wasn't re-

Sketch of Sherwood Anderson, Sinclair
Lewis, and Edgar Lee Masters by Frank D.
McSherry on the cover of August Derleth's
Three Literary Men, 1963.
© Candlelight Press, 1963

belling against the American small town
any more than I was" (49). Similarly, Lewis
rebutted Van Doren's essay in a long letter to
the critic, referenced in Van Doren's 1936
autobiography, *Three Worlds* (153–59), denying that he had ever read, let alone been
influenced by, *Spoon River Anthology*. Later
Lewis told Derleth:

I like Carl [Van Doren] but don't like some
of his theories. That's what they are, just theories, unsupported by fact. The trouble with
critics is that they like to create a horse and
ride it to death . . . .
*Then you didn't feel you were rebelling against
the village?*
Nothing of it. I disliked some things about
village life. I dislike some things about city life,
too. I got out of Sauk Center because there
weren't any opportunities for me there. Carl
said I couldn't stand the dull people. Well,

those people he named—I like those
people—maybe each one of them was dull
about some things—aren't we all—but I loved
those people—Carol Kennicott and Sam and
Champ and Will Kennicott and Bea. I put into
my book what I saw and what I felt. I didn't
think it was rebellious then. I don't think it is
now, either. (*Three Literary Men* 12–13)

Anderson's response was quite similar:

There wasn't anything to this revolting. I
liked Clyde [Ohio]. I saw it the way it was and
I put it down the way it was. I didn't run away
from Clyde. The time came, and I went. I sup-
pose you could say I grew away from it.
There's time for one kind of life and a time for
another. There's no such thing as "revolting"
or "rebelling" or whatever it is they want to
call it. (*Three Literary Men* 34)

While Derleth went to the horses'
mouths for his argument against the revolt
from the village, Barry Gross tackled its proponents head-on in his article "The Revolt
That Wasn't: The Legacies of Critical Myo-
pia," *CEA Critic* 39.2 (January 1977): 4–8. In
this essay Gross characterized the revolt as
a concept developed by urban eastern critics who "wanted to see the village revolted
from, who were convinced that provincial
life, especially in the Middle West, condemned America to the status of second-
class culture" (4). Gross said that these
critics knew little about the Midwest or its
literature and found in *Spoon River Anthology, Winesburg, Ohio,* and *Main Street* only
confirmations of the stereotypes of the
Midwest with which they were familiar. He
asserted that their biased readings of these
Midwestern classics influenced the way
these books were read and interpreted by
several generations of readers.

Gross argued that Masters, Anderson,
and Lewis were in revolt, not from the village itself, but from the myth of the village
as "the great good place, as simple and innocent, pure and virtuous, democratic and
egalitarian" (5) and that they were evoking
a preindustrial Midwest that was the great
good place. For example, in *Winesburg, Ohio*
Anderson was not writing as a realist or a
naturalist, but as an elegist: "His subject is
not the village one should revolt from but an
already vanished America, a time when 'the
factories had not come'" (6). Gross heavily

stressed the East Coast perspective of critics he held responsible for perpetuating the notion of a revolt-from-the-village movement, emphasizing that the outsider always misses the love and the tie that binds in the regionalist's text (8).

In a second essay, "In Another Country: The Revolt from the Village," *MidAmerica* 4 (1977): 101–11, Gross mentioned Van Doren's essay but primarily blamed Mencken, whom he designated the literary and cultural arbiter of the 1920s, for establishing the revolt from the village as a literary movement. "He saw the Midwest as America writ large, as the spiritual seat of everything that was most repressive and conventional, most drab and debilitating in American life" (103). Gross further indicted Kazin in *On Native Grounds* and Hoffman in *The Twenties* for perpetuating distorted views of Middle Western literature in their discussions of the revolt from the village. Gross pointed out that writers such as Gale, Suckow, Louis Bromfield (1896–1956), and Fisher, whom critics categorized as village rebels, actually praised the Midwest; Gross asserted that "abuse is balanced evenly with approbation" (104) in the works of the major Midwestern writers. Moreover, Gross argued that emphasis had been misplaced on the so-called revolt elements of these books. George Willard's departure from Winesburg is not a revolt; it is just a departure. Carol Kennicott, the outsider, is ridiculed in *Main Street* almost as much as are Gopher Prairie and its inhabitants. Cather is not revolting against the village but against "progress." The only real evidence of the revolt from the village in the major works of Midwestern literature, according to Gross, is found in *Sister Carrie* (1900) by (Herman) Theodore Dreiser (1871–1945) and in Fitzgerald's *The Great Gatsby* (1925). "Carrie Meeber and Jimmy Gatz revolt because they have nothing to lose by leaving and nothing to gain by staying" (107). Gross argued that the people who revolted, like Jimmy Gatz and Carrie Meeber, did not rebel against middle-class values but in fact aspired to them, and their abandonment of their Midwestern towns for eastern cities was a means to upward mobility. He maintained that the real revolt was not from the village but from "the citification of it, not from the Midwest but from

the progress that had robbed it of its romantic promise" (108).

David D(aniel) Anderson (1924–2011) wrote extensively against the notion of a revolt from the village as a defining characteristic of Midwestern literature. In his many essays and books on the work of Sherwood Anderson, he argued forcefully that *Winesburg, Ohio* is not a part of the literature of revolt, if indeed there is such a thing. In "The Search for a Living Past," in *Sherwood Anderson: Centennial Studies* (1976), edited by Hilbert H. Campbell and Charles E. Modlin, 212–23, he wrote, "One of the most persistent and most misleading attempts at interpreting Midwestern literature is the so-called 'Revolt from the Village' myth" (212). Anderson summarized Van Doren's argument and his influence on later critics, such as Hoffman and Hilfer, and stressed that "the conviction with which Van Doren stated his case has made that interpretation of Midwestern literature a fixture of modern American criticism" (212). Anderson criticized Hoffman and Hilfer for grounding their arguments in "the sandy interpretation originally constructed by Van Doren on the basis of a few isolated works" (213) and for not carefully analyzing the so-called revolt books or the Midwestern myths they perpetuate. What these authors were revolting against, he asserted, was not the village itself but the changes imposed on village life that resulted from an increasingly commercial and materialistic way of existence that came to the villages with modern times. The more fundamental myth of the Midwest, wrote Anderson, is not a myth of revolt but a myth of movement and search in response to the death of the Jeffersonian dream.

In his essay "The Midwestern Town in Midwestern Fiction," *MidAmerica* 6 (1979): 27–43, Anderson elaborated on his objections to the simplistic "revolt from the village" characterization of much early twentieth-century Midwestern literature. Anderson argued that the novels that describe the movement from the towns to the cities during the first two decades of the twentieth century contain no evidence to support Van Doren's assertion that they constitute a revolt from the village. Rather, novelists such as Tarkington, Anderson, and

Dreiser show that the Midwestern town has two dimensions: environmental reality and metaphorical point of departure for the continued search for a new dimension, which he characterized as a search that had begun on the Atlantic coast or in western Europe many generations ago and had continued as a search for fulfillment and personal advancement in an open society through the movement west. As the twentieth century beckoned, this search became a quest for the American Dream, the conviction that in America "the individual, no matter how humble his origins, may advance as far as his ability and virtue may take him" (43). Thus George Willard and his fictional contemporaries who leave the Midwestern small town for the big city are not revolting from the village; to the contrary, in their quest for self-fulfillment and success, they are taking with them the village and its ideals of progress, individualism, democracy, and education.

In a subsequent essay, "Sherwood Anderson and the Critics," published in his edited collection *Critical Essays on Sherwood Anderson* (1981), Anderson argued against the unquestioning acceptance of what he called "the most widespread and most widely accepted literary metaphor of the Midwest" (1). Anderson traced the literary genealogy of the revolt and exposed it as an oversimplified generalization unsupported by facts, pointing out that Van Doren and other eastern critics glossed over the affection and respect that the so-called revolt authors felt for the people in their respective villages while projecting their own eastern cultural biases into their readings.

In the waning decades of the twentieth century scholars of Midwestern literature sought to provide a more complex and nuanced discussion of the revolt-from-the-village phenomenon, as well as of the books that had traditionally been cited as exemplifying the movement, and sometimes situated the revolt within a larger theory of the region. In her essay "The Safe Middle West: Escape to and Escape from Home," *MidAmerica* 14 (1987): 18–27, Margaret Stuhr found the notion of "middleness" to be at the heart of what she called "the double-edged mythology of The Safe Middle West" (18) that centers on the diametrically opposed meanings of the adjective "safe." To explain "why the region has both attracted and alienated its native sons and daughters" (18), she showed how the notion of "safe" embodies both positive and negative values. Stuhr argued that the Midwest is "safe" simultaneously in negative and positive ways— beneficially safe in regard to its identity as a haven of harmony and stability and strong family values and at the same time safe in a bad way because these qualities make it "a cowardly retreat from the unknown and the challenging" (19). Stuhr related the revolt from the village to this second aspect of the safe Middle West, which has generated ambivalence in its writers, as well as to the many coming and goings that characterize the region and are reflected in the departure/return motif prominent in the works of Midwestern writers such as Lewis, Tarkington, Suckow, and Fitzgerald. She concluded by discussing in detail the functioning of this motif in the lives of Hamlin Garland, Nick Carraway, and Dorothy Gale.

For Stephen Enniss, as for Stuhr, ambiguity and ambivalence were central to discussion of the revolt from the village. Focusing on Anderson's landmark novel in his essay "The Implied Community of *Winesburg, Ohio,*" *Old Northwest* 11.1–2 (Spring– Summer 1985): 51–60, Enniss described the stigmatizing effect of Van Doren's classification of the book as part of the literature of revolt and analyzed the way in which this label has resulted in oversimplified interpretations of the novel as a critique of repressive small-town life. Enniss wrote that classifying the book in this way encourages readers to blame the town of Winesburg for the characters' communication problems and emotional handicaps. Moreover, the Winesburg residents who leave are motivated less by public pressure to conform than by their personal needs. Enniss further argued that just as many characters escaped to Winesburg as from Winesburg, and that not all of its residents were lonely and isolated.

Similarly, John T. Hallwas (b. 1945) introduced his 1992 critical edition, *Spoon River Anthology: An Annotated Edition,* with a seventy-nine-page essay in which he noted that "readers of American literature continue to associate the book with the so-called 'revolt from the village' movement that also produced Sherwood Anderson's *Winesburg, Ohio* (1919) and Sinclair Lewis's *Main Street* (1920)" (2), but he rejected that simplistic classification and instead argued for a more complex vision of the book as "a depiction of the struggle for self-realization in a society that has lost contact with the great democratic vision that once gave purpose and meaning to American lives" (2). In his emphasis on the main thrust of *Spoon River Anthology* as "a spiritual quest for 'the Petersburg environment,' an attempt to recover what had vanished—from his life and from American culture—by memorializing it in his poetry" (3), Hallwas echoed Anderson's analysis, as did David (Marion) Holman in *A Certain Slant of Light: Regionalism and the Form of Southern and Midwestern Fiction* (1995), arguing that the failure of Midwestern society to achieve the Jeffersonian dream resulted in disillusionment with the Midwestern small town (97).

In his essay "The Ambiguities of the Escape Theme in Midwestern Literature, 1918–1934," *MidAmerica* 26 (1999): 49–76, Matts Västå endeavored to complicate the traditional notion of the revolt from the village as an exodus and an estrangement from the village. Västå, like Stuhr and Enniss, emphasized the ambiguities of the escape theme in the literature of revolt, outlining several types of escape found in these books: the escape of no return, the conclusive escape, the open-ended escape, and the inconclusive escape. He asserted that the inconclusive escape "qualifies the revolt-from-the-village approach and makes the attitudes toward the Middle West much more complicated than merely looking at the Middle West as a 'metaphor of abuse'" (63). Västå concluded that the conflicting nuances of the escape motif, as well as the escape/return pattern frequently found in revolt literature, reflect the ambivalence and complexity of the characters' attitudes toward the Midwest.

With the coming of the new millennium, Gjerde sought in "Middleness and the Middle West" (2001) to theorize the region by means of the same double-edged sword of middleness that engaged Stuhr, asserting that the identity the Midwest derives arises largely from the middleness in

its name. After reviewing both positive and negative kinds of Midwestern middleness, Gjerde identified four defining characteristics that construct the Midwestern identity: revolt, nostalgia, condescension, and defensiveness. He stated that revolt was a more common and successful theme than nostalgia and cited Howe, Garland, Lewis, Cather, Masters, and WILLIAM DEAN HOWELLS (1837–1920) as authors of works that comprise complex mixtures of condemnation of and nostalgia for the Midwestern small town but that nevertheless have had the overall effect of foregrounding repressiveness, conformity, and stultification as key elements of the Midwestern identity. Another twenty-first-century observer, Tom Lutz, in his essay "The Revolt from the Village: Anderson, Lewis, Suckow," in *Cosmopolitan Vistas: American Regionalism and Literary Value* (2004), argued that the best "revolt" books, such as those by Anderson, Lewis, and Suckow, evince a kind of double consciousness that can articulate both the limitations and the advantages of small-town life. Lutz claimed that these works are characterized by a cosmopolitan outlook; they work on multiple levels, comprising both critique and celebration and valuing both the particular and the universal. In "The Myth of the Midwestern 'Revolt from the Village,'" *MidAmerica* 40 (2013): 39–85, historian Jon K. Lauck argued that the revolt became so widely and uncritically accepted because the concept was compatible with the mainly leftist political and intellectual forces of cultural rebellion that were dominant during the first half of the twentieth century.

Did Carl Van Doren discover the revolt from the village, or did he invent it? This may not be the most fruitful question to ask in the current climate of postmodern literary theory that problematizes the notion of any historical reality unmediated by language. The revolt from the village, seen from this perspective, becomes one of many socially constructed phenomena that make up our world. Rather than asking whether such a movement really did exist, it might be more useful to ask why Van Doren read *Winesburg, Ohio* and saw one sort of phenomenon while David D. Anderson read the same book and saw quite another. It may be more productive, therefore, to think of the revolt from the village not as a literary movement but as a prism through which one might view the literature from one of several perspectives. By examining these perspectives, we may be able to answer some questions that have been raised about the revolt from the village. Why did this notion catch on so quickly and endure so persistently while at the same time becoming a contested term? Why has it attached itself to Midwestern small-town literature rather than to that of any other American region? And, most important, how has it shaped the way we think and feel about the Midwest and its literature?

First of all, the revolt can be viewed as a projection of Van Doren's personal experiences with the rural Midwest, most particularly his need to transcend the limitations of his native region by moving on to a culturally richer life in New York City. Born on a farm near Hope, ILLINOIS, Van Doren moved with his family at age fifteen to nearby Urbana and received his undergraduate education at the University of Illinois, where he taught for a few years before leaving to do doctoral work at Columbia University. There he subsequently became a professor of literature and also served as literary editor of both the *Nation* and the *Century Magazine*, helped found the Literary Guild of America, and published over fifty books, including a Pulitzer Prize–winning biography of Benjamin Franklin (1706–1790). The structure of his autobiography, *Three Worlds* (1936), provides strong evidence of the influence of his Midwestern upbringing. The first world of the title, the prewar world, is divided into three sections: village, town, and university. Although Van Doren stated that "I remembered Hope with affection and I had not been made unhappy by anything Urbana had ever done to me" (152), some of the tales he related in the early part of the book would not be out of place in *Spoon River Anthology*. Further, he admitted that although he enjoyed his childhood on the farm in Hope, after he moved to Urbana, he became resentful of his country upbringing. "Ambition in me first took the form of snobbishness," he explained (1). Likewise, when Van Doren left Urbana for better opportunities in New York, he was also eager to distance himself from that small Illinois town. Thus the revolt from the village was, first and foremost, Van Doren's personal revolt against his Midwestern past, which led him to focus more directly on the negative elements of the books he reviewed in his 1921 essay, elements that resonated strongly with his own experiences, as well as with the zeitgeist.

Van Doren's effort to distance himself physically and intellectually from the provincialism and outdated pastoralism of the heartland where he grew up points to a very real pattern of migration from the villages and towns of the Midwest to CHICAGO and New York; thus the literature of revolt indubitably chronicled a pattern of migration that was a key part of America's cultural transition from a rural to an urban society. Between 1870 and 1920 over 11 million people left their native farms and villages and towns for the cities. By 1920, the year in which *Main Street, Moon-Calf,* and *Miss Lulu Bett* were published, only thirty percent of Americans were engaged in agricultural employment, a cultural development reflected in the large number of revolt-from-the-village books published during that year. As Herron noted in *The Small Town in American Drama*, "One dream of escapism frequently reflected in native drama tallies with the incessantly growing shift in population to the increasingly congested cities. In actuality the acceleration of life, as symbolized by urban multiplicity and giantism, continued to fascinate ambitious, restless youths on farms and in towns far and wide" (236). Similarly, John and Margaret Wrenn observed in *Edgar Lee Masters* (1983) that "Masters and Anderson were right in denying the validity of a revolt-from-the-village school which points to nothing more noteworthy than the long process of nineteenth- and twentieth-century urbanization" (182).

Another perspective on the revolt from the village emphasizes that it not only reflected a very real population shift but also the larger context of social revolt and rebellion in evidence at the beginning of the twentieth century. In *The End of American Innocence* (1959) Henry F. May (1915–2012) discussed "the innocent rebellion" (1912–1917) as a positive development, emphasizing not the literal escape from the village and the ensuing liberation from middle-class morality and small-town conventions and materialism but, more important and positively, the valorizing of spontaneity and the lure of the intellectual and cultural attractions of the urban centers, the embrace of new scientific theories, and the new music, art, and dance. Thus May and others saw the revolt less as a rejection of the village and more as a quest for self-fulfillment and wider cultural horizons that could be achieved only in the city.

A subset of May's "innocent rebellion" is the literary revolt of the realists and naturalists against the genteel tradition. In *The Story of American Literature* (1939) Ludwig Lewisohn (1882–1955) discussed the revolt-from-the-village writers within an analysis of a larger revolt against the idea that "literature was a decorous illustration of a system of ethics, manners and economics fixed and frozen for all time somewhere in England, sometime in the nineteenth century" (418). In an age in which expression had become divorced from experience by nineteenth-century literary conventions, Lewisohn viewed the naturalists as rescuers of art, as "the liberators of our cultural life" (465). Masters, Anderson, and Lewis, the writers whom Van Doren depicted as the leaders of the revolt from the village, were among those whom Lewisohn praised for their bold and risky innovations.

T(homas) K(ing) Whipple (1890–1939) similarly indicted the genteel tradition as "one form of the cult of respectability, which springs from dread of reality and which allies itself with practicality, is eminently hostile to fullness of life" (10); in *Spokesmen* (1928) he focused on realists and naturalists who rebelled against this tradition by writing "with special vigor and directness" (21). Of the ten writers he discussed, six were Midwesterners often associated with the revolt from the village: Dreiser, Anderson, Cather, Lewis, CARL (AUGUST) SANDBURG (1878–1967), and (NICHOLAS) VACHEL LINDSAY (1879–1931). One Midwestern writer whom he did not discuss, Masters, succinctly explained the new vogue for a more realistic literature:

The people were ready for Spoon River. They needed that kind of book. They'd had their fill of moonlight and silly love stories. They'd had enough of sentimentality and unreality. They wanted books like *Sister Carrie* and *Winesburg, Ohio* and *Spoon River* and *Main Street* because they were about flesh and blood men and women. (*Three Literary Men* 50)

The revolt from the village can also be viewed as a subset of the post–World War I modernist revolt against traditional literary ideals and conventions. The modernist's quest for new forms of language and structures is reflected in the imagery of Van Doren's 1921 essay. We are oriented to this mind-set from the very first words of the essay, "The newest style in American fiction" (407). Van Doren was looking for new forms of literature to write about, and books like *Main Street, Winesburg, Ohio,* and *Spoon River Anthology* more than met his expectations. Throughout the essay he situates the books he is reviewing within the modernist impulse to reject old forms and construct new ones, representing them as tearing down walls, breaking patterns, digging beneath surfaces, penetrating facades, and puncturing bubbles: "The roofs and walls of Spoon River were gone and the passerby saw into every bedroom; the closets were open and all the skeletons rattled undenied; brains and breasts had unlocked themselves and set their most private treasures out for the most public gaze" (407). He also uses metaphors of light and heat to articulate the capacity of these works to illuminate modern culture and energize readers, as seen in this approving characterization of Dell's style in *Moon-Calf:* "He writes with a candid lucidity which everywhere lets in the light" (412), and in this description of *This Side of Paradise:* "The narrative flares up now into delightful verse and now into glittering comic dialogue" (412).

Related to this perspective is the view of the revolt as a rebellion against middle-class values in general. During the first decades of the twentieth century Mencken, Brooks, and other critics excoriated the middle class as the bastion of Puritanism, an ideology that they blamed for the sterility and materialism of American culture. For many, the prime locus of puritanical middle-class values was the Middle Western village. This attitude was so ingrained that, in the minds of many, the Midwest became a synecdoche for middle-class values. The "revolt" authors were seen, therefore, not so much as revolting against the village as opposing what the village stood for: repression, conformity, intolerance. and other middle-class attitudes that inhibited cultural development and ostracized individuals who defied village norms. Thus Herron in *The Small Town in American Literature* praised Lewis for his "almost uncanny faculty for unmasking the middle-class mind, with satire, burlesque, and humor, which is sometimes genial, sometimes malicious" (384).

At the heart of the American Dream lies Thomas Jefferson's agrarian vision of the West, the "happy land of farms and simple industries" (336) that Dreiser rhapsodized about in *A Hoosier Holiday* (1916) as he drove through INDIANA. From Jefferson's day onward, many observers have situated this "happy land" in the abundant garden of the Midwest, whose vast, fertile lands would make anyone willing to work hard enough free, independent, and the equal of all. Thus the rural village of the West, comprising this natural aristocracy of freehold farmers, became enshrined in the American cultural imagination as the matrix of democracy, fostering democratic values such as egalitarianism, industry, and self-reliance, and, since its residents derived their living from nature, virtue and peace as well. Reinforced by poems such as *The American Village* (1772) by Philip Freneau and *Greenfield Hill* (1794) by Timothy Dwight, as well as by many popular novels, such as *Mabel Vaughan* (1857) by Maria Susanna Cummins (1827–1866) and *India: The Pearl of Pearl River* (1853) by Mrs. E. D. E. N. Southworth (1819–1899), the agrarian myth became deeply rooted in the American cultural imagination, and the idyllic notion of a rural utopia persisted for over two hundred years.

From one point of view, then, what the revolt-from-the-village authors were doing was not rejecting the village itself but rather exposing the reality behind the pastoral ideal of the village and recording the social changes that occurred as industrialization, commercialization, and urbanization transformed American culture. "Anderson was in revolt," wrote Arthur Hobson Quinn in *The Literature of the American People,* "not against the village, but against the swallowing up of the village as it had once been by the monster of industrialism" (873).

In *The Middle West: Its Meaning in American Culture* (1989), cultural geographer James R(obert) Shortridge (b. 1944) described this development as the coming of industry to what had been viewed as a utopian middle kingdom situated between the decadent cities of the eastern seaboard and the lawless and uncivilized Wild West. Shortridge observed that, as Lewis suggested in *Main Street,* this cultural change was seen by many as a betrayal: "In attempting to merge the pastoral and the technological, Middle-Western society had sacrificed its ideals" (45). In this context, the revolt from the village can be viewed more as a sensibility than as a literary movement; its central texts communicate this sense of the betrayal of the Jeffersonian dream as Midwestern towns and villages underwent the shift from an agrarian to a business- and industry-based economy. The works classified under the revolt-from-the-village rubric functioned, then, to establish a countermyth. Subscribing to this view, K. Narayana Chandran wrote in "Revolt from the Grave: *Spoon River Anthology* by Edgar Lee Masters," *Midwest Quarterly* 29.4 (Summer 1988): 438–47: "Masters only helps us realize how historical forces have favored the city and the machine against the country and nature in a combat deemed inevitable for the nation's progress" (440).

Scholars such as Anderson and Gross who have most vociferously rejected the notion of a revolt from the village argue that its proponents' focus on the small town's shortcomings is a misplaced emphasis. What is most significant in these books, they argue, is the positive rather than the negative: the protagonist's belief in the values of the Jeffersonian dream and his departure as signaling the next phase in his search for self-fulfillment rather than a sweeping rejection of his native village.

Why Midwestern readers have accentuated the positive aspects of the revolt literature while eastern-based critics have dwelt on the negative might be explained by viewing the revolt-from-the-village phenomenon from a postcolonial perspective. The ontological ironies inherent in the identity of a region that is geographically central but culturally marginal are perhaps nowhere more clearly apparent than in the writings of Van Doren, Kazin, Howe, Hoffman, and others whose perception of a revolt from the village reflected their changing attitudes toward the once culturally central pastoral ideals associated with the Midwest, attitudes that, with the modern rejection of Victorian values, transferred the more pejorative aspects of pastoralism to the heartland. Shortridge traces this changing image of the Midwest, noting that the good press that characterized the region as the most vital, vigorous, moral, mature, and, most important, American part of the nation peaked around 1920. Conversely, the image of the Midwest as parochial, conventional, and culturally backward reached its nadir around 1950 (39).

Shortridge's project was to examine how the regional identity of the Midwest changed over time. He argued that the region, despite its urban components, has always had a strongly pastoral identity and that Americans' changing attitudes toward pastoralism were reflected in their changing attitudes toward the Midwest. As pastoralism came to suggest a region that no longer conjured up the agrarian ideal but rather what Lewis referred to in *Main Street* as a bewildered empire, the image of the Midwest declined. As Shortridge saw it, *Main Street,* the most popular revolt-from-the-village book, "shook the twin pillars of Middle-western cultural identity" (46).

Lewis's best seller, as well as other books classified under the revolt-from-the-village rubric, encouraged readers from the more culturally advanced East to treat the Midwest hegemonically. *Winesburg, Ohio,* for example, was well received, but the condescending tone of Paul Rosenfeld's encomium of Sherwood Anderson's artistry, published in the *DIAL* in 1922 and reprinted in David D. Anderson's *Critical Essays on Sherwood Anderson,* reflects his perceived position of cultural superiority: "The quaint little mushroom-like heads of Anderson's tales, the unedu-

cated, the undignified village dreamers, with their queer hops and springs, straggly speech, ineffectual large gestures, they are the little mis-shapen humans in this towering machine-noisy inhuman land, the aged infants grown a little screw-loose with inarticulateness" (*Critical Essays on Sherwood Anderson* 82). Earlier in the essay Rosenfeld had praised Anderson's skillful use of language but had personified his words as quaint, small-town Midwesterners: "Aprons and overalls they still wear, for they are working-words. . . . They leave us freshened as gingham-clad country girls driving past in a buggy do. If they are a little old and a little weary, they hold themselves like certain old folk who wear threadbare shawls and shiny black trousers, and still make their self-regard felt by their port" (75).

Contemporary critics such as David Jordan, Edward M. Watts, Roberto Dainotto, Judith Fetterley, and Marjorie Pryse have taken a postcolonial approach to the relationship of region to nation, demonstrating the ways in which the internal region has been viewed as marginalized space subject to the cultural hegemony of the East. The latest of these, Ryan Poll, situates his discussion of the small town within the context of globalization. In *Main Street and Empire* (2012) he challenges essentialist notions of the small town as an icon of national identity that signifies stability, security, and community, and he analyzes its ideological function in furthering the spread of U.S. power and of global capitalism and conceptualizes the revolt from the village as a modernist critique of this ideological function.

Although Van Doren never formally defined the literary movement he heralded in 1921, he sounded a note that resonated throughout scholarly discussions of the Midwest and shaped subsequent notions of Midwestern literary identity throughout the twentieth century and beyond. Those who deny that there ever was a revolt from the village must certainly concede that the term has taken on a life of its own, much as have "political correctness" and "cultural literacy," however much one may disagree with the way these terms are used or the political positions they invoke. Although some nonnative observers may have eagerly embraced the revolt from the village to show their eastern sophistication or disavowal of middle-class values, it cannot be denied that much negativity exists in the early twentieth-century literature of the small-town Midwest. Moreover, the escape and estrangement motifs that dominate the classic novels of revolt continue to be prevalent in works by such contemporary Midwestern authors as JANE HAMILTON (b.1957), GARY EDWARD KEILLOR (b.1942), writing as Garrison Keillor, DAN GERBER (b.1940), JON (FRANCIS) HASSLER (1933–2008), and Jonathan Franzen (b. 1959), suggesting that these themes, if not essential elements of the Midwestern identity, have been enduring aspects of the way it has been constructed over the past century.

SELECTED WORKS: The big three revolt-from-the-village books that were emphasized in Van Doren's 1921 essay and that have garnered the most critical attention are Edgar Lee Masters's *Spoon River Anthology* (1915), Sherwood Anderson's *Winesburg, Ohio* (1919), and Sinclair Lewis's *Main Street* (1920). These authors' responses to Van Doren's characterization of their works can be found in August Derleth's *Three Literary Men* (1963), which contains his interviews with Masters, Anderson, and Lewis.

Readers wishing to experience other "revolt" books are directed to three novels: Willa Cather's *The Song of the Lark* (1915), Floyd Dell's *Moon-Calf* (1920), and Zona Gale's *Miss Lulu Bett* (1920). Early twentieth-century books that construct a more positive image of the rural Midwest include Zona Gale's *Friendship Village* (1908); Theodore Dreiser's *A Hoosier Holiday* (1916, republished by Indiana University Press in 1997); and Meredith Nicholson's *The Valley of Democracy* (1918).

Readers who wish to investigate the literary roots of the movement are directed to Edward Eggleston's *The Hoosier School-Master* (1871), *The Paper City* (1879) by DAVID ROSS LOCKE (1833–1888), E. W. Howe's *The Story of a Country Town* (1883), Joseph Kirkland's *Zury: The Meanest Man in Spring County* (1887), the stories in Hamlin Garland's MAIN-TRAVELLED ROADS (1891), and Theodore Dreiser's *Sister Carrie* (1900). Contemporary twists on the revolt theme can be seen in the following novels: Jon Hassler's *Grand Opening* (1987), Jane Hamilton's *A Map of the World* (1994), Garrison's Keillor's *Wobegon Boy*

(1997), and Jonathan Franzen's *The Corrections* (2001), as well as in Dan Gerber's collection of stories *Grass Fires* (1987).

FURTHER READING: Any scholar interested in the revolt from the village must begin with the writings of Carl Van Doren. His seminal essay "The Revolt from the Village: 1920," *Nation* 113 (October 12, 1921): 407–12, which is part of his series on contemporary American novelists, is required reading. Other essential readings are his essay "On Hating the Provinces," in *The Roving Critic* (1923), and his *Sinclair Lewis: A Biographical Sketch with a Bibliography by Harvey Taylor* (1933). Particularly interesting is his autobiography, *Three Worlds* (1936). Contemporaries of Van Doren who also critiqued the Midwestern village are George Jean Nathan and H. L. Mencken in *The American Credo: A Contribution toward the Interpretation of the National Mind* (1920) and Van Wyck Brooks in his collection of essays *Letters and Leadership* (1918) and "The Literary Life in America (1927), reprinted in *America's Coming-of-Age* (1958). Brooks's *The Ordeal of Mark Twain* (1920) also points to the village as a cause of cultural malaise.

A somewhat different slant on the cultural revolt discussed by Van Doren can be found in T. K. Whipple's *Spokesmen* (1928); Paul Rosenfeld's review of *Winesburg, Ohio,* reprinted in David D. Anderson's 1981 collection *Critical Essays on Sherwood Anderson;* Henry F. May's *The End of American Innocence* (1959); and K. Narayana Chandran's essay "Revolt from the Grave: *Spoon River Anthology* by Edgar Lee Masters," *Midwest Quarterly* 29.4 (Summer 1988): 438–47.

Significant treatments of the revolt from the village that reflect Van Doren's essay are Dorothy Dondore's *The Prairie and the Making of Middle America* (1926), Russell Blankenship's *American Literature as an Expression of the National Mind* (1931), Harlan Hatcher's *Creating the Modern American Novel* (1935), Ima Honaker Herron's *The Small Town in American Literature* (1939), and Ludwig Lewisohn's *The Story of American Literature* (1939).

Scholars who continued to pursue a line of inquiry into the revolt-from-the-village phenomenon similar to Van Doren's at mid-century are Alfred Kazin in *On Native Grounds* (1942), Frederick J. Hoffman in *The Twenties* (1955), Robert Spiller and others in

The Literary History of the United States (1948), Henry Steele Commager in *The American Mind* (1950), Arthur Hobson Quinn in *The Literature of the American People* (1951), and John Flanagan in his essay "Literary Protest in the Midwest," *Southwest Review* 34.2 (Spring 1949): 148–57.

Scholars in the second half of the twentieth century who continued to discuss the revolt from the village are Robert B(ingham) Downs in *Famous American Books* (1971), Roy W. Meyer in *The Middle Western Farm Novel in the Twentieth Century* (1965), George F. Day in *A Literary History of the American West* (1987), and Ronald Weber in *The Midwestern Ascendancy in American Writing* (1992).

Two scholars sought to locate the revolt's beginning in the literature of the nineteenth century: Philip H. Ford in his essay "Evidence of a Revolt from the Village in the Eighteen Nineties," *West Virginia University Bulletin* 10 (1956): 40–54, and Diane Dufva Quantic in her 1971 Kansas State University dissertation "Anticipations of the Revolt from the Village in Nineteenth Century Middle Western Fiction" and her essay "The Revolt from the Village and Middle Western Fiction, 1870–1915," *Kansas Quarterly* 5.6 (1973): 5–16. Others attempted to define or refine the notion of the revolt from the village more precisely. These include Thomas Tanselle in "Sinclair Lewis and Floyd Dell: Two Views of the Midwest," *Twentieth-Century Literature* 9 (1964): 175–84; Anthony Channell Hilfer in *The Revolt from the Village, 1915–1930* (1969); Park Dixon Goist in *From Main Street to State Street: Town, City and Community in America* (1977) and "Community and Self in the Midwest Town: Floyd Dell's *Moon-Calf*," *MidAmerica* 2 (1975): 88–92; and Charles Wordell in "The Revolt from the Village and the Exquisites: Carl Van Vechten's *The Tattooed Countess*," *Chu-Shikoku Studies in American Literature* 20 (1984): 5–18.

Two major attacks on the notion of the revolt from the village as a legitimate literary movement were launched in the 1970s by Barry Gross and David D. Anderson. Gross published "In Another Country: The Revolt from the Village," *MidAmerica* 4 (1977): 101–11, and "The Revolt That Wasn't," *CEA Critic* 39.2 (January 1977): 4–8. Anderson questioned the notion of a literary revolt from the village in three main essays: "The Mid-

western Town in Midwestern Fiction," *MidAmerica* 6 (1979): 27–43: "The Search for a Living Past," in *Sherwood Anderson: Centennial Studies*, edited by Hilbert Campbell and Charles E. Modlin (212–23); and "Sherwood Anderson and the Critics," in David Anderson's *Critical Essays on Sherwood Anderson* (1981). 1–17. See also John and Margaret Wrenn's "'T. M.': The Forgotten Muse of Sherwood Anderson and Edgar Lee Masters," in *Sherwood Anderson: Centennial Studies*, listed previously, 175–83.

Since then, the revolt debate has continued, mainly in essays such as Margaret Stuhr's "The Safe Middle West: Escape to and Escape from Home," *MidAmerica* 14 (1987): 18–27; Stephen Enniss's "The Implied Community of *Winesburg, Ohio*," *Old Northwest* 11.2 (Spring–Summer 1985): 51–60; Matts Västå's "The Ambiguities of the Escape Theme in Midwestern Literature, 1918–1934," *MidAmerica* 26 (1999): 49–76; and Jon Gjerde's "Middleness and the Middle West," in *The American Midwest: Essays on Regional History* (2001), edited by Andrew R. L. Cayton and Susan E. Gray, 180–95. See also David Holman's *A Certain Slant of Light: Regionalism and the Form of Southern and Midwestern Fiction* (1995), John Hallwas's introduction to his 1992 edition of *Spoon River Anthology*, and Tom Lutz's chapter "The Revolt from the Village: Anderson, Lewis, Suckow," in his *Cosmopolitan Vistas: American Regionalism and Literary Value* (2004).

Postcolonial perspectives include James Shortridge's *The Middle West: Its Meaning in American Culture* (1989); David M. Jordan's *New World Regionalism: Literature in the Americas* (1994); Roberto Dainotto's "'All the Regions Do Smilingly Revolt,'" *Critical Inquiry* 22.3 (1996): 486–505; Edward Watts's *An American Colony: Regionalism and the Roots of Midwestern Culture* (2002); and Judith Fetterley and Marjorie Pryse's *Writing Out of Place: Regionalism, Women, and American Literary Culture* (2003). Two analyses of the revolt from the village are offered in Ryan Poll's *Main Street and Empire: The Fictional Small Town in the Age of Globalization* (2012) and Jon K. Lauck's "The Myth of the Midwestern 'Revolt from the Village'" *MidAmerica* 40 (2013): 39–85.

MARCIA NOE

THE UNIVERSITY OF TENNESSEE AT CHATTANOOGA

RIVER LITERATURE

OVERVIEW: Many works of Midwestern nonfiction, fiction, and poetry portray the aesthetic, practical, and metaphoric value of rivers. The Ohio and Missouri Rivers help define the boundaries of the Midwest, and through the central Midwest runs the Mississippi, a prime focus of Midwestern river literature. Early European explorers closely described the rivers they traveled. Nineteenth-century Midwesterners surveyed further and deepened their insights into the rivers of their particular locales. See also EXPLORATION ACCOUNTS. *Life on the Mississippi* (1883) and *ADVENTURES OF HUCKLEBERRY FINN* (London 1884; New York 1885) by SAMUEL LANGHORNE CLEMENS (1835–1910), writing as Mark Twain, with their expansive and heady views of the magnificent river, helped raise the Mississippi to international literary eminence. Contemporary writers continue to explore the ongoing condition and significance of the Mississippi and other rivers, often attempting mythic themes and dramatic means to explore the sheer mystery and exuberance of life on Midwestern waters.

HISTORY AND SIGNIFICANCE: The first important European accounts of Midwestern rivers are the journals kept by French explorers. In 1661, for example, Pierre-Esprit Radisson (1636–1710) ascended the St. Mary's River, which drains Lake Superior to Lake Huron, with Médard des Groseilliers (1618–1696). In his *Voyages* (1885), edited by Gideon D. Scull, Radisson describes the rapids at what became Sault Ste. Marie, MICHIGAN, as well as the surrounding country. Also notable is the journal kept by Father Jacques Marquette (1637–1675) of his 1673 expedition with Louis Joliet (1645–1700) from St. Ignace via Lake Michigan, the Fox River, and the Wisconsin River to the Mississippi. See "The Mississippi Voyage of Jolliet and Marquette" in *Early Narratives of the Northwest, 1634–1699* (1917), edited by Louis P. Kellogg, 221–58. See also GREAT LAKES LITERATURE.

Among explorers of the early American republic, Meriwether Lewis (1774–1809) and William Clark (1770–1838) contributed their *History of the Expedition under the Command of Captains Lewis and Clark, to the Sources of the Missouri, Thence across the Rocky Mountains and down the River Columbia to the Pacific Ocean* (1814). Lewis and Clark recorded in fine detail, and sometimes with poetic flair, their observations of Indian cultures and of plant, animal, geographic, and geological phenomena along the route of the Corps of Discovery expedition they led to explore the lands of the Louisiana Purchase. Beginning in May 1804, they followed the entire course of the Missouri River from ST. LOUIS to the Great Falls in Montana. It did not take long for the Missouri's power to assert itself: on May 24 Clark wrote that the boat "passed a Verry bad part of the River called the Deavels race ground, this is where the Current sets against Some projecting rocks for half a mile on the Labd. Side. . . . We attempted to pass up under the Lbd. Bank which was falling in So fast . . . The Swiftness of the Current wheeled the boat, broke our Toe rope, and was nearly over Setting the boat" (the definitive Nebraska edition of the *Journals,* painstakingly edited under the direction of Gary E. Moulton, is now available online). The expedition continued across mountains to the Columbia River and the Pacific coast and then retraced its route, returning to St. Louis twenty-eight months later, the crew's sense of the Midwest having been sharpened by their knowledge of the different climates, terrains, and ecosystems to the west.

Later American explorers, most notably Zebulon Montgomery Pike (1779–1813) and HENRY ROWE SCHOOLCRAFT (1793–1864), also chronicled their Midwestern river travels. Pike's account is found in *Exploratory Travels through the Western Territories of North America: Comprising a Voyage from St. Louis, on the Mississippi, to the Source of That River . . .* (1811). Schoolcraft, a self-taught ethnographer, also transcribed indigenous stories, including river stories, in such works as *Narrative of an Expedition through the Upper Mississippi to Itasca Lake* (1834). Henry Wadsworth Longfellow (1807–1882) drew on these stories to produce *The Song of Hiawatha* (1855). A member of the party searching for the source of the Mississippi, Schoolcraft traveled northward on the Mississippi during 1832, the year of the Black Hawk War.

Recollections of the Last Ten Years, Passed in Occasional Residences and Journeyings in the Valley of the Mississippi (1826) by Timothy Flint

(1780–1840) records the struggles and accomplishments of frontier families, the Indian tribes, and aspects of Negro slavery they encountered and the Ohio, Mississippi, and Missouri Rivers they traveled. Flint's river observations are always acute, as in this comparison of the Ohio with the Mississippi: "The Ohio is calm and placid, and except when full, its waters are limpid to a degree. The face of the Mississippi is always turbid; the current every where sweeping and rapid; and it is full of singular boils. . . . The river seems always in wrath, tearing away the banks on one hand with gigantic fury, with all their woods, to deposit the spoils in another place" (87).

German Prince Maximilian von Wied (1782–1867) traveled up the Missouri River for scientific purposes with Karl (Charles) Bodmer (1809–1893), the Swiss artist generally acknowledged as the painter of the best of the early contact Indian scenes and portraits. Maximilian's account was published in German in 1839–1841, followed by an English translation, *Travels in the Interior of North America in the Years 1832–1834*, in 1843.

LIFE OF MA-KA-TAI-ME-SHE-KIA-KIAK, OR BLACK HAWK (1833) was written by BLACK HAWK (1767–1838) to defend his refusal to relinquish Sauk land. Although Black Hawk had to work through a translator and editor, his story is told in the first person and is thus the first indigenous American AUTOBIOGRAPHY. In this work Black Hawk highlights the advantages of traditional life in Saukenuk, the Sauk village at the site of present-day Rock Island. He also describes the flight of his band from the ILLINOIS militia and the U.S. Army. The band followed the Rock River toward Lake Koshkonong. Sensing defeat and weary and hungry, they turned west and followed the Wisconsin River to the Mississippi, giving up their hopes of settling again in Saukenuk. But their attempts to surrender went unrecognized. Attacked by both the army pursuing them and a Mississippi River steamboat guarding the river, many Sauk were killed as they tried to cross the Mississippi at its junction with the Bad Axe River. After a period of imprisonment, Black Hawk lived the remaining five years of his life with his people in southeast IOWA. When he died, he was buried near the Des Moines River. Written during this period,

this volume conveys a sense of the importance of rivers as boundary markers and as means of food, travel, and geographic orientation in the old Northwest.

In *Life on the Mississippi* (1883) Mark Twain refers to Black Hawk in a description of the upper river, but first he depicts virtually the entire length of the Mississippi. Unlike earlier exploration accounts, Twain is less concerned about documenting geographic detail than about weaving together facts of geography, history, and personal experience with opinion in an informal and personable narrative. The product of multiple trips on the most important river in the United States, *Life on the Mississippi* simultaneously portrays the river as an economic entity and as a powerful symbol of underlying characteristics of American life: movement, change, and the need for alertness and flexibility. Descriptive highlights of the book include Twain's account of his boyhood dreams to be a steamboatman and vivid memories of how the sleepy town of Hannibal came to life when the steamboats arrived from upstream and downstream. Twain portrays a sense of "the great Mississippi, the majestic, the magnificent Mississippi, rolling its mile-wide tide along, shining in the sun; the dense forest away on the other side" (28). Memorable too is Twain's account of the change that occurred in him when as a professional steamboatman he "had mastered the language of this water" and as a result had lost the innocent romance of the picturesque river: "A day came when I began to cease from noting the glories and the charms which the moon and the sun and the twilight wrought upon the river's face" (5). As a river pilot, he needed to translate aesthetic appreciation of the river's beauties into practical understanding of the flowing water's implications for safe navigation.

Twain eloquently examines the river's moods and mysteries in all his Mississippi River works. Of these, *Adventures of Huckleberry Finn* is the quintessential work of river literature, with the Mississippi functioning as setting, as symbol, and even perhaps as actor. Huckleberry Finn first enjoys freedom when he runs away to Jackson's Island in the middle of the river, where he finds Jim, who has fled from slavery and with whom he drifts down the river with the current.

La Crosse, Wisconsin, river scene, 1873.
Chromolithograph by George H. Ellsbury.
Image courtesy of the Library of Congress

Echoing his creator, Huck is occasionally eloquent in his descriptions of the beauty and serenity of the river and his observation that "it's lovely to live on a raft" (1996 Random House edition, 164). But the freedom of the river is complicated and compromised by the land values witnessed in the communities the river passes through, including thievery, cowardice, bigotry, class injustice, and slavery. Corruption even infects the river itself, as when the fleeing Duke and Dauphin commandeer Huck's raft and subjugate Huck and Jim. The search for freedom on the raft, as DAVID D(ANIEL) ANDERSON (1924–2011) concludes in the *Dictionary of Midwestern Literature*, volume 1, *The Authors* (2001), "is ultimately futile as rivers end and innocence is lost to experience" (115). The Mississippi River also plays an important role in Twain's *The Adventures of Tom Sawyer* (1876).

In his frequently anthologized early poem "The Negro Speaks of Rivers" (1921) LANGSTON (JAMES MERCER) HUGHES (1902–1967) assumes a collective voice for African Americans. The poem's speaker represents black history with symbolic images of African rivers (the Euphrates, the Congo, and the Nile) and the Mississippi as viewed near St. Louis. "The Negro Speaks of Rivers" was included in Hughes's first book, THE WEARY BLUES (1926).

T(HOMAS) S(TEARNS) ELIOT (1888–1965) also used the Mississippi River as a symbol. In "The Dry Salvages" (1941), one part of *Four Quartets* (1943), he alludes to the Mississippi in referring to the river as "a strong, brown god," a force within us. Insofar as it represents time, it is destructive (21).

Later, the Mississippi River figures in *Thomas and Beulah* (1986), a collection of poems by RITA DOVE (b. 1952). Most of these poems are set in Akron, OHIO, and that industrial landscape dominates the present, but the collection opens with a poem set on the Mississippi River. The pull of the river persists throughout Thomas's life and even affects Beulah, although she has no such direct river experience.

Another contemporary writer whose work evokes the Mississippi River is Winona LaDuke (b. 1959), a Los Angeles–born writer and a political, environmental, and American Indian rights activist, as well as an enrolled Ojibwa tribal member. Her novel *Last Standing Woman* (1997) is set on the White Earth Reservation, just west of the headwaters of the Mississippi River. It concludes joyfully with the tribal ancestors being reburied overlooking the Mississippi.

Mississippi downriver adventures, often solo performances, are ubiquitous and frequently emphasize the colorful characters populating the river's shores. Eddy L. Harris (b. 1956), a nonfiction writer, was living in St. Louis when he canoed the length of the Mississippi River. The result was *Mississippi Solo: A River Quest* (1988), which provides a thorough view of the river and its environs. Northern sections of the Mississippi were still wild and relatively untraveled, especially in the late fall, when Harris began his trip. His work describes the difficulties and delays involved with passing through the locks that make the upper river navigable, recounts the dangers of sharing a river with huge barges, and details economic and social conditions in river towns, including Clemens's Hannibal. An African American, Harris also reflects on the impact of race and racism on his river experience. He explores and exemplifies the American competitive spirit and reflects the Midwestern values of friendliness and compassion. *Mississippi Solo* thus provides an alternative ending to that of *Huckleberry Finn*. Rather than lighting out for the territory, Harris ends by toasting the river and returning to St. Louis.

Several other authors have penned Mississippi downriver accounts. Clarence Jonk (1906–1987) wrote *River Journey* (1964), which details the spirited author's Depression-era adventures in building a makeshift rudderless houseboat and attempting to take it to New Orleans, although Jonk did not get far before winter set in and ice gathered around him. Another such work is *Old Man River and Me: One Man's Journey down the Mighty Mississippi* (1998) by Mark A. Knudsen (b. 1939), which chronicles his trip from St. Paul (see MINNEAPOLIS/ST. PAUL) down the Mississippi on a motorized johnboat. An earlier account by an international writer, Jonathan Raban (b. 1942), is found in *Old Glory: A Voyage down the Mississippi* (1981), detailing a trip in a sixteen-foot motorboat.

In addition to personal accounts of one-time downriver trips, many memoirs and recollections of life on the Mississippi River exist. Two of these are *Old Times on the Upper Mississippi: The Recollections of a Steamboat Pilot from 1854 to 1868* (1909) by George Byron Merrick (1841–1931) and the humorous *My Life on the Mississippi; or, Why I Am Not Mark Twain* (1973) by RICHARD PIKE BISSELL (1913–1977). The latter includes a selective, lightly annotated bibliography of Mississippi River books. Bissell also wrote an autobiographical novel, *A Stretch on the River* (1950), concerning adventures on a Mississippi towboat.

A fine survey of Mississippi River lore appears in *Voices on the River: The Story of the Mississippi Waterways* (1964) by WALTER (EDWIN) HAVIGHURST (1901–1994). The book focuses on stories of the Mississippi River and the many rivers feeding it. Havighurst, born and reared in the Fox River valley city of Appleton, WISCONSIN, gained a sense of the importance of rivers as a child. The prologue presents an overview of the unique personalities who knew and made history on the Mississippi River and its branches. The extensive bibliography provides valuable sources for further research.

Given its centrality in American history and geography, the Mississippi River is the most important river in the United States. The upper river is essential to the Midwest, but the mystique of other Midwestern rivers is also explored in many literary works. For example, in addition to the numerous Mississippi downriver accounts, many works describe canoe trips on other rivers. Among these is *Canoeing with the Cree* (1935) by (Arnold) ERIC SEVAREID (1912–1992). This volume

recounts a youthful adventure in 1930 with a friend traveling the Red River of the North to Hudson Bay in Canada. *Dismal River* (1990) by Ron Block (b. 1955) is a book-length narrative poem about canoeing a Nebraska river. *The Drownt Boy: An Ozark Tale* (1994) by Art Homer (b. 1951) is the story of the poet's journey with his son on the flooded Current River in MISSOURI.

Other works of memorable river travels include *River Horse: The Logbook of a Boat across America* (1999) by WILLIAM LEAST HEAT-MOON (William Lewis Trogdon) (b. 1939), recounting his journey across the United States via America's inland waterways. The early stages of the trip took him and his crew from the Hudson River in New York through the Erie Canal to the Allegheny, Ohio, Mississippi, and Missouri Rivers. He reached the Missouri just as floods were about to crest, a sight he found intimidating but fascinating.

The poems of JAMES WRIGHT (1927–1980) often grieve for the former beauty of the now-polluted Ohio River. In "One Last Look at the Adige: Verona in the Rain," for example, this beautiful Italian river makes Wright think that "The Ohio must have looked / Something like this / To the people who loved it / Long before I was born" (284). In many other poems also found in *Above the River: The Complete Poems* (1990), especially those that originally appeared in the collection *Shall We Gather at the River* (1968), Wright often evokes rivers from his memory, as in "Living by the Red River," "The River down Home," and "Lifting Illegal Nets by Flashlight." In "Rip" he writes, "Close by a big river, I am alive in my own country, / I am home again" (162) suggesting the importance of rivers to his sense of identity.

For TONI MORRISON (b. CHLOE ARDELIA WOFFORD, 1931), the Ohio River is not so much a personal symbol as a social and political one. *Beloved* (1987), set in Ohio with flashbacks to slavery in Kentucky, presents the Ohio River as a crossable boundary between slavery and freedom. Over a century earlier, in *Uncle Tom's Cabin* (1852), Harriet Beecher Stowe (1811–1896) had invested the Ohio with a similar meaning.

For AUGUST (WILLIAM) DERLETH (1909–1971), born and raised in Sauk City, Wisconsin, the Wisconsin River provided an essential sense of place. His book *The*

Wisconsin: River of a Thousand Isles (1942) is a noteworthy entry in the Rivers of America series. Derleth includes lumberjack songs and stories and lists the best sources for descriptions of the Wisconsin River and life along its banks. For portraits of the river in his books, Derleth lists *Wind over Wisconsin* (1938), *Restless Is the River* (1939), *Sweet Genevieve* (1942), and *Bright Journey* (1955).

Midwestern forester, naturalist, and leader of the American ecological movement ALDO LEOPOLD (1887–1948) grew up on the Mississippi. *A SAND COUNTY ALMANAC* (1949) focuses on the same region as Derleth's work but puts stronger emphasis on the flora and fauna of the region and on concerns about the relationships between humans and the natural world. ZONA GALE (1874–1938) was foremost among the other writers Derleth cited as contributing to the literature of the Wisconsin River. Gale's work focuses on Portage, Wisconsin, her hometown, located between the Fox and the Wisconsin Rivers. Her writing emphasizes the community-centered values of the town. Derleth mentions Gale's *Papa La Fleur* (1933) as her work with the greatest focus on the river.

The Missouri River has also presented writers with significant subject matter. In *The River and I* (1910), for example, JOHN G(NEISENAU) NEIHARDT (1881–1973) details his trip down the Missouri River from Great Falls, Montana, to Sioux City, Iowa. In *Peace like a River* (2001), the first novel by Leif L. Enger (b. 1961), the Missouri serves as a literal and figurative dividing line separating the scene of Davey Land's crime at his home east of the river from the wilder Dakota badlands where he finds places to hide from the lawmen pursuing him.

The Grass Dancer (1994) by Susan Power (b. 1961) is set near the Missouri River on the Standing Rock Sioux Reservation straddling the border between NORTH DAKOTA and SOUTH DAKOTA. Here the river is a place of history and a source of imaginative power. The Missouri River also inspires Nebraska-born poet, novelist, and editor MICHAEL ANANIA (b. 1939). "Stops along the Western Bank of the Missouri River" in *The Color of Dust* (1970) and "The Riversongs of Arion" in *Riversongs* (1978) are two sequences of his poems that are especially successful in conveying closely observed river details and history in a personal voice and spare style.

In Illinois, JOHN (IGNATIUS) KNOEPFLE (b. 1923) deepened his interest in Midwestern rivers in the process of researching the history of Midwestern settlement and taping contemporary rivermen. His masterwork, *poems from the sangamon* (1985), is imbued with a keen sense of river life and exemplifies how myth and history can serve as a basis for poetry. EDGAR LEE MASTERS (1868–1950), best known for his *SPOON RIVER ANTHOLOGY* (1915), also wrote *The Sangamon* (1942), another work in the Rivers of America series. This volume combines family history with the life of the river in west central Illinois.

Michigan rivers figure in the early short stories of ERNEST (MILLER) HEMINGWAY (1899–1961). "Big Two-Hearted River" was written after a fishing trip on the Big and Little Fox Rivers in Michigan's Upper Peninsula. Along with the other Nick Adams stories published in *IN OUR TIME* (1925), this work conveys a deep sense of the region. For THEODORE ROETHKE (1908–1963), Michigan's Tittabawassee River provides a setting and evokes themes in poems such as "Moss Gathering" and the title poem in *THE LOST SON and Other Poems* (1948). Roethke returns to the Saginaw Valley of Michigan in such later poems as "Meditation at Oyster River." Among the best poems of another Michigan writer, JIM (JAMES THOMAS) HARRISON (1937–2016), are those in his collection *The Theory and Practice of Rivers* (1985). The title poem is partly set, like Hemingway's story and Harrison's novels *Wolf* (1971) and *Sundog* (1984), on rivers in Michigan's Upper Peninsula. Harrison explores themes similar to Hemingway's, especially the exploration of wild rivers as a spiritual exercise. The influence of both Hemingway and Harrison is evident in *Platte River* (1994), a collection of three novellas by Rick Bass (b. 1958). The protagonist of the title novella, a former football player from Montana, experiences a fleeting sense of grace while fishing with friends on Michigan's scenic Platte River, near Traverse City. *Once upon a River* (2011) by Bonnie Jo Campbell (b. 1962) treats a fictional tributary of Michigan's Kalamazoo River almost as a character in itself, describing both its wild and its polluted sections

BONNIE JO CAMPBELL
AUTHOR OF THE NATIONAL BOOK AWARD FINALIST
AMERICAN SALVAGE

ONCE
UPON A
RIVER

A NOVEL

Bonnie Jo Campbell's *Once upon a River*, 2011.
© W. W. Norton & Company. Reprinted by permission
of W. W. Norton & Company

River (1985) by John Madson (1923–1995). Madson's book is of particular interest for its often humorous exploration of human and animal denizens of the upper Mississippi, as well as "the moods of the River—its character and temper in starlight and storm, on August afternoons when water and sun flow together like molten brass . . . and transition seasons of gentleness and beauty: that special world of mud, scour holes, wild orchids, yorky nuts and fine pearls, of crowfoot bars, trammel nets and heron rookeries" (25).

SELECTED WORKS: Mark Twain's *Adventures of Huckleberry Finn* (1884, 1885) is the most celebrated work of Midwestern and American river literature. It is Midwestern in authorship and setting but international in its acclaim. Ernest Hemingway helped secure its supreme importance when he asserted that Twain's book was the beginning of American literature. Twain's place as the premier writer of river literature is enhanced by his nonfiction work *Life on the Mississippi* (1883). Eddie L. Harris's *Mississippi Solo* (1988) provides a twentieth-century counterpart to Twain's work. A notable overview is found in Walter Havighurst's *Voices on the River: The Story of the Mississippi Waterways* (1964). August Derleth's *Wisconsin: River of a Thousand Isles* (1942) and Edgar Lee Masters's *The Sangamon* (1942) are excellent on secondary but important Midwestern rivers. William Least Heat-Moon's *River Horse* (1999) is a more contemporary work detailing three important Midwestern rivers.

James Wright is among the poets for whom Midwestern rivers serve as important images and symbols. Wright's many poems evocative of rivers as geographic realities and memories are found in *Above the River: The Complete Poems* (1990). The works of other Midwestern poets significantly reflecting on rivers include Theodore Roethke in *The Lost Son and Other Poems* (1948), Michael Anania in *The Color of Dust* (1970) and *Riversongs* (1978), John Knoepfle in *poems from the sangamon* (1985), Jim Harrison in *The Theory and Practice of Rivers* (1985), and Rita Dove in *Thomas and Beulah* (1986). Midwestern novelists who emphasize rivers and river metaphors include Zona Gale in *Papa La Fleur* (1933), August Derleth in several novels, including *Restless Is the River* (1939), and Toni Morrison in *Beloved* (1987).

with poetic intensity. Set in the 1970s, the novel follows a teenage girl from a broken family as she takes to the river by boat, surviving by hunting and fishing as she searches for the mother who abandoned her.

Finally, in addition to NEBRASKA works by Neihardt and Ron Block previously noted, Paul A(ustin) Johnsgard (b. 1931), a naturalist and prolific writer with a graceful style, brings his keen scientific eye to describing two of Nebraska's rivers in *The Platte: Channels in Time* (1984) and *The Niobrara: A River Running through Time* (2007).

A few other publication highlights, replete with anecdotes and river lore, include *A-Rafting on the Mississippi* (1928), by Charles Edward Russell (1860–1941), an account of the logging and lumber industry on the upper Mississippi in the nineteenth century; *Steamboating on the Upper Mississippi, the Water Way to Iowa: Some River History* (1937) by William. J. Petersen (1901–1989); and *Up on the*

FURTHER READING: The books about Midwestern rivers in the Rivers of America series are foundational. They provide accounts of regional history and culture from the advent of European exploration through their dates of publication. The series consists of sixty-five volumes published between 1937 and 1974, each concentrating on one river and including illustrations by well-known artists. In addition to Derleth's book on the Wisconsin River and Masters's on the Sangamon, the series includes books on many Midwestern rivers: *The Upper Mississippi* (1938) by Walter Havighurst, *The Wabash* (1940) by William E. Wilson (1906–1988), *The Illinois* (1940) by James Gray (1899–1985), *The Kaw* (1941) by Floyd Benjamin Streeter (1888–1956), *The Chicago* (1942) by HARRY HANSEN (1884–1977), *The Missouri* (1945) by Stanley Vestal (1877–1957), *The Ohio* (1949) by R(ichard) E(lwell) Banta (1912–1977), *The Minnesota* (1962) by Evan Jones (1915–1996), and *The St. Croix: Midwest Border River* (1965) by James Taylor Dunn (1912–2002). Aimed at a wide audience, this series presents river history written from many personal perspectives. Often these volumes refer to or include short pieces of river-region folk literature and serve to make accessible materials that might otherwise be lost. The books of the series tend, however, to present the immigrant viewpoint as if it were universal and to refer to indigenous people in stereotypical terms. Gender bias in the language also marks several of these volumes as needing reediting.

Good backgrounds to literary study of Midwestern rivers begin with Reuben Gold Thwaites's (1853–1913) seventy-three-volume edition of *The Jesuit Relations and Allied Documents* (1896–1901), detailing the extent of French exploration in the new country in the seventeenth century. Also important is *The Definitive Journals of Lewis and Clark* (1983–2001) in thirteen volumes, edited by Gary E. Moulton. The set published by the University of Nebraska Press (1983–2001) includes documents either unknown or unavailable in earlier editions. Moulton's one-volume abridgment of this work, *The Lewis and Clark Journals: An American Epic of Discovery* (2003), provides a more compact account produced with the same scholarly care. The discoveries of Marquette and Jo-

liet are found in *An Account of the Discovery of Some New Countries and Nations in North America, in 1673, by Père Marquette and Sieur Joliet: Tr. from the French* (1850). Another important source is *Travels in the Interior of North America in the Years 1832–1834* by Prince Maximilian von Wied, including the superb paintings of Karl Bodmer. This work has often been reproduced in part. The definitive edition edited by Stephen S. Witte and Marsha V. Gallagher saw completion in 2012 with the publication by the University of Oklahoma Press of the third volume in a three-volume set, the culmination of a fifty-year project.

The bibliography of books on the Mississippi River is vast and multifaceted. *A Treasury of Mississippi River Folklore: Stories, Ballads, and Folkways of the Mid-American River Country* (1955), edited by Benjamin A. Botkin, features not only the Mississippi but also the Missouri, the Ohio, and other tributaries. A good source suggesting further reading is *The Mississippi River Reader* (1962), edited by WRIGHT MORRIS (1910–1998). The volume is a collection of short works and selections from longer works about the Mississippi River from the early European explorers through Mark Twain, (HAROLD) HART CRANE (1899–1932), and Scott Joplin (ca. 1867–1917). In his introduction, Morris emphasizes the Mississippi as a symbol of the American imagination. Contemporary evidence that interest in the Mississippi is still robust is found in the anthology *Big River Reader: Stories about the People, Wildlife and History of the Upper Mississippi River* (2003), edited by Pamela Eyden, Molly McGuire, and Reggie McLeod; all selections in this book were originally published in *Big River*, a magazine still in publication.

An interesting study by Michael Allen looks back to the Midwest in a crucial century of professional river travel: *Western Rivermen, 1763–1861: Ohio and Mississippi Boatmen and the Myth of the Alligator Horse* (1990). Informed by his love of river life, his extensive research on primary accounts of historic rivermen, including Mike Fink (ca. 1770–ca. 1823), the celebrated river braggart, and his own four-year experience working on various rivers, Allen presents an engaged and empathetic account.

Currents of Change: Art and Life along the Mississippi River, 1850–1861 (2004), compiled by Jason Busch, Christopher Monkhouse, and Janet Whitmore, resulted from an exhibition commemorating the 150th anniversary of the Grand Excursion in 1854 up the Mississippi after the completion of the first railroad to the Mississippi. In addition to the lavish illustrations, this volume includes an essay by Christopher Monkhouse on the impact of Longfellow's *Hiawatha* in defining this region. Another useful exhibition book is the profusely illustrated *Mississippi Panorama* (1950), edited by Perry T. Rathbone. This volume also includes works of art from the Missouri River and discussions of the scrolled Mississippi River panorama phenomenon, focusing on the Dickeson-Egan panorama (1850).

Although rivers are featured in the works of many Midwestern writers, critical studies of these writers are generally organized on other bases. As a result, no book-length studies approach the literature from this perspective. William Barillas's *The Midwestern Pastoral: Place and Landscape in Literature of the American Heartland* (2006) begins with a river-centered personal background statement, a lyrical account of childhood explorations along the Flint River and the undeveloped areas near his suburban Flint, Michigan, home. This book provides an excellent theoretical starting point in its first chapter's analysis of the complex components both of pastoralism and of concepts of the Midwest. The elements of nostalgia, utilitarianism, and Jeffersonian thought and policy are characteristic of much Midwestern river literature. Barillas also emphasizes literature's role in creating responsible relations between humans and the natural world. The most enduring Midwestern river literature takes on and works to fulfill just such a role.

In "The Midwest: Flowing against the Grid," a chapter in *America by Rivers* (1998), Tim Palmer surveys the region's rivers, commenting briefly on Midwestern writers and recounting a trip on the Minnesota River (111–36). Margaret Rozga argues in "Navigating the Mainstream: Metaphors and Multiethnic Literature," *MELUS* 30.2 (Summer 2005): 65–78, that the literature of the Mississippi River is worth studying as a significant and multicultural body of works. T. S. McMillin, a professor at Oberlin College in Ohio, provides both theoretical and personal perspectives in *The Meaning of Rivers: Flow and Reflection in American Literature* (2011).

MARGARET ROZGA

UNIVERSITY OF WISCONSIN–WAUKESHA

RURAL LITERATURE.
See Farm Literature

S

SALONS.
See Clubs, Salons, and Societies

SAND COUNTY ALMANAC, A

HISTORY: Few works of American literature have had the global impact of *A Sand
County Almanac* (1949) by ALDO LEOPOLD
(1887–1948). Part natural history, part philosophical exploration, and part radical manifesto, the text begins as a series of natural
history essays detailing Leopold's rehabilitation of a worn-out farm in central WISCON-
SIN and ends as a philosophical treatise calling for nothing short of complete realignment
of the ethical relationship between human
beings and nature.

Leopold was born on January 11, 1887,
in Burlington, IOWA, near the banks of the
Mississippi River. His boyhood was divided between the study of history and
literature inside the classroom and orni-
thology and woodlore outside. Hunting,
camping, and hiking trips across Iowa, IL-
LINOIS, and MICHIGAN inspired Leopold with
a passion for conservation as he tramped
the region's rapidly diminishing prairies
and river bottoms, seeing firsthand the
damaging effects of habitat destruction on
wildlife populations.

After earning a master's degree in for-
estry from Yale in 1909, Leopold entered
the U.S. Forest Service. His first job took him
to New Mexico, where he served for more
than a decade and in 1924 was instrumental
in establishing the Gila National Wilderness,
the nation's first official wilderness area. His
Midwestern roots drew him back to his home
region, however, and in 1924 he settled in
Madison, Wisconsin. There he continued to
work for the cause of conservation. Two early
publications, *Report on a Game Survey of the
North Central States* (1931) and *Game Management* (1933), drew heavily from field research
in the Midwest and established the author as
the nation's preeminent authority on wildlife conservation. As a result, in 1933 Leopold
was offered a position at the University of
Wisconsin in the nation's first graduate program in wildlife management.

In the spring of 1935, soon after his appointment at the university, Leopold purchased an abandoned, worn-out farm in
Sauk County on the banks of the Wisconsin
River for use as a deer-hunting camp. The
Leopold family renovated a run-down
chicken coop on the property and soon
called it their weekend home, dubbing it
"the Shack." The tract of abused land quickly

Aldo Leopold seated with his Shack in the background. Photo by Carl Leopold, ca. 1940.

Courtesy of the Aldo Leopold Foundation

became much more than a hunter's retreat. In the midst of the Dust Bowl, the depleted farm became a laboratory where Leopold could experiment with methods for reestablishing ecological health to a damaged landscape, and where he could endeavor to understand humanity's proper role in the natural world.

Leopold's experiences rehabilitating the land surrounding "the Shack" quickly found their way into his journals and published writings. Several of the sketches from the first section of *A Sand County Almanac* had been published earlier in slightly different versions in *Wisconsin Agriculturist and Farmer,* a regional farm newspaper, in the late 1930s and early 1940s. These include "Back from the Argentine," "Sky Dance," "The Geese Return," and others.

By 1941 Leopold planned to gather the essays into book form. Work on the project, including crafting additional essays, began in earnest. That year Leopold began correspondence with Alfred A. Knopf about the possibility of bringing out a collection of natural history essays with an ecological focus. The author worked steadily on the collection for the next three years, and in 1944 he sent a representative selection of the essays to Knopf and to the Macmillan Company. Macmillan summarily rejected the essays, almost without comment, within a week. Knopf was slightly more encouraging; but the editors there, too, rejected the work

in its current form. They worried that the collection's ecological concepts were too difficult for the lay reader and that the essays lacked a unity of tone: some were simple natural history essays, others ecological polemics. A prolonged correspondence about revision of the manuscript ensued between Leopold and Knopf, resulting in key changes in the book's tone and structure.

Leopold worked diligently to make the changes suggested by Knopf, and in September 1947 he submitted his revised manuscript, titled *Great Possessions.* Within two months, however, Knopf rejected Leopold's revision, still finding the book's ecological agenda too far-reaching. In March 1948 Leopold sent the manuscript to Oxford University Press, which accepted it a month later without critical comment.

Oxford's acceptance of the manuscript came only days before Leopold's death on April 21, 1948. The author's son, Luna Leopold, took over his father's work, along with several of Leopold's colleagues, and saw the project through its final editing. The publisher disliked the title *Great Possessions*, and the editorial team finally settled on calling Leopold's work *A Sand County Almanac.* The first Oxford edition was published in 1949, complemented by the simple but elegant wildlife art of Charles W. Schwartz on its cover and illustrating the text.

The book sold slowly in its initial printing, and in its first decade it realized sales of only about 20,000 copies. Although the book struck a chord within the conservation community, early reviewers in mainstream publications missed its philosophical and ethical points and found it to be little more than another collection of natural history essays.

SIGNIFICANCE: The most important contribution of *A Sand County Almanac* to American nature writing is its deft introduction of ecological concepts into the discussion of humanity's place in nature. Earlier writers who dealt with nature—Henry David Thoreau (1817–1862), as well as Leopold's fellow Midwesterners Liberty Hyde Bailey (1858–1954) and JOHN MUIR (1838–1914)— had intuited an intimate and interconnected relationship to the nonhuman world. Leopold, however, was able to use the emergent scientific discipline of ecology as the basis of his philosophical argument that each human should regard himself or herself as a "plain member and citizen" of a "land community" rather than a "conqueror" of nature (1966 Oxford edition (204).

Leopold's text is part of a tradition of American nature writing stretching back to Thoreau's *Walden* (1854), a tradition that blends an isolated narrator's first-person account of the workings of nature with broad social commentary. In both works a simplified, more nature-centered existence becomes the vehicle for a critique of an increasingly technological and misguided American society. Like Thoreau's earlier text, the first section of *A Sand County Almanac,* which contains the natural history essays that Leopold referred to as "the shack sketches," is arranged seasonally, compressing events observed over several years into a single calendar year (foreword).

As did Thoreau, Leopold illustrates his points with observations of the local landscape. An intimate sense of place is a hallmark of his writing; Leopold grounds many of his most complex ecological concepts in his daily meanderings on his farm and elsewhere in central Wisconsin. Thus, for example, his observation of the native prairie wildflower cutleaf silphium gives rise to a discussion of biodiversity, and the sawing and splitting of a single oak tree for firewood leads seamlessly into an engaging exploration of the concepts of forest succession, species extinction, and natural selection, all skillfully interwoven with a narrative of the Midwest's human history.

Leopold's work departs from the comfortable structure of seasonally sequenced natural history essays, however, in the book's second section, titled "Sketches Here and There." Linked to the shack sketches of the book's first section by the continuation of the key themes of nature's inherent value and the beauty of ecological wholeness, the second section explores environmental wreckage caused by human interference with natural systems. Recounting the mass draining of marshlands in Wisconsin, the extinction of the passenger pigeon in the Midwest, and his own role in the extirpation of wolves and grizzly bears in the Southwest, Leopold points out the root causes of environmental ruin: economic greed, anthropocentric hubris, and an educational

system badly out of step with the realities of nature.

In the book's final section, titled "The Upshot," Leopold addresses the ethical and philosophical changes he sees as necessary to reverse these losses. In the most ambitious and influential of the final essays, "The Land Ethic," Leopold calls for a radical rejection of land-use decisions based on economics and in their place suggests the extension of ethical consideration to all members of "the land-community" (204). Rather than evaluating interactions with nature in terms of human benefit, Leopold calls for a redefinition of proper conduct based on what is beneficial to the entire ecosystem: "A thing is right," he states, "when it tends to preserve the integrity, stability, and beauty of the entire biotic community. It is wrong when it tends otherwise" (224–25).

Although early critics may have missed the significance of these lines, later critics and environmentalists took note of Leopold's push toward a more biocentric view of the universe. *A Sand County Almanac* gained a broad readership during the 1960s and 1970s when it became a core text of the environmental movement. In 1978 Leopold was honored posthumously with the John Burroughs Medal for his accomplishments in the field of conservation, most notably in writing *A Sand County Almanac.* Often cited by experts in environmental ethics, public policy, game conservation, and ecological restoration, the book is also a standard high school and college text and a popular favorite among amateur naturalists.

What began as an introspective narrative of one man's interactions with 120 acres of the Wisconsin landscape has given rise to a number of ecologically grounded works steeped in a revitalized sense of place. Leopold's book has influenced many writers in the years since its publication. Among the most notable literary heirs of *A Sand County Almanac* are *Desert Solitaire* (1968) by Edward Abbey (1927–1989), *A Pilgrim at Tinker Creek* (1974) by Annie Dillard (b. 1945), and *Refuge: An Unnatural History of Family and Place* (1991) by Terry Tempest Williams (b. 1956). Midwestern nature writers directly influenced by Leopold and his book include PAUL GRUCHOW (1947–2004), Wes Jackson (b. 1936), Stephanie Mills (b. 1948), and SCOTT RUSSELL SANDERS (b. 1945).

IMPORTANT EDITIONS: The first edition of *A Sand County Almanac* was published by Oxford University Press in 1949. Several pieces from a second posthumously published collection of Aldo Leopold's essays, *Round River* (1953), were added to a second Oxford edition published in 1966, including "A Man's Leisure Time," "Goose Music," and "Natural History—The Forgotten Science." In 1970 Ballantine Books produced an inexpensive paperback version of the expanded second edition, a version of the text that has brought Leopold's words and ideas to millions of readers. Both the Oxford and Ballantine editions remain in print, but most scholars consider the Oxford edition the standard. Edited by Curt Meine and published by the Library of America, *A Sand County Almanac, and Other Writings on Ecology and Conservation* (2013) supplements the complete text with more than fifty additional writings, as well as photographs, drawings, and maps by Leopold and excerpts from his field journals. To date, Leopold's *A Sand County Almanac* has been published in twelve languages.

FURTHER READING: Leopold's other published writings often shed light on the ideas that ultimately converged to form *A Sand County Almanac*. His collection *Round River* (1953) includes selections from his journals dealing with many of the same conservation and land-use concerns explored in *A Sand County Almanac. For the Health of the Land: Previously Unpublished Essays and Other Writings* (1999), edited by J. Baird Callicott and Eric Freyfogle, offers readers a glimpse into Leopold's early writings on "land health" issues in Wisconsin during the 1930s and early 1940s.

Leopold's ties to the Midwest are best covered in William Barillas's *The Midwestern Pastoral: Place and Landscape in Literature of the American Heartland* (2006). Also useful is Susan Flader's "Aldo Leopold's Sand County," in J. Baird Callicott's collection *Companion to "A Sand County Almanac"* (1987), 40–62. Thomas K. Dean's entry on Leopold in volume 1 of *Dictionary of Midwestern Literature* (2001), 316, also provides a fine overview of the author's life as it relates to the Midwest.

Two excellent biographies of the author provide insight into the events that combined to produce *A Sand County Almanac*: environmental historian Curt Meine's *Aldo Leopold: His Life and Work* (1988) and Marybeth Lorbiecki's *Aldo Leopold: A Fierce Green Fire* (1996). Dennis Ribbens's essay "The Making of *A Sand County Almanac*," in Callicott's *Companion to "A Sand County Almanac,"* 91–109, explores in detail the years associated with the writing, revision, and publication of Leopold's text.

Perhaps the best overview of the impact of *A Sand County Almanac* on the American environmental movement is Roderick Nash's chapter "Aldo Leopold: Prophet" from *Wilderness and the American Mind* (1982). Nash's *The Rights of Nature: A History of Environmental Ethics* (1989) also explores the ethical and philosophical innovations of *A Sand County Almanac*. Also useful is James I. McClintock's *Kindred Spirits: Aldo Leopold, Joseph Wood Krutch, Edward Abbey, Annie Dillard, and Gary Snyder* (1994). For an intimate glimpse at how Leopold's example influenced later generations of environmentalist writers, see Terry Tempest Williams's essay "Wilderness and Intellectual Humility: Aldo Leopold," in *Red: Passion and Patience in the Desert* (2002).

The Aldo Leopold Foundation, located in Baraboo, Wisconsin, continues to maintain Leopold's beloved shack and carries on the author's work of fostering an ethical relationship to the natural world. The manuscript of *A Sand County Almanac* is housed with the Leopold Papers at the University of Wisconsin–Madison Archives.

ROD PHILLIPS   MICHIGAN STATE UNIVERSITY

SCANDINAVIAN AMERICAN LITERATURE

OVERVIEW: Scandinavian American literature of the Midwest may be defined as the literature—novels, short stories, plays, poetry, and essays—written and published by Midwesterners who were immigrants or children of immigrants from the present countries of Denmark, Finland, Iceland, Norway, and Sweden. The bulk of this literature was published from the 1870s to about the end of the 1940s. During this period Scandinavian immigrant groups produced an extensive body of literature in the Midwestern states, mostly written and published in the languages of their homelands. Many immigrants to the Midwest from Scandinavian countries were avid readers who were equipped with a literacy that had been shaped by reforms of public education in their homelands. Educational reforms vastly improved the reading and writing skills of those who immigrated to the Midwest, where the largest number of Scandinavian immigrants settled from the late 1830s through the 1870s and later, first in ILLINOIS, then in WISCONSIN, IOWA, and MINNESOTA, and finally in NORTH DAKOTA and SOUTH DAKOTA.

This entry proceeds first with a generalized history of Scandinavian writing in the Midwest, followed by specific individual sections on Danish American, Finnish American, Icelandic American, Norwegian American, and Swedish American contributions to that literature. A brief Selected Works section recommends some of the most important primary works, and a Further Reading section provides further critical information on the wide range of Scandinavian American literature.

HISTORY AND SIGNIFICANCE: The bulk of Scandinavian American literature was written and read in the upper Midwest. Working on farmland or in factories, immigrants nevertheless found time to read. Some of them also turned to writing, at least in writing letters home. In fact, the basis of literary activity for all these groups was letters sent from the Midwest to families and friends back home. For a long time such letters, often referred to as "America letters" and written in poor handwriting, constituted the writers' sole means of communication with "the old world." The experience of being immigrants in the Midwest led many Scandinavians who in their home countries would never have committed their thoughts to paper to become American letter writers. These letters make up a genre of folk literature produced by the people and for the people; many of these have been collected and made available both in English translations and, more extensively, in Scandinavian languages.

Scandinavian American letters from the Midwest were often private reports of the acquisition of new land, harvests accomplished, buying and selling of corn and cattle, brief references to commonly shared lines in the Bible or hymnals, and news of set-tlers from the same home community. Sometimes, at the end, the writer added a typical but oddly short sentence about having been blessed with the birth of a new child. There is often a brevity to these Midwestern letters that may baffle the modern reader. The documents do not appear today to be particularly private or personal; in fact, they are often constructed according to a common pattern of nineteenth-century letter writing. But when bundles of such letters were written by the same immigrant or by a family of immigrants, sometimes over several decades, they often serve as chronicles or family sagas of unusual quality.

Thus, like much American immigrant literature since the Puritans, the body of Midwestern Scandinavian texts had a distinctly epistolary beginning. Letters from the Midwest were sometimes reprinted in Scandinavian newspapers, where they served both to educate readers and to persuade others to emigrate as well. On a large scale, the letters prove that Midwestern immigrant writers participated in the modern experience of mass migration. But the basis for much of their literary endeavor was the romantic notion of the farmer-writer. It is no coincidence that *The Third Life of Per Smevik* (1912; English translation 1971), the first published novel by OLE EDVART RØLVAAG (1876–1931), was structured as a series of letters sent to a father in the old country from a young Midwestern immigrant.

Literature produced by Scandinavian immigrants grew in quantity as well as quality after the establishment of Scandinavian-language newspapers in the Midwest during the late 1800s. Newspapers in the Finnish, Dano-Norwegian, and Swedish languages were published in several Midwestern cities, catering to both urban and rural immigrants. A few of these papers, for instance, those printed in CHICAGO or MINNEAPOLIS, had by 1920 gained a circulation that could match that of city-based papers in the respective home countries. For a time Scandinavian languages were employed to such an extent in the Midwest that some writers hoped that their language would remain the communication medium of choice in their new country.

Although those hopes failed, Scandinavian-language newspapers in the Midwest were exceedingly important and had a three-fold function. First, they provided immigrant readers with news from the home country. Second, they informed their readers about American politics and regional cultural affairs. Finally, they helped establish a completely new literary context in the Midwest. Excerpts from both American and Scandinavian novels, as well as poetry and shorter fiction, were published by some of these papers.

The larger synods of various Scandinavian Lutheran churches also had centers of publishing and soon established colleges of higher education throughout the Midwest. On the shelves of the first generation of Scandinavian immigrants, books of Lutheran theology often replaced agricultural handbooks as the sons of immigrants were sent to prepare for the ministry in Midwestern churches. It is a remarkable feature of Scandinavian literary culture in the Midwest that institutions like the immigrant press and immigrant churches took responsibility for the production of literature, including serious fiction. Indeed, Rølvaag's first three novels were published by the Augsburg Publishing House, founded in 1891 in Minneapolis and from 1917 the major publisher for the Norwegian Lutheran Church of America. Likewise, volumes of Swedish American literature were published by the Augustana Book Concern of Rock Island, Illinois, founded in 1884 and owned by the Swedish Lutheran Augustana Synod. Many Scandinavian American writers in the Midwest worked for their respective immigrant churches or in church-related schools. This was a unique cultural situation unlike anything in the home countries.

Scandinavian American church colleges were essential in shaping a serious immigrant literature in the Midwest and produced both religious and secular texts. Their archives are full of Lutheran journals replete with essays of intense and subtle religious debates, now mostly inaccessible to American readers. These essays are part of a once-vibrant Scandinavian literature in the Midwest.

Before World War I Scandinavian immigrants and their descendants could pick up books published in languages other than English at railroad stations and stores in small Midwestern towns. Here they would find classic fiction such as *Uncle Tom's Cabin* (1852) by Harriet Beecher Stowe (1811–1896) and novels by James Fenimore Cooper (1789–1851) in Scandinavian translations. In the same places they could find Scandinavian novels printed in the Midwest, in the original language, often in cheap pirated editions. Several Scandinavian American writers were ambitious enough to produce their own texts for this market.

The Quota Acts of the 1920s and new prosperity in the Nordic countries halted mass emigration from these countries. Soon Midwestern Scandinavian newspapers folded, one after the other, while some of the institutions of higher learning expanded and assimilated beyond their original ethnic missions. Scandinavian churches merged and became American denominations where pastors no longer wrote passionate sermons in a Scandinavian language. Because there were few newcomers from Scandinavia, the language of new generations of Scandinavian Midwesterners became English. In spite of all the bustling life reported and imagined in what was once a Scandinavian Midwestern literature, it is now obsolete and may be studied only as a historical discipline. Only a few volumes of this literature, translated into English, linger today.

Contemporary Midwestern poets of Scandinavian background such as ROBERT (ELWOOD) BLY (b. 1926) and Phebe Hanson (b. 1928) may occasionally write poems pertaining to their Scandinavian heritage, but they would not be classified, nor would they think of themselves, as primarily Scandinavian American writers. Nevertheless, these and other Midwestern writers ought to be studied in light of the Scandinavian American literature of the past, to which they provide a link. Born to Swedish American parents in the Midwest, CARL (AUGUST) SANDBURG (1878–1967) may qualify as a member of this group, but he rarely used his ethnic background as a theme in his poetry, and he is generally considered an American writer outside the Scandinavian American fold. The well-known but fictional Minnesota place name Lake Wobegon, famous as the setting of thg national best-selling novel *Lake Wobegon Days* (1985), is peopled by GARY EDWARD KEILLOR (b. 1942), writing as Garrison Keillor, with imagined Norwegian immigrants and their descendants, but it cannot be defined as Scandinavian American literature.

Scandinavian writers wrote from the perspective of Midwestern American experience, not perspectives associated with their Scandinavian homelands. Swedish author (Karl Artur) Vilhelm Moberg (1898–1973) wrote a well-known series of novels about immigrant pioneers in the Midwest. These novels were later filmed, but neither the films nor the novels they are based on earned a place in Scandinavian literature arising from the Midwest. Finally, newer novels, like *Amalie's Story* (1970) by Julie Jensen McDonald (1929–2013), in which a poor woman achieves success in a Danish American community in Iowa, do not necessarily belong to Scandinavian American literature because they were written long after the period of immigration in which they are set. Even a Minnesota writer like WILLIAM JON (BILL) HOLM (1943–2009), who in a sense continued to write Icelandic American texts, and Jane Piirto (b. 1941), a Midwestern poet with a Finnish American background, may not be classified as Scandinavian American writers. Yet stories of Scandinavian immigrants continue to appear in the hundreds of family histories, biographies, documentaries, and memorabilia published in the Midwest every year. Popular books in this category are *Julia's Children: A Norwegian Immigrant Family in Minnesota, 1876–1947* (1987) by Margaret Chrislock Gilseth (1919–2007) and *Nothing to Do but Stay: My Pioneer Mother* (1991) by Carrie Ahdele Carrine Young (b. 1923), a memoir about a Norwegian American mother in pioneer North Dakota. Such books serve as links to the Scandinavian American past, but they are not necessarily part of a Scandinavian American literature, as is the classic *The Diary of Elisabeth Koren, 1853–1855* (1955).

The genre of Scandinavian American literature is now an important part of Midwestern literary history, sadly neglected and unexplored after it peaked during the 1910s and 1920s. In all likelihood Scandinavian American literature, despite its long persistence as a cultural force in Midwestern literary life, produced only one American novel writer of lasting fame, Ole E. Rølvaag.

English was not the mother tongue of most Scandinavian Midwestern writers, and only a few texts were originally published in English. Most often these writers focused on themes concerning aspects of migration from their home countries and assimilation into American culture. They often discussed language change and the conflicting values of the first and the second generation, as, for instance, in Ole Rølvaag's *Peder Victorious* (1929). By far, most of these writers stayed in the Midwest, but the few who returned to their homeland after they had made their contribution to American literature must still be included as Midwestern writers.

In the literary histories of their homelands, Midwestern writers of Scandinavian origin have been largely neglected or reduced to footnotes. In American literary histories they also remain, with a few exceptions, largely unknown. For instance, of the dozens of Scandinavian Midwestern writers, only Ole E. Rølvaag and THORSTEIN (BUNDE) VEBLEN (1857–1929), two vastly different Norwegian American writers, are discussed in the first volume of *Dictionary of Midwestern Literature* (2001). They were probably the only two Midwestern writers within the Scandinavian American fold to achieve international recognition.

The first standard critical work on Scandinavian American literature was Dorothy Burton Skårdal's *The Divided Heart: Scandinavian Immigrant Experience through Literary Sources* (1974). A student of historian Oscar Handlin (1915–2011), Skårdal was influenced by Handlin's idea of the uprootedness of the American immigrant. Hence she saw the Scandinavian immigrant as being "divided," and her conclusions have since been contested. Not primarily interested in the creative minds that produced this body of literature, she regarded their narratives as fictional but fairly trustworthy reports of social history. But she was the first scholar to peruse volumes of archived Scandinavian immigrant literature.

Inspired by New Historicism and newer general studies of American immigrant literature, later readers of Scandinavian American contributions to Midwestern literature emphasized the complexity of the double worlds in which these immigrant writers thrived. In his seminal study *The Minds of the West: Ethnocultural Evolution in the Rural Middle West, 1830–1917* (1997), historian Jon Gjerde (1953–2008) argues that Scandinavian immigrants in the Midwest were equipped with "a complementary identity" (8) comprising both the belief in American ideas of freedom and the desire to retain values from the old country. This double intellectual perspective is reflected in much Midwestern Scandinavian American literature. In his book on Norwegian American writers in the Midwest, *Twofold Identities* (2004), Øyvind T. Gulliksen (b. 1945) argues that the immigrant status of these writers gave many of them a sense of having become privileged and competent settlers of a double landscape rather than marginalized migrants afflicted by divided hearts.

In spite of common Scandinavian roots, immigrants from Scandinavian countries often settled in their own clusters, founded their own varieties of American immigrant culture, celebrated their own identity, established their own churches and publishing houses, and wrote their own literature in the Midwest. True, they felt that they had much in common, but the notion of a Scandinavian literature covering all five groups was largely an American construction. In the following the highlights of the literatures of all five specific groups will be presented briefly. References will be predominantly to texts available in English.

Danish American Literature: Adam Dan (1848–1931) emigrated from Denmark in 1871 to accept a pastor's job in a Danish American congregation in Racine, Wisconsin, the town with the largest population of Danish immigrants in the United States around 1900. Soon after Dan arrived, he came into serious conflict with some members of his congregation, who accused him of failing to preach scripture as the only way to salvation. When such conflicts occurred in immigrant Midwestern churches—and they were not rare—they quickened authorial energies. Characteristically, most of Dan's poetry and fiction is based on eighteenth-century conflicts in Danish Lu-

theran culture. He spent most of his life as a writer and pastor in Chicago before finally retiring to Clinton, Iowa, where he died. His tombstone reminds the observer that Dan was a pastor and a poet among Danish Americans for close to sixty years. Between the 1890s and the 1920s Dan published several collections of poetry and sketches, such as *Solglimt* (1899), *Vaarbud* (1902), and *Sommerløv* (1903). His most important work is the novel *Prærierosen* (1892) a depiction of the conflict between pietist and liberal forces in an Iowa Danish American community.

Kristian Østergaard (1855–1931) immigrated to Elkhorn, Iowa, in 1878 to become a teacher at the Danish American high school there. Later he became a Lutheran minister, serving in Ringsted, Iowa, and elsewhere in the Midwest. He retired to Tyler, Minnesota, where he died. The author of more than twenty volumes, Østergaard struggled to retain the Danish language. He helped edit a Danish American songbook, *Den Dansk-Amerikanske Højskolesangbog* (1906); collections of stories from early Midwestern farm life, like *Nybyggere* (1891); and a novel from pioneer days titled *Danby Folk* (1927). In his collection of poetry *Sange fra Prærien* (1912) he meditates on the idea that even if he will not be able to make the Midwest his home, his children will.

In a sense, Tyler, Minnesota, became a literary center of Danish American letters when Carl Hansen (1860–1916) settled there and soon established himself as an author, public speaker, and president of the Danish American Society before he left for the West Coast. Like Østergaard, Hansen is buried in Tyler. For a while he was also a teacher at the Danish school in Elkhorn, Iowa. His publications include several collections of stories of Midwestern immigrant farms: *Præriens Børn* (1895), *Præriefolk* (1907), and *Landsmænd* (1908). Hansen and most Danish American writers published extensively in Denmark, as well as in the Midwest, but very little of their writing exists in English translation. Sophus Winther (1893–1983), however, wrote three novels about Danish American life in English, titled *Take All to Nebraska* (1936), *Mortgage Your Heart* (1937), and *This Passion Never Dies* (1938), all based on his memories and knowledge of immigrant lives in rural NEBRASKA. The novels give a bleak picture of the hardships and economic exploitation of the Grimsen family in the 1890s. Born in Denmark, Winther grew up on farms in Nebraska, was educated at American universities, and published a book on playwright Eugene (Gladstone) O'Neill (1888–1953).

Other Danish American writers lived in larger cities and focused on urban immigrant life. Anton Kvist (1878–1965) was trained as a bricklayer in Denmark, attended Grand View College in Des Moines, and settled in Chicago, where he edited *Dansk Tidende,* a Danish paper, in the 1930s. He published several volumes of poetry and songs, among them *Fyr og Flamme* (1910), *Fred og Fejde* (1917), and *Sange fra Vejen* (1948). Enok Mortensen (1902–1984) was born in Denmark, emigrated to the Midwest in 1919, studied at Grand View College, worked as a pastor in Chicago from 1929 to 1936, and became president of the Danish school in Tyler, Minnesota. He published *Livets Lykke* (1933), a Danish American play, as well as a Chicago novel titled *Saaledes blev jeg hjemløs* (1934). His *Danish-American Life and Letters: A Bibliography* (1945) remains useful.

Finnish American Literature: Finnish immigration to the Midwest started later than that from the other Nordic countries, and assimilation was slower. This may be one reason that Finnish American literature in English was still thriving in the Midwest as late as the 1960s, when the literary production of the other Scandinavian groups had come to an end. Immigrants from Finland settled in northern Minnesota and the Upper Peninsula of MICHIGAN, where they worked in the mines and lumber industries, fished, and did small-scale farming. A majority of the first Finnish immigrants to the Midwest were unmarried men, some of whom left their home country to avoid being drafted into the Russian army. There is a profound sense of the woods and northern wildlife in Finnish American literature. For a time their language, linguistically not Scandinavian, and their isolated settlements may have set them apart not only from English-speaking Americans but also from other Midwestern Scandinavian groups.

Both hymnals and essays of political RADICALISM attracted Finnish American Midwestern readers. Loneliness handled with a stoic attitude was a much-repeated theme in the beginning but became less prevalent with assimilation to American life. Ruth Pitkanen Johnson (1908–1992) was born in Finland but moved with her parents to Michigan when she was three years old and later to Iowa, where she married and taught school. Some of her texts are included in anthologies of Finnish American literature. Aili L. Jarvenpa (1918–2002) was a Finnish American poet whose papers are held at the History Research Center in Minneapolis. Born to Finnish immigrant parents in Winton, Minnesota, she published books of her poetry. In several of her poems, like those published in *Half Immersed* (1978), she connects the old world and the new. Her collection of Finnish American stories was characteristically titled *In Two Cultures: The Stories of Second Generation Finnish-Americans* (1992). *Finns in Minnesota Midwinter* (1986), a book of poetry by James A. Johnson (b. 1947), also focuses on Finnish American immigrant experiences. Lauri Lemberg (1887–1965) wrote several plays for the Finnish American stage. His only novel, *St. Croix Avenue* (1992), focuses on a teenage immigrant from Finland who settles in a Finnish American community in Duluth. The best-known novel written by a Finnish American novelist raised in the Midwest remains *Mountain of Winter* (1965) by Shirley Schoonover (1936–2004). Jane Piirto has used her upbringing in Michigan as her source for a collection of poems and essays, *A Location in the Upper Peninsula* (1994), which includes an essay about going back to Finland in search of information connected to her grandmother and great-grandmother. This type of story, which takes the writer through old church records and cemeteries in the old country, may be typical among Midwestern writers today who seek to construct their own senses of self. Beth L. Virtanen (b. 1959), from Michigan's Upper Peninsula, has written short fiction and nonfiction in the same vein and has published a book of poetry titled *Guarding Passage* (2005) that explores her Finnish heritage and its impact on her intellectual life. Hanna Pylväinen's debut novel, *We Sinners* (2012), focuses on a Finnish American family whose lives are largely defined by a strict and pietistic Lutheran immigrant church in the Midwest.

Other important Midwestern Finnish American authors include Joseph David Damrell (b. 1944), whose novels *Gift* (1992) and *Billy Maki* (1997) examine the relationship of Finnish Americans to the land in which they live and to those who share it with them. Timo Koskinen (b. 1945) is a Midwestern transplant who was born in Finland and was sent while he was a baby to be raised by relatives in the United States. His *Bone Soup and a Lapland Wizard* (1984) depicts the hardship of immigrant life. A Finlandia University faculty member and a resident of Michigan's Upper Peninsula for more than thirty years, Lauri A(rvid) Anderson (b. 1942) has produced several collections of stories, including *Hunting Hemingway's Trout* (1990). Anderson has said that he does not consider himself a Finnish American writer but rather a writer who "happens to be Finnish-American." Of all the Nordic groups in the Midwest, the Finnish Americans are probably the only group to have established their own association for the study and continued production of literature within their own fold, the Finnish North American Literature Association.

Finnish American poetry in the Midwest has appeared in a variety of modes, from the deeply tragic to verse of folk humor. *Summer-Day Poems, and Other Stories* by Gordon Pekuri (b. 1951) appeared in 1973. Heino A. "Hap" Puotinen (1911–1991) wrote a series of humorous folk-poetry volumes incorporating the interlanguage formed in immigrant Finnish and English households, including *Bull Fight in the Sauna* (1969). Others also worked in this humorous vein of mixed-language texts; one example is *Tall Timber Tales: Sketches and Stories* (1973) by Jingo Wiitala Vachon (1918–2009). Two anthologies of Midwestern Finnish American writing are *Red, White and a Paler Shade of Blue: Poems on the Finnish-American Experience* (1996), edited by Mary Kinnunen; and *O Finland: Stories, Poems, and Illustrations by Americans of Finnish Origin* (1998), edited by Judith Harvala Henderson and David William Salmela.

Icelandic American Literature: Immigrants from Iceland were outnumbered by all the other Midwestern Scandinavian groups, and in the beginning they were counted as Danish immigrants. But they were fiercely independent, used their own language, and always viewed literature as a vital part of their identity. Wherever families of Icelanders clustered in the Midwest, a local bard was among them.

Most Icelandic immigrants settled in Canada, some after time spent in the United States. In the Midwest they lived as farmers and farmhands in two main settlements. One was close to Minneota, Minnesota; the second, larger settlement was in Pembina County, North Dakota, for some time the home of several Icelandic American poets. Kristjan N. Júlíus (1859–1936), nicknamed Káinn, was born in Akureyri, Iceland, and moved to the United States at the age of eighteen, living for many years in Mountain, North Dakota. A farmhand and self-taught poet, he had published poetry in Iceland. A monument in his honor was dedicated in North Dakota by the president of Iceland in 1999. In his writing he developed an Icelandic North Dakota sense of humor. Noting that pastors often instructed their congregation to sing only the first and the last stanzas of a hymn, Júlíus is reported to have said, "Therefore, I have acquired the habit only to compose the first and the last verse, so that they who look at it at all, will have to read the whole poem" (quoted from the speech by Olafur Ragnar Grimsson, the president of Iceland, at the Kristjan N. Júlíus Memorial dedication, 1999). He tended to write humorous and ironic verse, short poems, and sketches of barn dances, children's play, drinking habits, and church rituals.

Stephan Stephansson, ca. 1917.
Courtesy of Stephan V. Benediktson

Bjorn B(jornsson) Jonsson (1870–1938) worked as a minister and newspaper editor in Minneota, Minnesota, from 1894 to 1914, when he moved to Canada. He also wrote stories under the pseudonym Grimur Grimsson. Better known is the poet Stephan G(uðmundsson) Stephansson (1853–1927), who emigrated from Iceland with his parents. They settled first in Wisconsin but later joined the Icelandic community in Pembina County, North Dakota, where Stephansson remained a farmer and poet for nine years before leaving permanently for Canada. Bill Holm, a later Midwestern poet, meditates on his Icelandic American heritage in several of his books, most of all in *The Music of Failure* (1985) and *The Dead Get By with Everything* (1991). Walking across an Icelandic American cemetery in the Midwest, Holm offers a comment that illustrates the status of Scandinavian American writing in the Midwest as a whole: "What a relief to find a graveyard with stones that read Hallgrimur, Vigfus, Adalborg, Metusalem, Gottskalksson, Gislason, Isfeld! They say: we're not melted yet, or if so, the job is just finished, and the alloy still smoking" (*The Music of Failure* 7). In *The Windows of Brimnes: An American in Iceland* (2007) Holm tells of time he spent in northern Iceland. The book is a reflection on what it means to be genuinely in touch with the culture of the ancestral homeland. By returning for periods of time, Holm acquired a new version of the twofold identity that some Scandinavian American immigrant writers once enjoyed.

Drude Janson, ca. 1885–1890.
Courtesy of the Norwegian-American Historical Association, Northfield, Minnesota

Norwegian American Literature: No other Scandinavian group in the Midwest produced as many novels before the 1930s, some released in English translations, as did Norwegian Americans. Perhaps the earliest Midwestern voice in Norwegian American fiction in English comes from a woman writer, an immigrant to Minneapolis, Drude Krog Janson (1846–1934). Her novel *A Saloonkeeper's Daughter* (1889; English translation 2002) is a remarkable accomplishment in Scandinavian American writing, not only because it was written by the wife of a Unitarian pastor but also because the main character is a young female immigrant who grows to independence in the Scandinavian sections of Minneapolis and becomes a Unitarian minister in Chicago. This novel has generated a collection of essays, *To Become the Self One Is: A Critical Companion to Drude Krog Janson's "A Saloonkeper's Daughter"* (2005), edited by Asbjørn Grønstad and Lene Johannessen.

A serious novel, *A Saloonkeeper's Daughter* did not sell nearly as well as did the most popular of all Midwestern Norwegian American novels, *The Cotter's Son* (1885; English translation 1963), a Midwestern DIME NOVEL by Hans Andersen Foss (1851–1929), which cleverly combines a romantic Norwegian peasant tale with the Horatio Alger "from rags to riches" formula. This ideology was severely opposed by Waldemar Theodor Ager (1869–1941), a writer who emigrated from Norway when he was sixteen. He settled first in Chicago and then moved to Eau Claire, Wisconsin, in 1892. In Eau Claire, Ager became the editor of *Reform,* an immigrant newspaper in the Norwegian language. A prolific writer, he published four major novels of immigrant life in the

Midwest, all eventually translated into English. If Rølvaag constructed his immigrant South Dakota farmer from the ideals of the Jeffersonian yeoman, Ager turned his attention to Norwegian immigrants in a Wisconsin small-town setting. In his first novel, *Christ before Pilate: An American Story* (1910; English translation 1924), a pastor tries unsuccessfully to solve problems within local immigrant churches. *On the Way to the Melting Pot* (1917; English translation 1995) praises the Puritan work ethic but offers fierce criticism of the American politics of assimilation. *Sons of the Old Country* (1926; English translation 1983) is a collective novel of immigrants in the Midwestern sawmill industry, and in his novel *I Sit Alone* (1929; English translation 1931), the immigrant character, dismayed by American materialism, seeks refuge in a lonely North Dakota cabin. A good friend of Rølvaag, Ager labored for the continued use of the Norwegian language in the Midwest. The Norwegian-language program proved to be a losing battle, but Ager's arguments against the melting-pot ideology come close to those of Horace M(eyer) Kallen (1882–1974) in "Democracy versus the Melting Pot" (1915), reprinted in *Theories of Ethnicity: A Classical Reader* (1996), edited by Werner Sollors (67–92).

Because Rølvaag plays such a pivotal role in Scandinavian American literature, readers tend to think that he was a solitary figure in the field. In reality, he was surrounded by many writers who often corresponded, read, and reviewed one another's books. One of them, Simon Johnson (1874–1970), came to North Dakota as a child and later moved to work for the important Norwegian-language newspaper *Decorah-Posten* in Decorah, Iowa. Johnson wrote four major novels. One novel was translated as *From Fjord to Prairie; or, In the New Kingdom* (1914; English translation 1916). Johnson aptly illustrated the double landscape of Scandinavian American writers in the Midwest when he stated that "Ibsen and Bjørnson set the table for us, each in his special way. So do Whitman, Emerson, and Longfellow" (unpublished memoirs in the Archives of the National Library, Oslo, Norway, 114). This idea of a literary double consciousness filled him and other Midwestern

Waldemar Ager as a young man, ca. 1900.
Courtesy of Borgny Ager and the Ager Association of Eau Claire, Wisconsin

immigrant writers in the Scandinavian fold with gratitude because they were convinced that they would not have had careers as writers if they had remained at home.

Two other important writers were Jon Norstog (1877–1942) and Johannes Benjamin Wist (1864–1923). Jon Norstog wrote—as well as printed, bound, published, marketed, and sold—several long plays about Old Testament heroes. When the duties of his writing beckoned, he considered his farmwork of less importance. In 1915 a friend noticed that on the shelves in his one-room sod house near Watsford, North Dakota, were "Bibles and devotional books, Thomas á Kempis, Bunyan, Icelandic sagas, Milton, Byron, Shakespeare, Goethe . . . Luther, and some of the Norwegian poets" (Torkel Oftelie, quoted in Øyvind Gulliksen, "Jon Norstogs bibliotek," *Norwegian-American Essays, 2004* (2005): 127. Norstog also wrote a trilogy titled *Exodus* (1928–1931), in which the main character is a Norwegian American artist in the Midwest.

An immigrant from Norway in 1884, Johannes Wist worked as a journalist in Minneapolis and Wisconsin before becoming an editor in Decorah in 1901. He had the sense of humor that Norstog, and perhaps even Rølvaag, lacked, and his novels reflect other sides of Midwestern immigrant culture. His trilogy *The Rise of Jonas Olsen: A Norwegian Immigrant's Saga* (1920–1922; English translation 2006), about a fictional Norwegian immigrant who comes to Minneapolis in the 1880s and later establishes himself in a small town in the Red River valley, is a delightful description of assimilation to Midwestern life without the skepticism about the melting-pot concept expressed by Ager and Rølvaag. Educated as a minister, Peer O(lsen) Strømme (1856–1921) turned to work as an editor and writer. In his novel *Halvor: A Story of Pioneer Youth* (1893; English translation 1960) the protagonist is used as a foil to the author's educational experience at Luther College in Decorah, Iowa.

Ole E. Rølvaag, professor of Norwegian at St. Olaf College, Northfield, Minnesota, from 1906 until the year he died, remains the best-known Midwestern Scandinavian American writer. His reputation rests on the classic novel GIANTS IN THE EARTH (1924, 1925; English translation 1927), but as other city novels have come to the fore in Scandinavian American fiction, Rølvaag's novel set in Minneapolis, *The Boat of Longing* (1921; English translation 1933) has received renewed attention. His novel *Pure Gold* (1920; English translation 1930) is a satire of American materialism. His concluding volume in the series of Beret Holm and her pioneer family, *Their Fathers' God* (1931), may be read as a jeremiad against second-generation Norwegian Americans and their failure to retain and develop their inherited values as they assimilated into American culture.

Swedish American Literature: Immigrant writers within the Swedish American fold were more widespread than in the other groups, and many of them fell outside Midwestern literature. Many Swedish American writers worked for immigrant churches or newspapers, and they were also more city based than writers in the other Scandinavian Midwestern groups. Chicago soon became the second-largest "Swedish" city in the world, a center for Swedish immigrant literature and language and the publication of Swedish American newspapers, and the site of a Swedish theatre, well documented by Henriette C(hristiane K(oren) Naeseth (1899–1987) in *The Swedish Theatre of Chicago, 1868–1950* (1951).

Carl Sandburg's poem "Chicago," the lead poem of his 1916 collection CHICAGO POEMS, has become part of the Midwestern and American literary canon, but it has counterparts in a number of now-unknown poems about the city in Swedish American literature, for instance, the poems "Chicago i höstprakt" and "Pa Bremer Street i Chicago" by Magnus Henrik Elmblad (1848–1888). See THE CHANGING MIDWESTERN LITERARY CANON. Working for a Swedish American newspaper in Chicago, Elmblad also wrote a long poem about the Chicago fire, published in 1872. In 1878 a collection of his poems, *Samlade dikter,* was published in Swedish in Chicago. Sandburg came to an active use of his Swedish American roots late in life, whereas a number of Swedish American writers in Chicago wrote from within and for their fellow immigrants.

There is often a sentimental strain in Swedish American poetry; much of it was written to commemorate specific occasions, but as a body of Midwestern literature it covered themes of immigration, assimilation, and the change of language, issues not then found in Swedish literature at home. Carl Fredrik Peterson (1843–1901) settled in Chicago in 1877, where he became the editor of *Svenska Tribunen,* a Swedish-language newspaper in the city. He was one of the most prolific Swedish American writers in the Midwest and published several works including an American history in Swedish (1890), as well as the fictional *Kärlek och plikt* (1895). Signe Ankarfelt (1858–1926) was educated as a teacher in her homeland before she arrived in Chicago in 1881, where she wrote memories of her childhood, as well as essays and poetry for Swedish American publications. Her poem "A Flower in the Wreath, Laid at the Foot of the Statue of Linné, in Lincoln Park, Chicago, May 23rd, 1891," received special notice in the *Chicago Tribune* at the time; the paper stated that her poem had a quality comparable to Longfellow. In another poem, available in H. Arnold Burton's *A Folk Divided: Homeland Swedes and*

Swedish Americans, 1840–1940 (1994), she writes home to Sweden: "Thou art my brother, although distance / separates us now, our hands may yet reach out. / I am thy sister, who would wish that thou / some day couldst rightly understand me" (v). As an upper-middle-class immigrant to Chicago, Vilhelm Henning Berger (1867–1936) failed financially, and his Chicago stories reflect his failure to find the Promised Land. He wrote several short stories based on his experiences as an unemployed worker on the seedy side of that city. Jakob Bonggren (1854–1940), a journalist for the *Svenska Amerikanaren*, a Swedish newspaper in Chicago, also wrote poetry in which he promoted both assimilation and his Swedish heritage. Ernst William Olson (1870–1958) worked for the Augustana Book Concern for almost forty years. An editor of several Swedish American publications and a translator of hymns, Olson always supported a Swedish American literary culture in both languages. Ernst Skarstedt (1857–1929), author and journalist, published a bibliographic survey of Swedish American writers in 1897 that has been the basis for later work. *Prärieblomman*, published annually between 1900 and 1913 by the Augustana Book Concern, was at the time the most influential Swedish American literary magazine and again illustrates the connection between religion and immigrant culture. It helped establish a Swedish American literary culture and clearly operated within the concept of the double landscape in which the immigrant writer existed.

SELECTED WORKS: There is an abundance of Midwestern Scandinavian American literature, written and published in the Midwest, mostly in non-English languages and preserved in archives. Some of the best-known works of Midwestern Scandinavian American literature, most of them Norwegian, have been published in English translations and are listed here. They include Waldemar Ager's *Christ before Pilate: An American Story* (1910; English translation, 1924), *On the Way to the Melting Pot* (1917; English translation 1995), *Sons of the Old Country* (1926; English translation 1983), and *I Sit Alone* (1929; English translation 1931); Hans A. Foss's *The Cotter's Son* (1885; English translation 1963); Drude Krog Janson's *A Saloonkeeper's Daughter* (1889; English translation 2002); Aili Jarvenpa's *In Two Cultures: The Stories of Second Generation Finnish-Americans* (1992); Simon Johnson's *From Fjord to Prairie; or, In the New Kingdom* (1914; English translation 1916); Lauri Lemberg's *St. Croix Avenue* (1992); Jane Piirto's *A Location in the Upper Peninsula* (1994); Ole E. Rølvaag's *The Third Life of Per Smevik* (1912; English translation 1971), *Pure Gold* (1920; English translation 1930), *The Boat of Longing* (1921; English translation 1933), *Giants in the Earth* (1927), *Peder Victorious* (1929), and *Their Fathers' God* (1931); Peer O. Strømme's *Halvor: A Story of Pioneer Youth* (1893; English translation 1960); Sophus Keith Winther's *Take All to Nebraska* (1936), *Mortgage Your Heart* (1937), and *Their Passion Never Dies* (1938); and Johannes Wist's *The Rise of Jonas Olsen* (1920–1922; English translation 2006).

Anthologies of or including Scandinavian American literature of the Midwest include *Red, White and a Paler Shade of Blue: Poems on the Finnish-American Experience* (1996), edited by Mary Kinnunen; *O Finland: Stories, Poems, and Illustrations by Americans of Finnish Origin* (1998), edited by Judith Harvala Henderson and David William Salmela; *Western-Icelandic Short Stories* (1992), edited by Kirsten Wolf and Arny Hjaltadottir; *Sampo: The Magic Mill; A Collection of Finnish-American Writing* (1989), edited by Aili Jarvenpa and Michael G. Karni; *Connecting Souls: Finnish Voices in North America; An Anthology of Finnish-American and Finnish-Canadian Writings* (2000), edited by Varpu Lindström and Börje Vähämäki; and *Saunas: Short Stories, Poems, Illustrations, and Photographs* (2002), edited by David William Salmela.

FURTHER READING: Dorothy Burton Skårdal's pioneering study *The Divided Heart: Scandinavian Immigrant Experience through Literary Sources* (1974) includes a selected bibliography and an index of Scandinavian American writers excluding Finnish and Icelandic groups. Christer Mossberg's *Scandinavian Immigrant Literature* (1981) also treats Scandinavian immigrant writing as a whole but does not limit discussion to the Midwest. *Scandinavians in America: Literary Life* (1985), edited by J. R. Christianson, contains essays on Midwestern immigrant writers from all Nordic countries except Iceland. Maxine Schwartz Seller's *Ethnic Theatre in the United*

States (1983) includes chapters on Danish American theatre by Clinton M. Hyde, Finnish American theatre by Timo R. Riippa and Michael G. Karni, and Swedish American theatre by Anne-Charlotte Hanes Harvey. By far, most of these amateur theatres were in cities like Minneapolis and Chicago. Very few Scandinavian American plays were written, and fewer still were produced. *Selected Plays of Marcus Thrane* (2008), translated and introduced by Terje I. Leiren, presents six plays written from the 1860s to the 1880s for a Norwegian American theatre group in Chicago.

Not much has been written on contributions to Midwestern literature by Danish Americans. Dorothy Burton Skårdal has written an extensive essay, "Danish-American Literature: A Call to Action," *Scandinavian Studies* 48.4 (Autumn 1976): 405–25. There is also a chapter on Danish American literature in Johannes Knudsen and Enok Mortensen's *The Danish-American Immigrant: Phases of His Religion and Culture* (1950).

Anita Aukee Johnson's "Finnish-American Literature" in *New Immigrant Literatures in the United States: A Sourcebook to Our Multicultural Literary Heritage* (1996), edited by Alpana Sharma Knippling, paves new ground but does not give credit to the earliest writers. Paul Kauppila and Marianne Wargelin's entry on Finnish American literature in *The Greenwood Encyclopedia of Multiethnic American Literature* (2005), edited by Emmanuel S. Nelson, is a beginning to a larger history. This five-volume encyclopedia contains useful introductions to Scandinavian American literature in general. Raija Taramaa's *Stubborn and Silent Finns with "Sisu" in Finnish-American Literature: An Imagological Study of Finnishness in the Literary Production of Finnish-American Authors* (2007) deals mostly with second- and third-generation Finnish American writers. A. William Hoglund's *Finnish Immigrants in America, 1880–1920* (1960) provides a useful historical framework. His essay "Finnish-American Humor and Satire," in *Scandinavians in America* (1985), edited by J. R. Christianson, is a good short study up to the 1930s.

Playford V(ernon) Thorson (1925–2012) mentions Icelandic American writers in "Icelanders," in *American Immigrant Cultures:*

Builders of a Nation (1997), edited by David Levinson and Melvin Ember. Kristjana Gunnars's *Stephan G. Stephansson: Selected Prose and Poetry* (1988) includes the poet's "Autobiographical Fragments" about his life in Wisconsin and North Dakota before his move to Alberta, Canada. Some of his Midwestern poems are also included in the original Icelandic and in English translation. Jónas Thor's *Icelanders in North America: The First Settlers* (2002) gives essential information for further studies of the literary culture of this Midwestern group.

The most complete history of any section of Scandinavian American Literature in the Midwest is Orm Øverland's *The Western Home: A Literary History of Norwegian America* (1996). His study gives extensive and detailed insight into the literary culture of Norwegian Americans; so far, there is no parallel study of any other Scandinavian immigrant group in the Midwest. Norwegian American literature in the Midwest is also dealt with in Odd S. Lovoll's chapter "Cultural Growth" in his book *The Promise of America: A History of the Norwegian-American People* (1984). The major novels of Rølvaag and Ager are analyzed by Øyvind T. Gulliksen in *Twofold Identities: Norwegian-American Contributions to Midwestern Literature* (2004). The best study of Rølvaag's trilogy remains Harold P. Simonson's *Prairies Within: The Tragic Trilogy of Ole Rølvaag* (1987). Pauline Farseth and Theodore Blegen's *Frontier Mother: The Letters of Gro Svendsen* (1950) is an immigrant story told through letters home from Iowa. George T(obias) Flom (1871–1960) and Theodore C(hristian) Blegen (1891–1969), both historians, worked to save stories of Norwegian American experiences in the Midwest. See Flom's *A History of Norwegian Immigration to the United States* (1909) and Blegen's *Norwegian Migration: The American Transition* (1940). Einar I. Haugen's *The Norwegian Language in America* (1953) is not only a pioneering study in sociolinguistics but also a rich source of Midwestern stories. The best and most comprehensive collection of American letters sent to Norway, largely from the Midwest, is Orm Øverland's multivolume *From America to Norway: Norwegian-American Immigrant Letters, 1838–1914*. Volume 1 (2012) covers the years 1838–1870 and volume 2 (2015) covers 1871–1892.

In his *Letters from the Promised Land: Swedes in America, 1840–1914* (1975) H. A. Barton presents a collection of immigrant letters sent to Sweden. Anna Williams has published a book in Swedish on the poet and journalist (Olof) Jakob Bonggren (1854–1940), *Skribent i Svensk-Amerika: Jakob Bonggren, journalist och poet* (1991). Dag Blanck's *Becoming Swedish-American: The Construction of an Ethnic Identity in the Augustana Synod, 1860–1917* (1997) is very useful, as is the volume edited by Blanck and Philip J. Anderson, *Swedes in the Twin Cities: Immigrant Life and Minnesota's Urban Frontier* (2001). In the first chapters of his book *Literature and the Immigrant Community: The Case of Arthur Landfors* (1990), Alan Swanson treats Swedish American literature in general, with some relevance to the Midwest region. Minnesota historian George M. Stephenson's *Religious Aspects of Swedish Immigration* (1932) documents Swedish American experiences in the Midwest.

Scandinavian American literature, whether published in English or in the languages of the five Nordic countries, constitutes a significant body of literature. Even if it has largely come to a close, it has contributed to Midwestern literature in all genres, and new scholarship in the field is constantly appearing.

ØYVIND T. GULLIKSEN

TELEMARK UNIVERSITY COLLEGE, TELEMARK, NORWAY
LUTHER COLLEGE

SCIENCE FICTION AND FANTASY

OVERVIEW: Science fiction, as considered here, refers to fantasy texts, as well as to the genre typically designated in commercial publishing. Traditionally, science fiction includes works focused on the ways science affects real or imagined societies. Fantasy tends to focus on particularly imaginative or strange settings and characters. All discussions of Midwestern science fiction in this context must include substantial reference to the region's geologic, geographic, and scenic real "space," one of the principal themes of science fiction, which also appropriates the borderless inner psychological space as its other setting. Science fiction imagined by Midwestern writers tends to reflect a perspective more stereotypically traditional, conservative, insulated, domestic,

normal, and deliberate than those of the science-fiction cultures of the nation's continental coasts. Scholar Darko Ronald Suvin (b. 1930), in *Metamorphoses of Science Fiction* (1979), asserts that the ennui such traditional culture can engender begs for destabilization in discourses of "cognitive estrangement" (4). Representative Midwestern science-fiction authors also tend to project regional rhetorical and cultural subtexts in works that do not explicitly focus on the region or its people. Nonetheless, the history of Midwestern science fiction parallels and reflects the genre's continuing growth in the United States and around the world. Midwestern science fiction includes several significant writers recognized in *Dictionary of Midwestern Literature*, volume 1 (2001), as well as many others who must be read to understand fully the scale and significance of the region's science fiction.

HISTORY AND SIGNIFICANCE: Science fiction and fantasy began its remarkable rise as a specific genre in the United States in the 1920s. A 1904 immigrant from Luxembourg, Hugo Gernsback (1884–1967), born Hugo Gernsbacher, is often credited with coining the term "science fiction" in 1926. In magazines, books (especially paperbacks), radio, movies, and television, it experienced two periods of great growth. From the 1940s to the 1960s a "golden age" of writers codified the genre from the ur-works of such authors as Jules (Gabriel) Verne (1828–1905), Charles Lutwidge Dodgson (1832–1898), writing as Lewis Carroll, William Morris (1834–1896), L(YMAN) FRANK BAUM (1856–1919), and H(ubert) G(eorge) Wells (1866–1946). Two major causes produced the second period of growth. From the onset of the 1970s to the present, filmmakers have undertaken an impressive reification of certain science fiction themes. See FILM. That process has been ongoing since the premiere of Stanley Kubrick's *2001: A Space Odyssey* in 1968. The second cause was the recognition in the 1970s of science fiction as academically respectable in K–12 and university curricula, owing to publication of reference works by scholars who established a canon and critical appreciation of the genre. By 1980 most high schools and universities included science fiction as required reading in one or more literature courses, a trend that has continued. The rise of science fiction in the Midwest parallels this progress.

Some of the earliest examples of Midwestern science fiction appear in nineteenth-century DIME NOVELS. Edward S(ylvester) Ellis (1840–1916) wrote *The Huge Hunter; or, The Steam Man of the Prairies* (1868), in which the main character is a ST. LOUIS inventor who builds a mechanical man. *Under Five Lakes; or, The Cruise of the* Destroyer (1886) by Charles Bertrand Lewis (1842–1924), using the pseudonym M. Quad, focuses on a specially built submarine used to explore the Great Lakes. *The Deadwood Sports; or, Diamond Dick's Deliverance* (1888) and its sequel, *Josh's Boy Pards; or, The Mysterious Sky Stranger* (1888), are by an unknown person writing as Lieutenant S. G. Lansing. These stories are set in the Black Hills of SOUTH DAKOTA and involve a mysterious flying machine. *The Deadwood Sports* can be found in Beadle's Boy's Library of Sport, Story and Adventure (octavo edition, no. 228) and Pocket Library (no. 377). *Josh's Boy Pards* appears in Beadle's octavo edition (no. 238).

Other early appearances of Midwestern fantasy include the work of MINNESOTA writer IGNATIUS LOYOLA DONNELLY (1831–1901) with his futuristic, dystopian novel *Caesar's Column* (1890). MISSOURI writer SAMUEL LANGHORNE CLEMENS (1835–1910), writing as Mark Twain, is known for his time-traveling story *A Connecticut Yankee in King Arthur's Court* (1889). WILLIAM DEAN HOWELLS (1837–1920) also contributed to shaping early Midwestern science fiction with his utopian tale *A Traveler from Altruria* (1894), a critique of the Gilded Age's unchecked capitalist tendencies, first published in installments in the *Cosmopolitan* between November 1892 and October 1893. AMBROSE (GWINNETT) BIERCE (1842–ca. 1914) dabbled in alternative-reality stories, most notably in "An Occurrence at Owl Creek Bridge" (1890) and in other stories in *Tales of Soldiers and Civilians* (1891). James B. Alexander (b. 1831), a civil engineer, self-published *The Lunarian Professor and His Remarkable Revelations Concerning the Earth, the Moon, and Mars . . .* (1909), in which an extraterrestrial relates to a MINNEAPOLIS man the existence of utopian civilizations on various bodies of the solar system.

In the early twentieth century Midwestern writers deepened their interest in science fiction and fantasy. L. Frank Baum of CHICAGO combined Midwestern tornado realism with fantasy in *The WONDERFUL WIZARD OF OZ* (1900) and the many Oz stories that followed. UPTON (BEALL) SINCLAIR (JR.) (1878–1968) wrote *The Millennium* (1924), a utopian science-fiction history set in New York. *When Worlds Collide* (1933) and *After Worlds Collide* (1934) were novels co-written by EDWIN BALMER (1883–1959) and Philip (Gordon) Wylie (1902–1971). The first novel, adapted into a movie in 1951, is partially set in MICHIGAN and focuses on an end-of-the-world scenario caused by a planet colliding with Earth. The second novel deals with the aftermath of the surviving community. Although the fantasy world of Superman, with its Midwestern foundations, is most often associated with comic books (see COMIC STRIPS AND BOOKS), his first novelistic appearance was in *The*

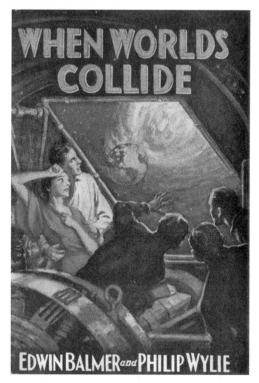

When Worlds Collide by Edwin Balmer and Philip Wylie.

© 1932, 1933 by Edwin Balmer and Philip Wylie.
Reprinted by permission of HarperCollins Publishers

Adventures of Superman (1942) by George F. Lowther (1913–1975).

The science-fiction and fantasy genres in the United States progressed significantly in the mid-twentieth century, with prominent contributions from many Midwestern writers. RAY (DOUGLAS) BRADBURY (1920–2012) was well known for novels such as *The Martian Chronicles* (1950), *Fahrenheit 451* (1953), and *Dandelion Wine* (1957), the last of which is set in fictional Green Town, ILLINOIS, based on his hometown, Waukegan, Illinois. Bradbury's sequel to *Dandelion Wine* is *Farewell Summer* (2006). INDIANA-born KURT VONNEGUT (JR.) (1922–2007) wrote works with science-fiction elements, including *Player Piano* (1952), *The Sirens of Titan* (1959), *Cat's Cradle* (1963), *Slaughterhouse-Five* (1969), and *Breakfast of Champions* (1973). All Vonnegut's novels have some Midwestern connection through the presence of individual characters or the expression of regional values and experiences. AUGUST (WILLIAM) DERLETH (1909–1971) and CLIFFORD D. SIMAK (1904–1988) created fantasy and science fiction drawing on the Midwest, and WISCONSIN in particular. Derleth, respected in science-fiction and fantasy circles for publishing the works of legendary writer H(oward) P(hillips) Lovecraft (1890–1937), was a talented author in the genre as well, producing collections of stories including *Someone in the Dark* (1941) and *Something Near* (1945). Simak transformed his hometown, Millville, Wisconsin, in much of his fiction, including novels such as *Way Station* (1963) and *All Flesh Is Grass* (1965) and many short stories.

Critics have noted the influence of pioneer history on the writing of Missouri-born Robert Heinlein (1907–1988), and some of his fiction contains portions set in the Midwest, including the landing of a flying saucer in Grinnell, IOWA, in *The Puppet Masters* (1951). Noted science-fiction writer Philip K(indred) Dick (1928–1982), connected personally to the Midwest through his birth in CHICAGO, has events from his novel *Ubik* (1969) take place in Des Moines, Iowa. Fritz (Reuter) Leiber (Jr.) (1910–1992), originally of Illinois, makes references to the Midwest or to his childhood there in many short stories.

The late twentieth century continued to see Midwestern writers influenced by the genre and Midwestern locations woven into works of science fiction and fantasy. Michigan has provided a rich landscape for writers and stories. The trilogy by Western Michigan University English professor Robert Stallman (1929–1980), *The Book of the Beast: The Orphan* (1980), *The Captive* (posthumously, 1981) and *The Beast* (posthumously, 1982), brilliantly reimagines the werewolf topos as a human/extraterrestrial life form. DETROIT-born MARGE PIERCY (b. 1936) places part of her novel *He, She, and It* (1991) in NEBRASKA. Writer Robert Charles Wilson (b. 1953) transports Two Rivers, Michigan, to an alternate earth in *Mysterium* (1994). OHIO has also served as a popular backdrop. Several fantasy or science-fiction elements appear in the writing of children's author VIRGINIA (ESTHER) HAMILTON (1936–2002). Many of her novels and stories draw inspiration from her hometown, Yellow Springs, Ohio, from her first novel, *Zeely* (1967), to her later novels, such as *Willie Bea and the Time the Martians Landed* (1983).

Other Midwestern states have their moments in the genre as well. Famed science-fiction writer Gene Wolfe (b. 1931) uses Chicago prominently in his novel *Free Live Free* (1984). Pete (Murray) Hautman (b. 1952) focuses on a time-traveling Illinois teen in *Mr. Was* (1996). The small fishing town of Lake Jellico, Minnesota, becomes the focus of a mysterious investigation of a lake monster in *News from the Edge: The Monster of Minnesota* (1997) by Mark Sumner (b. 1959). Thomas Disch (1940–2008) sets his science-fiction novel *On Wings of Song* (1979) in Iowa and New York.

The science-fiction and fantasy genre continues to have a place in the Midwest in the twenty-first century. *The Law of Nines* (2009) by Terry Goodkind (b. 1948) focuses on a Nebraska artist and contains numerous fantasy and science-fiction elements. *The Wannoshay Cycle* (2008) by Iowa-born Michael Jasper (b. 1970) revolves around three alien ships that crash-land in the Midwest and Canada. Fantasy elements shadow the novel *Distance Haze* (2000) by Jamil Nasir (b. 1955), focusing on a scientific religious institute built on a sacred burial ground in southwestern Michigan. English writer turned Midwesterner Neil Gaiman (b. 1960) wrote *American Gods* (2001), one of the strongest twenty-first-century fantasy novels set almost entirely in the Midwest. The novel emphasizes the supernatural possibilities in Wisconsin and Illinois towns and other prominent locations.

Midwestern universities produced the two most influential American scholarly journals for science fiction. Thomas D(ean) Clareson (1926–1993) started *Extrapolation* at Wooster College, Ohio, in 1959; it is still published but is currently based in Texas. R. D. Mullen and Darko Suvin founded *Science Fiction Studies* in 1973. It has been published ever since at De Pauw University, Indiana. Science-fiction fan clubs have existed since the 1940s. An informally organized Midwestern fan group calling itself General Technics began in the 1970s and has continued to the present, focusing on "hard sf," science fiction that follows scientific laws. It publishes an electronic fanzine, *Pyrotechnics*. The St. James guides to science-fiction and fantasy writers list about 950 authors who earn the attention of historians and critics. Of these, approximately 180 are associated with the Midwest by birth, residence, education, or subject matter.

SELECTED WORKS: Ray Bradbury's works are science-fiction standards; his *Dandelion Wine* (1957) has particularly strong Midwestern connections. August Derleth merges fantasy and science fiction with the Midwest in a particularly fluid way. Many of his short stories, including some collected in *Someone in the Dark* (1941), provide perspectives on place and genre. Works by these and other authors mentioned in this entry offer a strong introduction to Midwestern science fiction and fantasy.

FURTHER READING: No history of Midwestern science fiction exists, and no comprehensive appreciation of its meaning or achievement as literary art has yet appeared. The most immediately useful reference works are biobibliographic and encyclopedic: *St. James Guide to Science Fiction Writers* (1996), *St James Guide to Fantasy Writers* (1996), *The Cambridge Companion to Science Fiction* (2003), *The Greenwood Encyclopedia of Science Fiction and Fantasy: Themes, Works, and Wonders* (2005), and *The Oxford Handbook of Science Fiction* (2014). Three editions of *Anatomy of Wonder: A Critical Guide to Science Fiction* (second edition 1981; fourth edition 1995;

fifth edition 2004) are also helpful resources. The 1995 edition of *Anatomy* lists a number of histories of science fiction, but none is definitive. The monthly serial *Locus, the Magazine of the Science Fiction and Fantasy Field*, published since 1968, continues to attempt exhaustive coverage of all new publications, publishers, editorial migrations, prizes, writers' lives, vicissitudes, and obituaries associated with the field. The Gunn Center for the Study of Science Fiction at the University of Kansas also provides some detailed online resources on science fiction writers and texts.

JOHN R. PFEIFFER   CENTRAL MICHIGAN UNIVERSITY

SISTER CARRIE

HISTORY: (HERMAN) THEODORE DREISER (1871–1945) began writing *Sister Carrie* (1900), his first novel, in the autumn of 1899 when he was twenty-eight years old. It was published in early November 1900 by Doubleday, Page and Company in New York. In CHICAGO, ST. LOUIS, and Toledo, Dreiser had worked as a journalist writing dozens of articles in newspapers and periodicals on subjects ranging from city politics to immigrant life and labor strife and from the theatrical stage to religion and the Chicago World's Columbian Exposition of 1893. As a result, he was well equipped to express the hard facts and basic truths of American urban life at the turn of the twentieth century.

The heroine of the novel, Carrie Meeber, much like Dreiser, is a small-town Midwesterner who arrives by rail in Chicago alone, innocent, and on her own at the age of eighteen. Carrie pounds the pavement in a discouraging hunt for employment until, having been turned down a dozen times, she is forced to take the most menial of jobs in a shoe factory. The hard and humiliating times she suffers in Chicago correspond closely to Dreiser's own; Carrie's flight to New York, in turn, draws on the story of his sister Emma's elopement with her lover, a Chicago saloon cashier and embezzler.

His heroine's eventual career in the theatrical world also reflects Dreiser's youth and family history. When he moved to New York in 1894, he joined his brother John Paul Dreiser Jr. (1857–1906), who, under the name of Paul Dresser, had achieved fame as a composer of popular songs. Together the two brothers were to write the nostalgic and sentimental hymn to INDIANA, "On the Banks of the Wabash Far Away." As an actor and singer, Paul was positioned to introduce young Theodore to backstage life. That knowledge served Dreiser well in depicting Carrie's entry into musical theatre and her success on the stage in New York.

The action in the novel unfolds in an uncomplicated time sequence beginning in August 1889 with Carrie's arrival in Chicago on a train from WISCONSIN, as Dreiser himself had come by train from Indiana. The novel follows Carrie for roughly the next decade, ending with her climb up the ladder of fame and success. Since Carrie lives unmarried with one man and then another, her behavior conforms to the Victorian moral standard of the fallen woman. But Dreiser does not judge her actions as sinful, nor does he punish her with a melodramatic fall. Her life presents, in something of a parody of the American dream of success, the story of an individual with minimal talent rising above unpromising conditions.

A parallel plotline traces the declining fortunes of her second lover, George Hurstwood, a greeter at a swank Chicago saloon. When he meets Carrie, she is living with Drouet, a traveling salesman. Hurstwood is married, the father of adult children, socially prominent, and financially well off. When Hurstwood becomes infatuated with Carrie, he impulsively embezzles a small fortune from his employers and elopes with

Drawing by Reginald Marsh from Theodore Dreiser's *Sister Carrie*, 1939 edition.

© 2014 Estate of Reginald Marsh / Art Students League, New York. Artists Rights Society (ARS), New York

Carrie to New York. There, as he spends the remainder of the money he embezzled, he drifts into idleness and on to skid row and ends a penniless suicide. Carrie, meanwhile, enjoys a burgeoning popularity on the Broadway stage. Whereas Carrie is always guided strongly by self-interest, Hurstwood succumbs to his overpowering emotional desires. He represents the ever-present danger that a climber, through bad choices or accident—or both—might slip into a catastrophic fall.

A person, Dreiser suggests, can prosper or suffer from chance and accident, which more strongly affect one's fate than do any personal moral values, wishes, or plans. People are, at last, no more than wisps blown about in unfriendly winds, without control, without direction, and blinded by the illusion that their lives possess significance. This is Dreiser's great thematic message, and it dominates *Sister Carrie*. The novel was strongly influenced by the evolutionary theories of Charles Darwin (1809–1882), imbibed by Dreiser through his reading of the philosopher Herbert Spencer (1820–1903). Spencer's *First Principles* (1864) exploded the moral values and Victorian idealism Dreiser had once trusted and believed in. During his career as a reporter, he had observed Spencer's phrase "survival of the fittest" operating in a highly competitive and unforgiving world. In such a world morality has little, perhaps nothing, to do with prosperity or failure. Instead, success or failure is all too often determined by chance, obsessive desire, or an accidental circumstance.

Dreiser's espousal of that stark approach to life—with a new, fairly direct representation of his characters' sexual lives—provoked belated efforts by his publisher to cancel publication. For a time the fate of the novel hung in the balance as Doubleday, Page all but abandoned it, but it survived. Throughout his life Dreiser promoted the story that Frank Doubleday's wife had insisted on the suppression of the book. But Doubleday, to meet his contractual obligations, printed 1,000 copies and grudgingly filled some 400 orders from bookstores. (BENJAMIN) FRANK(LIN) NORRIS, (JR.) (1870–1902) aggressively backed Dreiser and sent out over a hundred review copies. Doubleday's qualms were confirmed to some extent when many reviewers stridently attacked what they saw as the book's immorality, its hopelessness, and its "dreary" deterministic philosophy. At the same time, some of the most critical reviews in 1900–1901, including many that found it "too realistic," granted the book's emotional power and acknowledged its flashes of insight. Jack Salzman, collecting these early reviews in *Theodore Dreiser: The Critical Reception* (1972), concludes that "there is little basis for the generally held belief" that the press accorded *Sister Carrie* an "overwhelmingly denunciatory" reception (xvii–xviii). Responding to the judgment of the American and British press, William Heinemann in London decided to republish *Sister Carrie* in an abridged form. In August 1901, with the chapters on Carrie in Chicago condensed, the book won still more favorable reviews, the beginnings of its international reputation, and about $100 in royalties for Dreiser.

SIGNIFICANCE: Writers of the *Chicago Renaissance* and the Midwest were to find in the legend of *Sister Carrie*'s suppression a symbol of liberation and a call to sexual freedom. In the novel itself, Dale Kramer asserts in *Chicago Renaissance: The Literary Life in the Midwest* (1966), they found a "major force" in literature (24). After Dreiser bought the printers' plates from the publisher, the book was reissued by the B. W. Dodge Company in 1907, launched this time with an advertising campaign and a flurry of favorable reviews. The dust jacket carried endorsements from Midwesterners (Joseph) Brand Whitlock (1869–1934), (Hannibal) Hamlin Garland (1860–1940), William Marion Reedy (1862–1920), and Edna Kenton (1876–1954). Their responses to the novel, culled from letters to Dreiser and earlier reviews, gave an intimation of what *Sister Carrie* would mean to writers like Floyd Dell (1887–1969) and others in the second wave of the Chicago Renaissance. In the years just before World War I, Dell championed it and Dreiser's liberated vision against genteel literary tastes. Writing in Chicago's *Friday Literary Review,* Dell, as quoted in F(rancis) O(tto) Matthiessen's *Theodore Dreiser* (1951), contended that "the poetry of Chicago has been adequately rendered so far, by only one writer, and in only one book—*Sister Carrie*" (26). The poet Edgar Lee Masters (1868–1950), another

member of Chicago's avant-garde, as quoted in Matthiesen's *Theodore Dreiser,* remembered *Sister Carrie* as the book that "set the pace for truth, and freed the young, and enlightened the old where they could be enlightened" (61). During Dreiser's lifetime his novel achieved the status of a modern classic, leading the way for many Midwestern writers, such as Sherwood Anderson (1876–1941), James T(homas) Farrell (1904–1979), Ernest (Miller) Hemingway (1899–1961), and Saul (C.) Bellow (1915–2005).

Responding to his critics in 1907, Dreiser said, as reprinted in Salzman's *Theodore Dreiser: The Critical Reception,* that in writing *Sister Carrie,* he had "intended" to present "a picture of conditions" (41). The conditions he described were produced by the Industrial Revolution, the mass immigration of the 1880s and 1890s, and the rapid growth of cities. Especially in the Midwest, the spectacular growth of industrial cities brought on immense changes from agriculture to manufacturing and a disruptive imbalance of wealth and power. Dreiser's opening chapters describe the staggering population growth of late nineteenth-century Chicago and, in depicting figuring the enormous scale of "the great city," express Carrie's wonder and terror in this new urban landscape. Through Carrie's innocent eyes and her sense of diminished identity, he also tabulated and probed the surface qualities of changing clothing styles, theatrical illusions, and the pervasive presence of sentimentality in popular culture. Her unfulfilled desires, set against the abundance and seductive wealth of the city, represent the workings of modern consumer culture—the transitory quality of social relationships that developed as populations shifted from the Midwest's rural areas to the region's cities, the decay of politics, the division of the population into rigid classes founded on wealth, and the beginnings of a pervasive celebrity-centered public life. All these conditions were there to be seen in the world presented by young Dreiser. He was soon recognized as an astute observer, a man possessed of an instinctive grasp of modern conditions and the changes affecting America. Aside from such important developments on the social scene, Dreiser was concerned also with the broader, more fundamental, questions that dealt with life in a rapidly industrializing America: the relationship of the individual to the masses to natural objects, and to the idea of God.

With practical examples from novelists such as Chicago's HENRY BLAKE FULLER (1857–1929), Émile Zola (1840–1902), and, most notably, Honoré de Balzac (1799–1850), Dreiser early on developed into a writer of the naturalistic school. See also REALISM AND NATURALISM. He viewed life as a continual, and too often losing, struggle of the individual against the tremendous forces that rule the universe. Under naturalism, despite periodic and momentary illusions of success, individuals over the long term fight a losing battle to succeed against the powers of an all-too-often hostile heredity or environment. Few, if any, genuine triumphs were to be gained. Eager to signal his agreement with naturalistic thinkers, Dreiser at various intervals injected throughout *Sister Carrie* brief notices of this philosophic viewpoint.

Dreiser drew as well on the examples and narrative conventions of popular literature. From the advice books and DIME NOVELS that warned against urban vice, from the Horatio Alger (1832–1899) novels that urged readers to strive and succeed in the city, and, of course, from newspaper stories like those of the Chicago columnist GEORGE ADE (1866–1944), Dreiser took inspiration, borrowed catchwords, and recast type characters. In *Sister Carrie*, as Amy Kaplan suggests in *The Social Construction of American Realism* (1988), Dreiser was both entrapped in and liberated by "mass culture," particularly the sentimentalism that tightly bound up popular stories of country innocents in the city (140). As F. O. Matthiessen suggested, Dreiser did not reject the vogue of Indiana folksiness or "geniality" associated with (NEWTON) BOOTH TARKINGTON (1869–1946) and JAMES WHITCOMB RILEY (1849–1916) (64). In presenting Chicago as a magnet, a tempting lure, and a dazzling wonder for those fresh from the region's farms and SMALL TOWNS, he recontextualized the literary conventions that framed the myth of the city and the Midwest as a hinterland. *Sister Carrie* stands among those rare volumes that have remained relevant a century and more after first publication.

IMPORTANT EDITIONS: Modern readers are likely to encounter *Sister Carrie* just as Dreiser published it, for he never revised the book. For scholars, there is the University of Pennsylvania scholarly edition edited by James L. W. West III, John C. Berkey, and Alice M. Winters (1981), which restores many words and passages cut from the manuscript before its 1900 publication. Donald Pizer, in his introduction to *New Essays on "Sister Carrie"* (1991), noted that over twenty translations of *Sister Carrie* had appeared (14). The number has grown since Pizer's tally: *Dreiser Studies* 33.1 (Spring 2002) devoted a large "Special Section" to "*Sister Carrie* in Translation" (27–75).

FURTHER READING: Perhaps the richest source for Dreiser's comments on *Sister Carrie* is the two volumes of the *Dreiser-Mencken Letters* (1986), edited by Thomas P. Riggio. Dreiser often confided in H(enry) L(ewis) Mencken (1880–1956), an early and indefatigable supporter. Of special interest is a letter to Mencken on May 13, 1916, where he recounts "the history" of the novel's composition and publication (231–34). The only full-length biography written by a scholar who knew and worked with Dreiser is Robert Elias's *Theodore Dreiser: Apostle of Nature* (1949), a much-admired study. W(illiam) A(ndrew) Swanberg's *Dreiser* (1965) is the most complete biography and is generally relied on for its immense factual detail concerning the novelist's life and career. The first volume of Richard (Roberts) Lingeman's biography, *Theodore Dreiser: At the Gates of the City* (1986), concentrates on the background and composition of *Sister Carrie*. Jack Salzman's *Theodore Dreiser: The Critical Reception* (1972) reprints a generous sampling of the reviews from 1900 and 1907.

An important contribution is "*Sister Carrie": Theodore Dreiser's Sociological Tragedy* (1992) by David E. E. Sloane. *Two Dreisers* (1969) by Ellen Moers (1928–1979) includes an astute examination of *Sister Carrie*. *New Essays on "Sister Carrie"* (1991), edited by Donald Pizer, presents critical views by a variety of scholars. Full-length critical works, sometimes placing *Sister Carrie* within a biographical framework, include *Hard Facts: Setting and Form in the American Novel* (1985) by Philip Fisher, *Theodore Dreiser Revisited* (1992) by Philip Gerber, *Theodore Dreiser: His World and His Novels* (1969) by Richard Lehan, and *The Novels of Theodore Dreiser* (1976) by Donald Pizer. In her closing chapters in *The So-cial Construction of American Realism* (1988) Amy Kaplan takes up "the problem of sentimentalism" and popular art in Dreiser's novel. For an understanding of Dreiser's relation to Chicago and Indiana writers, F. O. Matthiessen's brief comments in *Theodore Dreiser* (1951) are powerfully suggestive. Timothy Spears, in *Chicago Dreaming: Mid-westerners and the City* (2005), builds on Matthiessen's work, presenting *Sister Carrie* as a key to the way the "expectations and desires" of "rural Midwesterners" created the character of Chicago (xiii). For a sense of the novel's importance to the Chicago Renaissance, Bernard Duffey's *The Chicago Renaissance in American Letters* (1954), Dale Kramer's *Chicago Renaissance: The Literary Life in the Midwest* (1966), and Carl S. Smith's *Chicago and the American Literary Imagination, 1880–1920* (1984) are critical. *Dreiser Studies*, an ongoing journal published by the International Dreiser Society, includes reviews of books of interest concerning Dreiser, as well as articles from a broad spectrum of contributors whose common interests are Dreiser's life and fiction. H. L. Mencken placed the manuscript of *Sister Carrie* in the Manuscripts and Archives Division of the New York Public Library.

PHILIP GERBER

THE COLLEGE AT BROCKPORT, STATE UNIVERSITY
OF NEW YORK

GUY SZUBERLA   UNIVERSITY OF TOLEDO

SLAM POETRY.
See Poetry Slams

SLAVE NARRATIVES
OVERVIEW: A significant literary tradition known today as the African American slave-narrative tradition had its beginnings in the autobiographical narratives of fugitive and former slaves. These narratives came into existence in the United States around the mid-eighteenth century and remain significant historical documents today. Although most are associated with the South and focus on southern experiences, some significant narratives originated in other regions and carry specific imprints of the political, social, and cultural values of those regions. Midwestern slave narratives were written by those who

were slaves in the region, as well as by fugitive and former slaves who made the Midwest their home.

HISTORY AND SIGNIFICANCE: "Whatever else it is, autobiography stems more often than not from a need to explain and justify the self," states William Andrews in his 1986 study *To Tell a Free Story: The First Century of Afro-American Autobiography, 1760–1865* (1). Slave narratives that began surfacing in the United States around 1760 certainly embraced this motivation. Not only did these narrators feel a need to explain their individual existence, but they were also forced to justify their status as humans deserving full human rights.

Antebellum narratives, especially those written between 1830 and 1850, provided strong political weapons in describing the hard lives and abuses to which slaves were subject, as reflected in the *Narrative of the Life of Frederick Douglass, an American Slave* (1845) by Frederick Douglass (born Frederick Augustus Washington Bailey) (1818–1895) and the fictionalized *Uncle Tom's Cabin* (1852) by Harriet Beecher Stowe (1811–1896). The political value of these documents to abolitionists may be one of the reasons many slave narratives of this period disappeared. In his article "Black Message / White Envelope: Genre, Authenticity, and Authority in the Antebellum Slave Narrative," *Callaloo* 32 (Summer 1987), John Sekora reports that "after the Civil War and under the aegis of 'national reconciliation'" slave narratives were considered "irrelevant and outdated curiosities" (482). For that same reason, even those narratives that remained in print required validation by historians before being seriously considered for study by literary scholars.

The oral narratives collected under the aegis of the Works Progress Administration's FEDERAL WRITERS' PROJECT from 1936 through 1938 led to renewed literary interest in slave narratives. Sekora, in the same *Callaloo* article, indicates that in the 1950s revisionist historians authenticated the narratives as valuable historical documents, and literary scholars embraced them as major literary works (482–83).

Today African American slave narratives are esteemed for documenting the social fabric of a growing nation and for their ability to prompt readers to participate in the nation's ongoing racial dialogue. Writers of Midwestern slave narratives extended that same invitation to their readers. The Midwest's historical experiences and documents, including the Northwest Ordinances, the Missouri Compromise, the Underground Railroad, the Fugitive Slave Law, the Kansas-Nebraska Act, and the Dred Scott case, significantly affected the tone and nature of this dialogue.

Some Midwestern narrators, in works like *A Slave's Adventures toward Freedom: Not Fiction, but the True Story of a Struggle* (1918) by Peter Bruner (1845–1938) and *What Experience Has Taught Me: An Autobiography of Thomas William Burton* (1910) by Thomas William Burton (1860–1930), subscribed to and benefited from the Midwestern belief in progress and the recurring Midwestern motif of using education as a stepping-stone to success. In other works, such as *Book for the People! To Be Read by All Voters, Black and White, with Thrilling Events of the Life of Norvel Blair, of Grundy County, State of Illinois* (1880) by Norvel Blair (1825–1916) and *The New Man: Twenty-Nine Years a Slave, Twenty-Nine Years a Free Man* (1895) by Henry Clay Bruce (1836–1902), the narrators were quick to point out the injustices suffered by blacks in a region that was supposed to be their promised land.

Most slave narratives are spiritual in tone. However, Midwestern narrators rarely differentiated between what other narrators like Frederick Douglass label as "slave-holding religion" and their own religious practices (*Narrative of the Life of Frederick Douglass, an American Slave,* 1982 Penguin Classics edition, appendix, 153). Midwestern slave narrators typically upheld the version of religion practiced by their owners. Scholars like Mary W. Burger, in her article "I, Too, Sing America: The Black Autobiographer's Response to Life in the Midwest and Mid-Plains," *Kansas Quarterly* 7.3 (Summer 1975), attributes this attitude to "the masters' lax rules about religious instruction for blacks" because most slaves "were allowed to go to church and were preached to by a white minister" (46).

As literary texts, these narratives launched the African American literary tradition and a distinct genre, the African American slave-narrative tradition, which is still widely practiced today. Many renowned Midwestern African American writers, including RICHARD WRIGHT (1908–1960), author of *NATIVE SON* (1940); LANGSTON HUGHES (1902–1967), creator of many novels, short stories, poetry collections such as *THE WEARY BLUES* (1926), plays, and nonfiction works; Nobel Prize winner TONI MORRISON (b. CHLOE ARDELIA WOFFORD, 1931), author of nine novels, including *SONG OF SOLOMON* (1977); Poet Laureate / Consultant in Poetry to the Library of Congress RITA DOVE (b. 1952), author of nine volumes of poetry, as well as other works; Consultant in Poetry to the Library of Congress GWENDOLYN BROOKS (1917–2000), author of many volumes of poetry, including *A STREET IN BRONZEVILLE* (1945), as well as other works; and LORRAINE HANSBERRY (1930–1965), playwright author of *A RAISIN IN THE SUN* (1959), are deeply rooted in this tradition. It is a tradition of authenticity that gives the narrator a platform to highlight experiences that shaped the individual, as well as the nation as a whole.

According to Stephen Butterfield in his *Black Autobiography in America* (1974), "The structure of [Richard Wright's] *Black Boy* belongs to the slave narrative" (156). Indeed, there are several noticeable affinities between the *Narrative of the Life of Frederick Douglass* and *Black Boy,* starting with the protagonists. Jerry W. Ward Jr. in his introduction to *Black Boy* describes this affinity as the "use of the abused male prototype" (xvii). The two texts share the same structure as novels of ascent, as well as several themes, including valuing education and resisting oppression. Similarly, several Langston Hughes's poems, like his frequently anthologized "The Negro Speaks of Rivers," "Harlem [Dream Deferred]," "I Too," and "Theme for English B," are a continuation of America's dialogue on black identity, freedom, and African American citizenship that started in slave narratives. William Andrews in his online study *North American Slave Narratives,* developed in conjunction with the Documenting the American South program of the University Library of the University of North Carolina–Chapel Hill, asserts the importance of the tradition to the nation: "Slave and ex-slave narratives are important not only for what they tell us about African American history and literature, but also because they reveal to us the complexities of the dialogue between whites and blacks in this country in the last two centuries, particularly for African Americans."

Although Midwestern states are well represented in the Works Progress Administration's Federal Writers' Project via the multivolume series *Slave Narratives: A Folk History of Slavery in the United States, from Interviews with Former Slaves* (1936; reprinted 1976), more noticeable full-length narratives came out of ILLINOIS, KANSAS, MICHIGAN, MISSOURI, OHIO, and WISCONSIN. In *Book for the People!*, Norvel Blair highlighted racial relationships between African Americans and whites in Illinois and cautioned the former to be wary of northern whites pretending to be of help to them. *The New Man* by Henry Clay Bruce detailed slave life in Missouri and painted a clear picture of a fugitive slave's adventures in Kansas. Michigan was reflected in *Aunt Sally; or, The Cross the Way of Freedom: A Narrative of the Slave-Life and Purchase of the Mother of Rev. Isaac Williams, of Detroit, Michigan* (1858) by Isaac D. Williams (b. ca. 1821). This volume was a spiritual narrative for use in Sabbath schools to give young people a glimpse into slave struggles and the role of faith in redemption. In *Fifty*

Years of Slavery in the United States of America (1891) Harry Smith detailed his experiences as a slave in Kentucky and a free man in Indiana and Michigan. *Narrative of William W. Brown, a Fugitive Slave, Written by Himself* (1847) by William Wells Brown (ca. 1814–1884) provided a detailed description of slavery in Missouri.

Ohio was treated in the *Memoirs of Samuel Spottford Clement Relating Interesting Experiences in Days of Slavery and Freedom* (1908); the work was noticeable for the narrator's candid description of relationships between races in the Midwest's first state. *A Slave's Adventures toward Freedom*, by Peter Bruner was a religiously inspiring success story of a former slave working as a janitor at Miami University in Ohio. *His Promised Land: The Autobiography of John P. Parker* (1996), edited and published by Stuart Seely Sprague, detailed the relentless efforts of John P. Parker (1827–1900) to escape slavery and offered a valuable inside story of the Underground Railroad in Ripley, Ohio. In 2007 this story was made into an opera performed at the Aronoff Center in CINCINNATI, Ohio, *Rise for Freedom: The John P. Parker Story*. Wisconsin slave narratives included *Thirty Years a Slave: From Bondage to Freedom*

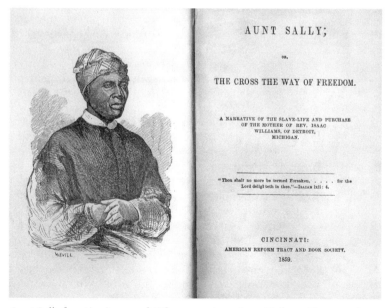

Aunt Sally frontispiece and title page. American Reform Tract and Book Society, 1859.

Image courtesy of Special Collections, Grand Valley State University Libraries

(1897) by Louis Hughes (1832–1913), the narration of a fugitive slave from Alabama who found success practicing as a nurse in Milwaukee.

The History of William Webb (1873) narrated the slave experience of William Webb (b. ca. 1836) and offered an optimistic view of life for former slaves once they reached the Promised Land. Webb recounted his experiences when he "was between nine and ten years of age" seeing slaves mistreated in the fields and mothers being parted from their children at the auction block and said, "I looked to the heavens and cried out Lord if you rule this earth, why do not you deliver us from this cruel bondage. I heard a voice say, I will be with you and your race of people." When young William asked his mother who the speaker was, his mother said, "My son, that was God who spoke to you" (3). Webb went on to explain how, whenever he was in despair, he held on to the promise of meeting both his mother and his father in heaven.

From the Darkness Cometh the Light; or, Struggles for Freedom (ca. 1890) was another spiritual narration exemplifying the devotion of Lucy Ann (Berry) Delaney (ca. 1828–ca. 1891) to faith. What Experience Has Taught Me: An Autobiography of Thomas William Burton reflected a belief in progress and success through education that is often expressed in Midwestern slave narratives. All these works, with the exception of the entries in the Works Progress Administration's Federal Writers' Project's Slave Narratives" and John P. Parker's narrative, are available on William Andrews's North American Slave Narratives website.

SELECTED WORKS: Readers interested in gaining insight into Midwestern slave narratives should consult the following works. Norvel Blair's Book for the People! To Be Read by All Voters (1880) highlights black people's struggles for freedom in Illinois. Henry Clay Bruce's The New Man: Twenty-Nine Years a Slave, Twenty-Nine Years a Free Man (1895) details slave life in Missouri and paints a clear picture of a fugitive slave's adventures in Kansas. Narrative of William W. Brown, a Fugitive Slave, Written by Himself (1847) offers insights into Missouri history and also introduces the reader to a narrator whose rhetorical skills clearly match those of Frederick Douglass. His Promised Land: The Autobiography of John P. Parker (1996) offers a valuable inside story of the Underground Railroad in Ripley, Ohio. In What Experience Has Taught Me: An Autobiography of Thomas William Burton (1910) the author enriches his narrative with photographs and poetry and highlights the Midwestern slave narrators' belief in progress and success through education.

FURTHER READING: Wilbur H. Siebert's study The Underground Railroad from Slavery to Freedom (1898) is often labeled the most carefully researched document on the topic. Mary W. Burger's Black Autobiography: A Literature of Celebration (1974), one of the earliest critical works, has a specific entry on Midwestern African American autobiographers. Closely following Burger's 1874 publication, Stephen Butterfield's Black Autobiography in America (1974) provides a comprehensive chronological survey of the genre that examines its development, importance and influence, themes, and place in American literature. Charles T. Davis and Henry Louis Gates's The Slave's Narrative (1985) is a convenient collection of essays critiquing the genre's development over three centuries. William L. Andrews's To Tell a Free Story: The First Century of Afro-American Autobiography, 1760–1865 (1986) offers a comprehensive study of the genre in its first century of existence. Marion Wilson Starling's The Slave Narrative: Its Place in American History (1988) details the historical and literary significance of the slave narratives.

Additional resources are available in the Schomburg Center for Research in Black Culture at the New York Public Library and in the Black Archives of Mid-America in KANSAS CITY (Missouri), which covers black life in Missouri, Kansas, Iowa, Oklahoma, and the Midwest. Duke University's Special Collections and its slave-narrative manuscripts are also valuable, as is the online American Memory Collection of the Manuscripts Division of the Library of Congress, which houses slave narratives collected under the aegis of the Federal Writers' Project, 1936–1938.

IMMACULATE KIZZA
THE UNIVERSITY OF TENNESSEE AT CHATTANOOGA

SMALL TOWN, THE

OVERVIEW: More than the coastal villages of the Northeast, the hamlets of the South, or the mining camps of the West, the Midwestern small town has served as an all-American literary setting. All these regional literary settings owe some of their cachet to the small-town mythos, a conception of the village as a close-knit, pastoral community where it seems that everyone knows everyone else. As Ima Honaker Herron points out in *The Small Town in American Literature* (1939), portrayals of village life in New England often relied on Old Europe's pastoral sensibilities to describe towns that provided the centers of religious, political, and social interaction (33). Midwestern authors have used and built on this small-town myth, making their small towns malleable backdrops against which to satisfy the varied desires of their readership.

The literary setting of the Midwestern town has functioned in diverse ways, by turns showing the strengths and weaknesses of American westward settlement, providing an exotic atmosphere for love stories, or acting as a small stage on which to play out larger American cultural debates, including those of race, class, wealth, and gender. Authors have often characterized the Midwestern small town as a stultifying place that artists yearn to escape from, but this characterization is tempered with nostalgia and longing for an idealized home, creating a tension between the pull away from and the pull toward the small town.

The reflection of the small town in Midwestern literature has followed the historical development of small-town life in the Midwest. In the mid to late nineteenth century Midwestern writers redefined the idyllic image of the small town imported from New England by superimposing on it the harsh realities of frontier settlement. By the early twentieth century the Midwestern small town had evolved into the symbol of everything middling and middlebrow in American culture. This perceived analogy led to the use of Midwestern small towns as the setting for authors' scathing literary REVOLT FROM THE VILLAGE. Since World War II, with the majority of Americans living in urban and suburban areas, the small town has increasingly been viewed in Midwest-ern literature as a mythic place that satisfies readers' nostalgic yearning for what they perceive as having been a simpler past. Set between the metropolis and the rural farm, the industrial and the pastoral, the cosmopolitan and the rustic, the Wild West frontier and the settled Eastern landscape, the small town as represented in Midwestern literature has been seen as a place to escape from and to retreat to, simultaneously containing all that America prizes and despises about itself.

HISTORY AND SIGNIFICANCE:

The Nineteenth Century—Frontier Towns and Country Towns: The waves of Midwestern settlement created two related but distinct types of small town, the frontier town and the country town. The literary depiction of the frontier town satisfied two simultaneous urges of the American reader: it embodied the reassuring village myth of neighborly community life while also reflecting the seemingly limitless opportunities of westward expansion. Texts about frontier communities also reflected darker aspects of westward expansion, echoing the fact that actual frontier towns often had little in common with the boosterish claims of their developers. Land speculators regularly platted idealized representations of still-unbuilt towns on paper and then sold plots of land to hopeful settlers, who often found their dreams undercut when the railroad line ran in a different direction or another village won the fight to be the county seat. If frontier settlements survived for a generation, they came to be portrayed as country towns, middle points between city and farm.

Although stories about country towns reflected the village myth of community, they also reflected the reality of the small-town middleman. These middlemen made their living off the farmer: merchants charging marked-up prices for goods, speculators and bankers selling and mortgaging land at inflated interest rates, and railway agents and commodity traders controlling farmers' means for transporting their harvest. Subsequently, farmers' political movements, like the Grange movement of the 1870s and Populism in the 1890s, found their way into portrayals of the country town.

The earliest portrayals of Midwestern frontier towns, like those by JAMES HALL (1793–1868) and CAROLINE KIRKLAND (1801–1864), often attempted to balance a romantic and heroic image of pioneers and their overall struggles with less flattering depictions of those settlers' daily lives and manners. Hall's account of his keelboat journey on the Ohio River, *Letters from the West* (1828), stands as one of the first depictions of Midwestern frontier life, focusing on life in the wilderness but also on the bustling economic growth in newly sprung-up river communities. The courthouse, crude as it was, often acted as the center of frontier life because, as James Hall observed in the preface to *Legends of the West* (1832), "in new counties, every body goes to court" (x). Settlers were drawn to town not necessarily out of a sense of community but to settle land-claim disputes. Similarly, in Kirkland's primarily autobiographical novel of frontier-town life *A NEW HOME—WHO'LL FOLLOW?* (1839), the depiction of a beautiful and wild MICHIGAN is balanced with the portrayal of settlements peopled by less palatable characters, including land sharks and unmannered rumormongers. Kirkland describes how land speculators in DETROIT promoted their towns to buyers with little consideration of facts, touting future rail or steamboat lines that would regularly fail to materialize.

Because many early Midwestern novels naturally took settlers and settlement as their topic, the small town often serves as the setting for a cast of characters—unscrupulous storeowners, lenders, and plain thieves—who take advantage of pioneer farmers. Two authors who took a dark view of the small town were EDWARD EGGLESTON (1837–1902) and JOSEPH KIRKLAND (1830–1894). Eggleston's *The Hoosier Schoolmaster* (1871) follows Ralph Hartsook as he travels from the relatively settled country town of Lewisburg, INDIANA, to the corrupt backwater of Flat Creek to become the schoolmaster. There Ralph finds that his greatest challenge is not educating and taming the rough youth of the frontier town but battling the corrupt group of thieves led by the elusive Dr. Small, a gambler who also hails from Lewisburg. Eggleston's narrator subtly mocks both the "civilized" characters of Lewisburg and the backcountry hicks of Flat Creek, but corruption ultimately comes out of the country town, not the frontier village. Eggleston's *The Mystery of Metropolisville* (1873) chronicles the boom-and-bust cycle of Metropolisville, a small town that fades quickly when the railroad expands along another route.

Kirkland's *Zury: The Meanest Man in Spring County* (1887) presents both rural and urban views of the frontier town of Wayback, ILLINOIS. To Anne Sparrow, a refined schoolteacher from Boston, Wayback is a backwater where all the trees have been cut to build sordid houses, the flies reign, and there is no intellectual conversation. To Zury Prouder, a miserly but clever settler, Wayback is a place to hold mortgages and take advantage of settlers. Anne's civilized upbringing intimidates the village hicks, and Zury's ability to outwit the small-town lenders makes him one of the few settlers in Spring County to thrive. Together, they get the better of the small town and build a successful and cultured farm.

The most critically recognized early Midwestern novel to focus on the small town is *The Story of a Country Town* (1883) by EDGAR WATSON HOWE (1853–1937). Howe's novel depicts the transition from the frontier town to the country town by describing not one but two towns: the barely formed Fairview, MISSOURI, a frontier town consisting only of a church, a graveyard, and a scattering of houses; and the bustling Twin Mounds, a country town of six hundred "very wicked people" (132). The novel's narrator, Ned Westlock, describes Fairview as a cold and gray setting of relentless toil, but the frontier town grows and thrives because of the interconnectedness and hardworking nature of its people. Twin Mounds, on the other hand, is peopled with merchants not clever enough to make it back East and farmers-turned-politicians too corrupt and lazy to work. Ned's father, Rev. John Westlock, is a cold but honest man when he lives and farms in Fairview, but upon his move to Twin Mounds the elder Westlock commences an adulterous affair that leads him to abandon his family and culminates in his eventual disgrace. Howe looks nostalgically back on the frontier town, a lifestyle that is quickly disappearing, while finding fault with the country town.

The novels of MARY HARTWELL CATHER-WOOD (1847–1902) balance a critique of small-town life with optimism for the opportunities these towns held. Her *Craque-o'Doom* (1881) is a dark and autobiographical account of her youth in a frontier town, but *The Spirit of an Illinois Town* (1897) balances critical and hopeful elements in its depiction of Trail City, a town whose bustling growth is threatened only by cutthroat competition among its districts. After becoming sick of his European travels, the novel's narrator, Seth Adams, journeys to Trail City and reflects on how American the country town is: "The only endearing characteristic of the town was its Americanness. The raw land, the unfinish, the glad rush, the high, clear air, the jolly insolence of independent human beings, how American they all were!" (6). Kate Keene, Seth's love interest and a native of Trail City, embodies a mix of this American spirit and an Old World classicism that allows her to be both a hard worker and, when giving one of her brilliant reading performances, a supple Greek goddess. When Kate is killed in a tornado that wipes out half of Trail City, she becomes the eponymous "spirit" of the town, a ghost watching over the growing village, nurturing its American vitality but tempering it with European culture and manners.

Although the six Mississippi Valley stories of the first edition of (HANNIBAL) HAMLIN GARLAND's (1860–1940) *MAIN-TRAVELLED ROADS* (1891) depict farm life, the stories he added to the collection in later editions (1899, 1922, 1930) shift his focus to the country town, a setting he characterized primarily as a stepping-stone between the rural and the metropolitan worlds. In "God's Ravens" a CHICAGO writer returns to the small town of his youth to regain his health but finds himself unable to connect with the small-town folk. Yet after he takes ill, the town rallies around him and nurses him back to health. In "A Day's Pleasure" a farm wife takes great pains to make a trip to town for a simple day's release from her dreary existence on the farm. Once there, however, she cannot find a way to fill her time and is stuck wandering aimlessly up and down the main street until a towns-woman takes mercy on her and invites her in for tea. In both stories the idealized town

fails initially to live up to the outsider's expectations, and only through charitable and fairly uncharacteristic actions of small-town residents are the outsider's dreams actualized. "The Fireplace" comments derisively on the domesticating quality of small-town life; the plot follows a farmer who retires to a cramped house in town to please his wife. Life in town comes to represent the death of his heroic pioneer lifestyle, for the retired farmer is unable to adjust to the inactivity of town life and longs for the rustic and impractical fireplace he loved in his pioneer homestead.

Over the course of his literary career, SAMUEL LANGHORNE CLEMENS (1835–1910), writing as Mark Twain, balanced a boy's vision of a happy river town as a playground with an adult understanding of the injustice of slavery and the stultifying small-town social life. His joyful depiction of St. Petersburg, Missouri, in *The Adventures of Tom Sawyer* (1876) is tempered by the complex moral tale presented in *ADVENTURES OF HUCKLEBERRY FINN* (London 1884; New York 1885). Huck's final decision to "light out for the territory" (405) despite the fact that Jim has been freed reflects his understanding of the corrupt underpinnings of supposedly "sivilized" (405) small-town life. Twain explores this dual nature further in *The Tragedy of Pudd'nhead Wilson* (1894), a story set in Dawson's Landing, "half a day's journey, per steamboat, below St. Louis" (17), inches away from the "true" South. The story about two children switched as babies—one white, the other one-sixteenth black—points out how incremental but minute racial differences point to larger moral problems, including how closely the Midwest is linked to the South through the slave trade. Twain's "The Man That Corrupted Hadleyburg" (1900) prefigures the twentieth-century Revolt from the Village movement, portraying a town whose self-satisfied motto reads "Lead us not into temptation" (23), but whose nineteen leading families are corrupt gossipmongers.

The Early Twentieth Century—The Revolt from the Village: The economic changes of the late nineteenth and early twentieth centuries signaled the end of the economic and political dominance of the Midwestern small town. As industrialism drew people from villages and farms to growing urban centers, the distance between the small town and the metropolis shrank; transportation via rail and communication via telegraph and later telephone made the small town more accessible and escapable than ever. At the same time, in American popular culture the small town—especially the Midwestern small town—became the personification of everything good, noble, and useful in the United States. As Anthony Channell Hilfer (1936–2008) points out in *The Revolt from the Village, 1915–1930* (1969), growing industrial cities like Chicago and Detroit were made up largely of people who held small-town values and who idealized small-town life, often the life they had led as children. The dual perspective on the small town as economically embattled and as emblematic of America elicited two contradictory and often simultaneous responses in authors. Authors like (NEWTON) BOOTH TARKINGTON (1869–1946) and (NICHOLAS) VACHEL LINDSAY (1879–1931) viewed small-town life as threatened by the forces of nationalism, modernity, and industrialization.

At the same time, the small town became the whipping boy of authors like (HARRY) SINCLAIR LEWIS (1885–1951), EDGAR LEE MASTERS (1868–1950), and SHERWOOD ANDERSON (1876–1941), not so much because of what it was, but because in their eyes the small town personified the American middle class and thus represented everything stultifying and middlebrow about America. In the October 12, 1921, issue of *The Nation*, CARL (CLINTON) VAN DOREN (1885–1950) termed the resulting literary portrayal of the small town the "Revolt from the Village." These authors, however, also saw in the Midwestern small town the hometowns of their youth and, therefore, often tempered their critiques of the American middle class with moments of nostalgia.

Tarkington and Lindsay, seeing the small town as increasingly besieged by the forces of industrialism and modernity, presented early twentieth-century portraits of the small town that were primarily idyllic. Tarkington's melodramatic *The Gentleman from Indiana* (1899), dramatized in 1905, describes a hometown of Plattville as a place where everyone knows and is kind to everyone else. A group of outsiders, the Six-Cross-Roads people, threaten to corrupt everything the small town values with their vigilante violence. Lindsay, in his oral performances of "The Illinois Village" and "On the Building of Springfield," both published in *Adventures While Preaching the Gospel of Beauty* (1914), celebrates small towns like the Springfield of his youth while lamenting the thundering commerce that erodes those charms.

ZONA GALE (1874–1938) and WILLA CATHER (1873–1947) illustrate how authors often modified their use of the Midwestern town over the course of their careers. In her *Friendship Village* (1908) and *Friendship Village Love Stories* (1909) Gale romanticizes her vision of a closely knit women's community in a WISCONSIN town that rights the wrongs of poverty and loneliness. Her later novels *Birth* (1918) and *Miss Lulu Bett* (1920), however, focus not on the community as a whole, but rather on the damage that a tight-knit community can inflict on the individual. This image of the outcast—usually identified with the author—as beset by the common, controlling front of the community is a recurrent theme in texts from the Revolt from the Village school.

Cather, on the other hand, used the image of the outcast artist early in her career. Her short story "The Sculptor's Funeral," published in *The Troll Garden* (1905), looks at the village of Sand City through the eyes of a student of deceased sculptor Harvey Merrick. The student, who has accompanied Merrick's body back to Sand City to be buried, finds the leading townsmen greedy and too narrow-minded to appreciate Merrick's art. In *My Ántonia* (1918) Cather sees the small town as a center point between city and country. The fictional town of Black Hawk acts as a stepping-stone between Jim Burden's idealistic vision of his youthful farm life and his complex modern life in the metropolis. Jim uses Black Hawk as a buffer between city and country, and therefore, he resists any attempts by Ántonia Shimerda to leave her place on the farm and become a part of the small town. Ántonia represents the lost farm life of his youth, and her difficulty in adjusting even to small-town life ensures that she will not become sophisticated and ruin his idealized memories.

Although both Howe and Twain wrote about the dark side of the small town in the nineteenth century, Masters and Anderson are generally credited with being in the forefront of the Revolt from the Village. Masters's SPOON RIVER ANTHOLOGY (1915) is a collection of dramatic monologues, accounts of the everyday sins and tragedies, loves and triumphs of the dead citizens of Spoon River. Although certain poems reflect on the simple joys and rewards of rural and small-town life, the individual narratives highlight larger social issues, bluntly portraying rape and prostitution and examining the social structure that enables such crimes. For example, Nellie Clark recounts her rape at age eight, as well as her desertion at the hands of her husband years later upon his discovery of it. Fiddler Jones, on the other hand, tells the story of a man whose life, though simple, is plainly one of joy and wisdom because of the relationships he establishes with his neighbors and his attitude toward life. In epitaphs like those of Jones, Spoon River, despite all its Midwestern affectations, comes to represent all that is good and bad in America.

Like Masters, Anderson centers each of his stories in WINESBURG, OHIO (1919) on a single character or "grotesque" who seems hopelessly isolated in the small village. The collection of short stories balances the perspective of the older, more urbane narrator with that of George Willard, a young reporter for the *Winesburg Eagle.* George's dreams and lusts drive his desire to leave the town even as they connect him to it. The narrator longs for the simplicity of small-town life and voices more sympathy for the townsfolk, characters with unrealized dreams, than for George Willard. George both feels that he belongs in the town and wishes to escape it; the narrator feels compassion and longing for the people in the town but has grown beyond it. Anderson's *Poor White* (1920) takes as its subject the town of Bidwell as it grows from a quaint village like Winesburg to an industrialized city. The small town of Bidwell contains an equal mix of positive and negative traits, but when it grows to be a center for industry, the negative aspects of greed and cronyism expand at the expense of tradition, honesty, and agrarianism.

Sinclair Lewis's MAIN STREET (1920), the story of Carol Kennicott's marriage and subsequent life in the small, repressed town of Gopher Prairie, has often been labeled the pinnacle of the Revolt from the Village movement. As an outsider continually trying to make a home for herself in the closed village, Carol is struck by the town's hideous ARCHITECTURE and drab setting. Throughout the novel, Carol attempts to reform Gopher Prairie, throwing extravagant parties, promoting urban reform, and making friends with the local Communist agitator. Each of her attempts further alienates the townsfolk from her and her outsider ideas. But Lewis's satire addresses more than the narrow-mindedness of a Midwestern small town. Carol, for example, is far from an idealized character: her ideas of high culture and reform are rarely well formed, and her principles are evidenced much more in word than in deed. Lewis portrays Carol's husband, Dr. Will Kennicott, not as a narrow-minded man but as one who manages to create a fulfilling existence through his work. And even when Carol escapes Gopher Prairie to do war work in Washington, she finds the same kind of small-mindedness in the country's capital as she did in the small town. Lewis uses his Midwestern backdrop to satirize the closed-mindedness of the entire nation, a narrowness that exists in every person, village, and even urban center. Although Midwestern small towns provided the setting for parts of Lewis's other novels, including *Arrowsmith* (1925) and *Elmer Gantry* (1927), only in *Main Street* did he deliver a full accounting of the small town.

Midwestern authors commonly wrote about their small-town experiences from more urbane vantage points such as Chicago and New York, but RING (GOLD WILMER) LARDNER (1885–1933) and CARL VAN VECHTEN (1880–1964) presented particularly compelling narratives of the conflicting feelings associated with leaving simple hometown life while enjoying the sophistication of the big city. Lardner's *You Know Me, Al* (1916) is made up of letters from Jack, an arrogant rookie baseball player for the Chicago White Sox, written to Al, a friend who still lives in Jack's small hometown. The narrative structure allows the reader to identify with the small-town Al while still enjoying Jack's foolish escapades. Lardner's short story "Haircut" follows much the same pattern: the small-town barber relates a local story to an outsider, allowing the reader to feel both within and without the community, being a part of the small town and simultaneously above it.

Van Vechten's *The Tattooed Countess* (1924) satirizes the Revolt theme rather than the small town itself by including exaggerated characters of both worldliness and small-town simplicity. In the book Countess Nattatorrini returns to her hometown of Maple Valley, IOWA, after twenty years of grand excitement in Europe. She bears a tattoo and finds the town both enamored of and shocked by her fast behavior, makeup, low-cut gowns, and cigarettes. The Countess becomes enamored of Gareth Johns, a teenager who in his intellectual and cultural pursuits already finds Maple Valley stultifying. Together they run off to Chicago, she finding in him her young paramour, he finding in her his ticket out of Maple Valley. Van Vechten disrespects all his characters: the worldly Countess acts like a teen in love, and Gareth Johns, while intellectually superior to his townsfolk, is willing to sell his soul to the Countess just to escape.

RUTH SUCKOW (1892–1960) took small-town Iowa as her primary focus, consistently implicating her characters in a pull both away from and toward the village. Her short story "A Rural Community," collected in *Iowa Interiors* (1926), balances the perspective of Ralph Chapin, a world traveler returning to visit his small hometown of Walnut, Iowa, with that of the Hockadays, his adoptive parents, who have never sought to leave their provincial setting. Ralph's wandering existence is enabled by the rooted quality of his family. Suckow's novels, including *The Odyssey of a Nice Girl* (1925), *The Bonney Family* (1928), *Cora* (1929), and *The Kramer Girls* (1930), present complex portraits of small-town life—a life comforting to her young female protagonists but offering few opportunities for self-fulfillment. *The Folks* (1934) depicts an idealized family that scatters over time, mirroring the dispersion of the Midwestern small town itself. And although *New Hope* (1942) seems like an idealized portrait of the small town, its per-

spective, that of a child, shows that Suckow understands the growing tendency to think of the small town as an idealized place of our youth, but no longer as an active, growing community.

The Postwar Period—Harsh Realities and Mythic Memories: By the beginning of World War II the tendency to use the Midwestern small town to represent all that was middlebrow in the United States ebbed, not so much because authors no longer found negative aspects in American society, but because the American population had been moving out of small towns since before the turn of the twentieth century, drawn by economic opportunity and the wide array of entertainment available in the modern urban metropolis. Many readers in the first half of the twentieth century thought of themselves as small-town folk despite living in the big city or its suburbs, but by the second half of the century the great majority of Americans had never lived in a small town. Small towns saw their once-vibrant Main Street businesses go bankrupt as shopping malls and large retailers in larger cities drew customers with low prices and a wider variety of goods and services. Also, with the decline in rail travel and the increased use of the automobile, a centralized station like that at the center of the small town became less important. Finally, national television broadcasting did much to erode the regional distinctiveness that had long been considered a part of small-town life. Partially because of these trends, authors began to look to another place to ground their satiric attacks on middle-class values: the growing suburb. Although they did not desert the small town as a backdrop, its depiction began a subtle change. To authors coming out of small towns, like GARY EDWARD KEILLOR (b. 1942), writing as Garrison Keillor, the small town assumed mythic proportions. Postwar literary portrayals of the Midwestern small town present a layered experience wherein the author superimposes an often dour present on an idealized past, a past embellished with tall tales and larger-than-life heroes. In taking on serious social issues like racism and economic decay, Midwestern authors have used a now larger-than-life small-town mythos as an antidote. As the complexity of modernity increases, so does the simplification and idealization of the Midwestern small town.

A series of authors in the 1940s and 1950s worked across genres to embellish the mythic quality of the small town. The epic novel RAINTREE COUNTY (1948) by ROSS (FRANKLIN) LOCKRIDGE JR. (1914–1948) consists of a series of flashbacks roughly following the life of John Wickliff Shawnessy. In depicting Shawnessy's life, Lockridge makes into legend the adventures of those Midwestern pioneers who founded the small town of Waycross in the mid-nineteenth century. In his popular musical *The Music Man* (1958), MEREDITH (ROBERT) WILLSON (1902–1984) creates a nostalgic portrait of a small Midwestern town in 1912.The simplicity of River City, Iowa, with its trusting townsfolk and barbershop quartet, eventually charms not only Harold Hill, the city slicker, but also the modern audience. In re-creating the small-town OHIO of his youth in the picture book *Lentil* (1940), as well as the children's stories in *Homer Price* (1943) and *Centerburg Tales* (1951), children's author (JOHN) ROBERT McCLOSKEY (1914–2003) does much to solidify readers' idealized image of the Midwestern small town. Lockridge, Willson, and McCloskey all look back in time, bolstering the all-American image of the small town to combat the tensions emerging from the social and economic upheavals of the postwar era.

Later authors like Keillor and JON HASSLER (1933–2008) have used the mythic backdrop of the small town to show a redeeming depth beneath the sometimes harsh realities of the modern small town. Keillor's *Lake Wobegon Days* (1985) builds on the sketches and stories he presents on his radio program *A Prairie Home Companion* and couples the historical with the fantastic and humorous, using actual historical trends in Midwestern towns to create quasi-historical characters. Through his characters, like the missionaries who hope to convert the Indians through interpretive dance, Keillor celebrates the actual history of the Midwestern small town while making light of his fictional Lake Wobegon. Keillor's other collection of Lake Wobegon stories, *Leaving Home* (1987), follows more of the format of his weekly broadcasts, mixing anecdote with reflection. Hassler uses the simplicity of his small-town

Flushing, Michigan, 2014. Photo by William Barillas.

setting of Staggerford to cope with the complicated issues he addresses. In his novels *Staggerford* (1977) and *The Love Hunter* (1981) Hassler studies the reverberations of adultery, divorce, alcoholism, and mercy killing, using the small town to ground the moral discussion. This theme recurs in his later novels, especially *Grand Opening* (1987), which highlights religious tensions between Catholics and Lutherans in a small MINNESOTA town.

Authors have also used the backdrop of the small town as a place to reflect ethnic and racial tension within American society. In the first novel by TONI MORRISON (b. CHLOE ARDELIA WOFFORD, 1931), *The Bluest Eye* (1970), the small-town setting creates interracial tensions as the social life of the close-knit community of Lorain consistently reminds African American characters of the social and economic inequities they are forced to live with. In her novels *The Beet Queen* (1986), *Tracks* (1988), and *The Master Butcher Singing Club* (2003), (KAREN) LOUISE ERDRICH (b. 1954) treats the small town as both a transitional and a confrontational place, one where races mix and passions come to a boil. In *Tracks,* Fleur, a young Ojibwa woman, comes to the small town of Argus to work at the butcher shop but eventually ends up card-sharping the white men in town. The men rape her to take revenge, and Fleur summons a tornado to destroy them, but the result of their union is Fleur's daughter, Lulu, whose strength symbolizes the power that can emerge after conflict.

DAVE (PEARSON) ETTER (1928–2015) and PATRICIA HAMPL (b. 1946) ground their poems and narratives in concrete descriptions of modern small towns, but both authors also reflect on the mythos of the Midwestern town. Etter's *Alliance, Illinois* (1983), a collection of dramatic monologues reminiscent of Masters's *Spoon River Anthology*, presents the small town as an eternally fixed point to return to. In the poem "Living in the Middle" the narrator hearkens back to the Midwestern small town acting as the center of U.S. culture on his being "in the middle of town, / in the middle of my life, / a self-confessed middlebrow, / a member of the middle class, / and of course middle western, / the middle, you see, the middle" (5).

Hampl's *Spillville* (1987) mixes a series of personal essays on her tour of small-town Iowa with a narrative retelling of Antonin Dvořák's summer spent in Spillville, a small Iowa town. By mixing her experience of visiting the rural Midwest with tales of Dvořák's stay in the town, she is able to make the town homelike and mysterious, smaller and greater than life.

SELECTED WORKS: Howe's *The Story of a Country Town* (1883) is an essential starting point for anyone interested in understanding the small town on the Midwestern frontier in that its dark portrayal of small-town gossip prefigures the later Revolt from the Village works. Hamlin Garland's *Main-Travelled Roads* (1891) and the added country-town stories of his later editions capture life in both frontier and country towns. Twain's oft-anthologized novella "The Man That Corrupted Hadleyburg" (1900) also provides a template for later portrayals of the small town in its vociferous attack on the town's leading citizens. Reading both *Friendship Village* (1908) and *Miss Lulu Bett* (1920) allows an understanding of Zona Gale's progression from a romantic to a dark portrayal of the small town. Cather's short story "The Sculptor's Funeral" (1905) is her most focused look at the small town. No reading list of small-town Midwestern literature would be complete without the triad of Masters's *Spoon River Anthology* (1915), Anderson's *Winesburg, Ohio* (1919), and, most important, Lewis's *Main Street* (1920), all works that have become central portrayals of the Midwest and the small town. Suckow's *New Hope* (1934) and Lockridge's *Raintree County* (1948) both artfully look back at the history of a small town. *Lake Wobegon Days* (1985) is Keillor's most entertaining and most complete novel about small-town life. The anthology *The Small Town in American Literature* (1971), edited by David M. Cook and Craig G. Swauger, collects much of the more important small-town fiction and poetry, including selections from the fiction of Masters, Cather, Anderson, and Lewis, among others; each selection includes an insightful introduction and commentary.

FURTHER READING: Ima Honaker Herron's detailed *The Small Town in American Literature* (1939) and its companion piece, *The Small Town in American Drama* (1969), are foundational surveys of the American small town. Lewis Atherton's *Main Street on the Middle Border* (1954) presents a celebratory but entertaining and informative history of the manners and traditions of Midwestern small-town life while dwelling briefly on literary depictions of it. Page Smith's *As a City upon a Hill: The Town in American History* (1966) considers the small town in American history and dedicates a chapter to a reading of the small town in literature. Anthony Channell Hilfer's *The Revolt from the Village, 1915–1930* (1969) is perhaps the most in-depth study of the "village virus" phenomenon. Robert Dorman addresses the characterization of the small town as the idealized republican community in his well-regarded *Revolt of the Provinces: The Regionalist Movement in America, 1920–1945* (1993). The collection of essays *The Small Town in America: A Multidisciplinary Revisit* (1995), edited by Hans Bak, Johannes Willem Bertens, and Theo d'Haen, provides both a literary and a sociological perspective on the small town. Two essays of special note in this volume are Walter Hölbling's "From *Main Street* to *Lake Wobegon* and Half-Way Back: The Ambiguous Myth of the Small Town in Recent American Literature," a study especially helpful in looking at postwar small-town literature in the Midwest, and William V. Miller's "Sherwood Anderson's 'Middletown': A Sociology of the Midwestern States," which provides an in-depth look at Anderson's small-town fiction. Matts Västå presents a useful reading of the pull to and away from the small town in "The Ambiguities of the Escape Theme in Midwestern Literature, 1918–1934,"

MidAmerica 26 (1999): 49–76. Finally, Timothy B. Spears's *Chicago Dreaming: Midwesterners and the City, 1871–1919* (2005) discusses the relationship between Chicago and small-town migrants such as Floyd Dell, Willa Cather, and Sherwood Anderson.

JEFFREY SWENSON   HIRAM COLLEGE

SOCIETIES.
See Clubs, Salons, and Societies

SOCIETY FOR THE STUDY OF MIDWESTERN LITERATURE, THE

OVERVIEW: Since its inception in 1971, the Society for the Study of Midwestern Literature has existed to encourage and assist the study of Midwestern literature. Its primary vehicles for achieving that goal include sponsorship of the society's annual conference, publication of scholarly journals and books, provision of awards and recognitions for creative and analytical writers and works, publication of an annual bibliography of Midwestern literature, sponsorship of sessions relating to Midwestern literature at the meetings of other professional societies, and mentoring of emerging scholars and writers.

In the mid- to late 1960s and early 1970s literary regionalism became an important focus, as marked by the creation of the Western Literature Association in 1965, the Society for the Study of Southern Literature in 1968, and the Society for the Study of Midwestern Literature in 1971. The Society for the Study of Midwestern Literature formalized Midwestern literary studies as an academic focus and encouraged and provided a forum for presentation, discussion, and analysis of Midwestern literature from many theoretical literary perspectives, as well as through interdisciplinary and multicultural approaches.

HISTORY AND SIGNIFICANCE: A Midwestern regional cultural identity began to emerge tentatively with the founding by JOHN T(OWNER) FREDERICK (1893–1975) of the literary journal the *Midland,* which first appeared in January 1915. Until its demise as a casualty of the Depression in 1933, the journal published and gave a sense of Midwestern identity to writers as diverse as JAMES T(HOMAS) FARRELL (1904–1979), RUTH SUCKOW

(1892–1960), PHIL(IP) (DUFFIELD) STONG (1899–1957), and dozens of others. By the mid-twentieth century the publication of two important literary anthologies, *Out of the Midwest* (1944), edited by Frederick, and *America Is West* (1945), edited by JOHN T. FLANAGAN (1906–1996), gave a new focus to the writing of what each saw as a unique literary region. The two anthologies became influential sources in ensuing years.

The literature with which Frederick and Flanagan were concerned was essentially that of a clearly identifiable Midwest from its emerging identity in the Ohio Valley in the early nineteenth century to an urban industrial-agricultural complex spread across the twelve states of Midwestern America by the twentieth century. The subtitle of Frederick's anthology is *A Collection of Present-Day Writing;* that of Flanagan's is *An Anthology of Middlewestern Life and Literature.* Together they define and illustrate the body of writing from the past that, combined with writings of the second half of the twentieth century and the early years of the twenty-first century, provide the substance of what can be called Midwestern literature.

Publication of these two anthologies was the first manifestation of the movement that was to lead to the founding of the Society for the Study of Midwestern Literature. On November 23–25, 1969, the Midwest Modern Language Association, a regional affiliate of the Modern Language Association, met at the Chase-Park Plaza Hotel in ST. LOUIS. Under the general theme "Criticism and Culture," one of the conference sections, chaired by W. Gordon Milne of Lake Forest College, consisted of three papers: "Howells and the Ghetto: 'The Mystery of Misery'" by Sanford E. Marovitz of Kent State University, "Dreiser and Fitzgerald as Social Critics" by Alexander C. Kern of the University of Iowa, and "Sherwood Anderson and the Coming of the New Deal" by DAVID D(ANIEL) ANDERSON (1924–2011) of Michigan State University. The later selection of two of the papers for publication in *Criticism and Culture: The Papers of the Midwest Modern Language Association* suggested their significance in explicating the theme of the meeting. However, before their publication, the three essays suggested an additional similarity, that of the region from which the authors being discussed came: the Midwest. Furthermore, the region provided the inspiration for many of their best works, works set in the Midwest. Beyond inspiration, the region had provided the substance of much of these writers' work.

Anderson thought that the region exhibited a similarity evident in the papers and saw that similarity as worthy of further critical exploration. He circulated a letter among colleagues, asking whether each thought that such a meeting would be successful. The invitation list included Russel B(laine) Nye (1913–1993) and C. Merton Babcock of Michigan State University, Bernard Duffey (1917–1994) of Duke University, William Thomas of Ohio State University–Marion, Robert R. Hubach of Bowling Green State University, and William B. McCann of East Lansing, MICHIGAN. All had published in the area of Midwestern literature, history, and culture, and all replied enthusiastically in the affirmative.

The idea for a meeting became an idea for an organization. The group consented to act as an organizing committee. Planning discussions continued, and in spring 1971 the first issue of the *Society for the Study of Midwestern Literature Newsletter* appeared. Actually an invitation to join, announcing dues of one dollar per year, it also set forth the goals of the society:

This Society will be dedicated to the study of the rich literary heritage of the area that Sherwood Anderson called "Mid-America"— the land between the Appalachians and the Rockies, the Canadian border and the Ohio River Valley. The Society will first of all recognize the fact that much of the literature in the mainstream of the American literary heritage is Midwestern in its influences, inception, origin and/or subject matter and that the relationship between the works and the region is both real and significant.

With that principle as a point of departure, the Society will exist to encourage and assist the study of that literature in whatever direction the insight, imagination, and curiosity of the members may lead.

Those principles remain the guiding purpose of the society.

The issue announced other plans: an organizational structure, dues, meetings,

The Society for the Study of Midwestern Literature

Design for a promotional brochure for the Society for the Study of Midwestern Literature.
© Society for the Study of Midwestern Literature, 1979

and a journal, all of which came to pass. The first meeting was held at Michigan State University on October 16, 1971. Subsequent annual meetings have continued there; meetings in conjunction with meetings of the Modern Language Association and the Midwestern Modern Language Association have also been held annually since 1976.

The society publishes two scholarly journals. *MidAmerica: The Yearbook of the Society for the Study of Midwestern Literature* is a peer-reviewed annual that first appeared in 1974. It contains critical essays, award-winning entries from the annual conferences, and the "Annual Bibliography of Midwestern Literature." *Midwestern Miscellany,* first published in 1974 as an annual, also publishes peer-reviewed critical essays. It often devotes special issues to single authors, topics, or themes. In 1998 *Midwestern Miscellany* became a semi-annual publication. The last number of the *SSML Newsletter* was issued in the fall of 1997; its successor, *SSML News and Opportunities,* began in August 1998 and appears irregularly.

The SSML's annual conference became a three-day meeting in 1976 commemorating the centenary of SHERWOOD ANDERSON's (1876–1941) birth. The symposium, the Cultural Heritage of the Midwest, continues in that format. Formal elements include scholarly papers and the Midwest Poetry

Festival. The conference features scholarship on Midwestern literature, as well as presentations of Midwestern poetry, fiction, DRAMA, and CREATIVE NONFICTION. Many members participate in multiple conference dimensions.

The society presents six major awards and prizes annually. The MidAmerica Award, begun in 1977, is given for distinguished contributions to the study of Midwestern literature; the Mark Twain Award, begun in 1980, recognizes distinguished contributions to Midwestern literature. The first MidAmerica Award was presented to John T. Flanagan of the University of Illinois; the first Mark Twain Award was presented to (JOHN WESLEY) "JACK" CONROY (1898–1990) of MISSOURI. The society also recognizes presentations at its annual symposium with four prizes: the Midwestern Heritage Prize, renamed in 2012 the David D. Anderson Heritage Prize for Literary Criticism; the Gwendolyn Brooks Poetry Prize; the Paul Somers Prize for Creative Prose; and the David Diamond Student Writing Prize. The society maintains an active role in supporting and initiating scholarship via its annual conference and its two journals.

In 2001 SSML members concluded the first phase of a major research and writing project, *Dictionary of Midwestern Literature*, volume 1, *The Authors,* containing nearly four hundred entries on individual poets, prose writers, journalists, and playwrights and a prefatory overview. The volume, edited by Philip A. Greasley of the University of Kentucky, was published by Indiana University Press. Volume 2, *Dimensions of the Midwestern Literary Imagination,* also under Greasley's editorship, provides entries on pivotal Midwestern literary works; the literatures of the twelve Midwestern states and their significant cities; the literatures of the region's major population groups; Midwestern experiences, perceptions, and movements of the past two hundred years; literary genres and types of the past and present; major literary periodicals; and sister arts and related disciplinary approaches, as well as a bibliographic survey. A third volume, *The Literary History of the Midwest,* is projected.

David D. Anderson was the Executive Secretary of the Society for the Study of Midwestern Literature until his death in 2011. A corporate board and an executive council now direct the activities of the society. Since its founding in 1971, Michigan State University has been the society's institutional home.

FURTHER READING: No history of the Society for the Study of Midwestern Literature has yet been written. David B. Schock has filmed *Distinct and Midwestern: Dave Anderson Talks about the History of SSML,* which was first screened at the May 2007 SSML conference. The record of the society and its activities are best reviewed in its publications: *SSML Newsletter* (Spring 1971–Fall 1997), *MidAmerica* (1974 to the present), and *Midwestern Miscellany* (1974 to the present). Two review entries in *MidAmerica,* the first by Roger Bresnahan, "*MidAmerica:* A Ten-Year Retrospective," *MidAmerica* 10 (1983): 9–23, and the second by Marcia Noe, "*MidAmerica:* The Second Decade," *MidAmerica* 21 (1994): 39–49, reflect the coverage, emphasis, and impact of that journal.

DAVID D. ANDERSON   MICHIGAN STATE UNIVERSITY
ROBERT BEASECKER

GRAND VALLEY STATE UNIVERSITY

SONG OF SOLOMON

HISTORY: With the publication of her third novel, *Song of Solomon* (1977), TONI MORRISON (b. CHLOE ARDELIA WOFFORD, 1931) gained the interest of critics and readers as a poetically charged author who depicted rich African American traditions in her fiction. The novel became a main selection of the Book-of-the-Month Club, the first novel by an African American writer to be chosen since Richard Wright's *NATIVE SON* in 1940, and also won both the National Book Critics' Circle Award and the American Academy and Institute of Arts and Letters Award, *Song of Solomon* details a black man's search for identity by discovering his family's history.

Song of Solomon has drawn critical acclaim for its use of African-centered themes and folklore. Although some critics found flaws in the novel, *Song of Solomon* became a best seller and attracted the admiration of critics and readers alike when it was initially published. A contemporary reviewer in the

Toni Morrison's *Song of Solomon*. Cover design by R. D. Scudellari.
© Knopf, 1977. Courtesy of the Knopf Group, Random House

Village Voice, Vivian Gornick, wrote in "Into the Dark Heart of Childhood" on August 29, 1977 that "Morrison's ability is not exercised to the *largest* degree. At a certain point one begins to feel a manipulativeness in the book's structure, and then to sense that the characters are moving to fulfill the requirements of that structure" (41). Reynolds Price, in the September 11, 1977, *New York Times Book Review* article "The Adventures of Macon Dead," praised *Song of Solomon* for its overall purpose, which seemed to him "to be communication of painfully discovered and powerfully held convictions about the possibility of transcendence within human life, on the time-scale of a single life" (48).

Wofford was born on February 18, 1931, in Lorain, OHIO, a western CLEVELAND suburb, to a family that had only recently migrated to the Midwest from the South in an effort to flee southern racism. Growing up in Lorain, a small steel town inhabited by Europeans, Mexicans, and southern black émigrés, Morrison spent her childhood avidly reading, from Leo (Lev Nikolayevich) Tolstoy (1828–1910) and Fyodor Mikhailovich Dostoyevsky (1821–1881) to Gustave Flaubert (1821–1880) and Jane Austen (1775–1817). After graduating from Howard University, she accepted an associate editor's position with a textbook subsidiary of Random House in Syracuse, New York. In 1967 Morrison transferred to New York to become a senior editor for Random House.

Working as a senior editor afforded Morrison the opportunity to edit books by African American writers and activists, including Andrew Young, Muhammad Ali, and Angela Davis. Meanwhile, Morrison was attempting to find a publisher for her first novel, *The Bluest Eye,* which was eventually published in 1970. Although it was not commercially successful, the novel did give Morrison the acclaim she was seeking. She followed in 1973 with her second novel, *Sula,* which was nominated for the National Book Award for Fiction. In 1977 Morrison published *Song of Solomon* with Alfred Knopf. New American Library purchased paperback rights for an estimated $115,000, and it quickly became a best seller. *Song of Solomon* was also selected for Oprah Winfrey's book club.

SIGNIFICANCE: The themes of Morrison's first two novels differ. In *The Bluest Eye* Morrison addresses standards of beauty in America, family victimization, and the effect of these issues on African American girls. *Sula* addresses bigotry, racism, and African American repression and portrays African American fortitude in surviving in a scornful world. In *Song of Solomon,* however, Morrison draws on African American oral narratives to create a richly textured novel that functions on several levels and incorporates a wide range of black communities across America, from the more liberal Midwest to the conservative South.

As a thematic concern, Morrison infuses *Song of Solomon* with allusions to flight. The most prevalent of these is the historical flight of black people from slavery, poverty, and cruelty at the hands of white oppressors and their belief in the West African legend that they could fly back to Africa. Morrison fictionalizes this legend through Solomon, the great-grandfather of Milkman Dead, the novel's protagonist. While uncovering the story of Solomon and his ability to fly, Milkman realizes the importance of pride in his heritage and appreciation of his relationship to his family and community. Other allusions to flight in the novel include Robert Smith's claiming to fly to the opposite shore of Lake Michigan, Solomon's mythological flight, and Pilate's allegorical flight when she transcends society's subjective limitations. Pilate is Macon's sister, a maker of home-brewed wine who lives with her daughter and granddaughter in Southside.

Morrison locates many of her novels in the Midwest. This geographic locale is essential to her for two reasons. First, having grown up in the Midwest, Morrison feels akin to this region. "No matter what I write," she explained in a 1983 interview quoted in Andrew R. L. Cayton's *Ohio: The History of a People* (2002), "I begin there" (287). In Lorain, for example, she learned about the importance of community and identity. Because Ohio, as Morrison stated in *Black Women Writers at Work* (1983), is an "interesting and complex state," partly because the Ohio River "has historically represented freedom . . . the state seems to be especially well suited for staging leaps in *Song of Solomon*" (158). Second, and more important, as Morrison reported in an interview with Elissa Schappnell published as "Toni Morrison: The Art of Fiction," in *Toni Morrison's "Song of Solomon": A Casebook*, edited by Jan Furman, the African American experience she intends to "dramatize is neither stereotypically inner-city ghetto nor Deep South plantation" (233–34).

Set during the 1950s and 1960s in an urban space of an unnamed industrialized MICHIGAN city, *Song of Solomon* focuses on the effects of events that occurred in the early twentieth century. Central to *Song of Solomon* is Morrison's concern with social changes, like the Great Migration, which disrupted the most cherished social unit, the family. The larger migration of African Americans from the South to the North, Midwest, and West over the past century may have involved as many as seven million people.

Some historians have made distinctions between the first Great Migration (1910–1940), during which it is estimated that 1.6 million migrants left the South, and the Second Great Migration (1940–1970), in which at least five million African Americans relocated. Although the Great Migration helped many educated African Americans acquire jobs and a measure of class mobility, these migrants were met with considerable discrimination and racism, including housing and mortgage discrimination and unethical working conditions.

In *Song of Solomon* Morrison portrays the experiences of one of those families, the Deads, showing their progression from Virginia to Pennsylvania and eventually to the unnamed Michigan town. Various clues, however, lead the reader to the conclusion that the unnamed city is probably DETROIT, "the Motor City," origin of the famous "Motown sound." Although these symbols point to Detroit, the story raises questions that may suggest that the unnamed locale could be elsewhere. Robert Smith, we learn, attempts to fly "to the other side of Lake Superior" (3). In *The Identifying Fictions of Toni Morrison: Modernist Authenticity and Postmodern Blackness* (2000) John N. Duvall suggests that this may imply that the unnamed locale would probably be in Michigan's Upper Peninsula, since this is the only area of the state bordered by Lake Superior. However, remaining true to the tradition that Africans felt that they could fly across the Atlantic Ocean back to Africa, flying from Detroit to the other side of Lake Superior would also be within the realm of possibility. Morrison also highlights the tribulations of Guitar, who moved to the North with his family after his father's death; no doubt many other inhabitants of Southside are relatively recent migrants from the rural South. When Guitar was a child, her father was killed in an accident at a sawmill. Unable to cope, Guitar's mother abandoned the family. After Guitar's grandmother took responsibility for him, Macon Dead evicted Guitar's family from their Southside home for nonpayment of rent. Although the Great Migration brought about significant economic development for African Americans, Morrison uses it to represent the loss of the rural culture of southern African Americans who migrated to the North. This loss is personified in her characterization of Macon Dead, who flees a farm in Pennsylvania called Lincoln's Heaven.

Song of Solomon confronts the varied definitions of achievement and progress as they relate to the African American family in the Midwest. For example, Macon, Milkman's father, has definitely attained a measure of material success in buying land on Honore Island and evicting tenants who cannot pay their rent. However, the push to advancement has left him morally and spiritually ruined and unable to relate to his family and community. Regardless of its increased opportunities and purported freedoms, the Midwest is still problematic for African Americans migrating from the South. As Milkman contextualizes the differences between the two spaces, he reflects movement as an important theme: "I live in the North now. So the first question comes to mind is North of what? Why, north of the South. So North exists because the South does. But does that mean North is different from South? No way! South is just south of North" (2004 Knopf/Doubleday edition, 114). The slight differences between the two geographic spaces and their inhabitants, Milkman suggests, are worth noticing: "Northerners, for example—born and bred ones, that is—are picky about their food. Well, not about the food. They actually don't give a shit about the food. What they're picky about is the trappings. You know what I mean? The pots and shit. Now, they're real funny about pots. But tea? They don't know Earl Grey from old man Lipton's instant" (114).

Although the setting in the novel moves from the industrialized North, profoundly affected by the materialistic ideals and customs of white America, to the rural South, the novel is nonetheless immersed in conventional ideals and marked by a strong sense of history. Pilate, Milkman's aunt, has lived in many states and has taken her love for geography on the road, including an island near Virginia where she joined a colony of farmers and found a lover. She settles, however, in the Midwest.

In *Song of Solomon* readers experience a variety of settings through characters' physical movement or their memories, including places like Boston, Massachusetts; Macon, Georgia; Birmingham, Alabama; Danville, Pennsylvania; Shalimar, Virginia; and Jacksonville, Florida. These shifts in locale are significant in presenting a distinction between the African American community in the North and the established African American community in the South. In the South, for example, racism was ingrained in every echelon of the African American community and was evidenced through Jim Crow laws, lynching, and other day-to-day acts to ensure that the black man remained in his place. Conversely, African Americans were finding that northern racism was more subtle as it reared its head in workplace and housing practices. This shift reverses the established freedom trail of subjugated black slaves in that Milkman achieves his freedom not by escaping to the North, as his ancestors had done, but by returning to the South to discover those roots.

Scholars have identified varying literary antecedents for *Song of Solomon*. In her article "Signifying Circe in Toni Morrison's *Song of Solomon*," *Classical World* 99.4 (Summer 2006): 415–418, Judith Fletcher explores the novel's "classical antecedents," revealing that *Song of Solomon* "shares with Homer's *Odyssey* a profound concern with naming" (405). In "William Faulkner Reprised: Isolation in Toni Morrison's *Song of Solomon*," *Mississippi Quarterly* 58.1–2 (Winter 2004/2005): 7–24, Lorie Watkins Fulton identifies the "Faulknerian influence" on Morrison's novels (8). According to Morrison in "Faulkner and Women," in *Faulkner and Yoknapatawpha* (1986), edited by Doreen Fowler and Ann J. Abadie, "William Faulkner had an enormous effect on me, an enormous effect" (295–96). Critics David Cowart in "Faulkner and Joyce in Morrison's *Song of Solomon*," *American Literature* 61.1 (March 1990): 87–100, John N. Duvall in "Doe Hunting and Masculinity: *Song of Solomon* and *Go Down, Moses*," *Arizona Quarterly* 47.1 (Spring 1991): 95–115, and Lucinda H. MacKethan in "The Grandfather Clause: Reading the Legacy from 'The Bear' to *Song of Solomon*," in *Unflinching Gaze: Morrison and Faulkner Reenvisioned* (1997), edited by Carol A. Kolmerten, Stephen M. Ross, and Judith Bryant Wittenberg, 99–114, have paired Faulkner's *Go Down, Moses* (1942) with *Song of Solomon* and have demonstrated how Morrison makes it her own in this novel that cele-brates community and vanquishes the de-structive isolation that she sees as the dark heart of Faulkner's fiction.

To date, no media adaptations of *Song of Solomon* are listed on the Official Website of the Toni Morrison Society; there are, however, over 150 doctoral dissertations on Morrison's works. Less than 5 percent of these dissertations are devoted to exploring *Song of Solomon*. One of the most notable is Therese E. Higgins's 2000 Kent State University dissertation, published in 2002 as *Religiosity, Cosmology and Folklore: The African Influence in the Novels of Toni Morrison*. By emphasizing the connections between the African origin and the African American product, Higgins explores the histories of the values, traditions, mores, and cosmologies of several of Africa's leading tribes and con-nects these findings to each of Morrison's seven novels published at the time she con-ducted research for *Religiosity, Cosmology and Folklore.*

IMPORTANT EDITIONS: Although well over half a million copies of *Song of Solomon* have been sold. The Vintage Books paper-back edition, first issued in 2004, remains in print. Translation rights have been sold in more than ten countries. In 1983 and again in 1993 Angela Praesent translated *Song of Solomon* into German. In 1994 Hayakawa Publishing released a Japanese version translated by Japanese author Masumi Kaneda. Tung-jung Chen translated *Song of Solomon* in to Chinese in 2008.

FURTHER READING: Morrison's fiction has received immense attention from schol-ars and critics alike, including criticism by scholars such as John N. Duvall, Trudier Harris, and Patrick Bryce Bjork. Harold Bloom's *Toni Morrison's "Song of Solomon"* (1999) characterizes the best existing criti-cism on *Song of Solomon*. Essays specifically on *Song of Solomon* appear in Jan Furman's *Toni Morrison's "Song of Solomon": A Casebook* (2003), offering analytical and interpretive frameworks for studying the novel. The essays in this indispensable collection rep-resent the most important issues concerning *Song of Solomon* to date. Furman's casebook also includes a noteworthy interview by Elissa Schappnell, "Toni Morrison: The Art of Fiction." Schappnell begins by discussing

Morrison's interest in the Midwest as a set-ting for her novels. Danille Taylor-Guthrie's *Conversations with Toni Morrison* (1994) in-cludes interviews with Morrison by such scholars as Robert Stepto, Nellie McKay, Claudia Tate, and Gloria Naylor. This collec-tion sheds light on the influences behind Morrison's premises concerning the role race plays in the construction of American arts and letters. The conversations offer an exhilarating opportunity to examine Morrison's development as a writer and a scholar. Numerous texts discuss Morrison's life and works. Perhaps one of the most noteworthy is Carolyn C. Denard's *Toni Mor-rison: Conversations* (2008). Denard includes interviews by such writers as A. J. Verdelle that bring to the foreground Morrison's comments on American literature and her own novels. In the interviews in this collec-tion, Morrison discusses her childhood in Lorain, Ohio, the continuing evolution of her style, and her novels *Jazz* (1992), *Paradise* (1999), and *Love* (2003). Claudia Tate's inter-view in *Black Women Writers at Work* (1983) also sheds light on Morrison's Midwestern focus. In *The Identifying Fictions of Toni Mor-rison: Modernist Authenticity and Postmodern Blackness* (2000) John N. Duvall considers the setting of *Song of Solomon* and points to the Upper Peninsula as the possible locale.

Other noteworthy discussions of *Song of Solomon*'s Midwestern importance include Bo G. Ekelund's "History and Other Places in Toni Morrison's Fiction," *Studia Neophilo-logica* 78.2 (Fall 2006): 138–52. Arguing that Morrison employs "a particular configura-tion of time and space in *Song of Solomon*" (144), Ekelund concludes that the novel draws up the "span between the evident poles of the South as the past and the north-ern city as modernity" (145). Jennifer Ter-ry's "Buried Perspectives: Narratives of Landscape in Toni Morrison's *Song of Solo-mon*," *Narrative Inquiry* 17. 1 (2007): 93–118, examines Morrison's efforts to give voice to the African American experience and identity and how Morrison revisits and challenges traditional stories of national be-longing. Taken as a whole, these discus-sions remain essential contributions to any conversation on *Song of Solomon*, especially in regard to understanding its Midwestern focus.

The manuscript of *Song of Solomon,* along with Morrison's other manuscripts, is held at Princeton University's Special Collections Department. However, these documents are not currently available to the public.

WILLIE J. HARRELL JR.   KENT STATE UNIVERSITY

SOUTH DAKOTA

South Dakota, along with its sister state NORTH DAKOTA, was admitted to the Union on November 2, 1889. Before that, it was part of Dakota Territory, which was established on March 2, 1861. Dakota Territory included North and South Dakota, most of Montana, which became a separate territory in 1864, and most of Wyoming, which became a territory in 1868. The region was part of the Louisiana Territory purchased from France in 1803.

Area: 77,116 square miles
Land: 75,811 square miles
Water: 1,305 square miles
Population (2010 census): 819,761

OVERVIEW: The literary heritage of South Dakota reaches back into the prewriting eras of rock paintings, winter counts, and the extensive oral traditions of American Indians. The landscape references and calls to mind stories of the events and people who occupied it over time. A significant portion of the state's writing is by Native people who preserve, interpret, and perpetuate indigenous traditions. Other literature grew predominantly out of experiences with the land by explorers, traders, pioneers, and settlers.

The state is divided by the Missouri River into areas conventionally known within the state as East River and West River. East River is a fertile area with the state's richest farmland. West River includes the Great Plains, a heavily glaciated, more arid region, and the Black Hills, a small mountain range that forms the western border of the state. The Great Plains region contains four of the largest of the state's nine Indian reservations: Pine Ridge, Rosebud, Cheyenne River, and Standing Rock. The Black Hills region has gold and other minerals, although gold has been largely depleted, and forests, which are managed and remain productive.

The Missouri River is as much a cultural as a geographic divide; the green, well-watered settlements of the east suggest a Midwestern flavor, while the west's semi-arid, rugged, and less populated terrain gives it a western orientation. A double perspective thus emerges when the authors of the state are grouped together into a single literary history: the state produced some of the nation's first western DIME NOVELS, as well as a long list of prairie homesteader narratives. Although South Dakota is officially part of the Midwest, it might best be understood as a transitional state. The literature of the state often reflects this regional transition.

The American Indian presence is markedly reflected in the state's literature in terms of the number of indigenous authors and the number of works by non-Indian authors who address that presence. The written record deals with the conflicts between tribes and the white people who displaced them through their enterprises and settlements and with the triumphs of settlers in opening the land to agriculture. In addition to the themes of pioneering, homesteading, and community formation are found the themes of aspiration and disaffection that prompted some to leave South Dakota.

HISTORY AND SIGNIFICANCE: Authorship in South Dakota has been an itinerant enterprise. Many writers who originated in the state have located elsewhere. Many writers from other places have lived in the state for a time to investigate subjects, have written about them, and then have moved on. Some writers have come and made South Dakota their home. Except for American Indian authors, transient writers have outnumbered those who have identified with South Dakota as residents.

Trying to integrate South Dakota's American Indian and non–American Indian literary history poses some particular challenges. In sharp contrast to the state's rela-

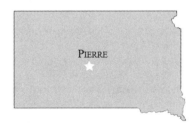

PIERRE

© Karen Greasley, 2014

tively short history of Euro-American literature, its indigenous literary history reaches back centuries to prewriting traditions. Formal differences also present challenges: many works by American Indians are mixtures of essays, stories, poems, and songs that do not always fit into traditional Euro-American *belles lettres* genres.

Given these formal and historical concerns, this entry begins with two sections devoted to American Indian literature. The first section focuses exclusively on literature written by American Indians; the second section is devoted to non-Indian writers whose works focus on tribal peoples and cultures. After these sections, the entry turns to the large numbers of Caucasians and other nonindigenous people who began producing literature in or about the state in conventional literary forms and traditions. Following the "Exploration" section is a lengthy "Settlement and Development" section that includes works of fiction, short stories, memoirs, and epistolary writings in the state. The succeeding sections present the literature of South Dakota in a manner paralleling the other state entries in this volume.

American Indian Literature: Numerous accounts of prewriting traditions and cultures in South Dakota are recorded in ethnological, anthropological, historical, and religious-affiliated publications. It was not until the turn of the twentieth century that a large number of American Indian authors began to publish their own stories and the stories of their people. Some wrote in English; others collaborated with English-language writers and scholars. One of the first to begin publishing accounts of his culture and traditions was CHARLES ALEXANDER EASTMAN (Ohiyesa; 1858–1939). Eastman was raised in the traditional Indian ways by his father's family in Canada. After obtaining a medical degree in Boston, Eastman was sent to the Pine Ridge agency, where he was physician in attendance during the Wounded Knee massacre. His first book, *Indian Boyhood* (1902), was directed toward juvenile readers but contained important ethnological information not known to white America. He followed with *Red Hunters and the Animal People* (1904) and *Old Indian Days* (1907). With his wife, Elaine Goodale East-

man (1863–1953), he collaborated on *Wigwam Evenings: Sioux Folk Tales* (1909) and *Smoky Day's Wigwam Evenings: Indian Stories Retold* (1910). Eastman's later works sought to create an understanding of tribal life and ways it could be maintained in the context of white culture: *The Soul of the Indian* (1911), *The Indian Today: The Past and Future of the First American* (1915), and *From the Deep Woods to Civilization: Chapters in the Autobiography of an Indian* (1916). Elaine Goodale Eastman continued her writing with *Yellow Star: A Story of East and West* (1931), *Pratt, the Red Man's Moses* (1935), and *Sister to the Sioux: The Memoirs of Elaine Goodale Eastman, 1885–91* (1978).

Marie L. McLaughlin (1842–1924) was one-fourth Sioux. For her book *Myths and Legends of the Sioux* (1916), she collected and rendered into English children's stories told to her by her mother, to whom the book is dedicated, and by elders on the Sioux reservations where she was stationed with her husband, a resident agent at Standing Rock Reservation.

A writer who attempted to portray Sioux culture authentically and respectfully, Ella Cara Deloria (1889–1971) has only recently become widely recognized. She was born on the Yankton Sioux Reservation and was given the Dakota name Beautiful Day Woman. She was working as a teacher at the Haskell Indian School when anthropologist Franz Boas (1858–1942) asked her to translate some Sioux texts. Her collaboration with Boas led to the publication of *Dakota Texts* (1932), a bilingual collection of legends of the Dakota, and *Dakota Grammar* (1941), a language study co-authored with Boas. She further described Sioux culture in *Speaking of Indians* (1944) and in a transcribed oral history, for which she was interviewed by Bea Medicine, *Reminiscences of Ella Deloria, Standing Rock Sioux Tribe of South Dakota* (1979). A collection of her narratives from memory was edited with commentary by Julian Rice in *Iron Hawk* (1993). *Waterlily* (1988), a posthumously published novel, provides a detailed portrayal of the customs and values by which the Sioux lived before they were put on reservations.

LUTHER STANDING BEAR (Sioux, 1868–1939) also worked intensively to provide authentic information in place of the misconceptions of tribal peoples that pervaded popular culture. His major works are *My People, the Sioux* (1928), *My Indian Boyhood* (1931), *The Land of the Spotted Eagle* (1933), and *Stories of the Sioux* (1934), a rendering in English of stories told to him by tribal storytellers.

ZITKALA-ŠA (RED BIRD, 1876–1938), also known as Gertrude Simmons, her name at birth, and Gertrude Bonnin, her married name, was born on the Yankton Reservation. She was a bilingual writer who was very influential in writing corrective portrayals of the Sioux and in making oral traditions available in writing. Her major contributions are *Old Indian Legends* (1901) and *American Indian Stories* (1921).

Although BLACK ELK (1863–1950) relied on English-language collaborators to tell his stories, his work in presenting Lakota life ways and beliefs has earned scriptural respect. With poet-novelist JOHN G(NEISENAU) NEIHARDT (1881–1973) he authored *BLACK ELK SPEAKS* (1932), and with Joseph Epes Brown (1920–2000) he wrote *The Sacred Pipe* (1953).

William J. Bordeaux (1884–1962), born on the Rosebud Reservation, a descendant of a French trader who married a Brule Sioux, published *Custer's Conqueror* (1952), an account of Crazy Horse gathered from relatives and tribal members.

John (Fire) Lame Deer (ca. 1903–1976) was born on the Rosebud Reservation and recounted how as a traditional Sioux he worked as a rancher, a rodeo rider, an Indian Police officer, and a holy man. He collaborated with Richard Erdoes (1912–2008) to produce *Lame Deer, Seeker of Visions* (1972) and contributed to Erdoes's *The Sounds of Flutes, and Other Indian Legends* (1976).

The state's Indian writers continued to produce quality works in the later decades of the twentieth century. Dallas Chief Eagle (1925–1980), a Teton Sioux leader, wrote *Winter Count* (1967), a historical novel of a newly married Indian couple kidnapped by white renegades during the time span 1874–1890.

Elizabeth (Bowed Head Irving) Cook-Lynn (b. 1930), an American Indian studies historian, a political theorist, and a leading writer of the twentieth-century Native American renaissance, is a member of the Crow Creek Sioux tribe of Fort Thompson, South Dakota. She is the founding editor of

Crow Creek Sioux writer Elizabeth Cook-Lynn, 2007. Photo by Felver.
Courtesy of Elizabeth Cook-Lynn, Oakland, California

the *Wičazo Ša Review*, a Native American studies journal now housed at the University of Minnesota Press. Her fiction includes *The Power of Horses, and Other Stories* (1990), *From the River's Edge* (1991), and *Aurelia: A Crow Creek Trilogy* (1999). Among her books of poetry are *Then Badger Said This* (1983) and *Seek the House of Relatives* (1983). She has also authored several nonfiction works, including *Why I Can't Read Wallace Stegner: A Tribal Voice* (1996), *Anti-Indianism in Modern America: A Voice from Tatekeya's Earth* (2001), *New Indians, Old Wars* (2007), and *A Separate Country: Postcoloniality and American Indian Nations* (2012).

Virginia Driving Hawk Sneve (b. 1933) continues the work of establishing accurate and respectful portrayals of American Indians. Among her multiple works of literature and tribal history for young readers is *The Trickster and the Troll* (1997), in which the Lakota trickster meets up with a Norwegian troll. She has also produced *Completing the*

Circle (1995), a valuable collection of biographies of Dakota women.

Ed McGaa (b. 1936), a Pine Ridge native who is a lawyer and a decorated Vietnam War fighter pilot, has written a number of prose works dealing with Oglala Sioux perceptions, including *Mother Earth Spirituality: Native American Paths to Healing Ourselves and Our World* (1990). Also noteworthy is the work of Dakota writer Allen Chuck Ross (b. 1940), who also identifies himself as Ehanamani, his Dakota name. His best-known work is *Mitakuye Oyasin: "We Are All Related"* (1989), in which he draws parallels between Jungian psychology and traditional Dakota and Lakota philosophy and thought.

Adrian C. Louis (b. 1946) is a member of the Lovelock Paiute tribe in Nevada; he lived for some time on the Pine Ridge Reservation. In addition to two books of poems with Pine Ridge settings, *Among the Dog Eaters: Poems* (1992) and *Blood Thirsty Savages* (1994), he is the author of the novel *Skins* (1995), which was made into a movie with the same title. Joseph Iron Eye Dudley (b. Joseph A. Dudley, 1940) is another South Dakota American Indian writer. He explores the spirituality of indigenous ways in *Choteau Creek: A Sioux Reminiscence* (1992).

In *Lakota Woman* (1990) Rosebud native Mary (Brave Bird) Crow Dog (1954–2013) collaborated with Richard Erdoes to chronicle her struggles with being a "mixed blood" on the reservation. The book also describes Crow Dog's development as an activist who joined the American Indian Movement and participated in the takeover of Wounded Knee in 1973. In addition, she and Erdoes collaborated on the sequel, *Ohitika Woman* (1993), published under her maiden name, Mary Brave Bird.

Vine Deloria Jr. (1933–2005), nephew of Ella Cara Deloria, was one of the country's most prolific critics of American culture, particularly as it impinged on Native America. Born in Martin, South Dakota, he was raised on the Standing Rock Reservation. His first book, *Custer Died for Your Sins: An Indian Manifesto* (1969), was published during the height of the civil rights era and was followed by *We Talk, You Listen: New Tribes, New Turf* (1970). He took up the issue of indigenous religion in *God Is Red: A Native View of Religion* (1973) and produced a series of fif-

teen books on events and policies in history. He challenged the presumptions of science and technology in two books: *Red Earth, White Lies: Native Americans and the Myth of Scientific Fact* (1995) and *Evolution, Creationism, and Other Modern Myths* (2002). His essays on spirituality and conventional western thought were collected in *Spirit and Reason: The Vine Deloria, Jr., Reader* (1999). Deloria celebrated white writers who presented the Native American view in *A Sender of Words: Essays in Memory of John G. Neihardt* (1984) and *Frank Waters: Man and Mystic* (1993). He wrote an ethnographic study of his people in *Singing for a Spirit: A Portrait of the Dakota Sioux* (1999).

Perhaps the most prolific American Indian writer in the state is Joseph M. Marshall III (b. 1946). *Hundred in the Hand: A Novel* (2007), the first work in Marshall's Lakota Western series, provides a fresh Lakota perspective on the Battle of the Hundred in Hand, also known as the Fetterman Fight of 1866. The second novel in the series, *The Long Knives Are Crying: A Novel* (2008) begins a decade later, in 1875. The narrator retells events especially significant to the Lakota people, including the Battle of the Little Bighorn (the Greasy Grass) and the Battle of the Rosebud, a bloody engagement that played a critical role for Lakotas as they fought to preserve their land and culture in the face of white incursion. Among his other well-regarded publications are *The Dance House: Stories from Rosebud* (1998), *The Lakota Way: Stories and Lessons for Living* (2001), and *The Journey of Crazy Horse: A Lakota History* (2004).

Lydia Whirlwind Soldier (b. 1942) is an enrolled member of the Rosebud Sioux Tribe. Her work has appeared in various magazines and anthologies. She has written a collection of poetry titled *Memory Songs* (1999).

Shaping Survival: Essays by Four American Indian Tribal Women (2001), edited by Jack W. Marken and Charles L. Woodard, is a powerful collection of essays by four twentieth-century tribal women. The firsthand experiences they share range from boarding school struggles to the devastating effects on tribal communities that followed construction of the Missouri River dams. Its contributors are Lanniko Lee (b. 1949), Karen Lone

Hill (b. 1956), Florestine Kiyukanpi Renville (b. 1946), and Lydia Whirlwind Soldier.

The Oak Lake Writers' Society is a society of Nakota, Dakota, and Lakota writers who seek to preserve and promote their cultures through writing. Since 1993 experienced and beginning writers alike have gathered each summer at South Dakota State University's Oak Lake Field Station for writing workshops. Members of the society have contributed to two noteworthy publications. In *This Stretch of the River: Lakota, Dakota, and Nakota Responses to the Lewis and Clark Expedition and Bicentennial* (2006), editors Craig Howe (b. 1959), a member of the Oglala Sioux tribe, and Kimberly TallBear (b. 1968), a member of the Sisseton-Wahpeton Oyate tribe, have collected poetry, fiction, memoirs, history, and literary criticism by Oak Lake Writers' Society members, who are also modern-day descendants of those Tetons depicted in the journals of Lewis and Clark. Their writings provide alternative ways of understanding the expedition and its implications. The society's second publication, *He Sapa Woihanble: Black Hills Dream* (2011), edited by Craig Howe, Lydia Whirlwind Soldier, and Lanniko Lee, contains written poetry, prose, and memoirs expressing spiritual relationships to He Sapa, the land known to many as the Black Hills of South Dakota.

Writing about American Indians by Non-Indian Writers: A number of non-Indian authors have written about South Dakota's tribal people's histories and cultures. Some of the most significant contributions to South Dakota literature are biographies of Lakota leaders by non-Indian authors from outside the state. These biographies were produced in the context of conflicting literary viewpoints between those who believed that a literary and historical tradition was established only through written documents and those who believed that a comprehensive tradition must acknowledge and include the spoken word, dances, ceremonies, and all other forms of cultural expression. In 1931 Black Elk collaborated with John G. Neihardt to write *Black Elk Speaks,* a seminal work of American Indian literature. Neihardt's interest in stories of the Great Plains grew out of his work on *The River and I* (1910), an account of a canoe trip

down the Missouri River from its headwaters; a collection, *Indian Tales and Others* (1926); and his five-part epic poem, *A Cycle of the West* (1949), many portions of which involve South Dakota themes and settings. Neihardt used material gained from many South Dakota sources besides Black Elk in writing the novel *When the Tree Flowered: The Fictional Autobiography of Eagle Voice, a Sioux Indian* (1951).

Mari(e) (Susette) Sandoz (1896–1966), a Nebraska native from the sand hills near the South Dakota border, grew up familiar with the Lakotas in the region. Although she wrote historical fiction, she was also acclaimed for her meticulous historical research. She drew heavily on her research for *Crazy Horse, the Strange Man of the Oglalas: A Biography* (1942), but she also employed her personal knowledge of the Lakota people to write the biography from their cultural perspective. She drew on her childhood experiences in *These Were the Sioux* (1961), a memoir of her relationship with people from the Pine Ridge and Rosebud Reservations who frequented the Sandoz homestead as they traveled the region to visit their ancestral lands.

Two later biographies of Crazy Horse are derivative. Larry (Jeff) McMurtry (b. 1936) wrote *Crazy Horse* (1999), and Kingsley M. Bray (b. 1956) provided *Crazy Horse, a Lakota Life* (2006).

Walter Stanley Campbell (1887–1957), who wrote both fiction and nonfiction under the pseudonym Stanley Vestal, produced the first extensive biography of Sitting Bull, *Sitting Bull: Champion of the Sioux* (1932). His interviews with Sitting Bull's South Dakota friends and relatives gave him materials based on oral accounts by Sitting Bull's nephew for *Warpath and Council Fire: The True Story of the Fighting Sioux as Told in a Biography of Chief White Bull* (1934, 1948). A later comprehensive biography of Sitting Bull, *The Lance and the Shield: The Life and Times of Sitting Bull* (1993), was written by Robert M(arshall) Utley (b. 1929), the former chief historian of the National Park Service.

Among the earliest efforts to record Sioux materials were those by missionaries Stephen Riggs (1812–1883) and his wife, Mary Ann Clark Longley Riggs (1813–1869). He published *Mary and I: Forty Years with the*

Sioux (1880). A collection of her letters written between 1832 and 1869, *A Small Bit of Bread and Butter* (1996), appeared posthumously. An early state historian and journalist, Jonah LeRoy "Doane" Robinson (1856–1946), most famous for conceiving the plan for sculpting Mount Rushmore, gathered native materials from field service workers on the reservations and published them in *Tales of the Dakota: One Hundred Anecdotes Illustrative of Sioux Life and Thinking* (1928).

Reneé Sansom Flood (b. 1945) wrote a number of works using South Dakota American Indian materials. They include *Remember Your Relatives: Yankton Sioux Images, 1851–1904* (1985), with Shirley Bernie (b. 1951); *Lessons from Chouteau Creek: Yankton Memories of Dakota Territorial Intrigue* (1986); and *Lost Bird of Wounded Knee: Spirit of the Lakota* (1995), the story of a child who survived the Wounded Knee massacre. *Lost Bird* was nominated for a Pulitzer Prize. She also edited *The Badlands Fox* (1991) by Margaret Lemley Warren (1916–1998), a memoir of Warren's father, Pete Warren, a horse rancher.

Pine Ridge writer and teacher Mark St. Pierre (b. 1950) wrote *Madonna Swan: A Lakota Woman's Story* (1991), a penetrating, insightful biography of a Cheyenne River woman's struggle to overcome tuberculosis as a child and create a life on the reservation, where she taught in the Head Start program. His book *Walking in the Sacred Manner: Healers, Dreamers, and Pipe Carriers* (1995) examines the way plains tribal women participated in the spiritual lives of their people. As with *Madonna Swan,* St. Pierre used extensive record searches and interviews with a young white, middle-class man and a Pine Ridge Indian who ended up in the violent chaos of the Vietnam War in writing *Of Uncommon Birth: Dakota Sons in Vietnam* (2003).

Mark W. McGinnis (b. 1950) produced *Lakota and Dakota Animal Wisdom Stories* (1994), illustrated with paintings on canvas. He used the same technique in published interviews of South Dakota religious denomination leaders, *Elders of the Faiths* (1996), for which he painted portraits of those he interviewed.

In his epilogue to the best seller *Lame Deer, Seeker of Visions,* Richard Erdoes recalls that his "first encounter with the American West" took place in the open plains of western South Dakota, which contrasted sharply with the Vienna, Austria, of his youth. Erdoes was a lifelong advocate for American Indian civil rights and eventually the author, editor, and illustrator of numerous books about American Indians. In addition to the collaborations listed earlier in this entry, he worked with anthropologist Alfonso Ortiz (1939–1997) to produce one of the foremost reference books on Indian folklore, *American Indian Myths and Legends* (1984), and its sequel, *American Indian Trickster Tales* (1998).

Another Euro-American author who has devoted much of his career to the study of Lakota culture is Ron D. Theisz (b. 1941). Born in Yugoslavia, Theisz was a professor at Sinte Gleska College on the Rosebud Reservation and at Black Hills State University. His publications include scholarly work on Lakota music, dance, art, and literature and creative work of his own. His collection of narratives, *Buckskin Tokens: Contemporary Oral Narratives of the Lakota* (1975), appeared when the different Sioux bands were not sufficiently represented in mainstream anthologies. Together with Ben Black Bear Sr. (1918–1982), Theisz also composed an informative introduction to the cultural significance of Lakota song and dance titled *Songs and Dances of the Lakota* (1976). In the summer of 1986 Theisz and his longtime friend, fellow musician, educator, and adoptive brother Severt Young Bear (b. ca. 1963) tape-recorded Young Bear's family history. Theisz transcribed these recordings and published them in a volume titled *Standing in the Light: A Lakota Way of Seeing* (1994).

Charles L. Woodard (b. 1942) is among the scholars in South Dakota who promote the contributions of its tribal and nontribal writers. Among the many works he has edited are *As Far as I Can See: Contemporary Writing of the Middle Plains* (1989) and, with Jack W. Marken (1922–2005), *Shaping Survival: Essays by Four American Indian Tribal Women* (2002). He also authored *Ancestral Voice: Conversations with N. Scott Momaday* (1989).

Exploration: Aside from some scattered records regarding the fur trade in the Louisiana and Dakota Territories, the first extensive account of what is now South Dakota was by Meriwether Lewis (1774–1809) and William Clark (1770–1838) as it appeared in the first edition of their journals, *The History of the Expedition under the Command of Captains Lewis and Clark* (1814). Lewis had asked a number of members of the expedition to keep journals, and that of Sgt. Patrick Gass (1771–1870), *A Journal of the Voyages and Travels of a Corps of Discovery, under the Command of Capt. Lewis and Capt. Clarke* [*sic*] (1807), was the first published account. Gass's journal, however, did not contain the meticulous observation or the detailed accounts of the land and people that Lewis set as the standard for recording the expedition. The first edition of the Lewis and Clark journals was rendered by Nicholas Biddle 1786–1844, who limited his work to the narrative and, although true to the original, abridged the content. In 1904 Reuben Gold Thwaites (1853–1913) of the Wisconsin State Historical Society published an eight-volume set of the complete journals. In 1962 Donald Jackson edited *Letters of the Lewis and Clark Expedition: 1783–1854*, which was published in an expanded version in 1978. Gary E. Moulton expanded the journals with new materials and scholarly notes in his thirteen-volume publication *The Definitive Journals of Lewis & Clark* (1983–2001).

Joseph Nicolas Nicollet (1786–1843) made three exploratory trips into the upper Mississippi Valley in the 1830s for the purpose of mapping the region. His second trip, in 1838, involved exploration of the territory between the Mississippi River and the Missouri River and took him into southeastern South Dakota, where he did extensive mapping. During this trip he was guided by members of the Wahpeton-Sisseton Sioux tribe and recorded extensive accounts of what he saw on his maps and in his notes and journals. The first publication of his work was *Report Intended to Illustrate a Map of the Hydrological Basin of the Upper Mississippi River* (1843). Accessible versions of his journals are *A Scientist on the Mississippi Headwaters with Notes on Indian Life* (1970), translated by André Fertey and edited by Martha Coleman Bray, and *Joseph N. Nicollet on the Plains and Prairies: The Expeditions of 1838–39 with Journals, Letters, and Notes on the Dakota Indi-*

ans (1976) by Edmund C. Bray and Martha Coleman Bray.

George Catlin (1796–1872) produced some of the most arresting works that deal extensively with South Dakota. His *Letters and Notes on the Manners, Customs, and Condition of the North American Indians* (1841) contains extensive notes on and portraits of Indians and Indian life, as well as observations on the landscape and its animal and geological features.

Settlement and Development: The Homestead Act of 1862 and the extension of the railroad into Dakota Territory in 1878 paved the way for new settlements across the state. This period of settlement and development has inspired over a century of writing, ranging from fiction to biography and memoir.

Fiction: (HANNIBAL) HAMLIN GARLAND (1860–1940) was one of the earliest South Dakota writers to gain national attention, and the six stories that make up his first major publication, MAIN-TRAVELLED ROADS (1891), were among the first works by a writer of fiction to use South Dakota as a setting. Garland spent only a brief period, 1883–1884, in South Dakota, but the experience stayed with him.

Garland launched his career with the publication of *Main-Travelled Roads*, which expressed many of his negative feelings about the area. After its publication Garland wrote additional works about those living on "the middle border," referring to the frontier communities in WISCONSIN, IOWA, and South Dakota where his family had lived. His semi-autobiographical narrative *A Son of the Middle Border* (1917) offers vivid details of Garland's early years in the rural Midwest, including chapters about his time in South Dakota's Brown and McPherson Counties. *A Daughter of the Middle Border* (1921) picks up where *A Son of the Middle Border* leaves off, describing his departure from the prairies of Dakota. His other works with an emphasis on South Dakota are *The Captain of Gray-Horse Troop* (1902), about an agent assigned to Pine Ridge to mediate between the Indians and the ranchers, and *The Book of the American Indian* (1923), which incorporates information Garland collected during visits and interviews on South Dakota reservations. It includes one of the most accurate accounts of the killing of Sitting Bull.

Many assume that L(YMAN) FRANK BAUM (1856–1919) found inspiration for his hugely successful THE WONDERFUL WIZARD OF OZ (1900) in KANSAS. In fact, the story has its origins farther north. Baum spent three years in South Dakota, from 1888 to 1891, enough time to experience the tornadoes and droughts he would eventually incorporate into his best-known work. Born in New York, Baum moved to Aberdeen, South Dakota, in 1888, where he operated a variety store, Baum's Bazaar, and edited the newspaper the *Aberdeen Saturday Pioneer.*

A native South Dakotan, William Otis Lillibridge (1878–1909) produced a national best seller with his first novel, *Ben Blair: The Story of a Plainsman* (1905). Several other books followed, two of them published after his death. They include *Where the Trail Divides* (1907), involving the Sioux uprising of 1862; *The Quest Eternal* (1908); *The Dissolving Circle* (1908), involving a love triangle; *Quercus Alba, the Veteran of the Ozarks* (1910); and *A Breath of Prairie* (1911), a collection of Lillibridge's short fiction.

The novel *A Prayer for Tomorrow* (1938) by J. Hyatt Downing (1888–1973) offers a grim view of central South Dakota farming conditions. Downing grew up in the rural community of Blunt, where he thought that plowing of the land was futile. He went on to write additional works of fiction, including *Hope for the Living* (1939) and *The Harvest Is Late* (1944).

A contemporary of Downing, Arvid Shulenberger (1919–1964), wrote *Roads from the Fort* (1954), a historical novel set near Fort Randall in 1857 and focusing on two soldiers caught between warring Sioux bands. He also published a book of poetry, *Ancient Music, and Other Poems* (1960).

Writers who found humor on the Dakota frontier include Kennett Harris (1864–1930). English by birth, Harris published *Meet Mr. Stegg* (1920), a collection of tall tales set in the Black Hills. The collection has been compared to the storytelling of SAMUEL LANGHORNE CLEMENS (1835–1910), who wrote as Mark Twain. Another, Archer B. Gilfillan (1886–1955), worked as a sheepherder and columnist in Harding County for many

years and provided entertaining details of his experiences in *A Shepherd's Holiday* (1936) and *A Goat's Eye View of the Black Hills* (1953). His best-known work, however, was his first, *Sheep* (1929).

By the end of the nineteenth century Germans and Scandinavians were moving into the upper Midwest. See SCANDINAVIAN LITERATURE. In 1896, twenty-year-old OLE EDVART RØLVAAG (1876–1931) left his Norwegian fishing village on the island of Dønna to join his uncle in Elk Point, South Dakota. Rølvaag soon lost interest in farming and left his uncle's farm for nearby education. Rølvaag's contact with South Dakota's immigrant homesteaders profoundly influenced him, and their experiences became his primary literary focus. He first published his works in Norwegian and played a key role in most of the English translations that followed. *GIANTS IN THE EARTH* (1927) offers a powerful representation of the hardships faced by a Norwegian pioneer family that settles in Dakota Territory during the 1870s. The second and third installments of this epic trilogy are *Peder Victorious* (1929) and *Their Fathers' God* (1931). Rølvaag's other works set in South Dakota include *The Third Life of Per Smevik* (1971), *Pure Gold* (1930), *The Boat of Longing* (1933), and a collection of his shorter prose works, *When the Wind Is in the South, and Other Stories* (1984).

Reuben Goertz (1918–1993) offers insight into the social life and customs of the many Germans who immigrated to South Dakota from Russia during the 1880s. His essays are collected in *Princes, Potentates, and Plain People* (1994). In *The Nunda Irish* (1990) William McDonald (b. 1924) provides a fictionalized history of the Irish of his hometown, Nunda, South Dakota.

African Americans also constituted a significant presence in South Dakota's early history. Before the Dakota boom of the 1880s, African Americans found work in small businesses in the eastern towns of Sioux Falls and Yankton, as well as in the many towns springing up in the Black Hills. But with the opening up of "free land," they came to the area as farmers and ranchers drawn by the prospect of wealth and independence they believed was available to them on the open frontier. Few of these

African American pioneers had as remarkable a career as writer, filmmaker, and South Dakota homesteader OSCAR MICHEAUX (1884–1951). Micheaux is best known for his more than forty films, starting with his silent film *The Homesteader* (1919) and ending with *The Betrayal* (1948). But he also wrote seven novels and self-published all his books, fearing that white publishers would reject his more rounded characterizations of African Americans. Three of these novels, *The Conquest: The Story of a Negro Pioneer* (1913), *The Homesteader: A Novel* (1917), and *The Wind from Nowhere* (1943), are based on his homesteading experience from 1905 to 1910 in Gregory, South Dakota. In 1919 he made *The Homesteader* into the previously mentioned film with the same title. Historians claim that it is the first feature-length African American film. His film *The Exile* (1931) was a remake of *The Homesteader,* and *The Wind from Nowhere* served as the basis for his final film, *The Betrayal.*

Of the authors who have written about the pioneers and settlers of early South Dakota, at least half were women. Many wrote works of romance and adventure. A refreshing departure from the glut of western romances at the turn of the twentieth century can be found in *Bachelor Bess: The Homesteading Letters of Elizabeth Corey, 1909–1919* (1990) by Elizabeth Corey (1887–1954). Written during the state's last land boom, the letters of Elizabeth Corey, also known as "Bachelor Bess," are as historically informative as they are entertaining.

When Eudora Edith Kohl (1884–1959) published *Land of the Burnt Thigh* (1938), she insisted that it was fiction; however, its story line of two single women homesteading near the Lower Brule Indian Reservation near Pierre bears a striking resemblance to the author's own life. Like her main characters, the two sisters Edith and Ida Mary Ammons, Kohl homesteaded with her sister near McClure, south of Pierre. Kohl's novel introduces a number of other single women homesteaders and highlights the importance of cooperative living as the sisters socialize and share food and other resources with their neighbors to overcome the difficulties of pioneer life.

Mary Worthy Breneman was the pen name of the mother-daughter team of Mary Worthy Thurston (1880–1969) and her daughter, Muriel R. Breneman (1914–2006). They are the co-authors of *The Land They Possessed* (1956). Roughly based on Thurston and her parents' homesteading experience in north central South Dakota, the book tells the story of John, Mavis, and daughter Michal Ward, an Anglo-American family that moves to the area during the Dakota boom period.

Few authors of fiction have covered as much South Dakota history as FREDERICK MANFRED (b. Feike Feikema, 1912–1994) and no other novel with a South Dakota setting has been more successful than his best seller *Lord Grizzly* (1954). His fiction draws from a region he referred to as Siouxland, which includes South Dakota, MINNESOTA, Iowa, and Nebraska. His Buckskin Man Tales include *Conquering Horse* (1959), which reaches back to the early 1800s, before white settlement, to tell the tale of No Name, a young Sioux warrior. *Lord Grizzly* focuses on the legendary mountain man Hugh Glass, who in 1823–1824 traveled with General William Ashley's expedition up the Missouri River and was attacked by a grizzly bear in northwestern South Dakota. *Scarlet Plume* (1964) is a CAPTIVITY NARRATIVE set in Minnesota during the Dakota Wars of 1862, and in *Riders of Judgment* (1957) Manfred recounts the history of the Johnson County, Wyoming, range wars. *King of Spades* (1966), the last in his series, takes place in Deadwood during the Black Hills gold rush. South Dakota is also the setting of his first novel, *The Golden Bowl* (1944), a story of those who survived South Dakota's 1930s Dust Bowl.

HERBERT KRAUSE (1905–1976) was the author of three novels, as well as several poems, essays, reviews, and an unpublished play. Although his three novels are set in Minnesota, where Krause was born, he wrote all of them during his tenure at Augustana College in Sioux Falls. *Wind without Rain* (1939) tells the story of the difficulties of German American immigrants who settled near Fergus Falls, Minnesota. His second novel, *The Thresher* (1946), is set in the wheat lands of Minnesota, where the wheat threshers struggle to adapt to twentieth-century agricultural technologies. In Krause's third novel, *The Oxcart Trail* (1954), he writes the story of O'Shaughnessy Dark, a man who helps African American slaves escape via the Underground Railroad. In 1970 Krause founded the Center for Western Studies at Augustana College, where he worked to promote the study and preservation of northern plains history. Krause's abundant contributions to the state earned him a place in the South Dakota Hall of Fame in 1976.

Ike Blasingame (1884–1962) provides a vivid depiction of his life as a cowboy on Matador Ranch in western South Dakota in *Dakota Cowboy: My Life in the Old Days* (1958). Born in Presho, South Dakota, and raised on a ranch, E(dward) R. Zietlow (b. 1932) wrote fiction that draws on his West River upbringing in South Dakota. His first novel, *These Same Hills* (1961), received critical notice. His further publications were a collection of short stories, *A Country for Old Men and Other Stories* (1977) and two novellas published together, *The Indian Maiden's Captivity* and *The Heart of the Country* (1978).

Among his many contributions to the state's literary culture, John R. Milton (1924–1995) published works of poetry and fiction, including "The Inheritance of Emmy One Horse," published in *The Best American Short Stories of 1969* (1970), edited by Martha Foley and David Burnett. Milton's other works related to South Dakota and the western region are *South Dakota: A Bicentennial History* (1977) and his scholarly book *The Novel of the American West* (1980).

Best known for *Paris Trout* (1988), a novel set in rural Georgia, Pete Dexter (b. 1943) has also written works with ties to South Dakota. He turned to nineteenth-century Black Hills history for the material of his novel *Deadwood* (1986). *Deadwood* centers on Wild Bill Hickok's (1837–1876) lesser-known companion, Charles H. Utter, "Colorado Charlie" (ca. 1838–ca. 1913), who provides a fresh perspective on Deadwood's colorful past.

David Diamond (b. S. I. Davison, 1936–2014) was a South Dakota native who was a radio personality in major markets and then became a professor of mass communications, retired from Black Hills State University in 2008, and received the Mark Twain Award for his writing from the SOCIETY FOR THE STUDY OF MIDWESTERN LITERATURE in 2006. Diamond wrote a novel, many short stories,

and poetry. His South Dakota short stories are collected in *Fire in the Badlands* (1997).

Kent Meyers (b. 1955) won the Mountain and Plains Booksellers' Association Award, the One Book South Dakota Award, and a *Christian Science Monitor* listing in its best novels of 2004 for *The Work of Wolves* (2004). *The Work of Wolves* is especially noteworthy and atypical for its cross-cultural dramatization of South Dakota life. Consisting of four parts, the novel integrates local legend and American Indian myth to tell the story of a new generation that must come to terms with the violence and greed of its predecessors. A later novel, *Twisted Tree* (2009), rich in description, deals with the consequences of murder in a small South Dakota town.

Brian Bedard (b. 1945) followed founder John Milton as the editor of South Dakota's premier literary journal, *South Dakota Review*, and remained in that position until his retirement in 2011. Bedard also coordinated the creative-writing program at the University of South Dakota during these years. He was among the first graduates of the University of Montana's MFA program, where he studied under Richard Hugo. Bedard's stories have appeared widely in such forums as *Quarterly West, Cimarron Review, Alaska Quarterly*, and *North American Review*. His two volumes of collected works are *Hour of the Beast, and Other Stories* (1984) and the award-winning *Grieving on the Run* (2007), both of which include South Dakota themes and settings. When asked to describe some of his interests in writing about this region, Bedard explained in an e-mail to Paul Baggett on September 14, 2011:

As I see it, all fiction writers seek a dramatic testing point for the values and beliefs of their time. For me that testing point is the intersection of Civilization and Nature. Thus my preoccupation [has been] with the Northern Plains and the American West, where the civilization/Nature negotiation is most dramatically acted out.

Steven Wingate (b. 1964) came to South Dakota State University in 2012, where he is a professor of English and the director of the Great Plains Writers' Conference. Wingate has experimented with a variety of forms in his award-winning collection of short stories, *Wifeshopping* (2008); two collections of prose poems, *The Birth of Trigonometry in the Bones of Olduvai* (2013) and *Thirty-One Octets: Incantations and Meditations* (2014); and a number of hybrid-genre pieces—"prose poems, non-narrative screenplays, lists of all kinds, and form-driven project[s]"—which, he reports on his website, "have appeared in such journals as *Witness, Mississippi Review, Sonora Review, Pank,* and the *Fiction Collective 2* anthology *Degenerative Prose: Writing Beyond Category.*" In an interview with Paul Baggett on July 23, 2014, Wingate explains, "My heart is going into the work that finds its own ways to express things."

Creative Nonfiction: Poet, essayist, and anthologist LINDA HASSELSTROM (b. 1943) lives on her family's cattle ranch near Hermosa, South Dakota, where she also runs Windbreak House, a retreat center for women writers. She captures the joys and hardships of life on the Great Plains in books such as *Going over East: Reflections of a Woman Rancher* (1987), *Windbreak: A Woman Rancher on the Northern Plains* (1987), *Land Circle: Writings Collected from the Land* (1991), *Feels like Far: A Rancher's Life on the Great Plains* (1999), and *Between Grass and Sky* (2002). Her *Roadside History of South Dakota* (1994) is a highly entertaining tour guide that brings to life many of the small towns and open landscapes of the state. In *No Place like Home: Notes on a Western Life* (2010) she challenges those who view South Dakota as empty space to be used for hazardous-waste dumping, uranium mining, ammunition testing, and shortsighted real estate development, insisting instead on our responsibilities as advocates for our communities and the land that sustains them and us.

KATHLEEN NORRIS (b. 1947) moved into her deceased grandmother's home in Lemmon, South Dakota, in 1974. In *Dakota: A Spiritual Geography* (1993) she embarks on a journey of spiritual reflection, calling her book "an invitation to a land of little rain and few trees, dry summer winds and harsh winters, a land rich in grass and sky and surprises" (2). That is not to say that she withholds criticism of the closed-mindedness she sometimes encounters in her small town. Nor does she avoid discussing the economic problems of the farmers and small-town businesses or the environmental challenges particular to the western

Dakotas. In *The Cloister Walk* (1996) she writes about her time spent among the Benedictines. Drawing on her experiences as a lay associate at Assumption Abbey in NORTH DAKOTA and during the two years she lived in a Benedictine monastery in Collegeville, Minnesota, Norris provides a thoughtful and inspirational description of monastic life. Additional memoirs told in Norris's poetic voice and with strong religious themes are *Amazing Grace: A Vocabulary of Faith* (1999) and *Acedia and Me* (2008).

Buffalo rancher, falconry enthusiast, rock climber, and naturalist Dan O'Brien (b. 1947) has written a number of works of fiction and nonfiction, many of them with South Dakota settings. *The Spirit of the Black Hills* (1987) is especially ambitious, bringing together many of the contemporary problems in the Black Hills: the hunting of gray wolves, drug-related violence, and tensions between federal agents and American Indians. O'Brien's *Buffalo for the Broken Heart: Restoring Life to a Black Hills Ranch* (2001) records his shift from cattle ranching to raising bison, during which he also discovered the economic, social, and environmental advantages of reintroducing native species and living locally.

Two authors who have continued to write about farm life are Robert "Bob" (Clayton) Amerson (1925–2006) and Douglas A(rthur) Unger (b. 1952). In *From the Hidewood: Memories of a Dakota Neighborhood* (1996) Amerson has written a coming-of-age memoir of 1930s farm life in eastern South Dakota. Unger's novel *Leaving the Land* (1984) depicts the plight of the South Dakota family farm in the face of the encroachment of big business and industry.

Formerly a freelance broadcaster for the BBC, British writer Fraser Harrison (b. 1944) came to the Great Plains to write *Infinite West: Travels in South Dakota* (2012). His travel narrative departs from travelogue convention. Rather than describe foreign locations for readers back home, his aim is to "describe the face that South Dakota showed to the tourist, but with this twist: that [he] would also be describing the face to its owner" (186). Harrison thus directs his impressions toward South Dakotans, particularly toward those who think that they have nothing new to learn about the state.

Poetry: Poetry was the preferred genre for many of South Dakota's earliest professional writers, including John Wallace Crawford (1847–1917). Also known as "Captain Jack: Poet Scout of the Black Hills," Crawford was a member of the Black Hills Rangers militia and eventually became the chief scout of the Fifth Cavalry, replacing William "Buffalo Bill" Cody (1846–1917), who held that position before him. Wearing his hair long and clad in a sombrero, buckskin pants, and a six-shooter around his waist, he would recite poems and recount adventures that contributed to the frontier myths his audiences had previously only read about. His earliest publication is *Poet Scout: Being a Selection of Incidental and Illustrative Verses and Songs* (1879).

In 1937 South Dakota's governor, Leslie Jensen, named Charles "Badger" Clark Jr. (1883–1957) the first Poet Laureate of the state. Humbled by such a "high-falutin" name, Clark quickly changed it to "poet lariat," a more fitting title for the prolific cowboy poet. While working on a ranch near Tombstone, Clark began composing poems in his letters home. After the appearance of his first poem in 1906, Clark's reputation took off. He published at least two hundred poems; the most comprehensive collection is *Badger Clark Ballads: Selected Works of a Cowboy Poet* (1982).

Rudolf G. Ruste (1892–1976) and Audrae Visser (1919–2001), former editors of *Pasque Petals,* the poetry journal of the South Dakota Poetry Society, worked to promote poetry across the state. Ruste's publications include *Day Dirt* (1925) and *Daddy's Poems* (1938). Visser was the state's third Poet Laureate and published multiple volumes of poetry, including *Rustic Roads* (1961), *Grass Roots Poetry* (1991), and *Prairie Poetry* (1998).

Linda Hasselstrom and Kathleen Norris are also accomplished poets. Hasselstrom has published a comprehensive collection of her poetry up to 1993, *Dakota Bones* (1993), and *Bitter Creek Junction* (1999). Her later poetry appears in *Dirt Songs: A Plains Duet* (2011), which also includes poetry by Nebraska poet Twyla M. Hansen. Norris's poetic works include *Falling Off* (1971), *The Middle of the World* (1981), *How I Came to Drink My Grandmother's Piano: Some Benedictine Poems* (1989), and *Little Girls in Church* (1995).

South Dakota Poet Laureate 2002–2015 David Allan Evans. Photo by Jan Evans.
Courtesy of David Allan Evans

Norris's husband, David Dwyer (1946–2003), was also a poet and former South Dakota resident. Among his published works is a collection of poetry titled *Other Men and Other Women* (1988).

Leo Dangel (b. 1941) provides colorful details of country life in western Minnesota and eastern South Dakota. His works include *Old Man Brunner Country* (1987), *Hogs and Personals: Poems* (1992), and *The Crow on the Golden Arches* (2004).

The poems of the fourth Poet Laureate of the state, David Allan Evans (b. 1940), reflect his interests in sports, nature, and experiences growing up in the meatpacking city of Sioux City, Iowa, although he certainly has not limited himself to these subjects. His poetry collections include *Among Athletes* (1970), *Train Windows* (1976), *Real and False Alarms* (1985), *Hanging Out with the Crows* (1991), *The Bull Rider's Advice* (2003), and *This Water, These Rocks* (2009).

Debra Nystrom (b. 1954) lives in Charlottesville, Virginia, and teaches at the University of Virginia, but the setting for much of her poetry is South Dakota, where she grew up. The people and places of the state are prominently featured in *Torn Sky* (2003). In this collection Nystrom takes on many of the ghosts from South Dakota's past, including imagined incidents omitted from Lewis and Clark's journals, a witness's account of the Wounded Knee massacre, and the cultural gap that persists between Native and non-native peoples. South Dakota is also the setting for a later work, *Bad River Road: Poems* (2009).

Although the newest generation of South Dakota poets continues to explore Midwestern themes and settings, some have also turned their attention to more distant terrain. A dual citizen of Ireland and the United States, Patrick Hicks (b. 1970)draws frequently on his bicultural roots, writing with what he has called his "hyphenated tongue." His first full-length collection, *Finding the Gossamer* (2008), features poems about his life in Minnesota and his career in South Dakota. *This London* (2010) captures some of the hidden history of the British capital. His first collection of short stories, *The Collector of Names* (2015), uses various locations in the Midwest for settings. Lee Ann Roripaugh (b. 1965), South Dakota Poet Laureate since 2015, finds inspiration in her Japanese American bicultural upbringing. Her first collection, *Beyond Heart Mountain* (1999), describes a relocation camp where Japanese Americans were interned following the bombing of Pearl Harbor. Her other published works include *Year of the Snake* (2004), *On the Cusp of a Dangerous Year* (2009), and *Dandarians* (2014).

Christine Stewart-Nunez (b. 1973) has written about Catherine of Siena, an Italian mystic and saint, in *The Love of Unreal Things* (2005), supermodel Kate Moss in *Unbound and Branded* (2006), and her experiences as a teacher in Turkey in *Postcards on Parchment* (2008). In her collection *Keeping Them Alive* (2011) she blends the 1984 death of her sister and the 2006 birth of her son within a series of poetic confessions, meditations, and celebrations.

Jim Reese (b. 1972) has lived and worked in both Nebraska and South Dakota, and material for his poetry often comes from both states. In *Ghost on 3rd* (2010) images range from South Dakota bumper stickers to a five-year-old playing on the monkey bars. Reese's most unusual subject matter in *Ghost* comes from his experiences as a writer-in-residence within the federal prison system.

Many other writers continue to produce quality poetry within or about the state. These poets include Darla D. Bielfeldt (b. 1967) with *Harvey Dunn: Feminine Images; Poems* (2004); Jerome Freeman (b. 1948) with *Easing the Edges* (1994); Charles Luden (b. 1949) with *West of Venus: Punk Love Poems* (1986); Bruce Roseland (b. 1951) with *A Prairie Prayer* (2008); and Dennis Sampson (b. 1949), author of *Needlegrass* (2005).

Drama: Drama in South Dakota, as in other Midwestern states, especially those in the western tier of states on the Great Plains, began with touring companies in 1869, bringing dramatic productions from the East, according to Arthur Huseboe in his invaluable 1989 volume *An Illustrated History of the Arts in South Dakota* (5; subsequent references to South Dakota drama are to this work). In South Dakota such productions were largely urban phenomena, taking place especially in cities like Sioux Falls, Rapid City, and Yankton (60). Perhaps the most important development was the emergence of the Sioux Falls Community Playhouse in 1945–1946, but theatres existed there as early as 1879. Such theatres included the Booth Grand Opera House (1886), the New Theatre (1897), and the Orpheum (1913) (60–61). The Civic Theatre Association was established in Sioux Falls in 1931 (62). By the late 1920s, however, live drama was facing serious competition from movies and vaudeville in popular culture. A movie theatre opened as early as 1906 in Aberdeen (45).

In the western part of the state, Rapid City offered several venues, including the Rapid City Group Theatre, which had its origins in 1968 (68). In the Black Hills, the Black Hills Passion Play, under the auspices of Josef Meier, played annually in Spearfish from 1938 to 2008. Also in the Black Hills, the Black Hills Playhouse, associated with the University of South Dakota, was established by Warren Lee in 1946 in Custer State Park; this playhouse is still in operation and is considered a huge success. In the eastern part of the state, the Prairie Repertory Theater, started in 1970, has provided summer theatre productions for over four decades. Beginning in Madison as an extension of South Dakota State University's theatre program, the Prairie Repertory Theatre now stages its shows in Brookings at South Dakota State University's Donor Auditorium and in Brandon Valley at the Brandon Valley Performing Arts Center. The Dakota Theatre Caravan, organized in 1977 in Yankton, has produced original South Dakota material, such as its first production, *Dakota Roads: The Story of a Prairie Family* (1977) (75–76). Other theatre groups in the state include the Lewis and Clark Theatre Company (1962) in Yankton and the South Dakota Theatre Association, begun in 1988 in Pierre (77–78).

South Dakota's earliest poet, John Wallace "Captain Jack" Crawford, was also one of the state's earliest dramatists, with four plays to his name. His first play, *Fonda; or, The Trapper's Dream* (1877; published in 1888), is an anti-Mormon melodrama, while his second, *The Mighty Truth; or, In Clouds or Sunshine* (1879; published in 1896), references many of the sociopolitical subjects of Crawford's time, including temperance, women's suffrage, the institution of Indian boarding schools, and lynch law. Crawford wrote two other plays toward the end of his life: *The Dregs: A Monologue* (1907), a one-act play about prohibition, and *Colonel Bob: A Western Pastoral* (1908).

Warren Marion Lee (1908–1978) founded the Black Hills Playhouse in 1946 and remained its director for nearly thirty years. His four plays, many of them historical fictions set during the Black Hills gold rush, include *Shave and Haircut, Six Bits!* (1940), *Trouble Shooter: A Farce-Comedy in Three Acts* (1946), *The Showmaker and the Wolves* (1976), and *Legend of Devils Gulch* (1980). Kenn Pierson (b. 1957) based *Mountain Thunder: The Ballad of Badger Clark* (1997) on the poems and journals of Clark. *Mountain Thunder* was then filmed by South Dakota Public Television.

Wayne S. Knutson (1926–2015) grew up on a farm near Sisseton, South Dakota, and incorporated his appreciation for the heroic qualities of the struggling South Dakota farmer into his tragedy *One Life to Spend* (1951), which he later rewrote. The updated version is titled *Dream Valley* (1960). The hero

of both these plays, Emil Ronnervig, reappears in his later play *The Dakota Descendants of Ola Rue* (1987). Now much older, Emil holds on to his dream of farming in a valley that many believe was better left unplowed.

Ronald Robinson (b. 1936) based his musical comedy *Aces and Eights* (1989) on the life of Deadwood legend Wild Bill Hickok. His musical comedy *What Ever Happened to Radio?* (1970), and his drama *Nation Invisible* (1991) are also set in South Dakota. Robinson also wrote fiction; his first novel, *Thunder Dreamer* (1996), features a voyage through South Dakota that has been compared to that of *ADVENTURES OF HUCKLEBERRY FINN* (1884, 1885).

Craig Volk (b. 1951) is an accomplished playwright with multiple productions to his credit, some of them with South Dakota connections. His stage play *Sodbusters* (1988) is set in 1880s Dakota Territory. In the process of "proving up" a quarter section of land, three bachelor brothers also develop kindred bonds for one another. Set on a run of rodeo fence outside the bull-riding chutes, *Chute Roosters* (1988) takes a satiric look at "might makes right" in contemporary America. Volk also wrote the script for the half-hour narrative film *Porch Light* (1995), which depicts a young man's attempt to return to the family farm after learning that he is dying of AIDS. The film concludes with documentary testimonies by South Dakotans who had also seen loved ones die of the disease.

A former professor of theatre and chair of the Performing and Visual Arts Department at Augustana College in Sioux Falls, playwright Ivan W. Fuller (b. 1960) has contributed significantly to the theatre culture of Sioux Falls. As the founder and artistic director of the Bare Bodkins Theatre Company, he staged numerous summer Shakespeare productions for the city. He also wrote and produced two original works while at Augustana: *Eating into the Fabric* (2010), based on stories from the World War II siege of Leningrad; and *Awake in Me* (2011), based on the life and writings of Soviet poet Olga Berggolts.

A graduate of the University of South Dakota and professor of creative writing at Pennsylvania State University, Toni Jensen (b. 1971) has written two plays. *Her Mother's*

Daughter (1994) is a one-act play that was turned into a script and televised on South Dakota Public Television. Her full-length documentary drama *Camp Happiness* (1995) is based on the 1988 murder of Cliff Hirocke outside Vermillion, South Dakota, a murder that was compared to the Wyoming murder of Matthew Shepard in both its motive and its execution. The play explores the connections between victims and perpetrators, as well as intersections between family members and friends. Jensen has also authored a number of short stories, including "Looking for Boll Weevil," published in *Best of the West: Stories from the Wide Side of the Missouri* (2011), and "At the Powwow Hotel," published in *Best Stories from the Southwest* (2008). In her short story collection *From the Hilltop* (2010) Jensen captures the lives of American Indians living off the reservation.

Film: FILM production by South Dakotans has been largely limited to documentaries. Among others cited by Arthur Huseboe, Charles Nauman (b. 1924) wrote and produced a number of films devoted to the difficulties of Native American life, including *Tahtonka* (1968), *Johnny Vik* (1977), and *Yes, I Am Not Iktomi* (1999). Nauman also published the novel *Pola* (2011). Nauman's former wife, H. Jane Nauman (b. 1928), the owner of Sun Dog Films in Custer, South Dakota, is perhaps best known for the documentary *Lakota Quillwork: Art and Legend* (1985). Another production company, Cottonwood Productions of Wakonda, produced the ecological *Let the Waters Run Free* in 1972, as well as *Paha Sapa: The Story of Custer State Park* (1975) and *The Rebirth of Whitewood Creek* (1987). A third film-production company is Unity Productions, organized by Tim Schwab (b. 1956) and Christina Craton (b. 1952) and responsible for the prairie studies *Home Land* (1984) and *Boom and Bust* (1985), as well as *Letters from America: The Life and Times of O. E. Rølvaag* (1989), *Ghosts along the Freeway* (1991), *The Artists and the Wolves* (1993), *The Burning Barrel* (1996), *Gateway* (1999), and *Being Osama* (2004). Since its move to national distribution in the early 1990s, the company has renamed itself First Light Films International. The state's most famous film writer, producer, and director was the African American Oscar Micheaux, who made more than forty films, including *The Homesteader* (1919), a film adaptation of his novel of the same title. Three noteworthy films set on the Pine Ridge Indian Reservation are director Michael Apted's *Thunderheart* (1992), director Chris Eyre's *Skins* (2002), and *Incident at Oglala* (1992), Michael Apted's documentary about the events and legal proceedings leading to the arrest of American Indian Movement activist Leonard Peltier. Some well-known films made at least partially in South Dakota include *North by Northwest* (1959), directed by Alfred Hitchcock and starring Cary Grant, Eva Marie Saint, and James Mason; Terrence Malick's *Badlands* (1973), with Martin Sheen and Sissy Spacek; and *Dances with Wolves* (1990), directed by and starring Kevin Costner.

Popular Literature:

Dime Novels: The 1870s gold rush to the Black Hills resulted in the production of some of South Dakota's earliest and most widely read fiction in the form of the dime novel. The author chiefly responsible was Edward L. Wheeler (ca. 1854–1885), who helped to make figures like Wild Bill Hickok, Calamity Jane, Deadwood Dick, and the town of Deadwood the stuff of western legend. Wheeler published over thirty Deadwood Dick novels between 1877 and 1884. The first of these western romances was *Deadwood Dick: The Prince of the Road* (1877).

The historical figure behind Wheeler's Deadwood Dick series was Nat Love (1854–1921), whose autobiography, *Life and Adventures of Nat Love* (1907), explains how he acquired his legendary status. An African American who was born a slave in Tennessee, Love eventually became a Texas cowboy respected for his riding abilities. After winning multiple contests at an 1876 rodeo in Deadwood, he gained the nickname "Deadwood Dick."

Romance, Juvenile, and Young Adult Fiction: South Dakota's prairies have served as the setting for a number of romance novels and have helped produce a long list of books for children and young adults. See CHILDREN'S AND YOUNG-ADULT LITERATURE. Three of the earliest works are *In Far Dakota* (1890) by Mary Locke, *Sara Dakota* (1894) by Mary E(lizabeth) Q(uakenbush) Brush (1857–1940), and *That Dakota Girl* (1900) by Stella Lucile Gilman (ca. 1869–1949). More successful was *The Biography of a Prairie Girl* (1902) by Eleanor Gates (1875–1951). Gates's semi-autobiographical novel is set in the Vermillion River valley, where she spent ten years of her childhood. She also wrote *The Plow Woman* (1906), *Cupid: The Cow-Punch* (1907), *A Poor Little Rich Girl* (1912), *We Are Seven: A Three-Act Whimsical Farce* (1915), *Apron Strings: A Story for All Mothers Who Have Daughters and for Daughters Who Have Mothers* (1917), *Out of the West* (1924), and *Fish Bait* (1928).

The most commercially successful of the early generation of romance novelists was Kate Boyles Bingham (1876–1959). Kate and her brother, Virgil Boyles (1872–1965), co-authored a series of westerns, although biographers have claimed that while her brother assisted with plot construction and historical research, Kate Bingham did the majority of the writing. Like many women of her generation, Kate advocated women's suffrage, and her political sentiments sometimes emerge in her writing. The siblings' first novel, *Langford of the Three Bars* (1907), borrows from the historic events surrounding the life and death of notorious cattle rustler Jack Sully.

In addition to her concerns for women, Kate grew increasingly sensitive to the difficulties facing the Sioux at the turn of the century. *The Homesteaders* (1909) and *The Spirit Trail* (1910) incorporate some of her sympathies. For instance, *The Spirit Trail* is set during the 1870s, when Custer led his infamous expedition into the Black Hills. She and her brother preface their book with a reprint of the Fort Laramie Treaty, which guaranteed Lakota ownership of the Black Hills and the surrounding region. Their final collaboration is titled *Daughter of the Badlands* (1922).

A number of authors who wrote for children and young adults made a name for themselves in the decades between the two world wars. The most famous was LAURA INGALLS WILDER (1867–1957). Wilder's novels provide some of the most extensive portrayals of pioneer life on the South Dakota frontier. Her Little House series of books chronicles her life through her father's restless moves as he homesteaded in many Midwestern states, her childhood in what was then Dakota Territory, and her growth to maturity and marriage. Especially vivid are descriptions of the challenges that meet the Ingalls family upon their arrival in what would soon become De Smet, South Dakota. Ingalls's narratives capture the difficulties family members faced in sustaining themselves during the long and difficult winters, as well as the beauty she found in the landscapes of eastern South Dakota. Those works with South Dakota settings are *By the Shores of Silver Lake* (1939), *The Long Winter* (1940), *Little Town on the Prairie* (1941), *These Happy Golden Years* (1943), *On the Way Home* (1962), and *The First Four Years* (1971). Laura Ingalls Wilder's daughter, ROSE WILDER LANE (1886–1968), assisted her mother and benefited greatly from their collaboration: Lane's two most successful novels, *Let the Hurricane Roar* (1933; reissued as *Young Pioneers* in 1961) and *Free Land* (1938), draw heavily on her mother's memories of her family's homesteading experiences in Dakota Territory.

By the 1930s the children's novel about the pioneer heroine had become a genre unto itself. *The Jumping-Off Place* (1929) by Marian Hurd McNeely (1877–1930) tells the story of four orphans' homesteading experiences in Tripp County, South Dakota. Set in 1910, when McNeely and her husband had homesteaded the same area, the book dramatizes the childrens' battles against blizzards, drought, rattlesnakes, and a family of squatters who claim title to the same parcel of land. Ethel Powelson Hueston (1887–1971) spent a short time in South Dakota, but it gave her enough material for *Blithe Baldwin* (1933), the story of a young cowgirl who finds work on a dude ranch in the Black Hills. Other works of hers with links to South Dakota include *That Hastings Girl* (1933), *Star of the West: The Romance of the Lewis and Clark Expedition* (1935), and *Calamity Jane of Deadwood Gulch* (1937). A young-adult novel by Francis Gilchrist Wood (1859–1944), *Turkey Red* (1932), is remarkable for its representation of the young Janet Craig, who proves herself more than capable of taking care of a farm and a printing press, while her injured husband, Allen Craig, finds the challenges of baby care and domestic responsibilities more than he bargained for.

In two semi-autobiographical narratives Lucile Foster Fargo (1880–1962) captures the experiences of a girl living in one of the many railroad towns in Dakota Territory: *Prairie Girl* (1937) and *Prairie Chautauqua* (1943). They draw on Fargo's experiences as a young girl when her family homesteaded for two years near Mitchell and then moved to Dell Rapids in eastern South Dakota. Fargo's heroine, Prairie, departs from convention by expressing many of the author's feminist sentiments.

Among the children's book writers who emerged just after World War II was Borghild Dahl (1890–1984), who became blind as an adult, an experience that led her to her best-known work, *I Wanted to See* (1944). Dahl went on to write fifteen children's books, most of them about the lives of Norwegian immigrants, including her novel *Karen* (1947), whose titular character is a strong Norwegian pioneer who homesteads with her husband, Arne, on the South Dakota prairie. In *Deborah* (1946) Marian Castle (1896–1993) stretches a novel across three generations, from the homesteading years of the 1890s to the economic collapse of the 1920s. The modern conveniences of the postwar generation do little to make life easier on the prairies of western South Dakota for Anne Holland, the heroine of *Wind 'til Sundown* (1954) by Verna Moxley (1901–1994). Having moved with her family from MICHIGAN to western South Dakota, she confronts the same challenges that earlier generations of pioneers faced, and she manages to overcome them. Another postwar children's author is William Harlowe Briggs (1876–1952). Briggs's homesteading novel *Dakota in the Morning* (1942) departs from the many stories centered on the lives of young girls by focusing on the experiences of Bub, a young boy.

Another writer, Vera Cleaver (1919–1992), created dozens of books for children and young readers during her lifetime, many of them with her husband, Bill Cleaver (1920–1981). Their novel *Dust of the Earth* (1975) has a South Dakota connection, telling the story of fourteen-year-old Fern and her family as they inherit and move to a farm in South Dakota's Badlands.

Two other noteworthy writers for young readers are Brett Harvey (b. 1936) and Nancy Veglahn (b. 1937). In *My Prairie Year* (1986) and *My Prairie Christmas* (1990) Harvey uses material from her grandmother's diaries to tell stories of the homesteading experience. Veglahn has written works of historical fiction, as well as biography, including *Follow the Golden Goose* (1970), a tale set during the Black Hills gold rush, and *The Buffalo King: The Story of Scotty Philip* (1971), a biography of a Scottish immigrant who worked to save the bison of the Dakota prairies during the late 1800s. Veglahn's other works are *Peter Cartwright, Pioneer Circuit Rider* (1968), *South Dakota* (1970), *Getting to Know the Missouri River* (1972), and *The South Dakota Story* (1985).

Born in Haslemere, England, Paul Goble (b. 1933) developed an interest in the Indians of the plains during his childhood. He wrote and illustrated *Red Hawk's Account of Custer's Last Battle* (1969), a story of the battle told by the fictional Red Hawk, whose narrative is a composite of the many published accounts of the Sioux and Cheyenne survivors, interwoven with italicized passages expressing the conventional historical account more familiar to white readers. Since then, Goble has written and illustrated over thirty children's books about plains Indians. Most of Goble's books reflect his interest in Indian spirituality, as well as those stories and cultural practices that express belief in the interdependency of all living things. Reminiscent of tribal ledger painting, Goble's colorful illustrations contribute to the cultural meaning of his texts. His works include the Caldecott Medal winner *The Girl Who Loved Wild Horses* (1978), *Star Boy* (1983), and *Tipi: Home of the Nomadic Buffalo Hunter* (2007).

Journalism and Literary Journal Publications: Before the official organization of Dakota Territory in 1861, a printing press had been set up in Sioux Falls as early as 1858 by Samuel J. Albright (1829–1913), and in July 1859 he began publication of the first South Dakota newspaper, the *Dakota Democrat.* By virtue of its being designated the territorial capital from 1861 to 1863, Yankton became the second town to have a newspaper, the *Weekly Dakotan,* which began in June 1861 under the direction of Frank M. Ziebach. Just two months later, T. Elwood Clark and James Bedwell established the *Dakota Republican* in Vermillion.

Journalism is a significant part of the literary history of South Dakota. L. Frank Baum made an early journalistic venture with the *Aberdeen Saturday Pioneer* (1888–1890). Tim Giago (b. 1934) established an American Indian journalistic voice as a columnist for the *Rapid City Journal* in 1979 and then started his own newspaper in 1981, the *Lakota Times,* which in 1992 became *Indian Country Today.* In 2000 he started the *Lakota Journal,* from which he retired in 2004, but in the spring of 2009 he started a new weekly, *Native Sun News.* Giago's books include *Notes from Indian Country* (1984) and *Children Left Behind: Dark Legacy of the Indian Mission Schools* (2006).

In 1985 Bernie Hunhoff (b. 1951) started *South Dakota Magazine,* which has a circulation of 45,000, to explore and promote the heritage, nature, culture, and arts of the state. The magazine's prominent writers are Hunhoff, Roger Holtzmann (b. 1954), and Paul Higbee (b. 1953). Many of the state's best-known writers, such as Linda Hasselstrom, Kathleen Norris, Dan O'Brien, and Bob Karolevitz (1922–2011), appear in the magazine.

Contributing more specifically to South Dakota's literary culture are *South Dakota Review, Pasque Petals,* and *Paddlefish. South Dakota Review,* founded by John R. Milton, has been publishing literary and scholarly works since its inception in 1963. The journal's early issues contributed significantly to the renaissance in American Indian literature. *Pasque Petals* is the semi-annual publication of the South Dakota Poetry Society. Its present editor is Francie Davis. *Paddlefish* is one of the newest literary journals in the state; Jim Reese founded and continues to edit the journal, bringing together writers from across the state and region.

South Dakota Federal Writers' Project: One of the FEDERAL WRITERS' PROJECT's lasting achievements was the American Guide Series, which surveyed the people, traditions, and resources of every state in the union. Under the direction of M. Lisle Reese, *A South Dakota Guide* (1938) includes a brief history of the state together with political, social, and cultural aspects of the population, recommended automobile tours, maps, and a bibliography. A revised second edition was published in 1952 as *South Dakota: A Guide to the State.*

SELECTED WORKS: Some of South Dakota's richest cultural contributions to literature come from its American Indian authors. The most famous of these texts is John Neihardt's interview of Black Elk, *Black Elk Speaks: Being the Life of a Holy Man of the Oglala Sioux* (1932). Other seminal works are Luther Standing Bear's *My People, the Sioux* (1928), Charles A. Eastman's *Indian Boyhood* (1902), Ella Cara Deloria's *Waterlily* (1988), and Zitkala-Ša's *Old Indian Legends* (1901). Later contributions include *Singing for the Spirit: A Portrait of the Dakota Sioux* (1999) by Vine Deloria Jr., *Aurelia: A Crow Creek Trilogy* (1999) by Elizabeth Cook-Lynn, and *The Long Knives Are Crying* (2008) by Joseph Marshall III.

A Son of the Middle Border (1917) by Hamlin Garland and *Giants in the Earth* (1927) by Ole Rølvaag provide striking accounts of pioneer experiences. Both Mary Worthy Breneman's *The Land They Possessed* (1956) and Edith Kohl's *Land of the Burnt Thigh* (1938) dramatize the particular challenges of women who homesteaded the area. *The Conquest: The Story of a Negro Pioneer* (1913) by Oscar Micheaux offers an early African American perspective. *The Long Winter* (1940) by Laura Ingalls Wilder is set during the particularly harsh winter months of 1880–1881.

Will Lillibridge's *Ben Blair* (1905) and Kate Boyles Bingham and Virgil Boyles's *Langford of the Three Bars* (1907) represent two of the state's best-known western romances. Frederick Manfred turned toward more realistic, historical fiction about the state in such books as *Lord Grizzly* (1954).

In nonfiction, Linda Hasselstrom's *Land Circle: Writings Collected from the Land* (1991) and Dan O'Brien's *Buffalo for the Broken Heart* (2001) are concerned with the condition of the land. Kathleen Norris in *Dakota: A Spiritual Geography* (1993) captures isolation and community in a small town.

Kent Meyers is perhaps the most accomplished novelist living in South Dakota today. His fiction captures both the particularity and universality of life on the plains. His novel *The Work of Wolves* (2004) remains his most admired work to date.

A sampling of the "cowboy poetry" of Charles "Badger" Clark Jr., South Dakota's first Poet Laureate, can be found in *Badger Clark Ballads* (1982). The characteristic work of David Allan Evans, South Dakota's fourth Poet Laureate, appears in *The Bull Rider's Advice.*

Literature of South Dakota (1976) edited by John R. Milton and *Horizons: The South Dakota Writers' Anthology* (1983) edited by Linda Hasselstrom and Nancy Iversen (b. 1942) are useful introductory sources to the literature of South Dakota, providing readers with an array of poetry and prose from across the state.

O. W. Coursey's *Literature of South Dakota* (1916) is the earliest state anthology. John R. Milton updated and expanded Coursey's work with the publication already mentioned, *The Literature of South Dakota* (1976). In addition to Linda Hasselstrom and Nancy Iversen's collection of contemporary poetry and prose, *Horizons: The South Dakota Writers' Anthology* (1983), Patrick Hicks has collected poetry from fourteen of South Dakota's best poets in a volume titled *A Harvest of Words: Contemporary South Dakota Poetry* (2010).

FURTHER READING:

Bibliographies and Guides: Arthur R. Huseboe edited *An Illustrated History of the Arts in South Dakota* (1989), which contains a chapter titled "The Literary Arts" and an equallinformative section written by Oglala Lakota artist and scholar Arthur Amiotte titled "An Appraisal of Sioux Arts." *A New South Dakota History* (2005), edited by Harry F. Thompson, includes Huseboe's history of literature in the state, an introductory essay by Vine Deloria Jr. that provides American Indian perspectives on South Dakota's landscape, and a valuable chapter by Ruth Ann Alexander about the contributions of women writers in the state.

To mark the state's centennial, the South Dakota Library Association sponsored the publication of *South Dakota: Changing, Changeless, 1889–1989: A Selected Annotated Bibliography* (1995), edited by Sue Laubersheimer. Also valuable is the annotated bibliography by Jack W. Marken and Herbert T. Hoover titled *Bibliography of the Sioux* (1980). Marken and Hoover include significant articles and books published through 1978 about the state's tribal cultures. Two online bibliographies are also available. From 1998 to 2002 high school teachers Donna Fisher and Sharon Olbertson worked with scholars from across the state to produce *The South Dakota Literary Map*. The map, which is available online, includes annotations for over 150 novelists, poets, playwrights,

and journalists. The University of Nebraska at Lincoln's Plains Humanities Alliance has created an online bibliography titled "Great Plains, Great Books" for five states in the region. Charles Woodard maintains the online "South Dakota Book List" of the Plains Humanities Alliance Great Books of the Great Plains, which provides annotations for over one hundred significant works in the state. Although dated, the basic source for the history of South Dakota PRINTING AND PUBLISHING is still Albert H. Allen's *Dakota Imprints, 1858–1889* (1947).

Libraries and Repositories: The University of South Dakota's Chilson Collection includes local histories, South Dakota history, material related to tribal cultures, and materials related to western expansion of the United States; the Richardson Collection contains chiefly manuscript collections focusing on South Dakota's cultural, political, and economic history. South Dakota State University's Hilton M. Briggs Library Special Collections includes a number of rare books and manuscripts pertaining to the state's literary history, including the papers of Elizabeth Cook-Lynn, Kathleen Norris, and Virginia Driving Hawk Sneve.

The Center for Western Studies at Augustana College in Sioux Falls includes the personal collections of Herbert Krause, Richard Cropp, Frederick Manfred, C. J. McDonald, John R. Milton, Alan Woolworth, and Miles Browne. Its holdings focus on the American West, American literature, and American Indian ethnology. The Oglala Lakota College Library and Archives on the Pine Ridge Reservation and the Sinte Gleska University Library on the Rosebud Reservation hold materials concerning the Lakotas and other indigenous peoples. Other libraries include the South Dakota State Archives in Pierre, Northern State University's Beulah Williams Library, Black Hills State University's E. Y. Berry Library, Dakota State University's Karl E. Mundt Library, and Dakota Wesleyan University's McGovern Library.

PAUL BAGGETT   SOUTH DAKOTA STATE UNIVERSITY
DAVID L. NEWQUIST   NORTHERN STATE UNIVERSITY

SPOON RIVER ANTHOLOGY

HISTORY: The poems of *Spoon River Anthology* (1915) changed forever the image of the Midwestern village in verse, as well as the life of their creator, EDGAR LEE MASTERS (1868–1950). Formatted as tombstone epitaphs of rural Illinoisans who had lived in the town of Spoon River, the epitaphs vaulted Masters to literary prominence after their serial appearance in the St. Louis–based *REEDY'S MIRROR* in 1914–1915. Publication of the poems in book form later in 1915 fueled a literary storm that lasted for the better part of a decade.

Masters was born in KANSAS but spent his formative years in ILLINOIS, first in Petersburg on the banks of the Sangamon River near New Salem—the home of ABRAHAM LINCOLN (1809–1865)—during his youth and young-adult years and then in Lewistown, near the Spoon River. These two rural county seats later provided Masters with many details and characters for *Spoon River Anthology.* After graduation from Lewistown High School, Masters worked on a local newspaper and spent one year in the preparatory unit of nearby Knox College in Galesburg, Illinois, before acquiescing to his father's demands to return home and study law. In 1891 Masters passed the Illinois bar exam and spent a year working in his father's law office before moving to CHICAGO in 1892. There he earned a living as an attorney and married before becoming a law partner of CLARENCE DARROW (1857–1938) in 1903.

The law firm prospered, but Masters was unhappy with both the law and his marriage and dreamed of becoming a famous author. He experimented with rhymed verses and prose articles on political and social themes and in 1896 generated his first separately published work, *Bimetallism,* a pamphlet in defense of free silver. Masters's first volume of poems, a derivative collection of juvenilia titled *A Book of Verses,* was published in 1898, followed by *Maximilian: A Play in Five Acts* in 1902. Nine more volumes of poems and plays filled the next decade, but none of these attracted attention, and Masters's editor friend WILLIAM MARION REEDY (1862–1920) chided him for his old-fashioned verses. In May 1914 Masters replied by forwarding to *Reedy's Mirror* the first of his Spoon River epitaphs. Masters regarded these first pieces as satires on the new free-verse movement, but Reedy recognized their merit and ultimately published more

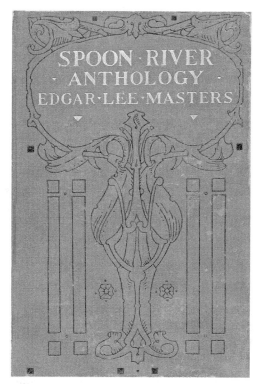

Edgar Lee Masters's *Spoon River Anthology.* Macmillan Co., 1915.
Image courtesy of Special Collections, Grand Valley State University Libraries

than two hundred of the epitaphs in his weekly *Mirror* before the Macmillan Company gathered them as *Spoon River Anthology* in April 1915.

The volume became that rarest of literary phenomena, a book of poetry that attracted attention from both popular and critical audiences. It stirred additional controversy in 1916 when the definitive edition added thirty-two more pieces. Through the remainder of World War I and into the 1920s, *Spoon River Anthology* remained an item of intense discussion. As Percy Boynton wrote in *Some Contemporary Americans* (1924), it became "the most read and most talked of volume of poetry that had ever been written in America" (52). *Spoon River Anthology* had lifted the veil of respectability from the American village and created a literary and social uproar.

Masters's village was populated with adulterous spouses, burdensome children, and stunted lives filled with poverty of spirit and purse. Greedy bankers, shyster lawyers, and lying editors sent many a villager to an early grave, carried there as often as not by hypocritical churchmen and corrupt civic leaders. Loveless marriages and meaningless work made matters worse. And always there were wagging tongues, the village gossips who passed along damaging information about their fellow townspeople, many of whom sought escape through sex, suicide, or alcohol.

In "Nellie Clark," for example, the subject dies of despair after the town finishes with her:

> I was only eight years old;
> And before I grew up and knew what it
>   meant
> I had no words for it, except
> That I was frightened and told my Mother;
> And that my Father got a pistol
> And would have killed Charlie, who was a
>   big boy,
> Fifteen years old, except for his Mother.
> Nevertheless the story clung to me.
> But the man who married me, a widower
>   of thirty-five,
> Was a newcomer and never heard it
> Till two years after we were married.
> Then he considered himself cheated,
> And the village agreed that I was not really
>   a virgin.
> Well, he deserted me, and I died
> The following winter. (2004 edition, 84)

Nellie Clark's story and those of Spoon River's other unquiet ghosts might be found in societies around the world, a detail that lends a universal quality to *Spoon River Anthology*, but Masters had discovered most of the details in his own backyard. Certainly, the themes are consistent with post–Civil War village life in Illinois, as is shown by a parallel reading of Masters's 1936 autobiography, *Across Spoon River*. In both books one finds a streak of frontier violence; naturalistic plundering wherein the strong rob the weak; the winless battle between the sexes that begins early and ends never; and the knowledge that the village knows all and repeats all, and that there is no closure except through death—and even that is tentative since the epitaph remains.

Masters's aggressively realistic and even sensational portrayal of mid-American village life strongly rejected dominant "genteel" American writing, particularly in poetry, which had clung tenaciously to a moralistic, romantic worldview, blank or rhymed syllabic verse, and elevated, connotatively charged language. Not unexpectedly, American literary traditionalists disliked Masters's poetic subject and form. East Coast literary modernist and imagist poet Amy (Lawrence) Lowell (1874–1925) in her *Tendencies in Modern American Poetry* (1917) wrote negatively about Masters's portrayal of life: "*Spoon River* is one long chronicle of rapes, seductions, liaisons, and perversions," and "One wonders, if life in our little Western cities is as bad as this, why everyone does not commit suicide" (174–75). Even the Midwestern realistic writer who had risen to national literary arbiter, WILLIAM DEAN HOWELLS (1837–1920), in his September 1915 *Harper's Magazine* "Editor's Easy Chair" book-review column, disparaged the poetic form of Masters's *Spoon River Anthology* as "shredded prose" (634–35).

Opposed to these were the literary radicals associated with the CHICAGO RENAISSANCE who defended Masters. HARRIET MONROE (1860–1936) implored Masters to send her some of the Spoon River poems for publication in *POETRY: A MAGAZINE OF VERSE*. CARL (AUGUST) SANDBURG (1878–1967) said that Masters had written about "the people of life itself" in his May 1915 article in *THE LITTLE REVIEW* (42). Ezra Pound (1885–1972) expressed even greater certainty about the importance of Masters's new book. "AT LAST," Pound wrote in *THE Egoist* for January 1915, "America has discovered a poet" (11).

The effect of such attention was to create an international poetic best seller. The first edition of *Spoon River Anthology* (1915) exhausted seven printings in seven months and went through nineteen printings before the augmented edition of 1916 added more poems, sales, and controversy. Remarkably, the momentum of this favorable beginning continued through Masters's death in 1950, the turbulent 1960s, the revisionist 1970s and 1980s, and into the twenty-first century. Masters's anthology has never been out of print and has been translated in whole or in part into dozens of foreign languages. It was the highlight of Masters's career. Subsequent volumes never achieved comparable success.

SIGNIFICANCE: *Spoon River Anthology* was the first realistic evaluation in verse of life in the Midwest, and the plainness of its free-verse language often reflected the plainness of the language spoken on the courthouse square. *Spoon River* became a literary watershed because it contrasted greatly with the placid iambics and rhymed images of village life popularized by earlier American poets, which *Spoon River Anthology*'s "Petit, the Poet" correctly characterizes as "seeds in a dry pod, tick, tick, tick" (109). The New England icons Henry Wadsworth Longfellow (1807–1882) and John Greenleaf Whittier (1807–1892), for example, had established their reputations by writing sentimental portrayals of American small-town life. In their orderly towns, village smithies labored for the common good; wives seldom strayed far from the hearth and the henhouse; and apple-cheeked elders said grace at Christian tables. Bad boys existed, but they were "good" little bad boys, not rapists. *Spoon River Anthology* grafted a sinister new realism onto this nineteenth-century view of Main Street.

The ensuing critical clamor and the status of *Spoon River Anthology* as a sensational book sometimes mask the reality that it makes use of several conventional literary devices and borrowings. It is modeled on *Epigrams from the Greek Anthology,* a collection of pithy sayings and epitaphs that date back more than one thousand years. Nor is the organization of individual epitaphs unique. Many follow the structure and brevity of a sonnet, two or three ideas followed by a summary statement. In only fifteen lines, for example, we learn that Nellie Clark was violated, the village told her husband, the husband deserted her, and Nellie died.

Masters's effective use of the dramatic monologue with its understood speaker and listener was also borrowed from its most famous popularizer, Robert Browning (1812–1889). Masters had discovered Browning while still in Lewistown and about 1912 printed an admiring pamphlet concerning him before creating the character Elijah Browning in *Spoon River Anthology.* And of course the vehicle of free verse as a means to discuss sexual subjects was not new

either, but was taken from another of Masters's favorite authors, Walt Whitman (1819–1892), who had joined the two in *Leaves of Grass* (1855–1892).

Nevertheless, the source materials for *Spoon River Anthology* were almost entirely Midwestern, as Masters explained in *Across Spoon River* and in his article "The Genesis of *Spoon River*" in the *American Mercury* for January 1933 (38–55). The materials Masters consulted to write *Spoon River* included boyhood and adult diaries; legal cases he or his lawyer father had tried or had known about in downstate Illinois and Chicago; family histories and lore from both sides of his family; schoolboy adventures; the stories Masters heard from village patriarchs in Petersburg and Lewistown; an occasional trip home to his rural roots during the composition of *Spoon River;* and, of course, his own voluminous reading that included, even during his village years, heartland prose realists such as SAMUEL LANGHORNE CLEMENS (1835–1910), writing as Mark Twain, EDGAR WATSON HOWE (1853–1937), and the Illinois iconoclast ROBERT GREEN INGERSOLL (1833–1899).

The literary ripples from *Spoon River Anthology* have touched all creative genres. The poems of confessional writers such as Robert (Traill Spence) Lowell (1917–1977) and Sylvia Plath (1932–1963) are visibly related to the epitaphs; SHERWOOD ANDERSON (1876–1941) began WINESBURG, OHIO (1919) shortly after staying up all night reading *Spoon River Anthology;* and MAIN STREET (1920) author (HARRY) SINCLAIR LEWIS (1885–1951) used his 1930 Nobel Prize address to thank Masters for creating "a new school of native American poetry," as reported in James Hutchisson's *The Rise of Sinclair Lewis, 1920–1930* (1996): 240. One of the most frequently presented plays in the United States, *Our Town* by THORNTON WILDER (1897–1975), sums up life by alluding to Masters and paraphrasing *Spoon River*'s "Lucinda Matlock": "It's like what one of those Middle West poets said: You got to love life to have life, and you got to have life to love life" (act 2).

Masters's *Spoon River Anthology* has been almost universally recognized as the primary text leading to the famous or infamous declaration by CARL VAN DOREN (1885–1950) of an early twentieth-century American literary movement rebelling against rural and small-town life and values, first expressed in his "The Revolt from the Village: 1920," *The Nation* 113 (October 12, 1921): 407–12. Citing works like *Spoon River Anthology*, Sherwood Anderson's *Winesburg, Ohio*, and Sinclair Lewis's *Main Street*, Van Doren proclaimed a Midwestern literary movement rejecting the nature and quality of rural and small-town life. That argument is discussed at length in this volume's REVOLT FROM THE VILLAGE entry, which considers the views of several twentieth-century Midwestern writers and discusses the philosophical and literary perspectives underlying "revolt from the village," as well as the critical counterarguments raised over the past ninety years.

IMPORTANT EDITIONS: There are three important editions of *Spoon River Anthology:* the first edition of 1915 and the augmented, definitive edition of 1916, both printed by the Macmillan Company, and *Spoon River Anthology: An Annotated Edition* (1992). The 1992 edition, with an introduction and annotations by John E. Hallwas, is an excellent handbook with microbiographies of the Midwesterners whose lives and deaths Masters used to create his famous work. The paperback with introduction by poet (Anna Thilda) May Swenson (1913–1989) has been the most readily accessible edition, first from the Macmillan Company and now Simon and Schuster (2004), and is the source of the quotations in this entry.

FURTHER READING: Ronald Primeau's *Beyond Spoon River: The Legacy of Edgar Lee Masters* (1981) offers critical commentary, as does the Twayne Series's *Edgar Lee Masters* (1983) by John H. and Margaret M. Wrenn. The Masters's family biography *Last Stands: Notes from Memory* (1982) by Hilary Masters (b. 1928) is a useful view by an insider. The only full-length life study is Herbert K. Russell's *Edgar Lee Masters: A Biography* (2001). There is no extant manuscript of *Spoon River Anthology*, the pages of which were discarded by William Marion Reedy or his staff as the poems were printed serially. The Harry Ransom Humanities Research Center at the University of Texas at Austin is the major repository of Masters's papers. Other significant collections are at Georgetown University's Lauinger Library, the Newberry Library in Chicago, and the University of Chicago's Regenstein Library.

HERBERT K. RUSSELL   CARBONDALE, ILLINOIS

ST. LOUIS

St. Louis was established as a river trading post in 1764, was acquired in the Louisiana Purchase in 1803, and was incorporated in 1809.

Area: 61.92 square miles

Population (2010 census): 319,294

OVERVIEW: St. Louis's literature has been shaped by its French Catholic origins, its mid-nineteenth-century European immigrants, its African American community, and its activists, city boosters, and beer barons. As a young gateway city at the frontier's edge, St. Louis collected and distributed the texts and tales of the West and established its own prolific newspaper culture. Spurred by Gilded Age river and rail industry, it reached its literary peak around the time of the 1904 Louisiana Purchase Exposition. Although a poorer midcentury city often watched its young literary talent depart for the coasts, recent decades have witnessed the return of a thriving local writing community supported by universities, presses, and renewed public interest in its literary archive.

HISTORY AND SIGNIFICANCE: Pierre (Liguest) Laclède (1729–1778) and (René) Auguste Chouteau (Jr.) (1750–1829) explored and settled the Mississippi River's western banks at the confluence with the Missouri River during the winter of 1763–1764. Colonial-era French and Spanish journals were followed by the Louisiana Purchase expedition writings of Meriwether Lewis

© Karen Greasley, 2014

(1774–1809) and William Clark (1770–1838). In 1808 Joseph Charless (1772–1834) founded the *Missouri Gazette,* the first newspaper west of the Mississippi, and published St. Louis's first book, *The Laws of the Territory of Louisiana.* Literary works featuring local settings first appeared in 1821: *The Pedlar,* a farce by playwright Alphonso Wetmore (1793–1849); and *Missourian Lays and Other Western Ditties* by Angus Umphraville (b. 1798), the first English poetry volume west of the Mississippi, which includes "The Old Maid of St. Louis."

The region's rough frontier character was portrayed in *Recollections of the Last Ten Years, Passed in Occasional Residences and Journeyings in the Valley of the Mississippi,* (1826) by missionary Timothy Flint (1780–1840). Later writers were nostalgic; JOHN G(NEISENAU) NEIHARDT (1881–1973) recalled St. Louis as the border of the 1820s West in *The Song of Three Friends* (1919), epic verse on frontier boatmen and fur traders.

An expanding nineteenth-century St. Louis saw a proliferation of newspapers. Early small papers like the *Gazette* (1808) and the *Western Journal* (1815) evolved into the larger-sheet news format as the Civil War approached. A local pastor, Elijah (Parish) Lovejoy (1802–1837), used his abolitionist *St. Louis Observer* (1833) to condemn local lynchings until he was shot to death in Alton, ILLINOIS, in an attack on his press. The immigration surge after 1840 resulted in several German-language papers. Radical Heinrich Börnstein (1805–1892) arrived to edit the weekly anti-slavery *Anzeiger des Westens* (1835), which also published his anti-Jesuit novel *The Mysteries of St. Louis* (English translation, 1852). German papers included *Amerika,* a Catholic daily (1872), and *Westliche Post,* a liberal daily (1857). Joseph Pulitzer (1847–1911) arrived in St. Louis without English or financial resources but reported for the *Westliche Post,* which he purchased and merged with the *St. Louis Dispatch* to form the *St. Louis Post-Dispatch* in 1879 His papers offered a new reformist pursuit of local scandals, frauds, and figures. (HERMAN) THEODORE DREISER (1871–1945) worked briefly at the *St. Louis Globe Democrat* in 1892 but jeopardized his career when his theatre review written from press clippings went to print, although

the company's actors, stranded by a flood, had never performed. St. Louis was home to two of the country's oldest African American newspapers: the *St. Louis Advance,* founded by P. H. Murray in 1880, and the *St. Louis Argus,* founded in 1912 by brothers J. E. and William Mitchell. See also NEWSPAPER JOURNALISM.

Nineteenth-century crimes and disasters were reflected in prose, verse, and popular ballads, such as those recounting the Meeks family murder. Works detailing the city's decades of cholera epidemics and its great fire of 1849 include Börnstein's *The Mysteries of St. Louis* and the epic poem *A Mournful Elegy* (1849) by John Russell (b. ca. 1808), which commemorated the Gravois coal-mine cholera epidemic. St. Louis witnessed numerous riots, but the worst was the Nativist riot of 1854, which targeted Irish and German communities. This riot was recorded in *Life on the Mississippi* (1883) by SAMUEL LANGHORNE CLEMENS (1835–1910), writing as Mark Twain, who arrived in St. Louis in 1853 as a newspaper typesetter and later returned as steamship pilot and lecturer.

As the most populous city of a slave state bordered by free states, St. Louis generated both pro-slavery and abolitionist writers, although more Civil War–era publications were unionist. The renowned anti-slavery lecturer William Wells Brown (ca. 1814–1884) published his local experience of slavery in his *Narrative of William W. Brown, a Fugitive Slave, Written by Himself* (1847). In his *American Notes* (1842) Charles (John Huffam) Dickens (1812–1870) cited St. Louis in his attack on the institution of slavery. Many locals wrote about the Civil War. William Greenleaf Eliot (1811–1887) published the biography of a man he had rescued and freed in *The Story of Archer Alexander* (1885). Jessie Benton Frémont (1824–1902) wrote *The Story of the Guard: A Chronicle of the War* (1863), and local pastor Galusha Anderson (1832–1918) narrated *The Story of a Border City during the Civil War* (1908). A visiting Anthony Trollope (1815–1882) described St. Louis under martial law in *North America* (1862), and Winston Churchill (1871–1947) set the love story *The Crisis* (1901) in Civil War–era St. Louis. Jefferson Barracks often hosted prominent generals, and while he was in town, Ulysses S(impson) Grant (1822–1885) composed

St. Louis street scene, 1890. Photoprint by Kilburn.
Image courtesy of the Library of Congress

Personal Memoirs of U. S. Grant (1885, 1886). Similarly, General William (Tecumseh) Sherman (1820–1891) wrote the *Memoirs of General W. T. Sherman* (1875).

After the Civil War, St. Louis experienced an industrial boom. By the turn of the century it was the nation's fourth-largest city and a literary center. The St. Louis Mercantile Library's guest lecturers included Clemens, Matthew Arnold (1822–1885), Oscar Wilde (1854–1900), and Ralph Waldo Emerson (1803–1882), while the Ethical Society hosted ERNEST (MILLER) HEMINGWAY (1899–1961), (HARRY) SINCLAIR LEWIS (1885–1951), and *POETRY* editor HARRIET MONROE (1860–1936). In 1867 William T(orrey) Harris (1835–1909) founded the landmark *Journal of Speculative Philosophy,* which published William James (1842–1910) and John Dewey (1859–1952), as well as Georg Wilhelm Friedrich Hegel (1770–1831), Johann Gottlieb Fichte (1762–1814), and Friedrich Wilhelm Joseph von Schelling (1775–1854). The city's World's Fair of 1904 drew millions of visitors and inspired a century of literary production. Sally Benson (1897–1972) recounts fair-era childhood stories in *Meet Me in St. Louis* (1942); Thomas (Clayton) Wolfe (1900–1938) presents *Lost Boy* (1937) through the eyes of siblings who visited the World's Fair city; and JANE (GRAVES) SMILEY (b. 1949) explores

the era's social contradictions in *Private Life* (2010).

Many local literary families and figures remember their St. Louis start, although some of these departed in the twentieth century. The Eliot family continued to produce writers; both Henry Ware Eliot (1843–1919) and his wife, Charlotte (Champe) Stearns Eliot (1843–1929), published. T(HOMAS) S(TEARNS) ELIOT (1888–1965) noted the St. Louis foundation of his cityscapes; the poetry of "The Dry Salvages" (1941) from *Four Quartets* (1943) begins with Eliot's famous characterization of the Mississippi River as "a strong brown god" (21). Characters inhabiting the city's Central West End appear in *At Fault* (1890) by Kate (Katherine O'Flaherty) Chopin (1850–1904), who was born and raised in St. Louis and began her writing career there upon her return as a widow. Local journalist, humorist, and "children's poet" EUGENE FIELD (SR.) (1850–1895) garnered fame for his "Wynken, Blynken, and Nod" (1889). WILLIAM MARION REEDY (1862–1920) edited the nationally recognized avant-garde *REEDY'S MIRROR,* in which he promoted Midwestern realism, naturalism, and new approaches to verse and published Dreiser, ORRICK (GLENDAY) JOHNS (1887–1946), SARA TEASDALE (1884–1933), ZOË AKINS (1886–1958), and FANNIE HURST (1885–1968). Reedy launched EDGAR LEE MASTERS (1868–1950) by eliciting, shaping, and publishing the early poems that would become his *SPOON RIVER ANTHOLOGY* (1915). Although Teasdale felt lonely and trapped in St. Louis by her health, the fine lyrical verse of her *Flame and Shadow* (1920) pays tribute in "Sunset: St. Louis." Johns's *Time of Our Lives: The Story of My Father and Myself* (1937) portrays two generations of the city's literary community.

Early twentieth-century St. Louis literature addressed the racism and poverty that plagued the region. Built in 1874, the Eads Bridge had been the site of a moonlit walk Walt Whitman (1819–1892) recorded in *Specimen Days* (1882), but in 1917 it became the site of one of America's worst race riots. When local African American workers replaced strikers from the Aluminum Ore Company, a deadly attack on the community of East St. Louis followed. The NAACP sent W. E. B. Du Bois and Martha Gruening to investigate and published their findings in the organization's magazine, *The Crisis* (September 1917). St. Louis writers often doubled as activists. Josephine (Winslow) Johnson (1910–1990) and Fannie (Frank) Cook (1893–1949) organized St. Louis support for the African American sharecroppers' protest of 1939. Cook wrote about local sharecroppers in *Boot-Heel Doctor* (1941) and about the African American Ville community in *Mrs. Palmer's Honey* (1946). First published in the *Mirror,* Fannie Hurst recounted her work in a local shoe factory for a *St. Louis Post-Dispatch* exposé. She went on to portray countless working women in short fiction filled with St. Louis sites and figures. (Thomas Lanier) Tennessee Williams (1911–1983) set the Wingfield family apartment in *The Glass Menagerie* (1945), as well as several of his other early plays, in St. Louis. Local writers also took on politics and corruption. Reedy covered a street railway strike in "The Story of the Strike" (1900); two years later Claude (Hazeltine) Wetmore (1862–1944) and Lincoln Steffens (1866–1936) published "Tweed Days in St. Louis" in *McClure's Magazine*. A century later Jonathan Franzen (b. 1959) narrated the city's fall from nineteenth-century glory and its contemporary political corruption in *The Twenty-Seventh City* (1988) and drew from his local childhood for *The Corrections* (2001).

St. Louis often appears as the remembered city of its literary children. Charles (Augustus) Lindbergh (1902–1974) named his famous plane and his autobiography *The Spirit of St. Louis* (1953) to honor the city's supporters of his famed flight. Hurst recounts her St. Louis childhood in her autobiography, *Anatomy of Me* (1958); Emily Hahn (1905–1997) relates hers fondly in *Times and Places* (1970). Chester (Bomar) Himes (1909–1984) includes his teen St. Louis years in his autobiographical *The Third Generation* (1954); and the brick apartment houses of the Delmar Loop appear in the fiction of Harold Brodkey (b. Aaron Roy Weintraub, 1930–1996). In her autobiography, *I Know Why the Caged Bird Sings* (1969), Marguerite Ann Johnson (1928–2014), writing as Maya Angelou, addresses rape, racism, and literature through an account of her St. Louis childhood. The 1985 novel *Betsey Brown* (1985) by Ntozake Shange (b. Paulette Williams in 1948) sketches a child's experience of city school integration and busing. The sites of a St. Louis childhood also appear in the fiction of WILLIAM S(EWARD) BURROUGHS (II) (1914–1997).

Local universities continue to host numerous writers. St. Louis University (1818) faculty have included (Herbert) Marshall McLuhan (1911–1980), Sigfried Giedion (1888–1968), and Walter (Jackson) Ong (1912–2003). Washington University (1853) hosted Jarvis Thurston (1914–2008) and MONA (JANE) VAN DUYN (1921–2004); the two launched *Perspective* together in 1947. Its faculty has also included Howard Nemerov (1920–1991), WILLIAM H(OWARD) GASS (b. 1924), and STANLEY (LAWRENCE) ELKIN (1930–1995), who praised St. Louis in his *Esquire* essay "Why I Live Where I Live" (1980). Current faculty members include Mary Jo Bang (b. 1946), Kathryn Davis (b.1946), and Carl Phillips (b. 1959).

SELECTED WORKS: Accounts of western expeditions that set out from St. Louis are numerous; the most famous is *The Definitive Journals of Lewis and Clark,* a 13-volume edition edited by Gary Moulton (1983–2001). The *Missouri Gazette* offers an early glimpse of the area in its record of conflicts and treaties with local tribes, early abolitionist views, and local politics and news. Neihardt's nostalgic *The Song of Three Friends* (1919) includes epic verses portraying a heroic Mike Fink, as well as trappers, traders, and boatmen. Civil war–era St. Louis is reflected in slavery narratives—*A Narrative of William W. Brown, a Fugitive Slave, Written by Himself* (1847) and William Greenleaf Eliot's *The Story of Archer Alexander* (1885)—and in the setting of Winston Churchill's *The Crisis* (1901). St. Louis appears in Twain's *Life on the Mississippi* (1883), as well in Thomas Wolfe's *Lost Boy* (1937). *Reedy's Mirror* had a national impact on poetry and prose from the 1890s to the 1920s and offered many writers their first publications. Orrick Johns's *Time of Our Lives: The Story of My Father and Myself* (1937) offers local recollections. Twentieth-century St. Louis provides the setting for diverse works, from Tennessee Williams's *The Glass Menagerie* (1944) to Jonathan Franzen's *The Corrections* (2001).

St. Louis literature has been well anthologized. Publications include *Germans for a*

Free Missouri: Translations from the St. Louis Radical Press, 1857–1862 (1983), edited by Steven Rowan; the Jewish Writing in St. Louis series, edited by Howard Schwartz and Barbara Raznick (1997, 2005); *Ain't but a Place: An Anthology of African American Writings about St. Louis* (1998), edited by Gerald Early; *Seeking St. Louis: Voices from a River City* (2000), edited by Lee Ann Sandweiss; *St. Louis Muse: An Anthology of Regional Poetry* (2002), edited by Chris Hayden; *Stories from Before: The New Voices of Immigrants in St. Louis* (2007), edited by Janet Morey and Gail Schafers; and *Flood Stage: An Anthology of Saint Louis Poets* (2010), edited by Matthew Freeman. Area literary journals include *Boulevard, Natural Bridge, Arch,* and *River Styx.* St. Louis hosts numerous writing clubs. Its Wednesday Club began as a post–Civil War reading group for women and awarded local Marianne (Craig) Moore (1887–1972) its first poetry prize in 1926. The St. Louis Writers Guild was formed in 1920 by local authors; the St. Louis Poetry Center followed in 1946.

FURTHER READING: St. Louis literature has been surveyed regularly. Print sources include *Literature of the Louisiana Territory* (1904) and *The St. Louis Book Authors* (1925) by Alexander DeMenil; *Joseph Charless, Pioneer Printer of St. Louis* (1931) by Douglas McMurtrie; *Important Firsts in Missouri Imprints, 1808–1858* (1967) by Viola A. Perotti; and *Saint Louis: A Chronological and Documentary History* (1974) by Robert Vexler. Local sites, history, and folklore are presented in Walter Schroeder and Howard Marshall's reissued WPA publication *Missouri; A Guide to the "Show Me" State* (orig. pub. 1941, 1998); Charles Van Ravenswaay's *Saint Louis: An Informal History of the City and Its People, 1764–1865* (1991); and *Passing It On: The Folklore of St. Louis* (2008) by John L. Oldani. Useful literary and biographical surveys include *Missouri Writers: A Literary History of Missouri, 1780–1955* (1955) by Elijah Jacobs and Forrest Wolverton and *Literary St. Louis* (2000), edited by Lorin Cuoco and William H. Gass. The St. Louis Public Library (1865) offers the Reedy Collection and local manuscripts. Washington University houses a significant modern literature archive, while the Missouri History Museum, established in 1866, holds the papers of Chopin, Cook, and Hurst and local literary correspondence. The University of Mis-

souri–St. Louis is home to the archives of the St. Louis Mercantile Library, begun in 1846, the oldest continuously operating general library west of the Mississippi.

KATHERINE FAMA   UNIVERSITY COLLEGE DUBLIN

ST. PAUL.

See Minneapolis/St. Paul

STREET IN BRONZEVILLE, A

HISTORY: *A Street in Bronzeville,* the first poetic volume by GWENDOLYN BROOKS (1917–2000), published by Harper and Brothers in 1945, details the lives, struggles, dreams, and triumphs of CHICAGO's African American community as it confronted discrimination and segregation in the years before and during World War II. Set in Chicago's South Side neighborhood labeled Bronzeville by *Chicago Bee* theatre editor James Gentry, the volume provides a microcosm of African American experience.

Brooks was born to David and Keziah Wims Brooks, educated, cultured Chicagoans, while Keziah was visiting her parents in Topeka, KANSAS. At that time the United States remained racially divided. Lynchings continued; the color line limited available jobs; the Supreme Court's 1897 *Plessy v. Ferguson* separate-but-equal ruling governed education; and statute legalized segregated housing. World War II increased interracial contact, boosted black self-confidence, and broadened African American perspectives, but blacks remained second-class citizens. The African American influx made black life in Chicago more difficult. In escaping the South's overt discrimination and racial violence, Chicago newcomers competed with residents for industrial jobs and housing. Surprisingly, young Gwendolyn Brooks remained positively grounded in family, church, and faith that reason and humanity would prevail. In that period integrationist-assimilationist strategies were considered appropriate for blacks, socially and literarily.

But American literature was changing, and the Midwest was leading the way. The CHICAGO RENAISSANCE'S first generation advanced realistic prose fiction while retaining genteel poetic orientations. The second generation, from approximately 1912 to the mid-1920s, rejected moralizing and romantic worldviews, poetic diction, and rhymed syllabic verse in favor of free verse and realistic subjects and language. It was pro-labor, anti-establishment, and anti-government. Chicago was the center of this poetic revolution, which gave way in time to the Harlem Renaissance's celebration of black beauty, primitivism, and exoticism. The Chicago Renaissance's third generation, often called the Black Chicago Renaissance, was active during the years when Brooks wrote and published *A Street in Bronzeville*. These Chicago writers advanced realistic presentation and sympathetically portrayed those whom white society oppressed racially, ethnically, and sociologically. Works like NATIVE SON (1940) by RICHARD WRIGHT (1908-1960) marked the Black Chicago Renaissance and critically depicted Chicago's black community.

Brooks's poetic inheritance owed much to white writing, and in addressing white editors, publishers, and audiences, she could realistically portray working-class black life, but direct narrative attacks on white society were not productive then. She centered her work, therefore, on graphic depiction, allowing white readers to vicariously experience black pain, frustration, and anger. Although the poems in *A Street in Bronzeville* adopt traditional literary forms and language, they juxtapose white literary ordering structures to the disorder and uncertainty of poverty-stricken, wartime black Chicago life.

Years of writing and revision preceded *A Street in Bronzeville*. As Brooks's poetic mastery grew, she achieved recognition. This recognition led Alfred A. Knopf editor Emily Morison to invite submission by Brooks, whom Knopf had previously rejected. Instead, Brooks submitted the *Bronzeville* poems to Harper and Brothers, which accepted it, partially on the basis of Richard Wright's very positive assessment. Harper recommended that Brooks fill out the volume, and Brooks followed Wright's prescription by adding a major anchor poem.

Publication came on August 15, 1945, days after World War II ended. Early reviews were congratulatory. PAUL ENGLE (1908-1991), director of the IOWA WRITERS' WORKSHOP, wrote the August 26, 1945, *Chicago Tribune* "Books" section review, "Chicago Can Take Pride in New, Young Voice in Poetry," lauded

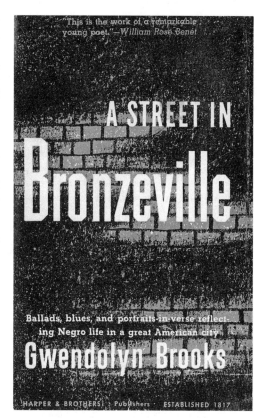

Gwendolyn Brooks's *A Street in Bronzeville*. © 1944, 1945 Gwendolyn Brooks Blakely. Reprinted by permission of HarperCollins Publishers. Image courtesy of University of Kentucky Special Collections Research Center

the publication, and asserted that "Miss Brooks is the first Negro poet to write wholly out of a deep and imaginative talent, without relying on the fact of color to draw sympathy and interest" (quoted in Stephen C. Wright, *On Gwendolyn Brooks: Reliant Contemplation*, 3). Engle further expressed his wish that Chicagoans would appreciate her writing and her talent (Wright 4).

SIGNIFICANCE: Brooks's aesthetically compelling, socially engaged, realistic poetry uses Chicago's Bronzeville as a microcosm of 1940s black America. She personalizes representative experiences and exemplifies African American social claims. Like the writings of earlier Chicago Renaissance writers EDGAR LEE MASTERS (1868-1950), CARL (AUGUST) SANDBURG (1878-1967), and SHERWOOD ANDERSON (1876-1941), her work asserts timeless, universal messages through a series of individual portraits. In her March 12, 1945, letter to Harper editor Elizabeth Lawrence, Brooks defined her initial concept for the volume: "To take some personality or event, or idea from each (or many) of the approximately thirty houses on a street in this vicinity" (quoted in George E. Kent, *A Life of Gwendolyn Brooks*, 71). Yet she intended more than abstract theorizing on racial justice, social change, and poetics. Gwendolyn Brooks was describing *her* home neighborhood. *Bronzeville* was a compilation of "family portraits," real and figurative.

Like earlier Chicago Renaissance writers, Brooks advanced American literary realism. *MAIN-TRAVELLED ROADS* (1891) by (HANNIBAL) HAMLIN GARLAND (1860–1940) had portrayed the physical hardships and psychic costs of western frontier life. Masters's *SPOON RIVER ANTHOLOGY* (1915) had portrayed previously taboo elements of Midwestern small-town life, shocking readers with psychological and sexual revelations, attacks on small-town life, and use of poetry for social criticism. Sandburg's *CHICAGO POEMS* (1916) had broken new ground by rejecting syllabic verse and rhyme and by using strong, direct anti-poetic diction, as in his volume's opening line, "Hog butcher to the world" (*Chicago Poems*, 1916 edition, 3). Brooks's *Bronzeville*, like Sandburg's volume, sets human worth, dignity, and spirit against naturalistic backdrops. She follows Sherwood Anderson in portraying those whom society has left behind. Her work is striking in using poetry to present Chicago black trauma. Her volume extends earlier Midwestern experiments in realistic poetry, portraying individuals lower in society, facing more difficult situations, and having fewer options. Her tone is often ironic and sardonic, but her characters cope and sometimes achieve moments of transcendence. Dignity, joy in small gains, and quiet heroism are their best possible outcomes.

In "the old-marrieds" a long-married couple makes love silently "in the crowding darkness" (3). In "kitchenette building" a Bronzeville mother captures the dichotomy between constraint and aspiration. Similarly, in "The Sundays of Satin-Legs Smith," Brooks portrays a man with unbroken spirit, luxuriating in his day of regal release from "shabby days . . . desertedness . . . intricate fear . . . postponed resentments, and . . . prim precautions" (26) before surrendering himself again to weekday realities. Satin-Legs Smith begins Sunday with an elaborate lavender-scented bubble bath, providing an olfactory counterpoint to "His heritage of cabbage and pigtails, / Old intimacy with alleys, garbage pails" (27). He dresses in exuberant clothes, ". . . wonder-suits in yellow and in wine, / Sarcastic green and zebra-striped cobalt" (28). He meets his similarly appointed date for Sunday dinner at a restaurant reflecting black limitations and ends the day with the promise of sex. Smith's conscious assertions of life and spirit make him king for the day. He lives without compromise, making the most of limited possibilities. His taste may be uninformed, his clothing garish, his date questionable, his restaurant third-rate, but he is actively living, not just surviving. He savors every moment. Satin-Legs Smith has aspirations and acts on them. He projects unvanquished hopes and dreams.

Not all *Bronzeville* images are positive. Brooks portrays the inescapable, permeating "onion fumes . . . fried potatoes / And yesterday's garbage ripening in the hall" in "kitchenette building" (4), multiple experiences of rejection and discrimination, and a mother's deep embarrassment at her son's fathering of an illegitimate child. Examples of need-driven violations of moral standards and lives devoid of spirit and hope are frequent. Desperation is palpable. Death is the central reality.

The most compelling of the volume's twenty-six poems is not one of the war poems or the many funereal poems—"southeast corner," "the funeral," "hunchback girl: she thinks of heaven," "obituary for a living lady," "the murder," or "of De Witt Williams on his way to Lincoln Cemetery." Rather, it is "the mother," the dramatic monologue capturing one mother's anguished and infinitely loving decision to abort to keep her children from daily degradation at the hands of white society.

Ultimately, Brooks moves beyond depiction of small, permitted dreams amid pervasive injustices and addresses timeless, cosmic themes. An intense sonnet cycle, "Gay Chaps at the Bar," closes the volume.

On the surface, these poems pose immediate questions, like why black men should suffer and die for the white society that oppresses them, and what they will be after the war if they are lucky enough to survive it. At a deeper level, these sonnets probe ultimate questions and raise central dilemmas. They oppose African American constraints to often naïve hopes and dreams and depict feelings of love overcome by realities of war, experiences of racial segregation contrasted with white realizations of black humanity, early faith in God contrasted with later perception of cosmic meaninglessness, and early certainty in a loved one contrasted with later doubts and reflections on war's carnage. These war sonnets ask central questions: Who am I? What do I believe in? What is the meaning of life? Is there a God? And, if so, what is his plan? The volume ends with the eternal quest for meaning unanswered. Juxtaposed to "firstly inclined to take what it is told," a poem depicting youthful readiness to believe in God, is the answering sonnet, "God works in a mysterious way," asking God for certainty but receiving none.

Brooks's content is powerful; her artistry is equally strong. She adopts traditional as well as jazzy contemporary poetic forms. Sonnets, ballads, and other stanzaic poems are juxtaposed to free verse. Some poems use refrains presented as blues lyrics. Although most lines are unrhymed, several adopt rhyme or slant rhyme. Diction varies widely, from the most refined to the aggressively slangy. Black dialect appears sparingly. Word choice is always careful, depicting worldview, defining characters, or creating mood or juxtaposition.

Two opposed poems in the war sonnet cycle "Gay Chaps at the Bar" epitomize Brooks's linguistic facility and ability to capture worldview through vocabulary, connotation, and syntax. She starts the William Blake–like "innocence" poem on religious belief, titled "firstly inclined to take what it is told," by addressing God with reverential language, "Thee sacrosanct," but she intersperses lines like "the narcotic milk of peace for men," suggesting that religious belief will not prevail. The companion Blakean "experience" poem, "God works in a mysterious way," replaces the earlier sonnet's language and connotation with words reflecting skepticism, empiricism, and naturalism. Brooks's language is direct and experiential, but elegant turn of phrase and expressiveness set it apart from normal speech, as in these lines from "kitchenette building": "We are things of dry hours and the involuntary plan, / Grayed in, and gray" (4). This language echoes the modernist language and experience of "The Waste Land" and "The Hollow Men" by T(HOMAS) S(TEARNS) ELIOT (1888-1965).

Brooks's influence has been powerful and enduring. She holds special significance for black poets like Lucille Clifton (1936-2010) and Major Jackson (b. 1968). Black Midwestern poets RITA DOVE (b. 1952), Patricia Smith (b. 1955), and Quraysh Ali Lansana (Ron Myles) (b. 1964) have all testified in writing about Brooks's personal and artistic influence. This influence often centers on A Street in Bronzeville, which established Brooks's aesthetic and social sensibility in many of her best-loved, most anthologized poems.

IMPORTANT EDITIONS: The standard edition is the original Harper and Brothers 1945 edition, which saw two reprintings that year. These poems are also available in The World of Gwendolyn Brooks (1971) and Blacks (1987). Bronzeville poems also appear in other Brooks collections, including Selected Poems (1963).

FURTHER READING: Brooks's memoirs include Report from Part One (1972) and Report from Part Two (1996). Biographies include George E. Kent's A Life of Gwendolyn Brooks (1990) and Harold Bloom's Gwendolyn Brooks (2003). Conversations with Gwendolyn Brooks (2003), edited by Gloria Jean Wade Gayles, contains several interviews.

Henry Louis Gates Jr.'s Life upon These Shores: Looking at African American History, 1513–2008 (2011) provides the broader context of the African American experience in this country, as well as specific references to Brooks and the events and accomplishments of her time. The first three chapters of Barbara Jean Bolden's Urban Rage in Bronzeville: Social Commentary in the Poetry of Gwendolyn Brooks, 1945–1960 (1998) include "A Historical Perspective: Gwendolyn Brooks, the Chicago Renaissance, and Bronzeville"; discussion and analysis of Brooks's Bronzeville poems;

and "The 1940s: A Milieu for Integrationist Poetics." Chapter 2 of *Gwendolyn Brooks: Poetry and the Heroic Voice* (1987) by D. H. Melhem describes *A Street in Bronzeville*'s publication history and provides discussion, commentary, and analysis (16–50). Henry B. Shaw's *Social Themes in the Poetry of Gwendolyn Brooks* (1973) examines early commentary on the volume's social statement.

Articles include Gary Smith's "Gwendolyn Brooks's *A Street in Bronzeville,* the Harlem Renaissance and the Mythologies of Black Women," *MELUS* 10.3 (Fall 1983): 33–46; and Janet Ruth Heller's "Gwendolyn Brooks's Dramatic Monologues in *A Street in Bronzeville,*" *MidAmerica* 29 (2002): 54–60. Book-length works of analysis and commentary include *Gwendolyn Brooks* (2000) and *Gwendolyn Brooks: Comprehensive Research and Study Guide* (2003), both edited by Harold Bloom. The latter contains analyses of the *Bronzeville* poems. *Gwendolyn Brooks* (2010), edited by Mildred Mickle, includes critical perspectives, as well as Kathy Rugoff's "The Critical Reception and Influence of Gwendolyn Brooks." Pages 3 to 5 of *On Gwendolyn Brooks: Reliant Contemplation* (1996), edited by Stephen C. Wright, reprint Paul Engle's August 26, 1945, *Chicago Tribune* book review; page 5 reprints the equally positive September 22, 1945, *New Yorker* review.

Princeton University Library holds some Gwendolyn Brooks materials, but the Bancroft Library at the University of California, Berkeley, has the largest collection.

PHILIP A. GREASLEY   UNIVERSITY OF KENTUCKY

STUDS LONIGAN: A TRILOGY

HISTORY: With the 1935 publication of *Studs Lonigan: A Trilogy,* JAMMES T(HOMAS) FARRELL (1904–1979) completed the story of a young Irish Catholic character whose spiritual and cultural deprivation reveals the urban problems of CHICAGO, especially those of the city's South Side. The works that make up the trilogy, *Young Lonigan: A Boyhood in Chicago Streets* (1932), *The Young Manhood of Studs Lonigan* (1934), and *Judgment Day* (1935), begin in 1916 and continue into the Depression. Collectively, they remain Farrell's best-known work.

Born and raised in Chicago, Farrell was the second surviving son of James Francis and Mary (Daly) Farrell, who struggled to raise their large family on meager salaries as a maid and a teamster. At the age of three, Farrell was sent to live with his maternal grandparents in their comfortable apartment in the South Side neighborhood immediately west of Washington Park, where he would set the Lonigan trilogy. He attended St. Cyril High School and worked summers as a telephone clerk at the Amalgamated Express Company until graduation, after which he was fully employed there. While enrolled in night classes at De Paul University, Farrell first read (HERMAN) THEODORE DREISER (1871–1945). He soon quit his dead-end job and his night classes to work as a gas-station attendant. By 1925 he had saved enough money to enter the University of Chicago.

The papers Farrell submitted in Professor James Weber Linn's composition class provided the foundation for *Studs Lonigan*. In these essays he gives detailed impressions of

James T. Farrell's *Studs Lonigan: A Trilogy,* 1938.
© Random House

his South Side neighborhood and its inhabitants, revealing their emotions, desires, and aspirations, and in a short story called "Studs," published in the July–September 1930 issue of *This Quarter,* he tells of a wake for the young Studs, prefiguring the trilogy's ending.

After the 1932 publication of *Young Lonigan,* Farrell met with critical acclaim, especially from editors of leftist publications such as the *New Masses,* the *New Republic,* and *The Nation.* The May 22, 1932, *New York Herald Tribune* review of *Young Lonigan,* titled "Some of the Most Recent Spring Fiction," called the novel a classic (8). In the *New Republic* 78 (March 21, 1934), Fred T. Marsh called *The Young Manhood of Studs Lonigan* "a distinguished and outstanding contemporary novel" and "a great piece of American realism" (165). In "Portrait of an Age" in the *Nation* 140 (May 1, 1935), William Troy, reviewing *Judgment Day,* called Farrell "the most terrifying novelist now writing in America," and although he felt that the book was not as outstanding as the first two volumes, he remarked that "the last quarter, which is devoted to Studs Lonigan's illness and death, brings the whole series to a brilliant and momentous close" (513). The trilogy, completed in 1935, remains the foundation of Farrell's reputation, although his O'Neill-O'Flaherty pentalogy (1936–1953) is also highly regarded.

SIGNIFICANCE: In the *Studs Lonigan* trilogy Farrell explores the cultural and spiritual poverty of his Chicago South Side neighborhood and its negative impact on its residents. To clarify the nature of this poverty, he deliberately portrays a middle-class protagonist whose family owns an apartment building and lives without financial worries until the Depression. Farrell suggests that the American Dream here is predicated on a sense of superiority to other ethnic groups and that Americans across the nation are caught up in the same spiritually hollow idea and become equally frustrated when it fails to materialize.

Through eight quarters at the University of Chicago, during which Farrell read widely, he learned from the naturalism of Dreiser and Émile Zola (1840–1902), the exploration of the mythical American Dream by (HARRY) SINCLAIR LEWIS (1885–1951), the

psychological insight of SHERWOOD ANDERSON (1876–1941), and the stream of consciousness of James Joyce (1882–1941). Critics agree, however, that Farrell's years growing up in Chicago's Washington Park were most important and that he portrays the city with an insider's perspective, incorporating aspects of his experience into his work.

Beginning with Studs's grammar school graduation at age fourteen on the day of President Wilson's nomination for a second term and ending with his death at twenty-nine during the early Depression, the trilogy follows him through sixty-five discontinuous days in two South Side neighborhoods. Farrell evokes the urban locale and its influence with an external reality, depicting street corners where neighborhood toughs congregate, poolrooms where they while away their days, and bars where they drink bootleg whiskey and jeopardize their futures. The massive looming brick apartment buildings and the unyielding fireplug on the street corner reinforce the outer view that young Studs projects to the world—defiance of anything not considered manly.

Some critics have deemed this trilogy naturalistic, intimating that environment controls the characters, but Farrell goes beyond earlier naturalism to show that environment and character interact, and that Studs chooses the negative values in his milieu. In his determination to "be a man"—a successful street fighter, a decorated soldier, or a brutal football champion—Studs makes unfortunate choices that return to haunt him in the last volume, *Judgment Day.* He chooses to skip school, hang around with the gang, drink to excess, fornicate, and fight. He hides any inner tenderness, which surfaces only in the more natural Washington Park, where the adolescent Studs sits in a tree with his only true love, Lucy, and, later, in Grant Park, where the young adult Studs proposes to Catherine.

In *James T. Farrell* (1971) Edgar M. Branch points out that Farrell uses traditional water imagery to suggest the choices open to Studs. The young boy feels as if a warm stream flows through him when he is with Lucy, and he is clean and removed from worldly concerns when he swims in the YMCA pool. In the last volume, however, Farrell demonstrates the effects of his protagonist's bad choices by connecting water to death. Studs experiences a heart attack while swimming in Lake Michigan with Catherine and is later drenched in rain as he plods from place to place desperately searching for employment (68–69).

Unlike most early naturalists, Farrell experiments with differing points of view. Although he tells much of the story from Studs's perspective, he intersperses short interior monologues comparing his protagonist's worldview to that of Davey Cohen, who derives his feelings of power from beating up Studs and visiting a brothel, and contrasting it with that of Danny O'Neill, who enjoys being alone and throwing a ball against a ledge and who wins a fight by breathing through his nose, saving his breath. Whereas Studs allows neighborhood myths to stunt his emotional and intellectual development, Danny O'Neill, in a later pentalogy, succeeds in spite of local influences. Framing this trilogy with reveries by Studs's father, Paddy Lonigan, Farrell situates Studs within a temporal continuum as the older man daydreams about his difficult past, congratulates himself on providing a good life for his children, and worries about the Depression. These narrative shifts allow Farrell to provide glimpses into the entire community and Studs's place within it.

Although earlier novelists had portrayed the results of economic poverty in the city, Farrell is the first to emphasize the negative impact of cultural poverty. In a 1948 letter to H(enry) L(ouis) Mencken (1880–1956) quoted in "James T. Farrell" in the *Dictionary of Literary Biography Documentary Series* 2, Farrell stated that "the background from which I came was not one which fostered and affirmed the values of sophisticated literary culture. It was one of spiritual poverty" (80). "What he wants for men," reviewer Joseph Warren Beach in his May 27, 1945, *New York Times Book Review* wrote of Farrell's *The League of Cultured Philistines* (1945), "is a way of life culturally sustaining and satisfying so that they may grow to full spiritual stature" (5). The institutions revered in Midwestern cities—the home and family, the neighborhood, the school, and the church—all fail Studs Lonigan, who makes choices influenced by the worst attributes of each group. He skips class and quits

school because he finds it boring. He emulates neighborhood bullies rather than boys like Danny O'Neill, who use their heads instead of their fists. Even when he is initiated into the Order of St. Christopher, he finds it a hoax. These institutions fail Studs by promoting shallow values of material success, ethnic superiority, and surface piety.

During his student years Farrell read Dreiser's *Sister Carrie* (1900), Lewis's *Babbitt* (1922), and Anderson's *Tar: A Midwest Childhood* (1926). Later, writing in this tradition of Midwestern literature in which urbanization and industrialization dealt a death blow to the agrarian dream of the West and resulted in these impoverished values, Farrell, like Dreiser, Henry Blake Fuller (1857–1929), Richard Wright (1908–1960), and Nelson Algren (1909–1981), set his story in Chicago, the city founded, as Fuller asserts in *With the Procession* (1895), "for the one common, avowed object of making money" (248). Carlo Rotella, in his entry "Literary Images of Chicago" in *The Encyclopedia of Chicago* (2004), edited by James R. Grossman, Ann Durkin Keating, and Janice L. Reiff, links Farrell to Wright and Algren as central figures in the development of Chicago realism because they "explored the social and literary consequences of the city's maturing as an industrial metropolis" (487). David D(aniel) Anderson (1924–2011) makes this point even more strongly in "Sherwood Anderson, Henry Blake Fuller, James T. Farrell, and the Midwestern City as Metaphor and Reality," *SSML Newsletter* 25.3 (Fall 1995); he writes that Anderson's *Poor White* (1920), Fuller's *The Cliff-Dwellers* (1893), and the Studs Lonigan trilogy "combine to make "a massive metaphor of money—the search for it, the accumulation of it, its loss. . . . Money and the city are one" (8). Anderson sees the trilogy as portraying a Chicago decaying physically and spiritually, dehumanizing its inhabitants as its neighborhoods crumble, and thus destroying Chicagoans' major source of identity (20).

Indeed, the works of the Lonigan trilogy can best be appreciated not only as Chicago novels but also as neighborhood novels. Rotella writes that Farrell, Wright, and Algren "brought the hard facts and human consequences of neighborhood life to literary center stage" (487). Robert Butler explores further the significance of the neighborhood in "Farrell's Ethnic Neighborhood and Wright's Urban Ghetto: Two Visions of Chicago's South Side," *MELUS* 18.1 (Spring 1993): 103–11. He notes that Farrell uses realistic and poetic techniques to portray his South Side neighborhood as complex and multivalent, offering possibilities for liberation as well as entrapment. In his 1963 monograph on Farrell for the University of Minnesota Pamphlets on American Writers series, Branch compares the literary neighborhood that Farrell creates in his trilogy to Cather's NEBRASKA and Faulkner's South: "It is especially meaningful to us because, through its rich details of urban manners, it shows the heavy cost exacted of people and institutions by the modern city" (45). In "James T. Farrell and Washington Park: The Novel as Social History," *Chicago History* 8.2 (Summer 1979): 81–91, Charles Fanning and Ellen Skerrett outline the coordinates of this neighborhood: the Street, the Park, the Church, and the Home, showing how Studs's destiny is shaped by his choice of locale.

A central element in the neighborhood dynamic of the Studs Lonigan trilogy is the neighborhood's changing ethnic composition. In the early pages of *Young Lonigan*, Farrell is among the earliest American novelists to explore the phenomenon of white flight along with other aspects of ethnic prejudice, as seen in Paddy's racist reflections about Jews and blacks moving into his neighborhood and Old Man O'Brien's anti-Semitic diatribe about Jewish interlopers ruining it. Near the end of *The Young Manhood of Studs Lonigan,* the Lonigan family flees the old neighborhood because African Americans are moving in, and Studs is astounded when he derives his identity from being the brother-in-law of a successful Jewish bookie, reinforcing both his cultural prejudices and his steadily declining power. In *Judgment Day* Studs attempts to change his old ways but finds that it is too late. The dance marathon he and Catherine watch suggests Studs's condition. As the audience seeks glamour and romance and tosses coins onto the dance floor, the drugged and debilitated dancers spend hours merely going through the motions in the contest. Studs's body has been severely weakened by years of degradation, but his mind still gravitates toward immediate gratification, as represented by his orgasm at a burlesque show shortly before his final physical collapse. On the day the bank fails and his father loses all his money, Studs dies as his mother reviles his pregnant fiancée, all the while "mumbling the rosary" (Modern Library edition 460).

Studs Lonigan is an American classic and was made into a United Artists movie in 1960 and a 1979 television miniseries. Although Farrell's reputation waned after World War II, when the leftist critics who had earlier praised him turned against him and his new anti-Communist political stance, and fell even more after his death in 1979, in the twenty-first century it has undergone a revival. In 2004 the centennial of his birth was celebrated at the New York Public Library, with Norman (Kingsley) Mailer (1923–2007), historian Arthur Schlesinger Jr., and hundreds of admirers in attendance; similar celebrations were held at Chicago's Newberry Library and in Paris, where a new French translation of his *Gas House McGinty* (1933) had been issued. In that same year Robert K. Landers's biography *An Honest Writer: The Life and Times of James T. Farrell* was published.

Although Farrell published over fifty books, he never again attained the literary success of this first trilogy. *Studs Lonigan* has secured a permanent place in American literature by critiquing the materialistic aspects of the American Dream and the misery that follows from pursuing it. This trilogy, with its exploration of spiritual impoverishment in a Chicago neighborhood, has influenced later writers across America. Richard Wright's NATIVE SON (1940) was directly inspired by Farrell's trilogy in his portrayal of Studs's African American counterpart, the economically and culturally deprived Bigger Thomas. Mailer and KURT VONNEGUT (JR.) (1922–2007) have openly acknowledged indebtedness to Farrell, specifically for the vivid texture he gives to real life. Today *Studs Lonigan* is enjoying something of a rebirth: in 1999 it was rated number twenty-nine in the Modern Library's top one hundred English-language novels of the twentieth century. In 2004 it was reissued by the Library of America.

IMPORTANT EDITIONS: *Studs Lonigan: The Trilogy* was published in one volume in 1935 by Vanguard Press, which also brought out the separate volumes: *Young Lonigan: A Boyhood in Chicago Streets* in 1932, *The Young Manhood of Studs Lonigan* in 1934, and *Judgment Day* in 1935. The first edition of *Young Lonigan* is significant for its introduction by Professor Frederic M. Thrasher, promoting the book as intended for educational purposes in order to deter censorship for its crude language, violence, and sex. The most widely available editions are the 1938 Modern Library volume, now out of print, with Farrell's introduction explaining the work's genesis, and the 2001 Penguin Classics paperback edition with an introduction by Ann Douglas. In 2004 the Library of America reissued the trilogy with the inclusion of "Boys and Girls," a short story derived from a *Young Lonigan* chapter omitted earlier because of its sexual realism. In 2007 a new novel, *Dreaming Baseball*, written by Farrell and edited posthumously by Ron Briley, Margaret Davidson, and James Barbour, was published by Kent State University Press. Using three newly discovered manuscript versions, these editors reduced the original 500-page novel about the 1919 Black Sox to a more readable 300-page publication. Although the novel has garnered mixed reviews, it remains a valuable contribution to the Farrell canon.

FURTHER READING: Farrell's *A Note on Literary Criticism* (1936) contains his theory of Marxist aesthetics underlying the writing of *Studs Lonigan*. Edgar M. Branch remains the premier Farrell scholar with his pamphlet *James T. Farrell* (1963), his Twayne book *James T. Farrell* (1971), *Studs Lonigan's Neighborhood and the Making of James T. Farrell* (1996), *A Paris Year: Dorothy and James T. Farrell, 1931–1932* (1998), and several articles. Alan M. Wald's *James T. Farrell: The Revolutionary Socialist Years* (1978) and Kathleen Farrell's *Literary Integrity and Political Action: The Public Argument of James T. Farrell* (2000) deal with Farrell's political development. Robert K. Landers's biography *An Honest Writer: The Life and Times of James T. Farrell* (2004) also emphasizes Farrell's political stances over the years. Mary Hricko's *The Genesis of the Chicago Renaissance: Theodore Dreiser, Langston Hughes, Richard Wright, and James T. Farrell* (2009) compares the work of Dreiser, Hughes, Wright, and Farrell in their contributions to the two periods of the CHICAGO RENAISSANCE (1890–1920 and 1930–1950). The work stresses the contributions of Chicago writing to American literature.

Scholarly book chapters that discuss *Studs Lonigan* include Joseph Warren Beach's "Tragedy of the Poolroom Loafer" in *American Fiction, 1920–1940* (1941) and Donald Pizer's "James T. Farrell and the 1930s" in *Literature at the Barricades: The American Writer in the 1930s* (1982), edited by Ralph F. Bogardus and Fred Hobson. Two excellent articles on the trilogy books as neighborhood novels are Robert Butler's "Farrell's Ethnic Neighborhood and Wright's Urban Ghetto: Two Visions of Chicago's South Side," *MELUS* 18.1 (Spring 1993): 103–11, and Charles Fanning and Ellen's Skerrett's "James T. Farrell and Washington Park: The Novel as Social History," *Chicago History* 8 (Summer 1979): 80–91. David D. Anderson's "Sherwood Anderson, Henry Blake Fuller, James T. Farrell, and the Midwestern City as Metaphor and Reality," *SSML Newsletter* 25.3 (Fall 1995): 16–23, offers an overview of the urban novel as a chronicle of cultural decline.

The University of Pennsylvania is the main repository of Farrell's manuscripts and letters.

JOYCE CALDWELL SMITH
THE UNIVERSITY OF TENNESSEE AT CHATTANOOGA

SUBURB, THE

OVERVIEW: The term "suburb" conjures up images of mass-produced developments, affluent cul-de-sacs, traffic jams, and vast shopping malls. The history of suburban development in the United States, however, dates back to the early nineteenth-century horse-and-carriage suburbs located at the edges of cities. The streetcar subdivisions that sprouted along rail lines after the Civil War, the onslaught of advertisements encouraging home ownership in the early 1900s, and the standardization of building materials in the 1920s paved the way for the mass-produced suburbs of the 1940s and 1950s. In the post–World War II era, federal policy and practice facilitated the rise of the suburban home as the primary embodiment of the white, middle-class American dream.

In Midwestern literary depictions, authors emphasize the role of consumerism and industrialization in the loss of traditional rural values as small towns give way to modern exurban centers. Authors present the suburban home as a source of identity as well as alienation, revealing the spiritually desolate interior concealed by a facade of middle-class decorum.

HISTORY AND SIGNIFICANCE: Borderlands dominated the early history of suburban development, and literary representations of the suburb during this era emphasized the indistinct spaces created by these border regions. Accessible by horsecar, private carriage, railroads, and streetcar lines, borderlands occupied a nebulous area between city and country.

WILLIAM DEAN HOWELLS (1837–1920) describes just such a location in *Suburban Sketches* (1871). Howells's narrator speaks with equal parts of fascination and dismay about the Boston suburb of Charlesbridge. He disdains the commute to the city, one moment complaining about the unseemly nature of the passengers and the next moment wishing for some interaction with these "strangers." Not unlike the way *The Rise of Silas Lapham* (1885) pits Midwestern origins against eastern sensibilities, *Suburban Sketches* conveys a distinct sense of displacement, and one can easily read Howells's Midwestern origins beneath his reaction to the nether region of suburban living.

Howells's frequent references to immigrants, building materials, and the often violent transformation of the natural environment highlight the entanglements of industry, commerce, and class in a history of suburban development driven by the demands of financial profit. Howells seems conflicted about this reality, but (HERMAN) THEODORE DREISER (1871–1945) and SHERWOOD ANDERSON (1876–1941) are more overtly derisive. Dreiser offers a glimpse of these complex class dynamics in *Jennie Gerhardt* (1911); the novel situates its protagonist within a naturalistic vision of survival and fate. In the end, even the luxury of Hyde Park does not allow Jennie to transcend the social system that demands separation of the classes. In *Poor White* (1920) Anderson shows the effects of urban sprawl and industry on the small town of Bidwell, OHIO. Rural land and traditional jobs surrender to the pressures of industrialization as the small town yields to the modern metropolis.

(NEWTON) BOOTH TARKINGTON (1869–1946) offers one of the first truly provocative depictions of Midwestern suburban development in *The Magnificent Ambersons* (1918). Of the Ambersons, Tarkington writes, "Their splendour lasted throughout all the years that saw their Midland town spread and darken into a city" (3). The novel features two key components of the nascent twentieth-century suburban revolution: the subdividing of large estates and the growing dominance of the automobile. After Wilbur Minafer dies, leaving the Amberson family in financial straits, Major Amberson subdivides the Amberson estate to help the family survive. The subdividing of large estates becomes an increasingly common practice and an essential element in the history of suburban sprawl. *The Magnificent Ambersons* also comments on the rise of the automobile. As the physical emblem of Eugene Morgan's success as an industrialist, the automobile represents the wave of the future in the novel and foreshadows the central role the automobile will play in American industry and the nation's suburban geography.

The 1920s were pivotal years for suburban construction and literary representations of suburbia. As secretary of commerce and later as president, Herbert (Clark) Hoover (1874–1964) actively advocated for home ownership and the standardization of building materials to increase the rate of new construction. An emergent critical discourse leveled against middle-class conformity and suburban alienation paralleled this call for standardized construction. Authors portrayed the suburban middle class in decidedly negative terms, notoriously captured by H(erbert) L(ouis) Mencken's (1880–1956) moniker the "booboisie." Writers and social critics viewed the middle-class "middle-man" as a narrow-minded, materialistic conformist, and behind the facade of his suburban house, authors inevitably discovered a decidedly hollow core.

No one presents this theme better than (HARRY) SINCLAIR LEWIS (1885–1951) in *Babbitt* (1922). More than just a literary character, Babbitt defined the "materialistic, self-complacent business man conforming to the standards of his set" (*Oxford English Dictionary*). See also BUSINESS. In the early twentieth century politicians and real estate builders forged a link between home ownership and responsible American citizenship, but it was not enough simply to own a home; the house must contain the most advanced appliances and state-of-the-art luxuries. The houses in Floral Heights display the best that money can buy, and Lewis exposes this materialism as a source of treacherous conformity: "In fact there was but one thing wrong with the Babbitt house: It was not a home" (15). This distinction between house and home embodies the tension in the novel between standardization and the individual. The novel oscillates between Babbitt's discontent with the trappings of middle-class life and his embrace of these very same trappings.

F(RANCIS) SCOTT (KEY) FITZGERALD (1896–1940) remains a significant literary figure for understanding the trope of the displaced Midwesterner. His emphasis on commuting and the automobile aligns THE GREAT GATSBY (1925) with the history of suburban sprawl. Eastern wealth and social elitism produce the exclusive suburbs of West and East Egg, and they offer tangible markers of the upper-class ideals toward which Fitzgerald's displaced Midwesterners aspire. They also produce the valley of ashes, however, described as "a fantastic farm where ashes grow like wheat into ridges and hills and grotesque gardens" (27). The valley of ashes symbolizes the industrial inversion of America's rural past.

By midcentury authors expressed their concerns about displacement and conformity in more fatalistic terms. In *Mr. Smith* (1951) LOUIS BROMFIELD (1896–1956) participated in the trend of exposing the potentially lethal fiction of the suburban ideal. From *Babbitt* to *Mr. Smith,* the stakes had been raised. Bromfield described the suburbs as a cancer of illusion and hypocrisy that threatened the entire nation. EVAN S(HELBY) CONNELL (JR.) (1924–2013) extended the line from *Babbitt* to *Mr. Smith* with *Mrs. Bridge* (1959) and

Mr. Bridge (1969). India Bridge finds her life as a wife and mother in an upper-middle-class suburb of KANSAS CITY banal and tedious, and Walter Bridge seems invested in nothing beyond the demands of financial security. Connell depicts the suburb as an isolating environment devoid of authentic human contact.

As documented by scholars across disciplines, suburban development in the twentieth century cannot be disentangled from the politics of race and space. From the 1930s through the 1950s the Home Owners' Loan Corporation and the Federal Housing Administration helped transform the suburban home into the normal expectation of the white middle class, subsidizing loans for new construction and condoning racial discrimination through prejudicial loan practices. The presence of a residential "color line"—whether merely implied or, as in areas of DETROIT, marked by a concrete wall—is a central component of suburban history. Sinclair Lewis's *Kingsblood Royal* (1947) is among the first wave of literary works to address the issue of the color line in the postwar era. Neil Kingsblood's African American heritage jeopardizes the reputation of his family and his standing in the suburb of Sylvan Park. Lewis emphasizes Kingsblood's status as a social trespasser within his suburban community, and "social prejudice" is how the Neighborhood Committee parses the problem when it forces the Kingsbloods to move. The novel culminates in a violent clash at the Sylvan Park home, where Lewis masterfully opposes the growing menace of racial conflict to the perceived serenity of the suburban landscape.

RICHARD WRIGHT (1908–1960) and LORRAINE (VIVIAN) HANSBERRY (1930–1965) explored the volatile nature of the color line in CHICAGO and the real estate practices that perpetuate racial prejudice. In the court scene in Wright's NATIVE SON (1940), Boris A. Max, Bigger Thomas's lawyer, articulates a compelling argument against the well-designed and intentional real estate practices that preserve America's urban ghettos and deny African Americans the sense of home essential to inclusive citizenship. The Dalton home in Hyde Park depends on keeping the Bigger Thomases of the world in their kitchenette apartments. The politics of racial containment in urban centers is essential to understanding how the suburbs continued to redraw the color line throughout the twentieth century.

The promise of the suburban ideal and the potential consequences of crossing the color line underlie Hansberry's *A RAISIN IN THE SUN* (1959). Hansberry never directly portrays the home in Clybourne Park, underscoring that the suburban ideal remains elusive for African Americans. The Youngers may leave behind their claustrophobic South Side tenement, but the threat of violence awaits them, the embodiment of which arrives in the form of Karl Linder, a representative of a segregationist homeowners' association. The relocation of the Youngers to Clybourne Park also speaks to the blockbusting practices of real estate agents who would sell homes to African Americans in the hopes of inciting further white flight. This practice allowed real estate agents and developers to reap heavy profits both from new home construction and from selling older suburban homes to African Americans at inflated prices.

The persistence of the color line is evident in the poetry of GWENDOLYN BROOKS (1917–2000). Brooks addresses the issue in her poem "Sammy Chester Leaves 'Godspell' and Visits *Upward Bound* on the Lake Forest Lawn, Bringing West Afrika." Published in *Beckonings* (1975), the poem juxtaposes the west side of Chicago to "West AFRIKA." Brooks undercuts the pastoral images of Lake Forest with her attention to the racial segregation that denies Sammy Chester a sense of home. The reference to the Upward Bound educational program also exposes Chicago's enduring segregation in the post-1954 *Brown v. Board of Education* era.

In the 1960s and 1970s a mass exodus of commercial and job centers followed the initial wave of postwar residential suburbanization, leaving behind economically blighted urban centers and exacerbating the insidious geography of racial segregation. Capitalizing on the Interstate Highway Act of 1956 and backed by federal subsidies and tax incentives, private developers built enormous shopping centers and strip malls on rural land that, in turn, served as catalysts for new residential construction.

The 1956 National System of Interstate and Defense Highways rhetorically linked national security to the highway system that would expedite the expansion of suburban sprawl. By the late 1950s the suburbs were enmeshed in discourses about the global threats of communism and nuclear war.

As the contemporary literature reflects, a sense of pervasive fear and violence amplified earlier concerns about race, alienation, and conformity. Increasingly, authors implicated the suburbs in political violence both within and outside the nation's borders. In *Expensive People* (1968) JOYCE CAROL OATES (b. 1938) suggests that the startling homogeneity of suburban neighborhoods breeds violence and indifference. HARRIETTE SIMPSON ARNOW (1908–1986) and (WILLIAM) TIM(OTHY) O'BRIEN (b. 1946) juxtapose suburban fear, intolerance, and superficiality to the violence of the Vietnam War era. Arnow's *The Weedkiller's Daughter* (1969) examines the racist, anti-Communist, and stultifying environment of upper-middle-class suburbia against Detroit's displaced rural past. Although O'Brien's *The Nuclear Age* (1985) is set outside the Midwest, it intersperses the contemporary story of William Cowling, who is digging a bomb shelter in his backyard, within a chronological narrative that moves from William's childhood fear of nuclear war through his years as a draft dodger and pseudorevolutionary during the Vietnam War.

In *The Bluest Eye* (1970) and *Sula* (1973) TONI MORRISON (CHLOE ARDELIA WOFFORD) (b. 1931) explores the topography of race in connection with modern urban development and the inherent "whiteness" of the suburban ideal. The opening of *The Bluest Eye* exposes the fictional construct of the suburban ideal even as it prepares the reader for the model against which Pecola Breedlove's demise plays out. In *Sula* economic disparity, the inflated price of land, television towers, and a golf course transform the Bottom into a modern suburb.

Real estate speculation, restrictive covenants, and racial antagonism are also at the center of a novel by Whitney Terrell (b. 1967), *The King of Kings County* (2005), which depicts the development of a suburban empire in rural Kansas City. The entrenched racial segregation of 1960s and 1970s Detroit inhabits the background of the first two novels by Jeffrey (Kent) Eugenides (b. 1960). *The Virgin Suicides* (1993) includes a reference to the 1967 Detroit riots and National Guardsmen parachuting into suburban backyards. The story of the ill-fated Lisbon daughters deconstructs the perceived threat from without by drawing attention to the threat within the suburban home. In *Middlesex* (2002) Eugenides covers the years 1922–2001. The city and suburbs of Detroit play a pivotal role in this story, narrated by the intersex Caliope (Callie/ Cal) Stephanides. Cal's father, Milton, loses his restaurant when it is burned to the ground during the 1967 riots, but the insurance policy allows him to open a chain of restaurants, and Cal grows up in relative financial comfort within the affluent suburbs of Detroit.

The impact of suburban sprawl on American geography and culture suffuses the work of Jonathan Franzen (b. 1959). Several essays in *How to Be Alone* (2003) address urban decline and suburban sprawl. Franzen's conspiracy-laden *The Twenty-Seventh City* (1988) revolves around a referendum to reunify the city of St. Louis with its economically prosperous suburbs. The novel suggests equivalence between real estate development and the terror tactics of the conspirators. Franzen opens *The Corrections* (2001) with a description of the Lamberts' Midwestern home: "The fiction of living in this house was that no one lived here" (5). As Alfred and Enid Lambert struggle to find items they have stored away and places to stash the evidence of daily life, the suburban home appears both too spacious and too illusory to inhabit. In a later novel, *Freedom* (2010), Franzen explores the intertwined issues of gentrification and suburban sprawl in St. Paul, Minnesota. See Minneapolis/St. Paul.

Two other novels offer cutting, witty perspectives on contemporary suburban life. Set in the Chicago suburbs, *The Middlesteins* (2012) by Jami Attenberg (b. 1971) depicts the inauspicious decline of Edie Middlestein, a morbidly obese and compulsive overeater, with a blend of dark humor and compassion. As the narrative moves across time and alternates among members of the Middlestein

family, Edith's personal tragedy and the disintegration of her thirty-year marriage provide the occasion to contemplate how this suburban Jewish family responds to the unfolding failures and disappointments in their lives. In his second novel, *Fallen Land* (2013), Patrick Flanery (b. 1975) describes the transformation of Poplar Farm into Dolores Woods, a failed community of Gothic suburban estates. Set on the outskirts of an unnamed Midwestern city, the novel begins in 1919 with race riots and a lynching and then jumps to the post-housing-bubble recession era. Allusions to a quasi-dystopian state, however, suggest a near-future setting where suburban privatism and neoliberal ideology run amok.

SELECTED WORKS: As a novel that focuses on the industrialization of the small town and early twentieth-century suburbanization, Booth Tarkington's *The Magnificent Ambersons* (1918) provides a useful entrée into Midwestern suburban literature. The most important work of suburban literature of the first half of the twentieth century, however, is Sinclair Lewis's *Babbitt* (1922), which set the terms for critiques of suburban alienation and conformity. Louis Bromfield's *Mr. Smith* (1951) offers an important follow-up to *Babbitt,* heightening a benign suburban malaise to the status of a malignant cancer. Richard Wright's *Native Son* (1940) and Lorraine Hansberry's *A Raisin in the Sun* (1959) are essential for understanding how race has influenced urban and suburban history. Jeffrey Eugenides's *The Virgin Suicides* (1993), Jonathan Franzen's *The Corrections* (2001) and *Freedom* (2010), Whitney Terrell's *The King of Kings County* (2005), Jami Attenberg's *The Middlesteins* (2012), and Patrick Flanery's *Fallen Land* (2013) offer innovative contemporary perspectives on Midwestern suburban culture.

FURTHER READING: The suburb in Midwestern literature remains fertile ground for future scholarly work. To date, three book-length studies of suburban literature have been published: Catherine Jurca's *White Diaspora: The Suburb and the Twentieth-Century Novel* (2001), Robert Beuka's *SuburbiaNation: Reading Suburban Landscape in Twentieth-Century American Fiction and Film* (2004), and Kathy Knapp's *American Unexceptionalism: The Everyman and the Suburban*

Novel after 9/11 (2014). Beuka offers a reading of *The Great Gatsby,* Jurca's study includes chapters on *Babbitt* and *Native Son,* and Knapp examines instances of failure and belonging in *Freedom.* Two essays in *Sinclair Lewis: New Essays in Criticism* (1997), edited by James M. Hutchisson, warrant mention for their treatment of Midwestern suburban history: Edward Watts's *"Kingsblood Royal, The God-Seeker,* and the Racial History of the Midwest" (94–109) and James Williams's "Gopher Prairie or Prairie Style? Wright and Wharton Help Dodsworth Find His Way Home" (125–46). The latter nicely discusses the architectural influence of FRANK LLOYD WRIGHT (1867–1959) on the development of the suburban home. Jayne Waterman offers a compelling reading of Midwestern suburban estrangement in "Suburban Self-Alienation: Louis Bromfield's *Mr. Smith," MidAmerica* 32 (2005): 61–66. In "Space, Property and the Psyche: Violent Topographies in Early Oates Novels," *Studies in the Novel* 38 (2006): 397–413, Susana Araújo discusses the place of violence in the affluent suburbs of Joyce Carol Oates's *Expensive People.* Numerous articles have been published on Jeffrey Eugenides and Jonathan Franzen, but few specifically focus on the suburb. Christian Long's "Running out of Gas: The Energy Crisis in 1970s Suburban Narratives," *Canadian Review of American Studies* 41 (2011): 342–69, includes a discussion of Eugenides's *The Virgin Suicides.* In "Contested Terrain: The Suburbs as Region," *American Literature* 84 (2012): 617–44, Keith Wilhite examines the connection between suburban narratives and regionalism in Franzen's *The Corrections.* Martin Dines explores how European pasts and ethnic difference haunt suburbia in "Suburban Gothic and the Ethnic Uncanny in Jeffrey Eugenides's *The Virgin Suicides," Journal of American Studies* 46 (2012): 959–75.

No major work has been specifically devoted to Midwestern suburban literature, but general histories and cultural studies are vital sources. The list of essential works begins with Kenneth Jackson's *Crabgrass Frontier: The Suburbanization of the United States* (1985). Jackson provides an exhaustive study of America's suburban history and includes substantive discussions of Chicago, Detroit, and St. Louis. In *Middletown: A Study in American Culture* (1929) Robert Staughton Lynd (1892–1970) and Helen Merrell Lynd (1896–1982) analyze the loss of small-town community in Muncie, INDIANA, as a result of consumerism and industrialization. In *The Organization Man* (1956) William Hollingsworth Whyte (1917–1999) harangues the loss of individuality among the suburbanites of Park Forest, ILLINOIS. Scott Donaldson (b. 1928) refutes this maligned image of suburbia in *The Suburban Myth* (1969), and Alan Ehrenhalt takes on critics of suburban conformity in *The Lost City: Discovering the Forgotten Virtues of Community in the Chicago of the 1950s* (1995). Arnold R. Hirsch's *Making the Second Ghetto: Race and Housing in Chicago, 1940–1960* (1983) and Thomas Sugrue's *The Origins of the Urban Crisis: Race and Inequality in Postwar Detroit* (1996; revised edition, 2005) discuss the role of prejudicial federal policies and real estate practices in urban decline. In *Borderland: Origins of the American Suburb, 1820–1939* (1988) John R. Stilgoe includes a chapter on real estate speculation and the railroad in the early development of Chicago; and Joel Garreau (b. 1948) discusses the central role of the automobile in edge-city development, using Detroit as a prototypical example, in *Edge City: Life on the New Frontier* (1961).

KEITH WILHITE   SIENA COLLEGE

SUNDAY MIRROR.
See *Reedy's Mirror*

T–Y

Technology and Industry

OVERVIEW: Throughout its history Midwestern literature has explored the impact of technology and industry on the experience and worldviews of the region's people. The evolving relationship among people, place, and technology is central to Midwestern literature, particularly in writing from the late nineteenth and early twentieth centuries as the United States evolved from a rural-agrarian to a technologically based urban-industrial society. The dominant views of technology and its impacts have changed over time, but consideration of the topic continues unabated.

Over the past two centuries Midwestern writers have differed significantly in their views of technology and industry. Some have celebrated the expanded opportunities and improved living standards associated with technological advances and urbanization; others have condemned oppressive labor conditions and the loss of individuality imposed by factories, assembly lines, and the regulation of individual action in the workplace.

Three perspectives on technology appear in Midwestern literature. One asserts the triumph of the human spirit in creating and using technology to its benefit; this perspective maintains theories of progress associated with the Enlightenment. Its antithesis maintains that technology and industry oppress the human body and spirit. Closely associated with romantic primitivism, religious orientations, and concepts of ecological sustainability, this second perspective typically rejects concepts of material progress in favor of human harmony with God and the natural world. The complement to both of these is the view that despite human pretensions to intellect and rising technological scope and power, the natural forces of the universe can and will prevail over human efforts and products. This fatalistic view rejects the association of technology with progress and underscores human fragility.

Midwestern literary considerations of industry and technology raise the related issues of control, dependency, identity, individualism, social class, gender, family, and labor. These issues are associated with agriculture, urbanization, transportation, communication, the factory system, manufacturing, and mass production during five distinct periods: the pre–Civil War or antebellum era, the post–Civil War Gilded

Age, the early twentieth-century Machine Age, the post–World War II era of technological optimism, and the postindustrial ecological era, often said to have begun with the first Earth Day in 1970.

HISTORY AND SIGNIFICANCE: Over the past two hundred years the introduction of new technologies, like electricity for lighting and power, canals, steam power, steamboats, railroads, automobiles, and telephones, as well as the factory system, the assembly line, and steel-frame skyscrapers, has significantly changed people's lives. From the pioneer era to the present day, Midwestern writers have concerned themselves with the experience and significance of these changes, documenting individual and community responses to increasingly urban-industrial-technological environments.

By the early nineteenth century the Industrial Revolution had inaugurated an age of technological progress unlike anything Americans had previously experienced. Although technology advanced at unprecedented speeds, as reflected in patent records and increasing numbers and types of factories, American society, especially in the Midwest, remained essentially agrarian in the antebellum era. The literature of the time reflects that reality.

A NEW HOME—WHO'LL FOLLOW? (1839) by CAROLINE KIRKLAND (1801–1864), for example, depicts the autobiographical Mrs. Mary Clavers, who moves with her husband to a remote village in southern MICHIGAN. Through Mrs. Clavers, Kirkland corrects the distorted picture of frontier life seen in popular romances, emphasizing the lack of material and aesthetic development among the pioneers. See also FRONTIER AND PIONEER ACCOUNTS. Kirkland embraces technological progress as a positive force that reinforces middle-class values in a rustic environment.

Midwestern values remained anchored in agrarian ideals throughout the Gilded Age, even as industrialism gained momentum after the Civil War. The increasing impact of technology and industry on nature and human dignity during this period became a major concern among writers. The early works of SAMUEL LANGHORNE CLEMENS (1835–1910), writing as Mark Twain, including ADVENTURES OF HUCKLEBERRY FINN (London 1884; New York 1885), reflect a view of enhanced independence, mobility, and opportunity during the heyday of steamboat technology. At the same time, Twain associates machines with danger and disruption, as in the scene in which a steamboat destroys Huck's raft and separates Huck from his companion, Jim. Concerns about technology's dangers are magnified in Twain's fable A Connecticut Yankee in King Arthur's Court (1889), the main character of which is a quintessential American technocrat. Innovations in transportation, communication, and manufacturing make Hank Morgan wealthy but also threaten his physical security. The Enlightenment concept of progress is overshadowed by negative trade-offs.

In The Rise of Silas Lapham (1885) WILLIAM DEAN HOWELLS (1837–1920) provides a cultural profile of the changing roles of men and women who embrace technological optimism. Howells depicts how a successful paint company makes and then breaks one man socially and economically. Men can rise and fall in this environment, but women are called on to stay at home or to serve in low positions created as charitable safe havens for them by dominant males, as in the case of Lapham's largely nonfunctional secretary, the daughter of his Civil War comrade.

As the Gilded Age gave way to the Machine Age, many writers viewed the encroachment of technological change as threatening. Female characters in particular are powerless before complex and increasingly dominant industrial-technological systems. SISTER CARRIE (1900) by (HERMAN) THEODORE DREISER (1871–1945) develops the roles open to women in Midwestern cities at the turn of the century: industrial work at the lowest social tier if they have the strength to meet its implacable demands; domestic work as wives and mothers; or the moral compromise of becoming the sexual property of men. Only through sexual service does Carrie Meeber, newly arrived in CHICAGO from small-town WISCONSIN, achieve opportunities to launch her career as an actress. There she is most successful in reflecting human need rather than production and consumption.

UPTON (BEALL) SINCLAIR (JR.) (1878–1968) dedicated THE JUNGLE (1906) to the

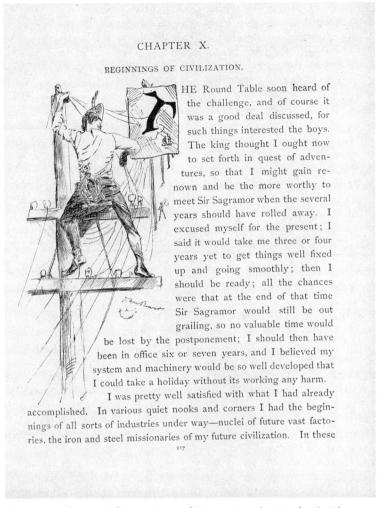

Illustration by Daniel Carter Beard in *A Connecticut Yankee in King Arthur's Court*. Charles L. Webster and Co., 1891.

Image courtesy of the University of Kentucky Special Collections Research Center

overworked, oppressed laborers of Chicago's turn-of-the-century meatpacking industry. The novel, which influenced public opinion in favor of food safety, depicts factories, railroads, and other technologies transforming people's lives, mostly for the worse.

WILLA CATHER (1873–1947) viewed technology with a mixture of cautious optimism and fear that positive human values were being subordinated or turned toward more negative materialistic alternatives. In *O PIONEERS!* (1913) Cather describes "three years of drought and failure" on the NE-

BRASKA frontier as "the last struggle of a wild soil against the encroaching plowshare" (47). Technology ultimately prevails. Alexandra, the novel's protagonist, succeeds in agriculture partly because of her willingness to experiment with new technology, including the first silo in her part of the country. Material gains come, however, at the cost of cultural homogenization, materialism, and loneliness. These concerns permeate Cather's *My Ántonia* (1918), in which the narrator, Nebraska-bred Jim Burden, has accepted an unhappy marriage in New York as the price of his economic success as a railroad lawyer. The principal joy in Burden's life is his renewed friendship with the title character, a Czech woman who represents the last stand of Old World values in the new Machine Age.

In CHICAGO POEMS (1916) and *Smoke and Steel* (1922) by CARL (AUGUST) SANDBURG (1878–1967), technology assumes its own life, underscoring the possibility that the technologically based human-created milieu may displace nature and human fellowship. Most negatively, in "Mill Doors" (1916) Sandburg presents a nightmarish vision of unregulated industry stealing the lives of the working class, often people originally from more traditional rural-agricultural communities. Similarly, in "They Will Say" (1916) the poet represents industrialism in images of working-class children pulled away from natural beauty and sustenance "to work, broken and smothered, for bread and wages, / To eat dust in their throats and die empty-hearted / For a little handful of pay on a few Saturday nights" (9).

Sandburg, however, also underscores the cultural excitement that accompanies the shift from preindustrial society to the new urban-industrial world. In "Skyscraper" from *Chicago Poems,* for example, the building assumes a soul, thoughts, and memories, thus personifying the blue-collar workers whose labor expresses their aspiration and pride in creation. Ultimately, in poems like "Prayers of Steel" from *Cornhuskers* (1918), Sandburg's working-class speaker's pride and prayerfulness become one with the industrial city: "Lay me on an anvil, O God. / . . . Let me be the great nail holding a skyscraper through blue nights into white stars" (65).

Another recurring motif in early twentieth-century Midwestern literature is the rural-to-industrial coming-of-age story. SHERWOOD ANDERSON (1876–1941) personifies the new life made possible through mechanization in Hugh McVey, the protagonist in *Poor White* (1920). Hugh grows up next to a lazy river, the son of a lazy man. But when he is fourteen, the railroad comes through, and "Hugh [begins] a little to awaken" (5). For Hugh, like other Midwesterners, the railroad does more than cover miles; it transports possibility. Coming of age in the industrial era means that Hugh can

"take hold of steel, wood, and iron" and visualize "a thousand new machines, formed by his hands and brain, doing the work that had been done by the hands of men" (70). The "success of his corn-cutting machine and the apparatus for unloading coal cars" gives Hugh a sense of purpose and a place in the community (227).

The experience of Anderson's inventor, Hugh McVey, suggests consideration of a larger issue: the impact of technology and industry on gender identity and opportunity. These are mediated by who uses, produces, or consumes specific types of technology. Literature of the Machine Age usually describes the technological world as oppressive for women because it excludes their participation and consequently isolates them from a world in motion. While American cultural myth celebrates the self-made man and Yankee ingenuity, women are socialized to marginal roles in the Machine Age. Anderson addresses these issues in *Perhaps Women* (1931), a collection of poetic essays about technology and gender drawing on his observations of labor conditions in the industrial South. According to Anderson, men have lost their manhood to the factory system, and any hope for cultural renewal lies with women. Woman, Anderson asserts, "will remain a being untouched by the machine" because even if it tires her physically, "it cannot paralyze or make impotent her spirit. She remains, as she will remain, a being with a hidden inner life" (140).

The automobile became a key image in literature of the Machine Age, and writers portrayed it both positively and negatively. In MAIN STREET (1920) (HARRY) SINCLAIR LEWIS (1885–1951) describes the residents of a small MINNESOTA town as a "savorless people . . . listening to mechanical music, saying mechanical things about the excellence of Ford automobiles, and viewing themselves as the greatest race in the world" (265). In Lewis's *Babbitt* (1922) white middle-class Midwesterners are thorough utilitarians who love machines, especially automobiles, for the status they confer as much as for the convenience they offer. George Babbitt sees his motorcar as "poetry and tragedy, love and heroism" (24). Most of all, he knows that "a family's motor indicated its rank as precisely

Women welding at the Lincoln Motor Company, Detroit, Michigan, 1914–1918. U.S. Army Signal Corps photo.
Image courtesy of the Library of Congress

as the grades of the peerage determined the rank of an English family" (74).

The formal experiments of literary modernism reflected, in part, changes brought about by technology and industry, including a faster pace of life and new modes of work and leisure. A strong example is the trilogy of novels written by JOHN DOS PASSOS (1896–1970), consisting of *The 42nd Parallel* (1930), *1919* (1932), and *The Big Money* (1936) and collected as *U.S.A.* in 1938. *U.S.A.* presents a portrait of early twentieth-century American society by means of collage, combining fictional narratives, "Newsreel" sections about current events, autobiographical "Camera Eye" segments, and short biographies of public figures, including leaders in technology and industry like Midwesterners Thomas Edison, Henry Ford, FRANK LLOYD WRIGHT (1867–1959), and the Wright brothers. Dos Passos portrays the era not only as experienced firsthand but also as mediated by the newspaper and FILM indus-

tries and as affected by urbanization and new technologies.

Midwestern literature often shows people as anxious in the face of life-changing technologies. Although popular culture in the era of technological optimism associated technology with freedom and individuality, literature increasingly came to reflect tensions about who is in control, humans or machines. Quality human life cannot be manufactured, as HARRIETTE SIMPSON ARNOW (1908–1986) illustrates in her novel *THE DOLLMAKER* (1954) by using simple natural images, such as lilacs and their lovely aroma. Such positive sensations are juxtaposed to the hellish red glow of a steel pour in a World War II–era DETROIT steel mill. Gertie Nevels's resistance to machine power makes a compelling condemnatory statement on the factory system. Uprooted from her beloved rural Kentucky, Gertie could assimilate like every other woman who "dreams of a ten-cubic-foot Icy Heart," the latest and greatest refrigerator, "in her kitchen" (273). But new domestic appliances cannot soften Gertie's alienation from her urban-industrial environment in this wrenching portrait of the American Dream turned nightmare.

The human-created environment, that which is shaped by technology driven by human needs and aspirations, stands opposed to the nonhuman power of the natural world. In many texts human will and technology prevail, and nature is tamed and subdued, at least for a time. In the writings of MARY FRANCES DONER (1893–1985), for example, life is connected at all levels to Great Lakes shipping. See GREAT LAKES LITERATURE. All manner of ships, from freighter to frigate, seem to subordinate nature as they ply the vast waters in scene after scene in *Glass Mountain* (1942). But no matter how large, powerful, or technologically advanced these ships may be, their crews quiver in terror at a falling barometer in November. As in the popular ballad "The Wreck of the *Edmund Fitzgerald*" (1976) by Gordon Lightfoot (b. 1938), the tanker *New Haven Socony,* the freighter *William B. Davock,* and other Great Lakes vessels are rendered powerless by nature's fury.

The automobile continues to play a defining role in many Midwestern literary works during the era of technological optimism and beyond, not only as subject matter but also as part of character identification. In the nonfiction *Driving to Detroit: An Automotive Odyssey* (1998) Leslie Hazleton (b. 1945) admits, "It was a pathetic illusion to see life in metal. Yet I'd done it many times" (63). Similarly, Rick Amery, the main character in *Motown* (1991) by LOREN D. ESTLEMAN (b. 1952), acknowledges that his love of cars is the "source of all his troubles" (4). The car is personified when Rick feels the "Z-28 filling its lungs and pure premium-leaded hammering in its veins," suggesting a transfer of power from machine to human when the gears engage (60). But as the plot of Estleman's novel emphasizes, power rests not with the individual but with the industrial system and its products, rendering Rick's personification illusory.

In some narratives the domination of the automobile industry results in wealth and status, success does not make people happy. This is the case in Estleman's Detroit series, which follows the development of the auto industry decade by decade. *Thunder City: A Novel of Detroit* (1999) highlights the change from horse-drawn carriages to automobiles between 1900 and 1910. This technological transition is a central catalyst in the lives of Detroit's Irish, Polish, German, African American, and Sicilian citizens, denizens of an entrenched industrial society in which people are less important than the products they produce.

A number of poets have continued the tradition begun by Sandburg, writing memorably about Midwestern workers and industrial landscapes. An important influence on such poets is THEODORE ROETHKE (1908–1963), who portrays technology positively in poems about his family's greenhouses in Saginaw, Michigan, but negatively in poems like "Highway: Michigan" (1948). JAMES WRIGHT (1927–1980) wrote some of his best-known poems about the often brutal effects of industry on both people and nature. These include "Autumn Begins in Martins Ferry, Ohio" (1963), a bleak description of factory workers at a high school football game. U.S. Poet Laureate Philip Levine (1928–2015) wrote vividly about Depression-era Detroit, his experience working in the city's factories, and the declining fortunes of the industrial Midwest. A much-anthologized poem is Levine's "Coming Home" (1972), a dark vision of the auto industry in Detroit. JIM (JAMES RAYMOND) DANIELS (b. 1956) has written a trilogy drawing on his early experiences as a Detroit autoworker. The poems in *Places/Everyone* (1985), *Punching Out* (1990), and *M-80* (1993) find dignity in industrial labor while acknowledging the toll it takes on the human body and spirit. In writing *Factory* (1980), a book-length poem about working in a Milwaukee can factory, Antler, born Brad Burdick (b. 1946), was inspired by the prophetic litanies of Walt Whitman (1819–1892) and Allen Ginsberg (1926–1997). In this and other poems Antler counters the power of industry with ecological utopianism and unabashed eroticism.

Technological themes are also found in song lyrics with Midwestern origins or themes. Railroads and trains, for example, have represented freedom and escape from oppressive situations, beginning with nineteenth-century folk songs and spirituals. "Rock Island Line" and "Wabash Cannonball" both refer to Midwestern railroad lines; some scholars have suggested that the former has roots in the Underground Railroad, the network of abolitionists helping slaves escape north to freedom. During the early twentieth century, African Americans migrating out of the South brought their music to northern cities like Chicago and Detroit, where blues and gospel reached a mass audience first through recording technology and then via radio. Trains, a dominant mode of transportation at the time, often figure in songs from that era.

Midwestern blues songs with railroad motifs include "Freight Train Blues" (1924), written by Thomas A. Dorsey (1899–1993) and recorded by Trixie Smith; "Through Train Blues" (1928) by Tampa Red (Hudson Whittaker, 1904–1981); "Detroit Special" (1936) by Big Bill Broonzy (Lee Conley Bradley, 1903–1958); "Hobo Blues" (1949) by John Lee Hooker (1917–2001); and "All Aboard" (1956) by Muddy Waters (McKinley Morganfield, 1913–1983). All these composers lived and worked in Chicago except for Hooker, who was the foremost figure in Detroit blues. The gospel-soul-style "People Get Ready" (1965), written by Chicago's Curtis Mayfield (1942–1999) and recorded by the Impressions, is one of the most notable songs associated with the civil rights movement. Mayfield envisions a train of righteousness and justice that all people are welcome to board.

Songs about automobiles were written almost as soon as cars appeared on American roads. Since Detroit has been the center of the U.S. auto industry for over a century, it is not surprising that many car songs refer either to Detroit or cars built there. Automobiles typically figure in these songs as symbols of individual freedom, self-expression, and sexuality. The car craze of the 1920s produced such songs as "In My Flivver Just for Two" (1925) by Gordon Taylor and Floyd Kendall and "Up and Down the 8 Mile Road" (1926) by Gus Kahn and Walter Donaldson. (Both are found in the online collections of the Smithsonian In-

stitution.) During the 1950s and 1960s, as Detroit manufactured large, aesthetically pleasing automobiles, popular musicians produced a steady stream of car songs, including "Maybelline" by Chuck (Charles Edward Anderson) Berry (b. 1926) of Missouri and "From a Buick 6" by Bob Dylan (Robert Allen Zimmerman) (b. 1941) of Minnesota. With the oil crisis of the 1970s and the subsequent decline of Detroit and the automobile industry, car songs dropped out of favor. Those that did appear were often marked by ambiguity and irony. Later examples include "One Piece at a Time" (1976) by Johnny Cash (1932–2003), "Little Red Corvette" (1983) by Prince (Rogers Nelson, 1958–2016) of Minnesota, and "The Big Three Killed My Baby" (1999), written by Jack White (b. 1975) and recorded by the White Stripes from Detroit.

Rust Belt literature, identified and discussed as a genre in the last decade, is not limited to the Midwest, but includes writing about industrial decline, working-class life, and urban renewal in CLEVELAND, Detroit, and other cities and towns in the lower Great Lakes region. As in Buffalo, Pittsburgh, and other cities to the east, these locations have declined since the 1970s as corporations have shut down factories and thrown thousands out of work. First-person nonfiction accounts about the human impact of industry include *Rivethead* (1991) by Ben (Bernard Egan) Hamper (b. 1956), about the author's experience working in a General Motors plant for many years. Charlie LeDuff (b. 1966), a Detroit native who became a Pulitzer Prize-winning journalist for the *New York Times*, wrote *Detroit: An American Autopsy* (2013), a narrative about returning to live and work in Detroit, where he investigated the causes and social effects of the city's decline. Other Rust Belt memoirs include *Teardown: Memoir of a Vanishing City* (2013) by Gordon Young (b. 1966), about Flint, Michigan and *The Hard Way on Purpose: Essays and Dispatches from the Rust Belt* (2014) by David Giffel (b. 1964), about Akron, OHIO. The short story collection *American Salvage* (2009) by Bonnie Jo Campbell (b. 1962) and the novels *Crooked River Burning* (2001) by Mark Winegardner (b. 1961), *The Keepers of Truth* (2000) by Michael Collins (b. 1964), and *The Insurgent* (2010) by Noah Cicero (b. 1980) are also referred to as works of Midwestern Rust Belt literature.

Finally, *A SAND COUNTY ALMANAC* (1949) by ALDO LEOPOLD (1887–1948) anticipates the postindustrial ecological rejection of progress through commercial and industrial strength and subjugation of nature by technology. Leopold instead advocates ecological values that place humans inside the environment and dependent on its well-being rather than outside nature in an observing and controlling role. Instead of dominance of nature by technology, Leopold asserts the need to conserve both natural and human communities by means of science and a land ethic. Leopold's influence is strongly evident in later ENVIRONMENTAL LITERATURE, which often addresses industrial abuses and the need for sustainable technology.

Technology, industry, and attendant social conflicts will continue to provoke literary responses in the Midwest. The world economic crisis that began in 2008 has brought new challenges to the region as jobs become valuable commodities regardless of their nature, as the middle class is pressed on all sides, and as American manufacturers, led by Detroit and the auto industry, struggle in a globalized economy. How writers will characterize the individual, human experience of these trends remains to be seen, but they may find inspiration in how their predecessors portrayed Midwesterners of earlier eras facing economic, industrial, and technological change.

SELECTED WORKS: Caroline Kirkland's *A New Home—Who'll Follow?* (1839) is a strong example of early Midwestern fiction about the frontier. Steamboat technology figures prominently in Mark Twain's *Life on the Mississippi* (1883) and *Adventures of Huckleberry Finn* (1884, 1885). *A Connecticut Yankee in King Arthur's Court* (1889) is Twain's fable on the social costs of industrialism. William Dean Howells concerns himself with social class and mass consumption in *The Rise of Silas Lapham* (1885).

Theodore Dreiser's *Sister Carrie* (1900) depicts both the material splendor and the social displacements brought about by the Industrial Revolution. Upton Sinclair's muckraking novel *The Jungle* (1906) remains the classic in its genre. Willa Cather's *O Pioneers!* (1913) and *My Ántonia* (1918) consider displacement and alienation from nature while celebrating individualism in the face of technological and social change. The central theme in Sherwood Anderson's *Poor White* (1920) and *Perhaps Women* (1931) is the impact of technological change on human relationships and communities. Sinclair Lewis's satirical novels *Main Street* (1920) and *Babbitt* (1922) detail the material circumstances and values of middle-class Midwesterners of the Machine Age.

Harriette Simpson Arnow's *The Dollmaker* (1954) portrays white southern migrants in the industrial Midwest. Mary Frances Doner's *Glass Mountain* (1942) and *The Salvager* (1958) depict the Great Lakes shipping industry. *Motown* (1991) and *Thunder City: A Novel of Detroit* (1999) are but two of Loren D. Estleman's hard-bitten detective novels concerned with the rise and fall of industrial Detroit.

Carl Sandburg inaugurated a Midwestern tradition of poetry about working-class industrial experience with his books *Chicago Poems* (1916), *Cornhuskers* (1918), and *Smoke and Steel* (1920), all reprinted in *The Complete Poems of Carl Sandburg* (1970). Later books continuing that tradition include Theodore Roethke's *THE LOST SON* (1948), James Wright's *THE BRANCH WILL NOT BREAK* (1963), Philip Levine's *They Feed They Lion* (1972), Jim Daniels's *Places/Everyone* (1985), and Antler's *Factory* (1980), reprinted in *The Selected Poems* (2000).

Ben Hamper's memoir *Rivethead* (1991) is considered a classic of Rust Belt literature. Aldo Leopold's *A Sand County Almanac* (1949) continues to inform the postindustrial ecological consciousness that began with antipollution activism in the late 1960s and early 1970s.

Anthologies include *Technology in American Literature* (2000), edited by Kathleen Nolan Monahan and James S. Nolan, which features Anderson, Howells, Twain, and other writers. *Working Classics: Poems on Industrial Life* (1990), edited by Peter Oresick and Nicolas Coles, includes Midwestern poets like Antler, Daniels, and Levine. In addition to the online *Belt Magazine*, Belt Publishing of Cleveland produces printed works of Rust Belt literature, including *Rust Belt Chic: The Cleveland Anthology* (2012), edited by Anne Trubek and Richey Piiparinen; *The Cincinnati Anthology* (2014), edited by Zan McQuade; *A Detroit Anthology* (2014), edited by Anna Clark; and *Car Bombs to Cookie Tables: The Youngstown Anthology* (2015), edited by Jacqueline Marino and Will Mille.

Readings in contemporary literature may be supplemented by such films as Michael Moore's documentary *Roger and Me* (1989), which assaults corporate greed as the basis for human losses in the automotive industry city of Flint, Michigan.

FURTHER READING: Leo Marx's *The Machine in the Garden: Technology and the Pastoral Ideal in America* (1964) is the classic study of American literary responses to the Industrial Revolution. Marx discusses Twain in *The Pilot and the Passenger: Essays on Literature, Technology, and Culture in the United States* (1988). In *Shifting Gears: Technology, Literature, Culture in Modernist America* (1987) Cecelia Tichi describes how writers, including such Midwesterners as Anderson, Cather, EDNA FERBER (1885–1968), and ERNEST (MILLER) HEMINGWAY (1899–1961), reacted to technological change, particularly in their use of language. Jon Teaford's *Cities of the Heartland: The Rise and Fall of the Industrial Midwest* (1993) treats writers of the CHICAGO RENAISSANCE as an expression of the "Windy City and the Midwest . . . at high noon, having achieved an industrial, political, and cultural zenith" (165). In *The Midwestern Pastoral: Place and Landscape in Literature of the American Heartland* (2006) William Barillas deals with technology in relation to utilitarian individualism and Midwestern archetypes like the "tinkerer," seen both in popular culture and in literary texts.

On Caroline Kirkland's *A New Home— Who'll Follow?*, consult Lori Merish's *Sentimental Materialism: Gender, Commodity Culture, and Nineteenth-Century American Literature* (2000). Jerry W. Thomason's entry on technology in *The Mark Twain Encyclopedia* (1993), edited by J. R. LeMaster and James D. Wilson, provides a starting point for inquiry that may lead to Sherwood Cummings's *Mark Twain and Science: Adventures of a Mind* (1988) and Jeffrey Steinbrink's "Mark Twain's Mechanical Marvels," in *Constructing Mark Twain: New Directions in Scholarship* (2001), edited by Laura E. Skandera-Trombley and Michael J. Kiskis (72–86). On *A Connecticut Yankee in King Arthur's Court*, consult Mary Lyndon Shanley's "Mark Twain, Technology, Social Change, and Political Power," in *The Artist and Political Vision* (1982), edited by Benjamin R. Barber and Michael J. Gargas McGrath (267–89); and "'We Should See Certain Things Yet, Let Us Hope and Believe': Technology, Sex, and Politics in Mark Twain's *Connecticut Yankee*" by Bernard J. Dobski Jr. and Benjamin A. Kleinerman, *Review of Politics* 69.4 (Fall 2007): 599–624. Dawn Henwood undertakes a gendered reading of Howells in "Complications of Heroinism: Gender, Power, and the Romance of Self-Sacrifice in *The Rise of Silas Lapham*," *American Literary Realism* 30.3 (Spring 1998): 14–30.

Sources on Dreiser include Stanley Corkin's "*Sister Carrie* and Industrial Life: Objects and the New American Self," *Modern Fiction Studies* 33.4 (Winter 1987): 605–19; and Laura Hapke's "Men Strike, Women Sew: Gendered Labor Worlds in Dreiser's Social Protest Art," in *Theodore Dreiser and American Culture: New Readings* (2000), edited by Yoshinobu Hakutani (104–14). On Sinclair, consult Steven Rosendale's "In Search of Left Ecology's Usable Past: *The Jungle*, Social Change, and the Class Character of Environmental Impairment," in *The Greening of Literary Scholarship: Literature, Theory, and the Environment* (2002), edited by Rosendale (59–76).

Eileen T. Bender addresses technological issues in "Pioneer or Gadgeteer: Bergsonian Metaphor in the Work of Willa Cather," *Midwest Quarterly* 28.1 (Autumn 1986): 130–40. William Conlogue offers "Managing the Farm, Educating the Farmer: *O Pioneers!* and the New Agriculture," *Great Plains Quarterly* 21.1 (Winter 2001): 3–15. Philip A. Greasley discusses Anderson and Sandburg in "Beyond Brutality: Forging Midwestern Urban-Industrial Mythology," *MidAmerica* 11 (1984): 9–19. In "Modeling, Diagramming, and Early Twentieth-Century Histories of Invention and Entrepreneurship: Henry Ford, Sherwood Anderson, Samuel Insull," *Journal of American Studies* 36.3 (December 2002): 491–512, Jeffory A. Clymer compares Anderson's view of invention in

Poor White to that of industrialists of the era. Also see DAVID D(ANIEL) ANDERSON'S "Sherwood Anderson's Technologically Displaced Persons," *Society for the Study of Midwestern Literature Newsletter* 12.3 (Fall 1982): 9–20.

Glen A. Love's "Babbitt's Dance: Technology, Power, and Art in the Novels of Sinclair Lewis" appears in *Sinclair Lewis at 100: Papers Presented at a Centennial Conference* (1985), edited by Michael Connaughton (75–85). Haeja K. Chung has edited *Harriette Simpson Arnow: Critical Essays on Her Work* (1995). In "Mary Frances Doner: Michigan Author," *MidAmerica* 26 (1999): 129–37, Mary DeJong Obuchowski reviews Doner's writings about the Great Lakes. Joseph Hynes discusses *Motown* and other Estleman novels about crime in Detroit in "Looking for Endings: The Fiction of Loren D. Estleman," *Journal of Popular Culture* 29.3 (Winter 1995): 121–27.

Kevin Stein has contributed " 'A Dark River of Labor': Work and Workers in James Wright's Poetry," *American Poetry Review* 22.6 (November–December 1993): 49–54. A good introduction to Philip Levine is Kate Daniels's "About Philip Levine: A Profile," *Ploughshares* 33.4 (Winter 2007): 191–97. Steven R. Luebke's "Pictures of Our People: Jim Daniels' 'Digger' Poems" appears in *Wascana Review of Contemporary Poetry and Short Fiction* 37.2 (Fall 2002): 158–74; see also Janet Ruth Heller's "Growing Up in Detroit: Jim Daniels's *M-80*," *MidAmerica* 24 (1997): 122–32. Howard Nelson's "The Work of Antler" appears in *Twayne Companion to Contemporary Literature in English*, volume 1 (2002), edited by R. H. W. Dillard and Amanda Cockrell, 21–34. Jim Daniels has much to say about Antler and other poets in "Work Poetry and Working-Class Poetry: The Zip Code of the Heart," in *New Working-Class Studies* (2005), edited by John Russo and Sherry Lee Linkon (113–36). On Rust Belt literature, see Steven High's *Industrial Sunset: The Making of North America's Rust Belt, 1969–1984* (2003) and Asynith Helen Palmer's 2014 University of Michigan dissertation "Re-Constructing the Rust Belt: An Exploration of Industrial Ruin in Blogs, Fiction, and Poetry." The extensive bibliography on Aldo Leopold includes Bryan Norton's "Beyond Positivist Ecology: Toward an Integrated Ecological Ethics," *Sci-*

ence and Engineering Ethics 14.4 (December 2008): 581–92.

DENISE PILATO   EASTERN MICHIGAN UNIVERSITY

THEATRE.
See Regional Theatre

TRANSGENDER LITERATURE.
See Lesbian, Gay, Bisexual, Transgender and Queer Literature

TRIFLES
HISTORY: When she first staged and acted in *Trifles* on August 8, 1916, at the Provincetown Players' wharf theatre, playing the key role of Mrs. Hale, SUSAN KEATING GLASPELL (1876–1948) had published three novels and over thirty short stories, but she was making her first solo attempt at theatre writing, inspired by a murder trial near Indianola, IOWA, that she had covered for the *Des Moines Daily News* at the turn of the century. An accomplished journalist and fiction writer, Glaspell became a first-time playwright and actress in her late thirties when she wrote *Suppressed Desires* (1914) with her husband, GEORGE CRAM COOK (1873–1924), and later acted in it with him during the Provincetown Players' first season in 1915. Glaspell wrote thirteen more dramas, including the Pulitzer Prize–winning *Alison's House* (1930), but none of them have been as frequently staged, anthologized, adapted, or taught as this one-act play about an uprooted, isolated, culturally deprived farmwife, Minnie Wright, who strangles her husband, John, in their bed and whose kitchen becomes a text that reveals the motive for the crime and creates sympathy for the murderess as two simultaneous investigations take place on stage: an unsuccessful one conducted by the sheriff and the county attorney as they search fruitlessly at the crime scene for clues to Minnie's motivation, and a successful one conducted by the sheriff's wife, Mrs. Peters, and a neighboring farmwife, Mrs. Hale, who piece together the story of the murder from the "trifles" in Minnie's kitchen.

A few months after the play's debut, Frank Shay published it in *The Washington Square Plays* (1916). Subsequently, the play enjoyed a number of well-received productions in both the United States and Great Britain. In *Susan Glaspell: A Research*

Early production of *Trifles*, ca. 1916.
Billy Rose Theatre Division, the New York Public
Library for the Performing Arts, Astor, Lenox, and
Tilden Foundations

and Production Sourcebook (1993) Mary E. Papke reports that *Trifles* was staged by New York's Washington Square Players in 1916, at King's Hall in London in 1919, and by London's Pioneer Players in 1920 and was revived by the Provincetown Players in 1921 (20). In 1926 it was first mounted professionally in England at the Playhouse in Liverpool and was performed by the Dublin Drama League in 1927 (20). Always a favorite of little theatres and college/university theatre programs, *Trifles* was produced by the Players Club of Columbus, OHIO, in 1928 and the London People's Theatre (1930 and 1932) (20), as well as by many other nonprofessional theatre groups, and became one of the most frequently produced one-act plays in the history of American theatre. It was adapted as a film by Martha Moran in 1979 and by Pamela Gay Walker in 2009. John Bilotta and John F. McGrew adapted it as an opera that debuted in San Francisco in 2010.

SIGNIFICANCE: The world premiere of *Trifles* took place amid a storm of rallies, parades, lobbying efforts, and media blitzes by suffragists just four years before American women won the vote. Thus the feminist thrust of the play resonated especially strongly in Greenwich Village and Provincetown, where Glaspell and Cook launched their little-theatre venture. Here, Linda Ben-Zvi asserts in *Susan Glaspell: Her Life and Times* (2005), the artists, actors, and playwrights of the Provincetown Players lived their politics through their art, supporting the Paterson strike with a pageant, writing plays that advocated companionate marriage and birth control, advocating pacifism, and protesting America's entry into World War I in the pages of the leftist magazine *The Masses* (126). As a feminist-themed play, *Trifles* complements Glaspell's later works for the Provincetown Players: *Woman's Honor* (1918), which satirizes the gendered double standard of morality that undergirds patriarchy; *Chains of Dew* (1922), in which one of the main characters promotes birth control; and *The Verge* (1921), in which the female protagonist defies her husband, friend, and lover in her quest for self-fulfillment.

Trifles packs a powerful punch for a number of reasons. First, in the experience of her central character, Minnie Wright, Glaspell marries two complementary themes: the devastating effect of isolation on the Midwestern prairie and the oppressive marginalization of women—within marriage, within the community, and within American society as a whole. These themes are echoed in *A Window to the South* (1919) by WISCONSIN playwright Mary Katharine Reely (1881–1959); in *WINESBURG, OHIO* (1919) by SHERWOOD ANDERSON (1876–1941); in *Miss Lulu Bett* (1920), a novel by Wisconsin's ZONA GALE (1874–1938) that she later adapted as a Pulitzer Prize–winning play with the same title; in *MAIN STREET* (1920) by SINCLAIR LEWIS (1885–1951); in *GIANTS IN THE EARTH* (1927) by OLE EDVART RØLVAAG (1876–1931); and in *Old Jules* (1935) and the short story "The Vine," published in *Prairie Schooner* in 1927 by Nebraskan MARI(E SUSETTE) SANDOZ (1896–1966). Antecedents include *The Story of a Country Town* (1883) by EDGAR WATSON HOWE (1853–1937), *MAIN-TRAVELLED ROADS* (1891) by (HANNIBAL) HAMLIN GARLAND (1860–1940), and *SPOON RIVER ANTHOLOGY* (1915) by EDGAR LEE MASTERS (1868–1950). These works emphasize the squalor, cultural sterility, and drudgery of daily life on farms and in Midwestern small towns. They are classified as prairie realism and are associated with the REVOLT FROM THE VILLAGE.

Second, by never allowing Minnie Wright to appear onstage, Glaspell underscores her alienation, marginalized status, and vulnerability, a device that wins audience sympathy for Minnie and, later, for Mrs. Peters's and Mrs. Hale's legally subversive acts. Although Minnie is not present and, therefore, never utters a word, her disorderly kitchen—with its unwashed pans, dirty roller towels, half-finished sewing, and strangled pet canary—speaks volumes about her miserable existence with a taciturn, frugal farmer on a lonely Iowa farmstead. The sheriff's and the county attorney's disparaging remarks about Minnie's poor housekeeping ironically emphasize their blindness to the real clues in the kitchen and help solidify the growing bonds of sisterhood between the female characters.

Third, by putting a twist on the conventional murder mystery and focusing the audience's attention not on "whodunit" but on why and how, Glaspell emphasizes the limitations of Minnie's life that drove her to her deadly deed rather than the sensationalism of the actual murder. Also, by focusing on the questions of why and how Minnie murdered John, Glaspell is able to unfold two parallel murder investigations, pitting the sheriff and the county attorney against Mrs. Peters and Mrs. Hale in a battle of the sexes that the women ultimately win. That battle situates Minnie's loneliness and frustration as parts of larger problems endemic to patriarchal marriage: gendered power inequities and a legal system that renders half of the citizenry invisible and unheard.

Fourth, by centering the play on the women's inquiry rather than on the official investigation conducted by the men, Glaspell is able to demonstrate how the two women, although one is from the town and the other from the country, bond through a mutual discovery process that builds sisterhood and links them in complicity as they discuss what they have found, share experiences, come to understand why Minnie killed her husband, and hide what they have discovered from the men, thus improving Minnie's chances of acquittal. As they share their experiences of loneliness and deprivation as pioneer wives, they move from the personal to the political and participate in the first feminist consciousness-raising session in American theatre history.

Fifth, Trifles also stresses the differences between male and female ways of thinking, perceiving, valuing, and speaking and endorses the validity of the latter. While Mrs. Peters and Mrs. Hale work inductively, clue by clue, until they reach their conclusion and use their shared experiences of isolation and deprivation to come to their decision, the sheriff and the county attorney employ a different logic, avoiding the kitchen, concentrating on the crime scene in the bedroom, and working deductively with known facts, direct evidence, and the letter of the law. Their statements are authoritative, assertive, direct, and sometimes officious and condescending, while indirection, fragmentation, non sequitur, hesitation, and ellipsis characterize the women's speech.

There was little scholarly discussion of Trifles until the 1970s. Subsequent decades have witnessed a veritable explosion of scholarship on Trifles and its analogue, the short story "A Jury of Her Peers," primarily from feminist and legal studies perspectives; the play and the short story are the subjects of over ninety journal articles. Notable among these are discussions of Trifles and "Jury" that have appeared in ten legal journals; these scholars share the belief that Glaspell's critique goes beyond demonstrating the inequities of patriarchy to show how the legal system itself is flawed. For Patricia L. Bryan, writing in the Stanford Law Review 49.6 (1997): 1293–1363, the Hossack trial on which "Jury" is based demonstrates how competing courtroom narratives use patriarchal social norms that elide the complexities of the case. Glaspell's story then raises questions about a legal system that allows some stories to be told and others not. In "Susan Glaspell's Trifles and 'A Jury of Her Peers': Woman Abuse in a Literary and Legal Context," Buffalo Law Review 45 (1997): 779–844, Marina Angel discusses the story as an enactment of what a group excluded from the legal system will do when that system threatens a member of the group. Angel points out that Mrs. Peters and Mrs. Hale use different facts to reach different moral and legal conclusions than do the sheriff and the county attorney, suggesting that the women's choice to hide the evidence of Minnie's motivation is an example of jury nullification. In "Invisible Victims: A Comparison of Susan Glaspell's 'A Jury of Her Peers' and Herman Melville's 'Bartleby the Scrivener,'" Cardozo Studies in Law and Literature 8 (1996): 203–49, Robin West argues that "Jury" demonstrates how the law makes certain kinds of suffering invisible, such as Minnie's emotional abuse by her husband; "Jury" brings this process of legitimation to the forefront and allows this victim of legitimated harm to be heard.

Feminist scholarship on *Trifles* is voluminous. In "Small Things Reconsidered: 'A Jury of Her Peers,'" in Linda Ben-Zvi's 1995 *Susan Glaspell: Essays on Her Theatre and Fiction* (49–69), Elaine Hedges provides a historical context for the play that emphasizes what life was like for rural women at the turn of the century in order to make *Trifles* more accessible to contemporary audiences. Linda Ben-Zvi's "'Murder, She Wrote': The Genesis of Susan Glaspell's *Trifles*" in the same collection analyzes the relationship between the newspaper stories Glaspell published on the trial and the play she wrote fifteen years later (19–48). In "Silent Justice in a Different Key: Glaspell's *Trifles*," *Midwest Quarterly* 44.3 (Spring 2003): 282–90, Suzy Holstein focuses on the conflict between the male and female modes of perception that governs the action of *Trifles,* arguing that because the male and female characters perceive the Wrights' home space differently, they come to different ethical positions and decisions about the case. In "Susan Glaspell's *Trifles* and 'A Jury of Her Peers': Feminine Reading and Communication," *Tennessee Philological Bulletin* 36 (1999): 37–48, Janet Grose compares *Trifles* and "Jury" and argues that the differences between the story and the play suggest that Glaspell intended to emphasize patriarchal oppression in *Trifles* and feminine communication in "Jury."

IMPORTANT EDITIONS: No typescript or manuscript of *Trifles* or "Jury" exists; the version of *Trifles* published in *Plays by Susan Glaspell* (1920) was considered the standard version until 2010, when Linda Ben-Zvi and J. Ellen Gainor published *Susan Glaspell: The Complete Plays,* which, of course, includes Glaspell's most famous play. *Trifles* was also published in London by Ernest Benn in *Trifles, and Six Other Short Plays* (1926). Since that time it has been included in over sixty anthologies and books on playwriting. It is taught in classes in play analysis, introduction to theatre, feminism and theatre, American drama, introduction to literature, and American women writers, as well as surveys of American literature.

Glaspell adapted *Trifles* as a short story, "A Jury of Her Peers," and published it in *Every Week* on March 5, 1917. Subsequently, the story appeared on pages 256–82 of Edward J. O'Brien's *Best Short Stories of 1917* (1917), in John Updike and Katrina Kenison's *The Best American Short Stories of the Century* (1999), and in over thirty other anthologies to date. It was published in book form by Ernest Benn in London in 1927 as part of Benn's Yellow Books series. In 1961 "Jury" was an episode on *Alfred Hitchcock Presents.* In 1980 Sally Heckel adapted the story as a film, which was nominated for an Academy Award. "Jury" is taught in criminal law, civil procedure, and law and literature classes in more than fifteen law schools.

FURTHER READING: Glaspell tells the story of how she came to write *Trifles* in her biography of George Cram Cook, *A Road to the Temple* (1927). Helene Deutsch and Stella Hanau (press agents for the Experimental Theatre, a group that evolved from the original Provincetown Players) also comment on the play's success in *The Provincetown: A Story of the Theatre* (1931), noting that "it has been translated into the language of every country where women murder their husbands" (14). Edna Kenton, a member of the Provincetown Players' Executive Committee, tells the story of how *Trifles* came to be written in her chronicle of the Provincetown Players, *The Provincetown Players and the Playwrights' Theatre, 1915–1922* (2004); the book features facsimiles of the group's original playbills, including that of its 1921 revival of *Trifles.*

Theatre critics of the era were enthusiastic about the play. Heywood Broun, reviewing the Washington Square Players' production for the November 14, 1916, *New York Times* in "Best Bill Seen at the Comedy: Washington Square Players Set New Mark in Skill," called the play "a striking illustration of the effect which may be produced by . . . indirection" (7); Arthur Hornblow in "Mr. Hornblow Goes to the Play: The Washington Square Players," *Theatre Magazine* 25 (January 1917): 21–24, called it "an ingenious study in feminine ability at inductive and deductive analysis. In *"Bushido* the Climax of the Washington Square Players' Finest Program,'" the *New York*

Times reviewer praised the play on November 14, 1916, as intensely moving but called it "a spare, little tragedy" and "a bleak little tragedy" (8). On November 25, 1916, in "New Attractions for New York Playgoers: Washington Square Players," the *New York Dramatic Mirror* critic remarked on Glaspell's skill in developing suspense and sustaining tension throughout the play (7).

Mary E. Papke's *Susan Glaspell: A Resource and Production Sourcebook* (1993) provides an excellent production and reception history of *Trifles,* as well as of Glaspell's other works. Marcia Noe's *Susan Glaspell: Voice from the Heartland* (1983), Barbara Ozieblo's *Susan Glaspell: A Critical Biography* (2000), and Linda Ben-Zvi's *Susan Glaspell: Her Life and Times* (2005) are three biographies that discuss *Trifles* within the context of Glaspell's life, Midwestern upbringing, and cultural milieu. Readers interested in the particulars of the Margaret Hossack murder trial on which *Trifles* is based can find them in Patricia L. Bryan and Thomas Wolf's *Midnight Assassin: A Murder in America's Heartland* (2005). J. Ellen Gainor's *Susan Glaspell in Context: American Theater, Culture, and Politics 1915–48* (2001), Kristina Hinz-Bode's *Susan Glaspell and the Anxiety of Expression: Language and Isolation in the Plays* (2006), and Barbara Ozieblo and Jerry R. Dickey's *Susan Glaspell and Sophie Treadwell* (2008) contain chapters on *Trifles.*

Key essays include Linda Ben-Zvi's "Murder She Wrote: The Genesis of Susan Glaspell's 'Trifles'" in the 1995 collection she edited, *Susan Glaspell: Essays on Her Theatre and Fiction,* 19–48; Elaine Hedges's "Small Things Reconsidered: 'A Jury of Her Peers'" in the same collection, 49–69; Janet Grose's "Susan Glaspell's *Trifles* and 'A Jury of Her Peers': Feminine Reading and Communication," *Tennessee Philological Bulletin* 36 (1999): 37–48; Suzy Holstein's "Silent Justice in a Different Key: Glaspell's *Trifles,*" *Midwest Quarterly* 44.3 (Spring 2003): 282–90; Marina Angel's "Susan Glaspell's *Trifles* and 'A Jury of Her Peers': Woman Abuse in a Literary and Legal Context," *Buffalo Law Review* 45 (1997): 779–844; Robin West's "Invisible Victims: A Comparison of Susan Glaspell's 'A Jury of Her Peers' and Herman Melville's 'Bartleby the Scrivener,'" *Cardozo Studies in Law and Literature* 8 (1996): 203–49; and Patricia L. Bryan's "Stories in Fiction and in Fact: Susan Glaspell's 'A Jury of Her Peers' and the 1901 Murder Trial of Margaret Hossack," *Stanford Law Review* 49.6 (1997): 1293–1363. The Susan Glaspell Society website includes news of current productions, notices of upcoming conferences that feature panels on Glaspell's work, and bibliographies of primary and secondary sources.

MARCIA NOE
THE UNIVERSITY OF TENNESSEE AT CHATTANOOGA

UNIVERSITY OF IOWA WRITERS' WORKSHOP.

See Iowa Writers' Workshop

URBAN LITERATURE

OVERVIEW: In the rich body of urban literature from the Midwest, the city is not a neutral setting; it is a powerful environment that strongly influences the destinies of its residents. In much of this literature the city, most often CHICAGO, is presented as a materialistic dynamo, a force that can corrupt or strengthen, enslave or liberate, destroy or enrich, but one that is not passive, gentle, or genteel. It is a setting where human beings can triumph or suffer defeat, but they cannot expect a life of repose. For better or worse, the urban Midwest in literature is a challenging environment, a crucible for success or failure.

This image of the Midwestern city is a major element in American literature of the late nineteenth and early twentieth centuries, most notably in the Chicago novels of (HERMAN) THEODORE DREISER (1871–1945), the poetry of CARL (AUGUST) SANDBURG (1878–1967), and the midland city works of (NEWTON) BOOTH TARKINGTON (1869–1946). During this era Americans questioned the benefits of unbridled capitalism and fast-paced industrialization, and Midwestern cities—unlike cultured Boston, staid Philadelphia, or even the aristocratic New York of Edith Wharton—were prime examples of the exciting and often dangerous dynamism of the rapidly changing nation. Thus authors striving to come to terms with America's transformation turned to the Midwest as a setting and subject for their work.

During the mid-twentieth century the Midwestern city survived as an element in the works of both African American and

European American authors who sought to depict the individual's struggle to survive in the urban environment. In the literature of NELSON ALGREN (1909–1981), RICHARD WRIGHT (1908–1960), and SAUL (C.) BELLOW (1915–2005), Chicago remains the raw edge of urbanism.

HISTORY AND SIGNIFICANCE: During the early nineteenth century residents of the Midwest's nascent cities sought to develop a literature that expressed the spirit of the lands west of the Appalachians and to prove to Easterners that civilization could flourish along the Ohio River and the Great Lakes. Lyceums, clubs dedicated to all manner of intellectual endeavors, and short-lived literary periodicals proliferated, especially in CINCINNATI, the hub of western American culture in the antebellum period. Pioneering Midwestern literature focuses, however, on the natural features of the region, its forests and prairies, or on its exciting frontier origins, as well as on the clash between Native Americans and the agents of transformation, the frontiersmen. Although trans-Appalachian authors wrote in cities, few of them wrote about cities. A number of guidebooks, directories, and early local histories, however, did extol the commercial progress and future material glories of Midwestern cities, thus anticipating the importance of BUSINESS and the entrepreneurial spirit in the later urban literature of the region. Moreover, early Midwestern poets occasionally presented themes repeated in future works. For example, "The Old Mound," a lengthy poem by Cincinnati's Charles A. Jones (1815–1851), describes a prehistoric earthwork set amid the encroaching city of Cincinnati, a remnant of the primeval past trapped in the bustling urban present. As in later Midwestern works, the city is an aggressive, profane entity, contrasting sharply with the sacred, ancient burial mound.

By the late nineteenth century the region's forests and prairies were fast yielding to its burgeoning cities, a phenomenon that Midwestern writers could not ignore. Chicago especially was the wonder of the nation, the world's greatest railroad center, famed for the lethal efficiency of its meatpacking houses and its cutthroat trading in agricultural commodities. The city's newspapers were the breeding ground for a new generation of writers whose job was to report the realities of this sprawling, brawling metropolis. The *Chicago Daily News* became famous for its staff of writers, led by the popular columnist EUGENE FIELD (SR.) (1850–1895), who is remembered today primarily as the author of children's poetry. In his witty column "Sharps and Flats" Field enjoyed puncturing pretensions and applying down-to-earth common sense rather than high-toned literary posturing to the emerging urban scene.

Also among Chicago's newspaper columnists were humorists FINLEY PETER DUNNE (1867–1936) and GEORGE ADE (1866–1944). Against the backdrop of urban labor conflict, political corruption, and capitalist greed, Dunne's Irish dialect-speaking character, Mr. Dooley, presents newspaper readers with cracker-barrel wisdom, though not in the setting of a crossroads general store but appropriately in an urban tavern frequented by Irish immigrants. Ade's short stories tell of the life of common folks attempting to carve out a niche for themselves in the big city. A striving office boy, a colorful purveyor of tall tales at a down-at-the-heels hotel, and an African American bootblack are all the stuff of his humor. Moreover, his immensely popular *Fables in Slang* (1900) and subsequent volumes express satiric insights in the argot of Chicago's masses. Although Ade's humor is warm and reassuring to urban readers, his language is as modern and fast paced as the Chicago packinghouses.

In the 1890s a number of novelists also attempted to interpret the new spirit of the Midwestern metropolis, creating a scenario that was repeated in one Chicago novel after another during the following quarter century. These novels describe the travails and triumphs of Chicagoans who seek success in the city but suffer the debilitating effects of their material pursuit. The making of money is a dominant theme, and Mammon's mecca is Chicago. *The Cliff-Dwellers* (1893) by HENRY BLAKE FULLER (1857–1929) is a notable example of the type. It deals with the denizens of the eighteen-story Clifton Building, a Chicago skyscraper whose "cliff-dwellers" are dedicated to making money. The novel's protagonist, George Ogden, is a recent arrival from New England who fails

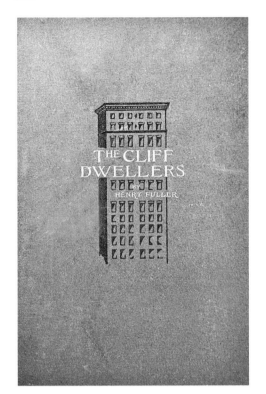

Henry Blake Fuller's *The Cliff-Dwellers*.
Harper & Bros., 1893.
Image courtesy of Special Collections, Grand Valley
State University Libraries

in his pursuit of financial success, in part because of the extravagance of a social-climbing wife. Among the characters is the ruthless financier Erastus Brainard, described by Fuller as "merely a financial appliance—one of the tools of the trade," a person for whom business is everything (38).

Fuller continued his indictment of Mammon-worshipping, social-climbing Chicagoans two years later in *With the Procession* (1895). This novel deals with an old, well-to-do Chicago family that has failed to keep up with the social procession and belatedly attempts to reestablish itself in the city's elite social circle. The effort proves disastrous for the family as Fuller once again computes the heavy toll materialism and vain ambition levy on Chicagoans. One of the novel's characters sums up Fuller's critical vision of the great Midwestern metropolis when he observes, "It is the only great city in the world to which all its citizens have come for the one common avowed object of making money. There you have its genesis, its growth, its end and object" (University of Chicago Press edition 203).

University of Chicago professor ROBERT HERRICK (1868-1938) agreed, describing the devastating effect of the city's materialism and acquisitive greed in a series of novels published during the first decade of the twentieth century. In *The Web of Life* (1900), *The Common Lot* (1904), and *The Memoirs of an American Citizen* (1905), Herrick views Chicago as a city dominated by an overpowering passion to succeed that corrupts the souls and erodes the morality of its residents. A character in *The Common Lot* concludes that Chicago "throttled the finer aspirations of men like a remorseless giant, converting its youth into iron-clawed beasts of prey, answering to one hoarse cry, 'Success, Success, Success!'"(406). In that same novel a critic of the prevailing materialism symbolized by Chicago proclaims, "We measure everything by one yardstick, and that is money" (55). Moreover, the product of this material striving is an ugly city. According to *The Web of Life*, "No other city on the globe could present quite this combination of tawdriness, slackness, dirt, vulgarity" (198-99).

With its reputation for fast-paced commercial growth and relentless pursuit of wealth, Chicago became a favorite subject for authors who sought to express America's growing doubts about the race for financial gain and worldly success. Novelists who had never lived in Chicago or had left the city chose the Midwestern metropolis as the appropriate setting for their tales of ambition and material survival. The most notable was Theodore Dreiser, who lived in Chicago for a short time as a teenager and returned as a young newspaper reporter before moving on to New York City. Although he was no longer a Chicago resident, Dreiser repeatedly turned to that great Midwestern hub as a locale for his novels of amoral striving.

In *SISTER CARRIE* (1900) Carrie Meeber comes to Chicago from a small town in WISCONSIN and finds a city of sharp material contrasts, with magnificent department stores full of tempting merchandise and harsh factories exploiting poorly paid workers who are barely able to survive. Rather than remain in the ranks of the downtrodden workers, Carrie becomes the mistress of a slick traveling salesman and then the lover of a wealthier married man. Her ultimate success comes as an actress in New York City after she leaves Chicago. But the Midwest metropolis opens her eyes to the material realities of the world and thus serves a vital purpose in her rise to success.

In Dreiser's *Jennie Gerhardt* (1911) the protagonist also finds material security in the Windy City by living out of wedlock with a wealthy man, and in *The Titan* (1914), as in *The Financier* (1912) and *The Stoic* (1947), Dreiser recounts the career of Chicago streetcar magnate Frank Cowperwood, a man who lives almost wholly for sex and success. *The Titan* alternates between tales of his sexual conquests and accounts of his shrewd triumphs over business foes, accomplished largely through political corruption. In each of the Dreiser novels, Chicago is portrayed as a city where characters are liberated from their pasts and are able to pursue their material goals with little concern for traditional morality.

(BENJAMIN) FRANK(LIN) NORRIS (JR.) (1870-1902) was born in Chicago but spent most of his adult life in California. Yet he too turned to Chicago as the setting for *The Pit* (1903), his novel on the corrupting mania of greed. In this work Norris's protagonist, Curtis Jadwin, falls prey to an addiction for dealing in wheat futures at Chicago's Board of Trade. In the novel Chicago is depicted as a city that crushes men with cruel indifference, and Norris describes "the pile of the Board of Trade Building" at night as "black, grave, monolithic, crouching on its foundations, like a monstrous sphinx with blind eyes" (41). In the minds of Norris and many of his contemporaries, the city and its financial institutions were monsters indiscriminately destroying unwary human victims drawn to them by a desire to make money.

Neither UPTON (BEALL) SINCLAIR (JR.) (1878-1968) nor WILLA CATHER (1873-1947) were Chicagoans, but both used the Midwestern metropolis as a setting for their works in which the protagonists strive to get ahead. Seeking to promote socialism, Sinclair set *THE JUNGLE* (1906) in Chicago's exploitative packinghouse district and described the tra-

vails of working-class Lithuanian immigrants. In Sinclair's work Chicago is a town that not only slaughters pigs and cattle but sacrifices human beings as well for the sake of satisfying the capitalist craving for profits. In Cather's *The Song of the Lark* (1915) Chicago is more benign. It does not destroy the protagonist but instead nurtures her desire for fame and fortune. As in Dreiser's *Sister Carrie,* Chicago is a setting in which one can escape the small-town past and take the decisive first steps toward fulfilling one's ambition. Cather's heroine, Thea Kronborg, is an ambitious young woman from a small town in Colorado who comes to Chicago to study music and while there forms a liaison with a married man. After moving on to New York City and Europe, Kronborg achieves fame as an opera singer. For Thea, as for Carrie, Chicago is the portal through which she must pass to achieve success, a fertile ground for ambition and a liberating atmosphere freeing one from the crippling limitations and traditional restraints of the village. See REVOLT FROM THE VILLAGE.

During the second decade of the twentieth century Americans were not only writing about Chicago; they were also writing in Chicago. This was the decade of the CHICAGO RENAISSANCE, when writers flocked to the Midwestern metropolis and achieved the success so many of their fictional characters seek. Chicagoan HARRIET MONROE (1860-1936) founded *POETRY: A MAGAZINE OF VERSE* in 1912, which became renowned for publishing some of the most distinguished poetry of the era. MARGARET C. ANDERSON (1886-1973) edited the *LITTLE REVIEW,* an avant-garde periodical that won a reputation for defying convention. During this same decade EDGAR LEE MASTERS (1868-1950), a Chicago lawyer, published *SPOON RIVER ANTHOLOGY* (1915), and poet (NICHOLAS) VACHEL LINDSAY (1879-1931) frequented the city. The literati gathered at the 57th Street studio-residence of critic-novelist FLOYD DELL (1887-1969) and his wife, Margery Currey (1877-1959), sharing in the intellectual ferment of the Windy City. By the close of the decade the critic H(enry) L(ewis) Mencken (1880-1956) was declaring Chicago the literary capital of America and the source of the nation's best and most innovative literature.

A number of authors living in Chicago during this second decade of the century continued to portray the city as a catalyst for ambition and material strife. Before achieving fame for his sketches of the Midwestern small town in WINESBURG, OHIO (1919), SHERWOOD ANDERSON (1876–1941) published two novels set in part in Chicago. In *Windy McPherson's Son* (1916) the protagonist, like many other fictional characters of the era, comes to Chicago from a small town, pursues his ambition, and makes a fortune, but he does not find satisfaction in his success. In *Marching Men* (1917) Anderson's chief character leaves his small-town home for a Chicago torn by class strife and labor unrest. The novel's protagonist leads a rising corps of marching men who might possibly impose a new order on the harsh, chaotic city. In both of these works Chicago is a divided, dissatisfying product of large-scale industrialization and cutthroat urbanization. It is the prime example of what is wrong with early twentieth-century America.

The preeminent poet of the Chicago Renaissance and the most significant molder of the city's image was Carl Sandburg. His *CHICAGO POEMS* (1916) expresses the spirit, squalor, and tough reality of the city in language that is simple and unpoetic and thus suitable to a metropolis seen as the antithesis of genteel. Most notably, his title poem, "Chicago," reiterates the city's image presented in the works of Dreiser and Norris but does so with straightforward force and vigor so memorable that its lines have become among the best known in American verse. Sandburg's Chicago is the "Hog Butcher for the World," the "City of the Big Shoulders," a proud, lively, coarse city, fierce, cunning, active, and savage (1). It can break weak souls, but at the same time it is a mecca for the strong and ambitious. Sandburg's poem transcends art and becomes an icon of the Midwestern metropolis. Just as Grant Wood's *American Gothic* became the renowned visual symbol of the rural Midwest, Sandburg's "Chicago" indelibly branded its image of the great heartland city on the American mind.

Although most of the Midwest's significant urban literature of the early twentieth century was set in Chicago, writers elsewhere in America's heartland were also attempting to interpret the urban scene. Most notably, Indianapolis's Booth Tarkington authored a series of novels that record the social history of the urbanizing Midwest. In his Growth trilogy he traces the trials of families adapting to the rapid urbanization of a Midwestern city, usually assumed to be Tarkington's lifelong home, Indianapolis. As in many Chicago novels, the making of money is seen as the engine that drives his midland city, and the inexorable advance of material "progress" mows down any resistant individual in its path. Growth and its by-product, profit, are the dominant goals of urban Midwesterners, a fact that characters in Tarkington's novels must accept.

Tarkington's symbol of urban growth is the smoke that hangs as a pall over the midland cities, a constant reminder that they are places where one makes money. In the opening line of the first novel in the trilogy, *The Turmoil* (1915), Tarkington describes his midland city as both wonderful and dirty, set in a fog of smoke. According to Tarkington, the smoke is the breath of a giant panting for ever more money, a monster created by the great American god of Bigness. Cities need to grow bigger; that is the imperative of American urbanization, for bigness means money. Never a dismal novelist, Tarkington did not present his characters as doomed to an intolerable urban existence; however, he saw that they must adapt and make their peace as best they can with the consuming drive for material bigness.

The finest and most famous novel in the trilogy, *The Magnificent Ambersons* (1918), tells of a prominent family whose fortunes decline as their midland town grows into an industrial city. Everyone acquainted with the family eagerly looks forward to spoiled, arrogant George Amberson Minafer getting his comeuppance, and by the end of the novel he has suffered this fate. But no individual gives George his comeuppance; instead, he is cut down by the growth of the city, which destroys the family's wealth and the genteel way of life characteristic of its magnificent heyday.

Tarkington's *Alice Adams* (1921) was originally intended to be part of the trilogy of the midland city, although in the finished novel the protagonist is primarily a victim of her overweening quest for social status rather than a hapless individual forced to adapt to bigness and growth. Yet the social aspirations of the lower-middle-class Adams family depend on the expected profits from a malodorous glue factory; smoke and stench mark the path to success. Once the glue factory fails, Alice is forced to relinquish her dreams of social magnificence and enroll in a secretarial school. As in *The Magnificent Ambersons,* expectations of gentility yield to the commercial realities of the Midwestern city.

In the urban works of Tarkington and other Midwestern writers before 1930, the fictional characters are generally native-born whites fighting a battle for money, fame, and social success. Ethnicity and inter-ethnic conflict are not prominent elements in the fictional urban melee. Even in Sinclair's *The Jungle* the Lithuanians are depicted as victims of capitalism rather than disadvantaged because of their ethnicity or immigrant status. After 1930, however, ethnic identity plays a larger role in Chicago novels; the participants in the harsh struggle for material survival or success speak with an accent.

This ethnic component is evident in the novels of JAMES T(HOMAS) FARRELL (1904–1979), most notably in his *STUDS LONIGAN* trilogy (1932-1935). It deals with a young lower-middle-class man from Chicago's South Side and covers his life from his parochial school graduation to his death fifteen years later. The Lonigan family holds on precariously to respectability and a modest prosperity in an insular world defined by Catholic parishes and threatened by Jews, blacks, and other non-Irish groups poised to move into the neighborhood. In the second volume of the trilogy young Studs's life centers on a neighborhood gang whose toughness, shallowness, vulgarity, and corruption are a reflection in microcosm of the attributes of the city of broad shoulders as a whole. Eventually the invasion of blacks displaces the Lonigans, who resettle in a new neighborhood farther south. Moreover, the Great Depression of the 1930s ruins both father and son financially. The Lonigans' parochial world succumbs to the inexorable change of the city and the worldwide collapse of capitalism. Just as urban growth patterns and economic change doom the magnificent Ambersons, leaving their mansion in a decaying neighborhood of boardinghouses and apartment buildings, so the outward spread of "undesirable" ethnic groups and the uncontrollable fortunes of the marketplace shatter the Lonigans' more modest American dream.

Studs Lonigan may be a tough guy, but he is not nearly as tough as the characters in the novels of another Chicagoan, Nelson Algren. Like Farrell, Algren focused on life in the ethnic neighborhoods, socially far removed from the players in Norris's Pit or the city's Frank Cowperwoods. Yet the same raw spirit of striving and exploitative sexuality prevails among Algren's working-class Polish Americans as is evident in Dreiser's Cowperwood. Most notably, in *Never Come Morning* (1942) and *The Man with the Golden Arm* (1949) the lives of Algren's white ethnics are as harsh and violent as those in the city's famed stockyards. The protagonists are young gang member and aspiring boxer Bruno Bicek and card dealer Frankie Machine, both of whom commit murder. At the end of *Never Come Morning* Bicek is headed for the electric chair, confirming his belief that he will never live to be twenty-one. In *The Man with the Golden Arm* Frankie commits suicide by hanging himself in a cheap flophouse. Although Algren was writing in the traditional Chicago spirit, he surpassed all his predecessors in his raw, brutal portrait of Chicago life. Studs Lonigan at least lives until he is twenty-nine; in Algren's Chicago few survive to twenty-one.

In *Chicago: City on the Make* (1951) Algren elaborates on his vision of the great Midwestern metropolis. Dedicated to Carl Sandburg, this prose poem perpetuates a Sandburgian image of Chicago as a hustler's town where the sharper's spirit of cunning and gouging is alive, a tough city that is typically American in its grit. Generations of Chicago writers have agreed with Algren. No other city seems a better setting for tales of those seeking, and often failing, to fulfill the American Dream.

Whereas Farrell wrote of Chicago's Irish and Algren of its Poles, Saul Bellow portrayed his fellow Jews in the Midwestern metropolis. A Chicagoan of immigrant parentage who viewed his hometown as the hub of harsh materialism, Bellow followed in Dreiser's footsteps in depicting the tough, moneymaking city on Lake Michigan. In the opening line of Bellow's THE ADVENTURES OF AUGIE MARCH (1953), the protagonist expresses the familiar spirit of Chicago literature, describing himself as an American, born in Chicago, who does things his own way. For Bellow, like many of his predecessors, no one was more American than a Chicagoan who strove to achieve with tough determination in the somber, often threatening, city. Although it was his home for much of his life and an integral part of his Nobel Prize–winning literature, Bellow's Chicago was no place for a devotee of high culture or a sensitive, contemplative soul. Instead, it was a city suited to the crass and corrupt. In his story "Zetland: By a Character Witness" Bellow depicts Chicago as empty, without substance, a stopover for the nation's trains and a place to fill mail orders but arid in art and intellect. As the intellectual protagonist reads Keats on the public lagoon, Polish children along the shore throw crab apples and stones. Throughout Bellow's work one finds this contrast between intellect and the brutal and material as represented by Chicago.

While Farrell, Algren, and Bellow depicted white ethnics in the mecca of brutal materialism, a number of African American writers were inserting their race into the Chicago formula and portraying the plight of blacks in a city that seemed to promise rewards but too often handed out only defeat. The most notable black Chicago novelist was Richard Wright, whose NATIVE SON (1940) is a classic portrayal of a young African American, Bigger Thomas, and his destruction in the white city of the big shoulders. Set in a bitterly cold Chicago winter when white snow smothers the black sooty slums, Native Son is a story of frustrated aspirations, murder, and desperate flight from punishment. In the end protagonist Bigger Thomas, like Algren's Bruno Bicek, is headed for the electric chair. He too does not survive Chicago until his twenty-first birthday.

Black poet GWENDOLYN BROOKS (1917–2000) and African American playwright LORRAINE HANSBERRY (1930–1965) did not present such a brutal or disheartening picture of Chicago, but their portrait of the city accorded with literary tradition. Brooks's A STREET IN BRONZEVILLE (1945) depicts the everyday material life of habitués of South Side taverns and pool halls and occupants of inexpensive kitchenette apartments who survive dry, gray lives devoted to paying the rent and feeding the family. The Younger family in Hansberry's A RAISIN IN THE SUN (1959) finds its dreams of a new home compromised by the corrupt greed of a black man the son had trusted and the racism of whites seeking to keep the family out of their neighborhood. Although race is the principal subject of the drama, Chicago plays its traditional role as an especially tough place for those striving to better themselves. Chicagoans are portrayed as especially bad "peckerwoods" who pose a particularly formidable threat to blacks attempting to get ahead.

White migrants from the South also found the Midwestern city a cold, harsh place destructive of their dreams. Although (Thomas Lanier) Tennessee Williams (III) (1911–1983) was a self-proclaimed Southerner, he was raised and educated in the Midwest, living for over two decades in ST. LOUIS, a town he loathed and called St. Pollution. The smoke-ridden MISSOURI metropolis was the setting for his most famous work set in the Midwest, *The Glass Menagerie* (1945) In this play the Wingfield family lives on an alley in St. Louis, inhabiting a grim tenement across from a cheap, gaudy urban dance hall. Far removed from their genteel origins in the South, they survive uneasily in the industrialized Midwest, working in a shoe warehouse, selling magazine subscriptions, and, like Alice Adams, reduced to attending secretarial school, that training ground for a common commercial existence. They await gentleman callers for the daughter, but there are no gentlemen in the hustling material world of the Midwestern city.

Williams's Laura Wingfield takes refuge in her menagerie of glass animals. Gertie Nevels, the Southern white protagonist of THE DOLLMAKER (1954), a novel by HARRIETTE SIMPSON ARNOW (1908–1986), finds herself equally misplaced in industrial DETROIT, a Midwestern monument to American capitalism second only to Chicago. In the hellish, exploitative atmosphere of the Motor City, Gertie finds escape whittling a Christ image from wood. For both authors, commercial gain is the business of the Midwestern city; it is no place for unassimilated souls from the preindustrial South who collect fragile glass or fashion spiritual symbols.

During the last third of the twentieth century Midwestern cities seemed a less appropriate setting for novels or dramas concerned with the battle to succeed and the realization of material dreams. Rust-belt Chicago's big shoulders were sagging, and few young people from small towns were converging on St. Louis or Detroit in search of their fortunes. Poet JIM (JAMES RAYMOND) DANIELS (b. 1956) worked in the Sandburg tradition by writing of the material realities of the working class in the Detroit region, and ELMORE (JOHN) LEONARD JR. (1925-2013) used Detroit as the locale for his urban crime novels that perpetuate the tough, corrupt image long associated with the Midwestern metropolis of Chicago. Playwright DAVID (ALAN) MAMET (b. 1947) is perhaps the most highly regarded Chicago writer of his generation, and in keeping with the tradition of Norris, Sinclair, and Dreiser, he uses the ILLINOIS metropolis as a setting for plays that portray the brutal, competitive avarice of American capitalism. Most notably, in *Glengarry Glen Ross* (1984) Mamet presents the dog-eat-dog struggle to survive and succeed among real estate salesmen. In this play Chicago remains the capital of brutal materialism, a place where so many writers have tested American capitalism and the much-vaunted American material Dream and found them wanting. See also *AMERICAN BUFFALO*.

SELECTED WORKS: Henry Blake Fuller's *The Cliff-Dwellers* (1893) and *With the Procession* (1895) are classic Chicago novels dealing with striving for financial and social success. The three most significant Chicago novels by Robert Welch Herrick (1868-1938) are *The Web of Life* (1900), *The Common Lot* (1904), and *The Memoirs of an American Citizen* (1905). Other significant early 1900s novels set in Chicago are Theodore Dreiser's *Sister Carrie* (1900) and *The Titan* (1914), Frank Norris's *The Pit* (1903), Upton Sinclair's *The Jungle* (1906), and Willa Cather's *The Song of*

the Lark (1915). Carl Sandburg's *Chicago Poems* (1916) presents a notable portrait of the city and its people. Booth Tarkington's Growth trilogy dealing with Midwestern urbanization and its impact consists of *The Turmoil* (1915), *The Magnificent Ambersons* (1918), and *The Midlander* (1924). The three novels in James T. Farrell's *Studs Lonigan* trilogy are *Young Lonigan* (1932), *The Young Manhood of Studs Lonigan* (1934), and *Judgment Day* (1935). The principal Chicago novels of Nelson Algren are *Never Come Morning* (1942) and *The Man with the Golden Arm* (1949). Among Saul Bellow's works with Chicago settings are *The Adventures of Augie March* (1953), *Herzog* (1964), *Humboldt's Gift* (1975), *The Dean's December* (1982), and the stories "Zetland: By a Character Witness," "A Silver Dish," and "Cousins" from *Him with His Foot in His Mouth, and Other Stories* (1984). The most important African American Chicago novel is Richard Wright's *Native Son* (1940). An important volume of Gwendolyn Brooks's Chicago poetry is *A Street in Bronzeville* (1945). Lorraine Hansberry's fame rests primarily on *A Raisin in the Sun* (1959). The most famous play set in the urban Midwest, however, is Tennessee Williams's *The Glass Menagerie* (1945). The most distinguished Chicago playwright of the late twentieth century is David Mamet; his works include *American Buffalo* (copyright in 1976 and published in 1977) and *Glengarry Glen Ross* (1984).

FURTHER READING: Ronald Weber's *The Midwestern Ascendancy in American Writing* (1992) provides an overview of Midwestern literature. Robert C. Bray's *Rediscoveries: Literature and Place in Illinois* (1982) and James Hurt's *Writing Illinois: The Prairie, Lincoln, and Chicago* (1992) discuss the literature of the Midwest's most populous state. Clarence Andrews's *Michigan in Literature* (1992) surveys the literary history of MICHIGAN and includes a chapter on Detroit literature. Kenny J. Williams's *Prairie Voices: A Literary History of Chicago from the Frontier to 1893* (1980) examines literary efforts in nineteenth-century Chicago.

For a discussion of Chicago humorists of the late nineteenth and early twentieth centuries, see James DeMuth's *Small Town Chicago: The Comic Perspective of Finley Peter Dunne, George Ade, and Ring Lardne*r (1980).

Bernard Duffey's *The Chicago Renaissance in American Letters: A Critical History* (1954) surveys Chicago's literary heyday of the early twentieth century, as do Dale Kramer's *Chicago Renaissance: The Literary Life in the Midwest, 1900–1930* (1966) and Carl S. Smith's *Chicago and the American Literary Imagination, 1880–1920* (1984). Also useful on this subject is Kenny J. Williams's *A Storyteller and a City: Sherwood Anderson's Chicago* (1988). A basic resource for information on the Chicago Renaissance is Jan Pinkerton and Randolph H. Hudson's *Encyclopedia of the Chicago Literary Renaissance* (2004). Carla Cappetti's *Writing Chicago: Modernism, Ethnography, and the Novel* (1993) emphasizes the significance of urban sociology in the works of Farrell, Algren, and Wright.

JON C. TEAFORD   PURDUE UNIVERSITY

UTOPIAN LITERATURE

OVERVIEW: Utopian communities sprang up among the earliest colonies in North America and have continued throughout the United States to the present. Although the term suggests a place constructed under circumstances so perfect as to be impossible to achieve, people persist in making the attempt. Such communities—groups within larger societies that profess ideal values and often live exclusively and according to communal principles and structure—have existed for millennia around the world. The variety of causes for development, leadership styles, and values makes utopian communities difficult to characterize, but most consist of groups that exist as more or less independent units within larger societies. The amount of literature from and about utopian settlements in the Midwest is limited but worth considering. The history of such communities, the stressful conditions under which they were formed, the labor involved, and the transient nature of many explain in part why so little literary activity arose from them. Historical accounts, explanatory material such as brochures, and political and sociological studies dominate the materials available on Midwestern communal activities. In general, accounts by members tend to present the communities in their most positive light. Outsiders and those who became disillusioned and left tend to render them satirically or represent them as confining and repressive. Some historical fiction and biographies exist, and utopias and dystopias set in the Midwest appear in science fiction. Such places also offer prime vehicles for satire. Although one would expect that the hippie and alternative-lifestyle communes of the 1960s would have been fertile ground for *belles lettres*, they apparently produced little besides ephemera.

Among the authors of note writing utopian literature is WILLIAM DEAN HOWELLS (1837–1920), who grew up in OHIO; another, MARGE PIERCY (b. 1936), was born in DETROIT and spent many years in the Midwest. Communities that have given rise to literature include the Mormon settlements at Nauvoo, ILLINOIS, and on Beaver Island, MICHIGAN, and those at Harmony and New Harmony, INDIANA. Larger numbers of fictional works have described events, real or otherwise, that might have occurred at locations in the Midwest.

HISTORY AND SIGNIFICANCE: The colonists who arrived along North America's east coast in the early seventeenth century experimented with communalism, in which religious and social elements were to have interacted in ways Christians believed had characterized the early church in Rome, though with limited success and duration. In fact, Roger Williams founded his Rhode Island democracy in reaction against the theocracies of the Massachusetts Bay Puritans and the even more radical separatists of Plymouth. More immigrants arrived, some as members of groups, including Quakers and millennialists of various kinds. Some groups remained together and founded settlements. As the colonies grew and became independent, other groups and sects formed and broke away. For example, Unitarians gave birth to transcendentalists, and people with some associations with them formed the short-lived Brook Farm and Fruitlands. Still more societies came from abroad. The country expanded westward, and so did utopian communities.

Many such communities came to the Midwest, but most were short lived. Often drawn by charismatic leaders, they moved from the East, arrived from across the Atlantic, or simply established themselves and grew, continued west, or failed in the middle states. Some still exist; most have dissolved, having left their mark.

In the 1830s revelations Joseph Smith said he received gave him the status of a prophet to those who believed, and he led his small group of Mormons from Palmyra, New York, to Kirtland, Ohio, where the band solidified its religious and social doctrines, acquired property, and increased. Internal tensions and friction with outsiders, based partly on the practice of polygamy, led most members to move to locations in MISSOURI and then to Nauvoo, Illinois, where further problems developed. When Joseph and his brother Hyrum were murdered there in 1844, the majority of their followers went farther west with Brigham Young, while one smaller group went to Independence, Missouri, as the Reorganized Church of Jesus Christ of Latter-Day Saints and another to WISCONSIN and then to Beaver Island in Lake Michigan. Its leader, James Strang, who called himself King, was also murdered, and the members scattered. The other Mormon groups, however, continue to grow in strength and numbers, though few remain in communal situations.

The Mormon settlements on Beaver Island, Michigan, and at Nauvoo, Illinois, stimulated books of historical fiction. Both the practice of polygamy and the violent events on Beaver Island prompted such authors as JAMES OLIVER CURWOOD (1878–1927) to dramatize the reign of James Strang and his breakaway Mormon group in *The Courage of Captain Plum* (1908). Less well-known books such as *Harem Island: The Astounding True Story of a Self-Proclaimed Saint Who Made Religion a Business and Turned Sin into a Virtue* (1961) by Eugene Lee Caesar (1927–1986), the juvenile novel *Pirate of the Pine Lands: Being the Adventures of Young Tom Lansing Afloat and Ashore on the Michigan Frontier in the Years 1852 to 1854, and Particularly His Part in the Historic Matter of King James Strang, the Notorious Great Lakes Pirate, Told Here by Himself from Memory* (1929) by Karl William Detzer (1891–1987), and *The Stranger on the Island* (1933) by (JOSEPH) BRAND WHITLOCK (1869–1934) sensationalize the rise and fall of the Beaver Island colony. Virginia Sorensen (1912–1991), who left the Mormon Church, portrays issues that Mormons face in *A Little*

Lower than the Angels (1942). Authors who are Mormons paint brighter pictures of Nauvoo's history. *Saints* (1984) by Orson Scott Card (b. 1951) takes place there; the *Trust Williams Trilogy* (1999–2000) by Robert Farrell Smith (b. 1970) begins there; and Tom Roulstone (b. 1939) chronicles the flight from Nauvoo in *One against the Wilderness* (1996).

Personal accounts and other archival materials abound and can be found in many collections. The most extensive body of material, however, resides in the Church Historian's Office in Salt Lake City, Utah.

Several idealistic communities began in Europe and moved to the New World. In 1774 Ann Lee brought eight members of the United Society of Believers in Christ's Second Appearing from England to New York. Celibate millennialists who had broken away from the Quakers, they were called Shakers because of their religious ecstasies. Although they were persecuted, they were effective evangelists and took advantage of religious revivals to recruit members. After establishing several communities in the East, in 1802 they founded societies in Kentucky, Ohio, and Indiana. Membership was voluntary, the probationary period was long, those who did not wish to stay left, and no person profited more than another. Rigidly governed by elders on communistic principles, they sustained themselves for a while, but they did not procreate. After 1850 their numbers dwindled to two or three by 2000, and none remain in the Midwest.

Most of the well-known Shaker songs were composed or "received" in the eastern villages. However, in *The Gift to Be Simple* (1940) Edward Deming Andrews has recorded a few that originated in the Midwestern communities, such as "Faithful Soldiers Travel On" by John Wood of Union Village, Ohio (277–78), and "Heaven Bound," by John Brown, also of Union Village (304–5).

Collections of Midwestern Shaker materials exist on the sites of the communities. A large Midwestern archive is in the Library of the Western Reserve Historical Society in CLEVELAND, Ohio, and there are also materials in the Clarke Historical Library at Central Michigan University in Mt. Pleasant, Michigan.

Religious principles caused Frederick (Reichert) Rapp (1775–1834) and his congregation to separate from the Lutheran Church in Württemberg. He brought six hundred followers to set up the Harmony Society, agricultural colonies that were communistic and celibate. They resided first in Maryland and Pennsylvania, in 1815 left for ten years on the Wabash River in Indiana, and then returned to Economy, Pennsylvania.

When he moved his community back to Pennsylvania, Frederick Rapp sold the Harmony property in Indiana to Robert Owen (1771–1858), who had begun social reform in the factories of New Lanark, Scotland. Owen set up an ideal community there called New Harmony, based on humane social principles. The assortment of Americans who joined the enterprise made an unfortunate mix, and several groups broke away and founded communities in Yellow Springs, Ohio, and elsewhere. Admiring Owen's principles, others imitated him and founded societies of their own in Indiana, Ohio, and New York, none of which lasted. By 1827 Owen was ready to withdraw, and the other communities were gone by 1830.

Robert Dale Owen (1801–1877), son of the founder of the New Harmony community, recorded his impressions of the colony in *Twenty-Seven Years of Autobiography: Threading My Way* (1874). He also wrote *Beyond the Breakers: A Story of the Present Day* (1870), a long and complicated romance set in the fictional village of Chiskauga in western Ohio. This novel dramatizes his concerns about the laws of inheritance and marital property as they apply to women. *Seth Way: A Romance of the New Harmony Community* (1917) and *The Beckoning Road* (1929) by Robert Owen's great-granddaughter, Caroline Dale Snedecker (1871–1956), writing as Caroline Dale Owen, drew on reminiscences of her grandmother to describe the successes and failures of New Harmony; the former stresses equality in marriage, while the latter is a work for young people. Both describe the form of education there. Another fictionalized rendering of the community is an impressionistic, sometimes sarcastic description of Harmony and New Harmony, *Angel in the Forest: A Fairy Tale of Two Utopias* (1945) by Marguerite Young (1908–1995). This volume draws on a multitude of sources: accounts by visitors, letters, biographies, and autobiographies of residents.

Correspondence and diaries include such accounts of New Harmony as *Partnership for Posterity: The Correspondence of William Maclure and Marie Duclos Fretageot, 1820–1933* (1994), edited by Josephine Mirabella Elliott. Many Harmonist and Owenist documents can be found in the Workingmen's Institute and Library in New Harmony, Indiana, and in the Harmony Society Archives of the Pennsylvania Historical and Museum Commission at Old Economy in Ambridge, Pennsylvania.

Three more groups of German immigrants shared with the Rappites both their benevolent communistic form of governance and their limited interaction with outsiders. Some Rappites left Economy and joined another German emigrant, the mystic and millennialist William Keil (1816–1877). Agricultural by skill, they looked for cheap land and founded Bethel in Missouri. Their numbers and prosperity increased, and in the 1850s Keil thought that some should move west. They did, establishing themselves in Aurora, Oregon. After Keil's death in 1877, members divided the land peacefully among themselves and dissolved the communities.

Motivated by persecution because they refused military service and by the general hardship of the time, a group of German pacifists settled Zoar, Ohio, in the early nineteenth century. Under their leader, Joseph Michael Bäumler (1778–1853), later called Bimeler, they embraced communism and celibacy. The Society of Separatists of Zoar benefited greatly from the industrialization of northeastern Ohio; its members participated in building the Ohio Canal and built factories of their own. However, evangelism was not part of their program, and after Bimeler's death in 1853, with industrialization increasing around them, the society gradually declined.

Yet another pacifist sect founded in Germany, the Community of True Inspiration, became the Amana Society in IOWA around 1859. The settlement remains active. Very much like the Amana Society in its pietistic beliefs, a colony in Bishop Hill, Illinois, was settled by Swedish emigrants under the leadership of Eric Janson (1808–1850) in 1846. However, Janson's fiery oratory and belligerent and adventurous nature belied his theology; he was shot by one of his congregation, and because his followers failed to maintain unity, the colony ended in acrimony.

Other socialist experiments called Fourierist Phalanxes were based in part on the theories of the Frenchman Charles Fourier and were organized by his disciple Albert Brisbane (1809–1890). Such well-known literary figures as Horace Greeley (1811–1872), George Ripley (1802–1880), and William Ellery Channing (1818–1901) became interested, if not involved. Brook Farm in Massachusetts was a phalanx for part of its short life; forty or fifty others developed and quickly waned in the East and in Ohio, Michigan, Illinois, Indiana, Wisconsin, and Iowa, victims, at least to some extent, of American individualism. The Wisconsin Phalanx in Fond du Lac County had the unusual distinction of dissolving without loss to its investors; it survived longer than most others, six years.

According to Robert P. Sutton in *Heartland Utopias* (2009), the Icarians, another group of long-lasting communistic settlements, was inspired by the novel *Voyage et aventures de lord William Carisdall en Icarie* (1840) of Étienne Cabet (1782–1852), a French writer and publisher. Cabet and his followers met disaster in Texas but successfully took over the Mormon property in Nauvoo, Illinois, in 1849. Rebellious members moved variously to Cloverdale, Missouri; Corning, Iowa; and California. The final group disbanded in 1898. Novelist Katherine Holland Brown 1857–1931 fictionalized both the virtues and flaws and the partial breakdown of the Nauvoo community in 1856 in *Diane: A Romance of the Icarian Settlement on the Mississippi* (1904).

In 1903 a group with seventeenth-century English roots settled in Benton Harbor, Michigan and became known there as the House of David. Wracked by scandals, it has nevertheless survived for over a century in its present location and was best known for a time for its bearded baseball teams. The title of one sensational novel about this group suggests one reason for its mixed reputation: *The King of the Harem Heaven: The Amazing True Story of a Daring Charlatan Who Ran a Virgin Love Cult in Amer-*

ica (1960) by Anthony Sterling, pseudonym of Eugene Lee Caesar. Laura Kasischke (b. 1961) published a novella, *Eden Springs* (2010), about this group; it incorporates court documents and selections from newspapers into the fictional narrative.

Hutterites are among the communities that have lasted into the twentieth century. These Anabaptist and pietistic groups originated in Germany and moved around eastern Europe and Russia before coming to North America, where they set up colonies in rather isolated areas in Canada and the northern United States, including NORTH DAKOTA and SOUTH DAKOTA. Their strong educational and economic principles are among the qualities that have enabled them to grow and survive. They have produced a body of writings, mostly historical, that are printed and used primarily by the membership of the communities.

Some books about two groups have achieved wide popularity: the Old Order Amish, pacifist Anabaptists closely related to the Mennonites, and the Amana community in Iowa. The Amish have thrived in loosely organized rural communities established first in Pennsylvania and now spread throughout the Midwest, but particularly in Ohio and Indiana. The denomination operates Pathway Publishers, which produces *Family Life* and other magazines, books on general Amish subjects, literature for young people, and Christian romances; its series of Ellie books by Ohio author Mary Christner Borntrager (b. 1921), like other similar wide-selling fiction on Amish and Amana subjects, focuses on customs, daily activities, and religious life, along with chaste love stories.

One might expect that insiders and critics of these communities and the many other exclusive settlements that also flourished briefly would produce works focused on their values, internal conflicts, and internal relationships. However, little in the way of *belles lettres* has emerged. Documents and other materials relating to them, fertile ground for fiction and drama, may be found in the archives on the sites of these organizations.

One community made up at least in part of literary figures, called the Portage Experiment or Witt Cottage, exemplifies the difficulties inherent in writing from or about utopian enterprises. It existed near Briggsville, Wisconsin, for about two months in 1931. There, Jean Toomer (1894–1967), Margery Latimer, and others studied the mysticism of George ïvanovitch Gurdjieff 1866–1949). It is notable only because the authors involved mention it in some of their works. For example, Jean Toomer's *Cane* (1923 raises some of the issues members discussed, and his unpublished monograph "Portage Potential: An Adventure in Human Development" (1931) describes them in detail. That document may be found among the Jean Toomer Papers in the Collection of American Literature at the Beinecke Rare Book and Manuscript Library, Yale University, New Haven, Connecticut.

The generation and founding of utopian communities in the Midwest, as well as elsewhere, were not conducive to the production of fiction, poetry, or drama. However, the utopian phenomenon was documented in literature in a number of ways. Accounts by visitors include those by John Humphrey Noyes (1811–1886), who recorded his theories, as well as his observations of communities he visited, in his *History of American Socialisms* (1870), and by Charles Nordhoff (1830–1901), who traveled extensively in the Midwest and elsewhere and presented his findings in *The Communistic Societies of the United States* (1875). Biographies and autobiographies of participants in utopian communities present a variety of opinions about them. In his autobiographical *My Year in a Log Cabin* (1893) William Dean Howells describes a short-lived utopian experiment his father conducted in southern Ohio around 1867.

During the second half of the nineteenth century and into the twentieth century, still more communities developed on other principles: spiritualism, anti-slavery, care for orphans, the New Deal, eastern religions, vegetarianism, and organic farming. Although free love characterized a small number, some of the longest lasting have been monastic, generally Roman Catholic or Episcopal, but also based on other religious and philosophical beliefs, such as Buddhism. In a useful appendix to his collection of essays *America's Communal Utopias* (1997), Donald E. Pitzer lists many of these (449–94).

Beginning in the mid-twentieth century, thousands of loosely organized groups, often called communes or "intentional communities," developed in response to numerous ideologies. Unlike those of the eighteenth and nineteenth centuries, when the founding principles tended to be religious or tied to major political theories, these later groups were likely to be secular, single-issue, and ephemeral. Countercultural groups based on such foci as beat values, drugs, opposition to the war in Vietnam, music, crafts, and organic farming proliferated but generally did not last very long. Some religious groups, such as those sponsored by Transcendental Meditation and Christian revival organizations, have persisted longer, and survivalists exist in small pockets. Many hippie communes existed only for short periods of time because of internal differences of opinion or conflicts in interests and values. Around the 1980s groups developed what is called cohousing. Members rent apartments in a single building or own homes in a common area, for example, but work elsewhere. Elements of lifestyle such as organic landscaping or intensive recycling draw them together, and they often share a combination of meals, facilities, and activities. Such cooperative ventures tend to be diverse in their values and often are short lived. The Fellowship for Intentional Community has periodically published *Communities Directory: A Guide to Cooperative Living*, which provides history, explanations, and options.

Literary works growing out of contemporary Midwestern communal enterprises appear to be few, if any. The situation of relatively small, hardworking, self-sustaining communities should be material for creative works. Utopias as they existed, and indeed as they occur now, have provided microcosms of potentially ideal societies and areas in which unified works could arise. In addition, the conflicts arising in a community of shared beliefs, the intensity of which might generate heated, even violent discussion, could be fertile ground for novel writers. Perhaps those factors, as well as the combination of hard work and devotion to the utopian cause, are not conducive to writing and publication. Still, in communities where celibacy, open marriage, or polygamy flourish, sexual issues might arise. Rivalry for leadership, division of labor, hostility from the outside, coercive tactics from within, and oppression on the grounds of religious or political tenets could supply yet more material for the fiction writer who might write of a dystopia as easily as a utopia. A case could be made for the role of a once-admired apartment building in Chicago as a decaying dystopia in *In the Mecca* (1968). In a poem with the same title in that collection, the poet GWENDOLYN BROOKS (1917–2000) describes the decline of the African American community there.

The mythologies that have grown out of the Midwest also make it a useful setting for imaginative renderings of fictional utopias. The abundant fertile land, the open, available spaces, the temperate climate, the sense of the possibilities of a fresh beginning in an untouched Eden, the isolation that is both imaginary and real, and the distance from the industrial East all make the Midwest a *tabula rasa* for an artist who has a political, philosophical, or religious agenda and needs a locus for an ideal community. However, relatively little fiction, drama, or poetry has arisen from these situations. Among the few authors is Charles Monroe Sheldon (1857–1946), who, as pastor of a Congregational church in Topeka, KANSAS, developed a novel from sermons he preached based on Christian Socialism, serialized them in a Christian magazine in 1896, and published them as a novel, *In His Steps: "What Would Jesus Do?,"* in 1897. William Dean Howells wrote novels including *The Leatherwood God* (1916), for which he used a true story of a charlatan who induced members of a village in eastern Ohio to regard him as God; even after opponents revealed his deception, he led his followers on a journey to what he called the New Jerusalem, which was really Philadelphia. Having accomplished nothing, he drowned, and his body disappeared, so his adherents persisted in believing that he had gone directly to heaven. Howells also based his novel *New Leaf Mills* (1913) on his father's short-lived attempt to create a utopia in southwestern Ohio.

Outsiders to utopian communities provided a few imaginative, if unfavorable, renderings. Among these is Marguerite Young's description of Harmony and New Harmony in *Angel in the Forest.*

On the other hand, a notable body of utopian literature by Midwestern writers has been set in real places that are fictionalized, simply because the societies they depict are drawn, at least in part, from the imagination. L(YMAN) FRANK BAUM (1856–1919) begins and ends *The Wonderful Wizard of Oz* (1900) in Kansas, and Midwestern farmworker characteristics and values, such as honesty and loyalty, turn up in the Scarecrow, the Lion, and the Tin Man. The Wizard himself represents the stock traveling salesman / con man figure. After all, they are based on people Dorothy knew in the Midwest, and the fantasy holds up a mirror to the characters and weather of her world. IGNATIUS LOYOLA DONNELLY (1831–1901) of Wisconsin set *The Golden Bottle* (1892) in Kansas, the center of the country, as a means of portraying his Populist beliefs.

Donnelly, however, placed one of his vehicles for his scientific theories, *Atlantis: The Antediluvian World* (1882), and his novel *Caesar's Column: A Story of the Twentieth Century* (1890), among others, in imaginary locales. Howells's Altrurian works, including his novel *A Traveller from Altruria* (1894), took their titles and mythical location from the concept of altruism and expressed his theories for solving the problems of poverty and inequality. Marge Piercy set the first part of her science-fiction novel *He, She, and It* (1991) in NEBRASKA, in a futuristic urban dystopia, socially repressive and politically suppressive, polluted, poverty-stricken in places, and riddled with violations of peace and person. Another futuristic novel by Piercy, *Dance the Eagle to Sleep* (1970), is set partly in CHICAGO.

"The Curious Republic of Gondour" (1870–1871), a story by SAMUEL LANGHORNE CLEMENS (1835–1910), writing as Mark Twain, on the other hand, attacks the political and social practices of his time by using an American traveler who does not understand the ideals in the fictitious Gondour; he uses a similar means in *A Connecticut Yankee in King Arthur's Court* (1889). Other Midwestern authors have written utopian and dystopian novels with settings outside the Midwest, for example, *Fahrenheit 451* (1953 by RAY (DOUGLAS) BRADBURY (1920–2012) and Marge Piercy's *Woman on the Edge of Time* (1976).

Perhaps for many, the term "Midwestern utopia" is an oxymoron, as is any effort to locate an ideal community in any real place. That does not mean that writers cannot attempt to construct such communities nor write about ideal places existing only in the mind or functioning on the basis of the single-minded devotion of their participants. However, such attempts in regard to Midwestern settings or characteristics have so far rarely been successful.

SELECTED WORKS: The Midwestern author who has contributed most to fiction based on personal experience about actual utopian communities is William Dean Howells. He expressed altruism in his *A Traveler from Altruria* (1894), wrote a fictionalized autobiography in *New Leaf Mills* (1913), and fictionalized true events in *The Leatherwood God* (1916).

Other books based on real people in real places are Caroline Dale Snedecker's *Seth Way: A Romance of the New Harmony Community* (1917) and *The Beckoning Road* (1929), Marguerite Young's *Angel in the Forest* (1945), and James Oliver Curwood's *The Courage of Captain Plum* (1908). Less well-known books such as *Harem Island: The Astounding True Story of a Self-Proclaimed Saint Who Made Religion a Business and Turned Sin into a Virtue* (1961) by Eugene Lee Caesar; the juvenile novel *Pirate of the Pine Lands: Being the Adventures of Young Tom Lansing Afloat and Ashore on the Michigan Frontier in the Years 1852 to 1854, and Particularly His Part in the Historic Matter of King James Strang, the Notorious Great Lakes Pirate, Told Here by Himself from Memory* (1929) by Karl William Detzer; *The Stranger on the Island* (1933) by Brand Whitlock; Virginia Sorenson's *A Little Lower than the Angels* (1942); Orson Scott Card's *Saints* (1984); Robert Farrell Smith's *Trust Williams Trilogy* (1999–2000); and Tom Roulstone in *One against the Wilderness* (1996) provide fictionalized histories. Eugene Lee Caesar sensationalized scandals in the House of David community in *The King of the Harem Heaven: The Amazing True Story of a Daring Charlatan Who Ran a Virgin Love Cult in America* (1960) under the pseudonym Anthony Sterling. Robert Dale Owen may have based Chiskauga, Ohio, in *Beyond the Breakers: A Story of the Present Day* (1870) on New Harmony.

Ignatius Loyola Donnelly's *The Golden Bottle* (1892) and L. Frank Baum's *The Wonderful Wizard of Oz* (1900) both have Kansas settings. Marge Piercy begins *He, She, and It* (1991) in Nebraska, and *Dance the Eagle to Sleep* (1970) is set partly in Chicago.

Among the Utopias or dystopias with fictional settings are Donnelly's novels *Atlantis: The Antediluvian World* (1882) and *Caesar's Column* (1890); Howells's *Letters of an Altrurian Traveller* (1893–1894), *Traveler from Altruria* (1894), and *Through the Eye of the Needle: A Romance with an Introduction* (1907); and Mark Twain's "The Curious Republic of Gondour" (1870–1871) and *A Connecticut Yankee in King Arthur's Court* (1889). Other dystopian novels by Midwestern authors that do not have Midwestern settings include Ray Bradbury's *Fahrenheit 451* (1953) and Marge Piercy's *Woman on the Edge of Time* (1976).

Nonfiction accounts of Midwestern utopian communities by travelers include observations such as those by John Humphrey Noyes in *History of American Socialisms* (1870) and Charles Nordhoff in *The Communistic Societies of the United States* (1875). Among autobiographies are Robert Dale Owen's *Twenty-Seven Years of Autobiography: Threading My Way* (1874) and William Dean Howells's *My Years in a Log Cabin* (1893). Diaries and correspondence include *Partnership for Posterity: The Correspondence of William Maclure and Marie Duclos Fretageot, 1820–1933* (1994), edited by Josephine Mirabella Elliott.

FURTHER READING: Robert P. Sutton's *Heartland Utopias* (2009) provides a scholarly overview of nineteenth- and twentieth-century utopian settlements in the Midwest. Alice Felt Tyler's *Freedom's Ferment: Phases of American Social History from the Colonial Period to the Outbreak of the Civil War* (1944), a standard early reference work, contains valuable sections on utopian communities, including those in the Midwest; and Mark Holloway's *Heavens on Earth: Utopian Communities in America, 1680–1880* (1966) remains a basic text on the subject. Studies of selected communities in more depth appear in Dolores Hayden's *Seven American Utopias: The Architecture of Communitarian Socialism (1790–1975)* (1976). Later works include Ira L. Mandeleker's *Religion, Society, and Utopia in Nineteenth-Century America* (1984) and *All*

Things New: American Communes and Utopian Movements, 1860–1914 (1990) by Robert S. Fogarty. *America's Communal Utopias* (1997), edited by Donald E. Pitzer, brings the topic up to the present and has a useful list of utopian communities, as does the current edition of *Communities Directory: A Guide to Cooperative Living.* On communes and communal movements in the 1960s, two books are particularly helpful: *Communes USA: A Personal Tour* (1972) by Richard Fairfield and *The 60s Communes: Hippies and Beyond* (1999) by Timothy Miller. See also Fairfield's edited collection *The Modern Utopian: Alternative Communities of the '60s and '70s* (2010). *The Cambridge Companion to Utopian Literature* (2012), edited by Gregory Claeys, is a valuable resource.

Vernon L. Parrington offers a survey of utopian writing, including fiction, in *American Dreams: A Study of American Utopias* (1947). *Daring to Dream: Utopian Fiction by United States Women before 1950* (second edition, 1995), edited by Carol Farley Kessler, includes a selection from Caroline Snedecker's *Seth Way* and provides an annotated bibliography of utopian literature written by women in the United States, including a few works set in the Midwest and some based on New Harmony principles. In *A Bibliographical Guide to Midwestern Literature* (1981) Gerald Nemanic includes a bibliography on utopian communities. Encyclopedias and bibliographies of literature pertaining to idealistic settlements include Mary Ellen Snodgrass's *Encyclopedia of Utopian Literature* (1995), *Index to Science Fiction Anthologies and Collections* (1978, 1984) by William Contento, *British and American Utopian Literature, 1516–1975: An Annotated Bibliography* (1979) and *British and American Utopian Literature, 1516–1985: An Annotated Chronological Bibliography* (1988), the latter two by Lyman Tower Sargent. These volumes reveal how little utopian literature has come out of the Midwest. A specialized work focusing exclusively on Shaker music, which notes the few songs that originated in the Midwest, is *The Shaker Spiritual* (1979) by Daniel W. Patterson.

Unpublished memoirs, correspondence, and other documents relating to utopian communities reside in large and small libraries throughout the country. Collections and archives such as the Harmony Society Archives of the Pennsylvania Historical and Museum Commission at Old Economy in Ambridge, Pennsylvania, and the New Harmony Workingmen's Institute in New Harmony, Indiana, may yield unpublished personal accounts of the colonies that existed there. Documents pertaining to the North Union Shaker settlement are collected in the Shaker Historical Society Museum in Shaker Heights, Ohio. The largest Midwestern archive of Shaker materials is in the Library of the Western Reserve Historical Society in Cleveland, Ohio, and there is also a collection in the Clarke Historical Library at Central Michigan University in Mt. Pleasant, Michigan. Mormon materials may also be found in the archives of the various settlements, but the most extensive archives are those in the Church Historian's Office in Salt Lake City, Utah. Libraries and museums at the sites of other settlements also contain valuable primary resources on the Mormons. Most of the well-known communities mentioned in this article have libraries and archives on their sites.

New information is available on the Internet under results of search terms such as "utopias," "utopian communities," and "intentional communities," as well as under the names of the various settlements. Sites are continually being updated.

MARY DEJONG OBUCHOWSKI

CENTRAL MICHIGAN UNIVERSITY

WEARY BLUES, THE

HISTORY: When LANGSTON HUGHES (1902–1967) published his first volume consisting primarily of verse poems in 1926, it received mixed critical reviews in spite of an introduction by CARL VAN VECHTEN (1880–1964), a key figure of the Harlem Renaissance. Although the book received positive notices in the *New York Times,* the *New Republic,* and the *New York Herald Tribune,* Emily Bernard, in *Remember Me to Harlem: The Letters of Langston Hughes and Carl Van Vechten, 1925–1964* (2001) cites Countee Cullen (1903–1946), a leading African American poet of the time, as being critical of the volume; in his review in *Opportunity,* Cullen stated that Hughes placed "too much emphasis on strictly Negro themes" (37).

The publication of Hughes's book had been aided by Van Vechten, who informed Hughes on May 14, 1925, "My news is this: that I handed *The Weary Blues* to Knopf yesterday with the proper incantation. I do not feel particularly dubious about the outcome: your poems are too beautiful to escape appreciation. (8). On May 15, 1925, Hughes wrote back, "I would be very, very much pleased if you would do the introduction to my poems (8). The collection became available in bookstores in mid-January 1926 and was reprinted four months later. At that point it had sold 12,000 copies (37). The volume was reprinted six more times by the 1939 edition, which was identified as the eighth printing. In his introduction to *The Weary Blues*, Van Vechten acknowledges Hughes's ties to the Midwest, stating that he had lived "before his twelfth year, in the City of Mexico, Topeka, Kansas, . . . Indiana, Kansas City . . . attended Central High School . . . at Cleveland, Ohio" and "worked in Chicago [as] delivery-and-dumb-boy in hat stores" (9). It is not clear whether this introduction was meant to highlight Hughes's social status or to present him as a transient and romantic figure. Whatever the purpose, Langston Hughes was nurtured by Midwestern educational systems and tempered by the Midwest's cultural, social, and political environments.

Langston Hughes's career spanned several decades between the 1920s Harlem Renaissance and the 1960s. He is often associated with the Harlem Renaissance because his poetry gave voice to the spirit of that movement and age. Although Hughes is associated with a literary movement centered in Harlem, he, like several members of that movement, migrated from elsewhere. Langston Hughes belonged to the American Midwest, and many of his poems evoke Midwestern imagery, experiences, and sounds, including blues music and jazz, which he first heard in Lawrence, KANSAS, and CHICAGO, ILLINOIS. Arnold Rampersad (b. 1941) indicates in *The Life of Langston Hughes,* volume 1, *1902–1941* (1986) that Hughes also experienced the religion and music of the "Holiness and Sanctified churches" in Chicago (27), whose jeremiad energy he reproduces in "Fire": "Fire, Lord! / Fire gonna burn ma soul! . I ain't been good, / I ain't

been clean— / I been stinkin', low-down, mean" (*Vintage Hughes* 27). In Hughes's 1940 autobiography, *The Big Sea,* he recalls his experience of being "saved from sin" in his "Auntie Reed's" church in Kansas City when he "was going on thirteen" (18).

SIGNIFICANCE: *The Weary Blues* reflects the presence of the Midwest in Hughes's consciousness and art because, like "Fire," several of the poems in the collection evoke the region through blues music and jazz or by recalling Hughes's childhood experiences there. *The Weary Blues* consists of sixty-nine poems divided into seven sections: "The Weary Blues," "Dream Variations," "The Negro Speaks of Rivers," "Black Pierrot," "Water-Front Streets," "Shadows in the Sun," and "Our Land." The poems are predominantly in free verse, though a few dialect poems echo the use of dialect by PAUL LAURENCE DUNBAR (1872–1906). Hughes read Dunbar's poetry while he was attending Central High School in CLEVELAND, OHIO. "Little Negro dialect poems like Paul Laurence Dunbar's and poems without rhymes like Sandburg's were the first real poems I tried to write," Hughes recalls in *The Big Sea* (28). In the same vein, Hughes's verse poems reflect the presence of Amy Lowell (1874–1925), CARL (AUGUST) SANDBURG (1878–1967), and (NICHOLAS) VACHEL LINDSAY (1879–1931), who introduced Hughes to the literary world, and all of whom Hughes read at Central High School (28). He also "began to write like Carl Sandburg" (28). Like Hughes, Sandburg and Lindsay were Midwesterners and had spent their childhood in Illinois. As a child, Hughes was fascinated with Chicago. While he was living with his Auntie Reed, he "used to walk to the Santa Fé station and stare at the railroad tracks becase the railroad tracks ran to Chicago and Chicago was the biggest town in the world to [him (23). It is not surprising that he "was glad" when his mother sent for him to join her in Lincoln, Illinois, because "Lincoln, Illinois . . . was not far from Chicago" (23). Perhaps it was also the rich cultural energy of Chicago that drew the young Hughes, for Chicago and its blues and jazz would later figure in his work.

The section "The Weary Blues" is dominated by jazz; nine of these fifteen poems deal with some aspect of that music, and there is a focus on Harlem jazz clubs and cabaret dancers in such poems as "Jazzonia," "Negro Dancers," "Cabaret," and "Harlem Nights." In these poems jazz syncopation is evident. But the poems also carry the spirit of Midwestern cities such as Chicago, DETROIT, KANSAS CITY, Lawrence, and Indianapolis, as if anticipating Hughes's later visits to some of those cities. In these poems jazz serves as a trope representing the African American cultural imprint on America, especially as Hughes attempts to emphasize the Americanness of jazz and of blacks. He makes this claim in his poem "I Too," published one year before the *Weary Blues*. "Jazzonia" can be seen as Hughes's homage to jazz and the dancing girls of Harlem and Chicago jazz and cabaret clubs. Whether real or imagined, Hughes's focus in the poem is on the music with its pulsating energy, colors, and rhythm, which he captures in references to colors in verses such as "Oh, silver tree! / Oh, shining rivers of the soul!" (25), making his childhood jazz influences part of his literary repertoire.

Similarly, blues music, rooted in black cultural experience and associated with Midwestern cities of Hughes's childhood, figures in some of this poetry, particularly "The Weary Blues," "To Midnight Nan at Leroy's," and "Blues Fantasy." Steven C(arl) Tracy (b. 1954), in his 1988 *Langston Hughes and the Blues*, asserts that in the blues poems Hughes "[presents] us with an ovserver of the blues singer or situation" (3–4). In a letter of May 15, 1925, Hughes tells Van Vechten, who was writing a paper on the blues, "I am going to type some old verse for you that I used to hear when I was a kid" (*Remember Me to Harlem* 9). In the poems identified here, Hughes deploys his knowledge of blues, not only using basic blues structure as an organizing device but also evoking its thematic content, the pain and suffering of the soul, addressing such experiences as disempowerment, abandonment, loneliness, frustration, and travel. These themes connect Hughes's poems to African American spirituals and work songs, which W(illiam) E(dward) B(urghardt) DuBois (1868–1963) named "Sorrow Songs" from which the blues originated (*The Souls of Black Folk*, 1903: 250) . Furthermore, the poems reveal Hughes's desolate soul to the reader,

underscoring the appeal of the musical form to Hughes, who "would make up" the blues "in [his] head and sing on [his] way to work" (*The Big Sea* 217).

In the title poem, "The Weary Blues," which won first prize at the *Opportunity Magazine* dinner in 1925, Hughes returns to the sorrowful yet determined tone of the blues. In this poem about a Harlem piano player, Hughes voices the pain of a "black man's soul" as if to exorcise the loneliness his soul felt as a child in Lawrence. Rampersad states that Hughes believed "in nothing but books and the wonderful world in books—where if people suffered, they suffered in beautiful language, not in monosyllables, as we did in Kansas" (*The Life of Langston Hughes*, volume l, *1902–1941*, 14). The title poem, according to Hughes in *The Big Sea*, includes "the first blues verse [he had] ever heard way back in Lawrence, Kansas, when [he] was a kid" (215). Steven C. Tracy, in "To the Tune of Those Weary Blues," *MELUS* 8.3 (Fall 1981), claims that Hughes's "The Weary Blues" was influenced by the "oral blues tradition, as by Texas songster Henry Thomas whose . . . 'Texas Worried Blues' makes the common substitution of 'worried' for 'weary'" as in Langston Hughes's poem (74). For Tracy, "It was the early blues of itinerant musicians of the first two decades of the twentieth century that influenced Hughes in his Lawrence, Kansas days, and the blues of that area were strongly influenced by slave and work songs" (76).

Moreover, in "The Weary Blues" the "Negro's" song "in this world / Ain't got nobody but ma self" is reminiscent of Hughes's dilemma while he was living alone in Cleveland during his high school years. Rampersad indicates that "where Langston himself spent Thanksgiving, 1918,is not known; he was still living alone" (*The Life of Langston Hughes*, volume 1, *1902–1941*, 28), having been abandoned by his mother, (Caroline) Carrie Mercer Langston Hughes, who had left to join her husband, Homer Clark, in Chicago. Throughout his childhood Langston Hughes was constantly abandoned; he was moved from one Midwestern location to another, from Joplin, MISSOURI, to Lawrence, Lincoln, Cleveland, and Chicago.

Hughes described "The Weary Blues" as his "lucky poem—because it won first prize"

(*The Big Sea* 215). Certainly that prize helped garner public attention, including that of Van Vechten. It is, therefore, significant that Hughes's first poetry collection takes its title from his "lucky poem." Although in *The Big Sea* Hughes simply states, "I called the book *The Weary Blues*" (216), another scholar claims that it was Van Vechten who suggested the volume's title (*Remember Me to Harlem*).

"Blues Fantasy" recalls the blues tradition in its repetition of lines and in the relationship between blues and travel, journey, or migration, especially by road and train. Several waves of migration to the North brought many southern blacks, including blues singers, to northern cities, several of them in the Midwest. "I got a railroad ticket" (*The Weary Blues* 37), the speaker says. "Got a railroad ticket, / Pack my trunk and ride" (37). Railroad tracks traverse the Midwest and continue to the West Coast. Chicago is a train hub and boasts a strong blues tradition that nurtured such southern artists as John Lee Hooker (1917–2001), Muddy Waters (McKinley Morganfield) (1915–1983), (Riley B.) B(lues) B(oy) King (1925–2015), Robert (Leroy) Johnson (1911–1938), and Gertrude (Pridgett) "Ma" Rainey (1886–1939). Hughes experienced a similar journey, having traveled by train from Lawrence to Lincoln to join his mother in the summer of 1915. When Hughes arrived that year, he was in the middle of American history, in the land of ABRAHAM LINCOLN (1809–1865), the great emancipator. It is not surprising that Lincoln figures in Hughes's poem "The Negro Speaks of Rivers."

In the section titled "The Negro Speaks of Rivers" Hughes shifts his tone to one of seriousness. The poems in this section use standard English devoid of any dialect and, like Dunbar's standard English poems, display a gravity not present in "The Weary Blues" section, for instance. In these poems Hughes addresses topics such as slavery and African diasporic connections. In 1919 Hughes traveled to Mexico City to spend a year with his father before returning to study at Columbia University. Hughes establishes a direct connection between his personal life in the Midwest and the genesis of the poem. He wrote his most popular poem, "The Negro Speaks of Rivers," "just outside

St. Louis" while crossing the Mississippi by train on his way to Mexico (*The Big Sea* 54–55). North America's largest river, the Mississippi, is an important Midwestern geographic marker, traversing and transforming the landscape each year from MINNESOTA through IOWA, WISCONSIN, Illinois, and Missouri. Although Hughes's poem connects the Mississippi with other great rivers of world civilization, as well as with the story of African slavery and its presence in the New World, it also, through its evocation of the great Mississippi, links the Midwest with the narrative of Africans in the United States and suggests the transformations they would bring to the Midwest, particularly through their post-Reconstruction migrations from the South. Hughes's poem also inscribes the Midwest and its favorite son, Abraham Lincoln, into history. Hughes indicates that while he was thinking of the significance of the Mississippi to "Negroes in the past," he recalled reading that Abraham Lincoln had traveled down the river and had seen slavery at its worst. Consequently, Lincoln "decided within himself that it should be removed from American life" (*The Big Sea* 55). Lincoln's feat, the emancipation of enslaved Africans, can be compared in stature to the mighty Mississippi.

The gravity of the issues addressed by the poems in this section is almost overwhelming. One can feel Hughes's pain and the frustration resulting from racism. Hughes experienced racial discrimination in the Midwest even as the area nurtured him. He was sometimes chased home after school by white schoolmates in Lawrence. One Sunday in Chicago "he wandered into a Polish neighbourhood" and was beaten by a "gang of boys" who told him, "We don't 'low no niggers in this street" (*The Life of Langston Hughes,* volume l, 1902–1941, 27). Hughes recalls this experience in "The White Ones" (106). Ironically, because of his race, his classmates at Central High unanimously elected him class poet (*The Big Sea* 24). "The South" addresses racial identity, underscoring the problematic nature of biracialism and the marginalizing of blacks by racism.

In "As I Grew Older" (55) Hughes explores racial disempowerment, anticipating the books *Black Boy* (1945) and NATIVE SON

(1940) by RICHARD WRIGHT (1908–1960), which are set in Chicago, as well as Wright's essay "The Ethics of Living Jim Crow" (1937). The poem presents a geography of despair and disappointment, and the speaker's "forgotten . . . dream" foreshadows the Youngers' anguish in A RAISIN IN THE SUN (1959) by LORRAINE (VIVIAN) HANSBERRY (1930–1965), which is also set in Chicago. Her title invokes a verse from Hughes's poem "Harlem." "Aunt Sue's Stories" (57) recalls Hughes's storytelling experience while living with his grandmother in Lawrence and connects him to the "sorrow songs" and African American oral traditions.

In the section titled "Our Land" Hughes pays tribute to black people while suggesting Midwestern geography. Most poems in this section recall his travels to Africa. Again, Hughes employs blues or some adaptation of the form as an organizing principle in several poems, such as "Lament for Dark Peoples." "Our Land: Poem for a Decorative Panel" describes landscapes hinting at Midwestern geography and simultaneously evokes some of the region's summer days with its "gorgeous sun" and "fragrant" or pungent "waters" of the Great Lakes and the frigid temperatures of a "land where life is cold" (99). Although the poem may be about warm or tropical lands suggested by the second stanza, where "thick trees / Bowed down with chattering parrots / Brilliant as the day" (99), Hughes's poem also hints at the climatic tension that the Midwest experiences yearly—warm, brilliant, humid, sunny summer days set against dramatically cold, gray winter days. The section also contains one of Hughes's frequently anthologized poems, "Mother to Son."

Other poems in the collection also reflect the Midwest. In "Troubled Woman" (86) Hughes revisits familiar landscapes, the autumn, and then the frozen rains that often plague the Midwest as aspects of this poem. Perhaps the "troubled woman" is one of those "workers and gamblers, prostitutes and pimps, church folks and sinners" (The Big Sea 33) who populated Chicago's "South State Street . . . in its glory" (33). Like "Troubled Woman," "Poème d'Automne" suggests a surfacing of memory, the memory of "winter winds" that "strip" bare the bodies of "slender trees" in the Midwest, an evoca-

tion of memories of Midwestern winters in the cold, windy cities of Chicago or Cleveland (45).

"Winter Moon" recalls the "ghostly" whiteness of the moon on a crisp wintry Midwestern night or after a snowfall. Similarly, "March Moon" (47) looks back at The Waste Land (1922) by T(HOMAS) S(TEARNS) ELIOT (1888–1965). The barrenness and nakedness of the landscape in the poem underscore the stark nakedness of the winter landscape.

IMPORTANT EDITIONS: At its publication in 1926, The Weary Blues went through four reprintings within a few months. Although several printings of this book exist, there are only a few editions. The title poem, "The Weary Blues," as well as "The Negro Speaks of Rivers," appears in most anthologies of African American and American literature. The 1939 publication used for this entry is identified as the eighth printing of the volume, and the 1931 printing as a "special cheaper edition." The 1944 and 1947 printings include notes identifying them as a Borzoi Book. A photo reprint of the 1926 edition was published in 1973, and a facsimile reprint in 2003. A few non-English editions exist: two Danish translations (1945 and 1964) by Ole Sarvig (1921–1981) published by UMI Books on Demand, a Czech edition published in 1957 by Státní nakladatelství krásné literatury, hudby a umění, and a Japanese translation (1958) by Saito Tadatoshi. LP and CD recordings of Langston Hughes reading his poems to musical accompaniment by Charles Mingus Jr. (1922–1979) exist under the title The Weary Blues. The CD recording, however, is not primarily of the poems of the 1926 edition.

FURTHER READING: Langston Hughes's autobiographies The Big Sea (1940) and I Wonder as I Wander (1956) provide extensive information. Additionally, Arnold Rampersad's two-volume biography—The Life of Langston Hughes, volume 1, 1902–1941: I, Too, Sing America (1986) and The Life of Langston Hughes, volume 2, 1941–1967: I Dream a World (1988)—is essential reading. Rampersad's edited volume The Collected Works of Langston Hughes, volume 1, The Poems: 1921–1940 (2001), contains the complete text of the 1926 Weary Blues. Emily Bernard's edited collection Remember Me to Harlem: The Letters of Langston

Hughes and Carl Van Vechten, 1925–1964 (2001) provides important background information on Hughes's relationship with Van Vechten and publication of *The Weary Blues*. Steven C. Tracy's *Langston Hughes and the Blues* (1988) contributes to better understanding of Hughes's fusion of blues and poetry. More biographical background information on Hughes's Midwestern childhood and his literary development can be culled from Faith Berry's *Langston Hughes, before and beyond Harlem* (1983).

MAUREEN N. EKE   CENTRAL MICHIGAN UNIVERSITY

WINESBURG, OHIO

HISTORY: When he published *Winesburg, Ohio* in 1919, SHERWOOD ANDERSON (1876–1941) revolutionized the short story genre and literary depictions of Midwestern small-town life. This collection of stories, related by their settings around a fictionalized OHIO town and by the recurrence of the character George Willard, transformed Anderson into an influential literary figure who, in this and subsequent works, chronicled America's transition from a rural, small-town culture into an urban, industrial, alienated early twentieth-century society.

Raised in Clyde, Ohio, during a period when Horatio Alger stories and the experiences of the Gilded Age helped shape the national myth of success, Anderson became a moderately prosperous businessman by the time he was thirty. However, as financial and marital pressures deepened, he turned to fiction writing as a release. In 1912 he suffered a nervous breakdown, which he and other writers would later elevate to the status of legend. Shortly afterward he settled in CHICAGO, where he became an advertising writer and began to mix with writers associated with the CHICAGO RENAISSANCE.

During this time Anderson enjoyed a supportive audience on which he tried out some of his early fiction. FLOYD DELL (1887–1969) helped get his first novel, *Windy McPherson's Son*, published in 1916. Anderson followed with *Marching Men* in 1917 and the poetry collection *Mid-American Chants* in 1918. These works garnered some praise when they were first published, but today most readers consider them apprentice works. While revising his first two novels in

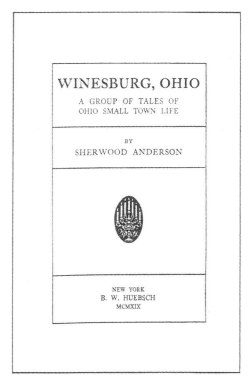

Sherwood Anderson's *Winesburg, Ohio*, first edition. B. W. Huebsch, 1919.
Image courtesy of Transylvania University Library

1915, Anderson composed "The Book of the Grotesque" and "Hands," the first tales of what would evolve into *Winesburg, Ohio*. He published nine of the Winesburg tales serially in *The Masses, Seven Arts,* and THE LITTLE REVIEW before arranging them with the other stories for Ben Huebsch, who published the book in New York in May 1919.

Although *Winesburg, Ohio* was not a best seller, it became a sensation among critics and writers. Anderson attracted attention for exploring psychological issues through fragmented glimpses of his characters, a radical shift from traditional plot-driven stories. Nonetheless, many popular reviewers dismissed the book as prurient. But this work and the short-story collections that followed, especially *The Triumph of the Egg* (1920) and *Horses and Men* (1922), greatly influenced his contemporaries and subsequent generations of writers.

SIGNIFICANCE: In his early novels Sherwood Anderson began depicting the milieu of the modern grotesque and showed a growing awareness of the indeterminacy of meaning in language. In *Winesburg, Ohio,* however, he successfully explores the close relationship of these two issues in the content and the telling of the tales. The physical setting, many character types, and the informal and intrusive narration have deep roots in the Midwest; and just as this region was a mélange of peoples and traditions from across the continent, Anderson repeatedly intimates that the frustrated, stagnant lives of people in Winesburg are indicative of the lives of Americans everywhere who were confronting the stifling constraints of modern industrial America.

In "The Book of the Grotesque" Anderson sketches a thematic backdrop in which he describes how individuals become "grotesques." No critical consensus exists concerning how Anderson turned his attention to grotesques; most acknowledge some indebtedness to SPOON RIVER ANTHOLOGY (1915) by EDGAR LEE MASTERS (1868–1950), the experimental play *Grotesques* (1915) by Cloyd Head (1886–1969), and possibly the poem "Ten Grotesques" (1915) by ARTHUR DAVISON FICKE (1883–1945), all of which appeared in Chicago only months before Anderson wrote "The Book of the Grotesque." Regardless of the influence, Anderson created a paradigm of human behavior that he believed characterized modern America.

One can approach *Winesburg, Ohio* as a series of case studies of the modern grotesque. Although the narrator of "The Book of the Grotesque" self-consciously backs away from a concrete definition of the term, his tentative rendering of the old writer's "elaborate theory" (1997 Love edition 9) suggests something akin to the diagnosis of a disease. Individuals snatch up truths— abstract concepts related to living in society—and become grotesques by trying to mold their lives rigidly by them. They may do this consciously or unconsciously, of their own accord or coerced by some component of society, but they practice their truths presumably in pursuit of contented, fulfilling lives.

The truths reflect a variety of experiences characterizing American life that had evolved during the nation's development into facile formulas and static cultural myths governing individual life expectations and societal norms. They touch on conventional ideals like success, respectability, and proper relations between men and women. But the characters inhabiting the town of Winesburg do not achieve the good life; most become failures by society's standards. They may feel cheated by conventional notions of success, like Wash Williams in "Respectability," or obsessed with an inflexible conception of RELIGION, like Jesse Bentley in "Godliness" or Curtis Hartman in "The Strength of God." They may be socially inert, like Seth Richmond in "The Thinker" or Enoch Robinson in "Loneliness," or suppressed by rigid gender roles, like Alice Hindman in "Adventure" or Belle Carpenter in "An Awakening."

In each case, as characters recognize their failure, they perceive a betrayal of sorts that includes the inability of language to facilitate the connections necessary to achieve wholeness and fulfillment. Language gives the truths the air of concrete substance, and when embracing individual truths reduces them to grotesques, these individuals intuitively think that language is a means of providing meaning. However, the plight that such characters experience involves their attempts to find empathy and understanding from others, seemingly as a way of transcending grotesqueness. As the tales show, these attempts regularly involve characters trying to communicate via language, often with George Willard, the town's young newspaper reporter. Nearly all of Anderson's characters in *Winesburg, Ohio* remain frustrated after such attempts.

Until this period American literary history was replete with characters who grappled with the meaning of their lives, struggled to achieve fulfillment in society, and embraced or rejected cherished American ideals. But following the lead of SAMUEL LANGHORNE CLEMENS (1835–1910), writing as Mark Twain, whom he acknowledged as a major influence, Anderson situated his characters in small-town middle America. In *Winesburg, Ohio* as in some of his other significant fiction, Anderson underscores the dignity of common people, showing in each tale that such individuals are not simplistic or pathetic but are imbued with the same aspirations and frustrations as "successful" individuals who swagger on a more public and powerful stage.

Early critics who dismissed the book as lewd failed to take into account that the Midwestern setting of *Winesburg, Ohio* epitomized sweeping changes affecting the nation as a whole. In *The Midwestern Ascendancy in American Writing* (1992) Ronald Weber discusses what he calls a "central ambivalence within Midwestern life" at the turn of the twentieth century that indeed may have served as a microcosm for the nation as a whole (23). Weber argues that the Midwest in this period was characterized by inherently contrary values: an elegiac memory for the promise of hope and innocence dating to the region's pioneering days, and the desire for the "full pursuit of progress and . . . refinement" that was to be found in burgeoning cities and industrial centers by the end of the nineteenth century (23). In *Winesburg, Ohio* Anderson displays an unabated sympathy for characters struggling in this milieu of social transformation. Rather than lead the REVOLT FROM THE VILLAGE with (HARRY) SINCLAIR LEWIS (1885–1951), he

Winesburg, Ohio

HANDS

UPON the half decayed veranda of a small frame house that stood near the edge of a ravine near the town of Winesburg, Ohio, a fat little old man walked nervously up and down. Across a long field that has been seeded for clover but that had produced only a dense crop of yellow mustard weeds, he could see the public highway along which went a wagon filled with berry pickers returning from the fields. The berry pickers, youths and maidens, laughed and shouted boisterously. A boy clad in a blue shirt leaped from the wagon and attempted to drag after him one of the maidens who screamed and protested shrilly. The feet of the boy in the road kicked up a cloud of dust that floated across the face of the departing sun. Over the long field came a thin girlish voice. "Oh, you Wing Biddlebaum, comb your hair, it's falling into your eyes," commanded the voice to the man, who was

7

Opening page of "Hands" from *Winesburg, Ohio*. B. W. Huebsch, 1919.
Image courtesy of Transylvania University Library

embraces the village because he was from the village and knew that in spite of its many faults, the simpler, more earnest agrarian values of the nation's Winesburgs could serve as a corrective to the industrialized, competitive lifestyle of modern America, represented by Chicago.

Anderson sketches many variant instances of grotesqueness throughout *Winesburg, Ohio*. But unlike his previous novels, in this work he refrains from setting down a definitive cure. In fact, consistent with the book's wariness of language, Anderson provides only an intuitive solution in the story "Sophistication" near the end of the book. There George Willard and Helen White seek each other out, intending to relate their newfound frustrations as maturing adults, but when they meet, they achieve an intuitive understanding not obfuscated or distorted by any spoken words. As the narrator aptly describes it, "for some reason they could not have explained they had both got from their silent evening together the thing needed" (200).

In much of his subsequent fiction and nonfiction, Anderson would recognize the modern grotesque in other locales. But with *Winesburg, Ohio*, his greatest achievement, Anderson helped secure the Midwest a significant place in the American literary canon and became a major influence on later writers. See THE CHANGING MIDWESTERN LITERARY CANON.

The Nick Adams stories by ERNEST (MILLER) HEMINGWAY (1899–1961), for instance, are directly influenced by Anderson's tales, as is much of the fiction by William Faulkner (1897–1962). Other twentieth-century writers such as Jean Toomer (1894–1967), Thomas (Clayton) Wolfe (1900–1938), (Mary) Flannery O'Connor (1925–1964), WRIGHT MORRIS (1910–1998), Raymond (Clevie) Carver (Jr.) (1938–1988), SAUL (C.) BELLOW (1915–2005), and John (Hoyer) Updike (1932–2009) acknowledged their indebtedness to Anderson, specifically for his experiments in the short-story form, writing from personal experience of local communities, studying society's have-nots, and capturing individuals' fleeting moments of insight. Today *Winesburg, Ohio* is enjoying something of a renaissance, evidenced by the many editions of it available in print and Random House's ranking it twenty-fourth on its list of the top one hundred literary works written in English in the twentieth century.

IMPORTANT EDITIONS: Originally published in 1919 by B. W. Huebsch, *Winesburg, Ohio* today can be found in nearly a dozen different editions in English and over a dozen translations. Ray Lewis White refers to his 1997 critical edition, *Sherwood Anderson's "Winesburg, Ohio,"* as an "expert text" of the book (lviii). Although this edition is interesting for its copious annotations that suggest models from Anderson's Ohio background for the characters and places appearing in the tales, its editorial methodology is seriously flawed, and occasional errors crop up in the annotations. Readers will be served best by either the 1996 Norton Critical Edition edited by Charles E. Modlin and Ray Lewis White or the 1997 Glen A. Love edition. Anderson adapted *Winesburg, Ohio* into an unsuccessful play, published in *Plays: "Winesburg" and Others* (1937).

FURTHER READING: Anderson often discussed *Winesburg, Ohio* in his letters and autobiographical works. His *Memoirs* (1942; critical edition edited by Ray Lewis White, 1969) includes an extended treatment; *A Story Teller's Story* (1924) also contains references to the book. The strongest edited collections of his letters on the subject are found in Howard Mumford Jones's 1953 *Letters of Sherwood Anderson* and William A. Sutton's 1985 *Letters to Bab*.

The first volume of Walter B. Rideout's *Sherwood Anderson: A Writer in America* (2006) provides valuable information on Anderson's life around the time he wrote *Winesburg, Ohio*. For a more detailed account of this period, see *A Storyteller and a City: Sherwood Anderson's Chicago* (1988) by Kenny Jackson Williams and Ronald Weber's *The Midwestern Ascendancy in American Writing* (1992). *Midwest Portraits* (1923) by HARRY HANSEN (1884–1977) and Floyd Dell's *Homecoming: An Autobiography* (1933) provide firsthand accounts of Anderson's experiences during the Chicago Renaissance.

Critical studies of *Winesburg, Ohio* are legion. Ray Lewis White's *"Winesburg, Ohio": An Exploration* (1990) provides a solid introduction. *Sherwood Anderson: An Introduction and Interpretation* (1967) by DAVID D(ANIEL) AN-

DERSON (1924–2011) and Robert Allen Pap-
inchak's *Sherwood Anderson: A Study of the
Short Fiction* (1992) are also noteworthy. William L. Phillips's "How Sherwood Anderson Wrote *Winesburg, Ohio*," originally published in 1951 and reprinted in Ray Lewis
White's 1966 collection *The Achievement of
Sherwood Anderson* (62–84) provides a close
examination of Anderson's composition of
the tales. Judy Jo Small's *A Reader's Guide to
the Short Stories of Sherwood Anderson* (1994)
is an excellent resource for detailing the
composition and publishing history of the
book and assessing the major critical studies on each tale.

Essays specifically on *Winesburg, Ohio*
exist in several general collections on Anderson's works, such as *The Achievement of
Sherwood Anderson*, edited by White; *Sherwood Anderson: A Collection of Critical Essays*
(1974), edited by Walter B. Rideout; *Sherwood
Anderson: Centennial Studies* (1976), edited by
Hilbert H. Campbell and Charles E. Modlin; and *Critical Essays on Sherwood Anderson*
(1981), edited by David D. Anderson. *New Essays on "Winesburg, Ohio"* (1990), edited by
John W. Crowley, offers a variety of theoretical perspectives on the book. David
Stouck's essay "Sherwood Anderson and the
Postmodern Novel," *Contemporary Literature*
26.3 (Fall 1985): 302–16, makes a compelling
case that *Winesburg, Ohio* and other works
are forerunners of postmodern fiction.
Robert Dunne's *A New Book of the Grotesques:
Contemporary Approaches to Sherwood Anderson's Early Fiction* (2005) provides extensive
interpretation of *Winesburg, Ohio* using postmodern theoretical approaches, as does
Clarence Lindsay's *Such a Rare Thing: The Art
of Sherwood Anderson's "Winesburg, Ohio"*
(2009). Mark P. Buechsel's *Sacred Land: Sherwood Anderson, Midwestern Modernism, and
the Sacramental Vision of Nature* (2014) also
demonstrates a contemporary perspective in
analyzing the work in the context of modernism and spirituality.

The *Sherwood Anderson Review*, published
by the Sherwood Anderson Society, was a
steady source for articles relating to Anderson's life until it ceased publication. The
manuscript of *Winesburg, Ohio* is held by the
Newberry Library in Chicago.

ROBERT DUNNE

CENTRAL CONNECTICUT STATE UNIVERSITY

WISCONSIN

Wisconsin was admitted to the Union as the
thirtieth state on May 29, 1848. Before statehood it was part of the Northwest Territory
from 1787 to 1800, Indiana Territory from
1800 to 1809, Illinois Territory from 1809 to
1818, Michigan Territory from 1818 to 1836,
and Wisconsin Territory from 1836 to 1848.

Area: 65,497 square miles

Land: 54,158 square miles

Water: 11,339 square miles

Population (2010 census): 5,686,986

OVERVIEW: Wisconsin's geography, Native
American peoples, and immigrant settlers
have combined to produce a vibrant, valuable, and distinctive literary heritage. The
forests and lakes of northern Wisconsin and
the farmland of southern Wisconsin have
directed the attention of many of its writers
to the landscape. Some have focused their
attention on the environment and have
written works of close natural observation,
showing either the influence of the environment on the lives of Wisconsin pioneers
and residents or how the harvesting of the
state's natural resources through logging or
other industries has changed individuals
and communities. The importance of agriculture to the state is reflected in the number of literary works with farm settings or
that recount the rural experience. Before
widespread European settlement and
after, Wisconsin's native tribes, Menominee,
Ojibwa, Ho-Chunk (formerly known as
Winnebago), Potawatomi, Stockbridge Mun-
see, Oneida, and Sauk, have sung their experience on the land. In the nineteenth

© Karen Greasley, 2014

century many Americans left their homes in New England and other eastern states to migrate to Wisconsin Territory. In addition, immigrants from across Europe, Asia, and Africa have settled in the state. Large numbers of Swedish, Swiss, Norwegian, English, Belgian, and Polish immigrants have made Wisconsin their home, but the largest cultural influence comes from Germany. The mass immigration of German settlers to the state that began during the middle of the nineteenth century had a dramatic effect on the state's intellectual and political life.

Wisconsin is a self-reflective state, and the themes and subjects of its literature are very often the natural landscape, the social movements taken up by its residents, and the ways of life of its cities, towns, farms, and countryside. The state's literary history coincides well with American literary movements. Since its settlement followed that of other Midwestern states, Wisconsin came later to the progression of American literary movements than did other states. Still, Wisconsin came to embrace both local color and regionalism as these movements found a congenial home amid the ethnic diversity of the state and the particular interest of the state's writers seeking their place in history. The large number of German freethinkers and intellectuals imprinted the state with a progressive stamp that continues to be visible today in the works of many of its writers.

Explorers described the Wisconsin landscape and its indigenous peoples as early as the seventeenth century, the period of the first European forays into the territory. The Fox and Wisconsin Rivers, which cross the state, assisted those early explorers in moving from the northeast to the southwest portion of the state and down the Mississippi, providing an efficient route for exportation of furs and timber while enhancing communication among settlers. Later, its excellent network of transportation waterways notwithstanding, its industrial center and port city, Milwaukee, was eclipsed by CHICAGO as a trading hub. Although Milwaukee remains a major business center, tourism and agriculture are the most fully developed economic enterprises in the state, and manufacturing and heavy industry are concentrated in the more populated southeast corner of the state and in the Fox River valley.

Wisconsin's writers have kept their eyes open, observing the natural environment, recording the historical events that have affected the state and the nation, and responding to the pressures of rural and urban life. They have left records of the ideas that intrigued them and the social forces at work in cities and on farms. Certainly, Wisconsin writers have much in common with Midwestern writers in general. If there are any areas that separate Wisconsin and its writers from those of other Midwestern states, they may be attributed to the state's natural landscape and its pattern of settlement. The many lakes and forests of the northern part of the state and the concentration of population in the southern urban centers give the state a wilderness quality that contrasts with the more heavily farmed states to the east, west, and south. The large numbers of nineteenth-century German immigrants who fled authoritarian repression after the failed German Revolution of 1848–1849 provided the state with a unique intellectual environment that remains alive even today. Although their numbers have declined over the years, Wisconsin continues to have active congregations of German freethinkers who have traditionally placed special emphasis on progressive inquiry. For example, Henrik Ibsen's *A Doll's House* (1879) was deemed so controversial that it could not easily find a venue or an audience in the United States, but the play's U.S. premiere took place in 1882 in Milwaukee, where an early adaptation of the play under the title *The Child Wife* opened to large audiences seven years before its New York premiere.

HISTORY AND SIGNIFICANCE:

Exploration and Travel: When Jean Nicolet became the first European to land on what would become Wisconsin soil in 1634, he was met at Green Bay by Winnebago Indians, now known as the Ho-Chunk. From the very first, European explorers and settlers shared Wisconsin with American Indian tribes. Like the Europeans, these tribes shifted locations across the territory in and out of the state as the result of political and tribal conflicts. Nicolet left no written record of his brief visit to Wisconsin, but other early French explorers did. Many of these accounts are included in *Early Narratives of the Northwest, 1634–1699* (1917), edited by Louise Phelps Kellogg. In 1673 a Jesuit priest, Jacques Marquette (1637–1675), joined with Louis Joliet (1645–1700) to travel across Wisconsin territory in the hopes that their exploration would discover a water route to the Pacific Ocean. The record of their travel in both French and English texts is contained in the 73 volume *The Jesuit Relations and Allied Documents: Travels and Explorations of the Jesuit Missionaries in New France, 1610–1791* (1896–1901), edited by Reuben Gold Thwaites (1853–1913).

The British presence in Wisconsin began with the French and Indian War in the mid-1700s and concluded with the War of 1812. During more than half a century, however, the British established no permanent settlements and exerted little influence in the territory.

The first British writer to describe Wisconsin was Jonathan Carver (1710–1780), who served as a mapmaker on Robert Rogers's 1767 expedition seeking a Northwest Passage. Carver crossed Wisconsin with Rogers and traveled up the Mississippi to a point north of MINNEAPOLIS. His account, *Travels through the Interior Parts of North-America, in the Years 1766, 1767, and 1768* (1778), generated a wide readership. Peter Pond (1740–ca. 1807) arrived in Wisconsin in 1773 to trade in furs. The account of his time in Wisconsin is published in *Five Fur Traders of the Northwest: Being the Narrative of Peter Pond and the Diaries of John Macdonell, Archibald N. McLeod, Hugh Faries, and Thomas Connor* (1933), edited by Charles Gates.

Even after the American Revolution, Wisconsin's wilderness attracted British attention. In 1836 the novelist Frederick Marryat (1792–1848) navigated the Fox and Wisconsin Rivers and recorded his trip in *A Diary in America, with Remarks on Its Institutions* (1839). British geologist and surveyor George William Featherstonhaugh (1780–1866) also crossed the Wisconsin territory via its rivers and recorded his observations in *A Canoe Voyage up the Minnay Sotor* (1847).

Americans also prepared works describing Wisconsin Territory. HENRY ROWE SCHOOLCRAFT (1793–1864), an early ethnologist and Indian agent, recorded his exploration of MICHIGAN, Wisconsin, and MINNESOTA in *Narrative Journal of Travels through the Northwestern Regions of the United States: Extending from Detroit through the Great Chain of American Lakes to the Sources of the Mississippi . . .* (1821) and *Narrative of an Expedition through the Upper Mississippi to Itasca Lake . . .* (1834). Juliette Kinzie (1806–1870), wife of the Indian agent at Fort Winnebago, described early settler life in *Wau-Bun, The "Early Day" in the North-West* (1856), based on her experiences from 1830 to 1833 in the early settlement at Portage. Wisconsin naturalist and archaeologist Increase Allen Lapham (1811–1875) also contributed to early accounts of the Wisconsin territory with his *Winter's Journey from Milwaukee to Green Bay* (1843).

Two important Wisconsin examples exist of the CAPTIVITY NARRATIVE, a popular genre that recorded experiences traveling and living with American Indians. The earlier account, *The Lost Child; or, The Child Claimed by Two Mothers: A Narrative of the Loss and Discovery of Casper A. Partridge among the Menominee Indians . . .* (1852) by Florus B. Plimpton (1830–1886) concerns the abduction of a six-year-old boy in Winnebago County. *Indian Massacre and Captivity of Hall Girls: Complete History of the Massacre of Sixteen Whites on Indian Creek, near Ottawa, Ill., and Sylvia Hall and Rachel Hall as Captives in Illinois and Wisconsin during the Black Hawk War, 1832* (1915) by Charles Martin Scanlan (1854–1940) recounts the events leading up to Sylvia and Rachel Hall's captivity, their travels through northern ILLINOIS to Black Hawk's Grove outside Janesville, Wisconsin, and their eventual ransom and return home after nine days with members of the Sauk tribe.

The first book printed in Wisconsin was published while it was still a territory. The fourteen-page publication, *Kikinawa-dendamoiwewin or Almanac, Wa Aiongin Obiboniman Debeniminang Iesos, 1834*, is an Ojibwa-language almanac printed in Green Bay in the offices of the first Wisconsin newspaper, the *Green-Bay Intelligencer,* probably in late 1833.

Fiction: An anonymous Milwaukee resident authored the first novel published in Wisconsin, *Garangula, the Ongua-Honwa Chief: A Tale of Indian Life among the Mohawks and Onondagas Two Hundred Years Ago* (1857). One of the earliest novels set in Wisconsin is *Out from the Shadows; or, Trial and Triumph* (1876) by Ella Giles Ruddy (1851–1917), a romance based on the Wisconsin murder of Daniel Ingersoll and the trial of his wife Sarah Ingersoll for the crime. Other romances by Ruddy include *Bachelor Ben* (1875), *Maiden Rachel* (1879), *Flowers of the Spirit* (1891), and *Club Etiquette* (1902).

Many Wisconsin authors have written historical fiction based on the exploration and settlement of the state. AUGUST (WILLIAM) DERLETH (1909–1971) is the foremost writer of Wisconsin historical novels and, thus far, Wisconsin's most prolific writer with over 150 works published during his lifetime. In *Bright Journey* (1940) he provides an account of the War of 1812 and the development of the fur trade using the historical figure Hercules Dousman (1800–1868) as his central character, recounting the life of that fur agent of John Jacob Astor to the point of his marriage proposal of 1842. In 1958 Derleth published *The House on the Mound,* a sequel and continuation of the fictionalized life of Dousman. Other historical novels by Derleth with Wisconsin settings include *The Hills Stand Watch* (1960), which traces a romance between a young Welsh woman and a Cornish man who settle in the Mineral Point lead-mining area, and *The Shadow in the Glass* (1963), a fictional biography of Nelson Dewey, Wisconsin's first governor. Derleth planned an ambitious Sac Prairie Saga, a collection of at least fifty works that would trace the changes in Sauk City and Prairie du Sac, the twin towns where he was born and raised, from the time of European settlement to the 1950s. In *Wind over Wisconsin* (1938) Derleth focuses on fur trader Chalfonte Pierneau, who in the early years of the 1830s experiences the loss of his wife, anticipates the end of the fur trade, and serves as a witness to the even greater loss and dispossession of the lands of Black Hawk and the Sauk Indians during the Black Hawk Indian War of 1832. *Restless Is the River* (1939)

traces the arrival of German immigrants to the Sac Prairie area and details the challenges they faced adapting to the harsh conditions after they left Germany following the failed revolution of 1848–1849. Derleth also published *Shadow of Night* (1943), a novel of revenge and forgiveness set in the early 1850s, once again drawing on the German intellectuals and freethinkers who were settling in Wisconsin in huge numbers. Finally, *Still Is the Summer Night* (1937) explores the love triangle among two brothers, Horatio and Alton Halder, and Horatio's wife, Julie. Set in the early 1880s, the novel investigates the relationship of these people while examining the life of a SMALL TOWN on the Wisconsin River.

Other Wisconsin writers have also published historical novels set in the state. In *The Landlooker* (1957) William Steuber (1904–2005) takes his main character, Emil Rohland, and his older brother, Rudolph, from Chicago to Wisconsin, where they plan to sell harnesses no longer needed by the government at the close of the Civil War. In the process the Rohlands experience life in a logging camp and arrive in Peshtigo shortly before the devastating fire of 1871. E. W. Lovell published *Legacy* (1934), a historical novel set in a disguised Green Bay that traces the history of the area through the lives of a family. Using the records of the Wisconsin, INDIANA, and Michigan Civil War units, John K. Driscoll (b. 1935) fictionalizes the history of the Black Hats of the Iron Brigade in his novel *The Baraboo Guards: A Novel of the American Civil War* (1995).

Small-town life in Wisconsin has been the subject of many writers who have directed their attention to the advantages of small towns, as well as to the scarcity of opportunities there. Among these writers, ZONA GALE (1874–1938) is perhaps the most distinguished. Gale transformed her native Portage, Wisconsin, into Friendship Village. In *Friendship Village* (1908), *Friendship Village Love Stories* (1909), *Neighborhood Stories* (1914), and *Peace in Friendship Village* (1919), Gale crafted optimistic, lighthearted fictions that present the village as a domestic utopia. A more realistic description of village life can be found in her novel *Birth* (1918) and in the novel *Miss Lulu Bett* (1920), which she transformed into an extremely successful play that was awarded a Pulitzer Prize for Drama in 1921.

Portage, Wisconsin, also produced Margery Latimer (1899–1932). Latimer came to the attention of Zona Gale when she was a teenager. Gale mentored Latimer and supported her through a scholarship while she was a student at the University of Wisconsin–Madison. Latimer's first novel, *We Are Incredible* (1928), contains an unflattering and sharply critical portrayal of Hester Linden, a thinly disguised version of Gale. Shortly afterward Latimer published a collection of short stories, *Nellie Bloom, and Other Stories* (1929). With Gale's continued support, Latimer published a second collection of short stories, *Guardian Angel, and Other Stories* (1932). The novella *Guardian Angel*, a Scribner's short-story-contest finalist, contains another savage portrait of Gale. Latimer married poet Jean Toomer (1894–1967) and died shortly after giving birth to their daughter in 1932.

Two contemporary writers focus on small-town Wisconsin, one through memoir and the other through the novel. Michael Perry (b. 1964) draws on his experience living in New Auburn, Wisconsin, and serving on its volunteer fire department in *Population 485: Meeting Your Neighbors One Siren at a Time* (2002). He gives an account of his courtship of his wife in *Truck: A Love Story* (2006) and of rural life in *Coop: A Year of Poultry, Pigs, and Parenting* (2009). David Rhodes (b. 1946), a graduate of the IOWA WRITERS' WORKSHOP, has set two novels in Words, a small town in Wisconsin's driftless region. *Driftless* (2008) and its sequel, *Jewelweed* (2013), trace the lives of the residents of this unincorporated town as they explore their identity and seek meaningful relationships with others tied to this small community.

As might be expected, Wisconsin produced many farm novels as part of its development. (HANNIBAL) HAMLIN GARLAND (1860–1940) gave American readers a realistic vision of the difficulties of farm life in the prairie states of his Middle Border: Wisconsin, IOWA, Minnesota, NEBRASKA, and the Dakotas. Wisconsin figures as a setting in only some of his short stories, among them several in *MAIN-TRAVELLED ROADS* (1891). *Rose of Dutcher's Coolly* (1895), generally considered

Garland's best novel, takes its central character, Rose, from the family's Wisconsin farm to Madison and eventually to Chicago. On its publication, many readers were shocked by Garland's frank treatment of the reproductive aspects of barnyard life. By 1898 Garland felt that he had lost touch with the Middle Border, and thereafter for a time his novels had western settings. He later returned to the Midwest and farm life in a series of popular autobiographical works partly set in Wisconsin: *A Son of the Middle Border* (1917), *A Daughter of the Middle Border* (1921), and *Trail-Makers of the Middle Border* (1926).

GLENWAY WESCOTT (1901–1987) was raised on a small farm outside Kewaskum in southeast Wisconsin, and his rural Wisconsin experience is reflected in his early work. His autobiographical first novel, *The Apple of the Eye* (1924), fictionalizes his childhood on the family farm and the complex and often painful relationships with his family members. *The Grandmothers: A Family Portrait* (1927) earned Wescott the Harper Prize. Reflecting from his home in Europe, Alwyn Tower, the central character, constructs a family chronicle of his ancestors' pioneer and farm experiences. The next year Wescott published a collection of short stories, *Good-bye, Wisconsin* (1928), set mostly in rural Wisconsin. The stories in the collection contrast the perceived limitations of the Midwestern rural experience with the cultural opportunities of urban and European life. *The Babe's Bed* (1930) concluded Wescott's treatment of Wisconsin in fic-

Hamlin Garland house, West Salem, Wisconsin, 2014. Photo by William Barillas.

tion, although he claimed throughout his life that his rural Midwestern experience was formative. Wescott was gay, and although homosexuality is not directly addressed in his Wisconsin fiction, the sensitive characters in this fiction are seen struggling to establish their identities. See also LESBIAN, GAY, BISEXUAL, TRANSGENDER, AND QUEER LITERATURE.

The attractions and the contemporary challenges of farm life are the subject of *A Map of the World* (1994) by JANE HAMILTON (b. 1957). Hamilton chronicles the loss of the Goodwin family farm, which suggests the loss of rural culture faced with a changing value system that results in a transformation of identity from rural to suburban. *The Short History of a Prince* (1998), a coming-of-age novel, focuses on the difficulty its central character, Walter McCloud, has in accepting his homosexuality, his failed goals as a ballet dancer, and his place both within a small Wisconsin community and in his family. Hamilton returns to the complexities of family relationships in *Disobedience* (2000), in which an adolescent boy discovers his mother's infidelity.

Other novelists have chosen to write about rural Wisconsin life. Margaret Ashmun (1875–1940), born in the Wisconsin town of Rural, set her novel *The Lake* (1924) along the Chain of Lakes in Waupaca County. Also born in Wisconsin, Ben Logan (1920–2014) returned to the state after a career writing for television and radio. *The Land Remembers: The Story of a Farm and Its People* (1975) recounts the life of a farm set against the changing seasons. *The Empty Meadow* (1983) presents Steve Carlson's coming into manhood during the Depression era. University of Wisconsin–Eau Claire writer John Hildebrand (b. 1949) has used fictional narrative techniques in his reflective, imagistic essay on his family's Minnesota farm in *Mapping the Farm* (1995). See also FARM LITERATURE.

In addition to farm and rural novels, Wisconsin has produced novels about urban life. Milwaukee and Madison, Wisconsin's two major urban centers, have been used as the settings for a number of novels that explore Wisconsin city life. Several Wisconsin novels are set in Milwaukee. William Henry Bishop (1847–1928) wrote *The Golden Justice* (1887), one of the first novels to use Milwaukee as its setting. See also URBAN LITERATURE.

Many Milwaukee novels focus on ethnicity, particularly Milwaukee's German American heritage. Among these are *Dawn O'Hara, the Girl Who Laughed* (1911) by EDNA FERBER (1885–1968) and *Bucket Boy: A Milwaukee Legend* (1947) by Ernest Meyer (1892–1953), a novel based on Meyer's boyhood experiences leading to his career in journalism. See NEWSPAPER JOURNALISM. August Derleth wrote about Milwaukee, as well as almost every other community in the state. His novel *The Wind Leans West* (1969) is set in Milwaukee and traces the development of the banking industry in the city beginning in 1839. Mary Helen Stefaniak (b. 1951) writes of Croatian American family life in 1930s Milwaukee in *The Turk and My Mother* (2004), while *Color of Law* (2000), a novel by David Milofsky (b. 1946), investigates a fictional case of racial injustice affecting that city's African American community. Milofsky has also written a coming-of-age novel, *A Friend of Kissinger* (2003), set in both Madison and Milwaukee. It treats the sexual awakening of its fourteen-year-old protagonist, Danny Meyer.

Madison, smaller than Milwaukee, has a surprising number of works set amid its four lakes. Wallace Stegner (1909–1993), better known for his writing about the West, uses Madison and the university campus in *Crossing to Safety* (1987). J. Allen Kirsch (b. 1955) has written two books, *Madlands* (1993) and *God's Little Isthmus: More Tales from Madlands* (1997), both of which poke fun at Madison's university and city politics, its reputation for left-leaning political correctness, and the bizarre behavior of many of its bohemian residents. *Birds of America* (1998), a collection of short stories by Lorrie Moore (b. 1957), contains a number of stories with Midwestern settings, including several with Madison connections. Her novel *A Gate at the Stairs* (2009), which was a finalist for the PEN/Faulkner Award, is set in a major university town closely resembling Madison. Kelly Cherry (b. 1940) sets her interconnected collection of short stories *The Society of Friends* (1999) in Madison. Madison novelist Jacquelyn Mitchard (b. 1955) uses Madison as part of the setting of her novel *The Deep End of the*

Ocean (1996). *The Dive from Clausen's Pier* (2002), the first novel by short-story writer Ann Packer (b. 1959), takes Carrie Bell, the central character, away from Madison and her paraplegic fiancé, Mike, to Manhattan. The novel compares New York and Madison; the East Coast is set against Midwestern culture as Carrie Bell confronts her future.

Many novels focus on Wisconsin's industries. Logging in Wisconsin began with European settlement but increased dramatically in the 1850s as the North Woods began to provide timber for the construction and expansion of Midwestern cities. By the 1890s logging had become Wisconsin's most profitable industry. One of the earliest novels to use the northern logging camps and shanties as its setting is *High Joe: The Logger's Story* (1892) by Jabez Burritt Smith (1852–1914). Smith's tale is more concerned with pointing out the dangers of drink and the virtues of temperance than it is with the lives of the loggers it depicts. The most significant novel of the logging industry is certainly Edna Ferber's *Come and Get It* (1935). Ferber tells the story of Barney Glasgow, a Wisconsin lumberman, and his family. Set amid the paper mills of the Fox River valley and in northern Wisconsin, the novel criticizes the excesses of these early entrepreneurs at the same time at which it recognizes the vision and determination they possessed, a situation that fueled the growth of the Midwest but devastated the North Woods environment. Ferber's novel was adapted for the screen in 1936. In 1941 Leslie Evan Schlytter (1896–1950) published *The Tall Brothers* (1941), a historical novel of the lumbering industry in Wisconsin. *Ballads and Songs of the Shanty Boy* (1926), edited by Franz Rickaby, though not a novel, conveys through the songs and biographical materials of logger William "Bill" Allen a sense of the life of the loggers who floated timber down Wisconsin rivers.

Novels and short fiction about fishing in Wisconsin, such as Victoria Houston's Loon Lake fishing mysteries, treated in the popular fiction section of this entry, are relatively common. For a state bounded on two sides by Lake Superior and Lake Michigan and on a third by the Mississippi River, Wisconsin novels examining commercial fishing are surprisingly rare. *Fisherman's Beach* (1962) by George Vukelich (1927–1995) may be the only novel to focus on a family of Great Lakes fishermen. See GREAT LAKES LITERATURE. Set in and around Two Rivers on Lake Michigan, the novel recounts the end of Old Man La Mere's life and the conflict over which of his sons will inherit his fishing business. Vukelich also wrote extensively about fishing in his essays collected in *North Country Notebook* (1987) and *North Country Notebook, volume 2* (1992).

Given the history of European migration into Wisconsin, a significant body of immigrant and ethnic literature exists in the state. Two novels by Edward Harris Heth (1909–1963) focus on Milwaukee's ethnic neighborhoods. In *Light over Ruby Street* (1940) Heth depicted the African American experience in Milwaukee. An earlier novel by Heth, *Told with a Drum* (1937), is set during World War I in Milwaukee and laments both the anti-German sentiment and the loss of German culture at that time. STERLING NORTH (1906–1974) treated similar themes in his novel *Night Outlasts the Whippoorwill* (1936). David Kherdian (b. 1931) has written about the Armenian American experience in Racine in two works for a young-adult audience, *The Road from Home: The Story of an Armenian Girl* (1979) and *Root River Run* (1984). See CHILDREN'S AND YOUNG-ADULT LITERATURE.

The experience of Polish immigrants in the Great Lakes region is the subject of the fiction of Anthony Bukoski (b. 1945). Bukoski has published four short-story collections, *Twelve below Zero* (1986), *Children of Strangers* (1993), *Polonaise* (1999), and *Time between Trains* (2003), with individual narratives set in Illinois, Michigan, and Wisconsin, especially the Superior, Wisconsin, area. Many of his stories illustrate the conflicts felt by immigrants who labored to maintain their Polish culture in the declining Lake Superior port community. Ken Parejko (b. 1945) treats similar themes in his novel *Remember Me Dancing* (1996), in which the central character, a young woman, must decide between accepting a marriage arranged by her mother and following her own heart. The experience of Norwegian immigrants to northern Wisconsin is chronicled by Muriel Halvorsen (1921–2013) in *With Trees on Either Hand* (1995).

The Indian tribes that lived in Wisconsin before the arrival of European immigrants had a rich oral tradition. The earliest literature of Wisconsin's tribes was passed down orally and is not associated with individual artists or writers. With the arrival of European settlers and a culture of individual rather than collective voices, a number of Wisconsin Native peoples saw their life experiences collected in print. See also NATIVE AMERICAN LITERATURE.

BLACK HAWK (1767–1838), or Ma-ka-tai-me-she-kia-kiak, attempted to reclaim land originally ceded to the Sauk but from which they were dispossessed as settlements in southern Wisconsin continued to make the Indian land desirable to whites. In 1832 Black Hawk and his followers, men, women, and children, were hunted down and many of them were slaughtered at the Bad Axe River along the southwest edge of the state. Imprisoned and eventually released, Black Hawk gave an account of his life published as *LIFE OF MA-KA-TAI-ME-SHE-KIA-KIAK, OR BLACK HAWK* (1833). A number of Black Hawk's uncollected speeches can be found in *Illinois Literature: The Nineteenth Century* (1986), edited by John E. Hallwas, and in Frank E. Stevens's *The Black Hawk War* (1903).

Like that of Black Hawk, the life story of Sam Blowsnake, or Hágaga (Ho-Chunk, 1875–1965), is filtered through the perspective of a white man. Ethnologist Paul Radin, who translated Blowsnake's *The Autobiography of a Winnebago Indian* (1920), later reshaped that book into *Crashing Thunder: The Autobiography of an American Indian* (1926). (Radin changed Blowsnake's name in the book to that of his brother, Crashing Thunder.) Both books provide information about Ho-Chunk cultural practices and stories while telling the story of Blowsnake's life. Mountain Wolf Woman (1884–1960), Blowsnake's sister, provides a perspective on the life and lifestyle of a traditional Ho-Chunk woman in her autobiography *Mountain Wolf Woman, Sister of Crashing Thunder: The Autobiography of a Winnebago Indian* (1961). Nancy Oestreich Lurie (b. 1924), an anthropologist at the University of Michigan, developed a close relationship with Mountain Wolf Woman and interviewed her in Ann Arbor, Michigan, for the autobiography.

Nonnative writers have also written novels chronicling the experience of Wisconsin's tribes. William Steuber's novel *Go Away, Thunder* (1972) focuses on the experiences of the Menominee Indians before the arrival of the Europeans. Phebe Jewell Nichols (1885–1964) published widely on Wisconsin's Menominee Indians, including biographies, cultural accounts, and one novel, *Sunrise of the Menominees* (1930).

Nature and Environmental Prose: Perhaps in no other area is the quality of Wisconsin writing as high as it is in its nature and ENVIRONMENTAL LITERATURE. Intellectually influenced by the transcendentalists and physically by the Wisconsin landscape in which he grew up, JOHN MUIR (1838–1914), though seen as a writer about the West, was Midwestern in origin and temperament. His autobiography, *The Story of My Boyhood and Youth* (1913), demonstrates how his love of the wild was fostered by his early days in Fountain Lake, northeast of Portage, Wisconsin, and led him to his achievements in wilderness protection. Also influenced by transcendentalism, particularly the works of Henry David Thoreau (1817–1862), was August Derleth. *Walden West* (1961) and *Return to Walden West* (1970) are prose poems that combine Derleth's observations on the natural environment along the Wisconsin River with the "lives of quiet desperation" lived by the inhabitants of his Sac Prairie. Like Muir, Derleth spent his youth largely outdoors in the meadows and bluffs along the Wisconsin River, an experience that helped him develop his environmental ethic.

A fervent conservationist and professor of wildlife management, ALDO LEOPOLD (1887–1948) is revered in Wisconsin and elsewhere as the father of environmental conservation. His most important work, *A SAND COUNTY ALMANAC* (1949), argues for a "land ethic," a proper relationship between humans and the environment, at the same time at which it focuses directly on a small, sandy piece of land northeast of Baraboo along the Wisconsin River, reinvesting that spent farmland with the importance Leopold felt humanity should ascribe to the land. Also of interest is *Round River: From the Journal of Aldo Leopold* (1953).

Transplanted Chicagoan NORBERT BLEI (1935–2013) follows in the tradition of these Wisconsin nature writers in a number of works, among them *Door Way: The People in the Landscape* (1981), *Door Steps: The Days, the Seasons* (1983), and *Meditations on a Small Lake (Requiem for a Diminishing Landscape)* (1987), all of which are infused with his understanding of the Door County environment, both human and natural.

Poetry: The first poem published in Wisconsin appeared in the first issue of the newspaper *Green-Bay Intelligencer* on December 11, 1833. All we know of the author of the elegy, "On the Death of Mrs. J. A. M. A.," is the author's initial, "E." In his preface Bernard I. Durward (1817–1902) identifies his book, *Wild Flowers of Wisconsin: Poems* (1872), as the first volume of poems published in the state; however, Rev. Noah Cressy's (1776–1867) *The Burning of the* Phoenix (1848), describing a marine disaster on Lake Michigan in 1847, was actually the first book-length publication. Many of the poems in Durward's collection contain references to Wisconsin settings, both rural and urban. Durward began dividing his time between his home in Milwaukee and a cabin he constructed in the Devil's Lake region, a location now known as Durward's Glen. He taught English at St. Francis Seminary in Milwaukee, and the religious references in his poetry reflect his Roman Catholic background.

ELLA WHEELER WILCOX (1850–1919) was a widely read poet at the close of the nineteenth century, writing sentimental poetry in quatrains after the fashion of Longfellow and the earlier Fireside Poets. Wilcox's first volume of poetry, *Drops of Water: A Selection of Temperance Poems and Reflections* (1872), was quickly followed by *Poems of Passion* (1883), which established her reputation. Other collections ensued, including *Poems of Pleasure* (1888), *Poems of Power* (1901), *The Collected Poems of Ella Wheeler Wilcox* (1917), and *Sonnets of Sorrow and Triumph* (1918). There is little Midwestern about her poetry, and less that could be identified as unconventional. Interest in her verse has yet to revive.

Born in Cumberland, Wisconsin, Mary Evaline Wolff (1887–1964) took the veil as SISTER MARY MADELEVA and published spiritual, introspective poetry of high quality. Among her poetry collections are *Knights Errant, and Other Poems* (1923), *A Question of Lovers, and Other Poems* (1935), *Gates, and Other Poems* (1938), *Selected Poems* (1939), and *The Last Four Things: Collected Poems* (1959). Sister Mary Madeleva's poetry demonstrates a remarkable control of poetic line.

LORINE NIEDECKER (1903–1970), Wisconsin's most distinguished poet, lived almost her entire life around her family home on Blackhawk Island on Lake Koshkonong. The natural world, Wisconsin history, and her life experience make up much of the subject matter of her poetry, and her spare poems communicate that subject matter with precision, clarity, and force. Niedecker's reputation has grown steadily since her death. The collections of poetry published in her lifetime, *New Goose* (1946), *My Friend Tree* (1961), *T and G: The Collected Poems, 1936–1966* (1968), and *My Life by Water: Collected Poems 1936–1968* (1970), have been followed by a number of posthumous collections,

Poet Lorine Niedecker, ca. 1920.
Courtesy of Hoard Historical Museum, Fort Atkinson, Wisconsin

including *Blue Chicory* (1976), *From This Condensery: The Complete Writing of Lorine Niedecker* (1985), *The Granite Pail: The Selected Poems of Lorine Niedecker* (1985), *Harpsichord and Salt Fish* (1991), and *Collected Works* (2002).

Wisconsin's ubiquitous and prolific August Derleth also made his mark in poetry, publishing roughly two dozen volumes. Derleth wrote nature, Wisconsin regional, and love poetry, showing a divided debt to Henry David Thoreau in theme and Robert Frost (1874–1963) in technique. Among his works are *Hawk on the Wind* (1938), *Rind of Earth* (1942), *Selected Poems* (1944), *The Edge of Night* (1945), *Elegy: On the Umbral Moon* (1957), *By Owl Light* (1967), *Collected Poems, 1937–1967* (1967), and *The Landscape of the Heart* (1970). Edna Meudt (1906–1989), a friend of Derleth, developed a statewide reputation as a poet. Her collections include *Round River Canticle* (1960), *In No Strange Land* (1964), and *The Ineluctable Sea* (1975), which contains a series of poems on the final years of August Derleth's life.

Although Ronald Wallace (b. 1945) was born in Cedar Rapids, Iowa, he spent well over a quarter of a century in Wisconsin until his retirement from directing the University of Wisconsin–Madison's creative-writing program. Some of his poems focus on south central Wisconsin locales; others look back to his earlier years in both Iowa and MISSOURI. A winner of the Hopwood Award in 1970 and the Cairn Poetry Prize in 1975, Wallace has published seven books of poetry, including *Long for This World: New and Selected Poems* (2003).

Wisconsin's governors have named four poet laureates. The first two, Ellen Kort (1936–2015) and Denise Sweet (b. 1952), are both Native Americans with Anishinaabe/Ojibwa tribal affiliations. Kort, Poet Laureate from 2000 to 2004, was the author of *There Is Something Ancient Here* (1986), *If Death Were a Woman* (1994), *Notes from a Small Island* (1994), and *Sing Back My Bones* (1996). Denise Sweet, appointed poet laureate for 2004 to 2008, was born in Minnesota but grew up in Wisconsin. Among her works are *Know by Heart* (1992) and *Songs for Discharming* (1997). In 2008, the tenure of Wisconsin Poet Laureate was changed to a two year term. The third Poet Laureate, Marilyn Taylor (b. 1939), served from 2009–2010. Taylor's

books include *Shadows like These* (1994), *Exit Only: Twenty-One Poems* (2001), and *Subject to Change* (2004). She also served as the Poet Laureate of Milwaukee from 2004 to 2006. Bruce Dethlefsen (b. 1948) served as the state's fourth Poet Laureate for 2011–2012. His poems "The House We Haunt is Ours" (*Free Verse*, June/July 2009) and "For the Time Being" (*Quill and Parchment*, June 2009) were both nominated for the Pushcart Prize. In 2011, the Wisconsin Academy of Sciences, Arts, and Letters assumed stewardship of the Poet Laureate program. Max Garland (b. 1954), author of *The Postal Confessions* (1995) and *Hunger Wide as Heaven* (2006), was Poet Laureate for 2013–2014. Kimberly Blaeser (b. 1955), a poet of Anishinaabe ancestry, serves a term as Poet Laureate for 2015–2016. Blaeser's work, including the collections *Absentee Indians and Other Poems* (2002) and *Apprenticed to Justice* (2007), has been highly acclaimed.

J(ohn) D(ennison) Whitney (b. 1940) teaches creative writing at the University of Wisconsin–Marathon County. His collection *sd* (1973; expanded edition, 1988) is a sequence of poems focusing on the relationship of a married couple. He has turned to American Indian themes, publishing *Grandmother Says* (2005), another sequence of poems of remarkable insight. Robert Schuler (b. 1939) has published extensively in Wisconsin; his collections include *Music for Monet* (1984) and *The Red Cedar Suite* (1999). Tom Montag (b. 1947) has focused his attention on Midwesternness, the subject of his Vagabond in the Middle project, which is intended to explore the Midwestern character. His earlier work is collected in *Middle Ground* (1982).

Wisconsin has produced many poets who have seen their work published in chapbooks and collections. Among them are Antler (born Brad Burdick) (b. 1946), with *Antler: The Selected Poems* (2000); Margaret Benbow (b. 1944), *Stalking Joy* (1997); Norbert Blei, *Paint Me a Picture, Make Me a Poem* (1987); Karl Elder (b. 1948), *A Man in Pieces* (1994); R. Virgil Ellis (b. 1933), *The Tenting Cantos* (2009); Jean Feraca (b. 1943), *Crossing the Great Divide* (1992); Susan Firer (b. 1948), *The Lives of the Saints and Everything* (1993); Doug Flaherty (b. 1939), *Good Thief Come Home: Selected Poems, 1970–1990* (1990); David Graham

(b. 1953), *Greatest Hits, 1975–2000* (2001); Horace Gregory (1898–1982), *Selected Poems* (1951); William Harrold (1936–2001), *Trails Filled with Lighted Notions* (1988); John Judson (b. 1930), *The Inardo Poems* (1996); Richard Kirkwood (1931–2013), *Dying like Keats* (1980); William Ellery Leonard (1876–1944), *Two Lives* (1925); Carl Lindner (b. 1940), *Angling into Light* (2001); William Meissner (b. 1948), *The Sleepwalker's Son* (1987); Lou B. "Bink" Noll (1927–1986), *The House* (1984); Mike O'Connell (b. 1943), *My Bucket's Got a Hole in It* (1995); Angela Peckenpaugh (b. 1942), *Remembering Rivers* (1991); Felix Pollak (1909–1987), *Say When* (1969); Sara Rath (b. 1941), *Remembering the Wilderness* (1983); Bruce Renner (b. 1944), *The Language of Light Ambits* (1988); Mary Shumway (1926–2000), *Legends and Other Voices: Selected and New Poems* (1992); David Steingass (b. 1940), *Fishing for Dynamite* (1998); Dennis Trudell (b. 1938), *Fragments in Us: Recent and Earlier Poems* (1996); Mark Turcotte (b. 1958), *The Feathered Heart* (1998); and Roberta Hill Whiteman (b. 1947), *Star Quilt* (1984).

Drama: The earliest dramatic work printed in Wisconsin was *The Drummer; or, New York Clerks and Country Merchants: A Local Play, in Two Acts* (1851). It was written by Benjamin Penhallow Shillaber (1814–1890) and printed in Milwaukee.

Although both THORNTON (NIVEN) WILDER (1897–1975) and BEN HECHT (1894–1964) were born and raised in Wisconsin, neither dramatist spent much of his productive career in the state or used Wisconsin as the setting for his plays. Wilder's *Our Town* (1938) may have a cast of characters steeped in Midwestern values, but the play's events are located in Grover's Corners, New Hampshire. The title of most celebrated Wisconsin dramatist falls to Zona Gale, who published *The Neighbors* in 1914 and won a Pulitzer Prize in 1921, the first for a woman dramatist, for *Miss Lula Bett* (1920). She followed the successful *Miss Lulu Bett* with *Uncle Jimmy* (1922) and *Mister Pitt* (1925), an adaptation of *Birth* (1918). See also DRAMA.

William Ellery Leonard, in addition to his poetry, published two plays, *Glory of the Morning* (1912) and *Red Bird: A Drama of Wisconsin History in Four Acts* (1923); both use the Ho-Chunk tribe as subject matter. Both Leonard and Gale supported the Wisconsin

Dramatic Society, a Milwaukee organization. The society published two collections of plays, *Wisconsin Plays* (1914) and *Wisconsin Plays: Second Series* (1920), in which the work of both authors is represented. The 1930s saw publication of two additional collections of plays for amateur performance: *Wisconsin Rural Plays* (1931) and *Wisconsin Community Plays* (1935).

As soon as he arrived in Wisconsin from KANSAS, ROBERT EDWARD GARD (1910–1992) became active in promoting regional plays and regional writing throughout the state. Gard wrote a number of regional plays, among them *The Freedom: A Wisconsin Comedy in Three Acts* (1948) and *River Boat* (1948), and his creation of the Wisconsin Idea Theatre and the Wisconsin Idea Theatre Conference in 1945 had a profound effect in encouraging dramatists and theatre groups across the state by providing a forum for the exchange of ideas.

Fred Alley (1963–2001), co-founder of the American Folklore Theatre in Door County, wrote a number of plays and musicals in the Robert Gard tradition. Best known among his works is *Guys on Ice* (1998), a musical set in an ice-fishing shanty on a Wisconsin lake. This play, *Lumberjacks in Love* (1996), and *The Bachelors* (2001), written with James Kaplan, make up Alley's musical trilogy. With James Valcq, he adapted *The Spitfire Grill* (1996) and set the play in Gilead, Wisconsin. Paul Muldoon (b. 1951) used Wisconsin as the setting for the libretto of his opera *Shining Brow* (1993), a treatment of Frank Lloyd Wright's affair with Mamah Cheney at Taliesin in Spring Green.

Printing and Journalism: Albert G. Ellis (1800–1885), known as General Ellis for his service as surveyor general for both Iowa and Wisconsin, improvised a printing press as early as 1827 in Green Bay, although it took until 1833 for him to secure printing equipment from DETROIT capable of producing a folio newspaper. That newspaper, Wisconsin Territory's first, the *Green-Bay Intelligencer,* published its initial issue on December 11, 1833, asserting that its goal was "the advancement of the country west of Lake Michigan." Only the *Chicago Democrat* preceded the *Intelligencer* in publishing west of Lake Michigan. Eighteen months later, reflecting its politics, Ellis changed the newspaper's name to the *Green-Bay Intelligencer and Wisconsin Democrat.*

Newspapers developed on both sides of the Milwaukee River before the City of Milwaukee was incorporated. Milwaukee's first newspaper, the *Milwaukee Advertiser,* represented the interests of Byron Kilbourn's west-side Kilbourntown and released its first issue on July 14, 1836. On the east side, Solomon Juneau lent his support to the *Milwaukee Sentinel,* which began publication in June 1837. Kilbourntown and Juneautown eventually combined with Walker's Point to form Milwaukee in 1846. The *Milwaukee Advertiser* ceased publication in 1841 and was immediately succeeded by the *Milwaukee Courier,* while the *Sentinel* continues as Wisconsin's longest-running daily newspaper, now the *Milwaukee Journal Sentinel* after merging with another newspaper, the *Milwaukee Journal,* in 1995. See also NEWSPAPER JOURNALISM.

Shortly after the turn of the twentieth century, Wisconsin boasted approximately 750 daily, weekly, or semi-weekly publications. Many of these reflected Wisconsin's European immigrants, particularly Germans and Scandinavians. In 1844 the *Wiskonsin-Banner* began publication in Milwaukee; it was soon followed by *Volksfreund,* which later combined with the *Wiskonsin-Banner* to form *Banner und Volksfreund.*

Mathilde Franziska Anneke (1817–1884) published *Deutsche Frauen-Zeitung,* a periodical advocating women's rights in Milwaukee, beginning in 1852. The first Norwegian-language newspaper in the United States, *Nordlyset,* was published in Racine County beginning in 1847. Additionally, La Crosse was the home of *Fædrelandet,* another Norwegian-language paper, which started in 1864. Eventually it merged with *Emigranten* to form *Fædrelandet og Emigranten* in Minneapolis in 1868.

A number of Wisconsin presses publish books of interest to local, regional, and national audiences. See also PRINTING AND PUBLISHING. The University of Wisconsin Press, a nonprofit division of the University of Wisconsin–Madison Graduate School, released its first book in 1937. Currently, it publishes over one hundred new books a year, including a significant number on the culture, history, and literature of Wisconsin and the upper Midwest. Since 1985 the University of Wisconsin Press has selected and published the work of the annual winner of its Brittingham Prize in Poetry.

Arkham House may be Wisconsin's most distinguished little press. Founded by August Derleth and Minnesotan writer Donald Wandrei (1908–1987) after the death of horror-fiction writer H. P. Lovecraft in 1937, Arkham House began publishing Lovecraft's work, which had previously seen print only in pulp magazines. Over the years Derleth and Wandrei expanded the press, publishing weird, ghost, and science-fiction books by new and established authors, many of them Midwesterners. The short stories of both RAY (DOUGLAS) BRADBURY (1920–2012) and Robert Bloch (1917–1994) were first collected in books published by Arkham House: Bloch in *The Opener of the Way* (1945) and Bradbury in *Dark Carnival* (1947). Derleth collected his own macabre short stories as well, a number of them set in Wisconsin, including *Someone in the Dark* (1941), *Something Near* (1945), and *Not Long for This World* (1948).

Founded as Waubesa Press in 1990, Badger Books focuses on publishing books on Midwestern subjects, primarily on Wisconsin. Its Famous Wisconsin series currently includes notable Wisconsin films, authors, mystics, artists and architects, and musicians.

Wisconsin Federal Writers' Project: Wisconsin writers participated in the FEDERAL WRITERS' PROJECT as part of the U.S. Works Progress Administration (WPA). The Federal Writers' Project was intended to support writers during the Depression because they were as hard hit by the Depression as workers in manufacturing and other sectors of the economy. An additional goal was to help writers maintain their professional skills. The Wisconsin Federal Writers' Project undertook a number of projects, including the Wisconsin volume of the American Guide Series, published as *Wisconsin: A Guide to the Badger State* (1941). Lorine Niedecker was employed as a writer on the project, as was wood engraver Frank Utpatel, who designed the chapter headpieces and tailpieces for the publication. Staff members as part of the Folklore Project undertook other assignments, including preparing typescripts on Wisconsin circus lore and Wisconsin Indian lore.

They also conducted interviews with Wisconsin residents on pioneer and early town life, as well as the immigrant experience. See IMMIGRANT AND MIGRANT LITERATURE. In 1998 faculty in the University of Wisconsin Anthropology Department discovered 167 notebooks written by Wisconsin Oneida Indians as part of the Oneida Ethnological Study, associated with the Oneida Language and Folklore Project of the WPA, which had been believed lost. Project members developed a nineteen-letter alphabet for the previously unwritten Oneida language, and Oneida Indians conducted interviews and wrote about Oneida life in Wisconsin. Sixty-six of the 167 notebooks are written in full or in part in Oneida.

Popular Literature:

Dime Novels: DIME NOVELS, inexpensive and often melodramatic adventure stories, gained an active readership in the last half of the nineteenth century. The unsettled wilderness frequently provided the backdrop for these popular novels, and Midwestern settings, including Wisconsin, were not unusual. Although Thomas C. Harbaugh (1849–1924) was not a Wisconsinite, he placed at least one of his novels, *Nightingale Nat; or, The Forest Captains* (1878) in the vicinity of Lake Superior. So, too, did William G. Patten (1866–1945), writing under the pseudonym Burt L. Standish. His Merriwell series includes *Frank Merriwell in Form; or, Wolfers, the Wonder from Wisconsin* (1905). Paul Bibbs, about whom little is known other than his residence in Madison, Wisconsin, wrote at least one novel set partly in Wisconsin, *Scarlet Moccasin; or, The Forest Fort's Queen* (1870). *The Silver Bugle; or, The Indian Maiden of St. Croix* (1864) treats Minnesota's Indian war of 1862 but also includes action set in Wisconsin and Iowa. About its author, Lieut.-Col. Hazeltine, nothing is known, including his real name. Researchers will find Wisconsin's dime novels a field entirely open to investigation.

Mystery and Detective Fiction: Wisconsin residents and localities have served as the inspiration and setting for much MYSTERY AND DETECTIVE FICTION. In the 1950s Ed Gein gained notoriety for a series of grisly murders and dismemberments in his rural Wisconsin farmhouse. Robert Bloch used Gein as the model for Norman Bates in his novel *Psycho* (1959), and almost three decades later Thomas Harris (b. 1940) reintroduced Gein to the reading public as the Buffalo Bill of *Silence of the Lambs* (1988). Although Bloch placed the Bates Motel in Illinois and used Wisconsin only infrequently in his settings, many mystery writers have located their works in cities and rural areas across Wisconsin.

August Derleth published ten Judge Peck mysteries during the 1930s and 1940s, including *Murder Stalks the Wakely Family* (1934), *The Man on All Fours* (1934), *Sign of Fear* (1935), and *Mischief in the Lane* (1944). These conventional whodunits follow Judge Ephraim Peabody Peck and Dr. Jasper Considine as they solve murders committed in Sac Prairie and neighboring towns, such as Madison, Baraboo, and Mineral Point.

Writing as Craig Rice, Georgia Ann Randolph Craig (1908–1957) created the hard-drinking lawyer John J. Malone. Although most of Craig's novels are set in Chicago, *Trial by Fury* (1941) is set in a fictionalized Fort Atkinson, Wisconsin. Craig partnered with Baraboo-born Stuart Palmer (1905–1968) to write a collection of stories, *People vs. Withers and Malone* (1963), which combined Craig's Malone with Palmer's popular spinster sleuth, Hildegarde Withers.

Milwaukee writer Jack Ritchie (1922–1983), born John George Reitci, published more than 350 detective stories in magazines such as *Manhunt, Alfred Hitchcock's Mystery Magazine,* and *Ellery Queen's Mystery Magazine* from the 1950s through the 1970s. His detective, Milwaukee police officer Henry Turnbuckle, figures prominently in a number of his stories using a Milwaukee setting. The Turnbuckle stories have been collected in *The Adventures of Henry Turnbuckle* (1987). Another writer who uses Milwaukee as a location for her mysteries is Kathleen Anne Barrett (b. 1954), who was born and raised in Milwaukee. She has produced a series of mysteries featuring Beth Hartley, a nonpracticing attorney doing legal research in the Milwaukee area. Barrett's works include *Milwaukee Winters Can Be Murder* (1996), *Milwaukee Summers Can Be Deadly* (1997), and *Milwaukee Autumns Can Be Lethal* (1998).

Three detective series explore crime in the small towns along the Mississippi River, in the Wisconsin North Woods, and on an

American Indian Reservation. Mary Logue (b. 1952) has created a series of detective novels featuring Claire Watkins, a widow who has left the Minneapolis area to become the deputy sheriff of Fort St. Antoine, Wisconsin. *Blood Country* (1999), *Dark Coulee* (2000), and *Bone Harvest* (2004) focus on Watkins's criminal investigations and her personal life as she solves mysteries and confronts the loss of her husband and the creation of her new life. In *Dead Angler* (2000), *Dead Creek* (2000), *Dead Water* (2001), *Dead Frenzy* (2003), and *Dead Hot Mama* (2004) by Victoria Houston (b. 1945), the Loon Lake, Wisconsin, sleuth is retired dentist Doc Paul Osborne, who teams up with the female police chief, Lew Ferris, to solve murders and hone their fishing skills. Houston's series captures the small-town culture of northern Wisconsin and focuses on that area's obsession with angling. Cherokee mystery writer Mardi Oakley Medawar (b. 1945) has turned from nineteenth-century Kiowa healer and sleuth Tay-bodal to begin a new series of mysteries set on the Ojibwa Red Cliff Reservation near Bayfield, Wisconsin. In *Murder on the Red Cliff Rez* (2002) Police Chief David Lameraux and "Rez Tracker" Karen Charboneau investigate the murder of the tribal attorney and eventually uncover illegal logging and crooked reservation leaders. Other Wisconsin mysteries include *Sunflower* (1998) and *Bleeding Heart* (2000) by Martha Powers (b. 1941).

Children's and Young-Adult Literature: Wisconsin's forests, lakes, rivers, and small towns have provided the backdrop for the work of a number of writers of juvenile and young-adult fiction. Certainly one of the most popular is CAROL RYRIE BRINK (1895–1981), who based her Caddie Woodlawn books on her grandmother's stories of pioneer life in Wisconsin and her own meticulous research. *Caddie Woodlawn* (1935) earned a Newbery Medal for its realistic description of life on the land in the 1860s. Brink followed her successful tale with *Magical Melons: More Stories about Caddie Woodlawn* (1944). Another work by her with a Wisconsin setting is *Winter Cottage* (1968). See also CHILDREN'S AND YOUNG ADULT LITERATURE.

Raised and educated in Wisconsin, MARIE HALL ETS (1893–1984) used her experiences in the state to write and illustrate a number of children's books. *Mr. Penny* (1935), *Mr. Penny's Horse Race* (1956), and *Mr. Penny's Circus* (1961), as well as *Mr. T. W. Anthony Woo* (1951), are set in rural Wisconsin. She places *In the Forest* (1944), *Another Day* (1953), and *Just Me* (1965) in Wisconsin's North Woods.

ELIZABETH ENRIGHT (GILLHAM) (1909–1968) also authored and illustrated children's books. A niece of FRANK LLOYD WRIGHT (1867–1959), with whose family she summered as a child, Enright learned from her grandmother about the experiences of Welsh immigrants to the state at the same time at which she explored the outdoors. The Wyoming Valley outside Spring Green, Wisconsin, is the setting for *Thimble Summer* (1938), in which Garnet Linden finds a magic thimble that provides for her a series of summer adventures. Also set in Wisconsin are *Gone-Away Lake* (1957) and *Return to Gone-Away* (1961). *Thimble Summer* earned a Newbery Medal, and *Gone-Away Lake* was recognized as a Newbery Honor Book.

August Derleth authored two series of juvenile books, one set along the Wisconsin River during the 1920s and the other set in Wisconsin and Michigan during the early years of exploration and settlement. The more popular of these two series is the Steve and Sim books, a series of ten novels that translate Tom Sawyer, Huckleberry Finn, and the Mississippi of SAMUEL LANGHORNE CLEMENS (1835–1910), writing as Mark Twain, into Stephen Grendon, Simolean Jones, and the Wisconsin River. In each of the novels Derleth's alter ego, Steve, leads his innocent friend Sim into trouble. The novels include *The Moon Tenders* (1958), *The Mill Creek Irregulars* (1959), *The Pinkertons Ride Again* (1960), *The Ghost of Black Hawk Island* (1961), and *Tent Show Summer* (1963). Novels in the American Heritage Series include *The Captive Island* (1952), *Empire of Fur* (1953), *Land of Gray Gold* (1954), and *Sweet Land of Michigan* (1962). *The Beast in Holger's Woods* (1968) is set around Rhinelander, Wisconsin, and features that lumber town's mythical beast, the Hodag.

Although he lived outside the Midwest for almost half his life, Sterling North created a number of memorable children's books linked to Wisconsin. His most famous work, *Rascal: A Memoir of a Better Era* (1963), uses the natural world around Edgerton, Wisconsin, to show a boy's growth and development, accompanied by the raccoon, Rascal. *The Wolfling: A Documentary Novel of the Eighteen-Seventies* (1969) is set during the era of North's father's youth in the Lake Koshkonong area. In this novel a young boy captures a young wolf-dog and makes the animal his own in spite of difficulties with his family and community.

Madison, Wisconsin, children's author and illustrator Kevin Henkes (b. 1960) has set a number of his works in Madison, as well as in fictional Wisconsin towns. *Return to Sender* (1984), *Two under Par* (1987), *The Zebra Wall* (1988), *Words of Stone* (1992), and *Protecting Marie* (1995) are notable works by this author.

Romance Novels: In its earlier days the romance novel often required an exotic setting or metropolitan locale for its hero. Since the dramatic increase in the number of romance novels during the last half of the twentieth century, romance writers have felt free to explore other locales, including ones in the Midwest. Romance novels are ephemeral, and dozens appear in and disappear from print from year to year.

In the early 1990s Harlequin created a miniseries of connected romances and romantic entanglements set in Tyler, Wisconsin, "America's favorite hometown." Titles include *Wisconsin Wedding* (1992) by Carla Neggers (b. 1955); *Bachelor's Puzzle* (1992) and *Courthouse Steps* (1993) by Ginger Chambers; *Blazing Star* (1992) by Suzanne Ellison; *Monkey Wrench* (1992) and *Whirlwind* (1992) by Nancy Martin (b. 1953); *Sunshine* (1992) and *Bright Hopes* (1992) by Pat Warren (b. 1936); and *Crossroads* (1992) and *Love Knot* (1993) by Marian L. Franz (b. 1949) and Carol I. Wagner (b. 1940), writing together as Marisa Carroll. The Return to Tyler series includes *Tyler Brides* (2001), a collection of three novelettes by Kristine Rolofson (b.1975), Jacqueline Diamond (Hyman) (b. 1949), and Heather MacAllister (b. 1953), as well as *Prescription for Seduction* (2001) by Darlene Scalera (b. 1958).

Lori Wick (b. 1958) has garnered a following for her faith-based Christian romances. *Sophie's Heart* (1995) investigates the difficulties of opening up to romantic relationships after the loss of a spouse. Wick's *A Song of Silas* (1990) is a historical romance set in the fictional farmland around Baxter, Wisconsin, during the 1880s. *The Long Road Home* (1991) is the sequel to *Song of Silas*. Set in Bayfield, Wisconsin, and the North Woods logging communities, the novel reintroduces Pastor Paul Cameron, who must come to terms with the loss of his wife, Corrine, and regain the faith that was shaken by her death.

Romance writers have turned to e-books as an alternative means of distributing their works. Christine DeSmet (b. 1954) has released her romance novel *Spirit Lake* (2001) in both e-book and traditional paperback formats. In this book, set in northern Wisconsin, wildlife rescuer Laurel Hastings discovers her former love, Cole Wescott, who has chosen to hide from killers in an empty Spirit Lake mansion.

Science Fiction: Wisconsin has its share of authors writing science, fantasy, and horror fiction. Perhaps the most widely read of Wisconsin's science-fiction writers is CLIFFORD D(ONALD) SIMAK (1904–1988). Although Simak left Wisconsin after his graduation from the University of Wisconsin–Madison, his fiction often uses his native Millville, Wisconsin, and the Wisconsin countryside for its settings. Notable works include *Way Station* (1963), in which the main character, a man well over one hundred years old, staffs an intergalactic way station in southwest Wisconsin, and *The Goblin Reservation* (1968), which uses the campus of his alma mater, the University of Wisconsin–Madison, as the location from which Professor Peter Maxwell undertakes his adventures in the future. See also SCIENCE FICTION AND FANTASY.

Once again, August Derleth exercised his considerable influence on Wisconsin writing, this time on science and horror fiction. He published several collections of horror fiction, including *Someone in the Dark* (1941), *Something Near* (1945), and *Lonesome Places* (1962). A collection of Derleth's science fiction featuring journalist Tex Harrigan was published posthumously as *Harrigan's File* (1975). Derleth worked within H. P. Lovecraft's Cthulhu Mythos in *The Mask of Cthulhu* (1958) and *The Trail of Cthulhu* (1962), applying a Wisconsin look and feel to Lovecraft's New England locales.

Peter (Francis) Straub (b. 1943) was born, raised, and educated in Wisconsin, although he has lived in Ireland and currently has residences in both New York and England. A number of his explorations of psychopathic behavior and tales of supernatural events have Wisconsin settings, often designed to heighten the effect. His thirteen-story collection *Houses without Doors* (1990) contains the Milwaukee-based short story "A Short Guide to the City," which employs the city's ethnic neighborhoods as parts of its setting. His early works, including *If You Could See Me Now* (1977) and his second novel, *Under Venus* (1985), are set in fictional Wisconsin towns. With Stephen King (b. 1947), Straub co-authored *The Talisman* (1984); *Black House* (2001) is set in another fictional town, Tamarack, Wisconsin, which suffers the depredations of a serial killer. He earned the Bram Stoker Award for his novel *A Dark Matter* (2010), set in Madison during the 1960s. The novel follows the lives of four young people who are induced to participate in an occult rite that affects their lives decades into the future.

Barry B. Longyear (b. 1942), though not a Midwestern writer, has crafted one novel, *City of Baraboo* (1980), worthy of mention for moving the Wisconsin circus tradition into the twenty-second century. Neil Gaiman (b. 1960) was born in England but lived a number of years in Wisconsin. His fantasy novel *American Gods* (2001) possesses a clear Midwestern orientation. It employs several Wisconsin locales and traces the impending conflict between the old gods of the immigrants to America and the new gods of our technological future.

Lesbian and Gay Fiction: Works with gay and lesbian themes are now being published with increasing frequency and are being read by larger audiences interested in issues of gender. See LESBIAN, GAY, BISEXUAL, TRANSGENDER, AND QUEER LITERATURE. In the 1920s some mainstream writers addressed issues of homosexuality but were obliged to do so obliquely. Glenway Wescott, for example, does not make sexual orientation an overt issue in either *The Apple of the Eye* (1924) or *Good-bye, Wisconsin* (1928), but he hints at the difficulties through the alienation of a number of his characters. Perhaps the most significant Wisconsin gay text is *Farm Boys: Lives of Gay Men from the Rural Midwest* (1996), a collection of personal narratives by gay

men edited by Will Fellows. These voices present a distinctly Midwestern viewpoint, contrasting their experiences with those of the culturally dominant East and West Coasts.

Writers of gay and lesbian fiction, like other Wisconsin fiction writers, explore issues of importance to them. Elizabeth Ridley (b. 1966) has published two novels of self-discovery, *Throwing Roses* (1993) and *Rainey's Lament* (1999), both set partially in Milwaukee. Both novels trace the healing process of their protagonists and investigate relationships between mothers and daughters. Nikki Rashan (1972–2015), an African American novelist, in *Double Pleasure, Double Pain* (2003), writes about the difficulty young women experience in coming to terms with their lesbianism. *Hodag Winter* (1991) by Deborah Wiese (b. ca. 1971) focuses on discrimination in the workplace. Her protagonist, Colleen O'Hara, is removed from her teaching position when the principal of her northern Wisconsin school discovers her sexual orientation. Writing under the name Jackie Calhoun, Jackie Calhoun Smith (b. 1934) has published a number of lesbian romance novels that also examine personal and social issues experienced by gay and lesbian individuals. Among her many works set in Wisconsin are *Lifestyles* (1990) and *Woman in the Mirror* (2004). Her second novel, *Second Chance* (1991), is partially set in the state.

Wisconsin has produced several gay mystery novelists. Michael Craft Johnson (b. 1950), writing as Michael Craft, created a seven-book series featuring journalist Mark Manning and his life partner, architect Neal Waite, amateur sleuths who solve mysteries with thematic ties to political and social themes significant to a gay audience. In the first two novels, *Flight Dreams* (1997) and *Eye Contact* (1998), Mark Manning is employed by a Chicago newspaper. In the third novel in the series, *Body Language* (1999), he moves from Chicago to Dumont, Wisconsin, to begin publishing a local newspaper. *Name Games* (2000), *Boy Toy* (2001), *Hot Spot* (2002), and *Bitch Slap* (2004), the concluding books in the series, are all set in Wisconsin. John Peyton Cooke (b. 1967) places his novel *The Chimney Sweeper* (1994) in Isthmus City, Wisconsin. Jesse James Colson, Cooke's protagonist, joins the Isthmus City police force, but as an individual guilty of murder himself, he feels pressure to acknowledge his former criminal life. Cooke's vampire novel *Out for Blood* (1991) is set in Chicago, Madison, and pre-Soviet Russia. In 1991 Wisconsin novelist Barbara Lindquist (1930–2013), writing as B. L. Holmes, published *Mega*, a dystopian novel set in a homophobic future. Finally, the novel *The Night Listener* (2000) by Armistead Maupin (b. 1944) is partially set in Wisconsin and explores the relationship between a public radio storyteller, Gabriel Noone, and one of his fans, an abused, HIV-infected, thirteen-year-old Wisconsin boy. It was made into a movie starring Robin Williams in 2006.

Graphic Novels: GRAPHIC NOVELS have increased in popularity around the turn of the twenty-first century. A development from manga, Japanese graphic books or visual novels, these works address serious themes in book-length comic-book format. Craig Thompson (b. 1975) has created an autobiographical coming-of-age graphic novel, *Blankets* (2003), partially set in a rural Wisconsin landscape. In the novel the protagonist confronts the difficulties of falling in love and growing up in a strictly religious family; the book traces the main character's movement toward adulthood and simultaneous loss of faith. The American Library Association named *Blankets* one of the best books for young adults published in 2003.

Literary Awards: The Wisconsin Library Association recognizes Wisconsin authors with two awards. The Notable Wisconsin Author Award is given to Wisconsin writers, past and present, who have lived for a significant amount of time in Wisconsin and have made a contribution to the state's literary and intellectual climate. As of 2008 the Wisconsin Library Association had identified 126 notable Wisconsin authors, including, RAY STANNARD BAKER (1870–1946), Norbert Blei, August Derleth, Marie Hall Ets, Edna Ferber, Zona Gale, Robert Gard, Hamlin Garland, Jane Hamilton, WALTER (EDWIN) HAVIGHURST (1901–1994), Aldo Leopold, John Muir, Lorine Niedecker, GEORGE W(ILBUR) PECK (1840–1916), FREDERICK JACKSON TURNER (1861–1932), Glenway Wescott, LAURA INGALLS WILDER (1867–1957), Thornton Wilder,

and Frank Lloyd Wright. Since 1974 the Banta Award has been given annually to a Wisconsin author for a book of significant literary or intellectual value published in the preceding calendar year. Winners of the award, presented with the support of the Banta Foundation of the Banta Corporation, include a number of established literary figures, among them Thornton Wilder, Ben Logan, Lorine Niedecker, Margaret George (b. 1943), Ellen M. Hunnicutt (1931–2013), Jane Hamilton, and Ronald Wallace.

Several other Wisconsin associations support literary award competitions. The Wisconsin Academy of Sciences, Arts, and Letters annually conducts the *Wisconsin People and Ideas* Fiction and Poetry Contests. Finalists in these contests have their works published in *Wisconsin People and Ideas*. The Council for Wisconsin Writers sponsors a number of award competitions, among the most significant of which are the Lynde and Harry Bradley Major Achievement Award, given to recognize a writer's most significant literary accomplishments, and the Christopher Latham Sholes Award for support of Wisconsin writers and writing. In 2002 Milwaukee poet Antler received the first Bradley Major Achievement Award, and Wisconsin's first poet laureate, Ellen Kort, received the first Christopher Latham Sholes Award. Finally, the Wisconsin Regional Writers' Association, a statewide group founded by Robert Gard as part of his commitment to supporting professional and amateur regional writing in Wisconsin, conducts a number of popular writing contests each year, among them the Jade Ring Contest, which includes winners in a number of genres, the Florence Lindemann Humor Contest, and the Al P. Nelson Feature Article Contest.

Literary Societies: A number of societies encourage literary endeavor in general, as well as individual Wisconsin writers. See CLUBS, SALONS, AND SOCIETIES. The most significant statewide organization supporting Wisconsin creative writers and scholars is the Wisconsin Academy of Sciences, Arts, and Letters, established in 1870. The academy publishes two periodicals, *Wisconsin People and Ideas*, formerly the *Wisconsin Academy Review*, and the peer-reviewed *Transactions*, which explore thought and culture from a Wisconsin perspective. The academy also conducts annual writing contests and publishes the work of winners in its periodicals.

Another organization is the Wisconsin Regional Writers' Association (WRWA), founded by Robert Gard in 1948 to assist amateur and professional writers in improving their craft. An inclusive organization reflective of the Wisconsin idea that the borders of the university are the borders of the state, the WRWA supports its members regardless of their level of expertise by publishing newsletters, holding regional conferences, and sponsoring annual writing contests. The Wisconsin Fellowship of Poets was organized in 1950 to foster a greater appreciation of poetry, support Wisconsin poets, and promote the study of poetry in Wisconsin schools. The fellowship conducts annual poetry contests.

Three individual Wisconsin writers have been the subject of organizations founded to promote their study. The Hamlin Garland Society, an affiliate of the American Literature Association, was formed in 1999 to encourage scholarly research on Hamlin Garland. The August Derleth Society first met in 1978 in Prairie du Sac, Wisconsin, and is dedicated to promoting the reading of Derleth's works. To that end, it supports writing contests at the elementary school level, as well as at fourteen University of Wisconsin campuses. Finally, the Sterling North Society was founded in 1989 to promote the work of Sterling North and the Edgerton, Wisconsin, area. All three societies issue newsletters and maintain digitized collections of images and text on their websites.

SELECTED WORKS: Some Wisconsin writers deserve special note as major figures in the state's literary history. The land has been the focus of Wisconsin's most significant and influential writers, beginning with Juliette Kinzie's *Wau-Bun, the "Early Day" in the North-West* (1856). In historical fiction, August Derleth wrote of the decline of the fur trade and Blackhawk's defeat in *Wind over Wisconsin* (1938), while in *The Landlooker* (1957) William Steuber re-created the experience of northern residents of the state after the Civil War at the time of the Peshtigo fire. John Muir's autobiographical *The Story of My*

Boyhood and Youth (1913) connects his development to the Wisconsin environment, and Aldo Leopold's *A Sand County Almanac* (1949) uses his family shack along the Wisconsin River as a springboard for creating a land ethic. The influence and importance of cultivated land has been addressed by Wisconsin writers as well, most significantly by Ben Logan in *The Land Remembers: The Story of a Farm and Its People* (1975) and in Jane Hamilton's poignant novel *A Map of the World* (1994). The lives of those who live on the land and the way their environment molds them have been subjects of Wisconsin's significant writers. Hamlin Garland's *Rose of Dutcher's Coolly* (1895) looks at the role of women in society, as does Zona Gale's *Miss Lulu Bett* (1920). Another early feminist writer, Margery Latimer (1899–1932), is also of interest, particularly for her short-story collection *Guardian Angel, and Other Stories* (1932). Edna Ferber's *Come and Get It* (1935) focuses on the lumber industry in the Fox River valley. Social and economic pressures are the subject matter of Glenway Wescott in *Good-bye, Wisconsin* (1928) and Zona Gale in *Birth* (1918). August Derleth's prose poem *Walden West* (1961) intersperses nature writing with considerations of the difficulties of small-town life.

Wisconsin lagged behind other Midwestern states in the production of an anthology of poetry by its state's writers. The first collection of Wisconsin poetry is very likely *Poetry out of Wisconsin* (1937), edited by August Derleth and Raymond E. F. Larsson. This anthology contains works by 198 poets, including established writers such as Zona Gale, Hamlin Garland, Lorine Niedecker, Sister Mary Madeleva, and Glenway Wescott, as well as single poems by minor poetic voices. Derleth and Larsson include a representative selection of nineteenth-century Wisconsin poetry in addition to some selections by German immigrants to the state. *The Journey Home: The Literature of Wisconsin through Four Centuries* (1989) in three volumes, edited by Jim Stephens, is a significant resource for students and researchers.

The Wisconsin Federation of Poets has sponsored publication of at least three collections of Wisconsin poetry: *Poems out of Wisconsin* (1961), edited by Maude Totten; *Po-*

ems out of Wisconsin III (1967), edited by Jo Bartels Alderson and J. Michael Alderson; and *New Poetry out of Wisconsin* (1969), edited by August Derleth. These three anthologies focus on the work of contemporary Wisconsin poets. *Brewing: 20 Milwaukee Poets* (1972), edited by Martin J. Rosenblum, contains the work of young, emerging poets living in the Milwaukee area and includes early work by Antler, Susan Firer, and Tom Montag. The anthology *Wisconsin Poetry* (1991), edited by Carl N. Haywood, is a special issue of *Transactions of the Wisconsin Academy of Sciences, Arts, and Letters*. Wisconsin writers submitted thousands of poems to the Wisconsin Academy, from which 213 poems by sixty-five poets were selected for publication, including work by Antler, Norbert Blei, Susan Firer, Ronald Wallace, and J. D. Whitney.

Several anthologies illustrate the breadth of Wisconsin's multicultural poets. *Dreaming History: A Collection of Wisconsin Native-American Writing* (1995), edited by Mary Anne Doan and Jim Stevens, contains poetry from American Indian poets with a variety of tribal affiliations, as well as a general bibliography of sources focused on Wisconsin's Indian tribes and their writers. *I Didn't Know There Were Latinos in Wisconsin: An Anthology of Hispanic Poetry* (1989), edited by Oscar Mireles, provides representative samples of the works of twenty Latino/Latina poets writing in both English and Spanish. See also LATINO/LATINA LITERATURE.

FURTHER READING:

Bibliographies: For over a century librarians and scholars have worked to compile bibliographies of Wisconsin writers. The first, *Bibliography of Wisconsin Authors* (1893) by Emma Alethea Hawley, includes books held in the collection of the State Historical Society of Wisconsin. In addition, it lists articles from periodicals and papers from scholarly or professional society transactions whether or not those materials were holdings of the society's library. In 1937 the Wisconsin Library Association supported Mary Emogene Hazeltine in the compilation of *One Hundred Years of Wisconsin Authorship, 1836–1937*. This bibliography lists the works of nine hundred Wisconsin authors who were born or lived for an extended period in Wisconsin. A later bibliography has added to

the earlier compilations: *Wisconsin Authors and Their Books, 1836–1975* (1976) by Orrilla T. Blackshear identifies the publications of 5,300 Wisconsin writers.

On Wisconsin: Books about the Badger State for Children and Young Adults (1997), compiled by the Cooperative Children's Book Center at the University of Wisconsin-Madison, provides an annotated bibliography of children's books written about Wisconsin. The bibliography is organized by subject area. Other resources in this area include Kathy Howard Latrobe's *Exploring the Great Lakes States through Literature* (1994) and *The Great Lakes Region in Children's Books: A Selected Annotated Bibliography* (1980), edited by Donna Taylor.

The only extended study of Wisconsin's literary history is August Derleth's *Wisconsin Writers and Writing* (1998), edited by Peter Ruber and Kenneth B. Grant. Derleth prepared a series of six lectures on the state's literary history and presented the lectures at the University of Wisconsin–Madison in the fall of 1963. *The State of Wisconsin 1977 Blue Book* contains an extended analysis by John O. Stark of nine Wisconsin authors: John Muir, Hamlin Garland, Zona Gale, Aldo Leopold, Horace Gregory, Glenway Wescott, Mark Schorer (1908–1977), August Derleth, and Ben Logan, all of whose work was influenced by their lives in the state.

For the study of early Wisconsin printing and publishers, the volumes of the American Imprints Inventory of the WPA for the state are the standard source. *A Check List of Wisconsin Imprints* was issued in four parts by the Wisconsin Historical Records Survey in 1942, covering 1833–1849, 1850–1854, 1855–1858, and 1859–1863; a fifth part covering the years 1864–1869 appeared in 1953. An important precursor, *Early Printing in Wisconsin, with a Bibliography of the Issues of the Press, 1833–1850* (1931) was written by Douglas C(rawford) McMurtrie (1888–1944). Besides the useful annotated bibliography, the book contains detailed historical and biographical information about the various early printing establishments and printers, as well as numerous facsimiles of the products of these presses.

A later work on the state's writers, *Famous Wisconsin Authors* (2002) by James P. Roberts, contains thirty-five sketches of

Wisconsin poets and fiction writers. The Wisconsin Library Association published *Wisconsin Literary Travel Guide* (1989), which contains an alphabetical listing of selected cities and towns along with literary connections for each locale.

Libraries and Repositories: The largest collection of published works on Wisconsin topics can be found in the University of Wisconsin–Madison Memorial Library collection. Memorial Library's holdings exceed 3 million volumes, the largest individual library collection in the state. As part of the University of Wisconsin system, the Memorial Library allows users to search electronically all the University of Wisconsin library collections on its twenty-six campuses. In addition, an increasing number of historical and literary works are being digitized and made available on the internet as part of the University of Wisconsin's Digital Collections: The State of Wisconsin Collection.

Although the State Historical Society of Wisconsin's library in Madison does not exclusively acquire Wisconsin literary texts for its holdings, it houses a large collection of Wisconsin historical materials. The Historical Society Archives contains extensive literary correspondence and manuscript collections of a number of Wisconsin authors, including Edna Ferber, Zona Gale, and August Derleth.

Wisconsin's Own Library, a collection begun in the 1940s by the wife of Governor Oscar Rennebohm and sponsored by the Wisconsin Federation of Women's Clubs, is currently housed in the Lane Library of Ripon College. The 4,697 volumes of the collection were written or edited by individuals who were born in Wisconsin or had an established residence in the state.

With over 2 million volumes, the Milwaukee Public Library is the largest public library in the state. Since its inception in 1878, the Milwaukee Public Library has aggressively acquired local- and state-authored texts and has established an archive of manuscripts by Milwaukee authors, among which are the historical novels of Anne Powers (Schwartz) (1913–1987).

KENNETH B. GRANT
UNIVERSITY OF WISCONSIN–BARABOO/SAUK COUNTY

WONDERFUL WIZARD OF OZ, THE

HISTORY: Written by L. FRANK BAUM (1856–1919), and published in 1900, *The Wonderful Wizard of Oz* ushered in not only a new century but also a new type of imaginative children's literature that Baum called a modernized fairy tale. His innovative form eliminated the heavy-handed didacticism rife in children's literature up to this time, as well as the fearsome moralizing evidenced in works like those of the Brothers Grimm. *The Wonderful Wizard of Oz*, as Baum states in his introduction to the book, "was written solely to pleasure children of today. . . . The wonderment and joy are retained and the heart-aches and nightmares are left out" (5).

The general story line is well known, if only through the 1939 MGM film version, *The Wizard of Oz*, which employed most elements of the original book with the notable exceptions of the beginning and ending segments. Dorothy, a little orphan girl, is transported by a tornado from her aunt and uncle's KANSAS farm to the fairyland of Oz. There she encounters strange inhabitants and talking animals, some of whom advise her that only the Wizard of Oz can help her get home. Along the way she meets a scarecrow, a tin woodman, and a cowardly lion. Together they travel to the Emerald City to ask the Wizard for his help. After many adventures, including the revelation that the great wizard is nothing more than a ventriloquist and sleight-of-hand artist from Omaha who had arrived in Oz some years before on a runaway balloon, Dorothy is finally returned to her Kansas farm by means of magic silver shoes that had belonged to a wicked witch. Although the 1939 film portrays Dorothy's time in Oz as merely something she dreamed, Baum's original story leaves no doubt that her magical journey was to a real place.

Baum and his illustrator-collaborator, W. W. Denslow (1856–1915), completed *The Wonderful Wizard of Oz* in October 1899, the work of only a few months after their acclaimed and best-selling 1899 debut with *Father Goose, His Book*. The manuscript of the new story about the magical fairyland of Oz carried a number of provisional titles, among them "The Emerald City," "From

Kansas to Fairyland," and "The Land of Oz," the last being the one under which Baum originally registered the copyright with the Library of Congress in January 1900. *The Wonderful Wizard of Oz* was first published during the third week of May 1900 by the Chicago firm of George M. Hill Company, but the first printing of 10,000 copies did not appear in bookstores until mid-September. Demand for the book was so great that three more printings were needed to satisfy the reading public. According to the publisher's claims, some 90,000 copies of *The Wonderful Wizard of Oz* had been issued by January 1901; however, evidence in Denslow's account books showing royalties received, as well as bankruptcy documents of the George M. Hill Company, indicate that the figure was around 35,000 copies. Whichever number is correct, the book was an unqualified best seller.

When the George M. Hill Company failed in 1902, Indianapolis publisher Bobbs-

Opening page of L. Frank Baum's *The Wonderful Wizard of Oz*. G. M. Hill Co., 1900.
Image courtesy of Special Collections, Grand Valley State University Libraries

Merrill obtained the printing plates and reissued the book in 1903 under the revised title *The New Wizard of Oz.* Other than the title, no significant changes were made to either Baum's text or Denslow's illustrations. Bobbs-Merrill seems to have kept the book in print continuously until 1956, when the copyright expired and the work entered the public domain. After the appearance of the 1939 movie, *The Wizard of Oz*, a number of abridged picture-book adaptations of Baum's book for young children appeared; however, these followed the story line of the film rather than Baum's text.

Baum initially intended *The Wonderful Wizard of Oz* to be a single stand-alone volume and had given no thought to writing sequels. Demand from his young readers for more stories about Oz and its denizens at last compelled him to write *The Marvelous Land of Oz*, which was published by Reilly & Britton in 1904. This book, as well as all subsequent Oz titles until 1942, was illustrated by John R. Neill. By the time of his death in 1919, Baum had written fourteen Oz books, and the series was so popular that the publisher engaged Ruth Plumly Thompson (1891–1976) to continue the stories. Thompson, as the "Royal Historian of Oz," contributed one book a year to the Oz canon from 1921 through 1939, when she ended her association with Reilly & Lee. From 1940 through 2015 no fewer than thirty additional Oz books appeared from various authors.

The initial critical reception of the Baum and Denslow collaboration was mostly positive. Many reviewers commented that the book was unique in the world of children's books, while others made favorable comparisons to Lewis Carroll's *Alice in Wonderland* (1865). The book sold well in 1900 because it was unlike anything on the market at the time, but aggressive, widespread marketing, particularly during the Christmas season, was also important.

From 1900 through 1930 the popularity of *The Wonderful Wizard of Oz* and its growing number of sequels remained high, but public libraries made attempts to remove the books from their children's shelves in the 1930s and again during the mid-1950s. The first series of attempts was instigated by the New York Public Library and the second by the Detroit Public Library. Both were widely emulated. In the first case, no reason was given for the censorship, but in DETROIT the rationale for removing the books was couched in vague and unconvincing terms that condemned them for poor writing, old-fashioned ideas, and, most ludicrously, lack of imagination. Although these attacks by librarians were without merit, they may partly explain the conspicuous absence of references to Baum or his works in the majority of critical works on children's literature until the mid-1970s.

SIGNIFICANCE: The Midwestern milieu of the first and last chapters of *The Wonderful Wizard of Oz* stems directly from Baum's experiences in Aberdeen, SOUTH DAKOTA. In 1888 he and his family moved there, hoping to find business opportunities in the West after his upstate New York lubricating-oil business failed. Unfortunately, they arrived in Aberdeen at the onset of an economic depression further exacerbated by long-term drought.

The dry, flat, featureless Great Plains of the Dakotas were thus relocated to the Kansas prairie that Baum so vividly describes in the first chapter of *The Wonderful Wizard of Oz*. Baum drew on his firsthand observations of the landscape and his knowledge of the families who worked the South Dakota land to juxtapose the colorless, hardscrabble Kansas farm to the verdant, wondrous plentitude of the Land of Oz.

The tornado is another Midwestern phenomenon that Baum employs. These devastating storms are common in the open Midwestern prairie, and the destructive 1890 tornado near Aberdeen impressed Baum. His memory of that storm was the source for the "cyclone" that carries the farmhouse and Dorothy from Kansas to Oz.

Baum's unsuccessful ventures as an Aberdeen general-store proprietor and newspaper editor caused him and his family to move to CHICAGO in 1891. There he finally made his name as a writer. Suzanne Rahn in *The Wizard of Oz: Shaping an Imaginary World* (1998) and Katharine Rogers in *L. Frank Baum: Creator of Oz* (2002) suggest that Chicago influenced the creation of *The Wonderful Wizard of Oz* in two important ways. The first was the World's Columbian Exposition, held in Chicago for six months in

1893. The exposition's famed White City with its mechanical innovations and electrical wonders was transmuted in Baum's imagination into the Emerald City, the major metropolis and capital of Oz.

The second influence was literary. Residing in Chicago at this time was novelist (HANNIBAL) HAMLIN GARLAND 1860–1940). His essay "The Literary Emancipation of the West," published in *Forum* in October 1893, called for a new Midwestern literary style that rejected current forms and instituted a new one that he would later term "veritism" in his *Crumbling Idols* (1894). Garland's veritism consciously combined local color and realism, as had his *MAIN-TRAVELLED ROADS* (1891). The opening chapter of *The Wonderful Wizard of Oz* echoes Garland, and Baum's unequivocal, unromanticized picture of the empty gray Kansas prairie is especially startling because it was unlike anything else in children's literature.

After the book's positive reception Baum began to prepare a substantially different musical comedy version called *The Wizard of Oz*. Opening in New York in mid-1902, this so-called extravaganza was a popular and financial success. It played for years on Broadway and with touring companies throughout the country. In 1975 another Broadway musical, *The Wiz*, appeared, also based on Baum's book.

At least four motion-picture adaptations of *The Wonderful Wizard of Oz* have appeared in addition to Baum's 1908 combined film and live-action production depicting scenes from several of his Oz books. Two silent films were produced in 1910 and 1925, and the iconic Judy Garland vehicle now considered an American classic appeared in 1939. The fourth was an indifferent 1978 film version of the stage musical *The Wiz*.

Besides the publisher-sanctioned sequels, *The Wonderful Wizard of Oz* has inspired other imaginative literature using the Oz universe. A four-book series by Gregory Maguire (b. 1954), the Wicked Years, has arisen from the reimagined and revisionist Oz milieu: *Wicked* (1995), a story of Dorothy's nemesis, the Wicked Witch of the West, and three sequels, *Son of a Witch* (2005), *A Lion among Men* (2008), and *Out of Oz* (2011). *Wicked* was adapted as a Broadway musical in 2003. Some film critics have noted that George Lucas's *Star Wars: A New Hope* (1977) can be seen as a *Wonderful Wizard of Oz* transported to a distant galaxy.

IMPORTANT EDITIONS: The first edition of *The Wonderful Wizard of Oz*, like those of many books written for children, is quite scarce and difficult to locate in collectible condition; when copies do appear in the marketplace, they can command high prices.

The Wizard of Oz and Who He Was (1957) by Martin Gardner and Russell B. Nye was the first critical edition of the *Wonderful Wizard of Oz*. It was published, ironically, at the height of the efforts to remove the book from American library shelves.

A later critical edition edited by Michael Patrick Hearn, *The Wizard of Oz* (1983), was published in Schocken's Critical Heritage Series. It contains not only the complete text of the book but also selected important critical essays, from early appreciations to later interpretations that view Oz as utopia or the book as an allegory of Populist thought. Hearn also edited *The Annotated Wizard of Oz* (1973). It was reissued, revised and expanded, as *The Annotated Wizard of Oz Centennial Edition* (2000), a volume in W. W. Norton's series of annotated classics. Besides copious notes and explications, this volume contains a full-color reproduction of the first edition's text and illustrations.

One other full-color facsimile of the first edition of *The Wonderful Wizard of Oz* is currently in print, published in 2000 by HarperCollins as part of its Books of Wonder series.

FURTHER READING: Baum's 180-word preface to *The Wonderful Wizard of Oz* is a clear authorial statement. In *The Annotated Wizard of Oz* Michael Patrick Hearn terms this a "manifesto for the liberation of American children's literature" that sets forth the author's intentions in writing the book (5). In subsequent interviews and other comments Hearn enlarges on these ideas.

Suzanne Rahn's *The Wizard of Oz: Shaping an Imaginary World* (1998), a volume in Twayne's Masterwork Studies, contains a useful survey of the literary and historical context of Baum's first Oz book, as well as a new critical reading of it. Rahn is also the editor of *L. Frank Baum's World of Oz: A Classic Series at 100* (2000), a collection of essays issued under the auspices of the Children's Literature Association to celebrate the centennial of the first publication of Baum's book. Rahn's introduction to the volume is a valuable survey of the public and critical reception of *The Wonderful Wizard of Oz* through the years.

Katharine M. Rogers's scholarly biography *L. Frank Baum: Creator of Oz* (2002) is the first since the hagiographic memoir *To Please a Child: A Biography of L. Frank Baum, Royal Historian of Oz* was published by Baum's eldest son Frank Joslyn Baum in 1961. Although Rogers breaks no new ground, she does provide three chapters on Baum's years in South Dakota and Chicago, as well as on the writing and publication of *The Wonderful Wizard of Oz*.

Detailed and indispensable bibliographic information about editions, states, and variants of the entire Oz series are found in the second edition of *Bibliographica Oziana: A Concise Bibliographical Checklist of the Oz Books by L. Frank Baum and His Successors*, compiled by Douglas Greene and Peter Hanff (1988). Two important works that deal with the book's initial publication are *A Bookbinder's Analysis of the First Edition of "The Wonderful Wizard of Oz"* (2011) by Michael O. Riley and Peter Hanff's *Cyclone on the Prairies: "The Wonderful Wizard of Oz" and the Arts & Crafts of Publishing in Chicago, 1900* (2011).

Fraser Sherman's *The Wizard of Oz Catalog* (2005) provides an exhaustive annotated list of the original Oz books and sequels; theatrical adaptations; comic-book versions; adaptations for audio, film, and television; and electronic formats and computer games.

The International Wizard of Oz Club, founded in 1957, is a flourishing society devoted to the study and appreciation of Baum and all his works. Its journal, *The Baum Bugle: A Journal of Oz*, appears three times a year and publishes popular and semischolarly articles. Its Spring 2000 issue (44.1) celebrates the one hundredth anniversary of *The Wonderful Wizard of Oz* and includes newspaper clippings from Baum's scrapbook that record the initial critical reception of the book.

The original manuscript of *The Wonderful Wizard of Oz* was allegedly destroyed after

Baum's death in 1919 by Maud Gage Baum, his wife.

ROBERT BEASECKER   GRAND VALLEY STATE UNIVERSITY

. . . *Y NO SE LO TRAGÓ LA TIERRA* / . . .
AND THE EARTH DID NOT DEVOUR HIM

HISTORY: With the 1971 publication of . . . *y no se lo tragó la tierra* / . . . *And the Earth Did Not Devour Him* by Tomás Rivera (1935–1984), an important new literary voice emerged in the United States. Awarded the Quinto Literary Prize, the first national award for Chicano/Chicana literature, the novel has become a classic of LATINO/LATINA LITERATURE, as well as of U.S. literature in general.

The young Chicano protagonist of this novel, initially unmoored and confused, comes to understand his story and sense of self as rooted in the collective narrative of Mexican Americans, especially those who, like him, labor in the fields. Work and life for Chicano/Chicana migrant workers in the Midwestern United States, including discrimination and appalling work conditions, as well as the promise of greater opportunity and the formation of new communities, are central not only to the action of Rivera's groundbreaking novel but also to its articulation of a Chicano/a collective experience that is also Midwestern. Rivera acknowledged the significance of the region in Chicano/a experience, and the publication of his first novel firmly established connections to the canons of Chicano/a and U.S. literature.

Rivera wrote the novel in Spanish. The first and most subsequent editions have been bilingual. Although it is set in the late 1940s and early 1950s, the volume was a literary milestone that paralleled political and social developments among Mexican Americans and the emergence of the Chicano Movement in the 1960s and 1970s.

For the first two decades of his life Rivera was a migrant worker, joining his family yearly on the journey as far north as MINNESOTA and back again to Crystal City, Texas, his birthplace and hometown. Rivera suggested in an interview with Juan Bruce-Novoa in *Chicano Authors: Inquiry by Interview* (1980) that his experiences in the Midwest were pivotal in his formation as a writer since it was there that he discovered reading and writing, the former with the help of a friendly librarian in Hampton, IOWA, at the age of ten and the latter when he composed his first short story, based on a car accident he experienced with his family in Bay City, MICHIGAN (141–42). Rivera also acknowledged his Texas background when he described the import of his discovery of Américo Paredes's *"With His Pistol in His Hand": A Border Ballad and Its Hero* (1958). Paredes's research on Mexican American literary traditions allowed Rivera to imagine both that he could write fiction that drew from Chicano/a experiences and that his work could get published.

The novel continued a long-submerged literary tradition among Mexican Americans and inaugurated a new era in that tradition. . . . *y no se lo tragó la tierra* was widely lauded for its exploration of the experiences of Mexican Americans and its stylistic and linguistic innovation. The novel was a landmark in Chicano/a literature in its use of colloquial expressions and syntax and its structural grace as a cyclical narrative of interrelated stories emphasizing the interplay between individual and collective identity. Rivera instantly became a major figure in Chicano/a letters. The novel influenced countless Chicano/a writers to follow and brought significant recognition to Chicano/a and Latino/a literature generally. Brenda Cárdenas (b. 1961), H. G. Carrillo (b. 1960), Ana Castillo (b. 1953), SANDRA CISNEROS (b. 1954), Hugo Martínez-Serros (b. 1930), Achy Obejas (b. 1956), and others have since added to the body of literature by and about Chicano/as and Latino/as in the Midwest, while such writers as Rigoberto González (b. 1970) and Helena Viramontes (b. 1954) have further mined the migrant worker experience in literature.

. . . *y no se lo tragó la tierra* was Rivera's first published work. As Julián Olivares notes, Rivera also published five short stories in journals and anthologies that by the early 1980s had been republished in multiple venues. These, along with two previously unpublished stories, are collected in the bilingual volume titled *The Harvest: Short Stories by Tomás Rivera* (1989), edited by Olivares. Rivera's poems appear in *The Searchers: Collected Poetry* (1990), also edited by Oli-

Migrant workers in the field in . . . *And the Earth Did Not Swallow Him* (1994), the film adaptation of Tomás Rivera's . . . *y no se lo tragó la tierra*.
© Severo Rene Perez, 1994. Severo Perez Archive Whitliff Collections, Texas State University-San Marcos

vares. Rivera's work on a second novel was left unfinished at his untimely death.

SIGNIFICANCE: Written from the perspective of Mexican American migrants, . . . *y no se lo tragó la tierra* expands our understanding of the Midwest and the visions of farms, immigrants, land, and small towns frequently associated with it by exploring the intersections of race, ethnicity, and class in the region. In contrast to the myth of ethnic assimilation, . . . *y no se lo tragó la tierra* imagines a community in formation that recognizes and respects its difference.

In "The Great Plains as Refuge in Chicano Literature" (1982), in *Tomás Rivera: The Complete Works* (1992), 319–32, Rivera notes the influence of GIANTS IN THE EARTH (1927) by OLE E(DVART) RØLVAAG (1876–1931) in inspiring him to create this novel about those he considered the Mexican American giants in the earth. He describes the challenges facing Chicano/a writers that he strove to overcome: to represent Mexican American life from the Mexican American perspective and thereby conserve it, and to shatter the

stereotypes of Mexican Americans created by Anglo American writers including William Sydney Porter (1862–1910), writing as O. Henry, (Francis) Bret Harte (1836–1902), and John (Ernst) Steinbeck (1902–1968).

As the Chicano narrator/protagonist of . . . *y no se lo tragó la tierra* remembers the events, stories, and voices of his past as a migrant worker, he awakens to his identity. The novel alternates chapters recounting the often tragic stories of characters limited by the demands of migrant labor and the low social status of Mexican Americans with thirteen vignettes of migrant life. In "The Children Couldn't Wait," set in Texas, a boy is murdered by an Anglo boss on a hot day for making too many trips to the water tank at the edge of the fields. In the title story the novel's protagonist, angry and frustrated by the inhumane working conditions that bring sickness on his family, curses God and in that action discovers the possibility and the power of questioning his cultural inheritance and religious instruction. In "When We Arrive" we are privy to the thoughts, prayers, dreams, hopes, and frustrations of a group of migrant workers crammed together in the back of a truck as they travel to the Midwest for the harvest.

The novel emphasizes the search for place, voice, and identity that Rivera found central to Chicano/a literature. Voice is particularly significant since the events of the novel unfold as a series of stories recounted among migrant workers, narratives composed with an ear for the cadences of everyday conversation that testify to the Mexican American migrant experience and suggest an oral collective memory. . . . *y no se lo tragó la tierra* appears to insist, as it tells us in one of its vignettes, that "the spoken word was the seed of love in the darkness" (1995 edition 147).

Set in Minnesota, Iowa, and WISCONSIN, as well as in Texas, the novel claims both regions as Chicano/a homelands. In doing so, it expands the notion of Aztlán—the physical, cultural, and spiritual home of Chicanos/as frequently associated with the Southwest—to include communities of Chicanos/as in the Midwest. This novel does not ignore the isolation and alienation that Chicano/a and Mexican migrant workers faced in the region. In the chapter "It's That It Hurts" the protagonist/narrator, a young boy attending school in an Anglo-dominated Midwestern town faces the racial insults and violence of an Anglo student. Shaken by these events, the narrator cannot clearly remember what happened: "I don't remember anymore how or when I hit him but I know I did because someone told the principal that we were fighting in the restroom" (94). At this point he can only recall what the Anglo janitor has verified. His own memory of the injustice is lost to him. The fourth vignette of the novel focuses on a character whose dawning recognition of the discrimination directed against him in a Midwestern town propels him to seek assistance from his father. Yet in another chapter, titled "When We Arrive," one speaker insists that he will join his uncle in Minneapolis (see also MINNEAPOLIS/ST. PAUL) and work in a hotel rather than remain a migrant worker (143). Rivera's novel ironically contrasts the desire to remake oneself in a new land with the limitations imposed by race and class, thereby drawing our attention to the interplay among divergent groups in the Midwest and between social and individual desires.

Four chapters that Rivera originally included in his manuscript but that were excluded from the novel represent Chicano/a characters in the Midwest. This editorial decision weakened the novel's recognition of the Midwest as a Chicano/a homeland. The four stories, published in *The Harvest: Short Stories by Tomás Rivera* (1989), are "Eva and Daniel," "The Harvest," "On the Road to Texas: Pete Fonseca," and "Zoo Island." They present characters in Minnesota and Iowa negotiating what it means to belong to a community. "Zoo Island" in particular portrays migrant workers acting in unison to define themselves in the face of Anglo attempts to dehumanize them in the Midwest. In this story Chicano/a migrant workers and families, isolated in a camp and continually subjected to the humiliating gaze of Anglo townspeople who drive out to indulge their curiosity, take a census and erect a town sign, a gesture, as Julián Olivares notes, that conveys their insistence on recognition as a community (*Harvest* 80). Their action reminds us of the presence of Chicanos/as in the Midwest dating back to the early twentieth century.

Since 1987 over 97,000 copies of . . . *y no se lo tragó la tierra* have been sold. A movie version written and directed by Severo Pérez appeared in 1994 and garnered numerous awards. . . . *And the Earth Did Not Swallow Him* is a feature-length drama originally produced for PBS's American Playhouse. Excerpts from the novel have appeared in numerous anthologies, including *The Heath Anthology of American Literature,* fourth edition (2002), edited by Paul Lauter. The novel is also included in *Tomás Rivera: The Complete Works* (1992) and Littell McDougal's textbook *Language of Literature* (1996).

IMPORTANT EDITIONS: The first edition of Rivera's novel appeared in 1971, translated by Herminio Ríos C. with the collaboration of the author and titled . . . *y no se lo tragó la tierra / . . . And the Earth Did Not Part.* The second edition in 1987 offered a new translation by Evangelina Vigil-Piñón and altered the English title to . . . *And the Earth Did Not Devour Him.* Vigil-Piñón updated her translation in a 1992 edition. The most widely

Migrant workers on the road in . . . *And the Earth Did Not Swallow Him* (1994), the film adaptation of Tomás Rivera's . . . *y no se lo tragó la tierra.*
© Severo Rene Perez, 1994. Severo Perez Archive Whitliff Collections, Texas State University–San Marcos

available text is the 1995 edition, which includes photo stills from the Severo Pérez film and uses . . . *And the Earth Did Not Devour Him* as its English title. The earliest translation maintains a formality of address and relation in language that conveys distance between generations, while the 1987 and 1992 translations reduce this distance with more colloquial and intimate language, often inflected with a Texas dialect that still remains faithful to the original. With the exception of a 1996 Spanish-language text and a 1987 English-language rendition by Rolando Hinojosa titled *This Migrant Earth,* every edition of the novel has been bilingual. Hinojosa's text departs significantly from the original, hence its status as rendition rather than translation. The first Latin American edition was published in 2012 by Ediciones Corregidor of Buenos Aires, Argentina. It features an extensive introduc-

tion by editors Julio Ramos and Gustavo Buenrostro and a concluding essay by French philosopher Jean-Luc Nancy.

FURTHER READING: Rivera discusses the influence of both Mexican and U.S. literary and cultural traditions on the novel's creation and its Midwestern emphasis in essays collected in *Tomás Rivera: The Complete Works* (1992), edited by Julián Olivares. Olivares provides valuable information on Rivera in his introductions to *The Harvest: Short Stories by Tomás Rivera* (1989), *The Searchers: Collected Poetry* (1990), and *Tomás Rivera: The Complete Works* (1992). *Tomás Rivera, 1935–1984: The Man and His Work* (1988), edited by Vernon E. Lattin, Rolando Hinojosa, and Gary D. Keller, examines Rivera's contributions as both writer and educator, including Santiago Daydí-Tolson's essay "Ritual and Religion in Tomás Rivera's Work." Significant interviews appear in Juan Bruce-Novoa's *Chicano Authors: Inquiry by Interview* (1980) and Javier Vázquez-Castro's *Acerca de literatura: Diálogo con tres autores chicanos* (1979). Critical studies of Rivera's work are numerous; over 125 articles are in circulation. *International Studies in Honor of Tomás Rivera* (1986), edited by Julián Olivares, collects important critical perspectives on Rivera's fiction and poetry, including articles by Luis Leal on memory, Nicolás Kanellos on dialogue, and Julián Olivares on identity. Ramón Saldívar's *Chicano Narrative: The Dialectics of Difference* (1990) and Teresa McKenna's *Migrant Song: Politics and Process in Contemporary Chicano Literature* (1997) read the novel as a key work in the Chicano/a literary tradition. The power of the spoken and the unspoken is analyzed in Joseph Sommers's "Interpreting Tomás Rivera," in *Modern Chicano Writers* (1979), edited by Sommers and Tomás Ybarra-Frausto, 94–107, and in Lauro Flores's "The Discourse of Silence in the Narrative of Tomás Rivera," *Revista Chicano-Riqueña* 13.3–4 (1985): 96–106. Theresa Delgadillo's "Exiles, Migrants, Settlers, and Natives: Literary Representations of Chicanos/as and Mexicans in the Midwest" first appeared online in 1999 and was reprinted in *Midwestern Miscellany* 30 (Fall 2002): 27–45; it discusses the centrality of the Midwestern locale in the novel, as does " 'Your Homeland Is Where You Live and Where

You Work': Challenging Midwestern Pastoral(ism) in Tomás Rivera's . . . *And the Earth Did Not Devour Him*" by William Barillas, in *Midwestern Literature* (2013), edited by Ronald Primeau (76–93). Rivera's novel is addressed in guides such as *U.S. Latino Literature: A Critical Guide for Students and Teachers* (2000), edited by Harold Augenbraum and Margarite Fernández Olmos. Manuel Martinez examines the communalist ethos of the novel in *Countering the Counterculture: Rereading Postwar American Dissent from Jack Kerouac to Tomás Rivera* (2003). Rivera's manuscripts and personal papers, including the manuscript of . . . *y no se lo tragó la tierra,* are collected in the Tomás Rivera Archive at the University of California–Riverside.

THERESA DELGADILLO   THE OHIO STATE UNIVERSITY

YOUNG ADULT LITERATURE.
See Children's and Young Adult Literature

Bibliography

The following is a list of critical articles, books, and anthologies that focus on the Midwest. Items included in this list were chosen for their focus on the region's literature, history, or culture in a broad context or because of a focus on particular Midwestern cities, states, or locations that contributes to an understanding of the region's dynamic content. These general resources serve as a starting point for students and scholars interested in researching and understanding the Midwest.

Abraham, Nabeel, and Andrew Shryock, eds. *Arab Detroit: From Margin to Mainstream.* Detroit: Wayne State University Press, 2000.

Agard, Walter R. "Classics on the Midwest Frontier." *Classical Journal* 51.3 (December 1955): 103–10.

Alexander, Ruth Ann. "Midwest Main Street in Literature: Symbol of Conformity." *Rocky Mountain Social Science Journal* 5.2 (1968): 1–12.

Aley, Ginette. "Dwelling within the Place Worth Seeking: The Midwest, Regional Identity, and Internal Histories." In *Regionalism and the Humanities*, edited by Timothy R. Mahoney and Wendy J. Katz, 95–109. Lincoln: University of Nebraska Press, 2008.

———. "'Knotted Together like Roots in the Darkness': Rural Midwestern Women and Region—A Bibliographic Guide." *Agricultural History* 77.3 (Summer 2003): 453–81.

Allen, Harold B. *The Linguistic Atlas of the Upper Midwest.* 3 vols. Minneapolis: University of Minnesota Press, 1973–1976.

ANDERSON, DAVID D(ANIEL). "The Art of the Midwestern Campaign Biography." *Midwestern Miscellany* 4 (1976): 34–43.

———. "The Chicago Renaissance in Fiction." *Midwestern Miscellany* 27.2 (1999): 7–16.

———. "The Dimensions of the Midwest." *MidAmerica* 1 (1974): 7–15.

———. "The Fiction of the Great Lakes." *Northwest Ohio Quarterly* 34.1 (Winter 1961–1962): 18–28.

———. "Mark Twain, Sherwood Anderson, and Midwestern Modernism." *MidAmerica* 21 (1994): 73–81.

———. "The Midwestern Town in Midwestern Fiction." *MidAmerica* 6 (1979): 27–42

———. "Midwestern Writers and the Myth of the Search." *Georgia Review* 34.1 (Spring 1980): 131–43.

———. "Notes toward a Definition of the Mind of the Midwest." *MidAmerica* 3 (1976): 7–16.

———. *Ohio: In Fact and Fiction; Further Essays on the Ohio Experience.* East Lansing, MI: Midwestern Press, 2006.

———. *Ohio: In Myth, Memory, and Imagination; Essays on the Ohio Experience.* East Lansing, MI: Midwestern Press, 2004.

———. "The Origins and Development of the Literature of the Middle West." In *Dictionary of Midwestern Literature*, 9–24. edited by Philip A. Greasley, vol. 1. Bloomington: Indiana University Press, 2001.

———. "Three Generations of Missouri Fiction." *Midwestern Miscellany* 9 (1981): 7–20.

Anderson, Kathie Ryckman. *Dakota: The Literary Heritage of the Northern Prairie State.* Grand Forks: University of North Dakota Press, 1990.

Anderson, Patricia A. "Everyday Life in the Midwest: Popular Preoccupations in Children's Books." *Midwestern Miscellany* 3 (1975): 39–43.

———. "Images of the Midwest in Children's Literature." *Midwestern Miscellany* 1 (1974): 15–20.

Andrews, Clarence A. ed. *Growing Up in the Midwest.* Ames: Iowa State University Press, 1981.

———. "Iowa Literary History, 1971–1991." *Books at Iowa* 56 (April 1992): 47–58.

———. *A Literary History of Iowa.* Iowa City: University of Iowa Press, 1972.

———. *Michigan in Literature.* Detroit: Wayne State University Press, 1992.

Anfinson, John O. *The River We Have Wrought: A History of the Upper Mississippi.* Minneapolis: University of Minnesota Press, 2005.

Archer, Marion Fuller, ed. *The Upper Midwest.* Chicago: American Library Association, 1981.

Ashworth, William. *The Late, Great Lakes: An Environmental History.* New York: Knopf, 1986.

Atherton, Lewis. *Main Street on the Middle Border.* Bloomington: Indiana University Press, 1954.

———. "The Midwestern Country Town: Myth and Reality." *Agricultural History* 26.3 (July 1952): 73–80.

Babnich, Judith. "Megan Terry's 100,001 Horror Stories of the Plains: Tall Tales and Stories from the People of the Midwest." *Mississippi Folklore Register* 22.1–2 (Spring–Fall 1988): 47–59.

Baldwin, Davarian L. *Chicago's New Negroes: Modernity, the Great Migration, and Black Urban Life.* Chapel Hill: University of North Carolina Press, 2007.

Balfour, Conrad. *The Butterfly Tree: An Anthology of Black Writing from the Upper Midwest.* St. Paul, MN: New Rivers Press, 1985.

Balken, Debra Bricker. *After Many Springs: Regionalism, Modernism, and the Midwest.* Des Moines, IA: Des Moines Art Center, 2009.

Banta, R. E., ed. *Indiana Authors and Their Books, 1816–1916.* Crawfordsville, IN: Wabash College, 1949.

Barillas, William. "Ecocriticism and Midwestern Literary Studies: Some Points of Departure (and Arrival)." *MidAmerica* 22 (1995): 128–38.

———. *The Midwestern Pastoral: Place and Landscape in Literature of the American Heartland.* Athens: Ohio University Press, 2006.

———. "Origins of the Midwestern Landscape: Survey and Settlement." *MidAmerica* 19 (1992): 36–47.

Barker, Nellie Garner. *Kansas Women in Literature.* Kansas City, KS: Meursall, 1915.

Barlow, Philip, and Mark Silk, eds. *Religion and Public Life in the Midwest: America's Common Denominator?* Walnut Creek, CA: Rowman Altamira, 2004.

Barron, Ron. *A Guide to Minnesota Writers.* Rev. ed. Mankato: Minnesota Council of Teachers of English, 1993.

Beasecker, Robert, ed. *Michigan in the Novel, 1816–1996: An Annotated Bibliography.* Detroit: Wayne State University Press, 1998.

Blackshear, Orrilla Thompson. *Wisconsin Authors and Their Books, 1836–1975.* Madison: Wisconsin Department of Public Instruction, 1976.

Blanke, David. *Sowing the American Dream: How Consumer Culture Took Root in the Rural Midwest.* Athens: Ohio University Press, 2000.

Blocker, Jack S. *A Little More Freedom: African Americans Enter the Urban Midwest, 1860–1930.* Columbus: Ohio State University Press, 2008.

Bodi, Russ. "Priestly Sleuths: Mystery in Midwestern Urban Settings." *Midwestern Miscellany* 27.1 (1999): 32–40.

Boehm, Lisa Krissoff. *Popular Culture and the Enduring Myth of Chicago, 1871–1968.* New York: Routledge, 2004.

Bond, Beverley W., Jr. *The Civilization of the Old Northwest.* New York: Macmillan, 1934.

Bone, Robert, and Richard A. Courage. *The Muse in Bronzeville: African American Creative 10Expression in Chicago, 1932–1950.* New Brunswick, NJ: Rutgers University Press, 2011.

Borchert, John R. *America's Northern Heartland.* Minneapolis: University of Minnesota Press, 1987.

Bradway, Becky, ed. *In the Middle of the Middle West: Literary Nonfiction from the Heartland.* Bloomington: Indiana University Press, 2003.

Bray, Robert C. *Rediscoveries: Literature and Place in Illinois.* Urbana: University of Illinois Press, 1982.

Bray, Robert C., and John Hallwas, eds. *A Reader's Guide to Illinois Literature.* 2nd ed. Springfield: Illinois State Library, 1987.

Bredahl, A. Carl, Jr. *New Ground: Western American Narrative and the Literary Canon.* Chapel Hill: University of North Carolina Press, 1989.

Brehm, Victoria. "Great Lakes Maritime Fiction." *MidAmerica* 16 (1989): 19–28.

Bresnahan, Roger J. "The Midwest as Metaphor: Four Asian Writers." *MidAmerica* 19 (1992): 138–44.

Brooks, H. Allen. *The Prairie School: Frank Lloyd Wright and His Midwest Contemporaries.* Toronto: University of Toronto Press, 1972.

Brown, Dale Patrick. *Literary Cincinnati: The Missing Chapter.* Athens: Ohio University Press, 2011.

Brown, David Scott. *Beyond the Frontier: The Midwestern Voice in American Historical Writing.* Chicago: University of Chicago Press, 2009.

Buckingham, Betty Jo, ed. *Iowa and Some Iowans: A Bibliography for Schools and Libraries.* 4th ed. Des Moines: Iowa Department of Education, 1996.

Buley, Roscoe Carlyle. *The Old Northwest: Pioneer Period, 1815–1840.* 2 vols. Indianapolis: Indiana Historical Society, 1950.

Bunkers, Suzanne L., ed. *Diaries of Girls and Women: A Midwestern American Sampler.* Madison: University of Wisconsin Press, 2001.

Cansler, Loman D. "Midwestern and British Children's Lore Compared." *Western Folklore* 27.1 (January 1968): 1–18.

Cárdenas, Brenda, and Johanny Vázquez Paz, eds. *Between the Heart and the Land / Entre el corazón y la tierra: Latina Poets in the Midwest.* Chicago: MARCH/Abrazo Press, 2001.

Cárdenas, Gilberto. *La Causa: Civil Rights, Social Justice and the Struggle for Equality in the Midwest.* Houston: Arte Público Press, 2004.

Carpenter, Allan, ed. *The Encyclopedia of the Midwest.* New York: Facts on File, 1989.

Caswell, Lucy. "The Midwestern School of Editorial Cartooning." In *Cartoon America: Comic Art in the Library of Congress,* edited by Harry Katz, 198–203. New York: Abrams, 2006.

Cayton, Andrew R. L. "The Middle West." In *A Companion to 19th-Century America,* edited by William L. Barney, 272–86. Malden, MA: Blackwell, 2001.

Cayton, Andrew R. L., and Susan E. Gray, eds. *The American Midwest: Essays on Regional History.* Bloomington: Indiana University Press, 2001.

Cayton, Andrew R. L., and Stuart D. Hobbs, eds. *The Center of a Great Empire: The Ohio Country in the Early American Republic.* Athens: Ohio University Press, 2005.

Cayton, Andrew R. L., and Peter S. Onuf. *The Midwest and the Nation: Rethinking the History of an American Region.* Bloomington: Indiana University Press, 1990.

Cella, Matthew J. C. *Bad Land Pastoralism in Great Plains Fiction.* Iowa City: University of Iowa Press, 2010.

Checkoway, Barry, and Carl V. Patton, eds. *The Metropolitan Midwest: Policy Problems and Prospects for Change.* Urbana: University of Illinois Press, 1985.

Clark, Dan Elbert. *The Middle West in American History.* 1931. New York: Thomas Y. Crowell, 1966.

Clark, Thomas D. *The Rampaging Frontier: Manners and Humors of Pioneer Days in the South and the Middle West.* Bloomington: Indiana University Press, 1964.

Cohen, Lizabeth. *Making a New Deal: Industrial Workers in Chicago, 1919–1939.* Cambridge: Cambridge University Press, 1990.

Cohen, Norm. "Folk Music of the Midwest and Great Lakes Region." In *Folk Music: A Regional Exploration,* 149–66. Westport, CT: Greenwood Press, 2005.

Comentale, Edward P. "'The Possibilities of Hard-Won Land': Midwestern Modernism and the Novel." In *A Companion to the Modern American Novel 1900–1950,* 240–65, edited by John T. Matthews. Oxford, England: Wiley-Blackwell, 2009.

Conzen, Kathleen Neils. *Immigrant Milwaukee, 1836–1860: Accommodation and Community in a Frontier City.* Cambridge, MA: Harvard University Press, 1976.

Cordier, Mary Hurlbut. *Schoolwomen of the Prairies and Plains: Personal Narratives from Iowa, Kansas, and Nebraska, 1860s–1920s.* Albuquerque: University of New Mexico Press, 1992.

Cox, Gerry, and Carol MacDaniels. *Guide to Nebraska Authors.* Lincoln, NE: Dageforde Publishing, 1998.

Coyle, William, ed. *Ohio Authors and Their Books, 1796–1950.* Cleveland: World, 1962.

Critchlow, Donald T. *Socialism in the Heartland: The Midwestern Experience, 1900–1925.* South Bend, IN: University of Notre Dame Press, 1988.

Cronon, William. *Nature's Metropolis: Chicago and the Great West.* New York: Norton, 1991.

Culture of the Middle West, The. Lawrence College Faculty Lecture Series. Appleton, WI: Lawrence College, 1944.

Cumbler, John T. *Northeast and Midwest United States: An Environmental History.* Santa Barbara, CA: ABC-CLIO, 2005.

Danziger, Edmund Jefferson, Jr. *Great Lakes Indian Accommodation and Resistance during the Early Reservation Years, 1850–1900.* Ann Arbor: University of Michigan Press, 2009.

Davies, Richard O., Joseph A. Amato, and David R. Pichaske, eds. *A Place Called Home: Writings on the Midwestern Small Town.* St. Paul: Minnesota Historical Society, 2003.

Day, George F. Introduction to section 3, "The Midwest." In *A Literary History of the American West,* edited by Western Literature Association, 636–63. Fort Worth: Texas Christian University Press, 1987.

Delgadillo, Theresa. "Exiles, Migrants, Settlers, and Natives: Literary Representations of Chicano/as and Mexicans in the Midwest." *Midwestern Miscellany* 30 (Fall 2002): 27–45.

Dempsey, Dave, and Jack Dempsey. *Ink Trails: Michigan's Famous and Forgotten Authors.* East Lansing: Michigan State University Press, 2012.

Dennison, Craig. "México de afuera in Northern Missouri: The Creation of Porfiriato Society in America's Heartland." *Rupkatha: Journal on Interdisciplinary Studies in Humanities* 2.3 (2010): 256–67.

DERLETH, AUGUST (WILLIAM). *Wisconsin Regional Literature.* Sauk City, WI: n.p., 1942.

Devens, Carol. *Countering Colonization: Native American Women and Great Lakes Missions, 1630–1900.* Berkeley: University of California Press, 1992.

Dondore, Dorothy Ann. *The Prairie and the Making of Middle America: Four Centuries of Description.* Cedar Rapids, IA: Torch Press, 1926.

Dorman, Robert L. "From the Middle of Nowhere to the Heartland: The Great Plains and American Regionalism." In *Literature and Place, 1800–2000,* edited by Peter Brown and Michael Irwin, 179–98. Bern, Switzerland: Peter Lang, 2008.

Dougherty, Charles T. "Novels of the Middle Border: A Critical Bibliography for Historians." *Historical Bulletin* 25 (May 1947): 77–78, 85–88.

Drake, St. Clair, and Horace Roscoe Cayton. *Black Metropolis: A Study of Negro Life in a Northern City.* 1945. Chicago: University of Chicago Press, 1970.

Duffey, Bernard. *The Chicago Renaissance in American Letters: A Critical History.* East Lansing: Michigan State College Press, 1954

Duncan, Hugh Dalziel. *Culture and Democracy: The Struggle for Form in Society and Architecture in Chicago and the Middle West during the Life and Times of Louis H. Sullivan.* Totowa, NJ: Bedminster Press, 1965.

Dunlop, M. H. *Sixty Miles from Contentment: Traveling the Nineteenth-Century American Interior.* New York: Basic Books, 1995.

Edmunds, Russell David, ed. *Enduring Nations: Native Americans in the Midwest.* Urbana: University of Illinois Press, 2008.

Emerson, Thomas E., and R. Barry Lewis, eds. *Cahokia and the Hinterlands: Middle Mississippian Cultures of the Midwest.* Urbana: University of Illinois Press, 1999.

Engel, Bernard F. "Muscular Innocence in the Midwestern Work Ethic." *MidAmerica* 10 (1983): 38–53.

———. "Poetry of the Early Midwest." *Midwestern Miscellany* 6 (1978): 21–29.

Engel, Bernard F., and Patricia W. Julius. *A New Voice for a New People: Midwestern Poetry, 1800–1910.* Lanham, MD: University Press of America, 1985.

Ervin, Jean. "A Sense of Place: The Upper Midwest in Fiction." *Upper Midwest History* 2 (1982): 45–51.

Etcheson, Nicole. *The Emerging Midwest: Upland Southerners and the Political Culture of the Old Northwest, 1787–1861.* Bloomington: Indiana University Press, 1996.

Evans, David Allan. "'Plow It and Find Out': Midwestern American Poetry." *South Dakota Review* 41.1–2 (Spring/Summer 2003): 33–41.

Faruque, Cathleen Jo. *Migration of Hmong to the Midwestern United States.* Lanham, MD: University Press of America, 2002.

Faulkner, Virginia, and Frederick C. Luebke, eds. *Vision and Refuge: Essays on the Literature of the Great Plains.* Lincoln: University of Nebraska Press, 1982.

Fenton, John H. *Midwest Politics.* New York: Holt, Rinehart and Winston, 1966.

Ferlazzo, Paul. "Midwestern Literary Periodicals." *Great Lakes Review* 1.2 (Winter 1975): 58–66.

Fernández, Lilia. "Latinas in the Midwest." In *Latinas in the United States: A Historical Encyclopedia,* vol. 1, edited by Vicki L. Ruiz and Virginia Sánchez Korrol, 14–18. Bloomington: Indiana University Press, 2006.

Feurer, Rosemary. *Radical Unionism in the Midwest, 1900–1950.* Urbana: University of Illinois Press, 2006.

Flanagan, John T., ed. *America Is West: An Anthology of Middlewestern Life and Literature.* Minneapolis: University of Minnesota Press, 1945.

———. "European Elements in Mid-Western Literature." *Kentucky Foreign Language Quarterly* 2 (Second Quarter 1955): 59–66.

———. "A Half-Century of Middlewestern Fiction." *Critique* 2 (Winter 1959): 16–34.

———. "Literary Protest in the Midwest." *Southwest Review* 34 (Spring 1949): 148–57.

———. "The Middle Western Farm Novel." *Minnesota History* 23.2 (June 1942): 113–25.

———. "The Middle Western Historical Novel." *Journal of the Illinois State Historical Society* 37.1 (March 1944): 7–47.

———. "Poetic Voices in the Early Middle West." *Centennial Review* 24.3 (Fall 1980): 269–83.

———. "The Reality of Midwestern Literature." In *The Midwest: Myth or Reality?* edited by Thomas T. McAvoy, 75–91. Notre Dame, IN: University of Notre Dame Press, 1961.

———. "A Soil for the Seeds of Literature." In *The Heritage of the Middle West,* edited by John J. Murray, 198–233. Norman: University of Oklahoma Press, 1958.

———. "Some Projects in Midwest Cultural History." *Indiana Magazine of History* 47.3 (September 1951): 241–50.

———. "Thirty Years of Minnesota Fiction." *Minnesota History* 31.3 (September 1950): 129–44.

Fox, Dixon Ryan, ed. *Sources of Culture in the Middle West.* 1934. New York: Russell and Russell, 1964.

Fox, Maynard. *Book-Length Fiction by Kansas Writers, 1915–1938.* Topeka: Kansas State Printing Plant, 1944.

Frazer, Timothy C., ed. *"Heartland" English: Variation and Transition in the American Midwest.* Tuscaloosa: University of Alabama Press, 1993.

FREDERICK, JOHN T(OWNER). *Out of the Midwest: A Collection of Present-Day Writing.* New York: Whittlesey House, 1944.

Frenz, Horst. "The German Drama in the Middle West." *American-German Review* 8 (June 1942): 15–17, 37.

Fuller, Wayne E. *The Old Country School: The Story of Rural Education in the Middle West.* Chicago: University of Chicago Press, 1982.

———. *One-Room Schools of the Middle West: An Illustrated History.* Lawrence: University Press of Kansas, 1994.

Fuson, Benjamin Willis. *Centennial Bibliography of Kansas Literature, 1854–1961.* Salina: Kansas Wesleyan University Print Shop, 1961.

———. *Kansas Literature of the Nineteen Sixties: A Bibliography.* Salina: Kansas Wesleyan University Print Shop, 1970.

Gallagher, Bernice E. *Illinois Women Novelists in the Nineteenth Century: An Analysis and Annotated Bibliography.* Urbana: University of Illinois Press, 1994.

García, Juan R. *Mexicans in the Midwest, 1900–1932.* Tucson: University of Arizona Press, 1996.

Garland, John Henry. *The North American Midwest: A Regional Geography.* New York: Wiley, 1955.

Garner, John S., ed. *The Midwest in American Architecture.* Urbana: University of Illinois Press, 1991.

Gates, Paul W. *Landlords and Tenants on the Prairie Frontier.* Ithaca, NY: Cornell University Press, 1973.

Gjerde, John. *The Minds of the West: Ethnocultural Evolution in the Rural Middle West, 1830–1917.* Chapel Hill: University of North Carolina Press, 1997.

Glazer, Sidney. *The Middle West: A Study of Progress.* New York: Bookman, 1962.

Goodrich, Madge Knevels. *A Bibliography of Michigan Authors.* Richmond, VA: Richmond Press, 1928.

Grady, Wayne *The Great Lakes: The Natural History of a Changing Region.* Vancouver, BC: Greystone Books, 2011.

Gray, Susan E. *The Yankee West: Community Life on the Michigan Frontier.* Chapel Hill: University of North Carolina Press, 1996.

Greasley, Philip A. "Beyond Brutality: Forging Midwestern Urban-Industrial Mythology." *MidAmerica* 11 (1984): 9–19.

———, ed. *Dictionary of Midwestern Literature.* Vol. 1, *The Authors.* Bloomington: Indiana University Press, 2001.

———. "Mid American Poetry in Midwestern Little Magazines." *MidAmerica* 5 (1978): 50–65.

Green, Adam. *Selling the Race: Culture, Community, and Black Chicago, 1940–1955.* Chicago: University of Chicago Press, 2007.

Greenberg, Joel. *A Natural History of the Chicago Region.* Chicago: University of Chicago Press, 2002.

Gridley, Roy E. "Some Versions of the Primitive and the Pastoral on the Great Plains of America." In *Survivals of Pastoral,* edited by Richard F. Hardin, 61–85. Lawrence: University of Kansas Press, 1979.

Grosh, Ronald M. "Early American Literary Realism II: The Midwestern Matrix." *MidAmerica* 16 (1989): 122–30.

———. "Provincialism and Cosmopolitanism: A Re-assessment of Early Midwestern Realism." *Midwestern Miscellany* 21 (1993): 9–18.

Gross, Barry. "In Another Country: The Revolt from the Village." *MidAmerica* 4 (1977): 101–11.

Grossman, James R. *Land of Hope: Chicago, Black Southerners, and the Great Migration.* Chicago: University of Chicago Press, 1989.

Grossman, James R., Ann Durkin Keating, and Janice L. Reiff, eds. *The Encyclopedia of Chicago.* Chicago: University of Chicago Press, 2004.

Grover, Dorys Crow. "Selected Midwestern Writers and the Populist Movement." *MidAmerica* 17 (1990): 83–90.

Gruenwald, Kim M. *River of Enterprise: The Commercial Origins of Regional Identity in the Ohio Valley, 1790–1850.* Bloomington: Indiana University Press, 2002.

Gulliksen, Øyvind T. *Twofold Identities: Norwegian-American Contributions to Mid-*

western Literature. New York: Peter Lang, 2004.

Gundy, Jeffrey. "Humility and Midwestern Literature: Is There a Plains Style?" *MidAmerica* 15 (1988): 19–26.

Hafen, P. Jane. "Native American Writers of the Midwest." in *Updating the Literary West*, 711–19. Western Literature Association, Fort Worth: Texas Christian University Press.

Hampsten, Elizabeth. *Read This Only to Yourself: The Private Writings of Midwestern Women, 1880–1910*. Bloomington: Indiana University Press, 1982.

Harkness, David James. *The Literary Midwest: A Manual for Schools and Clubs*. Knoxville: University of Tennessee for the Division of University Extension, 1958.

Hart, John Fraser. "The Middle West." *Annals of the Association of American Geographers* 62.2 (June 1972): 258–82.

HAVIGHURST, WALTER (EDWIN), ed. *Land of Promise: The Story of the Northwest Territory*. New York: Macmillan, 1946.

———. ed. *Land of the Long Horizons*. New York: Coward-McCann, 1960.

———. "Regional Writing in America." *Ohioana Quarterly* 20.4 (Winter 1977): 146–54.

———. "Regional Writing in America: II. Writing in the Midwest." *Ohioana Quarterly* 21.1 (Spring 1978): 8–13.

Hawley, Emma Alethea. *Bibliography of Wisconsin Authors: Being a List of Books and Other Publications Written by Wisconsin Authors, in the Library of the State Historical Society of Wisconsin*. Madison: Democrat Printing Company, 1893.

Hazeltine, Mary Emogene. *One Hundred Years of Wisconsin Authorship, 1836–1937: A Contribution to a Bibliography of Books by Wisconsin Authors*. Madison: Wisconsin Library Association, 1937.

Hendrickson, Walter B. "Science and Culture in the American Middle West." *Isis* 64.3 (September 1973): 326–40.

Herr, Cheryl Temple. *Critical Regionalism and Cultural Studies: From Ireland to the American Midwest*. Gainesville: University Press of Florida, 1996.

Herrera, Olga U. *Toward the Preservation of a Heritage: Latin American and Latino Art in the Midwestern United States*. Notre Dame, IN: Institute for Latino Studies, 2008.

Hicks, John D. "The 'Ecology' of Middle-Western Historians." *Wisconsin Magazine of History* 24.4 (June 1941): 377–84.

Higbie, Frank Tobias. *Indispensable Outcasts: Hobo Workers and Community in the American Midwest, 1880–1930*. Urbana: University of Illinois Press, 2003.

Hilfer, Anthony Channell. *The Revolt from the Village, 1915–1930*. Chapel Hill: University of North Carolina Press, 1969.

Hine, Darlene Clark. *Black Women in the Middle West: The Michigan Experience*. Ann Arbor: Historical Society of Michigan, 1990.

Hine, Darlene Clark, and Patrick Kay Bidelman. *The Black Women in the Middle West Project: A Comprehensive Resource Guide, Illinois and Indiana*. Indianapolis: Indiana Historical Bureau, 1986.

Hine, Darlene Clark, and John McCluskey Jr., eds. *The Black Chicago Renaissance*. Urbana: University of Illinois Press, 2012.

Hinman, Dorothy, and Ruth Zimmerman. *Reading for Young People: The Midwest*. Chicago: American Library Association, 1979.

Hoelscher, Steven D., and Robert C. Ostergren. "Old European Homelands in the American Middle West." *Journal of Cultural Geography* 13.2 (Spring/Summer 1993): 87–106.

Holden, Greg. *The Booklover's Guide to the Midwest: A Literary Tour*. Cincinnati: Clerisy Press, 2009.

———. *Literary Chicago: A Book Lover's Tour of the Windy City*. Chicago: Lake Claremont Press, 2001.

Holman, David Marion. *A Certain Slant of Light: Regionalism and the Form of Southern and Midwestern Fiction*. Baton Rouge: Louisiana State University Press, 1995.

Hubach, Robert R. *Early Midwestern Travel Narratives: An Annotated Bibliography, 1634–1850*. Detroit: Wayne State University Press, 1961.

Hubbart, Henry C. *The Older Middle West, 1840–1880*. New York: Russell and Russell, 1963.

Hudson, John C. *Making the Corn Belt: A Geographical History of Middle-Western Agriculture*. Bloomington: Indiana University Press, 1994.

———. "The Middle West as a Cultural Hybrid." *Pioneer America Society Transactions* 7 (1984): 35–45.

———. "North American Origins of Middlewestern Frontier Populations." *Annals of the Association of American Geographers* 78.3 (September 1988): 395–413.

Hurt, James. *Writing Illinois: The Prairie, Lincoln, and Chicago*. Urbana: University of Illinois Press, 1992.

Huseboe, Arthur R. *An Illustrated History of the Arts in South Dakota*. Sioux Falls, SD: Augustana College Center for Western Studies, 1989.

Huseboe, Arthur R., and William Geyer, eds. *Where the West Begins: Essays on Middle Border and Siouxland Writing, in Honor of Herbert*

Krause. Sioux Falls, SD: Center for Western Studies, 1978.

Hutton, Graham. *Midwest at Noon.* Chicago: University of Chicago Press, 1946.

Jacobson, Joanne. "The Quotidian in 20th Century Fiction by Midwestern Women." *Revue Française d'Etudes Américaines* 11.30 (November 1986): 481–90.

Jakle, John A. *My Kind of Midwest: Omaha to Ohio.* Chicago: Center for American Places at Columbia College Chicago, 2008.

Jensen, Richard J. *The Winning of the Midwest: Social and Political Conflict, 1888–96.* Chicago: University of Chicago Press, 1971.

Johnson, Hildegard Binder. *Order upon the Land: The U.S. Rectangular Land Survey and the Upper Mississippi Country.* New York: Oxford University Press, 1976.

Johnson, Victoria E. *Heartland TV: Prime Time Television and the Struggle for U.S. Identity.* New York: New York University Press, 2008.

Johnson, Yvonne J., ed. *Feminist Frontiers: Women Who Shaped the Midwest.* Kirksville, MO: Truman State University Press, 2010.

Johnstone, Barbara. "Community and Contest: Midwestern Men and Women Creating their Worlds in Conversational Storytelling." In *Gender and Conversational Interaction,* edited by Deborah Tannen, 62–80. New York: Oxford University Press, 1994.

———. "Variation in Discourse: Midwestern Narrative Style." *American Speech* 65.3 (Autumn 1990): 195–214.

Jones, Evan. *The Plains States: Iowa, Kansas, Minnesota, Missouri, Nebraska, North Dakota, South Dakota.* New York: Time-Life Books, 1968.

Judson, Katharine B., ed. *Native American Legends of the Great Lakes and the Mississippi Valley.* De Kalb: Northern Illinois University Press, 2000.

Kaser, James A. *The Chicago of Fiction: A Resource Guide.* Lanham, MD: Scarecrow Press, 2011.

Kellman, Steven G. "Food Fights in Iowa: The Vegetarian Stranger in Recent Midwest Fiction." *Virginia Quarterly Review* 71.3 (Summer 1995): 435–47.

Kilpatrick, Thomas L., and Patsy-Rose Hoshiko. *Illinois! Illinois! An Annotated Bibliography of Fiction.* Metuchen, NJ: Scarecrow Press, 1979.

Kinietz, W. Vernon. *The Indians of the Western Great Lakes, 1615–1760.* Ann Arbor: University of Michigan Press, 1940.

Kirby, Jack Temple. "Rural Culture in the American Middle West: Jefferson to Jane Smiley." *Agricultural History* 70.4 (Autumn 1996): 581–97.

Kleppner, Paul. *The Cross of Culture: A Social Analysis of Midwestern Politics, 1850–1900.* New York: Free Press, 1970.

KNOEPFLE, JOHN (IGNATIUS). "Crossing the Midwest." In *Regional Perspectives: An Examination of America's Literary Heritage,* edited by John Gordon Burke, 77–174. Chicago: American Library Association, 1973.

Knott, John R. *Imagining the Forest: Narratives of Michigan and the Upper Midwest.* Ann Arbor: University of Michigan Press, 2011.

Knupfer, Anne Meis. *The Chicago Black Renaissance and Women's Activism.* Urbana: University of Illinois Press, 2006.

Køhlert, Frederik Byrn. *The Chicago Literary Experience: Writing the City, 1893–1953.* Copenhagen, Denmark: Museum Tusculanum Press, 2011.

Konecky, Eugene. "Midwestern Writers: The Midlandish Mind." *Prairie Schooner* 4.3 (Summer 1930): 181–85.

Kramer, Dale. *Chicago Renaissance: The Literary Life in the Midwest, 1900–1930.* New York: Appleton-Century, 1966.

Kramer, Frank R. *Voices in the Valley: Mythmaking and Folk Belief in the Shaping of the Middle West.* Madison: University of Wisconsin Press, 1964.

LaGrand, James B. *Indian Metropolis: Native Americans in Chicago, 1945–75.* Urbana: University of Illinois Press, 2002.

Larrie, Reginald R. *Makin' Free: African-Americans in the Northwest Territory.* Detroit: B. Ethridge Books, 1981.

Lauck, Jon K. *The Lost Region: Toward a Revival of Midwestern History.* Iowa City: University of Iowa Press, 2013.

———. "Why the Midwest Matters." *Midwest Quarterly* 4.2 (Winter 2013): 165–85.

Leary, James P., ed. *Midwestern Folk Humor.* Little Rock: August House, 1991.

———, ed. *So Ole Says to Lena: Folk Humor of the Upper Midwest.* 2nd ed. Madison: University of Wisconsin Press, 2001.

Lee, Erika. "Asian American Studies in the Midwest: New Questions, Approaches, and Communities." *Journal of Asian American Studies* 12.3 (October 2009): 247–73.

Lesy, Michael. *Wisconsin Death Trip.* New York: Pantheon, 1973.

Lieberg, Carolyn S. *Calling the Midwest Home: A Lively Look at the Origins, Attitudes, Quirks, and Curiosities of America's Heartlanders.* Berkeley, CA: Wildcat Canyon Press, 1996.

Lookingbill, Brad. "Terror in the Heartland: Representations of the American Great Plains, 1930–1940." In *Literature of Nature: An International Sourcebook,* edited by

Patrick D. Murphy, 26–31. Chicago: Fitzroy Dearborn, 1998.

Low, Denise. *Natural Theologies: Essays about Literature of the New Middle West.* Omaha, NE: Backwaters Press, 2011.

Ludwig, G. M. *The Influence of the Pennsylvania Dutch in the Middle West.* Allentown: Pennsylvania Folklore Society, 1947.

Lutz, Tom. *Cosmopolitan Vistas: American Regionalism and Literary Value.* Ithaca, NY: Cornell University Press, 2004.

Madison, James H. "Diverging Trails: Why the Midwest Is Not the West." In *Frontier and Region: Essays in Honor of Martin Ridge,* edited by Robert C. Ritchie and Paul Andrew Hutton, 43–53. Albuquerque: University of New Mexico Press and Huntington Library Press, 1997.

———. *Heartland: Comparative Histories of the Midwestern States.* Bloomington: Indiana University Press, 1988.

Mahoney, Timothy R. *Provincial Lives: Middle-Class Experience in the Antebellum Middle West.* Cambridge: Cambridge University Press, 1999.

———. *River Towns in the Great West: The Structure of Provincial Urbanization in the American Midwest, 1820–1870.* Cambridge: Cambridge University Press, 1990.

Martinez, Rubén O., ed. *Latinos in the Midwest.* East Lansing: Michigan State University Press, 2011.

Martone, Michael A., ed. *Not Normal, Illinois: Peculiar Fictions from the Flyover.* Bloomington: Indiana University Press, 2009.

———, ed. *A Place of Sense: Essays in Search of the Midwest.* Iowa City: University of Iowa Press, 1988.

Mattingly, Paul H., and Edward W. Stevens Jr., eds. *"Schools and the Means of Education Shall Forever Be Encouraged": A History of Education in the Old Northwest, 1787–1880.* Athens: Ohio University Libraries, 1987.

Mattson, Jeremy. "The Comic Song in the American Midwest, 1825–1875." *MidAmerica* 4 (1977): 30–55.

Maxwell, Donald W. *Literature of the Great Lakes Region: An Annotated Bibliography.* New York: Garland, 1991.

McAvoy, Thomas T., et al., eds. *The Midwest: Myth or Reality?* Notre Dame, IN: University of Notre Dame Press, 1961.

McCluskey, John, Jr. "Paradise Valley: Black Writers and Midwestern Cities, 1910–1950." *Journal of American Culture* 5.3 (Fall 1982): 93–103.

McLaughlin, Robert. *The Heartland: Illinois, Indiana, Michigan, Ohio, Wisconsin.* New York: Time-Life Books, 1967.

McNeil, Brownie. "The Child Ballad in the Middle West and Lower Mississippi Valley." In *Mesquite and Willow,* edited by Mody C. Boatright, 23–77. Dallas: Southern Methodist University Press, 1956.

Mead, C. David. *Yankee Eloquence in the Middle West: The Ohio Lyceum, 1850–1870.* East Lansing: Michigan State College Press, 1951.

Meeks, Leslie H. "The Lyceum in the Middle West." *Indiana Magazine of History* 29.2 (June 1933): 87–95.

Merrill, Horace S. *Bourbon Democracy of the Middle West, 1865–1896.* Baton Rouge: Louisiana State University Press, 1953.

Meyer, Roy W. *The Middle Western Farm Novel in the Twentieth Century.* Lincoln: University of Nebraska Press, 1965.

Michaud, Joseph A. *Iowa City, City of the Book: Writing, Publishing, and Book Arts in the Heartland.* Iowa City: Camp Pope Publishing, 2011.

Middleton, Stephen. *The Black Laws in the Old Northwest: A Documentary History.* Westport, CT: Greenwood Press, 1993.

Millard, Ann V., Jorge Chapa, and Catalina Burillo. *Apple Pie and Enchiladas: Latino Newcomers in the Rural Midwest.* Austin: University of Texas Press, 2004.

Milton, John R., ed. *The Literature of South Dakota.* Vermillion: University of South Dakota Press, 1976.

Minnesota Centennial Literature Group. *Minnesota Authors: A Selected Bio-Bibliography.* St. Paul: Minnesota Statehood Centennial Commission, 1958.

Morser, Eric J. *Hinterland Dreams: The Political Economy of a Midwestern City.* Philadelphia: University of Pennsylvania Press, 2011.

Motz, Marilyn Ferris. "Folk Expression of Time and Place: 19th-Century Midwestern Rural Diaries." *Journal of American Folklore* 100.396 (April–June 1987): 131–47.

———. "Visual Autobiography: Photograph Albums of Turn-of-the-Century Midwestern Women." *American Quarterly* 41.1 (March 1989): 63–92.

Mueller, Lisel. "Midwestern Poetry: Goodbye to All That." 1971. In *In the Middle: Ten Midwestern Women Poets,* edited by Sylvia Griffith Wheeler, 69–72. Kansas City: BkMk / University of Missouri–Kansas City, 1985.

Murphy, Lucy Eldersveld. *A Gathering of Rivers: Indians, Métis, and Mining in the Western Great Lakes, 1737–1832.* Lincoln: University of Nebraska Press, 2004.

Murphy, Lucy Eldersveld, and Wendy Hamand Venet, eds. *Midwestern Women: Work, Community, and Leadership at the Crossroads.* Bloomington: Indiana University Press, 1998.

Murray, John J., ed. *The Heritage of the Middle West*. Norman: University of Oklahoma Press, 1958.

Murray, Thomas E., and Beth Lee Simon, eds. *Language Variation and Change in the American Midland: A New Look at "Heartland" English*. Amsterdam, Netherlands: Benjamins, 2006.

Naess, Harald S. *Norwegian Influence on the Upper Midwest*. Duluth: University of Minnesota–Duluth, Continuing Education and Extension, 1976.

Nelson, Daniel. *Farm and Factory: Workers in the Midwest, 1880–1990*. Bloomington: Indiana University Press, 1995.

Nemanic, Gerald, ed. *A Bibliographical Guide to Midwestern Literature*. Iowa City: University of Iowa Press, 1981.

Neth, Mary. *Preserving the Family Farm: Women, Community, and the Foundations of Agribusiness in the Midwest, 1900–1940*. Baltimore: Johns Hopkins University Press, 1998.

Ney, Jason, and Terri Nichols. *America's Natural Places: The Midwest*. Santa Barbara, CA: Greenwood Press / ABC-CLIO, 2010.

Nibbelink, Herman. "Novels of American Rural Life, 1963–1984." *North Dakota Quarterly* 53.4 (Fall 1985): 167–72.

Nichols, Jeannette P., and J. G. Randall. *Democracy in the Middle West, 1840–1940*. New York: D. Appleton-Century, 1941.

Niedzielski, Nancy. "Attitudes toward Midwestern American English." In *Handbook of Perceptual Dialectology*, vol. 2, edited by Daniel Long and Dennis R. Preston, 321–27. Amsterdam, Netherlands: Benjamins, 2002.

Noble, Allen G., and Hubert G. H. Wilhem, eds. *Barns of the Midwest*. Athens: Ohio University Press, 1995.

Noe, Marcia, ed. *Exploring the Midwestern Literary Imagination: Essays in Honor of David D. Anderson*. Troy, NY: Whitston, 1993.

Nordin, Dennis S., and Roy V. Scott. *From Prairie Farmer to Entrepreneur: The Transformation of Midwestern Agriculture*. Bloomington: Indiana University Press, 2005.

Noverr, Douglas A. "Midwestern Travel Literature of the Nineteenth Century: Romance and Reality." *MidAmerica* 4 (1977): 18–29.

Nye, Russel Blaine. *Midwestern Progressive Politics: A Historical Study of Its Origins and Development, 1870–1950*. East Lansing: Michigan State College Press, 1951.

Onuf, Peter S. *Statehood and Union: A History of the Northwest Ordinance*. Bloomington: Indiana University Press, 1987.

Orians, George Harrison. "Cannon through the Forest: Novels of the Land Battles of the War of 1812 in the Old Northwest." *Ohio History* 72.3 (July 1963): 195–215.

Osborne, Karen Lee, and William J. Spurlin, eds. *Reclaiming the Heartland: Lesbian and Gay Voices from the Midwest*. Minneapolis: University of Minnesota Press, 1996.

Page, Brian, and Richard Walker. "From Settlement to Fordism: The Agro-Industrial Revolution in the American Midwest." *Economic Geography* 67.4 (October 1991): 281–315.

Payne, Alma J. "The Midwest: Literary Resource and Refuge." *Old Northwest* 1.1 (March 1975): 1–9.

Penney, David W., ed. *Great Lakes Indian Art*. Detroit: Wayne State University Press and Detroit Institute of Arts, 1989.

Phelan, Raymond V. *Slavery in the Old Northwest*. Madison: State Historical Society of Wisconsin, 1906.

Pichaske, David R. *Rooted: Seven Midwest Writers of Place*. Iowa City: University of Iowa Press, 2006.

———. "Where Now 'Midwestern Literature'?" *Midwest Quarterly* 48.1 (Autumn 2006): 100–119.

Pickle, Linda S. *Contented among Strangers: Rural German-Speaking Women and Their Families in the Nineteenth-Century Midwest*. Urbana: University of Illinois Press, 1996.

Pinkerton, Jan, and Randolph H. Hudson. *Encyclopedia of the Chicago Literary Renaissance: The Essential Guide to the Lives and Works of the Chicago Renaissance Writers*. New York: Facts on File, 2004.

Pollack, Norman. *The Populist Response to Industrial America: Midwestern Populist Thought*. Cambridge, MA: Harvard University Press, 1962.

Popper, Deborah E. "The Middle West: Corn Belt and Industrial Belt United." *Journal of Cultural Geography* 30.1 (February 2013): 32–54.

Price, John T. "Midwestern Autobiographical Nonfiction." in *Updating the Literary West*, 701–10. Western Literature Association, Fort Worth: Texas Christian University Press.

Prince, Hugh C. *Wetlands of the American Midwest: A Historical Geography of Changing Attitudes*. Chicago: University of Chicago Press, 1997.

Prosterman, Leslie. *Ordinary Life, Festival Days: Aesthetics in the Midwestern County Fair*. Washington, DC: Smithsonian Institution Press, 1995.

Quaife, Milo Milton. *Chicago and the Old Northwest, 1673–1835*. 1913. Urbana: University of Illinois Press, 2001.

Quantic, Diane Dufva. *The Nature of the Place: A Study of Great Plains Fiction*. Lincoln: University of Nebraska Press, 1995.

———. "The Revolt from the Village and Middle Western Fiction, 1870–1915." *Kansas Quarterly* 5.4 (Fall 1973): 5–16.

Radavich, David. "Center Stage: Midwestern Plays and Playwrights." *Midwestern Miscellany* 30.1 (2002): 7–19.

———. "Rabe, Mamet, Shepard, and Wilson: Mid-American Male Dramatists in the 1970s and '80s." *Midwest Quarterly* 48.3 (Spring 2007): 342–68.

Ramos-Zayas, Ana Y. *National Performances: The Politics of Class, Race, and Space in Puerto Rican Chicago.* Chicago: University of Chicago Press, 2003.

Raymond, Elizabeth. "Learning the Land: The Development of a Sense of Place in the Prairie Midwest." *MidAmerica* 14 (1987): 28–40.

Read, Allen Walker. "The War of the Dictionaries in the Middle West." In *Papers on Lexicography in Honor of Warren N. Cordell,* edited by James Edmund Congleton, John Edward Gates, and Donald Hobar, 3–15. Terre Haute: Dictionary Society of North America, Indiana State University, 1979.

Recchia, Edward. "There's No Place Like Home: The Midwest in American Film Musicals." *Midwest Quarterly* 39.2 (Winter 1998): 202–14.

Reigelman, Milton M. *The "Midland": A Venture in Literary Regionalism.* Iowa City: University of Iowa Press, 1975.

Rhodes, Richard. *The Inland Ground: An Evocation of the American Middle West.* Lawrence: University Press of Kansas, 1991.

Rikoon, J. Sanford. *Threshing in the Midwest, 1820–1940: A Study of Traditional Culture and Technological Change.* Bloomington: Indiana University Press, 1988.

Riley, Glenda. *The Female Frontier: A Comparative View of Women on the Prairie and the Plains.* Lawrence: University Press of Kansas, 1988.

Riney-Kehrberg, Pamela. *Childhood on the Farm: Work, Play, and Coming of Age in the Midwest.* Lawrence: University Press of Kansas, 2005.

Robertson, Stacey M. *Hearts Beating for Liberty: Women Abolitionists in the Old Northwest.* Chapel Hill: University of North Carolina Press, 2010.

Robinson, Doane. *South Dakota Literature.* Pierre: South Dakota Historical Society, 1912.

Rosen, Michael J. "Is There a Midwestern Literature?" *Iowa Review* 20.3 (Fall 1990): 94–102.

Ross, Edward Alswort. "The Middle West: Being Studies of Its People in Comparison with those of the East." *Century Illustrated Monthly Magazine* 84.1 (May 1912): 142–48.

Rowe, Mike. *Chicago Blues: The City and the Music.* New York: Da Capo Press, 1975.

Rugh, Susan Sessions. *Our Common Country: Family Farming, Culture, and Community in the Nineteenth-Century Midwest.* Bloomington: Indiana University Press, 2001.

Rusk, Ralph Leslie. *The Literature of the Middle Western Frontier.* 2 vols. New York: Columbia University Press, 1925

Ryden, Kent C. "Writing the Midwest: History, Literature, and Regional Identity." *Geographical Review* 89.4 (October 1999): 511–32.

Salamon, Sonya. *Newcomers to Old Towns: Suburbanization of the Heartland.* Chicago: University of Chicago Press, 2003.

———. *Prairie Patrimony: Family, Farming, and Community in the Midwest.* Chapel Hill: University of North Carolina Press, 1992.

Sallquist, Sylvia Lea. "The Image of the Hired Girl in Literature: The Great Plains, 1860 to World War I." *Great Plains Quarterly* 4.3 (Summer 1984): 166–77.

Saloutos, Theodore, and John D. Hicks. *Agricultural Discontent in the Middle West, 1900–1939.* Madison: University of Wisconsin Press, 1951.

Sanders, Mark. *A Bibliographic Introduction to Poetry in Nebraska.* Ord, NE: Sandhills Press, 1992.

SANDERS, SCOTT RUSSELL. "Imagining the Midwest." In *Writing from the Center,* 22–51. Bloomington: Indiana University Press, 1995.

Saum, Lewis O. "The Success Theme in Great Plains Realism." *American Quarterly* 18.4 (Winter 1966): 579–98.

Sayre, Robert, ed. *Recovering the Prairie.* Madison: University of Wisconsin Press, 1999.

———. "Rethinking Midwestern Regionalism." *North Dakota Quarterly* 62.2 (Spring 1994–1995): 114–31.

Schumaker, Arthur W. *A History of Indiana Literature.* Indianapolis: Indiana Historical Society, 1962.

Schwalm, Leslie A. *Emancipation's Diaspora: Race and Reconstruction in the Upper Midwest.* Chapel Hill: University of North Carolina Press, 2009.

Sharp, Nancy W., and James R. Sharp. *American Legislative Leaders in the Midwest, 1911–1994.* Westport, CT: Greenwood Press, 1997.

Sherman, Caroline B. "The Development of American Rural Fiction." *Agricultural History* 12.1 (January 1938): 67–76.

———. "Farm Life Fiction." *South Atlantic Quarterly* 27 (July 1928): 310–24.

———. "Farm Life Fiction Reaches Maturity." *Sewanee Review* 39.4 (October–December 1931): 472–83.

Shortridge, James R. *The Middle West: Its Meaning in American Culture.* Lawrence: University Press of Kansas, 1989.

Sisson, Richard, Christian K. Zacher, and Andrew R. L. Cayton, eds. *The American Midwest: An Interpretive Encyclopedia.* Bloomington: Indiana University Press, 2007.

Slade, Joseph W., and Judith Yaross Lee, eds. *The Midwest.* Westport, CT: Greenwood Press, 2004.

Slaymaker, William. "The Ec(h)ological Conscience: Reflections on the Nature of Human Presence in Great Plains Environmental Writing." In *Regionalism and the Humanities,* edited by Timothy R. Mahoney and Wendy J. Katz, 26–42. Lincoln: University of Nebraska Press, 2008.

Sleeper-Smith, Susan. *Indian Women and French Men: Rethinking Cultural Encounter in the Western Great Lakes.* Amherst: University of Massachusetts Press, 2001.

Smallwood, Carol, ed. *Michigan Authors.* 3rd ed. Hillsdale, MI: Hillsdale Educational Publishers, 1993.

Smith, Henry Nash. "The Western Farmer in Imaginative Literature, 1818–1891." *Mississippi Valley Historical Review* 36.3 (December 1949): 479–90.

———. *Virgin Land: The American West as Symbol and Myth.* Cambridge, MA: Harvard University Press, 1950.

Smith, Suzanne E. *Dancing in the Street: Motown and the Cultural Politics of Detroit.* Cambridge, MA: Harvard University Press, 1999.

Smith, Timothy L., and Donald E. Pitzer. *The History of Education in the Middle West.* Indianapolis: Indiana Historical Society, 1978.

Sosin, Jack M. *Whitehall and the Wilderness: The Middle West in British Colonial Policy, 1760–1775.* Lincoln: University of Nebraska Press, 1961.

Spayde, Jon. "The Midwest." In *The Literary Guide to the United States,* edited by Stewart Benedict, 87–128. New York: Facts on File, 1981.

Spears, Timothy B. *Chicago Dreaming: Midwesterners and the City, 1871–1919.* Chicago: University of Chicago Press, 2005.

Sporn, Paul. *Against Itself: The Federal Theater and Writers' Projects in the Midwest.* Detroit: Wayne State University Press, 1995.

Spurlin, William J. "Remapping Same-Sex Desire: Queer Writing and Culture in the American Heartland." In *De-centering Sexualities: Politics and Representations beyond the Metropolis,* edited by Richard Phillips, Diane Watt, and David Shuttleton, 179–94. London: Routledge, 2000.

Streed, Sarah. *Leaving the House of Ghosts: Cambodian Refugees in the American Midwest.* Jefferson, NC: McFarland, 2002.

STRYK, LUCIEN, ed. *Heartland: Poets of the Midwest.* De Kalb: Northern Illinois University Press, 1967.

———. *Heartland II: Poets of the Midwest.* De Kalb: Northern Illinois University Press, 1975.

Stuhr, Margaret D. "The Safe Middle West: Escape to and Escape from Home." *MidAmerica* 14 (1987): 18–27.

SUCKOW, RUTH. "Middle Western Literature." *English Journal* 21.3 (March 1932): 175–82.

Suggs, Henry Lewis, ed. *The Black Press in the Middle West, 1865–1985.* Westport, CT: Greenwood Press, 1996.

Sugrue, Thomas J. *The Origins of the Urban Crisis: Race and Inequality in Postwar Detroit.* Princeton, NJ: Princeton University Press, 1996.

Sutton, Robert P. *Heartland Utopias.* De Kalb: Northern Illinois University Press, 2009.

Szymanski, Ronald, ed. *America in Literature: The Midwest.* New York: Scribners, 1979.

Tanner, Helen Hornbeck, ed. *Atlas of Great Lakes Indian History.* Norman: University of Oklahoma Press, 1987.

Taylor, Donna, ed. *The Great Lakes Region in Children's Books: A Selected Annotated Bibliography.* Brighton, MI: Green Oaks Press, 1980.

Teaford, Jon. *Cities of the Heartland: The Rise and Fall of the Industrial Midwest.* Bloomington: Indiana University Press, 1993.

Thacker, Robert. *The Great Prairie Fact and Literary Imagination.* Albuquerque: University of New Mexico Press, 1989.

Theobald, Paul. *Call School: Rural Education in the Midwest to 1918.* Carbondale: Southern Illinois University Press, 1995.

Thompson, Donald E., and Richard E. Banta, eds. *Indiana Authors and Their Books* 3 vols. Crawfordsville, IN: Wabash College, 1949–1981.

Thomson, Betty F. *The Shaping of America's Heartland: The Landscape of the Middle West.* Boston: Houghton Mifflin, 1977.

Thornton, Harrison John. "Chautauqua and the Midwest." *Wisconsin Magazine of History* 33.2 (December 1949): 152–63.

Tibbetts, John C. "The Midwest." In *The Columbia Companion to American History on Film: How the Movies Have Portrayed the American Past,* edited by Peter C. Rollins, 421–29. New York: Columbia University Press, 2003.

Tishler, William H., ed. *Midwestern Landscape Architecture.* Urbana: University of Illinois Press, 2000.

Torgerson, Lowell E. *Bibliography of North Dakota Authors and Poets.* Minot, ND: Torgerson, 1982.

Townsend, Richard F. *Hero, Hawk, and Open Hand: American Indian Art of the Ancient*

Midwest and South. Chicago: Art Institute of Chicago in association with Yale University Press, 2004.

Tracy, Steven C., ed. *Writers of the Black Chicago Renaissance.* Urbana: University of Illinois Press, 2011.

Turner, Frederick Jackson. "The Middle West." In *The Frontier in American History,* 126–59. New York: Henry Holt, 1920.

Uzendoski, Emily Jane. *A Handlist of Nebraska Authors.* Lincoln: Nebraska Department of Education, 1977.

Valdés, Dennis N. *Al Norte: Agricultural Workers in the Great Lakes Region, 1917–1970.* Austin: University of Texas Press, 1991.

Valdés, Dionicio Nodín. *Barrios Norteños: St. Paul and Midwestern Mexican Communities in the Twentieth Century.* Austin: University of Texas Press, 2000.

Vanausdall, Jeanette. *Pride and Protest: The Novel in Indiana.* Indianapolis: Indiana Historical Society, 1999.

Vargas, Zaragosa. *Proletarians of the North: A History of Mexican Industrial Workers in Detroit and the Midwest, 1917–1933.* Berkeley: University of California Press, 1993.

Västå, Matts. "The Ambiguities of the Escape Theme in Midwestern Literature, 1918–1934." *MidAmerica* 26 (1999): 49–76.

Vincent, Stephen A. *Southern Seed, Northern Soil: African-American Farm Communities in the Midwest, 1765–1900.* Bloomington: Indiana University Press, 2002.

Vinz, Mark, and Thom Tammaro, eds. *Imagining Home: Writing from the Midwest.* Minneapolis: University of Minnesota Press, 1995.

———, eds. *Inheriting the Land: Contemporary Voices from the Midwest.* Minneapolis: University of Minnesota Press, 1993.

Voegeli, V. Jacque. *Free but Not Equal: The Midwest and the Negro during the Civil War.* Chicago: University of Chicago Press, 1967.

Waitley, Douglas. *Portrait of the Midwest: From the Ice Age to the Industrial Era.* London: Abelard-Schuman, 1963.

Walker, Kenneth R. "Autumn on the Middle Border: A Bountiful Harvest of Literature in the Middle West in September, 1901." *Northwest Ohio Quarterly* 32.2 (Spring 1960): 51–60.

———. "Distinctively American: A Glimpse of Midwestern Culture in 1901." *Northwest Ohio Quarterly* 34.3 (Summer 1962): 138–54.

———. "The Era of Industrialization: Capital and Labor in the Midwest in 1901." *Northwest Ohio Quarterly* 37.2 (Spring 1965): 49–60.

———. "The Growing Political Significance of the United States Midwest in 1901." *Northwest Ohio Quarterly* 29.4 (Autumn 1957): 235–46.

———. *A History of the Middle West, from the Beginning to 1970.* Little Rock: Pioneer Press, 1972.

Wallace, Kathleen R. " 'Roots, Aren't They Supposed to Be Buried?': The Experience of Place in Midwestern Women's Autobiographies." In *Mapping American Culture,* edited by Wayne Franklin and Michael Steiner, 168–87. Iowa City: University of Iowa Press, 1992.

Watts, Edward. *An American Colony: Regionalism and the Roots of Midwestern Culture.* Athens: Ohio University Press, 2002.

———. "Hardly Flyover Country: Recent Developments in Midwestern Studies." *MidAmerica* 24 (1997): 36–45.

———. "The Midwest as a Colony: Transnational Regionalism." In *Regionalism and the Humanities,* edited by Timothy R. Mahoney and Wendy J. Katz, 166–89. Lincoln: University of Nebraska Press, 2008.

Watts, Edward, and David Rachels, eds. *The First West: Writing from the American Frontier, 1776–1860.* New York: Oxford University Press, 2002.

Weber, Ronald. *The Midwestern Ascendancy in American Writing.* Bloomington: Indiana University Press, 1992.

Wegelin, Oscar. "Wisconsin Verse: A Compilation of Volumes of Verse Written by Authors Born or Residing in the State of Wisconsin." *Papers of the Bibliographical Society of America* 7.3–4 (1912–13): 90–114.

Weisenberger, Francis P. "Urbanization of the Middle West: Town and Village in the Pioneer Period." *Indiana Magazine of History* 41.1 (March 1945): 19–30.

Wertenbaker, Thomas J. "The Molding of the Middle West." *American Historical Review* 53.2 (January 1948): 223–34.

Wertheim, Sally, and Alan D. Bennett, eds. *Remembering: Cleveland's Jewish Voices.* Kent, OH: Kent State University Press, 2011.

Western Literature Association, ed. *Updating the Literary West.* Fort Worth: Texas Christian University Press, 1997.

Wheeler, Kenneth. *Cultivating Regionalism: Higher Education and the Making of the American Midwest.* De Kalb: Northern Illinois University Press, 2011.

Whitaker, James W. *Farming in the Midwest, 1840–1900.* Washington: Agricultural History Society, 1974.

White, Richard. *The Middle Ground: Indians, Empires, and Republics in the Great Lakes Region, 1650–1815.* Cambridge: Cambridge University Press, 1991.

Whitney, Blair. "American Indian Literature of the Great Lakes." *Great Lakes Review* 2.2 (Winter 1976): 43–53.

Wiegand, Wayne A. *Main Street Public Library: Community Places and Reading Spaces in the Rural Heartland, 1876–1956.* Iowa City: University of Iowa Press, 2011.

Williams, Frederick D., ed. *The Northwest Ordinance: Essays on Its Formulation, Provisions, and Legacy.* East Lansing: Michigan State University Press, 1989.

Williams, Kenny J. "'Creative Defiance': An Overview of Chicago Literature." *Midwestern Miscellany* 14 (1986): 7–24.

———. *Prairie Voices: A Literary History of Chicago from the Frontier to 1893.* Nashville, TN: Townsend Press, 1980.

Wimberly, Lowry C. *Mid Country: Writings from the Heart of America.* Lincoln: University of Nebraska Press, 1945.

Winckler, Suzanne. *Smithsonian Guides to Historic America: The Great Lakes States.* Rev. ed. New York: Stewart, Tabori and Chang, 1998.

———. *Smithsonian Guides to Historic America: The Plains States.* Rev. ed. New York: Stewart, Tabori and Chang, 1998.

Wishart, David J., ed. *Encyclopedia of the Great Plains.* Lincoln: University of Nebraska Press, 2004.

Wixson, Douglas. *Worker-Writer in America: Jack Conroy and the Tradition of Midwestern Literary Radicalism, 1898–1990.* Urbana: University of Illinois Press, 1994.

Woolley, Lisa. *American Voices of the Chicago Renaissance.* De Kalb: Northern Illinois University Press, 2000.

Wuthnow, Robert. *Remaking the Heartland: Middle America since the 1950s.* Princeton, NJ: Princeton University Press, 2011.

Zivanovic, Judith. "Touring Melodramas and Midwest Frontier Values." *Heritage of the Great Plains* 23.2 (Spring 1990): 18–25.

SARA KOSIBA

TROY UNIVERSITY

Contributors

CRYSTAL S. ANDERSON is an Associate Professor of English at Elon University, where she teaches courses on the Harlem Renaissance and modern African American literature; she conducts research on modernist and contemporary African American writers, including Nella Larsen, John Edgar Wideman, Ishmael Reed, Gloria Naylor, Octavia Butler, and Paul Beatty.

Until his death in December 2011, DAVID D. ANDERSON was the leading scholar in the field of Midwestern literature. He founded the Society for the Study of Midwestern Literature, wrote many influential scholarly books, articles, and conference papers, and was an internationally known expert on Sherwood Anderson, contributing many articles; one book, *Sherwood Anderson: An Introduction and Interpretation* (1967); and three edited or co-edited volumes, *Sherwood Anderson, Dimensions of His Literary Art: A Collection of His Critical Essays* (1976), *Critical Essays on Sherwood Anderson* (1981), and, with Jack Salzman and Kichinosuke Ohashi, *Sherwood Anderson, The Writer at His Craft* (1979). Michigan State University named him a University Distinguished Professor. Wittenburg University and Bowling Green State University conferred honorary degrees on him, and the Ohioana Library honored him with its 2009 Ohioana Career Award. He founded the journals *MidAmerica* and *Midwestern Miscellany*, the scholarly publications of the Society for the Study of Midwestern Literature, and edited them for over thirty years.

KATHIE RYCKMAN ANDERSON, a sixth-generation North Dakotan, is the author of *Dakota: The Literary Heritage of the Northern Prairie State* (1990), one of four volumes published for the state's centennial.

PATRICIA A. ANDERSON was the archivist of the Society for the Study of Midwestern Literature. She graduated from Bowling Green State University, taught high school English in Ohio and Michigan, and, after receiving a Master of Science in Librarianship at Western Michigan University, served as a librarian for the Lansing, Michigan, school system until her retirement.

MARILYN JUDITH ATLAS is an Associate Professor of English at Ohio University, specializes in the American Renaissance, realism, naturalism, modernisms, the Chicago Renaissance, and Jewish, African American, Midwestern, and women's literature, and sees her place in the Midwest as a mirror of and window to the rest of her whirling world.

THOMAS FOX AVERILL is Writer-in-Residence and Professor of English at Washburn University in Topeka, where he has taught Kansas literature for more than thirty years; he is the founder of the Washburn Center for Kansas Studies and maintains a website, A Map of Kansas Literature. He is the author of three story collections, three novels, and two books of nonfiction.

PAUL BAGGETT is an Associate Professor of English and Coordinator of Peace and Conflict Studies at South Dakota State University. He specializes in nineteenth- and twentieth-century American literature and culture, with particular interests in Native American, African American, and immigrant writers and in literature of the Great Plains.

WILLIAM BARILLAS is the author of *The Midwestern Pastoral: Place and Landscape in Literature of the American Heartland* (2006) and many scholarly essays, poems, and works of creative nonfiction. A native of Michigan and a second-generation Guatemalan American, he teaches in the Department of English at the University of Wisconsin–La Crosse.

JILL BARNUM crossed the international date line on a U.S. Navy vessel as a young child and ever afterward was smitten by a love of the sea. The holder of a named chair at the University of Minnesota, she was widely known for excellent teaching and wide-ranging research. A romantic at heart, she relished life but died too young.

ROBERT BEASECKER, a member of the Society for the Study of Midwestern Literature since 1973, is Director of Special Collections at Grand Valley State University Libraries. He is the author of *Michigan in the Novel, 1816–1996: An Annotated Bibliography* (1998), has edited the Civil War letters of a Michigan regimental surgeon, and compiles the society's "Annual Bibliography of Midwestern Literature."

ANNE BECK has written about one-act farm plays of the early twentieth century by and about Midwestern farm women.

JAMES M. BOEHNLEIN has been a member of the Society for the Study of Midwestern Literature since 1993 and has delivered lectures and published essays treating American protest literature; he has also taught courses at both the undergraduate and graduate levels on the American protest movement.

SHEENA DENNEY BORAN is currently pursuing a PhD in English literature at the University of Mississippi, where she teaches in the Center for Writing and Rhetoric; her work has appeared in *Midwestern Miscellany.*

VICTORIA BREHM, a National Endowment for the Humanities Fellow who is listed in *Who's Who in the Midwest,* is a retired university professor who has written extensively about Great Lakes maritime and Native literatures and history.

As a graduate student at The University of Tennessee at Chattanooga, RACHEL BRENEMAN worked as a research assistant researching Midwestern periodicals; she is currently an Instructor in English at Hill College in Cleburne, Texas.

ROGER J. BRESNAHAN is a generalist scholar who has written and published on a wide range of topics. Early in his career he came to Michigan State University and was greatly influenced by David D. Anderson. He is currently a member of the corporate board of directors of the Society for the Study of Midwestern Literature and handles day-to-day affairs as Secretary-Treasurer.

EMILY THORNTON CALVO'S poetry has been published in *After Hours, Colere,* and other periodicals; for twenty years she has performed at libraries, schools, and festivals. She co-founded Chicago Slam Works and received a grant from the City of Chicago for her poetry collection *Lending Color to the Otherwise Absurd* (2014).

SHARON CARLSON is the Director of the Western Michigan University Archives and Regional History Collections. Her dissertation focused on the role of ladies' library associations in promoting reading and literacy.

JENNIFER CATHEY earned a Master of Arts in English at The University of Tennessee at Chattanooga.

ANDREW R. L. CAYTON, University Distinguished Professor of History at Miami University in Oxford, Ohio, was the editor with Susan E. Gray of *The American Midwest: Essays on Regional History* (2001) and with Richard Sisson and Christian Zacher of *The American Midwest: An Interpretive Encyclopedia* (2014).

HAEJA K. CHUNG taught interdisciplinary courses in the humanities and (Asian) American and English literature at Michigan State University. She has written widely on Harriette Simpson Arnow.

Born and raised in the northern Midwest, EMILY CHURILLA first encountered the Midwest's literature when she read James Oliver Curwood as a young adult; although her research has taken her outside this area, she continues to both read and teach its authors, from Sherwood Anderson to Richard Wright.

HANNAH COFFEY earned a Bachelor of Arts in Classical Languages and a Bachelor of Science in Environmental Science from the University of Maine and a Master of Arts in English from The University of Tennessee at Chattanooga; she teaches Western humanities at The University of Tennessee at Chattanooga and also writes for the *Chattanooga Times Free Press* and *Nooga.com*.

DANIEL P. COMPORA is an Associate Professor of English at the University of Toledo; his areas of expertise include folklore, particularly regional, urban, and local contemporary legends; science fiction and fantasy literature; and detective fiction.

SHEILA MARIE CONTRERAS directs the Chicano/Latino Studies Program at Michigan State University, where she is Associate Professor of English. Her book *Blood Lines: Myth, Indigenism, and Chicana/o Literature* was published by the University of Texas Press in 2008.

LESLIE CZECHOWSKI earned her master's degree in Liberal Studies at the University of Minnesota and served in the Peace Corps in Moldova, doing community development in a small village.

EDWARD DAUTERICH currently teaches, reads, and investigates Midwestern literature at Kent State University. His interests include Sinclair Lewis, Dawn Powell, Toni Morrison, and other writers with a tenuous but tangible connection to Ohio; he also studies working-class literature, African American literature, and cultural materialism.

TODD F. DAVIS is the author of four books of poems, including *In the Kingdom of the Ditch* (2013) and *The Least of These* (2012), both from Michigan State University Press, as well as scholarly work on Dan Gerber, Jeff Gundy, Jim Harrison, Janet Kauffman, Mary Swander, and Kurt Vonnegut.

THERESA DELGADILLO is Assistant Professor of Comparative Studies at Ohio State University. Her work has examined spirituality, Afro-Latinidad, and Latinos/as in the Midwest; her book *Spiritual Mestizaje: Religion, Gender, Race, and Nation in Contemporary Chicana Narrative* appeared in 2011.

JILL DOERFLER (White Earth Anishinaabe), Assistant Professor of American Indian Studies at the University of Minnesota–Duluth, teaches courses on Anishinaabe literature and American Indian literature and has published on the works of Gerald Vizenor, Louise Erdrich, and Kimberly Blaeser. Her book *Those Who Belong: Identity, Family, Blood, and Citizenship among the White Earth Anishinaabeg* was published in 2015.

ROBERT DUNNE, Professor of English at Central Connecticut State University, has published extensively on Sherwood Anderson, including *A New Book of the Grotesques: Contemporary Approaches to Sherwood Anderson's Early Fiction* (2005), and a number of essays in such journals as *MidAmerica*, *Midwest Quarterly*, and *Studies in Short Fiction*.

MAUREEN N. EKE is a Professor of English at Central Michigan University, where she teaches courses in African Diasporan literatures, postcolonial literatures and theory, and women's writing. Her courses include several Midwestern writers; she has presented papers at conferences of the Society for the Study of Midwestern Literature.

CAROL FADDA-CONREY is Assistant Professor of English at Syracuse University. Her research and teaching interests include a focus on Arab American cultures and literatures, evident in her book *Contemporary Arab-American Literature: Transnational Reconfigurations of Citizenship and Belonging* (2014).

KATHERINE FAMA is a Lecturer in the School of English, Drama, and Film at University College Dublin. She has recently published in *JML* and *MELUS* and is currently completing a book which explores urban domestic architecture and the emergence of the single woman in the modern American novel.

TIMOTHY C. FRAZER, Professor Emeritus at Western Illinois University, did fieldwork for the *Dictionary of American Regional English* in 1970 and has published widely on Midwestern language and geography. In retirement he is learning Spanish, biblical Hebrew, and Canadian French while researching a book on alcoholism in the White House and teaching English as a second language.

PHILIP GERBER was Professor of English at the College at Brockport, State University of New York, and a noted scholar of Theodore Dreiser and Willa Cather. A recipient of the MidAmerica Award, he was born in Aberdeen, South Dakota, and earned bachelor's, master's, and doctoral degrees from the University of Iowa.

KENNETH B. GRANT is Emeritus Professor of English at the University of Wisconsin–Baraboo/Sauk County; his research interests include August Derleth, Zona Gale, Margery Latimer, and Jane Hamilton.

KAREN M. GREASLEY lives in Frankfort, Kentucky, is trained in graphic arts and communications, and works in retail management.

MARSHA O. GREASLEY teaches in the Woodford County, Kentucky, schools and maintains a long-term interest in children's literature.

PHILIP A. GREASLEY is the General Editor of the Dictionary of Midwestern Literature

series; in 2013 he retired as Associate Professor of English and the Associate Provost / Associate Vice President for University Engagement at the University of Kentucky.

ØYVIND T. GULLIKSEN is Professor Emeritus of American studies at Telemark University College in Bø, Norway; he earned his PhD in American literature from the University of Bergen and has been Visiting Professor at Luther College in Decorah, Iowa, several times.

A graduate of the Iowa Writers' Workshop, BENJAMIN HALE is the author of the novel *The Evolution of Bruno Littlemore.*

WILLIE J. HARRELL JR. is the author of *Origins of the African American Jeremiad: The Rhetorical Strategies of Social Protest and Activism, 1760–1861* (2011) and editor of *We Wear the Mask: Paul Laurence Dunbar and the Politics of Representative Reality* (2010).

STEPHEN C. HOLDER is Professor Emeritus and past chair of the English Department at Central Michigan University. He has taught and published in the areas of American literature, American popular culture, and American studies.

ASHLEY HOPKINS holds a master's degree in American literature and spent a year and a half as the editorial assistant for both *MidAmerica* and *Midwestern Miscellany* academic journals.

JEFFREY HOTZ, Assistant Professor of English at East Stroudsburg University, has published articles and a book, *Divergent Visions, Contested Spaces: The Early United States through the Lens of Travel* (2006), that focus on depictions of place and travel in early American literature.

WILLIAM E. HUNTZICKER, a Minneapolis writer, teaches journalism and mass-media courses at St. Cloud State University in Minnesota and is the author of *The Popular Press, 1833–1865* (1999) and numerous articles and book chapters on nineteenth-century media.

KATHERINE JOSLIN is Professor of English and the founding Director of the University Center for the Humanities at Western Michigan University. She is the author of *Edith Wharton* (1991), *Jane Addams, A Writer's Life* (2004), and *Edith Wharton and the Making of Fashion* (2009); she teaches courses in American literature and culture.

IMMACULATE KIZZA is Professor of English at The University of Tennessee at Chattanooga; her research interests include African American literature, the slave-narrative tradition, African literature, and British modernism.

SARA KOSIBA is an Associate Professor of English at Troy University. A former member of the Executive Council of the Society for the Study of Midwestern Literature, she has published articles on Midwestern writers as varied as Dawn Powell, Ernest Hemingway, and Josephine Herbst.

JOYCE LADENSON was the long-term Director of the Michigan State University Women's Studies Program and has written on and taught U.S. feminist literature and culture.

CLARENCE B. LINDSAY retired from the University of Toledo, where he was Professor of English; in the 1980s the Society for the Study of Midwestern Literature and David D. Anderson nurtured his developing interest in Sherwood Anderson and Ernest Hemingway, on whom he published articles in leading journals in subsequent years. His book *Such a Rare Thing: The Art of Sherwood Anderson's "Winesburg, Ohio"* appeared in 2009.

LARRY LOCKRIDGE, Professor of English at New York University and a Guggenheim fellow, is the author of books on British romanticism and received the MidAmerica Award in 1998 for his biography of his father, Ross Lockridge Jr.

LOREN LOGSDON is a native of West Central Illinois with degrees from Eureka College, the University of Illinois, and Ohio University. He is completing his fifty-fourth year of college teaching, with editorial work on three Midwestern little magazines. He founded *Eureka Studies in Teaching Short Fiction*. His main scholarship is on Ray Bradbury, but he has also published two books on the history of Eureka College.

PAUL W. MILLER is Emeritus Professor of English at Wittenberg University. His literary and professional interests have included Renaissance poetry, Shakespeare, and Canadian and American literature, including the novels of Brand Whitlock and Ernest Hemingway.

DAVID L. NEWQUIST is Professor Emeritus at Northern State University, Aberdeen, South Dakota, with specialties in Native American literature and Midwestern regional literature.

MARCIA NOE is Professor of English and Director of Women's Studies at The University of Tennessee at Chattanooga; she chairs the Society for the Study of Midwestern Literature's Editorial Committee and edits *MidAmerica,* an annual publication of the Society for the Study of Midwestern Literature.

MARY DEJONG OBUCHOWSKI, Central Michigan University Professor Emerita in American literature and modern poetry, has been on the Editorial Board of the *Dictionary of Midwestern Literature* since 1991. She has special but not exclusive interests in Midwestern women writers and poets.

SALLY E. PARRY is an Associate Dean in the College of Arts and Sciences at Illinois State University and executive director of the Sinclair Lewis Society. She has published widely on Lewis and his contemporaries and has edited two collections of Lewis's short stories, *Go East Young Man: Sinclair Lewis on Class in America* (2005) and *The Minnesota Stories of Sinclair Lewis* (2005). She is the co-author, with Robert L. McLaughlin, of *We'll Always Have the Movies: American Cinema in World War II.*

STEVE PAUL is the former Editorial Page Editor of the *Kansas City Star*, where he toiled as a writer and editor for more than forty years. He is a former board member and officer of the National Book Critics Circle.

DAVID PERUSEK is Associate Professor of Anthropology at Kent State University at Ashtabula; an ethnographer and Cleveland-area native, he came to his interest in the study of Midwestern literature through David D. Anderson and Patricia A. Anderson.

JOHN R. PFEIFFER, English, Central Michigan University, created a course in Fantasy and Science Fiction in 1971 at the U.S. Air Force Academy and writes often about it; he co-authored "The Modern Period, 1938 to the Present" in *Anatomy of Wonder: Science Fiction,* first three editions, 1976, 1981, and 1987.

ROD PHILLIPS is a poet, scholar, and Associate Professor of Humanities, Culture, and Writing at Michigan State University's James Madison College. His current project explores the theme of hunting in postwar American literature and focuses extensively on the writings of Aldo Leopold.

DENISE PILATO is an Associate Professor in the School of Technology Studies at Eastern Michigan University. She holds master's and doctoral degrees in American studies from Michigan State University and is the author of *Retrieval of a Legacy: Nineteenth-Century American Women Inventors* (2000).

RONALD PRIMEAU taught Midwestern literature and has published on Paul Laurence Dunbar, Herbert Woodward Martin, Edgar Lee Masters, and others.

DAVID RADAVICH, Professor of English Emeritus at Eastern Illinois University, has published extensively on Midwestern drama and has authored poetry and plays set in the region.

KRISTY NELSON RAINE, Reference Librarian and Archivist at Mount Mercy University in Cedar Rapids, Iowa, maintains the web's definitive bibliography devoted to fiction with an Iowa setting.

After studying philosophy and communications at the College of William and Mary and the University of Pennsylvania, MILTON REIGELMAN received a PhD in English from the University of Iowa, where he first met John T. Frederick, editor of *The Midland* magazine. Reigelman, who teaches at Centre College, edited two anthologies on Melville.

GARYN G. ROBERTS has published a range of books, articles, essays, *Dictionary of Midwestern Literature* entries, and more on Midwestern literature and popular culture for almost thirty years.

JOHN ROHRKEMPER, a past president of the Society for the Study of Midwestern Literature and recipient of the society's 2011 MidAmerica Award for distinguished contribution to the study of Midwestern literature, currently is at work on several manuscripts regarding work, money, and technology in the life and writing of Mark Twain.

ROBERT ROOT, Professor Emeritus at Central Michigan University, teaches nonfiction in the Ashland University MFA Program. He is the editor of *Landscapes with Figures: The Nonfiction of Place* (2007) and the author of *The Nonfictionist's Guide: On Reading and Writing Creative Nonfiction* (2008), as well as several works of creative nonfiction.

MARGARET ROZGA'S books of poetry include *200 Nights and One Day* (2009), about the Milwaukee-based campaign for local and national fair-housing laws, and *Though I Haven't Been to Baghdad* (2012); she has published essays on Midwestern writers Gwendolyn Brooks and Martha Bergland.

A native Illinoisan, HERBERT K. RUSSELL has written *Edgar Lee Masters: A Biography* (University of Illinois Press, 2001), has edited *The Enduring River: Edgar Lee Masters' Uncollected Spoon River Poems* (Southern Illinois University Press, 1991), and has published several articles on Midwestern subjects in scholarly journals and reference works.

MIKE RYAN is an independent scholar and outdoorsman who teaches, farms, and hunts on the cusp of the Appalachian foothills in

Fairfield County, Ohio. He regularly contributes to the agricultural magazine *Ohio's Country Journal* and has published in *Ohioana Quarterly, Aethlon: The Journal of Sport Literature,* and *Ohio Outdoor News.*

DAVID K. SAUER is Professor Emeritus at the Jesuit College of Spring Hill, where he directed theatre and taught in the English Department. He has published *David Mamet: A Resource and Production Sourcebook* (2003), *David Mamet's "Oleanna"* (2009) and *American Drama and the Postmodern: Fragmenting the Realistic Stage* (2011) and is finishing *David Mamet.*

ANN LOUISH SEATON is Director of Media and Difference, Director of Multicultural Affairs, and Assistant Professor of Humanities at Bard College in Annandale-on-Hudson, New York.

JAMES SEATON is the winner of the 2008 MidAmerica Award from the Society for the Study of Midwestern Literature "for distinguished contributions to the study of Midwestern literature."

LAUREN BROWN SHEPHERD earned an MA in Literary Studies from The University of Tennessee at Chattanooga and has served as Executive Director of the Athens (Tennessee) Area Council for the Arts since 2013.

JOYCE CALDWELL SMITH specializes in American literature of the late nineteenth and early twentieth centuries. She has published articles on Stephen Crane, Erskine Caldwell, and other American authors and is the volume editor of *Stephen Crane: Bloom's Classic Critical Views* (2009) and the author of *Bloom's How to Write about Stephen Crane* (2011).

MARC KELLY SMITH is the founder of the international poetry slam movement and the catalyst for the engaging styles and immense popularity of performance poetry evident today. He was adviser to Mark Eleveld's best-selling *Spoken Word Revolution: Slam, Hip Hop and the Poetry of a New Generation* (2005) and is the President of Chicago Slam Works, a nonprofit organization that propels performance poetry to even higher peaks of excellence.

CRYSTAL STALLMAN, an Instructor at Hawkeye Community College in Waterloo, Iowa, and at Kirkwood Community College in Cedar Rapids, Iowa, became interested in Native Americans as depicted in literature and captivity narratives as a child; she grew up near the infamous site of the Spirit Lake massacre and began reading captivity narratives at a young age, sparking her continued interest in these subjects.

JEFFREY SWENSON teaches American literature, writing, and Midwestern regionalism at Hiram College. His current research concerns Ohio-born author Jim Tully, an Irish American hobo, boxer, and Hollywood writer.

GUY SZUBERLA has written and published frequently on Chicago and Midwestern writers, including George Ade, Saul Bellow, Theodore Dreiser, Henry Blake Fuller, and John T. McCutcheon. He taught American literature and American studies at the University of Toledo, where he is Professor Emeritus. He was President of the Great Lakes American Studies Association and the Society for the Study of Midwestern Literature and served for several years on the editorial boards of *The Old Northwest* and *Dictionary of Midwestern Literature.*

THOM TAMMARO is the co-editor of two award-winning anthologies of Midwestern literature, *Inheriting the Land: Contemporary Voices from the Midwest* (1993) and *Imagining Home: Writing from the Midwest* (1995), both published by the University of Minnesota Press. He is Professor of English and directs the MFA in Creative Writing Program at Minnesota State University–Moorhead.

JON C. TEAFORD is the author of *Cities of the Heartland: The Rise and Fall of the Industrial Midwest* (1993) and was a Senior Consulting Editor for *The American Midwest: An Interpretive Encyclopedia* (2007).

CATHERINE TOBIN has taught American history at Central Michigan University since 1988; her doctoral dissertation in history focused on Irish canal workers in the

Midwest and called for firsthand accounts from this region.

ELLEN SERLEN UFFEN has written on Midwesterners Edna Ferber, Herbert Gold, Fannie Hurst, Ben Hecht, Jo Sinclair, and others and is the author of *Strands of the Cable: The Place of the Past in Jewish American Women's Writing* (1992).

LANCE WELDY is an Associate Professor of English at Francis Marion University and has presented scholarly papers on the works of Laura Ingalls Wilder, Willa Cather, and Ole E. Rølvaag.

As a scholar and student of postmodern American literature, JOHNNIE WILCOX believes that American Midwestern literary and critical writers have contributed elements essential to American literary postmodernism, a conviction deepened by his research and teaching at Ohio University.

KEITH WILHITE is an assistant professor of English at Siena College. His teaching and scholarship focus on twentieth- and twenty-first-century American literature, including Midwestern writers such as Willa Cather, Jim Tully, Richard Wright, Jeffrey Eugenides, and Jonathan Franzen.

With degrees from MIT, Stanford, and the University of North Carolina–Chapel Hill, DOUGLAS WIXSON is a longtime member of the Society for the Study of Midwestern Literature who has published widely in scholarly journals. His five books include the award-winning *Worker-Writer in America: Jack Conroy and the Tradition of Midwestern Literary Radicalism, 1898–1990* (1994) and *On the Dirty Plate Trail: Remembering the Dust Bowl Refugee Camps* (2007). He received the Society for the Study of Midwestern Literature's MidAmerica Award in 1995.

JOSEPH J. WYDEVEN was Professor Emeritus of English and Humanities at Bellevue University. He specialized in novelist and photographer Wright Morris and was the author of *Wright Morris Revisited* (1998). Other interests included all varieties of Midwestern noir fiction, such as the works of Daniel Woodrell and Bonnie Jo Campbell.

SUSAN YANOS, a lifelong resident of rural east central Indiana, is a farmwife, writer, and teacher of writing and literature, including Indiana literature. She has taught at Indiana University East in Richmond, Ball State University in Muncie, and Earlham School of Religion in Richmond.

Entries by Author

Index

Please note: Author names in **bold** can also be found in *Dictionary of Midwestern Literature, Volume One*. Page numbers in **bold** indicate major discussions. *Italicized* page numbers refer to illustrations/images.

W